M·A·N·U·F·A·C·T·U·R·I·N·G
&·D·I·S·T·R·I·B·U·T·I·O·N
USA

Fifth Edition

Industry Analyses,
Statistics and Leading Companies

ISSN 1529-7659

M·A·N·U·F·A·C·T·U·R·I·N·G
&·D·I·S·T·R·I·B·U·T·I·O·N
USA

Fifth Edition

Industry Analyses,
Statistics and Leading Companies

Volume 2

Arsen J. Darnay, Managing Editor

Joyce P. Simkin, Editor

GALE
CENGAGE Learning

Detroit • New York • San Francisco • New Haven, Conn • Waterville, Maine • London

Manufacturing & Distribution USA, 5th Edition

Joyce P. Simkin

Project Editor: Julie A. Gough

Editorial: Arsen J. Darnay, Monique D. Magee

Editorial Support Services: Scott Flaugher

Manufacturing: Rita Wimberley

Product Management: Jenai Mynatt

Gale
27500 Drake Rd.
Farmington Hills, MI, 48331-3535

ISBN-13: 978-1-4144-0867-5 (3 vol. set)   ISBN-10: 1-4144-0867-6 (3 vol. set)
ISBN-13: 978-1-4144-0868-2 (vol. 1)   ISBN-10: 1-4144-0868-4 (vol. 1)
ISBN-13: 978-1-4144-0869-9 (vol. 2)   ISBN-10: 1-4144-0869-2 (vol. 2)
ISBN-13: 978-1-4144-0870-5 (vol. 3)   ISBN-10: 1-4144-0870-6 (vol. 3)

ISSN 1529-7659

This title is also available as an e-book.
ISBN-13: 978-1-4144-3829-0
ISBN-10: 1-4144-3829-X
Contact your Gale sales representative for ordering information.

Printed in the United States of America
1 2 3 4 5 6 7 13 12 11 10 09

TABLE OF CONTENTS

Preface

Manufacturing: The Big Picture

This section will provide an overview of the U.S. manufacturing sector. This will serve as the "big picture" of which the individual NAICS chapters are distinct views. In this section, the focus will be on changes between 1982 and 2006.

In recent years an important subject of political debate has been the loss of U.S. manufacturing jobs. Manufacturing jobs have long been the highest paying sources of income for many, especially for those who do not have an advanced college degree, a majority of the population. According to the U.S. Census Bureau, 72 percent of the population 25 years old and over had less than a bachelor's degree in 2006. Manufacturing jobs have been and continue to be outsourced to countries such as Mexico and China. Some consider this a signal of an economy in transition. Just as in the 19th century our economy switched from agrarian to industrial, the 20th century ushered in a transition from an economy based on manufacturing to one based on services and increasingly one based on high tech services. However, in the 21st century, information technology jobs, such as those held by computer programmers and analysts, were also being outsourced to foreign countries.

Those in favor of outsourcing argue that despite the loss of manufacturing jobs, the manufacturing sector and the economy as a whole are prospering. Productivity has been on the rise. A workforce with high skills using more advanced production processes allows industries to produce more output with fewer workers. Other sectors of the economy have been expanding. The overall unemployment rate declined in the past 25 years. Foreign investment in U.S. manufacturing now surpasses U.S. investment in manufacturing abroad.

Those opposed to outsourcing argue that the jobs created in the last 25 years do not pay as well as the manufacturing jobs that have been lost. The trade deficit continues to rise. Despite numerous free trade agreements, exports have not kept pace with imports. Many see the importing of goods, especially goods needed for national defense, as a dangerous trend.

In this section we will state the facts as they are reported in national statistics. The policy implications, of course, must be drawn by those charged with setting the nation's economic course.

To start, a note on the data used to analyze the U.S. manufacturing sector. Data in the section below entitled *Issues in Manufacturing* are drawn from governmental as well as non-governmental sources. All other data are drawn from five economic censuses. These are surveys of nearly all manufacturing establishments. Also included are data from the most recent *Annual Survey of Manufactures* (ASM), which is a partial sampling of industrial activity and not at the same level of precision as the other years. Gross Domestic Product (GDP) data have been taken from the Bureau of Economic Analysis website (http://www.bea.gov/).

Prior to 1997, data were classified using Standard Industrial Classification (SIC) coding. In 1997, data were reclassified using the North American Industrial Classification System (NAICS). As a result of this reclassification, 259 new manufacturing industries were created by merging two or more parts of SIC coded industries; 214 industries remained unchanged after this transition. However, this was not the first reclassification of industries. In 1987, the SIC coding system underwent a change from the 1972 SIC coding. As a result, data prior to 1987 for 35 of the 214 industries taken over without changes to the NAICS system only provide comparable data back to 1987.

In 2003, the U.S. Census Bureau made another important change in how it collects and reports data in the *Annual Survey of Manufactures*. Starting in 2003, the ASM no longer reports on all 6-digit NAICS manufacturing industries. Instead a subset of the total has been created by the Census Bureau and it is this subset on which it reports in the ASM. This change reflects the shrinking of U.S. manufacturing.

In preparing *MDUSA* the editors have done a great deal of work to restructure this title so that it adheres to the new, shorter ASM industry list. The ASM industry list contains 6-digit NAICS industries as well as industries made up of two or more 6-digit NAICS industries. For any ASM industry that is a combination of 6-digit NAICS industries, a new code is used. The new ASM code is a 5-digit number and a letter. Whenever such a new industry code is presented in this work, a list is provided for the user of the component NAICS industries that are covered by the new single ASM NAICS code. In addition, two new appendices are provided, one that offers a conversion from ASM NAICS codes to 2002 NAICS codes and the other providing a look-up guide in the other direction—2002 NAICS codes to ASM NAICS codes.

Of the 322 manufacturing industries presented in this work, 234 are "straight" 6-digit NAICS industries and 88 are new ASM industries (industries made up of more than one 6-digit NAICS industry).

When discussing the manufacturing sector as a whole, all 322 ASM industries are included in the statistics. Only the 137 ASM industries for which historical data are available are included when details about the manufacturing sector are discussed.

Sources for the graphics in this section are listed under *Graphics Sources*. An annotated source list follows.

The General State of Manufacturing

Figure 1. The Importance of Manufacturing to the U.S. Economy, 1947-2007

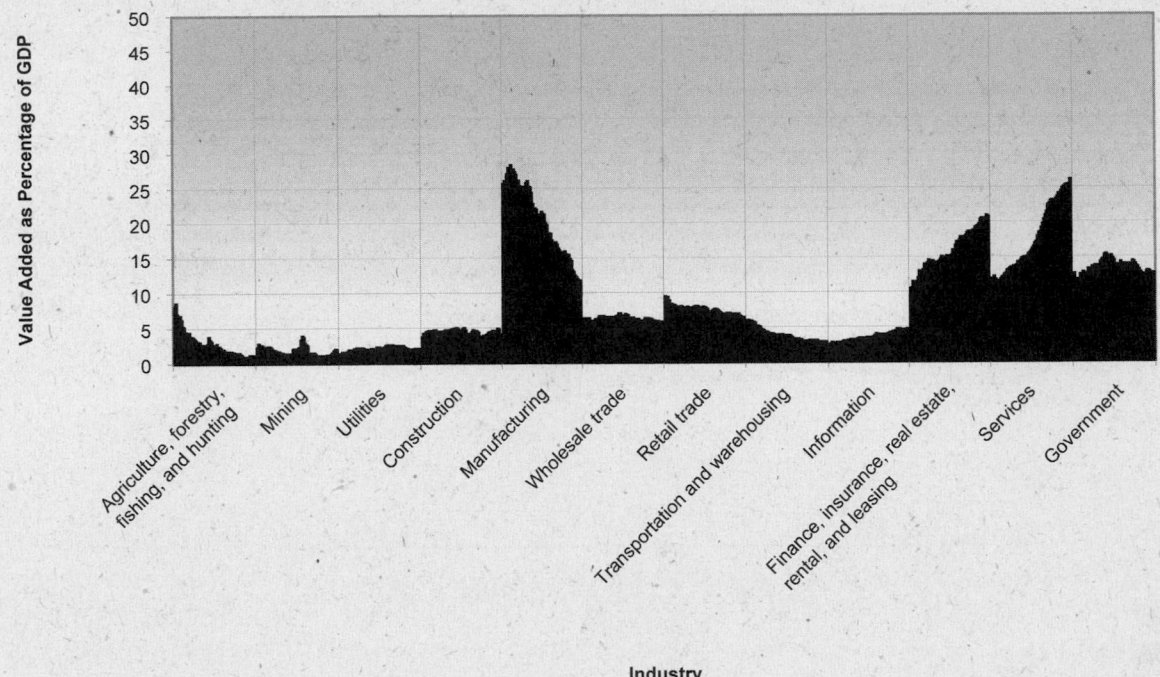

Manufacturing continues to slip in overall importance within the U.S. economy. As a percentage of Gross Domestic Product (GDP), Manufacturing, in terms of value added by labor, went from 25.6 percent in 1947 to 11.7 percent of GDP in 2007, a decline of 13.9 percent. Nearly half of that decline occurred in the years 1982 to 2007. In 1982, manufacturing was nearly 19 percent of GDP; in 2007, 11.7 percent. The slippage in share of GDP suggests that other sectors of the economy have been expanding more rapidly.

As Figure 1 shows, in the post-World War II era, the Service sector expanded the most rapidly (a 14.3 percent gain), followed by Finance, Insurance, Real Estate, Rental, and Leasing (+10.3 percent) and Information (+2.2 percent). From 1982 to 2007, the gains in these industries were 8.2 percent, 4.1 percent, and 0.9 percent, respectively. The year 1984 was pivitol, it was the first year that the Service sector surpassed the Manufacturing sector as the largest sector in the economy. By 2007, in terms of value added, Services outperformed Manufacturing by a ratio greater than 2 to 1. Finance, Insurance, Real Estate, Rental, and Leasing outperformed Manufacturing by a ratio of nearly 2 to 1. The gross domestic product value of Services was $3.6 trillion. Finance, Insurance, Real Estate, Rental, and Leasing GDP was $2.9 trillion. Manufacturing GDP was $1.6 trillion.

Note, however, that Manufacturing—along with agriculture, forestry, mining, transportation, and construction—are basic economic activities. All other sectors depend upon these. Therefore, the expansion of the services sector is in a real sense *enabled* by the productivity of these basic sectors.

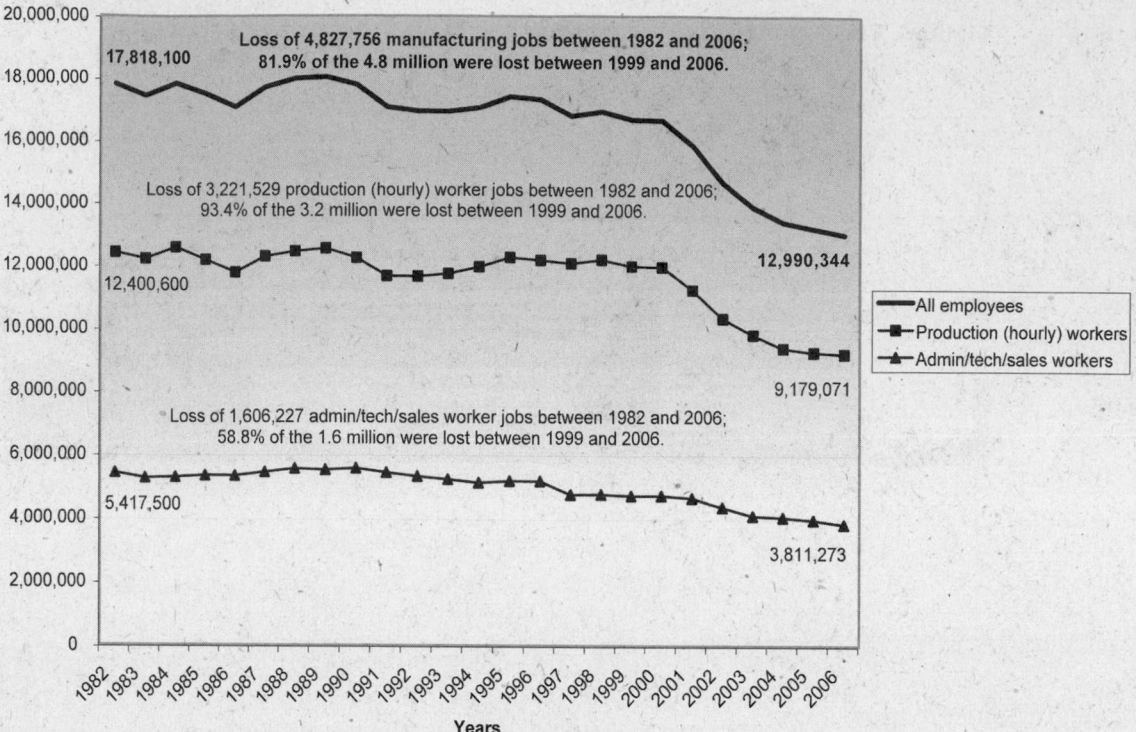

Figure 2. Employment in the Manufacturing Sector, 1982-2006

Manufacturing employment, as a percentage of total nonagricultural employment, declined from 18.5 percent in 1982 to 9.1 percent in 2006. Total employment in the economy increased. Manufacturing employment shrank by more than 4.8 million jobs, from 17.8 million in 1982 to 12.9 million in 2006.

Manufacturing output, measured in dollars, grew in the 1982 to 2006 period—but at a lower rate than GDP. Output per employee increased 251.3 percent in the period, compensation per employee increased by 137.9 percent.

Value added represents the *labor* contribution to this sector of the economy, which is aided by machines. Value added represents the value of shipments less the cost of materials, supplies, containers, fuel, purchased electrical power, and contract work and other services purchased. Part of capital investment includes investment in more efficient machinery allowing a worker to make more product in the same amount of time. From 1982 to 2006, growth in value added per employee (283.7 percent) was greater than growth in capital investment per employee (141.9 percent). This shows that technology played an important role in the manufacturing sector during this time period.

Indicators of Manufacturing

Establishments. Despite the decline in employment, the total number of manufacturing establishments increased from 348,000 in 1982 to 350,000 in 2002. Establishment counts in 2005 (last available year) were down from the 2002 level, but establishment data for non-census years come from the County Business Patterns, a statistical data collection system based on sampling rather than, as in census years, 100 percent reporting by manufacturers.

Employment. Manufacturing employment showed a decline in 2006 from 1982 (see Figure 2). Manufacturing employed more than 17.8 million people in 1982 and more than 12.9 million people in 2006. Manufacturing employment as a percentage of the total labor force dropped from 18.5 percent in 1982 to 9.1 percent in 2006 (nonagricultural payrolls). In the period 1982 to 2006, the total labor force rose 47.9 percent and manufacturing employment dropped by 27.1 percent.

Hourly production employment, representing most manufacturing jobs, decreased at a slightly lower rate (25.9 percent) than employment of administrative, sales, and technical forces (a decline of 29.6 percent), in the 1982 to 2006 period. The latter segment is relatively small and is also most subject to "outsourcing"—as, for instance, by purchasing contract services such as payroll support, computer support, and engineering services. The numbers suggest that corporate "downsizing" is continuing to show up in manufacturing statistics. This is the more probable because production labor actually *increased* from 1992 to 1997 while the administrative, sales, and technical segment continued to lose ground.

The picture was not so bleak for all industries in the manufacturing sector. Despite the decline in hourly production worker employment throughout the manufacturing sector, some industries gained hourly production worker jobs. Table 1 lists the employment gains and losses for the 137 unchanged ASM NAICS industries by major industrial category.

Table 1. Hourly Production Worker Employment Gains and Losses in Unchanged ASM NAICS Industries, 1987-2006

Industry category	Number of hourly production worker jobs:		Net job effect, 1987-2006
	Gained	Lost	
Apparel manufacturing	NA	NA	NA
Beverage and tobacco product manufacturing	13,800	15,700	-1,900
Chemical manufacturing	27,600	54,700	-27,100
Computer and electronic product manufacturing	63,400	264,700	-201,300
Electrical equipment, appliance, and component manufacturing	65,000	139,300	-73,800
Fabricated metal product manufacturing	25,900	70,900	-45,000
Food manufacturing	23,300	33,300	-10,000
Furniture and related product manufacturing	38,100	85,100	-47,000
Leather and allied product manufacturing	0	59,600	-59,600
Machinery manufacturing	38,600	63,700	-25,100
Nonmetallic mineral product manufacturing	47,500	79,300	-31,800
Paper manufacturing	22,800	63,100	-40,300
Petroleum and coal products manufacturing	7,200	18,200	-11,000
Plastics and rubber products manufacturing	29,000	34,900	-5,900
Primary metal manufacturing	34,500	57,400	-22,900
Printing and related support activities	NA	NA	NA

[Continued on next page]

Table 1. Hourly Production Worker Employment Gains and Losses in Unchanged ASM NAICS Industries, 1987-2006 [continued]

Industry	Number of hourly production worker jobs:		Net job effect, 1987-2006
	Gained	Lost	
Textile mills	NA	NA	NA
Textile product mills	NA	NA	NA
Transportation equipment manufacturing	38,100	244,300	-206,200
Wood product manufacturing	43,700	60,200	-16,500
Miscellaneous manufacturing	56,600	63,400	-6,800
Total	**575,100**	**1,407,800**	**-832,200**

Note: NA: historical data are not available because the *Annual Survey of Manufactures'* NAICS codes combine both unchanged industries and new industries within these categories.

Despite the recent hiring trend in some industry categories such as Nonmetallic Mineral Product Manufacturing (12,700 jobs gained from 2004 to 2006), Machinery Manufacturing (+11,200 jobs), and Fabricated Metal Product Manufacturing (+5,200 jobs) no industry category gained net hourly production workers during the 1987-2006 period. The types of industries that lost the most hourly production workers were Transportation Equipment Manufacturing (206,200 net jobs), Computer and Electronic Product Manufacturing (201,300 net jobs), and Electrical Equipment, Appliance, and Component Manufacturing (73,800 net jobs). Table 2 shows the top 5 specific industries that gained production workers and the top 5 that lost production workers.

Table 2. Top 5 Unchanged ASM NAICS Industries With Hourly Production Worker Gains in Employment and Top 5 Unchanged ASM NAICS Industries With Hourly Production Worker Losses in Employment, 1987-2006

NAICS	Industry description	Number of employees	NAICS	Industry description	Number of employees
332721	Precision turned product manufacturing	24,100	336411	Aircraft manufacturing	-60,100
327320	Ready-mix concrete manufacturing	17,100	31621M	Footwear manufacturing	-55,000
327991	Cut stone and stone product manufacturing	10,000	336414	Guided missile and space vehicle manufacturing	-47,600
33313M	Mining and oil and gas field machinery manufacturing	9,300	334111	Electronic computer manufacturing	-42,900
339950	Sign manufacturing	6,200	336412	Aircraft engine and engine parts manufacturing	-42,000

Compensation. Wages for manufacturing production workers over the period 1982 to 2006, after adjusting for inflation, grew 10.9 percent, slightly more than the growth rate for all U.S. hourly workers (8.5 percent). While average annual incomes for hourly workers in the service sector remained lower ($27,705 in 2006) than those of manufacturing production workers ($35,933 in 2006), the average wages in the service sector grew at a faster rate over the 1982 to 2006 period than did the wages of manufacturing sector production workers. The inflation adjusted growth in average service sector incomes for hourly workers was 13.8 percent while growth in manufacturing sector production worker incomes was 10.9 percent over the same twenty-six year period.

As shown in Figure 3, the average incomes of hourly workers in neither the manufacturing sector nor the service sector grew at the inflation adjusted rate of 54.1 percent seen for the overall U.S. workforce between 1982 and 2006. In fact, in 2006 the average manufacturing production worker made $1,584 less than the U.S. mean income of $37,517.

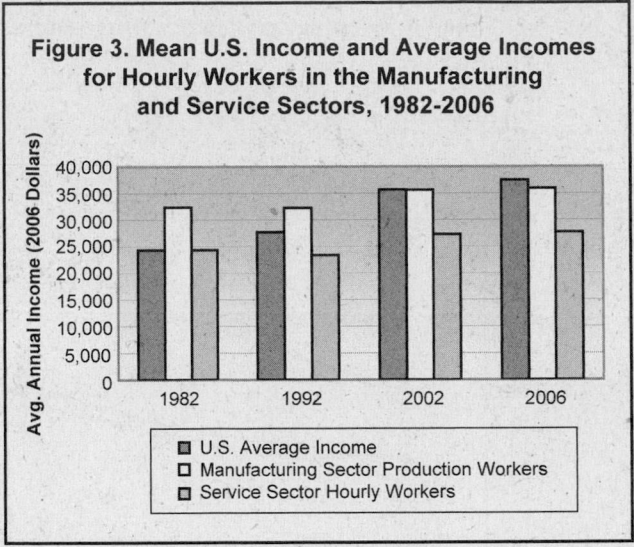

Figure 3. Mean U.S. Income and Average Incomes for Hourly Workers in the Manufacturing and Service Sectors, 1982-2006

From 1982 to 2006, aggregate hourly wages in the manufacturing sector increased at a lower rate than value of shipments. However, aggregate administrative/technical/sales salaries increased at a higher rate. Non-inflation adjusted aggregate hourly wages increased by 127.1 percent. Administrative/technical/sales salaries increased by 158.1 percent and value of shipments increased by 156.1 percent.

Table 3. Employee Compensation, 1982-2006

[Data in dollars per year. Numbers in **bold** show the highest values per category.]

	1982	1987	1992	1997	2002	2006	Growth (%) 1982-2006	Growth (%) 1987-2006
All employees								
All industries	$19,161	$24,183	$29,153	$33,907	$39,217	45,599	137.9	**88.6**
Unchanged ASM NAICS industries	-	**26,792**	**32,389**	**37,154**	**42,599**	**50,097**	-	86.9
New ASM NAICS industries	-	-	-	32,605	37,800	43,992	-	-
Hourly production worker wages								
All industries	16,514	20,476	24,185	28,036	32,598	37,508	127.1	83.2
Unchanged ASM NAICS industries	-	**22,551**	**26,567**	**30,569**	**35,349**	**41,328**		**83.3**
New ASM NAICS industries	-	-	-	27,120	31,437	36,195		
Administrative, technical, and sales employee salaries								
All industries	25,218	32,557	40,047	48,850	54,937	65,085	158.1	**99.9**
Unchanged ASM NAICS industries	-	**35,376**	**43,757**	**51,874**	**58,202**	**69,495**		96.4
New ASM NAICS industries	-	-	-	47,278	53,405	63,356		

Performance. In the 1982 to 2006 period, manufacturing shipments declined relative to GDP. Measured as a percent of GDP in 1982, manufacturing shipments (roughly equivalent to sales) represented 60.2 percent and in 2006 they represented 38.0 percent.

In current dollars, costs have grown at nearly twice the rate of capital investment. (See Figure 4). Cost of materials grew 142.2 percent, from $1.1 trillion to $2.7 trillion. Capital investment grew 76.5 percent, from $77 billion to $136 billion. Value added grew the most in this period, 23.7 percentage points higher than the growth in value of shipments. Value

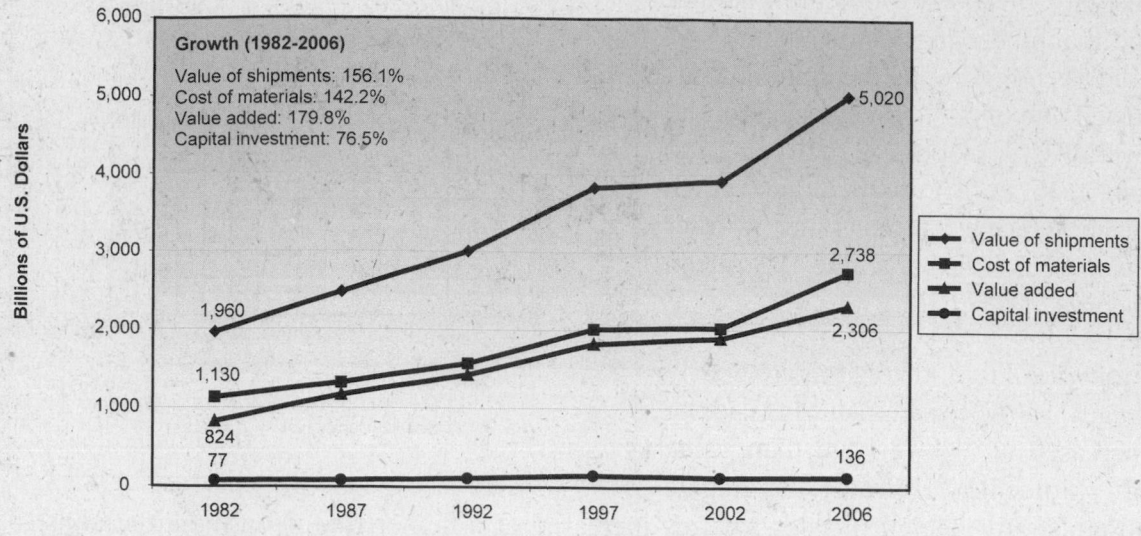

Figure 4. Manufacturing Performance and Growth, Current Dollars, 1982-2006

added grew 179.8 percent, from $824 billion to $2.3 trillion. Value of shipments rose 156.1 percent, from nearly $2.0 trillion to more than $5.0 trillion.

When analyzing only the industries for which historical data are available, value of shipments rose at a faster rate than capital investment, but at a slower rate than cost of materials. Value of shipments rose 123.9 percent from $790.7 billion in 1987 to $1.8 trillion in 2006. Capital investment rose 107.8 percent from $26.0 billion to $54.0 billion. Cost of materials rose 126.9 percent from $451.7 billion to $1.0 trillion. Growth in value added surpassed growth in capital investment. Value added rose 116.9 percent from $343.2 billion in 1987 to $744.7 billion in 2006.

Adjusting for inflation, in the manufacturing sector as a whole, only capital investment showed a decline. During the period 1982 to 2006, inflation adjusted growth rates for cost of materials, value of shipments, and value added were 11.0 percent, 17.4 percent, and 28.3 percent, respectively.

From 1987 to 2006, all performance factors outpaced inflation in the industries for which historical data are available. Cost of materials grew 29.8 percent, value added grew 24.1 percent, value of shipments grew 28.1 percent, and capital investment grew 18.9 percent.

Productivity. Productivity (output per hour) is expressed as an index (see Figure 5).[1] Wage and salary data are shown in constant 2006 dollars. From 1987 to 2006, productivity rose faster than aggregate wages and salaries and faster than wages and salaries per employee. In fact, aggregate wages and salaries fell an average of 1.2 percent yearly during this time period—from $749.0 billion to $592.3 billion. The average annual percentage increase in productivity was 3.7 percent. Average annual increase in wages and salaries per employee was 0.4 percent. Conventional wisdom links productivity increases to increases in pay, but the two, in practice, do not go hand in hand.

Productivity arises from human skills, technology and management. Aggregate wages and salaries declined during this time period while productivity increased. This may mean

Figure 5. Manufacturing Productivity, 1987-2006

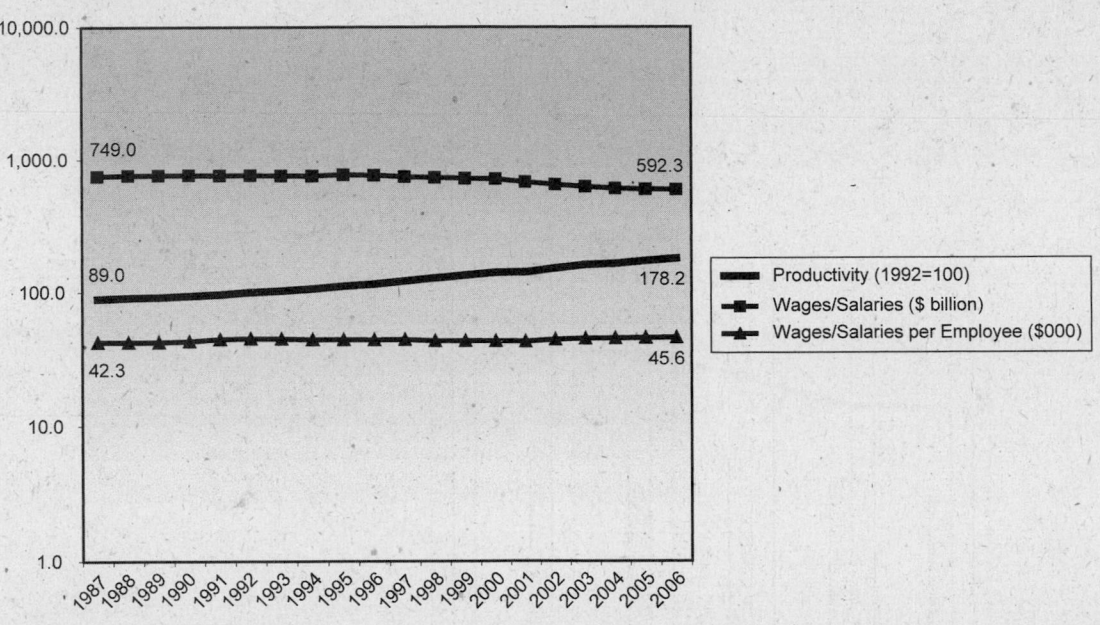

that technology played a bigger role in manufacturing during this time period than human skill. Other measures indicative of productivity are shown in Figure 6. These measurements confirm the effect of technology on manufacturing productivity. Capital investment, shipments, and value added per employee and per production worker increased from 1982 to 2006. During this period manufacturing jobs overall declined by more than 4.8 million and production worker jobs declined by more than 3.2 million. The manufacturing sector produced more with fewer workers.

Issues in Manufacturing

Free Trade. In 1993, in a debate with Al Gore over the North American Free Trade Agreement (NAFTA), Ross Perot coined the phrase "giant sucking sound" to describe the loss of U.S. jobs to Mexico if NAFTA was ratified. During the debate, he and Pat Choate, political economist and former vice presidential candidate, claimed that 5 million U.S. jobs would be lost. On January 1, 1994, NAFTA took effect and its consequences are still being debated fourteen years later.

The Central America-Dominican Republic-United States Free Trade Agreement (CAFTA-DR), took effect on March 1, 2006. This agreement includes the United States, Costa Rica, Dominican Republic, El Salvador, Guatemala, Honduras, and Nicaragua. Since this agreement took effect, the United States' trade balance with member countries has gone from a trade deficit of $1.2 billion in 2005 to a trade surplus of $3.7 billion in 2007. In contrast, the United States had a trade deficit of $90.0 billion with Canada and Mexico in 1993, a year before NAFTA. In 1995, two years after NAFTA took effect, the trade deficit decreased to $34.4 billion. However, by 2007, the trade deficit with NAFTA member countries increased to $138.9 billion.

Figure 6. Other Factors in Manufacturing Productivity, 1982-2006

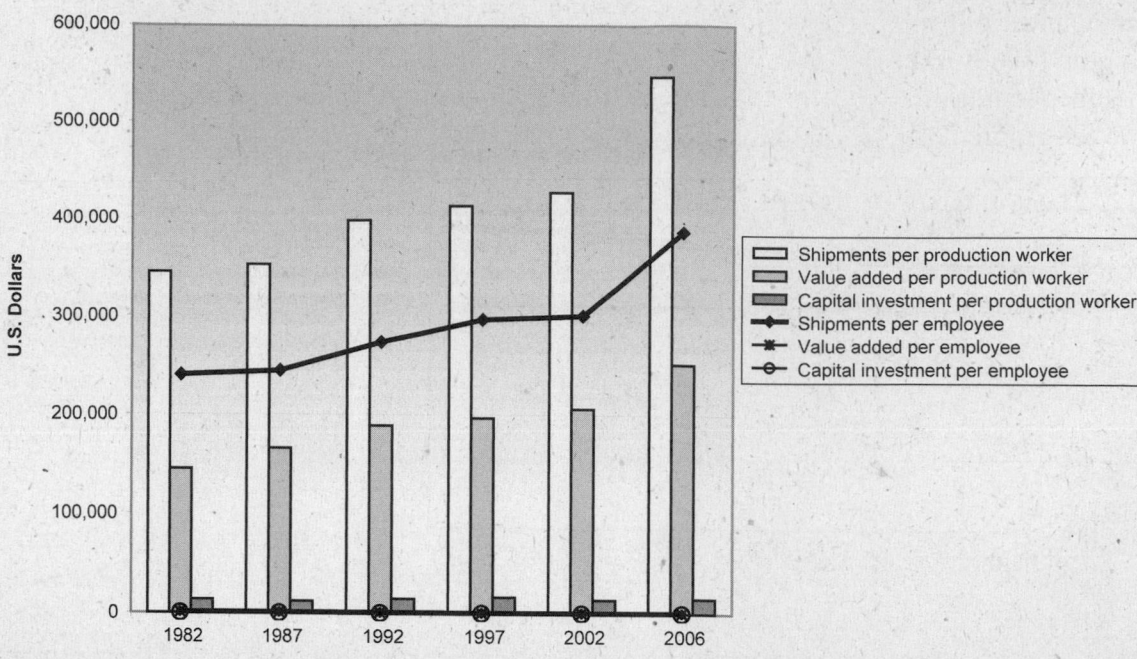

On January 1, 1995 the World Trade Organization (WTO) was founded. It is a successor to the General Agreement on Tariffs and Trade (GATT), which was first signed in 1947. The WTO's purpose is to "ensure that trade flows as smoothly, predictably and freely as possible" by negotiating trade agreements, resolving trade disputes, and providing technical assistance and training to developing countries. Member nations must adhere to a set of rules: agreements that were the result of negotiations between members. These agreements outline the rights and obligations of member nations in order to ensure a "non-discriminatory trading system".[2]

As of May 16, 2008, the WTO had 152 member countries, including the United States. In 2006, trade among WTO members represented the vast majority of all international trade, 94.8 percent of exports in the world and 95.3 percent of imports in the world. This equated to more than $11.4 trillion in exports and more than $11.8 trillion in imports.

From 1992 (first year of available comparable data) to 2007, export of goods from the United States and import of goods to the United States, on average, trended upward. However, once a country becomes a member of the WTO, the average yearly increase in exports to that country from the United States slows. From 1992 to the year a country becomes a member of the WTO, exports from the United States increased an average of 30.0 percent per year. After a country becomes a member of the WTO, exports from the United States slowed to an average increase of 20.4 percent per year. Imports of goods from individual countries to the United States also decreased from an average of 34.5 percent[3] per year before a country joins the WTO to an average of 33.5 percent per year after that country joins the WTO. Table 4 shows the top five WTO member countries the U.S. exports to and imports from.

The United States did not increase its exports and imports to all member countries during this time period, however. The United States shipped fewer goods to eleven member countries after their entry into the WTO, most notably Japan ($1.7 billion less) and Cyprus ($88.8 million less). The United States imported fewer goods from twenty two member countries after their entry into the WTO. The amount of imports from Hong Kong and Singapore decreased the most: $3.3 billion and $165.1 million, respectively.

Table 4. Top 5 WTO Member Countries the United States Exports To and Imports From, 1992 to 2007

	EXPORTS				IMPORTS		
Country (Year of WTO Entry)	Total, ($ mil)	Average Total Per Year ($ mil)	Average, Total Per Year, ($ mil)	Country (Year of WTO Entry)	Total, ($ mil)	Average Total Per Year, ($ mil)	Average Total Per Year, ($ mil)
	Year of Entry to 2007		1992 to Year of Entry		Year of Entry to 2007		1992 to Year of Entry
Canada (1995)	121,678.0.0	9,359.8	9,157.9	China (2001)	219,229.4	36,538.2	7,655.1
Mexico (1995)	90,249.2	6,942.2	1,424.9	Canada (1995)	168,741.0	12,980.1	11,435.0
China (2001)	46,056.0	7,676.0	1,176.3	Mexico (1995)	148,698.6	11,432.4	6,722.3
Germany (1995)	27,257.7	2,096.7	286.5	Germany (1995)	57,520.6	4,424.7	2,005.9
United Kingdom (1995)	21,439.7	1,649.2	1,514.2	Venezuela (1995)	30,132.7	2,317.9	365.7

Employment. Between 1982 and 1992, nearly 760,000 hourly production worker jobs were lost in the United States. In the next 5 years, from 1992 to 1997, more than 424,000 jobs were created. After one more year of upturn, production worker jobs declined again. From 1997 to 2006, more than 2.9 million production worker jobs were lost. Despite the slight upturn from 1992 to 1998, overall, the United States lost more than 3.2 million production worker jobs between 1982 and 2006. From 1982 to 2006, more than 1.6 million administrative, technical, and sales jobs were lost also, with the greatest loss during the 1992 to 1997 period. Overall, from 1982 to 2006, the manufacturing sector lost more than 4.8 million jobs.

Not all of these job losses can be attributed to companies exporting jobs to foreign countries. As discussed earlier, from 1982 to 2006, technology played an important role in manufacturing. Value added per employee increased while the number of workers decreased. However, job losses due to NAFTA were anticipated. The NAFTA-Transitional Adjustment Assistance Program (NAFTA-TAA) was established as part of the NAFTA Implementation Act of 1993. This program was set up to help workers whose companies were directly or indirectly affected by trade with or by production shifting to Mexico or Canada. This program provided up to 52 weeks of unemployment benefits and worker retraining. According to the U.S. Department of Labor, from 1994 to 2007, more than 1,822,000 workers were certified as eligible for this program and its successor, the Trade Adjustment Assistance Reform Act of 2002 (TAA).

In 2002, the NAFTA-TAA program was replaced by the TAA. This program added to the benefits of NAFTA-TAA by providing health care assistance to displaced workers. Under Section 113 of this act, "workers may be eligible to apply ... if they were laid off as a result of increased imports or if their companies shifted production out of the United States to

Figure 7. Countries with the Largest Trade Deficits with the United States, 1985-2007

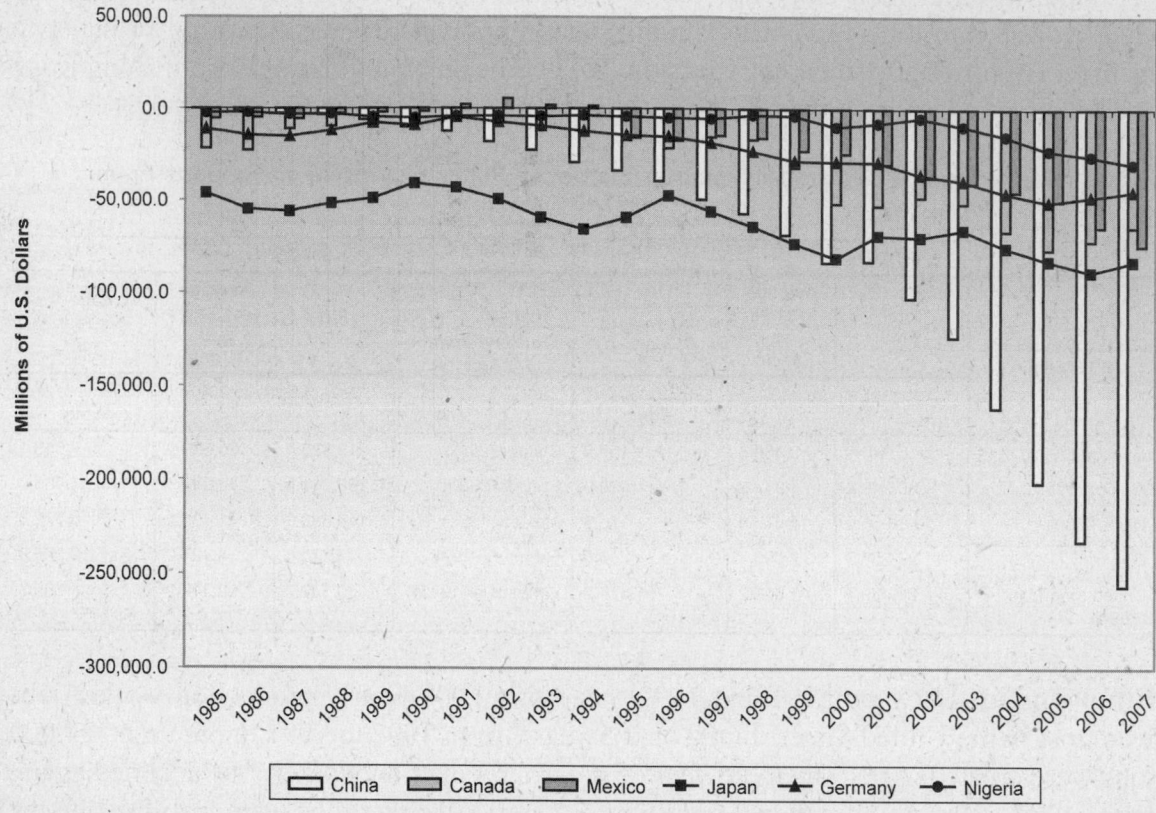

certain foreign countries."[4] The TAA also increased the number of foreign countries covered and included not only Canada and Mexico, but Israel, Jordan, most of the countries in Africa, and many countries in Central and South America and the Caribbean. However, China and Japan were not on the list. Yet, these two countries have had the highest and second highest merchandise trade deficit with the United States since 1991 (see Figure 7).

Merchandise trade deficit. Much debate in recent years has centered around the trade deficit. From 1982 to 2007 the trade deficit has grown more than 2,134 percent from $36.4 billion in 1982 to $815.4 billion in 2007.

World Trade. From 1982 to 2000, U.S. merchandise exports as a percentage of total world exports remained constant at around 11 to 12 percent. However, from 2001 to 2007, U.S. merchandise exports as a percentage of total world exports trended downward, from 11.7 percent to 8.4 percent. In contrast, merchandise imports into the United States as a percentage of total world imports trended upward from 13.1 percent in 1982 to 18.7 percent in 2000. From 2001 to 2007, U.S. merchandise imports as a percentage of total world imports trended downward from 18.2 percent to 14.2 percent.

Globalization. Companies closing their factories in the United States and moving their manufacturing plants overseas or across the border are growing in number. In the 1990s, some industrialized nations were offering multi-million dollar grants, tax holidays, and other financial incentives to entice American manufacturers to build plants in their countries. Because of this, some high-tech companies moved their manufacturing operations to countries like Ireland, Japan, and Malta.

But for many companies that have closed U.S. plants, and others that have not yet done so, outsourcing to foreign manufacturing companies offers a more economical alternative. Low labor costs and savings from eliminating factory overhead costs entice U.S. firms to outsource to countries such as Mexico, Singapore, Pakistan, Malaysia, Taiwan, Korea, and China.

In 2008, the government-mandated minimum wage for workers in Mexico was $4.85 per day, an increase of 15 percent from 1994 when NAFTA took effect. Production worker wages in Mexican maquiladoras in 2006 (the last year for which data are available) were $2.64 per hour, an increase of 45 percent from 1994. From 1994 to 2007, tortilla prices increased 126 percent.[5] In comparison, the Federal minimum wage in the United States was $5.85 per hour and, according to the Bureau of Labor Statistics, the median hourly wage for production workers was $13.53 in 2007. But, despite the comparatively low wages, by 2003, foreign companies who have done business in Mexico were looking to outsource to countries with lower wages still, such as China and Sri Lanka. The search for low wage workers continues. By 2006, U.S. corporations were contemplating relocation of their factories out of China to "lower-cost countries"[6] due to labor shortages, an average 14 percent employee turnover rate, and rising wages in China. At one factory in Dongguan, wages in 2005 rose 40 percent to an average of $160 a month. In 2007, Richard Ligus, president of Rockford Consulting, a company specializing in manufacturing distribution and supply chain strategies, stated "people tell me that we've probably got three years in China before their standard of living goes up. After that they'll probably go to India. And after that, to Viet Nam."[7]

In 2007, the Department of Commerce instituted the Invest in America program. Its purpose is to "provide support for state governments' investment promotion efforts."[8] Invest in America Week was inaugurated May 5-9, 2008. Thirteen states held activities promoting foreign investment in the United States.

In 2005, the last year for which data are available, subsidiaries of foreign companies in the United States employed nearly 5.1 million workers, 4.4 percent of the total U.S. workforce. The average wage paid was $66,042 per year, 25 percent higher than the average wage paid by U.S. companies. In the manufacturing sector, subsidiaries of foreign companies employed 1.9 million workers, 15 percent of the U.S. manufacturing workforce. The average wage was $73,790 per year, 47.3 percent higher than the average wage paid to manufacturing workers in the United States by U.S. companies.

As Table 5 shows, foreign investment in the manufacturing sector was concentrated in the traditionally higher-paying industries such as Transportation Equipment Manufacturing, Chemical Manufacturing, and Machinery Manufacturing. In contrast, U.S. manufacturing was concentrated in the traditionally lower-paying industries such as Miscellaneous Manufacturing, Fabricated Metal Products, and Food Manufacturing. However, as Figure 8 shows, subsidiaries of foreign-owned manufacturing companies in all industries paid their employees between 21.7 percent and 64.8 percent higher wages on average than U.S. manufacturing companies did in comparable industries.

According to the 2005 Georgia Manufacturing Survey, on average, manufacturing companies that based their competitive strategies on innovation of products and processes had higher profit margins and paid their employees higher wages than those manufacturing companies that based their competitive strategies on low price.

**Table 5. Top 5 Manufacturing Industries and Average Salary,
by Number of Employees, 2005**

U. S.-owned Companies	
Industry	**Average Yearly Salary**
Other Manufacturing	$33,770
Fabricated Metal Product Manufacturing	39,660
Food Manufacturing	38,815
Transportation Equipment Manufacturing	48,980
Computer & Electronic Product Manufacturing	57,471
Subsidiaries of Foreign-owned Companies	
Industry	**Average Yearly Salary**
Transportation Equipment Manufacturing	$69,557
Chemical Manufacturing	102,126
Machinery Manufacturing	80,239
Nonmetallic Mineral Manufacturing	63,555
Other Manufacturing	64,502

Globalization and the trade deficit. As U.S. companies outsource or move manufacturing plants across the border or overseas, the United States must import more goods. According to a February 24, 2000 statement made by Donald A. Manzullo, Chairman of the Committee on Small Business in the United States House of Representatives, "one estimate reveals that nearly 40 percent of all American imports are simply intra-company transactions by American multinational companies."[9] Therefore, with profits from imported goods going back to American companies, the trade deficit is not as large as originally thought. In June 2001, the Census Bureau reported that 47 percent of all U.S. imports in 2000 were related party imports. Related party imports, as defined by the Census Bureau, "includes [imports] by U.S. companies with their subsidiaries abroad as well as [imports] by U.S. subsidiaries of foreign companies with their parent companies."[10] That leaves the profits from the majority of imports, more than 53 percent, going to foreign-owned companies in 2000. In 2007, related party imports were 47 percent of all imports also. In 1992, the first year for which comparable data is available, related party imports comprised 45 percent of all imports.

The growing trade deficit is seen by some as a sign that the U.S. economy is strong. W. Michael Cox and Richard Alm of the Federal Reserve Bank of Dallas claim that big trade deficits, coupled with a large surplus in capital accounts (purchase and sale of stocks, bonds, and property) show that the United States is attractive to foreign investors. (See Figure 9). From 1982 to 1997, foreign investment in U.S. manufacturing lagged U.S. investment abroad. However, from 1998 to 2006, foreign investment in U.S. manufacturing far exceeded U.S. investment in manufacturing abroad. In 2006, foreign companies invested $90.2 billion more in the U.S. manufacturing sector than the United States invested

Figure 8. Average Salary of Employees at Foreign-owned Subsidiaries and U.S.-owned Manufacturing Companies, by Industry, 2005

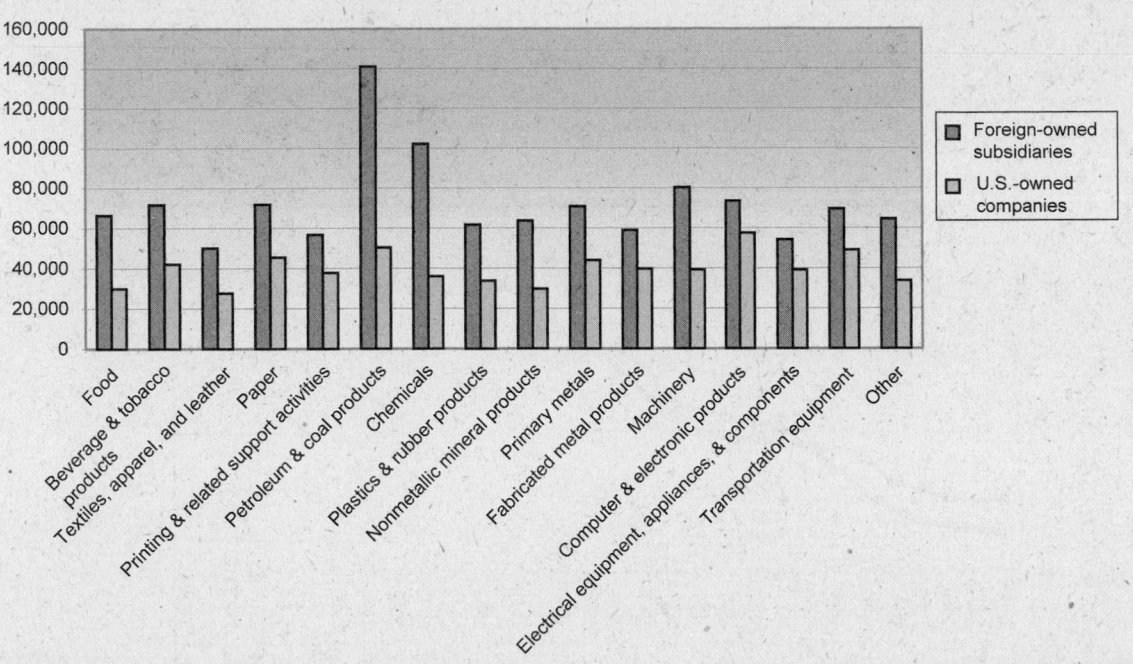

in the manufacturing sector abroad. However, as a percentage of total U.S. investment by foreign companies, manufacturing investment by foreign companies declined slightly from 35.3 percent in 1982 to 33.2 percent in 2006.

In comparison, U.S. investment in manufacturing abroad increased from more than $83 billion in 1982 to more than $503 billion in 2006. And, like foreign investment in U.S. manufacturing, U.S. manufacturing investment abroad as a percentage of total investment abroad declined. But this decline was more substantial, from 40.2 percent in 1982 to 21.1 percent in 2006. This decline signals an increase in investment into other sectors of foreign economies, most notably the Holding Companies (Nonbank) sector. By 2006, 29.8 percent of the U.S. investment dollars abroad went to this sector of foreign economies. The Finance and Insurance sector garnered 23.2 percent of the U.S. investment dollars abroad.

Those opposed to large trade deficits point to the loss of manufacturing jobs in the United States as a sign that the trade deficit and globalization are detrimental to the economy. However, total employment increased from 1982 to 2006 and the unemployment rate went from 9.7 in 1982 to 4.6 in 2006. Productivity also rose during this time period. Total corporate profits rose from $191.0 billion in 1982 to more than $1.8 trillion in 2006. Corporate profits in manufacturing rose from $67.1 billion in 1982 to $293.4 billion in 2006.

Opponents to globalization argue that the jobs that were created do not pay as well as the jobs that were lost. In a December 2006 editorial in the *Atlanta Journal-Constitution*, U.S. Senators Byron Dorgan and Sherrod Brown wrote that trade deficits, caused by unfair trade agreements, create "downward pressure on income and benefits for American workers."[11] Most often cited are jobs in the retail and service sector, such as the pay of retail sales personnel, of cashiers, and of waiters and waitresses. According to the U.S. Bureau

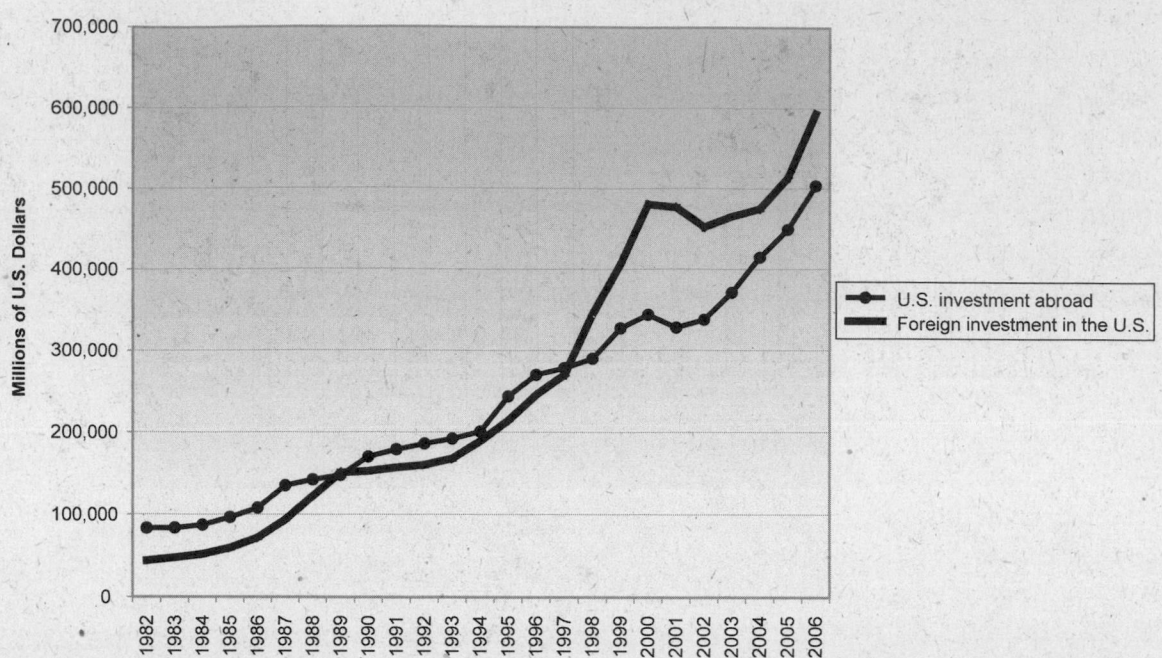

Figure 9. U.S. Investment in Manufacturing Abroad vs. Foreign Investment in Manufacturing in the U.S., 1982-2006

of Labor Statistics (BLS), in 2007, the median hourly wage for these workers ranged from $7.62 for waiters and waitresses up to $9.69 for retail sales persons. The median hourly wage for production workers was $13.53, half were paid more and half were paid less.

But, as Table 6 shows, not all jobs created were low paying. Many jobs created paid, on average, close to if not above the average hourly manufacturing wage. According to the BLS, from 1982 to 2007, the number of workers being paid at or below the Federal minimum wage dropped by 4.8 million. In 1982, almost 6.5 million workers (12.8 percent of hourly workers) were paid at or below the Federal minimum wage. Over the years, the Federal minimum wage failed to keep up with inflation and the number of workers earning at or below this wage dropped to 1.7 million in 2007 (2.3 percent of hourly workers).

Table 6. Change in Employment and Average Hourly Wages, by Economic Sector, 1982-2007

[Average hourly wages for manufacturing production workers was $17.26 in 2007]

Sector	Change in Employment, 1982-2007 (000)	Average Hourly Wage ($)		Hourly Wage Difference Between Current Sector and Manufacturing Sector, 2007
		1982	2007	
Education and health services	9,192.0	7.00	18.11	+0.85
Professional and business services	8,385.0	8.30	20.13	+2.87
Leisure and hospitality	5,927.0	4.63	10.41	-6.85
Retail trade	4,035.5	6.34	12.76	-4.50
Construction	2,661.0	11.04	20.95	+3.69
Financial activities	2,276.0	6.82	19.64	+2.38
Other services	2,117.0	6.11	15.42	-1.84
Transportation and warehousing	1,585.1	10.67	17.73	+0.47
Wholesale trade	1,199.2	8.81	19.59	+2.33
Information	837.0	10.76	23.94	+6.68

Buy American. In 1933, President Herbert Hoover signed the Buy American Act (BAA). The Act imposed restrictions on Federal government contracts. The Federal government was now obligated to buy products that were at least 50 percent manufactured in the United States. However, the Act exempted the Federal government if the government agency concerned determined American-made products "to be inconsistent with the public interest, or the cost to be unreasonable."[12] No clarification was given in the law as to what "inconsistent with the public interest" or "cost to be unreasonable" meant. Also, this law exempted government agencies from buying American products if the products would be used outside of the United States or if those American-made manufactured items would be unavailable "in sufficient and reasonably available commercial quantities and of a satisfactory quality."

Because of these exemptions, complying with the Buy American Act did not always result in the selection of American companies that employ a majority of American workers. Many American companies vying for government contracts, including Department of Defense contracts, have moved some or all of their manufacturing operations overseas. In response to this trend, U.S. Senator Russ Feingold of Wisconsin introduced the Buy American Improvement Act (BAIA) in 2003. A similar bill was introduced in the House of Representatives in 2004 by Ohio Representatives Sherrod Brown and Tim Ryan.

In an attempt to limit the Buy American Act waivers, the bill would require the U.S. Commerce Secretary to appoint a panel composed of industry, labor, and academic representatives in order to define "consistent with the public interest" and "cost to be unreasonable" as stated in the original 1933 bill. It would also increase the percentage of American made parts per product from 50 percent to 75 percent. U.S. companies would be granted preference for a government contract if their bids were comparable to foreign companies' bids or if they were the only U.S. company producing that particular product.

The BAIA would apply to Congress, the Legislative Branch, and U.S. agencies operating outside the U.S. (military bases, embassies, other government facilities), all of which were exempted from the BAA. Also under the BAIA, each agency must file an annual report with Congress providing an itemized list of BAA waivers and the dollar amount for each.

In a response to the findings in the Government Accountability Office (GAO) report *Federal Procurement: International Agreements Result in Waivers of Some U.S. Domestic Source Restrictions*, released January 2005, U.S. Senator Russ Feingold reintroduced the BAIA, renamed the Buy American Improvement Act of 2005. The GAO report found that "current trade agreements result in the waiver of the Buy American Act...for certain products from 45 countries.... [These] waivers...allow products from the countries involved to compete in a comparable manner [with U.S.-made products]."[13] On February 16, 2005, the Act was referred to the Committee on Homeland Security and Governmental Affairs.

In May 2005, U.S. Representative Donald A. Manzullo introduced a controversial amendment to the Homeland Security Authorization Act of 2006. The amendment, similar to the BAIA, would require "that more than 50 percent of the components in end products purchased by the Department of Homeland Security...be mined, produced or manufactured inside the U. S."[14] The amendment would also prevent waivers of the Buy American Act without approval of Congress. In a U.S. House of Representatives Press Release, Representative Manzullo declared: "when U.S. taxpayers' dollars are spent, we must make sure the federal government is buying as much of their goods and services as possible from U.S. manufacturers."[15]

The president of the Information Technology Association of America, Harris Miller, countered Representative Manzullo's statements by saying "... I guess (the department) will have to learn to do without computers and cell phones.... I cannot think of a single U.S. manufacturer that could meet this 50 percent threshold for these devices..." According to Miller, the amendment also would increase the government's cost and adversely affect global trade by opening up the possibility of other countries imposing trade restrictions on the United States.[16] U.S. Representative Tom Davis, in a statement opposing the amendment, expressed a similar viewpoint when he said "this restriction would have a devastating effect on the Department of Homeland Security's ability to buy the most high-tech and sophisticated products at a reasonable price to support our critical anti-terror efforts.... [T]his provision will require the Department to pay an artificially high price for products it needs to protect us against terror.... We should not be wasting our Homeland Security dollars...."[14]

In May 2005, the amendment passed in the United States House of Representatives. It was then attached to the Defense Department Reauthorization Act, in addition to becoming a part of the Department of Homeland Security Authorization Act. However, when these bills were passed by Congress they no longer contained the full amendment.

Senator Feingold again reintroduced the BAIA in February 2007. Ten months later, Congress approved a provision in the National Defense Authorization Act for Fiscal Year 2008 that relaxed the Buy American Act's "restrictions regulating the amount of domestic metal content in the U.S. military's weapons systems."[17] The bill became law on January 28, 2008.

Taking advantage of the exemption in the Buy American Act that allows companies from allied countries to be treated the same as companies from the United States, the U.S. Defense Department awarded a $35 billion contract to Northrop Grumman, based in Los Angeles, California, and Airbus, headquartered in Toulouse, France, to build a fleet of midair refueling tankers in March 2008. Boeing Co. of Chicago, Illinois also submitted a proposal to build the fleet, using Pratt & Whitney engines. Pratt & Whitney is headquartered in East Hartford, Connecticut. Shortly thereafter, U.S. Representative Todd Tiart started an online petition to overturn the contract, collecting more than 73,000 signatures by mid-April. U.S. Representative John Murtha, chairman of the House Defense Appropriations Subcommittee, stated that he would stop funding for the contract and Representative Duncan Hunter planned to reintroduce a bill that would prohibit the Defense Department from awarding contracts to companies that receive foreign subsidies. As for revising the Buy American Act legislation, Representative Murtha "doubted there was support for [it]."[18]

In response to Boeing's protest of the contract, the Government Accountability Office (GAO) issued a nonbinding ruling in June 2008 that stated "the Air Force had made a number of significant errors that could have affected the outcome of what was a close competition between Boeing and Northrop Grumman."[19] None of these errors, however, were related to violations of the Buy American Act. The GAO recommended the Air Force reopen the bidding process with a new decision based on the GAO's ruling.

[1] 1987-2006 data are based on the North American Industrial Classification System. Prior data are based on the Standard Industrial Classification; therefore, 1982-1986 data are not comparable to later data and are not included with the aggregate productivity statistics.

[2] *Source:* "The World Trade Organization In Brief," World Trade Organization, Geneva, Switzerland, 2007 [Online] http://www.wto.org/english/res_e/doload_e/inbr_e.pdf [accessed June 3, 2008]

[3] The import averages for 1992 to the year of entry into the WTO do not include Cambodia. In 1992, goods imported from Cambodia into the United States totalled $100,000. In 2004, when Cambodia entered the WTO, imports from Cambodia totalled nearly $1.5 billion, a total increase of 1,497,300 percent or an average increase of 115,176.9 percent per year.

[4] *Source:* "Trade Adjustment Assistance Reform Act of 2002: Free Trade Agreement and Trade Beneficiary Countries," U.S. Department of Labor, Employment & Training Administration, Washington, DC, March 27, 2004, updated January 9, 2008 [Online] http://www.doleta.gov/tradeact/2002act_freetradeagreements.cfm [accessed June 3, 2008]

[5] *Sources:* Bacon, David, "More Poverty as NAFTA Turns 10," Organic Consumers Association, Finland, MN, January 19, 2004, reprint of article in the *San Francisco Monitor*, January 14, 2004 [Online] http://www.organicconsumers.org/corp/nafta011904.cfm [accessed February 5, 2004]; Ross, John "NAFTA and Mexico's Agrarian Apocalypse Zero Hour," Organic Consumers Association, Finland, MN, reprint of article in *Counterpunch*, January 15, 2008 [Online] http://www.organicconsumers.org/articles/article_9730.cfm [accessed May 22, 2008]; "Mexico Raises Minimum Wages by 4 Percent, to Around US$4.85 (€3.37) a Day," Associated Press, *International Herald Tribune*, December 22, 2007 [Online] http://www.iht.com/articles/ap/2007/12/22/business/LA-FIN-Mexico-Minimum-Wage.php [accessed May 22, 2008] and "Table 1. Hourly Compensation Costs for Production Workers in Maquiladora Manufacturing, 1975-2006, U.S. Dollars," U.S. Department of Labor, Bureau of Labor Statistics, May 2008 [Online] ftp://ftp.bls.gov/pub/special.requests/ForeignLabor/pwusdmexmaq.txt [accessed May 30, 2008]

[6] *Source:* Roberts, Dexter "How Rising Wages Are Changing The Game in China," *BusinessWeek Online*, March 27, 2006 [Online] http://www.businessweek.com/magazine/content/06_13/b3977049.htm [accessed May 25, 2006]

[7] *Source:* Murray, Charles J., "Experts Say Outsourcing is Still Strong," *Design News*, September 25, 2007 [Online] http://www.designnews.com/index.asp?layout=article&articleID=CA6482762&industryid=43656 [accessed June 4, 2008]

[8] *Source:* Eck, Brittany, "Department of Commerce Announces Inaugural 'Invest in America' Week," U.S. Department of Commerce, International Trade Administration, Washington, DC, May 5, 2008 [Online] http://www.ita.doc.gov/press/press_releases/2008/invest-in-america_050508.asp [accessed May 23, 2008]

[9] *Source:* Manzullo, Donald A. and Carolyn McCarthy, "Remarks of the Honorable Donald A. Manzullo Before the Trade Deficit Review Commission," U.S. House of Representatives, Washington, DC, February 24, 2000 [Online] http://www.ustdrc.gov/hearings/24feb00/smanzullo.pdf [accessed February 4, 2004]

[10] *Source:* "U.S. Goods Trade: Imports & Exports by Related Parties: 2000," *United States Department of Commerce News,* Economics and Statistics Administration, U.S. Census Bureau, Washington, DC, June 26, 2001 [Online] http://www.census.gov/foreign-trade/Press-Release/2000pr/aip/related-party.html [accessed May 26, 2006]

[11] *Source:* Dorgan, Byron and Sherrod Brown, "Reform Trade Policies: U.S. Workers Robbed. (Editorial)." *The Atlanta Journal Constitution,* December 27, 2006, p. A13, *Infotrac Custom Newspapers,* Gale, Gale Cengage Learning Trial Site [Online] http://find.galegroup.com/ips/start.do?prodId=IPS [accessed May 30, 2008]

[12] *Source*: "§10a. American materials required for public use," *U.S. Code Collection,* Legal Information Institute, Cornell University Law School, Ithaca, NY [Online] http://www.law.cornell.edu/uscode/41/usc_sec_41_00000010---a000-.html [accessed June 6, 2008]

[13] *Source: Federal Procurement: International Agreements Result in Waivers of Some U.S. Domestic Source Restrictions,* GAO-05-188, United States Government Accountability Office, Washington, DC, January 2005 [Online] http://www.gao.gov/ htext/d05188.html [accessed May 30, 2006]

[14] *Source:* "Department of Homeland Security Authorization Act For Fiscal Year 2006 – (House of Representatives - May 18, 2005)," *Congressional Record for the 109th Congress – House,* U.S. Government Printing Office, Washington, DC, May 18, 2005 [Online] http://thomas.loc.gov/cgi-bin/query/C?r109:./temp/~r109pnNSvu [accessed June 10, 2008]

[15] *Source:* "U.S. House Approves Manzullo Amendment to Require Department of Homeland Security to Buy American," *Press Release,* U.S. House of Representatives, Washington, DC, May 18, 2005 [Online] http://manzullo.house.gov/News/DocumentSingle.aspx?DocumentID=55428 [accessed June 6, 2008]

[16] *Source:* Frauenheim, Ed, "'Buy American' Legislation Draws Fire," *CNET News.com,* May 20, 2005 [Online] http://news.cnet.com/Buy+American+legislation+draws+fire/2100-1022_3-5715486.html [accessed May 30, 2006]

[17] *Source*: Scully, Megan, "Congress Quietly Revises 'Buy America' Rule for Defense Materials," *Government Executive.com,* December 17, 2007 [Online] http://www.govexec.com/story_page_pf.cfm?articleid=38856 [accessed May 29, 2008]

[18] *Source*: Brodsky, Robert, "NEWS+ANALYSIS Buy American...Or Else," *Government Executive.com,* May 1, 2008 [Online] http://www.govexec.com/story_page_pf.cfm?articleid=39897 [accessed May 29, 2008]

[19] *Source:* Golden, Michael R., "GAO Sustains Boeing Bid Protest," *Press Release*, United States Government Accountability Office, Washington, DC, June 18, 2008 [Online] http://www.gao.gov/press/press_boeing2008jun18_3.pdf [accessed June 19, 2008]

Graphics Sources

Figure 1: Adapted from "Value Added by Industry as a Percentage of Gross Domestic Product 1947-2007," *Gross Domestic Product by Industry Accounts,* U.S. Department of Commerce, Bureau of Economic Analysis, Washington, DC, April 29, 2008 [Online] http://www.bea.gov/industry/gpotables/gpo_list.cfm?anon=71311&registered=0 [accessed June 2, 2008]

Figure 2, Table 1, Table 2, Figure 4, Figure 6: Adapted from "Table 1. Statistics for All Manufacturing Establishments: 2005 and Earlier Years," *Annual Survey of Manufactures*, U.S. Census Bureau, Washington, DC, November 2006 and "Sector 31: Annual Survey of Manufactures: General Statistics: Statistics for Industry Groups and Industries: 2006 and 2005," *Annual Survey of Manufactures,* U.S. Census Bureau, Washington, DC, December 31, 2006 [Online] http://factfinder.census.gov/servlet/IBQTable?_bm=y&ds_name=AM0631GS101 [accessed December 3, 2007]

Figure 3, Table 3: Adapted from *1982, 1987, 1992, 1997,* and *2002 Economic Census* and *Annual Survey of Manufactures*, U.S. Census Bureau, Washington, DC, various publication dates; "Average Weekly Earnings of Production Workers, Total Private: Not Seasonally Adjusted," *Employment, Hours, and Earnings from the Current Employment Statistics Survey (National),* U.S. Department of Labor, Bureau of Labor Statistics, Washington, DC [Online] http://www.bls.gov/ces/home.htm [accessed June 2, 2008]; "Historical Income Tables — People," U.S. Census Bureau, Washington DC, [Online] http://www.census.gov/hhes/www/income/histinc/p04.html [accessed June 13, 2008]

Figure 5: Adapted from "Table 1. Statistics for All Manufacturing Establishments: 2005 and Earlier Years," *Annual Survey of Manufactures*, U.S. Census Bureau, Washington, DC, November 2006; "Sector 31: Annual Survey of Manufactures: General Statistics: Statistics for Industry Groups and Industries: 2006 and 2005," *Annual Survey of Manufactures,* U.S. Census Bureau, Washington, DC, December 31, 2006 [Online] http://factfinder.census.gov/servlet/IBQTable?_bm=y&ds_name=AM0631GS101 [accessed December 31, 2007] and "Major Sector Productivity and Cost Index, 1987-2007," Series ID: PRS30006093, U.S. Department of Labor, Bureau of Labor Statistics, Washington, DC [Online] http://www.bls.gov/lpc/home.htm#tables [accessed February 20, 2008]

Table 4: Adapted from "U.S. Trade in Goods (Imports, Exports and Balance) by Country," *Foreign Trade Statistics*, U.S. Census Bureau, Washington, DC, May 9, 2008 [Online] http://www.census.gov/foreign-trade/balance/index.html [accessed May 19, 2008]; "Members and Observers," *Understanding the WTO: The Organization*, World Trade Organization, Geneva, Switzerland [Online] http://www.wto.org/english/thewto_e/whatis_e/tif_e/org6_e.htm [accessed May 19, 2008] and "NAFTA and GATT Intellectual Property Issues," *Ladas & Perry Bulletin*, December 2004, revised April 23, 1996 [Online] http://www.ladas.com/BULLETINS/1994/NAFTAGATT.html [accessed June 2, 2006]

Figure 7: Adapted from "Trade in Goods (Imports, Exports and Trade Balance) with China," "Trade in Goods (Imports, Exports and Trade Balance) with Canada," "Trade in Goods (Imports, Exports and Trade Balance) with Japan," "Trade in Goods (Imports, Exports and Trade Balance) with Germany," "Trade in Goods (Imports, Exports and Trade Balance) with Mexico," and "Trade in Goods (Imports, Exports and Trade Balance) with Nigeria," *Foreign Trade Statistics,* U.S. Census Bureau, Washington, DC, May 9, 2008 [Online] http://www.census.gov/foreign-trade/balance/ [accessed May 19, 2008]

Table 5, Figure 8: Adapted from "Sector 31: Annual Survey of Manufactures: General Statistics: Statistics for Industry Groups and Industries: 2006 and 2005," *2006 Annual Survey of Manufactures*, U.S. Census Bureau, Washington, DC, December 31, 2006 [Online] http://factfinder.census.gov/servlet/IBQTable?_bm=y&ds_name=AM0631GS101 [accessed December 3, 2007] and "Majority-Owned U.S. Affiliates: Selected Data by Industry 1999-2005," *Foreign Direct Investment in the U.S.: Financial and Operating Data for U.S. Affiliates of Foreign Multinational Companies*, Bureau of Economic Analysis, International Economic Accounts, Washington, DC [Online] http://www.bea.gov/international/di1fdiop.htm [accessed May 27, 2008]

Figure 9: Adapted from "U.S. Direct Investment Abroad: Balance of Payments and Direct Investment Position Data: Historical Data," *International Economic Accounts,* U.S. Department of Commerce, Bureau of Economic Analysis, Washington, DC, March 27, 2006 [Online] http://www.bea.doc.gov/bea/di/di1usdbal.htm [accessed May 25, 2006]; "Foreign Direct Investment in the US: Balance of Payments and Direct Investment Position Data: Historical Data," *International Economic Accounts,* U.S. Department of Commerce, Bureau of Economic Analysis, Washington, DC, March 27, 2006 [Online] http://www.bea.doc.gov/bea/di/di1fdibal.htm [accessed May 25, 2006]; "U.S. Direct Investment Abroad, U.S. Direct Investment Position Abroad on a Historical-Cost Basis, 1999-2006" and "Foreign Direct Investment in the U.S., Foreign Direct Investment Position in the United States on a Historical-Cost Basis," *International Economic Accounts,* U.S. Department of Commerce, Bureau of Economic Analysis, Washington, DC, April 8, 2008 [Online] http://www.bea.gov/international/index.html [accessed May 22, 2008]

Table 6: "Table B-1. Employees on nonfarm payrolls by major industry sector, 1958 to date," *Employment, Hours, and Earnings from the Current Employment Statistics Survey (National),* U.S. Department of Labor, Bureau of Labor Statistics, Washington, DC [Online] ftp://ftp.bls.gov/pub/suppl/empsit.ceseeb1.txt [accessed May 23, 2008]

Annotated Source List

"§10a. American materials required for public use," *U.S. Code Collection,* Legal Information Institute, Cornell University Law School, Ithaca, NY [Online] http://www.law.cornell.edu/uscode/41/usc_sec_41_00000010---a000-.html [accessed June 6, 2008]

"1. Employment status of the civilian noninstitutional population, 1940 to date," *Current Population Survey,* U.S. Department of Labor, Bureau of Labor Statistics, Washington, DC [Online] http://www.bls.gov/cps/cpsaat1.pdf [accessed January 7, 2008]

1982, 1987, 1992, 1997, and *2002 Economic Census,* U.S. Census Bureau, Washington, DC, various publication dates

Annual Survey of Manufactures, U.S. Census Bureau, Washington, DC, various publication dates

"Average Hourly Earnings of Production Workers: Not Seasonally Adjusted," *Employment, Hours, and Earnings from the Current Employment Statistics Survey (National),* U.S. Department of Labor, Bureau of Labor Statistics, Washington, DC [Online] http://www.bls.gov/ces/home.htm [accessed May 23, 2008]

"Average Weekly Earnings of Production Workers, Total Private: Not Seasonally Adjusted," *Employment, Hours, and Earnings from the Current Employment Statistics Survey (National),* U.S. Department of Labor, Bureau of Labor Statistics, Washington, DC [Online] http://www.bls.gov/ces/home.htm [accessed June 2, 2008]

"Background Note: Japan," U.S. Department of State, Bureau of East Asian and Pacific Affairs, Washington, DC, March 2008 [Online] http://www.state.gov/r/pa/ei/bgn/4142.htm [accessed June 4, 2008]

"Background Note: Malta," U.S. Department of State, Bureau of European and Eurasian Affairs, Washington, DC, November 2007 [Online] http://www.state.gov/r/pa/ei/bgn/ 5382.htm [accessed June 4, 2008]

Bacon, David, "More Poverty as NAFTA Turns 10," Organic Consumers Association, Little Marais, MN, January 19, 2004, reprint of article in the *San Francisco Monitor*, January 14, 2004 [Online] http://www.organicconsumers.org/corp/nafta011904.cfm [accessed February 5, 2004]

Bartlett, Bruce, "Trade Issues: Trade Deficit Reflects Strength of U.S. Economy," National Center or Policy Analysis, Dallas, TX, December 27, 1999 [Online] http://www,ncpa.org/ pd/trade/pd122899a.html [accessed June 5, 2008]

Brodsky, Robert, "NEWS+ANALYSIS Buy American...Or Else," *Government Executive.com*, May 1, 2008 [Online] http://www.govexec.com/story_page_pf.cfm?article id=39897 [accessed May 29, 2008]

"'Buy America' Activity Begins," National Defense Industrial Association, Arlington, VA, February 13, 2004 [Online] http://www.ndia.org/Content/NavigationMenu/Advocacy/ Action_Items/BAIA_04.htm [accessed June 6, 2008]

"Congressional Record Statement of Russ Feingold on the Buy American Improvement Act," February 16, 2005 [Online] http://feingold.senate.gov/statements/05/02/ 2005414B05.html [accessed May 30, 2006]

County Business Patterns, U.S. Census Bureau, Washington, DC, various publication dates

"Current-Dollar and 'Real' Gross Domestic Product," *National Economic Accounts*, U.S. Department of Commerce, Bureau of Economic Analysis, Washington, DC [Online] http://www.bea.gov/national/index.htm#gdp [accessed October 15, 2007]

DeLong, Chris, et. al., "NAFTA and Jobs: Remember the 'Giant Sucking Sound?'" [Online] http://www.j-bradford-delong.net/OpEd/naftaandjobs.html [accessed June 3, 2008]

"Department of Homeland Security Authorization Act For Fiscal Year 2006 – (House of Representatives - May 18, 2005)," *Congressional Record for the 109th Congress – House,* Government Printing Office, Washington, DC, May 18, 2005 [Online] http: //thomas.loc.gov/cgi-bin/query/C?r109:./temp/~r109pnNSvu [accessed June 10, 2008]

Dorgan, Byron and Sherrod Brown, "Reform Trade Policies: U.S. Workers Robbed. (Editorial)." *The Atlanta Journal Constitution,* December 27, 2006, p. A13, *Infotrac Custom Newspapers,* Gale, Gale Cengage Learning Trial Site [Online] http://find.galegroup.com/ ips/start.do?prodId=IPS [accessed May 30, 2008]

Eck, Brittany, "Department of Commerce Announces Inaugural 'Invest in America' Week," U.S. Department of Commerce, International Trade Administration, Washington, DC, May 5, 2008 [Online] http://www.ita.doc.gov/press/press_releases/2008/invest-in-america_050508.asp [accessed May 23, 2008]

"Exhibit 5. U.S. Trade in Goods," *FT900: U.S. International Trade in Goods and Services Current Release: March 2008,* U.S. Census Bureau, Bureau of Economic Analysis, Washington, DC, May 9, 2008 [Online] http://www.census.gov/foreign-trade/Press-Release/current_press_release/exh5.pdf [accessed May 20, 2008]

"Extended Mass Layoffs in the First Quarter of 2008," *News*, U.S. Department of Labor, Bureau of Labor Statistics, Washington, DC, May 15, 2008 [Online] http://www.bls.gov/news.release/archives/mslo_05152008.pdf [accessed May 30, 2008]

Federal Procurement: International Agreements Result in Waivers of Some U.S. Domestic Source Restrictions, GAO-05-188, United States Government Accountability Office, Washington, DC, January 2005 [Online] http://www.gao.gov/htext/d05188.html [accessed May 30, 2006]

"Feingold Urges Feds to 'Buy American'," *Small Business Times,* February 15, 2007 [Online] http://www.biztimes.com/daily/2007/2/15/feingold-urges-feds-to-buy-american [accessed May 29, 2008]

"Foreign Direct Investment in the US: Balance of Payments and Direct Investment Position Data: Historical Data," *International Economic Accounts,* U.S. Department of Commerce, Bureau of Economic Analysis, Washington, DC, March 27, 2006 [Online] http://www.bea.doc.gov/bea/di/di1fdibal.htm [accessed May 25, 2006]

"Foreign Direct Investment in the U.S., Foreign Direct Investment Position in the United States on a Historical-Cost Basis," *International Economic Accounts,* U.S. Department of Commerce, Bureau of Economic Analysis, Washington, DC, April 8, 2008 [Online] http://www.bea.gov/international/index.html [accessed May 22, 2008]

Frauenheim, Ed, "'Buy American' legislation draws fire," *CNET News.com,* May 20, 2005 [Online] http://news.com.com/Buy+American+legislation+draws+fire/2100-1022_3-5715486.html [accessed May 30, 2006]

"From Fortress Economy to Open Market, Foreign Companies Have Made Malta Their Home," *The Washington Times,* July 10-14, 2000 [Online] http://www.internationalspecial reports.com/archives/00/malta2000/6.htm [accessed June 4, 2008]

Golden, Michael R., "GAO Sustains Boeing Bid Protest," *Press Release*, United States Government Accountability Office, Washington, DC, June 18, 2008 [Online] http://www.gao.gov/press/press_boeing2008jun18_3.pdf [accessed June 19, 2008]

"Historical Income Tables — People," U.S. Census Bureau, Washington DC, [Online] http://www.census.gov/hhes/www/income/histinc/p04.html [accessed June 13, 2008]

"HS Total All Merchandise — 2007 Balance with Central Am.-Dominican Rep. Free Trade Agreement (CAFTA-DR)," *Trade Stats Express — National Trade Data* [Online] http://tse.export.gov/NTDChartPP.aspx?UniqueURL=qekz0seo2obod4e5vmihmnu-2008-5-19-9-8-26 [accessed May 19, 2008]

"HS Total All Merchandise — 2007 Balance with N. American Free Trade Agreement," *Trade Stats Express — National Trade Data* [Online] http://tse.export.gov/NTDChartPP.aspx?UniqueURL=vwmjtrbuaztpua55nzvc4hnk-2008-5-19-10-22-47 [accessed May 19, 2008]

International Trade Statistics 2007, World Trade Organization, Geneva, Switzerland, 2007 [Online] http://www.wto.org/english/res_e/statis_e/its2007_e/its07_toc_e.htm [accessed May 19, 2008]

"Japan Foreign Investment Incentives" [Online] http://www.worldwide-tax.com/japan/jap_invest.asp [accessed June 4, 2008]

Manzullo, Donald A. and Carolyn McCarthy, "Remarks of the Honorable Donald A. Manzullo Before the Trade Deficit Review Commission," U.S. House of Representatives, Washington, DC, February 24, 2000 [Online] http://www.ustdrc.gov/hearings/24feb00/smanzullo.pdf [accessed February 4, 2004]

"Major Sector Productivity and Cost Index, 1987-2007," Series ID: PRS30006093, U.S. Department of Labor, Bureau of Labor Statistics, Washington, DC [Online] http://www.bls.gov/lpc/home.htm#tables [accessed February 20, 2008]

"Majority-Owned U.S. Affiliates: Selected Data by Industry 1999-2005," *Foreign Direct Investment in the U.S.: Financial and Operating Data for U.S. Affiliates of Foreign Multinational Companies*, Bureau of Economic Analysis, International Economic Accounts, Washington, DC [Online] http://www.bea.gov/international/di1fdiop.htm [accessed May 27, 2008]

May 2007 National Occupational Employment and Wage Estimates: United States, U.S. Department of Labor, Bureau of Labor Statistics, Washington, DC, May 12, 2008 [Online] http://www.bls.gov/oes/current/oes_nat.htm [accessed May 23, 2008]

"Members and Observers," *Understanding the WTO: The Organization*, World Trade Organization, Geneva, Switzerland [Online] http://www.wto.org/english/thewto_e/whatis_e/tif_e/org6_e.htm [accessed May 19, 2008]

"Mexico Raises Minimum Wages by 4 Percent, to Around US$4.85 (€3.37) a Day," Associated Press, *International Herald Tribune*, December 22, 2007 [Online] http://www.iht.com/articles/ap/2007/12/22/business/LA-FIN-Mexico-Minimum-Wage.php [accessed May 22, 2008]

Morrissey, Jane, "Software Makers Flock to Ireland Lured by Generous Incentives," *PCWeek*, March 9, 1992, p. 152, *General OneFile*, Gale, Public Trial Site [Online] http://find.galegroup.com/ips/start.do?prodId=IPS [accessed June 4, 2008]

Murray, Charles J., "Experts Say Outsourcing is Still Strong," *Design News*, September 25, 2007 [Online] http://www.designnews.com/index.asp?layout=article&articleID=CA6 482762&industryid=43656 [accessed June 4, 2008]

"NAFTA and GATT Intellectual Property Issues," *Ladas & Perry Bulletin*, December 2004, revised April 23, 1996 [Online] http://www.ladas.com/BULLETINS/1994/ NAFTAGATT.html [accessed June 2, 2006]

"NAFTA-Transitional Adjustment Assistance," U.S. Department of Labor, Employment & Training Administration, Washington, DC, April 11, 2004 [Online] http://www.dolets.gov/ programs/factsht/nafta.cfm [accessed June 3, 2008]

"NAFTA-Transitional Adjustment Assistance (1994-2002)," Public Citizen, Washington, DC [Online] http://www.citizen.org/trade/forms/taa_search.cfm?dataset=1 [accessed February 4, 2004]

National Defense Authorization Act for Fiscal Year 2008, Public Law 110-181- Jan. 28, 2008, U.S. Government Printing Office, Washington, DC [Online] http:// frwebgate.access.gpo.gov/cgi-bin/getdoc.cgi?dbname=110_cong_public_laws&docid=f: publ181.110.pdf [accessed June 6, 2008]

Porteus, Liza, "'Buy American' Provisions Return for More Congressional Debate," *FoxNews.com*, June 5, 2005 [Online] http://www.foxnews.com/story/ 0,2933,158462,00.html [accessed May 30, 2005]

"Production Workers, Thousands: Not Seasonally Adjusted," *Employment, Hours, and Earnings from the Current Employment Statistics Survey (National)*, U.S. Department of Labor, Bureau of Labor Statistics, Washington, DC [Online] http://www.bls.gov/ces/ home.htm [accessed May 23, 2008]

Roberts, Dexter, "How Rising Wages Are Changing The Game in China," *BusinessWeek Online*, March 27, 2006 [Online] http://www.businessweek.com/magazine/content/06_13/ b3977049.htm [accessed May 25, 2006]

Ross, John "NAFTA and Mexico's Agrarian Apocalypse Zero Hour," Organic Consumers Association, Finland, MN, reprint of article in *Counterpunch*, January 15, 2008 [Online] http://www.organicconsumers.org/articles/article_9730.cfm [accessed May 22, 2008]

Scully, Megan, "Congress Quietly Revises 'Buy America' Rule for Defense Materials," *Government Executive.com*, December 17, 2007 [Online] http://www.govexec.com/story_ page_pf.cfm?articleid=38856 [accessed May 29, 2008]

"Table 1. Educational Attainment of the Population 18 Years and Over, by Age, Sex, Race, and Hispanic Origin: 2006," *Current Population Survey, 2006 Annual Social and Economic Supplement*, U.S. Census Bureau, Washington, DC, March 15, 2007 [Online] http://www.census.gov/population/socdemo/education/cps2006/tab01-01.xls [accessed February 12, 2008]

"Table 1. Hourly Compensation Costs for Production Workers in Maquiladora Manufacturing, 1975-2006, U.S. Dollars," U.S. Department of Labor, Bureau of Labor Statistics, May 2008 [Online] ftp://ftp.bls.gov/pub/special.requests/ForeignLabor/pwusdmexmaq.txt [accessed May 30, 2008]

"Table 10. Employed wage and salary workers paid hourly rates with earnings at or below the prevailing Federal minimum wage by sex, 1979-2007 annual averages," *Characteristics of Minimum Wage Workers: 2007*, U.S. Department of Labor, Bureau of Labor Statistics, Washington, DC [Online] http://www.bls.gov/cps/minwage2007tbls.htm#10 [accessed May 23, 2008]

"Table B-1. Employees on nonfarm payrolls by major industry sector, 1958 to date," *Employment, Hours, and Earnings from the Current Employment Statistics Survey (National)*, U.S. Department of Labor, Bureau of Labor Statistics, Washington, DC [Online] ftp://ftp.bls.gov/pub/suppl/empsit.ceseeb1.txt [accessed May 23, 2008]

"Table B-6. Chain-type quantity indexes for gross domestic product, 1959-2007," *Economic Report of the President: 2008*, U.S. Government Printing Office, Washington, DC, February 11, 2008 [Online] http://www.gpoaccess.gov/eop/2008/B6.xls [accessed February 20, 2008]

"Table B-91. Corporate profits by industry, 1959-2007," *Economic Report of the President: 2008*, U.S. Government Printing Office, Washington, DC, February 11, 2008 [Online] http://www.gpoaccess.gov/eop/2008/B91.xls [accessed June 6, 2008]

"Table B-103. U.S. international transactions, 1946-2007," *Economic Report of the President: 2008*, U.S. Government Printing Office, Washington, DC, February 11, 2008 [Online] http://www.gpoaccess.gov/eop/2008/B103.xls [accessed May 20, 2008]

"Total Merchandise Trade, 1948-2007," *World Trade Organization Statistics Database*, World Trade Organization, Geneva, Switzerland [Online] http://stat.wto.org/StatisticalProgram/WSDBViewData.aspx?Language=E [accessed June 3, 2008]

"Trade Adjustment Assistance Reform Act of 2002: Free Trade Agreement and Trade Beneficiary Countries," U.S. Department of Labor, Employment & Training Administration, Washington, DC, March 27, 2004, updated January 9, 2008 [Online] http://www.doleta.gov/tradeact/2002act_freetradeagreements.cfm [accessed June 3, 2008]

"Trade Adjustment Assistance (TAA) and Alternative Trade Adjustment Assistance (ATAA) Services and Benefits," U.S. Department of Labor, Employment & Training Administration, Washington, DC, March 27, 2004, updated July 20, 2007 [Online] http://www.doleta.gov/tradeact/benefits.cfm [accessed June 3, 2008]

"Trade Adjustment Assistance (TAA) Estimated Number of Workers Covered by Certifications," U.S. Department of Labor, Employment & Training Administration, Washington, DC [Online] http://www.doleta.gov/tradeact/taa_certs.cfm [accessed May 20, 2008]

"Trade Deficit Explained," National Center for Policy Analysis, Dallas, TX, 2001 [Online] http://www.ncpa.org/pd/trade/tradea4.html [accessed February 6, 2004]

"(Unadj) Employment Level," *Current Population Survey*, Series ID: LNU02000000, U.S. Department of Labor, Bureau of Labor Statistics, Washington, DC [Online] http://www.bls.gov/ces/home.htm [accessed May 23, 2008]

"(Unadj) Unemployment Rate," *Current Population Survey*, Series ID: LNU04000000, U.S. Department of Labor, Bureau of Labor Statistics, Washington, DC [Online] http://www.bls.gov/ces/home.htm [accessed May 23, 2008]

United States, Cong. House of Representatives, 108th Congress, 2nd Session, *H.R. 3741 Buy American Improvement Act of 2004*, Congressional Bills, GPO Access [Online] http://www.gpoaccess.gov/bills/index.html [accessed June 6, 2008]

United States, Cong. House of Representatives, 109th Congress, 1st Session, *H.R. 2360 An Act Making Appropriations for the Department of Homeland Security for the Fiscal Year Ending September 30, 2006, and for Other Purposes,* Congressional Bills, GPO Access [Online] http://www.gpoaccess.gov/bills/index.html [accessed June 13, 2006]

United States, Cong. House of Representatives, 109th Congress, 1st Session, *H.R. 2863 An Act Making Appropriations for the Department of Defense for the Fiscal Year Ending September 30, 2006, and for Other Purposes,* Congressional Bills, GPO Access [Online] http://www.gpoaccess.gov/bills/index.html [accessed June 13, 2006]

United States, Cong. Senate, 108th Congress, 1st Session, *S. 1480 Buy American Improvement Act of 2003,* Congressional Bills, GPO Access [Online] http://www.gpoaccess.gov/ bills/index.html [accessed June 6, 2008]

United States, Cong. Senate, 109th Congress, 1st Session, *S. 395 A Bill to Amend the Buy American Act to Increase the Requirement for American-made Content, to Tighten the Waiver Provisions, and for Other Purposes* [introduced in the Senate February 16, 2005], Congressional Bills, GPO Access [Online] http://www.gpoaccess.gov/bills/index.html [accessed May 30, 2006]

"U.S.-CAFTA-DR Free Trade Agreement: How Can U.S. Companies Benefit?" *Export.gov* [Online] http://www.export.gov/fta/CAFTA/ [accessed May 19, 2008]

"U.S. Direct Investment Abroad: Balance of Payments and Direct Investment Position Data: Historical Data," *International Economic Accounts,* U.S. Department of Commerce, Bureau of Economic Analysis, Washington, DC, March 27, 2006 [Online] http://www.bea.doc.gov/bea/di/di1usdbal.htm [accessed May 25, 2006]

"U.S. Direct Investment Abroad, U.S. Direct Investment Position Abroad on a Historical-Cost Basis, 1999-2006," *International Economic Accounts,* U.S. Department of Commerce, Bureau of Economic Analysis, Washington, DC, April 8, 2008 [Online] http://www.bea.gov/international/index.html [accessed May 22, 2008]

"U.S. Direct Investment Abroad, U.S. Direct Investment Position Abroad on a Historical-Cost Basis, by Industry of Affiliate Only (All Industries) (NAICS) for (1999, 2000, 2001, 2002, 2003, 2004, 2005, 2006)," *International Economic Accounts,* U.S. Department of Commerce, Bureau of Economic Analysis, Washington, DC, March 13, 2008 [Online] http://www.bea.gov/international/ii_web/timeseries7_2.cfm [accessed May 22, 2008]

"U.S. Goods Trade: Imports & Exports by Related Parties: 2000," *United States Department of Commerce News,* June 26, 2001 [Online] http://www.census.gov/foreign-trade/Press-Release/2000pr/aip/related-party.html [accessed May 26, 2006]

"U.S. Goods Trade: Imports & Exports by Related Parties: 2007," *U.S. Census Bureau News,* May 9, 2008 [Online] http://www.census.gov/foreign-trade/Press-Release/2007pr/aip/related_party/rp07-text.pdf [accessed May 23, 2008]

"U.S. House Approves Manzullo Amendment to Require Department of Homeland Security to Buy American," *Press Release,* U.S. House of Representatives, Washington, DC, May 18, 2005 [Online] http://manzullo.house.gov/News/DocumentSingle.aspx?DocumentID=55428 [accessed June 6, 2008]

"U.S. Manufacturers Decrease Overseas Investment," *Newsdesk,* Society of Manufacturing Engineers, Dearborn, MI, May 25, 2004 [Online] http://www.sme.org/cgi-bin/get-press.pl?&&20041131&ND&&SME& [accessed June 4, 2008]

"U.S. Senator Russ Feingold on the Buy American Act," *Russ Feingold Speech*, July 29, 2003 [Online] http://feingold.senate.gov/speeches/03/07/2003820902.html [accessed February 10, 2004]

"U.S. Trade in Goods (Imports, Exports and Balance) by Country," *Foreign Trade Statistics,* U.S. Census Bureau, Washington, DC, May 9, 2008 [Online] http://www.census.gov/foreign-trade/balance/index.html [accessed May 19, 2008]

"Value Added by Industry, 1947-2007," *Gross Domestic Product by Industry Accounts*, U.S. Department of Commerce, Bureau of Economic Analysis, Washington, DC, April 29, 2008 [Online] http://www.bea.gov/industry/gpotables/gpo_list.cfm?anon=71311&registered = 0 [accessed June 2, 2008]

"Wages: Minimum Wage," U.S. Department of Labor, Washington, DC [Online] http://www.dol.gov/dol/topic/wages/minimumwage.htm [accessed May 22, 2008]

"The World Trade Organization In Brief," World Trade Organization, Geneva, Switzerland [Online] http://www.wto.org/english/res_e/doload_e/inbr_e.pdf [accessed June 3, 2008]

Youtie, Jan, et. al., *Innovation in Manufacturing: Needs, Practices, and Performance in Georgia, 2002-2005,* Georgia Tech Policy Project on Industrial Modernization, Georgia Institute of Technology, Atlanta, GA, August 2005 [Online] http://www.cherry.gatech.edu/SURVEY/GMS-2005-final.pdf [accessed June 2, 2008]

Introduction

Manufacturing and Distribution USA (MDUSA) presents information on manufacturing, the wholesale trade, and the retail sector in a comprehensive 3-volume presentation. Data are drawn from a variety of federal statistical sources and are combined with information on leading public and private corporations obtained from the *Ward's Business Directory of U.S. Private and Public Companies*.

History

The "USA" series grew out of a need to present federal statistical data, from different agencies, in a more "user friendly" format and, at the same time, combined with data on corporate participation in various industries. The series features preanalyzed data, ratios, and projections — in a standard format — so that all the data are handily available to the analyst or student in one place. This approach continues with *MDUSA*.

MDUSA is a successor of the award-winning *Manufacturing USA* and also holds the contents heretofore published as *Wholesale and Retail Industries USA*. The first edition came at a time when the government's statistical systems were still, as it were, straddling between the old Standard Industrial Classification (SIC) coding and the new 1997 North American Industry Classification System (NAICS). The first edition of *MDUSA* contained data in both formats — and therefore, of necessity, did not have all of the information that users of this series are accustomed to getting. The second edition was entirely coded using the 1997 NAICS coding. Input-output data and occupational data were once more back in their usual places. The third edition followed the familiar layout of the second edition.

The fourth edition of *MDUSA* came at another time of transition. In 2002, the Federal Government restructured its 1997 NAICS coding. In 2003, the *Annual Survey of Manufactures (ASM)* restructured its data using codes based on the 2002 Federal Government NAICS codes. Many of these codes correspond directly with the 2002 Federal Government NAICS codes. Others, however, encompass two or more Federal Government NAICS codes. For example, ASM NAICS industry 31121M Flour Milling and Malt Manufacturing includes three 2002 NAICS industries: 311211 Flour Milling, 311212 Rice Milling, and 311213 Malt Manufacturing. As a result of the restructured *Annual Survey of Manufactures* data, this edition of *MDUSA* is coded using two different, though related, NAICS coding formats. The Manufacturing section is coded using ASM NAICS codes. The Wholesale and Retail section is coded using the 2002 Federal Government NAICS coding.

'The Most Current Data Available'

MDUSA reports the most current data available at the time of the book's preparation. The objective is to present hard information — data based on actual survey by authoritative bodies — for all manufacturing and distribution industries on a comparable basis. A few industries may collect more recent information through their industry associations or other bodies. Similarly, estimates are published on this or that industry based on the analyses and guesses of knowledgeable individuals. These data are rarely in the same format as the federal data and are not available for a large cross section of industry. Therefore, the data in *MDUSA* are, indeed, the most current at this level of detail and spanning the entirety of manufacturing and distribution activity. It is meant to serve as the foundation on which others can base their own projections.

In addition to presenting current survey data, the editors also provide projected data for most categories from 2007 to the year 2010.

Scope and Coverage

MDUSA presents statistical data on 460 distinct industries — 322 in the manufacturing sector, 138 in the wholesale and retail sectors. Within the manufacturing presentation, 234 industries correspond directly with NAICS-coded industries. Eighty-eight industries are combinations of NAICS-coded industries. These industries are marked with an asterisk and their corresponding NAICS codes are shown at the bottom of the page. One hundred eighteen industries are either identical to a single old SIC industry or are combinations of old SIC industries; consequently, a full time-series is available for these industries going back some period of time. The industries can also be found by ASM NAICS code by looking in the NAICS Index. Conversion guides have been included in this edition to assist the user in transitioning from NAICS to ASM NAICS and vice versa.

Data on 68 NAICS-coded wholesale industries are shown. Within this group, 40 are, again, equivalent to old SIC industries. These industries are marked with an asterisk and their old SIC code is shown at the bottom of the page. The retail sector is covered by 70 NAICS-coded industries; 27 of these have direct SIC equivalents.

Presentation. Data are typically for 1997 to 2006, with some elements taken from surveys for 1998 to 2001 and 2003 to 2006. The NAICS series began in 1997. Those industries that have remained essentially unchanged feature a full time series, from 1990 or 1991 forward, with projections to 2010.

ASM NAICS manufacturing tables additionally feature ratios (for 2002), company data, materials consumed (2002), product share details (2002) and state level data (2002). State data, for manufacturing, are still incomplete. This is noted in each table.

The NAICS wholesale and retail presentation (Part II) provides national and state-level data. State coverage is more complete.

SIC and NAICS

The transition between SIC and NAICS was implemented for the 1997 Economic Census. An updating of the industrial classification system was long overdue. Relatively minor modifications had last taken place in 1987. The new NAICS coding — which was used by the U.S., Canada, and Mexico — represented a major revamping. Additional sectors were created (e.g., Information) and the "services" categories greatly increased.

An updating of the 1997 NAICS codes was implemented for the 2002 Economic Census. Fourteen of the twenty sectors remained unchanged, including the Manufacturing sector. However, the 2002 NAICS changes were substantial for the Construction, Wholesale, Retail, and Information sectors. Minor adjustments were made to the Mining and Administrative and Support Services sectors.

In 2003, the *Annual Survey of Manufactures (ASM)* restructured its data into a combination of NAICS and NAICS-based industries. These industries are based on the 2002 Federal Government NAICS structure. Many ASM-coded industries correspond directly to 2002 NAICS-coded industries. Others correspond to two or more 2002 NAICS-coded industries. The ASM-coded industries that correspond to more than a single NAICS-coded industry include a letter in their code and the first page of the presentation on these industries includes a list of the individual NAICS industries that were combined in its creation.

In *MDUSA*, the organization of data is based on the "new order." Industries no longer classified as manufacturing under NAICS are excluded. Data on *Newspapers, Periodicals, Book Publishing, and Miscellaneous Publishing* do not appear in *MDUSA*. These industries, once in manufacturing, have been reclassified as NAICS Sector 51 - Information.

Major changes in the industrial classification system typically mean some loss of information. Restatement of past years in NAICS terms will require some time — provided budgets for it are available. In some cases, no data for years before 1997 will ever be available.

Under the NAICS coding, 6-digit industry codes replace the old 4-digit SIC codes. The first two digits indicate the sector, the last four specify the industry. The code 311110 - Animal Food Manufacturing, can be parsed as follows: 31 is the first sector code used for manufacturing; 311 is Food Manufacturing, the industry group; 1110 is the actual industry designation. In normal practice, all six digits are used to designate the industry. In the NAICS manual, a trailing zero in some codes is suppressed. The trailing zero appears in published data series, however, and is also used in *MDUSA*.

Organization and Content

MDUSA is now divided into three volumes, as follows:

- **Volume I** — includes *Part I - Manufacturing by ASM NAICS Code*. Included in this volume is the range from 311111 - Dog and Cat Food Manufacturing through 33211P – Crown, Closure, and Metal Stamping Manufacturing.

- **Volume II** — concludes Part I, ranging from 33221N – Cutlery, Kitchen Utensil, Pot and Pan Manufacturing through 339999 – Miscellaneous Manufacturing Not Elsewhere Classified.

- **Volume III** — presents Part II, Wholesale and Retail Industries by NAICS Code. The wholesale trade range extends from 423110 – Automobile and Other Motor Vehicle Merchant Wholesalers through 424990 – Other Miscellaneous Nondurable Goods Merchant Wholesalers. Retail begins with 441110 – New Car Dealers and concludes with 454390 – Other Direct Selling Establishments. Volume III concludes with the indexes and the appendices.

Presentation within each part is the same. Tables included are shown for each part below.

Part I - ASM NAICS Manufacturing

1	Trend Graphics	Provided when multiple years of data are available.
2	General Statistics	National statistics.
3	Indices of Change	National data in index format.
4	Selected Ratios	Twenty ratios for the industry.
5	Leading Companies	Up to 75 companies in this industry.
6	Materials Consumed	Purchases of materials and products by quantity and cost.
7	Product Share Details	Product categories within the industry in dollars.
8	Input-Output Table(s)	Industries this NAICS buys from, sells to.
9	Occupations Employed	Occupations employed by the industry group.
10	Maps	States and regions where the industry is active.
11	Industry Data by State	Data on those states available at publication time.

Part II - NAICS Wholesale and Retail

1	Trend Graphics	Provided when multiple years of data are available.
2	General Statistics	National statistics.
3	Indices of Change	National data in index format.
4	Selected Ratios	Six ratios for the industry.
5	Leading Companies	Up to 75 companies in this industry.
6	Occupations Employed	Occupations employed by the industry group.
7	Maps	States and regions where the industry is active.
8	Industry Data by State	State level statistics.

Each industry begins on a new page. The order of graphics and tables is invariable. In some instances, data may not be available in a category, e.g., company data or geographical data. The absence of data is indicated in each section.

Three indexes (found in Volume III) are:

- **NAICS Index**. Data are presented by number and then alphabetcally. Page references are provided for each entry. Volume numbers are shown in Roman numerals.

- **Product/Activity Index**. This index shows products and commercial activities (printing, stores, etc.). Presentation is alphabetical. References are provided to pages, with volume indication in Roman numerals.

- **Company Index**. All companies appearing in *MDUSA* are shown in alphabetical order. More than 16,300 companies are indexed. Entries show volume and page numbers. NAICS codes are also provided within brackets.

Two appendices (found in Volume III) are:

- **ASM NAICS To 2002 NAICS Conversion Guide.** All 322 ASM NAICS industries appearing in *MDUSA* are shown in ASM NAICS order. Entries show ASM NAICS codes and descriptions in bold, with corresponding 2002 NAICS codes and descriptions indented.

- **2002 NAICS To ASM NAICS Conversion Guide.** All 473 NAICS industries corresponding to the ASM NAICS industries appearing in *MDUSA* are shown in 2002 NAICS order. Entries show 2002 NAICS codes and descriptions in bold, with corresponding ASM NAICS codes and descriptions indented.

For more detailed information on *MDUSA*'s industry profiles, please consult the *Overview of Content and Sources*, which follows.

Comments and Suggestions are Welcome

Comments on or suggestions for improvement of the usefulness, format, and coverage of *MDUSA* are always welcome. Although every effort is made to maintain accuracy, errors may occasionally occur; the editors will be grateful if these are called to their attention. Please contact the editor below with comments and suggestions or, to have technical questions answered, call the editor directly at ECDI at (248) 926-5187.

> Editor
> Manufacturing and Distribution USA
> Gale
> 27500 Drake Road
> Farmington Hills, MI 48331-3535
> Toll-free: 800-347-GALE
> Fax: 248-699-8069
> E-mail: BusinessProducts@cengage.com
> URL: gale.cengage.com

Overview of Content and Sources

Industry Coding Structure

Manufacturing data in *MDUSA* are ordered in conformity with the *Annual Survey of Manufactures'* North American Industry Classification System (ASM NAICS). The codes are based on the 2002 North American Industry Classification System (NAICS). The Wholesale and Retail data in *MDUSA* are ordered in conformity with the 2002 NAICS.

The NAICS coding system was first used in the 1997 Economic Census and revised for the 2002 Economic Census. Many industries were reclassified so that they no longer resembled the former Standard Industrial Classification (SIC) codes. However, a fairly large number of NAICS codes correspond directly — without change — to the older SIC codes. Of the 460 industries presented in *MDUSA*, 118 either have direct SIC equivalents or are combinations of SIC industries. When the industries coincide, longer time series of data are provided. In the manufacturing section, the data are presented under ASM NAICS codes. When an industry is the equivalent of two or more 2002 NAICS industries, an asterisk is used to mark the industry, and the corresponding 2002 NAICS codes are supplied at the bottom of the page. In the wholesale and retail section, the data are presented under NAICS codes, but an asterisk is used to mark the industry, and the equivalent SIC code is supplied at the bottom of the page. New industries that have no SIC equivalent show data and projections from 1997 forward.

Industry Profiles

Each industry profile contains the tables and graphics listed in the *Introduction*. A detailed discussion of each graphic display and table follows; the meaning of each data element is explained, and the sources from which the data were obtained are cited.

Trends Graphics

At the beginning of each industry profile, two graphs are presented showing (1) industry shipments (manufacturing) or sales (wholesale/retail) and (2) employment plotted for the years 1991 to 2010 (or an earlier date) on logarithmic scale. The curves are provided primarily to give the user an at-a-glance assessment of important trends in the industry. The logarithmic scale ensures that the shipment trends and employment trends can be compared visually despite different magnitudes and denominations of the data (millions of dollars for shipments or sales and thousands of employees for employment); in this mode of presentation, if two curves have the same slope, the values are growing or declining at the same rate. If the values fit within a single cycle (1 to 9, 10 to 90, etc.), a single cycle is shown; if the values bridge two cycles, both are shown.

The data graphed are derived from the first table, *General Statistics*. All available years of data are plotted. If data gaps appear in the series, missing points are calculated using a least-squares curve fitting algorithm.

Those portions of curves based on projections by the editors are shown in a dotted-line format.

General Statistics

Manufacturing. This table shows national statistics for the industry for the years 1991-2010 under five groupings: Companies, Establishments, Employment, Compensation, and Production. The last four groupings are further subdivided, as described below.

Data for 1992, 1997, and 2002 are from the Economic Census held in each of those years. Data for other years, through and including 2006, are from the *Annual Survey of Manu-factures (ASM)*. Establishment counts in the *ASM* years are from the *County Business Pat-terns* for those years. New industries created in the 1997 NAICS reclassification will not show data earlier than 1997. New industries created in the 2002 NAICS reclassification will not show data earlier than 2002.

Data for the period 2007-2010 are projected by the editors. A discussion of the methods of projection is presented below. Projected data are followed by the letter "p".

Company counts are available only from the full *Census of Manufactures* conducted every five years.

Establishment data are provided for 1991 through 2006; projections are shown thereafter. Establishment counts in the Census years (1992, 1997, 2002) are from the Economic Census. In other years, values are from the *County Business Patterns*. Establishment counts are typically higher than company counts because many companies operate from more than one facility. Total establishments are shown together with establishments that employ 20 or more people. Comparing the number of large establishments with total establishments will tell the user whether the industry is populated by relatively small operations or is dominated by large facilities. Values shown are absolute numbers of establishments.

The **Employment** grouping is subdivided into total employment, shown in 1,000 employees (thus a value of 134.9 means that the industry employs 134,900 people), production workers (in thousands), and production hours worked (in millions of hours). Dividing hours worked by production workers produces hours worked by a production worker in the year. This value is precalculated for the user in the table of Selected Ratios. A value of around 1,940 hours indicates full-time employment — on average; obviously such aggregate data hide the finer details of day-to-day industrial operation: the presence of part-time workers, overtime clocked, etc.

The **Compensation** grouping shows the industry's total payroll (in millions of dollars) and wages (in dollars per hour). The payroll value includes all forms of compensation subject to federal taxes, including wages, salaries, commissions, bonuses, etc. The *Survey of Manufactures* provides payroll and wage data as aggregates. The wages per hour were calculated by dividing the Survey wage aggregate by the total hours worked in production.

The interested user can reverse this calculation ($/hour times hours will produce wages-in-the-aggregate). Additional calculations can be used to determine the salaries of those employees who are not production workers. The procedure is to calculate aggregate wages and to deduct the result from payroll to obtain salaries paid; next, salaried employees can be calculated by deducting production workers from total employment; finally, salaries paid divided by salaried employment will produce the average annual salary of the administrative/technical workforce in the industry.

The **Production** grouping shows cost of materials, value added in manufacturing, value of shipments, and capital investments, all in millions of dollars; thus a value of 0.9 means that the actual value is $900,000.

Cost of materials includes cost of raw materials, fuels, freight, and contract work associated with production and excludes costs of services (e.g., advertising, insurance), overhead, depreciation, rents, royalties, and capital expenditures.

Value Added by Manufacture represents Value of Shipments less cost of materials, supplies, containers, fuel, purchased electrical power, and contract work plus income for services rendered. The result is adjusted by adding the difference between the cost and sales price of the merchandise by merchandising operations plus net change in finished goods and work-in-process inventories between the beginning and the end of the year. Value Added is a good measure of net value of production because it avoids the duplications inherent in the Value of Shipments measure (below).

Value of Shipments is the net selling value of products leaving production plants in an industry. In industries where two or more production stages for a product are included under the same SIC, the Value of Shipments measure will tend to overstate the economic importance of the industry: the value of product shipments is usually lower than total Value of Shipments. Nonetheless, Value of Shipments corresponds to the sales volume of the industry.

The Capital Investments column shows capital expenditures for equipment and structures made by the industry provided that these expenditures are depreciated rather than expensed in the year of acquisition.

Wholesale and Retail. The General Statistics for the wholesale and retail sectors show four elements of data and three ratios. The data are Establishments and Employment (actual number) and Payroll and Sales (in millions of dollars). Ratios for Employees per Establishment (number), Sales per Establishment (dollars), and Payroll per Employee ($) are provided. Missing data elements are extrapolated, where possible, and marked with the letter "e". Projections, to the year 2010, are marked with the letter "p".

Indices of Change

The data presented in the *General Statistics* table are partially restated as indices for all industries where multiple years of data are available. The purpose of the table is to show the user rapidly how different categories of the industry have changed since 2002. Indices are shown for the census years (1992, 1997, and 2002) and for years beyond.

The year 2002 is used as the base and is therefore shown as 100 in every category. Other values are expressed in relation to the 2002 value.

Values of 100 indicate no change in relation to the base year; values above 100 mean better and values below 100 indicate worse performance — all relative to the 2002 base. Note, however, that these are indices rather than compounded annual rates of growth or decline.

Indices based on projections by the editors are followed by a "p".

Selected Ratios

To understand an industry, analysts calculate ratios of various kinds so that the absolute numbers can be placed in a more global perspective. Twenty important industrial ratios are precalculated for the user in the Selected Ratios table. Additionally, the same ratios are also provided for the average of all manufacturing, wholesale, or retail industries; an index, comparing the two categories, is also provided.

The ratios are calculated for the most recent complete year available; that year is usually the year of the most recent Economic Census. In this case, 2002.

The first column of values represents the **Average of All** . . . — be it manufacturing, wholesale, or retail. These ratios are calculated by (1) adding all categories for manufacturing, wholesale, or retail and (2) calculating the ratios based on the totals.

The second column of values shows the ratios for the **Analyzed Industry**, i.e., the industry currently under consideration.

The third column is an **Index** comparing the Analyzed Industry to the Average of All . . . Industries. The index is useful for determining quickly and consistently how the Analyzed Industry stands in relation to all manufacturing, all wholesale, or all retail. Index values of 100 mean that the Analyzed Industry, within a given ratio, is identical to the average of all industries. An index value of 500 means that the Analyzed Industry is five times the average — for instance, that it has five times as many employees per establishment or pays five times as much. An index value of 50 would indicate that the Analyzed Industry is half of the average of all industries (50 percent). Similarly, an index of 105 means 5 percent above average and 95 indicates 5 percent below.

Manufacturing presentations show 20 ratios. For the wholesale and retail sectors, on which less information is available, six ratios are provided.

Leading Companies

The table of *Leading Companies* shows up to 75 companies that participate in the industry. The listings are sorted in descending order of sales and show the company name, address, name of the Chief Executive Officer, telephone, company type, sales (in millions of dollars) and employment (in thousands of employees). The number of companies shown, their total sales, and total employment are summed at the top of the table for the user's convenience.

The data are from the *Ward's Business Directory of U.S. Private and Public Companies* for 2007, Volumes 1 and 2. Public and private corporations, divisions, subsidiaries, joint ventures, and corporate groups are shown. Thus a listing for an industry may show the parent company as well as important divisions and subsidiaries of the same company (usually in a different location).

While this method of presentation has the disadvantage of duplication (the sales of a parent corporation include the sales of any divisions listed separately), it has the advantage of providing the user with information on major components of an enterprise at different locations. In any event, the user should not assume that the sum of the sales (or employment) shown in the *Leading Companies* table represents the total sales (or employment) of an industry. The Shipments or Sales column of the *General Statistics* table is a better guide to industry sales.

The company's type (private, public, division, etc.) is shown on the table under the column headed "Co. Type," thus providing the user with a means of roughly determining the total "net" sales (or employment) represented in the table; this can be accomplished by adding the values and then deducting values corresponding to divisions and subsidiaries of parent organizations also shown in the table. The code used is as follows:

P	Public corporation
R	Private corporation
S	Subsidiary
D	Division
J	Joint venture
G	Corporate group

An asterisk (*) placed behind the sales volume indicates an estimate; the absence of an asterisk indicates that the sales value has been obtained from annual reports, other formal submissions to regulatory bodies, or from the corporation. The symbol "<" appears in front of some employment values to indicate that the actual value is "less than" the value shown. Thus the value of "<0.1" means that the company employs fewer than 100 people.

Materials Consumed

The *Materials Consumed* table is drawn from the 2002 Economic Census. This table reports the quantities of materials and products (e.g., containers, packaging) used by the industry. The delivered cost of the materials, in millions of dollars, is also shown. Data are not available for all industries. Where data are missing, the table header is reproduced with the notation that data are not available.

A number of symbols are used to indicate why data are omitted or their basis. (D) means that data are withheld to avoid disclosure of competitive information; "na" is used when data are "not available." (S) means that data are withheld because statistical norms were not met; (X) stands for "not applicable;" (Z) means that less than half of the unit quantity is consumed; "nec" means "not elsewhere classified," and "nsk" abbreviates "not specified by kind." A single asterisk (*) shows instances where 10-19 percent of the data were estimated; two asterisks (**) show a 20-29 percent estimate.

Product Share Details

The table of *Product Share Details* shows the products of the industry broken down by product classes and categories. Data are shown in millions of dollars of product shipments. The source of product data is the 2002 Economic Census.

This table highlights the difference between *industry shipments* and *product shipments*. In practice this means that total product shipments may be higher or lower than data for shipments shown in the General Statistics table. Product shipments will be higher when significant quantities of the product classified under this code are manufactured in other industries. Product shipments will be lower than industry shipments because industry shipments include miscellaneous receipts (e.g., sales of scrap, contract work) as well as product shipments. Duplication is also reflected in industry shipments but excluded from the product shipment data.

Multiple levels of product groups, products, and subcategories are combined to make a table. Product groups are shown in bold. Lower levels are indented.

In some instances, the symbol (D) will appear instead of a value; the symbol appears when data are withheld to prevent disclosure of competitive information. The abbreviation "nec" stands for "not elsewhere classified," and the abbreviation "nsk" stands for "not specified by kind."

Occupations Employed by Industry Group

MDUSA presents data on 132 occupation categories employed by manufacturing industries; since most of these categories combine two or three occupations, more than 260 occupations are covered. The information presented is an extract from the *Industry-Occupation Matrix* produced by the Bureau of Labor Statistics (BLS), Department of Labor.

The table on *Occupations Employed* presents an extract; showing the entire matrix would have required too much space. Thus only those occupations are included that represent 1% or more of total employment in an industry. The advantage of this method is that the data are kept manageable while most of an industry's employment is defined by occupation. The disadvantage is that certain occupations, although employed by an industry, do not make the "cutoff" of 1 percent of total employment.

The data are shown for 2006 (updated from 2004) in percent of Total Employment for an industry group (4-digit NAICS industry level or groupings of 4-digit NAICS industries). Also shown is the Bureau of Labor Statistics' projection of the anticipated growth or decline of the occupation to the year 2016. This value is reported as a percent change to 2016; a value of 5.5, for instance, means that overall employment, in the industry group, will increase 5.5 percent between 2006 and 2016; a negative value indicates a corresponding decline. Note that these are not rates of annual change.

The BLS produces most of the data in 4-digit NAICS format. Occupation data for the industries 332710 Machine Shops, 337121 Upholstered Household Furniture Manufacturing, 337122 Nonupholstered Wood Household Furniture Manufacturing, 337127 Institutional Furniture Manufacturing, 33712N Household Nonupholstered Furniture not elsewhere classified, 33991M Jewelry and Silverware Manufacturing, 446110 Pharmacies and Drug Stores, and 451110 Sporting Goods Stores are in 5-digit NAICS format. Data have been matched as closely as possible to the 6-digit NAICS codes. But the same table of *Occupations Employed* is reproduced for each industry which matches the BLS's 4-digit or 5-digit NAICS grouping. This approach has been adopted so that the user will find the occupations associated with an industry with other data on that industry.

The user should note the following:

- As already stated, the occupations shown are a subset of total occupations employed: those that account for 1 percent or more of employment in the industry group.

- Since the data are for groups, some occupations listed may appear out of place in a particular NAICS industry; that is because those occupations are employed by a related NAICS industry in the same group.

- Growth or decline indicated for an occupation within an industry group does not mean that the occupation is growing or declining overall. Also, changes introduced by BLS between editions of this series can be quite drastic. An occupation that grew by several percentage points in an industry two years ago is shown suddenly declining to the year 2016 now.

Map Graphics

The geographical presentation of data begins with two maps titled *Location by State* and *Regional Concentration*.

Manufacturing. In the first map, all states in which the industry is present are shaded. In the second, the industry's concentration is shown by Census region. The two maps, together, tell the user at a glance where the industry is active and which regions rank first, second, and third in value of shipments or in number of establishments; establishment counts are used for ranking in those industries where shipment data are withheld (the (D) symbol) for the majority of states. In the case of some industries, only one or two regions are shaded because the industry is concentrated in a few states. The data for ranking are taken from the table on *Industry Data by State* which immediately follows the maps.

Wholesale and Retail. The information above relates to these sectors as well, with one exception. Since wholesale and retail activity occurs most everywhere, only those states are highlighted on the state map where the activity is greater in the state than would be indicated by the state's share of total U.S. population. Shaded states mean intense wholesale or retail activity.

The regional boundaries are those of the Census Regions and are named, from left to right and top to bottom as follows:

Pacific (includes Alaska and Hawaii)	East South Central
Mountain	New England
West North Central	Middle Atlantic
West South Central	South Atlantic
East North Central	

In the case of the Pacific region, all parts of the region are shaded (including Alaska and Hawaii), even if the basis for the ranking is the industry's predominance in California (the usual case).

Although regional data are only graphed and not reported in a separate table, the table of *Industry Data by State* provides all the necessary information for constructing a regional table.

Industry Data by State

Manufacturing. The table on *Industry Data by State* provides ten data elements for each state in which the industry is active. They come from the 2002 Economic Census, the most recently available data set on states. Even in this series, certain data elements are suppressed by the Bureau of the Census to prevent disclosure of competitive information. This may come about in instances where only a few operations are present in the state or they are operated by a small number of companies. The states are shown in descending order of shipments. The categories of Establishments, Shipments, Total Employment, and Wages are identical to those in the table of *General Statistics*. In addition, six elements of information are provided so that the user can more easily compare the size, performance, and characteristics of the industry from one state to the next.

Shipments are expressed in millions of dollars and as a percent of the total U.S. shipments for the industry. This is useful for determining the relative importance of the state in the industry as a whole. Shipments per Establishment are also provided; this measure gives an insight into the relative size of the factories in the state.

Total employment is shown together with percent of total employment in the U.S. industry and employment per establishment. For some states, employment is shown as the midpoint of a range; these items are marked with an asterisk (*).

Cost data are expressed as percent of Shipments to facilitate the user's analysis of the relative cost advantages of one state over another. The lower the percentile, the lower the cost experience of the industry in the state. This information, however, must be viewed in light of the hourly wage experience in the state.

Investment data are shown as Investments per Employee, again to facilitate state-to-state comparisons.

The symbol (D) is used when data are withheld to prevent disclosure of proprietary information. Dashes are used to indicate that the corresponding data element cannot be calculated because some part of the ratio is missing or withheld.

Wholesale and Retail. State data, for these sectors, is organized slightly differently. Categories are Establishments, Employment, Payroll, and Sales. Total establishments are shown together with the percent of U.S. establishments that they represent. Employment is treated in the same way, but Employment per Establishment is also shown. Payroll is shown in millions of dollars and also per employee, in dollars. Sales are expressed in total (millions of dollars), as a percent of the U.S. total, and as Sales per Establishment (in dollars). Where employment is not provided by the Economic Census, a range of employment is provided.

Projected Data Series

As a service to the busy user of this book, *MDUSA* features trend projections of data — when a sufficient number of years of data is available.

How Projections Were Made

Projections are based on a curve-fitting algorithm using the least-squares method. In essence, the algorithm calculates a trend line for the data using existing data points. Extensions of the trend line are used to predict future years of data.

What Values Were Projected

Every category (column) reported under General Statistics has been subject to projection. In those cases where a coherent series exists from 1991 to the present in Part I and 1990 to the present in Part II, the entire series was used. In those cases where the industry definition underwent a change in 1997, trends are calculated from 1997 forward.

Cost of Materials and Value Added by Manufacturer (in the manufacturing industries) were calculated using the 2002 ratio of costs or value added to shipments in 2002 and then applying that ratio to other years using the projected shipment values for those years. Costs and value added were treated in this manner because averaging these data for a long period (1991-2001, for example) would not properly reflect cost savings and productivity changes achieved most recently. Therefore the use of a ratio, based on the most recent survey year, seemed more appropriate.

Limitations of Projections

Projections are simply means of detecting trends — that may or may not hold in the future. The projections in *MDUSA*, therefore, are not as reliable as actual survey data. Most analysts trying to project the future routinely turn to trend projection. In *MDUSA*, the work of doing the projections has been done for the user in advance.

NAICS 33221N - CUTLERY, KITCHEN UTENSIL, POT AND PAN MANUFACTURING*

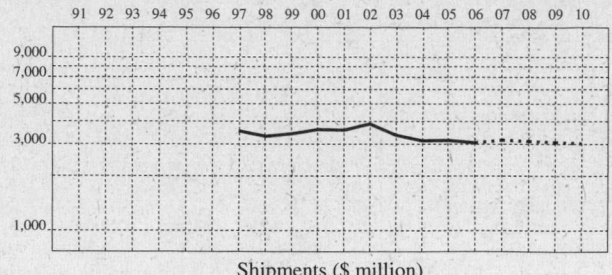

Shipments ($ million)

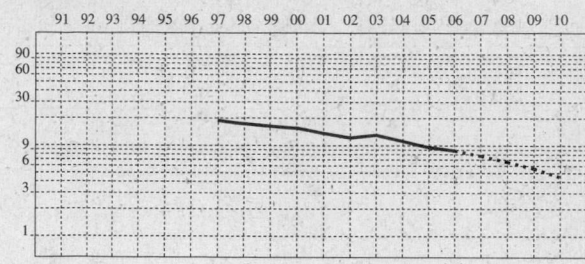

Employment (000)

GENERAL STATISTICS

Year	Com-panies	Establishments		Employment			Compensation		Production ($ million)			
		Total	with 20 or more employees	Total (000)	Production Workers (000)	Hours (Mil)	Payroll ($ mil)	Wages ($/hr)	Cost of Materials	Value Added by Manufacture	Value of Shipments	Capital Invest.
1997	235	250	101	18.8	14.6	28.7	584.2	13.17	1,119.8	2,463.8	3,541.9	235.7
1998		251	106	17.3	13.4	27.4	553.6	13.35	1,072.8	2,206.4	3,310.1	355.8
1999		253	107	16.3	12.6	27.3	548.1	13.37	1,153.9	2,252.0	3,420.5	202.0
2000		238	105	15.5	12.1	25.9	531.5	13.96	1,099.5	2,492.7	3,611.2	224.4
2001		233	106	13.7	10.7	21.9	492.5	15.21	1,060.2	2,497.0	3,586.8	75.9
2002	197	207	75	12.2	9.1	17.6	494.0	17.32	1,209.7	2,678.2	3,880.3	76.2
2003		212	80	13.1	10.0	19.3	523.6	17.37	1,410.4	1,963.8	3,364.6	99.9
2004		224	76	11.2	8.4	16.3	479.9	18.34	1,257.5	1,898.5	3,131.8	139.8
2005		228	71	9.6	7.2	14.4	419.8	18.17	1,446.5	1,681.6	3,147.4	53.1
2006		209P	67P	8.8	6.4	12.9	407.1	19.70	1,465.1	1,604.8	3,054.1	57.6
2007		205P	63P	7.7P	5.6P	10.8P	407.0P	20.32P	1,514.7P	1,659.2P	3,157.6P	5.2P
2008		200P	58P	6.6P	4.7P	8.9P	389.4P	21.11P	1,493.2P	1,635.5P	3,112.6P	
2009		195P	53P	5.6P	3.8P	7.0P	371.9P	21.89P	1,471.6P	1,611.9P	3,067.6P	
2010		191P	48P	4.5P	2.9P	5.1P	354.4P	22.68P	1,450.0P	1,588.3P	3,022.7P	

Sources: 1997 and 2002 *Economic Census*; other years, up to 2006, are from *Annual Survey of Manufactures*. Establishment counts for non-Census years are from *County Business Patterns*; 1997 and 2002 values are from the 1997 and 2002 censuses, respectively. 'P's show projections by the editors.

INDICES OF CHANGE

Year	Com-panies	Establishments		Employment			Compensation		Production ($ million)			
		Total	with 20 or more employees	Total (000)	Production Workers (000)	Hours (Mil)	Payroll ($ mil)	Wages ($/hr)	Cost of Materials	Value Added by Manufacture	Value of Shipments	Capital Invest.
1997	119	121	135	154	160	163	118	76	93	92	91	309
1998		121	141	142	147	156	112	77	89	82	85	467
1999		122	143	134	138	155	111	77	95	84	88	265
2000		115	140	127	133	147	108	81	91	93	93	294
2001		113	141	112	118	124	100	88	88	93	92	100
2002	100	100	100	100	100	100	100	100	100	100	100	100
2003		102	107	107	110	110	106	100	117	73	87	131
2004		108	101	92	92	93	97	106	104	71	81	183
2005		110	95	79	79	82	85	105	120	63	81	70
2006		101P	90P	72	70	73	82	114	121	60	79	76
2007		99P	83P	63P	62P	61P	82P	117P	125P	62P	81P	7P
2008		97P	77P	54P	52P	51P	79P	122P	123P	61P	80P	
2009		94P	70P	46P	42P	40P	75P	126P	122P	60P	79P	
2010		92P	64P	37P	32P	29P	72P	131P	120P	59P	78P	

Sources: Same as General Statistics. Values reflect change from the base year, 2002. Values above 100 mean greater than 2002, values below 100 mean less than 2002, and the values of 100 in other years means the same as 2002. 'P's show projections by the editors.

SELECTED RATIOS

For 2002	Avg. of All Manufact.	Analyzed Industry	Index	For 2002	Avg. of All Manufact.	Analyzed Industry	Index
Employees per Establishment	42	59	140	Value Added per Production Worker	182,367	294,308	161
Payroll per Establishment	1,639,184	2,386,473	146	Cost per Establishment	5,769,015	5,843,961	101
Payroll per Employee	39,053	40,492	104	Cost per Employee	137,446	99,156	72
Production Workers per Establishment	30	44	149	Cost per Production Worker	195,506	132,934	68
Wages per Establishment	694,845	1,472,618	212	Shipments per Establishment	11,158,348	18,745,411	168
Wages per Production Worker	23,548	33,498	142	Shipments per Employee	265,847	318,057	120
Hours per Production Worker	1,980	1,934	98	Shipments per Production Worker	378,144	426,407	113
Wages per Hour	11.89	17.32	146	Investment per Establishment	361,338	368,116	102
Value Added per Establishment	5,381,325	12,938,164	240	Investment per Employee	8,609	6,246	73
Value Added per Employee	128,210	219,525	171	Investment per Production Worker	12,245	8,374	68

Sources: Same as General Statistics. The 'Average of All Manufacturing' column represents the average of all manufacturing industries reported for the most recent complete year available. The Index shows the relationship between the Average and the Analyzed Industry. For example, 100 means that they are equal; 500 that the Analyzed Industry is five times the average; 50 means that the Analyzed Industry is half the national average. The abbreviation 'na' is used to show that data are 'not available'. Ratios shown for 2002, the last complete census year.

*Equivalent to Federal Government NAICS 332211, 332214.

LEADING COMPANIES   Number shown: 75   Total sales ($ mil): 47,424   Total employment (000): 119.8

Company Name	Address				CEO Name	Phone	Co. Type	Sales ($ mil)	Empl. (000)
Gillette Co.	PO Box 720	Boston	MA	02217	James M. Kilts	617-421-7000	S	10,477	28.7
Ball Corp.	PO Box 5000	Broomfield	CO	80021	R. David Hoover	303-469-3131	P	7,475	15.5
Kenwood Silver Company Inc.	163-181 Kenwood	Sherrill	NY	13461	Terry Westbrook	315-361-3000	S	3,586*	2.9
Snap-On Inc.	PO Box 1410	Kenosha	WI	53141	Tim Chambers	262-656-5200	P	2,841	11.6
Metaldyne Corp.	47603 Halyard Dr.	Plymouth	MI	48170	Thomas Amato	734-207-6200	S	1,886	8.0
Tang Industries Inc.	8960 Spanish Ridge	Las Vegas	NV	89148	Cyrus Tang	702-734-3700	R	1,500*	3.2
Rittal Corp.	1 Rittal Pl.	Springfield	OH	45504	Carie Ray	937-399-0500	R	1,268*	0.6
Plastech Engineered Products	835 Mason Ave.	Dearborn	MI	48124	Julie Nguyen Brown	313-791-3001	R	1,070	4.8
Robert Bosch Tool Corp.	1961 Bishop Ln.	Louisville	KY	40218	Timothy Shea	502-625-2050	D	1,057*	0.2
MTD Products Inc.	PO Box 368022	Cleveland	OH	44136	Curtis E. Moll	330-225-2600	R	1,015*	6.7
Alcoa Closure Systems Intl	6625 Network Way	Indianapolis	IN	46278	V. Lance Mitchell	317-390-5000	S	980*	3.0
Masonite Door Corp.	1 N D Mabry Hwy	Tampa	FL	33609	Fred Lynch	813-877-2726	R	876*	<0.1
Barden Corp.	PO Box 2449	Danbury	CT	06813	John McCloskey	203-744-2211	R	776*	0.3
Sub-Zero Inc.	4717 Hammersley	Madison	WI	53711	James Bakke	608-271-2233	R	758*	3.0
Oregon Cutting Systems Group	PO Box 22127	Portland	OR	97269	Jim Oscermanc	503-653-8881	D	674*	1.0
Bachman Machine Co.	4321 N Broadway	St. Louis	MO	63147	William Bachman	314-231-4221	R	656*	0.1
Shiloh Industries Inc.	880 Steel Dr.	Valley City	OH	44280	Curtis Moll	330-558-2600	P	590	1.8
WKI Holding Company Inc.	11911 Freedom Dr.	Reston	VA	20190		703-456-4700	R	515*	2.9
Matco Tools Corp.	4403 Allen Rd.	Stow	OH	44224		330-929-4949	D	467*	0.5
Ladish Company Inc.	5481 S Packard Ave.	Cudahy	WI	53110		414-747-2611	P	425	2.0
Bing Group L.L.C.	11500 Oakland St.	Detroit	MI	48211	David Bing	313-867-3700	R	411*	1.1
Northern Stamping Inc.	6600 Chapek Pkwy.	Cleveland	OH	44125		216-883-8888	R	410*	0.2
Feintool US Operations Inc.	11280 Cornell Park	Cincinnati	OH	45242	Richard Surico	513-247-0110	R	408*	0.3
Fiskars Brands Inc.	2537 Daniels St.	Madison	WI	53718	Heikki Allonen	608-259-1649	R	399*	<0.1
Skill Metalforming Technologies	16151 Puritas Ave.	Cleveland	OH	44135	Roger Kalski	216-267-8866	R	352*	0.1
Onedia Ltd.	PO Box 1	Oneida	NY	13421	James E. Joseph	315-361-3000	R	348	0.7
M. Kamenstein Corp.	1 Merrick Ave.	Westbury	NY	11590	Jeffrey Siegel	516-683-6000	S	308	1.0
C. Cowles and Co.	83 Water St.	New Haven	CT	06511	Lawrence C. Moon Jr.	203-865-3110	R	260*	0.2
American Safety Razor Co.	240 Cedar Knolls Rd	Cedar Knolls	NJ	07927	James D. Murphy	973-753-3000	R	254*	2.0
Elixir Industries	24800 Chrisanta Dr.	Mission Viejo	CA	92691	Christopher Sahm	949-860-5000	R	221*	<0.1
Defiance Metal Products Co.	PO Box 447	Defiance	OH	43512		419-784-5332	R	211*	1.7
General Dynamics Armament/Tech	4 LakePointe Plz.	Charlotte	NC	28217	Linda Hudson	703-714-8000	S	198*	1.2
Adrian Steel Co.	906 James Street	Adrian	MI	49221		517-265-6194	R	196*	<0.1
Anstro Manufacturing Inc.	238 Wolcott Rd.	Wolcott	CT	06716	Robert Bosco	203-879-1423	R	182*	0.2
Norfolk Iron and Metal Co.	PO Box 1129	Norfolk	NE	68702	Richard Robinson	402-371-1810	R	180*	0.3
Alcas Corp.	PO Box 810	Olean	NY	14760	Sandra Grey	716-372-3111	R	177*	<0.1
Wallace Silversmiths Inc.	175 McClellan Hwy.	East Boston	MA	02128	Bob Meers	617-561-2200	S	174*	0.3
Precision Resource Inc.	25 Forest Pkwy.	Shelton	CT	06484		203-925-0012	R	174*	0.2
MPI International Inc.	2129 Austin Ave.	Rochester	MI	48309		248-853-9010	R	157*	1.0
Rotary Corp.	PO Box 747	Glennville	GA	30427		912-654-3433	R	156*	0.4
Midwest Stamping Inc.	3455 Briarfield	Maumee	OH	43537	Ronald L. Thompson	419-724-6970	R	155*	0.6
FIC America Corp.	485 E Lies Rd.	Carol Stream	IL	60188	Itsuo Kozuka	630-871-7609	R	135*	0.7
American Trim L.L.C.	1005 W Grand Ave.	Lima	OH	45801	Jeffrey Hawk	419-739-4349	R	130*	<0.1
Northern Engraving Corp.	PO Box 377	Sparta	WI	54656		608-269-6911	R	130*	0.5
G and F Industries Inc.	PO Box 515	Sturbridge	MA	01566	John Argitis	508-347-9132	R	123*	0.2
Chestnut Group Inc.	115 Bloomingdale	Wayne	PA	19087	Park Blatchford	610-688-3300	R	122*	0.4
Duffy Tool & Stamping Ltd.	PO Box 2128	Muncie	IN	47307	Greggory Notestine	765-288-1941	R	113*	0.2
Wauconda Tool and Engineering	821 W Algonquin	Algonquin	IL	60102	Chuck Burnside	847-658-4588	R	112*	<0.1
Oberg Industries Inc.	PO Box 368	Freeport	PA	16229		724-295-2121	R	110*	0.5
Consolidated Fabricators Corp.	4600 S Santa Fe Ave	Los Angeles	CA	90058	Michael Melideo	323-586-4500	R	109*	0.1
TABC Inc.	PO Box 2140	Long Beach	CA	90801	Seiji Ikezaki	562-428-3604	S	109*	0.6
Waterloo Industries Inc.	PO Box 2095	Waterloo	IA	50703	John M. Trebel	319-235-7131	D	108*	1.0
GMP Metal Products	3883 Delor Street	Saint Louis	MO	63116		314-481-0300	S	100*	0.2
Ridgeview Industries Inc.	2727 3 Mile Rd. NW	Grand Rapids	MI	49534	David Nykamp	616-453-8636	R	100*	0.2
Wozniak Industries Inc.	2 Mid America Plz.	Villa Park	IL	60181	Edward Wozniak	630-954-3400	R	100*	<0.1
Schick Wilkinson Sword	10 Leighton Rd.	Milford	CT	06460	Joseph Lynch	203-882-2100	S	97*	0.6
Vulcan Inc.	PO Box 1850	Foley	AL	36536	Robert W. Lee	251-943-7000	R	96*	0.3
Major Die and Engineering Co.	1352 Industrial Dr.	Itasca	IL	60143		630-773-3444	R	95*	<0.1
Stack On Products Co.	PO Box 489	Wauconda	IL	60084			R	94*	0.3
Trans-Matic Manufacturing Co.	300 E 48th St.	Holland	MI	49423	Patrick Thompson	616-820-2500	R	94*	0.3
Mayville Engineering Company	715 S Street	Mayville	WI	53050	Bob Kamphuis	920-387-4500	R	90*	0.5
Pacific Manufacturing Ohio	8955 Seward Rd.	Fairfield	OH	45011	Toshiteru Ando	513-642-0055	R	89*	0.5
Penn United Technology Inc.	PO Box 399	Saxonburg	PA	16056	Carl Jones	724-352-1507	R	88*	0.7
Atlantic Tool and Die Company	19963 Progress Dr.	Strongsville	OH	44149	Frank Mehwald	440-238-6931	R	87*	0.2
Casey Tool and Machine Company	400 W Delaware	Casey	IL	62420	James Yates	217-932-2547	R	87*	0.5
Gill Manufacturing Inc.	5271 Plainfield Ave	Grand Rapids	MI	49525	Jack Shaffer	616-559-2700	R	79*	0.6
Innovance Inc.	505 W Front St.	Albert Lea	MN	56007	Mike Larson	507-377-8910	R	79*	<0.1
Heyco Metals Inc.	1069 Stinson Dr.	Reading	PA	19605	Michael Jemison	610-926-4131	R	75*	<0.1
Stanco Metal Products Inc.	PO Box 307	Grand Haven	MI	49417	Warren Stansberry	616-842-5000	R	69*	<0.1
Florence Corp.	5935 Corporate Dr.	Manhattan	KS	66503	David Dailey	785-323-4400	R	69*	0.2
Challenge Manufacturing Co.	PO Box 1049	Holland	MI	49422	Bruce Vor Broker	616-735-6500	R	66*	0.5
Mid-West Spring and Stamping	1404 Joliet Rd., C	Romeoville	IL	60446	Michael B. Curran		R	62*	0.5
Towle Manufacturing Co.	175 McClellan Hwy.	East Boston	MA	02128	Stuart Hemingway	617-561-2200	S	62*	0.2
Modineer Co.	PO Box 640	Niles	MI	49120	Michael Dreher	269-683-2550	R	62*	0.1
Zippo Manufacturing Company	PO Box 364	Bradford	PA	16701	Greg Booth	814-368-2700	R	62*	0.8

Source: Ward's Business Directory of U.S. Private and Public Companies, Volumes 1 and 2, 2008. The company type code used is as follows: P - Public, R - Private, S - Subsidiary, D - Division, J - Joint Venture, A - Affiliate, G - Group. Sales are in millions of dollars, employees are in thousands. An asterisk (*) indicates an estimated sales volume. The symbol < stands for 'less than'. Company names and addresses are truncated, in some cases, to fit into the available space.

MATERIALS CONSUMED FOR CUTLERY AND FLATWARE (EXCEPT PRECIOUS) MANUFACTURING

Material	Quantity	Delivered Cost ($ million)
Metal bolts, nuts, screws, and other screw machine products	(X)	6.5
Other fabricated metal products (exc. castings and forgings)	(X)	65.9
Iron and steel castings (rough and semifinished)	(X)	8.9
Aluminum and aluminum-base alloy castings (rough and semifinished)	(X)	0.4
Other nonferrous metal castings, rough or semifinished (inc. aluminum)	(X)	(D)
Iron and steel forgings	(X)	6.8
Steel bars, bar shapes, and plates (exc. castings, forgings, fabr. metal products)	(X)	0.6
Steel sheet, strip, and tin mill products	(X)	78.7
Steel wire and wire products	(X)	2.2
All other steel shapes and forms (exc. castings, forgings, fabr. metal products)	(X)	(D)
Copper and copper-base alloy shapes and forms (exc. castings, forgings, fabr. metal products)	(X)	1.3
Aluminum and aluminum-base alloy shapes and forms (exc. castings, forgings, fabr. metal products)	(X)	(D)
Other nonferrous shapes and forms (exc. castings, forgings, fabricated metal products)	(X)	(D)
Wood parts, including handles	(X)	3.3
Plastics resins consumed in the form of granules, pellets, etc.	(X)	61.5
Plastics products, incl. film, sheet, rod, tube, and fabricated shapes	(X)	79.0
Paper and paperboard containers (incl. shipping sacks and other paper packaging supplies)	(X)	84.4
All other materials, components, parts, containers, and supplies	(X)	55.4
Materials, ingredients, containers, and supplies, nsk	(X)	5.9

Source: 2002 Economic Census. Explanation of symbols used: (D): Withheld to avoid disclosure of competitive data; na: Not available; (S): Withheld because statistical norms were not met; (X): Not applicable; (Z): Less than half the unit shown; nec: Not elsewhere classified; nsk: Not specified by kind; - : zero; p : 10-19 percent estimated; q : 20-29 percent estimated.

MATERIALS CONSUMED FOR KITCHEN UTENSIL, POT, AND PAN MANUFACTURING

Material	Quantity	Delivered Cost ($ million)
Metal bolts, nuts, screws, and other screw machine products	(X)	5.6
Other fabricated metal products (exc. castings and forgings)	(X)	12.9
Castings, rough and semifinished	(X)	(D)
Steel sheet and strip (including tinplate)	(X)	34.2
Steel plate	(X)	(D)
All other steel shapes and forms (exc. castings, forgings, fabr. metal products)	(X)	37.7
Aluminum and aluminum-base alloy sheet, plate, foil, and welded tubing	(X)	65.7
Other aluminum and aluminum-base alloy shapes and forms (exc. castings, forgings, fabr. metal products)	(X)	112.5
Other nonferrous shapes and forms (exc. castings, forgings, fabricated metal products)	(X)	(D)
Plastics materials and resins	(X)	11.1
All other chemicals and allied products (exc. plastics materials and resins)	(X)	(D)
Paperboard containers, boxes, and corrugated paperboard	(X)	18.1
All other materials, components, parts, containers, and supplies	(X)	118.9
Materials, ingredients, containers, and supplies, nsk	(X)	14.8

Source: 2002 Economic Census. Explanation of symbols used: (D): Withheld to avoid disclosure of competitive data; na: Not available; (S): Withheld because statistical norms were not met; (X): Not applicable; (Z): Less than half the unit shown; nec: Not elsewhere classified; nsk: Not specified by kind; - : zero; p : 10-19 percent estimated; q : 20-29 percent estimated.

PRODUCT SHARE DETAILS FOR CUTLERY AND FLATWARE (EXCEPT PRECIOUS) MANUFACTURING

Product or Product Class Shipments	Mil. $	Product or Product Class Shipments	Mil. $
CUTLERY AND FLATWARE (EXCEPT PRECIOUS)	2,780.2	clad to nonprecious metal	(D)
Cutlery, scissors, shears, trimmers, and snips	**626.9**	Kitchen and other cutlery	158.6
Flatware and cutlery	109.1	Kitchen cutlery (including knives, forks, cleavers, butchers' and meat packing), except carving sets	117.7
Table cutlery for food serving and eating, with handles of materials other than metal	84.5	All other cutlery (including knife blades sold separately), except kitchen cutlery	41.0
Electrosilverplated flatware and cutlery, electrosilverplated to a nonprecious (except pewter) metal base	(D)	Scissors and shears	222.8
Flatware made of base metal clad with nonprecious metal	(D)	All other knives, including nonelectric hair clippers	134.9
Flatware and cutlery, precious and nonprecious metal plated to a nonprecious (except pewter) metal base, except electrosilverplated	(D)	Cutlery, scissors, shears, trimmers, and snips, nsk	1.4
		Razor blades and razors, except electric	**2,118.9**
		Razors, except electric	(D)
		Razor blades, single and double edge for shaving	(D)
Flatware and cutlery, solid nonprecious (except pewter) metal, except plated metal and nonprecious metal		Razor blades for all other uses	(D)
		Cutlery and flatware (except precious), nsk, total	**34.5**

Source: 2002 Economic Census. The values are product shipments in millions of dollars for 2002. Total product shipments may be lower or higher than industry shipments. See Introduction for a full discussion. Values of indented subcategories are summed in the main heading(s). The symbol (D) appears when data are withheld to prevent disclosure of competitive information. The abbreviation nsk stands for 'not specified by kind' and nec for 'not elsewhere classified'. A dash (-) means zero.

PRODUCT SHARE DETAILS FOR KITCHEN UTENSIL, POT, AND PAN MANUFACTURING

Product or Product Class Shipments	Mil. $	Product or Product Class Shipments	Mil. $
KITCHEN UTENSILS, POTS, AND PANS	1,111.4	**aluminum**	**378.4**
Stamped and spun utensils, cooking and kitchen, aluminum	**720.1**	Top of range household stamped and spun stainless steel utensils (items generally used directly on top of source of heat)	109.7
Top of range household stamped and spun aluminum utensils (items generally used directly on top of source of heat), including pressure cookers	364.3	Other stamped and spun cooking and kitchen utensils (including copper and vitreous enamel)	266.9
Other stamped and spun aluminum cooking and kitchen utensils, including commercial and hospital	355.5	Other stamped and spun stainless steel cooking and kitchen utensils, including commercial, hospital, and outdoor cooking equipment	169.9
Stamped and spun aluminum utensils, cooking and kitchen	233.1	Tinware (including household, commercial, hospital, and outdoor cooking equipment)	4.6
Camping and outdoor stamped and spun aluminum cooking equipment	21.3	Other stamped and spun cooking and kitchen utensils (including copper and vitreous enamel)	92.4
Other stamped and spun aluminum cooking and kitchen utensils, including commercial and hospital . . .	101.1	Stamped and spun utensils, cooking and kitchen, except aluminum, nsk	1.8
Stamped and spun utensils, cooking and kitchen, aluminum, nsk	0.3	**Kitchen utensils, pots, and pans, nsk, total**	**13.0**
Stamped and spun utensils, cooking and kitchen, except			

Source: 2002 *Economic Census*. The values are product shipments in millions of dollars for 2002. Total product shipments may be lower or higher than industry shipments. See Introduction for a full discussion. Values of indented subcategories are summed in the main heading(s). The symbol (D) appears when data are withheld to prevent disclosure of competitive information. The abbreviation nsk stands for 'not specified by kind' and nec for 'not elsewhere classified'. A dash (-) means zero.

INPUTS AND OUTPUTS FOR CUTLERY, UTENSIL, POT, AND PAN MANUFACTURING

Economic Sector or Industry Providing Inputs	%	Sector	Economic Sector or Industry Buying Outputs	%	Sector
Compensation of employees	22.1		Personal consumption expenditures	69.0	
Iron & steel mills & ferroalloys	4.4	Manufg.	Exports of goods & services	7.0	Cap Inv
Alumina refining & primary aluminum production	4.3	Manufg.	Personal care services	3.0	Services
Fabricated metals, nec	3.7	Manufg.	Colleges, universities, & professional schools	3.0	Services
Paperboard containers	2.5	Manufg.	Change in private inventories	2.7	In House
Wholesale trade	2.4	Trade	General S/L govt. services	2.3	S/L Govt
Aluminum products from purchased aluminum	2.3	Manufg.	Food services & drinking places	1.6	Services
Management of companies & enterprises	1.9	Services	Amusement & recreation, nec	0.6	Services
Plastics materials & resins	1.6	Manufg.	Hospitals	0.6	Services
Advertising & related services	0.9	Services	Educational services, nec	0.5	Services
Plastics packaging materials, film & sheet	0.9	Manufg.	Motor vehicle parts	0.5	Manufg.
Plastics products, nec	0.7	Manufg.	Machine shops	0.4	Manufg.
Truck transportation	0.7	Util.	Retail trade	0.3	Trade
Machine shops	0.7	Manufg.	Fabricated metals, nec	0.3	Manufg.
Power generation & supply	0.7	Util.	Light truck & utility vehicles	0.3	Manufg.
Securities, commodity contracts, investments	0.7	Fin/R.E.	Ornamental & architectural metal products	0.3	Manufg.
Architectural, engineering, & related services	0.6	Services	Industrial machinery, nec	0.3	Manufg.
Turned products & screws, nuts, & bolts	0.5	Manufg.	General Federal government services, defense	0.2	Fed Govt
Specialized design services	0.5	Services	Plate work & fabricated structural products	0.2	Manufg.
Semiconductors & related devices	0.5	Manufg.	Wholesale trade	0.2	Trade
Telecommunications	0.5	Services	Poultry processing	0.2	Manufg.
Employment services	0.4	Services	Civic, social, & professional organizations	0.2	Services
Natural gas distribution	0.4	Util.	Rubber products, nec	0.2	Manufg.
Cutting tools & machine tool accessories	0.4	Manufg.	Manufacturing, nec	0.2	Manufg.
Printed circuit assemblies (electronic assemblies)	0.4	Manufg.	General Federal government services, nondefense	0.2	Fed Govt
Coating, engraving, heat treating & allied activities	0.4	Manufg.	Automobiles	0.2	Manufg.
Real estate	0.4	Fin/R.E.	Metal cans, boxes, & other containers (light gauge)	0.2	Manufg.
Legal services	0.4	Services	Valve & fittings other than plumbing	0.1	Manufg.
Lessors of nonfinancial assets	0.4	Fin/R.E.	Coating, engraving, heat treating & allied activities	0.1	Manufg.
Business support services	0.4	Services	Hotels & motels, including casino hotels	0.1	Services
Chemical products & preparations, nec	0.3	Manufg.	Scientific research & development services	0.1	Services
Ferrous metal foundries	0.3	Manufg.	Crowns & closures & metal stamping	0.1	Manufg.
Monetary authorities/depository credit intermediation	0.3	Fin/R.E.	Child day care services	0.1	Services
Crowns & closures & metal stamping	0.2	Manufg.	Elementary & secondary schools	0.1	Services
Support services, nec	0.2	Services	Signs	0.1	Manufg.
Professional, scientific, technical services, nec	0.2	Services	Other Federal Government enterprises	0.1	Fed Govt
Noncomparable imports	0.2	Foreign	Mining & oil & gas field machinery	0.1	Manufg.
Maintenance/repair of nonresidential structures	0.2	Construct.	Commercial & service industry machinery, nec	0.1	Manufg.
Nonferrous metal foundries	0.2	Manufg.	Motorcycles, bicycles, & parts	0.1	Manufg.
Services to buildings & dwellings	0.2	Services	Accommodations, nec	0.1	Services
Abrasive products	0.2	Manufg.			
Retail trade	0.2	Trade			
Investigation & security services	0.2	Services			
Accounting, tax preparation, bookkeeping, & payroll	0.2	Services			
Warehousing & storage	0.2	Util.			
Forging, stamping, & sintering, nec	0.2	Manufg.			
Metal cans, boxes, & other containers (light gauge)	0.2	Manufg.			
Rail transportation	0.1	Util.			
Automotive equipment rental & leasing	0.1	Fin/R.E.			
Unlaminated plastics profile shapes	0.1	Manufg.			
Automotive repair & maintenance, ex. car washes	0.1	Services			
Basic organic chemicals, nec	0.1	Manufg.			
Valve & fittings other than plumbing	0.1	Manufg.			

Continued on next page.

INPUTS AND OUTPUTS FOR CUTLERY, UTENSIL, POT, AND PAN MANUFACTURING - Continued

Economic Sector or Industry Providing Inputs	%	Sector	Economic Sector or Industry Buying Outputs	%	Sector
Data processing, hosting, & related services	0.1	Services			
Scientific research & development services	0.1	Services			
Taxes on production & imports, less subsidies	0.1				
Commercial & industrial equipment repair/maintenance	0.1	Services			
Nonferrous metal (ex. copper & aluminum) processing	0.1	Manufg.			
Food services & drinking places	0.1	Services			
Custom roll forming	0.1	Manufg.			

Source: Benchmark Input-Output Accounts for the U.S. Economy, 2002, U.S. Department of Commerce, Washington, D.C., January 2008. The abbreviation nec stands for 'not elsewhere classified'.

OCCUPATIONS EMPLOYED BY CUTLERY & HANDTOOL MANUFACTURING

Occupation	% of Total 2006	Change to 2016	Occupation	% of Total 2006	Change to 2016
Team assemblers	7.9	-24.8	Helpers--Production workers	2.1	-24.8
Machinists	5.5	-21.1	Welders, cutters, solderers, & brazers	1.9	-20.1
Cutting, punching, & press machine operators	4.8	-32.4	Customer service representatives	1.7	-17.3
Grinding, lapping, polishing machine tool operators	4.8	-27.1	Tool grinders, filers, & sharpeners	1.7	-32.4
Packers & packagers, hand	4.4	-39.9	Multiple machine tool operators & tenders	1.6	-17.3
First-line supervisors/managers of production workers	3.9	-24.8	Forging machine operators & tenders	1.4	-39.9
Tool & die makers	3.1	-21.1	General & operations managers	1.4	-32.4
Computer-controlled machine tool operators	2.8	-17.3	Bookkeeping, accounting, & auditing clerks	1.4	-24.8
Packaging & filling machine operators & tenders	2.5	-32.4	Mechanical engineers	1.3	-24.8
Sales reps, wholesale & manufacturing, exc tech	2.5	-24.8	Lathe & turning machine tool operators & tenders	1.2	-32.4
Shipping, receiving, & traffic clerks	2.5	-27.7	Industrial truck & tractor operators	1.1	-32.4
Laborers & freight, stock, & material movers, hand	2.3	-32.4	Office clerks, general	1.1	-26.0
Inspectors, testers, sorters, samplers, & weighers	2.2	-29.1	Industrial engineers	1.1	-8.7
Maintenance & repair workers, general	2.1	-24.8			

Source: Industry-Occupation Matrix, Bureau of Labor Statistics, December 4, 2007. These data are reported based on 4-digit NAICS categories but have been matched to corresponding 6-digit NAICS industry codes. The change reported for each occupation to the year 2016 is a percent of growth or decline as estimated by the Bureau of Labor Statistics. The abbreviation nec stands for 'not elsewhere classified'.

LOCATION BY STATE AND REGIONAL CONCENTRATION

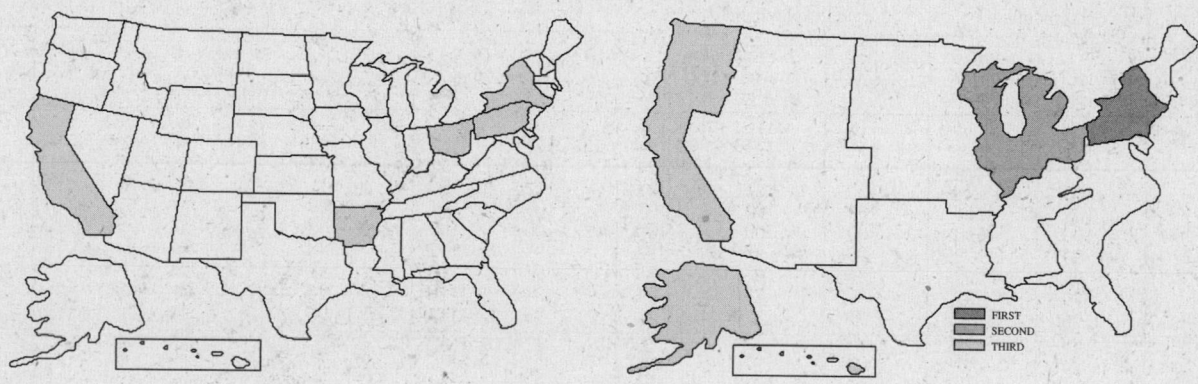

FIRST
SECOND
THIRD

INDUSTRY DATA BY STATE

State	Establish-ments	Shipments			Employment				Cost as % of Shipments	Investment per Employee ($)
		Total ($ mil)	% of U.S.	Per Establ.	Total Number	% of U.S.	Per Establ.	Wages ($/hour)		
New York	22	192.6	5.0	8,753.3	1,833	15.1	83	16.32	32.1	8,515
Pennsylvania	17	102.7	2.6	6,042.4	670	5.5	39	12.50	31.3	3,661
Ohio	16	81.2	2.1	5,074.3	558	4.6	35	12.86	46.5	4,964
California	15	77.1	2.0	5,143.0	537	4.4	36	20.89	32.3	2,270
Arkansas	6	12.1	0.3	2,019.5	118	1.0	20	13.14	39.1	407

Source: 2002 Economic Census. The states are in descending order of shipments or establishments (if shipment data are missing for the majority). The symbol (D) appears when data are withheld to prevent disclosure of competitive information. States marked with (D) are sorted by number of establishments. A dash (-) indicates that the data element cannot be calculated. Data may not show all states active in the NAICS category. All data available at the time of publication are shown.

NAICS 33221P - HAND TOOL AND SAW BLADE MANUFACTURING*

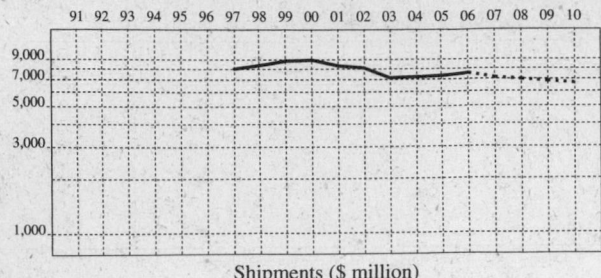

Shipments ($ million)

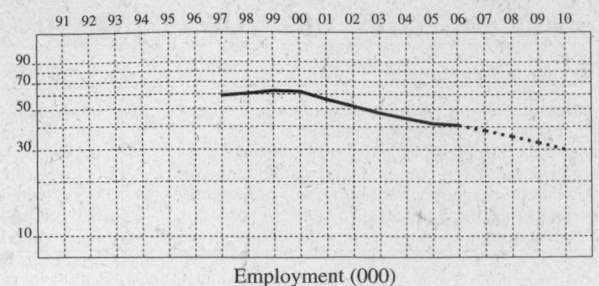

Employment (000)

GENERAL STATISTICS

Year	Companies	Establishments		Employment			Compensation		Production ($ million)			
		Total	with 20 or more employees	Total (000)	Production Workers (000)	Hours (Mil)	Payroll ($ mil)	Wages ($/hr)	Cost of Materials	Value Added by Manufacture	Value of Shipments	Capital Invest.
1997	1,326	1,438	494	59.1	43.6	88.7	1,923.8	13.12	2,966.2	5,037.5	8,017.4	304.2
1998		1,449	517	60.6	45.4	91.3	2,021.5	13.30	3,130.5	5,294.9	8,396.0	325.8
1999		1,434	519	62.5	46.3	91.0	2,060.2	13.91	3,275.2	5,613.3	8,850.8	344.6
2000		1,405	521	61.9	45.2	88.7	2,117.6	14.44	3,354.2	5,629.6	8,966.4	362.0
2001		1,365	482	56.1	40.3	78.8	1,948.5	14.49	3,304.1	5,020.0	8,329.6	240.4
2002	1,216	1,335	435	51.7	37.5	73.5	1,890.2	15.10	3,034.3	5,075.6	8,113.5	214.9
2003		1,325	429	47.5	34.7	67.7	1,754.5	15.40	2,665.3	4,466.3	7,150.2	181.6
2004		1,312	404	44.3	31.8	63.1	1,723.2	16.00	2,733.2	4,465.7	7,219.6	190.9
2005		1,322	412	41.6	29.6	59.6	1,722.6	16.67	2,901.1	4,451.8	7,314.6	157.3
2006		1,279P	390P	40.6	28.7	59.4	1,758.1	16.98	2,972.9	4,592.1	7,554.0	204.0
2007		1,260P	375P	38.0P	26.6P	53.1P	1,678.1P	17.35P	2,809.6P	4,339.9P	7,139.2P	138.7P
2008		1,240P	359P	35.3P	24.5P	48.9P	1,639.3P	17.79P	2,748.7P	4,245.8P	6,984.3P	118.0P
2009		1,221P	344P	32.7P	22.3P	44.7P	1,600.4P	18.23P	2,687.7P	4,151.6P	6,829.3P	97.3P
2010		1,202P	328P	30.0P	20.2P	40.5P	1,561.5P	18.66P	2,626.7P	4,057.4P	6,674.4P	76.6P

Sources: 1997 and 2002 *Economic Census*; other years, up to 2006, are from *Annual Survey of Manufactures*. Establishment counts for non-Census years are from *County Business Patterns*; 1997 and 2002 values are from the 1997 and 2002 censuses, respectively. 'P's show projections by the editors.

INDICES OF CHANGE

Year	Companies	Establishments		Employment			Compensation		Production ($ million)			
		Total	with 20 or more employees	Total (000)	Production Workers (000)	Hours (Mil)	Payroll ($ mil)	Wages ($/hr)	Cost of Materials	Value Added by Manufacture	Value of Shipments	Capital Invest.
1997	109	108	114	114	116	121	102	87	98	99	99	142
1998		109	119	117	121	124	107	88	103	104	103	152
1999		107	119	121	123	124	109	92	108	111	109	160
2000		105	120	120	121	121	112	96	111	111	111	168
2001		102	111	109	107	107	103	96	109	99	103	112
2002	100	100	100	100	100	100	100	100	100	100	100	100
2003		99	99	92	93	92	93	102	88	88	88	85
2004		98	93	86	85	86	91	106	90	88	89	89
2005		99	95	80	79	81	91	110	96	88	90	73
2006		96P	90P	79	77	81	93	112	98	90	93	95
2007		94P	86P	74P	71P	72P	89P	115P	93P	86P	88P	65P
2008		93P	83P	68P	65P	67P	87P	118P	91P	84P	86P	55P
2009		91P	79P	63P	59P	61P	85P	121P	89P	82P	84P	45P
2010		90P	75P	58P	54P	55P	83P	124P	87P	80P	82P	36P

Sources: Same as General Statistics. Values reflect change from the base year, 2002. Values above 100 mean greater than 2002, values below 100 mean less than 2002, and the values of 100 in other years means the same as 2002. 'P's show projections by the editors.

SELECTED RATIOS

For 2002	Avg. of All Manufact.	Analyzed Industry	Index	For 2002	Avg. of All Manufact.	Analyzed Industry	Index
Employees per Establishment	42	39	92	Value Added per Production Worker	182,367	135,349	74
Payroll per Establishment	1,639,184	1,415,880	86	Cost per Establishment	5,769,015	2,272,884	39
Payroll per Employee	39,053	36,561	94	Cost per Employee	137,446	58,691	43
Production Workers per Establishment	30	28	95	Cost per Production Worker	195,506	80,915	41
Wages per Establishment	694,845	831,348	120	Shipments per Establishment	11,158,348	6,077,528	54
Wages per Production Worker	23,548	29,596	126	Shipments per Employee	265,847	156,934	59
Hours per Production Worker	1,980	1,960	99	Shipments per Production Worker	378,144	216,360	57
Wages per Hour	11.89	15.10	127	Investment per Establishment	361,338	160,974	45
Value Added per Establishment	5,381,325	3,801,948	71	Investment per Employee	8,609	4,157	48
Value Added per Employee	128,210	98,174	77	Investment per Production Worker	12,245	5,731	47

Sources: Same as General Statistics. The 'Average of All Manufacturing' column represents the average of all manufacturing industries reported for the most recent complete year available. The Index shows the relationship between the Average and the Analyzed Industry. For example, 100 means that they are equal; 500 that the Analyzed Industry is five times the average; 50 means that the Analyzed Industry is half the national average. The abbreviation 'na' is used to show that data are 'not available'. Ratios shown for 2002, the last complete census year.

*Equivalent to Federal Government NAICS 332212, 332213.

LEADING COMPANIES
Number shown: **75**   Total sales ($ mil): **296,173**   Total employment (000): **607.6**

Company Name	Address				CEO Name	Phone	Co. Type	Sales ($ mil)	Empl. (000)
McKesson Corp.	1 Post St.	San Francisco	CA	94104	John H. Hammergren	415-983-8300	P	92,977	31.8
Caterpillar Inc.	100 NE Adams St.	Peoria	IL	61629		309-675-1000	P	44,958	101.3
Deere and Co.	1 John Deere Pl.	Moline	IL	61265		309-765-8000	P	24,082	52.0
CP and P Inc.	133 Peachtree St.	Atlanta	GA	30303	Jospeh Moller	404-652-4000	S	16,083*	55.0
Danaher Corp.	2099 Penn. Avenue	Washington	DC	20006	H. Lawrence Culp Jr.	202-828-0850	P	11,026	50.0
Seco Holding Company Inc.	11177 E 8 Mile Rd.	Warren	MI	48089	Bruce Belden	586-497-5000	R	9,960*	0.3
Saint-Gobain Abrasives Inc.	1 New Bond St.	Worcester	MA	01606	Jean Phelizon	508-795-5000	R	6,831*	2.5
AGCO Corp.	4205 River Green Pk	Duluth	GA	30096		770-813-9200	P	6,828	13.7
Black and Decker Corp.	101 Schilling Rd.	Hunt Valley	MD	21031	Nolan D. Archibald	410-716-3900	P	6,563	25.0
Cooper Industries Ltd.	PO Box 4446	Houston	TX	77210	Kirk S. Hachigian	713-209-8400	P	5,903	31.5
Stanley Works	PO Box 700	New Britain	CT	06053		860-225-5111	P	4,484	18.4
Carl Zeiss IMT Corp.	6250 Sycamore N	Osseo	MN	55369	Gregory Lee	763-744-2400	R	4,420*	0.1
Energizer Holdings Inc.	533 Maryville Univ.	St. Louis	MO	63141		314-985-2000	P	3,365	11.1
Milliken Chemical	PO Box 1926	Spartanburg	SC	29304	Ashley Allen	864-503-2200	R	3,317*	10.0
Snap-On Inc.	PO Box 1410	Kenosha	WI	53141	Tim Chambers	262-656-5200	P	2,841	11.6
GE Water and Process Tech.	4636 Somerton Rd.	Trevose	PA	19053	Jeff Garwood	215-355-3300	S	2,748*	8.0
Nordic Group of Companies Ltd.	414 Broadway, 200	Baraboo	WI	53913	William R. Sauey	608-356-0136	R	2,706*	2.5
International Game Technology	PO Box 10580	Reno	NV	89510	G. Thomas Baker	775-448-7777	P	2,621	5.4
Kennametal Inc.	PO Box 231	Latrobe	PA	15650	Carlos M. Cardoso	724-539-5000	P	2,386	14.0
Toro Co.	8111 Lyndale Ave. S	Bloomington	MN	55420		952-888-8801	P	1,877	5.3
Regal-Beloit Corp.	200 State St.	Beloit	WI	53511		608-364-8800	P	1,803	17.9
Polaris Industries Inc.	2100 Hwy. 55	Medina	MN	55340		763-542-0500	P	1,780	3.2
American Greetings Corp.	1 American Rd.	Cleveland	OH	44144		216-252-7300	P	1,745	28.9
CC Industries Inc.	222 N La Salle St.	Chicago	IL	60601	William H. Crown	312-855-4000	S	1,560*	6.0
Actuant Corp.	13000 W Slvr Spring	Butler	WI	53007	Bob Arzbaecher	414-352-4160	P	1,459	6.3
Tri-Con Industries Ltd.	4000 NW 44th St.	Lincoln	NE	68524		402-470-3311	R	1,450*	0.3
Danaher Tool Group	125 Pwdr Forest Dr.	Weatogue	CT	06089	H. Lawrence Culp	860-843-7300	S	1,380*	4.7
Federal Signal Corp.	1415 W 22nd St.	Oak Brook	IL	60523	James C. Janning	630-954-2000	P	1,268	5.5
Blyth Inc.	1 E Weaver St.	Greenwich	CT	06831		203-661-1926	P	1,221	4.0
Longaberger Co.	1500 E Main St.	Newark	OH	43055	Jim Klein	740-322-5000	R	1,206*	8.7
Lancaster Colony Corp.	37 W Broad St.	Columbus	OH	43215	John B. Gerlach, Jr.	614-224-7141	P	1,091	5.6
TriMas Corp.	39400 Woodward	Bloomfield Hls	MI	48304	Grant Beard	248-631-5450	P	1,068	5.1
Robert Bosch Tool Corp.	1961 Bishop Ln.	Louisville	KY	40218	Timothy Shea	502-625-2050	D	1,057*	0.2
Syngenta Seeds Inc. - NK	PO Box 959	Minneapolis	MN	55440	Jeff Cox	763-593-7333	S	1,044*	1.3
Brady Corp.	PO Box 571	Milwaukee	WI	53201		414-358-6600	P	1,018	8.0
MTD Products Inc.	PO Box 368022	Cleveland	OH	44136	Curtis E. Moll	330-225-2600	R	1,015*	6.7
MSC Industrial Supply Co.	75 Maxess Rd.	Melville	NY	11747	Mitchell Jacobson	516-812-2000	D	785*	2.8
Arctic Cat Inc.	PO Box 810	Thief River Fls	MN	56701		218-681-8558	P	782	1.8
Travel Tags Inc.	5842 Carmen Ave.	Inver Grove Hts	MN	55076	Barb Cederberg	651-450-1201	R	763*	0.3
Ceradyne Inc.	3169 Red Hill Ave.	Costa Mesa	CA	92626		714-549-0421	P	757	2.5
Westfaliasurge Inc.	1880 Country Frm	Naperville	IL	60563	Dirk Hejnal	630-369-8100	S	755*	0.1
Suntory Water Group Inc.	5660 New Northside	Atlanta	GA	30328	Stewart E. Allen	770-933-1400	R	688*	5.5
Yankee Candle Company Inc.	16 Yankee Candle	South Deerfield	MA	01373	Harlan M. Kent	413-665-8306	R	688	4.1
Alliance Gaming Corp.	6601 S Bermuda Rd.	Las Vegas	NV	89119	Richard M. Haddrill	702-584-7700	P	682	2.3
Oregon Cutting Systems Group	PO Box 22127	Portland	OR	97269	Jim Oscermanc	503-653-8881	D	674*	1.0
WMH Tool Group Inc.	2420 Vantage Dr.	Elgin	IL	60124	Peter Chatel	847-851-1000	R	627*	<0.1
Blount Inc.	PO Box 22127	Portland	OR	97269	James S. Osterman	503-653-8881	S	583*	3.0
NGK Spark Plugs (U.S.A.) Inc.	46929 Megellan	Wixom	MI	48393	Shinichi Oda	248-926-6900	D	567*	0.6
Mid-South Industries Inc.	PO Box 322	Gadsden	AL	35902	Larry Ferguson	256-494-1302	R	563*	1.6
LMT Fette Inc.	1997 Ohio St.	Lisle	IL	60532	Brian Nowicki	630-969-5412	R	558*	0.2
Chore-Time/Brock International	PO Box 2000	Milford	IN	46542	Warren E Buffett	547-658-4191	S	552*	1.0
WMS Industries Inc.	800 S Northpoint	Waukegan	IL	60085	Brian R. Gamache	847-785-3000	P	539	1.4
Alamo Group Inc.	PO Box 549	Seguin	TX	78155	Ronald Robinson	830-379-1480	P	504	2.3
Anchor Lamina America Inc.	PO Box 2540	Farmington Hls	MI	48333	Roy Verstraete	248-489-9122	R	500*	<0.1
Matco Tools Corp.	4403 Allen Rd.	Stow	OH	44224		330-929-4949	D	467*	0.5
Gehl Co.	PO Box 179	West Bend	WI	53095	William Gehl	262-334-9461	P	458	0.9
Koken Manufacturing Company	PO Box 265	Saint Louis	MO	63166	Masahiro Kanaya	314-231-7383	R	458*	<0.1
Arden Companies	18000 W 9 Mile Rd.	Southfield	MI	48075	Robert S. Sachs	248-355-1101	R	424*	1.2
James Hardie Transition Co.	26300 La Alameda	Mission Viejo	CA	92691	Donald Manson	949-348-1800	R	423*	<0.1
Metalworking Products	1 Teledyne Pl.	La Vergne	TN	37086	David M. Hogan	615-641-4200	S	402*	1.0
Fiskars Brands Inc.	2537 Daniels St.	Madison	WI	53718	Heikki Allonen	608-259-1649	R	399*	<0.1
WMS Gaming Inc.	3401 N California	Chicago	IL	60618	Brian R. Gamache	773-961-1620	S	398*	0.8
Amscan Holdings Inc.	80 Grasslands Rd.	Elmsford	NY	10523	James Harrison	914-345-2020	R	386*	2.0
Totes-Isotoner Corp.	9655 International	Cincinnati	OH	45246	Douglas Gernert	513-682-8200	R	358*	1.1
UNICEF	333 E 38th St., 6th	New York	NY	10016	Charles Lyons	212-326-7000	R	352*	1.0
Douglas Dynamics L.L.C.	915 Riverview Dr.	Johnson City	TN	37601	Jim Janik	423-928-3962	S	343*	0.5
Hardinge Inc.	PO Box 1507	Elmira	NY	14902	J. Patrick Ervin	607-734-2281	P	327	1.5
Kuhn Knight Inc.	1501 W 7th Ave.	Brodhead	WI	53520	Thierry Krier	608-897-2131	R	305*	0.2
Simplicity Manufacturing Inc.	PO Box 997	Port Washington	WI	53074	Warner Frazier	262-377-5450	R	305*	0.5
Russ Berrie and Company Inc.	111 Bauer Dr.	Oakland	NJ	07436	Andrew R. Gatto	201-337-9000	P	295	1.0
Lindsay Corp.	2707 N 108th St.	Omaha	NE	68164	M. N. Christodolou	402-428-2131	P	282	0.9
Trumpf Inc.	111 Hyde Rd.	Farmington	CT	06032	Rolf Biekert	860-255-6000	S	278*	0.6
Stanley Hand Tools	480 Myrtle St.	New Britain	CT	06053	Jeff Chen	860-225-5111	D	276*	0.3
Regal-Beloit Flight Services	200 State St.	Beloit	WI	53511	Henry W. Knueppel	608-364-8800	S	275*	1.0
Columbia Parcar Florida	PO Box 60	Reedsburg	WI	53959		608-524-8888	R	256*	<0.1

Source: Ward's Business Directory of U.S. Private and Public Companies, Volumes 1 and 2, 2008. The company type code used is as follows: P - Public, R - Private, S - Subsidiary, D - Division, J - Joint Venture, A - Affiliate, G - Group. Sales are in millions of dollars, employees are in thousands. An asterisk (*) indicates an estimated sales volume. The symbol < stands for 'less than'. Company names and addresses are truncated, in some cases, to fit into the available space.

MATERIALS CONSUMED FOR HAND AND EDGE TOOL MANUFACTURING

Material	Quantity	Delivered Cost ($ million)
Metal bolts, nuts, screws, and other screw machine products	(X)	57.1
Other fabricated metal products (exc. castings and forgings)	(X)	66.4
Iron and steel castings (rough and semifinished)	(X)	81.5
Aluminum and aluminum-base alloy castings (rough and semifinished)	(X)	30.9
Other nonferrous metal castings, rough or semifinished (inc. aluminum)	(X)	11.3
Iron and steel forgings	(X)	33.4
Steel bars, bar shapes, and plates (exc. castings, forgings, fabr. metal products)	(X)	136.4
Steel sheet, strip, and tin mill products	(X)	89.4
Steel wire and wire products	(X)	19.9
All other steel shapes and forms (exc. castings, forgings, fabr. metal products)	(X)	290.1
Copper and copper-base alloy shapes and forms (exc. castings, forgings, fabr. metal products)	(X)	2.9
Aluminum and aluminum-base alloy shapes and forms (exc. castings, forgings, fabr. metal products)	(X)	(D)
Other nonferrous shapes and forms (exc. castings, forgings, fabricated metal products)	(X)	(D)
Wood parts, including handles	(X)	67.3
Plastics resins consumed in the form of granules, pellets, etc.	(X)	55.1
Plastics products, incl. film, sheet, rod, tube, and fabricated shapes	(X)	94.0
Paper and paperboard containers (incl. shipping sacks and other paper packaging supplies)	(X)	83.7
Fluid power products	(X)	8.1
Electrical transmission, distribution, and control equipment	(X)	19.2
All other materials, components, parts, containers, and supplies	(X)	542.0
Materials, ingredients, containers, and supplies, nsk	(X)	235.3

Source: 2002 Economic Census. Explanation of symbols used: (D): Withheld to avoid disclosure of competitive data; na: Not available; (S): Withheld because statistical norms were not met; (X): Not applicable; (Z): Less than half the unit shown; nec: Not elsewhere classified; nsk: Not specified by kind; - : zero; p : 10-19 percent estimated; q : 20-29 percent estimated.

MATERIALS CONSUMED FOR SAW BLADE AND HANDSAW MANUFACTURING

Material	Quantity	Delivered Cost ($ million)
Iron and steel castings (rough and semifinished)	(X)	(D)
Nonferrous (aluminum, copper, etc.) castings (rough and semifinished)	(X)	(D)
Steel bars, bar shapes, and plates (exc. castings, forgings, fabr. metal products)	(X)	45.6
Steel sheet, strip, and tin mill products	(X)	62.1
Steel wire and wire products	(X)	12.6
All other steel shapes and forms (exc. castings, forgings, fabr. metal products)	(X)	43.1
Nonferrous shapes and forms	(X)	0.4
Fabricated metal products (excluding forgings)	(X)	3.7
Wood parts, including handles	(X)	(D)
Plastics products, incl. film, sheet, rod, tube, and fabricated shapes	(X)	6.8
Paper and paperboard containers (incl. shipping sacks and other paper packaging supplies)	(X)	15.7
All other materials, components, parts, containers, and supplies	(X)	104.3
Materials, ingredients, containers, and supplies, nsk	(X)	19.5

Source: 2002 Economic Census. Explanation of symbols used: (D): Withheld to avoid disclosure of competitive data; na: Not available; (S): Withheld because statistical norms were not met; (X): Not applicable; (Z): Less than half the unit shown; nec: Not elsewhere classified; nsk: Not specified by kind; - : zero; p : 10-19 percent estimated; q : 20-29 percent estimated.

PRODUCT SHARE DETAILS FOR HAND AND EDGE TOOL MANUFACTURING

Product or Product Class Shipments	Mil. $	Product or Product Class Shipments	Mil. $
HAND AND EDGE TOOLS.	6,179.3	Other handtools, including woodworking and metal working files and rasps, except edge tools	1,238.6
Mechanics' hand service tools	**2,404.5**	Shovels, spades, scoops, telegraph spoons, and scrapers	146.0
Mechanics' slip joint pliers	290.3	Light forged hammers, less than 4 lb (excluding ball peen hammers)	39.4
Mechanics' solid joint pliers	210.8	Heavy forged handtools, sledges (4 lb or more), picks, pick mattocks, and mauls	36.7
Other mechanics' hand service tools	567.5	Steel handtool goods (forks, hoes, rakes, weeders, etc.)	92.6
Mechanics' ball peen hammers	7.3	Soldering irons (electric)	(D)
Screwdrivers	165.2	Clamps and vises (except machine tool accessories)	74.1
Automobile jacks, mechanical (except hydraulic and pneumatic)	35.2	Wheelbarrows	(D)
Mechanics' tools for automotive use (except jacks)	139.1	Metal cutting shears (including aviation and tinners' strips, BX, and wire filament cutters)	67.9
Other mechanics' hand service tools (including blow torches and tape measures)	220.8	Tool-type scissors and shears	124.7
Mechanics' wrenches	1,335.8	Other handtools, including nonpowered lawnmovers, woodworking and metalworking files and rasps, and precision files, except edge tools	623.3
Mechanics' socket wrenches, including sockets, drives (ratchet and other), extensions, etc.	348.6	All other miscellaneous handtools, nsk	3.7
Mechanics' open-end and box wrenches	42.5	**Precision measuring tools (inspection, quality control, tool room, and machinists')**	**649.3**
Mechanics' torque wrenches	64.3	Precision measuring tools (inspection, quality control, tool room, and machinists')	335.7
Mechanics' adjustable wrenches, including pipe wrenches	99.5	Comparators (excluding optical) (inspection, quality control, tool room, and machinists' precision measuring tools)	73.8
Mechanics' combination open-end and box wrenches	99.1	Fixture type, fixed size precision measuring limit gauges (American Gauge Design Type C58-61) (inspection, quality control, tool room, and machinists')	23.1
Mechanics' wiring wrenches (including fish wire)	578.2	Thread type, fixed size precision measuring limit gauges (American Gauge Design Type C58-61) (inspection, quality control, tool room, and machinists')	23.8
All other mechanics' wrenches	103.7	Adjustable size precision measuring limit gauges	40.3
Edge tools, hand-operated	**642.5**	Precision measuring gauge blocks	8.7
Other hand-operated edge tools (including agricultural and forestry edge handtools)	630.6	Precision measuring dial indicators	19.4
Axes, adzes, hatchets, and chisels (hand-operated)	55.4	Precision measuring micrometers and calipers	18.8
Professional and craft edge handtools (including palette knives, paperhanger knives, putty knives, scrapers, trimmers, etc.)	373.1	Other precision measuring tools, including industrial quality control laser systems and equipment dividers, gear checking and surface texture measuring machines	127.9
Other hand-operated edge tools (including kitchen, animal hand clippers, agricultural, and forestry edge handtools)	202.0	Pneumatic and electronic precision measuring gauges	47.5
Edge tools, hand-operated, nsk	11.9	Coordinate and contour precision measuring machines	175.7
Dies and interchangeable cutting tools, for machines and power-driven handtools	**794.1**	Parts and accessories for machinists' precision measuring tools (sold separately)	8.0
Steel rule dies (except metal cutting), for machines and power-driven handtools	216.3	Precision measuring tools (inspection, quality control, tool room, and machinists'), nsk	82.4
Other cutting dies, for use in cutting cloth, paper, leathers, etc. (excluding dies for cutting metal), for machines and power-driven handtools	150.5	**Hand and edge tools, nsk, total**	**446.5**
All other woodcutting machine tools	406.5		
Dies and interchangeable woodcutting tools, for machine and power-driven hand	72.0		
Machines knives	92.5		
Countersink, drill, and router bits for woodcutting	146.0		
All other woodcutting machine tools	96.0		
Dies and interchangeable cutting tools, for machines and power-driven handtools, nsk	20.7		
All other handtools, nec	**1,242.3**		

Source: 2002 *Economic Census*. The values are product shipments in millions of dollars for 2002. Total product shipments may be lower or higher than industry shipments. See Introduction for a full discussion. Values of indented subcategories are summed in the main heading(s). The symbol (D) appears when data are withheld to prevent disclosure of competitive information. The abbreviation nsk stands for 'not specified by kind' and nec for 'not elsewhere classified'. A dash (-) means zero.

PRODUCT SHARE DETAILS FOR SAW BLADE AND HANDSAW MANUFACTURING

Product or Product Class Shipments	Mil. $	Product or Product Class Shipments	Mil. $
SAW BLADES AND HANDSAWS	1,154.9	metal teeth and cutting segments sold separately)	20.4
Handsaws, saw blades (hand and power), and saw accessories	**1,154.9**	Power band saw blades for metalworking (flexible back, spring temper metal cutting, and high-speed metal cutting)	108.1
Woodworking power saw blades and accessories	548.9	Other metalworking saw blades (saber, reciprocating, etc.), and hack (power only)	59.4
Power circular saw blades for woodworking, solid tooth	111.3	All other power saw blades	178.1
Power circular saw blades for woodworking, inserted tooth	59.3	All other hand-operated saws	188.5
Power band saw blades for woodworking	(D)	Hand-operated hacksaws	17.9
Teeth for inserted power woodworking saws, sold separately	11.6	Hand-operated carpenter crosscut saws and ripsaws	16.3
All other woodworking power saw blades (scroll, jig, etc.)	(D)	Other handsaws (heavy handsaws, crosscut, buck, miter, coping, pruning, compass, etc., including frames and blades)	154.3
Metalworking and other power saw blades and accessories	365.9	Saw blades and handsaws, nsk, total	51.5
Power circular saw blades for metalworking (including			

Source: 2002 *Economic Census*. The values are product shipments in millions of dollars for 2002. Total product shipments may be lower or higher than industry shipments. See Introduction for a full discussion. Values of indented subcategories are summed in the main heading(s). The symbol (D) appears when data are withheld to prevent disclosure of competitive information. The abbreviation nsk stands for 'not specified by kind' and nec for 'not elsewhere classified'. A dash (-) means zero.

INPUTS AND OUTPUTS FOR HANDTOOL MANUFACTURING

Economic Sector or Industry Providing Inputs	%	Sector	Economic Sector or Industry Buying Outputs	%	Sector
Compensation of employees	33.2		Personal consumption expenditures	17.0	
Iron & steel mills & ferroalloys	9.9	Manufg.	General S/L govt. services	11.1	S/L Govt
Wholesale trade	4.1	Trade	Exports of goods & services	10.1	Cap Inv
Management of companies & enterprises	3.3	Services	Retail trade	6.8	Trade
Nonferrous metal (ex. copper & aluminum) processing	1.9	Manufg.	Residential permanent site structures	5.3	Construct.
Advertising & related services	1.6	Services	General Federal government services, defense	4.6	Fed Govt
Paperboard containers	1.6	Manufg.	Motor vehicle parts	4.1	Manufg.
Securities, commodity contracts, investments	1.2	Fin/R.E.	Wholesale trade	3.6	Trade
Ferrous metal foundries	1.2	Manufg.	Private fixed investment	2.7	
Power generation & supply	1.1	Util.	Residential structures, nec	2.1	Construct.
Alumina refining & primary aluminum production	0.9	Manufg.	Change in private inventories	1.3	In House
Turned products & screws, nuts, & bolts	0.9	Manufg.	Cut stone & stone products	1.1	Manufg.
Truck transportation	0.9	Util.	Cattle	1.1	Agric.
Miscellaneous wood products	0.9	Manufg.	Owner-occupied dwellings	1.0	
Real estate	0.9	Fin/R.E.	Pipeline transportation	0.8	Util.
Lessors of nonfinancial assets	0.8	Fin/R.E.	Plastics products, nec	0.8	Manufg.
Plastics packaging materials, film & sheet	0.8	Manufg.	Community food, housing, relief, & rehabilitation	0.8	Services
Plastics materials & resins	0.8	Manufg.	Truck transportation	0.7	Util.
Monetary authorities/depository credit intermediation	0.8	Fin/R.E.	Dairy cattle & milk	0.7	Agric.
Nonferrous metal foundries	0.7	Manufg.	Periodical publishers	0.7	Services
Semiconductors & related devices	0.7	Manufg.	Packaging machinery	0.6	Manufg.
Plastics products, nec	0.7	Manufg.	Plate work & fabricated structural products	0.6	Manufg.
Printed circuit assemblies (electronic assemblies)	0.6	Manufg.	General Federal government services, nondefense	0.6	Fed Govt
Legal services	0.6	Services	Grains	0.5	Agric.
Professional, scientific, technical services, nec	0.6	Services	Ornamental & architectural metal products	0.5	Manufg.
Machine shops	0.6	Manufg.	Light truck & utility vehicles	0.5	Manufg.
Architectural, engineering, & related services	0.5	Services	Industrial machinery, nec	0.5	Manufg.
Forging, stamping, & sintering, nec	0.5	Manufg.	S/L govt. invest., education	0.4	S/L Govt
Transportation equipment, nec	0.5	Manufg.	Personal & household goods repair/maintenance	0.4	Services
Steel products from purchased steel	0.5	Manufg.	Paper mills	0.4	Manufg.
Motor vehicle parts	0.5	Manufg.	Civic, social, & professional organizations	0.4	Services
Accounting, tax preparation, bookkeeping, & payroll	0.4	Services	Commercial & industrial equipment repair/maintenance	0.4	Services
Taxes on production & imports, less subsidies	0.4		Greenhouse & nursery products	0.4	Agric.
Food services & drinking places	0.4	Services	Nonresidential structures, nec	0.4	Construct.
Telecommunications	0.3	Services	Vegetables and melons	0.4	Agric.
Abrasive products	0.3	Manufg.	Rubber products, nec	0.3	Manufg.
Natural gas distribution	0.3	Util.	Miscellaneous crops	0.3	Agric.
Management, scientific, & technical consulting	0.3	Services	Oilseeds	0.3	Agric.
Warehousing & storage	0.3	Util.	Poultry & eggs	0.3	Agric.
Scientific research & development services	0.3	Services	Federal government, investment, national defense	0.3	Fed Govt
Automotive equipment rental & leasing	0.3	Fin/R.E.	Manufacturing, nec	0.3	Manufg.
Data processing, hosting, & related services	0.3	Services	Metal cans, boxes, & other containers (light gauge)	0.3	Manufg.
Services to buildings & dwellings	0.3	Services	Automotive equipment rental & leasing	0.3	Fin/R.E.
Nondepository credit intermediation activities	0.3	Fin/R.E.	Automobiles	0.3	Manufg.
Coating, engraving, heat treating & allied activities	0.3	Manufg.	Machine shops	0.3	Manufg.
Maintenance/repair of nonresidential structures	0.3	Construct.	Signs	0.3	Manufg.
Rail transportation	0.3	Util.	Coating, engraving, heat treating & allied activities	0.2	Manufg.
Cutting tools & machine tool accessories	0.3	Manufg.	Rail transportation	0.2	Util.
Relay & industrial controls	0.3	Manufg.	Valve & fittings other than plumbing	0.2	Manufg.
Noncomparable imports	0.2	Foreign	Livestock, nec	0.2	Agric.
Handtools	0.2	Manufg.	Commercial & service industry machinery, nec	0.2	Manufg.
Business support services	0.2	Services	Crowns & closures & metal stamping	0.2	Manufg.
Employment services	0.2	Services	Fruit	0.2	Agric.
Hotels & motels, including casino hotels	0.2	Services	Real estate	0.2	Fin/R.E.
Specialized design services	0.2	Services	Internet publishing & broadcasting	0.2	Services
Retail trade	0.2	Trade	Automotive repair & maintenance, ex. car washes	0.2	Services
Chemical products & preparations, nec	0.2	Manufg.	Mining & oil & gas field machinery	0.2	Manufg.
Automotive repair & maintenance, ex. car washes	0.2	Services	Commercial & health care structures	0.2	Construct.
Commercial & industrial machinery rental & leasing	0.2	Fin/R.E.	Handtools	0.2	Manufg.
Air transportation	0.2	Util.	Motorcycles, bicycles, & parts	0.2	Manufg.
Commercial & industrial equipment repair/maintenance	0.1	Services	Aircraft parts & auxiliary equipment, nec	0.2	Manufg.
Paints & coatings	0.1	Manufg.	Cotton	0.2	Agric.
Other computer related services, including facilities	0.1	Services	S/L govt. invest., other	0.2	S/L Govt
Support services, nec	0.1	Services	Maintenance/repair of residential structures	0.2	Construct.
Unlaminated plastics profile shapes	0.1	Manufg.	Transportation equipment, nec	0.2	Manufg.
Paperboard mills	0.1	Manufg.	Engine equipment, nec	0.2	Manufg.
Valve & fittings other than plumbing	0.1	Manufg.	AC, refrigeration, and warm air heating equipment	0.1	Manufg.
			Hardware	0.1	Manufg.
			Surgical appliances & supplies	0.1	Manufg.
			Turned products & screws, nuts, & bolts	0.1	Manufg.
			Electronic & precision equipment repair/maintenance	0.1	Services
			Transit & ground passenger transportation	0.1	Util.
			Hotels & motels, including casino hotels	0.1	Services
			Maintenance/repair of nonresidential structures	0.1	Construct.
			Semiconductors & related devices	0.1	Manufg.
			Car washes	0.1	Services
			Jewelry & silverware	0.1	Manufg.
			Air transportation	0.1	Util.
			Power boilers & heat exchangers	0.1	Manufg.
			Scenic & sightseeing transport & related services	0.1	Util.

Continued on next page.

INPUTS AND OUTPUTS FOR HANDTOOL MANUFACTURING - Continued

Economic Sector or Industry Providing Inputs	%	Sector	Economic Sector or Industry Buying Outputs	%	Sector
			Construction machinery	0.1	Manufg.
			Fabricated pipes & pipe fittings	0.1	Manufg.
			Turbines & turbine generator set units	0.1	Manufg.
			Household cooking appliances	0.1	Manufg.
			Religious organizations	0.1	Services
			Farm machinery & equipment	0.1	Manufg.
			Semiconductor machinery	0.1	Manufg.
			Electromedical & electrotherapeutic apparatus	0.1	Manufg.
			Switchgear & switchboard apparatus	0.1	Manufg.

Source: Benchmark Input-Output Accounts for the U.S. Economy, 2002, U.S. Department of Commerce, Washington, D.C., January 2008. The abbreviation nec stands for 'not elsewhere classified'.

OCCUPATIONS EMPLOYED BY CUTLERY & HANDTOOL MANUFACTURING

Occupation	% of Total 2006	Change to 2016	Occupation	% of Total 2006	Change to 2016
Team assemblers	7.9	-24.8	Helpers--Production workers	2.1	-24.8
Machinists	5.5	-21.1	Welders, cutters, solderers, & brazers	1.9	-20.1
Cutting, punching, & press machine operators	4.8	-32.4	Customer service representatives	1.7	-17.3
Grinding, lapping, polishing machine tool operators	4.8	-27.1	Tool grinders, filers, & sharpeners	1.7	-32.4
Packers & packagers, hand	4.4	-39.9	Multiple machine tool operators & tenders	1.6	-17.3
First-line supervisors/managers of production workers	3.9	-24.8	Forging machine operators & tenders	1.4	-39.9
Tool & die makers	3.1	-21.1	General & operations managers	1.4	-32.4
Computer-controlled machine tool operators	2.8	-17.3	Bookkeeping, accounting, & auditing clerks	1.4	-24.8
Packaging & filling machine operators & tenders	2.5	-32.4	Mechanical engineers	1.3	-24.8
Sales reps, wholesale & manufacturing, exc tech	2.5	-24.8	Lathe & turning machine tool operators & tenders	1.2	-32.4
Shipping, receiving, & traffic clerks	2.5	-27.7	Industrial truck & tractor operators	1.1	-32.4
Laborers & freight, stock, & material movers, hand	2.3	-32.4	Office clerks, general	1.1	-26.0
Inspectors, testers, sorters, samplers, & weighers	2.2	-29.1	Industrial engineers	1.1	-8.7
Maintenance & repair workers, general	2.1	-24.8			

Source: Industry-Occupation Matrix, Bureau of Labor Statistics, December 4, 2007. These data are reported based on 4-digit NAICS categories but have been matched to corresponding 6-digit NAICS industry codes. The change reported for each occupation to the year 2016 is a percent of growth or decline as estimated by the Bureau of Labor Statistics. The abbreviation nec stands for 'not elsewhere classified'.

LOCATION BY STATE AND REGIONAL CONCENTRATION

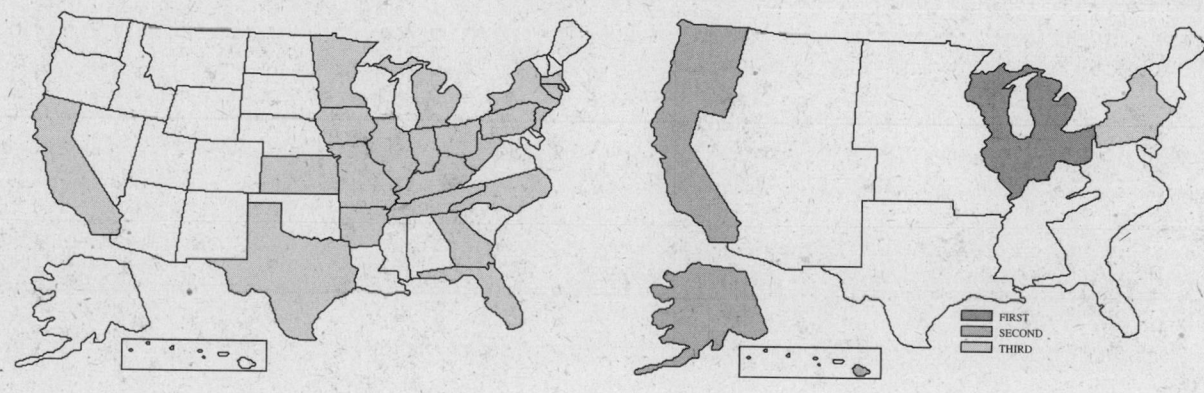

INDUSTRY DATA BY STATE

State	Establish-ments	Shipments			Employment				Cost as % of Shipments	Investment per Employee ($)
		Total ($ mil)	% of U.S.	Per Establ.	Total Number	% of U.S.	Per Establ.	Wages ($/hour)		
Ohio	92	762.9	9.4	8,292.2	4,316	8.3	47	15.98	37.5	8,884
California	181	669.6	8.3	3,699.7	4,665	9.0	26	13.45	40.2	5,634
Minnesota	33	546.6	6.7	16,564.3	2,205	4.3	67	20.18	59.0	1,838
Illinois	91	526.8	6.5	5,788.9	4,205	8.1	46	14.93	30.5	2,627
North Carolina	28	385.9	4.8	13,783.4	1,832	3.5	65	15.37	46.6	2,960
New York	71	305.8	3.8	4,306.5	1,991	3.8	28	15.32	48.0	3,827
Michigan	96	304.4	3.8	3,170.6	2,490	4.8	26	17.20	33.7	3,444

Continued on next page.

INDUSTRY DATA BY STATE - Continued

State	Establish-ments	Shipments			Employment				Cost as % of Shipments	Investment per Employee ($)
		Total ($ mil)	% of U.S.	Per Establ.	Total Number	% of U.S.	Per Establ.	Wages ($/hour)		
New Jersey	44	264.2	3.3	6,005.1	1,833	3.5	42	13.86	32.1	5,109
Massachusetts	4	257.1	3.2	64,265.0	1,170	2.3	292	17.53	31.7	5,324
Pennsylvania	60	255.4	3.1	4,256.2	1,788	3.5	30	15.07	34.6	4,076
Texas	36	253.4	3.1	7,040.1	1,675	3.2	47	14.33	37.7	2,603
Connecticut	36	215.6	2.7	5,988.9	1,573	3.0	44	17.48	38.8	2,388
Indiana	24	164.0	2.0	6,832.9	1,036	2.0	43	16.76	38.5	1,887
Missouri	34	149.3	1.8	4,391.1	483	0.9	14	15.50	18.8	6,455
Tennessee	27	146.6	1.8	5,429.6	1,407	2.7	52	15.04	53.2	6,717
Arkansas	8	143.6	1.8	17,952.2	1,017	2.0	127	12.99	32.4	1,531
Florida	30	121.5	1.5	4,048.5	598	1.2	20	13.65	41.2	3,692
West Virginia	6	116.6	1.4	19,427.0	746	1.4	124	20.03	28.8	1,206
Kentucky	24	103.7	1.3	4,321.6	919	1.8	38	14.90	40.5	3,350
Georgia	17	101.4	1.2	5,964.6	601	1.2	35	15.56	26.6	2,077
Iowa	14	75.4	0.9	5,383.6	458	0.9	33	17.95	35.4	7,793
Kansas	8	41.1	0.5	5,133.0	306	0.6	38	10.83	35.1	2,781
Rhode Island	11	20.7	0.3	1,880.8	164	0.3	15	13.34	34.4	1,207

Source: 2002 *Economic Census*. The states are in descending order of shipments or establishments (if shipment data are missing for the majority). The symbol (D) appears when data are withheld to prevent disclosure of competitive information. States marked with (D) are sorted by number of establishments. A dash (-) indicates that the data element cannot be calculated. Data may not show all states active in the NAICS category. All data available at the time of publication are shown.

NAICS 33231M - PLATE WORK AND FABRICATED STRUCTURAL PRODUCT MANUFACTURING*

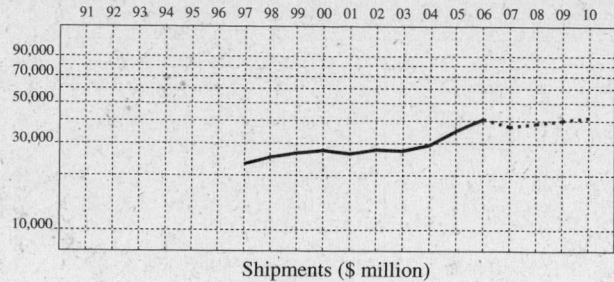

Shipments ($ million)

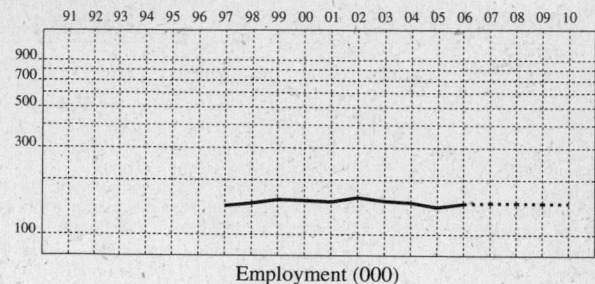

Employment (000)

GENERAL STATISTICS

Year	Com-panies	Establishments		Employment			Compensation		Production ($ million)			
		Total	with 20 or more employees	Total (000)	Production Workers (000)	Hours (Mil)	Payroll ($ mil)	Wages ($/hr)	Cost of Materials	Value Added by Manufacture	Value of Shipments	Capital Invest.
1997	4,438	4,677	1,774	143.6	103.9	211.0	4,500.2	12.98	12,636.0	10,518.9	23,038.5	446.5
1998		4,744	1,825	148.5	106.9	215.1	4,797.7	13.65	13,659.7	11,537.8	25,163.8	471.2
1999		4,595	1,842	155.5	112.4	231.2	5,161.3	13.56	13,958.0	12,619.9	26,513.2	606.1
2000		4,389	1,872	153.8	111.6	226.3	5,279.3	14.19	14,400.2	13,094.2	27,394.3	614.6
2001		4,648	1,935	151.4	109.7	222.7	5,290.5	14.42	13,639.6	12,596.3	26,272.4	608.4
2002	5,226	5,544	1,904	159.8	112.8	226.2	5,866.3	15.73	13,905.5	13,823.2	27,640.1	773.9
2003		5,322	1,801	152.8	106.8	218.5	5,753.3	15.99	13,918.7	13,420.9	27,268.2	496.0
2004		5,392	1,845	149.7	106.4	217.3	5,848.3	16.65	15,473.5	14,095.8	29,387.4	515.0
2005		5,407	1,863	141.4	99.7	209.7	5,895.5	17.25	18,467.5	17,046.6	35,248.4	603.8
2006		5,591P	1,882P	148.0	106.1	224.1	6,582.2	17.94	22,097.7	19,127.6	40,878.0	684.0
2007		5,716P	1,888P	149.3P	105.2P	219.9P	6,559.3P	18.30P	20,054.0P	17,358.6P	37,097.4P	662.6P
2008		5,841P	1,894P	149.1P	104.8P	219.8P	6,752.4P	18.86P	20,861.6P	18,057.6P	38,591.4P	677.3P
2009		5,965P	1,900P	148.9P	104.4P	219.8P	6,945.4P	19.42P	21,669.2P	18,756.7P	40,085.3P	691.9P
2010		6,090P	1,906P	148.7P	103.9P	219.7P	7,138.5P	19.98P	22,476.8P	19,455.8P	41,579.3P	706.6P

Sources: 1997 and 2002 *Economic Census*; other years, up to 2006, are from *Annual Survey of Manufactures*. Establishment counts for non-Census years are from *County Business Patterns*; 1997 and 2002 values are from the 1997 and 2002 censuses, respectively. 'P's show projections by the editors.

INDICES OF CHANGE

Year	Com-panies	Establishments		Employment			Compensation		Production ($ million)			
		Total	with 20 or more employees	Total (000)	Production Workers (000)	Hours (Mil)	Payroll ($ mil)	Wages ($/hr)	Cost of Materials	Value Added by Manufacture	Value of Shipments	Capital Invest.
1997	85	84	93	90	92	93	77	83	91	76	83	58
1998		86	96	93	95	95	82	87	98	83	91	61
1999		83	97	97	100	102	88	86	100	91	96	78
2000		79	98	96	99	100	90	90	104	95	99	79
2001		84	102	95	97	98	90	92	98	91	95	79
2002	100	100	100	100	100	100	100	100	100	100	100	100
2003		96	95	96	95	97	98	102	100	97	99	64
2004		97	97	94	94	96	100	106	111	102	106	67
2005		98	98	88	88	93	100	110	133	123	128	78
2006		101P	99P	93	94	99	112	114	159	138	148	88
2007		103P	99P	93P	93P	97P	112P	116P	144P	126P	134P	86P
2008		105P	99P	93P	93P	97P	115P	120P	150P	131P	140P	88P
2009		108P	100P	93P	93P	97P	118P	123P	156P	136P	145P	89P
2010		110P	100P	93P	92P	97P	122P	127P	162P	141P	150P	91P

Sources: Same as General Statistics. Values reflect change from the base year, 2002. Values above 100 mean greater than 2002, values below 100 mean less than 2002, and the values of 100 in other years means the same as 2002. 'P's show projections by the editors.

SELECTED RATIOS

For 2002	Avg. of All Manufact.	Analyzed Industry	Index	For 2002	Avg. of All Manufact.	Analyzed Industry	Index
Employees per Establishment	42	29	69	Value Added per Production Worker	182,367	122,546	67
Payroll per Establishment	1,639,184	1,058,135	65	Cost per Establishment	5,769,015	2,508,207	43
Payroll per Employee	39,053	36,710	94	Cost per Employee	137,446	87,018	63
Production Workers per Establishment	30	20	69	Cost per Production Worker	195,506	123,276	63
Wages per Establishment	694,845	641,798	92	Shipments per Establishment	11,158,348	4,985,588	45
Wages per Production Worker	23,548	31,544	134	Shipments per Employee	265,847	172,967	65
Hours per Production Worker	1,980	2,005	101	Shipments per Production Worker	378,144	245,036	65
Wages per Hour	11.89	15.73	132	Investment per Establishment	361,338	139,592	39
Value Added per Establishment	5,381,325	2,493,362	46	Investment per Employee	8,609	4,843	56
Value Added per Employee	128,210	86,503	67	Investment per Production Worker	12,245	6,861	56

Sources: Same as General Statistics. The 'Average of All Manufacturing' column represents the average of all manufacturing industries reported for the most recent complete year available. The Index shows the relationship between the Average and the Analyzed Industry. For example, 100 means that they are equal; 500 that the Analyzed Industry is five times the average; 50 means that the Analyzed Industry is half the national average. The abbreviation 'na' is used to show that data are 'not available'. Ratios shown for 2002, the last complete census year.

*Equivalent to Federal Government NAICS 332311, 332312, 332313.

LEADING COMPANIES   Number shown: **75**   Total sales ($ mil): **110,530**   Total employment (000): **273.3**

Company Name	Address				CEO Name	Phone	Co. Type	Sales ($ mil)	Empl. (000)
Nucor Corp.	1915 Rexford Rd.	Charlotte	NC	28211	Daniel R. DiMicco	704-366-7000	P	16,593	18.0
API Group Inc.	2366 Rose Pl.	St. Paul	MN	55113	Lee R. Anderson Sr.	651-636-4320	R	9,000	5.0
Commercial Metals Co.	6565 N MacArthur	Irving	TX	75039		214-689-4300	P	8,329	12.7
Dover Corp.	280 Park Ave.	New York	NY	10017		212-922-1640	P	7,226	33.4
McDermott International Inc.	757 N Eldridge Pky.	Houston	TX	77079	Robert Deason	281-870-5011	P	5,632	28.4
Allegheny Technologies Inc.	1000 Six PPG Pl.	Pittsburgh	PA	15222		412-394-2800	P	5,453	9.5
Trinity Industries Inc.	2525 Stemmons	Dallas	TX	75207		214-631-4420	P	3,833	14.4
Harsco Corp.	PO Box 8888	Camp Hill	PA	17001	S. D. Fazzolari	717-763-7064	P	3,688	21.5
Amsted Industries Inc.	2 Prudential Plaza	Chicago	IL	60601	W. Robert Reum	312-645-1700	R	3,050	9.9
Baltimore Aircoil Company Inc.	PO Box 7322	Baltimore	MD	21227	Steven Duerwachter	410-799-6200	R	2,510*	0.2
Consolidated Metco Inc.	PO Box 83201	Portland	OR	97283		503-286-5741	R	2,510*	0.1
Mechanical Construction Inc.	1500 Chester Pk.	Eddystone	PA	19022	Michael J. Hall	610-876-9292	S	2,370*	3.3
A.O. Smith Corp.	PO Box 245008	Milwaukee	WI	53224		414-359-4000	P	2,312	16.8
Valley Joist Inc.	PO Box 680718	Fort Payne	AL	35968		256-845-2330	R	2,100*	0.1
Hutchinson FTS Inc.	1835 Technology	Troy	MI	48083	Paul Campbell	248-589-7710	R	1,863*	<0.1
Silgan Containers Corp.	21800 Oxnard St.	Woodland Hills	CA	91367	James D. Beam	818-348-3700	S	1,648*	5.0
NCI Building Systems Inc.	PO Box 692055	Houston	TX	77269	Norman C. Chambers	281-897-7788	P	1,624	5.7
Mid-Atlantic Constructors Inc.	1500 Chester Pk.	Eddystone	PA	19022	Michael J. Hall	610-532-7831	S	1,607*	3.3
Tang Industries Inc.	8960 Spanish Ridge	Las Vegas	NV	89148	Cyrus Tang	702-734-3700	R	1,500*	3.2
Valmont Industries Inc.	1 Valmont Plz.	Omaha	NE	68154	Mogens C. Bay	402-963-1000	P	1,500	6.0
Williams Enterprise of Georgia	1285 Hawthorne	Smyrna	GA	30080	Dale Williams	770-436-1596	R	1,478*	0.6
EBSCO Industries Inc.	PO Box 1943	Birmingham	AL	35201	Dixon Brooke Jr.	205-991-6600	R	1,400*	5.0
Babcock and Wilcox Co.	PO Box 351	Barberton	OH	44203	John A. Fees	330-753-4511	S	1,080*	10.8
TriMas Corp.	39400 Woodward	Bloomfield Hls	MI	48304	Grant Beard	248-631-5450	P	1,068	5.1
C and D Zodiac Inc.	5701 Bolsa Ave.	Huntington Bch	CA	92647		714-934-0000	R	1,045*	0.5
Alberici Corp.	8800 Page Ave.	St. Louis	MO	63114	Gregory Kozicz	314-733-2000	R	1,033	0.5
EPE Industrial Filters Inc.	9250 Bloomington	Bloomington	MN	55431	William Cook	847-381-0860	R	1,024*	1.5
Texas Industries Inc.	1341 W Mckingbird	Dallas	TX	75247	Mel G. Brekhus	972-647-6700	P	996	2.7
McWane Corp.	PO Box 43327	Birmingham	AL	35243	G. Ruffner Page, Jr.	205-414-3100	R	944*	7.0
Manchester Tank and Equipment	1000 Corp Centre Dr	Franklin	TN	37067	Robert Richard	615-370-3833	R	926*	<0.1
Johnstown Holdings Inc.	545 Central Ave.	Johnstown	PA	15902	John Bolduc	814-535-9000	R	918*	0.2
Champion Home Builders Co.	2701 Cambridge Ct.	Auburn Hills	MI	48326	William Griffiths	248-340-9090	S	807*	2.0
Butler Manufacturing Co.	PO Box 419917	Kansas City	MO	64141		816-968-3000	S	796*	4.3
American Railcar Industries	100 Clark St.	St. Charles	MO	63301		636-940-6000	P	698	2.2
Chart Industries Inc.	One Infinity Corp.	Garfield Height	OH	44125	Samuel F. Thomas	440-753-1490	P	666	2.8
Riley Power Inc.	PO Box 15040	Worcester	MA	01615		508-852-7100	R	612*	0.4
American Cast Iron Pipe Co.	PO Box 2727	Birmingham	AL	35202		205-325-7701	R	596*	2.3
NATCO Group Inc.	2950 N Loop W, 700	Houston	TX	77092	John U. Clarke	713-683-9292	P	570	2.5
Gulf Island Fabrication Inc.	PO Box 310	Houma	LA	70361	Kerry J. Chauvin	985-872-2100	P	473	1.9
U.S. Foundry and Manufacturing	8351 NW 93rd St.	Medley	FL	33166	Alex DeBogory		R	468*	0.5
Suncoast Post-Tension L.P.	654 N Sam Houston	Houston	TX	77060		281-445-8886	R	464*	0.2
Alaskan Copper Co's Inc.	PO Box 3546	Seattle	WA	98124	Kermit Rosen	206-623-5800	R	392*	0.3
Mestek Inc.	260 N Elm St.	Westfield	MA	01085	R. Bruce Dewey	413-568-9571	R	372*	2.6
Skyline Corp.	PO Box 743	Elkhart	IN	46515	Arthur J. Decio	574-294-6521	P	366	2.3
Garlock Sealing Technologies	1666 Division St.	Palmyra	NY	14522	Ernest F. Schaub	315-597-4811	D	354*	1.5
Claymont Steel Holdings Inc.	4001 Philadelphia	Claymont	DE	19703	Jeff Bradley	302-792-5400	P	333	0.4
Mobile Mini Inc.	PO Box 79149	Phoenix	AZ	85062	Steven G. Bunger	480-894-6311	P	318	2.1
Maxcess Technologies Inc.	230 Deming Way	Summerville	SC	29483	Andy Miarka	843-821-1200	R	291*	<0.1
Duraloy Technologies Inc.	120 Bridge St.	Scottdale	PA	15683	Vincent Schiavoni	724-887-5100	R	271*	0.1
Kirk and Blum Manufacturing	3120 Forrer St.	Cincinnati	OH	45209	Richard J. Blum	513-458-2600	S	265*	0.4
CEI Enterprises Inc.	245 Woodward SE	Albuquerque	NM	87102		505-842-5556	S	264*	0.1
Southern Heat Exchanger Corp.	PO Box 1850	Tuscaloosa	AL	35403	Bill Laganke	205-345-5335	R	234*	0.2
Bohler Uddeholm America Inc.	4902 Tollview Dr.	Rolling Mdws	IL	60008	Erik Svendsen	847-577-2220	R	234*	0.2
Daman Industrial Services Inc.	PO Box 486	East Brady	PA	16028		724-526-5714	R	228*	<0.1
Alcan Composites USA Inc.	PO Box 507	Benton	KY	42025		270-527-4200	R	224*	0.1
Middle Atlantic Products Inc.	300 Fairfield Rd.	Fairfield	NJ	07004	Robert J. Schluter	973-839-1011	R	220*	0.3
General Atomics	PO Box 85608	San Diego	CA	92186	James Blue	858-455-3000	R	219*	1.0
Burnham Holdings Inc.	PO Box 3205	Lancaster	PA	17604	Albert Morrison III	717-397-4700	P	218	1.3
Raven Industries Inc.	PO Box 5107	Sioux Falls	SD	57117	Conrad J. Hoigaard	605-336-2750	P	217	0.9
Amtrol Inc.	1400 Division Rd.	West Warwick	RI	02893	Larry T. Guillemette	401-884-6300	R	213	1.3
Cleaver-Brooks Inc.	PO Box 421	Milwaukee	WI	53201	Welch Goggins	414-359-0600	R	210*	0.2
Owens Corning Fabric Solutions	PO Box 1366	Elkhart	IN	46515	Raymond Stout	574-522-8473	D	207	0.8
Poly Processing Co.	8055 Ash Street	French Camp	CA	95231	Dixon Abell	209-982-4904	R	204*	0.3
CCC Group Inc.	PO Box 200350	San Antonio	TX	78220	Dennis Hubner	210-661-4251	R	200*	2.0
Ameri-Forge Ltd.	13770 Industrial Rd	Houston	TX	77015	William Friel	713-393-4200	R	200*	0.2
Robinson Steel Company Inc.	4303 Kennedy Ave.	East Chicago	IN	46312		219-398-4600	R	200*	0.2
SMI Manufacturing Inc.	13312 E Hardy Rd.	Houston	TX	77039	Bo Eagles	281-449-0345	R	200*	<0.1
API Delevan	270 Quaker Rd.	East Aurora	NY	14052		716-652-3600	S	195*	1.8
ALSTOM Power Inc.	3020 Truax Rd.	Wellsville	NY	14895	E Bysiek	585-593-2700	S	191*	0.6
Ceco Door Products	9159 Telecom Dr.	Milan	TN	38358	Larry Denbrock	731-686-8345	S	190*	0.6
Chief Industries Inc.	PO Box 2078	Grand Island	NE	68802	Robert Eihusen	308-389-7200	R	185*	<0.1
Keppel Amfels Inc.	PO Box 3107	Brownsville	TX	78523	C Ho	956-831-8220	R	183*	1.5
Arrow Group Industries Inc.	PO Box 928	Wayne	NJ	07474	George Smith	973-696-6900	R	180*	<0.1
Frazier Industrial Company	PO Box F	Long Valley	NJ	07853	Donald Frazier	908-876-3001	R	173*	0.1
Morgan Buildings and Spas Inc.	PO Box 660280	Dallas	TX	75266	Guy Morgan	972-840-1200	R	169*	<0.1

Source: Ward's Business Directory of U.S. Private and Public Companies, Volumes 1 and 2, 2008. The company type code used is as follows: P - Public, R - Private, S - Subsidiary, D - Division, J - Joint Venture, A - Affiliate, G - Group. Sales are in millions of dollars, employees are in thousands. An asterisk (*) indicates an estimated sales volume. The symbol < stands for 'less than'. Company names and addresses are truncated, in some cases, to fit into the available space.

MATERIALS CONSUMED FOR PREFABRICATED METAL BUILDING AND COMPONENT MANUFACTURING

Material	Quantity	Delivered Cost ($ million)
Metal bolts, nuts, screws, and other screw machine products	(X)	31.8
Other fabricated metal products (exc. castings and forgings)	(X)	648.7
Castings, rough and semifinished	(X)	0.9
Steel bars, bar shapes, and plates (exc. castings, forgings, fabr. metal products)	(X)	238.0
Steel concrete reinforcing bars	(X)	0.7
Steel sheet and strip (including tinplate)	(X)	298.6
Steel structural shapes (exc. castings, forgings, fabr. metal products)	(X)	73.0
All other steel shapes and forms (exc. castings, forgings, fabr. metal products)	(X)	35.0
Aluminum and aluminum-base alloy sheet, plate, foil, and welded tubing	(X)	86.8
Aluminum and aluminum-base alloy extruded shapes (rod, bar, pipe, tube, etc.)	(X)	40.2
All other aluminum and aluminum-base alloy shapes and forms, incl. refinery shapes (exc. castings and forgings)	(X)	6.0
Other nonferrous shapes and forms (exc. castings, forgings, fabricated metal products)	(X)	2.1
Iron and steel scrap (excluding home scrap)	(X)	0.7
Paints, varnishes, stains, lacquers, shellacs, japans, enamels, etc.	(X)	14.9
All other materials, components, parts, containers, and supplies	(X)	302.7
Materials, ingredients, containers, and supplies, nsk	(X)	608.0

Source: 2002 *Economic Census*. Explanation of symbols used: (D): Withheld to avoid disclosure of competitive data; na: Not available; (S): Withheld because statistical norms were not met; (X): Not applicable; (Z): Less than half the unit shown; nec: Not elsewhere classified; nsk: Not specified by kind; - : zero; p : 10-19 percent estimated; q : 20-29 percent estimated.

MATERIALS CONSUMED FOR FABRICATED STRUCTURAL METAL MANUFACTURING

Material	Quantity	Delivered Cost ($ million)
Fabricated metal pipe (excluding castings and forgings)	(X)	75.7
Fabricated metal valves and pipe fittings	(X)	26.0
All other fabricated metal products (exc. castings and forgings)	(X)	373.7
Iron and steel castings (rough and semifinished)	(X)	187.3
Aluminum and aluminum-base alloy castings (rough and semifinished)	(X)	6.6
Other nonferrous metal castings, rough or semifinished (inc. aluminum)	(X)	5.9
Forgings	(X)	6.9
Steel bars and bar shapes (exc. concrete reinforcing bars, castings, forgings, and fabricated metal products)	(X)	343.8
Steel concrete reinforcing bars	(X)	403.9
Steel sheet and strip (including tinplate)	(X)	431.0
Steel plate	(X)	443.0
Wide flange steel structural beams	(X)	574.2
All other steel structural shapes (exc. sheet pilings, castings, forgings, and fabricated steel products)	(X)	341.6
All other steel shapes and forms, incl. sheet pilings	(X)	60.3
Nonferrous refinery shapes (exc. castings, forgings, fabr. metal products)	(X)	2.3
Copper and copper-base alloy pipe and tube (exc. castings, forgings, fabr. metal products)	(X)	30.4
All other copper and copper-base alloy shapes and forms (exc. castings, forgings, fabr. metal products)	(X)	4.9
Aluminum and aluminum-base alloy sheet, plate, foil, and welded tubing	(X)	35.8
All other aluminum and aluminum-base alloy shapes and forms (exc. castings, forgings, fabr. metal products)	(X)	18.8
All other nonferrous shapes and forms (exc. castings, forgings, fabr. metal products)	(X)	4.2
Paints, varnishes, stains, lacquers, shellacs, japans, enamels, etc.	(X)	111.0
Welding electrodes	(X)	36.9
Metal bolts, nuts, screws, and other screw machine products	(X)	83.6
All other materials, components, parts, containers, and supplies	(X)	926.9
Materials, ingredients, containers, and supplies, nsk	(X)	2,503.7

Source: 2002 *Economic Census*. Explanation of symbols used: (D): Withheld to avoid disclosure of competitive data; na: Not available; (S): Withheld because statistical norms were not met; (X): Not applicable; (Z): Less than half the unit shown; nec: Not elsewhere classified; nsk: Not specified by kind; - : zero; p : 10-19 percent estimated; q : 20-29 percent estimated.

MATERIALS CONSUMED FOR PLATE WORK MANUFACTURING

Material	Quantity	Delivered Cost ($ million)
Fabricated metal pipe (excluding castings and forgings)	(X)	6.0
Fabricated metal valves and pipe fittings	(X)	2.6
All other fabricated metal products (exc. castings and forgings)	(X)	55.5
Iron and steel castings (rough and semifinished)	(X)	27.3
Nonferrous (aluminum, copper, etc.) castings (rough and semifinished)	(X)	1.2
Forgings	(X)	4.4
Steel bars and bar shapes (exc. concrete reinforcing bars, castings, forgings, and fabricated metal products)	(X)	16.3
Steel concrete reinforcing bars	(X)	(D)
Steel sheet and strip (including tinplate)	(X)	93.9
Steel plate	(X)	83.7
Wide flange steel structural beams	(X)	4.3
All other steel structural shapes (exc. sheet pilings, castings, forgings, and fabricated steel products)	(X)	13.2
All other steel shapes and forms, incl. sheet pilings	(X)	(D)
Copper and copper-base alloy pipe and tube (exc. castings, forgings, fabr. metal products)	(X)	1.5
All other copper and copper-base alloy shapes and forms (exc. castings, forgings, fabr. metal products)	(X)	0.4
Aluminum and aluminum-base alloy sheet, plate, foil, and welded tubing	(X)	20.2

Continued on next page.

MATERIALS CONSUMED FOR PLATE WORK MANUFACTURING - Continued

Material	Quantity	Delivered Cost ($ million)
All other aluminum and aluminum-base alloy shapes and forms (exc. castings, forgings, fabr. metal products)	(X)	1.4
All other nonferrous shapes and forms (exc. castings, forgings, fabr. metal products)	(X)	1.9
Paints, varnishes, stains, lacquers, shellacs, japans, enamels, etc.	(X)	8.9
Welding electrodes	(X)	7.6
All other materials, components, parts, containers, and supplies	(X)	312.8
Materials, ingredients, containers, and supplies, nsk	(X)	464.9

Source: 2002 Economic Census. Explanation of symbols used: (D): Withheld to avoid disclosure of competitive data; na: Not available; (S): Withheld because statistical norms were not met; (X): Not applicable; (Z): Less than half the unit shown; nec: Not elsewhere classified; nsk: Not specified by kind; - : zero; p : 10-19 percent estimated; q : 20-29 percent estimated.

PRODUCT SHARE DETAILS FOR PREFABRICATED METAL BUILDING AND COMPONENT MANUFACTURING

Product or Product Class Shipments	Mil. $	Product or Product Class Shipments	Mil. $
PREFABRICATED METAL BUILDINGS AND COMPONENTS	4,717.7	Prefabricated and portable greenhouses, steel and aluminum	120.7
Prefabricated metal building and component systems, excluding farm service buildings, residential buildings, and parts	**2,896.5**	Prefabricated and portable grain storage buildings, including farm and commercial types, steel and aluminum	91.2
Prefabricated metal building systems, excluding farm service buildings, residential buildings, and parts	409.3	Other prefabricated and portable farm service buildings (livestock shelters, machinery storage, etc.), steel and aluminum	114.4
Institutional, medical, and religious prefabricated metal building systems, excluding farm service buildings, residential buildings, and parts . . .	169.1	Prefabricated and portable aluminum and steel buildings . .	790.7
Public and educational prefabricated metal building systems, excluding farm service buildings, residential buildings, and parts.	240.2	Prefabricated and portable small steel utility buildings, including toolsheds, cabanas, storage houses, etc. . . .	139.5
Industrial and commercial prefabricated metal building systems, excluding farm service buildings, residential buildings, and parts . . .	2,247.8	Other prefabricated and portable steel buildings . . . :	131.9
Prefabricated metal building and component systems, excluding farm service buildings, residental buildings, and parts, nsk	239.3	Prefabricated and portable dwellings, steel and aluminum, including vacation homes and camps . . .	59.0
Other prefabricated and portable metal buildings and parts .	**1,267.2**	Prefabricated and portable small aluminum utility buildings, including toolsheds, cabanas, storage houses, etc.	80.3
Prefabricated and portable farm services buildings, greenhouses, and grain storage buildings, steel and aluminum	326.3	Other prefabricated and portable aluminum buildings . .	10.0
		Panels, parts, or sections for prefabricated buildings, not sold as a complete unit, steel and aluminum	370.1
		Other prefabricated and portable metal buildings and parts, nsk	150.2
		Prefabricated metal buildings and components, nsk, total . .	**554.0**

Source: 2002 Economic Census. The values are product shipments in millions of dollars for 2002. Total product shipments may be lower or higher than industry shipments. See Introduction for a full discussion. Values of indented subcategories are summed in the main heading(s). The symbol (D) appears when data are withheld to prevent disclosure of competitive information. The abbreviation nsk stands for 'not specified by kind' and nec for 'not elsewhere classified'. A dash (-) means zero.

PRODUCT SHARE DETAILS FOR FABRICATED STRUCTURAL METAL MANUFACTURING

Product or Product Class Shipments	Mil. $	Product or Product Class Shipments	Mil. $
FABRICATED STRUCTURAL METAL	17,054.3	Other fabricated structural iron and steel, metal and aluminum	(D)
Fabricated structural metal bar joists and concrete reinforcing bars	**9,478.4**	Fabricated structural iron and steel for transmission towers, substations, radio antenna towers, and supporting structures	462.8
Fabricated structural iron and steel for industrial buildings, metal bar joists, short span (open web)	3,190.6	Fabricated structural iron and steel for offshore oil and gas platforms	738.5
Fabricated structural iron and steel for commerical, residential, institutional, and public buildings . . .	6,065.9	Fabricated structural iron and steel for tunneling and subway work	(D)
Fabricated structural iron and steel for commerical buildings, including metal bar joists, long span	3,534.7	Fabricated structural iron and steel for aerospace and defense	172.9
Fabricated structural iron and steel for residential buildings, including metal concrete reinforcing bars . . .	916.3	Other fabricated structural iron and steel	1,036.9
Fabricated structural iron and steel for institutional, medical, and religious buildings	475.0	Fabricated structural aluminum for ships, boats, barges, transmission towers, and other structures	64.5
Fabricated structural iron and steel for public and educational buildings	783.5	Fabricated structural metal other than iron, steel, or aluminum	112.2
Fabricated structural iron and steel for public utilities . .	277.2	Fabricated structural iron and steel for ships, boats, and barges	(D)
Fabricated structural aluminum for buildings (all types) . .	79.3	Other fabricated structural metal, nsk	435.3
Fabricated structural metal bar joists and concrete reinforcing bars, nsk	221.9	**Fabricated structural metal, nsk, total**	**3,005.9**
Fabricated structural metal for bridges	**1,023.4**		
Other fabricated structural metal	**3,546.7**		

Source: 2002 Economic Census. The values are product shipments in millions of dollars for 2002. Total product shipments may be lower or higher than industry shipments. See Introduction for a full discussion. Values of indented subcategories are summed in the main heading(s). The symbol (D) appears when data are withheld to prevent disclosure of competitive information. The abbreviation nsk stands for 'not specified by kind' and nec for 'not elsewhere classified'. A dash (-) means zero.

PRODUCT SHARE DETAILS FOR PLATE WORK MANUFACTURING

Product or Product Class Shipments	Mil. $	Product or Product Class Shipments	Mil. $
FABRICATED STEEL PLATE WORK	3,204.4	turbine sound systems (enclosed) (including natural gas compression, electric generation, marine propulsion, etc.)	(D)
Fabricated steel plate (stacks and weldments)	**3,204.4**		
Fabricated steel plate containers	222.0		
Fabricated steel plate containers (trash and other), less than 13 gal	51.4	Other fabricated steel plate sound control equipment (including sound panels, one piece enclosures, industrial silencers, and air duct silencers) . . .	(D)
Fabricated steel plate containers (trash and other), 13 gal to 79 gal	31.2	Weldments and fabricated steel plate for other purposes . . .	1,814.4
Fabricated steel plate containers (trash and other), more than 79 gal	139.3	Fabricated steel plate shielding for use in nuclear reactor buildings	(D)
Fabricated steel plate sound control equipment . .	198.5	Weldments and fabricated steel plate for other purposes . .	(D)
Fabricated steel plate sound control equipment for jet engine test facilites (including hush houses, demountable run-up silencers, demountable test cells, etc.)	(D)	Fabricated steel plate pipe, penstocks, tunnel lining, stacks, and breeching	100.5
Fabricated steel plate sound control equipment for gas		Fabricated steel plate work (stacks and weldments), nsk, total	869.0

Source: 2002 *Economic Census*. The values are product shipments in millions of dollars for 2002. Total product shipments may be lower or higher than industry shipments. See Introduction for a full discussion. Values of indented subcategories are summed in the main heading(s). The symbol (D) appears when data are withheld to prevent disclosure of competitive information. The abbreviation nsk stands for 'not specified by kind' and nec for 'not elsewhere classified'. A dash (-) means zero.

INPUTS AND OUTPUTS FOR PLATE WORK AND FABRICATED STRUCTURAL PRODUCTS

Economic Sector or Industry Providing Inputs	%	Sector	Economic Sector or Industry Buying Outputs	%	Sector
Compensation of employees	27.7		Nonresidential structures, nec	22.0	Construct.
Iron & steel mills & ferroalloys	15.9	Manufg.	Motor vehicle parts	13.8	Manufg.
Wholesale trade	4.4	Trade	Commercial & health care structures	11.9	Construct.
Plate work & fabricated structural products	2.7	Manufg.	Water transportation	5.5	Util.
Management of companies & enterprises	2.6	Services	Residential permanent site structures	3.6	Construct.
Steel products from purchased steel	2.2	Manufg.	Residential structures, nec	3.1	Construct.
Machine shops	1.5	Manufg.	Machine shops	2.7	Manufg.
Specialized design services	1.4	Services	Plate work & fabricated structural products	2.6	Manufg.
Aluminum products from purchased aluminum	1.2	Manufg.	Other S/L govt. enterprises	2.6	S/L Govt
Employment services	1.1	Services	Pipeline transportation	2.3	Util.
Coating, engraving, heat treating & allied activities	1.1	Manufg.	Exports of goods & services	2.1	Cap Inv
Turned products & screws, nuts, & bolts	1.1	Manufg.	Aircraft parts & auxiliary equipment, nec	1.8	Manufg.
Truck transportation	1.1	Util.	Maintenance/repair of nonresidential structures	1.8	Construct.
Securities, commodity contracts, investments	1.0	Fin/R.E.	Railroad rolling stock	1.7	Manufg.
Business support services	1.0	Services	Food services & drinking places	1.7	Services
Legal services	1.0	Services	Owner-occupied dwellings	1.5	
Paints & coatings	1.0	Manufg.	Wholesale trade	1.0	Trade
Architectural, engineering, & related services	0.9	Services	Construction machinery	0.9	Manufg.
Chemical products & preparations, nec	0.9	Manufg.	Semiconductors & related devices	0.7	Manufg.
Real estate	0.9	Fin/R.E.	Oil & gas extraction	0.6	Mining
Metal cutting & forming machine tools	0.8	Manufg.	Oil & gas well drilling	0.6	Mining
Lessors of nonfinancial assets	0.8	Fin/R.E.	Sporting & athletic goods	0.5	Manufg.
Monetary authorities/depository credit intermediation	0.8	Fin/R.E.	Facilities support services	0.5	Services
Power generation & supply	0.6	Util.	Architectural, engineering, & related services	0.5	Services
Support services, nec	0.6	Services	Engineered wood members & trusses	0.5	Manufg.
Professional, scientific, technical services, nec	0.6	Services	General S/L govt. services	0.5	S/L Govt
Semiconductors & related devices	0.6	Manufg.	Crowns & closures & metal stamping	0.4	Manufg.
Abrasive products	0.6	Manufg.	Ship building & repairing	0.4	Manufg.
Printed circuit assemblies (electronic assemblies)	0.5	Manufg.	AC, refrigeration, and warm air heating equipment	0.4	Manufg.
Fabricated pipes & pipe fittings	0.5	Manufg.	Guided missiles & space vehicles	0.4	Manufg.
Advertising & related services	0.5	Services	Manufacturing structures	0.4	Construct.
Crowns & closures & metal stamping	0.5	Manufg.	Industrial machinery, nec	0.4	Manufg.
Investigation & security services	0.5	Services	Material handling equipment	0.4	Manufg.
Metal cans, boxes, & other containers (light gauge)	0.5	Manufg.	Waste management & remediation services	0.3	Services
Telecommunications	0.5	Services	Engine equipment, nec	0.3	Manufg.
Ferrous metal foundries	0.5	Manufg.	Scientific research & development services	0.3	Services
Food services & drinking places	0.4	Services	Automotive equipment rental & leasing	0.3	Fin/R.E.
Taxes on production & imports, less subsidies	0.4		Boat building	0.3	Manufg.
Fabricated metals, nec	0.4	Manufg.	Private fixed investment	0.3	
Data processing, hosting, & related services	0.4	Services	Air & gas compressors	0.3	Manufg.
Accounting, tax preparation, bookkeeping, & payroll	0.4	Services	Pumps & pumping equipment	0.3	Manufg.
Automotive equipment rental & leasing	0.4	Fin/R.E.	Steel products from purchased steel	0.2	Manufg.
Management, scientific, & technical consulting	0.4	Services	Telecommunications	0.2	Services
Maintenance/repair of nonresidential structures	0.3	Construct.	Concrete products, nec	0.2	Manufg.
Hotels & motels, including casino hotels	0.3	Services	Personal consumption expenditures	0.2	
Services to buildings & dwellings	0.3	Services	Legal services	0.2	Services
Rail transportation	0.3	Util.	General Federal government services, nondefense	0.2	Fed Govt
Ball & roller bearings	0.3	Manufg.	Ornamental & architectural metal products	0.2	Manufg.
General purpose machinery, nec	0.3	Manufg.	Federal government, investment, nondefense	0.2	Fed Govt
Air transportation	0.3	Util.	Maintenance/repair of residential structures	0.2	Construct.
Natural gas distribution	0.3	Util.	Light truck & utility vehicles	0.2	Manufg.
Warehousing & storage	0.3	Util.	Fabricated metals, nec	0.2	Manufg.
Valve & fittings other than plumbing	0.2	Manufg.	Air purification & ventilation equipment	0.2	Manufg.

Continued on next page.

INPUTS AND OUTPUTS FOR PLATE WORK AND FABRICATED STRUCTURAL PRODUCTS - Continued

Economic Sector or Industry Providing Inputs	%	Sector	Economic Sector or Industry Buying Outputs	%	Sector
Custom roll forming	0.2	Manufg.	Professional, scientific, technical services, nec	0.2	Services
Facilities support services	0.2	Services	Turbines & turbine generator set units	0.2	Manufg.
Handtools	0.2	Manufg.	Aircraft	0.1	Manufg.
Commercial & industrial machinery rental & leasing	0.2	Fin/R.E.	Computer system design services	0.1	Services
Automotive repair & maintenance, ex. car washes	0.2	Services	Rubber products, nec	0.1	Manufg.
Scientific research & development services	0.2	Services	Mining & oil & gas field machinery	0.1	Manufg.
Commercial & industrial equipment repair/maintenance	0.2	Services	Change in private inventories	0.1	In House
Copper rolling, drawing, extruding, & alloying	0.2	Manufg.	General Federal government services, defense	0.1	Fed Govt
Ornamental & architectural metal products	0.2	Manufg.	Civic, social, & professional organizations	0.1	Services
Nondepository credit intermediation activities	0.1	Fin/R.E.	Prefabricated wood buildings	0.1	Manufg.
Paperboard containers	0.1	Manufg.	Real estate	0.1	Fin/R.E.
Other computer related services, including facilities	0.1	Services	Manufacturing, nec	0.1	Manufg.
Motor vehicle parts	0.1	Manufg.			
Plastics packaging materials, film & sheet	0.1	Manufg.			
Industrial molds	0.1	Manufg.			
Waste management & remediation services	0.1	Services			
Springs & wire products	0.1	Manufg.			

Source: Benchmark Input-Output Accounts for the U.S. Economy, 2002, U.S. Department of Commerce, Washington, D.C., January 2008. The abbreviation nec stands for 'not elsewhere classified'.

OCCUPATIONS EMPLOYED BY ARCHITECTURAL & STRUCTURAL METALS MANUFACTURING

Occupation	% of Total 2006	Change to 2016	Occupation	% of Total 2006	Change to 2016
Welders, cutters, solderers, & brazers	11.2	13.6	Cost estimators	1.4	15.4
Team assemblers	8.6	6.8	Office clerks, general	1.3	5.2
Structural metal fabricators & fitters	8.0	6.8	Assemblers & fabricators, nec	1.2	-3.9
Cutting, punching, & press machine operators	5.8	-3.9	Rolling machine operators & tenders	1.2	6.8
First-line supervisors/managers of production workers	4.2	6.8	Mechanical drafters	1.2	8.0
Sheet metal workers	4.2	4.8	Maintenance & repair workers, general	1.2	6.8
Helpers--Production workers	3.3	6.8	Industrial truck & tractor operators	1.2	-3.9
Laborers & freight, stock, & material movers, hand	2.8	-3.9	Truck drivers, heavy & tractor-trailer	1.1	6.8
Sales reps, wholesale & manufacturing, exc tech	2.5	6.8	Computer-controlled machine tool operators	1.1	17.5
General & operations managers	1.8	-3.9	Inspectors, testers, sorters, samplers, & weighers	1.1	0.7
Coating, painting, & spraying machine operators	1.6	1.5	Grinding, lapping, polishing machine tool operators	1.1	3.6
Shipping, receiving, & traffic clerks	1.5	2.8	Industrial production managers	1.0	6.8
Machinists	1.5	12.1	Multiple machine tool operators & tenders	1.0	17.5
Bookkeeping, accounting, & auditing clerks	1.4	6.8			

Source: Industry-Occupation Matrix, Bureau of Labor Statistics, December 4, 2007. These data are reported based on 4-digit NAICS categories but have been matched to corresponding 6-digit NAICS industry codes. The change reported for each occupation to the year 2016 is a percent of growth or decline as estimated by the Bureau of Labor Statistics. The abbreviation nec stands for 'not elsewhere classified'.

LOCATION BY STATE AND REGIONAL CONCENTRATION

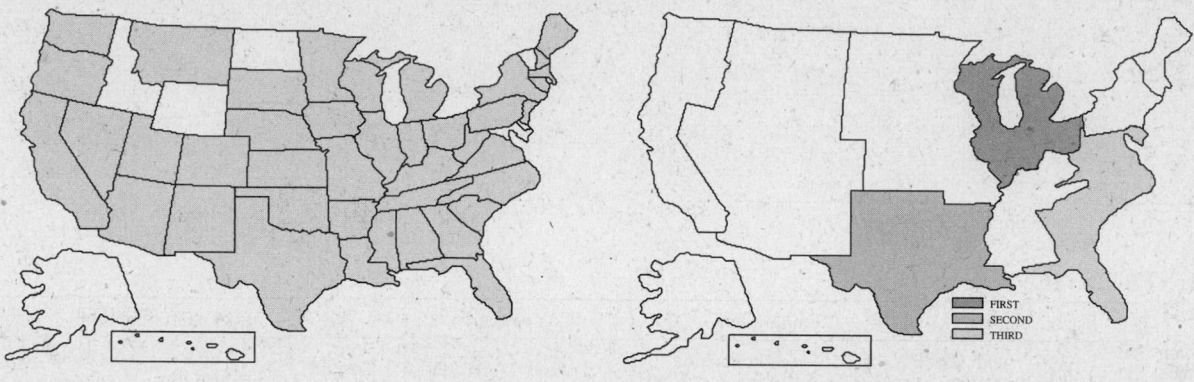

FIRST
SECOND
THIRD

INDUSTRY DATA BY STATE

| State | Establish-ments | Shipments | | | Employment | | | | Cost as % of Shipments | Investment per Employee ($) |
		Total ($ mil)	% of U.S.	Per Establ.	Total Number	% of U.S.	Per Establ.	Wages ($/hour)		
Texas	515	3,154.8	11.4	6,125.9	17,881	11.2	35	14.64	50.2	7,934
California	451	2,079.6	7.5	4,611.0	12,124	7.6	27	15.93	47.9	3,272
Pennsylvania	304	1,712.8	6.2	5,634.3	10,850	6.8	36	16.74	47.0	5,093
Illinois	196	1,163.5	4.2	5,936.1	6,583	4.1	34	15.99	49.1	3,616
Michigan	242	1,125.6	4.1	4,651.3	5,397	3.4	22	16.80	54.3	5,386
Ohio	293	1,100.2	4.0	3,755.0	6,754	4.2	23	15.50	47.9	6,762
Alabama	186	912.1	3.3	4,903.5	5,693	3.6	31	15.94	55.0	4,323
Florida	237	902.3	3.3	3,807.3	5,715	3.6	24	14.56	52.8	5,802
Georgia	146	878.3	3.2	6,015.5	4,643	2.9	32	14.40	53.4	4,933
Indiana	168	834.7	3.0	4,968.4	4,702	2.9	28	16.36	56.6	2,787
Louisiana	77	826.2	3.0	10,729.6	5,411	3.4	70	16.67	51.6	3,671
New York	213	762.9	2.8	3,581.9	3,696	2.3	17	17.85	54.0	5,632
North Carolina	134	758.3	2.7	5,659.3	3,830	2.4	29	15.63	50.1	6,351
Virginia	115	747.4	2.7	6,499.2	3,623	2.3	32	15.07	47.9	3,045
South Carolina	97	687.6	2.5	7,088.7	3,864	2.4	40	15.32	56.2	2,553
Wisconsin	157	656.2	2.4	4,179.4	4,219	2.6	27	15.92	49.7	6,506
Tennessee	144	623.9	2.3	4,332.6	3,971	2.5	28	15.44	48.4	2,556
Oklahoma	132	534.7	1.9	4,050.6	3,143	2.0	24	15.19	46.7	3,564
Missouri	115	530.8	1.9	4,615.3	3,178	2.0	28	14.99	50.5	7,643
Utah	83	477.3	1.7	5,750.2	2,531	1.6	30	17.76	53.8	3,120
Nebraska	43	473.0	1.7	10,999.2	2,754	1.7	64	13.31	54.8	2,199
New Jersey	103	464.3	1.7	4,508.1	1,734	1.1	17	16.48	52.2	5,885
Mississippi	62	451.8	1.6	7,287.6	2,168	1.4	35	13.28	62.0	4,262
Arizona	69	447.0	1.6	6,478.4	2,260	1.4	33	15.89	46.4	2,208
Arkansas	51	422.3	1.5	8,279.6	3,530	2.2	69	14.79	40.1	1,890
Minnesota	122	396.8	1.4	3,252.6	2,347	1.5	19	18.43	53.0	3,385
Washington	136	370.5	1.3	2,724.6	2,338	1.5	17	17.55	44.9	5,817
Iowa	84	360.7	1.3	4,294.0	2,127	1.3	25	13.47	54.8	1,797
Colorado	84	318.6	1.2	3,792.8	1,745	1.1	21	16.72	52.5	3,357
Oregon	103	308.3	1.1	2,993.2	1,879	1.2	18	17.09	51.6	4,548
Kansas	38	276.1	1.0	7,267.1	1,334	0.8	35	14.28	59.6	8,214
Kentucky	97	266.1	1.0	2,742.9	1,614	1.0	17	14.67	49.2	6,134
Connecticut	59	184.4	0.7	3,125.1	1,145	0.7	19	18.00	40.8	3,603
Nevada	27	177.6	0.6	6,579.4	1,051	0.7	39	18.43	45.6	2,452
New Hampshire	20	111.8	0.4	5,587.7	700	0.4	35	15.01	41.3	4,073
Maine	21	102.1	0.4	4,859.9	548	0.3	26	15.16	52.8	13,597
West Virginia	30	85.3	0.3	2,842.5	572	0.4	19	14.42	45.8	3,152
Montana	14	76.9	0.3	5,494.4	500	0.3	36	16.25	52.2	1,970
Massachusetts	19	69.8	0.3	3,671.1	607	0.4	32	16.96	37.9	3,249
South Dakota	16	65.3	0.2	4,082.7	522	0.3	33	13.41	48.4	2,402
New Mexico	20	42.6	0.2	2,130.8	251	0.2	13	15.05	63.4	3,892

Source: 2002 *Economic Census*. The states are in descending order of shipments or establishments (if shipment data are missing for the majority). The symbol (D) appears when data are withheld to prevent disclosure of competitive information. States marked with (D) are sorted by number of establishments. A dash (-) indicates that the data element cannot be calculated. Data may not show all states active in the NAICS category. All data available at the time of publication are shown.

NAICS 33232M - ORNAMENTAL, SHEET AND ARCHITECTURAL METAL WORK MANUFACTURING*

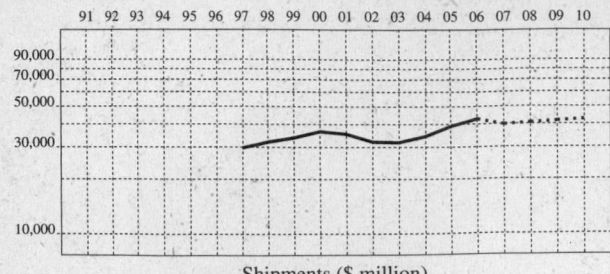

Shipments ($ million)

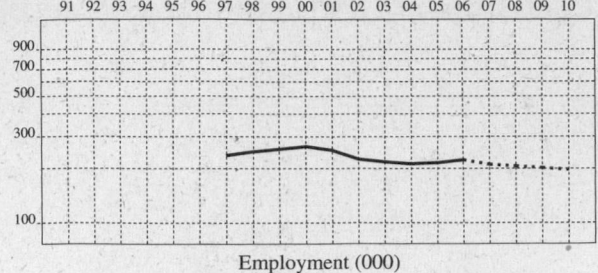

Employment (000)

GENERAL STATISTICS

| Year | Companies | Establishments | | Employment | | | Compensation | | Production ($ million) | | | |
		Total	with 20 or more employees	Total (000)	Production Workers (000)	Hours (Mil)	Payroll ($ mil)	Wages ($/hr)	Cost of Materials	Value Added by Manufacture	Value of Shipments	Capital Invest.
1997	7,274	7,745	2,729	236.1	172.4	349.3	6,924.9	12.11	14,334.1	15,425.7	29,670.4	821.6
1998		7,745	2,802	247.5	183.3	382.5	7,457.4	11.96	15,383.9	16,753.6	32,011.6	994.6
1999		7,654	2,821	255.7	188.5	386.9	7,772.0	12.38	16,217.4	17,687.3	33,789.5	1,024.6
2000		7,465	2,876	264.6	196.6	394.9	8,341.9	13.19	17,498.7	19,200.5	36,512.0	970.4
2001		7,715	2,892	252.2	187.1	372.3	8,023.6	13.24	16,959.6	18,325.0	35,393.9	908.5
2002	7,584	8,070	2,465	225.3	163.7	320.9	7,480.5	14.20	14,827.6	17,177.4	32,041.4	855.9
2003		7,858	2,392	217.7	160.1	325.4	7,384.7	14.01	15,070.5	16,698.1	31,818.6	658.4
2004		7,852	2,396	212.4	153.0	315.1	7,543.3	14.58	16,644.7	17,908.3	34,294.4	844.3
2005		7,942	2,370	214.9	154.2	319.5	7,954.4	15.04	19,687.5	19,471.5	39,060.2	991.9
2006		7,960P	2,311P	222.9	161.0	334.2	8,529.9	15.25	21,929.9	21,016.6	42,656.8	1,052.7
2007		7,995P	2,246P	210.6P	151.4P	310.2P	8,186.8P	15.74P	20,445.0P	19,593.6P	39,768.5P	918.0P
2008		8,031P	2,180P	206.1P	147.7P	303.0P	8,267.8P	16.13P	20,916.5P	20,045.4P	40,685.6P	919.0P
2009		8,066P	2,115P	201.7P	144.0P	295.7P	8,348.8P	16.52P	21,387.9P	20,497.2P	41,602.6P	920.1P
2010		8,101P	2,050P	197.3P	140.2P	288.5P	8,429.8P	16.91P	21,859.4P	20,949.0P	42,519.6P	921.1P

Sources: 1997 and 2002 *Economic Census*; other years, up to 2006, are from *Annual Survey of Manufactures*. Establishment counts for non-Census years are from *County Business Patterns*; 1997 and 2002 values are from the 1997 and 2002 censuses, respectively. 'P's show projections by the editors.

INDICES OF CHANGE

| Year | Companies | Establishments | | Employment | | | Compensation | | Production ($ million) | | | |
		Total	with 20 or more employees	Total (000)	Production Workers (000)	Hours (Mil)	Payroll ($ mil)	Wages ($/hr)	Cost of Materials	Value Added by Manufacture	Value of Shipments	Capital Invest.
1997	96	96	111	105	105	109	93	85	97	90	93	96
1998		96	114	110	112	119	100	84	104	98	100	116
1999		95	114	113	115	121	104	87	109	103	105	120
2000		93	117	117	120	123	112	93	118	112	114	113
2001		96	117	112	114	116	107	93	114	107	110	106
2002	100	100	100	100	100	100	100	100	100	100	100	100
2003		97	97	97	98	101	99	99	102	97	99	77
2004		97	97	94	93	98	101	103	112	104	107	99
2005		98	96	95	94	100	106	106	133	113	122	116
2006		99P	94P	99	98	104	114	107	148	122	133	123
2007		99P	91P	93P	92P	97P	109P	111P	138P	114P	124P	107P
2008		100P	88P	91P	90P	94P	111P	114P	141P	117P	127P	107P
2009		100P	86P	90P	88P	92P	112P	116P	144P	119P	130P	108P
2010		100P	83P	88P	86P	90P	113P	119P	147P	122P	133P	108P

Sources: Same as General Statistics. Values reflect change from the base year, 2002. Values above 100 mean greater than 2002, values below 100 mean less than 2002, and the values of 100 in other years means the same as 2002. 'P's show projections by the editors.

SELECTED RATIOS

For 2002	Avg. of All Manufact.	Analyzed Industry	Index	For 2002	Avg. of All Manufact.	Analyzed Industry	Index
Employees per Establishment	42	28	67	Value Added per Production Worker	182,367	104,932	58
Payroll per Establishment	1,639,184	926,952	57	Cost per Establishment	5,769,015	1,837,373	32
Payroll per Employee	39,053	33,202	85	Cost per Employee	137,446	65,813	48
Production Workers per Establishment	30	20	69	Cost per Production Worker	195,506	90,578	46
Wages per Establishment	694,845	564,657	81	Shipments per Establishment	11,158,348	3,970,434	36
Wages per Production Worker	23,548	27,836	118	Shipments per Employee	265,847	142,217	53
Hours per Production Worker	1,980	1,960	99	Shipments per Production Worker	378,144	195,732	52
Wages per Hour	11.89	14.20	119	Investment per Establishment	361,338	106,059	29
Value Added per Establishment	5,381,325	2,128,550	40	Investment per Employee	8,609	3,799	44
Value Added per Employee	128,210	76,242	59	Investment per Production Worker	12,245	5,228	43

Sources: Same as General Statistics. The 'Average of All Manufacturing' column represents the average of all manufacturing industries reported for the most recent complete year available. The Index shows the relationship between the Average and the Analyzed Industry. For example, 100 means that they are equal; 500 that the Analyzed Industry is five times the average; 50 means that the Analyzed Industry is half the national average. The abbreviation 'na' is used to show that data are 'not available'. Ratios shown for 2002, the last complete census year.

*Equivalent to Federal Government NAICS 332321, 332322, 332323.

LEADING COMPANIES Number shown: **75** Total sales ($ mil): **214,555** Total employment (000): **563.7**

Company Name	Address				CEO Name	Phone	Co. Type	Sales ($ mil)	Empl. (000)
Lowe's Companies Inc.	PO Box 1111	N Wilkesboro	NC	28656		704-758-1000	P	48,283	157.0
Caterpillar Inc.	100 NE Adams St.	Peoria	IL	61629		309-675-1000	P	44,958	101.3
Deere and Co.	1 John Deere Pl.	Moline	IL	61265		309-765-8000	P	24,082	52.0
API Group Inc.	2366 Rose Pl.	St. Paul	MN	55113	Lee R. Anderson Sr.	651-636-4320	R	9,000	5.0
AGCO Corp.	4205 River Green Pk	Duluth	GA	30096		770-813-9200	P	6,828	13.7
Allegheny Technologies Inc.	1000 Six PPG Pl.	Pittsburgh	PA	15222		412-394-2800	P	5,453	9.5
BorgWarner Inc.	3850 Hamlin Rd.	Auburn Hills	MI	48326		248-754-9200	P	5,329	17.7
Owens Corning	1 O Corning Pky	Toledo	OH	43659	David T. Brown	419-248-8000	P	4,978	20.0
Harsco Corp.	PO Box 8888	Camp Hill	PA	17001	S. D. Fazzolari	717-763-7064	P	3,688	21.5
Armstrong World Industries	PO Box 3001	Lancaster	PA	17604	Michael D. Lockhart	717-397-0611	P	3,550	12.9
Pentair Inc.	5500 Wayzata Blvd.	Golden Valley	MN	55416	Winslow H. Buxton	763-545-1730	P	3,399	16.0
Truth Hardware Corp.	700 W Bridge St.	Owatonna	MN	55060	Greg Wobschall	507-451-5620	R	3,218*	1.0
Alenco Holding Corp.	615 W Carson St.	Bryan	TX	77801		979-779-7770	R	2,960*	0.5
Metals USA Special Flat Rolled	2840 E Heartland Dr	Liberty	MO	64068	Lew Krausse	816-415-0004	S	2,639*	<0.1
JELD-WEN Inc.	PO Box 1329	Klamath Falls	OR	97601	Richard Wendt	541-882-3451	R	2,476*	23.8
Quanex Corp.	1900 W Loop S	Houston	TX	77027		713-961-4600	P	2,049	4.1
Henkel Consumer Adhesives Inc.	32150 Just Imagine	Avon	OH	44011	John Kahl	440-937-7000	S	1,978*	0.5
G-I Holdings Corp.	1361 Alps Rd.	Wayne	NJ	07470	Samuel Heyman	973-628-3000	R	1,970	3.6
Toro Co.	8111 Lyndale Ave. S	Bloomington	MN	55420		952-888-8801	P	1,877	5.3
Metals USA Inc.	1 Riverway, 1100	Houston	TX	77056	Laurenco Goncalves	713-965-0990	S	1,845	2.7
Griffon Corp.	100 Jericho Quadran	Jericho	NY	11753	Harvey R. Blau	516-938-5544	P	1,617	5.3
CC Industries Inc.	222 N La Salle St.	Chicago	IL	60601	William H. Crown	312-855-4000	S	1,560*	6.0
Pella Corp.	102 Main St.	Pella	IA	50219	Charles S. Farver	641-628-1000	R	1,531*	10.6
Tang Industries Inc.	8960 Spanish Ridge	Las Vegas	NV	89148	Cyrus Tang	702-734-3700	R	1,500*	3.2
Sierra Pacific Industries	PO Box 496028	Redding	CA	96049	A.A. Emmerson	530-378-8000	R	1,425*	3.9
EBSCO Industries Inc.	PO Box 1943	Birmingham	AL	35201	Dixon Brooke Jr.	205-991-6600	R	1,400*	5.0
Pemko Manufacturing Co.	PO Box 3780	Ventura	CA	93006	Phil Goossens	805-642-2600	R	1,240*	0.1
EMCO Enterprises Inc.	PO Box 853	Des Moines	IA	50304		515-265-6101	R	1,170*	0.6
Watkins Associated Industries	PO Box 1738	Atlanta	GA	30301	John Watkins	404-872-3841	R	1,153*	10.0
Amesbury Group Inc.	57 S Hunt Rd.	Amesbury	MA	01913		978-388-0581	R	1,140*	<0.1
MTD Products Inc.	PO Box 368022	Cleveland	OH	44136	Curtis E. Moll	330-225-2600	R	1,015*	6.7
Johnstown Holdings Inc.	545 Central Ave.	Johnstown	PA	15902	John Bolduc	814-535-9000	R	918*	0.2
Feralloy Corp.	8755 W Higgins Rd.	Chicago	IL	60631		773-380-1500	R	904*	<0.1
California Steel Industries	PO Box 5080	Fontana	CA	92335	Masakazu Kurushima	909-350-6300	R	846*	1.0
Simpson Manufacturing Company	5956 W Las Positas	Pleasanton	CA	94588	Thomas J. Fitzmyers	925-560-9000	P	817	2.7
Scott Company of California	1717 Doolittle Dr.	San Leandro	CA	94577	Joseph A. Guglielmo	510-895-2333	R	793*	1.2
Westfaliasurge Inc.	1880 Country Frm	Naperville	IL	60563	Dirk Hejnal	630-369-8100	S	755*	0.1
Drew Industries Inc.	200 Mamaroneck	White Plains	NY	10601	Leigh J. Abrams	914-428-9098	P	669	3.5
Int'l Extrusion Corp. - TX	202 Singleton Rd.	Waxahachie	TX	75165	Ronald L. Rudy	972-937-7032	S	639*	1.5
Blount Inc.	PO Box 22127	Portland	OR	97269	James S. Osterman	503-653-8881	S	583*	3.0
LMT Fette Inc.	1997 Ohio St.	Lisle	IL	60532	Brian Nowicki	630-969-5412	R	558*	0.2
Chore-Time/Brock International	PO Box 2000	Milford	IN	46542	Warren E Buffett	547-658-4191	S	552*	1.0
Windsor Republic Doors	155 Republic Dr.	Mc Kenzie	TN	38201	Mike Taylor	731-352-3383	R	514*	1.2
Overhead Door Corp.	2501 St. Hwy. 121	Lewisville	TX	75022	Howard Simons		R	508*	0.1
Alamo Group Inc.	PO Box 549	Seguin	TX	78155	Ronald Robinson	830-379-1480	P	504	2.3
Columbia Ventures Corp.	203 SE Park Plaza	Vancouver	WA	98684	K. D. Peterson Jr.	360-816-1840	R	502*	0.2
Thermal Industries Inc.	5450 2nd Ave.	Pittsburgh	PA	15207	David Rascoe	412-395-1900	R	501*	<0.1
Harvey Industries Inc.	1400 Main St., 3	Waltham	MA	02451	Thomas Bigony	781-899-3500	R	481*	0.1
Suncoast Post-Tension L.P.	654 N Sam Houston	Houston	TX	77060		281-445-8886	R	464*	0.2
Gehl Co.	PO Box 179	West Bend	WI	53095	William Gehl	262-334-9461	P	458	0.9
James Hardie Transition Co.	26300 La Alameda	Mission Viejo	CA	92691	Donald Manson	949-348-1800	R	423*	<0.1
ThyssenKrupp Safway Inc.	N19 Riverwood	Waukesha	WI	53188	Marc Wilson	262-523-6500	S	409*	3.5
General Aluminum Co. of TX	PO Box 819022	Dallas	TX	75381	Dean Guerin	972-242-5271	R	384*	0.2
Weather Shield Manufacturing	PO Box 309	Medford	WI	54451	Edward Schield	715-748-2100	R	375*	0.2
Mestek Inc.	260 N Elm St.	Westfield	MA	01085	R. Bruce Dewey	413-568-9571	R	372*	2.6
Alcoa	PO Box 40	Magnolia	AR	71754	Alain Belda	870-234-4260	R	324*	0.8
Team Inc.	PO Box 123	Alvin	TX	77512	Philip J. Hawk	281-331-6154	P	318	3.4
Champion Window Mfr & Supplies	12121 Champion	Cincinnati	OH	45241	Edward Levine	513-346-4600	R	313*	0.3
Eagle Window and Door Inc.	PO Box 1072	Dubuque	IA	52004	Dave Beeken	563-556-2270	S	311*	0.9
Linde BOC Process Plants	6100 S Yale Ave. St	Tulsa	OK	74136	Steven Bertone	918-477-1200	R	306*	0.3
Kuhn Knight Inc.	1501 W 7th Ave.	Brodhead	WI	53520	Thierry Krier	608-897-2131	R	305*	0.2
Simplicity Manufacturing Inc.	PO Box 997	Port Washington	WI	53074	Warner Frazier	262-377-5450	R	305*	0.5
Maxcess Technologies Inc.	230 Deming Way	Summerville	SC	29483	Andy Miarka	843-821-1200	R	291*	<0.1
Lindsay Corp.	2707 N 108th St.	Omaha	NE	68164	M. N. Christodolou	402-428-2131	P	282	0.9
PGT Inc.	1070 Technology	North Venice	FL	34275	Rodney Hershberger	941-480-1600	P	278	1.9
Therma-Tru Corp.	PO Box 8780	Maumee	OH	43537	Carl Hedlund	419-891-7400	S	273*	<0.1
Kirk and Blum Manufacturing	3120 Forrer St.	Cincinnati	OH	45209	Richard J. Blum	513-458-2600	S	265*	0.4
Consolidated Systems Inc.	PO Box 1756	Columbia	SC	29202	S Holtschlag	803-771-7920	R	262*	0.3
Vermeer Manufacturing Company	PO Box 200	Pella	IA	50219	Mary Andringa	641-628-3141	R	238*	2.0
Alcan Composites USA Inc.	PO Box 507	Benton	KY	42025		270-527-4200	R	224*	0.1
Tomkins Industries Inc.	PO Box 2327	Elkhart	IN	46515		574-296-0000	R	215*	0.5
Owens Corning Fabric Solutions	PO Box 1366	Elkhart	IN	46515	Raymond Stout	574-522-8473	D	207	0.8
CCC Group Inc.	PO Box 200350	San Antonio	TX	78220	Dennis Hubner	210-661-4251	R	200*	2.0
TRACO	71 Progress Ave.	Cranberry Twp	PA	16066	Robert P. Randall	724-776-7000	R	200*	2.0
Metalcraft of Mayville Inc.	PO Box 151	Mayville	WI	53050	Edwin Gallun	920-387-3150	R	200*	0.7

Source: Ward's Business Directory of U.S. Private and Public Companies, Volumes 1 and 2, 2008. The company type code used is as follows: P - Public, R - Private, S - Subsidiary, D - Division, J - Joint Venture, A - Affiliate, G - Group. Sales are in millions of dollars, employees are in thousands. An asterisk (*) indicates an estimated sales volume. The symbol < stands for 'less than'. Company names and addresses are truncated, in some cases, to fit into the available space.

MATERIALS CONSUMED FOR METAL WINDOW AND DOOR MANUFACTURING

Material	Quantity	Delivered Cost ($ million)
Flat glass (plate, float, and sheet)	(X)	285.5
Builders' hardware (door locks, locksets, lock trim, etc.)	(X)	231.2
Metal bolts, nuts, screws, and other screw machine products	(X)	75.0
Other fabricated metal products (exc. castings, forgings, bolts, etc.)	(X)	211.0
Iron and steel castings (rough and semifinished)	(X)	109.6
Nonferrous (aluminum, copper, etc.) castings (rough and semifinished)	(X)	26.2
Forgings	(X)	1.0
Steel bars, bar shapes, and plates (exc. castings, forgings, fabr. metal products)	(X)	36.9
Steel sheet and strip (including tinplate)	(X)	840.8
Steel structural shapes (exc. castings, forgings, fabr. metal products)	(X)	71.8
Steel wire and wire products	(X)	24.7
All other steel shapes and forms (exc. castings, forgings, fabr. metal products)	(X)	149.5
Copper and copper-base alloy shapes and forms (exc. castings, forgings, fabr. metal products)	(X)	0.6
Aluminum and aluminum-base alloy sheet, plate, foil, and welded tubing	(X)	80.7
Other nonferrous shapes and forms (exc. castings, forgings, fabricated metal products)	(X)	68.9
All other aluminum and aluminum-base alloy shapes and forms, incl. refinery shapes (exc. castings and forgings)	(X)	402.9
Aluminum and aluminum-base alloy scrap (exc. home scrap)	(X)	27.7
Plastics products consumed in the form of sheets, rods, etc.	(X)	109.5
All other materials, components, parts, containers, and supplies	(X)	1,955.9
Materials, ingredients, containers, and supplies, nsk	(X)	575.2

Source: 2002 *Economic Census*. Explanation of symbols used: (D): Withheld to avoid disclosure of competitive data; na: Not available; (S): Withheld because statistical norms were not met; (X): Not applicable; (Z): Less than half the unit shown; nec: Not elsewhere classified; nsk: Not specified by kind; - : zero; p : 10-19 percent estimated; q : 20-29 percent estimated.

MATERIALS CONSUMED FOR SHEET METAL WORK MANUFACTURING

Material	Quantity	Delivered Cost ($ million)
Metal bolts, nuts, screws, and other screw machine products	(X)	120.0
Other fabricated metal products (exc. castings and forgings)	(X)	528.3
Iron and steel castings (rough and semifinished)	(X)	64.0
Nonferrous (aluminum, copper, etc.) castings (rough and semifinished)	(X)	24.6
Forgings	(X)	(D)
Steel bars, bar shapes, and plates (exc. castings, forgings, fabr. metal products)	(X)	37.1
Steel concrete reinforcing bars	(X)	0.7
Steel sheet and strip (including tinplate)	(X)	1,236.7
Steel structural shapes (exc. castings, forgings, fabr. metal products)	(X)	117.0
All other steel shapes and forms (exc. castings, forgings, fabr. metal products)	(X)	0.0
Copper and copper-base alloy shapes and forms (exc. castings, forgings, fabr. metal products)	(X)	30.3
Aluminum and aluminum-base alloy sheet, plate, foil, and welded tubing	(X)	472.4
Aluminum and aluminum-base alloy extruded shapes (rod, bar, pipe, tube, etc.)	(X)	62.3
All other aluminum and aluminum-base alloy shapes and forms, incl. refinery shapes (exc. castings and forgings)	(X)	80.8
Other nonferrous shapes and forms (exc. castings, forgings, fabricated metal products)	(X)	82.6
Scrap, including iron, steel, aluminum and aluminum-base alloy (exc. home scrap)	(X)	(D)
Flat glass (plate, float, and sheet)	(X)	14.7
Paperboard containers, boxes, and corrugated paperboard	(X)	68.7
Paints, varnishes, stains, lacquers, shellacs, japans, etc.	(X)	55.1
All other materials, components, parts, containers, and supplies	(X)	1,157.4
Materials, ingredients, containers, and supplies, nsk	(X)	1,374.5

Source: 2002 *Economic Census*. Explanation of symbols used: (D): Withheld to avoid disclosure of competitive data; na: Not available; (S): Withheld because statistical norms were not met; (X): Not applicable; (Z): Less than half the unit shown; nec: Not elsewhere classified; nsk: Not specified by kind; - : zero; p : 10-19 percent estimated; q : 20-29 percent estimated.

MATERIALS CONSUMED FOR ORNAMENTAL & ARCHITECTURAL METAL WORK

Material	Quantity	Delivered Cost ($ million)
Metal bolts, nuts, screws, and other screw machine products	(X)	43.2
Other fabricated metal products (exc. castings and forgings)	(X)	124.7
Castings, rough and semifinished	(X)	24.0
Steel bars, bar shapes, and plates (exc. castings, forgings, fabr. metal products)	(X)	117.2
Steel concrete reinforcing bars	(X)	1.5
Steel sheet and strip (including tinplate)	(X)	203.3
Steel structural shapes (exc. castings, forgings, fabr. metal products)	(X)	86.1
All other steel shapes and forms (exc. castings, forgings, fabr. metal products)	(X)	159.7
Copper and copper-base alloy shapes and forms (exc. castings, forgings, fabr. metal products)	(X)	9.9
Aluminum and aluminum-base alloy sheet, plate, foil, and welded tubing	(X)	45.9
Aluminum and aluminum-base alloy extruded shapes (rod, bar, pipe, tube, etc.)	(X)	76.6
All other aluminum and aluminum-base alloy shapes and forms, incl. refinery shapes (exc. castings and forgings)	(X)	31.7
Other nonferrous shapes and forms (exc. castings, forgings, fabricated metal products)	(X)	32.0
Iron and steel scrap (excluding home scrap)	(X)	20.4
Paints, varnishes, stains, lacquers, shellacs, japans, enamels, etc.	(X)	29.9

Continued on next page.

MATERIALS CONSUMED FOR ORNAMENTAL & ARCHITECTURAL METAL WORK - Continued

Material	Quantity	Delivered Cost ($ million)
All other materials, components, parts, containers, and supplies	(X)	463.4
Materials, ingredients, containers, and supplies, nsk	(X)	431.2

Source: 2002 *Economic Census*. Explanation of symbols used: (D): Withheld to avoid disclosure of competitive data; na: Not available; (S): Withheld because statistical norms were not met; (X): Not applicable; (Z): Less than half the unit shown; nec: Not elsewhere classified; nsk: Not specified by kind; - : zero; p : 10-19 percent estimated; q : 20-29 percent estimated.

PRODUCT SHARE DETAILS FOR METAL WINDOW AND DOOR MANUFACTURING

Product or Product Class Shipments	Mil. $	Product or Product Class Shipments	Mil. $
METAL WINDOWS AND DOORS	10,408.8	Residential iron and steel garage doors	968.4
Metal doors (except storm doors)	**5,367.5**	Metal doors (except storm doors), nsk	105.3
Residential aluminum doors (including garage and closet doors, excluding shower doors, tub enclosures, and storm doors)	485.3	**Metal windows (except storm sash)**	**2,291.1**
		All other residential aluminum window sash and frames, including jalousie, excluding storm sash	309.5
Swinging residential aluminum doors	133.4	Steel window sash and frames	49.9
Sliding residential aluminum doors (glass, patio-type)	195.4	Aluminum awning window sash and frames	42.9
All other residential aluminum doors (including garage and closet doors)	115.0	Aluminum horizontal sliding window sash and frames	126.5
Overhead and sliding commercial and institutional aluminum doors	41.5	All other residential aluminum window sash and frames (including jalousie, excluding storm sash)	90.2
Commercial, institutional, and industrial aluminum doors, excluding shower doors, tub enclosures, and storm doors	762.0	Other metal window sash and frames (except storm sash)	947.4
Overhead industrial aluminum doors	20.6	Other steel window sash and frames	103.8
Sliding industrial aluminum doors	(D)	Other aluminum single and double hung sash and frames	316.5
All other industrial aluminum doors	(D)	Other aluminum awning window sash and frames	13.8
Swinging commercial and institutional aluminum doors	232.2	Other aluminum projected window sash and frames	89.1
All other commercial and institutional aluminum doors	310.0	Other aluminum window sash and frames	394.2
Industrial iron and steel doors	384.4	Metal window, other than steel or aluminum	30.1
Overhead industrial iron and steel doors	246.8	Residential aluminum single and double hung window sash and frames, except storm sash	808.1
Swing industrial iron and steel doors	65.7	Metal windows (except storm sash), nsk	226.1
All other industrial iron and steel doors (including sliding)	72.0	**Metal molding and trim and store fronts**	**989.0**
Residential iron and steel doors (except garage doors, shower doors, tub enclosures, and storm doors)	830.3	All other metal trim (including combination of metal)	955.6
		Aluminum moldings and trim	428.2
Residential steel composite doors (steel clad with foam wood components)	389.4	Steel molding and trim	12.3
Residential insulated steel entrance doors	264.8	Store fronts, sold complete at factory	30.4
All other residential iron and steel doors	176.1	Steel curtain walls (including stainless)	15.4
Commercial and institutional iron and steel doors, except shower doors, tub enclosures, and storm doors	1,032.3	Aluminum curtain walls	435.5
		All other curtain walls	33.8
Overhead and sliding commercial and institutional iron and steel doors	297.6	Metal molding and trim and store fronts, nsk	33.4
Swing commercial and institutional iron and steel doors	476.7	**Metal combination screen, storm sash, and storm doors**	**537.2**
All other commercial and institutional iron and steel doors	258.0	Metal storm sash (including combination)	521.7
		Storm sash (except combination)	13.4
Door frames (including trim sold as an intergral part of the door frame, except storm door frames)	363.3	Combination screen and storm sash	60.9
Aluminum door frames	128.8	Storm doors	447.4
Steel door frames, 16 gauge and heavier	157.9	Metal combination screen, storm sash, and storm doors, nsk	15.5
Steel door frames, lighter than 16 gauge	76.6	**Metal window and door screens (except combination) and metal weather strip**	**329.9**
Shower doors and tub enclosures and other metal doors not made of aluminum or steel	436.2	Metal door, window screens, and metal weather strip	318.2
		Metal door screens	62.9
Metal doors other than steel or aluminum, excluding shower doors, tub enclosures, and storm doors	39.1	Metal window screens, with metal frames (including tension and roll types)	171.7
Shower doors and tub enclosures (all metal)	397.1	Metal weather strip	83.6
		Metal window and door screens (except combination) and metal weather strip, nsk	11.7
		Metal windows and doors, nsk, total	**894.0**

Source: 2002 *Economic Census*. The values are product shipments in millions of dollars for 2002. Total product shipments may be lower or higher than industry shipments. See Introduction for a full discussion. Values of indented subcategories are summed in the main heading(s). The symbol (D) appears when data are withheld to prevent disclosure of competitive information. The abbreviation nsk stands for 'not specified by kind' and nec for 'not elsewhere classified'. A dash (-) means zero.

PRODUCT SHARE DETAILS FOR SHEET METAL WORK MANUFACTURING

Product or Product Class Shipments	Mil. $	Product or Product Class Shipments	Mil. $
SHEET METAL WORK	14,563.1	**Sheet metal awnings, canopies, cornices, and soffits**	**684.4**
Sheet metal air-conditioning ducts and stove pipe	**1,939.0**	Sheet metal awnings, canopies, carports, soffit, shutters, steel and aluminum	614.7
Sheet metal air-conditioning ducts, (including dust collection ducts)	1,485.0	Steel sheet metal awnings, canopies, carports, and patios	91.6
Sheet metal work (including dust collection ducts)	1,412.4	Aluminum sheet metal awnings, canopies, carports, and patios	165.7
Aluminum sheet metal work (including dust collection ducts)	72.6	Sheet metal cornices, skylights, domes, and copings (steel and aluminum)	236.3
Sheet metal stove pipe, furnace smoke pipe, and elbows	317.4	Sheet metal soffits, fascia, and shutters (steel and aluminum)	121.1
Steel sheet metal stove pipe, furnace smoke pipe, and elbows	279.1	Sheet metal awnings, canopies, cornices, and soffits, nsk	69.7
Aluminum sheet metal stove pipe, furnace smoke pipe, and elbows	38.4	**Sheet metal electronic enclosures**	**2,308.9**
Sheet metal air-conditioning ducts and stove pipe, nsk	136.6	Steel sheet metal computer and peripheral equipment enclosures	913.7
Sheet metal culverts, flumes, irrigation pipes, etc.	**538.9**	Aluminum sheet metal computer and peripheral equipment enclosures	320.7
Sheet metal culverts, flumes, irrigation pipes, etc.	511.1	Other sheet metal electronic enclosures (excluding computers), including machine and motor housings, panels, and guards, steel and aluminum	808.9
Steel sheet metal culverts, flumes, irrigation pipes, etc.	421.8	Sheet metal electronic enclosures, nsk	265.7
Aluminum sheet metal culverts, flumes, irrigation pipes, etc.	25.9	**Metal studs, nonload and load-bearing (iron, steel, and aluminum)**	**326.7**
Other sheet metal culverts, flumes, irrigation pipes, etc.	63.4	**Other sheet metal work**	**3,598.8**
Sheet metal culverts, flumes, irrigation pipes, etc., nsk	27.8	Sheet metal roof ventilators, louvers and dampers for heating, ventilation, and air-conditioning	815.8
Sheet metal roofing and roof drainage equipment	**1,432.6**	Steel and aluminum sheet metal roof ventilators	423.6
Sheet metal roofing, all types	774.9	Steel sheet metal work for heating, ventilation, and air-conditioning	286.2
Sheet metal roof drainage equipment (including eave troughs, etc.)	575.2	Aluminum sheet metal work for heating, ventilation, and air-conditioning	106.0
Aluminum and other sheet metal roofing, all types	164.1	Steel restaurant and hotel kitchen sheet metal equipment	335.4
Steel sheet metal roof drainage equipment (including eave troughs, etc.)	114.9	Aluminum and other sheet metal work	2,442.6
Aluminum sheet metal roof drainage equipment (including eave troughs, etc.)	234.8	Aluminum restaurant and hotel kitchen sheet metal equipment	35.1
All other sheet metal roof drainage equipment (including eave troughs, etc.)	61.3	Other steel sheet metal work	1,652.5
Sheet metal roofing and roof drainage equipment, nsk	82.6	Other aluminum sheet metal work	217.1
Sheet metal flooring and siding	**866.8**	Other sheet metal work, metals other than steel and aluminum	537.9
Sheet metal siding	612.0	Other steel metal work, nsk	5.0
Steel sheet metal siding	213.8	**Sheet metal work, nsk, total**	**2,867.1**
Residential aluminum sheet metal siding (including mobile homes)	238.7		
Other aluminum sheet metal siding (commercial, industrial, farm buildings, etc.)	69.3		
Other sheet metal siding	90.3		
Fabricated sheet metal flooring	191.0		
Sheet metal flooring and siding, nsk	63.8		

Source: 2002 Economic Census. The values are product shipments in millions of dollars for 2002. Total product shipments may be lower or higher than industry shipments. See Introduction for a full discussion. Values of indented subcategories are summed in the main heading(s). The symbol (D) appears when data are withheld to prevent disclosure of competitive information. The abbreviation nsk stands for 'not specified by kind' and nec for 'not elsewhere classified'. A dash (-) means zero.

PRODUCT SHARE DETAILS FOR ORNAMENTAL & ARCHITECTURAL METAL WORK

Product or Product Class Shipments	Mil. $	Product or Product Class Shipments	Mil. $
ORNAMENTAL AND ARCHITECTURAL METAL WORK . .	5,165.9	construction	314.1
Metal grilles, registers, and air diffusers	**575.9**	Open aluminum flooring and grating for building	
Other grills, including open mesh partitions	267.5	construction	50.7
Aluminum warm air or air-conditioning grills, registers,		**Metal scaffolding and shoring and forming for concrete work**	**564.3**
and air diffusers	201.4	Scaffolding, shoring, and forming for concrete work	551.3
Other iron and steel grills (including open mesh		Suspended scaffolding (including midpoint, two-point,	
partitions)	46.9	multilevel, boatswain chairs, etc.) (iron, steel, and	
Other aluminum grills (including open mesh partitions) . .	19.2	aluminum)	34.3
Iron and steel warm air or air-conditioning grills, registers,		Access scaffolding (including tube and coupler system,	
and air diffusers	307.0	prefabricated mobil scaffolds, etc.) (iron, steel, and	
Metal grilles, registers, and air diffusers, nsk	1.4	aluminum)	(D)
Ornamental and architectural metal work	**1,578.6**	Shoring (including flying forms, postshores, ellis	
Iron, steel, and aluminum stairs, staircases, and fire		clamps, reshores, etc.) (iron, steel, and aluminum) . . .	(D)
escapes	962.1	Forming (including modular, prefabricated custom	
Iron and steel stairs, staircases, fire escapes, and		design, etc.) (iron, steel, aluminum, and all other	
expanded metal plaster lath	804.4	material-metal combinations)	184.8
Aluminum stairs, staircases, fire escapes, and metal		Metal scaffolding and shoring and forming for concrete	
plaster base accessories (including corner beads,		work, nsk	13.0
screens, grounds, etc)	157.7	**Other architectural and ornamental work**	**1,207.5**
Steel and aluminum fences, gates (other than wire), and		Other aluminum and metal architectural and ornamental	
railings and window guards	535.2	work	314.9
Iron and steel fences and gates (other than wire) . . .	189.2	Other aluminum architectural and ornamental work . .	227.1
Aluminum fences and gates (other than wire)	114.4	Other metal architectural and ornamental work (other	
Iron, steel, and aluminum metal railings and window		than iron, steel, or aluminum)	87.9
guards (other than wire)	231.7	Other iron and steel architectural and ornamental work . .	717.7
Ornamental and architectural metal work, nsk	81.4	Metal stalls and corrals	39.7
Open metal flooring, grating, and studs	**364.7**	Other architectural and ornamental work, nsk	135.2
Open iron and steel flooring and grating for building		**Ornamental and architectural metal work, nsk, total** . .	**874.9**

Source: 2002 *Economic Census.* The values are product shipments in millions of dollars for 2002. Total product shipments may be lower or higher than industry shipments. See Introduction for a full discussion. Values of indented subcategories are summed in the main heading(s). The symbol (D) appears when data are withheld to prevent disclosure of competitive information. The abbreviation nsk stands for 'not specified by kind' and nec for 'not elsewhere classified'. A dash (-) means zero.

INPUTS AND OUTPUTS FOR ORNAMENTAL & ARCHITECTURAL METAL PRODUCTS

Economic Sector or Industry Providing Inputs	%	Sector	Economic Sector or Industry Buying Outputs	%	Sector
Compensation of employees	30.3		Residential permanent site structures	15.2	Construct.
Iron & steel mills & ferroalloys	11.2	Manufg.	Nonresidential structures, nec	10.6	Construct.
Wholesale trade	4.8	Trade	Commercial & health care structures	10.5	Construct.
Aluminum products from purchased aluminum	4.5	Manufg.	Residential structures, nec	6.9	Construct.
Management of companies & enterprises	2.9	Services	Owner-occupied dwellings	6.1	
Ornamental & architectural metal products	2.8	Manufg.	Food services & drinking places	4.7	Services
Chemical products & preparations, nec	1.8	Manufg.	Maintenance/repair of nonresidential structures	3.6	Construct.
Accounting, tax preparation, bookkeeping, & payroll	1.8	Services	Motor vehicle parts	3.1	Manufg.
Machine shops	1.5	Manufg.	Ornamental & architectural metal products	2.8	Manufg.
Advertising & related services	1.3	Services	Other S/L govt. enterprises	2.3	S/L Govt
Custom roll forming	1.3	Manufg.	Plastics products, nec	2.2	Manufg.
Real estate	1.3	Fin/R.E.	Metal cans, boxes, & other containers (light gauge)	1.8	Manufg.
Turned products & screws, nuts, & bolts	1.1	Manufg.	Telecommunications	1.6	Services
Paints & coatings	1.1	Manufg.	Exports of goods & services	1.3	Cap Inv
Semiconductors & related devices	1.0	Manufg.	Engine equipment, nec	1.3	Manufg.
Truck transportation	1.0	Util.	Search, detection, & navigation instruments	1.1	Manufg.
Telecommunications	1.0	Services	Printed circuit assemblies (electronic assembiles)	1.1	Manufg.
Securities, commodity contracts, investments	0.9	Fin/R.E.	Natural gas distribution	1.1	Util.
Nonferrous metal (ex. copper & aluminum) processing	0.9	Manufg.	Private fixed investment	1.1	
Hardware	0.8	Manufg.	Architectural, engineering, & related services	1.0	Services
Flat glass	0.7	Manufg.	Manufacturing structures	0.9	Construct.
Coating, engraving, heat treating & allied activities	0.7	Manufg.	Fabricated metals, nec	0.8	Manufg.
Lessors of nonfinancial assets	0.7	Fin/R.E.	Commercial & service industry machinery, nec	0.7	Manufg.
Alumina refining & primary aluminum production	0.7	Manufg.	Manufactured homes & mobile homes	0.7	Manufg.
Monetary authorities/depository credit intermediation	0.6	Fin/R.E.	Travel trailers & campers	0.7	Manufg.
Architectural, engineering, & related services	0.6	Services	Automobiles	0.7	Manufg.
Power generation & supply	0.6	Util.	Oil & gas operations services	0.6	Mining
Taxes on production & imports, less subsidies	0.6		Semiconductors & related devices	0.6	Manufg.
Ferrous metal foundries	0.6	Manufg.	Waste management & remediation services	0.6	Services
Professional, scientific, technical services, nec	0.5	Services	Computer system design services	0.6	Services
Legal services	0.5	Services	Maintenance/repair of residential structures	0.6	Construct.
Nonferrous metal foundries	0.5	Manufg.	Military armored vehicles, tanks, & tank components	0.6	Manufg.
Maintenance/repair of nonresidential structures	0.5	Construct.	General S/L govt. services	0.5	S/L Govt
Printed circuit assemblies (electronic assembiles)	0.5	Manufg.	Civic, social, & professional organizations	0.5	Services
Paperboard containers	0.5	Manufg.	Data processing, hosting, & related services	0.4	Services
Unlaminated plastics profile shapes	0.4	Manufg.	Construction machinery	0.4	Manufg.
Services to buildings & dwellings	0.4	Services	Prefabricated wood buildings	0.4	Manufg.
Automotive equipment rental & leasing	0.4	Fin/R.E.	Electromedical & electrotherapeutic apparatus	0.4	Manufg.
Specialized design services	0.4	Services	Analytical laboratory instruments	0.4	Manufg.
Plastics packaging materials, film & sheet	0.4	Manufg.	Retail trade	0.4	Trade
Food services & drinking places	0.4	Services	Motor vehicle bodies	0.4	Manufg.

Continued on next page.

INPUTS AND OUTPUTS FOR ORNAMENTAL & ARCHITECTURAL METAL PRODUCTS - Continued

Economic Sector or Industry Providing Inputs	%	Sector	Economic Sector or Industry Buying Outputs	%	Sector
Employment services	0.4	Services	Computer terminals & peripherals	0.4	Manufg.
Business support services	0.3	Services	Electronic computers	0.3	Manufg.
Data processing, hosting, & related services	0.3	Services	Scientific research & development services	0.3	Services
Warehousing & storage	0.3	Util.	Relay & industrial controls	0.3	Manufg.
Automotive repair & maintenance, ex. car washes	0.3	Services	Wood windows & doors & millwork	0.3	Manufg.
Management, scientific, & technical consulting	0.3	Services	Switchgear & switchboard apparatus	0.3	Manufg.
Rail transportation	0.3	Util.	Laboratory apparatus & furniture	0.3	Manufg.
Metal cans, boxes, & other containers (light gauge)	0.3	Manufg.	Broadcast & wireless communications equipment	0.3	Manufg.
Natural gas distribution	0.3	Util.	General Federal government services, defense	0.2	Fed Govt
Commercial & industrial equipment repair/maintenance	0.2	Services	Individual & family services	0.2	Services
Fabricated metals, nec	0.2	Manufg.	Computer storage devices	0.2	Manufg.
Hotels & motels, including casino hotels	0.2	Services	Basic organic chemicals, nec	0.2	Manufg.
Air transportation	0.2	Util.	Industrial process variable instruments	0.2	Manufg.
Basic organic chemicals, nec	0.2	Manufg.	Motor homes	0.2	Manufg.
Scrap	0.2	Scrap	Optical instruments & lenses	0.2	Manufg.
Crowns & closures & metal stamping	0.2	Manufg.	General Federal government services, nondefense	0.2	Fed Govt
Commercial & industrial machinery rental & leasing	0.2	Fin/R.E.	Electronic components, nec	0.2	Manufg.
Support services, nec	0.2	Services	Wholesale trade	0.2	Trade
Scientific research & development services	0.2	Services	Services to buildings & dwellings	0.2	Services
Plate work & fabricated structural products	0.2	Manufg.	Watches, clocks, & related devices	0.2	Manufg.
Ball & roller bearings	0.2	Manufg.	Child day care services	0.2	Services
Investigation & security services	0.2	Services	Commercial & industrial machinery rental & leasing	0.2	Fin/R.E.
Handtools	0.2	Manufg.	Electrical equipment & components, nec	0.2	Manufg.
Copper rolling, drawing, extruding, & alloying	0.2	Manufg.	Machine shops	0.1	Manufg.
Valve & fittings other than plumbing	0.2	Manufg.	Automatic environmental controls	0.1	Manufg.
Postal service	0.2	Util.	Telephone apparatus	0.1	Manufg.
Commercial & service industry machinery, nec	0.1	Manufg.	Amusement & recreation, nec	0.1	Services
Other computer related services, including facilities	0.1	Services	Plate work & fabricated structural products	0.1	Manufg.
Nondepository credit intermediation activities	0.1	Fin/R.E.	Bare printed circuit boards	0.1	Manufg.
Internet service providers & web search portals	0.1	Services	Surgical & medical instrument	0.1	Manufg.
Cutting tools & machine tool accessories	0.1	Manufg.	Surgical appliances & supplies	0.1	Manufg.
			Electricity & signal testing instruments	0.1	Manufg.
			Colleges, universities, & professional schools	0.1	Services
			Communications equipment, nec	0.1	Manufg.
			Totalizing fluid meters & counting devices	0.1	Manufg.

Source: Benchmark Input-Output Accounts for the U.S. Economy, 2002, U.S. Department of Commerce, Washington, D.C., January 2008. The abbreviation nec stands for 'not elsewhere classified'.

OCCUPATIONS EMPLOYED BY ARCHITECTURAL & STRUCTURAL METALS MANUFACTURING

Occupation	% of Total 2006	Change to 2016	Occupation	% of Total 2006	Change to 2016
Welders, cutters, solderers, & brazers	11.2	13.6	Cost estimators	1.4	15.4
Team assemblers	8.6	6.8	Office clerks, general	1.3	5.2
Structural metal fabricators & fitters	8.0	6.8	Assemblers & fabricators, nec	1.2	-3.9
Cutting, punching, & press machine operators	5.8	-3.9	Rolling machine operators & tenders	1.2	6.8
First-line supervisors/managers of production workers	4.2	6.8	Mechanical drafters	1.2	8.0
Sheet metal workers	4.2	4.8	Maintenance & repair workers, general	1.2	6.8
Helpers--Production workers	3.3	6.8	Industrial truck & tractor operators	1.2	-3.9
Laborers & freight, stock, & material movers, hand	2.8	-3.9	Truck drivers, heavy & tractor-trailer	1.1	6.8
Sales reps, wholesale & manufacturing, exc tech	2.5	6.8	Computer-controlled machine tool operators	1.1	17.5
General & operations managers	1.8	-3.9	Inspectors, testers, sorters, samplers, & weighers	1.1	0.7
Coating, painting, & spraying machine operators	1.6	1.5	Grinding, lapping, polishing machine tool operators	1.1	3.6
Shipping, receiving, & traffic clerks	1.5	2.8	Industrial production managers	1.0	6.8
Machinists	1.5	12.1	Multiple machine tool operators & tenders	1.0	17.5
Bookkeeping, accounting, & auditing clerks	1.4	6.8			

Source: Industry-Occupation Matrix, Bureau of Labor Statistics, December 4, 2007. These data are reported based on 4-digit NAICS categories but have been matched to corresponding 6-digit NAICS industry codes. The change reported for each occupation to the year 2016 is a percent of growth or decline as estimated by the Bureau of Labor Statistics. The abbreviation nec stands for 'not elsewhere classified'.

LOCATION BY STATE AND REGIONAL CONCENTRATION

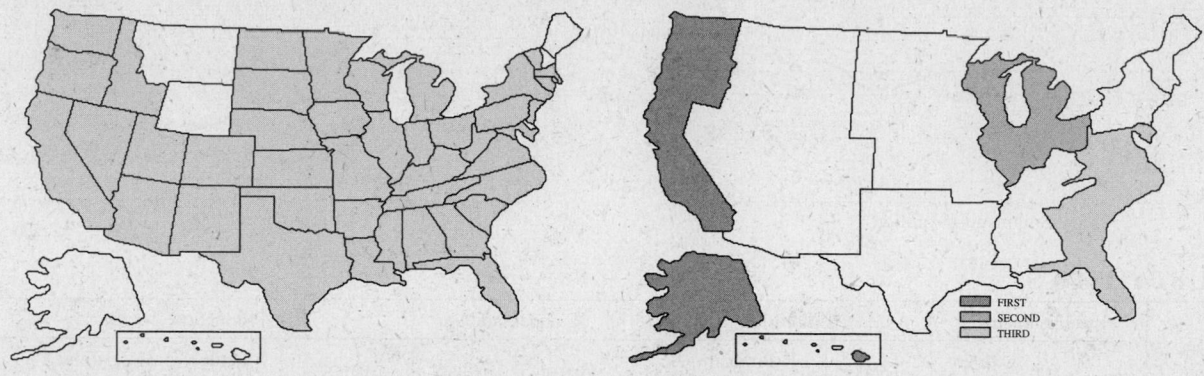

INDUSTRY DATA BY STATE

| State | Establish-ments | Shipments | | | Employment | | | | Cost as % of Shipments | Investment per Employee ($) |
		Total ($ mil)	% of U.S.	Per Establ.	Total Number	% of U.S.	Per Establ.	Wages ($/hour)		
California	1,122	3,682.3	11.5	3,281.9	28,022	12.4	25	14.64	41.7	3,502
Texas	627	2,760.3	8.6	4,402.4	19,807	8.8	32	12.68	47.5	4,462
Ohio	349	2,033.1	6.3	5,825.6	11,380	5.1	33	14.35	54.2	4,758
Pennsylvania	378	1,970.8	6.2	5,213.9	12,038	5.3	32	15.03	49.4	4,566
Florida	465	1,637.6	5.1	3,521.7	12,579	5.6	27	12.16	45.2	3,668
Illinois	275	1,534.4	4.8	5,579.5	10,229	4.5	37	14.78	42.8	4,278
New York	497	1,392.4	4.3	2,801.6	12,083	5.4	24	15.29	40.5	2,532
Wisconsin	174	1,247.3	3.9	7,168.1	8,301	3.7	48	15.58	47.3	3,199
Indiana	198	1,230.1	3.8	6,212.4	7,729	3.4	39	13.52	50.9	2,662
Georgia	214	1,147.1	3.6	5,360.3	7,468	3.3	35	13.71	52.4	4,656
New Jersey	263	1,062.3	3.3	4,039.1	7,701	3.4	29	14.43	48.2	3,504
North Carolina	207	1,013.9	3.2	4,898.2	6,712	3.0	32	12.40	51.4	4,760
Tennessee	147	822.1	2.6	5,592.3	5,507	2.4	37	13.40	49.1	7,475
Michigan	253	815.5	2.5	3,223.3	5,803	2.6	23	15.49	43.2	3,787
Massachusetts	216	614.8	1.9	2,846.1	4,691	2.1	22	16.24	41.3	2,189
Alabama	148	611.3	1.9	4,130.5	4,427	2.0	30	13.23	46.0	3,983
Iowa	68	564.1	1.8	8,295.5	3,526	1.6	52	16.06	44.1	4,434
Missouri	149	550.8	1.7	3,696.9	4,776	2.1	32	13.60	45.5	2,420
Minnesota	166	549.4	1.7	3,309.9	3,626	1.6	22	16.40	42.5	3,711
Washington	202	523.9	1.6	2,593.4	3,765	1.7	19	14.59	47.1	3,361
Arizona	180	511.9	1.6	2,844.1	4,140	1.8	23	14.01	45.8	3,953
Mississippi	61	446.9	1.4	7,325.4	2,935	1.3	48	13.11	45.2	4,657
Kansas	77	416.2	1.3	5,405.8	3,054	1.4	40	12.58	51.7	3,284
Connecticut	125	399.3	1.2	3,194.7	2,439	1.1	20	15.43	38.1	4,093
Oklahoma	107	391.9	1.2	3,662.9	2,809	1.2	26	13.49	41.6	3,215
Arkansas	72	380.3	1.2	5,281.4	2,766	1.2	38	14.96	44.3	2,580
Oregon	145	375.0	1.2	2,586.2	2,684	1.2	19	16.17	43.1	3,667
Maryland	107	329.1	1.0	3,076.0	2,295	1.0	21	15.88	35.3	3,010
Virginia	126	318.2	1.0	2,525.1	2,264	1.0	18	14.71	45.8	3,932
Colorado	138	315.9	1.0	2,288.8	2,634	1.2	19	14.01	44.6	4,326
Kentucky	111	305.8	1.0	2,755.1	2,084	0.9	19	14.68	45.8	2,804
Utah	101	268.4	0.8	2,657.4	1,951	0.9	19	15.09	47.6	3,866
South Carolina	83	208.6	0.7	2,513.6	1,592	0.7	19	13.92	46.3	2,952
Nevada	56	193.6	0.6	3,457.7	1,245	0.6	22	14.22	49.4	2,807
Nebraska	37	160.1	0.5	4,327.1	699	0.3	19	12.19	52.6	3,093
Louisiana	74	155.1	0.5	2,096.5	1,422	0.6	19	13.13	49.0	2,631
West Virginia	22	146.6	0.5	6,664.3	956	0.4	43	10.86	35.0	2,649
South Dakota	6	143.9	0.4	23,982.0	1,353	0.6	226	10.34	51.3	1,602
Idaho	19	77.3	0.2	4,069.3	606	0.3	32	15.54	37.6	2,535
New Mexico	45	62.3	0.2	1,384.3	517	0.2	11	14.97	38.8	1,896
Rhode Island	17	55.4	0.2	3,261.1	377	0.2	22	16.68	50.2	7,682
Vermont	12	48.8	0.2	4,069.6	511	0.2	43	12.65	36.3	1,642
North Dakota	4	13.6	<0.1	3,402.2	114	0.1	28	10.96	69.4	6,842

Source: 2002 *Economic Census*. The states are in descending order of shipments or establishments (if shipment data are missing for the majority). The symbol (D) appears when data are withheld to prevent disclosure of competitive information. States marked with (D) are sorted by number of establishments. A dash (-) indicates that the data element cannot be calculated. Data may not show all states active in the NAICS category. All data available at the time of publication are shown.

NAICS 332410 - POWER BOILER AND HEAT EXCHANGER MANUFACTURING

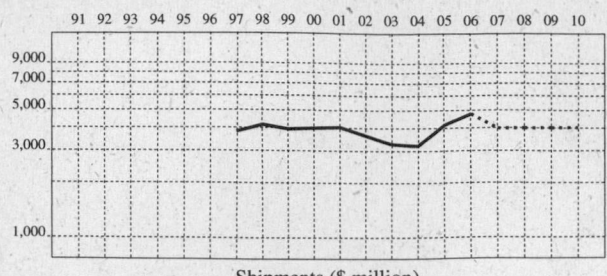

Shipments ($ million)

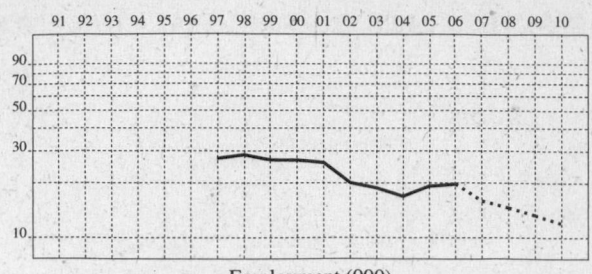

Employment (000)

GENERAL STATISTICS

| Year | Companies | Establishments | | Employment | | | Compensation | | Production ($ million) | | | |
		Total	with 20 or more employees	Total (000)	Production Workers (000)	Hours (Mil)	Payroll ($ mil)	Wages ($/hr)	Cost of Materials	Value Added by Manufacture	Value of Shipments	Capital Invest.
1997	433	466	267	27.3	19.5	40.6	936.3	14.15	1,796.1	2,041.6	3,812.6	99.8
1998		474	256	28.6	20.6	42.8	999.4	14.20	1,977.8	2,226.1	4,159.3	122.6
1999		467	260	26.8	19.1	38.0	940.6	14.98	1,893.9	2,017.8	3,935.2	137.6
2000		447	242	26.7	18.9	37.5	930.4	15.08	1,966.8	2,024.7	3,989.0	97.3
2001		413	234	25.9	18.7	37.1	917.4	15.45	1,991.2	2,040.8	4,043.1	111.8
2002	292	330	193	20.1	14.1	28.9	804.2	16.63	1,671.9	1,971.5	3,644.9	116.3
2003		320	180	18.8	13.2	26.9	789.7	17.46	1,350.2	1,935.7	3,276.5	124.3
2004		314	178	16.9	11.5	23.5	744.2	18.30	1,539.6	1,664.8	3,202.7	133.5
2005		301	182	19.2	12.8	26.7	960.2	19.79	2,169.4	2,000.3	4,162.8	82.4
2006		263P	156P	19.7	13.4	29.1	1,056.7	20.49	2,320.5	2,615.4	4,773.0	92.7
2007		237P	143P	15.9P	10.5P	22.2P	884.3P	20.69P	1,936.1P	2,182.1P	3,982.2P	102.5P
2008		212P	130P	14.6P	9.5P	20.2P	880.0P	21.42P	1,943.3P	2,190.3P	3,997.2P	100.8P
2009		186P	117P	13.3P	8.5P	18.2P	875.7P	22.16P	1,950.6P	2,198.5P	4,012.2P	99.1P
2010		160P	104P	12.0P	7.5P	16.2P	871.4P	22.89P	1,957.9P	2,206.7P	4,027.1P	97.4P

Sources: 1997 and 2002 *Economic Census*; other years, up to 2006, are from *Annual Survey of Manufactures*. Establishment counts for non-Census years are from *County Business Patterns*; 1997 and 2002 values are from the 1997 and 2002 censuses, respectively. 'P's show projections by the editors.

INDICES OF CHANGE

| Year | Companies | Establishments | | Employment | | | Compensation | | Production ($ million) | | | |
		Total	with 20 or more employees	Total (000)	Production Workers (000)	Hours (Mil)	Payroll ($ mil)	Wages ($/hr)	Cost of Materials	Value Added by Manufacture	Value of Shipments	Capital Invest.
1997	148	141	138	136	138	140	116	85	107	104	105	86
1998		144	133	142	146	148	124	85	118	113	114	105
1999		142	135	133	135	131	117	90	113	102	108	118
2000		135	125	133	134	130	116	91	118	103	109	84
2001		125	121	129	133	128	114	93	119	104	111	96
2002	100	100	100	100	100	100	100	100	100	100	100	100
2003		97	93	94	94	93	98	105	81	98	90	107
2004		95	92	84	82	81	93	110	92	84	88	115
2005		91	94	96	91	92	119	119	130	101	114	71
2006		80P	81P	98	95	101	131	123	139	133	131	80
2007		72P	74P	79P	74P	77P	110P	124P	116P	111P	109P	88P
2008		64P	67P	73P	67P	70P	109P	129P	116P	111P	110P	87P
2009		56P	61P	66P	60P	63P	109P	133P	117P	112P	110P	85P
2010		48P	54P	60P	53P	56P	108P	138P	117P	112P	110P	84P

Sources: Same as General Statistics. Values reflect change from the base year, 2002. Values above 100 mean greater than 2002, values below 100 mean less than 2002, and the values of 100 in other years means the same as 2002. 'P's show projections by the editors.

SELECTED RATIOS

For 2002	Avg. of All Manufact.	Analyzed Industry	Index	For 2002	Avg. of All Manufact.	Analyzed Industry	Index
Employees per Establishment	42	61	145	Value Added per Production Worker	182,367	139,823	77
Payroll per Establishment	1,639,184	2,436,970	149	Cost per Establishment	5,769,015	5,066,364	88
Payroll per Employee	39,053	40,010	102	Cost per Employee	137,446	83,179	61
Production Workers per Establishment	30	43	145	Cost per Production Worker	195,506	118,574	61
Wages per Establishment	694,845	1,456,385	210	Shipments per Establishment	11,158,348	11,045,152	99
Wages per Production Worker	23,548	34,086	145	Shipments per Employee	265,847	181,338	68
Hours per Production Worker	1,980	2,050	104	Shipments per Production Worker	378,144	258,504	68
Wages per Hour	11.89	16.63	140	Investment per Establishment	361,338	352,424	98
Value Added per Establishment	5,381,325	5,974,242	111	Investment per Employee	8,609	5,786	67
Value Added per Employee	128,210	98,085	77	Investment per Production Worker	12,245	8,248	67

Sources: Same as General Statistics. The 'Average of All Manufacturing' column represents the average of all manufacturing industries reported for the most recent complete year available. The Index shows the relationship between the Average and the Analyzed Industry. For example, 100 means that they are equal; 500 that the Analyzed Industry is five times the average; 50 means that the Analyzed Industry is half the national average. The abbreviation 'na' is used to show that data are 'not available'. Ratios shown for 2002, the last complete census year.

LEADING COMPANIES   Number shown: 75   Total sales ($ mil): 57,898   Total employment (000): 179.4

Company Name	Address				CEO Name	Phone	Co. Type	Sales ($ mil)	Empl. (000)
API Group Inc.	2366 Rose Pl.	St. Paul	MN	55113	Lee R. Anderson, Sr.	651-636-4320	R	9,000	5.0
Dover Corp.	280 Park Ave.	New York	NY	10017		212-922-1640	P	7,226	33.4
McDermott International Inc.	757 N Eldridge Pky.	Houston	TX	77079	Robert Deason	281-870-5011	P	5,632	28.4
Harsco Corp.	PO Box 8888	Camp Hill	PA	17001	S. D. Fazzolari	717-763-7064	P	3,688	21.5
Amsted Industries Inc.	2 Prudential Plaza	Chicago	IL	60601	W. Robert Reum	312-645-1700	R	3,050	9.9
Baltimore Aircoil Company Inc.	PO Box 7322	Baltimore	MD	21227	Steven Duerwachter	410-799-6200	R	2,510*	0.2
Consolidated Metco Inc.	PO Box 83201	Portland	OR	97283		503-286-5741	R	2,510*	0.1
Mechanical Construction Inc.	1500 Chester Pk.	Eddystone	PA	19022	Michael J. Hall	610-876-9292	S	2,370*	3.3
A.O. Smith Corp.	PO Box 245008	Milwaukee	WI	53224		414-359-4000	P	2,312	16.8
Hutchinson FTS Inc.	1835 Technology	Troy	MI	48083	Paul Campbell	248-589-7710	R	1,863*	<0.1
Williams Enterprise of Georgia	1285 Hawthorne	Smyrna	GA	30080	Dale Williams	770-436-1596	R	1,478*	0.6
Babcock and Wilcox Co.	PO Box 351	Barberton	OH	44203	John A. Fees	330-753-4511	S	1,080*	10.8
TriMas Corp.	39400 Woodward	Bloomfield Hls	MI	48304	Grant Beard	248-631-5450	P	1,068	5.1
C and D Zodiac Inc.	5701 Bolsa Ave.	Huntington Bch	CA	92647		714-934-0000	R	1,045*	0.5
EPE Industrial Filters Inc.	9250 Bloomington	Bloomington	MN	55431	William Cook	847-381-0860	R	1,024*	1.5
McWane Corp.	PO Box 43327	Birmingham	AL	35243	G. Ruffner Page, Jr.	205-414-3100	R	944*	7.0
Manchester Tank and Equipment	1000 Corp Centre Dr	Franklin	TN	37067	Robert Richard	615-370-3833	R	926*	<0.1
Chart Industries Inc.	One Infinity Corp.	Garfield Height	OH	44125	Samuel F. Thomas	440-753-1490	P	666	2.8
Riley Power Inc.	PO Box 15040	Worcester	MA	01615		508-852-7100	R	612*	0.4
American Cast Iron Pipe Co.	PO Box 2727	Birmingham	AL	35202		205-325-7701	R	596*	2.3
NATCO Group Inc.	2950 N Loop W, 700	Houston	TX	77092	John U. Clarke	713-683-9292	P	570	2.5
Alaskan Copper Co's Inc.	PO Box 3546	Seattle	WA	98124	Kermit Rosen	206-623-5800	R	392*	0.3
Mestek Inc.	260 N Elm St.	Westfield	MA	01085	R. Bruce Dewey	413-568-9571	R	372*	2.6
Mobile Mini Inc.	PO Box 79149	Phoenix	AZ	85062	Steven G. Bunger	480-894-6311	P	318	2.1
Maxcess Technologies Inc.	230 Deming Way	Summerville	SC	29483	Andy Miarka	843-821-1200	R	291*	<0.1
Kirk and Blum Manufacturing	3120 Forrer St.	Cincinnati	OH	45209	Richard J. Blum	513-458-2600	S	265*	0.4
CEI Enterprises Inc.	245 Woodward SE	Albuquerque	NM	87102		505-842-5556	S	264*	0.1
Southern Heat Exchanger Corp.	PO Box 1850	Tuscaloosa	AL	35403	Bill Laganke	205-345-5335	R	234*	0.2
General Atomics	PO Box 85608	San Diego	CA	92186	James Blue	858-455-3000	R	219*	1.0
Burnham Holdings Inc.	PO Box 3205	Lancaster	PA	17604	Albert Morrison III	717-397-4700	P	218	1.3
Raven Industries Inc.	PO Box 5107	Sioux Falls	SD	57117	Conrad J. Hoigaard	605-336-2750	P	217	0.9
Amtrol Inc.	1400 Division Rd.	West Warwick	RI	02893	Larry T. Guillemette	401-884-6300	R	213	1.3
Cleaver-Brooks Inc.	PO Box 421	Milwaukee	WI	53201	Welch Goggins	414-359-0600	R	210*	0.2
Poly Processing Co.	8055 Ash Street	French Camp	CA	95231	Dixon Abell	209-982-4904	R	204*	0.3
Ameri-Forge Ltd.	13770 Industrial Rd	Houston	TX	77015	William Friel	713-393-4200	R	200*	0.2
Robinson Steel Company Inc.	4303 Kennedy Ave.	East Chicago	IN	46312		219-398-4600	R	200*	0.2
API Delevan	270 Quaker Rd.	East Aurora	NY	14052		716-652-3600	S	195*	1.8
ALSTOM Power Inc.	3020 Truax Rd.	Wellsville	NY	14895	E Bysiek	585-593-2700	S	191*	0.6
Keppel Amfels Inc.	PO Box 3107	Brownsville	TX	78523	C Ho	956-831-8220	R	183*	1.5
Roberts Company Inc.	PO Box 1109	Winterville	NC	28590	John Roberts	252-355-9353	R	163*	0.3
Aluminum Precision Products	3333 W Warner	Santa Ana	CA	92704	Philip Keeler	714-546-8125	R	155*	0.7
Paul Mueller Co.	PO Box 828	Springfield	MO	65801	Paul Mueller	417-831-3000	P	153	1.2
Southeast Texas Industries	PO Box 1449	Buna	TX	77612	Richard Purkey	409-994-3570	R	146*	0.3
Taco Inc.	1160 Cranston St.	Cranston	RI	02920		401-942-8000	R	140*	0.4
Ultra Air Products Inc.	3309 John Conley	Lapeer	MI	48446	Don Swanson	810-667-6800	R	136*	0.7
Suspa Inc.	3970 Rgr B Chaffee	Grand Rapids	MI	49548	Steve Garvelink	616-241-4200	R	116*	0.2
Beall Trailers of Montana Inc.	PO Box 2543	Billings	MT	59103	Jerry Beall	406-252-7163	R	113*	0.8
ATCO Rubber Products Inc.	7101 Atco Dr.	Fort Worth	TX	76118	Charles Anderson	817-595-2894	R	113*	0.6
Consolidated Fabricators Corp.	4600 S Santa Fe Ave	Los Angeles	CA	90058	Michael Melideo	323-586-4500	R	109*	0.1
Structural Steel Services Inc.	PO Box 2929	Meridian	MS	39302	Tommy Dulaney	601-483-5381	R	108*	0.2
Mervis Industries Inc.	PO Box 827	Danville	IL	61834	Louis Mervis	217-442-5300	R	100*	0.3
Besser Co.	801 Johnson St.	Alpena	MI	49707	Kevin Curtis	989-354-4111	R	99*	0.4
EvapCo Inc.	5151 Allendale Ln.	Taneytown	MD	21787	Wilson Bradley	410-756-2600	R	96*	0.2
Apache Stainless Equipment	PO Box 538	Beaver Dam	WI	53916	Patrick Albregts	920-356-9900	S	96*	0.2
HTP Inc.	PO Box 429	East Freetown	MA	02717	David Davis	508-763-8071	R	87*	0.2
Enerfab Inc.	4955 Spring Grove	Cincinnati	OH	45232	Wendell Bell	513-641-0500	R	84*	0.1
Deltak L.L.C.	13330 12th Ave. N	Plymouth	MN	55441		763-557-7440	S	83*	0.1
Burger Iron Co.	3100 Gilchrist Rd.	Mogadore	OH	44260	Tom Fiocca	330-253-5121	R	79*	0.2
Super Steel Products Corp.	7900 W Twr. Ave.	Milwaukee	WI	53223		414-355-4800	R	79*	0.6
Manitowoc Ice Inc.	2110 S 26th St.	Manitowoc	WI	54220	Dan Brandel	920-682-0161	S	77*	0.4
McAbee Construction Inc.	PO Box 1460	Tuscaloosa	AL	35403	Leroy McAbee	205-349-2212	R	77*	0.5
Lyon Workspace Products L.L.C.	PO Box 671	Aurora	IL	60507		630-892-8941	R	76*	0.6
CST Industries Inc.	PO Box 2907	Kansas City	KS	66110		913-621-3700	R	76*	<0.1
Smithco Engineering Inc.	PO Box 571330	Tulsa	OK	74157	Judith Smith	918-446-4406	R	76*	<0.1
Tricon Metals and Services	PO Box 101447	Birmingham	AL	35210	J Cashio	205-956-2567	R	73*	0.2
McKenzie Tank Lines Inc.	PO Box 1200	Tallahassee	FL	32302	Joseph Audie	850-576-1221	R	72*	<0.1
Sioux City Foundry Co.	PO Box 3067	Sioux City	IA	51102	Andrew Galinsky	712-252-4181	R	71*	<0.1
Central Maintenance & Welding	2620 Keysville Rd.	Lithia	FL	33547	Conrad Varnam	813-737-1402	R	67*	0.3
Graham Corp.	PO Box 719	Batavia	NY	14021	Jerald D. Bidlack	585-343-2216	P	66	0.3
Taylor Forge Engineered System	208 N Iron St.	Paola	KS	66071	Michael Kilkenny	913-294-5331	R	61*	0.2
Modern Welding Company of TX	PO Box 85	Rhome	TX	76078	John Jones	817-636-2215	R	61*	0.6
Sweco Fab Inc.	PO Box 34546	Houston	TX	77234	Durga Agrawal	713-731-0030	R	61*	0.4
Slant Fin Corp.	100 Forest Dr.	Greenvale	NY	11548	Donald Brown	516-484-2600	R	60*	0.4
Astro Air Inc.	1653 N Bolton St.	Jacksonville	TX	75766	Rex Dacus	903-586-3691	R	59*	0.3
Saylor-Beall Manufacturing Co.	PO Box 40	Saint Johns	MI	48879	Bruce Mc Fee	989-224-2371	S	58*	0.3

Source: Ward's Business Directory of U.S. Private and Public Companies, Volumes 1 and 2, 2008. The company type code used is as follows: P - Public, R - Private, S - Subsidiary, D - Division, J - Joint Venture, A - Affiliate, G - Group. Sales are in millions of dollars, employees are in thousands. An asterisk (*) indicates an estimated sales volume. The symbol < stands for 'less than'. Company names and addresses are truncated, in some cases, to fit into the available space.

MATERIALS CONSUMED

Material	Quantity	Delivered Cost ($ million)
Fabricated metal pipe (excluding castings and forgings)	(X)	50.8
Fabricated metal valves and pipe fittings	(X)	15.9
All other miscellaneous fabricated metal parts designed for steel power boilers (exc. castings and forgings)	(X)	31.2
All other fabricated metal products (exc. castings, forgings, and all other parts designed for steel power boilers)	(X)	153.8
Iron and steel castings (rough and semifinished)	(X)	23.3
Nonferrous (aluminum, copper, etc.) castings (rough and semifinished)	(X)	6.1
Forgings	(X)	26.9
Steel bars and bar shapes (exc. concrete reinforcing bars, castings, forgings, and fabricated metal products)	(X)	18.1
Steel sheet and strip (including tinplate)	(X)	33.9
Steel plate	(X)	137.5
Wide flange steel structural beams	(X)	2.4
All other steel structural shapes (exc. sheet pilings, castings, forgings, and fabricated steel products)	(X)	1.9
All other steel shapes and forms, incl. sheet pilings	(X)	5.7
Copper and copper-base alloy pipe and tube (exc. castings, forgings, fabr. metal products)	(X)	45.9
All other copper and copper-base alloy shapes and forms (exc. castings, forgings, fabr. metal products)	(X)	14.6
Aluminum and aluminum-base alloy sheet, plate, foil, and welded tubing	(X)	31.9
All other aluminum and aluminum-base alloy shapes and forms (exc. castings, forgings, fabr. metal products)	(X)	9.6
All other nonferrous shapes and forms (exc. castings, forgings, fabr. metal products)	(X)	24.4
Paints, varnishes, stains, lacquers, shellacs, japans, enamels, etc.	(X)	11.8
Welding electrodes	(X)	7.3
All other materials, components, parts, containers, and supplies	(X)	238.8
Materials, ingredients, containers, and supplies, nsk	(X)	421.5

Source: 2002 Economic Census. Explanation of symbols used: (D): Withheld to avoid disclosure of competitive data; na: Not available; (S): Withheld because statistical norms were not met; (X): Not applicable; (Z): Less than half the unit shown; nec: Not elsewhere classified; nsk: Not specified by kind; - : zero; p: 10-19 percent estimated; q : 20-29 percent estimated.

PRODUCT SHARE DETAILS

Product or Product Class Shipments	Mil. $	Product or Product Class Shipments	Mil. $
POWER BOILERS AND HEAT EXCHANGERS	3,356.5	applications)	(D)
Fabricated heat exchangers and steam condensers (except nuclear applications)	**1,420.7**	Water tube steel power boilers (stationary and marine), more than 15 p.s.i. steam working pressure, 100,001 lb per hour or more super heated (except for nuclear applications)	(D)
Fabricated bar tube industrial heat exchangers, closed types (except nuclear applications)	467.4	Other water tube steel power boilers (stationary and marine), parts, and attachments (except for nuclear applications)	88.9
Fabricated fin tube industrial heat exchangers, closed types (except nuclear applications)	567.0	Steel power boilers (stationary and marine), parts, and attachments (except for nuclear applications)	25.4
Fabricated steam condensers (except nuclear applications)	219.3		
Fabricated heat exchangers and steam condensers (except nuclear applications), nsk	167.1	Fire tube steel power boilers (stationary and marine), scotch type pressure (except for nuclear applications)	(D)
Steel power boilers (stationary and marine), parts and attachments (except nuclear applications)	**933.1**	Vertical and other fire tube type steel power boilers (stationary and marine) (except for nuclear applications)	48.5
Water tube steel, fire tube steam and vertical and other power boilers	580.0	Other steel power boilers (stationary and marine) (except for nuclear applications)	123.6
Water tube steel power boilers (stationary and marine), more than 15 p.s.i. steam working pressure, 100,000 lb per hour or less, saturated (except for nuclear applications)	11.2	Parts and attachments for steel power boilers (sold separately) (except for nuclear applications)	302.5
Water tube steel power boilers (stationary and marine), more than 15 p.s.i. steam working pressure, 100,000 lb per hour or less, super heated (except for nuclear applications)	3.2	Steel power boilers (stationary and marine), parts and attachments (except for nuclear applications), nsk	50.5
Water tube steel power boilers (stationary and marine), more than 15 p.s.i. steam working pressure, 100,001 lb per hour or more saturated (except for nuclear		**Nuclear reactor steam supply systems, heat exchangers and condensers, pressurizers, components, and auxiliary equipment**	**204.3**
		Power boiler and heat exchangers, nsk, total	**798.4**

Source: 2002 Economic Census. The values are product shipments in millions of dollars for 2002. Total product shipments may be lower or higher than industry shipments. See Introduction for a full discussion. Values of indented subcategories are summed in the main heading(s). The symbol (D) appears when data are withheld to prevent disclosure of competitive information. The abbreviation nsk stands for 'not specified by kind' and nec for 'not elsewhere classified'. A dash (-) means zero.

INPUTS AND OUTPUTS FOR POWER BOILER AND HEAT EXCHANGER MANUFACTURING

Economic Sector or Industry Providing Inputs	%	Sector	Economic Sector or Industry Buying Outputs	%	Sector
Compensation of employees	32.0		Private fixed investment	28.1	
Iron & steel mills & ferroalloys	8.4	Manufg.	Exports of goods & services	13.2	Cap Inv
Wholesale trade	3.8	Trade	Food services & drinking places	9.2	Services
Management of companies & enterprises	2.7	Services	Nonresidential structures, nec	6.8	Construct.
Fabricated pipes & pipe fittings	2.4	Manufg.	Commercial & health care structures	6.1	Construct.
Aluminum products from purchased aluminum	2.1	Manufg.	Residential structures, nec	5.0	Construct.
Copper rolling, drawing, extruding, & alloying	1.9	Manufg.	AC, refrigeration, and warm air heating equipment	3.1	Manufg.
Machine shops	1.8	Manufg.	Other S/L govt. enterprises	3.1	S/L Govt
Power boilers & heat exchangers	1.7	Manufg.	Residential permanent site structures	2.9	Construct.

Continued on next page.

INPUTS AND OUTPUTS FOR POWER BOILER AND HEAT EXCHANGER MANUFACTURING - Continued

Economic Sector or Industry Providing Inputs	%	Sector	Economic Sector or Industry Buying Outputs	%	Sector
Chemical products & preparations, nec	1.4	Manufg.	General Federal government services, nondefense	2.1	Fed Govt
Coating, engraving, heat treating & allied activities	1.3	Manufg.	Waste management & remediation services	2.1	Services
Forging, stamping, & sintering, nec	1.2	Manufg.	Telecommunications	2.0	Services
Paints & coatings	1.1	Manufg.	Paints & coatings	1.4	Manufg.
Securities, commodity contracts, investments	0.9	Fin/R.E.	Maintenance/repair of nonresidential structures	1.4	Construct.
Metal cans, boxes, & other containers (light gauge)	0.9	Manufg.	Power boilers & heat exchangers	1.3	Manufg.
Power generation & supply	0.9	Util.	Manufacturing structures	1.3	Construct.
Ferrous metal foundries	0.9	Manufg.	Toilet preparations	1.2	Manufg.
Specialized design services	0.9	Services	Power generation & supply	1.1	Util.
Truck transportation	0.8	Util.	Machine shops	0.8	Manufg.
Turned products & screws, nuts, & bolts	0.8	Manufg.	Fabricated metals, nec	0.7	Manufg.
Automotive equipment rental & leasing	0.7	Fin/R.E.	Federal government, investment, nondefense	0.6	Fed Govt
Employment services	0.7	Services	Paper mills	0.6	Manufg.
Semiconductors & related devices	0.7	Manufg.	Scientific research & development services	0.5	Services
Plate work & fabricated structural products	0.7	Manufg.	Owner-occupied dwellings	0.5	
Fabricated metals, nec	0.7	Manufg.	Soap & cleaning compounds	0.5	Manufg.
Primary smelting & refining of copper	0.7	Manufg.	Industrial machinery, nec	0.4	Manufg.
Printed circuit assemblies (electronic assembles)	0.7	Manufg.	Chemical products & preparations, nec	0.4	Manufg.
Architectural, engineering, & related services	0.6	Services	Heating equipment (except warm air furnaces)	0.3	Manufg.
Lessors of nonfinancial assets	0.6	Fin/R.E.	Engine equipment, nec	0.3	Manufg.
Real estate	0.6	Fin/R.E.	Basic organic chemicals, nec	0.3	Manufg.
Business support services	0.6	Services	Turbines & turbine generator set units	0.2	Manufg.
Legal services	0.6	Services	Adhesives	0.2	Manufg.
Monetary authorities/depository credit intermediation	0.6	Fin/R.E.	Pharmaceutical preparations	0.2	Manufg.
Steel products from purchased steel	0.5	Manufg.	Printing inks	0.2	Manufg.
Noncomparable imports	0.5	Foreign	Architectural, engineering, & related services	0.2	Services
Professional, scientific, technical services, nec	0.5	Services	Real estate	0.2	Fin/R.E.
Natural gas distribution	0.5	Util.	Maintenance/repair of residential structures	0.2	Construct.
Valve & fittings other than plumbing	0.4	Manufg.	Petroleum lubricating oil & grease	0.2	Manufg.
Support services, nec	0.4	Services	Synthetic dyes & pigments	0.1	Manufg.
Custom roll forming	0.4	Manufg.	General purpose machinery, nec	0.1	Manufg.
Rolling mill & other metalworking machinery	0.4	Manufg.	Fats & oils refining & blending	0.1	Manufg.
Crowns & closures & metal stamping	0.4	Manufg.	Pesticides & other agricultural chemicals	0.1	Manufg.
Paperboard containers	0.4	Manufg.	Plastics & rubber industry machinery	0.1	Manufg.
Commercial & industrial machinery rental & leasing	0.4	Fin/R.E.	Semiconductor machinery	0.1	Manufg.
Advertising & related services	0.4	Services			
General purpose machinery, nec	0.3	Manufg.			
Ball & roller bearings	0.3	Manufg.			
Investigation & security services	0.3	Services			
Maintenance/repair of nonresidential structures	0.3	Construct.			
Handtools	0.3	Manufg.			
Services to buildings & dwellings	0.3	Services			
Taxes on production & imports, less subsidies	0.3				
Nonferrous metal foundries	0.3	Manufg.			
Food services & drinking places	0.3	Services			
Accounting, tax preparation, bookkeeping, & payroll	0.2	Services			
Warehousing & storage	0.2	Util.			
Telecommunications	0.2	Services			
Data processing, hosting, & related services	0.2	Services			
Automotive repair & maintenance, ex. car washes	0.2	Services			
Metal tanks (heavy gauge)	0.2	Manufg.			
Clay & nonclay refractory manufacturing	0.2	Manufg.			
Cutting tools & machine tool accessories	0.2	Manufg.			
Rail transportation	0.2	Util.			
Scientific research & development services	0.2	Services			
Plastics packaging materials, film & sheet	0.2	Manufg.			
Commercial & industrial equipment repair/maintenance	0.2	Services			
Springs & wire products	0.2	Manufg.			
Alumina refining & primary aluminum production	0.1	Manufg.			
Abrasive products	0.1	Manufg.			
Hotels & motels, including casino hotels	0.1	Services			
Facilities support services	0.1	Services			
Metal cutting & forming machine tools	0.1	Manufg.			
Air transportation	0.1	Util.			
Nonferrous metal (ex. copper & aluminum) processing	0.1	Manufg.			
Relay & industrial controls	0.1	Manufg.			
Other computer related services, including facilities	0.1	Services			
Management, scientific, & technical consulting	0.1	Services			
Paperboard mills	0.1	Manufg.			
Nondepository credit intermediation activities	0.1	Fin/R.E.			
Ornamental & architectural metal products	0.1	Manufg.			

Source: Benchmark Input-Output Accounts for the U.S. Economy, 2002, U.S. Department of Commerce, Washington, D.C., January 2008. The abbreviation nec stands for 'not elsewhere classified'.

OCCUPATIONS EMPLOYED BY BOILER, TANK, & SHIPPING CONTAINER MANUFACTURING

Occupation	% of Total 2006	Change to 2016	Occupation	% of Total 2006	Change to 2016
Welders, cutters, solderers, & brazers	13.8	-4.1	Sales reps, wholesale & manufacturing, exc tech	1.8	-9.9
Cutting, punching, & press machine operators	5.4	-18.9	Laborers & freight, stock, & material movers, hand	1.8	-18.9
Team assemblers	4.5	-9.9	Packaging & filling machine operators & tenders	1.6	-18.9
First-line supervisors/managers of production workers	4.0	-9.9	Welding, soldering, & brazing machine operators	1.4	1.3
Structural metal fabricators & fitters	3.7	-9.9	Industrial engineers	1.4	9.4
Coating, painting, & spraying machine operators	3.0	-14.4	Boilermakers	1.3	-1.6
Industrial truck & tractor operators	2.7	-18.9	Shipping, receiving, & traffic clerks	1.2	-13.3
Inspectors, testers, sorters, samplers, & weighers	2.6	-15.0	Packers & packagers, hand	1.2	-27.9
Helpers--Production workers	2.5	-9.9	Machine feeders & offbearers	1.2	-18.9
Maintenance & repair workers, general	2.4	-9.9	Bookkeeping, accounting, & auditing clerks	1.1	-9.9
Industrial machinery mechanics	2.1	3.6	Multiple machine tool operators & tenders	1.1	-0.9
Machinists	2.1	-5.4	Mechanical engineers	1.1	-9.9
General & operations managers	1.9	-18.9	Industrial production managers	1.1	-9.9
Sheet metal workers	1.9	-11.6	Grinding, lapping, polishing machine tool operators	1.1	-12.6

Source: *Industry-Occupation Matrix*, Bureau of Labor Statistics, December 4, 2007. These data are reported based on 4-digit NAICS categories but have been matched to corresponding 6-digit NAICS industry codes. The change reported for each occupation to the year 2016 is a percent of growth or decline as estimated by the Bureau of Labor Statistics. The abbreviation nec stands for 'not elsewhere classified'.

LOCATION BY STATE AND REGIONAL CONCENTRATION

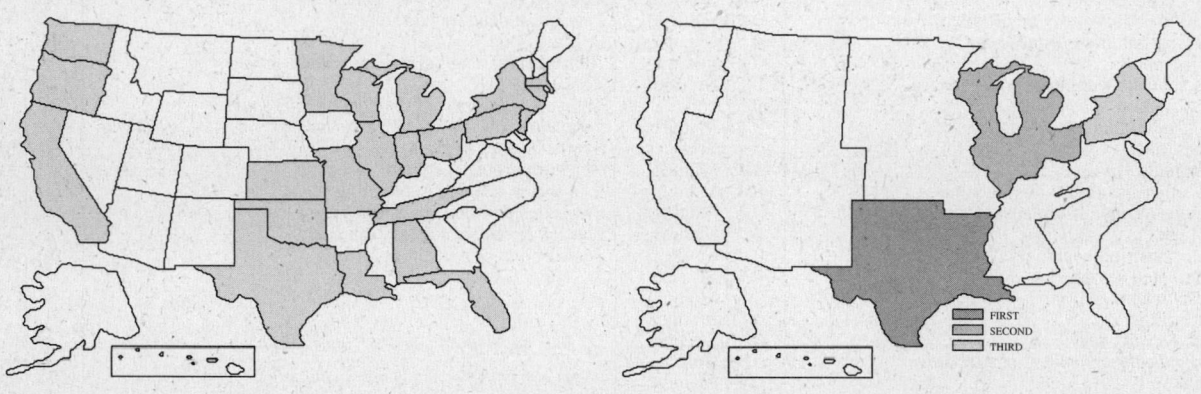

FIRST
SECOND
THIRD

INDUSTRY DATA BY STATE

State	Establish- ments	Shipments			Employment				Cost as % of Shipments	Investment per Employee ($)
		Total ($ mil)	% of U.S.	Per Establ.	Total Number	% of U.S.	Per Establ.	Wages ($/hour)		
New York	26	413.1	11.3	15,888.7	2,614	13.0	101	18.43	42.6	3,755
Texas	42	404.6	11.1	9,632.5	2,414	12.0	57	16.29	39.8	5,243
Oklahoma	38	357.1	9.8	9,396.6	2,377	11.8	63	16.24	47.0	4,859
Minnesota	8	339.8	9.3	42,477.9	438	2.2	55	15.86	74.1	2,539
Ohio	15	267.8	7.3	17,853.7	1,316	6.5	88	18.90	45.2	12,110
Pennsylvania	15	210.6	5.8	14,039.9	993	4.9	66	15.84	40.9	5,265
Tennessee	8	118.0	3.2	14,743.9	632	3.1	79	14.11	48.4	2,983
Wisconsin	13	112.2	3.1	8,629.1	785	3.9	60	16.40	32.7	1,645
California	21	108.2	3.0	5,151.4	617	3.1	29	18.18	35.5	2,741
Kansas	5	107.5	2.9	21,497.4	409	2.0	82	16.55	51.6	1,599
Oregon	4	95.8	2.6	23,944.0	338	1.7	84	18.83	69.1	11,109
Massachusetts	7	93.3	2.6	13,333.4	308	1.5	44	20.87	18.5	695
Illinois	19	91.6	2.5	4,821.9	704	3.5	37	15.00	38.0	4,605
New Jersey	9	68.1	1.9	7,572.0	338	1.7	38	16.11	40.9	2,831
Louisiana	8	63.4	1.7	7,919.5	486	2.4	61	16.05	43.0	4,535
Indiana	7	63.1	1.7	9,017.6	518	2.6	74	14.49	41.0	2,378
Missouri	4	60.0	1.6	15,012.5	345	1.7	86	17.75	42.3	(D)
Washington	7	31.9	0.9	4,556.4	229	1.1	33	14.96	43.4	1,459
Michigan	6	30.3	0.8	5,051.7	223	1.1	37	12.00	36.6	883
Connecticut	7	26.5	0.7	3,785.1	184	0.9	26	15.11	41.8	4,391
Florida	7	25.7	0.7	3,673.9	245	1.2	35	12.98	34.7	1,363
Alabama	5	25.6	0.7	5,122.2	194	1.0	39	15.89	48.2	1,943

Source: 2002 *Economic Census*. The states are in descending order of shipments or establishments (if shipment data are missing for the majority). The symbol (D) appears when data are withheld to prevent disclosure of competitive information. States marked with (D) are sorted by number of establishments. A dash (-) indicates that the data element cannot be calculated. Data may not show all states active in the NAICS category. All data available at the time of publication are shown.

NAICS 332420 - METAL TANK (HEAVY GAUGE) MANUFACTURING

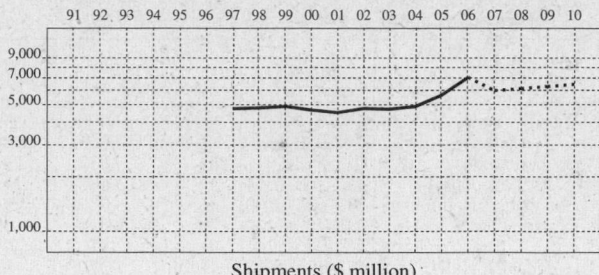

Shipments ($ million)

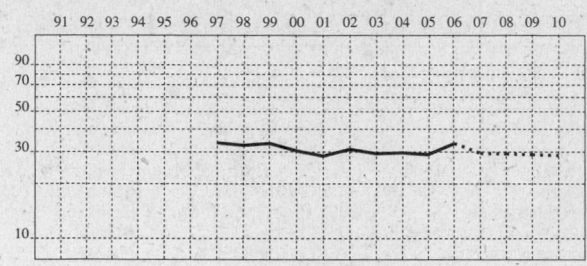

Employment (000)

GENERAL STATISTICS

Year	Com-panies	Establishments		Employment			Compensation		Production ($ million)			
		Total	with 20 or more employees	Total (000)	Production Workers (000)	Hours (Mil)	Payroll ($ mil)	Wages ($/hr)	Cost of Materials	Value Added by Manufacture	Value of Shipments	Capital Invest.
1997	552	613	394	33.7	24.2	49.3	1,132.8	14.18	2,356.1	2,402.9	4,755.4	122.4
1998		631	388	32.6	23.6	48.8	1,155.8	14.47	2,316.1	2,494.5	4,800.7	125.8
1999		633	384	33.4	24.1	49.6	1,228.4	15.36	2,363.3	2,482.5	4,891.0	133.4
2000		613	364	30.4	22.0	46.0	1,168.1	15.64	2,223.1	2,478.7	4,672.1	115.9
2001		608	358	28.5	20.6	41.4	1,087.5	16.13	1,963.9	2,567.6	4,524.3	93.2
2002	597	665	348	31.0	22.7	45.0	1,183.5	16.82	2,151.3	2,592.5	4,771.5	105.3
2003		647	351	29.4	21.7	44.0	1,155.9	16.95	2,096.8	2,655.9	4,725.3	58.4
2004		675	350	29.7	21.4	42.7	1,205.9	17.97	2,280.4	2,681.8	4,887.9	87.0
2005		654	334	29.0	21.7	43.9	1,223.3	18.08	2,575.3	3,122.7	5,640.8	105.6
2006		669P	327P	33.4	25.9	51.5	1,461.2	19.17	3,370.8	3,796.2	7,050.3	161.9
2007		675P	320P	29.5P	22.4P	44.5P	1,312.7P	19.41P	2,854.0P	3,214.2P	5,969.5P	104.9P
2008		682P	313P	29.3P	22.4P	44.2P	1,333.2P	19.94P	2,932.1P	3,302.1P	6,132.7P	103.9P
2009		688P	305P	29.0P	22.3P	43.9P	1,353.6P	20.47P	3,010.1P	3,390.0P	6,295.8P	102.8P
2010		694P	298P	28.7P	22.3P	43.6P	1,374.1P	21.00P	3,088.1P	3,477.8P	6,459.0P	101.7P

Sources: 1997 and 2002 *Economic Census*; other years, up to 2006, are from *Annual Survey of Manufactures*. Establishment counts for non-Census years are from *County Business Patterns*; 1997 and 2002 values are from the 1997 and 2002 censuses, respectively. 'P's show projections by the editors.

INDICES OF CHANGE

Year	Com-panies	Establishments		Employment			Compensation		Production ($ million)			
		Total	with 20 or more employees	Total (000)	Production Workers (000)	Hours (Mil)	Payroll ($ mil)	Wages ($/hr)	Cost of Materials	Value Added by Manufacture	Value of Shipments	Capital Invest.
1997	92	92	113	109	107	110	96	84	110	93	100	116
1998		95	111	105	104	108	98	86	108	96	101	119
1999		95	110	108	106	110	104	91	110	96	103	127
2000		92	105	98	97	102	99	93	103	96	98	110
2001		91	103	92	91	92	92	96	91	99	95	89
2002	100	100	100	100	100	100	100	100	100	100	100	100
2003		97	101	95	96	98	98	101	97	102	99	55
2004		102	101	96	94	95	102	107	106	103	102	83
2005		98	96	94	96	98	103	107	120	120	118	100
2006		101P	94P	108	114	114	123	114	157	146	148	154
2007		102P	92P	95P	99P	99P	111P	115P	133P	124P	125P	100P
2008		102P	90P	95P	99P	98P	113P	119P	136P	127P	129P	99P
2009		103P	88P	94P	98P	98P	114P	122P	140P	131P	132P	98P
2010		104P	86P	93P	98P	97P	116P	125P	144P	134P	135P	97P

Sources: Same as General Statistics. Values reflect change from the base year, 2002. Values above 100 mean greater than 2002, values below 100 mean less than 2002, and the values of 100 in other years means the same as 2002. 'P's show projections by the editors.

SELECTED RATIOS

For 2002	Avg. of All Manufact.	Analyzed Industry	Index	For 2002	Avg. of All Manufact.	Analyzed Industry	Index
Employees per Establishment	42	47	111	Value Added per Production Worker	182,367	114,207	63
Payroll per Establishment	1,639,184	1,779,699	109	Cost per Establishment	5,769,015	3,235,038	56
Payroll per Employee	39,053	38,177	98	Cost per Employee	137,446	69,397	50
Production Workers per Establishment	30	34	116	Cost per Production Worker	195,506	94,771	48
Wages per Establishment	694,845	1,138,195	164	Shipments per Establishment	11,158,348	7,175,188	64
Wages per Production Worker	23,548	33,344	142	Shipments per Employee	265,847	153,919	58
Hours per Production Worker	1,980	1,982	100	Shipments per Production Worker	378,144	210,198	56
Wages per Hour	11.89	16.82	141	Investment per Establishment	361,338	158,346	44
Value Added per Establishment	5,381,325	3,898,496	72	Investment per Employee	8,609	3,397	39
Value Added per Employee	128,210	83,629	65	Investment per Production Worker	12,245	4,639	38

Sources: Same as General Statistics. The 'Average of All Manufacturing' column represents the average of all manufacturing industries reported for the most recent complete year available. The Index shows the relationship between the Average and the Analyzed Industry. For example, 100 means that they are equal; 500 that the Analyzed Industry is five times the average; 50 means that the Analyzed Industry is half the national average. The abbreviation 'na' is used to show that data are 'not available'. Ratios shown for 2002, the last complete census year.

LEADING COMPANIES   Number shown: 75   Total sales ($ mil): 57,898   Total employment (000): 179.4

Company Name	Address				CEO Name	Phone	Co. Type	Sales ($ mil)	Empl. (000)
API Group Inc.	2366 Rose Pl.	St. Paul	MN	55113	Lee R. Anderson Sr.	651-636-4320	R	9,000	5.0
Dover Corp.	280 Park Ave.	New York	NY	10017		212-922-1640	P	7,226	33.4
McDermott International Inc.	757 N Eldridge Pky.	Houston	TX	77079	Robert Deason	281-870-5011	P	5,632	28.4
Harsco Corp.	PO Box 8888	Camp Hill	PA	17001	S. D. Fazzolari	717-763-7064	P	3,688	21.5
Amsted Industries Inc.	2 Prudential Plaza	Chicago	IL	60601	W. Robert Reum	312-645-1700	R	3,050	9.9
Baltimore Aircoil Company Inc.	PO Box 7322	Baltimore	MD	21227	Steven Duerwachter	410-799-6200	R	2,510*	0.2
Consolidated Metco Inc.	PO Box 83201	Portland	OR	97283		503-286-5741	R	2,510*	0.1
Mechanical Construction Inc.	1500 Chester Pk.	Eddystone	PA	19022	Michael J. Hall	610-876-9292	S	2,370*	3.3
A.O. Smith Corp.	PO Box 245008	Milwaukee	WI	53224		414-359-4000	P	2,312	16.8
Hutchinson FTS Inc.	1835 Technology	Troy	MI	48083	Paul Campbell	248-589-7710	R	1,863*	<0.1
Williams Enterprise of Georgia	1285 Hawthorne	Smyrna	GA	30080	Dale Williams	770-436-1596	R	1,478*	0.6
Babcock and Wilcox Co.	PO Box 351	Barberton	OH	44203	John A. Fees	330-753-4511	S	1,080*	10.8
TriMas Corp.	39400 Woodward	Bloomfield Hls	MI	48304	Grant Beard	248-631-5450	P	1,068	5.1
C and D Zodiac Inc.	5701 Bolsa Ave.	Huntington Bch	CA	92647		714-934-0000	R	1,045*	0.5
EPE Industrial Filters Inc.	9250 Bloomington	Bloomington	MN	55431	William Cook	847-381-0860	R	1,024*	1.5
McWane Corp.	PO Box 43327	Birmingham	AL	35243	G. Ruffner Page, Jr.	205-414-3100	R	944*	7.0
Manchester Tank and Equipment	1000 Corp Centre Dr	Franklin	TN	37067	Robert Richard	615-370-3833	R	926*	<0.1
Chart Industries Inc.	One Infinity Corp.	Garfield Height	OH	44125	Samuel F. Thomas	440-753-1490	P	666	2.8
Riley Power Inc.	PO Box 15040	Worcester	MA	01615		508-852-7100	R	612*	0.4
American Cast Iron Pipe Co.	PO Box 2727	Birmingham	AL	35202		205-325-7701	R	596*	2.3
NATCO Group Inc.	2950 N Loop W, 700	Houston	TX	77092	John U. Clarke	713-683-9292	P	570	2.5
Alaskan Copper Co's Inc.	PO Box 3546	Seattle	WA	98124	Kermit Rosen	206-623-5800	R	392*	0.3
Mestek Inc.	260 N Elm St.	Westfield	MA	01085	R. Bruce Dewey	413-568-9571	R	372*	2.6
Mobile Mini Inc.	PO Box 79149	Phoenix	AZ	85062	Steven G. Bunger	480-894-6311	P	318	2.1
Maxcess Technologies Inc.	230 Deming Way	Summerville	SC	29483	Andy Miarka	843-821-1200	R	291*	<0.1
Kirk and Blum Manufacturing	3120 Forrer St.	Cincinnati	OH	45209	Richard J. Blum	513-458-2600	S	265*	0.4
CEI Enterprises Inc.	245 Woodward SE	Albuquerque	NM	87102		505-842-5556	S	264*	0.1
Southern Heat Exchanger Corp.	PO Box 1850	Tuscaloosa	AL	35403	Bill Laganke	205-345-5335	R	234*	0.2
General Atomics	PO Box 85608	San Diego	CA	92186	James Blue	858-455-3000	R	219*	1.0
Burnham Holdings Inc.	PO Box 3205	Lancaster	PA	17604	Albert Morrison III	717-397-4700	P	218	1.3
Raven Industries Inc.	PO Box 5107	Sioux Falls	SD	57117	Conrad J. Hoigaard	605-336-2750	P	217	0.9
Amtrol Inc.	1400 Division Rd.	West Warwick	RI	02893	Larry T. Guillemette	401-884-6300	R	213	1.3
Cleaver-Brooks Inc.	PO Box 421	Milwaukee	WI	53201	Welch Goggins	414-359-0600	R	210*	0.2
Poly Processing Co.	8055 Ash Street	French Camp	CA	95231	Dixon Abell	209-982-4904	R	204*	0.3
Ameri-Forge Ltd.	13770 Industrial Rd	Houston	TX	77015	William Friel	713-393-4200	R	200*	0.2
Robinson Steel Company Inc.	4303 Kennedy Ave.	East Chicago	IN	46312		219-398-4600	R	200*	0.2
API Delevan	270 Quaker Rd.	East Aurora	NY	14052		716-652-3600	S	195*	1.8
ALSTOM Power Inc.	3020 Truax Rd.	Wellsville	NY	14895	E Bysiek	585-593-2700	S	191*	0.6
Keppel Amfels Inc.	PO Box 3107	Brownsville	TX	78523	C Ho	956-831-8220	R	183*	1.5
Roberts Company Inc.	PO Box 1109	Winterville	NC	28590	John Roberts	252-355-9353	R	163*	0.3
Aluminum Precision Products	3333 W Warner	Santa Ana	CA	92704	Philip Keeler	714-546-8125	R	155*	0.7
Paul Mueller Co.	PO Box 828	Springfield	MO	65801	Paul Mueller	417-831-3000	P	153	1.2
Southeast Texas Industries	PO Box 1449	Buna	TX	77612	Richard Purkey	409-994-3570	R	146*	0.3
Taco Inc.	1160 Cranston St.	Cranston	RI	02920		401-942-8000	R	140*	0.4
Ultra Air Products Inc.	3309 John Conley	Lapeer	MI	48446	Don Swanson	810-667-6800	R	136*	0.2
Suspa Inc.	3970 Rgr B Chaffee	Grand Rapids	MI	49548	Steve Garvelink	616-241-4200	R	116*	0.2
Beall Trailers of Montana Inc.	PO Box 2543	Billings	MT	59103	Jerry Beall	406-252-7163	S	113*	0.8
ATCO Rubber Products Inc.	7101 Atco Dr.	Fort Worth	TX	76118	Charles Anderson	817-595-2894	R	113*	0.6
Consolidated Fabricators Corp.	4600 S Santa Fe Ave	Los Angeles	CA	90058	Michael Melideo	323-586-4500	R	109*	0.1
Structural Steel Services Inc.	PO Box 2929	Meridian	MS	39302	Tommy Dulaney	601-483-5381	R	108*	0.2
Mervis Industries Inc.	PO Box 827	Danville	IL	61834	Louis Mervis	217-442-5300	R	100*	0.3
Besser Co.	801 Johnson St.	Alpena	MI	49707	Kevin Curtis	989-354-4111	R	99*	0.4
EvapCo Inc.	5151 Allendale Ln.	Taneytown	MD	21787	Wilson Bradley	410-756-2600	R	96*	0.2
Apache Stainless Equipment	PO Box 538	Beaver Dam	WI	53916	Patrick Albregts	920-356-9900	S	96*	0.2
HTP Inc.	PO Box 429	East Freetown	MA	02717	David Davis	508-763-8071	R	87*	0.2
Enerfab Inc.	4955 Spring Grove	Cincinnati	OH	45232	Wendell Bell	513-641-0500	R	84*	0.3
Deltak L.L.C.	13330 12th Ave. N	Plymouth	MN	55441		763-557-7440	S	83*	0.1
Burger Iron Co.	3100 Gilchrist Rd.	Mogadore	OH	44260	Tom Fiocca	330-253-5121	R	79*	0.2
Super Steel Products Corp.	7900 W Twr. Ave.	Milwaukee	WI	53223		414-355-4800	R	79*	0.6
Manitowoc Ice Inc.	2110 S 26th St.	Manitowoc	WI	54220	Dan Brandel	920-682-0161	S	77*	0.4
McAbee Construction Inc.	PO Box 1460	Tuscaloosa	AL	35403	Leroy McAbee	205-349-2212	R	77*	0.5
Lyon Workspace Products L.L.C.	PO Box 671	Aurora	IL	60507		630-892-8941	R	76*	0.6
CST Industries Inc.	PO Box 2907	Kansas City	KS	66110		913-621-3700	R	76*	<0.1
Smithco Engineering Inc.	PO Box 571330	Tulsa	OK	74157	Judith Smith	918-446-4406	R	76*	<0.1
Tricon Metals and Services	PO Box 101447	Birmingham	AL	35210	J Cashio	205-956-2567	R	73*	<0.1
McKenzie Tank Lines Inc.	PO Box 1200	Tallahassee	FL	32302	Joseph Audie	850-576-1221	R	72*	<0.1
Sioux City Foundry Co.	PO Box 3067	Sioux City	IA	51102	Andrew Galinsky	712-252-4181	R	71*	<0.1
Central Maintenance & Welding	2620 Keysville Rd.	Lithia	FL	33547	Conrad Varnam	813-737-1402	R	67*	0.3
Graham Corp.	PO Box 719	Batavia	NY	14021	Jerald D. Bidlack	585-343-2216	P	66	0.3
Taylor Forge Engineered System	208 N Iron St.	Paola	KS	66071	Michael Kilkenny	913-294-5331	R	61*	0.2
Modern Welding Company of TX	PO Box 85	Rhome	TX	76078	John Jones	817-636-2215	R	61*	0.6
Sweco Fab Inc.	PO Box 34546	Houston	TX	77234	Durga Agrawal	713-731-0030	R	61*	0.4
Slant Fin Corp.	100 Forest Dr.	Greenvale	NY	11548	Donald Brown	516-484-2600	R	60*	0.4
Astro Air Inc.	1653 N Bolton St.	Jacksonville	TX	75766	Rex Dacus	903-586-3691	R	59*	0.3
Saylor-Beall Manufacturing Co.	PO Box 40	Saint Johns	MI	48879	Bruce Mc Fee	989-224-2371	S	58*	0.3

Source: Ward's Business Directory of U.S. Private and Public Companies, Volumes 1 and 2, 2008. The company type code used is as follows: P - Public, R - Private, S - Subsidiary, D - Division, J - Joint Venture, A - Affiliate, G - Group. Sales are in millions of dollars, employees are in thousands. An asterisk (*) indicates an estimated sales volume. The symbol < stands for 'less than'. Company names and addresses are truncated, in some cases, to fit into the available space.

MATERIALS CONSUMED

Material	Quantity	Delivered Cost ($ million)
Fabricated metal pipe (excluding castings and forgings)	(X)	89.3
Fabricated metal valves and pipe fittings	(X)	145.4
All other miscellaneous fabricated metal parts designed for steel power boilers (exc. castings and forgings)	(X)	17.0
All other fabricated metal products (exc. castings, forgings, and all other parts designed for steel power boilers)	(X)	82.5
Iron and steel castings (rough and semifinished)	(X)	17.8
Nonferrous (aluminum, copper, etc.) castings (rough and semifinished)	(X)	(D)
Forgings	(X)	26.4
Steel bars and bar shapes (exc. concrete reinforcing bars, castings, forgings, and fabricated metal products)	(X)	54.0
Steel sheet and strip (including tinplate)	(X)	158.5
Steel plate	(X)	266.9
Wide flange steel structural beams	(X)	14.8
All other steel structural shapes (exc. sheet pilings, castings, forgings, and fabricated steel products)	(X)	41.9
All other steel shapes and forms, incl. sheet pilings	(X)	(D)
Copper and copper-base alloy pipe and tube (exc. castings, forgings, fabr. metal products)	(X)	2.9
All other copper and copper-base alloy shapes and forms (exc. castings, forgings, fabr. metal products)	(X)	0.7
Aluminum and aluminum-base alloy sheet, plate, foil, and welded tubing	(X)	30.3
All other aluminum and aluminum-base alloy shapes and forms (exc. castings, forgings, fabr. metal products)	(X)	14.2
All other nonferrous shapes and forms (exc. castings, forgings, fabr. metal products)	(X)	28.1
Paints, varnishes, stains, lacquers, shellacs, japans, enamels, etc.	(X)	24.6
Welding electrodes	(X)	12.1
All other materials, components, parts, containers, and supplies	(X)	324.3
Materials, ingredients, containers, and supplies, nsk	(X)	407.7

Source: 2002 *Economic Census*. Explanation of symbols used: (D): Withheld to avoid disclosure of competitive data; na: Not available; (S): Withheld because statistical norms were not met; (X): Not applicable; (Z): Less than half the unit shown; nec: Not elsewhere classified; nsk: Not specified by kind; - : zero; p : 10-19 percent estimated; q : 20-29 percent estimated.

PRODUCT SHARE DETAILS

Product or Product Class Shipments	Mil. $	Product or Product Class Shipments	Mil. $
METAL TANKS (HEAVY GAUGE)	4,432.9	Liquefied petroleum gas tanks, ferrous and nonferrous, custom fabricated at the factory	58.7
Gas cylinders	**492.4**	All other ferrous metal tanks and vessels, custom fabricated at the factory	424.7
Seamless ferrous and nonferrous gas cylinders	252.4	All other nonferrous metal tanks and vessels, custom fabricated at the factory	100.6
Welded ferrous and nonferrous gas cylinders	240.0	Metal tanks and vessels, custom fabricated at the factory and field erected, nsk	111.5
Metal tanks, complete at factory (standard line pressure)	**622.5**	**Metal tanks and vessels, custom fabricated and field erected**	**1,019.6**
Liquefied petroleum gas tanks (all types), complete at factory	258.1	Ferrous and nonferrous metal bulk storage tanks, custom fabricated and field erected, elevated and ground storage types	622.3
Air receivers (tanks), complete at factory	126.1	Ferrous metal bulk storage tanks, elevated type, for dry materials	34.9
Other pressure tanks (including anhydrous ammonia tanks) complete at factory	238.3	Ferrous metal bulk storage tanks, elevated type, for water	199.8
Metal tanks, complete at factory (standard line nonpressure)	**435.5**	Ferrous metal bulk storage tanks, elevated type, for other liquids	87.1
Ferrous and nonferrous metal storage tanks	435.0	Nonferrous metal bulk storage tanks, elevated type	(D)
Ferrous tanks, complete at factory, 4,000 gal capacity or less	140.8	Ferrous metal bulk storage tanks, ground storage type, for dry materials	(D)
Nonferrous tanks, complete at factory, 4,000 gal capacity or less	26.5	Ferrous metal bulk storage tanks, ground storage type, for petroleum products	84.7
Ferrous tanks, complete at factory, more than 4,000 gal capacity	138.1	Ferrous metal bulk storage tanks, ground storage type, for water	66.5
Nonferrous tanks, complete at factory, more than 4,000 gal capacity	21.7	Ferrous metal bulk storage tanks, ground storage type, for other materials	58.3
Other ferrous tanks, complete at factory (including tanks for trailers, metal septic tanks, etc.)	68.5	Nonferrous metal bulk storage tanks, ground storage type	35.8
Other nonferrous metal nonpressure storage tanks, complete at factory (including tanks for trailers, metal septic tanks, etc.)	39.3	Ferrous metal pressure vessels and tanks, custom fabricated and field erected, for refineries, chemical plants, and paper mills	130.7
Metal tanks, complete at factory (standard line nonpressure), nsk	0.6	Ferrous and nonferrous metal pressure vessels and tanks	219.0
Metal tanks and vessels, custom fabricated at the factory and field erected	**1,364.5**	Ferrous metal pressure vessels and tanks, custom fabricated and field erected, for other processing industries	136.8
Ferrous metal pressure tanks and vessels (more than 24 inch outside diameter and not less than 5 cu ft capacity)	551.3	Nonferrous metal pressure vessels and tanks custom fabricated and field erected	82.2
Custom fabricated at the factory, for refineries, chemical plants, and paper mills	307.8	Metal tanks and vessels, custom fabricated and field erected, nsk	47.6
Custom fabricated at the factory, for other processing industries	243.6	**Metal tanks (heavy gauge), nsk, total**	**498.4**
All other metal tanks and vessels, custom fabricated at the factory	701.7		
Nonferrous metal process pressure vessels, tanks, and kettles for refineries, chemical plants, paper mills (more than 24 inch o.d. and not less than 5 cu ft cap.), custom fabricated at the factory	117.7		

Source: 2002 *Economic Census*. The values are product shipments in millions of dollars for 2002. Total product shipments may be lower or higher than industry shipments. See Introduction for a full discussion. Values of indented subcategories are summed in the main heading(s). The symbol (D) appears when data are withheld to prevent disclosure of competitive information. The abbreviation nsk stands for 'not specified by kind' and nec for 'not elsewhere classified'. A dash (-) means zero.

INPUTS AND OUTPUTS FOR METAL TANK (HEAVY GAUGE) MANUFACTURING

Economic Sector or Industry Providing Inputs	%	Sector	Economic Sector or Industry Buying Outputs	%	Sector
Compensation of employees	32.5		Private fixed investment	41.2	
Iron & steel mills & ferroalloys	15.2	Manufg.	Nonresidential structures, nec	17.6	Construct.
Wholesale trade	4.8	Trade	Exports of goods & services	7.5	Cap Inv
Fabricated pipes & pipe fittings	4.7	Manufg.	Residential permanent site structures	7.0	Construct.
Management of companies & enterprises	3.1	Services	Residential structures, nec	5.7	Construct.
Aluminum products from purchased aluminum	1.4	Manufg.	Motor vehicle parts	2.9	Manufg.
Paints & coatings	1.3	Manufg.	Commercial & health care structures	2.6	Construct.
Valve & fittings other than plumbing	1.2	Manufg.	General Federal government services, nondefense	2.6	Fed Govt
Securities, commodity contracts, investments	1.2	Fin/R.E.	Owner-occupied dwellings	1.5	
Truck transportation	1.0	Util.	Maintenance/repair of nonresidential structures	1.5	Construct.
Metal tanks (heavy gauge)	0.9	Manufg.	Paints & coatings	1.5	Manufg.
Power generation & supply	0.8	Util.	Toilet preparations	1.2	Manufg.
Chemical products & preparations, nec	0.8	Manufg.	Metal tanks (heavy gauge)	0.8	Manufg.
Lessors of nonfinancial assets	0.8	Fin/R.E.	Machine shops	0.5	Manufg.
Monetary authorities/depository credit intermediation	0.8	Fin/R.E.	Soap & cleaning compounds	0.5	Manufg.
Real estate	0.8	Fin/R.E.	Fabricated metals, nec	0.5	Manufg.
Specialized design services	0.8	Services	Maintenance/repair of residential structures	0.5	Construct.
Architectural, engineering, & related services	0.8	Services	Other S/L govt. enterprises	0.4	S/L Govt
Machine shops	0.7	Manufg.	Industrial machinery, nec	0.4	Manufg.
Forging, stamping, & sintering, nec	0.7	Manufg.	Chemical products & preparations, nec	0.4	Manufg.
Professional, scientific, technical services, nec	0.7	Services	Manufacturing structures	0.4	Construct.
Employment services	0.6	Services	Real estate	0.3	Fin/R.E.
Legal services	0.6	Services	Basic organic chemicals, nec	0.3	Manufg.
Semiconductors & related devices	0.6	Manufg.	Engine equipment, nec	0.3	Manufg.
Business support services	0.6	Services	Turbines & turbine generator set units	0.2	Manufg.
Printed circuit assemblies (electronic assemblies)	0.6	Manufg.	Adhesives	0.2	Manufg.
Advertising & related services	0.5	Services	Pharmaceutical preparations	0.2	Manufg.
Coating, engraving, heat treating & allied activities	0.5	Manufg.	Printing inks	0.2	Manufg.
Automotive equipment rental & leasing	0.5	Fin/R.E.	Petroleum lubricating oil & grease	0.2	Manufg.
Steel products from purchased steel	0.4	Manufg.	Synthetic dyes & pigments	0.1	Manufg.
Food services & drinking places	0.4	Services	Power boilers & heat exchangers	0.1	Manufg.
Ferrous metal foundries	0.4	Manufg.	General purpose machinery, nec	0.1	Manufg.
Natural gas distribution	0.4	Util.	Fats & oils refining & blending	0.1	Manufg.
Support services, nec	0.4	Services	Pesticides & other agricultural chemicals	0.1	Manufg.
General purpose machinery, nec	0.4	Manufg.	Plastics & rubber industry machinery	0.1	Manufg.
Data processing, hosting, & related services	0.4	Services			
Services to buildings & dwellings	0.3	Services			
Maintenance/repair of nonresidential structures	0.3	Construct.			
Paperboard containers	0.3	Manufg.			
Metal cans, boxes, & other containers (light gauge)	0.3	Manufg.			
Plate work & fabricated structural products	0.3	Manufg.			
Scientific research & development services	0.3	Services			
Accounting, tax preparation, bookkeeping, & payroll	0.3	Services			
Nondepository credit intermediation activities	0.3	Fin/R.E.			
Rail transportation	0.3	Util.			
Rolling mill & other metalworking machinery	0.3	Manufg.			
Taxes on production & imports, less subsidies	0.3				
Telecommunications	0.3	Services			
Warehousing & storage	0.3	Util.			
Investigation & security services	0.3	Services			
Turned products & screws, nuts, & bolts	0.3	Manufg.			
Hotels & motels, including casino hotels	0.3	Services			
Fabricated metals, nec	0.2	Manufg.			
Commercial & industrial machinery rental & leasing	0.2	Fin/R.E.			
Air transportation	0.2	Util.			
Custom roll forming	0.2	Manufg.			
Automotive repair & maintenance, ex. car washes	0.2	Services			
Noncomparable imports	0.2	Foreign			
Commercial & industrial equipment repair/maintenance	0.2	Services			
Plastics packaging materials, film & sheet	0.2	Manufg.			
Cutting tools & machine tool accessories	0.1	Manufg.			
Alumina refining & primary aluminum production	0.1	Manufg.			
Clay & nonclay refractory manufacturing	0.1	Manufg.			
Motor vehicle parts	0.1	Manufg.			
Crowns & closures & metal stamping	0.1	Manufg.			
Other computer related services, including facilities	0.1	Services			
Facilities support services	0.1	Services			
Management, scientific, & technical consulting	0.1	Services			
Abrasive products	0.1	Manufg.			
Ball & roller bearings	0.1	Manufg.			
Metal cutting & forming machine tools	0.1	Manufg.			
Handtools	0.1	Manufg.			
Civic, social, & professional organizations	0.1	Services			

Source: Benchmark Input-Output Accounts for the U.S. Economy, 2002, U.S. Department of Commerce, Washington, D.C., January 2008. The abbreviation nec stands for 'not elsewhere classified'.

OCCUPATIONS EMPLOYED BY BOILER, TANK, & SHIPPING CONTAINER MANUFACTURING

Occupation	% of Total 2006	Change to 2016	Occupation	% of Total 2006	Change to 2016
Welders, cutters, solderers, & brazers	13.8	-4.1	Sales reps, wholesale & manufacturing, exc tech	1.8	-9.9
Cutting, punching, & press machine operators	5.4	-18.9	Laborers & freight, stock, & material movers, hand	1.8	-18.9
Team assemblers	4.5	-9.9	Packaging & filling machine operators & tenders	1.6	-18.9
First-line supervisors/managers of production workers	4.0	-9.9	Welding, soldering, & brazing machine operators	1.4	1.3
Structural metal fabricators & fitters	3.7	-9.9	Industrial engineers	1.4	9.4
Coating, painting, & spraying machine operators	3.0	-14.4	Boilermakers	1.3	-1.6
Industrial truck & tractor operators	2.7	-18.9	Shipping, receiving, & traffic clerks	1.2	-13.3
Inspectors, testers, sorters, samplers, & weighers	2.6	-15.0	Packers & packagers, hand	1.2	-27.9
Helpers--Production workers	2.5	-9.9	Machine feeders & offbearers	1.2	-18.9
Maintenance & repair workers, general	2.4	-9.9	Bookkeeping, accounting, & auditing clerks	1.1	-9.9
Industrial machinery mechanics	2.1	3.6	Multiple machine tool operators & tenders	1.1	-0.9
Machinists	2.1	-5.4	Mechanical engineers	1.1	-9.9
General & operations managers	1.9	-18.9	Industrial production managers	1.1	-9.9
Sheet metal workers	1.9	-11.6	Grinding, lapping, polishing machine tool operators	1.1	-12.6

Source: *Industry-Occupation Matrix*, Bureau of Labor Statistics, December 4, 2007. These data are reported based on 4-digit NAICS categories but have been matched to corresponding 6-digit NAICS industry codes. The change reported for each occupation to the year 2016 is a percent of growth or decline as estimated by the Bureau of Labor Statistics. The abbreviation nec stands for 'not elsewhere classified'.

LOCATION BY STATE AND REGIONAL CONCENTRATION

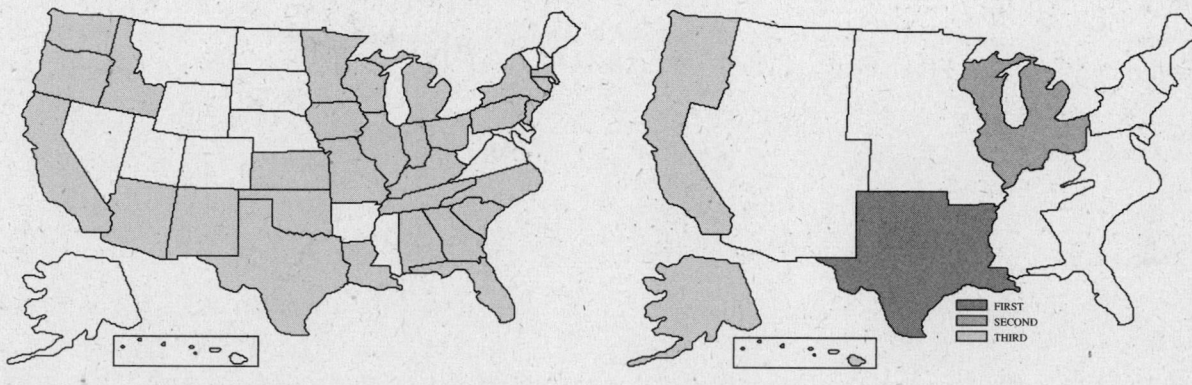

FIRST
SECOND
THIRD

INDUSTRY DATA BY STATE

State	Establish-ments	Shipments Total ($ mil)	Shipments % of U.S.	Shipments Per Establ.	Employment Total Number	Employment % of U.S.	Employment Per Establ.	Wages ($/hour)	Cost as % of Shipments	Investment per Employee ($)
Texas	81	393.1	8.2	4,853.2	2,615	8.4	32	15.57	50.5	3,923
Ohio	27	364.6	7.6	13,502.7	3,132	10.1	116	21.69	50.2	3,378
California	59	359.7	7.5	6,095.8	1,979	6.4	34	17.99	42.2	3,530
Pennsylvania	36	330.1	6.9	9,168.1	2,224	7.2	62	16.11	38.8	3,842
Wisconsin	29	247.3	5.2	8,528.6	1,806	5.8	62	18.42	45.3	2,633
Oklahoma	24	233.9	4.9	9,747.9	1,452	4.7	61	17.62	62.7	1,479
Georgia	23	203.1	4.3	8,831.7	936	3.0	41	16.25	47.7	2,908
Tennessee	20	201.5	4.2	10,075.5	1,119	3.6	56	15.28	52.7	5,500
Iowa	10	199.5	4.2	19,948.9	643	2.1	64	17.22	25.1	2,163
Kentucky	16	198.6	4.2	12,411.2	1,144	3.7	72	14.26	38.6	2,305
Minnesota	13	152.8	3.2	11,750.3	1,074	3.5	83	18.47	45.2	1,901
Indiana	23	149.9	3.1	6,518.0	1,157	3.7	50	16.45	44.4	1,576
Missouri	17	144.4	3.0	8,492.1	1,335	4.3	79	15.24	40.3	3,880
Louisiana	20	130.0	2.7	6,500.2	959	3.1	48	14.74	50.6	6,382
Alabama	19	127.0	2.7	6,682.7	760	2.5	40	16.61	51.4	5,504
Illinois	25	123.0	2.6	4,918.6	854	2.8	34	15.36	44.0	6,311
Kansas	12	114.9	2.4	9,575.2	618	2.0	52	13.50	55.9	2,299
Massachusetts	6	111.7	2.3	18,621.0	674	2.2	112	15.75	42.9	2,162
New Jersey	16	87.3	1.8	5,456.8	534	1.7	33	18.77	49.9	8,880
North Carolina	16	85.6	1.8	5,352.3	516	1.7	32	14.72	42.7	1,498
Florida	22	78.9	1.7	3,585.9	613	2.0	28	13.33	38.7	1,587
New York	18	67.6	1.4	3,756.6	547	1.8	30	17.19	32.0	1,868
Michigan	14	42.3	0.9	3,019.4	174	0.6	12	17.42	39.1	3,557
New Mexico	7	33.5	0.7	4,781.9	302	1.0	43	17.23	37.7	2,964
South Carolina	4	27.2	0.6	6,812.5	177	0.6	44	15.39	42.1	(D)
Idaho	7	25.8	0.5	3,681.3	214	0.7	31	14.89	40.5	5,925
Washington	11	25.7	0.5	2,337.7	207	0.7	19	16.03	28.2	652
Oregon	8	23.5	0.5	2,941.6	158	0.5	20	14.89	44.9	11,734

Continued on next page.

INDUSTRY DATA BY STATE - Continued

State	Establish-ments	Shipments			Employment				Cost as % of Shipments	Investment per Employee ($)
		Total ($ mil)	% of U.S.	Per Establ.	Total Number	% of U.S.	Per Establ.	Wages ($/hour)		
Connecticut	6	17.7	0.4	2,947.0	117	0.4	20	14.74	52.1	1,744
Arizona	12	16.8	0.4	1,399.1	164	0.5	14	10.31	42.1	1,341

Source: 2002 *Economic Census*. The states are in descending order of shipments or establishments (if shipment data are missing for the majority). The symbol (D) appears when data are withheld to prevent disclosure of competitive information. States marked with (D) are sorted by number of establishments. A dash (-) indicates that the data element cannot be calculated. Data may not show all states active in the NAICS category. All data available at the time of publication are shown.

NAICS 33243M - METAL CAN, BOX, AND OTHER METAL CONTAINER (LIGHT GAUGE) MANUFACTURING*

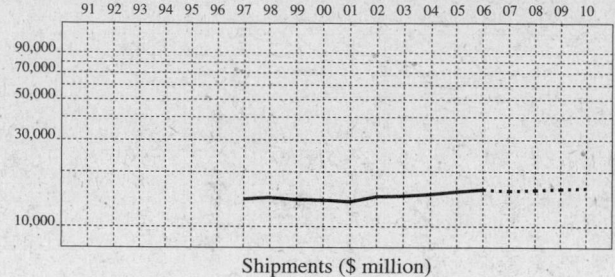

Shipments ($ million)

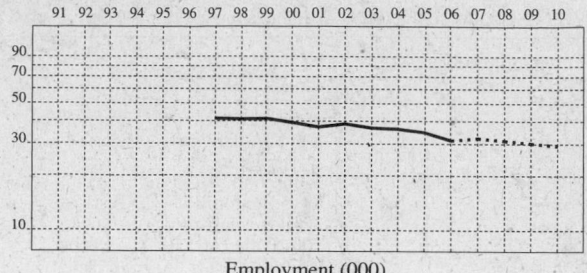

Employment (000)

GENERAL STATISTICS

Year	Com- panies	Establishments		Employment			Compensation		Production ($ million)			
		Total	with 20 or more employees	Total (000)	Production Workers (000)	Hours (Mil)	Payroll ($ mil)	Wages ($/hr)	Cost of Materials	Value Added by Manufacture	Value of Shipments	Capital Invest.
1997	562	764	371	41.3	34.0	71.0	1,595.6	17.48	9,818.8	4,402.0	14,154.5	361.4
1998		750	380	40.9	33.6	72.3	1,624.0	16.94	9,515.7	4,968.0	14,449.3	354.6
1999		705	364	41.2	33.7	71.8	1,637.1	17.01	9,134.3	4,898.8	14,053.5	331.9
2000		679	360	39.2	32.4	68.9	1,550.2	16.79	8,939.9	5,100.8	13,965.7	341.4
2001		681	347	37.1	30.6	64.6	1,505.6	17.42	8,644.8	4,943.2	13,704.8	324.7
2002	455	623	332	38.6	31.5	66.8	1,587.5	17.68	8,944.4	5,644.0	14,624.4	315.7
2003		616	344	36.7	30.2	68.0	1,592.9	17.59	9,043.0	5,639.0	14,720.4	309.4
2004		615	340	36.2	28.7	61.9	1,578.5	18.85	9,249.4	5,844.1	15,066.5	335.3
2005		611	321	34.7	27.5	59.0	1,545.2	19.63	9,886.5	5,708.9	15,567.2	436.0
2006		567P	319P	31.3	25.1	54.0	1,508.9	20.86	10,036.7	5,999.2	15,968.2	350.7
2007		547P	312P	32.2P	25.6P	56.0P	1,525.4P	20.06P	9,872.8P	5,901.2P	15,707.4P	359.0P
2008		526P	306P	31.2P	24.7P	54.2P	1,516.8P	20.43P	9,996.2P	5,975.0P	15,903.7P	361.3P
2009		505P	299P	30.2P	23.8P	52.4P	1,508.2P	20.80P	10,119.6P	6,048.7P	16,100.1P	363.6P
2010		484P	293P	29.3P	22.8P	50.6P	1,499.7P	21.17P	10,243.0P	6,122.5P	16,296.4P	366.0P

Sources: 1997 and 2002 *Economic Census*; other years, up to 2006, are from *Annual Survey of Manufactures*. Establishment counts for non-Census years are from *County Business Patterns*; 1997 and 2002 values are from the 1997 and 2002 censuses, respectively. 'P's show projections by the editors.

INDICES OF CHANGE

Year	Com- panies	Establishments		Employment			Compensation		Production ($ million)			
		Total	with 20 or more employees	Total (000)	Production Workers (000)	Hours (Mil)	Payroll ($ mil)	Wages ($/hr)	Cost of Materials	Value Added by Manufacture	Value of Shipments	Capital Invest.
1997	124	123	112	107	108	106	101	99	110	78	97	114
1998		120	114	106	107	108	102	96	106	88	99	112
1999		113	110	107	107	107	103	96	102	87	96	105
2000		109	108	102	103	103	98	95	100	90	95	108
2001		109	105	96	97	97	95	99	97	88	94	103
2002	100	100	100	100	100	100	100	100	100	100	100	100
2003		99	104	95	96	102	100	99	101	100	101	98
2004		99	102	94	91	93	99	107	103	104	103	106
2005		98	97	90	87	88	97	111	111	101	106	138
2006		91P	96P	81	80	81	95	118	112	106	109	111
2007		88P	94P	83P	81P	84P	96P	113P	110P	105P	107P	114P
2008		84P	92P	81P	78P	81P	96P	116P	112P	106P	109P	114P
2009		81P	90P	78P	76P	78P	95P	118P	113P	107P	110P	115P
2010		78P	88P	76P	72P	76P	94P	120P	115P	108P	111P	116P

Sources: Same as General Statistics. Values reflect change from the base year, 2002. Values above 100 mean greater than 2002, values below 100 mean less than 2002, and the values of 100 in other years means the same as 2002. 'P's show projections by the editors.

SELECTED RATIOS

For 2002	Avg. of All Manufact.	Analyzed Industry	Index	For 2002	Avg. of All Manufact.	Analyzed Industry	Index
Employees per Establishment	42	62	148	Value Added per Production Worker	182,367	179,175	98
Payroll per Establishment	1,639,184	2,548,154	155	Cost per Establishment	5,769,015	14,356,982	249
Payroll per Employee	39,053	41,127	105	Cost per Employee	137,446	231,720	169
Production Workers per Establishment	30	51	171	Cost per Production Worker	195,506	283,949	145
Wages per Establishment	694,845	1,895,705	273	Shipments per Establishment	11,158,348	23,474,157	210
Wages per Production Worker	23,548	37,493	159	Shipments per Employee	265,847	378,870	143
Hours per Production Worker	1,980	2,121	107	Shipments per Production Worker	378,144	464,267	123
Wages per Hour	11.89	17.68	149	Investment per Establishment	361,338	506,742	140
Value Added per Establishment	5,381,325	9,059,390	168	Investment per Employee	8,609	8,179	95
Value Added per Employee	128,210	146,218	114	Investment per Production Worker	12,245	10,022	82

Sources: Same as General Statistics. The 'Average of All Manufacturing' column represents the average of all manufacturing industries reported for the most recent complete year available. The Index shows the relationship between the Average and the Analyzed Industry. For example, 100 means that they are equal; 500 that the Analyzed Industry is five times the average; 50 means that the Analyzed Industry is half the national average. The abbreviation 'na' is used to show that data are 'not available'. Ratios shown for 2002, the last complete census year.

*Equivalent to Federal Government NAICS 332431, 332439.

LEADING COMPANIES   Number shown: 75   Total sales ($ mil): **461,982**   Total employment (000): **963.1**

Company Name	Address				CEO Name	Phone	Co. Type	Sales ($ mil)	Empl. (000)
Ford Motor Co.	1 American Rd.	Dearborn	MI	48126		313-322-3000	P	172,455	246.0
Caterpillar Inc.	100 NE Adams St.	Peoria	IL	61629		309-675-1000	P	44,958	101.3
Deere and Co.	1 John Deere Pl.	Moline	IL	61265		309-765-8000	P	24,082	52.0
Anheuser-Busch Companies Inc.	1 Busch Pl.	St. Louis	MO	63118	August Busch	314-577-2000	P	18,989	30.8
Nucor Corp.	1915 Rexford Rd.	Charlotte	NC	28211	Daniel R. DiMicco	704-366-7000	P	16,593	18.0
Novelis Inc.	3399 Peachtree Rd.	Atlanta	GA	30326	Martha Finn Brooks	416-814-4200	S	9,800	12.9
Terex Corp.	200 Nyala Farm Rd.	Westport	CT	06880		203-222-7170	P	9,138	21.0
API Group Inc.	2366 Rose Pl.	St. Paul	MN	55113	Lee R. Anderson Sr.	651-636-4320	R	9,000	5.0
Fortune Brands Inc.	520 Lake Cook Rd.	Deerfield	IL	60015	Bruce A. Carbonari	847-484-4400	P	8,563	31.0
Crown Holdings Inc.	1 Crown Way	Philadelphia	PA	19154	John W. Conway	215-698-5100	P	7,727	21.8
Ball Corp.	PO Box 5000	Broomfield	CO	80021	R. David Hoover	303-469-3131	P	7,475	15.5
Newell Rubbermaid Inc.	10B Glenlake Pkwy.	Atlanta	GA	30328		770-407-3800	P	6,407	22.0
Oshkosh Truck Corp.	PO Box 2566	Oshkosh	WI	54903	Robert G. Bohn	920-235-9150	P	6,307	14.2
Cooper Industries Ltd.	PO Box 4446	Houston	TX	77210	Kirk S. Hachigian	713-209-8400	P	5,903	31.5
BorgWarner Inc.	3850 Hamlin Rd.	Auburn Hills	MI	48326		248-754-9200	P	5,329	17.7
Stanley Works	PO Box 700	New Britain	CT	06053		860-225-5111	P	4,484	18.4
Trinity Industries Inc.	2525 Stemmons	Dallas	TX	75207		214-631-4420	P	3,833	14.4
Flowserve Corp.	5215 N O'Connor	Irving	TX	75039		972-443-6500	P	3,763	15.0
Coors Brewing Co.	PO Box 4030	Golden	CO	80401	Fritz Van Paasschen	303-279-6565	S	3,705*	8.3
Harsco Corp.	PO Box 8888	Camp Hill	PA	17001	S. D. Fazzolari	717-763-7064	P	3,688	21.5
NACCO Industries Inc.	5875 Landerbrook	Mayfield Hgts	OH	44124		440-449-9600	P	3,603	10.2
Pentair Inc.	5500 Wayzata Blvd.	Golden Valley	MN	55416	Winslow H. Buxton	763-545-1730	P	3,399	16.0
Greif Inc.	425 Winter Rd.	Delaware	OH	43015	David B. Fischer	740-549-6000	P	3,322	10.3
Kalmar Industries USA L.L.C.	415 E Dundee St.	Ottawa	KS	66067		785-242-2200	R	3,320*	0.3
Waltco Truck Equipment Company	PO Box 354	Tallmadge	OH	44278	Lennart Bohman	330-633-9191	R	3,320*	0.2
Truth Hardware Corp.	700 W Bridge St.	Owatonna	MN	55060	Greg Wobschall	507-451-5620	R	3,218*	1.0
Crosby Group Inc.	PO Box 3128	Tulsa	OK	74101	Larry Postelwait	918-834-4611	R	3,101*	<0.1
Arco Auto and Marine Products	3921 Navy Blvd.	Pensacola	FL	32507	Ron Miller	850-455-5476	R	3,015	<0.1
Silgan Holdings Inc.	4 Landmark Sq., 400	Stamford	CT	06901	Anthony J. Allott	203-975-7110	P	2,923	8.4
Snap-On Inc.	PO Box 1410	Kenosha	WI	53141	Tim Chambers	262-656-5200	P	2,841	11.6
Freightliner L.L.C.	PO Box 3849	Portland	OR	97208	Chris Patterson	503-745-8000	S	2,734*	14.0
Crown Cork and Seal Company	1 Crown Way	Philadelphia	PA	19154	John W. Conway	215-698-5100	S	2,640*	11.0
Metals USA Special Flat Rolled	2840 E Heartland Dr	Liberty	MO	64068	Lew Krausse	816-415-0004	S	2,639*	<0.1
HNI Corp.	PO Box 1109	Muscatine	IA	52761	Timothy Anderson	563-264-7400	P	2,571	14.2
JELD-WEN Inc.	PO Box 1329	Klamath Falls	OR	97601	Richard Wendt	541-882-3451	P	2,476*	23.8
True Value Co.	8600 W Bryn Mawr	Chicago	IL	60631	Bryan R. Ableidinger	773-695-5000	R	2,050	3.0
Hillenbrand Industries Inc.	1069 State Rte 46E	Batesville	IN	47006		812-934-7000	P	2,024	9.9
G-I Holdings Corp.	1361 Alps Rd.	Wayne	NJ	07470	Samuel Heyman	973-628-3000	R	1,970	3.6
Hutchinson FTS Inc.	1835 Technology	Troy	MI	48083	Paul Campbell	248-589-7710	R	1,863*	<0.1
Metals USA Inc.	1 Riverway, 1100	Houston	TX	77056	Laurenco Goncalves	713-965-0990	S	1,845	2.7
Volvo Trucks North America	PO Box 26115	Greensboro	NC	27402	Peter Karlsten	336-393-2000	S	1,737*	5.4
Silgan Containers Corp.	21800 Oxnard St.	Woodland Hills	CA	91367	James D. Beam	818-348-3700	S	1,648*	5.0
CC Industries Inc.	222 N La Salle St.	Chicago	IL	60601	William H. Crown	312-855-4000	S	1,560*	6.0
Ancra International L.L.C.	4880 W Rosecrans	Hawthorne	CA	90250	Steve Frediani	310-973-5000	S	1,560*	0.1
Pettibone Traverse Lift L.L.C.	PO Box 368	Baraga	MI	49908		906-353-6611	R	1,560*	0.1
Heico Holding Inc.	2626 Warrenville Rd	Downers Grove	IL	60515	Michael Heisley	630-353-5000	R	1,560*	<0.1
Barnes Group Inc.	PO Box 489	Bristol	CT	06011	Thomas Barnes	860-583-7070	P	1,539	6.7
Valmont Industries Inc.	1 Valmont Plz.	Omaha	NE	68154	Mogens C. Bay	402-963-1000	P	1,500	6.0
EBSCO Industries Inc.	PO Box 1943	Birmingham	AL	35201	Dixon Brooke Jr.	205-991-6600	R	1,400*	5.0
Dresser Inc.	15455 Dallas Pkwy.	Addison	TX	75001		972-361-9800	S	1,343*	6.0
Yale Security Inc.	1902 Airport Rd.	Monroe	NC	28110		704-283-2101	R	1,201*	0.2
Adams Rite Manufacturing Co.	260 W Santa Fe St.	Pomona	CA	91767	Peter Adams	909-632-2300	R	1,201*	0.2
AAR Corp.	1100 N Wood Dale	Wood Dale	IL	60191	Ira A. Eichner	630-227-2000	P	1,061	3.9
Robert Bosch Tool Corp.	1961 Bishop Ln.	Louisville	KY	40218	Timothy Shea	502-625-2050	D	1,057*	0.2
Crown Equipment Corp.	44 S Washington St.	New Bremen	OH	45869	James Dicke	419-629-2311	R	1,049*	7.6
BWAY Holding Co.	8607 Roberts Dr.	Atlanta	GA	30350	Jean-Pierre M. Ergas	770-645-4800	P	959	2.5
United Components Inc.	14601 Hwy 41 N	Evansville	IN	47725	Bruce Zorich	812-867-4156	S	906	6.8
Feralloy Corp.	8755 W Higgins Rd.	Chicago	IL	60631		773-380-1500	R	904*	<0.1
Johnson Controls Interiors	49200 Halyard Dr.	Plymouth	MI	48170	John Barth	734-254-5000	S	875*	5.0
California Steel Industries	PO Box 5080	Fontana	CA	92335	Masakazu Kurushima	909-350-6300	R	846*	1.0
International Industries Inc.	PO Box 1210	Gilbert	WV	25621		304-664-3227	R	835*	0.5
Simpson Manufacturing Company	5956 W Las Positas	Pleasanton	CA	94588	Thomas J. Fitzmyers	925-560-9000	P	817	2.7
Scott Company of California	1717 Doolittle Dr.	San Leandro	CA	94577	Joseph A. Guglielmo	510-895-2333	R	793*	1.2
American Auto Accessories Inc.	11201 Northern Blvd	Corona	NY	11368	Henry Hsu	347-625-8800	R	769*	1.2
Raybestos Products Co.	1204 Darlington Ave	Crawfordsville	IN	47933	Larry S. Singleton	765-362-3500	S	701*	5.3
Commercial Vehicle Group Inc.	6530 W Campus Ovl	New Albany	OH	43054	Gordon Boyd	614-289-5360	P	697	6.4
Ameron International Corp.	245 S Los Robles	Pasadena	CA	91101	James Marlen	626-683-4000	P	631	2.8
Kautex Textron North America	750 Stephenson	Troy	MI	48083	Robert K. Simpson	248-616-5100	D	625*	5.0
Performance Contracting Group	16400 College Blvd.	Lenexa	KS	66219	Craig Davis	913-888-8600	R	600*	5.7
LMT Fette Inc.	1997 Ohio St.	Lisle	IL	60532	Brian Nowicki	630-969-5412	R	558*	0.2
Overhead Door Corp.	2501 St. Hwy. 121	Lewisville	TX	75022	Howard Simons		R	508*	0.1
Columbia Ventures Corp.	203 SE Park Plaza	Vancouver	WA	98684	K. D. Peterson Jr.	360-816-1840	R	502*	0.2
McNeilus Companies Inc.	113 Conner Rd.	Villa Rica	GA	30180	Micheal Wuest	770-459-6005	S	485*	1.0
Cascade Corp.	PO Box 20187	Portland	OR	97294		503-669-6300	P	479	2.1
Advanced Accessory Holdings	12900 Hall Rd.	Sterling Hgts	MI	48313	Alan C. Johnson	586-997-2900	R	443	2.3

Source: Ward's Business Directory of U.S. Private and Public Companies, Volumes 1 and 2, 2008. The company type code used is as follows: P - Public, R - Private, S - Subsidiary, D - Division, J - Joint Venture, A - Affiliate, G - Group. Sales are in millions of dollars, employees are in thousands. An asterisk (*) indicates an estimated sales volume. The symbol < stands for 'less than'. Company names and addresses are truncated, in some cases, to fit into the available space.

MATERIALS CONSUMED FOR METAL CAN MANUFACTURING

Material	Quantity	Delivered Cost ($ million)
Lids, ends, and parts for metal cans	(X)	1,974.3
All other fabricated metal products (exc. castings and forgings)	(X)	(D)
Forgings	(X)	(D)
Steel sheet, strip, and tin mill products	(X)	443.2
Steel bars, bar shapes, and plates (exc. castings, forgings, fabr. metal products)	(X)	63.9
All other steel shapes and forms (exc. castings, forgings, fabr. metal products)	(X)	(D)
Aluminum and aluminum-base alloy sheet, plate, foil, and welded tubing	(X)	1,677.5
Other aluminum and aluminum-base alloy shapes and forms (exc. castings, forgings, fabr. metal products)	(X)	(D)
Other nonferrous shapes and forms (exc. castings, forgings, fabricated metal products)	(X)	(D)
Paints, varnishes, stains, lacquers, shellacs, japans, enamels, etc.	(X)	128.6
Adhesives and sealants	(X)	16.6
Printing inks	(X)	43.3
All other chemicals and allied products	(X)	18.1
Paperboard containers, boxes, and corrugated paperboard	(X)	31.7
All other materials, components, parts, containers, and supplies	(X)	224.6
Materials, ingredients, containers, and supplies, nsk	(X)	72.0

Source: 2002 Economic Census. Explanation of symbols used: (D): Withheld to avoid disclosure of competitive data; na: Not available; (S): Withheld because statistical norms were not met; (X): Not applicable; (Z): Less than half the unit shown; nec: Not elsewhere classified; nsk: Not specified by kind; - : zero; p : 10-19 percent estimated; q : 20-29 percent estimated.

MATERIALS CONSUMED FOR METAL CONTAINER MANUFACTURING NEC

Material	Quantity	Delivered Cost ($ million)
Lids, ends, and parts for metal cans	(X)	108.5
All other fabricated metal products (exc. castings and forgings)	(X)	47.7
Forgings	(X)	(D)
Steel sheet, strip, and tin mill products	(X)	336.7
Steel bars, bar shapes, and plates (exc. castings, forgings, fabr. metal products)	(X)	6.2
All other steel shapes and forms (exc. castings, forgings, fabr. metal products)	(X)	97.3
Aluminum and aluminum-base alloy sheet, plate, foil, and welded tubing	(X)	61.2
Other aluminum and aluminum-base alloy shapes and forms (exc. castings, forgings, fabr. metal products)	(X)	60.0
Other nonferrous shapes and forms (exc. castings, forgings, fabricated metal products)	(X)	(D)
Paints, varnishes, stains, lacquers, shellacs, japans, enamels, etc.	(X)	82.6
Adhesives and sealants	(X)	2.7
Printing inks	(X)	4.8
All other chemicals and allied products	(X)	2.7
Paperboard containers, boxes, and corrugated paperboard	(X)	41.4
All other materials, components, parts, containers, and supplies	(X)	360.1
Materials, ingredients, containers, and supplies, nsk	(X)	202.0

Source: 2002 Economic Census. Explanation of symbols used: (D): Withheld to avoid disclosure of competitive data; na: Not available; (S): Withheld because statistical norms were not met; (X): Not applicable; (Z): Less than half the unit shown; nec: Not elsewhere classified; nsk: Not specified by kind; - : zero; p : 10-19 percent estimated; q : 20-29 percent estimated.

PRODUCT SHARE DETAILS FOR METAL CAN MANUFACTURING

Product or Product Class Shipments	Mil. $	Product or Product Class Shipments	Mil. $
METAL CANS	11,045.4	excluding cooking and kitchen utensils	(D)
Steel cans and tinware products	**4,223.8**	Steel cans and tinware products, nsk	64.4
Steel cans, including lids, ends, and parts shipped separately	(D)	**Aluminum cans, including lids, ends, and parts shipped separately**	**6,745.7**
Tinware end products, including ice cream cans, but		**Metal cans, nsk, total**	**75.8**

Source: 2002 Economic Census. The values are product shipments in millions of dollars for 2002. Total product shipments may be lower or higher than industry shipments. See Introduction for a full discussion. Values of indented subcategories are summed in the main heading(s). The symbol (D) appears when data are withheld to prevent disclosure of competitive information. The abbreviation nsk stands for 'not specified by kind' and nec for 'not elsewhere classified'. A dash (-) means zero.

PRODUCT SHARE DETAILS FOR METAL CONTAINER MANUFACTURING NEC

Product or Product Class Shipments	Mil. $	Product or Product Class Shipments	Mil. $
OTHER METAL CONTAINERS	2,814.5	Vacuum and insulated bottles, jugs, and chests (except those made principally of foam plastics) and other sheet metal bins and vats (steel and aluminum)	52.8
Steel pails, 1 to 12 gallon capacity, and fabricated steel boxes	**774.3**	All other metal barrels and containers (including beer barrels, air cargo containers, and parts for metal barrels and pails)	223.3
Steel pails, 1 to 12 gallon capacity	353.0		
Fabricated steel boxes	384.6		
Fabricated steel boxes for packaging and shipping	142.8	Stamped and pressed metal end products, excluding spinning products and metal electric enclosures	551.8
Fabricated steel boxes other than for shipping (ammunition boxes, jewelry cases, etc.)	241.8	Stamped and pressed galvanized steel pails, ash cans, garbage cans, tubs, etc. (excluding shipping containers)	28.2
Steel pails (1 to 12 gallon capacity) and fabricated steel boxes, nsk	36.7	Other stamped and pressed metal pails, ash cans, garbage cans, tubs, etc. (excluding shipping containers)	5.7
Steel shipping barrels and drums, excluding beer barrels (more than 12 gallon capacity)	**596.8**		
All other metal containers	**1,107.0**	Stamped and pressed metal mailboxes (commercial and multiple unit residential)	47.4
Metal barrels, vacuum and insulated bottles, grain bins and vats, and other barrels	555.2	Stamped and pressed metal toolboxes	470.6
Metal fluid milk shipping and delivery containers (except crates) and sheet metal grain bins and vats (excluding drying floors, fans, and heaters) (steel and aluminum)	279.1	**Other metal containers, nsk, total**	**336.4**

Source: 2002 *Economic Census.* The values are product shipments in millions of dollars for 2002. Total product shipments may be lower or higher than industry shipments. See Introduction for a full discussion. Values of indented subcategories are summed in the main heading(s). The symbol (D) appears when data are withheld to prevent disclosure of competitive information. The abbreviation nsk stands for 'not specified by kind' and nec for 'not elsewhere classified'. A dash (-) means zero.

INPUTS AND OUTPUTS FOR METAL CAN, BOX, & OTHER METAL CONTAINER (LIGHT GAUGE)

Economic Sector or Industry Providing Inputs	%	Sector	Economic Sector or Industry Buying Outputs	%	Sector
Compensation of employees	15.0		Breweries	19.8	Manufg.
Aluminum products from purchased aluminum	13.8	Manufg.	Canned & dehydrated fruits & vegetables	16.2	Manufg.
Metal cans, boxes, & other containers (light gauge)	12.2	Manufg.	Metal cans, boxes, & other containers (light gauge)	12.3	Manufg.
Iron & steel mills & ferroalloys	10.1	Manufg.	Motor vehicle parts	4.4	Manufg.
Wholesale trade	4.8	Trade	Dog & cat food	4.0	Manufg.
Alumina refining & primary aluminum production	3.8	Manufg.	Soft drinks & ice	3.9	Manufg.
Ornamental & architectural metal products	3.8	Manufg.	Exports of goods & services	3.0	Cap Inv
Paints & coatings	1.8	Manufg.	Tobacco products	2.8	Manufg.
Truck transportation	1.4	Util.	Construction machinery	1.7	Manufg.
Management of companies & enterprises	1.4	Services	Paints & coatings	1.7	Manufg.
Power generation & supply	1.3	Util.	Coffee & tea	1.3	Manufg.
Machine shops	1.0	Manufg.	Dry, condensed, & evaporated dairy products	1.3	Manufg.
Securities, commodity contracts, investments	1.0	Fin/R.E.	Private fixed investment	1.2	
Coating, engraving, heat treating & allied activities	0.7	Manufg.	Fluid milk & butter	1.0	Manufg.
Lessors of nonfinancial assets	0.7	Fin/R.E.	Plate work & fabricated structural products	0.9	Manufg.
Custom roll forming	0.7	Manufg.	Industrial machinery, nec	0.9	Manufg.
Monetary authorities/depository credit intermediation	0.7	Fin/R.E.	Snack food	0.8	Manufg.
Semiconductors & related devices	0.6	Manufg.	Material handling equipment	0.7	Manufg.
Printed circuit assemblies (electronic assemblies)	0.6	Manufg.	Light truck & utility vehicles	0.6	Manufg.
Paperboard containers	0.6	Manufg.	Food, nec	0.6	Manufg.
Professional, scientific, technical services, nec	0.6	Services	Ornamental & architectural metal products	0.6	Manufg.
Natural gas distribution	0.5	Util.	Air & gas compressors	0.6	Manufg.
Maintenance/repair of nonresidential structures	0.5	Construct.	Pumps & pumping equipment	0.5	Manufg.
Turned products & screws, nuts, & bolts	0.4	Manufg.	Soap & cleaning compounds	0.5	Manufg.
Services to buildings & dwellings	0.4	Services	Engine equipment, nec	0.5	Manufg.
Real estate	0.4	Fin/R.E.	Wholesale trade	0.5	Trade
Taxes on production & imports, less subsidies	0.4		Frozen food	0.5	Manufg.
Nonferrous metal (ex. copper & aluminum) processing	0.4	Manufg.	Chemical products & preparations, nec	0.4	Manufg.
Food services & drinking places	0.3	Services	Rubber products, nec	0.4	Manufg.
Printing inks	0.3	Manufg.	Basic organic chemicals, nec	0.4	Manufg.
Architectural, engineering, & related services	0.3	Services	Turbines & turbine generator set units	0.4	Manufg.
Automotive repair & maintenance, ex. car washes	0.3	Services	Seasoning & dressing	0.4	Manufg.
Fabricated metals, nec	0.3	Manufg.	Seafood product preparation & processing	0.3	Manufg.
Data processing, hosting, & related services	0.3	Services	Mining & oil & gas field machinery	0.3	Manufg.
Rail transportation	0.3	Util.	Federal government, investment, national defense	0.3	Fed Govt
Commercial & industrial equipment repair/maintenance	0.2	Services	Automobiles	0.3	Manufg.
Advertising & related services	0.2	Services	Personal consumption expenditures	0.3	
Air transportation	0.2	Util.	Air purification & ventilation equipment	0.3	Manufg.
Hotels & motels, including casino hotels	0.2	Services	Manufacturing, nec	0.3	Manufg.
Ball & roller bearings	0.2	Manufg.	Machine shops	0.3	Manufg.
Handtools	0.2	Manufg.	S/L govt. invest., other	0.3	S/L Govt
Accounting, tax preparation, bookkeeping, & payroll	0.2	Services	Valve & fittings other than plumbing	0.3	Manufg.
Plate work & fabricated structural products	0.2	Manufg.	Toilet preparations	0.3	Manufg.
Automotive equipment rental & leasing	0.2	Fin/R.E.	Coating, engraving, heat treating & allied activities	0.3	Manufg.
Crowns & closures & metal stamping	0.2	Manufg.	Electronic components, nec	0.2	Manufg.
Telecommunications	0.2	Services	Animal food, nec	0.2	Manufg.
Legal services	0.2	Services	Poultry processing	0.2	Manufg.
Adhesives	0.1	Manufg.	Crowns & closures & metal stamping	0.2	Manufg.
Valve & fittings other than plumbing	0.1	Manufg.	Power boilers & heat exchangers	0.2	Manufg.

Continued on next page.

INPUTS AND OUTPUTS FOR METAL CAN, BOX, & OTHER METAL CONTAINER (LIGHT GAUGE) - Continued

Economic Sector or Industry Providing Inputs	%	Sector	Economic Sector or Industry Buying Outputs	%	Sector
Warehousing & storage	0.1	Util.	Adhesives	0.2	Manufg.
Nondepository credit intermediation activities	0.1	Fin/R.E.	Commercial & service industry machinery, nec	0.2	Manufg.
Scientific research & development services	0.1	Services	Signs	0.2	Manufg.
Other computer related services, including facilities	0.1	Services	Motorcycles, bicycles, & parts	0.2	Manufg.
			Semiconductor machinery	0.2	Manufg.
			Pharmaceutical preparations	0.2	Manufg.
			General purpose machinery, nec	0.2	Manufg.
			Printing inks	0.2	Manufg.
			Transportation equipment, nec	0.2	Manufg.
			Broadcast & wireless communications equipment	0.2	Manufg.
			AC, refrigeration, and warm air heating equipment	0.2	Manufg.
			Surgical appliances & supplies	0.2	Manufg.
			Turned products & screws, nuts, & bolts	0.2	Manufg.
			Petroleum lubricating oil & grease	0.2	Manufg.
			Hardware	0.2	Manufg.
			Aircraft parts & auxiliary equipment, nec	0.2	Manufg.
			Synthetic dyes & pigments	0.2	Manufg.
			Plastics products, nec	0.2	Manufg.
			General Federal government services, defense	0.2	Fed Govt.
			Jewelry & silverware	0.2	Manufg.
			Fats & oils refining & blending	0.2	Manufg.
			Pesticides & other agricultural chemicals	0.1	Manufg.
			Retail trade	0.1	Trade
			Farm machinery & equipment	0.1	Manufg.
			Packaging machinery	0.1	Manufg.
			Fabricated pipes & pipe fittings	0.1	Manufg.
			Fabricated metals, nec	0.1	Manufg.
			Lighting fixtures	0.1	Manufg.
			Electromedical & electrotherapeutic apparatus	0.1	Manufg.
			Household cooking appliances	0.1	Manufg.
			Switchgear & switchboard apparatus	0.1	Manufg.
			Aircraft	0.1	Manufg.
			Confectionery products from cacao beans	0.1	Manufg.
			Plastics & rubber industry machinery	0.1	Manufg.
			Arms, ordnance, & accessories	0.1	Manufg.
			Metal tanks (heavy gauge)	0.1	Manufg.
			Cheese	0.1	Manufg.
			Sporting & athletic goods	0.1	Manufg.

Source: Benchmark Input-Output Accounts for the U.S. Economy, 2002, U.S. Department of Commerce, Washington, D.C., January 2008. The abbreviation nec stands for 'not elsewhere classified'.

OCCUPATIONS EMPLOYED BY BOILER, TANK, & SHIPPING CONTAINER MANUFACTURING

Occupation	% of Total 2006	Change to 2016	Occupation	% of Total 2006	Change to 2016
Welders, cutters, solderers, & brazers	13.8	-4.1	Sales reps, wholesale & manufacturing, exc tech	1.8	-9.9
Cutting, punching, & press machine operators	5.4	-18.9	Laborers & freight, stock, & material movers, hand	1.8	-18.9
Team assemblers	4.5	-9.9	Packaging & filling machine operators & tenders	1.6	-18.9
First-line supervisors/managers of production workers	4.0	-9.9	Welding, soldering, & brazing machine operators	1.4	1.3
Structural metal fabricators & fitters	3.7	-9.9	Industrial engineers	1.4	9.4
Coating, painting, & spraying machine operators	3.0	-14.4	Boilermakers	1.3	-1.6
Industrial truck & tractor operators	2.7	-18.9	Shipping, receiving, & traffic clerks	1.2	-13.3
Inspectors, testers, sorters, samplers, & weighers	2.6	-15.0	Packers & packagers, hand	1.2	-27.9
Helpers--Production workers	2.5	-9.9	Machine feeders & offbearers	1.2	-18.9
Maintenance & repair workers, general	2.4	-9.9	Bookkeeping, accounting, & auditing clerks	1.1	-9.9
Industrial machinery mechanics	2.1	3.6	Multiple machine tool operators & tenders	1.1	-0.9
Machinists	2.1	-5.4	Mechanical engineers	1.1	-9.9
General & operations managers	1.9	-18.9	Industrial production managers	1.1	-9.9
Sheet metal workers	1.9	-11.6	Grinding, lapping, polishing machine tool operators	1.1	-12.6

Source: Industry-Occupation Matrix, Bureau of Labor Statistics, December 4, 2007. These data are reported based on 4-digit NAICS categories but have been matched to corresponding 6-digit NAICS industry codes. The change reported for each occupation to the year 2016 is a percent of growth or decline as estimated by the Bureau of Labor Statistics. The abbreviation nec stands for 'not elsewhere classified'.

LOCATION BY STATE AND REGIONAL CONCENTRATION

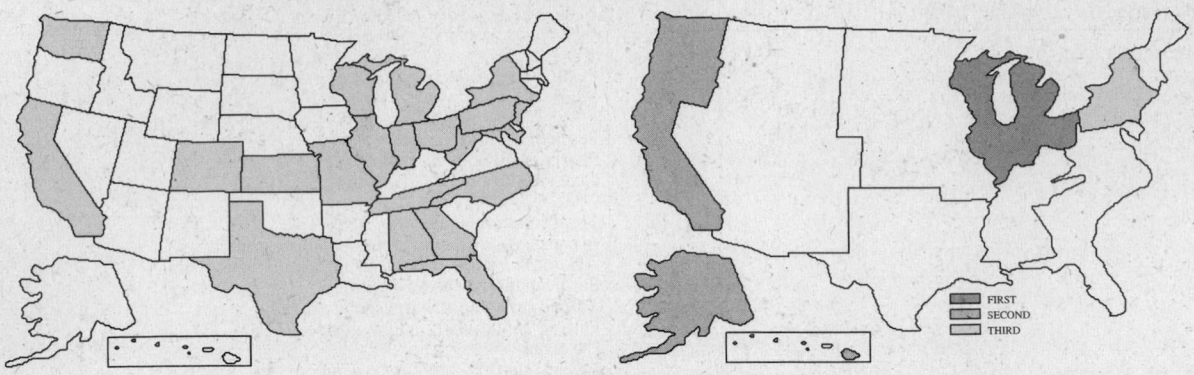

INDUSTRY DATA BY STATE

| State | Establish-ments | Shipments | | | Employment | | | | Cost as % of Shipments | Investment per Employee ($) |
		Total ($ mil)	% of U.S.	Per Establ.	Total Number	% of U.S.	Per Establ.	Wages ($/hour)		
California	69	1,757.9	12.0	25,476.6	3,804	9.8	55	20.80	60.0	13,463
Ohio	56	1,316.9	9.0	23,516.0	3,382	8.8	60	16.18	65.3	6,616
Illinois	47	1,276.0	8.7	27,149.1	5,355	13.9	114	15.64	52.9	9,301
Texas	36	812.0	5.6	22,554.3	2,200	5.7	61	16.81	63.3	9,020
Wisconsin	24	733.9	5.0	30,579.0	1,642	4.3	68	19.73	63.7	8,603
Pennsylvania	35	602.5	4.1	17,215.2	1,998	5.2	57	16.64	68.8	6,194
Indiana	22	587.7	4.0	26,715.0	1,108	2.9	50	17.94	62.1	7,560
New York	19	579.6	4.0	30,503.8	1,048	2.7	55	20.42	60.9	13,075
Florida	20	570.5	3.9	28,525.5	1,050	2.7	53	19.18	64.3	4,312
Missouri	21	511.1	3.5	24,337.8	1,448	3.7	69	18.30	57.7	7,924
Georgia	4	510.8	3.5	127,696.7	1,039	2.7	260	15.19	55.6	5,886
Colorado	4	378.7	2.6	94,673.0	595	1.5	149	24.48	61.0	3,783
Washington	13	292.8	2.0	22,520.2	635	1.6	49	21.35	57.9	4,970
Tennessee	13	266.6	1.8	20,504.4	1,147	3.0	88	15.68	68.5	4,074
New Jersey	15	190.7	1.3	12,711.4	577	1.5	38	18.57	59.5	4,276
Maryland	11	178.9	1.2	16,259.4	670	1.7	61	19.82	58.3	5,173
Michigan	19	131.2	0.9	6,905.7	621	1.6	33	14.69	51.6	3,019
Alabama	10	116.6	0.8	11,662.4	428	1.1	43	15.06	69.6	22,741
West Virginia	3	105.5	0.7	35,150.3	254	0.7	85	16.05	80.5	18,055
North Carolina	10	54.7	0.4	5,467.6	248	0.6	25	23.52	61.1	1,931
Kansas	5	14.9	0.1	2,972.0	105	0.3	21	12.06	49.9	1,105

Source: 2002 *Economic Census.* The states are in descending order of shipments or establishments (if shipment data are missing for the majority). The symbol (D) appears when data are withheld to prevent disclosure of competitive information. States marked with (D) are sorted by number of establishments. A dash (-) indicates that the data element cannot be calculated. Data may not show all states active in the NAICS category. All data available at the time of publication are shown.

NAICS 332510 - HARDWARE MANUFACTURING

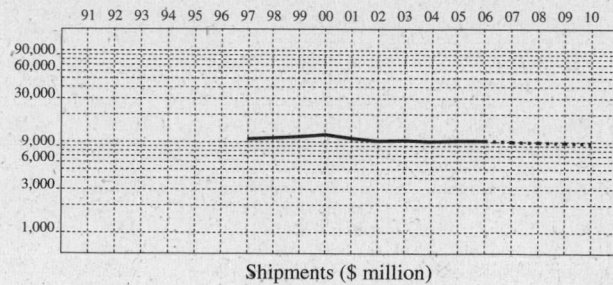

Shipments ($ million)

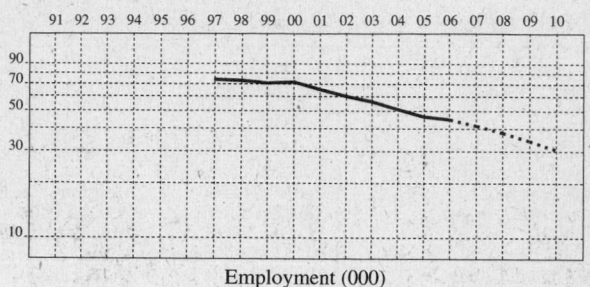

Employment (000)

GENERAL STATISTICS

| Year | Com-panies | Establishments | | Employment | | | Compensation | | Production ($ million) | | | |
		Total	with 20 or more employees	Total (000)	Production Workers (000)	Hours (Mil)	Payroll ($ mil)	Wages ($/hr)	Cost of Materials	Value Added by Manufacture	Value of Shipments	Capital Invest.
1997	903	1,007	488	74.0	57.0	113.8	2,270.2	12.99	4,797.7	6,008.0	10,775.2	383.5
1998		992	474	73.1	56.6	112.8	2,273.9	12.93	4,920.2	6,041.9	11,058.1	352.7
1999		981	473	70.8	54.0	108.4	2,284.9	13.04	4,862.7	6,633.1	11,408.9	350.9
2000		955	474	71.7	55.0	107.2	2,336.8	13.50	5,285.4	6,744.1	11,994.3	391.8
2001		939	463	65.4	49.2	95.3	2,156.1	13.65	4,839.6	6,000.6	10,942.3	291.1
2002	809	897	382	60.0	45.7	89.2	2,053.1	14.29	4,284.3	5,940.8	10,225.2	264.3
2003		856	381	56.3	42.2	82.8	1,986.7	14.62	4,334.1	5,959.7	10,351.0	202.8
2004		843	371	51.1	38.2	78.3	1,890.7	14.89	4,423.6	5,736.3	10,111.3	191.3
2005		830	370	46.6	34.3	69.1	1,798.6	15.44	4,610.0	5,625.9	10,254.0	208.9
2006		800P	343P	44.9	33.2	66.2	1,756.1	15.63	4,539.2	5,818.3	10,275.9	175.0
2007		776P	325P	41.5P	30.2P	60.2P	1,711.4P	15.92P	4,416.3P	5,660.8P	9,997.7P	138.7P
2008		752P	307P	37.9P	27.2P	54.3P	1,644.3P	16.25P	4,356.7P	5,584.4P	9,862.8P	112.8P
2009		727P	290P	34.2P	24.2P	48.5P	1,577.2P	16.58P	4,297.1P	5,508.0P	9,727.9P	86.9P
2010		703P	272P	30.6P	21.2P	42.6P	1,510.0P	16.91P	4,237.6P	5,431.7P	9,593.0P	61.0P

Sources: 1997 and 2002 Economic Census; other years, up to 2006, are from Annual Survey of Manufactures. Establishment counts for non-Census years are from County Business Patterns; 1997 and 2002 values are from the 1997 and 2002 censuses, respectively. 'P's show projections by the editors.

INDICES OF CHANGE

| Year | Com-panies | Establishments | | Employment | | | Compensation | | Production ($ million) | | | |
		Total	with 20 or more employees	Total (000)	Production Workers (000)	Hours (Mil)	Payroll ($ mil)	Wages ($/hr)	Cost of Materials	Value Added by Manufacture	Value of Shipments	Capital Invest.
1997	112	112	128	123	125	128	111	91	112	101	105	145
1998		111	124	122	124	126	111	90	115	102	108	133
1999		109	124	118	118	122	111	91	114	112	112	133
2000		106	124	120	120	120	114	94	123	114	117	148
2001		105	121	109	108	107	105	96	113	101	107	110
2002	100	100	100	100	100	100	100	100	100	100	100	100
2003		95	100	94	92	93	97	102	101	100	101	77
2004		94	97	85	84	88	92	104	103	97	99	72
2005		93	97	78	75	77	88	108	108	95	100	79
2006		89P	90P	75	73	74	86	109	106	98	100	66
2007		86P	85P	69P	66P	67P	83P	111P	103P	95P	98P	52P
2008		84P	80P	63P	60P	61P	80P	114P	102P	94P	96P	43P
2009		81P	76P	57P	53P	54P	77P	116P	100P	93P	95P	33P
2010		78P	71P	51P	46P	48P	74P	118P	99P	91P	94P	23P

Sources: Same as General Statistics. Values reflect change from the base year, 2002. Values above 100 mean greater than 2002, values below 100 mean less than 2002, and the values of 100 in other years means the same as 2002. 'P's show projections by the editors.

SELECTED RATIOS

For 2002	Avg. of All Manufact.	Analyzed Industry	Index	For 2002	Avg. of All Manufact.	Analyzed Industry	Index
Employees per Establishment	42	67	159	Value Added per Production Worker	182,367	129,996	71
Payroll per Establishment	1,639,184	2,288,852	140	Cost per Establishment	5,769,015	4,776,254	83
Payroll per Employee	39,053	34,218	88	Cost per Employee	137,446	71,405	52
Production Workers per Establishment	30	51	173	Cost per Production Worker	195,506	93,748	48
Wages per Establishment	694,845	1,421,035	205	Shipments per Establishment	11,158,348	11,399,331	102
Wages per Production Worker	23,548	27,892	118	Shipments per Employee	265,847	170,420	64
Hours per Production Worker	1,980	1,952	99	Shipments per Production Worker	378,144	223,746	59
Wages per Hour	11.89	14.29	120	Investment per Establishment	361,338	294,649	82
Value Added per Establishment	5,381,325	6,622,965	123	Investment per Employee	8,609	4,405	51
Value Added per Employee	128,210	99,013	77	Investment per Production Worker	12,245	5,783	47

Sources: Same as General Statistics. The 'Average of All Manufacturing' column represents the average of all manufacturing industries reported for the most recent complete year available. The Index shows the relationship between the Average and the Analyzed Industry. For example, 100 means that they are equal; 500 that the Analyzed Industry is five times the average; 50 means that the Analyzed Industry is half the national average. The abbreviation 'na' is used to show that data are 'not available'. Ratios shown for 2002, the last complete census year.

LEADING COMPANIES   Number shown: **75**   Total sales ($ mil): **96,735**   Total employment (000): **314.8**

Company Name	Address				CEO Name	Phone	Co. Type	Sales ($ mil)	Empl. (000)
Nucor Corp.	1915 Rexford Rd.	Charlotte	NC	28211	Daniel R. DiMicco	704-366-7000	P	16,593	18.0
Fortune Brands Inc.	520 Lake Cook Rd.	Deerfield	IL	60015	Bruce A. Carbonari	847-484-4400	P	8,563	31.0
Newell Rubbermaid Inc.	10B Glenlake Pkwy.	Atlanta	GA	30328		770-407-3800	P	6,407	22.0
Cooper Industries Ltd.	PO Box 4446	Houston	TX	77210	Kirk S. Hachigian	713-209-8400	P	5,903	31.5
BorgWarner Inc.	3850 Hamlin Rd.	Auburn Hills	MI	48326		248-754-9200	P	5,329	17.7
Stanley Works	PO Box 700	New Britain	CT	06053		860-225-5111	P	4,484	18.4
Flowserve Corp.	5215 N O'Connor	Irving	TX	75039		972-443-6500	P	3,763	15.0
Truth Hardware Corp.	700 W Bridge St.	Owatonna	MN	55060	Greg Wobschall	507-451-5620	R	3,218*	1.0
Crosby Group Inc.	PO Box 3128	Tulsa	OK	74101	Larry Postelwait	918-834-4611	R	3,101*	<0.1
Arco Auto and Marine Products	3921 Navy Blvd.	Pensacola	FL	32507	Ron Miller	850-455-5476	R	3,015	<0.1
HNI Corp.	PO Box 1109	Muscatine	IA	52761	Timothy Anderson	563-264-7400	P	2,571	14.2
JELD-WEN Inc.	PO Box 1329	Klamath Falls	OR	97601	Richard Wendt	541-882-3451	R	2,476*	23.8
True Value Co.	8600 W Bryn Mawr	Chicago	IL	60631	Bryan R. Ableidinger	773-695-5000	R	2,050	3.0
Hillenbrand Industries Inc.	1069 State Rte 46E	Batesville	IN	47006		812-934-7000	P	2,024	9.9
Hutchinson FTS Inc.	1835 Technology	Troy	MI	48083	Paul Campbell	248-589-7710	R	1,863*	<0.1
Barnes Group Inc.	PO Box 489	Bristol	CT	06011	Thomas Barnes	860-583-7070	P	1,539	6.7
Valmont Industries Inc.	1 Valmont Plz.	Omaha	NE	68154	Mogens C. Bay	402-963-1000	P	1,500	6.0
Dresser Inc.	15455 Dallas Pkwy.	Addison	TX	75001		972-361-9800	S	1,343*	6.0
Yale Security Inc.	1902 Airport Rd.	Monroe	NC	28110		704-283-2101	R	1,201*	0.2
Adams Rite Manufacturing Co.	260 W Santa Fe St.	Pomona	CA	91767	Peter Adams	909-632-2300	R	1,201*	0.2
Robert Bosch Tool Corp.	1961 Bishop Ln.	Louisville	KY	40218	Timothy Shea	502-625-2050	D	1,057*	0.2
BWAY Holding Co.	8607 Roberts Dr.	Atlanta	GA	30350	Jean-Pierre M. Ergas	770-645-4800	P	959	2.5
United Components Inc.	14601 Hwy 41 N	Evansville	IN	47725	Bruce Zorich	812-867-4156	S	906	6.8
Johnson Controls Interiors	49200 Halyard Dr.	Plymouth	MI	48170	John Barth	734-254-5000	S	875*	5.0
Simpson Manufacturing Company	5956 W Las Positas	Pleasanton	CA	94588	Thomas J. Fitzmyers	925-560-9000	P	817	2.7
American Auto Accessories Inc.	11201 Northern Blvd	Corona	NY	11368	Henry Hsu	347-625-8800	R	769*	1.2
Raybestos Products Co.	1204 Darlington Ave	Crawfordsville	IN	47933	Larry S. Singleton	765-362-3500	S	701*	5.3
Commercial Vehicle Group Inc.	6530 W Campus Ovl	New Albany	OH	43054	Gordon Boyd	614-289-5360	P	697	6.4
Ameron International Corp.	245 S Los Robles	Pasadena	CA	91101	James Marlen	626-683-4000	P	631	2.8
Kautex Textron North America	750 Stephenson	Troy	MI	48083	Robert K. Simpson	248-616-5100	D	625*	5.0
Performance Contracting Group	16400 College Blvd.	Lenexa	KS	66219	Craig Davis	913-888-8600	R	600*	5.7
Cascade Corp.	PO Box 20187	Portland	OR	97294		503-669-6300	P	479	2.1
Advanced Accessory Holdings	12900 Hall Rd.	Sterling Hgts	MI	48313	Alan C. Johnson	586-997-2900	R	443	2.3
Bing Group L.L.C.	11500 Oakland St.	Detroit	MI	48211	David Bing	313-867-3700	R	411*	1.1
Schlage Lock Co.	2315 Briargate Pky.	Colorado Spgs	CO	80920	Herbert Henkel	719-264-5300	S	397*	0.8
TECT Utica Corp.	2 Halsey Rd.	Whitesboro	NY	13492	Ron Cable	315-768-8070	R	356*	1.3
Royal Lock Corp.	290 Industrial Dr.	Wauconda	IL	60084	Larry Freck	847-526-0220	D	319*	0.7
O.C. Tanner Recognition Co.	1930 S State St.	Salt Lake City	UT	84115	Kent H. Murdock	801-486-2430	R	319*	1.8
Team Inc.	PO Box 123	Alvin	TX	77512	Philip J. Hawk	281-331-6154	P	318	3.4
ASC Inc.	1 ASC Ctr.	Southgate	MI	48195	Paul Wilbur	734-285-4911	S	300*	1.0
Maxcess Technologies Inc.	230 Deming Way	Summerville	SC	29483	Andy Miarka	843-821-1200	R	291*	<0.1
Simpson Strong-Tie Company	4120 Dublin Blvd.	Dublin	CA	94568	Tom Tetfzmer	925-560-9000	S	285*	1.2
Pall Aeropower Corp.	1054 Ridge Rd.	New Port Richey	FL	34654	Jim Wester	727-849-9999	R	271*	0.5
Intermagnetics General Corp.	PO Box 461	Latham	NY	12110	Leo Blecher	518-782-1122	R	265	1.1
Gunderson Rail Services	4012 NW Front St.	Portland	OR	97210		503-972-5950	S	260*	1.4
C. Cowles and Co.	83 Water St.	New Haven	CT	06511	Lawrence C. Moon Jr.	203-865-3110	R	260*	1.2
Thermos Co.	2550 Golf Rd., 800	Rolling Mdws	IL	60008		847-439-7821	R	232*	<0.1
Autocam Corp.	4070 E Paris Ave SE	Kentwood	MI	49512	John C. Kennedy	616-698-0707	S	230*	2.3
Raytech Corp.	4 Corporate Dr.	Shelton	CT	06484		203-925-8023	R	227	1.7
L.S. Starrett Co.	121 Crescent St.	Athol	MA	01331	Douglas A. Starrett	978-249-3551	P	222	2.1
Nielsen and Bainbridge	40 Eisenhower Dr.	Paramus	NJ	07653	Jack Forbes	201-368-9191	R	219*	0.9
Defiance Metal Products Co.	PO Box 447	Defiance	OH	43512		419-784-5332	R	211*	1.7
Hebco Products Inc.	1232 Whetstone St.	Bucyrus	OH	44820	Andrew Ason	419-562-7987	R	201*	0.9
Burgess-Norton Manufacturing	737 Peyton St.	Geneva	IL	60134	John Carroll	630-232-4100	S	199*	0.9
General Dynamics Armament/Tech	4 LakePointe Plz.	Charlotte	NC	28217	Linda Hudson	703-714-8000	S	198*	1.2
Playcore Inc.	430 Chestnut St.	Chattanooga	TN	37402	Frederic L. Contino	423-756-0015	R	197*	1.1
CompX International Inc.	5430 LBJ Fwy.	Dallas	TX	75240	David A. Bowers	972-448-1400	P	178	1.0
Rev-A-Shelf Company L.L.C.	PO Box 99585	Louisville	KY	40269		502-499-5835	S	173*	1.3
Strattec Security Corp.	3333 W Good Hope	Milwaukee	WI	53209		414-247-3333	P	168	2.2
Sun Hydraulics Corp.	1500 W Univ. Pkwy.	Sarasota	FL	34243	Allen J. Carlson	941-362-1200	P	167	0.7
Hager, C and Sons Hinge Mfg.	PO Box 12300	Saint Louis	MO	63157	August Hager	314-772-4400	R	165*	<0.1
Kaba Ilco Corp.	PO Box 2627	Rocky Mount	NC	27802	Frank Belflower	252-446-3321	R	163*	0.7
Morton Metalcraft Co.	PO Box 729	Welcome	NC	27374	William Morton	336-731-5700	S	161*	1.4
Eastern Inc.	PO Box 460	Naugatuck	CT	06770	Leonard F. Leganza	203-729-2255	P	156	0.7
Midwest Stamping Inc.	3455 Briarfield	Maumee	OH	43537	Ronald L. Thompson	419-724-6970	R	155*	0.6
Deloro Stellite Company Inc.	1201 Eisenhower Dr.	Goshen	IN	46526	Mark Aldridge	574-534-2585	R	153*	1.2
Hurd Corp.	PO Box 548	Upland	IN	46989	Leland Boren	423-787-8800	S	149*	1.1
Bridgewater Interiors L.L.C.	4617 W Fort St.	Detroit	MI	48209	John Barth	313-842-3300	J	147*	0.3
EFCO Corp.	1800 NE Broadway	Des Moines	IA	50313	Chris Fuldnet	515-266-1141	R	144*	1.0
Atek Manufacturing L.L.C.	PO Box 403	Brainerd	MN	56401	Christy Bieber Orris	218-829-1481	R	140*	0.3
Latrobe Specialty Steel Co.	PO Box 31	Latrobe	PA	15650	Hans J. Sack	724-537-7711	R	130*	0.8
A and B Process Systems Corp.	PO Box 86	Stratford	WI	54484	A. J. Hilgemann	715-687-4332	R	128*	0.2
Crotty Corp.	854 E Chicago Rd.	Quincy	MI	49082	Keith Boyle	517-639-8787	R	127*	0.3
Chestnut Group Inc.	115 Bloomingdale	Wayne	PA	19087	Park Blatchford	610-688-3300	R	122*	0.4
Manufacturers Industrial Group	PO Box 1048	Lexington	TN	38351		731-967-0001	R	120*	0.9

Source: Ward's Business Directory of U.S. Private and Public Companies, Volumes 1 and 2, 2008. The company type code used is as follows: P - Public, R - Private, S - Subsidiary, D - Division, J - Joint Venture, A - Affiliate, G - Group. Sales are in millions of dollars, employees are in thousands. An asterisk (*) indicates an estimated sales volume. The symbol < stands for 'less than'. Company names and addresses are truncated, in some cases, to fit into the available space.

MATERIALS CONSUMED

Material	Quantity	Delivered Cost ($ million)
Metal hardware (inc, hinges, handles, locks, casters, etc.)	(X)	326.6
Metal bolts, nuts, screws, and other screw machine products	(X)	128.0
Metal stampings	(X)	241.8
All other fabricated metal products (excluding forgings)	(X)	243.5
Iron and steel castings (rough and semifinished)	(X)	62.5
Aluminum and aluminum-base alloy castings (rough and semifinished)	(X)	52.3
Copper and copper-base alloy castings (rough and semifinished)	(X)	17.7
Zinc and zinc-base alloy castings (rough and semifinished)	(X)	88.9
All other nonferrous castings (rough and semifinished)	(X)	10.3
Forgings	(X)	26.0
Steel bars, bar shapes, and plates (exc. castings, forgings, fabr. metal products)	(X)	60.7
Steel sheet, strip, and tin mill products	(X)	292.5
Steel wire and wire products	(X)	40.0
All other steel shapes and forms (exc. castings, forgings, fabr. metal products)	(X)	77.9
Copper and copper-base alloy rod, bar, and mechanical wire	(X)	20.4
Copper and copper-base alloy sheet, strip, and plate	(X)	10.3
All other copper and copper-base alloy shapes and forms (exc. castings, forgings, fabr. metal products)	(X)	10.4
Aluminum and aluminum-base alloy sheet, plate, foil, and welded tubing	(X)	16.2
Aluminum and aluminum-base alloy extruded shapes (rod, bar, pipe, tube, etc.)	(X)	22.9
Other aluminum and aluminum-base alloy shapes and forms (exc. castings, forgings, fabr. metal products)	(X)	54.7
Zinc and zinc-base alloy shapes and forms (exc. castings, forgings, fabr. metal products)	(X)	24.7
All other nonferrous shapes and forms (exc. castings, forgings, fabr. metal products)	(X)	9.9
Metal powders	(X)	31.5
Fabricated rubber products (exc. tires, tubes, hoses, belting, and gaskets)	(X)	(D)
Plastics products, incl. film, sheet, rod, tube, and fabricated shapes	(X)	127.1
All other rubber and miscellaneous plastics products	(X)	14.5
Paperboard containers, boxes, and corrugated paperboard	(X)	100.3
Plastics resins consumed in the form of granules, pellets, etc.	(X)	43.0
Glass and glass products	(X)	(D)
Electric motors, generators, and parts	(X)	162.6
All other materials, components, parts, containers, and supplies	(X)	822.6
Materials, ingredients, containers, and supplies, nsk	(X)	489.9

Source: 2002 *Economic Census*. Explanation of symbols used: (D): Withheld to avoid disclosure of competitive data; na: Not available; (S): Withheld because statistical norms were not met; (X): Not applicable; (Z): Less than half the unit shown; nec: Not elsewhere classified; nsk: Not specified by kind; - : zero; p : 10-19 percent estimated; q : 20-29 percent estimated.

PRODUCT SHARE DETAILS

Product or Product Class Shipments	Mil. $	Product or Product Class Shipments	Mil. $
HARDWARE	9,632.2	Hangers, tracks, and related builders' hardware items (except sliding and folding door hardware), residential and commercial	303.0
Furniture hardware, except cabinet hardware	**718.0**	Sliding and folding door hardware, residential and commercial	107.7
Rotating and tilting furniture fixtures and bases	329.3	Door holders and stops (overhead, surface, and concealed), floor and wall mounted	44.7
Furniture hardware, including drawer pulls and handles, etc. (except furniture and drawer slides)	154.2	Rim locks and all other locking devices	38.7
Furniture and drawer slides	(D)	Other builders' hardware	305.0
Furniture casters	101.6	Padlocks and locksets	1,109.7
Other floor protective furniture hardware devices	(D)	Pin tumbler padlocks	183.9
Builders' hardware	**4,762.4**	All other padlocks	64.9
Bored doorlocks, locksets, and lock trim, cylindrical and tubular (except deadlocks)	790.2	Mortised doorlocks, locksets, and lock trim (except mortised deadlocks)	120.6
Architectural trim and other miscellaneous closet hardware	969.1	Tubular and mortised deadlocks	159.3
All other miscellaneous architectural trim (sold separately), including protection plates, push plates, pulls, push-pull bars, lock trim, etc.	128.2	Fabricated metal safe and vault locks	109.2
Key blanks	93.8	Electronically or electrically operated doorlocks, locksets, and lock trim	179.1
Exit devices, including fire exit hardware	381.3	All other doorlocks, locksets, and lock trim types	292.7
Miscellaneous closet hardware, including shelving other than wire and decorative shelving	47.2	Builders' hardware, nsk	13.4
Surface applied door controls, closers, and checking devices	265.5	**Motor vehicle hardware (lock units, door and window handles, window regulators, hinges, license plate brackets, etc.)**	**2,628.1**
Concealed (overhead, in the door, on the floor) door controls, closers, and checking devices	25.0	**Other transportation equipment hardware (except motor vehicle)**	**335.8**
Electromechanical-pneumatic door controls, closers, and checking devices with hold-open mechanism released by integral or remote smoke detector	28.2	Other transportation equipment hardware (including aircraft and railroad car hardware)	334.0
Screen and storm door hardware, including pneumatic and hydraulic closers and window locks	410.4	Marine hardware	110.9
Hinges and cabinet hardware	670.6	Aircraft hardware	128.9
Butt hinges, including spring hinges, 3 and 1/2 in. by 3 and 1/2 in. or less (excluding cabinet hinges)	41.7	Other transportation equipment hardware, including railroad car hardware	94.2
Butt hinges, including spring hinges, more than 3 and 1/2 in. by 3 and 1/2 in., either dimension (excluding cabinet hinges)	157.5	Other transportation equipment hardware (except motor vehicle), nsk	1.8
Other hinges, including spring hinges (excluding cabinet hinges)	66.3	**All other miscellaneous hardware**	**568.4**
Cabinet hinges	39.9	Casket and casket shell hardware	46.0
Cabinet locks	31.3	Casters and wheels for dollies and industrial handtrucks	170.7
Cabinet knobs, pulls, and catches	88.6	Refrigerator and stove hardware	55.4
Other cabinet hardware, including drawer slides, etc.	245.4	Pulleys, metal (except power transmission), and block and tackle	62.8
Other builders' hardware	799.0	Other hardware, including saddlery and harness hardware (excluding drapery hardware)	233.6
		Hardware, nsk, total	**619.5**

Source: 2002 *Economic Census*. The values are product shipments in millions of dollars for 2002. Total product shipments may be lower or higher than industry shipments. See Introduction for a full discussion. Values of indented subcategories are summed in the main heading(s). The symbol (D) appears when data are withheld to prevent disclosure of competitive information. The abbreviation nsk stands for 'not specified by kind' and nec for 'not elsewhere classified'. A dash (-) means zero.

INPUTS AND OUTPUTS FOR HARDWARE MANUFACTURING

Economic Sector or Industry Providing Inputs	%	Sector	Economic Sector or Industry Buying Outputs	%	Sector
Compensation of employees	27.8		Exports of goods & services	13.9	Cap Inv
Iron & steel mills & ferroalloys	5.4	Manufg.	Retail trade	8.6	Trade
Hardware	4.2	Manufg.	Residential permanent site structures	7.4	Construct.
Crowns & closures & metal stamping	4.0	Manufg.	Light truck & utility vehicles	5.1	Manufg.
Wholesale trade	3.6	Trade	Food services & drinking places	3.9	Services
Management of companies & enterprises	2.5	Services	Aircraft engine & engine parts	3.6	Manufg.
Nonferrous metal foundries	2.1	Manufg.	Automobiles	3.5	Manufg.
Motors & generators	1.8	Manufg.	Hardware	3.2	Manufg.
Turned products & screws, nuts, & bolts	1.7	Manufg.	Turned products & screws, nuts, & bolts	3.0	Manufg.
Paperboard containers	1.2	Manufg.	Wood windows & doors & millwork	2.9	Manufg.
Securities, commodity contracts, investments	1.2	Fin/R.E.	Residential structures, nec	2.4	Construct.
Advertising & related services	1.0	Services	Owner-occupied dwellings	2.4	
Machine shops	1.0	Manufg.	Personal consumption expenditures	2.3	
Aluminum products from purchased aluminum	0.9	Manufg.	Ornamental & architectural metal products	1.9	Manufg.
Truck transportation	0.8	Util.	Aircraft parts & auxiliary equipment, nec	1.8	Manufg.
Plastics packaging materials, film & sheet	0.8	Manufg.	Upholstered household furniture	1.7	Manufg.
Plastics products, nec	0.8	Manufg.	Toilet preparations	1.6	Manufg.
Lessors of nonfinancial assets	0.8	Fin/R.E.	Nonresidential structures, nec	1.6	Construct.
Steel products from purchased steel	0.8	Manufg.	Custom architectural woodwork & millwork	1.6	Manufg.
Monetary authorities/depository credit intermediation	0.8	Fin/R.E.	Private fixed investment	1.6	
Semiconductors & related devices	0.7	Manufg.	Aircraft	1.5	Manufg.
Power generation & supply	0.7	Util.	Telecommunications	1.2	Services
Printed circuit assemblies (electronic assemblies)	0.7	Manufg.	Maintenance/repair of nonresidential structures	1.1	Construct.
Ferrous metal foundries	0.7	Manufg.	Boat building	1.1	Manufg.
Professional, scientific, technical services, nec	0.6	Services	General Federal government services, defense	1.0	Fed Govt
Coating, engraving, heat treating & allied activities	0.6	Manufg.	Rubber & plastics hose & belting	1.0	Manufg.
Noncomparable imports	0.5	Foreign	Signs	1.0	Manufg.

Continued on next page.

INPUTS AND OUTPUTS FOR HARDWARE MANUFACTURING - Continued

Economic Sector or Industry Providing Inputs	%	Sector	Economic Sector or Industry Buying Outputs	%	Sector
Abrasive products	0.5	Manufg.	Motor vehicle parts	1.0	Manufg.
Real estate	0.5	Fin/R.E.	Community food, housing, relief, & rehabilitation	0.9	Services
Taxes on production & imports, less subsidies	0.5		Automotive repair & maintenance, ex. car washes	0.8	Services
Nonferrous metal (ex. copper & aluminum) processing	0.5	Manufg.	Wood kitchen cabinets & countertops	0.8	Manufg.
Food services & drinking places	0.5	Services	Nonupholstered wood household furniture	0.7	Manufg.
Copper rolling, drawing, extruding, & alloying	0.5	Manufg.	Other S/L govt. enterprises	0.6	S/L Govt
Legal services	0.5	Services	AC, refrigeration, and warm air heating equipment	0.6	Manufg.
Plastics materials & resins	0.5	Manufg.	Manufacturing, nec	0.6	Manufg.
Cutting tools & machine tool accessories	0.4	Manufg.	Natural gas distribution	0.6	Util.
Data processing, hosting, & related services	0.4	Services	Wholesale trade	0.5	Trade
Architectural, engineering, & related services	0.4	Services	Plastics products, nec	0.5	Manufg.
Specialized design services	0.4	Services	Engine equipment, nec	0.5	Manufg.
Business support services	0.4	Services	Computer terminals & peripherals	0.4	Manufg.
Employment services	0.3	Services	Commercial & health care structures	0.4	Construct.
Telecommunications	0.3	Services	Manufactured homes & mobile homes	0.4	Manufg.
Communication & energy wires & cables	0.3	Manufg.	Maintenance/repair of residential structures	0.4	Construct.
Forging, stamping, & sintering, nec	0.3	Manufg.	Leather products, nec	0.4	Manufg.
Hotels & motels, including casino hotels	0.3	Services	Fabricated metals, nec	0.3	Manufg.
Management, scientific, & technical consulting	0.3	Services	Prefabricated wood buildings	0.3	Manufg.
Accounting, tax preparation, bookkeeping, & payroll	0.3	Services	Semiconductors & related devices	0.3	Manufg.
Services to buildings & dwellings	0.3	Services	Heavy duty trucks	0.3	Manufg.
Maintenance/repair of nonresidential structures	0.3	Construct.	Fishing	0.3	Agric.
Metal cans, boxes, & other containers (light gauge)	0.2	Manufg.	Truck transportation	0.3	Util.
Natural gas distribution	0.2	Util.	Engineered wood members & trusses	0.3	Manufg.
Air transportation	0.2	Util.	Scientific research & development services	0.3	Services
Automotive equipment rental & leasing	0.2	Fin/R.E.	Machine shops	0.3	Manufg.
Warehousing & storage	0.2	Util.	Showcases, partitions, shelving, and lockers	0.2	Manufg.
Alumina refining & primary aluminum production	0.2	Manufg.	Civic, social, & professional organizations	0.2	Services
Retail trade	0.2	Trade	Motor vehicle bodies	0.2	Manufg.
Fabricated metals, nec	0.2	Manufg.	Architectural, engineering, & related services	0.2	Services
Paints & coatings	0.2	Manufg.	Medical & diagnostic labs & outpatient services	0.2	Services
Support services, nec	0.2	Services	Services to buildings & dwellings	0.2	Services
Scientific research & development services	0.2	Services	Individual & family services	0.2	Services
Automotive repair & maintenance, ex. car washes	0.2	Services	Specialized design services	0.2	Services
Plate work & fabricated structural products	0.2	Manufg.	S/L govt. passenger transit	0.2	S/L Govt
Investigation & security services	0.2	Services	Waste management & remediation services	0.2	Services
Commercial & industrial equipment repair/maintenance	0.1	Services	Construction machinery	0.2	Manufg.
Unlaminated plastics profile shapes	0.1	Manufg.	Institutional furniture	0.2	Manufg.
Ball & roller bearings	0.1	Manufg.	Rail transportation	0.1	Util.
Other computer related services, including facilities	0.1	Services	General S/L govt. services	0.1	S/L Govt
Handtools	0.1	Manufg.	Insurance carriers	0.1	Fin/R.E.
Motor vehicle parts	0.1	Manufg.	Truck trailers	0.1	Manufg.
Valve & fittings other than plumbing	0.1	Manufg.	Warehousing & storage	0.1	Util.
Nondepository credit intermediation activities	0.1	Fin/R.E.	Change in private inventories	0.1	In House
Rail transportation	0.1	Util.	Securities, commodity contracts, investments	0.1	Fin/R.E.
Commercial & industrial machinery rental & leasing	0.1	Fin/R.E.			
Custom roll forming	0.1	Manufg.			
Relay & industrial controls	0.1	Manufg.			
Paperboard mills	0.1	Manufg.			

Source: Benchmark Input-Output Accounts for the U.S. Economy, 2002, U.S. Department of Commerce, Washington, D.C., January 2008. The abbreviation nec stands for 'not elsewhere classified'.

OCCUPATIONS EMPLOYED BY HARDWARE MANUFACTURING

Occupation	% of Total 2006	Change to 2016	Occupation	% of Total 2006	Change to 2016
Team assemblers	13.6	-29.4	Helpers--Production workers	1.8	-29.4
Cutting, punching, & press machine operators	6.4	-36.5	Packaging & filling machine operators & tenders	1.7	-36.5
First-line supervisors/managers of production workers	3.7	-29.4	Multiple machine tool operators & tenders	1.7	-22.3
Machinists	3.1	-25.9	Customer service representatives	1.7	-22.3
Welders, cutters, solderers, & brazers	3.1	-24.9	Milling & planing machine operators & tenders	1.5	-36.5
Grinding, lapping, polishing machine tool operators	2.7	-31.5	Coating, painting, & spraying machine operators	1.5	-32.9
Assemblers & fabricators, nec	2.6	-36.5	Drilling & boring machine tool operators	1.5	-36.5
Shipping, receiving, & traffic clerks	2.5	-32.1	Maintenance & repair workers, general	1.4	-29.4
Packers & packagers, hand	2.4	-43.5	Industrial truck & tractor operators	1.3	-36.5
Laborers & freight, stock, & material movers, hand	2.4	-36.5	General & operations managers	1.3	-36.5
Computer-controlled machine tool operators	2.3	-22.3	Bookkeeping, accounting, & auditing clerks	1.2	-29.4
Sales reps, wholesale & manufacturing, exc tech	2.2	-29.4	Office clerks, general	1.1	-30.4
Structural metal fabricators & fitters	2.2	-29.4	Industrial production managers	1.1	-29.4
Tool & die makers	2.1	-25.9	Molding, coremaking, & casting machine operators	1.0	-36.5
Inspectors, testers, sorters, samplers, & weighers	1.9	-33.4			

Source: Industry-Occupation Matrix, Bureau of Labor Statistics, December 4, 2007. These data are reported based on 4-digit NAICS categories but have been matched to corresponding 6-digit NAICS industry codes. The change reported for each occupation to the year 2016 is a percent of growth or decline as estimated by the Bureau of Labor Statistics. The abbreviation nec stands for 'not elsewhere classified'.

LOCATION BY STATE AND REGIONAL CONCENTRATION

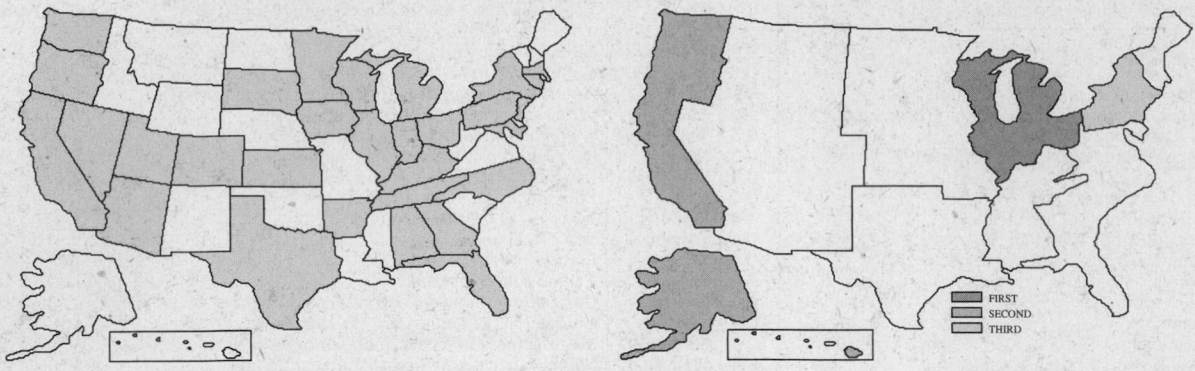

FIRST
SECOND
THIRD

INDUSTRY DATA BY STATE

State	Establish-ments	Shipments			Employment				Cost as % of Shipments	Investment per Employee ($)
		Total ($ mil)	% of U.S.	Per Establ.	Total Number	% of U.S.	Per Establ.	Wages ($/hour)		
Indiana	36	932.0	9.1	25,888.9	4,561	7.6	127	15.28	29.8	4,698
Ohio	55	925.0	9.0	16,818.4	4,120	6.9	75	17.15	38.2	4,769
Illinois	69	883.8	8.6	12,808.6	5,399	9.0	78	16.83	36.0	4,173
Tennessee	18	875.7	8.6	48,652.6	3,349	5.6	186	15.16	63.8	4,277
Michigan	56	765.0	7.5	13,660.1	6,802	11.3	121	13.98	47.6	3,048
California	134	742.1	7.3	5,537.8	4,876	8.1	36	13.06	34.2	5,486
Wisconsin	26	566.8	5.5	21,800.3	2,161	3.6	83	19.41	37.8	5,366
Connecticut	35	425.1	4.2	12,146.1	2,331	3.9	67	15.88	37.9	5,876
Pennsylvania	32	405.2	4.0	12,663.3	2,498	4.2	78	15.39	35.3	10,287
New York	48	394.1	3.9	8,211.3	2,137	3.6	45	15.28	38.4	2,897
North Carolina	27	389.8	3.8	14,436.7	3,018	5.0	112	12.43	38.9	2,754
Kentucky	15	378.2	3.7	25,211.6	2,079	3.5	139	12.91	52.8	5,212
Georgia	19	252.9	2.5	13,309.5	1,649	2.7	87	11.59	64.1	3,399
Texas	42	213.4	2.1	5,081.2	1,240	2.1	30	12.95	46.9	4,331
Minnesota	19	183.3	1.8	9,648.9	1,231	2.1	65	13.18	31.3	4,745
Colorado	10	159.3	1.6	15,929.4	1,045	1.7	105	12.39	57.0	1,233
Alabama	13	139.0	1.4	10,688.8	963	1.6	74	14.13	45.6	2,407
Arizona	20	137.5	1.3	6,873.4	486	0.8	24	14.09	51.7	6,628
Massachusetts	19	112.7	1.1	5,930.6	870	1.4	46	12.63	39.1	4,163
Florida	35	103.8	1.0	2,964.5	1,124	1.9	32	9.64	34.1	1,845
Iowa	10	99.5	1.0	9,952.9	720	1.2	72	11.53	57.8	3,161
Oregon	10	85.7	0.8	8,565.1	412	0.7	41	14.78	49.9	5,544
Arkansas	7	66.0	0.6	9,422.3	734	1.2	105	9.90	40.1	285
South Dakota	6	54.1	0.5	9,018.3	378	0.6	63	12.48	51.0	1,529
New Jersey	17	52.9	0.5	3,108.9	306	0.5	18	14.87	24.5	2,549
Washington	19	41.6	0.4	2,189.9	266	0.4	14	15.44	36.9	13,049
Maryland	6	36.8	0.4	6,131.2	330	0.5	55	13.43	21.5	2,515
Nevada	5	31.6	0.3	6,324.0	147	0.2	29	13.34	30.3	3,129
Rhode Island	6	18.4	0.2	3,068.5	139	0.2	23	10.92	21.4	4,353
Utah	6	16.4	0.2	2,730.5	120	0.2	20	11.50	47.8	2,100
Kansas	5	11.4	0.1	2,275.0	101	0.2	20	11.06	40.9	3,554

Source: 2002 *Economic Census*. The states are in descending order of shipments or establishments (if shipment data are missing for the majority). The symbol (D) appears when data are withheld to prevent disclosure of competitive information. States marked with (D) are sorted by number of establishments. A dash (-) indicates that the data element cannot be calculated. Data may not show all states active in the NAICS category. All data available at the time of publication are shown.

NAICS 33261M - SPRING AND WIRE PRODUCT MANUFACTURING*

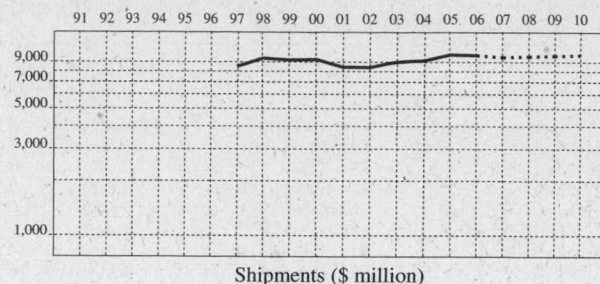

Shipments ($ million)

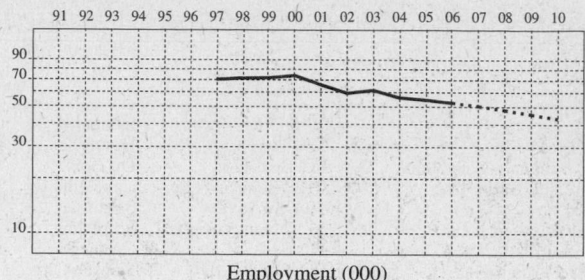

Employment (000)

GENERAL STATISTICS

Year	Companies	Establishments Total	Establishments with 20 or more employees	Employment Total (000)	Employment Production Workers (000)	Employment Hours (Mil)	Compensation Payroll ($ mil)	Compensation Wages ($/hr)	Production Cost of Materials	Production Value Added by Manufacture	Production Value of Shipments	Capital Invest.
1997	1,662	1,833	732	70.4	54.7	107.6	1,905.0	11.57	3,975.5	4,542.5	8,499.8	341.3
1998		1,888	744	71.5	55.6	112.1	2,067.4	12.28	4,364.0	5,079.2	9,427.5	346.4
1999		1,877	741	71.8	56.9	112.8	2,071.3	12.19	4,106.9	5,182.9	9,223.1	337.4
2000		1,839	762	73.9	58.2	115.0	2,161.7	12.45	4,213.4	5,149.0	9,286.4	297.9
2001		1,775	730	65.8	51.7	101.3	1,958.6	12.69	3,792.3	4,584.4	8,440.2	270.6
2002	1,867	2,038	650	59.2	46.4	92.0	1,874.1	13.52	3,673.2	4,745.1	8,421.0	238.4
2003		1,751	661	61.5	48.4	98.0	2,008.3	13.57	4,058.7	4,940.0	9,006.8	223.3
2004		1,788	679	56.1	42.7	90.7	1,923.8	13.73	4,392.5	4,836.1	9,165.7	208.2
2005		1,707	653	54.6	42.2	88.5	1,979.0	14.72	4,966.3	4,977.8	9,879.1	224.6
2006		1,762P	641P	52.6	41.0	86.3	1,989.0	15.15	5,145.8	4,696.4	9,801.7	295.3
2007		1,747P	628P	50.4P	39.0P	82.8P	1,955.7P	15.23P	5,025.7P	4,586.8P	9,572.9P	206.1P
2008		1,733P	614P	48.0P	37.1P	79.6P	1,948.7P	15.60P	5,069.4P	4,626.7P	9,656.1P	192.9P
2009		1,719P	601P	45.5P	35.1P	76.4P	1,941.8P	15.97P	5,113.1P	4,666.5P	9,739.4P	179.8P
2010		1,704P	588P	43.1P	33.2P	73.2P	1,934.8P	16.34P	5,156.8P	4,706.4P	9,822.6P	166.6P

Sources: 1997 and 2002 Economic Census; other years, up to 2006, are from Annual Survey of Manufactures. Establishment counts for non-Census years are from County Business Patterns; 1997 and 2002 values are from the 1997 and 2002 censuses, respectively. 'P's show projections by the editors.

INDICES OF CHANGE

Year	Companies	Establishments Total	Establishments with 20 or more employees	Employment Total (000)	Employment Production Workers (000)	Employment Hours (Mil)	Compensation Payroll ($ mil)	Compensation Wages ($/hr)	Production Cost of Materials	Production Value Added by Manufacture	Production Value of Shipments	Capital Invest.
1997	89	90	113	119	118	117	102	86	108	96	101	143
1998		93	114	121	120	122	110	91	119	107	112	145
1999		92	114	121	123	123	111	90	112	109	110	142
2000		90	117	125	125	125	115	92	115	109	110	125
2001		87	112	111	111	110	105	94	103	97	100	114
2002	100	100	100	100	100	100	100	100	100	100	100	100
2003		86	102	104	104	107	107	100	110	104	107	94
2004		88	104	95	92	99	103	102	120	102	109	87
2005		84	100	92	91	96	106	109	135	105	117	94
2006		86P	99P	89	88	94	106	112	140	99	116	124
2007		86P	97P	85P	84P	90P	104P	113P	137P	97P	114P	86P
2008		85P	95P	81P	80P	87P	104P	115P	138P	98P	115P	81P
2009		84P	93P	77P	76P	83P	104P	118P	139P	98P	116P	75P
2010		84P	91P	73P	72P	80P	103P	121P	140P	99P	117P	70P

Sources: Same as General Statistics. Values reflect change from the base year, 2002. Values above 100 mean greater than 2002, values below 100 mean less than 2002, and the values of 100 in other years means the same as 2002. 'P's show projections by the editors.

SELECTED RATIOS

For 2002	Avg. of All Manufact.	Analyzed Industry	Index	For 2002	Avg. of All Manufact.	Analyzed Industry	Index
Employees per Establishment	42	29	69	Value Added per Production Worker	182,367	102,265	56
Payroll per Establishment	1,639,184	919,578	56	Cost per Establishment	5,769,015	1,802,355	31
Payroll per Employee	39,053	31,657	81	Cost per Employee	137,446	62,047	45
Production Workers per Establishment	30	23	77	Cost per Production Worker	195,506	79,164	40
Wages per Establishment	694,845	610,324	88	Shipments per Establishment	11,158,348	4,131,992	37
Wages per Production Worker	23,548	26,807	114	Shipments per Employee	265,847	142,247	54
Hours per Production Worker	1,980	1,983	100	Shipments per Production Worker	378,144	181,487	48
Wages per Hour	11.89	13.52	114	Investment per Establishment	361,338	116,977	32
Value Added per Establishment	5,381,325	2,328,312	43	Investment per Employee	8,609	4,027	47
Value Added per Employee	128,210	80,154	63	Investment per Production Worker	12,245	5,138	42

Sources: Same as General Statistics. The 'Average of All Manufacturing' column represents the average of all manufacturing industries reported for the most recent complete year available. The Index shows the relationship between the Average and the Analyzed Industry. For example, 100 means that they are equal; 500 that the Analyzed Industry is five times the average; 50 means that the Analyzed Industry is half the national average. The abbreviation 'na' is used to show that data are 'not available'. Ratios shown for 2002, the last complete census year.

*Equivalent to Federal Government NAICS 332611, 332612, 332618.

LEADING COMPANIES   Number shown: **75**   Total sales ($ mil): **71,409**   Total employment (000): **154.7**

Company Name	Address				CEO Name	Phone	Co. Type	Sales ($ mil)	Empl. (000)
Praxair Inc.	39 Old Ridgebury	Danbury	CT	06810	Stephen F. Angel	716-879-4077	P	9,402	28.0
Fortune Brands Inc.	520 Lake Cook Rd.	Deerfield	IL	60015	Bruce A. Carbonari	847-484-4400	P	8,563	31.0
Triangle Suspension Systems	PO Box 425	Du Bois	PA	15801	Greg Maffia	814-375-7211	R	7,000*	0.2
Owl Wire and Cable Inc.	3127 Seneca Tpke.	Canastota	NY	13032	Philip Kemper	315-697-2011	R	7,000*	0.2
Kerite Co.	49 Day Street	Seymour	CT	06483	John Degray	203-888-2591	R	7,000*	<0.1
Quest Technology L.P.	6750 Nancy Ridge	San Diego	CA	92121	Stan Zalkind	858-558-1996	S	4,449*	1.4
Leggett and Platt Inc.	PO Box 757	Carthage	MO	64836		417-358-8131	P	4,306	24.0
Hallmark Cards Inc.	PO Box 419034	Kansas City	MO	64141		816-274-5111	R	4,100*	16.0
Heico Companies L.L.C.	70 W Madison St.	Chicago	IL	60602	M. E. Heisley, Sr.	312-419-8220	R	2,500	11.0
Bombardier Transport. Holdings	1501 Lebanon Ch.	Pittsburgh	PA	15236	Raymond Betler	412-655-5700	R	2,037*	0.9
Caribe General Electric Prods	PO Box 41306	San Juan	PR	00940		787-774-0202	R	1,558*	3.0
United States Surgical Corp.	150 Glover Ave.	Norwalk	CT	06850	Allen Panzer	203-845-1000	S	1,172*	5.8
Euramax International Inc.	5445 Triangle Pky.	Norcross	GA	30092	J. David Smith	770-449-7066	R	1,068	3.2
Bekaert Corp.	3200 W Market St.	Akron	OH	44333		330-867-3325	R	867*	1.6
Barden Corp.	PO Box 2449	Danbury	CT	06813	John McCloskey	203-744-2211	R	776*	0.3
LTV Copperweld	4 Gateway Ctr.	Pittsburgh	PA	15222	Dennis McGlone	412-263-3200	R	732*	3.0
Charter Manufacturing Company	PO Box 217	Thiensville	WI	53092		262-243-4700	R	720*	<0.1
U.S. Bronze Powders Inc.	PO Box 31	Flemington	NJ	08822		908-782-5454	R	574*	0.3
Haldex Garphyttan Corp.	4404 Nimitz Pkwy.	South Bend	IN	46628	Kirk Manning	574-232-8800	D	525*	0.4
Starck, H C Inc.	45 Industrial Pl.	Nwtn Highland	MA	02461	Olaff Schmidtpak	617-630-5880	D	522*	0.4
Suncoast Post-Tension L.P.	654 N Sam Houston	Houston	TX	77060		281-445-8886	R	464*	0.2
Insteel Industries Inc.	1373 Boggs Dr.	Mount Airy	NC	27030	Howard O. Woltz Jr.	336-786-2141	P	298	0.6
Davis Wire Corp.	PO Box 2145	Baldwin Park	CA	91706	Michael Heisley	626-969-7656	R	277*	0.2
Home Products International	4501 W 47th St.	Chicago	IL	60632		773-890-1010	R	234*	1.3
Pyrotek Inc.	9503 E Montgomery	Spokane	WA	99206	Allan Roy	509-926-6212	R	225*	1.5
Adrian Steel Co.	906 James Street	Adrian	MI	49221		517-265-6194	R	196*	<0.1
Insteel Wire Products Co.	1373 Boggs Dr.	Mount Airy	NC	27030	H.O. Woltz	336-786-2141	D	189*	0.7
Kern-Liebers USA Inc.	PO Box 396	Holland	OH	43528	Lothar Bauerle	419-865-2437	R	178*	<0.1
Phelps Dodge Magnet Wire Co.	806 Douglas Rd.	Coral Gables	FL	33134	Don Disque	305-648-8000	S	170*	1.3
Draka USA Corp.	9 Forge Park	Franklin	MA	02038	Joe Dixon	508-520-1200	S	170*	0.9
Central Wire Industries Ltd.	370 Franklin Tpke.	Mahwah	NJ	07430	Thierry Cremailh	201-529-0900	R	167*	<0.1
Dynamic Materials Corp.	5405 Spine Rd.	Boulder	CO	80301	Yvon P. Cariou	303-665-5700	P	165	0.4
Deloro Stellite Company Inc.	1201 Eisenhower Dr.	Goshen	IN	46526	Mark Aldridge	574-534-2585	R	153*	1.2
American Spring Wire Corp.	PO Box 46510	Cleveland	OH	44146		216-292-4620	R	153*	0.2
Tempel Steel Co.	5500 N Wolcott	Chicago	IL	60640	Vincent Buonanno	773-250-8000	R	152*	<0.1
Duo-Fast Corp.	2400 Galvin Dr.	Elgin	IL	60123		847-634-1900	S	136*	0.9
Enterprise Products Inc.	6846 Suva St.	Bell Gardens	CA	90201	Ron Spicer	562-927-2515	R	134*	0.2
South Bay Cable	PO Box 67	Idyllwild	CA	92549		951-659-2183	R	130*	1.3
Chestnut Group Inc.	115 Bloomingdale	Wayne	PA	19087	Park Blatchford	610-688-3300	R	122*	0.4
Nexans USA Inc.	PO Box 60339	Charlotte	NC	28260	Kevin Cyr	717-354-6200	R	121*	0.5
Schmidt Group Inc.	PO Box 25189	Greenville	SC	29616	Carl V. Schmidt	864-288-9460	R	113*	<0.1
Hoover Precision Products Inc.	PO Box 899	Cumming	GA	30028	Takanori Kondo	770-889-9223	R	113*	0.2
National-Standard Co.	1631 Lake St.	Niles	MI	49120	Frank Hagan	616-683-8100	S	110*	0.6
Clarion Sintered Metals Inc.	PO Box S	Ridgway	PA	15853	Howard Peterson	814-773-3124	R	106*	0.2
ITW Hobart Brothers Co.	101 Trade Sq. E	Troy	OH	45373		937-332-4000	S	102*	0.5
Bridon-American Corp.	PO Box 6000	Wilkes Barre	PA	18773	John Churchfield	570-822-3349	R	101*	0.4
Peterson American Co.	21200 Telegraph Rd.	Southfield	MI	48034	Eric C. Peterson	248-799-5400	R	100*	1.0
Taubensee Steel and Wire Co.	600 Diens Dr.	Wheeling	IL	60090		847-459-5100	R	100*	0.1
Eastern Wholesale Fence Co.	274 Middle Isl. Rd.	Medford	NY	11763	Peter Williams	631-698-0975	R	98*	0.3
Tuthill Transport Technologies	1205 Indu. Prk Dr.	Mount Vernon	MO	65712	Greg Rocque	417-466-2178	S	95*	0.4
Hyson Products	10367 Brecksvil Rd.	Brecksville	OH	44141	Regis Minerd	440-526-5900	D	91*	0.7
Engineered Sinterings/Plastics	140 Commercial St.	Watertown	CT	06795	Alexander Alves	860-274-8877	R	88*	0.2
Carl Stahl Sava Industries	PO Box 30	Riverdale	NJ	07457	Zdenek Fremund	973-835-0882	R	85*	<0.1
Atlantic Teleconnect Inc.	2529 Commerce	North Port	FL	34286	Ric Galberaith		R	84*	<0.1
Capstan Industries Inc.	10 Cushing Dr.	Wrentham	MA	02093	Chris Doughty	508-384-3100	R	84*	0.2
AFC Cable Systems Inc.	272 Duchaine Blvd.	New Bedford	MA	02745	Bob Tereira	508-998-1131	S	76*	1.3
BCS Industries, L.L.C.	1195 Harbert Ave.	Memphis	TN	38104	Joseph A. Higdon	901-946-1005	R	75*	0.2
Cambridge International Inc.	PO Box 399	Cambridge	MD	21613	William Colson	410-228-3000	R	74*	0.3
Loos and Company Inc.	PO Box 98	Pomfret	CT	06258	William Loos	860-928-7981	R	71*	0.4
Delta Scientific Corp.	40355 Delta Ln.	Palmdale	CA	93551	Harry D. Dickinson	661-575-1100	R	69*	0.3
Keystone Powdered Metal Co.	251 State St.	Saint Marys	PA	15857		814-781-1591	R	68*	0.5
Standard Steel Specialty Co.	PO Box 20	Beaver Falls	PA	15010	Robert Conley	724-846-7600	S	67*	0.3
Phifer Inc.	PO Box 1700	Tuscaloosa	AL	35403	Beverly Phifer	205-345-2120	R	66*	0.9
New York Wire Co.	PO Box 866	Mount Wolf	PA	17347	Barry Douglas	717-266-5626	R	65*	0.5
Mid-West Spring and Stamping	1404 Joliet Rd., C	Romeoville	IL	60446	Michael B. Curran		R	62*	0.5
Contours Ltd.	PO Box 608	Orrville	OH	44667		330-683-5060	R	61*	0.2
Elberta Crate and Box Co.	PO Box 760	Bainbridge	GA	39818	Thomas Simmons	229-246-2266	R	57*	0.7
Pegasus Manufacturing Inc.	422 Timber Ridge	Middletown	CT	06457		860-635-8811	R	57*	0.2
National Nail Corp.	PO Box 2434	Grand Rapids	MI	49501	Scott Baker	616-538-8000	R	56*	0.2
Tokusen USA Inc.	PO Box 1150	Conway	AR	72033	Ken Nagai	501-327-6800	R	54*	0.3
Hamrock Inc.	12521 Los Nietos Rd	Santa Fe Spgs	CA	90670	Stephen Hamrock	562-944-0255	R	52*	0.3
I. Schumann and Co.	22500 Alexander	Bedford	OH	44146	Michael Schumann	440-439-2300	R	52*	0.2
Horton Fan Sysems Inc.	201 W Carmel Dr.	Carmel	IN	46032		317-249-4001	R	51*	0.1
Rebco Inc.	650 Brandy Camp	Kersey	PA	15846	Kenneth Huey	814-885-8035	R	50*	0.1
Mueller Inc.	1915 Hutchins Ave.	Ballinger	TX	76821	David Davenport	325-365-3555	S	50*	0.2

Source: Ward's Business Directory of U.S. Private and Public Companies, Volumes 1 and 2, 2008. The company type code used is as follows: P - Public, R - Private, S - Subsidiary, D - Division, J - Joint Venture, A - Affiliate, G - Group. Sales are in millions of dollars, employees are in thousands. An asterisk (*) indicates an estimated sales volume. The symbol < stands for 'less than'. Company names and addresses are truncated, in some cases, to fit into the available space.

MATERIALS CONSUMED FOR SPRING (HEAVY GAUGE) MANUFACTURING

Material	Quantity	Delivered Cost ($ million)
Metal bolts, nuts, screws, and other screw machine products	(X)	2.7
Other fabricated metal products (exc. castings and forgings)	(X)	(D)
Castings, rough and semifinished	(X)	(D)
Steel bars and bar shapes (exc. castings, forgings, fabr. metal products)	(X)	44.2
Steel sheet and strip (including tinplate)	(X)	29.4
Steel wire and wire products	(X)	82.3
All other steel shapes and forms (exc. castings, forgings, fabr. metal products)	(X)	8.6
Nonferrous shapes and forms	(X)	(D)
All other materials, components, parts, containers, and supplies	(X)	20.4
Materials, ingredients, containers, and supplies, nsk	(X)	41.0

Source: 2002 Economic Census. Explanation of symbols used: (D): Withheld to avoid disclosure of competitive data; na: Not available; (S): Withheld because statistical norms were not met; (X): Not applicable; (Z): Less than half the unit shown; nec: Not elsewhere classified; nsk: Not specified by kind; - : zero; p : 10-19 percent estimated; q : 20-29 percent estimated.

MATERIALS CONSUMED FOR SPRING (LIGHT GAUGE) MANUFACTURING

Material	Quantity	Delivered Cost ($ million)
Metal bolts, nuts, screws, and other screw machine products	(X)	(D)
Other fabricated metal products (exc. castings and forgings)	(X)	14.7
Castings, rough and semifinished	(X)	1.5
Forgings	(X)	(D)
Steel bars and bar shapes (exc. castings, forgings, fabr. metal products)	(X)	26.5
Steel sheet and strip (including tinplate)	(X)	21.7
Steel wire and wire products	(X)	462.9
All other steel shapes and forms (exc. castings, forgings, fabr. metal products)	(X)	81.1
Nonferrous shapes and forms	(X)	8.1
All other materials, components, parts, containers, and supplies	(X)	74.0
Materials, ingredients, containers, and supplies, nsk	(X)	75.2

Source: 2002 Economic Census. Explanation of symbols used: (D): Withheld to avoid disclosure of competitive data; na: Not available; (S): Withheld because statistical norms were not met; (X): Not applicable; (Z): Less than half the unit shown; nec: Not elsewhere classified; nsk: Not specified by kind; - : zero; p : 10-19 percent estimated; q : 20-29 percent estimated.

MATERIALS CONSUMED FOR FABRICATED WIRE PRODUCT MANUFACTURING NEC

Material	Quantity	Delivered Cost ($ million)
Metal bolts, nuts, screws, and other screw machine products	(X)	14.5
Other fabricated metal products (exc. castings and forgings)	(X)	88.4
Forgings	(X)	9.1
Castings, rough and semifinished	(X)	2.2
Steel bars and bar shapes (exc. castings, forgings, fabr. metal products)	(X)	30.6
Steel sheet and strip (including tinplate)	(X)	57.7
Steel wire and wire products	(X)	596.4
All other steel shapes and forms (exc. castings, forgings, fabr. metal products)	(X)	143.4
Other nonferrous shapes and forms (exc. castings, forgings, fabricated metal products)	(X)	13.6
Plastics products consumed in the form of sheets, rods, etc.	(X)	61.5
All other materials, components, parts, containers, and supplies	(X)	420.6
Materials, ingredients, containers, and supplies, nsk	(X)	725.4

Source: 2002 Economic Census. Explanation of symbols used: (D): Withheld to avoid disclosure of competitive data; na: Not available; (S): Withheld because statistical norms were not met; (X): Not applicable; (Z): Less than half the unit shown; nec: Not elsewhere classified; nsk: Not specified by kind; - : zero; p : 10-19 percent estimated; q : 20-29 percent estimated.

PRODUCT SHARE DETAILS FOR SPRING (HEAVY GAUGE) MANUFACTURING

Product or Product Class Shipments	Mil. $	Product or Product Class Shipments	Mil. $
SPRINGS (HEAVY GAUGE)	676.0	steel springs for shipment to U.S. motor vehicle manufacturers or their suppliers for use in original equipment	15.8
Hot formed steel springs (except wire)	**314.1**	Other hot formed, hot wound, and helical steel springs	77.6
Hot formed, hot wound, helical steel automobile coil springs	180.0	Hot formed hot wound locomotive, railroad car, and other helical steel springs	22.8
Hot formed, hot wound, helical automobile coil steel springs for domestic replacement and shipments for export	37.0	Other hot formed steel springs, including torsion bar springs and leaf springs for tractors, farm equipment, locomotives, etc.	54.8
Hot formed, hot wound, helical automobile coil steel springs for shipment to U.S. motor vehicle manufacturers or their suppliers for use in original equipment	143.0	Hot formed steel springs, except wire, nsk	1.5
		Cold formed steel springs, except wire	**335.3**
		Cold formed steel springs, except wire	334.0
Hot formed steel automotive, truck, bus, trailer, etc., leaf springs	55.0	Cold formed flat springs made of sheet or strip	212.3
Hot formed automotive, truck, bus, trailer, etc., leaf steel springs for domestic replacement and shipments for export	39.2	Cold formed helical suspension steel springs	121.7
		Cold formed steel springs, except wire, nsk	1.3
Hot formed automotive, truck, bus, trailer, etc., leaf		**Springs (heavy gauge), nsk, total**	**26.7**

Source: 2002 *Economic Census*. The values are product shipments in millions of dollars for 2002. Total product shipments may be lower or higher than industry shipments. See Introduction for a full discussion. Values of indented subcategories are summed in the main heading(s). The symbol (D) appears when data are withheld to prevent disclosure of competitive information. The abbreviation nsk stands for 'not specified by kind' and nec for 'not elsewhere classified'. A dash (-) means zero.

PRODUCT SHARE DETAILS FOR SPRING (LIGHT GAUGE) MANUFACTURING

Product or Product Class Shipments	Mil. $	Product or Product Class Shipments	Mil. $
SPRINGS (LIGHT GAUGE)	2,180.5	**Other wire springs**	**1,274.1**
Precision mechanical wire springs	**830.6**	Spring units for box springs, innerspring mattresses, and dual-purpose sleep furniture	688.3
Precision mechanical extension- and torsion-type wire springs	333.6	Other wire springs	578.4
Precision mechanical extension-type wire springs	160.4	Seat and back springs for motor vehicles	97.5
Precision mechanical torsion-type wire springs	173.2	Spring units for upholstered furniture	37.2
Precision mechanical compression-type wire springs	463.6	Other springs for mattresses and bedsprings, upholstery and furniture springs (unassembled)	104.1
Precision mechanical compression-type wire springs, shipped to original equipment manufacturers	396.4	Valve springs	64.2
Other precision mechanical compression-type wire spring shipments	67.3	Other wire springs	275.4
		Other wire springs, nsk	7.4
Precision mechanical wire springs, nsk	33.4	**Springs (light gauge), nsk, total**	**75.8**

Source: 2002 *Economic Census*. The values are product shipments in millions of dollars for 2002. Total product shipments may be lower or higher than industry shipments. See Introduction for a full discussion. Values of indented subcategories are summed in the main heading(s). The symbol (D) appears when data are withheld to prevent disclosure of competitive information. The abbreviation nsk stands for 'not specified by kind' and nec for 'not elsewhere classified'. A dash (-) means zero.

PRODUCT SHARE DETAILS FOR FABRICATED WIRE PRODUCT MANUFACTURING NEC

Product or Product Class Shipments	Mil. $	Product or Product Class Shipments	Mil. $
OTHER FABRICATED WIRE PRODUCTS	5,572.1	fabricated wire products	202.9
Noninsulated ferrous wire rope, cable, forms, and strand, not made in plants that draw wire	**576.4**	Nonferrous nails, brads, tacks, and staples	14.7
		Other fabricated wire products, nec	188.2
Noninsulated ferrous wire rope, cable, forms, and strand, not made in plants that draw wire	567.6	Other fabricated wire products, nsk	10.2
Noninsulated ferrous wire rope, cable, and fabricated wire rope assemblies, not made in plants that draw wire	301.0	**Ferrous wire cloth and other ferrous woven wire products, not made in plants that draw wire**	**222.2**
Noninsulated ferrous wire forms and strand (including strand for prestressed concrete, composite wire strand (except ACSR), and guard rail cable)	266.6	**Nonferrous wire cloth and other nonferrous woven wire products, not made in plants that draw wire**	**64.6**
Noninsulated ferrous wire rope, cable, forms, and strand, nsk	8.8	**Steel fencing and fence gates, not made in plants that draw wire**	**263.0**
Other fabricated wire products, not made in plants that draw wire	**213.0**	**Steel nails, staples, tacks, spikes, and brads, not made in plants that draw wire**	**374.4**
		Other ferrous wire products (except springs), not made in plants that draw wire	**2,709.1**
Nonferrous nails, brads, tacks, and staples and other		**Other fabricated wire products, nsk, total**	**1,149.4**

Source: 2002 *Economic Census*. The values are product shipments in millions of dollars for 2002. Total product shipments may be lower or higher than industry shipments. See Introduction for a full discussion. Values of indented subcategories are summed in the main heading(s). The symbol (D) appears when data are withheld to prevent disclosure of competitive information. The abbreviation nsk stands for 'not specified by kind' and nec for 'not elsewhere classified'. A dash (-) means zero.

INPUTS AND OUTPUTS FOR SPRING AND WIRE PRODUCT MANUFACTURING

Economic Sector or Industry Providing Inputs	%	Sector	Economic Sector or Industry Buying Outputs	%	Sector
Compensation of employees	30.0		Mattresses	11.3	Manufg.
Steel products from purchased steel	16.0	Manufg.	Light truck & utility vehicles	9.9	Manufg.
Iron & steel mills & ferroalloys	6.5	Manufg.	Exports of goods & services	7.7	Cap Inv
Wholesale trade	3.3	Trade	Wholesale trade	4.0	Trade
Management of companies & enterprises	2.9	Services	Basic inorganic chemicals, nec	3.8	Manufg.
Truck transportation	1.4	Util.	Motor vehicle parts	3.6	Manufg.
Springs & wire products	1.2	Manufg.	Retail trade	3.3	Trade
Real estate	1.1	Fin/R.E.	Cattle	3.3	Agric.
Plastics packaging materials, film & sheet	1.1	Manufg.	Nonresidential structures, nec	3.1	Construct.
Securities, commodity contracts, investments	1.0	Fin/R.E.	Management of companies & enterprises	3.0	Services
Power generation & supply	1.0	Util.	Railroad rolling stock	2.6	Manufg.
Advertising & related services	0.8	Services	Architectural, engineering, & related services	2.6	Services
Machine shops	0.7	Manufg.	Automobiles	2.6	Manufg.
Lessors of nonfinancial assets	0.7	Fin/R.E.	Upholstered household furniture	2.4	Manufg.
Monetary authorities/depository credit intermediation	0.7	Fin/R.E.	Automotive repair & maintenance, ex. car washes	2.0	Services
Semiconductors & related devices	0.7	Manufg.	Truck transportation	2.0	Util.
Printed circuit assemblies (electronic assemblies)	0.6	Manufg.	Springs & wire products	1.9	Manufg.
Chemical products & preparations, nec	0.6	Manufg.	Other S/L govt. enterprises	1.6	S/L Govt
Professional, scientific, technical services, nec	0.6	Services	Electromedical & electrotherapeutic apparatus	1.5	Manufg.
Turned products & screws, nuts, & bolts	0.6	Manufg.	Personal consumption expenditures	1.4	
Natural gas distribution	0.5	Util.	Steel products from purchased steel	1.3	Manufg.
Coating, engraving, heat treating & allied activities	0.4	Manufg.	Motor vehicle bodies	1.1	Manufg.
Legal services	0.4	Services	Transit & ground passenger transportation	1.1	Util.
Food services & drinking places	0.4	Services	Gaskets, packing, & sealing devices	1.1	Manufg.
Paperboard containers	0.4	Manufg.	Owner-occupied dwellings	1.0	
Accounting, tax preparation, bookkeeping, & payroll	0.4	Services	Heavy duty trucks	0.8	Manufg.
Architectural, engineering, & related services	0.3	Services	Construction machinery	0.8	Manufg.
Taxes on production & imports, less subsidies	0.3		Turned products & screws, nuts, & bolts	0.7	Manufg.
Data processing, hosting, & related services	0.3	Services	Telecommunications	0.7	Services
Telecommunications	0.3	Services	General S/L govt. services	0.6	S/L Govt
Automotive equipment rental & leasing	0.3	Fin/R.E.	Waste management & remediation services	0.6	Services
Maintenance/repair of nonresidential structures	0.3	Construct.	Commercial & health care structures	0.6	Construct.
Copper, nickel, lead, and zinc	0.3	Mining	Couriers & messengers	0.5	Util.
Services to buildings & dwellings	0.3	Services	Major household appliances, nec	0.5	Manufg.
Gold, silver, & other metal ore	0.3	Mining	Residential structures, nec	0.5	Construct.
Warehousing & storage	0.3	Util.	Plate work & fabricated structural products	0.5	Manufg.
Specialized design services	0.3	Services	Machine shops	0.5	Manufg.
Business support services	0.3	Services	Pipeline transportation	0.5	Util.
Cutting tools & machine tool accessories	0.2	Manufg.	Services to buildings & dwellings	0.4	Services
Hotels & motels, including casino hotels	0.2	Services	Ornamental & architectural metal products	0.4	Manufg.
Employment services	0.2	Services	Residential permanent site structures	0.4	Construct.
Communication & energy wires & cables	0.2	Manufg.	Industrial machinery, nec	0.4	Manufg.
Custom roll forming	0.2	Manufg.	Warehousing & storage	0.4	Util.
Management, scientific, & technical consulting	0.2	Services	Scientific research & development services	0.4	Services
Scientific research & development services	0.2	Services	Computer system design services	0.3	Services
Copper rolling, drawing, extruding, & alloying	0.2	Manufg.	Fabricated metals, nec	0.3	Manufg.
Forging, stamping, & sintering, nec	0.2	Manufg.	Rubber products, nec	0.3	Manufg.
Rail transportation	0.2	Util.	Maintenance/repair of nonresidential structures	0.3	Construct.
Automotive repair & maintenance, ex. car washes	0.2	Services	Community food, housing, relief, & rehabilitation	0.2	Services
Air transportation	0.2	Util.	Manufacturing, nec	0.2	Manufg.
Unlaminated plastics profile shapes	0.2	Manufg.	Crowns & closures & metal stamping	0.2	Manufg.
Commercial & industrial equipment repair/maintenance	0.2	Services	Nonupholstered wood household furniture	0.2	Manufg.
Metal cans, boxes, & other containers (light gauge)	0.2	Manufg.	Food services & drinking places	0.2	Services
Commercial & industrial machinery rental & leasing	0.2	Fin/R.E.	S/L govt. passenger transit	0.2	S/L Govt
Fabricated metals, nec	0.2	Manufg.	Valve & fittings other than plumbing	0.2	Manufg.
Support services, nec	0.2	Services	Coating, engraving, heat treating & allied activities	0.2	Manufg.
Crowns & closures & metal stamping	0.1	Manufg.	Oil & gas well drilling	0.2	Mining
Nondepository credit intermediation activities	0.1	Fin/R.E.	AC, refrigeration, and warm air heating equipment	0.2	Manufg.
Valve & fittings other than plumbing	0.1	Manufg.	Personal & household goods repair/maintenance	0.2	Services
Industrial gases	0.1	Manufg.	Musical instruments	0.2	Manufg.
Investigation & security services	0.1	Services	Mining & oil & gas field machinery	0.2	Manufg.
Other computer related services, including facilities	0.1	Services	Hardware	0.2	Manufg.
Plate work & fabricated structural products	0.1	Manufg.	Oil & gas operations services	0.2	Mining
Relay & industrial controls	0.1	Manufg.	Signs	0.1	Manufg.
Paperboard mills	0.1	Manufg.	Air transportation	0.1	Util.
Aluminum products from purchased aluminum	0.1	Manufg.	Commercial & service industry machinery, nec	0.1	Manufg.
Ball & roller bearings	0.1	Manufg.	Motorcycles, bicycles, & parts	0.1	Manufg.
			Aircraft parts & auxiliary equipment, nec	0.1	Manufg.
			General purpose machinery, nec	0.1	Manufg.
			Coated & laminated paper & packaging materials	0.1	Manufg.
			Surgical appliances & supplies	0.1	Manufg.
			Real estate	0.1	Fin/R.E.
			Transportation equipment, nec	0.1	Manufg.
			Nonferrous metal foundries	0.1	Manufg.
			Hunting and trapping	0.1	Agric.
			Support services, nec	0.1	Services
			Metal cans, boxes, & other containers (light gauge)	0.1	Manufg.
			General Federal government services, defense	0.1	Fed Govt
			Maintenance/repair of residential structures	0.1	Construct.
			Jewelry & silverware	0.1	Manufg.

Continued on next page.

911

INPUTS AND OUTPUTS FOR SPRING AND WIRE PRODUCT MANUFACTURING - Continued

Economic Sector or Industry Providing Inputs	%	Sector	Economic Sector or Industry Buying Outputs	%	Sector
			Power boilers & heat exchangers	0.1	Manufg.
			Engine equipment, nec	0.1	Manufg.

Source: Benchmark Input-Output Accounts for the U.S. Economy, 2002, U.S. Department of Commerce, Washington, D.C., January 2008. The abbreviation nec stands for 'not elsewhere classified'.

OCCUPATIONS EMPLOYED BY SPRING & WIRE PRODUCT MANUFACTURING

Occupation	% of Total 2006	Change to 2016	Occupation	% of Total 2006	Change to 2016
Cutting, punching, & press machine operators	8.2	-33.4	Coating, painting, & spraying machine operators	1.9	-29.7
Team assemblers	6.7	-26.0	Metal workers & plastic workers, nec	1.8	-40.8
Extruding & drawing machine operators & tenders	5.4	-26.0	Packers & packagers, hand	1.6	-40.8
First-line supervisors/managers of production workers	4.6	-26.0	Welding, soldering, & brazing machine operators	1.6	-16.8
Welders, cutters, solderers, & brazers	4.2	-21.2	Laborers & freight, stock, & material movers, hand	1.6	-33.4
Helpers--Production workers	4.1	-26.0	Forging machine operators & tenders	1.5	-40.8
Sales reps, wholesale & manufacturing, exc tech	3.1	-26.0	Customer service representatives	1.5	-18.6
Machinists	2.8	-22.3	Grinding, lapping, polishing machine tool operators	1.4	-28.2
Multiple machine tool operators & tenders	2.5	-18.6	Assemblers & fabricators, nec	1.4	-33.4
Computer-controlled machine tool operators	2.5	-18.6	Bookkeeping, accounting, & auditing clerks	1.3	-26.0
Shipping, receiving, & traffic clerks	2.3	-28.8	Tool & die makers	1.2	-22.3
Machine feeders & offbearers	2.1	-33.4	Office clerks, general	1.2	-27.1
Inspectors, testers, sorters, samplers, & weighers	2.1	-30.2	Industrial machinery mechanics	1.2	-14.9
Industrial truck & tractor operators	2.0	-33.4	Industrial production managers	1.1	-26.0
General & operations managers	1.9	-33.4	Lathe & turning machine tool operators & tenders	1.1	-33.4
Maintenance & repair workers, general	1.9	-26.0	Rolling machine operators & tenders	1.1	-26.0

Source: Industry-Occupation Matrix, Bureau of Labor Statistics, December 4, 2007. These data are reported based on 4-digit NAICS categories but have been matched to corresponding 6-digit NAICS industry codes. The change reported for each occupation to the year 2016 is a percent of growth or decline as estimated by the Bureau of Labor Statistics. The abbreviation nec stands for 'not elsewhere classified'.

LOCATION BY STATE AND REGIONAL CONCENTRATION

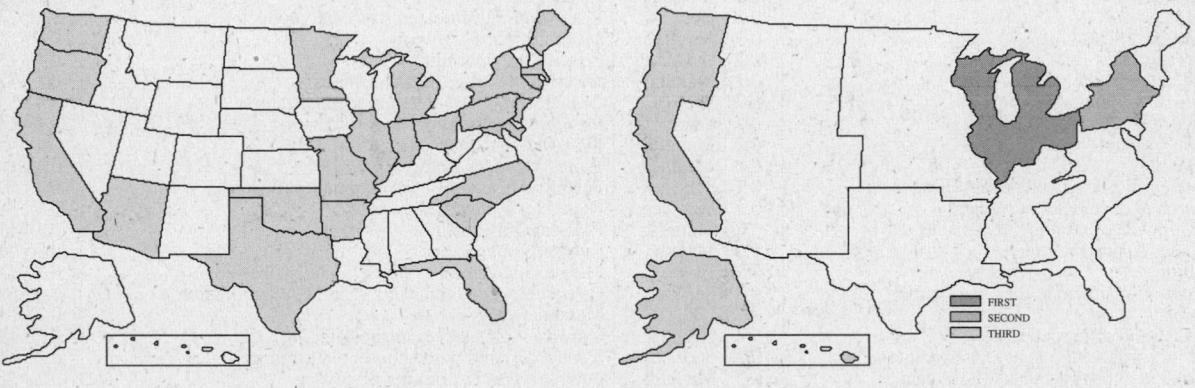

FIRST
SECOND
THIRD

INDUSTRY DATA BY STATE

State	Establish-ments	Shipments			Employment				Cost as % of Shipments	Investment per Employee ($)
		Total ($ mil)	% of U.S.	Per Establ.	Total Number	% of U.S.	Per Establ.	Wages ($/hour)		
Illinois	200	751.1	8.2	3,755.4	5,592	8.8	28	13.81	40.5	4,165
Pennsylvania	137	749.2	8.2	5,468.5	4,586	7.3	33	14.89	44.5	3,333
Ohio	135	730.5	8.0	5,410.9	5,237	8.3	39	14.09	42.1	3,262
California	233	674.1	7.4	2,893.1	4,435	7.0	19	13.21	47.8	3,194
Texas	159	602.1	6.6	3,786.9	3,770	6.0	24	12.60	46.9	3,670
Michigan	121	415.4	4.5	3,432.8	3,342	5.3	28	14.30	41.7	3,967
Missouri	35	332.5	3.6	9,499.6	2,008	3.2	57	11.63	48.6	3,110
Indiana	51	297.0	3.2	5,822.7	2,055	3.3	40	11.38	49.4	2,159
Florida	56	270.0	3.0	4,821.3	1,498	2.4	27	13.15	47.4	6,091
New Jersey	62	211.5	2.3	3,410.7	1,774	2.8	29	14.73	37.9	4,225
New York	87	203.9	2.2	2,343.7	1,750	2.8	20	12.33	40.7	3,383
North Carolina	41	189.3	2.1	4,617.9	1,268	2.0	31	13.07	48.3	2,523

Continued on next page.

INDUSTRY DATA BY STATE - Continued

| State | Establish-ments | Shipments | | | Employment | | | | Cost as % of Shipments | Investment per Employee ($) |
		Total ($ mil)	% of U.S.	Per Establ.	Total Number	% of U.S.	Per Establ.	Wages ($/hour)		
Maryland	28	172.9	1.9	6,173.6	1,338	2.1	48	13.68	27.6	2,307
Arkansas	18	135.9	1.5	7,551.1	1,002	1.6	56	13.47	51.7	7,587
Oklahoma	23	132.2	1.4	5,746.2	858	1.4	37	13.21	54.2	6,101
Minnesota	36	127.6	1.4	3,544.0	995	1.6	28	16.36	39.2	2,124
Massachusetts	42	121.9	1.3	2,901.3	1,503	2.4	36	11.19	39.9	6,052
Connecticut	34	79.8	0.9	2,347.3	682	1.1	20	13.81	36.4	2,248
Oregon	23	74.9	0.8	3,254.6	588	0.9	26	11.88	32.5	2,617
South Carolina	20	60.3	0.7	3,012.8	346	0.5	17	11.69	46.7	3,910
Arizona	20	38.8	0.4	1,937.6	236	0.4	12	13.61	52.6	4,788
Washington	27	37.0	0.4	1,372.2	340	0.5	13	13.28	47.2	2,241
Maine	16	11.2	0.1	697.1	126	0.2	8	12.16	40.8	2,683

Source: 2002 Economic Census. The states are in descending order of shipments or establishments (if shipment data are missing for the majority). The symbol (D) appears when data are withheld to prevent disclosure of competitive information. States marked with (D) are sorted by number of establishments. A dash (-) indicates that the data element cannot be calculated. Data may not show all states active in the NAICS category. All data available at the time of publication are shown.

NAICS 332710 - MACHINE SHOPS

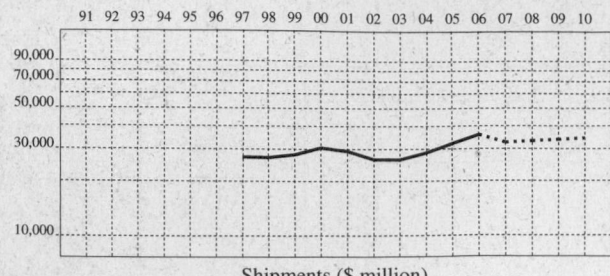

Shipments ($ million)

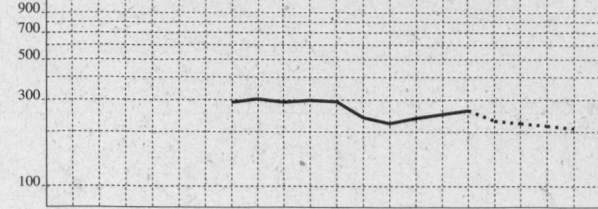

Employment (000)

GENERAL STATISTICS

| Year | Companies | Establishments | | Employment | | | Compensation | | Production ($ million) | | | |
		Total	with 20 or more employees	Total (000)	Production Workers (000)	Hours (Mil)	Payroll ($ mil)	Wages ($/hr)	Cost of Materials	Value Added by Manufacture	Value of Shipments	Capital Invest.
1997	23,438	23,616	3,773	290.8	225.8	429.1	9,491.0	14.78	8,765.8	18,460.2	27,131.5	1,552.6
1998		23,955	3,996	303.1	236.4	477.2	9,844.5	13.79	8,777.9	18,284.0	27,006.3	1,704.6
1999		23,233	3,786	291.5	224.8	434.1	9,744.7	15.07	9,252.8	18,833.8	27,995.4	1,736.8
2000		22,830	3,808	298.6	232.8	442.8	10,407.7	15.81	10,143.5	20,551.8	30,495.4	1,882.1
2001		22,756	3,828	293.7	224.7	448.2	10,191.7	15.17	9,743.2	19,447.3	29,217.1	1,624.5
2002	22,148	22,363	3,061	240.1	180.7	349.0	8,968.0	17.10	8,527.4	17,848.4	26,347.6	1,226.2
2003		21,375	3,037	222.8	169.6	342.2	8,882.4	17.58	8,711.1	17,744.8	26,256.9	984.4
2004		21,273	3,152	238.4	177.3	364.4	9,397.8	17.43	10,209.5	18,076.2	28,594.3	1,296.7
2005		21,240	3,273	250.0	187.5	390.1	10,130.7	17.69	12,090.1	20,478.1	32,187.3	1,424.5
2006		20,705P	2,959P	262.5	197.5	409.2	11,030.9	18.32	13,518.1	22,551.0	35,890.1	1,475.9
2007		20,342P	2,846P	230.1P	170.1P	357.4P	10,086.6P	18.88P	12,252.1P	20,439.1P	32,529.0P	1,226.1P
2008		19,980P	2,733P	222.9P	163.6P	348.0P	10,137.0P	19.35P	12,486.1P	20,829.4P	33,150.2P	1,177.9P
2009		19,618P	2,620P	215.8P	157.2P	338.7P	10,187.5P	19.83P	12,720.1P	21,219.8P	33,771.5P	1,129.8P
2010		19,256P	2,507P	208.7P	150.7P	329.4P	10,238.0P	20.30P	12,954.1P	21,610.1P	34,392.7P	1,081.7P

Sources: 1997 and 2002 *Economic Census*; other years, up to 2006, are from *Annual Survey of Manufactures*. Establishment counts for non-Census years are from *County Business Patterns*; 1997 and 2002 values are from the 1997 and 2002 censuses, respectively. 'P's show projections by the editors.

INDICES OF CHANGE

| Year | Companies | Establishments | | Employment | | | Compensation | | Production ($ million) | | | |
		Total	with 20 or more employees	Total (000)	Production Workers (000)	Hours (Mil)	Payroll ($ mil)	Wages ($/hr)	Cost of Materials	Value Added by Manufacture	Value of Shipments	Capital Invest.
1997	106	106	123	121	125	123	106	86	103	103	103	127
1998		107	131	126	131	137	110	81	103	102	103	139
1999		104	124	121	124	124	109	88	109	106	106	142
2000		102	124	124	129	127	116	92	119	115	116	153
2001		102	125	122	124	128	114	89	114	109	111	132
2002	100	100	100	100	100	100	100	100	100	100	100	100
2003		96	99	93	94	98	99	103	102	99	100	80
2004		95	103	99	98	104	105	102	120	101	109	106
2005		95	107	104	104	112	113	103	142	115	122	116
2006		93P	97P	109	109	117	123	107	159	126	136	120
2007		91P	93P	96P	94P	102P	112P	110P	144P	115P	123P	100P
2008		89P	89P	93P	91P	100P	113P	113P	146P	117P	126P	96P
2009		88P	86P	90P	87P	97P	114P	116P	149P	119P	128P	92P
2010		86P	82P	87P	83P	94P	114P	119P	152P	121P	131P	88P

Sources: Same as General Statistics. Values reflect change from the base year, 2002. Values above 100 mean greater than 2002, values below 100 mean less than 2002, and the values of 100 in other years means the same as 2002. 'P's show projections by the editors.

SELECTED RATIOS

For 2002	Avg. of All Manufact.	Analyzed Industry	Index	For 2002	Avg. of All Manufact.	Analyzed Industry	Index
Employees per Establishment	42	11	26	Value Added per Production Worker	182,367	98,774	54
Payroll per Establishment	1,639,184	401,020	24	Cost per Establishment	5,769,015	381,317	7
Payroll per Employee	39,053	37,351	96	Cost per Employee	137,446	35,516	26
Production Workers per Establishment	30	8	27	Cost per Production Worker	195,506	47,191	24
Wages per Establishment	694,845	266,865	38	Shipments per Establishment	11,158,348	1,178,178	11
Wages per Production Worker	23,548	33,027	140	Shipments per Employee	265,847	109,736	41
Hours per Production Worker	1,980	1,931	98	Shipments per Production Worker	378,144	145,809	39
Wages per Hour	11.89	17.10	144	Investment per Establishment	361,338	54,832	15
Value Added per Establishment	5,381,325	798,122	15	Investment per Employee	8,609	5,107	59
Value Added per Employee	128,210	74,337	58	Investment per Production Worker	12,245	6,786	55

Sources: Same as General Statistics. The 'Average of All Manufacturing' column represents the average of all manufacturing industries reported for the most recent complete year available. The Index shows the relationship between the Average and the Analyzed Industry. For example, 100 means that they are equal; 500 that the Analyzed Industry is five times the average; 50 means that the Analyzed Industry is half the national average. The abbreviation 'na' is used to show that data are 'not available'. Ratios shown for 2002, the last complete census year.

LEADING COMPANIES   Number shown: **75**   Total sales ($ mil): **81,728**   Total employment (000): **227.7**

Company Name	Address				CEO Name	Phone	Co. Type	Sales ($ mil)	Empl. (000)
General Dynamics Corp.	2941 Fairview Park	Falls Church	VA	22042	Nicholas D. Chabraja	703-876-3000	P	27,240	83.5
Applied Materials Inc.	PO Box 58039	Santa Clara	CA	95052		408-727-5555	P	9,735	15.3
Prager Inc.	PO Box 61670	New Orleans	LA	70161	Jennifer McKnight	504-524-2363	R	7,580*	<0.1
Harsco Corp.	PO Box 8888	Camp Hill	PA	17001	S. D. Fazzolari	717-763-7064	P	3,688	21.5
Diebold Inc.	PO Box 3077	North Canton	OH	44720		330-490-4000	P	2,906	15.5
O'Reilly Automotive Inc.	233 S Patterson Ave	Springfield	MO	65802	Greg Henslee	417-862-6708	P	2,522	18.5
American Power Conversion	132 Fairgrounds Rd.	West Kingston	RI	02892	Rodger B. Dowdell Jr.	401-789-5735	S	1,980	7.6
Teleflex Inc.	155 S Limerick Rd.	Limerick	PA	19468	Jeffrey P. Black	610-948-5100	P	1,934	14.0
Schuler Inc.	7145 Commerce	Canton	MI	48187	Timothy McCaughey	734-207-7200	R	1,874*	<0.1
Weir Spm	7701 Skyline Park	Fort Worth	TX	76108	Steve Noon	817-246-2461	R	1,770*	0.3
Curtiss-Wright Corp.	4 Becker Farm Rd.	Roseland	NJ	07068	Martin R. Benante	973-597-4700	P	1,592	6.2
Moog Inc.	Jamison Rd.	East Aurora	NY	14052		716-652-2000	P	1,558	8.4
Fulmer Company L.L.C.	3004 Venture Ct.	Export	PA	15632	Leo Eger	724-325-7140	R	1,320*	<0.1
Swagelok Co.	29500 Solon Rd.	Solon	OH	44139	Arthur F. Anton	440-248-4600	R	1,100*	3.3
NGK-Locke Inc.	2525 Insulator Dr.	Baltimore	MD	21230	Shun Matsushita	410-347-1700	S	941*	3.7
Intermec Inc.	6001 36th Ave. W	Everett	WA	98203	Patrick Byrne	425-348-2600	P	849	2.4
Senior Operations Inc.	300 E Devon Ave.	Bartlett	IL	60103	Graham Menzies	630-837-1811	R	733*	0.7
White Systems Inc.	30 Boright Ave.	Kenilworth	NJ	07033	Richard Paolino	908-272-6700	S	673*	0.3
Bachman Machine Co.	4321 N Broadway	St. Louis	MO	63147	William Bachman	314-231-4221	R	656*	0.1
Parker Drilling Co.	1401 Enclave Pky.	Houston	TX	77077		281-406-2000	P	655	3.1
Altra Holdings Inc.	14 Hayward St.	Quincy	MA	02171	Michael L. Hurt	617-328-3300	P	584	3.5
Cotton Goods Manufacturing Co.	259 N California	Chicago	IL	60612	Edward J. Lewis	773-265-0088	R	525*	<0.1
Omega Flex Inc.	451 Creamery Way	Exton	PA	19341	Kevin R. Hoben	610-524-7272	S	475*	0.1
CPI Products L.L.C.	12501 Taylor Rd.	Charlevoix	MI	49720	Doug Hellyar	231-547-6064	R	466*	<0.1
RMS Co.	8600 Evergreen Blvd	Coon Rapids	MN	55433	Arthur Mouyard	763-786-1520	S	400*	0.3
Cretex Co's Inc.	311 Lowell NW	Elk River	MN	55330	Albert Bailey	763-441-2121	R	400*	<0.1
Gleason Corp.	PO Box 22970	Rochester	NY	14692		585-473-1000	R	350*	2.6
Graphel Corp.	PO Box 369	West Chester	OH	45071	Cliff Kersker	513-779-6166	R	337*	0.1
Engineered Machined Products	3111 N 28th St.	Escanaba	MI	49829	Brian Larche	906-786-8404	R	333*	0.5
Magnetic Instruments Corp.	1801 Indu. Blvd.	Brenham	TX	77833	Nelson Byman	979-836-4481	R	331*	0.2
Systems Electro Coating	253 Old Jackson Rd.	Madison	MS	39110	Toni Cooley	601-407-2340	R	282*	<0.1
Pall Aeropower Corp.	1054 Ridge Rd.	New Port Richey	FL	34654	Jim Wester	727-849-9999	S	271*	0.5
Taurus Numeric Tool Inc.	213 Chelsea Rd.	Monticello	MN	55362	Mike Pudil	763-295-9202	S	252*	<0.1
Domaille Engineering Inc.	7100 Dresser Dr. NE	Rochester	MN	55906	Nancy Domaille	507-281-0275	R	238*	<0.1
Autocam Corp.	4070 E Paris Ave SE	Kentwood	MI	49512	John C. Kennedy	616-698-0707	S	230*	2.3
Daman Industrial Services Inc.	PO Box 486	East Brady	PA	16028		724-526-5714	R	228*	<0.1
Bollinger Shipyards Inc.	PO Box 250	Lockport	LA	70374	Donald Bollinger	985-532-2554	R	222*	0.6
Benedict-Miller L.L.C.	123 N 8th St.	Kenilworth	NJ	07033	John Benedict	908-497-1477	R	216*	0.1
Schaefers Enterprise Wolf Lake	PO Box 136	Wolf Lake	IL	62998		618-833-5498	R	214*	<0.1
Harlan Machinery Company Inc.	706 Wells Rd.	Boulder City	NV	89005	Paul E. Hassler	702-293-7723	S	195*	<0.1
Flowserve USA Inc.	225 W Foster Ave.	Bensenville	IL	60106	Luis M. Kling	630-595-0800	D	190*	<0.1
Stark Industrial Inc.	PO Box 3030	North Canton	OH	44720	Ray Wilkof	330-966-8108	R	190*	<0.1
Oerlikon USA Holding Inc.	615 Epsilon Dr.	Pittsburgh	PA	15238	James Brissenden	724-327-5700	R	172*	0.2
Alamo Iron Works	PO Box 231	San Antonio	TX	78291		210-223-6161	R	163*	0.4
Rotary Corp.	PO Box 747	Glennville	GA	30427		912-654-3433	R	156*	0.4
Maddox Foundry/Machine Wrks	PO Drawer 7	Archer	FL	32618	Monte Marchant	352-495-2121	R	154*	0.2
Zamperla Inc.	PO Box 5545	Parsippany	NJ	07054	Alberto Zamperla	973-334-8133	R	154*	<0.1
Ontario Corp.	PO Box 2757	Muncie	IN	47307		765-378-4100	R	140*	0.1
Tennessee Cummins Mid-South	PO Box 3080	Memphis	TN	38173	Ben Strafuss	901-577-0600	S	130*	0.5
Carolina Tractor/CAT	PO Box 1095	Charlotte	NC	28201	Edward Weisiger	704-596-6700	R	127*	0.7
Dana Corp. Plumley Div.	100 Plumley Dr.	Paris	TN	38242	Michael J. Burns	731-642-5582	J	123*	1.5
G and F Industries Inc.	PO Box 515	Sturbridge	MA	01566	John Argitis	508-347-9132	R	123*	0.2
Precision Strip Inc.	PO Box 104	Minster	OH	45865	Tom Compton	419-628-2343	S	122*	0.3
Main Tool and Manufacturing	7850 Beech St. NE	Minneapolis	MN	55432	Samual Jefferson	763-571-1772	R	119*	<0.1
K and N Engineering Inc.	PO Box 1329	Riverside	CA	92502	Jerry Mall	951-826-4100	R	109*	0.6
Cascade Machinery and Electric	PO Box 3575	Seattle	WA	98124	John Spring	206-762-0500	R	100	<0.1
Parker Hannifin Racor Div.	PO Box 3208	Modesto	CA	95353		209-521-7860	D	98*	0.8
CG Bretting Manufacturing Inc.	PO Box 113	Ashland	WI	54806	David Bretting	715-682-5231	R	96*	0.5
JK Manufacturing Co.	7301 W 66th St.	Bedford Park	IL	60638	Jozef Koniecko	708-563-2500	R	95*	<0.1
Major Die and Engineering Co.	1352 Industrial Dr.	Itasca	IL	60143		630-773-3444	R	95*	<0.1
Meyer Tool Inc.	PO Box 25098	Cincinnati	OH	45225	Arlyn Easton	513-853-4400	R	89*	0.7
Remmele Engineering Inc.	10 Old Hwy. 8 SW	New Brighton	MN	55112	Richard Pogue	651-635-4100	S	88*	0.5
Casey Tool and Machine Company	400 W Delaware	Casey	IL	62420	James Yates	217-932-2547	R	87*	0.5
Monroe Truck Equipment Inc.	1051 W 7th St.	Monroe	WI	53566	Richard Feller	608-328-8127	R	86*	0.3
Cummins Southeastern Power	PO Box 11737	Tampa	FL	33680	Richard Stohler	813-621-7202	S	86*	0.3
Diversified Group Inc.	PO Box 23890	New Orleans	LA	70183	Danny Hughes	504-733-2800	R	85*	0.3
H and L Tooth Co.	PO Box 48	Owasso	OK	74055	Richard Launder	918-272-0951	R	81*	<0.1
TSS Technologies Inc.	800 Global Way	West Chester	OH	45069	Brent Nichols	513-772-7000	R	80*	0.1
Triumph Engines - Tempe	2015 W Alameda	Tempe	AZ	85282		602-438-8760	S	79*	0.3
Burger Iron Co.	3100 Gilchrist Rd.	Mogadore	OH	44260	Tom Fiocca	330-253-5121	R	79*	0.2
Innovance Inc.	505 W Front St.	Albert Lea	MN	56007	Mike Larson	507-377-8910	R	79*	<0.1
B and C Corp.	PO Box 110	Barberton	OH	44203	Louis Bilinovich	330-848-3714	R	78*	0.3
Worthington Precision Metals	8229 Tyler Blvd.	Mentor	OH	44060	Joe Harden	440-255-6700	S	77*	0.3
WEDCO Technology Inc.	5333 Westheimer	Houston	TX	77056	John Knapp	713-351-4100	S	72*	0.8
Southern Fabricators Inc.	4768 Hungerford	Memphis	TN	38118	Greg Langston	901-363-1571	R	72*	0.7

Source: Ward's Business Directory of U.S. Private and Public Companies, Volumes 1 and 2, 2008. The company type code used is as follows: P - Public, R - Private, S - Subsidiary, D - Division, J - Joint Venture, A - Affiliate, G - Group. Sales are in millions of dollars, employees are in thousands. An asterisk (*) indicates an estimated sales volume. The symbol < stands for 'less than'. Company names and addresses are truncated, in some cases, to fit into the manufacturing space.

MATERIALS CONSUMED

Material	Quantity	Delivered Cost ($ million)
Metal bolts, nuts, screws, and other screw machine products	(X)	133.6
Other fabricated metal products (excluding forgings)	(X)	399.0
Forgings	(X)	157.6
Iron and steel castings (rough and semifinished)	(X)	708.0
Aluminum and aluminum-base alloy castings (rough and semifinished)	(X)	225.5
Other nonferrous metal castings, rough or semifinished (inc. aluminum)	(X)	26.3
Steel bars, bar shapes, and plates (exc. castings, forgings, fabr. metal products)	(X)	333.2
Steel sheet and strip (including tinplate)	(X)	96.8
Steel structural shapes and sheet piling (exc. castings, forgings, fabr. metal products)	(X)	13.3
All other steel shapes and forms (exc. castings, forgings, fabr. metal products)	(X)	89.4
Copper and copper-base alloy rod, bar, and mechanical wire	(X)	18.8
All other copper and copper-base alloy shapes and forms (exc. castings, forgings, fabr. metal products)	(X)	38.5
Aluminum and aluminum-base alloy sheet, plate, foil, and welded tubing	(X)	109.3
All other aluminum and aluminum-base alloy shapes and forms (exc. castings, forgings, fabr. metal products)	(X)	134.1
Other nonferrous shapes and forms (exc. castings, forgings, fabricated metal products)	(X)	38.1
Cutting tools for machine tools	(X)	150.0
Fluid power products	(X)	43.1
All other materials, components, parts, containers, and supplies	(X)	1,686.5
Materials, ingredients, containers, and supplies, nsk	(X)	1,897.9

Source: 2002 *Economic Census*. Explanation of symbols used: (D): Withheld to avoid disclosure of competitive data; na: Not available; (S): Withheld because statistical norms were not met; (X): Not applicable; (Z): Less than half the unit shown; nec: Not elsewhere classified; nsk: Not specified by kind; - : zero; p : 10-19 percent estimated; q : 20-29 percent estimated.

PRODUCT SHARE DETAILS

Product or Product Class Shipments	Mil. $	Product or Product Class Shipments	Mil. $
RECEIPTS FOR MACHINE SHOP WORK AND JOB ORDER REPAIRS	24,571.3		

Source: 2002 *Economic Census*. The values are product shipments in millions of dollars for 2002. Total product shipments may be lower or higher than industry shipments. See Introduction for a full discussion. Values of indented subcategories are summed in the main heading(s). The symbol (D) appears when data are withheld to prevent disclosure of competitive information. The abbreviation nsk stands for 'not specified by kind' and nec for 'not elsewhere classified'. A dash (-) means zero.

INPUTS AND OUTPUTS FOR MACHINE SHOPS

Economic Sector or Industry Providing Inputs	%	Sector	Economic Sector or Industry Buying Outputs	%	Sector
Compensation of employees	41.6		Motor vehicle parts	11.6	Manufg.
Management of companies & enterprises	4.2	Services	Machine shops	3.5	Manufg.
Machine shops	3.5	Manufg.	Federal government, investment, nondefense	3.4	Fed Govt
Plate work & fabricated structural products	2.8	Manufg.	Air transportation	2.6	Util.
Iron & steel mills & ferroalloys	2.4	Manufg.	Transit & ground passenger transportation	2.2	Util.
Nonferrous metal foundries	2.1	Manufg.	Residential structures, nec	1.9	Construct.
Wholesale trade	2.1	Trade	Aluminum products from purchased aluminum	1.9	Manufg.
Real estate	2.0	Fin/R.E.	Ornamental & architectural metal products	1.9	Manufg.
Aluminum products from purchased aluminum	1.3	Manufg.	Industrial machinery, nec	1.6	Manufg.
Securities, commodity contracts, investments	1.3	Fin/R.E.	Plate work & fabricated structural products	1.6	Manufg.
Power generation & supply	1.1	Util.	Manufacturing, nec	1.6	Manufg.
Professional, scientific, technical services, nec	1.0	Services	Management of companies & enterprises	1.5	Services
Ferrous metal foundries	0.9	Manufg.	Plastics products, nec	1.5	Manufg.
Turned products & screws, nuts, & bolts	0.9	Manufg.	Residential permanent site structures	1.4	Construct.
Automotive equipment rental & leasing	0.9	Fin/R.E.	Truck transportation	1.3	Util.
Monetary authorities/depository credit intermediation	0.9	Fin/R.E.	Other S/L govt. enterprises	1.2	S/L Govt
Lessors of nonfinancial assets	0.9	Fin/R.E.	Nonresidential structures, nec	1.2	Construct.
Custom computer programming services	0.7	Services	Oil & gas extraction	1.1	Mining
Taxes on production & imports, less subsidies	0.7		Telecommunications	1.1	Services
Cutting tools & machine tool accessories	0.7	Manufg.	Light truck & utility vehicles	1.1	Manufg.
Advertising & related services	0.7	Services	Printing	1.0	Manufg.
Food services & drinking places	0.7	Services	Commercial & health care structures	0.9	Construct.
Paints & coatings	0.7	Manufg.	Material handling equipment	0.8	Manufg.
Truck transportation	0.7	Util.	Rubber products, nec	0.8	Manufg.
Accounting, tax preparation, bookkeeping, & payroll	0.6	Services	Turned products & screws, nuts, & bolts	0.7	Manufg.
Legal services	0.6	Services	Coating, engraving, heat treating & allied activities	0.7	Manufg.
Nonferrous metal (ex. copper & aluminum) processing	0.6	Manufg.	AC, refrigeration, and warm air heating equipment	0.7	Manufg.
Hotels & motels, including casino hotels	0.5	Services	Automotive repair & maintenance, ex. car washes	0.6	Services
Specialized design services	0.5	Services	Paperboard containers	0.6	Manufg.
Coating, engraving, heat treating & allied activities	0.5	Manufg.	Automobiles	0.6	Manufg.
Telecommunications	0.5	Services	Valve & fittings other than plumbing	0.6	Manufg.
Business support services	0.5	Services	Ferrous metal foundries	0.6	Manufg.
Motors & generators	0.5	Manufg.	Mining & oil & gas field machinery	0.6	Manufg.
Employment services	0.5	Services	Metal cans, boxes, & other containers (light gauge)	0.6	Manufg.
Semiconductors & related devices	0.5	Manufg.	Semiconductors & related devices	0.6	Manufg.
Architectural, engineering, & related services	0.5	Services	Paper mills	0.6	Manufg.

Continued on next page.

INPUTS AND OUTPUTS FOR MACHINE SHOPS - Continued

Economic Sector or Industry Providing Inputs	%	Sector	Economic Sector or Industry Buying Outputs	%	Sector
Commercial & industrial machinery rental & leasing	0.4	Fin/R.E.	Basic organic chemicals, nec	0.5	Manufg.
Printed circuit assemblies (electronic assembiles)	0.4	Manufg.	Retail trade	0.5	Trade
Valve & fittings other than plumbing	0.4	Manufg.	Commercial & service industry machinery, nec	0.5	Manufg.
Warehousing & storage	0.4	Util.	General purpose machinery, nec	0.5	Manufg.
Industrial molds	0.4	Manufg.	Scenic & sightseeing transport & related services	0.5	Util.
Air transportation	0.4	Util.	Newspaper publishers	0.5	Services
Chemical products & preparations, nec	0.3	Manufg.	Signs	0.5	Manufg.
Services to buildings & dwellings	0.3	Services	Plastics materials & resins	0.5	Manufg.
Maintenance/repair of nonresidential structures	0.3	Construct.	Fluid power process machinery	0.5	Manufg.
Copper rolling, drawing, extruding, & alloying	0.3	Manufg.	Wholesale trade	0.5	Trade
Fluid power process machinery	0.3	Manufg.	Crowns & closures & metal stamping	0.5	Manufg.
Support services, nec	0.3	Services	Petroleum refineries	0.5	Manufg.
Fabricated metals, nec	0.3	Manufg.	Semiconductor machinery	0.5	Manufg.
Abrasive products	0.3	Manufg.	Plastics packaging materials, film & sheet	0.5	Manufg.
Scientific research & development services	0.3	Services	Exports of goods & services	0.5	Cap Inv
Alumina refining & primary aluminum production	0.2	Manufg.	Surgical appliances & supplies	0.4	Manufg.
Laminated plastics plates, sheets, & shapes	0.2	Manufg.	Aircraft parts & auxiliary equipment, nec	0.4	Manufg.
Investigation & security services	0.2	Services	Book publishers	0.4	Services
Natural gas distribution	0.2	Util.	Fabricated metals, nec	0.4	Manufg.
Automotive repair & maintenance, ex. car washes	0.2	Services	Nonferrous metal foundries	0.4	Manufg.
Primary smelting & refining of copper	0.2	Manufg.	Toilet preparations	0.4	Manufg.
Management, scientific, & technical consulting	0.2	Services	Owner-occupied dwellings	0.4	
Ornamental & architectural metal products	0.2	Manufg.	Pumps & pumping equipment	0.4	Manufg.
Paperboard containers	0.2	Manufg.	Engine equipment, nec	0.4	Manufg.
Unlaminated plastics profile shapes	0.2	Manufg.	Personal & household goods repair/maintenance	0.4	Services
Waste management & remediation services	0.2	Services	Special tools, dies, jigs, & fixtures	0.4	Manufg.
Commercial & industrial equipment repair/maintenance	0.2	Services	Hardware	0.4	Manufg.
Petroleum refineries	0.2	Manufg.	Maintenance/repair of nonresidential structures	0.4	Construct.
Metal cans, boxes, & other containers (light gauge)	0.2	Manufg.	Packaging machinery	0.4	Manufg.
Data processing, hosting, & related services	0.2	Services	Aircraft	0.4	Manufg.
Crowns & closures & metal stamping	0.2	Manufg.	Broadcast & wireless communications equipment	0.4	Manufg.
Flat glass	0.2	Manufg.	Directories, mailing lists, & other publishers	0.4	Services
Metal cutting & forming machine tools	0.2	Manufg.	Construction machinery	0.3	Manufg.
Nondepository credit intermediation activities	0.1	Fin/R.E.	Motorcycles, bicycles, & parts	0.3	Manufg.
Transit & ground passenger transportation	0.1	Util.	Turbines & turbine generator set units	0.3	Manufg.
Other computer related services, including facilities	0.1	Services	Transportation equipment, nec	0.3	Manufg.
Power boilers & heat exchangers	0.1	Manufg.	Iron & steel mills & ferroalloys	0.3	Manufg.
Hardware	0.1	Manufg.	Surgical & medical instrument	0.3	Manufg.
Communication & energy wires & cables	0.1	Manufg.	Steel products from purchased steel	0.3	Manufg.
Civic, social, & professional organizations	0.1	Services	Chemical products & preparations, nec	0.3	Manufg.
Springs & wire products	0.1	Manufg.	Farm machinery & equipment	0.3	Manufg.
Plastics packaging materials, film & sheet	0.1	Manufg.	Jewelry & silverware	0.3	Manufg.
Ball & roller bearings	0.1	Manufg.	Metal cutting & forming machine tools	0.3	Manufg.
			Search, detection, & navigation instruments	0.3	Manufg.
			Soap & cleaning compounds	0.3	Manufg.
			General S/L govt. services	0.3	S/L Govt
			Wood windows & doors & millwork	0.3	Manufg.
			Scientific research & development services	0.3	Services
			Paperboard mills	0.3	Manufg.
			Rail transportation	0.3	Util.
			Coated & laminated paper & packaging materials	0.3	Manufg.
			Wineries	0.3	Manufg.
			Air & gas compressors	0.3	Manufg.
			Artificial & synthetic fibers & filaments	0.3	Manufg.
			Power-driven handtools	0.3	Manufg.
			Guided missiles & space vehicles	0.3	Manufg.
			Electromedical & electrotherapeutic apparatus	0.3	Manufg.
			Power boilers & heat exchangers	0.3	Manufg.
			Industrial molds	0.3	Manufg.
			Industrial process variable instruments	0.3	Manufg.
			Communication & energy wires & cables	0.2	Manufg.
			Vending, commercial, industrial, office machinery	0.2	Manufg.
			Sporting & athletic goods	0.2	Manufg.
			Springs & wire products	0.2	Manufg.
			Ball & roller bearings	0.2	Manufg.
			Power generation & supply	0.2	Util.
			Nonferrous metal (ex. copper & aluminum) processing	0.2	Manufg.
			Pipeline transportation	0.2	Util.
			Lighting fixtures	0.2	Manufg.
			Fabricated pipes & pipe fittings	0.2	Manufg.
			Copper rolling, drawing, extruding, & alloying	0.2	Manufg.
			Periodical publishers	0.2	Services
			Switchgear & switchboard apparatus	0.2	Manufg.
			Electronic computers	0.2	Manufg.
			Electronic components, nec	0.2	Manufg.
			Custom architectural woodwork & millwork	0.2	Manufg.
			Wiring devices	0.2	Manufg.
			Oil & gas operations services	0.2	Mining
			Commercial & industrial equipment repair/maintenance	0.2	Services
			Heating equipment (except warm air furnaces)	0.2	Manufg.

Continued on next page.

INPUTS AND OUTPUTS FOR MACHINE SHOPS - Continued

Economic Sector or Industry Providing Inputs	%	Sector	Economic Sector or Industry Buying Outputs	%	Sector
			Plumbing fixture fittings & trim	0.2	Manufg.
			Telephone apparatus	0.2	Manufg.
			Paints & coatings	0.2	Manufg.
			Relay & industrial controls	0.2	Manufg.
			Coal	0.2	Mining
			Arms, ordnance, & accessories	0.2	Manufg.
			Computer terminals & peripherals	0.2	Manufg.
			Soft drinks & ice	0.2	Manufg.
			Household cooking appliances	0.2	Manufg.
			Wood kitchen cabinets & countertops	0.2	Manufg.
			Postal service	0.2	Util.
			Watches, clocks, & related devices	0.2	Manufg.
			Analytical laboratory instruments	0.2	Manufg.
			Heavy duty trucks	0.2	Manufg.
			Mechanical power transmission equipment	0.2	Manufg.
			Motor vehicle bodies	0.2	Manufg.
			Real estate	0.2	Fin/R.E.
			Sanitary paper products	0.2	Manufg.
			Cutting tools & machine tool accessories	0.2	Manufg.
			Motors & generators	0.2	Manufg.
			Rolling mill & other metalworking machinery	0.2	Manufg.
			Irradiation apparatus	0.2	Manufg.
			Showcases, partitions, shelving, and lockers	0.2	Manufg.
			Gaskets, packing, & sealing devices	0.2	Manufg.
			Printed circuit assemblies (electronic assembles)	0.2	Manufg.
			Ammunition	0.2	Manufg.
			Air purification & ventilation equipment	0.2	Manufg.
			Oil & gas well drilling	0.2	Mining
			Carpet & rug mills	0.2	Manufg.
			Electrical equipment & components, nec	0.2	Manufg.
			Bread & bakery products	0.2	Manufg.
			Basic inorganic chemicals, nec	0.2	Manufg.
			Ship building & repairing	0.2	Manufg.
			Handtools	0.2	Manufg.
			Maintenance/repair of residential structures	0.2	Construct.
			Metal & other household furniture	0.2	Manufg.
			Glass products from purchased glass	0.1	Manufg.
			Ready-mix concrete	0.1	Manufg.
			Synthetic dyes & pigments	0.1	Manufg.
			Plastics bottles	0.1	Manufg.
			Tires	0.1	Manufg.
			Metal tanks (heavy gauge)	0.1	Manufg.
			Architectural, engineering, & related services	0.1	Services
			Electricity & signal testing instruments	0.1	Manufg.
			Lawn & garden equipment	0.1	Manufg.
			Plastics & rubber industry machinery	0.1	Manufg.
			Laboratory apparatus & furniture	0.1	Manufg.
			Railroad rolling stock	0.1	Manufg.
			Computer storage devices	0.1	Manufg.
			Dolls, toys, & games	0.1	Manufg.
			Fiber, yarn, & thread mills	0.1	Manufg.
			Forging, stamping, & sintering, nec	0.1	Manufg.
			Tobacco products	0.1	Manufg.
			Software publishers	0.1	Services
			Concrete products, nec	0.1	Manufg.
			Adhesives	0.1	Manufg.
			Stationery products	0.1	Manufg.
			Curtain & linen mills	0.1	Manufg.
			Fertilizer	0.1	Manufg.
			Textile & fabric finishing mills	0.1	Manufg.
			Totalizing fluid meters & counting devices	0.1	Manufg.
			Cement	0.1	Manufg.
			Travel trailers & campers	0.1	Manufg.
			Ophthalmic goods	0.1	Manufg.
			Water transportation	0.1	Util.
			Alumina refining & primary aluminum production	0.1	Manufg.
			Canned & dehydrated fruits & vegetables	0.1	Manufg.
			Pesticides & other agricultural chemicals	0.1	Manufg.
			Electron tubes	0.1	Manufg.
			Primary batteries	0.1	Manufg.

Source: Benchmark Input-Output Accounts for the U.S. Economy, 2002, U.S. Department of Commerce, Washington, D.C., January 2008. The abbreviation nec stands for 'not elsewhere classified'.

OCCUPATIONS EMPLOYED BY MACHINE SHOPS

Occupation	% of Total 2006	Change to 2016	Occupation	% of Total 2006	Change to 2016
Machinists	27.6	-13.1	Milling & planing machine operators & tenders	1.7	-25.6
Computer-controlled machine tool operators	8.3	-9.0	Team assemblers	1.6	-17.3
First-line supervisors/managers of production workers	5.3	-17.3	Sales reps, wholesale & manufacturing, exc tech	1.6	-17.3
Welders, cutters, solderers, & brazers	4.7	-12.0	Drilling & boring machine tool operators	1.6	-25.6
Lathe & turning machine tool operators & tenders	3.2	-25.6	Shipping, receiving, & traffic clerks	1.5	-20.4
Helpers--Production workers	2.6	-17.3	Numerical tool & process control programmers	1.3	-14.7
Grinding, lapping, polishing machine tool operators	2.6	-19.8	Secretaries, exc legal, medical, & executive	1.2	-26.4
General & operations managers	2.3	-25.6	Industrial production managers	1.1	-17.3
Inspectors, testers, sorters, samplers, & weighers	2.2	-22.0	Tool & die makers	1.1	-13.1
Office clerks, general	2.1	-18.5	Multiple machine tool operators & tenders	1.1	-9.0
Cutting, punching, & press machine operators	1.8	-25.6	Janitors & cleaners, exc maids & housekeeping cleaners	1.0	-15.4
Bookkeeping, accounting, & auditing clerks	1.8	-17.3			

Source: Industry-Occupation Matrix, Bureau of Labor Statistics, December 4, 2007. These data are reported based on 4-digit NAICS categories but have been matched to corresponding 6-digit NAICS industry codes. The change reported for each occupation to the year 2016 is a percent of growth or decline as estimated by the Bureau of Labor Statistics. The abbreviation nec stands for 'not elsewhere classified'.

LOCATION BY STATE AND REGIONAL CONCENTRATION

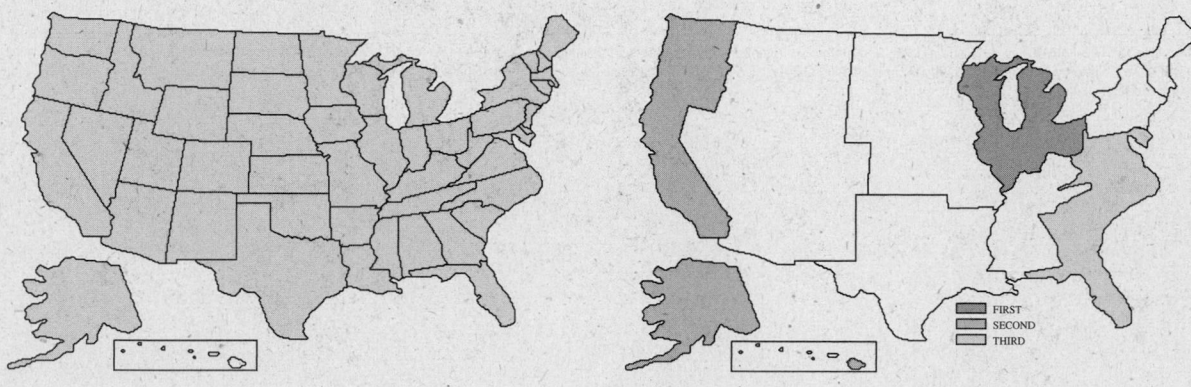

FIRST
SECOND
THIRD

INDUSTRY DATA BY STATE

State	Establish-ments	Shipments			Employment				Cost as % of Shipments	Investment per Employee ($)
		Total ($ mil)	% of U.S.	Per Establ.	Total Number	% of U.S.	Per Establ.	Wages ($/hour)		
California	2,982	3,249.7	12.3	1,089.8	29,282	12.2	10	18.18	29.7	5,167
Michigan	1,293	2,207.0	8.4	1,706.8	16,926	7.0	13	17.28	36.5	6,844
Ohio	1,587	1,992.9	7.6	1,255.8	18,881	7.9	12	16.33	31.3	4,160
Texas	1,564	1,881.0	7.1	1,202.7	17,273	7.2	11	16.09	29.6	5,677
Illinois	1,234	1,639.7	6.2	1,328.8	14,761	6.1	12	17.27	31.0	5,114
Pennsylvania	1,155	1,463.5	5.6	1,267.1	14,270	5.9	12	16.68	31.8	4,616
Wisconsin	709	1,438.4	5.5	2,028.8	11,577	4.8	16	16.56	41.4	4,920
New York	848	951.3	3.6	1,121.9	8,489	3.5	10	17.02	30.5	5,473
Minnesota	650	946.1	3.6	1,455.5	7,896	3.3	12	18.11	32.5	6,189
Massachusetts	634	835.5	3.2	1,317.8	7,009	2.9	11	19.40	29.8	4,840
Indiana	658	713.0	2.7	1,083.6	7,188	3.0	11	16.76	29.6	4,622
North Carolina	585	606.0	2.3	1,035.9	5,989	2.5	10	15.88	32.0	5,075
Connecticut	451	592.1	2.2	1,312.9	5,371	2.2	12	18.77	39.5	4,917
New Jersey	529	545.9	2.1	1,032.0	4,504	1.9	9	19.35	34.9	5,835
Washington	459	443.8	1.7	966.9	4,106	1.7	9	16.45	30.8	4,517
Missouri	416	423.0	1.6	1,016.9	4,122	1.7	10	17.46	28.5	5,707
Tennessee	404	418.8	1.6	1,036.7	3,951	1.6	10	17.40	31.0	3,522
Virginia	319	404.1	1.5	1,266.7	4,219	1.8	13	16.48	28.3	4,546
Kansas	212	396.1	1.5	1,868.4	3,388	1.4	16	15.59	43.1	4,168
Kentucky	258	355.3	1.3	1,376.9	3,408	1.4	13	15.66	30.6	2,954
Alabama	355	336.7	1.3	948.4	3,601	1.5	10	16.61	32.4	4,050
Louisiana	280	335.6	1.3	1,198.5	3,612	1.5	13	16.90	29.8	4,666
Georgia	417	335.2	1.3	803.9	3,119	1.3	7	17.07	33.7	3,962
Maryland	182	321.5	1.2	1,766.6	2,474	1.0	14	17.83	35.0	9,312
South Carolina	303	313.6	1.2	1,035.0	3,028	1.3	10	17.60	32.5	10,213
Arizona	311	311.8	1.2	1,002.6	3,147	1.3	10	17.70	30.3	3,402
Florida	593	306.3	1.2	516.5	3,294	1.4	6	16.25	31.5	4,132
Iowa	235	305.3	1.2	1,299.3	2,903	1.2	12	16.12	36.2	4,442
Oregon	341	291.5	1.1	854.9	2,894	1.2	8	16.19	31.2	4,404
Oklahoma	355	255.3	1.0	719.1	2,871	1.2	8	16.22	28.8	4,181

Continued on next page.

INDUSTRY DATA BY STATE - Continued

State	Establish-ments	Shipments			Employment				Cost as % of Shipments	Investment per Employee ($)
		Total ($ mil)	% of U.S.	Per Establ.	Total Number	% of U.S.	Per Establ.	Wages ($/hour)		
Colorado	310	224.2	0.9	723.2	2,173	0.9	7	17.27	31.6	3,929
New Hampshire	200	189.7	0.7	948.6	1,747	0.7	9	18.95	27.5	4,232
Maine	112	165.8	0.6	1,480.0	1,113	0.5	10	20.08	30.3	10,110
Utah	180	162.3	0.6	901.5	1,591	0.7	9	16.20	32.7	4,173
West Virginia	121	141.3	0.5	1,167.5	1,672	0.7	14	14.13	31.8	4,262
Arkansas	193	129.0	0.5	668.5	1,286	0.5	7	15.56	31.3	4,558
Rhode Island	85	102.0	0.4	1,199.4	892	0.4	10	17.39	31.6	9,299
Mississippi	134	101.2	0.4	755.2	1,012	0.4	8	15.30	36.0	4,112
Nebraska	113	85.5	0.3	756.9	885	0.4	8	16.06	31.5	2,579
Idaho	112	62.8	0.2	560.9	733	0.3	7	15.95	28.6	6,774
Delaware	36	59.6	0.2	1,655.9	405	0.2	11	20.08	31.3	4,432
New Mexico	86	59.0	0.2	686.6	613	0.3	7	19.20	33.2	3,372
Wyoming	42	47.6	0.2	1,132.2	484	0.2	12	17.91	33.4	3,667
Montana	75	43.6	0.2	580.9	347	0.1	5	17.25	42.5	3,775
Nevada	78	39.7	0.2	509.5	393	0.2	5	18.21	27.7	2,700
South Dakota	49	38.0	0.1	776.4	421	0.2	9	15.25	38.6	4,133
Vermont	45	32.2	0.1	715.3	362	0.2	8	15.45	23.5	4,008
North Dakota	41	21.7	0.1	528.8	259	0.1	6	15.46	31.8	4,417
Alaska	20	16.4	0.1	818.4	105	<0.1	5	17.32	31.1	4,857

Source: 2002 *Economic Census*. The states are in descending order of shipments or establishments (if shipment data are missing for the majority). The symbol (D) appears when data are withheld to prevent disclosure of competitive information. States marked with (D) are sorted by number of establishments. A dash (-) indicates that the data element cannot be calculated. Data may not show all states active in the NAICS category. All data available at the time of publication are shown.

NAICS 332721 - PRECISION TURNED PRODUCT MANUFACTURING

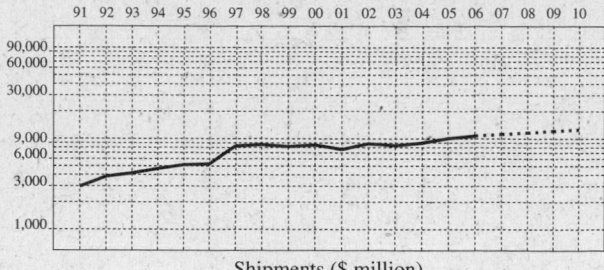

Shipments ($ million)

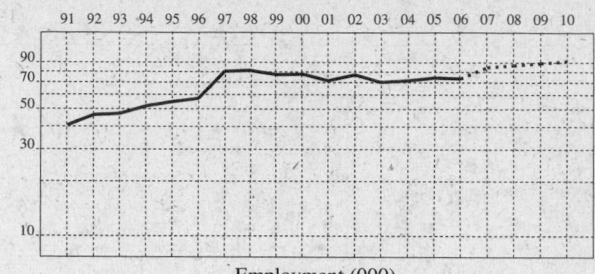

Employment (000)

GENERAL STATISTICS

Year	Com-panies	Establishments		Employment			Compensation		Production ($ million)			
		Total	with 20 or more employees	Total (000)	Production Workers (000)	Hours (Mil)	Payroll ($ mil)	Wages ($/hr)	Cost of Materials	Value Added by Manufacture	Value of Shipments	Capital Invest.
1991		1,492	577	40.6	32.3	70.5	1,017.0	10.23	1,110.3	1,888.1	2,974.7	101.4
1992	1,671	1,706	646	46.4	36.5	77.6	1,270.8	11.29	1,443.5	2,393.5	3,830.1	135.1
1993		1,667	655	47.1	38.5	81.5	1,334.0	11.36	1,524.2	2,655.8	4,169.6	152.2
1994		1,632	654	51.8	41.9	91.8	1,461.3	11.25	1,716.6	2,974.0	4,669.1	225.3
1995		1,620	691	54.7	44.4	95.7	1,574.1	11.60	1,964.6	3,230.3	5,130.9	253.7
1996		1,660	689	57.1	46.0	97.9	1,683.4	12.26	1,932.5	3,351.1	5,277.8	231.0
1997	2,696	2,745	1,125	80.4	63.7	136.6	2,634.0	13.28	2,849.0	5,512.9	8,326.1	578.2
1998		2,689	1,169	81.4	65.4	139.3	2,720.8	13.56	2,872.3	5,732.8	8,616.7	652.7
1999		2,616	1,110	77.2	61.2	128.3	2,690.5	14.39	2,717.2	5,477.7	8,210.7	582.4
2000		2,555	1,084	77.8	62.1	129.0	2,792.5	15.04	2,836.9	5,737.5	8,561.2	587.1
2001		2,487	1,070	71.7	57.2	116.9	2,557.1	15.06	2,515.0	5,082.7	7,655.1	431.9
2002	2,831	2,892	1,125	77.3	60.2	121.1	2,839.6	16.33	2,822.6	6,013.0	8,835.6	533.2
2003		2,832	1,047	70.3	55.5	122.9	2,737.9	15.88	2,805.2	5,674.2	8,425.5	412.2
2004		2,751	1,033	71.7	55.6	124.4	2,873.2	16.23	3,146.9	5,902.3	8,956.7	514.4
2005		2,665	1,058	74.5	58.8	129.4	3,052.6	16.59	3,796.5	6,381.6	10,099.7	553.4
2006		3,113P	1,243P	73.8	58.2	128.4	3,181.0	17.13	4,059.4	6,765.3	10,765.4	573.1
2007		3,219P	1,283P	84.9P	66.7P	143.6P	3,497.7P	17.85P	4,220.8P	7,034.3P	11,193.4P	671.0P
2008		3,325P	1,324P	87.1P	68.4P	147.3P	3,641.4P	18.33P	4,399.9P	7,332.7P	11,668.4P	702.1P
2009		3,430P	1,365P	89.3P	70.0P	151.1P	3,785.1P	18.80P	4,579.0P	7,631.2P	12,143.3P	733.1P
2010		3,536P	1,406P	91.6P	71.7P	154.8P	3,928.8P	19.27P	4,758.1P	7,929.7P	12,618.2P	764.1P

Sources: 1992, 1997, 2002 *Economic Census*; other years, up to 2006, are from the *Annual Survey of Manufactures*. Establishment counts for non-Census years are from *County Business Patterns*; 1997 and 2002 values are from the 1997 and 2002 censuses respectively, reported in the Federal Government's NAICS format. Other years were originally reported in equivalent SIC format. 'P's show projections by the editors.

INDICES OF CHANGE

Year	Com-panies	Establishments		Employment			Compensation		Production ($ million)			
		Total	with 20 or more employees	Total (000)	Production Workers (000)	Hours (Mil)	Payroll ($ mil)	Wages ($/hr)	Cost of Materials	Value Added by Manufacture	Value of Shipments	Capital Invest.
1992	59	59	57	60	61	64	45	69	51	40	43	25
1997	95	95	100	104	106	113	93	81	101	92	94	108
2001		86	95	93	95	97	90	92	89	85	87	81
2002	100	100	100	100	100	100	100	100	100	100	100	100
2003		98	93	91	92	101	96	97	99	94	95	77
2004		95	92	93	92	103	101	99	111	98	101	96
2005		92	94	96	98	107	108	102	135	106	114	104
2006		108P	110P	95	97	106	112	105	144	113	122	107
2007		111P	114P	110P	111P	119P	123P	109P	150P	117P	127P	126P
2008		115P	118P	113P	114P	122P	128P	112P	156P	122P	132P	132P
2009		119P	121P	116P	116P	125P	133P	115P	162P	127P	137P	137P
2010		122P	125P	118P	119P	128P	138P	118P	169P	132P	143P	143P

Sources: Same as General Statistics. Values reflect change from the base year, 2002. Values above 100 mean greater than 2002, values below 100 mean less than 2002, and the values of 100 in other years means the same as 2002. 'P's show projections by the editors.

SELECTED RATIOS

For 2002	Avg. of All Manufact.	Analyzed Industry	Index	For 2002	Avg. of All Manufact.	Analyzed Industry	Index
Employees per Establishment	42	27	64	Value Added per Production Worker	182,367	99,884	55
Payroll per Establishment	1,639,184	981,881	60	Cost per Establishment	5,769,015	976,003	17
Payroll per Employee	39,053	36,735	94	Cost per Employee	137,446	36,515	27
Production Workers per Establishment	30	21	71	Cost per Production Worker	195,506	46,887	24
Wages per Establishment	694,845	683,805	98	Shipments per Establishment	11,158,348	3,055,187	27
Wages per Production Worker	23,548	32,850	140	Shipments per Employee	265,847	114,303	43
Hours per Production Worker	1,980	2,012	102	Shipments per Production Worker	378,144	146,771	39
Wages per Hour	11.89	16.33	137	Investment per Establishment	361,338	184,371	51
Value Added per Establishment	5,381,325	2,079,184	39	Investment per Employee	8,609	6,898	80
Value Added per Employee	128,210	77,788	61	Investment per Production Worker	12,245	8,857	72

Sources: Same as General Statistics. The 'Average of All Manufacturing' column represents the average of all manufacturing industries reported for the most recent complete year available. The Index shows the relationship between the Average and the Analyzed Industry. For example, 100 means that they are equal; 500 that the Analyzed Industry is five times the average; 50 means that the Analyzed Industry is half the national average. The abbreviation 'na' is used to show that data are 'not available'. Ratios shown for 2002, the last complete census year.

LEADING COMPANIES   Number shown: **75**   Total sales ($ mil): **9,057**   Total employment (000): **13.2**

Company Name	Address				CEO Name	Phone	Co. Type	Sales ($ mil)	Empl. (000)
Bolton Metal Products Ltd.	PO Box 388	Bellefonte	PA	16823	Charles Doland	814-355-6217	R	7,000*	<0.1
Hebco Products Inc.	1232 Whetstone St.	Bucyrus	OH	44820	Andrew Ason	419-562-7987	R	201*	0.9
Melling Tool Co.	PO Box 1188	Jackson	MI	49204	David Horthrop	517-787-8172	R	100*	0.3
Worthington Precision Metals	8229 Tyler Blvd.	Mentor	OH	44060	Joe Harden	440-255-6700	S	77*	0.3
JJ Ryan Corp.	PO Box 39	Plantsville	CT	06479	Ronald Fontanella	860-628-0393	R	66*	0.2
Bonney Forge Corp.	PO Box 330	Mount Union	PA	17066	John Leone	814-542-2545	R	55*	0.3
SH Leggitt Co.	1000 Civic Ctr Loop	San Marcos	TX	78666	Don Leggitt	512-396-0707	R	52*	0.2
North American Acquisition	1875 Holmes Rd.	Elgin	IL	60123	George Dressel	847-695-8030	R	51*	0.3
Griffiths Holding Corp.	2717 Niagara Ln. N	Minneapolis	MN	55447	Harold Griffiths	763-557-8935	R	49*	<0.1
GP Companies Inc.	11174 Northland Dr.	Saint Paul	MN	55120	William Brown	651-454-6500	R	46*	0.1
Huron Inc.	6554 Lakeshore Rd.	Lexington	MI	48450	Robert Bales	810-359-5344	R	43*	0.5
Hy-Production Inc.	6000 Grafton Rd.	Valley City	OH	44280	William Kneebusch	330-273-2400	R	41*	0.1
Ashley F. Ward Inc.	7490 Easy St.	Mason	OH	45040		513-398-1414	R	40*	0.3
Defiance Precision Products	1125 Precision Way	Defiance	OH	43512		419-782-8955	S	40*	0.3
Standby Screw Machine Products	1122 W Bagley Rd.	Berea	OH	44017	Sal Caroniti	440-243-8200	R	39*	0.4
Precision Tube Inc.	1025 Fortune Dr.	Richmond	KY	40475	Mark Gentry	859-623-5595	R	39*	0.1
Wayne Wire Cloth Products Inc.	PO Box 550	Kalkaska	MI	49646	Michael Brown	231-258-9187	R	37*	0.2
Shane Group Inc.	200 Industrial Dr.	Hillsdale	MI	49242	D.C. Shaneour	517-439-4316	R	37*	0.2
Mitchel and Scott Machine Co.	1841 Ludlow Ave.	Indianapolis	IN	46201	Brett Pheffer	317-639-5331	R	35*	0.3
Curtis Screw Company L.L.C.	50 Thielman Dr.	Buffalo	NY	14206	Paul Hojnacki	716-885-0110	R	34*	0.2
Black River Manufacturing Inc.	2625 20th Street	Port Huron	MI	48060		810-982-9812	R	32*	0.2
Dexter Automatic Products Co.	2500 Bishop Cir. E	Dexter	MI	48130	Ronald Tupper	734-426-8900	R	28*	0.2
Morris Manufacturing and Sales	1015 E Mechanic St.	Brazil	IN	47834	Michael Morris	812-446-6141	R	27*	0.1
Kennametal Inc.	378 Main Street	Lyndonville	VT	05851	Carlos M. Cardoso	802-626-3331	D	26*	0.3
Microbest Inc.	670 Captain Neville	Waterbury	CT	06705	Steven Griffin	203-597-0355	R	25*	0.1
Creed Monarch Inc.	PO Box 550	New Britain	CT	06050	Clark Creed	860-225-7884	R	23*	0.3
Master Automatic Machine Co.	40485 Schoolcraft	Plymouth	MI	48170	John Evasic	734-414-0500	R	22*	0.3
Hy-Level Industries Inc.	PO Box 368015	Cleveland	OH	44136	Donald Rebar	440-572-1540	R	22*	0.2
Golden States Engineering Inc.	15338 Garfield Ave.	Paramount	CA	90723	Alexandra Rostovski	562-634-3125	R	22*	0.1
Supreme Machined Products Co.	18686 172nd Ave.	Spring Lake	MI	49456	Gregory Olson	616-842-6550	R	21*	0.1
Precisionform Inc.	148 W Airport Rd.	Lititz	PA	17543	James Corckran	717-560-7610	R	21*	0.2
Aircraft Gear Corp.	PO Box 2066	Loves Park	IL	61130	Dean Olson	815-877-7473	R	20*	<0.1
Charleston Metal Products Inc.	350 Grant St.	Waterloo	IN	46793		260-837-8211	R	20*	0.1
Gits Manufacturing Co.	1739 Commerce Rd.	Creston	IA	50801	Daryl Lilly	641-782-2105	S	19*	0.2
Len Industries Inc.	815 Rice St.	Leslie	MI	49251	Leonard Len	517-589-8241	R	19*	0.2
Herker Industries Inc.	N57 Carmen	Menomonee Fls	WI	53051	Robert Fancher	262-781-8270	R	19*	0.2
Manth-Brownell Inc.	PO Box 59	Kirkville	NY	13082	Wesley Skinner	315-687-7263	R	19*	0.2
Automatic Machine Products Co.	PO Box 1018	Attleboro	MA	02703	John Holden	508-222-2300	R	19*	0.1
Fraen Corp.	80 Newcrossing Rd.	Reading	MA	01867	Charles Fuller	781-942-2223	R	19*	0.1
IW Industries Inc.	35 Melville Park Rd	Melville	NY	11747		631-293-9494	R	18*	0.2
Sli Holdings Inc.	PO Box 780	Westfield	IN	46074	Scott Waddell	317-867-0100	R	18*	0.1
Metal Seal and Products Inc.	4323 Hamann Pkwy.	Willoughby	OH	44094	Edmund Diemer	440-946-8500	R	18*	0.2
Dawlen Corp.	PO Box 884	Jackson	MI	49204	Faith F. Small	517-787-2200	R	18*	<0.1
Onyx Industries Inc.	25311 Normandie	Harbor City	CA	90710	Vladimir Reil	310-539-8830	R	18*	0.1
Alpha Grainger Manufacturing	20 Discovery Way	Franklin	MA	02038	Jacob Grainger	508-520-4005	R	18*	0.2
R and R Manufacturing Company	95 Silvermine Rd.	Seymour	CT	06483	Larry Lapucia	203-888-6441	R	18*	0.2
Biddle Precision Components	701 S Main St.	Sheridan	IN	46069	Brian Myers	317-758-4451	R	17*	0.2
MKM Machine Tool Company Inc.	PO Box 2307	Jeffersonville	IN	47131	Robert Moore	812-282-6627	R	17*	0.1
AMC Manufacturing Inc.	10584 Middle Ave.	Elyria	OH	44035	Kevin Koepp	440-458-5165	R	17*	0.1
Header Products Inc.	PO Box 74188	Romulus	MI	48174	Michael Mc Manus	734-941-2220	R	17*	0.1
White Engineering Surfaces	1 Pheasant Run	Newtown	PA	18940	Christopher Nyland	215-968-5021	R	17*	0.1
Alger Manufacturing Company	724 S Bon View	Ontario	CA	91761	Duane Femrite	909-986-4591	R	17*	0.1
Jewel Vallorbs Co.	PO Box 958	Lancaster	PA	17608	Jeanette Steudler	717-392-3978	R	17*	0.2
Nook Industries Inc.	4950 E 49th St.	Cleveland	OH	44125	Ronald Domeck	216-271-7900	R	17*	0.2
Remke Brothers Inc.	PO Box 327	Delavan	WI	53115	Warren Bentley	262-728-5262	R	16*	0.1
National Cycle Inc.	PO Box 158	Maywood	IL	60153	Barry Willey	708-343-0400	R	16*	<0.1
Steuby Company, John J	6002 N Lindbergh	Hazelwood	MO	63042	John Steuby	314-895-1000	R	16*	0.2
R and B Grinding Company Inc.	1900 Clark St.	Racine	WI	53403	Raymond Biddle	262-634-5538	R	15*	0.2
Bracalente Manufacturing Co.	PO Box 570	Trumbauersville	PA	18970	Thomas Bracalente	215-536-3077	R	15*	0.2
Sorenson Engineering Inc.	32032 Dunlap Blvd.	Yucaipa	CA	92399	David Sorenson	909-795-2434	R	15*	0.2
S and S Screw Machine Company	1500 McMinnville	Sparta	TN	38583	Larry Battle	931-738-3631	R	15*	0.1
Griner Engineering Inc.	2500 N Curry Pke.	Bloomington	IN	47404	John Griner	812-332-2220	R	15*	<0.1
General Automation Inc.	3300 Oakton St.	Skokie	IL	60076	Ed Gajewski	847-676-4004	R	14*	0.1
Seastrom Manufacturing Company	456 Seastrom St.	Twin Falls	ID	83301		208-737-4300	R	14*	0.1
Northwest Automatic Products	501 Royalston Ave.	Minneapolis	MN	55405	Tom Hoffelder	612-339-7521	R	14*	0.1
Specialty Manufacturing Co.	5858 Centerville Rd	Saint Paul	MN	55127	Dan Keown	651-653-0599	R	14*	<0.1
Tomz Corp.	47 Episcopal Rd.	Berlin	CT	06037	Zbignew Matulaniec	860-829-0670	R	13*	0.1
Quality Control Corp.	7315 W Wilson Ave.	Chicago	IL	60706	Richard Michalek	708-887-5400	R	13*	0.3
Meaden Screw Products Co.	16W210 83rd St.	Burr Ridge	IL	60527	Thomas Meaden	630-655-0888	R	13*	<0.1
Betty Machine Company Inc.	324 Free Hill Rd.	Hendersonville	TN	37075	John Zobl	615-826-6004	R	13*	0.1
Lutco Bearings Inc.	677 Cambridge St.	Worcester	MA	01610	John Stowe	508-756-6296	R	13*	0.1
Rima Manufacturing Company	3850 Munson Hwy.	Hudson	MI	49247	Edward Engle	517-448-8921	R	13*	0.1
Highland Machine & Screw Prods	PO Box 329	Highland	IL	62249	Edwin Frisse	618-654-2103	R	13*	0.1
T and L Automatics Inc.	770 Emerson St.	Rochester	NY	14613	Thomas Hassett	585-647-3717	R	12*	0.1
Torco Inc.	PO Box 4070	Marietta	GA	30061	William Smith	770-427-3704	R	12*	0.1

Source: Ward's Business Directory of U.S. Private and Public Companies, Volumes 1 and 2, 2008. The company type code used is as follows: P - Public, R - Private, S - Subsidiary, D - Division, J - Joint Venture, A - Affiliate, G - Group. Sales are in millions of dollars, employees are in thousands. An asterisk (*) indicates an estimated sales volume. The symbol < stands for 'less than'. Company names and addresses are truncated, in some cases, to fit into the available space.

MATERIALS CONSUMED

Material	Quantity	Delivered Cost ($ million)
Forgings	(X)	109.9
All other fabricated metal products (exc. castings, forgings, bolts, nuts, screws, washers, rivets, etc.)	(X)	44.4
Nonferrous (aluminum, copper, etc.) castings (rough and semifinished)	(X)	35.4
Iron and steel castings (rough and semifinished)	(X)	110.9
Steel bars and bar shapes (exc. castings, forgings, fabr. metal products)	(X)	380.5
Steel sheet and strip (including tinplate)	(X)	25.4
Steel wire and wire products	(X)	20.8
All other steel shapes and forms (exc. castings, forgings, fabr. metal products)	(X)	20.4
Copper and copper-base alloy rod, bar, and bar shapes (exc. castings, forgings, fabr. metal products)	(X)	86.0
All other copper and copper-base alloy shapes and forms (exc. castings, forgings, fabr. metal products)	(X)	(D)
Aluminum and aluminum-base alloy extruded shapes (rod, bar, pipe, tube, etc.)	(X)	67.6
All other aluminum and aluminum-base alloy shapes and forms (exc. castings, forgings, fabr. metal products)	(X)	15.5
Other nonferrous shapes and forms (exc. castings, forgings, fabricated metal products)	(X)	33.9
Paperboard containers, boxes, and corrugated paperboard	(X)	11.7
Special dies, tools, die sets, jigs, and fixtures (exc. cutting tools)	(X)	(D)
Plastics products consumed in the form of sheets, rods, etc.	(X)	8.8
Metal bolts, nuts, screws, and other screw machine products	(X)	57.2
Cutting tools for machine tools	(X)	99.3
All other materials, components, parts, containers, and supplies	(X)	425.0
Materials, ingredients, containers, and supplies, nsk	(X)	546.0

Source: 2002 *Economic Census*. Explanation of symbols used: (D): Withheld to avoid disclosure of competitive data; na: Not available; (S): Withheld because statistical norms were not met; (X): Not applicable; (Z): Less than half the unit shown; nec: Not elsewhere classified; nsk: Not specified by kind; - : zero; p : 10-19 percent estimated; q : 20-29 percent estimated.

PRODUCT SHARE DETAILS

Product or Product Class Shipments	Mil. $	Product or Product Class Shipments	Mil. $
PRECISION TURNED PRODUCTS, MADE ON CNC EQUIPMENT OR SCREW MACHINES	8,534.9	Precision turned products for medical supplies	365.5
Precision-turned products, automotive	**2,129.2**	Precision turned products for machinery, nec	741.0
Precision-turned products, except automotive	**4,367.3**	Precision turned products, nec	1,358.4
Precision turned products, aircraft	576.5	Precision turned products for ordnance	79.1
Precision turned products for household appliances (including radio and television)	211.7	Precision turned products for all other end uses	1,279.3
		Precision turned products, except automotive, nsk	769.1
Precision turned products for electric and electronic equipment (except household appliances)	345.1	**Precision turned products, made on CNC equipment or screw machines, nsk, total**	**2,038.4**

Source: 2002 *Economic Census*. The values are product shipments in millions of dollars for 2002. Total product shipments may be lower or higher than industry shipments. See Introduction for a full discussion. Values of indented subcategories are summed in the main heading(s). The symbol (D) appears when data are withheld to prevent disclosure of competitive information. The abbreviation nsk stands for 'not specified by kind' and nec for 'not elsewhere classified'. A dash (-) means zero.

INPUTS AND OUTPUTS FOR TURNED PRODUCT AND SCREW, NUT, AND BOLT MANUFACTURING

Economic Sector or Industry Providing Inputs	%	Sector	Economic Sector or Industry Buying Outputs	%	Sector
Compensation of employees	36.3		Motor vehicle parts	20.7	Manufg.
Iron & steel mills & ferroalloys	6.3	Manufg.	Exports of goods & services	5.1	Cap Inv
Steel products from purchased steel	4.4	Manufg.	Light truck & utility vehicles	3.2	Manufg.
Wholesale trade	3.6	Trade	Automobiles	2.7	Manufg.
Management of companies & enterprises	3.6	Services	Valve & fittings other than plumbing	2.3	Manufg.
Hardware	2.5	Manufg.	Nonresidential structures, nec	2.3	Construct.
Industrial molds	1.6	Manufg.	Ornamental & architectural metal products	2.0	Manufg.
Turned products & screws, nuts, & bolts	1.3	Manufg.	Plate work & fabricated structural products	1.7	Manufg.
Real estate	1.3	Fin/R.E.	General purpose machinery, nec	1.5	Manufg.
Copper rolling, drawing, extruding, & alloying	1.3	Manufg.	Machine shops	1.3	Manufg.
Power generation & supply	1.2	Util.	Turned products & screws, nuts, & bolts	1.2	Manufg.
Machine shops	1.1	Manufg.	Heavy duty trucks	1.2	Manufg.
Securities, commodity contracts, investments	1.1	Fin/R.E.	Wiring devices	1.2	Manufg.
Cutting tools & machine tool accessories	1.1	Manufg.	Aircraft parts & auxiliary equipment, nec	1.1	Manufg.
Special tools, dies, jigs, & fixtures	1.0	Manufg.	Personal consumption expenditures	1.1	
Truck transportation	0.9	Util.	Truck transportation	1.1	Util.
Nonferrous metal foundries	0.9	Manufg.	Wholesale trade	1.0	Trade
Ferrous metal foundries	0.9	Manufg.	Construction machinery	1.0	Manufg.
Nonferrous metal (ex. copper & aluminum) processing	0.8	Manufg.	Material handling equipment	0.9	Manufg.
Semiconductors & related devices	0.8	Manufg.	AC, refrigeration, and warm air heating equipment	0.9	Manufg.
Aluminum products from purchased aluminum	0.8	Manufg.	Hardware	0.9	Manufg.
Lessors of nonfinancial assets	0.7	Fin/R.E.	Fluid power process machinery	0.9	Manufg.
Forging, stamping, & sintering, nec	0.7	Manufg.	Farm machinery & equipment	0.9	Manufg.
Printed circuit assemblies (electronic assemblies)	0.7	Manufg.	Aircraft	0.9	Manufg.
Monetary authorities/depository credit intermediation	0.7	Fin/R.E.	Engine equipment, nec	0.9	Manufg.
Advertising & related services	0.6	Services	Electromedical & electrotherapeutic apparatus	0.9	Manufg.
Taxes on production & imports, less subsidies	0.6		Sporting & athletic goods	0.8	Manufg.
Professional, scientific, technical services, nec	0.6	Services	Industrial machinery, nec	0.8	Manufg.
Automotive equipment rental & leasing	0.5	Fin/R.E.	Motors & generators	0.8	Manufg.

Continued on next page.

INPUTS AND OUTPUTS FOR TURNED PRODUCT AND SCREW, NUT, AND BOLT MANUFACTURING - Continued

Economic Sector or Industry Providing Inputs	%	Sector	Economic Sector or Industry Buying Outputs	%	Sector
Accounting, tax preparation, bookkeeping, & payroll	0.4	Services	Lighting fixtures	0.8	Manufg.
Abrasive products	0.4	Manufg.	Electronic components, nec	0.8	Manufg.
Coating, engraving, heat treating & allied activities	0.4	Manufg.	Surgical appliances & supplies	0.7	Manufg.
Food services & drinking places	0.4	Services	Search, detection, & navigation instruments	0.7	Manufg.
Telecommunications	0.4	Services	Crowns & closures & metal stamping	0.7	Manufg.
Maintenance/repair of nonresidential structures	0.4	Construct.	Switchgear & switchboard apparatus	0.7	Manufg.
Data processing, hosting, & related services	0.4	Services	Commercial & service industry machinery, nec	0.7	Manufg.
Services to buildings & dwellings	0.4	Services	Special tools, dies, jigs, & fixtures	0.6	Manufg.
Warehousing & storage	0.4	Util.	Surgical & medical instrument	0.6	Manufg.
Legal services	0.3	Services	Motor vehicle bodies	0.6	Manufg.
Paperboard containers	0.3	Manufg.	Electronic connectors	0.6	Manufg.
Natural gas distribution	0.3	Util.	Coal	0.5	Mining
Commercial & industrial machinery rental & leasing	0.3	Fin/R.E.	Lawn & garden equipment	0.5	Manufg.
Fabricated metals, nec	0.3	Manufg.	Broadcast & wireless communications equipment	0.5	Manufg.
Architectural, engineering, & related services	0.3	Services	Electrical equipment & components, nec	0.5	Manufg.
Springs & wire products	0.3	Manufg.	Residential permanent site structures	0.5	Construct.
Hotels & motels, including casino hotels	0.2	Services	Fabricated metals, nec	0.5	Manufg.
Scientific research & development services	0.2	Services	Communications equipment, nec	0.5	Manufg.
Automotive repair & maintenance, ex. car washes	0.2	Services	Telephone apparatus	0.5	Manufg.
Commercial & industrial equipment repair/maintenance	0.2	Services	Rubber products, nec	0.5	Manufg.
Air transportation	0.2	Util.	Retail trade	0.4	Trade
Management, scientific, & technical consulting	0.2	Services	Pumps & pumping equipment	0.4	Manufg.
Business support services	0.2	Services	Semiconductor machinery	0.4	Manufg.
Metal cans, boxes, & other containers (light gauge)	0.2	Manufg.	Turbines & turbine generator set units	0.4	Manufg.
Custom roll forming	0.2	Manufg.	Manufacturing, nec	0.4	Manufg.
Other computer related services, including facilities	0.1	Services	Plastics products, nec	0.4	Manufg.
Plastics packaging materials, film & sheet	0.1	Manufg.	Relay & industrial controls	0.4	Manufg.
Rail transportation	0.1	Util.	General S/L govt. services	0.4	S/L Govt
Employment services	0.1	Services	Automotive repair & maintenance, ex. car washes	0.4	Services
Nondepository credit intermediation activities	0.1	Fin/R.E.	Air & gas compressors	0.4	Manufg.
Paperboard mills	0.1	Manufg.	Irradiation apparatus	0.4	Manufg.
Specialized design services	0.1	Services	Printed circuit assemblies (electronic assembiles)	0.4	Manufg.
Crowns & closures & metal stamping	0.1	Manufg.	Petroleum refineries	0.4	Manufg.
Plate work & fabricated structural products	0.1	Manufg.	Household cooking appliances	0.4	Manufg.
Bare printed circuit boards	0.1	Manufg.	Handtools	0.4	Manufg.
Ornamental & architectural metal products	0.1	Manufg.	Oil & gas extraction	0.4	Mining
Showcases, partitions, shelving, and lockers	0.1	Manufg.	Metal cans, boxes, & other containers (light gauge)	0.4	Manufg.
Waste management & remediation services	0.1	Services	Industrial process variable instruments	0.3	Manufg.
			Custom roll forming	0.3	Manufg.
			Watches, clocks, & related devices	0.3	Manufg.
			Truck trailers	0.3	Manufg.
			Travel trailers & campers	0.3	Manufg.
			Manufactured homes & mobile homes	0.3	Manufg.
			Printing	0.3	Manufg.
			Industrial molds	0.3	Manufg.
			Coating, engraving, heat treating & allied activities	0.3	Manufg.
			Mining & oil & gas field machinery	0.3	Manufg.
			Commercial & industrial equipment repair/maintenance	0.3	Services
			Boat building	0.3	Manufg.
			Audio & video equipment	0.3	Manufg.
			Heating equipment (except warm air furnaces)	0.3	Manufg.
			Springs & wire products	0.3	Manufg.
			Signs	0.3	Manufg.
			Residential structures, nec	0.3	Construct.
			Ship building & repairing	0.3	Manufg.
			Military armored vehicles, tanks, & tank components	0.3	Manufg.
			Soft drinks & ice	0.3	Manufg.
			Aircraft engine & engine parts	0.2	Manufg.
			Major household appliances, nec	0.2	Manufg.
			Totalizing fluid meters & counting devices	0.2	Manufg.
			Motorcycles, bicycles, & parts	0.2	Manufg.
			Arms, ordnance, & accessories	0.2	Manufg.
			Metal cutting & forming machine tools	0.2	Manufg.
			Transportation equipment, nec	0.2	Manufg.
			Household laundry equipment	0.2	Manufg.
			Railroad rolling stock	0.2	Manufg.
			Power-driven handtools	0.2	Manufg.
			Magnetic & optical recording media	0.2	Manufg.
			Electron tubes	0.2	Manufg.
			Plastics & rubber industry machinery	0.2	Manufg.
			Small electrical appliances	0.2	Manufg.
			Owner-occupied dwellings	0.2	
			Basic organic chemicals, nec	0.2	Manufg.
			Analytical laboratory instruments	0.2	Manufg.
			Commercial & health care structures	0.2	Construct.
			Jewelry & silverware	0.2	Manufg.
			Scenic & sightseeing transport & related services	0.2	Util.
			Ball & roller bearings	0.2	Manufg.
			Wood windows & doors & millwork	0.2	Manufg.
			Food services & drinking places	0.2	Services

Continued on next page.

INPUTS AND OUTPUTS FOR TURNED PRODUCT AND SCREW, NUT, AND BOLT MANUFACTURING - Continued

Economic Sector or Industry Providing Inputs	%	Sector	Economic Sector or Industry Buying Outputs	%	Sector
			Household refrigerators & home freezers	0.2	Manufg.
			Power boilers & heat exchangers	0.2	Manufg.
			Newspaper publishers	0.2	Services
			Plastics packaging materials, film & sheet	0.2	Manufg.
			Rolling mill & other metalworking machinery	0.2	Manufg.
			Breweries	0.1	Manufg.
			Cutting tools & machine tool accessories	0.1	Manufg.
			Packaging machinery	0.1	Manufg.
			Paperboard containers	0.1	Manufg.
			Telecommunications	0.1	Services
			Fabricated pipes & pipe fittings	0.1	Manufg.
			Maintenance/repair of nonresidential structures	0.1	Construct.
			Personal & household goods repair/maintenance	0.1	Services
			Ammunition	0.1	Manufg.
			Iron & steel mills & ferroalloys	0.1	Manufg.
			Toilet preparations	0.1	Manufg.
			Mechanical power transmission equipment	0.1	Manufg.
			Power, distribution, & specialty transformers	0.1	Manufg.
			Automatic environmental controls	0.1	Manufg.
			Vending, commercial, industrial, office machinery	0.1	Manufg.
			Software publishers	0.1	Services
			Book publishers	0.1	Services
			Motor homes	0.1	Manufg.
			Plastics materials & resins	0.1	Manufg.
			Paper mills	0.1	Manufg.
			Custom architectural woodwork & millwork	0.1	Manufg.
			Community food, housing, relief, & rehabilitation	0.1	Services
			Computer terminals & peripherals	0.1	Manufg.
			Directories, mailing lists, & other publishers	0.1	Services
			Internet publishing & broadcasting	0.1	Services
			Air purification & ventilation equipment	0.1	Manufg.
			Warehousing & storage	0.1	Util.
			Optical instruments & lenses	0.1	Manufg.

Source: Benchmark Input-Output Accounts for the U.S. Economy, 2002, U.S. Department of Commerce, Washington D.C., January 2008. User should note that this Input-Output table is not for this particular narrowly defined industry but for a larger aggregate. Input and Output data for Turned Product and Screw, Nut, and Bolt Manufacturing include Input and Output data for the Annual Survey of Manufactures' NAICS industries 332721 and 332722. The abbreviation nec stands for 'not elsewhere classified'.

OCCUPATIONS EMPLOYED BY MACHINE SHOPS, TURNED PRODUCTS, & SCREWS, NUTS, & BOLTS

Occupation	% of Total 2006	Change to 2016	Occupation	% of Total 2006	Change to 2016
Machinists	23.5	-14.4	Maintenance & repair workers, general	1.2	-20.9
Computer-controlled machine tool operators	7.6	-10.9	Numerical tool & process control programmers	1.1	-16.4
First-line supervisors/managers of production workers	5.1	-19.6	Secretaries, exc legal, medical, & executive	1.0	-27.4
Lathe & turning machine tool operators & tenders	4.5	-29.8	Laborers & freight, stock, & material movers, hand	1.0	-28.9
Welders, cutters, solderers, & brazers	3.7	-12.4	Janitors & cleaners, exc maids & housekeeping cleaners	0.9	-17.2
Inspectors, testers, sorters, samplers, & weighers	2.7	-25.9	Mechanical engineers	0.9	-20.2
Cutting, punching, & press machine operators	2.6	-29.9	Executive secretaries & administrative assistants	0.8	-19.1
Grinding, lapping, polishing machine tool operators	2.6	-22.2	Purchasing agents, exc wholesale, retail, & farm	0.7	-19.7
Helpers--Production workers	2.4	-19.0	Forging machine operators & tenders	0.7	-40.5
General & operations managers	2.2	-27.4	Truck drivers, light or delivery services	0.7	-18.7
Office clerks, general	1.9	-20.1	Industrial machinery mechanics	0.7	-8.0
Drilling & boring machine tool operators	1.9	-28.9	Rolling machine operators & tenders	0.6	-25.9
Shipping, receiving, & traffic clerks	1.8	-24.1	Accountants & auditors	0.6	-20.2
Team assemblers	1.8	-20.3	Production, planning, & expediting clerks	0.6	-21.0
Sales reps, wholesale & manufacturing, exc tech	1.7	-20.1	Structural metal fabricators & fitters	0.6	-17.6
Bookkeeping, accounting, & auditing clerks	1.6	-19.1	Industrial engineers	0.6	-5.0
Milling & planing machine operators & tenders	1.6	-27.3	Packers & packagers, hand	0.5	-38.3
Multiple machine tool operators & tenders	1.5	-14.3	First-line supervisors/managers of office workers	0.5	-25.4
Tool & die makers	1.4	-17.6	Customer service representatives	0.5	-14.4
Industrial production managers	1.2	-20.3			

Source: Industry-Occupation Matrix, Bureau of Labor Statistics, December 4, 2007. These data are reported based on 4-digit NAICS categories but have been matched to corresponding 6-digit NAICS industry codes. The change reported for each occupation to the year 2016 is a percent of growth or decline as estimated by the Bureau of Labor Statistics. The abbreviation nec stands for 'not elsewhere classified'.

LOCATION BY STATE AND REGIONAL CONCENTRATION

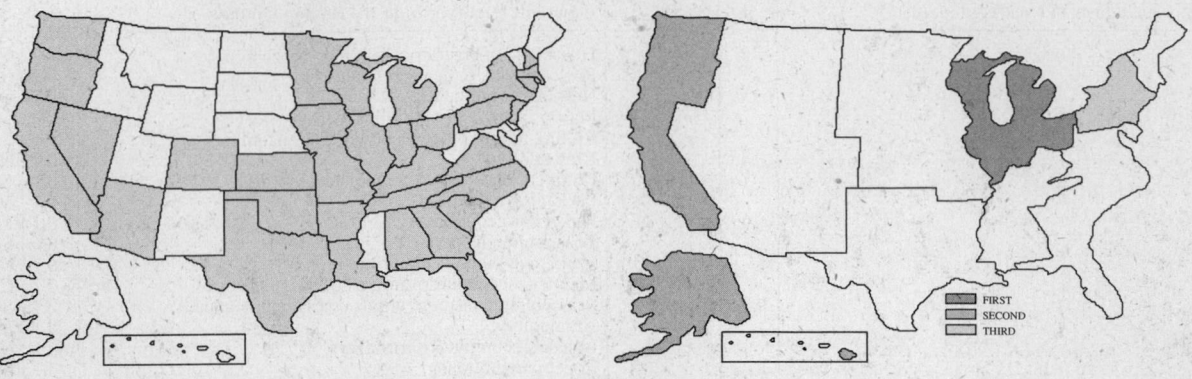

INDUSTRY DATA BY STATE

| State | Establish-ments | Shipments | | | Employment | | | | Cost as % of Shipments | Investment per Employee ($) |
		Total ($ mil)	% of U.S.	Per Establ.	Total Number	% of U.S.	Per Establ.	Wages ($/hour)		
Michigan	268	1,308.6	14.8	4,882.7	9,200	11.9	34	16.44	35.9	8,445
Ohio	246	950.7	10.8	3,864.5	8,000	10.3	33	15.52	32.9	6,252
California	386	857.9	9.7	2,222.5	8,121	10.5	21	16.43	27.0	4,550
Illinois	214	843.8	9.6	3,943.1	7,670	9.9	36	15.91	31.9	6,928
New York	165	499.2	5.6	3,025.4	4,873	6.3	30	16.00	37.1	7,530
Indiana	95	428.2	4.8	4,507.0	3,906	5.1	41	16.20	34.8	9,871
Pennsylvania	136	421.7	4.8	3,100.7	4,019	5.2	30	15.74	35.1	5,382
Connecticut	145	382.0	4.3	2,634.4	3,362	4.3	23	17.68	30.1	4,103
Texas	144	344.7	3.9	2,393.7	2,989	3.9	21	17.02	26.2	10,627
Wisconsin	113	340.0	3.8	3,008.7	2,895	3.7	26	16.66	34.0	6,730
Minnesota	89	293.9	3.3	3,302.2	2,491	3.2	28	17.67	33.3	6,820
Massachusetts	85	226.9	2.6	2,669.0	1,868	2.4	22	17.87	26.0	9,196
New Jersey	84	171.8	1.9	2,045.3	1,418	1.8	17	17.68	22.7	3,344
Missouri	54	169.6	1.9	3,140.1	1,620	2.1	30	16.40	34.9	3,327
Iowa	36	144.5	1.6	4,013.9	1,317	1.7	37	15.64	36.7	3,134
North Carolina	50	115.1	1.3	2,302.2	922	1.2	18	15.90	22.3	3,903
Florida	57	114.4	1.3	2,007.7	1,175	1.5	21	15.07	26.6	3,455
Arizona	37	106.6	1.2	2,879.8	1,053	1.4	28	16.21	32.8	12,020
Washington	46	101.9	1.2	2,215.2	838	1.1	18	22.35	32.0	3,317
South Carolina	21	88.6	1.0	4,219.3	585	0.8	28	15.46	35.1	8,137
Georgia	26	87.2	1.0	3,354.5	683	0.9	26	15.29	33.7	14,316
Tennessee	35	86.8	1.0	2,481.1	905	1.2	26	14.73	31.9	4,288
Kansas	21	60.4	0.7	2,876.5	544	0.7	26	14.96	26.8	9,127
Oregon	26	60.3	0.7	2,317.3	526	0.7	20	19.33	24.8	31,253
New Hampshire	24	58.9	0.7	2,453.2	559	0.7	23	17.96	20.2	11,662
Louisiana	17	54.2	0.6	3,186.0	450	0.6	26	13.91	28.4	16,384
Kentucky	25	53.7	0.6	2,149.9	604	0.8	24	13.73	33.5	5,227
Colorado	34	52.0	0.6	1,529.0	554	0.7	16	18.73	24.6	4,953
Oklahoma	28	45.2	0.5	1,615.2	485	0.6	17	18.79	37.1	3,186
Alabama	26	44.0	0.5	1,694.2	373	0.5	14	15.13	30.7	4,214
Virginia	17	40.3	0.5	2,367.9	399	0.5	23	18.29	23.6	2,762
Arkansas	12	19.8	0.2	1,654.1	189	0.2	16	15.51	38.8	6,878
Nevada	11	16.7	0.2	1,516.2	148	0.2	13	16.58	20.3	1,770
Rhode Island	23	15.8	0.2	686.9	183	0.2	8	14.61	29.2	4,962

Source: 2002 *Economic Census*. The states are in descending order of shipments or establishments (if shipment data are missing for the majority). The symbol (D) appears when data are withheld to prevent disclosure of competitive information. States marked with (D) are sorted by number of establishments. A dash (-) indicates that the data element cannot be calculated. Data may not show all states active in the NAICS category. All data available at the time of publication are shown.

NAICS 332722 - BOLT, NUT, SCREW, RIVET, AND WASHER MANUFACTURING

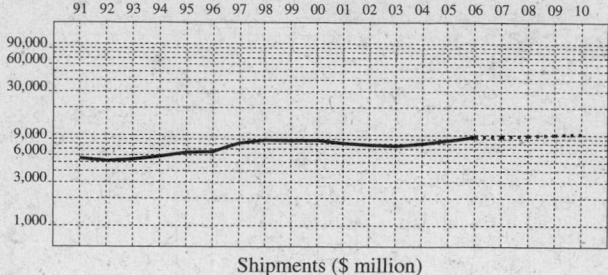

Shipments ($ million)

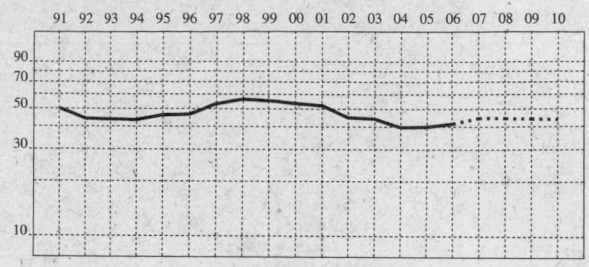

Employment (000)

GENERAL STATISTICS

Year	Companies	Establishments		Employment			Compensation		Production ($ million)			
		Total	with 20 or more employees	Total (000)	Production Workers (000)	Hours (Mil)	Payroll ($ mil)	Wages ($/hr)	Cost of Materials	Value Added by Manufacture	Value of Shipments	Capital Invest.
1991		911	479	50.0	36.3	77.4	1,419.5	11.83	2,402.0	3,108.8	5,508.8	174.6
1992	806	930	436	44.0	31.8	66.4	1,350.0	12.80	2,309.2	2,866.4	5,183.1	150.9
1993		914	439	43.7	32.0	68.2	1,361.1	12.74	2,351.3	3,008.2	5,373.2	163.0
1994		895	453	43.4	31.9	68.5	1,413.9	12.76	2,546.2	3,276.4	5,793.7	157.3
1995		893	472	46.1	34.2	72.2	1,530.6	13.58	2,888.2	3,541.4	6,393.1	386.6
1996		942	475	46.5	35.1	74.7	1,581.6	13.36	2,976.1	3,585.1	6,519.0	189.5
1997	911	1,040	529	53.0	39.6	84.3	1,939.4	14.56	3,507.3	4,649.8	8,130.5	396.4
1998		1,033	546	56.3	42.4	89.2	2,046.2	14.92	3,748.5	5,088.1	8,766.2	351.6
1999		1,009	537	55.3	41.9	88.5	2,087.2	15.47	3,663.3	4,980.0	8,654.8	374.7
2000		993	520	53.5	40.6	85.6	2,122.2	16.23	3,694.6	5,013.2	8,720.4	397.3
2001		973	503	52.1	39.7	82.0	1,990.2	15.84	3,382.8	4,622.6	8,109.5	273.3
2002	835	964	456	44.8	33.3	69.3	1,794.9	16.66	3,329.8	4,452.0	7,782.8	307.2
2003		944	458	44.2	32.0	70.5	1,790.7	16.31	3,244.7	4,385.9	7,586.0	306.1
2004		937	458	39.7	28.9	64.0	1,701.8	17.15	3,394.2	4,770.9	8,013.3	214.0
2005		924	460	39.9	29.1	62.5	1,768.5	17.84	3,883.5	4,960.6	8,709.9	215.5
2006		978P	490P	41.5	30.9	63.8	1,922.1	19.41	4,202.8	5,406.9	9,513.7	229.3
2007		981P	491P	44.6P	33.4P	70.9P	2,046.3P	18.83P	4,220.1P	5,429.1P	9,552.8P	311.1P
2008		985P	492P	44.4P	33.2P	70.5P	2,082.4P	19.27P	4,330.8P	5,571.6P	9,803.4P	316.1P
2009		988P	493P	44.1P	33.0P	70.1P	2,118.6P	19.71P	4,441.5P	5,714.0P	10,054.1P	321.2P
2010		991P	494P	43.8P	32.8P	69.7P	2,154.8P	20.15P	4,552.2P	5,856.4P	10,304.7P	326.3P

Sources: 1992, 1997, 2002 *Economic Census*; other years, up to 2006, are from the *Annual Survey of Manufactures*. Establishment counts for non-Census years are from *County Business Patterns*; 1997 and 2002 values are from the 1997 and 2002 censuses respectively, reported in the Federal Government's NAICS format. Other years were originally reported in equivalent SIC format. 'P's show projections by the editors.

INDICES OF CHANGE

Year	Companies	Establishments		Employment			Compensation		Production ($ million)			
		Total	with 20 or more employees	Total (000)	Production Workers (000)	Hours (Mil)	Payroll ($ mil)	Wages ($/hr)	Cost of Materials	Value Added by Manufacture	Value of Shipments	Capital Invest.
1992	97	96	96	98	95	96	75	77	69	64	67	49
1997	109	108	116	118	119	122	108	87	105	104	104	129
2001		101	110	116	119	118	111	95	102	104	104	89
2002	100	100	100	100	100	100	100	100	100	100	100	100
2003		98	100	99	96	102	100	98	97	99	97	100
2004		97	100	89	87	92	95	103	102	107	103	70
2005		96	101	89	87	90	99	107	117	111	112	70
2006		101P	107P	93	93	92	107	117	126	121	122	75
2007		102P	108P	100P	100P	102P	114P	113P	127P	122P	123P	101P
2008		102P	108P	99P	100P	102P	116P	116P	130P	125P	126P	103P
2009		102P	108P	98P	99P	101P	118P	118P	133P	128P	129P	105P
2010		103P	108P	98P	98P	101P	120P	121P	137P	132P	132P	106P

Sources: Same as General Statistics. Values reflect change from the base year, 2002. Values above 100 mean greater than 2002, values below 100 mean less than 2002, and the values of 100 in other years means the same as 2002. 'P's show projections by the editors.

SELECTED RATIOS

For 2002	Avg. of All Manufact.	Analyzed Industry	Index	For 2002	Avg. of All Manufact.	Analyzed Industry	Index
Employees per Establishment	42	46	111	Value Added per Production Worker	182,367	133,694	73
Payroll per Establishment	1,639,184	1,861,929	114	Cost per Establishment	5,769,015	3,454,149	60
Payroll per Employee	39,053	40,065	103	Cost per Employee	137,446	74,326	54
Production Workers per Establishment	30	35	117	Cost per Production Worker	195,506	99,994	51
Wages per Establishment	694,845	1,197,654	172	Shipments per Establishment	11,158,348	8,073,444	72
Wages per Production Worker	23,548	34,671	147	Shipments per Employee	265,847	173,723	65
Hours per Production Worker	1,980	2,081	105	Shipments per Production Worker	378,144	233,718	62
Wages per Hour	11.89	16.66	140	Investment per Establishment	361,338	318,672	88
Value Added per Establishment	5,381,325	4,618,257	86	Investment per Employee	8,609	6,857	80
Value Added per Employee	128,210	99,375	78	Investment per Production Worker	12,245	9,225	75

Sources: Same as General Statistics. The 'Average of All Manufacturing' column represents the average of all manufacturing industries reported for the most recent complete year available. The Index shows the relationship between the Average and the Analyzed Industry. For example, 100 means that they are equal; 500 that the Analyzed Industry is five times the average; 50 means that the Analyzed Industry is half the national average. The abbreviation 'na' is used to show that data are 'not available'. Ratios shown for 2002, the last complete census year.

LEADING COMPANIES   Number shown: 75   Total sales ($ mil): 85,038   Total employment (000): 155.4

Company Name	Address				CEO Name	Phone	Co. Type	Sales ($ mil)	Empl. (000)
Nucor Corp.	1915 Rexford Rd.	Charlotte	NC	28211	Daniel R. DiMicco	704-366-7000	P	16,593	18.0
Illinois Tool Works Inc.	3600 W Lake Ave.	Glenview	IL	60025		847-724-7500	P	16,171	60.0
Textron Inc.	40 Westminster St.	Providence	RI	02903		401-421-2800	P	13,225	44.0
Acument Global Technologies	840 W Long Lake	Troy	MI	48098	Joseph Gray	248-813-6329	S	10,080*	9.0
Triangle Suspension Systems	PO Box 425	Du Bois	PA	15801	Greg Maffia	814-375-7211	R	7,000*	0.2
Union Tank Car Co.	175 W Jackson Blvd.	Chicago	IL	60604	Kenneth Fischl	312-431-3111	R	7,000*	0.2
Bolton Metal Products Ltd.	PO Box 388	Bellefonte	PA	16823	Charles Doland	814-355-6217	R	7,000*	<0.1
ACCO Brands Corp.	300 Tower Pkwy.	Lincolnshire	IL	60069	David Campbell		P	1,939	6.0
Connell L.P.	1 International Pl.	Boston	MA	02110	Margot C. Connell	617-737-2700	R	1,429*	2.0
Fairchild Corp.	1750 Tysons Blvd.	McLean	VA	22102	Eric I. Steiner	703-478-5800	P	355	0.8
Saf-Holland USA Inc.	PO Box 425	Muskegon	MI	49443	Timothy Hemingway	231-773-3271	R	321*	0.3
Penn Engineering and Mfg.	PO Box 1000	Danboro	PA	18916	Charlie Grigg	215-766-8853	R	239*	1.4
T-3 Energy Services Inc.	7135 Ardmore	Houston	TX	77054	Gus D. Halas	713-996-4110	P	217	0.7
MNP Corp.	PO Box 189002	Utica	MI	48318	Larry Berman	586-254-1320	R	200*	0.6
Anstro Manufacturing Inc.	238 Wolcott Rd.	Wolcott	CT	06716	Robert Bosco	203-879-1423	R	182*	0.2
Pfi L.L.C.	PO Box 879	Pawtucket	RI	02862		401-725-3880	R	178*	<0.1
Cold Heading Co.	21777 Hoover Rd.	Warren	MI	48089		586-497-7000	R	150*	<0.1
H and L Tool Company Inc.	32701 Dequindre	Madison Heights	MI	48071	Michael Bourg	248-585-7474	S	148*	0.1
Tinnerman Palnut Engineer Prds	1060 W 130th St.	Brunswick	OH	44212	Todd Hemingway	330-220-5100	S	140*	0.6
Purchased Parts Group Inc.	2700 Summer Ave.	Memphis	TN	38112	A. Lee Mulkey	901-452-7491	R	139*	0.3
John Wagner Associates Inc.	205 Mason Cir.	Concord	CA	94520	Richard Holmberg	925-687-6606	R	120*	0.4
Integrated Logistics Solutions	23000 Euclid Ave.	Cleveland	OH	44117	Edward Crawford	216-692-7100	D	114*	0.3
ITW Bee Leitzke	2000 Industrial Rd.	Iron Ridge	WI	53035		920-625-2342	R	103*	0.2
Kamax L.P.	500 W Long Lake	Troy	MI	48098		248-879-0200	R	90*	0.3
Daniel Measurement and Control	PO Box 19097	Houston	TX	77224	Joe Vasvily	713-467-6000	S	79*	0.5
Emhart Teknologies Inc.	PO Box 868	Mount Clemens	MI	48046	Paul A. Gustafson	586-949-0440	S	70*	0.5
Standard Steel Specialty Co.	PO Box 20	Beaver Falls	PA	15010	Robert Conley	724-846-7600	S	67*	0.3
Huck International Aerospace	3724 E Columbia St.	Tucson	AZ	85714		520-519-7400	D	67*	0.2
Crest Electronics Inc.	PO Box 727	Dassel	MN	55325	Larry Lautt	320-275-3382	R	66*	<0.1
Limitorque Corp.	PO Box 11318	Lynchburg	VA	24506		434-528-4400	S	65*	0.3
Semblex Corp.	199 W Diversey	Elmhurst	IL	60126	Robert Rothkopf	630-833-2880	R	62*	0.1
Nelson Stud Welding Inc.	PO Box 4019	Elyria	OH	44036	Ken Caratelli	440-329-0400	R	54*	0.4
Strongwell Corp.	PO Box 580	Bristol	VA	24203		276-645-8000	R	50*	0.4
AAA Aircraft Supply L.L.C.	68 Shaker Rd.	Enfield	CT	06082	Charles W. Grigg	860-749-1116	S	50*	0.2
Arnold Engineering Co.	300 N West St.	Marengo	IL	60152	Charles W. Grigg	815-568-2000	S	50*	0.2
Greenville Metals Inc.	99 Crestview Dr.	Transfer	PA	16154	Charles W. Grigg	724-646-0654	S	50*	0.2
SPS International Investment	1105 N Market St.	Wilmington	DE	19801	Charles W. Grigg	302-478-9055	S	50*	0.2
Jergens Inc.	15700 S Waterloo	Cleveland	OH	44110		216-486-2100	R	49*	0.2
Detroit Heading L.L.C.	6421 Lynch Rd.	Detroit	MI	48234	Jeanette M. Abraham	313-267-2240	R	49	<0.1
Standco Industries Inc.	PO Box 87	Houston	TX	77001		713-224-6311	R	43*	0.3
Edwin B Stimpson Company Inc.	900 Sylvan Ave.	Bayport	NY	11705		631-472-2000	R	42*	0.2
Chicago Rivet and Machine Co.	PO Box 3061	Naperville	IL	60566	Michael J. Bourg	630-357-8500	P	40	0.3
ND Industries Inc.	1000 N Crooks Rd.	Clawson	MI	48017	Richard Wallace	248-655-2520	R	40*	0.1
Precision Tube Inc.	1025 Fortune Dr.	Richmond	KY	40475	Mark Gentry	859-623-5595	R	39*	0.1
Captive Fasteners Corp.	19 Thornton Rd.	Oakland	NJ	07436		201-337-6800	R	36*	0.3
Federal Screw Works	20229 Nine Mile Rd.	St. Clair Shore	MI	48080		586-443-4222	P	35	0.3
Accurate Threaded Fasteners	3550 W Pratt Ave.	Lincolnwood	IL	60712	Don Surber	847-677-1300	R	33*	0.3
Allfast Fastening Systems Inc.	15200 Don Julian Rd	Hacienda Hts	CA	91745	James Randall	626-968-9388	R	33*	0.3
Birmingham Fastener and Supply	PO Box 10323	Birmingham	AL	35202	Howard Tinney	205-595-3511	R	33*	0.2
Corpus Christi Gasket/Fastener	PO Box 4074	Corpus Christi	TX	78469	David Massie	361-884-6366	R	32*	0.1
JD Norman Industries Inc.	787 W Belden Ave.	Addison	IL	60101		630-458-3700	R	31*	<0.1
Dexter Fastener Technologies	2110 Bishop Cir. E	Dexter	MI	48130	Mike Frazier	734-426-5200	R	31*	0.2
Saegertown Manufacturing Corp.	PO Box 828	Saegertown	PA	16433	Chalmer Jordan	814-763-2655	R	30*	0.2
Southern Imperial Inc.	1400 Eddy Ave.	Rockford	IL	61103	Stanley Valiulis	815-877-7041	R	29*	0.2
Spirol International Corp.	30 Rock Ave.	Danielson	CT	06239	Hans Koehl	860-774-8571	R	29*	0.2
WICO Metal Products Company	23500 Sherwood	Warren	MI	48091	Richard Brodie	586-755-9600	R	28*	0.2
Deringer-Ney Inc.	616 Atrium Dr., 100	Vernon Hills	IL	60061		847-932-6800	R	28*	0.2
Paul R Briles Inc.	1700 W 132nd St.	Gardena	CA	90249	Robert Briles	310-323-6222	R	27*	0.2
Atlas Bolt and Screw Co.	1628 Troy Rd.	Ashland	OH	44805	Robert Moore	419-289-6171	R	27*	0.2
Ferry Cap and Set Screw Co.	2151 Scranton Rd.	Cleveland	OH	44113	Joseph Auliffe	216-771-2533	R	27*	0.2
MS Aerospace Inc.	13928 Balboa Blvd.	Sylmar	CA	91342	Michel Szostak	818-833-9095	R	26*	0.2
All American Products Co.	PO Box 190	San Fernando	CA	91341	Nathan O Shaw	818-361-0059	R	25*	0.1
Lehigh Consumer Products Corp.	2834 Schoeneck Rd.	Macungie	PA	18062	Fred Keller	610-966-9702	S	25*	0.2
Hargis Industries Inc.	PO Box 4515	Tyler	TX	75712	Joe Hargis	903-592-2826	R	24*	<0.1
Mayday Manufacturing Co.	1500 Interstate 35W	Denton	TX	76207	James Nelson	940-898-8301	R	24*	0.1
B and G Manufacturing Company	PO Box 904	Hatfield	PA	19440	Richard Edmonds	215-822-1925	R	23*	0.1
Polygon Co.	PO Box 176	Walkerton	IN	46574	Jim Shobert	574-586-3145	R	22*	0.3
Self Industries Inc.	3491 Mary Taylor	Birmingham	AL	35235	Michael McDowell	205-655-3284	R	22*	<0.1
Standard Die Supply Inc.	PO Box 2044	Indianapolis	IN	46206	Charles Wolfred	317-236-6200	R	22*	<0.1
Golden States Engineering Inc.	15338 Garfield Ave.	Paramount	CA	90723	Alexandra Rostovski	562-634-3125	R	22*	0.1
Ohio Nut and Bolt Co.	33 Lou Groza Blvd.	Berea	OH	44017	Patrick Finnegam	440-243-0200	S	21*	0.1
Mid-West Fabricating Co.	313 N Johns St.	Amanda	OH	43102	Jennifer Friel	740-969-4411	R	21*	0.2
Slidematic Industries Inc.	4520 W Addison St.	Chicago	IL	60641	David Magnuson	773-545-4213	R	21*	<0.1
Anchor Bolt and Screw Co.	1560 Frontenac Blvd	Naperville	IL	60563	Pat Henriksen	630-536-0700	R	20*	0.1
Mid-Park Inc.	PO Box 326	Leitchfield	KY	42755	Alan Bernard	270-259-3152	R	20*	<0.1

Source: Ward's Business Directory of U.S. Private and Public Companies, Volumes 1 and 2, 2008. The company type code used is as follows: P - Public, R - Private, S - Subsidiary, D - Division, J - Joint Venture, A - Affiliate, G - Group. Sales are in millions of dollars, employees are in thousands. An asterisk (*) indicates an estimated sales volume. The symbol < stands for 'less than'. Company names and addresses are truncated, in some cases, to fit into the available space.

MATERIALS CONSUMED

Material	Quantity	Delivered Cost ($ million)
Fabricated metal products, including forgings	(X)	177.0
Castings, rough and semifinished	(X)	2.5
Steel bars and bar shapes (exc. castings, forgings, fabr. metal products)	(X)	149.4
Steel sheet and strip (including tinplate)	(X)	74.9
Steel wire and wire products	(X)	580.0
All other steel shapes and forms (exc. castings, forgings, fabr. metal products)	(X)	150.1
Copper and copper-base alloy rod, bar, and bar shapes (exc. castings, forgings, fabr. metal products)	(X)	42.2
All other copper and copper-base alloy shapes and forms (exc. castings, forgings, fabr. metal products)	(X)	27.0
Aluminum and aluminum-base alloy extruded shapes (rod, bar, pipe, tube, etc.)	(X)	(D)
All other aluminum and aluminum-base alloy shapes and forms (wire, rolled rod and bar, powder, welded tubing, etc.)	(X)	25.8
Other nonferrous shapes and forms (exc. castings, forgings, fabricated metal products)	(X)	67.8
Paperboard containers, boxes, and corrugated paperboard	(X)	27.3
Special dies, tools, die sets, jigs, and fixtures (exc. cutting tools)	(X)	(D)
All other materials, components, parts, containers, and supplies	(X)	485.3
Materials, ingredients, containers, and supplies, nsk	(X)	470.3

Source: 2002 Economic Census. Explanation of symbols used: (D): Withheld to avoid disclosure of competitive data; na: Not available; (S): Withheld because statistical norms were not met; (X): Not applicable; (Z): Less than half the unit shown; nec: Not elsewhere classified; nsk: Not specified by kind; - : zero; p : 10-19 percent estimated; q : 20-29 percent estimated.

PRODUCT SHARE DETAILS

Product or Product Class Shipments	Mil. $	Product or Product Class Shipments	Mil. $
BOLTS, NUTS, SCREWS, RIVETS AND WASHERS	7,172.3	round) (except aircraft types)	379.9
Aircraft (including aerospace) fasteners other than plastics (meet specifications for flying vehicles)	**1,178.7**	Other externally threaded metal fasteners, including studs, except aircraft types	560.1
Aircraft (including aerospace) fasteners other than plastics (meet specifications for flying vehicles)	1,087.3	Externally threaded metal fasteners, except aircraft types, nsk	263.6
Aircraft bolts, except plastics (including aerospace), less than 161 KSI tensile (meets specifications for flying vehicles)	125.3	**Internally threaded metal fasteners, except aircraft types**	**651.2**
Aircraft bolts, except plastics (including aerospace), 161 KSI tensile or more (meets specifications for flying vehicles)	292.6	Internally threaded metal fasteners, except aircraft types	572.7
Aircraft screws and studs, except plastics (including aerospace) (meets specifications for flying vehicles)	121.1	Hex nuts, including flanges, double chamfered, washer face, flat, jam, slotted, thick, castle, heavy, machine, and locking (except aircraft types)	251.4
Aircraft locknuts, except plastics (including aerospace), including flanged locknuts (meets specifications for flying vehicles)	193.1	Square nuts (including flat, washer, crowned, heavy, track, sleeve, and machine), sheet metal nuts, weld nuts, wing nuts, nut retainers, etc. (except aircraft types)	28.7
Other internally threaded aircraft fasteners, except plastics (including aerospace), including flanged nuts (all types except flanged locknuts), hex square nuts (all types) and sheet metal fasteners	170.4	Other internally threaded metal fasteners, including flanged nuts and locknuts (except aircraft types)	292.6
Aircraft (including aerospace) washers, all types except plastics	25.2	Internally threaded metal fasteners, except aircraft types, nsk	78.5
Aircraft (including aerospace) rivets, all types except plastics	104.4	**Nonthreaded metal fasteners, except aircraft types**	**949.3**
Aircraft (including aerospace) pins, all types except plastics	55.2	Nonthreaded metal fasteners, except aircraft types	833.4
		Solid rivets, except aircraft types	89.0
Aircraft (including aerospace) fasteners other than plastics (meet specifications for flying vehicles), nsk	91.4	Tubular, split (including rivet caps) and blind rivets, except aircraft types	148.9
Externally threaded metal fasteners, except aircraft types	**2,781.7**	Washers, except aircraft types	157.9
Externally threaded metal fasteners, except aircraft types	2,518.1	Other nonthreaded metal fasteners, including pins (except aircraft types)	437.7
Mine roof bolts	110.8	Nonthreaded metal fasteners, except aircraft types, nsk	115.8
Hex bolts, including heavy, tap-and-joint, excluding high-strength structural and aircraft	426.7	**Products (except fasteners), made by cold-, warm-, or hot-heading processes**	**1,001.9**
Other metal bolts, including square, round, plow, high-strength structural, and bent bolts (except aircraft types)	538.0	Products (except fasteners), made by cold-, warm-, or hot-heading processes	1,001.9
		Aircraft parts, except fasteners	47.6
		Automotive parts, except fasteners	750.7
Cap, set, machine, lag, flange, and self-locking screws, except aircraft types	502.5	Parts for household appliances, including radio and television (except fasteners)	25.3
		Turnbuckles and hose clamps	115.8
		Other products (except fasteners), nec	62.5
Tapping screws (including fillister, flat, hex, oval, pan, and truss) and wood screws (including flat, oval, and		Products (except fasteners), made by cold-, warm-, or hot-heading processes, nsk	0.0
		Bolts, nuts, screws, rivets, and washers, nsk, total	**609.6**

Source: 2002 Economic Census. The values are product shipments in millions of dollars for 2002. Total product shipments may be lower or higher than industry shipments. See Introduction for a full discussion. Values of indented subcategories are summed in the main heading(s). The symbol (D) appears when data are withheld to prevent disclosure of competitive information. The abbreviation nsk stands for 'not specified by kind' and nec for 'not elsewhere classified'. A dash (-) means zero.

INPUTS AND OUTPUTS FOR TURNED PRODUCT AND SCREW, NUT, AND BOLT MANUFACTURING

Economic Sector or Industry Providing Inputs	%	Sector	Economic Sector or Industry Buying Outputs	%	Sector
Compensation of employees	36.3		Motor vehicle parts	20.7	Manufg.
Iron & steel mills & ferroalloys	6.3	Manufg.	Exports of goods & services	5.1	Cap Inv
Steel products from purchased steel	4.4	Manufg.	Light truck & utility vehicles	3.2	Manufg.
Wholesale trade	3.6	Trade	Automobiles	2.7	Manufg.
Management of companies & enterprises	3.6	Services	Valve & fittings other than plumbing	2.3	Manufg.
Hardware	2.5	Manufg.	Nonresidential structures, nec	2.3	Construct.
Industrial molds	1.6	Manufg.	Ornamental & architectural metal products	2.0	Manufg.
Turned products & screws, nuts, & bolts	1.3	Manufg.	Plate work & fabricated structural products	1.7	Manufg.
Real estate	1.3	Fin/R.E.	General purpose machinery, nec	1.5	Manufg.
Copper rolling, drawing, extruding, & alloying	1.3	Manufg.	Machine shops	1.3	Manufg.
Power generation & supply	1.2	Util.	Turned products & screws, nuts, & bolts	1.2	Manufg.
Machine shops	1.1	Manufg.	Heavy duty trucks	1.2	Manufg.
Securities, commodity contracts, investments	1.1	Fin/R.E.	Wiring devices	1.2	Manufg.
Cutting tools & machine tool accessories	1.1	Manufg.	Aircraft parts & auxiliary equipment, nec	1.1	Manufg.
Special tools, dies, jigs, & fixtures	1.0	Manufg.	Personal consumption expenditures	1.1	
Truck transportation	0.9	Util.	Truck transportation	1.1	Util.
Nonferrous metal foundries	0.9	Manufg.	Wholesale trade	1.0	Trade
Ferrous metal foundries	0.9	Manufg.	Construction machinery	1.0	Manufg.
Nonferrous metal (ex. copper & aluminum) processing	0.8	Manufg.	Material handling equipment	0.9	Manufg.
Semiconductors & related devices	0.8	Manufg.	AC, refrigeration, and warm air heating equipment	0.9	Manufg.
Aluminum products from purchased aluminum	0.8	Manufg.	Hardware	0.9	Manufg.
Lessors of nonfinancial assets	0.7	Fin/R.E.	Fluid power process machinery	0.9	Manufg.
Forging, stamping, & sintering, nec	0.7	Manufg.	Farm machinery & equipment	0.9	Manufg.
Printed circuit assemblies (electronic assembles)	0.7	Manufg.	Aircraft	0.9	Manufg.
Monetary authorities/depository credit intermediation	0.7	Fin/R.E.	Engine equipment, nec	0.9	Manufg.
Advertising & related services	0.6	Services	Electromedical & electrotherapeutic apparatus	0.9	Manufg.
Taxes on production & imports, less subsidies	0.6		Sporting & athletic goods	0.8	Manufg.
Professional, scientific, technical services, nec	0.6	Services	Industrial machinery, nec	0.8	Manufg.
Automotive equipment rental & leasing	0.5	Fin/R.E.	Motors & generators	0.8	Manufg.
Accounting, tax preparation, bookkeeping, & payroll	0.4	Services	Lighting fixtures	0.8	Manufg.
Abrasive products	0.4	Manufg.	Electronic components, nec	0.8	Manufg.
Coating, engraving, heat treating & allied activities	0.4	Manufg.	Surgical appliances & supplies	0.7	Manufg.
Food services & drinking places	0.4	Services	Search, detection, & navigation instruments	0.7	Manufg.
Telecommunications	0.4	Services	Crowns & closures & metal stamping	0.7	Manufg.
Maintenance/repair of nonresidential structures	0.4	Construct.	Switchgear & switchboard apparatus	0.7	Manufg.
Data processing, hosting, & related services	0.4	Services	Commercial & service industry machinery, nec	0.7	Manufg.
Services to buildings & dwellings	0.4	Services	Special tools, dies, jigs, & fixtures	0.6	Manufg.
Warehousing & storage	0.4	Util.	Surgical & medical instrument	0.6	Manufg.
Legal services	0.3	Services	Motor vehicle bodies	0.6	Manufg.
Paperboard containers	0.3	Manufg.	Electronic connectors	0.6	Manufg.
Natural gas distribution	0.3	Util.	Coal	0.5	Mining
Commercial & industrial machinery rental & leasing	0.3	Fin/R.E.	Lawn & garden equipment	0.5	Manufg.
Fabricated metals, nec	0.3	Manufg.	Broadcast & wireless communications equipment	0.5	Manufg.
Architectural, engineering, & related services	0.3	Services	Electrical equipment & components, nec	0.5	Manufg.
Springs & wire products	0.3	Manufg.	Residential permanent site structures	0.5	Construct.
Hotels & motels, including casino hotels	0.2	Services	Fabricated metals, nec	0.5	Manufg.
Scientific research & development services	0.2	Services	Communications equipment, nec	0.5	Manufg.
Automotive repair & maintenance, ex. car washes	0.2	Services	Telephone apparatus	0.5	Manufg.
Commercial & industrial equipment repair/maintenance	0.2	Services	Rubber products, nec	0.5	Manufg.
Air transportation	0.2	Util.	Retail trade	0.4	Trade
Management, scientific, & technical consulting	0.2	Services	Pumps & pumping equipment	0.4	Manufg.
Business support services	0.2	Services	Semiconductor machinery	0.4	Manufg.
Metal cans, boxes, & other containers (light gauge)	0.2	Manufg.	Turbines & turbine generator set units	0.4	Manufg.
Custom roll forming	0.2	Manufg.	Manufacturing, nec	0.4	Manufg.
Other computer related services, including facilities	0.1	Services	Plastics products, nec	0.4	Manufg.
Plastics packaging materials, film & sheet	0.1	Manufg.	Relay & industrial controls	0.4	Manufg.
Rail transportation	0.1	Util.	General S/L govt. services	0.4	S/L Govt
Employment services	0.1	Services	Automotive repair & maintenance, ex. car washes	0.4	Services
Nondepository credit intermediation activities	0.1	Fin/R.E.	Air & gas compressors	0.4	Manufg.
Paperboard mills	0.1	Manufg.	Irradiation apparatus	0.4	Manufg.
Specialized design services	0.1	Services	Printed circuit assemblies (electronic assemblies)	0.4	Manufg.
Crowns & closures & metal stamping	0.1	Manufg.	Petroleum refineries	0.4	Manufg.
Plate work & fabricated structural products	0.1	Manufg.	Household cooking appliances	0.4	Manufg.
Bare printed circuit boards	0.1	Manufg.	Handtools	0.4	Manufg.
Ornamental & architectural metal products	0.1	Manufg.	Oil & gas extraction	0.4	Mining
Showcases, partitions, shelving, and lockers	0.1	Manufg.	Metal cans, boxes, & other containers (light gauge)	0.4	Manufg.
Waste management & remediation services	0.1	Services	Industrial process variable instruments	0.3	Manufg.
			Custom roll forming	0.3	Manufg.
			Watches, clocks, & related devices	0.3	Manufg.
			Truck trailers	0.3	Manufg.
			Travel trailers & campers	0.3	Manufg.
			Manufactured homes & mobile homes	0.3	Manufg.
			Printing	0.3	Manufg.
			Industrial molds	0.3	Manufg.
			Coating, engraving, heat treating & allied activities	0.3	Manufg.
			Mining & oil & gas field machinery	0.3	Manufg.
			Commercial & industrial equipment repair/maintenance	0.3	Services
			Boat building	0.3	Manufg.
			Audio & video equipment	0.3	Manufg.
			Heating equipment (except warm air furnaces)	0.3	Manufg.

Continued on next page.

INPUTS AND OUTPUTS FOR TURNED PRODUCT AND SCREW, NUT, AND BOLT MANUFACTURING - Continued

Economic Sector or Industry Providing Inputs	%	Sector	Economic Sector or Industry Buying Outputs	%	Sector
			Springs & wire products	0.3	Manufg.
			Signs	0.3	Manufg.
			Residential structures, nec	0.3	Construct.
			Ship building & repairing	0.3	Manufg.
			Military armored vehicles, tanks, & tank components	0.3	Manufg.
			Soft drinks & ice	0.3	Manufg.
			Aircraft engine & engine parts	0.2	Manufg.
			Major household appliances, nec	0.2	Manufg.
			Totalizing fluid meters & counting devices	0.2	Manufg.
			Motorcycles, bicycles, & parts	0.2	Manufg.
			Arms, ordnance, & accessories	0.2	Manufg.
			Metal cutting & forming machine tools	0.2	Manufg.
			Transportation equipment, nec	0.2	Manufg.
			Household laundry equipment	0.2	Manufg.
			Railroad rolling stock	0.2	Manufg.
			Power-driven handtools	0.2	Manufg.
			Magnetic & optical recording media	0.2	Manufg.
			Electron tubes	0.2	Manufg.
			Plastics & rubber industry machinery	0.2	Manufg.
			Small electrical applicances	0.2	Manufg.
			Owner-occupied dwellings	0.2	
			Basic organic chemicals, nec	0.2	Manufg.
			Analytical laboratory instruments	0.2	Manufg.
			Commercial & health care structures	0.2	Construct.
			Jewelry & silverware	0.2	Manufg.
			Scenic & sightseeing transport & related services	0.2	Util.
			Ball & roller bearings	0.2	Manufg.
			Wood windows & doors & millwork	0.2	Manufg.
			Food services & drinking places	0.2	Services
			Household refrigerators & home freezers	0.2	Manufg.
			Power boilers & heat exchangers	0.2	Manufg.
			Newspaper publishers	0.2	Services
			Plastics packaging materials, film & sheet	0.2	Manufg.
			Rolling mill & other metalworking machinery	0.2	Manufg.
			Breweries	0.1	Manufg.
			Cutting tools & machine tool accessories	0.1	Manufg.
			Packaging machinery	0.1	Manufg.
			Paperboard containers	0.1	Manufg.
			Telecommunications	0.1	Services
			Fabricated pipes & pipe fittings	0.1	Manufg.
			Maintenance/repair of nonresidential structures	0.1	Construct.
			Personal & household goods repair/maintenance	0.1	Services
			Ammunition	0.1	Manufg.
			Iron & steel mills & ferroalloys	0.1	Manufg.
			Toilet preparations	0.1	Manufg,
			Mechanical power transmission equipment	0.1	Manufg.
			Power, distribution, & specialty transformers	0.1	Manufg.
			Automatic environmental controls	0.1	Manufg.
			Vending, commercial, industrial, office machinery	0.1	Manufg.
			Software publishers	0.1	Services
			Book publishers	0.1	Services
			Motor homes	0.1	Manufg.
			Plastics materials & resins	0.1	Manufg.
			Paper mills	0.1	Manufg.
			Custom architectural woodwork & millwork	0.1	Manufg.
			Community food, housing, relief, & rehabilitation	0.1	Services
			Computer terminals & peripherals	0.1	Manufg.
			Directories, mailing lists, & other publishers	0.1	Services
			Internet publishing & broadcasting	0.1	Services
			Air purification & ventilation equipment	0.1	Manufg.
			Warehousing & storage	0.1	Util.
			Optical instruments & lenses	0.1	Manufg.

Source: Benchmark Input-Output Accounts for the U.S. Economy, 2002, U.S. Department of Commerce, Washington D.C., January 2008. User should note that this Input-Output table is not for this particular narrowly defined industry but for a larger aggregate. Input and Output data for Turned Product and Screw, Nut, and Bolt Manufacturing include Input and Output data for the Annual Survey of Manufactures' NAICS industries 332721 and 332722. The abbreviation nec stands for 'not elsewhere classified'.

OCCUPATIONS EMPLOYED BY MACHINE SHOPS, TURNED PRODUCTS, & SCREWS, NUTS, & BOLTS

Occupation	% of Total 2006	Change to 2016	Occupation	% of Total 2006	Change to 2016
Machinists	23.5	-14.4	Maintenance & repair workers, general	1.2	-20.9
Computer-controlled machine tool operators	7.6	-10.9	Numerical tool & process control programmers	1.1	-16.4
First-line supervisors/managers of production workers	5.1	-19.6	Secretaries, exc legal, medical, & executive	1.0	-27.4
Lathe & turning machine tool operators & tenders	4.5	-29.8	Laborers & freight, stock, & material movers, hand	1.0	-28.9
Welders, cutters, solderers, & brazers	3.7	-12.4	Janitors & cleaners, exc maids & housekeeping cleaners	0.9	-17.2
Inspectors, testers, sorters, samplers, & weighers	2.7	-25.9	Mechanical engineers	0.9	-20.2
Cutting, punching, & press machine operators	2.6	-29.9	Executive secretaries & administrative assistants	0.8	-19.1
Grinding, lapping, polishing machine tool operators	2.6	-22.2	Purchasing agents, exc wholesale, retail, & farm	0.7	-19.7
Helpers--Production workers	2.4	-19.0	Forging machine operators & tenders	0.7	-40.5
General & operations managers	2.2	-27.4	Truck drivers, light or delivery services	0.7	-18.7
Office clerks, general	1.9	-20.1	Industrial machinery mechanics	0.7	-8.0
Drilling & boring machine tool operators	1.9	-28.9	Rolling machine operators & tenders	0.6	-25.9
Shipping, receiving, & traffic clerks	1.8	-24.1	Accountants & auditors	0.6	-20.2
Team assemblers	1.8	-20.3	Production, planning, & expediting clerks	0.6	-21.0
Sales reps, wholesale & manufacturing, exc tech	1.7	-20.1	Structural metal fabricators & fitters	0.6	-17.6
Bookkeeping, accounting, & auditing clerks	1.6	-19.1	Industrial engineers	0.6	-5.0
Milling & planing machine operators & tenders	1.6	-27.3	Packers & packagers, hand	0.5	-38.3
Multiple machine tool operators & tenders	1.5	-14.3	First-line supervisors/managers of office workers	0.5	-25.4
Tool & die makers	1.4	-17.6	Customer service representatives	0.5	-14.4
Industrial production managers	1.2	-20.3			

Source: Industry-Occupation Matrix, Bureau of Labor Statistics, December 4, 2007. These data are reported based on 4-digit NAICS categories but have been matched to corresponding 6-digit NAICS industry codes. The change reported for each occupation to the year 2016 is a percent of growth or decline as estimated by the Bureau of Labor Statistics. The abbreviation nec stands for 'not elsewhere classified'.

LOCATION BY STATE AND REGIONAL CONCENTRATION

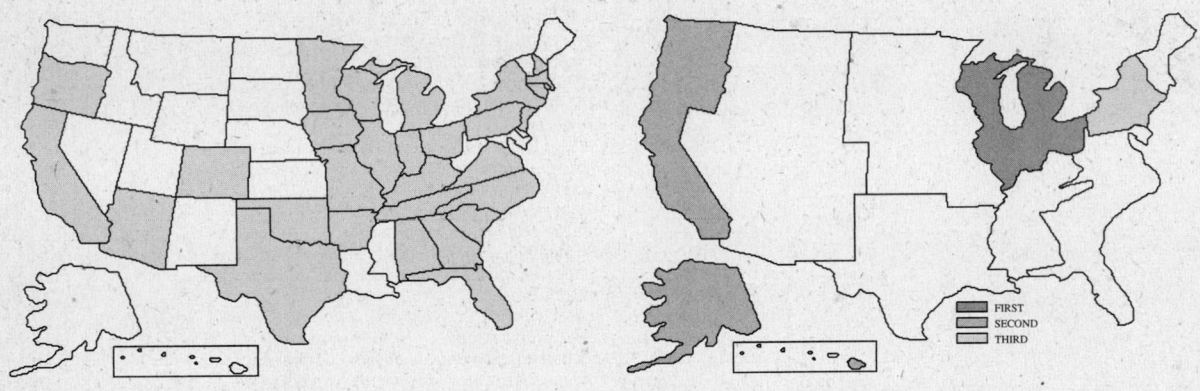

INDUSTRY DATA BY STATE

State	Establishments	Shipments Total ($ mil)	% of U.S.	Per Establ.	Employment Total Number	% of U.S.	Per Establ.	Wages ($/hour)	Cost as % of Shipments	Investment per Employee ($)
Illinois	126	1,315.8	16.9	10,442.5	7,362	16.4	58	17.17	43.7	10,095
Michigan	100	1,277.9	16.4	12,778.6	4,636	10.4	46	17.88	50.6	7,561
California	133	1,067.3	13.7	8,024.8	7,186	16.1	54	17.21	30.9	3,473
Ohio	84	659.9	8.5	7,855.4	4,205	9.4	50	16.34	49.3	13,896
Pennsylvania	50	503.1	6.5	10,061.7	3,391	7.6	68	19.18	31.8	3,143
Indiana	30	378.8	4.9	12,625.0	1,826	4.1	61	16.48	48.6	7,877
Wisconsin	31	268.7	3.5	8,668.9	1,266	2.8	41	16.76	49.8	6,930
Texas	43	237.5	3.1	5,522.9	1,652	3.7	38	15.73	42.4	5,372
Tennessee	20	186.0	2.4	9,297.9	1,166	2.6	58	15.24	47.2	4,572
New York	47	180.2	2.3	3,834.3	1,060	2.4	23	16.33	41.6	3,085
Alabama	12	178.6	2.3	14,879.8	685	1.5	57	12.86	55.2	18,902
Massachusetts	30	171.6	2.2	5,719.6	978	2.2	33	16.61	45.5	3,777
Kentucky	12	163.7	2.1	13,637.6	716	1.6	60	13.79	47.6	13,860
New Jersey	28	154.6	2.0	5,522.2	1,103	2.5	39	14.25	43.1	4,335
Connecticut	40	129.8	1.7	3,244.3	1,049	2.3	26	16.35	28.4	5,509
Virginia	6	106.1	1.4	17,684.3	683	1.5	114	12.30	48.6	3,877
Iowa	5	93.1	1.2	18,621.0	632	1.4	126	13.45	33.9	1,851
Florida	18	60.5	0.8	3,359.9	531	1.2	30	13.17	37.3	2,667
North Carolina	8	59.6	0.8	7,449.9	526	1.2	66	13.63	56.5	724
Minnesota	12	55.7	0.7	4,642.6	430	1.0	36	19.06	31.7	4,060
Oklahoma	5	54.6	0.7	10,921.6	313	0.7	63	19.86	44.2	7,115
Missouri	15	51.6	0.7	3,441.4	362	0.8	24	15.94	35.8	3,069
South Carolina	9	48.0	0.6	5,337.8	206	0.5	23	13.01	35.5	3,563
Colorado	7	46.1	0.6	6,581.7	307	0.7	44	15.02	40.3	6,564

Continued on next page.

INDUSTRY DATA BY STATE - Continued

| State | Establish-ments | Shipments | | | Employment | | | | Cost as % of Shipments | Investment per Employee ($) |
		Total ($ mil)	% of U.S.	Per Establ.	Total Number	% of U.S.	Per Establ.	Wages ($/hour)		
Arizona	8	45.0	0.6	5,621.7	272	0.6	34	17.61	31.1	2,460
Rhode Island	14	39.0	0.5	2,788.9	383	0.9	27	13.94	31.1	4,488
Georgia	8	33.7	0.4	4,208.6	204	0.5	25	17.98	33.1	3,387
Arkansas	7	22.6	0.3	3,232.4	167	0.4	24	13.38	45.1	1,263
New Hampshire	7	20.8	0.3	2,966.9	200	0.4	29	14.90	32.7	6,065
Oregon	10	20.2	0.3	2,020.3	138	0.3	14	18.35	41.3	3,101

Source: 2002 Economic Census. The states are in descending order of shipments or establishments (if shipment data are missing for the majority). The symbol (D) appears when data are withheld to prevent disclosure of competitive information. States marked with (D) are sorted by number of establishments. A dash (-) indicates that the data element cannot be calculated. Data may not show all states active in the NAICS category. All data available at the time of publication are shown.

NAICS 33281M - COATING, ENGRAVING, HEAT TREATING, AND ALLIED ACTIVITIES*

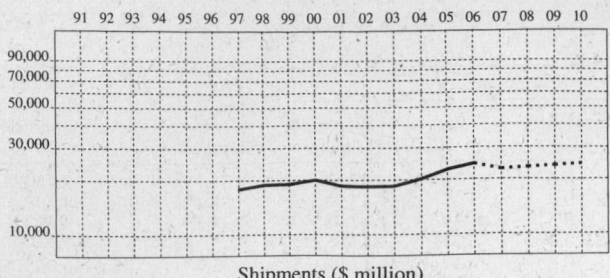

Shipments ($ million)

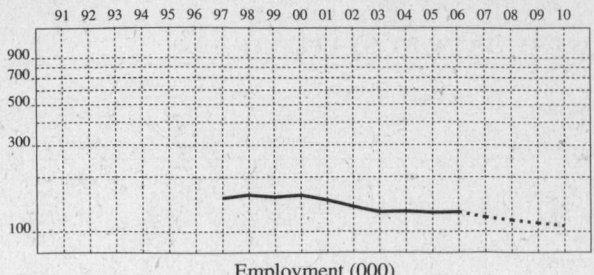

Employment (000)

GENERAL STATISTICS

Year	Companies	Establishments		Employment			Compensation		Production ($ million)			
		Total	with 20 or more employees	Total (000)	Production Workers (000)	Hours (Mil)	Payroll ($ mil)	Wages ($/hr)	Cost of Materials	Value Added by Manufacture	Value of Shipments	Capital Invest.
1997	5,927	6,360	2,223	153.1	120.1	240.7	4,522.3	12.21	7,563.7	10,288.5	17,855.4	899.9
1998		6,400	2,310	159.2	126.3	252.4	4,817.7	12.55	7,944.3	10,921.5	18,875.1	986.6
1999		6,278	2,248	155.1	123.5	249.2	4,780.2	12.67	8,147.7	10,925.1	18,987.6	746.8
2000		6,161	2,236	159.0	126.0	250.7	5,029.2	13.22	8,663.5	11,488.1	19,998.1	807.4
2001		6,116	2,208	148.8	117.0	236.5	4,718.5	13.16	8,060.8	10,408.0	18,551.8	823.0
2002	5,817	6,317	1,914	137.1	106.2	209.0	4,640.1	14.76	7,624.6	10,797.7	18,378.0	697.8
2003		6,175	1,935	128.2	99.6	202.7	4,452.3	14.69	7,909.0	10,576.7	18,490.2	645.1
2004		6,196	1,910	129.2	99.0	210.9	4,649.0	14.78	8,384.3	11,953.4	20,182.7	705.2
2005		6,215	1,948	127.3	98.0	207.4	4,808.0	15.59	9,807.9	13,047.1	22,739.2	503.6
2006		6,143P	1,833P	128.2	99.3	207.3	5,007.6	16.29	10,527.5	13,947.1	24,343.7	581.1
2007		6,122P	1,779P	119.8P	91.6P	194.1P	4,803.6P	16.48P	9,830.0P	13,023.1P	22,730.9P	504.0P
2008		6,102P	1,725P	115.7P	88.0P	188.1P	4,814.8P	16.93P	10,057.3P	13,324.2P	23,256.5P	461.1P
2009		6,081P	1,671P	111.6P	84.3P	182.2P	4,825.9P	17.38P	10,284.6P	13,625.3P	23,782.1P	418.3P
2010		6,060P	1,616P	107.4P	80.7P	176.3P	4,837.0P	17.83P	10,511.9P	13,926.4P	24,307.6P	375.4P

Sources: 1997 and 2002 *Economic Census*; other years, up to 2006, are from *Annual Survey of Manufactures*. Establishment counts for non-Census years are from *County Business Patterns*; 1997 and 2002 values are from the 1997 and 2002 censuses, respectively. 'P's show projections by the editors.

INDICES OF CHANGE

Year	Companies	Establishments		Employment			Compensation		Production ($ million)			
		Total	with 20 or more employees	Total (000)	Production Workers (000)	Hours (Mil)	Payroll ($ mil)	Wages ($/hr)	Cost of Materials	Value Added by Manufacture	Value of Shipments	Capital Invest.
1997	102	101	116	112	113	115	97	83	99	95	97	129
1998		101	121	116	119	121	104	85	104	101	103	141
1999		99	117	113	116	119	103	86	107	101	103	107
2000		98	117	116	119	120	108	90	114	106	109	116
2001		97	115	109	110	113	102	89	106	96	101	118
2002	100	100	100	100	100	100	100	100	100	100	100	100
2003		98	101	94	94	97	96	100	104	98	101	92
2004		98	100	94	93	101	100	100	110	111	110	101
2005		98	102	93	92	99	104	106	129	121	124	72
2006		97P	96P	94	94	99	108	110	138	129	132	83
2007		97P	93P	87P	86P	93P	104P	112P	129P	121P	124P	72P
2008		97P	90P	84P	83P	90P	104P	115P	132P	123P	127P	66P
2009		96P	87P	81P	79P	87P	104P	118P	135P	126P	129P	60P
2010		96P	84P	78P	76P	84P	104P	121P	138P	129P	132P	54P

Sources: Same as General Statistics. Values reflect change from the base year, 2002. Values above 100 mean greater than 2002, values below 100 mean less than 2002, and the values of 100 in other years means the same as 2002. 'P's show projections by the editors.

SELECTED RATIOS

For 2002	Avg. of All Manufact.	Analyzed Industry	Index	For 2002	Avg. of All Manufact.	Analyzed Industry	Index
Employees per Establishment	42	22	52	Value Added per Production Worker	182,367	101,673	56
Payroll per Establishment	1,639,184	734,542	45	Cost per Establishment	5,769,015	1,206,997	21
Payroll per Employee	39,053	33,845	87	Cost per Employee	137,446	55,613	40
Production Workers per Establishment	30	17	57	Cost per Production Worker	195,506	71,795	37
Wages per Establishment	694,845	488,339	70	Shipments per Establishment	11,158,348	2,909,292	26
Wages per Production Worker	23,548	29,047	123	Shipments per Employee	265,847	134,048	50
Hours per Production Worker	1,980	1,968	99	Shipments per Production Worker	378,144	173,051	46
Wages per Hour	11.89	14.76	124	Investment per Establishment	361,338	110,464	31
Value Added per Establishment	5,381,325	1,709,308	32	Investment per Employee	8,609	5,090	59
Value Added per Employee	128,210	78,758	61	Investment per Production Worker	12,245	6,571	54

Sources: Same as General Statistics. The 'Average of All Manufacturing' column represents the average of all manufacturing industries reported for the most recent complete year available. The Index shows the relationship between the Average and the Analyzed Industry. For example, 100 means that they are equal; 500 that the Analyzed Industry is five times the average; 50 means that the Analyzed Industry is half the national average. The abbreviation 'na' is used to show that data are 'not available'. Ratios shown for 2002, the last complete census year.

*Equivalent to Federal Government NAICS 332811, 332812, 332813.

LEADING COMPANIES   Number shown: 75   Total sales ($ mil): 37,154   Total employment (000): 113.0

Company Name	Address				CEO Name	Phone	Co. Type	Sales ($ mil)	Empl. (000)
Praxair Inc.	39 Old Ridgebury	Danbury	CT	06810	Stephen F. Angel	716-879-4077	P	9,402	28.0
Quest Technology L.P.	6750 Nancy Ridge	San Diego	CA	92121	Stan Zalkind	858-558-1996	S	4,449*	1.4
Hallmark Cards Inc.	PO Box 419034	Kansas City	MO	64141		816-274-5111	R	4,100*	16.0
Sequa Corp.	200 Park Ave.	New York	NY	10166	Gail Binderman	212-986-5500	P	2,183	10.2
H.B. Fuller Co.	PO Box 64683	St. Paul	MN	55164	Michele Volpi	651-236-5900	P	1,428	3.2
Turner Industries Ltd.	PO Box 2750	Baton Rouge	LA	70821	Roland M. Toups	225-922-5050	R	1,410	13.3
United States Surgical Corp.	150 Glover Ave.	Norwalk	CT	06850	Allen Panzer	203-845-1000	S	1,172*	5.8
Euramax International Inc.	5445 Triangle Pky.	Norcross	GA	30092	J. David Smith	770-449-7066	R	1,068	3.2
Feralloy Corp.	8755 W Higgins Rd.	Chicago	IL	60631		773-380-1500	R	904*	<0.1
Barden Corp.	PO Box 2449	Danbury	CT	06813	John McCloskey	203-744-2211	R	776*	0.3
Shachihata Incorporated USA	PO Box 2017	Torrance	CA	90505	Shinkitiro Funahashi		S	700*	0.9
U.S. Bronze Powders Inc.	PO Box 31	Flemington	NJ	08822		908-782-5454	R	574*	0.3
ICO Global Services Inc.	1811 Bering Dr, 200	Houston	TX	77057	A. John Knapp, Jr.	713-351-4100	S	380*	0.9
Metokote Corp.	1340 Neubrecht Rd.	Lima	OH	45801	DeWayne Pinkstaff	419-996-7800	R	364*	1.0
Crown Group Inc.	2111 Wltr P Reuther	Warren	MI	48091		586-575-9800	R	362*	1.0
Wall Colmonoy Corp.	101 West Girard	Madison Heights	MI	48071		248-585-6400	R	336*	0.3
Insteel Industries Inc.	1373 Boggs Dr.	Mount Airy	NC	27030	Howard O. Woltz Jr.	336-786-2141	P	298	0.6
Union Electric Steel Corp.	PO BOX 465	Carnegie	PA	15106	Robert Carothers	412-429-7655	S	277*	0.4
Material Sciences Corp.	2200 E Pratt Blvd.	Elk Grove Vlg	IL	60007		847-439-2210	P	263	0.6
Consolidated Systems Inc.	PO Box 1756	Columbia	SC	29202	S Holtschlag	803-771-7920	R	262*	0.3
AZZ Inc.	1300 S Universty Dr	Fort Worth	TX	76107	David H. Dingus	817-810-0095	P	260	1.0
C. Cowles and Co.	83 Water St.	New Haven	CT	06511	Lawrence C. Moon Jr.	203-865-3110	R	260*	0.2
Things Remembered Inc.	5500 Avion Park Dr.	Cleveland	OH	44143	Suzanne Sutter	440-473-2000	R	240*	3.0
Daman Industrial Services Inc.	PO Box 486	East Brady	PA	16028		724-526-5714	R	228*	<0.1
AMI Doduco Inc.	1003 Corporate Ln.	Export	PA	15632	James M. Papada	724-733-8332	S	225*	1.8
Pyrotek Inc.	9503 E Montgomery	Spokane	WA	99206	Allan Roy	509-926-6212	R	225*	1.5
Benedict-Miller L.L.C.	123 N 8th St.	Kenilworth	NJ	07033	John Benedict	908-497-1477	R	216*	0.1
Nicholas J Bouras Inc.	PO Box 662	Summit	NJ	07902	Nicholas Bouras	908-277-1617	R	204*	<0.1
Precoat Metals	1310 Papin St.	St. Louis	MO	63103	Gerard M. Dombek	314-436-7010	S	191*	0.7
Engineered Materials/Solutions	2200 E Pratt Blvd.	Elk Grove Vlg	IL	60007	Cliff Nastas	847-439-2210	S	189*	0.6
Keymark Corp.	PO Box 626	Fonda	NY	12068	William Keller	518-853-3421	R	183*	0.9
Oerlikon USA Holding Inc.	615 Epsilon Dr.	Pittsburgh	PA	15238	James Brissenden	724-327-5700	R	172*	0.2
Dynamic Materials Corp.	5405 Spine Rd.	Boulder	CO	80301	Yvon P. Cariou	303-665-5700	P	165	0.4
Acheson Colloids Co.	1600 Washington	Port Huron	MI	48060		810-984-5581	S	165*	0.9
Midwest Stamping Inc.	3455 Briarfield	Maumee	OH	43537	Ronald L. Thompson	419-724-6970	R	155*	0.6
Deloro Stellite Company Inc.	1201 Eisenhower Dr.	Goshen	IN	46526	Mark Aldridge	574-534-2585	R	153*	1.2
Tempel Steel Co.	5500 N Wolcott	Chicago	IL	60640	Vincent Buonanno	773-250-8000	R	152*	<0.1
Lapham-Hickey Steel Corp.	5500 W 73rd St.	Chicago	IL	60638	William Hickey	708-496-6111	R	140*	0.4
Duo-Fast Corp.	2400 Galvin Dr.	Elgin	IL	60123		847-634-1900	R	136*	0.9
Sapa Anodizing Inc.	PO Box 11263	Portland	OR	97211		503-802-3000	R	129*	0.5
Wausau Window & Wall Systems	1415 W Street	Wausau	WI	54401	Russ Huffer	715-845-2161	D	119*	1.0
Hoover Precision Products Inc.	PO Box 899	Cumming	GA	30028	Takanori Kondo	770-889-9223	R	113*	0.2
CB Manufacturing and Sales Co.	PO Box 37	West Carrollton	OH	45449	Charlie Biehn	937-866-5986	R	111*	0.1
Spraylat Corp.	143 Sparks Ave.	Pelham	NY	10803	James Borner	914-738-1600	R	110*	<0.1
Clarion Sintered Metals Inc.	PO Box S	Ridgway	PA	15853	Howard Peterson	814-773-3124	R	106*	0.2
Int'l Metals & Chemicals Grp.	165 Twnship Lane	Jenkintown	PA	19046	Peter A. Schorsch	215-517-6000	R	105*	0.2
Transco Products Erection Inc.	55 E Jackson Blvd.	Chicago	IL	60604	Edward Wolbert	312-427-2818	R	104*	<0.1
Bodine Aluminum Inc.	2100 Walton Rd.	St. Louis	MO	63114	Robert Lloyd	314-423-8200	S	94*	0.3
Engineered Sinterings/Plastics	140 Commercial St.	Watertown	CT	06795	Alexander Alves	860-274-8877	R	88*	0.2
Penn United Technology Inc.	PO Box 399	Saxonburg	PA	16056	Carl Jones	724-352-1507	R	88*	0.7
Umc Acquisition Corp.	9151 Imperial Hwy.	Downey	CA	90242	Dominick Baione	562-886-1750	R	88*	<0.1
Pacific Aerospace/Electronics	434 Olds Station Rd	Wenatchee	WA	98801	Donald A. Wright	509-667-9600	R	85*	0.8
Enerfab Inc.	4955 Spring Grove	Cincinnati	OH	45232	Wendell Bell	513-641-0500	R	84*	0.3
Capstan Industries Inc.	10 Cushing Dr.	Wrentham	MA	02093	Chris Doughty	508-384-3100	R	84*	0.2
T-L Irrigation Co.	PO Box 1047	Hastings	NE	68902	Leroy Thom	402-462-4128	R	78*	0.3
IN Kote L.L.P.	30755 Edison Rd.	New Carlisle	IN	46552		574-654-1000	R	76*	0.5
N Am Galvanizing & Coatings	5314 S Yale Ave.	Tulsa	OK	74135	Ronald J. Evans	918-488-9420	P	74	0.4
General Extrusions Inc.	PO Box 2669	Youngstown	OH	44507	Herbert Schuler	330-783-0270	R	71*	0.3
Smiths Tubular Systems-Laconia	PO Box 678	Laconia	NH	03247		603-524-2064	R	69*	0.3
Keystone Powdered Metal Co.	251 State St.	Saint Marys	PA	15857		814-781-1591	R	68*	0.5
Gordon Aluminum Industries	1000 Mason St.	Schofield	WI	54476	Alfred Gordon	715-359-6101	R	65*	0.3
Chemtool Inc.	PO Box 538	Crystal Lake	IL	60039	James Athans	815-459-1250	R	65*	0.1
Rust-Oleum Corp.	PO Box 1008	Hagerstown	MD	21741		301-223-8500	S	64*	0.2
Aluminum Casting & Engineering	2309 S Lenox St.	Milwaukee	WI	53207	Eckhart Grohmann	414-744-3902	R	62*	0.5
Jrlon Inc.	PO Box 244	Palmyra	NY	14522	James Redmond	315-597-4067	R	59*	<0.1
Donsco Inc.	PO Box 2001	Wrightsville	PA	17368	Arthur Mann	717-252-1561	R	57*	0.3
Concote Corp.	PO Box 35848	Dallas	TX	75235	Robert Hanton	214-956-0077	R	56*	0.1
Oliver Steel Plate Co.	7851 Bavaria Rd.	Twinsburg	OH	44087	Jim Stevenson	330-425-7000	S	55*	<0.1
Bemis Associates Inc.	1 Bemis Way	Shirley	MA	01464	Stephen Howard	978-425-6761	R	54*	0.2
Specialty Coating Systems Inc.	7645 Woodland Dr.	Indianapolis	IN	46278	John Fry	317-244-1200	R	53*	<0.1
I. Schumann and Co.	22500 Alexander	Bedford	OH	44146	Michael Schumann	440-439-2300	R	52*	0.2
Gentz Industries L.L.C.	25250 Easy St.	Warren	MI	48089	Donald Duckett	586-772-2500	R	51*	0.2
Rebco Inc.	650 Brandy Camp	Kersey	PA	15846	Kenneth Huey	814-885-8035	R	50*	0.1
Industrial Polishing Services	9465 Customhouse	San Diego	CA	92154		619-661-1691	R	50	1.5
Diamond Manufacturing Company	243 W 8th St.	Wyoming	PA	18644	Charles Flack	570-693-0300	R	50*	0.2

Source: Ward's Business Directory of U.S. Private and Public Companies, Volumes 1 and 2, 2008. The company type code used is as follows: P - Public, R - Private, S - Subsidiary, D - Division, J - Joint Venture, A - Affiliate, G - Group. Sales are in millions of dollars, employees are in thousands. An asterisk (*) indicates an estimated sales volume. The symbol < stands for 'less than'. Company names and addresses are truncated, in some cases, to fit into the available space.

MATERIALS CONSUMED FOR METAL COATING AND NONPRECIOUS ENGRAVING

Material	Quantity	Delivered Cost ($ million)
Fabricated metal products, including forgings	(X)	312.4
Castings, rough and semifinished	(X)	(D)
Steel shapes and forms (exc. castings, forgings, fabr. metal products)	(X)	1,640.4
Nonferrous shapes and forms	(X)	64.5
Plastics materials and resins	(X)	87.3
Paints, varnishes, stains, lacquers, shellacs, japans, enamels, etc.	(X)	475.1
Foundry chemicals, metal treating and plating compounds	(X)	350.3
Other chemicals and allied products	(X)	62.5
Grinding wheels and other abrasive products, exc. industrial diamonds	(X)	(D)
All other materials, components, parts, containers, and supplies	(X)	419.8
Materials, ingredients, containers, and supplies, nsk	(X)	619.9

Source: 2002 *Economic Census*. Explanation of symbols used: (D): Withheld to avoid disclosure of competitive data; na: Not available; (S): Withheld because statistical norms were not met; (X): Not applicable; (Z): Less than half the unit shown; nec: Not elsewhere classified; nsk: Not specified by kind; - : zero; p : 10-19 percent estimated; q : 20-29 percent estimated.

MATERIALS CONSUMED FOR ELECTROPLATING, PLATING, POLISHING, ANODIZING, AND COLORING

Material	Quantity	Delivered Cost ($ million)
Fabricated metal products, including forgings	(X)	102.7
Castings, rough and semifinished	(X)	2.1
Steel shapes and forms (exc. castings, forgings, fabr. metal products)	(X)	238.9
Nonferrous shapes and forms	(X)	27.4
Plastics materials and resins	(X)	23.5
Paints, varnishes, stains, lacquers, shellacs, japans, enamels, etc.	(X)	18.9
Foundry chemicals, metal treating and plating compounds	(X)	230.8
Other chemicals and allied products	(X)	136.8
Grinding wheels and other abrasive products, exc. industrial diamonds	(X)	26.5
All other materials, components, parts, containers, and supplies	(X)	176.8
Materials, ingredients, containers, and supplies, nsk	(X)	356.1

Source: 2002 *Economic Census*. Explanation of symbols used: (D): Withheld to avoid disclosure of competitive data; na: Not available; (S): Withheld because statistical norms were not met; (X): Not applicable; (Z): Less than half the unit shown; nec: Not elsewhere classified; nsk: Not specified by kind; - : zero; p : 10-19 percent estimated; q : 20-29 percent estimated.

PRODUCT SHARE DETAILS FOR METAL HEAT TREATING

Product or Product Class Shipments	Mil. $	Product or Product Class Shipments	Mil. $
METAL HEAT TREATING	3,379.6	annealing, brazing, shot peening, tempering, etc.)	3,271.6
Heat treating of metal for the trade (heat treating, pickling, annealing, brazing, shot peening, tempering, etc.)	**3,379.6**	Heat treating of metal for the trade (heat treating, pickling, annealing, brazing, shot peening, tempering, etc.), nsk,	
Heat treating of metal for the trade (heat treating, pickling,		total	108.0

Source: 2002 *Economic Census*. The values are product shipments in millions of dollars for 2002. Total product shipments may be lower or higher than industry shipments. See Introduction for a full discussion. Values of indented subcategories are summed in the main heading(s). The symbol (D) appears when data are withheld to prevent disclosure of competitive information. The abbreviation nsk stands for 'not specified by kind' and nec for 'not elsewhere classified'. A dash (-) means zero.

PRODUCT SHARE DETAILS FOR METAL COATING AND NONPRECIOUS ENGRAVING

Product or Product Class Shipments	Mil. $	Product or Product Class Shipments	Mil. $
METAL COATING, ENGRAVING, AND ALLIED SERVICES	9,247.3	wash coating (including organic coatings, enamels, lacquers, alkyds, plastics, etc.)	490.5
Metal etching, engraving, coating, and allied services	**9,247.3**	Inorganic metal coatings, including porcelain	311.9
All other metal coating, including curtain coating and wash coating (including organic coatings, enamels, lacquers, alkyds, plastics, etc.)	1,490.6	Metal galvanizing and other hot dip metal coating	2,808.6
		Metal coil coating (including organic coatings, enamels, lacquers, alkyds, plastics, etc.)	1,542.4
Electronic metal engraving, excluding metal nameplates	77.7	Metal liquid spray coating, including electrostatic coating (including organic coatings, enamels, lacquers, alkyds, plastics, etc.)	851.2
Photo chemical metal etching, including machining (excluding metal nameplates)	166.3		
Etching and engraving metal nameplates	103.1	Metal powder coating, including electrostatic and fluidized bed (including organic coatings, enamels, lacquers, alkyds, plastics, etc.)	907.5
Engraving and etching on nonprecious (except pewter) metal hollowware, flatware, and cutlery	77.2		
Other engraving and etching, except jewelry and silverware	263.8	Flocking metals and metal products for the trade	240.4
All other metal coating, including curtain coating and		Metal coating, engraving, and allied services, nsk, total	1,406.6

Source: 2002 *Economic Census*. The values are product shipments in millions of dollars for 2002. Total product shipments may be lower or higher than industry shipments. See Introduction for a full discussion. Values of indented subcategories are summed in the main heading(s). The symbol (D) appears when data are withheld to prevent disclosure of competitive information. The abbreviation nsk stands for 'not specified by kind' and nec for 'not elsewhere classified'. A dash (-) means zero.

PRODUCT SHARE DETAILS FOR ELECTROPLATING, PLATING, POLISHING, ANODIZING, AND COLORING

Product or Product Class Shipments	Mil. $	Product or Product Class Shipments	Mil. $
ELECTROPLATING, PLATING, POLISHING, ANODIZING, AND COLORING	5,662.2	coloring	5,152.3
Electroplating, plating, polishing, anodizing, and coloring	5,471.3	Laminating steel for the trade	319.0
Electroplating, plating, polishing, anodizing, and		Electroplating, plating, polishing, anodizing, and coloring, nsk, total	191.0

Source: 2002 *Economic Census*. The values are product shipments in millions of dollars for 2002. Total product shipments may be lower or higher than industry shipments. See Introduction for a full discussion. Values of indented subcategories are summed in the main heading(s). The symbol (D) appears when data are withheld to prevent disclosure of competitive information. The abbreviation nsk stands for 'not specified by kind' and nec for 'not elsewhere classified'. A dash (-) means zero.

INPUTS AND OUTPUTS FOR COATING, ENGRAVING, HEAT TREATING AND ALLIED ACTIVITIES

Economic Sector or Industry Providing Inputs	%	Sector	Economic Sector or Industry Buying Outputs	%	Sector
Compensation of employees	30.6		Motor vehicle parts	8.7	Manufg.
Iron & steel mills & ferroalloys	9.8	Manufg.	Truck transportation	3.6	Util.
Chemical products & preparations, nec	4.3	Manufg.	Residential structures, nec	3.5	Construct.
Paints & coatings	3.4	Manufg.	Telecommunications	3.5	Services
Wholesale trade	3.3	Trade	Coating, engraving, heat treating & allied activities	2.6	Manufg.
Management of companies & enterprises	3.0	Services	Residential permanent site structures	2.5	Construct.
Coating, engraving, heat treating & allied activities	2.7	Manufg.	Nonresidential structures, nec	2.1	Construct.
Power generation & supply	2.1	Util.	Petroleum refineries	2.1	Manufg.
Natural gas distribution	1.6	Util.	Oil & gas extraction	2.0	Mining
Real estate	1.6	Fin/R.E.	Water transportation	1.8	Util.
Securities, commodity contracts, investments	1.0	Fin/R.E.	Plate work & fabricated structural products	1.5	Manufg.
Dry-cleaning & laundry services	1.0	Services	Printing	1.5	Manufg.
Machine shops	0.9	Manufg.	Plastics products, nec	1.3	Manufg.
Petroleum refineries	0.9	Manufg.	Light truck & utility vehicles	1.3	Manufg.
Truck transportation	0.8	Util.	Soft drinks & ice	1.3	Manufg.
Lessors of nonfinancial assets	0.7	Fin/R.E.	Ornamental & architectural metal products	1.1	Manufg.
Professional, scientific, technical services, nec	0.7	Services	Automotive repair & maintenance, ex. car washes	1.0	Services
Taxes on production & imports, less subsidies	0.7		Retail trade	1.0	Trade
Monetary authorities/depository credit intermediation	0.7	Fin/R.E.	Basic organic chemicals, nec	1.0	Manufg.
Industrial process variable instruments	0.7	Manufg.	Industrial machinery, nec	0.9	Manufg.
Industrial gases	0.6	Manufg.	Aluminum products from purchased aluminum	0.9	Manufg.
Plastics materials & resins	0.6	Manufg.	Guided missiles & space vehicles	0.8	Manufg.
Custom roll forming	0.6	Manufg.	Plastics packaging materials, film & sheet	0.8	Manufg.
Advertising & related services	0.5	Services	Newspaper publishers	0.8	Services
Food services & drinking places	0.5	Services	Commercial & health care structures	0.8	Construct.
Semiconductors & related devices	0.5	Manufg.	Owner-occupied dwellings	0.8	
Basic organic chemicals, nec	0.5	Manufg.	Paperboard containers	0.8	Manufg.
Printed circuit assemblies (electronic assemblies)	0.5	Manufg.	Automobiles	0.8	Manufg.
Maintenance/repair of nonresidential structures	0.5	Construct.	Breweries	0.7	Manufg.
Data processing, hosting, & related services	0.5	Services	Iron & steel mills & ferroalloys	0.7	Manufg.
Accounting, tax preparation, bookkeeping, & payroll	0.5	Services	Toilet preparations	0.7	Manufg.
Hotels & motels, including casino hotels	0.4	Services	Maintenance/repair of nonresidential structures	0.7	Construct.
Services to buildings & dwellings	0.4	Services	Machine shops	0.7	Manufg.
Automotive equipment rental & leasing	0.4	Fin/R.E.	Rubber products, nec	0.7	Manufg.
Air transportation	0.4	Util.	Plastics materials & resins	0.7	Manufg.
Telecommunications	0.4	Services	Paper mills	0.7	Manufg.
Industrial process furnaces & ovens	0.4	Manufg.	Manufacturing, nec	0.7	Manufg.
Nonferrous metal (ex. copper & aluminum) processing	0.4	Manufg.	Book publishers	0.6	Services
Legal services	0.3	Services	Metal cans, boxes, & other containers (light gauge)	0.6	Manufg.
Scientific research & development services	0.3	Services	Soap & cleaning compounds	0.5	Manufg.
Cutting tools & machine tool accessories	0.3	Manufg.	Directories, mailing lists, & other publishers	0.5	Services
Rail transportation	0.3	Util.	Valve & fittings other than plumbing	0.5	Manufg.
Turned products & screws, nuts, & bolts	0.3	Manufg.	Chemical products & preparations, nec	0.5	Manufg.
Warehousing & storage	0.3	Util.	Postal service	0.5	Util.
Waste management & remediation services	0.3	Services	Air transportation	0.5	Util.
Automotive repair & maintenance, ex. car washes	0.3	Services	Wineries	0.5	Manufg.
Paperboard containers	0.3	Manufg.	Scenic & sightseeing transport & related services	0.4	Util.
Management, scientific, & technical consulting	0.3	Services	Ferrous metal foundries	0.4	Manufg.
Basic inorganic chemicals, nec	0.3	Manufg.	Personal & household goods repair/maintenance	0.4	Services
Commercial & industrial equipment repair/maintenance	0.3	Services	Commercial & industrial equipment repair/maintenance	0.4	Services
Miscellaneous wood products	0.2	Manufg.	Pipeline transportation	0.4	Util.
Commercial & industrial machinery rental & leasing	0.2	Fin/R.E.	Aircraft parts & auxiliary equipment, nec	0.4	Manufg.
Fabricated metals, nec	0.2	Manufg.	Nonferrous metal foundries	0.4	Manufg.
Metal cans, boxes, & other containers (light gauge)	0.2	Manufg.	Signs	0.4	Manufg.
Abrasive products	0.2	Manufg.	Crowns & closures & metal stamping	0.4	Manufg.
Architectural, engineering, & related services	0.2	Services	Periodical publishers	0.4	Services
Business support services	0.2	Services	Search, detection, & navigation instruments	0.4	Manufg.
General purpose machinery, nec	0.2	Manufg.	Mining & oil & gas field machinery	0.4	Manufg.
Material handling equipment	0.2	Manufg.	Surgical appliances & supplies	0.4	Manufg.
Artificial & synthetic fibers & filaments	0.1	Manufg.	Commercial & service industry machinery, nec	0.4	Manufg.
Forging, stamping, & sintering, nec	0.1	Manufg.	Power generation & supply	0.4	Util.
Crowns & closures & metal stamping	0.1	Manufg.	Motor vehicle bodies	0.4	Manufg.
Plate work & fabricated structural products	0.1	Manufg.	Software publishers	0.4	Services
Ball & roller bearings	0.1	Manufg.	Sporting & athletic goods	0.4	Manufg.
Handtools	0.1	Manufg.	AC, refrigeration, and warm air heating equipment	0.4	Manufg.

Continued on next page.

INPUTS AND OUTPUTS FOR COATING, ENGRAVING, HEAT TREATING AND ALLIED ACTIVITIES - Continued

Economic Sector or Industry Providing Inputs	%	Sector	Economic Sector or Industry Buying Outputs	%	Sector
Transit & ground passenger transportation	0.1	Util.	Wood windows & doors & millwork	0.4	Manufg.
Nondepository credit intermediation activities	0.1	Fin/R.E.	Aircraft	0.4	Manufg.
Other computer related services, including facilities	0.1	Services	Material handling equipment	0.4	Manufg.
Water, sewage and other systems	0.1	Util.	Oil & gas operations services	0.4	Mining
Copper, nickel, lead, and zinc	0.1	Mining	Paints & coatings	0.4	Manufg.
			Automotive equipment rental & leasing	0.4	Fin/R.E.
			Wholesale trade	0.4	Trade
			Fabricated metals, nec	0.3	Manufg.
			Turned products & screws, nuts, & bolts	0.3	Manufg.
			Coal	0.3	Mining
			Motorcycles, bicycles, & parts	0.3	Manufg.
			Paperboard mills	0.3	Manufg.
			Steel products from purchased steel	0.3	Manufg.
			Wood kitchen cabinets & countertops	0.3	Manufg.
			Transportation equipment, nec	0.3	Manufg.
			Engine equipment, nec	0.3	Manufg.
			Hardware	0.3	Manufg.
			Coated & laminated paper & packaging materials	0.3	Manufg.
			Basic inorganic chemicals, nec	0.3	Manufg.
			Oil & gas well drilling	0.3	Mining
			Investigation & security services	0.3	Services
			Semiconductors & related devices	0.3	Manufg.
			Carpet & rug mills	0.3	Manufg.
			Maintenance/repair of residential structures	0.3	Construct.
			Construction machinery	0.3	Manufg.
			Ready-mix concrete	0.3	Manufg.
			Glass products from purchased glass	0.3	Manufg.
			Jewelry & silverware	0.3	Manufg.
			General purpose machinery, nec	0.3	Manufg.
			Synthetic dyes & pigments	0.2	Manufg.
			Electromedical & electrotherapeutic apparatus	0.2	Manufg.
			Sanitary paper products	0.2	Manufg.
			Farm machinery & equipment	0.2	Manufg.
			Broadwoven fabric mills	0.2	Manufg.
			Surgical & medical instrument	0.2	Manufg.
			Semiconductor machinery	0.2	Manufg.
			Power boilers & heat exchangers	0.2	Manufg.
			Turbines & turbine generator set units	0.2	Manufg.
			Other S/L govt. enterprises	0.2	S/L Govt
			Packaging machinery	0.2	Manufg.
			Telephone apparatus	0.2	Manufg.
			Lighting fixtures	0.2	Manufg.
			Industrial process variable instruments	0.2	Manufg.
			Fabricated pipes & pipe fittings	0.2	Manufg.
			Fiber, yarn, & thread mills	0.2	Manufg.
			Switchgear & switchboard apparatus	0.2	Manufg.
			Copper rolling, drawing, extruding, & alloying	0.2	Manufg.
			Custom architectural woodwork & millwork	0.2	Manufg.
			Adhesives	0.2	Manufg.
			Concrete products, nec	0.2	Manufg.
			Broadcast & wireless communications equipment	0.2	Manufg.
			Tobacco products	0.2	Manufg.
			Electronic computers	0.2	Manufg.
			Nonferrous metal (ex. copper & aluminum) processing	0.2	Manufg.
			Curtain & linen mills	0.2	Manufg.
			Household cooking appliances	0.2	Manufg.
			Cement	0.2	Manufg.
			Springs & wire products	0.2	Manufg.
			Electronic components, nec	0.2	Manufg.
			Computer terminals & peripherals	0.2	Manufg.
			Textile & fabric finishing mills	0.2	Manufg.
			Heavy duty trucks	0.2	Manufg.
			Communication & energy wires & cables	0.2	Manufg.
			Artificial & synthetic fibers & filaments	0.2	Manufg.
			Pesticides & other agricultural chemicals	0.2	Manufg.
			Transit & ground passenger transportation	0.2	Util.
			Heating equipment (except warm air furnaces)	0.2	Manufg.
			Concrete pipe, brick, & block	0.2	Manufg.
			Plastics bottles	0.2	Manufg.
			Arms, ordnance, & accessories	0.2	Manufg.
			Fertilizer	0.2	Manufg.
			Metal & other household furniture	0.2	Manufg.
			Analytical laboratory instruments	0.2	Manufg.
			Polystyrene foam products	0.2	Manufg.
			Asphalt shingle & coating materials	0.2	Manufg.
			Fluid power process machinery	0.2	Manufg.
			Irradiation apparatus	0.2	Manufg.
			Special tools, dies, jigs, & fixtures	0.2	Manufg.
			Relay & industrial controls	0.2	Manufg.
			Showcases, partitions, shelving, and lockers	0.2	Manufg.

Continued on next page.

INPUTS AND OUTPUTS FOR COATING, ENGRAVING, HEAT TREATING AND ALLIED ACTIVITIES - Continued

Economic Sector or Industry Providing Inputs	%	Sector	Economic Sector or Industry Buying Outputs	%	Sector
			Watches, clocks, & related devices	0.2	Manufg.
			Clay & nonclay refractory manufacturing	0.2	Manufg.
			Vending, commercial, industrial, office machinery	0.2	Manufg.
			Power-driven handtools	0.1	Manufg.
			Unlaminated plastics profile shapes	0.1	Manufg.
			Miscellaneous mining services	0.1	Mining
			Radio & television broadcasting	0.1	Services
			Tires	0.1	Manufg.
			Plumbing fixture fittings & trim	0.1	Manufg.
			Motors & generators	0.1	Manufg.
			Air & gas compressors	0.1	Manufg.
			Ammunition	0.1	Manufg.
			Support activities for printing	0.1	Manufg.
			Alumina refining & primary aluminum production	0.1	Manufg.
			Gaskets, packing, & sealing devices	0.1	Manufg.
			Metal cutting & forming machine tools	0.1	Manufg.
			Software, audio, and video media reproducing	0.1	Manufg.
			Stationery products	0.1	Manufg.
			Mineral wool	0.1	Manufg.
			Printed circuit assemblies (electronic assemblies)	0.1	Manufg.
			Electrical equipment & components, nec	0.1	Manufg.
			Plastics pipe & pipe fittings	0.1	Manufg.
			Pressed & blown glass & glassware, nec	0.1	Manufg.
			Wiring devices	0.1	Manufg.
			Computer storage devices	0.1	Manufg.
			Metal tanks (heavy gauge)	0.1	Manufg.
			Engineered wood members & trusses	0.1	Manufg.
			Natural gas distribution	0.1	Util.
			Ship building & repairing	0.1	Manufg.
			Industrial molds	0.1	Manufg.
			Synthetic rubber	0.1	Manufg.
			Pumps & pumping equipment	0.1	Manufg.
			Dolls, toys, & games	0.1	Manufg.
			Travel trailers & campers	0.1	Manufg.
			Lawn & garden equipment	0.1	Manufg.
			Railroad rolling stock	0.1	Manufg.
			Urethane & other foam products (except polystrene)	0.1	Manufg.

Source: Benchmark Input-Output Accounts for the U.S. Economy, 2002, U.S. Department of Commerce, Washington, D.C., January 2008. The abbreviation nec stands for 'not elsewhere classified'.

OCCUPATIONS EMPLOYED BY COATING, ENGRAVING, HEAT TREATING, & ALLIED ACTIVITIES

Occupation	% of Total 2006	Change to 2016	Occupation	% of Total 2006	Change to 2016
Plating & coating machine operators & tenders	14.3	-14.5	Shipping, receiving, & traffic clerks	2.2	-21.1
Coating, painting, & spraying machine operators	6.9	-22.1	Grinding & polishing workers, hand	1.9	-18.0
Helpers--Production workers	6.1	-18.0	Machine feeders & offbearers	1.9	-26.2
Grinding, lapping, polishing machine tool operators	5.6	-20.5	Sales reps, wholesale & manufacturing, exc tech	1.5	-18.0
First-line supervisors/managers of production workers	5.3	-18.0	Office clerks, general	1.5	-19.2
Heat treating equipment operators & tenders	4.2	-18.0	Industrial production managers	1.4	-18.0
Inspectors, testers, sorters, samplers, & weighers	3.8	-22.7	Bookkeeping, accounting, & auditing clerks	1.3	-18.0
Laborers & freight, stock, & material movers, hand	3.5	-26.2	Team assemblers	1.2	-18.0
Packers & packagers, hand	2.9	-34.4	Industrial truck & tractor operators	1.2	-26.2
General & operations managers	2.3	-26.2	Machinists	1.1	-13.9
Maintenance & repair workers, general	2.3	-18.0	Truck drivers, light or delivery services	1.1	-18.0

Source: Industry-Occupation Matrix, Bureau of Labor Statistics, December 4, 2007. These data are reported based on 4-digit NAICS categories but have been matched to corresponding 6-digit NAICS industry codes. The change reported for each occupation to the year 2016 is a percent of growth or decline as estimated by the Bureau of Labor Statistics. The abbreviation nec stands for 'not elsewhere classified'.

LOCATION BY STATE AND REGIONAL CONCENTRATION

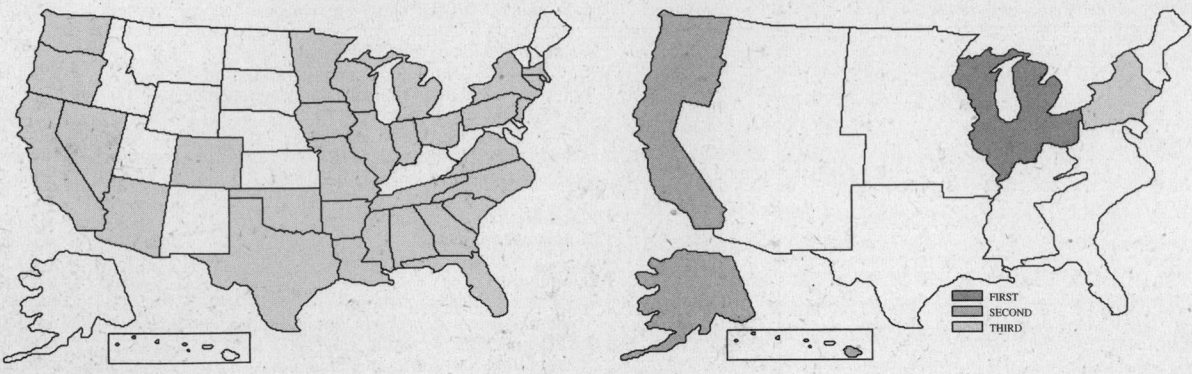

INDUSTRY DATA BY STATE

| State | Establish-ments | Shipments | | | Employment | | | | Cost as % of Shipments | Investment per Employee ($) |
		Total ($ mil)	% of U.S.	Per Establ.	Total Number	% of U.S.	Per Establ.	Wages ($/hour)		
Ohio	525	2,714.3	14.8	5,170.2	13,692	10.0	26	15.19	54.4	4,128
California	998	1,837.8	10.0	1,841.5	18,989	13.8	19	13.59	34.5	3,600
Indiana	234	1,618.4	8.8	6,916.1	6,988	5.1	30	16.34	28.7	5,703
Michigan	513	1,600.7	8.7	3,120.3	14,850	10.8	29	14.60	29.1	4,361
Illinois	444	1,433.2	7.8	3,227.9	10,885	7.9	25	15.02	37.2	3,758
Pennsylvania	264	1,192.4	6.5	4,516.6	4,882	3.6	18	16.29	61.5	4,931
Texas	378	805.5	4.4	2,130.9	7,697	5.6	20	14.34	36.1	3,110
Wisconsin	227	535.2	2.9	2,357.8	6,397	4.7	28	14.37	27.9	2,578
Connecticut	167	479.0	2.6	2,868.3	4,146	3.0	25	15.72	34.7	6,593
New York	244	471.4	2.6	1,932.1	4,336	3.2	18	14.02	34.7	2,619
Massachusetts	184	378.8	2.1	2,058.6	3,986	2.9	22	15.21	24.8	3,325
Minnesota	171	360.6	2.0	2,108.5	4,122	3.0	24	14.30	29.6	4,871
Washington	96	255.6	1.4	2,662.9	2,119	1.5	22	15.94	34.1	3,926
Louisiana	48	234.9	1.3	4,894.7	1,954	1.4	41	17.00	38.8	6,120
New Jersey	159	231.8	1.3	1,457.9	2,396	1.7	15	14.69	31.3	3,815
North Carolina	118	193.1	1.1	1,636.3	1,662	1.2	14	15.20	32.3	3,339
Alabama	27	127.9	0.7	4,735.8	1,118	0.8	41	14.03	38.4	2,482
Oklahoma	67	124.1	0.7	1,852.4	1,135	0.8	17	15.63	35.1	5,377
Arizona	106	123.6	0.7	1,165.7	1,478	1.1	14	13.07	27.0	3,264
Mississippi	14	120.1	0.7	8,579.1	474	0.3	34	19.59	55.3	2,806
Georgia	29	115.8	0.6	3,994.3	674	0.5	23	15.95	62.0	9,003
Rhode Island	69	107.9	0.6	1,564.3	1,256	0.9	18	13.73	33.0	2,131
Oregon	85	105.8	0.6	1,244.3	1,144	0.8	13	14.75	26.4	3,625
Tennessee	53	101.6	0.6	1,916.6	1,230	0.9	23	13.87	34.4	5,331
Colorado	65	94.5	0.5	1,453.6	621	0.5	10	13.85	52.4	2,770
Florida	68	87.1	0.5	1,280.6	807	0.6	12	16.86	27.3	2,519
Missouri	52	79.7	0.4	1,532.2	821	0.6	16	12.55	34.5	6,048
Iowa	41	79.0	0.4	1,926.5	875	0.6	21	13.82	27.7	4,661
Arkansas	14	73.1	0.4	5,222.5	600	0.4	43	14.36	35.0	2,223
Virginia	23	23.8	0.1	1,034.5	260	0.2	11	13.79	35.1	1,681
Nevada	14	18.3	0.1	1,304.6	271	0.2	19	11.51	18.4	1,114
South Carolina	9	14.1	0.1	1,561.8	146	0.1	16	14.73	16.5	3,596

Source: 2002 *Economic Census*. The states are in descending order of shipments or establishments (if shipment data are missing for the majority). The symbol (D) appears when data are withheld to prevent disclosure of competitive information. States marked with (D) are sorted by number of establishments. A dash (-) indicates that the data element cannot be calculated. Data may not show all states active in the NAICS category. All data available at the time of publication are shown.

NAICS 332913 - PLUMBING FIXTURE FITTING AND TRIM MANUFACTURING

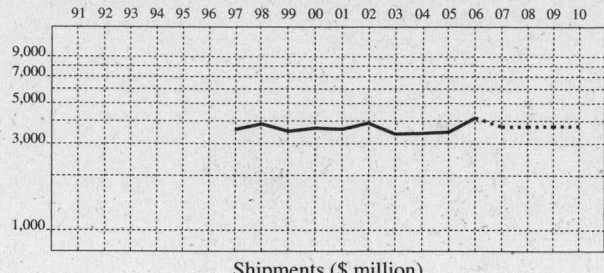

Shipments ($ million)

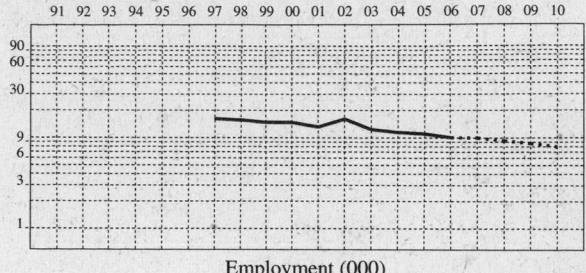

Employment (000)

GENERAL STATISTICS

Year	Com-panies	Establishments		Employment			Compensation		Production ($ million)			
		Total	with 20 or more employees	Total (000)	Production Workers (000)	Hours (Mil)	Payroll ($ mil)	Wages ($/hr)	Cost of Materials	Value Added by Manufacture	Value of Shipments	Capital Invest.
1997	93	110	94	16.2	11.7	23.8	498.3	13.23	1,775.3	1,832.2	3,584.0	85.5
1998		167	91	15.7	11.4	23.4	499.3	13.20	1,826.2	2,034.3	3,854.6	78.4
1999		173	92	14.8	10.9	21.2	463.8	14.31	1,686.8	1,845.9	3,512.8	68.8
2000		178	97	14.8	11.2	22.0	498.7	14.66	1,806.1	1,906.0	3,655.6	57.1
2001		172	87	13.2	9.7	19.5	462.4	15.21	1,684.0	1,925.3	3,602.6	56.4
2002	136	155	81	16.1	12.3	25.1	558.7	14.30	1,802.3	2,084.5	3,898.6	76.8
2003		152	80	12.4	9.3	18.3	463.2	15.55	1,730.1	1,676.6	3,392.8	60.0
2004		148	78	11.5	8.7	20.5	493.1	15.14	1,736.2	1,744.5	3,423.1	51.6
2005		146	77	11.1	8.0	16.4	468.1	15.95	1,881.8	1,600.3	3,481.4	54.9
2006		158P	74P	10.1	7.2	14.9	444.0	16.21	2,164.7	2,072.2	4,161.3	51.0
2007		158P	72P	10.0P	7.4P	15.9P	465.9P	16.51P	1,930.7P	1,848.2P	3,711.4P	46.3P
2008		158P	69P	9.3P	7.0P	15.1P	462.5P	16.82P	1,935.9P	1,853.1P	3,721.4P	43.1P
2009		159P	67P	8.7P	6.5P	14.2P	459.0P	17.14P	1,941.0P	1,858.1P	3,731.3P	39.9P
2010		159P	64P	8.0P	6.0P	13.4P	455.6P	17.45P	1,946.2P	1,863.0P	3,741.3P	36.6P

Sources: 1997 and 2002 *Economic Census*; other years, up to 2006, are from *Annual Survey of Manufactures*. Establishment counts for non-Census years are from *County Business Patterns*; 1997 and 2002 values are from the 1997 and 2002 censuses, respectively. 'P's show projections by the editors.

INDICES OF CHANGE

Year	Com-panies	Establishments		Employment			Compensation		Production ($ million)			
		Total	with 20 or more employees	Total (000)	Production Workers (000)	Hours (Mil)	Payroll ($ mil)	Wages ($/hr)	Cost of Materials	Value Added by Manufacture	Value of Shipments	Capital Invest.
1997	68	71	116	101	95	95	89	93	99	88	92	111
1998		108	112	98	93	93	89	92	101	98	99	102
1999		112	114	92	89	84	83	100	94	89	90	90
2000		115	120	92	91	88	89	103	100	91	94	74
2001		111	107	82	79	78	83	106	93	92	92	73
2002	100	100	100	100	100	100	100	100	100	100	100	100
2003		98	99	77	76	73	83	109	96	80	87	78
2004		95	96	71	71	82	88	106	96	84	88	67
2005		94	95	69	65	65	84	112	104	77	89	71
2006		102P	91P	63	59	59	79	113	120	99	107	66
2007		102P	88P	62P	60P	63P	83P	115P	107P	89P	95P	60P
2008		102P	85P	58P	57P	60P	83P	118P	107P	89P	95P	56P
2009		102P	82P	54P	53P	57P	82P	120P	108P	89P	96P	52P
2010		103P	79P	50P	49P	53P	82P	122P	108P	89P	96P	48P

Sources: Same as General Statistics. Values reflect change from the base year, 2002. Values above 100 mean greater than 2002, values below 100 mean less than 2002, and the values of 100 in other years means the same as 2002. 'P's show projections by the editors.

SELECTED RATIOS

For 2002	Avg. of All Manufact.	Analyzed Industry	Index	For 2002	Avg. of All Manufact.	Analyzed Industry	Index
Employees per Establishment	42	104	247	Value Added per Production Worker	182,367	169,472	93
Payroll per Establishment	1,639,184	3,604,516	220	Cost per Establishment	5,769,015	11,627,742	202
Payroll per Employee	39,053	34,702	89	Cost per Employee	137,446	111,944	81
Production Workers per Establishment	30	79	269	Cost per Production Worker	195,506	146,528	75
Wages per Establishment	694,845	2,315,677	333	Shipments per Establishment	11,158,348	25,152,258	225
Wages per Production Worker	23,548	29,181	124	Shipments per Employee	265,847	242,149	91
Hours per Production Worker	1,980	2,041	103	Shipments per Production Worker	378,144	316,959	84
Wages per Hour	11.89	14.30	120	Investment per Establishment	361,338	495,484	137
Value Added per Establishment	5,381,325	13,448,387	250	Investment per Employee	8,609	4,770	55
Value Added per Employee	128,210	129,472	101	Investment per Production Worker	12,245	6,244	51

Sources: Same as General Statistics. The 'Average of All Manufacturing' column represents the average of all manufacturing industries reported for the most recent complete year available. The Index shows the relationship between the Average and the Analyzed Industry. For example, 100 means that they are equal; 500 that the Analyzed Industry is five times the average; 50 means that the Analyzed Industry is half the national average. The abbreviation 'na' is used to show that data are 'not available'. Ratios shown for 2002, the last complete census year.

LEADING COMPANIES   Number shown: **75**   Total sales ($ mil): **47,408**   Total employment (000): **243.5**

Company Name	Address				CEO Name	Phone	Co. Type	Sales ($ mil)	Empl. (000)
Masco Corp.	21001 Van Born Rd.	Taylor	MI	48180	Ronald W. Ayers	313-274-7400	P	11,770	52.0
Fortune Brands Inc.	520 Lake Cook Rd.	Deerfield	IL	60015	Bruce A. Carbonari	847-484-4400	P	8,563	31.0
American Standard Inc.	PO Box 6820	Piscataway	NJ	08855		732-980-3000	S	7,614*	67.0
Trane Inc.	PO Box 6820	Piscataway	NJ	08855		732-980-6000	P	7,450	29.6
Kohler Co.	444 Highland Dr.	Kohler	WI	53044	Herbert Kohler	920-457-4441	R	4,061*	33.0
Jacuzzi Brands Inc.	777 S Flagler Dr.	W Palm Bch	FL	33401		561-514-3838	S	1,202	4.5
Viking Automatic Sprinkler Co.	1301 L Orient St.	Saint Paul	MN	55117	Lee Anderson	651-558-3300	R	1,150*	<0.1
Robert Bosch Tool Corp.	1961 Bishop Ln.	Louisville	KY	40218	Timothy Shea	502-625-2050	D	1,057*	0.2
NCH Corp.	PO Box 152170	Irving	TX	75015		972-438-0211	R	688*	8.5
Elkay Manufacturing Co.	2222 Camden Ct.	Oak Brook	IL	60523	Ronald Katz	630-574-8484	R	470*	3.6
NIBCO Inc.	PO Box 1167	Elkhart	IN	46515	Rex Martin	574-295-3000	R	292*	3.0
Gerber Plumbing Fixtures	2500 Intle. Pkwy.	Woodridge	IL	60517		630-679-1420	R	289*	<0.1
Davis-Ulmer Sprinkler Company	One Commerce Dr.	Amherst	NY	14228	R. Steven Ulmer	716-691-3200	R	179*	0.2
AY Mc Donald Industries Inc.	PO Box 508	Dubuque	IA	52004	John Mc Donald	563-583-7311	R	163*	0.4
Mueller Brass Co.	PO Box 5021	Port Huron	MI	48061	William O'Hagan	810-987-7770	S	151*	0.4
Keeney Manufacturing Co.	PO Box 310159	Newington	CT	06131		860-666-3342	R	132*	0.2
Chicago Faucet Co.	2100 Clearwater Dr.	Des Plaines	IL	60018	William Christensen	847-803-5000	R	121*	0.3
Wolverine Brass Inc.	2951 E Hwy. 501	Conway	SC	29526	Lloyd Coppedge	843-347-3121	R	111*	0.2
Parker Hannifin Brass Prods	300 Parker Dr.	Otsego	MI	49078		269-694-9411	D	104*	0.6
Zoeller Co.	PO Box 16347	Louisville	KY	40256		502-778-2731	R	100*	0.2
Milwaukee Valve Company Inc.	16550 W Stratton Dr	New Berlin	WI	53151	Richard Giannini	262-432-2700	R	100*	<0.1
Flowtronex PSI Inc.	10661 Newkirk St.	Dallas	TX	75220	Dan Driscoll	214-357-1320	S	98*	0.2
Suncast Corp.	701 N Kirk Rd.	Batavia	IL	60510	Thomas Tisbo	630-879-2050	R	88*	0.8
Mansfield Plumbing Products	150 W 1st St.	Perrysville	OH	44864		419-938-5211	R	87*	0.6
T-L Irrigation Co.	PO Box 1047	Hastings	NE	68902	Leroy Thom	402-462-4128	R	78*	0.3
Vanguard Industries Inc.	831 N Vanguard St.	McPherson	KS	67460	John Fraser	620-241-6369	R	74*	<0.1
Lee Supply Corp.	PO Box 681430	Indianapolis	IN	46268		317-290-2500	R	61*	0.2
Symmons Industries Inc.	31 Brooks Dr.	Braintree	MA	02184	William OKeeffe	781-848-2250	R	60*	0.3
Price Pfister Inc.	19701 Da Vinci	Foothill Ranch	CA	92610		949-672-4000	S	55	0.4
Zurn Plumbing Products Group	1801 Pittsburgh Ave	Erie	PA	16502		814-455-0921	R	52*	0.3
Sloan Valve Co.	10500 Seymour Ave.	Franklin Park	IL	60131	Charles Allen	847-671-4300	R	50*	<0.1
Wiginton Fire Sprinklers	699 Aero Ln.	Sanford	FL	32771	Donald Wiginton	407-936-1922	R	50*	<0.1
Delta Faucet Co.	PO Box 40980	Indianapolis	IN	46240	Reinhard Metzger	317-848-1812	D	48*	0.4
T.F. Hudgins Inc.	PO Box 920946	Houston	TX	77292	Ted Edwards	713-682-3651	R	45*	<0.1
Anderson Copper and Brass Co.	4325 Frontage Rd.	Oak Forest	IL	60452	Steve Anton	708-535-9030	S	40*	0.2
Starline Manufacturing Company	6060 W Douglas	Milwaukee	WI	53218	Keith Kramer	414-358-4060	S	40*	0.2
Royal Baths Manufacturing Co.	14635 Chrisman Rd.	Houston	TX	77039	George Dawson	281-442-3400	R	38*	0.5
Shane Group Inc.	200 Industrial Dr.	Hillsdale	MI	49242	D.C. Shaneour	517-439-4316	R	37*	0.2
Alson's Corp.	PO Box 282	Hillsdale	MI	49242		517-439-1411	S	35*	0.2
Coast Foundry and Mfg. Co.	PO Box 1788	Pomona	CA	91769	Armand Antunez	909-596-1883	R	34*	0.2
T and S Brass and Bronze Works	PO Box 1088	Travelers Rest	SC	29690	Claude Thiesen		R	34*	0.3
Fernco Inc.	300 S Dayton St.	Davison	MI	48423	Christoper Cooper	810-653-9626	R	31*	0.1
Creftcon Industries	PO Box 1269	La Puente	CA	91749	Leonard Freibott	626-964-6531	R	30*	0.2
Jay R. Smith Manufacturing Co.	PO Box 3237	Montgomery	AL	36109	Jay L. Smith	334-277-8520	R	30*	0.3
Brass-Craft Manufacturing Co.	39600 Orchard Hill	Novi	MI	48375	Todd Talbot	248-305-6000	S	28*	0.2
Water Saver Faucet Co.	701 W Erie Street	Chicago	IL	60610	Steven Kersten	312-666-5500	R	28*	0.1
Speakman Co.	PO Box 191	Wilmington	DE	19899	Rodman Ward	302-764-7100	R	27*	0.1
LDR Industries Inc.	600 N Kilbourn Ave.	Chicago	IL	60624	Lawrence Greenspon	773-265-3000	R	25*	0.1
American Granby Inc.	7652 Morgan Rd.	Liverpool	NY	13090	John Lowe	315-451-1100	R	25*	<0.1
Hago Manufacturing Company	1120 Globe Ave.	Mountainside	NJ	07092	Phil Emond	908-232-8687	R	24*	0.1
Telsco Industries Inc.	3301 W Kingsley	Garland	TX	75041	Mike Mason	972-278-6131	R	22*	0.1
William Steinen Manufacturing	29 E Halsey Rd.	Parsippany	NJ	07054	William Steinen	973-887-6400	R	21*	0.1
Bowles Fluidics Corp.	PO Box 6300	Columbia	MD	21045	Eric Koehler	410-381-0400	R	20*	0.3
Delafield Corp.	1548 Flower Ave.	Duarte	CA	91010	Nik Ray	626-303-0740	R	19*	0.1
IW Industries Inc.	35 Melville Park Rd	Melville	NY	11747		631-293-9494	R	18*	0.2
L and J Technologies Inc.	5911 Butterfield Rd.	Hillside	IL	60162	Lou Jannotta	708-236-6000	R	18*	0.1
Hydro Systems Inc.	29132 Ave. Paine	Valencia	CA	91355	Scott Steinhardt	661-775-0686	R	15*	<0.1
Dometic Corp.	PO Box 38	Big Prairie	OH	44611		330-496-3211	R	14*	0.1
Specialty Manufacturing Co.	5858 Centerville Rd	Saint Paul	MN	55127	Dan Keown	651-653-0599	R	14*	<0.1
Fisher Manufacturing Co.	PO Box 60	Tulare	CA	93275	Ray Fisher	559-685-5200	R	13*	<0.1
Guardian Equipment	660 N Union Ave.	Chicago	IL	60610	Steven Kersten	312-733-2626	R	13*	<0.1
Robert Manufacturing Co.	10667 Jersey Blvd.	R Cucamonga	CA	91730	Robert Hartwell	909-987-4654	R	12*	0.1
Anthony Wilcock Enterprises	2600 W Olive Ave.	Burbank	CA	91505	Anthony Wilcock	818-843-8117	R	11*	<0.1
Bead Industries Inc.	11 Cascade Blvd.	Milford	CT	06460	Kenneth Bryant	203-301-0270	R	11*	<0.1
Ametco Manufacturing Corp.	PO Box 1210	Willoughby	OH	44096	Steve Mitrovich	440-951-4300	R	8*	<0.1
Richway Industries Ltd.	PO Box 508	Janesville	IA	50647	Richard Borglum	319-987-2976	R	7*	<0.1
Change Parts Inc.	PO Box 587	Ludington	MI	49431	Doug Sarto	231-845-5107	R	7*	<0.1
Four Guys Stainless Tank/Equip	PO Box 90	Meyersdale	PA	15552	Alma Lauver	814-634-8373	R	7*	<0.1
Krendl Machine Company Inc.	1201 Spencervil Rd.	Delphos	OH	45833	John Krendl	419-692-3060	R	7*	<0.1
Productigear Inc.	1900 W 34th St.	Chicago	IL	60608	Richard Wieker	773-847-4505	R	6*	<0.1
Swan Black Manufacturing Co.	4540 W Thomas St.	Chicago	IL	60651	Jeff Lichten	773-227-3700	R	6*	<0.1
Ki Industries Inc.	5540 McDermott Dr.	Berkeley	IL	60163	David Goltermann	708-449-1990	R	6*	<0.1
Grace Composites L.L.C.	351 Ruth Rd.	Lonoke	AR	72086		501-676-9505	R	6*	<0.1
Josam Company Inc.	PO Box T	Michigan City	IN	46361	Barry Hodgekins	219-872-5531	R	5*	<0.1
Ind. Fiberglass Specialties	521 Kiser St.	Dayton	OH	45404	Theodore Morton	937-222-9000	R	5*	<0.1

Source: Ward's Business Directory of U.S. Private and Public Companies, Volumes 1 and 2, 2008. The company type code used is as follows: P - Public, R - Private, S - Subsidiary, D - Division, J - Joint Venture, A - Affiliate, G - Group. Sales are in millions of dollars, employees are in thousands. An asterisk (*) indicates an estimated sales volume. The symbol < stands for 'less than'. Company names and addresses are truncated, in some cases, to fit into the available space.

MATERIALS CONSUMED

Material	Quantity	Delivered Cost ($ million)
Metal stampings	(X)	24.2
All other fabricated metal products (excluding forgings)	(X)	98.9
Iron and steel castings (rough and semifinished)	(X)	9.1
Copper and copper-base alloy castings (rough and semifinished)	(X)	69.9
Other nonferrous metal castings, rough or semifinished (inc. aluminum)	(X)	18.7
Forgings	(X)	27.5
Steel shapes and forms (exc. castings, forgings, fabr. metal products)	(X)	7.2
Copper and copper-base alloy refinery shapes (exc. castings, forgings, fabr. metal products)	(X)	(D)
Copper and copper-base alloy rod, bar, and mechanical wire	(X)	56.3
Copper and copper-base alloy pipe and tube (exc. castings, forgings, fabr. metal products)	(X)	17.9
All other copper and copper-base alloy shapes and forms (exc. castings, forgings, fabr. metal products)	(X)	(D)
All other nonferrous shapes and forms (exc. castings, forgings, fabr. metal products)	(X)	43.4
Plastics resins consumed in the form of granules, pellets, etc.	(X)	10.7
Fabricated plastics products (excluding gaskets)	(X)	70.6
Paperboard containers, boxes, and corrugated paperboard	(X)	39.4
All other materials, components, parts, containers, and supplies	(X)	668.4
Materials, ingredients, containers, and supplies, nsk	(X)	265.6

Source: 2002 Economic Census. Explanation of symbols used: (D): Withheld to avoid disclosure of competitive data; na: Not available; (S): Withheld because statistical norms were not met; (X): Not applicable; (Z): Less than half the unit shown; nec: Not elsewhere classified; nsk: Not specified by kind; - : zero; p : 10-19 percent estimated; q : 20-29 percent estimated.

PRODUCT SHARE DETAILS

Product or Product Class Shipments	Mil. $	Product or Product Class Shipments	Mil. $
PLUMBING FIXTURE FITTINGS AND TRIM	3,318.4	without spray (metallic and nonmetallic)	11.0
Single lever plumbing fixture controls, two and three handle bath and shower fittings, and antiscald bath or shower valves (brass goods)	**1,110.9**	Deck faucet sink fittings, concealed type, with spray	(D)
		Deck faucet sink fittings, concealed type, without spray	19.4
Lavatory single lever controls (metallic and nonmetallic)	212.5	Other lavatory and sink fittings	257.9
Kitchen single lever controls, nonmetal	305.1	Metallic and nonmetallic lavatory fittings (except basin cocks and single control), 4-in. center-set with pop-up drain	106.4
Kitchen with spray single lever controls (metallic and nonmetallic)	246.6	Metallic and nonmetallic lavatory fittings (except basin cocks and single control), 4-in. center-set without pop-up drain	14.2
Kitchen without spray single lever controls (metallic and nonmetallic)	58.4	Metallic and nonmetallic lavatory fittings (except basin cocks and single control), greater than 4 in., with pop-up drain	39.2
Shower and shower-tub combination single lever controls, including mechanical tub filler and shower control only	106.4	Metallic and nonmetallic lavatory fittings (except basin cocks and single control), greater than 4 in., without pop-up drain	(D)
Shower combination single lever controls, mechanical	32.0	Lavatory and sink basin cocks (one supply line only)	1.0
Shower-tub combination single lever controls, mechanical	(D)	Wallmount combination sink faucet fittings	(D)
Other single lever controls, including mechanical tub filler and shower control only	(D)	Single sink faucet fittings (solid flanged female and adjustable male flange)	(D)
Two and three handle bath and shower fittings, and antiscald bath and shower valves (brass goods)	483.2	Other sink fittings (including sink strainers sold separately)	9.0
Two and three handle bathtub fillers	23.6	Drains and overflows (metallic and nonmetallic), including pop-up drains for bath and shower, lavatory, and sink	39.4
Two and three handle shower fittings with shower heads	54.8		
Two and three handle shower heads sold separately	46.8		
Two and three handle bathtub and shower diverter spout	4.6	Lavatory and sink fittings (except single control), including drains and overflows (brass goods), nsk	33.1
Two and three handle bathtub and shower three valve diverter	(D)	**Plumbing fixtures, fittings, and trim (brass goods), nec**	**1,321.5**
Two and three handle personal showers (handheld)	(D)	IPS mechanical connecting plumbing fixtures	(D)
Two and three handle tub and shower control only	(D)	Plumbing compression stops, including those with drains	57.7
Other two and three handle bath and shower fittings, including stall and gang	24.2	Sediment, hydrant, lawn, hose bibs, and sill cock faucets	20.2
Antiscald bath and shower valves, including thermostatic, thermo-pressure, and pressure balanced controlled fittings	232.1	Metallic P-traps	30.0
		Nonmetallic P-traps	(D)
Single lever plumbing fixture controls, two or three handle bath or shower fittings, and antiscald bath or shower valves (brass goods), nsk	3.9	Metalic S-traps	(D)
		Nonmetallic S-traps	(D)
Lavatory and sink fittings (except single control), including drains and overflows (brass goods)	**544.6**	Flushometer valves and flush valves (for gravity-type flush tanks)	137.0
Faucet deck sink fittings	253.6	Other items and accessories, including water closet tank, flushing controls, double laundry-tray faucets, and solder connecting fittings	747.6
3 in. to 4 in. deck faucet sink fittings, exposed type (rough or plated, with or without hose end), excluding double laundry-tray faucets	(D)	Lawn sprinklers	(D)
6 in. to 8 in. deck faucet sink fittings, exposed type, with spray (metallic and nonmetallic)	42.0	**Plumbing fixture fittings and trim, nsk, total**	**341.4**
6 in. to 8 in. deck faucet sink fittings, exposed type,			

Source: 2002 Economic Census. The values are product shipments in millions of dollars for 2002. Total product shipments may be lower or higher than industry shipments. See Introduction for a full discussion. Values of indented subcategories are summed in the main heading(s). The symbol (D) appears when data are withheld to prevent disclosure of competitive information. The abbreviation nsk stands for 'not specified by kind' and nec for 'not elsewhere classified'. A dash (-) means zero.

INPUTS AND OUTPUTS FOR PLUMBING FIXTURE FITTING AND TRIM MANUFACTURING

Economic Sector or Industry Providing Inputs	%	Sector	Economic Sector or Industry Buying Outputs	%	Sector
Compensation of employees	20.0		Residential permanent site structures	22.8	Construct.
Communication & energy wires & cables	6.4	Manufg.	Owner-occupied dwellings	14.4	
Wholesale trade	4.0	Trade	Nonresidential structures, nec	11.3	Construct.
Nonferrous metal foundries	3.9	Manufg.	Commercial & health care structures	9.8	Construct.
Primary smelting & refining of copper	3.5	Manufg.	Food services & drinking places	8.0	Services
Copper rolling, drawing, extruding, & alloying	3.1	Manufg.	Residential structures, nec	6.8	Construct.
Plastics products, nec	2.4	Manufg.	Maintenance/repair of nonresidential structures	4.4	Construct.
Management of companies & enterprises	2.1	Services	Exports of goods & services	3.1	Cap Inv
Paperboard containers	1.7	Manufg.	Plastics products, nec	2.3	Manufg.
Machine shops	1.6	Manufg.	Manufactured homes & mobile homes	1.7	Manufg.
Aluminum products from purchased aluminum	1.2	Manufg.	Telecommunications	1.5	Services
Forging, stamping, & sintering, nec	1.2	Manufg.	Motor vehicle parts	1.5	Manufg.
Management, scientific, & technical consulting	1.2	Services	Maintenance/repair of residential structures	1.4	Construct.
Crowns & closures & metal stamping	1.1	Manufg.	Engine equipment, nec	1.3	Manufg.
Securities, commodity contracts, investments	1.1	Fin/R.E.	Computer terminals & peripherals	1.3	Manufg.
Semiconductors & related devices	0.9	Manufg.	Semiconductors & related devices	0.9	Manufg.
Printed circuit assemblies (electronic assembles)	0.9	Manufg.	Civic, social, & professional organizations	0.9	Services
Coating, engraving, heat treating & allied activities	0.9	Manufg.	Data processing, hosting, & related services	0.7	Services
Plumbing fixture fittings & trim	0.8	Manufg.	Travel trailers & campers	0.7	Manufg.
Retail trade	0.8	Trade	Plumbing fixture fittings & trim	0.7	Manufg.
Power generation & supply	0.7	Util.	Motor homes	0.5	Manufg.
Lessors of nonfinancial assets	0.7	Fin/R.E.	Retail trade	0.5	Trade
Monetary authorities/depository credit intermediation	0.7	Fin/R.E.	Scientific research & development services	0.4	Services
Truck transportation	0.7	Util.	Manufacturing structures	0.4	Construct.
Advertising & related services	0.7	Services	Waste management & remediation services	0.4	Services
Cutting tools & machine tool accessories	0.7	Manufg.	Services to buildings & dwellings	0.3	Services
Abrasive products	0.6	Manufg.	Change in private inventories	0.3	In House
Professional, scientific, technical services, nec	0.6	Services	Individual & family services	0.3	Services
Maintenance/repair of nonresidential structures	0.5	Construct.	Wholesale trade	0.2	Trade
Turned products & screws, nuts, & bolts	0.5	Manufg.	Amusement & recreation, nec	0.2	Services
Services to buildings & dwellings	0.5	Services	Commercial & industrial machinery rental & leasing	0.2	Fin/R.E.
Custom roll forming	0.5	Manufg.	Elementary & secondary schools	0.1	Services
Legal services	0.4	Services	Colleges, universities, & professional schools	0.1	Services
Real estate	0.4	Fin/R.E.	Other S/L govt. enterprises	0.1	S/L Govt
Plastics materials & resins	0.4	Manufg.			
Taxes on production & imports, less subsidies	0.4				
Metal cans, boxes, & other containers (light gauge)	0.4	Manufg.			
Ferrous metal foundries	0.3	Manufg.			
Noncomparable imports	0.3	Foreign			
Fabricated metals, nec	0.3	Manufg.			
Automotive repair & maintenance, ex. car washes	0.3	Services			
Food services & drinking places	0.3	Services			
Natural gas distribution	0.3	Util.			
Business support services	0.3	Services			
Commercial & industrial equipment repair/maintenance	0.3	Services			
Iron & steel mills & ferroalloys	0.3	Manufg.			
Valve & fittings other than plumbing	0.3	Manufg.			
Architectural, engineering, & related services	0.3	Services			
Plate work & fabricated structural products	0.3	Manufg.			
Accounting, tax preparation, bookkeeping, & payroll	0.2	Services			
Data processing, hosting, & related services	0.2	Services			
Telecommunications	0.2	Services			
Ball & roller bearings	0.2	Manufg.			
Automotive equipment rental & leasing	0.2	Fin/R.E.			
Warehousing & storage	0.2	Util.			
Employment services	0.2	Services			
Nonferrous metal (ex. copper & aluminum) processing	0.2	Manufg.			
Handtools	0.2	Manufg.			
Hotels & motels, including casino hotels	0.2	Services			
Relay & industrial controls	0.2	Manufg.			
Scientific research & development services	0.2	Services			
Laminated plastics plates, sheets, & shapes	0.2	Manufg.			
Environmental & other technical consulting services	0.1	Services			
Specialized design services	0.1	Services			
Petroleum lubricating oil & grease	0.1	Manufg.			
Chemical products & preparations, nec	0.1	Manufg.			
Office administrative services	0.1	Services			
Air transportation	0.1	Util.			
Bare printed circuit boards	0.1	Manufg.			
Nondepository credit intermediation activities	0.1	Fin/R.E.			
Other computer related services, including facilities	0.1	Services			
Paperboard mills	0.1	Manufg.			
Support services, nec	0.1	Services			
Commercial & industrial machinery rental & leasing	0.1	Fin/R.E.			
Springs & wire products	0.1	Manufg.			

Source: Benchmark Input-Output Accounts for the U.S. Economy, 2002, U.S. Department of Commerce, Washington, D.C., January 2008. The abbreviation nec stands for 'not elsewhere classified'.

INPUTS AND OUTPUTS FOR VALVE AND FITTINGS OTHER THAN PLUMBING

Economic Sector or Industry Providing Inputs	%	Sector	Economic Sector or Industry Buying Outputs	%	Sector
Compensation of employees	30.1		Exports of goods & services	15.1	Cap Inv
Wholesale trade	4.4	Trade	Private fixed investment	7.3	
Ferrous metal foundries	4.2	Manufg.	Motor vehicle parts	5.6	Manufg.
Nonferrous metal foundries	3.4	Manufg.	Oil & gas extraction	5.2	Mining
Valve & fittings other than plumbing	3.3	Manufg.	Nonresidential structures, nec	4.6	Construct.
Iron & steel mills & ferroalloys	3.2	Manufg.	Other S/L govt. enterprises	4.3	S/L Govt
Management of companies & enterprises	2.8	Services	Light truck & utility vehicles	3.3	Manufg.
Turned products & screws, nuts, & bolts	2.4	Manufg.	Valve & fittings other than plumbing	2.6	Manufg.
Copper rolling, drawing, extruding, & alloying	2.0	Manufg.	Cable & other subscription programming	2.4	Services
Gaskets, packing, & sealing devices	1.3	Manufg.	Construction machinery	2.4	Manufg.
Fabricated pipes & pipe fittings	1.1	Manufg.	Aircraft	2.3	Manufg.
Alumina refining & primary aluminum production	1.0	Manufg.	Farm machinery & equipment	1.6	Manufg.
Communication & energy wires & cables	0.9	Manufg.	Commercial & service industry machinery, nec	1.5	Manufg.
Machine shops	0.9	Manufg.	Natural gas distribution	1.3	Util.
Securities, commodity contracts, investments	0.9	Fin/R.E.	Guided missiles & space vehicles	1.2	Manufg.
Power generation & supply	0.9	Util.	Industrial machinery, nec	1.2	Manufg.
Truck transportation	0.9	Util.	Toilet preparations	1.1	Manufg.
Primary smelting & refining of copper	0.8	Manufg.	Residential permanent site structures	1.1	Construct.
Forging, stamping, & sintering, nec	0.7	Manufg.	Ship building & repairing	1.1	Manufg.
Rubber & plastics hose & belting	0.6	Manufg.	Basic organic chemicals, nec	1.1	Manufg.
Advertising & related services	0.6	Services	Telecommunications	1.1	Services
Scrap	0.6	Scrap	Mining & oil & gas field machinery	1.0	Manufg.
Semiconductors & related devices	0.6	Manufg.	Material handling equipment	1.0	Manufg.
Coating, engraving, heat treating & allied activities	0.6	Manufg.	Commercial & health care structures	1.0	Construct.
Printed circuit assemblies (electronic assemblies)	0.6	Manufg.	Aircraft engine & engine parts	0.9	Manufg.
Lessors of nonfinancial assets	0.6	Fin/R.E.	Semiconductor machinery	0.9	Manufg.
Crowns & closures & metal stamping	0.5	Manufg.	Truck transportation	0.9	Util.
Taxes on production & imports, less subsidies	0.5		Maintenance/repair of nonresidential structures	0.9	Construct.
Real estate	0.5	Fin/R.E.	Automobiles	0.9	Manufg.
Monetary authorities/depository credit intermediation	0.5	Fin/R.E.	General purpose machinery, nec	0.8	Manufg.
Plastics products, nec	0.5	Manufg.	Engine equipment, nec	0.8	Manufg.
Legal services	0.4	Services	Wholesale trade	0.8	Trade
Professional, scientific, technical services, nec	0.4	Services	AC, refrigeration, and warm air heating equipment	0.8	Manufg.
Paperboard containers	0.4	Manufg.	Vending, commercial, industrial, office machinery	0.8	Manufg.
Specialized design services	0.4	Services	Federal government, investment, national defense	0.7	Fed Govt
Architectural, engineering, & related services	0.3	Services	Air & gas compressors	0.7	Manufg.
Telecommunications	0.3	Services	Residential structures, nec	0.6	Construct.
Employment services	0.3	Services	Waste management & remediation services	0.6	Services
Maintenance/repair of nonresidential structures	0.3	Construct.	Lawn & garden equipment	0.6	Manufg.
Services to buildings & dwellings	0.3	Services	Turbines & turbine generator set units	0.6	Manufg.
Business support services	0.3	Services	Architectural, engineering, & related services	0.5	Services
Cutting tools & machine tool accessories	0.3	Manufg.	Aircraft parts & auxiliary equipment, nec	0.5	Manufg.
Warehousing & storage	0.3	Util.	Machine shops	0.5	Manufg.
Data processing, hosting, & related services	0.3	Services	Chemical products & preparations, nec	0.5	Manufg.
Motors & generators	0.3	Manufg.	General Federal government services, defense	0.5	Fed Govt
Automotive equipment rental & leasing	0.3	Fin/R.E.	Air purification & ventilation equipment	0.4	Manufg.
Accounting, tax preparation, bookkeeping, & payroll	0.3	Services	Tobacco products	0.4	Manufg.
Food services & drinking places	0.3	Services	Paper mills	0.4	Manufg.
Metal cans, boxes, & other containers (light gauge)	0.2	Manufg.	Services to buildings & dwellings	0.4	Services
Management, scientific, & technical consulting	0.2	Services	Scientific research & development services	0.4	Services
Fabricated metals, nec	0.2	Manufg.	S/L govt. invest., other	0.4	S/L Govt
Natural gas distribution	0.2	Util.	Pumps & pumping equipment	0.4	Manufg.
Automotive repair & maintenance, ex. car washes	0.2	Services	Plastics & rubber industry machinery	0.3	Manufg.
Scientific research & development services	0.2	Services	Manufacturing structures	0.3	Construct.
Support services, nec	0.2	Services	Fabricated pipes & pipe fittings	0.3	Manufg.
Commercial & industrial equipment repair/maintenance	0.2	Services	Fabricated metals, nec	0.3	Manufg.
Other computer related services, including facilities	0.2	Services	Retail trade	0.3	Trade
Plate work & fabricated structural products	0.2	Manufg.	Automotive repair & maintenance, ex. car washes	0.3	Services
Ball & roller bearings	0.1	Manufg.	Commercial & industrial equipment repair/maintenance	0.3	Services
Noncomparable imports	0.1	Foreign	Heavy duty trucks	0.3	Manufg.
Investigation & security services	0.1	Services	Plate work & fabricated structural products	0.3	Manufg.
Hotels & motels, including casino hotels	0.1	Services	Basic inorganic chemicals, nec	0.3	Manufg.
Handtools	0.1	Manufg.	Metal tanks (heavy gauge)	0.3	Manufg.
Commercial & industrial machinery rental & leasing	0.1	Fin/R.E.	Motor vehicle bodies	0.2	Manufg.
Retail trade	0.1	Trade	Oil & gas well drilling	0.2	Mining
Nondepository credit intermediation activities	0.1	Fin/R.E.	Asphalt paving mixtures & blocks	0.2	Manufg.
Plastics packaging materials, film & sheet	0.1	Manufg.	Plastics products, nec	0.2	Manufg.
Rail transportation	0.1	Util.	Breweries	0.2	Manufg.
Nonferrous metal (ex. copper & aluminum) processing	0.1	Manufg.	Ornamental & architectural metal products	0.2	Manufg.
Air transportation	0.1	Util.	Paperboard mills	0.2	Manufg.
			Transit & ground passenger transportation	0.2	Util.
			Wood containers & pallets	0.2	Manufg.
			Owner-occupied dwellings	0.2	
			Rubber products, nec	0.2	Manufg.
			Soft drinks & ice	0.2	Manufg.
			Fluid power process machinery	0.2	Manufg.
			Food services & drinking places	0.2	Services
			Computer system design services	0.2	Services
			Metal cutting & forming machine tools	0.2	Manufg.
			Iron & steel mills & ferroalloys	0.2	Manufg.

Continued on next page.

INPUTS AND OUTPUTS FOR VALVE AND FITTINGS OTHER THAN PLUMBING - Continued

Economic Sector or Industry Providing Inputs	%	Sector	Economic Sector or Industry Buying Outputs	%	Sector
			Oil & gas operations services	0.2	Mining
			Plastics materials & resins	0.2	Manufg.
			Couriers & messengers	0.2	Util.
			Rolling mill & other metalworking machinery	0.2	Manufg.
			Synthetic dyes & pigments	0.1	Manufg.
			Railroad rolling stock	0.1	Manufg.
			Truck trailers	0.1	Manufg.
			Alkalies & chlorine	0.1	Manufg.
			Pesticides & other agricultural chemicals	0.1	Manufg.
			Surgical appliances & supplies	0.1	Manufg.
			Crowns & closures & metal stamping	0.1	Manufg.
			Paints & coatings	0.1	Manufg.
			S/L govt. electric utilities	0.1	S/L Govt

Source: *Benchmark Input-Output Accounts for the U.S. Economy, 2002*, U.S. Department of Commerce, Washington D.C., January 2008. *User should note that this Input-Output table is not for this particular narrowly defined industry but for a larger aggregate. Input and Output data for* Valve and Fittings Other Than Plumbing *include Input and Output data for the* Annual Survey of Manufactures' *NAICS industries 332913 and 33291N.* The abbreviation nec stands for 'not elsewhere classified'.

OCCUPATIONS EMPLOYED BY OTHER FABRICATED METAL PRODUCT MANUFACTURING

Occupation	% of Total 2006	Change to 2016	Occupation	% of Total 2006	Change to 2016
Team assemblers	11.0	-11.4	Structural metal fabricators & fitters	1.4	-11.4
Machinists	4.6	-7.0	Mechanical engineers	1.4	-11.4
Welders, cutters, solderers, & brazers	3.9	-5.7	General & operations managers	1.3	-20.3
First-line supervisors/managers of production workers	3.8	-11.4	Executive secretaries & administrative assistants	1.3	-11.4
Cutting, punching, & press machine operators	3.4	-20.3	Coating, painting, & spraying machine operators	1.3	-15.8
Inspectors, testers, sorters, samplers, & weighers	3.0	-16.4	Packers & packagers, hand	1.2	-29.1
Computer-controlled machine tool operators	2.8	-2.5	Customer service representatives	1.2	-2.5
Grinding, lapping, polishing machine tool operators	2.7	-14.0	Drilling & boring machine tool operators	1.2	-20.3
Sales reps, wholesale & manufacturing, exc tech	2.2	-11.4	Industrial machinery mechanics	1.1	1.9
Helpers--Production workers	2.2	-11.4	Assemblers & fabricators, nec	1.1	-20.3
Lathe & turning machine tool operators & tenders	2.0	-20.3	Industrial truck & tractor operators	1.1	-20.3
Laborers & freight, stock, & material movers, hand	2.0	-20.3	Bookkeeping, accounting, & auditing clerks	1.1	-11.4
Shipping, receiving, & traffic clerks	1.9	-14.7	Production, planning, & expediting clerks	1.0	-11.4
Industrial engineers	1.8	7.6	Molding, coremaking, & casting machine operators	1.0	-20.3
Maintenance & repair workers, general	1.7	-11.4	Office clerks, general	1.0	-12.7

Source: *Industry-Occupation Matrix*, Bureau of Labor Statistics, December 4, 2007. These data are reported based on 4-digit NAICS categories but have been matched to corresponding 6-digit NAICS industry codes. The change reported for each occupation to the year 2016 is a percent of growth or decline as estimated by the Bureau of Labor Statistics. The abbreviation nec stands for 'not elsewhere classified'.

LOCATION BY STATE AND REGIONAL CONCENTRATION

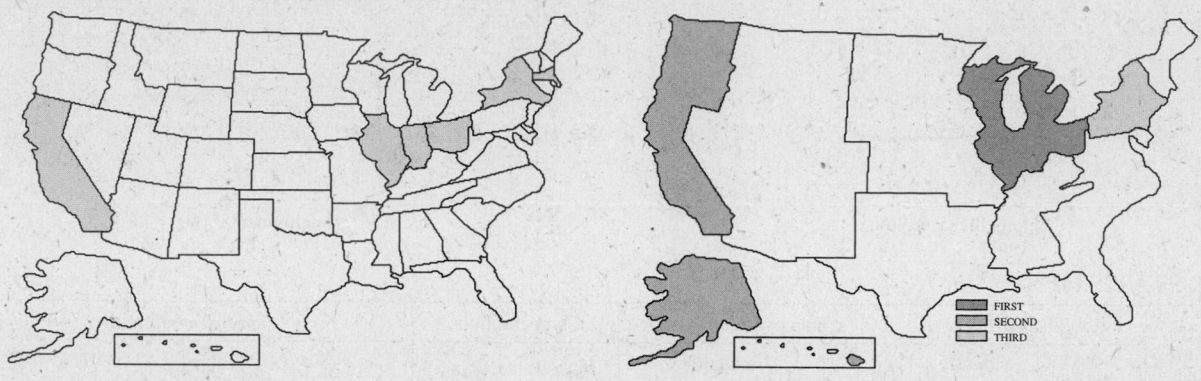

INDUSTRY DATA BY STATE

State	Establish-ments	Shipments			Employment				Cost as % of Shipments	Investment per Employee ($)
		Total ($ mil)	% of U.S.	Per Establ.	Total Number	% of U.S.	Per Establ.	Wages ($/hour)		
Indiana	9	554.7	14.2	61,629.4	1,719	10.7	191	12.08	35.9	4,196
Illinois	14	379.9	9.7	27,138.6	1,713	10.6	122	20.01	45.4	3,340
California	32	323.9	8.3	10,123.0	2,111	13.1	66	13.93	47.2	2,797
New York	13	82.9	2.1	6,374.7	293	1.8	23	15.39	50.3	4,150
Ohio	14	82.3	2.1	5,882.0	524	3.3	37	16.18	50.6	14,563
Massachusetts	4	68.0	1.7	16,997.7	340	2.1	85	11.99	27.3	5,932

Source: 2002 *Economic Census*. The states are in descending order of shipments or establishments (if shipment data are missing for the majority). The symbol (D) appears when data are withheld to prevent disclosure of competitive information. States marked with (D) are sorted by number of establishments. A dash (-) indicates that the data element cannot be calculated. Data may not show all states active in the NAICS category. All data available at the time of publication are shown.

NAICS 33291N - VALVES AND FITTINGS MANUFACTURING, NONPLUMBING*

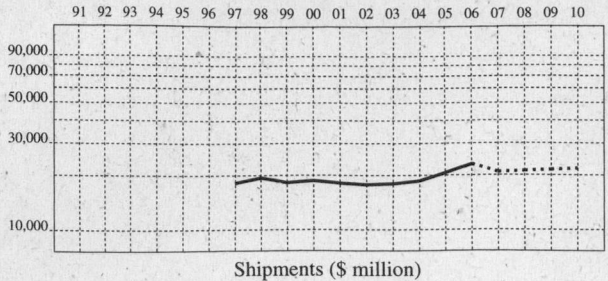

Shipments ($ million)

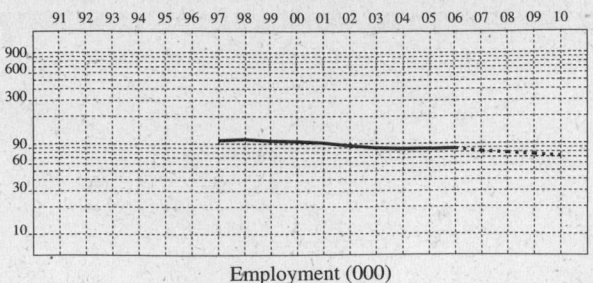

Employment (000)

GENERAL STATISTICS

Year	Companies	Establishments		Employment			Compensation		Production ($ million)			
		Total	with 20 or more employees	Total (000)	Production Workers (000)	Hours (Mil)	Payroll ($ mil)	Wages ($/hr)	Cost of Materials	Value Added by Manufacture	Value of Shipments	Capital Invest.
1997	1,005	1,205	702	109.0	74.0	153.5	3,817.8	14.02	7,511.7	10,607.9	18,178.8	670.6
1998		1,286	706	112.1	76.3	159.0	3,993.8	14.26	8,295.5	11,270.8	19,423.8	680.2
1999		1,308	705	107.7	73.4	149.9	3,974.5	14.80	7,654.0	10,641.9	18,239.3	603.7
2000		1,309	689	106.5	73.2	151.2	3,994.4	14.98	8,030.5	10,846.9	18,709.1	614.8
2001		1,247	677	102.2	69.4	141.0	3,898.8	15.53	7,680.6	10,471.7	18,149.1	582.7
2002	964	1,166	631	95.0	64.5	128.8	3,814.6	16.59	7,155.8	10,557.5	17,788.1	531.8
2003		1,167	630	89.8	60.7	123.6	3,740.1	16.78	7,123.8	10,859.3	18,021.7	428.3
2004		1,159	628	87.8	59.5	125.0	3,841.2	17.32	7,356.5	11,395.3	18,622.0	444.5
2005		1,127	637	87.8	60.8	129.2	3,950.8	17.60	8,409.0	12,456.2	20,685.0	442.9
2006		1,126P	609P	88.0	60.7	127.4	4,126.8	18.26	9,910.1	13,605.8	23,074.3	506.2
2007		1,108P	597P	81.4P	55.9P	116.8P	3,947.5P	18.70P	8,948.4P	12,285.4P	20,835.1P	399.0P
2008		1,089P	585P	78.3P	53.9P	112.7P	3,953.4P	19.19P	9,084.7P	12,472.6P	21,152.5P	371.4P
2009		1,070P	574P	75.1P	51.8P	108.7P	3,959.2P	19.68P	9,221.1P	12,659.8P	21,469.9P	343.9P
2010		1,052P	562P	72.0P	49.7P	104.7P	3,965.1P	20.17P	9,357.4P	12,847.0P	21,787.4P	316.3P

Sources: 1997 and 2002 *Economic Census*; other years, up to 2006, are from *Annual Survey of Manufactures*. Establishment counts for non-Census years are from *County Business Patterns*; 1997 and 2002 values are from the 1997 and 2002 censuses, respectively. 'P's show projections by the editors.

INDICES OF CHANGE

Year	Companies	Establishments		Employment			Compensation		Production ($ million)			
		Total	with 20 or more employees	Total (000)	Production Workers (000)	Hours (Mil)	Payroll ($ mil)	Wages ($/hr)	Cost of Materials	Value Added by Manufacture	Value of Shipments	Capital Invest.
1997	104	103	111	115	115	119	100	85	105	100	102	126
1998		110	112	118	118	123	105	86	116	107	109	128
1999		112	112	113	114	116	104	89	107	101	103	114
2000		112	109	112	113	117	105	90	112	103	105	116
2001		107	107	108	108	109	102	94	107	99	102	110
2002	100	100	100	100	100	100	100	100	100	100	100	100
2003		100	100	95	94	96	98	101	100	103	101	81
2004		99	100	92	92	97	101	104	103	108	105	84
2005		97	101	92	94	100	104	106	118	118	116	83
2006		97P	96P	93	94	99	108	110	138	129	130	95
2007		95P	95P	86P	87P	91P	103P	113P	125P	116P	117P	75P
2008		93P	93P	82P	84P	88P	104P	116P	127P	118P	119P	70P
2009		92P	91P	79P	80P	84P	104P	119P	129P	120P	121P	65P
2010		90P	89P	76P	77P	81P	104P	122P	131P	122P	122P	59P

Sources: Same as General Statistics. Values reflect change from the base year, 2002. Values above 100 mean greater than 2002, values below 100 mean less than 2002, and the values of 100 in other years means the same as 2002. 'P's show projections by the editors.

SELECTED RATIOS

For 2002	Avg. of All Manufact.	Analyzed Industry	Index	For 2002	Avg. of All Manufact.	Analyzed Industry	Index
Employees per Establishment	42	81	194	Value Added per Production Worker	182,367	163,682	90
Payroll per Establishment	1,639,184	3,271,527	200	Cost per Establishment	5,769,015	6,137,050	106
Payroll per Employee	39,053	40,154	103	Cost per Employee	137,446	75,324	55
Production Workers per Establishment	30	55	187	Cost per Production Worker	195,506	110,943	57
Wages per Establishment	694,845	1,832,583	264	Shipments per Establishment	11,158,348	15,255,660	137
Wages per Production Worker	23,548	33,129	141	Shipments per Employee	265,847	187,243	70
Hours per Production Worker	1,980	1,997	101	Shipments per Production Worker	378,144	275,784	73
Wages per Hour	11.89	16.59	140	Investment per Establishment	361,338	456,089	126
Value Added per Establishment	5,381,325	9,054,460	168	Investment per Employee	8,609	5,598	65
Value Added per Employee	128,210	111,132	87	Investment per Production Worker	12,245	8,245	67

Sources: Same as General Statistics. The 'Average of All Manufacturing' column represents the average of all manufacturing industries reported for the most recent complete year available. The Index shows the relationship between the Average and the Analyzed Industry. For example, 100 means that they are equal; 500 that the Analyzed Industry is five times the average; 50 means that the Analyzed Industry is half the national average. The abbreviation 'na' is used to show that data are 'not available'. Ratios shown for 2002, the last complete census year.

*Equivalent to Federal Government NAICS 332911, 332912, 332919.

LEADING COMPANIES   Number shown: **75**   Total sales ($ mil): **366,173**   Total employment (000): **1,086.0**

Company Name	Address				CEO Name	Phone	Co. Type	Sales ($ mil)	Empl. (000)
Boeing Co.	100 N Riverside Plz	Chicago	IL	60606		312-544-2000	P	66,387	159.3
Lockheed Martin Corp.	6801 Rockledge Dr.	Bethesda	MD	20817	Richard F. Ambrose	301-897-6000	P	41,862	140.0
Northrop Grumman Corp.	1840 Century Park E	Los Angeles	CA	90067		310-553-6262	P	32,018	122.6
Raytheon Co.	870 Winter St.	Waltham	MA	02451		781-522-3000	P	21,301	72.1
Nucor Corp.	1915 Rexford Rd.	Charlotte	NC	28211	Daniel R. DiMicco	704-366-7000	P	16,593	18.0
Textron Inc.	40 Westminster St.	Providence	RI	02903		401-421-2800	P	13,225	44.0
Parker Hannifin Corp.	6035 Parkland Blvd.	Cleveland	OH	44124	Lee Banks	216-896-3000	P	10,718	57.3
Fortune Brands Inc.	520 Lake Cook Rd.	Deerfield	IL	60015	Bruce A. Carbonari	847-484-4400	P	8,563	31.0
Pratt and Whitney	400 Main Street	East Hartford	CT	06108	Stephen Finger	860-565-4321	S	7,670*	30.0
Newell Rubbermaid Inc.	10B Glenlake Pkwy.	Atlanta	GA	30328		770-407-3800	P	6,407	22.0
Goodrich Corp.	4 Coliseum Centre	Charlotte	NC	28217		704-423-7000	P	6,392	23.4
Cooper Industries Ltd.	PO Box 4446	Houston	TX	77210	Kirk S. Hachigian	713-209-8400	P	5,903	31.5
Allegheny Technologies Inc.	1000 Six PPG Pl.	Pittsburgh	PA	15222		412-394-2800	P	5,453	9.5
BorgWarner Inc.	3850 Hamlin Rd.	Auburn Hills	MI	48326		248-754-9200	P	5,329	17.7
SPX Corp.	13515 Ballnyn Corp.	Charlotte	NC	28277		704-752-4400	P	4,822	17.8
Cameron International Corp.	1333 W Loop S	Houston	TX	77027	Sheldon R. Erikson	713-513-3300	P	4,666	15.4
Stanley Works	PO Box 700	New Britain	CT	06053		860-225-5111	P	4,484	18.4
Rockwell Collins Inc.	400 Collins Rd. NE	Cedar Rapids	IA	52498		319-295-1000	P	4,415	19.5
Spirit AeroSystems Holdings	3801 S Oliver	Wichita	KS	67210	Jeffrey L. Turner	316-526-9000	P	3,861	13.1
Flowserve Corp.	5215 N O'Connor	Irving	TX	75039		972-443-6500	P	3,763	15.0
Wood Group Pressure Control	PO Box 82	Houston	TX	77001	Scott Bender	832-325-4200	R	3,657*	0.1
Hamilton Sundstrand Corp.	1 Hamilton Rd.	Windsor Locks	CT	06096	Ronald F. McKenna	860-654-6000	S	3,600*	16.0
Pentair Inc.	5500 Wayzata Blvd.	Golden Valley	MN	55416	Winslow H. Buxton	763-545-1730	P	3,399	16.0
Truth Hardware Corp.	700 W Bridge St.	Owatonna	MN	55060	Greg Wobschall	507-451-5620	R	3,218*	1.0
Hi-Stat Manufacturing Company	28001 Cabot Dr.	Novi	MI	48377	John Corey	248-489-9300	D	3,194*	5.0
Crosby Group Inc.	PO Box 3128	Tulsa	OK	74101	Larry Postelwait	918-834-4611	R	3,101*	<0.1
Arco Auto and Marine Products	3921 Navy Blvd.	Pensacola	FL	32507	Ron Miller	850-455-5476	R	3,015	<0.1
Control Components Inc.	22591 Ave. Empresa	R St Margarita	CA	92688	Martin Lamb	949-858-1877	R	2,840*	0.2
Crane Co.	100 First Stamford	Stamford	CT	06902	Thomas Craney	203-363-7300	P	2,619	12.0
Apph Wichita Inc.	1445 S Sierra Dr.	Wichita	KS	67209	Dan Kilby	316-943-5752	P	2,590*	<0.1
HNI Corp.	PO Box 1109	Muscatine	IA	52761	Timothy Anderson	563-264-7400	P	2,571	14.2
JELD-WEN Inc.	PO Box 1329	Klamath Falls	OR	97601	Richard Wendt	541-882-3451	R	2,476*	23.8
Festo Corp.	PO Box 18023	Hauppauge	NY	11788		631-435-0800	R	2,452*	0.2
Smith Industries Inc.	14200 Roosevlt Blvd	Clearwater	FL	33762	Vic Bonneau	727-531-7781	R	2,125*	10.0
True Value Co.	8600 W Bryn Mawr	Chicago	IL	60631	Bryan R. Ableidinger	773-695-5000	R	2,050	3.0
Hillenbrand Industries Inc.	1069 State Rte 46E	Batesville	IN	47006		812-934-7000	P	2,024	9.9
Synalloy Metals Inc.	390 Bristol Metals	Bristol	TN	37621	Ronald H. Braam	423-989-4700	S	2,012*	0.4
Hutchinson FTS Inc.	1835 Technology	Troy	MI	48083	Paul Campbell	248-589-7710	R	1,863*	<0.1
Mueller Water Products Inc.	1200 Abernathy Rd.	Atlanta	GA	30328	Gregory E. Hyland	770-206-4200	P	1,849	6.8
Envirotech Pumpsystems Inc.	PO Box 209	Salt Lake City	UT	84110	Joseph Roark	801-359-8731	R	1,770*	0.3
Weir Valve and Controls USA	285 Canal St.	Salem	MA	01970		978-744-5690	R	1,770*	0.1
Precise Machine Co.	2215 River Hill Rd.	Irving	TX	75061	Ronald S. Saks	972-438-3995	S	1,708*	0.7
Precise Machine Partners	3600 Mueller Rd.	St. Charles	MO	63301	Ronald S. Saks	636-946-6525	S	1,708*	0.7
Hitachi Cable Indiana Inc.	5300 Grant Line Rd.	New Albany	IN	47150	Kenji Nakata	812-945-9011	R	1,590*	<0.1
Vought Aircraft Industries	PO Box 655907	Dallas	TX	75265	Elmer Doty	972-946-2011	S	1,577*	6.0
Barnes Group Inc.	PO Box 489	Bristol	CT	06011	Thomas Barnes	860-583-7070	P	1,539	6.7
AAR Manufacturing Inc.	1100 N Wood Dale	Wood Dale	IL	60191	David Storch	630-227-2000	S	1,526*	3.5
Valmont Industries Inc.	1 Valmont Plz.	Omaha	NE	68154	Mogens C. Bay	402-963-1000	P	1,500	6.0
Beckett Corp.	400 E Royal Ln.	Irving	TX	75039	Wingate Sung	972-871-8000	R	1,409*	0.1
Watts Water Technologies Inc.	815 Chestnut St.	North Andover	MA	01845		978-688-1811	P	1,382	7.8
Dresser Inc.	15455 Dallas Pkwy.	Addison	TX	75001		972-361-9800	S	1,343*	6.0
Yale Security Inc.	1902 Airport Rd.	Monroe	NC	28110		704-283-2101	R	1,201*	0.2
Adams Rite Manufacturing Co.	260 W Santa Fe St.	Pomona	CA	91767	Peter Adams	909-632-2300	R	1,201*	0.2
ASCO	50-60 Hanover Rd.	Florham Park	NJ	07932	Jean Pierre	973-966-2000	D	1,169*	1.0
Henry Pratt Co.	401 S Highland Ave.	Aurora	IL	60506		630-844-4000	S	1,146*	0.3
Parker Hannifin Skinner Valve	95 Edgewood Ave.	New Britain	CT	06051	D E. Washkewicz	860-827-2300	D	1,138*	0.3
Swagelok Co.	29500 Solon Rd.	Solon	OH	44139	Arthur F. Anton	440-248-4600	R	1,100*	3.3
AAR Corp.	1100 N Wood Dale	Wood Dale	IL	60191	Ira A. Eichner	630-227-2000	P	1,061	3.9
Robert Bosch Tool Corp.	1961 Bishop Ln.	Louisville	KY	40218	Timothy Shea	502-625-2050	D	1,057*	0.2
C and D Zodiac Inc.	5701 Bolsa Ave.	Huntington Bch	CA	92647		714-934-0000	R	1,045*	0.5
L-3 Display Systems	1355 Bluegrass Lake	Alpharetta	GA	30004		770-752-7000	S	998*	0.3
EFD Inc.	977 Waterman Ave.	East Providence	RI	02914	Peter Lambert	401-434-1680	S	972*	0.3
BWAY Holding Co.	8607 Roberts Dr.	Atlanta	GA	30350	Jean-Pierre M. Ergas	770-645-4800	P	959	2.5
Triumph Group Inc.	1550 Liberty Ridge	Wayne	PA	19087	John M. Brasch	610-251-1000	P	955	5.1
McWane Corp.	PO Box 43327	Birmingham	AL	35243	G. Ruffner Page, Jr.	205-414-3100	R	944*	7.0
United Components Inc.	14601 Hwy 41 N	Evansville	IN	47725	Bruce Zorich	812-867-4156	S	906	6.8
Dow-United Tech. Compos. Prods	3951 Al Hwy. 229 S	Tallassee	AL	36078	Anthony Cacace	334-283-9200	R	886*	0.7
Johnson Controls Interiors	49200 Halyard Dr.	Plymouth	MI	48170	John Barth	734-254-5000	S	875*	5.0
Simpson Manufacturing Company	5956 W Las Positas	Pleasanton	CA	94588	Thomas J. Fitzmyers	925-560-9000	P	817	2.7
American Auto Accessories Inc.	11201 Northern Blvd	Corona	NY	11368	Henry Hsu	347-625-8800	R	769*	1.2
Hoerbiger Corporation of Amer.	3350 Gateway Dr.	Pompano Beach	FL	33069	Franz Gruber	954-979-5700	R	765*	0.3
Sub-Zero Inc.	4717 Hammersley	Madison	WI	53711	James Bakke	608-271-2233	R	758*	3.0
Senior Operations Inc.	300 E Devon Ave.	Bartlett	IL	60103	Graham Menzies	630-837-1811	R	733*	0.7
Western Oilfields Supply Co.	PO Box 2248	Bakersfield	CA	93303	John Lake	661-399-9124	R	710*	1.0
Raybestos Products Co.	1204 Darlington Ave	Crawfordsville	IN	47933	Larry S. Singleton	765-362-3500	S	701*	5.3

Source: Ward's Business Directory of U.S. Private and Public Companies, Volumes 1 and 2, 2008. The company type code used is as follows: P - Public, R - Private, S - Subsidiary, D - Division, J - Joint Venture, A - Affiliate, G - Group. Sales are in millions of dollars, employees are in thousands. An asterisk (*) indicates an estimated sales volume. The symbol < stands for 'less than'. Company names and addresses are truncated, in some cases, to fit into the available space.

MATERIALS CONSUMED FOR INDUSTRIAL VALVE MANUFACTURING

Material	Quantity	Delivered Cost ($ million)
Metal bolts, nuts, screws, and other screw machine products	(X)	175.3
Metal stampings	(X)	57.6
Valves, fittings, and couplings purchased for further assembly	(X)	267.0
Other fabricated metal products (excluding forgings)	(X)	234.4
Iron castings (rough and semifinished)	(X)	239.8
Steel castings (rough and semifinished)	(X)	374.4
Aluminum and aluminum-base alloy castings (rough and semifinished)	(X)	63.1
Copper and copper-base alloy castings (rough and semifinished)	(X)	113.4
Other nonferrous castings (rough and semifinished)	(X)	63.6
Iron and steel forgings	(X)	89.3
Nonferrous forgings	(X)	61.6
Steel bars, bar shapes, and plates (exc. castings, forgings, fabr. metal products)	(X)	137.3
Steel sheet and strip (including tinplate)	(X)	41.5
All other steel shapes and forms (exc. castings, forgings, fabr. metal products)	(X)	55.9
Copper and copper-base alloy refinery shapes (exc. castings, forgings, fabr. metal products)	(X)	56.1
Copper and copper-base alloy rod, bar, and mechanical wire	(X)	113.3
Copper and copper-base alloy pipe and tube (exc. castings, forgings, fabr. metal products)	(X)	18.8
All other copper and copper-base alloy shapes and forms (exc. castings, forgings, fabr. metal products)	(X)	15.0
Aluminum and aluminum-base alloy shapes and forms (exc. castings, forgings, fabr. metal products)	(X)	45.7
Other nonferrous shapes and forms (exc. castings, forgings, fabricated metal products)	(X)	15.0
Scrap, including iron, steel, aluminum and aluminum-base alloy (exc. home scrap)	(X)	38.7
Fractional horsepower electric motors and generators (less than 1 hp)	(X)	18.7
Paperboard containers, boxes, and corrugated paperboard	(X)	26.3
Hydraulic and pneumatic hose, rubber and plastics inner tube type	(X)	6.2
Other rubber and plastics hose and belting	(X)	21.8
Gaskets (all types), and packing and sealing devices	(X)	66.9
Fabricated rubber products (exc. tires, tubes, hoses, belting, and gaskets)	(X)	39.0
Fabricated plastics products (excluding gaskets)	(X)	46.3
All other materials, components, parts, containers, and supplies	(X)	300.4
Materials, ingredients, containers, and supplies, nsk	(X)	300.0

Source: 2002 *Economic Census*. Explanation of symbols used: (D): Withheld to avoid disclosure of competitive data; na: Not available; (S): Withheld because statistical norms were not met; (X): Not applicable; (Z): Less than half the unit shown; nec: Not elsewhere classified; nsk: Not specified by kind; - : zero; p : 10-19 percent estimated; q : 20-29 percent estimated.

MATERIALS CONSUMED FOR FLUID POWER VALVE AND HOSE FITTING MANUFACTURING

Material	Quantity	Delivered Cost ($ million)
Metal bolts, nuts, screws, and other screw machine products	(X)	244.0
Metal stampings	(X)	15.8
Valves, fittings, and couplings purchased for further assembly	(X)	225.7
Other fabricated metal products (excluding forgings)	(X)	159.3
Iron castings (rough and semifinished)	(X)	69.7
Steel castings (rough and semifinished)	(X)	12.6
Aluminum and aluminum-base alloy castings (rough and semifinished)	(X)	38.4
Copper and copper-base alloy castings (rough and semifinished)	(X)	1.9
Other nonferrous castings (rough and semifinished)	(X)	37.6
Iron and steel forgings	(X)	34.1
Nonferrous forgings	(X)	7.6
Steel bars, bar shapes, and plates (exc. castings, forgings, fabr. metal products)	(X)	217.8
Steel sheet and strip (including tinplate)	(X)	20.8
All other steel shapes and forms (exc. castings, forgings, fabr. metal products)	(X)	40.2
Copper and copper-base alloy rod, bar, and mechanical wire	(X)	(D)
Copper and copper-base alloy pipe and tube (exc. castings, forgings, fabr. metal products)	(X)	28.3
All other copper and copper-base alloy shapes and forms (exc. castings, forgings, fabr. metal products)	(X)	21.2
Aluminum and aluminum-base alloy shapes and forms (exc. castings, forgings, fabr. metal products)	(X)	105.7
Other nonferrous shapes and forms (exc. castings, forgings, fabricated metal products)	(X)	4.8
Scrap, including iron, steel, aluminum and aluminum-base alloy (exc. home scrap)	(X)	(D)
Fractional horsepower electric motors and generators (less than 1 hp)	(X)	3.7
Paperboard containers, boxes, and corrugated paperboard	(X)	16.9
Hydraulic and pneumatic hose, rubber and plastics inner tube type	(X)	74.3
Other rubber and plastics hose and belting	(X)	0.7
Gaskets (all types), and packing and sealing devices	(X)	15.2
Fabricated rubber products (exc. tires, tubes, hoses, belting, and gaskets)	(X)	14.5
Fabricated plastics products (excluding gaskets)	(X)	21.0
All other materials, components, parts, containers, and supplies	(X)	323.6
Materials, ingredients, containers, and supplies, nsk	(X)	105.7

Source: 2002 *Economic Census*. Explanation of symbols used: (D): Withheld to avoid disclosure of competitive data; na: Not available; (S): Withheld because statistical norms were not met; (X): Not applicable; (Z): Less than half the unit shown; nec: Not elsewhere classified; nsk: Not specified by kind; - : zero; p : 10-19 percent estimated; q : 20-29 percent estimated.

MATERIALS CONSUMED FOR METAL VALVE AND PIPE FITTING MANUFACTURING NEC

Material	Quantity	Delivered Cost ($ million)
Metal bolts, nuts, screws, and other screw machine products	(X)	16.6
Metal stampings	(X)	3.8
Valves, fittings, and couplings purchased for further assembly	(X)	92.2
Other fabricated metal products (excluding forgings)	(X)	22.0
Iron castings (rough and semifinished)	(X)	29.7
Steel castings (rough and semifinished)	(X)	22.5
Aluminum and aluminum-base alloy castings (rough and semifinished)	(X)	(D)
Copper and copper-base alloy castings (rough and semifinished)	(X)	34.9
Other nonferrous castings (rough and semifinished)	(X)	4.0
Iron and steel forgings	(X)	47.2
Nonferrous forgings	(X)	7.3
Steel bars, bar shapes, and plates (exc. castings, forgings, fabr. metal products)	(X)	32.1
All other steel shapes and forms (exc. castings, forgings, fabr. metal products)	(X)	13.8
Copper and copper-base alloy rod, bar, and mechanical wire	(X)	56.9
Copper and copper-base alloy pipe and tube (exc. castings, forgings, fabr. metal products)	(X)	22.9
All other copper and copper-base alloy shapes and forms (exc. castings, forgings, fabr. metal products)	(X)	15.5
Other nonferrous shapes and forms (exc. castings, forgings, fabricated metal products)	(X)	3.4
Scrap, including iron, steel, aluminum and aluminum-base alloy (exc. home scrap)	(X)	36.5
Fractional horsepower electric motors and generators (less than 1 hp)	(X)	(D)
Paperboard containers, boxes, and corrugated paperboard	(X)	11.5
Gaskets (all types), and packing and sealing devices	(X)	15.0
All other materials, components, parts, containers, and supplies	(X)	216.9
Materials, ingredients, containers, and supplies, nsk	(X)	209.6

Source: 2002 *Economic Census*. Explanation of symbols used: (D): Withheld to avoid disclosure of competitive data; na: Not available; (S): Withheld because statistical norms were not met; (X): Not applicable; (Z): Less than half the unit shown; nec: Not elsewhere classified; nsk: Not specified by kind; - : zero; p : 10-19 percent estimated; q : 20-29 percent estimated.

PRODUCT SHARE DETAILS FOR INDUSTRIAL VALVE MANUFACTURING

Product or Product Class Shipments	Mil. $	Product or Product Class Shipments	Mil. $
INDUSTRIAL VALVES	8,135.7	Alloy steel and other metal ball valves	188.5
Gates, globes, angles, straightway (Y-type) check, stop and check, cross, 3-and 4-way, and other industrial valves	**1,471.7**	Actuators for industrial ball valves	68.3
Gates, globes, angles, straightway (Y-type) check, stop and check, cross, 3-and 4-way, and other industrial valves, except parts	1,265.8	Parts for industrial ball valves	109.1
		Industrial ball valves, nsk	26.9
		Industrial butterfly valves (all metals, pressures, and types), including manual and power-operated, on-off valves	**543.8**
Iron body gates, globes, angles, straightway (Y-type) check, stop and check, cross, 3-and 4-way, and other industrial valves, all pressures, except IBBM, AWWA, and UL	319.1	Industrial butterfly valves	485.5
		Iron (including ductile) butterfly valves, except high-pressure	131.0
Cast carbon steel gates, globes, angles, straightway (Y-type) check, stop and check, cross, 3-and 4-way and other industrial valves	281.3	Brass and bronze butterfly valves, except high-pressure types	113.1
		Carbon steel butterfly valves, except high-pressure	50.0
Forged carbon steel gates, globes, angles, straightway (Y-type) check, stop and check, cross, 3-and 4-way and other industrial valves	139.0	Alloy steel and other metal butterfly valves, except high-pressure	64.2
		High-pressure iron butterfly valves (shut-off to full ANSI class ratings)	25.0
Alloy steel and other metal gates, globes, angles, straightway (Y-type) check, stop and check, cross, 3-and 4-way and other industrial valves	289.8	High-pressure carbon steel butterfly valves (shut-off to full ANSI class ratings)	22.8
Brass and bronze (125 lb, w.s.p. or more) gates, globes, angles, straightway (Y-type) check, stop and check, cross, 3-and 4-way and other industrial valves	208.6	High-pressure alloy steel and other metal butterfly valves (shut-off to full ANSI class ratings)	54.1
		Butterfly valve actuators	25.4
Actuators (power-operated, on-off mounted) for gates, globes, angles, straightway (Y-type) check, stop and check, cross, 3-and 4-way and other industrial valves	28.0	Parts for industrial butterfly valves	23.3
		Industrial butterfly valves, nsk	35.0
		Industrial plug valves (all metals, pressures, and types), such as lubricated, cylindrical eccentric, and sleeve-lined	**260.4**
Parts for gates, globes, angles, straightway (Y-type) check, stop and check, cross, 3-and 4-way, and other industrial valves	79.3	Industrial plug valves, except parts	244.8
		Iron (including ductile) plug valves	101.6
Gates, globes, angles, straightway (Y-type) check, stop and check, cross, 3-and 4-way, and other industrial valves, nsk	126.7	Carbon steel plug valves	77.3
		Alloy steel and other metal plug valves	65.9
Industrial valves for water works and municipal equipment	**975.5**	Parts for industrial plug valves (all metals, pressures, all types), including lubricated, cylindrical eccentric, and sleeve-lined	15.0
Industrial valves for water works and municipal equipment, except parts	919.6	Industrial plug valves, nsk	0.7
Industrial IBBM gate line and tapping valves for water works and municipal equipment	401.8	**Industrial valves, nec**	**986.5**
		Other industrial valves	903.9
Industrial UL check valves (all pressures) for water works and municipal equipment	10.7	Valve cocks and stops	93.3
		Diaphragm and pinch valves, except automatic valves	103.1
All other industrial UL valves (all pressures), including pest indicators, for water works and municipal equipment	108.0	Iron and steel pop safety valves and relief valves (more than 15 lb, w.s.p.)	125.0
Tapping sleeves and crosses for industrial valves for water works and municipal equipment (IBBM, AWWA, and UL)	16.7	Brass and bronze pop safety valves and relief valves (more than 15 lb, w.s.p.)	78.7
		Compressed gas cylinder valves	78.3
Fire hydrants	243.7	Valve steam traps (more than 15 lb, w.s.p.)	49.7
Industrial AWWA check valves (all pressures) for water works and municipal equipment	29.0	Actuators for all other industrial valves, nec, sold separately	180.2
Industrial AWWA butterfly valves (all pressures) for water works and municipal equipment	109.7	All other industrial valves	195.6
		Industrial valves, nec, nsk	82.6
Parts for industrial valves for water works and municipal equipment (IBBM, AWWA, and UL)	50.1	**Nuclear valves (N-stamp only)**	**72.5**
		Nuclear valves, except parts	59.0
Industrial valves for water works and municipal equipment (IBBM, AWWA, and UL), nsk	5.8	Gate, globe, and check valves	19.5
		Valves	39.5
Industrial ball valves (all metals, pressures, and types), including manual and power-operated, on-off valves	**1,102.4**	Parts for nuclear valves (N-stamp only)	8.7
Industrial ball valves, except parts	966.4	Nuclear valves (N-stamp only), nsk	4.8
Iron ball valves	74.1	**Automatic regulating and control valves and parts (except nuclear), power-operated, designed for modulating (throttling) service**	**1,993.3**
Brass and bronze ball valves	229.4	**Solenoid-operated valves and parts, except nuclear and fluid power transfer**	**377.7**
Carbon steel ball valves	406.1	**Industrial valves, nsk, total**	**351.9**

Source: 2002 *Economic Census*. The values are product shipments in millions of dollars for 2002. Total product shipments may be lower or higher than industry shipments. See Introduction for a full discussion. Values of indented subcategories are summed in the main heading(s). The symbol (D) appears when data are withheld to prevent disclosure of competitive information. The abbreviation nsk stands for 'not specified by kind' and nec for 'not elsewhere classified'. A dash (-) means zero.

PRODUCT SHARE DETAILS FOR FLUID POWER VALVE AND HOSE FITTING MANUFACTURING

Product or Product Class Shipments	Mil. $	Product or Product Class Shipments	Mil. $
FLUID POWER VALVES AND HOSE FITTINGS	5,836.0	tube end fittings and assemblies	564.6
Aerospace type hydraulic fluid power valves	728.9	Nonaerospace type flared (metal) fittings, couplings for, and	
Aerospace type pneumatic fluid power valves	625.3	assemblies of tubing used in fluid power transfer systems	398.5
Nonaerospace type hydraulic directional control valves	385.8	Nonaerospace type flareless fittings and couplings, including	
Nonaerospace type hydraulic valves, except directional		nonmetal fittings, used in fluid power transfer systems	545.2
control	561.6	Nonaerospace type hydraulic and pneumatic fittings and	
Nonaerospace type pneumatic directional control valves	512.4	couplings for hose	645.5
Nonaerospace type pneumatic valves, except directional		Nonaerospace type hydraulic and pneumatic assemblies of	
control	142.1	hose	274.4
Parts for fluid power valves	218.2	Fluid power valves and hose fittings, nsk, total	233.4
Aerospace type hydraulic and pneumatic fluid power hose or			

Source: 2002 Economic Census. The values are product shipments in millions of dollars for 2002. Total product shipments may be lower or higher than industry shipments. See Introduction for a full discussion. Values of indented subcategories are summed in the main heading(s). The symbol (D) appears when data are withheld to prevent disclosure of competitive information. The abbreviation nsk stands for 'not specified by kind' and nec for 'not elsewhere classified'. A dash (-) means zero.

PRODUCT SHARE DETAILS FOR METAL VALVE AND PIPE FITTING MANUFACTURING NEC

Product or Product Class Shipments	Mil. $	Product or Product Class Shipments	Mil. $
OTHER METAL VALVES AND PIPE FITTINGS	2,536.1	and unions for piping systems	447.4
Plumbing and heating valves and specialties, except		Cast brass or bronze fittings, flanges, and unions for	
plumbers' brass goods	527.4	piping systems	94.0
Metal aerosol valves	145.8	Wrought copper and wrought copper alloy fittings,	
Plumbing and heating valves, including specialties and		flanges, and unions for piping systems	353.4
parts	381.6	Cast and forged carbon, alloy, stainless steel, and other	
Plumbing and heating check valves, except plumbers'		metal fittings, flanges, and unions	819.0
brass goods	39.8	Cast carbon and alloy steel fittings, flanges, and unions	
All other plumbing and heating valves (less than 125 lb		for piping systems	(D)
w.s.p.), except plumbers' brass goods	121.2	Forged carbon, alloy, and stainless steel fittings,	
Plumbing and heating valve specialties, except		flanges, and unions for piping systems, including	
plumbers' brass goods	206.3	socket-weld or threaded-type	125.0
Parts for plumbing and heating valves and specialties,		Forged carbon steel butt-welding type flanges for piping	
except plumbers' brass goods	14.2	systems	(D)
Plumbing and heating valves and specialties, except		Forged alloy steel butt-welding type flanges for piping	
plumbers' brass goods, nsk	-	systems	(D)
Metal fittings, flanges, and unions for piping systems	1,731.9	Forged stainless steel butt-welding type flanges for	
Iron fittings, flanges, and unions for piping systems,		piping systems	10.2
including gray, malleable and ductile types	464.8	Forged carbon steel butt-welding type fittings for piping	
Gray iron fittings, flanges, and unions for piping		systems	2.9
systems	144.7	Forged alloy steel butt-welding type fittings for piping	
Gray iron grooved fittings and couplings for piping		systems	1.7
systems	(D)	Forged stainless steel butt-welding type fittings for	
Metal fittings, grooved fittings, flanges, and unions for		piping systems	27.8
piping systems	136.6	Metal pipe couplings	169.8
Malleable iron unions and union fittings for piping		Fire hose nozzles	(D)
systems	(D)	Other metal fittings, flanges, and unions, incluidng	
Ductile iron fittings, flanges, and unions for piping		metal framing and fittings for mechanical and	
systems	(D)	electrical supports	247.1
Ductile iron grooved fittings and couplings for piping		Other metal valves and pipe fittings	199.0
systems	60.3	Metal fittings, flanges, and unions for piping systems, nsk	0.6
Copper, copper alloy brass and bronze fittings, flanges,		Other metal valves and pipe fittings, nsk, total	276.8

Source: 2002 Economic Census. The values are product shipments in millions of dollars for 2002. Total product shipments may be lower or higher than industry shipments. See Introduction for a full discussion. Values of indented subcategories are summed in the main heading(s). The symbol (D) appears when data are withheld to prevent disclosure of competitive information. The abbreviation nsk stands for 'not specified by kind' and nec for 'not elsewhere classified'. A dash (-) means zero.

INPUTS AND OUTPUTS FOR VALVE AND FITTINGS OTHER THAN PLUMBING

Economic Sector or Industry Providing Inputs	%	Sector	Economic Sector or Industry Buying Outputs	%	Sector
Compensation of employees	30.1		Exports of goods & services	15.1	Cap Inv
Wholesale trade	4.4	Trade	Private fixed investment	7.3	
Ferrous metal foundries	4.2	Manufg.	Motor vehicle parts	5.6	Manufg.
Nonferrous metal foundries	3.4	Manufg.	Oil & gas extraction	5.2	Mining
Valve & fittings other than plumbing	3.3	Manufg.	Nonresidential structures, nec	4.6	Construct.
Iron & steel mills & ferroalloys	3.2	Manufg.	Other S/L govt. enterprises	4.3	S/L Govt
Management of companies & enterprises	2.8	Services	Light truck & utility vehicles	3.3	Manufg.
Turned products & screws, nuts, & bolts	2.4	Manufg.	Valve & fittings other than plumbing	2.6	Manufg.
Copper rolling, drawing, extruding, & alloying	2.0	Manufg.	Cable & other subscription programming	2.4	Services
Gaskets, packing, & sealing devices	1.3	Manufg.	Construction machinery	2.4	Manufg.
Fabricated pipes & pipe fittings	1.1	Manufg.	Aircraft	2.3	Manufg.
Alumina refining & primary aluminum production	1.0	Manufg.	Farm machinery & equipment	1.6	Manufg.
Communication & energy wires & cables	0.9	Manufg.	Commercial & service industry machinery, nec	1.5	Manufg.
Machine shops	0.9	Manufg.	Natural gas distribution	1.3	Util.
Securities, commodity contracts, investments	0.9	Fin/R.E.	Guided missiles & space vehicles	1.2	Manufg.

Continued on next page.

INPUTS AND OUTPUTS FOR VALVE AND FITTINGS OTHER THAN PLUMBING - Continued

Economic Sector or Industry Providing Inputs	%	Sector	Economic Sector or Industry Buying Outputs	%	Sector
Power generation & supply	0.9	Util.	Industrial machinery, nec	1.2	Manufg.
Truck transportation	0.9	Util.	Toilet preparations	1.1	Manufg.
Primary smelting & refining of copper	0.8	Manufg.	Residential permanent site structures	1.1	Construct.
Forging, stamping, & sintering, nec	0.7	Manufg.	Ship building & repairing	1.1	Manufg.
Rubber & plastics hose & belting	0.6	Manufg.	Basic organic chemicals, nec	1.1	Manufg.
Advertising & related services	0.6	Services	Telecommunications	1.1	Services
Scrap	0.6	Scrap	Mining & oil & gas field machinery	1.0	Manufg.
Semiconductors & related devices	0.6	Manufg.	Material handling equipment	1.0	Manufg.
Coating, engraving, heat treating & allied activities	0.6	Manufg.	Commercial & health care structures	1.0	Construct.
Printed circuit assemblies (electronic assemblies)	0.6	Manufg.	Aircraft engine & engine parts	0.9	Manufg.
Lessors of nonfinancial assets	0.6	Fin/R.E.	Semiconductor machinery	0.9	Manufg.
Crowns & closures & metal stamping	0.5	Manufg.	Truck transportation	0.9	Util.
Taxes on production & imports, less subsidies	0.5		Maintenance/repair of nonresidential structures	0.9	Construct.
Real estate	0.5	Fin/R.E.	Automobiles	0.9	Manufg.
Monetary authorities/depository credit intermediation	0.5	Fin/R.E.	General purpose machinery, nec	0.8	Manufg.
Plastics products, nec	0.5	Manufg.	Engine equipment, nec	0.8	Manufg.
Legal services	0.4	Services	Wholesale trade	0.8	Trade
Professional, scientific, technical services, nec	0.4	Services	AC, refrigeration, and warm air heating equipment	0.8	Manufg.
Paperboard containers	0.4	Manufg.	Vending, commercial, industrial, office machinery	0.8	Manufg.
Specialized design services	0.4	Services	Federal government, investment, national defense	0.7	Fed Govt
Architectural, engineering, & related services	0.3	Services	Air & gas compressors	0.7	Manufg.
Telecommunications	0.3	Services	Residential structures, nec	0.6	Construct.
Employment services	0.3	Services	Waste management & remediation services	0.6	Services
Maintenance/repair of nonresidential structures	0.3	Construct.	Lawn & garden equipment	0.6	Manufg.
Services to buildings & dwellings	0.3	Services	Turbines & turbine generator set units	0.6	Manufg.
Business support services	0.3	Services	Architectural, engineering, & related services	0.5	Services
Cutting tools & machine tool accessories	0.3	Manufg.	Aircraft parts & auxiliary equipment, nec	0.5	Manufg.
Warehousing & storage	0.3	Util.	Machine shops	0.5	Manufg.
Data processing, hosting, & related services	0.3	Services	Chemical products & preparations, nec	0.5	Manufg.
Motors & generators	0.3	Manufg.	General Federal government services, defense	0.5	Fed Govt
Automotive equipment rental & leasing	0.3	Fin/R.E.	Air purification & ventilation equipment	0.4	Manufg.
Accounting, tax preparation, bookkeeping, & payroll	0.3	Services	Tobacco products	0.4	Manufg.
Food services & drinking places	0.3	Services	Paper mills	0.4	Manufg.
Metal cans, boxes, & other containers (light gauge)	0.2	Manufg.	Services to buildings & dwellings	0.4	Services
Management, scientific, & technical consulting	0.2	Services	Scientific research & development services	0.4	Services
Fabricated metals, nec	0.2	Manufg.	S/L govt. invest., other	0.4	S/L Govt
Natural gas distribution	0.2	Util.	Pumps & pumping equipment	0.4	Manufg.
Automotive repair & maintenance, ex. car washes	0.2	Services	Plastics & rubber industry machinery	0.3	Manufg.
Scientific research & development services	0.2	Services	Manufacturing structures	0.3	Construct.
Support services, nec	0.2	Services	Fabricated pipes & pipe fittings	0.3	Manufg.
Commercial & industrial equipment repair/maintenance	0.2	Services	Fabricated metals, nec	0.3	Manufg.
Other computer related services, including facilities	0.2	Services	Retail trade	0.3	Trade
Plate work & fabricated structural products	0.2	Manufg.	Automotive repair & maintenance, ex. car washes	0.3	Services
Ball & roller bearings	0.1	Manufg.	Commercial & industrial equipment repair/maintenance	0.3	Services
Noncomparable imports	0.1	Foreign	Heavy duty trucks	0.3	Manufg.
Investigation & security services	0.1	Services	Plate work & fabricated structural products	0.3	Manufg.
Hotels & motels, including casino hotels	0.1	Services	Basic inorganic chemicals, nec	0.3	Manufg.
Handtools	0.1	Manufg.	Metal tanks (heavy gauge)	0.3	Manufg.
Commercial & industrial machinery rental & leasing	0.1	Fin/R.E.	Motor vehicle bodies	0.2	Manufg.
Retail trade	0.1	Trade	Oil & gas well drilling	0.2	Mining
Nondepository credit intermediation activities	0.1	Fin/R.E.	Asphalt paving mixtures & blocks	0.2	Manufg.
Plastics packaging materials, film & sheet	0.1	Manufg.	Plastics products, nec	0.2	Manufg.
Rail transportation	0.1	Util.	Breweries	0.2	Manufg.
Nonferrous metal (ex. copper & aluminum) processing	0.1	Manufg.	Ornamental & architectural metal products	0.2	Manufg.
Air transportation	0.1	Util.	Paperboard mills	0.2	Manufg.
			Transit & ground passenger transportation	0.2	Util.
			Wood containers & pallets	0.2	Manufg.
			Owner-occupied dwellings	0.2	
			Rubber products, nec	0.2	Manufg.
			Soft drinks & ice	0.2	Manufg.
			Fluid power process machinery	0.2	Manufg.
			Food services & drinking places	0.2	Services
			Computer system design services	0.2	Services
			Metal cutting & forming machine tools	0.2	Manufg.
			Iron & steel mills & ferroalloys	0.2	Manufg.
			Oil & gas operations services	0.2	Mining
			Plastics materials & resins	0.2	Manufg.
			Couriers & messengers	0.2	Util.
			Rolling mill & other metalworking machinery	0.2	Manufg.
			Synthetic dyes & pigments	0.1	Manufg.
			Railroad rolling stock	0.1	Manufg.
			Truck trailers	0.1	Manufg.
			Alkalies & chlorine	0.1	Manufg.
			Pesticides & other agricultural chemicals	0.1	Manufg.
			Surgical appliances & supplies	0.1	Manufg.
			Crowns & closures & metal stamping	0.1	Manufg.
			Paints & coatings	0.1	Manufg.
			S/L govt. electric utilities	0.1	S/L Govt

Source: Benchmark Input-Output Accounts for the U.S. Economy, 2002, U.S. Department of Commerce, Washington D.C., January 2008. *User should note that this Input-Output table is not for this particular narrowly defined industry but for a larger aggregate. Input and Output data for* Valve and Fittings Other Than Plumbing *include Input and Output data for the* Annual Survey of Manufactures' *NAICS industries 332913 and 33291N.* The abbreviation nec stands for 'not elsewhere classified'.

OCCUPATIONS EMPLOYED BY OTHER FABRICATED METAL PRODUCT MANUFACTURING

Occupation	% of Total 2006	Change to 2016	Occupation	% of Total 2006	Change to 2016
Team assemblers	11.0	-11.4	Structural metal fabricators & fitters	1.4	-11.4
Machinists	4.6	-7.0	Mechanical engineers	1.4	-11.4
Welders, cutters, solderers, & brazers	3.9	-5.7	General & operations managers	1.3	-20.3
First-line supervisors/managers of production workers	3.8	-11.4	Executive secretaries & administrative assistants	1.3	-11.4
Cutting, punching, & press machine operators	3.4	-20.3	Coating, painting, & spraying machine operators	1.3	-15.8
Inspectors, testers, sorters, samplers, & weighers	3.0	-16.4	Packers & packagers, hand	1.2	-29.1
Computer-controlled machine tool operators	2.8	-2.5	Customer service representatives	1.2	-2.5
Grinding, lapping, polishing machine tool operators	2.7	-14.0	Drilling & boring machine tool operators	1.2	-20.3
Sales reps, wholesale & manufacturing, exc tech	2.2	-11.4	Industrial machinery mechanics	1.1	1.9
Helpers--Production workers	2.2	-11.4	Assemblers & fabricators, nec	1.1	-20.3
Lathe & turning machine tool operators & tenders	2.0	-20.3	Industrial truck & tractor operators	1.1	-20.3
Laborers & freight, stock, & material movers, hand	2.0	-20.3	Bookkeeping, accounting, & auditing clerks	1.1	-11.4
Shipping, receiving, & traffic clerks	1.9	-14.7	Production, planning, & expediting clerks	1.0	-11.4
Industrial engineers	1.8	7.6	Molding, coremaking, & casting machine operators	1.0	-20.3
Maintenance & repair workers, general	1.7	-11.4	Office clerks, general	1.0	-12.7

Source: Industry-Occupation Matrix, Bureau of Labor Statistics, December 4, 2007. These data are reported based on 4-digit NAICS categories but have been matched to corresponding 6-digit NAICS industry codes. The change reported for each occupation to the year 2016 is a percent of growth or decline as estimated by the Bureau of Labor Statistics. The abbreviation nec stands for 'not elsewhere classified'.

LOCATION BY STATE AND REGIONAL CONCENTRATION

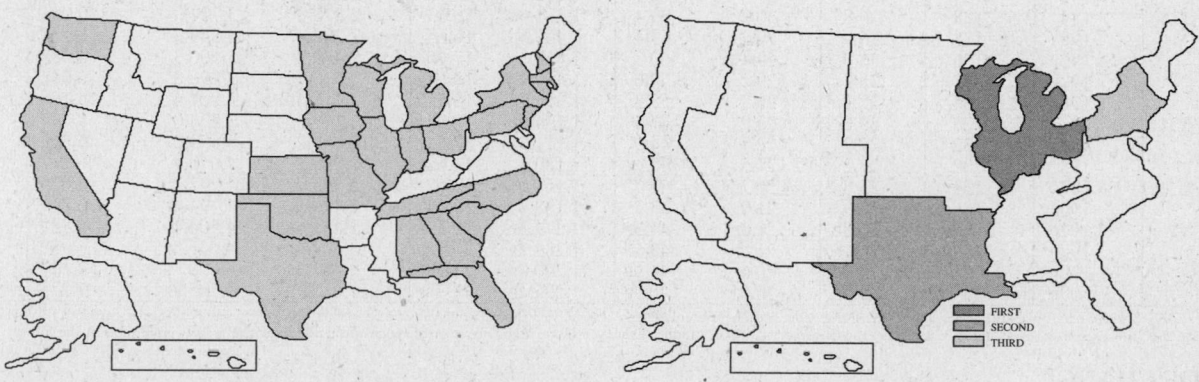

FIRST
SECOND
THIRD

INDUSTRY DATA BY STATE

State	Establish-ments	Shipments			Employment				Cost as % of Shipments	Investment per Employee ($)
		Total ($ mil)	% of U.S.	Per Establ.	Total Number	% of U.S.	Per Establ.	Wages ($/hour)		
Texas	129	1,641.8	9.2	12,727.2	7,656	8.1	59	16.00	39.8	6,133
Ohio	91	1,624.0	9.1	17,846.6	8,750	9.2	96	16.24	40.5	7,897
California	138	1,528.1	8.6	11,073.0	8,418	8.9	61	20.04	35.7	4,940
Pennsylvania	77	898.7	5.1	11,670.8	6,081	6.4	79	13.73	38.2	3,502
Illinois	67	846.7	4.8	12,636.7	4,468	4.7	67	17.05	47.0	3,842
Michigan	60	776.0	4.4	12,934.2	4,740	5.0	79	15.92	36.9	5,536
New York	42	553.3	3.1	13,174.8	3,484	3.7	83	17.49	30.9	5,993
Iowa	9	444.6	2.5	49,404.8	2,607	2.7	290	17.00	40.6	16,351
Minnesota	27	440.0	2.5	16,297.2	2,294	2.4	85	20.35	42.3	8,344
New Jersey	28	433.1	2.4	15,468.9	2,602	2.7	93	14.74	49.2	4,100
Connecticut	21	399.9	2.2	19,040.7	2,077	2.2	99	16.50	41.3	4,301
South Carolina	13	393.0	2.2	30,233.7	2,459	2.6	189	13.65	41.8	3,507
Indiana	18	323.5	1.8	17,971.9	1,163	1.2	65	15.92	42.9	5,011
Oklahoma	21	304.5	1.7	14,499.0	1,267	1.3	60	14.99	45.9	6,150
Massachusetts	14	302.4	1.7	21,602.8	1,417	1.5	101	19.79	58.4	2,989
Wisconsin	16	298.0	1.7	18,625.9	1,683	1.8	105	17.54	38.2	9,265
Missouri	11	281.7	1.6	25,611.9	1,682	1.8	153	16.27	36.0	3,089
Tennessee	7	273.4	1.5	39,056.7	1,232	1.3	176	18.46	34.9	9,952
North Carolina	12	254.0	1.4	21,164.9	1,227	1.3	102	14.23	33.0	2,386
Alabama	9	236.3	1.3	26,250.4	1,060	1.1	118	15.70	43.5	8,667
New Hampshire	7	167.7	0.9	23,963.4	679	0.7	97	10.99	42.4	5,614
Florida	10	152.3	0.9	15,233.3	1,218	1.3	122	15.18	34.7	5,540
Georgia	7	46.8	0.3	6,683.9	312	0.3	45	13.58	36.3	3,269
Washington	7	18.1	0.1	2,584.3	135	0.1	19	15.14	46.6	1,696
Kansas	11	17.3	0.1	1,577.1	124	0.1	11	12.60	39.3	8,895

Source: 2002 Economic Census. The states are in descending order of shipments or establishments (if shipment data are missing for the majority). The symbol (D) appears when data are withheld to prevent disclosure of competitive information. States marked with (D) are sorted by number of establishments. A dash (-) indicates that the data element cannot be calculated. Data may not show all states active in the NAICS category. All data available at the time of publication are shown.

NAICS 332991 - BALL AND ROLLER BEARING MANUFACTURING

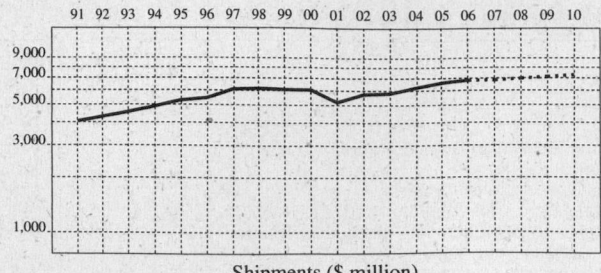

Shipments ($ million)

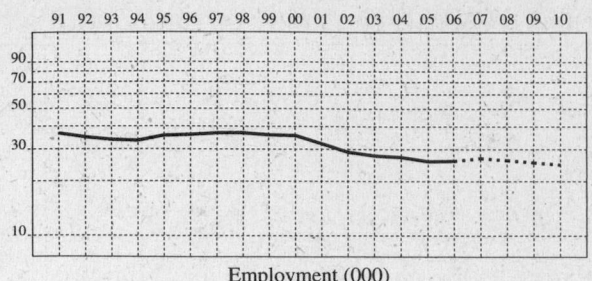

Employment (000)

GENERAL STATISTICS

| Year | Com-panies | Establishments | | Employment | | | Compensation | | Production ($ million) | | | |
		Total	with 20 or more employees	Total (000)	Production Workers (000)	Hours (Mil)	Payroll ($ mil)	Wages ($/hr)	Cost of Materials	Value Added by Manufacture	Value of Shipments	Capital Invest.
1991		181	126	36.6	29.8	57.3	1,054.0	13.85	1,540.3	2,451.9	4,051.2	305.7
1992	122	183	122	34.9	28.2	57.5	1,091.2	14.34	1,717.4	2,546.7	4,287.9	206.5
1993		185	126	33.8	27.3	57.2	1,081.5	14.48	1,778.0	2,746.6	4,557.4	205.5
1994		187	123	33.4	27.2	56.4	1,188.0	16.17	1,974.3	2,947.5	4,890.5	172.8
1995		186	122	35.6	29.2	60.7	1,239.0	15.65	2,101.7	3,234.0	5,281.1	248.1
1996		192	129	36.0	29.5	61.0	1,252.9	15.72	2,114.6	3,326.1	5,446.3	272.6
1997	115	184	128	36.8	30.0	63.4	1,378.6	16.43	2,378.8	3,724.9	6,091.2	309.0
1998		198	138	36.9	30.3	63.4	1,402.6	16.63	2,388.4	3,849.3	6,157.9	331.0
1999		192	136	36.0	29.4	60.3	1,427.8	17.76	2,489.7	3,600.3	6,082.5	295.1
2000		198	133	35.7	29.2	58.6	1,459.9	18.61	2,570.4	3,390.8	6,048.3	288.3
2001		198	135	32.2	26.3	53.3	1,332.7	18.51	2,111.3	3,007.6	5,186.1	270.1
2002	121	193	127	29.0	23.9	47.4	1,194.9	19.05	2,178.2	3,524.0	5,735.8	210.7
2003		189	132	27.7	22.7	44.9	1,111.2	18.54	2,058.2	3,699.0	5,802.0	247.7
2004		195	132	27.2	21.5	42.6	1,180.5	19.62	2,226.2	4,070.4	6,232.8	208.5
2005		187	134	25.8	20.7	42.7	1,169.0	19.62	2,365.7	4,292.7	6,624.2	225.6
2006		196P	136P	25.9	21.0	43.7	1,178.4	19.34	2,446.1	4,494.4	6,817.9	251.7
2007		197P	137P	26.8P	21.8P	44.3P	1,279.3P	20.57P	2,451.6P	4,504.4P	6,833.1P	250.2P
2008		198P	137P	26.1P	21.2P	43.1P	1,284.7P	20.98P	2,504.4P	4,601.5P	6,980.4P	249.9P
2009		198P	138P	25.4P	20.6P	41.9P	1,290.0P	21.38P	2,557.3P	4,698.7P	7,127.8P	249.6P
2010		199P	139P	24.7P	20.0P	40.7P	1,295.4P	21.78P	2,610.1P	4,795.8P	7,275.1P	249.2P

Sources: 1992, 1997, 2002 *Economic Census*; other years, up to 2006, are from the *Annual Survey of Manufactures*. Establishment counts for non-Census years are from *County Business Patterns*; 1997 and 2002 values are from the 1997 and 2002 censuses respectively, reported in the Federal Government's NAICS format. Other years were originally reported in equivalent SIC format. 'P's show projections by the editors.

INDICES OF CHANGE

| Year | Com-panies | Establishments | | Employment | | | Compensation | | Production ($ million) | | | |
		Total	with 20 or more employees	Total (000)	Production Workers (000)	Hours (Mil)	Payroll ($ mil)	Wages ($/hr)	Cost of Materials	Value Added by Manufacture	Value of Shipments	Capital Invest.
1992	101	95	96	120	118	121	91	75	79	72	75	98
1997	95	95	101	127	126	134	115	86	109	106	106	147
2001		103	106	111	110	112	112	97	97	85	90	128
2002	100	100	100	100	100	100	100	100	100	100	100	100
2003		98	104	96	95	95	93	97	94	105	101	118
2004		101	104	94	90	90	99	103	102	116	109	99
2005		97	106	89	87	90	98	103	109	122	115	107
2006		102P	107P	89	88	92	99	102	112	128	119	119
2007		102P	107P	92P	91P	93P	107P	108P	113P	128P	119P	119P
2008		102P	108P	90P	89P	91P	108P	110P	115P	131P	122P	119P
2009		103P	109P	88P	86P	88P	108P	112P	117P	133P	124P	118P
2010		103P	109P	85P	84P	86P	108P	114P	120P	136P	127P	118P

Sources: Same as General Statistics. Values reflect change from the base year, 2002. Values above 100 mean greater than 2002, values below 100 mean less than 2002, and the values of 100 in other years means the same as 2002. 'P's show projections by the editors.

SELECTED RATIOS

For 2002	Avg. of All Manufact.	Analyzed Industry	Index	For 2002	Avg. of All Manufact.	Analyzed Industry	Index
Employees per Establishment	42	150	358	Value Added per Production Worker	182,367	147,448	81
Payroll per Establishment	1,639,184	6,191,192	378	Cost per Establishment	5,769,015	11,286,010	196
Payroll per Employee	39,053	41,203	106	Cost per Employee	137,446	75,110	55
Production Workers per Establishment	30	124	420	Cost per Production Worker	195,506	91,138	47
Wages per Establishment	694,845	4,678,601	673	Shipments per Establishment	11,158,348	29,719,171	266
Wages per Production Worker	23,548	37,781	160	Shipments per Employee	265,847	197,786	74
Hours per Production Worker	1,980	1,983	100	Shipments per Production Worker	378,144	239,992	63
Wages per Hour	11.89	19.05	160	Investment per Establishment	361,338	1,091,710	302
Value Added per Establishment	5,381,325	18,259,067	339	Investment per Employee	8,609	7,266	84
Value Added per Employee	128,210	121,517	95	Investment per Production Worker	12,245	8,816	72

Sources: Same as General Statistics. The 'Average of All Manufacturing' column represents the average of all manufacturing industries reported for the most recent complete year available. The Index shows the relationship between the Average and the Analyzed Industry. For example, 100 means that they are equal; 500 that the Analyzed Industry is five times the average; 50 means that the Analyzed Industry is half the national average. The abbreviation 'na' is used to show that data are 'not available'. Ratios shown for 2002, the last complete census year.

LEADING COMPANIES Number shown: 63   Total sales ($ mil): 43,284   Total employment (000): 102.8

Company Name	Address				CEO Name	Phone	Co. Type	Sales ($ mil)	Empl. (000)
Nucor Corp.	1915 Rexford Rd.	Charlotte	NC	28211	Daniel R. DiMicco	704-366-7000	P	16,593	18.0
Rotek Inc.	1400 S Chillicothe	Aurora	OH	44202	Len Osborne	330-562-4000	R	7,625*	0.2
Federal-Mogul Corp.	PO Box 1966	Detroit	MI	48235	Jose Maria Alapont	248-354-7700	P	6,914	43.1
Timken Co.	PO Box 6932	Canton	OH	44706	James W. Griffith	330-438-3000	P	5,236	25.0
MRC Bearings	402 Chandler St.	Jamestown	NY	14701		716-661-2600	S	1,012*	1.6
Barden Corp.	PO Box 2449	Danbury	CT	06813	John McCloskey	203-744-2211	R	776*	0.3
Schaeffler Group USA Inc.	308 Springhill Farm	Fort Mill	SC	29715		803-548-8500	R	776*	0.3
F.A.G Bearings Corp.	PO Box 1933	Danbury	CT	06813	Dieter Kuetemeier	203-790-5474	R	776*	0.1
NTN-Bower Corp.	707 N Bower Rd.	Macomb	IL	61455	Yasunori Terada	309-837-0440	R	502*	<0.1
Kaydon Corp.	315 E Eisenhower	Ann Arbor	MI	48108		734-747-7025	P	451	2.1
NSK Corp.	PO Box 134007	Ann Arbor	MI	48113	Tsutomo Komori	734-913-7500	R	438*	0.4
NN Inc.	2000 Waters Edge	Johnson City	TN	37604	Roderick R. Baty	423-743-9151	P	421	2.2
RBC Bearings Inc.	1 Tribology Ctr.	Oxford	CT	06478	Michael J. Hartnett	203-267-7001	P	306	1.9
Peer Bearing Co.	2200 Norman Dr. S	Waukegan	IL	60085	Laurence Spungen	847-578-1000	R	200*	0.6
CompX International Inc.	5430 LBJ Fwy.	Dallas	TX	75240	David A. Bowers	972-448-1400	P	178	1.0
General Bearing Corp.	44 High St.	West Nyack	NY	10994		845-358-6000	P	120	1.0
Timken Aerospace/Super Precis.	7 Optical Ave.	Keene	NH	03431		603-352-0310	S	91*	0.6
New Hampshire Ball Bearings	155 Lexington Dr.	Laconia	NH	03246		603-524-0004	S	83*	0.5
Nachi America Inc.	715 Pushville Rd.	Greenwood	IN	46143	Steve Itoh	317-535-3675	S	76*	<0.1
Networks Electronic Corp.	9750 DeSoto Ave.	Chatsworth	CA	91311	Tamara Christen	818-341-0440	R	73*	0.1
NTN-BCA Corp.	401 W Lincoln Ave.	Lititz	PA	17543	Tom Kamachi	717-627-3623	R	66*	0.4
Kamatics Corp.	PO Box 1	Bloomfield	CT	06002	Paul Kuhn	860-243-7100	S	66*	0.5
Hub City Inc.	PO Box 1089	Aberdeen	SD	57402	Henry W. Knueppel	605-225-0360	S	40*	0.3
Defiance Precision Products	1125 Precision Way	Defiance	OH	43512		419-782-8955	S	40*	0.3
Aurora Bearing Company Inc.	970 S Lake St., 1	Aurora	IL	60506	Charles Richard	630-859-2030	R	36*	0.2
Virginia Industries Inc.	1022 Elm St.	Rocky Hill	CT	06067	Laura Grondin	860-571-3602	R	27*	<0.1
Carolina Forge Company L.L.C.	PO Box 370	Wilson	NC	27894	James Martin	252-237-8181	R	25*	0.2
Divine Brothers Co.	PO Box 438	Utica	NY	13503	Lees Divine	315-797-0470	R	23*	0.1
American Urethane Inc.	1905 Betson Ct.	Odenton	MD	21113	Jude Masters	410-672-2100	R	22*	<0.1
Pacific Bearing Corp.	PO Box 6980	Rockford	IL	61125	Robert Schroeder	815-389-5600	R	19*	0.1
Sli Holdings Inc.	PO Box 780	Westfield	IN	46074	Scott Waddell	317-867-0100	R	18*	0.1
Saginaw Products Corp.	68 Williamson St.	Saginaw	MI	48601	Nicolaos Rapanos	989-753-1411	R	15*	<0.1
Ashland Precision Tooling	1750 Baney Rd. S	Ashland	OH	44805		419-289-1736	R	15*	<0.1
Kendale Industries Inc.	7600 Hub Pkwy.	Cleveland	OH	44125	Dale Honroth	216-524-5400	R	14*	<0.1
TENTE Casters Inc.	2266 S Park Dr.	Hebron	KY	41048	Peter Fricke	859-586-5558	R	13*	<0.1
Bearing Service Company of PA	630 Alpha Dr.	Pittsburgh	PA	15238	Jacob Banks	412-963-7710	R	13*	<0.1
Fairbanks Company Inc.	PO Box 1871	Rome	GA	30162	Robert Lahre	706-234-6701	R	13*	<0.1
Schatz Bearing Corp.	10 Fairview Ave.	Poughkeepsie	NY	12601	Stephen Pomeroy	845-452-6000	R	12*	<0.1
National Bearings Inc.	PO Box 4726	Lancaster	PA	17604	Jessica May	717-569-0485	S	12*	0.1
Advanced Green Components	4005 Corporate Dr.	Winchester	KY	40391		859-737-4000	R	11*	<0.1
Del-Tron Precision Inc.	5 Trowbridge Dr.	Bethel	CT	06801	Ralph McIntosh	203-778-2727	R	10*	<0.1
Frost Inc.	2020 Bristol NW	Grand Rapids	MI	49504	Charles Frost	616-453-7781	R	9*	<0.1
Oconomowoc Manufacturing Corp.	PO Box 436	Oconomowoc	WI	53066	Kyle Stoehr	262-567-8383	R	9*	<0.1
Randall Bearings Inc.	PO Box 1258	Lima	OH	45802	Kent Morgan	419-223-1075	R	9*	<0.1
Roll Master Corp.	7432 Ranger Way	Fort Worth	TX	76133	Sandy Tucker	817-292-4319	R	9*	<0.1
MD Knowlton Co.	PO Box 29	Victor	NY	14564	Kent Fellows	585-924-3230	R	8*	<0.1
SN Precision Enterprises Inc.	145 Jordan Rd.	Troy	NY	12180	Augustine Sperrazza	518-283-8002	R	7*	<0.1
Jonathan Engineered Solutions	410 Exchange, 200	Irvine	CA	92602	Clark Higgins	714-665-4400	R	7*	<0.1
Miller Bearing Company Inc.	420 Portage Blvd.	Kent	OH	44240	Donald Miller	330-678-8844	R	7*	<0.1
Rotation Products Corp.	2849 N Catherwood	Indianapolis	IN	46219	Stuart Hansen	317-542-8563	R	7*	<0.1
Rymar Corp.	PO Box 156	Horsham	PA	19044	Pedro Rymar	215-443-5252	R	7*	<0.1
Keystone North Inc.	310 S Mn Street	Mansfield	PA	16933	Karen Hammer	570-662-3882	R	6*	<0.1
Triangle Manufacturing Co.	PO Box 1070	Oshkosh	WI	54903	Jack Sullivan	920-235-3710	R	6*	<0.1
JPM of Mississippi Inc.	PO Box 16449	Hattiesburg	MS	39404	William Taber	601-544-9950	R	5*	<0.1
C and S Engineering Inc.	956 Old Colony Rd.	Meriden	CT	06451	Alfred Cavallo	203-235-5727	R	5*	<0.1
Noonan Machine Co.	1091 E Green St.	Franklin Park	IL	60131	William Noonan	630-595-0144	R	5*	<0.1
Roller Service Corp.	23 McMillan Way	Newark	DE	19713	James Veacock	302-737-5000	R	4*	<0.1
MB Holdings Inc.	10385 Drummond	Philadelphia	PA	19154	Stanley Friedman	215-739-6880	R	4*	<0.1
Ketchie-Houston Inc.	201 Winecoff School	Concord	NC	28027	Edgar Ketchie	704-786-5101	R	4*	<0.1
American Metal Bearing Co.	7191 Acacia Ave.	Garden Grove	CA	92841	Mike Tornberg	714-892-5527	R	3*	<0.1
Emmco Development Corp.	243 Belmont Dr.	Somerset	NJ	08873		732-469-6464	R	2*	<0.1
Roysersford Foundry and Machine	PO Box 190	Royersford	PA	19468	Kurt Deisher	610-935-7200	R	2*	<0.1
Custom Metalizing and Machine	PO Box 2578	Sumter	SC	29151	Harold Weathersbee	803-773-1507	R	2*	<0.1

Source: Ward's Business Directory of U.S. Private and Public Companies, Volumes 1 and 2, 2008. The company type code used is as follows: P - Public, R - Private, S - Subsidiary, D - Division, J - Joint Venture, A - Affiliate, G - Group. Sales are in millions of dollars, employees are in thousands. An asterisk (*) indicates an estimated sales volume. The symbol < stands for 'less than'. Company names and addresses are truncated, in some cases, to fit into the available space.

MATERIALS CONSUMED

Material	Quantity	Delivered Cost ($ million)
Metal bolts, nuts, screws, and other screw machine products	(X)	28.3
Other fabricated metal products (exc. castings and forgings)	(X)	36.0
Cold iron and steel forgings	(X)	86.7
Other iron and steel forgings	(X)	145.1

Continued on next page.

MATERIALS CONSUMED - Continued

Material	Quantity	Delivered Cost ($ million)
Iron and steel castings (rough and semifinished)	(X)	79.9
Nonferrous (aluminum, copper, etc.) castings (rough and semifinished)	(X)	0.8
Steel bars, bar shapes, and plates (exc. castings, forgings, fabr. metal products)	(X)	164.7
Steel sheet and strip (including tinplate)	(X)	75.5
All other steel shapes and forms (exc. castings, forgings, fabr. metal products)	(X)	150.3
Nonferrous shapes and forms	(X)	4.5
Ball and roller bearings (mounted or unmounted)	(X)	(D)
Balls, rollers, cages, collars, races, and other antifriction bearing components and parts	(X)	551.6
Clutches, couplings, and other mechanical power transmission equipment	(X)	3.5
Electric motors, generators, and parts	(X)	13.3
Paperboard containers, boxes, and corrugated paperboard	(X)	12.4
Grinding wheels and other abrasive products, exc. industrial diamonds	(X)	32.5
Fluid power pumps, motors, and hydrostatic transmissions	(X)	16.1
Special dies, tools, die sets, jigs, and fixtures (exc. cutting tools)	(X)	(D)
All other materials, components, parts, containers, and supplies	(X)	354.3
Materials, ingredients, containers, and supplies, nsk	(X)	98.5

Source: 2002 Economic Census. Explanation of symbols used: (D): Withheld to avoid disclosure of competitive data; na: Not available; (S): Withheld because statistical norms were not met; (X): Not applicable; (Z): Less than half the unit shown; nec: Not elsewhere classified; nsk: Not specified by kind; - : zero; p : 10-19 percent estimated; q : 20-29 percent estimated.

PRODUCT SHARE DETAILS

Product or Product Class Shipments	Mil. $	Product or Product Class Shipments	Mil. $
BALL AND ROLLER BEARINGS	5,567.3	Mounted bearings, except plain	458.4
Ball bearings, complete, unmounted	1,920.1	Parts and components for ball and roller bearings, except	
Tapered roller bearings (including cups and cones),		cups and cones (including ball and rollers sold separately)	624.2
unmounted	1,465.0	Ball and roller bearings, nsk, total	56.7
Roller bearings, except tapered, unmounted	1,042.8		

Source: 2002 Economic Census. The values are product shipments in millions of dollars for 2002. Total product shipments may be lower or higher than industry shipments. See Introduction for a full discussion. Values of indented subcategories are summed in the main heading(s). The symbol (D) appears when data are withheld to prevent disclosure of competitive information. The abbreviation nsk stands for 'not specified by kind' and nec for 'not elsewhere classified'. A dash (-) means zero.

INPUTS AND OUTPUTS FOR BALL AND ROLLER BEARING MANUFACTURING

Economic Sector or Industry Providing Inputs	%	Sector	Economic Sector or Industry Buying Outputs	%	Sector
Compensation of employees	30.5		Motor vehicle parts	18.3	Manufg.
Ball & roller bearings	12.4	Manufg.	Exports of goods & services	12.7	Cap Inv
Iron & steel mills & ferroalloys	6.3	Manufg.	Ball & roller bearings	9.7	Manufg.
Wholesale trade	4.3	Trade	Telecommunications	7.4	Services
Forging, stamping, & sintering, nec	4.1	Manufg.	Material handling equipment	3.5	Manufg.
Management of companies & enterprises	2.7	Services	Oil & gas extraction	3.0	Mining
Power generation & supply	1.6	Util.	General Federal government services, defense	2.5	Fed Govt
Ferrous metal foundries	1.3	Manufg.	Industrial machinery, nec	2.3	Manufg.
Machine shops	1.1	Manufg.	Transit & ground passenger transportation	2.0	Util.
Truck transportation	0.9	Util.	Steel products from purchased steel	1.5	Manufg.
Securities, commodity contracts, investments	0.9	Fin/R.E.	Farm machinery & equipment	1.3	Manufg.
Maintenance/repair of nonresidential structures	0.8	Construct.	Construction machinery	1.3	Manufg.
Services to buildings & dwellings	0.7	Services	Mechanical power transmission equipment	1.3	Manufg.
Semiconductors & related devices	0.6	Manufg.	Aircraft	1.2	Manufg.
Special tools, dies, jigs, & fixtures	0.6	Manufg.	Wholesale trade	1.2	Trade
Printed circuit assemblies (electronic assemblies)	0.6	Manufg.	Automobiles	1.2	Manufg.
Lessors of nonfinancial assets	0.6	Fin/R.E.	Plate work & fabricated structural products	1.1	Manufg.
Cutting tools & machine tool accessories	0.5	Manufg.	Light truck & utility vehicles	1.1	Manufg.
Turned products & screws, nuts, & bolts	0.5	Manufg.	Fluid power process machinery	1.0	Manufg.
Abrasive products	0.5	Manufg.	Motors & generators	1.0	Manufg.
Monetary authorities/depository credit intermediation	0.5	Fin/R.E.	Railroad rolling stock	0.9	Manufg.
Automotive repair & maintenance, ex. car washes	0.5	Services	Aircraft parts & auxiliary equipment, nec	0.8	Manufg.
Natural gas distribution	0.5	Util.	Power-driven handtools	0.8	Manufg.
Taxes on production & imports, less subsidies	0.4		Speed changers, industrial high-speed drives, & gears	0.8	Manufg.
Professional, scientific, technical services, nec	0.4	Services	Air & gas compressors	0.7	Manufg.
Commercial & industrial equipment repair/maintenance	0.4	Services	Metal cutting & forming machine tools	0.7	Manufg.
Architectural, engineering, & related services	0.3	Services	Packaging machinery	0.7	Manufg.
Advertising & related services	0.3	Services	Mining & oil & gas field machinery	0.7	Manufg.
Specialized design services	0.3	Services	Ornamental & architectural metal products	0.7	Manufg.
Legal services	0.3	Services	Turbines & turbine generator set units	0.7	Manufg.
Employment services	0.3	Services	Rolling mill & other metalworking machinery	0.7	Manufg.
Management, scientific, & technical consulting	0.3	Services	Pipeline transportation	0.7	Util.
Business support services	0.2	Services	Commercial & industrial equipment repair/maintenance	0.6	Services
Food services & drinking places	0.2	Services	Aircraft engine & engine parts	0.6	Manufg.
Warehousing & storage	0.2	Util.	Lawn & garden equipment	0.6	Manufg.
Motors & generators	0.2	Manufg.	AC, refrigeration, and warm air heating equipment	0.6	Manufg.
Paperboard containers	0.2	Manufg.	Semiconductor machinery	0.5	Manufg.

Continued on next page.

INPUTS AND OUTPUTS FOR BALL AND ROLLER BEARING MANUFACTURING - Continued

Economic Sector or Industry Providing Inputs	%	Sector	Economic Sector or Industry Buying Outputs	%	Sector
Data processing, hosting, & related services	0.2	Services	Engine equipment, nec	0.5	Manufg.
Accounting, tax preparation, bookkeeping, & payroll	0.2	Services	Rubber products, nec	0.5	Manufg.
Coating, engraving, heat treating & allied activities	0.2	Manufg.	Pumps & pumping equipment	0.5	Manufg.
Real estate	0.2	Fin/R.E.	Manufacturing, nec	0.4	Manufg.
Automotive equipment rental & leasing	0.2	Fin/R.E.	Metal cans, boxes, & other containers (light gauge)	0.4	Manufg.
Scientific research & development services	0.2	Services	Machine shops	0.4	Manufg.
Fluid power process machinery	0.2	Manufg.	General purpose machinery, nec	0.4	Manufg.
Support services, nec	0.2	Services	Valve & fittings other than plumbing	0.3	Manufg.
Telecommunications	0.2	Services	Coating, engraving, heat treating & allied activities	0.3	Manufg.
Motor vehicle parts	0.1	Manufg.	Other S/L govt. enterprises	0.3	S/L Govt
Rail transportation	0.1	Util.	Crowns & closures & metal stamping	0.3	Manufg.
Electronic & precision equipment repair/maintenance	0.1	Services	Air purification & ventilation equipment	0.3	Manufg.
Other computer related services, including facilities	0.1	Services	Signs	0.3	Manufg.
Investigation & security services	0.1	Services	Commercial & service industry machinery, nec	0.3	Manufg.
Waste management & remediation services	0.1	Services	Heavy duty trucks	0.3	Manufg.
Hotels & motels, including casino hotels	0.1	Services	Plastics & rubber industry machinery	0.2	Manufg.
Noncomparable imports	0.1	Foreign	Motorcycles, bicycles, & parts	0.2	Manufg.
Air transportation	0.1	Util.	Electronic & precision equipment repair/maintenance	0.2	Services
			Surgical appliances & supplies	0.2	Manufg.
			Transportation equipment, nec	0.2	Manufg.
			Cable & other subscription programming	0.2	Services
			Turned products & screws, nuts, & bolts	0.2	Manufg.
			Hardware	0.2	Manufg.
			Jewelry & silverware	0.2	Manufg.
			Waste management & remediation services	0.2	Services
			Power boilers & heat exchangers	0.2	Manufg.
			Retail trade	0.2	Trade
			Fabricated pipes & pipe fittings	0.1	Manufg.
			Scientific research & development services	0.1	Services
			Industrial process variable instruments	0.1	Manufg.
			Automotive repair & maintenance, ex. car washes	0.1	Services
			Switchgear & switchboard apparatus	0.1	Manufg.
			Electromedical & electrotherapeutic apparatus	0.1	Manufg.
			Personal & household goods repair/maintenance	0.1	Services
			Household cooking appliances	0.1	Manufg.
			Fabricated metals, nec	0.1	Manufg.
			Arms, ordnance, & accessories	0.1	Manufg.
			Heating equipment (except warm air furnaces)	0.1	Manufg.
			Custom architectural woodwork & millwork	0.1	Manufg.
			Sporting & athletic goods	0.1	Manufg.
			Lighting fixtures	0.1	Manufg.
			Surgical & medical instrument	0.1	Manufg.
			Springs & wire products	0.1	Manufg.
			Irradiation apparatus	0.1	Manufg.
			Electronic components, nec	0.1	Manufg.
			Computer terminals & peripherals	0.1	Manufg.
			Search, detection, & navigation instruments	0.1	Manufg.

Source: Benchmark Input-Output Accounts for the U.S. Economy, 2002, U.S. Department of Commerce, Washington, D.C., January 2008. The abbreviation nec stands for 'not elsewhere classified'.

OCCUPATIONS EMPLOYED BY OTHER FABRICATED METAL PRODUCT MANUFACTURING

Occupation	% of Total 2006	Change to 2016	Occupation	% of Total 2006	Change to 2016
Team assemblers	11.0	-11.4	Structural metal fabricators & fitters	1.4	-11.4
Machinists	4.6	-7.0	Mechanical engineers	1.4	-11.4
Welders, cutters, solderers, & brazers	3.9	-5.7	General & operations managers	1.3	-20.3
First-line supervisors/managers of production workers	3.8	-11.4	Executive secretaries & administrative assistants	1.3	-11.4
Cutting, punching, & press machine operators	3.4	-20.3	Coating, painting, & spraying machine operators	1.3	-15.8
Inspectors, testers, sorters, samplers, & weighers	3.0	-16.4	Packers & packagers, hand	1.2	-29.1
Computer-controlled machine tool operators	2.8	-2.5	Customer service representatives	1.2	-2.5
Grinding, lapping, polishing machine tool operators	2.7	-14.0	Drilling & boring machine tool operators	1.2	-20.3
Sales reps, wholesale & manufacturing, exc tech	2.2	-11.4	Industrial machinery mechanics	1.1	1.9
Helpers--Production workers	2.2	-11.4	Assemblers & fabricators, nec	1.1	-20.3
Lathe & turning machine tool operators & tenders	2.0	-20.3	Industrial truck & tractor operators	1.1	-20.3
Laborers & freight, stock, & material movers, hand	2.0	-20.3	Bookkeeping, accounting, & auditing clerks	1.1	-11.4
Shipping, receiving, & traffic clerks	1.9	-14.7	Production, planning, & expediting clerks	1.0	-11.4
Industrial engineers	1.8	7.6	Molding, coremaking, & casting machine operators	1.0	-20.3
Maintenance & repair workers, general	1.7	-11.4	Office clerks, general	1.0	-12.7

Source: Industry-Occupation Matrix, Bureau of Labor Statistics, December 4, 2007. These data are reported based on 4-digit NAICS categories but have been matched to corresponding 6-digit NAICS industry codes. The change reported for each occupation to the year 2016 is a percent of growth or decline as estimated by the Bureau of Labor Statistics. The abbreviation nec stands for 'not elsewhere classified'.

LOCATION BY STATE AND REGIONAL CONCENTRATION

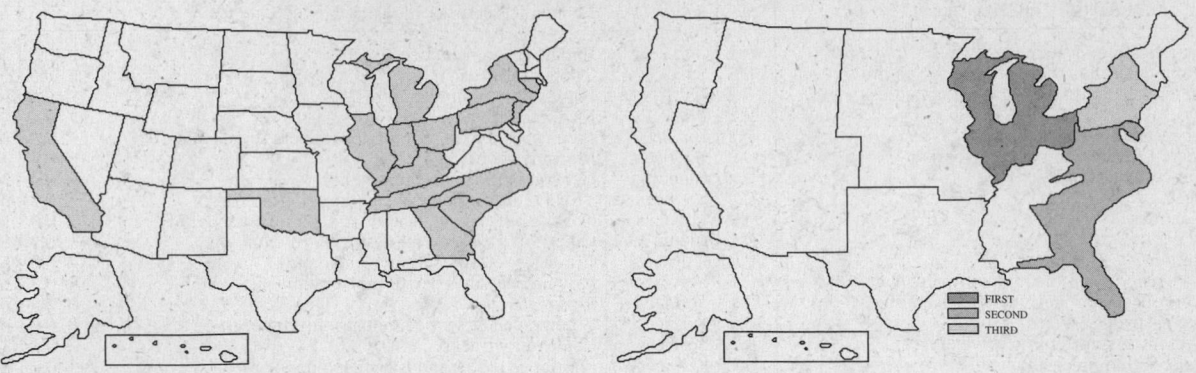

INDUSTRY DATA BY STATE

| State | Establish-ments | Shipments | | | Employment | | | | Cost as % of Shipments | Investment per Employee ($) |
		Total ($ mil)	% of U.S.	Per Establ.	Total Number	% of U.S.	Per Establ.	Wages ($/hour)		
Ohio	12	1,136.4	19.8	94,700.6	4,306	14.9	359	22.88	37.5	9,843
South Carolina	13	985.5	17.2	75,806.2	5,684	19.6	437	18.31	41.9	5,300
North Carolina	11	486.5	8.5	44,223.5	1,892	6.5	172	20.54	43.5	12,607
Illinois	16	386.9	6.7	24,178.6	1,977	6.8	124	20.30	40.8	14,433
Georgia	10	337.6	5.9	33,761.1	1,843	6.4	184	16.61	35.5	10,378
Tennessee	8	278.6	4.9	34,822.1	1,400	4.8	175	17.33	32.3	4,424
Indiana	10	273.3	4.8	27,334.4	1,912	6.6	191	18.30	26.7	3,908
Pennsylvania	9	267.6	4.7	29,732.2	1,134	3.9	126	19.17	30.8	5,183
Connecticut	15	205.4	3.6	13,695.0	1,356	4.7	90	18.92	29.3	3,200
Kentucky	8	169.7	3.0	21,208.3	531	1.8	66	18.87	31.4	6,638
New York	15	166.4	2.9	11,093.0	1,274	4.4	85	15.61	34.4	5,225
Michigan	8	138.6	2.4	17,322.1	613	2.1	77	19.48	64.4	4,225
California	14	104.1	1.8	7,434.1	746	2.6	53	17.42	25.2	3,741
New Jersey	5	57.9	1.0	11,586.6	426	1.5	85	17.56	26.1	2,808
Oklahoma	4	23.0	0.4	5,761.0	152	0.5	38	24.58	75.7	4,822

Source: 2002 *Economic Census*. The states are in descending order of shipments or establishments (if shipment data are missing for the majority). The symbol (D) appears when data are withheld to prevent disclosure of competitive information. States marked with (D) are sorted by number of establishments. A dash (-) indicates that the data element cannot be calculated. Data may not show all states active in the NAICS category. All data available at the time of publication are shown.

NAICS 332992 - SMALL ARMS AMMUNITION MANUFACTURING

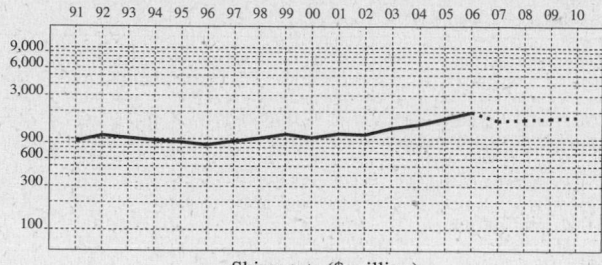

Shipments ($ million)

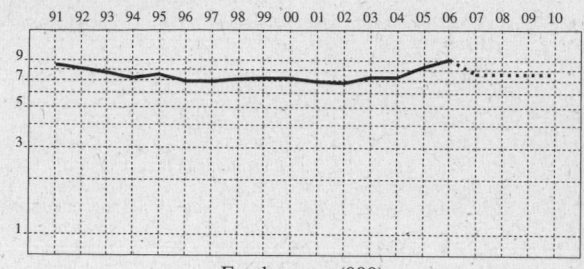

Employment (000)

GENERAL STATISTICS

Year	Companies	Establishments		Employment			Compensation		Production ($ million)			
		Total	with 20 or more employees	Total (000)	Production Workers (000)	Hours (Mil)	Payroll ($ mil)	Wages ($/hr)	Cost of Materials	Value Added by Manufacture	Value of Shipments	Capital Invest.
1991		85	22	8.5	6.4	12.7	249.6	13.38	369.5	520.3	941.5	24.0
1992	101	103	19	8.1	6.1	12.6	258.6	14.04	397.6	694.5	1,088.6	31.4
1993		102	18	7.7	5.8	11.5	251.5	15.02	367.4	640.0	1,021.8	31.8
1994		113	22	7.2	5.5	11.6	241.7	14.77	338.1	628.4	963.4	35.4
1995		106	20	7.5	5.7	11.7	252.2	15.14	372.2	586.3	919.5	30.1
1996		107	20	6.9	5.2	10.8	231.4	14.34	333.2	527.1	862.1	26.1
1997	108	113	19	6.9	5.2	10.3	242.1	16.15	360.9	584.8	938.8	26.7
1998		118	19	7.1	5.5	10.9	258.0	15.86	370.9	631.0	1,018.4	20.4
1999		117	23	7.2	5.5	11.4	277.6	16.48	437.7	672.9	1,124.9	33.8
2000		122	25	7.2	5.6	10.8	277.8	17.91	456.9	603.2	1,032.8	37.2
2001		111	25	6.9	5.2	10.7	258.1	16.52	425.3	697.6	1,139.6	20.1
2002	110	112	22	6.8	5.3	11.1	271.9	17.78	392.1	766.9	1,114.3	16.8
2003		112	24	7.3	5.8	12.3	312.9	17.95	431.9	880.7	1,311.4	20.9
2004		107	22	7.3	5.9	12.6	330.7	18.55	493.3	946.6	1,444.2	23.5
2005		109	24	8.3	6.8	13.9	354.7	18.44	598.0	1,082.8	1,683.6	28.7
2006		117P	24P	9.1	7.4	17.1	410.1	17.40	760.2	1,245.6	1,970.1	24.6
2007		118P	25P	7.6P	6.1P	13.2P	349.5P	18.99P	612.4P	1,003.4P	1,587.0P	22.9P
2008		119P	25P	7.6P	6.2P	13.4P	357.7P	19.31P	631.7P	1,035.0P	1,637.1P	22.4P
2009		120P	25P	7.6P	6.2P	13.5P	365.9P	19.63P	651.0P	1,066.7P	1,687.2P	21.9P
2010		121P	25P	7.6P	6.3P	13.7P	374.1P	19.96P	670.4P	1,098.4P	1,737.3P	21.5P

Sources: 1992, 1997, 2002 *Economic Census*; other years, up to 2006, are from the *Annual Survey of Manufactures*. Establishment counts for non-Census years are from *County Business Patterns*; 1997 and 2002 values are from the 1997 and 2002 censuses respectively, reported in the Federal Government's NAICS format. Other years were originally reported in equivalent SIC format. 'P's show projections by the editors.

INDICES OF CHANGE

Year	Companies	Establishments		Employment			Compensation		Production ($ million)			
		Total	with 20 or more employees	Total (000)	Production Workers (000)	Hours (Mil)	Payroll ($ mil)	Wages ($/hr)	Cost of Materials	Value Added by Manufacture	Value of Shipments	Capital Invest.
1992	92	92	86	119	115	114	95	79	101	91	98	187
1997	98	101	86	101	98	93	89	91	92	76	84	159
2001		99	114	101	98	96	95	93	108	91	102	120
2002	100	100	100	100	100	100	100	100	100	100	100	100
2003		100	109	107	109	111	115	101	110	115	118	124
2004		96	100	107	111	114	122	104	126	123	130	140
2005		97	109	122	128	125	130	104	153	141	151	171
2006		105P	110P	134	140	154	151	98	194	162	177	146
2007		106P	111P	112P	115P	119P	129P	107P	156P	131P	142P	136P
2008		107P	113P	112P	117P	121P	132P	109P	161P	135P	147P	133P
2009		108P	115P	112P	117P	122P	135P	110P	166P	139P	151P	130P
2010		108P	116P	112P	119P	123P	138P	112P	171P	143P	156P	128P

Sources: Same as General Statistics. Values reflect change from the base year, 2002. Values above 100 mean greater than 2002, values below 100 mean less than 2002, and the values of 100 in other years means the same as 2002. 'P's show projections by the editors.

SELECTED RATIOS

For 2002	Avg. of All Manufact.	Analyzed Industry	Index	For 2002	Avg. of All Manufact.	Analyzed Industry	Index
Employees per Establishment	42	61	145	Value Added per Production Worker	182,367	144,698	79
Payroll per Establishment	1,639,184	2,427,679	148	Cost per Establishment	5,769,015	3,500,893	61
Payroll per Employee	39,053	39,985	102	Cost per Employee	137,446	57,662	42
Production Workers per Establishment	30	47	160	Cost per Production Worker	195,506	73,981	38
Wages per Establishment	694,845	1,762,125	254	Shipments per Establishment	11,158,348	9,949,107	89
Wages per Production Worker	23,548	37,237	158	Shipments per Employee	265,847	163,868	62
Hours per Production Worker	1,980	2,094	106	Shipments per Production Worker	378,144	210,245	56
Wages per Hour	11.89	17.78	150	Investment per Establishment	361,338	150,000	42
Value Added per Establishment	5,381,325	6,847,321	127	Investment per Employee	8,609	2,471	29
Value Added per Employee	128,210	112,779	88	Investment per Production Worker	12,245	3,170	26

Sources: Same as General Statistics. The 'Average of All Manufacturing' column represents the average of all manufacturing industries reported for the most recent complete year available. The Index shows the relationship between the Average and the Analyzed Industry. For example, 100 means that they are equal; 500 that the Analyzed Industry is five times the average; 50 means that the Analyzed Industry is half the national average. The abbreviation 'na' is used to show that data are 'not available'. Ratios shown for 2002, the last complete census year.

LEADING COMPANIES   Number shown: 16   Total sales ($ mil): **10,275**   Total employment (000): **41.4**

Company Name	Address				CEO Name	Phone	Co. Type	Sales ($ mil)	Empl. (000)
Alliant Techsystems Inc.	5050 Lincoln Dr.	Edina	MN	55436	Daniel J. Murphy	952-351-3000	P	3,565	16.0
Pentair Inc.	5500 Wayzata Blvd.	Golden Valley	MN	55416	Winslow H. Buxton	763-545-1730	P	3,399	16.0
Olin Corp.	190 Carondelet Plz.	Clayton	MO	63105	Randall W. Larrimore	314-480-1400	P	1,277	3.6
Remington Arms Company Inc.	PO Box 700	Madison	NC	27025	Paul Cahan	336-548-8700	R	988*	0.2
Alliant Lk Cty Sm Caliber Amm.	MO Hwy. 7 and 78	Independence	MO	64057		816-796-7221	S	747*	3.0
Federal Cartridge Co.	900 Ehlen Dr.	Anoka	MN	55303	Gerald Bersett	763-323-2300	S	100*	1.0
Day and Zimmermann Lone Star	Hwy. 82 W	Texarkana	TX	75505	Hal Yoh	903-334-1210	D	53*	0.4
First Defense International	24843 Del Prado 323	Dana Point	CA	92629		949-366-6444	R	53*	0.4
Capco Inc.	PO Box 1028	Grand Junction	CO	81502		970-243-8750	R	31*	0.2
Hornady Manufacturing Co.	PO Box 1848	Grand Island	NE	68802	Steve Hornady	308-382-1390	R	19*	0.2
Nosler Inc.	PO Box 671	Bend	OR	97709	John Nosler	541-382-3921	R	14*	0.1
Sierra Bullets L.L.C.	PO Box 818	Sedalia	MO	65302		660-827-6300	R	14*	0.1
Crosman Corp.	PO Box 308	East Bloomfield	NY	14443	Ken D'Arcy	585-657-6161	R	12*	0.2
American Ammunition Inc.	3545 NW 71st St.	Miami	FL	33147	Andres F. Fernandez	305-835-7400	P	2	<0.1
HP White Laboratory Inc.	3114 Scarboro Rd.	Street	MD	21154	Donald Dunn	410-838-6550	R	2*	<0.1
Stoneco Inc.	PO Box 765	Trinidad	CO	81082	C. Stonebraker	719-846-2853	R	1*	<0.1

Source: Ward's Business Directory of U.S. Private and Public Companies, Volumes 1 and 2, 2008. The company type code used is as follows: P - Public, R - Private, S - Subsidiary, D - Division, J - Joint Venture, A - Affiliate, G - Group. Sales are in millions of dollars, employees are in thousands. An asterisk (*) indicates an estimated sales volume. The symbol < stands for 'less than'. Company names and addresses are truncated, in some cases, to fit into the available space.

MATERIALS CONSUMED

Material	Quantity	Delivered Cost ($ million)
Metal bolts, nuts, screws, and other screw machine products	(X)	0.3
Other fabricated metal products (exc. castings and forgings)	(X)	61.6
Iron and steel castings (rough and semifinished)	(X)	(D)
Aluminum and aluminum-base alloy castings (rough and semifinished)	(X)	(D)
Other nonferrous metal castings, rough or semifinished (inc. aluminum)	(X)	23.5
Steel shapes and forms (exc. castings, forgings, fabr. metal products)	(X)	11.2
Copper and copper-base alloy shapes and forms (exc. castings, forgings, fabr. metal products)	(X)	48.8
Aluminum and aluminum-base alloy shapes and forms (exc. castings, forgings, fabr. metal products)	(X)	(D)
Other nonferrous shapes and forms (exc. castings, forgings, fabricated metal products)	(X)	13.6
Smokeless powder	(X)	51.7
Plastics resins consumed in the form of granules, pellets, etc.	(X)	15.1
Other chemicals and allied products	(X)	9.9
Rough and dressed lumber	(X)	(D)
Paperboard containers, boxes, and corrugated paperboard	(X)	22.8
Fabricated plastics products (excluding gaskets)	(X)	(D)
Machine tool accessories, including cutting tools	(X)	7.2
Electronic, hydraulic, and mechanical subassemblies	(X)	(D)
All other materials, components, parts, containers, and supplies	(X)	56.8
Materials, ingredients, containers, and supplies, nsk	(X)	17.2

Source: 2002 *Economic Census*. Explanation of symbols used: (D): Withheld to avoid disclosure of competitive data; na: Not available; (S): Withheld because statistical norms were not met; (X): Not applicable; (Z): Less than half the unit shown; nec: Not elsewhere classified; nsk: Not specified by kind; - : zero; p : 10-19 percent estimated; q : 20-29 percent estimated.

PRODUCT SHARE DETAILS

Product or Product Class Shipments	Mil. $	Product or Product Class Shipments	Mil. $
SMALL ARMS AMMUNITION	1,097.5	Small arms ammunition primers (30 mm or less, 1.18 in. or less)	28.0
Rimfire rifle-pistol cartridges	257.4	All other small arms ammunition components	116.9
Centerfire rifle cartridges	135.8	Other small arms ammunition products, including industrial shells and cartridges, air gun ammunition, and percussion caps.	108.9
Centerfire pistols, including cartridges interchangeable between rifles and pistols (30 mm or less, 1.18 in. or less)	182.3		
Shotgun shells	218.1	Small arms ammunition, nsk, total	50.1

Source: 2002 *Economic Census*. The values are product shipments in millions of dollars for 2002. Total product shipments may be lower or higher than industry shipments. See Introduction for a full discussion. Values of indented subcategories are summed in the main heading(s). The symbol (D) appears when data are withheld to prevent disclosure of competitive information. The abbreviation nsk stands for 'not specified by kind' and nec for 'not elsewhere classified'. A dash (-) means zero.

INPUTS AND OUTPUTS FOR AMMUNITION MANUFACTURING

Economic Sector or Industry Providing Inputs	%	Sector	Economic Sector or Industry Buying Outputs	%	Sector
Compensation of employees	34.0		General Federal government services, defense	48.9	Fed Govt
Taxes on production & imports, less subsidies	3.5		Personal consumption expenditures	33.2	
Management of companies & enterprises	3.1	Services	Exports of goods & services	10.8	Cap Inv
Chemical products & preparations, nec	3.0	Manufg.	General S/L govt. services	5.0	S/L Govt
Wholesale trade	2.5	Trade	Change in private inventories	1.3	In House
Copper rolling, drawing, extruding, & alloying	2.3	Manufg.	Ammunition	0.4	Manufg.
Power, distribution, & specialty transformers	2.1	Manufg.	General Federal government services, nondefense	0.3	Fed Govt
Machine shops	1.8	Manufg.			
Nonferrous metal foundries	1.5	Manufg.			
Power generation & supply	1.5	Util.			
Coating, engraving, heat treating & allied activities	1.1	Manufg.			
Paperboard containers	1.1	Manufg.			
Turned products & screws, nuts, & bolts	1.1	Manufg.			
Custom computer programming services	1.0	Services			
Nonferrous metal (ex. copper & aluminum) processing	0.8	Manufg.			
Iron & steel mills & ferroalloys	0.8	Manufg.			
Plastics materials & resins	0.8	Manufg.			
Natural gas distribution	0.7	Util.			
Plastics products, nec	0.7	Manufg.			
Advertising & related services	0.6	Services			
Forging, stamping, & sintering, nec	0.6	Manufg.			
Real estate	0.6	Fin/R.E.			
Cutting tools & machine tool accessories	0.6	Manufg.			
Semiconductors & related devices	0.6	Manufg.			
Metal cans, boxes, & other containers (light gauge)	0.5	Manufg.			
Printed circuit assemblies (electronic assemblies)	0.5	Manufg.			
Truck transportation	0.5	Util.			
Fabricated metals, nec	0.5	Manufg.			
Crowns & closures & metal stamping	0.4	Manufg.			
Securities, commodity contracts, investments	0.4	Fin/R.E.			
Ammunition	0.4	Manufg.			
Valve & fittings other than plumbing	0.4	Manufg.			
Employment services	0.4	Services			
Abrasive products	0.4	Manufg.			
Legal services	0.4	Services			
Ferrous metal foundries	0.3	Manufg.			
Maintenance/repair of nonresidential structures	0.3	Construct.			
Plate work & fabricated structural products	0.3	Manufg.			
Specialized design services	0.3	Services			
Ball & roller bearings	0.3	Manufg.			
Handtools	0.3	Manufg.			
Warehousing & storage	0.3	Util.			
Services to buildings & dwellings	0.3	Services			
Management, scientific, & technical consulting	0.2	Services			
Business support services	0.2	Services			
Custom roll forming	0.2	Manufg.			
Automotive equipment rental & leasing	0.2	Fin/R.E.			
Architectural, engineering, & related services	0.2	Services			
Automotive repair & maintenance, ex. car washes	0.2	Services			
Lessors of nonfinancial assets	0.2	Fin/R.E.			
Alumina refining & primary aluminum production	0.2	Manufg.			
Commercial & industrial equipment repair/maintenance	0.2	Services			
Waste management & remediation services	0.2	Services			
Scientific research & development services	0.2	Services			
Telecommunications	0.2	Services			
Retail trade	0.2	Trade			
Basic organic chemicals, nec	0.1	Manufg.			
Support services, nec	0.1	Services			
Springs & wire products	0.1	Manufg.			
Accounting, tax preparation, bookkeeping, & payroll	0.1	Services			
Data processing, hosting, & related services	0.1	Services			
Investigation & security services	0.1	Services			
Commercial & industrial machinery rental & leasing	0.1	Fin/R.E.			
Paperboard mills	0.1	Manufg.			

Source: Benchmark Input-Output Accounts for the U.S. Economy, 2002, U.S. Department of Commerce, Washington D.C., January 2008. User should note that this Input-Output table is not for this particular narrowly defined industry but for a larger aggregate. Input and Output data for Ammunition Manufacturing include Input and Output data for the Annual Survey of Manufactures' NAICS industries 332992 and 332993. The abbreviation nec stands for 'not elsewhere classified'.

OCCUPATIONS EMPLOYED BY OTHER FABRICATED METAL PRODUCT MANUFACTURING

Occupation	% of Total 2006	Change to 2016	Occupation	% of Total 2006	Change to 2016
Team assemblers	11.0	-11.4	Structural metal fabricators & fitters	1.4	-11.4
Machinists	4.6	-7.0	Mechanical engineers	1.4	-11.4
Welders, cutters, solderers, & brazers	3.9	-5.7	General & operations managers	1.3	-20.3
First-line supervisors/managers of production workers	3.8	-11.4	Executive secretaries & administrative assistants	1.3	-11.4
Cutting, punching, & press machine operators	3.4	-20.3	Coating, painting, & spraying machine operators	1.3	-15.8
Inspectors, testers, sorters, samplers, & weighers	3.0	-16.4	Packers & packagers, hand	1.2	-29.1
Computer-controlled machine tool operators	2.8	-2.5	Customer service representatives	1.2	-2.5
Grinding, lapping, polishing machine tool operators	2.7	-14.0	Drilling & boring machine tool operators	1.2	-20.3
Sales reps, wholesale & manufacturing, exc tech	2.2	-11.4	Industrial machinery mechanics	1.1	1.9
Helpers--Production workers	2.2	-11.4	Assemblers & fabricators, nec	1.1	-20.3
Lathe & turning machine tool operators & tenders	2.0	-20.3	Industrial truck & tractor operators	1.1	-20.3
Laborers & freight, stock, & material movers, hand	2.0	-20.3	Bookkeeping, accounting, & auditing clerks	1.1	-11.4
Shipping, receiving, & traffic clerks	1.9	-14.7	Production, planning, & expediting clerks	1.0	-11.4
Industrial engineers	1.8	7.6	Molding, coremaking, & casting machine operators	1.0	-20.3
Maintenance & repair workers, general	1.7	-11.4	Office clerks, general	1.0	-12.7

Source: Industry-Occupation Matrix, Bureau of Labor Statistics, December 4, 2007. These data are reported based on 4-digit NAICS categories but have been matched to corresponding 6-digit NAICS industry codes. The change reported for each occupation to the year 2016 is a percent of growth or decline as estimated by the Bureau of Labor Statistics. The abbreviation nec stands for 'not elsewhere classified'.

LOCATION BY STATE AND REGIONAL CONCENTRATION

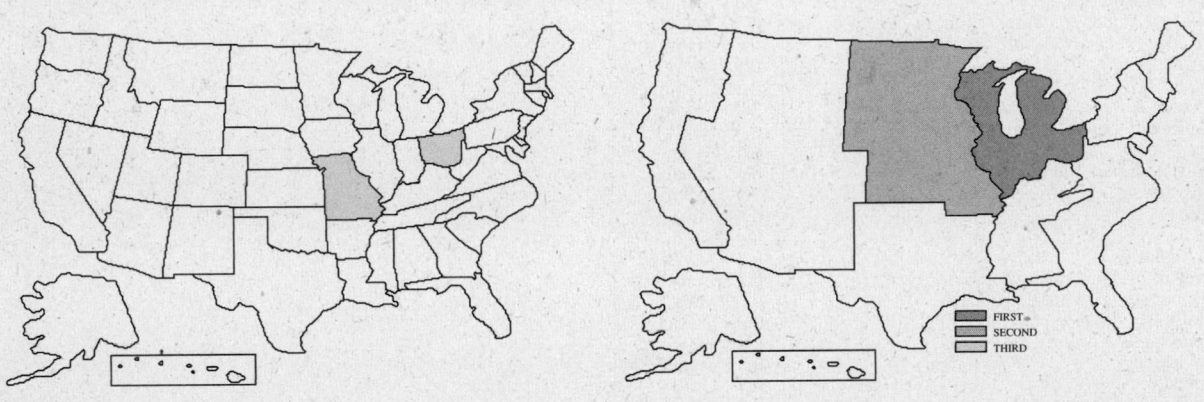

FIRST
SECOND
THIRD

INDUSTRY DATA BY STATE

State	Establish-ments	Shipments			Employment				Cost as % of Shipments	Investment per Employee ($)
		Total ($ mil)	% of U.S.	Per Establ.	Total Number	% of U.S.	Per Establ.	Wages ($/hour)		
Missouri	5	243.1	21.8	48,624.4	1,332	19.5	266	21.05	6.4	646
Ohio	6	10.6	1.0	1,773.8	100	1.5	17	11.50	37.0	1,310

Source: 2002 Economic Census. The states are in descending order of shipments or establishments (if shipment data are missing for the majority). The symbol (D) appears when data are withheld to prevent disclosure of competitive information. States marked with (D) are sorted by number of establishments. A dash (-) indicates that the data element cannot be calculated. Data may not show all states active in the NAICS category. All data available at the time of publication are shown.

NAICS 332993 - AMMUNITION (EXCEPT SMALL ARMS) MANUFACTURING

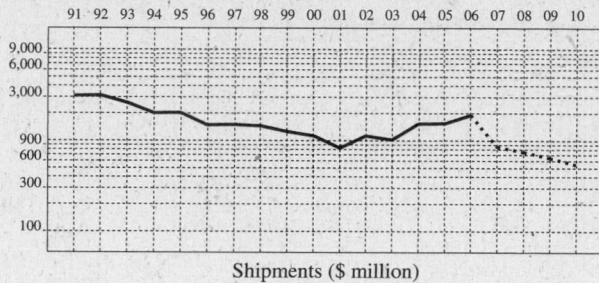

Shipments ($ million)

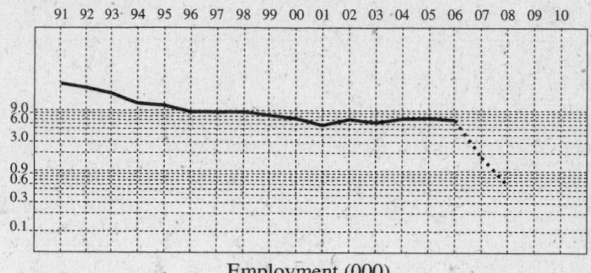

Employment (000)

GENERAL STATISTICS

Year	Com- panies	Establishments		Employment			Compensation		Production ($ million)			
		Total	with 20 or more employees	Total (000)	Production Workers (000)	Hours (Mil)	Payroll ($ mil)	Wages ($/hr)	Cost of Materials	Value Added by Manufacture	Value of Shipments	Capital Invest.
1991		79	62	27.2	14.9	25.9	775.2	13.34	1,121.2	1,870.3	3,102.9	37.2
1992	56	70	53	23.4	13.5	24.0	719.5	12.19	1,224.4	1,889.8	3,136.5	35.2
1993		76	49	18.9	10.7	19.3	556.4	12.79	776.0	1,686.8	2,601.8	21.4
1994		66	47	13.0	7.8	15.2	397.7	12.31	621.6	1,377.1	2,008.2	17.5
1995		63	42	12.0	6.7	13.5	407.5	13.27	800.5	1,138.8	2,024.1	15.5
1996		64	41	9.5	5.0	10.1	336.8	13.24	636.6	789.0	1,480.1	13.1
1997	45	53	31	9.4	5.0	9.0	379.5	15.68	621.0	831.8	1,497.0	28.0
1998		59	34	9.5	4.9	8.7	381.7	15.79	579.1	840.2	1,447.1	29.0
1999		55	34	8.3	4.3	7.7	341.6	15.45	471.8	795.0	1,254.4	26.9
2000		55	32	7.3	3.8	6.6	323.1	16.27	418.1	696.5	1,129.4	28.9
2001		56	26	5.7	3.4	5.7	245.4	16.81	201.0	625.6	829.0	14.7
2002	49	54	25	7.1	3.9	7.1	305.3	17.16	313.1	812.4	1,128.4	26.2
2003		47	24	6.3	3.2	6.4	279.3	16.42	311.2	731.8	1,019.8	15.5
2004		48	24	7.3	4.7	9.4	352.8	18.54	463.8	1,114.3	1,534.3	26.6
2005		45	27	7.5	4.4	8.4	348.4	18.20	435.1	1,026.3	1,545.1	29.3
2006		42P	17P	7.0	4.1	8.1	348.0	18.31	673.7	1,291.5	1,907.0	34.1
2007		40P	14P	1.7P	1.0P	2.4P	207.1P	19.10P	300.9P	576.8P	851.7P	24.9P
2008		38P	12P	0.6P	0.4P	1.3P	183.7P	19.54P	264.5P	507.0P	748.7P	24.9P
2009		36P	9P			0.3P	160.3P	19.98P	228.1P	437.2P	645.6P	24.9P
2010		34P	7P				136.9P	20.42P	191.7P	367.4P	542.5P	24.9P

Sources: 1992, 1997, 2002 *Economic Census*; other years, up to 2006, are from the *Annual Survey of Manufactures*. Establishment counts for non-Census years are from *County Business Patterns*; 1997 and 2002 values are from the 1997 and 2002 censuses respectively, reported in the Federal Government's NAICS format. Other years were originally reported in equivalent SIC format. 'P's show projections by the editors.

INDICES OF CHANGE

Year	Com- panies	Establishments		Employment			Compensation		Production ($ million)			
		Total	with 20 or more employees	Total (000)	Production Workers (000)	Hours (Mil)	Payroll ($ mil)	Wages ($/hr)	Cost of Materials	Value Added by Manufacture	Value of Shipments	Capital Invest.
1992	114	130	212	330	346	338	236	71	391	233	278	134
1997	92	98	124	132	128	127	124	91	198	102	133	107
2001		104	104	80	87	80	80	98	64	77	73	56
2002	100	100	100	100	100	100	100	100	100	100	100	100
2003		87	96	89	82	90	91	96	99	90	90	59
2004		89	96	103	121	132	116	108	148	137	136	102
2005		83	108	106	113	118	114	106	139	126	137	112
2006		78P	68P	99	105	114	114	107	215	159	169	130
2007		74P	58P	24P	26P	34P	68P	111P	96P	71P	75P	95P
2008		70P	48P	8P	10P	18P	60P	114P	84P	62P	66P	95P
2009		66P	38P			4P	53P	116P	73P	54P	57P	95P
2010		62P	28P				45P	119P	61P	45P	48P	95P

Sources: Same as General Statistics. Values reflect change from the base year, 2002. Values above 100 mean greater than 2002, values below 100 mean less than 2002, and the values of 100 in other years means the same as 2002. 'P's show projections by the editors.

SELECTED RATIOS

For 2002	Avg. of All Manufact.	Analyzed Industry	Index	For 2002	Avg. of All Manufact.	Analyzed Industry	Index
Employees per Establishment	42	131	313	Value Added per Production Worker	182,367	208,308	114
Payroll per Establishment	1,639,184	5,653,704	345	Cost per Establishment	5,769,015	5,798,148	101
Payroll per Employee	39,053	43,000	110	Cost per Employee	137,446	44,099	32
Production Workers per Establishment	30	72	245	Cost per Production Worker	195,506	80,282	41
Wages per Establishment	694,845	2,256,222	325	Shipments per Establishment	11,158,348	20,896,296	187
Wages per Production Worker	23,548	31,240	133	Shipments per Employee	265,847	158,930	60
Hours per Production Worker	1,980	1,821	92	Shipments per Production Worker	378,144	289,333	77
Wages per Hour	11.89	17.16	144	Investment per Establishment	361,338	485,185	134
Value Added per Establishment	5,381,325	15,044,444	280	Investment per Employee	8,609	3,690	43
Value Added per Employee	128,210	114,423	89	Investment per Production Worker	12,245	6,718	55

Sources: Same as General Statistics. The 'Average of All Manufacturing' column represents the average of all manufacturing industries reported for the most recent complete year available. The Index shows the relationship between the Average and the Analyzed Industry. For example, 100 means that they are equal; 500 that the Analyzed Industry is five times the average; 50 means that the Analyzed Industry is half the national average. The abbreviation 'na' is used to show that data are 'not available'. Ratios shown for 2002, the last complete census year.

LEADING COMPANIES Number shown: 11   Total sales ($ mil): **3,501**   Total employment (000): **28.5**

Company Name	Address				CEO Name	Phone	Co. Type	Sales ($ mil)	Empl. (000)
Day and Zimmermann Group Inc.	1818 Market St.	Philadelphia	PA	19103	Harold L. Yoh III	215-299-8000	R	1,900	23.0
Olin Corp.	190 Carondelet Plz.	Clayton	MO	63105	Randall W. Larrimore	314-480-1400	P	1,277	3.6
Special Devices Inc.	14370 White Sage	Moorpark	CA	93021	Tom W. Cresante	805-553-1200	R	163*	0.8
First Defense International	24843 Del Prado 323	Dana Point	CA	92629		949-366-6444	R	53*	0.4
Capco Inc.	PO Box 1028	Grand Junction	CO	81502		970-243-8750	R	31*	0.2
DSE Inc.	5201 S Westshore	Tampa	FL	33611	Dae Shin	813-831-0750	R	21*	0.1
Technical Ordnance Inc.	PO Box 800	St Bonifacius	MN	55375	Norman Hoffman	952-446-1526	R	21*	<0.1
Action Manufacturing Company	100 E Erie Ave.	Philadelphia	PA	19134	Arthur Mattia	215-739-6400	R	18*	0.2
Delfasco Inc.	PO Box 725	Greeneville	TN	37744	Philip Kadlecek	423-639-6191	R	15*	0.2
HP White Laboratory Inc.	3114 Scarboro Rd.	Street	MD	21154	Donald Dunn	410-838-6550	R	2*	<0.1
Philip Specialty Co.	3018 E Main St.	Grand Prairie	TX	75050	Philip Dyvig	972-264-5668	R	1*	<0.1

Source: *Ward's Business Directory of U.S. Private and Public Companies*, Volumes 1 and 2, 2008. The company type code used is as follows: P - Public, R - Private, S - Subsidiary, D - Division, J - Joint Venture, A - Affiliate, G - Group. Sales are in millions of dollars, employees are in thousands. An asterisk (*) indicates an estimated sales volume. The symbol < stands for 'less than'. Company names and addresses are truncated, in some cases, to fit into the available space.

MATERIALS CONSUMED

Material	Quantity	Delivered Cost ($ million)
Metal bolts, nuts, screws, and other screw machine products	(X)	(D)
Other fabricated metal products (exc. castings and forgings)	(X)	86.6
Iron and steel castings (rough and semifinished)	(X)	8.7
Aluminum and aluminum-base alloy castings (rough and semifinished)	(X)	4.0
Other nonferrous metal castings, rough or semifinished (inc. aluminum)	(X)	3.0
Iron and steel forgings	(X)	13.9
Steel shapes and forms (exc. castings, forgings, fabr. metal products)	(X)	9.4
Copper and copper-base alloy shapes and forms (exc. castings, forgings, fabr. metal products)	(X)	(D)
Aluminum and aluminum-base alloy shapes and forms (exc. castings, forgings, fabr. metal products)	(X)	3.3
Other nonferrous shapes and forms (exc. castings, forgings, fabricated metal products)	(X)	(D)
Smokeless powder	(X)	(D)
Other chemicals and allied products	(X)	(D)
Rough and dressed lumber	(X)	(D)
Paperboard containers, boxes, and corrugated paperboard	(X)	1.0
Fabricated plastics products (excluding gaskets)	(X)	2.6
Machine tool accessories, including cutting tools	(X)	6.3
Electronic, hydraulic, and mechanical subassemblies	(X)	40.8
All other materials, components, parts, containers, and supplies	(X)	36.4
Materials, ingredients, containers, and supplies, nsk	(X)	6.8

Source: 2002 *Economic Census*. Explanation of symbols used: (D): Withheld to avoid disclosure of competitive data; na: Not available; (S): Withheld because statistical norms were not met; (X): Not applicable; (Z): Less than half the unit shown; nec: Not elsewhere classified; nsk: Not specified by kind; - : zero; p : 10-19 percent estimated; q : 20-29 percent estimated.

PRODUCT SHARE DETAILS

Product or Product Class Shipments	Mil. $	Product or Product Class Shipments	Mil. $
AMMUNITION (EXCEPT SMALL ARMS)	780.8	primers, fuses, boosters, and nonsteel cases (more than 30 mm, more than 1.18 in.)	158.0
Artillery ammunition (more than 30 mm, more than 1.18 in.)	**387.1**	Receipts for artillery ammunition loading and assembly	(D)
Artillery ammunition	385.8	Artillery ammunition (more than 30 mm, more than 1.18 in.), nsk	1.3
Complete artillery rounds, loaded (more than 30 mm, more than 1.18 in.)	(D)	**Ammunition (except for small arms), nec**	**388.4**
Artillery ammunition steel cases only (more than 30 mm, more than 1.18 in.)	29.1	Bombs, depth charges, mines, torpedoes, etc., and parts	279.5
Artillery ammunition projectile metal parts (more than 30 mm, more than 1.18 in.)	2.3	Rockets (other than guided missiles) and parts	107.9
		Ammunition (except for small arms), nec, nsk	0.9
Other artillery ammunition components, including		**Ammunition (except small arms), nsk, total**	**5.4**

Source: 2002 *Economic Census*. The values are product shipments in millions of dollars for 2002. Total product shipments may be lower or higher than industry shipments. See Introduction for a full discussion. Values of indented subcategories are summed in the main heading(s). The symbol (D) appears when data are withheld to prevent disclosure of competitive information. The abbreviation nsk stands for 'not specified by kind' and nec for 'not elsewhere classified'. A dash (-) means zero.

INPUTS AND OUTPUTS FOR AMMUNITION MANUFACTURING

Economic Sector or Industry Providing Inputs	%	Sector	Economic Sector or Industry Buying Outputs	%	Sector
Compensation of employees	34.0		General Federal government services, defense	48.9	Fed Govt
Taxes on production & imports, less subsidies	3.5		Personal consumption expenditures	33.2	
Management of companies & enterprises	3.1	Services	Exports of goods & services	10.8	Cap Inv
Chemical products & preparations, nec	3.0	Manufg.	General S/L govt. services	5.0	S/L Govt
Wholesale trade	2.5	Trade	Change in private inventories	1.3	In House
Copper rolling, drawing, extruding, & alloying	2.3	Manufg.	Ammunition	0.4	Manufg.
Power, distribution, & specialty transformers	2.1	Manufg.	General Federal government services, nondefense	0.3	Fed Govt
Machine shops	1.8	Manufg.			
Nonferrous metal foundries	1.5	Manufg.			
Power generation & supply	1.5	Util.			
Coating, engraving, heat treating & allied activities	1.1	Manufg.			
Paperboard containers	1.1	Manufg.			
Turned products & screws, nuts, & bolts	1.1	Manufg.			
Custom computer programming services	1.0	Services			
Nonferrous metal (ex. copper & aluminum) processing	0.8	Manufg.			
Iron & steel mills & ferroalloys	0.8	Manufg.			
Plastics materials & resins	0.8	Manufg.			
Natural gas distribution	0.7	Util.			
Plastics products, nec	0.7	Manufg.			
Advertising & related services	0.6	Services			
Forging, stamping, & sintering, nec	0.6	Manufg.			
Real estate	0.6	Fin/R.E.			
Cutting tools & machine tool accessories	0.6	Manufg.			
Semiconductors & related devices	0.6	Manufg.			
Metal cans, boxes, & other containers (light gauge)	0.5	Manufg.			
Printed circuit assemblies (electronic assemblies)	0.5	Manufg.			
Truck transportation	0.5	Util.			
Fabricated metals, nec	0.5	Manufg.			
Crowns & closures & metal stamping	0.4	Manufg.			
Securities, commodity contracts, investments	0.4	Fin/R.E.			
Ammunition	0.4	Manufg.			
Valve & fittings other than plumbing	0.4	Manufg.			
Employment services	0.4	Services			
Abrasive products	0.4	Manufg.			
Legal services	0.4	Services			
Ferrous metal foundries	0.3	Manufg.			
Maintenance/repair of nonresidential structures	0.3	Construct.			
Plate work & fabricated structural products	0.3	Manufg.			
Specialized design services	0.3	Services			
Ball & roller bearings	0.3	Manufg.			
Handtools	0.3	Manufg.			
Warehousing & storage	0.3	Util.			
Services to buildings & dwellings	0.3	Services			
Management, scientific, & technical consulting	0.2	Services			
Business support services	0.2	Services			
Custom roll forming	0.2	Manufg.			
Automotive equipment rental & leasing	0.2	Fin/R.E.			
Architectural, engineering, & related services	0.2	Services			
Automotive repair & maintenance, ex. car washes	0.2	Services			
Lessors of nonfinancial assets	0.2	Fin/R.E.			
Alumina refining & primary aluminum production	0.2	Manufg.			
Commercial & industrial equipment repair/maintenance	0.2	Services			
Waste management & remediation services	0.2	Services			
Scientific research & development services	0.2	Services			
Telecommunications	0.2	Services			
Retail trade	0.2	Trade			
Basic organic chemicals, nec	0.1	Manufg.			
Support services, nec	0.1	Services			
Springs & wire products	0.1	Manufg.			
Accounting, tax preparation, bookkeeping, & payroll	0.1	Services			
Data processing, hosting, & related services	0.1	Services			
Investigation & security services	0.1	Services			
Commercial & industrial machinery rental & leasing	0.1	Fin/R.E.			
Paperboard mills	0.1	Manufg.			

Source: Benchmark Input-Output Accounts for the U.S. Economy, 2002, U.S. Department of Commerce, Washington D.C., January 2008. User should note that this Input-Output table is not for this particular narrowly defined industry but for a larger aggregate. Input and Output data for Ammunition Manufacturing include Input and Output data for the Annual Survey of Manufactures' NAICS industries 332992 and 332993. The abbreviation nec stands for 'not elsewhere classified'.

OCCUPATIONS EMPLOYED BY OTHER FABRICATED METAL PRODUCT MANUFACTURING

Occupation	% of Total 2006	Change to 2016	Occupation	% of Total 2006	Change to 2016
Team assemblers	11.0	-11.4	Structural metal fabricators & fitters	1.4	-11.4
Machinists	4.6	-7.0	Mechanical engineers	1.4	-11.4
Welders, cutters, solderers, & brazers	3.9	-5.7	General & operations managers	1.3	-20.3
First-line supervisors/managers of production workers	3.8	-11.4	Executive secretaries & administrative assistants	1.3	-11.4
Cutting, punching, & press machine operators	3.4	-20.3	Coating, painting, & spraying machine operators	1.3	-15.8
Inspectors, testers, sorters, samplers, & weighers	3.0	-16.4	Packers & packagers, hand	1.2	-29.1
Computer-controlled machine tool operators	2.8	-2.5	Customer service representatives	1.2	-2.5
Grinding, lapping, polishing machine tool operators	2.7	-14.0	Drilling & boring machine tool operators	1.2	-20.3
Sales reps, wholesale & manufacturing, exc tech	2.2	-11.4	Industrial machinery mechanics	1.1	1.9
Helpers--Production workers	2.2	-11.4	Assemblers & fabricators, nec	1.1	-20.3
Lathe & turning machine tool operators & tenders	2.0	-20.3	Industrial truck & tractor operators	1.1	-20.3
Laborers & freight, stock, & material movers, hand	2.0	-20.3	Bookkeeping, accounting, & auditing clerks	1.1	-11.4
Shipping, receiving, & traffic clerks	1.9	-14.7	Production, planning, & expediting clerks	1.0	-11.4
Industrial engineers	1.8	7.6	Molding, coremaking, & casting machine operators	1.0	-20.3
Maintenance & repair workers, general	1.7	-11.4	Office clerks, general	1.0	-12.7

Source: *Industry-Occupation Matrix*, Bureau of Labor Statistics, December 4, 2007. These data are reported based on 4-digit NAICS categories but have been matched to corresponding 6-digit NAICS industry codes. The change reported for each occupation to the year 2016 is a percent of growth or decline as estimated by the Bureau of Labor Statistics. The abbreviation nec stands for 'not elsewhere classified'.

INDUSTRY DATA BY STATE

State-level data are not available.

NAICS 332994 - SMALL ARMS MANUFACTURING

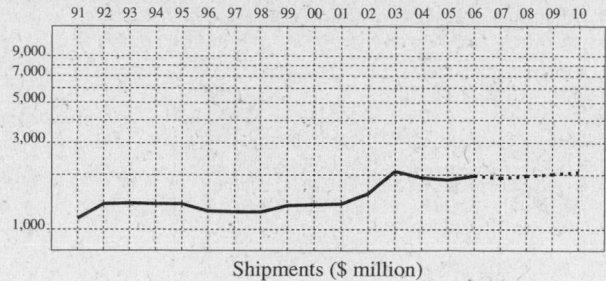

Shipments ($ million)

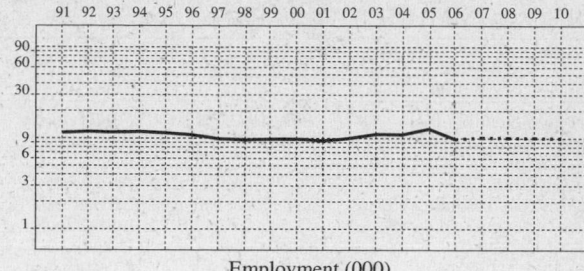

Employment (000)

GENERAL STATISTICS

Year	Com-panies	Establishments		Employment			Compensation		Production ($ million)			
		Total	with 20 or more employees	Total (000)	Production Workers (000)	Hours (Mil)	Payroll ($ mil)	Wages ($/hr)	Cost of Materials	Value Added by Manufacture	Value of Shipments	Capital Invest.
1991		137	48	11.5	8.5	16.4	321.1	13.39	389.1	745.9	1,148.5	26.5
1992	177	184	60	11.8	9.2	18.1	334.9	12.78	401.1	939.8	1,384.0	32.0
1993		188	59	11.6	9.2	19.2	342.1	12.70	401.9	973.5	1,396.2	93.6
1994		197	63	11.8	9.1	19.3	358.4	13.04	383.3	987.9	1,384.1	33.5
1995		187	64	11.4	9.0	17.8	350.5	13.75	390.4	1,020.6	1,385.8	34.4
1996		199	54	10.9	8.5	15.9	332.9	14.64	355.9	920.2	1,265.0	31.0
1997	191	198	55	9.9	7.5	14.0	320.6	14.32	354.8	879.9	1,251.8	32.6
1998		211	58	9.6	7.2	14.0	321.0	14.12	395.6	855.2	1,249.5	33.3
1999		220	58	9.8	7.4	13.9	325.4	14.58	423.0	925.9	1,356.3	25.9
2000		218	60	9.8	7.3	13.7	332.0	15.20	445.6	956.1	1,371.3	34.2
2001		213	56	9.4	6.9	13.1	314.1	14.72	421.6	975.7	1,384.6	21.7
2002	177	184	56	10.0	7.6	15.3	399.1	15.65	446.4	1,115.6	1,574.2	49.1
2003		189	59	11.1	8.2	16.1	439.3	15.64	595.8	1,414.7	2,093.9	46.9
2004		193	61	11.0	8.0	16.8	479.2	16.18	604.6	1,340.2	1,931.2	38.1
2005		194	59	12.7	8.7	17.6	523.0	16.48	640.7	1,252.1	1,877.6	39.9
2006		210P	59P	9.8	7.2	14.6	419.1	17.22	695.9	1,280.1	1,973.4	82.1
2007		212P	60P	10.2P	7.3P	14.5P	450.0P	16.95P	677.0P	1,245.3P	1,919.8P	47.2P
2008		214P	60P	10.1P	7.2P	14.3P	459.5P	17.22P	694.3P	1,277.2P	1,969.0P	47.9P
2009		215P	60P	10.1P	7.1P	14.1P	468.9P	17.49P	711.7P	1,309.1P	2,018.2P	48.7P
2010		217P	60P	10.0P	7.0P	13.9P	478.4P	17.76P	729.0P	1,341.0P	2,067.3P	49.4P

Sources: 1992, 1997, 2002 *Economic Census*; other years, up to 2006, are from the *Annual Survey of Manufactures*. Establishment counts for non-Census years are from *County Business Patterns*; 1997 and 2002 values are from the 1997 and 2002 censuses respectively, reported in the Federal Government's NAICS format. Other years were originally reported in equivalent SIC format. 'P's show projections by the editors.

INDICES OF CHANGE

Year	Com-panies	Establishments		Employment			Compensation		Production ($ million)			
		Total	with 20 or more employees	Total (000)	Production Workers (000)	Hours (Mil)	Payroll ($ mil)	Wages ($/hr)	Cost of Materials	Value Added by Manufacture	Value of Shipments	Capital Invest.
1992	100	100	107	118	121	118	84	82	90	84	88	65
1997	108	108	98	99	99	92	80	92	79	79	80	66
2001		116	100	94	91	86	79	94	94	87	88	44
2002	100	100	100	100	100	100	100	100	100	100	100	100
2003		103	105	111	108	105	110	100	133	127	133	96
2004		105	109	110	105	110	120	103	135	120	123	78
2005		105	105	127	114	115	131	105	144	112	119	81
2006		114P	106P	98	95	95	105	110	156	115	125	167
2007		115P	106P	102P	96P	95P	113P	108P	152P	112P	122P	96P
2008		116P	106P	101P	95P	93P	115P	110P	156P	114P	125P	98P
2009		117P	107P	101P	93P	92P	117P	112P	159P	117P	128P	99P
2010		118P	107P	100P	92P	91P	120P	113P	163P	120P	131P	101P

Sources: Same as General Statistics. Values reflect change from the base year, 2002. Values above 100 mean greater than 2002, values below 100 mean less than 2002, and the values of 100 in other years means the same as 2002. 'P's show projections by the editors.

SELECTED RATIOS

For 2002	Avg. of All Manufact.	Analyzed Industry	Index	For 2002	Avg. of All Manufact.	Analyzed Industry	Index
Employees per Establishment	42	54	129	Value Added per Production Worker	182,367	146,789	80
Payroll per Establishment	1,639,184	2,169,022	132	Cost per Establishment	5,769,015	2,426,087	42
Payroll per Employee	39,053	39,910	102	Cost per Employee	137,446	44,640	32
Production Workers per Establishment	30	41	140	Cost per Production Worker	195,506	58,737	30
Wages per Establishment	694,845	1,301,332	187	Shipments per Establishment	11,158,348	8,555,435	77
Wages per Production Worker	23,548	31,506	134	Shipments per Employee	265,847	157,420	59
Hours per Production Worker	1,980	2,013	102	Shipments per Production Worker	378,144	207,132	55
Wages per Hour	11.89	15.65	132	Investment per Establishment	361,338	266,848	74
Value Added per Establishment	5,381,325	6,063,043	113	Investment per Employee	8,609	4,910	57
Value Added per Employee	128,210	111,560	87	Investment per Production Worker	12,245	6,461	53

Sources: Same as General Statistics. The 'Average of All Manufacturing' column represents the average of all manufacturing industries reported for the most recent complete year available. The Index shows the relationship between the Average and the Analyzed Industry. For example, 100 means that they are equal; 500 that the Analyzed Industry is five times the average; 50 means that the Analyzed Industry is half the national average. The abbreviation 'na' is used to show that data are 'not available'. Ratios shown for 2002, the last complete census year.

LEADING COMPANIES   Number shown: **28**   Total sales ($ mil): **6,082**   Total employment (000): **12.1**

Company Name	Address				CEO Name	Phone	Co. Type	Sales ($ mil)	Empl. (000)
Modern Muzzleloading Inc.	21822 Hwy. J46	Centerville	IA	52544		641-856-2626	R	2,100*	<0.1
EBSCO Industries Inc.	PO Box 1943	Birmingham	AL	35201	Dixon Brooke Jr.	205-991-6600	R	1,400*	5.0
Remington Arms Company Inc.	PO Box 700	Madison	NC	27025	Paul Cahan	336-548-8700	R	988*	0.2
Beretta USA Corp.	17601 Beretta Dr.	Accokeek	MD	20607	Ugo Beretta	301-283-2191	R	633*	0.3
Smith and Wesson Holding Corp.	2100 Roosevelt Ave.	Springfield	MA	01104	Michael F. Golden	413-781-8300	P	235	1.5
Smith and Wesson Corp.	PO Box 2208	Springfield	MA	01102	Michael F. Golden		S	133*	1.0
Michaels of Oregon Co.	PO Box 1690	Oregon City	OR	97045		503-655-7964	S	111*	0.3
O.F. Mossberg and Sons Inc.	PO Box 497	North Haven	CT	06473	A. Iver Mossberg	203-230-5300	R	70*	0.8
Colt Defense Inc.	PO Box 118	Hartford	CT	06141	William M. Keyes	860-232-4489	R	69*	0.3
Colt's Manufacturing Company	PO Box 1868	Hartford	CT	06144	William Keys	860-236-6311	R	53*	0.5
First Defense International	24843 Del Prado 323	Dana Point	CA	92629		949-366-6444	R	53*	0.4
FN Manufacturing L.L.C.	PO Box 24257	Columbia	SC	29224	J-L Vanderstraeten	803-736-0522	R	51*	0.4
Marlin Firearms Co.	PO Box 248	North Haven	CT	06473	Robert Behn	203-239-5621	R	51*	0.4
Benjamin Sheridan Corp.	PO Box 308	E Bloomfield	NY	14443	Ken D'Arcy	585-657-6161	S	29*	0.3
Savage Arms Inc.	100 Springdale Rd.	Westfield	MA	01085	Ronald Coburn	413-568-7001	R	25*	0.2
Springfield Inc.	420 W Main St.	Geneseo	IL	61254	Dennis Reese	309-944-5631	R	17*	0.1
Crosman Corp.	PO Box 308	East Bloomfield	NY	14443	Ken D'Arcy	585-657-6161	R	12*	0.2
Glock Inc.	PO Box 369	Smyrna	GA	30081	Gaston Glock	770-432-1202	R	11*	<0.1
Weatherby Inc.	1605 Commerce	Paso Robles	CA	93446	Roy E. Weatherby Jr.	805-227-2600	R	8*	<0.1
Daisy Manufacturing Company	400 W Stribling Dr.	Rogers	AR	72756	Ray Hobbs	479-636-1200	R	8*	<0.1
Choate Machine and Tool Co.	PO Box 218	Bald Knob	AR	72010	Garth Choate	501-724-6193	R	5*	<0.1
KW Thompson Tool Company Inc.	PO Box 5002	Rochester	NH	03866	Gregg Ritz	603-332-2333	R	4*	<0.1
Burris Company Inc.	PO Box 1899	Greeley	CO	80632	John McCarty	970-356-1670	R	4*	<0.1
United States Fire Arms Mfg.	445 Ledyard St.	Hartford	CT	06114	Douglas Donnelly	860-724-1152	R	3*	<0.1
Aerospace America Inc.	PO Box 189	Bay City	MI	48707	Arthur Dore	989-684-2121	R	3*	<0.1
Redding Hunter Inc.	1089 Starr Rd.	Cortland	NY	13045	Richard Beebe	607-753-3331	R	3*	<0.1
HP White Laboratory Inc.	3114 Scarboro Rd.	Street	MD	21154	Donald Dunn	410-838-6550	R	2*	<0.1
Ransom International Corp.	PO Box 3845	Prescott	AZ	86302		928-778-7899	R	1*	<0.1

Source: *Ward's Business Directory of U.S. Private and Public Companies*, Volumes 1 and 2, 2008. The company type code used is as follows: P - Public, R - Private, S - Subsidiary, D - Division, J - Joint Venture, A - Affiliate, G - Group. Sales are in millions of dollars, employees are in thousands. An asterisk (*) indicates an estimated sales volume. The symbol < stands for 'less than'. Company names and addresses are truncated, in some cases, to fit into the available space.

MATERIALS CONSUMED

Material	Quantity	Delivered Cost ($ million)
Metal bolts, nuts, screws, and other screw machine products	(X)	12.6
Other fabricated metal products (exc. castings and forgings)	(X)	75.3
Iron and steel castings (rough and semifinished)	(X)	34.1
Aluminum and aluminum-base alloy castings (rough and semifinished)	(X)	6.2
Other nonferrous metal castings, rough or semifinished (inc. aluminum)	(X)	6.5
Iron and steel forgings	(X)	13.8
Steel shapes and forms (exc. castings, forgings, fabr. metal products)	(X)	47.0
Copper and copper-base alloy shapes and forms (exc. castings, forgings, fabr. metal products)	(X)	(D)
Aluminum and aluminum-base alloy shapes and forms (exc. castings, forgings, fabr. metal products)	(X)	3.9
Other nonferrous shapes and forms (exc. castings, forgings, fabricated metal products)	(X)	(D)
Smokeless powder	(X)	<0.1
Plastics resins consumed in the form of granules, pellets, etc.	(X)	0.2
Other chemicals and allied products	(X)	1.0
Rough and dressed lumber	(X)	12.2
Paperboard containers, boxes, and corrugated paperboard	(X)	7.7
Fabricated plastics products (excluding gaskets)	(X)	15.1
Machine tool accessories, including cutting tools	(X)	10.2
Electronic, hydraulic, and mechanical subassemblies	(X)	(D)
All other materials, components, parts, containers, and supplies	(X)	44.7
Materials, ingredients, containers, and supplies, nsk	(X)	26.6

Source: 2002 *Economic Census*. Explanation of symbols used: (D): Withheld to avoid disclosure of competitive data; na: Not available; (S): Withheld because statistical norms were not met; (X): Not applicable; (Z): Less than half the unit shown; nec: Not elsewhere classified; nsk: Not specified by kind; - : zero; p : 10-19 percent estimated; q : 20-29 percent estimated.

PRODUCT SHARE DETAILS

Product or Product Class Shipments	Mil. $	Product or Product Class Shipments	Mil. $
SMALL ARMS	1,532.7	Rimfire rifles	33.6
Machine guns (30 mm or less, 1.18 in. or less)	**(D)**	Single barrel shotguns and other small firearms, including	
Small arms (30 mm or less, 1.18 in. or less)	**(D)**	parts and attachments for small firearms	517.1
Centerfire pistols and revolvers	201.8	Single barrel shotguns	187.3
All other centerfire pistols and revolvers	(D)	Other small firearms (including double barrel shotguns,	
Rimfire pistols and revolvers	(D)	combination rifle-shotguns, and tranquilizer guns) . . .	179.9
Rifles	421.2	Parts and attachments for small firearms	149.9
Centerfire semiautomatic rifles	100.6	Small arms (30 mm or less, 1.18 in. or less), nsk	0.1
Centerfire bolt repeater rifles	148.9	**Small arms, nsk, total**	**66.6**
All other centerfire rifles	138.2		

Source: 2002 *Economic Census*. The values are product shipments in millions of dollars for 2002. Total product shipments may be lower or higher than industry shipments. See Introduction for a full discussion. Values of indented subcategories are summed in the main heading(s). The symbol (D) appears when data are withheld to prevent disclosure of competitive information. The abbreviation nsk stands for 'not specified by kind' and nec for 'not elsewhere classified'. A dash (-) means zero.

INPUTS AND OUTPUTS FOR ARMS, ORDNANCE, AND ACCESSORIES MANUFACTURING

Economic Sector or Industry Providing Inputs	%	Sector	Economic Sector or Industry Buying Outputs	%	Sector
Compensation of employees	31.2		Personal consumption expenditures	42.3	
Taxes on production & imports, less subsidies	4.9		Federal government, investment, national defense	29.2	Fed Govt
Management of companies & enterprises	3.0	Services	General Federal government services, defense	13.8	Fed Govt
Wholesale trade	2.7	Trade	Exports of goods & services	10.4	Cap Inv
Power, distribution, & specialty transformers	1.8	Manufg.	Personal & household goods repair/maintenance	2.5	Services
Machine shops	1.8	Manufg.	General S/L govt. services	0.7	S/L Govt
Custom computer programming services	1.8	Services	Arms, ordnance, & accessories	0.4	Manufg.
Iron & steel mills & ferroalloys	1.7	Manufg.	Investigation & security services	0.3	Services
Forging, stamping, & sintering, nec	1.6	Manufg.	General Federal government services, nondefense	0.1	Fed Govt
Sawmills & wood preservation	1.5	Manufg.			
Turned products & screws, nuts, & bolts	1.4	Manufg.			
Alumina refining & primary aluminum production	1.3	Manufg.			
Advertising & related services	1.2	Services			
Ferrous metal foundries	1.2	Manufg.			
Coating, engraving, heat treating & allied activities	1.2	Manufg.			
Copper rolling, drawing, extruding, & alloying	1.1	Manufg.			
Chemical products & preparations, nec	1.1	Manufg.			
Power generation & supply	0.8	Util.			
Real estate	0.6	Fin/R.E.			
Plastics products, nec	0.6	Manufg.			
Truck transportation	0.6	Util.			
Nonferrous metal foundries	0.6	Manufg.			
Metal cans, boxes, & other containers (light gauge)	0.5	Manufg.			
Arms, ordnance, & accessories	0.5	Manufg.			
Securities, commodity contracts, investments	0.5	Fin/R.E.			
Specialized design services	0.5	Services			
Semiconductors & related devices	0.5	Manufg.			
Legal services	0.5	Services			
Printed circuit assemblies (electronic assemblies)	0.5	Manufg.			
Employment services	0.5	Services			
Fabricated metals, nec	0.5	Manufg.			
Management, scientific, & technical consulting	0.4	Services			
Crowns & closures & metal stamping	0.4	Manufg.			
Cutting tools & machine tool accessories	0.4	Manufg.			
Nonferrous metal (ex. copper & aluminum) processing	0.4	Manufg.			
Valve & fittings other than plumbing	0.4	Manufg.			
Business support services	0.4	Services			
Plate work & fabricated structural products	0.4	Manufg.			
Architectural, engineering, & related services	0.3	Services			
Paperboard containers	0.3	Manufg.			
Ball & roller bearings	0.3	Manufg.			
Handtools	0.3	Manufg.			
Lessors of nonfinancial assets	0.3	Fin/R.E.			
Natural gas distribution	0.3	Util.			
Warehousing & storage	0.3	Util.			
Abrasive products	0.3	Manufg.			
Data processing, hosting, & related services	0.2	Services			
Support services, nec	0.2	Services			
Custom roll forming	0.2	Manufg.			
Telecommunications	0.2	Services			
Other computer related services, including facilities	0.2	Services			
Automotive equipment rental & leasing	0.2	Fin/R.E.			
Monetary authorities/depository credit intermediation	0.2	Fin/R.E.			
Accounting, tax preparation, bookkeeping, & payroll	0.2	Services			
Investigation & security services	0.2	Services			
Professional, scientific, technical services, nec	0.2	Services			
Maintenance/repair of nonresidential structures	0.2	Construct.			
Scientific research & development services	0.2	Services			
Services to buildings & dwellings	0.2	Services			

Continued on next page.

INPUTS AND OUTPUTS FOR ARMS, ORDNANCE, AND ACCESSORIES MANUFACTURING - Continued

Economic Sector or Industry Providing Inputs	%	Sector	Economic Sector or Industry Buying Outputs	%	Sector
Springs & wire products	0.2	Manufg.			
Computer system design services	0.1	Services			
Food services & drinking places	0.1	Services			
Automotive repair & maintenance, ex. car washes	0.1	Services			
Commercial & industrial machinery rental & leasing	0.1	Fin/R.E.			

Source: Benchmark Input-Output Accounts for the U.S. Economy, 2002, U.S. Department of Commerce, Washington D.C., January 2008. User should note that this Input-Output table is not for this particular narrowly defined industry but for a larger aggregate. Input and Output data for Arms, Ordnance, and Accessories Manufacturing include Input and Output data for the Annual Survey of Manufactures' NAICS industries 332994 and 332995. The abbreviation nec stands for 'not elsewhere classified'.

OCCUPATIONS EMPLOYED BY OTHER FABRICATED METAL PRODUCT MANUFACTURING

Occupation	% of Total 2006	Change to 2016	Occupation	% of Total 2006	Change to 2016
Team assemblers	11.0	-11.4	Structural metal fabricators & fitters	1.4	-11.4
Machinists	4.6	-7.0	Mechanical engineers	1.4	-11.4
Welders, cutters, solderers, & brazers	3.9	-5.7	General & operations managers	1.3	-20.3
First-line supervisors/managers of production workers	3.8	-11.4	Executive secretaries & administrative assistants	1.3	-11.4
Cutting, punching, & press machine operators	3.4	-20.3	Coating, painting, & spraying machine operators	1.3	-15.8
Inspectors, testers, sorters, samplers, & weighers	3.0	-16.4	Packers & packagers, hand	1.2	-29.1
Computer-controlled machine tool operators	2.8	-2.5	Customer service representatives	1.2	-2.5
Grinding, lapping, polishing machine tool operators	2.7	-14.0	Drilling & boring machine tool operators	1.2	-20.3
Sales reps, wholesale & manufacturing, exc tech	2.2	-11.4	Industrial machinery mechanics	1.1	1.9
Helpers--Production workers	2.2	-11.4	Assemblers & fabricators, nec	1.1	-20.3
Lathe & turning machine tool operators & tenders	2.0	-20.3	Industrial truck & tractor operators	1.1	-20.3
Laborers & freight, stock, & material movers, hand	2.0	-20.3	Bookkeeping, accounting, & auditing clerks	1.1	-11.4
Shipping, receiving, & traffic clerks	1.9	-14.7	Production, planning, & expediting clerks	1.0	-11.4
Industrial engineers	1.8	7.6	Molding, coremaking, & casting machine operators	1.0	-20.3
Maintenance & repair workers, general	1.7	-11.4	Office clerks, general	1.0	-12.7

Source: Industry-Occupation Matrix, Bureau of Labor Statistics, December 4, 2007. These data are reported based on 4-digit NAICS categories but have been matched to corresponding 6-digit NAICS industry codes. The change reported for each occupation to the year 2016 is a percent of growth or decline as estimated by the Bureau of Labor Statistics. The abbreviation nec stands for 'not elsewhere classified'.

LOCATION BY STATE AND REGIONAL CONCENTRATION

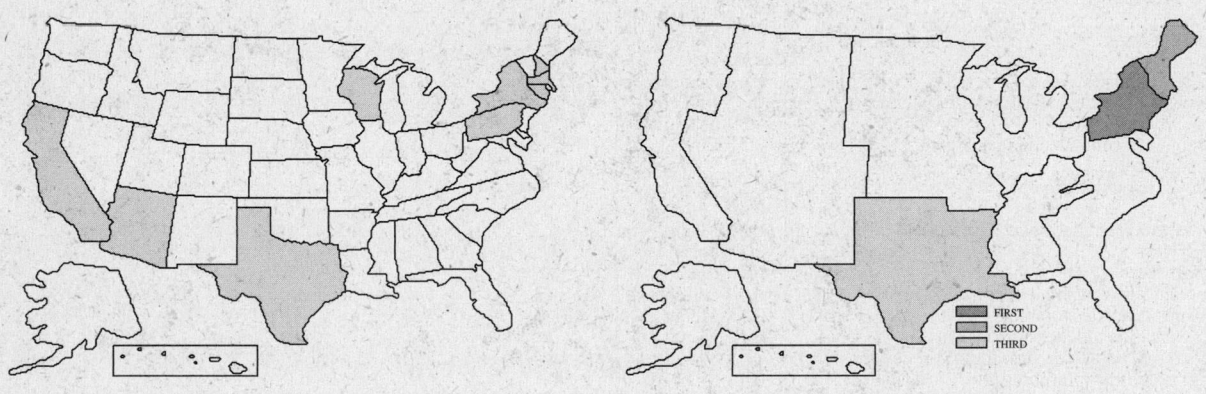

INDUSTRY DATA BY STATE

State	Establish-ments	Shipments			Employment				Cost as % of Shipments	Investment per Employee ($)
		Total ($ mil)	% of U.S.	Per Establ.	Total Number	% of U.S.	Per Establ.	Wages ($/hour)		
New York	7	245.5	15.6	35,069.6	1,424	14.3	203	17.87	23.7	2,804
New Hampshire	4	218.3	13.9	54,581.0	1,446	14.5	362	16.15	26.1	2,748
Connecticut	10	202.4	12.9	20,236.6	1,365	13.7	136	17.13	37.3	4,919
Massachusetts	4	127.5	8.1	31,871.0	1,077	10.8	269	15.52	38.3	5,305
Arizona	8	52.2	3.3	6,526.0	320	3.2	40	14.87	27.2	1,772
Texas	16	34.1	2.2	2,132.4	245	2.5	15	16.04	26.7	3,037
California	12	29.3	1.9	2,442.2	294	2.9	25	11.95	30.1	912
Pennsylvania	12	15.6	1.0	1,296.7	234	2.3	20	11.94	22.0	2,744
Wisconsin	8	11.8	0.7	1,470.1	117	1.2	15	10.60	23.8	2,803

Source: 2002 Economic Census. The states are in descending order of shipments or establishments (if shipment data are missing for the majority). The symbol (D) appears when data are withheld to prevent disclosure of competitive information. States marked with (D) are sorted by number of establishments. A dash (-) indicates that the data element cannot be calculated. Data may not show all states active in the NAICS category. All data available at the time of publication are shown.

NAICS 332995 - ORDNANCE AND ACCESSORIES MANUFACTURING NEC

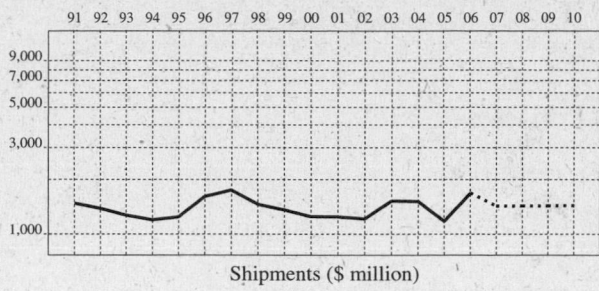

Shipments ($ million)

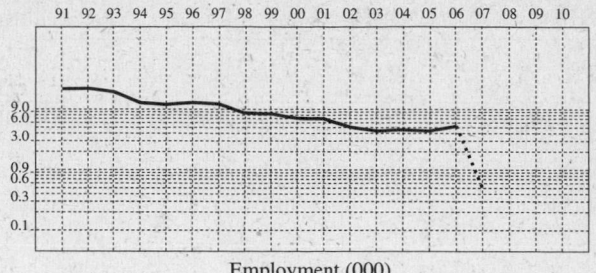

Employment (000)

GENERAL STATISTICS

Year	Com-panies	Establishments		Employment			Compensation		Production ($ million)			
		Total	with 20 or more employees	Total (000)	Production Workers (000)	Hours (Mil)	Payroll ($ mil)	Wages ($/hr)	Cost of Materials	Value Added by Manufacture	Value of Shipments	Capital Invest.
1991		61	33	21.5	9.3	19.1	858.6	16.45	196.3	1,241.5	1,480.2	13.2
1992	71	72	33	22.0	9.0	17.0	937.7	19.37	224.4	1,145.5	1,386.1	19.4
1993		67	29	19.3	8.5	16.4	882.8	19.33	356.5	873.8	1,272.0	25.5
1994		67	30	12.8	5.3	10.3	541.0	18.05	204.9	1,000.1	1,199.7	9.3
1995		63	26	12.0	4.9	10.0	521.6	18.40	198.1	1,089.1	1,244.2	12.3
1996		63	22	12.9	5.4	9.5	565.2	22.17	363.0	1,291.2	1,614.3	14.7
1997	67	70	31	12.3	4.8	8.9	547.1	24.17	366.7	1,397.5	1,750.5	18.0
1998		68	30	8.7	3.7	6.5	377.8	25.48	371.6	1,078.1	1,459.6	19.1
1999		65	30	8.4	2.9	6.1	383.9	23.82	402.0	937.9	1,360.9	19.4
2000		59	23	7.1	2.7	5.2	362.5	24.82	370.1	879.8	1,249.7	15.9
2001		57	22	7.0	2.7	5.1	366.1	25.87	400.0	873.3	1,246.6	19.7
2002	57	62	24	5.1	2.0	4.1	287.8	20.12	433.3	807.6	1,214.8	18.4
2003		65	24	4.4	2.0	3.8	268.2	20.79	546.3	1,017.9	1,524.5	25.8
2004		72	27	4.6	2.1	4.1	280.3	22.34	468.4	1,019.6	1,517.1	18.9
2005		82	30	4.4	1.8	3.6	291.3	24.20	385.3	820.3	1,177.3	14.9
2006		69P	24P	5.3	2.2	4.5	358.1	22.37	786.8	872.6	1,685.4	32.1
2007		69P	24P	0.5P	0.1P	0.1P	137.2P	24.74P	666.7P	739.4P	1,428.1P	23.1P
2008		69P	23P				95.8P	25,09P	668.3P	741.2P	1,431.6P	23.6P
2009		70P	23P				54.3P	25.44P	669.9P	743.0P	1,435.0P	24.1P
2010		70P	23P				12.9P	25.80P	671.5P	744.8P	1,438.5P	24.7P

Sources: 1992, 1997, 2002 *Economic Census*; other years, up to 2006, are from the *Annual Survey of Manufactures*. Establishment counts for non-Census years are from *County Business Patterns*; 1997 and 2002 values are from the 1997 and 2002 censuses respectively, reported in the Federal Government's NAICS format. Other years were originally reported in equivalent SIC format. 'P's show projections by the editors.

INDICES OF CHANGE

Year	Com-panies	Establishments		Employment			Compensation		Production ($ million)			
		Total	with 20 or more employees	Total (000)	Production Workers (000)	Hours (Mil)	Payroll ($ mil)	Wages ($/hr)	Cost of Materials	Value Added by Manufacture	Value of Shipments	Capital Invest.
1992	125	116	138	431	450	415	326	96	52	142	114	105
1997	118	113	129	241	240	217	190	120	85	173	144	98
2001		92	92	137	135	124	127	129	92	108	103	107
2002	100	100	100	100	100	100	100	100	100	100	100	100
2003		105	100	86	100	93	93	103	126	126	125	140
2004		116	113	90	105	100	97	111	108	126	125	103
2005		132	125	86	90	88	101	120	89	102	97	81
2006		111P	101P	104	110	110	124	111	182	108	139	174
2007		111P	99P	10P	5P	2P	48P	123P	154P	92P	118P	126P
2008		112P	98P				33P	125P	154P	92P	118P	128P
2009		112P	96P				19P	126P	155P	92P	118P	131P
2010		113P	94P				4P	128P	155P	92P	118P	134P

Sources: Same as General Statistics. Values reflect change from the base year, 2002. Values above 100 mean greater than 2002, values below 100 mean less than 2002, and the values of 100 in other years means the same as 2002. 'P's show projections by the editors.

SELECTED RATIOS

For 2002	Avg. of All Manufact.	Analyzed Industry	Index	For 2002	Avg. of All Manufact.	Analyzed Industry	Index
Employees per Establishment	42	82	196	Value Added per Production Worker	182,367	403,800	221
Payroll per Establishment	1,639,184	4,641,935	283	Cost per Establishment	5,769,015	6,988,710	121
Payroll per Employee	39,053	56,431	144	Cost per Employee	137,446	84,961	62
Production Workers per Establishment	30	32	109	Cost per Production Worker	195,506	216,650	111
Wages per Establishment	694,845	1,330,516	191	Shipments per Establishment	11,158,348	19,593,548	176
Wages per Production Worker	23,548	41,246	175	Shipments per Employee	265,847	238,196	90
Hours per Production Worker	1,980	2,050	104	Shipments per Production Worker	378,144	607,400	161
Wages per Hour	11.89	20.12	169	Investment per Establishment	361,338	296,774	82
Value Added per Establishment	5,381,325	13,025,806	242	Investment per Employee	8,609	3,608	42
Value Added per Employee	128,210	158,353	124	Investment per Production Worker	12,245	9,200	75

Sources: Same as General Statistics. The 'Average of All Manufacturing' column represents the average of all manufacturing industries reported for the most recent complete year available. The Index shows the relationship between the Average and the Analyzed Industry. For example, 100 means that they are equal; 500 that the Analyzed Industry is five times the average; 50 means that the Analyzed Industry is half the national average. The abbreviation 'na' is used to show that data are 'not available'. Ratios shown for 2002, the last complete census year.

LEADING COMPANIES   Number shown: 28   Total sales ($ mil): 43,832   Total employment (000): 168.1

Company Name	Address				CEO Name	Phone	Co. Type	Sales ($ mil)	Empl. (000)
Northrop Grumman Corp.	1840 Century Park E	Los Angeles	CA	90067	Daniel Murphy	310-553-6262	P	32,018	122.6
Alliant Holdings L.L.C.	5050 Lincoln Dr.	Edina	MN	55436	Daniel Murphy	952-351-3000	S	4,957*	14.8
Alliant Techsystems Inc.	5050 Lincoln Dr.	Edina	MN	55436	Daniel J. Murphy	952-351-3000	P	3,565	16.0
Orbital Sciences Corp.	21839 Atlantic Blvd	Dulles	VA	20166		703-406-5000	P	1,084	2.8
GenCorp Inc.	PO Box 537012	Sacramento	CA	95853	Terry L. Hall	916-355-4000	P	745	3.3
Blount International Inc.	PO Box 22127	Portland	OR	97269	Dennis Eagan	503-653-8881	P	516	3.2
AAI Corp.	PO Box 126	Hunt Valley	MD	21030		410-666-1400	S	219*	1.8
Sturm, Ruger and Company Inc.	Lacey Pl.	Southport	CT	06890	Michael Fifer	203-259-7843	P	168	1.1
Ellanef Manufacturing Corp.	9711 50th Ave.	Corona	NY	11368	Murray Edwards	718-699-4000	R	131*	0.2
Allied Defense Group Inc.	8000 Twrs. Crescent	Vienna	VA	22182		703-847-5268	P	129	0.7
Networks Electronic Corp.	9750 DeSoto Ave.	Chatsworth	CA	91311	Tamara Christen	818-341-0440	R	73*	0.1
Marlin Firearms Co.	PO Box 248	North Haven	CT	06473	Robert Behn	203-239-5621	R	51*	0.4
Gayston Corp.	200 S Pioneer Blvd.	Springboro	OH	45066		937-746-8500	R	36*	0.3
McLaughlin Research Corp.	PO Box 4132	Middletown	RI	02842	Warren Blakely	401-849-4010	R	26*	0.2
DSE Inc.	5201 S Westshore	Tampa	FL	33611	Dae Shin	813-831-0750	R	21*	0.1
Technical Ordnance Inc.	PO Box 800	St Bonifacius	MN	55375	Norman Hoffman	952-446-1526	R	21*	<0.1
Action Manufacturing Company	100 E Erie Ave.	Philadelphia	PA	19134	Arthur Mattia	215-739-6400	R	18*	0.2
Maine Machine Products Co.	PO Box 260	South Paris	ME	04281	Roland Sutton	207-743-6344	R	14*	0.2
Pyrotechnic Specialties Inc.	1661 Juniper Creek	Byron	GA	31008	Dave Karlson	478-956-5400	R	9*	<0.1
Alloy Surfaces Company Inc.	121 N Commerce	Aston	PA	19014		610-497-7979	R	9*	<0.1
R Stresau Laboratory Inc.	N8265 Medley Rd.	Spooner	WI	54801	Wayne Hanson	715-635-2777	R	7*	<0.1
Dewey Electronics Corp.	27 Muller Rd.	Oakland	NJ	07436	John H.D. Dewey	201-337-4700	P	5	<0.1
Fraser Manufacturing Corp.	PO Box 296	Lexington	MI	48450	Joseph Wilhelm	810-359-5338	R	4*	<0.1
United States Fire Arms Mfg.	445 Ledyard St.	Hartford	CT	06114	Douglas Donnelly	860-724-1152	R	3*	<0.1
Lonestar Couplings Inc.	8306 Northcourt Rd.	Houston	TX	77040	Titus Colaco	713-690-1873	R	2*	<0.1
HP White Laboratory Inc.	3114 Scarboro Rd.	Street	MD	21154	Donald Dunn	410-838-6550	R	2*	<0.1
Philip Specialty Co.	3018 E Main St.	Grand Prairie	TX	75050	Philip Dyvig	972-264-5668	R	1*	<0.1
Avant-Garde Technology Inc.	PO Box 276	Jamison	PA	18929	Richard Tems	215-345-8228	R	1*	<0.1

Source: *Ward's Business Directory of U.S. Private and Public Companies*, Volumes 1 and 2, 2008. The company type code used is as follows: P - Public, R - Private, S - Subsidiary, D - Division, J - Joint Venture, A - Affiliate, G - Group. Sales are in millions of dollars, employees are in thousands. An asterisk (*) indicates an estimated sales volume. The symbol < stands for 'less than'. Company names and addresses are truncated, in some cases, to fit into the available space.

MATERIALS CONSUMED

Material	Quantity	Delivered Cost ($ million)
Metal bolts, nuts, screws, and other screw machine products	(X)	8.3
Other fabricated metal products (exc. castings and forgings)	(X)	111.9
Iron and steel castings (rough and semifinished)	(X)	(D)
Aluminum and aluminum-base alloy castings (rough and semifinished)	(X)	(D)
Other nonferrous metal castings, rough or semifinished (inc. aluminum)	(X)	(D)
Iron and steel forgings	(X)	(D)
Steel shapes and forms (exc. castings, forgings, fabr. metal products)	(X)	4.9
Copper and copper-base alloy shapes and forms (exc. castings, forgings, fabr. metal products)	(X)	(D)
Aluminum and aluminum-base alloy shapes and forms (exc. castings, forgings, fabr. metal products)	(X)	(D)
Other nonferrous shapes and forms (exc. castings, forgings, fabricated metal products)	(X)	11.2
Smokeless powder	(X)	(D)
Other chemicals and allied products	(X)	(D)
Rough and dressed lumber	(X)	(D)
Paperboard containers, boxes, and corrugated paperboard	(X)	1.1
Fabricated plastics products (excluding gaskets)	(X)	2.2
Machine tool accessories, including cutting tools	(X)	(D)
Electronic, hydraulic, and mechanical subassemblies	(X)	(D)
All other materials, components, parts, containers, and supplies	(X)	45.6
Materials, ingredients, containers, and supplies, nsk	(X)	9.4

Source: 2002 *Economic Census*. Explanation of symbols used: (D): Withheld to avoid disclosure of competitive data; na: Not available; (S): Withheld because statistical norms were not met; (X): Not applicable; (Z): Less than half the unit shown; nec: Not elsewhere classified; nsk: Not specified by kind; - : zero; p : 10-19 percent estimated; q : 20-29 percent estimated.

PRODUCT SHARE DETAILS

Product or Product Class Shipments	Mil. $	Product or Product Class Shipments	Mil. $
ORDNANCE AND ACCESSORIES, NEC	1,281.7	Parts and other related equipment for heavy weapons (more than 30 mm, more than 1.18 in.)	65.6
Guns, howitzers, mortars, turrets, parts, and related equipment (more than 30 mm, more than 1.18 in.)	**739.9**	Guns, howitzers, mortars, turrets, parts, and related equipment (more than 30 mm, more than 1.18 in.), nsk	22.0
Guns, howitzers, mortars, turrets, parts, and related equipment (more than 30 mm, more than 1.18 in.)	717.9	**Other ordnance and accessories, nec (rocket projectors, line throwing guns, flame throwers, torpedo tubes, etc., and parts)**	**519.4**
Guns, howitzers, turrets (except aircraft turrets and turret drives), mounts, carriages (except self-propelled), mortars, and assembled and recoilless rifles (more than 30 mm, more than 1.18 in.).	652.2	**Ordnance and accessories, nec, nsk, total**	**22.3**

Source: 2002 *Economic Census*. The values are product shipments in millions of dollars for 2002. Total product shipments may be lower or higher than industry shipments. See Introduction for a full discussion. Values of indented subcategories are summed in the main heading(s). The symbol (D) appears when data are withheld to prevent disclosure of competitive information. The abbreviation nsk stands for 'not specified by kind' and nec for 'not elsewhere classified'. A dash (-) means zero.

INPUTS AND OUTPUTS FOR ARMS, ORDNANCE, AND ACCESSORIES MANUFACTURING

Economic Sector or Industry Providing Inputs	%	Sector	Economic Sector or Industry Buying Outputs	%	Sector
Compensation of employees	31.2		Personal consumption expenditures	42.3	
Taxes on production & imports, less subsidies	4.9		Federal government, investment, national defense	29.2	Fed Govt
Management of companies & enterprises	3.0	Services	General Federal government services, defense	13.8	Fed Govt
Wholesale trade	2.7	Trade	Exports of goods & services	10.4	Cap Inv
Power, distribution, & specialty transformers	1.8	Manufg.	Personal & household goods repair/maintenance	2.5	Services
Machine shops	1.8	Manufg.	General S/L govt. services	0.7	S/L Govt
Custom computer programming services	1.8	Services	Arms, ordnance, & accessories	0.4	Manufg.
Iron & steel mills & ferroalloys	1.7	Manufg.	Investigation & security services	0.3	Services
Forging, stamping, & sintering, nec	1.6	Manufg.	General Federal government services, nondefense	0.1	Fed Govt
Sawmills & wood preservation	1.5	Manufg.			
Turned products & screws, nuts, & bolts	1.4	Manufg.			
Alumina refining & primary aluminum production	1.3	Manufg.			
Advertising & related services	1.2	Services			
Ferrous metal foundries	1.2	Manufg.			
Coating, engraving, heat treating & allied activities	1.2	Manufg.			
Copper rolling, drawing, extruding, & alloying	1.1	Manufg.			
Chemical products & preparations, nec	1.1	Manufg.			
Power generation & supply	0.8	Util.			
Real estate	0.6	Fin/R.E.			
Plastics products, nec	0.6	Manufg.			
Truck transportation	0.6	Util.			
Nonferrous metal foundries	0.6	Manufg.			
Metal cans, boxes, & other containers (light gauge)	0.5	Manufg.			
Arms, ordnance, & accessories	0.5	Manufg.			
Securities, commodity contracts, investments	0.5	Fin/R.E.			
Specialized design services	0.5	Services			
Semiconductors & related devices	0.5	Manufg.			
Legal services	0.5	Services			
Printed circuit assemblies (electronic assemblies)	0.5	Manufg.			
Employment services	0.5	Services			
Fabricated metals, nec	0.5	Manufg.			
Management, scientific, & technical consulting	0.4	Services			
Crowns & closures & metal stamping	0.4	Manufg.			
Cutting tools & machine tool accessories	0.4	Manufg.			
Nonferrous metal (ex. copper & aluminum) processing	0.4	Manufg.			
Valve & fittings other than plumbing	0.4	Manufg.			
Business support services	0.4	Services			
Plate work & fabricated structural products	0.4	Manufg.			
Architectural, engineering, & related services	0.3	Services			
Paperboard containers	0.3	Manufg.			
Ball & roller bearings	0.3	Manufg.			
Handtools	0.3	Manufg.			
Lessors of nonfinancial assets	0.3	Fin/R.E.			
Natural gas distribution	0.3	Util.			
Warehousing & storage	0.3	Util.			
Abrasive products	0.3	Manufg.			
Data processing, hosting, & related services	0.2	Services			
Support services, nec	0.2	Services			
Custom roll forming	0.2	Manufg.			
Telecommunications	0.2	Services			
Other computer related services, including facilities	0.2	Services			
Automotive equipment rental & leasing	0.2	Fin/R.E.			
Monetary authorities/depository credit intermediation	0.2	Fin/R.E.			
Accounting, tax preparation, bookkeeping, & payroll	0.2	Services			
Investigation & security services	0.2	Services			
Professional, scientific, technical services, nec	0.2	Services			
Maintenance/repair of nonresidential structures	0.2	Construct.			
Scientific research & development services	0.2	Services			
Services to buildings & dwellings	0.2	Services			
Springs & wire products	0.2	Manufg.			
Computer system design services	0.1	Services			
Food services & drinking places	0.1	Services			
Automotive repair & maintenance, ex. car washes	0.1	Services			
Commercial & industrial machinery rental & leasing	0.1	Fin/R.E.			

Source: Benchmark Input-Output Accounts for the U.S. Economy, 2002, U.S. Department of Commerce, Washington D.C., January 2008. User should note that this Input-Output table is not for this particular narrowly defined industry but for a larger aggregate. Input and Output data for Arms, Ordnance, and Accessories Manufacturing include Input and Output data for the Annual Survey of Manufactures' NAICS industries 332994 and 332995. The abbreviation nec stands for 'not elsewhere classified'.

OCCUPATIONS EMPLOYED BY OTHER FABRICATED METAL PRODUCT MANUFACTURING

Occupation	% of Total 2006	Change to 2016	Occupation	% of Total 2006	Change to 2016
Team assemblers	11.0	-11.4	Structural metal fabricators & fitters	1.4	-11.4
Machinists	4.6	-7.0	Mechanical engineers	1.4	-11.4
Welders, cutters, solderers, & brazers	3.9	-5.7	General & operations managers	1.3	-20.3
First-line supervisors/managers of production workers	3.8	-11.4	Executive secretaries & administrative assistants	1.3	-11.4
Cutting, punching, & press machine operators	3.4	-20.3	Coating, painting, & spraying machine operators	1.3	-15.8
Inspectors, testers, sorters, samplers, & weighers	3.0	-16.4	Packers & packagers, hand	1.2	-29.1
Computer-controlled machine tool operators	2.8	-2.5	Customer service representatives	1.2	-2.5
Grinding, lapping, polishing machine tool operators	2.7	-14.0	Drilling & boring machine tool operators	1.2	-20.3
Sales reps, wholesale & manufacturing, exc tech	2.2	-11.4	Industrial machinery mechanics	1.1	1.9
Helpers--Production workers	2.2	-11.4	Assemblers & fabricators, nec	1.1	-20.3
Lathe & turning machine tool operators & tenders	2.0	-20.3	Industrial truck & tractor operators	1.1	-20.3
Laborers & freight, stock, & material movers, hand	2.0	-20.3	Bookkeeping, accounting, & auditing clerks	1.1	-11.4
Shipping, receiving, & traffic clerks	1.9	-14.7	Production, planning, & expediting clerks	1.0	-11.4
Industrial engineers	1.8	7.6	Molding, coremaking, & casting machine operators	1.0	-20.3
Maintenance & repair workers, general	1.7	-11.4	Office clerks, general	1.0	-12.7

Source: Industry-Occupation Matrix, Bureau of Labor Statistics, December 4, 2007. These data are reported based on 4-digit NAICS categories but have been matched to corresponding 6-digit NAICS industry codes. The change reported for each occupation to the year 2016 is a percent of growth or decline as estimated by the Bureau of Labor Statistics. The abbreviation nec stands for 'not elsewhere classified'.

LOCATION BY STATE AND REGIONAL CONCENTRATION

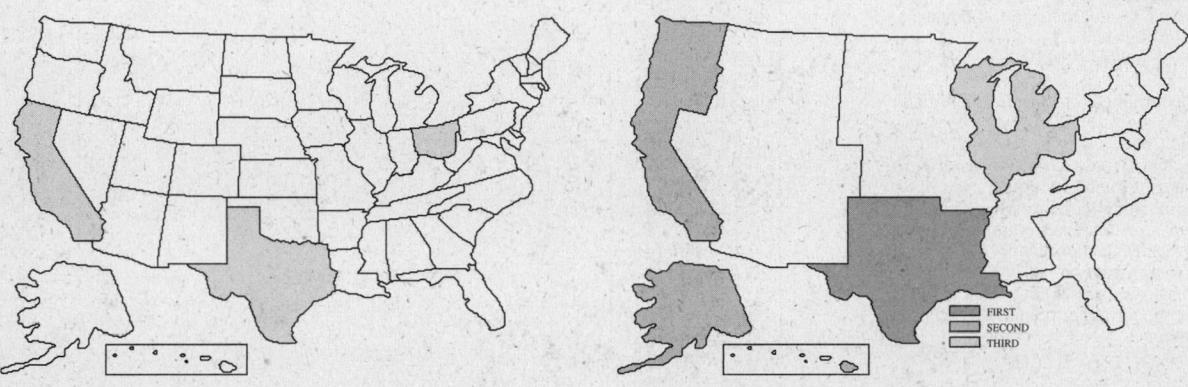

FIRST
SECOND
THIRD

INDUSTRY DATA BY STATE

State	Establish-ments	Shipments			Employment				Cost as % of Shipments	Investment per Employee ($)
		Total ($ mil)	% of U.S.	Per Establ.	Total Number	% of U.S.	Per Establ.	Wages ($/hour)		
Ohio	4	55.0	4.5	13,755.0	568	11.1	142	21.33	5.8	39
California	7	17.5	1.4	2,503.6	131	2.6	19	20.13	34.5	7,244
Texas	8	16.5	1.4	2,061.4	122	2.4	15	14.14	25.6	2,156

Source: 2002 *Economic Census.* The states are in descending order of shipments or establishments (if shipment data are missing for the majority). The symbol (D) appears when data are withheld to prevent disclosure of competitive information. States marked with (D) are sorted by number of establishments. A dash (-) indicates that the data element cannot be calculated. Data may not show all states active in the NAICS category. All data available at the time of publication are shown.

NAICS 332996 - FABRICATED PIPE AND PIPE FITTING MANUFACTURING

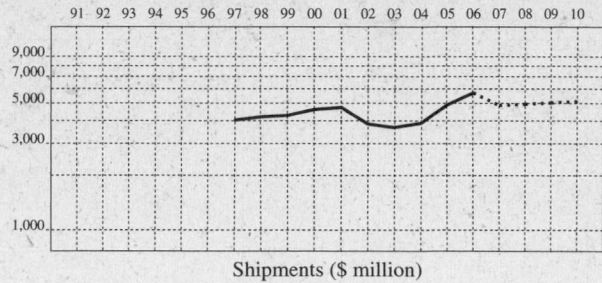

Shipments ($ million)

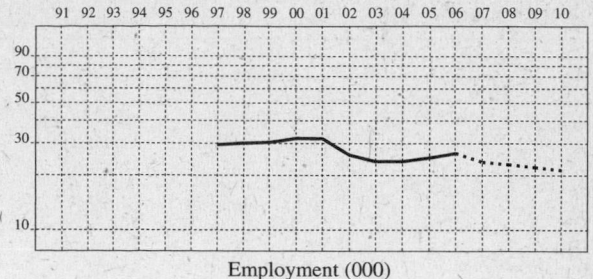

Employment (000)

GENERAL STATISTICS

Year	Com-panies	Establishments		Employment			Compensation		Production ($ million)			
		Total	with 20 or more employees	Total (000)	Production Workers (000)	Hours (Mil)	Payroll ($ mil)	Wages ($/hr)	Cost of Materials	Value Added by Manufacture	Value of Shipments	Capital Invest.
1997	805	857	321	29.5	22.3	45.7	874.3	12.41	1,966.6	2,087.8	4,032.7	146.9
1998		937	336	30.1	23.3	48.7	931.8	12.63	2,025.5	2,180.5	4,205.3	147.5
1999		957	347	30.4	23.2	47.2	954.0	13.10	2,005.8	2,288.3	4,281.5	111.2
2000		978	362	32.0	24.6	50.4	1,012.8	13.14	2,171.3	2,471.1	4,621.6	122.6
2001		934	363	31.9	24.8	50.8	1,045.4	13.67	2,232.4	2,527.8	4,742.8	117.6
2002	727	782	313	25.9	20.1	39.2	871.0	14.85	1,745.1	2,078.1	3,843.0	226.4
2003		780	293	23.9	18.4	38.7	837.2	14.22	1,712.0	1,949.1	3,679.0	97.8
2004		765	288	23.9	18.6	36.0	859.5	15.81	1,855.3	2,013.7	3,883.4	63.7
2005		751	292	25.0	18.6	38.0	988.3	16.85	2,424.5	2,455.8	4,901.7	97.0
2006		736P	289P	26.5	20.4	44.8	1,100.7	15.98	2,787.3	2,956.5	5,699.1	154.3
2007		711P	282P	23.7P	18.2P	37.8P	989.5P	16.92P	2,377.3P	2,521.6P	4,860.8P	112.2P
2008		686P	275P	23.0P	17.6P	36.6P	997.1P	17.40P	2,419.3P	2,566.1P	4,946.6P	109.2P
2009		661P	268P	22.2P	17.1P	35.5P	1,004.7P	17.89P	2,461.2P	2,610.6P	5,032.4P	106.2P
2010		637P	261P	21.4P	16.5P	34.4P	1,012.4P	18.37P	2,503.2P	2,655.1P	5,118.2P	103.3P

Sources: 1997 and 2002 *Economic Census*; other years, up to 2006, are from *Annual Survey of Manufactures*. Establishment counts for non-Census years are from *County Business Patterns*; 1997 and 2002 values are from the 1997 and 2002 censuses, respectively. 'P's show projections by the editors.

INDICES OF CHANGE

Year	Com-panies	Establishments		Employment			Compensation		Production ($ million)			
		Total	with 20 or more employees	Total (000)	Production Workers (000)	Hours (Mil)	Payroll ($ mil)	Wages ($/hr)	Cost of Materials	Value Added by Manufacture	Value of Shipments	Capital Invest.
1997	111	110	103	114	111	117	100	84	113	100	105	65
1998		120	107	116	116	124	107	85	116	105	109	65
1999		122	111	117	115	120	110	88	115	110	111	49
2000		125	116	124	122	129	116	88	124	119	120	54
2001		119	116	123	123	130	120	92	128	122	123	52
2002	100	100	100	100	100	100	100	100	100	100	100	100
2003		100	94	92	92	99	96	96	98	94	96	43
2004		98	92	92	93	92	99	106	106	97	101	28
2005		96	93	97	93	97	113	113	139	118	128	43
2006		94P	92P	102	101	114	126	108	160	142	148	68
2007		91P	90P	92P	91P	96P	114P	114P	136P	121P	126P	50P
2008		88P	88P	89P	88P	93P	114P	117P	139P	123P	129P	48P
2009		85P	86P	86P	85P	91P	115P	120P	141P	126P	131P	47P
2010		81P	83P	83P	82P	88P	116P	124P	143P	128P	133P	46P

Sources: Same as General Statistics. Values reflect change from the base year, 2002. Values above 100 mean greater than 2002, values below 100 mean less than 2002, and the values of 100 in other years means the same as 2002. 'P's show projections by the editors.

SELECTED RATIOS

For 2002	Avg. of All Manufact.	Analyzed Industry	Index	For 2002	Avg. of All Manufact.	Analyzed Industry	Index
Employees per Establishment	42	33	79	Value Added per Production Worker	182,367	103,388	57
Payroll per Establishment	1,639,184	1,113,811	68	Cost per Establishment	5,769,015	2,231,586	39
Payroll per Employee	39,053	33,629	86	Cost per Employee	137,446	67,378	49
Production Workers per Establishment	30	26	87	Cost per Production Worker	195,506	86,821	44
Wages per Establishment	694,845	744,399	107	Shipments per Establishment	11,158,348	4,914,322	44
Wages per Production Worker	23,548	28,961	123	Shipments per Employee	265,847	148,378	56
Hours per Production Worker	1,980	1,950	98	Shipments per Production Worker	378,144	191,194	51
Wages per Hour	11.89	14.85	125	Investment per Establishment	361,338	289,514	80
Value Added per Establishment	5,381,325	2,657,417	49	Investment per Employee	8,609	8,741	102
Value Added per Employee	128,210	80,236	63	Investment per Production Worker	12,245	11,264	92

Sources: Same as General Statistics. The 'Average of All Manufacturing' column represents the average of all manufacturing industries reported for the most recent complete year available. The Index shows the relationship between the Average and the Analyzed Industry. For example, 100 means that they are equal; 500 that the Analyzed Industry is five times the average; 50 means that the Analyzed Industry is half the national average. The abbreviation 'na' is used to show that data are 'not available'. Ratios shown for 2002, the last complete census year.

LEADING COMPANIES Number shown: 75   Total sales ($ mil): 23,705   Total employment (000): 93.5

Company Name	Address				CEO Name	Phone	Co. Type	Sales ($ mil)	Empl. (000)
Shaw Group Inc.	4171 Essen Ln.	Baton Rouge	LA	70809	James F. Barker	225-932-2500	P	5,724	27.0
Harsco Corp.	PO Box 8888	Camp Hill	PA	17001	S. D. Fazzolari	717-763-7064	P	3,688	21.5
VAM PTS Co.	19210 E Hardy Rd.	Houston	TX	77073		281-821-5510	R	2,993*	0.1
Dresser Inc.	15455 Dallas Pkwy.	Addison	TX	75001		972-361-9800	S	1,343*	6.0
Swagelok Co.	29500 Solon Rd.	Solon	OH	44139	Arthur F. Anton	440-248-4600	R	1,100*	3.3
United States Pipe and Foundry	PO Box 10406	Birmingham	AL	35222			S	985*	2.5
McWane Corp.	PO Box 43327	Birmingham	AL	35243	G. Ruffner Page, Jr.	205-414-3100	R	944*	7.0
Continental Disc Corp.	3160 W Heartland	Liberty	MO	64068	Kenneth Shaw	816-792-1500	R	523*	0.2
Aarque Steel Corp.	PO Box 109	Lakewood	NY	14750	Patrick Lavelle	716-763-4044	R	500*	3.0
Omega Flex Inc.	451 Creamery Way	Exton	PA	19341	Kevin R. Hoben	610-524-7272	S	475*	0.1
Lone Star Steel Co.	PO Box 803546	Dallas	TX	75380	Byron Dunn	972-386-3981	S	425*	1.5
Alaskan Copper Co's Inc.	PO Box 3546	Seattle	WA	98124	Kermit Rosen	206-623-5800	R	392*	0.3
Ward Manufacturing Inc.	PO Box 9	Blossburg	PA	16912	Doyne Chartrau	570-638-2131	S	337*	1.0
NIBCO Inc.	PO Box 1167	Elkhart	IN	46515	Rex Martin	574-295-3000	R	292*	3.0
MicroGroup Inc.	7 Industrial Park	Medway	MA	02053	Jay Carabiello	508-533-4925	R	278*	0.1
AZZ Inc.	1300 S Universty Dr	Fort Worth	TX	76107	David H. Dingus	817-810-0095	P	260	1.0
Trinity	2525 N Stemmons	Dallas	TX	75207	Tim Wallace	214-631-4420	S	248*	0.8
Contractors Steel Co.	PO Box 3364	Livonia	MI	48151	Donald Simon	734-464-4000	R	234*	0.8
Sunland Fabricating Inc.	30103 Sunland Dr.	Walker	LA	70785	Kent Shephard	225-667-1000	R	190*	0.5
Total Premier Services Inc.	654 N Sam Houston	Houston	TX	77060	Ron Dewan	832-300-8100	R	184*	<0.1
Mueller Brass Co.	PO Box 5021	Port Huron	MI	48061	William O'Hagan	810-987-7770	S	151*	0.4
Allied Tube and Conduit Corp.	16100 S Lathrop	Harvey	IL	60426	Rick Filetti	708-339-1610	S	113*	0.8
Performance Contractors Inc.	PO Box 83630	Baton Rouge	LA	70884	Art Favre	225-751-4156	R	109*	1.5
Jackson Tube Service Inc.	PO Box 1650	Piqua	OH	45356	Robert Jackson	937-773-8550	R	105*	0.3
Bristol Metals L.P.	PO Box 1589	Bristol	TN	37621	Ralph Matera	423-989-4700	S	100*	0.3
Pioneer Pipe Inc.	2021 Hanna Rd.	Marietta	OH	45750	David Archer	740-376-2400	S	95*	0.3
Superior Tube Co.	3900 Germantown	Collegeville	PA	19426	Scott Myers	610-489-5200	R	82*	0.3
Daniel Measurement and Control	PO Box 19097	Houston	TX	77224	Joe Vasvily	713-467-6000	S	79*	0.5
Atlas Industrial Holdings	5275 Sinclair Rd.	Columbus	OH	43229		614-841-4500	R	77*	0.2
Smiths Tubular Systems-Laconia	PO Box 678	Laconia	NH	03247		603-524-2064	R	69*	0.3
Atlantic States Cast Iron Pipe	183 Sitgreaves St.	Phillipsburg	NJ	08865		908-454-1161	S	69*	0.3
Curtis Maruyasu America Inc.	665 Metts Dr.	Lebanon	KY	40033		270-692-2109	R	64*	0.2
Global Tube Form Partners	3405 Engle Rd.	Fort Wayne	IN	46809		260-478-2363	R	60*	0.4
Pegasus Manufacturing Inc.	422 Timber Ridge	Middletown	CT	06457		860-635-8811	R	57*	0.2
Koyo Corp.	300 Fritz Keiper	Battle Creek	MI	49015	Toshio Uehara	269-962-9676	R	55*	0.3
Bonney Forge Corp.	PO Box 330	Mount Union	PA	17066	John Leone	814-542-2545	R	55*	0.3
Mission Clay Products Corp.	PO Box 549	Corona	CA	92878	Owen Garrett	951-277-4600	D	50*	0.2
Bombardier Transportation	151 Orchard St.	Auburn	NY	13021	Jean-Yves Leblanc	315-255-7800	S	50*	0.2
Howe-Baker Engineers Ltd.	3102 E 5th St.	Tyler	TX	75701	Luke Scorsony	903-597-0311	S	48*	0.3
Alex Products Inc.	PO Box 26	Ridgeville Cors	OH	43555	Dave Deylen	419-267-5240	R	47*	0.6
Texas Arai	8204 Fairbanks N	Houston	TX	77064	Barham Moss	713-937-1800	S	44*	0.3
Deublin Co.	2050 Norman Dr. W	Waukegan	IL	60085	Donald Deubler	847-689-8600	R	41*	0.2
Morton Welding Company Inc.	70 Commerce Dr.	Morton	IL	61550	Robert Dittmer	309-263-2590	R	37*	0.4
Alpha Wire Co.	711 Lidgerwood	Elizabeth	NJ	07207		908-925-8000	R	36*	0.2
Powerline Inc.	1400 Axtell Dr.	Troy	MI	48084	Richard Stewart	248-280-2040	R	36*	0.3
Deca Manufacturing Corp.	4210 116th Ter. N	Clearwater	FL	33762	Rob James	727-573-2910	R	35	0.2
Universal Tube Inc.	2607 Bond St.	Rochester Hills	MI	48309	William Henson	248-853-5100	R	34*	0.3
AAON Coil Products Inc.	203 Gum Springs	Longview	TX	75602	N H. Asbjornson	903-236-4403	S	34*	0.3
P.C. Campana Inc.	1374 E 28th St.	Lorain	OH	44055	Robert Campana	440-246-6500	R	33*	0.2
Blissfield Manufacturing Co.	626 Depot St.	Blissfield	MI	49228	Patrick Farver	517-486-2121	R	33*	0.1
Phillips Mfg. and Tower	PO Box 125	Shelby	OH	44875	Ralph Phillip	419-347-1720	R	33*	<0.1
Townley Engineering and Mfg.	PO Box 221	Candler	FL	32111	J Townley	352-687-3001	R	31*	0.2
Enduro Industries Inc.	PO Box 509	Hannibal	MO	63401	Henry Crute	573-248-2084	R	31*	<0.1
Fernco Inc.	300 S Dayton St.	Davison	MI	48423	Christoper Cooper	810-653-9626	R	31*	0.1
Whitley Products Inc.	PO Box 154	Pierceton	IN	46562	Jim Ciar	574-594-2112	R	30*	<0.1
Tube Specialties Company Inc.	PO Box 20608	Portland	OR	97294	Gary Weyhrich	503-618-8823	R	30*	0.3
Bohn and Dawson Inc.	3500 Tree Ct. Ind.	Saint Louis	MO	63122	Steven Hurster	636-225-5011	R	30*	0.2
Riker Products Inc.	PO Box 6976	Toledo	OH	43612	Gary Frye	419-729-1626	R	30*	0.2
Saegertown Manufacturing Corp.	PO Box 828	Saegertown	PA	16433	Chalmer Jordan	814-763-2655	R	30*	0.2
Mertz Inc.	PO Box 150	Ponca City	OK	74602	Steve Ballinger	580-762-5646	R	29*	0.2
Texas Steel Conversion Inc.	3101 Holmes Rd.	Houston	TX	77051	Brian Binau	713-733-6013	R	29*	0.3
Dynamic Products Inc.	16520 Peninsula St.	Houston	TX	77015	R Lindquist	281-457-3500	R	29*	0.2
Tube Fab Roman Engineering Co.	1715 M 68	Afton	MI	49705		231-238-9366	R	28*	0.2
Controls Southeast Inc.	PO Box 7500	Charlotte	NC	28241	Fred Stubblefield	704-588-3030	R	27*	0.2
Acme Cryogenics Inc.	PO Box 445	Allentown	PA	18105	Michael Fink	610-791-7909	R	27*	0.1
Saman Inc.	1628 W 139th St.	Gardena	CA	90249	Simon Khazani	310-515-1477	R	26*	0.1
Allied Studco	2525 N 27th Ave.	Phoenix	AZ	85009		602-272-6606	D	26*	0.2
Pennsylvania Machine Works	PO Box 2170	Boothwyn	PA	19061	Ronald Lafferty	610-497-3300	R	26*	0.2
Precision Tool, Die & Machine	6901 Preston Hwy.	Louisville	KY	40219	Tom Hudson	502-479-0800	R	26*	0.2
Globe Engineering Company Inc.	PO Box 12407	Wichita	KS	67277	Ronald Ross	316-943-1266	R	25*	0.2
Custom Alloy Corp.	3 Washington Ave.	High Bridge	NJ	08829	Adam Ambielli	908-638-6200	R	25*	0.2
Spinco Metal Products Inc.	1 Country Club Dr.	Newark	NY	14513	Robert Straubing	315-331-6285	R	25*	0.2
Kalkreuth Roofing/Sheet Metal	PO Box 6399	Wheeling	WV	26003	John Kalkreuth	304-232-8540	R	25*	0.2
Seal Tite Inc.	120 Moore Rd.	Hillsboro	OH	45133	Michael Kelley	937-393-4268	R	24*	0.2
Advanced Tubing Technology	150 Intercraft Dr.	Statesville	NC	28625	Doug Smyth	704-924-7020	R	23*	0.2

Source: *Ward's Business Directory of U.S. Private and Public Companies*, Volumes 1 and 2, 2008. The company type code used is as follows: P - Public, R - Private, S - Subsidiary, D - Division, J - Joint Venture, A - Affiliate, G - Group. Sales are in millions of dollars, employees are in thousands. An asterisk (*) indicates an estimated sales volume. The symbol < stands for 'less than'. Company names and addresses are truncated, in some cases, to fit into the available space.

MATERIALS CONSUMED

Material	Quantity	Delivered Cost ($ million)
Metal fittings, flanges, unions for piping systems (except forgings)	(X)	160.4
Metal stampings	(X)	4.0
Other fabricated metal products (exc. forgings, flanges, etc.)	(X)	161.9
Forgings	(X)	41.5
Iron and steel castings (rough and semifinished)	(X)	61.7
Aluminum and aluminum-base alloy castings (rough and semifinished)	(X)	1.5
Other nonferrous metal castings, rough or semifinished (inc. aluminum)	(X)	2.4
Steel bars and bar shapes (exc. castings, forgings, fabr. metal products)	(X)	40.2
Steel sheet and strip (including tinplate)	(X)	19.1
Other nonferrous shapes and forms (exc. castings, forgings, fabricated metal products)	(X)	4.0
Steel structural shapes (exc. castings, forgings, fabr. metal products)	(X)	6.3
Steel pipes (exc. castings, forgings, fabr. metal products)	(X)	319.6
All other steel shapes and forms (exc. castings, forgings, fabr. metal products)	(X)	55.8
Copper and copper-base alloy pipe and tube (exc. castings, forgings, fabr. metal products)	(X)	(D)
All other copper and copper-base alloy shapes and forms (exc. castings, forgings, fabr. metal products)	(X)	(D)
Aluminum and aluminum-base alloy sheet, plate, foil, and welded tubing	(X)	1.8
Aluminum and aluminum-base alloy extruded shapes (rod, bar, pipe, tube, etc.)	(S)	6.8
Other aluminum and aluminum-base alloy shapes and forms (exc. castings, forgings, fabr. metal products)	(X)	0.4
Metal powders	(X)	<0.1
Plastics resins consumed in the form of granules, pellets, etc.	(X)	5.8
All other materials, components, parts, containers, and supplies	(X)	203.3
Materials, ingredients, containers, and supplies, nsk	(X)	390.7

Source: 2002 Economic Census. Explanation of symbols used: (D): Withheld to avoid disclosure of competitive data; na: Not available; (S): Withheld because statistical norms were not met; (X): Not applicable; (Z): Less than half the unit shown; nec: Not elsewhere classified; nsk: Not specified by kind; - : zero; p : 10-19 percent estimated; q : 20-29 percent estimated.

PRODUCT SHARE DETAILS

Product or Product Class Shipments	Mil. $	Product or Product Class Shipments	Mil. $
FABRICATED PIPES AND PIPE FITTINGS	3,637.1	pipe fittings	47.0
Fabricated iron and steel pipes and pipe fittings made from purchased pipe	2,230.1	Fabricated copper and copper-base alloy pipe and pipe fittings.	38.3
All other nonferrous fabricated pipe and pipe fittings made from purchased pipe	424.3	All other nonferrous fabricated pipe and pipe fittings made from purchased pipe	339.0
Fabricated aluminum and aluminum-base alloy pipe and		Fabricated pipes and pipe fittings, nsk,total	982.8

Source: 2002 Economic Census. The values are product shipments in millions of dollars for 2002. Total product shipments may be lower or higher than industry shipments. See Introduction for a full discussion. Values of indented subcategories are summed in the main heading(s). The symbol (D) appears when data are withheld to prevent disclosure of competitive information. The abbreviation nsk stands for 'not specified by kind' and nec for 'not elsewhere classified'. A dash (-) means zero.

INPUTS AND OUTPUTS FOR FABRICATED PIPE AND PIPE FITTING MANUFACTURING

Economic Sector or Industry Providing Inputs	%	Sector	Economic Sector or Industry Buying Outputs	%	Sector
Compensation of employees	29.7		Residential permanent site structures	21.5	Construct.
Iron & steel mills & ferroalloys	14.5	Manufg.	Private fixed investment	10.7	
Fabricated pipes & pipe fittings	6.0	Manufg.	Nonresidential structures, nec	9.7	Construct.
Wholesale trade	4.8	Trade	Residential structures, nec	6.3	Construct.
Management of companies & enterprises	2.9	Services	Fabricated pipes & pipe fittings	6.0	Manufg.
Ferrous metal foundries	2.0	Manufg.	Metal tanks (heavy gauge)	5.9	Manufg.
Valve & fittings other than plumbing	1.9	Manufg.	Valve & fittings other than plumbing	5.1	Manufg.
Machine shops	1.6	Manufg.	Commercial & health care structures	4.8	Construct.
Forging, stamping, & sintering, nec	1.5	Manufg.	Owner-occupied dwellings	4.2	
Securities, commodity contracts, investments	1.2	Fin/R.E.	Plate work & fabricated structural products	3.8	Manufg.
Coating, engraving, heat treating & allied activities	1.1	Manufg.	Maintenance/repair of nonresidential structures	3.6	Construct.
Copper rolling, drawing, extruding, & alloying	1.0	Manufg.	Power boilers & heat exchangers	2.3	Manufg.
Truck transportation	1.0	Util.	Aircraft parts & auxiliary equipment, nec	2.3	Manufg.
Power generation & supply	0.9	Util.	Manufacturing structures	1.9	Construct.
Real estate	0.9	Fin/R.E.	Lighting fixtures	1.5	Manufg.
Lessors of nonfinancial assets	0.8	Fin/R.E.	Other S/L govt. enterprises	1.3	S/L Govt
Monetary authorities/depository credit intermediation	0.7	Fin/R.E.	Maintenance/repair of residential structures	1.2	Construct.
Turned products & screws, nuts, & bolts	0.7	Manufg.	Heating equipment (except warm air furnaces)	1.1	Manufg.
Semiconductors & related devices	0.7	Manufg.	Telecommunications	0.9	Services
Professional, scientific, technical services, nec	0.6	Services	AC, refrigeration, and warm air heating equipment	0.8	Manufg.
Printed circuit assemblies (electronic assemblies)	0.6	Manufg.	Commercial & service industry machinery, nec	0.6	Manufg.
Metal cans, boxes, & other containers (light gauge)	0.5	Manufg.	Architectural, engineering, & related services	0.6	Services
Aluminum products from purchased aluminum	0.4	Manufg.	Federal government, investment, national defense	0.5	Fed Govt
Advertising & related services	0.4	Services	Retail trade	0.5	Trade
Fabricated metals, nec	0.4	Manufg.	Commercial & industrial machinery rental & leasing	0.4	Fin/R.E.
Taxes on production & imports, less subsidies	0.4		S/L govt. invest., other	0.3	S/L Govt
Automotive equipment rental & leasing	0.4	Fin/R.E.	Individual & family services	0.3	Services
Food services & drinking places	0.4	Services	Computer system design services	0.2	Services
Paperboard containers	0.4	Manufg.	Fabricated metals, nec	0.2	Manufg.

Continued on next page.

INPUTS AND OUTPUTS FOR FABRICATED PIPE AND PIPE FITTING MANUFACTURING - Continued

Economic Sector or Industry Providing Inputs	%	Sector	Economic Sector or Industry Buying Outputs	%	Sector
Legal services	0.4	Services	Amusement & recreation, nec	0.2	Services
Laminated plastics plates, sheets, & shapes	0.4	Manufg.	Data processing, hosting, & related services	0.1	Services
Data processing, hosting, & related services	0.3	Services	Medical & diagnostic labs & outpatient services	0.1	Services
Plate work & fabricated structural products	0.3	Manufg.			
Telecommunications	0.3	Services			
Architectural, engineering, & related services	0.3	Services			
Accounting, tax preparation, bookkeeping, & payroll	0.3	Services			
Natural gas distribution	0.3	Util.			
Ball & roller bearings	0.3	Manufg.			
Rail transportation	0.3	Util.			
Handtools	0.3	Manufg.			
Warehousing & storage	0.3	Util.			
Services to buildings & dwellings	0.3	Services			
Hotels & motels, including casino hotels	0.3	Services			
Management, scientific, & technical consulting	0.2	Services			
Maintenance/repair of nonresidential structures	0.2	Construct.			
Business support services	0.2	Services			
Commercial & industrial machinery rental & leasing	0.2	Fin/R.E.			
Specialized design services	0.2	Services			
Cutting tools & machine tool accessories	0.2	Manufg.			
Employment services	0.2	Services			
Crowns & closures & metal stamping	0.2	Manufg.			
Custom roll forming	0.2	Manufg.			
Plastics materials & resins	0.2	Manufg.			
Scientific research & development services	0.2	Services			
Air transportation	0.2	Util.			
Nonferrous metal (ex. copper & aluminum) processing	0.2	Manufg.			
Nonferrous metal foundries	0.2	Manufg.			
Automotive repair & maintenance, ex. car washes	0.1	Services			
Support services, nec	0.1	Services			
Nondepository credit intermediation activities	0.1	Fin/R.E.			
Springs & wire products	0.1	Manufg.			
Commercial & industrial equipment repair/maintenance	0.1	Services			
Other computer related services, including facilities	0.1	Services			
Relay & industrial controls	0.1	Manufg.			
Primary smelting & refining of copper	0.1	Manufg.			
Paperboard mills	0.1	Manufg.			

Source: Benchmark Input-Output Accounts for the U.S. Economy, 2002, U.S. Department of Commerce, Washington, D.C., January 2008. The abbreviation nec stands for 'not elsewhere classified'.

OCCUPATIONS EMPLOYED BY OTHER FABRICATED METAL PRODUCT MANUFACTURING

Occupation	% of Total 2006	Change to 2016	Occupation	% of Total 2006	Change to 2016
Team assemblers	11.0	-11.4	Structural metal fabricators & fitters	1.4	-11.4
Machinists	4.6	-7.0	Mechanical engineers	1.4	-11.4
Welders, cutters, solderers, & brazers	3.9	-5.7	General & operations managers	1.3	-20.3
First-line supervisors/managers of production workers	3.8	-11.4	Executive secretaries & administrative assistants	1.3	-11.4
Cutting, punching, & press machine operators	3.4	-20.3	Coating, painting, & spraying machine operators	1.3	-15.8
Inspectors, testers, sorters, samplers, & weighers	3.0	-16.4	Packers & packagers, hand	1.2	-29.1
Computer-controlled machine tool operators	2.8	-2.5	Customer service representatives	1.2	-2.5
Grinding, lapping, polishing machine tool operators	2.7	-14.0	Drilling & boring machine tool operators	1.2	-20.3
Sales reps, wholesale & manufacturing, exc tech	2.2	-11.4	Industrial machinery mechanics	1.1	1.9
Helpers--Production workers	2.2	-11.4	Assemblers & fabricators, nec	1.1	-20.3
Lathe & turning machine tool operators & tenders	2.0	-20.3	Industrial truck & tractor operators	1.1	-20.3
Laborers & freight, stock, & material movers, hand	2.0	-20.3	Bookkeeping, accounting, & auditing clerks	1.1	-11.4
Shipping, receiving, & traffic clerks	1.9	-14.7	Production, planning, & expediting clerks	1.0	-11.4
Industrial engineers	1.8	7.6	Molding, coremaking, & casting machine operators	1.0	-20.3
Maintenance & repair workers, general	1.7	-11.4	Office clerks, general	1.0	-12.7

Source: Industry-Occupation Matrix, Bureau of Labor Statistics, December 4, 2007. These data are reported based on 4-digit NAICS categories but have been matched to corresponding 6-digit NAICS industry codes. The change reported for each occupation to the year 2016 is a percent of growth or decline as estimated by the Bureau of Labor Statistics. The abbreviation nec stands for 'not elsewhere classified'.

LOCATION BY STATE AND REGIONAL CONCENTRATION

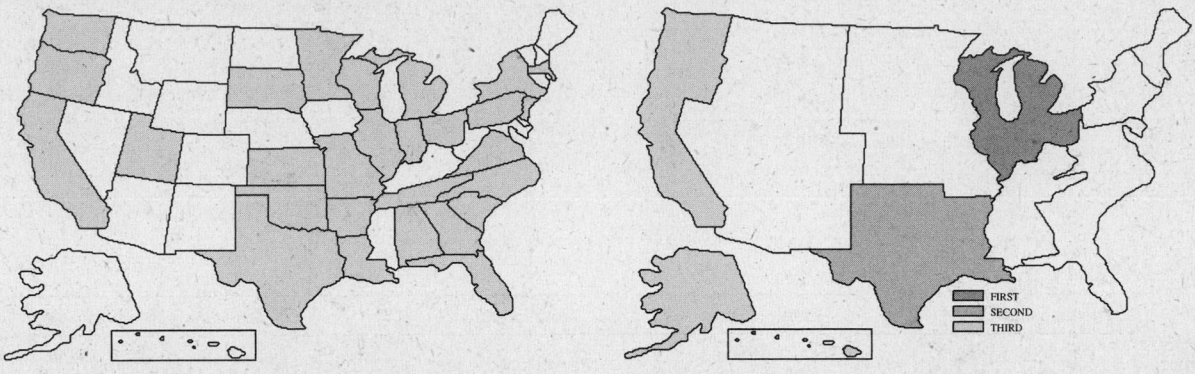

INDUSTRY DATA BY STATE

| State | Establish-ments | Shipments | | | Employment | | | | Cost as % of Shipments | Investment per Employee ($) |
		Total ($ mil)	% of U.S.	Per Establ.	Total Number	% of U.S.	Per Establ.	Wages ($/hour)		
Texas	97	941.0	24.5	9,701.1	5,459	21.0	56	15.15	46.8	25,571
Louisiana	22	328.3	8.5	14,924.4	2,272	8.8	103	16.32	44.4	4,117
California	92	275.4	7.2	2,993.2	2,042	7.9	22	13.76	50.2	3,608
Michigan	53	262.1	6.8	4,945.1	1,837	7.1	35	11.85	50.6	4,071
Pennsylvania	34	192.0	5.0	5,646.2	1,282	4.9	38	17.55	33.4	2,232
Ohio	44	179.1	4.7	4,069.4	1,555	6.0	35	13.75	46.8	3,575
Oklahoma	37	178.4	4.6	4,822.0	1,253	4.8	34	13.24	38.4	2,362
Wisconsin	23	136.9	3.6	5,953.0	933	3.6	41	14.10	43.1	2,832
Arkansas	13	131.3	3.4	10,103.2	811	3.1	62	14.42	36.9	3,009
Alabama	18	109.3	2.8	6,071.7	695	2.7	39	13.92	34.2	6,957
Indiana	28	104.5	2.7	3,732.7	830	3.2	30	21.05	32.6	4,220
North Carolina	19	101.9	2.7	5,365.1	737	2.8	39	13.17	50.0	2,693
Georgia	21	99.7	2.6	4,746.0	600	2.3	29	13.37	58.5	8,455
South Carolina	10	89.5	2.3	8,953.3	670	2.6	67	20.23	53.6	(D)
New Jersey	21	88.0	2.3	4,191.2	587	2.3	28	17.21	39.4	2,840
Tennessee	13	83.1	2.2	6,394.4	484	1.9	37	12.83	48.7	1,640
Minnesota	11	64.3	1.7	5,848.5	353	1.4	32	17.99	56.6	4,408
Illinois	34	56.6	1.5	1,665.0	480	1.9	14	12.53	41.5	5,871
New York	32	54.8	1.4	1,713.3	385	1.5	12	13.28	47.3	3,047
Oregon	11	49.4	1.3	4,494.5	371	1.4	34	15.27	44.9	3,957
Washington	17	42.2	1.1	2,483.4	278	1.1	16	12.89	51.1	1,345
Missouri	14	38.6	1.0	2,760.6	243	0.9	17	17.29	57.1	3,535
Kansas	8	29.2	0.8	3,652.6	159	0.6	20	13.41	59.9	3,006
Virginia	6	28.9	0.8	4,819.3	168	0.6	28	17.78	45.3	2,958
Utah	10	28.5	0.7	2,847.3	183	0.7	18	17.96	48.3	5,989
South Dakota	3	17.7	0.5	5,902.7	111	0.4	37	13.68	56.7	1,595
Florida	16	15.9	0.4	996.9	120	0.5	8	16.02	53.6	5,858
Massachusetts	8	10.7	0.3	1,332.1	108	0.4	14	22.79	27.4	3,009

Source: 2002 *Economic Census*. The states are in descending order of shipments or establishments (if shipment data are missing for the majority). The symbol (D) appears when data are withheld to prevent disclosure of competitive information. States marked with (D) are sorted by number of establishments. A dash (-) indicates that the data element cannot be calculated. Data may not show all states active in the NAICS category. All data available at the time of publication are shown.

NAICS 33299N - FABRICATED METAL PRODUCTS MANUFACTURING NEC*

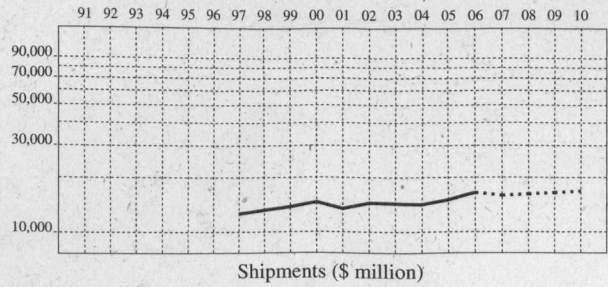

Shipments ($ million)

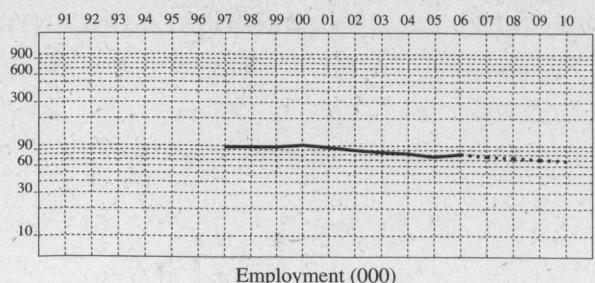

Employment (000)

GENERAL STATISTICS

Year	Com-panies	Establishments		Employment			Compensation		Production ($ million)			
		Total	with 20 or more employees	Total (000)	Production Workers (000)	Hours (Mil)	Payroll ($ mil)	Wages ($/hr)	Cost of Materials	Value Added by Manufacture	Value of Shipments	Capital Invest.
1997	3,720	3,784	998	96.5	72.6	141.6	2,912.8	13.17	5,755.5	6,931.7	12,640.2	436.4
1998		4,108	1,054	97.3	73.4	147.3	3,060.3	13.42	6,002.9	7,296.7	13,217.7	429.8
1999		4,123	1,033	97.1	72.8	146.3	3,178.7	13.71	6,165.6	7,633.4	13,777.9	463.3
2000		4,263	1,045	101.6	76.6	153.9	3,399.0	13.92	6,585.1	8,114.9	14,608.1	482.7
2001		3,984	1,026	95.9	71.9	144.8	3,216.8	13.79	6,008.0	7,447.4	13,461.2	453.1
2002	4,112	4,220	1,117	89.1	66.8	131.2	3,200.6	15.87	6,313.7	8,134.6	14,477.2	544.6
2003		3,687	1,067	84.9	64.3	126.9	3,150.0	16.21	6,138.6	8,245.8	14,394.5	370.1
2004		3,768	1,050	82.2	61.4	125.1	3,126.4	16.41	6,162.7	8,292.8	14,180.5	398.0
2005		3,637	1,000	76.1	56.5	117.5	3,051.1	16.77	6,799.6	8,569.5	15,073.9	382.0
2006		3,742P	1,055P	80.8	61.0	124.5	3,293.1	17.17	7,439.4	9,353.3	16,499.6	376.3
2007		3,700P	1,057P	76.1P	57.0P	117.1P	3,236.7P	17.77P	7,170.7P	9,015.5P	15,903.6P	385.4P
2008		3,658P	1,059P	73.6P	55.1P	113.7P	3,250.8P	18.27P	7,307.6P	9,187.6P	16,207.4P	376.6P
2009		3,616P	1,062P	71.0P	53.1P	110.3P	3,265.0P	18.77P	7,444.6P	9,359.8P	16,511.1P	367.8P
2010		3,574P	1,064P	68.5P	51.2P	106.9P	3,279.1P	19.26P	7,581.5P	9,532.0P	16,814.8P	359.0P

Sources: 1997 and 2002 *Economic Census*; other years, up to 2006, are from *Annual Survey of Manufactures*. Establishment counts for non-Census years are from *County Business Patterns*; 1997 and 2002 values are from the 1997 and 2002 censuses, respectively. 'P's show projections by the editors.

INDICES OF CHANGE

Year	Com-panies	Establishments		Employment			Compensation		Production ($ million)			
		Total	with 20 or more employees	Total (000)	Production Workers (000)	Hours (Mil)	Payroll ($ mil)	Wages ($/hr)	Cost of Materials	Value Added by Manufacture	Value of Shipments	Capital Invest.
1997	90	90	89	108	109	108	91	83	91	85	87	80
1998		97	94	109	110	112	96	85	95	90	91	79
1999		98	92	109	109	112	99	86	98	94	95	85
2000		101	94	114	115	117	106	88	104	100	101	89
2001		94	92	108	108	110	101	87	95	92	93	83
2002	100	100	100	100	100	100	100	100	100	100	100	100
2003		87	96	95	96	97	98	102	97	101	99	68
2004		89	94	92	92	95	98	103	98	102	98	73
2005		86	90	85	85	90	95	106	108	105	104	70
2006		89P	94P	91	91	95	103	108	118	115	114	69
2007		88P	95P	85P	85P	89P	101P	112P	114P	111P	110P	71P
2008		87P	95P	83P	82P	87P	102P	115P	116P	113P	112P	69P
2009		86P	95P	80P	79P	84P	102P	118P	118P	115P	114P	68P
2010		85P	95P	77P	77P	81P	102P	121P	120P	117P	116P	66P

Sources: Same as General Statistics. Values reflect change from the base year, 2002. Values above 100 mean greater than 2002, values below 100 mean less than 2002, and the values of 100 in other years means the same as 2002. 'P's show projections by the editors.

SELECTED RATIOS

For 2002	Avg. of All Manufact.	Analyzed Industry	Index	For 2002	Avg. of All Manufact.	Analyzed Industry	Index
Employees per Establishment	42	21	50	Value Added per Production Worker	182,367	121,775	67
Payroll per Establishment	1,639,184	758,436	46	Cost per Establishment	5,769,015	1,496,137	26
Payroll per Employee	39,053	35,921	92	Cost per Employee	137,446	70,861	52
Production Workers per Establishment	30	16	54	Cost per Production Worker	195,506	94,516	48
Wages per Establishment	694,845	493,399	71	Shipments per Establishment	11,158,348	3,430,616	31
Wages per Production Worker	23,548	31,170	132	Shipments per Employee	265,847	162,483	61
Hours per Production Worker	1,980	1,964	99	Shipments per Production Worker	378,144	216,725	57
Wages per Hour	11.89	15.87	133	Investment per Establishment	361,338	129,052	36
Value Added per Establishment	5,381,325	1,927,630	36	Investment per Employee	8,609	6,112	71
Value Added per Employee	128,210	91,297	71	Investment per Production Worker	12,245	8,153	67

Sources: Same as General Statistics. The 'Average of All Manufacturing' column represents the average of all manufacturing industries reported for the most recent complete year available. The Index shows the relationship between the Average and the Analyzed Industry. For example, 100 means that they are equal; 500 that the Analyzed Industry is five times the average; 50 means that the Analyzed Industry is half the national average. The abbreviation 'na' is used to show that data are 'not available'. Ratios shown for 2002, the last complete census year.

*Equivalent to Federal Government NAICS 332997, 332998, 332999.

LEADING COMPANIES   Number shown: 75   Total sales ($ mil): 573,333   Total employment (000): 1,266.2

Company Name	Address				CEO Name	Phone	Co. Type	Sales ($ mil)	Empl. (000)
Ford Motor Co.	1 American Rd.	Dearborn	MI	48126		313-322-3000	P	172,455	246.0
McKesson Corp.	1 Post St.	San Francisco	CA	94104	John H. Hammergren	415-983-8300	P	92,977	31.8
Caterpillar Inc.	100 NE Adams St.	Peoria	IL	61629		309-675-1000	P	44,958	101.3
General Dynamics Corp.	2941 Fairview Park	Falls Church	VA	22042	Nicholas D. Chabraja	703-876-3000	P	27,240	83.5
Deere and Co.	1 John Deere Pl.	Moline	IL	61265		309-765-8000	P	24,082	52.0
CP and P Inc.	133 Peachtree St.	Atlanta	GA	30303	Jospeh Moller	404-652-4000	S	16,083*	55.0
Masco Corp.	21001 Van Born Rd.	Taylor	MI	48180	Ronald W. Ayers	313-274-7400	P	11,770	52.0
Parker Hannifin Corp.	6035 Parkland Blvd.	Cleveland	OH	44124	Lee Banks	216-896-3000	P	10,718	57.3
Applied Materials Inc.	PO Box 58039	Santa Clara	CA	95052		408-727-5555	P	9,735	15.3
Terex Corp.	200 Nyala Farm Rd.	Westport	CT	06880		203-222-7170	P	9,138	21.0
Fortune Brands Inc.	520 Lake Cook Rd.	Deerfield	IL	60015	Bruce A. Carbonari	847-484-4400	P	8,563	31.0
American Standard Inc.	PO Box 6820	Piscataway	NJ	08855		732-980-3000	S	7,614*	67.0
Prager Inc.	PO Box 61670	New Orleans	LA	70161	Jennifer McKnight	504-524-2363	R	7,580*	<0.1
Trane Inc.	PO Box 6820	Piscataway	NJ	08855		732-980-6000	P	7,450	29.6
Saint-Gobain Abrasives Inc.	1 New Bond St.	Worcester	MA	01606	Jean Phelizon	508-795-5000	R	6,831*	2.5
Oshkosh Truck Corp.	PO Box 2566	Oshkosh	WI	54903	Robert G. Bohn	920-235-9150	P	6,307	14.2
BorgWarner Inc.	3850 Hamlin Rd.	Auburn Hills	MI	48326		248-754-9200	P	5,329	17.7
Kohler Co.	444 Highland Dr.	Kohler	WI	53044	Herbert Kohler	920-457-4441	R	4,061*	33.0
Flowserve Corp.	5215 N O'Connor	Irving	TX	75039		972-443-6500	P	3,763	15.0
Harsco Corp.	PO Box 8888	Camp Hill	PA	17001	S. D. Fazzolari	717-763-7064	P	3,688	21.5
NACCO Industries Inc.	5875 Landerbrook	Mayfield Hgts	OH	44124		440-449-9600	P	3,603	10.2
Energizer Holdings Inc.	533 Maryville Univ.	St. Louis	MO	63141		314-985-2000	P	3,365	11.1
Kalmar Industries USA L.L.C.	415 E Dundee St.	Ottawa	KS	66067		785-242-2200	R	3,320*	0.3
Waltco Truck Equipment Company	PO Box 354	Tallmadge	OH	44278	Lennart Bohman	330-633-9191	R	3,320*	0.2
Milliken Chemical	PO Box 1926	Spartanburg	SC	29304	Ashley Allen	864-503-2200	R	3,317*	10.0
Diebold Inc.	PO Box 3077	North Canton	OH	44720		330-490-4000	P	2,906	15.5
GE Water and Process Tech.	4636 Somerton Rd.	Trevose	PA	19053	Jeff Garwood	215-355-3300	S	2,748*	8.0
Freightliner L.L.C.	PO Box 3849	Portland	OR	97208	Chris Patterson	503-745-8000	S	2,734*	14.0
International Game Technology	PO Box 10580	Reno	NV	89510	G. Thomas Baker	775-448-7777	P	2,621	5.4
Crane Co.	100 First Stamford	Stamford	CT	06902	Thomas Craney	203-363-7300	P	2,619	12.0
HNI Corp.	PO Box 1109	Muscatine	IA	52761	Timothy Anderson	563-264-7400	P	2,571	14.2
O'Reilly Automotive Inc.	233 S Patterson Ave	Springfield	MO	65802	Greg Henslee	417-862-6708	P	2,522	18.5
JELD-WEN Inc.	PO Box 1329	Klamath Falls	OR	97601	Richard Wendt	541-882-3451	R	2,476*	23.8
Synalloy Metals Inc.	390 Bristol Metals	Bristol	TN	37621	Ronald H. Braam	423-989-4700	S	2,012*	0.4
American Power Conversion	132 Fairgrounds Rd.	West Kingston	RI	02892	Rodger B. Dowdell Jr.	401-789-5735	S	1,980	7.6
Teleflex Inc.	155 S Limerick Rd.	Limerick	PA	19468	Jeffrey P. Black	610-948-5100	P	1,934	14.0
Schuler Inc.	7145 Commerce	Canton	MI	48187	Timothy McCaughey	734-207-7200	R	1,874*	<0.1
Weir Spm	7701 Skyline Park	Fort Worth	TX	76108	Steve Noon	817-246-2461	R	1,770*	0.3
American Greetings Corp.	1 American Rd.	Cleveland	OH	44144		216-252-7300	P	1,745	28.9
Volvo Trucks North America	PO Box 26115	Greensboro	NC	27402	Peter Karlsten	336-393-2000	S	1,737*	5.4
Curtiss-Wright Corp.	4 Becker Farm Rd.	Roseland	NJ	07068	Martin R. Benante	973-597-4700	P	1,592	6.2
CC Industries Inc.	222 N La Salle St.	Chicago	IL	60601	William H. Crown	312-855-4000	S	1,560*	6.0
Ancra International L.L.C.	4880 W Rosecrans	Hawthorne	CA	90250	Steve Frediani	310-973-5000	S	1,560*	0.1
Pettibone Traverse Lift L.L.C.	PO Box 368	Baraga	MI	49908		906-353-6611	R	1,560*	0.1
Heico Holding Inc.	2626 Warrenville Rd	Downers Grove	IL	60515	Michael Heisley	630-353-5000	R	1,560*	<0.1
Moog Inc.	Jamison Rd.	East Aurora	NY	14052		716-652-2000	P	1,558	8.4
Barnes Group Inc.	PO Box 489	Bristol	CT	06011	Thomas Barnes	860-583-7070	P	1,539	6.7
Valmont Industries Inc.	1 Valmont Plz.	Omaha	NE	68154	Mogens C. Bay	402-963-1000	P	1,500	6.0
Beckett Corp.	400 E Royal Ln.	Irving	TX	75039	Wingate Sung	972-871-8000	R	1,409*	0.1
Watts Water Technologies Inc.	815 Chestnut St.	North Andover	MA	01845		978-688-1811	P	1,382	7.8
Dresser Inc.	15455 Dallas Pkwy.	Addison	TX	75001		972-361-9800	S	1,343*	6.0
Morgan Adv. Materials/Tech.	441 Hall Ave.	Saint Marys	PA	15857	David Cooper	814-781-1573	R	1,320*	0.3
Fulmer Company L.L.C.	3004 Venture Ct.	Export	PA	15632	Leo Eger	724-325-7140	R	1,320*	<0.1
Blyth Inc.	1 E Weaver St.	Greenwich	CT	06831		203-661-1926	P	1,221	4.0
Longaberger Co.	1500 E Main St.	Newark	OH	43055	Jim Klein	740-322-5000	R	1,206*	8.7
Jacuzzi Brands Inc.	777 S Flagler Dr.	W Palm Bch	FL	33401		561-514-3838	S	1,202	4.5
Viking Automatic Sprinkler Co.	1301 L Orient St.	Saint Paul	MN	55117	Lee Anderson	651-558-3300	R	1,150*	<0.1
Henry Pratt Co.	401 S Highland Ave.	Aurora	IL	60506		630-844-4000	S	1,146*	0.3
Parker Hannifin Skinner Valve	95 Edgewood Ave.	New Britain	CT	06051	D E. Washkewicz	860-827-2300	D	1,138*	0.3
Swagelok Co.	29500 Solon Rd.	Solon	OH	44139	Arthur F. Anton	440-248-4600	R	1,100*	3.3
Lancaster Colony Corp.	37 W Broad St.	Columbus	OH	43215	John B. Gerlach, Jr.	614-224-7141	P	1,091	5.6
AAR Corp.	1100 N Wood Dale	Wood Dale	IL	60191	Ira A. Eichner	630-227-2000	P	1,061	3.9
Robert Bosch Tool Corp.	1961 Bishop Ln.	Louisville	KY	40218	Timothy Shea	502-625-2050	D	1,057*	0.2
Crown Equipment Corp.	44 S Washington St.	New Bremen	OH	45869	James Dicke	419-629-2311	R	1,049*	7.6
Syngenta Seeds Inc. - NK	PO Box 959	Minneapolis	MN	55440	Jeff Cox	763-593-7333	S	1,044*	1.3
Brady Corp.	PO Box 571	Milwaukee	WI	53201	Peter Lambert	414-358-6600	P	1,018	8.0
EFD Inc.	977 Waterman Ave.	East Providence	RI	02914		401-434-1680	P	972*	0.3
BWAY Holding Co.	8607 Roberts Dr.	Atlanta	GA	30350	Jean-Pierre M. Ergas	770-645-4800	P	959	2.5
McWane Corp.	PO Box 43327	Birmingham	AL	35243	G. Ruffner Page, Jr.	205-414-3100	R	944*	7.0
NGK-Locke Inc.	2525 Insulator Dr.	Baltimore	MD	21230	Shun Matsushita	410-347-1700	S	941*	3.7
JW Aluminum Co.	PO Box 29419-05	Charleston	SC	29419	Don Kessing	843-572-1100	S	912*	0.8
United Components Inc.	14601 Hwy 41 N	Evansville	IN	47725	Bruce Zorich	812-867-4156	S	906	6.8
Intermec Inc.	6001 36th Ave. W	Everett	WA	98203	Patrick Byrne	425-348-2600	P	849	2.4
International Industries Inc.	PO Box 1210	Gilbert	WV	25621		304-664-3227	R	835*	0.5
P.R. Hoffman Machine Products	1517 Commerce	Carlisle	PA	17015		717-243-9900	S	812*	<0.1

Source: Ward's Business Directory of U.S. Private and Public Companies, Volumes 1 and 2, 2008. The company type code used is as follows: P - Public, R - Private, S - Subsidiary, D - Division, J - Joint Venture, A - Affiliate, G - Group. Sales are in millions of dollars, employees are in thousands. An asterisk (*) indicates an estimated sales volume. The symbol < stands for 'less than'. Company names and addresses are truncated, in some cases, to fit into the available space.

MATERIALS CONSUMED FOR INDUSTRIAL PATTERN MANUFACTURING

Material	Quantity	Delivered Cost ($ million)
Fabricated metal products (excluding forgings)	(X)	4.7
Iron and steel castings (rough and semifinished)	(X)	8.6
Aluminum and aluminum-base alloy castings (rough and semifinished)	(X)	5.7
Other nonferrous metal castings, rough or semifinished (inc. aluminum)	(X)	0.7
Steel shapes and forms (exc. castings, forgings, fabr. metal products)	(X)	1.4
Aluminum and aluminum-base alloy shapes and forms (exc. castings, forgings, fabr. metal products)	(X)	2.7
Other nonferrous shapes and forms (exc. castings, forgings, fabricated metal products)	(X)	0.9
Rough and dressed lumber	(X)	2.5
Plastics products consumed in the form of sheets, rods, etc.	(X)	2.3
All other materials, components, parts, containers, and supplies	(X)	43.5
Materials, ingredients, containers, and supplies, nsk	(X)	19.5

Source: 2002 *Economic Census*. Explanation of symbols used: (D): Withheld to avoid disclosure of competitive data; na: Not available; (S): Withheld because statistical norms were not met; (X): Not applicable; (Z): Less than half the unit shown; nec: Not elsewhere classified; nsk: Not specified by kind; - : zero; p : 10-19 percent estimated; q : 20-29 percent estimated.

MATERIALS CONSUMED FOR ENAMELED IRON AND METAL SANITARY WARE MANUFACTURING

Material	Quantity	Delivered Cost ($ million)
Metal stampings	(X)	13.9
All other fabricated metal products (excluding forgings)	(X)	(D)
Iron and steel castings (rough and semifinished)	(X)	46.5
Other nonferrous metal castings, rough or semifinished (inc. aluminum)	(X)	(D)
Steel shapes and forms (exc. castings, forgings, fabr. metal products)	(X)	97.2
Copper and copper-base alloy pipe and tube (exc. castings, forgings, fabr. metal products)	(X)	(D)
Plastics resins consumed in the form of granules, pellets, etc.	(X)	26.7
Fabricated plastics products (excluding gaskets)	(X)	(D)
Paperboard containers, boxes, and corrugated paperboard	(X)	20.4
All other materials, components, parts, containers, and supplies	(X)	126.5
Materials, ingredients, containers, and supplies, nsk	(X)	34.3

Source: 2002 *Economic Census*. Explanation of symbols used: (D): Withheld to avoid disclosure of competitive data; na: Not available; (S): Withheld because statistical norms were not met; (X): Not applicable; (Z): Less than half the unit shown; nec: Not elsewhere classified; nsk: Not specified by kind; - : zero; p : 10-19 percent estimated; q : 20-29 percent estimated.

MATERIALS CONSUMED FOR MISCELLANEOUS FABRICATED METAL PRODUCT MANUFACTURING NEC

Material	Quantity	Delivered Cost ($ million)
Metal bolts, nuts, screws, and other screw machine products	(X)	48.2
Metal fittings, flanges, unions for piping systems (except forgings)	(X)	8.8
Metal stampings	(X)	78.2
Other fabricated metal products (exc. unions, screws, etc.)	(X)	130.1
Forgings	(X)	7.9
Iron and steel castings (rough and semifinished)	(X)	39.9
Aluminum and aluminum-base alloy castings (rough and semifinished)	(X)	45.5
Other nonferrous metal castings, rough or semifinished (inc. aluminum)	(X)	7.6
Steel bars and bar shapes (exc. castings, forgings, fabr. metal products)	(X)	36.9
Steel sheet and strip (including tinplate)	(X)	443.5
Steel plate	(X)	58.4
Steel structural shapes (exc. castings, forgings, fabr. metal products)	(X)	21.2
Steel pipes (exc. castings, forgings, fabr. metal products)	(X)	23.9
All other steel shapes and forms (exc. castings, forgings, fabr. metal products)	(X)	25.7
Copper and copper-base alloy pipe and tube (exc. castings, forgings, fabr. metal products)	(X)	3.6
All other copper and copper-base alloy shapes and forms (exc. castings, forgings, fabr. metal products)	(X)	8.0
Aluminum and aluminum-base alloy sheet, plate, foil, and welded tubing	(X)	163.7
Aluminum and aluminum-base alloy extruded shapes (rod, bar, pipe, tube, etc.)	(X)	111.7
Aluminum and aluminum-base alloy foil, plain	(X)	195.3
Other aluminum and aluminum-base alloy shapes and forms (exc. castings, forgings, fabr. metal products)	(X)	43.2
Other nonferrous shapes and forms (exc. castings, forgings, fabricated metal products)	(X)	15.7
Metal powders	(X)	12.4
Plastics resins consumed in the form of granules, pellets, etc.	(X)	92.6
Plastics products consumed in the form of sheets, rods, etc.	(X)	32.8
Natural abrasive materials, excluding diamonds	(X)	(D)
Glues and adhesives	(X)	(D)
Paper and paperboard products (incl. paperboard boxes, etc.)	(X)	48.7
All other materials, components, parts, containers, and supplies	(X)	1,823.8
Materials, ingredients, containers, and supplies, nsk	(X)	1,093.4

Source: 2002 *Economic Census*. Explanation of symbols used: (D): Withheld to avoid disclosure of competitive data; na: Not available; (S): Withheld because statistical norms were not met; (X): Not applicable; (Z): Less than half the unit shown; nec: Not elsewhere classified; nsk: Not specified by kind; - : zero; p : 10-19 percent estimated; q : 20-29 percent estimated.

PRODUCT SHARE DETAILS FOR INDUSTRIAL PATTERN MANUFACTURING

Product or Product Class Shipments	Mil. $	Product or Product Class Shipments	Mil. $
INDUSTRIAL PATTERNS	616.5	All other industrial patterns (except shoe patterns)	131.7
Industrial patterns, except shoe patterns	**616.5**	Industrial patterns, nsk, total	94.5
Foundry patterns	390.3		

Source: 2002 Economic Census. The values are product shipments in millions of dollars for 2002. Total product shipments may be lower or higher than industry shipments. See Introduction for a full discussion. Values of indented subcategories are summed in the main heading(s). The symbol (D) appears when data are withheld to prevent disclosure of competitive information. The abbreviation nsk stands for 'not specified by kind' and nec for 'not elsewhere classified'. A dash (-) means zero.

PRODUCT SHARE DETAILS FOR ENAMELED IRON AND METAL SANITARY WARE MANUFACTURING

Product or Product Class Shipments	Mil. $	Product or Product Class Shipments	Mil. $
ENAMELED IRON AND METAL SANITARY WARE	1,285.7	including portable chemical toilets, water closet tanks, etc.	191.1
Metal plumbing fixtures	**1,285.7**	Enameled iron and metal sanitary ware, nsk, total	79.4
Enameled iron and metal plumbing fixtures	1,015.2		
Other enameled iron and metal plumbing fixtures,			

Source: 2002 Economic Census. The values are product shipments in millions of dollars for 2002. Total product shipments may be lower or higher than industry shipments. See Introduction for a full discussion. Values of indented subcategories are summed in the main heading(s). The symbol (D) appears when data are withheld to prevent disclosure of competitive information. The abbreviation nsk stands for 'not specified by kind' and nec for 'not elsewhere classified'. A dash (-) means zero.

PRODUCT SHARE DETAILS FOR MISCELLANEOUS FABRICATED METAL PRODUCT MANUFACTURING NEC

Product or Product Class Shipments	Mil. $	Product or Product Class Shipments	Mil. $
FABRICATED METAL PRODUCTS, NEC	11,863.1	Metal pipe hangers and supports (except metal framing)	143.7
Converted unmounted aluminum foil packaging products	**780.3**	Hardware	102.8
Converted unmounted aluminum foil for packaging products, not laminated to other materials	522.8	Electrosilverplated holloware, electrosilverplated to a nonprecious (except pewter) metal base	51.0
Coated foil .001 to .003 inch thickness	214.0	Holloware, precious and nonprecious metal plated to a nonprecious (except pewter) metal base, excluding	
Coated foil greater than .003 inch thickness	43.5	electrosilverplated holloware	40.2
Machinery products, nec	**1,286.7**	Electrosilverplated holloware, electrosilverplated to a precious metal or pewter base	(D)
Flexible copper and copper-base alloy hose and tubing	134.9	Unplated holloware of other metals, including	
Flexible aluminum and aluminum-base alloy hose and tubing	403.2	stainless steel	(D)
Flexible stainless steel hose and tubing	518.4	All other fabricated metal products, nec	4,826.7
Other flexible metal hose and tubing	230.2	Stamped metal wheels for golf carts, lawn mowers, etc. (disc type)	705.5
Fabricated metal collapsible tubes	**67.7**	Metal spools and reels	68.2
Fabricated collapsible metal tubes, including tin, tin-coated, tin-lead alloy, and lead	57.3	Metal pallets and skids, excluding wood and metal combinations	19.4
Fabricated collapsible aluminum tubes	50.7	Miscellaneous fabricated products, made primarily of metal (combs and hair curlers, etc.)	773.4
Other fabricated collapsible metal tubes, including tin, tin-coated, tin-lead alloy, and lead	6.6	Steel wool	(D)
Fabricated metal collapsible tubes, nsk	10.4	Metal scouring pads, including those with soap	(D)
Flat metal strapping	**396.0**	Fabricated metal safes and vaults (fire-resistive and burglary-resistive)	188.4
Metal ladders	**342.9**	Fabricated metal safe deposit boxes	35.1
Metal step, platform, and rung-type ladders, metal ladder-type step stools, and ladder accessories	342.9	All other fabricated metal bank and security vaults and equipment	59.6
Metal step and platform ladders	119.6	Fireplace fixtures and equipment (including irons, screens, tongs, and other fire tools)	63.5
Metal rung-type ladders (single, trestle, extension, sectional, etc.)	139.5	Traps, handcuffs, and leg irons	(D)
Metal ladder-type step stools	(D)	All other fabricated metal products (including metal ironing boards and metal memorial tablets and grave markers)	2,831.8
Metal ladder accessories, including levelors, ladder feet, ladder jacks, roof hooks, bucket shelves, etc.	(D)	All other fabricated metal products, nec, nsk	30.8
Metal ladder, nsk	0.0	**Fabricated metal products, nec, nsk, total**	**3,563.0**
All other miscellaneous fabricated metal products, nec	**5,426.5**		
Metal fittings, flanges, and unions for piping systems	466.2		
Permanent magnets, except ceramic permanent magnets	232.6		
Fabricated assemblies of railroad frogs, switches, and crossings	89.9		

Source: 2002 Economic Census. The values are product shipments in millions of dollars for 2002. Total product shipments may be lower or higher than industry shipments. See Introduction for a full discussion. Values of indented subcategories are summed in the main heading(s). The symbol (D) appears when data are withheld to prevent disclosure of competitive information. The abbreviation nsk stands for 'not specified by kind' and nec for 'not elsewhere classified'. A dash (-) means zero.

INPUTS AND OUTPUTS FOR OTHER FABRICATED METAL MANUFACTURING

Economic Sector or Industry Providing Inputs	%	Sector	Economic Sector or Industry Buying Outputs	%	Sector
Compensation of employees	29.9		Exports of goods & services	14.9	Cap Inv
Iron & steel mills & ferroalloys	6.5	Manufg.	Personal consumption expenditures	7.6	
Aluminum products from purchased aluminum	4.9	Manufg.	Food services & drinking places	4.1	Services
Wholesale trade	4.2	Trade	Motor vehicle parts	3.8	Manufg.
Management of companies & enterprises	2.8	Services	Nonresidential structures, nec	2.9	Construct.

Continued on next page.

INPUTS AND OUTPUTS FOR OTHER FABRICATED METAL MANUFACTURING - Continued

Economic Sector or Industry Providing Inputs	%	Sector	Economic Sector or Industry Buying Outputs	%	Sector
Ornamental & architectural metal products	1.7	Manufg.	Manufacturing structures	2.3	Construct.
Fabricated metals, nec	1.6	Manufg.	Residential permanent site structures	2.1	Construct.
Paints & coatings	1.4	Manufg.	Private fixed investment	2.0	
Real estate	1.2	Fin/R.E.	Transit & ground passenger transportation	1.9	Util.
Nonferrous metal foundries	1.1	Manufg.	Transportation equipment, nec	1.7	Manufg.
Power generation & supply	1.1	Util.	Retail trade	1.5	Trade
Crowns & closures & metal stamping	1.0	Manufg.	Owner-occupied dwellings	1.4	
Plastics materials & resins	1.0	Manufg.	Residential structures, nec	1.4	Construct.
Truck transportation	1.0	Util.	Concrete products, nec	1.3	Manufg.
Ferrous metal foundries	1.0	Manufg.	Basic inorganic chemicals, nec	1.2	Manufg.
Steel products from purchased steel	0.9	Manufg.	Wholesale trade	1.2	Trade
Securities, commodity contracts, investments	0.9	Fin/R.E.	Fabricated metals, nec	1.1	Manufg.
Motors & generators	0.8	Manufg.	Hotels & motels, including casino hotels	1.1	Services
Machine shops	0.8	Manufg.	Management of companies & enterprises	1.1	Services
Industrial molds	0.7	Manufg.	S/L govt. invest., education	1.0	S/L Govt
Natural gas distribution	0.6	Util.	Telecommunications	1.0	Services
Turned products & screws, nuts, & bolts	0.6	Manufg.	Other S/L govt. enterprises	0.9	S/L Govt
Semiconductors & related devices	0.6	Manufg.	Lawn & garden equipment	0.9	Manufg.
Lessors of nonfinancial assets	0.6	Fin/R.E.	Farm machinery & equipment	0.8	Manufg.
Printed circuit assemblies (electronic assemblies)	0.6	Manufg.	Steel products from purchased steel	0.8	Manufg.
Monetary authorities/depository credit intermediation	0.6	Fin/R.E.	Commercial & health care structures	0.8	Construct.
Advertising & related services	0.6	Services	Industrial machinery, nec	0.8	Manufg.
Communication & energy wires & cables	0.5	Manufg.	S/L govt. invest., other	0.8	S/L Govt
Chemical products & preparations, nec	0.5	Manufg.	General purpose machinery, nec	0.7	Manufg.
Abrasive products	0.5	Manufg.	Lessors of nonfinancial assets	0.7	Fin/R.E.
Valve & fittings other than plumbing	0.5	Manufg.	Maintenance/repair of nonresidential structures	0.7	Construct.
Professional, scientific, technical services, nec	0.5	Services	Manufacturing, nec	0.7	Manufg.
Coating, engraving, heat treating & allied activities	0.5	Manufg.	Plate work & fabricated structural products	0.6	Manufg.
Paperboard containers	0.5	Manufg.	Cutlery, utensils, pots, & pans	0.6	Manufg.
Paperboard mills	0.5	Manufg.	Chemical products & preparations, nec	0.6	Manufg.
Taxes on production & imports, less subsidies	0.4		Hospitals	0.6	Services
Automotive equipment rental & leasing	0.4	Fin/R.E.	Architectural, engineering, & related services	0.6	Services
Plastics packaging materials, film & sheet	0.4	Manufg.	Sanitary paper products	0.5	Manufg.
Hardware	0.3	Manufg.	Oil & gas extraction	0.5	Mining
Plate work & fabricated structural products	0.3	Manufg.	Plastics materials & resins	0.5	Manufg.
Accounting, tax preparation, bookkeeping, & payroll	0.3	Services	Ferrous metal foundries	0.5	Manufg.
Legal services	0.3	Services	Engine equipment, nec	0.4	Manufg.
Cutting tools & machine tool accessories	0.3	Manufg.	Machine shops	0.4	Manufg.
Maintenance/repair of nonresidential structures	0.3	Construct.	Confectionery products, chocolate	0.4	Manufg.
Services to buildings & dwellings	0.3	Services	Brick, tile & other structural clay products	0.4	Manufg.
Petroleum refineries	0.3	Manufg.	Clay & nonclay refractory manufacturing	0.4	Manufg.
Flat glass	0.3	Manufg.	Ornamental & architectural metal products	0.4	Manufg.
Warehousing & storage	0.3	Util.	Light truck & utility vehicles	0.4	Manufg.
Food services & drinking places	0.3	Services	Waste management & remediation services	0.4	Services
Metal cutting & forming machine tools	0.3	Manufg.	Material handling equipment	0.4	Manufg.
Telecommunications	0.3	Services	Nonferrous metal foundries	0.4	Manufg.
Data processing, hosting, & related services	0.2	Services	Concrete pipe, brick, & block	0.4	Manufg.
Nonferrous metal (ex. copper & aluminum) processing	0.2	Manufg.	Physician, dentist, other health practitioner offices	0.4	Services
Architectural, engineering, & related services	0.2	Services	Cheese	0.4	Manufg.
Power boilers & heat exchangers	0.2	Manufg.	Plastics products, nec	0.3	Manufg.
Rail transportation	0.2	Util.	Bread & bakery products	0.3	Manufg.
Industrial process variable instruments	0.2	Manufg.	Poultry processing	0.3	Manufg.
Commercial & industrial machinery rental & leasing	0.2	Fin/R.E.	Printing	0.3	Manufg.
Fluid power process machinery	0.2	Manufg.	Animal, except poultry, processing	0.3	Manufg.
Scientific research & development services	0.2	Services	Wineries	0.3	Manufg.
Alumina refining & primary aluminum production	0.2	Manufg.	Amusement & recreation, nec	0.3	Services
Automotive repair & maintenance, ex. car washes	0.2	Services	Canned & dehydrated fruits & vegetables	0.3	Manufg.
Noncomparable imports	0.2	Foreign	Tobacco products	0.3	Manufg.
Metal tanks (heavy gauge)	0.2	Manufg.	Scientific research & development services	0.3	Services
Employment services	0.2	Services	Plastics packaging materials, film & sheet	0.3	Manufg.
Hotels & motels, including casino hotels	0.2	Services	Rubber products, nec	0.3	Manufg.
Air transportation	0.2	Util.	Postal service	0.3	Util.
Commercial & industrial equipment repair/maintenance	0.1	Services	Federal government, investment, national defense	0.2	Fed Govt
Plastics products, nec	0.1	Manufg.	Real estate	0.2	Fin/R.E.
Business support services	0.1	Services	Paperboard containers	0.2	Manufg.
Copper rolling, drawing, extruding, & alloying	0.1	Manufg.	Dry, condensed, & evaporated dairy products	0.2	Manufg.
Specialized design services	0.1	Services	Paints & coatings	0.2	Manufg.
Metal cans, boxes, & other containers (light gauge)	0.1	Manufg.	Seasoning & dressing	0.2	Manufg.
Nonmetallic minerals, nec	0.1	Mining	Coal	0.2	Mining
Springs & wire products	0.1	Manufg.	Turned products & screws, nuts, & bolts	0.2	Manufg.
Management, scientific, & technical consulting	0.1	Services	Ice cream & frozen desserts	0.2	Manufg.
Industrial process furnaces & ovens	0.1	Manufg.	Warehousing & storage	0.2	Util.
Cutlery, utensils, pots, & pans	0.1	Manufg.	Metal cans, boxes, & other containers (light gauge)	0.2	Manufg.
Other computer related services, including facilities	0.1	Services	Snack food	0.2	Manufg.
Rubber & plastics hose & belting	0.1	Manufg.	Automobiles	0.2	Manufg.
			Semiconductors & related devices	0.2	Manufg.
			Coating, engraving, heat treating & allied activities	0.2	Manufg.
			Scenic & sightseeing transport & related services	0.2	Util.
			Services to buildings & dwellings	0.2	Services
			Computer terminals & peripherals	0.2	Manufg.

Continued on next page.

INPUTS AND OUTPUTS FOR OTHER FABRICATED METAL MANUFACTURING - Continued

Economic Sector or Industry Providing Inputs	%	Sector	Economic Sector or Industry Buying Outputs	%	Sector
			Surgical appliances & supplies	0.2	Manufg.
			Pottery, ceramics, and plumbing fixtures	0.2	Manufg.
			Computer system design services	0.2	Services
			Valve & fittings other than plumbing	0.2	Manufg.
			Truck transportation	0.2	Util.
			Cookies, crackers, & pasta	0.2	Manufg.
			Rail transportation	0.2	Util.
			Surgical & medical instrument	0.2	Manufg.
			Food, nec	0.2	Manufg.
			Crowns & closures & metal stamping	0.2	Manufg.
			Confectionery products from cacao beans	0.2	Manufg.
			Wet corn milling	0.2	Manufg.
			Maintenance/repair of residential structures	0.2	Construct.
			Federal government, investment, nondefense	0.2	Fed Govt
			Signs	0.2	Manufg.
			Mining & oil & gas field machinery	0.2	Manufg.
			Coffee & tea	0.2	Manufg.
			Commercial & service industry machinery, nec	0.1	Manufg.
			Educational services, nec	0.1	Services
			Mineral wool	0.1	Manufg.
			AC, refrigeration, and warm air heating equipment	0.1	Manufg.
			Nonmetallic mineral products, nec	0.1	Manufg.
			Aluminum products from purchased aluminum	0.1	Manufg.
			Asphalt paving mixtures & blocks	0.1	Manufg.
			General S/L govt. services	0.1	S/L Govt
			Turbines & turbine generator set units	0.1	Manufg.
			Civic, social, & professional organizations	0.1	Services
			Aircraft parts & auxiliary equipment, nec	0.1	Manufg.
			Motorcycles, bicycles, & parts	0.1	Manufg.
			Semiconductor machinery	0.1	Manufg.
			Boat building	0.1	Manufg.
			Power boilers & heat exchangers	0.1	Manufg.
			Cement	0.1	Manufg.
			Fertilizer	0.1	Manufg.
			Business support services	0.1	Services
			Natural gas distribution	0.1	Util.
			Animal food, nec	0.1	Manufg.
			Lighting fixtures	0.1	Manufg.
			Hardware	0.1	Manufg.
			Nondepository credit intermediation activities	0.1	Fin/R.E.
			Construction machinery	0.1	Manufg.
			Beet sugar	0.1	Manufg.
			Synthetic dyes & pigments	0.1	Manufg.
			Jewelry & silverware	0.1	Manufg.
			Asphalt shingle & coating materials	0.1	Manufg.
			Hunting and trapping	0.1	Agric.
			Internet publishing & broadcasting	0.1	Services
			Pipeline transportation	0.1	Util.
			Soybean & oilseed processing	0.1	Manufg.
			Wood kitchen cabinets & countertops	0.1	Manufg.
			Guided missiles & space vehicles	0.1	Manufg.

Source: Benchmark Input-Output Accounts for the U.S. Economy, 2002, U.S. Department of Commerce, Washington, D.C., January 2008. The abbreviation nec stands for 'not elsewhere classified'.

OCCUPATIONS EMPLOYED BY OTHER FABRICATED METAL PRODUCT MANUFACTURING

Occupation	% of Total 2006	Change to 2016	Occupation	% of Total 2006	Change to 2016
Team assemblers	11.0	-11.4	Structural metal fabricators & fitters	1.4	-11.4
Machinists	4.6	-7.0	Mechanical engineers	1.4	-11.4
Welders, cutters, solderers, & brazers	3.9	-5.7	General & operations managers	1.3	-20.3
First-line supervisors/managers of production workers	3.8	-11.4	Executive secretaries & administrative assistants	1.3	-11.4
Cutting, punching, & press machine operators	3.4	-20.3	Coating, painting, & spraying machine operators	1.3	-15.8
Inspectors, testers, sorters, samplers, & weighers	3.0	-16.4	Packers & packagers, hand	1.2	-29.1
Computer-controlled machine tool operators	2.8	-2.5	Customer service representatives	1.2	-2.5
Grinding, lapping, polishing machine tool operators	2.7	-14.0	Drilling & boring machine tool operators	1.2	-20.3
Sales reps, wholesale & manufacturing, exc tech	2.2	-11.4	Industrial machinery mechanics	1.1	1.9
Helpers--Production workers	2.2	-11.4	Assemblers & fabricators, nec	1.1	-20.3
Lathe & turning machine tool operators & tenders	2.0	-20.3	Industrial truck & tractor operators	1.1	-20.3
Laborers & freight, stock, & material movers, hand	2.0	-20.3	Bookkeeping, accounting, & auditing clerks	1.1	-11.4
Shipping, receiving, & traffic clerks	1.9	-14.7	Production, planning, & expediting clerks	1.0	-11.4
Industrial engineers	1.8	7.6	Molding, coremaking, & casting machine operators	1.0	-20.3
Maintenance & repair workers, general	1.7	-11.4	Office clerks, general	1.0	-12.7

Source: Industry-Occupation Matrix, Bureau of Labor Statistics, December 4, 2007. These data are reported based on 4-digit NAICS categories but have been matched to corresponding 6-digit NAICS industry codes. The change reported for each occupation to the year 2016 is a percent of growth or decline as estimated by the Bureau of Labor Statistics. The abbreviation nec stands for 'not elsewhere classified'.

LOCATION BY STATE AND REGIONAL CONCENTRATION

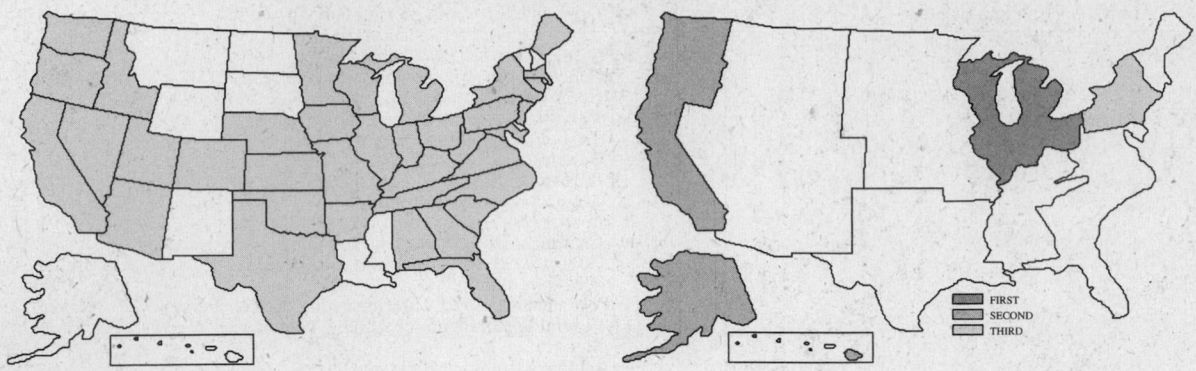

INDUSTRY DATA BY STATE

| State | Establish-ments | Shipments | | | Employment | | | | Cost as % of Shipments | Investment per Employee ($) |
		Total ($ mil)	% of U.S.	Per Establ.	Total Number	% of U.S.	Per Establ.	Wages ($/hour)		
California	477	1,318.5	9.1	2,764.1	8,857	9.9	19	15.54	44.6	4,906
Ohio	221	1,297.9	9.0	5,872.9	6,568	7.4	30	17.33	37.8	7,786
Illinois	268	1,233.0	8.5	4,600.7	6,064	6.8	23	18.90	49.0	13,085
Michigan	269	881.4	6.1	3,276.6	5,927	6.7	22	17.26	39.9	3,693
Indiana	103	838.5	5.8	8,140.8	3,621	4.1	35	14.70	60.1	3,657
Texas	219	821.9	5.7	3,752.8	4,780	5.4	22	14.24	38.0	8,949
Kentucky	54	708.8	4.9	13,126.3	1,854	2.1	34	17.81	52.6	6,894
Pennsylvania	211	697.3	4.8	3,304.9	4,716	5.3	22	15.17	41.2	5,732
Georgia	71	451.4	3.1	6,358.3	2,292	2.6	32	13.54	37.6	6,533
New York	173	411.0	2.8	2,376.0	2,853	3.2	16	14.57	42.2	5,480
North Carolina	106	396.5	2.7	3,740.4	2,277	2.6	21	15.56	44.0	10,073
Minnesota	93	309.5	2.1	3,327.5	1,842	2.1	20	16.61	40.1	7,836
Wisconsin	165	300.4	2.1	1,820.5	2,864	3.2	17	17.12	41.2	4,728
Alabama	48	295.5	2.0	6,157.3	1,478	1.7	31	12.49	51.1	5,002
Massachusetts	105	281.0	1.9	2,676.6	2,207	2.5	21	16.44	39.1	11,806
New Jersey	98	247.7	1.7	2,527.0	1,850	2.1	19	15.78	36.9	2,764
Virginia	48	202.1	1.4	4,211.1	1,315	1.5	27	14.39	41.4	3,401
Florida	117	201.9	1.4	1,725.3	1,828	2.1	16	15.62	42.1	3,323
Tennessee	61	193.3	1.3	3,168.4	1,312	1.5	22	14.79	47.2	5,439
Iowa	40	181.6	1.3	4,539.0	1,332	1.5	33	12.63	49.9	6,839
South Carolina	42	181.1	1.3	4,312.2	1,169	1.3	28	14.80	42.7	3,749
Nebraska	20	169.9	1.2	8,492.5	1,214	1.4	61	13.70	56.8	2,755
Washington	83	159.8	1.1	1,925.6	1,098	1.2	13	17.11	42.0	2,767
Oklahoma	46	153.2	1.1	3,331.0	1,357	1.5	30	13.93	40.9	2,681
Utah	38	137.5	0.9	3,617.2	1,168	1.3	31	13.18	40.3	9,673
Maryland	27	136.2	0.9	5,043.1	570	0.6	21	19.35	46.4	15,674
Connecticut	45	125.6	0.9	2,792.0	971	1.1	22	17.11	39.5	4,297
Rhode Island	25	122.9	0.8	4,916.6	1,107	1.2	44	13.29	45.1	1,671
Oregon	86	113.8	0.8	1,323.8	932	1.0	11	16.04	34.8	3,465
Arizona	54	110.5	0.8	2,047.1	922	1.0	17	14.39	40.7	2,685
Missouri	49	91.9	0.6	1,876.1	765	0.9	16	15.66	35.5	3,013
Colorado	70	81.6	0.6	1,166.1	754	0.8	11	14.88	33.2	2,625
Kansas	34	65.9	0.5	1,939.6	492	0.6	14	15.50	46.6	7,811
Nevada	19	64.5	0.4	3,395.4	554	0.6	29	14.34	44.6	2,466
Maine	14	49.3	0.3	3,520.6	364	0.4	26	17.04	46.7	9,956
Arkansas	37	46.2	0.3	1,249.6	419	0.5	11	13.00	48.2	16,468
West Virginia	15	42.7	0.3	2,847.2	335	0.4	22	12.38	41.7	1,466
Idaho	15	20.8	0.1	1,384.3	228	0.3	15	12.24	57.4	2,329

Source: 2002 *Economic Census*. The states are in descending order of shipments or establishments (if shipment data are missing for the majority). The symbol (D) appears when data are withheld to prevent disclosure of competitive information. States marked with (D) are sorted by number of establishments. A dash (-) indicates that the data element cannot be calculated. Data may not show all states active in the NAICS category. All data available at the time of publication are shown.

NAICS 333111 - FARM MACHINERY AND EQUIPMENT MANUFACTURING

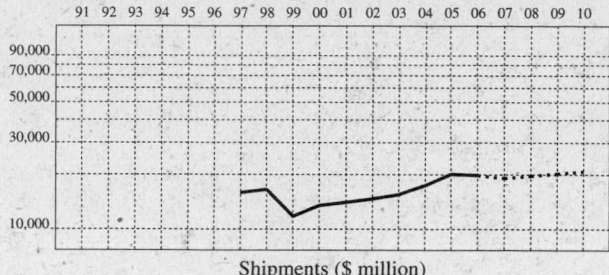

Shipments ($ million)

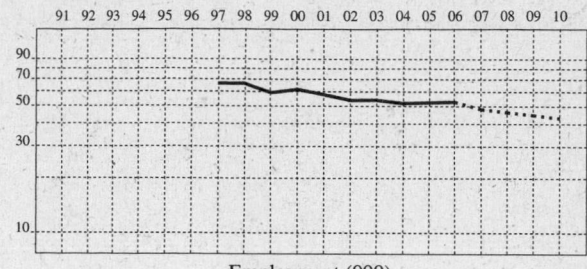

Employment (000)

GENERAL STATISTICS

Year	Companies	Establishments		Employment			Compensation		Production ($ million)			
		Total	with 20 or more employees	Total (000)	Production Workers (000)	Hours (Mil)	Payroll ($ mil)	Wages ($/hr)	Cost of Materials	Value Added by Manufacture	Value of Shipments	Capital Invest.
1997	1,263	1,337	460	66.2	47.8	95.4	2,368.9	16.24	8,456.6	7,541.4	15,899.4	508.9
1998		1,360	493	66.3	47.8	95.8	2,385.7	16.11	8,508.6	8,080.4	16,527.1	439.6
1999		1,318	460	59.1	42.3	76.5	2,093.8	16.85	6,445.7	5,164.8	11,771.6	332.3
2000		1,274	464	61.7	44.3	84.1	2,190.2	16.07	7,722.7	5,865.0	13,501.5	348.6
2001		1,243	445	57.7	41.1	79.9	2,149.2	16.57	7,648.0	6,303.9	14,059.9	332.2
2002	1,141	1,214	384	53.8	37.6	73.5	2,087.9	17.20	7,691.1	6,968.2	14,692.8	343.1
2003		1,138	400	53.9	36.1	71.8	2,113.0	17.42	8,108.0	7,285.6	15,504.7	322.5
2004		1,162	397	51.8	34.8	72.5	2,181.6	18.59	9,323.3	8,282.4	17,412.4	258.3
2005		1,185	404	52.3	36.0	72.5	2,196.0	18.58	10,495.0	9,623.5	20,113.9	305.1
2006		1,113P	375P	52.8	36.3	67.9	2,242.6	19.94	10,216.1	9,549.4	19,802.3	342.9
2007		1,086P	363P	48.1P	32.0P	63.2P	2,123.6P	19.49P	9,852.7P	9,209.7P	19,097.9P	257.6P
2008		1,059P	351P	46.4P	30.5P	60.3P	2,109.6P	19.88P	10,150.0P	9,487.6P	19,674.1P	240.2P
2009		1,032P	339P	44.7P	29.0P	57.4P	2,095.5P	20.26P	10,447.3P	9,765.5P	20,250.4P	222.8P
2010		1,005P	327P	43.0P	27.4P	54.6P	2,081.5P	20.65P	10,744.6P	10,043.4P	20,826.6P	205.4P

Sources: 1997 and 2002 *Economic Census*; other years, up to 2006, are from *Annual Survey of Manufactures*. Establishment counts for non-Census years are from *County Business Patterns*; 1997 and 2002 values are from the 1997 and 2002 censuses, respectively. 'P's show projections by the editors.

INDICES OF CHANGE

Year	Companies	Establishments		Employment			Compensation		Production ($ million)			
		Total	with 20 or more employees	Total (000)	Production Workers (000)	Hours (Mil)	Payroll ($ mil)	Wages ($/hr)	Cost of Materials	Value Added by Manufacture	Value of Shipments	Capital Invest.
1997	111	110	120	123	127	130	113	94	110	108	108	148
1998		112	128	123	127	130	114	94	111	116	112	128
1999		109	120	110	112	104	100	98	84	74	80	97
2000		105	121	115	118	114	105	93	100	84	92	102
2001		102	116	107	109	109	103	96	99	90	96	97
2002	100	100	100	100	100	100	100	100	100	100	100	100
2003		94	104	100	96	98	101	101	105	105	106	94
2004		96	103	96	93	99	104	108	121	119	119	75
2005		98	105	97	96	99	105	108	136	138	137	89
2006		92P	98P	98	97	92	107	116	133	137	135	100
2007		89P	95P	89P	85P	86P	102P	113P	128P	132P	130P	75P
2008		87P	91P	86P	81P	82P	101P	116P	132P	136P	134P	70P
2009		85P	88P	83P	77P	78P	100P	118P	136P	140P	138P	65P
2010		83P	85P	80P	73P	74P	100P	120P	140P	144P	142P	60P

Sources: Same as General Statistics. Values reflect change from the base year, 2002. Values above 100 mean greater than 2002, values below 100 mean less than 2002, and the values of 100 in other years means the same as 2002. 'P's show projections by the editors.

SELECTED RATIOS

For 2002	Avg. of All Manufact.	Analyzed Industry	Index	For 2002	Avg. of All Manufact.	Analyzed Industry	Index
Employees per Establishment	42	44	106	Value Added per Production Worker	182,367	185,324	102
Payroll per Establishment	1,639,184	1,719,852	105	Cost per Establishment	5,769,015	6,335,338	110
Payroll per Employee	39,053	38,809	99	Cost per Employee	137,446	142,957	104
Production Workers per Establishment	30	31	105	Cost per Production Worker	195,506	204,551	105
Wages per Establishment	694,845	1,041,351	150	Shipments per Establishment	11,158,348	12,102,801	108
Wages per Production Worker	23,548	33,622	143	Shipments per Employee	265,847	273,100	103
Hours per Production Worker	1,980	1,955	99	Shipments per Production Worker	378,144	390,766	103
Wages per Hour	11.89	17.20	145	Investment per Establishment	361,338	282,619	78
Value Added per Establishment	5,381,325	5,739,868	107	Investment per Employee	8,609	6,377	74
Value Added per Employee	128,210	129,520	101	Investment per Production Worker	12,245	9,125	75

Sources: Same as General Statistics. The 'Average of All Manufacturing' column represents the average of all manufacturing industries reported for the most recent complete year available. The Index shows the relationship between the Average and the Analyzed Industry. For example, 100 means that they are equal; 500 that the Analyzed Industry is five times the average; 50 means that the Analyzed Industry is half the national average. The abbreviation 'na' is used to show that data are 'not available'. Ratios shown for 2002, the last complete census year.

LEADING COMPANIES   Number shown: **75**   Total sales ($ mil): **88,629**   Total employment (000): **211.4**

Company Name	Address				CEO Name	Phone	Co. Type	Sales ($ mil)	Empl. (000)
Caterpillar Inc.	100 NE Adams St.	Peoria	IL	61629		309-675-1000	P	44,958	101.3
Deere and Co.	1 John Deere Pl.	Moline	IL	61265		309-765-8000	P	24,082	52.0
AGCO Corp.	4205 River Green Pk	Duluth	GA	30096		770-813-9200	P	6,828	13.7
Toro Co.	8111 Lyndale Ave. S	Bloomington	MN	55420		952-888-8801	P	1,877	5.3
CC Industries Inc.	222 N La Salle St.	Chicago	IL	60601	William H. Crown	312-855-4000	S	1,560*	6.0
MTD Products Inc.	PO Box 368022	Cleveland	OH	44136	Curtis E. Moll	330-225-2600	R	1,015*	6.7
Westfaliasurge Inc.	1880 Country Frm	Naperville	IL	60563	Dirk Hejnal	630-369-8100	S	755*	0.1
Blount Inc.	PO Box 22127	Portland	OR	97269	James S. Osterman	503-653-8881	S	583*	3.0
Chore-Time/Brock International	PO Box 2000	Milford	IN	46542	Warren E Buffett	547-658-4191	S	552*	1.0
Alamo Group Inc.	PO Box 549	Seguin	TX	78155	Ronald Robinson	830-379-1480	P	504	2.3
Gehl Co.	PO Box 179	West Bend	WI	53095	William Gehl	262-334-9461	P	458	0.9
James Hardie Transition Co.	26300 La Alameda	Mission Viejo	CA	92691	Donald Manson	949-348-1800	R	423*	<0.1
Kuhn Knight Inc.	1501 W 7th Ave.	Brodhead	WI	53520	Thierry Krier	608-897-2131	R	305*	0.2
Simplicity Manufacturing Inc.	PO Box 997	Port Washington	WI	53074	Warner Frazier	262-377-5450	R	305*	0.5
Lindsay Corp.	2707 N 108th St.	Omaha	NE	68164	M. N. Christodolou	402-428-2131	P	282	0.9
Vermeer Manufacturing Company	PO Box 200	Pella	IA	50219	Mary Andringa	641-628-3141	R	238*	2.0
Metalcraft of Mayville Inc.	PO Box 151	Mayville	WI	53050	Edwin Gallun	920-387-3150	R	200*	0.7
Chief Industries Inc.	PO Box 2078	Grand Island	NE	68802	Robert Eihusen	308-389-7200	R	185*	<0.1
Alamo Group (USA) Inc.	1502 E Walnut	Seguin	TX	78155	Ronald Robinson	830-379-1480	S	181*	0.3
Brillion Iron Works Inc.	200 Park Ave.	Brillion	WI	54110		920-756-2121	S	158*	1.0
Bobcat Co.	PO Box 6000	West Fargo	ND	58078		701-241-8700	S	154*	0.8
Blount Inc. Oregon Cutting Sys	PO Box 22127	Portland	OR	97269	James Osterman	503-653-8881	D	135*	1.0
Hog Slat Inc.	PO Box 300	Newton Grove	NC	28366	Tommy Herring	910-594-0219	R	130*	1.0
Farnam Companies Inc.	PO Box 34820	Phoenix	AZ	85067	Rick Blomquist	602-207-2179	S	126*	0.3
Priefert Manufacturing Company	PO Box 1540	Mount Pleasant	TX	75456	Sherri Fox	903-572-1741	R	120*	0.5
O and S America L.L.C.	777 8 Mile Rd.	Whitmore Lake	MI	48189	James M. Bonk	810-449-4401	R	119*	0.2
Flowtronex PSI Inc.	10661 Newkirk St.	Dallas	TX	75220	Dan Driscoll	214-357-1320	S	98*	0.2
Taylor-Dunn Corp.	2114 W Ball Rd.	Anaheim	CA	92804	Arthur J. Goodwin	714-956-4040	R	91*	0.2
Venchurs Inc.	800 Liberty St.	Adrian	MI	49221	Jeffery Wyatt	517-263-8937	R	90*	0.1
Alamo Group (SMC) Inc.	300 E 60th St. N	Sioux Falls	SD	57104		605-336-3628	S	85*	0.1
T-L Irrigation Co.	PO Box 1047	Hastings	NE	68902	Leroy Thom	402-462-4128	R	78*	0.3
Harsh International Inc.	600 Oak Ave.	Eaton	CO	80615	Robert Brown		R	78*	0.1
Southern Fabricators Inc.	4768 Hungerford	Memphis	TN	38118	Greg Langston	901-363-1571	R	72*	0.7
Bou-Matic L.L.C.	PO Box 8050	Madison	WI	53708		608-222-3484	R	72*	0.3
CNH Goodfield	PO Box 65	Goodfield	IL	61742	Harold Boyanovsky	309-965-2233	D	69*	0.4
P and H Manufacturing Company	PO Box 349	Shelbyville	IL	62565	Earl Peifer	217-774-2123	R	60*	0.3
Bush Hog L.L.C.	2501 Griffin Ave.	Selma	AL	36703	James Bearden	334-872-6261	R	60*	<0.1
Reynolds International Inc.	PO Box 550	McAllen	TX	78505	Paula Moore	956-687-7500	R	59*	0.2
Travis Pattern and Foundry	PO Box 6325	Spokane	WA	99217	Travis Garske	509-466-3545	R	58*	0.2
Unverferth Manufacturing Co.	27612 Temple Ave.	Shell Rock	IA	50670		319-885-6571	R	56*	0.2
Morbark Inc.	PO Box 1000	Winn	MI	48896	Lon Morey	989-866-2381	R	55*	0.6
WMI/TSH	28325 Vargo Ln.	Elberta	AL	36530	Eddie Warner	251-987-1236	R	53*	<0.1
Landoll Corp.	PO Box 111	Marysville	KS	66508	Donald Landoll	785-562-5381	R	50*	0.5
HCC Inc.	PO Box 952	Mendota	IL	61342	Donald Bickel	815-539-9371	R	48*	0.2
Howse Implement Company Inc.	PO Box 86	Laurel	MS	39441	Ben Howse	601-428-0841	R	48*	0.2
Philadelphia Tramrail Enterpr.	2207 E Ontario St.	Philadelphia	PA	19134	Robert Riethmiller	215-533-5100	R	47*	0.1
Sukup Manufacturing Co.	PO Box 677	Sheffield	IA	50475	Charles Sukup	641-892-4222	R	45*	0.3
M-E-C Co.	PO Box 330	Neodesha	KS	66757	David Parker	620-325-2673	R	45*	0.3
Rome Plow Co.	PO Box 48	Cedartown	GA	30125		770-748-4450	R	44*	<0.1
Sudenga Industries Inc.	PO Box 8	George	IA	51237	Larry Kruse	712-475-3301	R	43*	0.2
McLanahan Corp.	PO Box 229	Hollidaysburg	PA	16648	Michael Mc Lanahan	814-695-9807	R	43*	0.2
Dethmers Manufacturing Co.	PO Box 189	Boyden	IA	51234	James Koerselman	712-725-2311	R	42*	0.3
A.O. Smith Engineered Storage	345 Harvestore Dr.	Dekalb	IL	60115	Ron Stier	815-756-1551	D	41*	0.2
Farmtrac North America L.L.C.	PO Box 1139	Tarboro	NC	27886	Rajan Nanda	252-823-4151	R	41*	0.2
Ferris Industries Inc.	5375 N Main St.	Munnsville	NY	13409	Phillip Wenzel	315-495-0100	S	41*	0.2
Regen Technologies L.L.C.	4500 E Mustard	Springfield	MO	65803	Ron Guinn	417-829-2000	R	41*	0.2
Lor-AL Products Inc.	202 Industrial Park	Jackson	MN	56143	A.E. McQuinn	320-843-3954	R	39*	0.2
Northwestern Plastics Ltd.	1731 N Roosevlt	Burlington	IA	52601	Sam West	319-754-4000	R	38*	<0.1
Den Hartog Industries Inc.	PO Box 425	Hospers	IA	51238	John Den Hartog	712-752-8432	R	38*	0.3
KMW Ltd.	PO Box 327	Sterling	KS	67579	Michael Bender	620-278-3641	R	37*	0.2
Country Home Products Inc.	PO Box 25	Vergennes	VT	05491		802-877-1201	R	36*	0.1
KBH Corp.	395 Anderson Blvd.	Clarksdale	MS	38614	Buddy Bass	662-624-5471	R	36*	0.2
Kondex Corp.	274 S Pleasant Hill	Lomira	WI	53048	Scott Moon	920-269-4100	R	36*	0.2
Big Tex Trailer Manufacturing	850 Interest 30 E	Mount Pleasant	TX	75455	Ricky Baker	903-575-0300	R	36*	0.3
BC Supply	2008 E 50th St.	Lubbock	TX	79404	Breck Colquett	806-762-3227	R	35*	<0.1
Suburban Surgical Co.	275 12th St., A	Wheeling	IL	60090	James Pinkerman	847-537-9320	R	34*	0.2
T-Systems International Inc.	7545 Carroll Rd.	San Diego	CA	92121	Mark Huntley	858-578-1860	R	34*	0.1
M and W Gear Co.	1020 S Sangamon	Gibson City	IL	60936	Ronald A. Robinson	217-784-4261	S	33*	0.1
Auburn Consolidated Industries	PO Box 350	Auburn	NE	68305	Donna Skaggs	402-274-8600	R	32*	0.1
Fremont Plastic Products Inc.	2101 Cedar Street	Fremont	OH	43420	Brian Beth	419-332-6407	R	31*	0.3
Industrial Iron Works Inc.	PO Box 628	De Witt	AR	72042	Billy Adams	870-946-2494	R	31*	0.1
Ranco Fertiservice Inc.	PO Box 329	Sioux Rapids	IA	50585	Paul Krile	712-283-2525	R	30*	<0.1
Miller St. Nazianz Inc.	PO Box 127	St. Nazianz	WI	54232	John Miller	920-773-2121	R	30*	0.2
Tiger Corp.	3301 N Louise Ave.	Sioux Falls	SD	57107			S	30*	<0.1
Manitou North America Inc.	PO Box 21386	Waco	TX	76702	Serge Bosche	254-799-0232	R	30*	0.1

Source: Ward's Business Directory of U.S. Private and Public Companies, Volumes 1 and 2, 2008: The company type code used is as follows: P - Public, R - Private, S - Subsidiary, D - Division, J - Joint Venture, A - Affiliate, G - Group. Sales are in millions of dollars, employees are in thousands. An asterisk (*) indicates an estimated sales volume. The symbol < stands for 'less than'. Company names and addresses are truncated, in some cases, to fit into the available space.

MATERIALS CONSUMED

Material	Quantity	Delivered Cost ($ million)
Fluid power pumps, motors, and hydrostatic transmissions	(X)	179.3
Fluid power cylinders and rotary actuators (hydraulic and pneumatic)	(X)	102.9
Fluid power filters (hydraulic and pneumatic)	(X)	26.3
Fluid power hose, tube fittings, and assemblies (hydraulic and pneumatic)	(X)	85.3
Fluid power valves (hydraulic and pneumatic)	(X)	88.1
Metal bolts, nuts, screws, and other screw machine products	(X)	153.2
Metal stampings	(X)	225.0
All other fabricated metal products (excluding forgings)	(X)	228.1
Iron and steel forgings	(X)	63.8
Nonferrous forgings	(X)	1.0
Iron and steel castings (rough and semifinished)	(X)	254.1
Aluminum and aluminum-base alloy castings (rough and semifinished)	(X)	27.7
Other nonferrous metal castings, rough or semifinished (inc. aluminum)	(X)	3.5
Steel bars, bar shapes, and plates (exc. castings, forgings, fabr. metal products)	(X)	190.0
Steel sheet and strip (including tinplate)	(X)	218.2
Steel structural shapes and sheet piling (exc. castings, forgings, fabr. metal products)	(X)	35.4
All other steel shapes and forms (exc. castings, forgings, fabr. metal products)	(X)	365.4
Nonferrous shapes and forms	(X)	(D)
Metal powders	(X)	(D)
Diesel engines and parts specially designed for diesel engines	(X)	325.6
Gasoline engines and parts specially designed for gasoline engines	(X)	139.8
Engine electrical equipment (incl. spark plugs, magnetos, generators, starters, etc.)	(X)	93.9
Electric motors and generators	(X)	33.6
Ball bearings (mounted or unmounted)	(X)	49.1
Roller bearings (mounted or unmounted)	(X)	29.4
Mechanical speed changers, gears, and industrial high-speed drives	(X)	73.5
Pneumatic tires and inner tubes	(X)	166.0
Wheels, motor vehicle	(X)	31.1
Shocks, struts, and other suspension equipment and parts	(X)	29.3
Transmissions and parts	(X)	267.1
Rubber and plastics hose and belting	(X)	76.7
Fabricated plastics products (excluding gaskets)	(X)	129.4
Paints, varnishes, stains, lacquers, shellacs, japans, enamels, etc.	(X)	46.7
Cabs purchased for installation on farm machinery	(X)	86.9
All other materials, components, parts, containers, and supplies	(X)	2,529.0
Materials, ingredients, containers, and supplies, nsk	(X)	547.4

Source: 2002 *Economic Census*. Explanation of symbols used: (D): Withheld to avoid disclosure of competitive data; na: Not available; (S): Withheld because statistical norms were not met; (X): Not applicable; (Z): Less than half the unit shown; nec: Not elsewhere classified; nsk: Not specified by kind; - : zero; p : 10-19 percent estimated; q : 20-29 percent estimated.

PRODUCT SHARE DETAILS

Product or Product Class Shipments	Mil. $	Product or Product Class Shipments	Mil. $
FARM MACHINERY AND EQUIPMENT	13,542.3	for sale separately	599.5
Farm-type (power take-off hp) wheel tractors (2- and 4-wheel drive) (sold with or without attachments)	3,667.5	Other parts for farm machinery, including operator cabs, for sale separately	720.4
Farm dairy equipment, sprayers, and dusters (except aerial types), farm blowers, and attachments	616.9	Parts for farm machinery, for sale separately, nsk	34.0
Planting, seeding, and fertilizing machinery and attachments, excluding turf machinery	978.6	Farm plows (including plowshares, primary tillage), harrows, rollers, pulverizers, and cultivators and weeders, and attachments	343.7
Harvesting machinery (except hay and straw) and attachments	1,742.1	All other farm machinery and equipment, excluding parts, but including attachments	1,802.7
Haying machinery and attachments	945.6	Commercial turf and grounds care equipment, including parts and attachments	1,537.6
Parts for farm machinery, for sale separately	1,353.9	Farm machinery and equipment, nsk, total	553.6
Parts for farm-type wheel tractors (except operator cabs),			

Source: 2002 *Economic Census*. The values are product shipments in millions of dollars for 2002. Total product shipments may be lower or higher than industry shipments. See Introduction for a full discussion. Values of indented subcategories are summed in the main heading(s). The symbol (D) appears when data are withheld to prevent disclosure of competitive information. The abbreviation nsk stands for 'not specified by kind' and nec for 'not elsewhere classified'. A dash (-) means zero.

INPUTS AND OUTPUTS FOR FARM MACHINERY AND EQUIPMENT MANUFACTURING

Economic Sector or Industry Providing Inputs	%	Sector	Economic Sector or Industry Buying Outputs	%	Sector
Compensation of employees	20.5		Private fixed investment	70.6	
Wholesale trade	5.4	Trade	Exports of goods & services	17.5	Cap Inv
Iron & steel mills & ferroalloys	5.2	Manufg.	Forestry products	2.0	Agric.
Engine equipment, nec	4.2	Manufg.	General S/L govt. services	1.6	S/L Govt
Motor vehicle parts	3.7	Manufg.	Miscellaneous crops	1.1	Agric.
Management of companies & enterprises	3.6	Services	Grains	1.1	Agric.
Rubber products, nec	3.6	Manufg.	S/L govt. invest., other	0.9	S/L Govt
Plastics products, nec	3.4	Manufg.	Farm machinery & equipment	0.7	Manufg.
Crowns & closures & metal stamping	3.3	Manufg.	Other S/L govt. enterprises	0.6	S/L Govt

Continued on next page.

INPUTS AND OUTPUTS FOR FARM MACHINERY AND EQUIPMENT MANUFACTURING - Continued

Economic Sector or Industry Providing Inputs	%	Sector	Economic Sector or Industry Buying Outputs	%	Sector
Valve & fittings other than plumbing	2.5	Manufg.	Dairy cattle & milk	0.6	Agric.
Ferrous metal foundries	1.6	Manufg.	Oilseeds	0.6	Agric.
Fluid power process machinery	1.4	Manufg.	Livestock, nec	0.5	Agric.
Tires	1.2	Manufg.	Greenhouse & nursery products	0.3	Agric.
Fabricated metals, nec	1.2	Manufg.	Vegetables and melons	0.3	Agric.
Turned products & screws, nuts, & bolts	1.1	Manufg.	Cattle	0.2	Agric.
Truck transportation	0.9	Util.	Fruit	0.2	Agric.
Farm machinery & equipment	0.8	Manufg.	Scientific research & development services	0.2	Services
Retail trade	0.8	Trade	Sugar crops	0.1	Agric.
Paints & coatings	0.7	Manufg.	Cotton	0.1	Agric.
Advertising & related services	0.7	Services	Wholesale trade	0.1	Trade
Securities, commodity contracts, investments	0.7	Fin/R.E.	Hunting and trapping	0.1	Agric.
Ball & roller bearings	0.7	Manufg.	Poultry & eggs	0.1	Agric.
Speed changers, industrial high-speed drives, & gears	0.6	Manufg.			
Machine shops	0.6	Manufg.			
Rubber & plastics hose & belting	0.6	Manufg.			
Storage batteries	0.6	Manufg.			
Lessors of nonfinancial assets	0.5	Fin/R.E.			
Forging, stamping, & sintering, nec	0.5	Manufg.			
Monetary authorities/depository credit intermediation	0.5	Fin/R.E.			
Semiconductors & related devices	0.5	Manufg.			
Architectural, engineering, & related services	0.4	Services			
Electronic connectors	0.4	Manufg.			
Printed circuit assemblies (electronic assembiles)	0.4	Manufg.			
Power generation & supply	0.4	Util.			
Real estate	0.4	Fin/R.E.			
Noncomparable imports	0.4	Foreign			
Professional, scientific, technical services, nec	0.4	Services			
Coating, engraving, heat treating & allied activities	0.3	Manufg.			
Cutting tools & machine tool accessories	0.3	Manufg.			
Nonmetallic mineral products, nec	0.3	Manufg.			
Maintenance/repair of nonresidential structures	0.3	Construct.			
Services to buildings & dwellings	0.3	Services			
Construction machinery	0.3	Manufg.			
Mining & oil & gas field machinery	0.3	Manufg.			
Accounting, tax preparation, bookkeeping, & payroll	0.2	Services			
Data processing, hosting, & related services	0.2	Services			
Natural gas distribution	0.2	Util.			
Food services & drinking places	0.2	Services			
Motors & generators	0.2	Manufg.			
Legal services	0.2	Services			
Nonferrous metal foundries	0.2	Manufg.			
Telecommunications	0.2	Services			
Scientific research & development services	0.2	Services			
Automotive repair & maintenance, ex. car washes	0.2	Services			
General purpose machinery, nec	0.2	Manufg.			
Taxes on production & imports, less subsidies	0.2				
Automotive equipment rental & leasing	0.2	Fin/R.E.			
Warehousing & storage	0.2	Util.			
Commercial & industrial equipment repair/maintenance	0.2	Services			
Postal service	0.2	Util.			
Copper rolling, drawing, extruding, & alloying	0.2	Manufg.			
Air transportation	0.1	Util.			
Metal cans, boxes, & other containers (light gauge)	0.1	Manufg.			
Other computer related services, including facilities	0.1	Services			
Hotels & motels, including casino hotels	0.1	Services			
Rail transportation	0.1	Util.			
Relay & industrial controls	0.1	Manufg.			
Metal cutting & forming machine tools	0.1	Manufg.			
Business support services	0.1	Services			
Management, scientific, & technical consulting	0.1	Services			
Paperboard containers	0.1	Manufg.			
Custom roll forming	0.1	Manufg.			

Source: Benchmark Input-Output Accounts for the U.S. Economy, 2002, U.S. Department of Commerce, Washington, D.C., January 2008. The abbreviation nec stands for 'not elsewhere classified'.

OCCUPATIONS EMPLOYED BY AGRICULTURE, CONSTRUCTION, & MINING MACHINERY

Occupation	% of Total 2006	Change to 2016	Occupation	% of Total 2006	Change to 2016
Welders, cutters, solderers, & brazers	11.7	-0.7	Sales reps, wholesale & manufacturing, exc tech	1.6	-6.6
Team assemblers	10.3	-6.6	Helpers--Production workers	1.6	-6.6
First-line supervisors/managers of production workers	3.5	-6.6	Maintenance & repair workers, general	1.5	-6.6
Computer-controlled machine tool operators	3.4	2.7	Shipping, receiving, & traffic clerks	1.4	-10.2
Engine & other machine assemblers	3.2	-6.6	Welding, soldering, & brazing machine operators	1.4	5.0
Structural metal fabricators & fitters	2.4	-6.6	Production, planning, & expediting clerks	1.3	-6.6
Mechanical engineers	2.2	-6.6	General & operations managers	1.3	-16.0
Laborers & freight, stock, & material movers, hand	2.1	-16.0	Bookkeeping, accounting, & auditing clerks	1.3	-6.6
Cutting, punching, & press machine operators	2.1	-16.0	Purchasing agents, exc wholesale, retail, & farm	1.2	-6.6
Inspectors, testers, sorters, samplers, & weighers	2.0	-12.0	Industrial engineers	1.1	13.4
Industrial truck & tractor operators	1.8	-16.0	Mechanical drafters	1.1	-5.6

Source: *Industry-Occupation Matrix*, Bureau of Labor Statistics, December 4, 2007. These data are reported based on 4-digit NAICS categories but have been matched to corresponding 6-digit NAICS industry codes. The change reported for each occupation to the year 2016 is a percent of growth or decline as estimated by the Bureau of Labor Statistics. The abbreviation nec stands for 'not elsewhere classified'.

LOCATION BY STATE AND REGIONAL CONCENTRATION

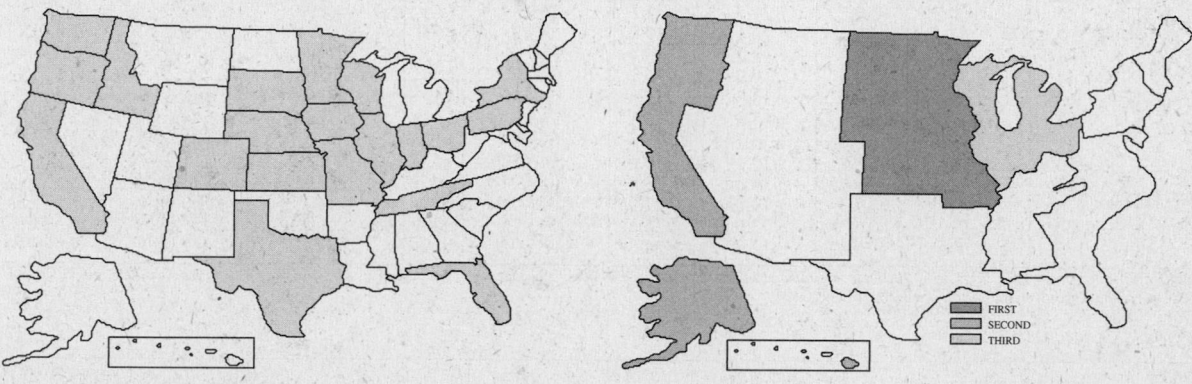

FIRST
SECOND
THIRD

INDUSTRY DATA BY STATE

State	Establishments	Shipments Total ($ mil)	Shipments % of U.S.	Shipments Per Establ.	Employment Total Number	Employment % of U.S.	Employment Per Establ.	Employment Wages ($/hour)	Cost as % of Shipments	Investment per Employee ($)
Iowa	90	3,685.7	25.1	40,952.4	8,560	15.9	95	19.86	44.6	10,870
Illinois	52	2,246.1	15.3	43,194.6	6,644	12.3	128	21.70	43.9	5,139
Nebraska	78	1,240.7	8.4	15,906.0	5,443	10.1	70	15.56	55.9	12,650
Wisconsin	52	946.6	6.4	18,204.5	4,394	8.2	84	25.14	71.1	5,355
Minnesota	76	896.5	6.1	11,796.3	3,260	6.1	43	14.07	51.2	4,671
Kansas	69	744.6	5.1	10,791.7	4,502	8.4	65	15.01	52.4	4,055
Indiana	29	359.9	2.4	12,410.7	1,080	2.0	37	16.35	55.4	6,860
California	104	284.3	1.9	2,733.7	1,729	3.2	17	15.34	52.9	3,653
Pennsylvania	40	262.5	1.8	6,562.0	1,098	2.0	27	22.75	48.8	4,557
Texas	67	161.2	1.1	2,405.9	1,327	2.5	20	13.28	44.4	4,366
Ohio	30	150.1	1.0	5,002.0	802	1.5	27	15.58	48.5	3,787
New York	14	102.1	0.7	7,293.7	565	1.0	40	12.67	42.8	1,609
Oregon	28	83.9	0.6	2,995.4	563	1.0	20	15.01	46.0	3,670
South Dakota	23	79.4	0.5	3,453.2	504	0.9	22	13.04	55.5	2,796
Colorado	17	79.2	0.5	4,658.5	442	0.8	26	14.58	51.8	10,448
Washington	31	76.1	0.5	2,454.2	464	0.9	15	16.66	50.3	4,194
Tennessee	18	68.8	0.5	3,824.3	481	0.9	27	11.82	48.7	5,154
Idaho	28	67.9	0.5	2,426.1	573	1.1	20	12.60	55.9	1,538
Missouri	25	63.9	0.4	2,555.3	422	0.8	17	12.34	61.1	3,678
Florida	29	39.6	0.3	1,364.3	284	0.5	10	14.97	51.4	2,595

Source: 2002 *Economic Census*. The states are in descending order of shipments or establishments (if shipment data are missing for the majority). The symbol (D) appears when data are withheld to prevent disclosure of competitive information. States marked with (D) are sorted by number of establishments. A dash (-) indicates that the data element cannot be calculated. Data may not show all states active in the NAICS category. All data available at the time of publication are shown.

NAICS 333112 - LAWN AND GARDEN TRACTOR AND HOME LAWN AND GARDEN EQUIPMENT MANUFACTURING

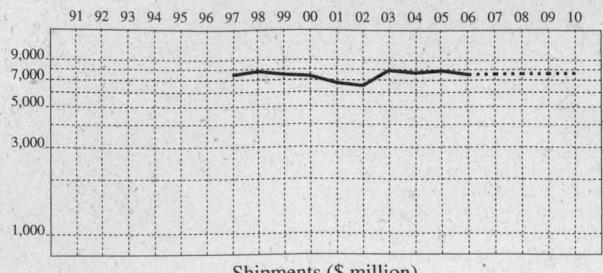

Shipments ($ million)

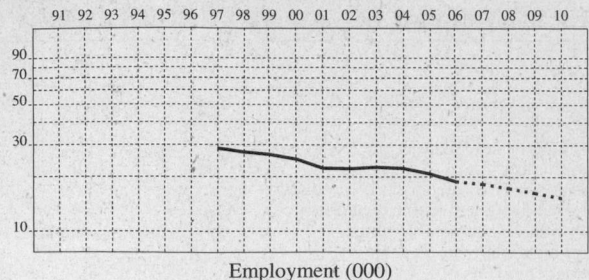

Employment (000)

GENERAL STATISTICS

Year	Com-panies	Establishments		Employment			Compensation		Production ($ million)			
		Total	with 20 or more employees	Total (000)	Production Workers (000)	Hours (Mil)	Payroll ($ mil)	Wages ($/hr)	Cost of Materials	Value Added by Manufacture	Value of Shipments	Capital Invest.
1997	127	145	75	28.6	22.9	45.6	734.4	11.17	4,757.5	2,779.6	7,464.5	184.4
1998		142	72	27.3	22.3	43.9	740.1	11.66	5,100.2	2,760.4	7,775.8	237.7
1999		136	69	26.5	21.7	43.1	755.5	11.66	4,689.0	2,892.5	7,483.9	130.5
2000		132	68	25.0	20.1	39.7	695.5	11.33	4,917.4	2,358.0	7,337.9	154.7
2001		134	67	22.3	18.2	35.4	650.7	11.83	4,347.0	2,261.0	6,733.4	159.5
2002	128	145	71	22.2	17.9	36.1	680.9	12.44	4,080.2	2,420.4	6,516.9	173.9
2003		161	67	22.6	18.3	35.8	703.4	13.15	5,356.9	2,660.4	7,905.3	146.7
2004		165	73	22.3	17.8	36.1	744.2	13.91	5,130.1	2,544.7	7,696.2	151.1
2005		161	75	20.8	16.7	33.9	669.8	13.22	5,477.7	2,533.6	7,872.3	148.8
2006		163P	71P	18.8	15.1	30.0	646.5	14.56	5,008.8	2,411.7	7,516.7	144.3
2007		166P	71P	18.2P	14.6P	29.4P	659.2P	14.45P	5,033.2P	2,423.5P	7,553.4P	133.5P
2008		170P	71P	17.3P	13.8P	27.9P	651.4P	14.81P	5,048.1P	2,430.6P	7,575.8P	128.1P
2009		173P	71P	16.3P	13.0P	26.3P	643.7P	15.16P	5,063.1P	2,437.8P	7,598.1P	122.7P
2010		176P	71P	15.3P	12.2P	24.8P	635.9P	15.52P	5,078.0P	2,445.0P	7,620.5P	117.3P

Sources: 1997 and 2002 *Economic Census*; other years, up to 2006, are from *Annual Survey of Manufactures*. Establishment counts for non-Census years are from *County Business Patterns*; 1997 and 2002 values are from the 1997 and 2002 censuses, respectively. 'P's show projections by the editors.

INDICES OF CHANGE

Year	Com-panies	Establishments		Employment			Compensation		Production ($ million)			
		Total	with 20 or more employees	Total (000)	Production Workers (000)	Hours (Mil)	Payroll ($ mil)	Wages ($/hr)	Cost of Materials	Value Added by Manufacture	Value of Shipments	Capital Invest.
1997	99	100	106	129	128	126	108	90	117	115	115	106
1998		98	101	123	125	122	109	94	125	114	119	137
1999		94	97	119	121	119	111	94	115	120	115	75
2000		91	96	113	112	110	102	91	121	97	113	89
2001		92	94	100	102	98	96	95	107	93	103	92
2002	100	100	100	100	100	100	100	100	100	100	100	100
2003		111	94	102	102	99	103	106	131	110	121	84
2004		114	103	100	99	100	109	112	126	105	118	87
2005		111	106	94	93	94	98	106	134	105	121	86
2006		112P	100P	85	84	83	95	117	123	100	115	83
2007		115P	100P	82P	82P	81P	97P	116P	123P	100P	116P	77P
2008		117P	100P	78P	77P	77P	96P	119P	124P	100P	116P	74P
2009		119P	100P	73P	73P	73P	95P	122P	124P	101P	117P	71P
2010		122P	100P	69P	68P	69P	93P	125P	124P	101P	117P	67P

Sources: Same as General Statistics. Values reflect change from the base year, 2002. Values above 100 mean greater than 2002, values below 100 mean less than 2002, and the values of 100 in other years means the same as 2002. 'P's show projections by the editors.

SELECTED RATIOS

For 2002	Avg. of All Manufact.	Analyzed Industry	Index	For 2002	Avg. of All Manufact.	Analyzed Industry	Index
Employees per Establishment	42	153	365	Value Added per Production Worker	182,367	135,218	74
Payroll per Establishment	1,639,184	4,695,862	286	Cost per Establishment	5,769,015	28,139,310	488
Payroll per Employee	39,053	30,671	79	Cost per Employee	137,446	183,793	134
Production Workers per Establishment	30	123	418	Cost per Production Worker	195,506	227,944	117
Wages per Establishment	694,845	3,097,131	446	Shipments per Establishment	11,158,348	44,944,138	403
Wages per Production Worker	23,548	25,088	107	Shipments per Employee	265,847	293,554	110
Hours per Production Worker	1,980	2,017	102	Shipments per Production Worker	378,144	364,073	96
Wages per Hour	11.89	12.44	105	Investment per Establishment	361,338	1,199,310	332
Value Added per Establishment	5,381,325	16,692,414	310	Investment per Employee	8,609	7,833	91
Value Added per Employee	128,210	109,027	85	Investment per Production Worker	12,245	9,715	79

Sources: Same as General Statistics. The 'Average of All Manufacturing' column represents the average of all manufacturing industries reported for the most recent complete year available. The Index shows the relationship between the Average and the Analyzed Industry. For example, 100 means that they are equal; 500 that the Analyzed Industry is five times the average; 50 means that the Analyzed Industry is half the national average. The abbreviation 'na' is used to show that data are 'not available'. Ratios shown for 2002, the last complete census year.

LEADING COMPANIES

Number shown: **75**   Total sales ($ mil): **36,010**   Total employment (000): **98.5**

Company Name	Address				CEO Name	Phone	Co. Type	Sales ($ mil)	Empl. (000)
Deere and Co.	1 John Deere Pl.	Moline	IL	61265		309-765-8000	P	24,082	52.0
Black and Decker Corp.	101 Schilling Rd.	Hunt Valley	MD	21031	Nolan D. Archibald	410-716-3900	P	6,563	25.0
Toro Co.	8111 Lyndale Ave. S	Bloomington	MN	55420		952-888-8801	P	1,877	5.3
MTD Products Inc.	PO Box 368022	Cleveland	OH	44136	Curtis E. Moll	330-225-2600	R	1,015*	6.7
Douglas Dynamics L.L.C.	915 Riverview Dr.	Johnson City	TN	37601	Jim Janik	423-928-3962	S	343*	0.5
Simplicity Manufacturing Inc.	PO Box 997	Port Washington	WI	53074	Warner Frazier	262-377-5450	R	305*	0.5
AFA Products Inc.	135 Pine St.	Forest City	NC	28043	Jim Wantuch	828-245-1160	R	195*	0.8
Exmark Manufacturing Company	PO Box 808	Beatrice	NE	68310	Mark Stinson	402-223-6300	D	117*	0.7
Magic Circle Corp.	6302 E County Rd.	Coatesville	IN	46121	Arthur Evans	765-246-6845	R	78*	0.2
Western Industries Inc.	W156 Pilgrim	Menomonee Fls	WI	53051	Tom Hall	262-251-1915	R	67*	0.6
Tuff Torq Corp.	5943 Commerce	Morristown	TN	37814	Koji Irikura	423-585-2000	R	65*	0.3
Commercial Turf Products Ltd.	1777 Miller Pkwy.	Streetsboro	OH	44241	Nick Cashier	330-995-7000	R	63*	0.2
G.L. Turner Co.	PO Box 5652	N Little Rock	AR	72119	Robert Hall, Jr.	501-945-0048	R	61*	<0.1
Aircap Industries Corp.	PO Box 2120	Tupelo	MS	38803	Ted Moll	662-566-2332	R	54*	0.5
Caterpillar Work Tools Inc.	PO Box 6	Wamego	KS	66547		785-456-2224	S	52*	0.3
Precision Products Inc.	316 Limit St.	Lincoln	IL	62656	Mort Kay	217-735-1590	R	52*	0.2
Swisher Mower and Machine Co.	PO Box 67	Warrensburg	MO	64093	Wayne Swisher	660-747-8183	R	52*	0.2
Walker Manufacturing Co.	5925 E Harmony Rd.	Fort Collins	CO	80528	Bob Walker	970-221-5614	R	37*	0.1
Country Home Products Inc.	PO Box 25	Vergennes	VT	05491		802-877-1201	R	36*	0.1
Kondex Corp.	274 S Pleasant Hill	Lomira	WI	53048	Scott Moon	920-269-4100	R	36*	0.2
AeroGrow International Inc.	6075 Longbow Dr.	Boulder	CO	80301	Michael Bissonnette	303-444-7755	R	35	<0.1
Hoffco/Comet Industries Inc.	358 NW F Street	Richmond	IN	47374	John Bratt	765-966-8161	R	35*	0.2
Systems Control	PO Box 788	Iron Mountain	MI	49801	Dave Brule, Sr.	906-774-0440	R	34*	0.2
Wright Manufacturing Inc.	4600 Wedgewood	Frederick	MD	21703	William Wright	301-360-9810	R	34*	0.1
M and W Gear Co.	1020 S Sangamon	Gibson City	IL	60936	Ronald A. Robinson	217-784-4261	S	33*	0.1
Auburn Consolidated Industries	PO Box 350	Auburn	NE	68305	Donna Skaggs	402-274-8600	R	32*	0.1
Alamo Group (KS) Inc.	1000 Vermont St.	Holton	KS	66436	Ronald A. Robinson	785-364-2186	R	30*	0.1
Manitou North America Inc.	PO Box 21386	Waco	TX	76702	Serge Bosche	254-799-0232	R	30*	0.1
Schmidt Engineering and Equip.	1905 S Moorland	New Berlin	WI	53151		262-784-6066	S	29*	0.1
Corona Clipper Inc.	22440 Temescal	Corona	CA	92883	Stephen Erickson	951-737-6515	R	26*	0.2
Wood-Mizer Products Inc.	8180 W 10th St.	Indianapolis	IN	46214	Jeffrey Laskowski	317-271-1542	R	26*	0.2
Shivvers Group Inc.	614 W English St.	Corydon	IA	50060	Carl Shivvers	641-872-1005	R	26*	0.1
Ardisam Inc.	PO Box 666	Cumberland	WI	54829	Ron Ruppel	715-822-2415	R	24*	0.1
Mid-West Fabricating Co.	313 N Johns St.	Amanda	OH	43102	Jennifer Friel	740-969-4411	R	21*	0.2
Haven Steel Products Inc.	PO Box 430	Haven	KS	67543	Marlon Cohn	620-465-2573	R	21*	<0.1
Maxim Holding Company Inc.	PO Box 110	Sebastopol	MS	39359	Albert Easom	601-625-7471	R	21*	<0.1
Femco Inc.	500 N US Hwy 81	McPherson	KS	67460	Rodney Borman	620-241-3513	R	20*	<0.1
Gilcrest Equipment Co.	618 N Enterprise Dr	Warrensburg	MO	64093	James Gilcrest	660-422-4272	R	18*	<0.1
Chapin Manufacturing Inc.	PO Box 549	Batavia	NY	14021	James Campbell	585-343-3140	R	17*	0.2
Whirltronics Inc.	208 Centennial Dr.	Buffalo	MN	55313	Steve Thul	763-682-1716	R	16*	<0.1
Pacific Topsoils Inc.	805 80th St. SW	Everett	WA	98203	Dave Forman	425-337-2700	R	15*	0.1
United Southern Industries	486 Vance Street	Forest City	NC	28043	Joe Bennett	828-245-6453	R	15*	0.2
Brown Manufacturing Corp.	6001 E Hwy. 27	Ozark	AL	36360	William Brown	334-795-6603	R	14*	<0.1
Tarrant Manufacturing Company	225 Excelsior Ave.	Saratoga Spgs	NY	12866	John Tarrant	518-584-4400	R	14*	<0.1
Wildcat Manufacturing Company	PO Box 1100	Freeman	SD	57029	Pat Dooey	605-925-4512	R	13*	<0.1
Root Spring Scraper Co.	527 W N Street	Kalamazoo	MI	49007	Frederick Root	269-382-2025	R	13*	<0.1
Hayes Products L.L.C.	6780 8th Street	Buena Park	CA	90620		714-523-1750	R	13*	0.1
Clarion Bathware Inc.	44 Amsler Ave.	Shippenville	PA	16254	David Groner	814-226-5374	R	12*	0.1
PECO Inc.	PO Box 1197	Arden	NC	28704	Peter Hall	828-684-1234	R	12*	<0.1
Fetzer W H and Sons Mfg.	PO Box 45	Plymouth	OH	44865	William Fetzer	419-687-8237	R	12*	<0.1
George Knotts Liquidating Co.	PO Box 111	Parker Ford	PA	19457	Richard Dhein	610-495-7181	R	11*	<0.1
Big John Tree Transplanter Mfg	PO Box 960	Heber Springs	AR	72543	Charles Blankenship	501-362-8161	R	10*	<0.1
Palmor Products Inc.	5225 Serum Plant	Thorntown	IN	46071	Stanley Morton	765-436-2496	R	10*	<0.1
Superior Cedar Products Inc.	PO Box 38	Carney	MI	49812	Dwaine Mellen	906-639-2132	R	10*	<0.1
Encore Manufacturing Company	PO Box 888	Beatrice	NE	68310	Douglas Tegtmeier	402-228-4255	R	10*	<0.1
Ashton Home Products Inc.	1150 S Patton St.	Xenia	OH	45385	John Kelch	937-374-3560	R	9*	<0.1
Precision Small Engine Company	2510 NW 16th Ln.	Pompano Beach	FL	33064	Andrew Masciarella	954-974-1960	R	9*	<0.1
National Mower Co.	700 Raymond Ave.	Saint Paul	MN	55114	Stan Kinkead	651-646-4079	R	9*	<0.1
Future Products Inc.	2100 Minnesota	Benson	MN	56215	Don Lenz	320-843-4614	R	9*	<0.1
Gledhill Road Machinery Co.	PO Box 567	Galion	OH	44833	Michelle Talbott	419-468-4400	R	9*	<0.1
Lorenz Manufacturing Co.	PO Box 127	Benson	MN	56215	Donn Lorenz	320-843-3210	R	8*	<0.1
Gandy Co.	PO Box 528	Owatonna	MN	55060	Dale Gandrud	507-451-5430	R	8*	<0.1
Valley View Industries, Hc	13834 Kostner Ave.	Midlothian	IL	60445	Howard Rynberk	708-597-0885	R	8*	<0.1
Lund Coating Technologies Inc.	PO Box 428	Collierville	TN	38027	John Schwanbeck	901-853-4761	R	8*	<0.1
Southland Mower Corp.	PO Box 347	Selma	AL	36702	Cater Lee	334-874-7405	R	8*	<0.1
American Road Machinery Inc.	401 Bridge St.	Minerva	OH	44657	David Hank	330-868-7724	R	7*	<0.1
Easy Lawn Inc.	9599 Nanticoke Bus	Greenwood	DE	19950	Robert Lisle	302-815-6500	R	7*	<0.1
Smithco West Inc.	PO Box 487	Cameron	WI	54822	Donald Smith	715-458-4192	R	7*	<0.1
Extrudex L.P.	310 Figgie Dr.	Painesville	OH	44077		440-352-7101	R	7*	<0.1
Erskine Attachments Inc.	PO Box 1083	Alexandria	MN	56308	Todd Olson	218-687-4045	R	7*	<0.1
MBTM Limited Inc.	PO Box 557	Leslie	MI	49251	Jack Lapinski	517-596-2210	R	6*	<0.1
Classen Manufacturing Inc.	PO Box 2401	Norfolk	NE	68702	Larry Classen	402-371-2294	R	6*	<0.1
Mercury Tool and Machine Inc.	PO Box 5190	Waco	TX	76708	Jack Peck	254-752-1639	R	6*	<0.1
Southern Green Inc.	21126 Plank Rd.	Zachary	LA	70791	Harry Knight	225-654-9888	R	5*	<0.1
Mo-Trim Inc.	PO Box 850	Cambridge	OH	43725	Jack Cartner	740-439-2725	R	5*	<0.1

Source: Ward's Business Directory of U.S. Private and Public Companies, Volumes 1 and 2, 2008. The company type code used is as follows: P - Public, R - Private, S - Subsidiary, D - Division, J - Joint Venture, A - Affiliate, G - Group. Sales are in millions of dollars, employees are in thousands. An asterisk (*) indicates an estimated sales volume. The symbol < stands for 'less than'. Company names and addresses are truncated, in some cases, to fit into the available space.

MATERIALS CONSUMED

Material	Quantity	Delivered Cost ($ million)
Fluid power pumps, motors, and hydrostatic transmissions	(X)	99.1
Fluid power cylinders and rotary actuators (hydraulic and pneumatic)	(X)	47.3
Fluid power filters (hydraulic and pneumatic)	(X)	6.5
Fluid power hose, tube fittings, and assemblies (hydraulic and pneumatic)	(X)	11.5
Fluid power valves (hydraulic and pneumatic)	(X)	10.8
Metal bolts, nuts, screws, and other screw machine products	(X)	96.7
Metal stampings	(X)	100.6
All other fabricated metal products (excluding forgings)	(X)	94.0
Iron and steel forgings	(X)	21.1
Nonferrous forgings	(X)	0.5
Iron and steel castings (rough and semifinished)	(X)	36.0
Aluminum and aluminum-base alloy castings (rough and semifinished)	(X)	68.2
Other nonferrous metal castings, rough or semifinished (inc. aluminum)	(X)	(D)
Steel bars, bar shapes, and plates (exc. castings, forgings, fabr. metal products)	(X)	18.4
Steel sheet and strip (including tinplate)	(X)	125.9
Steel structural shapes and sheet piling (exc. castings, forgings, fabr. metal products)	(X)	(D)
All other steel shapes and forms (exc. castings, forgings, fabr. metal products)	(X)	38.7
Nonferrous shapes and forms	(X)	0.5
Metal powders	(X)	27.3
Diesel engines and parts specially designed for diesel engines	(X)	4.5
Gasoline engines and parts specially designed for gasoline engines	(X)	815.7
Engine electrical equipment (incl. spark plugs, magnetos, generators, starters, etc.)	(X)	75.5
Electric motors and generators	(X)	4.7
Ball bearings (mounted or unmounted)	(X)	25.8
Roller bearings (mounted or unmounted)	(X)	10.0
Mechanical speed changers, gears, and industrial high-speed drives	(X)	23.2
Pneumatic tires and inner tubes	(X)	89.4
Wheels, motor vehicle	(X)	38.6
Shocks, struts, and other suspension equipment and parts	(X)	(D)
Transmissions and parts	(X)	90.5
Rubber and plastics hose and belting	(X)	35.6
Fabricated plastics products (excluding gaskets)	(X)	178.2
Paints, varnishes, stains, lacquers, shellacs, japans, enamels, etc.	(X)	66.9
Cabs purchased for installation on farm machinery	(X)	(D)
All other materials, components, parts, containers, and supplies	(X)	1,376.5
Materials, ingredients, containers, and supplies, nsk	(X)	110.1

Source: 2002 *Economic Census*. Explanation of symbols used: (D): Withheld to avoid disclosure of competitive data; na: Not available; (S): Withheld because statistical norms were not met; (X): Not applicable; (Z): Less than half the unit shown; nec: Not elsewhere classified; nsk: Not specified by kind; - : zero; p : 10-19 percent estimated; q : 20-29 percent estimated.

PRODUCT SHARE DETAILS

Product or Product Class Shipments	Mil. $	Product or Product Class Shipments	Mil. $
LAWN AND GARDEN EQUIPMENT	6,026.4	Parts and attachments for consumer lawn, garden, and snow equipment	747.5
Consumer nonriding lawn, garden, and snow equipment	2,699.3		
Consumer riding lawn, garden, and snow equipment	2,511.8	Lawn and garden equipment, nsk, total	67.7

Source: 2002 *Economic Census*. The values are product shipments in millions of dollars for 2002. Total product shipments may be lower or higher than industry shipments. See Introduction for a full discussion. Values of indented subcategories are summed in the main heading(s). The symbol (D) appears when data are withheld to prevent disclosure of competitive information. The abbreviation nsk stands for 'not specified by kind' and nec for 'not elsewhere classified'. A dash (-) means zero.

INPUTS AND OUTPUTS FOR LAWN AND GARDEN EQUIPMENT MANUFACTURING

Economic Sector or Industry Providing Inputs	%	Sector	Economic Sector or Industry Buying Outputs	%	Sector
Motor vehicle parts	15.4	Manufg.	Private fixed investment	76.0	
Compensation of employees	14.6		Personal consumption expenditures	10.8	
Engine equipment, nec	12.2	Manufg.	Owner-occupied dwellings	4.3	
Wholesale trade	6.8	Trade	Personal & household goods repair/maintenance	2.7	Services
Iron & steel mills & ferroalloys	3.0	Manufg.	Commercial & industrial machinery rental & leasing	1.7	Fin/R.E.
Fabricated metals, nec	2.7	Manufg.	Services to buildings & dwellings	0.7	Services
Management of companies & enterprises	2.5	Services	Retail trade	0.6	Trade
Plastics products, nec	2.4	Manufg.	Change in private inventories	0.6	In House
Valve & fittings other than plumbing	2.0	Manufg.	Agriculture & forestry services	0.5	Agric.
Crowns & closures & metal stamping	1.7	Manufg.	Exports of goods & services	0.4	Cap Inv
Tires	1.6	Manufg.	General S/L govt. services	0.3	S/L Govt
Fluid power process machinery	1.5	Manufg.	S/L govt. invest., other	0.3	S/L Govt
Turned products & screws, nuts, & bolts	1.4	Manufg.	Hunting and trapping	0.2	Agric.
Nonferrous metal foundries	1.2	Manufg.	Other S/L govt. enterprises	0.2	S/L Govt
Paints & coatings	1.2	Manufg.	Scientific research & development services	0.1	Services
Securities, commodity contracts, investments	0.9	Fin/R.E.	Investigation & security services	0.1	Services
Truck transportation	0.8	Util.	Federal government, investment, national defense	0.1	Fed Govt

Continued on next page.

INPUTS AND OUTPUTS FOR LAWN AND GARDEN EQUIPMENT MANUFACTURING - Continued

Economic Sector or Industry Providing Inputs	%	Sector	Economic Sector or Industry Buying Outputs	%	Sector
Gaskets, packing, & sealing devices	0.7	Manufg.			
Lessors of nonfinancial assets	0.7	Fin/R.E.			
Advertising & related services	0.6	Services			
Ball & roller bearings	0.6	Manufg.			
Rubber & plastics hose & belting	0.5	Manufg.			
Speed changers, industrial high-speed drives, & gears	0.5	Manufg.			
Monetary authorities/depository credit intermediation	0.5	Fin/R.E.			
Machine shops	0.5	Manufg.			
Semiconductors & related devices	0.5	Manufg.			
Ferrous metal foundries	0.5	Manufg.			
Printed circuit assemblies (electronic assembiles)	0.5	Manufg.			
Retail trade	0.4	Trade			
Professional, scientific, technical services, nec	0.4	Services			
Power generation & supply	0.4	Util.			
Architectural, engineering, & related services	0.3	Services			
Forging, stamping, & sintering, nec	0.3	Manufg.			
Coating, engraving, heat treating & allied activities	0.3	Manufg.			
Real estate	0.3	Fin/R.E.			
Legal services	0.3	Services			
Data processing, hosting, & related services	0.3	Services			
Maintenance/repair of nonresidential structures	0.2	Construct.			
Food services & drinking places	0.2	Services			
Nonferrous metal (ex. copper & aluminum) processing	0.2	Manufg.			
Services to buildings & dwellings	0.2	Services			
Farm machinery & equipment	0.2	Manufg.			
Scientific research & development services	0.2	Services			
Automotive equipment rental & leasing	0.2	Fin/R.E.			
Taxes on production & imports, less subsidies	0.2				
Rubber products, nec	0.1	Manufg.			
Accounting, tax preparation, bookkeeping, & payroll	0.1	Services			
Natural gas distribution	0.1	Util.			
Automotive repair & maintenance, ex. car washes	0.1	Services			
Laminated plastics plates, sheets, & shapes	0.1	Manufg.			
Rail transportation	0.1	Util.			
Air transportation	0.1	Util.			
Other computer related services, including facilities	0.1	Services			
Telecommunications	0.1	Services			
Management, scientific, & technical consulting	0.1	Services			
Warehousing & storage	0.1	Util.			
Metal cans, boxes, & other containers (light gauge)	0.1	Manufg.			
Postal service	0.1	Util.			
Commercial & industrial equipment repair/maintenance	0.1	Services			
Relay & industrial controls	0.1	Manufg.			
Business support services	0.1	Services			
Specialized design services	0.1	Services			
Hotels & motels, including casino hotels	0.1	Services			
Employment services	0.1	Services			
General purpose machinery, nec	0.1	Manufg.			

Source: Benchmark Input-Output Accounts for the U.S. Economy, 2002, U.S. Department of Commerce, Washington, D.C., January 2008. The abbreviation nec stands for 'not elsewhere classified'.

OCCUPATIONS EMPLOYED BY AGRICULTURE, CONSTRUCTION, & MINING MACHINERY

Occupation	% of Total 2006	Change to 2016	Occupation	% of Total 2006	Change to 2016
Welders, cutters, solderers, & brazers	11.7	-0.7	Sales reps, wholesale & manufacturing, exc tech	1.6	-6.6
Team assemblers	10.3	-6.6	Helpers--Production workers	1.6	-6.6
First-line supervisors/managers of production workers	3.5	-6.6	Maintenance & repair workers, general	1.5	-6.6
Computer-controlled machine tool operators	3.4	2.7	Shipping, receiving, & traffic clerks	1.4	-10.2
Engine & other machine assemblers	3.2	-6.6	Welding, soldering, & brazing machine operators	1.4	5.0
Structural metal fabricators & fitters	2.4	-6.6	Production, planning, & expediting clerks	1.3	-6.6
Mechanical engineers	2.2	-6.6	General & operations managers	1.3	-16.0
Laborers & freight, stock, & material movers, hand	2.1	-16.0	Bookkeeping, accounting, & auditing clerks	1.3	-6.6
Cutting, punching, & press machine operators	2.1	-16.0	Purchasing agents, exc wholesale, retail, & farm	1.2	-6.6
Inspectors, testers, sorters, samplers, & weighers	2.0	-12.0	Industrial engineers	1.1	13.4
Industrial truck & tractor operators	1.8	-16.0	Mechanical drafters	1.1	-5.6

Source: Industry-Occupation Matrix, Bureau of Labor Statistics, December 4, 2007. These data are reported based on 4-digit NAICS categories but have been matched to corresponding 6-digit NAICS industry codes. The change reported for each occupation to the year 2016 is a percent of growth or decline as estimated by the Bureau of Labor Statistics. The abbreviation nec stands for 'not elsewhere classified'.

LOCATION BY STATE AND REGIONAL CONCENTRATION

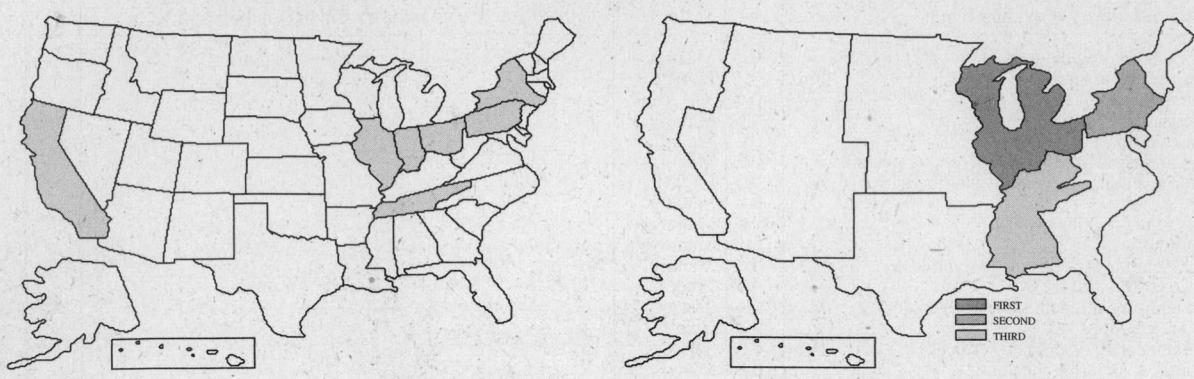

INDUSTRY DATA BY STATE

| State | Establish- ments | Shipments | | | Employment | | | | Cost as % of Shipments | Investment per Employee ($) |
		Total ($ mil)	% of U.S.	Per Establ.	Total Number	% of U.S.	Per Establ.	Wages ($/hour)		
Tennessee	7	1,122.0	17.2	160,279.3	3,371	15.2	482	12.20	70.6	11,534
Ohio	10	444.6	6.8	44,461.1	1,200	5.4	120	18.29	59.3	3,656
Illinois	8	308.1	4.7	38,512.2	1,281	5.8	160	9.92	79.6	3,738
Indiana	13	122.6	1.9	9,429.2	948	4.3	73	12.65	52.2	3,074
Pennsylvania	12	116.7	1.8	9,723.7	860	3.9	72	13.21	44.6	2,849
California	6	71.2	1.1	11,873.7	622	2.8	104	12.38	65.7	1,865
New York	5	25.0	0.4	5,005.8	109	0.5	22	12.34	66.8	5,028

Source: 2002 *Economic Census*. The states are in descending order of shipments or establishments (if shipment data are missing for the majority). The symbol (D) appears when data are withheld to prevent disclosure of competitive information. States marked with (D) are sorted by number of establishments. A dash (-) indicates that the data element cannot be calculated. Data may not show all states active in the NAICS category. All data available at the time of publication are shown.

NAICS 333120 - CONSTRUCTION MACHINERY MANUFACTURING

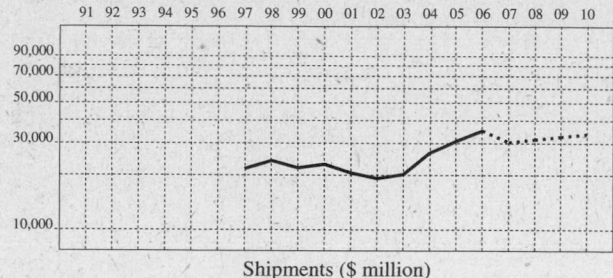

Shipments ($ million)

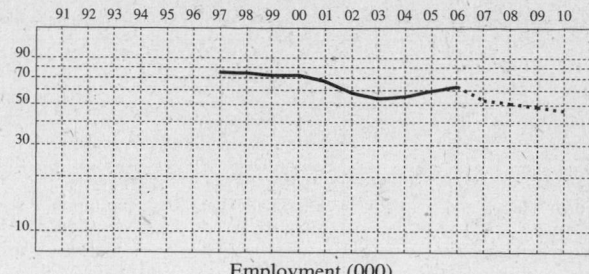

Employment (000)

GENERAL STATISTICS

| Year | Com-panies | Establishments | | Employment | | | Compensation | | Production ($ million) | | | |
		Total	with 20 or more employees	Total (000)	Production Workers (000)	Hours (Mil)	Payroll ($ mil)	Wages ($/hr)	Cost of Materials	Value Added by Manufacture	Value of Shipments	Capital Invest.
1997	721	784	394	74.9	50.6	102.6	2,994.8	17.39	12,851.3	8,659.0	21,667.1	492.5
1998		804	390	74.4	50.2	101.4	3,058.8	17.75	13,867.8	10,503.1	24,022.7	584.7
1999		814	400	72.2	48.5	97.3	2,923.8	17.65	13,441.2	8,462.7	21,920.7	572.7
2000		813	396	72.4	48.6	97.1	2,913.3	17.85	13,870.8	9,092.6	22,978.7	499.6
2001		793	385	67.1	43.7	85.6	2,753.5	18.00	12,095.5	8,373.5	20,587.8	399.7
2002	714	803	355	57.9	36.1	70.4	2,520.0	19.59	11,275.3	7,639.1	19,189.4	365.0
2003		784	361	54.0	34.6	70.7	2,363.0	19.17	12,634.1	7,421.3	20,185.0	209.7
2004		781	358	55.3	35.5	72.8	2,471.6	19.99	15,081.8	11,773.2	26,506.4	257.7
2005		774	377	59.3	39.0	78.5	2,693.2	20.70	19,810.2	11,417.7	30,819.6	496.1
2006		780P	356P	63.0	42.6	85.3	2,924.9	20.50	22,585.5	13,202.9	35,152.8	593.5
2007		777P	351P	53.0P	34.1P	68.4P	2,517.2P	21.06P	19,514.5P	11,407.7P	30,373.0P	374.1P
2008		774P	347P	50.8P	32.5P	65.2P	2,472.8P	21.45P	20,223.6P	11,822.2P	31,476.6P	360.8P
2009		771P	342P	48.6P	30.9P	61.9P	2,428.3P	21.85P	20,932.6P	12,236.7P	32,580.2P	347.5P
2010		768P	337P	46.4P	29.3P	58.7P	2,383.9P	22.25P	21,641.7P	12,651.2P	33,683.9P	334.3P

Sources: 1997 and 2002 *Economic Census*; other years, up to 2006, are from *Annual Survey of Manufactures*. Establishment counts for non-Census years are from *County Business Patterns*; 1997 and 2002 values are from the 1997 and 2002 censuses, respectively. 'P's show projections by the editors.

INDICES OF CHANGE

| Year | Com-panies | Establishments | | Employment | | | Compensation | | Production ($ million) | | | |
		Total	with 20 or more employees	Total (000)	Production Workers (000)	Hours (Mil)	Payroll ($ mil)	Wages ($/hr)	Cost of Materials	Value Added by Manufacture	Value of Shipments	Capital Invest.
1997	101	98	111	129	140	146	119	89	114	113	113	135
1998		100	110	128	139	144	121	91	123	137	125	160
1999		101	113	125	134	138	116	90	119	111	114	157
2000		101	112	125	135	138	116	91	123	119	120	137
2001		99	108	116	121	122	109	92	107	110	107	110
2002	100	100	100	100	100	100	100	100	100	100	100	100
2003		98	102	93	96	100	94	98	112	97	105	57
2004		97	101	96	98	103	98	102	134	154	138	71
2005		96	106	102	108	112	107	106	176	149	161	136
2006		97P	100P	109	118	121	116	105	200	173	183	163
2007		97P	99P	92P	94P	97P	100P	108P	173P	149P	158P	102P
2008		96P	98P	88P	90P	93P	98P	109P	179P	155P	164P	99P
2009		96P	96P	84P	86P	88P	96P	112P	186P	160P	170P	95P
2010		96P	95P	80P	81P	83P	95P	114P	192P	166P	176P	92P

Sources: Same as General Statistics. Values reflect change from the base year, 2002. Values above 100 mean greater than 2002, values below 100 mean less than 2002, and the values of 100 in other years means same as 2002. 'P's show projections by the editors.

SELECTED RATIOS

For 2002	Avg. of All Manufact.	Analyzed Industry	Index	For 2002	Avg. of All Manufact.	Analyzed Industry	Index
Employees per Establishment	42	72	172	Value Added per Production Worker	182,367	211,609	116
Payroll per Establishment	1,639,184	3,138,232	191	Cost per Establishment	5,769,015	14,041,469	243
Payroll per Employee	39,053	43,523	111	Cost per Employee	137,446	194,737	142
Production Workers per Establishment	30	45	152	Cost per Production Worker	195,506	312,335	160
Wages per Establishment	694,845	1,717,479	247	Shipments per Establishment	11,158,348	23,897,136	214
Wages per Production Worker	23,548	38,203	162	Shipments per Employee	265,847	331,423	125
Hours per Production Worker	1,980	1,950	98	Shipments per Production Worker	378,144	531,562	141
Wages per Hour	11.89	19.59	165	Investment per Establishment	361,338	454,545	126
Value Added per Establishment	5,381,325	9,513,200	177	Investment per Employee	8,609	6,304	73
Value Added per Employee	128,210	131,936	103	Investment per Production Worker	12,245	10,111	83

Sources: Same as General Statistics. The 'Average of All Manufacturing' column represents the average of all manufacturing industries reported for the most recent complete year available. The Index shows the relationship between the Average and the Analyzed Industry. For example, 100 means that they are equal; 500 that the Analyzed Industry is five times the average; 50 means that the Analyzed Industry is half the national average. The abbreviation 'na' is used to show that data are 'not available'. Ratios shown for 2002, the last complete census year.

LEADING COMPANIES   Number shown: **75**   Total sales ($ mil): **151,729**   Total employment (000): **291.8**

Company Name	Address				CEO Name	Phone	Co. Type	Sales ($ mil)	Empl. (000)
Caterpillar Inc.	100 NE Adams St.	Peoria	IL	61629		309-675-1000	P	44,958	101.3
APAC Inc.	900 Ashwood Pkwy.	Atlanta	GA	30338	Garry Higdem	770-392-5300	S	25,170*	1.5
Deere and Co.	1 John Deere Pl.	Moline	IL	61265		309-765-8000	P	24,082	52.0
PACCAR Inc.	PO Box 1518	Bellevue	WA	98009		425-468-7400	P	15,220	21.8
Terex Corp.	200 Nyala Farm Rd.	Westport	CT	06880		203-222-7170	P	9,138	21.0
Dover Corp.	280 Park Ave.	New York	NY	10017		212-922-1640	P	7,226	33.4
General Cable Corp.	4 Tesseneer Dr.	Highland Hgts	KY	41076	Gregory B. Kenny	859-572-8000	P	4,615	11.8
Manitowoc Company Inc.	PO Box 66	Manitowoc	WI	54221		920-684-4410	P	4,005	10.5
JLG Industries Inc.	1 Jlg Dr.	McConnellsburg	PA	17233		717-485-5161	S	2,289	4.1
Rowan Companies Inc.	2800 Post Oak Blvd.	Houston	TX	77056		713-621-7800	P	2,095	5.7
Heico Holding Inc.	2626 Warrenville Rd	Downers Grove	IL	60515	Michael Heisley	630-353-5000	R	1,560*	<0.1
Astec Industries Inc.	1725 Shepherd Rd.	Chattanooga	TN	37421	J. Don Brock	423-899-5898	P	869	1.0
Komatsu America International	1701 W Golf Rd.	Rolling Mdws	IL	60008	David W. Grzelak	847-437-5800	S	634*	4.6
Columbus McKinnon Corp.	140 J J Audubon Pky	Amherst	NY	14228	Herbert P. Ladds Jr.	716-689-5400	P	590	3.3
L.B. Foster Co.	415 Holiday Dr.	Pittsburgh	PA	15220	Stan Hasselbusch	412-928-3400	P	509	0.7
JCB Inc.	2000 Bamford Blvd.	Pooler	GA	31322	Helmut Peters	912-447-2000	R	501*	0.3
McNeilus Companies Inc.	113 Conner Rd.	Villa Rica	GA	30180	Micheal Wuest	770-459-6005	S	485*	1.0
Dayton Superior Corp.	7777 Washing. Vlg	Dayton	OH	45459	J.A. Ciccarelli	937-428-6360	P	483	1.6
Ballantine Inc.	840 McKinley St.	Anoka	MN	55303	Joe Newfield	763-427-3959	S	483*	<0.1
Schwing America Inc.	5900 Centerville Rd	Saint Paul	MN	55127	Thomas Anderson	651-429-0999	R	453*	0.6
Madill Equipment US Inc.	552 Hendrickson Dr.	Kalama	WA	98625	Gil Schmunk	360-673-5236	R	397*	<0.1
ESCO Corp.	PO Box 10123	Portland	OR	97296		503-228-2141	R	352*	0.8
Link-Belt Construction Equip.	PO Box 13600	Lexington	KY	40583	Chuck Martz	859-263-5200	R	349*	0.7
Multiquip Inc.	PO Box 6254	Carson	CA	90749	Roger Euliss	310-537-3700	R	317*	0.3
Kuhn Knight Inc.	1501 W 7th Ave.	Brodhead	WI	53520	Thierry Krier	608-897-2131	R	305*	0.2
Caterpillar Paving Products	PO Box 1362	Minneapolis	MN	55440	James Owens	763-425-4100	S	295*	0.6
P and H Mining Equipment Inc.	PO Box 310	Milwaukee	WI	53201	Mark Readinger	414-671-4400	S	272*	0.9
A.S.V. Inc.	PO Box 5160	Grand Rapids	MN	55744	Richard Benson	218-327-3434	P	246	0.3
Vermeer Manufacturing Company	PO Box 200	Pella	IA	50219	Mary Andringa	641-628-3141	R	238*	2.0
Coe Manufacturing Company Inc.	PO Box 520	Painesville	OH	44077	Shawn Casey	440-352-9381	R	236*	0.1
Altec Industries Inc.	PO Box 10264	Birmingham	AL	35202		205-991-7733	R	173*	<0.1
Wacker Corp.	N92 Anthony	Menomonee Fls	WI	53051	Christopher Barnard	262-255-0500	R	156*	0.5
Compaction America Inc.	2000 Kentville Rd.	Kewanee	IL	61443	Robert Patterson	309-853-3571	D	134*	0.4
Universal De Cristo	840 25th Ave.	Bellwood	IL	60104	Thomas Fahey	708-544-4255	R	134*	0.3
Charles Machine Works Inc.	PO Box 66	Perry	OK	73077	Ed Malzahn	580-336-4402	R	132*	1.2
Protection Services Inc.	635 Lucknow Rd.	Harrisburg	PA	17110	Douglas Danko	717-236-9307	R	127*	0.1
Hoge Warren Zimmermann Co.	40 W Crescentville	Cincinnati	OH	45246	Robert Hoge	513-618-0300	R	112*	<0.1
Psp Industries Inc.	9885 Doerr Ln.	Schertz	TX	78154	Andrew Easton	210-651-9595	R	105*	<0.1
Besser Co.	801 Johnson St.	Alpena	MI	49707	Kevin Curtis	989-354-4111	R	99*	0.4
Gardner Asphalt Inc.	PO Box 5449	Tampa	FL	33675	Raymond Hyer	813-248-2101	R	99*	<0.1
Angus Industries Inc.	PO Box 610	Watertown	SD	57201	Robert Kluver	605-886-5681	R	96*	0.3
Neil F Lampson Inc.	PO Box 6510	Kennewick	WA	99336	William Lampson	509-586-0411	R	96*	0.2
Godbersen-Smith Construction	PO Box 151	Ida Grove	IA	51445	Gary Godbersen	712-364-3347	R	90*	0.3
Deere-Hitachi Construct Mach.	PO Box 1187	Kernersville	NC	27285	Al Seeba	336-996-8100	J	89*	0.4
A.S.V. Distribution Inc.	PO Box 5160	Grand Rapids	MN	55744	Gary Lemke	218-327-3434	S	89*	0.2
White Construction Company	PO Box 790	Chiefland	FL	32644	Luther White	352-493-1444	R	83*	0.1
Dynapac	PO Box 615	Schertz	TX	78154	Bruce Trusedale	210-474-5770	R	83*	<0.1
H and L Tooth Co.	PO Box 48	Owasso	OK	74055	Richard Launder	918-272-0951	R	81*	<0.1
Patent Construction Systems	1 Mack Centre Dr.	Paramus	NJ	07652		201-261-5600	D	77*	0.7
Gencor Industries Inc.	5201 N Orng Blssm	Orlando	FL	32810	Marc G. Elliot	407-290-6000	P	75	0.3
Stone Construction Equipment	PO Box 150	Honeoye	NY	14471	Robert Fien	585-229-5141	R	69*	0.2
Braden Carco Gearmatic Winch	PO Box 547	Broken Arrow	OK	74013	Mark Pigott	918-251-8511	D	66*	0.3
TMF Center Inc.	300 W Washington	Williamsport	IN	47993	Lloyd Gowen	765-762-1000	R	62*	0.2
P.A. Landers Inc.	PO Box 217	Hanover	MA	02339	Preston Landers	781-826-8818	R	60*	<0.1
Allied Systems Co.	21433 SW Oregon	Sherwood	OR	97140		503-625-2560	R	59*	0.3
Reynolds International Inc.	PO Box 550	McAllen	TX	78505	Paula Moore	956-687-7500	R	59*	0.2
Johnson Gas Appliance Co.	520 E Ave. NW	Cedar Rapids	IA	52405	Barnes O'Donnell	319-365-5267	R	58*	<0.1
Bucyrus Blades Inc.	PO Box 628	Bucyrus	OH	44820	Larry Huget	419-562-6015	S	54*	0.2
Terex Mining	PO Box 998	Sherman	TX	75090		903-786-6405	D	53	0.1
MRL Equipment Company Inc.	PO Box 31154	Billings	MT	59107	John Gonitzke	406-869-9900	R	51*	<0.1
Hensley Attachments	800 S 5th Street	Mansfield	TX	76063	H. Kuribayashi	817-477-3167	S	49*	<0.1
Plasser American Corp.	PO Box 5464	Chesapeake	VA	23324	Joseph Neuhofer	757-543-3526	R	49*	0.2
Kress Corp.	227 W Illinois St.	Brimfield	IL	61517	Rita Kress	309-446-3395	R	47*	0.2
American Pecco Corp.	PO Box 670	Millwood	NY	10546	Ronald A. Yakin	914-762-0550	R	45*	0.2
Distribution Support Service	1860 Cmmnwealth	Boston	MA	02135	Steven Albanese	617-232-1234	R	44*	0.2
Rome Plow Co.	PO Box 48	Cedartown	GA	30125		770-748-4450	R	44*	<0.1
Ramsey Winch Co.	PO Box 581510	Tulsa	OK	74158	Robert Heffron	918-438-2760	R	44*	0.3
Hendrix Manufacturing Company	PO Box 919	Mansfield	LA	71052	Guy Hall	318-872-1660	R	42*	0.1
General Asphalt Company Inc.	PO Box 522306	Miami	FL	33152	Robert Lopez	305-592-3480	R	41*	0.1
Regen Technologies L.L.C.	4500 E Mustard	Springfield	MO	65803	Ron Guinn	417-829-2000	R	41*	0.2
General Equipment Co.	PO Box 334	Owatonna	MN	55060	Dennis Von Ruden	507-451-5510	R	40*	<0.1
Allen Engineering Corp.	PO Box 819	Paragould	AR	72451	Dewayne Allen	870-236-7751	R	39*	0.1
ACS Northwest Inc.	19602 60th Ave. NE	Arlington	WA	98223	Joseph Zeno	360-474-1940	R	38*	0.1
Weldall Manufacturing Inc.	2001 S Prairie Ave.	Waukesha	WI	53189	David Bahl	262-544-1155	R	38*	0.1
JLG Manufacturing L.L.C.	140 Hawbaker Ind	State College	PA	16801	Mike Houseknecht	814-237-9050	S	37*	0.1

Source: Ward's Business Directory of U.S. Private and Public Companies, Volumes 1 and 2, 2008. The company type code used is as follows: P - Public, R - Private, S - Subsidiary, D - Division, J - Joint Venture, A - Affiliate, G - Group. Sales are in millions of dollars, employees are in thousands. An asterisk (*) indicates an estimated sales volume. The symbol < stands for 'less than'. Company names and addresses are truncated, in some cases, to fit into the available space.

MATERIALS CONSUMED

Material	Quantity	Delivered Cost ($ million)
Fluid power pumps, motors, and hydrostatic transmissions	(X)	445.4
Fluid power cylinders and rotary actuators (hydraulic and pneumatic)	(X)	181.8
Fluid power hose, tube fittings, and assemblies (hydraulic and pneumatic)	(X)	123.9
Fluid power valves (hydraulic and pneumatic)	(X)	214.8
Metal bolts, nuts, screws, and other screw machine products	(X)	153.0
Fabricated structural metal products (excluding forgings)	(X)	459.6
Fabricated metal wire products (incl. wire rope, cable, springs, etc.)	(X)	31.6
All other fabricated metal products (excluding forgings)	(X)	216.4
Metal stampings	(X)	53.2
Forgings	(X)	119.5
Iron and steel castings (rough and semifinished)	(X)	499.4
Nonferrous (aluminum, copper, etc.) castings (rough and semifinished)	(X)	23.6
Steel bars, bar shapes, and plates (exc. castings, forgings, fabr. metal products)	(X)	363.9
Steel sheet and strip (including tinplate)	(X)	145.2
Steel structural shapes and sheet piling (exc. castings, forgings, fabr. metal products)	(X)	34.3
All other steel shapes and forms (exc. castings, forgings, fabr. metal products)	(X)	123.0
Nonferrous shapes and forms	(X)	10.8
Diesel engines and parts specially designed for diesel engines	(X)	516.6
Gasoline engines and parts specially designed for gasoline engines	(X)	67.7
Electric motors and generators	(X)	120.4
Ball bearings (mounted or unmounted)	(X)	28.6
Roller bearings (mounted or unmounted)	(X)	39.1
Mechanical speed changers, gears, and industrial high-speed drives	(X)	172.4
Pneumatic tires and inner tubes	(X)	231.2
Wheels, motor vehicle	(X)	47.1
Purchased chassis for vehicles (excluding passenger cars)	(X)	177.0
Transmissions and parts	(X)	245.4
Engine electrical equipment (incl. spark plugs, magnetos, generators, starters, etc.)	(X)	145.4
Shocks, struts, and other suspension equipment and parts	(X)	66.3
Rubber and plastics hose and belting	(X)	77.7
Fabricated plastics products (exc. gaskets, hoses, and belting)	(X)	42.1
Paints, varnishes, stains, lacquers, shellacs, japans, enamels, etc.	(X)	37.3
Electrical transmission, distribution, and control equipment	(X)	170.2
All other materials, components, parts, containers, and supplies	(X)	2,447.2
Materials, ingredients, containers, and supplies, nsk	(X)	1,790.0

Source: 2002 *Economic Census*. Explanation of symbols used: (D): Withheld to avoid disclosure of competitive data; na: Not available; (S): Withheld because statistical norms were not met; (X): Not applicable; (Z): Less than half the unit shown; nec: Not elsewhere classified; nsk: Not specified by kind; - : zero; p : 10-19 percent estimated; q : 20-29 percent estimated.

PRODUCT SHARE DETAILS

Product or Product Class Shipments	Mil. $	Product or Product Class Shipments	Mil. $
CONSTRUCTION MACHINERY	16,588.7	Digger-derricks (excluding parts)	(D)
Power cranes, excavation loaders, dozers, construction tractors, off-highway trucks and trailers, mixers, pavers, backhoes, and related equipment	**11,913.8**	Vertical earth augers and power posthole diggers, excluding water well and blasthole drills (excluding parts)	(D)
Power cranes, draglines, and shovels (excavators) (including surface mining equipment and attachments) (excluding parts)	2,561.6	Horizontal earth boring machines and accessories (excluding parts)	104.4
Mixers, pavers, and related equipment (excluding parts).	1,145.8	Pile driving equipment (including air, steam, and diesel pile hammers and impact pile or vibratory driver extractors) (excluding parts)	35.6
Off-highway trucks, coal haulers, truck-type tractor chassis, trailers and wagons, except parts	948.1	All other construction machinery and equipment, complete units	815.4
Tractor shovel loaders (skid steer, wheel, and crawler, and integral-design loader-backhoes)	1,288.1	Other construction machinery and equipment (excluding parts), nsk	12.3
Construction wheel and crawler tractors, dozers, and self-propelled log skidders	4,106.9	**Parts for construction machinery and equipment, sold separately**	**2,263.4**
Motor graders and light maintainers, rollers and compactors, rough-terrain forklifts, scraper bowls, and self-propelled continuous ditchers and trenchers, except parts	1,313.1	Parts for power cranes, draglines, and shovels (excavators) (including surface mining equipment) (sold separately)	617.7
Construction machinery for mounting on tractors and other prime movers (excluding parts, winches, and snow clearing attachments)	526.1	Parts for contractors' off-highway wheel tractors, crawler tractors, and tractor shovel loaders (sold separately)	618.4
Power cranes, excavation loaders, dozers, construction tractors, off-highway trucks and trailers, mixers, pavers, backhoes, and related equipment, nsk	24.0	Parts for other construction machinery	977.4
Other construction machinery and equipment (excluding parts)	**1,879.4**	Parts for mixers, pavers, and related equipment (sold separately)	158.9
Other construction machinery and equipment (excluding parts)	1,867.1	Parts for off-highway trucks, coal haulers, truck-type tractor chassis, trailers and wagons (sold separately)	114.9
Portable crushing plants, screening plants, washing plants, and combination plants (excluding parts)	153.0	Parts for motor graders and light maintainers, rollers and compactors, rough-terrain forklifts, scraper bowls, and self-propelled continuous ditchers and trenchers (sold separately)	177.5
Snow clearing attachments for mounting on tractors or trucks (except rotary snow blowers), including snow plows, etc. (excluding parts)	276.1	Parts for construction machinery (except winches) for mounting on tractors and other prime movers (sold separately)	160.6
Commercial brush, limb, and log chippers for waste wood reduction (excluding parts)	200.8	Parts for other construction machinery and equipment (except winches, hoists, and railroad rolling stock, sold separately)	365.5
Log splitters (excluding parts)	(D)	Parts for construction machinery and equipment, sold separately, nsk	49.8
Dredging machinery, hydraulic and other types (excluding parts)	15.0	**Construction machinery, nsk, total**	**532.1**

Source: 2002 *Economic Census*. The values are product shipments in millions of dollars for 2002. Total product shipments may be lower or higher than industry shipments. See Introduction for a full discussion. Values of indented subcategories are summed in the main heading(s). The symbol (D) appears when data are withheld to prevent disclosure of competitive information. The abbreviation nsk stands for 'not specified by kind' and nec for 'not elsewhere classified'. A dash (-) means zero.

INPUTS AND OUTPUTS FOR CONSTRUCTION MACHINERY MANUFACTURING

Economic Sector or Industry Providing Inputs	%	Sector	Economic Sector or Industry Buying Outputs	%	Sector
Compensation of employees	19.8		Private fixed investment	56.8	Cap Inv
Engine equipment, nec	6.5	Manufg.	Exports of goods & services	21.4	
Wholesale trade	6.5	Trade	S/L govt. invest., other	6.9	S/L Govt
Management of companies & enterprises	6.0	Services	Coal	2.7	Mining
Motor vehicle parts	5.1	Manufg.	Federal government, investment, national defense	2.5	Fed Govt
Iron & steel mills & ferroalloys	3.9	Manufg.	Residential structures, nec	2.2	Construct.
Valve & fittings other than plumbing	3.0	Manufg.	Residential permanent site structures	1.4	Construct.
Ferrous metal foundries	2.7	Manufg.	Construction machinery	1.3	Manufg.
Rubber products, nec	2.2	Manufg.	Nonresidential structures, nec	0.7	Construct.
Fluid power process machinery	2.1	Manufg.	Oil & gas well drilling	0.7	Mining
Retail trade	2.0	Trade	Commercial & health care structures	0.5	Construct.
Construction machinery	1.7	Manufg.	Oil & gas operations services	0.4	Mining
Tires	1.5	Manufg.	Waste management & remediation services	0.3	Services
Plastics products, nec	1.5	Manufg.	Ship building & repairing	0.3	Manufg.
Metal cans, boxes, & other containers (light gauge)	1.4	Manufg.	Miscellaneous mining services	0.3	Mining
Plate work & fabricated structural products	1.4	Manufg.	Maintenance/repair of nonresidential structures	0.2	Construct.
Speed changers, industrial high-speed drives, & gears	1.2	Manufg.	Nonmetallic minerals, nec	0.2	Mining
Noncomparable imports	1.1	Foreign	Sand, gravel, clay, & refractory minerals	0.2	Mining
Turned products & screws, nuts, & bolts	1.0	Manufg.	Farm machinery & equipment	0.2	Manufg.
Petroleum refineries	0.9	Manufg.	Architectural, engineering, & related services	0.2	Services
Truck transportation	0.9	Util.	Iron ore	0.1	Mining
Rubber & plastics hose & belting	0.9	Manufg.	Stone mining & quarrying	0.1	Mining
Heavy duty trucks	0.8	Manufg.			
Ornamental & architectural metal products	0.8	Manufg.			
Motors & generators	0.7	Manufg.			
Relay & industrial controls	0.7	Manufg.			
Ball & roller bearings	0.5	Manufg.			
Machine shops	0.5	Manufg.			
Railroad rolling stock	0.5	Manufg.			
Advertising & related services	0.5	Services			
Crowns & closures & metal stamping	0.5	Manufg.			

Continued on next page.

INPUTS AND OUTPUTS FOR CONSTRUCTION MACHINERY MANUFACTURING - Continued

Economic Sector or Industry Providing Inputs	%	Sector	Economic Sector or Industry Buying Outputs	%	Sector
Storage batteries	0.5	Manufg.			
Power generation & supply	0.4	Util.			
Paints & coatings	0.4	Manufg.			
Semiconductors & related devices	0.4	Manufg.			
Electronic components, nec	0.4	Manufg.			
Printed circuit assemblies (electronic assemblies)	0.4	Manufg.			
Real estate	0.3	Fin/R.E.			
Coating, engraving, heat treating & allied activities	0.3	Manufg.			
Motor vehicle bodies	0.3	Manufg.			
Natural gas distribution	0.3	Util.			
Automotive equipment rental & leasing	0.3	Fin/R.E.			
Legal services	0.3	Services			
General purpose machinery, nec	0.3	Manufg.			
Springs & wire products	0.2	Manufg.			
Securities, commodity contracts, investments	0.2	Fin/R.E.			
Telecommunications	0.2	Services			
Cutting tools & machine tool accessories	0.2	Manufg.			
Truck trailers	0.2	Manufg.			
Taxes on production & imports, less subsidies	0.2				
Management, scientific, & technical consulting	0.2	Services			
Maintenance/repair of nonresidential structures	0.2	Construct.			
Postal service	0.2	Util.			
Scientific research & development services	0.2	Services			
Warehousing & storage	0.2	Util.			
Plastics packaging materials, film & sheet	0.2	Manufg.			
Services to buildings & dwellings	0.2	Services			
Nonferrous metal foundries	0.2	Manufg.			
Lessors of nonfinancial assets	0.1	Fin/R.E.			
Commercial & industrial machinery rental & leasing	0.1	Fin/R.E.			
Hardware	0.1	Manufg.			
Fabricated metals, nec	0.1	Manufg.			
Rail transportation	0.1	Util.			
Accounting, tax preparation, bookkeeping, & payroll	0.1	Services			
Automotive repair & maintenance, ex. car washes	0.1	Services			
Air transportation	0.1	Util.			
Custom roll forming	0.1	Manufg.			

Source: Benchmark Input-Output Accounts for the U.S. Economy, 2002, U.S. Department of Commerce, Washington, D.C., January 2008. The abbreviation nec stands for 'not elsewhere classified'.

OCCUPATIONS EMPLOYED BY AGRICULTURE, CONSTRUCTION, & MINING MACHINERY

Occupation	% of Total 2006	Change to 2016	Occupation	% of Total 2006	Change to 2016
Welders, cutters, solderers, & brazers	11.7	-0.7	Sales reps, wholesale & manufacturing, exc tech	1.6	-6.6
Team assemblers	10.3	-6.6	Helpers--Production workers	1.6	-6.6
First-line supervisors/managers of production workers	3.5	-6.6	Maintenance & repair workers, general	1.5	-6.6
Computer-controlled machine tool operators	3.4	2.7	Shipping, receiving, & traffic clerks	1.4	-10.2
Engine & other machine assemblers	3.2	-6.6	Welding, soldering, & brazing machine operators	1.4	5.0
Structural metal fabricators & fitters	2.4	-6.6	Production, planning, & expediting clerks	1.3	-6.6
Mechanical engineers	2.2	-6.6	General & operations managers	1.3	-16.0
Laborers & freight, stock, & material movers, hand	2.1	-16.0	Bookkeeping, accounting, & auditing clerks	1.3	-6.6
Cutting, punching, & press machine operators	2.1	-16.0	Purchasing agents, exc wholesale, retail, & farm	1.2	-6.6
Inspectors, testers, sorters, samplers, & weighers	2.0	-12.0	Industrial engineers	1.1	13.4
Industrial truck & tractor operators	1.8	-16.0	Mechanical drafters	1.1	-5.6

Source: Industry-Occupation Matrix, Bureau of Labor Statistics, December 4, 2007. These data are reported based on 4-digit NAICS categories but have been matched to corresponding 6-digit NAICS industry codes. The change reported for each occupation to the year 2016 is a percent of growth or decline as estimated by the Bureau of Labor Statistics. The abbreviation nec stands for 'not elsewhere classified'.

LOCATION BY STATE AND REGIONAL CONCENTRATION

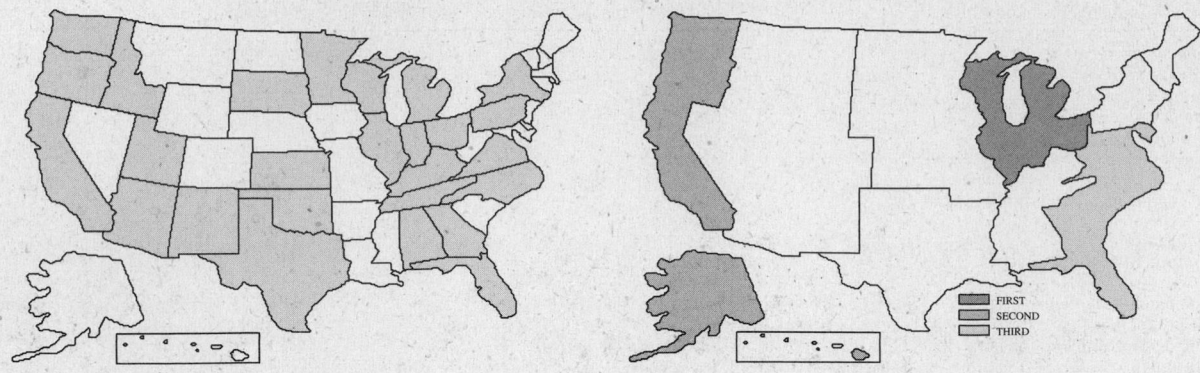

FIRST
SECOND
THIRD

INDUSTRY DATA BY STATE

State	Establish-ments	Shipments			Employment				Cost as % of Shipments	Investment per Employee ($)
		Total ($ mil)	% of U.S.	Per Establ.	Total Number	% of U.S.	Per Establ.	Wages ($/hour)		
Illinois	53	4,462.9	23.3	84,206.0	8,928	15.4	168	23.11	61.7	13,474
North Carolina	21	2,000.1	10.4	95,241.2	2,562	4.4	122	19.68	72.8	5,933
Wisconsin	53	1,673.5	8.7	31,574.9	5,989	10.3	113	25.59	54.2	6,217
Pennsylvania	33	921.0	4.8	27,909.3	3,339	5.8	101	19.16	63.6	4,896
Tennessee	19	743.0	3.9	39,107.6	2,328	4.0	123	19.09	64.9	4,335
Kansas	22	661.5	3.4	30,068.1	1,940	3.4	88	13.52	54.6	4,392
Oklahoma	23	552.8	2.9	24,034.7	2,573	4.4	112	15.44	52.0	3,383
Ohio	49	459.1	2.4	9,368.9	2,018	3.5	41	15.60	44.4	3,398
Texas	47	418.4	2.2	8,902.8	2,721	4.7	58	16.58	65.1	3,115
Minnesota	32	396.5	2.1	12,389.9	1,574	2.7	49	19.13	58.9	9,247
Georgia	14	342.5	1.8	24,465.4	647	1.1	46	17.85	61.3	10,686
Michigan	27	280.5	1.5	10,388.0	1,103	1.9	41	17.54	51.0	3,532
Kentucky	12	273.0	1.4	22,753.2	1,154	2.0	96	21.26	67.0	8,005
South Dakota	14	266.7	1.4	19,051.6	1,211	2.1	86	14.32	52.6	1,593
Indiana	29	249.5	1.3	8,604.0	1,083	1.9	37	21.24	61.7	3,427
Alabama	10	166.5	0.9	16,651.0	622	1.1	62	22.56	85.8	2,728
California	65	161.4	0.8	2,483.4	926	1.6	14	18.30	45.9	5,374
New York	28	133.0	0.7	4,750.4	714	1.2	25	19.94	56.1	5,371
Oregon	19	131.8	0.7	6,936.5	679	1.2	36	19.63	55.8	5,328
Florida	25	104.6	0.5	4,183.7	522	0.9	21	16.07	55.5	4,393
Virginia	11	99.2	0.5	9,018.7	443	0.8	40	14.80	62.6	4,289
Washington	23	70.5	0.4	3,067.0	372	0.6	16	17.82	47.2	5,175
Arizona	7	61.4	0.3	8,766.9	270	0.5	39	22.81	61.1	1,037
Idaho	9	53.2	0.3	5,911.2	339	0.6	38	15.26	64.0	2,460
Utah	7	27.0	0.1	3,858.4	128	0.2	18	15.58	36.0	6,648
New Mexico	6	15.5	0.1	2,591.3	106	0.2	18	16.31	53.2	1,764

Source: 2002 *Economic Census*. The states are in descending order of shipments or establishments (if shipment data are missing for the majority). The symbol (D) appears when data are withheld to prevent disclosure of competitive information. States marked with (D) are sorted by number of establishments. A dash (-) indicates that the data element cannot be calculated. Data may not show all states active in the NAICS category. All data available at the time of publication are shown.

NAICS 33313M - MINING AND OIL AND GAS FIELD MACHINERY MANUFACTURING*

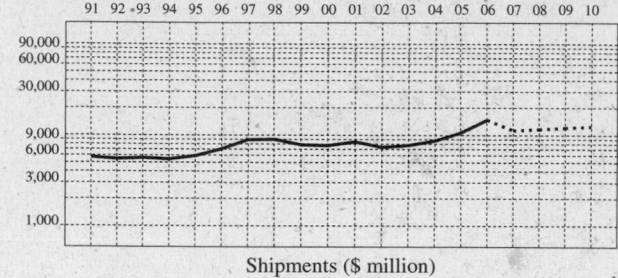

Shipments ($ million)

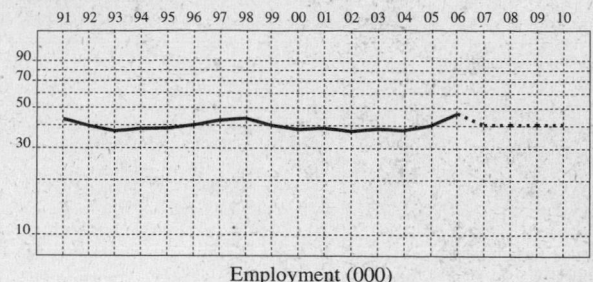

Employment (000)

GENERAL STATISTICS

| Year | Com-panies | Establishments | | Employment | | | Compensation | | Production ($ million) | | | |
		Total	with 20 or more employees	Total (000)	Production Workers (000)	Hours (Mil)	Payroll ($ mil)	Wages ($/hr)	Cost of Materials	Value Added by Manufacture	Value of Shipments	Capital Invest.
1991		884	379	43.2	24.5	50.4	1,289.4	12.59	2,680.4	2,920.2	5,716.1	132.2
1992	741	832	319	39.6	22.8	47.1	1,270.2	13.04	2,519.5	2,833.8	5,475.4	137.6
1993		815	302	37.1	21.5	43.7	1,185.9	13.47	2,614.0	2,927.4	5,620.9	138.7
1994		816	294	38.2	22.8	44.1	1,248.0	14.62	2,536.5	2,931.6	5,447.7	107.1
1995		802	310	38.4	24.3	47.7	1,249.3	14.25	2,685.9	3,354.6	5,904.2	151.7
1996		838	311	40.1	25.4	51.2	1,403.7	15.33	3,482.7	3,694.7	7,042.7	200.9
1997	760	854	354	42.7	28.4	56.2	1,641.9	16.14	4,136.6	5,038.8	8,881.7	292.0
1998		875	364	43.8	28.4	58.2	1,688.6	16.08	4,297.6	4,904.8	9,004.3	239.0
1999		842	338	40.1	25.2	50.1	1,549.3	15.83	3,878.3	3,697.8	7,839.8	220.4
2000		825	333	38.1	23.6	48.9	1,592.9	16.50	3,899.4	3,797.3	7,698.6	202.1
2001		794	330	38.8	24.2	49.7	1,717.6	17.19	4,575.2	3,990.8	8,477.7	253.9
2002	713	808	325	37.3	22.7	46.0	1,710.6	18.57	3,878.5	3,582.9	7,394.0	223.2
2003		805	319	38.4	24.2	51.1	1,795.0	17.36	4,227.4	3,526.9	7,731.4	192.8
2004		829	335	37.8	22.2	46.5	1,867.8	19.10	4,434.7	4,318.1	8,677.7	295.9
2005		833	349	40.2	25.6	54.8	1,981.5	19.86	5,606.6	5,333.3	10,697.7	234.6
2006		815P	336P	46.7	30.8	65.2	2,541.0	20.99	8,201.6	7,290.4	14,796.1	387.7
2007		814P	337P	40.5P	26.2P	55.3P	2,170.3P	20.58P	6,258.1P	5,562.8P	11,289.8P	314.0P
2008		812P	337P	40.6P	26.4P	55.8P	2,236.4P	21.08P	6,479.1P	5,759.3P	11,688.6P	325.9P
2009		810P	338P	40.6P	26.6P	56.3P	2,302.5P	21.58P	6,700.1P	5,955.7P	12,087.4P	337.7P
2010		808P	339P	40.7P	26.8P	56.9P	2,368.6P	22.08P	6,921.2P	6,152.2P	12,486.1P	349.6P

Sources: 1992, 1997, 2002 *Economic Census*; other years, up to 2006, are from the *Annual Survey of Manufactures*. Establishment counts for non-Census years are from *County Business Patterns*; 1997 and 2002 values are from the 1997 and 2002 censuses respectively, reported in the Federal Government's NAICS format. Other years were originally reported in equivalent SIC format. 'P's show projections by the editors.

INDICES OF CHANGE

| Year | Com-panies | Establishments | | Employment | | | Compensation | | Production ($ million) | | | |
		Total	with 20 or more employees	Total (000)	Production Workers (000)	Hours (Mil)	Payroll ($ mil)	Wages ($/hr)	Cost of Materials	Value Added by Manufacture	Value of Shipments	Capital Invest.
1992	104	103	98	106	100	102	74	70	65	79	74	62
1997	107	106	109	114	125	122	96	87	107	141	120	131
2001		98	102	104	107	108	100	93	118	111	115	114
2002	100	100	100	100	100	100	100	100	100	100	100	100
2003		100	98	103	107	111	105	93	109	98	105	86
2004		103	103	101	98	101	109	103	114	121	117	133
2005		103	107	108	113	119	116	107	145	149	145	105
2006		101P	103P	125	136	142	149	113	211	203	200	174
2007		101P	104P	109P	115P	120P	127P	111P	161P	155P	153P	141P
2008		100P	104P	109P	116P	121P	131P	114P	167P	161P	158P	146P
2009		100P	104P	109P	117P	122P	135P	116P	173P	166P	163P	151P
2010		100P	104P	109P	118P	124P	138P	119P	178P	172P	169P	157P

Sources: Same as General Statistics. Values reflect change from the base year, 2002. Values above 100 mean greater than 2002, values below 100 mean less than 2002, and the values of 100 in other years means the same as 2002. 'P's show projections by the editors.

SELECTED RATIOS

For 2002	Avg. of All Manufact.	Analyzed Industry	Index	For 2002	Avg. of All Manufact.	Analyzed Industry	Index
Employees per Establishment	42	46	110	Value Added per Production Worker	182,367	157,837	87
Payroll per Establishment	1,639,184	2,117,079	129	Cost per Establishment	5,769,015	4,800,124	83
Payroll per Employee	39,053	45,861	117	Cost per Employee	137,446	103,981	76
Production Workers per Establishment	30	28	95	Cost per Production Worker	195,506	170,859	87
Wages per Establishment	694,845	1,057,203	152	Shipments per Establishment	11,158,348	9,150,990	82
Wages per Production Worker	23,548	37,631	160	Shipments per Employee	265,847	198,231	75
Hours per Production Worker	1,980	2,026	102	Shipments per Production Worker	378,144	325,727	86
Wages per Hour	11.89	18.57	156	Investment per Establishment	361,338	276,238	76
Value Added per Establishment	5,381,325	4,434,282	82	Investment per Employee	8,609	5,984	70
Value Added per Employee	128,210	96,056	75	Investment per Production Worker	12,245	9,833	80

Sources: Same as General Statistics. The 'Average of All Manufacturing' column represents the average of all manufacturing industries reported for the most recent complete year available. The Index shows the relationship between the Average and the Analyzed Industry. For example, 100 means that they are equal; 500 that the Analyzed Industry is five times the average; 50 means that the Analyzed Industry is half the national average. The abbreviation 'na' is used to show that data are 'not available'. Ratios shown for 2002, the last complete census year.

*Equivalent to Federal Government NAICS 333131, 333132.

LEADING COMPANIES   Number shown: 75   Total sales ($ mil): 122,570   Total employment (000): 301.5

Company Name	Address				CEO Name	Phone	Co. Type	Sales ($ mil)	Empl. (000)
Halliburton Co.	5 Houston Ctr.	Houston	TX	77010		713-759-2600	P	15,264	51.0
Baker Hughes Inc.	PO Box 4740	Houston	TX	77210		713-439-8600	P	10,428	35.8
National Oilwell Varco Inc.	PO Box 4888	Houston	TX	77210		713-346-7500	P	9,789	26.7
Smith International Inc.	PO Box 60068	Houston	TX	77205		281-443-3370	P	8,764	19.9
Weatherford International Ltd.	515 Post Oak Blvd.	Houston	TX	77027	B. J. Duroc-Danner	713-693-4000	P	7,832	38.0
Penn Machine Co.	106 Station St.	Johnstown	PA	15905	H Wiegand	814-288-1547	R	7,000*	<0.1
Weatherford U S Inc.	PO Box 27706	Houston	TX	77227	B Duroc-Danner	713-693-4000	R	6,570*	0.3
Metso Minerals Industries Inc.	20965 Crossroads	Waukesha	WI	53186	Hannu Melarti	262-717-2500	R	6,340*	0.2
BJ Services Co.	4601 Westway Park	Houston	TX	77041		713-462-4239	P	4,820	16.7
Cameron International Corp.	1333 W Loop S	Houston	TX	77027	Sheldon R. Erikson	713-513-3300	P	4,666	15.4
FMC Technologies Inc.	1803 Gears Rd.	Houston	TX	77067		281-591-4000	P	4,615	11.0
General Cable Corp.	4 Tesseneer Dr.	Highland Hgts	KY	41076	Gregory B. Kenny	859-572-8000	P	4,615	11.8
Virginia Harbor Services Inc.	PO Box 98	Clear Brook	VA	22624	Michael Harper	540-667-5191	R	3,720*	<0.1
Wood Group Pressure Control	PO Box 82	Houston	TX	77001	Scott Bender	832-325-4200	R	3,657*	0.1
Joy Global Inc.	100 E Wisconsin	Milwaukee	WI	53202	Edward Doheny	414-319-8500	P	2,547	9.2
Kennametal Inc.	PO Box 231	Latrobe	PA	15650	Carlos M. Cardoso	724-539-5000	P	2,386	14.0
Oil States International Inc.	333 Clay St., 4620	Houston	TX	77002	Cindy B. Taylor	713-652-0582	P	2,088	6.6
Grant Prideco Inc.	400 N Sam Houston	Houston	TX	77060	John Deane	281-878-8000	P	1,909	5.1
Gardner Denver Inc.	PO Box 528	Quincy	IL	62306	Ross J. Centanni	217-222-5400	P	1,869	6.2
Weir Spm	7701 Skyline Park	Fort Worth	TX	76108	Steve Noon	817-246-2461	P	1,770*	0.3
W-H Energy Services Inc.	2000 W S Houston	Houston	TX	77042	Max Duncan	713-974-9071	P	1,127	3.5
Joy Mining Machinery	177 Thorn Hill Rd.	Warrendale	PA	15086	Mike Sutherlin	724-779-4500	D	865*	4.5
Range Resources Corp.	777 Main St., 800	Fort Worth	TX	76102	Charles L. Blackburn	817-870-2601	P	863	0.7
Bucyrus International Inc.	PO Box 500	S Milwaukee	WI	53172		414-768-4000	P	738	2.4
Oldenburg Group Inc.	1717 W Civic Dr.	Glendale	WI	53209	Wayne C. Oldenburg	414-977-1717	R	720*	1.2
Newpark Resources Inc.	2700 Research Forst	The Woodlands	TX	77381	William T. Ballantine	281-362-6800	P	613	2.0
Sandvik Mining & Construction	13500 NW Cnty Rd	Alachua	FL	32615		386-462-4100	R	503*	0.2
Hydril Co.	PO Box 60458	Houston	TX	77205	Paolo Rocco	281-449-2000	S	503	1.8
Dril-Quip Inc.	13550 Hempstead	Houston	TX	77040	Larry E. Reimert	713-939-7711	P	496	1.9
Gulf Island Fabrication Inc.	PO Box 310	Houma	LA	70361	Kerry J. Chauvin	985-872-2100	P	473	1.9
TIW Corp.	PO Box 35729	Houston	TX	77235		713-729-2110	R	410*	0.2
ESCO Corp.	PO Box 10123	Portland	OR	97296		503-228-2141	R	352*	0.8
GulfMark Offshore Inc.	10111 Richmond	Houston	TX	77042		713-963-9522	P	306	1.3
Frigoscandia Inc.	200 E Randolph Dr.	Chicago	IL	60601		312-861-6000	S	304*	0.4
P and H Mining Equipment Inc.	PO Box 310	Milwaukee	WI	53201	Mark Readinger	414-671-4400	S	272*	0.9
Blue Tee Corp.	250 Park Ave. S	New York	NY	10003	William M. Kelly	212-598-0880	R	250*	0.9
DBT America Inc.	2045 W Pke. St.	Houston	PA	15342		724-743-1200	R	209*	0.2
SMI Manufacturing Inc.	13312 E Hardy Rd.	Houston	TX	77039	Bo Eagles	281-449-0345	R	200*	<0.1
IPSCO Inc. (US)	650 Warrenville Rd.	Lisle	IL	60532	John Tulloch	630-810-4800	S	168*	<0.1
Maddox Foundry/Machine Wrks	PO Drawer 7	Archer	FL	32618	Monte Marchant	352-495-2121	R	154*	0.2
US. Filter/Johnson Screen	1950 Old Hwy 8	New Brighton	MN	55112	John Heeney	651-636-3900	R	149*	0.3
WWL Industries	PO Box 4574	Odessa	TX	79760	Billy D. White	432-362-0326	R	140*	<0.1
Owen Oil Tools Inc.	PO Box 40666	Fort Worth	TX	76140	Jeff West	817-551-0540	S	139*	0.2
Weatherford Oil Country Mfg.	300 W Stanley Ave.	Ventura	CA	93001		805-643-1200	S	135*	0.2
National Tank Co.	2950 N Loop W, 750	Houston	TX	77092	John Clarke	713-683-9292	S	125*	1.0
JH Fletcher and Co.	PO Box 2187	Huntington	WV	25722	Sammons Duncan	304-525-7811	R	120*	0.2
Boots & Coots Intl. Well Ctrl	7908 N S Houston	Houston	TX	77064		281-931-8884	P	105	0.4
Psp Industries Inc.	9885 Doerr Ln.	Schertz	TX	78154	Andrew Easton	210-651-9595	R	105*	<0.1
Martin Engineering	1 Martin Pl.	Neponset	IL	61345		309-594-2384	R	94*	0.5
Raleigh Mine and Ind. Supply	PO Box 72	Mount Hope	WV	25880	Stirl Smith	304-877-5503	R	93*	<0.1
Production Management Ind.	9761 Hwy. 90 E	Morgan City	LA	70380		985-631-3837	S	80*	0.8
Peerless Manufacturing Co.	PO Box 540667	Dallas	TX	75354	Peter Burlage	214-357-6181	P	75	0.2
T.D. Williamson Inc.	PO Box 2217	Tulsa	OK	74101	D. Bruce Binkley	918-447-5001	R	69*	0.4
TMF Center Inc.	300 W Washington	Williamsport	IN	47993	Lloyd Gowen	765-762-1000	R	62*	0.2
Reynolds International Inc.	PO Box 550	McAllen	TX	78505	Paula Moore	956-687-7500	R	59*	0.2
Ox Bodies Inc.	PO Box 886	Fayette	AL	35555	Lehman Pendley	205-932-5720	R	55*	0.2
Custom Chemicals Corp.	30 Paul Kohner Pl.	Elmwood Park	NJ	07407	Robert Veilee	201-791-5100	R	54*	<0.1
Worldwd Oilfield Machine, BOP	11809 Canemont St.	Houston	TX	77035	Sudhir Puranik	713-729-9200	R	53*	0.1
Caterpillar Work Tools Inc.	PO Box 6	Wamego	KS	66547		785-456-2224	S	52*	0.3
Caprock Pipe and Supply L.P.	PO Box 1535	Lovington	NM	88260		575-396-5881	R	51*	<0.1
Bolt Technology Corp.	4 Duke Pl.	Norwalk	CT	06854		203-853-0700	P	51	0.1
Howe-Baker Engineers Ltd.	3102 E 5th St.	Tyler	TX	75701	Luke Scorsony	903-597-0311	S	48*	0.3
Harbison-Fisher L.P.	PO Box 2477	Fort Worth	TX	76113	Charles Fischer	817-297-2211	R	45*	0.3
Dickirson Group Ltd.	PO Box 750	Ripley	WV	25271	David Dickirson	304-372-9111	R	44*	<0.1
Clinch River Corp.	521 Claypool Hill	Cedar Bluff	VA	24609	William Wampler	276-963-5271	R	44*	0.3
McLanahan Corp.	PO Box 229	Hollidaysburg	PA	16648	Michael Mc Lanahan	814-695-9807	R	43*	0.2
Derrick Corp.	590 Duke Rd.	Buffalo	NY	14225	James Derrick	716-683-9010	R	43*	0.2
Schramm Inc.	800 E Virginia Ave.	West Chester	PA	19380	Edward Breiner	610-696-2500	R	40*	0.2
Weatherford Specialty Machine	PO Box 1530	Scott	LA	70583		337-232-8198	R	34*	0.2
Kimray Inc.	PO Box 18949	Oklahoma City	OK	73154	Garman Kimmell	405-525-6601	R	34*	0.2
Weatherford Artif. Lift Sys.	905 S Grandview	Odessa	TX	79761		432-580-0178	R	33*	<0.1
Townley Engineering and Mfg.	PO Box 221	Candler	FL	32111	J Townley	352-687-3001	R	31*	0.2
Baker Truck Equipment Co.	PO Box 482	Hurricane	WV	25526	David Beltzeo	304-722-3814	R	31*	<0.1
Detroit Stoker Co.	PO Box 732	Monroe	MI	48161	Mark Eleniewski	734-241-9500	S	31*	0.3
Wood Group ESP	17420 Katy Fwy.	Houston	TX	77094	Joseph F. Brady	281-828-3500	S	31*	0.2

Source: Ward's Business Directory of U.S. Private and Public Companies, Volumes 1 and 2, 2008. The company type code used is as follows: P - Public, R - Private, S - Subsidiary, D - Division, J - Joint Venture, A - Affiliate, G - Group. Sales are in millions of dollars, employees are in thousands. An asterisk (*) indicates an estimated sales volume. The symbol < stands for 'less than'. Company names and addresses are truncated, in some cases, to fit into the available space.

MATERIALS CONSUMED FOR MINING MACHINERY AND EQUIPMENT MANUFACTURING

Material	Quantity	Delivered Cost ($ million)
Fluid power pumps, motors, and hydrostatic transmissions	(X)	4.8
Fluid power cylinders and rotary actuators (hydraulic and pneumatic)	(X)	7.7
Fluid power hose, tube fittings, and assemblies (hydraulic and pneumatic)	(X)	4.9
Fluid power valves (hydraulic and pneumatic)	(X)	4.8
Metal bolts, nuts, screws, and other screw machine products	(X)	8.3
Fabricated structural metal products (excluding forgings)	(X)	26.5
All other fabricated metal products (excluding forgings)	(X)	16.1
Metal stampings	(X)	10.2
Forgings	(X)	32.0
Iron and steel castings (rough and semifinished)	(X)	24.6
Nonferrous (aluminum, copper, etc.) castings (rough and semifinished)	(X)	2.0
Steel bars, bar shapes, and plates (exc. castings, forgings, fabr. metal products)	(X)	40.3
Steel sheet and strip (including tinplate)	(X)	(D)
Steel structural shapes and sheet piling (exc. castings, forgings, fabr. metal products)	(X)	(D)
All other steel shapes and forms (exc. castings, forgings, fabr. metal products)	(X)	11.0
Nonferrous shapes and forms	(X)	6.0
Diesel engines and parts specially designed for diesel engines	(X)	7.9
Gasoline engines and parts specially designed for gasoline engines	(X)	(D)
Electric motors and generators	(X)	27.7
Ball bearings (mounted or unmounted)	(X)	4.6
Roller bearings (mounted or unmounted)	(X)	7.7
Mechanical speed changers, gears, and industrial high-speed drives	(X)	28.9
Pneumatic tires and inner tubes	(X)	4.1
Wheels, motor vehicle	(X)	0.4
Purchased chassis for vehicles (excluding passenger cars)	(X)	5.9
Transmissions and parts	(X)	9.0
Engine electrical equipment (incl. spark plugs, magnetos, generators, starters, etc.)	(X)	1.1
Shocks, struts, and other suspension equipment and parts	(X)	1.5
Rubber and plastics hose and belting	(X)	5.0
Fabricated plastics products (exc. gaskets, hoses, and belting)	(X)	4.4
Paints, varnishes, stains, lacquers, shellacs, japans, enamels, etc.	(X)	3.1
Electrical transmission, distribution, and control equipment	(X)	32.3
All other materials, components, parts, containers, and supplies	(X)	195.3
Materials, ingredients, containers, and supplies, nsk	(X)	212.4

Source: 2002 *Economic Census*. Explanation of symbols used: (D): Withheld to avoid disclosure of competitive data; na: Not available; (S): Withheld because statistical norms were not met; (X): Not applicable; (Z): Less than half the unit shown; nec: Not elsewhere classified; nsk: Not specified by kind; - : zero; p : 10-19 percent estimated; q : 20-29 percent estimated.

MATERIALS CONSUMED FOR OIL AND GAS FIELD MACHINERY AND EQUIPMENT MANUFACTURING

Material	Quantity	Delivered Cost ($ million)
Fluid power valves (hydraulic and pneumatic)	(X)	50.0
All other valves	(X)	48.0
Fluid power pumps, motors, and hydrostatic transmissions	(X)	32.1
All other pumps	(X)	2.5
Fluid power cylinders and rotary actuators (hydraulic and pneumatic)	(X)	10.7
Fluid power filters (hydraulic and pneumatic)	(X)	5.5
Fluid power hose, tube fittings, and assemblies (hydraulic and pneumatic)	(X)	9.0
Fabricated metal products (exc. forgings and fluid power products)	(X)	195.3
Forgings	(X)	49.4
Iron and steel castings (rough and semifinished)	(X)	127.2
Nonferrous (aluminum, copper, etc.) castings (rough and semifinished)	(X)	3.5
Steel bars, bar shapes, and plates (exc. castings, forgings, fabr. metal products)	(X)	105.7
Steel structural shapes (exc. castings, forgings, fabr. metal products)	(X)	41.9
All other steel shapes and forms (exc. castings, forgings, fabr. metal products)	(X)	62.5
Nonferrous shapes and forms	(X)	2.6
Metal powders	(X)	18.1
Diesel and semidiesel engines	(X)	14.6
Integral horsepower electric motors and generators (1 hp or more)	(X)	4.2
Ball and roller bearings (mounted or unmounted)	(X)	6.8
Fabricated rubber products (exc. tires, tubes, hoses, belting, and gaskets)	(X)	18.1
Fabricated plastics products (excluding gaskets)	(X)	(D)
Industrial diamonds	(X)	(D)
Cutting tools for machine tools	(X)	10.4
All other materials, components, parts, containers, and supplies	(X)	919.4
Materials, ingredients, containers, and supplies, nsk	(X)	638.2

Source: 2002 *Economic Census*. Explanation of symbols used: (D): Withheld to avoid disclosure of competitive data; na: Not available; (S): Withheld because statistical norms were not met; (X): Not applicable; (Z): Less than half the unit shown; nec: Not elsewhere classified; nsk: Not specified by kind; - : zero; p : 10-19 percent estimated; q : 20-29 percent estimated.

PRODUCT SHARE DETAILS FOR MINING MACHINERY AND EQUIPMENT MANUFACTURING

Product or Product Class Shipments	Mil. $	Product or Product Class Shipments	Mil. $
MINING MACHINERY	1,955.0	carbide or cermets, and base metal parts thereof	(D)
Underground mining machinery (except parts sold separately)	**476.0**	Parts and attachments for mining machinery and equipment (except drill bits) for underground mining vehicles	77.1
Mineral processing and beneficiation machinery (except parts sold separately)	**(D)**	Parts and attachments for mining machinery and equipment (except drill bits) for minerals crushing, grinding, sorting, separating, or washing machines (except portable)	86.1
Crushing, pulverizing, and screening machinery (excluding portable combination plants), except parts sold separately	**258.4**		
Drills and other mining machinery (except parts sold separately)	**(D)**	Parts and attachments for mining machinery and equipment (except drill bits) for lifting, handling, loading, or unloading machinery for underground mines	2.8
Parts and attachments for mining machinery and equipment (sold separately)	**619.8**	Parts and attachments for mining machinery and equipment (except drill bits) for boring or sinking machinery other than coal or rock cutters and tunneling machinery	9.5
Mining and rock drill bits	290.1		
Percussion rock mining drill bits, with working part of sintered metal carbide or cermets, and base metal parts thereof	(D)	Parts and attachments for other mining machinery and equipment (except drill bits)	102.7
Rock mining drill bits other than percussion, with working part of sintered metal carbide or cermets, and base metal parts thereof	171.2	Parts and attachments for mining machinery and equipment (sold separately), nsk	20.9
Other mining drill bits with working part of sintered metal carbide or cermets, and base metal thereof	(D)	**Mining machinery and equipment, nsk, total**	**167.0**
Drill bits not having a working part of sintered metal			

Source: 2002 *Economic Census*. The values are product shipments in millions of dollars for 2002. Total product shipments may be lower or higher than industry shipments. See Introduction for a full discussion. Values of indented subcategories are summed in the main heading(s). The symbol (D) appears when data are withheld to prevent disclosure of competitive information. The abbreviation nsk stands for 'not specified by kind' and nec for 'not elsewhere classified'. A dash (-) means zero.

PRODUCT SHARE DETAILS FOR OIL AND GAS FIELD MACHINERY AND EQUIPMENT MANUFACTURING

Product or Product Class Shipments	Mil. $	Product or Product Class Shipments	Mil. $
OIL AND GAS FIELD MACHINERY	4,874.5	Oil and gas field production machinery and equipment, except pumps and parts	1,621.5
Rotary oil and gas field drilling machinery and equipment	**1,389.0**	Oil and gas field production well Christmas tree assemblies (surface and subsurface, excluding subsea)	110.9
Rotary oil and gas field drilling machinery and equipment, except parts	1,135.6		
Rotary drilling surface equipment, for blocks, crown, traveling, draw works and accessories, and rotary tables	(D)	Oil and gas field production well casings and tubing heads and supports (surface, subsurface, and subsea)	169.4
Rotary oil and gas field surface drilling well control equipment (blow-out preventers, etc.)	164.4	Oil and gas field production well chokes, manifolds, and other accessories (surface, subsurface, and subsea, excluding subsea manifolds and templates)	134.2
Other rotary oil and gas field surface drilling machinery and equipment (including kelly joints)	104.2	Oil and gas field production well rodless oil lifting machinery and equipment (except pumps)	(D)
Rotary oil and gas field subsurface drilling bits, with working part of sintered metal carbide or cermets	229.6	Oil and gas field production well subsea Christmas tree assemblies, manifolds, and templates	261.7
Rotary oil and gas field subsurface drilling bits, with working part of other material, including diamond	106.4	Oil and gas field surface rod lifting pumping units and accessories, including back crank equipment	(D)
Rotary oil and gas field subsurface drilling equipment for reamers, stabilizers, and coring equipment	(D)	Oil and gas field packers	120.8
Rotary oil and gas field subsurface drilling fishing and cutting tools	139.4	Oil and gas field screens, tubing, catchers, etc.	214.3
Rotary oil and gas field subsea drilling risers	45.2	Oil and gas field separating, metering, and treating equipment for use at the wellhead	157.5
Other rotary oil and gas field subsurface drilling equipment, nec	207.6	Other oil and gas field production machinery and tools, except pumps	445.4
Parts for rotary oil and gas field drilling equipment, sold separately (except for portable drilling rigs)	104.0	Parts for oil and gas field production machinery and tools, sold separately, except parts for portable drilling rigs and other drilling equipment	62.3
Rotary oil and gas field drilling machinery and equipment, nsk	149.4	Oil and gas field production machinery and equipment (except pumps), nsk	156.5
Other oil and gas field drilling machinery and equipment	**792.4**	**Portable drilling rigs and parts (above ground)**	**332.2**
Other oil and gas field drilling machinery and equipment, except parts	395.0	Portable drilling rigs used on the surface (above ground)	215.9
Other oil and gas field drilling cementing equipment	289.1	Parts for portable drilling rigs used on the surface (above ground)	116.3
Other oil and gas field drilling equipment, except rotary drilling equipment and portable drilling rigs	105.9	Portable drilling rigs and parts, nsk	0.1
Parts for other oil and gas field drilling equipment, sold separately	356.9	**Oil and gas field derricks and well surveying machinery**	**103.9**
Other oil and gas field drilling machinery and equipment, nsk	40.4	Oil and gas field derricks, substructures and accessories (regular and portable), except well logging equipment	49.9
Oil and gas field production machinery and equipment, except pumps	**1,840.3**	Oil and gas field well logging equipment	54.0
		Oil and gas field machinery and equipment, nsk, total	**416.8**

Source: 2002 *Economic Census*. The values are product shipments in millions of dollars for 2002. Total product shipments may be lower or higher than industry shipments. See Introduction for a full discussion. Values of indented subcategories are summed in the main heading(s). The symbol (D) appears when data are withheld to prevent disclosure of competitive information. The abbreviation nsk stands for 'not specified by kind' and nec for 'not elsewhere classified'. A dash (-) means zero.

INPUTS AND OUTPUTS FOR MINING AND OIL AND GAS FIELD MACHINERY MANUFACTURING

Economic Sector or Industry Providing Inputs	%	Sector	Economic Sector or Industry Buying Outputs	%	Sector
Compensation of employees	31.4		Exports of goods & services	61.1	Cap Inv
Iron & steel mills & ferroalloys	6.9	Manufg.	Private fixed investment	24.4	
Management of companies & enterprises	5.7	Services	Oil & gas operations services	3.4	Mining
Wholesale trade	5.6	Trade	Oil & gas extraction	3.1	Mining
Engine equipment, nec	4.4	Manufg.	Oil & gas well drilling	2.6	Mining
Ferrous metal foundries	3.4	Manufg.	Mining & oil & gas field machinery	1.1	Manufg.
Valve & fittings other than plumbing	3.1	Manufg.	Maintenance/repair of nonresidential structures	0.8	Construct.
Machine shops	2.1	Manufg.	Coal	0.8	Mining
Forging, stamping, & sintering, nec	1.9	Manufg.	Waste management & remediation services	0.7	Services
Gaskets, packing, & sealing devices	1.7	Manufg.	Farm machinery & equipment	0.5	Manufg.
Mining & oil & gas field machinery	1.3	Manufg.	General Federal government services, defense	0.4	Fed Govt
Semiconductors & related devices	1.2	Manufg.	Architectural, engineering, & related services	0.3	Services
Printed circuit assemblies (electronic assembles)	1.2	Manufg.	Miscellaneous mining services	0.3	Mining
Coating, engraving, heat treating & allied activities	1.1	Manufg.	Nonmetallic minerals, nec	0.2	Mining
Truck transportation	1.0	Util.	Stone mining & quarrying	0.2	Mining
Fluid power process machinery	1.0	Manufg.			
Food services & drinking places	0.8	Services			
Power generation & supply	0.8	Util.			
Nonmetallic mineral products, nec	0.8	Manufg.			
Speed changers, industrial high-speed drives, & gears	0.8	Manufg.			
Turned products & screws, nuts, & bolts	0.8	Manufg.			
Securities, commodity contracts, investments	0.8	Fin/R.E.			
Hotels & motels, including casino hotels	0.7	Services			
Motor vehicle parts	0.7	Manufg.			
Ball & roller bearings	0.7	Manufg.			
Metal cans, boxes, & other containers (light gauge)	0.7	Manufg.			
Taxes on production & imports, less subsidies	0.7				
Motors & generators	0.6	Manufg.			
Real estate	0.6	Fin/R.E.			
Plastics products, nec	0.6	Manufg.			
Plate work & fabricated structural products	0.5	Manufg.			
Crowns & closures & metal stamping	0.5	Manufg.			
Lessors of nonfinancial assets	0.5	Fin/R.E.			
Legal services	0.5	Services			
Telecommunications	0.5	Services			
Advertising & related services	0.5	Services			
Material handling equipment	0.5	Manufg.			
Specialized design services	0.4	Services			
Air transportation	0.4	Util.			
Architectural, engineering, & related services	0.4	Services			
Fabricated metals, nec	0.4	Manufg.			
Noncomparable imports	0.4	Foreign			
Employment services	0.4	Services			
Automotive equipment rental & leasing	0.4	Fin/R.E.			
Business support services	0.3	Services			
Custom roll forming	0.3	Manufg.			
Relay & industrial controls	0.3	Manufg.			
Maintenance/repair of nonresidential structures	0.3	Construct.			
Abrasive products	0.3	Manufg.			
Management, scientific, & technical consulting	0.3	Services			
Services to buildings & dwellings	0.3	Services			
Nonferrous metal (ex. copper & aluminum) processing	0.3	Manufg.			
Scientific research & development services	0.3	Services			
Cutting tools & machine tool accessories	0.3	Manufg.			
Warehousing & storage	0.3	Util.			
Data processing, hosting, & related services	0.2	Services			
Handtools	0.2	Manufg.			
Paperboard containers	0.2	Manufg.			
Accounting, tax preparation, bookkeeping, & payroll	0.2	Services			
Surgical appliances & supplies	0.2	Manufg.			
Transit & ground passenger transportation	0.2	Util.			
Support services, nec	0.2	Services			
Automotive repair & maintenance, ex. car washes	0.2	Services			
Natural gas distribution	0.2	Util.			
Commercial & industrial machinery rental & leasing	0.2	Fin/R.E.			
Other computer related services, including facilities	0.2	Services			
Plastics packaging materials, film & sheet	0.2	Manufg.			
General purpose machinery, nec	0.2	Manufg.			
Paperboard mills	0.2	Manufg.			
Commercial & industrial equipment repair/maintenance	0.2	Services			
Investigation & security services	0.2	Services			
Bare printed circuit boards	0.2	Manufg.			
Construction machinery	0.2	Manufg.			
Nonferrous metal foundries	0.1	Manufg.			
Monetary authorities/depository credit intermediation	0.1	Fin/R.E.			
Rail transportation	0.1	Util.			
Springs & wire products	0.1	Manufg.			
Chemical products & preparations, nec	0.1	Manufg.			
Paints & coatings	0.1	Manufg.			
Copper, nickel, lead, and zinc	0.1	Mining			

Continued on next page.

INPUTS AND OUTPUTS FOR MINING AND OIL AND GAS FIELD MACHINERY MANUFACTURING - Continued

Economic Sector or Industry Providing Inputs	%	Sector	Economic Sector or Industry Buying Outputs	%	Sector
Heavy duty trucks	0.1	Manufg.			
Rubber & plastics hose & belting	0.1	Manufg.			
Postal service	0.1	Util.			

Source: Benchmark Input-Output Accounts for the U.S. Economy, 2002, U.S. Department of Commerce, Washington, D.C., January 2008. The abbreviation nec stands for 'not elsewhere classified'.

OCCUPATIONS EMPLOYED BY AGRICULTURE, CONSTRUCTION, & MINING MACHINERY

Occupation	% of Total 2006	Change to 2016	Occupation	% of Total 2006	Change to 2016
Welders, cutters, solderers, & brazers	11.7	-0.7	Sales reps, wholesale & manufacturing, exc tech	1.6	-6.6
Team assemblers	10.3	-6.6	Helpers--Production workers	1.6	-6.6
First-line supervisors/managers of production workers	3.5	-6.6	Maintenance & repair workers, general	1.5	-6.6
Computer-controlled machine tool operators	3.4	2.7	Shipping, receiving, & traffic clerks	1.4	-10.2
Engine & other machine assemblers	3.2	-6.6	Welding, soldering, & brazing machine operators	1.4	5.0
Structural metal fabricators & fitters	2.4	-6.6	Production, planning, & expediting clerks	1.3	-6.6
Mechanical engineers	2.2	-6.6	General & operations managers	1.3	-16.0
Laborers & freight, stock, & material movers, hand	2.1	-16.0	Bookkeeping, accounting, & auditing clerks	1.3	-6.6
Cutting, punching, & press machine operators	2.1	-16.0	Purchasing agents, exc wholesale, retail, & farm	1.2	-6.6
Inspectors, testers, sorters, samplers, & weighers	2.0	-12.0	Industrial engineers	1.1	13.4
Industrial truck & tractor operators	1.8	-16.0	Mechanical drafters	1.1	-5.6

Source: Industry-Occupation Matrix, Bureau of Labor Statistics, December 4, 2007. These data are reported based on 4-digit NAICS categories but have been matched to corresponding 6-digit NAICS industry codes. The change reported for each occupation to the year 2016 is a percent of growth or decline as estimated by the Bureau of Labor Statistics. The abbreviation nec stands for 'not elsewhere classified'.

LOCATION BY STATE AND REGIONAL CONCENTRATION

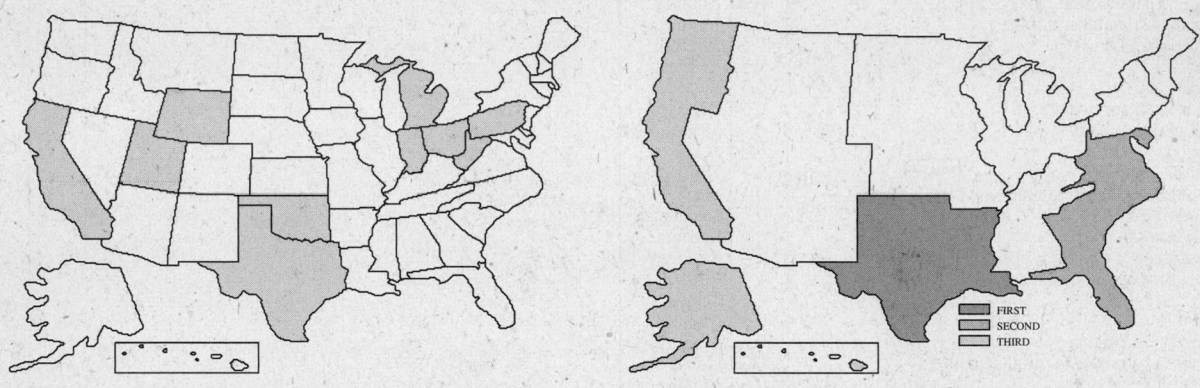

INDUSTRY DATA BY STATE

State	Establishments	Shipments Total ($ mil)	Shipments % of U.S.	Shipments Per Establ.	Employment Total Number	Employment % of U.S.	Employment Per Establ.	Wages ($/hour)	Cost as % of Shipments	Investment per Employee ($)
Texas	298	3,844.6	52.0	12,901.3	19,039	51.0	64	19.73	49.5	6,671
Oklahoma	67	742.1	10.0	11,076.7	3,368	9.0	50	17.63	61.8	6,041
Pennsylvania	32	392.7	5.3	12,270.4	2,086	5.6	65	18.61	59.1	4,104
West Virginia	46	208.3	2.8	4,528.3	1,401	3.8	30	16.64	53.1	3,248
Ohio	15	139.2	1.9	9,281.7	557	1.5	37	18.37	46.3	5,375
Utah	11	139.2	1.9	12,652.5	498	1.3	45	18.70	64.7	17,580
California	33	113.4	1.5	3,435.3	831	2.2	25	16.47	51.2	3,709
Michigan	9	56.9	0.8	6,324.4	304	0.8	34	15.03	52.4	2,151
Wyoming	9	37.8	0.5	4,196.4	192	0.5	21	20.22	40.5	6,120
Indiana	4	17.9	0.2	4,477.3	124	0.3	31	15.98	35.8	4,968

Source: 2002 Economic Census. The states are in descending order of shipments or establishments (if shipment data are missing for the majority). The symbol (D) appears when data are withheld to prevent disclosure of competitive information. States marked with (D) are sorted by number of establishments. A dash (-) indicates that the data element cannot be calculated. Data may not show all states active in the NAICS category. All data available at the time of publication are shown.

NAICS 333210 - SAWMILL AND WOODWORKING MACHINERY MANUFACTURING

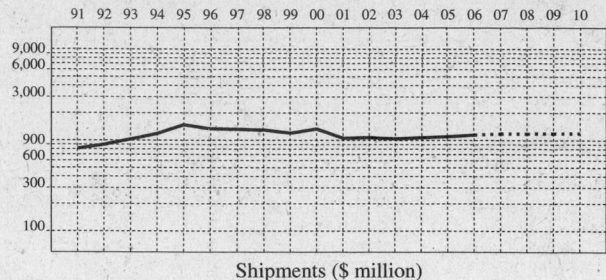

Shipments ($ million)

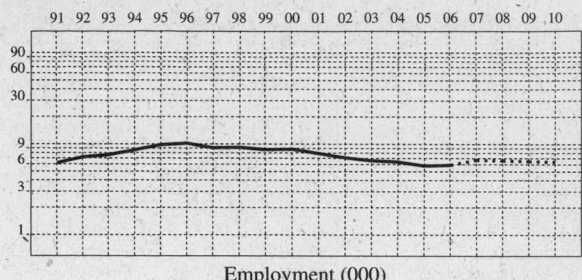

Employment (000)

GENERAL STATISTICS

Year	Com-panies	Establishments		Employment			Compensation		Production ($ million)			
		Total	with 20 or more employees	Total (000)	Production Workers (000)	Hours (Mil)	Payroll ($ mil)	Wages ($/hr)	Cost of Materials	Value Added by Manufacture	Value of Shipments	Capital Invest.
1991		291	97	6.2	3.9	8.1	184.7	11.15	368.9	420.3	811.4	7.2
1992	277	289	90	7.2	4.7	9.5	206.1	11.56	439.5	458.8	894.6	19.5
1993		291	93	7.6	5.1	10.7	221.0	11.62	507.0	548.8	1,028.2	20.0
1994		296	104	8.6	5.4	12.0	264.2	12.43	522.4	675.3	1,184.3	30.7
1995		307	109	9.8	6.3	13.9	307.6	12.45	711.2	788.2	1,482.6	28.2
1996		333	107	10.2	6.4	13.1	312.4	13.73	631.5	716.6	1,342.3	32.5
1997	314	327	98	9.1	5.8	11.7	302.2	13.59	628.6	690.6	1,321.8	18.1
1998		316	96	9.2	5.6	11.5	318.0	13.00	590.0	727.2	1,299.4	35.0
1999		327	92	8.7	5.5	10.8	312.0	14.64	586.6	622.1	1,202.2	41.0
2000		318	93	8.8	5.7	11.3	325.5	14.93	637.9	705.1	1,335.5	29.2
2001		302	91	7.9	5.0	9.6	284.4	15.15	480.3	566.8	1,054.7	20.0
2002	293	304	92	7.1	4.4	10.2	272.8	13.29	489.5	567.9	1,074.3	26.2
2003		298	88	6.6	3.9	7.9	263.9	16.10	456.2	596.2	1,040.2	20.8
2004		288	86	6.4	4.0	8.3	277.4	16.59	452.5	610.3	1,073.1	27.5
2005		287	86	5.8	3.5	7.0	263.8	18.55	506.4	602.0	1,101.8	15.8
2006		305P	87P	5.9	3.5	7.6	279.3	18.25	528.2	644.7	1,149.3	36.1
2007		305P	86P	6.7P	4.1P	8.3P	305.5P	17.99P	543.4P	663.2P	1,182.4P	29.8P
2008		305P	85P	6.6P	4.0P	8.1P	309.2P	18.43P	545.2P	665.4P	1,186.2P	30.3P
2009		305P	84P	6.5P	3.9P	7.9P	312.8P	18.88P	546.9P	667.5P	1,190.0P	30.8P
2010		304P	84P	6.4P	3.8P	7.7P	316.4P	19.33P	548.7P	669.7P	1,193.9P	31.3P

Sources: 1992, 1997, 2002 *Economic Census*; other years, up to 2006, are from the *Annual Survey of Manufactures*. Establishment counts for non-Census years are from *County Business Patterns*; 1997 and 2002 values are from the 1997 and 2002 censuses respectively, reported in the Federal Government's NAICS format. Other years were originally reported in equivalent SIC format. 'P's show projections by the editors.

INDICES OF CHANGE

Year	Com-panies	Establishments		Employment			Compensation		Production ($ million)			
		Total	with 20 or more employees	Total (000)	Production Workers (000)	Hours (Mil)	Payroll ($ mil)	Wages ($/hr)	Cost of Materials	Value Added by Manufacture	Value of Shipments	Capital Invest.
1992	95	95	98	101	107	93	76	87	90	81	83	74
1997	107	108	107	128	132	115	111	102	128	122	123	69
2001		99	99	111	114	94	104	114	98	100	98	76
2002	100	100	100	100	100	100	100	100	100	100	100	100
2003		98	96	93	89	77	97	121	93	105	97	79
2004		95	93	90	91	81	102	125	92	107	100	105
2005		94	93	82	80	69	97	140	103	106	103	60
2006		100P	95P	83	80	75	102	137	108	114	107	138
2007		100P	94P	94P	93P	81P	112P	135P	111P	117P	110P	114P
2008		100P	93P	93P	91P	79P	113P	139P	111P	117P	110P	116P
2009		100P	92P	92P	89P	77P	115P	142P	112P	118P	111P	118P
2010		100P	91P	90P	86P	75P	116P	145P	112P	118P	111P	119P

Sources: Same as General Statistics. Values reflect change from the base year, 2002. Values above 100 mean greater than 2002, values below 100 mean less than 2002, and the values of 100 in other years means the same as 2002. 'P's show projections by the editors.

SELECTED RATIOS

For 2002	Avg. of All Manufact.	Analyzed Industry	Index	For 2002	Avg. of All Manufact.	Analyzed Industry	Index
Employees per Establishment	42	23	56	Value Added per Production Worker	182,367	129,068	71
Payroll per Establishment	1,639,184	897,368	55	Cost per Establishment	5,769,015	1,610,197	28
Payroll per Employee	39,053	38,423	98	Cost per Employee	137,446	68,944	50
Production Workers per Establishment	30	14	49	Cost per Production Worker	195,506	111,250	57
Wages per Establishment	694,845	445,914	64	Shipments per Establishment	11,158,348	3,533,882	32
Wages per Production Worker	23,548	30,809	131	Shipments per Employee	265,847	151,310	57
Hours per Production Worker	1,980	2,318	117	Shipments per Production Worker	378,144	244,159	65
Wages per Hour	11.89	13.29	112	Investment per Establishment	361,338	86,184	24
Value Added per Establishment	5,381,325	1,868,092	35	Investment per Employee	8,609	3,690	43
Value Added per Employee	128,210	79,986	62	Investment per Production Worker	12,245	5,955	49

Sources: Same as General Statistics. The 'Average of All Manufacturing' column represents the average of all manufacturing industries reported for the most recent complete year available. The Index shows the relationship between the Average and the Analyzed Industry. For example, 100 means that they are equal; 500 that the Analyzed Industry is five times the average; 50 means that the Analyzed Industry is half the national average. The abbreviation 'na' is used to show that data are 'not available'. Ratios shown for 2002, the last complete census year.

LEADING COMPANIES   Number shown: 75   Total sales ($ mil): 6,035   Total employment (000): 23.9

Company Name	Address				CEO Name	Phone	Co. Type	Sales ($ mil)	Empl. (000)
Pentair Inc.	5500 Wayzata Blvd.	Golden Valley	MN	55416	Winslow H. Buxton	763-545-1730	P	3,399	16.0
Accu Systems Inc.	4964 S Redwood Rd.	Salt Lake City	UT	84123	Mel Hatch	480-948-7239	R	1,102*	<0.1
SCM Group USA Inc.	2475-B Satellite	Duluth	GA	30096	John Gangone	770-813-8820	R	420*	3.0
Coe Manufacturing Company Inc.	PO Box 520	Painesville	OH	44077	Shawn Casey	440-352-9381	R	236*	0.1
Unique Machine and Tool Co.	4232 E Magnolia St.	Phoenix	AZ	85034	Kenny Moffatt	602-470-1911	R	107*	<0.1
Morbark Inc.	PO Box 1000	Winn	MI	48896	Lon Morey	989-866-2381	R	55*	0.6
Diehl Machines Inc.	PO BOX 465	Wabash	IN	46992	Robert Rozman	260-563-2102	R	41*	0.1
Newman Machine Company Inc.	PO Box 5467	Greensboro	NC	27435	Frank York	336-273-8261	R	41*	0.1
Western Pneumatics Inc.	PO Box 21340	Eugene	OR	97402	Richard Nicol	541-461-2600	R	39*	0.2
Precision Husky Corp.	PO Box 507	Leeds	AL	35094		205-640-5181	R	29*	0.1
Wood-Mizer Products Inc.	8180 W 10th St.	Indianapolis	IN	46214	Jeffrey Laskowski	317-271-1542	R	26*	0.2
Nicholson Manufacturing Co.	200 S Orcas St.	Seattle	WA	98108	Scott Howell	206-682-2752	R	23*	0.2
Globe Machine Manufacturing	PO Box 2274	Tacoma	WA	98401	Calvin Bamford	253-383-2584	R	22*	0.1
Oregon Select Inc.	PO Box 10526	Eugene	OR	97440	Duncan Lean	541-342-5568	R	22*	<0.1
United Abrasives Inc.	PO Box 75	Willimantic	CT	06226	Aris Marziali	860-456-7131	R	21*	0.3
Grecon Dimter Inc.	PO Box 1784	Hickory	NC	28603	Jeff Davidon	704-799-0100	R	21*	<0.1
CR Onsrud Inc.	PO Box 419	Troutman	NC	28166	Charles Onsrud	704-528-4528	R	20*	<0.1
Fulghum Industries Inc.	PO Box 909	Wadley	GA	30477		478-252-5223	R	19*	<0.1
Kval Inc.	825 Petaluma Blvd.	Petaluma	CA	94952	Jerry Kvalheim	707-762-4363	R	18*	0.1
Ritter Manufacturing Company	1300B W 4th St.	Antioch	CA	94509	Ase Stornetta	925-757-7296	R	17*	<0.1
Reckart Equipment Co.	PO Box 216	Beverly	WV	26253	Darrell Reckart	304-338-4300	R	15*	<0.1
Komo Machine Inc.	11 Industrial Blvd.	Sauk Rapids	MN	56379	Charles Zajaczkowski	320-252-0580	R	14*	0.1
Tarrant Manufacturing Company	225 Excelsior Ave.	Saratoga Spgs	NY	12866	John Tarrant	518-584-4400	R	14*	<0.1
S.C. Industrial Resource Group	PO Box 473066	Garland	TX	75047	David Spencer	972-272-4521	R	13*	<0.1
Fletcher Machine Company Inc.	4305 E US Hwy. 64	South Lexington	NC	27292	Ray Fletcher	336-249-6101	R	12*	<0.1
Mereen-Johnson Machine Co.	4401 Lyndale N	Minneapolis	MN	55412	Charles Johnson	612-529-7791	R	12*	0.1
Great Lakes Custom Tool Mfg.	PO Box 152	Peshtigo	WI	54157	Russell Martin	715-582-3884	R	11*	<0.1
Voorwood Co.	PO Box 1127	Anderson	CA	96007	Larry Ackernecht	530-365-3311	R	11*	<0.1
Sherline Products Inc.	3235 Executive Rdg.	Vista	CA	92081	Joseph Martin	760-727-5857	R	11*	<0.1
Timesavers Inc.	11123 89th Ave. N	Osseo	MN	55369	Gregory Larson	763-488-6600	R	11*	<0.1
Ellington Industrial Supply	PO Box 128	Ellington	MO	63638	Ed Baker	573-663-7711	R	9*	<0.1
Joseph Machine Company Inc.	PO Box 121	Dillsburg	PA	17019	Joseph Pigliacampo	717-432-3442	R	9*	<0.1
Yanke Machine Shop Inc.	PO Box 5405	Boise	ID	83705	Ronald Yanke	208-342-8901	R	9*	0.1
Quality Fabric./Machine Wrks	PO Box 1949	Lake City	FL	32056	Dale Dryden	386-755-0220	R	9*	<0.1
Viking Engineering & Developm.	5750 Main St. NE	Fridley	MN	55432	Dean Bodem	763-571-2400	R	9*	<0.1
Pendu Manufacturing Inc.	718 N Shirk Rd.	New Holland	PA	17557	Marlin Hurst	717-354-4348	R	8*	<0.1
West Coast Industrial Systems	1995 W Airway Rd.	Lebanon	OR	97355	Blane Belveal	541-451-6677	R	8*	<0.1
Salem Equipment Inc.	PO Box 947	Salem	OR	97308	Lewis Judson	503-581-8411	R	8*	<0.1
Pneumech Systems Manufacturing	201 Pneu Mech Dr.	Statesville	NC	28625	David Brady	704-873-2475	R	6*	<0.1
Tannewitz Inc.	794 Chicago Dr.	Jenison	MI	49428	Morry Pysarchik	616-457-5999	R	6*	<0.1
L and L Machinery Inc.	5901 W Hwy. 22	Crestwood	KY	40014	Peter Nemeth	502-241-1502	R	6*	<0.1
Pistorius Machine Company Inc.	1785 Express Dr. N	Hauppauge	NY	11788	Robert Pistorius	631-582-6000	R	6*	<0.1
Weaver Manufacturing and Sales	1108 S 37th St.	Kansas City	KS	66106	Rick Weaver	913-831-1800	R	6*	<0.1
Sawing Systems Inc.	PO Box 3754	Knoxville	TN	37927	Joel Forker	865-525-0600	R	6*	<0.1
DuBois Machine Company Inc.	PO Box 470	Jasper	IN	47547	G Lang	812-482-3644	R	5*	<0.1
Acme Manufacturing Co.	4240 N Atlantic	Auburn Hills	MI	48326	Glen Carlson	248-393-7300	R	5*	<0.1
HMC Corp.	284 Maple St.	Contoocook	NH	03229	Peter Taylor	603-746-4691	R	5*	<0.1
Rayco Industries Inc.	1502 Valley Rd.	Richmond	VA	23222	Ray Poston	804-321-7111	R	5*	<0.1
Stringer Industries Inc.	PO Box 450	Tylertown	MS	39667	George Stringer	601-876-3376	R	5*	<0.1
Biesemeyer Manufacturing Corp.	216 S Alma Schl Rd	Mesa	AZ	85210		480-835-9300	S	5*	<0.1
Barr-Mullin Inc.	2506 Yonkers Rd.	Raleigh	NC	27604	Sandy Mullin	919-833-3334	R	5*	<0.1
Black Brothers Co.	PO Box 410	Mendota	IL	61342	James Carroll	815-539-7451	R	5*	<0.1
Meadows Mills Inc.	PO Box 1288	N Wilkesboro	NC	28659	Robert Hege	336-838-2282	R	5*	<0.1
Progress Industries Inc.	PO Box 29	Trussville	AL	35173	Iradj Tarassoli	205-655-8875	R	5*	<0.1
Kimwood Corp.	PO Box 97	Cottage Grove	OR	97424	Kim Woodard	541-942-4401	R	5*	<0.1
James L Taylor Manufacturing	108 Parker Ave. 128	Poughkeepsie	NY	12601	Michael Burdis	845-452-3780	R	5*	<0.1
Automated Lumber Handling Inc.	PO Box 796	Lenoir	NC	28645	William Dugger	828-754-4662	R	4*	<0.1
Brewco Inc.	PO Box 150	Central City	KY	42330	Clarence Brewer	270-754-5847	R	4*	<0.1
Morris Industrial Corp.	PO Box 249	Saraland	AL	36571	Harvey Morris	251-675-4636	R	4*	<0.1
Northwood Industrial Machinery	11610 Cwlth Dr.	Louisville	KY	40299	Behrouz Alizadeh	502-267-5504	R	4*	<0.1
Stapling Machines Inc.	41 Pine St., Ste 30	Rockaway	NJ	07866	Doug Halkenhauser	973-627-4400	R	4*	<0.1
Bowlin Company Inc.	PO Box 3007	Shreveport	LA	71133	Charles Bowlin	318-635-5344	R	4*	<0.1
Evans Machinery Inc.	PO Box 1406	Glendale	AZ	85311	Robert Perez	623-934-7294	R	4*	<0.1
Kasco Manufacturing Company	170 W 600 N	Shelbyville	IN	46176	Phil Kaster	317-398-4636	R	4*	<0.1
Premier Gear and Machine Works	1700 NW Thurman	Portland	OR	97209	Russel Cole	503-227-3514	R	4*	<0.1
Schuon Manufacturing Company	PO Box 1565	Hayden	ID	83835	Robert Schuon	208-664-3836	R	4*	<0.1
Yates-American Machine Co.	PO Box 958	Beloit	WI	53512	Darrell Borghi	608-364-0333	R	4*	<0.1
Accu-Router Inc.	634 Mt View Indust.	Morrison	TN	37357	Todd Herzog	931-668-7127	R	3*	<0.1
Columbia Construction Inc.	PO Box 2689	Columbia Falls	MT	59912	Larry Luce	406-892-3856	R	3*	<0.1
Merritt Plywood Machinery	10 Simonds St.	Lockport	NY	14094	David Mellor	716-434-5558	R	3*	<0.1
Ultimizers Inc.	28380 SE Stone Rd.	Boring	OR	97009	Leroy Cothrell	503-663-7263	R	3*	<0.1
LRH Enterprises Inc.	9250 Independence	Chatsworth	CA	91311	Ralph Hubert	818-782-0226	R	3*	<0.1
Peninsula Iron Works Inc.	PO Box 83067	Portland	OR	97283	James Johnson	503-286-4461	R	3*	<0.1
Price Systems Inc.	314 Reynolds Rd.	Malvern	AR	72104	James Harper	501-844-4260	R	3*	<0.1
Phantom Engineering Inc.	435 W 1000 N	Springville	UT	84663	Daryl Anderson	801-377-5757	R	3*	<0.1

Source: Ward's Business Directory of U.S. Private and Public Companies, Volumes 1 and 2, 2008. The company type code used is as follows: P - Public, R - Private, S - Subsidiary, D - Division, J - Joint Venture, A - Affiliate, G - Group. Sales are in millions of dollars, employees are in thousands. An asterisk (*) indicates an estimated sales volume. The symbol < stands for 'less than'. Company names and addresses are truncated, in some cases, to fit into the available space.

MATERIALS CONSUMED

Material	Quantity	Delivered Cost ($ million)
Fluid power pumps, motors, and hydrostatic transmissions	(X)	11.2
All other pumps	(X)	(D)
Fluid power valves (hydraulic and pneumatic)	(X)	(D)
Fluid power hose, tube fittings, and assemblies (hydraulic and pneumatic)	(X)	1.7
Fluid power cylinders and rotary actuators (hydraulic and pneumatic)	(X)	3.5
Fluid power filters (hydraulic and pneumatic)	(X)	0.8
Other fluid power products, hydraulic and pneumatic	(X)	2.2
Fabricated metal products (excluding forgings)	(X)	18.6
Forgings	(X)	1.6
Iron and steel castings (rough and semifinished)	(X)	18.7
Aluminum and aluminum-base alloy castings (rough and semifinished)	(X)	5.4
Other nonferrous metal castings, rough or semifinished (inc. aluminum)	(X)	0.7
Steel bars, bar shapes, and plates (exc. castings, forgings, fabr. metal products)	(X)	17.5
Steel sheet and strip (including tinplate)	(X)	14.8
All other steel shapes and forms (exc. castings, forgings, fabr. metal products)	(X)	32.8
Nonferrous shapes and forms	(X)	1.2
Fractional horsepower electric motors and generators (less than 1 hp)	(X)	8.3
Integral horsepower electric motors and generators (1 hp or more)	(X)	16.2
Ball bearings (mounted or unmounted)	(X)	6.1
Roller bearings (mounted or unmounted)	(X)	3.6
Fabricated plastics products (excluding gaskets)	(X)	5.0
Electrical transmission, distribution, and control equipment	(X)	13.4
Numerical controls for woodworking machinery and equipment	(X)	12.2
Paperboard containers, boxes, and corrugated paperboard	(X)	7.6
All other materials, components, parts, containers, and supplies	(X)	75.1
Materials, ingredients, containers, and supplies, nsk	(X)	106.5

Source: 2002 *Economic Census*. Explanation of symbols used: (D): Withheld to avoid disclosure of competitive data; na: Not available; (S): Withheld because statistical norms were not met; (X): Not applicable; (Z): Less than half the unit shown; nec: Not elsewhere classified; nsk: Not specified by kind; - : zero; p : 10-19 percent estimated; q : 20-29 percent estimated.

PRODUCT SHARE DETAILS

Product or Product Class Shipments	Mil. $	Product or Product Class Shipments	Mil. $
SAWMILL AND WOODWORKING MACHINERY	863.4	Woodworking shapers and profilers	12.7
Woodworking machinery, including parts, attachments, and accessories	**711.6**	Woodworking assembling, gluing, laminating, and finishing machines	27.6
Woodworking sawmill equipment	269.8	Multifunction woodworking machines	51.2
Woodworking sawmill circular saws (head rigs)	12.0	Other woodworking machines and equipment	93.6
Woodworking sawmill band saws (head rigs)	40.9	Parts, attachments, and accessories for woodworking machinery (sold separately), excluding saw blades and cutting tools	73.3
Woodworking sawmill equipment, removing bark from logs	26.2	Woodworking machinery, including parts, attachments, and accessories, nsk	19.3
Woodworking sawmill equipment, chipping or splitting wood	29.0	**Woodworking machinery for home workshops, garages, and service shops**	**85.3**
Woodworking sawmill equipment, specialized materials handling	43.7	Woodworking saws, machines, and equipment for home workshops, garages, and service shops	82.2
Other woodworking sawmill equipment	118.0	Woodworking saws, including circular saws and band saws (except chain saws), for home workshops, garages, and service shops	54.2
Woodworking machines and equipment, including moulders	349.2	Other woodworking machinery (except power-driven handtools) for home workshops, garages, and service shops	28.0
Woodworking sawing machines, except sawmill equipment	40.7	Woodworking machinery for home workshops, garages, and service shops, nsk	3.1
Woodworking planing machinery, including single and double planers, facers, jointers, and abrasive planers	25.6	**Sawmill and woodworking machinery, nsk, total**	**66.4**
Woodworking sanding machines	26.5		
Woodworking boring machines	3.7		
Woodworking mortising and tenoning machines	2.3		
Woodworking lathes or turning machines	11.0		
Woodworking routers	54.3		

Source: 2002 *Economic Census*. The values are product shipments in millions of dollars for 2002. Total product shipments may be lower or higher than industry shipments. See Introduction for a full discussion. Values of indented subcategories are summed in the main heading(s). The symbol (D) appears when data are withheld to prevent disclosure of competitive information. The abbreviation nsk stands for 'not specified by kind' and nec for 'not elsewhere classified'. A dash (-) means zero.

INPUTS AND OUTPUTS FOR OTHER INDUSTRIAL MACHINERY MANUFACTURING

Economic Sector or Industry Providing Inputs	%	Sector	Economic Sector or Industry Buying Outputs	%	Sector
Compensation of employees	34.5		Private fixed investment	62.8	
Management of companies & enterprises	6.4	Services	Exports of goods & services	15.5	Cap Inv
Wholesale trade	5.7	Trade	Printing	3.5	Manufg.
Iron & steel mills & ferroalloys	5.1	Manufg.	Industrial machinery, nec	2.4	Manufg.
Industrial machinery, nec	3.1	Manufg.	Personal consumption expenditures	2.3	
Machine shops	2.5	Manufg.	Basic organic chemicals, nec	1.9	Manufg.
Ferrous metal foundries	1.7	Manufg.	Paper mills	1.4	Manufg.

Continued on next page.

INPUTS AND OUTPUTS FOR OTHER INDUSTRIAL MACHINERY MANUFACTURING - Continued

Economic Sector or Industry Providing Inputs	%	Sector	Economic Sector or Industry Buying Outputs	%	Sector
Valve & fittings other than plumbing	1.5	Manufg.	Wholesale trade	1.2	Trade
Printed circuit assemblies (electronic assemblies)	1.3	Manufg.	Basic inorganic chemicals, nec	1.0	Manufg.
Motors & generators	1.2	Manufg.	Paperboard mills	0.9	Manufg.
Real estate	1.1	Fin/R.E.	S/L govt. invest., education	0.8	S/L Govt
Coating, engraving, heat treating & allied activities	1.1	Manufg.	Paints & coatings	0.8	Manufg.
Relay & industrial controls	1.1	Manufg.	Nonferrous metal foundries	0.7	Manufg.
Gaskets, packing, & sealing devices	1.0	Manufg.	Printed circuit assemblies (electronic assemblies)	0.5	Manufg.
Fluid power process machinery	1.0	Manufg.	Synthetic dyes & pigments	0.4	Manufg.
Ball & roller bearings	1.0	Manufg.	Alkalies & chlorine	0.4	Manufg.
Speed changers, industrial high-speed drives, & gears	1.0	Manufg.	General S/L govt. services	0.3	S/L Govt
Securities, commodity contracts, investments	1.0	Fin/R.E.	Plastics materials & resins	0.3	Manufg.
Semiconductors & related devices	1.0	Manufg.	Food services & drinking places	0.3	Services
Fabricated metals, nec	0.9	Manufg.	Retail trade	0.3	Trade
Turned products & screws, nuts, & bolts	0.9	Manufg.	Other S/L govt. enterprises	0.3	S/L Govt
Cutting tools & machine tool accessories	0.9	Manufg.	Alumina refining & primary aluminum production	0.2	Manufg.
Advertising & related services	0.8	Services	Specialized design services	0.2	Services
Truck transportation	0.8	Util.	Chemical products & preparations, nec	0.2	Manufg.
Power generation & supply	0.8	Util.	Federal government, investment, national defense	0.2	Fed Govt
Metal cans, boxes, & other containers (light gauge)	0.7	Manufg.	Fluid milk & butter	0.2	Manufg.
Nonferrous metal foundries	0.7	Manufg.	Petrochemicals	0.2	Manufg.
Aluminum products from purchased aluminum	0.7	Manufg.	Ferrous metal foundries	0.1	Manufg.
Custom computer programming services	0.6	Services	Civic, social, & professional organizations	0.1	Services
Lessors of nonfinancial assets	0.6	Fin/R.E.	Industrial gases	0.1	Manufg.
Air & gas compressors	0.6	Manufg.			
Plate work & fabricated structural products	0.6	Manufg.			
Monetary authorities/depository credit intermediation	0.5	Fin/R.E.			
Legal services	0.5	Services			
Taxes on production & imports, less subsidies	0.5				
Telecommunications	0.4	Services			
Crowns & closures & metal stamping	0.4	Manufg.			
Professional, scientific, technical services, nec	0.4	Services			
Accounting, tax preparation, bookkeeping, & payroll	0.4	Services			
Data processing, hosting, & related services	0.4	Services			
Abrasive products	0.4	Manufg.			
Scientific research & development services	0.4	Services			
Electronic components, nec	0.3	Manufg.			
Food services & drinking places	0.3	Services			
Warehousing & storage	0.3	Util.			
Automotive equipment rental & leasing	0.3	Fin/R.E.			
Plastics packaging materials, film & sheet	0.3	Manufg.			
Alumina refining & primary aluminum production	0.3	Manufg.			
Forging, stamping, & sintering, nec	0.3	Manufg.			
Custom roll forming	0.3	Manufg.			
Postal service	0.3	Util.			
Management, scientific, & technical consulting	0.3	Services			
Noncomparable imports	0.3	Foreign			
Handtools	0.3	Manufg.			
Paperboard containers	0.3	Manufg.			
Pumps & pumping equipment	0.2	Manufg.			
Plastics products, nec	0.2	Manufg.			
Architectural, engineering, & related services	0.2	Services			
Rubber products, nec	0.2	Manufg.			
Chemical products & preparations, nec	0.2	Manufg.			
Employment services	0.2	Services			
Hotels & motels, including casino hotels	0.2	Services			
Services to buildings & dwellings	0.2	Services			
Business support services	0.2	Services			
Natural gas distribution	0.2	Util.			
Maintenance/repair of nonresidential structures	0.2	Construct.			
Special tools, dies, jigs, & fixtures	0.2	Manufg.			
General purpose machinery, nec	0.2	Manufg.			
Commercial & industrial machinery rental & leasing	0.2	Fin/R.E.			
Specialized design services	0.2	Services			
Other computer related services, including facilities	0.2	Services			
Springs & wire products	0.1	Manufg.			
Paperboard mills	0.1	Manufg.			
Bare printed circuit boards	0.1	Manufg.			
Electronic capacitors, resistors, coils, transformers	0.1	Manufg.			
Steel products from purchased steel	0.1	Manufg.			
Metal tanks (heavy gauge)	0.1	Manufg.			
Air transportation	0.1	Util.			
Nondepository credit intermediation activities	0.1	Fin/R.E.			
Power boilers & heat exchangers	0.1	Manufg.			
Mechanical power transmission equipment	0.1	Manufg.			
Paper mills	0.1	Manufg.			
Automotive repair & maintenance, ex. car washes	0.1	Services			
Motor vehicle parts	0.1	Manufg.			
Rail transportation	0.1	Util.			

Source: Benchmark Input-Output Accounts for the U.S. Economy, 2002, U.S. Department of Commerce, Washington D.C., January 2008. User should note that this Input-Output table is not for this particular narrowly defined industry but for a larger aggregate. Input and Output data for Other Industrial Machinery Manufacturing *include Input and Output data for the* Annual Survey of Manufactures' *NAICS industries 333210 and 33329N. The abbreviation nec stands for 'not elsewhere classified'.*

OCCUPATIONS EMPLOYED BY INDUSTRIAL MACHINERY MANUFACTURING

Occupation	% of Total 2006	Change to 2016	Occupation	% of Total 2006	Change to 2016
Machinists	6.6	-14.0	Electrical engineers	1.6	-18.1
Team assemblers	5.5	-18.1	Structural metal fabricators & fitters	1.5	-18.1
Welders, cutters, solderers, & brazers	4.3	-12.8	Customer service representatives	1.5	-9.9
Mechanical engineers	4.0	-9.9	Grinding, lapping, polishing machine tool operators	1.4	-20.5
First-line supervisors/managers of production workers	3.8	-18.1	Office clerks, general	1.4	-19.3
Sales reps, wholesale & manufacturing, exc tech	2.5	-18.1	Cutting, punching, & press machine operators	1.4	-26.3
General & operations managers	2.3	-26.3	Engineering managers	1.4	-18.1
Electrical & electronic equipment assemblers	2.0	-34.5	Helpers--Production workers	1.3	-18.1
Computer-controlled machine tool operators	1.9	-9.9	Inspectors, testers, sorters, samplers, & weighers	1.2	-22.8
Shipping, receiving, & traffic clerks	1.8	-21.2	Sales representatives, wholesale & manufacturing, tech	1.2	-18.1
Electromechanical equipment assemblers	1.8	-18.1	Maintenance & repair workers, general	1.2	-18.1
Industrial machinery mechanics	1.8	-5.8	Accountants & auditors	1.1	-18.1
Purchasing agents, exc wholesale, retail, & farm	1.7	-18.1	Engine & other machine assemblers	1.1	-18.1
Bookkeeping, accounting, & auditing clerks	1.6	-18.1	Molding, coremaking, & casting machine operators	1.1	-26.3
Mechanical drafters	1.6	-17.1	Stock clerks & order fillers	1.1	-31.4
Industrial engineers	1.6	-0.5	Sales engineers	1.0	-18.1

Source: Industry-Occupation Matrix, Bureau of Labor Statistics, December 4, 2007. These data are reported based on 4-digit NAICS categories but have been matched to corresponding 6-digit NAICS industry codes. The change reported for each occupation to the year 2016 is a percent of growth or decline as estimated by the Bureau of Labor Statistics. The abbreviation nec stands for 'not elsewhere classified'.

LOCATION BY STATE AND REGIONAL CONCENTRATION

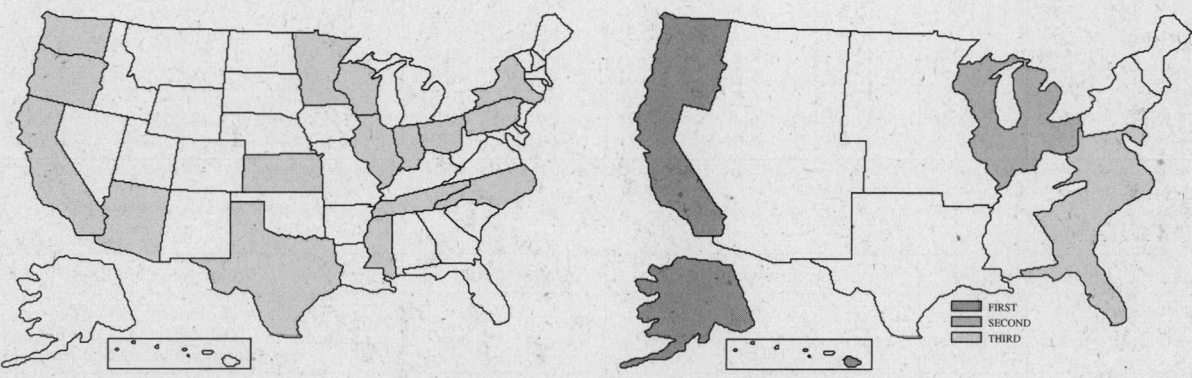

FIRST
SECOND
THIRD

INDUSTRY DATA BY STATE

State	Establish- ments	Shipments			Employment				Cost as % of Shipments	Investment per Employee ($)
		Total ($ mil)	% of U.S.	Per Establ.	Total Number	% of U.S.	Per Establ.	Wages ($/hour)		
Tennessee	9	113.2	10.5	12,583.2	426	6.0	47	11.56	57.8	1,937
Minnesota	13	107.9	10.0	8,299.7	517	7.2	40	13.92	57.1	3,503
Oregon	28	96.2	9.0	3,436.8	757	10.6	27	12.16	38.9	3,683
North Carolina	26	86.9	8.1	3,344.0	671	9.4	26	11.26	44.1	5,988
Indiana	13	73.4	6.8	5,644.6	512	7.2	39	12.91	47.6	2,277
Mississippi	5	69.8	6.5	13,963.4	339	4.8	68	15.92	37.8	1,392
California	23	59.8	5.6	2,598.3	475	6.7	21	13.24	35.0	4,507
Washington	12	36.0	3.3	2,997.5	274	3.8	23	17.25	33.3	1,964
Wisconsin	10	36.0	3.4	3,605.0	326	4.6	33	15.66	36.0	1,457
Ohio	14	31.0	2.9	2,212.1	303	4.2	22	14.13	19.1	3,023
Illinois	13	27.2	2.5	2,092.7	232	3.3	18	15.56	30.8	2,172
New York	11	20.1	1.9	1,828.8	154	2.2	14	12.88	39.7	2,662
Pennsylvania	13	17.0	1.6	1,307.2	155	2.2	12	15.13	22.4	5,019
Texas	15	11.9	1.1	790.4	100	1.4	7	15.90	47.6	9,150
Arizona	5	11.3	1.1	2,264.6	110	1.5	22	10.33	51.5	1,009
Kansas	5	9.8	0.9	1,966.2	104	1.5	21	15.23	35.7	1,462

Source: 2002 Economic Census. The states are in descending order of shipments or establishments (if shipment data are missing for the majority). The symbol (D) appears when data are withheld to prevent disclosure of competitive information. States marked with (D) are sorted by number of establishments. A dash (-) indicates that the data element cannot be calculated. Data may not show all states active in the NAICS category. All data available at the time of publication are shown.

NAICS 333220 - PLASTICS AND RUBBER INDUSTRY MACHINERY MANUFACTURING

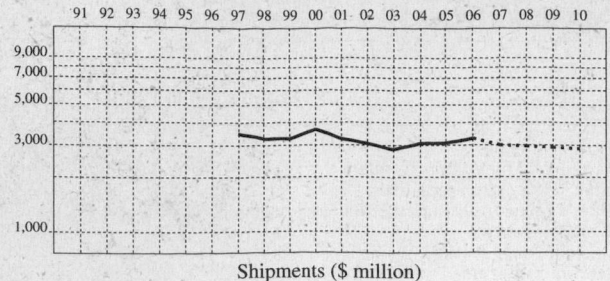

Shipments ($ million)

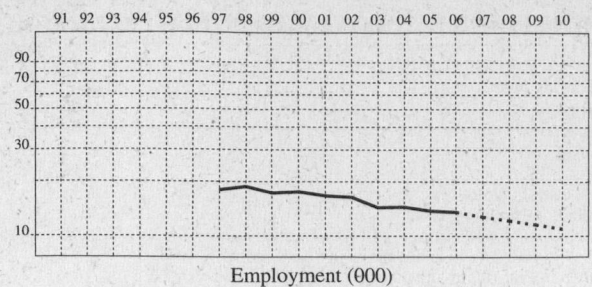

Employment (000)

GENERAL STATISTICS

Year	Com-panies	Establishments		Employment			Compensation		Production ($ million)			
		Total	with 20 or more employees	Total (000)	Production Workers (000)	Hours (Mil)	Payroll ($ mil)	Wages ($/hr)	Cost of Materials	Value Added by Manufacture	Value of Shipments	Capital Invest.
1997	424	452	168	18.0	10.1	20.4	723.2	16.69	1,612.3	1,903.6	3,481.9	92.8
1998		463	178	18.8	10.8	21.1	719.5	16.88	1,565.0	1,681.7	3,263.7	91.4
1999		503	190	17.3	10.5	21.3	720.2	17.05	1,646.3	1,627.4	3,258.2	106.1
2000		518	195	17.6	10.8	22.8	759.9	16.75	1,962.5	1,783.8	3,662.7	109.2
2001		524	200	16.7	9.9	20.2	696.1	16.18	1,449.5	1,751.8	3,246.9	96.9
2002	536	557	163	16.4	8.9	19.9	742.1	15.92	1,454.6	1,551.8	3,067.4	63.5
2003		563	176	14.4	7.8	15.5	688.8	18.75	1,340.4	1,501.8	2,843.7	36.1
2004		530	175	14.5	8.1	15.8	707.8	19.28	1,476.1	1,578.7	3,070.6	60.2
2005		500	171	13.8	7.9	15.3	689.2	19.33	1,483.1	1,609.7	3,085.5	56.0
2006		558P	175P	13.6	7.8	14.9	711.7	20.69	1,630.5	1,674.3	3,265.4	68.6
2007		567P	174P	12.8P	7.2P	14.1P	697.7P	20.09P	1,497.4P	1,537.7P	2,998.9P	46.5P
2008		577P	173P	12.2P	6.8P	13.2P	694.4P	20.51P	1,477.0P	1,516.6P	2,957.9P	40.7P
2009		586P	172P	11.6P	6.4P	12.4P	691.1P	20.94P	1,456.5P	1,495.6P	2,916.9P	35.0P
2010		595P	171P	11.0P	6.0P	11.5P	687.8P	21.36P	1,436.0P	1,474.5P	2,875.8P	29.3P

Sources: 1997 and 2002 *Economic Census*; other years, up to 2006, are from *Annual Survey of Manufactures*. Establishment counts for non-Census years are from *County Business Patterns*; 1997 and 2002 values are from the 1997 and 2002 censuses, respectively. 'P's show projections by the editors.

INDICES OF CHANGE

Year	Com-panies	Establishments		Employment			Compensation		Production ($ million)			
		Total	with 20 or more employees	Total (000)	Production Workers (000)	Hours (Mil)	Payroll ($ mil)	Wages ($/hr)	Cost of Materials	Value Added by Manufacture	Value of Shipments	Capital Invest.
1997	79	81	103	110	113	103	97	105	111	123	114	146
1998		83	109	115	121	106	97	106	108	108	106	144
1999		90	117	105	118	107	97	107	113	105	106	167
2000		93	120	107	121	115	102	105	135	115	119	172
2001		94	123	102	111	102	94	102	100	113	106	153
2002	100	100	100	100	100	100	100	100	100	100	100	100
2003		101	108	88	88	78	93	118	92	97	93	57
2004		95	107	88	91	79	95	121	101	102	100	95
2005		90	105	84	89	77	93	121	102	104	101	88
2006		100P	107P	83	88	75	96	130	112	108	106	108
2007		102P	107P	78P	81P	71P	94P	126P	103P	99P	98P	73P
2008		104P	106P	74P	76P	66P	94P	129P	102P	98P	96P	64P
2009		105P	106P	71P	72P	62P	93P	132P	100P	96P	95P	55P
2010		107P	105P	67P	67P	58P	93P	134P	99P	95P	94P	46P

Sources: Same as General Statistics. Values reflect change from the base year, 2002. Values above 100 mean greater than 2002, values below 100 mean less than 2002, and the values of 100 in other years means the same as 2002. 'P's show projections by the editors.

SELECTED RATIOS

For 2002	Avg. of All Manufact.	Analyzed Industry	Index	For 2002	Avg. of All Manufact.	Analyzed Industry	Index
Employees per Establishment	42	29	70	Value Added per Production Worker	182,367	174,360	96
Payroll per Establishment	1,639,184	1,332,316	81	Cost per Establishment	5,769,015	2,611,490	45
Payroll per Employee	39,053	45,250	116	Cost per Employee	137,446	88,695	65
Production Workers per Establishment	30	16	54	Cost per Production Worker	195,506	163,438	84
Wages per Establishment	694,845	568,776	82	Shipments per Establishment	11,158,348	5,507,002	49
Wages per Production Worker	23,548	35,596	151	Shipments per Employee	265,847	187,037	70
Hours per Production Worker	1,980	2,236	113	Shipments per Production Worker	378,144	344,652	91
Wages per Hour	11.89	15.92	134	Investment per Establishment	361,338	114,004	32
Value Added per Establishment	5,381,325	2,785,996	52	Investment per Employee	8,609	3,872	45
Value Added per Employee	128,210	94,622	74	Investment per Production Worker	12,245	7,135	58

Sources: Same as General Statistics. The 'Average of All Manufacturing' column represents the average of all manufacturing industries reported for the most recent complete year available. The Index shows the relationship between the Average and the Analyzed Industry. For example, 100 means that they are equal; 500 that the Analyzed Industry is five times the average; 50 means that the Analyzed Industry is half the national average. The abbreviation 'na' is used to show that data are 'not available'. Ratios shown for 2002, the last complete census year.

LEADING COMPANIES   Number shown: **75**   Total sales ($ mil): **88,937**   Total employment (000): **204.8**

Company Name	Address				CEO Name	Phone	Co. Type	Sales ($ mil)	Empl. (000)
Air Products & Chemicals	7201 Hamilton Blvd.	Allentown	PA	18195		610-481-4911	P	10,038	22.1
Applied Materials Inc.	PO Box 58039	Santa Clara	CA	95052		408-727-5555	P	9,735	15.3
Dover Corp.	280 Park Ave.	New York	NY	10017		212-922-1640	P	7,226	33.4
Etec Systems Inc.	PO Box 58039	Santa Clara	CA	95052		408-727-5555	S	6,992	12.2
Saint-Gobain Abrasives Inc.	1 New Bond St.	Worcester	MA	01606	Jean Phelizon	508-795-5000	R	6,831*	2.5
Metso Texas Shredder Inc.	11451 J. Maltsbergr	San Antonio	TX	78216	John Duncan	210-491-9521	P	6,340*	<0.1
Foster Wheeler Ltd.	Perryville Corp Prk	Clinton	NJ	08809	Umberto Dello Sala	908-730-4000	P	3,495	12.0
Parkson Corp.	PO Box 408399	Fort Lauderdale	FL	33340	William Acton	954-974-6610	R	3,330*	0.1
Fluid Management Operations	1023 Wheeling Rd.	Wheeling	IL	60090	Lawrence D. Kingsley	847-537-0880	S	1,935*	4.3
FM Delaware Inc.	1023 Wheeling Rd.	Wheeling	IL	60090	Lawrence D. Kingsley	847-537-0880	S	1,935*	4.3
Renco Group Inc.	30 Rockefeller Plz.	New York	NY	10112	Ira Leno Rennert	212-541-6000	R	1,900	9.4
Knight L.L.C.	20531 Crescent Bay	Lake Forest	CA	92630	George Noa	949-595-4800	S	1,889*	4.2
GE Infrastructure Water/Proc.	4636 Somerton Rd.	Trevose	PA	19053	George Oliver	215-355-3300	R	1,769*	4.0
Berwind L.L.C.	1500 Market St.	Philadelphia	PA	19102	Michael McClelland	215-563-2800	R	1,710	3.5
Lam Research Corp.	PO Box 5010	Fremont	CA	94537	James W. Bagley	510-572-0200	P	1,642	2.4
Novellus Systems Inc.	4000 N First St.	San Jose	CA	95134		408-943-9700	P	1,570	3.7
Nesco Inc.	6140 Parkland Blvd.	Mayfield Hgts	OH	44124	Robert J. Tomsich	440-461-6000	R	1,133*	10.3
ASM Lithography Holding Inc.	8555 S River Pkwy.	Tempe	AZ	85284	Eric Meurice	480-383-4422	R	1,022*	2.5
Sulzer Inc.	555 5th Ave., 15th	New York	NY	10017	Kelli Edell	212-949-0999	S	1,000*	4.5
Alcoa Closure Systems Intl	6625 Network Way	Indianapolis	IN	46278	V. Lance Mitchell	317-390-5000	S	980*	3.0
P.R. Hoffman Machine Products	1517 Commerce	Carlisle	PA	17015		717-243-9900	S	812*	<0.1
Milacron Inc.	PO Box 63716	Cincinnati	OH	45206	Ronald D. Brown	513-487-5000	P	808	3.5
Dover Diversified Inc.	Highland Oaks I	Downers Grove	IL	60515	William W. Spurgeon	630-725-9347	S	781*	4.0
Brooks Automation Inc.	15 Elizabeth Dr.	Chelmsford	MA	01824		978-262-2400	P	743	1.9
Progressive Tool & Ind./Wisne	21000 Telegraph Rd.	Southfield	MI	48034	Robert Stoutenburg	248-353-8888	D	733*	5.5
Kulicke and Soffa Industries	1005 Virginia Dr.	Fort Washington	PA	19034		215-784-6000	P	700	2.6
Bachman Machine Co.	4321 N Broadway	St. Louis	MO	63147	William Bachman	314-231-4221	R	656*	0.1
Riley Power Inc.	PO Box 15040	Worcester	MA	01615		508-852-7100	R	612*	0.4
FEI Co.	5350 NE Dawson	Hillsboro	OR	97124		503-726-7500	P	593	1.8
Gerber Scientific Inc.	83 Gerber Rd. W	South Windsor	CT	06074	Donald P. Aiken	860-644-1551	P	575	2.2
Cymer Inc.	17075 Thornmint Ct.	San Diego	CA	92127	Robert Akins	858-385-7300	P	521	1.0
UOP L.L.C.	25 E Algonquin Rd.	Des Plaines	IL	60017	Carlos Guimaraes	847-391-2000	R	500*	4.0
Universal Instruments Corp.	PO Box 825	Binghamton	NY	13902	Gerhard Meese	607-779-7689	S	424*	1.2
Axcelis Technologies Inc.	108 Cherry Hill Dr.	Beverly	MA	01915		978-787-4000	P	405	1.6
Veeco Instruments Inc.	100 Sunnyside Blvd.	Woodbury	NY	11797	Edward H. Braun	516-677-0200	P	403	1.3
FANUC Robotics America Inc.	3900 W Hamlin Rd.	Rochester Hills	MI	48309		248-377-7000	R	361*	0.9
Wall Colmonoy Corp.	101 West Girard	Madison Heights	MI	48071		248-585-6400	R	336*	0.3
Hardinge Inc.	PO Box 1507	Elmira	NY	14902	J. Patrick Ervin	607-734-2281	P	327	1.5
Gruber Systems Inc.	25636 Ave. Stanford	Valencia	CA	91355	John Hoskinson	661-257-4060	R	322*	0.3
Danieli Corp.	800 Cranberry Wds	Cranberry Twp	PA	16066	Mark Brandon	724-778-5400	R	306*	<0.1
Welex Inc.	850 Jolly Rd.	Blue Bell	PA	19422	Frank R. Nissel	215-542-8000	R	300*	0.1
Hitachi Metals America Limited	2 Manhattanville Rd	Purchase	NY	10577		914-694-9200	R	274*	<0.1
P and H Mining Equipment Inc.	PO Box 310	Milwaukee	WI	53201	Mark Readinger	414-671-4400	S	272*	0.9
Mattson Technology Inc.	47131 Bayside Pky.	Fremont	CA	94538	David Dutton		P	267	0.6
Pentaplast of America Inc.	PO Box 500	Gordonsville	VA	22942	Tom Goke	540-832-3600	S	237*	1.0
C-Tech Industries Inc.	4275 NW Pacif Rim	Camas	WA	98607		360-833-1600	R	234*	0.3
Intevac Inc.	3560 Bassett St.	Santa Clara	CA	95054	Kevin Fairbairn	408-986-9888	P	216	0.5
Semitool Inc.	655 W Reserve Dr.	Kalispell	MT	59901		406-752-2107	P	215	1.3
Datacard Group	11111 Bren Rd. W	Minnetonka	MN	55343	Kevin Gillick	952-933-1223	R	215*	1.4
LCI Corporation International	PO Box 16348	Charlotte	NC	28297	Richard Bearse	704-394-8341	R	198*	<0.1
Gerber Technology Inc.	24 Industrial Park	Tolland	CT	06084	John Hancock	860-871-8082	S	197	1.2
Celerity Group Inc.	1463 Centre Pnte Dr	Milpitas	CA	95035	David Shimmon	408-946-3100	S	190*	1.1
Stark Industrial Inc.	PO Box 3030	North Canton	OH	44720	Ray Wilkof	330-966-8108	R	190*	<0.1
Katy Industries Inc.	2461 S Clark St.	Arlington	VA	22202		703-236-4300	P	188	0.9
Emcore Corp.	10420 Research Rd.	Albuquerque	NM	87123		505-332-5000	P	170	0.7
SMC Corporation of America	PO Box 26640	Indianapolis	IN	46226	Yoshiki Takada	317-899-4440	R	151*	0.3
Evergreen Packaging Equipment	PO Box 3000	Cedar Rapids	IA	52406		319-399-3200	D	143*	0.3
SpeedFam-IPEC Inc.	PO Box 1585	Plainville	MA	02762			S	138*	0.6
ITOCHU International Inc.	335 Madison Ave.	New York	NY	10017	Satoshi Tanioka	212-818-8000	S	124*	0.3
Conair Group Inc.	1 Conair Dr.	Pittsburgh	PA	15202		412-312-6000	R	122*	0.6
VeriFone Inc.	300 Park Place Blvd	Clearwater	FL	33759	Douglas G. Bergeron	727-953-4000	S	121*	0.9
FSI International Inc.	3455 Lyman Blvd.	Chaska	MN	55318		952-448-5440	P	116	0.6
Ultratech Inc.	3050 Zanker Rd.	San Jose	CA	95134		408-321-8835	P	112	0.3
Wagstaff Inc.	3910 N Flora Rd.	Spokane	WA	99216	Paul May	509-922-1404	R	111*	0.3
Unique Machine and Tool Co.	4232 E Magnolia St.	Phoenix	AZ	85034	Kenny Moffatt	602-470-1911	R	107*	<0.1
Psp Industries Inc.	9885 Doerr Ln.	Schertz	TX	78154	Andrew Easton	210-651-9595	R	105*	<0.1
Electroglas Foreign Sales	5729 Fontanoso Way	San Jose	CA	95138	Thomas M. Rohrs	408-528-3000	S	104*	0.3
Angstrom Sciences Inc.	40 S Linden St.	Duquesne	PA	15110	Mark Bernick	412-469-8466	R	102*	<0.1
Besser Co.	801 Johnson St.	Alpena	MI	49707	Kevin Curtis	989-354-4111	R	99*	0.4
Global Industrial Equipment	11 Harbor Park Dr.	Port Washington	NY	11050	Richard Leeds	516-625-6200	S	93*	0.3
Pgp Corp.	7925 Beech Daly	Taylor	MI	48180	Paul Voss	313-291-7500	R	93*	<0.1
Phillips Service Industries	11878 Hubbard St.	Livonia	MI	48150	Scott Phillips	734-853-5000	R	92*	0.7
Talyst	21414 68th Ave. S	Kent	WA	98032		253-852-2023	R	86*	<0.1
Electroglas International Inc.	5729 Fontanoso Way	San Jose	CA	95138	Thomas M. Rohrs	408-528-3000	S	85*	0.2
ASM America Inc.	3440 E University	Phoenix	AZ	85034	Daniel G. Queyssac	602-470-5700	S	83*	0.5

Source: Ward's Business Directory of U.S. Private and Public Companies, Volumes 1 and 2, 2008. The company type code used is as follows: P - Public, R - Private, S - Subsidiary, D - Division, J - Joint Venture, A - Affiliate, G - Group. Sales are in millions of dollars, employees are in thousands. An asterisk (*) indicates an estimated sales volume. The symbol < stands for 'less than'. Company names and addresses are truncated, in some cases, to fit into the available space.

MATERIALS CONSUMED

Material	Quantity	Delivered Cost ($ million)
Electrical transmission, distribution, and control equipment	(X)	108.9
Fluid power pumps, motors, and hydrostatic transmissions	(X)	40.5
Other pumps and pump parts, excluding fluid power (complete assemblies)	(X)	7.8
Fluid power valves (hydraulic and pneumatic)	(X)	19.4
Fluid power cylinders and rotary actuators (hydraulic and pneumatic)	(X)	20.0
Fluid power hose, tube fittings, and assemblies (hydraulic and pneumatic)	(X)	11.2
Fluid power filters (hydraulic and pneumatic)	(X)	3.6
Other fluid power products, hydraulic and pneumatic	(X)	6.7
Metal bolts, nuts, screws, and other screw machine products	(X)	26.8
Metal tanks, heat exchangers, and other boiler products	(X)	30.6
Metal pipe, valves, and pipe fittings (excluding forgings)	(X)	8.8
Other fabricated metal products (exc. fluid power products and forgings)	(X)	47.4
Forgings	(X)	6.8
Iron and steel castings (rough and semifinished)	(X)	96.5
Aluminum and aluminum-base alloy castings (rough and semifinished)	(X)	8.6
Other nonferrous metal castings, rough or semifinished (inc. aluminum)	(X)	2.5
Steel bars, bar shapes, and plates (exc. castings, forgings, fabr. metal products)	(X)	65.2
Steel sheet and strip (including tinplate)	(X)	28.9
Steel structural shapes and sheet piling (exc. castings, forgings, fabr. metal products)	(X)	16.5
All other steel shapes and forms (exc. castings, forgings, fabr. metal products)	(X)	23.6
Aluminum and aluminum-base alloy sheet, plate, foil, and welded tubing	(X)	7.6
All other aluminum and aluminum-base alloy shapes and forms (exc. castings, forgings, fabr. metal products)	(X)	(D)
Other nonferrous shapes and forms (exc. castings, forgings, fabricated metal products)	(X)	3.5
Fractional horsepower electric motors and generators (less than 1 hp)	(X)	12.6
Integral horsepower electric motors and generators (1 hp or more)	(X)	36.2
Ball and roller bearings (mounted or unmounted)	(X)	11.6
Mechanical speed changers, gears, and industrial high-speed drives	(X)	37.5
Gold and other precious metals, all forms (incl. ingot, sheet, etc.)	(X)	(D)
Printed ciruit boards (without inserted components) for electronic circuitry	(X)	3.4
Printed circuit assemblies, loaded boards, and modules	(X)	41.0
Filter paper	(X)	(D)
All other materials, components, parts, containers, and supplies	(X)	227.7
Materials, ingredients, containers, and supplies, nsk	(X)	190.8

Source: 2002 *Economic Census*. Explanation of symbols used: (D): Withheld to avoid disclosure of competitive data; na: Not available; (S): Withheld because statistical norms were not met; (X): Not applicable; (Z): Less than half the unit shown; nec: Not elsewhere classified; nsk: Not specified by kind; - : zero; p : 10-19 percent estimated; q : 20-29 percent estimated.

PRODUCT SHARE DETAILS

Product or Product Class Shipments	Mil. $	Product or Product Class Shipments	Mil. $
RUBBER AND PLASTICS INDUSTRY MACHINERY	2,693.5	milling, slicing, grinding, etc., excluding patterns or molds	22.3
Plastics-working machinery and equipment, excluding patterns and molds	**2,382.7**	Machinery for treating plastics by means of a temperature change	139.2
Plastics screw extrusion machines, excluding patterns and molds	254.5	Other machinery for forming plastics	120.2
Plastics single screw extrusion machines, up to 2.49 in. screw diameter, excluding patterns and molds	63.3	Other machinery for working plastics or making products from plastics	412.5
Plastics single screw extrusion machines, 2.50 to 5.49 in. screw diameter, excluding patterns and molds	129.1	Other machinery for forming, working, or making products from plastics, and parts for plastics working machinery	382.7
Plastics single screw extrusion machines, 5.50 in. screw diameter or larger, excluding patterns and molds	34.0	Parts of machinery for treating plastics by means of a temperature change	(D)
Plastics multiple screw extrusion machines, excluding patterns and molds	28.0	Parts of calendering or rolling machines for plastics	(D)
Plastics molding machines, including blow, compression, and injections, excluding patterns and molds	839.1	Other parts for plastics working machinery	314.3
Plastics compression molding machines, excluding patterns and molds	45.0	Plastics working machinery and equipment, excluding patterns and molds, nsk	33.3
Plastics injection molding machines, 500 tons or less, excluding patterns and molds	322.9	**Rubber working machinery and equipment, excluding tire molds**	**210.0**
Plastics injection molding machines, more than 500 tons, excluding patterns and molds	205.9	Machinery for working rubber and making products of rubber, excluding tire molds	182.1
Plastics blow molding machines, excluding patterns and molds	265.2	High-intensity rubber solids mixers	25.4
Other machinery for working plastics and making products from plastics	873.2	Rubber extruding machines, excluding tire molds	28.4
		Rubber tire building equipment, except tire molds	47.0
Plastics granulators and pelletizers	91.5	Rubber tire recapping and repairing machinery and equipment, including recapping vulcanizers, excluding tire molds	21.6
Plastics thermoforming machines, excluding patterns and molds	75.8	Other machinery for working rubber and making products of rubber, excluding tire molds	59.7
Calendering or other rolling machines for working plastics, excluding patterns or molds	11.7	Parts for rubber working machinery, excluding tire molds	27.9
Machines for cold working plastics, including drilling,		**Rubber and plastics industry machinery, nsk, total**	**100.8**

Source: 2002 *Economic Census*. The values are product shipments in millions of dollars for 2002. Total product shipments may be lower or higher than industry shipments. See Introduction for a full discussion. Values of indented subcategories are summed in the main heading(s). The symbol (D) appears when data are withheld to prevent disclosure of competitive information. The abbreviation nsk stands for 'not specified by kind' and nec for 'not elsewhere classified'. A dash (-) means zero.

INPUTS AND OUTPUTS FOR PLASTICS AND RUBBER INDUSTRY MACHINERY MANUFACTURING

Economic Sector or Industry Providing Inputs	%	Sector	Economic Sector or Industry Buying Outputs	%	Sector
Compensation of employees	35.0		Private fixed investment	64.3	
Management of companies & enterprises	6.5	Services	Exports of goods & services	19.6	Cap Inv
Wholesale trade	5.4	Trade	Plastics products, nec	10.1	Manufg.
Iron & steel mills & ferroalloys	5.1	Manufg.	Plastics bottles	1.7	Manufg.
Ferrous metal foundries	3.7	Manufg.	Plastics & rubber industry machinery	1.3	Manufg.
Valve & fittings other than plumbing	2.8	Manufg.	Plastics pipe & pipe fittings	1.3	Manufg.
Relay & industrial controls	2.7	Manufg.	Plastics packaging materials, film & sheet	0.8	Manufg.
Plastics & rubber industry machinery	2.1	Manufg.	Unlaminated plastics profile shapes	0.2	Manufg.
Speed changers, industrial high-speed drives, & gears	2.1	Manufg.	Wholesale trade	0.2	Trade
Motors & generators	2.0	Manufg.	Federal government, investment, national defense	0.1	Fed Govt
Printed circuit assemblies (electronic assemblies)	1.7	Manufg.			
Fluid power process machinery	1.6	Manufg.			
Turned products & screws, nuts, & bolts	1.3	Manufg.			
Machine shops	1.2	Manufg.			
Real estate	1.0	Fin/R.E.			
Advertising & related services	1.0	Services			
Securities, commodity contracts, investments	1.0	Fin/R.E.			
Gaskets, packing, & sealing devices	0.9	Manufg.			
Taxes on production & imports, less subsidies	0.9				
Truck transportation	0.8	Util.			
Power generation & supply	0.7	Util.			
Custom computer programming services	0.7	Services			
Legal services	0.6	Services			
Lessors of nonfinancial assets	0.6	Fin/R.E.			
Ball & roller bearings	0.6	Manufg.			
Semiconductors & related devices	0.6	Manufg.			
Metal cans, boxes, & other containers (light gauge)	0.6	Manufg.			
Nonferrous metal foundries	0.5	Manufg.			
Plate work & fabricated structural products	0.5	Manufg.			
Monetary authorities/depository credit intermediation	0.5	Fin/R.E.			
Aluminum products from purchased aluminum	0.5	Manufg.			
Cutting tools & machine tool accessories	0.5	Manufg.			
Telecommunications	0.5	Services			
Automotive equipment rental & leasing	0.4	Fin/R.E.			
Coating, engraving, heat treating & allied activities	0.4	Manufg.			
Noncomparable imports	0.4	Foreign			
Motor vehicle parts	0.4	Manufg.			
Professional, scientific, technical services, nec	0.4	Services			
Fabricated metals, nec	0.4	Manufg.			
Electronic components, nec	0.4	Manufg.			
Pumps & pumping equipment	0.4	Manufg.			
Electronic capacitors, resistors, coils, transformers	0.4	Manufg.			
Scientific research & development services	0.4	Services			
Data processing, hosting, & related services	0.4	Services			
Accounting, tax preparation, bookkeeping, & payroll	0.3	Services			
Warehousing & storage	0.3	Util.			
Specialized design services	0.3	Services			
Forging, stamping, & sintering, nec	0.3	Manufg.			
Employment services	0.3	Services			
Food services & drinking places	0.3	Services			
Business support services	0.3	Services			
Architectural, engineering, & related services	0.3	Services			
Air & gas compressors	0.2	Manufg.			
Commercial & industrial machinery rental & leasing	0.2	Fin/R.E.			
Management, scientific, & technical consulting	0.2	Services			
Abrasive products	0.2	Manufg.			
Special tools, dies, jigs, & fixtures	0.2	Manufg.			
Postal service	0.2	Util.			
General purpose machinery, nec	0.2	Manufg.			
Metal tanks (heavy gauge)	0.2	Manufg.			
Services to buildings & dwellings	0.2	Services			
Maintenance/repair of nonresidential structures	0.2	Construct.			
Power boilers & heat exchangers	0.2	Manufg.			
Natural gas distribution	0.2	Util.			
Support services, nec	0.2	Services			
Other computer related services, including facilities	0.2	Services			
Hotels & motels, including casino hotels	0.1	Services			
Bare printed circuit boards	0.1	Manufg.			
Paperboard containers	0.1	Manufg.			
Chemical products & preparations, nec	0.1	Manufg.			
Rubber products, nec	0.1	Manufg.			
Crowns & closures & metal stamping	0.1	Manufg.			
Investigation & security services	0.1	Services			
Rail transportation	0.1	Util.			
Air transportation	0.1	Util.			
Automotive repair & maintenance, ex. car washes	0.1	Services			

Source: Benchmark Input-Output Accounts for the U.S. Economy, 2002, U.S. Department of Commerce, Washington, D.C., January 2008. The abbreviation nec stands for 'not elsewhere classified'.

OCCUPATIONS EMPLOYED BY INDUSTRIAL MACHINERY MANUFACTURING

Occupation	% of Total 2006	Change to 2016	Occupation	% of Total 2006	Change to 2016
Machinists	6.6	-14.0	Electrical engineers	1.6	-18.1
Team assemblers	5.5	-18.1	Structural metal fabricators & fitters	1.5	-18.1
Welders, cutters, solderers, & brazers	4.3	-12.8	Customer service representatives	1.5	-9.9
Mechanical engineers	4.0	-9.9	Grinding, lapping, polishing machine tool operators	1.4	-20.5
First-line supervisors/managers of production workers	3.8	-18.1	Office clerks, general	1.4	-19.3
Sales reps, wholesale & manufacturing, exc tech	2.5	-18.1	Cutting, punching, & press machine operators	1.4	-26.3
General & operations managers	2.3	-26.3	Engineering managers	1.4	-18.1
Electrical & electronic equipment assemblers	2.0	-34.5	Helpers--Production workers	1.3	-18.1
Computer-controlled machine tool operators	1.9	-9.9	Inspectors, testers, sorters, samplers, & weighers	1.2	-22.8
Shipping, receiving, & traffic clerks	1.8	-21.2	Sales representatives, wholesale & manufacturing, tech	1.2	-18.1
Electromechanical equipment assemblers	1.8	-18.1	Maintenance & repair workers, general	1.2	-18.1
Industrial machinery mechanics	1.8	-5.8	Accountants & auditors	1.1	-18.1
Purchasing agents, exc wholesale, retail, & farm	1.7	-18.1	Engine & other machine assemblers	1.1	-18.1
Bookkeeping, accounting, & auditing clerks	1.6	-18.1	Molding, coremaking, & casting machine operators	1.1	-26.3
Mechanical drafters	1.6	-17.1	Stock clerks & order fillers	1.1	-31.4
Industrial engineers	1.6	-0.5	Sales engineers	1.0	-18.1

Source: Industry-Occupation Matrix, Bureau of Labor Statistics, December 4, 2007. These data are reported based on 4-digit NAICS categories but have been matched to corresponding 6-digit NAICS industry codes. The change reported for each occupation to the year 2016 is a percent of growth or decline as estimated by the Bureau of Labor Statistics. The abbreviation nec stands for 'not elsewhere classified'.

LOCATION BY STATE AND REGIONAL CONCENTRATION

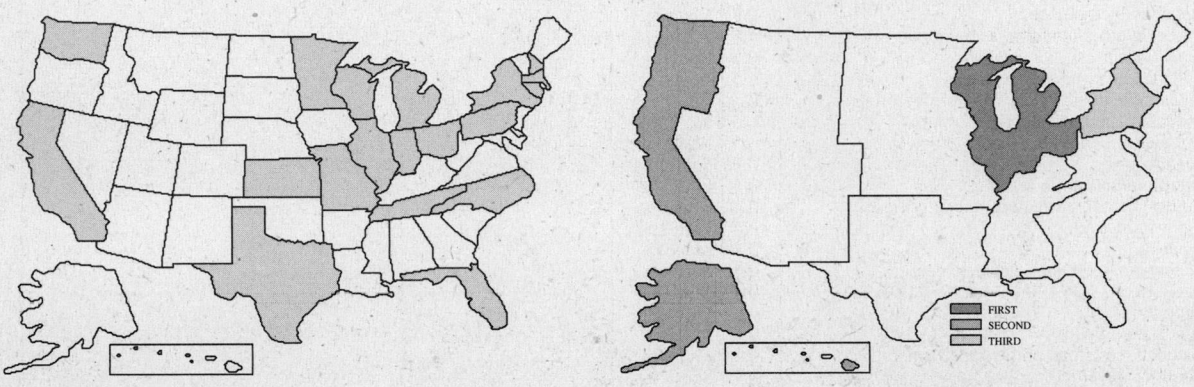

FIRST
SECOND
THIRD

INDUSTRY DATA BY STATE

State	Establish-ments	Shipments Total ($ mil)	Shipments % of U.S.	Shipments Per Establ.	Employment Total Number	Employment % of U.S.	Employment Per Establ.	Wages ($/hour)	Cost as % of Shipments	Investment per Employee ($)
Ohio	74	626.7	20.4	8,468.8	3,160	19.2	43	16.71	60.0	1,955
Pennsylvania	27	343.0	11.2	12,703.3	1,255	7.6	46	18.45	49.9	2,159
Michigan	57	341.6	11.1	5,993.5	1,897	11.5	33	19.66	41.2	3,048
Illinois	31	238.0	7.8	7,676.4	1,247	7.6	40	10.83	39.5	7,476
Massachusetts	27	198.8	6.5	7,364.3	1,284	7.8	48	17.52	43.7	2,657
New York	22	164.9	5.4	7,494.1	1,163	7.1	53	12.11	40.5	2,555
Connecticut	15	157.0	5.1	10,466.2	722	4.4	48	19.63	62.1	3,242
California	70	149.1	4.9	2,130.3	842	5.1	12	14.90	36.4	8,106
Wisconsin	19	93.3	3.0	4,910.7	561	3.4	30	15.91	32.3	4,203
Kansas	8	67.4	2.2	8,427.6	274	1.7	34	19.50	42.2	1,653
North Carolina	15	59.3	1.9	3,956.3	258	1.6	17	17.14	47.8	1,787
Minnesota	9	44.1	1.4	4,905.2	176	1.1	20	16.24	40.3	2,386
Texas	13	42.3	1.4	3,254.7	143	0.9	11	18.76	61.6	17,916
Washington	11	28.7	0.9	2,613.2	460	2.8	42	15.79	40.1	1,054
New Hampshire	4	23.4	0.8	5,854.0	104	0.6	26	16.68	62.0	1,442
Indiana	21	19.6	0.6	935.3	203	1.2	10	12.23	39.6	2,616
Tennessee	15	18.7	0.6	1,245.3	137	0.8	9	13.00	40.8	2,504
Missouri	8	10.8	0.4	1,355.0	101	0.6	13	9.21	38.2	505
Florida	15	10.7	0.3	714.0	126	0.8	8	10.49	43.4	1,230

Source: 2002 *Economic Census*. The states are in descending order of shipments or establishments (if shipment data are missing for the majority). The symbol (D) appears when data are withheld to prevent disclosure of competitive information. States marked with (D) are sorted by number of establishments. A dash (-) indicates that the data element cannot be calculated. Data may not show all states active in the NAICS category. All data available at the time of publication are shown.

NAICS 333295 - SEMICONDUCTOR MACHINERY MANUFACTURING

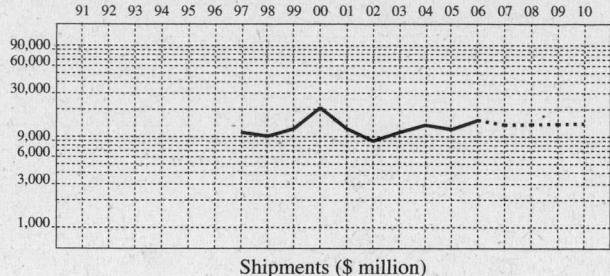

Shipments ($ million)

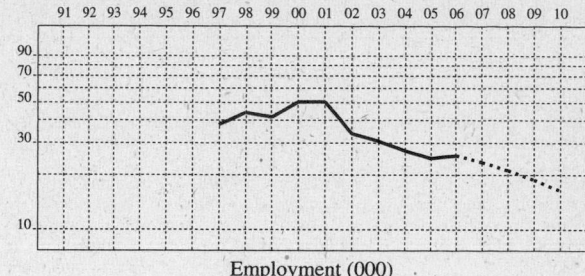

Employment (000)

GENERAL STATISTICS

| Year | Com-panies | Establishments | | Employment | | | Compensation | | Production ($ million) | | | |
		Total	with 20 or more employees	Total (000)	Production Workers (000)	Hours (Mil)	Payroll ($ mil)	Wages ($/hr)	Cost of Materials	Value Added by Manufacture	Value of Shipments	Capital Invest.
1997	242	256	151	37.8	20.9	42.1	1,590.3	14.49	5,354.0	6,004.3	11,152.2	683.6
1998		269	158	44.0	23.1	37.2	1,777.6	18.49	5,274.9	4,592.8	10,070.8	980.6
1999		269	149	41.6	21.3	42.5	2,105.5	19.31	5,696.0	6,890.9	12,223.5	664.2
2000		259	149	50.4	24.8	49.1	2,959.9	22.45	9,802.7	11,636.0	20,807.2	814.3
2001		257	153	50.5	24.7	49.4	2,784.3	19.65	6,050.4	5,647.4	12,206.2	823.9
2002	259	292	166	33.8	13.0	25.9	2,281.0	23.36	4,401.7	4,444.6	8,938.7	480.8
2003		285	150	30.7	13.3	25.7	2,025.5	21.62	4,917.0	5,747.1	11,100.9	365.2
2004		263	143	27.2	11.6	23.8	1,961.8	19.93	5,458.6	8,145.4	13,411.9	389.1
2005		244	128	24.7	10.5	21.0	1,950.6	20.81	5,540.6	6,331.1	12,000.1	351.9
2006		266P	140P	25.6	10.9	21.8	2,176.5	21.93	6,960.4	8,338.7	15,094.5	271.6
2007		266P	138P	23.5P	8.3P	17.7P	2,243.4P	23.12P	6,203.0P	7,431.3P	13,452.0P	210.0P
2008		266P	136P	21.2P	6.7P	14.8P	2,258.3P	23.65P	6,266.0P	7,506.8P	13,588.6P	142.3P
2009		266P	134P	18.8P	5.0P	11.9P	2,273.2P	24.18P	6,329.0P	7,582.3P	13,725.2P	74.6P
2010		266P	132P	16.4P	3.4P	9.0P	2,288.1P	24.71P	6,392.0P	7,657.7P	13,861.8P	6.8P

Sources: 1997 and 2002 *Economic Census*; other years, up to 2006, are from *Annual Survey of Manufactures*. Establishment counts for non-Census years are from *County Business Patterns*; 1997 and 2002 values are from the 1997 and 2002 censuses, respectively. 'P's show projections by the editors.

INDICES OF CHANGE

| Year | Com-panies | Establishments | | Employment | | | Compensation | | Production ($ million) | | | |
		Total	with 20 or more employees	Total (000)	Production Workers (000)	Hours (Mil)	Payroll ($ mil)	Wages ($/hr)	Cost of Materials	Value Added by Manufacture	Value of Shipments	Capital Invest.
1997	93	88	91	112	161	163	70	62	122	135	125	142
1998		92	95	130	178	144	78	79	120	103	113	204
1999		92	90	123	164	164	92	83	129	155	137	138
2000		89	90	149	191	190	130	96	223	262	233	169
2001		88	92	149	190	191	122	84	137	127	137	171
2002	100	100	100	100	100	100	100	100	100	100	100	100
2003		98	90	91	102	99	89	93	112	129	124	76
2004		90	86	80	89	92	86	85	124	183	150	81
2005		84	77	73	81	81	86	89	126	142	134	73
2006		91P	84P	76	84	84	95	94	158	188	169	56
2007		91P	83P	70P	64P	68P	98P	99P	141P	167P	150P	44P
2008		91P	82P	63P	52P	57P	99P	101P	142P	169P	152P	30P
2009		91P	81P	56P	38P	46P	100P	104P	144P	171P	154P	16P
2010		91P	80P	49P	26P	35P	100P	106P	145P	172P	155P	1P

Sources: Same as General Statistics. Values reflect change from the base year, 2002. Values above 100 mean greater than 2002, values below 100 mean less than 2002, and the values of 100 in other years means the same as 2002. 'P's show projections by the editors.

SELECTED RATIOS

For 2002	Avg. of All Manufact.	Analyzed Industry	Index	For 2002	Avg. of All Manufact.	Analyzed Industry	Index
Employees per Establishment	42	116	276	Value Added per Production Worker	182,367	341,892	187
Payroll per Establishment	1,639,184	7,811,644	477	Cost per Establishment	5,769,015	15,074,315	261
Payroll per Employee	39,053	67,485	173	Cost per Employee	137,446	130,228	95
Production Workers per Establishment	30	45	151	Cost per Production Worker	195,506	338,592	173
Wages per Establishment	694,845	2,072,000	298	Shipments per Establishment	11,158,348	30,611,986	274
Wages per Production Worker	23,548	46,540	198	Shipments per Employee	265,847	264,459	99
Hours per Production Worker	1,980	1,992	101	Shipments per Production Worker	378,144	687,592	182
Wages per Hour	11.89	23.36	196	Investment per Establishment	361,338	1,646,575	456
Value Added per Establishment	5,381,325	15,221,233	283	Investment per Employee	8,609	14,225	165
Value Added per Employee	128,210	131,497	103	Investment per Production Worker	12,245	36,985	302

Sources: Same as General Statistics. The 'Average of All Manufacturing' column represents the average of all manufacturing industries reported for the most recent complete year available. The Index shows the relationship between the Average and the Analyzed Industry. For example, 100 means that they are equal; 500 that the Analyzed Industry is five times the average; 50 means that the Analyzed Industry is half the national average. The abbreviation 'na' is used to show that data are 'not available'. Ratios shown for 2002, the last complete census year.

LEADING COMPANIES   Number shown: **75**   Total sales ($ mil): **88,937**   Total employment (000): **204.8**

Company Name	Address				CEO Name	Phone	Co. Type	Sales ($ mil)	Empl. (000)
Air Products & Chemicals	7201 Hamilton Blvd.	Allentown	PA	18195		610-481-4911	P	10,038	22.1
Applied Materials Inc.	PO Box 58039	Santa Clara	CA	95052		408-727-5555	P	9,735	15.3
Dover Corp.	280 Park Ave.	New York	NY	10017		212-922-1640	P	7,226	33.4
Etec Systems Inc.	PO Box 58039	Santa Clara	CA	95052		408-727-5555	S	6,992	12.2
Saint-Gobain Abrasives Inc.	1 New Bond St.	Worcester	MA	01606	Jean Phelizon	508-795-5000	R	6,831*	2.5
Metso Texas Shredder Inc.	11451 J. Maltsbergr	San Antonio	TX	78216	John Duncan	210-491-9521	R	6,340*	<0.1
Foster Wheeler Ltd.	Perryville Corp Prk	Clinton	NJ	08809	Umberto Dello Sala	908-730-4000	P	3,495	12.0
Parkson Corp.	PO Box 408399	Fort Lauderdale	FL	33340	William Acton	954-974-6610	R	3,330*	0.1
Fluid Management Operations	1023 Wheeling Rd.	Wheeling	IL	60090	Lawrence D. Kingsley	847-537-0880	S	1,935*	4.3
FM Delaware Inc.	1023 Wheeling Rd.	Wheeling	IL	60090	Lawrence D. Kingsley	847-537-0880	S	1,935*	4.3
Renco Group Inc.	30 Rockefeller Plz.	New York	NY	10112	Ira Leno Rennert	212-541-6000	R	1,900	9.4
Knight L.L.C.	20531 Crescent Bay	Lake Forest	CA	92630	George Noa	949-595-4800	S	1,889*	4.2
GE Infrastructure Water/Proc.	4636 Somerton Rd.	Trevose	PA	19053	George Oliver	215-355-3300	R	1,769*	4.0
Berwind L.L.C.	1500 Market St.	Philadelphia	PA	19102	Michael McClelland	215-563-2800	R	1,710	3.5
Lam Research Corp.	PO Box 5010	Fremont	CA	94537	James W. Bagley	510-572-0200	P	1,642	2.4
Novellus Systems Inc.	4000 N First St.	San Jose	CA	95134		408-943-9700	P	1,570	3.7
Nesco Inc.	6140 Parkland Blvd.	Mayfield Hgts	OH	44124	Robert J. Tomsich	440-461-6000	R	1,133*	10.3
ASM Lithography Holding Inc.	8555 S River Pkwy.	Tempe	AZ	85284	Eric Meurice	480-383-4422	R	1,022*	2.5
Sulzer Inc.	555 5th Ave., 15th	New York	NY	10017	Kelli Edell	212-949-0999	S	1,000*	4.5
Alcoa Closure Systems Intl	6625 Network Way	Indianapolis	IN	46278	V. Lance Mitchell	317-390-5000	S	980*	3.0
P.R. Hoffman Machine Products	1517 Commerce	Carlisle	PA	17015		717-243-9900	S	812*	<0.1
Milacron Inc.	PO Box 63716	Cincinnati	OH	45206	Ronald D. Brown	513-487-5000	P	808	3.5
Dover Diversified Inc.	Highland Oaks I	Downers Grove	IL	60515	William W. Spurgeon	630-725-9347	S	781*	4.0
Brooks Automation Inc.	15 Elizabeth Dr.	Chelmsford	MA	01824		978-262-2400	P	743	1.9
Progressive Tool & Ind./Wisne	21000 Telegraph Rd.	Southfield	MI	48034	Robert Stoutenburg	248-353-8888	D	733*	5.5
Kulicke and Soffa Industries	1005 Virginia Dr.	Fort Washington	PA	19034		215-784-6000	P	700	2.6
Bachman Machine Co.	4321 N Broadway	St. Louis	MO	63147	William Bachman	314-231-4221	R	656*	0.1
Riley Power Inc.	PO Box 15040	Worcester	MA	01615		508-852-7100	R	612*	0.4
FEI Co.	5350 NE Dawson	Hillsboro	OR	97124		503-726-7500	P	593	1.8
Gerber Scientific Inc.	83 Gerber Rd. W	South Windsor	CT	06074	Donald P. Aiken	860-644-1551	P	575	2.2
Cymer Inc.	17075 Thornmint Ct.	San Diego	CA	92127	Robert Akins	858-385-7300	P	521	1.0
UOP L.L.C.	25 E Algonquin Rd.	Des Plaines	IL	60017	Carlos Guimaraes	847-391-2000	R	500*	4.0
Universal Instruments Corp.	PO Box 825	Binghamton	NY	13902	Gerhard Meese	607-779-7689	S	424*	1.2
Axcelis Technologies Inc.	108 Cherry Hill Dr.	Beverly	MA	01915		978-787-4000	P	405	1.6
Veeco Instruments Inc.	100 Sunnyside Blvd.	Woodbury	NY	11797	Edward H. Braun	516-677-0200	P	403	1.3
FANUC Robotics America Inc.	3900 W Hamlin Rd.	Rochester Hills	MI	48309		248-377-7000	R	361*	0.9
Wall Colmonoy Corp.	101 West Girard	Madison Heights	MI	48071		248-585-6400	R	336*	0.3
Hardinge Inc.	PO Box 1507	Elmira	NY	14902	J. Patrick Ervin	607-734-2281	P	327	1.5
Gruber Systems Inc.	25636 Ave. Stanford	Valencia	CA	91355	John Hoskinson	661-257-4060	R	322*	0.3
Danieli Corp.	800 Cranberry Wds	Cranberry Twp	PA	16066	Mark Brandon	724-778-5400	R	306*	<0.1
Welex Inc.	850 Jolly Rd.	Blue Bell	PA	19422	Frank R. Nissel	215-542-8000	R	300*	0.1
Hitachi Metals America Limited	2 Manhattanville Rd	Purchase	NY	10577		914-694-9200	R	274*	<0.1
P and H Mining Equipment Inc.	PO Box 310	Milwaukee	WI	53201	Mark Readinger	414-671-4400	S	272*	0.9
Mattson Technology Inc.	47131 Bayside Pky.	Fremont	CA	94538	David Dutton		P	267	0.6
Pentaplast of America Inc.	PO Box 500	Gordonsville	VA	22942	Tom Goke	540-832-3600	S	237*	1.0
C-Tech Industries Inc.	4275 NW Pacif Rim	Camas	WA	98607		360-833-1600	R	234*	0.3
Intevac Inc.	3560 Bassett St.	Santa Clara	CA	95054	Kevin Fairbairn	408-986-9888	P	216	0.5
Semitool Inc.	655 W Reserve Dr.	Kalispell	MT	59901		406-752-2107	P	215	1.3
Datacard Group	11111 Bren Rd. W	Minnetonka	MN	55343	Kevin Gillick	952-933-1223	R	215*	1.4
LCI Corporation International	PO Box 16348	Charlotte	NC	28297	Richard Bearse	704-394-8341	R	198*	<0.1
Gerber Technology Inc.	24 Industrial Park	Tolland	CT	06084	John Hancock	860-871-8082	S	197	1.2
Celerity Group Inc.	1463 Centre Pnte Dr	Milpitas	CA	95035	David Shimmon	408-946-3100	S	190*	1.1
Stark Industrial Inc.	PO Box 3030	North Canton	OH	44720	Ray Wilkof	330-966-8108	R	190*	<0.1
Katy Industries Inc.	2461 S Clark St.	Arlington	VA	22202		703-236-4300	P	188	0.9
Emcore Corp.	10420 Research Rd.	Albuquerque	NM	87123		505-332-5000	P	170	0.7
SMC Corporation of America	PO Box 26640	Indianapolis	IN	46226	Yoshiki Takada	317-899-4440	R	151*	0.3
Evergreen Packaging Equipment	PO Box 3000	Cedar Rapids	IA	52406		319-399-3200	D	143*	0.3
SpeedFam-IPEC Inc.	PO Box 1585	Plainville	MA	02762			S	138*	0.6
ITOCHU International Inc.	335 Madison Ave.	New York	NY	10017	Satoshi Tanioka	212-818-8000	S	124*	0.3
Conair Group Inc.	1 Conair Dr.	Pittsburgh	PA	15202		412-312-6000	R	122*	0.6
VeriFone Inc.	300 Park Place Blvd	Clearwater	FL	33759	Douglas G. Bergeron	727-953-4000	S	121*	0.9
FSI International Inc.	3455 Lyman Blvd.	Chaska	MN	55318		952-448-5440	P	116	0.6
Ultratech Inc.	3050 Zanker Rd.	San Jose	CA	95134		408-321-8835	P	112	0.3
Wagstaff Inc.	3910 N Flora Rd.	Spokane	WA	99216	Paul May	509-922-1404	R	111*	0.3
Unique Machine and Tool Co.	4232 E Magnolia St.	Phoenix	AZ	85034	Kenny Moffatt	602-470-1911	R	107*	<0.1
Psp Industries Inc.	9885 Doerr Ln.	Schertz	TX	78154	Andrew Easton	210-651-9595	R	105*	<0.1
Electroglas Foreign Sales	5729 Fontanoso Way	San Jose	CA	95138	Thomas M. Rohrs	408-528-3000	S	104*	0.3
Angstrom Sciences Inc.	40 S Linden St.	Duquesne	PA	15110	Mark Bernick	412-469-8466	R	102*	<0.1
Besser Co.	801 Johnson St.	Alpena	MI	49707	Kevin Curtis	989-354-4111	R	99*	0.4
Global Industrial Equipment	11 Harbor Park Dr.	Port Washington	NY	11050	Richard Leeds	516-625-6200	S	93*	0.3
Pgp Corp.	7925 Beech Daly	Taylor	MI	48180	Paul Voss	313-291-7500	R	93*	<0.1
Phillips Service Industries	11878 Hubbard St.	Livonia	MI	48150	Scott Phillips	734-853-5000	R	92*	0.7
Talyst	21414 68th Ave. S	Kent	WA	98032		253-852-2023	R	86*	<0.1
Electroglas International Inc.	5729 Fontanoso Way	San Jose	CA	95138	Thomas M. Rohrs	408-528-3000	S	85*	0.2
ASM America Inc.	3440 E University	Phoenix	AZ	85034	Daniel G. Queyssac	602-470-5700	S	83*	0.5

Source: Ward's Business Directory of U.S. Private and Public Companies, Volumes 1 and 2, 2008. The company type code used is as follows: P - Public, R - Private, S - Subsidiary, D - Division, J - Joint Venture, A - Affiliate, G - Group. Sales are in millions of dollars, employees are in thousands. An asterisk (*) indicates an estimated sales volume. The symbol < stands for 'less than'. Company names and addresses are truncated, in some cases, to fit into the available space.

MATERIALS CONSUMED

Material	Quantity	Delivered Cost ($ million)
Electrical transmission, distribution, and control equipment	(X)	236.5
Fluid power pumps, motors, and hydrostatic transmissions	(X)	100.5
Other pumps and pump parts, excluding fluid power (complete assemblies)	(X)	157.6
Fluid power valves (hydraulic and pneumatic)	(X)	76.8
Fluid power cylinders and rotary actuators (hydraulic and pneumatic)	(X)	(D)
Fluid power hose, tube fittings, and assemblies (hydraulic and pneumatic)	(X)	53.7
Fluid power filters (hydraulic and pneumatic)	(X)	37.9
Other fluid power products, hydraulic and pneumatic	(X)	(D)
Metal bolts, nuts, screws, and other screw machine products	(X)	49.1
Metal tanks, heat exchangers, and other boiler products	(X)	30.8
Metal pipe, valves, and pipe fittings (excluding forgings)	(X)	38.8
Other fabricated metal products (exc. fluid power products and forgings)	(X)	192.3
Iron and steel castings (rough and semifinished)	(X)	(D)
Aluminum and aluminum-base alloy castings (rough and semifinished)	(X)	75.9
Other nonferrous metal castings, rough or semifinished (inc. aluminum)	(X)	(D)
Steel bars, bar shapes, and plates (exc. castings, forgings, fabr. metal products)	(X)	20.4
Steel structural shapes and sheet piling (exc. castings, forgings, fabr. metal products)	(X)	(D)
All other steel shapes and forms (exc. castings, forgings, fabr. metal products)	(X)	(D)
All other aluminum and aluminum-base alloy shapes and forms (exc. castings, forgings, fabr. metal products)	(X)	8.6
Other nonferrous shapes and forms (exc. castings, forgings, fabricated metal products)	(X)	(D)
Fractional horsepower electric motors and generators (less than 1 hp)	(X)	4.1
Integral horsepower electric motors and generators (1 hp or more)	(X)	(D)
Ball and roller bearings (mounted or unmounted)	(X)	(D)
Mechanical speed changers, gears, and industrial high-speed drives	(X)	3.8
Gold and other precious metals, all forms (incl. ingot, sheet, etc.)	(X)	(D)
Printed ciruit boards (without inserted components) for electronic circuitry	(X)	5.3
Printed circuit assemblies, loaded boards, and modules	(X)	48.8
Filter paper	(X)	(D)
All other materials, components, parts, containers, and supplies	(X)	2,038.8
Materials, ingredients, containers, and supplies, nsk	(X)	460.0

Source: 2002 *Economic Census*. Explanation of symbols used: (D): Withheld to avoid disclosure of competitive data; na: Not available; (S): Withheld because statistical norms were not met; (X): Not applicable; (Z): Less than half the unit shown; nec: Not elsewhere classified; nsk: Not specified by kind; - : zero; p : 10-19 percent estimated; q : 20-29 percent estimated.

PRODUCT SHARE DETAILS

Product or Product Class Shipments	Mil. $	Product or Product Class Shipments	Mil. $
SEMICONDUCTOR MANUFACTURING EQUIPMENT	8,403.4	Semiconductor assembly dicing machines, including saws and scribing-fracturing machines, die bonding, and wire bonding	12.9
Semiconductor wafer processing equipment, thin layer chemical vapor deposition	(D)	Parts and packaging equipment for semiconductor manufacturing machinery	1,767.4
Semiconductor wafer processing equipment, thin layer physical vapor deposition	700.3	Packaging equipment, including mold and seal equipment and finish and mark equipment	(D)
Semiconductor wafer processing equipment, plasma etch	(D)	Other assembly and packaging equipment, including lead frame inserting machines	103.8
Other semiconductor equipment	3,998.3	Parts for machine tools designed to produce or process semiconductor wafers	199.4
Microlithography, including aligners and other lithography systems	404.0	Parts for ion beam and plasma machines designed to process semiconductor wafers and designs by removal of material	(D)
Semiconductor wafer processing equipment, thin layer epitaxial growth deposition	128.6	Parts for ion implanters designed for doping semiconductor wafers	(D)
Semiconductor wafer processing equipment, wet etch	244.8	Parts for apparatus designed for the projection of circuit patterns on sensitized semiconductor materials	(D)
Semiconductor wafer processing equipment, reactive ion etch and stripping systems	(D)	Parts for pattern generating apparatus designed to produce masks and reticles from photoresist coated substrates	(D)
Ion implantation including current and voltage ion implanters	825.9	Other parts for semiconductor manufacturing machinery	1,091.0
Wafer processing equipment to saw (slice) blank wafers from crystal boules	(D)	Semiconductor manufacturing equipment(except furnaces and ovens, instruments, and photographics), nsk, total	152.4
Wafer processing equipment designed to grind and polish semiconductor wafers	5.7		
Wafer processing equipment, pattern generating apparatus to produce masks and reticles from photoresist coated substrates, except focused ion beam milling machines	250.6		
Other semiconductor wafer processing equipment	2,006.5		

Source: 2002 *Economic Census*. The values are product shipments in millions of dollars for 2002. Total product shipments may be lower or higher than industry shipments. See Introduction for a full discussion. Values of indented subcategories are summed in the main heading(s). The symbol (D) appears when data are withheld to prevent disclosure of competitive information. The abbreviation nsk stands for 'not specified by kind' and nec for 'not elsewhere classified'. A dash (-) means zero.

INPUTS AND OUTPUTS FOR SEMICONDUCTOR MACHINERY MANUFACTURING

Economic Sector or Industry Providing Inputs	%	Sector	Economic Sector or Industry Buying Outputs	%	Sector
Compensation of employees	31.1		Private fixed investment	51.4	
Semiconductor machinery	15.8	Manufg.	Exports of goods & services	26.8	Cap Inv
Management of companies & enterprises	5.9	Services	Semiconductor machinery	10.6	Manufg.
Wholesale trade	4.4	Trade	Change in private inventories	2.3	In House
Valve & fittings other than plumbing	2.2	Manufg.	Real estate	1.6	Fin/R.E.
Pumps & pumping equipment	1.9	Manufg.	Motion picture & video industries	1.2	Services
Relay & industrial controls	1.8	Manufg.	Semiconductors & related devices	1.1	Manufg.
Nonferrous metal foundries	1.4	Manufg.	Internet publishing & broadcasting	0.9	Services
Machine shops	1.3	Manufg.	Automotive equipment rental & leasing	0.8	Fin/R.E.
Management, scientific, & technical consulting	1.2	Services	Book publishers	0.5	Services
Securities, commodity contracts, investments	1.2	Fin/R.E.	Sound recording industries	0.5	Services
Fluid power process machinery	1.0	Manufg.	Radio & television broadcasting	0.4	Services
Legal services	1.0	Services	Scientific research & development services	0.4	Services
Real estate	1.0	Fin/R.E.	Computer system design services	0.3	Services
Truck transportation	1.0	Util.	Directories, mailing lists, & other publishers	0.3	Services
Gaskets, packing, & sealing devices	1.0	Manufg.	Newspaper publishers	0.3	Services
Aluminum products from purchased aluminum	0.9	Manufg.	Information services, nec	0.1	Services
Turned products & screws, nuts, & bolts	0.8	Manufg.	Architectural, engineering, & related services	0.1	Services
Lessors of nonfinancial assets	0.8	Fin/R.E.	Internet service providers & web search portals	0.1	Services
Custom computer programming services	0.8	Services			
Advertising & related services	0.8	Services			
Motors & generators	0.8	Manufg.			
Telecommunications	0.7	Services			
Monetary authorities/depository credit intermediation	0.7	Fin/R.E.			
Semiconductors & related devices	0.7	Manufg.			
Printed circuit assemblies (electronic assemblies)	0.7	Manufg.			
Iron & steel mills & ferroalloys	0.6	Manufg.			
Power generation & supply	0.6	Util.			
Data processing, hosting, & related services	0.6	Services			
Professional, scientific, technical services, nec	0.6	Services			
Cutting tools & machine tool accessories	0.5	Manufg.			
General purpose machinery, nec	0.5	Manufg.			
Coating, engraving, heat treating & allied activities	0.5	Manufg.			
Food services & drinking places	0.5	Services			
Warehousing & storage	0.5	Util.			
Accounting, tax preparation, bookkeeping, & payroll	0.4	Services			
Ball & roller bearings	0.4	Manufg.			
Primary nonferrous metal, ex. copper & aluminum	0.4	Manufg.			
Paper mills	0.3	Manufg.			
Scientific research & development services	0.3	Services			
Ferrous metal foundries	0.3	Manufg.			
Metal cans, boxes, & other containers (light gauge)	0.3	Manufg.			
Taxes on production & imports, less subsidies	0.3				
Hotels & motels, including casino hotels	0.3	Services			
Electronic components, nec	0.3	Manufg.			
Noncomparable imports	0.3	Foreign			
Fabricated metals, nec	0.3	Manufg.			
Air transportation	0.3	Util.			
Business support services	0.3	Services			
Plate-work & fabricated structural products	0.3	Manufg.			
Electronic capacitors, resistors, coils, transformers	0.2	Manufg.			
Services to buildings & dwellings	0.2	Services			
Abrasive products	0.2	Manufg.			
Special tools, dies, jigs, & fixtures	0.2	Manufg.			
Architectural, engineering, & related services	0.2	Services			
Plastics packaging materials, film & sheet	0.2	Manufg.			
Postal service	0.2	Util.			
Maintenance/repair of nonresidential structures	0.2	Construct.			
Other computer related services, including facilities	0.2	Services			
Air & gas compressors	0.2	Manufg.			
Automotive equipment rental & leasing	0.2	Fin/R.E.			
Environmental & other technical consulting services	0.2	Services			
Custom roll forming	0.2	Manufg.			
Paperboard containers	0.1	Manufg.			
Employment services	0.1	Services			
Crowns & closures & metal stamping	0.1	Manufg.			
Chemical products & preparations, nec	0.1	Manufg.			
Nondepository credit intermediation activities	0.1	Fin/R.E.			
Office administrative services	0.1	Services			
Automotive repair & maintenance, ex. car washes	0.1	Services			
Dry-cleaning & laundry services	0.1	Services			
Plastics products, nec	0.1	Manufg.			
Commercial & industrial equipment repair/maintenance	0.1	Services			
Handtools	0.1	Manufg.			
Paperboard mills	0.1	Manufg.			

Source: Benchmark Input-Output Accounts for the U.S. Economy, 2002, U.S. Department of Commerce, Washington, D.C., January 2008. The abbreviation nec stands for 'not elsewhere classified'.

OCCUPATIONS EMPLOYED BY INDUSTRIAL MACHINERY MANUFACTURING

Occupation	% of Total 2006	Change to 2016	Occupation	% of Total 2006	Change to 2016
Machinists	6.6	-14.0	Electrical engineers	1.6	-18.1
Team assemblers	5.5	-18.1	Structural metal fabricators & fitters	1.5	-18.1
Welders, cutters, solderers, & brazers	4.3	-12.8	Customer service representatives	1.5	-9.9
Mechanical engineers	4.0	-9.9	Grinding, lapping, polishing machine tool operators	1.4	-20.5
First-line supervisors/managers of production workers	3.8	-18.1	Office clerks, general	1.4	-19.3
Sales reps, wholesale & manufacturing, exc tech	2.5	-18.1	Cutting, punching, & press machine operators	1.4	-26.3
General & operations managers	2.3	-26.3	Engineering managers	1.4	-18.1
Electrical & electronic equipment assemblers	2.0	-34.5	Helpers--Production workers	1.3	-18.1
Computer-controlled machine tool operators	1.9	-9.9	Inspectors, testers, sorters, samplers, & weighers	1.2	-22.8
Shipping, receiving, & traffic clerks	1.8	-21.2	Sales representatives, wholesale & manufacturing, tech	1.2	-18.1
Electromechanical equipment assemblers	1.8	-18.1	Maintenance & repair workers, general	1.2	-18.1
Industrial machinery mechanics	1.8	-5.8	Accountants & auditors	1.1	-18.1
Purchasing agents, exc wholesale, retail, & farm	1.7	-18.1	Engine & other machine assemblers	1.1	-18.1
Bookkeeping, accounting, & auditing clerks	1.6	-18.1	Molding, coremaking, & casting machine operators	1.1	-26.3
Mechanical drafters	1.6	-17.1	Stock clerks & order fillers	1.1	-31.4
Industrial engineers	1.6	-0.5	Sales engineers	1.0	-18.1

Source: *Industry-Occupation Matrix*, Bureau of Labor Statistics, December 4, 2007. These data are reported based on 4-digit NAICS categories but have been matched to corresponding 6-digit NAICS industry codes. The change reported for each occupation to the year 2016 is a percent of growth or decline as estimated by the Bureau of Labor Statistics. The abbreviation nec stands for 'not elsewhere classified'.

LOCATION BY STATE AND REGIONAL CONCENTRATION

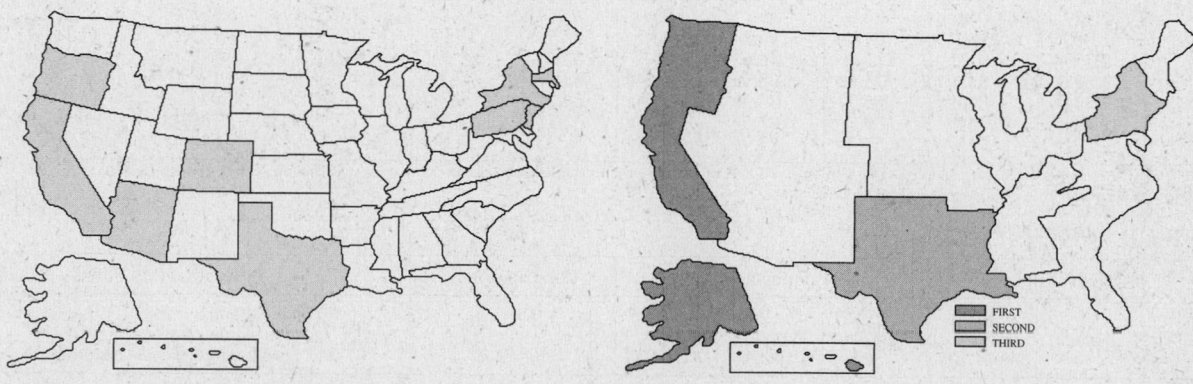

INDUSTRY DATA BY STATE

State	Establish-ments	Shipments Total ($ mil)	% of U.S.	Per Establ.	Employment Total Number	% of U.S.	Per Establ.	Wages ($/hour)	Cost as % of Shipments	Investment per Employee ($)
California	127	4,510.4	50.5	35,514.7	17,209	50.9	136	29.57	51.8	12,403
Massachusetts	19	1,149.0	12.9	60,473.6	4,787	14.2	252	30.72	47.7	11,438
Texas	34	1,106.2	12.4	32,534.4	2,835	8.4	83	17.78	52.5	33,581
Arizona	20	317.1	3.5	15,853.2	971	2.9	49	21.06	54.3	19,053
Oregon	6	283.0	3.2	47,172.3	979	2.9	163	15.22	48.3	24,760
New York	14	266.8	3.0	19,056.4	986	2.9	70	7.25	51.5	11,166
Colorado	6	165.2	1.8	27,537.5	482	1.4	80	13.70	71.1	13,774
Pennsylvania	9	128.9	1.4	14,322.1	612	1.8	68	20.09	53.4	8,191
New Jersey	9	44.2	0.5	4,912.8	200	0.6	22	16.64	55.2	14,015

Source: 2002 *Economic Census*. The states are in descending order of shipments or establishments (if shipment data are missing for the majority). The symbol (D) appears when data are withheld to prevent disclosure of competitive information. States marked with (D) are sorted by number of establishments. A dash (-) indicates that the data element cannot be calculated. Data may not show all states active in the NAICS category. All data available at the time of publication are shown.

NAICS 33329N - MACHINERY MANUFACTURING NEC*

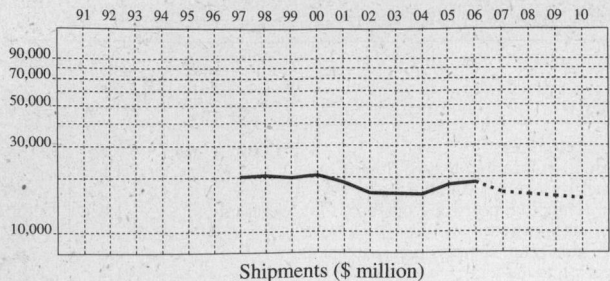

Shipments ($ million)

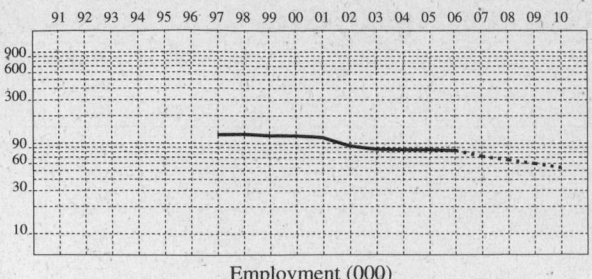

Employment (000)

GENERAL STATISTICS

| Year | Companies | Establishments | | Employment | | | Compensation | | Production ($ million) | | | |
		Total	with 20 or more employees	Total (000)	Production Workers (000)	Hours (Mil)	Payroll ($ mil)	Wages ($/hr)	Cost of Materials	Value Added by Manufacture	Value of Shipments	Capital Invest.
1997	3,487	3,658	1,309	124.2	71.9	144.9	4,777.8	15.76	9,636.2	10,638.2	20,214.6	645.2
1998		3,601	1,333	125.8	71.2	142.8	4,884.4	16.27	9,640.5	10,744.4	20,531.0	500.1
1999		3,575	1,289	121.5	70.5	139.1	4,887.7	16.23	9,490.6	10,458.6	19,951.0	574.5
2000		3,449	1,223	120.9	70.7	139.9	5,030.3	16.56	9,882.3	10,691.2	20,536.3	569.8
2001		3,325	1,180	115.4	65.5	128.8	4,768.2	16.54	8,938.6	9,481.9	18,703.0	486.7
2002	3,076	3,212	1,057	93.2	51.0	98.5	4,239.8	18.57	7,378.7	8,896.9	16,349.7	418.2
2003		3,050	1,038	85.8	47.7	93.3	4,074.0	18.91	7,622.7	8,605.3	16,267.6	293.2
2004		2,979	1,011	84.6	46.7	95.0	4,044.8	18.88	7,622.6	8,502.4	16,103.8	328.2
2005		2,920	980	84.8	46.8	94.7	4,299.0	19.55	8,992.6	9,217.3	18,151.4	339.8
2006		2,799P	912P	83.0	46.6	96.1	4,349.6	19.71	9,266.4	9,317.1	18,684.8	350.8
2007		2,697P	863P	71.6P	38.8P	78.4P	4,016.8P	20.39P	8,127.7P	8,172.1P	16,388.6P	253.9P
2008		2,595P	814P	65.7P	35.2P	71.4P	3,922.5P	20.88P	7,932.8P	7,976.2P	15,995.8P	218.2P
2009		2,494P	764P	59.8P	31.5P	64.3P	3,828.1P	21.37P	7,738.0P	7,780.3P	15,602.9P	182.4P
2010		2,392P	715P	54.0P	27.9P	57.2P	3,733.8P	21.86P	7,543.2P	7,584.4P	15,210.1P	146.6P

Sources: 1997 and 2002 *Economic Census*; other years, up to 2006, are from *Annual Survey of Manufactures*. Establishment counts for non-Census years are from *County Business Patterns*; 1997 and 2002 values are from the 1997 and 2002 censuses, respectively. 'P's show projections by the editors.

INDICES OF CHANGE

| Year | Companies | Establishments | | Employment | | | Compensation | | Production ($ million) | | | |
		Total	with 20 or more employees	Total (000)	Production Workers (000)	Hours (Mil)	Payroll ($ mil)	Wages ($/hr)	Cost of Materials	Value Added by Manufacture	Value of Shipments	Capital Invest.
1997	113	114	124	133	141	147	113	85	131	120	124	154
1998		112	126	135	140	145	115	88	131	121	126	120
1999		111	122	130	138	141	115	87	129	118	122	137
2000		107	116	130	139	142	119	89	134	120	126	136
2001		104	112	124	128	131	112	89	121	107	114	116
2002	100	100	100	100	100	100	100	100	100	100	100	100
2003		95	98	92	94	95	96	102	103	97	99	70
2004		93	96	91	92	96	95	102	103	96	98	78
2005		91	93	91	92	96	101	105	122	104	111	81
2006		87P	86P	89	91	98	103	106	126	105	114	84
2007		84P	82P	77P	76P	80P	95P	110P	110P	92P	100P	61P
2008		81P	77P	70P	69P	72P	93P	112P	108P	90P	98P	52P
2009		78P	72P	64P	62P	65P	90P	115P	105P	87P	95P	44P
2010		74P	68P	58P	55P	58P	88P	118P	102P	85P	93P	35P

Sources: Same as General Statistics. Values reflect change from the base year, 2002. Values above 100 mean greater than 2002, values below 100 mean less than 2002, and the values of 100 in other years means the same as 2002. 'P's show projections by the editors.

SELECTED RATIOS

For 2002	Avg. of All Manufact.	Analyzed Industry	Index	For 2002	Avg. of All Manufact.	Analyzed Industry	Index
Employees per Establishment	42	29	69	Value Added per Production Worker	182,367	174,449	96
Payroll per Establishment	1,639,184	1,319,988	81	Cost per Establishment	5,769,015	2,297,229	40
Payroll per Employee	39,053	45,491	116	Cost per Employee	137,446	79,171	58
Production Workers per Establishment	30	16	54	Cost per Production Worker	195,506	144,680	74
Wages per Establishment	694,845	569,472	82	Shipments per Establishment	11,158,348	5,090,193	46
Wages per Production Worker	23,548	35,866	152	Shipments per Employee	265,847	175,426	66
Hours per Production Worker	1,980	1,931	98	Shipments per Production Worker	378,144	320,582	85
Wages per Hour	11.89	18.57	156	Investment per Establishment	361,338	130,199	36
Value Added per Establishment	5,381,325	2,769,894	51	Investment per Employee	8,609	4,487	52
Value Added per Employee	128,210	95,460	74	Investment per Production Worker	12,245	8,200	67

Sources: Same as General Statistics. The 'Average of All Manufacturing' column represents the average of all manufacturing industries reported for the most recent complete year available. The Index shows the relationship between the Average and the Analyzed Industry. For example, 100 means that they are equal; 500 that the Analyzed Industry is five times the average; 50 means that the Analyzed Industry is half the national average. The abbreviation 'na' is used to show that data are 'not available'. Ratios shown for 2002, the last complete census year.

*Equivalent to Federal Government NAICS 333291, 333292, 333293, 333294, 333298.

LEADING COMPANIES

Number shown: **75**   Total sales ($ mil): **303,573**   Total employment (000): **621.1**

Company Name	Address				CEO Name	Phone	Co. Type	Sales ($ mil)	Empl. (000)
General Electric Co.	3135 Easton Tpk.	Fairfield	CT	06828		203-373-2211	P	172,738	327.0
Air Products & Chemicals	7201 Hamilton Blvd.	Allentown	PA	18195		610-481-4911	P	10,038	22.1
Applied Materials Inc.	PO Box 58039	Santa Clara	CA	95052		408-727-5555	P	9,735	15.3
Dover Corp.	280 Park Ave.	New York	NY	10017		212-922-1640	P	7,226	33.4
Silver King Refrigeration Inc.	1600 Xenium Ln. N	Plymouth	MN	55441	Korey Kohl	763-553-1881	S	7,000*	<0.1
Etec Systems Inc.	PO Box 58039	Santa Clara	CA	95052		408-727-5555	S	6,992	12.2
Saint-Gobain Abrasives Inc.	1 New Bond St.	Worcester	MA	01606	Jean Phelizon	508-795-5000	R	6,831*	2.5
Metso Power	3430 Toringdon	Charlotte	NC	28277	David King	704-541-1453	R	6,340*	<0.1
Metso Texas Shredder Inc.	11451 J. Maltsbergr	San Antonio	TX	78216	John Duncan	210-491-9521	R	6,340*	<0.1
Voith Paper Inc.	PO Box 2337	Appleton	WI	54912	Otto Heissenberger	920-731-7724	R	4,320*	0.2
Foster Wheeler Ltd.	Perryville Corp Prk	Clinton	NJ	08809	Umberto Dello Sala	908-730-4000	P	3,495	12.0
Parkson Corp.	PO Box 408399	Fort Lauderdale	FL	33340	William Acton	954-974-6610	R	3,330*	0.1
Cornelius IMI Inc.	101 Broadway St. W	Osseo	MN	55369	Richard Barkley	763-488-8200	R	2,840*	0.3
Schreiber Foods Inc.	PO Box 19010	Green Bay	WI	54307	David Pozniak	920-437-7601	R	2,500*	5.0
Volt Information Sciences Inc.	560 Lexington Ave.	New York	NY	10022		212-704-2400	P	2,353	43.0
A.O. Smith Corp.	PO Box 245008	Milwaukee	WI	53224		414-359-4000	P	2,312	16.8
NTK Holdings Inc.	50 Kennedy Plz.	Providence	RI	02903	Richard L. Bready	401-751-1600	S	2,218	9.8
Fluid Management Operations	1023 Wheeling Rd.	Wheeling	IL	60090	Lawrence D. Kingsley	847-537-0880	S	1,935*	4.3
FM Delaware Inc.	1023 Wheeling Rd.	Wheeling	IL	60090	Lawrence D. Kingsley	847-537-0880	S	1,935*	4.3
Renco Group Inc.	30 Rockefeller Plz.	New York	NY	10112	Ira Leno Rennert	212-541-6000	R	1,900	9.4
Knight L.L.C.	20531 Crescent Bay	Lake Forest	CA	92630	George Noa	949-595-4800	S	1,889*	4.2
Saurer Holding Inc.	1575 W 124th Ave.	Denver	CO	80234	Peter Kern	303-457-1234	R	1,850*	0.2
GE Infrastructure Water/Proc.	4636 Somerton Rd.	Trevose	PA	19053	George Oliver	215-355-3300	R	1,769*	4.0
Berwind L.L.C.	1500 Market St.	Philadelphia	PA	19102	Michael McClelland	215-563-2800	R	1,710	3.5
Lam Research Corp.	PO Box 5010	Fremont	CA	94537	James W. Bagley	510-572-0200	P	1,642	2.4
Rainin Instrument L.L.C.	PO Box 4026	Woburn	MA	01888	Kenneth Rainin	510-564-1600	R	1,590*	0.1
Novellus Systems Inc.	4000 N First St.	San Jose	CA	95134		408-943-9700	P	1,570	3.7
Sharp Manufacturing Co.	4050 S Mendenhall	Memphis	TN	38115	Saiko Hanatani	901-795-6510	S	1,508*	0.8
Rycoline Products L.L.C.	PO Box 97043	Chicago	IL	60690		773-775-6755	R	1,370*	<0.1
Goss International Corp.	3 Territorial Ct.	Bolingbrook	IL	60440	Robert A. Brown	630-755-9300	R	1,140	4.1
Nesco Inc.	6140 Parkland Blvd.	Mayfield Hgts	OH	44124	Robert J. Tomsich	440-461-6000	R	1,133*	10.3
ASM Lithography Holding Inc.	8555 S River Pkwy.	Tempe	AZ	85284	Eric Meurice	480-383-4422	R	1,022*	2.5
Sulzer Inc.	555 5th Ave., 15th	New York	NY	10017	Kelli Edell	212-949-0999	S	1,000*	4.5
Alcoa Closure Systems Intl	6625 Network Way	Indianapolis	IN	46278	V. Lance Mitchell	317-390-5000	S	980*	3.0
P.R. Hoffman Machine Products	1517 Commerce	Carlisle	PA	17015		717-243-9900	S	812*	<0.1
Milacron Inc.	PO Box 63716	Cincinnati	OH	45206	Ronald D. Brown	513-487-5000	P	808	3.5
Marquip L.L.C.	PO Box 28	Phillips	WI	54555		715-339-2191	R	786*	0.4
MKS Instruments Inc.	90 Industrial Way	Wilmington	MA	01887	Leo Berlinghieri	978-284-4000	P	783	3.0
Dover Diversified Inc.	Highland Oaks I	Downers Grove	IL	60515	William W. Spurgeon	630-725-9347	S	781*	4.0
Dawn Food Products Inc.	3333 Sargent Rd.	Jackson	MI	49201	Miles Jones	517-789-4400	R	751*	2.8
Brooks Automation Inc.	15 Elizabeth Dr.	Chelmsford	MA	01824		978-262-2400	P	743	1.9
Bakemark USA L.L.C.	7351 Crider Ave.	Pico Rivera	CA	90660		562-949-1054	R	733*	0.2
Progressive Tool & Ind./Wisne	21000 Telegraph Rd.	Southfield	MI	48034	Robert Stoutenburg	248-353-8888	D	733*	5.5
Kulicke and Soffa Industries	1005 Virginia Dr.	Fort Washington	PA	19034		215-784-6000	P	700	2.6
Freshflush L.L.C.	5980 Miami Lakes	Miami Lakes	FL	33014	Harry Shulman	305-362-2611	S	673*	0.3
Bachman Machine Co.	4321 N Broadway	St. Louis	MO	63147	William Bachman	314-231-4221	R	656*	0.1
Enodis Corp.	2227 Welbilt Blvd.	New Port Richey	FL	34655	Peter Brooks	727-375-7010	S	650*	3.0
Riley Power Inc.	PO Box 15040	Worcester	MA	01615		508-852-7100	R	612*	0.4
FEI Co.	5350 NE Dawson	Hillsboro	OR	97124		503-726-7500	P	593	1.8
Gerber Scientific Inc.	83 Gerber Rd. W	South Windsor	CT	06074	Donald P. Aiken	860-644-1551	P	575	2.2
J and J Snack Foods Corp.	6000 Central Hwy.	Pennsauken	NJ	08109		856-665-9534	P	569	2.6
Fisher Scientific	2000 Park Lane Dr.	Pittsburgh	PA	15275	David Dellapenta	412-490-8300	D	568	1.8
Salton Inc.	1955 W Field Ct.	Lake Forest	IL	60045	Leonhard Dreimann	847-803-4600	P	523	1.0
APV Americas	105 Crosspoint Pky.	Getzville	NY	14068	Haluk Drougan	716-692-3000	S	521*	2.5
Cymer Inc.	17075 Thornmint Ct.	San Diego	CA	92127	Robert Akins	858-385-7300	P	521	1.0
UOP L.L.C.	25 E Algonquin Rd.	Des Plaines	IL	60017	Carlos Guimaraes	847-391-2000	R	500*	4.0
Newport Corp.	1791 Deere Ave.	Irvine	CA	92606	Michael ONeill	949-863-3144	P	445	2.0
Devro Inc.	PO Box 11925	Columbia	SC	29211	Gordon Frame	803-796-9730	R	430*	0.3
Universal Instruments Corp.	PO Box 825	Binghamton	NY	13902	Gerhard Meese	607-779-7689	S	424*	1.2
Bottcher America Corp.	4600 Mercedes Dr.	Belcamp	MD	21017	Larry Lowe	410-273-7000	R	413*	0.1
Axcelis Technologies Inc.	108 Cherry Hill Dr.	Beverly	MA	01915		978-787-4000	P	405	1.6
Veeco Instruments Inc.	100 Sunnyside Blvd.	Woodbury	NY	11797	Edward H. Braun	516-677-0200	P	403	1.3
Kadant Inc.	1 Tec. Park Dr.	Westford	MA	01886		978-776-2000	P	367	2.0
FANUC Robotics America Inc.	3900 W Hamlin Rd.	Rochester Hills	MI	48309		248-377-7000	R	361*	0.9
Wall Colmonoy Corp.	101 West Girard	Madison Heights	MI	48071		248-585-6400	R	336*	0.3
Hardinge Inc.	PO Box 1507	Elmira	NY	14902	J. Patrick Ervin	607-734-2281	P	327	1.5
Gruber Systems Inc.	25636 Ave. Stanford	Valencia	CA	91355	John Hoskinson	661-257-4060	R	322*	0.3
Danieli Corp.	800 Cranberry Wds	Cranberry Twp	PA	16066	Mark Brandon	724-778-5400	R	306*	<0.1
Welex Inc.	850 Jolly Rd.	Blue Bell	PA	19422	Frank R. Nissel	215-542-8000	R	300*	0.1
American Water Heater Co.	PO Box 4056	Johnson City	TN	37602	Robert Trudeau	423-283-8000	R	278*	<0.1
Hitachi Metals America Limited	2 Manhattanville Rd	Purchase	NY	10577		914-694-9200	R	274*	<0.1
P and H Mining Equipment Inc.	PO Box 310	Milwaukee	WI	53201	Mark Readinger	414-671-4400	S	272*	0.9
Mattson Technology Inc.	47131 Bayside Pky.	Fremont	CA	94538	David Dutton		P	267	0.6
Presstek Inc.	55 Executive Dr.	Hudson	NH	03051		603-594-8585	P	266	0.9
Pentaplast of America Inc.	PO Box 500	Gordonsville	VA	22942	Tom Goke	540-832-3600	S	237*	1.0

Source: Ward's Business Directory of U.S. Private and Public Companies, Volumes 1 and 2, 2008. The company type code used is as follows: P - Public, R - Private, S - Subsidiary, D - Division, J - Joint Venture, A - Affiliate, G - Group. Sales are in millions of dollars, employees are in thousands. An asterisk (*) indicates an estimated sales volume. The symbol < stands for 'less than'. Company names and addresses are truncated, in some cases, to fit into the available space.

MATERIALS CONSUMED FOR PAPER INDUSTRY MACHINERY MANUFACTURING

Material	Quantity	Delivered Cost ($ million)
Electrical transmission, distribution, and control equipment	(X)	19.4
Fluid power pumps, motors, and hydrostatic transmissions	(X)	3.5
All other pumps	(X)	0.8
Fluid power valves (hydraulic and pneumatic)	(X)	(D)
Fluid power cylinders and rotary actuators (hydraulic and pneumatic)	(X)	(D)
Fluid power hose, tube fittings, and assemblies (hydraulic and pneumatic)	(X)	0.9
Fluid power filters (hydraulic and pneumatic)	(X)	0.4
Other fluid power products, hydraulic and pneumatic	(X)	1.7
Fabricated metal products (excluding forgings)	(X)	36.1
Forgings	(S)	3.0
Iron and steel castings (rough and semifinished)	(X)	47.0
Nonferrous (aluminum, copper, etc.) castings (rough and semifinished)	(X)	2.3
Steel bars, bar shapes, and plates (exc. castings, forgings, fabr. metal products)	(X)	29.6
Steel sheet and strip (including tinplate)	(S)	8.1
All other steel shapes and forms (exc. castings, forgings, fabr. metal products)	(X)	3.8
Nonferrous shapes and forms	(X)	2.0
Integral horsepower electric motors and generators (1 hp or more)	(X)	13.5
Ball bearings (mounted or unmounted)	(X)	4.5
Roller bearings (mounted or unmounted)	(X)	3.5
Plain bearings and bushings	(X)	4.1
Mechanical speed changers, gears, and industrial high-speed drives	(X)	11.6
Fabricated rubber products (exc. tires, tubes, hoses, belting, and gaskets)	(X)	8.6
All other materials, components, parts, containers, and supplies	(X)	203.5
Materials, ingredients, containers, and supplies, nsk	(X)	358.5

Source: 2002 *Economic Census*. Explanation of symbols used: (D): Withheld to avoid disclosure of competitive data; na: Not available; (S): Withheld because statistical norms were not met; (X): Not applicable; (Z): Less than half the unit shown; nec: Not elsewhere classified; nsk: Not specified by kind; - : zero; p : 10-19 percent estimated; q : 20-29 percent estimated.

MATERIALS CONSUMED FOR TEXTILE MACHINERY MANUFACTURING

Material	Quantity	Delivered Cost ($ million)
Fluid power products	(X)	10.4
Fabricated metal products (excluding forgings)	(X)	20.9
Forgings	(X)	3.4
Iron and steel castings (rough and semifinished)	(X)	7.4
Aluminum and aluminum-base alloy castings (rough and semifinished)	(X)	4.0
Other nonferrous metal castings, rough or semifinished (inc. aluminum)	(X)	2.1
Steel bars, bar shapes, and plates (exc. castings, forgings, fabr. metal products)	(X)	7.0
Steel sheet and strip (including tinplate)	(X)	3.1
Steel structural shapes and sheet piling (exc. castings, forgings, fabr. metal products)	(X)	(D)
Steel wire and wire products	(X)	12.0
All other steel shapes and forms (exc. castings, forgings, fabr. metal products)	(X)	2.9
Aluminum and aluminum-base alloy shapes and forms (exc. castings, forgings, fabr. metal products)	(X)	1.9
Other nonferrous shapes and forms (exc. castings, forgings, fabricated metal products)	(X)	1.2
Integral horsepower electric motors and generators (1 hp or more)	(X)	(D)
Ball bearings (mounted or unmounted)	(X)	3.8
Roller bearings (mounted or unmounted)	(X)	1.7
Speed reducers, gears, drives, and other mechanical power transmission equipment (exc. bearings)	(X)	4.2
Fabricated plastics products (excluding gaskets)	(X)	5.1
Electrical transmission, distribution, and control equipment	(X)	23.6
All other materials, components, parts, containers, and supplies	(X)	59.7
Materials, ingredients, containers, and supplies, nsk	(X)	148.6

Source: 2002 *Economic Census*. Explanation of symbols used: (D): Withheld to avoid disclosure of competitive data; na: Not available; (S): Withheld because statistical norms were not met; (X): Not applicable; (Z): Less than half the unit shown; nec: Not elsewhere classified; nsk: Not specified by kind; - : zero; p : 10-19 percent estimated; q : 20-29 percent estimated.

MATERIALS CONSUMED FOR PRINTING MACHINERY AND EQUIPMENT MANUFACTURING

Material	Quantity	Delivered Cost ($ million)
Fluid power products	(X)	13.4
Fabricated metal products (excluding forgings)	(X)	187.7
Forgings	(X)	4.1
Iron and steel castings (rough and semifinished)	(X)	29.5
Nonferrous (aluminum, copper, etc.) castings (rough and semifinished)	(X)	7.5
Steel bars, bar shapes, and plates (exc. castings, forgings, fabr. metal products)	(X)	20.4
All other steel shapes and forms (exc. castings, forgings, fabr. metal products)	(X)	11.6
Aluminum and aluminum-base alloy shapes and forms (exc. castings, forgings, fabr. metal products)	(X)	17.3
Other nonferrous shapes and forms (exc. castings, forgings, fabricated metal products)	(X)	3.5
Fractional horsepower electric motors and generators (less than 1 hp)	(X)	9.6
Integral horsepower electric motors and generators (1 hp or more)	(X)	6.6
Ball bearings (mounted or unmounted)	(X)	9.5

Continued on next page.

MATERIALS CONSUMED FOR PRINTING MACHINERY AND EQUIPMENT MANUFACTURING - Continued

Material	Quantity	Delivered Cost ($ million)
Roller bearings (mounted or unmounted)	(X)	6.1
Mechanical speed changers, gears, and industrial high-speed drives	(X)	11.8
Electrical transmission, distribution, and control equipment	(X)	26.7
All other materials, components, parts, containers, and supplies	(X)	342.9
Materials, ingredients, containers, and supplies, nsk	(X)	459.7

Source: 2002 Economic Census. Explanation of symbols used: (D): Withheld to avoid disclosure of competitive data; na: Not available; (S): Withheld because statistical norms were not met; (X): Not applicable; (Z): Less than half the unit shown; nec: Not elsewhere classified; nsk: Not specified by kind; - : zero; p : 10-19 percent estimated; q : 20-29 percent estimated.

MATERIALS CONSUMED FOR FOOD PRODUCT MACHINERY MANUFACTURING

Material	Quantity	Delivered Cost ($ million)
Fluid power pumps, motors, and hydrostatic transmissions	(X)	12.3
All other pumps	(X)	4.4
Fluid power valves (hydraulic and pneumatic)	(X)	8.3
Fluid power cylinders and rotary actuators (hydraulic and pneumatic)	(X)	3.9
Fluid power hose, tube fittings, and assemblies (hydraulic and pneumatic)	(X)	4.7
Fluid power filters (hydraulic and pneumatic)	(X)	1.5
Other fluid power products, hydraulic and pneumatic	(X)	3.1
Metal tanks, heat exchangers, and other boiler products	(X)	37.8
All other fabricated metal products (excluding forgings)	(X)	77.1
Forgings	(X)	4.1
Iron and steel castings (rough and semifinished)	(X)	17.4
Aluminum and aluminum-base alloy castings (rough and semifinished)	(X)	8.8
Other nonferrous metal castings, rough or semifinished (inc. aluminum)	(X)	4.6
Steel bars, bar shapes, and plates (exc. castings, forgings, fabr. metal products)	(X)	38.4
Steel sheet and strip (including tinplate)	(X)	34.8
All other steel shapes and forms (exc. castings, forgings, fabr. metal products)	(X)	15.9
Aluminum and aluminum-base alloy sheet, plate, foil, and welded tubing	(X)	9.5
All other aluminum and aluminum-base alloy shapes and forms (exc. castings, forgings, fabr. metal products)	(X)	2.2
Other nonferrous shapes and forms (exc. castings, forgings, fabricated metal products)	(X)	9.9
Fractional horsepower electric motors and generators (less than 1 hp)	(X)	9.3
Integral horsepower electric motors and generators (1 hp or more)	(X)	14.0
Ball and roller bearings (mounted or unmounted)	(X)	12.2
Mechanical speed changers, gears, and industrial high-speed drives	(X)	13.2
Electrical transmission, distribution, and control equipment	(X)	31.7
Aluminum and aluminum-base alloy shapes and forms (exc. castings, forgings, fabr. metal products)	(X)	(D)
Wood boxes, pallets, skids, and containers	(X)	4.3
Other nonferrous shapes and forms (exc. castings, forgings, fabricated metal products)	(X)	(D)
All other materials, components, parts, containers, and supplies	(X)	223.6
Materials, ingredients, containers, and supplies, nsk	(X)	397.4

Source: 2002 Economic Census. Explanation of symbols used: (D): Withheld to avoid disclosure of competitive data; na: Not available; (S): Withheld because statistical norms were not met; (X): Not applicable; (Z): Less than half the unit shown; nec: Not elsewhere classified; nsk: Not specified by kind; - : zero; p : 10-19 percent estimated; q : 20-29 percent estimated.

MATERIALS CONSUMED FOR INDUSTRIAL MACHINERY MANUFACTURING NEC

Material	Quantity	Delivered Cost ($ million)
Electrical transmission, distribution, and control equipment	(X)	88.5
Fluid power pumps, motors, and hydrostatic transmissions	(X)	37.7
Other pumps and pump parts, excluding fluid power (complete assemblies)	(X)	17.3
Fluid power valves (hydraulic and pneumatic)	(X)	32.1
Fluid power cylinders and rotary actuators (hydraulic and pneumatic)	(X)	10.4
Fluid power hose, tube fittings, and assemblies (hydraulic and pneumatic)	(X)	5.9
Fluid power filters (hydraulic and pneumatic)	(X)	5.4
Other fluid power products, hydraulic and pneumatic	(X)	4.0
Metal bolts, nuts, screws, and other screw machine products	(X)	22.5
Metal tanks, heat exchangers, and other boiler products	(X)	49.7
Metal pipe, valves, and pipe fittings (excluding forgings)	(X)	31.2
Other fabricated metal products (exc. fluid power products and forgings)	(X)	156.7
Forgings	(X)	4.9
Iron and steel castings (rough and semifinished)	(X)	46.5
Aluminum and aluminum-base alloy castings (rough and semifinished)	(X)	18.2
Other nonferrous metal castings, rough or semifinished (inc. aluminum)	(X)	13.3
Steel bars, bar shapes, and plates (exc. castings, forgings, fabr. metal products)	(X)	93.0
Steel sheet and strip (including tinplate)	(X)	98.3
Steel structural shapes and sheet piling (exc. castings, forgings, fabr. metal products)	(X)	22.5
All other steel shapes and forms (exc. castings, forgings, fabr. metal products)	(X)	44.7
Aluminum and aluminum-base alloy sheet, plate, foil, and welded tubing	(X)	13.2
All other aluminum and aluminum-base alloy shapes and forms (exc. castings, forgings, fabr. metal products)	(X)	8.5
Other nonferrous shapes and forms (exc. castings, forgings, fabricated metal products)	(X)	16.2

Continued on next page.

MATERIALS CONSUMED FOR INDUSTRIAL MACHINERY MANUFACTURING NEC - Continued

Material	Quantity	Delivered Cost ($ million)
Fractional horsepower electric motors and generators (less than 1 hp)	(X)	12.5
Integral horsepower electric motors and generators (1 hp or more)	(X)	26.1
Ball and roller bearings (mounted or unmounted)	(X)	9.7
Mechanical speed changers, gears, and industrial high-speed drives	(X)	17.7
Gold and other precious metals, all forms (incl. ingot, sheet, etc.)	(X)	0.6
Printed ciruit boards (without inserted components) for electronic circuitry	(X)	(D)
Printed circuit assemblies, loaded boards, and modules	(X)	52,8
Filter paper	(X)	(D)
All other materials, components, parts, containers, and supplies	(X)	894.1
Materials, ingredients, containers, and supplies, nsk	(X)	860.0

Source: 2002 Economic Census. Explanation of symbols used: (D): Withheld to avoid disclosure of competitive data; na: Not available; (S): Withheld because statistical norms were not met; (X): Not applicable; (Z): Less than half the unit shown; nec: Not elsewhere classified; nsk: Not specified by kind; - : zero; p : 10-19 percent estimated; q : 20-29 percent estimated.

PRODUCT SHARE DETAILS FOR PAPER INDUSTRY MACHINERY MANUFACTURING

Product or Product Class Shipments	Mil. $	Product or Product Class Shipments	Mil. $
PAPER INDUSTRIES MACHINERY	1,649.2	paper pulp, paper, and paperboard and paper and paperboard cutting machines, etc.	395.2
Paper industries machinery	**939.8**	Paper and paperboard cutting machines, except sheeters and winders	12.0
Paper industries wood preparations equipment and other paper industries pulp mill machinery, including pulp mill digesters and deckers, etc.	246.8	Machines for making paper and paperboard bags, sacks, or envelopes	19.4
Paper industries wood preparations equipment, including debarkers, chippers, knotters, splitters, chipscreens, water jet bark strippers, etc.	22.0	Paper and paperboard corrugated box making machines	138.7
Paper industries pulp mill grinders and refiners (TMP) for the manufacture of mechanical pulp	27.7	Machines for making paper and paperboard cartons, boxes, cases, tubes, drums, or similar containers, except by molding	69.3
Paper industries pulp mill deckers, thickeners, wet lap machines, bleaching equipment, pulp screens, washers, and save-alls	(D)	Other paper and paperboard converting equipment, nec, for finishing paper or paperboard	17.9
Paper mill stock preparation equipment, including refiners (chip, conical, deflaker, disk, etc.), pulpers, beaters, jordans, etc.	75.3	Other paper and paperboard converting equipment, nec, for converting paper and paperboard	138.1
Paper mill paper making machines	100.1	Paper industries machinery, nsk	66.7
Paper mill paper making machines, dryers for paper pulp, paper, or paperboard	44.1	**Parts and attachments for paper industries machinery (sold separately).**	**538.6**
Other paper mill paper making machines (including headbox forming area, presses, and reels)	55.9	Parts and attachments for paper industries wood preparation equipment (sold separately)	13.4
Paper mill coating machines, calendering and rolling machines, and other paper machines.	66.6	Parts and attachments for paper industries pulp mill machinery (sold separately)	51.1
Paper mill paper coating machines, including equipment for applying sizing and pigment coating to paper	3.5	Parts and attachments for paper industry machines for finishing paper (sold separately)	199.6
Paper mill paper calendering and similar rolling machines for finishing paper	12.2	Parts and attachments for paper mill machinery, except machines for finishing paper	78.0
Other paper mill paper machines	50.9	Parts and attachments for paper and paperboard converting equipment (sold separately)	150.1
Paper mill machines for finishing paper, except calendering or similar rolling	64.5	Parts and attachments for paper industries machinery (sold separately), nsk.	46.4
Machines for making bags, boxes, molding articles in		**Paper industries machinery, nsk, total**	**170.8**

Source: 2002 Economic Census. The values are product shipments in millions of dollars for 2002. Total product shipments may be lower or higher than industry shipments. See Introduction for a full discussion. Values of indented subcategories are summed in the main heading(s). The symbol (D) appears when data are withheld to prevent disclosure of competitive information. The abbreviation nsk stands for 'not specified by kind' and nec for 'not elsewhere classified'. A dash (-) means zero.

PRODUCT SHARE DETAILS FOR TEXTILE MACHINERY MANUFACTURING

Product or Product Class Shipments	Mil. $	Product or Product Class Shipments	Mil. $
TEXTILE MACHINERY	823.0	**Parts and attachments for textile machinery**	**285.1**
Textile machinery (except parts, attachments, and accessories)	**503.5**	Textile machinery turnings and shapes, including bobbins, shuttles, spools, picker sticks, caps, etc.	10.1
Fiber to fabric textile machinery, except parts, attachments, and accessories	198.2	Textile machinery turnings and shapes, shuttles	2.2
Cleaning and opening fiber-to-fabric textile machinery	3.0	Other textile machinery turnings and shapes, of plastics	0.4
Carding and combing fiber-to-fabric textile machines	9.8	Other textile machinery turnings and shapes, except plastics	7.5
Other fiber-to-fabrics textile machinery	(D)	Parts and attachments for fiber-to-fabric card clothing machinery	(D)
Fiber-to-fabric yarn winding machines (skein, spool, bobbin, quill, cone, etc.)	22.9	Parts and attachments for other fiber-to-fabric machinery, except card clothing	46.5
Other fiber-to-fabric yarn preparing machines (beaming, warping, warp tying, warp drawing in, slashing, etc.)	24.6	Dobbies and jacquards; card reducing, copy, punching, and assembling machines	0.2
Machines for extruding, drawing, texturing, or cutting manmade textile materials	103.7	Extruding, drawing, texturing and cutting manmade fibers, or for their auxiliary machines	22.9
Fabric weaving machinery, power-driven (including machinery for broad and narrow fabrics), shuttle and shuttleless	(D)	Preparing textile fibers or of their auxiliary machines	3.5
Fabric knitting machinery	22.0	Spindles, spindle flyers, spinning rings, and ring travelers	0.2
Other fabrics machinery, including lace, embroidery, braiding, and tufting machinery and hand looms	87.9	Other parts and attachments for fiber-to-fabric machinery and for their auxiliary machinery	19.5
Hand looms machinery	4.2	Parts and attachments for weaving machinery	74.0
Other fabrics machinery (including lace, embroidery, braiding, and tufting machinery)	83.6	Parts and attachments for weaving machinery, reeds for looms, healds and heald-frames	61.0
Textile bleaching, mercerizing, and dyeing machinery	30.3	Other parts and attachments of weaving machines or their auxiliary machinery	12.9
Textile printing machinery	71.0	Parts and attachments for knitting machinery	(D)
Industrial textile laser printing systems and equipment	(D)	Parts and attachments for knitting machinery, sinkers, and other articles used forming stitches, except needles	(D)
Textile printing machinery	65.4	Other parts and attachments for knitting machinery	2.7
Textile machinery for drying stocks, yarns, cloth, carpet, nonwoven, etc.	(D)	Parts and attachments for finishing machinery	40.4
Textile finishing machinery, including calendering or rolling	31.2	Parts and attachments for finishing machinery, calendering, and rolling machines	3.5
Finishing machinery, calendering or rolling machines	3.3	Other parts and attachments for finishing machines	36.9
Other finishing machinery	28.0	Other parts and attachments for textile machinery, nec (including printing)	90.9
Other textile machinery, nec	56.8	Parts and attachments for textile machinery, nsk	6.1
Machinery for the manufacture of finished felt and nonwovens in the piece or in shapes	(D)	**Textile machinery, nsk, total**	**34.4**
Textile rope and cablemaking machinery	(D)		
Other textile industries machinery, nec	49.8		
Textile machinery, nsk	28.1		

Source: 2002 *Economic Census*. The values are product shipments in millions of dollars for 2002. Total product shipments may be lower or higher than industry shipments. See Introduction for a full discussion. Values of indented subcategories are summed in the main heading(s). The symbol (D) appears when data are withheld to prevent disclosure of competitive information. The abbreviation nsk stands for 'not specified by kind' and nec for 'not elsewhere classified'. A dash (-) means zero.

PRODUCT SHARE DETAILS FOR PRINTING MACHINERY AND EQUIPMENT MANUFACTURING

Product or Product Class Shipments	Mil. $	Product or Product Class Shipments	Mil. $
PRINTING MACHINERY AND EQUIPMENT	2,711.6	Printing trades newspaper inserting equipment	(D)
Printing presses, offset lithographic	**373.5**	Other printing trades binding machinery and equipment, including stitchers and trimmers	37.8
Sheet-fed offset lithographic printing presses	32.2	Binding machinery and equipment, including paper cutting, collating, and gathering machines, nsk	45.1
Small sheet-fed offset lithographic printing presses, less than 14 inches	11.4	**Printing trades machinery, nec**	**1,428.5**
Other sheet-fed offset lithographic printing presses, 14 inches or more	20.9	Prepress preparatory equipment, excluding typesetting equipment and cameras, but including engravers materials and equipment	671.7
Offset roll-fed (web-fed) lithographic newspaper printing presses	130.0	Digital electronic prepress systems, components, and elements, including scanners, digitizers, recorders, digital previewers, etc..	326.6
Offset roll-fed (web-fed) lithographic printing presses for business forms and other uses	(D)	Other prepress preparatory equipment	27.5
Offset roll-fed (web-fed) lithographic commercial (including heat-set) printing presses	183.0	Industrial etching and engraving laser systems and equipment	79.8
Printing presses, offset lithographic, nsk	15.0	Engravers' materials and equipment, printing type, blocks, plates, cylinders, and other printing components	227.1
Printing presses, other than lithographic	**334.1**	Other printing trades engravers' materials and equipment	10.7
Sheet-fed and roll-fed (web-fed) flexographic printing presses	148.2	Parts, attachments, and accessories for printing presses, including flying pasters, dryers, folders, and reels	295.7
Other printing presses	128.3	Parts, attachments, and accessories for typesetting machines, all types, sold separately	(D)
Gravure printing machinery	57.3	Parts, attachments, and accessories for bindery equipment, all types, sold separately	18.5
Industrial laser printing press systems and equipment	(D)	Parts, attachments, and accessories for prepress preparatory equipment, excluding typesetting and camera parts, sold separately	(D)
Other printing presses, including metal decorating, proof, screen, pad printing, letterpress, and rebuilt printing presses	(D)	Parts, attachments, and accessories for other printing trades machinery and equipment, all types, sold separately	139.2
Printing presses, other than lithographic, nsk	57.5	Other printing trades machinery and equipment, including platens, except typewriters	200.1
Typesetting machinery, excluding justifying typewriters	**(D)**	Printing trades machinery, nec, nsk	87.0
Phototypesetting machines and other typesetting machinery	(D)	**Printing machinery and equipment, nsk, total**	**317.9**
Binding machinery and equipment, including paper cutting, collating, and gathering machines	**(D)**		
Binding machinery and equipment, including paper cutting, collating, and gathering machines	(D)		
Saddle, perfect-adhesive, and hard case (edition) printing trades binding equipment	(D)		
Printing trades paper cutting machines	15.1		
Printing trades collating and gathering machines (sold separately)	21.9		
Printing trades folding machines	29.6		

Source: 2002 *Economic Census*. The values are product shipments in millions of dollars for 2002. Total product shipments may be lower or higher than industry shipments. See Introduction for a full discussion. Values of indented subcategories are summed in the main heading(s). The symbol (D) appears when data are withheld to prevent disclosure of competitive information. The abbreviation nsk stands for 'not specified by kind' and nec for 'not elsewhere classified'. A dash (-) means zero.

PRODUCT SHARE DETAILS FOR FOOD PRODUCT MACHINERY MANUFACTURING

Product or Product Class Shipments	Mil. $	Product or Product Class Shipments	Mil. $
FOOD PRODUCTS MACHINERY	2,471.3	Industrial machinery, nec, for the preparation of fruits, vegetables, and nuts (not including the extraction or preparation of fixed vegetable oils)	34.4
Dairy and milk products plant machinery and equipment, except bottling and packaging	**299.2**	Industrial machinery and equipment for freezing and rapid chilling of food products	18.2
Industrial machinery and equipment for treating milk and dairy products by means of a change in temperature	215.9	Industrial driers for the manufacture of food products	9.3
Other dairy and milk products plant machinery and equipment	44.5	Industrial machinery and equipment, nec, for treating food products by a process involving a change in temperature (e.g., cooking or roasting)	69.0
Parts and attachments for dairy and milk products plant machinery and equipment, except for bottling and packaging equipment	38.8	Industrial machines for cleaning, sorting, or grading seed, grain, or dried leguminous vegetables	20.7
Commercial food products machinery, except packaging machinery and food cooking and warming equipment	**994.8**	Other industrial machinery used in the milling industry and for working of cereals or dried leguminous vegetables	(D)
Commercial food products slicers	88.1	Industrial machinery, nec, for the extraction or preparation of animal and fixed vegetable fats or oils	(D)
Commercial food products choppers, grinders, cutters, dicers, and similar machines	110.7	Other industrial food and feed products machinery	243.3
Commercial food products mixers and whippers, except drink mixers	88.4	Industrial machinery for sorting, grading, and cleaning fruits, vegetables, and eggs, and other machinery for processing and preparing meat and poultry	284.4
Other commercial food preparation machines, including tenderizers (power-driven), except packaging machinery and food cooking and warming equipment	135.8	Industrial machinery for sorting, grading, and cleaning fruits, vegetables, and eggs	74.9
Parts and attachments for commercial food preparation machines, except packaging machinery and food cooking and warming equipment	169.6	Industrial machinery and equipment, nec, for processing and preparing meat and poultry (not including the extraction and preparation of oils)	209.5
Industrial bakery machinery and equipment	374.4	Parts and attachments for industrial food and feed products machinery	169.8
Industrial bakery dough mixers, dividers, and molders	77.1	Parts and attachments for bakery furnaces and ovens	6.8
Industrial bakery bake ovens, including traveling tray	83.0	Parts and attachments for presses, crushers, and similar machinery used in the production of wine, cider, fruit juices, and similar beverages	0.8
Industrial rolling machines including pastry for the manufacture of bakery products	15.0	Parts and attachments for sorting, grading, or cleaning fruits, vegetables, and eggs	5.2
Other industrial bakery machinery and equipment	199.3	Other parts and attachments for industrial food products machinery, nec	157.0
Commercial food products machinery, except packaging machinery and food cooking and warming equipment, nsk	27.9	Industrial machinery and equipment for manufacturing or processing foods, beverages, and animal or fowl feed, nsk	78.0
Industrial machinery and equipment for manufacturing or processing foods, beverages, and animal and fowl feed	**990.3**	**Food products machinery, nsk, total**	**187.0**
Other industrial food and feed products machinery	458.2		
Industrial presses, crushers, and similar machinery used in the production of wine, cider, fruit juices, and similar beverages	48.5		

Source: 2002 *Economic Census*. The values are product shipments in millions of dollars for 2002. Total product shipments may be lower or higher than industry shipments. See Introduction for a full discussion. Values of indented subcategories are summed in the main heading(s). The symbol (D) appears when data are withheld to prevent disclosure of competitive information. The abbreviation nsk stands for 'not specified by kind' and nec for 'not elsewhere classified'. A dash (-) means zero.

PRODUCT SHARE DETAILS FOR INDUSTRIAL MACHINERY MANUFACTURING NEC

Product or Product Class Shipments	Mil. $	Product or Product Class Shipments	Mil. $
ALL OTHER INDUSTRIAL MACHINERY AND EQUIPMENT	6,667.6	Sawing machines for working stone, ceramics, or like materials (including glass)	32.0
Chemical manufacturing machinery, equipment, and parts	**1,249.1**	Grinding or polishing machines for glass working	22.7
Chemical manufacturing mixing, kneading, crushing, grinding, sifting, homogenizing (except dairy), emulsifying, or stirring machines	220.6	Grinding or polishing machines for working stone, ceramics, or like materials (except glass)	26.4
Other chemical manufacturing machines and equipment	791.7	Other special industry glass working machines	34.6
Distilling, rectifying, or fractionating machinery and equipment	72.6	Other special industry machines for working stone, ceramics, or like materials (except glass)	73.8
Heat exchange units	103.7	Clay products forming equipment (brick, tile, ceramic)	9.3
Dryers	63.0	Concrete block and other forming equipment, except parts	102.4
Gas or air liquefying machinery	74.4	Cement making machinery, except parts	41.3
Other chemical manufacturing machines and equipment	478.0	Cotton ginning machinery, except parts	74.8
Parts for chemical manufacturing machinery and equipment	226.6	Fuel fired kilns for cement, wood, and chemical processing and parts thereof	52.3
Parts for distilling, rectifying, fractionating, heat exchange, dryers, gas and air liquefying machinery and equipment	29.1	Distilling and rectifying equipment and heat exchange units for desalinization	(D)
Parts for other chemical manufacturing machinery and equipment	197.5	Filtering and purifying machinery and apparatus for desalinization	126.9
Chemical manufacturing machinery, equipment, and parts, nsk	10.1	Footware manufacturing and repairing machinery and parts (except shoe sole stitching machines)	8.2
Foundry machinery and equipment, excluding patterns and molds	**403.4**	Industrial sewing machine heads, including shoe sole stitching machine heads	27.9
Foundry machinery and equipment, including converters, excluding patterns and molds	263.0	Automatic industrial sewing machinery	9.6
Foundry pouring equipment, including ladles, crucibles, and pouring machines	24.1	Nonautomatic industrial sewing machinery	(D)
Foundry molding and core-making machines	19.6	Industrial sewing machine furniture, parts, and attachments	30.8
Foundry casting machines, except die casting machines, patterns, and molds	23.6	Machines and parts for insulating electrical wire for cable	11.0
Foundry blast cleaning machines	67.0	Electric battery manufacturing machinery, except parts	17.3
Other foundry machinery and equipment, including converters	128.7	Household sewing machines and parts	1.8
Parts for foundry machines and equipment	137.9	Parts for special industry machinery and equipment	255.2
Parts for foundry blast cleaning machines	8.2	Petroleum refining machinery	1.4
Other parts for foundry machinery and equipment	129.7	Ammunition and explosive loading machinery	(D)
Foundry machinery and equipment, excluding patterns and molds, nsk	2.5	Tobacco processing machinery	(D)
Printed circuit board manufacturing machinery, except testing	**977.6**	Machines for working stone, ceramics, or like materials (including glass)	7.7
Through-hole printed circuit board manufacturing machinery	235.8	Clay products forming equipment (brick, tile, ceramic)	(D)
Other printed circuit board manufacturing machinery and equipment, parts, accessories, and attachments	612.8	Concrete products forming equipment	120.9
Surface mount printed circuit board manufacturing machinery	401.9	Cement making machinery	(D)
Other printed circuit board manufacturing machinery and equipment	210.9	Glassmaking machinery and equipment	26.6
Parts, attachments, and accessories for printed circuit board manufacturing machinery and equipment	104.1	Cotton ginning machinery	22.0
Printed circuit board manufacturing machinery, nsk	24.9	Electroplating equipment	3.9
Special industry machinery and equipment, nec	**3,443.5**	Metal finishing equipment	24.3
Other special industry machines, including petroleum refining, ammunition, grinding or polishing machines for glass working, and other machines, nec	1,019.3	Desalinization equipment	16.6
Petroleum refining, distilling, or fractionating machinery and equipment	236.3	Electric battery making machines	7.9
Petroleum refining heat exchange units	(D)	Metal finishing, degreasing, and metal plating equipment, except rolling mill equipment, and parts	189.3
Other petroleum refining machinery	(D)	Electroplating equipment, except rolling mill lines and parts	22.1
Ammunition and explosive loading machinery	(D)	Vibratory metal finishing machines, except parts	2.4
Tobacco processing machinery, except parts	27.3	Metal plating equipment, except electroplating and parts	16.6
		Other metal finishing equipment, except electroplating and rolling mill equipment and parts	81.7
		Metal degreasing machines and parts	66.5
		Glassmaking machinery and equipment, including machines for hot working glass or glassware, except parts	156.7
		Special industry machinery and parts, nec	1,650.0
		Special industry machinery and equipment, nec, nsk	172.9
		All other industrial machinery, nsk, total	**594.1**

Source: 2002 *Economic Census*. The values are product shipments in millions of dollars for 2002. Total product shipments may be lower or higher than industry shipments. See Introduction for a full discussion. Values of indented subcategories are summed in the main heading(s). The symbol (D) appears when data are withheld to prevent disclosure of competitive information. The abbreviation nsk stands for 'not specified by kind' and nec for 'not elsewhere classified'. A dash (-) means zero.

INPUTS AND OUTPUTS FOR OTHER INDUSTRIAL MACHINERY MANUFACTURING

Economic Sector or Industry Providing Inputs	%	Sector	Economic Sector or Industry Buying Outputs	%	Sector
Compensation of employees	34.5		Private fixed investment	62.8	
Management of companies & enterprises	6.4	Services	Exports of goods & services	15.5	Cap Inv
Wholesale trade	5.7	Trade	Printing	3.5	Manufg.
Iron & steel mills & ferroalloys	5.1	Manufg.	Industrial machinery, nec	2.4	Manufg.
Industrial machinery, nec	3.1	Manufg.	Personal consumption expenditures	2.3	
Machine shops	2.5	Manufg.	Basic organic chemicals, nec	1.9	Manufg.
Ferrous metal foundries	1.7	Manufg.	Paper mills	1.4	Manufg.

Continued on next page.

INPUTS AND OUTPUTS FOR OTHER INDUSTRIAL MACHINERY MANUFACTURING - Continued

Economic Sector or Industry Providing Inputs	%	Sector	Economic Sector or Industry Buying Outputs	%	Sector
Valve & fittings other than plumbing	1.5	Manufg.	Wholesale trade	1.2	Trade
Printed circuit assemblies (electronic assemblies)	1.3	Manufg.	Basic inorganic chemicals, nec	1.0	Manufg.
Motors & generators	1.2	Manufg.	Paperboard mills	0.9	Manufg.
Real estate	1.1	Fin/R.E.	S/L govt. invest., education	0.8	S/L Govt
Coating, engraving, heat treating & allied activities	1.1	Manufg.	Paints & coatings	0.8	Manufg.
Relay & industrial controls	1.1	Manufg.	Nonferrous metal foundries	0.7	Manufg.
Gaskets, packing, & sealing devices	1.0	Manufg.	Printed circuit assemblies (electronic assemblies)	0.5	Manufg.
Fluid power process machinery	1.0	Manufg.	Synthetic dyes & pigments	0.4	Manufg.
Ball & roller bearings	1.0	Manufg.	Alkalies & chlorine	0.4	Manufg.
Speed changers, industrial high-speed drives, & gears	1.0	Manufg.	General S/L govt. services	0.3	S/L Govt
Securities, commodity contracts, investments	1.0	Fin/R.E.	Plastics materials & resins	0.3	Manufg.
Semiconductors & related devices	1.0	Manufg.	Food services & drinking places	0.3	Services
Fabricated metals, nec	0.9	Manufg.	Retail trade	0.3	Trade
Turned products & screws, nuts, & bolts	0.9	Manufg.	Other S/L govt. enterprises	0.3	S/L Govt
Cutting tools & machine tool accessories	0.9	Manufg.	Alumina refining & primary aluminum production	0.2	Manufg.
Advertising & related services	0.8	Services	Specialized design services	0.2	Services
Truck transportation	0.8	Util.	Chemical products & preparations, nec	0.2	Manufg.
Power generation & supply	0.8	Util.	Federal government, investment, national defense	0.2	Fed Govt
Metal cans, boxes, & other containers (light gauge)	0.7	Manufg.	Fluid milk & butter	0.2	Manufg.
Nonferrous metal foundries	0.7	Manufg.	Petrochemicals	0.2	Manufg.
Aluminum products from purchased aluminum	0.7	Manufg.	Ferrous metal foundries	0.1	Manufg.
Custom computer programming services	0.6	Services	Civic, social, & professional organizations	0.1	Services
Lessors of nonfinancial assets	0.6	Fin/R.E.	Industrial gases	0.1	Manufg.
Air & gas compressors	0.6	Manufg.			
Plate work & fabricated structural products	0.6	Manufg.			
Monetary authorities/depository credit intermediation	0.5	Fin/R.E.			
Legal services	0.5	Services			
Taxes on production & imports, less subsidies	0.5				
Telecommunications	0.4	Services			
Crowns & closures & metal stamping	0.4	Manufg.			
Professional, scientific, technical services, nec	0.4	Services			
Accounting, tax preparation, bookkeeping, & payroll	0.4	Services			
Data processing, hosting, & related services	0.4	Services			
Abrasive products	0.4	Manufg.			
Scientific research & development services	0.4	Services			
Electronic components, nec	0.3	Manufg.			
Food services & drinking places	0.3	Services			
Warehousing & storage	0.3	Util.			
Automotive equipment rental & leasing	0.3	Fin/R.E.			
Plastics packaging materials, film & sheet	0.3	Manufg.			
Alumina refining & primary aluminum production	0.3	Manufg.			
Forging, stamping, & sintering, nec	0.3	Manufg.			
Custom roll forming	0.3	Manufg.			
Postal service	0.3	Util.			
Management, scientific, & technical consulting	0.3	Services			
Noncomparable imports	0.3	Foreign			
Handtools	0.3	Manufg.			
Paperboard containers	0.3	Manufg.			
Pumps & pumping equipment	0.2	Manufg.			
Plastics products, nec	0.2	Manufg.			
Architectural, engineering, & related services	0.2	Services			
Rubber products, nec	0.2	Manufg.			
Chemical products & preparations, nec	0.2	Manufg.			
Employment services	0.2	Services			
Hotels & motels, including casino hotels	0.2	Services			
Services to buildings & dwellings	0.2	Services			
Business support services	0.2	Services			
Natural gas distribution	0.2	Util.			
Maintenance/repair of nonresidential structures	0.2	Construct.			
Special tools, dies, jigs, & fixtures	0.2	Manufg.			
General purpose machinery, nec	0.2	Manufg.			
Commercial & industrial machinery rental & leasing	0.2	Fin/R.E.			
Specialized design services	0.2	Services			
Other computer related services, including facilities	0.2	Services			
Springs & wire products	0.1	Manufg.			
Paperboard mills	0.1	Manufg.			
Bare printed circuit boards	0.1	Manufg.			
Electronic capacitors, resistors, coils, transformers	0.1	Manufg.			
Steel products from purchased steel	0.1	Manufg.			
Metal tanks (heavy gauge)	0.1	Manufg.			
Air transportation	0.1	Util.			
Nondepository credit intermediation activities	0.1	Fin/R.E.			
Power boilers & heat exchangers	0.1	Manufg.			
Mechanical power transmission equipment	0.1	Manufg.			
Paper mills	0.1	Manufg.			
Automotive repair & maintenance, ex. car washes	0.1	Services			
Motor vehicle parts	0.1	Manufg.			
Rail transportation	0.1	Util.			

Source: Benchmark Input-Output Accounts for the U.S. Economy, 2002, U.S. Department of Commerce, Washington D.C., January 2008. User should note that this Input-Output table is not for this particular, narrowly defined industry but for a larger aggregate. Input and Output data for Other Industrial Machinery Manufacturing include Input and Output data for the Annual Survey of Manufactures' NAICS industries 333210 and 33329N. The abbreviation nec stands for 'not elsewhere classified'.

OCCUPATIONS EMPLOYED BY INDUSTRIAL MACHINERY MANUFACTURING

Occupation	% of Total 2006	Change to 2016	Occupation	% of Total 2006	Change to 2016
Machinists	6.6	-14.0	Electrical engineers	1.6	-18.1
Team assemblers	5.5	-18.1	Structural metal fabricators & fitters	1.5	-18.1
Welders, cutters, solderers, & brazers	4.3	-12.8	Customer service representatives	1.5	-9.9
Mechanical engineers	4.0	-9.9	Grinding, lapping, polishing machine tool operators	1.4	-20.5
First-line supervisors/managers of production workers	3.8	-18.1	Office clerks, general	1.4	-19.3
Sales reps, wholesale & manufacturing, exc tech	2.5	-18.1	Cutting, punching, & press machine operators	1.4	-26.3
General & operations managers	2.3	-26.3	Engineering managers	1.4	-18.1
Electrical & electronic equipment assemblers	2.0	-34.5	Helpers--Production workers	1.3	-18.1
Computer-controlled machine tool operators	1.9	-9.9	Inspectors, testers, sorters, samplers, & weighers	1.2	-22.8
Shipping, receiving, & traffic clerks	1.8	-21.2	Sales representatives, wholesale & manufacturing, tech	1.2	-18.1
Electromechanical equipment assemblers	1.8	-18.1	Maintenance & repair workers, general	1.2	-18.1
Industrial machinery mechanics	1.8	-5.8	Accountants & auditors	1.1	-18.1
Purchasing agents, exc wholesale, retail, & farm	1.7	-18.1	Engine & other machine assemblers	1.1	-18.1
Bookkeeping, accounting, & auditing clerks	1.6	-18.1	Molding, coremaking, & casting machine operators	1.1	-26.3
Mechanical drafters	1.6	-17.1	Stock clerks & order fillers	1.1	-31.4
Industrial engineers	1.6	-0.5	Sales engineers	1.0	-18.1

Source: *Industry-Occupation Matrix*, Bureau of Labor Statistics, December 4, 2007. These data are reported based on 4-digit NAICS categories but have been matched to corresponding 6-digit NAICS industry codes. The change reported for each occupation to the year 2016 is a percent of growth or decline as estimated by the Bureau of Labor Statistics. The abbreviation nec stands for 'not elsewhere classified'.

LOCATION BY STATE AND REGIONAL CONCENTRATION

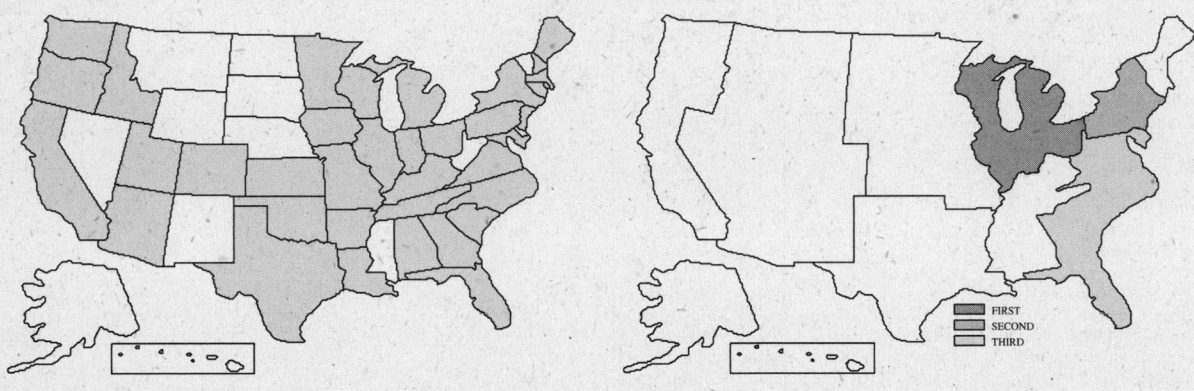

FIRST
SECOND
THIRD

INDUSTRY DATA BY STATE

State	Establish-ments	Shipments			Employment				Cost as % of Shipments	Investment per Employee ($)
		Total ($ mil)	% of U.S.	Per Establ.	Total Number	% of U.S.	Per Establ.	Wages ($/hour)		
Illinois	195	1,388.3	8.5	7,119.7	6,423	6.9	33	20.29	42.8	3,490
Wisconsin	146	1,213.5	7.4	8,311.6	6,805	7.3	47	20.04	47.5	3,545
California	305	1,153.9	7.1	3,783.2	7,512	8.1	25	17.52	41.2	6,370
New York	171	1,126.2	6.9	6,586.1	5,757	6.2	34	21.46	45.2	4,438
Ohio	198	1,086.9	6.6	5,489.3	5,923	6.4	30	17.61	47.8	4,799
Michigan	161	978.4	6.0	6,077.0	4,339	4.7	27	22.19	54.3	4,665
Texas	142	845.7	5.2	5,955.6	4,349	4.7	31	16.71	47.5	4,157
Pennsylvania	171	804.6	4.9	4,705.3	5,084	5.5	30	17.50	40.3	2,970
Massachusetts	95	662.7	4.1	6,975.5	4,082	4.4	43	20.74	40.1	3,578
New Jersey	146	602.4	3.7	4,126.0	2,974	3.2	20	20.53	49.9	4,135
North Carolina	148	563.3	3.4	3,805.9	3,616	3.9	24	15.39	41.3	10,594
Georgia	114	397.9	2.4	3,490.1	2,620	2.8	23	16.65	47.5	4,713
Minnesota	80	391.2	2.4	4,890.5	2,159	2.3	27	18.34	55.2	3,534
South Carolina	63	269.7	1.6	4,280.4	2,351	2.5	37	15.08	38.3	2,339
Iowa	33	249.0	1.5	7,546.5	1,443	1.5	44	18.59	41.0	8,021
Indiana	62	237.7	1.5	3,834.7	1,550	1.7	25	20.24	46.5	1,888
Connecticut	44	229.0	1.4	5,205.4	1,258	1.3	29	15.45	46.5	1,681
Oklahoma	23	227.4	1.4	9,885.1	1,051	1.1	46	16.14	43.8	16,009
Virginia	35	217.7	1.3	6,220.2	1,306	1.4	37	16.92	41.5	3,345
Missouri	37	205.8	1.3	5,563.4	1,362	1.5	37	22.23	39.2	1,952
Tennessee	33	143.3	0.9	4,343.8	911	1.0	28	17.84	51.8	3,123
Washington	26	132.5	0.8	5,096.4	648	0.7	25	18.09	35.9	3,363
Oregon	19	124.1	0.8	6,529.7	516	0.6	27	16.92	27.5	7,072
Florida	55	111.1	0.7	2,019.4	851	0.9	15	17.59	42.8	1,307
Colorado	28	107.4	0.7	3,834.9	520	0.6	19	18.94	38.9	5,704
Louisiana	15	97.3	0.6	6,485.3	429	0.5	29	23.31	45.5	1,650

Continued on next page.

INDUSTRY DATA BY STATE - Continued

State	Establish-ments	Shipments			Employment				Cost as % of Shipments	Investment per Employee ($)
		Total ($ mil)	% of U.S.	Per Establ.	Total Number	% of U.S.	Per Establ.	Wages ($/hour)		
Kansas	18	94.4	0.6	5,243.8	562	0.6	31	15.62	37.1	2,806
Alabama	13	74.9	0.5	5,762.0	613	0.7	47	18.06	40.8	1,922
Maryland	11	59.5	0.4	5,411.1	331	0.4	30	17.41	35.7	2,136
Arizona	12	49.9	0.3	4,154.2	493	0.5	41	14.35	47.4	2,168
Rhode Island	25	46.1	0.3	1,843.8	358	0.4	14	15.82	41.9	2,553
Maine	4	42.6	0.3	10,658.8	173	0.2	43	15.87	56.4	1,688
Utah	7	24.5	0.1	3,497.4	173	0.2	25	15.93	47.8	1,237
New Hampshire	7	22.0	0.1	3,139.4	117	0.1	17	15.95	32.3	932
Kentucky	10	20.8	0.1	2,080.9	185	0.2	19	16.64	40.9	1,778
Idaho	8	15.5	0.1	1,942.6	136	0.1	17	16.39	46.4	1,603
Arkansas	10	15.3	0.1	1,532.7	169	0.2	17	16.54	50.3	1,538

Source: 2002 Economic Census. The states are in descending order of shipments or establishments (if shipment data are missing for the majority). The symbol (D) appears when data are withheld to prevent disclosure of competitive information. States marked with (D) are sorted by number of establishments. A dash (-) indicates that the data element cannot be calculated. Data may not show all states active in the NAICS category. All data available at the time of publication are shown.

NAICS 333313 - OFFICE MACHINERY MANUFACTURING

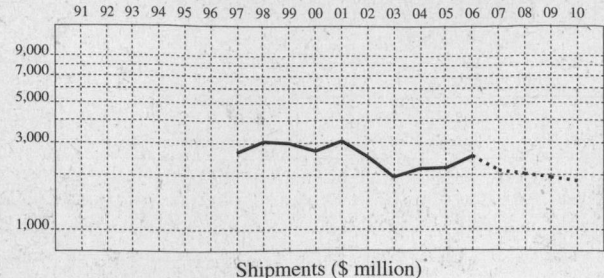

Shipments ($ million)

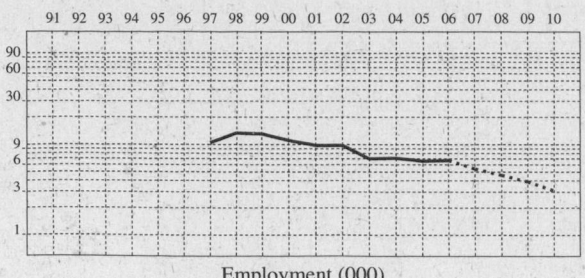

Employment (000)

GENERAL STATISTICS

Year	Com-panies	Establishments		Employment			Compensation		Production ($ million)			
		Total	with 20 or more employees	Total (000)	Production Workers (000)	Hours (Mil)	Payroll ($ mil)	Wages ($/hr)	Cost of Materials	Value Added by Manufacture	Value of Shipments	Capital Invest.
1997	131	137	72	10.5	4.9	9.5	327.9	11.73	1,180.5	1,488.2	2,667.9	113.6
1998		137	65	13.4	6.1	12.1	434.1	11.85	1,333.3	1,733.6	3,064.7	62.2
1999		157	79	13.1	6.0	11.9	409.3	11.87	1,268.3	1,466.5	2,993.3	52.1
2000		150	79	11.1	4.6	9.4	350.9	13.01	1,319.1	1,403.7	2,710.7	43.9
2001		144	78	9.8	4.5	9.2	344.0	13.55	1,631.0	1,403.6	3,071.5	54.7
2002	95	106	42	9.8	3.7	6.7	435.7	17.93	1,095.2	1,386.7	2,509.0	56.5
2003		110	48	7.0	3.0	5.5	332.8	15.61	871.5	1,064.4	1,940.7	68.9
2004		110	44	7.1	2.8	5.4	350.5	15.87	932.6	1,242.0	2,173.6	181.9
2005		108	42	6.6	2.6	5.4	340.6	15.67	911.5	1,287.5	2,192.8	143.3
2006		101P	38P	6.7	2.8	5.9	350.9	14.58	1,150.9	1,392.1	2,538.9	108.3
2007		95P	33P	5.4P	1.9P	3.9P	344.2P	16.99P	957.3P	1,157.9P	2,111.8P	130.1P
2008		90P	28P	4.6P	1.5P	3.1P	339.9P	17.50P	918.2P	1,110.6P	2,025.5P	137.6P
2009		84P	23P	3.9P	1.1P	2.4P	335.7P	18.01P	879.1P	1,063.3P	1,939.3P	145.2P
2010		79P	19P	3.1P	0.8P	1.6P	331.4P	18.52P	840.0P	1,016.0P	1,853.0P	152.7P

Sources: 1997 and 2002 *Economic Census*; other years, up to 2006, are from *Annual Survey of Manufactures*. Establishment counts for non-Census years are from *County Business Patterns*; 1997 and 2002 values are from the 1997 and 2002 censuses, respectively. 'P's show projections by the editors.

INDICES OF CHANGE

Year	Com-panies	Establishments		Employment			Compensation		Production ($ million)			
		Total	with 20 or more employees	Total (000)	Production Workers (000)	Hours (Mil)	Payroll ($ mil)	Wages ($/hr)	Cost of Materials	Value Added by Manufacture	Value of Shipments	Capital Invest.
1997	138	129	171	107	132	142	75	65	108	107	106	201
1998		129	155	137	165	181	100	66	122	125	122	110
1999		148	188	134	162	178	94	66	116	106	119	92
2000		142	188	113	124	140	81	73	120	101	108	78
2001		136	186	100	122	137	79	76	149	101	122	97
2002	100	100	100	100	100	100	100	100	100	100	100	100
2003		104	114	71	81	82	76	87	80	77	77	122
2004		104	105	72	76	81	80	89	85	90	87	322
2005		102	100	67	70	81	78	87	83	93	87	254
2006		95P	89P	68	76	88	81	81	105	100	101	192
2007		90P	78P	55P	51P	58P	79P	95P	87P	84P	84P	230P
2008		85P	67P	47P	41P	46P	78P	98P	84P	80P	81P	244P
2009		79P	56P	40P	30P	36P	77P	100P	80P	77P	77P	257P
2010		74P	45P	32P	22P	24P	76P	103P	77P	73P	74P	270P

Sources: Same as General Statistics. Values reflect change from the base year, 2002. Values above 100 mean greater than 2002, values below 100 mean less than 2002, and the values of 100 in other years means the same as 2002. 'P's show projections by the editors.

SELECTED RATIOS

For 2002	Avg. of All Manufact.	Analyzed Industry	Index	For 2002	Avg. of All Manufact.	Analyzed Industry	Index
Employees per Establishment	42	92	220	Value Added per Production Worker	182,367	374,784	206
Payroll per Establishment	1,639,184	4,110,377	251	Cost per Establishment	5,769,015	10,332,075	179
Payroll per Employee	39,053	44,459	114	Cost per Employee	137,446	111,755	81
Production Workers per Establishment	30	35	118	Cost per Production Worker	195,506	296,000	151
Wages per Establishment	694,845	1,133,311	163	Shipments per Establishment	11,158,348	23,669,811	212
Wages per Production Worker	23,548	32,468	138	Shipments per Employee	265,847	256,020	96
Hours per Production Worker	1,980	1,811	91	Shipments per Production Worker	378,144	678,108	179
Wages per Hour	11.89	17.93	151	Investment per Establishment	361,338	533,019	148
Value Added per Establishment	5,381,325	13,082,075	243	Investment per Employee	8,609	5,765	67
Value Added per Employee	128,210	141,500	110	Investment per Production Worker	12,245	15,270	125

Sources: Same as General Statistics. The 'Average of All Manufacturing' column represents the average of all manufacturing industries reported for the most recent complete year available. The Index shows the relationship between the Average and the Analyzed Industry. For example, 100 means that they are equal; 500 that the Analyzed Industry is five times the average; 50 means that the Analyzed Industry is half the national average. The abbreviation 'na' is used to show that data are 'not available'. Ratios shown for 2002, the last complete census year.

LEADING COMPANIES   Number shown: **75**   Total sales ($ mil): **92,533**   Total employment (000): **241.7**

Company Name	Address				CEO Name	Phone	Co. Type	Sales ($ mil)	Empl. (000)
Mars Inc.	6885 Elm Street	Mc Lean	VA	22101	John F. Mars	703-821-4900	R	18,462*	40.0
Xerox Corp.	PO Box 1600	Stamford	CT	06904		203-968-3000	P	17,288	57.4
Canon U.S.A. Inc.	1 Canon Plz.	Lake Success	NY	11042	Yoroku Adachi	516-328-5000	S	10,745*	11.0
Pitney Bowes Inc.	1 Elmcroft Rd.	Stamford	CT	06926	Michael J. Critelli	203-356-5000	P	6,130	26.3
Order-Matic Corp.	PO Box 25463	Oklahoma City	OK	73125	Bill Cunningham	405-672-1487	R	5,787	0.2
Lexmark International Inc.	740 New Circle Rd.	Lexington	KY	40550	Paul J. Curlander	859-232-2000	P	4,974	13.8
NCR Corp.	1700 S Patterson	Dayton	OH	45479		937-445-5000	P	4,970	23.2
Harris Corp.	1025 W NASA	Melbourne	FL	32919		321-727-9100	P	4,243	16.0
Oce-USA Inc.	5450 N Cumberland	Chicago	IL	60656	Jan Dix	773-714-8500	S	3,671*	3.1
Diebold Inc.	PO Box 3077	North Canton	OH	44720		330-490-4000	P	2,906	15.5
ACCO Brands Corp.	300 Tower Pkwy.	Lincolnshire	IL	60069	David Campbell		P	1,939	6.0
Stenograph L.L.C.	1500 Bishop Ct.	Mount Prospect	IL	60056		847-803-1400	R	1,560*	0.2
Fujitsu Transaction Solutions	2801 Network Blvd.	Frisco	TX	75034		972-963-2300	R	1,300*	0.3
Standard Register Co.	PO Box 1167	Dayton	OH	45401		937-221-1000	P	865	3.8
White Systems Inc.	30 Boright Ave.	Kenilworth	NJ	07033	Richard Paolino	908-272-6700	S	673*	0.3
Hypercom Arizona Inc.	2851 W Kathleen	Phoenix	AZ	85053	William Keiper	602-504-5000	S	606*	1.5
Hypercom Latino America Inc.	8880 NW 20th St.	Miami	FL	33172	William Keiper	305-477-0315	S	606*	1.5
Hypercom Mfg. Resources	2851 W Kathleen	Phoenix	AZ	85053	William Keiper	602-504-5000	S	606*	1.5
Hypercom Transaction Network	2851 W Kathleen	Phoenix	AZ	85053	William Keiper	602-504-5000	S	606*	1.5
Hypercom U.S.A. Inc.	2851 W Kathleen	Phoenix	AZ	85053	William Keiper	602-504-5000	S	606*	1.5
Coinstar Inc.	PO Box 91258	Bellevue	WA	98009	David W. Cole	425-943-8000	P	546	1.9
Hypercom Corp.	2851 W Kathleen	Phoenix	AZ	85053		602-504-5000	P	294	1.4
Toshiba America Info. Systems	PO Box 19724	Irvine	CA	92623		949-583-3000	S	290*	1.7
Ricoh Electronics Inc.	2320 Redhill Ave.	Santa Ana	CA	92705	Shunsuke Nakanishi	949-250-7440	R	276*	1.1
Brother Industries Inc.	7819 N Brother Blvd	Bartlett	TN	38133	Hiromi Gunji	901-377-7777	R	258*	1.2
PAR Technology Corp.	8383 Seneca Tpke.	New Hartford	NY	13413		315-738-0600	P	210	1.7
Great Northern Corp.	395 Stroebe Rd.	Appleton	WI	54914		920-739-3671	R	196*	0.2
Digi International Inc.	11001 Bren Rd. E	Minnetonka	MN	55343	Joseph T. Dunsmore	952-912-3444	P	173	0.6
American Changer Corp.	1400 NW 65th Pl.	Fort Lauderdale	FL	33309	Harry Steinbok	954-917-3009	R	127*	0.6
Bulman Products Inc.	1650 McReynolds	Grand Rapids	MI	49504		616-363-4416	R	124*	<0.1
VeriFone Inc.	300 Park Place Blvd	Clearwater	FL	33759	Douglas G. Bergeron	727-953-4000	S	121*	0.9
Mei Inc.	1301 Wilson Dr.	West Chester	PA	19380		610-430-2700	R	108*	0.5
Tokyo Electron America Inc.	PO Box 17200	Austin	TX	78760	Barry Rapozo	512-424-1136	R	102*	0.3
Cormark Inc.	1701 Winthrop Dr.	Des Plaines	IL	60018	Tom Conway	847-364-5900	R	101*	0.3
Cummins-Allison Corp.	PO Box 339	Mount Prospect	IL	60056	John Jones	847-299-9550	R	67*	0.2
ECRM Inc.	554 Clark Rd.	Tewksbury	MA	01876	Richard Black	978-851-0207	R	63*	0.2
Amano Cincinnati Inc.	140 Harrison Ave.	Roseland	NJ	07068	Osamu Okagaki	973-403-1900	R	56*	0.1
Koh-I-Noor Inc.	1 River Rd.	Leeds	MA	01053		413-584-5446	R	53*	0.4
Franklin Electronic Publishers	1 Franklin Plz.	Burlington	NJ	08016	Barry J. Lipsky	609-386-2500	P	52	0.2
Csi Acquisition Corp.	645 W 200 N	North Salt Lake	UT	84054		801-936-8082	R	52*	0.2
American Thermoform Corp.	1758 Brackett St.	La Verne	CA	91750		909-593-6711	R	45*	<0.1
Int'l Staple and Machine	PO Box 629	Butler	PA	16003	Farhad Gerannayeh		R	40*	0.2
Varitronic Systems Inc.	6835 Winnetka Cir.	Brooklyn Park	MN	55428	Frank Jaehnert	763-536-6400	D	38*	0.3
Graphic Enterprises Inc.	3874 Highland Park	North Canton	OH	44720	Jason Parikh		R	37*	0.3
Alpha Technology Inc.	PO Box 5408	Anderson	SC	29623	Dennis Tate	864-225-7245	R	36*	0.1
Newbold Corp.	450 Weaver St.	Rocky Mount	VA	24151	Robert Scott	540-489-4400	R	36*	0.2
Gunther International Ltd.	1 Winnenden Rd.	Norwich	CT	06360	Marc I. Perkins	860-823-1427	R	34	0.1
Ultimate Technology Corp.	100 Rawson Rd.	Victor	NY	14564		585-924-9500	R	26*	0.1
Control Module Inc.	227 Brainard Rd.	Enfield	CT	06082	Jana Moak	860-745-2433	R	25*	<0.1
QSI Systems Inc.	PO Box 718	Salem	NH	03079	Alfred Smilgis	603-893-7707	R	20*	<0.1
inc.jet Inc.	1 Winnenden Rd.	Norwich	CT	06360	Marc Perkins	860-823-3090	R	20*	<0.1
Real-Time Data Management Svcs	5400 Robin Hood	Norfolk	VA	23513	Ernest Sammons	757-855-2750	R	20*	<0.1
Happ Controls Inc.	106 Garlisch Dr.	Elk Grove Vlg	IL	60007	Tom Happ	847-593-6130	R	19*	0.3
Rowe International Inc.	1500 Union Ave. SE	Grand Rapids	MI	49507	Douglas Johnson	616-243-3633	R	19*	0.1
Heidelberg/Baumfolder Corp.	1660 Campbell Rd.	Sidney	OH	45365	Ulrik Nygaard	937-492-1281	S	19*	<0.1
Maro Display Inc.	112 Dillabur Ave.	N Kingstown	RI	02852	Steven Censo	401-294-5551	R	17*	<0.1
One Source Industries L.L.C.	15215 Alton Pky.	Irvine	CA	92618	Chris Tilton	949-784-7700	S	17*	<0.1
Gb Instruments Inc.	1143 W Newport	Deerfield Beach	FL	33442	Maurice Rochman	954-596-5000	R	17*	<0.1
Wand Corp.	7593 Corporate Way	Eden Prairie	MN	55344	John Perrill	952-361-6200	R	17*	0.1
Card Technology Corp.	70 Eisenhower Dr.	Paramus	NJ	07652		201-845-7373	R	16*	0.1
D and S Car Wash Equipment Co.	4200 Brandi Ln.	High Ridge	MO	63049	Jon Jansky	636-677-3442	R	16*	0.1
National Presort Inc.	3901 La Reunion	Dallas	TX	75212	Henry Daboub	214-634-2288	R	15*	<0.1
ID Technology Corp.	2051 Franklin Dr.	Fort Worth	TX	76101			R	15*	<0.1
Rapidprint	2055 S Main St.	Middletown	CT	06457	Donald Bidwell, Sr.	860-346-9283	D	15*	<0.1
Telestream Inc.	848 Gold Flat Rd.	Nevada City	CA	95959	Dan Castles	530-470-1300	R	15*	<0.1
Sanyo Fisher Corp.	21605 Plummer St.	Chatsworth	CA	91311	Shin Oka	818-998-7322	S	14*	0.1
Advanced Data Services Inc.	401 W Coleman	Mount Pleasant	SC	29464	Billie F. Attaway, Jr	843-852-3031	R	14*	<0.1
Fms Magnacraft Inc.	PO Box 11509	Milwaukee	WI	53211	Charles Bucolt	414-332-8466	R	13*	0.1
Doar Communications Inc.	170 Earle Ave.	Lynbrook	NY	11563		516-823-4000	R	13	0.2
Acroprint Time Recorder Co.	5640 Departure Dr.	Raleigh	NC	27616	Glenn Robbins	919-872-5800	R	13*	0.1
Deluxe Stitcher Company Inc.	6635 W Irving Park	Chicago	IL	60634	Frank Cangelosi	773-777-6500	R	13*	<0.1
Lathem Time Corp.	200 Selig Dr. SW	Atlanta	GA	30336	Bill Lathem		R	12*	0.2
Mercury Instruments Inc.	3940 Virginia Ave.	Cincinnati	OH	45227		513-272-1111	R	12*	<0.1
Global Payment Technologies	170 Wilbur Pl.	Bohemia	NY	11716	Richard Gerzoff	631-563-2500	P	12	<0.1
Special Service Systems Inc.	2007 E 11th St.	Tulsa	OK	74104	Gary Drummond	918-582-7777	R	12*	<0.1

Source: Ward's Business Directory of U.S. Private and Public Companies, Volumes 1 and 2, 2008. The company type code used is as follows: P - Public, R - Private, S - Subsidiary, D - Division, J - Joint Venture, A - Affiliate, G - Group. Sales are in millions of dollars, employees are in thousands. An asterisk (*) indicates an estimated sales volume. The symbol < stands for 'less than'. Company names and addresses are truncated, in some cases, to fit into the available space.

MATERIALS CONSUMED

Material	Quantity	Delivered Cost ($ million)
Cathode ray tubes (CRT) (excluding X-ray)	(X)	0.9
Printed ciruit boards (without inserted components) for electronic circuitry	(X)	2.4
Printed memory boards for electronic circuitry	(X)	0.4
Printed peripheral controllers for electronic circuitry	(X)	(D)
Printed computer processors for electronic circuitry	(X)	(D)
Printed communication boards for electronic circuitry	(X)	(D)
Other printed circuit boards for electronic circuitry	(X)	7.1
Semiconductors (incl. transistors, diodes, rectifiers, and integrated circuits), for electronic circuitry	(X)	0.3
Capacitors for electronic circuitry	(X)	0.1
Resistors for electronic circuitry	(X)	0.1
Connectors for electronic circuitry	(X)	0.2
Battery packs for electronic circuitry	(X)	(D)
Other power supply units for electronic circuitry	(X)	2.9
Other components and accessories, for electronic circuitry (coils, transformers, etc.), excluding tubes	(X)	(D)
Electrical transmission, distribution, and control equipment	(X)	(D)
Steel, aluminum, and other metal electronic enclosures	(X)	2.5
Plastics electronic enclosures	(X)	4.3
Sheet metal products, including stampings (exc. enclosures)	(X)	16.7
All other fabricated metal products (excluding forgings)	(X)	43.4
Forgings	(X)	0.2
Castings, rough and semifinished	(X)	(D)
Metal shapes and forms (exc. castings, forgings, fabr. metal products)	(X)	(D)
Insulated copper wire and cable (including magnet wire)	(X)	3.6
Fabricated plastics products (excluding enclosures)	(X)	5.5
Purchased software	(X)	8.5
Appliance outlets and other current-carrying wiring devices	(X)	(D)
Electric motors and generators	(X)	4.8
Paper and paperboard products (incl. paperboard boxes, etc.)	(X)	6.0
Purchased computers	(X)	18.2
Purchased peripheral storage devices	(X)	(D)
Purchased computer terminals	(X)	1.1
Purchased peripheral input devices (including keyboards, mouse devices, track balls, etc.)	(X)	(D)
Purchased peripheral printers	(X)	5.6
All other materials, components, parts, containers, and supplies	(X)	783.6
Materials, ingredients, containers, and supplies, nsk	(X)	21.1

Source: 2002 Economic Census. Explanation of symbols used: (D): Withheld to avoid disclosure of competitive data; na: Not available; (S): Withheld because statistical norms were not met; (X): Not applicable; (Z): Less than half the unit shown; nec: Not elsewhere classified; nsk: Not specified by kind; - : zero; p : 10-19 percent estimated; q : 20-29 percent estimated.

PRODUCT SHARE DETAILS

Product or Product Class Shipments	Mil. $	Product or Product Class Shipments	Mil. $
OFFICE MACHINES	2,453.4	Other electric office machines, including electric pencil sharpeners and electric staplers	77.7
Automatic typing and word processing machines, including parts and attachments	(D)	Other office machinery, nec	85.3
Duplicating machines, except parts and attachments	(D)	Parts and attachments for office machines	186.5
Mailing, letter handling, and addressing machines, except parts and attachments	1,983.8	Office machines, nsk, total	62.9

Source: 2002 Economic Census. The values are product shipments in millions of dollars for 2002. Total product shipments may be lower or higher than industry shipments. See Introduction for a full discussion. Values of indented subcategories are summed in the main heading(s). The symbol (D) appears when data are withheld to prevent disclosure of competitive information. The abbreviation nsk stands for 'not specified by kind' and nec for 'not elsewhere classified'. A dash (-) means zero.

INPUTS AND OUTPUTS FOR VENDING, COMMERCIAL, INDUSTRIAL, & OFFICE MACHINERY

Economic Sector or Industry Providing Inputs	%	Sector	Economic Sector or Industry Buying Outputs	%	Sector
Compensation of employees	24.8		Private fixed investment	48.0	
Wholesale trade	6.1	Trade	Exports of goods & services	13.6	Cap Inv
Management of companies & enterprises	4.6	Services	S/L govt. invest., other	10.1	S/L Govt
Valve & fittings other than plumbing	3.7	Manufg.	S/L govt. invest., education	7.4	S/L Govt
Real estate	3.4	Fin/R.E.	Personal consumption expenditures	5.5	
Iron & steel mills & ferroalloys	3.1	Manufg.	Management of companies & enterprises	4.6	Services
AC, refrigeration, and warm air heating equipment	2.8	Manufg.	Personal services, nec	2.1	Services
Wiring devices	2.3	Manufg.	Wholesale trade	1.6	Trade
Rubber products, nec	2.0	Manufg.	Dry-cleaning & laundry services	1.5	Services
Management, scientific, & technical consulting	2.0	Services	Vending, commercial, industrial, office machinery	1.1	Manufg.
Motors & generators	1.8	Manufg.	Federal government, investment, nondefense	0.9	Fed Govt
Vending, commercial, industrial, office machinery	1.6	Manufg.	General Federal government services, defense	0.7	Fed Govt
Lessors of nonfinancial assets	1.5	Fin/R.E.	Accounting, tax preparation, bookkeeping, & payroll	0.6	Services
Machine shops	1.4	Manufg.	Postal service	0.6	Util.
Plastics packaging materials, film & sheet	1.4	Manufg.	Change in private inventories	0.5	In House
Professional, scientific, technical services, nec	1.4	Services	Retail trade	0.4	Trade

Continued on next page.

INPUTS AND OUTPUTS FOR VENDING, COMMERCIAL, INDUSTRIAL, & OFFICE MACHINERY - Continued

Economic Sector or Industry Providing Inputs	%	Sector	Economic Sector or Industry Buying Outputs	%	Sector
Scientific research & development services	1.1	Services	Employment services	0.2	Services
Securities, commodity contracts, investments	1.1	Fin/R.E.			
Communication & energy wires & cables	1.0	Manufg.			
Forging, stamping, & sintering, nec	1.0	Manufg.			
Printed circuit assemblies (electronic assemblies)	1.0	Manufg.			
Coated & laminated paper & packaging materials	0.9	Manufg.			
Chemical products & preparations, nec	0.9	Manufg.			
Monetary authorities/depository credit intermediation	0.9	Fin/R.E.			
Synthetic rubber	0.9	Manufg.			
Computer terminals & peripherals	0.8	Manufg.			
Taxes on production & imports, less subsidies	0.8				
Crowns & closures & metal stamping	0.8	Manufg.			
Nonferrous metal (ex. copper & aluminum) processing	0.8	Manufg.			
Paints & coatings	0.8	Manufg.			
Truck transportation	0.7	Util.			
Support services, nec	0.7	Services			
Cutting tools & machine tool accessories	0.7	Manufg.			
Advertising & related services	0.7	Services			
Legal services	0.7	Services			
Coating, engraving, heat treating & allied activities	0.7	Manufg.			
Telecommunications	0.6	Services			
Glass products from purchased glass	0.6	Manufg.			
Petroleum refineries	0.6	Manufg.			
Semiconductors & related devices	0.5	Manufg.			
Turned products & screws, nuts, & bolts	0.5	Manufg.			
Noncomparable imports	0.5	Foreign			
Relay & industrial controls	0.5	Manufg.			
Data processing, hosting, & related services	0.5	Services			
Food services & drinking places	0.4	Services			
Abrasive products	0.4	Manufg.			
Business support services	0.4	Services			
Plastics products, nec	0.4	Manufg.			
Power generation & supply	0.4	Util.			
Accounting, tax preparation, bookkeeping, & payroll	0.4	Services			
Ornamental & architectural metal products	0.3	Manufg.			
Hotels & motels, including casino hotels	0.3	Services			
Automotive equipment rental & leasing	0.3	Fin/R.E.			
Employment services	0.3	Services			
Architectural, engineering, & related services	0.3	Services			
Electronic computers	0.3	Manufg.			
Metal cans, boxes, & other containers (light gauge)	0.3	Manufg.			
Fabricated metals, nec	0.3	Manufg.			
Custom roll forming	0.3	Manufg.			
Unlaminated plastics profile shapes	0.3	Manufg.			
Paperboard containers	0.3	Manufg.			
Air transportation	0.3	Util.			
Environmental & other technical consulting services	0.2	Services			
Nondepository credit intermediation activities	0.2	Fin/R.E.			
Travel arrangement & reservation services	0.2	Services			
Pressed & blown glass & glassware, nec	0.2	Manufg.			
Office administrative services	0.2	Services			
Warehousing & storage	0.2	Util.			
Waste management & remediation services	0.2	Services			
Software, audio, and video media reproducing	0.2	Manufg.			
Ferrous metal foundries	0.2	Manufg.			
Paperboard mills	0.2	Manufg.			
Nonferrous metal foundries	0.2	Manufg.			
Plate work & fabricated structural products	0.2	Manufg.			
Services to buildings & dwellings	0.2	Services			
Electronic capacitors, resistors, coils, transformers	0.2	Manufg.			
Electronic components, nec	0.2	Manufg.			
Laminated plastics plates, sheets, & shapes	0.2	Manufg.			
Maintenance/repair of nonresidential structures	0.2	Construct.			
Wood containers & pallets	0.2	Manufg.			
Photographic & photocopying equipment	0.2	Manufg.			
Commercial & industrial machinery rental & leasing	0.2	Fin/R.E.			
Ball & roller bearings	0.2	Manufg.			
Other computer related services, including facilities	0.2	Services			
Postal service	0.1	Util.			
Electrical equipment & components, nec	0.1	Manufg.			
Bare printed circuit boards	0.1	Manufg.			

Source: Benchmark Input-Output Accounts for the U.S. Economy, 2002, U.S. Department of Commerce, Washington D.C., January 2008. User should note that this Input-Output table is not for this particular narrowly defined industry but for a larger aggregate. Input and Output data for Vending, Commercial, Industrial, and Office Machinery Manufacturing include Input and Output data for the Annual Survey of Manufactures' NAICS industries 333313 and 33331N. The abbreviation nec stands for 'not elsewhere classified'.

OCCUPATIONS EMPLOYED BY COMMERCIAL & SERVICE INDUSTRY MACHINERY MANUFACTURING

Occupation	% of Total 2006	Change to 2016	Occupation	% of Total 2006	Change to 2016
Team assemblers	11.6	-12.3	Electrical engineers	1.4	-12.3
Welders, cutters, solderers, & brazers	3.4	-6.7	Maintenance & repair workers, general	1.4	-12.3
First-line supervisors/managers of production workers	3.3	-12.3	Engineering managers	1.4	-12.3
Inspectors, testers, sorters, samplers, & weighers	2.8	-17.3	Bookkeeping, accounting, & auditing clerks	1.4	-12.3
Sales reps, wholesale & manufacturing, exc tech	2.5	-12.3	Shipping, receiving, & traffic clerks	1.4	-15.6
Mechanical engineers	2.5	-12.3	Electromechanical equipment assemblers	1.4	-12.3
Computer software engineers, applications	2.3	5.3	Stock clerks & order fillers	1.3	-26.6
Electrical & electronic equipment assemblers	2.2	-29.8	Purchasing agents, exc wholesale, retail, & farm	1.3	-12.3
Machinists	1.9	-7.9	Accountants & auditors	1.2	-12.3
Assemblers & fabricators, nec	1.9	-21.0	Helpers--Production workers	1.1	-12.3
Cutting, punching, & press machine operators	1.8	-21.0	Executive secretaries & administrative assistants	1.1	-12.3
Industrial engineers	1.8	6.5	Office clerks, general	1.1	-13.6
General & operations managers	1.7	-21.0	Computer-controlled machine tool operators	1.0	-3.5
Coating, painting, & spraying machine operators	1.7	-16.7	Sales representatives, wholesale & manufacturing, tech	1.0	-12.3
Customer service representatives	1.6	-3.5	Laborers & freight, stock, & material movers, hand	1.0	-21.0
Ophthalmic laboratory technicians	1.4	-12.3			

Source: *Industry-Occupation Matrix*, Bureau of Labor Statistics, December 4, 2007. These data are reported based on 4-digit NAICS categories but have been matched to corresponding 6-digit NAICS industry codes. The change reported for each occupation to the year 2016 is a percent of growth or decline as estimated by the Bureau of Labor Statistics. The abbreviation nec stands for 'not elsewhere classified'.

LOCATION BY STATE AND REGIONAL CONCENTRATION

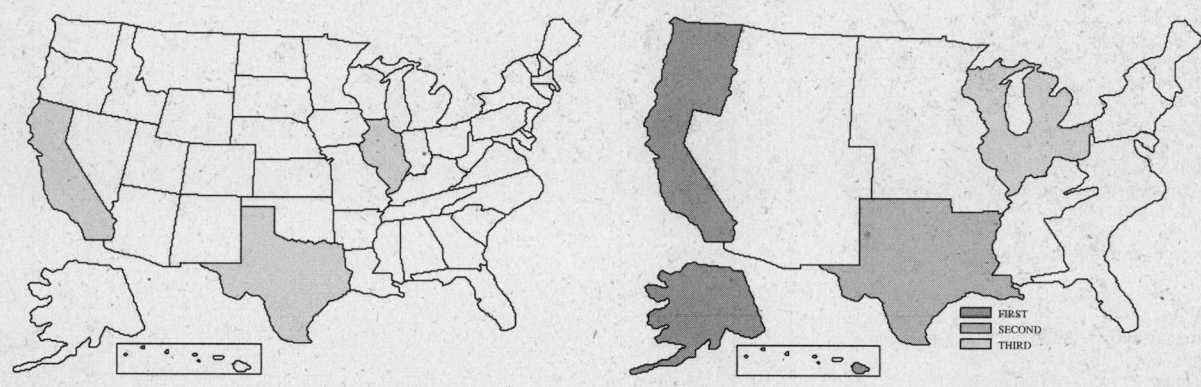

INDUSTRY DATA BY STATE

State	Establish-ments	Shipments			Employment				Cost as % of Shipments	Investment per Employee ($)
		Total ($ mil)	% of U.S.	Per Establ.	Total Number	% of U.S.	Per Establ.	Wages ($/hour)		
Texas	7	179.5	7.2	25,636.0	780	8.0	111	14.95	81.2	4,618
Illinois	6	89.6	3.6	14,929.2	433	4.4	72	18.46	40.6	1,141
California	18	24.6	1.0	1,366.7	134	1.4	7	9.71	46.3	4,455

Source: 2002 *Economic Census*. The states are in descending order of shipments or establishments (if shipment data are missing for the majority). The symbol (D) appears when data are withheld to prevent disclosure of competitive information. States marked with (D) are sorted by number of establishments. A dash (-) indicates that the data element cannot be calculated. Data may not show all states active in the NAICS category. All data available at the time of publication are shown.

NAICS 333314 - OPTICAL INSTRUMENT AND LENS MANUFACTURING

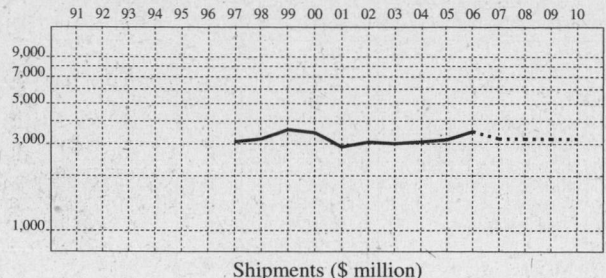

Shipments ($ million)

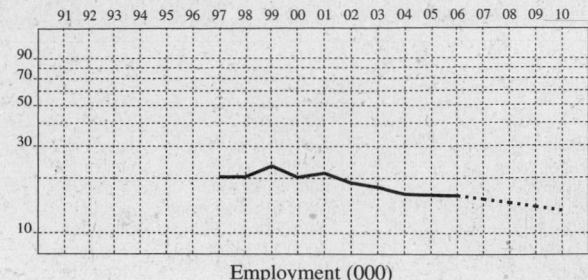

Employment (000)

GENERAL STATISTICS

Year	Companies	Establishments		Employment			Compensation		Production ($ million)			
		Total	with 20 or more employees	Total (000)	Production Workers (000)	Hours (Mil)	Payroll ($ mil)	Wages ($/hr)	Cost of Materials	Value Added by Manufacture	Value of Shipments	Capital Invest.
1997	480	497	190	20.4	12.1	24.0	809.9	14.67	1,151.8	1,951.4	3,080.2	172.2
1998		496	194	20.4	12.3	25.5	841.5	14.98	1,098.5	2,103.9	3,194.8	173.1
1999		490	182	23.4	12.4	25.2	948.2	14.81	1,335.9	2,295.7	3,595.7	214.0
2000		490	189	20.3	10.9	22.9	922.5	14.81	1,147.1	2,331.7	3,462.6	312.6
2001		496	193	21.4	11.2	23.1	940.9	15.47	908.2	1,977.2	2,891.1	474.7
2002	423	444	164	18.9	10.8	22.4	883.7	18.38	1,124.2	1,948.1	3,070.8	130.3
2003		445	164	17.9	10.3	22.0	900.4	19.28	1,179.7	1,804.1	3,011.8	97.0
2004		452	155	16.4	9.6	20.0	873.5	20.59	1,191.5	1,942.8	3,079.4	113.2
2005		441	148	16.2	9.5	19.4	917.3	21.00	1,272.2	1,894.2	3,161.7	119.3
2006		431P	147P	16.1	9.9	19.9	957.2	22.35	1,487.6	2,108.6	3,507.4	112.7
2007		423P	141P	15.4P	9.0P	18.8P	944.8P	22.85P	1,357.6P	1,924.3P	3,200.8P	111.7P
2008		415P	135P	14.7P	8.7P	18.1P	953.1P	23.80P	1,357.2P	1,923.8P	3,200.0P	97.1P
2009		407P	129P	14.0P	8.4P	17.5P	961.3P	24.75P	1,356.9P	1,923.3P	3,199.1P	82.5P
2010		399P	124P	13.3P	8.0P	16.8P	969.5P	25.70P	1,356.5P	1,922.8P	3,198.3P	67.9P

Sources: 1997 and 2002 *Economic Census*; other years, up to 2006, are from *Annual Survey of Manufactures*. Establishment counts for non-Census years are from *County Business Patterns*; 1997 and 2002 values are from the 1997 and 2002 censuses, respectively. 'P's show projections by the editors.

INDICES OF CHANGE

Year	Companies	Establishments		Employment			Compensation		Production ($ million)			
		Total	with 20 or more employees	Total (000)	Production Workers (000)	Hours (Mil)	Payroll ($ mil)	Wages ($/hr)	Cost of Materials	Value Added by Manufacture	Value of Shipments	Capital Invest.
1997	113	112	116	108	112	107	92	80	102	100	100	132
1998		112	118	108	114	114	95	82	98	108	104	133
1999		110	111	124	115	113	107	81	119	118	117	164
2000		110	115	107	101	102	104	81	102	120	113	240
2001		112	118	113	104	103	106	84	81	101	94	364
2002	100	100	100	100	100	100	100	100	100	100	100	100
2003		100	100	95	95	98	102	105	105	93	98	74
2004		102	95	87	89	89	99	112	106	100	100	87
2005		99	90	86	88	87	104	114	113	97	103	92
2006		97P	89P	85	92	89	108	122	132	108	114	86
2007		95P	86P	81P	83P	84P	107P	124P	121P	99P	104P	86P
2008		93P	82P	78P	81P	81P	108P	129P	121P	99P	104P	75P
2009		92P	79P	74P	78P	78P	109P	135P	121P	99P	104P	63P
2010		90P	75P	70P	74P	75P	110P	140P	121P	99P	104P	52P

Sources: Same as General Statistics. Values reflect change from the base year, 2002. Values above 100 mean greater than 2002, values below 100 mean less than 2002, and the values of 100 in other years means the same as 2002. 'P's show projections by the editors.

SELECTED RATIOS

For 2002	Avg. of All Manufact.	Analyzed Industry	Index	For 2002	Avg. of All Manufact.	Analyzed Industry	Index
Employees per Establishment	42	43	101	Value Added per Production Worker	182,367	180,380	99
Payroll per Establishment	1,639,184	1,990,315	121	Cost per Establishment	5,769,015	2,531,982	44
Payroll per Employee	39,053	46,757	120	Cost per Employee	137,446	59,481	43
Production Workers per Establishment	30	24	82	Cost per Production Worker	195,506	104,093	53
Wages per Establishment	694,845	927,279	133	Shipments per Establishment	11,158,348	6,916,216	62
Wages per Production Worker	23,548	38,121	162	Shipments per Employee	265,847	162,476	61
Hours per Production Worker	1,980	2,074	105	Shipments per Production Worker	378,144	284,333	75
Wages per Hour	11.89	18.38	155	Investment per Establishment	361,338	293,468	81
Value Added per Establishment	5,381,325	4,387,613	82	Investment per Employee	8,609	6,894	80
Value Added per Employee	128,210	103,074	80	Investment per Production Worker	12,245	12,065	99

Sources: Same as General Statistics. The 'Average of All Manufacturing' column represents the average of all manufacturing industries reported for the most recent complete year available. The Index shows the relation-ship between the Average and the Analyzed Industry. For example, 100 means that they are equal; 500 that the Analyzed Industry is five times the average; 50 means that the Analyzed Industry is half the national aver-age. The abbreviation 'na' is used to show that data are 'not available'. Ratios shown for 2002, the last complete census year.

LEADING COMPANIES   Number shown: **75**   Total sales ($ mil): **42,259**   Total employment (000): **122.1**

Company Name	Address				CEO Name	Phone	Co. Type	Sales ($ mil)	Empl. (000)
3M Co.	3M Ctr.	St. Paul	MN	55144	George W. Buckley	651-733-2204	P	24,462	76.2
Magna Donnelly Corp.	600 Wilshire Dr.	Troy	MI	48084	Carlos Mazzorin	248-729-2400	R	4,906*	<0.1
KLA-Tencor Corp.	160 Rio Robles	San Jose	CA	95134	Edward W. Barnholt	408-875-3000	P	2,731	6.0
PerkinElmer Inc.	940 Winter St.	Waltham	MA	02451	Robert F. Friel	781-663-6900	P	1,787	8.7
Ten X Technology Inc.	13091 Pond Springs	Austin	TX	78729	Jerry Wuest	512-918-9182	R	1,535*	<0.1
Cooper Companies Inc.	21062 Bake Pky.	Lake Forest	CA	92630	Thomas Bender	949-597-4700	P	951	7.6
3M Precision Optics Inc.	4000 McMann Rd.	Cincinnati	OH	45245		513-752-7000	S	690*	1.3
Ocean Optics Inc.	PO Box 2249	Dunedin	FL	34697	Michael Morris	727-733-2447	R	595*	<0.1
NeoPhotonics Corp.	2911 Zanker Rd.	San Jose	CA	95134	Tim Jenks	408-232-9200	R	448*	1.2
Optical Coating Laboratory	430 N McCarthy	Milpitas	CA	95035	Kevin Kennedy	408-546-5000	S	357*	1.5
Zeiss, Carl Inc.	1 Zeiss Dr.	Thornwood	NY	10594	Jim Kelly	914-681-7600	R	300*	1.7
II-VI Inc.	375 Saxonburg Blvd.	Saxonburg	PA	16056	Francis Kramer	724-352-4455	P	263	2.1
Welch Allyn Holdings Inc.	PO Box 220	Skaneateles Fls	NY	13153		315-685-4100	R	227*	1.4
Pentax of America Inc.	600 12th St.	Golden	CO	80403	Ikuzo Okamoto		S	224*	0.6
Zygo Corp.	PO Box 448	Middlefield	CT	06455		860-347-8506	P	181	0.6
AXSYS Technologies Inc.	175 Capital Blvd.	Rocky Hill	CT	06067	Stephen W. Bershad	860-257-0200	P	172	0.8
Nexans USA Inc.	PO Box 60339	Charlotte	NC	28260	Kevin Cyr	717-354-6200	R	121*	0.5
Gentex Corp.	324 Main Street	Simpson	PA	18407	L. Peter Frieder Jr.	570-282-3550	R	113*	0.6
Oplink Communications Inc.	46335 Landing Pky.	Fremont	CA	94538	Herbert Chang	510-933-7200	P	108	2.0
Meade Instruments Corp.	6001 Oak Canyon	Irvine	CA	92618	Harry L. Casari	949-451-1450	P	102	0.3
Titmus Optical Inc.	3811 Corporate Dr.	Petersburg	VA	23805	Thomas Goeltz	804-732-6121	S	88*	0.4
Suncoast Medical Clinic	601 7th St. S	St. Petersburg	FL	33701		727-894-1818	R	85*	0.3
Fujinon Inc.	10 Highpoint Dr.	Wayne	NJ	07470	Takeshi Higuchi	973-633-5600	R	85*	0.1
Topcon Technologies Inc.	37 W Century Rd.	Paramus	NJ	07652	Scott Hokari	201-261-9450	R	80*	<0.1
Insight Technology Inc.	9 Akira Way	Londonderry	NH	03053	Kenneth Solinsky	603-626-4800	R	76*	0.5
Leupold and Stevens Inc.	PO Box 688	Beaverton	OR	97075	Thomas Fruechtel	503-646-9171	R	76*	0.5
Synrad Inc.	4600 Campus Pl.	Mukilteo	WA	98275	Dave Clarke	425-349-3500	S	76*	0.2
Flents Products Company Inc.	5401 S Graham Rd.	St. Charles	MI	48655	Meredith Birrittella	989-865-8221	R	69*	0.1
CyberOptics Corp.	5900 Golden Hills	Minneapolis	MN	55416	Steven K. Case	763-542-5000	P	59	0.2
Pech Optical Corp.	PO Box 9100	Sioux City	IA	51102	Doug Pech	712-277-3937	R	54*	0.2
HACH Ultra Analytics	481 California Ave.	Grants Pass	OR	97526	Simon Appleby		S	54*	0.2
Cyoptics Inc.	9999 Hamilton Blvd.	Breinigsville	PA	18031	Ed Coringrato	484-397-2000	R	47*	0.1
DiCon Fiberoptics Inc.	1689 Regatta Blvd.	Richmond	CA	94804	Gilles Corcos	510-620-5000	R	46*	0.4
Ats Systems Oregon Inc.	2121 NE J London	Corvallis	OR	97330		541-758-3329	R	45*	0.3
Orange 21 Inc.	2070 Las Palmas Dr.	Carlsbad	CA	92009		760-804-8420	P	42	<0.1
Hilsinger Co.	PO Box 1538	Plainville	MA	02762	Robert Nahmias	508-699-4406	R	42*	0.2
David White Inc.	PO Box 359	Watseka	IL	60970	Ash Perry	815-432-9200	R	40*	0.2
Seiler Instrument and Mfg. Co.	170 E Kirkham Ave.	Saint Louis	MO	63119		314-968-2282	R	38*	0.1
Fiber Instrument Sales Inc.	161 Clear Rd.	Oriskany	NY	13424	Frank Giotto	315-736-2206	R	38*	0.2
Technical Wire Products L.L.C.	1505 W 3rd Ave.	Denver	CO	80223	Steven Ferrie	303-592-1903	R	38*	0.1
Testrite Instrument Company	216 S Newman St.	Hackensack	NJ	07601	Harold Rubin	201-543-0240	R	37*	0.1
Van Cort Instruments Inc.	PO Box 215	South Deerfield	MA	01373	L. Erik Van Cort	413-665-2000	R	35*	0.1
NEPTCO Inc.	PO Box 2323	Pawtucket	RI	02861	Gaetano Marini	401-722-5500	R	35*	<0.1
North American Enclosures Inc.	PO Box 850	Central Islip	NY	11722	Norman Grafstein	631-234-9500	R	34*	<0.1
Exotic Electro-Optics	36570 Briggs Rd.	Murrieta	CA	92563		951-926-2994	S	33*	0.3
Optical Gaging Products Inc.	850 Hudson Ave.	Rochester	NY	14621	Edward Polidor	585-544-0450	R	31*	0.2
Rigaku Innovative Technologies	1900 Taylor Rd.	Auburn Hills	MI	48326	John McGill	248-232-6400	S	31*	0.2
Awareness Technology Inc.	PO Box 1679	Palm City	FL	34991	Mary Freeman	772-283-6540	R	30*	0.1
Btx Technologies Inc.	5 Skyline Dr.	Hawthorne	NY	10532	Greg Schwartz	914-592-1800	R	29*	<0.1
Schott-Fostec L.L.C.	62 Columbus St.	Auburn	NY	13021	Doug Roberts	315-255-2791	S	28*	0.1
Optoplex Corp.	3390 Gateway Blvd.	Fremont	CA	94538	James Sha	510-490-9930	R	26*	<0.1
Kollmorgen Electro-Optical	347 King Street	Northampton	MA	01060	Ken Bixby	413-586-2330	D	25*	0.3
New Focus Inc.	39 Brighton Ave.	Allston	MA	02134	Nicola Pignati	617-783-0039	S	24	0.2
Westover Scientific Inc.	18421 Bothll-Evrett	Mill Creek	WA	98012	Steve Lytle	425-398-1298	R	24*	<0.1
Dolan-Jenner Industries Inc.	159 Swanson Rd.	Boxborough	MA	01719	Mike Balas	978-263-1400	S	22*	0.2
Xinetics Inc.	115 Jackson Rd.	Ayer	MA	01434	Mark Ealey	978-772-0352	R	21*	<0.1
Anorad Corp.	100 Precision Dr.	Shirley	NY	11967	Jim Smith	631-344-6600	D	20*	0.3
Moxtek Inc.	452 W 1260 N	Orem	UT	84057	Sanji Arisawa	801-225-0930	R	20*	0.1
Research Electro-Optics Inc.	5505 Airport Blvd.	Boulder	CO	80301	Robert Knollenberg	303-938-1960	R	20*	0.1
Trijicon Inc.	PO Box 930059	Wixom	MI	48393	Stephen Bindon	248-960-7700	R	20*	0.1
Michigan Development Corp.	3520 Green Ct. Ste.	Ann Arbor	MI	48105	Kenneth Baker	734-302-4600	R	19*	0.3
StockerYale Inc.	32 Hampshire Rd.	Salem	NH	03079	Mark W. Blodgett	603-893-8778	P	19	0.2
21st Century Optics Inc.	4700 33rd St.	Long Island Cty	NY	11101	Ralph Woythaler	718-392-2310	S	19*	0.1
Oerlikon Optics USA Inc.	16080 Table Mtn	Golden	CO	80403	Mike Cusier	303-273-9700	S	19*	<0.1
Forte Automation Systems Inc.	8155 Burden Rd.	Machesney Park	IL	61115	Toby Henderson	815-633-2300	R	19*	0.1
APA Enterprises Inc.	2950 NE 84th Ln.	Blaine	MN	55449	Anil K. Jain	763-784-4995	P	19	<0.1
American Technology Network	20 S Linden Ave.	S San Francisco	CA	94080	Marc Morgovsky	650-875-0130	R	19*	<0.1
Celestron Acquisition L.L.C.	2835 Columbia St.	Torrance	CA	90503		310-328-9560	R	18*	0.1
Reliance Medical Products Inc.	3535 Kings Mill Rd.	Mason	OH	45040	David Edenfield	513-398-3937	R	18*	0.1
Eyeonics	26970 Aliso Viejo	Aliso Viejo	CA	92656	Andy Corley	949-916-9352	S	17	0.1
Corning Tropel Corp.	60 O'Connor Rd.	Fairport	NY	14450	James Houghton	585-388-3500	S	17	0.1
Mir-Tec L.L.C.	1212 E Michigan St.	Indianapolis	IN	46202		317-686-4140	R	17*	0.1
Gurley Precision Instruments	514 Fulton St.	Troy	NY	12180	Patrick Brady	518-272-6300	R	16*	0.1
Spectro Inc.	160 Ayer Rd.	Littleton	MA	01460	Charles Hagedorn	978-486-0123	R	16*	<0.1
Sunoptic Technologies L.L.C.	6018 Bowdendale	Jacksonville	FL	32216		904-737-7611	R	15*	<0.1

Source: Ward's Business Directory of U.S. Private and Public Companies, Volumes 1 and 2, 2008. The company type code used is as follows: P - Public, R - Private, S - Subsidiary, D - Division, J - Joint Venture, A - Affiliate, G - Group. Sales are in millions of dollars, employees are in thousands. An asterisk (*) indicates an estimated sales volume. The symbol < stands for 'less than'. Company names and addresses are truncated, in some cases, to fit into the available space.

MATERIALS CONSUMED

Material	Quantity	Delivered Cost ($ million)
Printed ciruit boards (without inserted components) for electronic circuitry	(X)	6.8
Printed circuit assemblies, loaded boards, and modules	(X)	36.6
Semiconductors (incl. transistors, diodes, rectifiers, and integrated circuits), for electronic circuitry	(X)	11.4
Capacitors for electronic circuitry	(X)	(D)
Resistors for electronic circuitry	(X)	1.4
All other miscellaneous components and accessories for electronic circuitry (exc. tubes)	(X)	28.5
Current-carrying wiring devices	(X)	0.1
Fractional horsepower electric motors (less than 1 hp)	(X)	0.6
Electronic communication equipment	(X)	1.2
Electrical transmission, distribution, and control equipment	(X)	3.8
Electrical instrument mechanisms and meter movements	(X)	(D)
All other miscellaneous electrical measuring instruments and parts	(X)	5.1
Insulated wire and cable (including magnet wire)	(X)	1.8
Plastics resins consumed in the form of granules, pellets, etc.	(X)	14.6
Fabricated plastics products (exc. gaskets, hoses, and belting)	(X)	12.3
Paper and paperboard containers (incl. shipping sacks and other paper packaging supplies)	(X)	5.2
Sheet metal products (excluding stampings)	(X)	3.1
Metal stampings	(X)	1.6
Metal bolts, nuts, screws, and other screw machine products	(X)	6.2
Other fabricated metal products (exc. forgings, metal stampings, and sheet metal products)	(X)	23.8
Forgings	(X)	(D)
Castings, rough and semifinished	(X)	5.2
Aluminum and aluminum-base alloy shapes and forms (exc. castings, forgings, fabr. metal products)	(X)	3.0
Copper and copper-base alloy shapes and forms (exc. castings, forgings, fabr. metal products)	(X)	0.1
Steel shapes and forms (exc. castings, forgings, fabr. metal products)	(X)	0.5
Metal shapes and forms (exc. castings, forgings, fabr. metal products)	(X)	1.4
Other nonferrous shapes and forms (exc. castings, forgings, fabricated metal products)	(X)	0.5
Liquid crystal display screens (LCD), including LED	(X)	1.3
Glass and glass products (excluding windows and mirrors)	(X)	71.8
Optical instruments and lenses (exc. sighting, tracking, and fire control)	(X)	109.9
All other materials, components, parts, containers, and supplies	(X)	177.2
Materials, ingredients, containers, and supplies, nsk	(X)	445.1

Source: 2002 *Economic Census*. Explanation of symbols used: (D): Withheld to avoid disclosure of competitive data; na: Not available; (S): Withheld because statistical norms were not met; (X): Not applicable; (Z): Less than half the unit shown; nec: Not elsewhere classified; nsk: Not specified by kind; - : zero; p : 10-19 percent estimated; q : 20-29 percent estimated.

PRODUCT SHARE DETAILS

Product or Product Class Shipments	Mil. $	Product or Product Class Shipments	Mil. $
OPTICAL INSTRUMENTS AND LENSES	3,084.3	Other optical instruments and lenses (except sighting, tracking, and fire-control)	2,122.6
Sighting, tracking, and fire-control equipment, optical-type	**664.4**	Optical instruments and lenses, nec, nsk	4.8
Optical instruments and lenses, nec	**2,227.8**	**Optical instruments and lenses, nsk, total**	**192.1**
Binoculars and astronomical instruments	100.5		

Source: 2002 *Economic Census*. The values are product shipments in millions of dollars for 2002. Total product shipments may be lower or higher than industry shipments. See Introduction for a full discussion. Values of indented subcategories are summed in the main heading(s). The symbol (D) appears when data are withheld to prevent disclosure of competitive information. The abbreviation nsk stands for 'not specified by kind' and nec for 'not elsewhere classified'. A dash (-) means zero.

INPUTS AND OUTPUTS FOR OPTICAL INSTRUMENT AND LENS MANUFACTURING

Economic Sector or Industry Providing Inputs	%	Sector	Economic Sector or Industry Buying Outputs	%	Sector
Compensation of employees	36.9		Exports of goods & services	57.7	Cap Inv
Management of companies & enterprises	5.7	Services	Private fixed investment	24.4	
Wholesale trade	5.2	Trade	Ophthalmic goods	2.9	Manufg.
Optical instruments & lenses	3.7	Manufg.	Federal government, investment, national defense	2.5	Fed Govt
Printed circuit assemblies (electronic assemblies)	2.8	Manufg.	Optical instruments & lenses	2.2	Manufg.
Pressed & blown glass & glassware, nec	2.6	Manufg.	Personal consumption expenditures	2.2	
Advertising & related services	2.3	Services	Surgical appliances & supplies	1.8	Manufg.
Plastics products, nec	2.3	Manufg.	Change in private inventories	1.3	In House
Glass products from purchased glass	2.2	Manufg.	Medical & diagnostic labs & outpatient services	0.6	Services
Ornamental & architectural metal products	2.0	Manufg.	Analytical laboratory instruments	0.6	Manufg.
Electronic components, nec	1.8	Manufg.	Electronic components, nec	0.6	Manufg.
Noncomparable imports	1.5	Foreign	Electrical equipment & components, nec	0.5	Manufg.
Real estate	1.1	Fin/R.E.	S/L govt. invest., education	0.5	S/L Govt
Chemical products & preparations, nec	1.0	Manufg.	S/L govt. invest., other	0.4	S/L Govt
Securities, commodity contracts, investments	1.0	Fin/R.E.	Scientific research & development services	0.3	Services
Power generation & supply	1.0	Util.	Industrial process variable instruments	0.3	Manufg.
Dry-cleaning & laundry services	1.0	Services	Physician, dentist, other health practitioner offices	0.2	Services
Plastics materials & resins	0.9	Manufg.	Electronic connectors	0.1	Manufg.
Lessors of nonfinancial assets	0.8	Fin/R.E.	Electricity & signal testing instruments	0.1	Manufg.
Electricity & signal testing instruments	0.7	Manufg.			
Flat glass	0.7	Manufg.			

Continued on next page.

INPUTS AND OUTPUTS FOR OPTICAL INSTRUMENT AND LENS MANUFACTURING - Continued

Economic Sector or Industry Providing Inputs	%	Sector	Economic Sector or Industry Buying Outputs	%	Sector
Semiconductors & related devices	0.7	Manufg.			
Gaskets, packing, & sealing devices	0.7	Manufg.			
Plastics packaging materials, film & sheet	0.7	Manufg.			
Data processing, hosting, & related services	0.7	Services			
Monetary authorities/depository credit intermediation	0.7	Fin/R.E.			
Machine shops	0.7	Manufg.			
Turned products & screws, nuts, & bolts	0.6	Manufg.			
Food services & drinking places	0.6	Services			
Legal services	0.6	Services			
Truck transportation	0.6	Util.			
Telecommunications	0.5	Services			
Custom computer programming services	0.5	Services			
Professional, scientific, technical services, nec	0.5	Services			
Accounting, tax preparation, bookkeeping, & payroll	0.5	Services			
Coating, engraving, heat treating & allied activities	0.5	Manufg.			
Hotels & motels, including casino hotels	0.5	Services			
Warehousing & storage	0.4	Util.			
Bare printed circuit boards	0.4	Manufg.			
Management, scientific, & technical consulting	0.4	Services			
Scientific research & development services	0.4	Services			
Unlaminated plastics profile shapes	0.4	Manufg.			
Computer terminals & peripherals	0.4	Manufg.			
Business support services	0.4	Services			
Taxes on production & imports, less subsidies	0.4				
Architectural, engineering, & related services	0.3	Services			
Paperboard containers	0.3	Manufg.			
Air transportation	0.3	Util.			
Employment services	0.3	Services			
Specialized design services	0.3	Services			
Maintenance/repair of nonresidential structures	0.3	Construct.			
Retail trade	0.3	Trade			
Electronic capacitors, resistors, coils, transformers	0.3	Manufg.			
Services to buildings & dwellings	0.3	Services			
Alumina refining & primary aluminum production	0.2	Manufg.			
Fabricated metals, nec	0.2	Manufg.			
Automotive equipment rental & leasing	0.2	Fin/R.E.			
Iron & steel mills & ferroalloys	0.2	Manufg.			
Relay & industrial controls	0.2	Manufg.			
Other computer related services, including facilities	0.2	Services			
Support services, nec	0.2	Services			
Commercial & service industry machinery, nec	0.2	Manufg.			
Automotive repair & maintenance, ex. car washes	0.2	Services			
Valve & fittings other than plumbing	0.2	Manufg.			
Ferrous metal foundries	0.2	Manufg.			
Nonferrous metal foundries	0.2	Manufg.			
Commercial & industrial equipment repair/maintenance	0.2	Services			
Investigation & security services	0.1	Services			
Rubber products, nec	0.1	Manufg.			
Crowns & closures & metal stamping	0.1	Manufg.			
Nondepository credit intermediation activities	0.1	Fin/R.E.			
Transit & ground passenger transportation	0.1	Util.			
Ball & roller bearings	0.1	Manufg.			
Commercial & industrial machinery rental & leasing	0.1	Fin/R.E.			
Paperboard mills	0.1	Manufg.			

Source: Benchmark Input-Output Accounts for the U.S. Economy, 2002, U.S. Department of Commerce, Washington, D.C., January 2008. The abbreviation nec stands for 'not elsewhere classified'.

OCCUPATIONS EMPLOYED BY COMMERCIAL & SERVICE INDUSTRY MACHINERY MANUFACTURING

Occupation	% of Total 2006	Change to 2016	Occupation	% of Total 2006	Change to 2016
Team assemblers	11.6	-12.3	Electrical engineers	1.4	-12.3
Welders, cutters, solderers, & brazers	3.4	-6.7	Maintenance & repair workers, general	1.4	-12.3
First-line supervisors/managers of production workers	3.3	-12.3	Engineering managers	1.4	-12.3
Inspectors, testers, sorters, samplers, & weighers	2.8	-17.3	Bookkeeping, accounting, & auditing clerks	1.4	-12.3
Sales reps, wholesale & manufacturing, exc tech	2.5	-12.3	Shipping, receiving, & traffic clerks	1.4	-15.6
Mechanical engineers	2.5	-12.3	Electromechanical equipment assemblers	1.4	-12.3
Computer software engineers, applications	2.3	5.3	Stock clerks & order fillers	1.3	-26.6
Electrical & electronic equipment assemblers	2.2	-29.8	Purchasing agents, exc wholesale, retail, & farm	1.3	-12.3
Machinists	1.9	-7.9	Accountants & auditors	1.2	-12.3
Assemblers & fabricators, nec	1.9	-21.0	Helpers--Production workers	1.1	-12.3
Cutting, punching, & press machine operators	1.8	-21.0	Executive secretaries & administrative assistants	1.1	-12.3
Industrial engineers	1.8	6.5	Office clerks, general	1.1	-13.6
General & operations managers	1.7	-21.0	Computer-controlled machine tool operators	1.0	-3.5
Coating, painting, & spraying machine operators	1.7	-16.7	Sales representatives, wholesale & manufacturing, tech	1.0	-12.3
Customer service representatives	1.6	-3.5	Laborers & freight, stock, & material movers, hand	1.0	-21.0
Ophthalmic laboratory technicians	1.4	-12.3			

Source: Industry-Occupation Matrix, Bureau of Labor Statistics, December 4, 2007. These data are reported based on 4-digit NAICS categories but have been matched to corresponding 6-digit NAICS industry codes. The change reported for each occupation to the year 2016 is a percent of growth or decline as estimated by the Bureau of Labor Statistics. The abbreviation nec stands for 'not elsewhere classified'.

LOCATION BY STATE AND REGIONAL CONCENTRATION

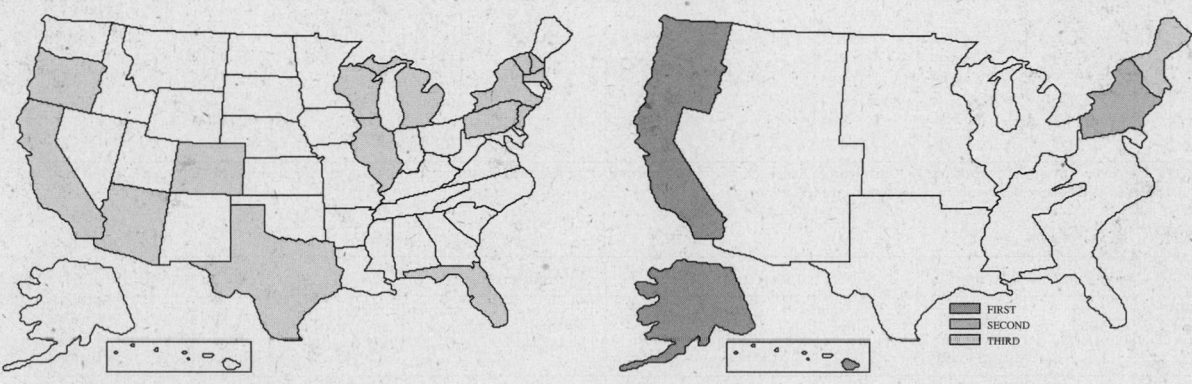

FIRST
SECOND
THIRD

INDUSTRY DATA BY STATE

State	Establish-ments	Shipments Total ($ mil)	Shipments % of U.S.	Shipments Per Establ.	Employment Total Number	Employment % of U.S.	Employment Per Establ.	Employment Wages ($/hour)	Cost as % of Shipments	Investment per Employee ($)
California	110	718.5	23.4	6,531.8	4,711	25.0	43	20.73	40.6	6,374
Florida	19	451.0	14.7	23,735.0	2,443	12.9	129	17.58	43.0	3,320
Massachusetts	46	276.9	9.0	6,019.2	2,170	11.5	47	17.80	33.1	3,054
New Hampshire	16	240.5	7.8	15,031.8	1,292	6.8	81	17.71	57.8	4,556
Pennsylvania	21	184.4	6.0	8,780.2	735	3.9	35	22.75	35.4	4,835
New York	47	177.7	5.8	3,781.5	1,407	7.5	30	19.65	39.5	10,526
Colorado	21	117.6	3.8	5,600.5	750	4.0	36	18.67	39.0	17,012
Oregon	7	102.9	3.3	14,694.7	669	3.5	96	16.43	27.1	3,259
New Jersey	18	102.6	3.3	5,697.4	433	2.3	24	19.30	17.9	6,349
Vermont	5	36.6	1.2	7,321.4	300	1.6	60	22.67	28.4	8,267
Michigan	6	34.6	1.1	5,772.8	257	1.4	43	15.26	39.1	46,035
Arizona	11	28.5	0.9	2,594.6	153	0.8	14	22.05	32.8	3,706
Illinois	12	22.9	0.7	1,908.9	131	0.7	11	20.08	34.8	3,702
Wisconsin	5	22.7	0.7	4,536.6	129	0.7	26	17.15	37.1	1,512
Texas	10	16.5	0.5	1,650.7	107	0.6	11	14.78	42.7	9,374

Source: 2002 Economic Census. The states are in descending order of shipments or establishments (if shipment data are missing for the majority). The symbol (D) appears when data are withheld to prevent disclosure of competitive information. States marked with (D) are sorted by number of establishments. A dash (-) indicates that the data element cannot be calculated. Data may not show all states active in the NAICS category. All data available at the time of publication are shown.

NAICS 333315 - PHOTOGRAPHIC AND PHOTOCOPYING EQUIPMENT MANUFACTURING

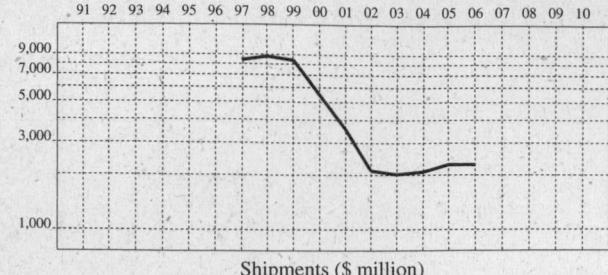

Shipments ($ million)

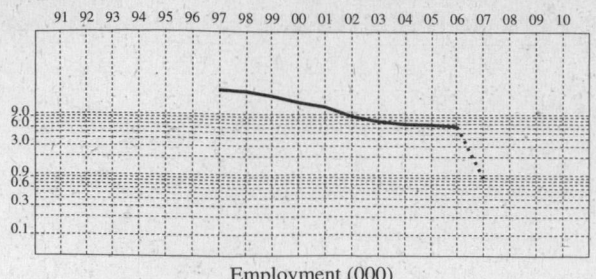

Employment (000)

GENERAL STATISTICS

| Year | Com-panies | Establishments | | Employment | | | Compensation | | Production ($ million) | | | |
		Total	with 20 or more employees	Total (000)	Production Workers (000)	Hours (Mil)	Payroll ($ mil)	Wages ($/hr)	Cost of Materials	Value Added by Manufacture	Value of Shipments	Capital Invest.
1997	419	428	131	24.7	14.8	26.7	1,099.9	18.55	3,828.2	4,542.6	8,410.1	281.6
1998		415	135	23.6	14.4	26.7	1,030.4	17.11	3,613.0	5,192.1	8,809.4	241.9
1999		410	122	19.8	11.8	21.8	876.8	17.71	3,238.7	5,141.5	8,396.7	125.8
2000		401	123	15.7	9.1	18.1	640.2	16.03	1,913.7	3,550.7	5,462.6	64.9
2001		377	120	13.3	7.8	14.7	539.8	15.92	1,487.7	2,071.6	3,567.1	59.4
2002	288	301	81	9.3	5.2	9.3	380.6	17.14	1,037.1	1,091.2	2,116.6	89.1
2003		303	78	7.7	4.6	8.9	332.6	16.94	996.8	1,048.8	2,020.7	14.1
2004		293	71	6.9	4.1	8.0	291.8	17.07	1,054.0	1,016.4	2,083.7	31.4
2005		276	68	6.8	4.0	8.0	299.8	16.58	1,055.6	1,234.1	2,287.2	26.2
2006		249P	55P	6.4	3.7	7.3	285.1	17.33	1,056.9	1,229.1	2,281.1	32.8
2007		227P	46P	0.9P	0.4P	1.4P	29.2P	16.57P				
2008		206P	36P					16.49P				
2009		184P	27P					16.40P				
2010		163P	17P					16.32P				

Sources: 1997 and 2002 *Economic Census*; other years, up to 2006, are from *Annual Survey of Manufactures*. Establishment counts for non-Census years are from *County Business Patterns*; 1997 and 2002 values are from the 1997 and 2002 censuses, respectively. 'P's show projections by the editors.

INDICES OF CHANGE

| Year | Com-panies | Establishments | | Employment | | | Compensation | | Production ($ million) | | | |
		Total	with 20 or more employees	Total (000)	Production Workers (000)	Hours (Mil)	Payroll ($ mil)	Wages ($/hr)	Cost of Materials	Value Added by Manufacture	Value of Shipments	Capital Invest.
1997	145	142	162	266	285	287	289	108	369	416	397	316
1998		138	167	254	277	287	271	100	348	476	416	271
1999		136	151	213	227	234	230	103	312	471	397	141
2000		133	152	169	175	195	168	94	185	325	258	73
2001		125	148	143	150	158	142	93	143	190	169	67
2002	100	100	100	100	100	100	100	100	100	100	100	100
2003		101	96	83	88	96	87	99	96	96	95	16
2004		97	88	74	79	86	77	100	102	93	98	35
2005		92	84	73	77	86	79	97	102	113	108	29
2006		83P	68P	69	71	78	75	101	102	113	108	37
2007		75P	57P	10P	8P	15P	8P	97P				
2008		68P	45P					96P				
2009		61P	33P					96P				
2010		54P	21P					95P				

Sources: Same as General Statistics. Values reflect change from the base year, 2002. Values above 100 mean greater than 2002, values below 100 mean less than 2002, and the values of 100 in other years means the same as 2002. 'P's show projections by the editors.

SELECTED RATIOS

For 2002	Avg. of All Manufact.	Analyzed Industry	Index	For 2002	Avg. of All Manufact.	Analyzed Industry	Index
Employees per Establishment	42	31	74	Value Added per Production Worker	182,367	209,846	115
Payroll per Establishment	1,639,184	1,264,452	77	Cost per Establishment	5,769,015	3,445,515	60
Payroll per Employee	39,053	40,925	105	Cost per Employee	137,446	111,516	81
Production Workers per Establishment	30	17	59	Cost per Production Worker	195,506	199,442	102
Wages per Establishment	694,845	529,575	76	Shipments per Establishment	11,158,348	7,031,894	63
Wages per Production Worker	23,548	30,654	130	Shipments per Employee	265,847	227,591	86
Hours per Production Worker	1,980	1,788	90	Shipments per Production Worker	378,144	407,038	108
Wages per Hour	11.89	17.14	144	Investment per Establishment	361,338	296,013	82
Value Added per Establishment	5,381,325	3,625,249	67	Investment per Employee	8,609	9,581	111
Value Added per Employee	128,210	117,333	92	Investment per Production Worker	12,245	17,135	140

Sources: Same as General Statistics. The 'Average of All Manufacturing' column represents the average of all manufacturing industries reported for the most recent complete year available. The Index shows the relationship between the Average and the Analyzed Industry. For example, 100 means that they are equal; 500 that the Analyzed Industry is five times the average; 50 means that the Analyzed Industry is half the national average. The abbreviation 'na' is used to show that data are 'not available'. Ratios shown for 2002, the last complete census year.

LEADING COMPANIES

Number shown: **75**   Total sales ($ mil): **65,906**   Total employment (000): **134.5**

Company Name	Address				CEO Name	Phone	Co. Type	Sales ($ mil)	Empl. (000)
Xerox Corp.	PO Box 1600	Stamford	CT	06904		203-968-3000	P	17,288	57.4
Canon U.S.A. Inc.	1 Canon Plz.	Lake Success	NY	11042	Yoroku Adachi	516-328-5000	S	10,745*	11.0
Eastman Kodak Co.	343 State St.	Rochester	NY	14650		716-724-4000	P	10,301	26.9
Arkwright Inc.	PO Box 139	Fiskeville	RI	02823		401-821-1000	R	7,179*	0.1
FUJIFILM Medical Systems USA	419 W Ave.	Stamford	CT	06902		203-324-2000	R	5,312*	0.2
Fujifilm Hunt Chemicals USA	40 Boroline Rd.	Allendale	NJ	07401	Albert Aerts	201-995-2200	R	3,432*	0.1
Konica Minolta Graphic Imaging	5800 Foremost Dr.	Grand Rapids	MI	49546	Peter Newton	616-575-2800	R	2,193*	0.2
Sony Music Entertainment Inc.	550 Madison Ave.	New York	NY	10022	Mike Bebel	212-833-8000	S	1,500*	10.0
Avid Technology Inc.	Avid Technology	Tewksbury	MA	01876	Gary Greenfield	978-640-6789	P	930	2.8
Lexar Media Inc.	47300 Bayside Pky.	Fremont	CA	94538	Eric B. Stang	510-413-1200	S	853*	0.3
Polaroid Holding Co.	1265 Main St.	Waltham	MA	02451	Jacque A. Nasser	781-386-2000	S	753	3.4
Polaroid Corp.	300 Baker Ave.	Concord	MA	01742	Bob Gregerson	781-386-2000	S	664*	3.0
Optical Coating Laboratory	430 N McCarthy	Milpitas	CA	95035	Kevin Kennedy	408-546-5000	S	357*	1.5
Pinnacle Systems Inc.	280 N Bernardo	Mountain View	CA	94043	Patti S. Hart	650-526-1600	D	347*	0.9
Recon Optical Inc.	550 W NW Hwy.	Barrington	IL	60010		847-381-2400	R	344*	0.2
Zeiss, Carl Inc.	1 Zeiss Dr.	Thornwood	NY	10594	Jim Kelly	914-681-7600	R	300*	1.7
Panavision International L.P.	6219 De Soto Ave.	Woodland Hills	CA	91367	Bob Beitcher	818-316-1000	S	194*	1.2
X-Rite Inc.	4300 44th St. SE	Grand Rapids	MI	49512	John Utley	616-803-2100	P	180	1.0
Da-Lite Screen Company Inc.	PO Box 137	Warsaw	IN	46581	Richard E. Lundin	574-267-8101	P	170*	0.6
Anacomp Inc.	15378 Ave Science	San Diego	CA	92128	Howard Dratler	858-716-3400	P	152	1.0
Regulus Integrated Solutions	860 Latour Ct.	Napa	CA	94558	Richard Long	707-254-4000	R	145*	0.1
Zondervan Corp.	5300 Patterson Ave.	Grand Rapids	MI	49530	Doug Lockhart	616-698-6900	S	133*	0.3
Proxima Corp.	27700B SW Pkwy.	Wilsonville	OR	97070	Kyle Ranson	503-685-8888	S	122*	0.3
Draper Inc.	411 S Pearl St.	Spiceland	IN	47385	John Pidgeon	765-987-7999	R	121*	0.5
Minco Manufacturing Inc.	855 Aeroplaza Dr.	Colorado Spgs	CO	80916	Ronald Eisele	719-550-1223	S	114*	0.1
Carotek Inc.	PO Box 1395	Matthews	NC	28106	Addison Bell	704-844-1100	R	94*	<0.1
NER Data Products Inc.	307 S Delsea Dr.	Glassboro	NJ	08028	Francis C. Oatway	856-881-5524	R	92*	0.5
PLUS Vision Corp. of America	9610 SW Sunshine	Beaverton	OR	97005		503-748-8700	S	90*	<0.1
Concord Camera Corp.	4000 Hollywood	Hollywood	FL	33021	Ira. B. Lampert	954-331-4200	P	87	0.1
ELXSI Corp.	3600 Rio Vista Ave.	Orlando	FL	32805	Alexander M. Milley	407-849-1090	P	86	2.4
Eye Communication Systems Inc.	PO Box 620	Hartland	WI	53029	John Bessent	262-367-1360	R	83*	<0.1
Deepsea Power and Light Inc.	3855 Ruffin Rd.	San Diego	CA	92123	Mark Olsson	858-576-1261	R	75*	0.2
Elcan Optical Technologies	1601 N Plano Rd.	Richardson	TX	75081		972-344-8000	R	68*	0.2
International Laser Group Inc.	PO Box 686	Woodland Hills	CA	91365	Cindy Michaels	818-888-0400	R	65*	0.2
Bretford Manufacturing Inc.	11000 Seymour Ave.	Schiller Park	IL	60131	Mikel Briggs	847-678-2545	R	61*	0.6
Ilford Imaging USA Inc.	115 W Century Rd.	Paramus	NJ	07652		201-265-6000	R	58*	<0.1
Electronic Imaging Service	7304 Kanis Rd.	Little Rock	AR	72204	Steve Bardwell	501-663-0100	R	57*	0.6
Nu-Kote International Inc.	200 Beasley Dr.	Franklin	TN	37064	Ron Baiocchi	615-794-9000	R	54*	0.2
Tiffen Acquisition L.L.C.	90 Oser Ave.	Hauppauge	NY	11788	Steve Tiffen	631-273-2500	R	51*	0.2
Ballantyne of Omaha Inc.	4350 McKinley St.	Omaha	NE	68112		402-453-4444	P	50	0.2
West Point Products L.L.C.	PO Box 50	Valley Grove	WV	26060		304-547-1360	R	50*	0.2
Macdermid Printing Solutions	260 S Pacific St.	San Marcos	CA	92069	Dan Lever	760-510-6277	S	46*	0.1
Tamron USA Inc.	10 Austin Blvd.	Commack	NY	11725	Tak Inoue	631-858-8400	S	43*	<0.1
Imaging and Sensing Technology	100 IST Ctr.	Horseheads	NY	14845	Donald Hartman	607-562-4300	R	38*	0.3
Testrite Instrument Company	216 S Newman St.	Hackensack	NJ	07601	Harold Rubin	201-543-0240	R	37*	0.1
Graphic Enterprises Inc.	3874 Highland Park	North Canton	OH	44720	Jason Parikh		R	37*	0.3
DeWAL Industries Inc.	PO Box 372	Saunderstown	RI	02874	Eric Walsh	401-789-9736	R	37*	0.1
Siemens Manufacturing Company	PO Box 61	Freeburg	IL	62243	John Siemens	618-539-3000	R	35*	<0.1
Anton Bauer Inc.	14 Progress Dr.	Shelton	CT	06484	Alexander Desorbo	203-929-1100	R	34*	0.1
Hollywood Film Co.	9265 Borden Ave.	Sun Valley	CA	91352	Vincent Carabello	818-683-1130	R	34*	0.1
Advanced Microsensors Inc.	333 S St. Bldg. 2	Shrewsbury	MA	01545		508-770-6600	R	32*	<0.1
Optical Gaging Products Inc.	850 Hudson Ave.	Rochester	NY	14621	Edward Polidor	585-544-0450	R	31*	0.2
Electronic Systems Engineering	1 E Eseco Rd.	Cushing	OK	74023	Arthur Kaminshine	918-225-1266	R	30*	<0.1
Solutek Corp.	94 Shirley St.	Boston	MA	02119	Marlowe A. Sigal	617-445-5335	R	29*	<0.1
AFP Imaging Corp.	250 Clearbrook Rd.	Elmsford	NY	10523		914-592-6100	P	29	0.1
Quality Manufacturing Company	PO Box 616	Winchester	KY	40392	James Barker	859-744-0420	R	28*	0.3
E Alko Inc.	20364 Plummer St.	Chatsworth	CA	91311	Eyal Alkoby	818-587-9700	R	28*	0.2
Advance Reproductions Corp.	100 Flagship Dr.	North Andover	MA	01845		978-685-2911	R	27*	<0.1
Cartridge Care Inc.	2256 Terminal Rd.	Roseville	MN	55113	Charles Pydych	612-331-7757	R	27*	<0.1
Chyron Corp.	5 Hub Dr.	Melville	NY	11747		631-845-2000	P	26	0.1
Myou Video Corp.	4783 Ruffner St.	San Diego	CA	92111	Terry Daffinrud	858-268-1100	R	25*	<0.1
La Vezzi Precision Inc.	999 Regency Dr.	Glendale Hts	IL	60139	Albert La Vezzi	630-582-1230	R	25*	<0.1
Turner Bellows Inc.	526 Child St.	Rochester	NY	14606	Marilyn Yeager	585-235-4456	R	24*	0.1
Vutec Corp.	2741 NE 4th Ave.	Pompano Beach	FL	33064	Howard Sinkoff	954-545-9000	R	24*	0.1
CRIS Camera Services	250 N 54th St.	Chandler	AZ	85226	Mark Treadwell	480-940-1103	R	23*	<0.1
Vishay Thin Film Inc.	2160 Liberty Dr.	Niagara Falls	NY	14304	Felix Zandman	716-283-4025	D	23*	0.2
Rosco Laboratories Inc.	52 Harbor Vw	Stamford	CT	06902	Stanford Miller	203-708-8900	R	23*	<0.1
AQC Group Corp.	200 Park Central	Pompano Beach	FL	33064	Mitch Howard	954-970-8899	R	22*	<0.1
Stewart Filmscreen Corp.	1161 W Sepulveda	Torrance	CA	90502	Grant Stewart	310-784-5300	R	22*	0.1
Consolidated International	4801 S Whipple St.	Chicago	IL	60632	C Meyers	773-376-5600	R	22*	<0.1
Shelton Technologies Inc.	1420 Stamy Rd.	Hiawatha	IA	52233	Gail Shelton	319-398-9898	R	20*	<0.1
JL Fisher Inc.	1000 W Isabel St.	Burbank	CA	91506	James Fisher	818-846-8366	R	20*	<0.1
Double M Laser Products Inc.	7201 Pinemont Dr.	Houston	TX	77040	Curtis Morris	713-956-9481	R	20*	<0.1
Metters Industries Inc.	8200 Greensboro Dr.	McLean	VA	22102	Samuel Metters	703-821-3300	R	19*	0.2
Sun Remanufacturing Corp.	1845 S McDonald	Mesa	AZ	85210	Robert Daggs	480-833-5600	R	19*	0.1

Source: Ward's Business Directory of U.S. Private and Public Companies, Volumes 1 and 2, 2008. The company type code used is as follows: P - Public, R - Private, S - Subsidiary, D - Division, J - Joint Venture, A - Affiliate, G - Group. Sales are in millions of dollars, employees are in thousands. An asterisk (*) indicates an estimated sales volume. The symbol < stands for 'less than'. Company names and addresses are truncated, in some cases, to fit into the available space.

MATERIALS CONSUMED

Material	Quantity	Delivered Cost ($ million)
All other fabricated metal products (excluding forgings)	(X)	22.7
Iron and steel castings (rough and semifinished)	(X)	2.8
Aluminum and aluminum-base alloy castings (rough and semifinished)	(X)	3.7
Other nonferrous metal castings, rough or semifinished (inc. aluminum)	(X)	(D)
Metal stampings	(X)	3.3
Steel shapes and forms (exc. castings, forgings, fabr. metal products)	(X)	4.8
Nonferrous shapes and forms	(X)	4.4
Resistors, capacitors, transformers, electron tubes, semiconductors, and other electronic components	(X)	89.1
Resistors for electronic circuitry	(X)	0.6
Capacitors for electronic circuitry	(X)	1.1
Semiconductors (incl. transistors, diodes, rectifiers, and integrated circuits), for electronic circuitry	(X)	2.1
All other miscellaneous components and accessories for electronic circuitry (exc. tubes)	(X)	8.4
Printed ciruit boards (without inserted components) for electronic circuitry	(X)	8.2
Printed circuit assemblies, loaded boards, and modules	(X)	6.3
Fractional horsepower electric motors (less than 1 hp)	(X)	8.7
Forgings	(X)	(D)
Prepared photographic chemicals	(X)	(D)
Synthetic organic chemicals (exc. prepared photographic chemicals)	(X)	(D)
All other miscellaneous inorganic chemicals	(X)	(D)
Paper and paperboard products	(X)	3.6
Photographic base papers	(X)	0.3
Paperboard containers, boxes, and corrugated paperboard	(X)	34.0
Plastics resins consumed in the form of granules, pellets, etc.	(X)	23.6
Fabricated plastics products (excluding gaskets)	(X)	10.2
Photographic and projection lenses and prisms	(X)	5.1
Light sensitive films and papers	(X)	1.3
All other materials, components, parts, containers, and supplies	(X)	310.8
Materials, ingredients, containers, and supplies, nsk	(X)	79.7

Source: 2002 Economic Census. Explanation of symbols used: (D): Withheld to avoid disclosure of competitive data; na: Not available; (S): Withheld because statistical norms were not met; (X): Not applicable; (Z): Less than half the unit shown; nec: Not elsewhere classified; nsk: Not specified by kind; - : zero; p : 10-19 percent estimated; q : 20-29 percent estimated.

PRODUCT SHARE DETAILS

Product or Product Class Shipments	Mil. $	Product or Product Class Shipments	Mil. $
PHOTOGRAPHIC AND PHOTOCOPYING EQUIPMENT	2,045.5	cameras, including computer output	16.2
Still picture photographic equipment	**837.9**	Microfilming equipment (including microfiche), microfilm readers, excluding handheld and service type	(D)
Still cameras (hand-type cameras, process cameras for photoengraving and photolithography, and other still cameras)	408.1	Microfilming equipment (including microfiche), microfilm reader-printers	(D)
Projectors, except rear screen viewers	27.7	Other microfilming equipment (including microfiche)	4.2
Still picture commercial-type processing equipment for film	40.5	Blueprinting and whiteprinting (direct process type) equipment	-
All other still picture commercial-type processing equipment (developing machines, motor-operated print washers and driers, etc.)	91.0	**Motion picture equipment**	**386.1**
		Motion picture equipment (all sizes 8 mm and greater), excluding projection screens and processing equipment	149.0
Other still picture equipment, parts, attachments, and accessories, including photographic laser systems and equipment (excluding projection screens)	266.5	Projection screens (for motion picture and-or still projection)	204.9
Still picture photographic equipment, nsk	4.2	Motion picture processing equipment, all types, excluding motion picture still type equipment and interchangeable types	23.0
Photocopying equipment, including diffusion transfer, dye transfer, electrostatic, light and heat sensitive types, etc.	**615.2**	Motion picture equipment, nsk	9.1
Microfilming, blueprinting, and whiteprinting equipment	**26.3**	**Photographic and photocopying equipment, nsk, total**	**180.0**
Microfilming equipment (including microfiche)	26.3		
Microfilming equipment (including microfiche),			

Source: 2002 Economic Census. The values are product shipments in millions of dollars for 2002. Total product shipments may be lower or higher than industry shipments. See Introduction for a full discussion. Values of indented subcategories are summed in the main heading(s). The symbol (D) appears when data are withheld to prevent disclosure of competitive information. The abbreviation nsk stands for 'not specified by kind' and nec for 'not elsewhere classified'. A dash (-) means zero.

INPUTS AND OUTPUTS FOR PHOTOGRAPHIC & PHOTOCOPYING EQUIPMENT

Economic Sector or Industry Providing Inputs	%	Sector	Economic Sector or Industry Buying Outputs	%	Sector
Compensation of employees	26.8		Personal consumption expenditures	31.0	
Wholesale trade	6.2	Trade	Private fixed investment	31.0	
Semiconductors & related devices	5.2	Manufg.	Exports of goods & services	17.5	Cap Inv
Management of companies & enterprises	4.7	Services	S/L govt. invest., education	6.0	S/L Govt
Coated & laminated paper & packaging materials	2.9	Manufg.	S/L govt. invest., other	5.5	S/L Govt
Chemical products & preparations, nec	2.4	Manufg.	Federal government, investment, national defense	3.1	Fed Govt
Paperboard containers	2.3	Manufg.	Personal services, nec	1.5	Services
Printed circuit assemblies (electronic assemblies)	2.2	Manufg.	Business support services	1.4	Services
Forging, stamping, & sintering, nec	1.7	Manufg.	Change in private inventories	0.8	In House

Continued on next page.

INPUTS AND OUTPUTS FOR PHOTOGRAPHIC & PHOTOCOPYING EQUIPMENT - Continued

Economic Sector or Industry Providing Inputs	%	Sector	Economic Sector or Industry Buying Outputs	%	Sector
Gaskets, packing, & sealing devices	1.7	Manufg.	Support activities for printing	0.7	Manufg.
Plastics materials & resins	1.5	Manufg.	Electronic & precision equipment repair/maintenance	0.3	Services
Basic organic chemicals, nec	1.5	Manufg.	Elementary & secondary schools	0.3	Services
Power generation & supply	1.0	Util.	Photographic & photocopying equipment	0.2	Manufg.
Real estate	0.9	Fin/R.E.	General S/L govt. services	0.2	S/L Govt
Advertising & related services	0.8	Services	Vending, commercial, industrial, office machinery	0.2	Manufg.
Basic inorganic chemicals, nec	0.7	Manufg.	Federal government, investment, nondefense	0.1	Fed Govt
Truck transportation	0.7	Util.	Telecommunications	0.1	Services
Plastics products, nec	0.7	Manufg.			
Noncomparable imports	0.6	Foreign			
Electronic capacitors, resistors, coils, transformers	0.5	Manufg.			
Motors & generators	0.5	Manufg.			
Electronic components, nec	0.5	Manufg.			
Bare printed circuit boards	0.5	Manufg.			
Photographic & photocopying equipment	0.5	Manufg.			
Unlaminated plastics profile shapes	0.4	Manufg.			
Machine shops	0.4	Manufg.			
Industrial gases	0.3	Manufg.			
Plastics packaging materials, film & sheet	0.3	Manufg.			
Custom roll forming	0.3	Manufg.			
Petrochemicals	0.3	Manufg.			
Iron & steel mills & ferroalloys	0.3	Manufg.			
Warehousing & storage	0.3	Util.			
Adhesives	0.3	Manufg.			
Coating, engraving, heat treating & allied activities	0.3	Manufg.			
Nonferrous metal foundries	0.3	Manufg.			
Paper mills	0.3	Manufg.			
Crowns & closures & metal stamping	0.2	Manufg.			
Scientific research & development services	0.2	Services			
Optical instruments & lenses	0.2	Manufg.			
Retail trade	0.2	Trade			
Automotive equipment rental & leasing	0.2	Fin/R.E.			
Turned products & screws, nuts, & bolts	0.2	Manufg.			
Accounting, tax preparation, bookkeeping, & payroll	0.2	Services			
Ferrous metal foundries	0.2	Manufg.			
Lighting fixtures	0.2	Manufg.			
Cutting tools & machine tool accessories	0.1	Manufg.			
Paperboard mills	0.1	Manufg.			
Natural gas distribution	0.1	Util.			
Postal service	0.1	Util.			
Legal services	0.1	Services			
Telecommunications	0.1	Services			
Alkalies & chlorine	0.1	Manufg.			
Fabricated metals, nec	0.1	Manufg.			
Metal cans, boxes, & other containers (light gauge)	0.1	Manufg.			
Data processing, hosting, & related services	0.1	Services			
Rail transportation	0.1	Util.			
Pressed & blown glass & glassware, nec	0.1	Manufg.			

Source: *Benchmark Input-Output Accounts for the U.S. Economy, 2002*, U.S. Department of Commerce, Washington, D.C., January 2008. The abbreviation nec stands for 'not elsewhere classified'.

OCCUPATIONS EMPLOYED BY COMMERCIAL & SERVICE INDUSTRY MACHINERY MANUFACTURING

Occupation	% of Total 2006	Change to 2016	Occupation	% of Total 2006	Change to 2016
Team assemblers	11.6	-12.3	Electrical engineers	1.4	-12.3
Welders, cutters, solderers, & brazers	3.4	-6.7	Maintenance & repair workers, general	1.4	-12.3
First-line supervisors/managers of production workers	3.3	-12.3	Engineering managers	1.4	-12.3
Inspectors, testers, sorters, samplers, & weighers	2.8	-17.3	Bookkeeping, accounting, & auditing clerks	1.4	-12.3
Sales reps, wholesale & manufacturing, exc tech	2.5	-12.3	Shipping, receiving, & traffic clerks	1.4	-15.6
Mechanical engineers	2.5	-12.3	Electromechanical equipment assemblers	1.4	-12.3
Computer software engineers, applications	2.3	5.3	Stock clerks & order fillers	1.3	-26.6
Electrical & electronic equipment assemblers	2.2	-29.8	Purchasing agents, exc wholesale, retail, & farm	1.3	-12.3
Machinists	1.9	-7.9	Accountants & auditors	1.2	-12.3
Assemblers & fabricators, nec	1.9	-21.0	Helpers--Production workers	1.1	-12.3
Cutting, punching, & press machine operators	1.8	-21.0	Executive secretaries & administrative assistants	1.1	-12.3
Industrial engineers	1.8	6.5	Office clerks, general	1.1	-13.6
General & operations managers	1.7	-21.0	Computer-controlled machine tool operators	1.0	-3.5
Coating, painting, & spraying machine operators	1.7	-16.7	Sales representatives, wholesale & manufacturing, tech	1.0	-12.3
Customer service representatives	1.6	-3.5	Laborers & freight, stock, & material movers, hand	1.0	-21.0
Ophthalmic laboratory technicians	1.4	-12.3			

Source: *Industry-Occupation Matrix*, Bureau of Labor Statistics, December 4, 2007. These data are reported based on 4-digit NAICS categories but have been matched to corresponding 6-digit NAICS industry codes. The change reported for each occupation to the year 2016 is a percent of growth or decline as estimated by the Bureau of Labor Statistics. The abbreviation nec stands for 'not elsewhere classified'.

LOCATION BY STATE AND REGIONAL CONCENTRATION

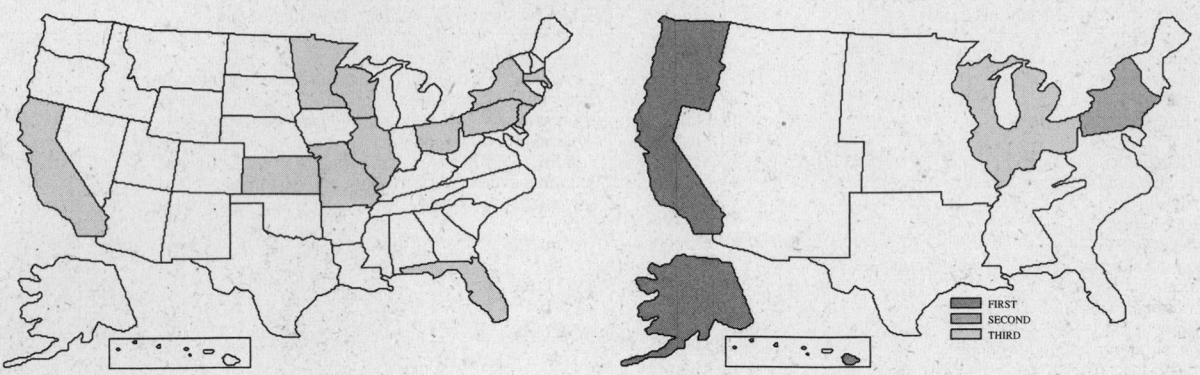

INDUSTRY DATA BY STATE

| State | Establish-ments | Shipments | | | Employment | | | | Cost as % of Shipments | Investment per Employee ($) |
		Total ($ mil)	% of U.S.	Per Establ.	Total Number	% of U.S.	Per Establ.	Wages ($/hour)		
California	77	955.7	45.2	12,411.5	3,246	35.1	42	20.41	51.8	19,277
Minnesota	10	181.8	8.6	18,182.3	449	4.8	45	16.12	59.4	1,154
Massachusetts	9	137.2	6.5	15,247.8	731	7.9	81	17.98	46.1	4,421
New York	23	99.6	4.7	4,331.0	721	7.8	31	10.92	37.5	2,173
New Jersey	17	93.4	4.4	5,495.4	464	5.0	27	11.25	58.0	3,681
Ohio	9	58.4	2.8	6,493.2	208	2.2	23	15.71	39.1	9,846
Illinois	18	42.1	2.0	2,338.4	284	3.1	16	17.55	33.7	2,254
Pennsylvania	13	32.4	1.5	2,494.3	215	2.3	17	12.76	49.2	5,600
Wisconsin	10	23.0	1.1	2,304.2	158	1.7	16	22.29	46.2	2,576
Florida	12	21.3	1.0	1,776.2	138	1.5	11	18.92	47.6	4,022
Kansas	5	17.8	0.8	3,564.0	157	1.7	31	14.44	24.0	3,338
Missouri	6	15.0	0.7	2,505.7	112	1.2	19	14.73	81.5	1,205

Source: 2002 *Economic Census*. The states are in descending order of shipments or establishments (if shipment data are missing for the majority). The symbol (D) appears when data are withheld to prevent disclosure of competitive information. States marked with (D) are sorted by number of establishments. A dash (-) indicates that the data element cannot be calculated. Data may not show all states active in the NAICS category. All data available at the time of publication are shown.

NAICS 33331N - COMMERCIAL AND SERVICE INDUSTRY MACHINERY MANUFACTURING NEC*

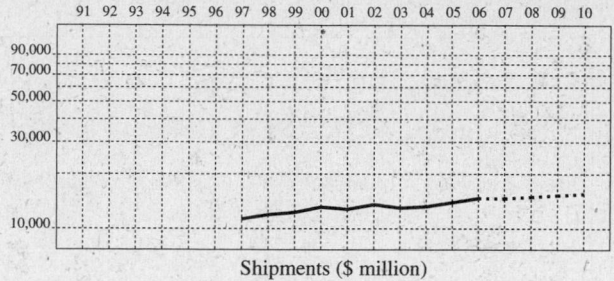

Shipments ($ million)

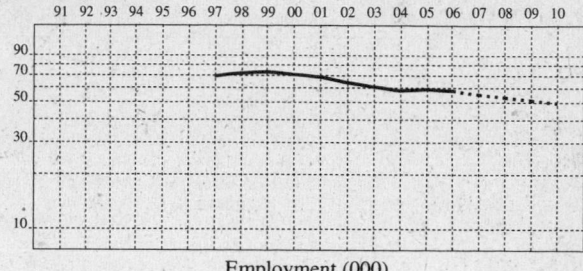

Employment (000)

GENERAL STATISTICS

Year	Com-panies	Establishments		Employment			Compensation		Production ($ million)			
		Total	with 20 or more employees	Total (000)	Production Workers (000)	Hours (Mil)	Payroll ($ mil)	Wages ($/hr)	Cost of Materials	Value Added by Manufacture	Value of Shipments	Capital Invest.
1997	1,448	1,536	568	69.4	41.7	83.1	2,319.5	12.58	5,364.0	5,877.6	11,271.8	285.2
1998		1,528	572	72.1	44.2	87.5	2,388.8	12.69	5,815.5	6,182.8	11,932.5	338.6
1999		1,493	571	73.3	44.1	87.6	2,540.6	12.70	5,907.7	6,324.8	12,275.7	387.2
2000		1,449	550	70.9	42.4	83.2	2,568.1	13.42	6,083.7	7,029.0	13,151.2	381.8
2001		1,440	529	68.7	40.1	78.2	2,547.8	13.64	6,359.8	6,361.6	12,794.1	356.3
2002	1,415	1,534	550	64.0	37.7	74.7	2,550.8	14.95	6,317.0	7,296.6	13,569.8	328.2
2003		1,499	563	60.8	35.7	71.0	2,502.1	15.18	5,935.3	7,060.9	13,001.1	310.6
2004		1,503	538	57.9	34.3	69.0	2,456.3	15.62	6,289.0	7,015.0	13,248.1	223.5
2005		1,485	545	58.9	34.6	70.5	2,613.0	16.12	6,767.3	7,210.2	13,942.3	215.1
2006		1,481P	537P	57.8	33.2	69.1	2,672.1	16.36	7,095.8	7,709.3	14,691.1	228.2
2007		1,478P	533P	55.1P	31.6P	64.8P	2,653.5P	16.97P	7,078.6P	7,690.6P	14,655.4P	224.2P
2008		1,475P	530P	53.2P	30.3P	62.5P	2,678.5P	17.45P	7,225.0P	7,849.7P	14,958.6P	209.4P
2009		1,472P	526P	51.3P	29.0P	60.2P	2,703.5P	17.93P	7,371.5P	8,008.8P	15,261.8P	194.7P
2010		1,469P	522P	49.5P	27.7P	57.9P	2,728.5P	18.41P	7,517.9P	8,167.9P	15,565.1P	179.9P

Sources: 1997 and 2002 *Economic Census*; other years, up to 2006, are from *Annual Survey of Manufactures*. Establishment counts for non-Census years are from *County Business Patterns*; 1997 and 2002 values are from the 1997 and 2002 censuses, respectively. 'P's show projections by the editors.

INDICES OF CHANGE

Year	Com-panies	Establishments		Employment			Compensation		Production ($ million)			
		Total	with 20 or more employees	Total (000)	Production Workers (000)	Hours (Mil)	Payroll ($ mil)	Wages ($/hr)	Cost of Materials	Value Added by Manufacture	Value of Shipments	Capital Invest.
1997	102	100	103	108	111	111	91	84	85	81	83	87
1998		100	104	113	117	117	94	85	92	85	88	103
1999		97	104	115	117	117	100	85	94	87	90	118
2000		94	100	111	112	111	101	90	96	96	97	116
2001		94	96	107	106	105	100	91	101	87	94	109
2002	100	100	100	100	100	100	100	100	100	100	100	100
2003		98	102	95	95	95	98	102	94	97	96	95
2004		98	98	90	91	92	96	104	100	96	98	68
2005		97	99	92	92	94	102	108	107	99	103	66
2006		97P	98P	90	88	93	105	109	112	106	108	70
2007		96P	97P	86P	84P	87P	104P	114P	112P	105P	108P	68P
2008		96P	96P	83P	80P	84P	105P	117P	114P	108P	110P	64P
2009		96P	96P	80P	77P	81P	106P	120P	117P	110P	112P	59P
2010		96P	95P	77P	73P	78P	107P	123P	119P	112P	115P	55P

Sources: Same as General Statistics. Values reflect change from the base year, 2002. Values above 100 mean greater than 2002, values below 100 mean less than 2002, and the values of 100 in other years means the same as 2002. 'P's show projections by the editors.

SELECTED RATIOS

For 2002	Avg. of All Manufact.	Analyzed Industry	Index	For 2002	Avg. of All Manufact.	Analyzed Industry	Index
Employees per Establishment	42	42	99	Value Added per Production Worker	182,367	193,544	106
Payroll per Establishment	1,639,184	1,662,842	101	Cost per Establishment	5,769,015	4,117,992	71
Payroll per Employee	39,053	39,856	102	Cost per Employee	137,446	98,703	72
Production Workers per Establishment	30	25	83	Cost per Production Worker	195,506	167,560	86
Wages per Establishment	694,845	728,008	105	Shipments per Establishment	11,158,348	8,846,023	79
Wages per Production Worker	23,548	29,622	126	Shipments per Employee	265,847	212,028	80
Hours per Production Worker	1,980	1,981	100	Shipments per Production Worker	378,144	359,942	95
Wages per Hour	11.89	14.95	126	Investment per Establishment	361,338	213,950	59
Value Added per Establishment	5,381,325	4,756,584	88	Investment per Employee	8,609	5,128	60
Value Added per Employee	128,210	114,009	89	Investment per Production Worker	12,245	8,706	71

Sources: Same as General Statistics. The 'Average of All Manufacturing' column represents the average of all manufacturing industries reported for the most recent complete year available. The Index shows the relationship between the Average and the Analyzed Industry. For example, 100 means that they are equal; 500 that the Analyzed Industry is five times the average; 50 means that the Analyzed Industry is half the national average. The abbreviation 'na' is used to show that data are 'not available'. Ratios shown for 2002, the last complete census year.

*Equivalent to Federal Government NAICS 333311, 333312, 333319.

LEADING COMPANIES　Number shown: 75　Total sales ($ mil): **424,071**　Total employment (000): **1,012.5**

Company Name	Address				CEO Name	Phone	Co. Type	Sales ($ mil)	Empl. (000)
General Electric Co.	3135 Easton Tpk.	Fairfield	CT	06828		203-373-2211	P	172,738	327.0
General Dynamics Corp.	2941 Fairview Park	Falls Church	VA	22042	Nicholas D. Chabraja	703-876-3000	P	27,240	83.5
Emerson Electric	PO Box 4100	St. Louis	MO	63136	L.C. Barrett	314-553-2000	P	22,572	137.7
Mars Inc.	6885 Elm Street	Mc Lean	VA	22101	John F. Mars	703-821-4900	R	18,462*	40.0
Air Products & Chemicals	7201 Hamilton Blvd.	Allentown	PA	18195		610-481-4911	P	10,038	22.1
Applied Materials Inc.	PO Box 58039	Santa Clara	CA	95052		408-727-5555	P	9,735	15.3
Prager Inc.	PO Box 61670	New Orleans	LA	70161	Jennifer McKnight	504-524-2363	R	7,580*	<0.1
Dover Corp.	280 Park Ave.	New York	NY	10017		212-922-1640	P	7,226	33.4
Boon Edam Tomsed	420 McKinney Pky.	Lillington	NC	27546	Tom DeVine	910-814-3800	R	7,005*	0.1
Prince Castle Inc.	355 Kehoe Blvd.	Carol Stream	IL	60188	Lance Cermainn	630-462-8800	R	7,000*	0.2
Graver Water Systems L.L.C.	750 Walnut Ave.	Cranford	NJ	07016		908-653-4200	R	7,000*	<0.1
Etec Systems Inc.	PO Box 58039	Santa Clara	CA	95052		408-727-5555	S	6,992	12.2
Saint-Gobain Abrasives Inc.	1 New Bond St.	Worcester	MA	01606	Jean Phelizon	508-795-5000	R	6,831*	2.5
Metso Texas Shredder Inc.	11451 J. Maltsbergr	San Antonio	TX	78216	John Duncan	210-491-9521	R	6,340*	<0.1
Cooper Industries Ltd.	PO Box 4446	Houston	TX	77210	Kirk S. Hachigian	713-209-8400	P	5,903	31.5
Culligan International Co.	1 Culligan Pkwy.	Northbrook	IL	60062	Mark Seals	847-205-6000	R	4,916*	5.5
Clorox Co.	PO Box 24305	Oakland	CA	94623		510-271-7000	P	4,847	7.8
Stanley Works	PO Box 700	New Britain	CT	06053		860-225-5111	P	4,484	18.4
Harsco Corp.	PO Box 8888	Camp Hill	PA	17001	S. D. Fazzolari	717-763-7064	P	3,688	21.5
Foster Wheeler Ltd.	Perryville Corp Prk	Clinton	NJ	08809	Umberto Dello Sala	908-730-4000	P	3,495	12.0
Parkson Corp.	PO Box 408399	Fort Lauderdale	FL	33340	William Acton	954-974-6610	R	3,330*	0.1
Arco Auto and Marine Products	3921 Navy Blvd.	Pensacola	FL	32507	Ron Miller	850-455-5476	R	3,015	<0.1
Exide Technologies	13000 Deerfield Pky	Alpharetta	GA	30004		678-566-9000	P	2,940	13.9
Diebold Inc.	PO Box 3077	North Canton	OH	44720		330-490-4000	P	2,906	15.5
Flow Systems	PO Box 1069	St. Helena Is	SC	29902	James Barrett	843-838-6699	R	2,681*	<0.1
O'Reilly Automotive Inc.	233 S Patterson Ave	Springfield	MO	65802	Greg Henslee	417-862-6708	P	2,522	18.5
Lockheed Martin Enterpr. Info.	12506 Lk Underhill	Orlando	FL	32825	Robert J. Stevens	407-306-1000	S	2,383*	4.0
NTK Holdings Inc.	50 Kennedy Plz.	Providence	RI	02903	Richard L. Bready	401-751-1600	S	2,218	9.8
AMETEK Inc.	PO Box 1764	Paoli	PA	19301	Frank S. Hermance	610-647-2121	P	2,137	10.4
American Power Conversion	132 Fairgrounds Rd.	West Kingston	RI	02892	Rodger B. Dowdell Jr.	401-789-5735	S	1,980	7.6
Fluid Management Operations	1023 Wheeling Rd.	Wheeling	IL	60090	Lawrence D. Kingsley	847-537-0880	S	1,935*	4.3
FM Delaware Inc.	1023 Wheeling Rd.	Wheeling	IL	60090	Lawrence D. Kingsley	847-537-0880	S	1,935*	4.3
Teleflex Inc.	155 S Limerick Rd.	Limerick	PA	19468	Jeffrey P. Black	610-948-5100	P	1,934	14.0
Scientific-Atlanta Inc.	PO Box 465447	Lawrenceville	GA	30042		770-236-5000	S	1,910	7.7
Renco Group Inc.	30 Rockefeller Plz.	New York	NY	10112	Ira Leno Rennert	212-541-6000	R	1,900	9.4
Knight L.L.C.	20531 Crescent Bay	Lake Forest	CA	92630	George Noa	949-595-4800	S	1,889*	4.2
Schuler Inc.	7145 Commerce	Canton	MI	48187	Timothy McCaughey	734-207-7200	R	1,874*	<0.1
Weir Spm	7701 Skyline Park	Fort Worth	TX	76108	Steve Noon	817-246-2461	R	1,770*	0.3
GE Infrastructure Water/Proc.	4636 Somerton Rd.	Trevose	PA	19053	George Oliver	215-355-3300	R	1,769*	4.0
Berwind L.L.C.	1500 Market St.	Philadelphia	PA	19102	Michael McClelland	215-563-2800	R	1,710	3.5
Global Industrial Technologies	400 Fairway Dr.	Coraopolis	PA	15108	Jon Allegretti	412-375-6600	R	1,680*	0.2
Lam Research Corp.	PO Box 5010	Fremont	CA	94537	James W. Bagley	510-572-0200	P	1,642	2.4
Curtiss-Wright Corp.	4 Becker Farm Rd.	Roseland	NJ	07068	Martin R. Benante	973-597-4700	P	1,592	6.2
Novellus Systems Inc.	4000 N First St.	San Jose	CA	95134		408-943-9700	P	1,570	3.7
Heico Holding Inc.	2626 Warrenville Rd	Downers Grove	IL	60515	Michael Heisley	630-353-5000	R	1,560*	<0.1
Moog Inc.	Jamison Rd.	East Aurora	NY	14052		716-652-2000	P	1,558	8.4
Sanden of America Inc.	601 Sanden Blvd.	Wylie	TX	75098	Kazuhiko Arai	972-442-8400	R	1,420*	<0.1
JDS Uniphase Corp.	430 N McCarthy	Milpitas	CA	95035	Martin A. Kaplan	408-546-5000	P	1,397*	7.0
Fulmer Company L.L.C.	3004 Venture Ct.	Export	PA	15632	Leo Eger	724-325-7140	R	1,320*	<0.1
Rittal Corp.	1 Rittal Pl.	Springfield	OH	45504	Carie Ray	937-399-0500	R	1,268*	0.6
Nesco Inc.	6140 Parkland Blvd.	Mayfield Hgts	OH	44124	Robert J. Tomsich	440-461-6000	R	1,133*	10.3
Swagelok Co.	29500 Solon Rd.	Solon	OH	44139	Arthur F. Anton	440-248-4600	R	1,100*	3.3
ASM Lithography Holding Inc.	8555 S River Pkwy.	Tempe	AZ	85284	Eric Meurice	480-383-4422	R	1,022*	2.5
Sulzer Inc.	555 5th Ave., 15th	New York	NY	10017	Kelli Edell	212-949-0999	S	1,000*	4.5
Alcoa Closure Systems Intl	6625 Network Way	Indianapolis	IN	46278	V. Lance Mitchell	317-390-5000	S	980*	3.0
NGK-Locke Inc.	2525 Insulator Dr.	Baltimore	MD	21230	Shun Matsushita	410-347-1700	S	941*	3.7
Scott Fetzer Co.	28800 Clemens Rd.	Westlake	OH	44145	K Semelsberger	440-892-3000	S	935*	14.5
Professional Chemicals Corp.	325 S Price Rd.	Chandler	AZ	85224	Bob Kline	480-899-7000	R	904*	<0.1
Intermec Inc.	6001 36th Ave. W	Everett	WA	98203	Patrick Byrne	425-348-2600	P	849	2.4
Graco Inc.	PO Box 1441	Minneapolis	MN	55440		612-623-6000	P	841	2.3
P.R. Hoffman Machine Products	1517 Commerce	Carlisle	PA	17015		717-243-9900	S	812*	<0.1
Milacron Inc.	PO Box 63716	Cincinnati	OH	45206	Ronald D. Brown	513-487-5000	P	808	3.5
Dover Diversified Inc.	Highland Oaks I	Downers Grove	IL	60515	William W. Spurgeon	630-725-9347	S	781*	4.0
Brooks Automation Inc.	15 Elizabeth Dr.	Chelmsford	MA	01824		978-262-2400	P	743	1.9
Progressive Tool & Ind./Wisne	21000 Telegraph Rd.	Southfield	MI	48034	Robert Stoutenburg	248-353-8888	D	733*	5.5
Senior Operations Inc.	300 E Devon Ave.	Bartlett	IL	60103	Graham Menzies	630-837-1811	R	733*	0.7
East Penn Manufacturing Co.	PO Box 147	Lyon Station	PA	19536			R	716*	5.0
Kulicke and Soffa Industries	1005 Virginia Dr.	Fort Washington	PA	19034		215-784-6000	P	700	2.6
White Systems Inc.	30 Boright Ave.	Kenilworth	NJ	07033	Richard Paolino	908-272-6700	S	673*	0.3
Tennant Co.	PO Box 1452	Minneapolis	MN	55440	Chris Killingstad	763-540-1200	P	664	2.8
Bachman Machine Co.	4321 N Broadway	St. Louis	MO	63147	William Bachman	314-231-4221	R	656*	0.1
Parker Drilling Co.	1401 Enclave Pky.	Houston	TX	77077		281-406-2000	P	655	3.1
Enodis Corp.	2227 Welbilt Blvd.	New Port Richey	FL	34655	Peter Brooks	727-375-7010	S	650*	3.0
Riley Power Inc.	PO Box 15040	Worcester	MA	01615		508-852-7100	R	612*	0.4
FEI Co.	5350 NE Dawson	Hillsboro	OR	97124		503-726-7500	P	593	1.8

Source: Ward's Business Directory of U.S. Private and Public Companies, Volumes 1 and 2, 2008. The company type code used is as follows: P - Public, R - Private, S - Subsidiary, D - Division, J - Joint Venture, A - Affiliate, G - Group. Sales are in millions of dollars, employees are in thousands. An asterisk (*) indicates an estimated sales volume. The symbol < stands for 'less than'. Company names and addresses are truncated, in some cases, to fit into the available space.

MATERIALS CONSUMED FOR AUTOMATIC VENDING MACHINE MANUFACTURING

Material	Quantity	Delivered Cost ($ million)
Fractional horsepower electric motors and generators (less than 1 hp)	(X)	36.3
Refrigeration compressors, compressor units, condensing units, and other heat transfer equipment	(X)	31.9
Current-carrying wiring devices	(X)	59.3
Metal bolts, nuts, screws, and other screw machine products	(X)	7.4
Metal stampings	(X)	10.2
Other fabricated metal products (exc. electrical enclosures and forgings)	(X)	40.0
Forgings	(X)	(D)
Castings, rough and semifinished	(X)	6.2
Steel shapes and forms (exc. castings, forgings, fabr. metal products)	(X)	59.1
Nonferrous shapes and forms	(X)	(D)
Plastics products consumed in the form of sheets, rods, etc.	(X)	37.6
Paints, varnishes, stains, lacquers, shellacs, japans, enamels, etc.	(X)	4.5
Paper and paperboard containers (incl. shipping sacks and other paper packaging supplies)	(X)	5.4
All other materials, components, parts, containers, and supplies	(X)	377.7
Materials, ingredients, containers, and supplies, nsk	(X)	82.7

Source: 2002 *Economic Census*. Explanation of symbols used: (D): Withheld to avoid disclosure of competitive data; na: Not available; (S): Withheld because statistical norms were not met; (X): Not applicable; (Z): Less than half the unit shown; nec: Not elsewhere classified; nsk: Not specified by kind; - : zero; p : 10-19 percent estimated; q : 20-29 percent estimated.

MATERIALS CONSUMED FOR COMMERCIAL LAUNDRY, DRYCLEANING, AND PRESSING MACHINERY

Material	Quantity	Delivered Cost ($ million)
Metal stampings	(X)	3.9
Metal pipe, valves, and pipe fittings (exc. plumbers' and forgings)	(X)	4.9
Other fabricated metal products (excluding forgings)	(X)	8.5
Forgings	(X)	(D)
Castings, rough and semifinished	(X)	4.0
Steel sheet and strip (including tinplate)	(X)	25.1
All other steel shapes and forms (exc. castings, forgings, fabr. metal products)	(X)	5.5
Fractional horsepower electric motors and generators (less than 1 hp)	(X)	(D)
Integral horsepower electric motors and generators (1 hp or more)	(X)	10.3
Current-carrying wiring devices	(X)	2.7
Electrical transmission, distribution, and control equipment	(X)	12.3
All other materials, components, parts, containers, and supplies	(X)	40.2
Materials, ingredients, containers, and supplies, nsk	(X)	84.8

Source: 2002 *Economic Census*. Explanation of symbols used: (D): Withheld to avoid disclosure of competitive data; na: Not available; (S): Withheld because statistical norms were not met; (X): Not applicable; (Z): Less than half the unit shown; nec: Not elsewhere classified; nsk: Not specified by kind; - : zero; p : 10-19 percent estimated; q : 20-29 percent estimated.

MATERIALS CONSUMED FOR COMMERCIAL & SERVICE INDUSTRY MACHINERY NEC

Material	Quantity	Delivered Cost ($ million)
Fluid power pumps, motors, and hydrostatic transmissions	(X)	279.6
Fluid power valves (hydraulic and pneumatic)	(X)	38.8
Fluid power cylinders and rotary actuators (hydraulic and pneumatic)	(X)	21.7
Fluid power hose, tube fittings, and assemblies (hydraulic and pneumatic)	(X)	36.6
Fluid power filters (hydraulic and pneumatic)	(X)	19.3
Other fluid power products, hydraulic and pneumatic	(X)	21.0
Metal bolts, nuts, screws, and other screw machine products	(X)	62.8
Other fabricated metal products (exc. electrical enclosures and forgings)	(X)	165.3
Forgings	(X)	3.1
Iron and steel castings (rough and semifinished)	(X)	37.9
Steel bars, bar shapes, and plates (exc. castings, forgings, fabr. metal products)	(X)	35.5
Steel sheet and strip (including tinplate)	(X)	72.7
Steel structural shapes and sheet piling (exc. castings, forgings, fabr. metal products)	(X)	18.6
All other steel shapes and forms (exc. castings, forgings, fabr. metal products)	(X)	34.4
Other nonferrous shapes and forms (exc. castings, forgings, fabricated metal products)	(X)	14.3
Fractional horsepower electric motors and generators (less than 1 hp)	(X)	39.5
Integral horsepower electric motors and generators (1 hp or more)	(X)	78.1
Mechanical speed changers, gears, and industrial high-speed drives	(X)	13.4
All other pumps	(X)	32.5
Metal pipe, valves, and pipe fittings (exc. plumbers' and forgings)	(X)	52.3
Other fabricated metal products (exc. fluid power products and forgings)	(X)	66.9
Nonferrous (aluminum, copper, etc.) castings (rough and semifinished)	(X)	21.9
Aluminum and aluminum-base alloy shapes and forms (exc. castings, forgings, fabr. metal products)	(X)	9.9
Aluminum and aluminum-base alloy sheet, plate, foil, and welded tubing	(X)	19.3
All other aluminum and aluminum-base alloy shapes and forms (exc. castings, forgings, fabr. metal products)	(X)	4.1
Sheet metal products (excluding stampings)	(X)	67.0
Plastics resins consumed in the form of granules, pellets, etc.	(X)	32.8
Plastics products consumed in the form of sheets, rods, etc.	(X)	50.2
Electrical enclosures (metal and plastics)	(X)	27.3

Continued on next page.

MATERIALS CONSUMED FOR COMMERCIAL & SERVICE INDUSTRY MACHINERY NEC - Continued

Material	Quantity	Delivered Cost ($ million)
Current-carrying wiring devices	(X)	86.9
Paper and paperboard containers (incl. shipping sacks and other paper packaging supplies)	(X)	34.0
All other materials, components, parts, containers, and supplies	(X)	1,204.3
Materials, ingredients, containers, and supplies, nsk	(X)	1,707.1

Source: 2002 *Economic Census*. Explanation of symbols used: (D): Withheld to avoid disclosure of competitive data; na: Not available; (S): Withheld because statistical norms were not met; (X): Not applicable; (Z): Less than half the unit shown; nec: Not elsewhere classified; nsk: Not specified by kind; - : zero; p : 10-19 percent estimated; q : 20-29 percent estimated.

PRODUCT SHARE DETAILS FOR AUTOMATIC VENDING MACHINE MANUFACTURING

Product or Product Class Shipments	Mil. $	Product or Product Class Shipments	Mil. $
AUTOMATIC VENDING MACHINES	1,300.0	Parts for automatic merchandising machines, money changing and dispensing machines	85.8
Automatic merchandising machines, coin-operated (vending), excluding money changing machines, coin-operated mechanisms	**823.6**	Parts for automatic merchandising machines, except coin-operated mechanisms	65.2
Automatic merchandising machines, coin-operated mechanisms, including time switches	**124.7**	Parts for money changing and dispensing machines	20.6
Coin-operated mechanisms for automatic merchandising machines, including parts	38.9	**Currency handling machines, including money changing and dispensing machines**	**317.9**
		Automatic vending machines, nsk, total	**33.9**

Source: 2002 *Economic Census*. The values are product shipments in millions of dollars for 2002. Total product shipments may be lower or higher than industry shipments. See Introduction for a full discussion. Values of indented subcategories are summed in the main heading(s). The symbol (D) appears when data are withheld to prevent disclosure of competitive information. The abbreviation nsk stands for 'not specified by kind' and nec for 'not elsewhere classified'. A dash (-) means zero.

PRODUCT SHARE DETAILS FOR COMMERCIAL LAUNDRY, DRYCLEANING, AND PRESSING MACHINERY

Product or Product Class Shipments	Mil. $	Product or Product Class Shipments	Mil. $
COMMERCIAL LAUNDRY, DRYCLEANING AND PRESSING MACHINES	574.4	Other commercial laundry equipment (more than 10 kg (22 lb) load capacity) including extractors only, except parts, attachments, and accessories	69.0
Commercial laundry equipment, washers, and washer-extractor combinations	142.2	Parts, attachments, and accessories for commercial laundry equipment and presses	90.4
Commercial laundry drying tumblers, except parts, attachments, and accessories	170.6	Parts, attachments, and accessories for commercial laundry equipment and presses, more than 10 kg (22 lb) load capacity	53.3
Commercial coin-operated laundry drying tumblers, more than 10 kg (22 lb) load capacity, except parts, attachments, and accessories	134.7	Parts, attachments, and accessories for commercial drycleaning equipment and clothing presses	37.2
Commercial laundry drying tumblers, centrifugal and compaction extractor	(D)	Commercial drycleaning machines and presses, including garment manufacturers' needle trades presses, reclaiming units, etc., except parts, attachments, and accessories	32.2
Commercial laundry drying tumblers, other than centrifugal dryers and coin-operated machines, more than 10 kg (22 lb.) load capacity, except parts, attachments, and accessories	(D)	Commercial drycleaning machines	7.8
Other commercial laundry equipment, except parts, attachments, and accessories	127.4	Commercial drycleaning presses and garment manufactures (needle trades) presses	14.3
Commercial laundry presses, more than 10 kg (22 lb) load capacity, except parts, attachments, and accessories	32.9	Other commercial drycleaning and presses machinery	10.1
Commercial laundry equipment, flatwork ironers	25.5	Commercial laundry, drycleaning, and pressing machines, nsk, total	11.6

Source: 2002 *Economic Census*. The values are product shipments in millions of dollars for 2002. Total product shipments may be lower or higher than industry shipments. See Introduction for a full discussion. Values of indented subcategories are summed in the main heading(s). The symbol (D) appears when data are withheld to prevent disclosure of competitive information. The abbreviation nsk stands for 'not specified by kind' and nec for 'not elsewhere classified'. A dash (-) means zero.

PRODUCT SHARE DETAILS FOR COMMERCIAL & SERVICE INDUSTRY MACHINERY NEC

Product or Product Class Shipments	Mil. $	Product or Product Class Shipments	Mil. $
OTHER COMMERCIAL AND SERVICE INDUSTRY MACHINERY	10,425.2	**Non-electrical machinery products, nec, including flexible metal hose and tubing, metal bellows, etc.**	**5,419.9**
Commercial cooking and food-warming equipment	**2,115.1**	Other service industry equipment	4,209.0
Commercial cooking equipment including ranges, deep-fat fryers, griddles, toasters, coffee urns, pressure cookers, etc., except electric	1,011.5	Instantaneous service industry water heaters, including parts	55.3
Commercial ranges, ovens, and broilers	523.3	All other service industry water heaters (including parts), more than 120 gallons (454.2 liters) capacity	53.6
Commercial deep-fat fryers	199.9	Industrial water softeners	247.3
Other commercial cooking equipment	219.9	Farm, household, and commercial water softeners	354.2
Commercial food-warming equipment, including steam tables	68.4	Conveyor-type commercial dishwashing machines	68.2
Commercial electric cooking equipment, including ranges, deep-fat fryers, griddles, toasters, coffee makers, coffee urns, etc.	900.4	All other commercial dishwashing machines	101.3
		Sewage treatment equipment, distilling or rectifying	15.2
Commercial electric ranges, ovens, and broilers	204.3	Sewage treatment equipment, filtering or purifying	479.4
Commercial microwave stoves and ovens	38.7	Sewage treatment equipment, centrifuges	26.6
Commercial electric deep-fat fryers	116.6	Other sewage treatment equipment	432.2
Other commercial electric cooking equipment, including griddles, toasters, coffee makers, etc.	327.9	Commercial car, truck, and bus washing machinery and equipment	279.9
Commercial electric food-warming equipment, including hot-food server units and steam tables	212.9	Service industry trash and garbage compactors	171.7
		Sewer pipe and drain cleaning equipment	120.7
Parts and accessories for commercial cooking and food-warming equipment	200.2	High-pressure (more than 1,000 p.s.i.) cleaning and blasting machinery and equipment (except foundry)	761.4
Commercial cooking and food-warming equipment, nsk	3.0	Barber and beauty shop furniture and equipment, excluding barber and beauty chairs	60.6
Commercial and industrial vacuum cleaners, including parts and attachments	**470.1**	Electric hand-drying apparatus	23.0
		Other service industry equipment	958.4
Commercial and industrial central and portable vacuum cleaner systems	332.5	All other parts and attachments for service industry equipment	400.9
Commercial and industrial portable vacuum cleaners	264.6	Parts for water softeners (excluding tanks)	36.0
Parts and attachments for commercial and industrial portable vacuum cleaners	67.8	Parts and attachments for commercial and industrial floor and carpet cleaning equipment	191.7
Commercial and industrial central vacuum cleaner systems, parts, and attachments	137.7	Parts for commercial dishwashing machines	36.4
Automotive maintenance equipment, parts, and attachments, except handtools	**632.4**	Parts for other service industry machines	136.8
Automotive maintenance equipment, except handtools	506.3	Commercial an industrial floor and carpet cleaning machines, except vacuum cleaners	791.1
Automotive frame and body alignment equipment	64.8	Carnival and amusement park equipment (ferris-wheels, merry-go-rounds, etc.), excluding electric equipment and coin-operated amusement machines	51.6
Automotive wheel alignment equipment	134.6	Commercial and industrial floor sanding and scrubbing machines	341.3
Automotive wheel balancing equipment	71.1		
Automotive tire and wheel mounting equipment	61.5	Commercial and industrial carpet cleaning equipment	304.2
Automotive brake service equipment	30.8	Other commercial and industrial floor and carpet cleaning machines, including waxing and polishing machines, except vacuum cleaners	94.0
All other automotive maintenance equipment	143.5		
Parts and attachments for automotive maintenance equipment	126.1	Non-electrical machinery products, nec, nsk	19.0
Electronic teaching machines, teaching aids, trainers, and simulators, including kits	**1,272.0**	**Other commercial and service industry machinery, nsk, total**	**515.6**

Source: 2002 *Economic Census.* The values are product shipments in millions of dollars for 2002. Total product shipments may be lower or higher than industry shipments. See Introduction for a full discussion. Values of indented subcategories are summed in the main heading(s). The symbol (D) appears when data are withheld to prevent disclosure of competitive information. The abbreviation nsk stands for 'not specified by kind' and nec for 'not elsewhere classified'. A dash (-) means zero.

INPUTS AND OUTPUTS FOR OTHER COMMERCIAL & SERVICE INDUSTRY MACHINERY

Economic Sector or Industry Providing Inputs	%	Sector	Economic Sector or Industry Buying Outputs	%	Sector
Compensation of employees	25.6		Private fixed investment	65.6	
Wholesale trade	5.2	Trade	Nonresidential structures, nec	8.7	Construct.
Management of companies & enterprises	4.7	Services	Residential permanent site structures	4.8	Construct.
Valve & fittings other than plumbing	2.9	Manufg.	General S/L govt. services	4.2	S/L Govt
Iron & steel mills & ferroalloys	2.3	Manufg.	Exports of goods & services	4.1	Cap Inv
Ornamental & architectural metal products	2.1	Manufg.	Federal government, investment, national defense	2.2	Fed Govt
Fluid power process machinery	1.8	Manufg.	S/L govt. invest., education	1.7	S/L Govt
Communication & energy wires & cables	1.7	Manufg.	S/L govt. invest., other	1.3	S/L Govt
Motors & generators	1.5	Manufg.	Elementary & secondary schools	1.3	Services
Synthetic rubber	1.4	Manufg.	Change in private inventories	1.1	In House
Advertising & related services	1.2	Services	Commercial & service industry machinery, nec	0.9	Manufg.
Machine shops	1.2	Manufg.	Commercial & health care structures	0.7	Construct.
Wiring devices	1.2	Manufg.	Services to buildings & dwellings	0.5	Services
Petroleum refineries	1.2	Manufg.	Wholesale trade	0.5	Trade
Electronic components, nec	1.1	Manufg.	Real estate	0.4	Fin/R.E.
Nonwoven fabric mills	1.1	Manufg.	Personal care services	0.4	Services
Turned products & screws, nuts, & bolts	1.1	Manufg.	Ornamental & architectural metal products	0.3	Manufg.
Gaskets, packing, & sealing devices	0.9	Manufg.	Commercial & industrial equipment repair/maintenance	0.3	Services
Semiconductors & related devices	0.9	Manufg.	Automotive repair & maintenance, ex. car washes	0.2	Services
Telecommunications	0.9	Services	Retail trade	0.1	Trade
Commercial & service industry machinery, nec	0.9	Manufg.			
Lessors of nonfinancial assets	0.8	Fin/R.E.			
Securities, commodity contracts, investments	0.8	Fin/R.E.			

Continued on next page.

INPUTS AND OUTPUTS FOR OTHER COMMERCIAL & SERVICE INDUSTRY MACHINERY - Continued

Economic Sector or Industry Providing Inputs	%	Sector	Economic Sector or Industry Buying Outputs	%	Sector
Real estate	0.8	Fin/R.E.			
Truck transportation	0.8	Util.			
Plastics packaging materials, film & sheet	0.7	Manufg.			
Coating, engraving, heat treating & allied activities	0.7	Manufg.			
Crowns & closures & metal stamping	0.6	Manufg.			
Monetary authorities/depository credit intermediation	0.6	Fin/R.E.			
Plastics products, nec	0.6	Manufg.			
Printed circuit assemblies (electronic assembiles)	0.6	Manufg.			
Motor vehicle parts	0.6	Manufg.			
Legal services	0.6	Services			
Relay & industrial controls	0.5	Manufg.			
Air purification & ventilation equipment	0.5	Manufg.			
Electronic connectors	0.5	Manufg.			
Professional, scientific, technical services, nec	0.5	Services			
Pumps & pumping equipment	0.5	Manufg.			
Paperboard containers	0.5	Manufg.			
Ferrous metal foundries	0.5	Manufg.			
Aluminum products from purchased aluminum	0.4	Manufg.			
Electronic capacitors, resistors, coils, transformers	0.4	Manufg.			
Plastics materials & resins	0.4	Manufg.			
Data processing, hosting, & related services	0.4	Services			
Power generation & supply	0.4	Util.			
Rubber products, nec	0.4	Manufg.			
Paints & coatings	0.4	Manufg.			
Cutting tools & machine tool accessories	0.4	Manufg.			
Nonferrous metal (ex. copper & aluminum) processing	0.4	Manufg.			
Management, scientific, & technical consulting	0.3	Services			
Nonferrous metal foundries	0.3	Manufg.			
Accounting, tax preparation, bookkeeping, & payroll	0.3	Services			
Food services & drinking places	0.3	Services			
Retail trade	0.3	Trade			
General purpose machinery, nec	0.3	Manufg.			
Metal cans, boxes, & other containers (light gauge)	0.3	Manufg.			
Taxes on production & imports, less subsidies	0.3				
Scientific research & development services	0.3	Services			
Automotive equipment rental & leasing	0.3	Fin/R.E.			
Fabricated metals, nec	0.3	Manufg.			
Electrical equipment & components, nec	0.3	Manufg.			
Warehousing & storage	0.3	Util.			
Fabricated pipes & pipe fittings	0.2	Manufg.			
Speed changers, industrial high-speed drives, & gears	0.2	Manufg.			
Other computer related services, including facilities	0.2	Services			
Architectural, engineering, & related services	0.2	Services			
Plate work & fabricated structural products	0.2	Manufg.			
Handtools	0.2	Manufg.			
Hotels & motels, including casino hotels	0.2	Services			
Ball & roller bearings	0.2	Manufg.			
Services to buildings & dwellings	0.2	Services			
Air transportation	0.2	Util.			
Maintenance/repair of nonresidential structures	0.2	Construct.			
Alumina refining & primary aluminum production	0.2	Manufg.			
Abrasive products	0.2	Manufg.			
Custom roll forming	0.2	Manufg.			
Commercial & industrial machinery rental & leasing	0.1	Fin/R.E.			
Natural gas distribution	0.1	Util.			
Unlaminated plastics profile shapes	0.1	Manufg.			
Automotive repair & maintenance, ex. car washes	0.1	Services			

Source: Benchmark Input-Output Accounts for the U.S. Economy, 2002, U.S. Department of Commerce, Washington, D.C., January 2008. The abbreviation nec stands for 'not elsewhere classified'.

INPUTS AND OUTPUTS FOR VENDING, COMMERCIAL, INDUSTRIAL, & OFFICE MACHINERY

Economic Sector or Industry Providing Inputs	%	Sector	Economic Sector or Industry Buying Outputs	%	Sector
Compensation of employees	24.8		Private fixed investment	48.0	
Wholesale trade	6.1	Trade	Exports of goods & services	13.6	Cap Inv
Management of companies & enterprises	4.6	Services	S/L govt. invest., other	10.1	S/L Govt
Valve & fittings other than plumbing	3.7	Manufg.	S/L govt. invest., education	7.4	S/L Govt
Real estate	3.4	Fin/R.E.	Personal consumption expenditures	5.5	
Iron & steel mills & ferroalloys	3.1	Manufg.	Management of companies & enterprises	4.6	Services
AC, refrigeration, and warm air heating equipment	2.8	Manufg.	Personal services, nec	2.1	Services
Wiring devices	2.3	Manufg.	Wholesale trade	1.6	Trade
Rubber products, nec	2.0	Manufg.	Dry-cleaning & laundry services	1.5	Services
Management, scientific, & technical consulting	2.0	Services	Vending, commercial, industrial, office machinery	1.1	Manufg.
Motors & generators	1.8	Manufg.	Federal government, investment, nondefense	0.9	Fed Govt
Vending, commercial, industrial, office machinery	1.6	Manufg.	General Federal government services, defense	0.7	Fed Govt

Continued on next page.

INPUTS AND OUTPUTS FOR VENDING, COMMERCIAL, INDUSTRIAL, & OFFICE MACHINERY - Continued

Economic Sector or Industry Providing Inputs	%	Sector	Economic Sector or Industry Buying Outputs	%	Sector
Lessors of nonfinancial assets	1.5	Fin/R.E.	Accounting, tax preparation, bookkeeping, & payroll	0.6	Services
Machine shops	1.4	Manufg.	Postal service	0.6	Util.
Plastics packaging materials, film & sheet	1.4	Manufg.	Change in private inventories	0.5	In House
Professional, scientific, technical services, nec	1.4	Services	Retail trade	0.4	Trade
Scientific research & development services	1.1	Services	Employment services	0.2	Services
Securities, commodity contracts, investments	1.1	Fin/R.E.			
Communication & energy wires & cables	1.0	Manufg.			
Forging, stamping, & sintering, nec	1.0	Manufg.			
Printed circuit assemblies (electronic assemblies)	1.0	Manufg.			
Coated & laminated paper & packaging materials	0.9	Manufg.			
Chemical products & preparations, nec	0.9	Manufg.			
Monetary authorities/depository credit intermediation	0.9	Fin/R.E.			
Synthetic rubber	0.9	Manufg.			
Computer terminals & peripherals	0.8	Manufg.			
Taxes on production & imports, less subsidies	0.8				
Crowns & closures & metal stamping	0.8	Manufg.			
Nonferrous metal (ex. copper & aluminum) processing	0.8	Manufg.			
Paints & coatings	0.8	Manufg.			
Truck transportation	0.7	Util.			
Support services, nec	0.7	Services			
Cutting tools & machine tool accessories	0.7	Manufg.			
Advertising & related services	0.7	Services			
Legal services	0.7	Services			
Coating, engraving, heat treating & allied activities	0.7	Manufg.			
Telecommunications	0.6	Services			
Glass products from purchased glass	0.6	Manufg.			
Petroleum refineries	0.6	Manufg.			
Semiconductors & related devices	0.5	Manufg.			
Turned products & screws, nuts, & bolts	0.5	Manufg.			
Noncomparable imports	0.5	Foreign			
Relay & industrial controls	0.5	Manufg.			
Data processing, hosting, & related services	0.5	Services			
Food services & drinking places	0.4	Services			
Abrasive products	0.4	Manufg.			
Business support services	0.4	Services			
Plastics products, nec	0.4	Manufg.			
Power generation & supply	0.4	Util.			
Accounting, tax preparation, bookkeeping, & payroll	0.4	Services			
Ornamental & architectural metal products	0.3	Manufg.			
Hotels & motels, including casino hotels	0.3	Services			
Automotive equipment rental & leasing	0.3	Fin/R.E.			
Employment services	0.3	Services			
Architectural, engineering, & related services	0.3	Services			
Electronic computers	0.3	Manufg.			
Metal cans, boxes, & other containers (light gauge)	0.3	Manufg.			
Fabricated metals, nec	0.3	Manufg.			
Custom roll forming	0.3	Manufg.			
Unlaminated plastics profile shapes	0.3	Manufg.			
Paperboard containers	0.3	Manufg.			
Air transportation	0.3	Util.			
Environmental & other technical consulting services	0.2	Services			
Nondepository credit intermediation activities	0.2	Fin/R.E.			
Travel arrangement & reservation services	0.2	Services			
Pressed & blown glass & glassware, nec	0.2	Manufg.			
Office administrative services	0.2	Services			
Warehousing & storage	0.2	Util.			
Waste management & remediation services	0.2	Services			
Software, audio, and video media reproducing	0.2	Manufg.			
Ferrous metal foundries	0.2	Manufg.			
Paperboard mills	0.2	Manufg.			
Nonferrous metal foundries	0.2	Manufg.			
Plate work & fabricated structural products	0.2	Manufg.			
Services to buildings & dwellings	0.2	Services			
Electronic capacitors, resistors, coils, transformers	0.2	Manufg.			
Electronic components, nec	0.2	Manufg.			
Laminated plastics plates, sheets, & shapes	0.2	Manufg.			
Maintenance/repair of nonresidential structures	0.2	Construct.			
Wood containers & pallets	0.2	Manufg.			
Photographic & photocopying equipment	0.2	Manufg.			
Commercial & industrial machinery rental & leasing	0.2	Fin/R.E.			
Ball & roller bearings	0.2	Manufg.			
Other computer related services, including facilities	0.2	Services			
Postal service	0.1	Util.			
Electrical equipment & components, nec	0.1	Manufg.			
Bare printed circuit boards	0.1	Manufg.			

Source: Benchmark Input-Output Accounts for the U.S. Economy, 2002, U.S. Department of Commerce, Washington D.C., January 2008. *User should note that this Input-Output table is* not *for this particular narrowly defined industry but for a larger aggregate. Input and Output data for* Vending, Commercial, Industrial, and Office Machinery Manufacturing *include Input and Output data for the* Annual Survey of Manufactures' *NAICS industries 333313 and 33331N.* The abbreviation nec stands for 'not elsewhere classified'.

OCCUPATIONS EMPLOYED BY COMMERCIAL & SERVICE INDUSTRY MACHINERY MANUFACTURING

Occupation	% of Total 2006	Change to 2016	Occupation	% of Total 2006	Change to 2016
Team assemblers	11.6	-12.3	Electrical engineers	1.4	-12.3
Welders, cutters, solderers, & brazers	3.4	-6.7	Maintenance & repair workers, general	1.4	-12.3
First-line supervisors/managers of production workers	3.3	-12.3	Engineering managers	1.4	-12.3
Inspectors, testers, sorters, samplers, & weighers	2.8	-17.3	Bookkeeping, accounting, & auditing clerks	1.4	-12.3
Sales reps, wholesale & manufacturing, exc tech	2.5	-12.3	Shipping, receiving, & traffic clerks	1.4	-15.6
Mechanical engineers	2.5	-12.3	Electromechanical equipment assemblers	1.4	-12.3
Computer software engineers, applications	2.3	5.3	Stock clerks & order fillers	1.3	-26.6
Electrical & electronic equipment assemblers	2.2	-29.8	Purchasing agents, exc wholesale, retail, & farm	1.3	-12.3
Machinists	1.9	-7.9	Accountants & auditors	1.2	-12.3
Assemblers & fabricators, nec	1.9	-21.0	Helpers--Production workers	1.1	-12.3
Cutting, punching, & press machine operators	1.8	-21.0	Executive secretaries & administrative assistants	1.1	-12.3
Industrial engineers	1.8	6.5	Office clerks, general	1.1	-13.6
General & operations managers	1.7	-21.0	Computer-controlled machine tool operators	1.0	-3.5
Coating, painting, & spraying machine operators	1.7	-16.7	Sales representatives, wholesale & manufacturing, tech	1.0	-12.3
Customer service representatives	1.6	-3.5	Laborers & freight, stock, & material movers, hand	1.0	-21.0
Ophthalmic laboratory technicians	1.4	-12.3			

Source: Industry-Occupation Matrix, Bureau of Labor Statistics, December 4, 2007. These data are reported based on 4-digit NAICS categories but have been matched to corresponding 6-digit NAICS industry codes. The change reported for each occupation to the year 2016 is a percent of growth or decline as estimated by the Bureau of Labor Statistics. The abbreviation nec stands for 'not elsewhere classified'.

LOCATION BY STATE AND REGIONAL CONCENTRATION

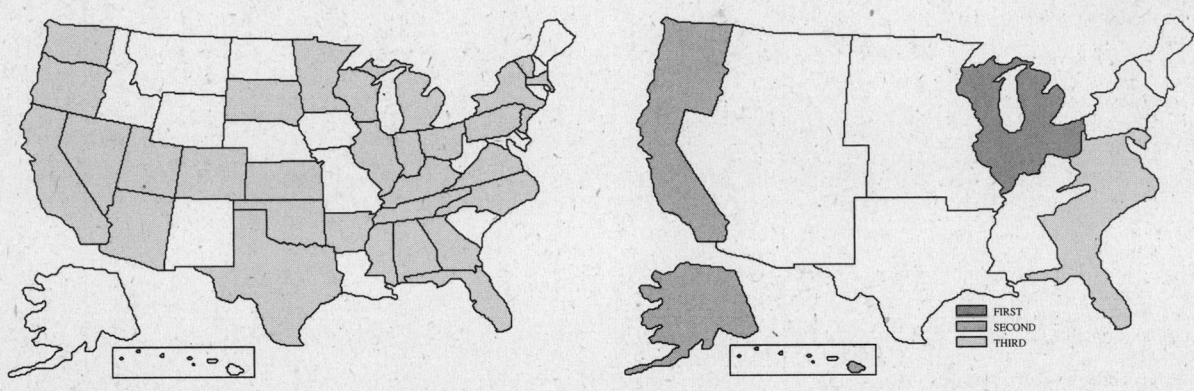

FIRST
SECOND
THIRD

INDUSTRY DATA BY STATE

State	Establish-ments	Shipments			Employment				Cost as % of Shipments	Investment per Employee ($)
		Total ($ mil)	% of U.S.	Per Establ.	Total Number	% of U.S.	Per Establ.	Wages ($/hour)		
Florida	86	1,301.0	9.6	15,127.8	3,827	6.0	44	17.27	46.1	6,352
California	195	1,109.1	8.2	5,687.9	5,292	8.3	27	15.01	47.0	3,611
Illinois	107	1,080.2	8.0	10,095.0	5,574	8.7	52	16.70	49.0	6,670
Minnesota	47	831.6	6.1	17,694.3	2,619	4.1	56	16.89	38.2	7,861
Ohio	81	605.3	4.5	7,472.8	3,060	4.8	38	14.17	42.9	5,059
Wisconsin	47	519.9	3.8	11,060.7	2,525	3.9	54	14.96	42.4	3,359
Texas	89	477.7	3.5	5,367.2	2,820	4.4	32	12.73	46.0	2,701
Michigan	55	451.1	3.3	8,202.3	2,079	3.3	38	15.30	50.1	4,971
Pennsylvania	56	353.6	2.6	6,313.4	1,439	2.2	26	17.59	48.4	3,425
Arkansas	13	335.5	2.5	25,807.9	749	1.2	58	13.41	68.9	3,150
Tennessee	21	316.2	2.3	15,055.8	1,008	1.6	48	13.78	46.1	6,700
Colorado	26	271.0	2.0	10,422.2	1,267	2.0	49	19.83	41.8	5,757
North Carolina	34	269.1	2.0	7,916.1	1,317	2.1	39	19.69	55.7	3,831
New York	52	263.4	1.9	5,066.3	1,601	2.5	31	15.32	42.1	2,646
Mississippi	8	207.0	1.5	25,873.6	841	1.3	105	13.49	46.8	10,650
Indiana	21	203.1	1.5	9,670.6	1,182	1.8	56	13.68	48.4	3,365
Oklahoma	18	187.3	1.4	10,405.4	889	1.4	49	15.74	49.9	1,299
Utah	17	184.3	1.4	10,842.1	883	1.4	52	18.64	40.4	3,606
Georgia	27	179.1	1.3	6,633.4	1,038	1.6	38	16.67	43.8	3,600
Massachusetts	32	164.8	1.2	5,150.8	880	1.4	28	15.45	45.0	4,099
Washington	21	154.6	1.1	7,360.0	846	1.3	40	19.17	42.7	2,994
New Jersey	32	140.5	1.0	4,389.6	601	0.9	19	13.34	52.6	4,453
Alabama	11	125.1	0.9	11,374.9	751	1.2	68	15.10	43.3	3,144
Kentucky	14	115.5	0.9	8,247.9	622	1.0	44	11.94	44.1	4,143
Arizona	29	105.0	0.8	3,620.3	879	1.4	30	10.23	46.9	2,709
Kansas	18	93.6	0.7	5,197.6	535	0.8	30	14.18	46.8	5,228

Continued on next page.

INDUSTRY DATA BY STATE - Continued

State	Establish-ments	Shipments			Employment				Cost as % of Shipments	Investment per Employee ($)
		Total ($ mil)	% of U.S.	Per Establ.	Total Number	% of U.S.	Per Establ.	Wages ($/hour)		
Vermont	6	90.3	0.7	15,048.8	474	0.7	79	15.74	32.1	1,633
Nevada	13	77.5	0.6	5,961.1	303	0.5	23	14.24	41.8	2,710
Virginia	19	69.3	0.5	3,645.8	1,065	1.7	56	9.56	39.2	1,468
Oregon	16	44.3	0.3	2,766.1	333	0.5	21	12.15	44.6	3,523
South Dakota	6	18.6	0.1	3,103.2	120	0.2	20	11.95	53.7	6,183

Source: 2002 *Economic Census*. The states are in descending order of shipments or establishments (if shipment data are missing for the majority). The symbol (D) appears when data are withheld to prevent disclosure of competitive information. States marked with (D) are sorted by number of establishments. A dash (-) indicates that the data element cannot be calculated. Data may not show all states active in the NAICS category. All data available at the time of publication are shown.

NAICS 333414 - HEATING EQUIPMENT MANUFACTURING

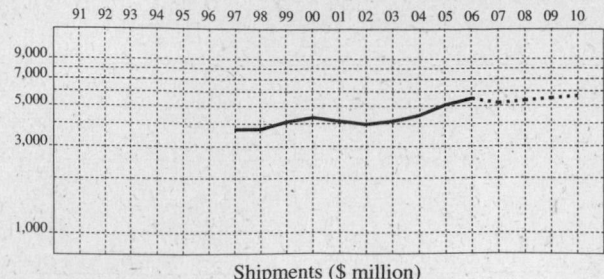

Shipments ($ million)

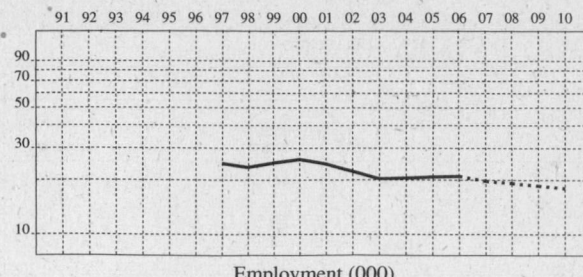

Employment (000)

GENERAL STATISTICS

Year	Com-panies	Establishments		Employment			Compensation		Production ($ million)			
		Total	with 20 or more employees	Total (000)	Production Workers (000)	Hours (Mil)	Payroll ($ mil)	Wages ($/hr)	Cost of Materials	Value Added by Manufacture	Value of Shipments	Capital Invest.
1997	442	469	181	24.7	16.1	32.0	757.0	11.78	1,656.3	2,071.1	3,716.7	89.6
1998		467	184	23.5	15.4	30.0	719.2	11.80	1,632.4	1,965.0	3,738.5	273.7
1999		452	176	24.9	16.7	32.5	808.5	12.72	1,869.2	2,237.2	4,099.8	140.3
2000		424	169	26.0	17.3	33.5	857.8	12.99	2,014.8	2,320.0	4,315.4	149.4
2001		419	172	24.5	16.1	32.0	839.0	13.38	1,937.4	2,148.2	4,113.9	143.8
2002	390	415	167	22.3	14.4	29.1	755.6	12.84	1,701.6	2,247.9	3,968.6	88.3
2003		403	165	20.3	13.0	26.6	745.6	13.94	1,692.9	2,360.3	4,121.9	74.7
2004		408	167	20.5	13.7	27.7	774.6	13.85	1,897.7	2,571.5	4,430.6	82.4
2005		405	162	20.8	13.8	28.4	815.1	14.21	2,314.4	2,782.7	5,070.2	64.8
2006		384P	159P	21.0	13.4	27.3	836.1	14.76	2,407.1	3,111.6	5,475.4	117.5
2007		375P	156P	19.7P	12.8P	26.5P	817.3P	14.95P	2,274.8P	2,940.5P	5,174.4P	63.1P
2008		366P	154P	19.2P	12.4P	25.9P	822.1P	15.26P	2,344.2P	3,030.4P	5,332.4P	52.3P
2009		357P	151P	18.6P	12.0P	25.3P	826.9P	15.57P	2,413.7P	3,120.2P	5,490.5P	41.5P
2010		348P	149P	18.0P	11.6P	24.7P	831.7P	15.89P	2,483.2P	3,210.0P	5,648.5P	30.7P

Sources: 1997 and 2002 *Economic Census*; other years, up to 2006, are from *Annual Survey of Manufactures*. Establishment counts for non-Census years are from *County Business Patterns*; 1997 and 2002 values are from the 1997 and 2002 censuses, respectively. 'P's show projections by the editors.

INDICES OF CHANGE

Year	Com-panies	Establishments		Employment			Compensation		Production ($ million)			
		Total	with 20 or more employees	Total (000)	Production Workers (000)	Hours (Mil)	Payroll ($ mil)	Wages ($/hr)	Cost of Materials	Value Added by Manufacture	Value of Shipments	Capital Invest.
1997	113	113	108	111	112	110	100	92	97	92	94	101
1998		113	110	105	107	103	95	92	96	87	94	310
1999		109	105	112	116	112	107	99	110	100	103	159
2000		102	101	117	120	115	114	101	118	103	109	169
2001		101	103	110	112	110	111	104	114	96	104	163
2002	100	100	100	100	100	100	100	100	100	100	100	100
2003		97	99	91	90	91	99	109	99	105	104	85
2004		98	100	92	95	95	103	108	112	114	112	93
2005		98	97	93	96	98	108	111	136	124	128	73
2006		93P	95P	94	93	94	111	115	141	138	138	133
2007		90P	94P	88P	89P	91P	108P	116P	134P	131P	130P	71P
2008		88P	92P	86P	86P	89P	109P	119P	138P	135P	134P	59P
2009		86P	91P	83P	83P	87P	109P	121P	142P	139P	138P	47P
2010		84P	89P	81P	81P	85P	110P	124P	146P	143P	142P	35P

Sources: Same as General Statistics. Values reflect change from the base year, 2002. Values above 100 mean greater than 2002, values below 100 mean less than 2002, and the values of 100 in other years means the same as 2002. 'P's show projections by the editors.

SELECTED RATIOS

For 2002	Avg. of All Manufact.	Analyzed Industry	Index	For 2002	Avg. of All Manufact.	Analyzed Industry	Index
Employees per Establishment	42	54	128	Value Added per Production Worker	182,367	156,104	86
Payroll per Establishment	1,639,184	1,820,723	111	Cost per Establishment	5,769,015	4,100,241	71
Payroll per Employee	39,053	33,883	87	Cost per Employee	137,446	76,305	56
Production Workers per Establishment	30	35	118	Cost per Production Worker	195,506	118,167	60
Wages per Establishment	694,845	900,347	130	Shipments per Establishment	11,158,348	9,562,892	86
Wages per Production Worker	23,548	25,948	110	Shipments per Employee	265,847	177,964	67
Hours per Production Worker	1,980	2,021	102	Shipments per Production Worker	378,144	275,597	73
Wages per Hour	11.89	12.84	108	Investment per Establishment	361,338	212,771	59
Value Added per Establishment	5,381,325	5,416,627	101	Investment per Employee	8,609	3,960	46
Value Added per Employee	128,210	100,803	79	Investment per Production Worker	12,245	6,132	50

Sources: Same as General Statistics. The 'Average of All Manufacturing' column represents the average of all manufacturing industries reported for the most recent complete year available. The Index shows the relationship between the Average and the Analyzed Industry. For example, 100 means that they are equal; 500 that the Analyzed Industry is five times the average; 50 means that the Analyzed Industry is half the national average. The abbreviation 'na' is used to show that data are 'not available'. Ratios shown for 2002, the last complete census year.

LEADING COMPANIES Number shown: **75**   Total sales ($ mil): **73,263**   Total employment (000): **229.8**

Company Name	Address				CEO Name	Phone	Co. Type	Sales ($ mil)	Empl. (000)
Raytheon Co.	870 Winter St.	Waltham	MA	02451		781-522-3000	P	21,301	72.1
TUTCO Inc.	500 Gould Dr.	Cookeville	TN	38506		931-432-4141	R	9,602*	0.5
Black and Decker Corp.	101 Schilling Rd.	Hunt Valley	MD	21031	Nolan D. Archibald	410-716-3900	P	6,563	25.0
Trane	4 Wood Hollow Rd.	Piscataway	NJ	08855		973-887-8800	S	6,020	27.1
Jarden Consumer Solutions	2381 Executive Ctr.	Boca Raton	FL	33431	Andrew Hill	561-912-4100	S	4,420*	13.0
Lennox International Inc.	PO Box 799900	Dallas	TX	75379	Todd M. Bluedorn	972-497-5000	P	3,750	15.0
NACCO Industries Inc.	5875 Landerbrook	Mayfield Hgts	OH	44124		440-449-9600	P	3,603	10.2
HNI Corp.	PO Box 1109	Muscatine	IA	52761	Timothy Anderson	563-264-7400	P	2,571	14.2
Dekko Technologies L.L.C.	PO Box 337	North Webster	IN	46555	Steven Hankinf	574-834-2818	R	2,130*	0.1
Scott Fetzer Co.	28800 Clemens Rd.	Westlake	OH	44145	K Semelsberger	440-892-3000	S	935*	14.5
Purolator Air Filtration	PO Box 32578	Louisville	KY	40232		502-969-2304	S	886*	6.7
Simmons Co.	1 Concourse Pky.	Atlanta	GA	30328	Charles R. Eitel	770-512-7700	R	855	3.0
Alpine Industries Inc.	310 T. Elmer Cox Dr	Greeneville	TN	37745	William Converse	423-638-7246	R	749*	1.0
Oregon Cutting Systems Group	PO Box 22127	Portland	OR	97269	Jim Oscermanc	503-653-8881	D	674*	1.0
Behr Heat Transfer Systems	4500 Leeds Ave.	Charleston	SC	29405	Hans Lange	843-745-1233	R	666*	0.7
Water Pik Technologies Inc.	1730 E Prospect Rd.	Fort Collins	CO	80553	Richard Bisson	970-484-1352	R	647*	0.6
Riley Power Inc.	PO Box 15040	Worcester	MA	01615		508-852-7100	R	612*	0.4
Applica Inc.	3633 Flamingo Rd.	Miramar	FL	33027		954-883-1000	S	556	0.3
Salton Inc.	1955 W Field Ct.	Lake Forest	IL	60045	Leonhard Dreimann	847-803-4600	P	523	1.0
Starck, H C Inc.	45 Industrial Pl.	Nwtn Highland	MA	02461	Olaff Schmidtpak	617-630-5880	D	522*	0.4
National Presto Industries	3925 N Hastings	Eau Claire	WI	54703	Maryjo Cohen	715-839-2121	P	421	1.0
Nordyne Inc.	8000 Phoenix Pkwy.	O Fallon	MO	63366	David Lagrand	636-561-7300	S	377*	1.8
Mestek Inc.	260 N Elm St.	Westfield	MA	01085	R. Bruce Dewey	413-568-9571	R	372*	2.6
Tatung Company of America Inc.	2850 El Presidio St	Long Beach	CA	90810	Andrew Sun	310-637-2105	S	355*	0.3
Aerus L.L.C.	300 E Valley Dr.	Bristol	VA	24201	Jim Scott		S	250*	5.0
iRobot Inc.	63 S Ave.	Burlington	MA	01803	Colin Angle	781-345-0200	P	249	0.4
Blendtec Inc.	1206 S 1680 W	Orem	UT	84058	Tom Dickson	801-222-0888	D	248*	0.1
Thermo Products L.L.C.	PO Box 217	North Judson	IN	46366		574-896-2133	R	218*	0.1
Cleaver-Brooks Inc.	PO Box 421	Milwaukee	WI	53201	Welch Goggins	414-359-0600	R	210*	0.2
ALSTOM Power Inc.	3020 Truax Rd.	Wellsville	NY	14895	E Bysiek	585-593-2700	S	191*	0.6
Ronco Inventions L.L.C.	PO Box 4052	Beverly Hills	CA	90213	Ron Popeil		R	173*	0.2
Melitta North America Inc.	13925 58th St. N	Clearwater	FL	33760	Martin Miller	727-535-2111	R	169*	0.1
Taco Inc.	1160 Cranston St.	Cranston	RI	02920		401-942-8000	R	140*	0.4
Bradford White Corp.	725 Talamore Dr.	Ambler	PA	19002	Robert Carnevale	215-641-9400	R	126*	<0.1
Tacony Corp.	1760 Gilsinn Ln.	Fenton	MO	63026		636-349-3000	R	120*	0.3
P and F Industries Inc.	445 Broadhollow	Melville	NY	11747	Richard A. Horowitz	631-694-9800	P	112	0.2
Dometic Corp.	PO Box 490	Elkhart	IN	46516	John Waters	574-294-2511	S	110*	0.6
Oasis Corp.	265 N Hamilton Rd.	Columbus	OH	43213	Romanie Gilliland	614-861-1350	R	92*	0.5
WFI Industries Ltd.	9000 Conservation	Fort Wayne	IN	46809	Bruce Ritchey	260-479-3224	P	91	0.3
Hamilton Beach/Proctor-Silex	234 Springs Rd.	Washington	NC	27889	Michael Morecroft		S	83*	0.3
Dacor Inc.	950 S Raymond	Pasadena	CA	91105	Ric Brutocao	626-799-1000	R	82*	0.5
Lakewood Engineering and Mfg.	501 N Sacramento	Chicago	IL	60612	D Hirschsield	773-722-4300	R	82*	0.4
Western Industries Inc.	W156 Pilgrim	Menomonee Fls	WI	53051	Tom Hall	262-251-1915	R	67*	0.6
Springfield Wire Inc.	PO Box 638	Springfield	MA	01102	William Bradford	413-781-6950	R	66*	0.3
Coen Company Inc.	PO Box 4267	Foster City	CA	94404	Antonio De La	650-638-0365	R	63*	<0.1
Slant Fin Corp.	100 Forest Dr.	Greenvale	NY	11548	Donald Brown	516-484-2600	R	60*	0.4
Boyd Coffee Co.	19730 NE Sandy	Portland	OR	97230	Richard Boyd	503-666-4545	R	59*	0.2
Johnson Gas Appliance Co.	520 E Ave. NW	Cedar Rapids	IA	52405	Barnes O'Donnell	319-365-5267	R	58*	<0.1
Eclipse Inc.	1665 Elmwood Rd.	Rockford	IL	61103	Campbell Perks	815-877-3031	R	53*	<0.1
ECR International Inc.	PO Box 4729	Utica	NY	13504		315-797-1310	R	51*	0.1
Remington Products Company	PO Box 44960	Madison	WI	53744	David Jones		S	51*	0.3
Wilbur Curtis Company Inc.	6913 W Acco Street	Montebello	CA	90640	Robert Curtis	323-837-2300	R	49*	0.3
Andis Co.	PO Box 85005	Racine	WI	53408	Matthew Andis	262-884-2600	R	45*	0.4
BMC Holdings Inc.	PO Box 607	Bryan	OH	43506	Richard Bard	419-636-1194	R	45*	0.3
Magic Aire	501 Galveston St.	Wichita Falls	TX	76301		940-397-2100	S	41*	0.3
Zeeco Inc.	22151 E 91st St. S	Broken Arrow	OK	74014		918-258-8551	R	41*	0.3
Ecoquest Manufacturing Inc.	310 T Elmer Cox	Greeneville	TN	37743	Michael Jackson	423-798-6488	R	41*	0.2
Farmtrac North America L.L.C.	PO Box 1139	Tarboro	NC	27886	Rajan Nanda	252-823-4151	R	41*	0.2
North American Manufacturing	4455 E 71st St.	Cleveland	OH	44105	James Neville	216-271-6000	R	40*	0.3
Cleveland Range Co.	1333 E 179th St.	Cleveland	OH	44110	Rick Cutler	216-481-4900	S	39*	0.2
Airtex Manufacturing Inc.	PO Box 650	De Soto	KS	66018	Richard Rambacher	913-583-3181	R	38*	0.2
ACME Manufacturing Co. Inc.	7601 State Rd.	Philadelphia	PA	19136	Roger Fix	215-338-2850	D	38*	0.5
Monessen Hearth Systems Co.	149 Cleveland Dr.	Paris	KY	40361	Dave Barett	859-987-0740	R	38*	0.3
Forney Corp.	3405 Wiley Post Rd.	Carrollton	TX	75006	John Conroy	972-458-6100	S	36*	0.2
Williams Comfort Products	250 W Laurel St.	Colton	CA	92324		909-825-0993	R	35*	0.3
Air System Components L.P.	1401 N Plano Rd.	Richardson	TX	75081	Terry O'Halloran	972-680-9126	S	35*	0.1
Beckett Gas Inc.	PO Box 4037	Elyria	OH	44036	John Beckett	440-327-3141	R	35*	0.2
T RAD North America Inc.	PO Box 2300	Hopkinsville	KY	42241	Yoshitaka Momose	270-885-9116	R	32*	0.2
Radac Corp.	1231 4th Ave.	Dayton	KY	41074	Richard Morris	859-581-7500	R	31*	0.1
Detroit Stoker Co.	PO Box 732	Monroe	MI	48161	Mark Eleniewski	734-241-9500	S	31*	0.3
EdgeCraft Corp.	825 Southwood Rd.	Avondale	PA	19311	Daniel Friel	610-268-0500	R	31*	0.2
Empire Comfort Systems Inc.	PO Box 529	Belleville	IL	62222	Brian Bauer	618-233-7420	R	30*	0.2
Des Champs Technologies Inc.	225 S Magnolia Ave.	Buena Vista	VA	24416	Nicholas Des Champs	540-291-1111	R	30*	<0.1
Thermal Solutions Products	PO Box 3244	Lancaster	PA	17605	Chris Drew	717-239-7642	S	30*	<0.1
Battle Creek Equipment Co.	307 W Jackson St.	Battle Creek	MI	49037	John Doty	269-962-6181	R	30*	<0.1

Source: Ward's Business Directory of U.S. Private and Public Companies, Volumes 1 and 2, 2008. The company type code used is as follows: P - Public, R - Private, S - Subsidiary, D - Division, J - Joint Venture, A - Affiliate, G - Group. Sales are in millions of dollars, employees are in thousands. An asterisk (*) indicates an estimated sales volume. The symbol < stands for 'less than'. Company names and addresses are truncated, in some cases, to fit into the available space.

MATERIALS CONSUMED

Material	Quantity	Delivered Cost ($ million)
Metal bolts, nuts, screws, and other screw machine products	(X)	28.5
Fabricated metal pipe (excluding castings and forgings)	(X)	11.9
Metal parts and attachments for heating equipment (exc. electric)	(X)	32.2
Fabricated metal valves and pipe fittings	(X)	40.6
Other fabricated metal products (excluding forgings)	(X)	138.2
Forgings	(X)	4.9
Iron and steel castings (rough and semifinished)	(X)	106.1
Aluminum and aluminum-base alloy castings (rough and semifinished)	(X)	9.9
Other nonferrous castings (rough and semifinished)	(X)	3.1
Steel bars, bar shapes, and plates (exc. castings, forgings, fabr. metal products)	(X)	22.2
Steel sheet and strip (including tinplate)	(X)	148.2
Steel structural shapes (exc. castings, forgings, fabr. metal products)	(X)	3.9
All other steel shapes and forms (exc. castings, forgings, fabr. metal products)	(X)	10.1
Aluminum and aluminum-base alloy shapes and forms (exc. castings, forgings, fabr. metal products)	(X)	5.3
Copper and copper-base alloy shapes and forms (exc. castings, forgings, fabr. metal products)	(X)	11.0
Other nonferrous shapes and forms (exc. castings, forgings, fabricated metal products)	(X)	3.4
Metal stampings	(X)	6.5
Integral horsepower electric motors and generators (1 hp or more)	(X)	38.7
Automatic temperature controls (thermostats, regulators, etc.)	(X)	101.7
Paperboard containers, boxes, and corrugated paperboard	(X)	37.5
All other materials, components, parts, containers, and supplies	(X)	512.9
Materials, ingredients, containers, and supplies, nsk	(X)	190.6

Source: 2002 Economic Census. Explanation of symbols used: (D): Withheld to avoid disclosure of competitive data; na: Not available; (S): Withheld because statistical norms were not met; (X): Not applicable; (Z): Less than half the unit shown; nec: Not elsewhere classified; nsk: Not specified by kind; - : zero; p : 10-19 percent estimated; q : 20-29 percent estimated.

PRODUCT SHARE DETAILS

Product or Product Class Shipments	Mil. $	Product or Product Class Shipments	Mil. $
HEATING EQUIPMENT, EXCEPT WARM AIR FURNACES	3,856.9	or less	119.4
Cast iron heating boilers, radiators, and convectors, except parts	**689.3**	Steel heating boilers (15 p.s.i. or less), and all hot water heating boilers, excluding parts, 400,001 Btu per hour or more, including scotch type and horizontal fire box	114.9
Cast iron boilers and radiators, and aluminum and other nonferrous metal radiators and convectors, incl. baseboard and finned tube type, residential, and special type (excl. electric)	660.0	Steel heating boilers (15 p.s.i. or less), and all hot water heating boilers, excluding parts, nsk	8.3
Gas-fired cast iron boilers, excluding parts	233.2	**Floor and wall furnaces, unit heaters, infrared heaters, and mechanical stokers**	**441.9**
Other cast iron boilers, excluding electric and parts	188.2	Floor and wall furnaces, unit heaters, gas-fired infrared heaters, and mechanical stokers, including parts	422.2
Cast iron and steel radiators and convectors, excluding parts	173.2	Floor and wall furnaces (gas and oil)	94.0
Aluminum and other nonferrous metal radiators and convectors, including baseboard and finned tube type, residential, industrial, and special type (excluding electric and parts)	65.4	Gas-fired unit heaters, 400,000 Btu per hour or less	175.0
		Steam and hot water heating element, centrifugal fan-type (blower) and propeller fan-type unit heaters (except electric)	19.8
Cast iron heating boilers, radiators, and convectors, except parts, nsk	29.3	Gas-fired infrared heaters	59.0
Domestic heating stoves, except electric and parts	**845.2**	Mechanical stokers, except electric	5.0
Heating stoves	844.5	Parts for floor and wall furnaces, unit heaters, gas-fired infrared heaters, and mechanical stokers	69.3
Gas fueled (all types) domestic hearth appliances (except electric and parts), B-vent, direct vent, vent-free (free-standing and fireplace insert)	195.7	Floor and wall furnaces, unit heaters, infrared heaters, and mechanical stokers (including parts), nsk	19.7
Vented log sets	36.1	**Other heating equipment, except electric (including parts for nonelectric heating equipment and oil burners)**	**1,416.6**
Ventless log sets	62.0	Oil burners	157.3
B-vent built-in appliances	15.5	Parts and attachments for oil burners	49.2
Direct vent built-in appliances	(D)	Gas burners and gas conversion burners (including parts), 400,000 Btu per hour or less	89.8
Vent-free built-in appliances	12.3	Gas burners and gas conversion burners (including parts), 400,000 Btu per hour or more	104.7
Coal, kerosene, gasoline, and fuel oil domestic heating stoves (excluding parts)	(D)	Parts and attachments for gas burners (sold separately)	35.5
Freestanding wood fireplaces and domestic heating stoves (all types), including circulating and radiants (excluding parts)	276.8	Heating unit ventilators, except electric	70.6
Wood pellet fuel-burning domestic heaters (excluding parts)	38.7	Nonelectric prefabricated metal fireplaces for commercial and industrial use	15.9
		Solar energy collectors (water or air)	35.3
Heat exchangers and zero clearance (factory built) domestic wood fireplaces	(D)	Electric swimming pool heaters	114.9
Domestic wood fireplace inserts	53.9	Wall and baseboard heating units for permanent installation	172.3
Domestic heating stoves, except electric (excluding parts), nsk	0.7	Parts, accessories, and attachments for wall and baseboard heating units	11.0
Steel heating boilers (15 psi or less) and all other hot water heating boilers, excluding parts	**242.6**	Other heating equipment, including dual-fired gas and oil burners, heat transfer (blast coils), range boilers, expansion tanks, direct-fired water heater tanks (incl. parts), except electric	560.1
Steel heating boilers	234.4	**Heating equipment (except warm air furnaces), nsk, total**	**221.3**
Steel heating boilers (15 p.s.i. or less), and all hot water heating boilers, excluding parts, 400,000 Btu per hour			

Source: 2002 Economic Census. The values are product shipments in millions of dollars for 2002. Total product shipments may be lower or higher than industry shipments. See Introduction for a full discussion. Values of indented subcategories are summed in the main heading(s). The symbol (D) appears when data are withheld to prevent disclosure of competitive information. The abbreviation nsk stands for 'not specified by kind' and nec for 'not elsewhere classified'. A dash (-) means zero.

INPUTS AND OUTPUTS FOR HEATING EQUIPMENT (EXCEPT WARM AIR FURNACES) MANUFACTURING

Economic Sector or Industry Providing Inputs	%	Sector	Economic Sector or Industry Buying Outputs	%	Sector
Compensation of employees	26.4		Personal consumption expenditures	27.4	
Iron & steel mills & ferroalloys	5.7	Manufg.	Residential permanent site structures	9.8	Construct.
Management of companies & enterprises	4.8	Services	Nonresidential structures, nec	8.1	Construct.
Paints & coatings	4.3	Manufg.	AC, refrigeration, and warm air heating equipment	6.1	Manufg.
Wholesale trade	4.3	Trade	Residential structures, nec	6.0	Construct.
Automatic environmental controls	3.5	Manufg.	Commercial & health care structures	5.9	Construct.
Ferrous metal foundries	3.0	Manufg.	Exports of goods & services	4.7	Cap Inv
Advertising & related services	2.6	Services	Elementary & secondary schools	4.2	Services
Securities, commodity contracts, investments	1.4	Fin/R.E.	Owner-occupied dwellings	3.5	
Machine shops	1.4	Manufg.	Other S/L govt. enterprises	2.6	S/L Govt
Turned products & screws, nuts, & bolts	1.3	Manufg.	Private fixed investment	2.5	
Heating equipment (except warm air furnaces)	1.3	Manufg.	Colleges, universities, & professional schools	2.4	Services
Plastics products, nec	1.3	Manufg.	Maintenance/repair of nonresidential structures	2.0	Construct.
Paperboard containers	1.2	Manufg.	Plastics materials & resins	1.5	Manufg.
Fabricated pipes & pipe fittings	1.1	Manufg.	Architectural, engineering, & related services	1.4	Services
Motors & generators	1.1	Manufg.	Food services & drinking places	1.3	Services
Truck transportation	1.0	Util.	General S/L govt. services	1.3	S/L Govt
Lessors of nonfinancial assets	1.0	Fin/R.E.	Waste management & remediation services	1.1	Services
Gaskets, packing, & sealing devices	0.9	Manufg.	Heating equipment (except warm air furnaces)	1.1	Manufg.
Coating, engraving, heat treating & allied activities	0.9	Manufg.	Asphalt paving mixtures & blocks	1.0	Manufg.
Monetary authorities/depository credit intermediation	0.9	Fin/R.E.	Wood containers & pallets	1.0	Manufg.
Semiconductors & related devices	0.7	Manufg.	Travel trailers & campers	0.8	Manufg.
Real estate	0.7	Fin/R.E.	Maintenance/repair of residential structures	0.7	Construct.
Professional, scientific, technical services, nec	0.7	Services	Manufacturing structures	0.7	Construct.
Printed circuit assemblies (electronic assemblies)	0.7	Manufg.	Telecommunications	0.6	Services
Power generation & supply	0.7	Util.	Change in private inventories	0.6	In House
Data processing, hosting, & related services	0.6	Services	Scientific research & development services	0.5	Services
Food services & drinking places	0.5	Services	Automotive equipment rental & leasing	0.3	Fin/R.E.
Legal services	0.5	Services	Data processing, hosting, & related services	0.2	Services
Nonferrous metal foundries	0.4	Manufg.	Motor homes	0.2	Manufg.
Telecommunications	0.4	Services	Real estate	0.1	Fin/R.E.
Scientific research & development services	0.4	Services	Services to buildings & dwellings	0.1	Services
Power boilers & heat exchangers	0.4	Manufg.			
Valve & fittings other than plumbing	0.4	Manufg.			
Architectural, engineering, & related services	0.4	Services			
Accounting, tax preparation, bookkeeping, & payroll	0.4	Services			
Copper rolling, drawing, extruding, & alloying	0.3	Manufg.			
Fabricated metals, nec	0.3	Manufg.			
Hotels & motels, including casino hotels	0.3	Services			
Nondepository credit intermediation activities	0.3	Fin/R.E.			
Taxes on production & imports, less subsidies	0.3				
Air transportation	0.3	Util.			
Automotive equipment rental & leasing	0.3	Fin/R.E.			
Natural gas distribution	0.3	Util.			
Cutting tools & machine tool accessories	0.3	Manufg.			
Postal service	0.3	Util.			
Warehousing & storage	0.3	Util.			
Plate work & fabricated structural products	0.3	Manufg.			
Crowns & closures & metal stamping	0.2	Manufg.			
Services to buildings & dwellings	0.2	Services			
Ball & roller bearings	0.2	Manufg.			
Maintenance/repair of nonresidential structures	0.2	Construct.			
Management, scientific, & technical consulting	0.2	Services			
Handtools	0.2	Manufg.			
Retail trade	0.2	Trade			
Other computer related services, including facilities	0.2	Services			
Forging, stamping, & sintering, nec	0.2	Manufg.			
Nonmetallic minerals, nec	0.2	Mining			
Noncomparable imports	0.2	Foreign			
Rail transportation	0.2	Util.			
Abrasive products	0.2	Manufg.			
Alumina refining & primary aluminum production	0.2	Manufg.			
Rubber products, nec	0.2	Manufg.			
Commercial & industrial machinery rental & leasing	0.2	Fin/R.E.			
Custom roll forming	0.2	Manufg.			
Business support services	0.1	Services			
Automotive repair & maintenance, ex. car washes	0.1	Services			
Commercial & industrial equipment repair/maintenance	0.1	Services			
Relay & industrial controls	0.1	Manufg.			
Springs & wire products	0.1	Manufg.			
Ornamental & architectural metal products	0.1	Manufg.			
Paperboard mills	0.1	Manufg.			
Civic, social, & professional organizations	0.1	Services			
Petroleum lubricating oil & grease	0.1	Manufg.			

Source: Benchmark Input-Output Accounts for the U.S. Economy, 2002, U.S. Department of Commerce, Washington, D.C., January 2008. The abbreviation nec stands for 'not elsewhere classified'.

OCCUPATIONS EMPLOYED BY VENTILATION, HEATING, AC, & COMMERCIAL REFRIGERATION

Occupation	% of Total 2006	Change to 2016	Occupation	% of Total 2006	Change to 2016
Team assemblers	19.2	-8.0	Machinists	1.6	-3.4
Welders, cutters, solderers, & brazers	6.1	-2.1	Shipping, receiving, & traffic clerks	1.5	-11.5
Cutting, punching, & press machine operators	5.0	-17.2	Heating, AC, & refrigeration mechanics & installers	1.4	-8.0
Sheet metal workers	3.4	-9.8	Mechanical engineers	1.4	-8.0
First-line supervisors/managers of production workers	3.1	-8.0	Maintenance & repair workers, general	1.3	-8.0
Helpers--Production workers	2.9	-8.0	Sales reps, wholesale & manufacturing, exc tech	1.3	-8.0
Assemblers & fabricators, nec	2.7	-17.2	Welding, soldering, & brazing machine operators	1.3	3.4
Inspectors, testers, sorters, samplers, & weighers	2.3	-13.3	Electrical & electronic equipment assemblers	1.2	-26.4
Laborers & freight, stock, & material movers, hand	2.2	-17.2	Production, planning, & expediting clerks	1.1	-8.0
Industrial truck & tractor operators	2.1	-17.2	Coating, painting, & spraying machine operators	1.1	-12.6
Structural metal fabricators & fitters	2.0	-8.0	Customer service representatives	1.1	1.2
Multiple machine tool operators & tenders	1.9	1.2	General & operations managers	1.1	-17.2

Source: Industry-Occupation Matrix, Bureau of Labor Statistics, December 4, 2007. These data are reported based on 4-digit NAICS categories but have been matched to corresponding 6-digit NAICS industry codes. The change reported for each occupation to the year 2016 is a percent of growth or decline as estimated by the Bureau of Labor Statistics. The abbreviation nec stands for 'not elsewhere classified'.

LOCATION BY STATE AND REGIONAL CONCENTRATION

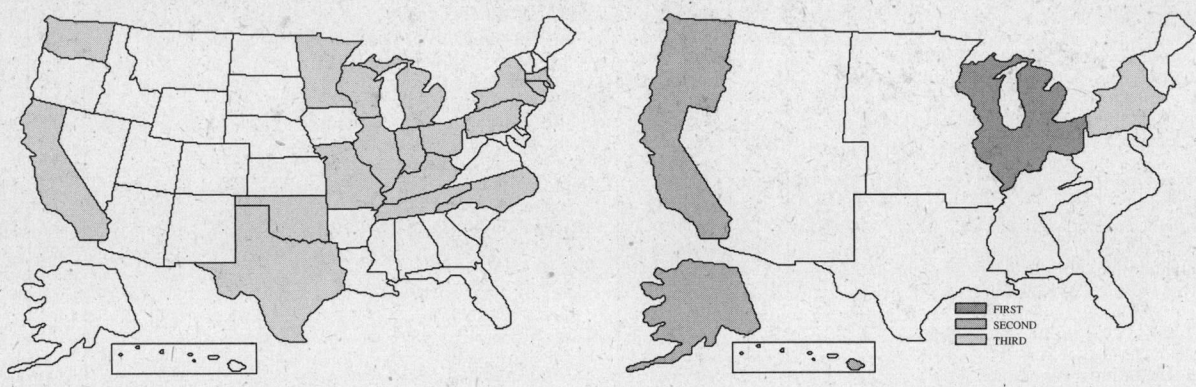

FIRST
SECOND
THIRD

INDUSTRY DATA BY STATE

State	Establish-ments	Shipments			Employment				Cost as % of Shipments	Investment per Employee ($)
		Total ($ mil)	% of U.S.	Per Establ.	Total Number	% of U.S.	Per Establ.	Wages ($/hour)		
Indiana	17	494.0	12.4	29,056.4	1,852	8.3	109	14.96	45.2	2,096
California	54	487.0	12.3	9,018.6	3,070	13.8	57	11.70	43.7	2,797
Pennsylvania	32	406.6	10.2	12,707.4	2,005	9.0	63	15.05	45.0	8,648
Minnesota	26	228.5	5.8	8,787.2	917	4.1	35	13.28	40.2	8,418
New York	22	219.0	5.5	9,952.4	1,191	5.3	54	10.83	42.1	2,103
Kentucky	3	187.9	4.7	62,635.7	1,058	4.7	353	11.18	45.5	4,393
Ohio	18	180.7	4.6	10,036.3	1,123	5.0	62	13.81	50.0	4,255
Tennessee	11	163.0	4.1	14,821.5	1,218	5.5	111	11.47	40.3	2,245
Texas	12	155.4	3.9	12,952.5	533	2.4	44	13.01	19.5	2,555
Washington	14	147.0	3.7	10,500.1	988	4.4	71	14.18	46.6	1,619
Illinois	16	113.3	2.9	7,080.0	700	3.1	44	16.21	38.9	3,939
Missouri	9	112.1	2.8	12,457.3	538	2.4	60	11.25	57.4	3,338
Massachusetts	11	102.5	2.6	9,322.0	739	3.3	67	13.16	42.4	2,414
Wisconsin	15	87.7	2.2	5,847.8	543	2.4	36	13.01	39.2	1,823
North Carolina	9	81.5	2.1	9,050.4	588	2.6	65	13.26	42.4	1,621
Michigan	17	62.4	1.6	3,669.5	309	1.4	18	15.03	43.5	1,612
Connecticut	7	49.8	1.3	7,119.7	240	1.1	34	11.63	39.4	2,883
Rhode Island	3	25.4	0.6	8,475.7	168	0.8	56	8.28	32.8	2,143
Oklahoma	6	20.0	0.5	3,335.7	125	0.6	21	13.18	39.2	2,120

Source: 2002 *Economic Census*. The states are in descending order of shipments or establishments (if shipment data are missing for the majority). The symbol (D) appears when data are withheld to prevent disclosure of competitive information. States marked with (D) are sorted by number of establishments. A dash (-) indicates that the data element cannot be calculated. Data may not show all states active in the NAICS category. All data available at the time of publication are shown.

NAICS 333415 - AIR-CONDITIONING AND WARM AIR HEATING EQUIPMENT

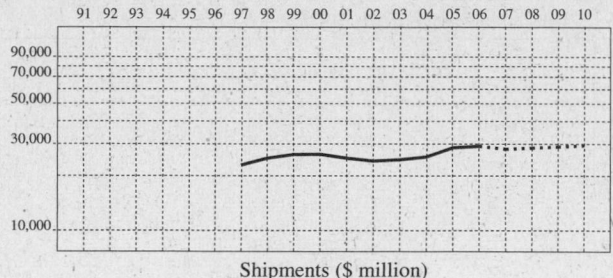

Shipments ($ million)

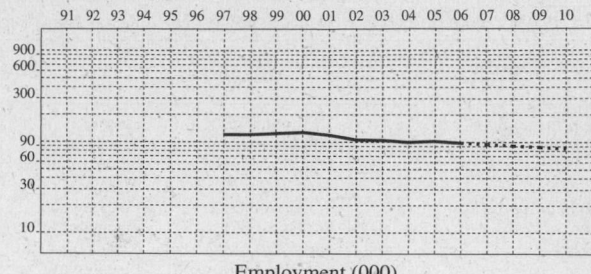

Employment (000)

GENERAL STATISTICS

Year	Companies	Establishments		Employment			Compensation		Production ($ million)			
		Total	with 20 or more employees	Total (000)	Production Workers (000)	Hours (Mil)	Payroll ($ mil)	Wages ($/hr)	Cost of Materials	Value Added by Manufacture	Value of Shipments	Capital Invest.
1997	645	799	503	120.3	91.8	185.3	3,699.5	12.64	12,509.0	10,268.7	22,941.0	565.8
1998		812	498	120.0	92.0	184.6	3,844.7	13.43	13,736.5	11,265.4	25,007.9	630.8
1999		810	497	124.0	95.9	190.9	4,043.1	13.45	14,002.2	12,376.4	26,220.7	822.2
2000		806	491	127.4	98.0	197.1	4,267.9	13.67	14,149.9	12,221.5	26,294.1	798.5
2001		848	498	118.9	89.0	183.4	3,950.5	13.42	13,152.5	11,622.4	25,025.5	748.4
2002	702	890	499	105.7	78.5	150.8	3,722.9	15.25	11,909.0	12,020.9	24,165.7	453.8
2003		843	468	104.6	77.5	151.4	3,775.8	15.44	12,412.0	12,272.6	24,535.1	376.5
2004		874	470	99.7	73.6	146.7	3,708.0	15.60	13,186.6	12,348.1	25,451.1	701.7
2005		916	493	102.4	76.0	151.3	3,942.8	16.12	15,388.5	13,281.4	28,612.8	540.8
2006		911P	476P	98.1	74.9	150.6	4,021.1	17.16	15,494.7	13,821.3	29,140.2	494.9
2007		925P	473P	94.6P	69.8P	138.0P	3,904.4P	17.20P	14,945.6P	13,331.5P	28,107.5P	499.0P
2008		938P	471P	91.4P	67.1P	132.3P	3,905.6P	17.67P	15,174.5P	13,535.7P	28,538.0P	478.2P
2009		951P	468P	88.2P	64.4P	126.7P	3,906.8P	18.14P	15,403.5P	13,739.9P	28,968.6P	457.4P
2010		965P	465P	85.0P	61.7P	121.0P	3,908.0P	18.61P	15,632.4P	13,944.1P	29,399.2P	436.6P

Sources: 1997 and 2002 *Economic Census*; other years, up to 2006, are from *Annual Survey of Manufactures*. Establishment counts for non-Census years are from *County Business Patterns*; 1997 and 2002 values are from the 1997 and 2002 censuses, respectively. 'P's show projections by the editors.

INDICES OF CHANGE

Year	Companies	Establishments		Employment			Compensation		Production ($ million)			
		Total	with 20 or more employees	Total (000)	Production Workers (000)	Hours (Mil)	Payroll ($ mil)	Wages ($/hr)	Cost of Materials	Value Added by Manufacture	Value of Shipments	Capital Invest.
1997	92	90	101	114	117	123	99	83	105	85	95	125
1998		91	100	114	117	122	103	88	115	94	103	139
1999		91	100	117	122	127	109	88	118	103	109	181
2000		91	98	121	125	131	115	90	119	102	109	176
2001		95	100	112	113	122	106	88	110	97	104	165
2002	100	100	100	100	100	100	100	100	100	100	100	100
2003		95	94	99	99	100	101	101	104	102	102	83
2004		98	94	94	94	97	100	102	111	103	105	155
2005		103	99	97	97	100	106	106	129	110	118	119
2006		102P	95P	93	95	100	108	113	130	115	121	109
2007		104P	95P	89P	89P	92P	105P	113P	125P	111P	116P	110P
2008		105P	94P	86P	85P	88P	105P	116P	127P	113P	118P	105P
2009		107P	94P	83P	82P	84P	105P	1.19P	129P	114P	120P	101P
2010		108P	93P	80P	79P	80P	105P	122P	131P	116P	122P	96P

Sources: Same as General Statistics. Values reflect change from the base year, 2002. Values above 100 mean greater than 2002, values below 100 mean less than 2002, and the values of 100 in other years means the same as 2002. 'P's show projections by the editors.

SELECTED RATIOS

For 2002	Avg. of All Manufact.	Analyzed Industry	Index	For 2002	Avg. of All Manufact.	Analyzed Industry	Index
Employees per Establishment	42	119	283	Value Added per Production Worker	182,367	153,132	84
Payroll per Establishment	1,639,184	4,183,034	255	Cost per Establishment	5,769,015	13,380,899	232
Payroll per Employee	39,053	35,221	90	Cost per Employee	137,446	112,668	82
Production Workers per Establishment	30	88	299	Cost per Production Worker	195,506	151,707	78
Wages per Establishment	694,845	2,583,933	372	Shipments per Establishment	11,158,348	27,152,472	243
Wages per Production Worker	23,548	29,296	124	Shipments per Employee	265,847	228,625	86
Hours per Production Worker	1,980	1,921	97	Shipments per Production Worker	378,144	307,843	81
Wages per Hour	11.89	15.25	128	Investment per Establishment	361,338	509,888	141
Value Added per Establishment	5,381,325	13,506,629	251	Investment per Employee	8,609	4,293	50
Value Added per Employee	128,210	113,727	89	Investment per Production Worker	12,245	5,781	47

Sources: Same as General Statistics. The 'Average of All Manufacturing' column represents the average of all manufacturing industries reported for the most recent complete year available. The Index shows the relationship between the Average and the Analyzed Industry. For example, 100 means that they are equal; 500 that the Analyzed Industry is five times the average; 50 means that the Analyzed Industry is half the national average. The abbreviation 'na' is used to show that data are 'not available'. Ratios shown for 2002, the last complete census year.

LEADING COMPANIES   Number shown: 75   Total sales ($ mil): 198,802   Total employment (000): 746.6

Company Name	Address				CEO Name	Phone	Co. Type	Sales ($ mil)	Empl. (000)
United Technologies Corp.	1 Financial Plz.	Hartford	CT	06101	Mario Abajo	860-728-7000	P	47,829	225.6
Danaher Corp.	2099 Penn. Avenue	Washington	DC	20006	H. Lawrence Culp Jr.	202-828-0850	P	11,026	50.0
Carrier Corp.	One Carrier Pl.	Farmington	CT	06034	Geraud Darnis		S	10,600	4.3
API Group Inc.	2366 Rose Pl.	St. Paul	MN	55113	Lee R. Anderson Sr.	651-636-4320	R	9,000	5.0
American Standard Inc.	PO Box 6820	Piscataway	NJ	08855		732-980-3000	S	7,614*	67.0
Trane Inc.	PO Box 6820	Piscataway	NJ	08855		732-980-6000	P	7,450	29.6
Dover Corp.	280 Park Ave.	New York	NY	10017		212-922-1640	P	7,226	33.4
Trane	4 Wood Hollow Rd.	Piscataway	NJ	08855		973-887-8800	S	6,020	27.1
McDermott International Inc.	757 N Eldridge Pky.	Houston	TX	77009	Robert Deason	281-870-5011	P	5,632	28.4
Hussmann Corp.	12999 St. Chrles Rd	Bridgeton	MO	63044	Dennis Gibson	314-291-2000	S	4,623*	8.0
York International Corp.	PO Box 1592	York	PA	17405		717-771-7890	S	4,510	23.2
PepsiAmericas Inc.	4000 Dain Rauscher	Minneapolis	MN	55402		612-661-4000	P	4,480	20.7
Marley-Wylain Co.	13515 Ballnyn Corp.	Charlotte	NC	28277	C. J. Kearney	704-752-4400	S	4,372*	23.8
Manitowoc Company Inc.	PO Box 66	Manitowoc	WI	54221		920-684-4410	P	4,005	10.5
Lennox International Inc.	PO Box 799900	Dallas	TX	75379	Todd M. Bluedorn	972-497-5000	P	3,750	15.0
Harsco Corp.	PO Box 8888	Camp Hill	PA	17001	S. D. Fazzolari	717-763-7064	P	3,688	21.5
Siemens Power Generation Inc.	4400 N Alafaya Trl.	Orlando	FL	32826	Randy Zwirn	407-736-2000	R	3,081*	3.0
Amsted Industries Inc.	2 Prudential Plaza	Chicago	IL	60601	W. Robert Reum	312-645-1700	R	3,050	9.9
Cornelius IMI Inc.	101 Broadway St. W	Osseo	MN	55369	Richard Barkley	763-488-8200	R	2,840*	0.3
Baltimore Aircoil Company Inc.	PO Box 7322	Baltimore	MD	21227	Steven Duerwachter	410-799-6200	R	2,510*	0.2
Consolidated Metco Inc.	PO Box 83201	Portland	OR	97283		503-286-5741	R	2,510*	0.1
Mechanical Construction Inc.	1500 Chester Pk.	Eddystone	PA	19022	Michael J. Hall	610-876-9292	S	2,370*	3.3
A.O. Smith Corp.	PO Box 245008	Milwaukee	WI	53224		414-359-4000	P	2,312	16.8
NTK Holdings Inc.	50 Kennedy Plz.	Providence	RI	02903	Richard L. Bready	401-751-1600	S	2,218	9.8
Hutchinson FTS Inc.	1835 Technology	Troy	MI	48083	Paul Campbell	248-589-7710	R	1,863*	<0.1
Goodman Global Inc.	2550 North Loop W	Houston	TX	77092	Charles A. Carroll	713-861-2500	S	1,795	4.9
Engineered Support Systems	201 Evans Ln.	St. Louis	MO	63121	Nicholas Innerbichler	314-553-4000	S	1,736	5.7
Rainin Instrument L.L.C.	PO Box 4026	Woburn	MA	01888	Kenneth Rainin	510-564-1600	R	1,590*	0.1
Formtek Inc.	260 N Elm St.	Westfield	MA	01085	John E. Reed	413-568-9571	S	1,530*	2.6
Williams Enterprise of Georgia	1285 Hawthorne	Smyrna	GA	30080	Dale Williams	770-436-1596	R	1,478*	0.6
Connell L.P.	1 International Pl.	Boston	MA	02110	Margot C. Connell	617-737-2700	R	1,429*	2.0
Sanden of America Inc.	601 Sanden Blvd.	Wylie	TX	75098	Kazuhiko Arai	972-442-8400	R	1,420*	<0.1
Tecumseh Products Co.	100 E Patterson St.	Tecumseh	MI	49286	Edwin Bunker	517-423-8411	P	1,133	10.3
Babcock and Wilcox Co.	PO Box 351	Barberton	OH	44203	John A. Fees	330-753-4511	S	1,080*	10.8
TriMas Corp.	39400 Woodward	Bloomfield Hls	MI	48304	Grant Beard	248-631-5450	P	1,068	5.1
C and D Zodiac Inc.	5701 Bolsa Ave.	Huntington Bch	CA	92647		714-934-0000	R	1,045*	0.5
EPE Industrial Filters Inc.	9250 Bloomington	Bloomington	MN	55431	William Cook	847-381-0860	R	1,024*	1.5
McWane Corp.	PO Box 43327	Birmingham	AL	35243	G. Ruffner Page, Jr.	205-414-3100	R	944*	7.0
Manchester Tank and Equipment	1000 Corp Centre Dr	Franklin	TN	37067	Robert Richard	615-370-3833	R	926*	<0.1
Behr Climate Systems Inc.	5020 Augusta Dr.	Fort Worth	TX	76106		817-624-7273	R	885*	0.2
McQuay International	13600 Indu Prk Blvd	Minneapolis	MN	55441	Ho Nyuk Chow	763-553-5330	S	838*	5.0
MKS Instruments Inc.	90 Industrial Way	Wilmington	MA	01887	Leo Berlinghieri	978-284-4000	P	783	3.0
Chart Industries Inc.	One Infinity Corp.	Garfield Height	OH	44125	Samuel F. Thomas	440-753-1490	P	666	2.8
Enodis Corp.	2227 Welbilt Blvd.	New Port Richey	FL	34655	Peter Brooks	727-375-7010	S	650*	3.0
Axair Nortec Inc.	PO Box 698	Ogdensburg	NY	13669	URS Schenk	315-425-1255	R	627*	<0.1
Standex International Corp.	6 Manor Pky.	Salem	NH	03079	Roger L. Fix	603-893-9701	P	621	5.4
Riley Power Inc.	PO Box 15040	Worcester	MA	01615		508-852-7100	R	612*	0.4
American Cast Iron Pipe Co.	PO Box 2727	Birmingham	AL	35202		205-325-7701	R	596*	2.3
NATCO Group Inc.	2950 N Loop W, 700	Houston	TX	77092	John U. Clarke	713-683-9292	P	570	2.5
Fisher Scientific	2000 Park Lane Dr.	Pittsburgh	PA	15275	David Dellapenta	412-490-8300	D	568	1.8
Middleby Corp.	1400 Toastmaster Dr	Elgin	IL	60120	Selim A. Bassoul	847-741-3300	P	501	1.7
LSB Industries Inc.	16 S Penn. Avenue	Oklahoma City	OK	73107	Jack E. Golsen	405-235-4546	P	492	1.6
Elkay Manufacturing Co.	2222 Camden Ct.	Oak Brook	IL	60523	Ronald Katz	630-574-8484	R	470*	3.6
Luwa Inc.	3901 Westpoint Blvd	Winston-Salem	NC	27103		336-760-3111	R	448*	0.1
Newport Corp.	1791 Deere Ave.	Irvine	CA	92606	Michael ONeill	949-863-3144	P	445	2.0
Liebert Corp.	PO Box 29186	Columbus	OH	43229	Robert Bauer	614-888-0246	S	440*	5.0
Proliance International Inc.	100 Gando Dr.	New Haven	CT	06513	Barry R. Banducci	203-401-6450	P	416	2.0
Alaskan Copper Co's Inc.	PO Box 3546	Seattle	WA	98124	Kermit Rosen	206-623-5800	R	392*	0.3
Lan-Leasing Inc.	6655 Lancer Blvd.	San Antonio	TX	78219	Chris Hughes	210-310-7000	S	386*	0.7
Nordyne Inc.	8000 Phoenix Pkwy.	O Fallon	MO	63366	David Lagrand	636-561-7300	S	377*	1.8
Mestek Inc.	260 N Elm St.	Westfield	MA	01085	R. Bruce Dewey	413-568-9571	P	372*	2.6
FES Systems Inc.	PO Box 2306	York	PA	17405	Ronald Eberhard	717-767-6411	R	347*	0.2
Reddy Ice Holdings Inc.	8750 N Central Expy	Dallas	TX	75231	William P. Brick	214-526-6740	P	339	1.5
Mobile Mini Inc.	PO Box 79149	Phoenix	AZ	85062	Steven G. Bunger	480-894-6311	P	318.	2.1
TOPP Portable Air	12 Crozerville Rd.	Aston	PA	19014	Dan Topp	610-459-5515	R	303*	<0.1
Mammoth Inc.	101 W 82nd St.	Chaska	MN	55318	David J. Huntley	952-361-2711	S	299*	0.4
Maxcess Technologies Inc.	230 Deming Way	Summerville	SC	29483	Andy Miarka	843-821-1200	R	291*	<0.1
Fedders Corp.	PO Box 813	Liberty Corner	NJ	07938	Michael Giordano	908-604-8686	P	279	2.0
Kirk and Blum Manufacturing	3120 Forrer St.	Cincinnati	OH	45209	Richard J. Blum	513-458-2600	S	265*	0.4
CEI Enterprises Inc.	245 Woodward SE	Albuquerque	NM	87102		505-842-5556	S	264*	0.1
AAON Inc.	2425 S Yukon Ave.	Tulsa	OK	74107	N H. Asbjornson	918-583-2266	P	263	1.4
Southern Heat Exchanger Corp.	PO Box 1850	Tuscaloosa	AL	35403	Bill Laganke	205-345-5335	R	234*	0.2
Michigan Automotive Compressor	2400 N Dearing Rd.	Parma	MI	49269	Hiroyo Kono	517-622-7000	R	231*	0.8
General Atomics	PO Box 85608	San Diego	CA	92186	James Blue	858-455-3000	R	219*	1.0
Burnham Holdings Inc.	PO Box 3205	Lancaster	PA	17604	Albert Morrison III	717-397-4700	P	218	1.3

Source: *Ward's Business Directory of U.S. Private and Public Companies*, Volumes 1 and 2, 2008. The company type code used is as follows: P - Public, R - Private, S - Subsidiary, D - Division, J - Joint Venture, A - Affiliate, G - Group. Sales are in millions of dollars, employees are in thousands. An asterisk (*) indicates an estimated sales volume. The symbol < stands for 'less than'. Company names and addresses are truncated, in some cases, to fit into the available space.

MATERIALS CONSUMED

Material	Quantity	Delivered Cost ($ million)
Refrigeration compressors, compressor units, condensing units, and other heat transfer equipment	(X)	1,915.8
Fractional horsepower electric timing motors (less than 1 hp)	(X)	313.9
Fractional horsepower electric motors (less than 1 hp), exc. timing motors	(X)	228.1
Integral horsepower electric motors and generators (1 hp or more)	(X)	475.7
Fans and blowers	(X)	180.4
Electrical transmission, distribution, and control equipment	(X)	347.7
Current-carrying wiring devices	(X)	149.7
Automatic temperature controls (thermostats, regulators, etc.)	(X)	267.9
Ball and roller bearings (mounted or unmounted)	(X)	22.7
Metal bolts, nuts, screws, and other screw machine products	(X)	186.1
Metal stampings	(X)	141.5
Metal hardware (inc. hinges, handles, locks, casters, etc.)	(X)	71.2
Metal pipe, valves, and pipe fittings (excluding forgings)	(X)	158.2
All other fabricated metal products (excluding forgings)	(X)	304.2
Forgings	(X)	23.7
Iron and steel castings (rough and semifinished)	(X)	377.6
Aluminum and aluminum-base alloy castings (rough and semifinished)	(X)	118.6
Other nonferrous metal castings, rough or semifinished (inc. aluminum)	(X)	22.9
Steel bars, bar shapes, and plates (exc. castings, forgings, fabr. metal products)	(X)	247.4
Steel sheet and strip (including tinplate)	(X)	667.1
Steel wire and wire products	(X)	53.5
All other steel shapes and forms (exc. castings, forgings, fabr. metal products)	(X)	123.4
Copper and copper-base alloy pipe and tube (exc. castings, forgings, fabr. metal products)	(X)	495.5
All other copper and copper-base alloy shapes and forms (exc. castings, forgings, fabr. metal products)	(X)	52.1
Aluminum and aluminum-base alloy sheet, plate, foil, and welded tubing	(X)	285.2
All other aluminum and aluminum-base alloy shapes and forms (exc. castings, forgings, fabr. metal products)	(X)	46.5
Other nonferrous shapes and forms (exc. castings, forgings, fabricated metal products)	(X)	35.2
Paper and paperboard containers (incl. shipping sacks and other paper packaging supplies)	(X)	146.5
Wooden containers, complete (incl. combination wood and paperboard)	(X)	43.5
Paints, varnishes, stains, lacquers, shellacs, japans, enamels, etc.	(X)	44.0
Refrigerant gases and other synthetic organic chemicals	(X)	68.2
Plastics resins consumed in the form of granules, pellets, etc.	(X)	78.9
Plastics products consumed in the form of sheets, rods, etc.	(X)	90.0
Fabricated plastics products (exc. gaskets, hoses, and belting)	(X)	164.0
Rubber and plastics hose and belting	(X)	37.1
Gaskets (all types) and asbestos packing	(X)	45.7
Mineral wool insulation (fibrous glass, rock wool, etc.)	(X)	65.3
All other materials, components, parts, containers, and supplies	(X)	1,817.3
Materials, ingredients, containers, and supplies, nsk	(X)	1,131.5

Source: 2002 *Economic Census*. Explanation of symbols used: (D): Withheld to avoid disclosure of competitive data; na: Not available; (S): Withheld because statistical norms were not met; (X): Not applicable; (Z): Less than half the unit shown; nec: Not elsewhere classified; nsk: Not specified by kind; - : zero; p : 10-19 percent estimated; q : 20-29 percent estimated.

PRODUCT SHARE DETAILS

Product or Product Class Shipments	Mil. $	Product or Product Class Shipments	Mil. $
AIR-CONDITIONING AND WARM AIR HEATING EQUIPMENT AND COMMERCIAL AND INDUSTRIAL REFRIGERATION EQUIPMENT	23,279.0	Other commercial refrigerators and related equipment	325.9
Heat transfer equipment (except electrically operated dehumidifiers), mechanically refrigerated, self-contained, except motor vehicle mechanical air-conditioning systems	**4,775.3**	Commercial refrigerators and related equipment, nsk	21.9
		Refrigeration condensing units, all refrigerants, except ammonia (complete)	**326.2**
Commercial refrigerators and related equipment	**2,740.8**	**Room air-conditioners and dehumidifiers, except portable dehumidifiers**	**1,013.3**
Commercial refrigerators and related equipment	2,718.9	**Refrigeration and air-conditioning equipment, nec**	**927.8**
Commercial refrigerated sectional coolers and cooling rooms of the prefabricated (factory produced) type, including self-contained and remote units	719.7	Refrigeration and air-conditioning equipment, nec	904.5
		Soda fountain refrigeration equipment (cooler box, fountainette, and similar equipment)	266.6
Commercial reach-in refrigerators and reach-in verticle display cabinets for normal temperature applications (not intended for frozen foods, ice cream, etc.), incl. self-contained and remote units	465.6	Beer dispensing refrigeration equipment	7.9
		Evaporative air coolers	125.8
		Other refrigeration equipment, nec	192.2
Commercial reach-in refrigerators and reach-in type verticle display cabinets for low temperature application, including self-contained and remote units	259.1	Other air-conditioning equipment, nec	312.0
		Refrigeration and air-conditioning equipment, nec, nsk	23.3
Commercial closed refrigerated display cases, operated at normal temperatures, including self-contained and remote units	50.6	**Compressors and compressor units, all refrigerants, except automotives**	**2,412.4**
Commercial open, one level, self-service refrigerated display cases, operated at normal temperatures, including self-contained and remote units	89.6	**Warm air furnaces, including duct furnaces and humidifiers, and electric comfort heating equipment**	**1,915.5**
Commercial open, multilevel, self-service refrigerated display cases, operated at normal temperatures, including self-contained and remote units	341.5	**Parts and accessories for air-conditioning and heat transfer equipment**	**1,697.4**
		Parts for heat transfer and air-conditioning equipment, nec	1,673.0
Commercial open, self-service refrigerated frozen food display cases, including self-contained and remote units	11.5	Parts for heat transfer equipment, including parts for air-conditioning condensing units	652.3
		Parts for unitary air-conditioners	191.0
Commercial closed, refrigerated frozen food cabinets, other than reach-in type, including self-contained and remote units	20.6	Parts for commercial refrigeration and related equipment	248.0
		Parts for compressors and compressor units	222.1
Other commercial refrigerated display cases operated at low temperatures, including self-contained and remote units	58.5	Parts for condensing units, excluding air-conditioning condensing units	3.5
Commercial mechanical refrigerated drinking water coolers	203.7	Parts for dehumidifiers and room air-conditioners	13.1
		Other parts for refrigeration equipment, nec	73.8
Commercial mechanical refrigerated bottled beverage coolers, dry and wet types, except coin-operated	(D)	Other parts for air-conditioning equipment, nec	172.5
		Parts for warm air furnaces, including duct furnaces (excluding complete humidifiers)	96.8
Commercial mechanical refrigerated bulk beverage dispensers, including malt dispensers and precooler cabinets, except coin-operated	(D)	Parts and accessories for air-conditioning and heat transfer equipment, nsk	24.4
		Unitary air-conditioners, except air source heat pumps	**5,403.8**
		Air source heat pumps, except room air-conditioners	**1,150.8**
		Ground and ground water source heat pumps	**127.8**
		Air-conditioning and warm air heating equipment and commercial and industrial refrigeration equipment, nsk, total	**787.8**

Source: 2002 *Economic Census*. The values are product shipments in millions of dollars for 2002. Total product shipments may be lower or higher than industry shipments. See Introduction for a full discussion. Values of indented subcategories are summed in the main heading(s). The symbol (D) appears when data are withheld to prevent disclosure of competitive information. The abbreviation nsk stands for 'not specified by kind' and nec for 'not elsewhere classified'. A dash (-) means zero.

INPUTS AND OUTPUTS FOR AC, REFRIGERATION, & HEATING EQUIPMENT

Economic Sector or Industry Providing Inputs	%	Sector	Economic Sector or Industry Buying Outputs	%	Sector
Compensation of employees	22.0		Private fixed investment	18.6	
AC, refrigeration, and warm air heating equipment	8.4	Manufg.	Exports of goods & services	13.3	Cap Inv
Wholesale trade	6.6	Trade	Residential permanent site structures	7.8	Construct.
Motors & generators	4.3	Manufg.	AC, refrigeration, and warm air heating equipment	7.3	Manufg.
Iron & steel mills & ferroalloys	4.1	Manufg.	Commercial & health care structures	5.8	Construct.
Management of companies & enterprises	3.8	Services	Residential structures, nec	5.1	Construct.
Copper rolling, drawing, extruding, & alloying	2.1	Manufg.	Owner-occupied dwellings	4.5	
Ferrous metal foundries	1.5	Manufg.	Nonresidential structures, nec	4.2	Construct.
Aluminum products from purchased aluminum	1.4	Manufg.	Personal consumption expenditures	3.9	
Automatic environmental controls	1.3	Manufg.	Pipeline transportation	3.6	Util.
Heating equipment (except warm air furnaces)	1.2	Manufg.	Maintenance/repair of nonresidential structures	2.5	Construct.
Plastics products, nec	1.1	Manufg.	General S/L govt. services	2.2	S/L Govt
Truck transportation	0.9	Util.	Food services & drinking places	1.4	Services
Relay & industrial controls	0.9	Manufg.	Household refrigerators & home freezers	1.2	Manufg.
Air purification & ventilation equipment	0.9	Manufg.	Maintenance/repair of residential structures	1.2	Construct.
Advertising & related services	0.8	Services	Wholesale trade	1.0	Trade
Crowns & closures & metal stamping	0.7	Manufg.	Federal government, investment, national defense	1.0	Fed Govt
Machine shops	0.7	Manufg.	Light truck & utility vehicles	0.9	Manufg.
Valve & fittings other than plumbing	0.7	Manufg.	Other S/L govt. enterprises	0.9	S/L Govt
Turned products & screws, nuts, & bolts	0.7	Manufg.	Heavy duty trucks	0.9	Manufg.
Wiring devices	0.7	Manufg.	Retail trade	0.7	Trade
Nonferrous metal foundries	0.7	Manufg.	S/L govt. invest., education	0.6	S/L Govt
Paperboard containers	0.6	Manufg.	Automobiles	0.6	Manufg.
Power boilers & heat exchangers	0.6	Manufg.	Travel trailers & campers	0.6	Manufg.
Securities, commodity contracts, investments	0.5	Fin/R.E.	Motor homes	0.5	Manufg.

Continued on next page.

INPUTS AND OUTPUTS FOR AC, REFRIGERATION, & HEATING EQUIPMENT - Continued

Economic Sector or Industry Providing Inputs	%	Sector	Economic Sector or Industry Buying Outputs	%	Sector
Power generation & supply	0.5	Util.	Vending, commercial, industrial, office machinery	0.5	Manufg.
Maintenance/repair of nonresidential structures	0.5	Construct.	Colleges, universities, & professional schools	0.5	Services
Semiconductors & related devices	0.5	Manufg.	Oil & gas extraction	0.5	Mining
Plate work & fabricated structural products	0.5	Manufg.	Urethane & other foam products (except polystrene)	0.4	Manufg.
Plastics packaging materials, film & sheet	0.5	Manufg.	Manufactured homes & mobile homes	0.4	Manufg.
Real estate	0.5	Fin/R.E.	Canned & dehydrated fruits & vegetables	0.4	Manufg.
Lessors of nonfinancial assets	0.5	Fin/R.E.	Cable & other subscription programming	0.4	Services
Taxes on production & imports, less subsidies	0.4		Motor vehicle parts	0.4	Manufg.
Printed circuit assemblies (electronic assemblies)	0.4	Manufg.	Computer system design services	0.3	Services
Services to buildings & dwellings	0.4	Services	Commercial & industrial equipment repair/maintenance	0.3	Services
Monetary authorities/depository credit intermediation	0.4	Fin/R.E.	Civic, social, & professional organizations	0.3	Services
Gaskets, packing, & sealing devices	0.4	Manufg.	Hospitals	0.3	Services
Hardware	0.3	Manufg.	Truck trailers	0.2	Manufg.
Mineral wool	0.3	Manufg.	Wood windows & doors & millwork	0.2	Manufg.
Plastics materials & resins	0.3	Manufg.	Chemical products & preparations, nec	0.2	Manufg.
Professional, scientific, technical services, nec	0.3	Services	Waste management & remediation services	0.2	Services
Coating, engraving, heat treating & allied activities	0.3	Manufg.	Manufacturing structures	0.2	Construct.
Automotive repair & maintenance, ex. car washes	0.3	Services	Data processing, hosting, & related services	0.2	Services
Basic organic chemicals, nec	0.3	Manufg.	Tobacco products	0.2	Manufg.
Automotive equipment rental & leasing	0.3	Fin/R.E.	Telecommunications	0.1	Services
Legal services	0.3	Services	Real estate	0.1	Fin/R.E.
Telecommunications	0.3	Services	Plastics products, nec	0.1	Manufg.
Commercial & industrial equipment repair/maintenance	0.3	Services	S/L govt. invest., other	0.1	S/L Govt
Noncomparable imports	0.3	Foreign	Air purification & ventilation equipment	0.1	Manufg.
Primary smelting & refining of copper	0.3	Manufg.	Nursing & residential care facilities	0.1	Services
Wood containers & pallets	0.2	Manufg.	Prefabricated wood buildings	0.1	Manufg.
Food services & drinking places	0.2	Services	General Federal government services, nondefense	0.1	Fed Govt
Cutting tools & machine tool accessories	0.2	Manufg.			
Retail trade	0.2	Trade			
Data processing, hosting, & related services	0.2	Services			
Scientific research & development services	0.2	Services			
Electronic components, nec	0.2	Manufg.			
Management, scientific, & technical consulting	0.2	Services			
Steel products from purchased steel	0.2	Manufg.			
Warehousing & storage	0.2	Util.			
Paints & coatings	0.2	Manufg.			
Ball & roller bearings	0.2	Manufg.			
Rubber & plastics hose & belting	0.2	Manufg.			
Air transportation	0.2	Util.			
Accounting, tax preparation, bookkeeping, & payroll	0.2	Services			
Abrasive products	0.2	Manufg.			
Hotels & motels, including casino hotels	0.2	Services			
Communication & energy wires & cables	0.2	Manufg.			
Nonferrous metal (ex. copper & aluminum) processing	0.1	Manufg.			
Commercial & industrial machinery rental & leasing	0.1	Fin/R.E.			
Natural gas distribution	0.1	Util.			
Fabricated pipes & pipe fittings	0.1	Manufg.			
Electronic capacitors, resistors, coils, transformers	0.1	Manufg.			
Motor vehicle parts	0.1	Manufg.			
Chemical products & preparations, nec	0.1	Manufg.			
Rail transportation	0.1	Util.			
Fabricated metals, nec	0.1	Manufg.			
Metal cans, boxes, & other containers (light gauge)	0.1	Manufg.			
Other computer related services, including facilities	0.1	Services			
Forging, stamping, & sintering, nec	0.1	Manufg.			

Source: Benchmark Input-Output Accounts for the U.S. Economy, 2002, U.S. Department of Commerce, Washington, D.C., January 2008. The abbreviation nec stands for 'not elsewhere classified'.

OCCUPATIONS EMPLOYED BY VENTILATION, HEATING, AC, & COMMERCIAL REFRIGERATION

Occupation	% of Total 2006	Change to 2016	Occupation	% of Total 2006	Change to 2016
Team assemblers	19.2	-8.0	Machinists	1.6	-3.4
Welders, cutters, solderers, & brazers	6.1	-2.1	Shipping, receiving, & traffic clerks	1.5	-11.5
Cutting, punching, & press machine operators	5.0	-17.2	Heating, AC, & refrigeration mechanics & installers	1.4	-8.0
Sheet metal workers	3.4	-9.8	Mechanical engineers	1.4	-8.0
First-line supervisors/managers of production workers	3.1	-8.0	Maintenance & repair workers, general	1.3	-8.0
Helpers--Production workers	2.9	-8.0	Sales reps, wholesale & manufacturing, exc tech	1.3	-8.0
Assemblers & fabricators, nec	2.7	-17.2	Welding, soldering, & brazing machine operators	1.3	3.4
Inspectors, testers, sorters, samplers, & weighers	2.3	-13.3	Electrical & electronic equipment assemblers	1.2	-26.4
Laborers & freight, stock, & material movers, hand	2.2	-17.2	Production, planning, & expediting clerks	1.1	-8.0
Industrial truck & tractor operators	2.1	-17.2	Coating, painting, & spraying machine operators	1.1	-12.6
Structural metal fabricators & fitters	2.0	-8.0	Customer service representatives	1.1	1.2
Multiple machine tool operators & tenders	1.9	1.2	General & operations managers	1.1	-17.2

Source: Industry-Occupation Matrix, Bureau of Labor Statistics, December 4, 2007. These data are reported based on 4-digit NAICS categories but have been matched to corresponding 6-digit NAICS industry codes. The change reported for each occupation to the year 2016 is a percent of growth or decline as estimated by the Bureau of Labor Statistics. The abbreviation nec stands for 'not elsewhere classified'.

LOCATION BY STATE AND REGIONAL CONCENTRATION

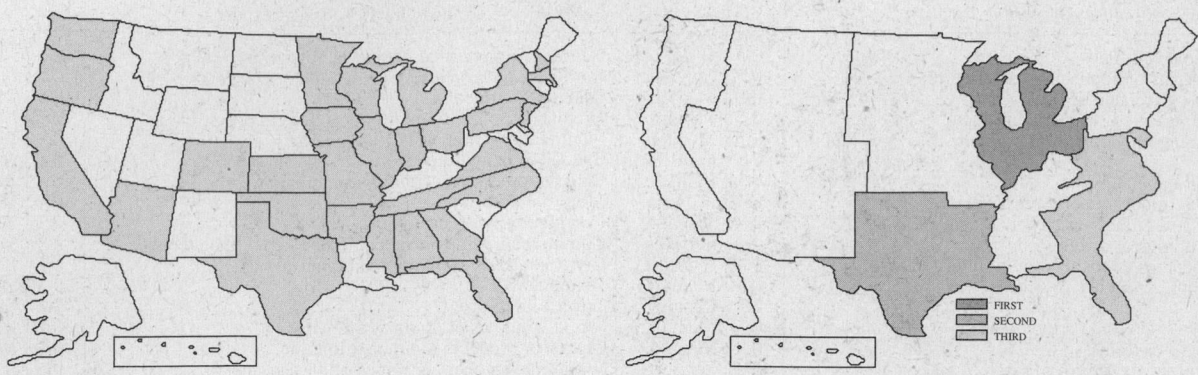

INDUSTRY DATA BY STATE

| State | Establish-ments | Shipments | | | Employment | | | | Cost as % of Shipments | Investment per Employee ($) |
		Total ($ mil)	% of U.S.	Per Establ.	Total Number	% of U.S.	Per Establ.	Wages ($/hour)		
Texas	99	2,806.9	11.6	28,352.3	11,926	11.3	120	14.32	51.0	4,918
Tennessee	27	2,175.4	9.0	80,568.9	7,267	6.9	269	15.67	51.9	3,623
Arkansas	17	1,375.9	5.7	80,936.0	4,260	4.0	251	17.15	37.8	4,358
Missouri	16	1,344.1	5.6	84,009.1	6,861	6.5	429	15.67	49.6	3,141
Georgia	32	1,338.4	5.5	41,823.9	6,727	6.4	210	14.37	54.0	2,134
Iowa	12	1,169.5	4.8	97,459.2	2,006	1.9	167	16.36	33.7	3,417
New York	47	1,109.4	4.6	23,605.3	4,200	4.0	89	16.88	55.9	2,284
Ohio	37	1,069.4	4.4	28,903.8	4,926	4.7	133	17.03	50.9	3,537
Wisconsin	30	1,009.3	4.2	33,643.8	5,170	4.9	172	16.43	54.9	4,589
Illinois	47	1,000.9	4.1	21,295.3	3,740	3.5	80	13.92	37.9	9,731
Indiana	25	978.5	4.0	39,140.8	3,671	3.5	147	19.86	45.7	12,871
Oklahoma	23	664.2	2.7	28,878.9	3,563	3.4	155	14.41	53.8	2,584
Pennsylvania	47	642.3	2.7	13,665.4	3,527	3.3	75	18.52	55.8	2,617
New Jersey	18	637.5	2.6	35,416.7	2,624	2.5	146	13.96	51.4	3,823
North Carolina	23	620.9	2.6	26,995.0	2,343	2.2	102	13.87	55.4	3,442
California	91	611.5	2.5	6,719.8	3,633	3.4	40	17.44	43.5	2,687
Mississippi	8	515.7	2.1	64,462.9	3,432	3.2	429	12.53	42.9	2,473
Kansas	7	482.6	2.0	68,943.9	1,867	1.8	267	13.69	57.2	17,061
Virginia	17	470.6	1.9	27,682.6	2,413	2.3	142	15.75	51.8	2,722
Florida	56	424.6	1.8	7,581.6	1,878	1.8	34	12.84	45.3	2,757
Colorado	6	405.2	1.7	67,530.2	1,188	1.1	198	12.88	52.1	2,848
Minnesota	23	390.5	1.6	16,976.6	2,591	2.5	113	17.26	47.4	1,997
Alabama	9	365.3	1.5	40,592.6	1,624	1.5	180	12.04	63.3	3,366
Michigan	34	365.0	1.5	10,736.1	2,711	2.6	80	15.79	45.5	1,412
Arizona	19	272.6	1.1	14,346.5	1,508	1.4	79	11.93	43.7	1,611
Massachusetts	11	132.9	0.6	12,086.0	960	0.9	87	14.41	53.1	2,080
Washington	14	76.7	0.3	5,478.1	332	0.3	24	15.05	55.5	2,831
New Hampshire	6	23.9	0.1	3,976.7	235	0.2	39	15.34	32.0	2,328
Oregon	7	17.3	0.1	2,468.4	111	0.1	16	15.34	50.3	8,099

Source: 2002 *Economic Census*. The states are in descending order of shipments or establishments (if shipment data are missing for the majority). The symbol (D) appears when data are withheld to prevent disclosure of competitive information. States marked with (D) are sorted by number of establishments. A dash (-) indicates that the data element cannot be calculated. Data may not show all states active in the NAICS category. All data available at the time of publication are shown.

NAICS 33341N - VENTILATION EQUIPMENT MANUFACTURING*

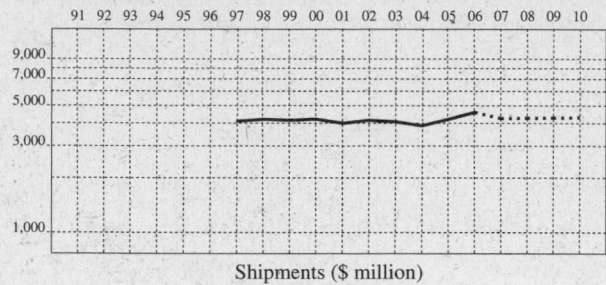

Shipments ($ million)

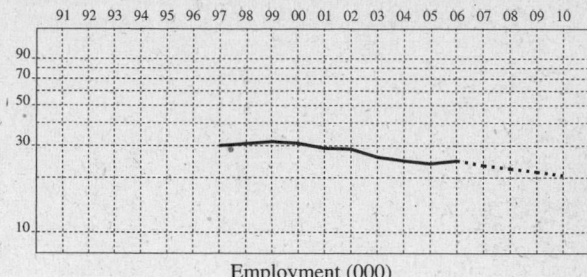

Employment (000)

GENERAL STATISTICS

| Year | Companies | Establishments | | Employment | | | Compensation | | Production ($ million) | | | |
		Total	with 20 or more employees	Total (000)	Production Workers (000)	Hours (Mil)	Payroll ($ mil)	Wages ($/hr)	Cost of Materials	Value Added by Manufacture	Value of Shipments	Capital Invest.
1997	505	573	277	30.0	20.9	42.3	908.3	12.00	1,902.9	2,185.5	4,100.9	125.1
1998		589	276	30.8	22.5	43.9	940.4	12.70	1,910.4	2,283.1	4,203.8	143.8
1999		557	275	31.6	22.4	45.4	958.6	12.05	1,803.4	2,348.7	4,151.6	116.3
2000		549	284	30.9	22.3	44.1	993.6	13.10	1,942.8	2,284.1	4,214.3	125.8
2001		547	275	29.1	20.7	41.3	955.9	13.18	1,899.3	2,084.5	3,999.3	112.0
2002	456	537	281	28.8	19.4	40.6	948.2	12.89	1,883.5	2,258.4	4,155.1	100.2
2003		549	278	26.0	18.7	38.0	904.0	13.33	1,753.9	2,356.2	4,080.4	60.6
2004		531	269	24.8	17.6	36.1	860.2	13.40	1,852.8	2,044.8	3,877.0	75.8
2005		524	265	23.9	17.2	35.6	874.4	13.61	2,078.0	2,161.8	4,207.1	56.3
2006		518P	270P	24.8	17.9	37.2	908.0	13.85	2,248.2	2,379.9	4,597.9	69.7
2007		511P	269P	23.3P	16.6P	34.8P	884.1P	14.02P	2,080.4P	2,202.2P	4,254.6P	47.9P
2008		504P	268P	22.4P	16.0P	33.8P	876.6P	14.20P	2,088.9P	2,211.3P	4,272.1P	38.6P
2009		498P	267P	21.5P	15.4P	32.7P	869.1P	14.38P	2,097.4P	2,220.3P	4,289.5P	29.4P
2010		491P	266P	20.6P	14.8P	31.7P	861.6P	14.57P	2,105.9P	2,229.3P	4,307.0P	20.2P

Sources: 1997 and 2002 *Economic Census*; other years, up to 2006, are from *Annual Survey of Manufactures*. Establishment counts for non-Census years are from *County Business Patterns*; 1997 and 2002 values are from the 1997 and 2002 censuses, respectively. 'P's show projections by the editors.

INDICES OF CHANGE

| Year | Companies | Establishments | | Employment | | | Compensation | | Production ($ million) | | | |
		Total	with 20 or more employees	Total (000)	Production Workers (000)	Hours (Mil)	Payroll ($ mil)	Wages ($/hr)	Cost of Materials	Value Added by Manufacture	Value of Shipments	Capital Invest.
1997	111	107	99	104	108	104	96	93	101	97	99	125
1998		110	98	107	116	108	99	99	101	101	101	144
1999		104	98	110	115	112	101	93	96	104	100	116
2000		102	101	107	115	109	105	102	103	101	101	126
2001		102	98	101	107	102	101	102	101	92	96	112
2002	100	100	100	100	100	100	100	100	100	100	100	100
2003		102	99	90	96	94	95	103	93	104	98	60
2004		99	96	86	91	89	91	104	98	91	93	76
2005		98	94	83	89	88	92	106	110	96	101	56
2006		96P	96P	86	92	92	96	107	119	105	111	70
2007		95P	96P	81P	86P	86P	93P	109P	110P	98P	102P	48P
2008		94P	95P	78P	82P	83P	92P	110P	111P	98P	103P	39P
2009		93P	95P	75P	79P	81P	92P	112P	111P	98P	103P	29P
2010		91P	95P	72P	76P	78P	91P	113P	112P	99P	104P	20P

Sources: Same as General Statistics. Values reflect change from the base year, 2002. Values above 100 mean greater than 2002, values below 100 mean less than 2002; and the values of 100 in other years means the same as 2002. 'P's show projections by the editors.

SELECTED RATIOS

For 2002	Avg. of All Manufact.	Analyzed Industry	Index	For 2002	Avg. of All Manufact.	Analyzed Industry	Index
Employees per Establishment	42	54	128	Value Added per Production Worker	182,367	116,412	64
Payroll per Establishment	1,639,184	1,765,736	108	Cost per Establishment	5,769,015	3,507,449	61
Payroll per Employee	39,053	32,924	84	Cost per Employee	137,446	65,399	48
Production Workers per Establishment	30	36	122	Cost per Production Worker	195,506	97,088	50
Wages per Establishment	694,845	974,551	140	Shipments per Establishment	11,158,348	7,737,616	69
Wages per Production Worker	23,548	26,976	115	Shipments per Employee	265,847	144,274	54
Hours per Production Worker	1,980	2,093	106	Shipments per Production Worker	378,144	214,180	57
Wages per Hour	11.89	12.89	108	Investment per Establishment	361,338	186,592	52
Value Added per Establishment	5,381,325	4,205,587	78	Investment per Employee	8,609	3,479	40
Value Added per Employee	128,210	78,417	61	Investment per Production Worker	12,245	5,165	42

Sources: Same as General Statistics. The 'Average of All Manufacturing' column represents the average of all manufacturing industries reported for the most recent complete year available. The Index shows the relationship between the Average and the Analyzed Industry. For example, 100 means that they are equal; 500 that the Analyzed Industry is five times the average; 50 means that the Analyzed Industry is half the national average. The abbreviation 'na' is used to show that data are 'not available'. Ratios shown for 2002, the last complete census year.

*Equivalent to Federal Government NAICS 333411, 333412.

LEADING COMPANIES   Number shown: **75**   Total sales ($ mil): **27,771**   Total employment (000): **111.5**

Company Name	Address				CEO Name	Phone	Co. Type	Sales ($ mil)	Empl. (000)
Tosoh SMD Inc.	3600 Gantz Rd.	Grove City	OH	43123	Mark Gore	614-875-7912	R	3,680*	<0.1
Pall Corp.	2200 Northern Blvd.	East Hills	NY	11548	Eric Krasnoff	516-484-5400	P	2,250	10.8
NTK Holdings Inc.	50 Kennedy Plz.	Providence	RI	02903	Richard L. Bready	401-751-1600	S	2,218	9.8
AMETEK Inc.	PO Box 1764	Paoli	PA	19301	Frank S. Hermance	610-647-2121	P	2,137	10.4
Johns Manville Corp.	PO Box 5108	Denver	CO	80217	Steve Hochhauser	303-978-2000	S	2,125*	8.5
Donaldson Company Inc.	PO Box 1299	Minneapolis	MN	55440	William M. Cook	952-887-3131	P	1,919	12.0
Gardner Denver Inc.	PO Box 528	Quincy	IL	62306	Ross J. Centanni	217-222-5400	P	1,869	6.2
Babcock and Wilcox Co.	PO Box 351	Barberton	OH	44203	John A. Fees	330-753-4511	S	1,080*	10.8
Purolator Air Filtration	PO Box 32578	Louisville	KY	40232		502-969-2304	S	886*	6.7
Fleetguard Inc.	1200 Fleetguard Rd.	Cookeville	TN	38506	Rick Mills	931-526-9551	S	828*	6.0
Alpine Industries Inc.	310 T. Elmer Cox Dr	Greeneville	TN	37745	William Converse	423-638-7246	R	749*	1.0
Riley Power Inc.	PO Box 15040	Worcester	MA	01615		508-852-7100	R	612*	0.4
EBM-Papst Inc.	PO Box 4009	Farmington	CT	06034	Robert Sobolewski	860-674-1515	R	465*	0.4
Luwa Inc.	3901 Westpoint Blvd	Winston-Salem	NC	27103		336-760-3111	R	448*	0.1
Mestek Inc.	260 N Elm St.	Westfield	MA	01085	R. Bruce Dewey	413-568-9571	R	372*	2.6
Kaman Aerospace Corp.	PO Box 2	Bloomfield	CT	06002	Sal Bordanelero	860-242-4461	D	349*	1.4
Cme L.L.C.	2945 Three Leaves	Mount Pleasant	MI	48858		989-773-0377	R	317*	0.4
Continental Conveyor & Equip.	PO Box 400	Winfield	AL	35594		205-487-6492	R	286*	0.3
Kirk and Blum Manufacturing	3120 Forrer St.	Cincinnati	OH	45209	Richard J. Blum	513-458-2600	S	265*	0.4
Flanders Corp.	PO Box 7568	St. Petersburg	FL	33734	Robert R. Amerson	727-822-4411	P	245	2.8
CECO Environmental Corp.	3120 Forrer St.	Cincinnati	OH	45209	Phillip DeZwirek	513-458-2600	P	236	0.7
MFRI Inc.	7720 N Lehigh Ave.	Niles	IL	60714		847-966-1000	P	213	1.1
Baldwin Filters	PO Box 6010	Kearney	NE	68848	Sam Ferrise	308-234-1951	S	213*	1.1
Avox Systems Inc.	225 Erie Street	Lancaster	NY	14086		716-683-5100	S	201*	1.0
Hayward Industrial Products	PO Box 18	Elizabeth	NJ	07207	Oscar Davis	908-351-5400	R	200*	0.3
BHA Group Holdings Inc.	8800 E 63rd St.	Raytown	MO	64133	James E. Lund	816-356-8400	S	179	1.0
Precisionaire Inc.	PO Box 7568	St Petersburg	FL	33734	Robert R. Amerson		S	170*	<0.1
Venturedyne Ltd.	600 College Ave.	Pewaukee	WI	53072		262-691-9900	R	147*	1.3
Air Vent Inc.	4117 Pinnacle Pnt.	Dallas	TX	75211	Cliff Tucker	214-630-7377	S	141*	0.1
TBDN Tennessee Co.	PO Box 1887	Jackson	TN	38302	Tokuja Yamauchi	731-421-4800	S	126*	0.5
Sundyne Corp.	14845 W 64th Ave.	Arvada	CO	80007	Phil Ruffner	303-425-0800	S	118*	0.7
General Resource Corp.	5909 Baker Rd.	Minnetonka	MN	55345	Tim Masterman	952-933-7474	R	112*	0.2
Delfield Co.	980 S Isabella Rd.	Mt. Pleasant	MI	48858	Kevin Clark	989-773-7981	D	108*	0.7
Psp Industries Inc.	9885 Doerr Ln.	Schertz	TX	78154	Andrew Easton	210-651-9595	R	105*	<0.1
Besser Co.	801 Johnson St.	Alpena	MI	49707	Kevin Curtis	989-354-4111	R	99*	0.4
Parker Hannifin Racor Div.	PO Box 3208	Modesto	CA	95353		209-521-7860	D	98*	0.8
Nidec America Corp.	318 Industrial Ln.	Torrington	CT	06790	Thomas Keenan	860-482-4422	R	97*	0.1
Lau Industries Inc.	4509 Springfield St	Dayton	OH	45431	Tom Edwards	937-476-6500	S	95*	1.1
Met-Pro Corp.	PO Box 144	Harleysville	PA	19438	Raymond J. De Hont	215-723-6751	P	91	0.4
Environmental Air Systems Inc.	PO Box 13006	Greensboro	NC	27415	James Bullock	336-273-1975	R	87*	0.4
USUI International Corp.	1045 Reed Dr.	Monroe	OH	45050	Takanobu Ihara	513-539-4591	R	86*	0.1
TPI Corp.	PO Box 4973	Johnson City	TN	37602	Robert Henry	423-477-4131	R	84*	<0.1
Fuel-Tech Inc.	512 Kingsland Dr.	Batavia	IL	60510	Ralph E. Bailey	630-845-4500	P	80	0.2
Loren Cook Co.	PO Box 4047	Springfield	MO	65808	Gerald Cook	417-869-6474	R	75*	0.9
Lasko Products Inc.	820 Lincoln Ave.	West Chester	PA	19380	Oscar Lasko	610-692-7400	R	74*	0.2
Twin City Fan Co's Ltd.	5959 Trenton Ln. N	Minneapolis	MN	55442	Charles Barry	763-551-7600	R	72*	0.1
Buffalo Air Handling Co.	467 Zane Snead Dr.	Amherst	VA	24521	William Phelps	434-946-7455	S	68*	0.5
Peerless-Winsmith Inc.	172 Eaton St.	Springville	NY	14141	David McCann	716-592-9310	R	64*	0.8
Henry Technologies Inc.	1 ABC Pkwy.	Beloit	WI	53511	Charlie Graham	608-361-4400	R	62*	<0.1
Dantherm Filtration Inc.	PO Box 429	Thomasville	NC	27361	Niels Petersen	336-889-5599	R	59*	0.1
Acme Engineering & Mfg.	PO Box 978	Muskogee	OK	74402	Lee Buddrus	918-682-7791	R	59*	0.5
Robinson Industries Inc.	PO Box 100	Zelienople	PA	16063	H Gutzwiller	724-452-6121	R	57*	0.2
Aerotech Inc.	4215 Legion Dr.	Mason	MI	48854	Robert Mitchell	517-676-7070	S	56*	<0.1
Revcor Inc.	251 Edwards Ave.	Carpentersville	IL	60110	John Reichwein	847-428-4411	R	55*	0.3
Eclipse Inc.	1665 Elmwood Rd.	Rockford	IL	61103	Campbell Perks	815-877-3031	R	53*	<0.1
Super Vacuum Manufacturing Co.	PO Box 87	Loveland	CO	80539	Roger Weinmeister	970-667-5146	R	51*	0.1
Horton Fan Sysems Inc.	201 W Carmel Dr.	Carmel	IN	46032		317-249-4001	R	51*	0.1
Hilliard Corp.	PO Box 866	Elmira	NY	14902	N. Mooers Den Blin	607-733-7121	R	50*	0.4
BHA Technologies Inc.	8800 East 63rd St.	Kansas City	MO	64133	James E. Lund	816-356-5515	S	49*	<0.1
Metal-Fab Inc.	3025 May St.	Wichita	KS	67213	Kenneth Shannon	316-943-2351	R	45*	0.4
Filtertek Inc.	PO Box 310	Hebron	IL	60034	Stephen Soltwedel	815-648-2416	S	44*	0.9
Nor-Lake Inc.	727 2nd Street	Hudson	WI	54016	Charles Dullea	715-386-2323	R	43*	0.3
Altair Corp.	350 Barclay Blvd.	Lincolnshire	IL	60069	Garry Brainin	847-634-9540	R	43*	<0.1
Ecoquest Manufacturing Inc.	310 T Elmer Cox	Greeneville	TN	37743	Michael Jackson	423-798-6488	R	41*	0.2
Hurst Boiler and Welding Co.	PO Box 530	Coolidge	GA	31738	Clifton Hurst	229-346-3545	R	41*	0.3
Precipitator Services Group	1625 Broad St.	Elizabethton	TN	37643	Carl Nidiffer	423-543-7331	R	40*	0.3
Dynasteel Corp.	PO Box 27640	Memphis	TN	38167	James Russell	901-358-6231	R	40*	0.1
Loranger International Corp.	817 4th Ave.	Warren	PA	16365	Albert Loranger	814-723-2250	R	39*	0.1
Airtex Manufacturing Inc.	PO Box 650	De Soto	KS	66018	Richard Rambacher	913-583-3181	R	38*	0.2
Ellis and Watts International	4400 Glen Willow	Batavia	OH	45103	Andrew Pike	513-752-9000	R	38*	0.2
Warren Technology Inc.	PO Box 5347	Hialeah	FL	33014	Winfield Kelley	305-556-6933	R	38*	0.2
Wayne Wire Cloth Products Inc.	PO Box 550	Kalkaska	MI	49646	Michael Brown	231-258-9187	R	37*	0.2
Parker Hannifin Pneumatic Div.	8676 M 89	Richland	MI	49083		269-629-5000	D	36*	0.3
Semco Duct & Acoustical Prods	1800 E Pointe Dr.	Columbia	MO	65201		573-443-1481	R	35*	0.1
Microdyne Products Co.	PO Box 910	Ballwin	MO	63011	Lee Witengier	314-291-5600	R	34*	<0.1

Source: Ward's Business Directory of U.S. Private and Public Companies, Volumes 1 and 2, 2008. The company type code used is as follows: P - Public, R - Private, S - Subsidiary, D - Division, J - Joint Venture, A - Affiliate, G - Group. Sales are in millions of dollars, employees are in thousands. An asterisk (*) indicates an estimated sales volume. The symbol < stands for 'less than'. Company names and addresses are truncated, in some cases, to fit into the available space.

MATERIALS CONSUMED FOR AIR PURIFICATION EQUIPMENT MANUFACTURING

Material	Quantity	Delivered Cost ($ million)
Metal bolts, nuts, screws, and other screw machine products	(X)	2.7
Metal pipe, valves, and pipe fittings (excluding forgings)	(X)	15.2
Other fabricated metal products (exc. fluid power products and forgings)	(X)	20.3
Fabricated structural metal products (excluding forgings)	(X)	30.9
Fluid power products	(X)	3.3
Iron and steel castings (rough and semifinished)	(X)	3.0
Nonferrous (aluminum, copper, etc.) castings (rough and semifinished)	(X)	1.4
Steel bars, bar shapes, and plates (exc. castings, forgings, fabr. metal products)	(X)	9.3
Steel sheet and strip (including tinplate)	(X)	37.0
All other steel shapes and forms (exc. castings, forgings, fabr. metal products)	(X)	7.1
Other nonferrous shapes and forms (exc. castings, forgings, fabricated metal products)	(X)	6.1
Aluminum and aluminum-base alloy shapes and forms (exc. castings, forgings, fabr. metal products)	(X)	8.3
Electric motors and generators	(X)	6.5
Ball and roller bearings (mounted or unmounted)	(X)	0.8
Flexible packaging materials, paperboard containers and boxes, and corrugated paperboard	(X)	12.9
All other materials, components, parts, containers, and supplies	(X)	483.4
Materials, ingredients, containers, and supplies, nsk	(X)	300.2

Source: 2002 *Economic Census*. Explanation of symbols used: (D): Withheld to avoid disclosure of competitive data; na: Not available; (S): Withheld because statistical norms were not met; (X): Not applicable; (Z): Less than half the unit shown; nec: Not elsewhere classified; nsk: Not specified by kind; - : zero; p : 10-19 percent estimated; q : 20-29 percent estimated.

MATERIALS CONSUMED FOR INDUSTRIAL AND COMMERCIAL FAN AND BLOWER MANUFACTURING

Material	Quantity	Delivered Cost ($ million)
Metal bolts, nuts, screws, and other screw machine products	(X)	11.2
Metal pipe, valves, and pipe fittings (excluding forgings)	(X)	0.8
Other fabricated metal products (exc. fluid power products and forgings)	(X)	11.5
Fabricated structural metal products (excluding forgings)	(X)	47.6
Fluid power products	(X)	2.1
Forgings	(X)	5.5
Iron and steel castings (rough and semifinished)	(X)	17.1
Nonferrous (aluminum, copper, etc.) castings (rough and semifinished)	(X)	16.2
Steel bars, bar shapes, and plates (exc. castings, forgings, fabr. metal products)	(X)	16.3
Steel sheet and strip (including tinplate)	(X)	59.7
All other steel shapes and forms (exc. castings, forgings, fabr. metal products)	(X)	7.6
Other nonferrous shapes and forms (exc. castings, forgings, fabricated metal products)	(X)	4.6
Aluminum and aluminum-base alloy shapes and forms (exc. castings, forgings, fabr. metal products)	(X)	16.5
Electric motors and generators	(X)	103.8
Ball and roller bearings (mounted or unmounted)	(X)	14.9
Flexible packaging materials, paperboard containers and boxes, and corrugated paperboard	(X)	10.8
All other materials, components, parts, containers, and supplies	(X)	361.6
Materials, ingredients, containers, and supplies, nsk	(X)	13.2

Source: 2002 *Economic Census*. Explanation of symbols used: (D): Withheld to avoid disclosure of competitive data; na: Not available; (S): Withheld because statistical norms were not met; (X): Not applicable; (Z): Less than half the unit shown; nec: Not elsewhere classified; nsk: Not specified by kind; - : zero; p : 10-19 percent estimated; q : 20-29 percent estimated.

PRODUCT SHARE DETAILS FOR AIR PURIFICATION EQUIPMENT MANUFACTURING

Product or Product Class Shipments	Mil. $	Product or Product Class Shipments	Mil. $
AIR PURIFICATION EQUIPMENT	2,149.2	CFM or less, except parts	707.7
Dust collection and other air purification equipment for industrial gas cleaning systems	**721.7**	Other dust collection and other air purification equipment, except parts	559.1
Dust collection and other air purification equipment for industrial gas cleaning systems (for cleaning outgoing air)	663.0	Air washers (purification equipment for cleaning incoming air), except parts	85.1
Dust collection and other air purification equipment for industrial gas cleaning systems (for cleaning outgoing air), except parts	594.3	Electrostatic precipitation dust collection and air purification equipment, except parts	99.5
Parts for industrial air purification equipment	68.7	Other dust collection and other air purification equipment (including air filters for air-conditioners and furnaces), except parts	374.4
Dust collection and other air purification equipment for industrial gas cleaning systems, nsk	58.7	Parts for dust collection and air purification equipment	59.4
Dust collection and other air purification equipment and parts for cleaning incoming air	**1,375.5**	Dust collection and other air purification equipment for cleaning incoming air, nsk	49.2
Air filters for air-conditioners and furnaces, etc., of 2400		**Air purification equipment, nsk, total**	**52.1**

Source: 2002 *Economic Census*. The values are product shipments in millions of dollars for 2002. Total product shipments may be lower or higher than industry shipments. See Introduction for a full discussion. Values of indented subcategories are summed in the main heading(s). The symbol (D) appears when data are withheld to prevent disclosure of competitive information. The abbreviation nsk stands for 'not specified by kind' and nec for 'not elsewhere classified'. A dash (-) means zero.

PRODUCT SHARE DETAILS FOR INDUSTRIAL AND COMMERCIAL FAN AND BLOWER MANUFACTURING

Product or Product Class Shipments	Mil. $	Product or Product Class Shipments	Mil. $
INDUSTRIAL AND COMMERCIAL FANS AND BLOWERS	1,669.7	Positive displacement centrifugal blowers, excluding turboblowers	24.5
Power roof ventilators and parts	103.3	Multistage centrifugal blowers	93.3
Axial and propeller type power roof ventilators, except parts	25.9	Industrial and commercial fans and blowers, and attic fans	354.6
Centrifugal type power roof ventilators, except parts	71.4	Axial fans, except parts	224.0
Parts for power roof ventilators	5.9	Axial fans directly connected to driver	164.5
Centrifugal blower-filter units, and classes I-IV centrifugal fans, except parts	507.7	Belt-driven axial fans	59.5
Centrifugal blower-filter units	315.5	Industrial propeller fans, except parts	58.8
Centrifugal classes I and II fans (more than 1 one-half in. to 6 three-fourth in. maximum total pressure)	106.5	Industrial propeller fans directly connected to driver	33.5
Centrifugal classes III and IV fans (more than 6 three-fourth in. maximum total pressure)	85.7	Industrial belt-driven propeller fans	25.3
Other centrifugal fans and blowers, except parts	653.5	Penthouses, shutters, guards, and other parts and accessories for industrial centrifugal, axial, and propeller fans and blowers (except power roof ventilators)	55.3
Industrial centrifugal fans, excluding blowers, turboblowers, and multistage blowers	181.1	Industrial and commercial fans and blowers, nsk, total	67.1

Source: 2002 Economic Census. The values are product shipments in millions of dollars for 2002. Total product shipments may be lower or higher than industry shipments. See Introduction for a full discussion. Values of indented subcategories are summed in the main heading(s). The symbol (D) appears when data are withheld to prevent disclosure of competitive information. The abbreviation nsk stands for 'not specified by kind' and nec for 'not elsewhere classified'. A dash (-) means zero.

INPUTS AND OUTPUTS FOR AIR PURIFICATION AND VENTILATION EQUIPMENT

Economic Sector or Industry Providing Inputs	%	Sector	Economic Sector or Industry Buying Outputs	%	Sector
Compensation of employees	30.0		Private fixed investment	44.8	
Management of companies & enterprises	5.9	Services	Exports of goods & services	9.0	Cap Inv
Wholesale trade	4.9	Trade	Commercial & health care structures	5.6	Construct.
Iron & steel mills & ferroalloys	4.5	Manufg.	Nonresidential structures, nec	5.2	Construct.
Motors & generators	3.8	Manufg.	Computer system design services	4.8	Services
Copper rolling, drawing, extruding, & alloying	3.5	Manufg.	AC, refrigeration, and warm air heating equipment	4.5	Manufg.
Nonwoven fabric mills	3.0	Manufg.	Waste management & remediation services	3.7	Services
Valve & fittings other than plumbing	2.5	Manufg.	Basic organic chemicals, nec	3.6	Manufg.
Air purification & ventilation equipment	1.8	Manufg.	Other S/L govt. enterprises	2.7	S/L Govt
Paints & coatings	1.8	Manufg.	Services to buildings & dwellings	1.7	Services
Metal cans, boxes, & other containers (light gauge)	1.2	Manufg.	Air purification & ventilation equipment	1.5	Manufg.
Plate work & fabricated structural products	1.1	Manufg.	Manufacturing structures	1.3	Construct.
Machine shops	1.1	Manufg.	Wholesale trade	1.3	Trade
Real estate	1.0	Fin/R.E.	Commercial & service industry machinery, nec	1.2	Manufg.
Truck transportation	0.9	Util.	Architectural, engineering, & related services	1.2	Services
Securities, commodity contracts, investments	0.8	Fin/R.E.	General S/L govt. services	1.0	S/L Govt
Cutting tools & machine tool accessories	0.8	Manufg.	Residential permanent site structures	0.8	Construct.
Alumina refining & primary aluminum production	0.8	Manufg.	Real estate	0.7	Fin/R.E.
AC, refrigeration, and warm air heating equipment	0.7	Manufg.	Plastics products, nec	0.6	Manufg.
Wiring devices	0.7	Manufg.	Plastics materials & resins	0.5	Manufg.
Advertising & related services	0.7	Services	Motor vehicle parts	0.5	Manufg.
Semiconductors & related devices	0.7	Manufg.	Scientific research & development services	0.5	Services
Power generation & supply	0.7	Util.	Chemical products & preparations, nec	0.4	Manufg.
Lessors of nonfinancial assets	0.6	Fin/R.E.	S/L govt. electric utilities	0.4	S/L Govt
Printed circuit assemblies (electronic assemblies)	0.6	Manufg.	Rail transportation	0.4	Util.
Plastics products, nec	0.6	Manufg.	Ferrous metal foundries	0.4	Manufg.
Ferrous metal foundries	0.5	Manufg.	Commercial & industrial equipment repair/maintenance	0.3	Services
Nonferrous metal foundries	0.5	Manufg.	Apparel knitting mills	0.3	Manufg.
Ball & roller bearings	0.5	Manufg.	Industrial gases	0.3	Manufg.
Gaskets, packing, & sealing devices	0.5	Manufg.	Elementary & secondary schools	0.2	Services
Electronic connectors	0.5	Manufg.	Warehousing & storage	0.2	Util.
Aluminum products from purchased aluminum	0.5	Manufg.	Scenic & sightseeing transport & related services	0.2	Util.
Turned products & screws, nuts, & bolts	0.5	Manufg.			
Monetary authorities/depository credit intermediation	0.5	Fin/R.E.			
Wood containers & pallets	0.5	Manufg.			
Ornamental & architectural metal products	0.4	Manufg.			
Professional, scientific, technical services, nec	0.4	Services			
Relay & industrial controls	0.4	Manufg.			
Data processing, hosting, & related services	0.3	Services			
Telecommunications	0.3	Services			
Legal services	0.3	Services			
Scientific research & development services	0.3	Services			
Taxes on production & imports, less subsidies	0.3				
Warehousing & storage	0.3	Util.			
Noncomparable imports	0.3	Foreign			
Accounting, tax preparation, bookkeeping, & payroll	0.3	Services			
Automotive equipment rental & leasing	0.3	Fin/R.E.			
Coating, engraving, heat treating & allied activities	0.3	Manufg.			
Plastics packaging materials, film & sheet	0.3	Manufg.			
Rubber & plastics hose & belting	0.3	Manufg.			
Abrasive products	0.2	Manufg.			

Continued on next page.

INPUTS AND OUTPUTS FOR AIR PURIFICATION AND VENTILATION EQUIPMENT - Continued

Economic Sector or Industry Providing Inputs	%	Sector	Economic Sector or Industry Buying Outputs	%	Sector
Food services & drinking places	0.2	Services			
Natural gas distribution	0.2	Util.			
Forging, stamping, & sintering, nec	0.2	Manufg.			
Communication & energy wires & cables	0.2	Manufg.			
Primary nonferrous metal, ex. copper & aluminum	0.2	Manufg.			
Industrial gases	0.2	Manufg.			
Nonferrous metal (ex. copper & aluminum) processing	0.2	Manufg.			
Services to buildings & dwellings	0.2	Services			
Maintenance/repair of nonresidential structures	0.2	Construct.			
Paperboard containers	0.2	Manufg.			
Architectural, engineering, & related services	0.2	Services			
Rubber products, nec	0.2	Manufg.			
Other computer related services, including facilities	0.2	Services			
Paper mills	0.2	Manufg.			
Commercial & industrial machinery rental & leasing	0.1	Fin/R.E.			
Hotels & motels, including casino hotels	0.1	Services			
Unlaminated plastics profile shapes	0.1	Manufg.			
Air transportation	0.1	Util.			
Management, scientific, & technical consulting	0.1	Services			
Paper bag & coated paper, nec	0.1	Manufg.			
Fabricated metals, nec	0.1	Manufg.			
Rail transportation	0.1	Util.			
Automotive repair & maintenance, ex. car washes	0.1	Services			
Custom roll forming	0.1	Manufg.			
Paperboard mills	0.1	Manufg.			

Source: Benchmark Input-Output Accounts for the U.S. Economy, 2002, U.S. Department of Commerce, Washington, D.C., January 2008. The abbreviation nec stands for 'not elsewhere classified'.

OCCUPATIONS EMPLOYED BY VENTILATION, HEATING, AC, & COMMERCIAL REFRIGERATION

Occupation	% of Total 2006	Change to 2016	Occupation	% of Total 2006	Change to 2016
Team assemblers	19.2	-8.0	Machinists	1.6	-3.4
Welders, cutters, solderers, & brazers	6.1	-2.1	Shipping, receiving, & traffic clerks	1.5	-11.5
Cutting, punching, & press machine operators	5.0	-17.2	Heating, AC, & refrigeration mechanics & installers	1.4	-8.0
Sheet metal workers	3.4	-9.8	Mechanical engineers	1.4	-8.0
First-line supervisors/managers of production workers	3.1	-8.0	Maintenance & repair workers, general	1.3	-8.0
Helpers--Production workers	2.9	-8.0	Sales reps, wholesale & manufacturing, exc tech	1.3	-8.0
Assemblers & fabricators, nec	2.7	-17.2	Welding, soldering, & brazing machine operators	1.3	3.4
Inspectors, testers, sorters, samplers, & weighers	2.3	-13.3	Electrical & electronic equipment assemblers	1.2	-26.4
Laborers & freight, stock, & material movers, hand	2.2	-17.2	Production, planning, & expediting clerks	1.1	-8.0
Industrial truck & tractor operators	2.1	-17.2	Coating, painting, & spraying machine operators	1.1	-12.6
Structural metal fabricators & fitters	2.0	-8.0	Customer service representatives	1.1	1.2
Multiple machine tool operators & tenders	1.9	1.2	General & operations managers	1.1	-17.2

Source: Industry-Occupation Matrix, Bureau of Labor Statistics, December 4, 2007. These data are reported based on 4-digit NAICS categories but have been matched to corresponding 6-digit NAICS industry codes. The change reported for each occupation to the year 2016 is a percent of growth or decline as estimated by the Bureau of Labor Statistics. The abbreviation nec stands for 'not elsewhere classified'.

LOCATION BY STATE AND REGIONAL CONCENTRATION

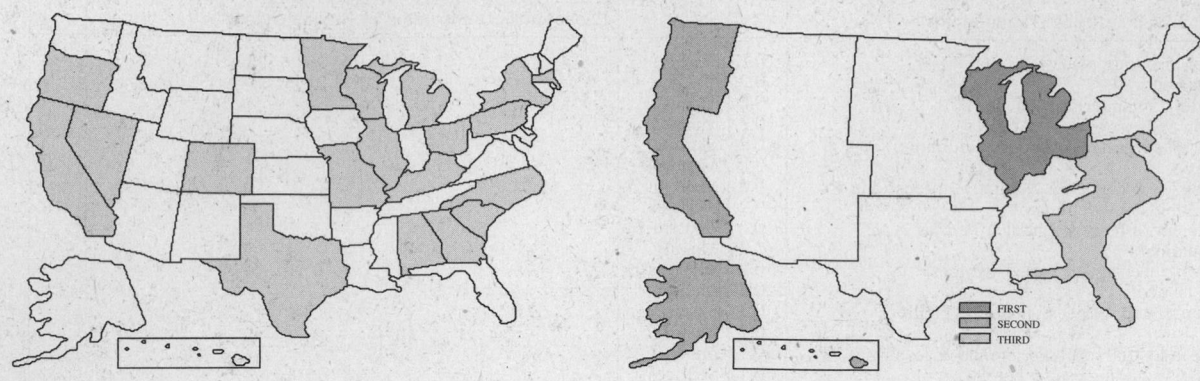

INDUSTRY DATA BY STATE

State	Establish-ments	Shipments			Employment				Cost as % of Shipments	Investment per Employee ($)
		Total ($ mil)	% of U.S.	Per Establ.	Total Number	% of U.S.	Per Establ.	Wages ($/hour)		
Illinois	39	325.3	7.8	8,340.5	2,389	8.3	61	14.46	44.1	2,864
Ohio	32	292.9	7.0	9,153.3	1,942	6.7	61	10.10	42.3	9,508
North Carolina	35	277.3	6.7	7,923.7	2,331	8.1	67	10.97	50.9	1,654
Wisconsin	18	270.7	6.5	15,040.8	1,484	5.2	82	16.78	39.2	1,253
Missouri	12	254.8	6.1	21,236.6	1,812	6.3	151	14.09	43.7	7,588
Texas	40	245.0	5.9	6,126.1	1,892	6.6	47	11.12	42.7	2,561
California	54	181.9	4.4	3,369.3	1,387	4.8	26	13.97	42.4	3,107
Michigan	27	145.1	3.5	5,374.4	947	3.3	35	14.28	52.1	1,668
Pennsylvania	19	95.1	2.3	5,007.4	519	1.8	27	14.05	41.7	1,746
Georgia	9	92.1	2.2	10,231.9	357	1.2	40	13.23	43.6	3,616
Kentucky	11	85.5	2.1	7,770.8	702	2.4	64	10.47	47.4	3,548
New York	17	84.9	2.0	4,993.1	642	2.2	38	17.51	36.5	992
Minnesota	16	62.5	1.5	3,903.8	450	1.6	28	14.27	42.9	1,622
Oregon	4	61.3	1.5	15,336.0	387	1.3	97	13.93	50.3	1,328
Massachusetts	7	50.4	1.2	7,197.4	334	1.2	48	13.06	43.7	2,769
Colorado	9	19.9	0.5	2,213.6	127	0.4	14	15.87	53.6	1,583
South Carolina	8	18.4	0.4	2,298.4	193	0.7	24	9.61	48.5	1,606
Alabama	6	17.1	0.4	2,852.8	181	0.6	30	11.19	48.1	939
Nevada	5	14.0	0.3	2,797.4	127	0.4	25	10.21	37.7	858

Source: 2002 *Economic Census*. The states are in descending order of shipments or establishments (if shipment data are missing for the majority). The symbol (D) appears when data are withheld to prevent disclosure of competitive information. States marked with (D) are sorted by number of establishments. A dash (-) indicates that the data element cannot be calculated. Data may not show all states active in the NAICS category. All data available at the time of publication are shown.

NAICS 333511 - INDUSTRIAL MOLD MANUFACTURING

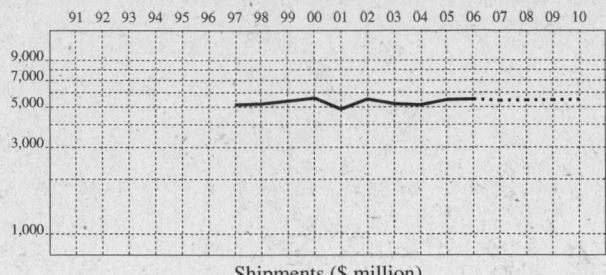

Shipments ($ million)

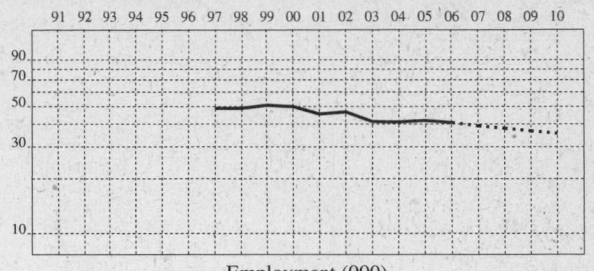

Employment (000)

GENERAL STATISTICS

| Year | Com-panies | Establishments | | Employment | | | Compensation | | Production ($ million) | | | |
		Total	with 20 or more employees	Total (000)	Production Workers (000)	Hours (Mil)	Payroll ($ mil)	Wages ($/hr)	Cost of Materials	Value Added by Manufacture	Value of Shipments	Capital Invest.
1997	2,487	2,535	706	48.9	38.6	82.7	2,096.3	18.07	1,423.6	3,721.6	5,140.0	357.1
1998		2,592	764	48.9	38.6	84.1	2,072.8	17.52	1,408.1	3,842.4	5,195.0	371.4
1999		2,465	705	50.8	40.4	83.2	2,120.9	18.02	1,515.7	3,933.9	5,384.4	396.4
2000		2,336	686	49.9	39.8	82.9	2,182.9	18.58	1,558.3	4,034.8	5,595.3	344.0
2001		2,263	639	45.5	35.8	74.5	1,964.3	18.25	1,406.2	3,382.4	4,862.6	222.6
2002	2,417	2,468	624	46.7	35.6	71.2	2,028.8	19.64	1,674.2	3,836.1	5,527.6	262.8
2003		2,359	585	41.4	31.6	64.9	1,888.5	20.21	1,542.1	3,586.8	5,196.2	176.1
2004		2,301	589	41.1	30.9	66.1	1,890.7	20.11	1,660.1	3,422.1	5,130.5	245.3
2005		2,201	554	41.9	32.1	69.8	1,978.2	20.07	1,794.7	3,710.9	5,481.4	302.5
2006		2,200P	531P	40.8	31.5	67.2	1,931.7	20.43	1,841.8	3,672.1	5,517.7	253.0
2007		2,162P	507P	39.1P	29.4P	61.9P	1,878.4P	20.95P	1,810.2P	3,609.2P	5,423.1P	205.2P
2008		2,124P	483P	37.9P	28.3P	59.6P	1,853.5P	21.29P	1,817.5P	3,623.7P	5,445.0P	189.2P
2009		2,086P	459P	36.7P	27.2P	57.3P	1,828.5P	21.63P	1,824.8P	3,638.2P	5,466.8P	173.2P
2010		2,048P	435P	35.6P	26.1P	55.0P	1,803.6P	21.97P	1,832.1P	3,652.8P	5,488.6P	157.2P

Sources: 1997 and 2002 *Economic Census*; other years, up to 2006, are from *Annual Survey of Manufactures*. Establishment counts for non-Census years are from *County Business Patterns*; 1997 and 2002 values are from the 1997 and 2002 censuses, respectively. 'P's show projections by the editors.

INDICES OF CHANGE

| Year | Com-panies | Establishments | | Employment | | | Compensation | | Production ($ million) | | | |
		Total	with 20 or more employees	Total (000)	Production Workers (000)	Hours (Mil)	Payroll ($ mil)	Wages ($/hr)	Cost of Materials	Value Added by Manufacture	Value of Shipments	Capital Invest.
1997	103	103	113	105	108	116	103	92	85	97	93	136
1998		105	122	105	108	118	102	89	84	100	94	141
1999		100	113	109	113	117	105	92	91	103	97	151
2000		95	110	107	112	116	108	95	93	105	101	131
2001		92	102	97	101	105	97	93	84	88	88	85
2002	100	100	100	100	100	100	100	100	100	100	100	100
2003		96	94	89	89	91	93	103	92	94	94	67
2004		93	94	88	87	93	93	102	99	89	93	93
2005		89	89	90	90	98	98	102	107	97	99	115
2006		89P	85P	87	88	94	95	104	110	96	100	96
2007		88P	81P	84P	83P	87P	93P	107P	108P	94P	98P	78P
2008		86P	77P	81P	79P	84P	91P	108P	109P	94P	99P	72P
2009		85P	74P	79P	76P	80P	90P	110P	109P	95P	99P	66P
2010		83P	70P	76P	73P	77P	89P	112P	109P	95P	99P	60P

Sources: Same as General Statistics. Values reflect change from the base year, 2002. Values above 100 mean greater than 2002, values below 100 mean less than 2002, and the values of 100 in other years means the same as 2002. 'P's show projections by the editors.

SELECTED RATIOS

For 2002	Avg. of All Manufact.	Analyzed Industry	Index	For 2002	Avg. of All Manufact.	Analyzed Industry	Index
Employees per Establishment	42	19	45	Value Added per Production Worker	182,367	107,756	59
Payroll per Establishment	1,639,184	822,042	50	Cost per Establishment	5,769,015	678,363	12
Payroll per Employee	39,053	43,443	111	Cost per Employee	137,446	35,850	26
Production Workers per Establishment	30	14	49	Cost per Production Worker	195,506	47,028	24
Wages per Establishment	694,845	566,600	82	Shipments per Establishment	11,158,348	2,239,708	20
Wages per Production Worker	23,548	39,280	167	Shipments per Employee	265,847	118,364	45
Hours per Production Worker	1,980	2,000	101	Shipments per Production Worker	378,144	155,270	41
Wages per Hour	11.89	19.64	165	Investment per Establishment	361,338	106,483	29
Value Added per Establishment	5,381,325	1,554,335	29	Investment per Employee	8,609	5,627	65
Value Added per Employee	128,210	82,143	64	Investment per Production Worker	12,245	7,382	60

Sources: Same as General Statistics. The 'Average of All Manufacturing' column represents the average of all manufacturing industries reported for the most recent complete year available. The Index shows the relationship between the Average and the Analyzed Industry. For example, 100 means that they are equal; 500 that the Analyzed Industry is five times the average; 50 means that the Analyzed Industry is half the national average. The abbreviation 'na' is used to show that data are 'not available'. Ratios shown for 2002, the last complete census year.

LEADING COMPANIES   Number shown: **75**   Total sales ($ mil): **16,265**   Total employment (000): **39.0**

Company Name	Address				CEO Name	Phone	Co. Type	Sales ($ mil)	Empl. (000)
Precise Technology Inc.	501 Mosside Blvd.	N Versailles	PA	15137	Michael Farrell	412-823-2100	R	3,422*	0.3
Connell L.P.	1 International Pl.	Boston	MA	02110	Margot C. Connell	617-737-2700	R	1,429*	2.0
United Plastics Group Inc.	900 Oakmont Ln.	Westmont	IL	60559	Shannon M. White	630-706-5500	R	1,206*	1.7
MTD Products Inc.	PO Box 368022	Cleveland	OH	44136	Curtis E. Moll	330-225-2600	R	1,015*	6.7
Dickten Masch Plastics L.L.C.	N44 Watertown	Nashotah	WI	53058	Douglas Gray	262-367-5200	R	951*	0.2
Progressive Tool & Ind./Wisne	21000 Telegraph Rd.	Southfield	MI	48034	Robert Stoutenburg	248-353-8888	D	733*	5.5
Stahl Specialty Co.	PO Box 6	Kingsville	MO	64061	Kevin Daugherty	816-597-3322	S	681*	0.8
Bachman Machine Co.	4321 N Broadway	St. Louis	MO	63147	William Bachman	314-231-4221	R	656*	0.1
LMT Fette Inc.	1997 Ohio St.	Lisle	IL	60532	Brian Nowicki	630-969-5412	R	558*	0.2
Anchor Lamina America Inc.	PO Box 2540	Farmington Hls	MI	48333	Roy Verstraete	248-489-9122	R	500*	<0.1
Skill Metalforming Technologies	16151 Puritas Ave.	Cleveland	OH	44135	Roger Kalski	216-267-8866	R	352*	0.1
Gruber Systems Inc.	25636 Ave. Stanford	Valencia	CA	91355	John Hoskinson	661-257-4060	R	322*	0.3
Flambeau Inc.	801 Lynn Ave.	Baraboo	WI	53913	Jason C. Souey	608-356-5551	R	212*	3.0
Defiance Metal Products Co.	PO Box 447	Defiance	OH	43512		419-784-5332	R	211*	1.7
MPI International Inc.	2129 Austin Ave.	Rochester	MI	48309		248-853-9010	S	157*	1.0
A. Finkl and Sons Co.	2011 N Southport	Chicago	IL	60614	Joseph Curci	773-975-2510	R	140*	0.4
Northern Engraving Corp.	PO Box 377	Sparta	WI	54656		608-269-6911	R	130*	0.5
G and F Industries Inc.	PO Box 515	Sturbridge	MA	01566	John Argitis	508-347-9132	R	123*	0.2
Duffy Tool & Stamping Ltd.	PO Box 2128	Muncie	IN	47307	Greggory Notestine	765-288-1941	R	113*	0.2
Oberg Industries Inc.	PO Box 368	Freeport	PA	16229		724-295-2121	R	110*	0.5
Trend Technologies L.L.C.	4626 Eucalyptus	Chino	CA	91710		909-597-7861	R	105*	0.1
Dayton Progress Corp.	PO Box 39	Dayton	OH	45405		937-859-5111	S	105*	1.1
GMP Metal Products	3883 Delor Street	Saint Louis	MO	63116		314-481-0300	S	100*	0.2
Major Die and Engineering Co.	1352 Industrial Dr.	Itasca	IL	60143		630-773-3444	R	95*	<0.1
Minster Machine Co.	PO Box 120	Minster	OH	45865	John Winch	419-628-2331	R	91*	0.6
Penn United Technology Inc.	PO Box 399	Saxonburg	PA	16056	Carl Jones	724-352-1507	R	88*	0.7
Gill Industries Inc.	5271 Plainfield Ave	Grand Rapids	MI	49525		616-559-2700	R	88*	0.1
Atlantic Tool and Die Company	19963 Progress Dr.	Strongsville	OH	44149	Frank Mehwald	440-238-6931	R	87*	0.2
Motor City Stampings Inc.	47783 Gratiot Ave.	Chesterfield	MI	48051	Judith Kucway	586-949-8420	R	84*	0.5
Le Sueur Inc.	PO Box 149	Le Sueur	MN	56058	Mark Mueller	507-665-6204	R	82*	0.6
Kop-Flex Inc.	PO Box 1696	Baltimore	MD	21203	Dale Skoch	410-768-2000	S	82*	0.2
Aquarius Brands Inc.	PO Box 3760	Ontario	CA	91761	Dave Abrams	909-395-5200	S	80*	0.1
Innovance Inc.	505 W Front St.	Albert Lea	MN	56007	Mike Larson	507-377-8910	R	79*	<0.1
Toledo Molding and Die Inc.	PO Box 6760	Toledo	OH	43612	Donald Harbaugh	419-470-3950	R	75*	<0.1
American Drill Bushing Co.	7141 Paramount	Pico Rivera	CA	90660	A Steele	323-725-1515	R	70*	0.1
Mold-Rite Tool Inc.	33830 Riviera	Fraser	MI	48026	Patrick Greene	586-296-3970	R	68*	0.7
American Household Products	PO Box 310	Leeds	AL	35094	Burns Roensch	205-699-5144	R	68*	<0.1
Kelco Industries Inc.	9210 Country Club	Woodstock	IL	60098	Kevin Kelly	815-338-5521	R	66*	<0.1
A.J.L. Manufacturing Corp.	100 Holleder Pkwy.	Rochester	NY	14615		585-254-1128	R	64*	0.2
Hatch Stamping Co.	635 E Industrial Dr	Chelsea	MI	48118	Daniel Craig	734-475-8628	R	63*	0.2
Aluminum Casting & Engineering	2309 S Lenox St.	Milwaukee	WI	53207	Eckhart Grohmann	414-744-3902	R	62*	0.5
Modineer Co.	PO Box 640	Niles	MI	49120	Michael Dreher	269-683-2550	R	62*	0.1
Victor Plastics Inc.	1125 240th St. NE	North Liberty	IA	52317		319-626-7500	R	58*	0.3
Modern Drop Forge Co.	PO Box 429	Blue Island	IL	60406	Gregory Heim	708-388-1806	R	58*	0.4
LTC Roll and Engineering Co.	23500 John Gorsuch	Clinton Twp	MI	48036	Andrew Ligda	586-465-1023	R	58*	0.2
Tenere Inc.	700 Kelly Ave.	Dresser	WI	54009	Trent Jenson	715-755-2158	R	56*	0.1
Concote Corp.	PO Box 35848	Dallas	TX	75235	Robert Hanton	214-956-0077	R	56*	0.1
Triumph Twist Drill Company	PO Box 9000	Crystal Lake	IL	60039	Arthur Beck	815-459-6250	R	56*	0.5
Mate Precision Tooling Inc.	1295 Lund Blvd.	Anoka	MN	55303	Jack Schneider	763-421-0230	R	56*	0.3
Xaloy Inc.	PO Box 7359	New Castle	PA	16107	Walter Cox	724-656-5600	R	51*	0.2
PME Co's Inc.	13870 E 11 Mile Rd.	Warren	MI	48089	Geoff O'Brien	586-779-8787	R	50*	0.2
Elizabeth Carbide Die Company	PO Box 95	McKeesport	PA	15135	D Keefer	412-751-3000	R	50*	0.1
Jergens Inc.	15700 S Waterloo	Cleveland	OH	44110		216-486-2100	R	49*	0.2
Griffiths Holding Corp.	2717 Niagara Ln. N	Minneapolis	MN	55447	Harold Griffiths	763-557-8935	R	49*	<0.1
Alpha Technology Corp.	PO Box 168	Howell	MI	48844	Stephen Sweda	517-546-9700	R	49*	0.3
Century Mold Company Inc.	25 Vantage Pnt. Dr.	Rochester	NY	14624	Ronald Ricotta	585-352-8600	R	49*	0.3
Alinabal Inc.	28 Woodmont Rd.	Milford	CT	06460	Sam Bergami	203-877-3241	R	49*	0.3
Delta Tooling Co.	1350 Harmon Rd.	Auburn Hills	MI	48326	Peter Mozer	248-391-6800	R	47*	0.1
General Tool Co.	101 Landy Ln.	Cincinnati	OH	45215	William Kramer	513-733-5500	R	45*	0.2
C and A Tool Engineering Inc.	PO Box 94	Churubusco	IN	46723	Richard Conrow	260-693-2167	R	44*	0.3
Landmark Manufacturing Corp.	28100 Quick Ave.	Gallatin	MO	64640	Donald Critten	660-663-2185	R	43*	0.3
Paslin Co.	25411 Ryan Rd.	Warren	MI	48091	Charles Pasque	586-758-0200	R	43*	0.3
Ever Fab Inc.	12928 Big Tree Rd.	East Aurora	NY	14052	Alan Everett	716-652-0772	R	40*	<0.1
Parkview Metal Products Inc.	1275 Ensell Rd.	Lake Zurich	IL	60047	Charles Leutwiler	847-540-2323	R	39*	0.3
Aircom Manufacturing Inc.	PO Box 18054	Indianapolis	IN	46218	Gregory Lyon	317-545-5383	R	38*	0.3
Steinmetz Inc.	PO Box 393	Moscow	PA	18444	Michael Steinmetz	570-842-6161	R	37*	<0.1
Hammill Manufacturing Company	PO Box 1450	Maumee	OH	43537	John Hammill	419-476-0789	R	36*	0.1
Roto-Die Company Inc.	800 Howerton Ln.	Eureka	MO	63025		636-587-3600	R	35*	0.6
Composidie Inc.	1295 State Rte. 380	Apollo	PA	15613	Ted Wohlin	724-727-3466	R	35*	0.2
PTI Engineered Plastics Inc.	44850 Centre Ct. E	Clinton Twp	MI	48038		586-263-5100	R	35*	0.1
Industry Products Co.	PO Box 1158	Piqua	OH	45356	Linda Cleveland	937-778-0585	R	34*	0.3
BTD Manufacturing Inc.	1111 13th Ave. SE	Detroit Lakes	MN	56501	Paul Gitner	218-847-4446	S	34*	0.4
West Troy Tool and Machine	155 Marybill Dr. S	Troy	OH	45373	Earl Davidson	937-339-2192	R	34*	<0.1
Ferriot Inc.	PO Box 7670	Akron	OH	44306	Gordon Keeler	330-786-3000	R	34*	0.3
GW Plastics Inc.	239 Pleasant St.	Bethel	VT	05032	Brenan Riehl	802-234-9941	R	34*	0.3

Source: Ward's Business Directory of U.S. Private and Public Companies, Volumes 1 and 2, 2008. The company type code used is as follows: P - Public, R - Private, S - Subsidiary, D - Division, J - Joint Venture, A - Affiliate, G - Group. Sales are in millions of dollars, employees are in thousands. An asterisk (*) indicates an estimated sales volume. The symbol < stands for 'less than'. Company names and addresses are truncated, in some cases, to fit into the available space.

MATERIALS CONSUMED

Material	Quantity	Delivered Cost ($ million)
Metal bolts, nuts, screws, and other screw machine products	(X)	40.0
Other fabricated metal products (exc. castings and forgings)	(X)	81.4
Forgings	(X)	14.2
Iron and steel castings (rough and semifinished)	(X)	66.9
Nonferrous (aluminum, copper, etc.) castings (rough and semifinished)	(X)	37.3
Steel bars, bar shapes, and plates (exc. castings, forgings, fabr. metal products)	(X)	188.5
Steel sheet and strip (including tinplate)	(X)	38.0
All other steel shapes and forms (exc. castings, forgings, fabr. metal products)	(X)	55.9
Aluminum and aluminum-base alloy sheet, plate, foil, and welded tubing	(X)	9.6
All other aluminum and aluminum-base alloy shapes and forms (exc. castings, forgings, fabr. metal products)	(X)	25.2
Other nonferrous shapes and forms (exc. castings, forgings, fabricated metal products)	(X)	12.8
Tungsten carbide metal powders	(X)	(D)
All other metal powders	(X)	2.7
Industrial diamonds	(X)	(D)
Electrical transmission, distribution, and control equipment	(X)	17.8
Grinding wheels and other abrasive products, exc. industrial diamonds	(X)	25.0
Fluid power products	(X)	12.1
Cutting tools for machine tools	(X)	28.1
All other materials, components, parts, containers, and supplies	(X)	290.0
Materials, ingredients, containers, and supplies, nsk	(X)	269.8

Source: 2002 Economic Census. Explanation of symbols used: (D): Withheld to avoid disclosure of competitive data; na: Not available; (S): Withheld because statistical norms were not met; (X): Not applicable; (Z): Less than half the unit shown; nec: Not elsewhere classified; nsk: Not specified by kind; - : zero; p : 10-19 percent estimated; q : 20-29 percent estimated.

PRODUCT SHARE DETAILS

Product or Product Class Shipments	Mil. $	Product or Product Class Shipments	Mil. $
INDUSTRIAL MOLDS	5,859.5	of metal for rubber	297.8
Industrial molds made of metal, for die-casting of metal or metal carbides (except ingot	655.4	Other industrial molds made of metal for rubber	49.9
Industrial molds made of metal, for low-pressure die-casting of metal or metal carbides (except ingot molds)	193.8	Industrial molds made of metal for other materials, nec	78.4
		Industrial mold bases made of metal	127.9
Industrial molds made of metal, for high-pressure die-casting of metal or metal carbides (except ingot molds)	461.6	Industrial molds made of materials other than metal for metal, metal carbides, glass, mineral materials, rubber, and plastics	87.2
Industrial molds made of metal and other materials, except industrial injection or compression molds made of metal for plastics	1,207.0	Other industrial molds made of materials other than metal, nec	95.5
Industrial permanent molds made of metal for gravity casting (except ingot molds)	75.8	Industrial mold boxes and flasks for use with patterns and sand molds in foundries	52.0
		Industrial injection-type molds made of metal for plastics	3,372.5
Other industrial molds made of metal for metal or metal carbides (except ingot molds)	82.8	Industrial injection-type molds made of metal for plastics	3,010.3
Industrial molds made of metal for wax	75.9	Industrial compression-type molds (including matched metal molds) made of metal for plastics	189.5
Industrial molds made of metal for mineral materials	16.2	Other industrial molds (including transfer, plunger, and rotational molds) made of metal for plastics	172.7
Industrial molds made of metal for glass	167.7	Industrial molds and mold boxes, nsk	624.6
Industrial injection and compression-type molds made			

Source: 2002 Economic Census. The values are product shipments in millions of dollars for 2002. Total product shipments may be lower or higher than industry shipments. See Introduction for a full discussion. Values of indented subcategories are summed in the main heading(s). The symbol (D) appears when data are withheld to prevent disclosure of competitive information. The abbreviation nsk stands for 'not specified by kind' and nec for 'not elsewhere classified'. A dash (-) means zero.

INPUTS AND OUTPUTS FOR INDUSTRIAL MOLD MANUFACTURING

Economic Sector or Industry Providing Inputs	%	Sector	Economic Sector or Industry Buying Outputs	%	Sector
Compensation of employees	46.3		Private fixed investment	78.4	
Iron & steel mills & ferroalloys	6.1	Manufg.	Exports of goods & services	9.1	Cap Inv
Management of companies & enterprises	5.4	Services	Turned products & screws, nuts, & bolts	3.6	Manufg.
Wholesale trade	3.2	Trade	Other S/L govt. enterprises	1.5	S/L Govt
Plastics products, nec	2.5	Manufg.	Machine shops	1.5	Manufg.
Real estate	1.7	Fin/R.E.	Fabricated metals, nec	1.3	Manufg.
Custom computer programming services	1.5	Services	Industrial molds	0.8	Manufg.
Ferrous metal foundries	1.4	Manufg.	Nonferrous metal foundries	0.8	Manufg.
Power generation & supply	1.4	Util.	Architectural, engineering, & related services	0.8	Services
Machine shops	1.2	Manufg.	Special tools, dies, jigs, & fixtures	0.6	Manufg.
Industrial molds	1.1	Manufg.	Plate work & fabricated structural products	0.4	Manufg.
Special tools, dies, jigs, & fixtures	1.1	Manufg.	Warehousing & storage	0.3	Util.
Aluminum products from purchased aluminum	1.1	Manufg.	Glass containers	0.2	Manufg.
Turned products & screws, nuts, & bolts	1.1	Manufg.	Scientific research & development services	0.2	Services
Nonferrous metal foundries	0.9	Manufg.	Iron & steel mills & ferroalloys	0.2	Manufg.
Securities, commodity contracts, investments	0.9	Fin/R.E.	Heavy duty trucks	0.1	Manufg.
Maintenance/repair of nonresidential structures	0.8	Construct.	Ferrous metal foundries	0.1	Manufg.

Continued on next page.

INPUTS AND OUTPUTS FOR INDUSTRIAL MOLD MANUFACTURING - Continued

Economic Sector or Industry Providing Inputs	%	Sector	Economic Sector or Industry Buying Outputs	%	Sector
Advertising & related services	0.8	Services			
Truck transportation	0.7	Util.			
Services to buildings & dwellings	0.7	Services			
Taxes on production & imports, less subsidies	0.7				
Lessors of nonfinancial assets	0.7	Fin/R.E.			
Automotive equipment rental & leasing	0.7	Fin/R.E.			
Cutting tools & machine tool accessories	0.6	Manufg.			
Semiconductors & related devices	0.6	Manufg.			
Printed circuit assemblies (electronic assemblies)	0.6	Manufg.			
Accounting, tax preparation, bookkeeping, & payroll	0.5	Services			
Abrasive products	0.5	Manufg.			
Monetary authorities/depository credit intermediation	0.5	Fin/R.E.			
Automotive repair & maintenance, ex. car washes	0.5	Services			
Telecommunications	0.5	Services			
Scientific research & development services	0.5	Services			
Warehousing & storage	0.5	Util.			
Professional, scientific, technical services, nec	0.4	Services			
Commercial & industrial equipment repair/maintenance	0.4	Services			
Data processing, hosting, & related services	0.4	Services			
Coating, engraving, heat treating & allied activities	0.4	Manufg.			
Legal services	0.4	Services			
Nonmetallic mineral products, nec	0.4	Manufg.			
Forging, stamping, & sintering, nec	0.3	Manufg.			
Commercial & industrial machinery rental & leasing	0.3	Fin/R.E.			
Power, distribution, & specialty transformers	0.3	Manufg.			
Food services & drinking places	0.3	Services			
Nonferrous metal (ex. copper & aluminum) processing	0.3	Manufg.			
Natural gas distribution	0.2	Util.			
Management, scientific, & technical consulting	0.2	Services			
Alumina refining & primary aluminum production	0.2	Manufg.			
Valve & fittings other than plumbing	0.2	Manufg.			
Other computer related services, including facilities	0.2	Services			
Noncomparable imports	0.2	Foreign			
Fabricated metals, nec	0.2	Manufg.			
Fluid power process machinery	0.2	Manufg.			
Electronic & precision equipment repair/maintenance	0.2	Services			
Metal cans, boxes, & other containers (light gauge)	0.2	Manufg.			
Architectural, engineering, & related services	0.1	Services			
Hotels & motels, including casino hotels	0.1	Services			
Chemical products & preparations, nec	0.1	Manufg.			
Rail transportation	0.1	Util.			
Crowns & closures & metal stamping	0.1	Manufg.			
Paperboard containers	0.1	Manufg.			
Plastics packaging materials, film & sheet	0.1	Manufg.			
Custom roll forming	0.1	Manufg.			
Plate work & fabricated structural products	0.1	Manufg.			
Ball & roller bearings	0.1	Manufg.			
Personal & household goods repair/maintenance	0.1	Services			
Paperboard mills	0.1	Manufg.			

Source: Benchmark Input-Output Accounts for the U.S. Economy, 2002, U.S. Department of Commerce, Washington, D.C., January 2008. The abbreviation nec stands for 'not elsewhere classified'.

OCCUPATIONS EMPLOYED BY METALWORKING MACHINERY MANUFACTURING

Occupation	% of Total 2006	Change to 2016	Occupation	% of Total 2006	Change to 2016
Machinists	12.8	-14.0	Office clerks, general	1.7	-19.3
Tool & die makers	11.0	-14.0	Shipping, receiving, & traffic clerks	1.6	-21.2
Computer-controlled machine tool operators	5.4	-9.9	Welders, cutters, solderers, & brazers	1.6	-12.9
First-line supervisors/managers of production workers	4.6	-18.1	Bookkeeping, accounting, & auditing clerks	1.5	-18.1
Grinding, lapping, polishing machine tool operators	3.3	-20.6	Helpers--Production workers	1.4	-18.1
Cutting, punching, & press machine operators	3.2	-26.3	Sales reps, wholesale & manufacturing, exc tech	1.4	-18.1
Team assemblers	2.9	-18.1	Tool grinders, filers, & sharpeners	1.4	-26.3
Molding, coremaking, & casting machine operators	2.8	-26.3	Numerical tool & process control programmers	1.3	-15.6
Mechanical engineers	2.2	-18.1	Milling & planing machine operators & tenders	1.3	-26.3
General & operations managers	2.0	-26.3	Maintenance & repair workers, general	1.3	-18.1
Inspectors, testers, sorters, samplers, & weighers	2.0	-22.8	Industrial production managers	1.1	-18.1
Mechanical drafters	1.8	-17.2	Janitors & cleaners, exc maids & housekeeping cleaners	1.1	-16.3
Lathe & turning machine tool operators & tenders	1.8	-26.3	Multiple machine tool operators & tenders	1.0	-9.9

Source: Industry-Occupation Matrix, Bureau of Labor Statistics, December 4, 2007. These data are reported based on 4-digit NAICS categories but have been matched to corresponding 6-digit NAICS industry codes. The change reported for each occupation to the year 2016 is a percent of growth or decline as estimated by the Bureau of Labor Statistics. The abbreviation nec stands for 'not elsewhere classified'.

LOCATION BY STATE AND REGIONAL CONCENTRATION

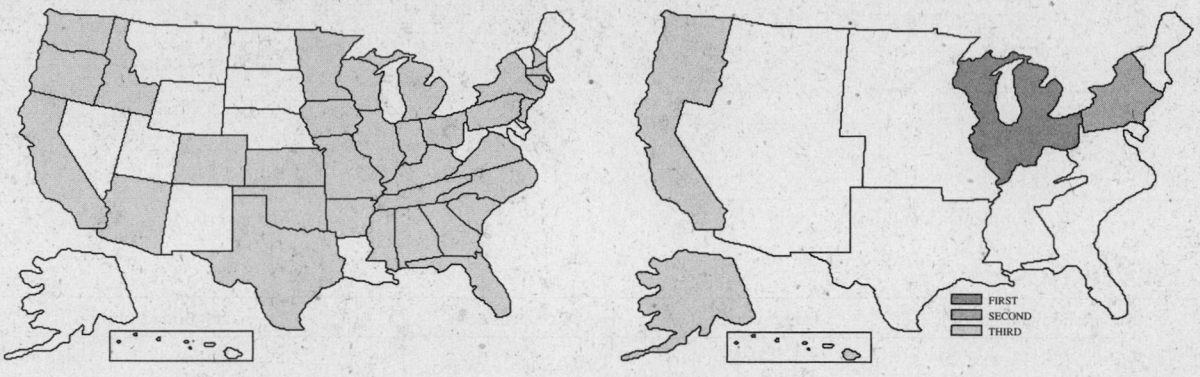

INDUSTRY DATA BY STATE

| State | Establish-ments | Shipments | | | Employment | | | | Cost as % of Shipments | Investment per Employee ($) |
		Total ($ mil)	% of U.S.	Per Establ.	Total Number	% of U.S.	Per Establ.	Wages ($/hour)		
Michigan	312	1,018.0	18.4	3,262.7	7,580	16.2	24	22.97	28.6	4,423
Ohio	254	578.1	10.5	2,275.8	5,204	11.1	20	20.26	28.6	4,416
Pennsylvania	162	402.1	7.3	2,481.9	3,353	7.2	21	19.86	30.9	5,312
Illinois	236	399.2	7.2	1,691.6	3,354	7.2	14	22.13	26.2	5,383
California	204	373.0	6.7	1,828.4	3,290	7.0	16	19.69	28.3	9,532
Texas	63	284.3	5.1	4,512.0	2,309	4.9	37	12.37	52.7	5,483
Wisconsin	126	281.5	5.1	2,234.4	2,485	5.3	20	21.61	25.5	7,250
Indiana	137	275.9	5.0	2,013.9	2,493	5.3	18	19.77	24.8	5,019
Massachusetts	68	222.8	4.0	3,276.3	1,747	3.7	26	18.03	38.9	6,657
New Jersey	83	161.8	2.9	1,949.8	1,222	2.6	15	20.00	35.8	5,331
Minnesota	101	129.9	2.3	1,286.0	1,157	2.5	11	23.13	26.9	5,041
Kentucky	37	129.0	2.3	3,485.2	864	1.8	23	14.99	27.8	6,407
New York	99	128.2	2.3	1,295.3	1,307	2.8	13	19.22	22.7	3,788
Tennessee	39	123.5	2.2	3,166.0	1,313	2.8	34	13.33	33.7	2,600
Missouri	45	120.0	2.2	2,666.1	1,061	2.3	24	18.34	22.7	4,490
Florida	70	107.1	1.9	1,530.0	961	2.1	14	17.46	32.6	2,766
North Carolina	39	91.4	1.7	2,344.4	702	1.5	18	19.25	38.6	3,433
Oklahoma	16	76.8	1.4	4,797.4	585	1.3	37	9.43	49.0	4,781
Connecticut	50	75.2	1.4	1,504.8	624	1.3	12	24.31	26.3	7,146
South Carolina	17	71.7	1.3	4,217.8	606	1.3	36	22.21	30.1	12,584
Colorado	30	59.9	1.1	1,997.8	481	1.0	16	16.74	22.9	7,952
Arizona	25	53.3	1.0	2,133.0	502	1.1	20	20.09	29.6	4,926
Iowa	20	46.2	0.8	2,307.9	494	1.1	25	19.30	24.2	4,704
Alabama	24	44.0	0.8	1,832.0	351	0.8	15	17.80	28.7	13,254
Virginia	15	35.4	0.6	2,361.6	267	0.6	18	16.67	27.7	7,536
Washington	27	32.9	0.6	1,219.7	423	0.9	16	19.82	29.6	10,149
Oregon	29	31.2	0.6	1,074.5	319	0.7	11	20.31	24.6	13,727
Georgia	17	23.7	0.4	1,392.9	204	0.4	12	15.32	31.9	26,000
Rhode Island	15	18.3	0.3	1,218.1	172	0.4	11	16.09	25.7	1,047
New Hampshire	18	18.2	0.3	1,009.7	226	0.5	13	20.78	23.7	3,642
Idaho	7	14.9	0.3	2,130.0	133	0.3	19	16.52	42.5	2,880
Kansas	7	14.4	0.3	2,060.4	146	0.3	21	24.49	20.3	5,671
Mississippi	8	11.0	0.2	1,378.4	135	0.3	17	14.49	32.6	1,119
Arkansas	18	9.8	0.2	543.7	117	0.3	7	20.15	20.5	1,632

Source: 2002 *Economic Census*. The states are in descending order of shipments or establishments (if shipment data are missing for the majority). The symbol (D) appears when data are withheld to prevent disclosure of competitive information. States marked with (D) are sorted by number of establishments. A dash (-) indicates that the data element cannot be calculated. Data may not show all states active in the NAICS category. All data available at the time of publication are shown.

NAICS 333512 - MACHINE TOOL (METAL CUTTING TYPES) MANUFACTURING

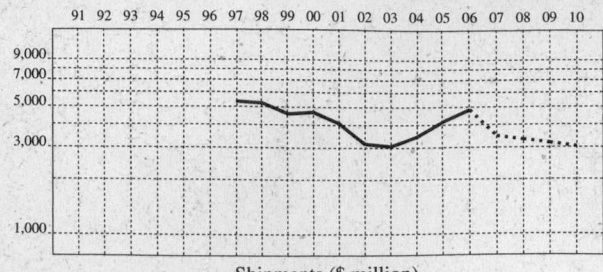

Shipments ($ million)

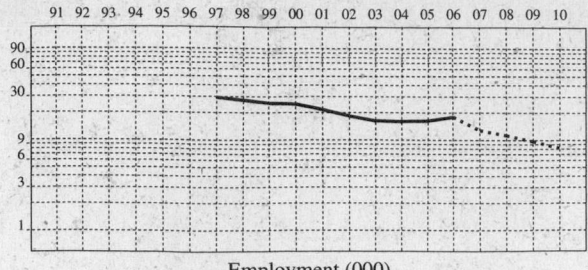

Employment (000)

GENERAL STATISTICS

Year	Companies	Establishments		Employment			Compensation		Production ($ million)			
		Total	with 20 or more employees	Total (000)	Production Workers (000)	Hours (Mil)	Payroll ($ mil)	Wages ($/hr)	Cost of Materials	Value Added by Manufacture	Value of Shipments	Capital Invest.
1997	369	401	262	29.4	16.9	35.0	1,268.4	17.83	2,819.7	2,609.4	5,334.9	142.2
1998		460	259	27.5	16.0	32.4	1,196.4	18.30	2,866.8	2,410.2	5,244.0	224.5
1999		456	255	25.5	14.9	30.2	1,159.4	17.90	2,483.5	2,081.0	4,601.6	186.1
2000		487	245	24.9	13.9	28.8	1,152.9	18.74	2,510.5	2,175.3	4,694.9	146.9
2001		519	246	21.6	11.6	23.8	1,035.2	18.52	2,236.1	1,699.4	4,090.1	106.8
2002	342	372	202	18.4	9.4	17.5	875.4	21.15	1,618.7	1,431.9	3,154.0	61.5
2003		557	209	16.3	8.0	17.5	821.6	19.69	1,577.0	1,438.0	3,060.4	45.8
2004		477	194	16.1	8.2	17.6	862.9	20.91	1,803.2	1,639.7	3,442.4	42.4
2005		504	188	16.3	8.8	18.6	917.6	21.79	2,292.4	1,963.2	4,158.1	70.8
2006		516P	177P	18.0	10.0	20.7	1,034.8	22.29	2,753.3	2,195.3	4,830.8	125.3
2007		525P	166P	12.8P	6.2P	13.3P	809.5P	22.55P	1,977.0P	1,576.3P	3,468.7P	38.7P
2008		535P	156P	11.3P	5.2P	11.3P	768.9P	23.06P	1,894.8P	1,510.8P	3,324.6P	24.8P
2009		544P	145P	9.7P	4.2P	9.3P	728.4P	23.58P	1,812.7P	1,445.3P	3,180.5P	10.9P
2010		553P	135P	8.2P	3.2P	7.3P	687.8P	24.10P	1,730.6P	1,379.9P	3,036.4P	

Sources: 1997 and 2002 *Economic Census*; other years, up to 2006, are from *Annual Survey of Manufactures*. Establishment counts for non-Census years are from *County Business Patterns*; 1997 and 2002 values are from the 1997 and 2002 censuses, respectively. 'P's show projections by the editors.

INDICES OF CHANGE

Year	Companies	Establishments		Employment			Compensation		Production ($ million)			
		Total	with 20 or more employees	Total (000)	Production Workers (000)	Hours (Mil)	Payroll ($ mil)	Wages ($/hr)	Cost of Materials	Value Added by Manufacture	Value of Shipments	Capital Invest.
1997	108	108	130	160	180	200	145	84	174	182	169	231
1998		124	128	149	170	185	137	87	177	168	166	365
1999		123	126	139	159	173	132	85	153	145	146	303
2000		131	121	135	148	165	132	89	155	152	149	239
2001		140	122	117	123	136	118	88	138	119	130	174
2002	100	100	100	100	100	100	100	100	100	100	100	100
2003		150	103	89	85	100	94	93	97	100	97	74
2004		128	96	88	87	101	99	99	111	115	109	69
2005		135	93	89	94	106	105	103	142	137	132	115
2006		139P	87P	98	106	118	118	105	170	153	153	204
2007		141P	82P	70P	66P	76P	92P	107P	122P	110P	110P	63P
2008		144P	77P	61P	55P	65P	88P	109P	117P	106P	105P	40P
2009		146P	72P	53P	45P	53P	83P	111P	112P	101P	101P	18P
2010		149P	67P	45P	34P	42P	79P	114P	107P	96P	96P	

Sources: Same as General Statistics. Values reflect change from the base year, 2002. Values above 100 mean greater than 2002, values below 100 mean less than 2002, and the values of 100 in other years means the same as 2002. 'P's show projections by the editors.

SELECTED RATIOS

For 2002	Avg. of All Manufact.	Analyzed Industry	Index	For 2002	Avg. of All Manufact.	Analyzed Industry	Index
Employees per Establishment	42	49	118	Value Added per Production Worker	182,367	152,330	84
Payroll per Establishment	1,639,184	2,353,226	144	Cost per Establishment	5,769,015	4,351,344	75
Payroll per Employee	39,053	47,576	122	Cost per Employee	137,446	87,973	64
Production Workers per Establishment	30	25	86	Cost per Production Worker	195,506	172,202	88
Wages per Establishment	694,845	994,960	143	Shipments per Establishment	11,158,348	8,478,495	76
Wages per Production Worker	23,548	39,375	167	Shipments per Employee	265,847	171,413	64
Hours per Production Worker	1,980	1,862	94	Shipments per Production Worker	378,144	335,532	89
Wages per Hour	11.89	21.15	178	Investment per Establishment	361,338	165,323	46
Value Added per Establishment	5,381,325	3,849,194	72	Investment per Employee	8,609	3,342	39
Value Added per Employee	128,210	77,821	61	Investment per Production Worker	12,245	6,543	53

Sources: Same as General Statistics. The 'Average of All Manufacturing' column represents the average of all manufacturing industries reported for the most recent complete year available. The Index shows the relationship between the Average and the Analyzed Industry. For example, 100 means that they are equal; 500 that the Analyzed Industry is five times the average; 50 means that the Analyzed Industry is half the national average. The abbreviation 'na' is used to show that data are 'not available'. Ratios shown for 2002, the last complete census year.

LEADING COMPANIES   Number shown: **75**   Total sales ($ mil): **19,695**   Total employment (000): **82.8**

Company Name	Address				CEO Name	Phone	Co. Type	Sales ($ mil)	Empl. (000)
Black and Decker Corp.	101 Schilling Rd.	Hunt Valley	MD	21031	Nolan D. Archibald	410-716-3900	P	6,563	25.0
Kennametal Inc.	PO Box 231	Latrobe	PA	15650	Carlos M. Cardoso	724-539-5000	P	2,386	14.0
Regal-Beloit Corp.	200 State St.	Beloit	WI	53511		608-364-8800	P	1,803	17.9
Johnstown Holdings Inc.	545 Central Ave.	Johnstown	PA	15902	John Bolduc	814-535-9000	R	918*	0.2
P.R. Hoffman Machine Products	1517 Commerce	Carlisle	PA	17015		717-243-9900	S	812*	<0.1
Giddings & Lewis Machine Tools	PO Box 590	Fond du Lac	WI	54936		920-921-9400	R	757*	0.4
Makino Inc.	7680 Innovation	Mason	OH	45040		513-573-7200	R	595*	0.2
Thermadyne Holdings Corp.	16052 Swingley	St. Louis	MO	63017	John Michael Bobyck	636-728-3000	P	494	2.9
Gleason Corp.	PO Box 22970	Rochester	NY	14692		585-473-1000	R	350*	2.6
Hercules Energy Manufacturing	16 S Penn. Avenue	Oklahoma City	OK	73107	Jack E. Golsen	405-235-4546	S	332*	1.3
Summit Machinery Co.	PO Box 1402	Oklahoma City	OK	73101	Jack E. Golsen	405-235-2075	R	332*	1.3
Haas Automation Inc.	2800 Sturgis Ave.	Oxnard	CA	93030	Gene Haas	805-278-1800	R	327*	0.8
Hardinge Inc.	PO Box 1507	Elmira	NY	14902	J. Patrick Ervin	607-734-2281	P	327	1.5
Morey Machinery Manufacturing	PO Box 4827	Middletown	NY	10941	Jack E. Golsen	845-343-1851	S	309*	1.2
Gerber Technology Inc.	24 Industrial Park	Tolland	CT	06084	John Hancock	860-871-8082	S	197	1.2
Mazak Corp.	PO Box 970	Florence	KY	41022	Brian Papke	859-342-1222	R	192*	0.5
Manan Medical Products	241 W Palatine Rd.	Wheeling	IL	60090	Werner Mittermeier	847-637-3333	R	191*	1.1
Stark Industrial Inc.	PO Box 3030	North Canton	OH	44720	Ray Wilkof	330-966-8108	R	190*	<0.1
Duo-Fast Corp.	2400 Galvin Dr.	Elgin	IL	60123		847-634-1900	S	136*	0.9
OSG Tap and Die Inc.	676 E Fullerton Ave	Glendale Hts	IL	60139	Gohei Osawa	630-790-1400	R	133*	<0.1
Clausing Industrial Inc.	1819 N Pitcher St.	Kalamazoo	MI	49007		269-345-7155	R	125*	<0.1
JH Fletcher and Co.	PO Box 2187	Huntington	WV	25722	Sammons Duncan	304-525-7811	R	120*	0.2
P and F Industries Inc.	445 Broadhollow	Melville	NY	11747	Richard A. Horowitz	631-694-9800	P	112	0.2
CB Manufacturing and Sales Co.	PO Box 37	West Carrollton	OH	45449	Charlie Biehn	937-866-5986	R	111*	0.1
Iscar Metals Inc.	300 Westway Pl.	Arlington	TX	76018	Jacob Harpaz	817-258-3200	R	95*	<0.1
Networks Electronic Corp.	9750 DeSoto Ave.	Chatsworth	CA	91311	Tamara Christen	818-341-0440	R	73*	0.1
Loos and Company Inc.	PO Box 98	Pomfret	CT	06258	William Loos	860-928-7981	R	71*	0.4
Hypertherm Inc.	PO Box 5010	Hanover	NH	03755	Richard Couch	603-643-3441	R	64*	0.5
Vulcan Engineering Co.	PO Box 307	Helena	AL	35080		205-663-0732	R	62*	0.2
Brinkman Products Inc.	167 Ames Street	Rochester	NY	14611	Robert Brinkman	585-235-4545	R	62*	0.3
A.K. Allen Inc.	PO Box 350	Mineola	NY	11501	A.K. Allen	516-747-5450	R	56*	0.2
Sunnen Products Co.	7910 Manchester	Saint Louis	MO	63143	Matt Kreider	314-781-2100	R	52*	0.5
Regal Cutting Tools	5330 E Rockton Rd.	South Beloit	IL	61080	Gene Zumba		D	50*	0.3
AGIE Ltd.	9009 Perimeter	Charlotte	NC	28216	Glynn Fletcher	704-927-8900	S	46*	<0.1
Fadal Machining Centers L.L.C.	PO Box 2477	Chatsworth	CA	91313	Peter Mosher	818-407-1400	S	45*	0.3
Thielenhaus Microfinish Corp.	42925 W 9 Mile Rd.	Novi	MI	48375	Manfred Sieringhaus	248-349-9450	R	45*	0.3
Continental Machines Inc.	5505 W 123rd St.	Savage	MN	55378	M Johnson	952-890-3300	R	45*	0.2
Mosey Manufacturing Company	262 Fort Wayne	Richmond	IN	47374	George Mosey	765-983-8800	R	43*	<0.1
New York Twist Drill Inc.	PO Box 368	South Beloit	IL	61080	Gene Zimbea		D	42*	0.2
Fastcut Tool Corp.	200 Front St.	Millersburg	PA	17061	Bill Coyle	717-692-8232	S	42*	<0.1
Ashley F. Ward Inc.	7490 Easy St.	Mason	OH	45040		513-398-1414	R	40*	0.3
IMPCO Machine Tools	PO Box 10156	Lansing	MI	48901	Dave Houghton	517-484-9411	R	38*	0.2
Airmar Technology Corp.	35 Meadowbrook	Milford	NH	03055	Stephen Boucher	603-673-9570	R	37*	0.2
Composidie Inc.	1295 State Rte. 380	Apollo	PA	15613	Ted Wohlin	724-727-3466	R	35*	0.2
CRC-Evans Pipeline Int'l	PO Box 50368	Tulsa	OK	74150		918-438-2100	R	35*	0.1
Picut Manufacturing Company	140 Mount Bethel	Warren	NJ	07059	Frederick Picut	908-754-1333	R	35*	<0.1
DTI Lebanon Subsidiary Inc.	PO Box 512	Lebanon	MO	65536	Tom Kowall	417-532-2142	R	33*	0.3
W.A. Whitney Co.	PO Box 1206	Rockford	IL	61105	Gary Geller	815-964-6771	S	33*	0.2
MC Machinery Systems Inc.	1500 Michael Dr.	Wood Dale	IL	60191	Tetsuji Koike	630-860-4210	R	32*	0.2
Kingsbury Corp.	80 Laurel St.	Keene	NH	03431		603-352-5212	R	32*	0.2
Magnetrol International Inc.	5300 Belmont Rd.	Downers Grove	IL	60515		630-969-4000	R	31*	0.3
PMC Industries Corp.	29100 Lakeland	Wickliffe	OH	44092		440-943-3300	S	31*	0.1
Reed-Rico	18 Industrial Dr.	Holden	MA	01520	Bruce Hutchinson	508-829-4491	D	30*	0.3
Moore Tool Company Inc.	PO Box 4088	Bridgeport	CT	06607	Newman Marsilius	203-366-3224	S	29*	0.1
Pmt Group Inc.	800 Union Ave.	Bridgeport	CT	06607	Newman Marsilius	203-367-8675	Pmt	29*	0.1
Hunt Valve Company Inc.	1913 E State St.	Salem	OH	44460	Gerald Bogner	330-337-9535	R	29*	0.2
Rollway Bearing International	PO Box 4827	Syracuse	NY	13221	Bill Eames		S	29*	0.2
Howmet TMP Corp.	3960 S Marginal Rd.	Cleveland	OH	44114	Ray Mitchell	216-391-3885	R	28*	0.2
Romac Industries Inc.	21919 20th Ave. SE	Bothell	WA	98021		425-951-6200	R	28*	0.2
Robbins Co.	29100 Hall St.	Solon	OH	44139	Lok Home	440-248-3303	R	27*	0.1
Tool-Flo Manufacturing Inc.	7803 Hansen Rd.	Houston	TX	77061	Dennis Flolo	713-941-1080	R	26*	0.1
Electronic Hardware Ltd.	PO Box 15039	N Hollywood	CA	91615	Richard Degn	818-982-6100	R	26*	<0.1
Marvel Manufacturing Company	3501 Marvel Dr.	Oshkosh	WI	54902	John Petek	920-236-7200	R	25*	0.2
PMC - Colinet Inc.	29100 Lakeland	Wickliffe	OH	44092	Dwight Perry	440-943-3300	S	25*	0.1
Microbest Inc.	670 Captain Neville	Waterbury	CT	06705	Steven Griffin	203-597-0355	S	25*	0.1
Channel Products Inc.	7100 Wilson Mills	Chesterland	OH	44026		440-423-0113	S	24*	0.1
Carolina Energy Solutions Inc.	244 E Mt Gallant Rd	Rock Hill	SC	29730	Richard Bryant	803-980-3060	R	23*	0.2
Peddinghaus Corp.	300 N Wash. Ave.	Bradley	IL	60915	Michael Sharp	815-937-3800	R	23*	0.2
Gehring Corp.	24800 Drake Rd.	Farmington Hls	MI	48335	Robert Dermolen	248-478-8060	R	23*	<0.1
Hy-Level Industries Inc.	PO Box 368015	Cleveland	OH	44136	Donald Rebar	440-572-1540	R	22*	0.2
Centricut L.L.C.	2 Technology Dr.	West Lebanon	NH	03784		603-298-7849	S	22*	0.1
Self Industries Inc.	3491 Mary Taylor	Birmingham	AL	35235	Michael McDowell	205-655-3284	R	22*	<0.1
Golden States Engineering Inc.	15338 Garfield Ave.	Paramount	CA	90723	Alexandra Rostovski	562-634-3125	R	22*	0.1
Cable West Inc.	276 Preuit Rd.	Wheatland	WY	82201	Donald Nichols	307-322-9214	R	22*	0.1
Wright-K Technology Inc.	2025 E Genesee	Saginaw	MI	48601	John Sivey	989-752-3103	R	22*	0.1

Source: Ward's Business Directory of U.S. Private and Public Companies, Volumes 1 and 2, 2008. The company type code used is as follows: P - Public, R - Private, S - Subsidiary, D - Division, J - Joint Venture, A - Affiliate, G - Group. Sales are in millions of dollars, employees are in thousands. An asterisk (*) indicates an estimated sales volume. The symbol < stands for 'less than'. Company names and addresses are truncated, in some cases, to fit into the available space.

MATERIALS CONSUMED

Material	Quantity	Delivered Cost ($ million)
Fluid power pumps, motors, and hydrostatic transmissions	(X)	13.8
Fluid power cylinders and rotary actuators (hydraulic and pneumatic)	(X)	8.1
Fluid power filters (hydraulic and pneumatic)	(X)	2.4
Fluid power hose, tube fittings, and assemblies (hydraulic and pneumatic)	(X)	7.3
Fluid power valves (hydraulic and pneumatic)	(X)	5.8
Metal bolts, nuts, screws, and other screw machine products	(X)	13.8
Other fabricated metal products (exc. fluid power products and forgings)	(X)	50.0
Forgings	(X)	2.5
Iron and steel castings (rough and semifinished)	(X)	50.2
Nonferrous (aluminum, copper, etc.) castings (rough and semifinished)	(X)	2.8
Steel bars, bar shapes, and plates (exc. castings, forgings, fabr. metal products)	(X)	43.5
Steel sheet and strip (including tinplate)	(X)	(D)
Steel structural shapes (exc. castings, forgings, fabr. metal products)	(X)	(D)
All other steel shapes and forms (exc. castings, forgings, fabr. metal products)	(X)	13.3
Nonferrous shapes and forms	(X)	3.6
Fractional horsepower electric timing motors (less than 1 hp)	(X)	9.0
Other fractional horsepower electric motors (less than 1 hp)	(X)	2.2
Integral horsepower electric motors and generators (1 hp or more)	(X)	12.6
Electrical transmission, distribution, and control equipment	(X)	16.7
Electrical industrial capacitors, resistors, rheostats, and coil windings	(X)	3.3
Numerical controls, metalworking machinery (exc. programmable)	(X)	28.7
Programmable controllers for metalworking machinery	(X)	27.7
Printed circuit assemblies, loaded boards, and modules	(X)	16.2
Printed ciruit boards (without inserted components) for electronic circuitry	(X)	2.3
Semiconductors (incl. transistors, diodes, rectifiers, and integrated circuits), for electronic circuitry	(X)	0.4
All other miscellaneous components and accessories for electronic circuitry (exc. tubes)	(X)	5.4
Electrical instrument mechanisms and meter movements	(X)	6.8
Electronic communication equipment	(X)	0.2
Optical instruments and lenses (exc. sighting, tracking, and fire control)	(X)	0.1
Ball bearings (mounted or unmounted)	(X)	13.7
Roller bearings (mounted or unmounted)	(X)	6.2
Mechanical speed changers, gears, and industrial high-speed drives	(X)	10.2
Wood boxes, pallets, skids, and containers	(X)	4.4
Cutting tools for machine tools	(X)	17.3
Fabricated plastics products (exc. gaskets, hoses, and belting)	(X)	2.9
Paper and paperboard containers (incl. shipping sacks and other paper packaging supplies)	(X)	1.5
All other materials, components, parts, containers, and supplies	(X)	332.9
Materials, ingredients, containers, and supplies, nsk	(X)	382.0

Source: 2002 Economic Census. Explanation of symbols used: (D): Withheld to avoid disclosure of competitive data; na: Not available; (S): Withheld because statistical norms were not met; (X): Not applicable; (Z): Less than half the unit shown; nec: Not elsewhere classified; nsk: Not specified by kind; - : zero; p : 10-19 percent estimated; q : 20-29 percent estimated.

PRODUCT SHARE DETAILS

Product or Product Class Shipments	Mil. $	Product or Product Class Shipments	Mil. $
MACHINE TOOLS, METAL CUTTING TYPES	2,561.0	nsk	6.0
Metal gear cutting machines	**80.2**	**Parts for metal cutting machine tools (sold separately) and rebuilt and remanufactured metal cutting machine tools**	**566.2**
Metal grinding, polishing, buffing, honing, and lapping machines, except gear-tooth grinding, lapping, polishing, and buffing	**312.5**	Parts for metal cutting machine tools (sold separately) and rebuilt	505.6
Metal lathes (turning machines) numerically and nonnumerically controlled	**182.1**	Parts for metal cutting machine tools, sold separately	388.6
Metal milling machines (excluding machining centers)	**51.3**	Rebuilt metal cutting type machine tools (including machines returned to same configuration they were in when new from factory)	49.5
Machine tools designed primarily for home workshops, labs, garages, etc. (metalworking and primarily metalworking)	**78.3**	Remanufactured metal cutting type machine tools (including machines in which the original carcass is reused and all possible modern improvements have been incorporated)	67.6
Metal drilling machines designed primarily for home workshops, labs, garages, etc.	(D)	Parts for metal cutting machine tools (sold separately) and rebuilt and remanufactured metal cutting machine tools, nsk	60.6
Metal grinding and polishing machines designed primarily for home workshops, labs, garages, etc., including crankshaft regrinding and valve grinding machines	(D)	**Metal machining centers (multifunction numerically controlled machines)**	**382.3**
Metal sawing and cut-off machines designed primarily for home workshops, labs, garages, etc.	2.9	**Metal station type machines**	**138.5**
Other metalworking (or primarily metalworking) machines for home workshops, labs, garages, etc., including automotive cylinder reboring machines and lathes	15.9	**Other metal cutting machine tools (except those designed primarily for home workshops, laboratories, garages, etc.)**	**458.4**
Machine tools designed primarily for home workshops, labs, etc. (metalworking and primarily metalworking),		**Metal boring machines and drilling machines (excluding machining centers)**	**114.7**
		Machine tools, metal cutting types, nsk, total	**196.5**

Source: 2002 Economic Census. The values are product shipments in millions of dollars for 2002. Total product shipments may be lower or higher than industry shipments. See Introduction for a full discussion. Values of indented subcategories are summed in the main heading(s). The symbol (D) appears when data are withheld to prevent disclosure of competitive information. The abbreviation nsk stands for 'not specified by kind' and nec for 'not elsewhere classified'. A dash (-) means zero.

INPUTS AND OUTPUTS FOR METAL CUTTING AND FORMING MACHINE TOOL MANUFACTURING

Economic Sector or Industry Providing Inputs	%	Sector	Economic Sector or Industry Buying Outputs	%	Sector
Compensation of employees	38.8		Private fixed investment	50.8	
Management of companies & enterprises	7.2	Services	Exports of goods & services	27.5	Cap Inv
Wholesale trade	4.7	Trade	S/L govt. invest., other	4.7	S/L Govt
Iron & steel mills & ferroalloys	4.5	Manufg.	Plate work & fabricated structural products	3.2	Manufg.
Relay & industrial controls	2.7	Manufg.	Nonferrous metal foundries	1.7	Manufg.
Ferrous metal foundries	2.3	Manufg.	General purpose machinery, nec	1.4	Manufg.
Metal cutting & forming machine tools	2.3	Manufg.	Metal cutting & forming machine tools	1.3	Manufg.
Machine shops	1.9	Manufg.	S/L govt. invest., education	1.3	S/L Govt
Paints & coatings	1.9	Manufg.	Rolling mill & other metalworking machinery	1.3	Manufg.
Ball & roller bearings	1.3	Manufg.	Motor vehicle parts	1.2	Manufg.
Securities, commodity contracts, investments	1.3	Fin/R.E.	Sporting & athletic goods	1.2	Manufg.
Advertising & related services	1.2	Services	Educational services, nec	0.8	Services
Motors & generators	1.1	Manufg.	Federal government, investment, national defense	0.7	Fed Govt
Fluid power process machinery	1.0	Manufg.	Machine shops	0.6	Manufg.
Real estate	1.0	Fin/R.E.	Personal consumption expenditures	0.6	
Valve & fittings other than plumbing	1.0	Manufg.	Fabricated metals, nec	0.5	Manufg.
Speed changers, industrial high-speed drives, & gears	1.0	Manufg.	General S/L govt. services	0.5	S/L Govt
Turned products & screws, nuts, & bolts	1.0	Manufg.	Farm machinery & equipment	0.2	Manufg.
Abrasive products	1.0	Manufg.	Warehousing & storage	0.2	Util.
Custom computer programming services	0.9	Services			
Cutting tools & machine tool accessories	0.8	Manufg.			
Power generation & supply	0.8	Util.			
Printed circuit assemblies (electronic assemblies)	0.8	Manufg.			
Truck transportation	0.7	Util.			
Lessors of nonfinancial assets	0.7	Fin/R.E.			
Coating, engraving, heat treating & allied activities	0.6	Manufg.			
Noncomparable imports	0.6	Foreign			
Taxes on production & imports, less subsidies	0.6				
Monetary authorities/depository credit intermediation	0.5	Fin/R.E.			
Electronic components, nec	0.5	Manufg.			
Telecommunications	0.5	Services			
Legal services	0.5	Services			
Data processing, hosting, & related services	0.5	Services			
Food services & drinking places	0.5	Services			
Professional, scientific, technical services, nec	0.5	Services			
Postal service	0.5	Util.			
Scientific research & development services	0.4	Services			
Custom roll forming	0.4	Manufg.			
Accounting, tax preparation, bookkeeping, & payroll	0.4	Services			
Warehousing & storage	0.4	Util.			
Automotive equipment rental & leasing	0.4	Fin/R.E.			
Electricity & signal testing instruments	0.3	Manufg.			
Wood containers & pallets	0.3	Manufg.			
Fabricated metals, nec	0.3	Manufg.			
Gold, silver, & other metal ore	0.3	Mining			
Hotels & motels, including casino hotels	0.2	Services			
Metal cans, boxes, & other containers (light gauge)	0.2	Manufg.			
Forging, stamping, & sintering, nec	0.2	Manufg.			
Rubber products, nec	0.2	Manufg.			
Services to buildings & dwellings	0.2	Services			
Plastics products, nec	0.2	Manufg.			
Maintenance/repair of nonresidential structures	0.2	Construct.			
Commercial & industrial machinery rental & leasing	0.2	Fin/R.E.			
Management, scientific, & technical consulting	0.2	Services			
Nonmetallic minerals, nec	0.2	Mining			
Air transportation	0.2	Util.			
Natural gas distribution	0.2	Util.			
Crowns & closures & metal stamping	0.2	Manufg.			
Other computer related services, including facilities	0.2	Services			
Architectural, engineering, & related services	0.2	Services			
Plastics packaging materials, film & sheet	0.2	Manufg.			
General purpose machinery, nec	0.2	Manufg.			
Rail transportation	0.2	Util.			
Business support services	0.2	Services			
Plate work & fabricated structural products	0.1	Manufg.			
Chemical products & preparations, nec	0.1	Manufg.			
Handtools	0.1	Manufg.			
Nonferrous metal foundries	0.1	Manufg.			
Nondepository credit intermediation activities	0.1	Fin/R.E.			
Employment services	0.1	Services			
Motor vehicle parts	0.1	Manufg.			
Paperboard mills	0.1	Manufg.			
Automotive repair & maintenance, ex. car washes	0.1	Services			
Specialized design services	0.1	Services			
Bare printed circuit boards	0.1	Manufg.			
Electronic capacitors, resistors, coils, transformers	0.1	Manufg.			
Paperboard containers	0.1	Manufg.			
Commercial & industrial equipment repair/maintenance	0.1	Services			

Source: Benchmark Input-Output Accounts for the U.S. Economy, 2002, U.S. Department of Commerce, Washington D.C., January 2008. User should note that this Input-Output table is not for this particular narrowly defined industry but for a larger aggregate. Input and Output data for Metal Cutting and Forming Machine Tool Manufacturing include Input and Output data for the Annual Survey of Manufactures' NAICS industries 333512 and 333513. The abbreviation nec stands for 'not elsewhere classified'.

OCCUPATIONS EMPLOYED BY METALWORKING MACHINERY MANUFACTURING

Occupation	% of Total 2006	Change to 2016	Occupation	% of Total 2006	Change to 2016
Machinists	12.8	-14.0	Office clerks, general	1.7	-19.3
Tool & die makers	11.0	-14.0	Shipping, receiving, & traffic clerks	1.6	-21.2
Computer-controlled machine tool operators	5.4	-9.9	Welders, cutters, solderers, & brazers	1.6	-12.9
First-line supervisors/managers of production workers	4.6	-18.1	Bookkeeping, accounting, & auditing clerks	1.5	-18.1
Grinding, lapping, polishing machine tool operators	3.3	-20.6	Helpers--Production workers	1.4	-18.1
Cutting, punching, & press machine operators	3.2	-26.3	Sales reps, wholesale & manufacturing, exc tech	1.4	-18.1
Team assemblers	2.9	-18.1	Tool grinders, filers, & sharpeners	1.4	-26.3
Molding, coremaking, & casting machine operators	2.8	-26.3	Numerical tool & process control programmers	1.3	-15.6
Mechanical engineers	2.2	-18.1	Milling & planing machine operators & tenders	1.3	-26.3
General & operations managers	2.0	-26.3	Maintenance & repair workers, general	1.3	-18.1
Inspectors, testers, sorters, samplers, & weighers	2.0	-22.8	Industrial production managers	1.1	-18.1
Mechanical drafters	1.8	-17.2	Janitors & cleaners, exc maids & housekeeping cleaners	1.1	-16.3
Lathe & turning machine tool operators & tenders	1.8	-26.3	Multiple machine tool operators & tenders	1.0	-9.9

Source: *Industry-Occupation Matrix*, Bureau of Labor Statistics, December 4, 2007. These data are reported based on 4-digit NAICS categories but have been matched to corresponding 6-digit NAICS industry codes. The change reported for each occupation to the year 2016 is a percent of growth or decline as estimated by the Bureau of Labor Statistics. The abbreviation nec stands for 'not elsewhere classified'.

LOCATION BY STATE AND REGIONAL CONCENTRATION

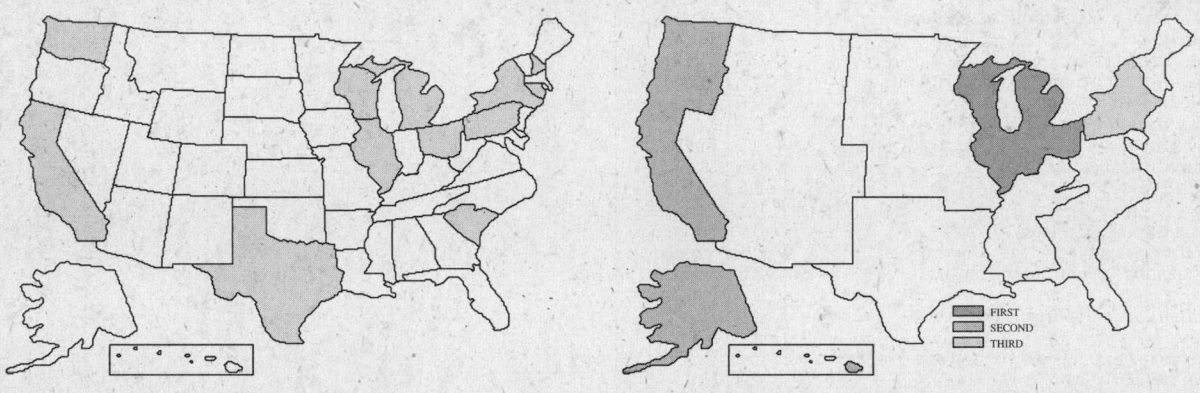

FIRST
SECOND
THIRD

INDUSTRY DATA BY STATE

State	Establish-ments	Shipments			Employment				Cost as % of Shipments	Investment per Employee ($)
		Total ($ mil)	% of U.S.	Per Establ.	Total Number	% of U.S.	Per Establ.	Wages ($/hour)		
Michigan	90	574.7	18.2	6,386.1	3,136	17.1	35	21.78	48.9	2,992
California	30	362.6	11.5	12,087.7	2,469	13.4	82	35.39	48.6	1,170
New York	16	314.6	10.0	19,659.5	2,019	11.0	126	21.05	60.6	3,618
Ohio	35	259.8	8.2	7,423.7	1,778	9.7	51	23.97	58.1	1,985
Illinois	30	222.1	7.0	7,402.5	1,237	6.7	41	18.19	46.6	5,201
Connecticut	12	218.2	6.9	18,187.1	905	4.9	75	18.09	52.8	10,109
Wisconsin	28	199.1	6.3	7,111.6	1,242	6.8	44	19.22	46.2	3,527
Pennsylvania	14	115.0	3.6	8,215.7	675	3.7	48	20.78	34.4	1,313
Washington	5	65.1	2.1	13,017.8	292	1.6	58	22.29	39.2	4,092
South Carolina	6	34.0	1.1	5,667.8	247	1.3	41	17.84	42.8	1,405
New Hampshire	4	30.9	1.0	7,721.7	246	1.3	62	18.77	47.2	2,028
Texas	5	23.5	0.7	4,699.0	151	0.8	30	18.53	48.3	4,000

Source: 2002 *Economic Census*. The states are in descending order of shipments or establishments (if shipment data are missing for the majority). The symbol (D) appears when data are withheld to prevent disclosure of competitive information. States marked with (D) are sorted by number of establishments. A dash (-) indicates that the data element cannot be calculated. Data may not show all states active in the NAICS category. All data available at the time of publication are shown.

NAICS 333513 - MACHINE TOOL (METAL FORMING TYPES) MANUFACTURING

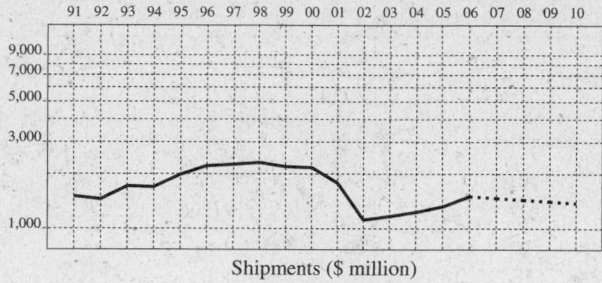

Shipments ($ million)

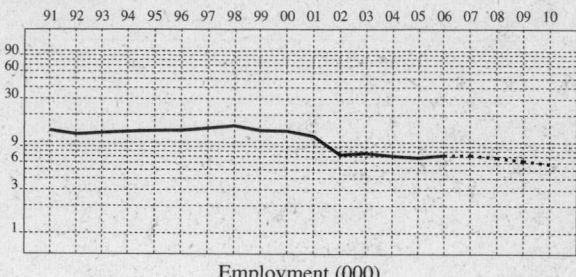

Employment (000)

GENERAL STATISTICS

Year	Companies	Establishments		Employment			Compensation		Production ($ million)			
		Total	with 20 or more employees	Total (000)	Production Workers (000)	Hours (Mil)	Payroll ($ mil)	Wages ($/hr)	Cost of Materials	Value Added by Manufacture	Value of Shipments	Capital Invest.
1991		280	125	13.5	8.5	17.7	443.5	14.30	746.5	636.4	1,505.5	31.6
1992	211	217	114	12.2	7.8	15.8	417.6	14.99	700.1	728.6	1,450.9	40.4
1993		229	109	12.7	7.8	16.7	461.9	15.68	833.4	872.4	1,712.7	32.7
1994		258	112	13.1	8.3	17.5	475.3	15.91	769.8	922.0	1,694.3	25.4
1995		277	117	13.4	8.5	18.5	511.5	16.22	910.3	1,165.9	1,982.2	56.1
1996		343	124	13.5	8.5	18.6	524.7	16.52	940.9	1,262.4	2,213.3	52.0
1997	220	225	144	14.2	9.1	18.8	598.6	18.37	961.5	1,289.6	2,255.0	92.0
1998		257	150	15.2	9.6	19.0	640.7	19.16	951.1	1,439.6	2,308.9	102.9
1999		257	154	13.5	8.7	18.0	596.0	18.32	909.9	1,274.5	2,190.7	68.1
2000		269	149	13.3	8.6	18.0	598.4	18.69	938.4	1,248.1	2,169.4	54.2
2001		287	135	11.7	7.2	14.8	504.4	18.22	758.4	961.2	1,784.9	36.8
2002	169	178	98	7.3	4.2	8.4	341.2	20.72	479.7	637.8	1,117.4	28.6
2003		311	118	7.6	4.5	9.2	368.7	20.20	510.7	654.4	1,168.2	14.1
2004		279	104	7.1	4.4	9.5	368.4	20.73	534.7	709.3	1,231.7	23.8
2005		288	110	6.8	4.5	9.8	354.1	19.54	580.5	756.4	1,325.2	34.0
2006		276P	122P	7.2	4.7	10.1	375.8	20.73	683.2	815.8	1,503.1	22.3
2007		278P	122P	7.2P	4.5P	9.5P	409.2P	21.64P	669.3P	799.2P	1,472.5P	34.2P
2008		279P	122P	6.8P	4.2P	8.9P	401.6P	22.07P	655.7P	783.0P	1,442.7P	33.0P
2009		281P	122P	6.3P	3.9P	8.2P	394.0P	22.49P	642.2P	766.8P	1,412.9P	31.7P
2010		282P	122P	5.8P	3.6P	7.6P	386.4P	22.92P	628.7P	750.7P	1,383.1P	30.5P

Sources: 1992, 1997, 2002 *Economic Census*; other years, up to 2006, are from the *Annual Survey of Manufactures*. Establishment counts for non-Census years are from *County Business Patterns*; 1997 and 2002 values are from the 1997 and 2002 censuses respectively, reported in the Federal Government's NAICS format. Other years were originally reported in equivalent SIC format. 'P's show projections by the editors.

INDICES OF CHANGE

Year	Companies	Establishments		Employment			Compensation		Production ($ million)			
		Total	with 20 or more employees	Total (000)	Production Workers (000)	Hours (Mil)	Payroll ($ mil)	Wages ($/hr)	Cost of Materials	Value Added by Manufacture	Value of Shipments	Capital Invest.
1992	125	122	116	167	186	188	122	72	146	114	130	141
1997	130	126	147	195	217	224	175	89	200	202	202	322
2001		161	138	160	171	176	148	88	158	151	160	129
2002	100	100	100	100	100	100	100	100	100	100	100	100
2003		175	120	104	107	110	108	97	106	103	105	49
2004		157	106	97	105	113	108	100	111	111	110	83
2005		162	112	93	107	117	104	94	121	119	119	119
2006		155P	125P	99	112	120	110	100	142	128	135	78
2007		156P	125P	99P	107P	113P	120P	104P	140P	125P	132P	120P
2008		157P	124P	93P	100P	106P	118P	107P	137P	123P	129P	115P
2009		158P	124P	86P	93P	98P	115P	109P	134P	120P	126P	111P
2010		159P	124P	79P	86P	90P	113P	111P	131P	118P	124P	107P

Sources: Same as General Statistics. Values reflect change from the base year, 2002. Values above 100 mean greater than 2002, values below 100 mean less than 2002, and the values of 100 in other years means the same as 2002. 'P's show projections by the editors.

SELECTED RATIOS

For 2002	Avg. of All Manufact.	Analyzed Industry	Index	For 2002	Avg. of All Manufact.	Analyzed Industry	Index
Employees per Establishment	42	41	98	Value Added per Production Worker	182,367	151,857	83
Payroll per Establishment	1,639,184	1,916,854	117	Cost per Establishment	5,769,015	2,694,944	47
Payroll per Employee	39,053	46,740	120	Cost per Employee	137,446	65,712	48
Production Workers per Establishment	30	24	80	Cost per Production Worker	195,506	114,214	58
Wages per Establishment	694,845	977,798	141	Shipments per Establishment	11,158,348	6,277,528	56
Wages per Production Worker	23,548	41,440	176	Shipments per Employee	265,847	153,068	58
Hours per Production Worker	1,980	2,000	101	Shipments per Production Worker	378,144	266,048	70
Wages per Hour	11.89	20.72	174	Investment per Establishment	361,338	160,674	44
Value Added per Establishment	5,381,325	3,583,146	67	Investment per Employee	8,609	3,918	46
Value Added per Employee	128,210	87,370	68	Investment per Production Worker	12,245	6,810	56

Sources: Same as General Statistics. The 'Average of All Manufacturing' column represents the average of all manufacturing industries reported for the most recent complete year available. The Index shows the relationship between the Average and the Analyzed Industry. For example, 100 means that they are equal; 500 that the Analyzed Industry is five times the average; 50 means that the Analyzed Industry is half the national average. The abbreviation 'na' is used to show that data are 'not available'. Ratios shown for 2002, the last complete census year.

LEADING COMPANIES   Number shown: **75**   Total sales ($ mil): **6,824**   Total employment (000): **22.6**

Company Name	Address				CEO Name	Phone	Co. Type	Sales ($ mil)	Empl. (000)
Metaldyne Corp.	47603 Halyard Dr.	Plymouth	MI	48170	Thomas Amato	734-207-6200	S	1,886	8.0
Saurer Holding Inc.	1575 W 124th Ave.	Denver	CO	80234	Peter Kern	303-457-1234	R	1,850*	0.2
Gleason Corp.	PO Box 22970	Rochester	NY	14692		585-473-1000	R	350*	2.6
Haas Automation Inc.	2800 Sturgis Ave.	Oxnard	CA	93030	Gene Haas	805-278-1800	R	327*	0.8
Danieli Corp.	800 Cranberry Wds	Cranberry Twp	PA	16066	Mark Brandon	724-778-5400	R	306*	<0.1
Trumpf Inc.	111 Hyde Rd.	Farmington	CT	06032	Rolf Biekert	860-255-6000	S	278*	0.6
Duo-Fast Corp.	2400 Galvin Dr.	Elgin	IL	60123		847-634-1900	S	136*	0.9
Minster Machine Co.	PO Box 120	Minster	OH	45865	John Winch	419-628-2331	R	91*	0.6
Astro Air Inc.	1653 N Bolton St.	Jacksonville	TX	75766	Rex Dacus	903-586-3691	R	59*	0.3
Angelus Sanitary Can Machine	4900 Pacific Blvd.	Los Angeles	CA	90058	Maury Koeberle	323-583-2171	R	56*	0.5
Mate Precision Tooling Inc.	1295 Lund Blvd.	Anoka	MN	55303	Jack Schneider	763-421-0230	R	56*	0.3
Magnetic Metals Corp.	1900 Hayes Ave.	Camden	NJ	08105	Frank Raneiro	856-964-7842	R	50*	0.4
Elizabeth Carbide Die Company	PO Box 95	McKeesport	PA	15135	D Keefer	412-751-3000	R	50*	0.1
Sterling Inc.	2900 S 160th St.	New Berlin	WI	53151	Tom Breslin	414-354-0970	R	45*	0.1
Murata Machinery USA Inc.	PO Box 667609	Charlotte	NC	28266	Masahiko Hattori	704-394-8331	R	43*	0.1
National Machinery L.L.C.	PO Box 747	Tiffin	OH	44883		419-447-5211	R	43*	0.3
General Electro-Mechanical	100 Gemcor Dr.	West Seneca	NY	14224	Thomas H. Speller Jr.	716-674-9300	R	41*	<0.1
Ntm Inc.	PO Box 1247	Mauldin	SC	29662	Curtis Harper	864-675-9376	R	41*	<0.1
Chicago Rivet and Machine Co.	PO Box 3061	Naperville	IL	60566	Michael J. Bourg	630-357-8500	P	40	0.3
Pines Manufacturing Inc.	30505 Clemens Rd.	Westlake	OH	44145	Donald Rebar	440-835-5553	R	39*	<0.1
Lummus Corp.	PO Box 4259	Savannah	GA	31407	Dikran Izmirlian	912-447-9000	R	37*	0.2
Composidie Inc.	1295 State Rte. 380	Apollo	PA	15613	Ted Wohlin	724-727-3466	R	35*	0.2
W.A. Whitney Co.	PO Box 1206	Rockford	IL	61105	Gary Geller	815-964-6771	S	33*	0.2
Sun Microstamping Technologies	14055 US Hwy 19	Clearwater	FL	33764	Bryan Clark	727-536-8822	R	32*	0.3
MC Machinery Systems Inc.	1500 Michael Dr.	Wood Dale	IL	60191	Tetsuji Koike	630-860-4210	R	32*	0.2
American GFM Corp.	1200 Cavalier Blvd.	Chesapeake	VA	23323	Robert Kralowetz	757-487-2442	R	32*	0.2
Strippit Inc.	12975 Clarence Ctr.	Akron	NY	14001	John Lesebbre	716-542-4511	R	32*	0.2
Charles E Jarrell Contracting	4208 Rider Trl. N	Earth City	MO	63045	Michael Jarrell	314-291-0100	R	32*	0.3
Martin Rea Industries Inc.	603 E Church Ave.	Reed City	MI	49677		231-832-5504	R	30*	0.1
Taylor's Industrial Services	820 W Marion Rd.	Mount Gilead	OH	43338		419-946-0222	R	29*	0.2
Deringer-Ney Inc.	616 Atrium Dr., 100	Vernon Hills	IL	60061		847-932-6800	R	28*	0.2
Buhler Inc.	PO Box 9497	Minneapolis	MN	55440		763-847-9900	R	27*	0.2
Schmiede Corp.	PO Box 1630	Tullahoma	TN	37388	Bozena Schmiede	931-455-4801	R	27*	0.1
Anderson Cook Inc.	17650 15 Mile Rd.	Fraser	MI	48026	Kim Anderson	586-293-0800	R	26*	<0.1
Mechanical Tool & Engineering	PO Box 5906	Rockford	IL	61125	Richard Nordlof	815-397-4701	R	26*	0.2
Centricut L.L.C.	2 Technology Dr.	West Lebanon	NH	03784		603-298-7849	S	22*	0.1
Gasbarre Products Inc.	PO Box 1011	Du Bois	PA	15801	Thomas Gasbarre	814-371-3015	R	21*	0.1
ASC Machine Tools Inc.	PO Box 11619	Spokane	WA	99211	Ray Griff	509-534-6600	R	21*	0.2
Williams White and Co.	600 River Dr.	Moline	IL	61265	Sunder Subbaroyan	309-797-7650	R	21*	0.1
Fabco-Air Inc.	PO Box 5159	Gainesville	FL	32627	William Schmidt	352-373-3578	R	20*	0.1
Jesse Engineering Co.	5225 7th St. E	Tacoma	WA	98424	Jeff Gellert	253-922-7433	R	18*	<0.1
Iverson Industries Inc.	580 Hillsdale St.	Wyandotte	MI	48192	Thomas Iverson	734-284-5301	R	18*	<0.1
Twist Inc.	PO Box 177	Jamestown	OH	45335	Joe Wright	937-675-9581	R	18*	0.1
Custom Engineering Co.	PO Box 10008	Erie	PA	16514	Thomas Hagen	814-898-2800	R	18*	0.2
MTD Technologies Inc.	5201 102nd Ave.	Pinellas Park	FL	33782	Dennis Ruppel	727-546-2446	R	17*	0.1
Advance Manufacturing Co. Inc.	PO Box 726	Westfield	MA	01086	Anthony Amanti	413-568-2411	R	17*	0.2
Amada Manufacturing America	14646 Northam St.	La Mirada	CA	90638	Sadashi Kiyooka	714-690-5600	R	17*	<0.1
Roper Whitney of Rockford Inc.	2833 Huffman Blvd.	Rockford	IL	61103	David Casazza	815-962-3011	R	17*	0.1
Erie Press Systems Inc.	PO Box 4061	Erie	PA	16512	Gary Lunger	814-455-3941	R	17*	<0.1
Clark Granco Inc.	7298 Storey Rd.	Belding	MI	48809	Lawrence Difatta	616-794-2600	R	16*	0.1
DADCO Inc.	43850 Plym Oaks	Plymouth	MI	48170	Michael Diebolt	734-207-1100	R	16*	0.1
Press Repair Engineering Sales	PO Box 1381	Morristown	TN	37816	Dennis Christian	423-586-2406	R	15*	<0.1
Qualex Manufacturing L.L.C.	PO Box 807	Georgetown	KY	40324		502-863-6348	R	15*	0.1
Baldauf Enterprises	1321 S Vly Ctr Dr.	Bay City	MI	48706	Harold Baldauf	989-686-0399	R	14*	<0.1
Wabash Metal Products Inc.	PO Box 298	Wabash	IN	46992	Bruce Freeman	260-563-1184	S	14*	<0.1
Rocky Mtn Welding & Fabric.	PO Box 397	Pleasant Grove	UT	84062	Marcel Roest	801-785-5990	R	13*	0.1
Jorban-Riscoe Associates Inc.	9808 Alden St.	Lenexa	KS	66215	Mark Riscoe	913-438-1244	R	13*	<0.1
HMS Products Co.	1200 E Big Beaver	Troy	MI	48083	Dave Sofy	248-689-8120	R	13*	<0.1
Baltec Corp.	130 Technology Dr.	Canonsburg	PA	15317	Fritz Boesch	724-873-5757	R	13*	<0.1
Pannier Corp.	207 Sandusky St.	Pittsburgh	PA	15212	Scott Heddaeus	412-323-4900	R	13*	<0.1
Kobelco Stewart Bolling Inc.	1600 Terex Road	Hudson	OH	44236	Toshio Yanagihara	330-655-3111	R	13*	<0.1
Daugherty Tool and Die Inc.	325 Industry Rd.	Buena Vista	PA	15018	Timothy Beringer	412-754-0200	R	12*	<0.1
Galland Henning Nopak Inc.	1025 S 40th St.	Milwaukee	WI	53215	H Nunnemacher	414-645-6000	R	12*	<0.1
Rogers Industrial Products	532 S Main Street	Akron	OH	44311	John Cole	330-535-3331	R	12*	<0.1
Hi-Tech Tool Industries Inc.	6701 Ctr. Dr.	Sterling Hgts	MI	48312	Arno Rabin	586-826-8346	R	12*	<0.1
Prim Hall Enterprises Inc.	11 Spellman Rd.	Plattsburgh	NY	12901	John Prim	518-561-7408	R	12*	<0.1
Technical Machine Products	5500 Walworth Ave.	Cleveland	OH	44102	Ted Soberay	216-281-9500	R	11*	<0.1
Taber Industries	455 Bryant Street	N Tonawanda	NY	14120	Dan Slawson	716-694-4000	R	11*	<0.1
Arnold's Welding Service	1405 Waterless St.	Fayetteville	NC	28306	Bill Arnold	910-485-6618	R	11*	<0.1
Winfield Taylor Corp.	PO Box 500	Brookfield	OH	44403	John Anderson	330-448-4464	R	11*	<0.1
Miller Tool and Die Co.	829 Belden Rd.	Jackson	MI	49203	Emmanuel Miller	517-782-0347	R	10*	<0.1
TENNSMITH Inc.	6926 Smithville	Mc Minnville	TN	37110	Douglas Smith	931-934-2211	R	10*	<0.1
Moore's Machine Company	13120 Nc Hwy. 902	Bear Creek	NC	27207	Eugene Moore	919-837-5354	R	10*	0.1
Edmunds Manufacturing Co.	PO Box 385	Farmington	CT	06034	R.F. Edmunds Jr.	860-677-2813	R	10*	0.1
Egenolf Machine Inc.	2916 Bluff Rd.	Indianapolis	IN	46225	James Egenolf	317-787-5301	R	10*	<0.1

Source: *Ward's Business Directory of U.S. Private and Public Companies*, Volumes 1 and 2, 2008. The company type code used is as follows: P - Public, R - Private, S - Subsidiary, D - Division, J - Joint Venture, A - Affiliate, G - Group. Sales are in millions of dollars, employees are in thousands. An asterisk (*) indicates an estimated sales volume. The symbol < stands for 'less than'. Company names and addresses are truncated, in some cases, to fit into the available space.

MATERIALS CONSUMED

Material	Quantity	Delivered Cost ($ million)
Fluid power pumps, motors, and hydrostatic transmissions	(X)	8.0
Fluid power cylinders and rotary actuators (hydraulic and pneumatic)	(X)	2.5
Fluid power filters (hydraulic and pneumatic)	(X)	0.4
Fluid power hose, tube fittings, and assemblies (hydraulic and pneumatic)	(X)	3.0
Fluid power valves (hydraulic and pneumatic)	(X)	3.0
Metal bolts, nuts, screws, and other screw machine products	(X)	2.9
Other fabricated metal products (exc. fluid power products and forgings)	(X)	16.6
Forgings	(X)	1.8
Iron and steel castings (rough and semifinished)	(X)	10.7
Nonferrous (aluminum, copper, etc.) castings (rough and semifinished)	(X)	0.3
Steel bars, bar shapes, and plates (exc. castings, forgings, fabr. metal products)	(X)	14.4
Steel sheet and strip (including tinplate)	(X)	1.4
Steel structural shapes (exc. castings, forgings, fabr. metal products)	(X)	2.9
All other steel shapes and forms (exc. castings, forgings, fabr. metal products)	(X)	3.7
Nonferrous shapes and forms	(X)	2.9
Fractional horsepower electric timing motors (less than 1 hp)	(X)	2.0
Other fractional horsepower electric motors (less than 1 hp)	(X)	0.2
Integral horsepower electric motors and generators (1 hp or more)	(X)	2.7
Electrical transmission, distribution, and control equipment	(X)	4.5
Electrical industrial capacitors, resistors, rheostats, and coil windings	(X)	0.9
Numerical controls, metalworking machinery (exc. programmable)	(X)	2.0
Programmable controllers for metalworking machinery	(X)	6.2
Printed circuit assemblies, loaded boards, and modules	(X)	1.0
Printed circuit boards (without inserted components) for electronic circuitry	(X)	0.3
Semiconductors (incl. transistors, diodes, rectifiers, and integrated circuits), for electronic circuitry	(X)	0.6
All other miscellaneous components and accessories for electronic circuitry (exc. tubes)	(X)	5.1
Electrical instrument mechanisms and meter movements	(X)	1.5
Electronic communication equipment	(X)	0.1
Optical instruments and lenses (exc. sighting, tracking, and fire control)	(X)	0.9
Ball bearings (mounted or unmounted)	(X)	2.3
Roller bearings (mounted or unmounted)	(X)	2.5
Mechanical speed changers, gears, and industrial high-speed drives	(X)	1.8
Wood boxes, pallets, skids, and containers	(X)	1.5
Cutting tools for machine tools	(X)	2.8
Fabricated plastics products (exc. gaskets, hoses, and belting)	(X)	0.2
Paper and paperboard containers (incl. shipping sacks and other paper packaging supplies)	(X)	0.7
All other materials, components, parts, containers, and supplies	(X)	102.8
Materials, ingredients, containers, and supplies, nsk	(X)	181.7

Source: 2002 *Economic Census*. Explanation of symbols used: (D): Withheld to avoid disclosure of competitive data; na: Not available; (S): Withheld because statistical norms were not met; (X): Not applicable; (Z): Less than half the unit shown; nec: Not elsewhere classified; nsk: Not specified by kind; - : zero; p : 10-19 percent estimated; q : 20-29 percent estimated.

PRODUCT SHARE DETAILS

Product or Product Class Shipments	Mil. $	Product or Product Class Shipments	Mil. $
MACHINE TOOLS, METAL FORMING TYPES	1,146.7	Other parts for metal forming machine tools	182.7
Metal punching and shearing machines (including power and manual) and bending and forming machines (power only)	**351.5**	Rebuilt metal forming machine tools (including machines returned to same configuration they were in when new from factory)	9.8
Metalworking presses (except forging and die-stamping presses)	**204.7**	Remanufactured metal forming machine tools (including machines in which the basic carcass is reused and all possible modern improvements have been incorporated)	14.9
Other metal forming machine tools, including forging and die-stamping machines (except metalworking presses)	**228.4**	Parts for metal forming machine tools (sold separately) and rebuilt and remanufactured metal forming machine tools, nsk	7.9
Parts for metal forming machine tools (sold separately) and rebuilt and remanufactured metal forming machine tools	**242.3**	**Machine tools, metal forming types, nsk, total**	**119.8**
Parts for metal forming machine tools (sold separately), rebuilt and remanufactured metal forming machine tools, and die-casting machines	234.4		
Parts for die-casting machines	27.0		

Source: 2002 *Economic Census*. The values are product shipments in millions of dollars for 2002. Total product shipments may be lower or higher than industry shipments. See Introduction for a full discussion. Values of indented subcategories are summed in the main heading(s). The symbol (D) appears when data are withheld to prevent disclosure of competitive information. The abbreviation nsk stands for 'not specified by kind' and nec for 'not elsewhere classified'. A dash (-) means zero.

INPUTS AND OUTPUTS FOR METAL CUTTING AND FORMING MACHINE TOOL MANUFACTURING

Economic Sector or Industry Providing Inputs	%	Sector	Economic Sector or Industry Buying Outputs	%	Sector
Compensation of employees	38.8		Private fixed investment	50.8	
Management of companies & enterprises	7.2	Services	Exports of goods & services	27.5	Cap Inv
Wholesale trade	4.7	Trade	S/L govt. invest., other	4.7	S/L Govt
Iron & steel mills & ferroalloys	4.5	Manufg.	Plate work & fabricated structural products	3.2	Manufg.
Relay & industrial controls	2.7	Manufg.	Nonferrous metal foundries	1.7	Manufg.
Ferrous metal foundries	2.3	Manufg.	General purpose machinery, nec	1.4	Manufg.
Metal cutting & forming machine tools	2.3	Manufg.	Metal cutting & forming machine tools	1.3	Manufg.

Continued on next page.

INPUTS AND OUTPUTS FOR METAL CUTTING AND FORMING MACHINE TOOL MANUFACTURING - Continued

Economic Sector or Industry Providing Inputs	%	Sector	Economic Sector or Industry Buying Outputs	%	Sector
Machine shops	1.9	Manufg.	S/L govt. invest., education	1.3	S/L Govt
Paints & coatings	1.9	Manufg.	Rolling mill & other metalworking machinery	1.3	Manufg.
Ball & roller bearings	1.3	Manufg.	Motor vehicle parts	1.2	Manufg.
Securities, commodity contracts, investments	1.3	Fin/R.E.	Sporting & athletic goods	1.2	Manufg.
Advertising & related services	1.2	Services	Educational services, nec	0.8	Services
Motors & generators	1.1	Manufg.	Federal government, investment, national defense	0.7	Fed Govt
Fluid power process machinery	1.0	Manufg.	Machine shops	0.6	Manufg.
Real estate	1.0	Fin/R.E.	Personal consumption expenditures	0.6	
Valve & fittings other than plumbing	1.0	Manufg.	Fabricated metals, nec	0.5	Manufg.
Speed changers, industrial high-speed drives, & gears	1.0	Manufg.	General S/L govt. services	0.5	S/L Govt
Turned products & screws, nuts, & bolts	1.0	Manufg.	Farm machinery & equipment	0.2	Manufg.
Abrasive products	1.0	Manufg.	Warehousing & storage	0.2	Util.
Custom computer programming services	0.9	Services			
Cutting tools & machine tool accessories	0.8	Manufg.			
Power generation & supply	0.8	Util.			
Printed circuit assemblies (electronic assemblies)	0.8	Manufg.			
Truck transportation	0.7	Util.			
Lessors of nonfinancial assets	0.7	Fin/R.E.			
Coating, engraving, heat treating & allied activities	0.6	Manufg.			
Noncomparable imports	0.6	Foreign			
Taxes on production & imports, less subsidies	0.6				
Monetary authorities/depository credit intermediation	0.5	Fin/R.E.			
Electronic components, nec	0.5	Manufg.			
Telecommunications	0.5	Services			
Legal services	0.5	Services			
Data processing, hosting, & related services	0.5	Services			
Food services & drinking places	0.5	Services			
Professional, scientific, technical services, nec	0.5	Services			
Postal service	0.5	Util.			
Scientific research & development services	0.4	Services			
Custom roll forming	0.4	Manufg.			
Accounting, tax preparation, bookkeeping, & payroll	0.4	Services			
Warehousing & storage	0.4	Util.			
Automotive equipment rental & leasing	0.4	Fin/R.E.			
Electricity & signal testing instruments	0.3	Manufg.			
Wood containers & pallets	0.3	Manufg.			
Fabricated metals, nec	0.3	Manufg.			
Gold, silver, & other metal ore	0.3	Mining			
Hotels & motels, including casino hotels	0.2	Services			
Metal cans, boxes, & other containers (light gauge)	0.2	Manufg.			
Forging, stamping, & sintering, nec	0.2	Manufg.			
Rubber products, nec	0.2	Manufg.			
Services to buildings & dwellings	0.2	Services			
Plastics products, nec	0.2	Manufg.			
Maintenance/repair of nonresidential structures	0.2	Construct.			
Commercial & industrial machinery rental & leasing	0.2	Fin/R.E.			
Management, scientific, & technical consulting	0.2	Services			
Nonmetallic minerals, nec	0.2	Mining			
Air transportation	0.2	Util.			
Natural gas distribution	0.2	Util.			
Crowns & closures & metal stamping	0.2	Manufg.			
Other computer related services, including facilities	0.2	Services			
Architectural, engineering, & related services	0.2	Services			
Plastics packaging materials, film & sheet	0.2	Manufg.			
General purpose machinery, nec	0.2	Manufg.			
Rail transportation	0.2	Util.			
Business support services	0.2	Services			
Plate work & fabricated structural products	0.1	Manufg.			
Chemical products & preparations, nec	0.1	Manufg.			
Handtools	0.1	Manufg.			
Nonferrous metal foundries	0.1	Manufg.			
Nondepository credit intermediation activities	0.1	Fin/R.E.			
Employment services	0.1	Services			
Motor vehicle parts	0.1	Manufg.			
Paperboard mills	0.1	Manufg.			
Automotive repair & maintenance, ex. car washes	0.1	Services			
Specialized design services	0.1	Services			
Bare printed circuit boards	0.1	Manufg.			
Electronic capacitors, resistors, coils, transformers	0.1	Manufg.			
Paperboard containers	0.1	Manufg.			
Commercial & industrial equipment repair/maintenance	0.1	Services			

Source: Benchmark Input-Output Accounts for the U.S. Economy, 2002, U.S. Department of Commerce, Washington D.C., January 2008. User should note that this Input-Output table is not for this particular narrowly defined industry but for a larger aggregate. Input and Output data for Metal Cutting and Forming Machine Tool Manufacturing include Input and Output data for the Annual Survey of Manufactures' NAICS industries 333512 and 333513. The abbreviation nec stands for 'not elsewhere classified'.

OCCUPATIONS EMPLOYED BY METALWORKING MACHINERY MANUFACTURING

Occupation	% of Total 2006	Change to 2016	Occupation	% of Total 2006	Change to 2016
Machinists	12.8	-14.0	Office clerks, general	1.7	-19.3
Tool & die makers	11.0	-14.0	Shipping, receiving, & traffic clerks	1.6	-21.2
Computer-controlled machine tool operators	5.4	-9.9	Welders, cutters, solderers, & brazers	1.6	-12.9
First-line supervisors/managers of production workers	4.6	-18.1	Bookkeeping, accounting, & auditing clerks	1.5	-18.1
Grinding, lapping, polishing machine tool operators	3.3	-20.6	Helpers--Production workers	1.4	-18.1
Cutting, punching, & press machine operators	3.2	-26.3	Sales reps, wholesale & manufacturing, exc tech	1.4	-18.1
Team assemblers	2.9	-18.1	Tool grinders, filers, & sharpeners	1.4	-26.3
Molding, coremaking, & casting machine operators	2.8	-26.3	Numerical tool & process control programmers	1.3	-15.6
Mechanical engineers	2.2	-18.1	Milling & planing machine operators & tenders	1.3	-26.3
General & operations managers	2.0	-26.3	Maintenance & repair workers, general	1.3	-18.1
Inspectors, testers, sorters, samplers, & weighers	2.0	-22.8	Industrial production managers	1.1	-18.1
Mechanical drafters	1.8	-17.2	Janitors & cleaners, exc maids & housekeeping cleaners	1.1	-16.3
Lathe & turning machine tool operators & tenders	1.8	-26.3	Multiple machine tool operators & tenders	1.0	-9.9

Source: Industry-Occupation Matrix, Bureau of Labor Statistics, December 4, 2007. These data are reported based on 4-digit NAICS categories but have been matched to corresponding 6-digit NAICS industry codes. The change reported for each occupation to the year 2016 is a percent of growth or decline as estimated by the Bureau of Labor Statistics. The abbreviation nec stands for 'not elsewhere classified'.

LOCATION BY STATE AND REGIONAL CONCENTRATION

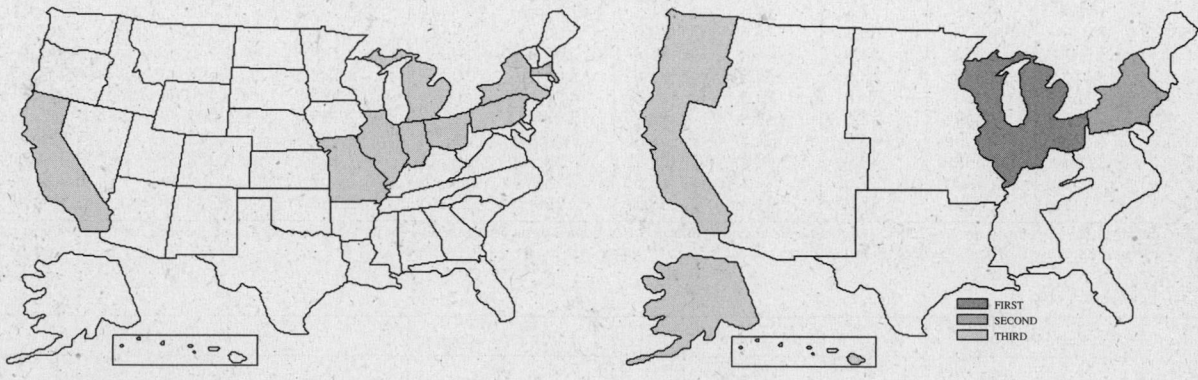

INDUSTRY DATA BY STATE

State	Establish-ments	Shipments Total ($ mil)	Shipments % of U.S.	Shipments Per Establ.	Employment Total Number	Employment % of U.S.	Employment Per Establ.	Wages ($/hour)	Cost as % of Shipments	Investment per Employee ($)
Ohio	20	248.8	22.3	12,438.2	1,684	23.2	84	25.92	43.2	1,977
Michigan	26	179.1	16.0	6,889.9	1,173	16.2	45	21.68	39.9	5,530
Illinois	14	100.1	9.0	7,153.4	584	8.0	42	20.92	44.5	8,284
New York	10	63.1	5.6	6,306.6	401	5.5	40	18.03	44.7	4,554
Pennsylvania	12	62.6	5.6	5,216.1	473	6.5	39	18.60	39.5	10,070
California	14	53.7	4.8	3,832.7	360	5.0	26	18.47	44.7	2,572
Massachusetts	8	38.5	3.4	4,810.3	263	3.6	33	20.07	38.6	5,038
Indiana	9	20.0	1.8	2,220.6	149	2.1	17	17.93	32.2	2,201
Missouri	6	18.8	1.7	3,135.0	153	2.1	25	20.68	37.5	1,072

Source: 2002 *Economic Census*. The states are in descending order of shipments or establishments (if shipment data are missing for the majority). The symbol (D) appears when data are withheld to prevent disclosure of competitive information. States marked with (D) are sorted by number of establishments. A dash (-) indicates that the data element cannot be calculated. Data may not show all states active in the NAICS category. All data available at the time of publication are shown.

NAICS 333514 - SPECIAL DIE AND TOOL, DIE SET, JIG, AND FIXTURE MANUFACTURING

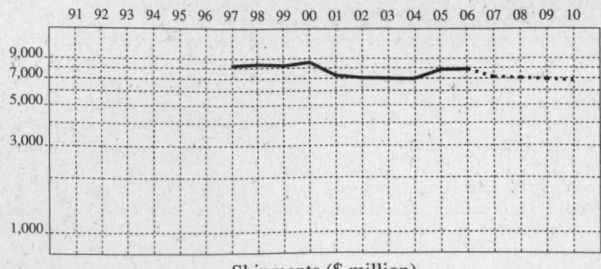

Shipments ($ million)

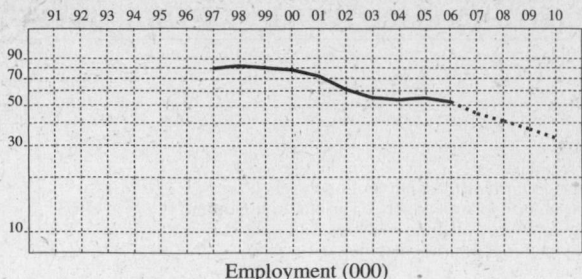

Employment (000)

GENERAL STATISTICS

| Year | Com-panies | Establishments | | Employment | | | Compensation | | Production ($ million) | | | |
		Total	with 20 or more employees	Total (000)	Production Workers (000)	Hours (Mil)	Payroll ($ mil)	Wages ($/hr)	Cost of Materials	Value Added by Manufacture	Value of Shipments	Capital Invest.
1997	4,658	4,735	1,064	79.8	61.9	128.2	3,216.7	17.58	2,373.7	5,924.5	8,217.0	500.7
1998		4,741	1,118	82.3	63.7	135.2	3,274.2	16.85	2,388.8	5,952.4	8,366.5	500.9
1999		4,532	1,057	80.2	61.0	128.6	3,227.4	17.53	2,415.4	5,813.3	8,225.3	543.4
2000		4,368	1,058	78.0	60.0	121.6	3,234.4	18.55	2,611.6	5,933.6	8,565.8	554.0
2001		4,237	995	71.8	54.3	111.7	2,854.1	17.60	2,165.2	5,025.6	7,270.4	351.0
2002	3,660	3,729	800	60.8	44.6	89.0	2,666.5	19.95	2,198.4	4,846.0	7,043.2	270.3
2003		3,531	752	54.9	41.0	85.3	2,563.1	20.59	2,189.6	4,746.6	7,005.1	261.4
2004		3,415	736	53.5	39.0	86.8	2,611.0	20.51	2,199.5	4,698.4	6,968.8	284.3
2005		3,351	740	54.8	39.3	86.6	2,746.3	20.91	2,685.2	5,170.6	7,831.6	334.4
2006		3,058P	649P	52.0	38.0	81.7	2,686.5	21.97	2,737.6	5,008.0	7,858.4	263.8
2007		2,856P	593P	44.9P	31.5P	68.8P	2,449.7P	22.25P	2,483.8P	4,543.7P	7,129.8P	201.4P
2008		2,653P	538P	40.9P	28.1P	62.2P	2,366.3P	22.80P	2,445.4P	4,473.5P	7,019.7P	167.7P
2009		2,450P	483P	37.0P	24.7P	55.5P	2,283.0P	23.35P	2,407.1P	4,403.3P	6,909.6P	134.1P
2010		2,248P	428P	33.0P	21.3P	48.8P	2,199.7P	23.91P	2,368.7P	4,333.2P	6,799.5P	100.4P

Sources: 1997 and 2002 *Economic Census*; other years, up to 2006, are from *Annual Survey of Manufactures*. Establishment counts for non-Census years are from *County Business Patterns*; 1997 and 2002 values are from the 1997 and 2002 censuses, respectively. 'P's show projections by the editors.

INDICES OF CHANGE

| Year | Com-panies | Establishments | | Employment | | | Compensation | | Production ($ million) | | | |
		Total	with 20 or more employees	Total (000)	Production Workers (000)	Hours (Mil)	Payroll ($ mil)	Wages ($/hr)	Cost of Materials	Value Added by Manufacture	Value of Shipments	Capital Invest.
1997	127	127	133	131	139	144	121	88	108	122	117	185
1998		127	140	135	143	152	123	84	109	123	119	185
1999		122	132	132	137	144	121	88	110	120	117	201
2000		117	132	128	135	137	121	93	119	122	122	205
2001		114	124	118	122	126	107	88	98	104	103	130
2002	100	100	100	100	100	100	100	100	100	100	100	100
2003		95	94	90	92	96	96	103	100	98	99	97
2004		92	92	88	87	98	98	103	100	97	99	105
2005		90	93	90	88	97	103	105	122	107	111	124
2006		82P	81P	86	85	92	101	110	125	103	112	98
2007		77P	74P	74P	71P	77P	92P	112P	113P	94P	101P	75P
2008		71P	67P	67P	63P	70P	89P	114P	111P	92P	100P	62P
2009		66P	60P	61P	55P	62P	86P	117P	109P	91P	98P	50P
2010		60P	53P	54P	48P	55P	82P	120P	108P	89P	97P	37P

Sources: Same as General Statistics. Values reflect change from the base year, 2002. Values above 100 mean greater than 2002, values below 100 mean less than 2002, and the values of 100 in other years means the same as 2002. 'P's show projections by the editors.

SELECTED RATIOS

For 2002	Avg. of All Manufact.	Analyzed Industry	Index	For 2002	Avg. of All Manufact.	Analyzed Industry	Index
Employees per Establishment	42	16	39	Value Added per Production Worker	182,367	108,655	60
Payroll per Establishment	1,639,184	715,071	44	Cost per Establishment	5,769,015	589,541	10
Payroll per Employee	39,053	43,857	112	Cost per Employee	137,446	36,158	26
Production Workers per Establishment	30	12	41	Cost per Production Worker	195,506	49,291	25
Wages per Establishment	694,845	476,146	69	Shipments per Establishment	11,158,348	1,888,764	17
Wages per Production Worker	23,548	39,811	169	Shipments per Employee	265,847	115,842	44
Hours per Production Worker	1,980	1,996	101	Shipments per Production Worker	378,144	157,919	42
Wages per Hour	11.89	19.95	168	Investment per Establishment	361,338	72,486	20
Value Added per Establishment	5,381,325	1,299,544	24	Investment per Employee	8,609	4,446	52
Value Added per Employee	128,210	79,704	62	Investment per Production Worker	12,245	6,061	49

Sources: Same as General Statistics. The 'Average of All Manufacturing' column represents the average of all manufacturing industries reported for the most recent complete year available. The Index shows the relationship between the Average and the Analyzed Industry. For example, 100 means that they are equal; 500 that the Analyzed Industry is five times the average; 50 means that the Analyzed Industry is half the national average. The abbreviation 'na' is used to show that data are 'not available'. Ratios shown for 2002, the last complete census year.

LEADING COMPANIES
Number shown: **75**   Total sales ($ mil): **16,265**   Total employment (000): **39.0**

Company Name	Address				CEO Name	Phone	Co. Type	Sales ($ mil)	Empl. (000)
Precise Technology Inc.	501 Mosside Blvd.	N Versailles	PA	15137	Michael Farrell	412-823-2100	R	3,422*	0.3
Connell L.P.	1 International Pl.	Boston	MA	02110	Margot C. Connell	617-737-2700	R	1,429*	2.0
United Plastics Group Inc.	900 Oakmont Ln.	Westmont	IL	60559	Shannon M. White	630-706-5500	R	1,206*	1.7
MTD Products Inc.	PO Box 368022	Cleveland	OH	44136	Curtis E. Moll	330-225-2600	R	1,015*	6.7
Dickten Masch Plastics L.L.C.	N44 Watertown	Nashotah	WI	53058	Douglas Gray	262-367-5200	R	951*	0.2
Progressive Tool & Ind./Wisne	21000 Telegraph Rd.	Southfield	MI	48034	Robert Stoutenburg	248-353-8888	D	733*	5.5
Stahl Specialty Co.	PO Box 6	Kingsville	MO	64061	Kevin Daugherty	816-597-3322	S	681*	0.8
Bachman Machine Co.	4321 N Broadway	St. Louis	MO	63147	William Bachman	314-231-4221	R	656*	0.1
LMT Fette Inc.	1997 Ohio St.	Lisle	IL	60532	Brian Nowicki	630-969-5412	R	558*	0.2
Anchor Lamina America Inc.	PO Box 2540	Farmington Hls	MI	48333	Roy Verstraete	248-489-9122	R	500*	<0.1
Skill Metalforming Technologies	16151 Puritas Ave.	Cleveland	OH	44135	Roger Kalski	216-267-8866	R	352*	0.1
Gruber Systems Inc.	25636 Ave. Stanford	Valencia	CA	91355	John Hoskinson	661-257-4060	R	322*	0.3
Flambeau Corp.	801 Lynn Ave.	Baraboo	WI	53913	Jason C. Souey	608-356-5551	R	212*	3.0
Defiance Metal Products Co.	PO Box 447	Defiance	OH	43512		419-784-5332	R	211*	1.7
MPI International Inc.	2129 Austin Ave.	Rochester	MI	48309		248-853-9010	S	157*	1.0
A. Finkl and Sons Co.	2011 N Southport	Chicago	IL	60614	Joseph Curci	773-975-2510	R	140*	0.4
Northern Engraving Corp.	PO Box 377	Sparta	WI	54656		608-269-6911	R	130*	0.5
G and F Industries Inc.	PO Box 515	Sturbridge	MA	01566	John Argitis	508-347-9132	R	123*	0.2
Duffy Tool & Stamping Ltd.	PO Box 2128	Muncie	IN	47307	Greggory Notestine	765-288-1941	R	113*	0.2
Oberg Industries Inc.	PO Box 368	Freeport	PA	16229		724-295-2121	R	110*	0.5
Trend Technologies L.L.C.	4626 Eucalyptus	Chino	CA	91710		909-597-7861	R	105*	0.1
Dayton Progress Corp.	PO Box 39	Dayton	OH	45405		937-859-5111	S	105*	1.1
GMP Metal Products	3883 Delor Street	Saint Louis	MO	63116		314-481-0300	R	100*	0.2
Major Die and Engineering Co.	1352 Industrial Dr.	Itasca	IL	60143		630-773-3444	R	95*	<0.1
Minster Machine Co.	PO Box 120	Minster	OH	45865	John Winch	419-628-2331	R	91*	0.6
Penn United Technology Inc.	PO Box 399	Saxonburg	PA	16056	Carl Jones	724-352-1507	R	88*	0.7
Gill Industries Inc.	5271 Plainfield Ave	Grand Rapids	MI	49525		616-559-2700	R	88*	0.1
Atlantic Tool and Die Company	19963 Progress Dr.	Strongsville	OH	44149	Frank Mehwald	440-238-6931	R	87*	0.2
Motor City Stampings Inc.	47783 Gratiot Ave.	Chesterfield	MI	48051	Judith Kucway	586-949-8420	R	84*	0.5
Le Sueur Inc.	PO Box 149	Le Sueur	MN	56058	Mark Mueller	507-665-6204	R	82*	0.6
Kop-Flex Inc.	PO Box 1696	Baltimore	MD	21203	Dale Skoch	410-768-2000	R	82*	0.2
Aquarius Brands Inc.	PO Box 3760	Ontario	CA	91761	Dave Abrams	909-395-5200	S	80*	0.1
Innovance Inc.	505 W Front St.	Albert Lea	MN	56007	Mike Larson	507-377-8910	R	79*	<0.1
Toledo Molding and Die Inc.	PO Box 6760	Toledo	OH	43612	Donald Harbaugh	419-470-3950	R	75*	0.1
American Drill Bushing Co.	7141 Paramount	Pico Rivera	CA	90660	A Steele	323-725-1515	R	70*	0.1
Mold-Rite Tool Inc.	33830 Riviera	Fraser	MI	48026	Patrick Greene	586-296-3970	R	68*	0.7
American Household Products	PO Box 310	Leeds	AL	35094	Burns Roensch	205-699-5144	R	68*	<0.1
Kelco Industries Inc.	9210 Country Club	Woodstock	IL	60098	Kevin Kelly	815-338-5521	R	66*	<0.1
A.J.L. Manufacturing Corp.	100 Holleder Pkwy.	Rochester	NY	14615		585-254-1128	R	64*	0.2
Hatch Stamping Co.	635 E Industrial Dr	Chelsea	MI	48118	Daniel Craig	734-475-8628	R	63*	0.2
Aluminum Casting & Engineering	2309 S Lenox St.	Milwaukee	WI	53207	Eckhart Grohmann	414-744-3902	R	62*	0.5
Modineer Co.	PO Box 640	Niles	MI	49120	Michael Dreher	269-683-2550	R	62*	0.1
Victor Plastics Inc.	1125 240th St. NE	North Liberty	IA	52317		319-626-7500	R	58*	0.3
Modern Drop Forge Co.	PO Box 429	Blue Island	IL	60406	Gregory Heim	708-388-1806	R	58*	0.4
LTC Roll and Engineering Co.	23500 John Gorsuch	Clinton Twp	MI	48036	Andrew Ligda	586-465-1023	R	58*	0.2
Tenere Inc.	700 Kelly Ave.	Dresser	WI	54009	Trent Jenson	715-755-2158	R	56*	0.1
Concote Corp.	PO Box 35848	Dallas	TX	75235	Robert Hanton	214-956-0077	R	56*	0.1
Triumph Twist Drill Company	PO Box 9000	Crystal Lake	IL	60039	Arthur Beck	815-459-6250	R	56*	0.5
Mate Precision Tooling Inc.	1295 Lund Blvd.	Anoka	MN	55303	Jack Schneider	763-421-0230	R	56*	0.3
Xaloy Inc.	PO Box 7359	New Castle	PA	16107	Walter Cox	724-656-5600	R	51*	0.2
PME Co's Inc.	13870 E 11 Mile Rd.	Warren	MI	48089	Geoff O'Brien	586-779-8787	R	50*	0.2
Elizabeth Carbide Die Company	PO Box 95	McKeesport	PA	15135	D Keefer	412-751-3000	R	50*	0.1
Jergens Inc.	15700 S Waterloo	Cleveland	OH	44110		216-486-2100	R	49*	0.2
Griffiths Holding Corp.	2717 Niagara Ln. N	Minneapolis	MN	55447	Harold Griffiths	763-557-8935	R	49*	<0.1
Alpha Technology Corp.	PO Box 168	Howell	MI	48844	Stephen Sweda	517-546-9700	R	49*	0.3
Century Mold Company Inc.	25 Vantage Pnt. Dr.	Rochester	NY	14624	Ronald Ricotta	585-352-8600	R	49*	0.2
Alinabal Inc.	28 Woodmont Rd.	Milford	CT	06460	Sam Bergami	203-877-3241	R	49*	0.3
Delta Tooling Co.	1350 Harmon Rd.	Auburn Hills	MI	48326	Peter Mozer	248-391-6800	R	47*	0.1
General Tool Co.	101 Landy Ln.	Cincinnati	OH	45215	William Kramer	513-733-5500	R	45*	0.2
C and A Tool Engineering Inc.	PO Box 94	Churubusco	IN	46723	Richard Conrow	260-693-2167	R	44*	0.3
Landmark Manufacturing Corp.	28100 Quick Ave.	Gallatin	MO	64640	Donald Critten	660-663-2185	R	43*	0.3
Paslin Co.	25411 Ryan Rd.	Warren	MI	48091	Charles Pasque	586-758-0200	R	43*	0.3
Ever Fab Inc.	12928 Big Tree Rd.	East Aurora	NY	14052	Alan Everett	716-652-0772	R	40*	<0.1
Parkview Metal Products Inc.	1275 Ensell Rd.	Lake Zurich	IL	60047	Charles Leutwiler	847-540-2323	R	39*	0.3
Aircom Manufacturing Inc.	PO Box 18054	Indianapolis	IN	46218	Gregory Lyon	317-545-5383	R	38*	0.3
Steinmetz Inc.	PO Box 393	Moscow	PA	18444	Michael Steinmetz	570-842-6161	R	37*	<0.1
Hammill Manufacturing Company	PO Box 1450	Maumee	OH	43537	John Hammill	419-476-0789	R	36*	0.1
Roto-Die Company Inc.	800 Howerton Ln.	Eureka	MO	63025		636-587-3600	R	35*	0.6
Composidie Inc.	1295 State Rte. 380	Apollo	PA	15613	Ted Wohlin	724-727-3466	R	35*	0.2
PTI Engineered Plastics Inc.	44850 Centre Ct. E	Clinton Twp	MI	48038		586-263-5100	R	35*	0.1
Industry Products Co.	PO Box 1158	Piqua	OH	45356	Linda Cleveland	937-778-0585	R	34*	0.3
BTD Manufacturing Inc.	1111 13th Ave. SE	Detroit Lakes	MN	56501	Paul Gitner	218-847-4446	S	34*	0.4
West Troy Tool and Machine	155 Marybill Dr. S	Troy	OH	45373	Earl Davidson	937-339-2192	R	34*	<0.1
Ferriot Inc.	PO Box 7670	Akron	OH	44306	Gordon Keeler	330-786-3000	R	34*	0.3
GW Plastics Inc.	239 Pleasant St.	Bethel	VT	05032	Brenan Riehl	802-234-9941	R	34*	0.4

Source: Ward's Business Directory of U.S. Private and Public Companies, Volumes 1 and 2, 2008. The company type code used is as follows: P - Public, R - Private, S - Subsidiary, D - Division, J - Joint Venture, A - Affiliate, G - Group. Sales are in millions of dollars, employees are in thousands. An asterisk (*) indicates an estimated sales volume. The symbol < stands for 'less than'. Company names and addresses are truncated, in some cases, to fit into the available space.

MATERIALS CONSUMED

Material	Quantity	Delivered Cost ($ million)
Metal bolts, nuts, screws, and other screw machine products	(X)	78.7
Other fabricated metal products (exc. castings and forgings)	(X)	100.5
Forgings	(X)	4.2
Iron and steel castings (rough and semifinished)	(X)	87.7
Nonferrous (aluminum, copper, etc.) castings (rough and semifinished)	(X)	18.4
Steel bars, bar shapes, and plates (exc. castings, forgings, fabr. metal products)	(X)	348.6
Steel sheet and strip (including tinplate)	(X)	28.4
All other steel shapes and forms (exc. castings, forgings, fabr. metal products)	(X)	36.2
Aluminum and aluminum-base alloy sheet, plate, foil, and welded tubing	(X)	13.3
All other aluminum and aluminum-base alloy shapes and forms (exc. castings, forgings, fabr. metal products)	(X)	7.4
Other nonferrous shapes and forms (exc. castings, forgings, fabricated metal products)	(X)	13.1
Tungsten carbide metal powders	(X)	24.4
All other metal powders	(X)	2.5
Industrial diamonds	(X)	7.2
Electrical transmission, distribution, and control equipment	(X)	17.9
Grinding wheels and other abrasive products, exc. industrial diamonds	(X)	11.4
Fluid power products	(X)	25.8
Cutting tools for machine tools	(X)	28.6
All other materials, components, parts, containers, and supplies	(X)	442.3
Materials, ingredients, containers, and supplies, nsk	(X)	368.3

Source: 2002 Economic Census. Explanation of symbols used: (D): Withheld to avoid disclosure of competitive data; na: Not available; (S): Withheld because statistical norms were not met; (X): Not applicable; (Z): Less than half the unit shown; nec: Not elsewhere classified; nsk: Not specified by kind; - : zero; p : 10-19 percent estimated; q : 20-29 percent estimated.

PRODUCT SHARE DETAILS

Product or Product Class Shipments	Mil. $	Product or Product Class Shipments	Mil. $
SPECIAL DIES, TOOLS, JIGS, AND FIXTURES	7,580.5	wiredrawing, and straightening dies	1,020.0
Jigs and fixtures	1,175.0	Metalworking stamping dies (including lamination and blanking), progressive-type, high-speed steel	659.6
Gauging and checking jigs and fixtures, less than 1,000 lb weight	476.4	Metalworking stamping dies (including lamination and blanking), progressive-type, carbide	168.8
Gauging and checking jigs and fixtures, 1,000 lb weight or more	224.3	Metalworking open-type forging dies, including cold forging and heading	53.0
Other than work holding fixtures	99.4	Metalworking closed-type forging dies, including cold forging and heading	(D)
Work holding fixtures	190.3	Metalworking ceramic and ceramic composite extrusion and wiredrawing and straightening dies	(D)
Other jigs and fixtures, 1,000 lb weight or more (holding, positioning, layout, assembly, etc.)	184.6	Metalworking high-speed steel extrusion and wiredrawing and straightening dies	67.1
Standard catalog components and parts for jigs and fixtures, including drill bushings	125.2	All other metalworking dies	517.4
Metalworking forming and drawing dies, all sizes	738.0	Other metalworking extrusion and wiredrawing and straightening dies	156.5
Press brake metalworking dies	72.0	Metalworking carbide extrusion and wiredrawing and straightening dies	38.0
Metalworking forming and drawing dies, 500 lb weight or less	119.1	All other high-speed steel metalworking dies	87.1
Metalworking forming and drawing dies, 501 to 3,000 lb weight	178.1	All other carbide metalworking dies	31.5
Metalworking forming and drawing dies, more than 3,000 lb weight	368.8	All other metalworking dies	114.1
All other metalworking stamping-type dies, lamination and blanking dies (punch, trim, notch, pierce, perforate, etc.)	953.3	Standard and special metalworking die sets	90.1
		Punches for dies	167.9
All other metalworking stamping-type dies, including lamination and blanking dies (punch, trim, notch, pierce, perforate, etc.)	716.4	Standard steel punches for dies	125.3
		Standard carbide punches for dies	24.7
Other metalworking stamping dies (including lamination and blanking), progressive-type	236.9	Other standard punches for dies	17.9
		Industrial models and prototypes	465.8
		Other specially designed tooling	780.9
Metalworking stamping, forging, extrusion, and		Special dies, tools, jigs, and fixtures, nsk, total	1,637.0

Source: 2002 Economic Census. The values are product shipments in millions of dollars for 2002. Total product shipments may be lower or higher than industry shipments. See Introduction for a full discussion. Values of indented subcategories are summed in the main heading(s). The symbol (D) appears when data are withheld to prevent disclosure of competitive information. The abbreviation nsk stands for 'not specified by kind' and nec for 'not elsewhere classified'. A dash (-) means zero.

INPUTS AND OUTPUTS FOR SPECIAL TOOL, DIE, JIG, AND FIXTURE MANUFACTURING

Economic Sector or Industry Providing Inputs	%	Sector	Economic Sector or Industry Buying Outputs	%	Sector
Compensation of employees	46.9		Private fixed investment	81.4	
Iron & steel mills & ferroalloys	7.7	Manufg.	Exports of goods & services	4.4	Cap Inv
Management of companies & enterprises	6.1	Services	Nonferrous metal foundries	2.6	Manufg.
Wholesale trade	3.2	Trade	Special tools, dies, jigs, & fixtures	2.4	Manufg.
Special tools, dies, jigs, & fixtures	3.0	Manufg.	Turned products & screws, nuts, & bolts	1.8	Manufg.
Real estate	1.7	Fin/R.E.	Glass containers	1.0	Manufg.
Turned products & screws, nuts, & bolts	1.6	Manufg.	Motor vehicle parts	0.9	Manufg.

Continued on next page.

INPUTS AND OUTPUTS FOR SPECIAL TOOL, DIE, JIG, AND FIXTURE MANUFACTURING - Continued

Economic Sector or Industry Providing Inputs	%	Sector	Economic Sector or Industry Buying Outputs	%	Sector
Ferrous metal foundries	1.6	Manufg.	Iron & steel mills & ferroalloys	0.9	Manufg.
Rolling mill & other metalworking machinery	1.5	Manufg.	Forging, stamping, & sintering, nec	0.8	Manufg.
Machine shops	1.4	Manufg.	Industrial molds	0.7	Manufg.
Power generation & supply	1.0	Util.	Ferrous metal foundries	0.5	Manufg.
Securities, commodity contracts, investments	1.0	Fin/R.E.	Semiconductors & related devices	0.5	Manufg.
Truck transportation	0.8	Util.	Ball & roller bearings	0.4	Manufg.
Advertising & related services	0.8	Services	Crowns & closures & metal stamping	0.3	Manufg.
Taxes on production & imports, less subsidies	0.8		Industrial machinery, nec	0.3	Manufg.
Semiconductors & related devices	0.8	Manufg.	Semiconductor machinery	0.2	Manufg.
Printed circuit assemblies (electronic assemblies)	0.8	Manufg.	AC, refrigeration, and warm air heating equipment	0.2	Manufg.
Lessors of nonfinancial assets	0.7	Fin/R.E.	Steel products from purchased steel	0.1	Manufg.
Industrial molds	0.6	Manufg.	General S/L govt. services	0.1	S/L Govt
Aluminum products from purchased aluminum	0.6	Manufg.			
Automotive equipment rental & leasing	0.6	Fin/R.E.			
Nonferrous metal (ex. copper & aluminum) processing	0.6	Manufg.			
Cutting tools & machine tool accessories	0.6	Manufg.			
Monetary authorities/depository credit intermediation	0.5	Fin/R.E.			
Accounting, tax preparation, bookkeeping, & payroll	0.5	Services			
Custom computer programming services	0.5	Services			
Food services & drinking places	0.5	Services			
Scientific research & development services	0.5	Services			
Telecommunications	0.5	Services			
Warehousing & storage	0.4	Util.			
Coating, engraving, heat treating & allied activities	0.4	Manufg.			
Data processing, hosting, & related services	0.4	Services			
Professional, scientific, technical services, nec	0.4	Services			
Nonferrous metal foundries	0.4	Manufg.			
Maintenance/repair of nonresidential structures	0.4	Construct.			
Hotels & motels, including casino hotels	0.4	Services			
Services to buildings & dwellings	0.3	Services			
Legal services	0.3	Services			
Valve & fittings other than plumbing	0.3	Manufg.			
Commercial & industrial machinery rental & leasing	0.3	Fin/R.E.			
Fluid power process machinery	0.3	Manufg.			
Management, scientific, & technical consulting	0.3	Services			
Relay & industrial controls	0.2	Manufg.			
Air transportation	0.2	Util.			
Automotive repair & maintenance, ex. car washes	0.2	Services			
Abrasive products	0.2	Manufg.			
Commercial & industrial equipment repair/maintenance	0.2	Services			
Fabricated metals, nec	0.2	Manufg.			
Natural gas distribution	0.2	Util.			
Other computer related services, including facilities	0.2	Services			
Rail transportation	0.2	Util.			
Chemical products & preparations, nec	0.2	Manufg.			
Metal cans, boxes, & other containers (light gauge)	0.2	Manufg.			
Plastics packaging materials, film & sheet	0.2	Manufg.			
Paperboard containers	0.2	Manufg.			
Crowns & closures & metal stamping	0.1	Manufg.			
Nonmetallic mineral products, nec	0.1	Manufg.			
Nonmetallic minerals, nec	0.1	Mining			
Paperboard mills	0.1	Manufg.			
Plate work & fabricated structural products	0.1	Manufg.			
Custom roll forming	0.1	Manufg.			
Bare printed circuit boards	0.1	Manufg.			
Forging, stamping, & sintering, nec	0.1	Manufg.			
Electronic & precision equipment repair/maintenance	0.1	Services			

Source: Benchmark Input-Output Accounts for the U.S. Economy, 2002, U.S. Department of Commerce, Washington, D.C., January 2008. The abbreviation nec stands for 'not elsewhere classified'.

OCCUPATIONS EMPLOYED BY METALWORKING MACHINERY MANUFACTURING

Occupation	% of Total 2006	Change to 2016	Occupation	% of Total 2006	Change to 2016
Machinists	12.8	-14.0	Office clerks, general	1.7	-19.3
Tool & die makers	11.0	-14.0	Shipping, receiving, & traffic clerks	1.6	-21.2
Computer-controlled machine tool operators	5.4	-9.9	Welders, cutters, solderers, & brazers	1.6	-12.9
First-line supervisors/managers of production workers	4.6	-18.1	Bookkeeping, accounting, & auditing clerks	1.5	-18.1
Grinding, lapping, polishing machine tool operators	3.3	-20.6	Helpers--Production workers	1.4	-18.1
Cutting, punching, & press machine operators	3.2	-26.3	Sales reps, wholesale & manufacturing, exc tech	1.4	-18.1
Team assemblers	2.9	-18.1	Tool grinders, filers, & sharpeners	1.4	-26.3
Molding, coremaking, & casting machine operators	2.8	-26.3	Numerical tool & process control programmers	1.3	-15.6
Mechanical engineers	2.2	-18.1	Milling & planing machine operators & tenders	1.3	-26.3
General & operations managers	2.0	-26.3	Maintenance & repair workers, general	1.3	-18.1
Inspectors, testers, sorters, samplers, & weighers	2.0	-22.8	Industrial production managers	1.1	-18.1
Mechanical drafters	1.8	-17.2	Janitors & cleaners, exc maids & housekeeping cleaners	1.1	-16.3
Lathe & turning machine tool operators & tenders	1.8	-26.3	Multiple machine tool operators & tenders	1.0	-9.9

Source: *Industry-Occupation Matrix*, Bureau of Labor Statistics, December 4, 2007. These data are reported based on 4-digit NAICS categories but have been matched to corresponding 6-digit NAICS industry codes. The change reported for each occupation to the year 2016 is a percent of growth or decline as estimated by the Bureau of Labor Statistics. The abbreviation nec stands for 'not elsewhere classified'.

LOCATION BY STATE AND REGIONAL CONCENTRATION

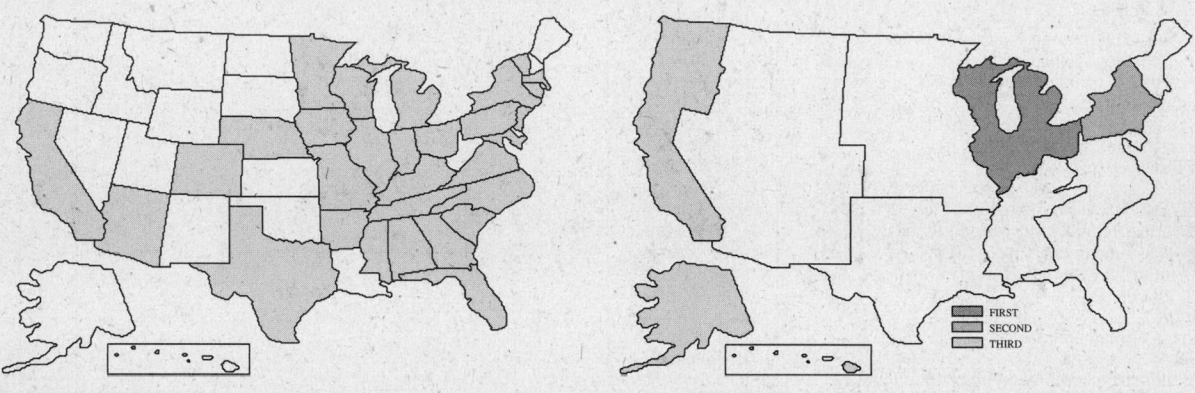

FIRST
SECOND
THIRD

INDUSTRY DATA BY STATE

State	Establishments	Shipments Total ($ mil)	Shipments % of U.S.	Shipments Per Establ.	Employment Total Number	Employment % of U.S.	Employment Per Establ.	Wages ($/hour)	Cost as % of Shipments	Investment per Employee ($)
Michigan	748	2,466.2	35.0	3,297.0	18,413	30.3	25	22.34	31.9	5,228
Ohio	380	823.3	11.7	2,166.7	6,828	11.2	18	19.12	32.9	4,860
Illinois	288	502.3	7.1	1,744.2	4,217	6.9	15	19.56	31.0	4,224
Pennsylvania	234	369.3	5.2	1,578.1	3,836	6.3	16	19.14	26.0	2,909
Wisconsin	180	366.7	5.2	2,037.0	3,264	5.4	18	19.90	25.7	4,566
California	266	331.2	4.7	1,245.0	2,942	4.8	11	17.32	35.9	5,158
Indiana	207	312.4	4.4	1,509.2	3,203	5.3	15	19.01	29.6	3,910
Minnesota	81	224.3	3.2	2,768.9	1,994	3.3	25	21.24	25.2	2,073
Vermont	11	189.5	2.7	17,231.5	1,169	1.9	106	19.76	64.3	6,020
New York	138	166.7	2.4	1,208.0	1,763	2.9	13	18.70	29.4	3,727
Missouri	64	125.0	1.8	1,953.7	1,037	1.7	16	15.33	30.3	4,163
Tennessee	107	125.0	1.8	1,168.2	1,330	2.2	12	20.40	28.8	3,795
Connecticut	108	115.1	1.6	1,066.0	1,147	1.9	11	20.44	28.3	3,311
Texas	90	80.9	1.1	899.4	882	1.4	10	19.47	24.2	7,211
Florida	71	69.4	1.0	978.1	651	1.1	9	15.66	26.3	2,095
Alabama	30	63.6	0.9	2,120.4	871	1.4	29	13.69	27.7	5,319
New Jersey	92	62.1	0.9	674.6	565	0.9	6	19.77	25.0	5,156
North Carolina	59	61.4	0.9	1,041.1	632	1.0	11	16.32	20.1	2,679
Georgia	44	55.1	0.8	1,252.8	462	0.8	10	19.77	27.4	2,208
Massachusetts	75	52.4	0.7	698.7	544	0.9	7	21.37	24.9	2,502
Iowa	38	49.2	0.7	1,295.8	518	0.9	14	19.74	29.6	5,533
Kentucky	53	48.1	0.7	908.3	581	1.0	11	17.73	25.4	5,718
Virginia	22	46.2	0.7	2,100.5	363	0.6	16	15.44	20.7	1,444
South Carolina	30	36.6	0.5	1,221.1	362	0.6	12	20.08	28.0	2,334
Rhode Island	30	30.9	0.4	1,031.1	286	0.5	10	17.76	24.2	5,311
Nebraska	12	28.2	0.4	2,350.8	419	0.7	35	13.63	36.0	1,950
Arkansas	29	24.4	0.3	840.4	304	0.5	10	17.69	30.7	1,711
Arizona	29	23.0	0.3	794.4	270	0.4	9	21.24	27.2	3,456
Mississippi	23	22.5	0.3	979.1	281	0.5	12	15.15	35.5	3,648

Continued on next page.

INDUSTRY DATA BY STATE - Continued

| State | Establish-ments | Shipments | | | Employment | | | | Cost as % of Shipments | Investment per Employee ($) |
		Total ($ mil)	% of U.S.	Per Establ.	Total Number	% of U.S.	Per Establ.	Wages ($/hour)		
Colorado	25	19.7	0.3	788.6	210	0.3	8	21.29	28.4	2,543
Maryland	15	18.2	0.3	1,212.9	174	0.3	12	17.70	28.7	3,333

Source: 2002 *Economic Census*. The states are in descending order of shipments or establishments (if shipment data are missing for the majority). The symbol (D) appears when data are withheld to prevent disclosure of competitive information. States marked with (D) are sorted by number of establishments. A dash (-) indicates that the data element cannot be calculated. Data may not show all states active in the NAICS category. All data available at the time of publication are shown.

NAICS 333515 - CUTTING TOOL AND MACHINE TOOL ACCESSORY MANUFACTURING

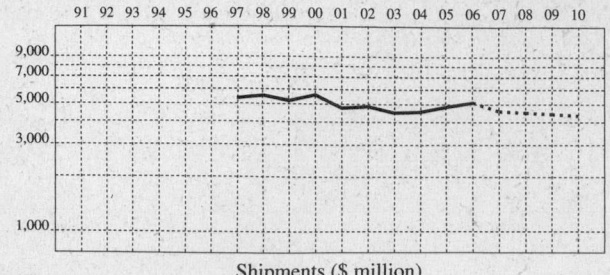

Shipments ($ million)

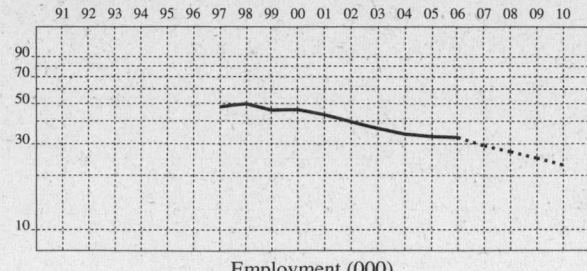

Employment (000)

GENERAL STATISTICS

Year	Com-panies	Establishments		Employment			Compensation		Production ($ million)			
		Total	with 20 or more employees	Total (000)	Production Workers (000)	Hours (Mil)	Payroll ($ mil)	Wages ($/hr)	Cost of Materials	Value Added by Manufacture	Value of Shipments	Capital Invest.
1997	1,816	1,916	499	47.8	34.7	70.6	1,639.9	14.76	1,795.0	3,581.0	5,335.8	275.9
1998		1,912	517	49.7	35.8	72.0	1,712.6	15.11	1,930.4	3,709.1	5,531.4	301.1
1999		1,892	496	45.9	32.5	66.5	1,634.7	15.49	1,882.5	3,299.3	5,197.8	300.1
2000		1,872	508	46.2	32.7	65.4	1,721.5	16.31	1,945.3	3,685.2	5,597.6	283.3
2001		1,837	497	43.3	30.4	60.3	1,568.9	16.05	1,582.7	3,146.2	4,766.1	202.1
2002	1,803	1,890	441	39.6	27.5	53.3	1,536.0	17.68	1,492.2	3,333.0	4,859.4	196.7
2003		1,503	383	36.4	25.4	50.6	1,455.5	17.33	1,409.7	3,057.7	4,499.0	228.1
2004		1,591	416	33.9	23.6	46.7	1,447.8	18.15	1,514.4	3,056.7	4,544.9	184.0
2005		1,592	414	32.9	23.3	47.0	1,439.5	18.42	1,690.9	3,126.1	4,840.8	183.3
2006		1,527P	385P	32.5	23.4	47.5	1,464.6	18.95	1,901.9	3,197.3	5,112.4	235.3
2007		1,476P	370P	29.2P	20.3P	40.2P	1,386.9P	19.45P	1,705.6P	2,867.3P	4,584.8P	174.3P
2008		1,426P	354P	27.1P	18.7P	37.0P	1,355.1P	19.93P	1,675.6P	2,816.9P	4,504.1P	162.5P
2009		1,376P	339P	25.0P	17.2P	33.7P	1,323.2P	20.41P	1,645.6P	2,766.4P	4,423.4P	150.7P
2010		1,325P	323P	22.9P	15.6P	30.5P	1,291.4P	20.89P	1,615.6P	2,716.0P	4,342.8P	139.0P

Sources: 1997 and 2002 *Economic Census*; other years, up to 2006, are from *Annual Survey of Manufactures*. Establishment counts for non-Census years are from *County Business Patterns*; 1997 and 2002 values are from the 1997 and 2002 censuses, respectively. 'P's show projections by the editors.

INDICES OF CHANGE

Year	Com-panies	Establishments		Employment			Compensation		Production ($ million)			
		Total	with 20 or more employees	Total (000)	Production Workers (000)	Hours (Mil)	Payroll ($ mil)	Wages ($/hr)	Cost of Materials	Value Added by Manufacture	Value of Shipments	Capital Invest.
1997	101	101	113	121	126	132	107	83	120	107	110	140
1998		101	117	126	130	135	111	85	129	111	114	153
1999		100	112	116	118	125	106	88	126	99	107	153
2000		99	115	117	119	123	112	92	130	111	115	144
2001		97	113	109	111	113	102	91	106	94	98	103
2002	100	100	100	100	100	100	100	100	100	100	100	100
2003		80	87	92	92	95	95	98	94	92	93	116
2004		84	94	86	86	88	94	103	101	92	94	94
2005		84	94	83	85	88	94	104	113	94	100	93
2006		81P	87P	82	85	89	95	107	127	96	105	120
2007		78P	84P	74P	74P	75P	90P	110P	114P	86P	94P	89P
2008		75P	80P	68P	68P	69P	88P	113P	112P	85P	93P	83P
2009		73P	77P	63P	63P	63P	86P	115P	110P	83P	91P	77P
2010		70P	73P	58P	57P	57P	84P	118P	108P	81P	89P	71P

Sources: Same as General Statistics. Values reflect change from the base year, 2002. Values above 100 mean greater than 2002, values below 100 mean less than 2002, and the values of 100 in other years means the same as 2002. 'P's show projections by the editors.

SELECTED RATIOS

For 2002	Avg. of All Manufact.	Analyzed Industry	Index	For 2002	Avg. of All Manufact.	Analyzed Industry	Index
Employees per Establishment	42	21	50	Value Added per Production Worker	182,367	121,200	66
Payroll per Establishment	1,639,184	812,698	50	Cost per Establishment	5,769,015	789,524	14
Payroll per Employee	39,053	38,788	99	Cost per Employee	137,446	37,682	27
Production Workers per Establishment	30	15	49	Cost per Production Worker	195,506	54,262	28
Wages per Establishment	694,845	498,595	72	Shipments per Establishment	11,158,348	2,571,111	23
Wages per Production Worker	23,548	34,267	146	Shipments per Employee	265,847	122,712	46
Hours per Production Worker	1,980	1,938	98	Shipments per Production Worker	378,144	176,705	47
Wages per Hour	11.89	17.68	149	Investment per Establishment	361,338	104,074	29
Value Added per Establishment	5,381,325	1,763,492	33	Investment per Employee	8,609	4,967	58
Value Added per Employee	128,210	84,167	66	Investment per Production Worker	12,245	7,153	58

Sources: Same as General Statistics. The 'Average of All Manufacturing' column represents the average of all manufacturing industries reported for the most recent complete year available. The Index shows the relationship between the Average and the Analyzed Industry. For example, 100 means that they are equal; 500 that the Analyzed Industry is five times the average; 50 means that the Analyzed Industry is half the national average. The abbreviation 'na' is used to show that data are 'not available'. Ratios shown for 2002, the last complete census year.

LEADING COMPANIES   Number shown: 75   Total sales ($ mil): **47,434**   Total employment (000): **126.2**

Company Name	Address				CEO Name	Phone	Co. Type	Sales ($ mil)	Empl. (000)
Danaher Corp.	2099 Penn. Avenue	Washington	DC	20006	H. Lawrence Culp Jr.	202-828-0850	P	11,026	50.0
Seco Holding Company Inc.	11177 E 8 Mile Rd.	Warren	MI	48089	Bruce Belden	586-497-5000	R	9,960*	0.3
Saint-Gobain Abrasives Inc.	1 New Bond St.	Worcester	MA	01606	Jean Phelizon	508-795-5000	R	6,831*	2.5
Carl Zeiss IMT Corp.	6250 Sycamore N	Osseo	MN	55369	Gregory Lee	763-744-2400	R	4,420*	0.1
Kennametal Inc.	PO Box 231	Latrobe	PA	15650	Carlos M. Cardoso	724-539-5000	P	2,386	14.0
Regal-Beloit Corp.	200 State St.	Beloit	WI	53511		608-364-8800	P	1,803	17.9
Actuant Corp.	13000 W Slvr Spring	Butler	WI	53007	Bob Arzbaecher	414-352-4160	P	1,459	6.3
Federal Signal Corp.	1415 W 22nd St.	Oak Brook	IL	60523	James C. Janning	630-954-2000	P	1,268	5.5
TriMas Corp.	39400 Woodward	Bloomfield Hls	MI	48304	Grant Beard	248-631-5450	P	1,068	5.1
MSC Industrial Supply Co.	75 Maxess Rd.	Melville	NY	11747	Mitchell Jacobson	516-812-2000	D	785*	2.8
Blount Inc.	PO Box 22127	Portland	OR	97269	James S. Osterman	503-653-8881	S	583*	3.0
NGK Spark Plugs (U.S.A.) Inc.	46929 Megellan	Wixom	MI	48393	Shinichi Oda	248-926-6900	D	567*	0.6
LMT Fette Inc.	1997 Ohio St.	Lisle	IL	60532	Brian Nowicki	630-969-5412	R	558*	0.2
Anchor Lamina America Inc.	PO Box 2540	Farmington Hls	MI	48333	Roy Verstraete	248-489-9122	R	500*	<0.1
Metalworking Products	1 Teledyne Pl.	La Vergne	TN	37086	David M. Hogan	615-641-4200	S	402*	1.0
Hardinge Inc.	PO Box 1507	Elmira	NY	14902	J. Patrick Ervin	607-734-2281	P	327	1.5
Trumpf Inc.	111 Hyde Rd.	Farmington	CT	06032	Rolf Biekert	860-255-6000	S	278*	0.6
Regal-Beloit Flight Services	200 State St.	Beloit	WI	53511	Henry W. Knueppel	608-364-8800	S	275*	1.0
Mitutoyo America Corp.	965 Corporate Blvd.	Aurora	IL	60504		630-820-9666	R	198*	0.2
Charles Machine Works Inc.	PO Box 66	Perry	OK	73077	Ed Malzahn	580-336-4402	R	132*	1.2
Powers Fasteners Inc.	200 Petersville Rd.	New Rochelle	NY	10801		914-235-6300	R	130*	0.3
CB Manufacturing and Sales Co.	PO Box 37	West Carrollton	OH	45449	Charlie Biehn	937-866-5986	R	111*	0.1
Oberg Industries Inc.	PO Box 368	Freeport	PA	16229		724-295-2121	R	110*	0.5
Kurt Manufacturing Company	5280 Main St. NE	Fridley	MN	55421		763-572-1500	R	101*	0.3
Kyocera Tycom North America	17862 Fitch	Irvine	CA	92614	Scott Yardley	949-955-0800	S	81*	0.3
Hexagon Metrology Inc.	250 Circuit Dr.	N Kingstown	RI	02852	William Gruber	401-886-2000	R	78*	0.7
Nachi America Inc.	715 Pushville Rd.	Greenwood	IN	46143	Steve Itoh	317-535-3675	S	76*	<0.1
American Drill Bushing Co.	7141 Paramount	Pico Rivera	CA	90660	A Steele	323-725-1515	R	70*	0.1
US Tool Grinding Inc.	701 S Desloge Dr.	Flat River	MO	63601	Bruce Williams	573-431-3856	R	63*	0.3
Henry Technologies Inc.	1 ABC Pkwy.	Beloit	WI	53511	Charlie Graham	608-361-4400	R	62*	<0.1
Thomas G Faria Corp.	PO Box 983	Uncasville	CT	06382	David Blackburn	860-848-9271	R	57*	0.3
PHB Inc.	7900 W Ridge Rd.	Fairview	PA	16415	William Hilbert	814-474-5511	R	57*	0.6
Triumph Twist Drill Company	PO Box 9000	Crystal Lake	IL	60039	Arthur Beck	815-459-6250	R	56*	0.5
Mate Precision Tooling Inc.	1295 Lund Blvd.	Anoka	MN	55303	Jack Schneider	763-421-0230	R	56*	0.3
Designatronics Inc.	PO Box 5416	New Hyde Park	NY	11042		516-328-3300	R	51*	0.3
Freud America Inc.	PO Box 7187	High Point	NC	27264	Russell Kohl	336-434-3171	R	51*	0.1
Regal Cutting Tools	5330 E Rockton Rd.	South Beloit	IL	61080	Gene Zumba		D	50*	0.3
Small Precision Tools Inc.	1330 Clegg St.	Petaluma	CA	94954		707-765-4545	S	49*	0.2
Estwing Manufacturing Company	2647 8th St.	Rockford	IL	61109		815-397-9521	R	47*	0.4
Tawas Tool Company Inc.	756 Aulerich Rd.	East Tawas	MI	48730	Bradley Lawton	989-362-6121	R	47*	<0.1
Thielenhaus Microfinish Corp.	42925 W 9 Mile Rd.	Novi	MI	48375	Manfred Sieringhaus	248-349-9450	R	45*	0.3
Continental Machines Inc.	5505 W 123rd St.	Savage	MN	55378	M Johnson	952-890-3300	R	45*	0.2
C and A Tool Engineering Inc.	PO Box 94	Churubusco	IN	46723	Richard Conrow	260-693-2167	R	44*	0.3
Apex-Cooper Tools Div.	PO Box 952	Dayton	OH	45401	Kirk Hachigian	937-222-7871	D	44*	0.4
Auto Meter Products Inc.	413 W Elm St.	Sycamore	IL	60178	Jeff King	815-895-8141	R	43*	0.2
Galaxy Industries Inc.	231 Jandus Rd.	Cary	IL	60013	Joseph Lebar	847-639-8580	R	43*	0.1
Royal Oak Industries Inc.	PO Box 127	Lake Orion	MI	48361	Daniel Carroll	248-340-9200	R	43*	0.4
Paslin Co.	25411 Ryan Rd.	Warren	MI	48091	Charles Pasque	586-758-0200	R	43*	0.3
Fastcut Tool Corp.	200 Front St.	Millersburg	PA	17061	Bill Coyle	717-692-8232	S	42*	<0.1
Ever Fab Inc.	12928 Big Tree Rd.	East Aurora	NY	14052	Alan Everett	716-652-0772	R	40*	<0.1
Hycalog	7211 N Gessner Dr.	Houston	TX	77036	John Deane	713-934-6600	D	40*	0.3
US Union Tool Inc.	6955 Aragon Cir.	Buena Park	CA	90620		714-521-6242	R	37*	0.2
Hammill Manufacturing Company	PO Box 1450	Maumee	OH	43537	John Hammill	419-476-0789	R	36*	0.1
LE Jones Co.	1200 34th Ave.	Menominee	MI	49858		906-863-4411	R	35*	0.2
EHR Enterprises Inc.	1604 Michigan Ave.	New Holstein	WI	53061	Edward Jones	920-898-2180	R	35*	<0.1
NC Industries Inc.	200 J J Audubon	Amherst	NY	14228	Roger Bollier	716-689-8400	R	34*	<0.1
DTI Lebanon Subsidiary Inc.	PO Box 512	Lebanon	MO	65536	Tom Kowall	417-532-2142	R	33*	0.3
Strippit Inc.	12975 Clarence Ctr.	Akron	NY	14001	John Lesebbre	716-542-4511	R	32*	0.2
Kurt J Lesker Co.	1925 Rte. 51 Ste. 1	Clairton	PA	15025	Kurt Lesker	412-233-0801	R	32*	0.2
Ingersoll Cutting Tool Co.	845 S Lyford Rd.	Rockford	IL	61108	Ilan Geri	815-387-6600	R	31*	0.3
PMC Industries Corp.	29100 Lakeland	Wickliffe	OH	44092		440-943-3300	S	31*	0.2
SS White Technologies Inc.	151 O New Brnswck	Piscataway	NJ	08854	Rahul Shukla	732-752-8300	R	31*	0.2
Reed-Rico	18 Industrial Dr.	Holden	MA	01520	Bruce Hutchinson	508-829-4491	D	30*	0.3
Guhring Inc.	PO Box 643	Brookfield	WI	53008	Jorg Guhring	262-784-6730	R	30*	0.3
Saegertown Manufacturing Corp.	PO Box 828	Saegertown	PA	16433	Chalmer Jordan	814-763-2655	R	30*	0.2
Moore Tool Company Inc.	PO Box 4088	Bridgeport	CT	06607	Newman Marsilius	203-366-3224	S	29*	0.1
Pmt Group Inc.	800 Union Ave.	Bridgeport	CT	06607	Newman Marsilius	203-367-8675	S	29*	0.1
Regal Cutting Tools	5330 E Rockton Rd.	Roscoe	IL	61073		815-389-3461	R	29*	0.3
Rollway Bearing International	PO Box 4827	Syracuse	NY	13221	Bill Eames		S	29*	0.2
E and E Engineering Inc.	PO Box 67000	Detroit	MI	48267	Matthew Hirzel	586-978-3800	R	28*	<0.1
Allied Machine & Engineering	PO Box 36	Dover	OH	44622	William Stokey	330-343-4283	R	28*	0.3
Excellon Automation Co.	20001 S Rancho	R Dominguez	CA	90220	David Balsbough	310-668-7700	S	27*	0.3
Husqvarna Construction Prods	10250 Two Notch	Columbia	SC	29229		803-788-8860	S	27*	0.2
Anderson Cook Inc.	17650 15 Mile Rd.	Fraser	MI	48026	Kim Anderson	586-293-0800	R	26*	<0.1
Tool-Flo Manufacturing Inc.	7803 Hansen Rd.	Houston	TX	77061	Dennis Flolo	713-941-1080	R	26*	0.1

Source: Ward's Business Directory of U.S. Private and Public Companies, Volumes 1 and 2, 2008. The company type code used is as follows: P - Public, R - Private, S - Subsidiary, D - Division, J - Joint Venture, A - Affiliate, G - Group. Sales are in millions of dollars, employees are in thousands. An asterisk (*) indicates an estimated sales volume. The symbol < stands for 'less than'. Company names and addresses are truncated, in some cases, to fit into the available space.

MATERIALS CONSUMED

Material	Quantity	Delivered Cost ($ million)
Metal bolts, nuts, screws, and other screw machine products	(X)	18.0
Other fabricated metal products (exc. castings and forgings)	(X)	47.0
Forgings	(X)	2.0
Iron and steel castings (rough and semifinished)	(X)	29.7
Nonferrous (aluminum, copper, etc.) castings (rough and semifinished)	(X)	6.0
Steel bars, bar shapes, and plates (exc. castings, forgings, fabr. metal products)	(X)	172.2
Steel sheet and strip (including tinplate)	(X)	7.0
All other steel shapes and forms (exc. castings, forgings, fabr. metal products)	(X)	30.2
Aluminum and aluminum-base alloy sheet, plate, foil, and welded tubing	(X)	2.0
All other aluminum and aluminum-base alloy shapes and forms (exc. castings, forgings, fabr. metal products)	(X)	6.5
Other nonferrous shapes and forms (exc. castings, forgings, fabricated metal products)	(X)	13.3
Tungsten carbide metal powders	(X)	203.5
All other metal powders	(X)	3.2
Industrial diamonds	(X)	31.0
Electrical transmission, distribution, and control equipment	(X)	11.1
Grinding wheels and other abrasive products, exc. industrial diamonds	(X)	38.7
Fluid power products	(X)	11.4
Cutting tools for machine tools	(X)	37.4
All other materials, components, parts, containers, and supplies	(X)	225.5
Materials, ingredients, containers, and supplies, nsk	(X)	228.3

Source: 2002 *Economic Census*. Explanation of symbols used: (D): Withheld to avoid disclosure of competitive data; na: Not available; (S): Withheld because statistical norms were not met; (X): Not applicable; (Z): Less than half the unit shown; nec: Not elsewhere classified; nsk: Not specified by kind; - : zero; p : 10-19 percent estimated; q : 20-29 percent estimated.

PRODUCT SHARE DETAILS

Product or Product Class Shipments	Mil. $	Product or Product Class Shipments	Mil. $
CUTTING TOOL AND MACHINE TOOL ACCESSORIES	4,455.0	Other carbide indexible and throwaway inserts	123.6
Small cutting tools for machine tools and metalworking machinery	**2,863.3**	Carbide inserts, other than indexible and throwaway types	42.5
Other cutting tools for machine tools, nec, except tips and blanks sold separately	794.9	Thread-rolling dies, including circular, flat, and planetary	11.3
Broaches (except holders and burnishing bars)	303.5	Other threading tools, including screw plates and threading sets	15.0
Carbon steel and high-speed steel reamers (except gun reamers), including blades sold separately	45.2	Other carbon steel cutting tools, nec	81.7
Solid and tipped carbide reamers, except gun reamers and tips and blanks sold separately, but including replaceable blades sold separately	135.0	Other high-speed steel cutting tools, nec	68.0
		Ceramic indexible and throwaway inserts	54.4
Hobs (all types)	36.3	Indexible and throwaway inserts other than carbide and ceramic	18.0
Gear shaper cutters and gear shaving cutters	27.0	Ceramic inserts, other than indexible and throwaway types	0.2
Single and double point cutting tools	53.4		
Circular form cutting tools, including semifinished blanks	36.5	Inserts, other than carbide and ceramic, other than indexible and throwaway	15.0
Other solid and tipped carbide cutting tools, nec, except tips and blanks sold separately	158.0	Taps (excluding taps in threading sets and screw plates and inserted chaser types)	122.2
Carbon steel and high-speed steel shank twist drills for machine tools and metalworking machinery (excluding combined drills, countersinks, and gun drills)	262.3	Precision ground carbide indexible and throwaway inserts	217.4
		Small cutting tools, nsk	86.0
Taper shank twist drills	13.8	**Other attachments and accessories**	**962.8**
Straight shank twist drills	248.5	Other attachments and accessories	910.0
Twist drills, gun drills, combined drills, countersinks, and counterbores	302.2	Holders for turning tools, mechanically clamping for inserts and bits (except box tools and screw machine tool holders)	127.1
Masonry twist drill bits	38.7	Holders for boring bars and heads	25.5
Solid and tipped carbide twist drills	144.1	Holders for drilling, reaming, and tapping chucks	59.7
Gun drills and gun reamers	31.7	Holders for special tooling and attachments for screw and automatic machines (box tools, tool holders, turrets, rollers, etc.)	144.9
Combination drills and countersinks	57.1		
Countersinks	19.7		
Counterbores	10.8	Holders for die heads and tap bodies for chaser-type threading and thread-rolling heads (excluding hand-type die stocks)	18.7
End mills and milling cutters	457.9		
High-speed steel end mills, except inserted blade types and shell mills	139.9	Other tool holders, including other chucks, drill heads, tool posts, turrets, sleeves, sockets, etc.	68.5
Solid and tipped carbide end mills, except inserted blade types, shell mills, and blades sold separately	143.0	Tracer and tapering attachments, safety devices, centers, dogs, work rests, chutes, etc.	26.4
Nonindexible inserted blade type milling cutters	25.6	Lathe chucks	18.5
Indexible and throwaway insert type milling cutters	99.1	Rotary tables, including numerically controlled	21.0
High-speed steel milling cutters, nec	43.0	Indexing work holders, excluding rotary tables	29.2
Solid and tipped carbide milling cutters, nec, except tips and blades sold separately	7.2	Collets, jaws, vises	75.5
Threading tools, including blanks, tips, and inserts	620.4	Tool room specialties (including levels, angle plates, parallels, sine bars, V-blocks, flats, etc.)	21.4
Dies, with two or more thread-forming edges integral with the body, except metalworking dies	33.2	Collets, jaws, or vises such as mandrels, feeding fingers clamps, stops, etc.	33.3
Chasers, single edge thread-cutting, circular blade and tangent types for mount in-on holders, die heads, and tap bodies	64.9	Other attachments and accessories	240.1
		Other attachments and accessories, nsk	52.8
Molded blanks and tips, except press-to-size inserts	92.3	**Cutting tool and machine tool accessories, nsk, total**	**628.8**

Source: 2002 *Economic Census*. The values are product shipments in millions of dollars for 2002. Total product shipments may be lower or higher than industry shipments. See Introduction for a full discussion. Values of indented subcategories are summed in the main heading(s). The symbol (D) appears when data are withheld to prevent disclosure of competitive information. The abbreviation nsk stands for 'not specified by kind' and nec for 'not elsewhere classified'. A dash (-) means zero.

INPUTS AND OUTPUTS FOR CUTTING TOOL AND MACHINE TOOL ACCESSORY MANUFACTURING

Economic Sector or Industry Providing Inputs	%	Sector	Economic Sector or Industry Buying Outputs	%	Sector
Compensation of employees	41.7		Exports of goods & services	11.6	Cap Inv
Management of companies & enterprises	7.6	Services	Motor vehicle parts	4.5	Manufg.
Nonferrous metal (ex. copper & aluminum) processing	5.6	Manufg.	Wholesale trade	3.4	Trade
Iron & steel mills & ferroalloys	4.7	Manufg.	Machine shops	3.4	Manufg.
Cutting tools & machine tool accessories	2.6	Manufg.	Turned products & screws, nuts, & bolts	3.0	Manufg.
Wholesale trade	2.5	Trade	Plastics products, nec	2.6	Manufg.
Truck transportation	2.3	Util.	Industrial machinery, nec	2.5	Manufg.
Power generation & supply	1.3	Util.	Cutting tools & machine tool accessories	2.3	Manufg.
Real estate	1.1	Fin/R.E.	Engine equipment, nec	2.0	Manufg.
Advertising & related services	1.0	Services	Light truck & utility vehicles	1.5	Manufg.
Machine shops	0.9	Manufg.	Rail transportation	1.5	Util.
Securities, commodity contracts, investments	0.9	Fin/R.E.	General purpose machinery, nec	1.5	Manufg.
Abrasive products	0.8	Manufg.	Retail trade	1.3	Trade
Nonmetallic minerals, nec	0.8	Mining	Semiconductors & related devices	1.3	Manufg.
Nonmetallic mineral products, nec	0.7	Manufg.	Power-driven handtools	1.2	Manufg.
Ferrous metal foundries	0.7	Manufg.	Sporting & athletic goods	1.2	Manufg.
Lessors of nonfinancial assets	0.6	Fin/R.E.	Material handling equipment	1.1	Manufg.
Semiconductors & related devices	0.6	Manufg.	Coating, engraving, heat treating & allied activities	1.0	Manufg.
Taxes on production & imports, less subsidies	0.6		Aircraft	1.0	Manufg.
Automotive equipment rental & leasing	0.6	Fin/R.E.	Plastics packaging materials, film & sheet	1.0	Manufg.
Printed circuit assemblies (electronic assemblies)	0.6	Manufg.	Manufacturing, nec	1.0	Manufg.
Turned products & screws, nuts, & bolts	0.5	Manufg.	Fluid power process machinery	1.0	Manufg.
Custom computer programming services	0.5	Services	AC, refrigeration, and warm air heating equipment	0.9	Manufg.
Monetary authorities/depository credit intermediation	0.5	Fin/R.E.	Packaging machinery	0.9	Manufg.
Professional, scientific, technical services, nec	0.4	Services	Semiconductor machinery	0.9	Manufg.
Telecommunications	0.4	Services	Valve & fittings other than plumbing	0.8	Manufg.
Scientific research & development services	0.4	Services	Wiring devices	0.8	Manufg.
Aluminum products from purchased aluminum	0.4	Manufg.	Farm machinery & equipment	0.8	Manufg.
Data processing, hosting, & related services	0.4	Services	Commercial & industrial equipment repair/maintenance	0.8	Services
Warehousing & storage	0.4	Util.	Motor vehicle bodies	0.8	Manufg.
Legal services	0.4	Services	Hardware	0.7	Manufg.
Accounting, tax preparation, bookkeeping, & payroll	0.4	Services	Fabricated metals, nec	0.7	Manufg.
Maintenance/repair of nonresidential structures	0.3	Construct.	Ferrous metal foundries	0.7	Manufg.
Services to buildings & dwellings	0.3	Services	Nonferrous metal foundries	0.7	Manufg.
Commercial & industrial machinery rental & leasing	0.3	Fin/R.E.	Commercial & service industry machinery, nec	0.7	Manufg.
Food services & drinking places	0.3	Services	General S/L govt. services	0.7	S/L Govt
Coating, engraving, heat treating & allied activities	0.3	Manufg.	Special tools, dies, jigs, & fixtures	0.7	Manufg.
Rail transportation	0.2	Util.	Signs	0.7	Manufg.
Management, scientific, & technical consulting	0.2	Services	Construction machinery	0.6	Manufg.
Relay & industrial controls	0.2	Manufg.	Industrial molds	0.6	Manufg.
Automotive repair & maintenance, ex. car washes	0.2	Services	Metal cutting & forming machine tools	0.6	Manufg.
Natural gas distribution	0.2	Util.	Vending, commercial, industrial, office machinery	0.6	Manufg.
Valve & fittings other than plumbing	0.2	Manufg.	Chemical products & preparations, nec	0.6	Manufg.
Commercial & industrial equipment repair/maintenance	0.2	Services	Ornamental & architectural metal products	0.6	Manufg.
Fluid power process machinery	0.2	Manufg.	Air purification & ventilation equipment	0.5	Manufg.
Nonferrous metal foundries	0.2	Manufg.	Ball & roller bearings	0.5	Manufg.
Hotels & motels, including casino hotels	0.1	Services	Paperboard containers	0.5	Manufg.
Other computer related services, including facilities	0.1	Services	Forging, stamping, & sintering, nec	0.5	Manufg.
Noncomparable imports	0.1	Foreign	Search, detection, & navigation instruments	0.5	Manufg.
Chemical products & preparations, nec	0.1	Manufg.	Scenic & sightseeing transport & related services	0.5	Util.
Paperboard containers	0.1	Manufg.	Broadcast & wireless communications equipment	0.5	Manufg.
Plastics packaging materials, film & sheet	0.1	Manufg.	Aircraft engine & engine parts	0.5	Manufg.
Fabricated metals, nec	0.1	Manufg.	Crowns & closures & metal stamping	0.4	Manufg.
			Printed circuit assemblies (electronic assemblies)	0.4	Manufg.
			Surgical & medical instrument	0.4	Manufg.
			Printing	0.4	Manufg.
			Electronic computers	0.4	Manufg.
			Jewelry & silverware	0.4	Manufg.
			Plumbing fixture fittings & trim	0.4	Manufg.
			Springs & wire products	0.4	Manufg.
			Relay & industrial controls	0.4	Manufg.
			Communication & energy wires & cables	0.4	Manufg.
			Glass products from purchased glass	0.4	Manufg.
			Plastics bottles	0.3	Manufg.
			Plate work & fabricated structural products	0.3	Manufg.
			Mining & oil & gas field machinery	0.3	Manufg.
			Aircraft parts & auxiliary equipment, nec	0.3	Manufg.
			Basic organic chemicals, nec	0.3	Manufg.
			Handtools	0.3	Manufg.
			Paper mills	0.3	Manufg.
			Surgical appliances & supplies	0.3	Manufg.
			Electricity & signal testing instruments	0.3	Manufg.
			Nonferrous metal (ex. copper & aluminum) processing	0.3	Manufg.
			Air transportation	0.3	Util.
			Copper rolling, drawing, extruding, & alloying	0.3	Manufg.
			Unlaminated plastics profile shapes	0.3	Manufg.
			Polystyrene foam products	0.3	Manufg.
			Soft drinks & ice	0.3	Manufg.
			Electrical equipment & components, nec	0.3	Manufg.
			Rubber products, nec	0.3	Manufg.

Continued on next page.

INPUTS AND OUTPUTS FOR CUTTING TOOL AND MACHINE TOOL ACCESSORY MANUFACTURING - Continued

Economic Sector or Industry Providing Inputs	%	Sector	Economic Sector or Industry Buying Outputs	%	Sector
			Cut stone & stone products	0.3	Manufg.
			Rolling mill & other metalworking machinery	0.3	Manufg.
			Motors & generators	0.3	Manufg.
			Turbines & turbine generator set units	0.3	Manufg.
			Watches, clocks, & related devices	0.3	Manufg.
			Automotive repair & maintenance, ex. car washes	0.3	Services
			Scientific research & development services	0.3	Services
			Ship building & repairing	0.3	Manufg.
			Bread & bakery products	0.3	Manufg.
			Electronic components, nec	0.3	Manufg.
			Petroleum refineries	0.2	Manufg.
			Totalizing fluid meters & counting devices	0.2	Manufg.
			Automobiles	0.2	Manufg.
			Other S/L govt. enterprises	0.2	S/L Govt
			Cutlery, utensils, pots, & pans	0.2	Manufg.
			Natural gas distribution	0.2	Util.
			Directories, mailing lists, & other publishers	0.2	Services
			Industrial process variable instruments	0.2	Manufg.
			Plastics materials & resins	0.2	Manufg.
			Oil & gas extraction	0.2	Mining
			Ammunition	0.2	Manufg.
			Plastics & rubber industry machinery	0.2	Manufg.
			Laboratory apparatus & furniture	0.2	Manufg.
			Ophthalmic goods	0.2	Manufg.
			Amusement & recreation, nec	0.2	Services
			Office supplies (except paper)	0.2	Manufg.
			Steel products from purchased steel	0.2	Manufg.
			Pumps & pumping equipment	0.2	Manufg.
			Gaskets, packing, & sealing devices	0.2	Manufg.
			Pressed & blown glass & glassware, nec	0.2	Manufg.
			Wineries	0.2	Manufg.
			Architectural, engineering, & related services	0.2	Services
			Bare printed circuit boards	0.2	Manufg.
			Telephone apparatus	0.2	Manufg.
			Lighting fixtures	0.2	Manufg.
			Arms, ordnance, & accessories	0.2	Manufg.
			Canned & dehydrated fruits & vegetables	0.2	Manufg.
			Pottery, ceramics, and plumbing fixtures	0.2	Manufg.
			Plastics pipe & pipe fittings	0.2	Manufg.
			Coated & laminated paper & packaging materials	0.2	Manufg.
			Heating equipment (except warm air furnaces)	0.2	Manufg.
			Communications equipment, nec	0.2	Manufg.
			Primary batteries	0.2	Manufg.
			Boat building	0.2	Manufg.
			Paperboard mills	0.2	Manufg.
			Truck transportation	0.2	Util.
			Electromedical & electrotherapeutic apparatus	0.2	Manufg.
			Metal cans, boxes, & other containers (light gauge)	0.2	Manufg.
			Urethane & other foam products (except polystrene)	0.2	Manufg.
			Motor homes	0.2	Manufg.
			Aluminum products from purchased aluminum	0.2	Manufg.
			Automatic environmental controls	0.2	Manufg.
			Wood windows & doors & millwork	0.1	Manufg.
			Book publishers	0.1	Services
			Mineral wool	0.1	Manufg.
			Personal services, nec	0.1	Services
			Toilet preparations	0.1	Manufg.
			Fabricated pipes & pipe fittings	0.1	Manufg.
			Snack food	0.1	Manufg.
			Switchgear & switchboard apparatus	0.1	Manufg.
			Analytical laboratory instruments	0.1	Manufg.
			Railroad rolling stock	0.1	Manufg.
			Breweries	0.1	Manufg.
			Business support services	0.1	Services
			Metal tanks (heavy gauge)	0.1	Manufg.
			Magnetic & optical recording media	0.1	Manufg.
			Power boilers & heat exchangers	0.1	Manufg.
			Sand, gravel, clay, & refractory minerals	0.1	Mining
			Showcases, partitions, shelving, and lockers	0.1	Manufg.
			Small electrical applicances	0.1	Manufg.
			Heavy duty trucks	0.1	Manufg.
			Basic inorganic chemicals, nec	0.1	Manufg.
			Dolls, toys, & games	0.1	Manufg.
			Asphalt paving mixtures & blocks	0.1	Manufg.

Source: Benchmark Input-Output Accounts for the U.S. Economy, 2002, U.S. Department of Commerce, Washington, D.C., January 2008. The abbreviation nec stands for 'not elsewhere classified'.

OCCUPATIONS EMPLOYED BY METALWORKING MACHINERY MANUFACTURING

Occupation	% of Total 2006	Change to 2016	Occupation	% of Total 2006	Change to 2016
Machinists	12.8	-14.0	Office clerks, general	1.7	-19.3
Tool & die makers	11.0	-14.0	Shipping, receiving, & traffic clerks	1.6	-21.2
Computer-controlled machine tool operators	5.4	-9.9	Welders, cutters, solderers, & brazers	1.6	-12.9
First-line supervisors/managers of production workers	4.6	-18.1	Bookkeeping, accounting, & auditing clerks	1.5	-18.1
Grinding, lapping, polishing machine tool operators	3.3	-20.6	Helpers--Production workers	1.4	-18.1
Cutting, punching, & press machine operators	3.2	-26.3	Sales reps, wholesale & manufacturing, exc tech	1.4	-18.1
Team assemblers	2.9	-18.1	Tool grinders, filers, & sharpeners	1.4	-26.3
Molding, coremaking, & casting machine operators	2.8	-26.3	Numerical tool & process control programmers	1.3	-15.6
Mechanical engineers	2.2	-18.1	Milling & planing machine operators & tenders	1.3	-26.3
General & operations managers	2.0	-26.3	Maintenance & repair workers, general	1.3	-18.1
Inspectors, testers, sorters, samplers, & weighers	2.0	-22.8	Industrial production managers	1.1	-18.1
Mechanical drafters	1.8	-17.2	Janitors & cleaners, exc maids & housekeeping cleaners	1.1	-16.3
Lathe & turning machine tool operators & tenders	1.8	-26.3	Multiple machine tool operators & tenders	1.0	-9.9

Source: Industry-Occupation Matrix, Bureau of Labor Statistics, December 4, 2007. These data are reported based on 4-digit NAICS categories but have been matched to corresponding 6-digit NAICS industry codes. The change reported for each occupation to the year 2016 is a percent of growth or decline as estimated by the Bureau of Labor Statistics. The abbreviation nec stands for 'not elsewhere classified'.

LOCATION BY STATE AND REGIONAL CONCENTRATION

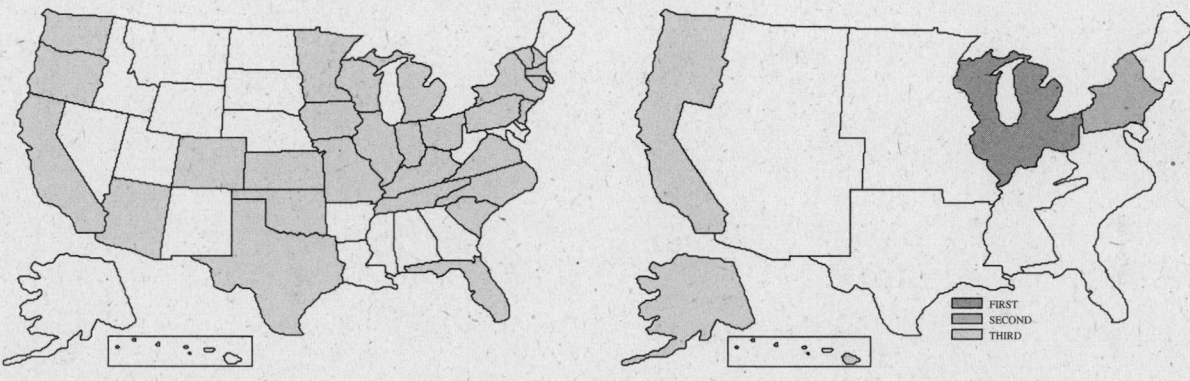

FIRST
SECOND
THIRD

INDUSTRY DATA BY STATE

State	Establish-ments	Shipments			Employment				Cost as % of Shipments	Investment per Employee ($)
		Total ($ mil)	% of U.S.	Per Establ.	Total Number	% of U.S.	Per Establ.	Wages ($/hour)		
Michigan	347	882.8	18.2	2,544.0	7,368	18.6	21	18.34	30.5	4,162
Illinois	167	423.7	8.7	2,537.2	3,487	8.8	21	17.73	35.9	6,407
Ohio	172	421.8	8.7	2,452.4	3,903	9.9	23	17.16	26.0	2,956
Pennsylvania	112	306.4	6.3	2,735.7	2,460	6.2	22	18.54	26.7	4,047
California	186	297.2	6.1	1,598.0	2,583	6.5	14	17.00	24.9	6,101
Wisconsin	69	256.0	5.3	3,709.8	1,997	5.0	29	16.43	41.0	6,914
South Carolina	45	180.9	3.7	4,019.7	1,514	3.8	34	16.41	40.7	8,226
Texas	57	171.1	3.5	3,002.1	1,049	2.6	18	17.94	32.1	3,283
Missouri	29	156.2	3.2	5,386.4	1,559	3.9	54	16.23	35.0	2,769
Tennessee	28	153.4	3.2	5,478.5	1,074	2.7	38	17.60	11.1	1,426
Massachusetts	57	134.2	2.8	2,354.0	1,222	3.1	21	18.96	30.0	5,881
New York	80	124.6	2.6	1,557.5	1,020	2.6	13	17.94	30.0	3,525
Washington	16	119.2	2.5	7,452.1	649	1.6	41	19.22	29.9	10,328
Connecticut	77	113.6	2.3	1,475.4	1,139	2.9	15	16.26	30.1	2,743
North Carolina	28	105.3	2.2	3,760.9	776	2.0	28	15.52	22.7	20,365
New Jersey	34	90.5	1.9	2,661.3	437	1.1	13	18.96	20.2	3,471
Florida	44	86.9	1.8	1,975.4	690	1.7	16	18.39	34.8	3,778
Indiana	55	85.3	1.8	1,550.3	795	2.0	14	17.52	30.4	3,887
Vermont	15	61.2	1.3	4,078.2	704	1.8	47	16.17	23.0	4,033
Minnesota	39	60.7	1.2	1,557.2	551	1.4	14	20.80	29.1	2,381
Iowa	18	55.6	1.1	3,090.0	462	1.2	26	17.01	39.1	3,405
Rhode Island	17	55.0	1.1	3,234.1	516	1.3	30	25.11	42.0	1,298
Oregon	12	44.4	0.9	3,703.1	249	0.6	21	17.98	35.7	2,751
Virginia	7	38.6	0.8	5,514.9	196	0.5	28	17.89	33.7	617
Kansas	10	37.2	0.8	3,720.1	165	0.4	16	17.98	19.1	5,291
Kentucky	14	21.8	0.4	1,557.6	152	0.4	11	19.10	40.8	5,921
Oklahoma	21	16.9	0.3	805.4	150	0.4	7	17.88	27.3	18,993
Arizona	23	15.2	0.3	659.3	147	0.4	6	17.10	33.6	1,633

Continued on next page.

INDUSTRY DATA BY STATE - Continued

| State | Establish-ments | Shipments | | | Employment | | | | Cost as % of Shipments | Investment per Employee ($) |
		Total ($ mil)	% of U.S.	Per Establ.	Total Number	% of U.S.	Per Establ.	Wages ($/hour)		
New Hampshire	11	13.6	0.3	1,233.9	129	0.3	12	20.37	24.7	953
Colorado	17	11.4	0.2	672.2	110	0.3	6	20.12	22.1	3,082

Source: 2002 *Economic Census*. The states are in descending order of shipments or establishments (if shipment data are missing for the majority). The symbol (D) appears when data are withheld to prevent disclosure of competitive information. States marked with (D) are sorted by number of establishments. A dash (-) indicates that the data element cannot be calculated. Data may not show all states active in the NAICS category. All data available at the time of publication are shown.

NAICS 333516 - ROLLING MILL MACHINERY AND EQUIPMENT MANUFACTURING

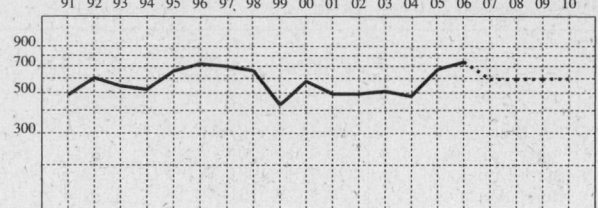

Shipments ($ million)

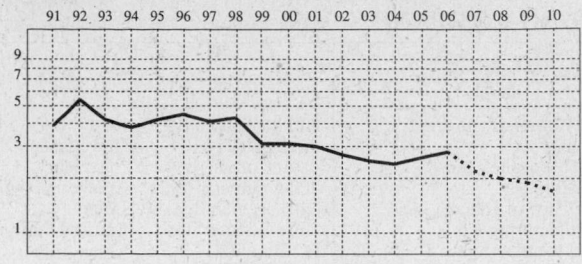

Employment (000)

GENERAL STATISTICS

| Year | Com-panies | Establishments | | Employment | | | Compensation | | Production ($ million) | | | |
		Total	with 20 or more employees	Total (000)	Production Workers (000)	Hours (Mil)	Payroll ($ mil)	Wages ($/hr)	Cost of Materials	Value Added by Manufacture	Value of Shipments	Capital Invest.
1991		87	36	3.9	2.3	4.9	138.1	13.35	228.5	260.6	486.8	11.5
1992	87	89	40	5.4	3.0	6.3	186.8	13.52	288.6	313.2	602.8	13.7
1993		92	36	4.2	2.4	4.9	154.9	14.88	262.1	284.2	545.3	7.2
1994		88	36	3.8	2.1	4.4	139.3	14.59	241.9	282.4	521.3	9.9
1995		87	34	4.2	2.3	4.8	156.1	15.56	324.2	340.8	658.2	13.0
1996		98	34	4.5	2.4	5.1	166.7	14.80	385.1	355.3	722.3	21.1
1997	98	100	40	4.1	2.2	4.7	167.3	15.93	323.5	363.6	700.1	17.3
1998		100	36	4.3	2.3	4.7	179.1	17.94	310.2	342.2	661.7	13.8
1999		95	33	3.1	1.6	3.4	127.4	16.17	201.1	218.1	429.7	21.5
2000		81	29	3.1	1.8	3.9	158.0	19.68	259.1	323.0	579.2	21.3
2001		88	30	3.0	1.8	3.6	146.2	19.30	249.9	242.7	494.0	14.6
2002	73	79	33	2.7	1.6	3.5	138.4	18.71	238.0	245.1	493.7	17.8
2003		72	30	2.5	1.4	3.0	123.6	20.10	232.9	270.1	510.7	11.5
2004		78	32	2.4	1.5	3.2	127.6	20.40	209.9	278.1	479.1	14.8
2005		80	32	2.6	1.6	3.6	150.0	21.48	342.2	349.0	672.4	15.2
2006		79P	30P	2.8	1.7	3.9	163.0	21.93	405.0	348.8	738.9	15.2
2007		78P	29P	2.2P	1.3P	3.0P	140.8P	22.35P	325.1P	280.0P	593.2P	17.4P
2008		77P	29P	2.0P	1.3P	2.8P	139.5P	22.94P	325.9P	280.7P	594.6P	17.7P
2009		76P	28P	1.9P	1.2P	2.7P	138.2P	23.52P	326.7P	281.4P	596.1P	18.0P
2010		75P	28P	1.7P	1.1P	2.5P	137.0P	24.10P	327.5P	282.1P	597.5P	18.2P

Sources: 1992, 1997, 2002 *Economic Census*; other years, up to 2006, are from the *Annual Survey of Manufactures*. Establishment counts for non-Census years are from *County Business Patterns*; 1997 and 2002 values are from the 1997 and 2002 censuses respectively, reported in the Federal Government's NAICS format. Other years were originally reported in equivalent SIC format. 'P's show projections by the editors.

INDICES OF CHANGE

| Year | Com-panies | Establishments | | Employment | | | Compensation | | Production ($ million) | | | |
		Total	with 20 or more employees	Total (000)	Production Workers (000)	Hours (Mil)	Payroll ($ mil)	Wages ($/hr)	Cost of Materials	Value Added by Manufacture	Value of Shipments	Capital Invest.
1992	119	113	121	200	188	180	135	72	121	128	122	77
1997	134	127	121	152	138	134	121	85	136	148	142	97
2001		111	91	111	113	103	106	103	105	99	100	82
2002	100	100	100	100	100	100	100	100	100	100	100	100
2003		91	91	93	87	86	89	107	98	110	103	65
2004		99	97	89	94	91	92	109	88	113	97	83
2005		101	97	96	100	103	108	115	144	142	136	85
2006		101P	91P	104	106	111	118	117	170	142	150	85
2007		99P	89P	81P	81P	86P	102P	119P	137P	114P	120P	98P
2008		98P	87P	74P	81P	80P	101P	123P	137P	115P	120P	99P
2009		97P	86P	70P	75P	77P	100P	126P	137P	115P	121P	101P
2010		95P	84P	63P	69P	71P	99P	129P	138P	115P	121P	102P

Sources: Same as General Statistics. Values reflect change from the base year, 2002. Values above 100 mean greater than 2002, values below 100 mean less than 2002, and the values of 100 in other years means the same as 2002. 'P's show projections by the editors.

SELECTED RATIOS

For 2002	Avg. of All Manufact.	Analyzed Industry	Index	For 2002	Avg. of All Manufact.	Analyzed Industry	Index
Employees per Establishment	42	34	81	Value Added per Production Worker	182,367	153,188	84
Payroll per Establishment	1,639,184	1,751,899	107	Cost per Establishment	5,769,015	3,012,658	52
Payroll per Employee	39,053	51,259	131	Cost per Employee	137,446	88,148	64
Production Workers per Establishment	30	20	69	Cost per Production Worker	195,506	148,750	76
Wages per Establishment	694,845	828,924	119	Shipments per Establishment	11,158,348	6,249,367	56
Wages per Production Worker	23,548	40,928	174	Shipments per Employee	265,847	182,852	69
Hours per Production Worker	1,980	2,188	110	Shipments per Production Worker	378,144	308,563	82
Wages per Hour	11.89	18.71	157	Investment per Establishment	361,338	225,316	62
Value Added per Establishment	5,381,325	3,102,532	58	Investment per Employee	8,609	6,593	77
Value Added per Employee	128,210	90,778	71	Investment per Production Worker	12,245	11,125	91

Sources: Same as General Statistics. The 'Average of All Manufacturing' column represents the average of all manufacturing industries reported for the most recent complete year available. The Index shows the relationship between the Average and the Analyzed Industry. For example, 100 means that they are equal; 500 that the Analyzed Industry is five times the average; 50 means that the Analyzed Industry is half the national average. The abbreviation 'na' is used to show that data are 'not available'. Ratios shown for 2002, the last complete census year.

LEADING COMPANIES   Number shown: 74   Total sales ($ mil): 8,990   Total employment (000): 5.3

Company Name	Address				CEO Name	Phone	Co. Type	Sales ($ mil)	Empl. (000)
RB and W Manufacturing L.L.C.	800 Mogadore Rd.	Kent	OH	44240		330-673-3446	S	6,375*	<0.1
Foseco Inc.	PO Box 81227	Cleveland	OH	44181	Lee Plutshack	440-826-4548	R	772*	<0.1
Cleveland Formtek Inc.	4899 Commerce	Cleveland	OH	44128	Joe Mayer	216-292-6300	R	372*	<0.1
Danieli Corp.	800 Cranberry Wds	Cranberry Twp	PA	16066	Mark Brandon	724-778-5400	R	306*	<0.1
Welded Tube of Canada Inc.	6401 Rogers Rd. A	Delta	OH	43515	Barry Sonshine	419-822-3333	R	96*	0.3
JK Manufacturing Co.	7301 W 66th St.	Bedford Park	IL	60638	Jozef Koniecko	708-563-2500	R	95*	<0.1
Bradbury Company Inc.	PO Box 667	Moundridge	KS	67107	David Bradbury	620-345-6394	R	90*	0.3
Arkansas Steel Associates	2803 Van Dyke Rd.	Newport	AR	72112	Toshinori Nakanishi	870-523-3693	R	89*	0.2
Vulcan Engineering Co.	PO Box 307	Helena	AL	35080		205-663-0732	R	62*	0.2
Dantherm Filtration Inc.	PO Box 429	Thomasville	NC	27361	Niels Petersen	336-889-5599	R	59*	0.1
Morgan Construction Company	15 Belmont St., 1	Worcester	MA	01605	Philip Morgan	508-755-6111	R	41*	0.4
Pines Manufacturing Inc.	30505 Clemens Rd.	Westlake	OH	44145	Donald Rebar	440-835-5553	R	39*	<0.1
IMPCO Machine Tools	PO Box 10156	Lansing	MI	48901	Dave Houghton	517-484-9411	R	38*	0.2
CRC-Evans Pipeline Int'l	PO Box 50368	Tulsa	OK	74150		918-438-2100	R	35*	0.1
Xtek Inc.	11451 Reading Rd.	Cincinnati	OH	45241	Kyle Seymour	513-733-7800	R	34*	0.2
Yoder Manufacturing Co.	26800 Richmond	Cleveland	OH	44146	Roger Steel	216-591-2180	S	31*	0.2
Intergrated Industrial Systems	475 Main St.	Yalesville	CT	06492	John Herbst	203-265-5684	R	30*	0.2
United Foundries Inc.	1400 Grace Ave. NE	Canton	OH	44705	Ronald Martin	330-456-2761	R	24*	0.2
Roto-Finish Company Inc.	1600 Douglas Ave.	Kalamazoo	MI	49007	Robert E. Hammond	269-345-7151	S	24*	<0.1
New Tech Machinery Corp.	1300 40th St.	Denver	CO	80205	Larry Coben	303-294-0538	R	22*	<0.1
J and J Manufacturing	PO Box 6295	Beaumont	TX	77725	James Hayes	409-833-8951	R	22*	<0.1
Bud Red Industries Inc.	200 B & E Ind. Dr.	Red Bud	IL	62278	Kalin Liefer	618-282-3801	R	21*	0.1
Bardons and Oliver Inc.	5800 Harper Rd.	Cleveland	OH	44139	Heath Oliver	440-498-5800	R	19*	0.1
Cannon Equipment Southeast	PO Box 1446	Chattanooga	TN	37401	Wayne Whitney	423-752-1000	R	19*	0.2
DP Manufacturing Inc.	PO Box 471710	Tulsa	OK	74147	Steve Oden	918-250-2450	R	19*	0.2
Mark One Corp.	517 Alpine Rd.	Gaylord	MI	49735	Francis Kestler	989-731-3800	R	18*	0.1
T and H Lemont	5,118 Dansher Rd.	Countryside	IL	60525	John Hillis	708-482-1800	S	14*	<0.1
Amerifab Inc.	2075 S Belmont	Indianapolis	IN	46221	Gabe Carinci	317-231-0100	R	12*	<0.1
Mc Ginnis Brothers Inc.	PO Box 2047	Huntington	WV	25720	Dave Ferguson	304-523-6428	R	12*	<0.1
Addison Machine Engineering	1301 Industrial St.	Reedsburg	WI	53959	Gerald Brunken	608-524-6454	R	11*	<0.1
Pandjiris Inc.	PO Box 790100	Saint Louis	MO	63179	Robert Mann	314-776-6893	R	10*	<0.1
Steward Machine Company Inc.	PO Box 11008	Birmingham	AL	35202	W Debardeleben	205-841-6461	R	9*	0.1
Capco Machinery Systems Inc.	PO Box 11945	Roanoke	VA	24022	Edward West	540-977-0404	R	8*	<0.1
Dalton Industries L.L.C.	PO Box 300888	Drayton Plains	MI	48330		248-673-0755	R	8*	<0.1
Perfecto Industries Inc.	1567 Calkins Dr.	Gaylord	MI	49735	Kevin Roberts	989-732-2941	R	8*	<0.1
Industrial Plastic Systems	PO Box 6280	Lakeland	FL	33807	Barron Burhans	863-646-8551	R	7*	<0.1
Wauseon Machine and Mfg.	995 Enterprise Ave.	Wauseon	OH	43567	Russell Dominique	419-337-0940	R	7*	<0.1
Bonell Manufacturing Co.	13521 S Halsted St.	Riverdale	IL	60827	Thomas Okleshen	708-849-1770	R	7*	<0.1
Future-All Inc.	PO Box 528	Carnegie	PA	15106	Charles King	412-279-2670	R	7*	<0.1
Medart Inc.	199 Clyde St.	Ellwood City	PA	16117	David Pierce	724-752-2900	R	6*	<0.1
Union Tool Corp.	PO Box 935	Warsaw	IN	46581		574-267-3211	R	6*	<0.1
Konrad Marine Inc.	1421 Hanley Rd.	Hudson	WI	54016	Ken Konrad	715-386-4203	R	6*	<0.1
UFF Machine Co.	PO Box 1081	Brookhaven	PA	19015	Richard Clure	610-876-7157	R	6*	<0.1
Finzer Roller of Illinois Inc.	9003 Yellow Brick	Baltimore	MD	21237		410-687-7188	S	5*	<0.1
J Horst Manufacturing Co.	PO Box 507	Dalton	OH	44618	James Horst	330-828-2216	R	5*	<0.1
Rafter Equipment Corp.	12430 Alameda Dr.	Strongsville	OH	44149	Walter Krenz	440-572-3700	R	5*	<0.1
Michigan Roll Form Inc.	33946 Doreka Dr.	Fraser	MI	48026	Cornelis Arens	586-294-7600	R	5*	<0.1
Feed-Lease Corp.	2600 Crooks Rd.	Rochester Hills	MI	48309	John Stretten	248-852-6660	R	5*	<0.1
Testa Machine Company Inc.	PO Box 416	Slovan	PA	15078	Richard Lounder	724-947-9397	R	4*	<0.1
Owens Research Inc.	13541 Lk Newman	Jacksonville	FL	32221	Carl Owens	904-448-1355	R	4*	<0.1
George L Kovacs	1810 W Business Ctr	Orange	CA	92867	George Kovacs	714-538-8026	R	4*	<0.1
Fab-Art Inc.	PO Box 2270	Youngstown	OH	44504	Daniel Tufaro	330-746-4628	R	4*	<0.1
Gega Corp.	4853 Campbells Run	Pittsburgh	PA	15205	Horst Lotz	412-787-2832	R	4*	<0.1
Laneko Roll Form Inc.	3003 Unionville Pke	Hatfield	PA	19440	Ernest Pfeiffer	215-822-1930	R	4*	<0.1
Dalhart R and R Machine Works	PO Box 1330	Dalhart	TX	79022	Wesley Wood	806-244-5686	R	4*	<0.1
Grover Machine Co.	207 Prospect Ave.	Saint Louis	MO	63122	Jean Micouleau	314-965-6808	R	3*	<0.1
Sticker Corp.	37877 Elm Street	Willoughby	OH	44094	Douglas Reighart	440-946-2100	R	3*	<0.1
Leman Machine Co.	PO Box 269	Portage	PA	15946	Stuart Leman	814-736-9696	R	3*	<0.1
George A Mitchell Co.	PO Box 3727	Youngstown	OH	44513	George Mitchell	330-758-5777	R	3*	<0.1
Konrad Corp.	1421 Hanley Rd.	Hudson	WI	54016	Ken Konrad	715-386-4200	R	3*	<0.1
Steel Plant Equipment Corp.	3360 Ridge Pke.	Eagleville	PA	19403	Gerard Marinari	610-539-0980	R	3*	<0.1
Mill Assist Services Inc.	141 N Farmer St.	Otsego	MI	49078	Denis Gloede	269-692-3211	R	3*	<0.1
Roller Equipment Manufacturing	13903 Norby Rd.	Grandview	MO	64030	Dean Armstrong	816-966-8717	R	3*	<0.1
Winchester Roll Products Inc.	41 Hildreth St.	Winchester	NH	03470	Barry Bordner	603-239-6326	R	2*	<0.1
Nor Service Inc.	215 S State Ave.	Freeport	IL	61032	Neil Rouse	815-232-8379	R	2*	<0.1
Grinding Equipment and Machine	15 S Worthington St	Youngstown	OH	44502	James Johnson	330-747-2313	R	2*	<0.1
S2F Engineering Inc.	324 Sherman St.	Blissfield	MI	49228	Steve Dobson	517-486-5737	R	2*	<0.1
Bendco Machine and Tool Co.	PO Box 6	Minster	OH	45865	Kenneth Wolaver	419-628-3802	R	2*	<0.1
Tube Forming and Machin Inc.	4614 Industrial Row	Oscoda	MI	48750	Jerome Orefice	989-739-3323	R	2*	<0.1
Western Technologies Inc.	4404 S Maybelle	Tulsa	OK	74107	Russell Patterson	918-712-2406	R	2*	<0.1
Indemax Inc.	PO Box 544	Sparta	NJ	07871	Alphonse Infurna	973-209-2424	R	2*	<0.1
Pacific Roller Die Company	1321 W Winton	Hayward	CA	94545		510-782-7242	R	1*	<0.1
Fontijne Grotnes Inc.	1025 W Thrndale	Itasca	IL	60143	Andrew Fontijne	630-875-1111	R	1*	<0.1
Criterion Machinery Inc.	7655 Hub 201	Cleveland	OH	44125	Rose Prescott	216-573-0311	R	1*	<0.1

Source: Ward's Business Directory of U.S. Private and Public Companies, Volumes 1 and 2, 2008. The company type code used is as follows: P - Public, R - Private, S - Subsidiary, D - Division, J - Joint Venture, A - Affiliate, G - Group. Sales are in millions of dollars, employees are in thousands. An asterisk (*) indicates an estimated sales volume. The symbol < stands for 'less than'. Company names and addresses are truncated, in some cases, to fit into the available space.

MATERIALS CONSUMED

Material	Quantity	Delivered Cost ($ million)
Fluid power pumps, motors, and hydrostatic transmissions	(X)	4.3
Fluid power cylinders and rotary actuators (hydraulic and pneumatic)	(X)	(D)
Fluid power filters (hydraulic and pneumatic)	(X)	0.7
Fluid power hose, tube fittings, and assemblies (hydraulic and pneumatic)	(X)	2.1
Fluid power valves (hydraulic and pneumatic)	(X)	2.4
Metal bolts, nuts, screws, and other screw machine products	(X)	0.4
Other fabricated metal products (exc. fluid power products and forgings)	(X)	18.0
Forgings	(X)	(D)
Iron and steel castings (rough and semifinished)	(X)	11.7
Nonferrous (aluminum, copper, etc.) castings (rough and semifinished)	(X)	(D)
Steel bars, bar shapes, and plates (exc. castings, forgings, fabr. metal products)	(X)	15.3
Steel sheet and strip (including tinplate)	(X)	1.3
Steel structural shapes (exc. castings, forgings, fabr. metal products)	(X)	2.1
All other steel shapes and forms (exc. castings, forgings, fabr. metal products)	(X)	1.8
Nonferrous shapes and forms	(X)	<0.1
Fractional horsepower electric timing motors (less than 1 hp)	(X)	0.1
Other fractional horsepower electric motors (less than 1 hp)	(X)	(D)
Integral horsepower electric motors and generators (1 hp or more)	(X)	(D)
Electrical transmission, distribution, and control equipment	(X)	(D)
Electrical industrial capacitors, resistors, rheostats, and coil windings	(X)	<0.1
Electrical instrument mechanisms and meter movements	(X)	<0.1
Numerical controls, metalworking machinery (exc. programmable)	(X)	<0.1
Programmable controllers for metalworking machinery	(X)	3.3
Ball bearings (mounted or unmounted)	(X)	(D)
Roller bearings (mounted or unmounted)	(X)	(D)
Mechanical speed changers, gears, and industrial high-speed drives	(X)	12.0
Wood boxes, pallets, skids, and containers	(X)	0.8
Cutting tools for machine tools	(X)	2.1
Printed circuit assemblies, loaded boards, and modules	(X)	(D)
Semiconductors (incl. transistors, diodes, rectifiers, and integrated circuits), for electronic circuitry	(X)	(D)
All other miscellaneous components and accessories for electronic circuitry (exc. tubes)	(X)	(D)
Paper and paperboard containers (incl. shipping sacks and other paper packaging supplies)	(X)	0.1
Fabricated plastics products (exc. gaskets, hoses, and belting)	(X)	(D)
Electronic communication equipment	(X)	(D)
All other materials, components, parts, containers, and supplies	(X)	54.4
Materials, ingredients, containers, and supplies, nsk	(X)	14.6

Source: 2002 *Economic Census*. Explanation of symbols used: (D): Withheld to avoid disclosure of competitive data; na: Not available; (S): Withheld because statistical norms were not met; (X): Not applicable; (Z): Less than half the unit shown; nec: Not elsewhere classified; nsk: Not specified by kind; - : zero; p : 10-19 percent estimated; q : 20-29 percent estimated.

PRODUCT SHARE DETAILS

Product or Product Class Shipments	Mil. $	Product or Product Class Shipments	Mil. $
ROLLING MILL MACHINERY	489.3	Processing lines (including pickling and cleaning, tinning, galvanizing, etc.), scarfing units, and press feed lines	31.1
Hot rolling mill machinery (including combination hot and cold) (except tube rolling)	**133.3**		
Cold rolling mill machinery	**71.7**	Other rolling mill machinery and equipment, except parts	12.6
Tandem cold rolling mill machinery	17.7	Machined rolls for rolling mills	98.2
Single stand cold rolling mill machinery	36.9	Parts, except rolls, for rolling mill machinery (sold separately)	43.8
Other cold rolling mill machinery and equipment	17.1		
Other rolling mill machinery (including tube mill machinery) and parts for all rolling mill machinery	**271.6**	Other rolling mill machinery (including tube mill machinery) and parts for all rolling mill machinery, nsk	0.4
Other rolling mill machinery (including tube mill machinery) and parts for all rolling mill machinery	271.2	**Rolling mill machinery, nsk, total**	**12.7**
Tube rolling mill machinery	85.5		

Source: 2002 *Economic Census*. The values are product shipments in millions of dollars for 2002. Total product shipments may be lower or higher than industry shipments. See Introduction for a full discussion. Values of indented subcategories are summed in the main heading(s). The symbol (D) appears when data are withheld to prevent disclosure of competitive information. The abbreviation nsk stands for 'not specified by kind' and nec for 'not elsewhere classified'. A dash (-) means zero.

INPUTS AND OUTPUTS FOR ROLLING MILL & OTHER METALWORKING MACHINERY

Economic Sector or Industry Providing Inputs	%	Sector	Economic Sector or Industry Buying Outputs	%	Sector
Compensation of employees	36.0		Private fixed investment	84.6	
Management of companies & enterprises	7.0	Services	Educational services, nec	4.4	Services
Wholesale trade	5.3	Trade	Exports of goods & services	3.2	Cap Inv
Iron & steel mills & ferroalloys	3.3	Manufg.	Special tools, dies, jigs, & fixtures	3.1	Manufg.
Relay & industrial controls	3.0	Manufg.	Rolling mill & other metalworking machinery	2.8	Manufg.
Rolling mill & other metalworking machinery	2.8	Manufg.	Plate work & fabricated structural products	0.5	Manufg.
Metal cutting & forming machine tools	2.8	Manufg.	Metal tanks (heavy gauge)	0.4	Manufg.
Motors & generators	2.3	Manufg.	Power boilers & heat exchangers	0.4	Manufg.
Ferrous metal foundries	2.0	Manufg.	Manufacturing, nec	0.3	Manufg.

Continued on next page.

INPUTS AND OUTPUTS FOR ROLLING MILL & OTHER METALWORKING MACHINERY - Continued

Economic Sector or Industry Providing Inputs	%	Sector	Economic Sector or Industry Buying Outputs	%	Sector
Speed changers, industrial high-speed drives, & gears	1.7	Manufg.			
Ball & roller bearings	1.5	Manufg.			
Fluid power process machinery	1.4	Manufg.			
Machine shops	1.3	Manufg.			
Real estate	1.2	Fin/R.E.			
Valve & fittings other than plumbing	1.1	Manufg.			
Securities, commodity contracts, investments	1.0	Fin/R.E.			
Turned products & screws, nuts, & bolts	0.9	Manufg.			
Printed circuit assemblies (electronic assembiles)	0.8	Manufg.			
Plastics products, nec	0.8	Manufg.			
Electronic components, nec	0.7	Manufg.			
Lessors of nonfinancial assets	0.6	Fin/R.E.			
Advertising & related services	0.6	Services			
Power generation & supply	0.6	Util.			
Abrasive products	0.6	Manufg.			
Custom computer programming services	0.6	Services			
Truck transportation	0.5	Util.			
Coating, engraving, heat treating & allied activities	0.5	Manufg.			
Monetary authorities/depository credit intermediation	0.5	Fin/R.E.			
Legal services	0.5	Services			
Architectural, engineering, & related services	0.5	Services			
Taxes on production & imports, less subsidies	0.5				
Cutting tools & machine tool accessories	0.5	Manufg.			
Broadcast & wireless communications equipment	0.5	Manufg.			
Scientific research & development services	0.4	Services			
Professional, scientific, technical services, nec	0.4	Services			
Data processing, hosting, & related services	0.4	Services			
Electronic capacitors, resistors, coils, transformers	0.4	Manufg.			
Telecommunications	0.4	Services			
Accounting, tax preparation, bookkeeping, & payroll	0.4	Services			
Automotive equipment rental & leasing	0.3	Fin/R.E.			
Semiconductors & related devices	0.3	Manufg.			
Warehousing & storage	0.3	Util.			
Plastics packaging materials, film & sheet	0.3	Manufg.			
Chemical products & preparations, nec	0.3	Manufg.			
Food services & drinking places	0.3	Services			
Management, scientific, & technical consulting	0.3	Services			
Forging, stamping, & sintering, nec	0.3	Manufg.			
Motor vehicle parts	0.2	Manufg.			
Fabricated metals, nec	0.2	Manufg.			
Wood containers & pallets	0.2	Manufg.			
Custom roll forming	0.2	Manufg.			
Metal cans, boxes, & other containers (light gauge)	0.2	Manufg.			
Unlaminated plastics profile shapes	0.2	Manufg.			
Electricity & signal testing instruments	0.2	Manufg.			
Hotels & motels, including casino hotels	0.2	Services			
Nonferrous metal foundries	0.2	Manufg.			
Natural gas distribution	0.2	Util.			
Services to buildings & dwellings	0.2	Services			
Maintenance/repair of nonresidential structures	0.2	Construct.			
Rubber products, nec	0.2	Manufg.			
Commercial & industrial machinery rental & leasing	0.2	Fin/R.E.			
Postal service	0.2	Util.			
Other computer related services, including facilities	0.2	Services			
Business support services	0.2	Services			
Electrical equipment & components, nec	0.1	Manufg.			
Plate work & fabricated structural products	0.1	Manufg.			
Nondepository credit intermediation activities	0.1	Fin/R.E.			
Air transportation	0.1	Util.			
Crowns & closures & metal stamping	0.1	Manufg.			
Paperboard containers	0.1	Manufg.			
Employment services	0.1	Services			
Handtools	0.1	Manufg.			
Paperboard mills	0.1	Manufg.			
Specialized design services	0.1	Services			
Automotive repair & maintenance, ex. car washes	0.1	Services			
Bare printed circuit boards	0.1	Manufg.			
General purpose machinery, nec	0.1	Manufg.			

Source: Benchmark Input-Output Accounts for the U.S. Economy, 2002, U.S. Department of Commerce, Washington D.C., January 2008. User should note that this Input-Output table is not for this particular narrowly defined industry but for a larger aggregate. Input and Output data for Rolling Mill & Other Metal Working Machinery include Input and Output data for the Annual Survey of Manufactures' NAICS industries 333516 and 333518. The abbreviation nec stands for 'not elsewhere classified'.

OCCUPATIONS EMPLOYED BY METALWORKING MACHINERY MANUFACTURING

Occupation	% of Total 2006	Change to 2016	Occupation	% of Total 2006	Change to 2016
Machinists	12.8	-14.0	Office clerks, general	1.7	-19.3
Tool & die makers	11.0	-14.0	Shipping, receiving, & traffic clerks	1.6	-21.2
Computer-controlled machine tool operators	5.4	-9.9	Welders, cutters, solderers, & brazers	1.6	-12.9
First-line supervisors/managers of production workers	4.6	-18.1	Bookkeeping, accounting, & auditing clerks	1.5	-18.1
Grinding, lapping, polishing machine tool operators	3.3	-20.6	Helpers--Production workers	1.4	-18.1
Cutting, punching, & press machine operators	3.2	-26.3	Sales reps, wholesale & manufacturing, exc tech	1.4	-18.1
Team assemblers	2.9	-18.1	Tool grinders, filers, & sharpeners	1.4	-26.3
Molding, coremaking, & casting machine operators	2.8	-26.3	Numerical tool & process control programmers	1.3	-15.6
Mechanical engineers	2.2	-18.1	Milling & planing machine operators & tenders	1.3	-26.3
General & operations managers	2.0	-26.3	Maintenance & repair workers, general	1.3	-18.1
Inspectors, testers, sorters, samplers, & weighers	2.0	-22.8	Industrial production managers	1.1	-18.1
Mechanical drafters	1.8	-17.2	Janitors & cleaners, exc maids & housekeeping cleaners	1.1	-16.3
Lathe & turning machine tool operators & tenders	1.8	-26.3	Multiple machine tool operators & tenders	1.0	-9.9

Source: Industry-Occupation Matrix, Bureau of Labor Statistics, December 4, 2007. These data are reported based on 4-digit NAICS categories but have been matched to corresponding 6-digit NAICS industry codes. The change reported for each occupation to the year 2016 is a percent of growth or decline as estimated by the Bureau of Labor Statistics. The abbreviation nec stands for 'not elsewhere classified'.

LOCATION BY STATE AND REGIONAL CONCENTRATION

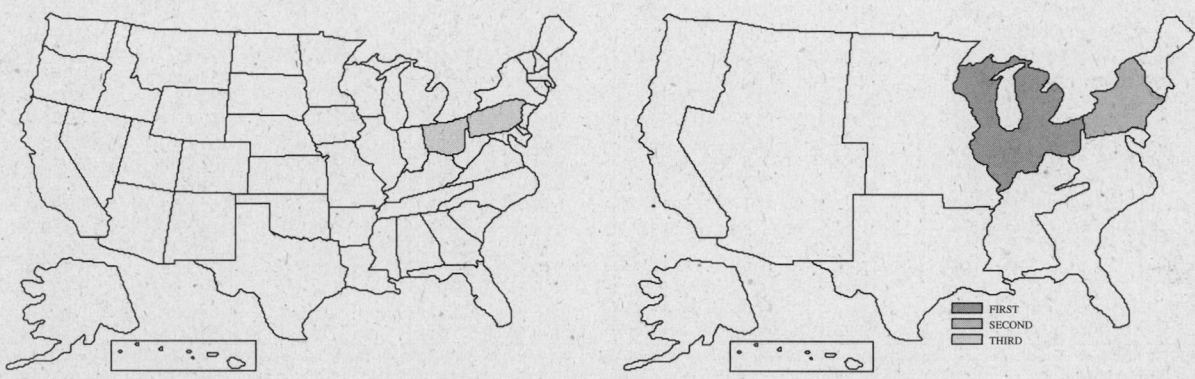

FIRST
SECOND
THIRD

INDUSTRY DATA BY STATE

State	Establish-ments	Shipments			Employment				Cost as % of Shipments	Investment per Employee ($)
		Total ($ mil)	% of U.S.	Per Establ.	Total Number	% of U.S.	Per Establ.	Wages ($/hour)		
Ohio	20	125.9	25.5	6,295.0	822	30.1	41	19.58	44.7	2,965
Pennsylvania	12	124.4	25.2	10,362.7	448	16.4	37	19.24	50.3	7,446

Source: 2002 *Economic Census.* The states are in descending order of shipments or establishments (if shipment data are missing for the majority). The symbol (D) appears when data are withheld to prevent disclosure of competitive information. States marked with (D) are sorted by number of establishments. A dash (-) indicates that the data element cannot be calculated. Data may not show all states active in the NAICS category. All data available at the time of publication are shown.

NAICS 333518 - METALWORKING MACHINERY MANUFACTURING NEC

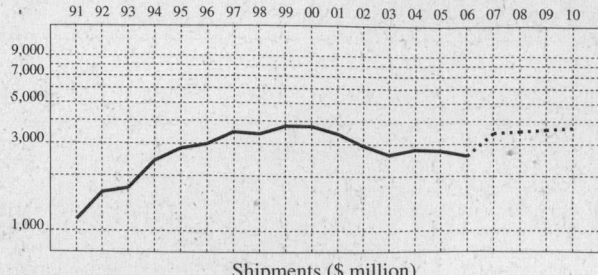

Shipments ($ million)

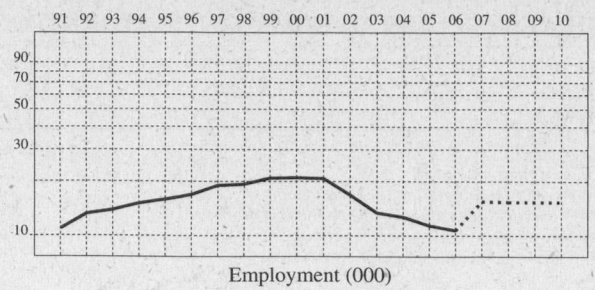

Employment (000)

GENERAL STATISTICS

| Year | Com-panies | Establishments | | Employment | | | Compensation | | Production ($ million) | | | |
		Total	with 20 or more employees	Total (000)	Production Workers (000)	Hours (Mil)	Payroll ($ mil)	Wages ($/hr)	Cost of Materials	Value Added by Manufacture	Value of Shipments	Capital Invest.
1991		297	143	10.9	6.5	14.8	358.9	12.41	505.1	702.0	1,150.8	32.5
1992	389	400	167	13.2	7.9	17.6	487.5	14.05	687.6	942.7	1,618.3	27.6
1993		390	171	13.9	8.6	18.9	514.8	13.77	739.8	1,003.3	1,711.4	17.2
1994		378	169	15.1	9.8	22.5	593.7	13.88	1,147.9	1,400.4	2,411.9	48.5
1995		377	173	15.9	9.9	22.4	655.8	15.48	1,364.0	1,551.4	2,822.3	62.9
1996		407	180	16.9	10.4	22.7	727.5	16.02	1,422.3	1,553.3	2,976.3	46.9
1997	448	474	225	19.0	11.3	25.0	857.3	17.60	1,624.7	1,790.5	3,463.8	79.2
1998		476	221	19.3	11.3	24.6	926.2	19.03	1,616.2	1,543.8	3,395.5	81.8
1999		471	224	20.9	12.8	27.1	970.1	17.89	1,851.3	1,799.6	3,763.1	76.4
2000		460	220	21.0	12.5	26.9	994.6	18.29	1,810.9	1,874.2	3,748.9	74.1
2001		460	210	20.8	11.9	24.3	982.3	18.51	1,778.0	1,572.4	3,415.7	68.6
2002	414	455	180	16.8	9.6	20.0	803.3	19.93	1,242.5	1,621.0	2,941.4	61.0
2003		444	181	13.4	7.7	16.1	679.0	20.53	1,131.1	1,487.4	2,629.1	36.4
2004		406	165	12.7	7.1	14.7	694.9	22.84	1,172.7	1,691.6	2,798.8	58.1
2005		401	163	11.4	6.5	14.0	691.1	24.58	1,266.3	1,517.4	2,755.3	43.6
2006		468P	198P	10.7	6.0	13.5	651.3	23.35	1,220.7	1,346.2	2,584.4	33.4
2007		474P	199P	15.5P	8.7P	18.2P	881.1P	24.32P	1,625.9P	1,793.1P	3,442.4P	61.0P
2008		480P	201P	15.4P	8.7P	17.9P	899.5P	25.07P	1,663.8P	1,834.8P	3,522.5P	61.9P
2009		486P	202P	15.4P	8.6P	17.7P	918.0P	25.81P	1,701.6P	1,876.5P	3,602.5P	62.8P
2010		492P	204P	15.4P	8.5P	17.4P	936.4P	26.55P	1,739.4P	1,918.3P	3,682.6P	63.8P

Sources: 1992, 1997, 2002 *Economic Census*; other years, up to 2006, are from the *Annual Survey of Manufactures*. Establishment counts for non-Census years are from *County Business Patterns*; 1997 and 2002 values are from the 1997 and 2002 censuses respectively, reported in the Federal Government's NAICS format. Other years were originally reported in equivalent SIC format. 'P's show projections by the editors.

INDICES OF CHANGE

| Year | Com-panies | Establishments | | Employment | | | Compensation | | Production ($ million) | | | |
		Total	with 20 or more employees	Total (000)	Production Workers (000)	Hours (Mil)	Payroll ($ mil)	Wages ($/hr)	Cost of Materials	Value Added by Manufacture	Value of Shipments	Capital Invest.
1992	94	88	93	79	82	88	61	70	55	58	55	45
1997	108	104	125	113	118	125	107	88	131	110	118	130
2001		101	117	124	124	122	122	93	143	97	116	112
2002	100	100	100	100	100	100	100	100	100	100	100	100
2003		98	101	80	80	81	85	103	91	92	89	60
2004		89	92	76	74	74	87	115	94	104	95	95
2005		88	91	68	68	70	86	123	102	94	94	71
2006		103P	110P	64	63	68	81	117	98	83	88	55
2007		104P	111P	92P	91P	91P	110P	122P	131P	111P	117P	100P
2008		106P	112P	92P	91P	89P	112P	126P	134P	113P	120P	101P
2009		107P	112P	92P	90P	89P	114P	130P	137P	116P	122P	103P
2010		108P	113P	92P	89P	87P	117P	133P	140P	118P	125P	105P

Sources: Same as General Statistics. Values reflect change from the base year, 2002. Values above 100 mean greater than 2002, values below 100 mean less than 2002, and the values of 100 in other years means the same as 2002. 'P's show projections by the editors.

SELECTED RATIOS

For 2002	Avg. of All Manufact.	Analyzed Industry	Index	For 2002	Avg. of All Manufact.	Analyzed Industry	Index
Employees per Establishment	42	37	88	Value Added per Production Worker	182,367	168,854	93
Payroll per Establishment	1,639,184	1,765,495	108	Cost per Establishment	5,769,015	2,730,769	47
Payroll per Employee	39,053	47,815	122	Cost per Employee	137,446	73,958	54
Production Workers per Establishment	30	21	72	Cost per Production Worker	195,506	129,427	66
Wages per Establishment	694,845	876,044	126	Shipments per Establishment	11,158,348	6,464,615	58
Wages per Production Worker	23,548	41,521	176	Shipments per Employee	265,847	175,083	66
Hours per Production Worker	1,980	2,083	105	Shipments per Production Worker	378,144	306,396	81
Wages per Hour	11.89	19.93	168	Investment per Establishment	361,338	134,066	37
Value Added per Establishment	5,381,325	3,562,637	66	Investment per Employee	8,609	3,631	42
Value Added per Employee	128,210	96,488	75	Investment per Production Worker	12,245	6,354	52

Sources: Same as General Statistics. The 'Average of All Manufacturing' column represents the average of all manufacturing industries reported for the most recent complete year available. The Index shows the relationship between the Average and the Analyzed Industry. For example, 100 means that they are equal; 500 that the Analyzed Industry is five times the average; 50 means that the Analyzed Industry is half the national average. The abbreviation 'na' is used to show that data are 'not available'. Ratios shown for 2002, the last complete census year.

LEADING COMPANIES   Number shown: **75**   Total sales ($ mil): **29,053**   Total employment (000): **104.5**

Company Name	Address				CEO Name	Phone	Co. Type	Sales ($ mil)	Empl. (000)
Dover Corp.	280 Park Ave.	New York	NY	10017		212-922-1640	P	7,226	33.4
Leggett and Platt Inc.	PO Box 757	Carthage	MO	64836		417-358-8131	P	4,306	24.0
Lincoln Electric Holdings Inc.	22801 St. Clair Ave	Cleveland	OH	44117		216-481-8100	P	2,281	9.0
Stoody Co.	5557 Nashville Rd.	Bowling Green	KY	42101	Paul D. Melnuk	270-781-9777	S	1,537*	3.0
Thermadyne Manufacturing	101 S Hanley Rd.	St. Louis	MO	63105	Paul D. Melnuk	314-721-5573	S	1,537*	3.0
Marison Cylinder Co.	101 S Hanley Rd.	St. Louis	MO	63105	Paul D. Melnuk	314-721-5573	S	1,530*	3.0
Modern Engineering Company	US Highway I-55 S	Gallman	MS	39077	Paul D. Melnuk	601-892-3500	S	1,530*	3.0
Thermadyne Industries Inc.	16052 Swingley	Chesterfield	MO	63017	Paul D. Melnuk	314-721-5573	S	1,530*	3.0
Thermal Dynamics Corp.	Industrial Part #D	West Lebanon	NH	03784	Paul D. Melnuk	603-298-5711	S	1,530*	3.0
Victor Coyne International	101 S Hanley Rd.	St. Louis	MO	63105	Paul D. Melnuk	314-721-5573	S	1,530*	3.0
Victor Gas Systems Inc.	960 Brookroad, 1	Conshohocken	PA	19428	Paul D. Melnuk	314-721-5573	S	1,530*	3.0
Cleveland Formtek Inc.	4899 Commerce	Cleveland	OH	44128	Joe Mayer	216-292-6300	R	372*	<0.1
Hardinge Inc.	PO Box 1507	Elmira	NY	14902	J. Patrick Ervin	607-734-2281	P	327.	1.5
Danieli Corp.	800 Cranberry Wds	Cranberry Twp	PA	16066	Mark Brandon	724-778-5400	R	306*	<0.1
Park Corp.	6200 Riverside Dr.	Cleveland	OH	44135	Daniel K. Park	216-267-4870	R	271*	3.2
Bradbury Company Inc.	PO Box 667	Moundridge	KS	67107	David Bradbury	620-345-6394	R	90*	0.3
Almco	507 W Front St.	Albert Lea	MN	56007	Richard Rocklin	507-377-2102	S	79*	<0.1
Ged Integrated Solutions Inc.	9280 Dutton Dr.	Twinsburg	OH	44087	Ronald Auletta	330-963-5401	R	71*	0.1
Weldmation Inc.	31720 Stephenson	Madison Heights	MI	48071	Arthur Kelsey	248-585-0010	R	71*	0.4
Evana Tool and Engineering	5825 Old Boonville	Evansville	IN	47715	William Phillips	812-479-8246	R	56*	0.3
Morbark Inc.	PO Box 1000	Winn	MI	48896	Lon Morey	989-866-2381	R	55*	0.6
Sunnen Products Co.	7910 Manchester	Saint Louis	MO	63143	Matt Kreider	314-781-2100	R	52*	0.5
Veri-Tek International Corp.	7402 W 100th Pl.	Bridgeview	IL	60455	David Langevin	708-237-2060	P	46	0.3
Thielenhaus Microfinish Corp.	42925 W 9 Mile Rd.	Novi	MI	48375	Manfred Sieringhaus	248-349-9450	R	45*	0.3
Tessy Plastics Corp.	PO Box 160	Elbridge	NY	13060	Henry Beck	315-689-3924	R	45*	0.5
Van Blarcom Closures Inc.	156 Sandford St.	Brooklyn	NY	11205	Vincent Scuderi	718-855-3810	R	44*	0.2
Assembly and Test Worldwide	313 Mound St.	Dayton	OH	45402	Richard Glennon	937-586-5600	R	40*	0.2
Herr-Voss	PO Box AB	Callery	PA	16024	Walter Stasik	724-538-3180	D	40*	0.2
Pines Manufacturing Inc.	30505 Clemens Rd.	Westlake	OH	44145	Donald Rebar	440-835-5553	R	39*	<0.1
Fori Automation Inc.	50955 Wing Dr.	Shelby Twp	MI	48315	Bernd Koerner	586-247-2336	R	35*	0.2
W.A. Whitney Co.	PO Box 1206	Rockford	IL	61105	Gary Geller	815-964-6771	S	33*	0.2
Automatic Feed Co.	476 E Riverview	Napoleon	OH	43545	Kim Beck	419-592-0050	R	32*	<0.1
Strippit Inc.	12975 Clarence Ctr.	Akron	NY	14001	John Lesebbre	716-542-4511	R	32*	0.2
Delta Brands Inc.	2204 Century Ctr. B	Irving	TX	75062	Samuel Savariego	972-438-7150	R	28*	0.2
JR Automation Technologies	13365 Tyler St.	Holland	MI	49424	Stephen Klotz	616-399-2168	R	27*	0.2
Anderson Cook Inc.	17650 15 Mile Rd.	Fraser	MI	48026	Kim Anderson	586-293-0800	R	26*	<0.1
Starting USA Corp.	1676 Rowe Pkwy.	Poplar Bluff	MO	63901	Allen Redfearn	573-686-9430	R	25*	0.1
Chapman/Leonard Studio Equip.	12950 Raymer St.	N Hollywood	CA	91605	Leonard Chapman	818-764-6726	R	25*	0.2
MIC Industries Inc.	PO Box 17369	Washington	DC	20041	Michael Ansari	703-318-1900	R	25*	<0.1
American Amer. Pulverizer Co.	5540 W Park Ave.	Saint Louis	MO	63110	Chris Griesedieck	314-781-6100	R	25*	<0.1
B and K Corp.	PO Box 1968	Saginaw	MI	48605		989-777-2111	R	24*	0.2
Riviera Tool Co.	5460 Executive Pky.	Grand Rapids	MI	49512	John C. Kennedy	616-698-2100	P	24	0.1
Systems, Machines, Automation	5807 Van Allen Way	Carlsbad	CA	92008	Edward Neff	760-929-7575	R	24*	0.1
Advanced Tubing Technology	150 Intercraft Dr.	Statesville	NC	28625	Doug Smyth	704-924-7020	R	23*	0.2
Aerial Machine & Tool	PO Box 222	Vesta	VA	24177	John Marcaccio	276-952-2006	R	23*	0.2
Golden States Engineering Inc.	15338 Garfield Ave.	Paramount	CA	90723	Alexandra Rostovski	562-634-3125	R	22*	0.1
Wright-K Technology Inc.	2025 N Genesee	Saginaw	MI	48601	John Sivey	989-752-3103	R	22*	0.1
Bud Red Industries Inc.	200 B & E Ind. Dr.	Red Bud	IL	62278	Kalin Liefer	618-282-3801	R	21*	0.1
RP Gatta Inc.	435 Gentry Dr.	Aurora	OH	44202	Raymond Gatta	330-562-2288	R	21*	<0.1
C.A. Litzler Co.	4800 W 160th St.	Cleveland	OH	44135	Matthew Litzler	216-267-8020	R	21*	<0.1
ASC Machine Tools Inc.	PO Box 11619	Spokane	WA	99211	Ray Griff	509-534-6600	R	21*	0.2
Wright Industries Inc.	PO Box 17914	Nashville	TN	37217	David Takes	615-361-6600	R	20*	0.2
Brenton Engineering Co.	4750 Cnty Rd 13	Alexandria	MN	56308	Jeff Bigger	320-852-7705	R	20*	0.1
Bardons and Oliver Inc.	5800 Harper Rd.	Cleveland	OH	44139	Heath Oliver	440-498-5800	R	19*	0.1
Mold-A-Matic Corp.	147 River St.	Oneonta	NY	13820	Jack Stanley	607-433-2121	R	19*	0.2
WSI Industries Inc.	213 Chelsea Rd.	Monticello	MN	55362		763-295-9202	P	19	<0.1
Mark One Corp.	517 Alpine Rd.	Gaylord	MI	49735	Francis Kestler	989-731-3800	R	18*	0.1
Clemco Industries Corp.	1 Cable Car Dr.	Washington	MO	63090	Arnie Sallaverry	636-239-0300	R	18*	0.1
Bartell Machinery Systems	6321 Elmer Hill Rd.	Rome	NY	13440		315-336-7600	R	17*	<0.1
MAC Products Inc.	PO Box 469	Kearny	NJ	07032	Edward Gollob	973-344-0700	R	17*	0.1
TA Systems Inc.	1842 Rochester Ind.	Rochester Hills	MI	48309	Tim Gale	248-656-5150	R	17*	<0.1
Jessup Engineering Inc.	2745 Bond St.	Rochester Hills	MI	48309	Ran Jessup	248-853-5600	R	16*	<0.1
Dane Systems Inc.	7275 Red Arrow	Stevensville	MI	49127	Stephen Klotz	269-465-3263	R	16*	<0.1
Manchester Tool and Die Inc.	PO Box 326	N Manchester	IN	46962	Barry Blocher	260-982-8524	R	15*	0.1
RWC Inc.	PO Box 920	Bay City	MI	48707	William Perlberg	989-684-4030	R	15*	0.2
ID Technology Corp.	2051 Franklin Dr.	Fort Worth	TX	76106			S	15*	<0.1
Auto Con Corp.	18901 15 Mile Rd.	Clinton Twp	MI	48035	Ronald Matheson	586-791-7474	R	15*	<0.1
Metro Machine and Engineering	8001 Wallace Rd.	Eden Prairie	MN	55344	Robert Midness	952-937-2800	R	14*	<0.1
Omega Automation Inc.	2850 Needmore Rd.	Dayton	OH	45414	Alan King	937-277-2929	R	14*	<0.1
Haumiller Engineering Co.	445 Renner Dr.	Elgin	IL	60123	Russ Holmer	847-695-9111	R	13*	0.1
Rowe Machinery and Mfg. Co.	76 Hinckley Rd.	Clinton	ME	04927		207-426-2351	D	13*	0.1
HMS Products Co.	1200 E Big Beaver	Troy	MI	48083	Dave Sofy	248-689-8120	R	13*	<0.1
Merrill Tool and Machine Inc.	21659 W Gratiot Rd.	Merrill	MI	48637	Jeff Merrill	989-643-7981	R	13*	<0.1
Pannier Corp.	207 Sandusky St.	Pittsburgh	PA	15212	Scott Heddaeus	412-323-4900	R	13*	<0.1
Deluxe Stitcher Company Inc.	6635 W Irving Park	Chicago	IL	60634	Frank Cangelosi	773-777-6500	R	13*	<0.1

Source: Ward's Business Directory of U.S. Private and Public Companies, Volumes 1 and 2, 2008. The company type code used is as follows: P - Public, R - Private, S - Subsidiary, D - Division, J - Joint Venture, A - Affiliate, G - Group. Sales are in millions of dollars, employees are in thousands. An asterisk (*) indicates an estimated sales volume. The symbol < stands for 'less than'. Company names and addresses are truncated, in some cases, to fit into the available space.

MATERIALS CONSUMED

Material	Quantity	Delivered Cost ($ million)
Fluid power pumps, motors, and hydrostatic transmissions	(X)	17.8
Fluid power cylinders and rotary actuators (hydraulic and pneumatic)	(X)	11.5
Fluid power filters (hydraulic and pneumatic)	(X)	1.1
Fluid power hose, tube fittings, and assemblies (hydraulic and pneumatic)	(X)	4.0
Fluid power valves (hydraulic and pneumatic)	(X)	12.0
Metal bolts, nuts, screws, and other screw machine products	(X)	11.7
Other fabricated metal products (exc. fluid power products and forgings)	(X)	35.6
Forgings	(X)	1.4
Iron and steel castings (rough and semifinished)	(X)	34.5
Nonferrous (aluminum, copper, etc.) castings (rough and semifinished)	(X)	2.8
Steel bars, bar shapes, and plates (exc. castings, forgings, fabr. metal products)	(X)	27.3
Steel sheet and strip (including tinplate)	(X)	14.2
Steel structural shapes (exc. castings, forgings, fabr. metal products)	(X)	6.0
All other steel shapes and forms (exc. castings, forgings, fabr. metal products)	(X)	5.6
Nonferrous shapes and forms	(X)	3.0
Fractional horsepower electric timing motors (less than 1 hp)	(X)	9.6
Other fractional horsepower electric motors (less than 1 hp)	(X)	10.0
Integral horsepower electric motors and generators (1 hp or more)	(X)	16.8
Electrical transmission, distribution, and control equipment	(X)	75.6
Electrical industrial capacitors, resistors, rheostats, and coil windings	(X)	5.9
Numerical controls, metalworking machinery (exc. programmable)	(X)	2.6
Programmable controllers for metalworking machinery	(X)	20.4
Printed circuit assemblies, loaded boards, and modules	(X)	11.6
Printed ciruit boards (without inserted components) for electronic circuitry	(X)	2.1
Semiconductors (incl. transistors, diodes, rectifiers, and integrated circuits), for electronic circuitry	(X)	3.7
All other miscellaneous components and accessories for electronic circuitry (exc. tubes)	(X)	7.1
Electrical instrument mechanisms and meter movements	(X)	4.1
Electronic communication equipment	(X)	10.0
Optical instruments and lenses (exc. sighting, tracking, and fire control)	(X)	1.8
Ball bearings (mounted or unmounted)	(X)	9.3
Roller bearings (mounted or unmounted)	(X)	6.0
Mechanical speed changers, gears, and industrial high-speed drives	(X)	12.1
Wood boxes, pallets, skids, and containers	(X)	3.2
Cutting tools for machine tools	(X)	7.8
Fabricated plastics products (exc. gaskets, hoses, and belting)	(X)	11.2
Paper and paperboard containers (incl. shipping sacks and other paper packaging supplies)	(X)	2.6
All other materials, components, parts, containers, and supplies	(X)	225.3
Materials, ingredients, containers, and supplies, nsk	(X)	361.8

Source: 2002 *Economic Census*. Explanation of symbols used: (D): Withheld to avoid disclosure of competitive data; na: Not available; (S): Withheld because statistical norms were not met; (X): Not applicable; (Z): Less than half the unit shown; nec: Not elsewhere classified; nsk: Not specified by kind; - : zero; p : 10-19 percent estimated; q : 20-29 percent estimated.

PRODUCT SHARE DETAILS

Product or Product Class Shipments	Mil. $	Product or Product Class Shipments	Mil. $
METALWORKING MACHINERY, NEC	2,677.0	(except dies, handheld, and ultrasonic)	7.9
Assembly machines	**1,829.9**	Wire rope and wire cable making machines (except handheld and ultrasonic)	5.6
Rotary transfer metalworking assembly machines (dial and rotary, trunnion, center column)	213.1	Other metalworking machines for working wire (except handheld and ultasonic)	79.8
Synchronous inline transfer metalworking assembly machines	288.9	Cut-to-length coil handling lines (conversion or straightening) (except handheld and ultrasonic)	172.3
Nonsynchronous inline transfer metalworking assembly machines	238.0	Slitting coil handling lines (conversion or straightening) (except handheld and ultrasonic)	40.9
Special-purpose and other types of metalworking assembly machines	865.0	Other metalworking machinery (except handheld and ultrasonic)	347.4
Parts and attachments for metalworking assembly machines (sold separately)	135.4	Parts and attachments for other metalworking machinery (except handheld and ultrasonic) (sold separately)	53.5
Assembly machines, nsk	89.5		
Other metalworking machinery (except handheld and ultrasonic)	**738.3**	Other metalworking machinery (except handheld and ultrasonic), nsk	31.0
Other metalworking machinery (except handheld and ultrasonic)	707.4	**Metalworking machinery, nec, nsk, total**	**108.8**
Metalworking draw benches and wiredrawing machines			

Source: 2002 *Economic Census*. The values are product shipments in millions of dollars for 2002. Total product shipments may be lower or higher than industry shipments. See Introduction for a full discussion. Values of indented subcategories are summed in the main heading(s). The symbol (D) appears when data are withheld to prevent disclosure of competitive information. The abbreviation nsk stands for 'not specified by kind' and nec for 'not elsewhere classified'. A dash (-) means zero.

INPUTS AND OUTPUTS FOR ROLLING MILL & OTHER METALWORKING MACHINERY

Economic Sector or Industry Providing Inputs	%	Sector	Economic Sector or Industry Buying Outputs	%	Sector
Compensation of employees	36.0		Private fixed investment	84.6	
Management of companies & enterprises	7.0	Services	Educational services, nec	4.4	Services
Wholesale trade	5.3	Trade	Exports of goods & services	3.2	Cap Inv
Iron & steel mills & ferroalloys	3.3	Manufg.	Special tools, dies, jigs, & fixtures	3.1	Manufg.
Relay & industrial controls	3.0	Manufg.	Rolling mill & other metalworking machinery	2.8	Manufg.
Rolling mill & other metalworking machinery	2.8	Manufg.	Plate work & fabricated structural products	0.5	Manufg.
Metal cutting & forming machine tools	2.8	Manufg.	Metal tanks (heavy gauge)	0.4	Manufg.
Motors & generators	2.3	Manufg.	Power boilers & heat exchangers	0.4	Manufg.
Ferrous metal foundries	2.0	Manufg.	Manufacturing, nec	0.3	Manufg.
Speed changers, industrial high-speed drives, & gears	1.7	Manufg.			
Ball & roller bearings	1.5	Manufg.			
Fluid power process machinery	1.4	Manufg.			
Machine shops	1.3	Manufg.			
Real estate	1.2	Fin/R.E.			
Valve & fittings other than plumbing	1.1	Manufg.			
Securities, commodity contracts, investments	1.0	Fin/R.E.			
Turned products & screws, nuts, & bolts	0.9	Manufg.			
Printed circuit assemblies (electronic assemblies)	0.8	Manufg.			
Plastics products, nec	0.8	Manufg.			
Electronic components, nec	0.7	Manufg.			
Lessors of nonfinancial assets	0.6	Fin/R.E.			
Advertising & related services	0.6	Services			
Power generation & supply	0.6	Util.			
Abrasive products	0.6	Manufg.			
Custom computer programming services	0.6	Services			
Truck transportation	0.5	Util.			
Coating, engraving, heat treating & allied activities	0.5	Manufg.			
Monetary authorities/depository credit intermediation	0.5	Fin/R.E.			
Legal services	0.5	Services			
Architectural, engineering, & related services	0.5	Services			
Taxes on production & imports, less subsidies	0.5				
Cutting tools & machine tool accessories	0.5	Manufg.			
Broadcast & wireless communications equipment	0.5	Manufg.			
Scientific research & development services	0.4	Services			
Professional, scientific, technical services, nec	0.4	Services			
Data processing, hosting, & related services	0.4	Services			
Electronic capacitors, resistors, coils, transformers	0.4	Manufg.			
Telecommunications	0.4	Services			
Accounting, tax preparation, bookkeeping, & payroll	0.4	Services			
Automotive equipment rental & leasing	0.3	Fin/R.E.			
Semiconductors & related devices	0.3	Manufg.			
Warehousing & storage	0.3	Util.			
Plastics packaging materials, film & sheet	0.3	Manufg.			
Chemical products & preparations, nec	0.3	Manufg.			
Food services & drinking places	0.3	Services			
Management, scientific, & technical consulting	0.3	Services			
Forging, stamping, & sintering, nec	0.3	Manufg.			
Motor vehicle parts	0.2	Manufg.			
Fabricated metals, nec	0.2	Manufg.			
Wood containers & pallets	0.2	Manufg.			
Custom roll forming	0.2	Manufg.			
Metal cans, boxes, & other containers (light gauge)	0.2	Manufg.			
Unlaminated plastics profile shapes	0.2	Manufg.			
Electricity & signal testing instruments	0.2	Manufg.			
Hotels & motels, including casino hotels	0.2	Services			
Nonferrous metal foundries	0.2	Manufg.			
Natural gas distribution	0.2	Util.			
Services to buildings & dwellings	0.2	Services			
Maintenance/repair of nonresidential structures	0.2	Construct.			
Rubber products, nec	0.2	Manufg.			
Commercial & industrial machinery rental & leasing	0.2	Fin/R.E.			
Postal service	0.2	Util.			
Other computer related services, including facilities	0.2	Services			
Business support services	0.2	Services			
Electrical equipment & components, nec	0.1	Manufg.			
Plate work & fabricated structural products	0.1	Manufg.			
Nondepository credit intermediation activities	0.1	Fin/R.E.			
Air transportation	0.1	Util.			
Crowns & closures & metal stamping	0.1	Manufg.			
Paperboard containers	0.1	Manufg.			
Employment services	0.1	Services			
Handtools	0.1	Manufg.			
Paperboard mills	0.1	Manufg.			
Specialized design services	0.1	Services			
Automotive repair & maintenance, ex. car washes	0.1	Services			
Bare printed circuit boards	0.1	Manufg.			
General purpose machinery, nec	0.1	Manufg.			

Source: Benchmark Input-Output Accounts for the U.S. Economy, 2002, U.S. Department of Commerce, Washington D.C., January 2008. User should note that this Input-Output table is not for this particular narrowly defined industry but for a larger aggregate. Input and Output data for Rolling Mill & Other Metal Working Machinery include Input and Output data for the Annual Survey of Manufactures' NAICS industries 333516 and 333518. The abbreviation nec stands for 'not elsewhere classified'.

OCCUPATIONS EMPLOYED BY METALWORKING MACHINERY MANUFACTURING

Occupation	% of Total 2006	Change to 2016	Occupation	% of Total 2006	Change to 2016
Machinists	12.8	-14.0	Office clerks, general	1.7	-19.3
Tool & die makers	11.0	-14.0	Shipping, receiving, & traffic clerks	1.6	-21.2
Computer-controlled machine tool operators	5.4	-9.9	Welders, cutters, solderers, & brazers	1.6	-12.9
First-line supervisors/managers of production workers	4.6	-18.1	Bookkeeping, accounting, & auditing clerks	1.5	-18.1
Grinding, lapping, polishing machine tool operators	3.3	-20.6	Helpers--Production workers	1.4	-18.1
Cutting, punching, & press machine operators	3.2	-26.3	Sales reps, wholesale & manufacturing, exc tech	1.4	-18.1
Team assemblers	2.9	-18.1	Tool grinders, filers, & sharpeners	1.4	-26.3
Molding, coremaking, & casting machine operators	2.8	-26.3	Numerical tool & process control programmers	1.3	-15.6
Mechanical engineers	2.2	-18.1	Milling & planing machine operators & tenders	1.3	-26.3
General & operations managers	2.0	-26.3	Maintenance & repair workers, general	1.3	-18.1
Inspectors, testers, sorters, samplers, & weighers	2.0	-22.8	Industrial production managers	1.1	-18.1
Mechanical drafters	1.8	-17.2	Janitors & cleaners, exc maids & housekeeping cleaners	1.1	-16.3
Lathe & turning machine tool operators & tenders	1.8	-26.3	Multiple machine tool operators & tenders	1.0	-9.9

Source: Industry-Occupation Matrix, Bureau of Labor Statistics, December 4, 2007. These data are reported based on 4-digit NAICS categories but have been matched to corresponding 6-digit NAICS industry codes. The change reported for each occupation to the year 2016 is a percent of growth or decline as estimated by the Bureau of Labor Statistics. The abbreviation nec stands for 'not elsewhere classified'.

LOCATION BY STATE AND REGIONAL CONCENTRATION

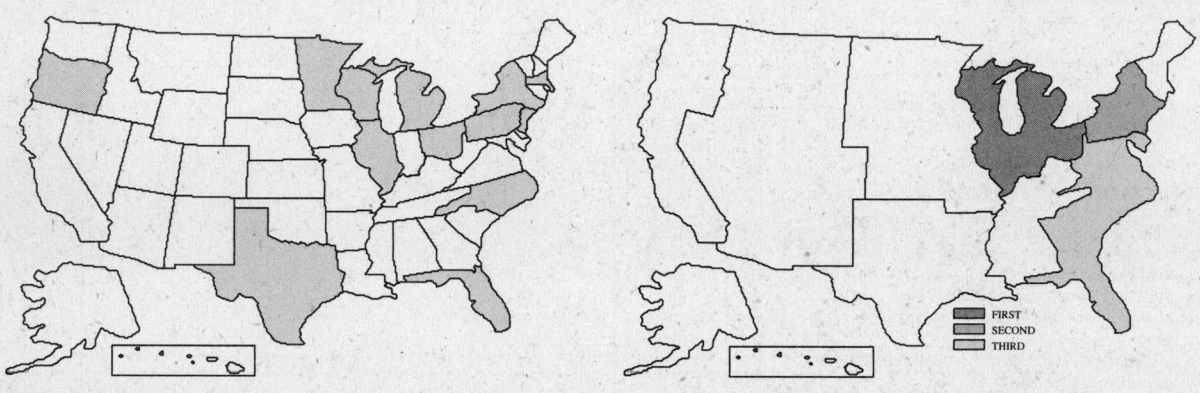

FIRST
SECOND
THIRD

INDUSTRY DATA BY STATE

State	Establish-ments	Shipments			Employment				Cost as % of Shipments	Investment per Employee ($)
		Total ($ mil)	% of U.S.	Per Establ.	Total Number	% of U.S.	Per Establ.	Wages ($/hour)		
Michigan	91	1,063.5	36.2	11,687.3	5,011	29.9	55	21.44	42.0	2,838
Illinois	45	369.8	12.6	8,217.8	1,697	10.1	38	19.08	37.9	5,202
Ohio	41	248.0	8.4	6,048.4	1,538	9.2	38	21.15	39.7	3,102
New York	18	126.7	4.3	7,037.2	990	5.9	55	19.64	45.1	2,380
Wisconsin	19	91.5	3.1	4,816.2	736	4.4	39	16.69	45.5	1,704
Massachusetts	16	88.4	3.0	5,525.4	405	2.4	25	17.02	49.0	12,679
Pennsylvania	22	72.3	2.5	3,285.8	681	4.1	31	16.86	32.4	2,617
Minnesota	12	65.2	2.2	5,430.3	368	2.2	31	24.40	49.7	856
Texas	13	58.9	2.0	4,530.2	393	2.3	30	13.35	40.3	2,249
Florida	10	55.4	1.9	5,543.1	306	1.8	31	16.85	43.2	3,101
Oregon	6	42.5	1.4	7,079.7	338	2.0	56	21.80	43.6	1,109
New Jersey	10	36.3	1.2	3,625.3	187	1.1	19	16.84	28.3	11,059
North Carolina	7	25.1	0.9	3,588.7	235	1.4	34	11.62	39.6	5,545

Source: 2002 Economic Census. The states are in descending order of shipments or establishments (if shipment data are missing for the majority). The symbol (D) appears when data are withheld to prevent disclosure of competitive information. States marked with (D) are sorted by number of establishments. A dash (-) indicates that the data element cannot be calculated. Data may not show all states active in the NAICS category. All data available at the time of publication are shown.

NAICS 333611 - TURBINE AND TURBINE GENERATOR SET UNIT MANUFACTURING

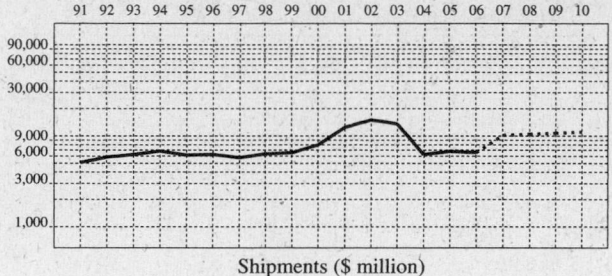

Shipments ($ million)

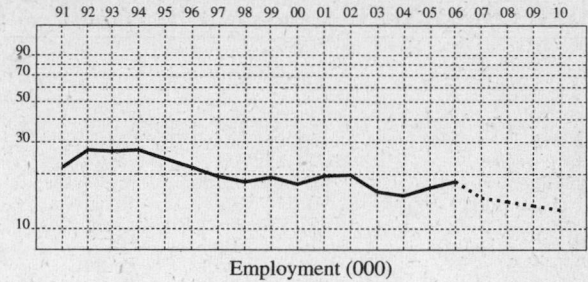

Employment (000)

GENERAL STATISTICS

| Year | Companies | Establishments | | Employment | | | Compensation | | Production ($ million) | | | |
		Total	with 20 or more employees	Total (000)	Production Workers (000)	Hours (Mil)	Payroll ($ mil)	Wages ($/hr)	Cost of Materials	Value Added by Manufacture	Value of Shipments	Capital Invest.
1991		76	41	21.8	13.0	27.4	962.8	18.54	2,674.4	2,882.9	5,093.0	182.5
1992	64	79	48	27.1	15.0	30.1	1,106.5	18.38	2,690.9	2,952.8	5,842.6	312.0
1993		81	50	26.7	15.0	30.4	1,126.6	18.62	2,684.2	3,808.6	6,234.0	310.1
1994		89	50	27.1	15.1	30.0	1,237.1	19.67	3,049.8	3,947.2	6,801.6	246.5
1995		91	51	24.3	14.8	28.8	1,050.8	19.03	3,028.4	2,700.7	6,143.8	161.9
1996		93	48	21.8	13.2	26.9	948.3	19.44	3,049.3	3,167.9	6,267.7	150.1
1997	67	85	53	19.4	11.0	23.1	905.4	20.54	2,825.0	2,786.6	5,767.2	177.4
1998		98	53	18.1	10.0	21.2	837.2	20.64	3,152.9	3,234.5	6,338.2	305.9
1999		103	61	19.2	10.4	21.1	912.4	21.42	3,188.0	3,435.8	6,529.9	309.0
2000		104	63	17.6	9.8	19.7	941.5	23.63	4,589.8	3,499.1	7,990.4	322.2
2001		110	62	19.5	11.8	23.9	1,109.5	23.77	6,325.9	6,329.6	12,449.4	358.8
2002	93	112	74	19.8	11.6	23.4	1,025.1	24.39	5,640.2	9,300.5	15,017.9	172.4
2003		131	74	16.0	9.9	21.1	924.5	23.52	6,478.1	7,011.6	13,631.0	209.7
2004		130	68	15.2	8.3	17.3	860.5	26.07	3,126.7	3,067.2	6,255.1	128.1
2005		133	69	16.8	9.4	20.1	928.5	24.12	3,671.0	2,903.3	6,762.1	178.2
2006		134P	75P	18.2	9.8	20.4	1,019.4	23.17	3,816.3	2,835.5	6,566.4	213.4
2007		138P	77P	14.8P	8.3P	17.5P	913.6P	25.68P	5,914.2P	4,394.3P	10,176.1P	208.0P
2008		142P	79P	14.1P	7.9P	16.8P	904.2P	26.17P	6,081.4P	4,518.5P	10,463.8P	204.9P
2009		146P	81P	13.4P	7.5P	16.0P	894.7P	26.65P	6,248.7P	4,642.7P	10,751.6P	201.9P
2010		150P	84P	12.7P	7.1P	15.2P	885.3P	27.14P	6,415.9P	4,767.0P	11,039.3P	198.9P

Sources: 1992, 1997, 2002 *Economic Census*; other years, up to 2006, are from the *Annual Survey of Manufactures*. Establishment counts for non-Census years are from *County Business Patterns*; 1997 and 2002 values are from the 1997 and 2002 censuses respectively, reported in the Federal Government's NAICS format. Other years were originally reported in equivalent SIC format. 'P's show projections by the editors.

INDICES OF CHANGE

| Year | Companies | Establishments | | Employment | | | Compensation | | Production ($ million) | | | |
		Total	with 20 or more employees	Total (000)	Production Workers (000)	Hours (Mil)	Payroll ($ mil)	Wages ($/hr)	Cost of Materials	Value Added by Manufacture	Value of Shipments	Capital Invest.
1992	69	71	65	137	129	129	108	75	48	32	39	181
1997	72	76	72	98	95	99	88	84	50	30	38	103
2001		98	84	98	102	102	108	97	112	68	83	208
2002	100	100	100	100	100	100	100	100	100	100	100	100
2003		117	100	81	85	90	90	96	115	75	91	122
2004		116	92	77	72	74	84	107	55	33	42	74
2005		119	93	85	81	86	91	99	65	31	45	103
2006		119P	101P	92	84	87	99	95	68	30	44	124
2007		123P	104P	75P	72P	75P	89P	105P	105P	47P	68P	121P
2008		127P	107P	71P	68P	72P	88P	107P	108P	49P	70P	119P
2009		130P	110P	68P	65P	68P	87P	109P	111P	50P	72P	117P
2010		134P	113P	64P	61P	65P	86P	111P	114P	51P	74P	115P

Sources: Same as General Statistics. Values reflect change from the base year, 2002. Values above 100 mean greater than 2002, values below 100 mean less than 2002, and the values of 100 in other years means the same as 2002. 'P's show projections by the editors.

SELECTED RATIOS

For 2002	Avg. of All Manufact.	Analyzed Industry	Index	For 2002	Avg. of All Manufact.	Analyzed Industry	Index
Employees per Establishment	42	177	421	Value Added per Production Worker	182,367	801,767	440
Payroll per Establishment	1,639,184	9,152,679	558	Cost per Establishment	5,769,015	50,358,929	873
Payroll per Employee	39,053	51,773	133	Cost per Employee	137,446	284,859	207
Production Workers per Establishment	30	104	351	Cost per Production Worker	195,506	486,224	249
Wages per Establishment	694,845	5,095,768	733	Shipments per Establishment	11,158,348	134,088,393	1,202
Wages per Production Worker	23,548	49,201	209	Shipments per Employee	265,847	758,480	285
Hours per Production Worker	1,980	2,017	102	Shipments per Production Worker	378,144	1,294,647	342
Wages per Hour	11.89	24.39	205	Investment per Establishment	361,338	1,539,286	426
Value Added per Establishment	5,381,325	83,040,179	1,543	Investment per Employee	8,609	8,707	101
Value Added per Employee	128,210	469,722	366	Investment per Production Worker	12,245	14,862	121

Sources: Same as General Statistics. The 'Average of All Manufacturing' column represents the average of all manufacturing industries reported for the most recent complete year available. The Index shows the relationship between the Average and the Analyzed Industry. For example, 100 means that they are equal; 500 that the Analyzed Industry is five times the average; 50 means that the Analyzed Industry is half the national average. The abbreviation 'na' is used to show that data are 'not available'. Ratios shown for 2002, the last complete census year.

LEADING COMPANIES   Number shown: 75   Total sales ($ mil): 22,715   Total employment (000): 64.3

Company Name	Address				CEO Name	Phone	Co. Type	Sales ($ mil)	Empl. (000)
Cameron International Corp.	1333 W Loop S	Houston	TX	77027	Sheldon R. Erikson	713-513-3300	P	4,666	15.4
Siemens Power Generation Inc.	4400 N Alafaya Trl.	Orlando	FL	32826	Randy Zwirn	407-736-2000	R	3,081*	3.0
Sequa Corp.	200 Park Ave.	New York	NY	10166	Gail Binderman	212-986-5500	P	2,183	10.2
Briggs and Stratton Corp.	PO Box 702	Milwaukee	WI	53201		414-259-5333	P	2,157	3.7
Elliott Overseas Corp.	901 N Fourth St.	Jeannette	PA	15644	Donald Maloney	724-527-2811	S	2,023*	2.0
Teleflex Inc.	155 S Limerick Rd.	Limerick	PA	19468	Jeffrey P. Black	610-948-5100	P	1,934	14.0
Dresser-Rand Group Inc.	1200 W S Houston	Houston	TX	77043	Vince Volpe	713-467-2221	P	1,665	6.0
Vestas Americas	1881 SW Naito	Portland	OR	97201	Jens Sobey	503-327-2000	S	870*	0.1
Riley Power Inc.	PO Box 15040	Worcester	MA	01615		508-852-7100	R	612*	0.4
Tuthill Corp.	8500 S Madison St.	Burr Ridge	IL	60527		630-382-4900	R	388*	0.9
TECT Utica Corp.	2 Halsey Rd.	Whitesboro	NY	13492	Ron Cable	315-768-8070	R	356*	1.3
Elliott Co.	901 N 4th St.	Jeannette	PA	15644	Antonio Casillo	724-527-2811	R	334*	0.7
Voith Siemens Hydro Power Gen.	PO Box 712	York	PA	17405	Mark Garner	717-792-7000	R	327*	0.4
Louisiana Compressor Maint.	PO Box 668	Houma	LA	70361	Stephen Snider	985-868-7232	S	269*	0.1
Rolls-Royce Energy Systems	105 N Sandusky St.	Mt. Vernon	OH	43050		740-393-8888	S	208*	0.1
Revak Turbomachinery Services	PO Box 1645	La Porte	TX	77572	Lynn Revak	281-474-4458	R	207*	0.1
QUANTUM Fuel Sys. Tech. WW	17872 Cartwright Rd	Irvine	CA	92614	Alan P. Niedzwiecki	949-399-4500	P	147	0.5
Cooper Turbocompressor Inc.	PO Box 209	Buffalo	NY	14225	Sheldon Erikson	716-896-6600	S	130	0.5
Valley Power Systems Inc.	425 S Hacienda Blvd	City of Industry	CA	91745	Sam Hill	626-333-1243	S	100*	0.3
Pfpc Enterprises Inc.	5750 Hillside Ave.	Cincinnati	OH	45233	James Coffaro	513-941-6200	R	91*	0.3
Stork H and E Turbo Blading	PO Box 177	Ithaca	NY	14851	John Berry	607-277-4968	R	56*	0.2
Chromalloy Castings Tampa	7030 Anderson Rd.	Tampa	FL	33634	Norman Alexander	813-885-4781	S	51*	0.2
Parker Hannifin HPD	14249 Indu. Pkwy.	Marysville	OH	43040	David Weir	937-644-3915	S	49*	0.2
Continental Machines Inc.	5505 W 123rd St.	Savage	MN	55378	M Johnson	952-890-3300	R	45*	0.2
Turbocam Inc.	PO Box 830	Barrington	NH	03825	Marian Noronha	603-905-0220	R	41*	0.1
Pratt and Whitney Auto-Air	5640 Enterprise Dr.	Lansing	MI	48911	Louis Chenevert	517-393-4040	S	36*	0.3
Microdyne Products Co.	PO Box 910	Ballwin	MO	63011	Lee Witengier	314-291-5600	R	34*	<0.1
M and W Gear Co.	1020 S Sangamon	Gibson City	IL	60936	Ronald A. Robinson	217-784-4261	S	33*	0.1
Lm Glasfiber Inc.	PO Box 5637	Grand Forks	ND	58206	Craig Hoiseth	701-780-9910	R	30*	0.1
Rich Technology International	28 Pond View Dr.	Scarborough	ME	04074	Allen Estes	207-883-7424	R	30*	0.1
Katolight Corp.	PO Box 3229	Mankato	MN	56002		507-625-7973	R	30*	0.2
Hunt Valve Company Inc.	1913 E State St.	Salem	OH	44460	Gerald Bogner	330-337-9535	R	29*	0.2
Arcturus Marine Systems Inc.	517 Martin Ave. A	Rohnert Park	CA	94928	D'Milo Hallerberg	707-586-3155	R	28*	<0.1
RHM Fluid Power Inc.	375 Manufacturers	Westland	MI	48186	W. W. Tulloch III	734-326-5400	R	27*	<0.1
Hardie-Tynes Company Inc.	PO Box 12166	Birmingham	AL	35202		205-252-5191	R	25*	<0.1
Clayton Industries	17477 Hurley St.	City of Industry	CA	91744	John Clayton	626-435-1200	R	25*	0.1
Tech Development Inc.	PO Box 13557	Dayton	OH	45413		937-898-9600	R	24*	<0.1
Capstone Turbine Corp.	21211 Nordhoff St.	Chatsworth	CA	91311		818-734-5300	P	21	0.2
Precision Rebuilders Inc.	350 N Commercial	Saint Clair	MO	63077	Mike Hill	636-629-1444	R	20*	<0.1
Btec Turbines L.P.	16730 Jacintoport	Houston	TX	77015		281-864-9122	R	19*	<0.1
Baker Energy	16340 Park Ten Pl.	Houston	TX	77084		281-579-7850	S	18*	0.1
Gilcrest Equipment Co.	618 N Enterprise Dr	Warrensburg	MO	64093	James Gilcrest	660-422-4272	R	18*	<0.1
Service Hydraulic and Supply	615 Airport Dr.	Shreveport	LA	71107	Robert Millan	318-226-1000	R	15*	<0.1
ACD Inc.	2321 S Pullman St.	Santa Ana	CA	92705		949-261-7533	S	14*	<0.1
Field Controls L.L.C.	2630 Airport Rd.	Kinston	NC	28504		252-522-3031	R	14*	<0.1
Precision Aerospace L.L.C.	3011 W Windsor	Phoenix	AZ	85009		602-352-8658	R	13*	<0.1
Aero Propulsion Support Inc.	108 May Dr. Ste. A	Harrison	OH	45030	Allan Slattery	513-367-9452	R	13*	<0.1
American Hydro Corp.	PO Box 3628	York	PA	17402	Selim Chacour	717-755-5300	R	13*	0.1
R and D Dynamics Corp.	15 Barber Pond Rd.	Bloomfield	CT	06002	Giri Agrawal	860-726-1204	R	12*	<0.1
Hoerbiger Auto. Comfort Sys.	284 Enterprise Dr.	Auburn	AL	36830	Gerhard Schoell	334-321-2292	R	11*	<0.1
Yanke Energy Inc.	PO Box 5405	Boise	ID	83705	Sheldon Schultz	208-338-2205	R	11*	<0.1
MI-TECH Inc.	PO Box 62499	N Charleston	SC	29419	William Totten	843-553-2743	R	10*	<0.1
Oliver Equipment Co.	PO Box 41145	Houston	TX	77241	Gale Oliver	713-856-9206	R	10*	<0.1
Turbo Dynamics Corp.	150 Express St.	Plainview	NY	11803	Mansour Lavi	516-349-8012	R	10*	<0.1
Steam Turbine Alt. Resources	PO Box 862	Marion	OH	43301	Sue Flaherty	740-387-5535	R	9*	<0.1
Alturdyne	660 Steel Street	El Cajon	CA	92020	Frank Verbeke	619-440-5531	R	9*	0.1
Hydro Dynamics Inc.	6200 Delfield Dr.	Waterford	MI	48329	Robert Newell	248-623-4700	R	9*	<0.1
Pacific Fluid Systems Inc.	12403 NE Marx St.	Portland	OR	97230		503-222-3295	R	9*	<0.1
Wmh Fluidpower Inc.	862 Lenox Ave.	Portage	MI	49024	Dave Gruss	269-327-7011	R	9*	<0.1
Industrial Governors/Ignition	19 20th St. S	Texas City	TX	77590	Ron Frefehour	409-945-0070	R	9*	<0.1
Alin Machining Company Inc.	3131 W Soffel Ave.	Melrose Park	IL	60160	Manny Gandhi	708-345-8600	R	8*	<0.1
Trireme Manufacturing Company	245 Boston St.	Topsfield	MA	01983	John Tsiplakis	978-887-2132	R	6*	<0.1
Engineered Sales Inc.	18 Progress Pkwy.	Maryland Hgts	MO	63043	Warren Hoffner	314-878-4500	S	6*	<0.1
LKM Industries Inc.	44 6th Rd.	Woburn	MA	01801	Salvatore Colucciello	781-935-9210	R	6*	<0.1
Tendaire Industries Inc.	1100 W Cedar St.	Beresford	SD	57004	Leon Lease	605-763-5500	R	6*	<0.1
Mary Mullen	1414 S Yellw Sprgs	Springfield	OH	45506	Mary Mullen	937-322-1861	R	6*	<0.1
Turbo City Inc.	1137 W Katella Ave.	Orange	CA	92867	Tom Miller	714-639-4933	R	5*	<0.1
Becon Inc.	46 Schweir Rd.	South Windsor	CT	06074	Brian Nutt	860-528-9641	R	5*	<0.1
Marsh Plating Corp.	103 N Grove St.	Ypsilanti	MI	48198	David Marsh	734-483-5767	R	5*	0.1
Newton Manufacturing Co.	4249 Delemere	Royal Oak	MI	48073	Noel Cook	248-549-9600	R	5*	<0.1
Rife Hydraulic Engine Mfg. Co.	PO Box 95	Nanticoke	PA	18634	N Gupta	570-740-1100	R	5*	<0.1
SRS Crisafulli Inc.	1610 Crisafulli Dr.	Glendive	MT	59330	Richard Memhard	406-365-3392	R	5*	<0.1
Electro-Hydraulic Automation	PO Box 10495	Cedar Rapids	IA	52410	Donald Kaas	319-395-0005	R	4*	<0.1
Converta Kiln Inc.	PO Box 341362	Memphis	TN	38184	Patrick Plass	901-358-4596	R	4*	<0.1
ROC Industries Inc.	1605 Brittmoore Rd.	Houston	TX	77043	Pamela Carlson	713-468-7744	R	4*	<0.1

Source: *Ward's Business Directory of U.S. Private and Public Companies*, Volumes 1 and 2, 2008. The company type code used is as follows: P - Public, R - Private, S - Subsidiary, D - Division, J - Joint Venture, A - Affiliate, G - Group. Sales are in millions of dollars, employees are in thousands. An asterisk (*) indicates an estimated sales volume. The symbol < stands for 'less than'. Company names and addresses are truncated, in some cases, to fit into the available space.

MATERIALS CONSUMED

Material	Quantity	Delivered Cost ($ million)
Fluid power pumps, motors, and hydrostatic transmissions	(X)	83.6
Fluid power cylinders and rotary actuators (hydraulic and pneumatic)	(X)	9.3
Fluid power filters (hydraulic and pneumatic)	(X)	39.8
Fluid power hose, tube fittings, and assemblies (hydraulic and pneumatic)	(X)	56.3
Fluid power valves (hydraulic and pneumatic)	(X)	87.9
Metal bolts, nuts, screws, and other screw machine products	(X)	58.8
Metal stampings	(X)	1.6
Metal tanks, heat exchangers, and other boiler products	(X)	75.5
Fabricated structural metal products (excluding forgings)	(X)	(D)
All other fabricated metal products (excluding forgings)	(X)	202.4
Iron and steel forgings	(X)	813.8
Nonferrous forgings	(X)	(D)
Iron and steel castings (rough and semifinished)	(X)	676.3
Aluminum and aluminum-base alloy castings (rough and semifinished)	(X)	11.0
Other nonferrous metal castings, rough or semifinished (inc. aluminum)	(X)	28.2
Steel bars, bar shapes, and plates (exc. castings, forgings, fabr. metal products)	(X)	197.6
Steel sheet and strip (including tinplate)	(X)	39.1
All other steel shapes and forms (exc. castings, forgings, fabr. metal products)	(X)	42.0
Nonferrous shapes and forms	(X)	(D)
Pistons, piston rings, carburetors, and valves (intake and exhaust only)	(X)	(D)
Engine electrical equipment (incl. spark plugs, magnetos, generators, starters, etc.)	(X)	(D)
Integral horsepower electric motors and generators (1 hp or more)	(X)	(D)
Injection fuel pumps	(X)	(D)
Machined engine blocks	(X)	(D)
Ball bearings (mounted or unmounted)	(X)	0.4
Roller bearings (mounted or unmounted)	(X)	(D)
Plain bearings and bushings	(X)	26.8
Mechanical speed changers, gears, and industrial high-speed drives	(X)	42.5
Turbines purchased for incorporation into turbine generator sets	(X)	12.4
Generators purchased for incorporation into turbine generator sets	(X)	6.1
Gaskets (all types), and packing and sealing devices	(X)	8.0
Fabricated plastics products (excluding gaskets)	(X)	0.7
Rubber and plastics hose and belting	(X)	(D)
Cutting tools for machine tools	(X)	16.0
All other materials, components, parts, containers, and supplies	(X)	473.9
Materials, ingredients, containers, and supplies, nsk	(X)	67.1

Source: 2002 *Economic Census*. Explanation of symbols used: (D): Withheld to avoid disclosure of competitive data; na: Not available; (S): Withheld because statistical norms were not met; (X): Not applicable; (Z): Less than half the unit shown; nec: Not elsewhere classified; nsk: Not specified by kind; - : zero; p : 10-19 percent estimated; q : 20-29 percent estimated.

PRODUCT SHARE DETAILS

Product or Product Class Shipments	Mil. $	Product or Product Class Shipments	Mil. $
TURBINES, TURBINE GENERATORS, AND TURBINE GENERATOR SETS	13,775.1	(sold separately)	1,210.4
Turbine generator sets	(D)	Parts and accessories for wind turbines (sold separately)	(D)
Steam turbines and other vapor turbines	880.5	Turbine generator parts and accessories (sold	
Accessories for turbines, turbine generators, and turbine		separately)	132.0
generator sets	1,817.2	Other turbines and turbine generators	1,521.5
Parts and accessories for hydraulic turbines (sold		Hydraulic turbines (all sizes)	(D)
separately)	(D)	Wind turbines	(D)
Parts and accessories for steam and other vapor turbines		Turbine generators	(D)
(sold separately)	404.6	Gas turbines, except aircraft (all sizes)	(D)
Parts and accessories for gas turbines, except aircraft		Turbines, turbine generators, and turbine generator sets	
		(including parts), nsk, total	96.9

Source: 2002 *Economic Census*. The values are product shipments in millions of dollars for 2002. Total product shipments may be lower or higher than industry shipments. See Introduction for a full discussion. Values of indented subcategories are summed in the main heading(s). The symbol (D) appears when data are withheld to prevent disclosure of competitive information. The abbreviation nsk stands for 'not specified by kind' and nec for 'not elsewhere classified'. A dash (-) means zero.

INPUTS AND OUTPUTS FOR TURBINE AND TURBINE GENERATOR SET UNITS MANUFACTURING

Economic Sector or Industry Providing Inputs	%	Sector	Economic Sector or Industry Buying Outputs	%	Sector
Compensation of employees	10.3		Private fixed investment	54.9	
Forging, stamping, & sintering, nec	5.9	Manufg.	Exports of goods & services	23.8	Cap Inv
Ferrous metal foundries	4.4	Manufg.	Power generation & supply	10.3	Util.
Wholesale trade	2.1	Trade	Natural gas distribution	3.4	Util.
Specialized design services	2.0	Services	Federal government, investment, national defense	2.3	Fed Govt
Management of companies & enterprises	1.9	Services	Federal government, investment, nondefense	1.3	Fed Govt
Iron & steel mills & ferroalloys	1.8	Manufg.	Ship building & repairing	1.1	Manufg.
Employment services	1.5	Services	Federal electric utilities	0.9	Fed Govt
Engine equipment, nec	1.5	Manufg.	S/L govt. invest., other	0.8	S/L Govt

Continued on next page.

INPUTS AND OUTPUTS FOR TURBINE AND TURBINE GENERATOR SET UNITS MANUFACTURING - Continued

Economic Sector or Industry Providing Inputs	%	Sector	Economic Sector or Industry Buying Outputs	%	Sector
Noncomparable imports	1.3	Foreign	Other S/L govt. enterprises	0.4	S/L Govt
Business support services	1.2	Services	Waste management & remediation services	0.2	Services
Legal services	1.1	Services	Turbines & turbine generator set units	0.2	Manufg.
Architectural, engineering, & related services	1.0	Services	Services to buildings & dwellings	0.1	Services
Valve & fittings other than plumbing	1.0	Manufg.	Hunting and trapping	0.1	Agric.
Support services, nec	0.9	Services			
Truck transportation	0.8	Util.			
Investigation & security services	0.7	Services			
Machine shops	0.7	Manufg.			
Motor vehicle parts	0.6	Manufg.			
Semiconductors & related devices	0.6	Manufg.			
Turned products & screws, nuts, & bolts	0.6	Manufg.			
Printed circuit assemblies (electronic assemblies)	0.5	Manufg.			
Fluid power process machinery	0.4	Manufg.			
Metal cans, boxes, & other containers (light gauge)	0.4	Manufg.			
Ball & roller bearings	0.4	Manufg.			
Speed changers, industrial high-speed drives, & gears	0.4	Manufg.			
Coating, engraving, heat treating & allied activities	0.3	Manufg.			
Facilities support services	0.3	Services			
Plate work & fabricated structural products	0.3	Manufg.			
Nonferrous metal foundries	0.3	Manufg.			
General purpose machinery, nec	0.3	Manufg.			
Rubber & plastics hose & belting	0.3	Manufg.			
Mechanical power transmission equipment	0.3	Manufg.			
Custom roll forming	0.3	Manufg.			
Motors & generators	0.3	Manufg.			
Real estate	0.2	Fin/R.E.			
Power generation & supply	0.2	Util.			
Fabricated metals, nec	0.2	Manufg.			
Securities, commodity contracts, investments	0.2	Fin/R.E.			
Abrasive products	0.2	Manufg.			
Lessors of nonfinancial assets	0.2	Fin/R.E.			
Turbines & turbine generator set units	0.2	Manufg.			
Postal service	0.1	Util.			
Automotive equipment rental & leasing	0.1	Fin/R.E.			
Advertising & related services	0.1	Services			
Maintenance/repair of nonresidential structures	0.1	Construct.			
Rubber products, nec	0.1	Manufg.			
Services to buildings & dwellings	0.1	Services			
Gaskets, packing, & sealing devices	0.1	Manufg.			
Cutting tools & machine tool accessories	0.1	Manufg.			
Paperboard containers	0.1	Manufg.			
Warehousing & storage	0.1	Util.			
Crowns & closures & metal stamping	0.1	Manufg.			

Source: Benchmark Input-Output Accounts for the U.S. Economy, 2002, U.S. Department of Commerce, Washington, D.C., January 2008. The abbreviation nec stands for 'not elsewhere classified'.

OCCUPATIONS EMPLOYED BY ENGINE, TURBINE, & POWER TRANSMISSION EQUIPMENT

Occupation	% of Total 2006	Change to 2016	Occupation	% of Total 2006	Change to 2016
Team assemblers	10.8	-16.1	Welders, cutters, solderers, & brazers	1.5	-10.7
Engine & other machine assemblers	7.0	-16.1	Industrial machinery mechanics	1.5	-3.5
Machinists	6.7	-11.9	Laborers & freight, stock, & material movers, hand	1.4	-24.5
First-line supervisors/managers of production workers	3.7	-16.1	Drilling & boring machine tool operators	1.4	-24.5
Inspectors, testers, sorters, samplers, & weighers	3.3	-20.9	General & operations managers	1.3	-24.5
Computer-controlled machine tool operators	3.2	-7.7	Cutting, punching, & press machine operators	1.2	-24.5
Assemblers & fabricators, nec	3.2	-24.5	Production, planning, & expediting clerks	1.2	-16.1
Mechanical engineers	2.9	-16.1	Stock clerks & order fillers	1.1	-29.8
Lathe & turning machine tool operators & tenders	2.8	-24.5	Electricians	1.1	-13.0
Maintenance & repair workers, general	2.6	-16.1	Shipping, receiving, & traffic clerks	1.1	-19.2
Multiple machine tool operators & tenders	2.4	-7.7	Customer service representatives	1.1	-7.7
Grinding, lapping, polishing machine tool operators	1.9	-18.6			

Source: Industry-Occupation Matrix, Bureau of Labor Statistics, December 4, 2007. These data are reported based on 4-digit NAICS categories but have been matched to corresponding 6-digit NAICS industry codes. The change reported for each occupation to the year 2016 is a percent of growth or decline as estimated by the Bureau of Labor Statistics. The abbreviation nec stands for 'not elsewhere classified'.

LOCATION BY STATE AND REGIONAL CONCENTRATION

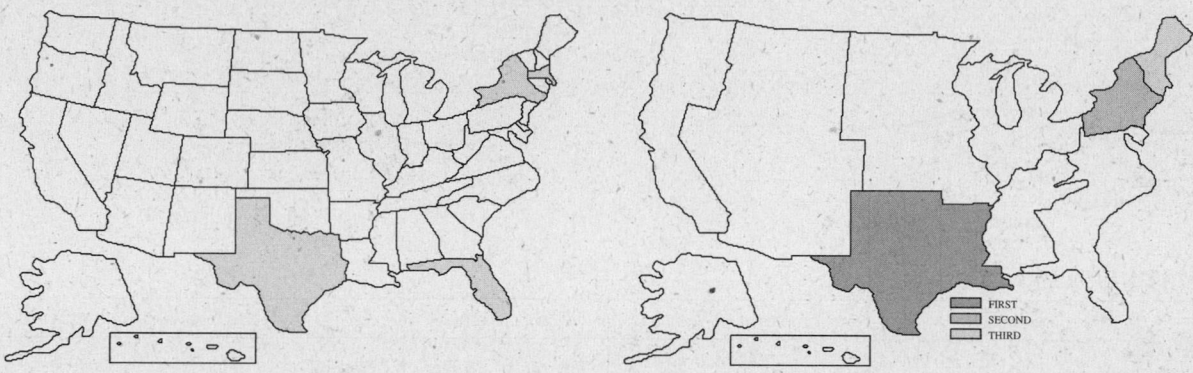

INDUSTRY DATA BY STATE

| State | Establish-ments | Shipments | | | Employment | | | | Cost as % of Shipments | Investment per Employee ($) |
		Total ($ mil)	% of U.S.	Per Establ.	Total Number	% of U.S.	Per Establ.	Wages ($/hour)		
New York	10	3,247.7	21.6	324,772.1	3,617	18.3	362	29.80	45.4	11,280
Texas	11	337.4	2.2	30,676.1	1,448	7.3	132	23.70	40.4	5,598
Massachusetts	6	80.7	0.5	13,449.7	455	2.3	76	26.11	34.3	5,064
Florida	6	30.3	0.2	5,057.5	190	1.0	32	16.80	57.7	1,732

Source: 2002 *Economic Census*. The states are in descending order of shipments or establishments (if shipment data are missing for the majority). The symbol (D) appears when data are withheld to prevent disclosure of competitive information. States marked with (D) are sorted by number of establishments. A dash (-) indicates that the data element cannot be calculated. Data may not show all states active in the NAICS category. All data available at the time of publication are shown.

NAICS 333612 - SPEED CHANGER, INDUSTRIAL HIGH-SPEED DRIVE, AND GEAR MANUFACTURING

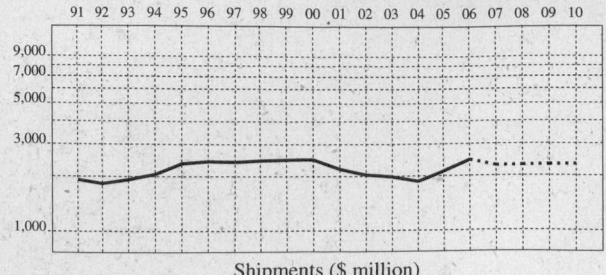

Shipments ($ million)

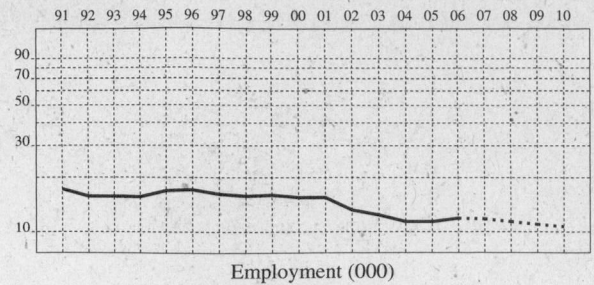

Employment (000)

GENERAL STATISTICS

Year	Companies	Establishments		Employment			Compensation		Production ($ million)			
		Total	with 20 or more employees	Total (000)	Production Workers (000)	Hours (Mil)	Payroll ($ mil)	Wages ($/hr)	Cost of Materials	Value Added by Manufacture	Value of Shipments	Capital Invest.
1991		266	156	17.2	11.5	23.1	509.5	12.84	703.8	1,194.1	1,916.5	63.2
1992	256	287	145	15.7	10.4	20.6	495.8	13.77	646.3	1,160.5	1,823.1	69.8
1993		277	141	15.7	10.6	22.1	526.0	14.33	696.4	1,229.5	1,921.5	55.4
1994		268	138	15.6	10.9	23.2	541.1	14.66	710.0	1,361.3	2,054.0	72.8
1995		261	145	16.9	12.1	24.7	598.5	15.46	895.5	1,510.6	2,351.2	81.5
1996		266	153	17.1	12.2	24.9	596.5	15.19	870.3	1,545.8	2,416.1	105.0
1997	235	266	141	16.2	11.2	22.8	596.4	15.90	938.0	1,467.8	2,399.6	116.2
1998		260	148	15.8	11.0	22.4	607.5	16.65	952.4	1,511.0	2,442.2	85.3
1999		265	140	16.0	11.4	22.8	623.5	16.88	952.3	1,470.3	2,467.5	95.6
2000		256	137	15.5	10.9	21.0	613.6	18.30	959.3	1,512.0	2,476.5	79.3
2001		248	133	15.5	11.0	19.9	609.5	18.44	822.2	1,359.5	2,189.9	59.4
2002	209	240	123	13.2	9.2	17.6	547.2	18.60	762.3	1,261.5	2,036.9	59.5
2003		245	123	12.4	8.6	16.5	522.9	19.09	787.1	1,204.5	1,986.2	41.6
2004		242	118	11.4	8.2	16.4	493.6	19.04	806.2	1,081.2	1,865.7	50.6
2005		233	114	11.4	8.2	16.7	532.2	19.73	946.8	1,193.4	2,121.6	64.2
2006		235p	118p	11.9	8.7	17.6	580.1	20.83	1,072.6	1,401.9	2,452.7	97.7
2007		232p	115p	11.8p	8.6p	16.6p	571.9p	21.04p	996.1p	1,302.0p	2,277.9p	70.2p
2008		229p	113p	11.4p	8.4p	16.1p	573.1p	21.53p	1,001.1p	1,308.4p	2,289.1p	69.6p
2009		226p	111p	11.0p	8.1p	15.6p	574.2p	22.02p	1,006.0p	1,314.8p	2,300.3p	69.1p
2010		223p	108p	10.7p	7.9p	15.1p	575.4p	22.52p	1,010.9p	1,321.2p	2,311.5p	68.5p

Sources: 1992, 1997, 2002 *Economic Census*; other years, up to 2006, are from the *Annual Survey of Manufactures*. Establishment counts for non-Census years are from *County Business Patterns*; 1997 and 2002 values are from the 1997 and 2002 censuses respectively, reported in the Federal Government's NAICS format. Other years were originally reported in equivalent SIC format. 'P's show projections by the editors.

INDICES OF CHANGE

Year	Companies	Establishments		Employment			Compensation		Production ($ million)			
		Total	with 20 or more employees	Total (000)	Production Workers (000)	Hours (Mil)	Payroll ($ mil)	Wages ($/hr)	Cost of Materials	Value Added by Manufacture	Value of Shipments	Capital Invest.
1992	122	120	118	119	113	117	91	74	85	92	90	117
1997	112	111	115	123	122	130	109	85	123	116	118	195
2001		103	108	117	120	113	111	99	108	108	108	100
2002	100	100	100	100	100	100	100	100	100	100	100	100
2003		102	100	94	93	94	96	103	103	95	98	70
2004		101	96	86	89	93	90	102	106	86	92	85
2005		97	93	86	89	95	97	106	124	95	104	108
2006		98p	96p	90	95	100	106	112	141	111	120	164
2007		97p	94p	89p	93p	94p	105p	113p	131p	103p	112p	118p
2008		95p	92p	86p	91p	91p	105p	116p	131p	104p	112p	117p
2009		94p	90p	83p	88p	89p	105p	118p	132p	104p	113p	116p
2010		93p	88p	81p	86p	86p	105p	121p	133p	105p	113p	115p

Sources: Same as General Statistics. Values reflect change from the base year, 2002. Values above 100 mean greater than 2002, values below 100 mean less than 2002, and the values of 100 in other years means the same as 2002. 'P's show projections by the editors.

SELECTED RATIOS

For 2002	Avg. of All Manufact.	Analyzed Industry	Index	For 2002	Avg. of All Manufact.	Analyzed Industry	Index
Employees per Establishment	42	55	131	Value Added per Production Worker	182,367	137,120	75
Payroll per Establishment	1,639,184	2,280,000	139	Cost per Establishment	5,769,015	3,176,250	55
Payroll per Employee	39,053	41,455	106	Cost per Employee	137,446	57,750	42
Production Workers per Establishment	30	38	130	Cost per Production Worker	195,506	82,859	42
Wages per Establishment	694,845	1,364,000	196	Shipments per Establishment	11,158,348	8,487,083	76
Wages per Production Worker	23,548	35,583	151	Shipments per Employee	265,847	154,311	58
Hours per Production Worker	1,980	1,913	97	Shipments per Production Worker	378,144	221,402	59
Wages per Hour	11.89	18.60	156	Investment per Establishment	361,338	247,917	69
Value Added per Establishment	5,381,325	5,256,250	98	Investment per Employee	8,609	4,508	52
Value Added per Employee	128,210	95,568	75	Investment per Production Worker	12,245	6,467	53

Sources: Same as General Statistics. The 'Average of All Manufacturing' column represents the average of all manufacturing industries reported for the most recent complete year available. The Index shows the relationship between the Average and the Analyzed Industry. For example, 100 means that they are equal; 500 that the Analyzed Industry is five times the average; 50 means that the Analyzed Industry is half the national average. The abbreviation 'na' is used to show that data are 'not available'. Ratios shown for 2002, the last complete census year.

LEADING COMPANIES   Number shown: **75**   Total sales ($ mil): **18,411**   Total employment (000): **18.1**

Company Name	Address				CEO Name	Phone	Co. Type	Sales ($ mil)	Empl. (000)
Amarillo Gear Co.	PO Box 1789	Amarillo	TX	79105	Steve Chaloupka	806-622-1273	S	7,000*	0.1
Twin Disc SouthEast Inc.	11700 NW 101 Rd.	Medley	FL	33178	Michael E. Batten	541-485-2203	S	5,317*	0.9
Festo Corp.	PO Box 18023	Hauppauge	NY	11788		631-435-0800	R	2,452*	0.2
Horsburgh and Scott Co.	5114 Hamilton Ave.	Cleveland	OH	44114	Ray Albertini	216-431-3900	R	477*	0.6
Colfax Corp.	8730 Stony Pnt Pky	Richmond	VA	23235	John A. Young	804-560-4070	R	394	2.0
Gleason Corp.	PO Box 22970	Rochester	NY	14692		585-473-1000	R	350*	2.6
Twin Disc Inc.	1328 Racine St.	Racine	WI	53403	Michael E. Batten	262-638-4000	P	317	0.9
Nidec-Shimpo America Corp.	1701 Glenlake Ave.	Itasca	IL	60143	Yoshio Takahara	630-924-7138	R	256*	<0.1
Luk Clutch Systems L.L.C.	PO Box 798	Wooster	OH	44691		330-264-4383	R	193*	1.0
Centrilift	200 W Stuart Roosa	Claremore	OK	74017	Chad Deaton	918-341-9600	D	115*	1.5
Cleveland Motion Controls Inc.	7550 Hub Pkwy.	Cleveland	OH	44125	Wayne Foley	216-524-8800	S	95*	0.1
RAM Industries Inc.	PO Box 629	Leesport	PA	19533		610-916-3939	R	75*	0.3
Keb America Inc.	5100 Valley Indust.	Shakopee	MN	55379	Andy Delius	952-224-1400	R	68*	<0.1
Von Weise Gear Co.	1401 E N St.	Eldon	MO	65026	Davin Moore		R	62*	0.3
Jrlon Inc.	PO Box 244	Palmyra	NY	14522	James Redmond	315-597-4067	R	59*	<0.1
Columbia Gear Corp.	530 County Rd. 50	Avon	MN	56310	Dana Lynch	320-356-7301	R	57*	0.4
Bunting Bearings L.L.C.	PO Box 729	Holland	OH	43528	Keith Brown	419-866-7000	R	50*	<0.1
Auburn Gear Inc.	400 E Auburn Dr.	Auburn	IN	46706	George Callas	260-925-3200	R	45*	0.2
Gast Manufacturing Inc.	PO Box 97	Benton Harbor	MI	49022	Ivy B. Suter	269-926-6171	D	40*	0.6
Hub City Inc.	PO Box 1089	Aberdeen	SD	57402	Henry W. Knueppel	605-225-0360	S	40*	0.3
Koellmann Gear Corp.	PO Box 101	Waldwick	NJ	07463	Michael Rasovic	201-447-0200	R	37*	0.3
Milwaukee Gear Co.	5150 N Prt Washing.	Milwaukee	WI	53217	Richard Fullington	414-962-3532	R	37*	0.3
Hoffco/Comet Industries Inc.	358 NW F Street	Richmond	IN	47374	John Bratt	765-966-8161	R	35*	0.2
Tol-O-Matic Inc.	3800 Cnty Rd 116	Hamel	MN	55340	William Toles	763-478-8000	R	31*	0.2
Pittman Inc.	343 Godshall Dr.	Harleysville	PA	19438	Ron Bean	215-256-6601	S	30*	0.2
Intergrated Industrial Systems	475 Main St.	Yalesville	CT	06492	John Herbst	203-265-5684	R	30*	0.2
Rostra Precision Controls Inc.	2519 Dana Dr.	Laurinburg	NC	28352	Raymond Ford	910-276-4853	R	30*	0.2
Bison Gear and Engineering	3850 Ohio Ave.	Saint Charles	IL	60174	Norman Bullock	630-377-4327	R	26*	0.2
Progress Instruments Inc.	807 NW Commerce	Lees Summit	MO	64086		816-524-4442	R	26*	0.1
AMI Arc Machines Inc.	10500 Orbital Way	Pacoima	CA	91331	M. E. Gedgaudas	818-896-9556	R	25*	0.2
Guyan International Inc.	PO Box 2068	Streetsboro	OH	44241	Richard Olszewski	330-626-2801	R	25*	0.1
Arrow Gear Company Inc.	2301 Curtiss St.	Downers Grove	IL	60515	Joseph Arvin	630-969-7640	R	23*	0.2
Overton Gear and Tool Corp.	530 Westgate Dr.	Addison	IL	60101	Lou Ertel	630-543-9570	R	23*	0.2
AC Technology Corp.	630 Douglas St.	Uxbridge	MA	01569	Allen Ottoson	508-278-9100	R	22*	0.2
Mamco Corp.	PO Box 510	Franksville	WI	53126	William Meltzer	262-886-9069	R	22*	0.2
Regal-Beloit Corp. Durst Div.	PO Box 298	Beloit	WI	53512		608-365-2563	D	22*	0.2
Morris Bean and Co.	777 E Hyde Rd.	Yellow Springs	OH	45387	Edward Myers	937-767-7301	R	20*	0.2
Smith Jones Inc.	PO Box 340	Kellogg	IA	50135	John Flintham	641-526-8211	R	20*	0.1
Harold Beck and Sons Inc.	2300 Terry Dr.	Newtown	PA	18940	Douglas Beck	215-968-4600	R	20*	0.1
Matlock Electric Company Inc.	2780 Highland Ave.	Cincinnati	OH	45212	Joseph Geoppinger	513-731-9600	R	20*	<0.1
Eastern Air Devices Inc.	1 Progress Dr.	Dover	NH	03820	James Elsner	603-742-3330	R	19*	0.1
Process Industries Consortium	3860 River Rd.	Schiller Park	IL	60176	Jeff Monger	847-671-1631	R	18*	0.1
Gilcrest Equipment Co.	618 N Enterprise Dr	Warrensburg	MO	64093	James Gilcrest	660-422-4272	R	18*	<0.1
Merkle-Korff Industries Inc.	25 NW Point Blvd.	Elk Grove Vlg	IL	60007		847-296-8800	R	16*	0.1
Chicago Gear - D O James Corp.	2823 W Fulton St.	Chicago	IL	60612	Frank Romans	773-638-0508	R	16*	0.1
Motor Technology Inc.	2796 Culver Ave.	Dayton	OH	45429	Robert Buckwalder	937-294-1041	R	16*	<0.1
Renold Inc.	100 Bourne St.	Westfield	NY	14787	Thomas Murrer	716-326-3121	R	15*	0.1
Nord Gear Corp.	PO Box 367	Waunakee	WI	53597	Terry Schadeberg	608-849-7300	R	15*	<0.1
PIC Design L.L.C.	PO Box 1004	Middlebury	CT	06762		203-758-8272	R	15*	<0.1
American Autogard Corp.	5173 26th Ave.	Rockford	IL	61109	Derek Gold	815-229-3190	R	15*	0.1
Cleveland Gear Company Inc.	3249 E 80th St.	Cleveland	OH	44104	Dana Lynch	216-641-9000	R	15*	0.1
Gear Works Seattle Inc.	PO Box 80886	Seattle	WA	98108	Jay Hamilton	206-762-3333	R	15*	0.1
Graetz Manufacturing Inc.	W11094 St Hwy. 64	Pound	WI	54161	Alton Graetz	920-897-4041	R	14*	<0.1
RAM-Gear Manufacturing Inc.	PO Box 1369	Alice	TX	78333	Ramiro Tagle	361-668-0235	R	14*	<0.1
Reuland Electric Co.	PO Box 1464	La Puente	CA	91749	Noel Reuland	626-964-6411	R	13*	<0.1
Acme Gear Company Inc.	PO Box 779	Englewood	NJ	07631	Joseph Gelles	201-568-2245	R	13*	<0.1
Superior Gearbox Co.	PO Box 645	Stockton	MO	65785	Richard Carr	417-276-5191	R	13*	<0.1
JG Kern Enterprises Inc.	44044 Merrill Rd.	Sterling Hgts	MI	48314	Brian Kern	586-726-1040	R	12*	<0.1
Lone Star Racing Inc.	1424 E Broadway	Phoenix	AZ	85040	Tom Fisher	602-243-7437	R	12*	<0.1
Max Zero Inc.	13200 6th Ave. N	Plymouth	MN	55441	Lyle Gerads	763-546-4300	R	11*	<0.1
MI-TECH Inc.	PO Box 62499	N Charleston	SC	29419	William Totten	843-553-2743	R	10*	<0.1
Schafer Gear Works Inc.	4701 Nimtz Pkwy.	South Bend	IN	46628	Bipin Doshi	574-234-4116	R	10*	0.1
Joseph Industries Inc.	10039 A Hudson	Streetsboro	OH	44241	Patrick Finnegan	330-528-0091	R	10*	<0.1
Hart Design and Manufacturing	1940 Radisson St.	Green Bay	WI	54302	John Adams	920-468-5927	R	10*	<0.1
Reliance Gear Corp.	205 W Factory Rd.	Addison	IL	60101	Leroy Maros	630-543-6640	R	9*	<0.1
Force Control Industries Inc.	PO Box 18366	Fairfield	OH	45018	James Besl	513-868-0900	R	9*	<0.1
Appliance Controls of Texas	PO Box 1068	Rowlett	TX	75030	Edward Gray	972-475-4180	R	9*	<0.1
VanAir Manufacturing Inc.	19015 US Hwy., 12	New Buffalo	MI	49117	Ralph Kokot	269-469-4461	R	9*	<0.1
Kem Equipment Inc.	PO Box 546	Tualatin	OR	97062	Travis Garske	503-692-5012	R	9*	<0.1
Steward Machine Company Inc.	PO Box 11008	Birmingham	AL	35202	W Debardeleben	205-841-6461	R	9*	0.1
De'ran Gear Inc.	9405 N County Rd.	Lubbock	TX	79415	Douglas Randolph	806-746-6926	R	9*	<0.1
JW Performance Transmission	1826 Baldwin St.	Rockledge	FL	32955	John Winters	321-632-6205	R	8*	<0.1
Wilkie Brothers Conveyors Inc.	PO Box 219	Marysville	MI	48040	Robert Wilkie	810-364-4820	R	8*	<0.1
Predator Systems Inc.	600 Psi Dr.	Boca Raton	FL	33431	Gordon Yowell	561-394-9991	R	8*	<0.1
St Louis Gear Company Inc.	PO Box 880	Keokuk	IA	52632	Daniel Hodges	319-524-5042	R	7*	<0.1

Source: Ward's Business Directory of U.S. Private and Public Companies, Volumes 1 and 2, 2008. The company type code used is as follows: P - Public, R - Private, S - Subsidiary, D - Division, J - Joint Venture, A - Affiliate, G - Group. Sales are in millions of dollars, employees are in thousands. An asterisk (*) indicates an estimated sales volume. The symbol < stands for 'less than'. Company names and addresses are truncated, in some cases, to fit into the available space.

MATERIALS CONSUMED

Material	Quantity	Delivered Cost ($ million)
Metal bolts, nuts, screws, and other screw machine products	(X)	13.7
Other fabricated metal products (exc. castings and forgings)	(X)	12.5
Cold iron and steel forgings	(X)	13.8
Other iron and steel forgings	(X)	31.2
Nonferrous forgings	(X)	4.8
Iron and steel castings (rough and semifinished)	(X)	56.6
Nonferrous (aluminum, copper, etc.) castings (rough and semifinished)	(X)	15.3
Steel bars, bar shapes, and plates (exc. castings, forgings, fabr. metal products)	(X)	42.3
Steel sheet and strip (including tinplate)	(X)	(D)
All other steel shapes and forms (exc. castings, forgings, fabr. metal products)	(X)	12.8
Copper and copper-base alloy shapes and forms (exc. castings, forgings, fabr. metal products)	(X)	6.0
All other nonferrous shapes and forms (exc. castings, forgings, fabr. metal products)	(X)	3.1
Scrap, including iron, steel, aluminum and aluminum-base alloy (exc. home scrap)	(X)	2.1
Ball bearings (mounted or unmounted)	(X)	9.7
Roller bearings (mounted or unmounted)	(X)	22.7
Balls, rollers, cages, collars, races, and other antifriction bearing components and parts	(X)	8.2
Clutches, couplings, and other mechanical power transmission equipment	(X)	84.1
Electric motors, generators, and parts	(X)	29.1
Paperboard containers, boxes, and corrugated paperboard	(X)	8.8
Grinding wheels and other abrasive products, exc. industrial diamonds	(X)	2.1
Fluid power pumps, motors, and hydrostatic transmissions	(X)	6.1
Special dies, tools, die sets, jigs, and fixtures (exc. cutting tools)	(X)	(D)
All other materials, components, parts, containers, and supplies	(X)	107.1
Materials, ingredients, containers, and supplies, nsk	(X)	123.4

Source: 2002 *Economic Census*. Explanation of symbols used: (D): Withheld to avoid disclosure of competitive data; na: Not available; (S): Withheld because statistical norms were not met; (X): Not applicable; (Z): Less than half the unit shown; nec: Not elsewhere classified; nsk: Not specified by kind; - : zero; p : 10-19 percent estimated; q : 20-29 percent estimated.

PRODUCT SHARE DETAILS

Product or Product Class Shipments	Mil. $	Product or Product Class Shipments	Mil. $
SPEED CHANGERS, INDUSTRIAL HIGH-SPEED DRIVES, AND GEARS	1,949.0	epicyclic, etc.) shaft speed reducers and motor-reducers, center distance 6 in. (15.24 cm) or less	94.9
Gears	**583.4**	Enclosed concentric and parallel as above, center distance greater than 6 in. (15.24 cm)	51.3
Gears, pinions, racks, and worms, sold separately	583.4	Concentric and parallel (planetary, cycloid, epicyclic, etc.) gearmotors (shaft motor-reducers), less than 1 hp (746 watts)	76.8
Loose gears, coarse pitch (diametral pitch less than 20), helical and spur (and herringbone), diameter 24 in. (60.96 cm) or less, hard finished	159.1	Concentric and parallel as above, least 1 hp (746 watts), up through 5 hp (3.73 kW)	53.9
Loose gears, as above, diameter 24 in. (60.96 cm) or less, other than hard finished	86.6	Concentric and parallel as above, 5 hp (3.73 kW), up through 20 hp (14.9 kW)	14.5
Loose gears, as above, diameter more than 24 in. (60.96 cm), up through 72 in. (182.88 cm)	52.8	Concentric and parallel as above, more than 20 hp (14.9 kW)	(D)
Loose gears, as above, diameter more than 72 in. (182.88 cm)	15.1	Planetary, cycloidal, epicyclic, chain, and cam reducers and gearmotors	127.7
Coarse pitch (diametral pitch less than 20) worms and worm gearing, sold separately	48.8	Replacement parts for concentric and parallel shaft speed reducer, motor-reducer, and gearmotor products	(D)
Loose gears, coarse pitch (diametral pitch less than 20), bevel (straight, spiral, and other)	91.1	Shaft-mounted speed reducers and screw conveyor drives and parts	113.0
Loose gearing, coarse pitch (diametral pitch less than 20), nec, including racks	31.7	Maximum bore of hollow shaft 2.756 in. (70 mm) or less in diameter	46.9
Loose gears, fine pitch (diametral pitch 20 or more), helical and spur (and herringbone)	60.7	Maximum bore of hollow shaft more than 2.756 in. (70 mm) in diameter	61.5
Fine pitch (diametral pitch 20 or more) worms and worm gearing, sold separately	6.6	Replacement parts	4.5
Loose gearing, fine pitch (diametral pitch 20 or more), nec, including bevel gears and racks	30.8	Industrial high-speed drives, fixed ratio, pitch line velocity of 5000 feet (1525 meters) per minute or more	(D)
Speed changers and industrial high-speed drives, and parts other than loose gearing	**1,289.4**	Offset parallel shaft and right angle speed reducers, except parts	256.9
Worm speed reducers	192.9	Offset parallel shaft speed reducers (including helical, herringbone, and spur), low-speed center 15 in. (38.10 cm) or less	29.5
Single reduction, center distance less than 3 in. (7.62 cm), with C-face, flange, or scoop mount	72.8	Offset parallel shaft speed reducers (including helical, herringbone, and spur), low-speed center more than 15 in. (38.10 cm)	19.8
Single reduction, center distance less than 3 in. (7.62 cm), without C-face, flange, or scoop mount	31.4	Right angle, single reduction speed reducers, other than worm	207.6
Single reduction, center distance 3 in. (7.62 cm) or more	68.4	Replacement parts for offset parallel and right angle speed reducers	24.2
Double or multiple reduction (worm/worm or helical/worm)	20.2	Mechanical adjustable speed drives (nonhydraulic variable speed changers), excluding parts	41.7
Right angle worm gearmotors (enclosed right angle worm gear drive in common support with an electric motor, having an exclusive and dependent, or interrelated, design)	(D)	Parts for mechanical adjustable speed drives (nonhydraulic variable speed changers)	6.5
Right angle worm gearmotors, less than 1 hp (746 watts)	18.0	Other geared speed changers, industrial high-speed drives, and mechanical variable speed drives (gearboxes and allied products), nec, and parts	88.8
Right angle worm gearmotors, at least 1 hp (746 watts)	(D)	**Speed changers, industrial high-speed drives, and gears, nsk, total**	**76.2**
Replacement parts for worm gear products (except for worms and worm gears)	25.2		
Planetary, cycloid, epicyclic, chain, cam, and allied concentric and parallel shaft speed reducers, motor-reducers, and gearmotor products, including parts	444.4		
Enclosed concentric and parallel (planetary, cycloid,			

Source: 2002 *Economic Census*. The values are product shipments in millions of dollars for 2002. Total product shipments may be lower or higher than industry shipments. See Introduction for a full discussion. Values of indented subcategories are summed in the main heading(s). The symbol (D) appears when data are withheld to prevent disclosure of competitive information. The abbreviation nsk stands for 'not specified by kind' and nec for 'not elsewhere classified'. A dash (-) means zero.

INPUTS AND OUTPUTS FOR SPEED CHANGER, INDUSTRIAL HIGH-SPEED DRIVE, & GEAR

Economic Sector or Industry Providing Inputs	%	Sector	Economic Sector or Industry Buying Outputs	%	Sector
Compensation of employees	37.1		Motor vehicle parts	17.7	Manufg.
Management of companies & enterprises	6.6	Services	Exports of goods & services	14.2	Cap Inv
Mechanical power transmission equipment	4.7	Manufg.	Construction machinery	6.3	Manufg.
Wholesale trade	3.9	Trade	Material handling equipment	6.2	Manufg.
Iron & steel mills & ferroalloys	3.2	Manufg.	Wholesale trade	5.1	Trade
Ferrous metal foundries	3.2	Manufg.	Industrial machinery, nec	4.9	Manufg.
Forging, stamping, & sintering, nec	3.0	Manufg.	Electromedical & electrotherapeutic apparatus	4.2	Manufg.
Ball & roller bearings	2.7	Manufg.	Engine equipment, nec	3.5	Manufg.
Noncomparable imports	2.6	Foreign	Other S/L govt. enterprises	3.0	S/L Govt
Motors & generators	2.2	Manufg.	Commercial & industrial equipment repair/maintenance	2.9	Services
Engine equipment, nec	1.4	Manufg.	Farm machinery & equipment	2.4	Manufg.
Power generation & supply	1.0	Util.	Search, detection, & navigation instruments	2.0	Manufg.
Nonferrous metal foundries	1.0	Manufg.	Packaging machinery	1.9	Manufg.
Taxes on production & imports, less subsidies	1.0		Waste management & remediation services	1.8	Services
Specialized design services	0.9	Services	Plastics & rubber industry machinery	1.6	Manufg.
Turned products & screws, nuts, & bolts	0.9	Manufg.	Mining & oil & gas field machinery	1.6	Manufg.
Employment services	0.8	Services	Ship building & repairing	1.6	Manufg.
Machine shops	0.8	Manufg.	Rolling mill & other metalworking machinery	1.6	Manufg.
Advertising & related services	0.7	Services	Tobacco products	1.5	Manufg.
Legal services	0.7	Services	Turbines & turbine generator set units	1.4	Manufg.
Truck transportation	0.7	Util.	Power-driven handtools	1.4	Manufg.

Continued on next page.

INPUTS AND OUTPUTS FOR SPEED CHANGER, INDUSTRIAL HIGH-SPEED DRIVE, & GEAR - Continued

Economic Sector or Industry Providing Inputs	%	Sector	Economic Sector or Industry Buying Outputs	%	Sector
Automotive equipment rental & leasing	0.6	Fin/R.E.	Metal cutting & forming machine tools	1.2	Manufg.
Semiconductors & related devices	0.6	Manufg.	Railroad rolling stock	1.1	Manufg.
Real estate	0.6	Fin/R.E.	General purpose machinery, nec	1.1	Manufg.
Securities, commodity contracts, investments	0.6	Fin/R.E.	Periodical publishers	1.0	Services
Business support services	0.6	Services	Motors & generators	1.0	Manufg.
Printed circuit assemblies (electronic assemblies)	0.6	Manufg.	Lawn & garden equipment	1.0	Manufg.
Architectural, engineering, & related services	0.6	Services	Services to buildings & dwellings	0.7	Services
Paperboard containers	0.6	Manufg.	Commercial & service industry machinery, nec	0.7	Manufg.
Natural gas distribution	0.5	Util.	Fluid power process machinery	0.7	Manufg.
Maintenance/repair of nonresidential structures	0.4	Construct.	Architectural, engineering, & related services	0.6	Services
Support services, nec	0.4	Services	Asphalt paving mixtures & blocks	0.5	Manufg.
Lessors of nonfinancial assets	0.4	Fin/R.E.	Personal & household goods repair/maintenance	0.5	Services
Copper rolling, drawing, extruding, & alloying	0.4	Manufg.	Mechanical power transmission equipment	0.5	Manufg.
Services to buildings & dwellings	0.4	Services	Wood containers & pallets	0.4	Manufg.
Telecommunications	0.4	Services	Scientific research & development services	0.4	Services
Scientific research & development services	0.3	Services	S/L govt. passenger transit	0.2	S/L Govt
Accounting, tax preparation, bookkeeping, & payroll	0.3	Services	Commercial & industrial machinery rental & leasing	0.2	Fin/R.E.
Investigation & security services	0.3	Services	Semiconductor machinery	0.2	Manufg.
Commercial & industrial machinery rental & leasing	0.3	Fin/R.E.	Scenic & sightseeing transport & related services	0.2	Util.
Warehousing & storage	0.3	Util.	Electronic & precision equipment repair/maintenance	0.2	Services
Management, scientific, & technical consulting	0.3	Services	Rail transportation	0.1	Util.
Automotive repair & maintenance, ex. car washes	0.3	Services	Investigation & security services	0.1	Services
Data processing, hosting, & related services	0.2	Services			
Monetary authorities/depository credit intermediation	0.2	Fin/R.E.			
Commercial & industrial equipment repair/maintenance	0.2	Services			
Fluid power process machinery	0.2	Manufg.			
Coating, engraving, heat treating & allied activities	0.2	Manufg.			
Professional, scientific, technical services, nec	0.2	Services			
Food services & drinking places	0.2	Services			
Facilities support services	0.2	Services			
Abrasive products	0.1	Manufg.			
Aluminum products from purchased aluminum	0.1	Manufg.			
Rubber products, nec	0.1	Manufg.			
Chemical products & preparations, nec	0.1	Manufg.			
Other computer related services, including facilities	0.1	Services			
Paperboard mills	0.1	Manufg.			

Source: Benchmark Input-Output Accounts for the U.S. Economy, 2002, U.S. Department of Commerce, Washington, D.C., January 2008. The abbreviation nec stands for 'not elsewhere classified'.

OCCUPATIONS EMPLOYED BY ENGINE, TURBINE, & POWER TRANSMISSION EQUIPMENT

Occupation	% of Total 2006	Change to 2016	Occupation	% of Total 2006	Change to 2016
Team assemblers	10.8	-16.1	Welders, cutters, solderers, & brazers	1.5	-10.7
Engine & other machine assemblers	7.0	-16.1	Industrial machinery mechanics	1.5	-3.5
Machinists	6.7	-11.9	Laborers & freight, stock, & material movers, hand	1.4	-24.5
First-line supervisors/managers of production workers	3.7	-16.1	Drilling & boring machine tool operators	1.4	-24.5
Inspectors, testers, sorters, samplers, & weighers	3.3	-20.9	General & operations managers	1.3	-24.5
Computer-controlled machine tool operators	3.2	-7.7	Cutting, punching, & press machine operators	1.2	-24.5
Assemblers & fabricators, nec	3.2	-24.5	Production, planning, & expediting clerks	1.2	-16.1
Mechanical engineers	2.9	-16.1	Stock clerks & order fillers	1.1	-29.8
Lathe & turning machine tool operators & tenders	2.8	-24.5	Electricians	1.1	-13.0
Maintenance & repair workers, general	2.6	-16.1	Shipping, receiving, & traffic clerks	1.1	-19.2
Multiple machine tool operators & tenders	2.4	-7.7	Customer service representatives	1.1	-7.7
Grinding, lapping, polishing machine tool operators	1.9	-18.6			

Source: Industry-Occupation Matrix, Bureau of Labor Statistics, December 4, 2007. These data are reported based on 4-digit NAICS categories but have been matched to corresponding 6-digit NAICS industry codes. The change reported for each occupation to the year 2016 is a percent of growth or decline as estimated by the Bureau of Labor Statistics. The abbreviation nec stands for 'not elsewhere classified'.

LOCATION BY STATE AND REGIONAL CONCENTRATION

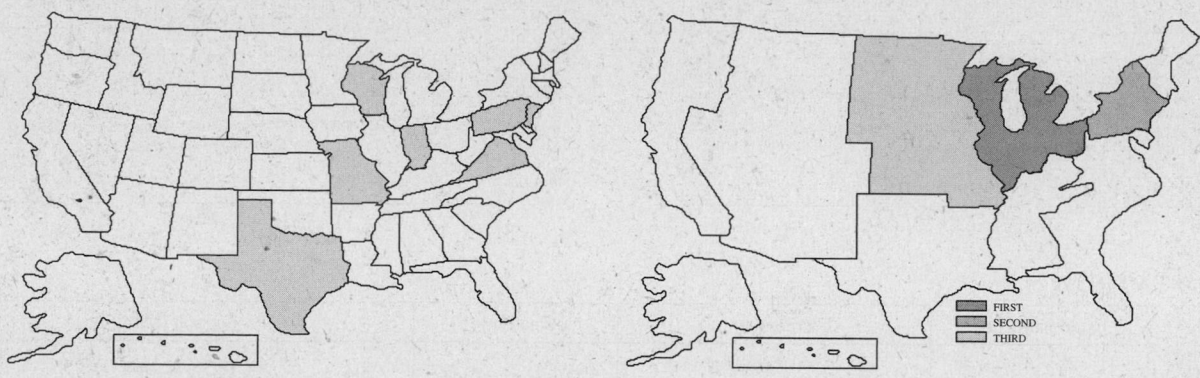

FIRST
SECOND
THIRD

INDUSTRY DATA BY STATE

| State | Establish-ments | Shipments | | | Employment | | | | Cost as % of Shipments | Investment per Employee ($) |
		Total ($ mil)	% of U.S.	Per Establ.	Total Number	% of U.S.	Per Establ.	Wages ($/hour)		
Wisconsin	21	244.4	12.0	11,639.2	1,854	14.0	88	21.25	38.2	3,859
Indiana	7	220.9	10.8	31,550.1	1,394	10.5	199	19.62	36.5	5,274
Texas	12	112.7	5.5	9,389.9	683	5.2	57	22.81	46.8	6,859
Missouri	12	105.7	5.2	8,807.1	671	5.1	56	12.35	44.1	2,404
Virginia	3	98.9	4.9	32,969.3	342	2.6	114	17.30	44.7	2,544
New Jersey	10	46.4	2.3	4,638.8	290	2.2	29	18.34	42.4	1,638
Pennsylvania	10	40.4	2.0	4,038.9	267	2.0	27	20.77	37.9	2,423

Source: 2002 *Economic Census*. The states are in descending order of shipments or establishments (if shipment data are missing for the majority). The symbol (D) appears when data are withheld to prevent disclosure of competitive information. States marked with (D) are sorted by number of establishments. A dash (-) indicates that the data element cannot be calculated. Data may not show all states active in the NAICS category. All data available at the time of publication are shown.

NAICS 333613 - MECHANICAL POWER TRANSMISSION EQUIPMENT MANUFACTURING

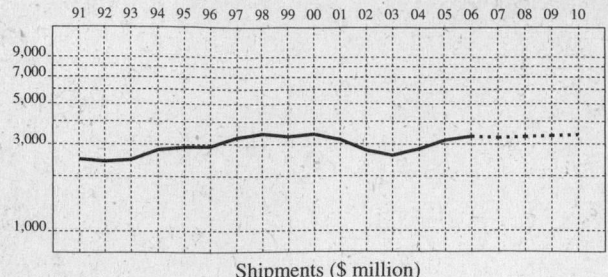

Shipments ($ million)

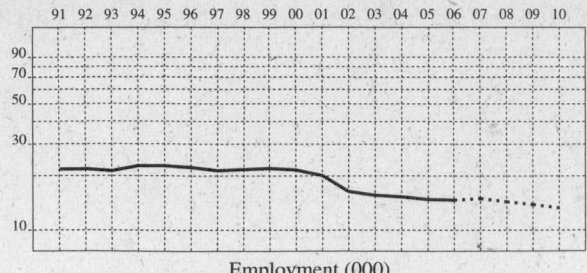

Employment (000)

GENERAL STATISTICS

| Year | Com-panies | Establishments | | Employment | | | Compensation | | Production ($ million) | | | |
		Total	with 20 or more employees	Total (000)	Production Workers (000)	Hours (Mil)	Payroll ($ mil)	Wages ($/hr)	Cost of Materials	Value Added by Manufacture	Value of Shipments	Capital Invest.
1991		290	179	21.7	14.8	29.8	606.0	11.84	1,049.8	1,442.4	2,479.1	61.9
1992	270	311	171	21.8	14.6	29.6	679.0	13.05	922.0	1,493.0	2,411.4	72.5
1993		306	167	21.3	14.6	30.3	693.5	13.53	1,016.6	1,462.6	2,462.3	72.6
1994		303	170	22.7	15.5	32.5	734.9	13.31	1,162.4	1,648.1	2,796.3	72.3
1995		300	168	22.7	15.7	31.5	747.6	14.36	1,221.4	1,702.3	2,897.1	85.6
1996		310	170	22.3	15.4	30.9	753.8	14.60	1,233.1	1,696.6	2,912.8	85.0
1997	262	299	151	21.4	15.1	30.3	763.7	15.37	1,389.9	1,886.5	3,254.8	132.1
1998		293	150	21.7	15.1	31.0	788.6	15.56	1,459.4	1,984.3	3,421.5	119.3
1999		293	149	22.0	14.9	29.8	783.0	15.64	1,405.8	1,902.6	3,301.6	148.7
2000		295	153	21.6	14.7	28.7	823.3	16.78	1,451.4	1,981.8	3,401.1	115.1
2001		292	149	20.1	13.6	26.5	778.9	16.96	1,355.5	1,799.7	3,173.7	122.4
2002	202	251	135	16.4	11.5	23.4	657.7	17.14	1,110.2	1,639.7	2,769.5	85.5
2003		261	135	15.6	11.1	21.7	649.7	17.21	982.7	1,616.6	2,601.8	87.3
2004		238	134	15.3	10.5	21.6	684.2	18.71	1,060.9	1,744.7	2,822.6	63.0
2005		235	128	14.8	10.4	21.5	698.8	19.52	1,230.8	1,942.5	3,156.6	78.0
2006		248P	126P	14.7	10.4	21.1	704.6	19.63	1,345.1	2,008.2	3,311.7	101.6
2007		243P	123P	15.0P	10.6P	21.1P	728.4P	19.93P	1,325.1P	1,978.3P	3,262.4P	104.7P
2008		238P	119P	14.4P	10.2P	20.3P	729.2P	20.42P	1,340.1P	2,000.7P	3,299.3P	106.0P
2009		233P	116P	13.9P	9.8P	19.6P	730.0P	20.90P	1,355.1P	2,023.1P	3,336.2P	107.2P
2010		229P	112P	13.3P	9.5P	18.8P	730.8P	21.38P	1,370.1P	2,045.5P	3,373.2P	108.5P

Sources: 1992, 1997, 2002 *Economic Census*; other years, up to 2006, are from the *Annual Survey of Manufactures*. Establishment counts for non-Census years are from *County Business Patterns*; 1997 and 2002 values are from the 1997 and 2002 censuses respectively, reported in the Federal Government's NAICS format. Other years were originally reported in equivalent SIC format. 'P's show projections by the editors.

INDICES OF CHANGE

| Year | Com-panies | Establishments | | Employment | | | Compensation | | Production ($ million) | | | |
		Total	with 20 or more employees	Total (000)	Production Workers (000)	Hours (Mil)	Payroll ($ mil)	Wages ($/hr)	Cost of Materials	Value Added by Manufacture	Value of Shipments	Capital Invest.
1992	134	124	127	133	127	126	103	76	83	91	87	85
1997	130	119	112	130	131	129	116	90	125	115	118	155
2001		116	110	123	118	113	118	99	122	110	115	143
2002	100	100	100	100	100	100	100	100	100	100	100	100
2003		104	100	95	97	93	99	100	89	99	94	102
2004		95	99	93	91	92	104	109	96	106	102	74
2005		94	95	90	90	92	106	114	111	118	114	91
2006		99P	93P	90	90	90	107	115	121	122	120	119
2007		97P	91P	91P	92P	90P	111P	116P	119P	121P	118P	122P
2008		95P	88P	88P	89P	87P	111P	119P	121P	122P	119P	124P
2009		93P	86P	85P	85P	84P	111P	122P	122P	123P	120P	125P
2010		91P	83P	81P	83P	80P	111P	125P	123P	125P	122P	127P

Sources: Same as General Statistics. Values reflect change from the base year, 2002. Values above 100 mean greater than 2002, values below 100 mean less than 2002, and the values of 100 in other years means the same as 2002. 'P's show projections by the editors.

SELECTED RATIOS

For 2002	Avg. of All Manufact.	Analyzed Industry	Index	For 2002	Avg. of All Manufact.	Analyzed Industry	Index
Employees per Establishment	42	65	156	Value Added per Production Worker	182,367	142,583	78
Payroll per Establishment	1,639,184	2,620,319	160	Cost per Establishment	5,769,015	4,423,108	77
Payroll per Employee	39,053	40,104	103	Cost per Employee	137,446	67,695	49
Production Workers per Establishment	30	46	155	Cost per Production Worker	195,506	96,539	49
Wages per Establishment	694,845	1,597,912	230	Shipments per Establishment	11,158,348	11,033,865	99
Wages per Production Worker	23,548	34,876	148	Shipments per Employee	265,847	168,872	64
Hours per Production Worker	1,980	2,035	103	Shipments per Production Worker	378,144	240,826	64
Wages per Hour	11.89	17.14	144	Investment per Establishment	361,338	340,637	94
Value Added per Establishment	5,381,325	6,532,669	121	Investment per Employee	8,609	5,213	61
Value Added per Employee	128,210	99,982	78	Investment per Production Worker	12,245	7,435	61

Sources: Same as General Statistics. The 'Average of All Manufacturing' column represents the average of all manufacturing industries reported for the most recent complete year available. The Index shows the relationship between the Average and the Analyzed Industry. For example, 100 means that they are equal; 500 that the Analyzed Industry is five times the average; 50 means that the Analyzed Industry is half the national average. The abbreviation 'na' is used to show that data are 'not available'. Ratios shown for 2002, the last complete census year.

LEADING COMPANIES   Number shown: **75**   Total sales ($ mil): **52,121**   Total employment (000): **160.0**

Company Name	Address				CEO Name	Phone	Co. Type	Sales ($ mil)	Empl. (000)
Neapco L.L.C.	PO Box 399	Pottstown	PA	19464		610-323-6000	R	7,580*	0.3
Perfection Hy-Test Company	100 Perfection Way	Timmonsville	SC	29161		843-326-5544	R	7,000*	0.2
Federal-Mogul Corp.	PO Box 1966	Detroit	MI	48235	Jose Maria Alapont	248-354-7700	P	6,914	43.1
ArvinMeritor Inc.	2135 W Maple Rd.	Troy	MI	48084		248-435-1000	P	6,449	18.0
Goodrich Corp.	4 Coliseum Centre	Charlotte	NC	28217		704-423-7000	P	6,392	23.4
Timken Co.	PO Box 6932	Canton	OH	44706	James W. Griffith	330-438-3000	P	5,236	25.0
Rockwell Automation Inc.	777 E Wisconsin	Milwaukee	WI	53202		414-212-5800	P	5,004	20.0
TriMas Corp.	39400 Woodward	Bloomfield Hls	MI	48304	Grant Beard	248-631-5450	P	1,068	5.1
Lufkin Industries Inc.	PO Box 849	Lufkin	TX	75902		936-634-2211	P	597	2.7
NSK Corp.	PO Box 134007	Ann Arbor	MI	48113	Tsutomo Komori	734-913-7500	S	438*	0.4
LSA Technologies Inc.	16 S Penn. Avenue	Oklahoma City	OK	73107	Jack E. Golsen	405-235-4546	S	392*	1.2
Tuthill Corp.	8500 S Madison St.	Burr Ridge	IL	60527		630-382-4900	R	388*	0.9
Engineered Machined Products	3111 N 28th St.	Escanaba	MI	49829	Brian Larche	906-786-8404	R	333*	0.5
Saf-Holland USA Inc.	PO Box 425	Muskegon	MI	49443	Timothy Hemingway	231-773-3271	R	321*	0.3
Twin Disc Inc.	1328 Racine St.	Racine	WI	53403	Michael E. Batten	262-638-4000	P	317	0.9
GKN Automotive Inc.	6400 Durham Rd.	Timberlake	NC	27583	Phillip Cabossol	336-364-6200	S	280*	3.0
Michigan Automotive Compressor	2400 N Dearing Rd.	Parma	MI	49269	Hiroyo Kono	517-622-7000	R	231*	0.8
Peer Bearing Co.	2200 Norman Dr. S	Waukegan	IL	60085	Laurence Spungen	847-578-1000	R	200*	0.6
Luk Clutch Systems L.L.C.	PO Box 798	Wooster	OH	44691		330-264-4383	R	193*	1.0
US Tsubaki Inc.	PO Box 665	Wheeling	IL	60090	Yoshinobu Miyazaki	847-459-9500	R	136*	0.1
Jeffrey Chain L.P.	2307 Maden Dr.	Morristown	TN	37813	George Graham	423-586-1951	R	134*	0.3
NTN Driveshaft Inc.	8251 S Intl. Dr.	Columbus	IN	47201	Nobuo Satoh	812-342-7000	R	119*	0.8
O and S America L.L.C.	777 8 Mile Rd.	Whitmore Lake	MI	48189	James M. Bonk	810-449-4401	R	119*	0.2
Magnetic Power Systems Inc.	PO Box 26508	Oklahoma City	OK	73126	Bruce Ryan	405-755-1600	R	105*	0.7
Melling Tool Co.	PO Box 1188	Jackson	MI	49204	David Horthrop	517-787-8172	R	100*	0.3
Timken Aerospace/Super Precis.	7 Optical Ave.	Keene	NH	03431		603-352-0310	S	91*	0.6
Alto Products Corp.	PO Box 1088	Atmore	AL	36504	David Landa	251-368-7777	R	82*	0.2
Kop-Flex Inc.	PO Box 1696	Baltimore	MD	21203	Dale Skoch	410-768-2000	S	82*	0.2
Elkhart Products Corp.	PO Box 1008	Elkhart	IN	46515	Dale Dieckbernd	574-264-3181	S	73*	0.6
Networks Electronic Corp.	9750 DeSoto Ave.	Chatsworth	CA	91311	Tamara Christen	818-341-0440	R	73*	0.1
American Drill Bushing Co.	7141 Paramount	Pico Rivera	CA	90660	A Steele	323-725-1515	R	70*	0.1
Keb America Inc.	5100 Valley Indust.	Shakopee	MN	55379	Andy Delius	952-224-1400	R	68*	<0.1
Keystone Powdered Metal Co.	251 State St.	Saint Marys	PA	15857		814-781-1591	R	68*	0.5
Kamatics Corp.	PO Box 1	Bloomfield	CT	06002	Paul Kuhn	860-243-7100	S	66*	0.5
Funk Manufacturing Co.	PO Box 577	Coffeyville	KS	67337		620-251-3400	S	63*	0.5
Caterpillar Work Tools Inc.	PO Box 6	Wamego	KS	66547		785-456-2224	S	52*	0.3
Huron Precision Inc.	55025 Gratiot Ave.	Chesterfield	MI	48051	Chriohir Cakaishi	586-749-1900	R	50*	<0.1
Hooper Corporation	PO Box 7455	Madison	WI	53707	Fred Davie	608-249-0451	R	50*	0.4
Weasler Engineering Inc.	PO Box 558	West Bend	WI	53095		262-338-2161	R	46*	0.3
Wellman Products Group	920 Lake Rd.	Medina	OH	44256	Steve Campbell		S	45*	0.3
Auburn Gear Inc.	400 E Auburn Dr.	Auburn	IN	46706	George Callas	260-925-3200	R	45*	0.2
Apex-Cooper Tools Div.	PO Box 952	Dayton	OH	45401	Kirk Hachigian	937-222-7871	D	44*	0.4
Texas Arai	8204 Fairbanks N	Houston	TX	77064	Barham Moss	713-937-1800	S	44*	0.3
Rail Bearing Service Inc.	PO Box 6932	Canton	OH	44706	James Griffith	330-438-3000	R	42*	0.3
AJ Rose Manufacturing Co.	38000 Chester Rd.	Avon	OH	44011	John Warnkey	440-934-7700	R	42*	0.2
Deublin Co.	2050 Norman Dr. W	Waukegan	IL	60085	Donald Deubler	847-689-8600	R	41*	0.2
Orion Corp.	PO Box 84	Grafton	WI	53024	Charles Bahn	262-377-2210	R	40*	0.1
Hub City Inc.	PO Box 1089	Aberdeen	SD	57402	Henry W. Knueppel	605-225-0360	S	40*	0.3
Reell Precision Manufacturing	1259 Willow Lk	Saint Paul	MN	55110	Eric Donaldson	651-484-2447	R	40*	0.2
Allied Locke Industries Inc.	PO Box 509	Dixon	IL	61021	William Crowson	815-288-1471	R	38*	0.3
Bucyrus Precision Tech Inc.	200 Crossroads Blvd	Bucyrus	OH	44820	Keiji Nishio	419-563-9950	R	37*	0.2
Eaton Corp. Airflex Div.	9919 Clinton Rd.	Cleveland	OH	44144		216-281-2211	D	37*	0.2
Force America Inc.	501 Cliff Rd. E	Burnsville	MN	55337	Gerard Budzien	952-707-1300	R	36*	<0.1
Machine Service Inc.	PO Box 10265	Green Bay	WI	54307	Edward Fowles	920-339-3000	R	36*	0.1
Aurora Bearing Company Inc.	970 S Lake St., 1	Aurora	IL	60506	Charles Richard	630-859-2030	R	36*	0.2
Goodrich Fuel and Utility Sys.	104 Otis St.	Rome	NY	13441	Bob Shoemaker	315-838-1200	D	34*	0.2
Xtek Inc.	11451 Reading Rd.	Cincinnati	OH	45241	Kyle Seymour	513-733-7800	R	34*	0.2
Tol-O-Matic Inc.	3800 Cnty Rd 116	Hamel	MN	55340	William Toles	763-478-8000	R	31*	0.2
SS White Technologies Inc.	151 O New Brnswck	Piscataway	NJ	08854	Rahul Shukla	732-752-8300	R	31*	0.2
Hyspan Precision Products Inc.	1685 Brandywine	Chula Vista	CA	91911	Donald Heye	619-421-1355	R	30*	0.1
Metallized Carbon Corp.	19 S Water St.	Ossining	NY	10562	Bruce Neri	914-941-3738	R	29*	0.1
Upco Inc.	PO Box 725	Claremore	OK	74018	William Ridenour	918-342-1270	R	26*	0.1
La Vezzi Precision Inc.	999 Regency Dr.	Glendale Hts	IL	60139	Albert La Vezzi	630-582-1230	R	25*	<0.1
Grover Corp.	PO Box 340080	Milwaukee	WI	53234	Stuart Banghart	414-384-9472	R	24*	<0.1
Lovejoy Inc.	2655 Wisconsin	Downers Grove	IL	60515	Michael Hennessy	630-852-0500	R	24*	0.2
EC Styberg Engineering Co.	PO Box 788	Racine	WI	53401	Ernest Styberg	262-637-9301	R	24*	0.2
Regal-Beloit Corp. Durst Div.	PO Box 298	Beloit	WI	53512		608-365-2563	D	22*	0.2
Kingsbury Inc.	10385 Drummond	Philadelphia	PA	19154	Woods Brown	215-824-4000	R	22*	0.1
Beemer Precision Inc.	PO Box 3080	Fort Washington	PA	19034	Harold Myer	215-646-8440	R	22*	<0.1
ENM Company Inc.	5617 N NW Hwy.	Chicago	IL	60646	Nicholas Polydoris	773-775-8400	R	22*	0.1
Leedy Manufacturing Company	210 Hall St. SW	Grand Rapids	MI	49507		616-245-0517	R	21*	<0.1
Aircraft Gear Corp.	PO Box 2066	Loves Park	IL	61130	Dean Olson	815-877-7473	R	20*	<0.1
DuPont Vespel Parts and Shapes	6200 Hillcrest Dr.	Valley View	OH	44125		216-901-3600	S	20*	0.2
Taiho Corporation of America	194 Heritage Dr.	Tiffin	OH	44883		419-443-1645	R	20*	0.1
Webb-Stiles Co.	PO Box 464	Valley City	OH	44280	Donald Stiles	330-225-7761	R	19*	<0.1

Source: Ward's Business Directory of U.S. Private and Public Companies, Volumes 1 and 2, 2008. The company type code used is as follows: P - Public, R - Private, S - Subsidiary, D - Division, J - Joint Venture, A - Affiliate, G - Group. Sales are in millions of dollars, employees are in thousands. An asterisk (*) indicates an estimated sales volume. The symbol < stands for 'less than'. Company names and addresses are truncated, in some cases, to fit into the available space.

MATERIALS CONSUMED

Material	Quantity	Delivered Cost ($ million)
Metal bolts, nuts, screws, and other screw machine products	(X)	13.1
Other fabricated metal products (exc. castings and forgings)	(X)	84.8
Cold iron and steel forgings	(X)	31.9
Other iron and steel forgings	(X)	14.6
Nonferrous forgings	(X)	(D)
Iron and steel castings (rough and semifinished)	(X)	92.0
Nonferrous (aluminum, copper, etc.) castings (rough and semifinished)	(X)	13.9
Steel bars, bar shapes, and plates (exc. castings, forgings, fabr. metal products)	(X)	106.6
Steel sheet and strip (including tinplate)	(X)	34.8
All other steel shapes and forms (exc. castings, forgings, fabr. metal products)	(X)	16.8
Copper and copper-base alloy shapes and forms (exc. castings, forgings, fabr. metal products)	(X)	9.1
All other nonferrous shapes and forms (exc. castings, forgings, fabr. metal products)	(X)	6.0
Scrap, including iron, steel, aluminum and aluminum-base alloy (exc. home scrap)	(X)	2.6
Ball bearings (mounted or unmounted)	(X)	10.6
Roller bearings (mounted or unmounted)	(X)	6.8
Balls, rollers, cages, collars, races, and other antifriction bearing components and parts	(X)	56.1
Clutches, couplings, and other mechanical power transmission equipment	(X)	54.4
Electric motors, generators, and parts	(X)	(D)
Paperboard containers, boxes, and corrugated paperboard	(X)	4.9
Grinding wheels and other abrasive products, exc. industrial diamonds	(X)	2.5
Fluid power pumps, motors, and hydrostatic transmissions	(X)	4.7
Engines (diesel, semidiesel, gasoline, and other carburetor-type engines)	(X)	(D)
Special dies, tools, die sets, jigs, and fixtures (exc. cutting tools)	(X)	(D)
All other materials, components, parts, containers, and supplies	(X)	283.6
Materials, ingredients, containers, and supplies, nsk	(X)	32.2

Source: 2002 *Economic Census*. Explanation of symbols used: (D): Withheld to avoid disclosure of competitive data; na: Not available; (S): Withheld because statistical norms were not met; (X): Not applicable; (Z): Less than half the unit shown; nec: Not elsewhere classified; nsk: Not specified by kind; - : zero; p : 10-19 percent estimated; q : 20-29 percent estimated.

PRODUCT SHARE DETAILS

Product or Product Class Shipments	Mil. $	Product or Product Class Shipments	Mil. $
MECHANICAL POWER TRANSMISSION EQUIPMENT	2,688.6	Other chains for sprocket drives	67.5
Plain bearings and bushings	**588.0**	Sheaves	126.4
Plain bearings and bushings, unmounted, machined (except engine)	569.8	Single drive sheaves	80.9
		Multiple drive sheaves	45.5
Plain bearings, mounted (except engine)	18.2	Other mechanical power transmission equipment, nec, except speed changers, drives, gears, and bearings	1,170.7
Mechanical power transmission equipment, except speed changers, drives, and gears	**2,095.6**	Universal joints	68.9
Friction-type clutches and brakes	152.2	Sprockets	191.1
Other clutches and brakes, including hydraulic couplings	114.0	Pulleys	72.9
Hydraulic-type clutches and brakes, including hydraulic couplings	36.2	Marine propulsion gear transmissions and drives	171.8
All other clutches and brakes	77.8	Mechanical power transmission equipment, nec, except parts	475.2
Flexible couplings	197.5	Parts for mechanical power transmission equipment	190.8
Gear-type flexible couplings	58.8	Mechanical power transmission equipment, except speed changers, drives, and gears, nec, nsk	37.1
Flexible couplings other than gear-type	138.7		
Roller chains for sprocket drives, meeting any ASME or ANSI standard	230.2	**Mechanical power transmission equipment, nsk, total**	**5.1**

Source: 2002 *Economic Census*. The values are product shipments in millions of dollars for 2002. Total product shipments may be lower or higher than industry shipments. See Introduction for a full discussion. Values of indented subcategories are summed in the main heading(s). The symbol (D) appears when data are withheld to prevent disclosure of competitive information. The abbreviation nsk stands for 'not specified by kind' and nec for 'not elsewhere classified'. A dash (-) means zero.

INPUTS AND OUTPUTS FOR MECHANICAL POWER TRANSMISSION EQUIPMENT

Economic Sector or Industry Providing Inputs	%	Sector	Economic Sector or Industry Buying Outputs	%	Sector
Compensation of employees	33.7		Heavy duty trucks	20.3	Manufg.
Iron & steel mills & ferroalloys	6.2	Manufg.	Engine equipment, nec	19.5	Manufg.
Management of companies & enterprises	6.0	Services	Exports of goods & services	13.9	Cap Inv
Wholesale trade	4.6	Trade	Material handling equipment	6.5	Manufg.
Ferrous metal foundries	3.6	Manufg.	Light truck & utility vehicles	6.4	Manufg.
Ball & roller bearings	3.4	Manufg.	Ship building & repairing	4.9	Manufg.
Mechanical power transmission equipment	2.9	Manufg.	Automobiles	4.4	Manufg.
Engine equipment, nec	2.1	Manufg.	Other S/L govt. enterprises	3.7	S/L Govt
Forging, stamping, & sintering, nec	2.0	Manufg.	Speed changers, industrial high-speed drives, & gears	2.6	Manufg.
Noncomparable imports	1.7	Foreign	Mechanical power transmission equipment	2.2	Manufg.
Machine shops	1.7	Manufg.	Motor vehicle parts	2.1	Manufg.
Power generation & supply	1.3	Util.	Tobacco products	1.7	Manufg.
Employment services	1.1	Services	Waste management & remediation services	1.6	Services
Securities, commodity contracts, investments	1.1	Fin/R.E.	Asphalt paving mixtures & blocks	1.6	Manufg.
Turned products & screws, nuts, & bolts	0.9	Manufg.	Wood containers & pallets	1.5	Manufg.
Semiconductors & related devices	0.9	Manufg.	Turbines & turbine generator set units	1.0	Manufg.

Continued on next page.

1130

INPUTS AND OUTPUTS FOR MECHANICAL POWER TRANSMISSION EQUIPMENT - Continued

Economic Sector or Industry Providing Inputs	%	Sector	Economic Sector or Industry Buying Outputs	%	Sector
Printed circuit assemblies (electronic assembiles)	0.9	Manufg.	Motors & generators	0.9	Manufg.
Lessors of nonfinancial assets	0.8	Fin/R.E.	Packaging machinery	0.9	Manufg.
Coating, engraving, heat treating & allied activities	0.7	Manufg.	S/L govt. passenger transit	0.6	S/L Govt
Truck transportation	0.7	Util.	Urethane & other foam products (except polystrene)	0.6	Manufg.
Monetary authorities/depository credit intermediation	0.6	Fin/R.E.	Scientific research & development services	0.6	Services
Nonferrous metal foundries	0.6	Manufg.	Architectural, engineering, & related services	0.6	Services
Speed changers, industrial high-speed drives, & gears	0.6	Manufg.	Fluid power process machinery	0.6	Manufg.
Architectural, engineering, & related services	0.6	Services	Industrial machinery, nec	0.5	Manufg.
Data processing, hosting, & related services	0.6	Services	Railroad rolling stock	0.4	Manufg.
Advertising & related services	0.5	Services	Educational services, nec	0.2	Services
Professional, scientific, technical services, nec	0.5	Services			
Real estate	0.5	Fin/R.E.			
Maintenance/repair of nonresidential structures	0.5	Construct.			
Taxes on production & imports, less subsidies	0.5				
Food services & drinking places	0.5	Services			
Services to buildings & dwellings	0.5	Services			
Telecommunications	0.4	Services			
Copper rolling, drawing, extruding, & alloying	0.4	Manufg.			
Legal services	0.4	Services			
Natural gas distribution	0.4	Util.			
Accounting, tax preparation, bookkeeping, & payroll	0.3	Services			
Scientific research & development services	0.3	Services			
Metal cans, boxes, & other containers (light gauge)	0.3	Manufg.			
Management, scientific, & technical consulting	0.3	Services			
Hotels & motels, including casino hotels	0.3	Services			
Automotive repair & maintenance, ex. car washes	0.3	Services			
Fabricated metals, nec	0.3	Manufg.			
Warehousing & storage	0.3	Util.			
Commercial & industrial equipment repair/maintenance	0.3	Services			
Plastics packaging materials, film & sheet	0.2	Manufg.			
Crowns & closures & metal stamping	0.2	Manufg.			
Other computer related services, including facilities	0.2	Services			
Plate work & fabricated structural products	0.2	Manufg.			
Special tools, dies, jigs, & fixtures	0.2	Manufg.			
Valve & fittings other than plumbing	0.2	Manufg.			
Paperboard containers	0.2	Manufg.			
Automotive equipment rental & leasing	0.2	Fin/R.E.			
Air transportation	0.2	Util.			
Rubber products, nec	0.2	Manufg.			
Aluminum products from purchased aluminum	0.2	Manufg.			
Custom roll forming	0.2	Manufg.			
Handtools	0.2	Manufg.			
Chemical products & preparations, nec	0.1	Manufg.			
Motors & generators	0.1	Manufg.			
Business support services	0.1	Services			
Rail transportation	0.1	Util.			
Relay & industrial controls	0.1	Manufg.			
Bare printed circuit boards	0.1	Manufg.			
Fluid power process machinery	0.1	Manufg.			
Nondepository credit intermediation activities	0.1	Fin/R.E.			
Paperboard mills	0.1	Manufg.			
Waste management & remediation services	0.1	Services			
Commercial & industrial machinery rental & leasing	0.1	Fin/R.E.			

Source: Benchmark Input-Output Accounts for the U.S. Economy, 2002, U.S. Department of Commerce, Washington, D.C., January 2008. The abbreviation nec stands for 'not elsewhere classified'.

OCCUPATIONS EMPLOYED BY ENGINE, TURBINE, & POWER TRANSMISSION EQUIPMENT

Occupation	% of Total 2006	Change to 2016	Occupation	% of Total 2006	Change to 2016
Team assemblers	10.8	-16.1	Welders, cutters, solderers, & brazers	1.5	-10.7
Engine & other machine assemblers	7.0	-16.1	Industrial machinery mechanics	1.5	-3.5
Machinists	6.7	-11.9	Laborers & freight, stock, & material movers, hand	1.4	-24.5
First-line supervisors/managers of production workers	3.7	-16.1	Drilling & boring machine tool operators	1.4	-24.5
Inspectors, testers, sorters, samplers, & weighers	3.3	-20.9	General & operations managers	1.3	-24.5
Computer-controlled machine tool operators	3.2	-7.7	Cutting, punching, & press machine operators	1.2	-24.5
Assemblers & fabricators, nec	3.2	-24.5	Production, planning, & expediting clerks	1.2	-16.1
Mechanical engineers	2.9	-16.1	Stock clerks & order fillers	1.1	-29.8
Lathe & turning machine tool operators & tenders	2.8	-24.5	Electricians	1.1	-13.0
Maintenance & repair workers, general	2.6	-16.1	Shipping, receiving, & traffic clerks	1.1	-19.2
Multiple machine tool operators & tenders	2.4	-7.7	Customer service representatives	1.1	-7.7
Grinding, lapping, polishing machine tool operators	1.9	-18.6			

Source: Industry-Occupation Matrix, Bureau of Labor Statistics, December 4, 2007. These data are reported based on 4-digit NAICS categories but have been matched to corresponding 6-digit NAICS industry codes. The change reported for each occupation to the year 2016 is a percent of growth or decline as estimated by the Bureau of Labor Statistics. The abbreviation nec stands for 'not elsewhere classified'.

LOCATION BY STATE AND REGIONAL CONCENTRATION

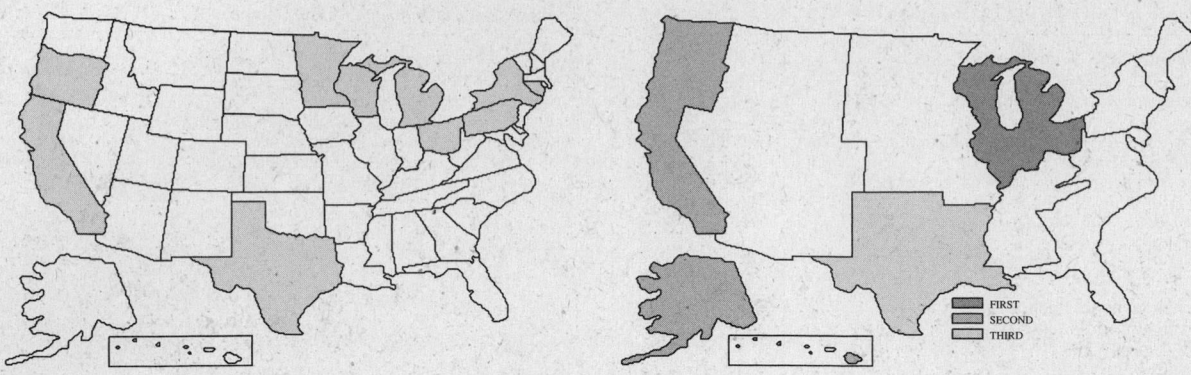

INDUSTRY DATA BY STATE

State	Establish-ments	Shipments			Employment				Cost as % of Shipments	Investment per Employee ($)
		Total ($ mil)	% of U.S.	Per Establ.	Total Number	% of U.S.	Per Establ.	Wages ($/hour)		
Wisconsin	23	419.6	15.1	18,241.4	2,232	13.6	97	20.75	38.2	4,791
Ohio	18	237.1	8.6	13,172.4	1,006	6.1	56	16.61	32.5	5,424
Texas	22	143.5	5.2	6,524.7	1,036	6.3	47	14.26	43.3	972
Michigan	19	142.3	5.1	7,491.7	950	5.8	50	19.92	31.9	6,385
Pennsylvania	9	123.8	4.5	13,759.3	702	4.3	78	20.99	28.5	2,537
New York	8	96.5	3.5	12,061.4	662	4.0	83	15.13	30.9	2,927
California	21	85.1	3.1	4,050.9	636	3.9	30	15.20	32.7	3,335
Connecticut	7	68.6	2.5	9,797.1	507	3.1	72	19.12	26.0	5,085
Minnesota	5	48.8	1.8	9,764.0	347	2.1	69	13.55	34.9	4,700
Oregon	7	14.8	0.5	2,121.3	159	1.0	23	14.57	28.0	1,742

Source: 2002 Economic Census. The states are in descending order of shipments or establishments (if shipment data are missing for the majority). The symbol (D) appears when data are withheld to prevent disclosure of competitive information. States marked with (D) are sorted by number of establishments. A dash (-) indicates that the data element cannot be calculated. Data may not show all states active in the NAICS category. All data available at the time of publication are shown.

NAICS 333618 - ENGINE EQUIPMENT MANUFACTURING NEC

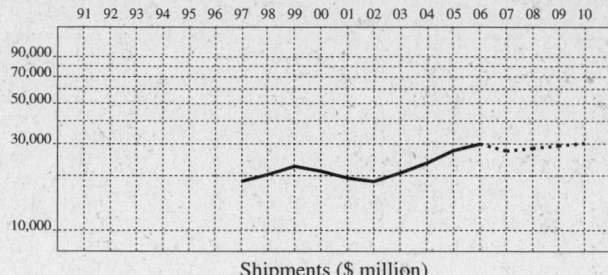

Shipments ($ million)

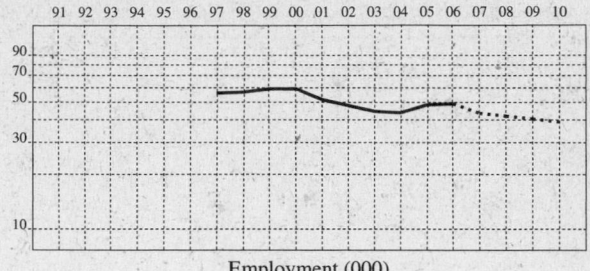

Employment (000)

GENERAL STATISTICS

Year	Companies	Establishments		Employment			Compensation		Production ($ million)			
		Total	with 20 or more employees	Total (000)	Production Workers (000)	Hours (Mil)	Payroll ($ mil)	Wages ($/hr)	Cost of Materials	Value Added by Manufacture	Value of Shipments	Capital Invest.
1997	243	300	164	56.1	40.7	81.4	2,326.1	18.16	10,473.4	8,006.9	18,614.6	630.7
1998		307	161	56.8	40.8	83.9	2,471.1	18.81	11,962.6	8,376.8	20,311.8	681.8
1999		310	161	59.2	41.1	86.3	2,690.6	18.54	12,426.6	10,204.8	22,537.6	794.7
2000		306	153	59.3	40.9	84.1	2,630.2	18.32	12,270.6	9,086.1	21,177.8	875.8
2001		299	154	51.6	34.6	70.2	2,313.3	18.58	9,774.2	9,473.2	19,417.4	692.2
2002	266	317	155	48.0	34.7	68.7	2,144.8	18.33	11,800.0	6,764.3	18,585.9	729.9
2003		301	148	44.6	33.1	67.1	2,139.4	20.24	14,163.7	6,409.4	20,696.3	625.0
2004		302	144	43.8	32.7	67.9	2,225.6	21.15	16,036.2	7,670.2	23,504.2	497.3
2005		298	152	48.5	35.6	72.1	2,352.3	21.23	19,744.7	8,130.3	27,547.2	818.7
2006		302P	144P	49.1	35.3	74.0	2,502.0	21.65	21,133.4	8,974.9	29,903.5	1,049.1
2007		301P	142P	43.5P	31.9P	65.8P	2,272.4P	21.73P	19,356.9P	8,220.5P	27,389.8P	823.6P
2008		301P	140P	42.0P	31.0P	64.0P	2,252.9P	22.14P	20,020.0P	8,502.0P	28,328.0P	838.9P
2009		300P	138P	40.5P	30.1P	62.2P	2,233.4P	22.54P	20,683.0P	8,783.6P	29,266.2P	854.2P
2010		300P	136P	39.0P	29.2P	60.4P	2,213.9P	22.95P	21,346.1P	9,065.2P	30,204.4P	869.5P

Sources: 1997 and 2002 *Economic Census*; other years, up to 2006, are from *Annual Survey of Manufactures*. Establishment counts for non-Census years are from *County Business Patterns*; 1997 and 2002 values are from the 1997 and 2002 censuses, respectively. 'P's show projections by the editors.

INDICES OF CHANGE

Year	Companies	Establishments		Employment			Compensation		Production ($ million)			
		Total	with 20 or more employees	Total (000)	Production Workers (000)	Hours (Mil)	Payroll ($ mil)	Wages ($/hr)	Cost of Materials	Value Added by Manufacture	Value of Shipments	Capital Invest.
1997	91	95	106	117	117	118	108	99	89	118	100	86
1998		97	104	118	118	122	115	103	101	124	109	93
1999		98	104	123	118	126	125	101	105	151	121	109
2000		97	99	124	118	122	123	100	104	134	114	120
2001		94	99	108	100	102	108	101	83	140	104	95
2002	100	100	100	100	100	100	100	100	100	100	100	100
2003		95	95	93	95	98	100	110	120	95	111	86
2004		95	93	91	94	99	104	115	136	113	126	68
2005		94	98	101	103	105	110	116	167	120	148	112
2006		95P	93P	102	102	108	117	118	179	133	161	144
2007		95P	92P	91P	92P	96P	106P	119P	164P	122P	147P	113P
2008		95P	91P	88P	89P	93P	105P	121P	170P	126P	152P	115P
2009		95P	89P	84P	87P	91P	104P	123P	175P	130P	157P	117P
2010		95P	88P	81P	84P	88P	103P	125P	181P	134P	163P	119P

Sources: Same as General Statistics. Values reflect change from the base year, 2002. Values above 100 mean greater than 2002, values below 100 mean less than 2002, and the values of 100 in other years means the same as 2002. 'P's show projections by the editors.

SELECTED RATIOS

For 2002	Avg. of All Manufact.	Analyzed Industry	Index	For 2002	Avg. of All Manufact.	Analyzed Industry	Index
Employees per Establishment	42	151	361	Value Added per Production Worker	182,367	194,937	107
Payroll per Establishment	1,639,184	6,765,931	413	Cost per Establishment	5,769,015	37,223,975	645
Payroll per Employee	39,053	44,683	114	Cost per Employee	137,446	245,833	179
Production Workers per Establishment	30	109	371	Cost per Production Worker	195,506	340,058	174
Wages per Establishment	694,845	3,972,464	572	Shipments per Establishment	11,158,348	58,630,599	525
Wages per Production Worker	23,548	36,290	154	Shipments per Employee	265,847	387,206	146
Hours per Production Worker	1,980	1,980	100	Shipments per Production Worker	378,144	535,617	142
Wages per Hour	11.89	18.33	154	Investment per Establishment	361,338	2,302,524	637
Value Added per Establishment	5,381,325	21,338,486	397	Investment per Employee	8,609	15,206	177
Value Added per Employee	128,210	140,923	110	Investment per Production Worker	12,245	21,035	172

Sources: Same as General Statistics. The 'Average of All Manufacturing' column represents the average of all manufacturing industries reported for the most recent complete year available. The Index shows the relationship between the Average and the Analyzed Industry. For example, 100 means that they are equal; 500 that the Analyzed Industry is five times the average; 50 means that the Analyzed Industry is half the national average. The abbreviation 'na' is used to show that data are 'not available'. Ratios shown for 2002, the last complete census year.

LEADING COMPANIES   Number shown: 75   Total sales ($ mil): 350,650   Total employment (000): 894.0

Company Name	Address				CEO Name	Phone	Co. Type	Sales ($ mil)	Empl. (000)
General Electric Co.	3135 Easton Tpk.	Fairfield	CT	06828		203-373-2211	P	172,738	327.0
Caterpillar Inc.	100 NE Adams St.	Peoria	IL	61629		309-675-1000	P	44,958	101.3
Emerson Electric	PO Box 4100	St. Louis	MO	63136	L.C. Barrett	314-553-2000	P	22,572	137.7
Cummins Inc.	PO Box 3005	Columbus	IN	47202		812-377-5000	P	13,048	37.8
Navistar International Corp.	PO Box 1488	Warrenville	IL	60555		630-753-5000	P	12,153	14.8
GE Aircraft Engines	1 Neumann Way	Cincinnati	OH	45215	Scott C. Donnelly	513-243-2000	D	11,181*	26.5
Boon Edam Tomsed	420 McKinney Pky.	Lillington	NC	27546	Tom DeVine	910-814-3800	R	7,005*	0.1
Etec Systems Inc.	PO Box 58039	Santa Clara	CA	95052		408-727-5555	S	6,992	12.2
Cooper Industries Ltd.	PO Box 4446	Houston	TX	77210	Kirk S. Hachigian	713-209-8400	P	5,903	31.5
Brunswick Corp.	1 N Field Ct.	Lake Forest	IL	60045		847-735-4700	P	5,671	27.1
Cameron International Corp.	1333 W Loop S	Houston	TX	77027	Sheldon R. Erikson	713-513-3300	P	4,666	15.4
Stanley Works	PO Box 700	New Britain	CT	06053		860-225-5111	P	4,484	18.4
Kohler Co.	444 Highland Dr.	Kohler	WI	53044	Herbert Kohler	920-457-4441	R	4,061*	33.0
Arco Auto and Marine Products	3921 Navy Blvd.	Pensacola	FL	32507	Ron Miller	850-455-5476	R	3,015	<0.1
Exide Technologies	13000 Deerfield Pky	Alpharetta	GA	30004		678-566-9000	P	2,940	13.9
Diebold Inc.	PO Box 3077	North Canton	OH	44720		330-490-4000	P	2,906	15.5
Flow Systems	PO Box 1069	St. Helena Is	SC	29920	James Barrett	843-838-6699	R	2,681*	<0.1
Lockheed Martin Enterpr. Info.	12506 Lk Underhill	Orlando	FL	32825	Robert J. Stevens	407-306-1000	S	2,383*	4.0
NTK Holdings Inc.	50 Kennedy Plz.	Providence	RI	02903	Richard L. Bready	401-751-1600	S	2,218	9.8
Scientific-Atlanta Inc.	PO Box 465447	Lawrenceville	GA	30042		770-236-5000	S	1,910	7.7
Detroit Diesel Corp.	13400 W Outer Dr.	Detroit	MI	48239	Robert R. Allran	313-592-5266	S	1,787*	5.0
JDS Uniphase Corp.	430 N McCarthy	Milpitas	CA	95035	Martin A. Kaplan	408-546-5000	PDS	1,397*	7.0
Rittal Corp.	1 Rittal Pl.	Springfield	OH	45504	Carie Ray	937-399-0500	R	1,268*	0.6
Tecumseh Products Co.	100 E Patterson St.	Tecumseh	MI	49286	Edwin Bunker	517-423-8411	P	1,133	10.3
International Truck and Engine	PO Box 1488	Warrenville	IL	60555	Daniel C. Ustian	630-753-5000	S	1,114*	1.7
ASMO North Carolina Inc.	470 Crawford Rd.	Statesville	NC	28625	Yutaka Kuroyanagi	704-878-6663	R	812*	0.8
East Penn Manufacturing Co.	PO Box 147	Lyon Station	PA	19536			R	716*	5.0
United Industrial Corp.	PO Box 126	Hunt Valley	MD	21030	W. G. Lichtenstein	410-628-3500	S	564	2.3
Lamson and Sessions Co.	25701 Science Park	Cleveland	OH	44122		216-464-3400	S	561	1.3
C and D Technologies Inc.	PO Box 3053	Blue Bell	PA	19422	Jeffrey A. Graves	215-619-2700	P	525	2.9
Overhead Door Corp.	2501 St. Hwy. 121	Lewisville	TX	75022	Howard Simons		R	508*	0.1
Camber Corp.	22289 Exploration	Lexington Park	MD	20653	Joseph Alexander	301-862-4577	R	447*	0.8
Rofin-Sinar Technologies Inc.	40984 Concept Dr.	Plymouth	MI	48170	Gunther Braun	734-455-5400	P	421	1.4
Link Simulation and Training	PO Box 5328	Arlington	TX	76005	John McNellis	817-619-3536	D	415*	0.8
Rofin-Sinar Inc.	40984 Concept Dr.	Plymouth	MI	48170	Gunther Braun	734-455-5400	S	375	1.4
Engineered Machined Products	3111 N 28th St.	Escanaba	MI	49829	Brian Larche	906-786-8404	R	333*	0.5
Consolidated Diesel Co.	PO Box 670	Whitakers	NC	27891		252-437-6611	J	326*	1.2
Deere Power Systems Group	PO Box 5100	Waterloo	IA	50704	Pierre E. Leroy	319-292-5643	D	271*	1.0
Electro Scientific Industries	13900 NW Sci Pk	Portland	OR	97229		503-641-4141	P	251	0.6
Preformed Line Products Co.	660 Beta Dr.	Cleveland	OH	44101	Robert Ruhlman	440-461-5200	P	217	1.5
FlightSafety International	Marine Air Terminal	Flushing	NY	11371	A.L. Ueltschi	718-565-4100	D	200*	1.5
IPG Photonics Corp.	50 Old Webster Rd.	Oxford	MA	01540	V. P. Gapontsev	508-373-1100	P	189	1.3
Spectra-Physics Lasers Inc.	PO Box 7013	Mountain View	CA	94039	Bruce Craig	650-961-2550	S	175*	1.0
FlightSafety International	PO Box 12304	Wichita	KS	67209	Albert Ueltschi	316-220-3100	S	170*	1.2
IPSCO Inc. (US)	650 Warrenville Rd.	Lisle	IL	60532	John Tulloch	630-810-4800	S	168*	<0.1
Paige Electric Company L.P.	PO Box 368	Union	NJ	07083		908-687-7810	R	165*	<0.1
Excel Technology Inc.	41 Research Way	East Setauket	NY	11733	Antoine Dominic	631-784-6175	P	160	0.7
Techko Inc.	9767 Research Dr.	Irvine	CA	92618	Joseph Ko	949-486-0678	R	154*	1.0
Penn Detroit Diesel Allison	PO Box 517830	Philadelphia	PA	19175	Christopher Cannon	215-335-0500	R	150*	<0.1
Micro Craft Inc.	41129 Jo Dr.	Novi	MI	48375	William Brown	248-476-6510	R	143*	<0.1
Zero Manufacturing Inc.	500 W 200 N	North Salt Lake	UT	84054	Stephen Henderson	801-298-5900	S	123*	0.3
Fisher Pierce	54 Commercial St.	Raynham	MA	02767	H. Lawerence Culp, Jr	508-821-1579	S	117*	0.2
Piller Inc.	45 Turner Rd.	Middletown	NY	10941	Michael Barron	845-695-5300	R	105*	<0.1
Mining Controls Inc.	PO Box 1141	Beckley	WV	25802	Randall Hurst	304-252-6243	R	104*	0.6
MCG Inc.	1500 N Front St.	New Ulm	MN	56073	Francis Tedesco	507-233-7000	R	103*	<0.1
Cubic Defense Systems Inc.	PO Box 85587	San Diego	CA	92186	Gerald Dinkel	858-277-6780	S	100*	0.9
Tri-Star Electronics Int'l	2201 Rosecrans Ave.	El Segundo	CA	90245	Terry Jarnigan	310-536-0444	D	90*	0.3
Aubrey Silvey Enterprises Inc.	371 Hamp Jones Rd.	Carrollton	GA	30117	Tommy Muse	770-834-0738	R	89*	0.2
Acme Electric Corp.	4815 W 5th St.	Lumberton	NC	28358	Robert J. McKenna	910-738-4251	S	89*	0.7
Jacobs Vehicle Systems	22 E Dudley Town	Bloomfield	CT	06002	Scott Wine	860-243-1441	S	89	0.4
Carlon Chimes Co.	25701 Science Park	Cleveland	OH	44122	M. J. Merriman, Jr.	216-464-3400	S	86*	0.2
Tracy Industries Inc.	PO Box 1260	La Puente	CA	91749	Thomas Tracy	562-692-9033	R	82*	0.2
Firearms Training Systems Inc.	7340 McGinnis Fry	Suwanee	GA	30024	Ronovan R. Mohling	770-813-0180	S	79	0.4
Synrad Inc.	4600 Campus Pl.	Mukilteo	WA	98275	Dave Clarke	425-349-3500	S	76*	0.2
Carrier Access Corp.	5395 Pearl Pky	Boulder	CO	80301		303-442-5455	P	75	0.3
Sonatech Inc.	879 Ward Dr.	Santa Barbara	CA	93111	Robert Carlson	805-683-1431	S	73*	0.5
Biolase Technology Inc.	4 Cromwell	Irvine	CA	92618		949-361-1200	P	70	0.2
Sling Media Inc.	1051 E Hillsdale	Foster City	CA	94404	Blake Krikorian	650-293-8000	R	69*	0.1
Cain Electrical Supply Corp.	PO Box 2158	Big Spring	TX	79721	Tom R. Ross	432-263-8421	R	67*	0.3
International Laser Group Inc.	PO Box 686	Woodland Hills	CA	91365	Cindy Michaels	818-888-0400	R	65*	0.2
Gale Banks Engineering	546 S Duggan Ave.	Azusa	CA	91702	Gale Banks	626-969-9600	R	64*	0.2
PI Manufacturing Corp.	20732 Currier Rd.	Walnut	CA	91789	Bill Chang	909-598-3718	R	61*	<0.1
Austin International Inc.	7 Ross Cannon St.	York	SC	29745	Randy Austin	803-628-0035	R	61*	0.1
Automotive Remanufacturers	3250 S 76th St.	Philadelphia	PA	19153	Carol Mancini	215-492-6330	R	59*	0.3
GMI Holdings Inc.	22790 Lake Park	Alliance	OH	44601	Carl Adrien	330-821-5360	S	54*	0.3

Source: Ward's Business Directory of U.S. Private and Public Companies, Volumes 1 and 2, 2008. The company type code used is as follows: P - Public, R - Private, S - Subsidiary, D - Division, J - Joint Venture, A - Affiliate, G - Group. Sales are in millions of dollars, employees are in thousands. An asterisk (*) indicates an estimated sales volume. The symbol < stands for 'less than'. Company names and addresses are truncated, in some cases, to fit into the available space.

MATERIALS CONSUMED

Material	Quantity	Delivered Cost ($ million)
Fluid power pumps, motors, and hydrostatic transmissions	(X)	198.4
Fluid power cylinders and rotary actuators (hydraulic and pneumatic)	(X)	(D)
Fluid power filters (hydraulic and pneumatic)	(X)	99.2
Fluid power hose, tube fittings, and assemblies (hydraulic and pneumatic)	(X)	72.0
Fluid power valves (hydraulic and pneumatic)	(X)	30.8
Metal bolts, nuts, screws, and other screw machine products	(X)	193.5
Metal stampings	(X)	41.6
Metal tanks, heat exchangers, and other boiler products	(X)	(D)
Fabricated structural metal products (excluding forgings)	(X)	38.5
All other fabricated metal products (excluding forgings)	(X)	290.4
Iron and steel forgings	(X)	486.0
Nonferrous forgings	(X)	0.6
Iron and steel castings (rough and semifinished)	(X)	835.8
Aluminum and aluminum-base alloy castings (rough and semifinished)	(X)	301.0
Other nonferrous metal castings, rough or semifinished (inc. aluminum)	(X)	70.9
Steel bars, bar shapes, and plates (exc. castings, forgings, fabr. metal products)	(X)	85.9
Steel sheet and strip (including tinplate)	(X)	16.5
All other steel shapes and forms (exc. castings, forgings, fabr. metal products)	(X)	24.6
Nonferrous shapes and forms	(X)	4.5
Pistons, piston rings, carburetors, and valves (intake and exhaust only)	(X)	398.2
Engine electrical equipment (incl. spark plugs, magnetos, generators, starters, etc.)	(X)	391.0
Integral horsepower electric motors and generators (1 hp or more)	(X)	2.0
Turbochargers	(X)	277.4
Injection fuel pumps	(X)	616.3
Machined engine blocks	(X)	377.2
Ball bearings (mounted or unmounted)	(X)	12.1
Roller bearings (mounted or unmounted)	(X)	8.0
Plain bearings and bushings	(X)	83.7
Mechanical speed changers, gears, and industrial high-speed drives	(X)	112.1
Generators purchased for incorporation into turbine generator sets	(X)	(D)
Gaskets (all types), and packing and sealing devices	(X)	95.2
Fabricated plastics products (excluding gaskets)	(X)	61.0
Rubber and plastics hose and belting	(X)	44.9
Cutting tools for machine tools	(X)	123.4
All other materials, components, parts, containers, and supplies	(X)	4,993.6
Materials, ingredients, containers, and supplies, nsk	(X)	541.4

Source: 2002 *Economic Census*. Explanation of symbols used: (D): Withheld to avoid disclosure of competitive data; na: Not available; (S): Withheld because statistical norms were not met; (X): Not applicable; (Z): Less than half the unit shown; nec: Not elsewhere classified; nsk: Not specified by kind; - : zero; p : 10-19 percent estimated; q : 20-29 percent estimated.

PRODUCT SHARE DETAILS

Product or Product Class Shipments	Mil. $	Product or Product Class Shipments	Mil. $
OTHER ENGINE EQUIPMENT	18,292.0	Oil pumps, new, for internal combustion engines, except aircraft and gasoline automotive engines and gas turbines	62.7
Gasoline and gas-gasoline engines (except aircraft, automobile, highway truck, bus, tank, and outboard marine)	2,276.3	Fuel pumps, new, for internal combustion engines, except aircraft and gasoline automotive engines and gas turbines	98.3
Diesel, semidiesel, and dual-fuel engines (except automobile, highway truck, bus, and tank)	2,769.5	Water pumps, new, for internal combustion engines, except aircraft and gasoline automotive engines and gas turbines	97.0
Diesel, semidiesel, and dual-fuel engines for automobiles, highway trucks, and buses	6,566.6	Engine blocks for internal combustion engines, except aircraft and gasoline automotive engines and gas turbines	67.4
Piston-type natural gas engines, including LPG engines (excluding gas turbines)	283.1	Cylinder liners (sleeves) for internal combustion engines, except aircraft and gasoline automotive engines and gas turbines	46.2
Engine equipment, nec	1,025.2	Cylinder heads for internal combustion engines, except aircraft and gasoline automotive engines and gas turbines	396.5
Tank engines, except gas turbines	-		
Converted internal combustion engines (basic engines, short blocks purchased or intracompany transfer and converted to marine or other uses)	(D)	Intake manifolds and exhaust manifolds for internal combustion engines, except aircraft and gasoline automotive engines and gas turbines	110.1
Outboard motors (including electric)	756.7	Valve guides, seats, and tappets for internal combustion engines, except aircraft and gasoline automotive engines and gas turbines	63.6
Other engine equipment, nec	(D)		
Engine equipment, nec, nsk	1.3	Rocker arms and parts for internal combustion engines, except aircraft and gasoline automotive engines and gas turbines	138.9
Parts and accessories for internal combustion engines, except aircraft and gasoline automotive engines and gas turbines	5,175.8	Engine speed governors for internal combustion engines, except aircraft and gasoline automotive engines and gas turbines	189.5
Electrical machinery, equipment, and supplies, excluding fuel injection systems	4,169.6	Superchargers, including turbochargers, for internal combustion engines, except aircraft and gasoline automotive engines and gas turbines	414.5
Connecting rods for internal combustion engines, except aircraft and gasoline automotive engines and gas turbines	65.3	Other parts and accessories for internal combustion engines, except aircraft and gasoline automotive engines and gas turbines	2,122.8
Engine crankshafts for internal combustion engines, except aircraft and gasoline automotive engines and gas turbines	35.6	Fuel injection systems (multipoint) for internal combustion engines, except aircraft and gasoline automotive engines and gas turbines	956.5
Engine camshafts for internal combustion engines, except aircraft and gasoline automotive engines and gas turbines	165.4	Parts and accessories for internal combustion engines, except aircraft and gas automotive engines and turbines, nsk	49.7
Flywheels for internal combustion engines, except aircraft and gasoline automotive engines and gas turbines	39.7	**Other engine equipment manufacturing, nsk, total**	**195.5**
Main (crankshaft) engine bearings (halves) for internal combustion engines, except aircraft and gasoline automotive engines and gas turbines	8.4		
Connecting rod bearings (halves) for internal combustion engines, except aircraft and gasoline automotive engines and gas turbines	12.7		
Other engine bearings (halves) (camshaft, balance shaft, etc.) for internal combustion engines, except aircraft and gasoline automotive engines and gas turbines	35.0		

Source: 2002 *Economic Census*. The values are product shipments in millions of dollars for 2002. Total product shipments may be lower or higher than industry shipments. See Introduction for a full discussion. Values of indented subcategories are summed in the main heading(s). The symbol (D) appears when data are withheld to prevent disclosure of competitive information. The abbreviation nsk stands for 'not specified by kind' and nec for 'not elsewhere classified'. A dash (-) means zero.

INPUTS AND OUTPUTS FOR OTHER ENGINE EQUIPMENT MANUFACTURING

Economic Sector or Industry Providing Inputs	%	Sector	Economic Sector or Industry Buying Outputs	%	Sector
Compensation of employees	17.1		Exports of goods & services	25.0	Cap Inv
Engine equipment, nec	9.4	Manufg.	Heavy duty trucks	13.4	Manufg.
Wholesale trade	7.0	Trade	Light truck & utility vehicles	8.8	Manufg.
Motor vehicle parts	4.5	Manufg.	Engine equipment, nec	7.1	Manufg.
Ferrous metal foundries	4.0	Manufg.	Private fixed investment	4.9	
Mechanical power transmission equipment	3.8	Manufg.	Construction machinery	4.8	Manufg.
Management of companies & enterprises	2.8	Services	Automobiles	3.8	Manufg.
Forging, stamping, & sintering, nec	2.5	Manufg.	S/L govt. invest., other	3.4	S/L Govt
Ornamental & architectural metal products	2.2	Manufg.	Lawn & garden equipment	3.3	Manufg.
Motors & generators	2.1	Manufg.	Ship building & repairing	2.8	Manufg.
Nonferrous metal foundries	2.1	Manufg.	Farm machinery & equipment	2.5	Manufg.
Noncomparable imports	1.7	Foreign	Automotive repair & maintenance, ex. car washes	2.1	Services
Truck transportation	1.5	Util.	Retail trade	2.0	Trade
Valve & fittings other than plumbing	1.0	Manufg.	Boat building	1.5	Manufg.
Wood kitchen cabinets & countertops	0.9	Manufg.	Wholesale trade	1.3	Trade
Gaskets, packing, & sealing devices	0.9	Manufg.	Mining & oil & gas field machinery	1.3	Manufg.
Communication & energy wires & cables	0.9	Manufg.	Motor vehicle parts	1.3	Manufg.
Turned products & screws, nuts, & bolts	0.9	Manufg.	Motors & generators	1.1	Manufg.
Iron & steel mills & ferroalloys	0.8	Manufg.	Personal consumption expenditures	1.1	
Rubber & plastics hose & belting	0.8	Manufg.	Transit & ground passenger transportation	1.0	Util.
Plastics products, nec	0.7	Manufg.	General S/L govt. services	0.8	S/L Govt
Concrete products, nec	0.7	Manufg.	Turbines & turbine generator set units	0.8	Manufg.
Speed changers, industrial high-speed drives, & gears	0.7	Manufg.	Commercial & industrial equipment repair/maintenance	0.7	Services
Rubber products, nec	0.6	Manufg.	General Federal government services, defense	0.5	Fed Govt
Cutting tools & machine tool accessories	0.6	Manufg.	Air & gas compressors	0.5	Manufg.

Continued on next page.

INPUTS AND OUTPUTS FOR OTHER ENGINE EQUIPMENT MANUFACTURING - Continued

Economic Sector or Industry Providing Inputs	%	Sector	Economic Sector or Industry Buying Outputs	%	Sector
Sawmills & wood preservation	0.6	Manufg.	Truck transportation	0.4	Util.
Fluid power process machinery	0.6	Manufg.	Other S/L govt. enterprises	0.4	S/L Govt
Machine shops	0.6	Manufg.	Personal & household goods repair/maintenance	0.4	Services
Power generation & supply	0.6	Util.	S/L govt. passenger transit	0.3	S/L Govt
Semiconductors & related devices	0.6	Manufg.	Electronic & precision equipment repair/maintenance	0.3	Services
General purpose machinery, nec	0.5	Manufg.	Transportation equipment, nec	0.3	Manufg.
Miscellaneous wood products	0.5	Manufg.	Material handling equipment	0.3	Manufg.
Plate work & fabricated structural products	0.5	Manufg.	Pumps & pumping equipment	0.3	Manufg.
Fabricated metals, nec	0.5	Manufg.	Natural gas distribution	0.2	Util.
Printed circuit assemblies (electronic assemblies)	0.5	Manufg.	Mechanical power transmission equipment	0.2	Manufg.
Securities, commodity contracts, investments	0.4	Fin/R.E.	Architectural, engineering, & related services	0.1	Services
Engineered wood members & trusses	0.4	Manufg.	Speed changers, industrial high-speed drives, & gears	0.1	Manufg.
Metal cans, boxes, & other containers (light gauge)	0.4	Manufg.	S/L govt. invest., education	0.1	S/L Govt
Nonferrous metal (ex. copper & aluminum) processing	0.4	Manufg.			
Wood windows & doors & millwork	0.4	Manufg.			
Lessors of nonfinancial assets	0.4	Fin/R.E.			
Crowns & closures & metal stamping	0.4	Manufg.			
Coating, engraving, heat treating & allied activities	0.3	Manufg.			
Automotive equipment rental & leasing	0.3	Fin/R.E.			
Switchgear & switchboard apparatus	0.3	Manufg.			
Hardware	0.3	Manufg.			
Veneer & plywood	0.3	Manufg.			
Adhesives	0.3	Manufg.			
Lighting fixtures	0.3	Manufg.			
Paints & coatings	0.3	Manufg.			
Lime & gypsum products	0.3	Manufg.			
Advertising & related services	0.3	Services			
Monetary authorities/depository credit intermediation	0.3	Fin/R.E.			
Plastics pipe & pipe fittings	0.3	Manufg.			
Legal services	0.3	Services			
Wiring devices	0.3	Manufg.			
Brick, tile & other structural clay products	0.3	Manufg.			
Plumbing fixture fittings & trim	0.3	Manufg.			
Cement	0.3	Manufg.			
Maintenance/repair of nonresidential structures	0.2	Construct.			
Professional, scientific, technical services, nec	0.2	Services			
Services to buildings & dwellings	0.2	Services			
Plastics packaging materials, film & sheet	0.2	Manufg.			
Data processing, hosting, & related services	0.2	Services			
Food services & drinking places	0.2	Services			
Ball & roller bearings	0.2	Manufg.			
Taxes on production & imports, less subsidies	0.2				
Retail trade	0.2	Trade			
Commercial & industrial machinery rental & leasing	0.2	Fin/R.E.			
Natural gas distribution	0.2	Util.			
Electronic components, nec	0.2	Manufg.			
Air transportation	0.2	Util.			
Real estate	0.2	Fin/R.E.			
Architectural, engineering, & related services	0.2	Services			
Specialized design services	0.2	Services			
Business support services	0.2	Services			
Scientific research & development services	0.2	Services			
Management, scientific, & technical consulting	0.1	Services			
Employment services	0.1	Services			
Automotive repair & maintenance, ex. car washes	0.1	Services			
Telecommunications	0.1	Services			
Hotels & motels, including casino hotels	0.1	Services			
Warehousing & storage	0.1	Util.			
Paperboard containers	0.1	Manufg.			
Commercial & industrial equipment repair/maintenance	0.1	Services			
Electronic connectors	0.1	Manufg.			
Abrasive products	0.1	Manufg.			
Rail transportation	0.1	Util.			
Accounting, tax preparation, bookkeeping, & payroll	0.1	Services			
Other computer related services, including facilities	0.1	Services			
AC, refrigeration, and warm air heating equipment	0.1	Manufg.			

Source: Benchmark Input-Output Accounts for the U.S. Economy, 2002, U.S. Department of Commerce, Washington, D.C., January 2008. The abbreviation nec stands for 'not elsewhere classified'.

OCCUPATIONS EMPLOYED BY ENGINE, TURBINE, & POWER TRANSMISSION EQUIPMENT

Occupation	% of Total 2006	Change to 2016	Occupation	% of Total 2006	Change to 2016
Team assemblers	10.8	-16.1	Welders, cutters, solderers, & brazers	1.5	-10.7
Engine & other machine assemblers	7.0	-16.1	Industrial machinery mechanics	1.5	-3.5
Machinists	6.7	-11.9	Laborers & freight, stock, & material movers, hand	1.4	-24.5
First-line supervisors/managers of production workers	3.7	-16.1	Drilling & boring machine tool operators	1.4	-24.5
Inspectors, testers, sorters, samplers, & weighers	3.3	-20.9	General & operations managers	1.3	-24.5
Computer-controlled machine tool operators	3.2	-7.7	Cutting, punching, & press machine operators	1.2	-24.5
Assemblers & fabricators, nec	3.2	-24.5	Production, planning, & expediting clerks	1.2	-16.1
Mechanical engineers	2.9	-16.1	Stock clerks & order fillers	1.1	-29.8
Lathe & turning machine tool operators & tenders	2.8	-24.5	Electricians	1.1	-13.0
Maintenance & repair workers, general	2.6	-16.1	Shipping, receiving, & traffic clerks	1.1	-19.2
Multiple machine tool operators & tenders	2.4	-7.7	Customer service representatives	1.1	-7.7
Grinding, lapping, polishing machine tool operators	1.9	-18.6			

Source: Industry-Occupation Matrix, Bureau of Labor Statistics, December 4, 2007. These data are reported based on 4-digit NAICS categories but have been matched to corresponding 6-digit NAICS industry codes. The change reported for each occupation to the year 2016 is a percent of growth or decline as estimated by the Bureau of Labor Statistics. The abbreviation nec stands for 'not elsewhere classified'.

LOCATION BY STATE AND REGIONAL CONCENTRATION

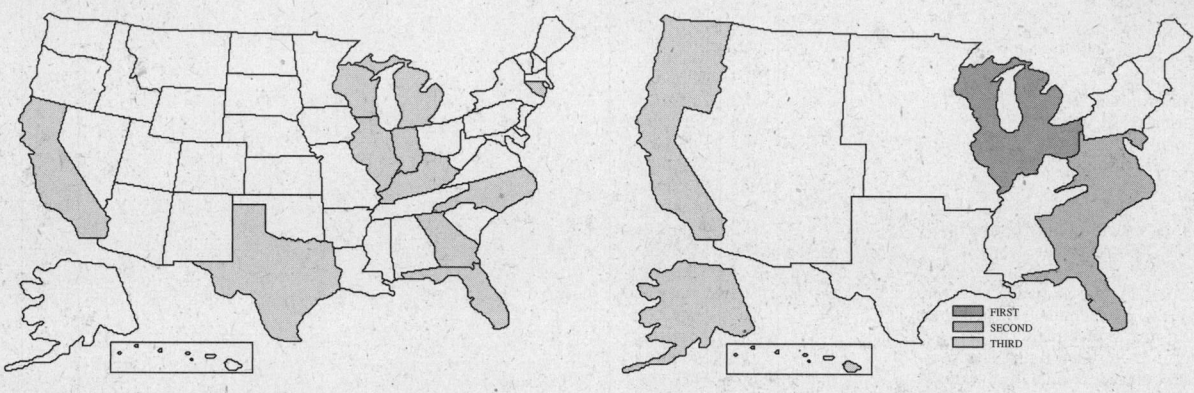

FIRST
SECOND
THIRD

INDUSTRY DATA BY STATE

State	Establish-ments	Shipments			Employment				Cost as % of Shipments	Investment per Employee ($)
		Total ($ mil)	% of U.S.	Per Establ.	Total Number	% of U.S.	Per Establ.	Wages ($/hour)		
Indiana	20	3,422.1	18.4	171,104.8	5,788	12.1	289	24.55	70.4	20,074
Illinois	20	2,662.2	14.3	133,109.3	6,238	13.0	312	16.19	59.0	15,579
Michigan	23	2,250.3	12.1	97,837.0	6,052	12.6	263	18.32	55.7	18,001
Wisconsin	18	1,732.8	9.3	96,267.3	5,998	12.5	333	23.13	55.3	11,283
North Carolina	12	834.2	4.5	69,516.5	2,205	4.6	184	16.18	65.8	11,287
Georgia	7	637.7	3.4	91,101.9	2,146	4.5	307	14.11	66.8	11,093
Kentucky	5	297.5	1.6	59,502.0	1,213	2.5	243	17.26	72.7	2,710
Connecticut	3	267.7	1.4	89,240.7	1,306	2.7	435	22.49	29.6	5,250
California	31	166.8	0.9	5,380.8	951	2.0	31	11.58	44.6	6,759
Florida	22	95.5	0.5	4,343.1	327	0.7	15	14.41	54.8	6,697
Texas	10	24.1	0.1	2,411.8	138	0.3	14	18.30	43.4	3,522

Source: 2002 *Economic Census*. The states are in descending order of shipments or establishments (if shipment data are missing for the majority). The symbol (D) appears when data are withheld to prevent disclosure of competitive information. States marked with (D) are sorted by number of establishments. A dash (-) indicates that the data element cannot be calculated. Data may not show all states active in the NAICS category. All data available at the time of publication are shown.

NAICS 333911 - PUMP AND PUMPING EQUIPMENT MANUFACTURING

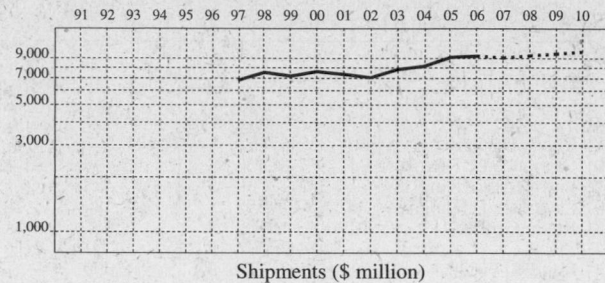
Shipments ($ million)

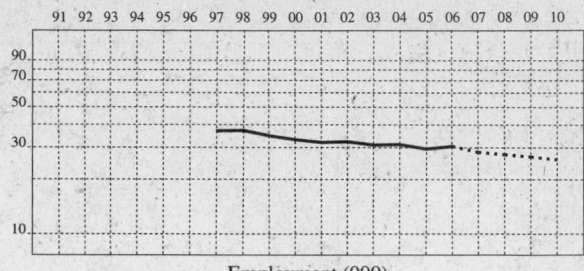
Employment (000)

GENERAL STATISTICS

Year	Com-panies	Establishments		Employment			Compensation		Production ($ million)			
		Total	with 20 or more employees	Total (000)	Production Workers (000)	Hours (Mil)	Payroll ($ mil)	Wages ($/hr)	Cost of Materials	Value Added by Manufacture	Value of Shipments	Capital Invest.
1997	408	489	250	37.0	21.3	43.9	1,443.7	15.60	3,395.2	3,442.1	6,825.0	187.5
1998		487	247	37.2	21.5	44.4	1,491.5	15.95	3,957.2	3,721.0	7,552.3	227.4
1999		475	235	34.8	19.5	39.9	1,432.1	16.03	3,509.4	3,595.2	7,210.2	190.5
2000		466	233	33.1	18.5	38.5	1,409.8	16.41	3,743.7	3,889.9	7,629.8	237.3
2001		458	237	32.0	18.0	36.5	1,362.1	16.74	3,631.8	3,646.4	7,378.4	186.5
2002	399	487	237	32.3	18.5	36.7	1,408.0	17.68	3,421.2	3,624.9	7,071.5	148.7
2003		486	233	31.0	17.9	38.3	1,393.3	16.47	3,737.4	4,130.8	7,834.2	153.7
2004		491	226	31.2	16.9	35.5	1,445.3	19.02	3,898.9	4,261.4	8,167.5	155.9
2005		490	226	29.5	17.4	35.4	1,492.3	19.92	4,404.5	4,732.7	9,136.6	139.1
2006		486P	223P	30.5	16.4	34.2	1,504.1	20.35	4,571.7	4,779.2	9,282.1	151.0
2007		487P	220P	28.3P	15.7P	32.6P	1,458.6P	20.30P	4,474.8P	4,677.9P	9,085.3P	130.8P
2008		488P	217P	27.5P	15.2P	31.5P	1,462.3P	20.83P	4,589.1P	4,797.4P	9,317.4P	122.3P
2009		489P	215P	26.7P	14.6P	30.5P	1,466.0P	21.35P	4,703.4P	4,916.9P	9,549.5P	113.8P
2010		490P	212P	25.8P	14.1P	29.4P	1,469.7P	21.88P	4,817.7P	5,036.4P	9,781.6P	105.2P

Sources: 1997 and 2002 *Economic Census*; other years, up to 2006, are from *Annual Survey of Manufactures*. Establishment counts for non-Census years are from *County Business Patterns*; 1997 and 2002 values are from the 1997 and 2002 censuses, respectively. 'P's show projections by the editors.

INDICES OF CHANGE

Year	Com-panies	Establishments		Employment			Compensation		Production ($ million)			
		Total	with 20 or more employees	Total (000)	Production Workers (000)	Hours (Mil)	Payroll ($ mil)	Wages ($/hr)	Cost of Materials	Value Added by Manufacture	Value of Shipments	Capital Invest.
1997	102	100	105	115	115	120	103	88	99	95	97	126
1998		100	104	115	116	121	106	90	116	103	107	153
1999		98	99	108	105	109	102	91	103	99	102	128
2000		96	98	102	100	105	100	93	109	107	108	160
2001		94	100	99	97	99	97	95	106	101	104	125
2002	100	100	100	100	100	100	100	100	100	100	100	100
2003		100	98	96	97	104	99	93	109	114	111	103
2004		101	95	97	91	97	103	108	114	118	115	105
2005		101	95	91	94	96	106	113	129	131	129	94
2006		100P	94P	94	89	93	107	115	134	132	131	102
2007		100P	93P	88P	85P	89P	104P	115P	131P	129P	128P	88P
2008		100P	92P	85P	82P	86P	104P	118P	134P	132P	132P	82P
2009		100P	91P	83P	79P	83P	104P	121P	137P	136P	135P	77P
2010		101P	89P	80P	76P	80P	104P	124P	141P	139P	138P	71P

Sources: Same as General Statistics. Values reflect change from the base year, 2002. Values above 100 mean greater than 2002, values below 100 mean less than 2002, and the values of 100 in other years means the same as 2002. 'P's show projections by the editors.

SELECTED RATIOS

For 2002	Avg. of All Manufact.	Analyzed Industry	Index	For 2002	Avg. of All Manufact.	Analyzed Industry	Index
Employees per Establishment	42	66	158	Value Added per Production Worker	182,367	195,941	107
Payroll per Establishment	1,639,184	2,891,170	176	Cost per Establishment	5,769,015	7,025,051	122
Payroll per Employee	39,053	43,591	112	Cost per Employee	137,446	105,920	77
Production Workers per Establishment	30	38	129	Cost per Production Worker	195,506	184,930	95
Wages per Establishment	694,845	1,332,353	192	Shipments per Establishment	11,158,348	14,520,534	130
Wages per Production Worker	23,548	35,073	149	Shipments per Employee	265,847	218,932	82
Hours per Production Worker	1,980	1,984	100	Shipments per Production Worker	378,144	382,243	101
Wages per Hour	11.89	17.68	149	Investment per Establishment	361,338	305,339	85
Value Added per Establishment	5,381,325	7,443,326	138	Investment per Employee	8,609	4,604	53
Value Added per Employee	128,210	112,226	88	Investment per Production Worker	12,245	8,038	66

Sources: Same as General Statistics. The 'Average of All Manufacturing' column represents the average of all manufacturing industries reported for the most recent complete year available. The Index shows the relationship between the Average and the Analyzed Industry. For example, 100 means that they are equal; 500 that the Analyzed Industry is five times the average; 50 means that the Analyzed Industry is half the national average. The abbreviation 'na' is used to show that data are 'not available'. Ratios shown for 2002, the last complete census year.

LEADING COMPANIES Number shown: 75   Total sales ($ mil): 497,177   Total employment (000): 490.3

Company Name	Address				CEO Name	Phone	Co. Type	Sales ($ mil)	Empl. (000)
General Motors Corp.	300 Renaissance Ctr	Detroit	MI	48265		313-556-5000	P	181,122	266.0
FE Petro Inc.	3760 Marsh Rd.	Madison	WI	53718	Chuck Franklin	608-838-8786	S	88,896*	0.1
FAST and Fluid Management Srl	1023 Wheeling Rd.	Wheeling	IL	60090	Lawrence D. Kingsley	847-537-0880	S	42,499*	4.2
Pumper Parts L.L.C.	6017 Enterprise Dr.	Export	PA	15632	Lawrence D. Kingsley	724-387-1776	S	42,488*	4.2
Wright Pump Inc.	S84 Enterprise	Muskego	WI	53150	Lawrence D. Kingsley	262-650-1925	S	42,488*	4.2
Depco Pump Company Inc.	PO Box 6820	Clearwater	FL	33758	Kevin Griffith	727-446-1656	R	23,868*	<0.1
ITT Corp.	4 W Red Oak Ln.	White Plains	NY	10604		914-641-2000	P	9,003	39.7
Union Tank Car Co.	175 W Jackson Blvd.	Chicago	IL	60604	Kenneth Fischl	312-431-3111	R	7,000*	0.2
Metso Minerals Industries Inc.	20965 Crossroads	Waukesha	WI	53186	Hannu Melarti	262-717-2500	R	6,340*	0.2
EMSAR Ventures Inc.	125 Access Rd.	Stratford	CT	06615	Francesco Mascitelli	203-377-8100	S	4,818*	0.5
Seaquist Closures L.L.C.	711 Fox Street	Mukwonago	WI	53149	Eric S. Ruskoski	262-363-7191	S	4,628*	0.5
Trinity Industries Inc.	2525 Stemmons	Dallas	TX	75207		214-631-4420	P	3,833	14.4
Flowserve Corp.	5215 N O'Connor	Irving	TX	75039		972-443-6500	P	3,763	15.0
Pentair Inc.	5500 Wayzata Blvd.	Golden Valley	MN	55416	Winslow H. Buxton	763-545-1730	P	3,399	16.0
Washington Group International	PO Box 73	Boise	ID	83729		208-386-5000	D	3,398	25.0
Bombardier Transport. Holdings	1501 Lebanon Ch.	Pittsburgh	PA	15236	Raymond Betler	412-655-5700	R	2,037*	0.9
Gardner Denver Inc.	PO Box 528	Quincy	IL	62306	Ross J. Centanni	217-222-5400	P	1,869	6.2
Envirotech Pumpsystems Inc.	PO Box 209	Salt Lake City	UT	84110	Joseph Roark	801-359-8731	R	1,770*	0.3
Beckett Corp.	400 E Royal Ln.	Irving	TX	75039	Wingate Sung	972-871-8000	R	1,409*	0.1
Westinghouse Air Brake Techn.	1001 Air Brake Ave.	Wilmerding	PA	15148	William E. Kassling	412-825-1000	P	1,360	6.0
IDEX Corp.	630 Dundee Rd.	Northbrook	IL	60062	Robert Brinley	847-498-7070	P	1,359	5.0
Greenbrier Companies Inc.	1 Centerpointe Dr.	Lake Oswego	OR	97035	Alejandro Centurion	503-684-7000	P	1,224	4.2
Progress Rail Services Corp.	PO Box 1037	Albertville	AL	35950		256-593-1260	S	1,200	3.8
Tecumseh Products Co.	100 E Patterson St.	Tecumseh	MI	49286	Edwin Bunker	517-423-8411	P	1,133	10.3
Procon Products	910 Ridgely Rd.	Murfreesboro	TN	37129	Roger Fix	615-890-5710	S	989*	0.1
Scott Fetzer Co.	28800 Clemens Rd.	Westlake	OH	44145	K Semelsberger	440-892-3000	S	935*	14.5
Graco Inc.	PO Box 1441	Minneapolis	MN	55440		612-623-6000	P	841	2.3
GE Transportation Systems	2901 East Lake Rd.	Erie	PA	16531	William Yuskovic	814-875-2234	S	747*	8.0
Robbins and Myers Inc.	51 Plum Street	Dayton	OH	45440		937-458-6600	P	695	3.3
Franklin Electric Company Inc.	400 E Spring St.	Bluffton	IN	46714		219-824-2900	P	602	3.2
Lufkin Industries Inc.	PO Box 849	Lufkin	TX	75902		936-634-2211	P	597	2.7
ACF Industries Inc.	101 Clark St.	St. Charles	MO	63301	Carl C. Icahn	636-949-2399	R	579*	0.5
Goulds Pumps Inc.	2881 East Bayard St	Seneca Falls	NY	13148	Bill Taylor	315-568-7123	S	558*	5.0
Motive Power, Inc.	4600 Apple St.	Boise	ID	83716	Albert Neupaver	208-947-4800	S	544*	0.3
Freedom Forge Corp.	500 N Walnut St.	Burnham	PA	17009	Michael Farrell	717-248-4911	S	480*	3.3
Schwing America Inc.	5900 Centerville Rd	Saint Paul	MN	55127	Thomas Anderson	651-429-0999	R	453*	0.6
Colfax Corp.	8730 Stony Pnt Pky	Richmond	VA	23235	John A. Young	804-560-4070	R	394	2.0
Tuthill Corp.	8500 S Madison St.	Burr Ridge	IL	60527		630-382-4900	R	388*	0.9
Sterling Fluid Systems Inc.	PO Box 7026	Indianapolis	IN	46207	Dean Douglas	317-925-9661	R	373*	0.3
Sihi Pumps Inc.	PO Box 460	Grand Island	NY	14072		716-773-6450	S	373*	<0.1
Beach-Russ Co.	544 Union Ave.	Brooklyn	NY	11211	C. A. Beach	718-388-4090	R	362*	<0.1
Engineered Machined Products	3111 N 28th St.	Escanaba	MI	49829	Brian Larche	906-786-8404	R	333*	0.5
Gruber Systems Inc.	25636 Ave. Stanford	Valencia	CA	91355	John Hoskinson	661-257-4060	R	322*	0.3
Multiquip Inc.	PO Box 6254	Carson	CA	90749	Roger Euliss	310-537-3700	R	317*	0.3
Gorman-Rupp Co.	PO Box 1217	Mansfield	OH	44901	James C. Gorman	419-755-1011	P	306	1.0
Ampco-Pittsburgh Corp.	600 Grant St.	Pittsburgh	PA	15219	Louis Berkman	412-456-4400	P	302	1.3
eProduction Solutions Inc.	22001 N Park Dr.	Kingwood	TX	77339	Dharmesh Mehta	281-348-1000	R	298*	1.0
Putzmeister America Inc.	1733 90th St.	Sturtevant	WI	53177	Dave Adams	262-886-3200	R	280*	0.3
Ebara International Corp.	350 Salomon Cir.	Sparks	NV	89434	Joel Madison	775-356-2796	R	275*	0.2
Waterous Co.	125 Hardman Ave. S	South St Paul	MN	55075	Donald Haugen	651-450-5000	R	267*	0.4
Gunderson Rail Services	4012 NW Front St.	Portland	OR	97210		503-972-5950	S	260*	1.4
Metaullics Systems Div/Pyrotek	31935 Aurora Rd.	Cleveland	OH	44139	Alan Roy	440-349-8800	S	250*	<0.1
BLD Products Ltd.	534 E 48th St.	Holland	MI	49423	Scott Bye	616-395-5600	S	213*	0.2
Cleaver-Brooks Inc.	PO Box 421	Milwaukee	WI	53201	Welch Goggins	414-359-0600	R	210*	0.2
Revak Turbomachinery Services	PO Box 1645	La Porte	TX	77572	Lynn Revak	281-474-4458	R	207*	0.1
QED Environmental Systems Inc.	PO Box 3726	Ann Arbor	MI	48106	Michael Cross	734-995-2547	R	192*	<0.1
Vmv Enterprises Inc.	1300 Kentucky Ave.	Paducah	KY	42003	Robert Pedersen	270-444-4555	R	189*	1.0
Pump Star Inc.	PO Box 3047	Enid	OK	73702	Soubhi Naddaf	580-548-2723	R	168*	0.9
Ampco UES Sub Inc.	600 Grant St.	Pittsburgh	PA	15219	Robert Paul	412-456-4400	R	164*	<0.1
AY Mc Donald Industries Inc.	PO Box 508	Dubuque	IA	52004	John Mc Donald	563-583-7311	R	163*	0.4
Wacker Corp.	N92 Anthony	Menomonee Fls	WI	53051	Christopher Barnard	262-255-0500	R	156*	0.5
Taco Inc.	1160 Cranston St.	Cranston	RI	02920		401-942-8000	R	140*	0.4
JH Fletcher and Co.	PO Box 2187	Huntington	WV	25722	Sammons Duncan	304-525-7811	R	120*	0.2
Sundyne Corp.	14845 W 64th Ave.	Arvada	CO	80007	Phil Ruffner	303-425-0800	S	118*	0.7
Centrilift	200 W Stuart Roosa	Claremore	OK	74017	Chad Deaton	918-341-9600	D	115*	1.5
Associated Fuel Pump Systems	PO Box 1326	Anderson	SC	29622		864-224-0012	R	112*	0.3
Myers, F E Co.	1101 Myers Pkwy.	Ashland	OH	44805	Randall J. Hogan	419-289-1144	D	101*	0.6
Zoeller Co.	PO Box 16347	Louisville	KY	40256		502-778-2731	R	100*	0.3
Melling Tool Co.	PO Box 1188	Jackson	MI	49204	David Horthrop	517-787-8172	R	100*	0.3
Valley Power Systems Inc.	425 S Hacienda Blvd	City of Industry	CA	91745	Sam Hill	626-333-1243	S	100*	0.3
Loram Maintenance of Way Inc.	PO Box 188	Hamel	MN	55340	Paul Wilson	763-478-6014	R	100*	0.2
Hornerxpress Inc.	5755 Powerline Rd.	Fort Lauderdale	FL	33309	William Kent	954-772-6966	R	100*	0.2
Portec Rail Products Inc.	PO Box 38250	Pittsburgh	PA	15238	Richard Jarosinsk	412-782-6000	P	99	0.3
Flowtronex PSI Inc.	10661 Newkirk St.	Dallas	TX	75220	Dan Driscoll	214-357-1320	S	98*	0.2
ITT Industries Bell & Gossett	8200 N Austin Ave.	Morton Grove	IL	60053	Pat DePalma	847-966-3700	S	89	0.8

Source: *Ward's Business Directory of U.S. Private and Public Companies*, Volumes 1 and 2, 2008. The company type code used is as follows: P - Public, R - Private, S - Subsidiary, D - Division, J - Joint Venture, A - Affiliate, G - Group. Sales are in millions of dollars, employees are in thousands. An asterisk (*) indicates an estimated sales volume. The symbol < stands for 'less than'. Company names and addresses are truncated, in some cases, to fit into the available space.

MATERIALS CONSUMED

Material	Quantity	Delivered Cost ($ million)
Fluid power pumps, motors, and hydrostatic transmissions	(X)	81.9
Fluid power valves, hose and tube fittings and assemblies	(X)	7.1
Other fluid power products, hydraulic and pneumatic	(X)	1.8
Metal bolts, nuts, screws, and other screw machine products	(X)	53.4
Metal pipe, valves, and pipe fittings (excluding forgings)	(X)	41.4
Fabricated structural metal products (excluding forgings)	(X)	116.4
Other fabricated metal products (exc. fluid power products and forgings)	(X)	45.6
Iron and steel forgings	(X)	32.3
Nonferrous forgings	(X)	3.8
Iron and steel castings (rough and semifinished)	(X)	359.9
Aluminum and aluminum-base alloy castings (rough and semifinished)	(X)	29.2
Other nonferrous metal castings, rough or semifinished (inc. aluminum)	(X)	58.4
Steel bars, bar shapes, and plates (exc. castings, forgings, fabr. metal products)	(X)	91.0
Steel sheet and strip (including tinplate)	(X)	9.1
All other steel shapes and forms (exc. castings, forgings, fabr. metal products)	(X)	40.4
Other nonferrous shapes and forms (exc. castings, forgings, fabricated metal products)	(X)	15.0
Aluminum and aluminum-base alloy shapes and forms (exc. castings, forgings, fabr. metal products)	(X)	5.1
Engines (diesel, semidiesel, gasoline, and other carburetor-type engines)	(X)	37.8
Fractional horsepower electric motors (less than 1 hp)	(X)	211.4
Integral horsepower electric motors and generators (1 hp or more)	(X)	202.4
Ball and roller bearings (mounted or unmounted)	(X)	22.2
Paperboard containers, boxes, and corrugated paperboard	(X)	34.6
Fabricated rubber products (excluding gaskets)	(X)	41.5
Fabricated plastics products (excluding gaskets)	(X)	104.8
Gaskets (all types), and packing and sealing devices	(X)	66.6
Electrical transmission, distribution, and control equipment	(X)	61.3
Paints, varnishes, stains, lacquers, shellacs, japans, enamels, etc.	(X)	6.4
All other materials, components, parts, containers, and supplies	(X)	823.9
Materials, ingredients, containers, and supplies, nsk	(X)	312.9

Source: 2002 *Economic Census*. Explanation of symbols used: (D): Withheld to avoid disclosure of competitive data; na: Not available; (S): Withheld because statistical norms were not met; (X): Not applicable; (Z): Less than half the unit shown; nec: Not elsewhere classified; nsk: Not specified by kind; - : zero; p : 10-19 percent estimated; q : 20-29 percent estimated.

PRODUCT SHARE DETAILS

Product or Product Class Shipments	Mil. $	Product or Product Class Shipments	Mil. $
PUMPS AND PUMPING EQUIPMENT	6,493.6	Pumps, except packaged pumps, hand pumps, automotive circulating pumps, locomotive pumps, hydraulic fluid power pumps, measuring and dispensing pumps, and industrial spraying equipment, nsk	14.7
Pumps (excexpt packaged, hand, automotive circulating, locomotive, hydraulic fluid power, measuring and dispensing, industrial spraying etc.)	**5,062.0**	**Parts and attachments for pumps and pumping equipment (except for hydraulic, fluid power, and air and gas compressors)**	**1,140.2**
Domestic water systems (pumps for farm and home use), excluding irrigation pumps	662.1	Locomotive fuel lubricating or cooling medium pumps, including parts and attachments	1,138.6
Domestic sump pumps (1 hp or less) (including the value of the driver if shipped as a complete unit)	298.4	Locomotive fuel lubricating or cooling medium pumps	10.0
Oil-well and oil-field pumps, except boiler feed (including the value of the driver if shipped as a complete unit)	652.8	Parts and attachments for pumps and pumping equipment (except for hydraulic fluid power, and air and gas compressors), and packaged pumps	1,128.5
Industrial pumps, except hydraulic fluid power pumps, automotive circulating pumps, and measuring and dispensing pumps	2,785.0	Parts and attachments for pumps and pumping equipment (except for hydraulic fluid power, and air and gas compressors), and locomotive and packaged pumps, nsk	1.6
Other pumps, except packaged pumps, hand pumps, automotive circulating pumps, locomotive pumps, hydraulic fluid power pumps, measuring and dispensing pumps, and industrial spraying equipment	649.1	**Pumps and pumping equipment, nsk, total**	**291.4**

Source: 2002 *Economic Census*. The values are product shipments in millions of dollars for 2002. Total product shipments may be lower or higher than industry shipments. See Introduction for a full discussion. Values of indented subcategories are summed in the main heading(s). The symbol (D) appears when data are withheld to prevent disclosure of competitive information. The abbreviation nsk stands for 'not specified by kind' and nec for 'not elsewhere classified'. A dash (-) means zero.

INPUTS AND OUTPUTS FOR PUMP AND PUMPING EQUIPMENT MANUFACTURING

Economic Sector or Industry Providing Inputs	%	Sector	Economic Sector or Industry Buying Outputs	%	Sector
Compensation of employees	27.3		Private fixed investment	49.5	
Motors & generators	6.5	Manufg.	Exports of goods & services	17.7	Cap Inv
Wholesale trade	5.6	Trade	Federal government, investment, national defense	6.4	Fed Govt
Ferrous metal foundries	5.4	Manufg.	Residential permanent site structures	3.3	Construct.
Management of companies & enterprises	5.0	Services	S/L govt. invest., other	2.6	S/L Govt
Gaskets, packing, & sealing devices	2.8	Manufg.	Residential structures, nec	2.1	Construct.
Iron & steel mills & ferroalloys	2.4	Manufg.	Semiconductor machinery	2.0	Manufg.
Nonferrous metal foundries	2.1	Manufg.	General S/L govt. services	1.9	S/L Govt
Plastics products, nec	2.0	Manufg.	Owner-occupied dwellings	1.6	
Machine shops	1.3	Manufg.	Nonresidential structures, nec	1.4	Construct.

Continued on next page.

1141

INPUTS AND OUTPUTS FOR PUMP AND PUMPING EQUIPMENT MANUFACTURING - Continued

Economic Sector or Industry Providing Inputs	%	Sector	Economic Sector or Industry Buying Outputs	%	Sector
Pumps & pumping equipment	1.3	Manufg.	Pumps & pumping equipment	1.1	Manufg.
Turned products & screws, nuts, & bolts	1.0	Manufg.	Maintenance/repair of nonresidential structures	1.1	Construct.
Advertising & related services	1.0	Services	Oil & gas well drilling	1.0	Mining
Valve & fittings other than plumbing	1.0	Manufg.	Rail transportation	0.9	Util.
Metal cans, boxes, & other containers (light gauge)	1.0	Manufg.	Steel products from purchased steel	0.7	Manufg.
Truck transportation	1.0	Util.	Commercial & service industry machinery, nec	0.6	Manufg.
Fluid power process machinery	1.0	Manufg.	Oil & gas extraction	0.6	Mining
Relay & industrial controls	0.9	Manufg.	General purpose machinery, nec	0.5	Manufg.
Plate work & fabricated structural products	0.9	Manufg.	Real estate	0.5	Fin/R.E.
Engine equipment, nec	0.9	Manufg.	Industrial machinery, nec	0.5	Manufg.
Semiconductors & related devices	0.9	Manufg.	Wholesale trade	0.4	Trade
Forging, stamping, & sintering, nec	0.9	Manufg.	Other S/L govt. enterprises	0.4	S/L Govt
Printed circuit assemblies (electronic assemblies)	0.8	Manufg.	Maintenance/repair of residential structures	0.4	Construct.
Power generation & supply	0.8	Util.	Commercial & health care structures	0.3	Construct.
Securities, commodity contracts, investments	0.7	Fin/R.E.	S/L govt. passenger transit	0.3	S/L Govt
Paints & coatings	0.7	Manufg.	Federal government, investment, nondefense	0.2	Fed Govt
Paperboard containers	0.7	Manufg.	Air & gas compressors	0.2	Manufg.
Management, scientific, & technical consulting	0.7	Services	Boat building	0.2	Manufg.
Lessors of nonfinancial assets	0.5	Fin/R.E.	Commercial & industrial equipment repair/maintenance	0.2	Services
Retail trade	0.5	Trade	Services to buildings & dwellings	0.2	Services
Real estate	0.5	Fin/R.E.	Oil & gas operations services	0.1	Mining
Ball & roller bearings	0.4	Manufg.	Plastics & rubber industry machinery	0.1	Manufg.
Monetary authorities/depository credit intermediation	0.4	Fin/R.E.	Scenic & sightseeing transport & related services	0.1	Util.
Alumina refining & primary aluminum production	0.4	Manufg.			
Abrasive products	0.3	Manufg.			
Professional, scientific, technical services, nec	0.3	Services			
Legal services	0.3	Services			
Telecommunications	0.3	Services			
Electronic components, nec	0.3	Manufg.			
Automotive equipment rental & leasing	0.3	Fin/R.E.			
Coating, engraving, heat treating & allied activities	0.3	Manufg.			
Rubber products, nec	0.3	Manufg.			
Taxes on production & imports, less subsidies	0.3				
Scientific research & development services	0.3	Services			
Plastics packaging materials, film & sheet	0.3	Manufg.			
Postal service	0.3	Util.			
Data processing, hosting, & related services	0.3	Services			
Warehousing & storage	0.2	Util.			
Aluminum products from purchased aluminum	0.2	Manufg.			
Noncomparable imports	0.2	Foreign			
Accounting, tax preparation, bookkeeping, & payroll	0.2	Services			
Maintenance/repair of nonresidential structures	0.2	Construct.			
Services to buildings & dwellings	0.2	Services			
Motor vehicle parts	0.2	Manufg.			
Food services & drinking places	0.2	Services			
Cutting tools & machine tool accessories	0.2	Manufg.			
Natural gas distribution	0.2	Util.			
Commercial & industrial machinery rental & leasing	0.2	Fin/R.E.			
Other computer related services, including facilities	0.1	Services			
Architectural, engineering, & related services	0.1	Services			
Automotive repair & maintenance, ex. car washes	0.1	Services			
Paperboard mills	0.1	Manufg.			
Fabricated metals, nec	0.1	Manufg.			
Laminated plastics plates, sheets, & shapes	0.1	Manufg.			
Business support services	0.1	Services			
Commercial & industrial equipment repair/maintenance	0.1	Services			
Bare printed circuit boards	0.1	Manufg.			
Electronic capacitors, resistors, coils, transformers	0.1	Manufg.			
Chemical products & preparations, nec	0.1	Manufg.			

Source: *Benchmark Input-Output Accounts for the U.S. Economy, 2002*, U.S. Department of Commerce, Washington D.C., January 2008. *User should note that this Input-Output table is not for this particular narrowly defined industry but for a larger aggregate. Input and Output data for* Pump and Pumping Equipment Manufacturing *include Input and Output data for the* Annual Survey of Manufactures' *NAICS industries 333911 and 333913.* The abbreviation nec stands for "not elsewhere classified".

OCCUPATIONS EMPLOYED BY OTHER GENERAL-PURPOSE MACHINERY MANUFACTURING

Occupation	% of Total 2006	Change to 2016	Occupation	% of Total 2006	Change to 2016
Team assemblers	11.0	-9.7	Multiple machine tool operators & tenders	1.4	-0.7
Machinists	5.9	-5.2	Lathe & turning machine tool operators & tenders	1.4	-18.8
Welders, cutters, solderers, & brazers	5.7	-4.0	Maintenance & repair workers, general	1.4	-9.7
First-line supervisors/managers of production workers	3.6	-9.7	Structural metal fabricators & fitters	1.4	-9.7
Mechanical engineers	2.8	-0.7	Industrial engineers	1.3	9.6
Computer-controlled machine tool operators	2.5	-0.7	Electrical & electronic equipment assemblers	1.3	-27.8
Sales reps, wholesale & manufacturing, exc tech	2.3	-9.7	Industrial machinery mechanics	1.3	3.8
Engine & other machine assemblers	2.0	-9.7	Mechanical drafters	1.3	-8.7
Inspectors, testers, sorters, samplers, & weighers	1.9	-14.9	Customer service representatives	1.3	-0.7
Cutting, punching, & press machine operators	1.8	-18.8	Coating, painting, & spraying machine operators	1.2	-14.2
Shipping, receiving, & traffic clerks	1.8	-13.1	Office clerks, general	1.2	-11.1
Helpers--Production workers	1.6	-9.7	Industrial production managers	1.1	-9.7
General & operations managers	1.6	-18.8	Electrical engineers	1.1	-9.7
Laborers & freight, stock, & material movers, hand	1.5	-18.8	Production, planning, & expediting clerks	1.1	-9.7
Purchasing agents, exc wholesale, retail, & farm	1.5	-18.8	Stock clerks & order fillers	1.0	-24.5
Bookkeeping, accounting, & auditing clerks	1.5	-9.7			

Source: Industry-Occupation Matrix, Bureau of Labor Statistics, December 4, 2007. These data are reported based on 4-digit NAICS categories but have been matched to corresponding 6-digit NAICS industry codes. The change reported for each occupation to the year 2016 is a percent of growth or decline as estimated by the Bureau of Labor Statistics. The abbreviation nec stands for 'not elsewhere classified'.

LOCATION BY STATE AND REGIONAL CONCENTRATION

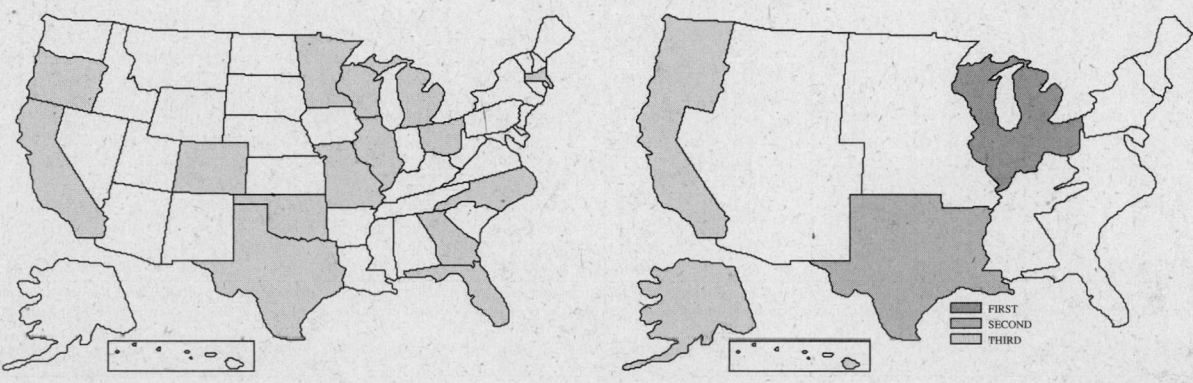

FIRST
SECOND
THIRD

INDUSTRY DATA BY STATE

State	Establish-ments	Shipments			Employment				Cost as % of Shipments	Investment per Employee ($)
		Total ($ mil)	% of U.S.	Per Establ.	Total Number	% of U.S.	Per Establ.	Wages ($/hour)		
California	63	812.6	11.5	12,898.6	3,742	11.6	59	13.39	52.4	6,086
Oklahoma	25	747.1	10.6	29,883.3	2,690	8.3	108	13.04	45.1	4,710
Ohio	30	644.3	9.1	21,475.9	3,564	11.0	119	16.83	50.9	2,725
Texas	56	556.0	7.9	9,928.2	2,664	8.2	48	23.06	48.1	4,831
Wisconsin	19	550.1	7.8	28,950.0	1,963	6.1	103	21.37	49.2	4,387
Illinois	24	420.8	6.0	17,534.9	1,960	6.1	82	17.59	44.7	4,892
Minnesota	7	297.1	4.2	42,443.4	960	3.0	137	23.61	39.3	4,477
North Carolina	7	229.3	3.2	32,758.3	765	2.4	109	12.93	30.7	1,864
Michigan	13	174.5	2.5	13,419.8	1,271	3.9	98	21.87	38.6	2,672
Georgia	11	167.0	2.4	15,180.4	905	2.8	82	15.99	47.7	2,707
Colorado	5	126.2	1.8	25,246.2	494	1.5	99	22.69	34.9	7,431
Florida	20	123.2	1.7	6,160.8	512	1.6	26	16.24	48.2	4,846
Oregon	7	122.1	1.7	17,444.1	434	1.3	62	23.12	71.8	2,931
Massachusetts	8	107.1	1.5	13,387.1	410	1.3	51	18.48	41.1	3,295
Missouri	9	35.2	0.5	3,912.6	169	0.5	19	18.64	40.9	3,485

Source: 2002 *Economic Census*. The states are in descending order of shipments or establishments (if shipment data are missing for the majority). The symbol (D) appears when data are withheld to prevent disclosure of competitive information. States marked with (D) are sorted by number of establishments. A dash (-) indicates that the data element cannot be calculated. Data may not show all states active in the NAICS category. All data available at the time of publication are shown.

NAICS 333912 - AIR AND GAS COMPRESSOR MANUFACTURING

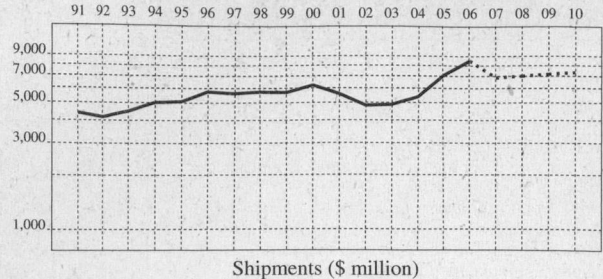

Shipments ($ million)

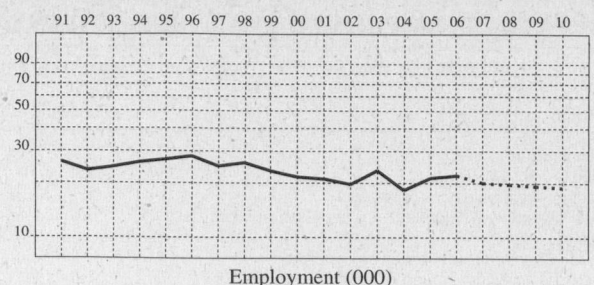

Employment (000)

GENERAL STATISTICS

Year	Companies	Establishments		Employment			Compensation		Production ($ million)			
		Total	with 20 or more employees	Total (000)	Production Workers (000)	Hours (Mil)	Payroll ($ mil)	Wages ($/hr)	Cost of Materials	Value Added by Manufacture	Value of Shipments	Capital Invest.
1991		244	137	26.1	14.8	30.1	837.0	13.80	2,305.0	2,016.5	4,389.7	96.8
1992	220	258	120	23.4	13.5	27.4	777.5	13.95	2,120.2	2,069.8	4,170.3	138.0
1993		283	118	24.5	14.2	28.9	831.6	13.88	2,137.8	2,310.8	4,493.2	122.2
1994		278	127	26.0	16.3	32.9	886.2	13.81	2,593.2	2,385.1	5,019.2	129.4
1995		293	134	26.9	16.8	34.5	948.1	13.77	2,685.3	2,522.4	5,087.0	128.1
1996		318	137	28.1	17.3	34.7	1,016.7	14.36	2,973.6	2,848.4	5,749.0	123.2
1997	269	314	138	24.8	14.8	30.1	940.3	15.21	3,044.6	2,659.9	5,633.0	169.5
1998		330	142	25.9	15.0	30.4	947.3	15.10	3,088.2	2,491.7	5,735.7	192.2
1999		325	139	23.3	13.9	26.6	917.9	16.01	2,952.1	2,636.4	5,695.5	207.6
2000		312	143	21.6	12.5	25.0	884.4	16.39	3,298.4	2,941.7	6,229.6	178.0
2001		312	140	21.1	11.1	22.0	837.7	17.39	3,003.8	2,595.4	5,567.2	149.3
2002	269	311	127	19.7	10.4	20.0	887.2	18.22	2,735.0	2,110.5	4,819.5	84.0
2003		306	130	23.5	10.5	20.9	989.5	18.85	2,792.1	2,098.2	4,874.9	105.8
2004		328	150	18.3	9.6	19.3	927.2	17.51	2,895.8	2,523.3	5,372.1	90.2
2005		328	144	21.4	12.4	25.3	1,125.6	19.53	3,369.3	3,834.3	7,079.6	159.4
2006		340P	144P	22.1	13.0	26.3	1,163.9	21.32	3,903.6	4,724.7	8,513.8	214.6
2007		345P	145P	20.1P	10.7P	21.1P	1,056.0P	20.21P	3,147.4P	3,809.5P	6,864.6P	159.8P
2008		350P	147P	19.7P	10.3P	20.4P	1,070.6P	20.68P	3,219.6P	3,896.8P	7,022.0P	161.8P
2009		354P	148P	19.3P	10.0P	19.7P	1,085.1P	21.16P	3,291.7P	3,984.1P	7,179.3P	163.8P
2010		359P	149P	18.9P	9.7P	19.0P	1,099.7P	21.63P	3,363.9P	4,071.5P	7,336.7P	165.7P

Sources: 1992, 1997, 2002 *Economic Census*; other years, up to 2006, are from the *Annual Survey of Manufactures*. Establishment counts for non-Census years are from *County Business Patterns*; 1997 and 2002 values are from the 1997 and 2002 censuses respectively, reported in the Federal Government's NAICS format. Other years were originally reported in equivalent SIC format. 'P's show projections by the editors.

INDICES OF CHANGE

Year	Companies	Establishments		Employment			Compensation		Production ($ million)			
		Total	with 20 or more employees	Total (000)	Production Workers (000)	Hours (Mil)	Payroll ($ mil)	Wages ($/hr)	Cost of Materials	Value Added by Manufacture	Value of Shipments	Capital Invest.
1992	82	83	94	119	130	137	88	77	78	98	87	164
1997	100	101	109	126	142	151	106	83	111	126	117	202
2001		100	110	107	107	110	94	95	110	123	116	178
2002	100	100	100	100	100	100	100	100	100	100	100	100
2003		98	102	119	101	104	112	103	102	99	101	126
2004		105	118	93	92	97	105	96	106	120	111	107
2005		105	113	109	119	127	127	107	123	182	147	190
2006		109P	114P	112	125P	132	131	117	143	224	177	255
2007		111P	114P	102P	103P	106P	119P	111P	115P	181P	142P	190P
2008		112P	115P	100P	99P	102P	121P	114P	118P	185P	146P	193P
2009		114P	116P	98P	96P	99P	122P	116P	120P	189P	149P	195P
2010		115P	117P	96P	93P	95P	124P	119P	123P	193P	152P	197P

Sources: Same as General Statistics. Values reflect change from the base year, 2002. Values above 100 mean greater than 2002, values below 100 mean less than 2002, and the values of 100 in other years means the same as 2002. 'P's show projections by the editors.

SELECTED RATIOS

For 2002	Avg. of All Manufact.	Analyzed Industry	Index	For 2002	Avg. of All Manufact.	Analyzed Industry	Index
Employees per Establishment	42	63	151	Value Added per Production Worker	182,367	202,933	111
Payroll per Establishment	1,639,184	2,852,733	174	Cost per Establishment	5,769,015	8,794,212	152
Payroll per Employee	39,053	45,036	115	Cost per Employee	137,446	138,832	101
Production Workers per Establishment	30	33	113	Cost per Production Worker	195,506	262,981	135
Wages per Establishment	694,845	1,171,704	169	Shipments per Establishment	11,158,348	15,496,785	139
Wages per Production Worker	23,548	35,038	149	Shipments per Employee	265,847	244,645	92
Hours per Production Worker	1,980	1,923	97	Shipments per Production Worker	378,144	463,413	123
Wages per Hour	11.89	18.22	153	Investment per Establishment	361,338	270,096	75
Value Added per Establishment	5,381,325	6,786,174	126	Investment per Employee	8,609	4,264	50
Value Added per Employee	128,210	107,132	84	Investment per Production Worker	12,245	8,077	66

Sources: Same as General Statistics. The 'Average of All Manufacturing' column represents the average of all manufacturing industries reported for the most recent complete year available. The Index shows the relationship between the Average and the Analyzed Industry. For example, 100 means that they are equal; 500 that the Analyzed Industry is five times the average; 50 means that the Analyzed Industry is half the national average. The abbreviation 'na' is used to show that data are 'not available'. Ratios shown for 2002, the last complete census year.

LEADING COMPANIES   Number shown: **75**   Total sales ($ mil): **24,308**   Total employment (000): **96.6**

Company Name	Address				CEO Name	Phone	Co. Type	Sales ($ mil)	Empl. (000)
Goodrich Corp.	4 Coliseum Centre	Charlotte	NC	28217	Sheldon R. Erikson	704-423-7000	P	6,392	23.4
Cameron International Corp.	1333 W Loop S	Houston	TX	77027	Sheldon R. Erikson	713-513-3300	P	4,666	15.4
Gardner Denver Inc.	PO Box 528	Quincy	IL	62306	Ross J. Centanni	217-222-5400	P	1,869	6.2
Dresser-Rand Group Inc.	1200 W S Houston	Houston	TX	77043	Vince Volpe	713-467-2221	P	1,665	6.0
Tecumseh Products Co.	100 E Patterson St.	Tecumseh	MI	49286	Edwin Bunker	517-423-8411	P	1,133	10.3
Ariel Corp.	35 Blackjack Rd.	Mount Vernon	OH	43050		740-397-0311	R	985*	0.7
Compressor Systems Inc.	PO Box 60760	Midland	TX	79711	Richard Folger	432-563-1170	R	980*	0.3
Scott Fetzer Co.	28800 Clemens Rd.	Westlake	OH	44145	K Semelsberger	440-892-3000	S	935*	14.5
Graco Inc.	PO Box 1441	Minneapolis	MN	55440		612-623-6000	P	841	2.3
Bristol Compressors Inc.	15185 Indu Prk Rd.	Bristol	VA	24202		276-466-4121	S	483*	2.5
Thomas Industries Inc.	211 Industrial Ct.	Wabasha	MN	55981	Jim Beckner	651-565-3395	S	410	2.2
Arrow Pneumatics Inc.	2111 W 21st Street	Broadview	IL	60155		708-343-9595	R	404*	0.1
Elliott Co.	901 N 4th St.	Jeannette	PA	15644	Antonio Casillo	724-527-2811	R	334*	0.7
Homax Products Inc.	PO Box 5643	Bellingham	WA	98227	Ross Clawson	360-733-9029	R	307*	<0.1
Louisiana Compressor Maint.	PO Box 668	Houma	LA	70361	Stephen Snider	985-868-7232	S	269*	0.1
Michigan Automotive Compressor	2400 N Dearing Rd.	Parma	MI	49269	Hiroyo Kono	517-622-7000	R	231*	0.8
AFA Products Inc.	135 Pine St.	Forest City	NC	28043	Jim Wantuch	828-245-1160	R	195*	0.8
Oerlikon USA Holding Inc.	615 Epsilon Dr.	Pittsburgh	PA	15238	James Brissenden	724-327-5700	R	172*	0.2
Sullair Corp.	3700 E Michigan	Michigan City	IN	46360	Henry Brook	219-879-5451	S	140*	0.7
Cooper Turbocompressor Inc.	PO Box 209	Buffalo	NY	14225	Sheldon Erikson	716-896-6600	S	130	0.5
Sundyne Corp.	14845 W 64th Ave.	Arvada	CO	80007	Phil Ruffner	303-425-0800	S	118*	0.7
Myers, F E Co.	1101 Myers Pkwy.	Ashland	OH	44805	Randall J. Hogan	419-289-1144	D	101*	0.6
Scroll Technologies	1 Scroll Dr.	Arkadelphia	AR	71923	Jorgen Clausen	870-246-0700	S	100*	0.5
Oxy-Dry Corp.	185 Hansen Court	Itasca	IL	60143	Martin Haver	630-595-3651	S	72*	<0.1
Wagner Spray Tech Corp.	PO Box 9362	Minneapolis	MN	55440	Richard Swenson	763-553-7000	R	68*	0.3
Graham Corp.	PO Box 719	Batavia	NY	14021	Jerald D. Bidlack	585-343-2216	P	66	0.3
Compressed Air Systems Inc.	9303 Stannum St.	Tampa	FL	33619	Richard Hall	813-626-8177	R	62*	<0.1
Automotive Remanufacturers	3250 S 76th St.	Philadelphia	PA	19153	Carol Mancini	215-492-6330	R	59*	0.3
Saylor-Beall Manufacturing Co.	PO Box 40	Saint Johns	MI	48879	Bruce Mc Fee	989-224-2371	S	58*	0.3
Iowa Mold Tooling Company Inc.	106 E 6th St.	Des Moines	IA	50309	Richard Long	641-923-3711	S	54*	0.4
Riley Industrial Services Inc.	PO Box 2014	Farmington	NM	87499	G Sonny Riley	505-327-4947	R	45*	0.2
Rogers Machinery Company Inc.	PO Box 230429	Portland	OR	97281	Walt Novak	503-639-6151	R	43*	0.2
Stellar Industries Inc.	PO Box 169	Garner	IA	50438	Barbara Beyer	641-923-3741	R	41*	0.2
Mitsub. Heavy Ind Climate Ctrl	1200 N Mitsubishi	Franklin	IN	46131	Kiyonobu Toma	317-346-5000	R	41*	0.4
Gssc Inc.	5148 113th Ave. N	Clearwater	FL	33760	James Hedger	727-573-2955	R	41*	<0.1
Gast Manufacturing Inc.	PO Box 97	Benton Harbor	MI	49022	Ivy B. Suter	269-926-6171	D	40*	0.6
Bauer Compressors Inc.	1328 Azalea Garden	Norfolk	VA	23502	Heinz Bauer	757-855-6006	R	40*	0.2
Tolco Corp.	1920 Linwood Ave.	Toledo	OH	43604	William Spengler	419-241-1113	R	37*	<0.1
Quincy Compressor Div.	PO Box C2	Quincy	IL	62305	John Thompson	217-222-7700	D	34*	0.5
Blissfield Manufacturing Co.	626 Depot St.	Blissfield	MI	49228	Patrick Farver	517-486-2121	R	33*	0.1
Champion Air Compressors	PO Box 4024	Quincy	IL	62305		815-875-3321	S	32*	0.2
Gulf Electroquip Management	PO Box 745	Houston	TX	77001		713-675-2525	R	31*	<0.1
FL Smidth Inc.	236 S Cherry St.	Manheim	PA	17545		717-665-2224	R	30*	0.1
Climate Control Inc.	2120 N 22nd Street	Decatur	IL	62526	Richard Demirjian	217-422-0055	D	27*	0.1
Hardie-Tynes Company Inc.	PO Box 12166	Birmingham	AL	35202		205-252-5191	R	25*	<0.1
Auto Crane Co.	PO Box 580692	Tulsa	OK	74158	Robert Heffron	918-836-0463	R	23*	0.1
Total Compression/Measurement	PO Box 11211	Midland	TX	79702		432-563-7999	R	23*	0.1
Fountainhead Group Inc.	23 Garden St.	New York Mills	NY	13417	Eugene Romano	315-736-0037	R	22*	0.1
Ralph A Hiller Company Inc.	6005 Enterprise Dr.	Export	PA	15632	Randolph Hiller	724-325-1200	R	21*	<0.1
Sullivan-Palatek Inc.	386 River Rd., A	Claremont	NH	03743	Bruce McFee	603-543-3131	S	20*	<0.1
Curtis-Toledo Inc.	1905 Kienlen Ave.	Saint Louis	MO	63133	K Carpenter	314-383-1300	R	19*	0.1
Associate Engineering Corp.	PO Box 346	Hustisford	WI	53034	Timothy Kelley	920-349-3281	R	19*	<0.1
Fleet Equipment Corp.	567 Commerce St.	Franklin Lakes	NJ	07417	Richard Pearson	201-337-7332	R	19*	<0.1
Baker Energy	16340 Park Ten Pl.	Houston	TX	77084		281-579-7850	S	18*	0.1
Chapin Manufacturing Inc.	PO Box 549	Batavia	NY	14021	James Campbell	585-343-3140	R	17*	0.2
Exline Inc.	PO Box 1487	Salina	KS	67402	Robert Exline	785-825-4683	R	17*	0.1
W Meyer William and Sons Inc.	1700 Franklin Blvd.	Libertyville	IL	60048	William Meyer	847-918-0111	R	16*	0.1
KNF Neuberger Inc.	2 Black Forest Rd.	Trenton	NJ	08691	Martin Becker	609-890-8889	R	16*	<0.1
Travaini Pumps USA Inc.	200 Newsome Dr.	Yorktown	VA	23692	Mario Travaini	757-988-3930	R	15*	<0.1
Belco Industries Inc.	115 E Main St.	Belding	MI	48809	Michael Kohn	616-794-0410	R	15*	0.1
Grimmer Industries Inc.	1015 Hurricane Rd.	Franklin	IN	46131	John Grimmer	317-736-3800	R	15*	<0.1
GVM Inc.	PO Box 358	Biglerville	PA	17307	Mark Anderson	717-677-6197	R	14*	<0.1
Engineering Designs Transfer	301 N Smith Ave.	Corona	CA	92880	Mohammad Gauhar	951-279-9400	R	14*	<0.1
Scales Industrial Technologies	110 Voice Rd.	Carle Place	NY	11514	William Scalchunes	516-248-9096	R	14*	<0.1
Rhino Linings USA Inc.	9151 Rehco Rd.	San Diego	CA	92121	Russell Lewis	858-450-0441	R	13*	<0.1
Independent Components Corp.	528 Hempstead	West Hempstead	NY	11552	Richard Sirow	516-481-5100	R	13*	<0.1
Somarakis Inc.	PO Box 1948	Vancouver	WA	98668	John Somarakis	360-574-6722	R	13*	<0.1
Kobelco Compressors Inc.	3000 Hammond	Elkhart	IN	46516	Kevin O'Neill	574-295-3145	R	12*	<0.1
Crosman Corp.	PO Box 308	East Bloomfield	NY	14443	Ken D'Arcy	585-657-6161	R	12*	0.2
Artisan Industries Inc.	73 Pond Street	Waltham	MA	02451	Richard Giberti	781-893-6800	R	12*	<0.1
ITW DeVilbiss	195 Intle. Blvd.	Glendale Hts	IL	60139		630-237-5000	R	12*	<0.1
Precision Plus Vacuum Parts	2055 Niagara Falls	Niagara Falls	NY	14304		716-297-2039	R	11*	<0.1
Con-Vey Keystone Inc.	PO Box 1399	Roseburg	OR	97470	Donald Goeckner	541-672-5506	R	11*	<0.1
Thomas Energy Systems Inc.	PO Box 471453	Tulsa	OK	74147	Vince Thomas	918-665-0031	R	11*	<0.1
Paasche Airbrush Co.	4311 N Normandy	Chicago	IL	60634	John Pettersen	773-867-9191	R	11*	<0.1

Source: Ward's Business Directory of U.S. Private and Public Companies, Volumes 1 and 2, 2008. The company type code used is as follows: P - Public, R - Private, S - Subsidiary, D - Division, J - Joint Venture, A - Affiliate, G - Group. Sales are in millions of dollars, employees are in thousands. An asterisk (*) indicates an estimated sales volume. The symbol < stands for 'less than'. Company names and addresses are truncated, in some cases, to fit into the available space.

MATERIALS CONSUMED

Material	Quantity	Delivered Cost ($ million)
Fluid power pumps, motors, and hydrostatic transmissions	(X)	23.2
Fluid power valves, hose and tube fittings and assemblies	(X)	41.1
Other fluid power products, hydraulic and pneumatic	(X)	30.3
Metal bolts, nuts, screws, and other screw machine products	(X)	44.1
Metal pipe, valves, and pipe fittings (excluding forgings)	(X)	66.6
Fabricated structural metal products (excluding forgings)	(X)	116.4
Other fabricated metal products (exc. fluid power products and forgings)	(X)	105.7
Iron and steel forgings	(X)	30.7
Nonferrous forgings	(X)	(D)
Iron and steel castings (rough and semifinished)	(X)	136.6
Aluminum and aluminum-base alloy castings (rough and semifinished)	(X)	35.2
Other nonferrous metal castings, rough or semifinished (inc. aluminum)	(X)	(D)
Steel bars, bar shapes, and plates (exc. castings, forgings, fabr. metal products)	(X)	36.7
Steel sheet and strip (including tinplate)	(X)	15.0
All other steel shapes and forms (exc. castings, forgings, fabr. metal products)	(X)	9.9
Other nonferrous shapes and forms (exc. castings, forgings, fabricated metal products)	(X)	1.8
Aluminum and aluminum-base alloy shapes and forms (exc. castings, forgings, fabr. metal products)	(X)	7.0
Engines (diesel, semidiesel, gasoline, and other carburetor-type engines)	(X)	86.0
Fractional horsepower electric motors (less than 1 hp)	(X)	61.2
Integral horsepower electric motors and generators (1 hp or more)	(X)	55.9
Ball and roller bearings (mounted or unmounted)	(X)	34.4
Paperboard containers, boxes, and corrugated paperboard	(X)	17.3
Fabricated rubber products (excluding gaskets)	(X)	8.9
Fabricated plastics products (excluding gaskets)	(X)	36.5
Gaskets (all types), and packing and sealing devices	(X)	38.5
Electrical transmission, distribution, and control equipment	(X)	98.2
Paints, varnishes, stains, lacquers, shellacs, japans, enamels, etc.	(X)	15.1
All other materials, components, parts, containers, and supplies	(X)	438.1
Materials, ingredients, containers, and supplies, nsk	(X)	413.3

Source: 2002 Economic Census. Explanation of symbols used: (D): Withheld to avoid disclosure of competitive data; na: Not available; (S): Withheld because statistical norms were not met; (X): Not applicable; (Z): Less than half the unit shown; nec: Not elsewhere classified; nsk: Not specified by kind; - : zero; p : 10-19 percent estimated; q : 20-29 percent estimated.

PRODUCT SHARE DETAILS

Product or Product Class Shipments	Mil. $	Product or Product Class Shipments	Mil. $
AIR AND GAS COMPRESSORS	4,181.0	**for refrigeration, ice making, and air-conditioning equipment), and packaged compressors**	**583.6**
Air and gas compressors and vacuum pumps	**2,608.3**	**Industrial spraying equipment**	**823.5**
Air and gas compressors (except compressors for ice making, refrigeration, or air-conditioning equipment), including air motors and packaged compressors	2,244.8	Industrial power paint spraying outfits and other liquid power sprayers, except agricultural	453.4
Vacuum pumps (compressors) (including value of the driver if shipped as a complete unit), except laboratory	316.1	Industrial hand sprayers, except agricultural and flame	134.8
Air and gas compressors and vacuum pumps, nsk	47.4	Parts and attachments for industrial spraying equipment, sold separately	235.3
Parts and attachments for air and gas compressors (except		**Air and gas compressors, nsk, total**	**165.6**

Source: 2002 Economic Census. The values are product shipments in millions of dollars for 2002. Total product shipments may be lower or higher than industry shipments. See Introduction for a full discussion. Values of indented subcategories are summed in the main heading(s). The symbol (D) appears when data are withheld to prevent disclosure of competitive information. The abbreviation nsk stands for 'not specified by kind' and nec for 'not elsewhere classified'. A dash (-) means zero.

INPUTS AND OUTPUTS FOR AIR AND GAS COMPRESSOR MANUFACTURING

Economic Sector or Industry Providing Inputs	%	Sector	Economic Sector or Industry Buying Outputs	%	Sector
Compensation of employees	28.6		Private fixed investment	60.2	
Wholesale trade	6.7	Trade	Exports of goods & services	24.2	Cap Inv
Management of companies & enterprises	4.5	Services	Air & gas compressors	2.6	Manufg.
Ferrous metal foundries	3.8	Manufg.	Residential permanent site structures	2.4	Construct.
Valve & fittings other than plumbing	3.6	Manufg.	Food services & drinking places	2.0	Services
Air & gas compressors	3.4	Manufg.	Industrial machinery, nec	1.9	Manufg.
Motors & generators	3.4	Manufg.	Residential structures, nec	0.9	Construct.
Gaskets, packing, & sealing devices	2.7	Manufg.	Nonresidential structures, nec	0.8	Construct.
Engine equipment, nec	2.6	Manufg.	Federal government, investment, national defense	0.6	Fed Govt
Metal cans, boxes, & other containers (light gauge)	1.9	Manufg.	Chemical products & preparations, nec	0.6	Manufg.
Iron & steel mills & ferroalloys	1.8	Manufg.	Telecommunications	0.6	Services
Plate work & fabricated structural products	1.8	Manufg.	Motor vehicle parts	0.5	Manufg.
Relay & industrial controls	1.7	Manufg.	Plastics products, nec	0.5	Manufg.
Advertising & related services	1.7	Services	Semiconductor machinery	0.4	Manufg.
Machine shops	1.6	Manufg.	Owner-occupied dwellings	0.3	
Turned products & screws, nuts, & bolts	1.6	Manufg.	Maintenance/repair of nonresidential structures	0.3	Construct.
Securities, commodity contracts, investments	1.3	Fin/R.E.	Change in private inventories	0.3	In House
Ball & roller bearings	1.3	Manufg.	Other S/L govt. enterprises	0.2	S/L Govt

Continued on next page.

INPUTS AND OUTPUTS FOR AIR AND GAS COMPRESSOR MANUFACTURING - Continued

Economic Sector or Industry Providing Inputs	%	Sector	Economic Sector or Industry Buying Outputs	%	Sector
Nonferrous metal foundries	1.3	Manufg.	Maintenance/repair of residential structures	0.2	Construct.
Plastics products, nec	1.1	Manufg.	Urethane & other foam products (except polystrene)	0.1	Manufg.
Forging, stamping, & sintering, nec	1.1	Manufg.	Pipeline transportation	0.1	Util.
Truck transportation	1.0	Util.	Plastics & rubber industry machinery	0.1	Manufg.
Lessors of nonfinancial assets	0.9	Fin/R.E.	Commercial & health care structures	0.1	Construct.
Monetary authorities/depository credit intermediation	0.8	Fin/R.E.			
Semiconductors & related devices	0.7	Manufg.			
Printed circuit assemblies (electronic assembiles)	0.7	Manufg.			
Power generation & supply	0.7	Util.			
Coating, engraving, heat treating & allied activities	0.7	Manufg.			
Paints & coatings	0.7	Manufg.			
Professional, scientific, technical services, nec	0.7	Services			
Fluid power process machinery	0.7	Manufg.			
Real estate	0.6	Fin/R.E.			
Telecommunications	0.6	Services			
Paperboard containers	0.5	Manufg.			
Legal services	0.5	Services			
Data processing, hosting, & related services	0.5	Services			
Food services & drinking places	0.5	Services			
Pumps & pumping equipment	0.5	Manufg.			
Management, scientific, & technical consulting	0.4	Services			
Noncomparable imports	0.4	Foreign			
Taxes on production & imports, less subsidies	0.4				
Architectural, engineering, & related services	0.4	Services			
Retail trade	0.3	Trade			
Accounting, tax preparation, bookkeeping, & payroll	0.3	Services			
Scientific research & development services	0.3	Services			
Services to buildings & dwellings	0.3	Services			
Fabricated metals, nec	0.3	Manufg.			
Maintenance/repair of nonresidential structures	0.3	Construct.			
Business support services	0.3	Services			
Hotels & motels, including casino hotels	0.3	Services			
Electronic components, nec	0.3	Manufg.			
Abrasive products	0.3	Manufg.			
Specialized design services	0.3	Services			
Automotive equipment rental & leasing	0.2	Fin/R.E.			
Employment services	0.2	Services			
Other computer related services, including facilities	0.2	Services			
Warehousing & storage	0.2	Util.			
Alumina refining & primary aluminum production	0.2	Manufg.			
Electronic capacitors, resistors, coils, transformers	0.2	Manufg.			
Nondepository credit intermediation activities	0.2	Fin/R.E.			
Air transportation	0.2	Util.			
Motor vehicle parts	0.2	Manufg.			
Natural gas distribution	0.2	Util.			
Crowns & closures & metal stamping	0.2	Manufg.			
Rubber products, nec	0.2	Manufg.			
Automotive repair & maintenance, ex. car washes	0.2	Services			
Support services, nec	0.2	Services			
Handtools	0.1	Manufg.			
Commercial & industrial equipment repair/maintenance	0.1	Services			
Postal service	0.1	Util.			
Commercial & industrial machinery rental & leasing	0.1	Fin/R.E.			
Custom roll forming	0.1	Manufg.			
Investigation & security services	0.1	Services			
Civic, social, & professional organizations	0.1	Services			
Paperboard mills	0.1	Manufg.			
Plastics packaging materials, film & sheet	0.1	Manufg.			

Source: Benchmark Input-Output Accounts for the U.S. Economy, 2002, U.S. Department of Commerce, Washington, D.C., January 2008. The abbreviation nec stands for 'not elsewhere classified'.

OCCUPATIONS EMPLOYED BY OTHER GENERAL-PURPOSE MACHINERY MANUFACTURING

Occupation	% of Total 2006	Change to 2016	Occupation	% of Total 2006	Change to 2016
Team assemblers	11.0	-9.7	Multiple machine tool operators & tenders	1.4	-0.7
Machinists	5.9	-5.2	Lathe & turning machine tool operators & tenders	1.4	-18.8
Welders, cutters, solderers, & brazers	5.7	-4.0	Maintenance & repair workers, general	1.4	-9.7
First-line supervisors/managers of production workers	3.6	-9.7	Structural metal fabricators & fitters	1.4	-9.7
Mechanical engineers	2.8	-0.7	Industrial engineers	1.3	9.6
Computer-controlled machine tool operators	2.5	-0.7	Electrical & electronic equipment assemblers	1.3	-27.8
Sales reps, wholesale & manufacturing, exc tech	2.3	-9.7	Industrial machinery mechanics	1.3	3.8
Engine & other machine assemblers	2.0	-9.7	Mechanical drafters	1.3	-8.7
Inspectors, testers, sorters, samplers, & weighers	1.9	-14.9	Customer service representatives	1.3	-0.7
Cutting, punching, & press machine operators	1.8	-18.8	Coating, painting, & spraying machine operators	1.2	-14.2
Shipping, receiving, & traffic clerks	1.8	-13.1	Office clerks, general	1.2	-11.1
Helpers--Production workers	1.6	-9.7	Industrial production managers	1.1	-9.7
General & operations managers	1.6	-18.8	Electrical engineers	1.1	-9.7
Laborers & freight, stock, & material movers, hand	1.5	-18.8	Production, planning, & expediting clerks	1.1	-9.7
Purchasing agents, exc wholesale, retail, & farm	1.5	-18.8	Stock clerks & order fillers	1.0	-24.5
Bookkeeping, accounting, & auditing clerks	1.5	-9.7			

Source: *Industry-Occupation Matrix*, Bureau of Labor Statistics, December 4, 2007. These data are reported based on 4-digit NAICS categories but have been matched to corresponding 6-digit NAICS industry codes. The change reported for each occupation to the year 2016 is a percent of growth or decline as estimated by the Bureau of Labor Statistics. The abbreviation nec stands for 'not elsewhere classified'.

LOCATION BY STATE AND REGIONAL CONCENTRATION

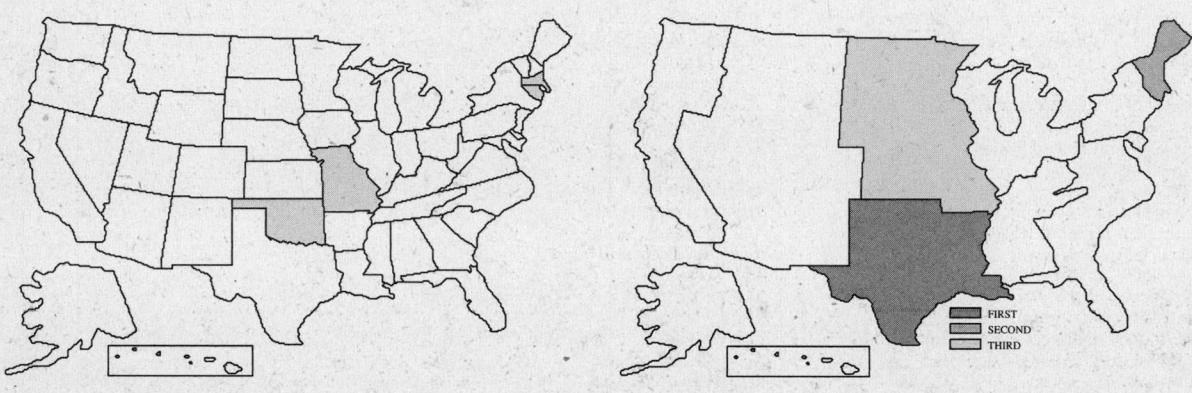

FIRST
SECOND
THIRD

INDUSTRY DATA BY STATE

State	Establish-ments	Shipments			Employment				Cost as % of Shipments	Investment per Employee ($)
		Total ($ mil)	% of U.S.	Per Establ.	Total Number	% of U.S.	Per Establ.	Wages ($/hour)		
Massachusetts	6	225.7	4.7	37,616.3	872	4.4	145	25.12	66.7	2,116
Oklahoma	13	173.9	3.6	13,377.5	745	3.8	57	16.51	54.9	5,471
Missouri	8	151.9	3.2	18,989.6	493	2.5	62	14.66	35.3	6,012
Connecticut	5	76.3	1.6	15,268.4	286	1.5	57	15.27	56.8	4,287

Source: 2002 *Economic Census*. The states are in descending order of shipments or establishments (if shipment data are missing for the majority). The symbol (D) appears when data are withheld to prevent disclosure of competitive information. States marked with (D) are sorted by number of establishments. A dash (-) indicates that the data element cannot be calculated. Data may not show all states active in the NAICS category. All data available at the time of publication are shown.

NAICS 333913 - MEASURING AND DISPENSING PUMP MANUFACTURING

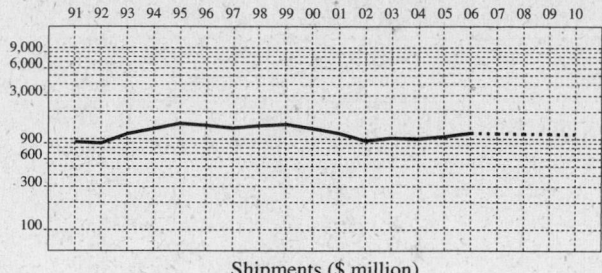

Shipments ($ million)

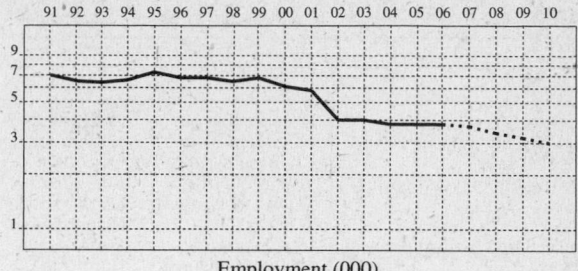

Employment (000)

GENERAL STATISTICS

| Year | Com-panies | Establishments | | Employment | | | Compensation | | Production ($ million) | | | |
		Total	with 20 or more employees	Total (000)	Production Workers (000)	Hours (Mil)	Payroll ($ mil)	Wages ($/hr)	Cost of Materials	Value Added by Manufacture	Value of Shipments	Capital Invest.
1991		73	40	7.0	4.5	8.1	192.8	11.93	426.4	493.5	927.7	22.2
1992	71	77	41	6.5	4.1	8.2	196.6	12.02	451.4	422.0	896.3	27.1
1993		76	41	6.4	4.7	9.2	208.4	13.79	582.4	585.5	1,137.6	31.8
1994		76	44	6.6	4.8	10.1	223.3	14.36	679.7	635.4	1,295.0	27.5
1995		76	43	7.3	4.9	9.4	238.1	13.65	774.9	700.3	1,479.0	26.8
1996		75	41	6.8	4.4	8.7	234.8	13.92	762.7	651.2	1,413.2	25.8
1997	65	71	35	6.8	4.3	8.0	251.4	15.15	713.6	601.1	1,320.2	32.4
1998		72	37	6.5	4.1	7.8	252.3	15.38	693.2	694.6	1,398.9	29.2
1999		67	32	6.8	4.2	7.8	265.2	16.14	800.5	660.2	1,448.3	40.1
2000		66	32	6.1	3.6	6.5	232.8	16.46	657.6	639.1	1,304.1	26.7
2001		67	31	5.8	3.3	6.1	239.5	16.58	592.6	552.7	1,152.1	30.5
2002	29	33	23	4.0	2.2	4.1	176.7	16.89	463.6	476.3	952.3	14.1
2003		52	23	4.0	2.1	4.1	184.4	17.31	470.2	551.5	1,022.9	10.0
2004		38	21	3.8	1.8	3.7	184.0	17.93	509.9	474.6	1,001.7	10.5
2005		42	21	3.8	1.8	3.8	196.6	18.21	706.0	353.9	1,063.2	17.1
2006		41P	20P	3.8	1.8	3.7	198.2	17.46	778.4	395.8	1,158.3	12.0
2007		39P	18P	3.7P	1.6P	3.2P	204.9P	18.90P	769.0P	391.0P	1,144.3P	14.7P
2008		36P	16P	3.4P	1.4P	2.7P	203.4P	19.31P	765.8P	389.4P	1,139.5P	13.6P
2009		33P	15P	3.2P	1.2P	2.3P	202.0P	19.71P	762.5P	387.7P	1,134.6P	12.5P
2010		30P	13P	3.0P	0.9P	1.9P	200.5P	20.12P	759.2P	386.0P	1,129.8P	11.4P

Sources: 1992, 1997, 2002 *Economic Census;* other years, up to 2006, are from the *Annual Survey of Manufactures.* Establishment counts for non-Census years are from *County Business Patterns;* 1997 and 2002 values are from the 1997 and 2002 censuses respectively, reported in the Federal Government's NAICS format. Other years were originally reported in equivalent SIC format. 'P's show projections by the editors.

INDICES OF CHANGE

| Year | Com-panies | Establishments | | Employment | | | Compensation | | Production ($ million) | | | |
		Total	with 20 or more employees	Total (000)	Production Workers (000)	Hours (Mil)	Payroll ($ mil)	Wages ($/hr)	Cost of Materials	Value Added by Manufacture	Value of Shipments	Capital Invest.
1992	245	233	178	163	186	200	111	71	97	89	94	192
1997	224	215	152	170	195	195	142	90	154	126	139	230
2001		203	135	145	150	149	136	98	128	116	121	216
2002	100	100	100	100	100	100	100	100	100	100	100	100
2003		158	100	100	95	100	104	102	101	116	107	71
2004		115	91	95	82	90	104	106	110	100	105	74
2005		127	91	95	82	93	111	108	152	74	112	121
2006		125P	86P	95	82	90	112	103	168	83	122	85
2007		117P	79P	93P	73P	78P	116P	112P	166P	82P	120P	104P
2008		108P	71P	85P	64P	66P	115P	114P	165P	82P	120P	96P
2009		100P	64P	80P	55P	56P	114P	117P	164P	81P	119P	89P
2010		91P	56P	75P	41P	46P	113P	119P	164P	81P	119P	81P

Sources: Same as General Statistics. Values reflect change from the base year, 2002. Values above 100 mean greater than 2002, values below 100 mean less than 2002, and the values of 100 in other years means the same as 2002. 'P's show projections by the editors.

SELECTED RATIOS

For 2002	Avg. of All Manufact.	Analyzed Industry	Index	For 2002	Avg. of All Manufact.	Analyzed Industry	Index
Employees per Establishment	42	121	289	Value Added per Production Worker	182,367	216,500	119
Payroll per Establishment	1,639,184	5,354,545	327	Cost per Establishment	5,769,015	14,048,485	244
Payroll per Employee	39,053	44,175	113	Cost per Employee	137,446	115,900	84
Production Workers per Establishment	30	67	226	Cost per Production Worker	195,506	210,727	108
Wages per Establishment	694,845	2,098,455	302	Shipments per Establishment	11,158,348	28,857,576	259
Wages per Production Worker	23,548	31,477	134	Shipments per Employee	265,847	238,075	90
Hours per Production Worker	1,980	1,864	94	Shipments per Production Worker	378,144	432,864	114
Wages per Hour	11.89	16.89	142	Investment per Establishment	361,338	427,273	118
Value Added per Establishment	5,381,325	14,433,333	268	Investment per Employee	8,609	3,525	41
Value Added per Employee	128,210	119,075	93	Investment per Production Worker	12,245	6,409	52

Sources: Same as General Statistics. The 'Average of All Manufacturing' column represents the average of all manufacturing industries reported for the most recent complete year available. The Index shows the relationship between the Average and the Analyzed Industry. For example, 100 means that they are equal; 500 that the Analyzed Industry is five times the average; 50 means that the Analyzed Industry is half the national average. The abbreviation 'na' is used to show that data are 'not available'. Ratios shown for 2002, the last complete census year.

LEADING COMPANIES   Number shown: 64   Total sales ($ mil): 25,449   Total employment (000): 23.5

Company Name	Address				CEO Name	Phone	Co. Type	Sales ($ mil)	Empl. (000)
Liquid Controls L.L.C.	105 Albrecht Dr.	Lake Bluff	IL	60044	Lawrence D. Kingsley	847-295-1050	S	11,215*	4.2
Culligan International Co.	1 Culligan Pkwy.	Northbrook	IL	60062	Mark Seals	847-205-6000	R	4,916*	5.5
Cornelius IMI Inc.	101 Broadway St. W	Osseo	MN	55369	Richard Barkley	763-488-8200	R	2,840*	0.3
Schwan's Technology Group Inc.	5140 Moundview	Red Wing	MN	55066	David Paskach	651-388-1821	R	2,040*	<0.1
EFD Inc.	977 Waterman Ave.	East Providence	RI	02914	Peter Lambert	401-434-1680	S	972*	0.3
Graco Inc.	PO Box 1441	Minneapolis	MN	55440		612-623-6000	P	841	2.3
Franklin Electric Company Inc.	400 E Spring St.	Bluffton	IN	46714		219-824-2900	P	602	3.2
Tuthill Corp.	8500 S Madison St.	Burr Ridge	IL	60527		630-382-4900	R	388*	0.9
Gorman-Rupp Co.	PO Box 1217	Mansfield	OH	44901	James C. Gorman	419-755-1011	P	306	1.0
Knight Inc.	20531 Crescent Bay	Lake Forest	CA	92630	George Noa	949-595-4800	S	189*	0.1
Bulman Products Inc.	1650 McReynolds	Grand Rapids	MI	49504		616-363-4416	R	124*	<0.1
Delfield Co.	980 S Isabella Rd.	Mt. Pleasant	MI	48858	Kevin Clark	989-773-7981	D	108*	0.7
Berg Company L.L.C.	PO Box 7065	Madison	WI	53707		608-221-4281	R	91*	0.5
GOJO Industries Inc.	PO Box 991	Akron	OH	44309	Joseph Kanfer	330-255-6000	R	83*	0.2
Great Plains Industries Inc.	PO Box 8901	Wichita	KS	67208	Grant Nutter	316-686-7361	R	54*	0.3
Pulsafeeder Inc.	2883 Brghtn-Henrtta	Rochester	NY	14623	Paul Beldham	585-292-8000	S	51*	0.3
Asymtek	2762 Loker Ave. W	Carlsbad	CA	92008	John Byers	760-431-1919	S	48*	0.3
Gasboy International Inc.	PO Box 22087	Greensboro	NC	27420	Greg Beason	336-547-5000	S	47*	0.3
Tolco Corp.	1920 Linwood Ave.	Toledo	OH	43604	William Spengler	419-241-1113	R	37*	<0.1
Federal APD Inc.	42775 W Nine Mile	Novi	MI	48375	Mark Cassens	248-374-9600	S	36*	0.2
Milton Roy Co.	201 Ivyland Road	Ivyland	PA	18974	Jean Pharamond	215-441-0800	S	34*	0.2
Fluid Management Inc.	1023 Wheeling Rd.	Wheeling	IL	60090	Suzanne Burns	847-537-0880	D	33*	0.2
Standard Machine and Mfg. Co.	10014 Big Bend Rd.	Saint Louis	MO	63122	Jack Deutsch	314-966-4500	R	33*	0.2
Parrot-Ice Drink Prods of Am.	13738 FM 529 Rd.	Houston	TX	77041	Greg Johnson	713-896-8798	R	24*	<0.1
Vitality Food Service Inc.	400 N Tampa St.	Tampa	FL	33602		813-301-4600	R	21*	0.3
Valco Cincinnati Inc.	PO Box 465619	Cincinnati	OH	45246	Gregory Amend	513-874-6550	R	18*	0.2
Clayton Corp.	866 Horan Dr.	Fenton	MO	63026	Byron Lapin	636-349-5333	R	17*	0.1
D and S Car Wash Equipment Co.	4200 Brandi Ln.	High Ridge	MO	63049	Jon Jansky	636-677-3442	R	16*	0.1
Technical Concepts L.L.C.	1301 Allanson Rd.	Mundelein	IL	60060		847-837-4100	R	16*	<0.1
March Manufacturing Inc.	1819 Pickwick Ln.	Glenview	IL	60026	Fred Zimmermann	847-729-5300	R	15*	<0.1
Charles Ross and Son Co.	PO Box 12308	Hauppauge	NY	11788	Richard Ross	631-234-0500	R	15*	<0.1
O'Day Equipment Inc.	1301 40th St. NW	Fargo	ND	58108	Jim O'Day	701-282-9260	R	14*	<0.1
Edge Industries Inc.	2887 3 Mile Rd. NW	Grand Rapids	MI	49534	Richard Hungerford	616-453-5458	R	13*	<0.1
Fittings Inc.	3300 Fisher Ave.	Fort Worth	TX	76111	Lewis Graves	817-332-3300	R	13*	<0.1
Newton Tool and Manufacturing	500 Pedricktown Rd.	Swedesboro	NJ	08085	Otto Del Prado	856-241-1500	R	11*	<0.1
Accumetric L.L.C.	350 Ring Rd.	Elizabethtown	KY	42701		270-769-3385	R	11*	<0.1
Apex Precision Technologies	8824 Union Mills Dr	Camby	IN	46113	Robert Oswald	317-821-1000	R	11*	<0.1
Alfred Conhagen Inc.	2035 Lincoln Hwy.	Edison	NJ	08817	Alfred Conhagen	732-287-4565	R	11*	<0.1
Bergstrom Company L.P.	PO Box 46579	Bedford	OH	44146		440-232-2282	R	11*	<0.1
Norwalk Company Inc.	PO Box 447	Stratford	CT	06615	Arthur McCauley	203-386-1234	R	10*	<0.1
Alwin Manufacturing Co.	PO Box 2126	Green Bay	WI	54306	Donald Krueger	920-499-1424	R	10*	<0.1
Sealant Equipment/Engineering	PO Box 701460	Plymouth	MI	48170	James Schultz	734-459-8600	R	10*	<0.1
Suntec Industries Inc.	PO Box 5000	Glasgow	KY	42142	Lucient Goldaorts	270-651-7116	R	10*	<0.1
Kutol Products Company Inc.	7650 Camargo Rd.	Cincinnati	OH	45243	Joseph Rhodenbaugh	513-527-5500	R	7*	<0.1
Tucs Equipment Inc.	5301 Indust Blvd.	Minneapolis	MN	55421	Marty Tucs	763-574-7475	R	7*	<0.1
Gertler Industries Inc.	914 W 17th St.	Costa Mesa	CA	92627	Bernard Gertler	949-631-4474	R	5*	<0.1
Prinzing Enterprises Inc.	PO Box 2131	Milwaukee	WI	53201	Frank M. Jaehnert		S	5*	<0.1
Ashby-Cross Company Inc.	28 Parker St.	Newburyport	MA	01950	Wayne Sturtevant	978-463-0202	R	5*	<0.1
American Fabricating Engineers	PO Box 38428	Germantown	TN	38183	Larry Lynch	662-893-3501	R	5*	<0.1
Fluid Management Systems Inc.	56 Felton St.	Waltham	MA	02453	Hamid Shirkhan	781-891-6522	R	5*	<0.1
HE Anderson Company Inc.	PO Box 1006	Muskogee	OK	74402	Herbert Anderson	918-687-4426	R	5*	<0.1
S.C.A. Schucker Company L.P.	46805 Magellan Dr.	Novi	MI	48377		248-669-3399	R	4*	<0.1
Anniston Pump Shop Inc.	PO Box 1198	Anniston	AL	36202	Margaret Turner	256-820-2980	R	4*	<0.1
Indco Inc.	PO Box 589	New Albany	IN	47151	James Sims	812-945-4383	R	4*	<0.1
E and E Custom Products Inc.	PO Box 339	Grant Park	IL	60940	Elliott Ewoldt	815-465-6591	R	4*	<0.1
Stenner Sales Inc.	3174 Desalvo Rd.	Jacksonville	FL	32246	Timothy Ware	904-641-1666	R	4*	<0.1
Velter Products Inc.	22 N 27th Street	Harrisburg	PA	17103	Eric Keller	717-234-4262	R	3*	<0.1
Harvard Clinical Technology	22 Pleasant St. N	North Natick	MA	01760	Diane Gargano	508-655-2000	R	3*	<0.1
PDC Machines Inc.	PO Box 2733	Warminster	PA	18974	Syed Afzal	215-443-9442	R	3*	<0.1
Adhesive Systems Technology	9000 Science Ctr.	New Hope	MN	55428	Steven Anderson	763-592-2060	R	3*	<0.1
Seventy-Three Manufacturing	136 Stauffer Rd.	Bechtelsville	PA	19505	Richard Croyle	610-845-7823	R	3*	<0.1
Encynova International Inc.	2322 W 25th Rd.	Greeley	CO	80634	John Beard	303-465-4800	R	3*	<0.1
Meters Inc.	PO Box 2109	Cartersville	GA	30120	Douglas Duncan	770-386-0080	R	2*	<0.1
Sensing Systems Corp.	PO Box 50180	New Bedford	MA	02745	Laverne Wallace	508-992-0872	R	2*	<0.1

Source: Ward's Business Directory of U.S. Private and Public Companies, Volumes 1 and 2, 2008. The company type code used is as follows: P - Public, R - Private, S - Subsidiary, D - Division, J - Joint Venture, A - Affiliate, G - Group. Sales are in millions of dollars, employees are in thousands. An asterisk (*) indicates an estimated sales volume. The symbol < stands for 'less than'. Company names and addresses are truncated, in some cases, to fit into the available space.

MATERIALS CONSUMED

Material	Quantity	Delivered Cost ($ million)
Fluid power pumps, motors, and hydrostatic transmissions	(X)	(D)
Fluid power valves, hose and tube fittings and assemblies	(X)	3.0
Other fluid power products, hydraulic and pneumatic	(X)	(D)
Metal bolts, nuts, screws, and other screw machine products	(X)	9.2
Metal pipe, valves, and pipe fittings (excluding forgings)	(X)	(D)
Fabricated structural metal products (excluding forgings)	(X)	3.7
Other fabricated metal products (exc. fluid power products and forgings)	(X)	(D)
Iron and steel forgings	(X)	(D)
Nonferrous forgings	(X)	(D)
Iron and steel castings (rough and semifinished)	(X)	8.5
Aluminum and aluminum-base alloy castings (rough and semifinished)	(X)	(D)
Other nonferrous metal castings, rough or semifinished (inc. aluminum)	(X)	(D)
Steel bars, bar shapes, and plates (exc. castings, forgings, fabr. metal products)	(X)	(D)
Steel sheet and strip (including tinplate)	(X)	(D)
All other steel shapes and forms (exc. castings, forgings, fabr. metal products)	(X)	1.3
Other nonferrous shapes and forms (exc. castings, forgings, fabricated metal products)	(X)	0.3
Aluminum and aluminum-base alloy shapes and forms (exc. castings, forgings, fabr. metal products)	(X)	(D)
Engines (diesel, semidiesel, gasoline, and other carburetor-type engines)	(X)	(D)
Fractional horsepower electric motors (less than 1 hp)	(X)	13.7
Integral horsepower electric motors and generators (1 hp or more)	(X)	0.5
Ball and roller bearings (mounted or unmounted)	(X)	0.7
Paperboard containers, boxes, and corrugated paperboard	(X)	(D)
Fabricated rubber products (excluding gaskets)	(X)	(D)
Fabricated plastics products (excluding gaskets)	(X)	21.5
Gaskets (all types), and packing and sealing devices	(X)	2.7
Electrical transmission, distribution, and control equipment	(X)	(D)
Paints, varnishes, stains, lacquers, shellacs, japans, enamels, etc.	(X)	(D)
All other materials, components, parts, containers, and supplies	(X)	87.1
Materials, ingredients, containers, and supplies, nsk	(X)	93.7

Source: 2002 *Economic Census*. Explanation of symbols used: (D): Withheld to avoid disclosure of competitive data; na: Not available; (S): Withheld because statistical norms were not met; (X): Not applicable; (Z): Less than half the unit shown; nec: Not elsewhere classified; nsk: Not specified by kind; - : zero; p : 10-19 percent estimated; q : 20-29 percent estimated.

PRODUCT SHARE DETAILS

Product or Product Class Shipments	Mil. $	Product or Product Class Shipments	Mil. $
MEASURING AND DISPENSING PUMPS	867.8	Multiple unit gasoline dispensing pumps, computing type (filling station type), without suction pumping unit, except parts and attachments	(D)
Single unit gasoline dispensing pumps, computing type (filling station type), except parts and attachments	127.3	Other gasoline service station measuring and dispensing pumping equipment, including lubricating oil pumps, barrel pumps, and grease guns and parts, and parts for gasoline pumps	(D)
Single unit gasoline dispensing pumps, computing type (filling station type), with suction pumping unit, except parts and attachments	104.8	Lubricating oil pumps, barrel pumps, grease guns, and other measuring and dispensing pumps for service station use, nec, complete units	274.3
Single unit gasoline dispensing pumps, computing type (filling station type), without suction pumping unit, except parts and attachments	22.5	Parts and attachments for measuring and dispensing pumps	(D)
Multiple unit gasoline dispensing pumps, computing type (filling station type), except parts and attachments	(D)	Measuring and dispensing pumps, nsk, total	4.2
Multiple unit gasoline dispensing pumps, computing type (filling station type), with suction pumping unit, except parts and attachments	(D)		

Source: 2002 *Economic Census*. The values are product shipments in millions of dollars for 2002. Total product shipments may be lower or higher than industry shipments. See Introduction for a full discussion. Values of indented subcategories are summed in the main heading(s). The symbol (D) appears when data are withheld to prevent disclosure of competitive information. The abbreviation nsk stands for 'not specified by kind' and nec for 'not elsewhere classified'. A dash (-) means zero.

INPUTS AND OUTPUTS FOR PUMP AND PUMPING EQUIPMENT MANUFACTURING

Economic Sector or Industry Providing Inputs	%	Sector	Economic Sector or Industry Buying Outputs	%	Sector
Compensation of employees	27.3		Private fixed investment	49.5	
Motors & generators	6.5	Manufg.	Exports of goods & services	17.7	Cap Inv
Wholesale trade	5.6	Trade	Federal government, investment, national defense	6.4	Fed Govt
Ferrous metal foundries	5.4	Manufg.	Residential permanent site structures	3.3	Construct.
Management of companies & enterprises	5.0	Services	S/L govt. invest., other	2.6	S/L Govt
Gaskets, packing, & sealing devices	2.8	Manufg.	Residential structures, nec	2.1	Construct.
Iron & steel mills & ferroalloys	2.4	Manufg.	Semiconductor machinery	2.0	Manufg.
Nonferrous metal foundries	2.1	Manufg.	General S/L govt. services	1.9	S/L Govt
Plastics products, nec	2.0	Manufg.	Owner-occupied dwellings	1.6	
Machine shops	1.3	Manufg.	Nonresidential structures, nec	1.4	Construct.
Pumps & pumping equipment	1.3	Manufg.	Pumps & pumping equipment	1.1	Manufg.
Turned products & screws, nuts, & bolts	1.0	Manufg.	Maintenance/repair of nonresidential structures	1.1	Construct.
Advertising & related services	1.0	Services	Oil & gas well drilling	1.0	Mining
Valve & fittings other than plumbing	1.0	Manufg.	Rail transportation	0.9	Util.

Continued on next page.

INPUTS AND OUTPUTS FOR PUMP AND PUMPING EQUIPMENT MANUFACTURING - Continued

Economic Sector or Industry Providing Inputs	%	Sector	Economic Sector or Industry Buying Outputs	%	Sector
Metal cans, boxes, & other containers (light gauge)	1.0	Manufg.	Steel products from purchased steel	0.7	Manufg.
Truck transportation	1.0	Util.	Commercial & service industry machinery, nec	0.6	Manufg.
Fluid power process machinery	1.0	Manufg.	Oil & gas extraction	0.6	Mining
Relay & industrial controls	0.9	Manufg.	General purpose machinery, nec	0.5	Manufg.
Plate work & fabricated structural products	0.9	Manufg.	Real estate	0.5	Fin/R.E.
Engine equipment, nec	0.9	Manufg.	Industrial machinery, nec	0.5	Manufg.
Semiconductors & related devices	0.9	Manufg.	Wholesale trade	0.4	Trade
Forging, stamping, & sintering, nec	0.9	Manufg.	Other S/L govt. enterprises	0.4	S/L Govt
Printed circuit assemblies (electronic assemblies)	0.8	Manufg.	Maintenance/repair of residential structures	0.4	Construct.
Power generation & supply	0.8	Util.	Commercial & health care structures	0.3	Construct.
Securities, commodity contracts, investments	0.7	Fin/R.E.	S/L govt. passenger transit	0.3	S/L Govt
Paints & coatings	0.7	Manufg.	Federal government, investment, nondefense	0.2	Fed Govt
Paperboard containers	0.7	Manufg.	Air & gas compressors	0.2	Manufg.
Management, scientific, & technical consulting	0.7	Services	Boat building	0.2	Manufg.
Lessors of nonfinancial assets	0.5	Fin/R.E.	Commercial & industrial equipment repair/maintenance	0.2	Services
Retail trade	0.5	Trade	Services to buildings & dwellings	0.2	Services
Real estate	0.5	Fin/R.E.	Oil & gas operations services	0.1	Mining
Ball & roller bearings	0.4	Manufg.	Plastics & rubber industry machinery	0.1	Manufg.
Monetary authorities/depository credit intermediation	0.4	Fin/R.E.	Scenic & sightseeing transport & related services	0.1	Util.
Alumina refining & primary aluminum production	0.4	Manufg.			
Abrasive products	0.3	Manufg.			
Professional, scientific, technical services, nec	0.3	Services			
Legal services	0.3	Services			
Telecommunications	0.3	Services			
Electronic components, nec	0.3	Manufg.			
Automotive equipment rental & leasing	0.3	Fin/R.E.			
Coating, engraving, heat treating & allied activities	0.3	Manufg.			
Rubber products, nec	0.3	Manufg.			
Taxes on production & imports, less subsidies	0.3				
Scientific research & development services	0.3	Services			
Plastics packaging materials, film & sheet	0.3	Manufg.			
Postal service	0.3	Util.			
Data processing, hosting, & related services	0.3	Services			
Warehousing & storage	0.2	Util.			
Aluminum products from purchased aluminum	0.2	Manufg.			
Noncomparable imports	0.2	Foreign			
Accounting, tax preparation, bookkeeping, & payroll	0.2	Services			
Maintenance/repair of nonresidential structures	0.2	Construct.			
Services to buildings & dwellings	0.2	Services			
Motor vehicle parts	0.2	Manufg.			
Food services & drinking places	0.2	Services			
Cutting tools & machine tool accessories	0.2	Manufg.			
Natural gas distribution	0.2	Util.			
Commercial & industrial machinery rental & leasing	0.2	Fin/R.E.			
Other computer related services, including facilities	0.1	Services			
Architectural, engineering, & related services	0.1	Services			
Automotive repair & maintenance, ex. car washes	0.1	Services			
Paperboard mills	0.1	Manufg.			
Fabricated metals, nec	0.1	Manufg.			
Laminated plastics plates, sheets, & shapes	0.1	Manufg.			
Business support services	0.1	Services			
Commercial & industrial equipment repair/maintenance	0.1	Services			
Bare printed circuit boards	0.1	Manufg.			
Electronic capacitors, resistors, coils, transformers	0.1	Manufg.			
Chemical products & preparations, nec	0.1	Manufg.			

Source: Benchmark Input-Output Accounts for the U.S. Economy, 2002, U.S. Department of Commerce, Washington D.C., January 2008. User should note that this Input-Output table is not for this particular narrowly defined industry but for a larger aggregate. Input and Output data for Pump and Pumping Equipment Manufacturing include Input and Output data for the Annual Survey of Manufactures' NAICS industries 333911 and 333913. The abbreviation nec stands for 'not elsewhere classified'.

OCCUPATIONS EMPLOYED BY OTHER GENERAL-PURPOSE MACHINERY MANUFACTURING

Occupation	% of Total 2006	Change to 2016	Occupation	% of Total 2006	Change to 2016
Team assemblers	11.0	-9.7	Multiple machine tool operators & tenders	1.4	-0.7
Machinists	5.9	-5.2	Lathe & turning machine tool operators & tenders	1.4	-18.8
Welders, cutters, solderers, & brazers	5.7	-4.0	Maintenance & repair workers, general	1.4	-9.7
First-line supervisors/managers of production workers	3.6	-9.7	Structural metal fabricators & fitters	1.4	-9.7
Mechanical engineers	2.8	-0.7	Industrial engineers	1.3	9.6
Computer-controlled machine tool operators	2.5	-0.7	Electrical & electronic equipment assemblers	1.3	-27.8
Sales reps, wholesale & manufacturing, exc tech	2.3	-9.7	Industrial machinery mechanics	1.3	3.8
Engine & other machine assemblers	2.0	-9.7	Mechanical drafters	1.3	-8.7
Inspectors, testers, sorters, samplers, & weighers	1.9	-14.9	Customer service representatives	1.3	-0.7
Cutting, punching, & press machine operators	1.8	-18.8	Coating, painting, & spraying machine operators	1.2	-14.2
Shipping, receiving, & traffic clerks	1.8	-13.1	Office clerks, general	1.2	-11.1
Helpers--Production workers	1.6	-9.7	Industrial production managers	1.1	-9.7
General & operations managers	1.6	-18.8	Electrical engineers	1.1	-9.7
Laborers & freight, stock, & material movers, hand	1.5	-18.8	Production, planning, & expediting clerks	1.1	-9.7
Purchasing agents, exc wholesale, retail, & farm	1.5	-18.8	Stock clerks & order fillers	1.0	-24.5
Bookkeeping, accounting, & auditing clerks	1.5	-9.7			

Source: *Industry-Occupation Matrix*, Bureau of Labor Statistics, December 4, 2007. These data are reported based on 4-digit NAICS categories but have been matched to corresponding 6-digit NAICS industry codes. The change reported for each occupation to the year 2016 is a percent of growth or decline as estimated by the Bureau of Labor Statistics. The abbreviation nec stands for 'not elsewhere classified'.

INDUSTRY DATA BY STATE

State-level data are not available.

NAICS 33392M - MATERIAL HANDLING EQUIPMENT MANUFACTURING*

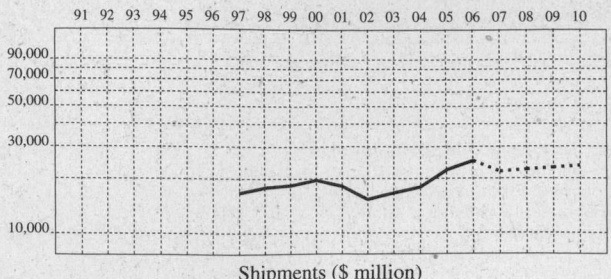

Shipments ($ million)

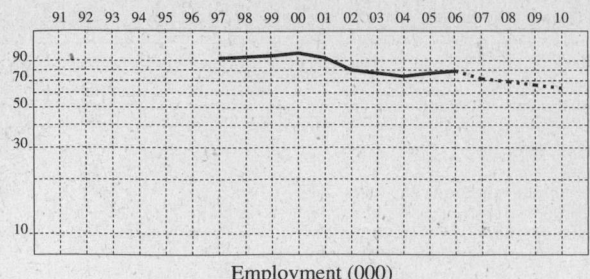

Employment (000)

GENERAL STATISTICS

Year	Com-panies	Establishments		Employment			Compensation		Production ($ million)			
		Total	with 20 or more employees	Total (000)	Production Workers (000)	Hours (Mil)	Payroll ($ mil)	Wages ($/hr)	Cost of Materials	Value Added by Manufacture	Value of Shipments	Capital Invest.
1997	1,756	1,855	826	92.9	59.8	123.6	3,335.6	13.99	9,515.2	7,188.3	16,660.5	415.1
1998		1,834	833	94.4	60.5	127.1	3,447.5	13.62	10,209.5	7,645.3	17,876.0	342.0
1999		1,816	813	96.0	62.2	129.7	3,661.8	14.43	10,063.4	8,226.4	18,345.1	442.7
2000		1,809	815	99.1	64.0	128.2	3,811.3	15.13	11,154.5	8,536.6	19,596.3	409.2
2001		1,799	806	93.4	59.4	116.1	3,542.0	15.71	10,125.9	7,881.5	18,115.5	395.7
2002	1,627	1,778	745	80.1	48.4	96.3	3,246.2	16.69	8,439.9	6,801.5	15,324.5	347.3
2003		1,752	739	76.9	48.1	97.9	3,290.9	16.50	9,410.8	7,129.9	16,606.8	295.3
2004		1,717	740	73.9	45.6	97.3	3,271.7	17.03	10,365.6	7,718.2	17,928.6	309.2
2005		1,705	756	76.8	48.4	103.8	3,555.1	18.12	13,038.3	9,393.5	22,304.3	271.9
2006		1,693P	721P	79.0	50.2	108.8	3,864.4	18.95	14,408.3	10,765.0	25,008.8	434.4
2007		1,674P	708P	71.6P	44.2P	93.9P	3,559.5P	19.16P	12,590.2P	9,406.6P	21,853.0P	320.5P
2008		1,656P	695P	69.0P	42.3P	90.5P	3,569.8P	19.73P	12,912.4P	9,647.4P	22,412.3P	312.1P
2009		1,637P	682P	66.3P	40.4P	87.0P	3,580.1P	20.30P	13,234.7P	9,888.1P	22,971.7P	303.8P
2010		1,619P	669P	63.7P	38.5P	83.6P	3,590.5P	20.87P	13,556.9P	10,128.9P	23,531.0P	295.5P

Sources: 1997 and 2002 *Economic Census*; other years, up to 2006, are from *Annual Survey of Manufactures*. Establishment counts for non-Census years are from *County Business Patterns*; 1997 and 2002 values are from the 1997 and 2002 censuses, respectively. 'P's show projections by the editors.

INDICES OF CHANGE

Year	Com-panies	Establishments		Employment			Compensation		Production ($ million)			
		Total	with 20 or more employees	Total (000)	Production Workers (000)	Hours (Mil)	Payroll ($ mil)	Wages ($/hr)	Cost of Materials	Value Added by Manufacture	Value of Shipments	Capital Invest.
1997	108	104	111	116	124	128	103	84	113	106	109	120
1998		103	112	118	125	132	106	82	121	112	117	98
1999		102	109	120	129	135	113	86	119	121	120	127
2000		102	109	124	132	133	117	91	132	126	128	118
2001		101	108	117	123	121	109	94	120	116	118	114
2002	100	100	100	100	100	100	100	100	100	100	100	100
2003		99	99	96	99	102	101	99	112	105	108	85
2004		97	99	92	94	101	101	102	123	113	117	89
2005		96	101	96	100	108	110	109	154	138	146	78
2006		95P	97P	99	104	113	119	114	171	158	163	125
2007		94P	95P	89P	91P	98P	110P	115P	149P	138P	143P	92P
2008		93P	93P	86P	87P	94P	110P	118P	153P	142P	146P	90P
2009		92P	92P	83P	83P	90P	110P	122P	157P	145P	150P	87P
2010		91P	90P	80P	80P	87P	111P	125P	161P	149P	154P	85P

Sources: Same as General Statistics. Values reflect change from the base year, 2002. Values above 100 mean greater than 2002, values below 100 mean less than 2002, and the values of 100 in other years means the same as 2002. 'P's show projections by the editors.

SELECTED RATIOS

For 2002	Avg. of All Manufact.	Analyzed Industry	Index	For 2002	Avg. of All Manufact.	Analyzed Industry	Index
Employees per Establishment	42	45	107	Value Added per Production Worker	182,367	140,527	77
Payroll per Establishment	1,639,184	1,825,759	111	Cost per Establishment	5,769,015	4,746,850	82
Payroll per Employee	39,053	40,527	104	Cost per Employee	137,446	105,367	77
Production Workers per Establishment	30	27	92	Cost per Production Worker	195,506	174,378	89
Wages per Establishment	694,845	903,963	130	Shipments per Establishment	11,158,348	8,618,954	77
Wages per Production Worker	23,548	33,208	141	Shipments per Employee	265,847	191,317	72
Hours per Production Worker	1,980	1,990	100	Shipments per Production Worker	378,144	316,622	84
Wages per Hour	11.89	16.69	140	Investment per Establishment	361,338	195,332	54
Value Added per Establishment	5,381,325	3,825,366	71	Investment per Employee	8,609	4,336	50
Value Added per Employee	128,210	84,913	66	Investment per Production Worker	12,245	7,176	59

Sources: Same as General Statistics. The 'Average of All Manufacturing' column represents the average of all manufacturing industries reported for the most recent complete year available. The Index shows the relationship between the Average and the Analyzed Industry. For example, 100 means that they are equal; 500 that the Analyzed Industry is five times the average; 50 means that the Analyzed Industry is half the national average. The abbreviation 'na' is used to show that data are 'not available'. Ratios shown for 2002, the last complete census year.

*Equivalent to Federal Government NAICS 333921, 333922, 333923, 333924.

LEADING COMPANIES   Number shown: **75**   Total sales ($ mil): **447,532**   Total employment (000): **942.9**

Company Name	Address				CEO Name	Phone	Co. Type	Sales ($ mil)	Empl. (000)
Ford Motor Co.	1 American Rd.	Dearborn	MI	48126		313-322-3000	P	172,455	246.0
United Technologies Corp.	1 Financial Plz.	Hartford	CT	06101	Mario Abajo	860-728-7000	P	47,829	225.6
Caterpillar Inc.	100 NE Adams St.	Peoria	IL	61629		309-675-1000	P	44,958	101.3
APAC Inc.	900 Ashwood Pkwy.	Atlanta	GA	30338	Garry Higdem	770-392-5300	S	25,170*	1.5
Deere and Co.	1 John Deere Pl.	Moline	IL	61265		309-765-8000	P	24,082	52.0
PACCAR Inc.	PO Box 1518	Bellevue	WA	98009		425-468-7400	P	15,220	21.8
Terex Corp.	200 Nyala Farm Rd.	Westport	CT	06880		203-222-7170	P	9,138	21.0
Schindler Elevator Corp.	20 Whippany Rd.	Morristown	NJ	07960	Scott Stadelman	973-397-6500	R	8,990*	0.3
Dover Corp.	280 Park Ave.	New York	NY	10017		212-922-1640	P	7,226	33.4
AGCO Corp.	4205 River Green Pk	Duluth	GA	30096		770-813-9200	P	6,828	13.7
Metso Minerals Industries Inc.	20965 Crossroads	Waukesha	WI	53186	Hannu Melarti	262-717-2500	R	6,340*	0.2
Oshkosh Truck Corp.	PO Box 2566	Oshkosh	WI	54903	Robert G. Bohn	920-235-9150	P	6,307	14.2
Otis Elevator Co.	10 Farm Springs Rd.	Farmington	CT	06032	Mario Abajo	860-676-6000	S	4,743*	61.0
General Cable Corp.	4 Tesseneer Dr.	Highland Hgts	KY	41076	Gregory B. Kenny	859-572-8000	P	4,615	11.8
KONE Inc.	1 Kone Ct.	Moline	IL	61265		309-764-6771	R	4,610*	0.6
Manitowoc Company Inc.	PO Box 66	Manitowoc	WI	54221		920-684-4410	P	4,005	10.5
NACCO Industries Inc.	5875 Landerbrook	Mayfield Hgts	OH	44124		440-449-9600	P	3,603	10.2
Kalmar Industries USA L.L.C.	415 E Dundee St.	Ottawa	KS	66067		785-242-2200	R	3,320*	0.3
Waltco Truck Equipment Company	PO Box 354	Tallmadge	OH	44278	Lennart Bohman	330-633-9191	R	3,320*	0.2
Freightliner L.L.C.	PO Box 3849	Portland	OR	97208	Chris Patterson	503-745-8000	S	2,734*	14.0
JLG Industries Inc.	1 Jlg Dr.	McConnellsburg	PA	17233		717-485-5161	S	2,289	4.1
Rowan Companies Inc.	2800 Post Oak Blvd.	Houston	TX	77056		713-621-7800	S	2,095	5.7
Heil Co.	5751 Cornelison Rd.	Chattanooga	TN	37411	Michael G. Jobe	423-899-9100	S	2,085*	1.6
Toro Co.	8111 Lyndale Ave. S	Bloomington	MN	55420		952-888-8801	P	1,877	5.3
Saurer Holding Inc.	1575 W 124th Ave.	Denver	CO	80234	Peter Kern	303-457-1234	R	1,850*	0.2
Volvo Trucks North America	PO Box 26115	Greensboro	NC	27402	Peter Karlsten	336-393-2000	S	1,737*	5.4
CC Industries Inc.	222 N La Salle St.	Chicago	IL	60601	William H. Crown	312-855-4000	S	1,560*	6.0
Ancra International L.L.C.	4880 W Rosecrans	Hawthorne	CA	90250	Steve Frediani	310-973-5000	S	1,560*	0.1
Pettibone Traverse Lift L.L.C.	PO Box 368	Baraga	MI	49908		906-353-6611	R	1,560*	0.1
Heico Holding Inc.	2626 Warrenville Rd	Downers Grove	IL	60515	Michael Heisley	630-353-5000	R	1,560*	<0.1
ThyssenKrupp Elevator	1995 N Park Pl.	Atlanta	GA	30339	Barry Pletch	770-799-0400	R	1,234*	10.5
Nesco Inc.	6140 Parkland Blvd.	Mayfield Hgts	OH	44124	Robert J. Tomsich	440-461-6000	R	1,133*	10.3
AAR Corp.	1100 N Wood Dale	Wood Dale	IL	60191	Ira A. Eichner	630-227-2000	P	1,061	3.9
Crown Equipment Corp.	44 S Washington St.	New Bremen	OH	45869	James Dicke	419-629-2311	R	1,049*	7.6
MTD Products Inc.	PO Box 368022	Cleveland	OH	44136	Curtis E. Moll	330-225-2600	R	1,015*	6.7
Astec Industries Inc.	1725 Shepherd Rd.	Chattanooga	TN	37421	J. Don Brock	423-899-5898	P	869	1.0
International Industries Inc.	PO Box 1210	Gilbert	WV	25621		304-664-3227	R	835*	0.5
Pneumatic Scale Corp.	10 Ascot Pkwy.	Cuyahoga Falls	OH	44223	Robert Chapman	330-923-0491	S	786*	0.2
AmBec Inc.	10330 S Dolfield Rd	Owings Mills	MD	21117	Tom Spangenberg	410-363-4400	S	786*	0.1
Westfaliasurge Inc.	1880 Country Frm	Naperville	IL	60563	Dirk Hejnal	630-369-8100	S	755*	0.1
Komatsu America International	1701 W Golf Rd.	Rolling Mdws	IL	60008	David W. Grzelak	847-437-5800	S	634*	4.6
Columbus McKinnon Corp.	140 J J Audubon Pky	Amherst	NY	14228	Herbert P. Ladds Jr.	716-689-5400	P	590	3.3
Blount Inc.	PO Box 22127	Portland	OR	97269	James S. Osterman	503-653-8881	S	583*	3.0
Chore-Time/Brock International	PO Box 2000	Milford	IN	46542	Warren E Buffett	547-658-4191	S	552*	1.0
L.B. Foster Co.	415 Holiday Dr.	Pittsburgh	PA	15220	Stan Hasselbusch	412-928-3400	P	509	0.7
Overhead Door Corp.	2501 St. Hwy. 121	Lewisville	TX	75022	Howard Simons		R	508*	0.1
Alamo Group Inc.	PO Box 549	Seguin	TX	78155	Ronald Robinson	830-379-1480	P	504	2.3
Ricon Corp.	7900 Nelson Rd.	Panorama City	CA	91402	William Baldwin	818-267-3000	R	502*	0.3
JCB Inc.	2000 Bamford Blvd.	Pooler	GA	31322	Helmut Peters	912-447-2000	R	501*	0.3
McNeilus Companies Inc.	113 Conner Rd.	Villa Rica	GA	30180	Micheal Wuest	770-459-6005	S	485*	1.0
Dayton Superior Corp.	7777 Washing. Vlg	Dayton	OH	45459	J.A. Ciccarelli	937-428-6360	P	483	1.6
Ballantine Inc.	840 McKinley St.	Anoka	MN	55303	Joe Newfield	763-427-3959	S	483*	<0.1
Cascade Corp.	PO Box 20187	Portland	OR	97294		503-669-6300	P	479	2.1
Gehl Co.	PO Box 179	West Bend	WI	53095	William Gehl	262-334-9461	P	458	0.9
Schwing America Inc.	5900 Centerville Rd	Saint Paul	MN	55127	Thomas Anderson	651-429-0999	R	453*	0.6
James Hardie Transition Co.	26300 La Alameda	Mission Viejo	CA	92691	Donald Manson	949-348-1800	R	423*	<0.1
Madill Equipment US Inc.	552 Hendrickson Dr.	Kalama	WA	98625	Gil Schmunk	360-673-5236	R	397*	<0.1
Mitsub. Caterpillar Forklift	2121 W S Houston	Houston	TX	77043		713-365-1000	R	374*	0.9
Raymond Corp.	PO Box 130	Greene	NY	13778		607-656-2311	R	372*	0.8
Cleveland Formtek Inc.	4899 Commerce	Cleveland	OH	44128	Joe Mayer	216-292-6300	R	372*	<0.1
Mestek Inc.	260 N Elm St.	Westfield	MA	01085	R. Bruce Dewey	413-568-9571	R	372*	2.6
ESCO Corp.	PO Box 10123	Portland	OR	97296		503-228-2141	R	352*	0.8
Link-Belt Construction Equip.	PO Box 13600	Lexington	KY	40583	Chuck Martz	859-263-5200	R	349*	0.7
Reinke Manufacturing Company	PO Box 566	Deshler	NE	68340	Chris Roth	402-365-7251	R	335*	0.4
Gruber Systems Inc.	25636 Ave. Stanford	Valencia	CA	91355	John Hoskinson	661-257-4060	R	322*	0.3
Saf-Holland USA Inc.	PO Box 425	Muskegon	MI	49443	Timothy Hemingway	231-773-3271	R	321*	0.3
Multiquip Inc.	PO Box 6254	Carson	CA	90749	Roger Euliss	310-537-3700	R	317*	0.3
Kuhn Knight Inc.	1501 W 7th Ave.	Brodhead	WI	53520	Thierry Krier	608-897-2131	R	305*	0.2
Simplicity Manufacturing Inc.	PO Box 997	Port Washington	WI	53074	Warner Frazier	262-377-5450	R	305*	0.5
Dexter Axle	PO Box 250	Elkhart	IN	46515	William Jones	574-295-7888	S	299*	1.7
Caterpillar Paving Products	PO Box 1362	Minneapolis	MN	55440	James Owens	763-425-4100	S	295*	0.6
Continental Conveyor & Equip.	PO Box 400	Winfield	AL	35594		205-487-6492	R	286*	0.3
Lindsay Corp.	2707 N 108th St.	Omaha	NE	68164	M. N. Christodolou	402-428-2131	P	282	0.9
P and H Mining Equipment Inc.	PO Box 310	Milwaukee	WI	53201	Mark Readinger	414-671-4400	S	272*	0.9
Pressure Vessel Service Inc.	10900 Harper Ave.	Detroit	MI	48213		313-921-1200	R	271*	<0.1

Source: Ward's Business Directory of U.S. Private and Public Companies, Volumes 1 and 2, 2008. The company type code used is as follows: P - Public, R - Private, S - Subsidiary, D - Division, J - Joint Venture, A - Affiliate, G - Group. Sales are in millions of dollars, employees are in thousands. An asterisk (*) indicates an estimated sales volume. The symbol < stands for 'less than'. Company names and addresses are truncated, in some cases, to fit into the available space.

MATERIALS CONSUMED FOR ELEVATOR AND MOVING STAIRWAY MANUFACTURING

Material	Quantity	Delivered Cost ($ million)
Fluid power pumps, motors, and hydrostatic transmissions	(X)	35.8
Fluid power cylinders and rotary actuators (hydraulic and pneumatic)	(X)	37.7
Fluid power filters (hydraulic and pneumatic)	(X)	0.5
Fluid power hose, tube fittings, and assemblies (hydraulic and pneumatic)	(X)	7.4
Fluid power valves (hydraulic and pneumatic)	(X)	2.2
Metal bolts, nuts, screws, and other screw machine products	(X)	40.5
Iron and steel forgings	(X)	3.5
Nonferrous forgings	(X)	(D)
Metal stampings	(X)	2.6
Iron and steel castings (rough and semifinished)	(X)	37.6
Steel bars, bar shapes, and plates (exc. castings, forgings, fabr. metal products)	(X)	59.9
Steel sheet and strip (including tinplate)	(X)	79.9
Steel structural shapes and sheet piling (exc. castings, forgings, fabr. metal products)	(X)	19.0
All other steel shapes and forms (exc. castings, forgings, fabr. metal products)	(X)	31.0
Fractional horsepower electric motors (less than 1 hp), exc. timing motors	(X)	2.6
Integral horsepower electric motors and generators (1 hp or more)	(X)	11.5
Ball bearings (mounted or unmounted)	(X)	1.5
Roller bearings (mounted or unmounted)	(X)	(D)
Mechanical speed changers, gears, and industrial high-speed drives	(X)	14.7
Rubber and plastics hose and belting	(X)	(D)
Nonferrous (aluminum, copper, etc.) castings (rough and semifinished)	(X)	0.9
Copper and copper-base alloy shapes and forms (exc. castings, forgings, fabr. metal products)	(X)	1.7
Aluminum and aluminum-base alloy shapes and forms (exc. castings, forgings, fabr. metal products)	(X)	15.7
Other nonferrous shapes and forms (exc. castings, forgings, fabricated metal products)	(X)	2.7
Electrical transmission, distribution, and control equipment	(X)	56.4
Storage batteries	(X)	0.1
Pneumatic tires and inner tubes	(X)	(D)
Paints, varnishes, stains, lacquers, shellacs, japans, enamels, etc.	(X)	7.0
All other materials, components, parts, containers, and supplies	(X)	381.8
Materials, ingredients, containers, and supplies, nsk	(X)	75.8

Source: 2002 *Economic Census*. Explanation of symbols used: (D): Withheld to avoid disclosure of competitive data; na: Not available; (S): Withheld because statistical norms were not met; (X): Not applicable; (Z): Less than half the unit shown; nec: Not elsewhere classified; nsk: Not specified by kind; - : zero; p : 10-19 percent estimated; q : 20-29 percent estimated.

MATERIALS CONSUMED FOR CONVEYOR AND CONVEYING EQUIPMENT MANUFACTURING

Material	Quantity	Delivered Cost ($ million)
Fluid power pumps, motors, and hydrostatic transmissions	(X)	17.0
Fluid power cylinders and rotary actuators (hydraulic and pneumatic)	(X)	11.0
Fluid power filters (hydraulic and pneumatic)	(X)	1.4
Fluid power hose, tube fittings, and assemblies (hydraulic and pneumatic)	(X)	7.9
Fluid power valves (hydraulic and pneumatic)	(X)	14.9
Metal bolts, nuts, screws, and other screw machine products	(X)	33.6
Iron and steel forgings	(X)	31.2
Nonferrous forgings	(X)	0.9
Metal stampings	(X)	32.3
Iron and steel castings (rough and semifinished)	(X)	54.5
Steel bars, bar shapes, and plates (exc. castings, forgings, fabr. metal products)	(X)	131.8
Steel sheet and strip (including tinplate)	(X)	132.5
Steel structural shapes and sheet piling (exc. castings, forgings, fabr. metal products)	(X)	32.9
All other steel shapes and forms (exc. castings, forgings, fabr. metal products)	(X)	64.5
Gasoline and other carburetor engines	(X)	0.6
Fractional horsepower electric motors (less than 1 hp), exc. timing motors	(X)	25.3
Integral horsepower electric motors and generators (1 hp or more)	(X)	41.2
Ball bearings (mounted or unmounted)	(X)	32.9
Roller bearings (mounted or unmounted)	(X)	60.0
Mechanical speed changers, gears, and industrial high-speed drives	(X)	53.6
Rubber and plastics hose and belting	(X)	54.6
Nonferrous (aluminum, copper, etc.) castings (rough and semifinished)	(X)	11.2
Copper and copper-base alloy shapes and forms (exc. castings, forgings, fabr. metal products)	(X)	(D)
Aluminum and aluminum-base alloy shapes and forms (exc. castings, forgings, fabr. metal products)	(X)	18.4
Other nonferrous shapes and forms (exc. castings, forgings, fabricated metal products)	(X)	4.9
Electrical transmission, distribution, and control equipment	(X)	60.5
Storage batteries	(X)	(D)
Pneumatic tires and inner tubes	(X)	3.8
Paints, varnishes, stains, lacquers, shellacs, japans, enamels, etc.	(X)	11.0
All other materials, components, parts, containers, and supplies	(X)	674.8
Materials, ingredients, containers, and supplies, nsk	(X)	341.3

Source: 2002 *Economic Census*. Explanation of symbols used: (D): Withheld to avoid disclosure of competitive data; na: Not available; (S): Withheld because statistical norms were not met; (X): Not applicable; (Z): Less than half the unit shown; nec: Not elsewhere classified; nsk: Not specified by kind; - : zero; p : 10-19 percent estimated; q : 20-29 percent estimated.

MATERIALS CONSUMED FOR OVERHEAD TRAVELING CRANES, HOISTS, AND MONORAIL SYSTEMS

Material	Quantity	Delivered Cost ($ million)
Fluid power pumps, motors, and hydrostatic transmissions	(X)	134.6
Fluid power cylinders and rotary actuators (hydraulic and pneumatic)	(X)	48.7
Fluid power hose, tube fittings, and assemblies (hydraulic and pneumatic)	(X)	24.1
Fluid power valves (hydraulic and pneumatic)	(X)	9.7
Fluid power filters (hydraulic and pneumatic)	(X)	1.4
Metal bolts, nuts, screws, and other screw machine products	(X)	29.2
Fabricated structural metal products (excluding forgings)	(X)	140.3
All other fabricated metal products (excluding forgings)	(X)	29.5
Metal stampings	(X)	3.4
Iron and steel forgings	(X)	5.9
Nonferrous forgings	(X)	0.1
Iron and steel castings (rough and semifinished)	(X)	91.7
Nonferrous (aluminum, copper, etc.) castings (rough and semifinished)	(X)	11.5
Steel bars, bar shapes, and plates (exc. castings, forgings, fabr. metal products)	(X)	83.9
Steel sheet and strip (including tinplate)	(X)	11.5
Steel structural shapes and sheet piling (exc. castings, forgings, fabr. metal products)	(X)	17.7
All other steel shapes and forms (exc. castings, forgings, fabr. metal products)	(X)	(D)
Aluminum and aluminum-base alloy shapes and forms (exc. castings, forgings, fabr. metal products)	(X)	9.4
Other nonferrous shapes and forms (exc. castings, forgings, fabricated metal products)	(X)	(D)
Integral horsepower electric motors and generators (1 hp or more)	(X)	28.1
Mechanical speed changers, gears, and industrial high-speed drives	(X)	33.8
Rubber and plastics hose and belting	(X)	6.4
Paints, varnishes, stains, lacquers, shellacs, japans, enamels, etc.	(X)	23.3
Electrical transmission, distribution, and control equipment	(X)	64.4
Ball and roller bearings (mounted or unmounted)	(X)	13.1
All other materials, components, parts, containers, and supplies	(X)	286.2
Materials, ingredients, containers, and supplies, nsk	(X)	457.4

Source: 2002 *Economic Census*. Explanation of symbols used: (D): Withheld to avoid disclosure of competitive data; na: Not available; (S): Withheld because statistical norms were not met; (X): Not applicable; (Z): Less than half the unit shown; nec: Not elsewhere classified; nsk: Not specified by kind; - : zero; p : 10-19 percent estimated; q : 20-29 percent estimated.

MATERIALS CONSUMED FOR INDUSTRIAL TRUCK, TRACTOR, TRAILER, & STACKER MACHINERY

Material	Quantity	Delivered Cost ($ million)
Fluid power pumps, motors, and hydrostatic transmissions	(X)	102.8
Fluid power cylinders and rotary actuators (hydraulic and pneumatic)	(X)	94.5
Fluid power filters (hydraulic and pneumatic)	(X)	11.0
Fluid power hose, tube fittings, and assemblies (hydraulic and pneumatic)	(X)	76.7
Fluid power valves (hydraulic and pneumatic)	(X)	47.7
Metal bolts, nuts, screws, and other screw machine products	(X)	39.7
Iron and steel forgings	(X)	26.2
Nonferrous forgings	(X)	(D)
Metal stampings	(X)	36.7
Iron and steel castings (rough and semifinished)	(X)	120.9
Steel bars, bar shapes, and plates (exc. castings, forgings, fabr. metal products)	(X)	109.5
Steel sheet and strip (including tinplate)	(X)	127.2
Steel structural shapes and sheet piling (exc. castings, forgings, fabr. metal products)	(X)	76.8
All other steel shapes and forms (exc. castings, forgings, fabr. metal products)	(X)	39.9
Gasoline and other carburetor engines	(X)	162.5
Fractional horsepower electric motors (less than 1 hp), exc. timing motors	(X)	3.9
Integral horsepower electric motors and generators (1 hp or more)	(X)	50.6
Ball bearings (mounted or unmounted)	(X)	24.8
Roller bearings (mounted or unmounted)	(X)	52.5
Mechanical speed changers, gears, and industrial high-speed drives	(X)	28.7
Rubber and plastics hose and belting	(X)	25.2
Nonferrous (aluminum, copper, etc.) castings (rough and semifinished)	(X)	(D)
Copper and copper-base alloy shapes and forms (exc. castings, forgings, fabr. metal products)	(X)	2.5
Aluminum and aluminum-base alloy shapes and forms (exc. castings, forgings, fabr. metal products)	(X)	24.3
Other nonferrous shapes and forms (exc. castings, forgings, fabricated metal products)	(X)	6.1
Electrical transmission, distribution, and control equipment	(X)	189.9
Storage batteries	(X)	71.7
Pneumatic tires and inner tubes	(X)	68.8
Paints, varnishes, stains, lacquers, shellacs, japans, enamels, etc.	(X)	17.3
All other materials, components, parts, containers, and supplies	(X)	589.4
Materials, ingredients, containers, and supplies, nsk	(X)	387.4

Source: 2002 *Economic Census*. Explanation of symbols used: (D): Withheld to avoid disclosure of competitive data; na: Not available; (S): Withheld because statistical norms were not met; (X): Not applicable; (Z): Less than half the unit shown; nec: Not elsewhere classified; nsk: Not specified by kind; - : zero; p : 10-19 percent estimated; q : 20-29 percent estimated.

PRODUCT SHARE DETAILS FOR ELEVATOR AND MOVING STAIRWAY MANUFACTURING

Product or Product Class Shipments	Mil. $	Product or Product Class Shipments	Mil. $
ELEVATORS AND MOVING STAIRWAYS	1,854.9	Moving stairways, escalators, and moving walkways	145.2
Elevators and moving stairways	**1,445.9**	Other nonfarm elevators, including sidewalk elevators, dumb waiters, man lifts, etc. (except portable elevator-stackers)	108.8
Geared and gearless electric passenger elevators (except farm, portable, and residential lifts)	422.8	Elevators and moving stairways, nsk	11.2
Geared electric passenger elevators (except farm, portable, and residential lifts)	282.9	**Parts and attachments for elevators and moving stairways (sold separately)**	**342.1**
Gearless electric passenger elevators (except farm, portable, and residential lifts)	139.9	Parts for automobile lifts (service station), passenger and freight elevators and escalators	342.1
Hydraulic passenger elevators (except farm and portable)	523.6	Parts for automobile lifts (service station and garage type)	32.1
Other elevators and moving stairways, except parts and attachments	488.3	Parts for passenger and freight elevators and escalators	309.9
Electric freight elevators (except farm and portable)	12.1	**Elevators and moving stairways, nsk, total**	**67.0**
Hydraulic freight elevators (except farm and portable)	21.5		
Automobile lifts (service station and garage type)	200.8		

Source: 2002 *Economic Census*. The values are product shipments in millions of dollars for 2002. Total product shipments may be lower or higher than industry shipments. See Introduction for a full discussion. Values of indented subcategories are summed in the main heading(s). The symbol (D) appears when data are withheld to prevent disclosure of competitive information. The abbreviation nsk stands for 'not specified by kind' and nec for 'not elsewhere classified'. A dash (-) means zero.

PRODUCT SHARE DETAILS FOR CONVEYOR AND CONVEYING EQUIPMENT MANUFACTURING

Product or Product Class Shipments	Mil. $	Product or Product Class Shipments	Mil. $
CONVEYORS AND CONVEYING EQUIPMENT	5,030.6	Bulk material handling screw conveyors and conveying systems, except hoists	(D)
Unit handling conveyors and conveying systems, except hoists and farm elevators	**2,223.5**	Bulk material handling bucket elevators and elevator systems, except hoists	38.2
Unit handling gravity and trolley conveyors and conveying systems, except hoists and farm elevators	250.9	Bulk material handling portable conveyors and conveying systems, except hoists	8.7
Unit handling gravity conveyors and conveying systems (skate wheel and roller), except hoists and farm elevators	178.2	Bulk material handling en masse conveyors and conveying systems, except hoists	34.8
Light- to medium-duty unit handling trolley (overhead) conveyors and conveying systems, except hoists and farm elevators	72.7	Bulk material handling vibrating conveyors and conveying systems, except hoists	78.4
Heavy-duty unit handling trolley (overhead) conveyors and conveying systems, except hoists and farm elevators	254.6	Bulk handling conveyors and conveying systems specially designed for underground use	(D)
Unit handling tow, belt, roller, pneumatic, portable, carousel, and other nonbelt conveyors and conveying systems	1,682.9	Other bulk handling conveyors and conveying systems, nec	322.1
Unit handling tow conveyors and conveying systems (under floor systems), except hoists and farm elevators	25.6	Farm conveyors, elevators, and stackers, single and double chain type	15.4
Light- to-medium-duty unit handling powered conveyors and conveying systems, belt	465.6	Farm conveyors, elevators, and stackers, auger type	46.3
Light- to-medium-duty unit handling powered conveyors and conveying systems, roller	400.0	Other farm conveyors, elevators, and stackers, nec	70.8
Heavy-duty unit handling powered conveyors and conveying systems, belt	173.6	Bulk material handling loading and storing traveling stackers	29.9
Heavy-duty unit handling powered conveyors and conveying systems, roller	141.7	Other bulk material handling loading and storing systems, including trippers, centrifugal throwers, etc.	26.0
Unit handling pneumatic tube conveyors and conveying systems, except hoists and farm elevators	91.6	Bulk material handling pneumatic conveyors and conveying systems, except hoists	97.8
Unit handling portable conveyors and conveying systems, except hoists and farm elevators	6.0	Bulk material handling unloading and reclaiming systems	70.8
Unit handling carousel conveyors and conveying systems, except hoists and farm elevators	41.1	Bulk material handling unloading and reclaiming vibrating feeders	37.6
All other unit handling conveyors and conveying systems, belt	163.9	Other bulk material handling unloading and reclaiming systems, including bins, apron feeders, gates, etc.	33.2
All other unit handling conveyors and conveying systems, except belt	173.9	Bulk material handling conveyors and conveying systems, except hoists and farm elevators, nsk	17.1
Unit handling conveyors and conveying systems, except hoists and farm elevators, nsk	35.1	**Parts, attachments, and accessories for bulk material handling conveyors and conveying systems (sold separately)**	**550.8**
Parts, attachments, and accessories for unit handling conveyors and conveying systems (sold separately)	**251.0**	Belt conveyor idlers, pulleys for bulk material handling	162.0
Bulk handling conveyors and conveying systems, except hoists and farm elevators	**1,590.9**	Belt conveyor idlers for bulk material handling conveyors and conveying systems (sold separately)	94.5
Bulk material handling conveyors and conveying systems, except hoists and farm elevators	554.9	Belt conveyor pulleys for bulk material handling conveyors and conveying systems (sold separarely)	67.5
Other bulk handling conveyors and conveying systems	850.3	All other parts, attachments, and accessories for bulk material handling conveyors and conveying systems (sold separately)	379.7
		Parts, attachments, and accessories for bulk material handling conveyors and conveying systems (sold separately), nsk	9.1
		Conveyors and conveying equipment, nsk, total	**414.4**

Source: 2002 *Economic Census*. The values are product shipments in millions of dollars for 2002. Total product shipments may be lower or higher than industry shipments. See Introduction for a full discussion. Values of indented subcategories are summed in the main heading(s). The symbol (D) appears when data are withheld to prevent disclosure of competitive information. The abbreviation nsk stands for 'not specified by kind' and nec for 'not elsewhere classified'. A dash (-) means zero.

PRODUCT SHARE DETAILS FOR OVERHEAD TRAVELING CRANES, HOISTS, AND MONORAIL SYSTEMS

Product or Product Class Shipments	Mil. $	Product or Product Class Shipments	Mil. $
OVERHEAD TRAVELING CRANES, HOISTS, AND MONORAIL SYSTEMS	2,819.5	Double top running bridge type overhead traveling cranes (except construction power cranes)	61.9
Hoists	**462.9**	Parts and attachments for overhead traveling cranes and monorail	68.8
Hoists, all types	341.2	Other parts and attachments for overhead traveling cranes	50.1
Chain hand hoists	27.9		
Ratchet lever hand hoists	17.6	Parts and attachments for monorail systems (sold separately)	18.6
Wire rope puller hand hoists	23.7	Overhead traveling cranes and monorail systems, nsk	31.1
Electric (roller and link) chain hoists	(D)	**Winches, aerial work platforms, and automotive wrecker hoists**	**1,815.6**
Other hoists, powered by electric motor	87.4	Personnel aerial work platforms (excluding parts)	1,473.5
Electric wire rope hoists (excluding hand, mine shaft, and slope wire rope hoists)	43.0	Winches for mounting on wheel and crawler tractors and other prime movers, complete units	51.0
Air or other nonelectric chain hoists, except hand	18.9	Electric and other winches, including marine use and automobile hoists used on tow trucks	180.4
Air and other nonelectric wire rope hoists (excluding hand, mine shaft, and slope wire rope hoists)	(D)	Electric winches, including marine use (excluding winches for tractor mounting and parts)	71.2
Other hoists, not powered by electric motor	47.8	Other winches, including automobile hoists used on tow trucks (excluding winches for mounting on wheel or crawler trailers)	109.2
Parts and attachments for hoists (sold separately)	73.3		
Hoists, nsk	48.4	Parts for winches, aerial work platforms, and automobile hoists (sold separately)	98.7
Overhead traveling cranes and monorail systems	**475.6**	Parts for winches for mounting on tractors and other prime movers (sold separately)	15.7
Overhead traveling cranes and monrail systems, including parts	313.9	Parts for winches for aerial work platforms and automobile hoists (sold separately)	83.0
Single top running bridge type overhead traveling cranes (except construction power cranes)	43.2	Winches, aerial work platforms, and automotive wrecker hoists, nsk	12.1
Under running bridge type overhead traveling cranes (except construction power cranes)	31.2	**Overhead traveling cranes, hoists, and monorail systems, nsk, total**	**65.4**
Gantry type overhead traveling cranes (except construction power cranes)	24.5		
Stacker-storage type overhead traveling cranes (except construction power cranes)	3.9		
Other overhead traveling cranes on fixed support	33.4		
Other overhead traveling cranes	86.0		
Buckets, grabs, and grips	42.2		
Monorail systems (manual and powered)	49.5		

Source: 2002 *Economic Census*. The values are product shipments in millions of dollars for 2002. Total product shipments may be lower or higher than industry shipments. See Introduction for a full discussion. Values of indented subcategories are summed in the main heading(s). The symbol (D) appears when data are withheld to prevent disclosure of competitive information. The abbreviation nsk stands for 'not specified by kind' and nec for 'not elsewhere classified'. A dash (-) means zero.

PRODUCT SHARE DETAILS FOR INDUSTRIAL TRUCK, TRACTOR, TRAILER, & STACKER MACHINERY

Product or Product Class Shipments	Mil. $	Product or Product Class Shipments	Mil. $
INDUSTRIAL TRUCKS, TRACTORS, TRAILERS, AND STACKER MACHINERY	4,521.8	internal combustion engine or other nonelectric powered	108.7
Industrial trucks, tractors, mobile straddle carriers and cranes, and automatic stacking machines	**3,422.7**	Other work trucks and tractors not fitted with lifting or handling equipment, self-propelled, internal combustion engine or other nonelectric powered	(D)
Work trucks, operator riding, self-propelled, electric motor powered	1,028.3	Work trucks and tractors not fitted with lifting and handling equipment, not self-propelled	11.2
Fork lift work trucks, operator riding, self-propelled, electric motor powered	858.3	Bulk powered material moving equipment, dock boards and metal pallets and skids	714.2
Other work trucks fitted with lifting or handling equipment, operator riding, self-propelled, electric motor powered	170.0	Mobile straddle carriers and cranes	35.2
Fork lift riding and nonriding work trucks, self-propelled, electric, gasoline, and other nonelectric motor powered	717.8	Portable elevators-stackers, except farm type	3.3
Nonriding fork lift and other work trucks fitted with lifting and handling equipment, self-propelled, electric motor powered	256.2	Palletizers and depalletizers (pallet loaders and unloaders), including industrial truck and related equipment used on smooth surfaces around depots, terminals, warehouses, etc.	98.7
Fork lift work trucks, operator riding, self-propelled, gasoline motor powered	438.7	Scissors type hydraulic lift tables (electrohydraulic lift platforms)	138.7
Fork lift and other work trucks, operator riding, self-propelled, internal combustion engine and other nonelectric powered	22.9	Other hydraulic lift tables (electrohydraulic lift platforms)	52.1
Fork lift work trucks, operator riding, self-propelled, diesel motor powered	(D)	Dock boards (industrial loading ramps, hinged loading ramps)	139.2
Work trucks, fork lifts, and tractors, self-propelled, electric, gasoline, and other power system	661.3	Automatic stacking machines	13.8
		Trailers and semitrailers for use with work tractors	61.6
Fork lift work trucks, operator riding, self-propelled, LPG (liquid petroleum gas) motor powered	413.8	Other hand carts and vehicles	133.5
		Other related articles	38.1
Fork lift work trucks, operator riding, self-propelled, other internal combustion engine and other nonelectric powered, incuding CNG (compresed natural gas)	(D)	Industrial trucks, tractors, mobile straddle carriers and cranes, and automatic stacking machines, nsk	9.4
		Parts and attachments for industrial trucks and tractors (sold separately)	**983.3**
Not self-propelled fork lift and other work trucks fitted with lifting and handling equipment (hand lift, etc.)	21.4	Parts and attachments for industrial work trucks fitted with lifting or handling equipment and all other vehicles	976.3
Work trucks and tractors not fitted with lifting or handling equipment, operator riding, self-propelled, electric motor powered	47.3	Parts and attachments for industrial work trucks fitted with lifting or handling equipment	570.2
Other work trucks and tractors not fitted with lifting or handling equipment, self-propelled, electric motor powered	(D)	Parts and attachments for other industrial stacker vehicles	292.4
		Parts and attachments for stacker machinery other than vehicles	113.7
Work trucks and tractors not fitted with lifting and handling equipment, operator riding, self-propelled,		Parts and attachments for industrial trucks and tractors (sold separately), nsk	7.1
		Industrial trucks, tractors, trailers, and stacker machinery, nsk, total	**115.8**

Source: 2002 *Economic Census*. The values are product shipments in millions of dollars for 2002. Total product shipments may be lower or higher than industry shipments. See Introduction for a full discussion. Values of indented subcategories are summed in the main heading(s). The symbol (D) appears when data are withheld to prevent disclosure of competitive information. The abbreviation nsk stands for 'not specified by kind' and nec for 'not elsewhere classified'. A dash (-) means zero.

INPUTS AND OUTPUTS FOR MATERIAL HANDLING EQUIPMENT MANUFACTURING

Economic Sector or Industry Providing Inputs	%	Sector	Economic Sector or Industry Buying Outputs	%	Sector
Compensation of employees	29.2		Private fixed investment	58.8	
Iron & steel mills & ferroalloys	8.3	Manufg.	Exports of goods & services	9.6	Cap Inv
Wholesale trade	7.2	Trade	Commercial & health care structures	6.4	Construct.
Management of companies & enterprises	5.3	Services	Nonresidential structures, nec	3.5	Construct.
Fluid power process machinery	2.7	Manufg.	Iron & steel mills & ferroalloys	3.4	Manufg.
Material handling equipment	2.4	Manufg.	Material handling equipment	1.9	Manufg.
Ferrous metal foundries	2.4	Manufg.	S/L govt. invest., other	1.6	S/L Govt
Relay & industrial controls	1.9	Manufg.	Oil & gas well drilling	0.9	Mining
Motor vehicle parts	1.8	Manufg.	Oil & gas operations services	0.8	Mining
Ball & roller bearings	1.7	Manufg.	Automotive repair & maintenance, ex. car washes	0.8	Services
Mechanical power transmission equipment	1.6	Manufg.	Wholesale trade	0.8	Trade
Valve & fittings other than plumbing	1.5	Manufg.	Retail trade	0.8	Trade
Speed changers, industrial high-speed drives, & gears	1.4	Manufg.	Warehousing & storage	0.8	Util.
Machine shops	1.4	Manufg.	Coal	0.7	Mining
Motors & generators	1.3	Manufg.	Manufacturing structures	0.6	Construct.
Turned products & screws, nuts, & bolts	1.1	Manufg.	Plastics materials & resins	0.5	Manufg.
Gaskets, packing, & sealing devices	1.1	Manufg.	Residential permanent site structures	0.5	Construct.
Truck transportation	1.1	Util.	Oil & gas extraction	0.4	Mining
Rubber & plastics hose & belting	0.9	Manufg.	Federal government, investment, national defense	0.3	Fed Govt
Real estate	0.9	Fin/R.E.	Sand, gravel, clay, & refractory minerals	0.3	Mining
Semiconductors & related devices	0.8	Manufg.	Stone mining & quarrying	0.3	Mining
Printed circuit assemblies (electronic assemblies)	0.7	Manufg.	Truck transportation	0.2	Util.
Crowns & closures & metal stamping	0.7	Manufg.	Colleges, universities, & professional schools	0.2	Services
Securities, commodity contracts, investments	0.7	Fin/R.E.	Waste management & remediation services	0.2	Services
Advertising & related services	0.7	Services	Motor vehicle parts	0.2	Manufg.
Metal cans, boxes, & other containers (light gauge)	0.7	Manufg.	Mining & oil & gas field machinery	0.2	Manufg.
Plate work & fabricated structural products	0.7	Manufg.	Gold, silver, & other metal ore	0.2	Mining

Continued on next page.

INPUTS AND OUTPUTS FOR MATERIAL HANDLING EQUIPMENT MANUFACTURING - Continued

Economic Sector or Industry Providing Inputs	%	Sector	Economic Sector or Industry Buying Outputs	%	Sector
Paints & coatings	0.6	Manufg.	Residential structures, nec	0.2	Construct.
Tires	0.6	Manufg.	Coating, engraving, heat treating & allied activities	0.2	Manufg.
Alumina refining & primary aluminum production	0.6	Manufg.	Iron ore	0.2	Mining
Forging, stamping, & sintering, nec	0.6	Manufg.	Scenic & sightseeing transport & related services	0.1	Util.
Nonferrous metal foundries	0.6	Manufg.	Miscellaneous mining services	0.1	Mining
Storage batteries	0.6	Manufg.	Canned & dehydrated fruits & vegetables	0.1	Manufg.
Lessors of nonfinancial assets	0.5	Fin/R.E.	Scientific research & development services	0.1	Services
Fabricated metals, nec	0.5	Manufg.	Soft drinks & ice	0.1	Manufg.
Legal services	0.5	Services	Nonmetallic minerals, nec	0.1	Mining
Coating, engraving, heat treating & allied activities	0.5	Manufg.			
Engine equipment, nec	0.5	Manufg.			
Electronic components, nec	0.5	Manufg.			
Power generation & supply	0.5	Util.			
Cutting tools & machine tool accessories	0.4	Manufg.			
Packaging machinery	0.4	Manufg.			
Monetary authorities/depository credit intermediation	0.4	Fin/R.E.			
Automotive equipment rental & leasing	0.3	Fin/R.E.			
Telecommunications	0.3	Services			
Professional, scientific, technical services, nec	0.3	Services			
Accounting, tax preparation, bookkeeping, & payroll	0.3	Services			
Plastics packaging materials, film & sheet	0.3	Manufg.			
Natural gas distribution	0.3	Util.			
Scientific research & development services	0.3	Services			
Taxes on production & imports, less subsidies	0.3				
Data processing, hosting, & related services	0.3	Services			
Warehousing & storage	0.3	Util.			
Architectural, engineering, & related services	0.2	Services			
Electronic capacitors, resistors, coils, transformers	0.2	Manufg.			
Rubber products, nec	0.2	Manufg.			
Noncomparable imports	0.2	Foreign			
Employment services	0.2	Services			
Food services & drinking places	0.2	Services			
Aluminum products from purchased aluminum	0.2	Manufg.			
Management, scientific, & technical consulting	0.2	Services			
Commercial & industrial machinery rental & leasing	0.2	Fin/R.E.			
Rail transportation	0.2	Util.			
Services to buildings & dwellings	0.2	Services			
Maintenance/repair of nonresidential structures	0.2	Construct.			
Postal service	0.2	Util.			
Specialized design services	0.2	Services			
Business support services	0.2	Services			
Chemical products & preparations, nec	0.1	Manufg.			
Other computer related services, including facilities	0.1	Services			
General purpose machinery, nec	0.1	Manufg.			
Abrasive products	0.1	Manufg.			
Paperboard containers	0.1	Manufg.			
Power, distribution, & specialty transformers	0.1	Manufg.			
Nonferrous metal (ex. copper & aluminum) processing	0.1	Manufg.			
Paperboard mills	0.1	Manufg.			
Automotive repair & maintenance, ex. car washes	0.1	Services			

Source: Benchmark Input-Output Accounts for the U.S. Economy, 2002, U.S. Department of Commerce, Washington, D.C., January 2008. The abbreviation nec stands for 'not elsewhere classified'.

OCCUPATIONS EMPLOYED BY OTHER GENERAL-PURPOSE MACHINERY MANUFACTURING

Occupation	% of Total 2006	Change to 2016	Occupation	% of Total 2006	Change to 2016
Team assemblers	11.0	-9.7	Multiple machine tool operators & tenders	1.4	-0.7
Machinists	5.9	-5.2	Lathe & turning machine tool operators & tenders	1.4	-18.8
Welders, cutters, solderers, & brazers	5.7	-4.0	Maintenance & repair workers, general	1.4	-9.7
First-line supervisors/managers of production workers	3.6	-9.7	Structural metal fabricators & fitters	1.4	-9.7
Mechanical engineers	2.8	-0.7	Industrial engineers	1.3	9.6
Computer-controlled machine tool operators	2.5	-0.7	Electrical & electronic equipment assemblers	1.3	-27.8
Sales reps, wholesale & manufacturing, exc tech	2.3	-9.7	Industrial machinery mechanics	1.3	3.8
Engine & other machine assemblers	2.0	-9.7	Mechanical drafters	1.3	-8.7
Inspectors, testers, sorters, samplers, & weighers	1.9	-14.9	Customer service representatives	1.3	-0.7
Cutting, punching, & press machine operators	1.8	-18.8	Coating, painting, & spraying machine operators	1.2	-14.2
Shipping, receiving, & traffic clerks	1.8	-13.1	Office clerks, general	1.2	-11.1
Helpers--Production workers	1.6	-9.7	Industrial production managers	1.1	-9.7
General & operations managers	1.6	-18.8	Electrical engineers	1.1	-9.7
Laborers & freight, stock, & material movers, hand	1.5	-18.8	Production, planning, & expediting clerks	1.1	-9.7
Purchasing agents, exc wholesale, retail, & farm	1.5	-18.8	Stock clerks & order fillers	1.0	-24.5
Bookkeeping, accounting, & auditing clerks	1.5	-9.7			

Source: Industry-Occupation Matrix, Bureau of Labor Statistics, December 4, 2007. These data are reported based on 4-digit NAICS categories but have been matched to corresponding 6-digit NAICS industry codes. The change reported for each occupation to the year 2016 is a percent of growth or decline as estimated by the Bureau of Labor Statistics. The abbreviation nec stands for 'not elsewhere classified'.

LOCATION BY STATE AND REGIONAL CONCENTRATION

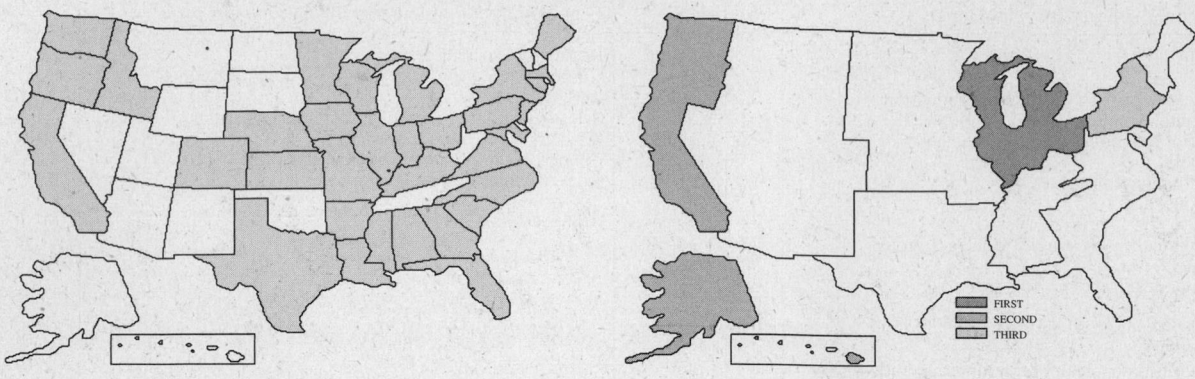

FIRST
SECOND
THIRD

INDUSTRY DATA BY STATE

| State | Establish- ments | Shipments | | | Employment | | | | Cost as % of Shipments | Investment per Employee ($) |
		Total ($ mil)	% of U.S.	Per Establ.	Total Number	% of U.S.	Per Establ.	Wages ($/hour)		
Michigan	137	1,809.8	11.8	13,210.6	8,722	10.9	64	20.53	50.1	3,870
Texas	111	1,102.1	7.2	9,928.4	5,242	6.5	47	17.18	64.7	6,598
Ohio	102	1,004.5	6.6	9,848.2	6,137	7.7	60	16.78	56.0	2,189
Pennsylvania	63	783.9	5.1	12,442.7	3,851	4.8	61	15.59	68.1	2,803
Illinois	93	754.5	4.9	8,113.3	3,946	4.9	42	16.90	54.3	6,869
Indiana	52	629.8	4.1	12,111.2	2,727	3.4	52	15.55	65.2	6,770
California	137	619.9	4.0	4,524.6	3,554	4.4	26	14.65	47.4	2,316
Washington	41	609.8	4.0	14,873.1	2,452	3.1	60	21.63	57.7	1,686
North Carolina	27	514.7	3.4	19,061.5	1,754	2.2	65	16.08	59.0	2,526
Missouri	45	395.1	2.6	8,779.5	2,248	2.8	50	15.11	38.8	2,641
Wisconsin	57	351.2	2.3	6,161.2	2,217	2.8	39	14.74	45.0	5,659
New Jersey	52	317.8	2.1	6,111.0	1,765	2.2	34	16.52	54.9	2,487
Florida	67	308.2	2.0	4,600.2	1,639	2.0	24	16.10	49.7	3,023
Georgia	23	282.6	1.8	12,288.0	971	1.2	42	15.89	64.8	3,652
Kentucky	22	267.4	1.7	12,155.2	1,314	1.6	60	21.35	54.7	2,570
New York	55	260.4	1.7	4,734.3	1,699	2.1	31	16.46	43.1	2,546
Alabama	24	206.6	1.3	8,607.9	1,238	1.5	52	16.35	45.5	2,457
South Carolina	13	184.0	1.2	14,155.4	686	0.9	53	14.96	63.9	1,606
Minnesota	43	182.6	1.2	4,247.3	1,298	1.6	30	14.09	44.3	2,136
Colorado	21	174.0	1.1	8,285.1	829	1.0	39	16.75	34.5	6,509
Iowa	24	165.2	1.1	6,882.7	1,295	1.6	54	16.61	46.0	3,918
Mississippi	8	149.9	1.0	18,733.3	1,058	1.3	132	16.88	55.0	1,037
Arkansas	15	147.9	1.0	9,860.1	1,337	1.7	89	13.98	47.7	4,647
Virginia	21	143.3	0.9	6,825.7	885	1.1	42	14.95	51.8	5,733
Kansas	14	129.3	0.8	9,232.3	614	0.8	44	15.18	58.5	3,990
Oregon	14	93.3	0.6	6,665.9	587	0.7	42	19.44	54.5	4,359
Louisiana	10	44.1	0.3	4,413.2	426	0.5	43	13.78	40.9	5,915
Maryland	6	35.6	0.2	5,930.0	110	0.1	18	15.52	53.8	1,564
Nebraska	8	30.2	0.2	3,773.5	244	0.3	30	12.62	47.0	1,193
Maine	3	27.3	0.2	9,094.7	160	0.2	53	15.81	41.5	2,737
Connecticut	6	21.9	0.1	3,650.7	137	0.2	23	18.90	40.9	2,445
Massachusetts	11	21.7	0.1	1,968.6	168	0.2	15	15.75	38.5	2,185
Idaho	4	11.7	0.1	2,925.5	105	0.1	26	14.02	58.0	4,600

Source: 2002 *Economic Census.* The states are in descending order of shipments or establishments (if shipment data are missing for the majority). The symbol (D) appears when data are withheld to prevent disclosure of competitive information. States marked with (D) are sorted by number of establishments. A dash (-) indicates that the data element cannot be calculated. Data may not show all states active in the NAICS category. All data available at the time of publication are shown.

NAICS 333991 - POWER-DRIVEN HAND TOOL MANUFACTURING

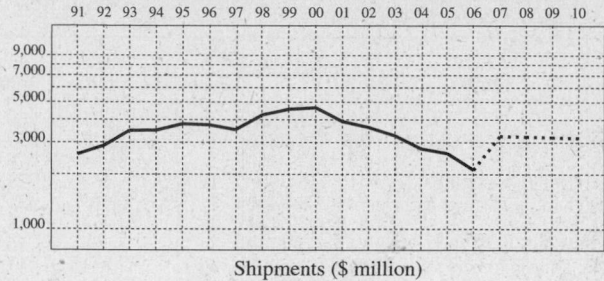

Shipments ($ million)

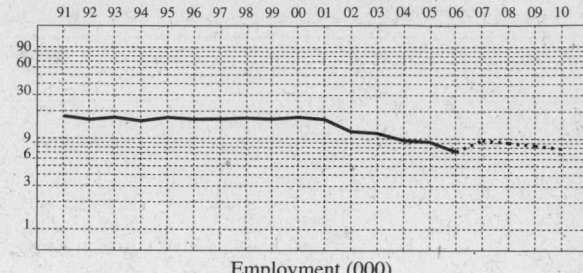

Employment (000)

GENERAL STATISTICS

| Year | Com-panies | Establishments | | Employment | | | Compensation | | Production ($ million) | | | |
		Total	with 20 or more employees	Total (000)	Production Workers (000)	Hours (Mil)	Payroll ($ mil)	Wages ($/hr)	Cost of Materials	Value Added by Manufacture	Value of Shipments	Capital Invest.
1991		212	75	17.5	11.4	21.5	429.1	10.86	1,276.7	1,310.9	2,580.7	74.7
1992	214	226	69	16.1	10.6	21.7	440.6	11.08	1,359.9	1,506.8	2,872.5	72.3
1993		230	74	17.0	11.7	24.4	471.6	10.98	1,721.7	1,758.3	3,480.1	112.2
1994		231	71	15.6	10.9	23.5	449.0	11.19	1,734.8	1,786.0	3,495.2	103.9
1995		230	88	17.0	11.9	24.6	500.7	12.13	1,771.1	2,030.6	3,790.8	117.8
1996		234	80	16.3	11.3	22.7	493.5	12.17	1,786.3	1,949.4	3,744.3	118.2
1997	195	214	63	16.4	12.2	23.9	512.2	12.95	1,620.8	1,938.0	3,523.9	129.2
1998		214	70	16.8	12.3	24.0	553.4	13.44	1,954.6	2,349.7	4,252.3	100.5
1999		218	72	16.4	12.1	22.9	523.4	12.98	2,121.7	2,451.2	4,570.8	103.9
2000		218	69	17.2	12.5	23.0	565.5	13.76	2,214.6	2,493.5	4,656.1	116.8
2001		220	75	16.3	11.0	20.6	517.4	14.19	1,935.6	1,931.9	3,912.2	90.6
2002	108	125	55	12.0	8.9	16.3	428.4	15.30	1,822.7	1,804.9	3,635.7	59.4
2003		197	60	11.5	8.1	15.2	446.0	16.21	1,658.1	1,600.2	3,270.7	72.0
2004		146	57	9.6	6.9	13.9	402.7	16.08	1,545.7	1,243.7	2,771.4	38.8
2005		148	57	9.2	6.3	11.7	370.9	17.30	1,396.1	1,223.0	2,609.3	47.3
2006		159P	58P	7.2	5.0	10.0	342.6	19.79	1,292.9	810.4	2,117.9	31.7
2007		154P	57P	9.6P	7.0P	12.9P	424.9P	18.16P	1,981.8P	1,242.2P	3,246.4P	53.8P
2008		148P	55P	9.0P	6.7P	12.1P	420.1P	18.67P	1,966.8P	1,232.8P	3,221.8P	49.9P
2009		142P	54P	8.4P	6.3P	11.3P	415.3P	19.19P	1,951.8P	1,223.4P	3,197.2P	46.0P
2010		137P	53P	7.8P	5.9P	10.4P	410.6P	19.70P	1,936.8P	1,214.0P	3,172.6P	42.1P

Sources: 1992, 1997, 2002 *Economic Census*; other years, up to 2006, are from the *Annual Survey of Manufactures*. Establishment counts for non-Census years are from *County Business Patterns*; 1997 and 2002 values are from the 1997 and 2002 censuses respectively, reported in the Federal Government's NAICS format. Other years were originally reported in equivalent SIC format. 'P's show projections by the editors.

INDICES OF CHANGE

| Year | Com-panies | Establishments | | Employment | | | Compensation | | Production ($ million) | | | |
		Total	with 20 or more employees	Total (000)	Production Workers (000)	Hours (Mil)	Payroll ($ mil)	Wages ($/hr)	Cost of Materials	Value Added by Manufacture	Value of Shipments	Capital Invest.
1992	198	181	125	134	119	133	103	72	75	83	79	122
1997	181	171	115	137	137	147	120	85	89	107	97	218
2001		176	136	136	124	126	121	93	106	107	108	153
2002	100	100	100	100	100	100	100	100	100	100	100	100
2003		158	109	96	91	93	104	106	91	89	90	121
2004		117	104	80	78	85	94	105	85	69	76	65
2005		118	104	77	71	72	87	113	77	68	72	80
2006		127P	105P	60	56	61	80	129	71	45	58	53
2007		123P	103P	80P	79P	79P	99P	119P	109P	69P	89P	91P
2008		118P	101P	75P	75P	74P	98P	122P	108P	68P	89P	84P
2009		114P	98P	70P	71P	69P	97P	125P	107P	68P	88P	77P
2010		109P	95P	65P	66P	64P	96P	129P	106P	67P	87P	71P

Sources: Same as General Statistics. Values reflect change from the base year, 2002. Values above 100 mean greater than 2002, values below 100 mean less than 2002, and the values of 100 in other years means the same as 2002. 'P's show projections by the editors.

SELECTED RATIOS

For 2002	Avg. of All Manufact.	Analyzed Industry	Index	For 2002	Avg. of All Manufact.	Analyzed Industry	Index
Employees per Establishment	42	96	229	Value Added per Production Worker	182,367	202,798	111
Payroll per Establishment	1,639,184	3,427,200	209	Cost per Establishment	5,769,015	14,581,600	253
Payroll per Employee	39,053	35,700	91	Cost per Employee	137,446	151,892	111
Production Workers per Establishment	30	71	241	Cost per Production Worker	195,506	204,798	105
Wages per Establishment	694,845	1,995,120	287	Shipments per Establishment	11,158,348	29,085,600	261
Wages per Production Worker	23,548	28,021	119	Shipments per Employee	265,847	302,975	114
Hours per Production Worker	1,980	1,831	92	Shipments per Production Worker	378,144	408,506	108
Wages per Hour	11.89	15.30	129	Investment per Establishment	361,338	475,200	132
Value Added per Establishment	5,381,325	14,439,200	268	Investment per Employee	8,609	4,950	57
Value Added per Employee	128,210	150,408	117	Investment per Production Worker	12,245	6,674	55

Sources: Same as General Statistics. The 'Average of All Manufacturing' column represents the average of all manufacturing industries reported for the most recent complete year available. The Index shows the relationship between the Average and the Analyzed Industry. For example, 100 means that they are equal; 500 that the Analyzed Industry is five times the average; 50 means that the Analyzed Industry is half the national average. The abbreviation 'na' is used to show that data are 'not available'. Ratios shown for 2002, the last complete census year.

LEADING COMPANIES   Number shown: **75**   Total sales ($ mil): **63,108**   Total employment (000): **247.2**

Company Name	Address				CEO Name	Phone	Co. Type	Sales ($ mil)	Empl. (000)
Illinois Tool Works Inc.	3600 W Lake Ave.	Glenview	IL	60025		847-724-7500	P	16,171	60.0
Danaher Corp.	2099 Penn. Avenue	Washington	DC	20006	H. Lawrence Culp Jr.	202-828-0850	P	11,026	50.0
Smith International Inc.	PO Box 60068	Houston	TX	77205		281-443-3370	P	8,764	19.9
Black and Decker Corp.	101 Schilling Rd.	Hunt Valley	MD	21031	Nolan D. Archibald	410-716-3900	P	6,563	25.0
Cooper Industries Ltd.	PO Box 4446	Houston	TX	77210	Kirk S. Hachigian	713-209-8400	P	5,903	31.5
Stanley Works	PO Box 700	New Britain	CT	06053		860-225-5111	P	4,484	18.4
Pentair Inc.	5500 Wayzata Blvd.	Golden Valley	MN	55416	Winslow H. Buxton	763-545-1730	P	3,399	16.0
Snap-On Inc.	PO Box 1410	Kenosha	WI	53141	Tim Chambers	262-656-5200	P	2,841	11.6
Blount Inc.	PO Box 22127	Portland	OR	97269	James S. Osterman	503-653-8881	S	583*	3.0
Anchor Lamina America Inc.	PO Box 2540	Farmington Hls	MI	48333	Roy Verstraete	248-489-9122	R	500*	<0.1
Matco Tools Corp.	4403 Allen Rd.	Stow	OH	44224		330-929-4949	D	467*	0.5
Wacker Corp.	N92 Anthony	Menomonee Fls	WI	53051	Christopher Barnard	262-255-0500	R	156*	0.5
Sullair Corp.	3700 E Michigan	Michigan City	IN	46360	Henry Brook	219-879-5451	S	140*	0.7
Great Neck Saw Manufacturers	PO Box 3	Mineola	NY	11501		516-746-5352	R	138*	0.4
Duo-Fast Corp.	2400 Galvin Dr.	Elgin	IL	60123		847-634-1900	S	136*	0.9
Charles Machine Works Inc.	PO Box 66	Perry	OK	73077	Ed Malzahn	580-336-4402	R	132*	1.2
Clausing Industrial Inc.	1819 N Pitcher St.	Kalamazoo	MI	49007		269-345-7155	R	125*	<0.1
JH Fletcher and Co.	PO Box 2187	Huntington	WV	25722	Sammons Duncan	304-525-7811	R	120*	0.2
P and F Industries Inc.	445 Broadhollow	Melville	NY	11747	Richard A. Horowitz	631-694-9800	P	112	0.2
Sioux Tools Inc.	250 Snap-On Dr.	Murphy	NC	28906	Mark Pozzoni	828-835-9765	S	100*	0.5
Ryobi Technologies Inc.	1428 Pearman Dairy	Anderson	SC	29625	Jeffrey Dils	864-226-6511	R	64*	0.3
Dynabrade Inc.	8989 Sheridan Dr.	Clarence	NY	14031	Walter Welsch	716-631-0100	R	56*	0.2
Triumph Twist Drill Company	PO Box 9000	Crystal Lake	IL	60039	Arthur Beck	815-459-6250	R	56*	0.5
Caterpillar Work Tools Inc.	PO Box 6	Wamego	KS	66547		785-456-2224	S	52*	0.3
Freud America Inc.	PO Box 7187	High Point	NC	27264	Russell Kohl	336-434-3171	R	51*	0.1
Continental Machines Inc.	5505 W 123rd St.	Savage	MN	55378	M Johnson	952-890-3300	R	45*	0.2
Stature Electric Inc.	PO Box 6660	Watertown	NY	13601	Richard D. Smith	315-782-5910	S	42*	0.3
Hycalog	7211 N Gessner Dr.	Houston	TX	77036	John Deane	713-934-6600	D	40*	0.3
Int'l Staple and Machine	PO Box 629	Butler	PA	16003	Farhad Gerannayeh		R	40*	0.2
Hoffco/Comet Industries Inc.	358 NW F Street	Richmond	IN	47374	John Bratt	765-966-8161	R	35*	0.2
Zircon Corp.	1580 Dell Ave.	Campbell	CA	95008		408-866-8600	R	31*	<0.1
Micro-Aire Surgical Instrument	Lock Box 96565	Chicago	IL	60693	Frank Altenhofen	434-975-8000	R	28*	0.2
Olympia Group Inc.	PO Box 90490	City of Industry	CA	91715	David Cartwright	626-336-4999	R	26*	0.2
Kennametal Inc.	378 Main Street	Lyndonville	VT	05851	Carlos M. Cardoso	802-626-3331	D	26*	0.3
Brunner and Lay Inc.	PO Box 1190	Springdale	AR	72765	Fred Brunner	479-756-0880	R	25*	0.1
Saw Daily Service Inc.	4481 Firestone Blvd	South Gate	CA	90280	Greg Daily	323-564-1791	R	24*	<0.1
Saw Southern Service L.P.	PO Box 11000	Atlanta	GA	30310	Peter Boyle	404-752-7000	R	24*	0.2
Ardisam Inc.	PO Box 666	Cumberland	WI	54829	Ron Ruppel	715-822-2415	R	24*	0.1
Jefferson City Tool Co.	6530 Poe Ave.	Dayton	OH	45377	John R. Folkerth	937-898-6070	S	23*	<0.1
Shopsmith Woodworking Centers	6530 Poe Ave.	Dayton	OH	45414	John R. Folkerth	937-898-6070	S	23*	<0.1
Diamond Z Trailer Inc.	11299 Bass Ln.	Caldwell	ID	83605	Robert Marshall	208-585-2929	R	23*	0.1
Powernail Co.	1300 Rose Rd.	Lake Zurich	IL	60047	Tom Anstett	847-634-3000	R	22*	<0.1
Carlton Co.	PO Box 68309	Portland	OR	97268	Russ German	503-659-8911	R	21*	0.1
Zephyr Manufacturing Company	PO Box 759	Inglewood	CA	90307	Bernard Kersulis	310-410-4907	R	20*	0.1
Broderson Manufacturing Corp.	PO Box 14770	Shawnee Msn	KS	66285	Polly Broderson	913-888-0606	R	20*	<0.1
Daniels Manufacturing Corp.	PO Box 593872	Orlando	FL	32859	George Daniels	407-855-6161	R	20*	0.2
Fabco-Air Inc.	PO Box 5159	Gainesville	FL	32627	William Schmidt	352-373-3578	R	20*	<0.1
Alden Corp.	PO Box 6262	Wolcott	CT	06716	Yvon Desaulniers	203-879-4889	R	19*	<0.1
Florida Pneumatic Mfg. Corp.	851 Jupiter Park Ln	Jupiter	FL	33458	Bart Swank	561-744-9500	S	18*	<0.1
Diamond Mk Products Inc.	PO Box 2803	Torrance	CA	90509	Robert Delahaut	310-539-5221	R	18*	0.2
Roper Whitney of Rockford Inc.	2833 Huffman Blvd.	Rockford	IL	61103	David Casazza	815-962-3011	R	17*	0.1
Vulcan Company Inc.	PO Box 36	Hingham	MA	02043	Alexander Clark	781-337-5970	R	16*	<0.1
Williams Tool Company Inc.	PO Box 180310	Fort Smith	AR	72918		479-646-8866	S	16*	<0.1
American Pneumatic Tool Inc.	14710 Maple Ave.	Gardena	CA	90248	Ken Evans	310-538-2600	R	15*	0.1
George Jue Manufacturing Co.	8140 Rosecrans Ave.	Paramount	CA	90723	George Jue	562-634-8180	R	15*	<0.1
Gougler Industries Inc.	PO Box 807	Kent	OH	44240	Larry Wittensoldner	330-673-5821	R	14*	<0.1
Carbide Technologies Inc.	18101 Malyn Blvd.	Fraser	MI	48026	Bernice Souris	586-296-5200	R	14*	0.1
Wisconsin Machine Tool Corp.	3225 Gateway Rd.	Brookfield	WI	53045	Patrick Cherone	262-317-3048	R	14*	0.1
Merrick Machine Co.	PO Box 188	Alda	NE	68810	Richard Merrick	308-384-1780	R	14*	<0.1
Thomas C Wilson Inc.	2111 44th Ave.	Long Island Cty	NY	11101	Charles Hanley	718-729-3360	R	14*	<0.1
NNT Corp.	1320 Norwood Ave.	Itasca	IL	60143	David Nyc	630-875-9600	R	14*	<0.1
Adhesive Technologies Inc.	3 Merrill Indu. Dr.	Hampton	NH	03842		603-926-1616	R	13*	<0.1
Hougen Manufacturing Inc.	PO Box 2005	Flint	MI	48501	Randall Hougen	810-635-7111	R	13*	0.1
S and G Tool Aid Corp.	43 E Alpine St.	Newark	NJ	07114	George Gering	973-824-7730	R	13*	<0.1
Garden Valley Coop.	PO Box 338	Alma	WI	54610	Joel Fenbobach	608-685-4481	R	13*	<0.1
Ace Drill Corp.	PO Box 160	Adrian	MI	49221	Alfred Brown	517-265-5184	R	12*	<0.1
Master Tool Company Inc.	PO Box 189	Grand River	OH	44045	John Cirino	440-354-0600	R	11*	<0.1
Hannibal Carbide Tool Inc.	PO Box 954	Hannibal	MO	63401	Kathryn Kapfer	573-221-2775	R	11*	0.1
Lie-Nielsen Toolworks Inc.	PO Box 9	Warren	ME	04864	Thomas Lie-Nielsen	207-273-2520	R	10*	<0.1
Pan American Tool Corp.	5990 NW 31st Ave.	Fort Lauderdale	FL	33309	Bert Leon	954-735-8665	R	10*	<0.1
Ohio Drill and Tool Co.	23255 Georgetown	Homeworth	OH	44634	Connie Hallman	330-525-7717	R	10*	<0.1
Apex Machine Tool Co.	1790 New Britain	Farmington	CT	06034	Edward McNerney	860-677-2884	D	9*	0.1
Stanley Fastening Systems Inc.	1 Briggs Dr., Rt. 2	East Greenwich	RI	02818	John H. Garlock, Jr	401-884-2500	D	9*	<0.1
Diedrich Drill Inc.	5 Fisher St.	La Porte	IN	46350	James Lange	219-326-7788	R	9*	<0.1
Relton Corp.	PO Box 60019	Arcadia	CA	91066	Craig Kinard	626-446-8201	R	9*	<0.1

Source: *Ward's Business Directory of U.S. Private and Public Companies*, Volumes 1 and 2, 2008. The company type code used is as follows: P - Public, R - Private, S - Subsidiary, D - Division, J - Joint Venture, A - Affiliate, G - Group. Sales are in millions of dollars, employees are in thousands. An asterisk (*) indicates an estimated sales volume. The symbol < stands for 'less than'. Company names and addresses are truncated, in some cases, to fit into the available space.

MATERIALS CONSUMED

Material	Quantity	Delivered Cost ($ million)
Metal bolts, nuts, screws, and other screw machine products	(X)	19.9
Other fabricated metal products (exc. fluid power products and forgings)	(X)	139.5
Forgings	(X)	45.6
Iron and steel castings (rough and semifinished)	(X)	89.3
Aluminum and aluminum-base alloy castings (rough and semifinished)	(X)	101.0
Other nonferrous metal castings, rough or semifinished (inc. aluminum)	(X)	9.7
Steel bars, bar shapes, and plates (exc. castings, forgings, fabr. metal products)	(X)	25.0
All other steel shapes and forms (exc. castings, forgings, fabr. metal products)	(X)	49.7
Nonferrous shapes and forms	(X)	2.3
Insulated copper wire and cable (excluding magnet wire)	(X)	16.0
Magnet wire	(X)	26.9
Electric motors and generators	(X)	146.2
Storage batteries	(X)	(D)
Ball and roller bearings (mounted or unmounted)	(X)	(D)
Mechanical speed changers, gears, and industrial high-speed drives	(X)	33.9
Fabricated plastics products (excluding gaskets)	(X)	138.9
Paperboard containers, boxes, and corrugated paperboard	(X)	39.2
Packaging paper and plastics film, coated and laminated	(X)	20.6
All other materials, components, parts, containers, and supplies	(X)	609.6
Materials, ingredients, containers, and supplies, nsk	(X)	5.0

Source: 2002 *Economic Census*. Explanation of symbols used: (D): Withheld to avoid disclosure of competitive data; na: Not available; (S): Withheld because statistical norms were not met; (X): Not applicable; (Z): Less than half the unit shown; nec: Not elsewhere classified; nsk: Not specified by kind; - : zero; p : 10-19 percent estimated; q : 20-29 percent estimated.

PRODUCT SHARE DETAILS

Product or Product Class Shipments	Mil. $	Product or Product Class Shipments	Mil. $
POWER-DRIVEN HAND TOOLS	3,276.7	Electric hand jig and saber saws, armature mounted on other than ball bearings (except battery powered)	(D)
Power-driven handtools, pneumatic, hydraulic, and power-actuated	**1,086.1**	Electric hand reciprocating saws (except battery-powered)	(D)
Power-driven handtools, pneumatic, hydraulic and power-actuated	1,073.3	Electric hand circular saws, armature mounted primarily on other than sleeve bearings, 7 in. (177.80 mm) blade or less (except battery-powered)	3.8
Pneumatic percussion handtools (such as runners, riveters, chippers, scalers)	71.2	Electric hand circular saws, armature mounted primarily on other than sleeve bearings, more than 7 in. (177.80 mm) to less than 8 in. (203.20 mm) blade (except battery-powered)	107.8
Pneumatic drills, screwdrivers, and nut-runners	77.6		
Pneumatic hand impact wrenches	(D)	Electric hand circular saws, armature mounted primarily on other than sleeve bearings, 8 in. (203.20 mm) blade or more (except battery-powered)	29.6
Pneumatic rotary hand grinders, polishers, and sanders	43.0		
Other pneumatic hand grinders, polishers, and sanders	19.6	Electric hammers, percussion and rotary, without drill chuck (except battery-powered)	2.5
Pneumatic hand staplers	51.0		
Pneumatic hand nailers	265.9	Electric screwdrivers and nut-runners (except battery-powered)	34.4
Other pneumatic-powered handtools	114.5		
Parts, attachments, and accessories for pneumatic-powered handtools (sold separately)	167.4	Electric hand right angle polishers, circular sanders, and grinders, less than 7 in. wheel drive (except battery-powered)	65.3
Power-actuated handtools and parts	(D)		
Hydraulic power-driven handtools	77.9	Electric hand impact wrenches (except battery-powered)	23.0
Parts, attachments, and accessories for hydraulic handtools	(D)	Electric hand right angle polishers, circular sanders, and grinders, 7 in. wheel drive or more (except battery-powered)	(D)
Power-driven handtools, pneumatic, hydraulic, and powder-actuated, nsk	12.8		
Power-driven handtools, internal combustion engine driven, including parts	**(D)**	Electric hand shears and nibblers (except battery-powered)	11.4
Internal combustion engine driven chain saws	(D)	All other electric hand polishers, circular sanders, and grinders (including die grinders, but excluding bench) (except battery-powered)	5.9
Other internal combustion engine-driven handtools, including cut-off saws and drills	(D)		
Parts, attachments, and accessories for internal combustion engine-driven chain saws	(D)	Electric hand planers (except battery-powered)	12.3
		Electric hand belt sanders (except battery-powered)	33.5
Parts, attachments, and accessories for internal combustion engine-driven tools, nec	(D)	Parts, attachments, and accessories for electric-powered handtools (except battery powered) (sold separately)	105.4
Power-driven handtools, battery-powered (cordless), including parts	**(D)**	Electric hand chain saws (except battery-powered)	(D)
Battery-powered (cordless) screwdrivers (without 3-jaw chuck)	(D)	Electric hand oscillating, reciprocating, vibrating, and random orbit sanders (except battery powered)	(D)
Battery-powered (cordless) driver-drills	352.6	Other electric-powered handtools (except battery-powered)	334.0
Battery-powered (cordless) drills	(D)		
Battery-powered, cordless handsaws	(D)		
Other battery-powered (cordless) handtools	204.0		
Parts, attachments, and accessories for battery-powered (cordless) handtools (sold separately)	10.4	Electric hand routers, less than one-half inch collet size (maximum collet capacity) (except battery-powered)	68.5
Power-driven handtools, electric (excluding battery-powered), including parts	**1,329.8**	Electric hand routers, one-half inch collet size (maximum collet capacity) or more (except battery-powered)	63.1
Drills (excluding battery powered)	122.5		
Electric hand jig and saber saws, armature mounted on ball bearings (except battery-powered)	39.0	**Power-driven handtools, nsk, total**	**29.5**
Electric hand circular saws, armature mounted primarily on sleeve bearings (except battery-powered)	(D)		

Source: 2002 *Economic Census*. The values are product shipments in millions of dollars for 2002. Total product shipments may be lower or higher than industry shipments. See Introduction for a full discussion. Values of indented subcategories are summed in the main heading(s). The symbol (D) appears when data are withheld to prevent disclosure of competitive information. The abbreviation nsk stands for 'not specified by kind' and nec for 'not elsewhere classified'. A dash (-) means zero.

INPUTS AND OUTPUTS FOR POWER-DRIVEN HANDTOOL MANUFACTURING

Economic Sector or Industry Providing Inputs	%	Sector	Economic Sector or Industry Buying Outputs	%	Sector
Compensation of employees	16.8		Private fixed investment	51.9	
Wholesale trade	5.1	Trade	Personal consumption expenditures	27.9	
Motors & generators	4.1	Manufg.	Exports of goods & services	9.5	Cap Inv
Plastics products, nec	4.0	Manufg.	General S/L govt. services	2.0	S/L Govt
Plastics packaging materials, film & sheet	3.7	Manufg.	Nonresidential structures, nec	1.8	Construct.
Nonferrous metal foundries	3.5	Manufg.	Change in private inventories	1.5	In House
Storage batteries	3.2	Manufg.	Residential structures, nec	0.9	Construct.
Management of companies & enterprises	2.9	Services	S/L govt. invest., education	0.7	S/L Govt
Ferrous metal foundries	2.5	Manufg.	Telecommunications	0.5	Services
Iron & steel mills & ferroalloys	2.0	Manufg.	Residential permanent site structures	0.5	Construct.
Cutting tools & machine tool accessories	2.0	Manufg.	Food services & drinking places	0.4	Services
Machine shops	1.9	Manufg.	Commercial & health care structures	0.3	Construct.
Ball & roller bearings	1.6	Manufg.	Natural gas distribution	0.3	Util.
Forging, stamping, & sintering, nec	1.4	Manufg.	Owner-occupied dwellings	0.3	
Speed changers, industrial high-speed drives, & gears	1.3	Manufg.	Maintenance/repair of nonresidential structures	0.3	Construct.
Paperboard containers	1.2	Manufg.	Oil & gas extraction	0.2	Mining
Copper rolling, drawing, extruding, & alloying	1.1	Manufg.	S/L govt. invest., other	0.2	S/L Govt
Turned products & screws, nuts, & bolts	1.0	Manufg.	Dairy cattle & milk	0.1	Agric.
Truck transportation	1.0	Util.	Miscellaneous crops	0.1	Agric.
Semiconductors & related devices	0.9	Manufg.			
Coating, engraving, heat treating & allied activities	0.8	Manufg.			
Printed circuit assemblies (electronic assembiles)	0.8	Manufg.			
Advertising & related services	0.7	Services			
Abrasive products	0.7	Manufg.			
Power generation & supply	0.5	Util.			
Real estate	0.5	Fin/R.E.			
Metal cans, boxes, & other containers (light gauge)	0.4	Manufg.			
Fabricated metals, nec	0.3	Manufg.			
Converted paper products, nec	0.3	Manufg.			
Specialized design services	0.3	Services			
Maintenance/repair of nonresidential structures	0.3	Construct.			
Securities, commodity contracts, investments	0.3	Fin/R.E.			
Valve & fittings other than plumbing	0.2	Manufg.			
Plate work & fabricated structural products	0.2	Manufg.			
Crowns & closures & metal stamping	0.2	Manufg.			
Taxes on production & imports, less subsidies	0.2				
Motor vehicle parts	0.2	Manufg.			
Services to buildings & dwellings	0.2	Services			
Laminated plastics plates, sheets, & shapes	0.2	Manufg.			
Legal services	0.2	Services			
Rubber products, nec	0.2	Manufg.			
Custom roll forming	0.2	Manufg.			
Handtools	0.2	Manufg.			
Custom computer programming services	0.2	Services			
Communication & energy wires & cables	0.2	Manufg.			
Noncomparable imports	0.2	Foreign			
Postal service	0.2	Util.			
Automotive equipment rental & leasing	0.2	Fin/R.E.			
Employment services	0.2	Services			
Lessors of nonfinancial assets	0.2	Fin/R.E.			
Automotive repair & maintenance, ex. car washes	0.2	Services			
Telecommunications	0.2	Services			
Scientific research & development services	0.2	Services			
Commercial & industrial equipment repair/maintenance	0.1	Services			
Warehousing & storage	0.1	Util.			
Business support services	0.1	Services			
Architectural, engineering, & related services	0.1	Services			
Relay & industrial controls	0.1	Manufg.			
Bare printed circuit boards	0.1	Manufg.			
Paperboard mills	0.1	Manufg.			

Source: Benchmark Input-Output Accounts for the U.S. Economy, 2002, U.S. Department of Commerce, Washington, D.C., January 2008. The abbreviation nec stands for 'not elsewhere classified'.

OCCUPATIONS EMPLOYED BY OTHER GENERAL-PURPOSE MACHINERY MANUFACTURING

Occupation	% of Total 2006	Change to 2016	Occupation	% of Total 2006	Change to 2016
Team assemblers	11.0	-9.7	Multiple machine tool operators & tenders	1.4	-0.7
Machinists	5.9	-5.2	Lathe & turning machine tool operators & tenders	1.4	-18.8
Welders, cutters, solderers, & brazers	5.7	-4.0	Maintenance & repair workers, general	1.4	-9.7
First-line supervisors/managers of production workers	3.6	-9.7	Structural metal fabricators & fitters	1.4	-9.7
Mechanical engineers	2.8	-0.7	Industrial engineers	1.3	9.6
Computer-controlled machine tool operators	2.5	-0.7	Electrical & electronic equipment assemblers	1.3	-27.8
Sales reps, wholesale & manufacturing, exc tech	2.3	-9.7	Industrial machinery mechanics	1.3	3.8
Engine & other machine assemblers	2.0	-9.7	Mechanical drafters	1.3	-8.7
Inspectors, testers, sorters, samplers, & weighers	1.9	-14.9	Customer service representatives	1.3	-0.7
Cutting, punching, & press machine operators	1.8	-18.8	Coating, painting, & spraying machine operators	1.2	-14.2
Shipping, receiving, & traffic clerks	1.8	-13.1	Office clerks, general	1.2	-11.1
Helpers--Production workers	1.6	-9.7	Industrial production managers	1.1	-9.7
General & operations managers	1.6	-18.8	Electrical engineers	1.1	-9.7
Laborers & freight, stock, & material movers, hand	1.5	-18.8	Production, planning, & expediting clerks	1.1	-9.7
Purchasing agents, exc wholesale, retail, & farm	1.5	-18.8	Stock clerks & order fillers	1.0	-24.5
Bookkeeping, accounting, & auditing clerks	1.5	-9.7			

Source: Industry-Occupation Matrix, Bureau of Labor Statistics, December 4, 2007. These data are reported based on 4-digit NAICS categories but have been matched to corresponding 6-digit NAICS industry codes. The change reported for each occupation to the year 2016 is a percent of growth or decline as estimated by the Bureau of Labor Statistics. The abbreviation nec stands for 'not elsewhere classified'.

LOCATION BY STATE AND REGIONAL CONCENTRATION

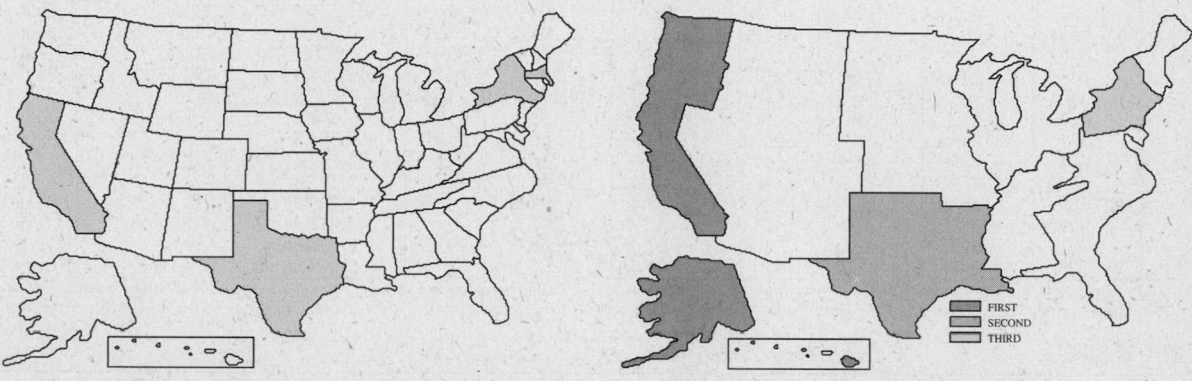

FIRST
SECOND
THIRD

INDUSTRY DATA BY STATE

State	Establish-ments	Shipments			Employment				Cost as % of Shipments	Investment per Employee ($)
		Total ($ mil)	% of U.S.	Per Establ.	Total Number	% of U.S.	Per Establ.	Wages ($/hour)		
New York	6	55.9	1.5	9,312.3	311	2.6	52	16.59	39.6	2,543
Texas	7	47.1	1.3	6,722.3	293	2.4	42	19.52	34.1	1,082
Massachusetts	5	39.1	1.1	7,818.0	192	1.6	38	18.07	42.3	6,063
California	14	31.2	0.9	2,228.5	219	1.8	16	19.31	28.2	1,950

Source: 2002 Economic Census. The states are in descending order of shipments or establishments (if shipment data are missing for the majority). The symbol (D) appears when data are withheld to prevent disclosure of competitive information. States marked with (D) are sorted by number of establishments. A dash (-) indicates that the data element cannot be calculated. Data may not show all states active in the NAICS category. All data available at the time of publication are shown.

NAICS 333993 - PACKAGING MACHINERY MANUFACTURING

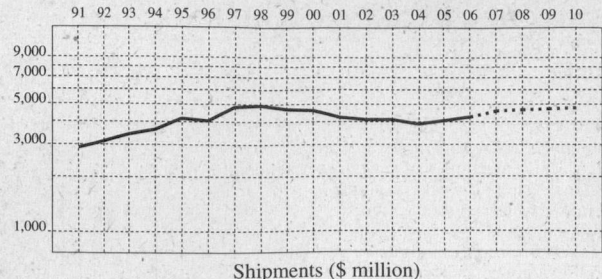

Shipments ($ million)

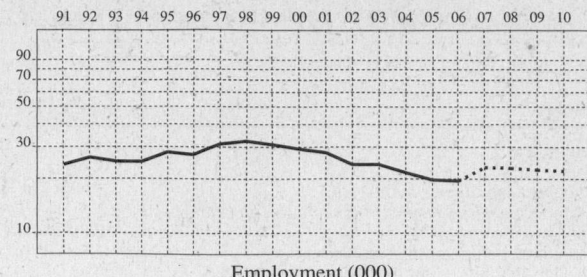

Employment (000)

GENERAL STATISTICS

Year	Companies	Establishments		Employment			Compensation		Production ($ million)			
		Total	with 20 or more employees	Total (000)	Production Workers (000)	Hours (Mil)	Payroll ($ mil)	Wages ($/hr)	Cost of Materials	Value Added by Manufacture	Value of Shipments	Capital Invest.
1991		478	241	23.9	13.7	28.1	797.2	13.99	1,222.4	1,627.0	2,879.9	68.4
1992	590	631	264	26.2	15.4	31.0	894.4	13.79	1,252.4	1,913.5	3,126.9	70.1
1993		633	265	24.9	14.2	29.2	899.5	14.29	1,378.4	2,010.0	3,418.2	90.2
1994		626	270	24.8	14.9	30.2	895.4	14.52	1,563.2	2,120.2	3,620.9	98.6
1995		629	271	28.0	16.9	34.3	1,013.0	14.69	1,831.7	2,447.4	4,184.7	87.0
1996		647	277	27.2	16.3	33.3	1,015.0	14.68	1,726.0	2,304.6	4,055.8	111.4
1997	643	688	306	31.2	16.9	34.0	1,242.8	15.96	2,086.0	2,657.3	4,820.2	122.3
1998		684	302	32.4	17.2	34.6	1,307.9	15.83	2,171.4	2,730.7	4,928.3	113.2
1999		655	292	31.0	16.3	33.7	1,294.4	15.91	2,220.0	2,488.4	4,689.8	92.1
2000		646	288	29.3	16.1	33.0	1,263.4	16.17	2,090.0	2,528.7	4,615.6	87.4
2001		643	274	27.9	14.7	30.1	1,207.9	16.89	1,894.4	2,259.1	4,229.6	73.7
2002	624	660	258	24.0	11.8	23.7	1,141.2	19.06	1,752.1	2,341.0	4,107.8	80.1
2003		668	267	24.0	12.1	24.6	1,138.3	18.31	1,680.2	2,460.9	4,113.0	54.8
2004		651	246	21.7	10.6	21.6	1,087.7	19.02	1,594.3	2,324.9	3,889.8	44.2
2005		641	249	19.8	10.3	21.2	1,016.5	19.61	1,757.4	2,353.3	4,064.3	76.7
2006		684P	269P	19.5	10.2	21.6	1,054.5	19.84	1,843.8	2,382.7	4,249.8	156.3
2007		689P	269P	23.2P	11.3P	23.4P	1,224.5P	20.06P	1,989.2P	2,570.7P	4,585.0P	90.9P
2008		695P	269P	22.9P	11.0P	22.7P	1,241.6P	20.49P	2,015.9P	2,605.1P	4,646.5P	91.1P
2009		701P	269P	22.5P	10.7P	22.0P	1,258.6P	20.92P	2,042.6P	2,639.6P	4,708.1P	91.3P
2010		706P	268P	22.2P	10.3P	21.4P	1,275.7P	21.35P	2,069.3P	2,674.1P	4,769.6P	91.5P

Sources: 1992, 1997, 2002 *Economic Census*; other years, up to 2006, are from the *Annual Survey of Manufactures*. Establishment counts for non-Census years are from *County Business Patterns*; 1997 and 2002 values are from the 1997 and 2002 censuses respectively, reported in the Federal Government's NAICS format. Other years were originally reported in equivalent SIC format. 'P's show projections by the editors.

INDICES OF CHANGE

Year	Companies	Establishments		Employment			Compensation		Production ($ million)			
		Total	with 20 or more employees	Total (000)	Production Workers (000)	Hours (Mil)	Payroll ($ mil)	Wages ($/hr)	Cost of Materials	Value Added by Manufacture	Value of Shipments	Capital Invest.
1992	95	96	102	109	131	131	78	72	71	82	76	88
1997	103	104	119	130	143	143	109	84	119	114	117	153
2001		97	106	116	125	127	106	89	108	97	103	92
2002	100	100	100	100	100	100	100	100	100	100	100	100
2003		101	103	100	103	104	100	96	96	105	100	68
2004		99	95	90	90	91	95	100	91	99	95	55
2005		97	97	83	87	89	89	103	100	101	99	96
2006		104P	104P	81	86	91	92	104	105	102	103	195
2007		104P	104P	97P	96P	99P	107P	105P	114P	110P	112P	113P
2008		105P	104P	95P	93P	96P	109P	108P	115P	111P	113P	114P
2009		106P	104P	94P	91P	93P	110P	110P	117P	113P	115P	114P
2010		107P	104P	93P	87P	90P	112P	112P	118P	114P	116P	114P

Sources: Same as General Statistics. Values reflect change from the base year, 2002. Values above 100 mean greater than 2002, values below 100 mean less than 2002, and the values of 100 in other years means the same as 2002. 'P's show projections by the editors.

SELECTED RATIOS

For 2002	Avg. of All Manufact.	Analyzed Industry	Index	For 2002	Avg. of All Manufact.	Analyzed Industry	Index
Employees per Establishment	42	36	87	Value Added per Production Worker	182,367	198,390	109
Payroll per Establishment	1,639,184	1,729,091	105	Cost per Establishment	5,769,015	2,654,697	46
Payroll per Employee	39,053	47,550	122	Cost per Employee	137,446	73,004	53
Production Workers per Establishment	30	18	61	Cost per Production Worker	195,506	148,483	76
Wages per Establishment	694,845	684,427	99	Shipments per Establishment	11,158,348	6,223,939	56
Wages per Production Worker	23,548	38,282	163	Shipments per Employee	265,847	171,158	64
Hours per Production Worker	1,980	2,008	101	Shipments per Production Worker	378,144	348,119	92
Wages per Hour	11.89	19.06	160	Investment per Establishment	361,338	121,364	34
Value Added per Establishment	5,381,325	3,546,970	66	Investment per Employee	8,609	3,338	39
Value Added per Employee	128,210	97,542	76	Investment per Production Worker	12,245	6,788	55

Sources: Same as General Statistics. The 'Average of All Manufacturing' column represents the average of all manufacturing industries reported for the most recent complete year available. The Index shows the relationship between the Average and the Analyzed Industry. For example, 100 means that they are equal; 500 that the Analyzed Industry is five times the average; 50 means that the Analyzed Industry is half the national average. The abbreviation 'na' is used to show that data are 'not available'. Ratios shown for 2002, the last complete census year.

LEADING COMPANIES   Number shown: 75   Total sales ($ mil): 43,109   Total employment (000): 146.7

Company Name	Address				CEO Name	Phone	Co. Type	Sales ($ mil)	Empl. (000)
Illinois Tool Works Inc.	3600 W Lake Ave.	Glenview	IL	60025		847-724-7500	P	16,171	60.0
Dover Corp.	280 Park Ave.	New York	NY	10017		212-922-1640	P	7,226	33.4
Avery Dennison Corp.	150 N Orange Grove	Pasadena	CA	91103	Kent Kresa	626-304-2000	P	6,308	22.7
Bemis Company Inc.	PO Box 669	Neenah	WI	54957	Jeffrey H. Curler	920-727-4100	P	3,649	15.7
Huhtamaki Consumer Packaging	9201 Packaging Dr.	De Soto	KS	66018	Kalle Tanhuanpaa	913-583-3025	R	2,910*	0.3
Elopak Inc.	30000 S Hill Rd.	New Hudson	MI	48165	Robert Gillis	248-486-4600	R	1,000*	0.1
Pneumatic Scale Corp.	10 Ascot Pkwy.	Cuyahoga Falls	OH	44223	Robert Chapman	330-923-0491	S	786*	0.2
Accraply Inc.	PO Box 95635	Chicago	IL	60694	Gregory Tschida	763-557-1313	S	786*	<0.1
Sub-Zero Inc.	4717 Hammersley	Madison	WI	53711	James Bakke	608-271-2233	R	758*	3.0
Lepel Corp.	200 Executive Dr.	Edgewood	NY	11717	Vladimir Pilic	631-586-3300	R	556*	<0.1
Tegrant Alloyd Brands Inc.	PO Box 627	Dekalb	IL	60115	Ron Leach	815-756-8451	R	325*	0.3
KHS-Bartelt	5501 N Washington	Sarasota	FL	34243	Mike Brancato	941-359-4000	R	251*	0.6
Sumitomo Heavy Ind. (USA)	4200 Holland Blvd.	Chesapeake	VA	23322	Yoshio Hinoh	757-485-3355	S	150*	0.3
Evergreen Packaging Equipment	PO Box 3000	Cedar Rapids	IA	52406		319-399-3200	D	143*	0.3
NYX Inc.	30111 Schoolcraft	Livonia	MI	48150		734-421-3850	R	136*	0.2
Bulman Products Inc.	1650 McReynolds	Grand Rapids	MI	49504		616-363-4416	R	124*	<0.1
Winpak Portion Packaging Inc.	828A N Yardley	Newtown	PA	18940	Thomas Herlihy	267-685-8200	R	119*	<0.1
Centis Custom Products	205 S Puente St.	Brea	CA	92821	Bill Stemph	714-626-2218	R	113*	0.2
Fres-co System USA Inc.	3005 State Rd.	Telford	PA	18969	Tullio Vigano	215-721-4600	R	100*	0.3
CG Bretting Manufacturing Inc.	PO Box 113	Ashland	WI	54806	David Bretting	715-682-5231	R	96*	0.5
RA Jones and Company Inc.	2701 Crescent Sprng	Covington	KY	41017	Gordon Bonfield	859-344-7120	R	63*	0.4
Hartness International Inc.	PO Box 26509	Greenville	SC	29616	Thomas Hartness	864-297-1200	R	58*	0.4
Angelus Sanitary Can Machine	4900 Pacific Blvd.	Los Angeles	CA	90058	Maury Koeberle	323-583-2171	R	56*	0.5
Doboy Inc.	869 S Knowles Ave.	New Richmond	WI	54017	William Heilhecker	715-246-6511	R	50*	0.2
Lantechcom L.L.C.	11000 Bluegrass Pky	Louisville	KY	40299	James Lancaster	502-267-4200	R	46*	0.3
Douglas Machine Inc.	3404 Iowa St.	Alexandria	MN	56308	Vernon Anderson	320-763-6587	R	44*	0.4
Sekisui Ta Industries L.L.C.	7100 Belgrave Ave.	Garden Grove	CA	92841		714-890-3340	R	42*	0.2
Hayssen Inc.	225 Spartangreen	Duncan	SC	29334	Robert Chapman	864-486-4000	S	40*	0.3
Hollymatic Corp.	600 E Plainfield Rd	La Grange	IL	60525	James Azzar	708-579-3700	R	37*	<0.1
Tolco Corp.	1920 Linwood Ave.	Toledo	OH	43604	William Spengler	419-241-1113	R	37*	<0.1
Acma USA Inc.	501 Southlake Blvd.	Richmond	VA	23236		804-794-9777	D	36*	0.2
Nercon Eng and Manufacturing	PO Box 2288	Oshkosh	WI	54903	James Nerenhausen	920-233-3268	R	34*	0.1
Univenture Inc.	13311 Indu. Pkwy.	Marysville	OH	43040	Michele Cole	937-645-4600	R	33*	0.2
Packaging Technologies Inc.	PO Box 3848	Davenport	IA	52808	Barry Shoulders	563-391-1100	R	30*	0.2
Chantland-Pvs Co.	PO Box 69	Humboldt	IA	50548	Don Sosnoski	515-332-4040	R	28*	0.2
Klikwood Corp.	5224 Snapfinger	Decatur	GA	30035	Peter Black	770-981-5200	R	28*	0.2
Martin Automatic Inc.	1661 Northrock Ct.	Rockford	IL	61103	Roger Cederholm	815-654-4800	R	28*	0.2
Great Lakes L.L.C.	9511 River St.	Schiller Park	IL	60176		847-678-3668	S	26*	0.2
Heisler Industries Inc.	224 Passaic Ave.	Fairfield	NJ	07004	Richard Heisler	973-227-6300	R	25*	<0.1
Sancoa International Co.	11000 Midlantic Dr.	Mount Laurel	NJ	08054	Joseph Sanski	856-273-0700	R	25*	0.3
WASP Inc.	PO Box 249	Glenwood	MN	56334	Merle Wagner	320-634-5126	R	24*	0.2
Adco Manufacturing Inc.	2170 Academy Ave.	Sanger	CA	93657	Frank Hoffman	559-875-5563	R	24*	0.1
Solid State Equipment Corp.	185 Gibraltar Rd.	Horsham	PA	19044	Richard Richardson	215-328-0700	R	24*	<0.1
R.A. Pearson Company Inc.	8120 W Sunset Hwy.	Spokane	WA	99224	Michael A. Senske	509-838-6226	R	23*	0.2
B and H Manufacturing Company	PO Box 247	Ceres	CA	95307	Calvin Bright	209-537-5785	R	23*	0.2
W.B. McGuire Company Inc.	1 Hudson Ave.	Hudson	NY	12534		518-828-7652	D	23*	0.2
US DigitalMedia	1929 W Lone Cactus	Phoenix	AZ	85027	Chris Pignotti	623-587-4900	R	23*	<0.1
Arpac L.P.	9511 River St.	Schiller Park	IL	60176		847-678-9034	R	21*	0.2
Enviro-Cote Inc.	1350 Home Ave.	Akron	OH	44310	Brian Tavolier	330-633-4700	R	21*	<0.1
Hybricon Corp.	12 Willow Rd.	Ayer	MA	01432	Paul Freve	978-772-5422	R	21*	<0.1
Trans World Services Inc.	PO Box 162	Melrose	MA	02176	Thomas Ford	781-665-9200	R	20*	<0.1
Bedford Ind. of Worthington	PO Box 39	Worthington	MN	56187	Robert Ludlow	507-376-4136	R	20*	0.2
MAF Industries Inc.	PO Box 218	Traver	CA	93673	Thomas Blanc	559-897-2905	R	20*	<0.1
Brenton Engineering Co.	4750 Cnty Rd 13	Alexandria	MN	56308	Jeff Bigger	320-852-7705	R	20*	0.1
Goldco Industries Inc.	5605 Goldco Dr.	Loveland	CO	80538	Richard Vandermeer	970-663-4770	R	19*	<0.1
Nilpeter USA Inc.	11550 Goldcoast Dr.	Cincinnati	OH	45249	Andrew Colletta	513-489-4400	R	18*	0.1
ATMI Packaging Inc.	10851 Louisiana	Bloomington	MN	55438		952-942-0855	S	18*	0.1
Taylor Products Company Inc.	2205 Jothi Ave.	Parsons	KS	67357	Lewis Ribich	620-421-5550	R	18*	<0.1
Specialty Enterprises Co.	6909 Wash. Blvd.	Montebello	CA	90640	Charles Heras	323-726-9721	R	18*	0.1
Paxar International Holdings	105 Corp. Park Dr.	White Plains	NY	10604	Arthur Hershaft	914-697-6800	S	17*	<0.1
Busse Brothers Inc.	124 N Columbus St.	Randolph	WI	53956	Thomas Young	920-326-3131	R	17*	0.1
Heat Seal L.L.C.	4580 E 71st St.	Cleveland	OH	44125	R Skalsky	216-341-2022	R	17*	0.1
Aylward Enterprises Inc.	401 Industrial Dr.	New Bern	NC	28562	John T. Aylward	252-633-5757	R	16*	<0.1
Gdm Electronic Assembly	562 S Milpitas Blvd	Milpitas	CA	95035		408-945-4100	R	15*	0.1
Lane Winpak Inc.	998 S Sierra Way	San Bernardino	CA	92408	William Lane	909-885-0715	R	15*	0.1
Weiler Engineering Inc.	1395 Gateway Dr.	Elgin	IL	60124	Gerhard Weiler	847-697-4900	R	15*	<0.1
Sohn Manufacturing Inc.	544 Sohn Dr.	Elkhart Lake	WI	53020	Wallace Beaudry	920-876-3361	R	15*	<0.1
Ro-An Industries Corp.	6420 Admiral Ave.	Middle Village	NY	11379	Angelo Cervera	718-821-1115	R	15*	<0.1
Computype Inc.	2285 W County Rd.	St. Paul	MN	55113	W.E. Roach	651-633-0633	R	15*	0.3
ID Technology Corp.	2051 Franklin Dr.	Fort Worth	TX	76106			S	15*	<0.1
Euclid Spiral Paper Tube Corp.	PO Box 458	Apple Creek	OH	44606	Leonard Buckner	330-698-4711	R	14*	<0.1
Osgood Industries Inc.	601 Burbank Rd.	Oldsmar	FL	34677	Martin Mueller	813-855-7337	R	14*	<0.1
Metro Machine and Engineering	8001 Wallace Rd.	Eden Prairie	MN	55344	Robert Midness	952-937-2800	R	14*	<0.1
MRM Inc.	102 Cabot St.	Holyoke	MA	01040	William Gregory	413-533-7141	R	13*	<0.1
Haumiller Engineering Co.	445 Renner Dr.	Elgin	IL	60123	Russ Holmer	847-695-9111	R	13*	<0.1

Source: Ward's Business Directory of U.S. Private and Public Companies, Volumes 1 and 2, 2008. The company type code used is as follows: P - Public, R - Private, S - Subsidiary, D - Division, J - Joint Venture, A - Affiliate, G - Group. Sales are in millions of dollars, employees are in thousands. An asterisk (*) indicates an estimated sales volume. The symbol < stands for 'less than'. Company names and addresses are truncated, in some cases, to fit into the available space.

MATERIALS CONSUMED

Material	Quantity	Delivered Cost ($ million)
Fluid power pumps, motors, and hydrostatic transmissions	(X)	9.7
Other fluid power products, hydraulic and pneumatic	(X)	34.9
Mechanical speed changers, gears, and industrial high-speed drives	(X)	27.2
Ball and roller bearings (mounted or unmounted)	(X)	22.0
Other mechanical power transmission equipment	(X)	18.4
Fabricated metal products, including forgings	(X)	129.2
Iron and steel castings (rough and semifinished)	(X)	50.8
Nonferrous (aluminum, copper, etc.) castings (rough and semifinished)	(X)	6.4
Stainless steel shapes and forms (exc. castings, forgings, fabr. metal products)	(X)	17.0
All other steel shapes and forms (exc. castings, forgings, fabr. metal products)	(X)	11.5
Aluminum and aluminum-base alloy shapes and forms (exc. castings, forgings, fabr. metal products)	(X)	12.2
Other nonferrous shapes and forms (exc. castings, forgings, fabricated metal products)	(X)	4.6
Relays and industrial controls (incl. programmable controllers) for drives, clutches, brakes, motors, etc.	(X)	54.3
Transformers (exc. electronic-type) and other electric power transmission and distribution equipment	(X)	11.0
Electric motors and generators	(X)	33.4
Purchased packaging machinery devices for incorporation into complete finished products	(X)	59.2
Other purchased devices for incorporation into complete finished products (exc. packaging machinery devices)	(X)	20.7
All other materials, components, parts, containers, and supplies	(X)	430.9
Materials, ingredients, containers, and supplies, nsk	(X)	491.0

Source: 2002 Economic Census. Explanation of symbols used: (D): Withheld to avoid disclosure of competitive data; na: Not available; (S): Withheld because statistical norms were not met; (X): Not applicable; (Z): Less than half the unit shown; nec: Not elsewhere classified; nsk: Not specified by kind; - : zero; p : 10-19 percent estimated; q : 20-29 percent estimated.

PRODUCT SHARE DETAILS

Product or Product Class Shipments	Mil. $	Product or Product Class Shipments	Mil. $
PACKAGING MACHINERY	3,646.6	Glass and plastics container and can capping, sealing, and lidding machinery (excluding all filling, bottling, and canning machinery, and parts)	76.8
Packing, packaging, and bottling machinery, except parts	**2,910.4**	Labeling machinery (all types of applications and methods), except parts	197.2
Cartoning, multipacking, and leaflet-coupon placing machinery, except parts	262.6	Coding, dating, imprinting, jet printing, marking, and stamping machinery, except parts	263.7
Thermoforming, blister, and skin machinery, including carded display machinery, except parts	22.1	Corrugated and solid fibre case and tray forming, loading, and sealing machinery, except parts	202.0
Bagging machines (pre-form opening, filling, and closing; modified atmosphere laminating; and form-fill-seal machines), except parts	255.8	Accumulating, collating, feeding, and unscrambling machinery; and testing, inspecting, detecting, checkweighing, and other quality control devices; except parts	168.2
Bag (pre-form) opening, filling, and closing machinery and systems, except parts	114.1	Accumulating, collating, feeding, and unscrambling machinery, except parts	128.8
Vacuum, gas, and other modified atmosphere laminating and bagging machines, except parts	30.1	Testing, inspecting, detecting, checkweighing, and other quality control devices, except parts	39.4
Horizontal bag and pouch form, fill, and seal machinery (performs all three functions)	50.7	Paper, film, and foil wrapping machines; shrink & stretch overwrapping, banding, & bundling machinery; & palletizing, depalletizing, and pallet unitizing machinery for packaging applications; excl. parts	248.1
Vertical bag and pouch form, fill, and seal machinery (performs all three functions)	60.9	Paper, film, and foil wrapping machines (all types, except shrink and stretch film equipment, and parts)	48.8
Machinery for bottling, canning, cleaning, drying bottles and containers, and adhesive devices for packing, packaging, and bottling; except parts	500.4	Shrink and stretch film overwrapping, banding, and bundling machinery (excluding pallet unitizing and parts)	162.1
Adhesive devices for packing, packaging, and bottling machinery (hot melt and cold glue), except parts	(D)	Palletizing, depalletizing, and pallet unitizing machinery with stretch film, adhesive, or strapping, except parts	37.1
Machinery for cleaning and drying bottles and other containers, except parts	8.8	Other packing, packaging, and bottling machinery or systems and combination of equipment nec, except parts	336.5
Bottling and canning machinery (including fillers, all types of closers, and accessory equipment), except parts	(D)	Packing, packaging, and bottling machinery, except parts, nsk	148.6
Liquids, dry, and viscous products filling machinery, including by count machinery, except bags and parts	228.6	**Parts for packing, packaging, and bottling machinery**	**651.6**
Dry products filling machinery (free and nonfree flowing), including by count machinery, except bags and parts	94.8	**Packaging machinery, nsk, total**	**84.5**
Liquids and viscous products filling machinery (very heavy liquids, slurries, and pumpable semisolids), except parts	133.8		

Source: 2002 Economic Census. The values are product shipments in millions of dollars for 2002. Total product shipments may be lower or higher than industry shipments. See Introduction for a full discussion. Values of indented subcategories are summed in the main heading(s). The symbol (D) appears when data are withheld to prevent disclosure of competitive information. The abbreviation nsk stands for 'not specified by kind' and nec for 'not elsewhere classified'. A dash (-) means zero.

INPUTS AND OUTPUTS FOR PACKAGING MACHINERY MANUFACTURING

Economic Sector or Industry Providing Inputs	%	Sector	Economic Sector or Industry Buying Outputs	%	Sector
Compensation of employees	36.9		Private fixed investment	68.6	
Management of companies & enterprises	6.8	Services	Wineries	13.7	Manufg.
Wholesale trade	4.9	Trade	Exports of goods & services	12.0	Cap Inv
Packaging machinery	3.7	Manufg.	Packaging machinery	2.8	Manufg.
Machine shops	2.4	Manufg.	Toilet preparations	1.6	Manufg.
Ferrous metal foundries	2.1	Manufg.	Material handling equipment	1.1	Manufg.
Fluid power process machinery	2.0	Manufg.	Federal government, investment, nondefense	0.2	Fed Govt
Relay & industrial controls	1.9	Manufg.			
Power, distribution, & specialty transformers	1.8	Manufg.			
Speed changers, industrial high-speed drives, & gears	1.6	Manufg.			
Securities, commodity contracts, investments	1.5	Fin/R.E.			
Handtools	1.4	Manufg.			
Nonwoven fabric mills	1.4	Manufg.			
Motors & generators	1.4	Manufg.			
Ball & roller bearings	1.3	Manufg.			
Cutting tools & machine tool accessories	1.2	Manufg.			
Iron & steel mills & ferroalloys	1.1	Manufg.			
Real estate	1.1	Fin/R.E.			
Coating, engraving, heat treating & allied activities	1.1	Manufg.			
Semiconductors & related devices	1.0	Manufg.			
Advertising & related services	1.0	Services			
Printed circuit assemblies (electronic assembles)	1.0	Manufg.			
Lessors of nonfinancial assets	0.9	Fin/R.E.			
Monetary authorities/depository credit intermediation	0.8	Fin/R.E.			
Mechanical power transmission equipment	0.7	Manufg.			
Truck transportation	0.7	Util.			
Data processing, hosting, & related services	0.7	Services			
Turned products & screws, nuts, & bolts	0.7	Manufg.			
Professional, scientific, technical services, nec	0.6	Services			
Telecommunications	0.6	Services			
Food services & drinking places	0.6	Services			
Alumina refining & primary aluminum production	0.6	Manufg.			
Scientific research & development services	0.5	Services			
Power generation & supply	0.5	Util.			
Accounting, tax preparation, bookkeeping, & payroll	0.5	Services			
Legal services	0.5	Services			
Metal cans, boxes, & other containers (light gauge)	0.5	Manufg.			
Fabricated metals, nec	0.5	Manufg.			
Taxes on production & imports, less subsidies	0.4				
Hotels & motels, including casino hotels	0.4	Services			
Noncomparable imports	0.4	Foreign			
Abrasive products	0.4	Manufg.			
Architectural, engineering, & related services	0.4	Services			
Plastics packaging materials, film & sheet	0.4	Manufg.			
Warehousing & storage	0.4	Util.			
Gaskets, packing, & sealing devices	0.4	Manufg.			
Nondepository credit intermediation activities	0.4	Fin/R.E.			
Automotive equipment rental & leasing	0.4	Fin/R.E.			
Forging, stamping, & sintering, nec	0.3	Manufg.			
Plate work & fabricated structural products	0.3	Manufg.			
Chemical products & preparations, nec	0.3	Manufg.			
Crowns & closures & metal stamping	0.3	Manufg.			
Nonferrous metal foundries	0.3	Manufg.			
Air transportation	0.3	Util.			
Postal service	0.2	Util.			
Rubber products, nec	0.2	Manufg.			
Other computer related services, including facilities	0.2	Services			
Custom roll forming	0.2	Manufg.			
Paperboard containers	0.2	Manufg.			
Management, scientific, & technical consulting	0.2	Services			
Valve & fittings other than plumbing	0.2	Manufg.			
Services to buildings & dwellings	0.2	Services			
Commercial & industrial machinery rental & leasing	0.2	Fin/R.E.			
Maintenance/repair of nonresidential structures	0.2	Construct.			
Paperboard mills	0.1	Manufg.			
Aluminum products from purchased aluminum	0.1	Manufg.			
Bare printed circuit boards	0.1	Manufg.			
Business support services	0.1	Services			
Springs & wire products	0.1	Manufg.			
Surgical appliances & supplies	0.1	Manufg.			
Transit & ground passenger transportation	0.1	Util.			
Civic, social, & professional organizations	0.1	Services			
Natural gas distribution	0.1	Util.			

Source: Benchmark Input-Output Accounts for the U.S. Economy, 2002, U.S. Department of Commerce, Washington, D.C., January 2008. The abbreviation nec stands for 'not elsewhere classified'.

OCCUPATIONS EMPLOYED BY OTHER GENERAL-PURPOSE MACHINERY MANUFACTURING

Occupation	% of Total 2006	Change to 2016	Occupation	% of Total 2006	Change to 2016
Team assemblers	11.0	-9.7	Multiple machine tool operators & tenders	1.4	-0.7
Machinists	5.9	-5.2	Lathe & turning machine tool operators & tenders	1.4	-18.8
Welders, cutters, solderers, & brazers	5.7	-4.0	Maintenance & repair workers, general	1.4	-9.7
First-line supervisors/managers of production workers	3.6	-9.7	Structural metal fabricators & fitters	1.4	-9.7
Mechanical engineers	2.8	-0.7	Industrial engineers	1.3	9.6
Computer-controlled machine tool operators	2.5	-0.7	Electrical & electronic equipment assemblers	1.3	-27.8
Sales reps, wholesale & manufacturing, exc tech	2.3	-9.7	Industrial machinery mechanics	1.3	3.8
Engine & other machine assemblers	2.0	-9.7	Mechanical drafters	1.3	-8.7
Inspectors, testers, sorters, samplers, & weighers	1.9	-14.9	Customer service representatives	1.3	-0.7
Cutting, punching, & press machine operators	1.8	-18.8	Coating, painting, & spraying machine operators	1.2	-14.2
Shipping, receiving, & traffic clerks	1.8	-13.1	Office clerks, general	1.2	-11.1
Helpers--Production workers	1.6	-9.7	Industrial production managers	1.1	-9.7
General & operations managers	1.6	-18.8	Electrical engineers	1.1	-9.7
Laborers & freight, stock, & material movers, hand	1.5	-18.8	Production, planning, & expediting clerks	1.1	-9.7
Purchasing agents, exc wholesale, retail, & farm	1.5	-18.8	Stock clerks & order fillers	1.0	-24.5
Bookkeeping, accounting, & auditing clerks	1.5	-9.7			

Source: Industry-Occupation Matrix, Bureau of Labor Statistics, December 4, 2007. These data are reported based on 4-digit NAICS categories but have been matched to corresponding 6-digit NAICS industry codes. The change reported for each occupation to the year 2016 is a percent of growth or decline as estimated by the Bureau of Labor Statistics. The abbreviation nec stands for 'not elsewhere classified'.

LOCATION BY STATE AND REGIONAL CONCENTRATION

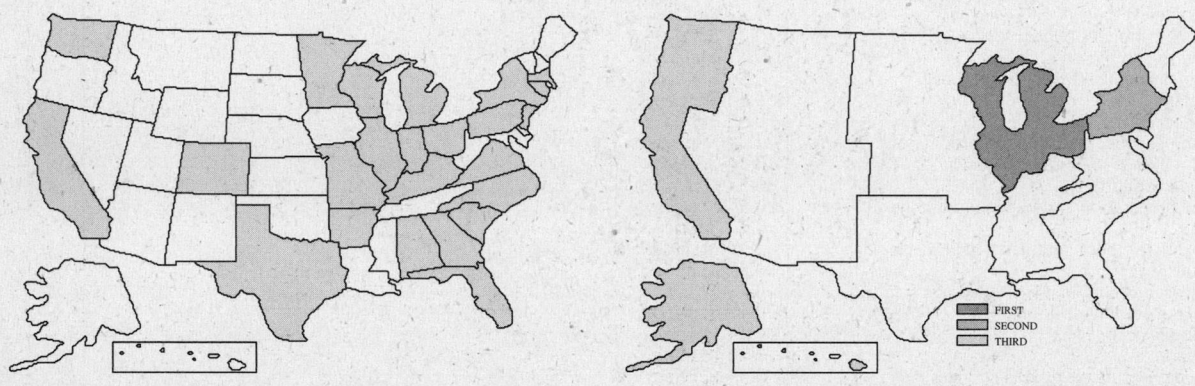

INDUSTRY DATA BY STATE

State	Establish-ments	Shipments			Employment				Cost as % of Shipments	Investment per Employee ($)
		Total ($ mil)	% of U.S.	Per Establ.	Total Number	% of U.S.	Per Establ.	Wages ($/hour)		
Illinois	50	510.9	12.4	10,218.1	2,344	9.8	47	20.48	43.9	4,045
Ohio	39	412.8	10.1	10,585.7	2,290	9.5	59	17.93	47.6	6,738
California	88	402.2	9.8	4,569.9	2,529	10.5	29	18.59	46.3	3,014
Wisconsin	39	329.6	8.0	8,452.4	1,824	7.6	47	19.28	40.5	3,847
Minnesota	36	299.9	7.3	8,331.4	2,417	10.1	67	17.85	43.8	3,444
Georgia	23	249.0	6.1	10,824.6	654	2.7	28	15.71	27.4	1,422
Kentucky	8	165.3	4.0	20,658.5	904	3.8	113	22.70	43.9	3,997
New Jersey	44	158.3	3.9	3,597.0	1,030	4.3	23	23.09	36.2	1,695
Pennsylvania	39	149.6	3.6	3,836.6	974	4.1	25	18.51	46.9	3,576
Florida	33	119.3	2.9	3,615.4	872	3.6	26	18.45	42.9	3,310
South Carolina	7	115.0	2.8	16,429.6	1,221	5.1	174	19.51	42.8	1,080
New York	35	108.2	2.6	3,091.4	688	2.9	20	22.17	39.7	1,560
North Carolina	21	105.8	2.6	5,039.8	378	1.6	18	18.56	46.9	4,156
Michigan	25	103.0	2.5	4,120.8	625	2.6	25	22.45	52.2	2,672
Virginia	10	101.4	2.5	10,139.0	585	2.4	58	18.35	47.0	2,056
Missouri	15	88.9	2.2	5,929.9	366	1.5	24	18.53	40.4	2,508
Washington	18	74.1	1.8	4,118.9	599	2.5	33	16.38	43.2	3,701
Massachusetts	16	69.1	1.7	4,318.9	488	2.0	30	17.84	35.6	5,256
Alabama	5	46.9	1.1	9,379.0	191	0.8	38	19.46	31.8	1,838
Texas	19	44.0	1.1	2,314.6	302	1.3	16	17.18	44.4	2,026
Connecticut	12	41.5	1.0	3,459.0	265	1.1	22	21.24	49.6	2,868
Colorado	8	26.9	0.7	3,368.5	250	1.0	31	13.60	56.3	2,564
Indiana	10	26.8	0.7	2,679.8	214	0.9	21	21.90	38.9	5,243
Arkansas	8	20.9	0.5	2,606.7	183	0.8	23	25.56	46.6	2,049

Source: 2002 *Economic Census*. The states are in descending order of shipments or establishments (if shipment data are missing for the majority). The symbol (D) appears when data are withheld to prevent disclosure of competitive information. States marked with (D) are sorted by number of establishments. A dash (-) indicates that the data element cannot be calculated. Data may not show all states active in the NAICS category. All data available at the time of publication are shown.

NAICS 333994 - INDUSTRIAL PROCESS FURNACE AND OVEN MANUFACTURING

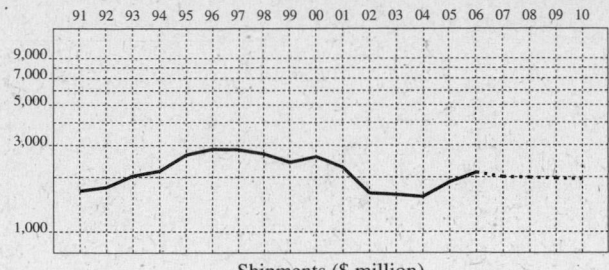

Shipments ($ million)

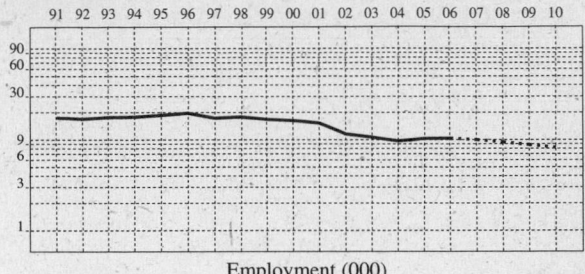

Employment (000)

GENERAL STATISTICS

| Year | Com- panies | Establishments | | Employment | | | Compensation | | Production ($ million) | | | |
		Total	with 20 or more employees	Total (000)	Production Workers (000)	Hours (Mil)	Payroll ($ mil)	Wages ($/hr)	Cost of Materials	Value Added by Manufacture	Value of Shipments	Capital Invest.
1991		353	171	17.5	10.9	22.1	472.3	10.40	714.3	940.0	1,679.6	29.0
1992	377	409	181	17.0	10.3	20.1	529.4	11.49	764.2	982.1	1,757.7	27.6
1993		407	176	17.7	11.4	22.5	550.6	11.99	869.1	1,190.5	2,033.0	36.7
1994		401	187	17.9	10.8	20.8	550.3	11.38	903.9	1,261.9	2,163.4	40.8
1995		403	194	18.7	10.7	22.2	584.9	11.07	1,165.4	1,521.9	2,654.7	51.7
1996		414	186	19.7	11.0	23.6	631.2	10.43	1,262.9	1,637.0	2,850.9	41.9
1997	378	403	179	17.4	10.2	23.1	648.8	12.35	1,349.1	1,499.0	2,837.0	65.4
1998		411	179	17.9	11.1	24.6	670.3	13.23	1,324.9	1,439.9	2,685.9	46.8
1999		402	175	16.8	9.8	20.4	624.8	14.06	1,159.5	1,212.5	2,413.8	100.5
2000		385	170	16.3	10.0	20.1	632.9	14.35	1,249.6	1,330.5	2,595.3	74.7
2001		378	165	15.3	9.1	17.6	622.6	15.11	1,077.5	1,118.6	2,267.0	47.5
2002	328	354	143	11.6	6.7	13.1	474.5	15.70	690.1	935.2	1,635.0	37.2
2003		348	138	10.7	6.3	12.8	466.0	16.07	682.2	930.2	1,607.1	26.1
2004		356	135	9.7	5.7	11.4	441.0	16.25	659.7	903.9	1,560.7	31.3
2005		341	136	10.3	6.3	12.5	473.7	17.07	837.5	1,056.4	1,880.1	23.9
2006		355P	139P	10.4	6.4	12.9	503.1	16.95	926.4	1,193.5	2,125.0	30.6
2007		352P	135P	10.0P	5.9P	12.0P	515.6P	17.65P	876.0P	1,128.5P	2,009.3P	41.9P
2008		348P	132P	9.4P	5.5P	11.2P	511.0P	18.12P	867.7P	1,117.8P	1,990.2P	41.6P
2009		344P	128P	8.8P	5.1P	10.4P	506.4P	18.60P	859.3P	1,107.1P	1,971.1P	41.3P
2010		341P	124P	8.2P	4.7P	9.6P	501.7P	19.07P	851.0P	1,096.4P	1,952.0P	41.0P

Sources: 1992, 1997, 2002 *Economic Census*; other years, up to 2006, are from the *Annual Survey of Manufactures*. Establishment counts for non-Census years are from *County Business Patterns*; 1997 and 2002 values are from the 1997 and 2002 censuses respectively, reported in the Federal Government's NAICS format. Other years were originally reported in equivalent SIC format. 'P's show projections by the editors.

INDICES OF CHANGE

| Year | Com- panies | Establishments | | Employment | | | Compensation | | Production ($ million) | | | |
		Total	with 20 or more employees	Total (000)	Production Workers (000)	Hours (Mil)	Payroll ($ mil)	Wages ($/hr)	Cost of Materials	Value Added by Manufacture	Value of Shipments	Capital Invest.
1992	115	116	127	147	154	153	112	73	111	105	108	74
1997	115	114	125	150	152	176	137	79	195	160	174	176
2001		107	115	132	136	134	131	96	156	120	139	128
2002	100	100	100	100	100	100	100	100	100	100	100	100
2003		98	97	92	94	98	98	102	99	99	98	70
2004		101	94	84	85	87	93	104	96	97	95	84
2005		96	95	89	94	95	100	109	121	113	115	64
2006		100P	97P	90	96	98	106	108	134	128	130	82
2007		99P	95P	86P	88P	92P	109P	112P	127P	121P	123P	113P
2008		98P	92P	81P	82P	85P	108P	115P	126P	120P	122P	112P
2009		97P	90P	76P	76P	79P	107P	118P	125P	118P	121P	111P
2010		96P	87P	71P	70P	73P	106P	121P	123P	117P	119P	110P

Sources: Same as General Statistics. Values reflect change from the base year, 2002. Values above 100 mean greater than 2002, values below 100 mean less than 2002, and the values of 100 in other years means the same as 2002. 'P's show projections by the editors.

SELECTED RATIOS

For 2002	Avg. of All Manufact.	Analyzed Industry	Index	For 2002	Avg. of All Manufact.	Analyzed Industry	Index
Employees per Establishment	42	33	78	Value Added per Production Worker	182,367	139,582	77
Payroll per Establishment	1,639,184	1,340,395	82	Cost per Establishment	5,769,015	1,949,435	34
Payroll per Employee	39,053	40,905	105	Cost per Employee	137,446	59,491	43
Production Workers per Establishment	30	19	64	Cost per Production Worker	195,506	103,000	53
Wages per Establishment	694,845	580,989	84	Shipments per Establishment	11,158,348	4,618,644	41
Wages per Production Worker	23,548	30,697	130	Shipments per Employee	265,847	140,948	53
Hours per Production Worker	1,980	1,955	99	Shipments per Production Worker	378,144	244,030	65
Wages per Hour	11.89	15.70	132	Investment per Establishment	361,338	105,085	29
Value Added per Establishment	5,381,325	2,641,808	49	Investment per Employee	8,609	3,207	37
Value Added per Employee	128,210	80,621	63	Investment per Production Worker	12,245	5,552	45

Sources: Same as General Statistics. The 'Average of All Manufacturing' column represents the average of all manufacturing industries reported for the most recent complete year available. The Index shows the relationship between the Average and the Analyzed Industry. For example, 100 means that they are equal; 500 that the Analyzed Industry is five times the average; 50 means that the Analyzed Industry is half the national average. The abbreviation 'na' is used to show that data are 'not available'. Ratios shown for 2002, the last complete census year.

LEADING COMPANIES   Number shown: 75   Total sales ($ mil): 25,014   Total employment (000): 41.1

Company Name	Address				CEO Name	Phone	Co. Type	Sales ($ mil)	Empl. (000)
Carrier Corp.	One Carrier Pl.	Farmington	CT	06034	Geraud Darnis		S	10,600	4.3
Dekko Technologies L.L.C.	PO Box 337	North Webster	IN	46555	Steven Hankinf	574-834-2818	R	2,130*	0.1
Hutchinson FTS Inc.	1835 Technology	Troy	MI	48083	Paul Campbell	248-589-7710	R	1,863*	<0.1
Rainin Instrument L.L.C.	PO Box 4026	Woburn	MA	01888	Kenneth Rainin	510-564-1600	R	1,590*	0.1
Ipsen Inc.	PO Box 6266	Rockford	IL	61125		815-332-4941	R	1,456*	0.1
Babcock and Wilcox Co.	PO Box 351	Barberton	OH	44203	John A. Fees	330-753-4511	S	1,080*	10.8
MKS Instruments Inc.	90 Industrial Way	Wilmington	MA	01887	Leo Berlinghieri	978-284-4000	P	783	3.0
Stahl Specialty Co.	PO Box 6	Kingsville	MO	64061	Kevin Daugherty	816-597-3322	S	681*	0.8
Fisher Scientific	2000 Park Lane Dr.	Pittsburgh	PA	15275	David Dellapenta	412-490-8300	D	568	1.8
Newport Corp.	1791 Deere Ave.	Irvine	CA	92606	Michael ONeill	949-863-3144	P	445	2.0
Proliance International Inc.	100 Gando Dr.	New Haven	CT	06513	Barry R. Banducci	203-401-6450	P	416	2.0
Nordyne Inc.	8000 Phoenix Pkwy.	O Fallon	MO	63366	David Lagrand	636-561-7300	S	377*	1.8
Templeton Coal Company Inc.	701 Wabash Ave.	Terre Haute	IN	47807	John Templeton	812-232-7037	R	166*	<0.1
Venturedyne Ltd.	600 College Ave.	Pewaukee	WI	53072		262-691-9900	R	147*	1.3
Sullair Corp.	3700 E Michigan	Michigan City	IN	46360	Henry Brook	219-879-5451	S	140*	0.7
Ultra Air Products Inc.	3309 John Conley	Lapeer	MI	48446	Don Swanson	810-667-6800	R	136*	0.7
Alltech Inc.	3031 Catnip Hill Rd	Nicholasville	KY	40356		859-885-9613	R	121*	0.2
Sarstedt Inc.	PO Box 468	Newton	NC	28658		828-465-4000	R	103*	0.2
TPI Corp.	PO Box 4973	Johnson City	TN	37602	Robert Henry	423-477-4131	R	84*	<0.1
Kewaunee Scientific Corp.	PO Box 1842	Statesville	NC	28687		704-873-7202	P	81	0.6
New Brunswick Scientific Co.	PO Box 4005	Edison	NJ	08818		732-287-1200	P	76	0.4
Barnstead-Thermolyne Corp.	PO Box 797	Dubuque	IA	52004		563-556-2241	S	70*	0.5
Buffalo Air Handling Co.	467 Zane Snead Dr.	Amherst	VA	24521	William Phelps	434-946-7455	S	68*	0.5
Ircon Inc.	7300 N Natchez	Niles	IL	60714	M Fay	847-967-5151	R	68*	<0.1
Electric Furnace Co.	435 W Wilson St.	Salem	OH	44460	Phillip Greenisen	330-332-4661	R	62*	0.4
Henry Technologies Inc.	1 ABC Pkwy.	Beloit	WI	53511	Charlie Graham	608-361-4400	R	62*	<0.1
Gt Solar Inc.	243 Daniel Webster	Merrimack	NH	03054	Thomas Zarrella	603-883-5200	R	60	0.1
Evans Tempcon Inc.	701 Ann St. NW	Grand Rapids	MI	49504		616-361-2681	R	59*	0.4
Saylor-Beall Manufacturing Co.	PO Box 40	Saint Johns	MI	48879	Bruce Mc Fee	989-224-2371	R	58*	0.3
Johnson Gas Appliance Co.	520 E Ave. NW	Cedar Rapids	IA	52405	Barnes O'Donnell	319-365-5267	R	58*	<0.1
CEM Corp.	PO Box 200	Matthews	NC	28106	Michael J. Collins	704-821-7015	R	55	0.2
Tempco Electric Heater Corp.	607 N Central Ave.	Wood Dale	IL	60191	Fermin Adames	630-350-2252	R	54*	0.3
Ebner Furnaces Inc.	224 Quadral Dr.	Wadsworth	OH	44281	Peter Ebner	330-335-1600	S	53*	0.2
Intricon Corp.	1260 Red Fox Rd.	Arden Hills	MN	55112	Mark S. Gorder	651-636-9770	P	52	0.6
Pacific Industrial Furnace Co.	49630 Pontiac Trl.	Wixom	MI	48393	Bill Keough	248-624-8191	D	47*	0.1
IKA-Works Inc.	2635 Northchase	Wilmington	NC	28405		910-452-7059	R	46*	<0.1
Bioanalytical Systems Inc.	2701 Kent Ave.	West Lafayette	IN	47906		765-463-4527	P	45	0.3
Restek Corp.	110 Benner Cir.	Bellefonte	PA	16823	Don Chandless	814-353-1300	R	43	0.2
Misonix Inc.	1938 New Hwy.	Farmingdale	NY	11735	Gary Gelman	631-694-9555	P	42	0.2
Zeeco Inc.	22151 E 91st St. S	Broken Arrow	OK	74014		918-258-8551	R	41*	0.3
Commerce Controls Inc.	41069 Vincenti Ct.	Novi	MI	48375	Harold Gardynik	248-476-1442	R	37*	0.2
Molecular Bio-Products Inc.	9880 Mesa Rim Rd.	San Diego	CA	92121	Larry Scaramella		S	36*	0.3
George Koch Sons L.L.C.	10 S 11th Ave.	Evansville	IN	47744	Steve Church	812-465-9600	S	36*	0.2
NuAire Inc.	2100 Fernbrook Ln.	Plymouth	MN	55447		763-553-1270	R	36*	0.2
CerCo L.L.C.	PO Box 35	Shreve	OH	44676		330-567-2145	R	35*	0.2
Seasons-4 Inc.	4500 Indust. Access	Douglasville	GA	30134		770-489-0716	R	34*	0.2
Consolidated Engineering Co.	1971 McCollum	Kennesaw	GA	30144	Paul Crafton	770-422-5100	R	33*	0.2
Rhea Campbell Manufacturing	1865 Hwy. 641 N	Paris	TN	38242		731-642-4251	R	32*	0.3
Kurt J Lesker Co.	1925 Rte. 51 Ste. 1	Clairton	PA	15025	Kurt Lesker	412-233-0801	R	32*	0.2
Detroit Stoker Co.	PO Box 732	Monroe	MI	48161	Mark Eleniewski	734-241-9500	S	31*	0.3
Atlas Material Testing Tech	4114 N Ravenswood	Chicago	IL	60613	William Lane	773-327-4520	R	30*	0.2
Bel-Art Products Inc.	6 Industrial Rd.	Pequannock	NJ	07440	David Landsberger	973-694-0500	R	29*	0.1
CG Electrodes L.L.C.	800 Theresia St.	Saint Marys	PA	15857	David Jardini	814-834-2801	R	29*	0.1
Dako Colorado Inc.	4850 Innovation Dr.	Fort Collins	CO	80525	Patrik Dahlen	970-226-2200	R	28*	0.2
Shenandoah Manufacturing Co.	720 Industrial Park	Anderson	MO	64831		417-845-6065	S	28*	0.1
Durex International Corp.	190 Detroit St.	Cary	IL	60013	Edward Hinz	847-639-5600	R	26*	0.2
Eisenmann Corp.	150 E Dartmoor Dr.	Crystal Lake	IL	60014	Peter Eisenmann	815-455-4100	R	26*	0.2
Crescent Metal Products Inc.	5925 Heisley Rd.	Mentor	OH	44060	Clifford Baggott	440-350-1100	R	26*	0.2
Callidus Technologies L.L.C.	7130 S Lewis, 335	Tulsa	OK	74136	William Bartlett	918-496-7599	D	25*	0.2
Labcon, North America	3700 Lakeville Hwy.	Petaluma	CA	94954		707-766-2100	S	25*	0.2
Fast Heat Inc.	776 Oaklawn Ave.	Elmhurst	IL	60126	Tim Stojka	630-833-5400	R	23*	0.1
Chromalox Inc.	103 Gamma Dr. Ext.	Pittsburgh	PA	15238		412-967-3800	D	23*	<0.1
Thermo Wisconsin Inc.	PO Box 5030	De Pere	WI	54115	Mohit Uberoi	920-766-7200	S	22*	0.2
Chemineer Inc.	PO Box 1123	Dayton	OH	45401		937-454-3200	S	22*	0.2
International Thermoproducts	11015 Mission Park	Santee	CA	92071	Randall Newcomb	619-562-7001	R	22*	<0.1
Boekel Industries Inc.	855 Penn. Blvd.	Feastrvl Trevose	PA	19053	Leo Synnestvedt	215-396-8200	R	21*	0.2
Buehler Ltd.	PO Box 1	Lake Bluff	IL	60044	David N. Farr	847-295-6500	S	21	0.2
Rapid Engineering Inc.	1100 7 Mile Rd. NW	Comstock Park	MI	49321	Steve Parker	616-784-0500	R	21*	0.1
C.A. Litzler Co.	4800 W 160th St.	Cleveland	OH	44135	Matthew Litzler	216-267-8020	R	21*	<0.1
Gasbarre Products Inc.	PO Box 1011	Du Bois	PA	15801	Thomas Gasbarre	814-371-3015	R	21*	0.1
Mechanical Equipment Company	12505 Reed Rd.	Sugar Land	TX	77478	George Gsell	281-276-7600	R	21*	<0.1
International Thermal Systems	4697 W Greenfield	Milwaukee	WI	53214		414-672-7700	R	20*	0.1
Parr Instrument Co.	211 53rd Street	Moline	IL	61265	Michael Steffenson	309-762-7716	R	20*	<0.1
Surface Combustion Inc.	PO Box 428	Maumee	OH	43537	William Bernard	419-891-7150	R	20*	0.1
Rama Corp.	600 W Esplanade	San Jacinto	CA	92583	Marco Renshaw	951-654-7351	R	20*	0.1

Source: *Ward's Business Directory of U.S. Private and Public Companies*, Volumes 1 and 2, 2008. The company type code used is as follows: P - Public, R - Private, S - Subsidiary, D - Division, J - Joint Venture, A - Affiliate, G - Group. Sales are in millions of dollars, employees are in thousands. An asterisk (*) indicates an estimated sales volume. The symbol < stands for 'less than'. Company names and addresses are truncated, in some cases, to fit into the available space.

MATERIALS CONSUMED

Material	Quantity	Delivered Cost ($ million)
Fluid power products	(X)	19.7
Fabricated metal products, including forgings	(X)	45.9
Iron and steel castings (rough and semifinished)	(X)	14.6
Nonferrous (aluminum, copper, etc.) castings (rough and semifinished)	(X)	6.2
Steel bars, bar shapes, and plates (exc. castings, forgings, fabr. metal products)	(X)	15.7
Steel sheet and strip (including tinplate)	(X)	13.1
All other steel shapes and forms (exc. castings, forgings, fabr. metal products)	(X)	10.1
Other nonferrous shapes and forms (exc. castings, forgings, fabricated metal products)	(X)	11.9
Aluminum and aluminum-base alloy shapes and forms (exc. castings, forgings, fabr. metal products)	(X)	2.2
Electrical transmission, distribution, and control equipment	(X)	42.8
Electric heating elements for industrial furnaces, ovens, and kilns	(X)	38.0
All other materials, components, parts, containers, and supplies	(X)	122.6
Materials, ingredients, containers, and supplies, nsk	(X)	231.0

Source: 2002 *Economic Census*. Explanation of symbols used: (D): Withheld to avoid disclosure of competitive data; na: Not available; (S): Withheld because statistical norms were not met; (X): Not applicable; (Z): Less than half the unit shown; nec: Not elsewhere classified; nsk: Not specified by kind; - : zero; p : 10-19 percent estimated; q : 20-29 percent estimated.

PRODUCT SHARE DETAILS

Product or Product Class Shipments	Mil. $	Product or Product Class Shipments	Mil. $
INDUSTRIAL FURNACES AND OVENS	1,512.2	excluding parts and attachments	55.0
Fuel-fired industrial process furnaces, ovens, and kilns	377.6	Electric (except high-frequency induction and dielectric and resistance-heated) metal processing and heat	
Fuel-fired industrial metal processing and heat treating furnaces (such as annealing, hardening, carburizing, and porcelain enameling furnaces), except parts and attachments	247.5	treating furnaces, except parts and attachments	31.9
		Other electric industrial furnaces, ovens, and kilns (complete units)	104.9
Fuel-fired metal processing and heat treating furnaces, ovens, and kilns for the melting, roasting, or other heat treatment of ores, pyrites, or metals, nec, except parts and attachments	52.8	Electric (except high-frequency induction and dielectric and resistance-heated) furnaces and ovens for diffusion, oxidation, or annealing of semiconductor wafers; except parts and attachments	20.3
Fuel-fired industrial furnaces, ovens, and kilns, nec	77.3	Electric industrial furnaces, ovens, and kilns, nec, excluding parts	84.6
Parts and attachments for industrial fuel-fired furnaces, ovens, and kilns	109.4	Parts and attachments for electric industrial furnaces, ovens, and kilns, and high-frequency induction and	
High-frequency induction and dielectric heating equipment, including furnaces, ovens, and kilns; except parts and attachments	167.5	dielectric heating equipment	92.1
		Other electrical heating equipment for industrial use, except parts and attachments and soldering irons	267.4
Electric resistance-heated furnaces, ovens, and kilns (except parts and attachments)	113.5	Industrial electric tubular heaters	99.7
Electric resistance-heated metal processing and heat treating furnaces (as for annealing, hardening, carburizing, and porcelain enameling), except parts and attachments	58.5	Electrical heating equipment for industrial use, nec, except parts and attachments and soldering irons	167.7
Electric resistance-heated furnaces, ovens, and kilns, except for metal processing and heat treating, and		Parts and attachments for electric industrial tubular heaters and other electrical heating equipment, nec, for industrial use	86.3
		Industrial furnaces and ovens, nsk, total	161.7

Source: 2002 *Economic Census*. The values are product shipments in millions of dollars for 2002. Total product shipments may be lower or higher than industry shipments. See Introduction for a full discussion. Values of indented subcategories are summed in the main heading(s). The symbol (D) appears when data are withheld to prevent disclosure of competitive information. The abbreviation nsk stands for 'not specified by kind' and nec for 'not elsewhere classified'. A dash (-) means zero.

INPUTS AND OUTPUTS FOR INDUSTRIAL PROCESS FURNACE AND OVEN MANUFACTURING

Economic Sector or Industry Providing Inputs	%	Sector	Economic Sector or Industry Buying Outputs	%	Sector
Compensation of employees	38.9		Exports of goods & services	45.9	Cap Inv
Industrial process furnaces & ovens	12.3	Manufg.	Private fixed investment	38.9	
Management of companies & enterprises	7.2	Services	Industrial process furnaces & ovens	9.7	Manufg.
Wholesale trade	3.3	Trade	Coating, engraving, heat treating & allied activities	3.8	Manufg.
Iron & steel mills & ferroalloys	2.8	Manufg.	Machine shops	0.9	Manufg.
Relay & industrial controls	1.5	Manufg.	Fabricated metals, nec	0.8	Manufg.
Securities, commodity contracts, investments	1.5	Fin/R.E.			
Real estate	1.5	Fin/R.E.			
Advertising & related services	1.2	Services			
Machine shops	1.1	Manufg.			
Ferrous metal foundries	1.0	Manufg.			
Fluid power process machinery	0.9	Manufg.			
Lessors of nonfinancial assets	0.8	Fin/R.E.			
Power generation & supply	0.8	Util.			
Architectural, engineering, & related services	0.7	Services			
Valve & fittings other than plumbing	0.7	Manufg.			
Coating, engraving, heat treating & allied activities	0.7	Manufg.			
Monetary authorities/depository credit intermediation	0.7	Fin/R.E.			
Taxes on production & imports, less subsidies	0.6				
Aluminum products from purchased aluminum	0.6	Manufg.			

Continued on next page.

INPUTS AND OUTPUTS FOR INDUSTRIAL PROCESS FURNACE AND OVEN MANUFACTURING - Continued

Economic Sector or Industry Providing Inputs	%	Sector	Economic Sector or Industry Buying Outputs	%	Sector
Food services & drinking places	0.6	Services			
Truck transportation	0.6	Util.			
Data processing, hosting, & related services	0.6	Services			
Professional, scientific, technical services, nec	0.6	Services			
Telecommunications	0.6	Services			
Legal services	0.6	Services			
Nonferrous metal foundries	0.5	Manufg.			
Noncomparable imports	0.5	Foreign			
Turned products & screws, nuts, & bolts	0.4	Manufg.			
Accounting, tax preparation, bookkeeping, & payroll	0.4	Services			
Scientific research & development services	0.4	Services			
Warehousing & storage	0.4	Util.			
Hotels & motels, including casino hotels	0.3	Services			
Automotive equipment rental & leasing	0.3	Fin/R.E.			
Management, scientific, & technical consulting	0.3	Services			
Custom roll forming	0.3	Manufg.			
Fabricated metals, nec	0.3	Manufg.			
Metal cans, boxes, & other containers (light gauge)	0.3	Manufg.			
Air transportation	0.2	Util.			
General purpose machinery, nec	0.2	Manufg.			
Crowns & closures & metal stamping	0.2	Manufg.			
Forging, stamping, & sintering, nec	0.2	Manufg.			
Cutting tools & machine tool accessories	0.2	Manufg.			
Electronic capacitors, resistors, coils, transformers	0.2	Manufg.			
Natural gas distribution	0.2	Util.			
Other computer related services, including facilities	0.2	Services			
Semiconductors & related devices	0.2	Manufg.			
Ball & roller bearings	0.2	Manufg.			
Electronic components, nec	0.2	Manufg.			
Plate work & fabricated structural products	0.2	Manufg.			
Services to buildings & dwellings	0.2	Services			
Alumina refining & primary aluminum production	0.2	Manufg.			
Handtools	0.2	Manufg.			
Nondepository credit intermediation activities	0.2	Fin/R.E.			
Maintenance/repair of nonresidential structures	0.2	Construct.			
Printed circuit assemblies (electronic assembles)	0.2	Manufg.			
Commercial & industrial machinery rental & leasing	0.2	Fin/R.E.			
Business support services	0.1	Services			
Nonferrous metal (ex. copper & aluminum) processing	0.1	Manufg.			
Automotive repair & maintenance, ex. car washes	0.1	Services			
Waste management & remediation services	0.1	Services			

Source: Benchmark Input-Output Accounts for the U.S. Economy, 2002, U.S. Department of Commerce, Washington, D.C., January 2008. The abbreviation nec stands for 'not elsewhere classified'.

OCCUPATIONS EMPLOYED BY OTHER GENERAL-PURPOSE MACHINERY MANUFACTURING

Occupation	% of Total 2006	Change to 2016	Occupation	% of Total 2006	Change to 2016
Team assemblers	11.0	-9.7	Multiple machine tool operators & tenders	1.4	-0.7
Machinists	5.9	-5.2	Lathe & turning machine tool operators & tenders	1.4	-18.8
Welders, cutters, solderers, & brazers	5.7	-4.0	Maintenance & repair workers, general	1.4	-9.7
First-line supervisors/managers of production workers	3.6	-9.7	Structural metal fabricators & fitters	1.4	-9.7
Mechanical engineers	2.8	-0.7	Industrial engineers	1.3	9.6
Computer-controlled machine tool operators	2.5	-0.7	Electrical & electronic equipment assemblers	1.3	-27.8
Sales reps, wholesale & manufacturing, exc tech	2.3	-9.7	Industrial machinery mechanics	1.3	3.8
Engine & other machine assemblers	2.0	-9.7	Mechanical drafters	1.3	-8.7
Inspectors, testers, sorters, samplers, & weighers	1.9	-14.9	Customer service representatives	1.3	-0.7
Cutting, punching, & press machine operators	1.8	-18.8	Coating, painting, & spraying machine operators	1.2	-14.2
Shipping, receiving, & traffic clerks	1.8	-13.1	Office clerks, general	1.2	-11.1
Helpers--Production workers	1.6	-9.7	Industrial production managers	1.1	-9.7
General & operations managers	1.6	-18.8	Electrical engineers	1.1	-9.7
Laborers & freight, stock, & material movers, hand	1.5	-18.8	Production, planning, & expediting clerks	1.1	-9.7
Purchasing agents, exc wholesale, retail, & farm	1.5	-18.8	Stock clerks & order fillers	1.0	-24.5
Bookkeeping, accounting, & auditing clerks	1.5	-9.7			

Source: Industry-Occupation Matrix, Bureau of Labor Statistics, December 4, 2007. These data are reported based on 4-digit NAICS categories but have been matched to corresponding 6-digit NAICS industry codes. The change reported for each occupation to the year 2016 is a percent of growth or decline as estimated by the Bureau of Labor Statistics. The abbreviation nec stands for 'not elsewhere classified'.

LOCATION BY STATE AND REGIONAL CONCENTRATION

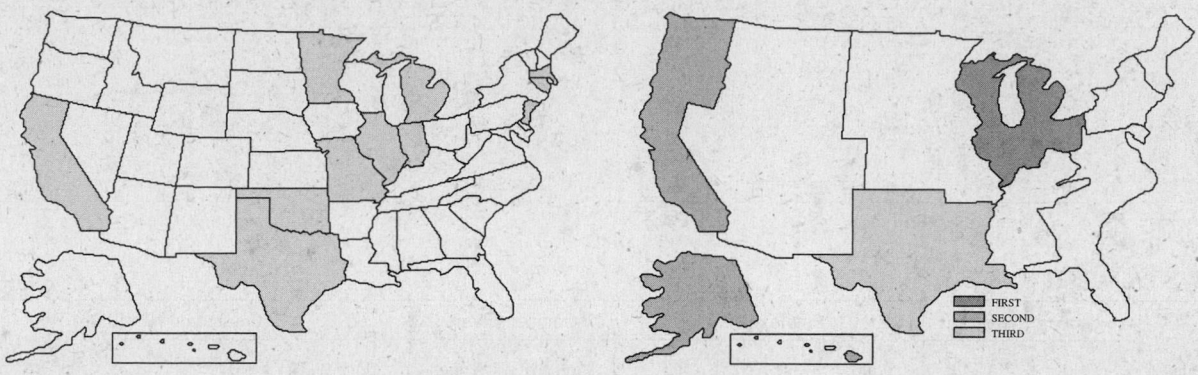

FIRST
SECOND
THIRD

INDUSTRY DATA BY STATE

| State | Establish-ments | Shipments | | | Employment | | | | Cost as % of Shipments | Investment per Employee ($) |
		Total ($ mil)	% of U.S.	Per Establ.	Total Number	% of U.S.	Per Establ.	Wages ($/hour)		
Illinois	20	172.5	10.6	8,625.2	1,022	8.8	51	15.62	37.3	3,474
Michigan	34	143.2	8.8	4,210.5	948	8.2	28	16.35	43.1	6,532
New Jersey	19	136.5	8.4	7,186.8	723	6.2	38	22.57	46.7	1,414
Missouri	11	113.4	6.9	10,305.5	1,142	9.9	104	13.33	28.1	1,873
California	35	91.6	5.6	2,617.3	639	5.5	18	15.48	38.8	3,061
Massachusetts	16	65.0	4.0	4,061.6	604	5.2	38	20.20	36.5	767
Indiana	14	62.4	3.8	4,457.9	422	3.6	30	14.07	41.3	2,220
Minnesota	7	39.2	2.4	5,606.4	282	2.4	40	19.69	45.8	2,759
Oklahoma	7	38.1	2.3	5,442.6	278	2.4	40	17.29	46.4	3,129
Texas	16	32.8	2.0	2,049.9	321	2.8	20	15.16	40.5	2,829
Connecticut	6	11.6	0.7	1,938.8	110	1.0	18	11.87	51.1	836

Source: 2002 *Economic Census*. The states are in descending order of shipments or establishments (if shipment data are missing for the majority). The symbol (D) appears when data are withheld to prevent disclosure of competitive information. States marked with (D) are sorted by number of establishments. A dash (-) indicates that the data element cannot be calculated. Data may not show all states active in the NAICS category. All data available at the time of publication are shown.

NAICS 33399N - FLUID POWER EQUIPMENT MANUFACTURING*

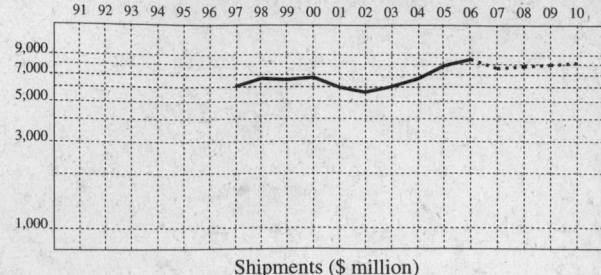

Shipments ($ million)

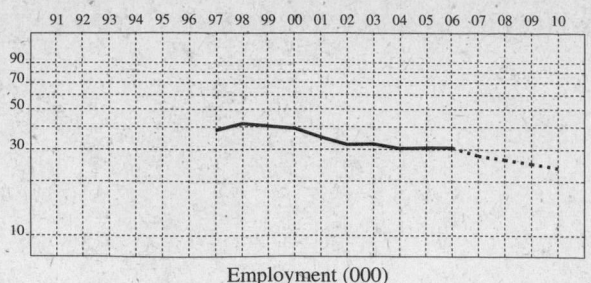

Employment (000)

GENERAL STATISTICS

Year	Companies	Establishments Total	Establishments with 20 or more employees	Employment Total (000)	Employment Production Workers (000)	Employment Hours (Mil)	Compensation Payroll ($ mil)	Compensation Wages ($/hr)	Production Cost of Materials	Production Value Added by Manufacture	Production Value of Shipments	Production Capital Invest.
1997	433	489	222	38.3	25.7	53.1	1,493.1	16.43	2,576.7	3,481.3	6,047.9	223.8
1998		489	227	41.7	28.3	59.0	1,637.7	16.55	2,954.3	3,822.0	6,669.2	302.2
1999		475	224	40.4	27.1	54.2	1,614.0	17.14	2,861.4	3,692.2	6,575.7	265.7
2000		470	233	39.2	26.5	54.4	1,609.2	16.76	3,076.2	3,732.2	6,767.0	245.3
2001		467	220	35.0	23.9	47.4	1,432.3	16.83	2,569.6	3,359.5	5,960.1	175.0
2002	395	474	223	31.9	20.5	40.9	1,366.2	16.92	2,411.6	3,135.1	5,617.2	201.1
2003		491	238	32.2	20.8	43.8	1,403.8	17.18	2,615.2	3,397.8	6,028.9	131.1
2004		496	235	30.4	19.5	43.0	1,394.7	17.83	2,970.0	3,783.6	6,655.9	171.0
2005		504	238	30.7	19.6	43.9	1,512.7	18.93	3,669.5	4,234.7	7,846.8	227.7
2006		494P	238P	30.7	20.4	44.8	1,546.4	19.01	4,175.5	4,458.3	8,535.4	237.8
2007		496P	240P	27.7P	17.7P	39.3P	1,428.5P	18.85P	3,727.5P	3,979.9P	7,619.6P	178.6P
2008		497P	241P	26.4P	16.6P	37.6P	1,415.4P	19.12P	3,811.9P	4,070.1P	7,792.1P	171.4P
2009		500P	243P	25.1P	15.6P	36.0P	1,402.2P	19.39P	3,896.3P	4,160.2P	7,964.7P	164.2P
2010		501P	245P	23.7P	14.6P	34.3P	1,389.0P	19.66P	3,980.7P	4,250.3P	8,137.3P	157.0P

Sources: 1997 and 2002 *Economic Census*; other years, up to 2006, are from *Annual Survey of Manufactures*. Establishment counts for non-Census years are from *County Business Patterns*; 1997 and 2002 values are from the 1997 and 2002 censuses, respectively. 'P's show projections by the editors.

INDICES OF CHANGE

Year	Companies	Establishments Total	Establishments with 20 or more employees	Employment Total (000)	Employment Production Workers (000)	Employment Hours (Mil)	Compensation Payroll ($ mil)	Compensation Wages ($/hr)	Production Cost of Materials	Production Value Added by Manufacture	Production Value of Shipments	Production Capital Invest.
1997	110	103	100	120	125	130	109	97	107	111	108	111
1998		103	102	131	138	144	120	98	123	122	119	150
1999		100	100	127	132	133	118	101	119	118	117	132
2000		99	104	123	129	133	118	99	128	119	120	122
2001		99	99	110	117	116	105	99	107	107	106	87
2002	100	100	100	100	100	100	100	100	100	100	100	100
2003		104	107	101	101	107	103	102	108	108	107	65
2004		105	105	95	95	105	102	105	123	121	118	85
2005		106	107	96	96	107	111	112	152	135	140	113
2006		104P	107P	96	100	110	113	112	173	142	152	118
2007		105P	107P	87P	86P	96P	105P	111P	155P	127P	136P	89P
2008		105P	108P	83P	81P	92P	104P	113P	158P	130P	139P	85P
2009		105P	109P	79P	76P	88P	103P	115P	162P	133P	142P	82P
2010		106P	110P	74P	71P	84P	102P	116P	165P	136P	145P	78P

Sources: Same as General Statistics. Values reflect change from the base year, 2002. Values above 100 mean greater than 2002, values below 100 mean less than 2002, and the values of 100 in other years means the same as 2002. 'P's show projections by the editors.

SELECTED RATIOS

For 2002	Avg. of All Manufact.	Analyzed Industry	Index	For 2002	Avg. of All Manufact.	Analyzed Industry	Index
Employees per Establishment	42	67	160	Value Added per Production Worker	182,367	152,932	84
Payroll per Establishment	1,639,184	2,882,278	176	Cost per Establishment	5,769,015	5,087,764	88
Payroll per Employee	39,053	42,828	110	Cost per Employee	137,446	75,599	55
Production Workers per Establishment	30	43	147	Cost per Production Worker	195,506	117,639	60
Wages per Establishment	694,845	1,459,975	210	Shipments per Establishment	11,158,348	11,850,633	106
Wages per Production Worker	23,548	33,757	143	Shipments per Employee	265,847	176,088	66
Hours per Production Worker	1,980	1,995	101	Shipments per Production Worker	378,144	274,010	72
Wages per Hour	11.89	16.92	142	Investment per Establishment	361,338	424,262	117
Value Added per Establishment	5,381,325	6,614,135	123	Investment per Employee	8,609	6,304	73
Value Added per Employee	128,210	98,279	77	Investment per Production Worker	12,245	9,810	80

Sources: Same as General Statistics. The 'Average of All Manufacturing' column represents the average of all manufacturing industries reported for the most recent complete year available. The Index shows the relationship between the Average and the Analyzed Industry. For example, 100 means that they are equal; 500 that the Analyzed Industry is five times the average; 50 means that the Analyzed Industry is half the national average. The abbreviation 'na' is used to show that data are 'not available'. Ratios shown for 2002, the last complete census year.

*Equivalent to Federal Government NAICS 333995, 333996.

LEADING COMPANIES Number shown: **75**   Total sales ($ mil): **45,920**   Total employment (000): **160.3**

Company Name	Address				CEO Name	Phone	Co. Type	Sales ($ mil)	Empl. (000)
Parker Hannifin Corp.	6035 Parkland Blvd.	Cleveland	OH	44124	Lee Banks	216-896-3000	P	10,718	57.3
ITT Corp.	4 W Red Oak Ln.	White Plains	NY	10604		914-641-2000	P	9,003	39.7
Flowserve Corp.	5215 N O'Connor	Irving	TX	75039		972-443-6500	P	3,763	15.0
Waltco Truck Equipment Company	PO Box 354	Tallmadge	OH	44278	Lennart Bohman	330-633-9191	R	3,320*	0.2
Crane Co.	100 First Stamford	Stamford	CT	06902	Thomas Craney	203-363-7300	P	2,619	12.0
Apph Wichita Inc.	1445 S Sierra Dr.	Wichita	KS	67209	Dan Kilby	316-943-5752	R	2,590*	<0.1
Festo Corp.	PO Box 18023	Hauppauge	NY	11788		631-435-0800	R	2,452*	0.2
Applied Ind. Technologies	PO Box 6925	Cleveland	OH	44101	David L. Pugh	216-426-4000	P	2,014	4.6
Sulzer Pumps Inc.	PO Box 10247	Portland	OR	97296	Cesar Montenegro	503-226-5200	R	1,576*	0.3
Mark IV Industries Inc.	PO Box 810	Amherst	NY	14226		716-689-4972	R	1,215*	8.1
Swagelok Co.	29500 Solon Rd.	Solon	OH	44139	Arthur F. Anton	440-248-4600	R	1,100*	3.3
TriMas Corp.	39400 Woodward	Bloomfield Hls	MI	48304	Grant Beard	248-631-5450	P	1,068	5.1
Cascade Corp.	PO Box 20187	Portland	OR	97294		503-669-6300	P	479	2.1
NSK Corp.	PO Box 134007	Ann Arbor	MI	48113	Tsutomo Komori	734-913-7500	R	438*	0.4
PHD Inc.	PO Box 9070	Fort Wayne	IN	46899	Joseph Oberlin	260-747-6151	R	218*	0.3
Bosch Rexroth Corp/Mobile Hydr	PO Box 25407	Lehigh Valley	PA	18002	Berend Bracht	610-694-8300	D	200*	0.5
Hyco International Inc.	100 Galleria Pkwy.	Atlanta	GA	30339	Ronald C. Whitaker	770-980-1935	R	189	1.2
Knight Inc.	20531 Crescent Bay	Lake Forest	CA	92630	George Noa	949-595-4800	S	189*	0.1
SMC Corporation of America	PO Box 26640	Indianapolis	IN	46226	Yoshiki Takada	317-899-4440	R	151*	0.3
Cross Manufacturing Inc.	11011 King St.	Overland Park	KS	66210	John Cross	913-451-1233	R	132*	0.3
Suspa Inc.	3970 Rgr B Chaffee	Grand Rapids	MI	49548	Steve Garvelink	616-241-4200	R	116*	0.2
Oilgear Co.	PO Box 343924	Milwaukee	WI	53234	David A. Zuege	414-327-1700	R	103	0.7
Power-Packer U.S.	516 Hillcrest Dr.	Westfield	WI	53964	Robert C. Arzbaecher	608-296-2118	S	95*	<0.1
International Motion Control	369 Franklin St.	Buffalo	NY	14202	Patrick Lee	716-855-2500	R	95*	<0.1
Bosch Rexroth Corp.	5150 Prairie Stone	Hoffman Estates	IL	60192	Wolfgang Dangel	847-645-3600	R	92*	<0.1
Pfpc Enterprises Inc.	5750 Hillside Ave.	Cincinnati	OH	45233	James Coffaro	513-941-6200	R	91*	0.3
Deere-Hitachi Construct Mach.	PO Box 1187	Kernersville	NC	27285	Al Seeba	336-996-8100	J	89*	0.4
Poclain Hydraulics Inc.	PO Box 801	Sturtevant	WI	53177	Laurent Bataille	262-321-0676	R	78*	0.2
Harsh International Inc.	600 Oak Ave.	Eaton	CO	80615	Robert Brown		R	78*	0.1
Emerson Proc Management Bettis	PO Box 508	Waller	TX	77484		281-727-5300	D	75*	0.6
Networks Electronic Corp.	9750 DeSoto Ave.	Chatsworth	CA	91311	Tamara Christen	818-341-0440	R	73*	0.1
Monarch Hydraulics Inc.	1363 Michigan NE	Grand Rapids	MI	49503		616-458-1306	R	70*	0.1
W-Industries Inc.	11500 Charles Rd.	Houston	TX	77041	Rick Lynn	713-466-9463	R	70*	0.2
L and H Technologies Inc.	PO Box 7207	Charlotte	NC	28241	Clifton Vann	704-588-3670	R	69*	<0.1
Limitorque Corp.	PO Box 11318	Lynchburg	VA	24506		434-528-4400	S	65*	0.3
Young and Franklin Inc.	942 Old Liverpool	Liverpool	NY	13088	Dudley Johnson	315-457-3110	R	60*	0.1
Ramrod Industries L.L.C.	800 S Monroe St.	Spencer	WI	54479		715-659-4996	R	59*	<0.1
Crysteel Manufacturing Inc.	PO Box 178	Lake Crystal	MN	56055	Dale Pilger	507-726-2728	R	55*	0.2
Linak US Inc.	2200 Stanley Gault	Louisville	KY	40223	Soren Stig-Nielsen	502-253-5595	R	48*	<0.1
Continental Machines Inc.	5505 W 123rd St.	Savage	MN	55378	M Johnson	952-890-3300	R	45*	0.2
Precision Hydraulic Cylinders	196 N Nc Hwy. 41	Beulaville	NC	28518	Christopher Barclay	910-298-0100	R	44*	0.1
Hy-Production Inc.	6000 Grafton Rd.	Valley City	OH	44280	William Kneebusch	330-273-2400	R	41*	0.1
Regen Technologies L.L.C.	4500 E Mustard	Springfield	MO	65803	Ron Guinn	417-829-2000	R	41*	0.2
Precision Tube Inc.	1025 Fortune Dr.	Richmond	KY	40475	Mark Gentry	859-623-5595	R	39*	0.1
Whittaker Controls Inc.	12838 Saticoy St.	N Hollywood	CA	91605		818-765-8160	R	37*	0.2
ITT Industries Flojet Div.	666 E Eyer Rd.	Santa Ana	CA	92705		949-859-4945	S	37*	0.3
Parker Hannifin Pneumatic Div.	8676 M 89	Richland	MI	49083		269-629-5000	D	36*	0.3
Machine Service Inc.	PO Box 10265	Green Bay	WI	54307	Edward Fowles	920-339-3000	R	36*	0.1
Goodrich Fuel and Utility Sys.	104 Otis St.	Rome	NY	13441	Bob Shoemaker	315-838-1200	D	34*	0.2
Teleflex Marine Inc.	640 N Lewis Rd.	Limerick	PA	19468	Paul Smith	610-495-7011	D	34*	0.2
Terex Telelect Inc.	PO Box 1150	Watertown	SD	57201	Pat Carroll	605-882-4000	S	33*	0.2
Tol-O-Matic Inc.	3800 Cnty Rd 116	Hamel	MN	55340	William Toles	763-478-8000	R	31*	0.2
Manitou North America Inc.	PO Box 21386	Waco	TX	76702	Serge Bosche	254-799-0232	R	30*	0.1
ITT Industries Aerospace Ctrls	28150 Industry Dr.	Valencia	CA	91355	Bob Briggs	661-295-4000	D	29	0.5
Leslie Controls Inc.	12501 Telecom Dr.	Tampa	FL	33637		813-978-1000	D	29*	0.2
RHM Fluid Power Inc.	375 Manufacturers	Westland	MI	48186	W. W. Tulloch III	734-326-5400	R	27*	<0.1
Mechanical Tool & Engineering	PO Box 5906	Rockford	IL	61125	Richard Nordlof	815-397-4701	R	26*	0.1
Crissair Inc.	PO Box 4000	Palmdale	CA	93590	Linda Bradley	661-273-5411	R	25*	0.1
Guyan International Inc.	PO Box 2068	Streetsboro	OH	44241	Richard Olszewski	330-626-2801	R	25*	0.1
Helac Corp.	PO Box 398	Enumclaw	WA	98022	Dean Weyer	360-825-1601	R	24*	0.1
Jarp Industries Inc.	PO Box 923	Wausau	WI	54402	John Kraft	715-359-4241	R	24*	0.2
Grover Corp.	PO Box 340080	Milwaukee	WI	53234	Stuart Banghart	414-384-9472	R	24*	<0.1
Indian Head Industries Inc.	8530 Cliff Cameron	Charlotte	NC	28269	Ronald Parker	704-547-7411	R	24*	<0.1
Bobalee Inc.	PO Box 151	Ida Grove	IA	51445	Gary Godbersen	712-845-4554	S	23*	0.2
Ralph A Hiller Company Inc.	6005 Enterprise Dr.	Export	PA	15632	Randolph Hiller	724-325-1200	R	21*	<0.1
Amot Controls Corp.	401 1st St.	Richmond	CA	94801		510-307-8300	S	21*	0.2
Broderson Manufacturing Corp.	PO Box 14770	Shawnee Msn	KS	66285	Polly Broderson	913-888-0606	R	20*	<0.1
Alliance Remanufacturing Inc.	450 E Luzerne St.	Philadelphia	PA	19124	Roger Tarno	215-425-7779	R	20*	0.1
Hannon Hydraulics L.P.	625 N Loop 12	Irving	TX	75061		972-438-2870	R	19*	<0.1
Schmidt Machine Company Inc.	7013 State Hwy. 199	Upper Sandusky	OH	43351	Randy Schmidt	419-294-3814	R	19*	<0.1
West Craft Manufacturing Inc.	PO Box 596	Alto	TX	75925	Gerald West	936-858-4426	R	18*	<0.1
Robeck Fluid Power Inc.	350 Lena Dr.	Aurora	OH	44202	Peter Becker	330-562-1140	R	18*	<0.1
Attica Hydraulic Exchange	48175 Gratiot Ave.	Chesterfield	MI	48051	William Wildner	586-949-4240	R	18*	0.1
Oil-Air Products Inc.	PO Box 129	Hamel	MN	55340	Robert Pierce	763-478-8744	R	17*	<0.1
Mdh Acquisition L.L.C.	3315 Haseley Dr.	Niagara Falls	NY	14304		716-297-0652	R	17*	0.2

Source: Ward's Business Directory of U.S. Private and Public Companies, Volumes 1 and 2, 2008. The company type code used is as follows: P - Public, R - Private, S - Subsidiary, D - Division, J - Joint Venture, A - Affiliate, G - Group. Sales are in millions of dollars, employees are in thousands. An asterisk (*) indicates an estimated sales volume. The symbol < stands for 'less than'. Company names and addresses are truncated, in some cases, to fit into the available space.

MATERIALS CONSUMED FOR FLUID POWER CYLINDER AND ACTUATOR MANUFACTURING

Material	Quantity	Delivered Cost ($ million)
Fluid power pumps purchased for incorporation into manufacturing products	(X)	12.2
Metal bolts, nuts, screws, and other screw machine products	(X)	22.7
Metal pipe, valves, and pipe fittings (excluding forgings)	(X)	10.3
Other fabricated metal products (excluding forgings)	(X)	49.3
Forgings	(X)	36.2
Iron and steel castings (rough and semifinished)	(X)	47.7
Aluminum and aluminum-base alloy castings (rough and semifinished)	(X)	4.8
Other nonferrous metal castings, rough or semifinished (inc. aluminum)	(X)	3.7
Steel bars, bar shapes, and plates (exc. castings, forgings, fabr. metal products)	(X)	84.7
Steel sheet and strip (including tinplate)	(X)	1.4
Steel tubing	(X)	81.4
All other steel shapes and forms (exc. castings, forgings, fabr. metal products)	(X)	29.6
Aluminum and aluminum-base alloy extruded shapes (rod, bar, pipe, tube, etc.)	(X)	23.1
Other aluminum and aluminum-base alloy shapes and forms (exc. castings, forgings, fabr. metal products)	(X)	3.4
Other nonferrous shapes and forms (exc. castings, forgings, fabricated metal products)	(X)	0.8
Metal powders	(X)	0.1
Lubricating and cutting oils	(X)	6.1
Paints, varnishes, stains, lacquers, shellacs, japans, enamels, etc.	(X)	5.2
Electric motors and generators	(X)	9.5
Ball bearings (mounted or unmounted)	(X)	7.1
Roller bearings (mounted or unmounted)	(X)	1.3
Plain bearings and bushings	(X)	5.3
Mechanical speed changers, gears, and industrial high-speed drives	(X)	4.8
Gaskets (all types), and packing and sealing devices	(X)	25.4
Cutting tools for machine tools	(X)	20.4
All other materials, components, parts, containers, and supplies	(X)	420.4
Materials, ingredients, containers, and supplies, nsk	(X)	187.2

Source: 2002 *Economic Census*. Explanation of symbols used: (D): Withheld to avoid disclosure of competitive data; na: Not available; (S): Withheld because statistical norms were not met; (X): Not applicable; (Z): Less than half the unit shown; nec: Not elsewhere classified; nsk: Not specified by kind; - : zero; p : 10-19 percent estimated; q : 20-29 percent estimated.

MATERIALS CONSUMED FOR FLUID POWER PUMP AND MOTOR MANUFACTURING

Material	Quantity	Delivered Cost ($ million)
Fluid power pumps purchased for incorporation into manufacturing products	(X)	26.7
Metal bolts, nuts, screws, and other screw machine products	(X)	64.4
Metal pipe, valves, and pipe fittings (excluding forgings)	(X)	13.4
Other fabricated metal products (excluding forgings)	(X)	59.0
Forgings	(X)	26.9
Iron and steel castings (rough and semifinished)	(X)	61.4
Aluminum and aluminum-base alloy castings (rough and semifinished)	(X)	47.9
Other nonferrous metal castings, rough or semifinished (inc. aluminum)	(X)	3.0
Steel bars, bar shapes, and plates (exc. castings, forgings, fabr. metal products)	(X)	23.1
Steel sheet and strip (including tinplate)	(X)	4.9
Steel tubing	(X)	(D)
All other steel shapes and forms (exc. castings, forgings, fabr. metal products)	(X)	2.3
Aluminum and aluminum-base alloy extruded shapes (rod, bar, pipe, tube, etc.)	(X)	8.0
Other aluminum and aluminum-base alloy shapes and forms (exc. castings, forgings, fabr. metal products)	(X)	(D)
Other nonferrous shapes and forms (exc. castings, forgings, fabricated metal products)	(X)	(D)
Metal powders	(X)	18.4
Lubricating and cutting oils	(X)	6.0
Paints, varnishes, stains, lacquers, shellacs, japans, enamels, etc.	(X)	0.8
Electric motors and generators	(X)	34.7
Ball bearings (mounted or unmounted)	(X)	9.5
Roller bearings (mounted or unmounted)	(X)	30.0
Plain bearings and bushings	(X)	5.1
Mechanical speed changers, gears, and industrial high-speed drives	(X)	9.6
Gaskets (all types), and packing and sealing devices	(X)	12.5
Cutting tools for machine tools	(X)	20.5
All other materials, components, parts, containers, and supplies	(X)	318.1
Materials, ingredients, containers, and supplies, nsk	(X)	122.9

Source: 2002 *Economic Census*. Explanation of symbols used: (D): Withheld to avoid disclosure of competitive data; na: Not available; (S): Withheld because statistical norms were not met; (X): Not applicable; (Z): Less than half the unit shown; nec: Not elsewhere classified; nsk: Not specified by kind; - : zero; p : 10-19 percent estimated; q : 20-29 percent estimated.

PRODUCT SHARE DETAILS FOR FLUID POWER CYLINDER AND ACTUATOR MANUFACTURING

Product or Product Class Shipments	Mil. $	Product or Product Class Shipments	Mil. $
FLUID POWER CYLINDERS AND ACTUATORS	3,080.3	cylinders and actuators, including accumulators, cushions, etc.	369.1
Nonaerospace type hydraulic fluid power cylinders and actuators, linear and rotary	956.8	Aerospace type fluid power cylinders and actuators, hydraulic and pneumatic	987.7
Nonaerospace type pneumatic fluid power cylinders and actuators, linear and rotary	520.7	Fluid power cylinders and actuators, nsk, total	246.0
Parts for nonaerospace hydraulic and pneumatic fluid power			

Source: 2002 *Economic Census*. The values are product shipments in millions of dollars for 2002. Total product shipments may be lower or higher than industry shipments. See Introduction for a full discussion. Values of indented subcategories are summed in the main heading(s). The symbol (D) appears when data are withheld to prevent disclosure of competitive information. The abbreviation nsk stands for 'not specified by kind' and nec for 'not elsewhere classified'. A dash (-) means zero.

PRODUCT SHARE DETAILS FOR FLUID POWER PUMP AND MOTOR MANUFACTURING

Product or Product Class Shipments	Mil. $	Product or Product Class Shipments	Mil. $
FLUID POWER PUMPS AND MOTORS	2,388.5	Aerospace type fluid power pumps and motors	212.9
Nonaerospace type reciprocating fluid power pumps . . .	632.9	Parts for fluid power pumps, motors, and hydrostatic	
Nonaerospace type rotary and other fluid power pumps . .	492.2	transmissions	510.0
Nonaerospace type fluid power motors	369.8	Fluid power pump and motors, nsk, total	170.7

Source: 2002 *Economic Census*. The values are product shipments in millions of dollars for 2002. Total product shipments may be lower or higher than industry shipments. See Introduction for a full discussion. Values of indented subcategories are summed in the main heading(s). The symbol (D) appears when data are withheld to prevent disclosure of competitive information. The abbreviation nsk stands for 'not specified by kind' and nec for 'not elsewhere classified'. A dash (-) means zero.

INPUTS AND OUTPUTS FOR FLUID POWER PROCESS MACHINERY

Economic Sector or Industry Providing Inputs	%	Sector	Economic Sector or Industry Buying Outputs	%	Sector
Compensation of employees	34.1		Motor vehicle parts	15.8	Manufg.
Iron & steel mills & ferroalloys	6.0	Manufg.	Exports of goods & services	9.5	Cap Inv
Management of companies & enterprises	6.0	Services	Light truck & utility vehicles	6.1	Manufg.
Wholesale trade	5.3	Trade	Material handling equipment	5.8	Manufg.
Turned products & screws, nuts, & bolts	3.0	Manufg.	Aircraft	5.8	Manufg.
Gaskets, packing, & sealing devices	2.5	Manufg.	Construction machinery	5.5	Manufg.
Ferrous metal foundries	2.5	Manufg.	Automobiles	3.9	Manufg.
Machine shops	2.4	Manufg.	Private fixed investment	3.3	
Fluid power process machinery	1.8	Manufg.	Commercial & service industry machinery, nec	2.9	Manufg.
Forging, stamping, & sintering, nec	1.6	Manufg.	General Federal government services, defense	2.9	Fed Govt
Nonferrous metal foundries	1.5	Manufg.	Farm machinery & equipment	2.9	Manufg.
Ball & roller bearings	1.4	Manufg.	Printing	2.5	Manufg.
Motors & generators	1.0	Manufg.	Industrial machinery, nec	2.5	Manufg.
Truck transportation	1.0	Util.	Wholesale trade	2.1	Trade
Semiconductors & related devices	1.0	Manufg.	General purpose machinery, nec	1.8	Manufg.
Cutting tools & machine tool accessories	1.0	Manufg.	Engine equipment, nec	1.6	Manufg.
Aluminum products from purchased aluminum	1.0	Manufg.	Fluid power process machinery	1.5	Manufg.
Power generation & supply	1.0	Util.	Aircraft engine & engine parts	1.4	Manufg.
Printed circuit assemblies (electronic assemblies)	1.0	Manufg.	Railroad rolling stock	1.4	Manufg.
Abrasive products	0.9	Manufg.	Lawn & garden equipment	1.4	Manufg.
Valve & fittings other than plumbing	0.8	Manufg.	Semiconductor machinery	1.4	Manufg.
Securities, commodity contracts, investments	0.8	Fin/R.E.	Ship building & repairing	1.4	Manufg.
Coating, engraving, heat treating & allied activities	0.6	Manufg.	Motor vehicle bodies	1.3	Manufg.
Advertising & related services	0.5	Services	Machine shops	1.2	Manufg.
Lessors of nonfinancial assets	0.5	Fin/R.E.	Packaging machinery	1.2	Manufg.
Real estate	0.4	Fin/R.E.	Pumps & pumping equipment	1.1	Manufg.
Management, scientific, & technical consulting	0.4	Services	Mining & oil & gas field machinery	1.0	Manufg.
Speed changers, industrial high-speed drives, & gears	0.4	Manufg.	Heavy duty trucks	0.9	Manufg.
Custom computer programming services	0.4	Services	Federal government, investment, national defense	0.9	Fed Govt
Monetary authorities/depository credit intermediation	0.4	Fin/R.E.	Truck trailers	0.9	Manufg.
Taxes on production & imports, less subsidies	0.4		Turbines & turbine generator set units	0.8	Manufg.
Legal services	0.4	Services	Rolling mill & other metalworking machinery	0.7	Manufg.
Mechanical power transmission equipment	0.4	Manufg.	Plastics & rubber industry machinery	0.6	Manufg.
Data processing, hosting, & related services	0.3	Services	Metal cutting & forming machine tools	0.6	Manufg.
Professional, scientific, technical services, nec	0.3	Services	Guided missiles & space vehicles	0.6	Manufg.
Scientific research & development services	0.3	Services	Aircraft parts & auxiliary equipment, nec	0.6	Manufg.
Paperboard containers	0.3	Manufg.	Warehousing & storage	0.5	Util.
Architectural, engineering, & related services	0.3	Services	Fabricated metals, nec	0.4	Manufg.
Nonferrous metal (ex. copper & aluminum) processing	0.3	Manufg.	Other S/L govt. enterprises	0.4	S/L Govt
Warehousing & storage	0.3	Util.	Air & gas compressors	0.4	Manufg.
Accounting, tax preparation, bookkeeping, & payroll	0.3	Services	Commercial & industrial equipment repair/maintenance	0.4	Services
Maintenance/repair of nonresidential structures	0.3	Construct.	Special tools, dies, jigs, & fixtures	0.3	Manufg.
Petroleum lubricating oil & grease	0.3	Manufg.	Retail trade	0.3	Trade
Fabricated metals, nec	0.3	Manufg.	Industrial process furnaces & ovens	0.2	Manufg.
Services to buildings & dwellings	0.3	Services	General Federal government services, nondefense	0.2	Fed Govt
Telecommunications	0.3	Services	Water transportation	0.1	Util.
Paints & coatings	0.2	Manufg.	Ball & roller bearings	0.1	Manufg.

Continued on next page.

INPUTS AND OUTPUTS FOR FLUID POWER PROCESS MACHINERY - Continued

Economic Sector or Industry Providing Inputs	%	Sector	Economic Sector or Industry Buying Outputs	%	Sector
Metal cans, boxes, & other containers (light gauge)	0.2	Manufg.	Industrial molds	0.1	Manufg.
Rubber products, nec	0.2	Manufg.	Scientific research & development services	0.1	Services
Automotive equipment rental & leasing	0.2	Fin/R.E.	Cutting tools & machine tool accessories	0.1	Manufg.
Noncomparable imports	0.2	Foreign			
Other computer related services, including facilities	0.2	Services			
Employment services	0.2	Services			
Business support services	0.2	Services			
Food services & drinking places	0.2	Services			
Specialized design services	0.2	Services			
Automotive repair & maintenance, ex. car washes	0.2	Services			
Natural gas distribution	0.2	Util.			
Plate work & fabricated structural products	0.2	Manufg.			
Crowns & closures & metal stamping	0.2	Manufg.			
Commercial & industrial equipment repair/maintenance	0.2	Services			
Relay & industrial controls	0.1	Manufg.			
Chemical products & preparations, nec	0.1	Manufg.			
Bare printed circuit boards	0.1	Manufg.			
Paperboard mills	0.1	Manufg.			
Custom roll forming	0.1	Manufg.			
Handtools	0.1	Manufg.			
Rail transportation	0.1	Util.			
Support services, nec	0.1	Services			
Commercial & industrial machinery rental & leasing	0.1	Fin/R.E.			

Source: Benchmark Input-Output Accounts for the U.S. Economy, 2002, U.S. Department of Commerce, Washington, D.C., January 2008. The abbreviation nec stands for 'not elsewhere classified'.

OCCUPATIONS EMPLOYED BY OTHER GENERAL-PURPOSE MACHINERY MANUFACTURING

Occupation	% of Total 2006	Change to 2016	Occupation	% of Total 2006	Change to 2016
Team assemblers	11.0	-9.7	Multiple machine tool operators & tenders	1.4	-0.7
Machinists	5.9	-5.2	Lathe & turning machine tool operators & tenders	1.4	-18.8
Welders, cutters, solderers, & brazers	5.7	-4.0	Maintenance & repair workers, general	1.4	-9.7
First-line supervisors/managers of production workers	3.6	-9.7	Structural metal fabricators & fitters	1.4	-9.7
Mechanical engineers	2.8	-0.7	Industrial engineers	1.3	9.6
Computer-controlled machine tool operators	2.5	-0.7	Electrical & electronic equipment assemblers	1.3	-27.8
Sales reps, wholesale & manufacturing, exc tech	2.3	-9.7	Industrial machinery mechanics	1.3	3.8
Engine & other machine assemblers	2.0	-9.7	Mechanical drafters	1.3	-8.7
Inspectors, testers, sorters, samplers, & weighers	1.9	-14.9	Customer service representatives	1.3	-0.7
Cutting, punching, & press machine operators	1.8	-18.8	Coating, painting, & spraying machine operators	1.2	-14.2
Shipping, receiving, & traffic clerks	1.8	-13.1	Office clerks, general	1.2	-11.1
Helpers--Production workers	1.6	-9.7	Industrial production managers	1.1	-9.7
General & operations managers	1.6	-18.8	Electrical engineers	1.1	-9.7
Laborers & freight, stock, & material movers, hand	1.5	-18.8	Production, planning, & expediting clerks	1.1	-9.7
Purchasing agents, exc wholesale, retail, & farm	1.5	-18.8	Stock clerks & order fillers	1.0	-24.5
Bookkeeping, accounting, & auditing clerks	1.5	-9.7			

Source: Industry-Occupation Matrix, Bureau of Labor Statistics, December 4, 2007. These data are reported based on 4-digit NAICS categories but have been matched to corresponding 6-digit NAICS industry codes. The change reported for each occupation to the year 2016 is a percent of growth or decline as estimated by the Bureau of Labor Statistics. The abbreviation nec stands for 'not elsewhere classified'.

LOCATION BY STATE AND REGIONAL CONCENTRATION

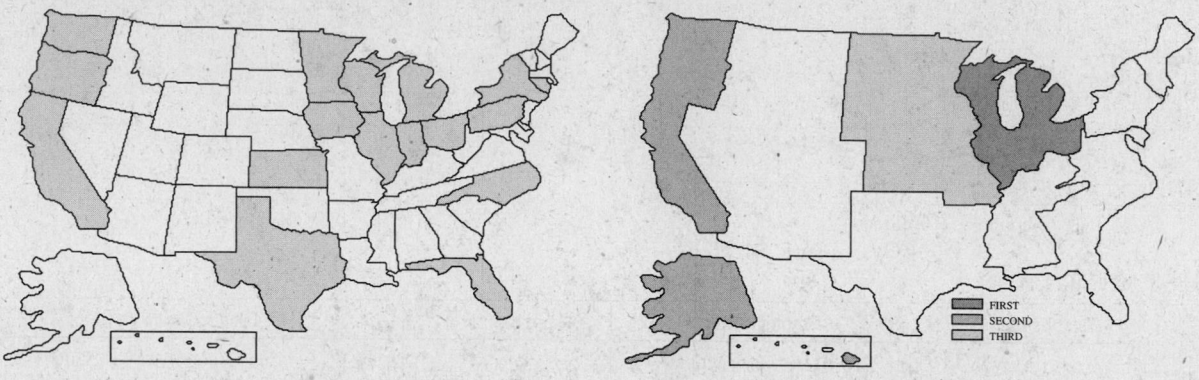

FIRST
SECOND
THIRD

INDUSTRY DATA BY STATE

| State | Establish-ments | Shipments | | | Employment | | | | Cost as % of Shipments | Investment per Employee ($) |
		Total ($ mil)	% of U.S.	Per Establ.	Total Number	% of U.S.	Per Establ.	Wages ($/hour)		
New York	14	549.3	9.8	39,235.2	3,093	9.7	221	23.10	23.4	6,240
Ohio	49	488.8	8.7	9,975.3	3,034	9.5	62	18.03	48.2	6,179
California	51	429.7	7.6	8,425.4	2,426	7.6	48	21.65	43.8	2,852
Illinois	12	380.8	6.8	31,729.9	1,788	5.6	149	19.18	59.6	5,945
Michigan	29	299.1	5.3	10,315.0	1,719	5.4	59	19.93	46.0	5,876
Wisconsin	26	232.5	4.1	8,941.8	1,524	4.8	59	15.32	46.7	4,407
Kansas	11	200.5	3.6	18,231.7	957	3.0	87	15.39	34.1	4,844
Texas	30	177.9	3.2	5,931.0	1,257	3.9	42	15.00	43.2	1,681
Minnesota	16	128.7	2.3	8,046.5	740	2.3	46	19.09	49.2	3,808
Iowa	7	124.4	2.2	17,769.4	1,075	3.4	154	13.77	40.9	3,118
North Carolina	5	106.8	1.9	21,350.8	535	1.7	107	19.10	47.4	11,675
Indiana	9	76.4	1.4	8,483.4	419	1.3	47	16.13	31.3	6,346
Washington	14	70.9	1.3	5,062.7	543	1.7	39	25.14	51.5	1,967
Florida	12	66.1	1.2	5,512.1	480	1.5	40	15.31	44.9	1,994
Oregon	9	46.6	0.8	5,180.6	341	1.1	38	16.98	27.0	3,413
Connecticut	8	33.6	0.6	4,195.7	244	0.8	30	19.17	28.7	3,631
Pennsylvania	9	30.4	0.5	3,375.3	189	0.6	21	15.29	50.4	5,323

Source: 2002 *Economic Census*. The states are in descending order of shipments or establishments (if shipment data are missing for the majority). The symbol (D) appears when data are withheld to prevent disclosure of competitive information. States marked with (D) are sorted by number of establishments. A dash (-) indicates that the data element cannot be calculated. Data may not show all states active in the NAICS category. All data available at the time of publication are shown.

NAICS 33399P - GENERAL PURPOSE MACHINERY MANUFACTURING NEC*

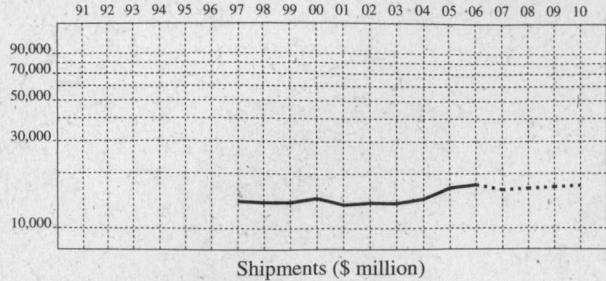

Shipments ($ million)

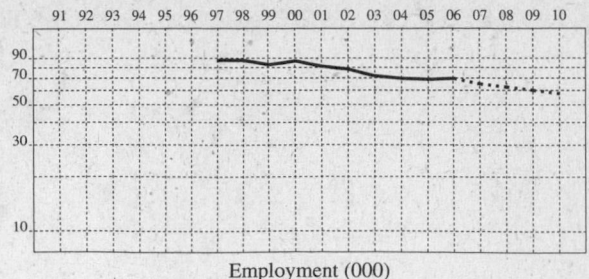

Employment (000)

GENERAL STATISTICS

| Year | Companies | Establishments | | Employment | | | Compensation | | Production ($ million) | | | |
		Total	with 20 or more employees	Total (000)	Production Workers (000)	Hours (Mil)	Payroll ($ mil)	Wages ($/hr)	Cost of Materials	Value Added by Manufacture	Value of Shipments	Capital Invest.
1997	2,333	2,457	789	87.5	53.9	105.3	3,208.9	14.73	6,750.8	7,447.6	14,091.7	419.0
1998		2,533	787	87.6	53.3	105.1	3,252.4	14.61	6,540.3	7,306.7	13,889.2	413.3
1999		2,452	787	82.9	49.4	96.1	3,227.7	14.96	6,742.2	7,207.7	13,938.5	415.5
2000		2,379	779	86.8	52.4	101.5	3,436.3	15.41	7,293.2	7,538.7	14,687.6	417.4
2001		2,295	771	81.2	47.7	94.3	3,294.4	15.84	6,555.4	6,720.4	13,524.4	416.2
2002	2,234	2,364	726	78.2	44.0	81.6	3,365.4	17.72	6,047.2	7,884.6	13,810.9	399.1
2003		2,208	683	71.8	40.7	81.1	3,189.7	17.08	6,199.7	7,611.6	13,741.7	360.8
2004		2,187	688	69.8	38.9	79.4	3,231.3	17.42	6,631.7	7,597.3	14,516.3	374.6
2005		2,149	678	68.9	39.5	83.4	3,318.3	16.97	7,798.3	9,006.3	16,697.4	458.0
2006		2,105P	660P	69.6	41.2	86.6	3,421.1	17.54	8,403.8	8,874.0	17,364.6	359.2
2007		2,059P	643P	64.9P	36.0P	75.5P	3,351.9P	18.26P	7,876.3P	8,317.0P	16,274.6P	382.8P
2008		2,013P	626P	62.5P	34.2P	72.6P	3,362.3P	18.63P	8,021.3P	8,470.1P	16,574.3P	379.0P
2009		1,966P	610P	60.0P	32.4P	69.7P	3,372.7P	19.00P	8,166.4P	8,623.3P	16,874.0P	375.3P
2010		1,920P	593P	57.5P	30.5P	66.8P	3,383.2P	19.37P	8,311.4P	8,776.5P	17,173.7P	371.5P

Sources: 1997 and 2002 *Economic Census*; other years, up to 2006, are from *Annual Survey of Manufactures*. Establishment counts for non-Census years are from *County Business Patterns*; 1997 and 2002 values are from the 1997 and 2002 censuses, respectively. 'P's show projections by the editors.

INDICES OF CHANGE

| Year | Companies | Establishments | | Employment | | | Compensation | | Production ($ million) | | | |
		Total	with 20 or more employees	Total (000)	Production Workers (000)	Hours (Mil)	Payroll ($ mil)	Wages ($/hr)	Cost of Materials	Value Added by Manufacture	Value of Shipments	Capital Invest.
1997	104	104	109	112	122	129	95	83	112	94	102	105
1998		107	108	112	121	129	97	82	108	93	101	104
1999		104	108	106	112	118	96	84	111	91	101	104
2000		101	107	111	119	124	102	87	121	96	106	105
2001		97	106	104	108	116	98	89	108	85	98	104
2002	100	100	100	100	100	100	100	100	100	100	100	100
2003		93	94	92	93	99	95	96	103	97	99	90
2004		93	95	89	88	97	96	98	110	96	105	94
2005		91	93	88	90	102	99	96	129	114	121	115
2006		89P	91P	89	94	106	102	99	139	113	126	90
2007		87P	89P	83P	82P	93P	100P	103P	130P	105P	118P	96P
2008		85P	86P	80P	78P	89P	100P	105P	133P	107P	120P	95P
2009		83P	84P	77P	74P	85P	100P	107P	135P	109P	122P	94P
2010		81P	82P	74P	69P	82P	101P	109P	137P	111P	124P	93P

Sources: Same as General Statistics. Values reflect change from the base year, 2002. Values above 100 mean greater than 2002, values below 100 mean less than 2002, and the values of 100 in other years means the same as 2002. 'P's show projections by the editors.

SELECTED RATIOS

For 2002	Avg. of All Manufact.	Analyzed Industry	Index	For 2002	Avg. of All Manufact.	Analyzed Industry	Index
Employees per Establishment	42	33	79	Value Added per Production Worker	182,367	179,195	98
Payroll per Establishment	1,639,184	1,423,604	87	Cost per Establishment	5,769,015	2,558,037	44
Payroll per Employee	39,053	43,036	110	Cost per Employee	137,446	77,330	56
Production Workers per Establishment	30	19	63	Cost per Production Worker	195,506	137,436	70
Wages per Establishment	694,845	611,655	88	Shipments per Establishment	11,158,348	5,842,174	52
Wages per Production Worker	23,548	32,863	140	Shipments per Employee	265,847	176,610	66
Hours per Production Worker	1,980	1,855	94	Shipments per Production Worker	378,144	313,884	83
Wages per Hour	11.89	17.72	149	Investment per Establishment	361,338	168,824	47
Value Added per Establishment	5,381,325	3,335,279	62	Investment per Employee	8,609	5,104	59
Value Added per Employee	128,210	100,826	79	Investment per Production Worker	12,245	9,070	74

Sources: Same as General Statistics. The 'Average of All Manufacturing' column represents the average of all manufacturing industries reported for the most recent complete year available. The Index shows the relationship between the Average and the Analyzed Industry. For example, 100 means that they are equal; 500 that the Analyzed Industry is five times the average; 50 means that the Analyzed Industry is half the national average. The abbreviation 'na' is used to show that data are 'not available'. Ratios shown for 2002, the last complete census year.

*Equivalent to Federal Government NAICS 333992, 333997, 333999.

LEADING COMPANIES   Number shown: 75   Total sales ($ mil): 172,386   Total employment (000): 473.8

Company Name	Address				CEO Name	Phone	Co. Type	Sales ($ mil)	Empl. (000)
General Dynamics Corp.	2941 Fairview Park	Falls Church	VA	22042	Nicholas D. Chabraja	703-876-3000	P	27,240	83.5
Illinois Tool Works Inc.	3600 W Lake Ave.	Glenview	IL	60025		847-724-7500	P	16,171	60.0
Applied Materials Inc.	PO Box 58039	Santa Clara	CA	95052		408-727-5555	P	9,735	15.3
API Group Inc.	2366 Rose Pl.	St. Paul	MN	55113	Lee R. Anderson Sr.	651-636-4320	R	9,000	5.0
Crown Holdings Inc.	1 Crown Way	Philadelphia	PA	19154	John W. Conway	215-698-5100	P	7,727	21.8
Prager Inc.	PO Box 61670	New Orleans	LA	70161	Jennifer McKnight	504-524-2363	R	7,580*	<0.1
Newell Rubbermaid Inc.	10B Glenlake Pkwy.	Atlanta	GA	30328		770-407-3800	P	6,407	22.0
Lincoln Electric Co.	22801 St. Clair Ave	Cleveland	OH	44117		216-481-8100	S	5,398*	7.0
Rockwell Automation Inc.	777 E Wisconsin	Milwaukee	WI	53202		414-212-5800	P	5,004	20.0
Culligan International Co.	1 Culligan Pkwy.	Northbrook	IL	60062	Mark Seals	847-205-6000	R	4,916*	5.5
Flowserve Corp.	5215 N O'Connor	Irving	TX	75039		972-443-6500	P	3,763	15.0
Harsco Corp.	PO Box 8888	Camp Hill	PA	17001	S. D. Fazzolari	717-763-7064	P	3,688	21.5
Diebold Inc.	PO Box 3077	North Canton	OH	44720		330-490-4000	P	2,906	15.5
Crown Cork and Seal Company	1 Crown Way	Philadelphia	PA	19154	John W. Conway	215-698-5100	S	2,640*	11.0
O'Reilly Automotive Inc.	233 S Patterson Ave	Springfield	MO	65802	Greg Henslee	417-862-6708	P	2,522	18.5
Heico Companies L.L.C.	70 W Madison St.	Chicago	IL	60602	M. E. Heisley, Sr.	312-419-8220	R	2,500	11.0
Pall Corp.	2200 Northern Blvd.	East Hills	NY	11548	Eric Krasnoff	516-484-5400	P	2,250	10.8
American Power Conversion	132 Fairgrounds Rd.	West Kingston	RI	02892	Rodger B. Dowdell Jr.	401-789-5735	S	1,980	7.6
Teleflex Inc.	155 S Limerick Rd.	Limerick	PA	19468	Jeffrey P. Black	610-948-5100	P	1,934	14.0
Schuler Inc.	7145 Commerce	Canton	MI	48187	Timothy McCaughey	734-207-7200	R	1,874*	<0.1
Weir Spm	7701 Skyline Park	Fort Worth	TX	76108	Steve Noon	817-246-2461	R	1,770*	0.3
Kawasaki Motors Manufacturing	PO Box 81469	Lincoln	NE	68501		402-476-6600	S	1,758*	1.3
Curtiss-Wright Corp.	4 Becker Farm Rd.	Roseland	NJ	07068	Martin R. Benante	973-597-4700	P	1,592	6.2
Rainin Instrument L.L.C.	PO Box 4026	Woburn	MA	01888	Kenneth Rainin	510-564-1600	R	1,590*	0.1
Moog Inc.	Jamison Rd.	East Aurora	NY	14052		716-652-2000	P	1,558	8.4
Stoody Co.	5557 Nashville Rd.	Bowling Green	KY	42101	Paul D. Melnuk	270-781-9777	S	1,537*	3.0
Thermadyne Manufacturing	101 S Hanley Rd.	St. Louis	MO	63105	Paul D. Melnuk	314-721-5573	S	1,537*	3.0
Marison Cylinder Co.	101 S Hanley Rd.	St. Louis	MO	63105	Paul D. Melnuk	314-721-5573	S	1,530*	3.0
Modern Engineering Company	US Highway I-55 S	Gallman	MS	39077	Paul D. Melnuk	601-892-3500	S	1,530*	3.0
Thermadyne Industries Inc.	16052 Swingley	Chesterfield	MO	63017	Paul D. Melnuk	314-721-5573	S	1,530*	3.0
Thermal Dynamics Corp.	Industrial Part #D	West Lebanon	NH	03784	Paul D. Melnuk	603-298-5711	S	1,530*	3.0
Victor Coyne International	101 S Hanley Rd.	St. Louis	MO	63105	Paul D. Melnuk	314-721-5573	S	1,530*	3.0
Victor Gas Systems Inc.	960 Brookroad, 1	Conshohocken	PA	19428	Paul D. Melnuk	314-721-5573	S	1,530*	3.0
Beckett Corp.	400 E Royal Ln.	Irving	TX	75039	Wingate Sung	972-871-8000	R	1,409*	0.1
Fulmer Company L.L.C.	3004 Venture Ct.	Export	PA	15632	Leo Eger	724-325-7140	R	1,320*	<0.1
Swagelok Co.	29500 Solon Rd.	Solon	OH	44139	Arthur F. Anton	440-248-4600	R	1,100*	3.3
TriMas Corp.	39400 Woodward	Bloomfield Hls	MI	48304	Grant Beard	248-631-5450	P	1,068	5.1
Nordson Corp.	28601 Clemens Rd.	Westlake	OH	44145	Edward P. Campbell	440-892-1580	P	994	4.1
Madison Filter Inc.	PO Box 238	Skaneateles Fls	NY	13153		315-685-3466	R	991*	0.1
EFD Inc.	977 Waterman Ave.	East Providence	RI	02914	Peter Lambert	401-434-1680	S	972*	0.3
NGK-Locke Inc.	2525 Insulator Dr.	Baltimore	MD	21230	Shun Matsushita	410-347-1700	S	941*	3.7
Intermec Inc.	6001 36th Ave. W	Everett	WA	98203	Patrick Byrne	425-348-2600	P	849	2.4
Graco Inc.	PO Box 1441	Minneapolis	MN	55440		612-623-6000	P	841	2.3
Pneumatic Scale Corp.	10 Ascot Pkwy.	Cuyahoga Falls	OH	44223	Robert Chapman	330-923-0491	S	786*	0.2
MKS Instruments Inc.	90 Industrial Way	Wilmington	MA	01887	Leo Berlinghieri	978-284-4000	P	783	3.0
Dover Diversified Inc.	Highland Oaks I	Downers Grove	IL	60515	William W. Spurgeon	630-725-9347	S	781*	4.0
Foseco Inc.	PO Box 81227	Cleveland	OH	44181	Lee Plutshack	440-826-4548	R	772*	<0.1
Progressive Tool & Ind./Wisne	21000 Telegraph Rd.	Southfield	MI	48034	Robert Stoutenburg	248-353-8888	D	733*	5.5
Senior Operations Inc.	300 E Devon Ave.	Bartlett	IL	60103	Graham Menzies	630-837-1811	R	733*	0.7
NCH Corp.	PO Box 152170	Irving	TX	75015		972-438-0211	R	688*	8.5
White Systems Inc.	30 Boright Ave.	Kenilworth	NJ	07033	Richard Paolino	908-272-6700	S	673*	0.3
Bachman Machine Co.	4321 N Broadway	St. Louis	MO	63147	William Bachman	314-231-4221	R	656*	0.1
Parker Drilling Co.	1401 Enclave Pky.	Houston	TX	77077		281-406-2000	P	655	3.1
Altra Holdings Inc.	14 Hayward St.	Quincy	MA	02171	Michael L. Hurt	617-328-3300	P	584	3.5
KOCH Enterprises Inc.	14 S Eleventh Ave.	Evansville	IN	47744	Robert L. Koch II	812-465-9800	R	577*	3.2
Fisher Scientific	2000 Park Lane Dr.	Pittsburgh	PA	15275	David Dellapenta	412-490-8300	D	568	1.8
National Filter Media Corp.	691 N 400 W	Salt Lake City	UT	84103	John Eugster	801-363-6736	R	526*	<0.1
Cotton Goods Manufacturing Co.	259 N California	Chicago	IL	60612	Edward J. Lewis	773-265-0088	R	525*	<0.1
Omega Flex Inc.	451 Creamery Way	Exton	PA	19341	Kevin R. Hoben	610-524-7272	S	475*	0.1
CPI Products L.L.C.	12501 Taylor Rd.	Charlevoix	MI	49720	Doug Hellyar	231-547-6064	R	466*	<0.1
Kaydon Corp.	315 E Eisenhower	Ann Arbor	MI	48108		734-747-7025	P	451	2.1
Newport Corp.	1791 Deere Ave.	Irvine	CA	92606	Michael ONeill	949-863-3144	P	445	2.0
RMS Co.	8600 Evergreen Blvd	Coon Rapids	MN	55433	Arthur Mouyard	763-786-1520	S	400*	0.3
Cretex Co's Inc.	311 Lowell NW	Elk River	MN	55330	Albert Bailey	763-441-2121	R	400*	<0.1
FANUC Robotics America Inc.	3900 W Hamlin Rd.	Rochester Hills	MI	48309		248-377-7000	R	361*	0.9
Cuno Inc.	400 Research Pky.	Meriden	CT	06450	Chris O'Connor	203-237-5541	S	352*	2.2
Gleason Corp.	PO Box 22970	Rochester	NY	14692		585-473-1000	R	350*	2.6
Graphel Corp.	PO Box 369	West Chester	OH	45071	Cliff Kersker	513-779-6166	R	337*	0.1
Engineered Machined Products	3111 N 28th St.	Escanaba	MI	49829	Brian Larche	906-786-8404	R	333*	0.5
Magnetic Instruments Corp.	1801 Indu. Blvd.	Brenham	TX	77833	Nelson Byman	979-836-4481	R	331*	0.2
Multiquip Inc.	PO Box 6254	Carson	CA	90749	Roger Euliss	310-537-3700	R	317*	0.3
Veeder-Root Co.	PO Box 2003	Simsbury	CT	06070	Brian Burnett	860-651-2700	S	282*	0.6
Systems Electro Coating	253 Old Jackson Rd.	Madison	MS	39110	Toni Cooley	601-407-2340	R	282*	<0.1
Pall Aeropower Corp.	1054 Ridge Rd.	New Port Richey FL		34654	Jim Wester	727-849-9999	S	271*	0.5
Taurus Numeric Tool Inc.	213 Chelsea Rd.	Monticello	MN	55362	Mike Pudil	763-295-9202	S	252*	<0.1

Source: Ward's Business Directory of U.S. Private and Public Companies, Volumes 1 and 2, 2008. The company type code used is as follows: P - Public, R - Private, S - Subsidiary, D - Division, J - Joint Venture, A - Affiliate, G - Group. Sales are in millions of dollars, employees are in thousands. An asterisk (*) indicates an estimated sales volume. The symbol < stands for 'less than'. Company names and addresses are truncated, in some cases, to fit into the available space.

MATERIALS CONSUMED FOR WELDING AND SOLDERING EQUIPMENT MANUFACTURING

Material	Quantity	Delivered Cost ($ million)
Metal bolts, nuts, screws, and other screw machine products	(X)	21.1
Other fabricated metal products (exc. castings and forgings)	(X)	23.1
Forgings	(X)	7.4
Iron and steel castings (rough and semifinished)	(X)	(D)
Copper and copper-base alloy castings (rough and semifinished)	(X)	4.7
Other nonferrous metal castings, rough or semifinished (exc. copper)	(X)	10.6
Steel bars, bar shapes, and plates (exc. castings, forgings, fabr. metal products)	(X)	48.1
Steel sheet and strip (including tinplate)	(X)	73.5
Steel wire and wire products	(X)	62.8
All other steel shapes and forms (exc. castings, forgings, fabr. metal products)	(X)	(D)
Copper and copper-base alloy shapes and forms (exc. castings, forgings, fabr. metal products)	(X)	60.6
Aluminum and aluminum-base alloy shapes and forms (exc. castings, forgings, fabr. metal products)	(X)	41.8
Other nonferrous shapes and forms (exc. castings, forgings, fabricated metal products)	(X)	12.0
Insulated copper wire and cable (excluding magnet wire)	(X)	7.5
Fractional horsepower electric timing motors (less than 1 hp)	(X)	9.6
Fractional horsepower electric motors (less than 1 hp), exc. timing motors	(X)	6.1
Integral horsepower electric motors and generators (1 hp or more)	(X)	(D)
Electrical transmission, distribution, and control equipment	(X)	57.1
Electrical industrial capacitors, resistors, rheostats, and coil windings	(X)	42.2
Pressure gauges	(X)	2.9
Ball bearings (mounted or unmounted)	(X)	2.0
Roller bearings (mounted or unmounted)	(X)	1.1
Paperboard containers, boxes, and corrugated paperboard	(X)	36.4
Industrial robots purchased for fabrication with welding equipment	(X)	47.6
All other materials, components, parts, containers, and supplies	(X)	882.7
Materials, ingredients, containers, and supplies, nsk	(X)	20.5

Source: 2002 Economic Census. Explanation of symbols used: (D): Withheld to avoid disclosure of competitive data; na: Not available; (S): Withheld because statistical norms were not met; (X): Not applicable; (Z): Less than half the unit shown; nec: Not elsewhere classified; nsk: Not specified by kind; - : zero; p : 10-19 percent estimated; q : 20-29 percent estimated.

MATERIALS CONSUMED FOR SCALE AND BALANCE (EXCEPT LABORATORY) MANUFACTURING

Material	Quantity	Delivered Cost ($ million)
Sheet metal products (excluding stampings)	(X)	13.8
Metal bolts, nuts, screws, and other screw machine products	(X)	3.7
All other fabricated metal products (excluding forgings)	(X)	6.2
Forgings	(X)	(D)
Iron and steel castings (rough and semifinished)	(X)	(D)
Nonferrous (aluminum, copper, etc.) castings (rough and semifinished)	(X)	1.5
Steel bars, bar shapes, and plates (exc. castings, forgings, fabr. metal products)	(X)	13.3
Steel structural shapes and sheet piling (exc. castings, forgings, fabr. metal products)	(X)	3.9
All other steel shapes and forms (exc. castings, forgings, fabr. metal products)	(X)	0.6
Nonferrous shapes and forms	(X)	(D)
Aluminum and aluminum-base alloy shapes and forms (exc. castings, forgings, fabr. metal products)	(X)	(D)
Copper and copper-base alloy shapes and forms (exc. castings, forgings, fabr. metal products)	(X)	(D)
Semiconductors (incl. transistors, diodes, rectifiers, and integrated circuits), for electronic circuitry	(X)	10.7
Resistors, capacitors, transformers, transducers, and other electronic-type components	(X)	18.4
Printed ciruit boards (without inserted components) for electronic circuitry	(X)	10.1
Electric motors and generators	(X)	3.0
Industrial controls	(X)	1.4
Purchased peripheral printers	(X)	2.4
Insulated wire and cable (including magnet wire)	(X)	3.9
Appliance outlets and other current-carrying wiring devices	(X)	(D)
Electrical transmission, distribution, and control equipment	(X)	2.8
Paperboard containers, boxes, and corrugated paperboard	(X)	3.4
Purchased peripheral input devices (including keyboards, mouse devices, track balls, etc.)	(X)	1.2
Liquid crystal display screens (LCD), including LED	(X)	5.2
Fabricated plastics products (excluding gaskets)	(X)	5.7
Fabricated rubber products (excluding gaskets)	(X)	0.6
All other materials, components, parts, containers, and supplies	(X)	73.4
Materials, ingredients, containers, and supplies, nsk	(X)	57.0

Source: 2002 Economic Census. Explanation of symbols used: (D): Withheld to avoid disclosure of competitive data; na: Not available; (S): Withheld because statistical norms were not met; (X): Not applicable; (Z): Less than half the unit shown; nec: Not elsewhere classified; nsk: Not specified by kind; - : zero; p : 10-19 percent estimated; q : 20-29 percent estimated.

MATERIALS CONSUMED FOR MISCELLANEOUS GENERAL PURPOSE MACHINERY NEC

Material	Quantity	Delivered Cost ($ million)
Electric motors and generators	(X)	44.2
Electrical transmission, distribution, and control equipment	(X)	32.1
Fluid power pumps, motors, and hydrostatic transmissions	(X)	49.5
Fluid power cylinders and rotary actuators (hydraulic and pneumatic)	(X)	42.2
Fluid power filters (hydraulic and pneumatic)	(X)	79.9
Fluid power valves (hydraulic and pneumatic)	(X)	12.0
Fluid power hose, tube fittings, and assemblies (hydraulic and pneumatic)	(X)	47.7
Other fluid power products, hydraulic and pneumatic	(X)	5.3
Mechanical speed changers, gears, and industrial high-speed drives	(X)	18.6
Ball and roller bearings (mounted or unmounted)	(X)	6.3
Other pumps and pump parts, excluding fluid power (complete assemblies)	(X)	25.4
Metal bolts, nuts, screws, and other screw machine products	(X)	64.6
Metal tanks, heat exchangers, and other boiler products	(X)	24.3
Metal pipe, valves, and pipe fittings (excluding forgings)	(X)	39.2
Other fabricated metal products (exc. fluid power products and forgings)	(X)	87.3
Forgings	(X)	12.8
Iron and steel castings (rough and semifinished)	(X)	115.0
Nonferrous (aluminum, copper, etc.) castings (rough and semifinished)	(X)	26.3
Steel bars, bar shapes, and plates (exc. castings, forgings, fabr. metal products)	(X)	49.2
Steel sheet and strip (including tinplate)	(X)	28.4
All other steel shapes and forms (exc. castings, forgings, fabr. metal products)	(X)	32.9
Aluminum and aluminum-base alloy shapes and forms (exc. castings, forgings, fabr. metal products)	(X)	26.4
Other nonferrous shapes and forms (exc. castings, forgings, fabricated metal products)	(X)	36.8
Filter paper	(X)	53.6
All other materials, components, parts, containers, and supplies	(X)	973.1
Materials, ingredients, containers, and supplies, nsk	(X)	1,405.4

Source: 2002 *Economic Census*. Explanation of symbols used: (D): Withheld to avoid disclosure of competitive data; na: Not available; (S): Withheld because statistical norms were not met; (X): Not applicable; (Z): Less than half the unit shown; nec: Not elsewhere classified; nsk: Not specified by kind; - : zero; p : 10-19 percent estimated; q : 20-29 percent estimated.

PRODUCT SHARE DETAILS FOR WELDING AND SOLDERING EQUIPMENT MANUFACTURING

Product or Product Class Shipments	Mil. $	Product or Product Class Shipments	Mil. $
WELDING AND SOLDERING EQUIPMENT	3,524.6	other than hard facing	47.6
Arc welding machines, components, and accessories (except electrodes), excluding stud welding equipment	**1,261.7**	Arc welding electrodes, metal, nsk	8.9
		Resistance welders, components, accessories, and electrodes	**565.9**
Arc welding apparatus and related equipment	1,261.7	Resistance welders	565.2
Direct current arc welding generators	107.2	Spot and projection resistance welders, single electrode	107.1
Rectifier-type direct current arc welders, fully or partly automatic	323.9	Spot and projection resistance welders, multielectrode	65.7
Rectifier-type direct current arc welders, not fully or partly automatic	(D)	Seam resistance welders	(D)
Automatic and semiautomatic wire drive apparatus	158.6	Other resistance welders, including flash, upset, and butt welders	13.2
Special-purpose automatic arc welding apparatus	84.9	Resistance welder transformers (sold separately)	(D)
Automatic and semiautomatic welding torches, guns and cables, and related accessories for arc welding machines	104.4	Resistance welder electrodes	103.8
Circuit welding accessories	47.4	Resistance welder components and accessories, including electrode holders, etc.	68.1
Positioning and manipulating arc welding equipment	98.9	Resistance welders, components, accessories, and electrodes, nsk	0.7
Alternating current transformer arc welding machines,	(D)	**Gas welding and cutting equipment, parts, attachments, and accessories**	**311.6**
Complete direct current arc welding units	226.2	Spare parts, accessories, attachments, adaptors, etc.	311.5
All other components and accessories for arc welding machinery, except welding rods, electrodes, and stud welding equipment	72.3	Gas welding and cutting torches (including gas air torches)	84.1
Arc welding electrodes, metal	**682.2**	Gas cutting machines and carriages, stationary and portable	13.7
Electrodes for welding	673.3	Other gas welding and cutting equipment, excluding pressure containers	(D)
Mild steel arc welding stick electrodes, other than hard facing	(D)	Tips for gas welding and cutting equipment (sold separately)	(D)
Low alloy steel arc welding stick electrodes, other than hard facing	(D)	Pressure regulators for gas welding and cutting equipment (sold separately)	43.9
Stainless steel (chromium, 4 percent or more) low alloy steel arc welding stick electrodes, other than hard facing	(D)	All other spare parts, accessories, attachments, adaptors, etc. for gas welding and cutting equipment (sold separately)	75.3
Nonferrous metal arc welding stick electrodes, other than hard facing	11.5	Gas welding and cutting equipment, parts, attachments, and accessories, nsk	0.2
Hard facing metal arc welding stick electrodes	16.4	**Other welding equipment, components, and accessories (excluding arc, resistance, and gas)**	**601.8**
Mild steel coiled and spooled continuous solid wire electrodes for automatic arc and inert gas welding, other than hard facing	(D)	Components and accessories for welding equipment	594.7
		Stud welding equipment	41.2
Low alloy steel coiled and spooled continuous solid wire electrodes for automatic arc and inert gas welding, other than hard facing	(D)	Industrial welding laser systems and equipment	33.5
		Plasma welding and cutting equipment, fully or partly automatic	190.6
Stainless steel (chromium, 4 percent or more) coiled and spooled continuous solid wire electrodes for automatic arc and inert gas welding, other than hard facing	20.4	Plasma welding and cutting equipment, not fully or partly automatic	153.9
		Welding equipment, nec	89.4
Nonferrous metal coiled and spooled continuous solid wire electrodes for automatic arc and inert gas welding, other than hard facing	34.1	Soldering equipment (except hand and ultrasonic)	10.5
		Components and accessories for all other welding equipment	75.5
Hard facing coiled and spooled continuous metal wire electrodes for automatic arc and inert gas welding	32.0	Other welding equipment, components, and accessories, nsk	7.2
Coiled and spooled continuous cored metal wire electrodes for automatic arc and inert gas welding,		**Welding and soldering equipment, nsk, total**	**101.3**

Source: 2002 *Economic Census*. The values are product shipments in millions of dollars for 2002. Total product shipments may be lower or higher than industry shipments. See Introduction for a full discussion. Values of indented subcategories are summed in the main heading(s). The symbol (D) appears when data are withheld to prevent disclosure of competitive information. The abbreviation nsk stands for 'not specified by kind' and nec for 'not elsewhere classified'. A dash (-) means zero.

PRODUCT SHARE DETAILS FOR SCALE AND BALANCE (EXCEPT LABORATORY) MANUFACTURING

Product or Product Class Shipments	Mil. $	Product or Product Class Shipments	Mil. $
SCALES AND BALANCES, EXCEPT LABORATORY	633.3	bathroom, coin-operated, free weighing, kitchen, and baby scales)	49.0
Vehicle and industrial scales	**316.5**	Mailing and parcel post scales (including handheld scales)	57.2
Motor truck and railroad track scales	73.7	Balances with or without weights (of all sensitivities), except laboratory	(D)
Motor truck scales	64.5	**Parts, attachments, and accessories for scales and balances, except laboratory**	**98.9**
Railroad track scales	9.2		
Industrial scales	131.9	Printers for scales and balances, except laboratory (sold separately)	3.0
Industrial bench and portable scales	11.9	Digital indicators for scales and balances, except laboratory (sold separately)	30.7
Industrial floor scales, dormant, pitless	23.1		
Automatic checkweigher and bulkweigher scales	46.0	Other accessories and attachments for scales and balances, except laboratory (sold separately)	12.6
Industrial over-under (predetermined weight) scales	1.1		
Industrial counting scales	49.8	Parts for scales and balances, except laboratory (sold for assembly elsewhere, repair, service, etc.)	52.6
Miscellaneous industrial scales (crane, suspension, tank, hopper, force measuring devices, bulk conveyor, etc.)	109.5	**Scales and balances, except laboratory, nsk, total**	**22.6**
Vehicle and industrial scales, nsk	1.4		
Retail, commercial, household, and mailing scales	**195.3**		
Retail and commercial scales, including delicatessen, checkstand, and automatic prepack	(D)		
Household and person-weighing scales (including			

Source: 2002 *Economic Census*. The values are product shipments in millions of dollars for 2002. Total product shipments may be lower or higher than industry shipments. See Introduction for a full discussion. Values of indented subcategories are summed in the main heading(s). The symbol (D) appears when data are withheld to prevent disclosure of competitive information. The abbreviation nsk stands for 'not specified by kind' and nec for 'not elsewhere classified'. A dash (-) means zero.

PRODUCT SHARE DETAILS FOR MISCELLANEOUS GENERAL PURPOSE MACHINERY NEC

Product or Product Class Shipments	Mil. $	Product or Product Class Shipments	Mil. $
ALL OTHER GENERAL PURPOSE MACHINERY	8,792.3	Steam and vapor separators	8.2
Filters and strainers, except fluid power	**2,373.0**	Sifting and screening machines	101.9
Industrial filters and strainers, except fluid power (assemblies (containment or housing devices) and reusable (cleanable) media)	1,748.3	Separatory products for general indursial use, nec	120.6
Filter and strainer assemblies (containment or housing devices; except for fluid power systems), with or without filter element installed, for water; except parts and accessories	990.9	Parts for products used for separating solids, liquids, and gases (except parts for filters and strainers and fluid power products)	72.5
		Gas generating equipment	40.2
Filter and strainer assemblies (containment or housing devices; except for fluid power systems), with or without filter element installed, for fluids other than water; except parts and accessories	513.2	Mixers for general industrial processes, solids or liquids	98.6
		Automatic fire sprinklers	172.2
Reusable (cleanable) media for filters and strainers, except for fluid power	244.2	Compressed air and gas dryers and centralized automatic lubricating system for pneumatic fluid power systems	207.1
Nonreusable media for filters and strainers, including disposable (throw away) litter cartridges, except for fluid power	544.1	Compressed air and gas dryers (refrigerant, desiccant, deliquescent, etc.)	99.0
		Lubricating systems, industrial, centralized and automatic, for pneumatic systems (sold separately)	108.1
Parts and accessories for filters and strainers (except for fluid power systems), sold separately	69.0	All other machinery for general industry use	1,080.3
Filters and strainers, except fluid power, nsk	11.6	Lubricating systems, industrial, centralized and automatic, for other than pneumatic system (complete systems)	42.1
Filters for hydraulic fluid power systems, nonaerospace	**291.4**	Metal bailing presses	50.9
Filters for pneumatic fluid power systems, nonaerospace	**126.8**	Hydraulic jacks	41.2
Filters for hydraulic and pneumatic fluid power systems, aerospace	**85.2**	Screwjacks (except automotive)	16.9
General purpose machinery, nec	**3,242.1**	All other miscellaneous machinery for general industrial use (complete units)	585.8
Industrial robots, attachments and parts	1,128.5	Metal bellows	113.3
Gas separating equipment	172.5	Parts for all other miscellaneous general industrial machinery and equipment	230.1
Centrifugals and separators (except cream, grain, and berry)	39.6	**All other miscellaneous machinery products, except electrical**	**906.3**
All other separatory products for general industry use	303.3	**All other general purpose machinery, nsk, total**	**1,767.4**

Source: 2002 *Economic Census.* The values are product shipments in millions of dollars for 2002. Total product shipments may be lower or higher than industry shipments. See Introduction for a full discussion. Values of indented subcategories are summed in the main heading(s). The symbol (D) appears when data are withheld to prevent disclosure of competitive information. The abbreviation nsk stands for 'not specified by kind' and nec for 'not elsewhere classified'. A dash (-) means zero.

INPUTS AND OUTPUTS FOR OTHER GENERAL PURPOSE MACHINERY MANUFACTURING

Economic Sector or Industry Providing Inputs	%	Sector	Economic Sector or Industry Buying Outputs	%	Sector
Compensation of employees	32.3		Exports of goods & services	40.6	Cap Inv
Management of companies & enterprises	6.0	Services	Private fixed investment	36.2	
Wholesale trade	5.2	Trade	Manufacturing structures	5.8	Construct.
Iron & steel mills & ferroalloys	3.5	Manufg.	Wholesale trade	1.9	Trade
Plastics products, nec	2.9	Manufg.	General purpose machinery, nec	1.5	Manufg.
General purpose machinery, nec	2.3	Manufg.	Personal consumption expenditures	1.1	
Turned products & screws, nuts, & bolts	2.0	Manufg.	Commercial & industrial equipment repair/maintenance	0.7	Services
Ferrous metal foundries	1.8	Manufg.	Oil & gas extraction	0.7	Mining
Valve & fittings other than plumbing	1.4	Manufg.	Other S/L govt. enterprises	0.7	S/L Govt
Synthetic rubber	1.2	Manufg.	Residential permanent site structures	0.7	Construct.
Motors & generators	1.1	Manufg.	Motor vehicle parts	0.7	Manufg.
Fabricated metals, nec	1.1	Manufg.	Paints & coatings	0.6	Manufg.
Real estate	1.1	Fin/R.E.	Engine equipment, nec	0.5	Manufg.
Printed circuit assemblies (electronic assemblies)	1.0	Manufg.	Commercial & health care structures	0.5	Construct.
Machine shops	1.0	Manufg.	Motor vehicle bodies	0.4	Manufg.
Semiconductors & related devices	1.0	Manufg.	Change in private inventories	0.4	In House
Advertising & related services	0.9	Services	S/L govt. invest., other	0.4	S/L Govt
Fluid power process machinery	0.9	Manufg.	Aircraft	0.4	Manufg.
Securities, commodity contracts, investments	0.9	Fin/R.E.	Nonresidential structures, nec	0.4	Construct.
Nonwoven fabric mills	0.8	Manufg.	Federal government, investment, national defense	0.4	Fed Govt
Alumina refining & primary aluminum production	0.8	Manufg.	Plate work & fabricated structural products	0.4	Manufg.
Truck transportation	0.8	Utl.	Semiconductor machinery	0.2	Manufg.
Power generation & supply	0.7	Util.	Personal & household goods repair/maintenance	0.2	Services
Relay & industrial controls	0.7	Manufg.	Construction machinery	0.2	Manufg.
Lessors of nonfinancial assets	0.7	Fin/R.E.	Turbines & turbine generator set units	0.2	Manufg.
Metal cutting & forming machine tools	0.7	Manufg.	Coating, engraving, heat treating & allied activities	0.2	Manufg.
Copper rolling, drawing, extruding, & alloying	0.7	Manufg.	Commercial & industrial machinery rental & leasing	0.2	Fin/R.E.
Paper mills	0.6	Manufg.	Commercial & service industry machinery, nec	0.2	Manufg.
Noncomparable imports	0.6	Foreign	Industrial machinery, nec	0.1	Manufg.
Paints & coatings	0.6	Manufg.	Farm machinery & equipment	0.1	Manufg.
Cutting tools & machine tool accessories	0.6	Manufg.	Maintenance/repair of nonresidential structures	0.1	Construct.
Monetary authorities/depository credit intermediation	0.6	Fin/R.E.	Material handling equipment	0.1	Manufg.
Steel products from purchased steel	0.6	Manufg.	Chemical products & preparations, nec	0.1	Manufg.
Nonferrous metal foundries	0.5	Manufg.			
Legal services	0.5	Services			
Aluminum products from purchased aluminum	0.5	Manufg.			
Paperboard containers	0.5	Manufg.			
Professional, scientific, technical services, nec	0.5	Services			
Telecommunications	0.5	Services			

Continued on next page.

INPUTS AND OUTPUTS FOR OTHER GENERAL PURPOSE MACHINERY MANUFACTURING - Continued

Economic Sector or Industry Providing Inputs	%	Sector	Economic Sector or Industry Buying Outputs	%	Sector
Data processing, hosting, & related services	0.4	Services			
Plastics packaging materials, film & sheet	0.4	Manufg.			
Coating, engraving, heat treating & allied activities	0.4	Manufg.			
Electronic components, nec	0.4	Manufg.			
Accounting, tax preparation, bookkeeping, & payroll	0.4	Services			
Scientific research & development services	0.3	Services			
Pumps & pumping equipment	0.3	Manufg.			
Taxes on production & imports, less subsidies	0.3				
Food services & drinking places	0.3	Services			
Automotive equipment rental & leasing	0.3	Fin/R.E.			
Warehousing & storage	0.3	Util.			
Chemical products & preparations, nec	0.3	Manufg.			
Speed changers, industrial high-speed drives, & gears	0.3	Manufg.			
Management, scientific, & technical consulting	0.3	Services			
Forging, stamping, & sintering, nec	0.3	Manufg.			
Electronic capacitors, resistors, coils, transformers	0.3	Manufg.			
Architectural, engineering, & related services	0.3	Services			
Abrasive products	0.3	Manufg.			
Bare printed circuit boards	0.2	Manufg.			
Rubber products, nec	0.2	Manufg.			
Custom computer programming services	0.2	Services			
Services to buildings & dwellings	0.2	Services			
Metal cans, boxes, & other containers (light gauge)	0.2	Manufg.			
Hotels & motels, including casino hotels	0.2	Services			
Maintenance/repair of nonresidential structures	0.2	Construct.			
Natural gas distribution	0.2	Util.			
Ball & roller bearings	0.2	Manufg.			
Motor vehicle parts	0.2	Manufg.			
Electrical equipment & components, nec	0.2	Manufg.			
Other computer related services, including facilities	0.2	Services			
Ornamental & architectural metal products	0.2	Manufg.			
Plate work & fabricated structural products	0.2	Manufg.			
Nonferrous metal (ex. copper & aluminum) processing	0.2	Manufg.			
Postal service	0.2	Util.			
Employment services	0.2	Services			
Business support services	0.2	Services			
Air transportation	0.2	Util.			
Commercial & industrial machinery rental & leasing	0.2	Fin/R.E.			
Custom roll forming	0.2	Manufg.			
Specialized design services	0.1	Services			
Automotive repair & maintenance, ex. car washes	0.1	Services			
Paperboard mills	0.1	Manufg.			
Commercial & industrial equipment repair/maintenance	0.1	Services			
Retail trade	0.1	Trade			

Source: *Benchmark Input-Output Accounts for the U.S. Economy, 2002*, U.S. Department of Commerce, Washington, D.C., January 2008. The abbreviation nec stands for 'not elsewhere classified'.

OCCUPATIONS EMPLOYED BY OTHER GENERAL-PURPOSE MACHINERY MANUFACTURING

Occupation	% of Total 2006	Change to 2016	Occupation	% of Total 2006	Change to 2016
Team assemblers	11.0	-9.7	Multiple machine tool operators & tenders	1.4	-0.7
Machinists	5.9	-5.2	Lathe & turning machine tool operators & tenders	1.4	-18.8
Welders, cutters, solderers, & brazers	5.7	-4.0	Maintenance & repair workers, general	1.4	-9.7
First-line supervisors/managers of production workers	3.6	-9.7	Structural metal fabricators & fitters	1.4	-9.7
Mechanical engineers	2.8	-0.7	Industrial engineers	1.3	9.6
Computer-controlled machine tool operators	2.5	-0.7	Electrical & electronic equipment assemblers	1.3	-27.8
Sales reps, wholesale & manufacturing, exc tech	2.3	-9.7	Industrial machinery mechanics	1.3	3.8
Engine & other machine assemblers	2.0	-9.7	Mechanical drafters	1.3	-8.7
Inspectors, testers, sorters, samplers, & weighers	1.9	-14.9	Customer service representatives	1.3	-0.7
Cutting, punching, & press machine operators	1.8	-18.8	Coating, painting, & spraying machine operators	1.2	-14.2
Shipping, receiving, & traffic clerks	1.8	-13.1	Office clerks, general	1.2	-11.1
Helpers--Production workers	1.6	-9.7	Industrial production managers	1.1	-9.7
General & operations managers	1.6	-18.8	Electrical engineers	1.1	-9.7
Laborers & freight, stock, & material movers, hand	1.5	-18.8	Production, planning, & expediting clerks	1.1	-9.7
Purchasing agents, exc wholesale, retail, & farm	1.5	-18.8	Stock clerks & order fillers	1.0	-24.5
Bookkeeping, accounting, & auditing clerks	1.5	-9.7			

Source: *Industry-Occupation Matrix*, Bureau of Labor Statistics, December 4, 2007. These data are reported based on 4-digit NAICS categories but have been matched to corresponding 6-digit NAICS industry codes. The change reported for each occupation to the year 2016 is a percent of growth or decline as estimated by the Bureau of Labor Statistics. The abbreviation nec stands for 'not elsewhere classified'.

LOCATION BY STATE AND REGIONAL CONCENTRATION

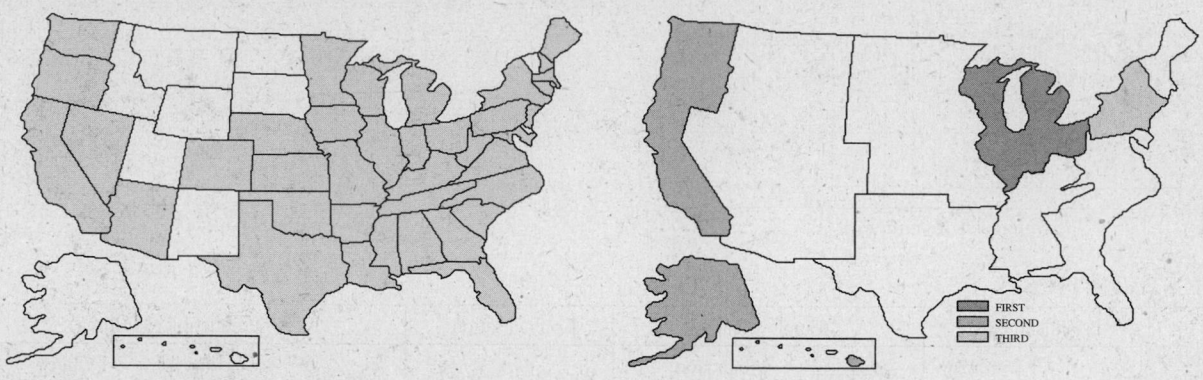

FIRST
SECOND
THIRD

INDUSTRY DATA BY STATE

| State | Establish-ments | Shipments | | | Employment | | | | Cost as % of Shipments | Investment per Employee ($) |
		Total ($ mil)	% of U.S.	Per Establ.	Total Number	% of U.S.	Per Establ.	Wages ($/hour)		
Michigan	199	2,089.4	15.1	10,499.5	9,476	12.1	48	19.97	54.4	3,214
Ohio	166	1,655.0	12.0	9,969.6	6,965	8.9	42	25.72	44.0	5,882
California	245	855.5	6.2	3,491.9	5,918	7.6	24	15.58	44.7	3,413
Pennsylvania	126	728.3	5.3	5,780.3	4,551	5.8	36	16.55	35.6	3,678
Texas	140	661.5	4.8	4,724.7	4,107	5.2	29	14.43	44.2	3,262
Missouri	31	644.7	4.7	20,797.5	4,144	5.3	134	27.60	20.1	11,698
Wisconsin	79	636.4	4.6	8,056.1	3,002	3.8	38	21.64	57.3	2,612
Illinois	155	620.8	4.5	4,005.3	3,959	5.1	26	15.64	44.8	4,621
Minnesota	57	581.7	4.2	10,205.4	3,103	4.0	54	17.15	41.0	7,016
New York	84	412.8	3.0	4,914.6	2,518	3.2	30	14.72	47.0	4,452
Florida	86	410.4	3.0	4,772.6	2,857	3.7	33	15.21	39.0	2,950
Connecticut	64	404.6	2.9	6,321.9	2,102	2.7	33	16.87	35.8	7,775
Massachusetts	69	387.8	2.8	5,619.9	1,892	2.4	27	20.99	34.8	10,422
New Hampshire	21	281.9	2.0	13,423.3	1,638	2.1	78	14.55	42.6	5,046
North Carolina	55	260.3	1.9	4,732.3	1,604	2.1	29	15.37	47.7	4,349
Indiana	61	238.8	1.7	3,914.8	1,457	1.9	24	15.95	45.1	3,093
Maryland	18	211.3	1.5	11,739.4	1,445	1.8	80	16.71	34.5	4,796
New Jersey	64	211.2	1.5	3,299.5	1,434	1.8	22	16.89	38.4	4,294
Tennessee	46	159.7	1.2	3,470.7	1,273	1.6	28	21.11	36.7	2,660
Kentucky	32	159.1	1.2	4,972.1	928	1.2	29	15.60	43.4	2,608
Georgia	31	127.2	0.9	4,104.7	728	0.9	23	14.23	54.3	4,135
Alabama	23	94.6	0.7	4,112.7	610	0.8	27	18.08	33.7	2,272
Virginia	23	91.2	0.7	3,963.1	696	0.9	30	15.29	39.2	2,191
Oklahoma	28	88.7	0.6	3,167.2	688	0.9	25	14.90	47.2	1,972
Rhode Island	11	82.5	0.6	7,503.7	448	0.6	41	15.86	28.4	3,469
Arizona	21	71.9	0.5	3,424.0	426	0.5	20	16.21	51.2	4,676
Arkansas	16	70.8	0.5	4,422.1	426	0.5	27	12.54	30.3	6,014
Washington	30	61.5	0.4	2,049.5	380	0.5	13	15.48	46.4	1,458
Kansas	18	49.9	0.4	2,771.5	434	0.6	24	14.96	32.7	3,256
Colorado	29	48.1	0.3	1,657.8	336	0.4	12	12.93	22.6	1,185
Oregon	30	47.8	0.3	1,592.8	417	0.5	14	13.77	41.6	2,825
Louisiana	20	34.5	0.2	1,726.2	258	0.3	13	16.51	38.2	3,783
Maine	11	28.4	0.2	2,577.8	212	0.3	19	15.87	49.2	3,575
Nevada	6	27.4	0.2	4,566.2	270	0.3	45	9.14	54.2	711
South Carolina	27	23.7	0.2	877.6	231	0.3	9	15.00	42.1	1,247
Iowa	18	21.0	0.2	1,168.9	206	0.3	11	15.29	38.8	1,553
Nebraska	10	17.5	0.1	1,750.0	114	0.1	11	14.46	49.1	3,939
West Virginia	8	12.1	0.1	1,507.6	111	0.1	14	14.21	34.8	2,757
Mississippi	10	12.0	0.1	1,202.9	142	0.2	14	13.59	38.7	3,261

Source: 2002 *Economic Census*. The states are in descending order of shipments or establishments (if shipment data are missing for the majority). The symbol (D) appears when data are withheld to prevent disclosure of competitive information. States marked with (D) are sorted by number of establishments. A dash (-) indicates that the data element cannot be calculated. Data may not show all states active in the NAICS category. All data available at the time of publication are shown.

NAICS 334111 - ELECTRONIC COMPUTER MANUFACTURING

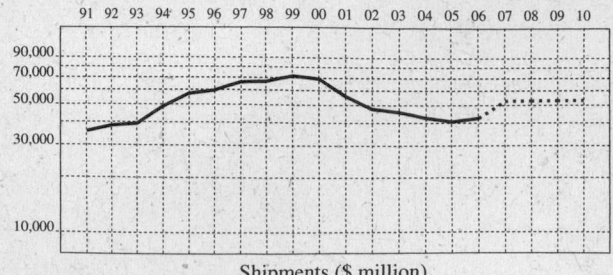

Shipments ($ million)

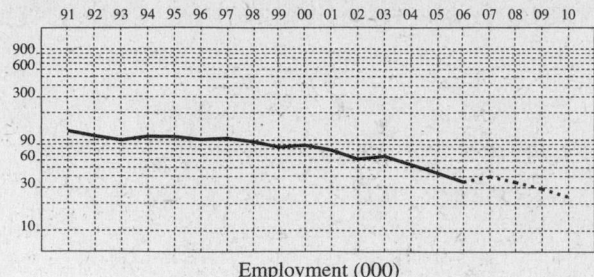

Employment (000)

GENERAL STATISTICS

| Year | Companies | Establishments | | Employment | | | Compensation | | Production ($ million) | | | |
		Total	with 20 or more employees	Total (000)	Production Workers (000)	Hours (Mil)	Payroll ($ mil)	Wages ($/hr)	Cost of Materials	Value Added by Manufacture	Value of Shipments	Capital Invest.
1991		766	377	126.0	38.1	78.7	5,343.7	12.80	19,078.4	16,877.5	35,572.9	1,153.5
1992	803	834	289	110.8	31.2	65.5	4,855.9	12.51	21,388.9	16,137.4	38,205.9	1,242.4
1993		747	278	99.5	28.8	60.2	4,514.7	13.49	23,498.6	16,218.4	39,176.8	1,042.9
1994		657	238	109.4	30.4	62.7	5,073.9	13.54	27,046.1	21,066.4	48,546.9	932.7
1995		539	207	108.7	35.1	71.3	4,846.4	13.12	35,684.2	22,173.6	57,054.0	907.2
1996		558	210	101.8	31.0	62.9	4,499.6	12.68	35,086.3	23,152.8	59,413.6	845.9
1997	536	563	213	105.4	37.8	67.7	4,251.7	13.99	40,239.7	25,516.2	65,923.7	1,065.7
1998		570	201	95.8	31.8	57.5	4,277.8	15.89	35,105.6	31,206.1	66,864.6	696.2
1999		590	175	83.7	28.8	57.8	4,715.1	17.68	41,845.7	29,402.7	71,679.7	717.9
2000		617	178	87.7	27.9	44.1	4,572.4	23.83	44,260.7	24,723.7	69,299.0	823.6
2001		546	174	77.3	21.3	34.2	3,548.5	26.39	38,030.0	17,516.2	55,869.1	470.4
2002	463	485	148	61.9	18.2	36.4	3,261.6	20.26	26,536.8	20,902.0	47,643.9	1,320.2
2003		530	159	66.2	15.9	30.6	4,870.2	25.15	26,265.4	19,543.7	45,876.2	1,168.5
2004		502	146	53.7	12.1	28.6	3,391.3	21.38	21,009.2	21,735.7	42,727.1	527.7
2005		449	121	43.6	12.4	23.9	2,532.4	23.33	18,289.3	22,446.1	40,694.1	376.2
2006		431P	99P	34.5	11.8	22.2	1,870.9	22.08	19,487.8	22,930.0	42,507.7	907.2
2007		410P	85P	39.7P	11.4P	19.2P	2,764.9P	25.77P	24,172.0P	28,441.6P	52,725.1P	660.0P
2008		389P	72P	34.3P	9.7P	15.6P	2,601.8P	26.68P	24,227.8P	28,507.2P	52,846.8P	633.2P
2009		368P	58P	29.0P	8.0P	11.9P	2,438.6P	27.60P	24,283.6P	28,572.9P	52,968.5P	606.5P
2010		348P	45P	23.6P	6.3P	8.3P	2,275.5P	28.51P	24,339.3P	28,638.5P	53,090.1P	579.7P

Sources: 1992, 1997, 2002 *Economic Census*; other years, up to 2006, are from the *Annual Survey of Manufactures*. Establishment counts for non-Census years are from *County Business Patterns*; 1997 and 2002 values are from the 1997 and 2002 censuses respectively, reported in the Federal Government's NAICS format. Other years were originally reported in equivalent SIC format. 'P's show projections by the editors.

INDICES OF CHANGE

| Year | Companies | Establishments | | Employment | | | Compensation | | Production ($ million) | | | |
		Total	with 20 or more employees	Total (000)	Production Workers (000)	Hours (Mil)	Payroll ($ mil)	Wages ($/hr)	Cost of Materials	Value Added by Manufacture	Value of Shipments	Capital Invest.
1992	173	172	195	179	171	180	149	62	81	77	80	94
1997	116	116	144	170	208	186	130	69	152	122	138	81
2001		113	118	125	117	94	109	130	143	84	117	36
2002	100	100	100	100	100	100	100	100	100	100	100	100
2003		109	107	107	87	84	149	124	99	94	96	89
2004		104	99	87	66	79	104	106	79	104	90	40
2005		93	82	70	68	66	78	115	69	107	85	28
2006		89P	67P	56	65	61	57	109	73	110	89	69
2007		85P	58P	64P	63P	53P	85P	127P	91P	136P	111P	50P
2008		80P	48P	55P	53P	43P	80P	132P	91P	136P	111P	48P
2009		76P	39P	47P	44P	33P	75P	136P	92P	137P	111P	46P
2010		72P	30P	38P	35P	23P	70P	141P	92P	137P	111P	44P

Sources: Same as General Statistics. Values reflect change from the base year, 2002. Values above 100 mean greater than 2002, values below 100 mean less than 2002, and the values of 100 in other years means the same as 2002. 'P's show projections by the editors.

SELECTED RATIOS

For 2002	Avg. of All Manufact.	Analyzed Industry	Index	For 2002	Avg. of All Manufact.	Analyzed Industry	Index
Employees per Establishment	42	128	304	Value Added per Production Worker	182,367	1,148,462	630
Payroll per Establishment	1,639,184	6,724,948	410	Cost per Establishment	5,769,015	54,715,052	948
Payroll per Employee	39,053	52,691	135	Cost per Employee	137,446	428,704	312
Production Workers per Establishment	30	38	127	Cost per Production Worker	195,506	1,458,066	746
Wages per Establishment	694,845	1,520,544	219	Shipments per Establishment	11,158,348	98,234,845	880
Wages per Production Worker	23,548	40,520	172	Shipments per Employee	265,847	769,691	290
Hours per Production Worker	1,980	2,000	101	Shipments per Production Worker	378,144	2,617,797	692
Wages per Hour	11.89	20.26	170	Investment per Establishment	361,338	2,722,062	753
Value Added per Establishment	5,381,325	43,096,907	801	Investment per Employee	8,609	21,328	248
Value Added per Employee	128,210	337,674	263	Investment per Production Worker	12,245	72,538	592

Sources: Same as General Statistics. The 'Average of All Manufacturing' column represents the average of all manufacturing industries reported for the most recent complete year available. The Index shows the relationship between the Average and the Analyzed Industry. For example, 100 means that they are equal; 500 that the Analyzed Industry is five times the average; 50 means that the Analyzed Industry is half the national average. The abbreviation 'na' is used to show that data are 'not available'. Ratios shown for 2002, the last complete census year.

LEADING COMPANIES   Number shown: **75**   Total sales ($ mil): **492,081**   Total employment (000): **1,019.8**

Company Name	Address				CEO Name	Phone	Co. Type	Sales ($ mil)	Empl. (000)
Hewlett-Packard Co.	3000 Hanover St.	Palo Alto	CA	94304		650-857-1501	P	104,286	172.0
International Bus. Machines	1 New Orchard Rd.	Armonk	NY	10504		914-499-1900	P	98,786	329.4
Dell Inc.	1 Dell Way	Round Rock	TX	78682	Michael R. Cannon	512-338-4400	P	57,420	90.5
Siemens IT Solutions & Service	101 Merritt 7	Norwalk	CT	06851	John McKenna Jr.	203-642-2300	S	39,634*	43.0
Intel Corp.	2200 Mission Clg.	Santa Clara	CA	95054	Craig R. Barrett	408-765-8080	P	38,334	86.3
Motorola Inc.	1303 E Algonquin	Schaumburg	IL	60196	Greg Brown	847-576-5000	P	36,622	66.0
Apple Inc.	1 Infinite Loop	Cupertino	CA	95014	Bill Campbell	408-996-1010	P	24,006	21.6
Lenovo Group Ltd.	1009 Think Pl.	Morrisville	NC	27560	Sotaro Amano		P	14,590	2.9
Sun Microsystems Inc.	4150 Network Cir.	Santa Clara	CA	95054		650-960-1300	P	13,873	34.2
Hitachi Global Storage Tech.	5600 Cottle Rd.	San Jose	CA	95193	Hiroaki Nakanishi	408-717-5000	J	9,450*	21.0
SYNNEX Corp.	44201 Nobel Dr.	Fremont	CA	94538		510-656-3333	P	7,004	6.1
Acer America Corp.	2641 Orchard Pky.	San Jose	CA	95134		408-432-6200	S	6,300*	5.4
Micron Technology Inc.	PO Box 6	Boise	ID	83707	Steven R. Appleton	208-368-4000	P	5,688	23.5
Unisys Corp.	Unisys Way	Blue Bell	PA	19424		215-986-4011	P	5,653	30.0
NCR Corp.	1700 S Patterson	Dayton	OH	45479		937-445-5000	P	4,970	23.2
RadioShack Corp.	300 RadioShack Cir.	Fort Worth	TX	76102	Julian C. Day	817-415-3700	P	4,252	35.8
Gateway Inc.	7565 Irvine Center	Irvine	CA	92618		949-471-7000	S	3,981	1.7
Hitachi America Ltd.	2000 Sierra Pnt Pky	Brisbane	CA	94005	Masahide Tanigahi	650-589-8300	S	2,127*	4.4
Hyperdata	817 S Lemon Ave.	Walnut	CA	91789	Toku Lee	909-468-2933	R	2,014*	<0.1
Embedded Communic. Computing	2900 S Diablo Way	Tempe	AZ	85282		602-438-5720	D	1,732*	1.5
Diversified Technology Inc.	476 Highland Col	Ridgeland	MS	39157		601-856-4121	R	1,380*	0.1
Fujitsu Transaction Solutions	2801 Network Blvd.	Frisco	TX	75034		972-963-2300	R	1,300*	0.3
Autotote Lottery Corp.	750 Lexington Ave.	New York	NY	10022	A. Lorne Weil	212-754-2233	S	926*	1.0
Micro Electronics Inc.	4119 Leap Rd.	Hilliard	OH	43026	John Baker	614-850-3000	R	797*	2.0
White Systems Inc.	30 Boright Ave.	Kenilworth	NJ	07033	Richard Paolino	908-272-6700	S	673*	0.3
GE Fanuc Embedded Systems Inc.	12090 S Memorial	Huntsville	AL	35803		256-880-0444	R	396*	0.2
Silicon Graphics Inc.	1140 E Arques Ave.	Sunnyvale	CA	94085	Robert Ewald	650-960-1980	P	341	1.6
Toshiba America Info. Systems	PO Box 19724	Irvine	CA	92623		949-583-3000	S	290*	1.7
Itronix Corp.	12825 E Mirabeau	Spokane Valley	WA	99216		509-624-6600	S	285*	0.5
Ruggedtronics Inc.	24711 Redlands	Loma Linda	CA	92354	Don Parker	909-796-5374	R	281*	<0.1
Government Micro Resources	7421 Gateway Ct.	Manassas	VA	20109	Humberto Pujais	703-594-8100	R	246*	0.2
Astronautics Corp. of America	PO Box 523	Milwaukee	WI	53201	Michael Russek	414-449-4000	R	233*	0.5
Autocam Corp.	4070 E Paris Ave SE	Kentwood	MI	49512	John C. Kennedy	616-698-0707	S	230*	2.3
Cognex Corp.	1 Vision Dr.	Natick	MA	01760	Jerald Fishman	508-650-3000	P	226	0.8
Wyse Technology Inc.	3471 N First St.	San Jose	CA	95134	Tarkan Maner	408-473-1200	P	221*	0.9
Cray Inc.	411 1st Ave. S, 600	Seattle	WA	98104		206-701-2000	P	221	0.8
EXFO America Inc.	3701 Plano Pkwy.	Plano	TX	75075	Germain Lamonde	972-907-1505	R	197*	0.2
Gerber Technology Inc.	24 Industrial Park	Tolland	CT	06084	John Hancock	860-871-8082	S	197	1.2
Force Computers Inc.	14643 Dallas Pky.	Dallas	TX	75254	Paul Mercadante	510-624-5300	S	180*	0.3
AAEON Technology Inc.	3 Crown Plz.	Hazlet	NJ	07730	Yung-Shun Chuang	732-203-9300	R	173*	0.3
Omnicell Inc.	1201 Charleston Rd.	Mountain View	CA	94043		650-251-6100	P	155	0.6
Vocollect Inc.	703 Rodi Rd.	Pittsburgh	PA	15235	Jack LeVan	412-829-8145	R	150*	0.3
Xycom Automation Inc.	750 N Maple Rd.	Saline	MI	48176	Jerry Tubbs		R	150*	0.1
WIN Enterprise Inc.	300 Willow St. S	North Andover	MA	01845	Chiman Patel	978-688-2000	R	133*	0.2
Lockheed Martin Tactical Def.	1210 Massillon Rd.	Akron	OH	44315	James W. Dunn	330-796-2800	S	116*	0.8
Alienware Corp.	14591 SW 120 St.	Miami	FL	33186	Alex Aguila	305-251-9797	S	111*	0.5
Neoware Inc.	3200 Horizon Dr.	King of Prussia	PA	19406	Klaus P. Besier	610-277-8300	S	107	0.2
Clear Cube Technology Inc.	8834 N Cap. of TX	Austin	TX	78759	Bruce Cohen	512-652-3500	R	106*	0.2
Mack Technologies Inc.	27 Carlisle Rd.	Westford	MA	01886	Donald Kendall	978-392-5500	R	105*	0.2
Radix Corp.	4855 Wiley Post	Salt Lake City	UT	84116	James H. Benson	801-537-1717	S	99*	0.2
Fargo Electronics Inc.	6533 Flying Cloud	Eden Prairie	MN	55344	Gary R. Holland	952-941-9470	S	81*	0.2
Edimax Computer Co.	10807 NW 29th St.	Miami	FL	33172	Danny Awhang	786-845-8099	R	75*	0.3
Granite Microsystems Inc.	10202 N Entrprs Dr.	Mequon	WI	53092	Daniel Armbrust	262-242-8800	R	70*	0.1
Concurrent Computer Corp.	4375 Rivr Green Pky	Duluth	GA	30096		678-258-4000	P	69	0.4
NCS Technologies Inc.	9490 Innovation Dr.	Manassas	VA	20110	An Nguyen	703-621-1700	R	66*	0.1
Root Group Inc.	1790 30th Street	Boulder	CO	80301	Bill Calderwood	303-447-8093	R	64*	<0.1
Advanced Control Systems Inc.	PO Box 922548	Norcross	GA	30010	John Muench	770-446-8854	R	64*	<0.1
Syn-Tech Systems Inc.	PO Box 5258	Tallahassee	FL	32314	Douglas Dunlap	850-878-2558	R	64*	<0.1
National Hybrid Inc.	2200 Smithtown	Ronkonkoma	NY	11779	Carol Klemm	631-981-2400	R	61*	0.1
Elitegroup Computer Systems	45401 Research	Fremont	CA	94539		510-226-7333	R	57*	<0.1
SOYO Group Inc.	1420 S Vintage Ave.	Ontario	CA	91761	Ming Tung Chok	909-292-2500	P	57	<0.1
Datalux Corp.	155 Aviation Dr.	Winchester	VA	22602		540-662-4500	R	56*	0.1
Golden Star Technology Inc.	2929 E Imperial	Brea	CA	92821	Alice Wang	714-572-8020	R	47*	0.1
Tangent Computer Inc.	191 Airport Blvd.	Burlingame	CA	94010	Doug Monsour		R	47*	<0.1
Koutech Systems Inc.	9314 Norwalk Blvd.	Santa Fe Spgs	CA	90670	Roger Kae	562-699-5340	S	47*	<0.1
I/OMagic Corp.	4 Marconi	Irvine	CA	92618	Tony Shahbaz	949-707-4800	P	46	<0.1
Wen Technology Corp.	22 Saw Mill River	Hawthorne	NY	10532	Sheree Wen	914-592-1145	R	45*	<0.1
HETRA Secure Solutions Corp.	2350 Commerce	Palm Bay	FL	32905	Michael Adamcheck	321-953-3033	R	44	<0.1
Aydin Displays Inc.	1 Riga Ln.	Birdsboro	PA	19508		610-404-7400	S	43*	<0.1
Hard Drives Northwest Inc.	14504 NE 20th St.	Bellevue	WA	98007	Hugh Stewart	425-644-6474	R	42*	<0.1
Advanced Programs Inc.	7125 Riverwood Dr.	Columbia	MD	21046	Steve Rice	410-312-5800	R	42*	<0.1
Aberdeen L.L.C.	9130 Norwalk Blvd.	Santa Fe Spgs	CA	90670	Moshe Ovadya	562-699-6998	R	39*	<0.1
Bermo Inc.	4501 Ball Rd. NE	Circle Pines	MN	55014	Daniel Berdass	763-786-7676	R	39*	0.3
Graphic Enterprises Inc.	3874 Highland Park	North Canton	OH	44720	Jason Parikh		R	37*	0.3
BT Technologies Inc.	1602 NE 205th Ter.	Miami	FL	33179	Brian D. Feldman	305-652-3115	R	37*	<0.1

Source: Ward's Business Directory of U.S. Private and Public Companies, Volumes 1 and 2, 2008. The company type code used is as follows: P - Public, R - Private, S - Subsidiary, D - Division, J - Joint Venture, A - Affiliate, G - Group. Sales are in millions of dollars, employees are in thousands. An asterisk (*) indicates an estimated sales volume. The symbol < stands for 'less than'. Company names and addresses are truncated, in some cases, to fit into the available space.

MATERIALS CONSUMED

Material	Quantity	Delivered Cost ($ million)
Cathode ray tubes (CRT) (excluding X-ray)	(X)	1.8
Printed ciruit boards (without inserted components) for electronic circuitry	(X)	(D)
Printed memory boards for electronic circuitry	(X)	2,406.5
Printed peripheral controllers for electronic circuitry	(X)	156.4
Printed computer processors for electronic circuitry	(X)	3,759.2
Printed communication boards for electronic circuitry	(X)	262.6
Other printed circuit boards for electronic circuitry	(X)	417.9
Semiconductors (incl. transistors, diodes, rectifiers, and integrated circuits), for electronic circuitry	(X)	163.9
Capacitors for electronic circuitry	(X)	7.8
Resistors for electronic circuitry	(X)	8.1
Connectors for electronic circuitry	(X)	11.0
Battery packs for electronic circuitry	(X)	18.1
Other power supply units for electronic circuitry	(X)	217.1
Other components and accessories, for electronic circuitry (coils, transformers, etc.), excluding tubes	(X)	(D)
Electrical transmission, distribution, and control equipment	(X)	4.1
Steel, aluminum, and other metal electronic enclosures	(X)	112.6
Plastics electronic enclosures	(X)	27.6
Sheet metal products, including stampings (exc. enclosures)	(X)	17.5
All other fabricated metal products (excluding forgings)	(X)	1.6
Forgings	(X)	(D)
Castings, rough and semifinished	(X)	0.5
Metal shapes and forms (exc. castings, forgings, fabr. metal products)	(X)	(D)
Insulated copper wire and cable (including magnet wire)	(X)	12.1
Fabricated plastics products (excluding enclosures)	(X)	(D)
Purchased software	(X)	280.2
Appliance outlets and other current-carrying wiring devices	(X)	(D)
Electric motors and generators	(X)	(D)
Paper and paperboard products (incl. paperboard boxes, etc.)	(X)	45.9
Purchased computers	(X)	1,332.6
Purchased peripheral storage devices	(X)	3,393.9
Purchased computer terminals	(X)	507.5
Purchased peripheral input devices (including keyboards, mouse devices, track balls, etc.)	(X)	864.3
Purchased peripheral printers	(X)	17.3
Other purchased electronic computing and peripheral equipment	(X)	(D)
All other materials, components, parts, containers, and supplies	(X)	5,850.0
Materials, ingredients, containers, and supplies, nsk	(X)	3,092.7

Source: 2002 Economic Census. Explanation of symbols used: (D): Withheld to avoid disclosure of competitive data; na: Not available; (S): Withheld because statistical norms were not met; (X): Not applicable; (Z): Less than half the unit shown; nec: Not elsewhere classified; nsk: Not specified by kind; - : zero; p : 10-19 percent estimated; q : 20-29 percent estimated.

PRODUCT SHARE DETAILS

Product or Product Class Shipments	Mil. $	Product or Product Class Shipments	Mil. $
ELECTRONIC COMPUTERS	40,939.6	**workstations, portable computers)**	**26,357.1**
Host computers, multiusers (mainframes, super computers, medium scale systems, UNIX servers, PC servers)	**12,967.4**	**Other computers, (array, analog, hybrid, or special-use computers)**	792.7
Single user computers, microprocessor-based, capable of supporting attached peripherals (personal computers,		**Electronic computers, nsk, total**	822.3

Source: 2002 Economic Census. The values are product shipments in millions of dollars for 2002. Total product shipments may be lower or higher than industry shipments. See Introduction for a full discussion. Values of indented subcategories are summed in the main heading(s). The symbol (D) appears when data are withheld to prevent disclosure of competitive information. The abbreviation nsk stands for 'not specified by kind' and nec for 'not elsewhere classified'. A dash (-) means zero.

INPUTS AND OUTPUTS FOR ELECTRONIC COMPUTER MANUFACTURING

Economic Sector or Industry Providing Inputs	%	Sector	Economic Sector or Industry Buying Outputs	%	Sector
Computer storage devices	14.3	Manufg.	Private fixed investment	56.8	
Wholesale trade	10.2	Trade	Personal consumption expenditures	19.1	
Printed circuit assemblies (electronic assemblies)	9.1	Manufg.	Exports of goods & services	12.6	Cap Inv
Compensation of employees	8.7		S/L govt. invest., other	2.6	S/L Govt
Semiconductors & related devices	7.7	Manufg.	S/L govt. invest., education	2.3	S/L Govt
Management of companies & enterprises	6.9	Services	Electronic computers	2.1	Manufg.
Software publishers	6.9	Services	Federal government, investment, nondefense	1.9	Fed Govt
Computer terminals & peripherals	4.7	Manufg.	Federal government, investment, national defense	1.2	Fed Govt
Electronic computers	2.5	Manufg.	Light truck & utility vehicles	0.4	Manufg.
Scientific research & development services	1.8	Services	Change in private inventories	0.3	In House
Software, audio, and video media reproducing	0.8	Manufg.	Automobiles	0.3	Manufg.
Electronic components, nec	0.5	Manufg.	Computer terminals & peripherals	0.2	Manufg.
Truck transportation	0.4	Util.	General Federal government services, nondefense	0.1	Fed Govt
Electronic capacitors, resistors, coils, transformers	0.4	Manufg.			
Noncomparable imports	0.4	Foreign			
Bare printed circuit boards	0.4	Manufg.			
Forging, stamping, & sintering, nec	0.3	Manufg.			

Continued on next page.

INPUTS AND OUTPUTS FOR ELECTRONIC COMPUTER MANUFACTURING - Continued

Economic Sector or Industry Providing Inputs	%	Sector	Economic Sector or Industry Buying Outputs	%	Sector
Ornamental & architectural metal products	0.2	Manufg.			
Paperboard containers	0.2	Manufg.			
Advertising & related services	0.2	Services			
Plastics packaging materials, film & sheet	0.2	Manufg.			
Real estate	0.2	Fin/R.E.			
Motor vehicle parts	0.2	Manufg.			
Electrical equipment & components, nec	0.2	Manufg.			
Chemical products & preparations, nec	0.1	Manufg.			
Plastics products, nec	0.1	Manufg.			
Automotive equipment rental & leasing	0.1	Fin/R.E.			
Machine shops	0.1	Manufg.			
Warehousing & storage	0.1	Util.			
Paperboard mills	0.1	Manufg.			
Air transportation	0.1	Util.			

Source: Benchmark Input-Output Accounts for the U.S. Economy, 2002, U.S. Department of Commerce, Washington, D.C., January 2008. The abbreviation nec stands for 'not elsewhere classified'.

OCCUPATIONS EMPLOYED BY COMPUTER & PERIPHERAL EQUIPMENT MANUFACTURING

Occupation	% of Total 2006	Change to 2016	Occupation	% of Total 2006	Change to 2016
Computer software engineers, systems software	10.1	-28.0	Computer & information systems managers	1.5	-34.5
Electrical & electronic equipment assemblers	7.4	-47.6	Financial analysts	1.4	-28.0
Computer hardware engineers	6.5	-28.0	Purchasing agents, exc wholesale, retail, & farm	1.4	-34.5
Computer software engineers, applications	5.5	-21.4	Engineers, nec	1.3	-34.5
Sales representatives, wholesale & manufacturing, tech	2.5	-34.5	Computer programmers	1.3	-47.6
Computer support specialists	2.4	-34.5	Accountants & auditors	1.3	-34.5
Computer systems analysts	2.4	-28.0	Executive secretaries & administrative assistants	1.3	-34.5
Engineering managers	2.3	-34.5	Inspectors, testers, sorters, samplers, & weighers	1.3	-38.3
Electrical & electronic engineering technicians	2.3	-34.5	Electrical engineers	1.2	-34.5
Business operation specialists, nec	2.1	-28.0	Team assemblers	1.2	-34.5
Industrial engineers	1.8	-20.5	Logisticians	1.1	-28.0
Marketing managers	1.7	-34.5	General & operations managers	1.1	-41.1
Office clerks, general	1.6	-35.5	Shipping, receiving, & traffic clerks	1.1	-37.0
Market research analysts	1.6	-34.5	Production, planning, & expediting clerks	1.0	-34.5
Electronics engineers, exc computer	1.5	-34.5			

Source: Industry-Occupation Matrix, Bureau of Labor Statistics, December 4, 2007. These data are reported based on 4-digit NAICS categories but have been matched to corresponding 6-digit NAICS industry codes. The change reported for each occupation to the year 2016 is a percent of growth or decline as estimated by the Bureau of Labor Statistics. The abbreviation nec stands for 'not elsewhere classified'.

LOCATION BY STATE AND REGIONAL CONCENTRATION

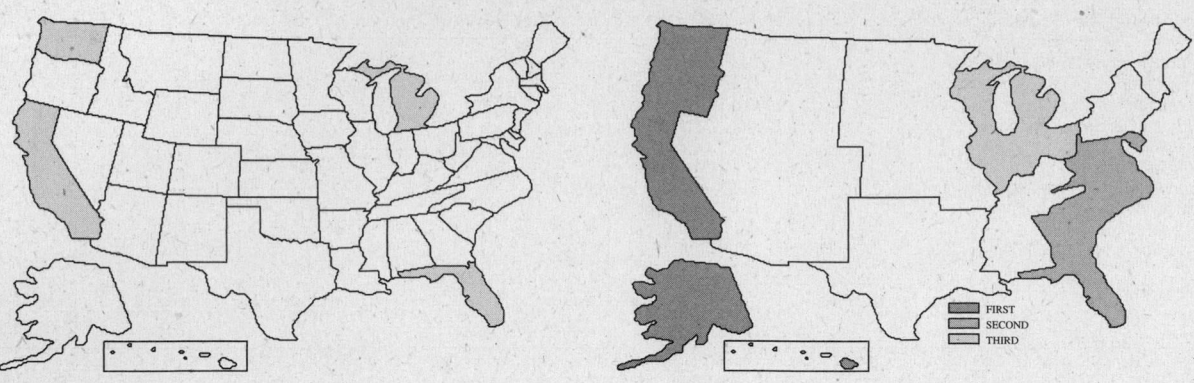

FIRST
SECOND
THIRD

INDUSTRY DATA BY STATE

| State | Establish-ments | Shipments | | | Employment | | | | Cost as % of Shipments | Investment per Employee ($) |
		Total ($ mil)	% of U.S.	Per Establ.	Total Number	% of U.S.	Per Establ.	Wages ($/hour)		
California	149	16,038.4	33.7	107,640.0	21,252	34.4	143	19.16	56.1	27,963
Florida	26	245.5	0.5	9,440.7	1,056	1.7	41	19.78	52.7	8,503
Michigan	16	224.5	0.5	14,031.3	1,466	2.4	92	23.10	23.6	2,734
Washington	13	190.2	0.4	14,629.2	1,017	1.6	78	23.36	61.3	5,849

Source: 2002 *Economic Census*. The states are in descending order of shipments or establishments (if shipment data are missing for the majority). The symbol (D) appears when data are withheld to prevent disclosure of competitive information. States marked with (D) are sorted by number of establishments. A dash (-) indicates that the data element cannot be calculated. Data may not show all states active in the NAICS category. All data available at the time of publication are shown.

NAICS 334112 - COMPUTER STORAGE DEVICE MANUFACTURING

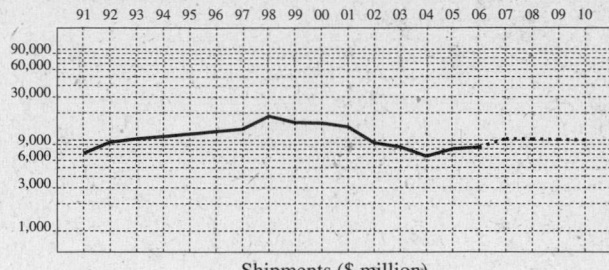

Shipments ($ million)

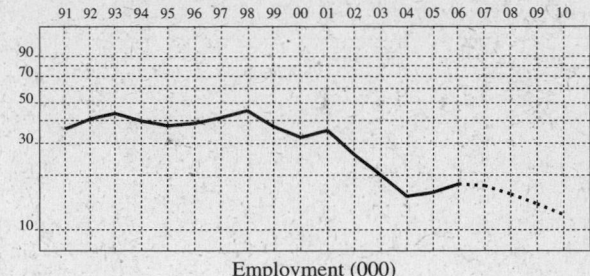

Employment (000)

GENERAL STATISTICS

Year	Com-panies	Establishments		Employment			Compensation		Production ($ million)			
		Total	with 20 or more employees	Total (000)	Production Workers (000)	Hours (Mil)	Payroll ($ mil)	Wages ($/hr)	Cost of Materials	Value Added by Manufacture	Value of Shipments	Capital Invest.
1991		126	71	36.0	12.2	27.1	1,444.1	13.01	3,674.2	3,600.2	7,188.6	392.8
1992	163	179	96	40.8	15.2	31.3	1,795.4	13.64	4,991.7	4,658.8	9,544.3	455.6
1993		178	91	43.8	17.6	34.9	1,796.0	13.72	6,110.0	4,294.8	10,395.3	557.7
1994		164	83	39.8	19.7	44.0	1,650.5	14.83	6,759.4	4,364.6	11,004.5	521.9
1995		175	84	37.5	17.0	38.3	1,779.4	16.05	7,110.3	4,559.9	11,725.6	614.4
1996		180	78	38.6	17.2	37.7	1,871.6	15.72	7,349.0	5,035.7	12,511.1	956.3
1997	199	209	85	41.4	19.4	40.4	1,922.5	14.67	7,399.3	5,923.4	13,278.5	1,386.6
1998		207	95	45.4	19.8	52.3	2,066.6	12.78	10,415.2	7,983.0	18,420.1	1,200.6
1999		210	88	37.0	18.5	37.5	1,712.8	16.25	8,611.9	7,225.8	15,711.0	916.1
2000		202	79	32.3	15.0	30.5	1,731.3	16.34	7,704.2	7,987.6	15,502.1	680.1
2001		193	79	35.3	14.5	29.8	1,617.2	16.10	6,396.9	7,291.8	14,062.8	592.1
2002	156	170	68	26.0	9.9	20.1	1,578.0	18.38	4,723.7	4,687.9	9,379.5	485.7
2003		168	63	20.0	9.4	19.7	1,319.6	17.49	4,775.2	3,565.0	8,443.3	450.3
2004		169	65	15.3	7.7	15.9	915.0	17.52	3,471.3	3,166.5	6,679.7	272.7
2005		148	60	16.1	8.3	17.6	1,026.8	16.87	4,335.7	3,902.2	8,032.0	386.7
2006		183P	66P	17.9	9.0	18.9	1,125.4	17.51	4,433.9	4,035.6	8,400.4	404.2
2007		184P	64P	17.5P	9.2P	19.2P	1,196.4P	18.20P	5,484.6P	4,991.9P	10,391.1P	521.7P
2008		185P	62P	15.7P	8.6P	17.9P	1,150.7P	18.50P	5,430.2P	4,942.4P	10,288.0P	507.6P
2009		185P	60P	13.9P	8.0P	16.5P	1,105.1P	18.80P	5,375.8P	4,892.9P	10,184.9P	493.4P
2010		186P	59P	12.1P	7.3P	15.1P	1,059.4P	19.09P	5,321.4P	4,843.3P	10,081.8P	479.3P

Sources: 1992, 1997, 2002 *Economic Census*; other years, up to 2006, are from the *Annual Survey of Manufactures*. Establishment counts for non-Census years are from *County Business Patterns*; 1997 and 2002 values are from the 1997 and 2002 censuses respectively, reported in the Federal Government's NAICS format. Other years were originally reported in equivalent SIC format. 'P's show projections by the editors.

INDICES OF CHANGE

Year	Com-panies	Establishments		Employment			Compensation		Production ($ million)			
		Total	with 20 or more employees	Total (000)	Production Workers (000)	Hours (Mil)	Payroll ($ mil)	Wages ($/hr)	Cost of Materials	Value Added by Manufacture	Value of Shipments	Capital Invest.
1992	104	105	141	157	154	156	114	74	106	99	102	94
1997	128	123	125	159	196	201	122	80	157	126	142	285
2001		114	116	136	146	148	102	88	135	156	150	122
2002	100	100	100	100	100	100	100	100	100	100	100	100
2003		99	93	77	95	98	84	95	101	76	90	93
2004		99	96	59	78	79	58	95	73	68	71	56
2005		87	88	62	84	88	65	92	92	83	86	80
2006		108P	96P	69	91	94	71	95	94	86	90	83
2007		108P	94P	67P	93P	96P	76P	99P	116P	106P	111P	107P
2008		109P	91P	60P	87P	89P	73P	101P	115P	105P	110P	105P
2009		109P	89P	53P	81P	82P	70P	102P	114P	104P	109P	102P
2010		109P	86P	47P	74P	75P	67P	104P	113P	103P	107P	99P

Sources: Same as General Statistics. Values reflect change from the base year, 2002. Values above 100 mean greater than 2002, values below 100 mean less than 2002, and the values of 100 in other years means the same as 2002. 'P's show projections by the editors.

SELECTED RATIOS

For 2002	Avg. of All Manufact.	Analyzed Industry	Index	For 2002	Avg. of All Manufact.	Analyzed Industry	Index
Employees per Establishment	42	153	364	Value Added per Production Worker	182,367	473,525	260
Payroll per Establishment	1,639,184	9,282,353	566	Cost per Establishment	5,769,015	27,786,471	482
Payroll per Employee	39,053	60,692	155	Cost per Employee	137,446	181,681	132
Production Workers per Establishment	30	58	197	Cost per Production Worker	195,506	477,141	244
Wages per Establishment	694,845	2,173,165	313	Shipments per Establishment	11,158,348	55,173,529	494
Wages per Production Worker	23,548	37,317	158	Shipments per Employee	265,847	360,750	136
Hours per Production Worker	1,980	2,030	103	Shipments per Production Worker	378,144	947,424	251
Wages per Hour	11.89	18.38	155	Investment per Establishment	361,338	2,857,059	791
Value Added per Establishment	5,381,325	27,575,882	512	Investment per Employee	8,609	18,681	217
Value Added per Employee	128,210	180,304	141	Investment per Production Worker	12,245	49,061	401

Sources: Same as General Statistics. The 'Average of All Manufacturing' column represents the average of all manufacturing industries reported for the most recent complete year available. The Index shows the relationship between the Average and the Analyzed Industry. For example, 100 means that they are equal; 500 that the Analyzed Industry is five times the average; 50 means that the Analyzed Industry is half the national average. The abbreviation 'na' is used to show that data are 'not available'. Ratios shown for 2002, the last complete census year.

LEADING COMPANIES   Number shown: **75**   Total sales ($ mil): **181,283**   Total employment (000): **545.5**

Company Name	Address				CEO Name	Phone	Co. Type	Sales ($ mil)	Empl. (000)
International Bus. Machines	1 New Orchard Rd.	Armonk	NY	10504		914-499-1900	P	98,786	329.4
EMC Corp.	176 South St.	Hopkinton	MA	01748		508-435-1000	P	13,230	31.1
Seagate Technology	920 Disc Dr.	Scotts Valley	CA	95066	Stephen Luczo	831-438-6550	P	11,360	54.0
Hitachi Global Storage Tech.	5600 Cottle Rd.	San Jose	CA	95193	Hiroaki Nakanishi	408-717-5000	J	9,450*	21.0
SYNNEX Corp.	44201 Nobel Dr.	Fremont	CA	94538		510-656-3333	P	7,004	6.1
Western Digital Corp.	20511 Lk Forest Dr.	Lake Forest	CA	92630	John Coyne	949-672-7000	P	5,468	29.6
NCR Corp.	1700 S Patterson	Dayton	OH	45479		937-445-5000	P	4,970	23.2
Oki Data Americas Inc.	2000 Bishops Gate	Mount Laurel	NJ	08054	Stewart Krentzman	856-235-2600	S	4,260*	0.5
SanDisk Corp.	601 McCarthy Blvd.	Milpitas	CA	95035		408-801-1000	P	3,896	3.2
Kingston Technology Company	17600 Newhope St.	Fountain Valley	CA	92708		714-435-2600	R	3,536*	3.3
Hitachi Data Systems Holding	750 Central Expy.	Santa Clara	CA	95050		408-970-1000	S	3,333*	3.4
Network Appliance Inc.	495 E Java Dr.	Sunnyvale	CA	94089		408-822-6000	P	2,804	6.6
Storage Technology Corp.	1 StorageTek Dr.	Louisville	CO	80028		303-673-5151	S	2,224	7.1
Tektronix Inc.	PO Box 500	Beaverton	OR	97077		503-627-7111	S	1,105	4.4
Hewlett-Packard Puerto Rico	PO Box 4048	Aguadilla	PR	00605		787-890-6000	R	1,052*	1.7
Quantum Corp.	1650 Technology	San Jose	CA	95110	Richard E. Belluzzo	408-944-4000	P	1,016	2.9
SMART Modular Technologies	4211 Starboard Dr.	Fremont	CA	94538	Ian MacKenzie	510-623-1231	P	828	1.4
Wintec Industries Inc.	4280 Technology	Fremont	CA	94538	Chu-Hui Jeng	510-360-6300	R	745*	0.3
White Systems Inc.	30 Boright Ave.	Kenilworth	NJ	07033	Richard Paolino	908-272-6700	S	673*	0.3
Advantek Inc.	5801 Clearwater Dr.	Minnetonka	MN	55343	Bruce Batten	952-938-6800	R	523*	<0.1
Engenio Information Tech.	670 N McCarthy	Milpitas	CA	95035	Thomas Georgens		S	519*	1.1
Advanced Digital Information	PO Box 97057	Redmond	WA	98073			S	454	1.1
FileNet Corp.	3565 Harbor Blvd.	Costa Mesa	CA	92626	Lee D. Roberts	714-327-3400	S	422	1.7
Astronautics Corp. of America	PO Box 523	Milwaukee	WI	53201	Michael Russek	414-449-4000	R	233*	0.5
Iomega Corp.	10955 Vsta Sorrento	San Diego	CA	92130	John Huberman	858-314-7000	P	230	0.3
Cray Inc.	411 1st Ave. S, 600	Seattle	WA	98104		206-701-2000	P	221	0.8
STEC, Inc.	3001 Daimler St.	Santa Ana	CA	92705	Manouch Moshayedi	949-476-1180	P	189	0.6
Dot Hill Systems Corp.	2200 Faraday Ave.	Carlsbad	CA	92008	Charles Christ	760-931-5500	P	188	0.3
Blue Coat Systems Inc.	420 N Mary Ave.	Sunnyvale	CA	94085	David W. Hanna	408-220-2200	P	178	0.7
MTI Technology Corp.	17595 Cartwright Rd	Irvine	CA	92614		949-251-1101	P	166	0.4
Overland Storage Inc.	4820 Overland Ave.	San Diego	CA	92123		858-571-5555	P	160	0.3
Xycom Automation Inc.	750 N Maple Rd.	Saline	MI	48176	Jerry Tubbs		R	150*	0.1
Optimus Solutions Inc.	22 Technology Park	Norcross	GA	30092	Mark Metz	770-447-1951	R	122	0.3
Hitachi Computer Products	1800 E Imhoff Rd.	Norman	OK	73071	George Wilson	405-360-5500	S	102*	0.5
NovaStor Corp.	80B W Cochran	Simi Valley	CA	93065	Peter Means	805-579-6700	R	96*	<0.1
Exabyte Corp.	2108 55th Street	Boulder	CO	80301	Gudmundur Einarsson	303-442-4333	S	91	0.2
Pillar Data Systems Inc.	2840 Jct. Ave.	San Jose	CA	95134	Nancy Holleran	408-503-4000	R	90*	0.3
Visiontek Products L.L.C.	1610 Colonial Pky.	Inverness	IL	60067		224-836-3900	R	75*	<0.1
Plasmon LMS Inc.	4425 Arrowswest	Colorado Spgs	CO	80907	Christopher Harris	719-593-7900	R	74*	0.2
TEAC America Inc. Data Storage	PO Box 750	Montebello	CA	90640	Koichiro Nakamura	323-726-0303	D	73*	0.3
ATP Electronics Inc.	750 N Mary Ave.	Sunnyvale	CA	94085	Tim Hsieh	408-732-5000	R	72*	0.2
3PAR Inc.	4209 Technology	Fremont	CA	94538	David C. Scott	510-413-5999	P	66	0.4
DataDirect Networks Inc.	9351 Deering Ave.	Chatsworth	CA	91311	Paul Bloch	818-700-7600	R	63*	0.2
Transpower Technologies Inc.	980 Sandhill Rd	Reno	NV	89511	Tom Lynch	775-852-0140	S	61*	2.2
APS Tech Inc.	22985 NW Evergrn	Hillsboro	OR	97124		503-844-4500	S	61*	<0.1
SAN Holdings Inc.	9800 Mount Pyramid	Englewood	CO	80112		303-495-6300	P	59	0.1
Memtech SSD Corp.	2107 North First St	San Jose	CA	95131	Manouch Moshayedi	408-452-1277	R	56*	0.5
Allot Communications Inc.	7664 Goldn Triangle	Eden Prairie	MN	55344	Rami Hadar	952-944-3100	R	49*	<0.1
Bluearc Corp.	50 Rio Robles Dr.	San Jose	CA	95134	Mike Gustafson	408-576-6600	R	42	0.2
Advanced Programs Inc.	7125 Riverwood Dr.	Columbia	MD	21046	Steve Rice	410-312-5800	R	42*	<0.1
Dataram Corp.	186 Princeton Rd.	West Windsor	NJ	08550		609-799-0071	P	38	<0.1
Xtera Communications Inc.	500 W Bethany, 100	Allen	TX	75013	John Hopper	972-649-5000	R	38*	0.4
TeraStor Corp.	930 Wrigley Way	Milpitas	CA	95035	Amyl Ahola	408-957-8990	R	34*	0.1
TechWorks Inc.	4030 W Braker Ln.	Austin	TX	78759			R	34*	<0.1
Spectra Logic Corp.	1700 N 55th St.	Boulder	CO	80301	Nathan C. Thompson	303-449-6400	R	33*	0.3
Taiyo Yuden (U.S.A.) Inc.	1770 La Costa Mdw.	San Marcos	CA	92069	Tomiji Kobayashi	760-510-3200	S	33*	0.2
LaserCard Corp.	1875 N Shoreline	Mountain View	CA	94043	Christopher J. Dyball	650-969-4428	P	32	0.2
Rorke Data Inc.	9700 W 76th St.	Eden Prairie	MN	55344		952-829-0300	S	30*	<0.1
Microland Electronics Corp.	1883 Ringwood	San Jose	CA	95131	Abraham Chen	408-441-1688	R	30*	<0.1
Contemporary Cybernetics Group	111 Cybernetics	Yorktown	VA	23693	Maria Lennman	757-833-9000	R	28*	0.1
IMC Networks Corp.	19772 Pauling	Foothill Ranch	CA	92610	Michael Dailey	949-465-3000	R	25*	<0.1
Mercom Systems Inc.	9 Polito Ave.	Lyndhurst	NJ	07071	Avi Margolin	201-507-8800	S	25*	<0.1
Progressive Computer Services	4250 Wissahickon	Philadelphia	PA	19129	Martin Becker	215-226-2220	R	23*	<0.1
ENM Company Inc.	5617 N NW Hwy.	Chicago	IL	60646	Nicholas Polydoris	773-775-8400	R	22*	0.1
Qualstar Corp.	3990-B Heritg Oak	Simi Valley	CA	93063	William J. Gervais	805-583-7744	P	21	<0.1
Kintronics Inc.	500 Executive Blvd.	Ossining	NY	10562	Bob Memisnik	914-944-3425	R	20*	<0.1
Alanco Technologies Inc.	15575 N 83rd	Scottsdale	AZ	85260		480-607-1010	P	19	<0.1
Vertical Circuits Inc.	10 Victor Sq., 100	Scotts Valley	CA	95066		831-438-3887	R	19*	<0.1
Surgient Inc.	8303 Mopac, Ste. C3	Austin	TX	78759	Bill Daniel	512-241-4600	R	18*	0.2
GST Inc.	20902 Bake Pkwy.	Lake Forest	CA	92630	David Breisacher	949-900-1090	R	17*	<0.1
Appro International Inc.	446 S Abbott Ave.	Milpitas	CA	95035	Daniel Kim	408-941-8100	R	16*	<0.1
DOME Imaging Systems Inc.	1195 NW Compton	Beaverton	OR	97006	Gerald K. Perkel		S	16*	<0.1
Mudlogging Company USA L.P.	6741 Satsuma Dr.	Houston	TX	77041		713-466-7400	R	16*	0.1
Micro Memory Inc.	9540 Vassar Ave.	Chatsworth	CA	91311	Mose Jadon	818-998-0070	R	15*	<0.1
P.C. Peripherals Inc.	927 Cinnamon Ln.	Louisville	CO	80027	Bob Wing	303-665-0330	R	15*	<0.1

Source: Ward's Business Directory of U.S. Private and Public Companies, Volumes 1 and 2, 2008. The company type code used is as follows: P - Public, R - Private, S - Subsidiary, D - Division, J - Joint Venture, A - Affiliate, G - Group. Sales are in millions of dollars, employees are in thousands. An asterisk (*) indicates an estimated sales volume. The symbol < stands for 'less than'. Company names and addresses are truncated, in some cases, to fit into the available space.

MATERIALS CONSUMED

Material	Quantity	Delivered Cost ($ million)
Cathode ray tubes (CRT) (excluding X-ray)	(X)	(D)
Printed ciruit boards (without inserted components) for electronic circuitry	(X)	41.8
Printed memory boards for electronic circuitry	(X)	20.1
Printed peripheral controllers for electronic circuitry	(X)	21.6
Printed computer processors for electronic circuitry	(X)	(D)
Printed communication boards for electronic circuitry	(X)	(D)
Other printed circuit boards for electronic circuitry	(X)	(D)
Semiconductors (incl. transistors, diodes, rectifiers, and integrated circuits), for electronic circuitry	(X)	227.1
Capacitors for electronic circuitry	(X)	(D)
Resistors for electronic circuitry	(X)	1.7
Connectors for electronic circuitry	(X)	1.6
Battery packs for electronic circuitry	(X)	0.7
Other power supply units for electronic circuitry	(X)	37.2
Other components and accessories, for electronic circuitry (coils, transformers, etc.), excluding tubes	(X)	(D)
Electrical transmission, distribution, and control equipment	(X)	(D)
Steel, aluminum, and other metal electronic enclosures	(X)	56.9
Plastics electronic enclosures	(X)	1.2
Sheet metal products, including stampings (exc. enclosures)	(X)	8.0
All other fabricated metal products (excluding forgings)	(X)	(D)
Castings, rough and semifinished	(X)	(D)
Metal shapes and forms (exc. castings, forgings, fabr. metal products)	(X)	(D)
Insulated copper wire and cable (including magnet wire)	(X)	11.2
Fabricated plastics products (excluding enclosures)	(X)	(D)
Purchased software	(X)	(D)
Appliance outlets and other current-carrying wiring devices	(X)	(D)
Electric motors and generators	(X)	14.5
Paper and paperboard products (incl. paperboard boxes, etc.)	(X)	29.3
Purchased computers	(X)	(D)
Purchased peripheral storage devices	(X)	893.5
Purchased computer terminals	(X)	(D)
Purchased peripheral input devices (including keyboards, mouse devices, track balls, etc.)	(X)	1.5
Purchased peripheral printers	(X)	(D)
All other materials, components, parts, containers, and supplies	(X)	1,249.7
Materials, ingredients, containers, and supplies, nsk	(X)	392.6

Source: 2002 *Economic Census*. Explanation of symbols used: (D): Withheld to avoid disclosure of competitive data; na: Not available; (S): Withheld because statistical norms were not met; (X): Not applicable; (Z): Less than half the unit shown; nec: Not elsewhere classified; nsk: Not specified by kind; - : zero; p : 10-19 percent estimated; q : 20-29 percent estimated.

PRODUCT SHARE DETAILS

Product or Product Class Shipments	Mil. $	Product or Product Class Shipments	Mil. $
COMPUTER STORAGE DEVICES	7,574.5	Parts, attachments, and accessories for computer storage devices	1,722.7
Computer storage devices (except parts, attachments, and accessories)	5,414.0	Computer storage devices, nsk, total	437.7

Source: 2002 *Economic Census*. The values are product shipments in millions of dollars for 2002. Total product shipments may be lower or higher than industry shipments. See Introduction for a full discussion. Values of indented subcategories are summed in the main heading(s). The symbol (D) appears when data are withheld to prevent disclosure of competitive information. The abbreviation nsk stands for 'not specified by kind' and nec for 'not elsewhere classified'. A dash (-) means zero.

INPUTS AND OUTPUTS FOR COMPUTER STORAGE DEVICE MANUFACTURING

Economic Sector or Industry Providing Inputs	%	Sector	Economic Sector or Industry Buying Outputs	%	Sector
Compensation of employees	23.7		Electronic computers	35.3	Manufg.
Computer storage devices	11.0	Manufg.	Private fixed investment	26.8	
Software publishers	9.9	Services	Exports of goods & services	10.1	Cap Inv
Management of companies & enterprises	9.5	Services	Computer storage devices	4.9	Manufg.
Wholesale trade	9.5	Trade	General S/L govt. services	4.7	S/L Govt
Semiconductors & related devices	3.2	Manufg.	General Federal government services, defense	4.5	Fed Govt
Scientific research & development services	2.7	Services	Personal consumption expenditures	3.5	
Computer terminals & peripherals	2.4	Manufg.	Other computer related services, including facilities	1.5	Services
Printed circuit assemblies (electronic assemblies)	1.3	Manufg.	Electromedical & electrotherapeutic apparatus	1.3	Manufg.
Noncomparable imports	1.0	Foreign	Change in private inventories	1.1	In House
Advertising & related services	0.9	Services	Wholesale trade	0.8	Trade
Software, audio, and video media reproducing	0.8	Manufg.	S/L govt. invest., education	0.7	S/L Govt
Power generation & supply	0.8	Util.	Federal government, investment, national defense	0.6	Fed Govt
Electronic capacitors, resistors, coils, transformers	0.8	Manufg.	Architectural, engineering, & related services	0.6	Services
Electron tubes	0.8	Manufg.	General Federal government services, nondefense	0.5	Fed Govt
Ornamental & architectural metal products	0.7	Manufg.	Data processing, hosting, & related services	0.4	Services
Wiring devices	0.7	Manufg.	Management, scientific, & technical consulting	0.4	Services
Plastics products, nec	0.7	Manufg.	Federal government, investment, nondefense	0.3	Fed Govt
Bare printed circuit boards	0.6	Manufg.	Irradiation apparatus	0.3	Manufg.

Continued on next page.

INPUTS AND OUTPUTS FOR COMPUTER STORAGE DEVICE MANUFACTURING - Continued

Economic Sector or Industry Providing Inputs	%	Sector	Economic Sector or Industry Buying Outputs	%	Sector
Automotive equipment rental & leasing	0.6	Fin/R.E.	Watches, clocks, & related devices	0.2	Manufg.
Real estate	0.6	Fin/R.E.	S/L govt. invest., other	0.2	S/L Govt
Paperboard containers	0.5	Manufg.	Broadcast & wireless communications equipment	0.1	Manufg.
Electronic components, nec	0.5	Manufg.	Computer terminals & peripherals	0.1	Manufg.
Management, scientific, & technical consulting	0.4	Services	Monetary authorities/depository credit intermediation	0.1	Fin/R.E.
Paperboard mills	0.4	Manufg.			
Electronic computers	0.4	Manufg.			
Iron & steel mills & ferroalloys	0.4	Manufg.			
Truck transportation	0.4	Util.			
Machine shops	0.4	Manufg.			
Warehousing & storage	0.4	Util.			
Taxes on production & imports, less subsidies	0.3				
Chemical products & preparations, nec	0.3	Manufg.			
Commercial & industrial machinery rental & leasing	0.3	Fin/R.E.			
Electrical equipment & components, nec	0.3	Manufg.			
Coating, engraving, heat treating & allied activities	0.3	Manufg.			
Maintenance/repair of nonresidential structures	0.3	Construct.			
Plastics packaging materials, film & sheet	0.2	Manufg.			
Services to buildings & dwellings	0.2	Services			
Legal services	0.2	Services			
Motor vehicle parts	0.2	Manufg.			
Telecommunications	0.2	Services			
Motors & generators	0.2	Manufg.			
Data processing, hosting, & related services	0.2	Services			
Accounting, tax preparation, bookkeeping, & payroll	0.2	Services			
Employment services	0.2	Services			
Retail trade	0.2	Trade			
Automotive repair & maintenance, ex. car washes	0.2	Services			
Business support services	0.1	Services			
Commercial & industrial equipment repair/maintenance	0.1	Services			
Specialized design services	0.1	Services			
Aluminum products from purchased aluminum	0.1	Manufg.			
Turned products & screws, nuts, & bolts	0.1	Manufg.			

Source: Benchmark Input-Output Accounts for the U.S. Economy, 2002, U.S. Department of Commerce, Washington, D.C., January 2008. The abbreviation nec stands for 'not elsewhere classified'.

OCCUPATIONS EMPLOYED BY COMPUTER & PERIPHERAL EQUIPMENT MANUFACTURING

Occupation	% of Total 2006	Change to 2016	Occupation	% of Total 2006	Change to 2016
Computer software engineers, systems software	10.1	-28.0	Computer & information systems managers	1.5	-34.5
Electrical & electronic equipment assemblers	7.4	-47.6	Financial analysts	1.4	-28.0
Computer hardware engineers	6.5	-28.0	Purchasing agents, exc wholesale, retail, & farm	1.4	-34.5
Computer software engineers, applications	5.5	-21.4	Engineers, nec	1.3	-34.5
Sales representatives, wholesale & manufacturing, tech	2.5	-34.5	Computer programmers	1.3	-47.6
Computer support specialists	2.4	-34.5	Accountants & auditors	1.3	-34.5
Computer systems analysts	2.4	-28.0	Executive secretaries & administrative assistants	1.3	-34.5
Engineering managers	2.3	-34.5	Inspectors, testers, sorters, samplers, & weighers	1.3	-38.3
Electrical & electronic engineering technicians	2.3	-34.5	Electrical engineers	1.2	-34.5
Business operation specialists, nec	2.1	-28.0	Team assemblers	1.2	-34.5
Industrial engineers	1.8	-20.5	Logisticians	1.1	-28.0
Marketing managers	1.7	-34.5	General & operations managers	1.1	-41.1
Office clerks, general	1.6	-35.5	Shipping, receiving, & traffic clerks	1.1	-37.0
Market research analysts	1.6	-34.5	Production, planning, & expediting clerks	1.0	-34.5
Electronics engineers, exc computer	1.5	-34.5			

Source: Industry-Occupation Matrix, Bureau of Labor Statistics, December 4, 2007. These data are reported based on 4-digit NAICS categories but have been matched to corresponding 6-digit NAICS industry codes. The change reported for each occupation to the year 2016 is a percent of growth or decline as estimated by the Bureau of Labor Statistics. The abbreviation nec stands for 'not elsewhere classified'.

LOCATION BY STATE AND REGIONAL CONCENTRATION

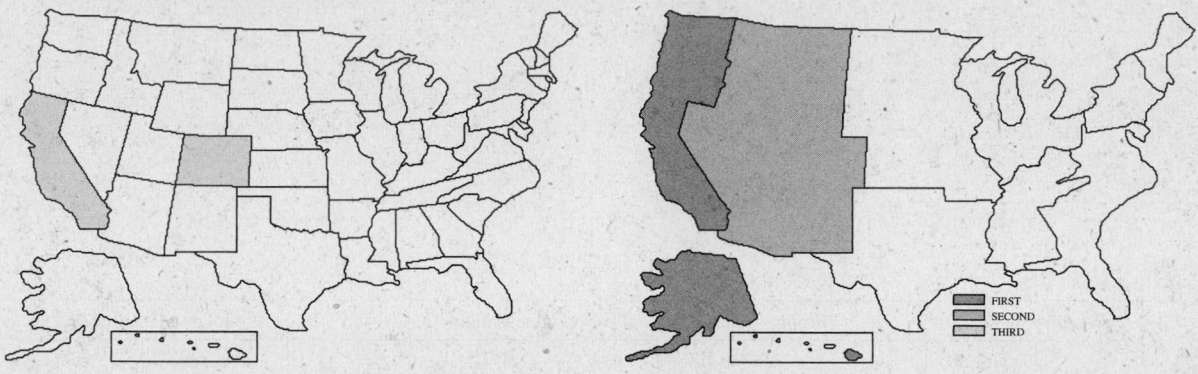

FIRST
SECOND
THIRD

INDUSTRY DATA BY STATE

| State | Establish-ments | Shipments | | | Employment | | | | Cost as % of Shipments | Investment per Employee ($) |
		Total ($ mil)	% of U.S.	Per Establ.	Total Number	% of U.S.	Per Establ.	Wages ($/hour)		
California	71	4,233.5	45.1	59,626.7	10,945	42.0	154	24.18	46.9	25,951
Colorado	12	1,123.2	12.0	93,600.7	3,005	11.5	250	12.99	52.4	17,374

Source: 2002 *Economic Census*. The states are in descending order of shipments or establishments (if shipment data are missing for the majority). The symbol (D) appears when data are withheld to prevent disclosure of competitive information. States marked with (D) are sorted by number of establishments. A dash (-) indicates that the data element cannot be calculated. Data may not show all states active in the NAICS category. All data available at the time of publication are shown.

NAICS 334113 - COMPUTER TERMINAL MANUFACTURING

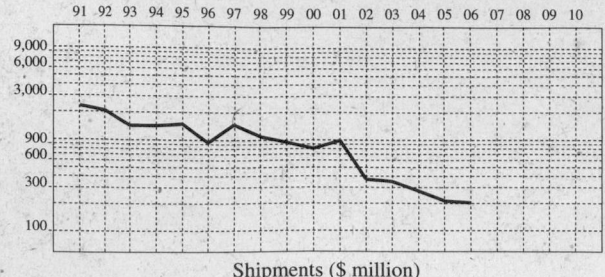

Shipments ($ million)

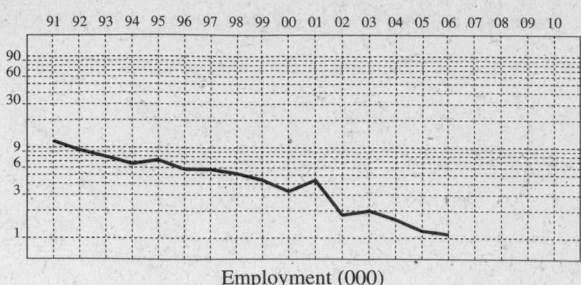

Employment (000)

GENERAL STATISTICS

| Year | Com-panies | Establishments | | Employment | | | Compensation | | Production ($ million) | | | |
		Total	with 20 or more employees	Total (000)	Production Workers (000)	Hours (Mil)	Payroll ($ mil)	Wages ($/hr)	Cost of Materials	Value Added by Manufacture	Value of Shipments	Capital Invest.
1991		154	70	11.7	5.2	10.3	386.1	11.99	1,429.5	865.0	2,326.5	42.4
1992	186	190	63	9.3	4.2	8.0	344.1	12.84	1,288.2	800.2	2,070.7	44.4
1993		177	61	7.9	3.5	6.8	307.2	12.25	807.8	615.8	1,435.0	29.3
1994		169	67	6.6	2.7	5.2	260.4	12.85	894.7	516.2	1,427.5	41.7
1995		157	59	7.3	3.2	6.0	284.4	13.43	1,001.5	522.1	1,498.7	54.0
1996		148	57	5.8	2.7	5.5	221.4	12.51	590.8	352.4	938.6	26.0
1997	141	142	45	5.8	2.8	5.9	253.1	15.31	941.9	528.6	1,483.5	34.7
1998		154	39	5.2	2.2	5.0	218.2	14.83	651.3	444.5	1,096.2	30.7
1999		134	34	4.4	2.2	4.4	183.7	14.76	544.6	388.8	941.2	67.4
2000		132	34	3.3	1.5	3.1	149.6	16.83	410.7	390.3	808.2	59.3
2001		133	41	4.4	1.7	2.8	167.5	16.97	503.9	498.2	988.0	37.1
2002	70	71	17	1.8	0.9	1.7	80.5	16.21	149.8	218.3	370.2	15.0
2003		70	25	2.0	0.9	1.7	93.9	16.82	151.2	188.0	350.7	13.6
2004		62	20	1.6	0.7	1.3	76.0	18.48	121.5	151.5	275.0	5.7
2005		52	14	1.2	0.5	1.0	62.5	18.13	80.8	128.8	213.6	4.3
2006		58P	11P	1.1	0.5	0.9	60.6	18.16	73.6	132.6	203.8	4.1
2007		49P	6P				14.0P	19.05P				10.4P
2008		40P	2P					19.50P				7.9P
2009		31P						19.96P				5.4P
2010		22P						20.42P				2.8P

Sources: 1992, 1997, 2002 *Economic Census*; other years, up to 2006, are from the *Annual Survey of Manufactures*. Establishment counts for non-Census years are from *County Business Patterns*; 1997 and 2002 values are from the 1997 and 2002 censuses respectively, reported in the Federal Government's NAICS format. Other years were originally reported in equivalent SIC format. 'P's show projections by the editors.

INDICES OF CHANGE

| Year | Com-panies | Establishments | | Employment | | | Compensation | | Production ($ million) | | | |
		Total	with 20 or more employees	Total (000)	Production Workers (000)	Hours (Mil)	Payroll ($ mil)	Wages ($/hr)	Cost of Materials	Value Added by Manufacture	Value of Shipments	Capital Invest.
1992	266	268	371	517	467	471	427	79	860	367	559	296
1997	201	200	265	322	311	347	314	94	629	242	401	231
2001		187	241	244	189	165	208	105	336	228	267	247
2002	100	100	100	100	100	100	100	100	100	100	100	100
2003		99	147	111	100	100	117	104	101	86	95	91
2004		87	118	89	78	76	94	114	81	69	74	38
2005		73	82	67	56	59	78	112	54	59	58	29
2006		81P	62P	61	56	53	75	112	49	61	55	27
2007		68P	38P				17P	118P				69P
2008		56P	14P					120P				53P
2009		43P						123P				36P
2010		30P						126P				19P

Sources: Same as General Statistics. Values reflect change from the base year, 2002. Values above 100 mean greater than 2002, values below 100 mean less than 2002, and the values of 100 in other years means the same as 2002. 'P's show projections by the editors.

SELECTED RATIOS

For 2002	Avg. of All Manufact.	Analyzed Industry	Index	For 2002	Avg. of All Manufact.	Analyzed Industry	Index
Employees per Establishment	42	25	60	Value Added per Production Worker	182,367	242,556	133
Payroll per Establishment	1,639,184	1,133,803	69	Cost per Establishment	5,769,015	2,109,859	37
Payroll per Employee	39,053	44,722	115	Cost per Employee	137,446	83,222	61
Production Workers per Establishment	30	13	43	Cost per Production Worker	195,506	166,444	85
Wages per Establishment	694,845	388,127	56	Shipments per Establishment	11,158,348	5,214,085	47
Wages per Production Worker	23,548	30,619	130	Shipments per Employee	265,847	205,667	77
Hours per Production Worker	1,980	1,889	95	Shipments per Production Worker	378,144	411,333	109
Wages per Hour	11.89	16.21	136	Investment per Establishment	361,338	211,268	58
Value Added per Establishment	5,381,325	3,074,648	57	Investment per Employee	8,609	8,333	97
Value Added per Employee	128,210	121,278	95	Investment per Production Worker	12,245	16,667	136

Sources: Same as General Statistics. The 'Average of All Manufacturing' column represents the average of all manufacturing industries reported for the most recent complete year available. The Index shows the relationship between the Average and the Analyzed Industry. For example, 100 means that they are equal; 500 that the Analyzed Industry is five times the average; 50 means that the Analyzed Industry is half the national average. The abbreviation 'na' is used to show that data are 'not available'. Ratios shown for 2002, the last complete census year.

LEADING COMPANIES Number shown: **75**   Total sales ($ mil): **129,018**   Total employment (000): **406.8**

Company Name	Address				CEO Name	Phone	Co. Type	Sales ($ mil)	Empl. (000)
International Bus. Machines	1 New Orchard Rd.	Armonk	NY	10504		914-499-1900	P	98,786	329.4
Sun Microsystems Inc.	4150 Network Cir.	Santa Clara	CA	95054		650-960-1300	P	13,873	34.2
SYNNEX Corp.	44201 Nobel Dr.	Fremont	CA	94538		510-656-3333	P	7,004	6.1
Unisys Corp.	Unisys Way	Blue Bell	PA	19424		215-986-4011	P	5,653	30.0
Palm Inc.	950 W Maude Ave.	Sunnyvale	CA	94085	Eric Benhamou	408-617-7000	P	1,561	1.2
Marquardt Switches Inc.	2711 US Rte. 20	Cazenovia	NY	13035	Michael Beckett	315-655-8050	R	338*	0.2
Wyse Technology Inc.	3471 N First St.	San Jose	CA	95134	Tarkan Maner	408-473-1200	R	221*	0.9
Smartronix Inc.	22685 Three Notch	California	MD	20619	M. Arshed Javaid	301-737-2800	R	221*	0.4
KDS USA	7373 Hunt Ave.	Garden Grove	CA	92841	John Hui	714-379-5599	R	192*	0.1
Optimus Solutions Inc.	22 Technology Park	Norcross	GA	30092	Mark Metz	770-447-1951	R	122	0.3
Princeton Digital (USA) Corp.	3300 Irvine Ave.	Newport Beach	CA	92660	Si-Chung Chang	949-777-3379	R	111*	0.2
Interstate Electronics Corp.	PO Box 3117	Anaheim	CA	92803	Robert Huffman	714-758-0500	S	90*	0.6
Grayhill Inc.	PO Box 10373	La Grange	IL	60525	Gene Hill	708-354-1040	R	56*	0.5
Aydin Displays Inc.	1 Riga Ln.	Birdsboro	PA	19508		610-404-7400	S	43*	<0.1
Advanced Programs Inc.	7125 Riverwood Dr.	Columbia	MD	21046	Steve Rice	410-312-5800	R	42*	<0.1
Follett Software Co.	1391 Corporate Dr.	McHenry	IL	60050	Tom Schenk	815-344-8700	S	39*	0.3
Crystal Group Inc.	850 Kacena Rd.	Hiawatha	IA	52233		319-378-1636	R	36*	<0.1
Rorke Data Inc.	9700 W 76th St.	Eden Prairie	MN	55344		952-829-0300	S	30*	<0.1
Two Technologies Inc.	419 Sargon Way, A	Horsham	PA	19044		215-441-5305	R	30*	<0.1
Ind. Electronic Engineers	7740 Lemona Ave.	Van Nuys	CA	91405	Donald Gumpertz	818-787-0311	R	29*	0.1
Electronic Monitoring Systems	30201 Aventura	R St Margarita	CA	92688	Fiona Walters	949-635-1600	R	27*	0.1
Ultimate Technology Corp.	100 Rawson Rd.	Victor	NY	14564		585-924-9500	R	26*	0.1
Linx Data Terminals Inc.	625 Digital Dr.	Plano	TX	75075	Marvin Kline	972-964-7090	R	26*	<0.1
Kristel L.P.	555 Kirk Rd.	Saint Charles	IL	60174		630-443-1290	R	26*	0.1
Global Data Granite Communic.	13 Columbia Dr.	Amherst	NH	03031	Robert St	603-881-8666	R	22*	<0.1
Milwaukee P.C. Incorporated	6013 W Bluemound	Milwaukee	WI	53213	Jim Petr	414-258-2275	R	15*	<0.1
Annapolis Micro Systems Inc.	190 Adm Cochran	Annapolis	MD	21401	Jane Donaldson	410-841-2514	R	14*	<0.1
Electronic Systems Services	22515 Gateway Ctr.	Clarksburg	MD	20871	Bill Kisse	301-944-2300	R	14*	0.1
Ezenia! Inc.	14 Celina Ave., 17	Nashua	NH	03063		781-505-2100	P	13	<0.1
Duratab Corp.	PO Box 2187	Abington	MA	02351	Mark Burns	508-944-3818	R	13*	<0.1
Verity Instruments Inc.	2901 Eisenhower St.	Carrollton	TX	75007	Mike Whelan	972-446-9990	R	13*	<0.1
Acroprint Time Recorder Co.	5640 Departure Dr.	Raleigh	NC	27616	Glenn Robbins	919-872-5800	R	13*	0.1
MCF Industries Inc.	39 1st Street	Lowell	MA	01850	Richard Mailloux	978-459-0127	R	13*	<0.1
New England Keyboard Inc.	1 Princeton Rd.	Fitchburg	MA	01420	David Myers	978-345-8332	R	13*	<0.1
Transparent Products Inc.	28064 Ave. Stanford	Valencia	CA	91355		661-294-9787	R	13*	<0.1
Quadrant Components Inc.	4378 Enterprise St.	Fremont	CA	94538	Chad Yau	510-656-9988	R	12*	<0.1
Universal Display Corp.	375 Phillips Blvd.	Ewing	NJ	08618	Steven V. Abramson	609-671-0980	P	12	<0.1
Giraffics	115 S State St.	Lindon	UT	84042	Leonard Lee	801-785-5000	R	12*	0.1
GraphOn Corp.	5400 Soquel Ave.	Santa Cruz	CA	95062	Robert P. Dilworth	603-225-3525	P	12	<0.1
Peripheral Systems Inc.	257 W 2950 S	Salt Lake City	UT	84115		801-474-2214	R	11*	<0.1
Telco Intercontinental Corp.	9812 Whithorn Dr.	Houston	TX	77095	Frank Liang	281-855-2218	R	11*	<0.1
Teledata Communications Inc.	100 Engineers Rd.	Hauppauge	NY	11788	George Nagrodsky	631-231-6700	R	10*	<0.1
Digitron Electronics	7801 E Telegraph	Montebello	CA	90640		323-887-0777	R	10*	<0.1
Elec-Tron Inc.	2050 E Northern St.	Wichita	KS	67216	Rose Rohleder	316-522-3401	R	9*	<0.1
CSI Keyboards Inc.	56 Pulaski St., 1	Peabody	MA	01960	Peter Castner	978-532-8181	R	9*	<0.1
AB Electronics Inc.	61 Commerce Dr.	Brookfield	CT	06804	Armando Bernardo	203-740-2793	R	9*	<0.1
Behemoth Corp.	202 Reynolds Ave.	League City	TX	77573	Luanne Edelman	281-332-4798	R	9*	<0.1
Jupiter Systems	31015 Huntwood	Hayward	CA	94544		510-675-1000	R	9*	<0.1
Westrex International	25 Denby Rd.	Boston	MA	02134	Dom Emello	617-254-1200	R	8*	<0.1
Tate Technology Inc.	3102 E Trent Ave.	Spokane	WA	99202	Lee Tate	509-534-2500	R	8*	<0.1
Continuum Technology Corp.	220 Continuum Dr.	Fletcher	NC	28732	Stephen Hafer	828-684-8682	S	7*	<0.1
Bartizan Data Systems L.L.C.	217 Riverdale Ave.	Yonkers	NY	10705	Lew Hoff	914-965-7977	R	7*	<0.1
Martech Computers	5235 Cottage Frm	Alpharetta	GA	30022	Marvin Tedjamulia	770-418-0101	R	7*	<0.1
N American Technology Exchg.	PO Box 7510	Broomfield	CO	80021	Wade Luther	303-443-1984	R	7*	<0.1
All Technics Products Inc.	216 Gates Rd.	Little Ferry	NJ	07643	David Wu	201-440-2225	R	6*	<0.1
Nortech Engineering Inc.	15 Commerce Way	Norton	MA	02766	Bob Davis	508-285-7831	R	6*	<0.1
Comark Corp.	93 West St.	Medfield	MA	02052	Steve Schott	508-359-8161	R	6*	<0.1
Dynasys Technologies Inc.	800 Belleair Rd.	Clearwater	FL	33756	Bob Scher	727-443-6600	R	6*	<0.1
Megadata Corp.	47 Arch Street	Greenwich	CT	06830	James T. Barry	631-589-6800	P	6	<0.1
OCP Group Inc.	7130 Engineer Rd.	San Diego	CA	92111	Neil Gleason	858-279-7400	R	6*	<0.1
SGB Enterprises Inc.	25327 Ave. Stanford	Santa Clarita	CA	91355	William Blowers	661-294-8306	R	6*	<0.1
Marco Manufacturing Company	1701 15 S 26th St.	Philadelphia	PA	19145	Anthony Simiriglio	215-463-2332	R	5*	<0.1
Computerwise Inc.	302 N Winchester	Olathe	KS	66062		913-829-0600	R	5*	<0.1
Genovation Inc.	17741 Mitchell N	Irvine	CA	92614	Max Rahim	949-833-3355	R	5*	<0.1
Pixelink Corp.	753 Forest St., 100	Marlborough	MA	01752	John Bowab	978-562-4803	D	5*	<0.1
Portable Warehouse Corp.	4430 E Miraloma	Anaheim	CA	92807	Kenny Le	714-701-1830	R	5*	<0.1
Custom Board Design Ltd.	609 Rte. 109	West Babylon	NY	11704	Tony Marasco	631-884-2700	R	5*	<0.1
Modular Industrial Solutions	1729 Little Orchard	San Jose	CA	95125	William Carey	408-971-0910	R	5*	<0.1
3b Technologies Corp.	5475 Peoria St.	Denver	CO	80239	Wen Liu	303-373-5718	R	4*	<0.1
Ind. Data Entry Automation Sys	27 Fennell St.	Skaneateles	NY	13152	John Hattersley	315-685-8311	R	4*	<0.1
Comcept Solutions L.L.C.	13770 58th St. N	Clearwater	FL	33760		727-497-1757	R	4*	<0.1
Westport Research Associates	7001 Blue Ridge	Kansas City	MO	64133	Don Cartner	816-358-8990	R	4*	<0.1
CECORP	8 Chrysler	Irvine	CA	92618	Alex Hagen	949-583-0792	R	4*	<0.1
Esprit Systems Inc.	6723 Mowry Ave.	Newark	CA	94560	Jason Barnes	510-438-3500	R	4*	<0.1
Technology Alternatives Corp.	1950 NE 208 Ter.	Miami	FL	33179	Lincoln Russin	305-933-2026	R	4*	<0.1

Source: Ward's Business Directory of U.S. Private and Public Companies, Volumes 1 and 2, 2008. The company type code used is as follows: P - Public, R - Private, S - Subsidiary, D - Division, J - Joint Venture, A - Affiliate, G - Group. Sales are in millions of dollars, employees are in thousands. An asterisk (*) indicates an estimated sales volume. The symbol < stands for 'less than'. Company names and addresses are truncated, in some cases, to fit into the available space.

MATERIALS CONSUMED

Material	Quantity	Delivered Cost ($ million)
Cathode ray tubes (CRT) (excluding X-ray)	(X)	(D)
Printed ciruit boards (without inserted components) for electronic circuitry	(X)	0.5
Printed memory boards for electronic circuitry	(X)	(D)
Printed peripheral controllers for electronic circuitry	(X)	(D)
Printed computer processors for electronic circuitry	(X)	(D)
Printed communication boards for electronic circuitry	(X)	(D)
Other printed circuit boards for electronic circuitry	(X)	(D)
Semiconductors (incl. transistors, diodes, rectifiers, and integrated circuits), for electronic circuitry	(X)	6.9
Capacitors for electronic circuitry	(X)	3.9
Resistors for electronic circuitry	(X)	0.3
Connectors for electronic circuitry	(X)	2.3
Battery packs for electronic circuitry	(X)	(D)
Other power supply units for electronic circuitry	(X)	0.3
Other components and accessories, for electronic circuitry (coils, transformers, etc.), excluding tubes	(X)	(D)
Electrical transmission, distribution, and control equipment	(X)	(D)
Steel, aluminum, and other metal electronic enclosures	(X)	0.4
Plastics electronic enclosures	(X)	(D)
Sheet metal products, including stampings (exc. enclosures)	(X)	4.0
Castings, rough and semifinished	(X)	(D)
Insulated copper wire and cable (including magnet wire)	(X)	(D)
Fabricated plastics products (excluding enclosures)	(X)	0.2
Purchased software	(X)	(D)
Appliance outlets and other current-carrying wiring devices	(X)	(D)
Paper and paperboard products (incl. paperboard boxes, etc.)	(X)	0.4
Purchased computers	(X)	(D)
Purchased peripheral storage devices	(X)	(D)
Purchased computer terminals	(X)	(D)
Purchased peripheral input devices (including keyboards, mouse devices, track balls, etc.)	(X)	0.6
Purchased peripheral printers	(X)	(D)
All other materials, components, parts, containers, and supplies	(X)	84.4
Materials, ingredients, containers, and supplies, nsk	(X)	18.8

Source: 2002 Economic Census. Explanation of symbols used: (D): Withheld to avoid disclosure of competitive data; na: Not available; (S): Withheld because statistical norms were not met; (X): Not applicable; (Z): Less than half the unit shown; nec: Not elsewhere classified; nsk: Not specified by kind; - : zero; p : 10-19 percent estimated; q : 20-29 percent estimated.

PRODUCT SHARE DETAILS

Product or Product Class Shipments	Mil. $	Product or Product Class Shipments	Mil. $
COMPUTER TERMINALS	348.3	Parts, attachments, and accessories for computer terminals (excluding point-of-sale and funds-transfer devices)	54.8
Computer terminals (excluding point-of-sale and funds-transfer devices, parts, attachments, and accessories)	258.9	Computer terminals, nsk, total	34.6

Source: 2002 Economic Census. The values are product shipments in millions of dollars for 2002. Total product shipments may be lower or higher than industry shipments. See Introduction for a full discussion. Values of indented subcategories are summed in the main heading(s). The symbol (D) appears when data are withheld to prevent disclosure of competitive information. The abbreviation nsk stands for 'not specified by kind' and nec for 'not elsewhere classified'. A dash (-) means zero.

INPUTS AND OUTPUTS FOR COMPUTER TERMINALS & OTHER COMPUTER PERIPHERALS

Economic Sector or Industry Providing Inputs	%	Sector	Economic Sector or Industry Buying Outputs	%	Sector
Compensation of employees	27.0		Private fixed investment	35.1	
Wholesale trade	10.2	Trade	Personal consumption expenditures	14.3	
Management of companies & enterprises	8.9	Services	Exports of goods & services	12.1	Cap Inv
Software publishers	5.7	Services	Electronic computers	4.6	Manufg.
Forging, stamping, & sintering, nec	4.1	Manufg.	Management of companies & enterprises	4.0	Services
Semiconductors & related devices	3.4	Manufg.	General S/L govt. services	2.8	S/L Govt
Printed circuit assemblies (electronic assemblies)	2.9	Manufg.	Nondepository credit intermediation activities	2.6	Fin/R.E.
Computer terminals & peripherals	2.7	Manufg.	Telecommunications	1.9	Services
Scientific research & development services	2.4	Services	S/L govt. invest., other	1.6	S/L Govt
Noncomparable imports	2.2	Foreign	S/L govt. invest., education	1.6	S/L Govt
Plastics products, nec	1.5	Manufg.	Retail trade	1.1	Trade
Advertising & related services	1.4	Services	Computer terminals & peripherals	0.9	Manufg.
Unlaminated plastics profile shapes	1.3	Manufg.	Change in private inventories	0.7	In House
Real estate	1.0	Fin/R.E.	Physician, dentist, other health practitioner offices	0.7	Services
Telecommunications	0.9	Services	Legal services	0.7	Services
Lessors of nonfinancial assets	0.8	Fin/R.E.	Irradiation apparatus	0.7	Manufg.
Ornamental & architectural metal products	0.7	Manufg.	Federal government, investment, national defense	0.7	Fed Govt
Truck transportation	0.7	Util.	Monetary authorities/depository credit intermediation	0.6	Fin/R.E.
Plastics pipe & pipe fittings	0.6	Manufg.	Federal government, investment, nondefense	0.6	Fed Govt
Legal services	0.6	Services	Light truck & utility vehicles	0.6	Manufg.
Electronic computers	0.5	Manufg.	Accounting, tax preparation, bookkeeping, & payroll	0.5	Services
Electronic connectors	0.5	Manufg.	Search, detection, & navigation instruments	0.4	Manufg.

Continued on next page.

INPUTS AND OUTPUTS FOR COMPUTER TERMINALS & OTHER COMPUTER PERIPHERALS - Continued

Economic Sector or Industry Providing Inputs	%	Sector	Economic Sector or Industry Buying Outputs	%	Sector
Motors & generators	0.5	Manufg.	Computer storage devices	0.4	Manufg.
Switchgear & switchboard apparatus	0.5	Manufg.	Management, scientific, & technical consulting	0.4	Services
Power generation & supply	0.5	Util.	Automobiles	0.4	Manufg.
Relay & industrial controls	0.5	Manufg.	Architectural, engineering, & related services	0.4	Services
Wiring devices	0.5	Manufg.	General Federal government services, nondefense	0.3	Fed Govt
Management, scientific, & technical consulting	0.4	Services	Securities, commodity contracts, investments	0.3	Fin/R.E.
Crowns & closures & metal stamping	0.4	Manufg.	Truck transportation	0.3	Util.
Electronic capacitors, resistors, coils, transformers	0.4	Manufg.	Newspaper publishers	0.3	Services
Nonferrous metal (ex. copper & aluminum) processing	0.4	Manufg.	Other computer related services, including facilities	0.3	Services
Petroleum refineries	0.4	Manufg.	Other S/L govt. enterprises	0.2	S/L Govt
Other computer related services, including facilities	0.4	Services	Professional, scientific, technical services, nec	0.2	Services
Wood kitchen cabinets & countertops	0.4	Manufg.	Elementary & secondary schools	0.2	Services
Bare printed circuit boards	0.4	Manufg.	Printing	0.2	Manufg.
Hardware	0.4	Manufg.	General Federal government services, defense	0.2	Fed Govt
Concrete pipe, brick, & block	0.4	Manufg.	Scientific research & development services	0.2	Services
Concrete products, nec	0.4	Manufg.	Hotels & motels, including casino hotels	0.2	Services
Sawmills & wood preservation	0.3	Manufg.	Advertising & related services	0.2	Services
Pottery, ceramics, and plumbing fixtures	0.3	Manufg.	Employment services	0.2	Services
Wood windows & doors & millwork	0.3	Manufg.	Nursing & residential care facilities	0.2	Services
Data processing, hosting, & related services	0.3	Services	Owner-occupied dwellings	0.2	
Electron tubes	0.3	Manufg.	Telephone apparatus	0.2	Manufg.
Machine shops	0.3	Manufg.	Computer system design services	0.2	Services
Taxes on production & imports, less subsidies	0.3		Broadcast & wireless communications equipment	0.2	Manufg.
Brick, tile & other structural clay products	0.3	Manufg.	Urethane & other foam products (except polystrene)	0.2	Manufg.
Plumbing fixture fittings & trim	0.3	Manufg.	Data processing, hosting, & related services	0.1	Services
Automotive equipment rental & leasing	0.3	Fin/R.E.	Colleges, universities, & professional schools	0.1	Services
Warehousing & storage	0.3	Util.	Business support services	0.1	Services
Accounting, tax preparation, bookkeeping, & payroll	0.3	Services	Services to buildings & dwellings	0.1	Services
Paperboard containers	0.3	Manufg.	Printed circuit assemblies (electronic assembiles)	0.1	Manufg.
Communication & energy wires & cables	0.3	Manufg.	Periodical publishers	0.1	Services
Fabricated metals, nec	0.2	Manufg.	Petroleum refineries	0.1	Manufg.
Coating, engraving, heat treating & allied activities	0.2	Manufg.	Analytical laboratory instruments	0.1	Manufg.
Securities, commodity contracts, investments	0.2	Fin/R.E.	Watches, clocks, & related devices	0.1	Manufg.
Electronic components, nec	0.2	Manufg.	Custom computer programming services	0.1	Services
Computer system design services	0.2	Services	Office administrative services	0.1	Services
Natural gas distribution	0.2	Util.			
Electrical equipment & components, nec	0.2	Manufg.			
Computer storage devices	0.2	Manufg.			
Iron & steel mills & ferroalloys	0.2	Manufg.			
Maintenance/repair of nonresidential structures	0.2	Construct.			
Commercial & industrial machinery rental & leasing	0.1	Fin/R.E.			
Services to buildings & dwellings	0.1	Services			
Chemical products & preparations, nec	0.1	Manufg.			
Paperboard mills	0.1	Manufg.			
Employment services	0.1	Services			
Turned products & screws, nuts, & bolts	0.1	Manufg.			
Retail trade	0.1	Trade			
Business support services	0.1	Services			
Plastics packaging materials, film & sheet	0.1	Manufg.			
Motor vehicle parts	0.1	Manufg.			

Source: *Benchmark Input-Output Accounts for the U.S. Economy, 2002*, U.S. Department of Commerce, Washington D.C., January 2008. *User should note that this Input-Output table is not for this particular narrowly defined industry but for a larger aggregate. Input and Output data for* Computer Terminals & Other Computer Peripherals *include Input and Output data for the* Annual Survey of Manufactures' *NAICS industries 334113 and 334119.* The abbreviation nec stands for 'not elsewhere classified'.

OCCUPATIONS EMPLOYED BY COMPUTER & PERIPHERAL EQUIPMENT MANUFACTURING

Occupation	% of Total 2006	Change to 2016	Occupation	% of Total 2006	Change to 2016
Computer software engineers, systems software	10.1	-28.0	Computer & information systems managers	1.5	-34.5
Electrical & electronic equipment assemblers	7.4	-47.6	Financial analysts	1.4	-28.0
Computer hardware engineers	6.5	-28.0	Purchasing agents, exc wholesale, retail, & farm	1.4	-34.5
Computer software engineers, applications	5.5	-21.4	Engineers, nec	1.3	-34.5
Sales representatives, wholesale & manufacturing, tech	2.5	-34.5	Computer programmers	1.3	-47.6
Computer support specialists	2.4	-34.5	Accountants & auditors	1.3	-34.5
Computer systems analysts	2.4	-28.0	Executive secretaries & administrative assistants	1.3	-34.5
Engineering managers	2.3	-34.5	Inspectors, testers, sorters, samplers, & weighers	1.3	-38.3
Electrical & electronic engineering technicians	2.3	-34.5	Electrical engineers	1.2	-34.5
Business operation specialists, nec	2.1	-28.0	Team assemblers	1.2	-34.5
Industrial engineers	1.8	-20.5	Logisticians	1.1	-28.0
Marketing managers	1.7	-34.5	General & operations managers	1.1	-41.1
Office clerks, general	1.6	-35.5	Shipping, receiving, & traffic clerks	1.1	-37.0
Market research analysts	1.6	-34.5	Production, planning, & expediting clerks	1.0	-34.5
Electronics engineers, exc computer	1.5	-34.5			

Source: *Industry-Occupation Matrix*, Bureau of Labor Statistics, December 4, 2007. These data are reported based on 4-digit NAICS categories but have been matched to corresponding 6-digit NAICS industry codes. The change reported for each occupation to the year 2016 is a percent of growth or decline as estimated by the Bureau of Labor Statistics. The abbreviation nec stands for 'not elsewhere classified'.

INDUSTRY DATA BY STATE

State-level data are not available.

NAICS 334119 - COMPUTER PERIPHERAL EQUIPMENT MANUFACTURING NEC

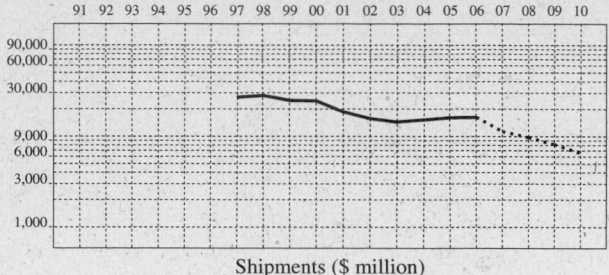

Shipments ($ million)

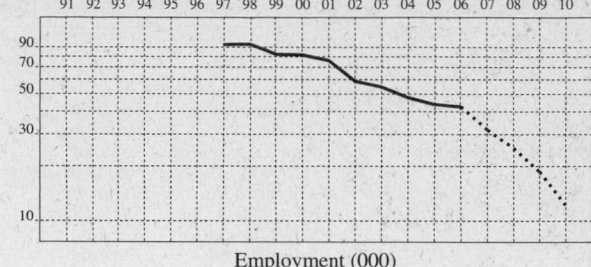

Employment (000)

GENERAL STATISTICS

Year	Com-panies	Establishments		Employment			Compensation		Production ($ million)			
		Total	with 20 or more employees	Total (000)	Production Workers (000)	Hours (Mil)	Payroll ($ mil)	Wages ($/hr)	Cost of Materials	Value Added by Manufacture	Value of Shipments	Capital Invest.
1997	1,014	1,061	354	93.1	41.0	86.2	4,563.9	18.30	16,981.2	10,151.8	26,897.3	968.1
1998		1,119	361	93.6	37.9	67.2	4,670.8	23.20	17,698.2	10,381.5	28,100.7	1,461.6
1999		1,108	386	82.5	31.2	67.4	4,372.4	17.10	14,667.5	10,039.4	24,829.6	976.5
2000		1,126	373	81.8	32.2	62.6	4,211.4	18.60	14,146.3	10,379.2	24,632.7	938.5
2001		1,044	372	76.2	27.6	58.3	3,832.0	16.89	9,413.8	9,087.9	18,608.6	787.6
2002	826	860	263	58.8	19.4	36.2	3,248.7	20.55	7,484.5	8,170.4	15,719.1	580.4
2003		794	279	54.7	16.9	31.7	3,140.2	21.53	7,523.8	6,909.8	14,420.3	361.7
2004		768	268	47.9	15.2	30.1	3,001.0	21.55	8,104.8	7,290.4	15,212.3	439.6
2005		722	255	43.9	14.2	28.4	2,810.1	21.12	8,431.1	7,526.6	16,065.1	586.4
2006		681P	240P	42.6	13.9	27.0	2,746.6	20.44	8,434.8	7,849.2	16,213.0	421.6
2007		626P	224P	31.7P	6.8P	12.7P	2,325.2P	21.24P	5,897.5P	5,488.0P	11,335.8P	230.0P
2008		570P	207P	25.2P	3.5P	6.0P	2,082.6P	21.48P	5,071.3P	4,719.2P	9,747.8P	135.0P
2009		515P	190P	18.7P	0.2P		1,840.0P	21.72P	4,245.1P	3,950.4P	8,159.8P	40.1P
2010		460P	174P	12.2P			1,597.3P	21.96P	3,419.0P	3,181.6P	6,571.8P	

Sources: 1997 and 2002 *Economic Census*; other years, up to 2006, are from *Annual Survey of Manufactures*. Establishment counts for non-Census years are from *County Business Patterns*; 1997 and 2002 values are from the 1997 and 2002 censuses, respectively. 'P's show projections by the editors.

INDICES OF CHANGE

Year	Com-panies	Establishments		Employment			Compensation		Production ($ million)			
		Total	with 20 or more employees	Total (000)	Production Workers (000)	Hours (Mil)	Payroll ($ mil)	Wages ($/hr)	Cost of Materials	Value Added by Manufacture	Value of Shipments	Capital Invest.
1997	123	123	135	158	211	238	140	89	227	124	171	167
1998		130	137	159	195	186	144	113	236	127	179	252
1999		129	147	140	161	186	135	83	196	123	158	168
2000		131	142	139	166	173	130	91	189	127	157	162
2001		121	141	130	142	161	118	82	126	111	118	136
2002	100	100	100	100	100	100	100	100	100	100	100	100
2003		92	106	93	87	88	97	105	101	85	92	62
2004		89	102	81	78	83	92	105	108	89	97	76
2005		84	97	75	73	78	86	103	113	92	102	101
2006		79P	91P	72	72	75	85	99	113	96	103	73
2007		73P	85P	54P	35P	35P	72P	103P	79P	67P	72P	40P
2008		66P	79P	43P	18P	17P	64P	105P	68P	58P	62P	23P
2009		60P	72P	32P	1P		57P	106P	57P	48P	52P	7P
2010		54P	66P	21P			49P	107P	46P	39P	42P	

Sources: Same as General Statistics. Values reflect change from the base year, 2002. Values above 100 mean greater than 2002, values below 100 mean less than 2002, and the values of 100 in other years means the same as 2002. 'P's show projections by the editors.

SELECTED RATIOS

For 2002	Avg. of All Manufact.	Analyzed Industry	Index	For 2002	Avg. of All Manufact.	Analyzed Industry	Index
Employees per Establishment	42	68	163	Value Added per Production Worker	182,367	421,155	231
Payroll per Establishment	1,639,184	3,777,558	230	Cost per Establishment	5,769,015	8,702,907	151
Payroll per Employee	39,053	55,250	141	Cost per Employee	137,446	127,287	93
Production Workers per Establishment	30	23	76	Cost per Production Worker	195,506	385,799	197
Wages per Establishment	694,845	865,012	124	Shipments per Establishment	11,158,348	18,278,023	164
Wages per Production Worker	23,548	38,346	163	Shipments per Employee	265,847	267,332	101
Hours per Production Worker	1,980	1,866	94	Shipments per Production Worker	378,144	810,263	214
Wages per Hour	11.89	20.55	173	Investment per Establishment	361,338	674,884	187
Value Added per Establishment	5,381,325	9,500,465	177	Investment per Employee	8,609	9,871	115
Value Added per Employee	128,210	138,952	108	Investment per Production Worker	12,245	29,918	244

Sources: Same as General Statistics. The 'Average of All Manufacturing' column represents the average of all manufacturing industries reported for the most recent complete year available. The Index shows the relationship between the Average and the Analyzed Industry. For example, 100 means that they are equal; 500 that the Analyzed Industry is five times the average; 50 means that the Analyzed Industry is half the national average. The abbreviation 'na' is used to show that data are 'not available'. Ratios shown for 2002, the last complete census year.

LEADING COMPANIES   Number shown: 75   Total sales ($ mil): 851,299   Total employment (000): 1,855.3

Company Name	Address				CEO Name	Phone	Co. Type	Sales ($ mil)	Empl. (000)
General Electric Co.	3135 Easton Tpk.	Fairfield	CT	06828		203-373-2211	P	172,738	327.0
Hewlett-Packard Co.	3000 Hanover St.	Palo Alto	CA	94304		650-857-1501	P	104,286	172.0
International Bus. Machines	1 New Orchard Rd.	Armonk	NY	10504		914-499-1900	P	98,786	329.4
Dell Inc.	1 Dell Way	Round Rock	TX	78682	Michael R. Cannon	512-338-4400	P	57,420	90.5
Microsoft Corp.	1 Microsoft Way	Redmond	WA	98052	Steven A. Ballmer		P	51,122	79.0
Intel Corp.	2200 Mission Clg.	Santa Clara	CA	95054	Craig R. Barrett	408-765-8080	P	38,334	86.3
Cisco Systems Inc.	170 W Tasman Dr.	San Jose	CA	95134		408-526-4000	P	34,922	61.5
Apple Inc.	1 Infinite Loop	Cupertino	CA	95014	Bill Campbell	408-996-1010	P	24,006	21.6
Emerson Electric	PO Box 4100	St. Louis	MO	63136	L.C. Barrett	314-553-2000	P	22,572	137.7
Mars Inc.	6885 Elm Street	Mc Lean	VA	22101	John F. Mars	703-821-4900	R	18,462*	40.0
Xerox Corp.	PO Box 1600	Stamford	CT	06904		203-968-3000	P	17,288	57.4
Lenovo Group Ltd.	1009 Think Pl.	Morrisville	NC	27560	Sotaro Amano		P	14,590	2.9
RISO Inc.	300 Rosewood Dr.	Danvers	MA	01923	Akira Hayama	978-777-7377	R	13,721*	0.4
Canon U.S.A. Inc.	1 Canon Plz.	Lake Success	NY	11042	Yoroku Adachi	516-328-5000	S	10,745*	11.0
Eastman Kodak Co.	343 State St.	Rochester	NY	14650		716-724-4000	P	10,301	26.9
Boon Edam Tomsed	420 McKinney Pky.	Lillington	NC	27546	Tom DeVine	910-814-3800	R	7,005*	0.1
SYNNEX Corp.	44201 Nobel Dr.	Fremont	CA	94538		510-656-3333	P	7,004	6.1
Etec Systems Inc.	PO Box 58039	Santa Clara	CA	95052		408-727-5555	S	6,992	12.2
Acer America Corp.	2641 Orchard Pky.	San Jose	CA	95134		408-432-6200	S	6,300*	5.4
Pitney Bowes Inc.	1 Elmcroft Rd.	Stamford	CT	06926	Michael J. Critelli	203-356-5000	P	6,130	26.3
Cooper Industries Ltd.	PO Box 4446	Houston	TX	77210	Kirk S. Hachigian	713-209-8400	P	5,903	31.5
Order-Matic Corp.	PO Box 25463	Oklahoma City	OK	73125	Bill Cunningham	405-672-1487	R	5,787	0.2
Micron Technology Inc.	PO Box 6	Boise	ID	83707	Steven R. Appleton	208-368-4000	P	5,688	23.5
Unisys Corp.	Unisys Way	Blue Bell	PA	19424		215-986-4011	P	5,653	30.0
Western Digital Corp.	20511 Lk Forest Dr.	Lake Forest	CA	92630	John Coyne	949-672-7000	P	5,468	29.6
Symantec Corp.	20330 Stevens Creek	Cupertino	CA	95014		408-517-8000	P	5,199	17.1
Lexmark International Inc.	740 New Circle Rd.	Lexington	KY	40550	Paul J. Curlander	859-232-2000	P	4,974	13.8
NCR Corp.	1700 S Patterson	Dayton	OH	45479		937-445-5000	P	4,970	23.2
Stanley Works	PO Box 700	New Britain	CT	06053		860-225-5111	P	4,484	18.4
Oki Data Americas Inc.	2000 Bishops Gate	Mount Laurel	NJ	08054	Stewart Krentzman	856-235-2600	S	4,260*	0.5
NVIDIA Corp.	2701 San Tomas	Santa Clara	CA	95050		408-486-2000	P	4,098	4.1
Kingston Technology Company	17600 Newhope St.	Fountain Valley	CA	92708		714-435-2600	R	3,536*	3.3
Pearson Assessments	5601 Green Vly Dr.	Bloomington	MN	55437	John Harnett		S	3,252*	6.0
Arco Auto and Marine Products	3921 Navy Blvd.	Pensacola	FL	32507	Ron Miller	850-455-5476	R	3,015	<0.1
Exide Technologies	13000 Deerfield Pky	Alpharetta	GA	30004		678-566-9000	P	2,940	13.9
Diebold Inc.	PO Box 3077	North Canton	OH	44720		330-490-4000	P	2,906	15.5
Juniper Networks Inc.	1194 N Mathilda	Sunnyvale	CA	94089		408-745-2000	P	2,836	5.9
Flow Systems	PO Box 1069	St. Helena Is	SC	29920	James Barrett	843-838-6699	R	2,681*	<0.1
LSI Corp.	1621 Barber Ln.	Milpitas	CA	95035		408-954-3108	P	2,604	6.2
UTStarcom Inc.	1275 Harbor Bay	Alameda	CA	94502		510-864-8800	P	2,466	5.1
Lockheed Martin Enterpr. Info.	12506 Lk Underhill	Orlando	FL	32825	Robert J. Stevens	407-306-1000	S	2,383*	4.0
Metal Management Inc.	500 N Dearborn St.	Chicago	IL	60610	Daniel W. Dienst	312-645-0700	P	2,229	1.8
Storage Technology Corp.	1 StorageTek Dr.	Louisville	CO	80028		303-673-5151	S	2,224	7.1
NTK Holdings Inc.	50 Kennedy Plz.	Providence	RI	02903	Richard L. Bready	401-751-1600	S	2,218	9.8
Hitachi America Ltd.	2000 Sierra Pnt Pky	Brisbane	CA	94005	Masahide Tanigahi	650-589-8300	S	2,127*	4.4
Hyperdata	817 S Lemon Ave.	Walnut	CA	91789	Toku Lee	909-468-2933	R	2,014*	<0.1
ACCO Brands Corp.	300 Tower Pkwy.	Lincolnshire	IL	60069	David Campbell		P	1,939	6.0
Scientific-Atlanta Inc.	PO Box 465447	Lawrenceville	GA	30042		770-236-5000	S	1,910	7.7
Embedded Communic. Computing	2900 S Diablo Way	Tempe	AZ	85282		602-438-5720	D	1,732*	1.5
Ergon Inc.	PO Box 1639	Jackson	MS	39215	Leslie B. Lampton, Sr	601-933-3000	R	1,725*	2.5
Spansion Inc.	PO Box 3453	Sunnyvale	CA	94088	Bertrand Cambou	408-962-2500	P	1,627	9.3
ViewSonic Corp.	381 Brea Canyon	Walnut	CA	91789	James Chu	909-444-8888	R	1,589	0.8
JDS Uniphase Corp.	430 N McCarthy	Milpitas	CA	95035	Martin A. Kaplan	408-546-5000	P	1,397*	7.0
Northstar Systems Inc.	9070 Rancho Pk Ct	R Cucamonga	CA	91730	Bob Thunell	909-483-9900	R	1,322*	3.5
Media Sciences Inc.	8 Allerman Rd.	Oakland	NJ	07436	Mike Levin	201-677-9311	S	1,311*	<0.1
Fujitsu Transaction Solutions	2801 Network Blvd.	Frisco	TX	75034		972-963-2300	R	1,300*	0.3
Rittal Corp.	1 Rittal Pl.	Springfield	OH	45504	Carie Ray	937-399-0500	R	1,268*	0.6
3Com Corp.	350 Campus Dr.	Marlborough	MA	01752	Eric A. Benhamou	508-323-5000	P	1,268	6.3
Brocade Communications Systems	1745 Technology	San Jose	CA	95110		408-333-8000	P	1,237	2.4
Tektronix Inc.	PO Box 500	Beaverton	OR	97077		503-627-7111	S	1,105	4.4
Harland Clarke	2939 Miller Rd.	Decatur	GA	30035	John Heald	770-981-9460	S	1,050	5.4
Black Box Corp.	1000 Park Dr.	Lawrence	PA	15055	William F. Andrews	724-746-5500	P	1,016	5.0
Quantum Corp.	1650 Technology	San Jose	CA	95110	Richard E. Belluzzo	408-944-4000	P	1,016	2.9
Newegg .com	16839 E Gale Ave.	City of Industry	CA	91745		909-395-9046	R	884*	1.5
Videojet Technologies Inc.	1500 Mittel Blvd.	Wood Dale	IL	60191	Craig Purse	630-860-7300	S	856*	1.3
SMART Modular Technologies	4211 Starboard Dr.	Fremont	CA	94538	Ian MacKenzie	510-623-1231	P	828	1.4
Hypercom Network Systems	2851 W Kathleen	Phoenix	AZ	85053	William Keiper	732-774-2485	S	823*	1.5
Zebra Technologies Corp.	333 Corp. Woods	Vernon Hills	IL	60061	Edward L. Kaplan	847-634-6700	P	760	2.8
National Instruments Corp.	11500 N MoPac	Austin	TX	78759		512-338-9119	P	740	4.1
Netgear Inc.	4500 Great America	Santa Clara	CA	95054		408-907-8000	P	728	0.5
East Penn Manufacturing Co.	PO Box 147	Lyon Station	PA	19536			R	716*	5.0
OPTIA	2032 E Pleasant Vly	Altoona	PA	16602	Hok S. Yau	814-943-1133	D	669*	<0.1
Electronics For Imaging Inc.	303 Velocity Way	Foster City	CA	94404	Guy Gecht	650-357-3500	P	621	2.0
Compix Media Inc.	26 Edelman	Irvine	CA	92618		949-585-0055	R	616*	<0.1
Foundry Networks Inc.	4980 Gr American	Santa Clara	CA	95054	Bobby R. Johnson Jr.	408-207-1700	P	607	1.0

Source: *Ward's Business Directory of U.S. Private and Public Companies*, Volumes 1 and 2, 2008. The company type code used is as follows: P - Public, R - Private, S - Subsidiary, D - Division, J - Joint Venture, A - Affiliate, G - Group. Sales are in millions of dollars, employees are in thousands. An asterisk (*) indicates an estimated sales volume. The symbol < stands for 'less than'. Company names and addresses are truncated, in some cases, to fit into the available space.

MATERIALS CONSUMED

Material	Quantity	Delivered Cost ($ million)
Cathode ray tubes (CRT) (excluding X-ray)	(X)	29.0
Printed ciruit boards (without inserted components) for electronic circuitry	(X)	54.9
Printed memory boards for electronic circuitry	(X)	142.1
Printed peripheral controllers for electronic circuitry	(X)	39.7
Printed computer processors for electronic circuitry	(X)	161.1
Printed communication boards for electronic circuitry	(X)	5.0
Other printed circuit boards for electronic circuitry	(X)	64.3
Semiconductors (incl. transistors, diodes, rectifiers, and integrated circuits), for electronic circuitry	(X)	63.2
Capacitors for electronic circuitry	(X)	12.4
Resistors for electronic circuitry	(X)	8.7
Connectors for electronic circuitry	(X)	63.5
Battery packs for electronic circuitry	(X)	(D)
Other power supply units for electronic circuitry	(X)	31.4
Other components and accessories, for electronic circuitry (coils, transformers, etc.), excluding tubes	(X)	31.4
Electrical transmission, distribution, and control equipment	(X)	7.2
Steel, aluminum, and other metal electronic enclosures	(X)	22.2
Plastics electronic enclosures	(X)	33.9
Sheet metal products, including stampings (exc. enclosures)	(X)	107.6
All other fabricated metal products (excluding forgings)	(X)	13.3
Forgings	(X)	(D)
Castings, rough and semifinished	(X)	3.2
Metal shapes and forms (exc. castings, forgings, fabr. metal products)	(X)	32.8
Insulated copper wire and cable (including magnet wire)	(X)	17.6
Fabricated plastics products (excluding enclosures)	(X)	70.1
Purchased software	(X)	4.9
Appliance outlets and other current-carrying wiring devices	(X)	0.8
Electric motors and generators	(X)	23.4
Paper and paperboard products (incl. paperboard boxes, etc.)	(X)	18.1
Purchased computers	(X)	(D)
Purchased peripheral storage devices	(X)	(D)
Purchased computer terminals	(X)	29.6
Purchased peripheral input devices (including keyboards, mouse devices, track balls, etc.)	(X)	27.1
Purchased peripheral printers	(X)	310.7
Other purchased electronic computing and peripheral equipment	(X)	(D)
All other materials, components, parts, containers, and supplies	(X)	2,527.9
Materials, ingredients, containers, and supplies, nsk	(X)	1,106.9

Source: 2002 *Economic Census*. Explanation of symbols used: (D): Withheld to avoid disclosure of competitive data; na: Not available; (S): Withheld because statistical norms were not met; (X): Not applicable; (Z): Less than half the unit shown; nec: Not elsewhere classified; nsk: Not specified by kind; - : zero; p : 10-19 percent estimated; q : 20-29 percent estimated.

PRODUCT SHARE DETAILS

Product or Product Class Shipments	Mil. $	Product or Product Class Shipments	Mil. $
OTHER COMPUTER PERIPHERAL EQUIPMENT	15,356.7	Point-of-sale terminals and funds-transfer devices	809.7
Computer peripheral (input-output) equipment, nec, except parts, attachments, and accessories	10,358.0	Parts and attachments for point-of-sale terminals and funds-transfer devices	81.1
Parts, subassemblies, and accessories for computer peripheral equipment	2,322.3	Other computer peripheral equipment, nsk, total	1,785.5

Source: 2002 *Economic Census*. The values are product shipments in millions of dollars for 2002. Total product shipments may be lower or higher than industry shipments. See Introduction for a full discussion. Values of indented subcategories are summed in the main heading(s). The symbol (D) appears when data are withheld to prevent disclosure of competitive information. The abbreviation nsk stands for 'not specified by kind' and nec for 'not elsewhere classified'. A dash (-) means zero.

INPUTS AND OUTPUTS FOR COMPUTER TERMINALS & OTHER COMPUTER PERIPHERALS

Economic Sector or Industry Providing Inputs	%	Sector	Economic Sector or Industry Buying Outputs	%	Sector
Compensation of employees	27.0		Private fixed investment	35.1	
Wholesale trade	10.2	Trade	Personal consumption expenditures	14.3	
Management of companies & enterprises	8.9	Services	Exports of goods & services	12.1	Cap Inv
Software publishers	5.7	Services	Electronic computers	4.6	Manufg.
Forging, stamping, & sintering, nec	4.1	Manufg.	Management of companies & enterprises	4.0	Services
Semiconductors & related devices	3.4	Manufg.	General S/L govt. services	2.8	S/L Govt
Printed circuit assemblies (electronic assembles)	2.9	Manufg.	Nondepository credit intermediation activities	2.6	Fin/R.E.
Computer terminals & peripherals	2.7	Manufg.	Telecommunications	1.9	Services
Scientific research & development services	2.4	Services	S/L govt. invest., other	1.6	S/L Govt
Noncomparable imports	2.2	Foreign	S/L govt. invest., education	1.6	S/L Govt
Plastics products, nec	1.5	Manufg.	Retail trade	1.1	Trade
Advertising & related services	1.4	Services	Computer terminals & peripherals	0.9	Manufg.
Unlaminated plastics profile shapes	1.3	Manufg.	Change in private inventories	0.7	In House
Real estate	1.0	Fin/R.E.	Physician, dentist, other health practitioner offices	0.7	Services
Telecommunications	0.9	Services	Legal services	0.7	Services
Lessors of nonfinancial assets	0.8	Fin/R.E.	Irradiation apparatus	0.7	Manufg.
Ornamental & architectural metal products	0.7	Manufg.	Federal government, investment, national defense	0.7	Fed Govt

Continued on next page.

INPUTS AND OUTPUTS FOR COMPUTER TERMINALS & OTHER COMPUTER PERIPHERALS - Continued

Economic Sector or Industry Providing Inputs	%	Sector	Economic Sector or Industry Buying Outputs	%	Sector
Truck transportation	0.7	Util.	Monetary authorities/depository credit intermediation	0.6	Fin/R.E.
Plastics pipe & pipe fittings	0.6	Manufg.	Federal government, investment, nondefense	0.6	Fed Govt
Legal services	0.6	Services	Light truck & utility vehicles	0.6	Manufg.
Electronic computers	0.5	Manufg.	Accounting, tax preparation, bookkeeping, & payroll	0.5	Services
Electronic connectors	0.5	Manufg.	Search, detection, & navigation instruments	0.4	Manufg.
Motors & generators	0.5	Manufg.	Computer storage devices	0.4	Manufg.
Switchgear & switchboard apparatus	0.5	Manufg.	Management, scientific, & technical consulting	0.4	Services
Power generation & supply	0.5	Util.	Automobiles	0.4	Manufg.
Relay & industrial controls	0.5	Manufg.	Architectural, engineering, & related services	0.4	Services
Wiring devices	0.5	Manufg.	General Federal government services, nondefense	0.3	Fed Govt
Management, scientific, & technical consulting	0.4	Services	Securities, commodity contracts, investments	0.3	Fin/R.E.
Crowns & closures & metal stamping	0.4	Manufg.	Truck transportation	0.3	Util.
Electronic capacitors, resistors, coils, transformers	0.4	Manufg.	Newspaper publishers	0.3	Services
Nonferrous metal (ex. copper & aluminum) processing	0.4	Manufg.	Other computer related services, including facilities	0.3	Services
Petroleum refineries	0.4	Manufg.	Other S/L govt. enterprises	0.2	S/L Govt
Other computer related services, including facilities	0.4	Services	Professional, scientific, technical services, nec	0.2	Services
Wood kitchen cabinets & countertops	0.4	Manufg.	Elementary & secondary schools	0.2	Services
Bare printed circuit boards	0.4	Manufg.	Printing	0.2	Manufg.
Hardware	0.4	Manufg.	General Federal government services, defense	0.2	Fed Govt
Concrete pipe, brick, & block	0.4	Manufg.	Scientific research & development services	0.2	Services
Concrete products, nec	0.4	Manufg.	Hotels & motels, including casino hotels	0.2	Services
Sawmills & wood preservation	0.3	Manufg.	Advertising & related services	0.2	Services
Pottery, ceramics, and plumbing fixtures	0.3	Manufg.	Employment services	0.2	Services
Wood windows & doors & millwork	0.3	Manufg.	Nursing & residential care facilities	0.2	Services
Data processing, hosting, & related services	0.3	Services	Owner-occupied dwellings	0.2	
Electron tubes	0.3	Manufg.	Telephone apparatus	0.2	Manufg.
Machine shops	0.3	Manufg.	Computer system design services	0.2	Services
Taxes on production & imports, less subsidies	0.3		Broadcast & wireless communications equipment	0.2	Manufg.
Brick, tile & other structural clay products	0.3	Manufg.	Urethane & other foam products (except polystrene)	0.2	Manufg.
Plumbing fixture fittings & trim	0.3	Manufg.	Data processing, hosting, & related services	0.1	Services
Automotive equipment rental & leasing	0.3	Fin/R.E.	Colleges, universities, & professional schools	0.1	Services
Warehousing & storage	0.3	Util.	Business support services	0.1	Services
Accounting, tax preparation, bookkeeping, & payroll	0.3	Services	Services to buildings & dwellings	0.1	Services
Paperboard containers	0.3	Manufg.	Printed circuit assemblies (electronic assemblies)	0.1	Manufg.
Communication & energy wires & cables	0.3	Manufg.	Periodical publishers	0.1	Services
Fabricated metals, nec	0.2	Manufg.	Petroleum refineries	0.1	Manufg.
Coating, engraving, heat treating & allied activities	0.2	Manufg.	Analytical laboratory instruments	0.1	Manufg.
Securities, commodity contracts, investments	0.2	Fin/R.E.	Watches, clocks, & related devices	0.1	Manufg.
Electronic components, nec	0.2	Manufg.	Custom computer programming services	0.1	Services
Computer system design services	0.2	Services	Office administrative services	0.1	Services
Natural gas distribution	0.2	Util.			
Electrical equipment & components, nec	0.2	Manufg.			
Computer storage devices	0.2	Manufg.			
Iron & steel mills & ferroalloys	0.2	Manufg.			
Maintenance/repair of nonresidential structures	0.2	Construct.			
Commercial & industrial machinery rental & leasing	0.1	Fin/R.E.			
Services to buildings & dwellings	0.1	Services			
Chemical products & preparations, nec	0.1	Manufg.			
Paperboard mills	0.1	Manufg.			
Employment services	0.1	Services			
Turned products & screws, nuts, & bolts	0.1	Manufg.			
Retail trade	0.1	Trade			
Business support services	0.1	Services			
Plastics packaging materials, film & sheet	0.1	Manufg.			
Motor vehicle parts	0.1	Manufg.			

Source: Benchmark Input-Output Accounts for the U.S. Economy, 2002, U.S. Department of Commerce, Washington D.C., January 2008. User should note that this Input-Output table is not for this particular narrowly defined industry but for a larger aggregate. Input and Output data for Computer Terminals & Other Computer Peripherals include Input and Output data for the Annual Survey of Manufactures' NAICS industries 334113 and 334119. The abbreviation nec stands for 'not elsewhere classified'.

OCCUPATIONS EMPLOYED BY COMPUTER & PERIPHERAL EQUIPMENT MANUFACTURING

Occupation	% of Total 2006	Change to 2016	Occupation	% of Total 2006	Change to 2016
Computer software engineers, systems software	10.1	-28.0	Computer & information systems managers	1.5	-34.5
Electrical & electronic equipment assemblers	7.4	-47.6	Financial analysts	1.4	-28.0
Computer hardware engineers	6.5	-28.0	Purchasing agents, exc wholesale, retail, & farm	1.4	-34.5
Computer software engineers, applications	5.5	-21.4	Engineers, nec	1.3	-34.5
Sales representatives, wholesale & manufacturing, tech	2.5	-34.5	Computer programmers	1.3	-47.6
Computer support specialists	2.4	-34.5	Accountants & auditors	1.3	-34.5
Computer systems analysts	2.4	-28.0	Executive secretaries & administrative assistants	1.3	-34.5
Engineering managers	2.3	-34.5	Inspectors, testers, sorters, samplers, & weighers	1.3	-38.3
Electrical & electronic engineering technicians	2.3	-34.5	Electrical engineers	1.2	-34.5
Business operation specialists, nec	2.1	-28.0	Team assemblers	1.2	-34.5
Industrial engineers	1.8	-20.5	Logisticians	1.1	-28.0
Marketing managers	1.7	-34.5	General & operations managers	1.1	-41.1
Office clerks, general	1.6	-35.5	Shipping, receiving, & traffic clerks	1.1	-37.0
Market research analysts	1.6	-34.5	Production, planning, & expediting clerks	1.0	-34.5
Electronics engineers, exc computer	1.5	-34.5			

Source: Industry-Occupation Matrix, Bureau of Labor Statistics, December 4, 2007. These data are reported based on 4-digit NAICS categories but have been matched to corresponding 6-digit NAICS industry codes. The change reported for each occupation to the year 2016 is a percent of growth or decline as estimated by the Bureau of Labor Statistics. The abbreviation nec stands for 'not elsewhere classified'.

LOCATION BY STATE AND REGIONAL CONCENTRATION

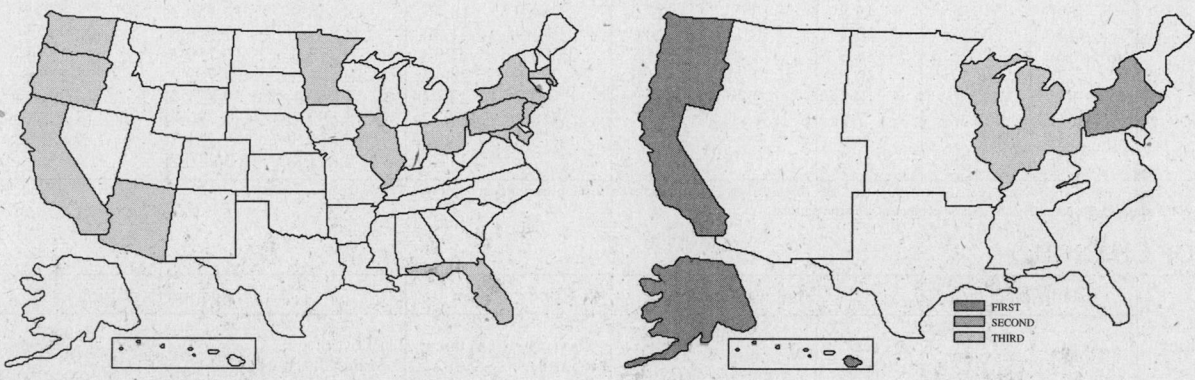

FIRST
SECOND
THIRD

INDUSTRY DATA BY STATE

State	Establish-ments	Shipments			Employment				Cost as % of Shipments	Investment per Employee ($)
		Total ($ mil)	% of U.S.	Per Establ.	Total Number	% of U.S.	Per Establ.	Wages ($/hour)		
Minnesota	27	2,463.0	15.7	91,221.6	9,087	15.4	337	20.14	51.2	7,594
New York	45	2,203.2	14.0	48,960.9	9,120	15.5	203	18.47	50.1	5,593
California	223	1,556.9	9.9	6,981.5	8,248	14.0	37	17.38	48.0	15,770
Oregon	20	1,309.3	8.3	65,463.2	7,612	12.9	381	38.44	55.3	8,409
Washington	29	840.3	5.3	28,974.6	1,976	3.4	68	16.13	46.1	5,226
Massachusetts	60	627.4	4.0	10,456.3	2,581	4.4	43	17.38	48.9	12,162
Illinois	36	562.8	3.6	15,632.8	1,994	3.4	55	17.74	46.5	5,990
Ohio	28	418.1	2.7	14,932.0	1,286	2.2	46	13.96	44.1	9,566
Rhode Island	3	225.8	1.4	75,260.3	545	0.9	182	14.20	60.4	13,945
Pennsylvania	36	224.5	1.4	6,235.4	1,125	1.9	31	23.36	44.5	8,022
New Jersey	18	172.5	1.1	9,584.7	916	1.6	51	11.06	52.6	8,505
Florida	31	161.1	1.0	5,195.3	748	1.3	24	17.11	47.0	7,295
Arizona	21	95.3	0.6	4,540.4	515	0.9	25	25.48	58.2	5,979
Maryland	13	86.7	0.6	6,668.6	423	0.7	33	20.15	43.3	8,948

Source: 2002 Economic Census. The states are in descending order of shipments or establishments (if shipment data are missing for the majority). The symbol (D) appears when data are withheld to prevent disclosure of competitive information. States marked with (D) are sorted by number of establishments. A dash (-) indicates that the data element cannot be calculated. Data may not show all states active in the NAICS category. All data available at the time of publication are shown.

NAICS 334210 - TELEPHONE APPARATUS MANUFACTURING

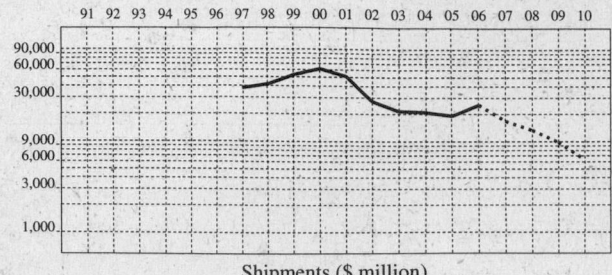

Shipments ($ million)

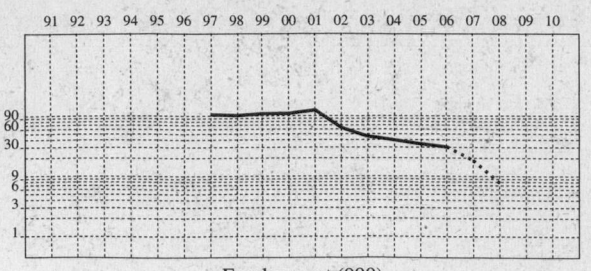

Employment (000)

GENERAL STATISTICS

| Year | Companies | Establishments | | Employment | | | Compensation | | Production ($ million) | | | |
		Total	with 20 or more employees	Total (000)	Production Workers (000)	Hours (Mil)	Payroll ($ mil)	Wages ($/hr)	Cost of Materials	Value Added by Manufacture	Value of Shipments	Capital Invest.
1997	547	598	329	105.4	41.9	78.5	5,266.2	19.07	14,701.8	23,276.1	37,809.9	1,220.4
1998		615	321	101.4	41.5	78.4	5,378.8	19.92	17,110.8	25,415.7	41,790.9	1,329.9
1999		609	320	108.5	42.8	81.1	6,261.8	20.28	20,264.7	32,744.8	52,767.4	1,643.9
2000		616	303	109.1	40.9	79.1	7,008.9	21.32	26,938.7	35,843.0	61,524.5	1,748.1
2001		574	294	124.1	41.6	76.9	7,985.3	22.90	22,497.7	28,005.2	51,098.9	2,832.6
2002	450	518	276	63.7	18.1	34.3	3,735.5	20.77	11,648.5	14,909.0	27,539.4	669.8
2003		469	260	45.8	13.2	27.5	2,944.9	18.46	8,454.9	13,156.9	21,539.1	592.4
2004		440	228	39.7	10.7	20.9	2,283.9	21.30	8,867.2	11,946.8	20,944.5	245.7
2005		436	225	34.3	11.4	21.7	2,073.3	21.98	8,273.0	10,759.1	19,156.8	191.6
2006		412P	214P	30.5	11.3	21.5	1,922.9	23.17	10,604.6	14,752.2	25,230.3	736.1
2007		387P	200P	18.3P	2.2P	5.0P	1,500.8P	22.44P	7,060.1P	9,821.4P	16,797.3P	289.5P
2008		361P	186P	7.8P			958.0P	22.72P	5,597.2P	7,786.4P	13,316.8P	138.3P
2009		335P	172P				415.3P	22.99P	4,134.3P	5,751.3P	9,836.3P	
2010		309P	158P					23.27P	2,671.4P	3,716.2P	6,355.8P	

Sources: 1997 and 2002 *Economic Census*; other years, up to 2006, are from *Annual Survey of Manufactures*. Establishment counts for non-Census years are from *County Business Patterns*; 1997 and 2002 values are from the 1997 and 2002 censuses, respectively. 'P's show projections by the editors.

INDICES OF CHANGE

| Year | Companies | Establishments | | Employment | | | Compensation | | Production ($ million) | | | |
		Total	with 20 or more employees	Total (000)	Production Workers (000)	Hours (Mil)	Payroll ($ mil)	Wages ($/hr)	Cost of Materials	Value Added by Manufacture	Value of Shipments	Capital Invest.
1997	122	115	119	165	231	229	141	92	126	156	137	182
1998		119	116	159	229	229	144	96	147	170	152	199
1999		118	116	170	236	236	168	98	174	220	192	245
2000		119	110	171	226	231	188	103	231	240	223	261
2001		111	107	195	230	224	214	110	193	188	186	423
2002	100	100	100	100	100	100	100	100	100	100	100	100
2003		91	94	72	73	80	79	89	73	88	78	88
2004		85	83	62	59	61	61	103	76	80	76	37
2005		84	82	54	63	63	56	106	71	72	70	29
2006		80P	77P	48	62	63	51	112	91	99	92	110
2007		75P	72P	29P	12P	15P	40P	108P	61P	66P	61P	43P
2008		70P	67P	12P			26P	109P	48P	52P	48P	21P
2009		65P	62P				11P	111P	35P	39P	36P	
2010		60P	57P					112P	23P	25P	23P	

Sources: Same as General Statistics. Values reflect change from the base year, 2002. Values above 100 mean greater than 2002, values below 100 mean less than 2002, and the values of 100 in other years means the same as 2002. 'P's show projections by the editors.

SELECTED RATIOS

For 2002	Avg. of All Manufact.	Analyzed Industry	Index	For 2002	Avg. of All Manufact.	Analyzed Industry	Index
Employees per Establishment	42	123	293	Value Added per Production Worker	182,367	823,702	452
Payroll per Establishment	1,639,184	7,211,390	440	Cost per Establishment	5,769,015	22,487,452	390
Payroll per Employee	39,053	58,642	150	Cost per Employee	137,446	182,865	133
Production Workers per Establishment	30	35	118	Cost per Production Worker	195,506	643,564	329
Wages per Establishment	694,845	1,375,311	198	Shipments per Establishment	11,158,348	53,164,865	476
Wages per Production Worker	23,548	39,360	167	Shipments per Employee	265,847	432,330	163
Hours per Production Worker	1,980	1,895	96	Shipments per Production Worker	378,144	1,521,514	402
Wages per Hour	11.89	20.77	175	Investment per Establishment	361,338	1,293,050	358
Value Added per Establishment	5,381,325	28,781,853	535	Investment per Employee	8,609	10,515	122
Value Added per Employee	128,210	234,050	183	Investment per Production Worker	12,245	37,006	302

Sources: Same as General Statistics. The 'Average of All Manufacturing' column represents the average of all manufacturing industries reported for the most recent complete year available. The Index shows the relationship between the Average and the Analyzed Industry. For example, 100 means that they are equal; 500 that the Analyzed Industry is five times the average; 50 means that the Analyzed Industry is half the national average. The abbreviation 'na' is used to show that data are 'not available'. Ratios shown for 2002, the last complete census year.

LEADING COMPANIES Number shown: **75** Total sales ($ mil): **201,180** Total employment (000): **609.5**

Company Name	Address				CEO Name	Phone	Co. Type	Sales ($ mil)	Empl. (000)
AT and T Inc.	175 E Houston	San Antonio	TX	78205	James W. Callaway	210-821-4105	P	68,256	310.0
Motorola Inc.	1303 E Algonquin	Schaumburg	IL	60196	Greg Brown	847-576-5000	P	36,622	66.0
Cisco Systems Inc.	170 W Tasman Dr.	San Jose	CA	95134		408-526-4000	P	34,922	61.5
Ball Corp.	PO Box 5000	Broomfield	CO	80021	R. David Hoover	303-469-3131	P	7,475	15.5
Corning Inc.	1 Riverfront Plz.	Corning	NY	14831	James R. Houghton	607-974-9000	P	5,860	24.5
JVC America Inc.	1700 Valley Rd.	Wayne	NJ	07470	Shigeharu Tsuchitani	973-317-5000	J	4,306*	0.3
Oki Data Americas Inc.	2000 Bishops Gate	Mount Laurel	NJ	08054	Stewart Krentzman	856-235-2600	S	4,260*	0.5
Harris Corp.	1025 W NASA	Melbourne	FL	32919		321-727-9100	P	4,243	16.0
Brightstar Corp.	2010 NW 84th Ave.	Miami	FL	33122	R. Marcelo Claure	305-421-6000	R	3,590	1.7
Fujitsu Network Communications	2801 Telecom Pkwy.	Richardson	TX	75082	George Chase	972-479-6000	R	2,969*	1.0
Hubbell Inc.	584 Derby Milford	Orange	CT	06477		203-799-4100	P	2,534	11.5
Tellabs Inc.	1 Tellabs Ctr.	Naperville	IL	60563	Michael J. Birck	630-798-8800	P	2,041	3.7
Griffon Corp.	100 Jericho Quadran	Jericho	NY	11753	Harvey R. Blau	516-938-5544	P	1,617	5.3
Comverse Technology Inc.	810 7th Ave.	New York	NY	10019	Andre Dahan	212-739-1000	P	1,589	5.1
JDS Uniphase Corp.	430 N McCarthy	Milpitas	CA	95035	Martin A. Kaplan	408-546-5000	P	1,397*	7.0
ADC Telecommunications Inc.	PO Box 1101	Minneapolis	MN	55440		952-938-8080	P	1,322	9.1
3Com Corp.	350 Campus Dr.	Marlborough	MA	01752	Eric A. Benhamou	508-323-5000	P	1,268	6.3
General Dynamics Network Sys.	77 A Street	Needham	MA	02494	Nicholas Chabraja	781-449-2000	S	1,237*	7.0
Teradyne Inc.	600 Riverpark Dr.	North Reading	MA	01864	James Bagley	978-370-2700	P	1,102	3.6
RF Micro Devices Inc.	7628 Thorndike Rd.	Greensboro	NC	27409	R A. Bruggeworth	336-664-1233	P	1,024	3.3
Hughes Network Systems Inc.	11717 Exploratn Ln.	Germantown	MD	20876	Pradman P. Kaul	301-428-5500	S	975*	1.5
Polycom Inc.	4750 Willow Rd.	Pleasanton	CA	94588	Robert C. Hagerty	925-924-6000	P	930	2.5
Plantronics Inc.	345 Encinal St.	Santa Cruz	CA	95060	SK Kannappan	831-426-5858	P	800	6.0
CIENA Corp.	1201 Winterson Rd.	Linthicum	MD	21090		410-694-5700	P	780	1.8
Kyocera Wireless Corp.	10300 Campus Pnt	San Diego	CA	92121	Rodney N. Lanthorne	858-882-2000	S	538*	0.9
IPC Systems Holdings Corp.	1500 Plaza Ten	Jersey City	NJ	07311	Lance B. Boxer	201-253-2000	R	485	1.4
ADTRAN Inc.	901 Explorer Blvd.	Huntsville	AL	35806	Thomas Stanton	256-963-8000	P	477	1.6
Alcatel Submarine Network Inc.	15036 Conf. Ctr.	Chantilly	VA	20151		703-679-3600	D	465*	0.8
Oce Printing Systems USA Inc.	5600 Broken Sound	Boca Raton	FL	33487	Joseph D. Skrzypczak		S	461*	0.9
Inter-Tel Inc.	1615 S 52nd St.	Tempe	AZ	85281	Alexander Cappello	480-449-8900	S	458	1.9
JBL Professional Inc.	8400 Balboa Blvd.	Northridge	CA	91329	John Carpanini	818-894-8850	S	443*	1.8
Allied Telesyn International	19800 N Creek Pky.	Bothell	WA	98011			S	350*	1.2
Sonus Networks Inc.	7 Technology Park	Westford	MA	01886	Hassan Ahmed	978-614-8100	P	320	0.9
ADC Broadband Access Systems	PO Box 1181	Minneapolis	MN	55440		952-938-8080	S	316*	7.5
Harmonic Inc.	549 Baltic Way	Sunnyvale	CA	94089	Patrick Harshman	408-542-2500	P	312	0.6
Telex Communications Inc.	12000 Portland Ave.	Burnsville	MN	55337	R V. Malpocher	952-884-4051	R	308*	3.0
Westell Technologies Inc.	750 N Commons Dr.	Aurora	IL	60504	Thomas E. Mader	630-898-2500	P	260	0.9
2Wire Inc.	1704 Automation	San Jose	CA	95131		408-428-9500	R	220	0.3
Genesys Telecommunications Lab	2001 Junipero Serra	Daly City	CA	94014			S	209*	1.1
SymmetriCom Inc.	2300 Orchard Pky	San Jose	CA	95131	Robert T. Clarkson	408-433-0910	P	208	0.9
Intervoice Inc.	17811 Waterview	Dallas	TX	75252		972-454-8000	P	196	0.8
Epic Technologies L.L.C.	200 Bluegrass Dr. E	Norwalk	OH	44857		419-668-8117	R	188*	0.2
Cirrus Logic Inc.	2901 Via Fortuna	Austin	TX	78746		512-851-4000	P	182	0.5
DDI Corp.	1220 Simon Cir.	Anaheim	CA	92806		714-688-7200	P	181	1.3
Zhone Technologies Inc.	7001 Oakport St.	Oakland	CA	94621	Mory Ejabat	510-777-7000	P	175	0.5
Advanced Concepts Inc.	9861 Broken Lnd	Columbia	MD	21046	Arnold Crater	301-596-2712	R	175*	0.3
Porta Systems Leasing Corp.	575 Underhill Blvd.	Syosset	NY	11791		516-364-9300	S	172*	0.3
Sycamore Networks Inc.	220 Mill Rd.	Chelmsford	MA	01824	Gururaj Deshpande	978-250-2900	P	156	0.4
Kentrox L.L.C.	20010 Tanasbourn	Hillsboro	OR	97124	Charles Vogt	503-350-6007	R	146*	0.3
Suttle Caribe Inc.	Carretera 3 Km 82.3	Humacao	PR	00791		787-852-0643	R	144*	0.3
MPI Technologies Inc.	4952 Warner Ave.	Huntington Bch	CA	92649	Gerard Logel	714-840-8077	R	142*	<0.1
TTG Acquisition Corp.	2150 Whitfield Ind.	Sarasota	FL	34243	Ewen R. Cameron	941-753-5000	S	141*	0.5
Flextronics International NC	130 Mosswood	Youngsville	NC	27596	Richard L. Sharp	919-556-7881	S	138*	0.5
Radyne Corp.	3138 E Elwood St.	Phoenix	AZ	85034		602-437-9620	P	134	0.3
SFA Inc.	2200 Defense Hwy.	Crofton	MD	21114		301-858-1230	R	124*	<0.1
Trillion Communications Corp.	4000 Farr Rd.	Bessemer	AL	35022	Ralph E. Brown	205-481-1678	R	120*	0.2
Communications Systems Inc.	PO Box 777	Hector	MN	55342	Jeffrey K. Berg	320-848-6231	P	115	0.5
ePUREDATA Inc.	572 E Green St.	Pasadena	CA	91101		626-683-8337	R	115*	0.2
Oplink Communications Inc.	46335 Landing Pky.	Fremont	CA	94538	Herbert Chang	510-933-7200	P	108	2.0
Frontrunner Network Systems	412 Linden Ave.	Rochester	NY	14625	Don Hauschild		S	107*	0.2
Pegasus Wireless Corp.	277 Royal Poinciana	Palm Beach	FL	33480	Jasper Knabb	510-490-8288	P	104	0.5
Hitachi Computer Products	1800 E Imhoff Rd.	Norman	OK	73071	George Wilson	405-360-5500	S	102*	0.5
Plant Equipment Inc.	PO Box 9007	Temecula	CA	92589	Timothy Fuller	951-719-2100	R	100*	0.2
Shoretel Inc.	960 Stewart Dr.	Sunnyvale	CA	94085	John W. Combs	408-331-3300	P	98	0.3
NEC Transmission Systems Inc.	14040 Park Ctr Rd.	Herndon	VA	20171		703-834-4000	S	87*	0.2
Palco Telecom Service Inc.	2914 Green Cove	Huntsville	AL	35803	Janice Migliore	256-883-3400	R	84*	0.2
NMS Communications Corp.	100 Crossing Blvd.	Framingham	MA	01702		508-271-1000	P	82	0.4
Total Communications Inc.	333 Burnham St.	East Hartford	CT	06108	Richard Lennon	860-282-9999	R	82*	0.1
Ditech Networks Inc.	825 E Middlefield	Mountain View	CA	94043	Todd Simpson	650-623-1300	P	80	0.2
Telect Inc.	PO Box 665	Liberty Lake	WA	99019	Bill Williams	509-926-6000	R	78*	0.3
Terayon Communications Systems	2450 Walsh Ave.	Santa Clara	CA	95054	Jerry Chase	408-235-5500	S	76	0.1
Carrier Access Corp.	5395 Pearl Pky	Boulder	CO	80301		303-442-5455	P	75	0.3
WatchGuard Technologies Inc.	505 5th Ave. S.	Seattle	WA	98104		206-521-8340	R	75*	0.3
Pyott-Boone Electronics Inc.	PO Box 809	Tazewell	VA	24651	Donald Fetterolf	276-988-5505	R	73*	0.2
Valcom Inc.	5614 Hollins Rd.	Roanoke	VA	24019	John Mason	540-563-2000	R	73*	0.2

Source: Ward's Business Directory of U.S. Private and Public Companies, Volumes 1 and 2, 2008. The company type code used is as follows: P - Public, R - Private, S - Subsidiary, D - Division, J - Joint Venture, A - Affiliate, G - Group. Sales are in millions of dollars, employees are in thousands. An asterisk (*) indicates an estimated sales volume. The symbol < stands for 'less than'. Company names and addresses are truncated, in some cases, to fit into the available space.

MATERIALS CONSUMED

Material	Quantity	Delivered Cost ($ million)
Printed ciruit boards (without inserted components) for electronic circuitry	(X)	248.0
Printed circuit assemblies, loaded boards, and modules	(X)	776.6
Semiconductors (incl. transistors, diodes, rectifiers, and integrated circuits), for electronic circuitry	(X)	682.1
Capacitors for electronic circuitry	(X)	63.5
Resistors for electronic circuitry	(X)	38.9
All other miscellaneous components and accessories for electronic circuitry (exc. tubes)	(X)	(D)
Electronic communication equipment	(X)	3,013.3
Electrical instrument mechanisms and meter movements	(X)	5.5
Electronic computer equipment	(X)	(D)
Purchased peripheral storage devices	(X)	2.1
Current-carrying wiring devices	(X)	25.8
Insulated wire and cable (including magnet wire)	(X)	50.3
Loudspeakers, microphones, and tuners (all types)	(X)	6.6
Fractional horsepower electric motors (less than 1 hp)	(X)	(D)
Plastics resins consumed in the form of granules, pellets, etc.	(X)	14.4
Fabricated plastics products (exc. gaskets, hoses, and belting)	(X)	31.5
Sheet metal products (excluding stampings)	(X)	50.0
Metal stampings	(X)	18.0
Metal bolts, nuts, screws, and other screw machine products	(X)	17.6
Other fabricated metal products (excluding forgings)	(X)	16.3
Forgings	(X)	(D)
Castings, rough and semifinished	(X)	2.8
Steel shapes and forms (exc. castings, forgings, fabr. metal products)	(X)	5.9
Aluminum and aluminum-base alloy shapes and forms (exc. castings, forgings, fabr. metal products)	(X)	14.6
Other nonferrous shapes and forms (exc. castings, forgings, fabricated metal products)	(X)	0.4
Paper and paperboard containers (incl. shipping sacks and other paper packaging supplies)	(X)	67.0
All other materials, components, parts, containers, and supplies	(X)	3,482.0
Materials, ingredients, containers, and supplies, nsk	(X)	1,120.6

Source: 2002 *Economic Census*. Explanation of symbols used: (D): Withheld to avoid disclosure of competitive data; na: Not available; (S): Withheld because statistical norms were not met; (X): Not applicable; (Z): Less than half the unit shown; nec: Not elsewhere classified; nsk: Not specified by kind; - : zero; p : 10-19 percent estimated; q : 20-29 percent estimated.

PRODUCT SHARE DETAILS

Product or Product Class Shipments	Mil. $	Product or Product Class Shipments	Mil. $
TELEPHONE SWITCHING, CARRIER, LINE TELEGRAPH, AND DATA COMMUNICATIONS EQUIPMENT	26,283.4	carrier equipment) and nonconsumer modems, including auxiliary sets	4,515.1
Telephone switching and switchboard equipment	7,084.7	All other telephone and telegraph (wire) apparatus, including telephone sets, telephone answering, and fax machines	12,771.8
Telephone and telegraph (wire) apparatus, carrier line equipment (office and line repeaters and line terminating		Telephone switching, carrier, line telegraph, and data communications equipment, nsk, total	1,911.9

Source: 2002 *Economic Census*. The values are product shipments in millions of dollars for 2002. Total product shipments may be lower or higher than industry shipments. See Introduction for a full discussion. Values of indented subcategories are summed in the main heading(s). The symbol (D) appears when data are withheld to prevent disclosure of competitive information. The abbreviation nsk stands for 'not specified by kind' and nec for 'not elsewhere classified'. A dash (-) means zero.

INPUTS AND OUTPUTS FOR TELEPHONE APPARATUS MANUFACTURING

Economic Sector or Industry Providing Inputs	%	Sector	Economic Sector or Industry Buying Outputs	%	Sector
Compensation of employees	18.1		Private fixed investment	57.2	
Broadcast & wireless communications equipment	9.9	Manufg.	Exports of goods & services	21.5	Cap Inv
Semiconductors & related devices	8.5	Manufg.	Telecommunications	7.4	Services
Management of companies & enterprises	7.3	Services	Management of companies & enterprises	2.7	Services
Wholesale trade	6.3	Trade	Personal consumption expenditures	2.4	
Electronic components, nec	5.8	Manufg.	S/L govt. invest., other	1.7	S/L Govt
Printed circuit assemblies (electronic assemblies)	3.7	Manufg.	S/L govt. invest., education	1.6	S/L Govt
Software publishers	2.1	Services	Federal government, investment, nondefense	1.3	Fed Govt
Scientific research & development services	2.1	Services	Federal government, investment, national defense	1.3	Fed Govt
Plastics products, nec	1.2	Manufg.	Telephone apparatus	0.7	Manufg.
Telephone apparatus	1.0	Manufg.	General S/L govt. services	0.3	S/L Govt
Real estate	1.0	Fin/R.E.	Cable & other subscription programming	0.2	Services
Bare printed circuit boards	0.9	Manufg.	Other S/L govt. enterprises	0.1	S/L Govt
Forging, stamping, & sintering, nec	0.9	Manufg.	General Federal government services, nondefense	0.1	Fed Govt
Noncomparable imports	0.8	Foreign	Data processing, hosting, & related services	0.1	Services
Communication & energy wires & cables	0.8	Manufg.	Internet service providers & web search portals	0.1	Services
Truck transportation	0.7	Util.	Nondepository credit intermediation activities	0.1	Fin/R.E.
Advertising & related services	0.6	Services	Periodical publishers	0.1	Services
Chemical products & preparations, nec	0.6	Manufg.			
Automotive equipment rental & leasing	0.5	Fin/R.E.			
Custom computer programming services	0.5	Services			
Telecommunications	0.4	Services			
Management, scientific, & technical consulting	0.4	Services			

Continued on next page.

INPUTS AND OUTPUTS FOR TELEPHONE APPARATUS MANUFACTURING - Continued

Economic Sector or Industry Providing Inputs	%	Sector	Economic Sector or Industry Buying Outputs	%	Sector
Electronic capacitors, resistors, coils, transformers	0.4	Manufg.			
Legal services	0.4	Services			
Motors & generators	0.3	Manufg.			
Turned products & screws, nuts, & bolts	0.3	Manufg.			
Computer terminals & peripherals	0.3	Manufg.			
Commercial & industrial machinery rental & leasing	0.3	Fin/R.E.			
Paperboard containers	0.3	Manufg.			
Warehousing & storage	0.2	Util.			
Natural gas distribution	0.2	Util.			
Lessors of nonfinancial assets	0.2	Fin/R.E.			
Accounting, tax preparation, bookkeeping, & payroll	0.2	Services			
Taxes on production & imports, less subsidies	0.2				
Machine shops	0.2	Manufg.			
Power generation & supply	0.2	Util.			
Ornamental & architectural metal products	0.2	Manufg.			
Coating, engraving, heat treating & allied activities	0.2	Manufg.			
Nonmetallic minerals, nec	0.2	Mining			
Maintenance/repair of nonresidential structures	0.2	Construct.			
Data processing, hosting, & related services	0.2	Services			
Plastics packaging materials, film & sheet	0.1	Manufg.			
Air transportation	0.1	Util.			
Services to buildings & dwellings	0.1	Services			
Crowns & closures & metal stamping	0.1	Manufg.			
Copper rolling, drawing, extruding, & alloying	0.1	Manufg.			
Wiring devices	0.1	Manufg.			
Other computer related services, including facilities	0.1	Services			
Motor vehicle parts	0.1	Manufg.			

Source: Benchmark Input-Output Accounts for the U.S. Economy, 2002, U.S. Department of Commerce, Washington, D.C., January 2008. The abbreviation nec stands for 'not elsewhere classified'.

OCCUPATIONS EMPLOYED BY COMMUNICATIONS EQUIPMENT MANUFACTURING

Occupation	% of Total 2006	Change to 2016	Occupation	% of Total 2006	Change to 2016
Electrical & electronic equipment assemblers	9.6	-19.4	General & operations managers	1.6	-9.3
Team assemblers	5.3	0.8	Purchasing agents, exc wholesale, retail, & farm	1.6	0.8
Computer software engineers, systems software	3.9	10.9	Electromechanical equipment assemblers	1.5	0.8
Electrical & electronic engineering technicians	3.8	0.8	Executive secretaries & administrative assistants	1.4	0.8
Computer software engineers, applications	3.4	21.0	Shipping, receiving, & traffic clerks	1.4	-3.0
Electronics engineers, exc computer	3.2	0.8	Accountants & auditors	1.3	0.8
Electrical engineers	2.9	0.8	Mechanical engineers	1.2	0.8
Industrial engineers	2.5	22.4	Electrical & electronics repairers, commercial/industry	1.1	7.4
First-line supervisors/managers of production workers	2.4	0.8	Production, planning, & expediting clerks	1.1	0.8
Computer hardware engineers	2.3	10.9	Sales engineers	1.1	0.8
Engineering managers	2.3	0.8	Marketing managers	1.1	0.8
Inspectors, testers, sorters, samplers, & weighers	2.0	-5.0	Computer support specialists	1.1	0.8
Customer service representatives	1.8	10.9	Bookkeeping, accounting, & auditing clerks	1.0	0.8
Sales representatives, wholesale & manufacturing, tech	1.8	0.8	Aerospace engineers	1.0	5.8
Sales reps, wholesale & manufacturing, exc tech	1.7	0.8			

Source: Industry-Occupation Matrix, Bureau of Labor Statistics, December 4, 2007. These data are reported based on 4-digit NAICS categories but have been matched to corresponding 6-digit NAICS industry codes. The change reported for each occupation to the year 2016 is a percent of growth or decline as estimated by the Bureau of Labor Statistics. The abbreviation nec stands for 'not elsewhere classified'.

LOCATION BY STATE AND REGIONAL CONCENTRATION

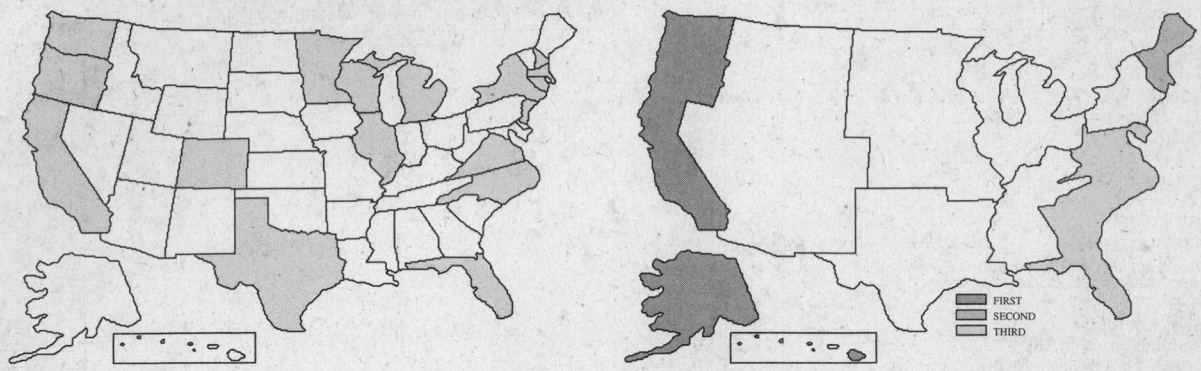

INDUSTRY DATA BY STATE

| State | Establish-ments | Shipments | | | Employment | | | | Cost as % of Shipments | Investment per Employee ($) |
		Total ($ mil)	% of U.S.	Per Establ.	Total Number	% of U.S.	Per Establ.	Wages ($/hour)		
California	134	12,136.6	44.1	90,571.3	16,454	25.8	123	24.34	39.9	14,124
Massachusetts	32	2,838.0	10.3	88,685.9	5,720	9.0	179	22.78	44.7	6,994
Florida	28	1,413.0	5.1	50,462.8	5,806	9.1	207	13.64	14.5	4,100
Illinois	25	1,364.0	5.0	54,561.8	6,895	10.8	276	17.90	46.1	5,754
Texas	37	1,109.9	4.0	29,997.2	5,391	8.5	146	20.68	40.9	4,409
New Hampshire	16	815.3	3.0	50,958.9	1,237	1.9	77	23.47	39.6	15,303
Colorado	15	803.8	2.9	53,588.4	2,886	4.5	192	20.44	64.6	35,702
Minnesota	13	712.7	2.6	54,821.0	1,110	1.7	85	17.46	45.0	3,536
North Carolina	11	570.7	2.1	51,886.1	793	1.2	72	20.56	47.2	10,074
Connecticut	21	331.5	1.2	15,787.5	1,083	1.7	52	19.37	43.8	4,361
Washington	15	312.9	1.1	20,859.1	1,038	1.6	69	12.48	50.8	2,895
New York	29	273.9	1.0	9,445.8	1,594	2.5	55	16.00	44.1	8,848
New Jersey	20	250.7	0.9	12,532.7	1,058	1.7	53	20.58	35.9	13,864
Virginia	14	142.2	0.5	10,157.9	983	1.5	70	13.94	48.6	2,314
Wisconsin	9	93.6	0.3	10,401.1	498	0.8	55	14.10	35.0	2,428
Michigan	8	48.3	0.2	6,039.0	352	0.6	44	12.71	57.6	2,091
Oregon	5	21.0	0.1	4,193.8	154	0.2	31	12.03	39.6	5,870

Source: 2002 *Economic Census*. The states are in descending order of shipments or establishments (if shipment data are missing for the majority). The symbol (D) appears when data are withheld to prevent disclosure of competitive information. States marked with (D) are sorted by number of establishments. A dash (-) indicates that the data element cannot be calculated. Data may not show all states active in the NAICS category. All data available at the time of publication are shown.

NAICS 334220 - RADIO AND TELEVISION BROADCASTING AND WIRELESS COMMUNICATIONS EQUIPMENT MANUFACTURING

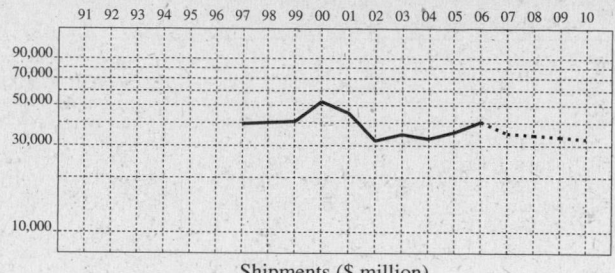

Shipments ($ million)

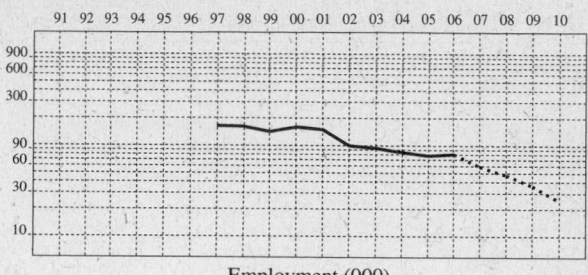

Employment (000)

GENERAL STATISTICS

Year	Com-panies	Establishments		Employment			Compensation		Production ($ million)			
		Total	with 20 or more employees	Total (000)	Production Workers (000)	Hours (Mil)	Payroll ($ mil)	Wages ($/hr)	Cost of Materials	Value Added by Manufacture	Value of Shipments	Capital Invest.
1997	1,089	1,215	637	163.9	79.9	157.3	7,374.6	16.43	18,166.3	21,616.7	39,515.7	1,841.1
1998		1,215	629	161.3	79.3	156.1	7,514.1	16.96	19,785.5	20,446.6	40,138.9	1,749.4
1999		1,182	595	141.7	67.0	131.2	7,155.4	17.63	19,621.4	20,482.7	40,647.1	1,334.0
2000		1,200	599	159.2	76.7	152.1	8,681.7	18.53	29,367.2	23,961.5	52,305.9	2,107.2
2001		1,158	582	149.5	65.8	126.6	7,954.1	18.58	26,470.7	19,331.1	45,334.4	1,778.6
2002	929	1,041	491	99.5	42.0	79.6	5,341.8	19.08	17,664.7	14,679.2	31,879.8	883.2
2003		1,029	500	93.5	37.3	70.6	5,326.1	17.92	19,729.5	15,061.8	34,574.0	829.7
2004		1,023	459	84.6	34.0	67.2	5,229.8	19.06	17,588.3	15,731.2	32,718.3	686.5
2005		994	463	77.6	31.9	66.8	5,178.6	20.22	17,340.7	18,574.5	35,522.3	791.0
2006		957P	425P	80.3	32.7	64.7	5,550.0	20.95	18,873.2	19,616.1	40,491.8	1,233.8
2007		925P	400P	58.7P	19.2P	38.2P	4,694.7P	20.85P	16,306.6P	16,948.5P	34,985.3P	652.1P
2008		893P	375P	47.4P	12.8P	25.7P	4,360.9P	21.27P	15,939.9P	16,567.3P	34,198.5P	530.1P
2009		861P	350P	36.1P	6.3P	13.1P	4,027.1P	21.69P	15,573.1P	16,186.2P	33,411.7P	408.0P
2010		829P	325P	24.7P		0.6P	3,693.3P	22.11P	15,206.4P	15,805.0P	32,624.8P	285.9P

Sources: 1997 and 2002 *Economic Census*; other years, up to 2006, are from *Annual Survey of Manufactures*. Establishment counts for non-Census years are from *County Business Patterns*; 1997 and 2002 values are from the 1997 and 2002 censuses, respectively. 'P's show projections by the editors.

INDICES OF CHANGE

Year	Com-panies	Establishments		Employment			Compensation		Production ($ million)			
		Total	with 20 or more employees	Total (000)	Production Workers (000)	Hours (Mil)	Payroll ($ mil)	Wages ($/hr)	Cost of Materials	Value Added by Manufacture	Value of Shipments	Capital Invest.
1997	117	117	130	165	190	198	138	86	103	147	124	208
1998		117	128	162	189	196	141	89	112	139	126	198
1999		114	121	142	160	165	134	92	111	140	128	151
2000		115	122	160	183	191	163	97	166	163	164	239
2001		111	119	150	157	159	149	97	150	132	142	201
2002	100	100	100	100	100	100	100	100	100	100	100	100
2003		99	102	94	89	89	100	94	112	103	108	94
2004		98	93	85	81	84	98	100	100	107	103	78
2005		95	94	78	76	84	97	106	98	127	111	90
2006		92P	87P	81	78	81	104	110	107	134	127	140
2007		89P	82P	59P	46P	48P	88P	109P	92P	115P	110P	74P
2008		86P	76P	48P	30P	32P	82P	111P	90P	113P	107P	60P
2009		83P	71P	36P	15P	16P	75P	114P	88P	110P	105P	46P
2010		80P	66P	25P		1P	69P	116P	86P	108P	102P	32P

Sources: Same as General Statistics. Values reflect change from the base year, 2002. Values above 100 mean greater than 2002, values below 100 mean less than 2002, and the values of 100 in other years means the same as 2002. 'P's show projections by the editors.

SELECTED RATIOS

For 2002	Avg. of All Manufact.	Analyzed Industry	Index	For 2002	Avg. of All Manufact.	Analyzed Industry	Index
Employees per Establishment	42	96	228	Value Added per Production Worker	182,367	349,505	192
Payroll per Establishment	1,639,184	5,131,412	313	Cost per Establishment	5,769,015	16,968,972	294
Payroll per Employee	39,053	53,686	137	Cost per Employee	137,446	177,535	129
Production Workers per Establishment	30	40	137	Cost per Production Worker	195,506	420,588	215
Wages per Establishment	694,845	1,458,951	210	Shipments per Establishment	11,158,348	30,624,207	274
Wages per Production Worker	23,548	36,161	154	Shipments per Employee	265,847	320,400	121
Hours per Production Worker	1,980	1,895	96	Shipments per Production Worker	378,144	759,043	201
Wages per Hour	11.89	19.08	160	Investment per Establishment	361,338	848,415	235
Value Added per Establishment	5,381,325	14,101,057	262	Investment per Employee	8,609	8,876	103
Value Added per Employee	128,210	147,530	115	Investment per Production Worker	12,245	21,029	172

Sources: Same as General Statistics. The 'Average of All Manufacturing' column represents the average of all manufacturing industries reported for the most recent complete year available. The Index shows the relationship between the Average and the Analyzed Industry. For example, 100 means that they are equal; 500 that the Analyzed Industry is five times the average; 50 means that the Analyzed Industry is half the national average. The abbreviation 'na' is used to show that data are 'not available'. Ratios shown for 2002, the last complete census year.

LEADING COMPANIES   Number shown: 75   Total sales ($ mil): **533,569**   Total employment (000): **1,252.8**

Company Name	Address				CEO Name	Phone	Co. Type	Sales ($ mil)	Empl. (000)
Technitrol Delaware Inc.	3411 Silverside Rd.	Wilmington	DE	19810	James M. Papada	302-478-8271	S	67,716*	22.8
Chrysler L.L.C.	1000 Chrysler Dr.	Auburn Hills	MI	48326	Thomas W. LaSorda	248-576-5741	S	45,237*	84.4
DIRECTV Global Inc.	2230 E Imperial	El Segundo	CA	90245	Roxanne Austin	310-535-5000	S	43,057*	116.0
Lockheed Martin Corp.	6801 Rockledge Dr.	Bethesda	MD	20817	Richard F. Ambrose	301-897-6000	P	41,862	140.0
Motorola Inc.	1303 E Algonquin	Schaumburg	IL	60196	Greg Brown	847-576-5000	P	36,622	66.0
Honeywell International Inc.	PO Box 4000	Morristown	NJ	07962	Adriane M. Brown	973-455-2000	P	34,589	122.0
General Dynamics Corp.	2941 Fairview Park	Falls Church	VA	22042	Nicholas D. Chabraja	703-876-3000	P	27,240	83.5
Raytheon Co.	870 Winter St.	Waltham	MA	02451		781-522-3000	P	21,301	72.1
ITT Federal Services Corp.	4410 E Fountain	Colorado Spgs	CO	80916	Steven Loranger	719-591-3600	S	20,690*	7.0
Mars Inc.	6885 Elm Street	Mc Lean	VA	22101	John F. Mars	703-821-4900	R	18,462*	40.0
Computer Sciences Corp.	2100 E Grand Ave.	El Segundo	CA	90245		310-615-0311	P	14,855	79.0
L-3 Communications Holdings	600 3rd Ave.	New York	NY	10016		212-697-1111	P	13,961	63.7
ITT Corp.	4 W Red Oak Ln.	White Plains	NY	10604		914-641-2000	P	9,003	39.7
QUALCOMM Inc.	5775 Morehouse Dr.	San Diego	CA	92121	Paul E. Jacobs	858-587-1121	P	8,871	12.8
Ball Corp.	PO Box 5000	Broomfield	CO	80021	R. David Hoover	303-469-3131	P	7,475	15.5
Order-Matic Corp.	PO Box 25463	Oklahoma City	OK	73125	Bill Cunningham	405-672-1487	R	5,787	0.2
Allegheny Technologies Inc.	1000 Six PPG Pl.	Pittsburgh	PA	15222		412-394-2800	P	5,453	9.5
Agilent Technologies Inc.	5301 Stevens Creek	Santa Clara	CA	95051	Patrick J. Byrne	408-345-8886	P	5,420	19.2
SPX Corp.	13515 Ballnyn Corp.	Charlotte	NC	28277		704-752-4400	P	4,822	17.8
Flextronics	2090 Fortune Dr.	San Jose	CA	95131	Mike McNamara	408-576-7000	S	4,699*	1.5
LSI Marcole Inc.	1108 Oakdale St.	Manchester	TN	37355	Robert J. Ready	931-723-4442	S	4,643*	1.4
Rockwell Collins Inc.	400 Collins Rd. NE	Cedar Rapids	IA	52498		319-295-1000	P	4,415	19.5
Oki Data Americas Inc.	2000 Bishops Gate	Mount Laurel	NJ	08054	Stewart Krentzman	856-235-2600	S	4,260*	0.5
Harris Corp.	1025 W NASA	Melbourne	FL	32919		321-727-9100	P	4,243	16.0
Sparton Electronics	PO Box 788	De Leon Springs	FL	32130	D W. Hockenbrocht	386-985-4631	S	3,491*	1.0
Philips Accessor./Comp. Periph	215 Entin Rd.	Clifton	NJ	07014		973-471-9050	A	3,113*	0.4
Fujitsu Network Communications	2801 Telecom Pkwy.	Richardson	TX	75082	George Chase	972-479-6000	R	2,969*	1.0
Benchmark Electronics Inc.	3000 Technology	Angleton	TX	77515		979-849-6550	P	2,916	10.9
Crane Co.	100 First Stamford	Stamford	CT	06902	Thomas Craney	203-363-7300	P	2,619	12.0
I/O Marine Systems Inc.	5200 Toler St.	Harahan	LA	70123	Robert P. Peebler	504-733-6061	S	2,610*	0.8
I/O Nevada L.L.C.	12300 Parc Crest Dr	Stafford	TX	77477	Robert P. Peebler	281-933-3339	S	2,610*	0.8
I/O Texas L.P.	12300 Parc Crest Dr	Stafford	TX	77477	Robert P. Peebler	281-933-3339	S	2,610*	0.8
Hubbell Inc.	584 Derby Milford	Orange	CT	06477		203-799-4100	P	2,534	11.5
Wakefield Thermal Solutions	33 Bridge St.	Pelham	NH	03076	Robert Streiter	603-635-2800	S	2,398*	0.1
Red Rocket Inc.	5217 Verdugo Way	Camarillo	CA	93012	James B. Schutz	805-409-0909	R	2,146*	0.7
Hitachi America Ltd.	2000 Sierra Pnt Pky	Brisbane	CA	94005	Masahide Tanigahi	650-589-8300	S	2,127*	4.4
CommScope Inc.	PO Box 1729	Hickory	NC	28603	Frank M. Drendel	828-324-2200	P	1,931	15.5
Scientific-Atlanta Inc.	PO Box 465447	Lawrenceville	GA	30042		770-236-5000	S	1,910	7.7
ACT Electronics Inc.	2 Cabot Rd.	Hudson	MA	01749		978-567-4000	R	1,870*	0.1
Opex Corp.	305 Commerce Dr.	Moorestown	NJ	08057	Jeff Bowen	856-727-1100	R	1,857*	0.7
Bose Corp.	The Mountain	Framingham	MA	01701	Amar G. Bose	508-879-7330	R	1,800	8.0
PerkinElmer Inc.	940 Winter St.	Waltham	MA	02451	Robert F. Friel	781-663-6900	P	1,787	8.7
Advanced Interconnection Tech	85 Adams Ave.	Hauppauge	NY	11788	Phillip A. Harris	631-968-1591	S	1,776*	0.6
Siemens VDO Automotive Corp.	2400 Executive Hill	Auburn Hills	MI	48326	John Sanderson	248-209-4000	S	1,738*	10.0
ECS. Inc International	1105 S Ridgeview	Olathe	KS	66062	Patricia S. Taylor	913-782-7787	R	1,689*	0.5
Stratos Optical Technologies	7444 W Wilson Ave.	Chicago	IL	60706	Phillip A. Harris	708-867-9600	S	1,645*	0.6
Stratos Lightwave Inc.	1335 Gateway Dr.	Melbourne	FL	32901	Phillip A. Harris	321-308-4100	S	1,633*	0.6
CC Industries Inc.	222 N La Salle St.	Chicago	IL	60601	William H. Crown	312-855-4000	S	1,560*	6.0
I/O General L.L.C.	12300 Parc Crest Dr	Stafford	TX	77477	Robert P. Peebler	281-933-3339	S	1,555*	0.5
Sony Music Entertainment Inc.	550 Madison Ave.	New York	NY	10022	Mike Bebel	212-833-8000	S	1,500*	10.0
Itron Inc.	2111 N Molter Rd.	Liberty Lake	WA	99019		509-924-9900	P	1,464	2.4
Rooney Holdings Inc.	1400 Gulf Shre Blvd	Naples	FL	34102	Jim Cavanaugh	239-403-0375	R	1,443*	2.6
K and L Microwave Inc.	2250 Northwood Dr.	Salisbury	MD	21801	Darby Kruger	410-749-2424	S	1,339*	0.5
AVX Corp.	PO Box 867	Myrtle Beach	SC	29578	John S. Gilbertson	843-448-9411	P	1,333	13.0
Radio Satellite Integrators	19144 Van Ness	Torrance	CA	90501	Jonathan Michels	310-787-7700	R	1,280*	<0.1
Olin Corp.	190 Carondelet Plz.	Clayton	MO	63105	Randall W. Larrimore	314-480-1400	P	1,277	3.6
Teradyne Inc.	600 Riverpark Dr.	North Reading	MA	01864	James Bagley	978-370-2700	P	1,102	3.6
Academy Precision Materials	5520 Midway Park	Albuquerque	NM	87109	Mike McCay	505-343-9440	R	1,096*	0.3
Orbital Sciences Corp.	21839 Atlantic Blvd	Dulles	VA	20166		703-406-5000	P	1,084	2.8
Technitrol Inc.	1210 Northbrook Dr.	Trevose	PA	19053		215-355-2900	P	1,027	26.1
Thales Communications Inc.	22605 Gateway Ctr.	Clarksburg	MD	20871	Mitchell Herbets	240-864-7000	R	800*	0.3
Loral Space and Communications	600 3rd Ave.	New York	NY	10016		212-697-1105	P	797	2.3
Powerwave Technologies Inc.	1801 E St. Andrew	Santa Ana	CA	92705	Ronald Buschur	714-466-1000	P	781	4.2
Emerson Netw. Pwr Emb Comp.	8310 Excelsior Dr.	Madison	WI	53717			S	774*	0.3
Sub-Zero Inc.	4717 Hammersley	Madison	WI	53711	James Bakke	608-271-2233	R	758*	3.0
Hutchinson Technology Inc.	40 W Highland Park	Hutchinson	MN	55350	Wayne M. Fortun	320-587-3797	P	716	4.7
Space Systems/Loral	3825 Fabian Way	Palo Alto	CA	94303	Robert E. Berry	650-852-4000	S	714*	1.8
Syntax-Brillian Corp.	1600 N Desert Dr.	Tempe	AZ	85281	James Li	602-389-8888	P	698	0.3
CTS Corp.	905 N West Blvd.	Elkhart	IN	46514	R R. Hemminghaus	574-293-7511	P	686	4.7
Ball Aerospace & Technologies	PO Box 1062	Boulder	CO	80306		303-939-4000	S	672*	3.0
Kaiser Systems Inc.	126 Sohier Rd.	Beverly	MA	01915	Kenneth Kaiser	978-922-9300	R	556*	<0.1
Aeroflex Inc.	PO Box 6022	Plainview	NY	11803	Harvey R. Blau	516-694-6700	R	537*	2.0
Varian Semiconductor Equipment	35 Dory Rd.	Gloucester	MA	01930	Richard Aurelio	978-281-2000	S	530*	1.0
ViaSat Inc.	6155 El Cam Real	Carlsbad	CA	92009		760-476-2200	P	517	1.5
Power-One Inc.	740 Calle Plano	Camarillo	CA	93012		805-987-8741	P	512	4.2

Source: Ward's Business Directory of U.S. Private and Public Companies, Volumes 1 and 2, 2008. The company type code used is as follows: P - Public, R - Private, S - Subsidiary, D - Division, J - Joint Venture, A - Affiliate, G - Group. Sales are in millions of dollars, employees are in thousands. An asterisk (*) indicates an estimated sales volume. The symbol < stands for 'less than'. Company names and addresses are truncated, in some cases, to fit into the available space.

MATERIALS CONSUMED

Material	Quantity	Delivered Cost ($ million)
Printed ciruit boards (without inserted components) for electronic circuitry	(X)	308.1
Printed circuit assemblies, loaded boards, and modules	(X)	442.7
Semiconductors (incl. transistors, diodes, rectifiers, and integrated circuits), for electronic circuitry	(X)	452.3
Capacitors for electronic circuitry	(X)	46.6
Resistors for electronic circuitry	(X)	26.5
All other miscellaneous components and accessories for electronic circuitry (exc. tubes)	(X)	208.0
Electronic communication equipment	(X)	4,171.1
Electrical instrument mechanisms and meter movements	(X)	89.9
Electronic computer equipment	(X)	81.3
Purchased peripheral storage devices	(X)	24.2
Current-carrying wiring devices	(X)	32.2
Insulated wire and cable (including magnet wire)	(X)	70.2
Loudspeakers, microphones, and tuners (all types)	(X)	7.3
Fractional horsepower electric motors (less than 1 hp)	(X)	6.3
Plastics resins consumed in the form of granules, pellets, etc.	(X)	12.0
Fabricated plastics products (exc. gaskets, hoses, and belting)	(X)	48.0
Sheet metal products (excluding stampings)	(X)	75.8
Metal stampings	(X)	13.9
Metal bolts, nuts, screws, and other screw machine products	(X)	45.5
Other fabricated metal products (excluding forgings)	(X)	48.9
Forgings	(X)	(D)
Castings, rough and semifinished	(X)	(D)
Steel shapes and forms (exc. castings, forgings, fabr. metal products)	(X)	53.0
Aluminum and aluminum-base alloy shapes and forms (exc. castings, forgings, fabr. metal products)	(X)	25.8
Other nonferrous shapes and forms (exc. castings, forgings, fabricated metal products)	(X)	12.0
Paper and paperboard containers (incl. shipping sacks and other paper packaging supplies)	(X)	28.4
All other materials, components, parts, containers, and supplies	(X)	4,804.0
Materials, ingredients, containers, and supplies, nsk	(X)	4,352.0

Source: 2002 Economic Census. Explanation of symbols used: (D): Withheld to avoid disclosure of competitive data; na: Not available; (S): Withheld because statistical norms were not met; (X): Not applicable; (Z): Less than half the unit shown; nec: Not elsewhere classified; nsk: Not specified by kind; - : zero; p : 10-19 percent estimated; q : 20-29 percent estimated.

PRODUCT SHARE DETAILS

Product or Product Class Shipments	Mil. $	Product or Product Class Shipments	Mil. $
RADIO AND TELEVISION BROADCASTING AND WIRELESS COMMUNICATIONS EQUIPMENT	30,083.6	Broadcast, studio, and related electronic equipment	3,192.4
Communication systems and equipment, except broadcast, but including microwave equipment, and space satellites	**24,556.4**	**Radio and television broadcasting and wireless communications equipment, nsk, total**	**2,334.9**

Source: 2002 Economic Census. The values are product shipments in millions of dollars for 2002. Total product shipments may be lower or higher than industry shipments. See Introduction for a full discussion. Values of indented subcategories are summed in the main heading(s). The symbol (D) appears when data are withheld to prevent disclosure of competitive information. The abbreviation nsk stands for 'not specified by kind' and nec for 'not elsewhere classified'. A dash (-) means zero.

INPUTS AND OUTPUTS FOR BROADCAST AND WIRELESS COMMUNICATIONS EQUIPMENT

Economic Sector or Industry Providing Inputs	%	Sector	Economic Sector or Industry Buying Outputs	%	Sector
Compensation of employees	22.1		Private fixed investment	56.0	
Broadcast & wireless communications equipment	13.1	Manufg.	Exports of goods & services	9.6	Cap Inv
Semiconductors & related devices	9.1	Manufg.	Broadcast & wireless communications equipment	8.8	Manufg.
Management of companies & enterprises	8.8	Services	Personal consumption expenditures	5.4	
Wholesale trade	8.0	Trade	Telephone apparatus	5.3	Manufg.
Electronic components, nec	5.3	Manufg.	Federal government, investment, national defense	3.4	Fed Govt
Software publishers	4.8	Services	Aircraft	2.6	Manufg.
Scientific research & development services	2.5	Services	Federal government, investment, nondefense	2.1	Fed Govt
Electronic connectors	2.0	Manufg.	General Federal government services, defense	1.0	Fed Govt
Printed circuit assemblies (electronic assemblies)	1.9	Manufg.	S/L govt. invest., other	0.7	S/L Govt
Advertising & related services	1.2	Services	Telecommunications	0.6	Services
Bare printed circuit boards	1.2	Manufg.	Change in private inventories	0.4	In House
Noncomparable imports	1.1	Foreign	Wholesale trade	0.4	Trade
Specialized design services	1.0	Services	Search, detection, & navigation instruments	0.3	Manufg.
Telecommunications	1.0	Services	Guided missiles & space vehicles	0.3	Manufg.
Employment services	0.8	Services	Communications equipment, nec	0.2	Manufg.
Real estate	0.8	Fin/R.E.	Management of companies & enterprises	0.2	Services
Legal services	0.7	Services	Electronic & precision equipment repair/maintenance	0.2	Services
Business support services	0.7	Services	S/L govt. invest., education	0.2	S/L Govt
Management, scientific, & technical consulting	0.6	Services	Aircraft engine & engine parts	0.2	Manufg.
Lessors of nonfinancial assets	0.6	Fin/R.E.	Electronic components, nec	0.1	Manufg.
Architectural, engineering, & related services	0.5	Services	Retail trade	0.1	Trade
Motor vehicle parts	0.5	Manufg.			
Truck transportation	0.4	Util.			
Support services, nec	0.4	Services			

Continued on next page.

INPUTS AND OUTPUTS FOR BROADCAST AND WIRELESS COMMUNICATIONS EQUIPMENT - Continued

Economic Sector or Industry Providing Inputs	%	Sector	Economic Sector or Industry Buying Outputs	%	Sector
Plastics products, nec	0.4	Manufg.			
Electricity & signal testing instruments	0.4	Manufg.			
Investigation & security services	0.3	Services			
Power generation & supply	0.3	Util.			
Warehousing & storage	0.3	Util.			
Custom computer programming services	0.3	Services			
Machine shops	0.3	Manufg.			
Automotive equipment rental & leasing	0.3	Fin/R.E.			
Turned products & screws, nuts, & bolts	0.3	Manufg.			
Taxes on production & imports, less subsidies	0.3				
Electronic capacitors, resistors, coils, transformers	0.3	Manufg.			
Accounting, tax preparation, bookkeeping, & payroll	0.3	Services			
Data processing, hosting, & related services	0.3	Services			
Ornamental & architectural metal products	0.3	Manufg.			
Other computer related services, including facilities	0.2	Services			
Computer terminals & peripherals	0.2	Manufg.			
Crowns & closures & metal stamping	0.2	Manufg.			
Maintenance/repair of nonresidential structures	0.2	Construct.			
Iron & steel mills & ferroalloys	0.2	Manufg.			
Services to buildings & dwellings	0.2	Services			
Air transportation	0.2	Util.			
Copper rolling, drawing, extruding, & alloying	0.2	Manufg.			
Facilities support services	0.2	Services			
Plastics packaging materials, film & sheet	0.2	Manufg.			
Food services & drinking places	0.2	Services			
Commercial & industrial machinery rental & leasing	0.1	Fin/R.E.			
Wiring devices	0.1	Manufg.			
Hotels & motels, including casino hotels	0.1	Services			
Automotive repair & maintenance, ex. car washes	0.1	Services			
Securities, commodity contracts, investments	0.1	Fin/R.E.			
Coating, engraving, heat treating & allied activities	0.1	Manufg.			
Computer system design services	0.1	Services			
Commercial & industrial equipment repair/maintenance	0.1	Services			
Paperboard containers	0.1	Manufg.			
Communication & energy wires & cables	0.1	Manufg.			
Alumina refining & primary aluminum production	0.1	Manufg.			
Metal & other household furniture	0.1	Manufg.			

Source: Benchmark Input-Output Accounts for the U.S. Economy, 2002, U.S. Department of Commerce, Washington, D.C., January 2008. The abbreviation nec stands for 'not elsewhere classified'.

OCCUPATIONS EMPLOYED BY COMMUNICATIONS EQUIPMENT MANUFACTURING

Occupation	% of Total 2006	Change to 2016	Occupation	% of Total 2006	Change to 2016
Electrical & electronic equipment assemblers	9.6	-19.4	General & operations managers	1.6	-9.3
Team assemblers	5.3	0.8	Purchasing agents, exc wholesale, retail, & farm	1.6	0.8
Computer software engineers, systems software	3.9	10.9	Electromechanical equipment assemblers	1.5	0.8
Electrical & electronic engineering technicians	3.8	0.8	Executive secretaries & administrative assistants	1.4	0.8
Computer software engineers, applications	3.4	21.0	Shipping, receiving, & traffic clerks	1.4	-3.0
Electronics engineers, exc computer	3.2	0.8	Accountants & auditors	1.3	0.8
Electrical engineers	2.9	0.8	Mechanical engineers	1.2	0.8
Industrial engineers	2.5	22.4	Electrical & electronics repairers, commercial/industry	1.1	7.4
First-line supervisors/managers of production workers	2.4	0.8	Production, planning, & expediting clerks	1.1	0.8
Computer hardware engineers	2.3	10.9	Sales engineers	1.1	0.8
Engineering managers	2.3	0.8	Marketing managers	1.1	0.8
Inspectors, testers, sorters, samplers, & weighers	2.0	-5.0	Computer support specialists	1.1	0.8
Customer service representatives	1.8	10.9	Bookkeeping, accounting, & auditing clerks	1.0	0.8
Sales representatives, wholesale & manufacturing, tech	1.8	0.8	Aerospace engineers	1.0	5.8
Sales reps, wholesale & manufacturing, exc tech	1.7	0.8			

Source: Industry-Occupation Matrix, Bureau of Labor Statistics, December 4, 2007. These data are reported based on 4-digit NAICS categories but have been matched to corresponding 6-digit NAICS industry codes. The change reported for each occupation to the year 2016 is a percent of growth or decline as estimated by the Bureau of Labor Statistics. The abbreviation nec stands for 'not elsewhere classified'.

LOCATION BY STATE AND REGIONAL CONCENTRATION

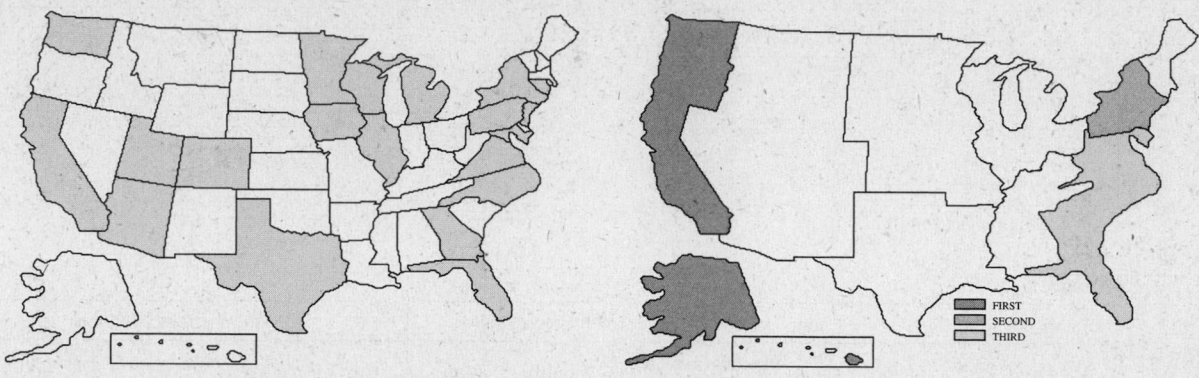

INDUSTRY DATA BY STATE

| State | Establish-ments | Shipments | | | Employment | | | | Cost as % of Shipments | Investment per Employee ($) |
		Total ($ mil)	% of U.S.	Per Establ.	Total Number	% of U.S.	Per Establ.	Wages ($/hour)		
California	281	10,467.2	32.8	37,249.7	36,549	36.7	130	22.84	53.7	13,004
Texas	62	5,712.8	17.9	92,141.6	7,038	7.1	114	17.60	67.9	7,008
Florida	57	3,321.4	10.4	58,269.6	7,853	7.9	138	19.31	45.9	7,206
Illinois	40	2,514.4	7.9	62,859.8	3,215	3.2	80	20.70	49.1	3,789
Maryland	37	1,893.3	5.9	51,170.7	6,595	6.6	178	22.41	71.6	11,040
New York	61	1,270.2	4.0	20,822.6	6,556	6.6	107	16.51	52.3	3,444
New Jersey	54	706.1	2.2	13,075.8	3,516	3.5	65	16.68	41.7	3,592
Pennsylvania	52	584.3	1.8	11,236.0	3,399	3.4	65	19.76	56.3	5,038
North Carolina	21	542.4	1.7	25,829.2	1,734	1.7	83	16.51	48.7	6,231
Georgia	22	348.4	1.1	15,834.9	1,291	1.3	59	17.39	53.4	4,664
Virginia	17	254.6	0.8	14,977.1	815	0.8	48	10.89	65.3	4,234
Iowa	7	253.4	0.8	36,193.9	1,248	1.3	178	12.51	62.9	10,833
Arizona	21	218.7	0.7	10,413.6	1,055	1.1	50	15.41	47.1	4,830
Connecticut	18	216.9	0.7	12,050.7	1,171	1.2	65	14.58	46.7	2,128
Colorado	19	164.2	0.5	8,643.5	906	0.9	48	19.31	46.6	3,480
Washington	24	115.0	0.4	4,792.9	729	0.7	30	16.31	40.1	1,401
Minnesota	11	73.9	0.2	6,721.5	481	0.5	44	13.06	57.9	2,349
Utah	8	65.0	0.2	8,129.1	380	0.4	48	14.42	40.7	2,071
Wisconsin	10	43.6	0.1	4,357.2	234	0.2	23	16.56	51.3	2,380
Michigan	7	18.8	0.1	2,679.3	148	0.1	21	9.62	50.0	3,196

Source: 2002 *Economic Census*. The states are in descending order of shipments or establishments (if shipment data are missing for the majority). The symbol (D) appears when data are withheld to prevent disclosure of competitive information. States marked with (D) are sorted by number of establishments. A dash (-) indicates that the data element cannot be calculated. Data may not show all states active in the NAICS category. All data available at the time of publication are shown.

NAICS 334290 - COMMUNICATIONS EQUIPMENT MANUFACTURING NEC

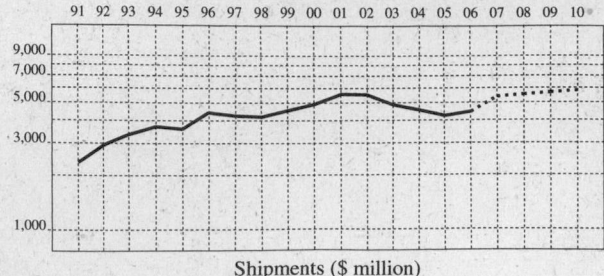

Shipments ($ million)

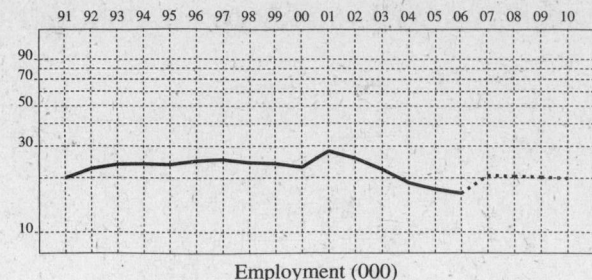

Employment (000)

GENERAL STATISTICS

Year	Com-panies	Establishments		Employment			Compensation		Production ($ million)			
		Total	with 20 or more employees	Total (000)	Production Workers (000)	Hours (Mil)	Payroll ($ mil)	Wages ($/hr)	Cost of Materials	Value Added by Manufacture	Value of Shipments	Capital Invest.
1991		421	177	20.0	8.8	18.2	530.7	9.72	926.2	1,444.6	2,356.1	63.3
1992	502	517	174	22.5	10.8	21.3	650.2	10.36	1,167.5	1,767.0	2,923.9	65.0
1993		523	185	23.7	11.7	22.6	698.4	10.19	1,412.5	1,939.5	3,349.7	83.8
1994		510	176	23.9	12.3	23.0	745.3	10.44	1,492.8	2,241.0	3,703.4	99.6
1995		488	177	23.7	12.0	23.1	762.0	10.34	1,425.4	2,203.1	3,595.6	124.9
1996		527	179	24.8	12.4	24.3	851.4	10.73	1,758.7	2,666.3	4,425.3	179.5
1997	465	499	161	25.3	12.1	23.3	917.4	11.66	1,669.0	2,567.6	4,242.7	148.8
1998		496	159	24.3	11.7	22.4	911.4	12.05	1,781.2	2,393.3	4,189.5	224.9
1999		475	158	24.0	11.6	21.6	842.3	12.85	1,935.6	2,640.2	4,539.0	147.0
2000		489	156	22.9	11.4	21.5	861.4	13.52	2,113.0	2,795.4	4,904.7	132.5
2001		468	167	28.1	12.9	24.9	1,149.7	14.59	2,223.5	3,420.5	5,571.0	146.5
2002	471	503	180	25.7	11.5	22.1	1,142.9	15.15	2,311.2	3,261.7	5,534.6	101.0
2003		486	178	22.3	9.6	19.4	1,003.5	14.94	2,097.1	2,733.8	4,874.5	72.2
2004		494	177	18.8	8.6	16.7	903.7	16.78	1,875.6	2,669.2	4,549.9	43.7
2005		481	171	17.3	8.0	16.2	865.5	16.37	1,800.1	2,426.8	4,235.0	64.5
2006		489P	168P	16.4	7.4	14.6	859.2	17.43	1,977.0	2,520.1	4,451.6	69.5
2007		489P	168P	20.6P	9.3P	18.1P	1,058.8P	17.52P	2,393.1P	3,050.5P	5,388.6P	97.2P
2008		489P	167P	20.4P	9.1P	17.8P	1,082.7P	18.06P	2,454.4P	3,128.7P	5,526.6P	95.6P
2009		488P	167P	20.2P	9.0P	17.4P	1,106.5P	18.60P	2,515.7P	3,206.8P	5,664.7P	94.0P
2010		488P	166P	19.9P	8.8P	17.1P	1,130.4P	19.14P	2,577.0P	3,285.0P	5,802.7P	92.5P

Sources: 1992, 1997, 2002 *Economic Census*; other years, up to 2006, are from the *Annual Survey of Manufactures*. Establishment counts for non-Census years are from *County Business Patterns*; 1997 and 2002 values are from the 1997 and 2002 censuses respectively, reported in the Federal Government's NAICS format. Other years were originally reported in equivalent SIC format. 'P's show projections by the editors.

INDICES OF CHANGE

Year	Com-panies	Establishments		Employment			Compensation		Production ($ million)			
		Total	with 20 or more employees	Total (000)	Production Workers (000)	Hours (Mil)	Payroll ($ mil)	Wages ($/hr)	Cost of Materials	Value Added by Manufacture	Value of Shipments	Capital Invest.
1992	107	103	97	88	94	96	57	68	51	54	53	64
1997	99	99	89	98	105	105	80	77	72	79	77	147
2001		93	93	109	112	113	101	96	96	105	101	145
2002	100	100	100	100	100	100	100	100	100	100	100	100
2003		97	99	87	83	88	88	99	91	84	88	71
2004		98	98	73	75	76	79	111	81	82	82	43
2005		96	95	67	70	73	76	108	78	74	77	64
2006		97P	93P	64	64	66	75	115	86	77	80	69
2007		97P	93P	80P	81P	82P	93P	116P	104P	94P	97P	96P
2008		97P	93P	79P	79P	81P	95P	119P	106P	96P	100P	95P
2009		97P	93P	79P	78P	79P	97P	123P	109P	98P	102P	93P
2010		97P	92P	77P	77P	77P	99P	126P	112P	101P	105P	92P

Sources: Same as General Statistics. Values reflect change from the base year, 2002. Values above 100 mean greater than 2002, values below 100 mean less than 2002, and the values of 100 in other years means the same as 2002. 'P's show projections by the editors.

SELECTED RATIOS

For 2002	Avg. of All Manufact.	Analyzed Industry	Index	For 2002	Avg. of All Manufact.	Analyzed Industry	Index
Employees per Establishment	42	51	122	Value Added per Production Worker	182,367	283,626	156
Payroll per Establishment	1,639,184	2,272,167	139	Cost per Establishment	5,769,015	4,594,831	80
Payroll per Employee	39,053	44,471	114	Cost per Employee	137,446	89,930	65
Production Workers per Establishment	30	23	77	Cost per Production Worker	195,506	200,974	103
Wages per Establishment	694,845	665,636	96	Shipments per Establishment	11,158,348	11,003,181	99
Wages per Production Worker	23,548	29,114	124	Shipments per Employee	265,847	215,354	81
Hours per Production Worker	1,980	1,922	97	Shipments per Production Worker	378,144	481,270	127
Wages per Hour	11.89	15.15	127	Investment per Establishment	361,338	200,795	56
Value Added per Establishment	5,381,325	6,484,493	120	Investment per Employee	8,609	3,930	46
Value Added per Employee	128,210	126,914	99	Investment per Production Worker	12,245	8,783	72

Sources: Same as General Statistics. The 'Average of All Manufacturing' column represents the average of all manufacturing industries reported for the most recent complete year available. The Index shows the relationship between the Average and the Analyzed Industry. For example, 100 means that they are equal; 500 that the Analyzed Industry is five times the average; 50 means that the Analyzed Industry is half the national average. The abbreviation 'na' is used to show that data are 'not available'. Ratios shown for 2002, the last complete census year.

LEADING COMPANIES   Number shown: 75   Total sales ($ mil): 115,407   Total employment (000): 420.8

Company Name	Address				CEO Name	Phone	Co. Type	Sales ($ mil)	Empl. (000)
Lockheed Martin Corp.	6801 Rockledge Dr.	Bethesda	MD	20817	Richard F. Ambrose	301-897-6000	P	41,862	140.0
Tyco International Ltd.	1 Tyco Park	Exeter	NH	03833	Edward D. Breen	441-292-8674	P	18,800	118.0
API Group Inc.	2366 Rose Pl.	St. Paul	MN	55113	Lee R. Anderson Sr.	651-636-4320	R	9,000	5.0
Rockwell Collins Inc.	400 Collins Rd. NE	Cedar Rapids	IA	52498		319-295-1000	P	4,415	19.5
Harris Corp.	1025 W NASA	Melbourne	FL	32919		321-727-9100	P	4,243	16.0
Diebold Inc.	PO Box 3077	North Canton	OH	44720		330-490-4000	P	2,906	15.5
Juniper Networks Inc.	1194 N Mathilda	Sunnyvale	CA	94089		408-745-2000	P	2,836	5.9
Hubbell Inc.	584 Derby Milford	Orange	CT	06477		203-799-4100	P	2,534	11.5
UTStarcom Inc.	1275 Harbor Bay	Alameda	CA	94502		510-864-8800	P	2,466	5.1
PerkinElmer Inc.	940 Winter St.	Waltham	MA	02451	Robert F. Friel	781-663-6900	P	1,787	8.7
Teledyne Technologies Inc.	1049 Dos Rios	Thousand Oaks	CA	91360		805-373-4545	P	1,622	8.1
NES Traffic Safety L.P.	12225 Disk Dr.	Romeoville	IL	60446	Andrew P. Studdert	815-372-2300	S	1,593*	2.5
Stenograph L.L.C.	1500 Bishop Ct.	Mount Prospect	IL	60056		847-803-1400	R	1,560*	0.2
3Com Corp.	350 Campus Dr.	Marlborough	MA	01752	Eric A. Benhamou	508-323-5000	P	1,268	6.3
General Dynamics Network Sys.	77 A Street	Needham	MA	02494	Nicholas Chabraja	781-449-2000	S	1,237*	7.0
Sensormatic del Caribe Inc.	Cortec Bldg., 104	Guayanabo	PR	00968	Ronald Assaf	787-783-7373	R	1,123*	1.5
ARRIS Group Inc.	3871 Lakefield Dr.	Suwanee	GA	30024		678-473-8400	P	992	0.6
Hughes Network Systems Inc.	11717 Exploratn Ln.	Germantown	MD	20876	Pradman P. Kaul	301-428-5500	S	975*	1.5
Checkpoint Systems Inc.	101 Wolf Dr.	Thorofare	NJ	08086		856-848-1800	P	834	3.9
CIENA Corp.	1201 Winterson Rd.	Linthicum	MD	21090		410-694-5700	P	780	1.8
Comverse Inc.	100 Quannapowitt	Wakefield	MA	01880	Andre Dahan	781-224-8888	S	767*	5.0
GE Security Inc.	8985 Town Ctr Pky.	Bradenton	FL	34202	Dean Seavers		S	640*	3.3
Siemens Building Technologies	1000 Deerfield Pkwy	Buffalo Grove	IL	60089	Daryl Dulaney	847-215-1000	S	583*	1.2
Stratus Technologies Inc.	111 Powdermill Rd.	Maynard	MA	01754	Stephen Kiely	978-461-7000	R	569*	2.3
ViaSat Inc.	6155 El Cam Real	Carlsbad	CA	92009		760-476-2200	P	517	1.5
IPC Systems Holdings Corp.	1500 Plaza Ten	Jersey City	NJ	07311	Lance B. Boxer	201-253-2000	R	485	1.4
Dolby Laboratories Inc.	100 Potrero Ave.	San Francisco	CA	94103		415-558-0200	P	482	1.0
Union Switch and Signal Inc.	1000 Technology	Pittsburgh	PA	15219	Ken Burk	412-688-2400	S	436*	0.5
Tekelec	5200 Paramount	Morrisville	NC	27560	Mark Floyd	919-460-5500	P	432	1.4
Finisar Corp.	1389 Moffett Prk Dr	Sunnyvale	CA	94089		408-548-1000	P	418	3.9
Pace Micro Technology	3701 FAU Blvd.	Boca Raton	FL	33431	John Dyson	561-995-6000	S	351*	0.6
Picolight Inc.	1480 Arthur Ave.	Louisville	CO	80027	Steve Hane	303-530-3189	R	346	0.1
Silicon Laboratories Inc.	400 W Cesar Chavez	Austin	TX	78701		512-416-8500	P	338	0.6
Alps Electric	30 Las Colinas Ln.	San Jose	CA	95119	Toru Usami	408-361-6400	R	328*	0.6
Telex Communications Inc.	12000 Portland Ave.	Burnsville	MN	55337	R V. Malpocher	952-884-4051	R	308*	3.0
ATX Technologies Inc.	8550 Freeport Pky.	Irving	TX	75063	Steve Millstein	972-753-6200	R	294*	0.4
Behavior Tech Computer (BTC)	4180 Business Ctr.	Fremont	CA	94538		510-657-3956	R	290*	0.6
Sentry Products Inc.	2225 Martin Ave.	Santa Clara	CA	95050	Ken Bays	408-727-1866	R	270	<0.1
EDO Reconnaissance/Surveillan.	18705 Madrone Pky.	Morgan Hill	CA	95037	James Smith	408-201-8000	S	267*	0.3
Sarnoff Corp.	201 Washington Rd.	Princeton	NJ	08540	Don Newsome	609-734-2000	R	230*	0.5
Raritan Computer Inc.	400 Cottontail Ln.	Somerset	NJ	08873		732-764-8886	R	227*	0.2
LoJack Corp.	200 Lowder Brook	Westwood	MA	02090	Joseph Abely	781-251-4700	P	223	0.9
Innovation Products Inc.	3381 Chicago Ave.	Riverside	CA	92507	Albert Johnson	951-682-8506	R	221*	0.3
Teledyne Brown Engineering	300 Sparkman NW	Huntsville	AL	35805	Rex D. Geveden	256-726-5555	S	187*	2.0
PECO II Global Services Inc.	PO Box 910	Galion	OH	44833	John Heindel	419-468-7600	S	184*	0.3
Applied Signal Technology Inc.	400 W California	Sunnyvale	CA	94086	Gary L. Yancey	408-749-1888	P	170	0.5
Norment Security Group	3224 Mobile Hwy.	Montgomery	AL	36108		334-281-8440	S	158*	0.7
Telephonics Inc.	815 Broad Hollow	Farmingdale	NY	11735	Joseph Battaglia	631-755-7000	S	154*	1.1
RedBack Networks Inc.	100 Headquarters Dr	San Jose	CA	95134		408-750-5000	S	153	0.5
Curbell Inc.	7 Cobham Dr.	Orchard Park	NY	14127	Shuhartha Ghose	716-667-3377	R	153*	<0.1
SpectraLink Corp.	5755 Central Ave.	Boulder	CO	80301	Bob Nugent	303-440-5330	S	145	0.4
NewTek Partners	5131 Beckwith Blvd.	San Antonio	TX	78249	Jim Plant	210-370-8000	R	140*	0.4
Electronic Warfare Associates	13873 Park Ctr. Rd.	Herndon	VA	20171	Doug Armstrong	703-904-5700	R	129*	1.0
Net Optics Inc.	1130 Mtn Vw Alvis	Sunnyvale	CA	94089	Eldad Matityahu	408-737-7777	R	122*	<0.1
Applied Digital Solutions Inc.	1690 S Congress	Delray Beach	FL	33445	Michael Krawitz	561-805-8000	P	118	0.4
Novar Controls Corp.	6060 Rockside Wds	Cleveland	OH	44131	Dean Lindstorm		R	113*	0.1
Titan Global Holdings Inc.	407 Intl. Pkwy.	Richardson	TX	75081	David Marks	972-470-9100	P	111	0.2
Channell Commercial Corp.	PO Box 9022	Temecula	CA	92591	W. H. Channell Jr.	951-719-2600	P	109	0.6
NetLogic Microsystems Inc.	1875 Charleston Rd.	Mountain View	CA	94043	Ron Jankov	650-961-6676	P	109	0.1
Adaptive Optics Associates	10 Wilson Rd.	Cambridge	MA	02138	Jeffrey Yorsz	617-806-1400	S	107*	0.2
Ansul Inc.	One Stanton St.	Marinette	WI	54143		715-735-7411	S	101*	0.7
Sypris Electronics L.L.C.	10901 N McKinley	Tampa	FL	33612	Bob Sanders	813-972-6000	S	100*	0.7
ICx Technologies Inc.	2100 Crystal Dr.	Arlington	VA	22202	Hans C. Kobler	703-678-2111	P	90	0.8
Interstate Electronics Corp.	PO Box 3117	Anaheim	CA	92803	Robert Huffman	714-758-0500	S	90*	0.6
Cornet Technology Inc.	6800 Versar Ctr.	Springfield	VA	22151	Natarajan Kumar	703-658-3400	R	82*	0.1
Adesta Communications Inc.	1200 Landmark Ctr.	Omaha	NE	68102	Bob Sommerfeld	402-233-7700	R	78*	0.2
3M Touch Systems	300 Griffin Brook	Methuen	MA	01844	George Buckley	978-659-9000	S	77*	0.1
Zenith Electronics	2000 Millbrook Dr.	Lincolnshire	IL	60069	Michael Ahn	847-941-8000	R	74*	0.2
Clover Systems	26241 Enterprise Ct	Lake Forest	CA	92630	Gordon Rudd	949-598-0800	R	74*	0.1
technotrans america Inc.	2181 S Foster Ave.	Wheeling	IL	60090	Heinz Harling	847-259-3330	R	74*	0.1
Union Metal Corp.	PO Box 9920	Canton	OH	44711	Darryl Dillenback	330-456-7653	R	74*	0.4
Vicon Industries Inc.	89 Arkay Dr.	Hauppauge	NY	11788	Kenneth M. Darby	631-952-2288	P	69	0.2
Microboards Technology L.L.C.	PO Box 846	Chanhassen	MN	55317	Mitch Akman	952-556-1600	R	69*	0.1
Aurora Networks	2803 Mission Clg.	Santa Clara	CA	95054		408-235-7000	R	69	<0.1
Numerex Corp.	1600 Parkwood Cir.	Atlanta	GA	30339		770-693-5950	P	68	0.1

Source: Ward's Business Directory of U.S. Private and Public Companies, Volumes 1 and 2, 2008. The company type code used is as follows: P - Public, R - Private, S - Subsidiary, D - Division, J - Joint Venture, A - Affiliate, G - Group. Sales are in millions of dollars, employees are in thousands. An asterisk (*) indicates an estimated sales volume. The symbol < stands for 'less than'. Company names and addresses are truncated, in some cases, to fit into the available space.

MATERIALS CONSUMED

Material	Quantity	Delivered Cost ($ million)
Printed ciruit boards (without inserted components) for electronic circuitry	(X)	71.8
Printed circuit assemblies, loaded boards, and modules	(X)	47.9
Semiconductors (incl. transistors, diodes, rectifiers, and integrated circuits), for electronic circuitry	(X)	59.9
Capacitors for electronic circuitry	(X)	24.8
Resistors for electronic circuitry	(X)	12.8
All other miscellaneous components and accessories for electronic circuitry (exc. tubes)	(X)	42.2
Electronic communication equipment	(X)	91.1
Electrical instrument mechanisms and meter movements	(X)	13.9
Electronic computer equipment	(X)	13.5
Purchased peripheral storage devices	(X)	0.2
Current-carrying wiring devices	(X)	2.4
Insulated wire and cable (including magnet wire)	(X)	12.2
Loudspeakers, microphones, and tuners (all types)	(X)	13.3
Fractional horsepower electric motors (less than 1 hp)	(X)	(D)
Plastics resins consumed in the form of granules, pellets, etc.	(X)	4.2
Fabricated plastics products (exc. gaskets, hoses, and belting)	(X)	21.7
Sheet metal products (excluding stampings)	(X)	21.6
Metal stampings	(X)	5.4
Metal bolts, nuts, screws, and other screw machine products	(X)	10.7
Other fabricated metal products (excluding forgings)	(X)	14.4
Forgings	(X)	(D)
Castings, rough and semifinished	(X)	20.2
Steel shapes and forms (exc. castings, forgings, fabr. metal products)	(X)	8.0
Aluminum and aluminum-base alloy shapes and forms (exc. castings, forgings, fabr. metal products)	(X)	9.9
Other nonferrous shapes and forms (exc. castings, forgings, fabricated metal products)	(X)	0.5
Paper and paperboard containers (incl. shipping sacks and other paper packaging supplies)	(X)	13.4
All other materials, components, parts, containers, and supplies	(X)	789.0
Materials, ingredients, containers, and supplies, nsk	(X)	603.4

Source: 2002 *Economic Census*. Explanation of symbols used: (D): Withheld to avoid disclosure of competitive data; na: Not available; (S): Withheld because statistical norms were not met; (X): Not applicable; (Z): Less than half the unit shown; nec: Not elsewhere classified; nsk: Not specified by kind; - : zero; p : 10-19 percent estimated; q : 20-29 percent estimated.

PRODUCT SHARE DETAILS

Product or Product Class Shipments	Mil. $	Product or Product Class Shipments	Mil. $
ALARM SYSTEMS, TRAFFIC CONTROL EQUIPMENT, AND INTERCOMMUNICATION AND PAGING SYSTEMS	4,876.2	**railway signals and attachments**	**895.9**
Alarm systems, including electric sirens and horns	**2,981.5**	**Intercommunications systems, including inductive paging systems (selective paging), except telephone and telegraph**	**305.5**
Vehicular and pedestrian traffic control equipment, electric		**Other communications equipment, nsk, total**	**693.3**

Source: 2002 *Economic Census*. The values are product shipments in millions of dollars for 2002. Total product shipments may be lower or higher than industry shipments. See Introduction for a full discussion. Values of indented subcategories are summed in the main heading(s). The symbol (D) appears when data are withheld to prevent disclosure of competitive information. The abbreviation nsk stands for 'not specified by kind' and nec for 'not elsewhere classified'. A dash (-) means zero.

INPUTS AND OUTPUTS FOR OTHER COMMUNICATIONS EQUIPMENT MANUFACTURING

Economic Sector or Industry Providing Inputs	%	Sector	Economic Sector or Industry Buying Outputs	%	Sector
Compensation of employees	27.7		Private fixed investment	13.9	
Software publishers	12.1	Services	Nonresidential structures, nec	11.7	Construct.
Management of companies & enterprises	10.6	Services	Telecommunications	9.3	Services
Wholesale trade	6.3	Trade	Management of companies & enterprises	8.2	Services
Scientific research & development services	3.0	Services	Residential structures, nec	8.2	Construct.
Plastics products, nec	2.7	Manufg.	Exports of goods & services	7.3	Cap Inv
Bare printed circuit boards	2.2	Manufg.	Residential permanent site structures	5.5	Construct.
Electronic components, nec	2.1	Manufg.	Investigation & security services	5.2	Services
Broadcast & wireless communications equipment	2.0	Manufg.	S/L govt. invest., other	2.9	S/L Govt
Printed circuit assemblies (electronic assembiles)	1.9	Manufg.	Maintenance/repair of nonresidential structures	2.6	Construct.
Semiconductors & related devices	1.9	Manufg.	Commercial & health care structures	2.5	Construct.
Turned products & screws, nuts, & bolts	1.6	Manufg.	Elementary & secondary schools	1.9	Services
Lessors of nonfinancial assets	1.5	Fin/R.E.	Rail transportation	1.6	Util.
Electronic capacitors, resistors, coils, transformers	1.1	Manufg.	Data processing, hosting, & related services	1.5	Services
Advertising & related services	1.1	Services	Nondepository credit intermediation activities	1.3	Fin/R.E.
Real estate	0.9	Fin/R.E.	Periodical publishers	1.3	Services
Taxes on production & imports, less subsidies	0.7		Owner-occupied dwellings	1.2	
Ornamental & architectural metal products	0.6	Manufg.	General Federal government services, defense	0.9	Fed Govt
Power generation & supply	0.6	Util.	Securities, commodity contracts, investments	0.8	Fin/R.E.
Telecommunications	0.5	Services	Book publishers	0.8	Services
Paperboard containers	0.4	Manufg.	Directories, mailing lists, & other publishers	0.7	Services
Electricity & signal testing instruments	0.4	Manufg.	Change in private inventories	0.6	In House
Audio & video equipment	0.4	Manufg.	Retail trade	0.6	Trade
Truck transportation	0.4	Util.	Physician, dentist, other health practitioner offices	0.5	Services
Noncomparable imports	0.4	Foreign	Cable & other subscription programming	0.5	Services

Continued on next page.

INPUTS AND OUTPUTS FOR OTHER COMMUNICATIONS EQUIPMENT MANUFACTURING - Continued

Economic Sector or Industry Providing Inputs	%	Sector	Economic Sector or Industry Buying Outputs	%	Sector
Legal services	0.4	Services	Federal government, investment, national defense	0.5	Fed Govt
Machine shops	0.4	Manufg.	Personal consumption expenditures	0.5	
Iron & steel mills & ferroalloys	0.4	Manufg.	Internet service providers & web search portals	0.5	Services
Ferrous metal foundries	0.3	Manufg.	Sound recording industries	0.4	Services
Management, scientific, & technical consulting	0.3	Services	Truck transportation	0.3	Util.
Alumina refining & primary aluminum production	0.3	Manufg.	Legal services	0.3	Services
Warehousing & storage	0.3	Util.	Automotive equipment rental & leasing	0.3	Fin/R.E.
Nonferrous metal foundries	0.3	Manufg.	Employment services	0.3	Services
Custom computer programming services	0.3	Services	Food services & drinking places	0.3	Services
Computer terminals & peripherals	0.3	Manufg.	Funds, trusts, & other financial vehicles	0.3	Fin/R.E.
Plastics packaging materials, film & sheet	0.3	Manufg.	Federal government, investment, nondefense	0.3	Fed Govt
Securities, commodity contracts, investments	0.3	Fin/R.E.	Real estate	0.2	Fin/R.E.
Automotive equipment rental & leasing	0.2	Fin/R.E.	Civic, social, & professional organizations	0.2	Services
Accounting, tax preparation, bookkeeping, & payroll	0.2	Services	Management, scientific, & technical consulting	0.2	Services
Copper rolling, drawing, extruding, & alloying	0.2	Manufg.	Scientific research & development services	0.2	Services
Crowns & closures & metal stamping	0.2	Manufg.	Accounting, tax preparation, bookkeeping, & payroll	0.2	Services
Coating, engraving, heat treating & allied activities	0.2	Manufg.	Maintenance/repair of residential structures	0.2	Construct.
Retail trade	0.2	Trade	Architectural, engineering, & related services	0.2	Services
Data processing, hosting, & related services	0.2	Services	Hotels & motels, including casino hotels	0.1	Services
Architectural, engineering, & related services	0.2	Services	Internet publishing & broadcasting	0.1	Services
Metal & other household furniture	0.2	Manufg.	Services to buildings & dwellings	0.1	Services
Employment services	0.2	Services	Grantmaking, giving, & social advocacy organizations	0.1	Services
Cutting tools & machine tool accessories	0.2	Manufg.	Religious organizations	0.1	Services
Business support services	0.2	Services	Amusement & recreation, nec	0.1	Services
Specialized design services	0.2	Services	Computer system design services	0.1	Services
Food services & drinking places	0.2	Services	Business support services	0.1	Services
Motor vehicle parts	0.2	Manufg.			
Monetary authorities/depository credit intermediation	0.2	Fin/R.E.			
Natural gas distribution	0.2	Util.			
Metal cans, boxes, & other containers (light gauge)	0.2	Manufg.			
Hotels & motels, including casino hotels	0.2	Services			
Other computer related services, including facilities	0.2	Services			
Communication & energy wires & cables	0.2	Manufg.			
Paperboard mills	0.2	Manufg.			
Relay & industrial controls	0.1	Manufg.			
Chemical products & preparations, nec	0.1	Manufg.			
Air transportation	0.1	Util.			
Plastics materials & resins	0.1	Manufg.			
Aluminum products from purchased aluminum	0.1	Manufg.			
Commercial & industrial machinery rental & leasing	0.1	Fin/R.E.			
Services to buildings & dwellings	0.1	Services			
Maintenance/repair of nonresidential structures	0.1	Construct.			
Professional, scientific, technical services, nec	0.1	Services			

Source: Benchmark Input-Output Accounts for the U.S. Economy, 2002, U.S. Department of Commerce, Washington, D.C., January 2008. The abbreviation nec stands for 'not elsewhere classified'.

OCCUPATIONS EMPLOYED BY COMMUNICATIONS EQUIPMENT MANUFACTURING

Occupation	% of Total 2006	Change to 2016	Occupation	% of Total 2006	Change to 2016
Electrical & electronic equipment assemblers	9.6	-19.4	General & operations managers	1.6	-9.3
Team assemblers	5.3	0.8	Purchasing agents, exc wholesale, retail, & farm	1.6	0.8
Computer software engineers, systems software	3.9	10.9	Electromechanical equipment assemblers	1.5	0.8
Electrical & electronic engineering technicians	3.8	0.8	Executive secretaries & administrative assistants	1.4	0.8
Computer software engineers, applications	3.4	21.0	Shipping, receiving, & traffic clerks	1.4	-3.0
Electronics engineers, exc computer	3.2	0.8	Accountants & auditors	1.3	0.8
Electrical engineers	2.9	0.8	Mechanical engineers	1.2	0.8
Industrial engineers	2.5	22.4	Electrical & electronics repairers, commercial/industry	1.1	7.4
First-line supervisors/managers of production workers	2.4	0.8	Production, planning, & expediting clerks	1.1	0.8
Computer hardware engineers	2.3	10.9	Sales engineers	1.1	0.8
Engineering managers	2.3	0.8	Marketing managers	1.1	0.8
Inspectors, testers, sorters, samplers, & weighers	2.0	-5.0	Computer support specialists	1.1	0.8
Customer service representatives	1.8	10.9	Bookkeeping, accounting, & auditing clerks	1.0	0.8
Sales representatives, wholesale & manufacturing, tech	1.8	0.8	Aerospace engineers	1.0	5.8
Sales reps, wholesale & manufacturing, exc tech	1.7	0.8			

Source: Industry-Occupation Matrix, Bureau of Labor Statistics, December 4, 2007. These data are reported based on 4-digit NAICS categories but have been matched to corresponding 6-digit NAICS industry codes. The change reported for each occupation to the year 2016 is a percent of growth or decline as estimated by the Bureau of Labor Statistics. The abbreviation nec stands for 'not elsewhere classified'.

1225

LOCATION BY STATE AND REGIONAL CONCENTRATION

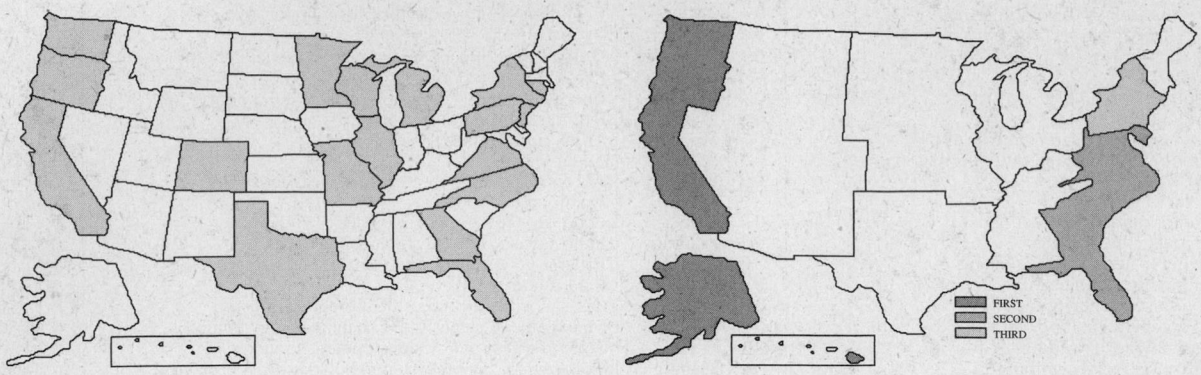

INDUSTRY DATA BY STATE

State	Establish-ments	Shipments			Employment				Cost as % of Shipments	Investment per Employee ($)
		Total ($ mil)	% of U.S.	Per Establ.	Total Number	% of U.S.	Per Establ.	Wages ($/hour)		
California	84	812.8	14.7	9,675.6	3,360	13.1	40	15.14	45.7	3,179
New York	31	671.5	12.1	21,660.9	2,918	11.4	94	16.11	43.6	4,109
Illinois	24	346.0	6.3	14,418.7	2,331	9.1	97	16.12	42.7	2,277
Connecticut	10	322.8	5.8	32,275.2	880	3.4	88	13.16	38.4	4,917
Missouri	11	279.6	5.1	25,421.1	1,721	6.7	156	13.71	45.1	3,891
Florida	39	225.9	4.1	5,791.7	1,582	6.2	41	15.88	42.2	4,623
Minnesota	8	213.9	3.9	26,734.4	830	3.2	104	15.38	38.0	2,563
Texas	35	179.4	3.2	5,126.9	1,166	4.5	33	11.85	49.2	1,984
New Jersey	22	158.3	2.9	7,194.1	635	2.5	29	13.94	28.1	3,613
Oregon	13	141.6	2.6	10,889.2	664	2.6	51	15.28	48.7	2,828
Michigan	15	103.0	1.9	6,863.9	589	2.3	39	20.11	46.1	2,613
North Carolina	13	94.7	1.7	7,282.5	404	1.6	31	10.79	36.4	1,020
Pennsylvania	16	89.5	1.6	5,593.7	555	2.2	35	18.73	45.8	1,404
Colorado	15	78.1	1.4	5,203.5	336	1.3	22	14.87	43.9	33,202
Virginia	14	70.9	1.3	5,067.4	367	1.4	26	13.70	52.2	1,913
Georgia	10	55.7	1.0	5,566.6	270	1.1	27	15.09	44.9	2,993
Washington	16	41.5	0.8	2,596.2	273	1.1	17	19.26	36.1	2,172
Wisconsin	13	17.3	0.3	1,332.2	143	0.6	11	14.40	34.9	5,783

Source: 2002 *Economic Census*. The states are in descending order of shipments or establishments (if shipment data are missing for the majority). The symbol (D) appears when data are withheld to prevent disclosure of competitive information. States marked with (D) are sorted by number of establishments. A dash (-) indicates that the data element cannot be calculated. Data may not show all states active in the NAICS category. All data available at the time of publication are shown.

NAICS 334310 - AUDIO AND VIDEO EQUIPMENT MANUFACTURING

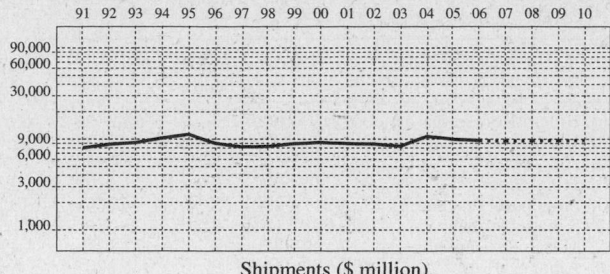

Shipments ($ million)

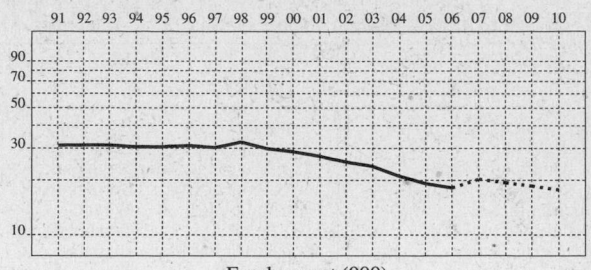

Employment (000)

GENERAL STATISTICS

Year	Com-panies	Establishments		Employment			Compensation		Production ($ million)			
		Total	with 20 or more employees	Total (000)	Production Workers (000)	Hours (Mil)	Payroll ($ mil)	Wages ($/hr)	Cost of Materials	Value Added by Manufacture	Value of Shipments	Capital Invest.
1991		401	170	31.1	21.7	41.9	732.4	9.36	5,893.8	2,122.4	7,993.6	277.5
1992	400	427	163	31.2	22.3	44.3	736.6	9.52	6,444.2	2,280.1	8,769.3	252.9
1993		439	164	31.2	22.6	45.0	774.8	9.60	6,596.7	2,567.4	9,159.3	211.5
1994		454	164	30.5	23.3	46.6	798.2	9.64	7,617.4	2,756.3	10,285.6	225.8
1995		477	167	30.5	22.5	43.7	847.1	10.38	9,208.9	2,343.0	11,278.0	270.3
1996		537	173	31.0	23.3	43.4	839.9	10.17	6,769.9	2,028.9	8,988.1	276.0
1997	524	554	195	30.2	20.7	40.3	936.9	11.74	5,816.7	2,371.3	8,214.8	207.9
1998		572	194	32.4	23.0	43.8	958.7	11.74	5,588.5	2,663.0	8,326.5	167.1
1999		539	173	29.8	20.3	37.7	990.8	12.73	6,152.9	2,855.0	8,927.2	174.8
2000		560	185	28.7	19.0	36.4	975.3	12.36	6,113.0	3,221.2	9,178.5	188.0
2001		561	184	27.1	17.6	34.5	963.0	12.27	5,638.5	3,143.0	8,941.5	256.4
2002	546	571	165	25.2	15.5	30.2	950.9	12.98	5,397.1	3,422.1	8,823.5	145.6
2003		568	168	23.9	14.6	28.9	936.6	13.18	4,818.8	3,529.2	8,361.7	131.0
2004		546	162	21.1	12.4	25.7	911.1	14.05	7,387.6	3,414.1	10,718.4	173.6
2005		518	145	19.2	11.1	22.6	849.7	14.79	6,878.3	3,084.5	9,969.3	117.5
2006		599P	169P	18.2	10.8	21.6	839.3	16.20	6,324.4	3,293.2	9,633.0	143.7
2007		609P	168P	20.3P	11.5P	22.7P	968.9P	15.46P	6,269.5P	3,264.6P	9,549.3P	125.5P
2008		620P	168P	19.4P	10.6P	21.1P	979.7P	15.88P	6,294.7P	3,277.7P	9,587.7P	116.6P
2009		630P	167P	18.6P	9.8P	19.4P	990.4P	16.30P	6,319.9P	3,290.8P	9,626.1P	107.6P
2010		641P	167P	17.7P	8.9P	17.8P	1,001.2P	16.71P	6,345.1P	3,304.0P	9,664.5P	98.7P

Sources: 1992, 1997, 2002 Economic Census; other years, up to 2006, are from the Annual Survey of Manufactures. Establishment counts for non-Census years are from County Business Patterns; 1997 and 2002 values are from the 1997 and 2002 censuses respectively, reported in the Federal Government's NAICS format. Other years were originally reported in equivalent SIC format. 'P's show projections by the editors.

INDICES OF CHANGE

Year	Com-panies	Establishments		Employment			Compensation		Production ($ million)			
		Total	with 20 or more employees	Total (000)	Production Workers (000)	Hours (Mil)	Payroll ($ mil)	Wages ($/hr)	Cost of Materials	Value Added by Manufacture	Value of Shipments	Capital Invest.
1992	73	75	99	124	144	147	77	73	119	67	99	174
1997	96	97	118	120	134	133	99	90	108	69	93	143
2001		98	112	108	114	114	101	95	104	92	101	176
2002	100	100	100	100	100	100	100	100	100	100	100	100
2003		99	102	95	94	96	98	102	89	103	95	90
2004		96	98	84	80	85	96	108	137	100	121	119
2005		91	88	76	72	75	89	114	127	90	113	81
2006		105P	102P	72	70	72	88	125	117	96	109	99
2007		107P	102P	81P	74P	75P	102P	119P	116P	95P	108P	86P
2008		108P	102P	77P	68P	70P	103P	122P	117P	96P	109P	80P
2009		110P	101P	74P	63P	64P	104P	126P	117P	96P	109P	74P
2010		112P	101P	70P	57P	59P	105P	129P	118P	97P	110P	68P

Sources: Same as General Statistics. Values reflect change from the base year, 2002. Values above 100 mean greater than 2002, values below 100 mean less than 2002, and the values of 100 in other years means the same as 2002. 'P's show projections by the editors.

SELECTED RATIOS

For 2002	Avg. of All Manufact.	Analyzed Industry	Index	For 2002	Avg. of All Manufact.	Analyzed Industry	Index
Employees per Establishment	42	44	105	Value Added per Production Worker	182,367	220,781	121
Payroll per Establishment	1,639,184	1,665,324	102	Cost per Establishment	5,769,015	9,452,014	164
Payroll per Employee	39,053	37,734	97	Cost per Employee	137,446	214,171	156
Production Workers per Establishment	30	27	92	Cost per Production Worker	195,506	348,200	178
Wages per Establishment	694,845	686,508	99	Shipments per Establishment	11,158,348	15,452,715	138
Wages per Production Worker	23,548	25,290	107	Shipments per Employee	265,847	350,139	132
Hours per Production Worker	1,980	1,948	98	Shipments per Production Worker	378,144	569,258	151
Wages per Hour	11.89	12.98	109	Investment per Establishment	361,338	254,991	71
Value Added per Establishment	5,381,325	5,993,170	111	Investment per Employee	8,609	5,778	67
Value Added per Employee	128,210	135,798	106	Investment per Production Worker	12,245	9,394	77

Sources: Same as General Statistics. The 'Average of All Manufacturing' column represents the average of all manufacturing industries reported for the most recent complete year available. The Index shows the relationship between the Average and the Analyzed Industry. For example, 100 means that they are equal; 500 that the Analyzed Industry is five times the average; 50 means that the Analyzed Industry is half the national average. The abbreviation 'na' is used to show that data are 'not available'. Ratios shown for 2002, the last complete census year.

LEADING COMPANIES   Number shown: 75   Total sales ($ mil): 109,692   Total employment (000): 240.8

Company Name	Address				CEO Name	Phone	Co. Type	Sales ($ mil)	Empl. (000)
Sony Electronics Inc.	1 Sony Dr.	Park Ridge	NJ	07656	Hideki Komiyama	201-930-1000	S	65,200*	163.0
Canon U.S.A. Inc.	1 Canon Plz.	Lake Success	NY	11042	Yoroku Adachi	516-328-5000	S	10,745*	11.0
Toshiba America Inc.	1251 Ave of the Am.	New York	NY	10020	Hideo Ito	212-596-0600	S	6,995	10.0
Pioneer Automotive Tech.	100 S Pioneer Blvd.	Springboro	OH	45066	Steve Moerner	937-746-6600	R	4,610*	0.3
JVC America Inc.	1700 Valley Rd.	Wayne	NJ	07470	Shigeharu Tsuchitani	973-317-5000	S	4,306*	0.3
Harman International Ind.	1101 Penn. Ave.	Washington	DC	20004	Sidney Harman	202-393-1101	P	3,551	11.7
Hitachi America Ltd.	2000 Sierra Pnt Pky	Brisbane	CA	94005	Masahide Tanigahi	650-589-8300	S	2,127*	4.4
Bose Corp.	The Mountain	Framingham	MA	01701	Amar G. Bose	508-879-7330	R	1,800	8.0
Sony Music Entertainment Inc.	550 Madison Ave.	New York	NY	10022	Mike Bebel	212-833-8000	S	1,500*	10.0
BD Biosciences	2350 Qume Dr.	San Jose	CA	95131	William Kozy			S	1,034	<0.1
Avid Technology Worldwide Inc.	Avid Technology	Tewksbury	MA	01876	David Krall	978-640-6789	S	698*	1.6
3M Precision Optics Inc.	4000 McMann Rd.	Cincinnati	OH	45245		513-752-7000	S	690*	1.3
JBL Professional Inc.	8400 Balboa Blvd.	Northridge	CA	91329	John Carpanini	818-894-8850	S	443*	1.8
Mitsubishi Electric Automotive	4773 Bethany Rd.	Mason	OH	45040	Takeo Sasaki	513-398-2220	R	434*	0.4
Rockford Sales.Com Inc.	546 S Rockford Dr.	Tempe	AZ	85281	Gary W. Suttle	480-967-3565	S	326*	0.7
Behavior Tech Computer (BTC)	4180 Business Ctr.	Fremont	CA	94538		510-657-3956	R	290*	0.6
Emerson Radio Corp.	PO Box 430	Parsippany	NJ	07054		973-884-5800	P	284	0.1
Universal Electronics Inc.	6101 Gateway Dr.	Cypress	CA	90630	Arling Arling	714-820-1000	P	273	0.4
TiVo Inc.	PO Box 2160	Alviso	CA	95002		408-519-9100	P	259	0.5
Sarnoff Corp.	201 Washington Rd.	Princeton	NJ	08540	Don Newsome	609-734-2000	S	230*	0.5
LOUD Technologies Inc.	16220 Wood-Red	Woodinville	WA	98072	Jamie Engen	425-892-6500	P	215	0.7
Crown International Inc.	1718 W Mishawaka	Elkhart	IN	46517	Blake Augsburger	574-294-8000	S	208*	0.7
JBL Consumer Products	8400 Balboa Blvd.	Northridge	CA	91329	John Carpanini	818-894-8850	S	202*	1.8
Fender Musical Instruments	8860 E Chaparral Rd	Scottsdale	AZ	85250		480-596-9690	R	196*	0.3
Altec Lansing Technologies	PO Box 277	Milford	PA	18337	Bob Garthwaite	570-296-4434	R	170*	1.5
Da-Lite Screen Company Inc.	PO Box 137	Warsaw	IN	46581	Richard E. Lundin	574-267-8101	R	170*	0.6
Hittite Microwave Corp.	20 Alpha Rd.	Chelmsford	MA	01824	Yalcin Ayasli	978-250-3343	P	156	0.3
Zondervan Corp.	5300 Patterson Ave.	Grand Rapids	MI	49530	Doug Lockhart	616-698-6900	S	133*	0.3
Harman Music Group Inc.	8760 Sandy Pky.	Sandy	UT	84070	Rob Urry	801-566-8800	D	127*	0.4
Alienware Corp.	14591 SW 120 St.	Miami	FL	33186	Alex Aguila	305-251-9797	S	111*	0.5
MPO Videotronics Inc.	5069 Maureen Ln.	Moorpark	CA	93021	Larry Kaiser	805-499-8513	R	98	0.2
Winegard Co.	3000 Kirkwood St.	Burlington	IA	52601		319-754-0600	R	96*	0.4
Rockford Corp.	600 S Rockford Dr.	Tempe	AZ	85281	Jerry E. Goldress	480-967-3565	P	89	0.2
3M Touch Systems	300 Griffin Brook	Methuen	MA	01844	George Buckley	978-659-9000	S	77*	0.1
Zenith Electronics	2000 Millbrook Dr.	Lincolnshire	IL	60069	Michael Ahn	847-941-8000	R	74*	0.2
Valcom Inc.	5614 Hollins Rd.	Roanoke	VA	24019	John Mason	540-563-2000	R	73*	0.2
TEAC America Inc. Data Storage	PO Box 750	Montebello	CA	90640	Koichiro Nakamura	323-726-0303	D	73*	0.3
Switchcraft Inc.	5555 N Elston Ave.	Chicago	IL	60630	Keith Bandolik	773-792-2700	R	64*	0.5
Immersive Media Co.	2407 SE 10th Ave.	Portland	OR	97214	Myles McGovern	503-231-2656	R	62*	<0.1
Eminence Speaker L.L.C.	PO Box 360	Eminence	KY	40019		502-845-5622	R	61*	0.2
Bretford Manufacturing Inc.	11000 Seymour Ave.	Schiller Park	IL	60131	Mikel Briggs	847-678-2545	R	61*	0.6
Toshiba America Consumer Prods	82 Totawa Rd.	Wayne	NJ	07470	Tadashi Okamura	973-628-8000	R	59*	0.1
SMM USA Inc.	4055 Calle Platino	Oceanside	CA	92056		760-941-4500	R	56*	0.2
Amplifier Research Corp.	160 Schoolhouse Rd.	Souderton	PA	18964	Donald Shepherd	215-723-8181	R	54*	0.1
Hitachi Kokusai Electric Amer.	PO Box 512408	Philadelphia	PA	19175	Masahiko Momose	516-921-7200	R	53*	<0.1
Cambridge SoundWorks Inc.	100 Brickstone Sq.	Andover	MA	01810		978-623-4400	S	52*	0.3
Digital Theater Systems Inc.	5171 Clareton Dr.	Agoura Hills	CA	91301	Jon Kirchner	818-706-3525	P	52	0.2
Lectrosonics Inc.	PO Box 15900	Rio Rancho	NM	87174	John Arasim	505-892-4501	R	51*	0.2
Russound Fmp Inc.	5 Forbes Rd. Ste. 1	Newmarket	NH	03857	Maureen Baldwin	603-659-5170	R	51*	0.2
Industrial Acoustics Company	1160 Commerce	Bronx	NY	10462	Micheal Mancuso	718-931-8000	R	48*	0.3
Harman Consumer Products	250 Crossways Park	Woodbury	NY	11797	Sidney Harman	516-496-3400	S	48*	0.2
Meyer Sound Laboratories Inc.	2832 San Pablo Ave.	Berkeley	CA	94702		510-486-1166	R	48*	0.1
Koss Corp.	4129 N Port Wash	Milwaukee	WI	53212	John C. Koss	414-964-5000	P	46	<0.1
Whelen Engineering Company	PO Box 1236	Charlestown	NH	03603	John Olson	860-526-9504	R	44*	0.3
Pacific Digital Corp.	17811 Mitchell N	Irvine	CA	92614	John Parsa	949-252-1111	R	43*	0.1
Credence Speakers Inc.	13075 Ogden Lndg	Kevil	KY	42053	Eugene Brandt	270-462-2161	R	43*	0.1
Line 6 Inc.	29901 Agoura Rd.	Agoura Hills	CA	91301	Mike Meunch	818-575-3600	R	40*	0.2
Micronas USA Inc.	2805 Mission Clg.	Santa Clara	CA	95054	Rainer Hoffmann	408-625-1200	R	39*	0.1
Mitek Corp.	704 30th St.	Monroe	WI	53566		608-328-5560	R	38*	0.1
Quam-Nichols Co.	234 E Marquette Rd.	Chicago	IL	60637	William Little	773-488-5800	R	37*	0.1
DivXNetworks Inc.	4780 Eastgate Mall	San Diego	CA	92121	Kevin Hall	858-882-0600	R	35*	0.2
Leitch Inc.	920 Corporate Ln.	Chesapeake	VA	23320	Timothy Thorsteinson	757-548-2300	S	35*	<0.1
Community Light and Sound Inc.	333 E 5th St.	Chester	PA	19013	Bruce Howze	610-876-3400	R	34*	0.1
Mesa Boogie Ltd.	1317 Ross St.	Petaluma	CA	94954	Randall Smith	707-778-6565	R	34*	0.1
SpeakerCraft Inc.	940 Columbia Ave.	Riverside	CA	92507	Jeremy Burkhardt	951-787-0543	R	34*	0.1
Whirlwind Music Distributors	99 Ling Rd.	Rochester	NY	14612	Michael Laiacona	585-663-8820	R	34*	0.1
Tech Products Corp.	2215 Lyons Rd.	Miamisburg	OH	45342	Dan Rork	937-438-1100	S	33*	<0.1
Phoenix Gold International	9300 N Decatur St.	Portland	OR	97203	Jonathan Cooley	503-286-9300	R	33*	0.2
Optical Gaging Products Inc.	850 Hudson Ave.	Rochester	NY	14621	Edward Polidor	585-544-0450	R	31*	0.2
HT Electronics Inc.	50 E Greg St., 112	Sparks	NV	89431		775-331-5401	R	31*	<0.1
Tierney Brothers Inc.	3300 University Ave	Minneapolis	MN	55414		612-331-5500	R	29*	<0.1
Biamp Systems Corp.	10074 SW Arctic Dr.	Beaverton	OR	97005	Graeme Harrison	503-641-7287	R	29*	<0.1
Nady Systems Inc.	6701 Shellmound St.	Emeryville	CA	94608	John Nady	510-652-2411	R	29*	<0.1
Phase Technology Corp.	6400 Youngerman	Jacksonville	FL	32244	Ken Hecht	904-777-0700	R	29*	<0.1
Snader and Associates Inc.	PO Box 8444	San Rafael	CA	94912	John Beritzhoff	415-257-8480	R	29*	<0.1

Source: Ward's Business Directory of U.S. Private and Public Companies, Volumes 1 and 2, 2008. The company type code used is as follows: P - Public, R - Private, S - Subsidiary, D - Division, J - Joint Venture, A - Affiliate, G - Group. Sales are in millions of dollars, employees are in thousands. An asterisk (*) indicates an estimated sales volume. The symbol < stands for 'less than'. Company names and addresses are truncated, in some cases, to fit into the available space.

MATERIALS CONSUMED

Material	Quantity	Delivered Cost ($ million)
Cabinets (wood, metal, and plastics)	(X)	221.0
Tuners	(X)	17.9
Speakers and speaker systems	(X)	283.9
Cathode ray picture tubes	(X)	997.5
Printed ciruit boards (without inserted components) for electronic circuitry	(X)	162.1
Printed circuit assemblies, loaded boards, and modules	(X)	376.4
Semiconductors (incl. transistors, diodes, rectifiers, and integrated circuits), for electronic circuitry	(X)	105.7
Capacitors for electronic circuitry	(X)	73.4
Resistors for electronic circuitry	(X)	15.6
All other miscellaneous components and accessories for electronic circuitry (exc. tubes)	(X)	254.3
Plastics products consumed in the form of sheets, rods, etc.	(X)	223.2
Paper and paperboard containers (incl. shipping sacks and other paper packaging supplies)	(X)	43.8
Current-carrying wiring devices	(X)	62.0
Metal stampings	(X)	13.8
Metal bolts, nuts, screws, and other screw machine products	(X)	14.8
All other fabricated metal products (excluding forgings)	(X)	36.8
Forgings	(X)	2.5
Castings, rough and semifinished	(X)	(D)
Steel shapes and forms (exc. castings, forgings, fabr. metal products)	(X)	4.5
Nonferrous shapes and forms	(X)	(D)
Insulated wire and cable (including magnet wire)	(X)	28.6
Liquid crystal display screens (LCD), including LED	(X)	33.6
All other materials, components, parts, containers, and supplies	(X)	408.6
Materials, ingredients, containers, and supplies, nsk	(X)	1,323.5

Source: 2002 *Economic Census*. Explanation of symbols used: (D): Withheld to avoid disclosure of competitive data; na: Not available; (S): Withheld because statistical norms were not met; (X): Not applicable; (Z): Less than half the unit shown; nec: Not elsewhere classified; nsk: Not specified by kind; - : zero; p : 10-19 percent estimated; q : 20-29 percent estimated.

PRODUCT SHARE DETAILS

Product or Product Class Shipments	Mil. $	Product or Product Class Shipments	Mil. $
AUDIO AND VIDEO EQUIPMENT	9,673.8	sold separately, and commercial sound equipment	1,769.5
Home, portable, and automobile radios and radio-phonograph-tape recorder-compact disc combinations	2,459.4	Other consumer audio and video equipment, including audio and video recorders and players (camcorders)	1,652.6
Television receivers, including combination models	3,391.1	Audio and video equipment, nsk, total	401.3
Speakers, including loudspeaker systems and loudspeakers			

Source: 2002 *Economic Census*. The values are product shipments in millions of dollars for 2002. Total product shipments may be lower or higher than industry shipments. See Introduction for a full discussion. Values of indented subcategories are summed in the main heading(s). The symbol (D) appears when data are withheld to prevent disclosure of competitive information. The abbreviation nsk stands for 'not specified by kind' and nec for 'not elsewhere classified'. A dash (-) means zero.

INPUTS AND OUTPUTS FOR AUDIO AND VIDEO EQUIPMENT MANUFACTURING

Economic Sector or Industry Providing Inputs	%	Sector	Economic Sector or Industry Buying Outputs	%	Sector
Compensation of employees	15.0		Personal consumption expenditures	76.8	
Electron tubes	12.2	Manufg.	Exports of goods & services	8.5	Cap Inv
Wholesale trade	8.8	Trade	Light truck & utility vehicles	3.5	Manufg.
Printed circuit assemblies (electronic assemblies)	5.7	Manufg.	Private fixed investment	3.0	
Custom computer programming services	5.4	Services	Automobiles	2.3	Manufg.
Management of companies & enterprises	5.4	Services	Change in private inventories	1.8	In House
Audio & video equipment	4.8	Manufg.	Retail trade	1.4	Trade
Electronic components, nec	3.9	Manufg.	Audio & video equipment	1.0	Manufg.
Plastics packaging materials, film & sheet	3.0	Manufg.	General S/L govt. services	0.4	S/L Govt
Office furnitures	3.0	Manufg.	Semiconductors & related devices	0.3	Manufg.
Plastics products, nec	2.4	Manufg.	Electronic components, nec	0.2	Manufg.
Bare printed circuit boards	2.4	Manufg.	Management of companies & enterprises	0.2	Services
Software publishers	1.9	Services			
Semiconductors & related devices	1.5	Manufg.			
Scientific research & development services	1.5	Services			
Electronic capacitors, resistors, coils, transformers	1.2	Manufg.			
Truck transportation	1.1	Util.			
Wiring devices	1.0	Manufg.			
Metal & other household furniture	0.8	Manufg.			
Advertising & related services	0.8	Services			
Noncomparable imports	0.7	Foreign			
Paperboard containers	0.7	Manufg.			
Real estate	0.6	Fin/R.E.			
Turned products & screws, nuts, & bolts	0.6	Manufg.			
Unlaminated plastics profile shapes	0.5	Manufg.			
Taxes on production & imports, less subsidies	0.4				
Power generation & supply	0.4	Util.			
Motor vehicle parts	0.4	Manufg.			
Crowns & closures & metal stamping	0.3	Manufg.			

Continued on next page.

INPUTS AND OUTPUTS FOR AUDIO AND VIDEO EQUIPMENT MANUFACTURING - Continued

Economic Sector or Industry Providing Inputs	%	Sector	Economic Sector or Industry Buying Outputs	%	Sector
Automotive equipment rental & leasing	0.3	Fin/R.E.			
Copper rolling, drawing, extruding, & alloying	0.3	Manufg.			
Legal services	0.2	Services			
Management, scientific, & technical consulting	0.2	Services			
Machine shops	0.2	Manufg.			
Communication & energy wires & cables	0.2	Manufg.			
Coating, engraving, heat treating & allied activities	0.2	Manufg.			
Warehousing & storage	0.2	Util.			
Laminated plastics plates, sheets, & shapes	0.2	Manufg.			
Commercial & industrial machinery rental & leasing	0.1	Fin/R.E.			
Relay & industrial controls	0.1	Manufg.			
Telecommunications	0.1	Services			
Custom roll forming	0.1	Manufg.			
Accounting, tax preparation, bookkeeping, & payroll	0.1	Services			
Employment services	0.1	Services			

Source: Benchmark Input-Output Accounts for the U.S. Economy, 2002, U.S. Department of Commerce, Washington, D.C., January 2008. The abbreviation nec stands for 'not elsewhere classified'.

OCCUPATIONS EMPLOYED BY AUDIO & VIDEO EQUIPMENT MANUFACTURING

Occupation	% of Total 2006	Change to 2016	Occupation	% of Total 2006	Change to 2016
Team assemblers	9.3	-19.1	Helpers--Production workers	1.6	-19.1
Assemblers & fabricators, nec	4.9	-27.2	General & operations managers	1.5	-27.2
Electrical engineers	3.1	-19.1	Computer-controlled machine tool operators	1.5	-11.0
Electronics engineers, exc computer	2.9	-19.1	Electronic home entertainment installers & repairers	1.4	-22.1
Inspectors, testers, sorters, samplers, & weighers	2.8	-23.7	Purchasing agents, exc wholesale, retail, & farm	1.3	-19.1
Electrical & electronic engineering technicians	2.7	-19.1	Computer systems analysts	1.3	-11.0
First-line supervisors/managers of production workers	2.6	-19.1	Sales reps, wholesale & manufacturing, exc tech	1.3	-19.1
Shipping, receiving, & traffic clerks	2.5	-22.1	Secretaries, exc legal, medical, & executive	1.3	-28.0
Mechanical engineers	2.2	-19.1	Bookkeeping, accounting, & auditing clerks	1.2	-19.1
Customer service representatives	2.0	-11.0	Accountants & auditors	1.0	-19.1
Sales representatives, wholesale & manufacturing, tech	1.8	-19.1	Computer software engineers, systems software	1.0	-11.0
Industrial engineers	1.7	-1.7			

Source: Industry-Occupation Matrix, Bureau of Labor Statistics, December 4, 2007. These data are reported based on 4-digit NAICS categories but have been matched to corresponding 6-digit NAICS industry codes. The change reported for each occupation to the year 2016 is a percent of growth or decline as estimated by the Bureau of Labor Statistics. The abbreviation nec stands for 'not elsewhere classified'.

LOCATION BY STATE AND REGIONAL CONCENTRATION

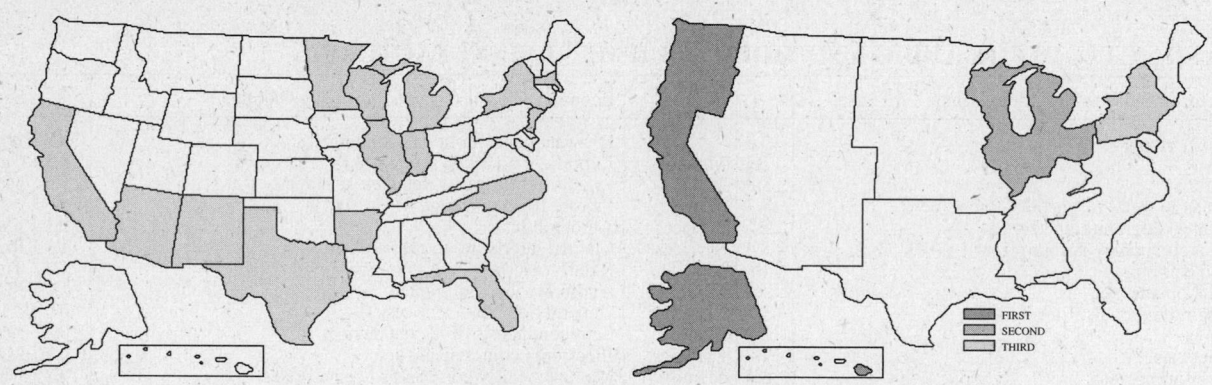

FIRST
SECOND
THIRD

INDUSTRY DATA BY STATE

State	Establish-ments	Shipments			Employment				Cost as % of Shipments	Investment per Employee ($)
		Total ($ mil)	% of U.S.	Per Establ.	Total Number	% of U.S.	Per Establ.	Wages ($/hour)		
California	157	964.9	10.9	6,145.9	5,251	20.8	33	12.46	44.6	4,355
Arkansas	7	591.9	6.7	84,561.9	1,432	5.7	205	11.14	77.7	4,766
Illinois	24	563.2	6.4	23,465.8	1,518	6.0	63	13.49	66.3	4,969

Continued on next page.

INDUSTRY DATA BY STATE - Continued

| State | Establish-ments | Shipments | | | Employment | | | | Cost as % of Shipments | Investment per Employee ($) |
		Total ($ mil)	% of U.S.	Per Establ.	Total Number	% of U.S.	Per Establ.	Wages ($/hour)		
Indiana	15	492.7	5.6	32,846.0	1,276	5.1	85	10.80	61.8	11,681
Massachusetts	18	367.2	4.2	20,401.8	924	3.7	51	13.22	32.1	5,504
Michigan	14	231.2	2.6	16,513.1	829	3.3	59	15.87	53.0	1,930
Florida	30	173.0	2.0	5,767.7	684	2.7	23	11.86	40.3	2,554
Arizona	13	118.3	1.3	9,098.0	285	1.1	22	10.87	28.0	1,874
New York	34	91.5	1.0	2,692.6	623	2.5	18	12.58	60.3	2,047
Texas	23	65.7	0.7	2,857.1	440	1.7	19	12.27	64.2	2,114
Wisconsin	11	58.4	0.7	5,311.4	327	1.3	30	8.11	40.4	3,924
Minnesota	12	48.1	0.5	4,010.3	364	1.4	30	10.93	66.6	6,357
New Jersey	14	34.8	0.4	2,484.2	212	0.8	15	12.38	61.0	1,632
North Carolina	13	32.1	0.4	2,465.5	196	0.8	15	11.94	57.3	3,434
New Mexico	6	29.5	0.3	4,921.2	173	0.7	29	15.36	40.4	1,688

Source: 2002 *Economic Census*. The states are in descending order of shipments or establishments (if shipment data are missing for the majority). The symbol (D) appears when data are withheld to prevent disclosure of competitive information. States marked with (D) are sorted by number of establishments. A dash (-) indicates that the data element cannot be calculated. Data may not show all states active in the NAICS category. All data available at the time of publication are shown.

NAICS 334411 - ELECTRON TUBE MANUFACTURING

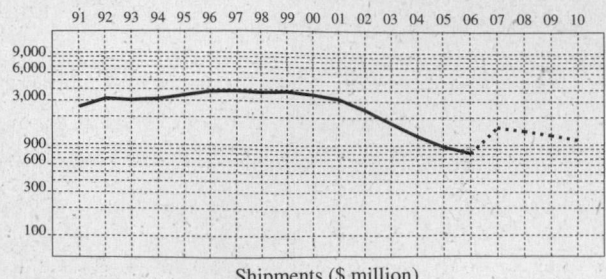

Shipments ($ million)

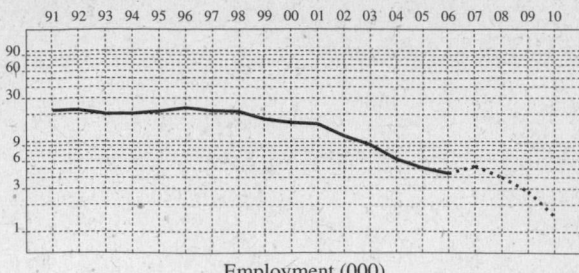

Employment (000)

GENERAL STATISTICS

| Year | Companies | Establishments | | Employment | | | Compensation | | Production ($ million) | | | |
		Total	with 20 or more employees	Total (000)	Production Workers (000)	Hours (Mil)	Payroll ($ mil)	Wages ($/hr)	Cost of Materials	Value Added by Manufacture	Value of Shipments	Capital Invest.
1991		185	100	22.1	16.3	32.2	630.3	12.90	1,454.6	1,131.0	2,568.3	77.3
1992	174	189	69	22.2	16.8	33.5	677.4	13.21	1,883.6	1,280.4	3,144.9	61.7
1993		195	73	20.2	15.3	30.9	628.9	13.73	1,912.9	1,135.8	3,051.5	85.5
1994		188	71	20.4	15.8	31.7	629.8	13.25	1,798.6	1,357.3	3,148.1	132.3
1995		175	71	21.5	16.6	33.3	663.6	13.10	1,987.8	1,472.9	3,447.7	141.6
1996		173	75	23.3	17.9	35.1	727.9	12.95	2,194.0	1,620.4	3,778.7	181.4
1997	148	158	58	21.7	16.7	34.1	730.1	14.32	2,297.6	1,580.7	3,825.1	159.6
1998		151	63	21.4	16.7	34.2	736.8	14.44	2,094.0	1,619.4	3,730.0	121.7
1999		151	60	17.6	13.6	28.3	663.3	15.86	2,089.4	1,758.0	3,821.7	104.8
2000		150	61	16.2	12.7	26.8	633.3	16.17	2,214.5	1,362.1	3,560.2	84.6
2001		147	62	15.6	12.3	24.5	633.0	18.05	1,878.3	1,180.6	3,199.4	162.0
2002	92	102	39	11.5	8.9	18.8	486.5	18.00	1,500.7	919.4	2,445.1	41.0
2003		103	37	9.2	6.9	13.4	381.2	19.50	988.2	769.8	1,757.0	41.4
2004		92	39	6.4	4.5	9.5	287.3	19.57	681.4	558.5	1,264.3	21.2
2005		83	34	5.1	3.6	7.5	240.5	20.76	456.6	502.8	958.1	16.8
2006		86P	32P	4.4	3.1	6.3	222.5	22.84	345.2	442.4	811.8	35.7
2007		78P	29P	5.3P	4.0P	8.6P	312.4P	21.60P	664.3P	851.4P	1,562.3P	44.6P
2008		70P	25P	4.0P	3.1P	6.7P	283.2P	22.24P	603.3P	773.2P	1,418.8P	39.0P
2009		62P	21P	2.8P	2.1P	4.8P	254.0P	22.87P	542.3P	695.0P	1,275.4P	33.5P
2010		54P	18P	1.5P	1.1P	2.9P	224.7P	23.51P	481.3P	616.8P	1,131.9P	27.9P

Sources: 1992, 1997, 2002 *Economic Census*; other years, up to 2006, are from the *Annual Survey of Manufactures*. Establishment counts for non-Census years are from *County Business Patterns*; 1997 and 2002 values are from the 1997 and 2002 censuses respectively, reported in the Federal Government's NAICS format. Other years were originally reported in equivalent SIC format. 'P's show projections by the editors.

INDICES OF CHANGE

| Year | Companies | Establishments | | Employment | | | Compensation | | Production ($ million) | | | |
		Total	with 20 or more employees	Total (000)	Production Workers (000)	Hours (Mil)	Payroll ($ mil)	Wages ($/hr)	Cost of Materials	Value Added by Manufacture	Value of Shipments	Capital Invest.
1992	189	185	177	193	189	178	139	73	126	139	129	150
1997	161	155	149	189	188	181	150	80	153	172	156	389
2001		144	159	136	138	130	130	100	125	128	131	395
2002	100	100	100	100	100	100	100	100	100	100	100	100
2003		101	95	80	78	71	78	108	66	84	72	101
2004		90	100	56	51	51	59	109	45	61	52	52
2005		81	87	44	40	40	49	115	30	55	39	41
2006		84P	82P	38	35	34	46	127	23	48	33	87
2007		76P	73P	46P	45P	46P	64P	120P	44P	93P	64P	109P
2008		68P	64P	35P	35P	36P	58P	124P	40P	84P	58P	95P
2009		60P	55P	24P	24P	26P	52P	127P	36P	76P	52P	82P
2010		53P	46P	13P	12P	15P	46P	131P	32P	67P	46P	68P

Sources: Same as General Statistics. Values reflect change from the base year, 2002. Values above 100 mean greater than 2002, values below 100 mean less than 2002, and the values of 100 in other years means the same as 2002. 'P's show projections by the editors.

SELECTED RATIOS

For 2002	Avg. of All Manufact.	Analyzed Industry	Index	For 2002	Avg. of All Manufact.	Analyzed Industry	Index
Employees per Establishment	42	113	269	Value Added per Production Worker	182,367	103,303	57
Payroll per Establishment	1,639,184	4,769,608	291	Cost per Establishment	5,769,015	14,712,745	255
Payroll per Employee	39,053	42,304	108	Cost per Employee	137,446	130,496	95
Production Workers per Establishment	30	87	296	Cost per Production Worker	195,506	168,618	86
Wages per Establishment	694,845	3,317,647	477	Shipments per Establishment	11,158,348	23,971,569	215
Wages per Production Worker	23,548	38,022	161	Shipments per Employee	265,847	212,617	80
Hours per Production Worker	1,980	2,112	107	Shipments per Production Worker	378,144	274,730	73
Wages per Hour	11.89	18.00	151	Investment per Establishment	361,338	401,961	111
Value Added per Establishment	5,381,325	9,013,725	168	Investment per Employee	8,609	3,565	41
Value Added per Employee	128,210	79,948	62	Investment per Production Worker	12,245	4,607	38

Sources: Same as General Statistics. The 'Average of All Manufacturing' column represents the average of all manufacturing industries reported for the most recent complete year available. The Index shows the relationship between the Average and the Analyzed Industry. For example, 100 means that they are equal; 500 that the Analyzed Industry is five times the average; 50 means that the Analyzed Industry is half the national average. The abbreviation 'na' is used to show that data are 'not available'. Ratios shown for 2002, the last complete census year.

LEADING COMPANIES   Number shown: **28**   Total sales ($ mil): **1,843**   Total employment (000): **3.4**

Company Name	Address				CEO Name	Phone	Co. Type	Sales ($ mil)	Empl. (000)
Hitachi Electronic Devices	PO Box 2203	Greenville	SC	29602	Yoshimichi Shibuya	864-299-2600	S	1,305	1.1
Thales Components Corp.	PO Box 540	Totowa	NJ	07511	Stephen Shapock	973-812-9000	S	181*	<0.1
Maxwell Technologies Inc.	9244 Balboa Ave.	San Diego	CA	92123	Richard D. Balanson	858-503-3300	P	57	0.3
Noble-Met Ltd.	200 S Yorkshire St.	Salem	VA	24153		540-389-7860	R	38*	0.1
Imaging and Sensing Technology	100 IST Ctr.	Horseheads	NY	14845	Donald Hartman	607-562-4300	R	38*	0.3
Hamamatsu Corp.	PO Box 6910	Bridgewater	NJ	08807	Akira Hiruma	908-231-0960	R	29*	<0.1
MPD Inc.	316 E 9th St.	Owensboro	KY	42303	Gary Braswell	270-685-6200	R	24*	0.2
Communications and Power Ind.	150 Sohier Rd.	Beverly	MA	01915	Robert A. Fickett	978-922-6000	S	19*	0.1
Bicron Bus. Unit of St-Gobain	12345 Kinsman Rd.	Newbury	OH	44065	Tom Kinisky	440-564-2251	S	19*	0.2
Thomas Electronics of New York	208 Davis Pkwy.	Clyde	NY	14433		315-923-2051	S	18*	0.1
Westrex Corporation of DE	1465 Howell Mill	Atlanta	GA	30318	Charles Whitener	404-352-2000	R	16*	<0.1
Amglo Kemlite Laboratories	215 Gateway Rd.	Bensenville	IL	60106	James Hyland	630-350-9470	R	15*	0.1
Thomas Electronics	100 Riverview Dr.	Wayne	NJ	07470	David Ketchum	973-696-5200	S	12*	0.2
Thomas Electronics	330 S La Londe	Addison	IL	60101	David Ketchum	630-543-6444	R	12*	<0.1
Union City Filament Corp.	PO Box 777	Ridgefield	NJ	07657	Joseph Celia	201-945-3366	R	11*	<0.1
Tfi Telemark	20936 Cabot Blvd.	Hayward	CA	94545	Gerald Henderson	510-887-2225	R	9*	<0.1
Troy-Onic Inc.	PO Box 494	Kenvil	NJ	07847	Michael Murphy	973-584-6830	R	7*	<0.1
Advanced Manufacturing Inc.	12205 28th St. N	St Petersburg	FL	33716	Gary Kinley	727-573-3300	S	6*	<0.1
Remtec Inc.	100 Morse St.	Norwood	MA	02062	Nahum Rapoport	781-762-9191	R	4*	<0.1
Connecticut Coining Inc.	10 Trowbridge Dr.	Bethel	CT	06801	Gregory Marciano	203-743-3861	R	4*	<0.1
Suntronic Inc.	10501 Kipp Way Dr.	Houston	TX	77099	John Ly	281-879-9562	R	4*	<0.1
Detector Technology Inc.	9 3rd Street	Palmer	MA	01069	Jay Ray	413-284-9975	R	3*	<0.1
Teltron Technologies Inc.	2 RIGA Ln.	Birdsboro	PA	19508		610-582-9450	S	3*	<0.1
Vacuum Tube Logic of America	PO Box 2604	Sunnyvale	CA	94087	Luke Manley	909-627-5944	R	3*	<0.1
Micacraft Products Inc.	PO Box 5699	Newark	NJ	07105	Bob Blanchard	973-589-3006	R	2*	<0.1
World Electronics Inc.	37 Hanover Pl.	Glen Rock	NJ	07452	Murray Rinzler	201-670-1177	R	2*	<0.1
Filtech Inc.	6 Pinckney St.	Boston	MA	02114	Paul Becker	617-227-1133	R	2*	<0.1
Spiral Designs Inc.	5775 Arapahoe Ave.	Boulder	CO	80303	Daniel Pringle	303-442-6553	R	1*	<0.1

Source: Ward's Business Directory of U.S. Private and Public Companies, Volumes 1 and 2, 2008. The company type code used is as follows: P - Public, R - Private, S - Subsidiary, D - Division, J - Joint Venture, A - Affiliate, G - Group. Sales are in millions of dollars, employees are in thousands. An asterisk (*) indicates an estimated sales volume. The symbol < stands for 'less than'. Company names and addresses are truncated, in some cases, to fit into the available space.

MATERIALS CONSUMED

Material	Quantity	Delivered Cost ($ million)
Tube blanks	(X)	2.6
Printed ciruit boards (without inserted components) for electronic circuitry	(X)	(D)
Printed circuit assemblies, loaded boards, and modules	(X)	9.0
Semiconductors (incl. transistors, diodes, rectifiers, and integrated circuits), for electronic circuitry	(X)	11.8
Capacitors for electronic circuitry	(X)	4.9
Resistors for electronic circuitry	(X)	(D)
All other miscellaneous components and accessories for electronic circuitry (exc. tubes)	(X)	108.6
Gold and other precious metals, all forms (incl. ingot, sheet, etc.)	(X)	4.7
Doped chemicals and other doped materials for electronic use	(X)	(D)
Ferrites (powder and paste)	(X)	(D)
Metal powders	(X)	3.1
Electronic computer equipment	(X)	(D)
Current-carrying wiring devices	(X)	0.8
Electronic communication equipment	(X)	(D)
Electrical instrument mechanisms and meter movements	(X)	(D)
All other miscellaneous electrical measuring instruments and parts	(X)	(D)
Fractional horsepower electric motors (less than 1 hp)	(X)	(D)
Electrical transmission, distribution, and control equipment	(X)	52.1
Loudspeakers, microphones, and tuners (all types)	(X)	(D)
Glass and glass products (excluding windows and mirrors)	(X)	563.2
Optical instruments and lenses (exc. sighting, tracking, and fire control)	(X)	(D)
Plastics resins consumed in the form of granules, pellets, etc.	(X)	(D)
Fabricated plastics products (excluding gaskets)	(X)	6.4
Sheet metal products (excluding stampings)	(X)	(D)
Metal stampings	(X)	33.7
Metal bolts, nuts, screws, and other screw machine products	(X)	24.4
Other fabricated metal products (excluding forgings)	(X)	90.4
Forgings	(X)	0.2
Castings, rough and semifinished	(X)	13.8
Steel shapes and forms (exc. castings, forgings, fabr. metal products)	(X)	(D)
Copper and copper-base alloy shapes and forms (exc. castings, forgings, fabr. metal products)	(X)	5.7
Aluminum and aluminum-base alloy shapes and forms (exc. castings, forgings, fabr. metal products)	(X)	1.1
Other nonferrous shapes and forms (exc. castings, forgings, fabricated metal products)	(X)	1.2
Insulated wire and cable (including magnet wire)	(X)	3.7
Paper and paperboard containers (incl. shipping sacks and other paper packaging supplies)	(X)	4.2
Resists (photosensitive resin films applied to surface of wafer)	(X)	(D)
Commodity gases	(X)	27.3
Masks	(X)	<0.1
Solvents	(X)	(D)

Continued on next page.

MATERIALS CONSUMED - Continued

Material	Quantity	Delivered Cost ($ million)
Cleaning compounds	(X)	(D)
All other materials, components, parts, containers, and supplies	(X)	264.5
Materials, ingredients, containers, and supplies, nsk	(X)	23.9

Source: 2002 *Economic Census*. Explanation of symbols used: (D): Withheld to avoid disclosure of competitive data; na: Not available; (S): Withheld because statistical norms were not met; (X): Not applicable; (Z): Less than half the unit shown; nec: Not elsewhere classified; nsk: Not specified by kind; - : zero; p : 10-19 percent estimated; q : 20-29 percent estimated.

PRODUCT SHARE DETAILS

Product or Product Class Shipments	Mil. $	Product or Product Class Shipments	Mil. $
ELECTRON TUBES	3,237.1	and rebuilt)	2,515.6
Transmittal, industrial, and special-purpose electron tubes (except x-ray)	586.6	Electron tube parts . . . . Electron tubes, nsk, total	92.9 41.9
Receiving-type electron tubes, including cathode ray (new			

Source: 2002 *Economic Census*. The values are product shipments in millions of dollars for 2002. Total product shipments may be lower or higher than industry shipments. See Introduction for a full discussion. Values of indented subcategories are summed in the main heading(s). The symbol (D) appears when data are withheld to prevent disclosure of competitive information. The abbreviation nsk stands for 'not specified by kind' and nec for 'not elsewhere classified'. A dash (-) means zero.

INPUTS AND OUTPUTS FOR ELECTRON TUBE MANUFACTURING

Economic Sector or Industry Providing Inputs	%	Sector	Economic Sector or Industry Buying Outputs	%	Sector
Compensation of employees	26.4		Exports of goods & services	43.5	Cap Inv
Glass products from purchased glass	10.0	Manufg.	Audio & video equipment	26.5	Manufg.
Pressed & blown glass & glassware, nec	8.7	Manufg.	General Federal government services, defense	7.0	Fed Govt
Electron tubes	8.2	Manufg.	Telecommunications	5.4	Services
Wholesale trade	8.2	Trade	Electron tubes	5.1	Manufg.
Electronic components, nec	3.8	Manufg.	Irradiation apparatus	3.2	Manufg.
Flat glass	3.4	Manufg.	Computer storage devices	1.7	Manufg.
Scientific research & development services	2.6	Services	Computer terminals & peripherals	1.3	Manufg.
Crowns & closures & metal stamping	1.7	Manufg.	Colleges, universities, & professional schools	1.0	Services
Power generation & supply	1.6	Util.	Wholesale trade	0.8	Trade
Relay & industrial controls	1.5	Manufg.	Electrical equipment & components, nec	0.6	Manufg.
Turned products & screws, nuts, & bolts	1.5	Manufg.	Printed circuit assemblies (electronic assemblies)	0.6	Manufg.
Truck transportation	1.4	Util.	General Federal government services, nondefense	0.6	Fed Govt
Management of companies & enterprises	1.3	Services	General S/L govt. services	0.5	S/L Govt
Machine shops	1.1	Manufg.	Electromedical & electrotherapeutic apparatus	0.4	Manufg.
Industrial gases	1.0	Manufg.	Electronic components, nec	0.3	Manufg.
Ornamental & architectural metal products	1.0	Manufg.	Bare printed circuit boards	0.3	Manufg.
Coating, engraving, heat treating & allied activities	0.8	Manufg.	Commercial & service industry machinery, nec	0.3	Manufg.
Natural gas distribution	0.6	Util.	Retail trade	0.2	Trade
Real estate	0.5	Fin/R.E.	Electronic & precision equipment repair/maintenance	0.2	Services
Printed circuit assemblies (electronic assemblies)	0.5	Manufg.	Surgical appliances & supplies	0.2	Manufg.
Metal & other household furniture	0.5	Manufg.	Magnetic & optical recording media	0.2	Manufg.
Electricity & signal testing instruments	0.4	Manufg.	Electronic connectors	0.1	Manufg.
Semiconductors & related devices	0.4	Manufg.			
Advertising & related services	0.4	Services			
Primary nonferrous metal, ex. copper & aluminum	0.4	Manufg.			
Metal cans, boxes, & other containers (light gauge)	0.4	Manufg.			
Electronic capacitors, resistors, coils, transformers	0.4	Manufg.			
Taxes on production & imports, less subsidies	0.4				
Noncomparable imports	0.4	Foreign			
Management, scientific, & technical consulting	0.4	Services			
Maintenance/repair of nonresidential structures	0.4	Construct.			
Iron & steel mills & ferroalloys	0.3	Manufg.			
Copper rolling, drawing, extruding, & alloying	0.3	Manufg.			
Warehousing & storage	0.3	Util.			
Fabricated metals, nec	0.3	Manufg.			
Services to buildings & dwellings	0.3	Services			
Ferrous metal foundries	0.3	Manufg.			
Basic organic chemicals, nec	0.3	Manufg.			
Plastics packaging materials, film & sheet	0.3	Manufg.			
Motors & generators	0.3	Manufg.			
Computer terminals & peripherals	0.3	Manufg.			
Audio & video equipment	0.3	Manufg.			
Securities, commodity contracts, investments	0.3	Fin/R.E.			
Nonferrous metal foundries	0.2	Manufg.			
Soap & cleaning compounds	0.2	Manufg.			
Office furnitures	0.2	Manufg.			
Plate work & fabricated structural products	0.2	Manufg.			
Automotive repair & maintenance, ex. car washes	0.2	Services			
Chemical products & preparations, nec	0.2	Manufg.			

Continued on next page.

INPUTS AND OUTPUTS FOR ELECTRON TUBE MANUFACTURING - Continued

Economic Sector or Industry Providing Inputs	%	Sector	Economic Sector or Industry Buying Outputs	%	Sector
Plastics products, nec	0.2	Manufg.			
Ball & roller bearings	0.2	Manufg.			
Commercial & industrial equipment repair/maintenance	0.2	Services			
Waste management & remediation services	0.2	Services			
Accounting, tax preparation, bookkeeping, & payroll	0.2	Services			
Paperboard containers	0.2	Manufg.			
Employment services	0.2	Services			
Cutting tools & machine tool accessories	0.1	Manufg.			
Custom roll forming	0.1	Manufg.			
Legal services	0.1	Services			
Valve & fittings other than plumbing	0.1	Manufg.			
Data processing, hosting, & related services	0.1	Services			
Business support services	0.1	Services			
Nonferrous metal (ex. copper & aluminum) processing	0.1	Manufg.			
Optical instruments & lenses	0.1	Manufg.			
Specialized design services	0.1	Services			
Automotive equipment rental & leasing	0.1	Fin/R.E.			
Rail transportation	0.1	Util.			

Source: Benchmark Input-Output Accounts for the U.S. Economy, 2002, U.S. Department of Commerce, Washington, D.C., January 2008. The abbreviation nec stands for 'not elsewhere classified'.

OCCUPATIONS EMPLOYED BY SEMICONDUCTOR & OTHER ELECTRONIC COMPONENT MANUFACTURING

Occupation	% of Total 2006	Change to 2016	Occupation	% of Total 2006	Change to 2016
Electrical & electronic equipment assemblers	10.9	-30.1	Computer software engineers, systems software	1.5	-3.8
Semiconductor processors	8.2	-12.6	Production workers, nec	1.3	-14.2
Team assemblers	4.5	-12.6	Shipping, receiving, & traffic clerks	1.3	-15.9
Electrical & electronic engineering technicians	4.1	-12.6	Purchasing agents, exc wholesale, retail, & farm	1.3	-12.6
Inspectors, testers, sorters, samplers, & weighers	3.9	-17.6	Production, planning, & expediting clerks	1.2	-12.6
Electronics engineers, exc computer	3.9	-12.6	General & operations managers	1.2	-21.3
First-line supervisors/managers of production workers	2.8	-12.6	Coil winders, tapers, & finishers	1.1	-30.1
Electrical engineers	2.6	-12.6	Machinists	1.1	-8.2
Industrial engineers	2.5	6.2	Industrial production managers	1.0	-12.6
Engineering managers	2.3	-3.8	Maintenance & repair workers, general	1.0	-12.6
Electromechanical equipment assemblers	1.7	-12.6			

Source: Industry-Occupation Matrix, Bureau of Labor Statistics, December 4, 2007. These data are reported based on 4-digit NAICS categories but have been matched to corresponding 6-digit NAICS industry codes. The change reported for each occupation to the year 2016 is a percent of growth or decline as estimated by the Bureau of Labor Statistics. The abbreviation nec stands for 'not elsewhere classified'.

LOCATION BY STATE AND REGIONAL CONCENTRATION

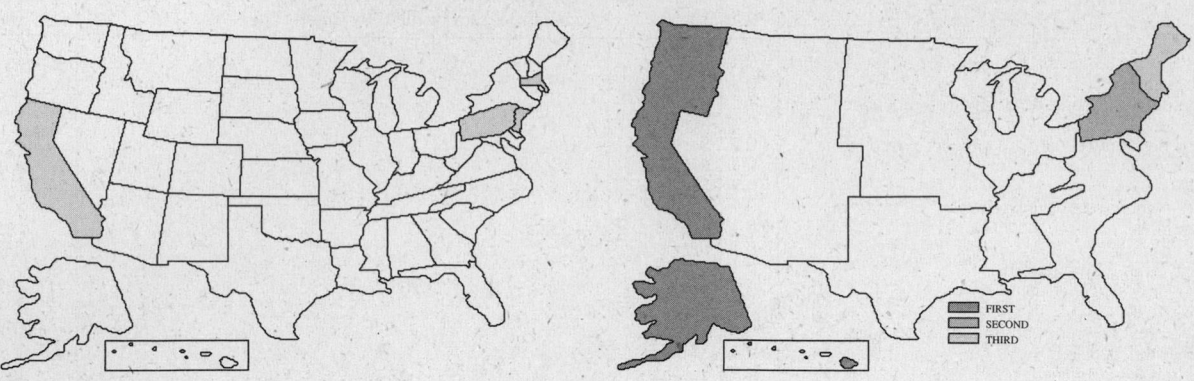

INDUSTRY DATA BY STATE

State	Establish-ments	Shipments			Employment				Cost as % of Shipments	Investment per Employee ($)
		Total ($ mil)	% of U.S.	Per Establ.	Total Number	% of U.S.	Per Establ.	Wages ($/hour)		
California	23	347.4	14.2	15,102.6	2,156	18.8	94	22.14	32.3	3,003
Pennsylvania	7	84.8	3.5	12,117.1	639	5.6	91	17.49	41.1	5,552
Massachusetts	6	46.7	1.9	7,777.0	630	5.5	105	19.44	30.9	1,868
New Jersey	7	31.3	1.3	4,467.6	376	3.3	54	11.72	36.6	888

Source: 2002 *Economic Census*. The states are in descending order of shipments or establishments (if shipment data are missing for the majority). The symbol (D) appears when data are withheld to prevent disclosure of competitive information. States marked with (D) are sorted by number of establishments. A dash (-) indicates that the data element cannot be calculated. Data may not show all states active in the NAICS category. All data available at the time of publication are shown.

NAICS 334412 - BARE PRINTED CIRCUIT BOARD MANUFACTURING

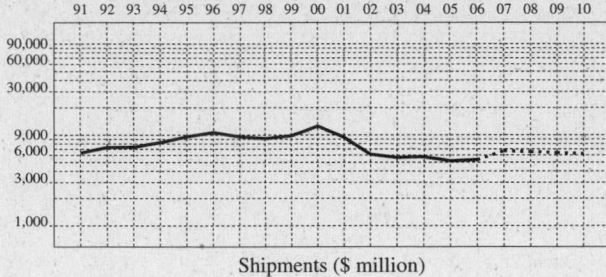

Shipments ($ million)

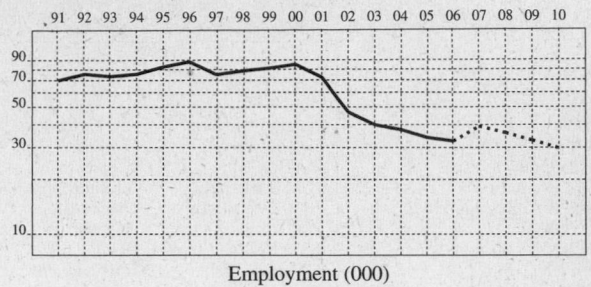

Employment (000)

GENERAL STATISTICS

| Year | Com- panies | Establishments | | Employment | | | Compensation | | Production ($ million) | | | |
		Total	with 20 or more employees	Total (000)	Production Workers (000)	Hours (Mil)	Payroll ($ mil)	Wages ($/hr)	Cost of Materials	Value Added by Manufacture	Value of Shipments	Capital Invest.
1991		1,187	598	69.9	47.1	99.4	1,920.7	9.92	2,678.0	3,443.9	6,352.9	311.1
1992	1,261	1,324	589	75.8	50.8	104.8	2,110.6	10.17	2,972.8	4,348.3	7,311.8	316.8
1993		1,346	609	73.6	50.5	105.0	2,129.4	10.58	3,151.2	4,160.0	7,377.6	282.8
1994		1,396	607	75.7	53.1	112.6	2,162.6	10.49	3,376.9	4,947.3	8,262.4	365.9
1995		1,409	639	82.8	59.6	126.9	2,384.1	10.32	3,944.4	5,718.5	9,577.9	455.3
1996		1,491	678	88.3	63.9	135.0	2,531.4	10.75	4,231.0	6,563.7	10,701.6	585.4
1997	1,315	1,389	588	75.1	56.8	114.6	2,274.1	11.92	3,827.7	5,789.1	9,595.8	609.1
1998		1,390	597	78.8	62.5	130.8	2,395.8	12.03	4,144.5	5,047.7	9,144.3	747.6
1999		1,374	571	81.4	65.2	137.9	2,661.2	13.04	4,413.2	5,557.1	9,832.1	687.6
2000		1,362	590	85.1	68.4	146.4	2,982.5	13.87	6,073.4	6,626.8	12,532.1	738.8
2001		1,314	598	72.3	55.6	107.6	2,359.2	14.16	4,484.4	4,731.7	9,413.6	575.8
2002	878	936	390	46.9	33.2	73.4	1,653.2	12.82	2,718.1	3,373.5	6,128.8	205.0
2003		907	395	40.1	28.8	59.2	1,440.3	14.31	2,326.9	3,345.1	5,651.9	123.9
2004		836	357	37.6	26.5	52.3	1,442.5	15.31	2,238.5	3,539.7	5,758.6	174.6
2005		781	343	34.1	24.2	48.3	1,344.2	16.22	1,912.5	3,256.6	5,182.4	134.7
2006		933P	388P	32.6	23.9	47.4	1,370.5	17.38	1,996.1	3,380.9	5,335.3	191.4
2007		896P	369P	39.2P	31.1P	62.8P	1,624.4P	16.69P	2,504.1P	4,241.4P	6,693.2P	294.1P
2008		859P	349P	36.1P	29.1P	58.4P	1,571.7P	17.15P	2,446.2P	4,143.2P	6,538.3P	280.8P
2009		822P	330P	32.9P	27.0P	54.0P	1,518.9P	17.62P	2,388.2P	4,045.1P	6,383.4P	267.6P
2010		785P	311P	29.8P	25.0P	49.6P	1,466.2P	18.09P	2,330.3P	3,946.9P	6,228.5P	254.4P

Sources: 1992, 1997, 2002 *Economic Census*; other years, up to 2006, are from the *Annual Survey of Manufactures*. Establishment counts for non-Census years are from *County Business Patterns*; 1997 and 2002 values are from the 1997 and 2002 censuses respectively, reported in the Federal Government's NAICS format. Other years were originally reported in equivalent SIC format. 'P's show projections by the editors.

INDICES OF CHANGE

| Year | Com- panies | Establishments | | Employment | | | Compensation | | Production ($ million) | | | |
		Total	with 20 or more employees	Total (000)	Production Workers (000)	Hours (Mil)	Payroll ($ mil)	Wages ($/hr)	Cost of Materials	Value Added by Manufacture	Value of Shipments	Capital Invest.
1992	144	141	151	162	153	143	128	79	109	129	119	155
1997	150	148	151	160	171	156	138	93	141	172	157	297
2001		140	153	154	167	147	143	110	165	140	154	281
2002	100	100	100	100	100	100	100	100	100	100	100	100
2003		97	101	86	87	81	87	112	86	99	92	60
2004		89	92	80	80	71	87	119	82	105	94	85
2005		83	88	73	73	66	81	127	70	97	85	66
2006		100P	100P	70	72	65	83P	136	73P	100	87P	93
2007		96P	95P	84P	94P	86R	98P	130P	92P	126P	109P	143P
2008		92P	90P	77P	88P	80P	95P	134P	90P	123P	107P	137P
2009		88P	85P	70P	81P	74P	92P	137P	88P	120P	104P	131P
2010		84P	80P	64P	75P	68P	89P	141P	86P	117P	102P	124P

Sources: Same as General Statistics. Values reflect change from the base year, 2002. Values above 100 mean greater than 2002, values below 100 mean less than 2002, and the values of 100 in other years means the same as 2002. 'P's show projections by the editors.

SELECTED RATIOS

For 2002	Avg. of All Manufact.	Analyzed Industry	Index	For 2002	Avg. of All Manufact.	Analyzed Industry	Index
Employees per Establishment	42	50	119	Value Added per Production Worker	182,367	101,611	56
Payroll per Establishment	1,639,184	1,766,239	108	Cost per Establishment	5,769,015	2,903,953	50
Payroll per Employee	39,053	35,249	90	Cost per Employee	137,446	57,955	42
Production Workers per Establishment	30	35	120	Cost per Production Worker	195,506	81,870	42
Wages per Establishment	694,845	1,005,329	145	Shipments per Establishment	11,158,348	6,547,863	59
Wages per Production Worker	23,548	28,343	120	Shipments per Employee	265,847	130,678	49
Hours per Production Worker	1,980	2,211	112	Shipments per Production Worker	378,144	184,602	49
Wages per Hour	11.89	12.82	108	Investment per Establishment	361,338	219,017	61
Value Added per Establishment	5,381,325	3,604,167	67	Investment per Employee	8,609	4,371	51
Value Added per Employee	128,210	71,930	56	Investment per Production Worker	12,245	6,175	50

Sources: Same as General Statistics. The 'Average of All Manufacturing' column represents the average of all manufacturing industries reported for the most recent complete year available. The Index shows the relationship between the Average and the Analyzed Industry. For example, 100 means that they are equal; 500 that the Analyzed Industry is five times the average; 50 means that the Analyzed Industry is half the national average. The abbreviation 'na' is used to show that data are 'not available'. Ratios shown for 2002, the last complete census year.

LEADING COMPANIES   Number shown: 75   Total sales ($ mil): 49,539   Total employment (000): 241.4

Company Name	Address				CEO Name	Phone	Co. Type	Sales ($ mil)	Empl. (000)
Jabil Circuit Inc.	10560 M L King Jr.	St. Petersburg	FL	33716		727-577-9749	P	12,291	61.0
Sanmina-SCI Corp.	2700 N 1st St.	San Jose	CA	95134	Joe Bronson	408-964-3555	P	10,384	52.6
Micron Technology Inc.	PO Box 6	Boise	ID	83707	Steven R. Appleton	208-368-4000	P	5,688	23.5
ECM Inc.	1515 259th St.	Harbor City	CA	90710	James M. Papada III	310-530-3456	S	4,855*	22.8
Benchmark Electronics Inc.	3000 Technology	Angleton	TX	77515		979-849-6550	P	2,916	10.9
Plexus Corp.	PO Box 156	Neenah	WI	54957		920-722-3451	P	1,546	7.8
Diversified Technology Inc.	476 Highland Col	Ridgeland	MS	39157		601-856-4121	R	1,380*	0.1
Cookson Electronics	1 Cookson Pl.	Providence	RI	02903	David Zerfoss	401-228-8820	D	1,103	5.0
Multi-Fineline Electronix Inc.	3140 E Coronado St.	Anaheim	CA	92806	Philip Harding	714-238-1488	P	1,082	17.2
Methode Development Co.	7401 W Wilson Ave.	Chicago	IL	60706	Donald W. Duda	708-867-6777	S	700*	3.2
TTM Technologies Inc.	2630 S Harbor Blvd.	Santa Ana	CA	92704	Kenton K. Alder	714-241-0303	P	670	4.0
Express Manufacturing Inc.	3519 West Warner	Santa Ana	CA	92704	C.P. Chin	714-979-2228	R	446*	0.5
Merix Corp.	PO Box 3000	Forest Grove	OR	97116	Michael Burger	503-359-9300	P	401	4.1
GE Fanuc Embedded Systems Inc.	12090 S Memorial	Huntsville	AL	35803		256-880-0444	R	396*	0.2
Saturn Electronics & Engineer.	255 Rex Blvd.	Auburn Hills	MI	48326	Wallace K. Tsuha, Jr.	248-853-5724	R	360*	4.0
Radian Corp.	PO Box 201088	Austin	TX	78720	Martin Koffel	512-419-6500	S	330*	2.2
Park Electrochemical Corp.	48 S Service Rd.	Melville	NY	11747		631-465-3600	P	257	1.0
Americor Electronics Ltd.	675 S Lively Blvd.	Elk Grove Vlg	IL	60007	Troy Gunnin	847-956-6200	R	247*	<0.1
Raven Industries Inc.	PO Box 5107	Sioux Falls	SD	57117	Conrad J. Hoigaard	605-336-2750	P	217	0.9
Reptron Manufacturing Services	13750 Reptron Blvd.	Tampa	FL	33626		813-814-5069	S	209*	1.0
DDI Corp.	1220 Simon Cir.	Anaheim	CA	92806		714-688-7200	P	181	1.3
SigmaTron International Inc.	2201 Landmeier Rd.	Elk Grove Vlg	IL	60007	Gary R. Fairhead	847-956-8000	P	166	2.1
Transistor Devices Inc.	36 Newburgh Rd.	Hackettstown	NJ	07840	Richard Blake	973-267-1900	R	151*	0.1
Dynamic Details Inc.	1220 Simon Cir.	Anaheim	CA	92806	Mikel Williams	714-688-7200	S	143*	1.3
Reptron Electronics Inc.	13700 Reptron Blvd.	Tampa	FL	33626	Paul J. Plante	813-854-2000	S	139	1.0
Palomar Medical Technologies	82 Cambridge St.	Burlington	MA	01803	Joseph P. Caruso	781-993-2300	P	124	0.3
Flash Electronics Inc.	4050 Starboard Dr.	Fremont	CA	94538	Bob Dean	510-440-2840	R	114*	0.5
Mid-South Electronics Inc.	2600 E Meighan	Gadsden	AL	35903	Harold Weaver	256-492-8997	R	111*	0.4
m-Audio	5795 Martin Rd.	Irwindale	CA	91706	Tim Ryan	626-633-9050	S	107*	0.1
Parlex Corp.	1 Parlex Pl.	Methuen	MA	01844		978-685-4341	S	106	1.9
Sypris Electronics L.L.C.	10901 N McKinley	Tampa	FL	33612	Bob Sanders	813-972-6000	S	100*	0.7
Compeq International Corp.	620 John Glenn Rd.	Salt Lake City	UT	84116	Webb Chang	801-990-2000	R	100*	0.4
Apsco Inc.	3700 Ln. Rd. Ext.	Perry	OH	44081	Steven Schmidt	440-352-8961	R	94*	0.4
SMTEK International Inc.	200 Science Dr.	Moorpark	CA	93021	Edward J. Smith	805-532-2800	S	93	0.5
Alstom Power Conversion	610 Epsilon Dr.	Pittsburgh	PA	15238	Torspen Astrom	412-967-0765	S	93*	0.2
International Control Services	606 W Imboden Dr.	Decatur	IL	62521	Dennis Espinoza	217-422-6700	R	91*	0.1
Phoenix International	1441 44th St. NW	Fargo	ND	58102			R	87*	0.2
MC Test Service Inc.	2725 Kirby Cir. NE	Palm Bay	FL	32905	Charles Rossi	321-253-0541	R	86*	0.4
NACOM Corp.	375 Airport Rd.	Griffin	GA	30224	Riku Yakazi	770-467-9545	R	85*	0.5
Amitron Inc.	2001 Landmeier Rd.	Elk Grove Vlg	IL	60007		847-290-9800	R	76*	0.3
Reliant Manufacturing L.L.C.	455 Weaver Park	Longmont	CO	80501		303-682-1000	R	74*	0.1
Pyott-Boone Electronics Inc.	PO Box 809	Tazewell	VA	24651	Donald Fetterolf	276-988-5505	R	73*	0.2
Ramp Industries Inc.	1 N Floral Ave.	Binghamton	NY	13905	Michael Pandich	607-729-5256	R	68*	0.3
Avg Advanced Technologies L.P.	343 Saint Paul Blvd	Carol Stream	IL	60188		630-668-3900	R	65*	<0.1
Riverside Electronics Ltd.	One Riverside Dr.	Lewiston	MN	55952	Stephen H. Craney	507-523-3220	R	65*	0.3
Micro Dynamics Corp.	6201 Bury Dr.	Eden Prairie	MN	55346	Michael Brown	952-941-8071	R	63*	<0.1
Paramit Corp.	18735 Madrone	Morgan Hill	CA	95037	Thanh Nguyen	408-782-5600	R	61*	0.3
National Hybrid Inc.	2200 Smithtown	Ronkonkoma	NY	11779	Carol Klemm	631-981-2400	R	61*	0.1
Jaton Corp.	556 S Milpitas Blvd	Milpitas	CA	95035	J Chiang	408-942-9888	R	60*	0.3
Corwil Technology Corp.	1635 McCarthy	Milpitas	CA	95035	Robert Corrao	408-321-6404	R	59*	0.2
ARC-Tronics Inc.	1150 Pagni Dr.	Elk Grove Vlg	IL	60007	Conrad Goeringer	847-437-0211	R	59*	0.3
Quality Systems Integrated	6720 Cobra Way	San Diego	CA	92121	Kiem Le	858-587-9797	R	58*	0.2
Sonic Manufacturing Technolog.	48133 Warm Springs	Fremont	CA	94539	Kenneth Raab	510-492-0900	R	54*	0.2
Victron Inc.	6600 Stevenson Blvd	Fremont	CA	94538	Chris Lee	510-360-2222	R	54*	0.2
Advanced Circuits Inc.	21100 E 32nd Pkwy.	Aurora	CO	80011	John Yacoub	303-576-6610	R	53*	0.2
Arizona Precision Sheet Metal	2140 W Pinncle	Phoenix	AZ	85027	John Thul	623-516-3700	R	52*	0.4
Electronic Evolution Tech.	9455 Double R Blvd.	Reno	NV	89511	Sonny Newman	775-355-9191	R	50*	0.2
UltraSource Inc.	22 Clinton Dr.	Hollis	NH	03049	Michael Casper	603-881-7799	R	49*	<0.1
Performance Technologies Inc.	205 Indigo Creek Dr	Rochester	NY	14626		585-256-0200	P	48	0.2
S.A.E. Circuits Colorado Inc.	4820 63rd St., 100	Boulder	CO	80301	Ervin Hammen	303-530-1900	R	48*	<0.1
Microboard Processing Inc.	4 Progress Ave.	Seymour	CT	06483	Mike Ellis	203-881-4300	R	48*	0.2
Tyan Computer Corp.	3288 Laurelview Ct.	Fremont	CA	94538	Symon Chang	510-651-8868	R	48*	<0.1
Electrotek Corp.	7745 S 10th St.	Oak Creek	WI	53154	Larry Petersen	414-762-1390	R	47*	0.2
Innova Electronics L.P.	8383 N S Houston	Houston	TX	77064	Trey Cook	281-897-0422	R	47*	0.2
Teknetix Inc.	2501 Garfield Ave.	Parkersburg	WV	26101	Joseph Florence	304-424-9400	R	47*	0.2
Holaday Circuits Inc.	11126 Bren Rd. W	Minnetonka	MN	55343	Marshall Lewis	952-933-3303	R	43*	0.2
Cal-Quality Electronics Inc.	2700 S Fairview St.	Santa Ana	CA	92704	Brock Koren	714-545-8886	R	42*	0.2
Hytel Group Inc.	290 Industrial Dr.	Hampshire	IL	60140	Scott Johansen	847-683-9800	R	41*	0.1
Altron Inc.	6700 Bunker Lk	Anoka	MN	55303	Alan Phillips	763-427-7735	R	41*	0.2
Fabricated Components Corp.	130 W Bristol Ln.	Orange	CA	92865	Jack Evans	714-974-8590	R	41*	0.2
IEC Electronics Corp.	PO Box 271	Newark	NY	14513	Barry Gilbert	315-331-7742	P	41	0.2
Loranger International Corp.	817 4th Ave.	Warren	PA	16365	Albert Loranger	814-723-2250	R	39*	0.1
Printed Circuits Assembly	13221 SE 26th St.	Bellevue	WA	98005	Sim Taing	425-644-7754	R	39*	0.2
Tech-Etch Inc.	45 Aldrin Rd.	Plymouth	MA	02360	George Keeler	508-747-0300	R	39*	0.4
Tri-Phase Inc.	6190 San Ignacio	San Jose	CA	95119	Beth Kendrick	408-284-7700	R	38*	0.2

Source: *Ward's Business Directory of U.S. Private and Public Companies*, Volumes 1 and 2, 2008. The company type code used is as follows: P - Public, R - Private, S - Subsidiary, D - Division, J - Joint Venture, A - Affiliate, G - Group. Sales are in millions of dollars, employees are in thousands. An asterisk (*) indicates an estimated sales volume. The symbol < stands for 'less than'. Company names and addresses are truncated, in some cases, to fit into the available space.

MATERIALS CONSUMED

Material	Quantity	Delivered Cost ($ million)
Tube blanks	(X)	(D)
Printed ciruit boards (without inserted components) for electronic circuitry	(X)	306.6
Printed circuit assemblies, loaded boards, and modules	(X)	189.5
Semiconductors (incl. transistors, diodes, rectifiers, and integrated circuits), for electronic circuitry	(X)	283.0
Capacitors for electronic circuitry	(X)	81.9
Resistors for electronic circuitry	(X)	74.1
All other miscellaneous components and accessories for electronic circuitry (exc. tubes)	(X)	77.6
Silicon, hyperpure	(X)	(D)
Gold and other precious metals, all forms (incl. ingot, sheet, etc.)	(X)	62.5
Doped chemicals and other doped materials for electronic use	(X)	31.7
Ferrites (powder and paste)	(X)	(D)
Metal powders	(X)	0.8
Electronic computer equipment	(X)	11.8
Current-carrying wiring devices	(X)	6.0
Electronic communication equipment	(X)	0.3
Electrical instrument mechanisms and meter movements	(X)	4.0
All other miscellaneous electrical measuring instruments and parts	(X)	1.7
Fractional horsepower electric motors (less than 1 hp)	(X)	3.5
Electrical transmission, distribution, and control equipment	(X)	12.0
Loudspeakers, microphones, and tuners (all types)	(X)	0.1
Glass and glass products (excluding windows and mirrors)	(X)	80.7
Optical instruments and lenses (exc. sighting, tracking, and fire control)	(X)	(D)
Plastics resins consumed in the form of granules, pellets, etc.	(X)	26.7
Fabricated plastics products (excluding gaskets)	(X)	49.6
Sheet metal products (excluding stampings)	(X)	33.4
Metal stampings	(X)	2.0
Metal bolts, nuts, screws, and other screw machine products	(X)	9.0
Other fabricated metal products (excluding forgings)	(X)	18.3
Castings, rough and semifinished	(X)	(D)
Steel shapes and forms (exc. castings, forgings, fabr. metal products)	(X)	(D)
Copper and copper-base alloy shapes and forms (exc. castings, forgings, fabr. metal products)	(X)	60.8
Aluminum and aluminum-base alloy shapes and forms (exc. castings, forgings, fabr. metal products)	(D)	(D)
Other nonferrous shapes and forms (exc. castings, forgings, fabricated metal products)	(X)	3.7
Insulated wire and cable (including magnet wire)	(X)	6.8
Paper and paperboard containers (incl. shipping sacks and other paper packaging supplies)	(X)	12.1
Resists (photosensitive resin films applied to surface of wafer)	(X)	45.4
Commodity gases	(X)	2.8
Speciality gases	(X)	1.2
Masks	(X)	2.3
Silicon chips	(X)	10.9
Solvents	(X)	5.7
Cleaning compounds	(X)	1.3
All other materials, components, parts, containers, and supplies	(X)	526.4
Materials, ingredients, containers, and supplies, nsk	(X)	286.5

Source: 2002 *Economic Census*. Explanation of symbols used: (D): Withheld to avoid disclosure of competitive data; na: Not available; (S): Withheld because statistical norms were not met; (X): Not applicable; (Z): Less than half the unit shown; nec: Not elsewhere classified; nsk: Not specified by kind; - : zero; p : 10-19 percent estimated; q : 20-29 percent estimated.

PRODUCT SHARE DETAILS

Product or Product Class Shipments	Mil. $	Product or Product Class Shipments	Mil. $
BARE PRINTED CIRCUIT BOARDS	6,457.5	Bare printed circuit (wiring) boards	5,794.8
Bare printed circuit boards	**6,457.5**	Bare printed circuit boards, nsk, total	662.7

Source: 2002 *Economic Census*. The values are product shipments in millions of dollars for 2002. Total product shipments may be lower or higher than industry shipments. See Introduction for a full discussion. Values of indented subcategories are summed in the main heading(s). The symbol (D) appears when data are withheld to prevent disclosure of competitive information. The abbreviation nsk stands for 'not specified by kind' and nec for 'not elsewhere classified'. A dash (-) means zero.

INPUTS AND OUTPUTS FOR BARE PRINTED CIRCUIT BOARD MANUFACTURING

Economic Sector or Industry Providing Inputs	%	Sector	Economic Sector or Industry Buying Outputs	%	Sector
Compensation of employees	32.0		Exports of goods & services	20.6	Cap Inv
Wholesale trade	7.1	Trade	Motor vehicle parts	9.1	Manufg.
Management of companies & enterprises	5.8	Services	Software publishers	6.0	Services
Bare printed circuit boards	5.7	Manufg.	Bare printed circuit boards	4.4	Manufg.
Semiconductors & related devices	5.2	Manufg.	Broadcast & wireless communications equipment	4.4	Manufg.
Printed circuit assemblies (electronic assembiles)	3.8	Manufg.	Other computer related services, including facilities	3.3	Services
Lessors of nonfinancial assets	3.0	Fin/R.E.	Electricity & signal testing instruments	3.1	Manufg.
Electronic capacitors, resistors, coils, transformers	2.6	Manufg.	Telephone apparatus	2.9	Manufg.
Scientific research & development services	2.4	Services	Totalizing fluid meters & counting devices	2.5	Manufg.
Power generation & supply	1.8	Util.	Search, detection, & navigation instruments	2.5	Manufg.
Primary nonferrous metal, ex. copper & aluminum	1.6	Manufg.	Semiconductors & related devices	2.4	Manufg.

Continued on next page.

INPUTS AND OUTPUTS FOR BARE PRINTED CIRCUIT BOARD MANUFACTURING - Continued

Economic Sector or Industry Providing Inputs	%	Sector	Economic Sector or Industry Buying Outputs	%	Sector
Real estate	1.3	Fin/R.E.	Audio & video equipment	2.3	Manufg.
Electronic components, nec	1.3	Manufg.	Relay & industrial controls	2.1	Manufg.
Chemical products & preparations, nec	1.2	Manufg.	Wholesale trade	2.1	Trade
Copper rolling, drawing, extruding, & alloying	1.2	Manufg.	Electronic computers	1.9	Manufg.
Plastics packaging materials, film & sheet	1.1	Manufg.	Printed circuit assemblies (electronic assemblies)	1.5	Manufg.
Plastics products, nec	0.8	Manufg.	Communications equipment, nec	1.4	Manufg.
Securities, commodity contracts, investments	0.7	Fin/R.E.	Custom computer programming services	1.2	Services
Glass products from purchased glass	0.7	Manufg.	Industrial process variable instruments	1.0	Manufg.
Legal services	0.6	Services	Electronic components, nec	1.0	Manufg.
Advertising & related services	0.6	Services	Computer system design services	1.0	Services
Pressed & blown glass & glassware, nec	0.6	Manufg.	Analytical laboratory instruments	1.0	Manufg.
Ornamental & architectural metal products	0.5	Manufg.	Electromedical & electrotherapeutic apparatus	0.9	Manufg.
Architectural, engineering, & related services	0.5	Services	Laboratory apparatus & furniture	0.8	Manufg.
Truck transportation	0.5	Util.	Computer terminals & peripherals	0.7	Manufg.
Maintenance/repair of nonresidential structures	0.5	Construct.	Switchgear & switchboard apparatus	0.6	Manufg.
Automotive equipment rental & leasing	0.5	Fin/R.E.	Computer storage devices	0.6	Manufg.
Telecommunications	0.5	Services	Plastics products, nec	0.6	Manufg.
Plastics materials & resins	0.5	Manufg.	Electrical equipment & components, nec	0.5	Manufg.
Basic inorganic chemicals, nec	0.4	Manufg.	Soft drinks & ice	0.5	Manufg.
Services to buildings & dwellings	0.4	Services	Automatic environmental controls	0.5	Manufg.
Alumina refining & primary aluminum production	0.4	Manufg.	Basic organic chemicals, nec	0.5	Manufg.
Monetary authorities/depository credit intermediation	0.4	Fin/R.E.	Watches, clocks, & related devices	0.5	Manufg.
Motor vehicle parts	0.4	Manufg.	Surgical appliances & supplies	0.4	Manufg.
Iron & steel mills & ferroalloys	0.4	Manufg.	Plastics packaging materials, film & sheet	0.4	Manufg.
Natural gas distribution	0.4	Util.	General purpose machinery, nec	0.4	Manufg.
Noncomparable imports	0.4	Foreign	Toilet preparations	0.3	Manufg.
Taxes on production & imports, less subsidies	0.4		Iron & steel mills & ferroalloys	0.3	Manufg.
Relay & industrial controls	0.4	Manufg.	Irradiation apparatus	0.3	Manufg.
Warehousing & storage	0.3	Util.	Plastics materials & resins	0.3	Manufg.
Specialized design services	0.3	Services	Industrial machinery, nec	0.3	Manufg.
Professional, scientific, technical services, nec	0.3	Services	Printing	0.3	Manufg.
Other computer related services, including facilities	0.3	Services	Software, audio, and video media reproducing	0.2	Manufg.
Machine shops	0.3	Manufg.	Plate work & fabricated structural products	0.2	Manufg.
Employment services	0.3	Services	Wiring devices	0.2	Manufg.
Automotive repair & maintenance, ex. car washes	0.3	Services	Chemical products & preparations, nec	0.2	Manufg.
Food services & drinking places	0.3	Services	Architectural, engineering, & related services	0.2	Services
Accounting, tax preparation, bookkeeping, & payroll	0.3	Services	General S/L govt. services	0.2	S/L Govt
Management, scientific, & technical consulting	0.3	Services	Aluminum products from purchased aluminum	0.2	Manufg.
Business support services	0.3	Services	Turned products & screws, nuts, & bolts	0.2	Manufg.
Custom computer programming services	0.3	Services	Machine shops	0.2	Manufg.
Commercial & industrial equipment repair/maintenance	0.3	Services	Construction machinery	0.2	Manufg.
Commercial & industrial machinery rental & leasing	0.2	Fin/R.E.	AC, refrigeration, and warm air heating equipment	0.2	Manufg.
Data processing, hosting, & related services	0.2	Services	Data processing, hosting, & related services	0.2	Services
Turned products & screws, nuts, & bolts	0.2	Manufg.	Electronic connectors	0.2	Manufg.
Waste management & remediation services	0.2	Services	Valve & fittings other than plumbing	0.2	Manufg.
Flat glass	0.2	Manufg.	Coating, engraving, heat treating & allied activities	0.2	Manufg.
Paperboard containers	0.2	Manufg.	Paints & coatings	0.2	Manufg.
Retail trade	0.2	Trade	Steel products from purchased steel	0.2	Manufg.
Ferrous metal foundries	0.2	Manufg.	Wood kitchen cabinets & countertops	0.2	Manufg.
Hotels & motels, including casino hotels	0.2	Services	Rubber products, nec	0.2	Manufg.
Nonferrous metal foundries	0.2	Manufg.	Asphalt shingle & coating materials	0.2	Manufg.
Air transportation	0.2	Util.	Material handling equipment	0.1	Manufg.
Coating, engraving, heat treating & allied activities	0.2	Manufg.	Lighting fixtures	0.1	Manufg.
Cutting tools & machine tool accessories	0.2	Manufg.	Optical instruments & lenses	0.1	Manufg.
Semiconductor machinery	0.2	Manufg.	Ornamental & architectural metal products	0.1	Manufg.
Computer terminals & peripherals	0.2	Manufg.	Wood windows & doors & millwork	0.1	Manufg.
Electron tubes	0.2	Manufg.	Mining & oil & gas field machinery	0.1	Manufg.
Support services, nec	0.1	Services	Surgical & medical instrument	0.1	Manufg.
Investigation & security services	0.1	Services	Aircraft parts & auxiliary equipment, nec	0.1	Manufg.
Paperboard mills	0.1	Manufg.	Carpet & rug mills	0.1	Manufg.
Computer system design services	0.1	Services	Glass products from purchased glass	0.1	Manufg.
Wiring devices	0.1	Manufg.	Synthetic dyes & pigments	0.1	Manufg.
Basic organic chemicals, nec	0.1	Manufg.	Coated & laminated paper & packaging materials	0.1	Manufg.
Metal cans, boxes, & other containers (light gauge)	0.1	Manufg.	Turbines & turbine generator set units	0.1	Manufg.
Electronic & precision equipment repair/maintenance	0.1	Services	Photographic & photocopying equipment	0.1	Manufg.
Electricity & signal testing instruments	0.1	Manufg.	Signs	0.1	Manufg.
			Commercial & service industry machinery, nec	0.1	Manufg.
			Hardware	0.1	Manufg.
			Ready-mix concrete	0.1	Manufg.
			Sporting & athletic goods	0.1	Manufg.
			Sanitary paper products	0.1	Manufg.
			Ship building & repairing	0.1	Manufg.
			Electronic capacitors, resistors, coils, transformers	0.1	Manufg.
			Heavy duty trucks	0.1	Manufg.
			Nonferrous metal (ex. copper & aluminum) processing	0.1	Manufg.

Source: Benchmark Input-Output Accounts for the U.S. Economy, 2002, U.S. Department of Commerce, Washington, D.C., January 2008. The abbreviation nec stands for 'not elsewhere classified'.

OCCUPATIONS EMPLOYED BY SEMICONDUCTOR & OTHER ELECTRONIC COMPONENT MANUFACTURING

Occupation	% of Total 2006	Change to 2016	Occupation	% of Total 2006	Change to 2016
Electrical & electronic equipment assemblers	10.9	-30.1	Computer software engineers, systems software	1.5	-3.8
Semiconductor processors	8.2	-12.6	Production workers, nec	1.3	-14.2
Team assemblers	4.5	-12.6	Shipping, receiving, & traffic clerks	1.3	-15.9
Electrical & electronic engineering technicians	4.1	-12.6	Purchasing agents, exc wholesale, retail, & farm	1.3	-12.6
Inspectors, testers, sorters, samplers, & weighers	3.9	-17.6	Production, planning, & expediting clerks	1.2	-12.6
Electronics engineers, exc computer	3.9	-12.6	General & operations managers	1.2	-21.3
First-line supervisors/managers of production workers	2.8	-12.6	Coil winders, tapers, & finishers	1.1	-30.1
Electrical engineers	2.6	-12.6	Machinists	1.1	-8.2
Industrial engineers	2.5	6.2	Industrial production managers	1.0	-12.6
Engineering managers	2.3	-3.8	Maintenance & repair workers, general	1.0	-12.6
Electromechanical equipment assemblers	1.7	-12.6			

Source: Industry-Occupation Matrix, Bureau of Labor Statistics, December 4, 2007. These data are reported based on 4-digit NAICS categories but have been matched to corresponding 6-digit NAICS industry codes. The change reported for each occupation to the year 2016 is a percent of growth or decline as estimated by the Bureau of Labor Statistics. The abbreviation nec stands for 'not elsewhere classified'.

LOCATION BY STATE AND REGIONAL CONCENTRATION

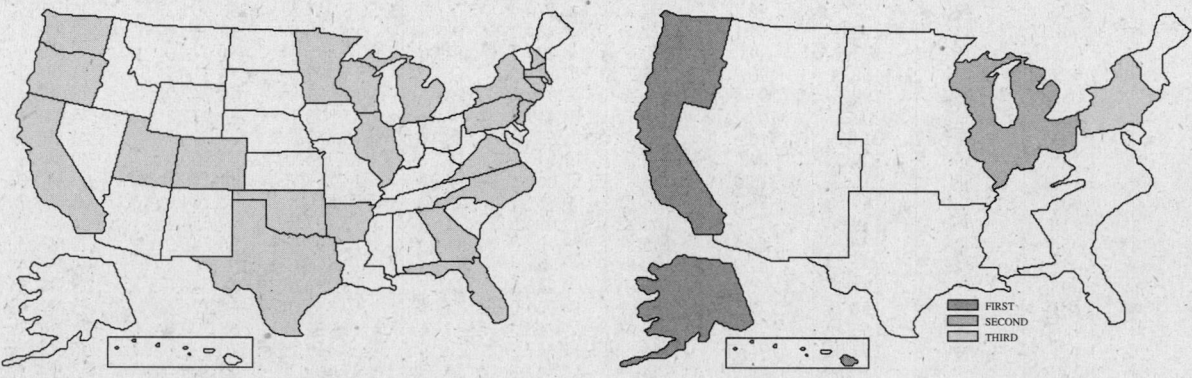

FIRST
SECOND
THIRD

INDUSTRY DATA BY STATE

State	Establish-ments	Shipments			Employment				Cost as % of Shipments	Investment per Employee ($)
		Total ($ mil)	% of U.S.	Per Establ.	Total Number	% of U.S.	Per Establ.	Wages ($/hour)		
California	264	1,360.3	22.2	5,152.8	10,444	22.3	40	13.37	45.7	4,883
Massachusetts	50	513.4	8.4	10,267.8	3,384	7.2	68	14.81	57.3	2,720
New York	49	465.3	7.6	9,495.5	3,513	7.5	72	11.91	36.5	1,211
New Hampshire	14	426.9	7.0	30,493.6	2,930	6.2	209	13.84	73.0	8,312
Minnesota	44	352.0	5.7	8,000.9	2,687	5.7	61	11.28	39.5	6,392
Florida	31	311.6	5.1	10,052.3	2,097	4.5	68	13.98	49.8	4,553
Illinois	64	235.5	3.8	3,679.7	2,313	4.9	36	9.75	40.2	5,715
Oregon	15	177.4	2.9	11,828.7	1,585	3.4	106	19.74	37.9	7,833
Wisconsin	14	163.9	2.7	11,706.3	1,523	3.2	109	14.49	39.5	2,207
Connecticut	18	162.2	2.6	9,012.4	1,105	2.4	61	14.46	41.0	11,119
Texas	57	147.7	2.4	2,591.4	1,259	2.7	22	11.32	36.7	4,096
Michigan	23	136.8	2.2	5,947.5	1,118	2.4	49	10.84	49.7	3,021
Georgia	11	120.0	2.0	10,911.5	911	1.9	83	12.08	37.0	1,159
Washington	22	102.3	1.7	4,650.5	976	2.1	44	15.27	38.2	6,036
Utah	13	98.1	1.6	7,547.5	1,092	2.3	84	13.05	50.4	1,005
Pennsylvania	28	64.0	1.0	2,284.4	799	1.7	29	10.53	39.2	925
Colorado	27	54.1	0.9	2,002.7	479	1.0	18	14.18	33.6	12,553
Arkansas	5	45.3	0.7	9,065.6	318	0.7	64	11.33	50.5	1,063
New Jersey	19	34.3	0.6	1,807.1	308	0.7	16	10.57	43.9	2,461
Virginia	8	29.1	0.5	3,641.3	307	0.7	38	11.97	27.7	3,404
North Carolina	15	17.3	0.3	1,152.9	194	0.4	13	16.32	36.3	1,155
Oklahoma	9	16.0	0.3	1,774.1	176	0.4	20	7.45	38.6	631

Source: 2002 Economic Census. The states are in descending order of shipments or establishments (if shipment data are missing for the majority). The symbol (D) appears when data are withheld to prevent disclosure of competitive information. States marked with (D) are sorted by number of establishments. A dash (-) indicates that the data element cannot be calculated. Data may not show all states active in the NAICS category. All data available at the time of publication are shown.

NAICS 334413 - SEMICONDUCTOR AND RELATED DEVICE MANUFACTURING

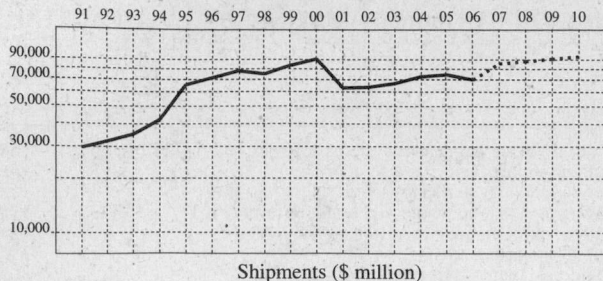

Shipments ($ million)

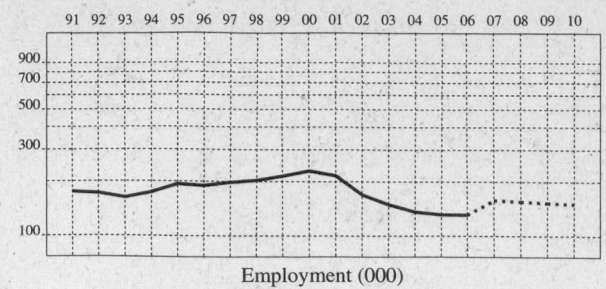

Employment (000)

GENERAL STATISTICS

Year	Companies	Establishments		Employment			Compensation		Production ($ million)			
		Total	with 20 or more employees	Total (000)	Production Workers (000)	Hours (Mil)	Payroll ($ mil)	Wages ($/hr)	Cost of Materials	Value Added by Manufacture	Value of Shipments	Capital Invest.
1991		901	449	175.0	86.2	177.4	6,490.8	12.69	9,197.7	20,151.9	29,668.1	2,945.0
1992	823	921	438	171.9	84.7	172.2	6,879.8	13.55	9,823.3	22,299.7	32,157.0	3,118.0
1993		930	436	162.5	82.2	167.2	6,770.4	14.08	8,937.5	26,465.2	35,151.5	3,838.5
1994		940	436	173.6	89.1	177.5	7,464.2	14.48	10,388.9	32,083.6	42,252.1	5,697.8
1995		938	452	193.4	99.0	200.6	8,803.1	14.86	14,895.4	51,272.0	65,622.9	9,181.7
1996		1,052	479	189.6	96.2	195.7	9,042.2	15.29	15,399.9	56,311.3	71,413.4	11,991.4
1997	980	1,082	491	198.1	105.8	214.5	9,994.4	16.36	14,967.8	63,747.2	78,009.4	11,531.8
1998		1,153	523	203.1	108.2	213.7	10,449.3	17.38	15,303.1	59,977.2	75,048.4	9,267.5
1999		1,155	527	214.7	116.6	237.4	11,651.3	18.16	15,853.5	68,021.7	83,535.6	9,155.5
2000		1,190	550	229.5	124.3	253.2	12,976.6	18.67	23,715.1	67,896.6	90,880.1	14,583.6
2001		1,177	580	216.2	118.3	233.8	11,660.8	19.27	18,767.7	44,118.2	63,173.0	12,159.6
2002	898	1,032	480	169.6	86.1	168.5	9,882.1	22.62	16,560.8	47,264.0	63,658.7	4,779.2
2003		1,016	460	149.8	72.1	146.2	9,094.5	22.26	17,197.3	49,654.6	66,627.9	4,288.9
2004		955	427	136.3	64.2	135.8	8,738.8	21.98	16,598.3	56,245.2	72,693.3	5,363.2
2005		951	417	131.7	61.7	129.8	9,041.3	23.51	15,560.6	59,412.7	74,597.4	8,740.6
2006		1,095P	493P	131.1	62.1	129.0	9,236.2	24.57	15,792.0	54,049.8	69,964.8	6,111.7
2007		1,104P	495P	157.7P	79.5P	162.0P	10,966.0P	24.94P	19,335.0P	66,176.1P	85,661.7P	8,969.0P
2008		1,113P	497P	155.4P	78.1P	159.4P	11,166.6P	25.74P	19,926.1P	68,199.0P	88,280.3P	9,121.6P
2009		1,121P	499P	153.0P	76.7P	156.8P	11,367.2P	26.55P	20,517.1P	70,222.0P	90,898.9P	9,274.2P
2010		1,130P	501P	150.6P	75.4P	154.1P	11,567.8P	27.35P	21,108.2P	72,245.0P	93,517.5P	9,426.8P

Sources: 1992, 1997, 2002 *Economic Census*; other years, up to 2006, are from the *Annual Survey of Manufactures*. Establishment counts for non-Census years are from *County Business Patterns*; 1997 and 2002 values are from the 1997 and 2002 censuses respectively, reported in the Federal Government's NAICS format. Other years were originally reported in equivalent SIC format. 'P's show projections by the editors.

INDICES OF CHANGE

Year	Companies	Establishments		Employment			Compensation		Production ($ million)			
		Total	with 20 or more employees	Total (000)	Production Workers (000)	Hours (Mil)	Payroll ($ mil)	Wages ($/hr)	Cost of Materials	Value Added by Manufacture	Value of Shipments	Capital Invest.
1992	92	89	91	101	98	102	70	60	59	47	51	65
1997	109	105	102	117	123	127	101	72	90	135	123	241
2001		114	121	127	137	139	118	85	113	93	99	254
2002	100	100	100	100	100	100	100	100	100	100	100	100
2003		98	96	88	84	87	92	98	104	105	105	90
2004		93	89	80	75	81	88	97	100	119	114	112
2005		92	87	78	72	77	91	104	94	126	117	183
2006		106P	103P	77	72	77	93	109	95	114	110	128
2007		107P	103P	93P	92P	96P	111P	110P	117P	140P	135P	188P
2008		108P	103P	92P	91P	95P	113P	114P	120P	144P	139P	191P
2009		109P	104P	90P	89P	93P	115P	117P	124P	149P	143P	194P
2010		109P	104P	89P	88P	91P	117P	121P	127P	153P	147P	197P

Sources: Same as General Statistics. Values reflect change from the base year, 2002. Values above 100 mean greater than 2002, values below 100 mean less than 2002, and the values of 100 in other years means the same as 2002. 'P's show projections by the editors.

SELECTED RATIOS

For 2002	Avg. of All Manufact.	Analyzed Industry	Index	For 2002	Avg. of All Manufact.	Analyzed Industry	Index
Employees per Establishment	42	164	392	Value Added per Production Worker	182,367	548,943	301
Payroll per Establishment	1,639,184	9,575,678	584	Cost per Establishment	5,769,015	16,047,287	278
Payroll per Employee	39,053	58,267	149	Cost per Employee	137,446	97,646	71
Production Workers per Establishment	30	83	283	Cost per Production Worker	195,506	192,344	98
Wages per Establishment	694,845	3,693,285	532	Shipments per Establishment	11,158,348	61,684,787	553
Wages per Production Worker	23,548	44,268	188	Shipments per Employee	265,847	375,346	141
Hours per Production Worker	1,980	1,957	99	Shipments per Production Worker	378,144	739,358	196
Wages per Hour	11.89	22.62	190	Investment per Establishment	361,338	4,631,008	1,282
Value Added per Establishment	5,381,325	45,798,450	851	Investment per Employee	8,609	28,179	327
Value Added per Employee	128,210	278,679	217	Investment per Production Worker	12,245	55,508	453

Sources: Same as General Statistics. The 'Average of All Manufacturing' column represents the average of all manufacturing industries reported for the most recent complete year available. The Index shows the relationship between the Average and the Analyzed Industry. For example, 100 means that they are equal; 500 that the Analyzed Industry is five times the average; 50 means that the Analyzed Industry is half the national average. The abbreviation 'na' is used to show that data are 'not available'. Ratios shown for 2002, the last complete census year.

LEADING COMPANIES   Number shown: **75**   Total sales ($ mil): **392,914**   Total employment (000): **1,168.2**

Company Name	Address				CEO Name	Phone	Co. Type	Sales ($ mil)	Empl. (000)
International Bus. Machines	1 New Orchard Rd.	Armonk	NY	10504		914-499-1900	P	98,786	329.4
Intel Corp.	2200 Mission Clg.	Santa Clara	CA	95054	Craig R. Barrett	408-765-8080	P	38,334	86.3
Motorola Inc.	1303 E Algonquin	Schaumburg	IL	60196	Greg Brown	847-576-5000	P	36,622	66.0
Raytheon Co.	870 Winter St.	Waltham	MA	02451		781-522-3000	P	21,301	72.1
Tyco International Ltd.	1 Tyco Park	Exeter	NH	03833	Edward D. Breen	441-292-8674	P	18,800	118.0
Avnet Inc.	2211 S 47th St.	Phoenix	AZ	85034		480-643-2000	P	15,681	11.7
Texas Instruments Inc.	PO Box 660199	Dallas	TX	75266	Thomas Engibous	972-995-2011	P	13,835	30.2
Jabil Circuit Inc.	10560 M L King Jr.	St. Petersburg	FL	33716		727-577-9749	P	12,291	61.0
Medtronic AVE Inc.	3576 Unocal Pl.	Santa Rosa	CA	95403	William Hawkins	707-525-0111	S	10,054	21.5
Epson Electronics America Inc.	2580 Orchard Pkwy.	San Jose	CA	95131	Toshio Akahane	408-922-0200	R	9,460*	<0.1
Advanced Micro Devices Inc.	PO Box 3453	Sunnyvale	CA	94088		408-749-4000	P	6,013	16.4
Freescale Semiconductor Inc.	6501 Wm Cannon	Austin	TX	78735	Richard Beyer	512-895-2000	P	5,722	23.2
Micron Technology Inc.	PO Box 6	Boise	ID	83707	Steven R. Appleton	208-368-4000	P	5,688	23.5
Western Digital Corp.	20511 Lk Forest Dr.	Lake Forest	CA	92630	John Coyne	949-672-7000	P	5,468	29.6
Agilent Technologies Inc.	5301 Stevens Creek	Santa Clara	CA	95051	Patrick J. Byrne	408-345-8886	P	5,420	19.2
Siltronic AG	4010 Moorprk Ave.	San Jose	CA	95117	Wilhelm Sittenthaler	408-296-7887	S	5,183*	5.6
Harris Corp.	1025 W NASA	Melbourne	FL	32919		321-727-9100	P	4,243	16.0
NVIDIA Corp.	2701 San Tomas	Santa Clara	CA	95050		408-486-2000	P	4,098	4.1
Broadcom Corp.	16215 Alton Pky.	Irvine	CA	92618		949-450-8700	P	3,776	4.7
Kingston Technology Company	17600 Newhope St.	Fountain Valley	CA	92708		714-435-2600	R	3,536*	3.3
United Microelectronics Corp.	488 De Guigne Dr.	Sunnyvale	CA	94085	Jackson Hu	408-523-7800	P	3,437	11.9
Siemens Power Generation Inc.	4400 N Alafaya Trl.	Orlando	FL	32826	Randy Zwirn	407-736-2000	R	3,081*	3.0
Amkor Technology Inc.	1900 S Price Rd.	Chandler	AZ	85286	James J. Kim	480-821-5000	P	2,739	21.6
LSI Corp.	1621 Barber Ln.	Milpitas	CA	95035		408-954-3108	P	2,604	6.2
Analog Devices Inc.	PO Box 9106	Norwood	MA	02062	Jerald G. Fishman	781-329-4700	P	2,546	9.6
Wakefield Thermal Solutions	33 Bridge St.	Pelham	NH	03076	Robert Streiter	603-635-2800	S	2,398*	0.1
AMI Semiconductor Inc.	2300 W Buckskin	Pocatello	ID	83201	Christine King	208-233-4690	S	2,323*	2.5
Samsung Semiconductor Inc.	3655 N 1st St.	San Jose	CA	95134	Young Hwan Park	408-544-4000	S	2,148	1.2
Hitachi America Ltd.	2000 Sierra Pnt Pky	Brisbane	CA	94005	Masahide Tanigahi	650-589-8300	S	2,127*	4.4
National Semiconductor Corp.	PO Box 58090	Santa Clara	CA	95052		408-721-5000	P	1,930	7.6
Sand Video Inc.	200 Brickstone Sq.	Andover	MA	01810	Peter Besen		S	1,861*	3.7
Maxim Integrated Products Inc.	120 San Gabriel Dr.	Sunnyvale	CA	94086	Tunc Doluca	408-737-7600	P	1,859	8.0
Xilinx Inc.	2100 Logic Dr.	San Jose	CA	95124		408-559-7778	P	1,843	3.4
Fairchild Semiconductor Int'l	82 Running Hill Rd.	South Portland	ME	04106		207-775-8100	P	1,670	9.7
Marvell Technology Group Ltd.	5488 Marvell Ln.	Santa Clara	CA	95054		408-222-2500	P	1,670	2.5
Atmel Corp.	2325 Orchard Pky.	San Jose	CA	95131		408-441-0311	P	1,639	7.4
Cypress Semiconductor Corp.	198 Champion Ct.	San Jose	CA	95134	Eric A. Benhamou	408-943-2600	P	1,596	7.9
ON Semiconductor Corp.	5005 E McDowell	Phoenix	AZ	85008		602-244-6600	P	1,566	11.7
Avago Technologies Pte	350 W Trimble Rd.	San Jose	CA	95131	Dick Chang	408-435-7400	S	1,527	6.5
MEMC Electronic Materials Inc.	PO Box 8	St. Peters	MO	63376	Nabeel Gareeb	636-474-5000	P	1,434	4.9
JDS Uniphase Corp.	430 N McCarthy	Milpitas	CA	95035	Martin A. Kaplan	408-546-5000	P	1,397*	7.0
AVX Corp.	PO Box 867	Myrtle Beach	SC	29578	John S. Gilbertson	843-448-9411	P	1,333	13.0
Altera Corp.	101 Innovation Dr.	San Jose	CA	95134	John P. Daane	408-544-7000	P	1,264	2.7
EaglePicher Corp.	2424 John Daly Rd.	Inkster	MI	48141	Donald L. Runkle	313-278-5956	R	1,244*	4.2
International Rectifier Corp.	233 Kansas St.	El Segundo	CA	90245	Donald Dancer		P	1,171	6.3
Linear Technology Corp.	1630 McCarthy	Milpitas	CA	95035	David Bell	408-432-1900	P	1,083	3.8
Varian Semiconductor Equipment	35 Dory Rd.	Gloucester	MA	01930	Richard A. Aurelio	978-282-2000	P	1,055	1.7
Microchip Technology Inc.	2355 W Chandler	Chandler	AZ	85224		480-792-7200	P	1,040	4.6
RF Micro Devices Inc.	7628 Thorndike Rd.	Greensboro	NC	27409	R A. Bruggeworth	336-664-1233	P	1,024	3.3
SMART Modular Technologies	4211 Starboard Dr.	Fremont	CA	94538	Ian MacKenzie	510-623-1231	P	828	1.4
Conexant Systems Inc.	4000 MacArthur	Newport Beach	CA	92660	Dwight Decker	949-483-4600	P	809	2.2
Integrated Device Technology	6024 Silver Crk Vly	San Jose	CA	95138		408-284-8200	P	804	2.1
Leviton Manufacturing Company	PO Box 630087	Little Neck	NY	11363	Donald Hendler	718-229-4040	R	800*	0.7
Intersil Corp.	1001 Murphy Ranch	Milpitas	CA	95035	David B. Bell	408-432-8888	P	757	1.5
Brooks Automation Inc.	15 Elizabeth Dr.	Chelmsford	MA	01824		978-262-2400	P	743	1.9
Skyworks Solutions Inc.	20 Sylvan Rd.	Woburn	MA	01801	David J. Aldrich	781-376-3000	P	742	3.4
Microsemi Corp.-Colorado	800 Hoyt St.	Broomfield	CO	80020	Jim Peterson	303-469-2161	S	735*	1.5
Microsemi Corp.-Integr. Prods	11861 Western Ave.	Garden Grove	CA	92841	Jim Peterson	714-898-8121	S	735*	1.5
Microsemi Corp.-Santa Ana	2830 S Fairview St.	Santa Ana	CA	92704	Jim Peterson	714-979-8220	S	735*	1.5
PMC Global Inc.	PO Box 1367	Sun Valley	CA	91353	Gary Kamins	818-896-1101	R	729*	4.0
AMIS Holdings Inc.	2300 W Buckskin	Pocatello	ID	83201	Christine King	208-233-4690	P	606	2.9
QLogic Corp.	26650 Aliso Viejo	Aliso Viejo	CA	92656	H.K. Desai	949-389-6000	P	587	1.0
Comdel Inc.	11 Kondelin Rd.	Gloucester	MA	01930	Theodore Johnson	978-282-0620	R	556*	<0.1
Aeroflex Inc.	PO Box 6022	Plainview	NY	11803	Harvey R. Blau	516-694-6700	R	537*	2.6
OSI Systems Inc.	12525 Chadron Ave.	Hawthorne	CA	90250	Deepak Chopra	310-978-0516	P	532	3.5
OmniVision Technologies Inc.	1341 Orleans Dr.	Sunnyvale	CA	94089	Shaw Hong	408-542-3000	P	528	2.1
Zoran Corp.	1390 Kifer Rd.	Sunnyvale	CA	94086	Levy Gerzberg	408-523-6500	P	507	1.4
First Solar Inc.	4050 E Cotton Ctr.	Phoenix	AZ	85040	Michael J. Ahearn	602-414-9300	P	504	1.5
TriQuint Semiconductor Inc.	2300 NE Brookwood	Hillsboro	OR	97124		503-615-9000	P	476	1.8
Hynix Semiconductor Mfg. Amer.	1830 Willow Crk Cir	Eugene	OR	97402	Deong Kim	541-338-5000	R	469*	1.2
Siliconix Inc.	PO Box 54951	Santa Clara	CA	95056	King Owyang	408-988-8000	S	466	2.0
FormFactor Inc.	7005 Southfront Rd.	Livermore	CA	94551	William H. Davidow	925-290-4000	P	462	1.1
Silicon Storage Technology	1171 Sonora Ct.	Sunnyvale	CA	94086		408-735-9110	P	452	0.6
PMC-Sierra Inc.	3975 Freedom Cir.	Santa Clara	CA	95054	Robert L. Bailey	408-239-8000	P	449	1.0
MRV Communications Inc.	20415 Nordhoff St.	Chatsworth	CA	91311	Noam Lotan	818-773-0900	P	448	1.5

Source: *Ward's Business Directory of U.S. Private and Public Companies*, Volumes 1 and 2, 2008. The company type code used is as follows: P - Public, R - Private, S - Subsidiary, D - Division, J - Joint Venture, A - Affiliate, G - Group. Sales are in millions of dollars, employees are in thousands. An asterisk (*) indicates an estimated sales volume. The symbol < stands for 'less than'. Company names and addresses are truncated, in some cases, to fit into the available space.

MATERIALS CONSUMED

Material	Quantity	Delivered Cost ($ million)
Tube blanks	(X)	2.1
Printed ciruit boards (without inserted components) for electronic circuitry	(X)	219.2
Printed circuit assemblies, loaded boards, and modules	(X)	136.7
Semiconductors (incl. transistors, diodes, rectifiers, and integrated circuits), for electronic circuitry	(X)	1,079.1
Capacitors for electronic circuitry	(X)	(D)
Resistors for electronic circuitry	(X)	12.4
All other miscellaneous components and accessories for electronic circuitry (exc. tubes)	(X)	238.7
Silicon, hyperpure	(X)	2,204.0
Gold and other precious metals, all forms (incl. ingot, sheet, etc.)	(X)	289.5
Doped chemicals and other doped materials for electronic use	(X)	1,952.2
Ferrites (powder and paste)	(X)	18.7
Metal powders	(X)	17.4
Electronic computer equipment	(X)	24.1
Current-carrying wiring devices	(X)	(D)
Electronic communication equipment	(X)	57.4
Electrical instrument mechanisms and meter movements	(X)	(D)
All other miscellaneous electrical measuring instruments and parts	(X)	5.1
Fractional horsepower electric motors (less than 1 hp)	(X)	(D)
Electrical transmission, distribution, and control equipment	(X)	22.4
Loudspeakers, microphones, and tuners (all types)	(X)	(D)
Glass and glass products (excluding windows and mirrors)	(X)	114.1
Optical instruments and lenses (exc. sighting, tracking, and fire control)	(X)	6.5
Plastics resins consumed in the form of granules, pellets, etc.	(X)	38.0
Fabricated plastics products (excluding gaskets)	(X)	20.5
Sheet metal products (excluding stampings)	(X)	(D)
Metal stampings	(X)	115.5
Metal bolts, nuts, screws, and other screw machine products	(X)	5.4
Other fabricated metal products (excluding forgings)	(X)	33.9
Forgings	(X)	(D)
Castings, rough and semifinished	(X)	(D)
Steel shapes and forms (exc. castings, forgings, fabr. metal products)	(X)	3.7
Copper and copper-base alloy shapes and forms (exc. castings, forgings, fabr. metal products)	(X)	18.9
Aluminum and aluminum-base alloy shapes and forms (exc. castings, forgings, fabr. metal products)	(X)	37.2
Other nonferrous shapes and forms (exc. castings, forgings, fabricated metal products)	(X)	11.7
Insulated wire and cable (including magnet wire)	(X)	27.6
Paper and paperboard containers (incl. shipping sacks and other paper packaging supplies)	(X)	28.9
Resists (photosensitive resin films applied to surface of wafer)	(X)	194.7
Commodity gases	(X)	436.1
Speciality gases	(X)	340.2
Masks	(X)	386.8
Silicon chips	(X)	1,310.2
Solvents	(X)	34.6
Cleaning compounds	(X)	(D)
All other materials, components, parts, containers, and supplies	(X)	2,528.5
Materials, ingredients, containers, and supplies, nsk	(X)	445.0

Source: 2002 *Economic Census*. Explanation of symbols used: (D): Withheld to avoid disclosure of competitive data; na: Not available; (S): Withheld because statistical norms were not met; (X): Not applicable; (Z): Less than half the unit shown; nec: Not elsewhere classified; nsk: Not specified by kind; - : zero; p : 10-19 percent estimated; q : 20-29 percent estimated.

PRODUCT SHARE DETAILS

Product or Product Class Shipments	Mil. $	Product or Product Class Shipments	Mil. $
SEMICONDUCTORS AND RELATED DEVICES	61,545.8	**Diodes and rectifiers**	**396.4**
Integrated microcircuits, including semiconductor networks, microprocessors, and MOS memories	**51,381.9**	**Other semiconductor devices, including semiconductor parts, such as chips, wafers, and heat sinks**	**6,870.6**
Transistors	**857.8**	**Semiconductors and related devices, nsk, total**	**2,039.2**

Source: 2002 *Economic Census*. The values are product shipments in millions of dollars for 2002. Total product shipments may be lower or higher than industry shipments. See Introduction for a full discussion. Values of indented subcategories are summed in the main heading(s). The symbol (D) appears when data are withheld to prevent disclosure of competitive information. The abbreviation nsk stands for 'not specified by kind' and nec for 'not elsewhere classified'. A dash (-) means zero.

INPUTS AND OUTPUTS FOR SEMICONDUCTOR AND RELATED DEVICE MANUFACTURING

Economic Sector or Industry Providing Inputs	%	Sector	Economic Sector or Industry Buying Outputs	%	Sector
Compensation of employees	20.6		Exports of goods & services	34.7	Cap Inv
Management of companies & enterprises	9.2	Services	Printed circuit assemblies (electronic assembiles)	5.7	Manufg.
Wholesale trade	6.2	Trade	Electronic computers	4.6	Manufg.
Basic inorganic chemicals, nec	4.1	Manufg.	Wholesale trade	4.0	Trade
Semiconductors & related devices	4.1	Manufg.	Telecommunications	3.8	Services
Primary nonferrous metal, ex. copper & aluminum	3.5	Manufg.	Broadcast & wireless communications equipment	3.8	Manufg.
Scientific research & development services	2.4	Services	Light truck & utility vehicles	3.3	Manufg.
Power generation & supply	1.3	Util.	Semiconductors & related devices	3.2	Manufg.

Continued on next page.

INPUTS AND OUTPUTS FOR SEMICONDUCTOR AND RELATED DEVICE MANUFACTURING - Continued

Economic Sector or Industry Providing Inputs	%	Sector	Economic Sector or Industry Buying Outputs	%	Sector
Advertising & related services	0.8	Services	General Federal government services, defense	2.9	Fed Govt
Legal services	0.7	Services	Telephone apparatus	2.9	Manufg.
Electronic components, nec	0.7	Manufg.	Motor vehicle parts	1.8	Manufg.
Industrial gases	0.7	Manufg.	Automobiles	1.5	Manufg.
Taxes on production & imports, less subsidies	0.6		Search, detection, & navigation instruments	1.4	Manufg.
Automotive equipment rental & leasing	0.6	Fin/R.E.	Aircraft	1.4	Manufg.
Chemical products & preparations, nec	0.6	Manufg.	Aluminum products from purchased aluminum	1.0	Manufg.
Lessors of nonfinancial assets	0.6	Fin/R.E.	Retail trade	0.7	Trade
Printed circuit assemblies (electronic assemblies)	0.6	Manufg.	Computer terminals & peripherals	0.7	Manufg.
Real estate	0.5	Fin/R.E.	Printing	0.6	Manufg.
Specialized design services	0.5	Services	Soft drinks & ice	0.5	Manufg.
Truck transportation	0.4	Util.	Plastics products, nec	0.5	Manufg.
Management, scientific, & technical consulting	0.4	Services	Custom computer programming services	0.4	Services
Employment services	0.4	Services	Bare printed circuit boards	0.4	Manufg.
Other computer related services, including facilities	0.4	Services	Ornamental & architectural metal products	0.4	Manufg.
Plastics packaging materials, film & sheet	0.4	Manufg.	Electromedical & electrotherapeutic apparatus	0.4	Manufg.
Maintenance/repair of nonresidential structures	0.4	Construct.	Electronic & precision equipment repair/maintenance	0.4	Services
Noncomparable imports	0.4	Foreign	Automotive repair & maintenance, ex. car washes	0.4	Services
Business support services	0.4	Services	Basic organic chemicals, nec	0.4	Manufg.
Data processing, hosting, & related services	0.4	Services	Computer storage devices	0.3	Manufg.
Electronic capacitors, resistors, coils, transformers	0.3	Manufg.	Software publishers	0.3	Services
Bare printed circuit boards	0.3	Manufg.	Plastics packaging materials, film & sheet	0.3	Manufg.
Services to buildings & dwellings	0.3	Services	Paperboard containers	0.3	Manufg.
Telecommunications	0.3	Services	Breweries	0.3	Manufg.
Plate work & fabricated structural products	0.3	Manufg.	Guided missiles & space vehicles	0.3	Manufg.
Ornamental & architectural metal products	0.3	Manufg.	Electricity & signal testing instruments	0.3	Manufg.
Commercial & industrial machinery rental & leasing	0.3	Fin/R.E.	Iron & steel mills & ferroalloys	0.3	Manufg.
Architectural, engineering, & related services	0.3	Services	Toilet preparations	0.3	Manufg.
Warehousing & storage	0.3	Util.	Totalizing fluid meters & counting devices	0.3	Manufg.
Semiconductor machinery	0.2	Manufg.	Paper mills	0.3	Manufg.
Automotive repair & maintenance, ex. car washes	0.2	Services	Plastics materials & resins	0.2	Manufg.
Machine shops	0.2	Manufg.	Electronic components, nec	0.2	Manufg.
Support services, nec	0.2	Services	Wiring devices	0.2	Manufg.
Computer system design services	0.2	Services	Industrial machinery, nec	0.2	Manufg.
Crowns & closures & metal stamping	0.2	Manufg.	Plate work & fabricated structural products	0.2	Manufg.
Commercial & industrial equipment repair/maintenance	0.2	Services	Computer system design services	0.2	Services
Wiring devices	0.2	Manufg.	Wineries	0.2	Manufg.
Motors & generators	0.2	Manufg.	Management of companies & enterprises	0.2	Services
Investigation & security services	0.2	Services	Manufacturing, nec	0.2	Manufg.
Audio & video equipment	0.2	Manufg.	General purpose machinery, nec	0.2	Manufg.
Forging, stamping, & sintering, nec	0.2	Manufg.	Audio & video equipment	0.2	Manufg.
Soap & cleaning compounds	0.2	Manufg.	Hospitals	0.2	Services
Electricity & signal testing instruments	0.2	Manufg.	Turned products & screws, nuts, & bolts	0.2	Manufg.
Natural gas distribution	0.2	Util.	Machine shops	0.2	Manufg.
Accounting, tax preparation, bookkeeping, & payroll	0.2	Services	Surgical & medical instrument	0.2	Manufg.
Plastics products, nec	0.2	Manufg.	Chemical products & preparations, nec	0.2	Manufg.
Rail transportation	0.2	Util.	Material handling equipment	0.1	Manufg.
Plastics pipe & pipe fittings	0.2	Manufg.	AC, refrigeration, and warm air heating equipment	0.1	Manufg.
Securities, commodity contracts, investments	0.1	Fin/R.E.	Aircraft parts & auxiliary equipment, nec	0.1	Manufg.
Electronic connectors	0.1	Manufg.	Wood windows & doors & millwork	0.1	Manufg.
Custom computer programming services	0.1	Services	Household cooking appliances	0.1	Manufg.
Industrial process variable instruments	0.1	Manufg.	Valve & fittings other than plumbing	0.1	Manufg.
Petroleum refineries	0.1	Manufg.	Paints & coatings	0.1	Manufg.
Unlaminated plastics profile shapes	0.1	Manufg.	Coating, engraving, heat treating & allied activities	0.1	Manufg.
Cutting tools & machine tool accessories	0.1	Manufg.	Artificial & synthetic fibers & filaments	0.1	Manufg.
Wood kitchen cabinets & countertops	0.1	Manufg.	Engine equipment, nec	0.1	Manufg.
Concrete pipe, brick, & block	0.1	Manufg.	Commercial & service industry machinery, nec	0.1	Manufg.
Concrete products, nec	0.1	Manufg.	Photographic & photocopying equipment	0.1	Manufg.
			Communications equipment, nec	0.1	Manufg.
			Paperboard mills	0.1	Manufg.
			Steel products from purchased steel	0.1	Manufg.
			Food services & drinking places	0.1	Services
			Wood kitchen cabinets & countertops	0.1	Manufg.
			Irradiation apparatus	0.1	Manufg.
			Rubber products, nec	0.1	Manufg.
			Household laundry equipment	0.1	Manufg.
			Lighting fixtures	0.1	Manufg.
			Coated & laminated paper & packaging materials	0.1	Manufg.
			Metal cans, boxes, & other containers (light gauge)	0.1	Manufg.
			Heavy duty trucks	0.1	Manufg.
			Fabricated metals, nec	0.1	Manufg.
			Mining & oil & gas field machinery	0.1	Manufg.
			Advertising & related services	0.1	Services
			Automatic environmental controls	0.1	Manufg.
			Carpet & rug mills	0.1	Manufg.
			Other computer related services, including facilities	0.1	Services
			Software, audio, and video media reproducing	0.1	Manufg.
			Glass products from purchased glass	0.1	Manufg.
			Aircraft engine & engine parts	0.1	Manufg.
			Sanitary paper products	0.1	Manufg.

Source: Benchmark Input-Output Accounts for the U.S. Economy, 2002, U.S. Department of Commerce, Washington, D.C., January 2008. The abbreviation nec stands for 'not elsewhere classified'.

OCCUPATIONS EMPLOYED BY SEMICONDUCTOR & OTHER ELECTRONIC COMPONENT MANUFACTURING

Occupation	% of Total 2006	Change to 2016	Occupation	% of Total 2006	Change to 2016
Electrical & electronic equipment assemblers	10.9	-30.1	Computer software engineers, systems software	1.5	-3.8
Semiconductor processors	8.2	-12.6	Production workers, nec	1.3	-14.2
Team assemblers	4.5	-12.6	Shipping, receiving, & traffic clerks	1.3	-15.9
Electrical & electronic engineering technicians	4.1	-12.6	Purchasing agents, exc wholesale, retail, & farm	1.3	-12.6
Inspectors, testers, sorters, samplers, & weighers	3.9	-17.6	Production, planning, & expediting clerks	1.2	-12.6
Electronics engineers, exc computer	3.9	-12.6	General & operations managers	1.2	-21.3
First-line supervisors/managers of production workers	2.8	-12.6	Coil winders, tapers, & finishers	1.1	-30.1
Electrical engineers	2.6	-12.6	Machinists	1.1	-8.2
Industrial engineers	2.5	6.2	Industrial production managers	1.0	-12.6
Engineering managers	2.3	-3.8	Maintenance & repair workers, general	1.0	-12.6
Electromechanical equipment assemblers	1.7	-12.6			

Source: Industry-Occupation Matrix, Bureau of Labor Statistics, December 4, 2007. These data are reported based on 4-digit NAICS categories but have been matched to corresponding 6-digit NAICS industry codes. The change reported for each occupation to the year 2016 is a percent of growth or decline as estimated by the Bureau of Labor Statistics. The abbreviation nec stands for 'not elsewhere classified'.

LOCATION BY STATE AND REGIONAL CONCENTRATION

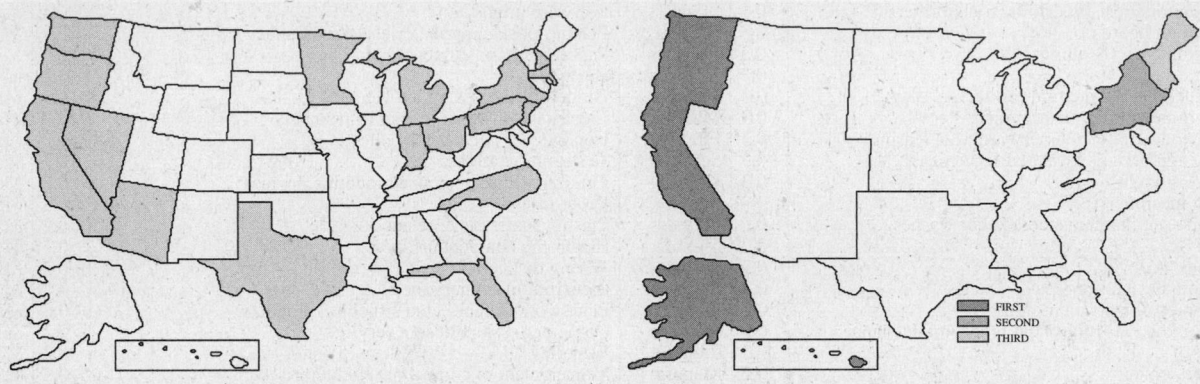

FIRST
SECOND
THIRD

INDUSTRY DATA BY STATE

State	Establish-ments	Shipments			Employment				Cost as % of Shipments	Investment per Employee ($)
		Total ($ mil)	% of U.S.	Per Establ.	Total Number	% of U.S.	Per Establ.	Wages ($/hour)		
California	388	11,936.9	18.8	30,765.3	42,924	25.3	111	22.52	24.4	27,911
Arizona	45	10,226.2	16.1	227,249.1	13,385	7.9	297	21.95	13.3	7,871
Oregon	27	9,184.9	14.4	340,181.7	6,999	4.1	259	24.71	11.4	16,902
Texas	78	9,167.0	14.4	117,525.3	29,530	17.4	379	21.38	54.1	33,093
Massachusetts	67	4,336.7	6.8	64,727.4	7,998	4.7	119	21.28	28.7	19,109
New York	37	1,297.7	2.0	35,073.9	9,333	5.5	252	17.51	22.4	2,434
Florida	26	926.9	1.5	35,650.0	3,703	2.2	142	23.71	21.4	19,162
Washington	24	866.8	1.4	36,115.7	3,484	2.1	145	20.06	39.7	11,167
North Carolina	17	729.7	1.1	42,923.1	2,607	1.5	153	28.46	42.8	74,892
Pennsylvania	44	643.7	1.0	14,630.7	5,242	3.1	119	24.89	37.0	14,196
New Jersey	35	376.9	0.6	10,769.3	1,827	1.1	52	22.49	33.7	6,617
Minnesota	17	339.8	0.5	19,987.6	1,730	1.0	102	27.39	31.2	17,361
Ohio	12	136.2	0.2	11,345.9	1,009	0.6	84	18.23	32.7	34,813
New Hampshire	19	107.6	0.2	5,665.6	749	0.4	39	18.18	30.9	2,522
Michigan	16	55.7	0.1	3,478.8	354	0.2	22	15.34	30.3	2,929
Indiana	7	17.7	<0.1	2,532.4	201	0.1	29	7.22	28.7	1,478
Nevada	4	14.6	<0.1	3,648.5	137	0.1	34	12.19	41.5	1,788

Source: 2002 *Economic Census*. The states are in descending order of shipments or establishments (if shipment data are missing for the majority). The symbol (D) appears when data are withheld to prevent disclosure of competitive information. States marked with (D) are sorted by number of establishments. A dash (-) indicates that the data element cannot be calculated. Data may not show all states active in the NAICS category. All data available at the time of publication are shown.

NAICS 334414 - ELECTRONIC CAPACITOR MANUFACTURING

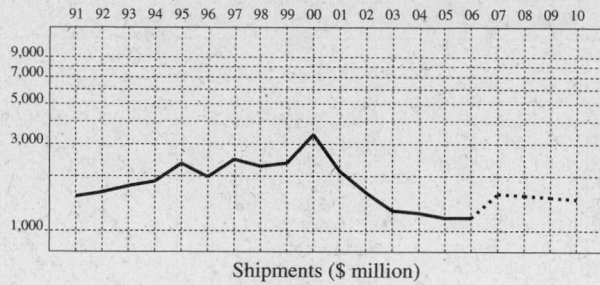

Shipments ($ million)

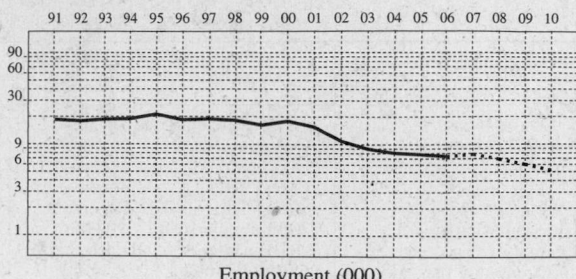

Employment (000)

GENERAL STATISTICS

Year	Companies	Establishments Total	Establishments with 20 or more employees	Employment Total (000)	Employment Production Workers (000)	Employment Hours (Mil)	Compensation Payroll ($ mil)	Compensation Wages ($/hr)	Production Cost of Materials	Production Value Added by Manufacture	Production Value of Shipments	Production Capital Invest.
1991		125	94	18.5	13.5	27.2	417.8	8.82	618.6	926.3	1,546.1	57.1
1992	99	117	80	17.9	13.4	26.3	415.7	9.43	703.0	930.0	1,630.1	64.0
1993		115	81	18.7	13.7	27.9	438.7	9.37	788.2	979.0	1,762.8	63.9
1994		115	77	18.8	14.2	29.4	474.2	9.99	879.8	1,002.3	1,871.9	78.5
1995		117	78	21.2	16.8	34.7	514.3	9.38	1,047.6	1,333.8	2,346.0	156.6
1996		120	75	18.4	14.2	28.3	472.1	9.57	984.6	1,004.8	1,977.9	212.3
1997	111	128	81	18.8	13.1	25.4	528.4	11.12	1,141.6	1,374.0	2,473.4	127.9
1998		125	81	18.2	12.7	25.0	510.4	10.91	1,033.1	1,239.5	2,265.6	158.7
1999		128	78	16.2	11.1	22.3	482.0	11.75	1,088.8	1,258.2	2,361.1	122.0
2000		120	79	17.9	12.9	24.9	576.5	12.36	1,533.0	1,919.4	3,385.9	281.5
2001		119	80	15.5	10.8	20.6	518.3	12.80	1,101.3	979.8	2,130.3	144.1
2002	84	104	60	10.9	7.5	14.8	383.5	12.53	840.9	720.5	1,628.2	125.1
2003		95	56	9.0	6.3	13.3	323.0	13.43	625.4	648.3	1,291.8	53.8
2004		94	52	8.1	5.6	11.3	305.5	13.90	618.9	639.3	1,251.3	56.0
2005		87	47	7.8	5.1	10.2	303.5	13.98	482.8	680.7	1,179.1	36.6
2006		98P	54P	7.4	4.7	9.8	302.6	14.04	442.6	740.0	1,178.6	42.5
2007		97P	51P	7.8P	4.9P	9.7P	353.1P	14.72P	599.7P	1,002.6P	1,596.9P	98.5P
2008		95P	49P	6.9P	4.2P	8.3P	343.5P	15.11P	586.6P	980.8P	1,562.1P	97.0P
2009		93P	47P	6.0P	3.5P	6.8P	333.8P	15.49P	573.5P	958.9P	1,527.3P	95.5P
2010		91P	44P	5.2P	2.8P	5.4P	324.1P	15.88P	560.5P	937.1P	1,492.5P	94.0P

Sources: 1992, 1997, 2002 *Economic Census*; other years, up to 2006, are from the *Annual Survey of Manufactures*. Establishment counts for non-Census years are from *County Business Patterns*; 1997 and 2002 values are from the 1997 and 2002 censuses respectively, reported in the Federal Government's NAICS format. Other years were originally reported in equivalent SIC format. 'P's show projections by the editors.

INDICES OF CHANGE

Year	Companies	Establishments Total	Establishments with 20 or more employees	Employment Total (000)	Employment Production Workers (000)	Employment Hours (Mil)	Compensation Payroll ($ mil)	Compensation Wages ($/hr)	Production Cost of Materials	Production Value Added by Manufacture	Production Value of Shipments	Production Capital Invest.
1992	118	113	133	164	179	178	108	75	84	129	100	51
1997	132	123	135	172	175	172	138	89	136	191	152	102
2001		114	133	142	144	139	135	102	131	136	131	115
2002	100	100	100	100	100	100	100	100	100	100	100	100
2003		91	93	83	84	90	84	107	74	90	79	43
2004		90	87	74	75	76	80	111	74	89	77	45
2005		84	78	72	68	69	79	112	57	94	72	29
2006		95P	90P	68	63	66	79	112	53	103	72	34
2007		93P	86P	72P	65P	66P	92P	117P	71P	139P	98P	79P
2008		91P	82P	63P	56P	56P	90P	121P	70P	136P	96P	78P
2009		89P	78P	55P	47P	46P	87P	124P	68P	133P	94P	76P
2010		87P	74P	48P	37P	36P	85P	127P	67P	130P	92P	75P

Sources: Same as General Statistics. Values reflect change from the base year, 2002. Values above 100 mean greater than 2002, values below 100 mean less than 2002, and the values of 100 in other years means the same as 2002. 'P's show projections by the editors.

SELECTED RATIOS

For 2002	Avg. of All Manufact.	Analyzed Industry	Index	For 2002	Avg. of All Manufact.	Analyzed Industry	Index
Employees per Establishment	42	105	250	Value Added per Production Worker	182,367	96,067	53
Payroll per Establishment	1,639,184	3,687,500	225	Cost per Establishment	5,769,015	8,085,577	140
Payroll per Employee	39,053	35,183	90	Cost per Employee	137,446	77,147	56
Production Workers per Establishment	30	72	244	Cost per Production Worker	195,506	112,120	57
Wages per Establishment	694,845	1,783,115	257	Shipments per Establishment	11,158,348	15,655,769	140
Wages per Production Worker	23,548	24,726	105	Shipments per Employee	265,847	149,376	56
Hours per Production Worker	1,980	1,973	100	Shipments per Production Worker	378,144	217,093	57
Wages per Hour	11.89	12.53	105	Investment per Establishment	361,338	1,202,885	333
Value Added per Establishment	5,381,325	6,927,885	129	Investment per Employee	8,609	11,477	133
Value Added per Employee	128,210	66,101	52	Investment per Production Worker	12,245	16,680	136

Sources: Same as General Statistics. The 'Average of All Manufacturing' column represents the average of all manufacturing industries reported for the most recent complete year available. The Index shows the relationship between the Average and the Analyzed Industry. For example, 100 means that they are equal; 500 that the Analyzed Industry is five times the average; 50 means that the Analyzed Industry is half the national average. The abbreviation 'na' is used to show that data are 'not available'. Ratios shown for 2002, the last complete census year.

LEADING COMPANIES   Number shown: 71   Total sales ($ mil): 11,162   Total employment (000): 82.0

Company Name	Address				CEO Name	Phone	Co. Type	Sales ($ mil)	Empl. (000)
Vishay Vitramon Inc.	One Greenwich Place	Shelton	CT	06484	Gerald Paul	402-563-6866	P	4,995	27.9
Vishay Intertechnology Inc.	PO Box 4004	Malvern	PA	19355	Gerald Paul	610-644-1300	P	2,833	27.9
AVX Corp.	PO Box 867	Myrtle Beach	SC	29578	John S. Gilbertson	843-448-9411	P	1,333	13.0
KEMET Corp.	PO Box 5928.	Greenville	SC	29606		864-963-6300	P	659	9.1
United Chemi-Con Inc.	9801 W Higgins Rd.	Rosemont	IL	60018		847-696-2000	R	510*	<0.1
Murata Electronics N America	2200 Lake Park Dr.	Smyrna	GA	30080	Hiroshi Jozuka	770-436-1300	R	175*	0.2
Micro Dynamics Corp.	6201 Bury Dr.	Eden Prairie	MN	55346	Michael Brown	952-941-8071	R	63*	<0.1
Johanson Technology Inc.	PO Box 923697	Sylmar	CA	91392	Eric Johanson	818-364-9800	R	60*	0.3
Novacap Inc.	25136 Anza Dr.	Valencia	CA	91355		661-295-5920	S	51	0.5
Beckwith Electric Company Inc.	6190-118th Ave. N	Largo	FL	33773	Bob Beckwith	727-544-2326	R	41*	0.1
Elpac Electronics Inc.	1562 Reynolds Ave.	Irvine	CA	92614		949-476-6070	R	29*	0.2
TDK Corporation of America	1600 Feehanville Dr	Mount Prospect	IL	60056	Frank Avant	847-803-6100	S	24*	0.2
Electrocube Inc.	PO Box 889	Monrovia	CA	91017	Clay Parrill	626-301-0122	R	24	<0.1
Cornell-Dubilier Electronics	140 Technology Pl.	Liberty	SC	29657	James Kaplan	864-843-2626	R	22*	<0.1
Steinerfilm Inc.	987 Simonds Rd.	Williamstown	MA	01267	Else Steiner	413-458-9525	R	21*	0.2
Nemco Electronics Corp.	675 Mariners Island	San Mateo	CA	94404	John Nolan	650-571-1234	R	20*	0.2
Vertical Circuits Inc.	10 Victor Sq., 100	Scotts Valley	CA	95066	Sunil Kaul	831-438-3887	R	19*	<0.1
Presidio Components Inc.	PO Box 81576	San Diego	CA	92138	Violet Devoe	858-578-9390	R	16*	0.1
ASC Capacitors	301 W O Street	Ogallala	NE	69153		308-284-3611	S	15*	0.2
Johanson Manufacturing Corp.	301 Rockaway Vly	Boonton	NJ	07005	Nancy Johanson	973-334-2676	R	14*	0.1
ASJ Components Inc.	451 E Patagonia	Nogales	AZ	85621		520-287-4731	R	14*	<0.1
General Assembly Corp.	140 Indu. Park Way	West Jefferson	NC	28694	Tom Lane	336-246-5143	R	13*	<0.1
AVX Tantalum Corp.	401 Hill St.	Biddeford	ME	04005		207-282-5111	S	12*	0.1
Dearborn Electronics Inc.	1221 N US Hwy 17	Longwood	FL	32750		407-695-6562	R	12*	<0.1
Tusonix Inc.	PO Box 37144	Tucson	AZ	85740		520-744-0400	S	12*	<0.1
Mpulse Microwave Inc.	576 Charcot Ave.	San Jose	CA	95131	Billy Long	408-432-1480	R	11*	<0.1
Electronic Concepts Inc.	PO Box 1278	Eatontown	NJ	07724	Bill Levin	732-542-7880	R	9*	0.1
Electron Coil Inc.	PO Box 71	Norwich	NY	13815	Douglas Marchant	607-336-7414	R	9*	<0.1
Knox Semiconductor Inc.	PO Box 609	Rockport	ME	04856	John Williams	207-236-6076	R	9*	<0.1
TSC Electronics Ltd.	1610 Lockness Pl.	Torrance	CA	90501	Shi Tsai	310-534-2738	R	8*	<0.1
Custom Electronics Inc.	87 Browne St.	Oneonta	NY	13820	Peter Dokuchitz	607-432-3880	R	8*	<0.1
ZF Array Technology Inc.	1965 Concourse Dr.	San Jose	CA	95131	Robert Zinn	408-433-9920	R	7*	<0.1
Viking Technologies Ltd.	80 Montauk Hwy.	Lindenhurst	NY	11757	David Kjeldsen	631-957-8000	R	7*	<0.1
Steelman Industries Inc.	PO Box 1461	Kilgore	TX	75663	Danny Bell	903-984-3061	R	7*	<0.1
Bishop Electronics Corp.	3729 San Gabriel	Pico Rivera	CA	90660	William Bishop	562-695-0446	R	6*	<0.1
Electronic Film Capacitors	41 Interstate Ln.	Waterbury	CT	06705	Jay Weiner	203-755-5629	R	6*	<0.1
Voltronics Corp.	100 Ford Rd., 10	Denville	NJ	07834	Aaron Goldberg	973-586-8585	R	6*	<0.1
F-Dyne Electronics	10443 Peach Ave.	Mission Hills	CA	91345	John Strickland	818-893-6068	R	6*	<0.1
FW Capacitors Inc.	PO Box 12636	Florence	SC	29504	Joseph Falcone	843-662-4728	R	5*	<0.1
Metuchen Capacitors Inc.	2139 State Rte. 35	Holmdel	NJ	07733	Stephen Ficsor	732-888-9700	R	5*	<0.1
Sigma Probe Inc.	1054 Yosemite Dr.	Milpitas	CA	95035	Thang Vo	408-441-8183	R	5*	<0.1
Union Technology Corp.	718 Monterey Pass	Monterey Park	CA	91754	David Chu	323-266-6603	R	5*	<0.1
Capax Technologies Inc.	24842 Ave. Tibbitts	Valencia	CA	91355	Jagdish Patel	661-257-7666	R	4*	<0.1
Polyflon Co.	1 Willard Rd.	Norwalk	CT	06851	Will Larusso	203-840-7555	S	4*	<0.1
Virgil Walker Inc.	27555 Ave. Scott	Valencia	CA	91355	Virgil Walker	661-257-9282	R	4*	<0.1
Corry Micronics Inc.	1 Plastics Rd.	Corry	PA	16407	Don Pavlek	814-664-7728	R	4*	<0.1
American Capacitor Corp.	5367 3rd Street	Irwindale	CA	91706	Joseph Latourelle	626-814-4444	R	3*	<0.1
Electro Ceramic Industries	75 Kennedy St.	Hackensack	NJ	07601	Herbert Schlomann	201-342-2630	R	3*	<0.1
Wright Capacitors Inc.	2610 Oak Street	Santa Ana	CA	92707	Casey Crandall	714-546-2490	R	3*	<0.1
Bycap Inc.	5505 N Wolcott	Chicago	IL	60640	Kenneth Yahiro	773-561-4976	R	3*	<0.1
Custom Capacitors Inc.	PO Box 15026	Brooksville	FL	34604	Jeffrey Fielder	352-796-3561	R	3*	<0.1
Tantalum Pellet Company Inc.	21421 N 14th Ave.	Phoenix	AZ	85027	Todd Knowles	623-582-5555	R	3*	<0.1
Tdl Inc.	550 Tpke. Street	Canton	MA	02021	Tobe Deutschmann	781-828-3366	R	3*	<0.1
Motor Capacitors Inc.	6455 N Avondale	Chicago	IL	60631	Terry Noon	773-774-6666	R	3*	<0.1
CSI Technologies Inc.	2595 Commerce	Vista	CA	92081	Narendra Soni	760-682-2222	R	2*	<0.1
Rtron Corp.	PO Box 743	Skokie	IL	60076	Bryan McLean	847-679-7180	R	2*	<0.1
Oren Elliott Products Inc.	PO Box 638	Edgerton	OH	43517	June Elliott	419-298-2306	R	2*	<0.1
Arco Electronics Inc.	4690 Calle Quetzal	Camarillo	CA	93012	John Drake	818-707-6465	R	2*	<0.1
Pacific Capacitor Co.	288 Digital Dr.	Morgan Hill	CA	95037	Harold Francis	408-778-6670	R	2*	<0.1
Richey Capacitor Inc.	PO Box 100296	Nashville	TN	37224	Royce Richey	615-254-3561	R	2*	<0.1
Gemini Controls L.L.C.	PO Box 380	Cedarburg	WI	53012		262-377-8585	R	1*	<0.1
High Voltage Components Inc.	PO Box 223	Cedarburg	WI	53012	Ronald Nielsen	262-375-0172	R	1*	<0.1
Standard Condenser Corp.	PO Box 1484	Skokie	IL	60076	Bryan Lean	847-675-3133	R	1*	<0.1
Myron Zucker Inc.	36825 Metro Ct.	Sterling Hgts	MI	48312	Donna Zobel	586-979-9955	R	1*	<0.1
Capcon International Inc.	23 Nassau Ave.	Inwood	NY	11096	Mario Irizarry	516-371-5600	R	1*	<0.1
Quality Components Inc.	103 Bridge St.	Ridgway	PA	15853	Judson Porter, Jr.	814-834-2817	S	1*	<0.1
Diablo Industries	2245 Meridian Blvd.	Minden	NV	89423	Jim Gibson	775-782-1041	R	1	<0.1
Phillips Components Inc.	23142 Alcalde Dr.	Laguna Hills	CA	92653	Stu Phillips	949-855-4263	R	1*	<0.1
HVC Inc.	7374 Sycamore Dr.	Cedarburg	WI	53012	Clifford Zahn	262-375-4955	R	1*	<0.1
Kemet Management/Development	3809 4th St. W	Birmingham	AL	35207	Carlos Spratt	205-323-6281	R	1*	<0.1
Tronser Inc.	3066 John Trush	Cazenovia	NY	13035	Michael Tronser	315-655-9528	R	1*	<0.1

Source: Ward's Business Directory of U.S. Private and Public Companies, Volumes 1 and 2, 2008. The company type code used is as follows: P - Public, R - Private, S - Subsidiary, D - Division, J - Joint Venture, A - Affiliate, G - Group. Sales are in millions of dollars, employees are in thousands. An asterisk (*) indicates an estimated sales volume. The symbol < stands for 'less than'. Company names and addresses are truncated, in some cases, to fit into the available space.

MATERIALS CONSUMED

Material	Quantity	Delivered Cost ($ million)
Tube blanks	(X)	(D)
Printed ciruit boards (without inserted components) for electronic circuitry	(X)	(D)
Printed circuit assemblies, loaded boards, and modules	(X)	(D)
Semiconductors (incl. transistors, diodes, rectifiers, and integrated circuits), for electronic circuitry	(X)	1.2
Capacitors for electronic circuitry	(X)	69.7
Resistors for electronic circuitry	(X)	0.6
All other miscellaneous components and accessories for electronic circuitry (exc. tubes)	(X)	17.2
Gold and other precious metals, all forms (incl. ingot, sheet, etc.)	(X)	65.0
Doped chemicals and other doped materials for electronic use	(X)	(D)
Ferrites (powder and paste)	(X)	(D)
Metal powders	(X)	119.7
Electronic computer equipment	(X)	<0.1
Current-carrying wiring devices	(X)	(D)
Electrical instrument mechanisms and meter movements	(X)	(D)
All other miscellaneous electrical measuring instruments and parts	(X)	(D)
Glass and glass products (excluding windows and mirrors)	(X)	(D)
Plastics resins consumed in the form of granules, pellets, etc.	(X)	7.9
Fabricated plastics products (excluding gaskets)	(X)	1.1
Sheet metal products (excluding stampings)	(X)	1.3
Metal stampings	(X)	17.9
Metal bolts, nuts, screws, and other screw machine products	(X)	0.9
Other fabricated metal products (excluding forgings)	(X)	2.0
Castings, rough and semifinished	(X)	(D)
Steel shapes and forms (exc. castings, forgings, fabr. metal products)	(X)	(D)
Copper and copper-base alloy shapes and forms (exc. castings, forgings, fabr. metal products)	(X)	0.5
Aluminum and aluminum-base alloy shapes and forms (exc. castings, forgings, fabr. metal products)	(X)	34.9
Other nonferrous shapes and forms (exc. castings, forgings, fabricated metal products)	(X)	5.8
Insulated wire and cable (including magnet wire)	(X)	0.1
Paper and paperboard containers (incl. shipping sacks and other paper packaging supplies)	(X)	11.8
Resists (photosensitive resin films applied to surface of wafer)	(X)	(D)
Commodity gases	(X)	3.0
Speciality gases	(X)	(D)
Masks	(X)	(D)
Solvents	(X)	1.2
Cleaning compounds	(X)	<0.1
All other materials, components, parts, containers, and supplies	(X)	160.5
Materials, ingredients, containers, and supplies, nsk	(X)	27.8

Source: 2002 Economic Census. Explanation of symbols used: (D): Withheld to avoid disclosure of competitive data; na: Not available; (S): Withheld because statistical norms were not met; (X): Not applicable; (Z): Less than half the unit shown; nec: Not elsewhere classified; nsk: Not specified by kind; - : zero; p : 10-19 percent estimated; q : 20-29 percent estimated.

PRODUCT SHARE DETAILS

Product or Product Class Shipments	Mil. $	Product or Product Class Shipments	Mil. $
ELECTRONIC CAPACITORS	1,366.0	**Capacitors for electronic circuitry**	**1,366.0**

Source: 2002 Economic Census. The values are product shipments in millions of dollars for 2002. Total product shipments may be lower or higher than industry shipments. See Introduction for a full discussion. Values of indented subcategories are summed in the main heading(s). The symbol (D) appears when data are withheld to prevent disclosure of competitive information. The abbreviation nsk stands for 'not specified by kind' and nec for 'not elsewhere classified'. A dash (-) means zero.

INPUTS AND OUTPUTS FOR ELECTRONIC CAPACITORS & OTHER INDUCTORS

Economic Sector or Industry Providing Inputs	%	Sector	Economic Sector or Industry Buying Outputs	%	Sector
Compensation of employees	37.8		Exports of goods & services	28.5	Cap Inv
Management of companies & enterprises	10.4	Services	Software publishers	5.5	Services
Wholesale trade	8.2	Trade	Motor vehicle parts	4.2	Manufg.
Iron & steel mills & ferroalloys	3.1	Manufg.	Semiconductors & related devices	4.0	Manufg.
Scientific research & development services	2.8	Services	Printed circuit assemblies (electronic assembiles)	3.5	Manufg.
Electronic capacitors, resistors, coils, transformers	2.3	Manufg.	Electronic computers	3.4	Manufg.
Nonferrous metal (ex. copper & aluminum) processing	2.0	Manufg.	Bare printed circuit boards	3.2	Manufg.
Primary nonferrous metal, ex. copper & aluminum	1.8	Manufg.	Electromedical & electrotherapeutic apparatus	2.8	Manufg.
Lessors of nonfinancial assets	1.7	Fin/R.E.	Telecommunications	2.3	Services
Power generation & supply	1.6	Util.	Search, detection, & navigation instruments	2.2	Manufg.
Copper rolling, drawing, extruding, & alloying	1.5	Manufg.	Electronic components, nec	2.0	Manufg.
Crowns & closures & metal stamping	1.2	Manufg.	Audio & video equipment	1.9	Manufg.
Alumina refining & primary aluminum production	1.0	Manufg.	Data processing, hosting, & related services	1.9	Services
Electronic components, nec	0.9	Manufg.	Telephone apparatus	1.8	Manufg.
Real estate	0.9	Fin/R.E.	Electrical equipment & components, nec	1.7	Manufg.
Paperboard containers	0.9	Manufg.	Electricity & signal testing instruments	1.7	Manufg.

Continued on next page.

INPUTS AND OUTPUTS FOR ELECTRONIC CAPACITORS & OTHER INDUCTORS - Continued

Economic Sector or Industry Providing Inputs	%	Sector	Economic Sector or Industry Buying Outputs	%	Sector
Communication & energy wires & cables	0.7	Manufg.	Broadcast & wireless communications equipment	1.6	Manufg.
Plastics products, nec	0.7	Manufg.	Other computer related services, including facilities	1.5	Services
Noncomparable imports	0.7	Foreign	Basic organic chemicals, nec	1.4	Manufg.
Truck transportation	0.7	Util.	Electronic capacitors, resistors, coils, transformers	1.3	Manufg.
Advertising & related services	0.7	Services	Computer storage devices	1.3	Manufg.
Taxes on production & imports, less subsidies	0.6		Computer terminals & peripherals	1.2	Manufg.
Printed circuit assemblies (electronic assemblies)	0.6	Manufg.	Communications equipment, nec	1.1	Manufg.
Securities, commodity contracts, investments	0.5	Fin/R.E.	Watches, clocks, & related devices	1.0	Manufg.
Chemical products & preparations, nec	0.5	Manufg.	Custom computer programming services	0.9	Services
Turned products & screws, nuts, & bolts	0.5	Manufg.	Power, distribution, & specialty transformers	0.9	Manufg.
Wiring devices	0.5	Manufg.	General Federal government services, defense	0.9	Fed Govt
Plastics materials & resins	0.4	Manufg.	Motors & generators	0.9	Manufg.
Telecommunications	0.4	Services	Commercial & service industry machinery, nec	0.8	Manufg.
Semiconductors & related devices	0.4	Manufg.	Industrial process variable instruments	0.7	Manufg.
Legal services	0.4	Services	Surgical appliances & supplies	0.7	Manufg.
Maintenance/repair of nonresidential structures	0.4	Construct.	Totalizing fluid meters & counting devices	0.7	Manufg.
Management, scientific, & technical consulting	0.4	Services	Material handling equipment	0.7	Manufg.
Services to buildings & dwellings	0.3	Services	Investigation & security services	0.7	Services
Warehousing & storage	0.3	Util.	General purpose machinery, nec	0.7	Manufg.
Accounting, tax preparation, bookkeeping, & payroll	0.3	Services	AC, refrigeration, and warm air heating equipment	0.6	Manufg.
Data processing, hosting, & related services	0.3	Services	Irradiation apparatus	0.6	Manufg.
Bare printed circuit boards	0.3	Manufg.	Educational services, nec	0.5	Services
Other computer related services, including facilities	0.3	Services	Wholesale trade	0.5	Trade
Automotive equipment rental & leasing	0.3	Fin/R.E.	Automatic environmental controls	0.5	Manufg.
Natural gas distribution	0.3	Util.	Analytical laboratory instruments	0.5	Manufg.
Employment services	0.3	Services	Semiconductor machinery	0.4	Manufg.
Automotive repair & maintenance, ex. car washes	0.2	Services	Industrial machinery, nec	0.4	Manufg.
Specialized design services	0.2	Services	Household cooking appliances	0.3	Manufg.
Architectural, engineering, & related services	0.2	Services	Engine equipment, nec	0.3	Manufg.
Ornamental & architectural metal products	0.2	Manufg.	General S/L govt. services	0.3	S/L Govt
Business support services	0.2	Services	Plastics materials & resins	0.3	Manufg.
Commercial & industrial equipment repair/maintenance	0.2	Services	Construction machinery	0.3	Manufg.
Basic inorganic chemicals, nec	0.2	Manufg.	Electronic & precision equipment repair/maintenance	0.3	Services
Pressed & blown glass & glassware, nec	0.2	Manufg.	Household refrigerators & home freezers	0.3	Manufg.
Relay & industrial controls	0.2	Manufg.	Internet service providers & web search portals	0.3	Services
Plastics packaging materials, film & sheet	0.2	Manufg.	Rolling mill & other metalworking machinery	0.2	Manufg.
Machine shops	0.2	Manufg.	Monetary authorities/depository credit intermediation	0.2	Fin/R.E.
Monetary authorities/depository credit intermediation	0.2	Fin/R.E.	Nondepository credit intermediation activities	0.2	Fin/R.E.
Electricity & signal testing instruments	0.2	Manufg.	Household laundry equipment	0.2	Manufg.
Waste management & remediation services	0.2	Services	Securities, commodity contracts, investments	0.2	Fin/R.E.
Coating, engraving, heat treating & allied activities	0.1	Manufg.	Aircraft	0.2	Manufg.
Professional, scientific, technical services, nec	0.1	Services	Photographic & photocopying equipment	0.2	Manufg.
Commercial & industrial machinery rental & leasing	0.1	Fin/R.E.	Plastics & rubber industry machinery	0.2	Manufg.
Motors & generators	0.1	Manufg.	Electron tubes	0.2	Manufg.
Food services & drinking places	0.1	Services	Air & gas compressors	0.2	Manufg.
Computer system design services	0.1	Services	Optical instruments & lenses	0.2	Manufg.
Industrial gases	0.1	Manufg.	Pumps & pumping equipment	0.2	Manufg.
Support services, nec	0.1	Services	Air transportation	0.1	Util.
Custom computer programming services	0.1	Services	Magnetic & optical recording media	0.1	Manufg.
			Farm machinery & equipment	0.1	Manufg.
			Vending, commercial, industrial, office machinery	0.1	Manufg.
			Commercial & industrial equipment repair/maintenance	0.1	Services
			Industrial gases	0.1	Manufg.

Source: Benchmark Input-Output Accounts for the U.S. Economy, 2002, U.S. Department of Commerce, Washington D.C., January 2008. User should note that this Input-Output table is not for this particular narrowly defined industry but for a larger aggregate. Input and Output data for Electronic Capacitors & Other Inductors include Input and Output data for the Annual Survey of Manufactures' NAICS industries 334414, 334415, and 334416. The abbreviation nec stands for 'not elsewhere classified'.

OCCUPATIONS EMPLOYED BY SEMICONDUCTOR & OTHER ELECTRONIC COMPONENT MANUFACTURING

Occupation	% of Total 2006	Change to 2016	Occupation	% of Total 2006	Change to 2016
Electrical & electronic equipment assemblers	10.9	-30.1	Computer software engineers, systems software	1.5	-3.8
Semiconductor processors	8.2	-12.6	Production workers, nec	1.3	-14.2
Team assemblers	4.5	-12.6	Shipping, receiving, & traffic clerks	1.3	-15.9
Electrical & electronic engineering technicians	4.1	-12.6	Purchasing agents, exc wholesale, retail, & farm	1.3	-12.6
Inspectors, testers, sorters, samplers, & weighers	3.9	-17.6	Production, planning, & expediting clerks	1.2	-12.6
Electronics engineers, exc computer	3.9	-12.6	General & operations managers	1.2	-21.3
First-line supervisors/managers of production workers	2.8	-12.6	Coil winders, tapers, & finishers	1.1	-30.1
Electrical engineers	2.6	-12.6	Machinists	1.1	-8.2
Industrial engineers	2.5	6.2	Industrial production managers	1.0	-12.6
Engineering managers	2.3	-3.8	Maintenance & repair workers, general	1.0	-12.6
Electromechanical equipment assemblers	1.7	-12.6			

Source: Industry-Occupation Matrix, Bureau of Labor Statistics, December 4, 2007. These data are reported based on 4-digit NAICS categories but have been matched to corresponding 6-digit NAICS industry codes. The change reported for each occupation to the year 2016 is a percent of growth or decline as estimated by the Bureau of Labor Statistics. The abbreviation nec stands for 'not elsewhere classified'.

LOCATION BY STATE AND REGIONAL CONCENTRATION

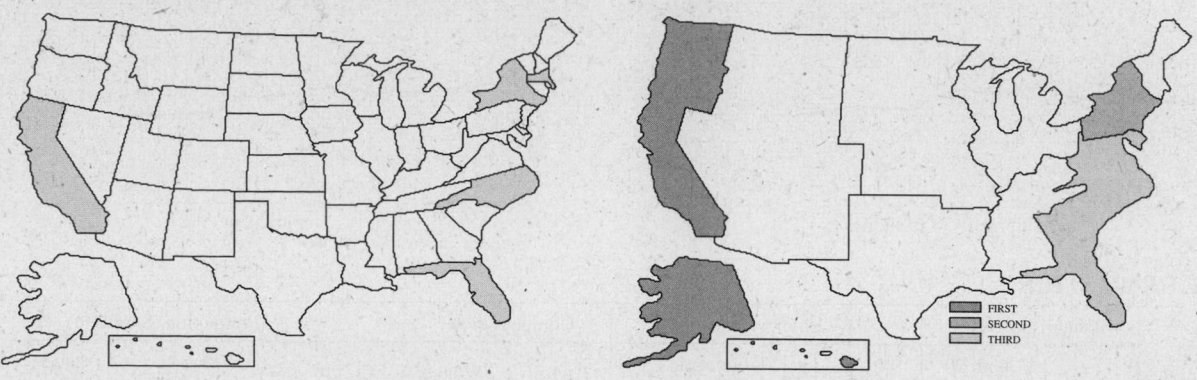

INDUSTRY DATA BY STATE

| State | Establish-ments | Shipments | | | Employment | | | | Cost as % of Shipments | Investment per Employee ($) |
		Total ($ mil)	% of U.S.	Per Establ.	Total Number	% of U.S.	Per Establ.	Wages ($/hour)		
North Carolina	4	194.1	11.9	48,524.5	851	7.8	213	15.21	56.5	8,818
California	24	150.6	9.2	6,274.5	1,678	15.4	70	12.89	29.7	3,061
New York	10	115.7	7.1	11,567.1	1,026	9.4	103	11.86	20.7	8,001
Massachusetts	8	65.0	4.0	8,120.1	628	5.8	78	10.75	52.7	5,266
Florida	5	40.0	2.5	7,998.0	452	4.1	90	9.31	51.7	3,469

Source: 2002 *Economic Census*. The states are in descending order of shipments or establishments (if shipment data are missing for the majority). The symbol (D) appears when data are withheld to prevent disclosure of competitive information. States marked with (D) are sorted by number of establishments. A dash (-) indicates that the data element cannot be calculated. Data may not show all states active in the NAICS category. All data available at the time of publication are shown.

NAICS 334415 - ELECTRONIC RESISTOR MANUFACTURING

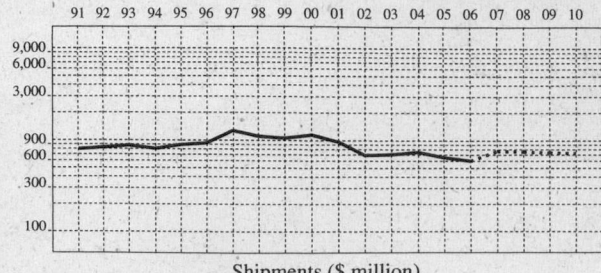

Shipments ($ million)

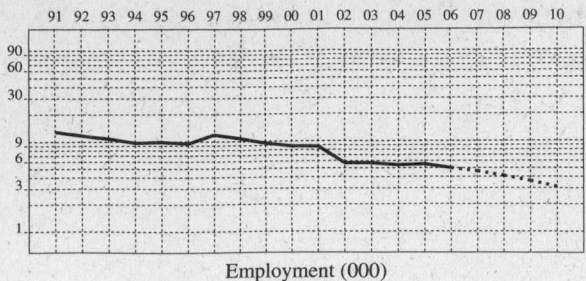

Employment (000)

GENERAL STATISTICS

| Year | Companies | Establishments | | Employment | | | Compensation | | Production ($ million) | | | |
		Total	with 20 or more employees	Total (000)	Production Workers (000)	Hours (Mil)	Payroll ($ mil)	Wages ($/hr)	Cost of Materials	Value Added by Manufacture	Value of Shipments	Capital Invest.
1991		99	81	12.9	8.6	16.2	244.4	7.16	277.7	510.4	797.1	33.6
1992	87	105	80	11.7	8.3	16.1	258.7	8.34	258.3	562.6	827.2	21.3
1993		102	77	10.8	7.9	16.1	249.9	8.76	277.8	598.7	870.5	25.7
1994		101	76	9.7	6.9	14.3	237.2	9.26	258.7	558.5	806.0	53.0
1995		96	76	9.9	7.0	13.8	244.6	9.41	303.1	596.4	890.7	40.6
1996		105	75	9.5	6.7	13.7	241.8	9.73	295.5	633.6	927.0	42.1
1997	91	118	84	11.9	8.6	16.6	310.4	10.73	448.9	806.5	1,273.1	55.4
1998		111	82	10.8	7.7	14.8	288.2	11.44	429.6	674.6	1,106.3	58.1
1999		109	75	9.5	6.7	13.6	268.3	10.83	388.2	673.3	1,058.2	32.6
2000		102	74	8.8	6.1	13.2	254.7	11.09	452.2	720.2	1,155.1	42.3
2001		99	75	8.7	6.0	12.5	251.9	11.17	371.7	583.0	964.4	43.7
2002	59	79	57	5.7	3.9	7.5	185.8	12.56	254.2	413.9	690.2	29.3
2003		74	55	5.7	3.9	7.4	186.3	13.18	241.0	452.9	704.1	43.2
2004		73	54	5.4	3.5	7.3	185.7	13.14	272.1	480.0	747.6	31.7
2005		69	52	5.5	3.6	7.0	186.4	14.61	226.4	426.0	653.7	21.8
2006		78P	56P	5.0	3.5	7.0	186.4	15.52	204.7	411.1	601.0	22.5
2007		76P	54P	4.6P	3.1P	6.4P	192.3P	15.06P	260.9P	523.9P	766.0P	33.3P
2008		73P	52P	4.1P	2.7P	5.7P	187.1P	15.53P	256.3P	514.8P	752.6P	32.9P
2009		71P	50P	3.6P	2.4P	5.0P	181.9P	16.00P	251.8P	505.7P	739.2P	32.4P
2010		69P	48P	3.1P	2.0P	4.3P	176.7P	16.47P	247.2P	496.5P	725.9P	31.9P

Sources: 1992, 1997, 2002 *Economic Census*; other years, up to 2006, are from the *Annual Survey of Manufactures*. Establishment counts for non-Census years are from *County Business Patterns*; 1997 and 2002 values are from the 1997 and 2002 censuses respectively, reported in the Federal Government's NAICS format. Other years were originally reported in equivalent SIC format. 'P's show projections by the editors.

INDICES OF CHANGE

| Year | Companies | Establishments | | Employment | | | Compensation | | Production ($ million) | | | |
		Total	with 20 or more employees	Total (000)	Production Workers (000)	Hours (Mil)	Payroll ($ mil)	Wages ($/hr)	Cost of Materials	Value Added by Manufacture	Value of Shipments	Capital Invest.
1992	147	133	140	205	213	215	139	66	102	136	120	73
1997	154	149	147	209	221	221	167	85	177	195	184	189
2001		125	132	153	154	167	136	89	146	141	140	149
2002	100	100	100	100	100	100	100	100	100	100	100	100
2003		94	96	100	100	99	100	105	95	109	102	147
2004		92	95	95	90	97	100	105	107	116	108	108
2005		87	91	96	92	93	100	116	89	103	95	74
2006		99P	98P	88	90	93	100	124	81	99	87	77
2007		96P	94P	81P	79P	85P	103P	120P	103P	127P	111P	114P
2008		93P	91P	72P	69P	76P	101P	124P	101P	124P	109P	112P
2009		90P	87P	63P	62P	67P	98P	127P	99P	122P	107P	111P
2010		87P	84P	54P	51P	57P	95P	131P	97P	120P	105P	109P

Sources: Same as General Statistics. Values reflect change from the base year, 2002. Values above 100 mean greater than 2002, values below 100 mean less than 2002, and the values of 100 in other years means the same as 2002. 'P's show projections by the editors.

SELECTED RATIOS

For 2002	Avg. of All Manufact.	Analyzed Industry	Index	For 2002	Avg. of All Manufact.	Analyzed Industry	Index
Employees per Establishment	42	72	172	Value Added per Production Worker	182,367	106,128	58
Payroll per Establishment	1,639,184	2,351,899	143	Cost per Establishment	5,769,015	3,217,722	56
Payroll per Employee	39,053	32,596	83	Cost per Employee	137,446	44,596	32
Production Workers per Establishment	30	49	167	Cost per Production Worker	195,506	65,179	33
Wages per Establishment	694,845	1,192,405	172	Shipments per Establishment	11,158,348	8,736,709	78
Wages per Production Worker	23,548	24,154	103	Shipments per Employee	265,847	121,088	46
Hours per Production Worker	1,980	1,923	97	Shipments per Production Worker	378,144	176,974	47
Wages per Hour	11.89	12.56	106	Investment per Establishment	361,338	370,886	103
Value Added per Establishment	5,381,325	5,239,241	97	Investment per Employee	8,609	5,140	60
Value Added per Employee	128,210	72,614	57	Investment per Production Worker	12,245	7,513	61

Sources: Same as General Statistics. The 'Average of All Manufacturing' column represents the average of all manufacturing industries reported for the most recent complete year available. The Index shows the relationship between the Average and the Analyzed Industry. For example, 100 means that they are equal; 500 that the Analyzed Industry is five times the average; 50 means that the Analyzed Industry is half the national average. The abbreviation 'na' is used to show that data are 'not available'. Ratios shown for 2002, the last complete census year.

LEADING COMPANIES　Number shown: **55**　Total sales ($ mil): **1,932**　Total employment (000): **3.7**

Company Name	Address				CEO Name	Phone	Co. Type	Sales ($ mil)	Empl. (000)
TT Electronics I R C	736 Greenway Rd.	Boone	NC	28607	R Fletcher	828-264-8861	R	1,287*	0.3
Vishay Dale Electronics Inc.	1122 23rd St.	Columbus	NE	68601	Gerald Paul	402-564-3131	S	162*	0.5
Carbone Lorraine North America	400 Myrtle Ave.	Boonton	NJ	07005	Michel Coniglio	973-541-4720	R	50*	<0.1
RCD Components Inc.	520 E Indust Prk Dr	Manchester	NH	03109	Louis Arcidy	603-669-0054	R	43*	0.4
Caddock Electronics Inc.	1717 Chicago Ave.	Riverside	CA	92507	Richard Caddock	951-788-1700	R	24*	0.1
Vishay Thin Film Inc.	2160 Liberty Dr.	Niagara Falls	NY	14304	Felix Zandman	716-283-4025	D	23*	0.2
Electro-Flex Heat Inc.	PO Box 88	Bloomfield	CT	06002	Jari Jariwala	860-242-6287	R	23*	<0.1
Two In One Manufacturing Inc.	51 Lake St., Ste. 4	Nashua	NH	03060	Mui Nguyen	603-595-8212	R	20*	<0.1
Vertical Circuits Inc.	10 Victor Sq., 100	Scotts Valley	CA	95066	Sunil Kaul	831-438-3887	R	19*	<0.1
Mini-Systems Inc.	PO Box 69	North Attleboro	MA	02761	Glen Robertson	508-695-0203	R	17*	<0.1
State Electronics Parts Corp.	36 State Rte. 10	East Hanover	NJ	07936	Louis Premock	973-887-2550	R	16*	<0.1
Prime Technology L.L.C.	PO Box 185	North Branford	CT	06471	Andrew Sadlon	203-481-5721	R	16*	0.2
Riedon Inc.	300 Cypress Ave.	Alhambra	CA	91801	Michael Zoeller	626-284-9901	R	16*	0.2
State of the Art Inc.	2470 Fox Hill Rd.	State College	PA	16803	Bob Hufnagel	814-355-8004	R	14*	0.2
ASJ Components Inc.	451 E Patagonia	Nogales	AZ	85621		520-287-4731	R	14*	<0.1
Huntington Electric Inc.	PO Box 366	Huntington	IN	46750	Michael Khorshid	260-356-0756	R	14*	0.1
Ohmcraft Inc.	93 Papermill St.	Honeoye Falls	NY	14472	Frank Collins	585-624-2610	R	13*	<0.1
Sensor Systems L.L.C.	PO Box 44000	St. Petersburg	FL	33743	Nancy Preis	727-347-2181	R	12*	0.1
Betatronix Inc.	110 Nicon Ct.	Hauppauge	NY	11788	Joseph Yanosik	631-582-6740	R	11*	<0.1
US Sensor Corp.	1832 W Collins Ave.	Orange	CA	92867	Roger Dankert	714-639-1000	R	11*	0.1
Milwaukee Resistor Corp.	8920 W Heather	Milwaukee	WI	53224	Brian Jonas	414-362-8900	S	9*	<0.1
Wilbrecht Electronics Inc.	1400 Energy Pk Dr.	Saint Paul	MN	55108	Jon Wilbrecht	651-659-0919	R	8*	<0.1
Phoenix Electric Corp.	PO Box 53	Readville	MA	02137	Thomas Clark	781-821-0200	R	8*	<0.1
Powerohm Resistors Inc.	PO Box 537	Katy	TX	77492	Vance Hinton	281-391-6800	R	7*	<0.1
Martinez Electronics	PO Box 21447	Long Beach	CA	90801		562-595-5462	R	7*	<0.1
Mills Resistor Co.	3651 Business Dr.	Sacramento	CA	95820	Ted Mills	916-453-7590	R	6*	<0.1
Precision Resistive Products	PO Box 189	Mediapolis	IA	52637	Oscar Cline	319-394-9131	R	6*	<0.1
Carter Manufacturing Corp.	237 Sugar Rd.	Bolton	MA	01740	Ahren Cohen	978-779-5501	R	5*	<0.1
Bantry Components Inc.	160 Bouchard St.	Manchester	NH	03103	Bernard Perry	603-668-3210	R	5*	<0.1
Servo Instrument Corp.	PO Box 43	Baraboo	WI	53913	Gordon R. Glorch	608-356-6623	R	5*	<0.1
Tepro Florida Inc.	PO Box 1260	Clearwater	FL	33763	Roger C. Mayo	727-796-1044	S	5*	<0.1
Precision Resistor Company	10601 75th St.	Largo	FL	33777	Fred Dusenberry	727-541-5771	R	5*	<0.1
Ametherm Inc.	3111 N Deer Run	Carson City	NV	89701	Eric Rauch	775-884-2434	R	4*	<0.1
Int'l Manufacturing Services	50 Schoolhouse Ln.	Portsmouth	RI	02871	Henry Liiv	401-683-9700	R	4*	<0.1
Able Coil and Electronics Co.	PO Box 9127	Bolton	CT	06043	Kenneth Rockfeller	860-646-5686	R	4*	<0.1
Component General Inc.	2445 Success Dr.	Odessa	FL	33556	James Cook	727-376-6655	R	4*	<0.1
ETI Systems	1954 Kellogg Ave.	Carlsbad	CA	92008	Bill Tice	760-929-0749	R	3*	<0.1
Voltronics Inc.	7746 W Addison St.	Chicago	IL	60634	Edwin Hedeen	773-625-1779	R	3*	<0.1
Novotechnik US Inc.	155 Northboro Rd.	Southborough	MA	01772	Matt Pietro	508-485-2244	R	3*	<0.1
Altronic Research Inc.	PO Box 249	Yellville	AR	72687	John Dyess	870-449-4093	R	3*	<0.1
Questech Services Corp.	2201 Executive Dr.	Garland	TX	75041	Robert Chapman	972-278-8006	R	3*	<0.1
Micro-Ohm Corp.	1088 Hamilton Rd.	Duarte	CA	91010	Byron Ritchey	626-357-5377	R	3*	<0.1
Stackpole Electronics Inc.	PO Box 58789	Raleigh	NC	27658	Jim Mollene	919-850-9500	R	2*	<0.1
Bel-Tronics Corp.	344 Interstate Rd.	Addison	IL	60101	James Rubenstein	630-543-7777	R	2*	<0.1
Vishay Angstrohm	PO Box 1827	Hagerstown	MD	21742		301-739-8722	D	2*	<0.1
Maurey Instrument Corp.	5959 W 115	Alsip	IL	60803	M Maurey	773-388-9898	R	2*	<0.1
Power Film Systems Inc.	PO Box 249	Yellville	AR	72687	John Dyess	870-449-4091	R	2*	<0.1
K-Tronics Inc.	PO Box 4398	Bisbee	AZ	85603	Robert Kidder	520-432-5388	R	2*	<0.1
Stetron International Inc.	90 Broadway St.	Buffalo	NY	14203	Edward Steger	716-854-3443	R	2*	<0.1
Gemini Controls L.L.C.	PO Box 380	Cedarburg	WI	53012		262-377-8585	R	1*	<0.1
Mining Resistors Inc.	PO Box 1020	Logan	WV	25601	Harry Slater	304-752-4681	R	1*	<0.1
Diablo Industries	2245 Meridian Blvd.	Minden	NV	89423	Jim Gibson	775-782-1041	R	1	<0.1
Phillips Components Inc.	23142 Alcalde Dr.	Laguna Hills	CA	92653	Stu Phillips	949-855-4263	R	1*	<0.1
RPF Components Inc.	215 Research Dr.	Milford	CT	06460	Robert Furst	203-877-4874	R	1*	<0.1
Isotek Corp.	1199 G A R Hwy.	Swansea	MA	02777	William Poisson	508-673-2900	R	1*	<0.1

Source: Ward's Business Directory of U.S. Private and Public Companies, Volumes 1 and 2, 2008. The company type code used is as follows: P - Public, R - Private, S - Subsidiary, D - Division, J - Joint Venture, A - Affiliate, G - Group. Sales are in millions of dollars, employees are in thousands. An asterisk (*) indicates an estimated sales volume. The symbol < stands for 'less than'. Company names and addresses are truncated, in some cases, to fit into the available space.

MATERIALS CONSUMED

Material	Quantity	Delivered Cost ($ million)
Tube blanks	(X)	2.4
Printed ciruit boards (without inserted components) for electronic circuitry	(X)	6.6
Printed circuit assemblies, loaded boards, and modules	(X)	2.2
Semiconductors (incl. transistors, diodes, rectifiers, and integrated circuits), for electronic circuitry	(X)	4.4
Capacitors for electronic circuitry	(X)	12.3
Resistors for electronic circuitry	(X)	5.9
All other miscellaneous components and accessories for electronic circuitry (exc. tubes)	(X)	6.7
Silicon, hyperpure	(X)	(D)
Gold and other precious metals, all forms (incl. ingot, sheet, etc.)	(X)	6.4
Doped chemicals and other doped materials for electronic use	(X)	2.3
Ferrites (powder and paste)	(X)	5.6
Metal powders	(X)	(D)

Continued on next page.

MATERIALS CONSUMED - Continued

Material	Quantity	Delivered Cost ($ million)
Electronic computer equipment	(X)	0.2
Current-carrying wiring devices	(X)	2.1
Electronic communication equipment	(X)	(D)
Electrical instrument mechanisms and meter movements	(X)	(D)
All other miscellaneous electrical measuring instruments and parts	(X)	(D)
Fractional horsepower electric motors (less than 1 hp)	(X)	(D)
Electrical transmission, distribution, and control equipment	(X)	(D)
Glass and glass products (excluding windows and mirrors)	(X)	(D)
Optical instruments and lenses (exc. sighting, tracking, and fire control)	(X)	(D)
Plastics resins consumed in the form of granules, pellets, etc.	(X)	5.8
Fabricated plastics products (excluding gaskets)	(X)	15.4
Sheet metal products (excluding stampings)	(X)	4.6
Metal stampings	(X)	7.6
Metal bolts, nuts, screws, and other screw machine products	(X)	4.9
Other fabricated metal products (excluding forgings)	(X)	7.3
Castings, rough and semifinished	(X)	(D)
Steel shapes and forms (exc. castings, forgings, fabr. metal products)	(X)	(D)
Copper and copper-base alloy shapes and forms (exc. castings, forgings, fabr. metal products)	(X)	0.7
Aluminum and aluminum-base alloy shapes and forms (exc. castings, forgings, fabr. metal products)	(X)	(D)
Other nonferrous shapes and forms (exc. castings, forgings, fabricated metal products)	(X)	1.4
Insulated wire and cable (including magnet wire)	(X)	3.5
Paper and paperboard containers (incl. shipping sacks and other paper packaging supplies)	(X)	2.7
Resists (photosensitive resin films applied to surface of wafer)	(X)	1.6
Commodity gases	(X)	1.2
Speciality gases	(X)	(D)
Masks	(X)	(D)
Silicon chips	(X)	0.4
Solvents	(X)	0.4
Cleaning compounds	(X)	(D)
All other materials, components, parts, containers, and supplies	(X)	6.2
Materials, ingredients, containers, and supplies, nsk	(X)	2.7

Source: 2002 *Economic Census*. Explanation of symbols used: (D): Withheld to avoid disclosure of competitive data; na: Not available; (S): Withheld because statistical norms were not met; (X): Not applicable; (Z): Less than half the unit shown; nec: Not elsewhere classified; nsk: Not specified by kind; - : zero; p : 10-19 percent estimated; q : 20-29 percent estimated.

PRODUCT SHARE DETAILS

Product or Product Class Shipments	Mil. $	Product or Product Class Shipments	Mil. $
ELECTRONIC RESISTORS	682.1	**Resistors for electronic circuitry**	**682.1**

Source: 2002 *Economic Census*. The values are product shipments in millions of dollars for 2002. Total product shipments may be lower or higher than industry shipments. See Introduction for a full discussion. Values of indented subcategories are summed in the main heading(s). The symbol (D) appears when data are withheld to prevent disclosure of competitive information. The abbreviation nsk stands for 'not specified by kind' and nec for 'not elsewhere classified'. A dash (-) means zero.

INPUTS AND OUTPUTS FOR ELECTRONIC CAPACITORS & OTHER INDUCTORS

Economic Sector or Industry Providing Inputs	%	Sector	Economic Sector or Industry Buying Outputs	%	Sector
Compensation of employees	37.8		Exports of goods & services	28.5	Cap Inv
Management of companies & enterprises	10.4	Services	Software publishers	5.5	Services
Wholesale trade	8.2	Trade	Motor vehicle parts	4.2	Manufg.
Iron & steel mills & ferroalloys	3.1	Manufg.	Semiconductors & related devices	4.0	Manufg.
Scientific research & development services	2.8	Services	Printed circuit assemblies (electronic assemblies)	3.5	Manufg.
Electronic capacitors, resistors, coils, transformers	2.3	Manufg.	Electronic computers	3.4	Manufg.
Nonferrous metal (ex. copper & aluminum) processing	2.0	Manufg.	Bare printed circuit boards	3.2	Manufg.
Primary nonferrous metal, ex. copper & aluminum	1.8	Manufg.	Electromedical & electrotherapeutic apparatus	2.8	Manufg.
Lessors of nonfinancial assets	1.7	Fin/R.E.	Telecommunications	2.3	Services
Power generation & supply	1.6	Util.	Search, detection, & navigation instruments	2.2	Manufg.
Copper rolling, drawing, extruding, & alloying	1.5	Manufg.	Electronic components, nec	2.0	Manufg.
Crowns & closures & metal stamping	1.2	Manufg.	Audio & video equipment	1.9	Manufg.
Alumina refining & primary aluminum production	1.0	Manufg.	Data processing, hosting, & related services	1.9	Services
Electronic components, nec	0.9	Manufg.	Telephone apparatus	1.8	Manufg.
Real estate	0.9	Fin/R.E.	Electrical equipment & components, nec	1.7	Manufg.
Paperboard containers	0.9	Manufg.	Electricity & signal testing instruments	1.7	Manufg.
Communication & energy wires & cables	0.7	Manufg.	Broadcast & wireless communications equipment	1.6	Manufg.
Plastics products, nec	0.7	Manufg.	Other computer related services, including facilities	1.5	Services
Noncomparable imports	0.7	Foreign	Basic organic chemicals, nec	1.4	Manufg.
Truck transportation	0.7	Util.	Electronic capacitors, resistors, coils, transformers	1.3	Manufg.
Advertising & related services	0.7	Services	Computer storage devices	1.3	Manufg.
Taxes on production & imports, less subsidies	0.6		Computer terminals & peripherals	1.2	Manufg.
Printed circuit assemblies (electronic assemblies)	0.6	Manufg.	Communications equipment, nec	1.1	Manufg.
Securities, commodity contracts, investments	0.5	Fin/R.E.	Watches, clocks, & related devices	1.0	Manufg.

Continued on next page.

INPUTS AND OUTPUTS FOR ELECTRONIC CAPACITORS & OTHER INDUCTORS - Continued

Economic Sector or Industry Providing Inputs	%	Sector	Economic Sector or Industry Buying Outputs	%	Sector
Chemical products & preparations, nec	0.5	Manufg.	Custom computer programming services	0.9	Services
Turned products & screws, nuts, & bolts	0.5	Manufg.	Power, distribution, & specialty transformers	0.9	Manufg.
Wiring devices	0.5	Manufg.	General Federal government services, defense	0.9	Fed Govt
Plastics materials & resins	0.4	Manufg.	Motors & generators	0.9	Manufg.
Telecommunications	0.4	Services	Commercial & service industry machinery, nec	0.8	Manufg.
Semiconductors & related devices	0.4	Manufg.	Industrial process variable instruments	0.7	Manufg.
Legal services	0.4	Services	Surgical appliances & supplies	0.7	Manufg.
Maintenance/repair of nonresidential structures	0.4	Construct.	Totalizing fluid meters & counting devices	0.7	Manufg.
Management, scientific, & technical consulting	0.4	Services	Material handling equipment	0.7	Manufg.
Services to buildings & dwellings	0.3	Services	Investigation & security services	0.7	Services
Warehousing & storage	0.3	Util.	General purpose machinery, nec	0.7	Manufg.
Accounting, tax preparation, bookkeeping, & payroll	0.3	Services	AC, refrigeration, and warm air heating equipment	0.6	Manufg.
Data processing, hosting, & related services	0.3	Services	Irradiation apparatus	0.6	Manufg.
Bare printed circuit boards	0.3	Manufg.	Educational services, nec	0.5	Services
Other computer related services, including facilities	0.3	Services	Wholesale trade	0.5	Trade
Automotive equipment rental & leasing	0.3	Fin/R.E.	Automatic environmental controls	0.5	Manufg.
Natural gas distribution	0.3	Util.	Analytical laboratory instruments	0.5	Manufg.
Employment services	0.3	Services	Semiconductor machinery	0.4	Manufg.
Automotive repair & maintenance, ex. car washes	0.2	Services	Industrial machinery, nec	0.4	Manufg.
Specialized design services	0.2	Services	Household cooking appliances	0.3	Manufg.
Architectural, engineering, & related services	0.2	Services	Engine equipment, nec	0.3	Manufg.
Ornamental & architectural metal products	0.2	Manufg.	General S/L govt. services	0.3	S/L Govt
Business support services	0.2	Services	Plastics materials & resins	0.3	Manufg.
Commercial & industrial equipment repair/maintenance	0.2	Services	Construction machinery	0.3	Manufg.
Basic inorganic chemicals, nec	0.2	Manufg.	Electronic & precision equipment repair/maintenance	0.3	Services
Pressed & blown glass & glassware, nec	0.2	Manufg.	Household refrigerators & home freezers	0.3	Manufg.
Relay & industrial controls	0.2	Manufg.	Internet service providers & web search portals	0.3	Services
Plastics packaging materials, film & sheet	0.2	Manufg.	Rolling mill & other metalworking machinery	0.2	Manufg.
Machine shops	0.2	Manufg.	Monetary authorities/depository credit intermediation	0.2	Fin/R.E.
Monetary authorities/depository credit intermediation	0.2	Fin/R.E.	Nondepository credit intermediation activities	0.2	Fin/R.E.
Electricity & signal testing instruments	0.2	Manufg.	Household laundry equipment	0.2	Manufg.
Waste management & remediation services	0.2	Services	Securities, commodity contracts, investments	0.2	Fin/R.E.
Coating, engraving, heat treating & allied activities	0.1	Manufg.	Aircraft	0.2	Manufg.
Professional, scientific, technical services, nec	0.1	Services	Photographic & photocopying equipment	0.2	Manufg.
Commercial & industrial machinery rental & leasing	0.1	Fin/R.E.	Plastics & rubber industry machinery	0.2	Manufg.
Motors & generators	0.1	Manufg.	Electron tubes	0.2	Manufg.
Food services & drinking places	0.1	Services	Air & gas compressors	0.2	Manufg.
Computer system design services	0.1	Services	Optical instruments & lenses	0.2	Manufg.
Industrial gases	0.1	Manufg.	Pumps & pumping equipment	0.2	Manufg.
Support services, nec	0.1	Services	Air transportation	0.1	Util.
Custom computer programming services	0.1	Services	Magnetic & optical recording media	0.1	Manufg.
			Farm machinery & equipment	0.1	Manufg.
			Vending, commercial, industrial, office machinery	0.1	Manufg.
			Commercial & industrial equipment repair/maintenance	0.1	Services
			Industrial gases	0.1	Manufg.

Source: Benchmark Input-Output Accounts for the U.S. Economy, 2002, U.S. Department of Commerce, Washington D.C., January 2008. User should note that this Input-Output table is not for this particular narrowly defined industry but for a larger aggregate. Input and Output data for Electronic Capacitors & Other Inductors include Input and Output data for the Annual Survey of Manufactures' NAICS industries 334414, 334415, and 334416. The abbreviation nec stands for 'not elsewhere classified'.

OCCUPATIONS EMPLOYED BY SEMICONDUCTOR & OTHER ELECTRONIC COMPONENT MANUFACTURING

Occupation	% of Total 2006	Change to 2016	Occupation	% of Total 2006	Change to 2016
Electrical & electronic equipment assemblers	10.9	-30.1	Computer software engineers, systems software	1.5	-3.8
Semiconductor processors	8.2	-12.6	Production workers, nec	1.3	-14.2
Team assemblers	4.5	-12.6	Shipping, receiving, & traffic clerks	1.3	-15.9
Electrical & electronic engineering technicians	4.1	-12.6	Purchasing agents, exc wholesale, retail, & farm	1.3	-12.6
Inspectors, testers, sorters, samplers, & weighers	3.9	-17.6	Production, planning, & expediting clerks	1.2	-12.6
Electronics engineers, exc computer	3.9	-12.6	General & operations managers	1.2	-21.3
First-line supervisors/managers of production workers	2.8	-12.6	Coil winders, tapers, & finishers	1.1	-30.1
Electrical engineers	2.6	-12.6	Machinists	1.1	-8.2
Industrial engineers	2.5	6.2	Industrial production managers	1.0	-12.6
Engineering managers	2.3	-3.8	Maintenance & repair workers, general	1.0	-12.6
Electromechanical equipment assemblers	1.7	-12.6			

Source: Industry-Occupation Matrix, Bureau of Labor Statistics, December 4, 2007. These data are reported based on 4-digit NAICS categories but have been matched to corresponding 6-digit NAICS industry codes. The change reported for each occupation to the year 2016 is a percent of growth or decline as estimated by the Bureau of Labor Statistics. The abbreviation nec stands for 'not elsewhere classified'.

LOCATION BY STATE AND REGIONAL CONCENTRATION

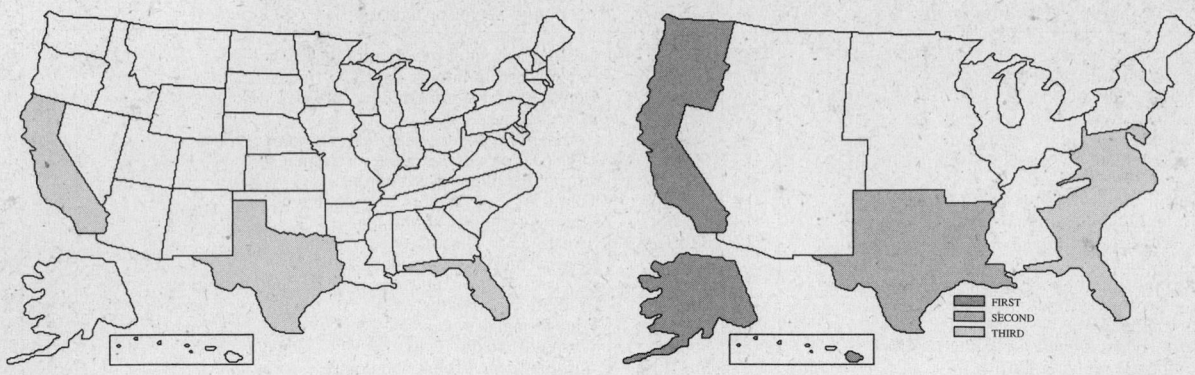

INDUSTRY DATA BY STATE

State	Establish-ments	Shipments			Employment				Cost as % of Shipments	Investment per Employee ($)
		Total ($ mil)	% of U.S.	Per Establ.	Total Number	% of U.S.	Per Establ.	Wages ($/hour)		
California	16	96.3	13.9	6,017.2	892	15.6	56	11.87	31.7	1,795
Texas	5	68.9	10.0	13,771.0	458	8.0	92	11.08	29.0	5,223
Florida	4	7.2	1.0	1,806.0	124	2.2	31	12.64	23.3	726

Source: 2002 *Economic Census*. The states are in descending order of shipments or establishments (if shipment data are missing for the majority). The symbol (D) appears when data are withheld to prevent disclosure of competitive information. States marked with (D) are sorted by number of establishments. A dash (-) indicates that the data element cannot be calculated. Data may not show all states active in the NAICS category. All data available at the time of publication are shown.

NAICS 334416 - ELECTRONIC COIL, TRANSFORMER, AND OTHER INDUCTORS

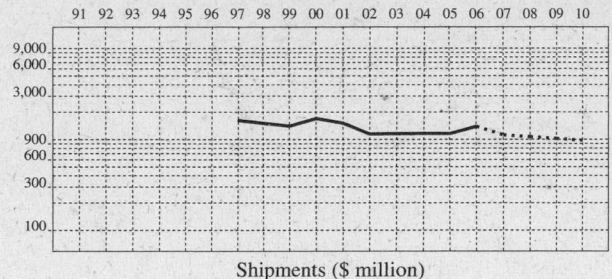

Shipments ($ million)

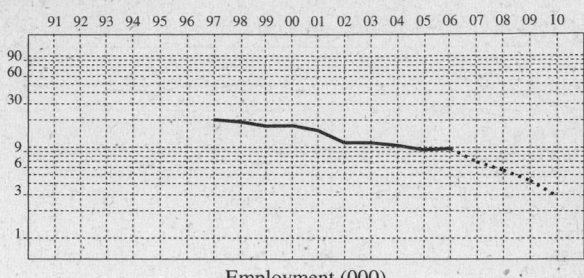

Employment (000)

GENERAL STATISTICS

| Year | Companies | Establishments | | Employment | | | Compensation | | Production ($ million) | | | |
		Total	with 20 or more employees	Total (000)	Production Workers (000)	Hours (Mil)	Payroll ($ mil)	Wages ($/hr)	Cost of Materials	Value Added by Manufacture	Value of Shipments	Capital Invest.
1997	425	448	220	20.1	15.3	30.6	494.6	8.96	600.8	1,027.8	1,623.7	36.9
1998		456	222	19.0	14.7	29.2	467.1	9.17	554.7	956.8	1,507.6	58.1
1999		447	222	17.1	13.2	25.5	429.6	9.78	545.6	865.9	1,405.8	50.3
2000		435	216	17.3	13.2	26.1	463.5	10.50	632.7	1,089.5	1,700.6	52.4
2001		408	213	15.3	11.3	21.4	426.8	10.86	558.5	951.7	1,512.8	28.4
2002	332	355	157	11.2	8.1	15.9	324.9	11.14	483.6	657.5	1,147.9	26.7
2003		357	157	11.2	8.5	16.9	344.3	11.48	451.0	707.0	1,153.8	8.8
2004		332	149	10.5	7.8	16.2	334.6	11.53	486.8	696.3	1,163.4	32.3
2005		318	143	9.4	6.8	14.3	315.2	12.38	519.5	622.7	1,156.1	9.7
2006		299P	129P	9.7	7.1	15.0	348.2	13.37	689.1	702.3	1,389.4	26.2
2007		280P	117P	6.9P	4.8P	10.3P	284.4P	13.39P	553.8P	564.4P	1,116.6P	11.1P
2008		261P	105P	5.6P	3.8P	8.3P	264.3P	13.84P	530.4P	540.5P	1,069.4P	7.1P
2009		242P	93P	4.3P	2.7P	6.4P	244.2P	14.29P	507.0P	516.7P	1,022.2P	3.1P
2010		222P	81P	2.9P	1.7P	4.4P	224.1P	14.74P	483.6P	492.8P	975.0P	

Sources: 1997 and 2002 *Economic Census*; other years, up to 2006, are from *Annual Survey of Manufactures*. Establishment counts for non-Census years are from *County Business Patterns*; 1997 and 2002 values are from the 1997 and 2002 censuses, respectively. 'P's show projections by the editors.

INDICES OF CHANGE

| Year | Companies | Establishments | | Employment | | | Compensation | | Production ($ million) | | | |
		Total	with 20 or more employees	Total (000)	Production Workers (000)	Hours (Mil)	Payroll ($ mil)	Wages ($/hr)	Cost of Materials	Value Added by Manufacture	Value of Shipments	Capital Invest.
1997	128	126	140	179	189	192	152	80	124	156	141	138
1998		128	141	170	181	184	144	82	115	146	131	218
1999		126	141	153	163	160	132	88	113	132	122	188
2000		123	138	154	163	164	143	94	131	166	148	196
2001		115	136	137	140	135	131	97	115	145	132	106
2002	100	100	100	100	100	100	100	100	100	100	100	100
2003		101	100	100	105	106	106	103	93	108	101	33
2004		94	95	94	96	102	103	104	101	106	101	121
2005		90	91	84	84	90	97	111	107	95	101	36
2006		84P	82P	87	88	94	107	120	142	107	121	98
2007		79P	75P	62P	59P	65P	88P	120P	115P	86P	97P	42P
2008		73P	67P	50P	47P	52P	81P	124P	110P	82P	93P	27P
2009		68P	59P	38P	33P	40P	75P	128P	105P	79P	89P	12P
2010		63P	52P	26P	21P	28P	69P	132P	100P	75P	85P	

Sources: Same as General Statistics. Values reflect change from the base year, 2002. Values above 100 mean greater than 2002, values below 100 mean less than 2002, and the values of 100 in other years means the same as 2002. 'P's show projections by the editors.

SELECTED RATIOS

For 2002	Avg. of All Manufact.	Analyzed Industry	Index	For 2002	Avg. of All Manufact.	Analyzed Industry	Index
Employees per Establishment	42	32	75	Value Added per Production Worker	182,367	81,173	45
Payroll per Establishment	1,639,184	915,211	56	Cost per Establishment	5,769,015	1,362,254	24
Payroll per Employee	39,053	29,009	74	Cost per Employee	137,446	43,179	31
Production Workers per Establishment	30	23	77	Cost per Production Worker	195,506	59,704	31
Wages per Establishment	694,845	498,946	72	Shipments per Establishment	11,158,348	3,233,521	29
Wages per Production Worker	23,548	21,867	93	Shipments per Employee	265,847	102,491	39
Hours per Production Worker	1,980	1,963	99	Shipments per Production Worker	378,144	141,716	37
Wages per Hour	11.89	11.14	94	Investment per Establishment	361,338	75,211	21
Value Added per Establishment	5,381,325	1,852,113	34	Investment per Employee	8,609	2,384	28
Value Added per Employee	128,210	58,705	46	Investment per Production Worker	12,245	3,296	27

Sources: Same as General Statistics. The 'Average of All Manufacturing' column represents the average of all manufacturing industries reported for the most recent complete year available. The Index shows the relationship between the Average and the Analyzed Industry. For example, 100 means that they are equal; 500 that the Analyzed Industry is five times the average; 50 means that the Analyzed Industry is half the national average. The abbreviation 'na' is used to show that data are 'not available'. Ratios shown for 2002, the last complete census year.

LEADING COMPANIES   Number shown: 75   Total sales ($ mil): 260,550   Total employment (000): 820.6

Company Name	Address				CEO Name	Phone	Co. Type	Sales ($ mil)	Empl. (000)
AT and T Inc.	175 E Houston	San Antonio	TX	78205	James W. Callaway	210-821-4105	P	68,256	310.0
Motorola Inc.	1303 E Algonquin	Schaumburg	IL	60196	Greg Brown	847-576-5000	P	36,622	66.0
Cisco Systems Inc.	170 W Tasman Dr.	San Jose	CA	95134		408-526-4000	P	34,922	61.5
L-3 Communications Holdings	600 3rd Ave.	New York	NY	10016		212-697-1111	P	13,961	63.7
Eastman Kodak Co.	343 State St.	Rochester	NY	14650		716-724-4000	P	10,301	26.9
ITT Corp.	4 W Red Oak Ln.	White Plains	NY	10604		914-641-2000	P	9,003	39.7
Ball Corp.	PO Box 5000	Broomfield	CO	80021	R. David Hoover	303-469-3131	P	7,475	15.5
Corning Inc.	1 Riverfront Plz.	Corning	NY	14831	James R. Houghton	607-974-9000	P	5,860	24.5
Agilent Technologies Inc.	5301 Stevens Creek	Santa Clara	CA	95051	Patrick J. Byrne	408-345-8886	P	5,420	19.2
Carl Zeiss IMT Corp.	6250 Sycamore N	Osseo	MN	55369	Gregory Lee	763-744-2400	R	4,420*	0.1
JVC America Inc.	1700 Valley Rd.	Wayne	NJ	07470	Shigeharu Tsuchitani	973-317-5000	S	4,306*	0.3
Oki Data Americas Inc.	2000 Bishops Gate	Mount Laurel	NJ	08054	Stewart Krentzman	856-235-2600	S	4,260*	0.5
Harris Corp.	1025 W NASA	Melbourne	FL	32919		321-727-9100	P	4,243	16.0
Brightstar Corp.	2010 NW 84th Ave.	Miami	FL	33122	R. Marcelo Claure	305-421-6000	R	3,590	1.7
Fujitsu Network Communications	2801 Telecom Pkwy.	Richardson	TX	75082	George Chase	972-479-6000	R	2,969*	1.0
Snap-On Inc.	PO Box 1410	Kenosha	WI	53141	Tim Chambers	262-656-5200	P	2,841	11.6
Vishay Intertechnology Inc.	PO Box 4004	Malvern	PA	19355	Gerald Paul	610-644-1300	P	2,833	27.9
Hubbell Inc.	584 Derby Milford	Orange	CT	06477		203-799-4100	P	2,534	11.5
Wakefield Thermal Solutions	33 Bridge St.	Pelham	NH	03076	Robert Streiter	603-635-2800	S	2,398*	0.1
DENSO Manufacturing Tennessee	1720 Rbrt C Jackson	Maryville	TN	37801	Mack Hattori	865-982-7000	S	2,231*	2.0
Tellabs Inc.	1 Tellabs Ctr.	Naperville	IL	60563	Michael J. Birck	630-798-8800	P	2,041	3.7
ECS. Inc International	1105 S Ridgeview	Olathe	KS	66062	Patricia S. Taylor	913-782-7787	R.S	1,689*	0.5
Griffon Corp.	100 Jericho Quadran	Jericho	NY	11753	Harvey R. Blau	516-938-5544	P	1,617	5.3
Comverse Technology Inc.	810 7th Ave.	New York	NY	10019	Andre Dahan	212-739-1000	P	1,589	5.1
JDS Uniphase Corp.	430 N McCarthy	Milpitas	CA	95035	Martin A. Kaplan	408-546-5000	P	1,397*	7.0
ADC Telecommunications Inc.	PO Box 1101	Minneapolis	MN	55440		952-938-8080	P	1,322	9.1
3Com Corp.	350 Campus Dr.	Marlborough	MA	01752	Eric A. Benhamou	508-323-5000	P	1,268	6.3
General Dynamics Network Sys.	77 A Street	Needham	MA	02494	Nicholas Chabraja	781-449-2000	S	1,237*	7.0
Tektronix Inc.	PO Box 500	Beaverton	OR	97077		503-627-7111	S	1,105	4.4
Teradyne Inc.	600 Riverpark Dr.	North Reading	MA	01864	James Bagley	978-370-2700	P	1,102	3.6
RF Micro Devices Inc.	7628 Thorndike Rd.	Greensboro	NC	27409	R A. Bruggeworth	336-664-1233	P	1,024	3.3
Hughes Network Systems Inc.	11717 Exploratn Ln.	Germantown	MD	20876	Pradman P. Kaul	301-428-5500	S	975*	1.5
Polycom Inc.	4750 Willow Rd.	Pleasanton	CA	94588	Robert C. Hagerty	925-924-6000	P	930	2.5
Plantronics Inc.	345 Encinal St.	Santa Cruz	CA	95060	SK Kannappan	831-426-5858	P	800	6.0
CIENA Corp.	1201 Winterson Rd.	Linthicum	MD	21090		410-694-5700	P	780	1.8
GenCorp Inc.	PO Box 537012	Sacramento	CA	95853	Terry L. Hall	916-355-4000	P	745	3.3
FlexStar Technology Inc.	47323 Warm Springs	Fremont	CA	94539	Eric Vergari	510-440-0170	R	622*	<0.1
Kyocera Wireless Corp.	10300 Campus Pnt	San Diego	CA	92121	Rodney N. Lanthorne	858-882-2000	S	538*	0.9
UOP L.L.C.	25 E Algonquin Rd.	Des Plaines	IL	60017	Carlos Guimaraes	847-391-2000	R	500*	4.0
IPC Systems Holdings Corp.	1500 Plaza Ten	Jersey City	NJ	07311	Lance B. Boxer	201-253-2000	R	485	1.4
ADTRAN Inc.	901 Explorer Blvd.	Huntsville	AL	35806	Thomas Stanton	256-963-8000	P	477	1.6
Anritsu Co.	490 Jarvis Dr.	Morgan Hill	CA	95037		408-778-2000	R	472*	0.5
Alcatel Submarine Network Inc.	15036 Conf. Ctr.	Chantilly	VA	20151		703-679-3600	D	465*	0.8
Credence Systems Corp.	1421 California	Milpitas	CA	95035		408-635-4300	P	461	1.5
Oce Printing Systems USA Inc.	5600 Broken Sound	Boca Raton	FL	33487	Joseph D. Skrzypczak		S	461*	0.9
Inter-Tel Inc.	1615 S 52nd St.	Tempe	AZ	85281	Alexander Cappello	480-449-8900	S	458	1.9
JBL Professional Inc.	8400 Balboa Blvd.	Northridge	CA	91329	John Carpanini	818-894-8850	S	443*	1.8
Core Laboratories Inc.	6316 Windfern Rd.	Houston	TX	77040	David M. Demshur	713-328-2673	S	427	4.0
Data Device Corp.	105 Wilbur Pl.	Bohemia	NY	11716	Clifford Lane	631-567-5600	R	388*	0.4
Allied Telesyn International	19800 N Creek Pky.	Bothell	WA	98011			S	350*	1.2
Analogic Corp.	8 Centennial Dr.	Peabody	MA	01960	Bernard Gordon	978-977-3000	P	341	1.5
Sonus Networks Inc.	7 Technology Park	Westford	MA	01886	Hassan Ahmed	978-614-8100	P	320	0.9
ADC Broadband Access Systems	PO Box 1181	Minneapolis	MN	55440		952-938-8080	S	316*	7.5
Harmonic Inc.	549 Baltic Way	Sunnyvale	CA	94089	Patrick Harshman	408-542-2500	P	312	0.6
Telex Communications Inc.	12000 Portland Ave.	Burnsville	MN	55337	R V. Malpocher	952-884-4051	R	308*	3.0
Westell Technologies Inc.	750 N Commons Dr.	Aurora	IL	60504	Thomas E. Mader	630-898-2500	P	260	0.9
Bel Fuse Inc.	206 Van Vorst St.	Jersey City	NJ	07302	Daniel Bernstein	201-432-0463	P	259	2.0
Nidec-Shimpo America Corp.	1701 Glenlake Ave.	Itasca	IL	60143	Yoshio Takahara	630-924-7138	R	256*	<0.1
Electro Rent Corporation Data	6060 Sepulveda	Van Nuys	CA	91411	William Weitzman	818-787-2100	D	256*	0.4
ABB Industrial Systems Inc.	579 Exec Campus	Westerville	OH	43082	Fred Kindle	614-818-6300	S	250*	1.5
Heraeus Electro-Nite Co.	1 Summit Sq.	Langhorne	PA	19047	Michael Midash	215-944-9000	R	246*	0.4
Cohu Inc.	12367 Crosthwaite	Poway	CA	92064	James A. Donahue	858-848-8100	P	245*	1.0
2Wire Inc.	1704 Automation	San Jose	CA	95131		408-428-9500	R	220	0.3
Raven Industries Inc.	PO Box 5107	Sioux Falls	SD	57117	Conrad J. Hoigaard	605-336-2750	P	217	0.9
Genesys Telecommunications Lab	2001 Junipero Serra	Daly City	CA	94014			S	209*	1.1
SymmetriCom Inc.	2300 Orchard Pky	San Jose	CA	95131	Robert T. Clarkson	408-433-0910	P	208	0.9
Mitutoyo America Corp.	965 Corporate Blvd.	Aurora	IL	60504		630-820-9666	R	198*	0.2
EXFO America Inc.	3701 Plano Pkwy.	Plano	TX	75075	Germain Lamonde	972-907-1505	R	197*	0.2
Intervoice Inc.	17811 Waterview	Dallas	TX	75252		972-454-8000	P	196	0.8
API Delevan	270 Quaker Rd.	East Aurora	NY	14052		716-652-3600	S	195*	1.8
Ideal Industries Inc.	Becker Pl.	Sycamore	IL	60178	Dave Juday		R	192*	1.7
Epic Technologies L.L.C.	200 Bluegrass Dr. E	Norwalk	OH	44857		419-668-8117	R	188*	0.2
Cirrus Logic Inc.	2901 Via Fortuna	Austin	TX	78746		512-851-4000	P	182	0.5
Simpson Electric Co.	PO Box 99	Lac d Flambeau	WI	54538	Richard Schermetzler	715-588-3311	R	182*	0.1
DDI Corp.	1220 Simon Cir.	Anaheim	CA	92806		714-688-7200	P	181	1.3

Source: Ward's Business Directory of U.S. Private and Public Companies, Volumes 1 and 2, 2008. The company type code used is as follows: P - Public, R - Private, S - Subsidiary, D - Division, J - Joint Venture, A - Affiliate, G - Group. Sales are in millions of dollars, employees are in thousands. An asterisk (*) indicates an estimated sales volume. The symbol < stands for 'less than'. Company names and addresses are truncated, in some cases, to fit into the available space.

MATERIALS CONSUMED

Material	Quantity	Delivered Cost ($ million)
Tube blanks	(X)	0.7
Printed ciruit boards (without inserted components) for electronic circuitry	(X)	2.1
Printed circuit assemblies, loaded boards, and modules	(X)	14.7
Semiconductors (incl. transistors, diodes, rectifiers, and integrated circuits), for electronic circuitry	(X)	5.3
Capacitors for electronic circuitry	(X)	5.6
Resistors for electronic circuitry	(X)	3.4
All other miscellaneous components and accessories for electronic circuitry (exc. tubes)	(X)	12.0
Silicon, hyperpure	(X)	(D)
Gold and other precious metals, all forms (incl. ingot, sheet, etc.)	(X)	1.2
Doped chemicals and other doped materials for electronic use	(X)	0.2
Ferrites (powder and paste)	(X)	5.1
Metal powders	(X)	0.6
Electronic computer equipment	(X)	0.1
Current-carrying wiring devices	(X)	11.1
Electronic communication equipment	(X)	(D)
Electrical instrument mechanisms and meter movements	(X)	(D)
All other miscellaneous electrical measuring instruments and parts	(X)	0.1
Fractional horsepower electric motors (less than 1 hp)	(X)	(D)
Electrical transmission, distribution, and control equipment	(X)	6.7
Loudspeakers, microphones, and tuners (all types)	(X)	(D)
Glass and glass products (excluding windows and mirrors)	(X)	(D)
Optical instruments and lenses (exc. sighting, tracking, and fire control)	(X)	(D)
Plastics resins consumed in the form of granules, pellets, etc.	(X)	3.2
Fabricated plastics products (excluding gaskets)	(X)	8.1
Sheet metal products (excluding stampings)	(X)	(D)
Metal stampings	(X)	9.8
Metal bolts, nuts, screws, and other screw machine products	(X)	5.2
Other fabricated metal products (excluding forgings)	(X)	2.7
Forgings	(X)	(D)
Castings, rough and semifinished	(X)	0.1
Steel shapes and forms (exc. castings, forgings, fabr. metal products)	(X)	53.1
Copper and copper-base alloy shapes and forms (exc. castings, forgings, fabr. metal products)	(X)	9.4
Aluminum and aluminum-base alloy shapes and forms (exc. castings, forgings, fabr. metal products)	(X)	1.3
Other nonferrous shapes and forms (exc. castings, forgings, fabricated metal products)	(X)	4.1
Insulated wire and cable (including magnet wire)	(X)	52.5
Paper and paperboard containers (incl. shipping sacks and other paper packaging supplies)	(X)	14.4
Resists (photosensitive resin films applied to surface of wafer)	(X)	(D)
Commodity gases	(X)	0.2
Masks	(X)	(D)
Silicon chips	(X)	(D)
Solvents	(X)	0.5
Cleaning compounds	(X)	0.1
All other materials, components, parts, containers, and supplies	(X)	87.1
Materials, ingredients, containers, and supplies, nsk	(X)	36.4

Source: 2002 *Economic Census*. Explanation of symbols used: (D): Withheld to avoid disclosure of competitive data; na: Not available; (S): Withheld because statistical norms were not met; (X): Not applicable; (Z): Less than half the unit shown; nec: Not elsewhere classified; nsk: Not specified by kind; - : zero; p : 10-19 percent estimated; q : 20-29 percent estimated.

PRODUCT SHARE DETAILS

Product or Product Class Shipments	Mil. $	Product or Product Class Shipments	Mil. $
ELECTRONIC COILS, TRANSFORMERS, AND OTHER INDUCTORS	1,237.4		

Source: 2002 *Economic Census*. The values are product shipments in millions of dollars for 2002. Total product shipments may be lower or higher than industry shipments. See Introduction for a full discussion. Values of indented subcategories are summed in the main heading(s). The symbol (D) appears when data are withheld to prevent disclosure of competitive information. The abbreviation nsk stands for 'not specified by kind' and nec for 'not elsewhere classified'. A dash (-) means zero.

INPUTS AND OUTPUTS FOR ELECTRONIC CAPACITORS & OTHER INDUCTORS

Economic Sector or Industry Providing Inputs	%	Sector	Economic Sector or Industry Buying Outputs	%	Sector
Compensation of employees	37.8		Exports of goods & services	28.5	Cap Inv
Management of companies & enterprises	10.4	Services	Software publishers	5.5	Services
Wholesale trade	8.2	Trade	Motor vehicle parts	4.2	Manufg.
Iron & steel mills & ferroalloys	3.1	Manufg.	Semiconductors & related devices	4.0	Manufg.
Scientific research & development services	2.8	Services	Printed circuit assemblies (electronic assembles)	3.5	Manufg.
Electronic capacitors, resistors, coils, transformers	2.3	Manufg.	Electronic computers	3.4	Manufg.
Nonferrous metal (ex. copper & aluminum) processing	2.0	Manufg.	Bare printed circuit boards	3.2	Manufg.
Primary nonferrous metal, ex. copper & aluminum	1.8	Manufg.	Electromedical & electrotherapeutic apparatus	2.8	Manufg.
Lessors of nonfinancial assets	1.7	Fin/R.E.	Telecommunications	2.3	Services
Power generation & supply	1.6	Util.	Search, detection, & navigation instruments	2.2	Manufg.
Copper rolling, drawing, extruding, & alloying	1.5	Manufg.	Electronic components, nec	2.0	Manufg.

Continued on next page,

INPUTS AND OUTPUTS FOR ELECTRONIC CAPACITORS & OTHER INDUCTORS - Continued

Economic Sector or Industry Providing Inputs	%	Sector	Economic Sector or Industry Buying Outputs	%	Sector
Crowns & closures & metal stamping	1.2	Manufg.	Audio & video equipment	1.9	Manufg.
Alumina refining & primary aluminum production	1.0	Manufg.	Data processing, hosting, & related services	1.9	Services
Electronic components, nec	0.9	Manufg.	Telephone apparatus	1.8	Manufg.
Real estate	0.9	Fin/R.E.	Electrical equipment & components, nec	1.7	Manufg.
Paperboard containers	0.9	Manufg.	Electricity & signal testing instruments	1.7	Manufg.
Communication & energy wires & cables	0.7	Manufg.	Broadcast & wireless communications equipment	1.6	Manufg.
Plastics products, nec	0.7	Manufg.	Other computer related services, including facilities	1.5	Services
Noncomparable imports	0.7	Foreign	Basic organic chemicals, nec	1.4	Manufg.
Truck transportation	0.7	Util.	Electronic capacitors, resistors, coils, transformers	1.3	Manufg.
Advertising & related services	0.7	Services	Computer storage devices	1.3	Manufg.
Taxes on production & imports, less subsidies	0.6		Computer terminals & peripherals	1.2	Manufg.
Printed circuit assemblies (electronic assemblies)	0.6	Manufg.	Communications equipment, nec	1.1	Manufg.
Securities, commodity contracts, investments	0.5	Fin/R.E.	Watches, clocks, & related devices	1.0	Manufg.
Chemical products & preparations, nec	0.5	Manufg.	Custom computer programming services	0.9	Services
Turned products & screws, nuts, & bolts	0.5	Manufg.	Power, distribution, & specialty transformers	0.9	Manufg.
Wiring devices	0.5	Manufg.	General Federal government services, defense	0.9	Fed Govt
Plastics materials & resins	0.4	Manufg.	Motors & generators	0.9	Manufg.
Telecommunications	0.4	Services	Commercial & service industry machinery, nec	0.8	Manufg.
Semiconductors & related devices	0.4	Manufg.	Industrial process variable instruments	0.7	Manufg.
Legal services	0.4	Services	Surgical appliances & supplies	0.7	Manufg.
Maintenance/repair of nonresidential structures	0.4	Construct.	Totalizing fluid meters & counting devices	0.7	Manufg.
Management, scientific, & technical consulting	0.4	Services	Material handling equipment	0.7	Manufg.
Services to buildings & dwellings	0.3	Services	Investigation & security services	0.7	Services
Warehousing & storage	0.3	Util.	General purpose machinery, nec	0.7	Manufg.
Accounting, tax preparation, bookkeeping, & payroll	0.3	Services	AC, refrigeration, and warm air heating equipment	0.6	Manufg.
Data processing, hosting, & related services	0.3	Services	Irradiation apparatus	0.6	Manufg.
Bare printed circuit boards	0.3	Manufg.	Educational services, nec	0.5	Services
Other computer related services, including facilities	0.3	Services	Wholesale trade	0.5	Trade
Automotive equipment rental & leasing	0.3	Fin/R.E.	Automatic environmental controls	0.5	Manufg.
Natural gas distribution	0.3	Util.	Analytical laboratory instruments	0.5	Manufg.
Employment services	0.3	Services	Semiconductor machinery	0.4	Manufg.
Automotive repair & maintenance, ex. car washes	0.2	Services	Industrial machinery, nec	0.4	Manufg.
Specialized design services	0.2	Services	Household cooking appliances	0.3	Manufg.
Architectural, engineering, & related services	0.2	Services	Engine equipment, nec	0.3	Manufg.
Ornamental & architectural metal products	0.2	Manufg.	General S/L govt. services	0.3	S/L Govt
Business support services	0.2	Services	Plastics materials & resins	0.3	Manufg.
Commercial & industrial equipment repair/maintenance	0.2	Services	Construction machinery	0.3	Manufg.
Basic inorganic chemicals, nec	0.2	Manufg.	Electronic & precision equipment repair/maintenance	0.3	Services
Pressed & blown glass & glassware, nec	0.2	Manufg.	Household refrigerators & home freezers	0.3	Manufg.
Relay & industrial controls	0.2	Manufg.	Internet service providers & web search portals	0.3	Services
Plastics packaging materials, film & sheet	0.2	Manufg.	Rolling mill & other metalworking machinery	0.2	Manufg.
Machine shops	0.2	Manufg.	Monetary authorities/depository credit intermediation	0.2	Fin/R.E.
Monetary authorities/depository credit intermediation	0.2	Fin/R.E.	Nondepository credit intermediation activities	0.2	Fin/R.E.
Electricity & signal testing instruments	0.2	Manufg.	Household laundry equipment	0.2	Manufg.
Waste management & remediation services	0.2	Services	Securities, commodity contracts, investments	0.2	Fin/R.E.
Coating, engraving, heat treating & allied activities	0.1	Manufg.	Aircraft	0.2	Manufg.
Professional, scientific, technical services, nec	0.1	Services	Photographic & photocopying equipment	0.2	Manufg.
Commercial & industrial machinery rental & leasing	0.1	Fin/R.E.	Plastics & rubber industry machinery	0.2	Manufg.
Motors & generators	0.1	Manufg.	Electron tubes	0.2	Manufg.
Food services & drinking places	0.1	Services	Air & gas compressors	0.2	Manufg.
Computer system design services	0.1	Services	Optical instruments & lenses	0.2	Manufg.
Industrial gases	0.1	Manufg.	Pumps & pumping equipment	0.2	Manufg.
Support services, nec	0.1	Services	Air transportation	0.1	Util.
Custom computer programming services	0.1	Services	Magnetic & optical recording media	0.1	Manufg.
			Farm machinery & equipment	0.1	Manufg.
			Vending, commercial, industrial, office machinery	0.1	Manufg.
			Commercial & industrial equipment repair/maintenance	0.1	Services
			Industrial gases	0.1	Manufg.

Source: Benchmark Input-Output Accounts for the U.S. Economy, 2002, U.S. Department of Commerce, Washington D.C., January 2008. User should note that this Input-Output table is not for this particular narrowly defined industry but for a larger aggregate. Input and Output data for Electronic Capacitors & Other Inductors *include Input and Output data for the* Annual Survey of Manufactures' *NAICS industries 334414, 334415, and 334416.* The abbreviation nec stands for 'not elsewhere classified'.

OCCUPATIONS EMPLOYED BY SEMICONDUCTOR & OTHER ELECTRONIC COMPONENT MANUFACTURING

Occupation	% of Total 2006	Change to 2016	Occupation	% of Total 2006	Change to 2016
Electrical & electronic equipment assemblers	10.9	-30.1	Computer software engineers, systems software	1.5	-3.8
Semiconductor processors	8.2	-12.6	Production workers, nec	1.3	-14.2
Team assemblers	4.5	-12.6	Shipping, receiving, & traffic clerks	1.3	-15.9
Electrical & electronic engineering technicians	4.1	-12.6	Purchasing agents, exc wholesale, retail, & farm	1.3	-12.6
Inspectors, testers, sorters, samplers, & weighers	3.9	-17.6	Production, planning, & expediting clerks	1.2	-12.6
Electronics engineers, exc computer	3.9	-12.6	General & operations managers	1.2	-21.3
First-line supervisors/managers of production workers	2.8	-12.6	Coil winders, tapers, & finishers	1.1	-30.1
Electrical engineers	2.6	-12.6	Machinists	1.1	-8.2
Industrial engineers	2.5	6.2	Industrial production managers	1.0	-12.6
Engineering managers	2.3	-3.8	Maintenance & repair workers, general	1.0	-12.6
Electromechanical equipment assemblers	1.7	-12.6			

Source: *Industry-Occupation Matrix*, Bureau of Labor Statistics, December 4, 2007. These data are reported based on 4-digit NAICS categories but have been matched to corresponding 6-digit NAICS industry codes. The change reported for each occupation to the year 2016 is a percent of growth or decline as estimated by the Bureau of Labor Statistics. The abbreviation nec stands for 'not elsewhere classified'.

LOCATION BY STATE AND REGIONAL CONCENTRATION

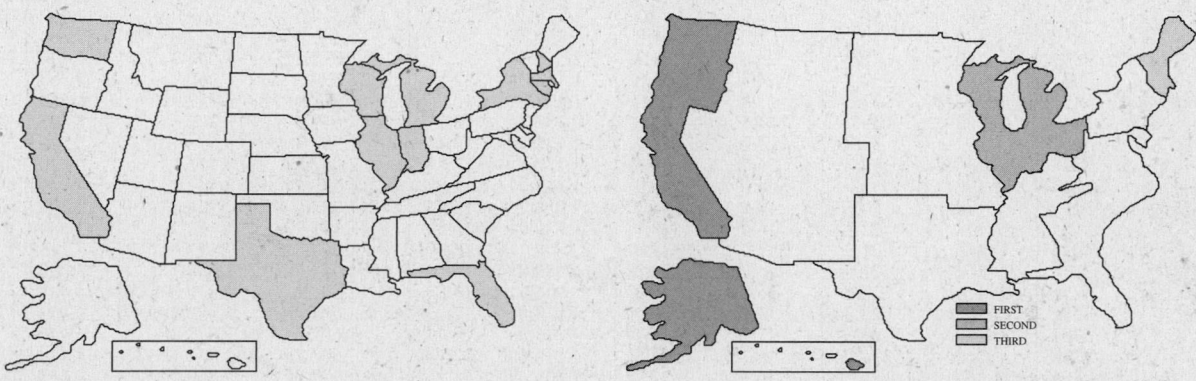

INDUSTRY DATA BY STATE

State	Establish- ments	Shipments			Employment				Cost as % of Shipments	Investment per Employee ($)
		Total ($ mil)	% of U.S.	Per Establ.	Total Number	% of U.S.	Per Establ.	Wages ($/hour)		
California	68	137.3	12.0	2,018.6	1,492	13.4	22	12.60	34.1	1,178
Illinois	40	109.5	9.5	2,737.8	1,290	11.6	32	10.99	39.2	1,850
Washington	7	94.7	8.3	13,529.4	277	2.5	40	12.48	64.3	1,419
New York	32	88.7	7.7	2,770.7	1,371	12.3	43	10.19	21.3	1,619
Texas	17	60.6	5.3	3,562.1	353	3.2	21	9.92	48.0	5,728
Indiana	10	48.7	4.2	4,868.6	470	4.2	47	11.92	42.9	3,847
New Hampshire	7	43.3	3.8	6,186.6	469	4.2	67	12.03	33.2	1,077
Wisconsin	10	37.9	3.3	3,787.4	352	3.2	35	10.37	41.3	889
Florida	17	34.1	3.0	2,004.8	442	4.0	26	9.25	38.6	631
Connecticut	17	29.6	2.6	1,743.9	453	4.1	27	10.22	35.5	801
Massachusetts	15	25.4	2.2	1,694.3	232	2.1	15	12.74	36.1	991
Michigan	11	22.2	1.9	2,022.2	200	1.8	18	9.08	42.9	1,500

Source: 2002 *Economic Census*. The states are in descending order of shipments or establishments (if shipment data are missing for the majority). The symbol (D) appears when data are withheld to prevent disclosure of competitive information. States marked with (D) are sorted by number of establishments. A dash (-) indicates that the data element cannot be calculated. Data may not show all states active in the NAICS category. All data available at the time of publication are shown.

NAICS 334417 - ELECTRONIC CONNECTOR MANUFACTURING

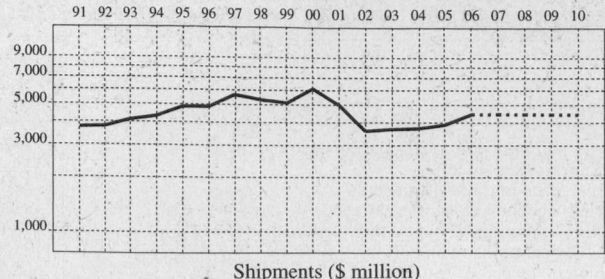

Shipments ($ million)

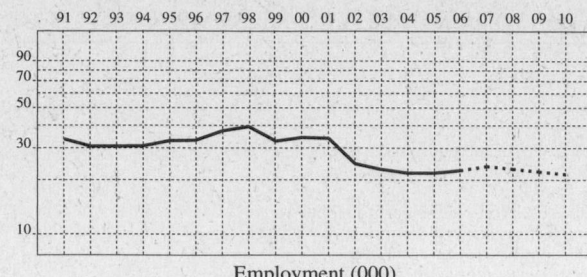

Employment (000)

GENERAL STATISTICS

Year	Com-panies	Establishments		Employment			Compensation		Production ($ million)			
		Total	with 20 or more employees	Total (000)	Production Workers (000)	Hours (Mil)	Payroll ($ mil)	Wages ($/hr)	Cost of Materials	Value Added by Manufacture	Value of Shipments	Capital Invest.
1991		251	183	33.6	23.7	48.3	887.5	10.94	1,321.3	2,334.7	3,751.2	142.2
1992	240	285	188	30.7	21.1	42.4	909.2	11.92	1,390.2	2,385.9	3,773.5	144.3
1993		283	188	30.7	20.9	42.2	916.3	12.22	1,514.5	2,600.0	4,112.3	210.7
1994		281	189	30.8	21.7	45.8	954.3	12.29	1,686.2	2,637.0	4,304.3	200.4
1995		280	190	32.9	23.8	51.3	1,090.1	12.36	1,871.5	3,046.7	4,860.2	207.1
1996		309	191	33.1	24.3	51.8	1,118.0	12.89	1,899.5	2,960.9	4,863.2	228.1
1997	283	347	216	37.3	27.8	56.3	1,177.4	12.74	1,818.9	3,853.9	5,666.4	233.3
1998		344	202	39.4	27.6	56.6	1,187.4	12.79	1,619.3	3,706.8	5,325.7	338.2
1999		333	197	32.8	24.2	50.2	1,128.4	13.41	1,591.3	3,533.7	5,125.3	237.2
2000		322	184	34.3	25.7	53.6	1,234.4	14.41	2,052.5	4,112.1	6,120.2	301.5
2001		330	190	33.9	24.0	45.9	1,245.0	15.81	1,777.7	3,142.2	4,989.5	274.2
2002	281	321	170	24.6	17.5	34.5	920.9	15.44	1,282.6	2,264.0	3,597.5	144.7
2003		312	178	22.9	16.4	33.8	889.9	15.50	1,191.7	2,462.7	3,684.1	134.8
2004		294	165	21.9	16.0	32.3	878.2	15.90	1,279.3	2,417.6	3,715.7	105.1
2005		278	162	21.9	16.2	32.8	888.0	16.16	1,413.0	2,538.7	3,899.4	102.1
2006		325P	174P	22.6	16.8	33.8	946.9	16.83	1,603.2	2,879.6	4,447.3	107.0
2007		328P	172P	23.8P	17.7P	35.5P	1,013.0P	17.03P	1,605.4P	2,883.5P	4,453.3P	157.8P
2008		330P	170P	23.0P	17.2P	34.4P	1,011.8P	17.41P	1,602.8P	2,878.8P	4,446.1P	153.5P
2009		333P	169P	22.2P	16.7P	33.3P	1,010.6P	17.78P	1,600.2P	2,874.1P	4,438.9P	149.2P
2010		335P	167P	21.5P	16.3P	32.3P	1,009.4P	18.16P	1,597.6P	2,869.5P	4,431.7P	144.9P

Sources: 1992, 1997, 2002 *Economic Census*; other years, up to 2006, are from the *Annual Survey of Manufactures*. Establishment counts for non-Census years are from *County Business Patterns*; 1997 and 2002 values are from the 1997 and 2002 censuses respectively, reported in the Federal Government's NAICS format. Other years were originally reported in equivalent SIC format. 'P's show projections by the editors.

INDICES OF CHANGE

Year	Com-panies	Establishments		Employment			Compensation		Production ($ million)			
		Total	with 20 or more employees	Total (000)	Production Workers (000)	Hours (Mil)	Payroll ($ mil)	Wages ($/hr)	Cost of Materials	Value Added by Manufacture	Value of Shipments	Capital Invest.
1992	85	89	111	125	121	123	99	77	108	105	105	100
1997	101	108	127	152	159	163	128	83	142	170	158	161
2001		103	112	138	137	133	135	102	139	139	139	189
2002	100	100	100	100	100	100	100	100	100	100	100	100
2003		97	105	93	94	98	97	100	93	109	102	93
2004		92	97	89	91	94	95	103	100	107	103	73
2005		87	95	89	93	95	96	105	110	112	108	71
2006		101P	102P	92	96	98	103	109	125	127	124	74
2007		102P	101P	97P	101P	103P	110P	110P	125P	127P	124P	109P
2008		103P	100P	93P	98P	100P	110P	113P	125P	127P	124P	106P
2009		104P	99P	90P	95P	97P	110P	115P	125P	127P	123P	103P
2010		104P	98P	87P	93P	94P	110P	118P	125P	127P	123P	100P

Sources: Same as General Statistics. Values reflect change from the base year, 2002. Values above 100 mean greater than 2002, values below 100 mean less than 2002, and the values of 100 in other years means the same as 2002. 'P's show projections by the editors.

SELECTED RATIOS

For 2002	Avg. of All Manufact.	Analyzed Industry	Index	For 2002	Avg. of All Manufact.	Analyzed Industry	Index
Employees per Establishment	42	77	183	Value Added per Production Worker	182,367	129,371	71
Payroll per Establishment	1,639,184	2,868,847	175	Cost per Establishment	5,769,015	3,995,639	69
Payroll per Employee	39,053	37,435	96	Cost per Employee	137,446	52,138	38
Production Workers per Establishment	30	55	185	Cost per Production Worker	195,506	73,291	37
Wages per Establishment	694,845	1,659,439	239	Shipments per Establishment	11,158,348	11,207,165	100
Wages per Production Worker	23,548	30,439	129	Shipments per Employee	265,847	146,240	55
Hours per Production Worker	1,980	1,971	100	Shipments per Production Worker	378,144	205,571	54
Wages per Hour	11.89	15.44	130	Investment per Establishment	361,338	450,779	125
Value Added per Establishment	5,381,325	7,052,960	131	Investment per Employee	8,609	5,882	68
Value Added per Employee	128,210	92,033	72	Investment per Production Worker	12,245	8,269	68

Sources: Same as General Statistics. The 'Average of All Manufacturing' column represents the average of all manufacturing industries reported for the most recent complete year available. The Index shows the relationship between the Average and the Analyzed Industry. For example, 100 means that they are equal; 500 that the Analyzed Industry is five times the average; 50 means that the Analyzed Industry is half the national average. The abbreviation 'na' is used to show that data are 'not available'. Ratios shown for 2002, the last complete census year.

LEADING COMPANIES

Number shown: **75**   Total sales ($ mil): **32,847**   Total employment (000): **188.7**

Company Name	Address				CEO Name	Phone	Co. Type	Sales ($ mil)	Empl. (000)
ITT Corp.	4 W Red Oak Ln.	White Plains	NY	10604		914-641-2000	P	9,003	39.7
Phoenix Contact Services Inc.	PO Box 4100	Harrisburg	PA	17111	Jack Nehlig	717-944-1300	R	3,873*	0.3
Molex Inc.	2222 Wellington Ct.	Lisle	IL	60532		630-969-4550	P	3,266	33.2
Amphenol Corp.	358 Hall Ave.	Wallingford	CT	06492		203-265-8900	P	2,851	32.0
Vishay Intertechnology Inc.	PO Box 4004	Malvern	PA	19355	Gerald Paul	610-644-1300	P	2,833	27.9
Hubbell Inc.	584 Derby Milford	Orange	CT	06477		203-799-4100	P	2,534	11.5
Thomas and Betts Corp.	8155 T and B Blvd.	Memphis	TN	38125	T. Kevin Dunnigan	901-252-8000	P	2,137	11.0
AVX Corp.	PO Box 867	Myrtle Beach	SC	29578	John S. Gilbertson	843-448-9411	P	1,333	13.0
Teradyne Inc.	600 Riverpark Dr.	North Reading	MA	01864	James Bagley	978-370-2700	P	1,102	3.6
Leviton Manufacturing Company	PO Box 630087	Little Neck	NY	11363	Donald Hendler	718-229-4040	R	800*	0.7
Methode Electronics Inc.	7401 W Wilson Ave.	Chicago	IL	60706	Warren L. Batts	708-867-6777	P	448	3.2
Cinch Connectors Inc.	1700 S Finley Rd.	Lombard	IL	60148	Michael Murray	630-705-6000	R	406*	0.1
Everett Charles Technologies	700 E Harrison Ave.	Pomona	CA	91767	Patrick T. Flynn	909-625-5551	S	216*	0.9
Ideal Industries Inc.	Becker Pl.	Sycamore	IL	60178	Dave Juday		R	192*	1.7
Spectrum Control Inc.	8031 Avonia Rd.	Fairview	PA	16415		814-474-2207	P	126	1.5
Tri-Star Electronics Int'l	2201 Rosecrans Ave.	El Segundo	CA	90245	Terry Jarnigan	310-536-0444	D	90*	0.3
Wago Corp.	PO Box 1015	Germantown	WI	53022	Thomas Artman	262-255-6222	R	90*	0.1
Lemo USA Inc.	PO Box 2408	Rohnert Park	CA	94927	Tim Hassett	707-578-8811	R	74*	<0.1
Deutsch Engin. Connecting Dev.	700 S Hathaway St.	Banning	CA	92220		951-849-7844	R	72*	0.5
Switchcraft Inc.	5555 N Elston Ave.	Chicago	IL	60630	Keith Bandolik	773-792-2700	R	64*	0.5
JAE Electronics Inc.	142 Technology Dr.	Irvine	CA	92618	Shinsuke Takahashi	949-753-2600	R	60*	<0.1
Radiall Inc.	3611 NE 112th Ave.	Vancouver	WA	98682	Dominique Pellizzari	360-944-7551	R	60*	<0.1
ENI Products Group	100 Highpower Rd.	Rochester	NY	14623	Leo Berlinghieri	585-427-8300	S	49*	0.3
FCI Electronics Inc.	825 Old Trail Rd.	Etters	PA	17319	Alain Bugat	717-938-7200	S	48*	0.2
WPI Inc.	90 W Broadway	Salem	NJ	08079	Henry Barbera	856-935-7370	R	45*	0.5
Hi Rel Connectors Inc.	760 Wharton Dr.	Claremont	CA	91711	Fred Baumann	909-626-1820	R	39*	0.3
Audio Authority Corp.	2048 Mercer Rd.	Lexington	KY	40511	Jonathan Sisk	859-233-4599	R	39*	<0.1
Fiber Instrument Sales Inc.	161 Clear Rd.	Oriskany	NY	13424	Frank Giotto	315-736-2206	R	38*	0.2
Alpha Wire Co.	711 Lidgerwood	Elizabeth	NJ	07207		908-925-8000	R	36*	0.2
Conxall Corp.	601 E Wildwood	Villa Park	IL	60181	Keith Bandliok	630-834-7504	S	34*	0.2
Whirlwind Music Distributors	99 Ling Rd.	Rochester	NY	14612	Michael Laiacona	585-663-8820	R	34*	0.1
Component Enterprises Company	PO Box 189	Norristown	PA	19404	Michael Hoffman	610-272-7900	R	32*	<0.1
Mill-Max Manufacturing Corp.	PO Box 300	Oyster Bay	NY	11771	Roger Bahnik	516-922-6000	R	32*	0.2
Synergetix	310 S 51st St.	Kansas City	KS	66106	Tanis Carey	913-342-0404	R	31	0.2
Cooper Industries Bussmann Div	PO Box 14460	St. Louis	MO	63178	H. John Riley Jr.	630-394-2877	D	30*	0.3
Harting Inc. of North America	1370 Bowes Rd.	Elgin	IL	60123	Allan Dickson	847-741-2700	R	30*	<0.1
Btx Technologies Inc.	5 Skyline Dr.	Hawthorne	NY	10532	Greg Schwartz	914-592-1800	R	29*	<0.1
Valwest Technolgies Inc.	430 N 47th Ave.	Phoenix	AZ	85043	Lorenzo Valenzuela	623-435-9778	R	28*	<0.1
CS Business Systems Inc.	1236 Main St.	Buffalo	NY	14209	Michael Choo	716-886-6521	R	27*	<0.1
Micro Mode Products Inc.	1870 John Towers	El Cajon	CA	92020	Michael Cuban	619-449-3844	R	26*	0.1
Mason Industries Inc.	PO Box 410	Smithtown	NY	11787	Norman Mason	631-348-0282	R	26*	0.2
Aero-Electric Connector Inc.	548 Amapola Ave.	Torrance	CA	90501		310-618-3737	R	25*	0.3
Radiall Aep Inc.	PO Box 510	New Haven	CT	06513	Andre Hernandez	203-776-2813	R	25*	0.2
Virginia Panel Corp.	1400 New Hope Rd.	Waynesboro	VA	22980	Gloria Stowers	540-932-3300	R	24*	0.2
Southwest Microwave Inc.	9055 S McKemy St.	Tempe	AZ	85284	Richard McCormick	480-783-0201	R	23*	0.1
Unicorp Inc.	291 Cleveland St.	Orange	NJ	07050	Steven Mercadante	973-674-1700	R	23*	0.2
Unicom Electric Inc.	908 Canada Ct.	City of Industry	CA	91748	Jeffrey Lo	626-964-7873	R	22*	<0.1
Hybricon Corp.	12 Willow Rd.	Ayer	MA	01432	Paul Freve	978-772-5422	R	21*	<0.1
J-T E C H	1631 E St Andrew	Santa Ana	CA	92705	Walter Naubauer	714-665-2080	R	20*	0.1
Continental-Wirt Electronics	130 James Way	Southampton	PA	18966	Burton Lifson	215-355-7080	R	20*	0.2
Cristek Interconnects Inc.	5395 E Hunter Ave.	Anaheim	CA	92807	Cristi Cristich	714-696-5200	R	20*	0.1
Reinforced Structures For Elec	50 Suffolk St.	Worcester	MA	01604	Edward Romeo	508-754-5316	R	20*	<0.1
Keystone Electronics Corp.	3107 20th Rd.	Astoria	NY	11105	Richard David	718-956-8900	R	20*	0.1
Abelconn L.L.C.	9210 Science Ctr.	New Hope	MN	55428		763-533-3533	R	19*	0.1
Calrad Electronics Inc.	819 N Highland	Los Angeles	CA	90038	Robert Shupper	323-465-2131	R	16*	<0.1
Xponet Inc.	20 Elberta Rd.	Painesville	OH	44077	Don Barber	440-354-6617	R	16*	<0.1
Bryant Rubber Corp.	1112 Lomita Blvd.	Harbor City	CA	90710	Steven Bryant	310-530-2530	R	16*	0.1
Component Equipment Company	3050 Cam Del Sol	Oxnard	CA	93030	Bill Rigby	805-484-0149	R	16*	0.1
Richards Manufacturing Sales	517 Lyons Ave.	Irvington	NJ	07111	Bruce Bier	973-371-1771	R	16*	<0.1
Phoenix Company of Chicago	555 Pond Dr.	Wood Dale	IL	60191	Bernard Machura	630-595-2300	R	15*	0.2
Communication Con Connectors	1855 Business Ctr.	Duarte	CA	91010	Robert Farnum	626-301-4200	R	15*	0.1
RF Industries Ltd.	7610 Miramar Rd.	San Diego	CA	92126	Howard F. Hill	858-549-6340	P	15	<0.1
Continental Connector Co.	53 La France Ave.	Bloomfield	NJ	07003	Lou Kilian	973-429-8500	R	14*	<0.1
Stewart Connector Systems Inc.	11118 Susquehanna	Glen Rock	PA	17327	Dan Bernstein	717-235-7512	S	13*	<0.1
US Conec Ltd.	PO Box 2306	Hickory	NC	28603	Bill Blubaugh	828-323-8883	R	13*	<0.1
Johnstech International Corp.	1210 New Brighton	Minneapolis	MN	55413	David Johnson	612-378-2020	R	13*	<0.1
Omnetics Connector Corp.	7260 Commerce Cir.	Minneapolis	MN	55432	Gerald Simonson	763-572-0656	R	13*	<0.1
Libra Industries Inc.	7770 Division Dr.	Mentor	OH	44060		440-974-7770	R	12*	0.2
Pico Macom Inc.	6260 Sequence Dr.	San Diego	CA	92121	Pepe Zyman	858-546-5050	S	12*	0.1
Array Connector Corp.	12400 SW 134th Ct.	Miami	FL	33186	William McPherson	305-234-1000	R	12*	<0.1
RF Connectors	7610 Miramar Rd.	San Diego	CA	92126		858-549-6340	D	12*	<0.1
PAVE Technology Co.	2751 Thunderhawk	Dayton	OH	45414		937-890-1100	R	12*	<0.1
MegaPhase L.L.C.	2098 W Main St., 3	Stroudsburg	PA	18360	William Pote	570-424-8400	R	12*	<0.1
Circuit Assembly Corp.	18 Thomas	Irvine	CA	92618	Roger Lang	949-855-7887	R	11*	<0.1
Kemlon Products & Development	PO Box 2189	Pearland	TX	77588	Russell Ring	281-997-3300	R	11*	0.2

Source: Ward's Business Directory of U.S. Private and Public Companies, Volumes 1 and 2, 2008. The company type code used is as follows: P - Public, R - Private, S - Subsidiary, D - Division, J - Joint Venture, A - Affiliate, G - Group. Sales are in millions of dollars, employees are in thousands. An asterisk (*) indicates an estimated sales volume. The symbol < stands for 'less than'. Company names and addresses are truncated, in some cases, to fit into the available space.

MATERIALS CONSUMED

Material	Quantity	Delivered Cost ($ million)
Tube blanks	(X)	(D)
Printed ciruit boards (without inserted components) for electronic circuitry	(X)	12.7
Printed circuit assemblies, loaded boards, and modules	(X)	30.4
Semiconductors (incl. transistors, diodes, rectifiers, and integrated circuits), for electronic circuitry	(X)	(D)
Capacitors for electronic circuitry	(X)	2.2
Resistors for electronic circuitry	(X)	(D)
All other miscellaneous components and accessories for electronic circuitry (exc. tubes)	(X)	175.3
Silicon, hyperpure	(X)	(D)
Gold and other precious metals, all forms (incl. ingot, sheet, etc.)	(X)	60.2
Doped chemicals and other doped materials for electronic use	(X)	0.1
Ferrites (powder and paste)	(X)	(D)
Metal powders	(X)	(D)
Electronic computer equipment	(X)	0.2
Current-carrying wiring devices	(X)	8.3
Electronic communication equipment	(X)	(D)
Electrical instrument mechanisms and meter movements	(X)	(D)
All other miscellaneous electrical measuring instruments and parts	(X)	(D)
Fractional horsepower electric motors (less than 1 hp)	(X)	(D)
Electrical transmission, distribution, and control equipment	(X)	0.6
Glass and glass products (excluding windows and mirrors)	(X)	0.4
Optical instruments and lenses (exc. sighting, tracking, and fire control)	(X)	(D)
Plastics resins consumed in the form of granules, pellets, etc.	(X)	42.4
Fabricated plastics products (excluding gaskets)	(X)	41.1
Sheet metal products (excluding stampings)	(X)	13.5
Metal stampings	(X)	22.2
Metal bolts, nuts, screws, and other screw machine products	(X)	66.5
Other fabricated metal products (excluding forgings)	(X)	38.9
Forgings	(X)	(D)
Castings, rough and semifinished	(X)	4.5
Steel shapes and forms (exc. castings, forgings, fabr. metal products)	(X)	23.9
Copper and copper-base alloy shapes and forms (exc. castings, forgings, fabr. metal products)	(X)	49.1
Aluminum and aluminum-base alloy shapes and forms (exc. castings, forgings, fabr. metal products)	(X)	44.7
Other nonferrous shapes and forms (exc. castings, forgings, fabricated metal products)	(X)	4.3
Insulated wire and cable (including magnet wire)	(X)	33.0
Paper and paperboard containers (incl. shipping sacks and other paper packaging supplies)	(X)	15.3
Resists (photosensitive resin films applied to surface of wafer)	(X)	(D)
Commodity gases	(X)	(D)
Speciality gases	(X)	(D)
Solvents	(X)	0.2
Cleaning compounds	(X)	0.3
All other materials, components, parts, containers, and supplies	(X)	240.2
Materials, ingredients, containers, and supplies, nsk	(X)	59.9

Source: 2002 *Economic Census*. Explanation of symbols used: (D): Withheld to avoid disclosure of competitive data; na: Not available; (S): Withheld because statistical norms were not met; (X): Not applicable; (Z): Less than half the unit shown; nec: Not elsewhere classified; nsk: Not specified by kind; - : zero; p : 10-19 percent estimated; q : 20-29 percent estimated.

PRODUCT SHARE DETAILS

Product or Product Class Shipments	Mil. $	Product or Product Class Shipments	Mil. $
ELECTRONIC CONNECTORS	3,803.6	circuitry	283.7
Coaxial (RF) connectors for electronic circuitry	485.5	Printed circuit connectors for electronic circuitry	788.2
Cylindrical connectors for electronic circuitry	530.7	Other connectors for electronic circuitry, including parts	1,495.7
Rack and panel (rectangular) connectors for electronic		Electronic connectors, nsk, total	219.7

Source: 2002 *Economic Census*. The values are product shipments in millions of dollars for 2002. Total product shipments may be lower or higher than industry shipments. See Introduction for a full discussion. Values of indented subcategories are summed in the main heading(s). The symbol (D) appears when data are withheld to prevent disclosure of competitive information. The abbreviation nsk stands for 'not specified by kind' and nec for 'not elsewhere classified'. A dash (-) means zero.

INPUTS AND OUTPUTS FOR ELECTRONIC CONNECTOR MANUFACTURING

Economic Sector or Industry Providing Inputs	%	Sector	Economic Sector or Industry Buying Outputs	%	Sector
Compensation of employees	33.4		Exports of goods & services	34.7	Cap Inv
Management of companies & enterprises	13.2	Services	Broadcast & wireless communications equipment	11.0	Manufg.
Electronic components, nec	5.2	Manufg.	Search, detection, & navigation instruments	6.5	Manufg.
Wholesale trade	4.6	Trade	Telecommunications	6.1	Services
Scientific research & development services	3.7	Services	Plastics products, nec	5.4	Manufg.
Turned products & screws, nuts, & bolts	2.9	Manufg.	Software publishers	4.2	Services
Copper rolling, drawing, extruding, & alloying	2.3	Manufg.	Retail trade	4.1	Trade
Lessors of nonfinancial assets	2.1	Fin/R.E.	Automotive repair & maintenance, ex. car washes	3.9	Services
Primary nonferrous metal, ex. copper & aluminum	1.8	Manufg.	Wholesale trade	2.8	Trade
Alumina refining & primary aluminum production	1.5	Manufg.	Scientific research & development services	2.7	Services
Chemical products & preparations, nec	1.4	Manufg.	Electrical equipment & components, nec	1.9	Manufg.

Continued on next page.

INPUTS AND OUTPUTS FOR ELECTRONIC CONNECTOR MANUFACTURING - Continued

Economic Sector or Industry Providing Inputs	%	Sector	Economic Sector or Industry Buying Outputs	%	Sector
Plastics materials & resins	1.3	Manufg.	Aircraft parts & auxiliary equipment, nec	1.8	Manufg.
Printed circuit assemblies (electronic assemblies)	1.2	Manufg.	Electromedical & electrotherapeutic apparatus	1.7	Manufg.
Power generation & supply	1.1	Util.	Data processing, hosting, & related services	1.5	Services
Plastics products, nec	1.1	Manufg.	Computer terminals & peripherals	1.4	Manufg.
Real estate	1.0	Fin/R.E.	Electronic & precision equipment repair/maintenance	1.3	Services
Advertising & related services	0.9	Services	Semiconductors & related devices	1.3	Manufg.
Communication & energy wires & cables	0.9	Manufg.	Other computer related services, including facilities	1.1	Services
Crowns & closures & metal stamping	0.9	Manufg.	Farm machinery & equipment	1.0	Manufg.
Iron & steel mills & ferroalloys	0.8	Manufg.	Commercial & service industry machinery, nec	1.0	Manufg.
Wiring devices	0.8	Manufg.	Custom computer programming services	0.7	Services
Securities, commodity contracts, investments	0.6	Fin/R.E.	General Federal government services, nondefense	0.5	Fed Govt
Noncomparable imports	0.6	Foreign	General S/L govt. services	0.5	S/L Govt
Basic inorganic chemicals, nec	0.6	Manufg.	Engine equipment, nec	0.4	Manufg.
Truck transportation	0.6	Util.	Air purification & ventilation equipment	0.3	Manufg.
Machine shops	0.5	Manufg.	Aircraft	0.2	Manufg.
Paperboard containers	0.5	Manufg.	Electronic computers	0.2	Manufg.
Plastics packaging materials, film & sheet	0.5	Manufg.	Investigation & security services	0.2	Services
Warehousing & storage	0.5	Util.	Irradiation apparatus	0.2	Manufg.
Bare printed circuit boards	0.4	Manufg.	Educational services, nec	0.2	Services
Ornamental & architectural metal products	0.4	Manufg.	Accounting, tax preparation, bookkeeping, & payroll	0.2	Services
Coating, engraving, heat treating & allied activities	0.4	Manufg.	Electronic connectors	0.2	Manufg.
Maintenance/repair of nonresidential structures	0.3	Construct.	Commercial & industrial equipment repair/maintenance	0.1	Services
Specialized design services	0.3	Services	Magnetic & optical recording media	0.1	Manufg.
Employment services	0.3	Services			
Nonferrous metal (ex. copper & aluminum) processing	0.3	Manufg.			
Retail trade	0.3	Trade			
Services to buildings & dwellings	0.3	Services			
Taxes on production & imports, less subsidies	0.3				
Pressed & blown glass & glassware, nec	0.3	Manufg.			
Industrial gases	0.3	Manufg.			
Legal services	0.3	Services			
Telecommunications	0.3	Services			
Accounting, tax preparation, bookkeeping, & payroll	0.3	Services			
Motors & generators	0.3	Manufg.			
Forging, stamping, & sintering, nec	0.3	Manufg.			
Semiconductors & related devices	0.3	Manufg.			
Electricity & signal testing instruments	0.3	Manufg.			
Electronic connectors	0.3	Manufg.			
Architectural, engineering, & related services	0.2	Services			
Data processing, hosting, & related services	0.2	Services			
Waste management & remediation services	0.2	Services			
Automotive repair & maintenance, ex. car washes	0.2	Services			
Business support services	0.2	Services			
Metal cans, boxes, & other containers (light gauge)	0.2	Manufg.			
Automotive equipment rental & leasing	0.2	Fin/R.E.			
Relay & industrial controls	0.2	Manufg.			
Food services & drinking places	0.2	Services			
Broadcast & wireless communications equipment	0.2	Manufg.			
Natural gas distribution	0.2	Util.			
Commercial & industrial equipment repair/maintenance	0.2	Services			
Monetary authorities/depository credit intermediation	0.2	Fin/R.E.			
Management, scientific, & technical consulting	0.2	Services			
Optical instruments & lenses	0.2	Manufg.			
Professional, scientific, technical services, nec	0.2	Services			
Cutting tools & machine tool accessories	0.1	Manufg.			
Paperboard mills	0.1	Manufg.			
Support services, nec	0.1	Services			
Electron tubes	0.1	Manufg.			
Investigation & security services	0.1	Services			
Hotels & motels, including casino hotels	0.1	Services			
Fabricated metals, nec	0.1	Manufg.			
Electronic & precision equipment repair/maintenance	0.1	Services			
Other computer related services, including facilities	0.1	Services			
Commercial & industrial machinery rental & leasing	0.1	Fin/R.E.			

Source: Benchmark Input-Output Accounts for the U.S. Economy, 2002, U.S. Department of Commerce, Washington, D.C., January 2008. The abbreviation nec stands for 'not elsewhere classified'.

OCCUPATIONS EMPLOYED BY SEMICONDUCTOR & OTHER ELECTRONIC COMPONENT MANUFACTURING

Occupation	% of Total 2006	Change to 2016	Occupation	% of Total 2006	Change to 2016
Electrical & electronic equipment assemblers	10.9	-30.1	Computer software engineers, systems software	1.5	-3.8
Semiconductor processors	8.2	-12.6	Production workers, nec	1.3	-14.2
Team assemblers	4.5	-12.6	Shipping, receiving, & traffic clerks	1.3	-15.9
Electrical & electronic engineering technicians	4.1	-12.6	Purchasing agents, exc wholesale, retail, & farm	1.3	-12.6
Inspectors, testers, sorters, samplers, & weighers	3.9	-17.6	Production, planning, & expediting clerks	1.2	-12.6
Electronics engineers, exc computer	3.9	-12.6	General & operations managers	1.2	-21.3
First-line supervisors/managers of production workers	2.8	-12.6	Coil winders, tapers, & finishers	1.1	-30.1
Electrical engineers	2.6	-12.6	Machinists	1.1	-8.2
Industrial engineers	2.5	6.2	Industrial production managers	1.0	-12.6
Engineering managers	2.3	-3.8	Maintenance & repair workers, general	1.0	-12.6
Electromechanical equipment assemblers	1.7	-12.6			

Source: *Industry-Occupation Matrix*, Bureau of Labor Statistics, December 4, 2007. These data are reported based on 4-digit NAICS categories but have been matched to corresponding 6-digit NAICS industry codes. The change reported for each occupation to the year 2016 is a percent of growth or decline as estimated by the Bureau of Labor Statistics. The abbreviation nec stands for 'not elsewhere classified'.

LOCATION BY STATE AND REGIONAL CONCENTRATION

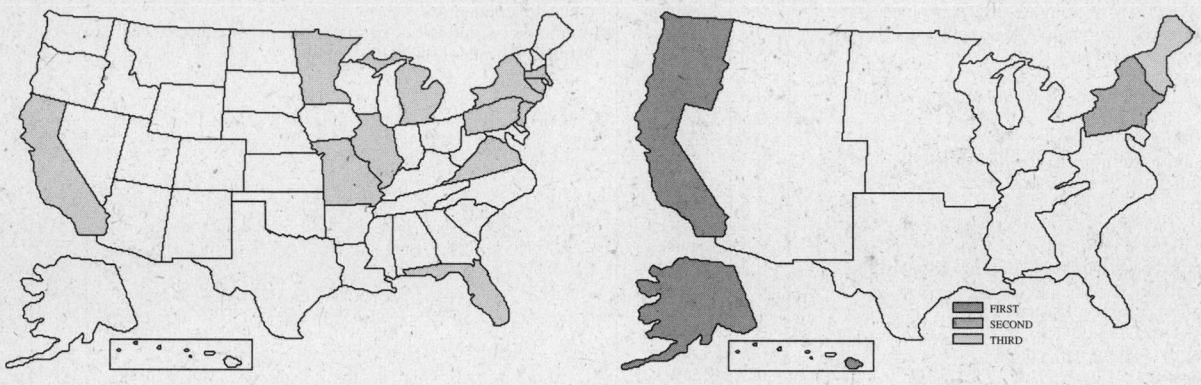

INDUSTRY DATA BY STATE

State	Establish-ments	Shipments			Employment				Cost as % of Shipments	Investment per Employee ($)
		Total ($ mil)	% of U.S.	Per Establ.	Total Number	% of U.S.	Per Establ.	Wages ($/hour)		
California	98	1,014.3	28.2	10,349.9	8,276	33.6	84	14.17	38.9	3,932
Pennsylvania	20	420.7	11.7	21,037.2	3,039	12.3	152	16.81	38.0	18,153
New York	14	354.4	9.9	25,312.4	2,032	8.2	145	19.23	26.6	2,674
Minnesota	11	160.6	4.5	14,596.8	416	1.7	38	19.59	38.1	2,685
Illinois	15	109.4	3.0	7,296.4	868	3.5	58	13.93	37.3	3,260
Massachusetts	18	97.7	2.7	5,429.7	775	3.1	43	13.88	29.5	1,232
Connecticut	9	93.8	2.6	10,418.0	506	2.1	56	16.12	52.7	3,374
Florida	14	61.7	1.7	4,405.7	615	2.5	44	14.33	32.1	4,951
New Jersey	13	36.9	1.0	2,840.2	341	1.4	26	12.03	34.5	4,592
Missouri	4	25.2	0.7	6,292.8	443	1.8	111	7.99	20.7	1,847
Virginia	5	15.2	0.4	3,040.4	123	0.5	25	17.63	25.8	2,919
Michigan	7	12.2	0.3	1,742.6	180	0.7	26	15.89	22.8	717

Source: 2002 *Economic Census*. The states are in descending order of shipments or establishments (if shipment data are missing for the majority). The symbol (D) appears when data are withheld to prevent disclosure of competitive information. States marked with (D) are sorted by number of establishments. A dash (-) indicates that the data element cannot be calculated. Data may not show all states active in the NAICS category. All data available at the time of publication are shown.

NAICS 334418 - PRINTED CIRCUIT ASSEMBLY MANUFACTURING

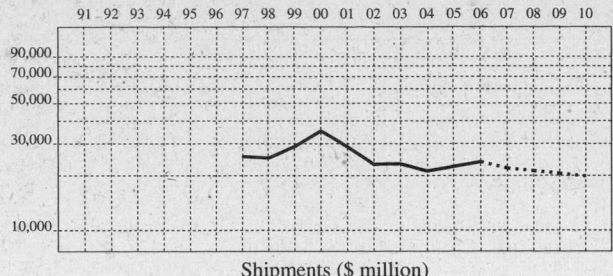

Shipments ($ million)

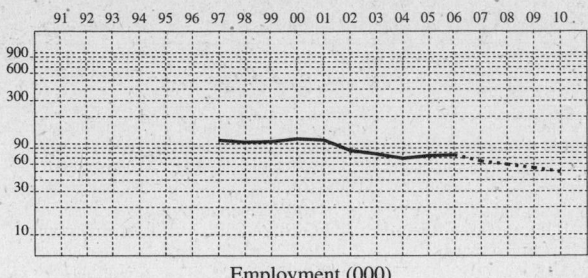

Employment (000)

GENERAL STATISTICS

Year	Com-panies	Establishments		Employment			Compensation		Production ($ million)			
		Total	with 20 or more employees	Total (000)	Production Workers (000)	Hours (Mil)	Payroll ($ mil)	Wages ($/hr)	Cost of Materials	Value Added by Manufacture	Value of Shipments	Capital Invest.
1997	657	714	547	110.0	65.4	131.6	3,821.5	11.65	13,840.6	11,338.3	25,573.4	862.2
1998		719	523	105.0	66.7	132.5	3,549.1	12.66	14,493.9	10,082.3	24,994.7	706.6
1999		730	501	106.0	65.6	133.6	3,865.5	13.41	15,662.3	13,739.6	28,920.3	701.6
2000		708	480	114.0	70.5	138.1	4,220.0	13.17	20,866.8	14,978.3	35,274.2	923.3
2001		716	459	110.6	65.2	124.5	4,140.2	13.35	17,880.2	10,221.4	28,844.5	691.1
2002	783	868	572	84.9	47.3	97.2	3,424.5	13.56	12,839.4	10,082.6	23,123.4	477.4
2003		855	534	77.6	42.8	93.6	3,391.5	13.74	13,240.0	10,044.1	23,244.9	411.2
2004		890	526	69.4	35.9	75.3	3,171.2	14.66	13,386.4	7,909.3	21,183.5	352.1
2005		906	534	74.0	40.8	85.0	3,402.5	14.94	14,096.7	8,386.8	22,446.9	358.5
2006		931P	529P	75.5	43.3	90.8	3,570.6	15.09	16,570.2	7,403.5	23,817.3	317.6
2007		959P	531P	64.5P	33.4P	71.8P	3,323.8P	15.46P	15,262.7P	6,819.3P	21,937.9P	219.0P
2008		987P	533P	59.4P	29.5P	64.8P	3,263.4P	15.79P	14,781.4P	6,604.3P	21,246.2P	153.3P
2009		1,015P	535P	54.3P	25.7P	57.9P	3,203.1P	16.13P	14,300.2P	6,389.3P	20,554.5P	87.6P
2010		1,043P	537P	49.1P	21.9P	50.9P	3,142.7P	16.46P	13,818.9P	6,174.2P	19,862.8P	22.0P

Sources: 1997 and 2002 *Economic Census*; other years, up to 2006, are from *Annual Survey of Manufactures*. Establishment counts for non-Census years are from *County Business Patterns*; 1997 and 2002 values are from the 1997 and 2002 censuses, respectively. 'P's show projections by the editors.

INDICES OF CHANGE

Year	Com-panies	Establishments		Employment			Compensation		Production ($ million)			
		Total	with 20 or more employees	Total (000)	Production Workers (000)	Hours (Mil)	Payroll ($ mil)	Wages ($/hr)	Cost of Materials	Value Added by Manufacture	Value of Shipments	Capital Invest.
1997	84	82	96	130	138	135	112	86	108	112	111	181
1998		83	91	124	141	136	104	93	113	100	108	148
1999		84	88	125	139	137	113	99	122	136	125	147
2000		82	84	134	149	142	123	97	163	149	153	193
2001		82	80	130	138	128	121	98	139	101	125	145
2002	100	100	100	100	100	100	100	100	100	100	100	100
2003		99	93	91	90	96	99	101	103	100	101	86
2004		103	92	82	76	77	93	108	104	78	92	74
2005		104	93	87	86	87	99	110	110	83	97	75
2006		107P	93P	89	92	93	104	111	129	73	103	67
2007		110P	93P	76P	71P	74P	97P	114P	119P	68P	95P	46P
2008		114P	93P	70P	62P	67P	95P	116P	115P	66P	92P	32P
2009		117P	94P	64P	54P	60P	94P	119P	111P	63P	89P	18P
2010		120P	94P	58P	46P	52P	92P	121P	108P	61P	86P	5P

Sources: Same as General Statistics. Values reflect change from the base year, 2002. Values above 100 mean greater than 2002, values below 100 mean less than 2002, and the values of 100 in other years means the same as 2002. 'P's show projections by the editors.

SELECTED RATIOS

For 2002	Avg. of All Manufact.	Analyzed Industry	Index	For 2002	Avg. of All Manufact.	Analyzed Industry	Index
Employees per Establishment	42	98	233	Value Added per Production Worker	182,367	213,163	117
Payroll per Establishment	1,639,184	3,945,276	241	Cost per Establishment	5,769,015	14,791,935	256
Payroll per Employee	39,053	40,336	103	Cost per Employee	137,446	151,230	110
Production Workers per Establishment	30	54	185	Cost per Production Worker	195,506	271,446	139
Wages per Establishment	694,845	1,518,470	219	Shipments per Establishment	11,158,348	26,639,862	239
Wages per Production Worker	23,548	27,865	118	Shipments per Employee	265,847	272,360	102
Hours per Production Worker	1,980	2,055	104	Shipments per Production Worker	378,144	488,867	129
Wages per Hour	11.89	13.56	114	Investment per Establishment	361,338	550,000	152
Value Added per Establishment	5,381,325	11,615,899	216	Investment per Employee	8,609	5,623	65
Value Added per Employee	128,210	118,759	93	Investment per Production Worker	12,245	10,093	82

Sources: Same as General Statistics. The 'Average of All Manufacturing' column represents the average of all manufacturing industries reported for the most recent complete year available. The Index shows the relationship between the Average and the Analyzed Industry. For example, 100 means that they are equal; 500 that the Analyzed Industry is five times the average; 50 means that the Analyzed Industry is half the national average. The abbreviation 'na' is used to show that data are 'not available'. Ratios shown for 2002, the last complete census year.

LEADING COMPANIES   Number shown: **75**   Total sales ($ mil): **525,035**   Total employment (000): **1,262.2**

Company Name	Address				CEO Name	Phone	Co. Type	Sales ($ mil)	Empl. (000)
AT and T Inc.	175 E Houston	San Antonio	TX	78205	James W. Callaway	210-821-4105	P	68,256	310.0
Technitrol Delaware Inc.	3411 Silverside Rd.	Wilmington	DE	19810	James M. Papada	302-478-8271	S	67,716*	22.8
Chrysler L.L.C.	1000 Chrysler Dr.	Auburn Hills	MI	48326	Thomas W. LaSorda	248-576-5741	S	45,237*	84.4
Motorola Inc.	1303 E Algonquin	Schaumburg	IL	60196	Greg Brown	847-576-5000	P	36,622	66.0
Cisco Systems Inc.	170 W Tasman Dr.	San Jose	CA	95134		408-526-4000	P	34,922	61.5
Honeywell International Inc.	PO Box 4000	Morristown	NJ	07962	Adriane M. Brown	973-455-2000	P	34,589	122.0
General Dynamics Corp.	2941 Fairview Park	Falls Church	VA	22042	Nicholas D. Chabraja	703-876-3000	P	27,240	83.5
Raytheon Co.	870 Winter St.	Waltham	MA	02451		781-522-3000	P	21,301	72.1
ITT Federal Services Corp.	4410 E Fountain	Colorado Spgs	CO	80916	Steven Loranger	719-591-3600	S	20,690*	7.0
Mars Inc.	6885 Elm Street	Mc Lean	VA	22101	John F. Mars	703-821-4900	R	18,462*	40.0
Computer Sciences Corp.	2100 E Grand Ave.	El Segundo	CA	90245		310-615-0311	P	14,855	79.0
ITT Corp.	4 W Red Oak Ln.	White Plains	NY	10604		914-641-2000	P	9,003	39.7
Ball Corp.	PO Box 5000	Broomfield	CO	80021	R. David Hoover	303-469-3131	P	7,475	15.5
Corning Inc.	1 Riverfront Plz.	Corning	NY	14831	James R. Houghton	607-974-9000	P	5,860	24.5
Order-Matic Corp.	PO Box 25463	Oklahoma City	OK	73125	Bill Cunningham	405-672-1487	R	5,787	0.2
Allegheny Technologies Inc.	1000 Six PPG Pl.	Pittsburgh	PA	15222		412-394-2800	P	5,453	9.5
Flextronics	2090 Fortune Dr.	San Jose	CA	95131	Mike McNamara	408-576-7000	S	4,699*	1.5
LSI Marcole Inc.	1108 Oakdale St.	Manchester	TN	37355	Robert J. Ready	931-723-4442	S	4,643*	1.4
JVC America Inc.	1700 Valley Rd.	Wayne	NJ	07470	Shigeharu Tsuchitani	973-317-5000	S	4,306*	0.3
Oki Data Americas Inc.	2000 Bishops Gate	Mount Laurel	NJ	08054	Stewart Krentzman	856-235-2600	S	4,260*	0.5
Harris Corp.	1025 W NASA	Melbourne	FL	32919		321-727-9100	P	4,243	16.0
Brightstar Corp.	2010 NW 84th Ave.	Miami	FL	33122	R. Marcelo Claure	305-421-6000	R	3,590	1.7
Sparton Electronics	PO Box 788	De Leon Springs	FL	32130	D W. Hockenbrocht	386-985-4631	S	3,491*	1.0
Fujitsu Network Communications	2801 Telecom Pkwy.	Richardson	TX	75082	George Chase	972-479-6000	R	2,969*	1.0
Benchmark Electronics Inc.	3000 Technology	Angleton	TX	77515		979-849-6550	P	2,916	10.9
Crane Co.	100 First Stamford	Stamford	CT	06902	Thomas Craney	203-363-7300	P	2,619	12.0
I/O Marine Systems Inc.	5200 Toler St.	Harahan	LA	70123	Robert P. Peebler	504-733-6061	S	2,610*	0.8
I/O Nevada L.L.C.	12300 Parc Crest Dr	Stafford	TX	77477	Robert P. Peebler	281-933-3339	S	2,610*	0.8
I/O Texas L.P.	12300 Parc Crest Dr	Stafford	TX	77477	Robert P. Peebler	281-933-3339	S	2,610*	0.8
Hubbell Inc.	584 Derby Milford	Orange	CT	06477		203-799-4100	P	2,534	11.5
Wakefield Thermal Solutions	33 Bridge St.	Pelham	NH	03076	Robert Streiter	603-635-2800	S	2,398*	0.1
Red Rocket Inc.	5217 Verdugo Way	Camarillo	CA	93012	James B. Schutz	805-409-0909	R	2,146*	0.7
Tellabs Inc.	1 Tellabs Ctr.	Naperville	IL	60563	Michael J. Birck	630-798-8800	P	2,041	3.7
ACT Electronics Inc.	2 Cabot Rd.	Hudson	MA	01749		978-567-4000	R	1,870*	0.1
Opex Corp.	305 Commerce Dr.	Moorestown	NJ	08057	Jeff Bowen	856-727-1100	S	1,857*	0.7
PerkinElmer Inc.	940 Winter St.	Waltham	MA	02451	Robert F. Friel	781-663-6900	P	1,787	8.7
Advanced Interconnection Tech	85 Adams Ave.	Hauppauge	NY	11788	Phillip A. Harris	631-968-1591	S	1,776*	0.6
Siemens VDO Automotive Corp.	2400 Executive Hill	Auburn Hills	MI	48326	John Sanderson	248-209-4000	S	1,738*	10.0
ECS. Inc International	1105 S Ridgeview	Olathe	KS	66062	Patricia S. Taylor	913-782-7787	S	1,689*	0.5
Stratos Optical Technologies	7444 W Wilson Ave.	Chicago	IL	60706	Phillip A. Harris	708-867-9600	S	1,645*	0.6
Stratos Lightwave Inc.	1335 Gateway Dr.	Melbourne	FL	32901	Phillip A. Harris	321-308-4100	S	1,633*	0.6
Griffon Corp.	100 Jericho Quadran	Jericho	NY	11753	Harvey R. Blau	516-938-5544	P	1,617	5.3
Comverse Technology Inc.	810 7th Ave.	New York	NY	10019	Andre Dahan	212-739-1000	P	1,589	5.1
CC Industries Inc.	222 N La Salle St.	Chicago	IL	60601	William H. Crown	312-855-4000	S	1,560*	6.0
I/O General L.L.C.	12300 Parc Crest Dr	Stafford	TX	77477	Robert P. Peebler	281-933-3339	S	1,555*	0.5
Rooney Holdings Inc.	1400 Gulf Shre Blvd	Naples	FL	34102	Jim Cavanaugh	239-403-0375	R	1,443*	2.6
JDS Uniphase Corp.	430 N McCarthy	Milpitas	CA	95035	Martin A. Kaplan	408-546-5000	P	1,397*	7.0
K and L Microwave Inc.	2250 Northwood Dr.	Salisbury	MD	21801	Darby Kruger	410-749-2424	S	1,339*	0.5
AVX Corp.	PO Box 867	Myrtle Beach	SC	29578	John S. Gilbertson	843-448-9411	P	1,333	13.0
ADC Telecommunications Inc.	PO Box 1101	Minneapolis	MN	55440		952-938-8080	P	1,322	9.1
Olin Corp.	190 Carondelet Plz.	Clayton	MO	63105	Randall W. Larrimore	314-480-1400	P	1,277	3.6
3Com Corp.	350 Campus Dr.	Marlborough	MA	01752	Eric A. Benhamou	508-323-5000	P	1,268	6.3
General Dynamics Network Sys.	77 A Street	Needham	MA	02494	Nicholas Chabraja	781-449-2000	S	1,237*	7.0
Teradyne Inc.	600 Riverpark Dr.	North Reading	MA	01864	James Bagley	978-370-2700	P	1,102	3.6
Academy Precision Materials	5520 Midway Park	Albuquerque	NM	87109	Mike McCay	505-343-9440	R	1,096*	0.3
Technitrol Inc.	1210 Northbrook Dr.	Trevose	PA	19053		215-355-2900	P	1,027	26.1
RF Micro Devices Inc.	7628 Thorndike Rd.	Greensboro	NC	27409	R A. Bruggeworth	336-664-1233	P	1,024	3.3
Hughes Network Systems Inc.	11717 Exploratn Ln.	Germantown	MD	20876	Pradman P. Kaul	301-428-5500	S	975*	1.5
Polycom Inc.	4750 Willow Rd.	Pleasanton	CA	94588	Robert C. Hagerty	925-924-6000	P	930	2.5
Plantronics Inc.	345 Encinal St.	Santa Cruz	CA	95060	SK Kannappan	831-426-5858	P	800	6.0
CIENA Corp.	1201 Winterson Rd.	Linthicum	MD	21090		410-694-5700	P	780	1.8
Emerson Netw. Pwr Emb Comp.	8310 Excelsior Dr.	Madison	WI	53717			S	774*	0.3
Sub-Zero Inc.	4717 Hammersley	Madison	WI	53711	James Bakke	608-271-2233	R	758*	3.0
Hutchinson Technology Inc.	40 W Highland Park	Hutchinson	MN	55350	Wayne M. Fortun	320-587-3797	P	716	4.7
CTS Corp.	905 N West Blvd.	Elkhart	IN	46514	R R. Hemminghaus	574-293-7511	P	686	4.7
Ball Aerospace & Technologies	PO Box 1062	Boulder	CO	80306		303-939-4000	S	672*	3.0
Kaiser Systems Inc.	126 Sohier Rd.	Beverly	MA	01915	Kenneth Kaiser	978-922-9300	R	556*	<0.1
Kyocera Wireless Corp.	10300 Campus Pnt	San Diego	CA	92121	Rodney N. Lanthorne	858-882-2000	S	538*	0.9
Aeroflex Inc.	PO Box 6022	Plainview	NY	11803	Harvey R. Blau	516-694-6700	P	537*	2.6
Varian Semiconductor Equipment	35 Dory Rd.	Gloucester	MA	01930	Richard Aurelio	978-281-2000	S	530*	1.0
Power-One Inc.	740 Calle Plano	Camarillo	CA	93012		805-987-8741	P	512	4.2
MtronPTI	100 Douglas Ave.	Yankton	SD	57078	Bob Zylstra	605-665-9321	S	487*	0.2
IPC Systems Holdings Corp.	1500 Plaza Ten	Jersey City	NJ	07311	Lance B. Boxer	201-253-2000	R	485	1.4
Micro-Coax Inc.	206 Jones Blvd.	Pottstown	PA	19464	Chris Kneiyzs	610-495-0110	R	485*	0.1
Dolby Laboratories Inc.	100 Potrero Ave.	San Francisco	CA	94103		415-558-0200	P	482	1.0

Source: Ward's Business Directory of U.S. Private and Public Companies, Volumes 1 and 2, 2008. The company type code used is as follows: P - Public, R - Private, S - Subsidiary, D - Division, J - Joint Venture, A - Affiliate, G - Group. Sales are in millions of dollars, employees are in thousands. An asterisk (*) indicates an estimated sales volume. The symbol < stands for 'less than'. Company names and addresses are truncated, in some cases, to fit into the available space.

MATERIALS CONSUMED

Material	Quantity	Delivered Cost ($ million)
Tube blanks	(X)	(D)
Printed ciruit boards (without inserted components) for electronic circuitry	(X)	1,572.5
Printed circuit assemblies, loaded boards, and modules	(X)	2,731.9
Semiconductors (incl. transistors, diodes, rectifiers, and integrated circuits), for electronic circuitry	(X)	3,234.5
Capacitors for electronic circuitry	(X)	524.7
Resistors for electronic circuitry	(X)	361.1
All other miscellaneous components and accessories for electronic circuitry (exc. tubes)	(X)	549.2
Silicon, hyperpure	(X)	95.6
Gold and other precious metals, all forms (incl. ingot, sheet, etc.)	(X)	4.7
Doped chemicals and other doped materials for electronic use	(X)	1.4
Ferrites (powder and paste)	(X)	3.4
Metal powders	(X)	1.9
Electronic computer equipment	(X)	71.6
Current-carrying wiring devices	(X)	17.1
Electronic communication equipment	(X)	20.6
Electrical instrument mechanisms and meter movements	(X)	3.7
All other miscellaneous electrical measuring instruments and parts	(X)	1.7
Fractional horsepower electric motors (less than 1 hp)	(X)	0.7
Electrical transmission, distribution, and control equipment	(X)	74.8
Loudspeakers, microphones, and tuners (all types)	(X)	0.9
Glass and glass products (excluding windows and mirrors)	(X)	(D)
Optical instruments and lenses (exc. sighting, tracking, and fire control)	(X)	3.5
Plastics resins consumed in the form of granules, pellets, etc.	(X)	2.3
Fabricated plastics products (excluding gaskets)	(X)	46.4
Sheet metal products (excluding stampings)	(X)	360.1
Metal stampings	(X)	15.9
Metal bolts, nuts, screws, and other screw machine products	(X)	48.7
Other fabricated metal products (excluding forgings)	(X)	35.1
Forgings	(X)	0.9
Castings, rough and semifinished	(X)	5.9
Steel shapes and forms (exc. castings, forgings, fabr. metal products)	(X)	1.0
Copper and copper-base alloy shapes and forms (exc. castings, forgings, fabr. metal products)	(X)	0.8
Aluminum and aluminum-base alloy shapes and forms (exc. castings, forgings, fabr. metal products)	(X)	2.1
Other nonferrous shapes and forms (exc. castings, forgings, fabricated metal products)	(X)	0.9
Insulated wire and cable (including magnet wire)	(X)	45.0
Paper and paperboard containers (incl. shipping sacks and other paper packaging supplies)	(X)	81.6
Resists (photosensitive resin films applied to surface of wafer)	(X)	(D)
Commodity gases	(X)	2.6
Speciality gases	(X)	0.1
Masks	(X)	0.3
Silicon chips	(X)	24.0
Solvents	(X)	3.0
Cleaning compounds	(X)	2.1
All other materials, components, parts, containers, and supplies	(X)	1,143.7
Materials, ingredients, containers, and supplies, nsk	(X)	1,016.5

Source: 2002 *Economic Census*. Explanation of symbols used: (D): Withheld to avoid disclosure of competitive data; na: Not available; (S): Withheld because statistical norms were not met; (X): Not applicable; (Z): Less than half the unit shown; nec: Not elsewhere classified; nsk: Not specified by kind; - : zero; p : 10-19 percent estimated; q : 20-29 percent estimated.

PRODUCT SHARE DETAILS

Product or Product Class Shipments	Mil. $	Product or Product Class Shipments	Mil. $
PRINTED CIRCUITS (ELECTRONIC ASSEMBLIES)	22,514.7	(printed circuit boards with inserted electronic	
External modems, consumer	505.6	components)	20,695.5
Printed circuit assemblies, loaded boards and modules		Printed circuits (electronic assemblies), nsk, total	1,313.6

Source: 2002 *Economic Census*. The values are product shipments in millions of dollars for 2002. Total product shipments may be lower or higher than industry shipments. See Introduction for a full discussion. Values of indented subcategories are summed in the main heading(s). The symbol (D) appears when data are withheld to prevent disclosure of competitive information. The abbreviation nsk stands for 'not specified by kind' and nec for 'not elsewhere classified'. A dash (-) means zero.

INPUTS AND OUTPUTS FOR PRINTED CIRCUIT ASSEMBLY MANUFACTURING

Economic Sector or Industry Providing Inputs	%	Sector	Economic Sector or Industry Buying Outputs	%	Sector
Compensation of employees	19.2		Exports of goods & services	21.3	Cap Inv
Printed circuit assemblies (electronic assemblies)	19.1	Manufg.	Printed circuit assemblies (electronic assemblies)	10.6	Manufg.
Semiconductors & related devices	19.1	Manufg.	Electronic computers	10.2	Manufg.
Wholesale trade	9.9	Trade	Wholesale trade	3.6	Trade
Management of companies & enterprises	7.2	Services	Telephone apparatus	2.3	Manufg.
Electronic components, nec	3.8	Manufg.	Motor vehicle parts	1.9	Manufg.
Scientific research & development services	2.0	Services	Broadcast & wireless communications equipment	1.5	Manufg.
Ornamental & architectural metal products	1.5	Manufg.	Search, detection, & navigation instruments	1.4	Manufg.

Continued on next page.

INPUTS AND OUTPUTS FOR PRINTED CIRCUIT ASSEMBLY MANUFACTURING - Continued

Economic Sector or Industry Providing Inputs	%	Sector	Economic Sector or Industry Buying Outputs	%	Sector
Electronic capacitors, resistors, coils, transformers	0.8	Manufg.	Telecommunications	1.4	Services
Chemical products & preparations, nec	0.7	Manufg.	Relay & industrial controls	1.2	Manufg.
Real estate	0.7	Fin/R.E.	Audio & video equipment	1.2	Manufg.
Noncomparable imports	0.7	Foreign	Electricity & signal testing instruments	1.1	Manufg.
Bare printed circuit boards	0.6	Manufg.	Retail trade	1.1	Trade
Power generation & supply	0.5	Util.	Computer terminals & peripherals	1.1	Manufg.
Truck transportation	0.5	Util.	Electronic components, nec	1.0	Manufg.
Industrial machinery, nec	0.5	Manufg.	Electronic & precision equipment repair/maintenance	1.0	Services
Advertising & related services	0.4	Services	Electromedical & electrotherapeutic apparatus	1.0	Manufg.
Basic inorganic chemicals, nec	0.4	Manufg.	Printing	1.0	Manufg.
Paperboard containers	0.4	Manufg.	Personal consumption expenditures	1.0	
Automotive equipment rental & leasing	0.3	Fin/R.E.	Plastics products, nec	0.8	Manufg.
Turned products & screws, nuts, & bolts	0.3	Manufg.	Semiconductors & related devices	0.8	Manufg.
Computer terminals & peripherals	0.3	Manufg.	Basic organic chemicals, nec	0.6	Manufg.
Relay & industrial controls	0.3	Manufg.	Bare printed circuit boards	0.6	Manufg.
Taxes on production & imports, less subsidies	0.2		Plastics packaging materials, film & sheet	0.6	Manufg.
Warehousing & storage	0.2	Util.	Totalizing fluid meters & counting devices	0.6	Manufg.
Plastics products, nec	0.2	Manufg.	Automotive repair & maintenance, ex. car washes	0.6	Services
Lessors of nonfinancial assets	0.2	Fin/R.E.	Industrial process variable instruments	0.5	Manufg.
Telecommunications	0.2	Services	Breweries	0.5	Manufg.
Machine shops	0.2	Manufg.	Electrical equipment & components, nec	0.5	Manufg.
Legal services	0.2	Services	Industrial machinery, nec	0.5	Manufg.
Maintenance/repair of nonresidential structures	0.2	Construct.	Paperboard containers	0.5	Manufg.
Commercial & industrial machinery rental & leasing	0.2	Fin/R.E.	Iron & steel mills & ferroalloys	0.5	Manufg.
Accounting, tax preparation, bookkeeping, & payroll	0.1	Services	Soft drinks & ice	0.5	Manufg.
Services to buildings & dwellings	0.1	Services	Toilet preparations	0.5	Manufg.
Data processing, hosting, & related services	0.1	Services	Irradiation apparatus	0.5	Manufg.
Copper rolling, drawing, extruding, & alloying	0.1	Manufg.	Watches, clocks, & related devices	0.5	Manufg.
Air transportation	0.1	Util.	Computer system design services	0.5	Services
Cutting tools & machine tool accessories	0.1	Manufg.	Analytical laboratory instruments	0.4	Manufg.
Coating, engraving, heat treating & allied activities	0.1	Manufg.	Aircraft	0.4	Manufg.
			Plastics materials & resins	0.4	Manufg.
			Paper mills	0.4	Manufg.
			Chemical products & preparations, nec	0.4	Manufg.
			Ornamental & architectural metal products	0.3	Manufg.
			Plate work & fabricated structural products	0.3	Manufg.
			Wineries	0.3	Manufg.
			General purpose machinery, nec	0.3	Manufg.
			Ferrous metal foundries	0.3	Manufg.
			Switchgear & switchboard apparatus	0.3	Manufg.
			Turned products & screws, nuts, & bolts	0.3	Manufg.
			Aluminum products from purchased aluminum	0.3	Manufg.
			Machine shops	0.3	Manufg.
			Legal services	0.3	Services
			Computer storage devices	0.3	Manufg.
			Material handling equipment	0.3	Manufg.
			AC, refrigeration, and warm air heating equipment	0.2	Manufg.
			Communications equipment, nec	0.2	Manufg.
			Valve & fittings other than plumbing	0.2	Manufg.
			Paints & coatings	0.2	Manufg.
			Steel products from purchased steel	0.2	Manufg.
			Coating, engraving, heat treating & allied activities	0.2	Manufg.
			Wood windows & doors & millwork	0.2	Manufg.
			Rubber products, nec	0.2	Manufg.
			Wood kitchen cabinets & countertops	0.2	Manufg.
			Lighting fixtures	0.2	Manufg.
			Paperboard mills	0.2	Manufg.
			Metal cans, boxes, & other containers (light gauge)	0.2	Manufg.
			Wiring devices	0.2	Manufg.
			Mining & oil & gas field machinery	0.2	Manufg.
			Coated & laminated paper & packaging materials	0.2	Manufg.
			Engine equipment, nec	0.2	Manufg.
			Surgical appliances & supplies	0.2	Manufg.
			Fabricated metals, nec	0.2	Manufg.
			Optical instruments & lenses	0.2	Manufg.
			Professional, scientific, technical services, nec	0.2	Services
			Carpet & rug mills	0.2	Manufg.
			Glass products from purchased glass	0.2	Manufg.
			Surgical & medical instrument	0.2	Manufg.
			Synthetic dyes & pigments	0.2	Manufg.
			Broadwoven fabric mills	0.2	Manufg.
			Sanitary paper products	0.2	Manufg.
			Signs	0.2	Manufg.
			Construction machinery	0.2	Manufg.
			Dolls, toys, & games	0.2	Manufg.
			Hardware	0.2	Manufg.
			Sporting & athletic goods	0.2	Manufg.
			Commercial & service industry machinery, nec	0.2	Manufg.
			Ready-mix concrete	0.2	Manufg.
			Turbines & turbine generator set units	0.2	Manufg.

Continued on next page.

INPUTS AND OUTPUTS FOR PRINTED CIRCUIT ASSEMBLY MANUFACTURING - Continued

Economic Sector or Industry Providing Inputs	%	Sector	Economic Sector or Industry Buying Outputs	%	Sector
			Nonferrous metal (ex. copper & aluminum) processing	0.2	Manufg.
			Pumps & pumping equipment	0.2	Manufg.
			Ship building & repairing	0.2	Manufg.
			Nonferrous metal foundries	0.2	Manufg.
			Heavy duty trucks	0.2	Manufg.
			Automatic environmental controls	0.1	Manufg.
			Custom architectural woodwork & millwork	0.1	Manufg.
			Motors & generators	0.1	Manufg.
			Manufacturing, nec	0.1	Manufg.
			Semiconductor machinery	0.1	Manufg.
			Accounting, tax preparation, bookkeeping, & payroll	0.1	Services
			Farm machinery & equipment	0.1	Manufg.
			Fiber, yarn, & thread mills	0.1	Manufg.
			Adhesives	0.1	Manufg.
			Light truck & utility vehicles	0.1	Manufg.
			Automobiles	0.1	Manufg.
			Curtain & linen mills	0.1	Manufg.
			Textile & fabric finishing mills	0.1	Manufg.
			Copper rolling, drawing, extruding, & alloying	0.1	Manufg.
			Tires	0.1	Manufg.
			Concrete products, nec	0.1	Manufg.
			Cement	0.1	Manufg.
			Springs & wire products	0.1	Manufg.
			Fertilizer	0.1	Manufg.
			Special tools, dies, jigs, & fixtures	0.1	Manufg.
			Musical instruments	0.1	Manufg.
			General Federal government services, defense	0.1	Fed Govt
			Fluid power process machinery	0.1	Manufg.
			Laboratory apparatus & furniture	0.1	Manufg.
			Soap & cleaning compounds	0.1	Manufg.
			Communication & energy wires & cables	0.1	Manufg.
			Showcases, partitions, shelving, and lockers	0.1	Manufg.
			Custom computer programming services	0.1	Services
			Institutional furniture	0.1	Manufg.
			Pesticides & other agricultural chemicals	0.1	Manufg.
			Crowns & closures & metal stamping	0.1	Manufg.
			Aircraft parts & auxiliary equipment, nec	0.1	Manufg.
			Concrete pipe, brick, & block	0.1	Manufg.
			Petroleum refineries	0.1	Manufg.
			Plastics & rubber industry machinery	0.1	Manufg.
			Internet service providers & web search portals	0.1	Services
			Boat building	0.1	Manufg.
			Asphalt shingle & coating materials	0.1	Manufg.
			Polystyrene foam products	0.1	Manufg.
			Handtools	0.1	Manufg.
			Transportation equipment, nec	0.1	Manufg.
			Electronic connectors	0.1	Manufg.
			Unlaminated plastics profile shapes	0.1	Manufg.
			Vending, commercial, industrial, office machinery	0.1	Manufg.
			Artificial & synthetic fibers & filaments	0.1	Manufg.
			Photographic & photocopying equipment	0.1	Manufg.
			Motor vehicle bodies	0.1	Manufg.

Source: Benchmark Input-Output Accounts for the U.S. Economy, 2002, U.S. Department of Commerce, Washington, D.C., January 2008. The abbreviation nec stands for 'not elsewhere classified'.

OCCUPATIONS EMPLOYED BY SEMICONDUCTOR & OTHER ELECTRONIC COMPONENT MANUFACTURING

Occupation	% of Total 2006	Change to 2016	Occupation	% of Total 2006	Change to 2016
Electrical & electronic equipment assemblers	10.9	-30.1	Computer software engineers, systems software	1.5	-3.8
Semiconductor processors	8.2	-12.6	Production workers, nec	1.3	-14.2
Team assemblers	4.5	-12.6	Shipping, receiving, & traffic clerks	1.3	-15.9
Electrical & electronic engineering technicians	4.1	-12.6	Purchasing agents, exc wholesale, retail, & farm	1.3	-12.6
Inspectors, testers, sorters, samplers, & weighers	3.9	-17.6	Production, planning, & expediting clerks	1.2	-12.6
Electronics engineers, exc computer	3.9	-12.6	General & operations managers	1.2	-21.3
First-line supervisors/managers of production workers	2.8	-12.6	Coil winders, tapers, & finishers	1.1	-30.1
Electrical engineers	2.6	-12.6	Machinists	1.1	-8.2
Industrial engineers	2.5	.6.2	Industrial production managers	1.0	-12.6
Engineering managers	2.3	-3.8	Maintenance & repair workers, general	1.0	-12.6
Electromechanical equipment assemblers	1.7	-12.6			

Source: Industry-Occupation Matrix, Bureau of Labor Statistics, December 4, 2007. These data are reported based on 4-digit NAICS categories but have been matched to corresponding 6-digit NAICS industry codes. The change reported for each occupation to the year 2016 is a percent of growth or decline as estimated by the Bureau of Labor Statistics. The abbreviation nec stands for 'not elsewhere classified'.

LOCATION BY STATE AND REGIONAL CONCENTRATION

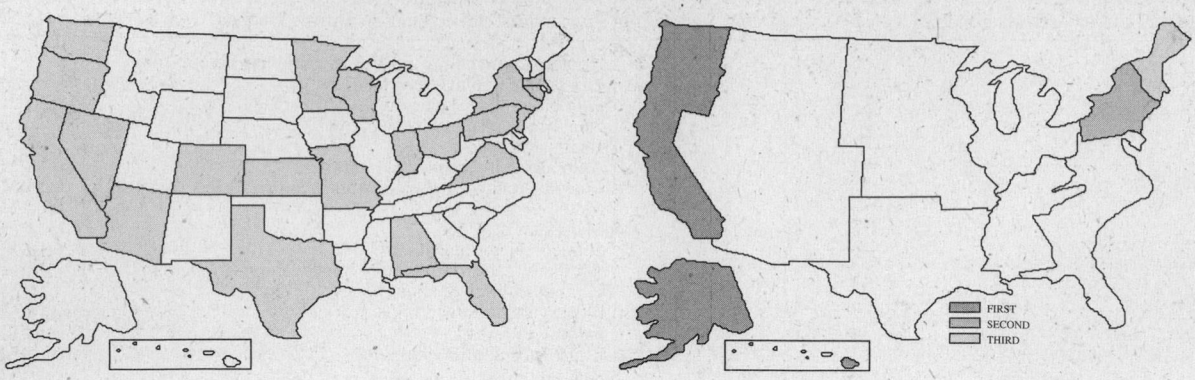

INDUSTRY DATA BY STATE

| State | Establish-ments | Shipments | | | Employment | | | | Cost as % of Shipments | Investment per Employee ($) |
		Total ($ mil)	% of U.S.	Per Establ.	Total Number	% of U.S.	Per Establ.	Wages ($/hour)		
California	208	5,165.7	22.3	24,835.0	17,269	20.3	83	14.05	57.4	8,709
New York	41	3,475.0	15.0	84,756.3	9,739	11.5	238	15.86	39.8	4,981
Texas	53	1,690.7	7.3	31,899.7	8,045	9.5	152	11.92	56.2	6,443
New Jersey	23	1,361.1	5.9	59,177.9	1,805	2.1	78	13.76	32.8	2,504
Minnesota	25	1,180.3	5.1	47,212.1	4,187	4.9	167	14.64	63.7	4,735
Florida	32	1,063.5	4.6	33,235.6	4,142	4.9	129	14.40	66.9	4,630
Wisconsin	26	777.0	3.4	29,883.0	3,353	3.9	129	13.79	75.7	1,458
Alabama	15	724.7	3.1	48,311.7	1,192	1.4	79	15.16	78.7	5,551
Massachusetts	51	644.4	2.8	12,635.6	3,183	3.7	62	12.12	57.4	5,780
Arizona	22	639.7	2.8	29,077.0	3,307	3.9	150	15.49	49.4	10,432
Colorado	16	453.6	2.0	28,350.6	1,105	1.3	69	13.81	68.0	7,636
Pennsylvania	38	382.7	1.7	10,069.8	1,999	2.4	53	12.33	56.1	4,811
Indiana	13	354.4	1.5	27,259.7	1,672	2.0	129	13.97	62.0	4,958
Ohio	25	215.4	0.9	8,616.6	1,544	1.8	62	12.97	52.2	1,900
Oregon	18	159.3	0.7	8,849.9	925	1.1	51	13.82	55.7	3,586
Washington	15	157.0	0.7	10,465.8	879	1.0	59	12.80	54.9	3,542
Connecticut	17	145.6	0.6	8,566.5	793	0.9	47	14.63	60.4	3,507
Missouri	9	104.3	0.5	11,584.8	411	0.5	46	13.50	72.4	1,426
Virginia	13	87.0	0.4	6,693.2	769	0.9	59	16.19	43.7	5,506
Nevada	6	46.4	0.2	7,725.2	344	0.4	57	9.51	60.2	5,974
Kansas	5	32.0	0.1	6,408.6	259	0.3	52	7.48	65.0	815

Source: 2002 *Economic Census*. The states are in descending order of shipments or establishments (if shipment data are missing for the majority). The symbol (D) appears when data are withheld to prevent disclosure of competitive information. States marked with (D) are sorted by number of establishments. A dash (-) indicates that the data element cannot be calculated. Data may not show all states active in the NAICS category. All data available at the time of publication are shown.

NAICS 334419 - ELECTRONIC COMPONENT MANUFACTURING NEC

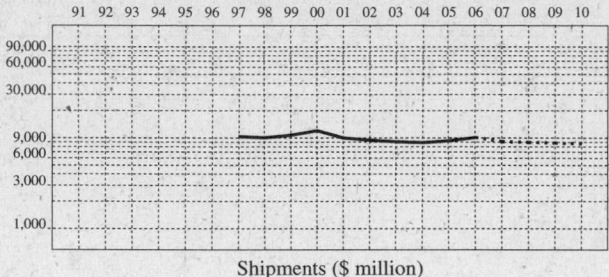

Shipments ($ million)

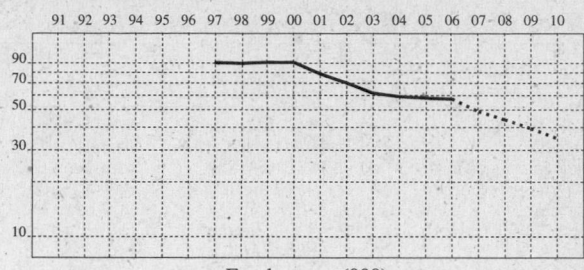

Employment (000)

GENERAL STATISTICS

| Year | Com-panies | Establishments | | Employment | | | Compensation | | Production ($ million) | | | |
		Total	with 20 or more employees	Total (000)	Production Workers (000)	Hours (Mil)	Payroll ($ mil)	Wages ($/hr)	Cost of Materials	Value Added by Manufacture	Value of Shipments	Capital Invest.
1997	1,762	1,835	709	90.7	60.7	117.2	2,730.1	11.35	4,385.8	5,984.6	10,375.6	417.0
1998		1,792	746	89.8	59.8	118.3	2,736.7	11.40	4,270.5	5,773.5	10,070.6	322.8
1999		1,754	725	91.0	61.7	121.5	2,894.2	11.93	4,449.1	6,326.6	10,738.6	381.4
2000		1,715	734	90.9	63.3	119.5	3,046.4	12.45	5,111.1	6,937.4	12,062.6	459.6
2001		1,663	750	78.6	52.0	99.5	2,709.4	12.96	4,161.0	5,380.5	9,987.9	480.2
2002	1,537	1,627	662	70.2	42.6	93.3	2,638.5	12.68	3,812.2	5,556.6	9,452.4	423.0
2003		1,474	623	61.8	37.4	76.4	2,445.5	14.34	3,736.0	5,352.2	9,104.0	389.4
2004		1,410	622	59.2	37.0	73.5	2,471.3	15.31	3,556.3	5,388.4	8,882.2	228.7
2005		1,355	615	58.1	36.0	72.0	2,481.4	16.07	3,805.1	5,490.1	9,305.4	244.1
2006		1,315P	602P	57.4	36.0	71.3	2,520.2	16.36	4,158.9	6,025.8	10,117.6	206.4
2007		1,254P	585P	48.9P	28.7P	59.2P	2,411.9P	16.82P	3,753.2P	5,438.0P	9,130.6P	239.3P
2008		1,192P	568P	44.2P	25.0P	52.4P	2,365.4P	17.43P	3,687.5P	5,342.8P	8,970.8P	218.3P
2009		1,130P	551P	39.5P	21.4P	45.7P	2,319.0P	18.03P	3,621.8P	5,247.6P	8,811.0P	197.2P
2010		1,068P	534P	34.8P	17.8P	38.9P	2,272.5P	18.64P	3,556.1P	5,152.4P	8,651.1P	176.1P

Sources: 1997 and 2002 *Economic Census*; other years, up to 2006, are from *Annual Survey of Manufactures*. Establishment counts for non-Census years are from *County Business Patterns*; 1997 and 2002 values are from the 1997 and 2002 censuses, respectively. 'P's show projections by the editors.

INDICES OF CHANGE

| Year | Com-panies | Establishments | | Employment | | | Compensation | | Production ($ million) | | | |
		Total	with 20 or more employees	Total (000)	Production Workers (000)	Hours (Mil)	Payroll ($ mil)	Wages ($/hr)	Cost of Materials	Value Added by Manufacture	Value of Shipments	Capital Invest.
1997	115	113	107	129	142	126	103	90	115	108	110	99
1998		110	113	128	140	127	104	90	112	104	107	76
1999		108	110	130	145	130	110	94	117	114	114	90
2000		105	111	129	149	128	115	98	134	125	128	109
2001		102	113	112	122	107	103	102	109	97	106	114
2002	100	100	100	100	100	100	100	100	100	100	100	100
2003		91	94	88	88	82	93	113	98	96	96	92
2004		87	94	84	87	79	94	121	93	97	94	54
2005		83	93	83	85	77	94	127	100	99	98	58
2006		81P	91P	82	85	76	96	129	109	108	107	49
2007		77P	88P	70P	67P	63P	91P	133P	98P	98P	97P	57P
2008		73P	86P	63P	59P	56P	90P	137P	97P	96P	95P	52P
2009		69P	83P	56P	50P	49P	88P	142P	95P	94P	93P	47P
2010		66P	81P	50P	42P	42P	86P	147P	93P	93P	92P	42P

Sources: Same as General Statistics. Values reflect change from the base year, 2002. Values above 100 mean greater than 2002, values below 100 mean less than 2002, and the values of 100 in other years means the same as 2002. 'P's show projections by the editors.

SELECTED RATIOS

For 2002	Avg. of All Manufact.	Analyzed Industry	Index	For 2002	Avg. of All Manufact.	Analyzed Industry	Index
Employees per Establishment	42	43	103	Value Added per Production Worker	182,367	130,437	72
Payroll per Establishment	1,639,184	1,621,696	99	Cost per Establishment	5,769,015	2,343,085	41
Payroll per Employee	39,053	37,585	96	Cost per Employee	137,446	54,305	40
Production Workers per Establishment	30	26	89	Cost per Production Worker	195,506	89,488	46
Wages per Establishment	694,845	727,132	105	Shipments per Establishment	11,158,348	5,809,711	52
Wages per Production Worker	23,548	27,771	118	Shipments per Employee	265,847	134,650	51
Hours per Production Worker	1,980	2,190	111	Shipments per Production Worker	378,144	221,887	59
Wages per Hour	11.89	12.68	107	Investment per Establishment	361,338	259,988	72
Value Added per Establishment	5,381,325	3,415,243	63	Investment per Employee	8,609	6,026	70
Value Added per Employee	128,210	79,154	62	Investment per Production Worker	12,245	9,930	81

Sources: Same as General Statistics. The 'Average of All Manufacturing' column represents the average of all manufacturing industries reported for the most recent complete year available. The Index shows the relationship between the Average and the Analyzed Industry. For example, 100 means that they are equal; 500 that the Analyzed Industry is five times the average; 50 means that the Analyzed Industry is half the national average. The abbreviation 'na' is used to show that data are 'not available'. Ratios shown for 2002, the last complete census year.

LEADING COMPANIES   Number shown: 75   Total sales ($ mil): 359,551   Total employment (000): 758.7

Company Name	Address				CEO Name	Phone	Co. Type	Sales ($ mil)	Empl. (000)
Technitrol Delaware Inc.	3411 Silverside Rd.	Wilmington	DE	19810	James M. Papada	302-478-8271	S	67,716*	22.8
Chrysler L.L.C.	1000 Chrysler Dr.	Auburn Hills	MI	48326	Thomas W. LaSorda	248-576-5741	S	45,237*	84.4
Honeywell International Inc.	PO Box 4000	Morristown	NJ	07962	Adriane M. Brown	973-455-2000	P	34,589	122.0
General Dynamics Corp.	2941 Fairview Park	Falls Church	VA	22042	Nicholas D. Chabraja	703-876-3000	P	27,240	83.5
Raytheon Co.	870 Winter St.	Waltham	MA	02451		781-522-3000	P	21,301	72.1
ITT Federal Services Corp.	4410 E Fountain	Colorado Spgs	CO	80916	Steven Loranger	719-591-3600	S	20,690*	7.0
Mars Inc.	6885 Elm Street	Mc Lean	VA	22101	John F. Mars	703-821-4900	R	18,462*	40.0
Computer Sciences Corp.	2100 E Grand Ave.	El Segundo	CA	90245		310-615-0311	P	14,855	79.0
ITT Corp.	4 W Red Oak Ln.	White Plains	NY	10604		914-641-2000	P	9,003	39.7
Ball Corp.	PO Box 5000	Broomfield	CO	80021	R. David Hoover	303-469-3131	P	7,475	15.5
Order-Matic Corp.	PO Box 25463	Oklahoma City	OK	73125	Bill Cunningham	405-672-1487	R	5,787	0.2
Allegheny Technologies Inc.	1000 Six PPG Pl.	Pittsburgh	PA	15222		412-394-2800	P	5,453	9.5
Flextronics	2090 Fortune Dr.	San Jose	CA	95131	Mike McNamara	408-576-7000	S	4,699*	1.5
LSI Marcole Inc.	1108 Oakdale St.	Manchester	TN	37355	Robert J. Ready	931-723-4442	S	4,643*	1.4
Oki Data Americas Inc.	2000 Bishops Gate	Mount Laurel	NJ	08054	Stewart Krentzman	856-235-2600	S	4,260*	0.5
Harris Corp.	1025 W NASA	Melbourne	FL	32919		321-727-9100	P	4,243	16.0
Sparton Electronics	PO Box 788	De Leon Springs	FL	32130	D W. Hockenbrocht	386-985-4631	S	3,491*	1.0
Benchmark Electronics Inc.	3000 Technology	Angleton	TX	77515		979-849-6550	P	2,916	10.9
Crane Co.	100 First Stamford	Stamford	CT	06902	Thomas Craney	203-363-7300	P	2,619	12.0
I/O Marine Systems Inc.	5200 Toler St.	Harahan	LA	70123	Robert P. Peebler	504-733-6061	S	2,610*	0.8
I/O Nevada L.L.C.	12300 Parc Crest Dr	Stafford	TX	77477	Robert P. Peebler	281-933-3339	S	2,610*	0.8
I/O Texas L.P.	12300 Parc Crest Dr	Stafford	TX	77477	Robert P. Peebler	281-933-3339	S	2,610*	0.8
Hubbell Inc.	584 Derby Milford	Orange	CT	06477		203-799-4100	P	2,534	11.5
Wakefield Thermal Solutions	33 Bridge St.	Pelham	NH	03076	Robert Streiter	603-635-2800	S	2,398*	0.1
Red Rocket Inc.	5217 Verdugo Way	Camarillo	CA	93012	James B. Schutz	805-409-0909	R	2,146*	0.7
ACT Electronics Inc.	2 Cabot Rd.	Hudson	MA	01749		978-567-4000	R	1,870*	0.1
Opex Corp.	305 Commerce Dr.	Moorestown	NJ	08057	Jeff Bowen	856-727-1100	R	1,857*	0.7
PerkinElmer Inc.	940 Winter St.	Waltham	MA	02451	Robert F. Friel	781-663-6900	P	1,787	8.7
Advanced Interconnection Tech	85 Adams Ave.	Hauppauge	NY	11788	Phillip A. Harris	631-968-1591	S	1,776*	0.6
Siemens VDO Automotive Corp.	2400 Executive Hill	Auburn Hills	MI	48326	John Sanderson	248-209-4000	S	1,738*	10.0
ECS. Inc International	1105 S Ridgeview	Olathe	KS	66062	Patricia S. Taylor	913-782-7787	R	1,689*	0.5
Stratos Optical Technologies	7444 W Wilson Ave.	Chicago	IL	60706	Phillip A. Harris	708-867-9600	S	1,645*	0.6
Stratos Lightwave Inc.	1335 Gateway Dr.	Melbourne	FL	32901	Phillip A. Harris	321-308-4100	S	1,633*	0.6
CC Industries Inc.	222 N La Salle St.	Chicago	IL	60601	William H. Crown	312-855-4000	S	1,560*	6.0
I/O General L.L.C.	12300 Parc Crest Dr	Stafford	TX	77477	Robert P. Peebler	281-933-3339	S	1,555*	0.5
Rooney Holdings Inc.	1400 Gulf Shre Blvd	Naples	FL	34102	Jim Cavanaugh	239-403-0375	R	1,443*	2.6
K and L Microwave Inc.	2250 Northwood Dr.	Salisbury	MD	21801	Darby Kruger	410-749-2424	S	1,339*	0.5
AVX Corp.	PO Box 867	Myrtle Beach	SC	29578	John S. Gilbertson	843-448-9411	P	1,333	13.0
Olin Corp.	190 Carondelet Plz.	Clayton	MO	63105	Randall W. Larrimore	314-480-1400	P	1,277	3.6
Teradyne Inc.	600 Riverpark Dr.	North Reading	MA	01864	James Bagley	978-370-2700	P	1,102	3.6
Academy Precision Materials	5520 Midway Park	Albuquerque	NM	87109	Mike McCay	505-343-9440	R	1,096*	0.3
Technitrol Inc.	1210 Northbrook Dr.	Trevose	PA	19053		215-355-2900	P	1,027	26.1
Emerson Netw. Pwr Emb Comp.	8310 Excelsior Dr.	Madison	WI	53717			S	774*	0.3
Sub-Zero Inc.	4717 Hammersley	Madison	WI	53711	James Bakke	608-271-2233	R	758*	3.0
Hutchinson Technology Inc.	40 W Highland Park	Hutchinson	MN	55350	Wayne M. Fortun	320-587-3797	P	716	4.7
CTS Corp.	905 N West Blvd.	Elkhart	IN	46514	R R. Hemminghaus	574-293-7511	P	686	4.7
Ball Aerospace & Technologies	PO Box 1062	Boulder	CO	80306		303-939-4000	S	672*	3.0
Kaiser Systems Inc.	126 Sohier Rd.	Beverly	MA	01915	Kenneth Kaiser	978-922-9300	R	556*	<0.1
Aeroflex Inc.	PO Box 6022	Plainview	NY	11803	Harvey R. Blau	516-694-6700	R	537*	2.6
Varian Semiconductor Equipment	35 Dory Rd.	Gloucester	MA	01930	Richard Aurelio	978-281-2000	S	530*	1.0
Power-One Inc.	740 Calle Plano	Camarillo	CA	93012		805-987-8741	P	512	4.2
MtronPTI	100 Douglas Ave.	Yankton	SD	57078	Bob Zylstra	605-665-9321	S	487*	0.2
Micro-Coax Inc.	206 Jones Blvd.	Pottstown	PA	19464	Chris Kneiyzs	610-495-0110	R	485*	0.1
Dolby Laboratories Inc.	100 Potrero Ave.	San Francisco	CA	94103		415-558-0200	P	482	1.0
Belkin Corp.	PO Box 5649	Compton	CA	90220	Chet Pipkin	310-604-2347	R	460*	1.0
Express Manufacturing Inc.	3519 West Warner	Santa Ana	CA	92704	C.P. Chin	714-979-2228	R	446*	0.5
JBL Professional Inc.	8400 Balboa Blvd.	Northridge	CA	91329	John Carpanini	818-894-8850	S	443*	1.8
CoorsTek Inc.	16000 Table Mtn	Golden	CO	80403	John K. Coors	303-271-7000	R	400*	2.4
Fiskars Brands Inc.	2537 Daniels St.	Madison	WI	53718	Heikki Allonen	608-259-1649	R	399*	<0.1
Advanced Energy Industries	1625 Sharp Point Dr	Fort Collins	CO	80525	Hans-Georg Betz	970-221-4670	P	385	1.6
Panamax	1690 Corporate Cir.	Petaluma	CA	94954	Bill Pollock		R	372*	0.1
Saturn Electronics & Engineer.	255 Rex Blvd.	Auburn Hills	MI	48326	Wallace K. Tsuha, Jr.	248-853-5724	R	360*	4.0
Tatung Company of America Inc.	2850 El Presidio St	Long Beach	CA	90810	Andrew Sun	310-637-2105	S	355*	0.3
M/A-COM Inc.	PO Box 3295	Lowell	MA	01853	David Coughlan	978-442-5000	S	339*	3.9
Van Meter Industrial Inc.	240 33rd. Ave. SW	Cedar Rapids	IA	52404		319-366-5301	R	329*	0.2
Silicon Image Inc.	1060 E Arques Ave.	Sunnyvale	CA	94085	Peter Hanelt	408-616-4000	P	321	0.6
Electronic Assembly Corp.	12515 E 55th St.	Tulsa	OK	74112		918-834-1837	R	320	<0.1
Telex Communications Inc.	12000 Portland Ave.	Burnsville	MN	55337	R V. Malpocher	952-884-4051	R	308*	3.0
OKI Semiconductor	1173 Borregas Ave.	Sunnyvale	CA	94085	Takaburni Asahi	408-720-1900	S	283*	0.1
Planar Systems Inc.	1195 NW Compton	Beaverton	OR	97006		503-748-1100	P	272	0.7
Artesyn North America Inc.	7575 Market Place	Eden Prairie	MN	55344		952-941-1100	S	271*	<0.1
Americor Electronics Ltd.	675 S Lively Blvd.	Elk Grove Vlg	IL	60007	Troy Gunnin	847-956-6200	R	247*	<0.1
Government Micro Resources	7421 Gateway Ct.	Manassas	VA	20109	Humberto Pujais	703-594-8100	R	246*	0.2
Intercon 1	1120 Wayzata E	Wayzata	MN	55391	M. J. Degen	218-828-3157	D	245*	1.0
Korry Electronics Co.	901 Dexter Ave. N	Seattle	WA	98109	Frank Houston	206-281-1300	S	242*	0.6

Source: Ward's Business Directory of U.S. Private and Public Companies, Volumes 1 and 2, 2008. The company type code used is as follows: P - Public, R - Private, S - Subsidiary, D - Division, J - Joint Venture, A - Affiliate, G - Group. Sales are in millions of dollars, employees are in thousands. An asterisk (*) indicates an estimated sales volume. The symbol < stands for 'less than'. Company names and addresses are truncated, in some cases, to fit into the available space.

MATERIALS CONSUMED

Material	Quantity	Delivered Cost ($ million)
Tube blanks	(X)	3.9
Printed ciruit boards (without inserted components) for electronic circuitry	(X)	70.3
Printed circuit assemblies, loaded boards, and modules	(X)	248.2
Semiconductors (incl. transistors, diodes, rectifiers, and integrated circuits), for electronic circuitry	(X)	144.1
Capacitors for electronic circuitry	(X)	60.8
Resistors for electronic circuitry	(X)	33.1
All other miscellaneous components and accessories for electronic circuitry (exc. tubes)	(X)	(D)
Silicon, hyperpure	(X)	(D)
Gold and other precious metals, all forms (incl. ingot, sheet, etc.)	(X)	14.7
Doped chemicals and other doped materials for electronic use	(X)	0.6
Ferrites (powder and paste)	(X)	16.2
Metal powders	(X)	11.1
Electronic computer equipment	(X)	13.2
Current-carrying wiring devices	(X)	28.6
Electronic communication equipment	(X)	66.8
Electrical instrument mechanisms and meter movements	(X)	15.4
All other miscellaneous electrical measuring instruments and parts	(X)	7.0
Fractional horsepower electric motors (less than 1 hp)	(X)	1.0
Electrical transmission, distribution, and control equipment	(X)	22.0
Loudspeakers, microphones, and tuners (all types)	(X)	(D)
Glass and glass products (excluding windows and mirrors)	(X)	10.9
Optical instruments and lenses (exc. sighting, tracking, and fire control)	(X)	(D)
Plastics resins consumed in the form of granules, pellets, etc.	(X)	29.8
Fabricated plastics products (excluding gaskets)	(X)	37.3
Sheet metal products (excluding stampings)	(X)	50.3
Metal stampings	(X)	32.2
Metal bolts, nuts, screws, and other screw machine products	(X)	47.2
Other fabricated metal products (excluding forgings)	(X)	110.6
Forgings	(X)	0.5
Castings, rough and semifinished	(X)	9.6
Steel shapes and forms (exc. castings, forgings, fabr. metal products)	(X)	30.8
Copper and copper-base alloy shapes and forms (exc. castings, forgings, fabr. metal products)	(X)	4.6
Aluminum and aluminum-base alloy shapes and forms (exc. castings, forgings, fabr. metal products)	(X)	40.3
Other nonferrous shapes and forms (exc. castings, forgings, fabricated metal products)	(X)	8.9
Insulated wire and cable (including magnet wire)	(X)	104.9
Paper and paperboard containers (incl. shipping sacks and other paper packaging supplies)	(X)	14.3
Resists (photosensitive resin films applied to surface of wafer)	(X)	1.3
Commodity gases	(X)	5.8
Speciality gases	(X)	0.6
Masks	(X)	1.6
Silicon chips	(X)	7.4
Solvents	(X)	1.9
Cleaning compounds	(X)	1.3
All other materials, components, parts, containers, and supplies	(X)	928.1
Materials, ingredients, containers, and supplies, nsk	(X)	561.4

Source: 2002 *Economic Census*. Explanation of symbols used: (D): Withheld to avoid disclosure of competitive data; na: Not available; (S): Withheld because statistical norms were not met; (X): Not applicable; (Z): Less than half the unit shown; nec: Not elsewhere classified; nsk: Not specified by kind; - : zero; p : 10-19 percent estimated; q : 20-29 percent estimated.

PRODUCT SHARE DETAILS

Product or Product Class Shipments	Mil. $	Product or Product Class Shipments	Mil. $
OTHER ELECTRONIC COMPONENTS	9,988.4	Microwave components and devices, except antennae, tubes, and semiconductors	1,524.4
Crystals, filters, piezoelectric, and other related electronic devices, except microwave filters	747.6	Electronic components, nec	4,317.2
Transducers, electrical-electronic input or output, nec	1,208.2	Other electronic components, nsk, total	1,426.3
Switches, mechanical, for electronic circuitry	764.7		

Source: 2002 *Economic Census*. The values are product shipments in millions of dollars for 2002. Total product shipments may be lower or higher than industry shipments. See Introduction for a full discussion. Values of indented subcategories are summed in the main heading(s). The symbol (D) appears when data are withheld to prevent disclosure of competitive information. The abbreviation nsk stands for 'not specified by kind' and nec for 'not elsewhere classified'. A dash (-) means zero.

INPUTS AND OUTPUTS FOR OTHER ELECTRONIC COMPONENT MANUFACTURING

Economic Sector or Industry Providing Inputs	%	Sector	Economic Sector or Industry Buying Outputs	%	Sector
Compensation of employees	35.2		Exports of goods & services	19.3	Cap Inv
Management of companies & enterprises	11.5	Services	Motor vehicle parts	11.4	Manufg.
Wholesale trade	8.9	Trade	Broadcast & wireless communications equipment	10.4	Manufg.
Printed circuit assemblies (electronic assembiles)	4.4	Manufg.	Telephone apparatus	9.3	Manufg.
Electronic components, nec	4.2	Manufg.	Printed circuit assemblies (electronic assembiles)	5.3	Manufg.
Scientific research & development services	3.2	Services	Search, detection, & navigation instruments	5.2	Manufg.
Semiconductors & related devices	1.9	Manufg.	Semiconductors & related devices	2.7	Manufg.
Real estate	1.5	Fin/R.E.	Electronic components, nec	2.5	Manufg.

Continued on next page.

INPUTS AND OUTPUTS FOR OTHER ELECTRONIC COMPONENT MANUFACTURING - Continued

Economic Sector or Industry Providing Inputs	%	Sector	Economic Sector or Industry Buying Outputs	%	Sector
Turned products & screws, nuts, & bolts	1.5	Manufg.	Audio & video equipment	2.0	Manufg.
Electronic capacitors, resistors, coils, transformers	1.1	Manufg.	Personal consumption expenditures	2.0	
Lessors of nonfinancial assets	1.1	Fin/R.E.	Electricity & signal testing instruments	1.9	Manufg.
Advertising & related services	1.1	Services	Electronic computers	1.4	Manufg.
Chemical products & preparations, nec	1.1	Manufg.	S/L govt. invest., other	1.3	S/L Govt
Power generation & supply	1.0	Util.	General Federal government services, nondefense	1.2	Fed Govt
Basic inorganic chemicals, nec	0.9	Manufg.	Wholesale trade	1.2	Trade
Bare printed circuit boards	0.9	Manufg.	Electronic connectors	1.1	Manufg.
Copper rolling, drawing, extruding, & alloying	0.9	Manufg.	Electrical equipment & components, nec	1.0	Manufg.
Audio & video equipment	0.9	Manufg.	Electromedical & electrotherapeutic apparatus	1.0	Manufg.
Motor vehicle parts	0.8	Manufg.	Totalizing fluid meters & counting devices	1.0	Manufg.
Iron & steel mills & ferroalloys	0.6	Manufg.	Computer system design services	0.9	Services
Broadcast & wireless communications equipment	0.6	Manufg.	Industrial process variable instruments	0.8	Manufg.
Noncomparable imports	0.6	Foreign	Commercial & service industry machinery, nec	0.8	Manufg.
Crowns & closures & metal stamping	0.6	Manufg.	Communications equipment, nec	0.7	Manufg.
Machine shops	0.6	Manufg.	Analytical laboratory instruments	0.7	Manufg.
Ornamental & architectural metal products	0.6	Manufg.	Residential permanent site structures	0.6	Construct.
Alumina refining & primary aluminum production	0.6	Manufg.	Electron tubes	0.6	Manufg.
Communication & energy wires & cables	0.5	Manufg.	Electronic & precision equipment repair/maintenance	0.6	Services
Plastics products, nec	0.5	Manufg.	Bare printed circuit boards	0.5	Manufg.
Telecommunications	0.4	Services	Construction machinery	0.5	Manufg.
Truck transportation	0.4	Util.	Material handling equipment	0.4	Manufg.
Legal services	0.4	Services	Watches, clocks, & related devices	0.4	Manufg.
Management, scientific, & technical consulting	0.4	Services	Petroleum refineries	0.4	Manufg.
Warehousing & storage	0.4	Util.	Industrial machinery, nec	0.3	Manufg.
Automotive equipment rental & leasing	0.4	Fin/R.E.	Optical instruments & lenses	0.3	Manufg.
Coating, engraving, heat treating & allied activities	0.4	Manufg.	AC, refrigeration, and warm air heating equipment	0.3	Manufg.
Wiring devices	0.4	Manufg.	General purpose machinery, nec	0.3	Manufg.
Taxes on production & imports, less subsidies	0.4		Computer storage devices	0.3	Manufg.
Plastics materials & resins	0.4	Manufg.	Light truck & utility vehicles	0.2	Manufg.
Metal cans, boxes, & other containers (light gauge)	0.4	Manufg.	General Federal government services, defense	0.2	Fed Govt
Accounting, tax preparation, bookkeeping, & payroll	0.4	Services	Computer terminals & peripherals	0.2	Manufg.
Optical instruments & lenses	0.3	Manufg.	Automatic environmental controls	0.2	Manufg.
Maintenance/repair of nonresidential structures	0.3	Construct.	Engine equipment, nec	0.2	Manufg.
Electricity & signal testing instruments	0.3	Manufg.	Soft drinks & ice	0.2	Manufg.
Securities, commodity contracts, investments	0.3	Fin/R.E.	Semiconductor machinery	0.2	Manufg.
Data processing, hosting, & related services	0.3	Services	Electronic capacitors, resistors, coils, transformers	0.2	Manufg.
Services to buildings & dwellings	0.3	Services	Other S/L govt. enterprises	0.2	S/L Govt
Relay & industrial controls	0.2	Manufg.	Aircraft	0.2	Manufg.
Nonferrous metal (ex. copper & aluminum) processing	0.2	Manufg.	Automobiles	0.1	Manufg.
Commercial & industrial machinery rental & leasing	0.2	Fin/R.E.	Retail trade	0.1	Trade
Plastics packaging materials, film & sheet	0.2	Manufg.	Pumps & pumping equipment	0.1	Manufg.
Paperboard containers	0.2	Manufg.	Hospitals	0.1	Services
Primary nonferrous metal, ex. copper & aluminum	0.2	Manufg.	Elementary & secondary schools	0.1	Services
Other computer related services, including facilities	0.2	Services	Rolling mill & other metalworking machinery	0.1	Manufg.
Automotive repair & maintenance, ex. car washes	0.2	Services	Metal cutting & forming machine tools	0.1	Manufg.
Employment services	0.2	Services	Printing	0.1	Manufg.
Aluminum products from purchased aluminum	0.2	Manufg.	Basic organic chemicals, nec	0.1	Manufg.
Commercial & industrial equipment repair/maintenance	0.2	Services	Poultry processing	0.1	Manufg.
Cutting tools & machine tool accessories	0.1	Manufg.	Architectural, engineering, & related services	0.1	Services
Business support services	0.1	Services	Plastics products, nec	0.1	Manufg.
Electron tubes	0.1	Manufg.	Canned & dehydrated fruits & vegetables	0.1	Manufg.
Natural gas distribution	0.1	Util.	Federal government, investment, nondefense	0.1	Fed Govt
Specialized design services	0.1	Services	Tobacco products	0.1	Manufg.
Computer terminals & peripherals	0.1	Manufg.	Paperboard containers	0.1	Manufg.
Fabricated metals, nec	0.1	Manufg.			
Retail trade	0.1	Trade			
Architectural, engineering, & related services	0.1	Services			
Paperboard mills	0.1	Manufg.			
Pressed & blown glass & glassware, nec	0.1	Manufg.			
Food services & drinking places	0.1	Services			

Source: Benchmark Input-Output Accounts for the U.S. Economy, 2002, U.S. Department of Commerce, Washington, D.C., January 2008. The abbreviation nec stands for 'not elsewhere classified'.

OCCUPATIONS EMPLOYED BY SEMICONDUCTOR & OTHER ELECTRONIC COMPONENT MANUFACTURING

Occupation	% of Total 2006	Change to 2016	Occupation	% of Total 2006	Change to 2016
Electrical & electronic equipment assemblers	10.9	-30.1	Computer software engineers, systems software	1.5	-3.8
Semiconductor processors	8.2	-12.6	Production workers, nec	1.3	-14.2
Team assemblers	4.5	-12.6	Shipping, receiving, & traffic clerks	1.3	-15.9
Electrical & electronic engineering technicians	4.1	-12.6	Purchasing agents, exc wholesale, retail, & farm	1.3	-12.6
Inspectors, testers, sorters, samplers, & weighers	3.9	-17.6	Production, planning, & expediting clerks	1.2	-12.6
Electronics engineers, exc computer	3.9	-12.6	General & operations managers	1.2	-21.3
First-line supervisors/managers of production workers	2.8	-12.6	Coil winders, tapers, & finishers	1.1	-30.1
Electrical engineers	2.6	-12.6	Machinists	1.1	-8.2
Industrial engineers	2.5	6.2	Industrial production managers	1.0	-12.6
Engineering managers	2.3	-3.8	Maintenance & repair workers, general	1.0	-12.6
Electromechanical equipment assemblers	1.7	-12.6			

Source: Industry-Occupation Matrix, Bureau of Labor Statistics, December 4, 2007. These data are reported based on 4-digit NAICS categories but have been matched to corresponding 6-digit NAICS industry codes. The change reported for each occupation to the year 2016 is a percent of growth or decline as estimated by the Bureau of Labor Statistics. The abbreviation nec stands for 'not elsewhere classified'.

LOCATION BY STATE AND REGIONAL CONCENTRATION

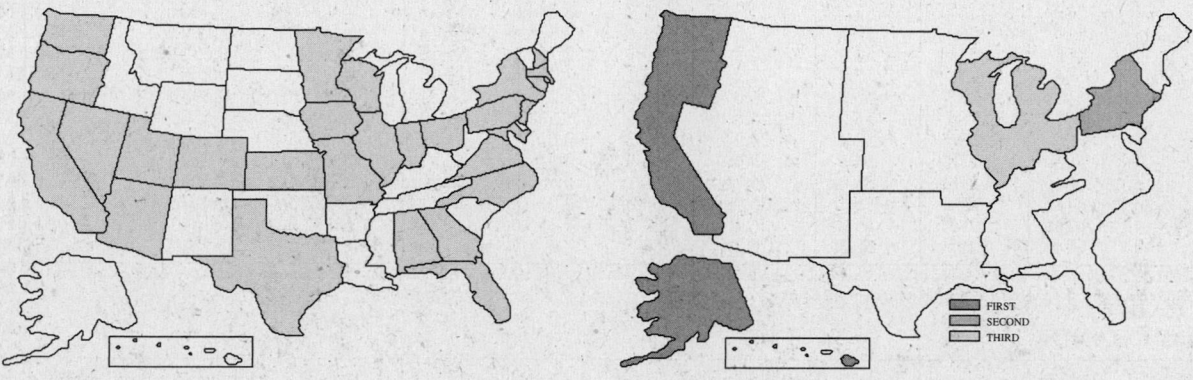

FIRST
SECOND
THIRD

INDUSTRY DATA BY STATE

State	Establish-ments	Shipments			Employment				Cost as % of Shipments	Investment per Employee ($)
		Total ($ mil)	% of U.S.	Per Establ.	Total Number	% of U.S.	Per Establ.	Wages ($/hour)		
California	409	2,391.9	25.3	5,848.1	16,819	23.9	41	13.21	40.2	11,141
Texas	82	744.2	7.9	9,075.6	3,296	4.7	40	14.25	51.9	3,601
New York	83	655.4	6.9	7,896.4	4,563	6.5	55	14.13	39.7	4,197
Massachusetts	80	611.7	6.5	7,645.9	3,919	5.6	49	15.45	37.9	5,238
Florida	63	454.7	4.8	7,217.8	3,310	4.7	53	10.42	49.6	5,747
Illinois	83	432.8	4.6	5,214.3	3,142	4.5	38	12.88	35.6	5,156
Pennsylvania	89	374.2	4.0	4,205.0	3,542	5.0	40	12.23	34.7	5,044
New Jersey	68	366.1	3.9	5,383.3	3,037	4.3	45	12.36	35.1	2,812
Colorado	33	290.4	3.1	8,800.4	1,672	2.4	51	16.80	37.0	10,894
North Carolina	31	243.3	2.6	7,848.0	1,375	2.0	44	11.91	49.5	5,504
Connecticut	38	232.5	2.5	6,118.8	1,534	2.2	40	14.82	37.8	2,874
Minnesota	34	223.6	2.4	6,577.6	2,042	2.9	60	11.68	34.6	3,035
Ohio	60	200.1	2.1	3,335.7	2,062	2.9	34	12.71	41.7	2,615
Maryland	24	193.5	2.0	8,060.8	1,600	2.3	67	14.34	44.8	6,304
Washington	35	190.9	2.0	5,453.6	2,004	2.9	57	14.73	30.5	3,317
Arizona	35	158.9	1.7	4,540.0	1,134	1.6	32	13.06	36.4	1,840
Indiana	35	147.6	1.6	4,217.1	1,452	2.1	41	9.56	48.1	1,818
Wisconsin	29	141.6	1.5	4,883.7	1,341	1.9	46	10.04	41.2	6,289
New Hampshire	33	136.6	1.4	4,138.4	1,022	1.5	31	10.69	37.5	6,062
Oregon	26	115.1	1.2	4,428.5	872	1.2	34	10.17	36.5	5,594
Virginia	22	111.1	1.2	5,051.8	864	1.2	39	12.62	24.2	5,147
Utah	17	86.9	0.9	5,113.4	756	1.1	44	9.42	31.0	4,097
Missouri	11	63.5	0.7	5,772.5	767	1.1	70	11.49	47.8	1,339
Nevada	12	56.4	0.6	4,701.7	255	0.4	21	9.20	45.1	2,275
Kansas	19	52.6	0.6	2,768.9	424	0.6	22	10.35	37.5	2,828
Rhode Island	7	44.7	0.5	6,380.0	383	0.5	55	10.77	25.3	2,817
Georgia	17	44.5	0.5	2,616.5	411	0.6	24	7.21	35.5	1,623
Iowa	7	21.1	0.2	3,012.9	173	0.2	25	17.07	28.1	2,306
Alabama	16	17.3	0.2	1,079.6	152	0.2	10	12.21	39.8	3,257

Source: 2002 *Economic Census*. The states are in descending order of shipments or establishments (if shipment data are missing for the majority). The symbol (D) appears when data are withheld to prevent disclosure of competitive information. States marked with (D) are sorted by number of establishments. A dash (-) indicates that the data element cannot be calculated. Data may not show all states active in the NAICS category. All data available at the time of publication are shown.

NAICS 334510 - ELECTROMEDICAL AND ELECTROTHERAPEUTIC APPARATUS

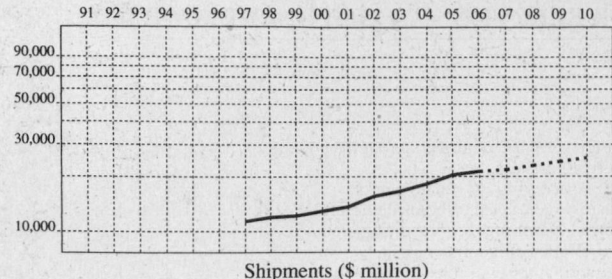

Shipments ($ million)

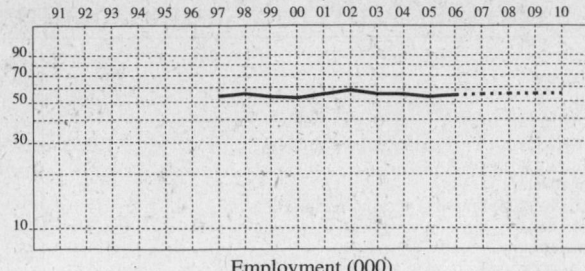

Employment (000)

GENERAL STATISTICS

Year	Com- panies	Establishments		Employment			Compensation		Production ($ million)			
		Total	with 20 or more employees	Total (000)	Production Workers (000)	Hours (Mil)	Payroll ($ mil)	Wages ($/hr)	Cost of Materials	Value Added by Manufacture	Value of Shipments	Capital Invest.
1997	485	543	267	53.7	24.4	50.6	2,562.5	14.29	3,877.7	7,545.5	11,370.0	432.2
1998		546	277	55.3	24.1	48.8	2,670.2	15.51	4,156.2	7,886.3	11,959.0	440.8
1999		512	264	53.2	22.8	45.7	2,588.0	15.64	4,409.0	8,406.5	12,166.1	351.7
2000		510	260	52.3	23.5	47.6	2,675.4	15,49	4,709.8	8,269.6	12,909.5	363.0
2001		475	238	54.9	24.8	49.7	2,769.1	15.62	5,041.9	8,631.2	13,642.6	374.9
2002	480	546	278	57.7	27.2	55.1	3,061.5	17.66	5,635.6	9,856.5	15,587.4	455.4
2003		577	275	55.0	26.0	55.2	3,214.3	18.74	5,785.8	10,696.2	16,587.9	370.6
2004		602	286	55.0	24.8	53.6	3,508.3	20.10	6,511.3	11,580.2	18,179.3	450.5
2005		605	276	53.4	24.2	49.3	3,611.0	21.65	6,286.5	14,260.4	20,446.7	1,081.3
2006		595P	278P	54.6	25.4	51.0	3,817.8	22.37	7,230.0	14,299.4	21,343.6	657.0
2007		604P	279P	55.0P	25.7P	53.2P	3,860.9P	22.70P	7,393.6P	14,623.0P	21,826.6P	734.5P
2008		614P	281P	55.1P	25.9P	53.6P	4,008.8P	23.61P	7,788.3P	15,403.5P	22,991.6P	777.6P
2009		624P	283P	55.2P	26.1P	54.1P	4,156.6P	24.52P	8,182.9P	16,184.0P	24,156.6P	820.6P
2010		634P	285P	55.3P	26.2P	54.5P	4,304.5P	25.42P	8,577.5P	16,964.5P	25,321.6P	863.7P

Sources: 1997 and 2002 *Economic Census*; other years, up to 2006, are from *Annual Survey of Manufactures*. Establishment counts for non-Census years are from *County Business Patterns*; 1997 and 2002 values are from the 1997 and 2002 censuses, respectively. 'P's show projections by the editors.

INDICES OF CHANGE

Year	Com- panies	Establishments		Employment			Compensation		Production ($ million)			
		Total	with 20 or more employees	Total (000)	Production Workers (000)	Hours (Mil)	Payroll ($ mil)	Wages ($/hr)	Cost of Materials	Value Added by Manufacture	Value of Shipments	Capital Invest.
1997	101	99	96	93	90	92	84	81	69	77	73	95
1998		100	100	96	89	89	87	88	74	80	77	97
1999		94	95	92	84	83	85	89	78	45	78	77
2000		93	94	91	86	86	87	88	84	84	83	80
2001		87	86	95	91	90	90	88	89	88	88	82
2002	100	100	100	100	100	100	100	100	100	100	100	100
2003		106	99	95	96	100	105	106	103	109	106	81
2004		110	103	95	91	97	115	114	116	117	117	99
2005		111	99	93	89	89	118	123	112	145	131	237
2006		109P	100P	95	93	93	125	127	128	145	137	144
2007		111P	100P	95P	94P	97P	126P	129P	131P	148P	140P	161P
2008		112P	101P	95P	95P	97P	131P	134P	138P	156P	148P	171P
2009		114P	102P	96P	96P	98P	136P	139P	145P	164P	155P	180P
2010		116P	102P	96P	96P	99P	141P	144P	152P	172P	162P	190P

Sources: Same as General Statistics. Values reflect change from the base year, 2002. Values above 100 mean greater than 2002, values below 100 mean less than 2002, and the values of 100 in other years means the same as 2002. 'P's show projections by the editors.

SELECTED RATIOS

For 2002	Avg. of All Manufact.	Analyzed Industry	Index	For 2002	Avg. of All Manufact.	Analyzed Industry	Index
Employees per Establishment	42	106	252	Value Added per Production Worker	182,367	362,371	199
Payroll per Establishment	1,639,184	5,607,143	342	Cost per Establishment	5,769,015	10,321,612	179
Payroll per Employee	39,053	53,059	136	Cost per Employee	137,446	97,671	71
Production Workers per Establishment	30	50	169	Cost per Production Worker	195,506	207,191	106
Wages per Establishment	694,845	1,782,172	256	Shipments per Establishment	11,158,348	28,548,352	256
Wages per Production Worker	23,548	35,774	152	Shipments per Employee	265,847	270,146	102
Hours per Production Worker	1,980	2,026	102	Shipments per Production Worker	378,144	573,066	152
Wages per Hour	11.89	17.66	149	Investment per Establishment	361,338	834,066	231
Value Added per Establishment	5,381,325	18,052,198	335	Investment per Employee	8,609	7,893	92
Value Added per Employee	128,210	170,823	133	Investment per Production Worker	12,245	16,743	137

Sources: Same as General Statistics. The 'Average of All Manufacturing' column represents the average of all manufacturing industries reported for the most recent complete year available. The Index shows the relationship between the Average and the Analyzed Industry. For example, 100 means that they are equal; 500 that the Analyzed Industry is five times the average; 50 means that the Analyzed Industry is half the national average. The abbreviation 'na' is used to show that data are 'not available'. Ratios shown for 2002, the last complete census year.

LEADING COMPANIES
Number shown: **75**   Total sales ($ mil): **305,372**   Total employment (000): **821.0**

Company Name	Address				CEO Name	Phone	Co. Type	Sales ($ mil)	Empl. (000)
Johnson & Johnson	1 Johnsn & Johnsn	New Brunswick	NJ	08901		732-524-0400	P	61,095	119.2
Pfizer Inc.	235 E 42nd St.	New York	NY	10017		212-573-2323	P	48,418	86.6
3M Co.	3M Ctr.	St. Paul	MN	55144	George W. Buckley	651-733-2204	P	24,462	76.2
Kimberly-Clark Corp.	PO Box 619100	Dallas	TX	75261		972-281-1200	P	18,266	53.0
Schering-Plough Corp.	2000 Galloping Hill	Kenilworth	NJ	07033		908-298-4000	P	12,690	55.0
Medtronic Inc.	710 Medtronic Pky.	Minneapolis	MN	55432		763-514-4000	P	12,299	38.0
Baxter International Inc.	1 Baxter Pky.	Deerfield	IL	60015		847-948-2000	P	11,263	46.0
Eastman Kodak Co.	343 State St.	Rochester	NY	14650		716-724-4000	P	10,301	26.9
Medtronic AVE Inc.	3576 Unocal Pl.	Santa Rosa	CA	95403	William Hawkins	707-525-0111	S	10,054	21.5
Covidien	15 Hampshire St.	Mansfield	MA	02048	Richard Meelia	508-261-8000	R	10,000	43.0
Siemens Medical Solutions USA	51 Valley Stream Pk	Malvern	PA	19355	Thomas McCausland	610-219-6300	S	9,135*	13.0
Encon Safety Products	PO Box 3826	Houston	TX	77253	David Key	713-466-1449	R	7,970*	<0.1
Becton, Dickinson and Co.	1 Becton Dr.	Franklin Lakes	NJ	07417		201-847-6800	P	6,360	28.0
Stryker Corp.	PO Box 4085	Kalamazoo	MI	49003		616-385-2600	P	6,001	16.0
Zimmer Holdings Inc.	PO Box 708	Warsaw	IN	46580	David Dvorak	574-267-6131	P	3,898	7.6
St. Jude Medical Inc.	1 Lillehei Plz.	St. Paul	MN	55117		651-483-2000	P	3,779	12.0
Cintas Corp.	PO Box 625737	Cincinnati	OH	45262		513-459-1200	P	3,707	34.0
Guidant Corp.	PO Box 44906	St. Paul	MN	55112	James M. Cornelius	651-582-4000	S	3,551	13.0
Medline Industries Inc.	1 Medline Pl.	Mundelein	IL	60060	Charles S. Mills	847-949-5500	R	2,450	4.9
Bausch and Lomb Inc.	1 Bausch Lomb Pl.	Rochester	NY	14604		585-338-6000	P	2,292	13.0
C.R. Bard Inc.	730 Central Ave.	Murray Hill	NJ	07974		908-277-8000	P	2,202	10.2
Biomet Inc.	PO Box 587	Warsaw	IN	46581	Jeffrey R. Binder	574-267-6639	R	2,026	4.1
DENTSPLY International Inc.	PO Box 872	York	PA	17405		717-845-7511	P	1,811	8.5
Varian Medical Systems Inc.	3100 Hansen Way	Palo Alto	CA	94304	Timothy Guertin	650-493-4000	P	1,777	4.5
Invacare Corp.	PO Box 4028	Elyria	OH	44036	Gerald B. Blouch	440-329-6000	P	1,602	5.7
Cadwell Laboratories Inc.	909 N Kellogg St.	Kennewick	WA	99336	Carl Cadwell	509-735-6481	R	1,583*	<0.1
GF Health Products Inc.	2935 Northeast Pky.	Atlanta	GA	30360	Michael A. Joffred		R	1,457*	2.2
Hartmann-Conco Inc.	481 Lakeshore	Rock Hill	SC	29730	John Gilbert	803-325-7600	R	1,431*	<0.1
STERIS Corp.	5960 Heisley Rd.	Mentor	OH	44060	Charles Immel	440-354-2600	P	1,197	5.1
Respironics Inc.	1010 Murry Ridge	Murrysville	PA	15668	Gerald E. McGinnis	724-387-5200	P	1,195	4.9
United States Surgical Corp.	150 Glover Ave.	Norwalk	CT	06850	Allen Panzer	203-845-1000	S	1,172*	5.8
Guidant's Cardiac Rhythm Manag	4100 Hamline	St. Paul	MN	55112	Fred McCoy	651-582-4000	S	1,130*	5.0
Sulzer Inc.	555 5th Ave., 15th	New York	NY	10017	Kelli Edell	212-949-0999	S	1,000*	4.5
Mine Safety Appliances Co.	PO Box 426	Pittsburgh	PA	15230		412-967-3000	P	914	4.9
Omron Healthcare Inc.	1200 Lakeside Dr.	Deerfield	IL	60015		847-680-6200	R	872*	0.1
Acuson Corp.	1220 Charleston Rd.	Mountain View	CA	94043	Klaus Hambuechen	650-969-9112	R	782*	1.0
Barden Corp.	PO Box 2449	Danbury	CT	06813	John McCloskey	203-744-2211	R	776*	0.3
CONMED Corp.	525 French Rd.	Utica	NY	13502	Eugene R. Corasanti	315-797-8375	P	694	3.2
Hanger Orthopedic Group Inc.	2 Bethesda Mtro Ctr	Bethesda	MD	20814	Thomas F. Kirk	301-986-0701	P	637	3.4
B. Braun Inc.	PO Box 4027	Bethlehem	PA	18018	Carroll Neubauer	610-997-4253	S	630*	1.6
Cook Group Inc.	PO Box 489	Bloomington	IN	47402	William A. Cook	812-339-2235	R	615	4.0
Coherent Inc.	PO Box 54980	Santa Clara	CA	95056	John R. Ambroseo	408-764-4000	P	601	2.3
Intuitive Surgical Inc.	950 Kifer Rd.	Sunnyvale	CA	94086		408-523-2100	P	601	0.8
Cotton Goods Manufacturing Co.	259 N California	Chicago	IL	60612	Edward J. Lewis	773-565-0088	R	525*	<0.1
Gambro Renal Products Inc.	10810 W Collins	Lakewood	CO	80215	Kevin Smith	303-232-6800	R	482*	<0.1
Terumo Cardiovascular Systems	6200 Jackson Rd.	Ann Arbor	MI	48103	Mark Sutter	734-663-4145	R	481*	0.3
Medtronic Sofamor Danek Inc.	1800 Pyramid Pl.	Memphis	TN	38132	Michael Demane	901-396-2695	S	470*	1.5
Amer. Med. Systems Holdings	10700 Bren Rd. W	Minnetonka	MN	55343		952-930-6000	P	464	1.2
Aearo Technologies Inc.	5457 W 79th St.	Indianapolis	IN	46268	Michael A. McLain	317-692-6666	R	423	1.7
Ethicon Johnson/Johnson Prof.	Rd. 183 KM 8.3	San Lorenzo	PR	00754		787-783-7070	P	400*	1.2
DJ Orthopedics L.L.C.	1430 Decision St.	Vista	CA	92081	Leslie H. Cross	760-727-1280	S	400*	1.2
Synthes USA L.P.	1302 Wrights Ln. E	West Chester	PA	19380		610-719-5000	R	393*	0.3
Datascope Corp.	14 Philips Pky.	Montvale	NJ	07645		201-391-8100	P	379	1.2
FLA Orthopedics Inc.	2881 Corporate Way	Miramar	FL	33025	E Slautterback	954-704-4484	R	370*	0.1
TECT Utica Corp.	2 Halsey Rd.	Whitesboro	NY	13492	Ron Cable	315-768-8070	R	356*	1.3
Wright Medical Group Inc.	5677 Airline Rd.	Arlington	TN	38002	F. Barry Bays	901-867-9971	P	339	1.1
Ethicon Endo-Surgery Inc.	4545 Creek Rd.	Cincinnati	OH	45242	Bob Salerno		S	324*	2.0
DHB Industries Inc.	2102 SW 2nd Street	Pompano Beach	FL	33069	Larry Ellis	954-630-0900	P	321	1.3
ZOLL Medical Corp.	269 Mill Rd.	Chelmsford	MA	01824		978-421-9655	P	310	1.3
ArthroCare Corp.	7500 Rialto Blvd.	Austin	TX	78735	Michael A. Baker	512-391-3900	P	308	1.1
Mentor Corp.	201 Mentor Dr.	Santa Barbara	CA	93111		805-879-6000	P	302	1.0
Zeiss, Carl Inc.	1 Zeiss Dr.	Thornwood	NY	10594	Jim Kelly	914-681-7600	R	300*	1.7
GE OEC Medical Systems Inc.	384 Wright Brothers	Salt Lake City	UT	84116	Ruben Beruman	801-328-9300	S	298*	1.0
Kayser-Roth Corp.	PO Box 26530	Greensboro	NC	27415		336-852-2030	R	288*	0.2
Medtronic MiniMed Inc.	18000 Devonshire St	Northridge	CA	91325	Jeff McCaulley	818-362-5958	S	287*	1.5
Align Technology Inc.	881 Martin Ave.	Santa Clara	CA	95050		408-470-1000	P	284	1.3
Getinge USA Inc.	1777 E Henrietta Rd	Rochester	NY	14623	Andrew Csery	585-475-1400	R	263*	0.2
Olympus America Inc.	3500 Corporate	Center Valley	PA	18034	F. Mark Gumz	484-896-5000	R	259*	1.7
Hoveround Corp.	2151 Whitfield Ind.	Sarasota	FL	34243	Thomas Kruse	941-739-6200	R	257*	0.3
Linvatec Corp.	11311 Concept Blvd.	Largo	FL	33773	Gerald Woodard		S	248*	1.1
SpaceLabs Medical Inc.	PO Box 7018	Issaquah	WA	98027	Deepak Chopra	425-657-7200	D	246*	1.2
Smith and Nephew Inc.	1450 E Brooks Rd.	Memphis	TN	38116	Davin Illingsworth	901-396-2121	R	235*	0.1
Thoratec Corp.	6101 Stoneridge Dr.	Pleasanton	CA	94588	Gary F. Burbach	925-847-8600	P	235	1.2
Medical Action Industries Inc.	800 Prime Pl.	Hauppauge	NY	11788	Paul D. Meringolo	631-231-4600	P	217	0.7
Roche Diagnostics Corp.	9115 Hague Rd.	Indianapolis	IN	46250	Tiffany Olson	317-521-2000	S	215	2.0

Source: Ward's Business Directory of U.S. Private and Public Companies, Volumes 1 and 2, 2008. The company type code used is as follows: P - Public, R - Private, S - Subsidiary, D - Division, J - Joint Venture, A - Affiliate, G - Group. Sales are in millions of dollars, employees are in thousands. An asterisk (*) indicates an estimated sales volume. The symbol < stands for 'less than'. Company names and addresses are truncated, in some cases, to fit into the available space.

MATERIALS CONSUMED

Material	Quantity	Delivered Cost ($ million)
Metal bolts, nuts, screws, and other screw machine products	(X)	107.1
Metal stampings	(X)	32.6
All other fabricated metal products (excluding forgings)	(X)	180.8
Forgings	(X)	36.9
Castings, rough and semifinished	(X)	17.7
Stainless steel shapes and forms (exc. castings, forgings, fabr. metal products)	(X)	13.3
Other steel shapes and forms (exc. castings, forgings, fabr. metal products)	(X)	(D)
Nonferrous shapes and forms	(X)	139.6
Transmittal, industrial, and special-purpose electron tubes (exc. X-ray)	(X)	(D)
Semiconductors (incl. transistors, diodes, rectifiers, and integrated circuits), for electronic circuitry	(X)	273.8
Capacitors for electronic circuitry	(X)	86.3
Resistors for electronic circuitry	(X)	72.6
Connectors for electronic circuitry	(X)	76.9
Other electronic components and accessories	(X)	378.7
Insulated wire and cable (excluding magnet wire)	(X)	119.2
Plastics products consumed in the form of sheets, rods, etc.	(X)	179.4
Paperboard containers, boxes, and corrugated paperboard	(X)	101.3
All other materials, components, parts, containers, and supplies	(X)	2,599.8
Materials, ingredients, containers, and supplies, nsk	(X)	680.0

Source: 2002 *Economic Census*. Explanation of symbols used: (D): Withheld to avoid disclosure of competitive data; na: Not available; (S): Withheld because statistical norms were not met; (X): Not applicable; (Z): Less than half the unit shown; nec: Not elsewhere classified; nsk: Not specified by kind; - : zero; p : 10-19 percent estimated; q : 20-29 percent estimated.

PRODUCT SHARE DETAILS

Product or Product Class Shipments	Mil. $	Product or Product Class Shipments	Mil. $
ELECTROMEDICAL AND ELECTROTHERAPEUTIC APPARATUS	14,995.1	**monitoring, etc.), excluding ionizing radiation equipment**	**13,613.4**
Electromedical equipment (diagnostic, therapeutic, patient		**Electronic hearing aids, complete units**	**833.2**
		Electromedical and electrotherapeutic apparatus, nsk, total	**548.5**

Source: 2002 *Economic Census*. The values are product shipments in millions of dollars for 2002. Total product shipments may be lower or higher than industry shipments. See Introduction for a full discussion. Values of indented subcategories are summed in the main heading(s). The symbol (D) appears when data are withheld to prevent disclosure of competitive information. The abbreviation nsk stands for 'not specified by kind' and nec for 'not elsewhere classified'. A dash (-) means zero.

INPUTS AND OUTPUTS FOR ELECTROMEDICAL & ELECTROTHERAPEUTIC APPARATUS

Economic Sector or Industry Providing Inputs	%	Sector	Economic Sector or Industry Buying Outputs	%	Sector
Compensation of employees	25.4		Private fixed investment	57.0	
Management of companies & enterprises	10.1	Services	Exports of goods & services	19.5	Cap Inv
Wholesale trade	5.5	Trade	Hospitals	6.6	Services
Software publishers	3.1	Services	Personal consumption expenditures	6.5	
Scientific research & development services	2.9	Services	Physician, dentist, other health practitioner offices	2.5	Services
Printed circuit assemblies (electronic assemblies)	2.7	Manufg.	General Federal government services, nondefense	2.1	Fed Govt
Semiconductors & related devices	2.1	Manufg.	Federal government, investment, nondefense	1.5	Fed Govt
Lessors of nonfinancial assets	1.9	Fin/R.E.	Electromedical & electrotherapeutic apparatus	1.2	Manufg.
Computer storage devices	1.6	Manufg.	Federal government, investment, national defense	1.2	Fed Govt
Electromedical & electrotherapeutic apparatus	1.5	Manufg.	Search, detection, & navigation instruments	0.5	Manufg.
Motors & generators	1.3	Manufg.	Surgical appliances & supplies	0.5	Manufg.
Plastics packaging materials, film & sheet	1.2	Manufg.	S/L govt. invest., education	0.5	S/L Govt
Electronic components, nec	1.1	Manufg.	Change in private inventories	0.3	In House
Custom roll forming	1.0	Manufg.			
Synthetic rubber	1.0	Manufg.			
Advertising & related services	1.0	Services			
Turned products & screws, nuts, & bolts	1.0	Manufg.			
Electronic capacitors, resistors, coils, transformers	0.9	Manufg.			
Real estate	0.9	Fin/R.E.			
Speed changers, industrial high-speed drives, & gears	0.9	Manufg.			
Power, distribution, & specialty transformers	0.9	Manufg.			
Paints & coatings	0.8	Manufg.			
Adhesives	0.8	Manufg.			
Electrical equipment & components, nec	0.8	Manufg.			
Ornamental & architectural metal products	0.8	Manufg.			
Paperboard containers	0.7	Manufg.			
Electronic connectors	0.6	Manufg.			
Springs & wire products	0.6	Manufg.			
Chemical products & preparations, nec	0.5	Manufg.			
Truck transportation	0.5	Util.			
Copper rolling, drawing, extruding, & alloying	0.5	Manufg.			
Bare printed circuit boards	0.5	Manufg.			
Relay & industrial controls	0.5	Manufg.			
Management, scientific, & technical consulting	0.5	Services			

Continued on next page.

INPUTS AND OUTPUTS FOR ELECTROMEDICAL & ELECTROTHERAPEUTIC APPARATUS - Continued

Economic Sector or Industry Providing Inputs	%	Sector	Economic Sector or Industry Buying Outputs	%	Sector
Basic organic chemicals, nec	0.5	Manufg.			
Machine shops	0.4	Manufg.			
Legal services	0.4	Services			
Crowns & closures & metal stamping	0.4	Manufg.			
Nonferrous metal (ex. copper & aluminum) processing	0.4	Manufg.			
Telecommunications	0.3	Services			
Communication & energy wires & cables	0.3	Manufg.			
Power generation & supply	0.3	Util.			
Warehousing & storage	0.3	Util.			
Securities, commodity contracts, investments	0.3	Fin/R.E.			
Coating, engraving, heat treating & allied activities	0.3	Manufg.			
Specialized design services	0.3	Services			
Forging, stamping, & sintering, nec	0.3	Manufg.			
Architectural, engineering, & related services	0.3	Services			
Automotive equipment rental & leasing	0.3	Fin/R.E.			
Monetary authorities/depository credit intermediation	0.3	Fin/R.E.			
Taxes on production & imports, less subsidies	0.3				
Accounting, tax preparation, bookkeeping, & payroll	0.3	Services			
Data processing, hosting, & related services	0.2	Services			
Other computer related services, including facilities	0.2	Services			
Food services & drinking places	0.2	Services			
Air transportation	0.2	Util.			
Professional, scientific, technical services, nec	0.2	Services			
Unlaminated plastics profile shapes	0.2	Manufg.			
Hotels & motels, including casino hotels	0.2	Services			
Iron & steel mills & ferroalloys	0.2	Manufg.			
Noncomparable imports	0.2	Foreign			
Employment services	0.2	Services			
Business support services	0.1	Services			
Commercial & industrial machinery rental & leasing	0.1	Fin/R.E.			
Motor vehicle parts	0.1	Manufg.			
Services to buildings & dwellings	0.1	Services			
Rubber & plastics hose & belting	0.1	Manufg.			
Maintenance/repair of nonresidential structures	0.1	Construct.			
Metal cans, boxes, & other containers (light gauge)	0.1	Manufg.			

Source: Benchmark Input-Output Accounts for the U.S. Economy, 2002, U.S. Department of Commerce, Washington, D.C., January 2008. The abbreviation nec stands for 'not elsewhere classified'.

OCCUPATIONS EMPLOYED BY NAVIGATIONAL, MEASURING, MEDICAL, & CONTROL INSTRUMENTS

Occupation	% of Total 2006	Change to 2016	Occupation	% of Total 2006	Change to 2016
Electrical & electronic equipment assemblers	7.1	-23.4	First-line supervisors/managers of production workers	2.1	-4.3
Team assemblers	5.3	-4.3	Engineers, nec	1.9	-4.3
Electromechanical equipment assemblers	3.6	-4.3	Purchasing agents, exc wholesale, retail, & farm	1.9	-4.3
Electrical engineers	3.3	-4.3	Machinists	1.8	0.5
Computer software engineers, applications	2.9	14.9	General & operations managers	1.7	-13.8
Aerospace engineers	2.9	0.5	Sales representatives, wholesale & manufacturing, tech	1.6	-4.3
Mechanical engineers	2.8	-4.3	Executive secretaries & administrative assistants	1.5	-4.3
Electrical & electronic engineering technicians	2.7	-4.3	Customer service representatives	1.3	5.3
Computer software engineers, systems software	2.7	5.3	Office clerks, general	1.2	-5.7
Industrial engineers	2.5	16.3	Shipping, receiving, & traffic clerks	1.2	-7.9
Inspectors, testers, sorters, samplers, & weighers	2.4	-9.7	Accountants & auditors	1.2	-4.3
Engineering managers	2.4	-4.3	Production, planning, & expediting clerks	1.2	-4.3
Electronics engineers, exc computer	2.2	-4.3			

Source: Industry-Occupation Matrix, Bureau of Labor Statistics, December 4, 2007. These data are reported based on 4-digit NAICS categories but have been matched to corresponding 6-digit NAICS industry codes. The change reported for each occupation to the year 2016 is a percent of growth or decline as estimated by the Bureau of Labor Statistics. The abbreviation nec stands for 'not elsewhere classified'.

LOCATION BY STATE AND REGIONAL CONCENTRATION

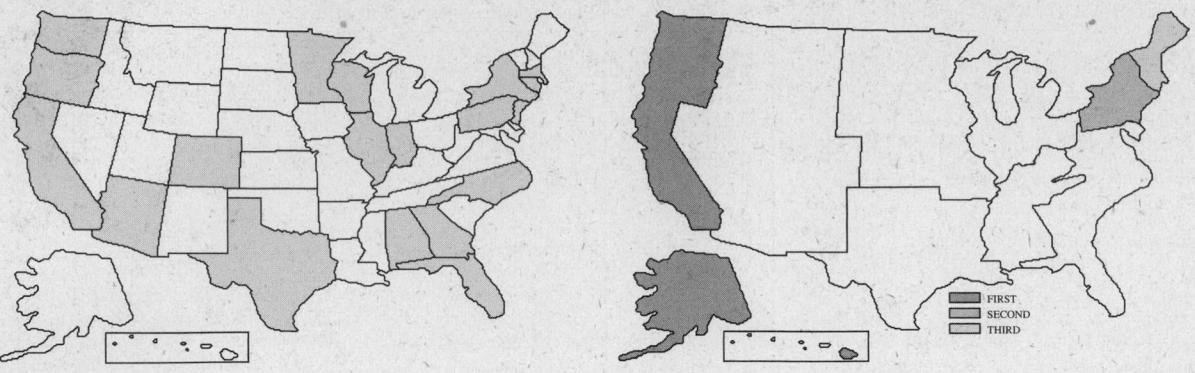

INDUSTRY DATA BY STATE

| State | Establish-ments | Shipments | | | Employment | | | | Cost as % of Shipments | Investment per Employee ($) |
		Total ($ mil)	% of U.S.	Per Establ.	Total Number	% of U.S.	Per Establ.	Wages ($/hour)		
California	120	2,933.5	18.8	24,446.2	11,605	20.1	97	20.74	34.8	5,875
Minnesota	42	2,785.5	17.9	66,321.7	8,771	15.2	209	17.24	20.0	9,776
Washington	19	1,638.7	10.5	86,245.9	5,127	8.9	270	16.63	55.8	7,439
Wisconsin	19	1,612.7	10.3	84,879.4	3,216	5.6	169	31.68	59.0	8,018
Massachusetts	42	1,450.7	9.3	34,541.6	4,248	7.4	101	20.19	17.1	13,548
Colorado	12	665.7	4.3	55,477.1	2,897	5.0	241	14.94	34.7	5,129
New Jersey	18	553.5	3.6	30,750.3	2,089	3.6	116	18.94	38.7	7,086
Pennsylvania	19	447.6	2.9	23,556.4	2,292	4.0	121	15.39	32.9	4,441
Illinois	20	371.2	2.4	18,560.3	1,536	2.7	77	14.20	40.5	3,253
Texas	20	357.1	2.3	17,856.4	1,851	3.2	93	14.17	16.8	8,656
Connecticut	16	321.3	2.1	20,080.6	1,285	2.2	80	15.33	28.9	5,016
Florida	31	265.9	1.7	8,578.6	1,604	2.8	52	13.01	49.7	3,757
New York	29	258.9	1.7	8,927.7	1,051	1.8	36	14.60	31.8	7,138
Oregon	12	251.9	1.6	20,994.4	1,361	2.4	113	35.18	39.4	2,705
Arizona	6	86.2	0.6	14,364.0	694	1.2	116	21.01	80.6	5,278
Alabama	5	65.4	0.4	13,089.0	408	0.7	82	22.29	36.5	9,284
Georgia	8	44.0	0.3	5,503.5	222	0.4	28	17.75	37.3	2,144
Indiana	6	21.9	0.1	3,651.3	186	0.3	31	20.11	29.9	6,022
North Carolina	8	18.1	0.1	2,257.2	104	0.2	13	14.95	32.7	3,625

Source: 2002 *Economic Census*. The states are in descending order of shipments or establishments (if shipment data are missing for the majority). The symbol (D) appears when data are withheld to prevent disclosure of competitive information. States marked with (D) are sorted by number of establishments. A dash (-) indicates that the data element cannot be calculated. Data may not show all states active in the NAICS category. All data available at the time of publication are shown.

NAICS 334511 - SEARCH, DETECTION, NAVIGATION, GUIDANCE SYSTEMS

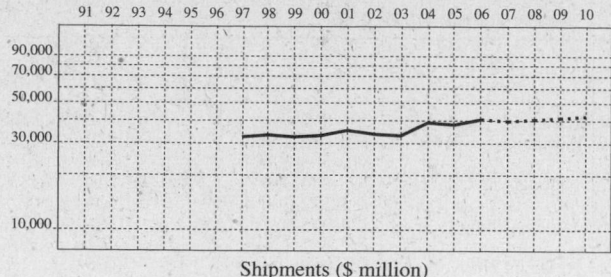

Shipments ($ million)

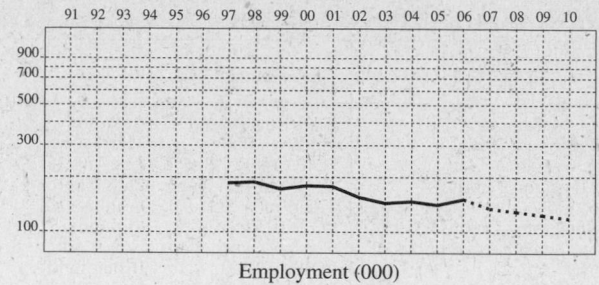

Employment (000)

GENERAL STATISTICS

Year	Com-panies	Establishments		Employment			Compensation		Production ($ million)			
		Total	with 20 or more employees	Total (000)	Production Workers (000)	Hours (Mil)	Payroll ($ mil)	Wages ($/hr)	Cost of Materials	Value Added by Manufacture	Value of Shipments	Capital Invest.
1997	577	688	317	185.9	64.8	123.9	9,422.2	20.62	8,950.8	23,119.9	32,473.3	1,021.0
1998		704	335	188.3	69.5	134.4	10,257.9	21.65	9,192.2	23,941.7	33,265.4	1,158.0
1999		678	334	172.5	60.5	116.7	9,571.9	22.14	10,421.6	22,107.6	32,486.0	1,011.5
2000		665	318	179.7	64.9	119.3	9,751.7	23.29	11,359.8	21,440.5	33,081.8	1,022.2
2001		668	327	178.1	63.3	112.2	10,042.3	26.06	11,941.5	23,374.9	35,345.5	1,104.8
2002	505	653	305	155.5	52.4	96.2	9,715.4	26.14	10,511.1	22,930.4	33,657.6	865.2
2003		659	335	144.2	44.0	85.5	9,911.0	25.80	10,174.2	23,779.9	33,023.8	1,389.7
2004		624	329	147.5	42.8	82.6	10,549.3	26.86	12,141.4	27,206.3	39,001.9	1,073.0
2005		634	320	141.3	43.9	86.9	10,128.1	26.35	12,552.8	26,419.7	38,019.8	1,005.6
2006		622P	323P	151.7	47.1	91.1	11,077.9	26.68	13,646.4	27,370.8	40,660.7	1,027.7
2007		613P	323P	134.8P	38.6P	74.4P	10,677.1P	28.51P	13,321.0P	26,718.1P	39,691.1P	1,073.3P
2008		605P	323P	129.4P	35.6P	68.8P	10,792.5P	29.23P	13,601.0P	27,279.8P	40,525.5P	1,074.3P
2009		596P	322P	124.0P	32.6P	63.3P	10,907.8P	29.95P	13,881.1P	27,841.5P	41,360.0P	1,075.3P
2010		588P	322P	118.6P	29.5P	57.7P	11,023.1P	30.67P	14,161.1P	28,403.2P	42,194.4P	1,076.3P

Sources: 1997 and 2002 *Economic Census*; other years, up to 2006, are from *Annual Survey of Manufactures*. Establishment counts for non-Census years are from *County Business Patterns*; 1997 and 2002 values are from the 1997 and 2002 censuses, respectively. 'P's show projections by the editors.

INDICES OF CHANGE

Year	Com-panies	Establishments		Employment			Compensation		Production ($ million)			
		Total	with 20 or more employees	Total (000)	Production Workers (000)	Hours (Mil)	Payroll ($ mil)	Wages ($/hr)	Cost of Materials	Value Added by Manufacture	Value of Shipments	Capital Invest.
1997	114	105	104	120	124	129	97	79	85	101	96	118
1998		108	110	121	133	140	106	83	87	104	99	134
1999		104	110	111	115	121	99	85	99	96	97	117
2000		102	104	116	124	124	100	89	108	94	98	118
2001		102	107	115	121	117	103	100	114	102	105	128
2002	100	100	100	100	100	100	100	100	100	100	100	100
2003		101	110	93	84	89	102	99	97	104	98	161
2004		96	108	95	82	86	109	103	116	119	116	124
2005		97	105	91	84	90	104	101	119	115	113	116
2006		95P	106P	98	90	95	114	102	130	119	121	119
2007		94P	106P	87P	74P	77P	110P	109P	127P	117P	118P	124P
2008		93P	106P	83P	68P	72P	111P	112P	129P	119P	120P	124P
2009		91P	106P	80P	62P	66P	112P	115P	132P	121P	123P	124P
2010		90P	106P	76P	56P	60P	113P	117P	135P	124P	125P	124P

Sources: Same as General Statistics. Values reflect change from the base year, 2002. Values above 100 mean greater than 2002, values below 100 mean less than 2002, and the values of 100 in other years means the same as 2002. 'P's show projections by the editors.

SELECTED RATIOS

For 2002	Avg. of All Manufact.	Analyzed Industry	Index	For 2002	Avg. of All Manufact.	Analyzed Industry	Index
Employees per Establishment	42	238	567	Value Added per Production Worker	182,367	437,603	240
Payroll per Establishment	1,639,184	14,878,101	908	Cost per Establishment	5,769,015	16,096,631	279
Payroll per Employee	39,053	62,478	160	Cost per Employee	137,446	67,595	49
Production Workers per Establishment	30	80	272	Cost per Production Worker	195,506	200,594	103
Wages per Establishment	694,845	3,850,946	554	Shipments per Establishment	11,158,348	51,543,032	462
Wages per Production Worker	23,548	47,990	204	Shipments per Employee	265,847	216,448	81
Hours per Production Worker	1,980	1,836	93	Shipments per Production Worker	378,144	642,321	170
Wages per Hour	11.89	26.14	220	Investment per Establishment	361,338	1,324,962	367
Value Added per Establishment	5,381,325	35,115,467	653	Investment per Employee	8,609	5,564	65
Value Added per Employee	128,210	147,462	115	Investment per Production Worker	12,245	16,511	135

Sources: Same as General Statistics. The 'Average of All Manufacturing' column represents the average of all manufacturing industries reported for the most recent complete year available. The Index shows the relationship between the Average and the Analyzed Industry. For example, 100 means that they are equal; 500 that the Analyzed Industry is five times the average; 50 means that the Analyzed Industry is half the national average. The abbreviation 'na' is used to show that data are 'not available'. Ratios shown for 2002, the last complete census year.

LEADING COMPANIES   Number shown: **75**   Total sales ($ mil): **232,707**   Total employment (000): **832.4**

Company Name	Address				CEO Name	Phone	Co. Type	Sales ($ mil)	Empl. (000)
Lockheed Martin Corp.	6801 Rockledge Dr.	Bethesda	MD	20817	Richard F. Ambrose	301-897-6000	P	41,862	140.0
Honeywell International Inc.	PO Box 4000	Morristown	NJ	07962	Adriane M. Brown	973-455-2000	P	34,589	122.0
Northrop Grumman Corp.	1840 Century Park E	Los Angeles	CA	90067		310-553-6262	P	32,018	122.6
General Dynamics Corp.	2941 Fairview Park	Falls Church	VA	22042	Nicholas D. Chabraja	703-876-3000	P	27,240	83.5
Raytheon Co.	870 Winter St.	Waltham	MA	02451		781-522-3000	P	21,301	72.1
Boeing Integrated Defense Sys.	PO Box 516	St. Louis	MO	63166	James Albaugh	314-232-0232	D	17,354*	72.0
L-3 Communications Holdings	600 3rd Ave.	New York	NY	10016		212-697-1111	P	13,961	63.7
Ball Corp.	PO Box 5000	Broomfield	CO	80021	R. David Hoover	303-469-3131	P	7,475	15.5
Rockwell Collins Inc.	400 Collins Rd. NE	Cedar Rapids	IA	52498		319-295-1000	P	4,415	19.5
Hamilton Sundstrand Corp.	1 Hamilton Rd.	Windsor Locks	CT	06096	Ronald F. McKenna	860-654-6000	S	3,600*	16.0
Hi-Stat Manufacturing Company	28001 Cabot Dr.	Novi	MI	48377	John Corey	248-489-9300	D	3,194*	5.0
Learjet Inc.	PO Box 7707	Wichita	KS	67277	Jim Ziegler	316-946-2000	R	2,867*	0.8
DRS Technologies Inc.	5 Sylvan Way	Parsippany	NJ	07054		973-898-1500	P	2,821	9.7
Crane Co.	100 First Stamford	Stamford	CT	06902	Thomas Craney	203-363-7300	P	2,619	12.0
Sequa Corp.	200 Park Ave.	New York	NY	10166	Gail Binderman	212-986-5500	P	2,183	10.2
Teleflex Inc.	155 S Limerick Rd.	Limerick	PA	19468	Jeffrey P. Black	610-948-5100	P	1,934	14.0
AAR Defense Systems	1100 N Wood Dale	Wood Dale	IL	60191	David Storch	630-227-2000	D	1,101*	3.5
Orbital Sciences Corp.	21839 Atlantic Blvd	Dulles	VA	20166		703-406-5000	P	1,084	2.8
FLIR Systems Inc.	27700A SW Pkwy.	Wilsonville	OR	97070	Earl R. Lewis	503-684-3731	P	779	1.7
EDO Corp.	60 E 42nd St., 42nd	New York	NY	10165		212-716-2000	S	715	4.0
Ball Aerospace & Technologies	PO Box 1062	Boulder	CO	80306		303-939-4000	S	672*	3.0
ESCO Technologies Inc.	9900A Clayton Rd.	St. Louis	MO	63124	V. Richey	314-213-7200	P	528	2.7
Link Simulation and Training	PO Box 5328	Arlington	TX	76005	John McNellis	817-619-3536	D	415*	0.8
DRS Sensors and Targeting Sys.	10600 Vly View St.	Cypress	CA	90630	Mark S Newman	714-220-3800	S	404*	1.5
Flightline Electronics Inc.	7625 Omnitech Pl.	Victor	NY	14564	Carlos Santiago	585-924-4000	R	358*	0.1
Sierra Nevada Corp.	444 Salomon Cir.	Sparks	NV	89434	Eren Ozmen	775-331-0222	R	344*	0.3
SiRF Technology Holdings Inc.	217 Devcon Dr.	San Jose	CA	95112	Diosdado Banatao	408-467-0410	P	329	0.8
Endicott Interconnect Tech.	PO Box 658	Endicott	NY	13761			R	294*	1.7
Argon ST Inc.	12701 Fair Lks Cir.	Fairfax	VA	22033	Terry L. Collins	703-322-0881	P	282	1.0
Northrop Grumman Electronics	PO Box 9650	Melbourne	FL	32902	Allen Dosier	321-951-5000	R	280*	2.0
Raytheon Electronic Systems	PO Box 902	El Segundo	CA	90245	Jack Kelbe	310-647-0445	R	255*	1.6
Heraeus Electro-Nite Co.	1 Summit Sq.	Langhorne	PA	19047	Michael Midash	215-944-9000	R	246*	0.4
LaBarge Inc.	PO Box 14499	St. Louis	MO	63178		314-997-0800	P	235	1.2
Astronautics Corp. of America	PO Box 523	Milwaukee	WI	53201	Michael Russek	414-449-4000	R	233*	0.5
AAI Corp.	PO Box 126	Hunt Valley	MD	21030		410-666-1400	S	219*	1.8
Raven Industries Inc.	PO Box 5107	Sioux Falls	SD	57117	Conrad J. Hoigaard	605-336-2750	P	217	0.9
Sparton Corp.	2400 E Ganson St.	Jackson	MI	49202	D W. Hockenbrocht	517-787-8600	P	200	1.2
FlightSafety International	Marine Air Terminal	Flushing	NY	11371	A.L. Ueltschi	718-565-4100	D	200*	1.5
Garmin International Inc.	1200 E 151st St.	Olathe	KS	66062	Min Kao	913-397-8200	R	196*	1.0
Teledyne Brown Engineering	300 Sparkman NW	Huntsville	AL	35805	Rex D. Geveden	256-726-5555	S	187*	2.0
Lee Co.	PO Box 424	Westbrook	CT	06498		860-399-6281	R	183*	0.8
Aerostructures Corp.	1431 Vultee Blvd.	Nashville	TN	37217	Elmer Doty	615-361-2000	S	181*	1.4
Aerovironment Inc.	181 W Huntington	Monrovia	CA	91016	Tim Conver	626-357-9983	P	174	0.5
NGK Spark Plugs Inc.	46929 Magellan	Wixom	MI	48393	Chikanori Abe	248-926-6900	R	172*	0.2
Herley Industries Inc.	101 North Pnt Blvd	Lancaster	PA	17601	Lee N. Blatt	717-735-8117	P	163	0.9
Transistor Devices Inc.	36 Newburgh Rd.	Hackettstown	NJ	07840	Richard Blake	973-267-1900	R	151*	0.1
B.A. E Sys. Land & Armaments	PO Box 15512	York	PA	17405		717-225-8000	R	148*	0.8
CompuDyne Corp.	2530 Riva Rd., 201	Annapolis	MD	21401		410-224-4415	P	148	0.7
Ellanef Manufacturing Corp.	9711 50th Ave.	Corona	NY	11368	Murray Edwards	718-699-4000	R	131*	0.2
MCL Inc.	PO Box 3287	Chicago	IL	60678	Arthur Faverio	630-759-9500	R	122*	0.5
Meggitt-U.S.A. Inc.	1955 N Surveyor	Simi Valley	CA	93063	John Stobie	805-526-5700	S	120*	1.2
Lockheed Martin Tactical Def.	1210 Massillon Rd.	Akron	OH	44315	James W. Dunn	330-796-2800	S	116*	0.8
HR Textron Inc.	25200 Rye Cyn. Rd.	Santa Clarita	CA	91355	Richard Millman	661-294-6000	S	112*	0.9
Crane Aerospace & Electronics	3000 Winona Ave.	Burbank	CA	91504	Gregory Ward	818-526-2600	S	104*	0.6
International Transducer Corp.	869 Ward Dr.	Santa Barbara	CA	93111		805-683-2575	S	104*	0.5
Aim Aviation Inc.	PO Box 9011	Renton	WA	98057	Mark Potensky	425-235-2750	R	104*	0.1
Cubic Defense Systems Inc.	PO Box 85587	San Diego	CA	92186	Gerald Dinkel	858-277-6780	S	100*	0.9
Interstate Electronics Corp.	PO Box 3117	Anaheim	CA	92803	Robert Huffman	714-758-0500	S	90*	0.6
Audio International Inc.	7300 Industry Dr.	N Little Rock	AR	72117		501-955-2929	R	86*	0.1
Universal Avionics Systems	3260 E Universal	Tucson	AZ	85706	Joachim Naimer	520-295-2300	R	82*	0.6
ITT Gilfillan Inc.	PO Box 7713	Van Nuys	CA	91409		818-988-2600	D	81	0.5
Topcon Technologies Inc.	37 W Century Rd.	Paramus	NJ	07652	Scott Hokari	201-261-9450	R	80*	<0.1
Meggitt Safety Systems	1955 N Surveyor	Simi Valley	CA	93063		805-526-5700	S	69*	0.5
Hoya Corporation USA Inc.	101 Metro Dr.	San Jose	CA	95110	Gerry Bottero	408-441-3300	R	67*	<0.1
DRS Systems Inc.	5 Sylvan Way	Parsippany	NJ	07054	Mark S. Newman	973-898-6019	S	67*	0.3
EADS Sogerma Barfield Inc.	4101 NW 29th St.	Miami	FL	33142	Francois Amat	305-871-3900	S	62*	0.2
Ametek Drexelbrook	205 Keith Valley Rd	Horsham	PA	19044	Frank Hermance	215-674-1234	D	60*	0.2
Dayton-Granger Inc.	PO Box 350550	Fort Lauderdale	FL	33335	Gibbons Cline	954-768-0224	R	60*	0.3
System Planning Corp.	1000 Wilson Blvd.	Arlington	VA	22209	Ronald Easley	703-351-8200	R	57*	<0.1
Electro-Methods Inc.	PO Box 54	South Windsor	CT	06074	Randy Fries	860-289-8661	R	55*	0.2
First Defense International	24843 Del Prado 323	Dana Point	CA	92629		949-366-6444	R	53*	0.4
EADS Barfield Inc.	PO Box 25367	Miami	FL	33102	Frederic Denise	305-876-1678	S	52*	0.3
Herley-MPX Inc.	3061 Industry Dr.	Lancaster	PA	17603	Lee N. Blatt	717-397-2777	D	51*	0.3
Niles Precision Co.	PO Box 548	Niles	MI	49120	James Skalla	269-683-0585	R	48*	0.2
Avtech Corp.	3400 Wallingford	Seattle	WA	98103	Jack Decrane	206-695-8000	R	47*	0.3

Source: *Ward's Business Directory of U.S. Private and Public Companies*, Volumes 1 and 2, 2008. The company type code used is as follows: P - Public, R - Private, S - Subsidiary, D - Division, J - Joint Venture, A - Affiliate, G - Group. Sales are in millions of dollars, employees are in thousands. An asterisk (*) indicates an estimated sales volume. The symbol < stands for 'less than'. Company names and addresses are truncated, in some cases, to fit into the available space.

MATERIALS CONSUMED

Material	Quantity	Delivered Cost ($ million)
Printed ciruit boards (without inserted components) for electronic circuitry	(X)	229.4
Printed circuit assemblies, loaded boards, and modules	(X)	574.4
Semiconductors (incl. transistors, diodes, rectifiers, and integrated circuits), for electronic circuitry	(X)	504.6
Capacitors for electronic circuitry	(X)	67.8
Resistors for electronic circuitry	(X)	36.2
All other miscellaneous components and accessories for electronic circuitry (exc. tubes)	(X)	915.7
Electronic communication equipment	(X)	259.3
Electrical instrument mechanisms and meter movements	(X)	131.1
Electronic computer equipment	(X)	(D)
Purchased peripheral storage devices	(X)	6.1
Current-carrying wiring devices	(X)	119.9
Insulated wire and cable (including magnet wire)	(X)	61.0
Loudspeakers, microphones, and tuners (all types)	(X)	2.5
Fractional horsepower electric motors (less than 1 hp)	(X)	65.7
Plastics resins consumed in the form of granules, pellets, etc.	(X)	10.9
Fabricated plastics products (exc. gaskets, hoses, and belting)	(X)	25.9
Sheet metal products (excluding stampings)	(X)	424.2
Metal stampings	(X)	13.0
Metal bolts, nuts, screws, and other screw machine products	(X)	81.0
Other fabricated metal products (excluding forgings)	(X)	133.8
Forgings	(X)	16.2
Castings, rough and semifinished	(X)	49.5
Steel shapes and forms (exc. castings, forgings, fabr. metal products)	(X)	18.7
Aluminum and aluminum-base alloy shapes and forms (exc. castings, forgings, fabr. metal products)	(X)	27.8
Other nonferrous shapes and forms (exc. castings, forgings, fabricated metal products)	(X)	12.2
Paper and paperboard containers (incl. shipping sacks and other paper packaging supplies)	(X)	(D)
All other materials, components, parts, containers, and supplies	(X)	4,173.6
Materials, ingredients, containers, and supplies, nsk	(X)	623.5

Source: 2002 *Economic Census*. Explanation of symbols used: (D): Withheld to avoid disclosure of competitive data; na: Not available; (S): Withheld because statistical norms were not met; (X): Not applicable; (Z): Less than half the unit shown; nec: Not elsewhere classified; nsk: Not specified by kind; - : zero; p : 10-19 percent estimated; q : 20-29 percent estimated.

PRODUCT SHARE DETAILS

Product or Product Class Shipments	Mil. $	Product or Product Class Shipments	Mil. $
SEARCH, DETECTION, NAVIGATION, GUIDANCE, AERONAUTICAL, AND NAUTICAL SYSTEMS AND INSTRUMENTS	31,566.3	instruments	3,221.5
Aeronautical, nautical, and navigational instruments, not sending or receiving radio signals, except engine		Search, detection, navigation, and guidance systems and equipment	27,404.7
		Search, detection, navigation, guidance, aeronautical, and nautical systems and instruments, nsk, total	940.2

Source: 2002 *Economic Census*. The values are product shipments in millions of dollars for 2002. Total product shipments may be lower or higher than industry shipments. See Introduction for a full discussion. Values of indented subcategories are summed in the main heading(s). The symbol (D) appears when data are withheld to prevent disclosure of competitive information. The abbreviation nsk stands for 'not specified by kind' and nec for 'not elsewhere classified'. A dash (-) means zero.

INPUTS AND OUTPUTS FOR SEARCH, DETECTION, AND NAVIGATION INSTRUMENTS

Economic Sector or Industry Providing Inputs	%	Sector	Economic Sector or Industry Buying Outputs	%	Sector
Compensation of employees	38.8		Private fixed investment	33.7	
Management of companies & enterprises	12.6	Services	Federal government, investment, national defense	26.5	Fed Govt
Wholesale trade	4.1	Trade	General Federal government services, defense	13.9	Fed Govt
Scientific research & development services	3.5	Services	Aircraft	12.1	Manufg.
Semiconductors & related devices	3.4	Manufg.	Exports of goods & services	8.3	Cap Inv
Electronic components, nec	2.6	Manufg.	Federal government, investment, nondefense	1.8	Fed Govt
Software publishers	1.9	Services	Aircraft engine & engine parts	0.7	Manufg.
Lessors of nonfinancial assets	1.9	Fin/R.E.	General Federal government services, nondefense	0.7	Fed Govt
Printed circuit assemblies (electronic assembiles)	1.8	Manufg.	S/L govt. invest., other	0.5	S/L Govt
Electronic connectors	1.2	Manufg.	Aircraft parts & auxiliary equipment, nec	0.3	Manufg.
Ornamental & architectural metal products	1.1	Manufg.	Ship building & repairing	0.3	Manufg.
Other computer related services, including facilities	1.0	Services	Search, detection, & navigation instruments	0.3	Manufg.
Advertising & related services	0.9	Services	Guided missiles & space vehicles	0.2	Manufg.
Relay & industrial controls	0.9	Manufg.	Boat building	0.2	Manufg.
Custom computer programming services	0.8	Services			
Communication & energy wires & cables	0.8	Manufg.			
Data processing, hosting, & related services	0.8	Services			
Power generation & supply	0.7	Util.			
Specialized design services	0.7	Services			
Bare printed circuit boards	0.7	Manufg.			
Computer terminals & peripherals	0.6	Manufg.			
Legal services	0.6	Services			
Employment services	0.6	Services			

Continued on next page.

INPUTS AND OUTPUTS FOR SEARCH, DETECTION, AND NAVIGATION INSTRUMENTS - Continued

Economic Sector or Industry Providing Inputs	%	Sector	Economic Sector or Industry Buying Outputs	%	Sector
Electricity & signal testing instruments	0.6	Manufg.			
Architectural, engineering, & related services	0.6	Services			
Real estate	0.6	Fin/R.E.			
Business support services	0.5	Services			
Broadcast & wireless communications equipment	0.5	Manufg.			
Computer system design services	0.5	Services			
Wiring devices	0.4	Manufg.			
Warehousing & storage	0.4	Util.			
Turned products & screws, nuts, & bolts	0.4	Manufg.			
Truck transportation	0.4	Util.			
Securities, commodity contracts, investments	0.4	Fin/R.E.			
Watches, clocks, & related devices	0.4	Manufg.			
Electronic capacitors, resistors, coils, transformers	0.4	Manufg.			
Plastics products, nec	0.4	Manufg.			
Telecommunications	0.3	Services			
Electromedical & electrotherapeutic apparatus	0.3	Manufg.			
Support services, nec	0.3	Services			
Accounting, tax preparation, bookkeeping, & payroll	0.3	Services			
Automotive equipment rental & leasing	0.3	Fin/R.E.			
Search, detection, & navigation instruments	0.3	Manufg.			
Forging, stamping, & sintering, nec	0.3	Manufg.			
Monetary authorities/depository credit intermediation	0.3	Fin/R.E.			
Management, scientific, & technical consulting	0.3	Services			
Investigation & security services	0.3	Services			
Industrial process variable instruments	0.3	Manufg.			
Taxes on production & imports, less subsidies	0.3				
Coating, engraving, heat treating & allied activities	0.2	Manufg.			
Machine shops	0.2	Manufg.			
Speed changers, industrial high-speed drives, & gears	0.2	Manufg.			
Professional, scientific, technical services, nec	0.2	Services			
Food services & drinking places	0.2	Services			
Synthetic rubber	0.2	Manufg.			
Motors & generators	0.2	Manufg.			
Maintenance/repair of nonresidential structures	0.2	Construct.			
Nonferrous metal (ex. copper & aluminum) processing	0.2	Manufg.			
Paints & coatings	0.2	Manufg.			
Services to buildings & dwellings	0.2	Services			
Analytical laboratory instruments	0.2	Manufg.			
Electrical equipment & components, nec	0.2	Manufg.			
Natural gas distribution	0.2	Util.			
Commercial & industrial machinery rental & leasing	0.2	Fin/R.E.			
Motor vehicle parts	0.2	Manufg.			
Hotels & motels, including casino hotels	0.2	Services			
Air transportation	0.2	Util.			
Facilities support services	0.1	Services			
Automotive repair & maintenance, ex. car washes	0.1	Services			
Copper rolling, drawing, extruding, & alloying	0.1	Manufg.			

Source: Benchmark Input-Output Accounts for the U.S. Economy, 2002, U.S. Department of Commerce, Washington, D.C., January 2008. The abbreviation nec stands for 'not elsewhere classified'.

OCCUPATIONS EMPLOYED BY NAVIGATIONAL, MEASURING, MEDICAL, & CONTROL INSTRUMENTS

Occupation	% of Total 2006	Change to 2016	Occupation	% of Total 2006	Change to 2016
Electrical & electronic equipment assemblers	7.1	-23.4	First-line supervisors/managers of production workers	2.1	-4.3
Team assemblers	5.3	-4.3	Engineers, nec	1.9	-4.3
Electromechanical equipment assemblers	3.6	-4.3	Purchasing agents, exc wholesale, retail, & farm	1.9	-4.3
Electrical engineers	3.3	-4.3	Machinists	1.8	0.5
Computer software engineers, applications	2.9	14.9	General & operations managers	1.7	-13.8
Aerospace engineers	2.9	0.5	Sales representatives, wholesale & manufacturing, tech	1.6	-4.3
Mechanical engineers	2.8	-4.3	Executive secretaries & administrative assistants	1.5	-4.3
Electrical & electronic engineering technicians	2.7	-4.3	Customer service representatives	1.3	5.3
Computer software engineers, systems software	2.7	5.3	Office clerks, general	1.2	-5.7
Industrial engineers	2.5	16.3	Shipping, receiving, & traffic clerks	1.2	-7.9
Inspectors, testers, sorters, samplers, & weighers	2.4	-9.7	Accountants & auditors	1.2	-4.3
Engineering managers	2.4	-4.3	Production, planning, & expediting clerks	1.2	-4.3
Electronics engineers, exc computer	2.2	-4.3			

Source: Industry-Occupation Matrix, Bureau of Labor Statistics, December 4, 2007. These data are reported based on 4-digit NAICS categories but have been matched to corresponding 6-digit NAICS industry codes. The change reported for each occupation to the year 2016 is a percent of growth or decline as estimated by the Bureau of Labor Statistics. The abbreviation nec stands for 'not elsewhere classified'.

LOCATION BY STATE AND REGIONAL CONCENTRATION

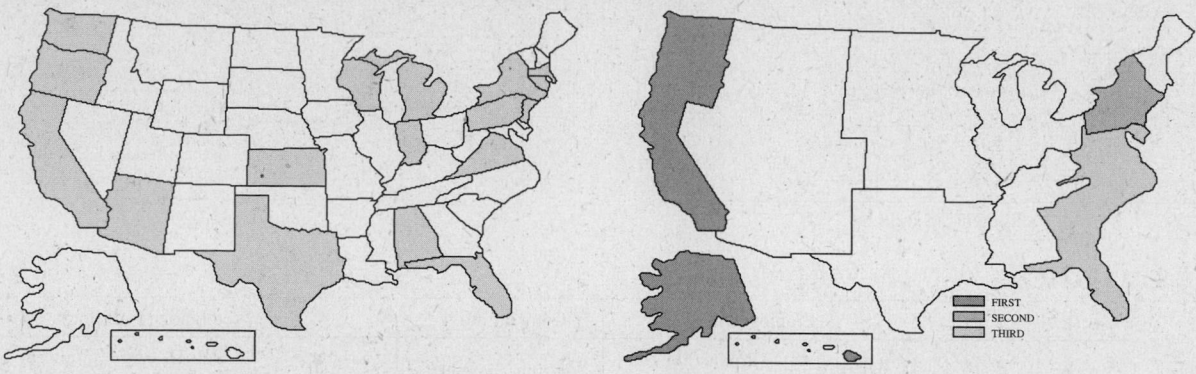

FIRST
SECOND
THIRD

INDUSTRY DATA BY STATE

| State | Establish-ments | Shipments | | | Employment | | | | Cost as % of Shipments | Investment per Employee ($) |
		Total ($ mil)	% of U.S.	Per Establ.	Total Number	% of U.S.	Per Establ.	Wages ($/hour)		
California	124	6,667.5	19.8	53,770.3	25,012	16.1	202	27.16	30.4	5,181
Florida	60	3,565.5	10.6	59,425.8	16,034	10.3	267	21.28	29.6	3,711
Massachusetts	43	3,225.8	9.6	75,019.6	11,853	7.6	276	25.32	31.8	4,954
Washington	22	2,176.4	6.5	98,925.3	15,848	10.2	720	23.02	16.4	3,136
New Jersey	32	2,019.0	6.0	63,095.2	8,929	5.7	279	35.09	38.4	5,819
Texas	47	1,963.3	5.8	41,771.6	10,883	7.0	232	30.24	37.7	5,485
Virginia	19	1,495.5	4.4	78,711.3	6,689	4.3	352	15.80	22.3	4,251
Arizona	22	1,358.9	4.0	61,770.1	4,870	3.1	221	22.03	33.0	7,100
New York	33	816.4	2.4	24,738.2	3,975	2.6	120	33.11	22.1	10,160
Kansas	13	733.9	2.2	56,454.9	2,372	1.5	182	17.74	52.0	5,702
Pennsylvania	26	409.0	1.2	15,730.0	2,217	1.4	85	18.39	48.3	8,696
Connecticut	16	376.1	1.1	23,508.3	2,592	1.7	162	23.91	41.9	2,880
Michigan	15	328.2	1.0	21,881.7	2,032	1.3	135	26.60	24.5	15,223
Oregon	10	151.7	0.5	15,170.9	629	0.4	63	17.60	37.4	5,800
Alabama	10	116.8	0.3	11,679.6	582	0.4	58	14.92	36.9	4,732
Indiana	6	70.7	0.2	11,789.0	348	0.2	58	13.86	46.9	1,247
Wisconsin	7	68.8	0.2	9,824.4	234	0.2	33	14.84	30.1	1,786

Source: 2002 *Economic Census*. The states are in descending order of shipments or establishments (if shipment data are missing for the majority). The symbol (D) appears when data are withheld to prevent disclosure of competitive information. States marked with (D) are sorted by number of establishments. A dash (-) indicates that the data element cannot be calculated. Data may not show all states active in the NAICS category. All data available at the time of publication are shown.

NAICS 334512 - AUTOMATIC ENVIRONMENTAL SYSTEMS

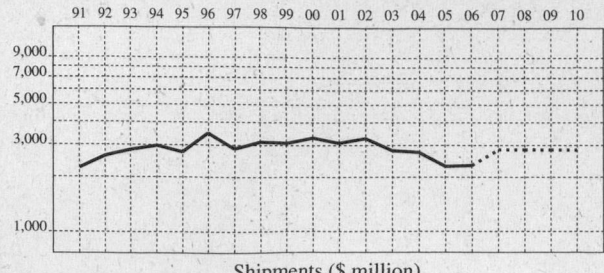

Shipments ($ million)

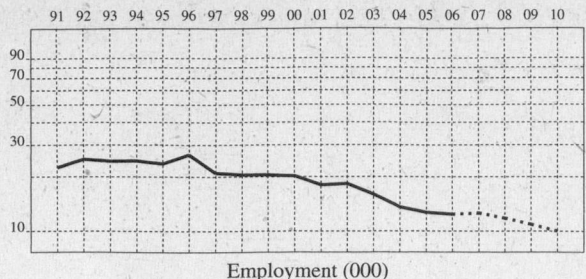

Employment (000)

GENERAL STATISTICS

Year	Com-panies	Establishments		Employment			Compensation		Production ($ million)			
		Total	with 20 or more employees	Total (000)	Production Workers (000)	Hours (Mil)	Payroll ($ mil)	Wages ($/hr)	Cost of Materials	Value Added by Manufacture	Value of Shipments	Capital Invest.
1991		258	118	22.5	14.9	27.7	615.2	11.29	892.4	1,297.7	2,243.7	56.0
1992	294	318	130	25.0	16.8	32.1	685.4	11.09	997.1	1,633.0	2,607.1	81.3
1993		329	144	24.4	17.2	33.2	697.0	11.29	1,069.2	1,732.9	2,812.9	87.6
1994		323	133	24.5	17.2	33.7	691.7	11.30	1,122.1	1,840.1	2,967.9	75.9
1995		316	134	23.6	16.3	32.7	675.2	11.29	1,097.7	1,626.7	2,738.9	93.0
1996		330	127	26.5	17.8	35.1	830.1	11.30	1,442.8	2,045.3	3,487.7	112.9
1997	293	314	120	21.0	14.6	29.3	651.2	12.45	1,174.2	1,667.1	2,860.6	115.0
1998		339	141	20.5	14.5	27.2	670.5	13.50	1,261.2	1,898.6	3,133.5	115.2
1999		331	125	20.5	13.7	28.4	697.6	12.94	1,173.4	1,880.9	3,089.5	85.9
2000		319	120	20.2	13.4	27.3	720.0	13.58	1,319.1	1,972.3	3,301.8	88.7
2001		329	115	18.0	11.8	23.7	646.2	13.51	1,299.1	1,789.0	3,091.1	86.0
2002	320	339	127	18.3	11.7	23.0	678.6	14.06	1,249.0	1,982.9	3,271.8	61.7
2003		338	110	16.0	10.3	21.4	583.9	13.40	1,120.4	1,661.1	2,806.7	49.6
2004		329	110	13.6	8.5	18.1	524.8	13.81	957.1	1,750.0	2,745.0	55.5
2005		310	106	12.7	8.0	16.3	537.0	15.27	887.4	1,410.2	2,293.9	57.9
2006		338P	111P	12.4	7.6	15.5	551.5	15.42	1,006.9	1,331.5	2,325.6	57.4
2007		340P	109P	12.6P	7.8P	16.6P	573.4P	15.30P	1,227.9P	1,623.7P	2,835.9P	63.3P
2008		342P	107P	11.8P	7.1P	15.4P	563.9P	15.58P	1,226.6P	1,622.0P	2,833.0P	61.3P
2009		344P	106P	10.9P	6.5P	14.3P	554.5P	15.87P	1,225.3P	1,620.3P	2,830.0P	59.4P
2010		346P	104P	10.0P	5.8P	13.1P	545.1P	16.16P	1,224.0P	1,618.6P	2,827.0P	57.4P

Sources: 1992, 1997, 2002 *Economic Census*; other years, up to 2006, are from the *Annual Survey of Manufactures*. Establishment counts for non-Census years are from *County Business Patterns*; 1997 and 2002 values are from the 1997 and 2002 censuses respectively, reported in the Federal Government's NAICS format. Other years were originally reported in equivalent SIC format. 'P's show projections by the editors.

INDICES OF CHANGE

Year	Com-panies	Establishments		Employment			Compensation		Production ($ million)			
		Total	with 20 or more employees	Total (000)	Production Workers (000)	Hours (Mil)	Payroll ($ mil)	Wages ($/hr)	Cost of Materials	Value Added by Manufacture	Value of Shipments	Capital Invest.
1992	92	94	102	137	144	140	101	79	80	82	80	132
1997	92	93	94	115	125	127	96	89	94	84	87	186
2001		97	91	98	101	103	95	96	104	90	94	139
2002	100	100	100	100	100	100	100	100	100	100	100	100
2003		100	87	87	88	93	86	95	90	84	86	80
2004		97	87	74	73	79	77	98	77	88	84	90
2005		91	83	69	68	71	79	109	71	71	70	94
2006		100P	87P	68	65	67	81	110	81	67	71	93
2007		100P	86P	69P	67P	72P	84P	109P	98P	82P	87P	103P
2008		101P	85P	64P	61P	67P	83P	111P	98P	82P	87P	99P
2009		101P	83P	60P	56P	62P	82P	113P	98P	82P	86P	96P
2010		102P	82P	55P	50P	57P	80P	115P	98P	82P	86P	93P

Sources: Same as General Statistics. Values reflect change from the base year, 2002. Values above 100 mean greater than 2002, values below 100 mean less than 2002, and the values of 100 in other years means the same as 2002. 'P's show projections by the editors.

SELECTED RATIOS

For 2002	Avg. of All Manufact.	Analyzed Industry	Index	For 2002	Avg. of All Manufact.	Analyzed Industry	Index
Employees per Establishment	42	54	129	Value Added per Production Worker	182,367	169,479	93
Payroll per Establishment	1,639,184	2,001,770	122	Cost per Establishment	5,769,015	3,684,366	64
Payroll per Employee	39,053	37,082	95	Cost per Employee	137,446	68,251	50
Production Workers per Establishment	30	35	117	Cost per Production Worker	195,506	106,752	55
Wages per Establishment	694,845	953,923	137	Shipments per Establishment	11,158,348	9,651,327	86
Wages per Production Worker	23,548	27,639	117	Shipments per Employee	265,847	178,787	67
Hours per Production Worker	1,980	1,966	99	Shipments per Production Worker	378,144	279,641	74
Wages per Hour	11.89	14.06	118	Investment per Establishment	361,338	182,006	50
Value Added per Establishment	5,381,325	5,849,263	109	Investment per Employee	8,609	3,372	39
Value Added per Employee	128,210	108,355	85	Investment per Production Worker	12,245	5,274	43

Sources: Same as General Statistics. The 'Average of All Manufacturing' column represents the average of all manufacturing industries reported for the most recent complete year available. The Index shows the relationship between the Average and the Analyzed Industry. For example, 100 means that they are equal; 500 that the Analyzed Industry is five times the average; 50 means that the Analyzed Industry is half the national average. The abbreviation 'na' is used to show that data are 'not available'. Ratios shown for 2002, the last complete census year.

LEADING COMPANIES   Number shown: **75**   Total sales ($ mil): **77,160**   Total employment (000): **318.6**

Company Name	Address				CEO Name	Phone	Co. Type	Sales ($ mil)	Empl. (000)
Johnson Controls Inc.	PO Box 591	Milwaukee	WI	53201		414-524-1200	P	34,624	140.0
L-3 Communications Holdings	600 3rd Ave.	New York	NY	10016		212-697-1111	P	13,961	63.7
Danaher Corp.	2099 Penn. Avenue	Washington	DC	20006	H. Lawrence Culp Jr.	202-828-0850	P	11,026	50.0
Culligan International Co.	1 Culligan Pkwy.	Northbrook	IL	60062	Mark Seals	847-205-6000	R	4,916*	5.5
Teleflex Inc.	155 S Limerick Rd.	Limerick	PA	19468	Jeffrey P. Black	610-948-5100	P	1,934	14.0
Donaldson Company Inc.	PO Box 1299	Minneapolis	MN	55440	William M. Cook	952-887-3131	P	1,919	12.0
Watsco Inc.	2665 S Bayshore Dr.	Coconut Grove	FL	33133		305-714-4100	P	1,758	3.3
Heico Holding Inc.	2626 Warrenville Rd	Downers Grove	IL	60515	Michael Heisley	630-353-5000	R	1,560*	<0.1
Steiner Corp.	PO Box 2317	Salt Lake City	UT	84110	Kevin Steiner	801-328-8831	R	855*	12.0
Siemens Building Technologies	1000 Deerfield Pkwy	Buffalo Grove	IL	60089	Daryl Dulaney	847-215-1000	R	583*	1.2
TAC L.L.C.	PO Box 2940	Loves Park	IL	61132	Enrique Santacana	815-637-3000	S	444*	0.5
TAC Americas Inc.	PO Box 951681	Dallas	TX	75395		972-323-1111	R	444*	0.4
Liebert Corp.	PO Box 29186	Columbus	OH	43229	Robert Bauer	614-888-0246	S	440*	5.0
Winona Watlow Inc.	PO Box 5580	Winona	MN	55987	Peter Desloge	507-454-5300	R	202*	0.3
Gold Line Controls Inc.	61 Whitecap Dr.	N Kingstown	RI	02852	Gilbert Conover	401-583-1100	R	200*	<0.1
Simpson Electric Co.	PO Box 99	Lac d Flambeau	WI	54538	Richard Schermetzler	715-588-3311	R	182*	0.1
NORESCO L.L.C.	One Research Dr.	Westborough	MA	01581	Neil Petchers	508-614-1000	S	160*	0.3
Taco Inc.	1160 Cranston St.	Cranston	RI	02920		401-942-8000	R	140*	0.4
Danfoss Inc.	7941 Corporate Dr.	Baltimore	MD	21236	Jorgen Clausen	410-931-8250	R	125*	0.1
KDC Systems/Dynalectric	4462 Corporate Ctr.	Los Alamitos	CA	90720	Chris Pesavento	714-828-7000	S	114*	0.5
Dwyer Instruments Inc.	PO Box 373	Michigan City	IN	46361	Stephen Clark	219-879-8868	R	69*	0.2
Avg Advanced Technologies L.P.	343 Saint Paul Blvd	Carol Stream	IL	60188		630-668-3900	R	65*	<0.1
Therm-O-Disc Inc.	1320 S Main St.	Mansfield	OH	44907	Peter Loconto	419-525-8500	S	61*	1.0
Evans Tempcon Inc.	701 Ann St. NW	Grand Rapids	MI	49504		616-361-2681	R	59*	0.4
Eclipse Inc.	1665 Elmwood Rd.	Rockford	IL	61103	Campbell Perks	815-877-3031	R	53*	<0.1
Nailer Industries	4714 Winfield Rd.	Houston	TX	77039	Mike Nailer	281-590-1172	R	50*	0.4
Omega Engineering Inc.	PO Box 4047	Stamford	CT	06906	Betty Ruth Hollander	203-359-1660	R	50*	0.4
INFICON Inc.	2 Technology Pl.	East Syracuse	NY	13057	Lukas Winkler	315-434-1100	S	48*	0.2
Siemens Building Technologies	8 Fernwood Rd.	Florham Park	NJ	07932		973-593-2600	S	48*	0.3
Mitsub. Heavy Ind Climate Ctrl	1200 N Mitsubishi	Franklin	IN	46131	Kiyonobu Toma	317-346-5000	R	41*	0.4
Beckwith Electric Company Inc.	6190-118th Ave. N	Largo	FL	33773	Bob Beckwith	727-544-2326	R	41*	0.1
Tech/Ops Sevcon Inc.	155 Northboro Rd.	Southborough	MA	01772	Matthew Boyle	508-281-5500	P	39	0.2
Standard-Thomson Corp.	PO Box 9109	Waltham	MA	02454		781-392-3508	S	36*	0.3
Forney Corp.	3405 Wiley Post Rd.	Carrollton	TX	75006	John Conroy	972-458-6100	S	36*	0.2
Electro-Mechanical Corp.	PO Box 8200	Bristol	VA	24203	Morris Arnold	276-466-8200	R	35*	0.1
Kimray Inc.	PO Box 18949	Oklahoma City	OK	73154	Garman Kimmell	405-525-6601	R	34*	0.2
Cox and Company Inc.	200 Varick St., 4	New York	NY	10014	Warren Achenbaum	212-366-0200	R	31*	0.2
Nailor Industries of Texas	4714 Winfield Rd.	Houston	TX	77039	Mike Nailor	281-590-1172	R	31*	0.2
PECO Manufacturing Company	PO Box 82189	Portland	OR	97282		503-233-6401	R	31*	0.3
Control Products Inc.	1724 Lake Dr. W	Chanhassen	MN	55317	Chris Berghoff	952-448-2217	R	31*	0.2
Portage Electric Products Inc.	PO Box 2170	Canton	OH	44720	Brandon Wehl	330-499-2727	R	30*	0.2
Leslie Controls Inc.	12501 Telecom Dr.	Tampa	FL	33637		813-978-1000	D	29*	0.2
Liquid Controls Corp.	105 Albrecht Dr.	Lake Bluff	IL	60044	Michael Schneider	847-295-1050	D	29*	0.2
Vibro-Meter Inc.	144 Harvey Rd.	Londonderry	NH	03053	Ronald Vadas	603-669-0940	R	28*	0.2
NovaTech L.L.C.	15541 W 110th St.	Shawnee Msn	KS	66219	Aubrey Zey	913-451-1880	R	28*	<0.1
Arens Controls Company L.L.C.	855 Commerce	Carpentersville	IL	60110		847-844-4700	R	25*	0.1
Channel Products Inc.	7100 Wilson Mills	Chesterland	OH	44026		440-423-0113	S	24*	0.1
Pyromation Inc.	5211 Industrial Rd.	Fort Wayne	IN	46825	Peter Wilson	260-484-2580	R	23*	0.1
Fast Heat Inc.	776 Oaklawn Ave.	Elmhurst	IL	60126	Tim Stojka	630-833-5400	R	23*	0.1
Chromalox Inc.	103 Gamma Dr. Ext.	Pittsburgh	PA	15238		412-967-3800	D	23*	<0.1
Pepperl Fuchs Inc.	1600 Enterprise Pky	Twinsburg	OH	44087		330-425-3555	R	23*	0.1
Naztec Inc.	PO Box 765	Sugar Land	TX	77487	Henry Beyer	281-240-7233	R	22*	<0.1
Ssac Inc.	PO Box 1000	Baldwinsville	NY	13027	Franck Chapeaux	315-638-1300	R	22*	0.1
Amot Controls Corp.	401 1st St.	Richmond	CA	94801		510-307-8300	S	21*	0.2
WahlcoMetroflex Inc.	29 Lexington St.	Lewiston	ME	04240		207-784-2338	R	21*	0.1
Hotwatt Inc.	128 Maple St.	Danvers	MA	01923	Robert Lee	978-777-0070	R	20*	0.1
ADA Environmental Solutions	8100 Southpark Way	Littleton	CO	80120	Michael D. Durham	303-734-1727	R	19	<0.1
Tork Inc.	1 Grove St.	Mount Vernon	NY	10550	Sam Shankar	914-664-3542	R	18*	0.1
Electro Industries Inc.	PO Box 538	Monticello	MN	55362		763-295-4138	R	18*	<0.1
Mixer Systems Inc.	PO Box 10	Pewaukee	WI	53072	William Boles	262-691-3100	R	17*	<0.1
Precision Speed Equipment Inc.	PO Box 7036	Sturgis	MI	49091	Robert Griffioen	269-651-4303	R	17*	0.1
Nexus Custom Electronics Inc.	PO Box 250	Brandon	VT	05733		802-247-6811	D	17*	0.1
Hansen Technologies Corp.	6827 High Grove	Burr Ridge	IL	60527	Jeff Nank	630-325-1565	S	17*	0.1
J and D Sales of Eau Claire	6200 US Hwy. 12	Eau Claire	WI	54701	Don Redetzke	715-834-1439	R	17*	<0.1
Food Automation - Service Tech	905 Honeyspot Rd.	Stratford	CT	06615	Bernard Koether	203-377-4414	R	16*	0.1
Nason Company Inc.	PO Box 505	West Union	SC	29696	Steve Mihaly	864-638-9521	R	15*	0.1
Phoenix Controls Corp.	75 Discovery Wy.	Acton	MA	01720	Bob Munro	978-795-3439	S	15*	0.1
Qualitrol Corp.	1385 Fairport Rd.	Fairport	NY	14450	Ron Meyr	585-586-1515	S	15*	0.1
ITT Industries Conoflow Div.	PO Box 768	St. George	SC	29477	Steven Loranger	843-563-9281	D	14*	<0.1
EWC Controls Inc.	385 Highway 33	Englishtown	NJ	07726	Chris Hiotis	732-446-3110	R	14*	0.1
Advantage Engineering Inc.	PO Box 407	Greenwood	IN	46142	Harold Short	317-887-0729	R	14*	<0.1
Elliott-Williams Company Inc.	3500 E 20th St.	Indianapolis	IN	46218	Michael Elliott	317-453-2295	R	13*	<0.1
Automation Components Inc.	2305 Pleasant View	Middleton	WI	53562	Troy Schwenn	608-831-2585	R	13*	<0.1
Norriseal	11122 W Little York	Houston	TX	77041	Jerry Sanderlin	713-466-3552	D	13*	<0.1
Dickson Co.	930 S Westwood	Addison	IL	60101	Michael Unger		R	13*	<0.1

Source: *Ward's Business Directory of U.S. Private and Public Companies*, Volumes 1 and 2, 2008. The company type code used is as follows: P - Public, R - Private, S - Subsidiary, D - Division, J - Joint Venture, A - Affiliate, G - Group. Sales are in millions of dollars, employees are in thousands. An asterisk (*) indicates an estimated sales volume. The symbol < stands for 'less than'. Company names and addresses are truncated, in some cases, to fit into the available space.

MATERIALS CONSUMED

Material	Quantity	Delivered Cost ($ million)
Printed ciruit boards (without inserted components) for electronic circuitry	(X)	25.6
Printed circuit assemblies, loaded boards, and modules	(X)	35.8
Semiconductors (incl. transistors, diodes, rectifiers, and integrated circuits), for electronic circuitry	(X)	52.7
Capacitors for electronic circuitry	(X)	11.1
Resistors for electronic circuitry	(X)	4.5
All other miscellaneous components and accessories for electronic circuitry (exc. tubes)	(X)	7.5
Current-carrying wiring devices	(X)	17.4
Electrical transmission, distribution, and control equipment	(X)	(D)
Electrical instrument mechanisms and meter movements	(X)	1.1
All other miscellaneous electrical measuring instruments and parts	(X)	10.7
Plastics resins consumed in the form of granules, pellets, etc.	(X)	18.8
Fabricated plastics products (exc. gaskets, hoses, and belting)	(X)	15.9
Sheet metal products (excluding stampings)	(X)	31.5
Metal stampings	(X)	25.5
Other fabricated metal products (exc. forgings, metal stampings, and sheet metal products)	(X)	8.9
Forgings	(X)	(D)
Castings, rough and semifinished	(X)	5.4
Metal shapes and forms (exc. castings, forgings, fabr. metal products)	(X)	3.0
Steel shapes and forms (exc. castings, forgings, fabr. metal products)	(X)	6.7
Aluminum and aluminum-base alloy shapes and forms (exc. castings, forgings, fabr. metal products)	(X)	4.1
Other nonferrous shapes and forms (exc. castings, forgings, fabricated metal products)	(X)	10.4
Copper and copper-base alloy shapes and forms (exc. castings, forgings, fabr. metal products)	(X)	(D)
Glass and glass products (excluding windows and mirrors)	(X)	0.9
Insulated wire and cable (including magnet wire)	(X)	15.1
Metal bolts, nuts, screws, and other screw machine products	(X)	14.2
Optical instruments and lenses (exc. sighting, tracking, and fire control)	(X)	2.7
Electronic communication equipment	(X)	(D)
Fractional horsepower electric motors (less than 1 hp)	(X)	1.8
Liquid crystal display screens (LCD), including LED	(X)	6.8
Paper and paperboard containers (incl. shipping sacks and other paper packaging supplies)	(X)	10.2
All other materials, components, parts, containers, and supplies	(X)	199.2
Materials, ingredients, containers, and supplies, nsk	(X)	341.2

Source: 2002 Economic Census. Explanation of symbols used: (D): Withheld to avoid disclosure of competitive data; na: Not available; (S): Withheld because statistical norms were not met; (X): Not applicable; (Z): Less than half the unit shown; nec: Not elsewhere classified; nsk: Not specified by kind; - : zero; p : 10-19 percent estimated; q : 20-29 percent estimated.

PRODUCT SHARE DETAILS

Product or Product Class Shipments	Mil. $	Product or Product Class Shipments	Mil. $
ENVIRONMENTAL CONTROLS. **Automatic environmental controls for monitoring residential**	2,827.7	**and commercial environments, and appliances**	2,827.7

Source: 2002 Economic Census. The values are product shipments in millions of dollars for 2002. Total product shipments may be lower or higher than industry shipments. See Introduction for a full discussion. Values of indented subcategories are summed in the main heading(s). The symbol (D) appears when data are withheld to prevent disclosure of competitive information. The abbreviation nsk stands for 'not specified by kind' and nec for 'not elsewhere classified'. A dash (-) means zero.

INPUTS AND OUTPUTS FOR AUTOMATIC ENVIRONMENTAL CONTROL MANUFACTURING

Economic Sector or Industry Providing Inputs	%	Sector	Economic Sector or Industry Buying Outputs	%	Sector
Compensation of employees	28.4		Residential structures, nec	15.9	Construct.
Management of companies & enterprises	11.3	Services	Nonresidential structures, nec	9.7	Construct.
Software publishers	3.8	Services	AC, refrigeration, and warm air heating equipment	9.4	Manufg.
Wholesale trade	3.7	Trade	Exports of goods & services	6.9	Cap Inv
Scientific research & development services	3.2	Services	Residential permanent site structures	6.5	Construct.
Semiconductors & related devices	2.7	Manufg.	Motor vehicle parts	6.1	Manufg.
Plastics products, nec	2.2	Manufg.	Wholesale trade	6.0	Trade
Printed circuit assemblies (electronic assemblies)	2.0	Manufg.	Commercial & health care structures	5.8	Construct.
Copper rolling, drawing, extruding, & alloying	1.9	Manufg.	Owner-occupied dwellings	4.2	
Crowns & closures & metal stamping	1.6	Manufg.	Major household appliances, nec	4.1	Manufg.
Ornamental & architectural metal products	1.5	Manufg.	Heating equipment (except warm air furnaces)	4.1	Manufg.
Bare printed circuit boards	1.3	Manufg.	Other S/L govt. enterprises	2.6	S/L Govt
Forging, stamping, & sintering, nec	1.3	Manufg.	Household cooking appliances	2.6	Manufg.
Electronic components, nec	1.1	Manufg.	Household laundry equipment	2.3	Manufg.
Wiring devices	1.0	Manufg.	Maintenance/repair of nonresidential structures	2.2	Construct.
Plastics materials & resins	0.9	Manufg.	Commercial & industrial equipment repair/maintenance	1.7	Services
Broadcast & wireless communications equipment	0.9	Manufg.	Household refrigerators & home freezers	1.3	Manufg.
Iron & steel mills & ferroalloys	0.8	Manufg.	Maintenance/repair of residential structures	1.3	Construct.
Electronic capacitors, resistors, coils, transformers	0.8	Manufg.	Small electrical applicances	1.1	Manufg.
Management, scientific, & technical consulting	0.8	Services	Legal services	1.1	Services
Turned products & screws, nuts, & bolts	0.8	Manufg.	Electronic & precision equipment repair/maintenance	0.8	Services
Lessors of nonfinancial assets	0.8	Fin/R.E.	Architectural, engineering, & related services	0.8	Services
Real estate	0.7	Fin/R.E.	Professional, scientific, technical services, nec	0.8	Services

Continued on next page.

INPUTS AND OUTPUTS FOR AUTOMATIC ENVIRONMENTAL CONTROL MANUFACTURING - Continued

Economic Sector or Industry Providing Inputs	%	Sector	Economic Sector or Industry Buying Outputs	%	Sector
Advertising & related services	0.7	Services	Accounting, tax preparation, bookkeeping, & payroll	0.5	Services
Custom computer programming services	0.7	Services	Computer system design services	0.3	Services
Power generation & supply	0.7	Util.	Search, detection, & navigation instruments	0.3	Manufg.
Electricity & signal testing instruments	0.6	Manufg.	Employment services	0.3	Services
Paperboard containers	0.5	Manufg.	Automatic environmental controls	0.2	Manufg.
Relay & industrial controls	0.5	Manufg.	Office administrative services	0.2	Services
Machine shops	0.5	Manufg.	Business support services	0.2	Services
Truck transportation	0.4	Util.	Management, scientific, & technical consulting	0.2	Services
Alumina refining & primary aluminum production	0.4	Manufg.	Waste management & remediation services	0.1	Services
Telecommunications	0.4	Services	General Federal government services, defense	0.1	Fed Govt
Architectural, engineering, & related services	0.3	Services			
Communication & energy wires & cables	0.3	Manufg.			
Warehousing & storage	0.3	Util.			
Aluminum products from purchased aluminum	0.3	Manufg.			
Monetary authorities/depository credit intermediation	0.3	Fin/R.E.			
Automotive equipment rental & leasing	0.3	Fin/R.E.			
Cutting tools & machine tool accessories	0.3	Manufg.			
Retail trade	0.3	Trade			
Automatic environmental controls	0.2	Manufg.			
Business support services	0.2	Services			
Taxes on production & imports, less subsidies	0.2				
Employment services	0.2	Services			
Coating, engraving, heat treating & allied activities	0.2	Manufg.			
Legal services	0.2	Services			
Maintenance/repair of nonresidential structures	0.2	Construct.			
Food services & drinking places	0.2	Services			
Accounting, tax preparation, bookkeeping, & payroll	0.2	Services			
Fabricated metals, nec	0.2	Manufg.			
Services to buildings & dwellings	0.2	Services			
Specialized design services	0.2	Services			
Data processing, hosting, & related services	0.2	Services			
Commercial & industrial machinery rental & leasing	0.2	Fin/R.E.			
Professional, scientific, technical services, nec	0.2	Services			
Ferrous metal foundries	0.1	Manufg.			
Hotels & motels, including casino hotels	0.1	Services			
Nonferrous metal foundries	0.1	Manufg.			
Motor vehicle parts	0.1	Manufg.			
Natural gas distribution	0.1	Util.			
Automotive repair & maintenance, ex. car washes	0.1	Services			
Air transportation	0.1	Util.			
Noncomparable imports	0.1	Foreign			
Other computer related services, including facilities	0.1	Services			
Paperboard mills	0.1	Manufg.			
Commercial & industrial equipment repair/maintenance	0.1	Services			
Chemical products & preparations, nec	0.1	Manufg.			

Source: Benchmark Input-Output Accounts for the U.S. Economy, 2002, U.S. Department of Commerce, Washington, D.C., January 2008. The abbreviation nec stands for 'not elsewhere classified'.

OCCUPATIONS EMPLOYED BY NAVIGATIONAL, MEASURING, MEDICAL, & CONTROL INSTRUMENTS

Occupation	% of Total 2006	Change to 2016	Occupation	% of Total 2006	Change to 2016
Electrical & electronic equipment assemblers	7.1	-23.4	First-line supervisors/managers of production workers	2.1	-4.3
Team assemblers	5.3	-4.3	Engineers, nec	1.9	-4.3
Electromechanical equipment assemblers	3.6	-4.3	Purchasing agents, exc wholesale, retail, & farm	1.9	-4.3
Electrical engineers	3.3	-4.3	Machinists	1.8	0.5
Computer software engineers, applications	2.9	14.9	General & operations managers	1.7	-13.8
Aerospace engineers	2.9	0.5	Sales representatives, wholesale & manufacturing, tech	1.6	-4.3
Mechanical engineers	2.8	-4.3	Executive secretaries & administrative assistants	1.5	-4.3
Electrical & electronic engineering technicians	2.7	-4.3	Customer service representatives	1.3	5.3
Computer software engineers, systems software	2.7	5.3	Office clerks, general	1.2	-5.7
Industrial engineers	2.5	16.3	Shipping, receiving, & traffic clerks	1.2	-7.9
Inspectors, testers, sorters, samplers, & weighers	2.4	-9.7	Accountants & auditors	1.2	-4.3
Engineering managers	2.4	-4.3	Production, planning, & expediting clerks	1.2	-4.3
Electronics engineers, exc computer	2.2	-4.3			

Source: Industry-Occupation Matrix, Bureau of Labor Statistics, December 4, 2007. These data are reported based on 4-digit NAICS categories but have been matched to corresponding 6-digit NAICS industry codes. The change reported for each occupation to the year 2016 is a percent of growth or decline as estimated by the Bureau of Labor Statistics. The abbreviation nec stands for 'not elsewhere classified'.

LOCATION BY STATE AND REGIONAL CONCENTRATION

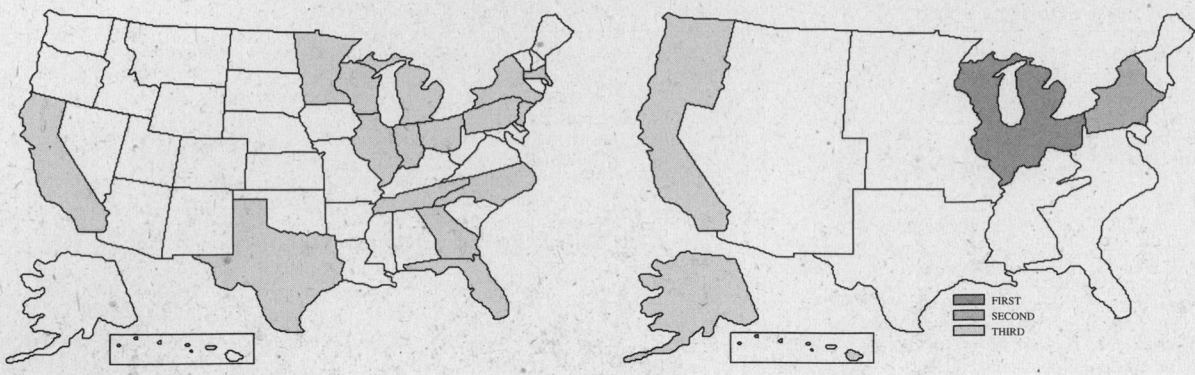

INDUSTRY DATA BY STATE

| State | Establish-ments | Shipments | | | Employment | | | | Cost as % of Shipments | Investment per Employee ($) |
		Total ($ mil)	% of U.S.	Per Establ.	Total Number	% of U.S.	Per Establ.	Wages ($/hour)		
California	47	518.5	15.8	11,031.2	1,476	8.1	31	15.45	43.5	6,974
Minnesota	13	447.5	13.7	34,426.2	1,916	10.5	147	22.82	19.3	2,269
Illinois	19	381.6	11.7	20,085.4	1,690	9.2	89	13.43	36.6	1,998
Ohio	21	305.4	9.3	14,543.0	2,909	15.9	139	11.76	35.7	2,562
Indiana	10	287.6	8.8	28,760.6	1,795	9.8	180	11.54	44.7	3,206
Tennessee	10	141.4	4.3	14,139.2	1,363	7.4	136	12.98	42.5	2,406
Massachusetts	8	116.1	3.5	14,514.5	482	2.6	60	12.86	44.6	10,635
Michigan	12	109.7	3.4	9,143.6	544	3.0	45	17.27	46.2	1,925
Georgia	8	102.3	3.1	12,787.0	379	2.1	47	13.22	36.0	5,668
Wisconsin	12	100.5	3.1	8,375.0	662	3.6	55	12.86	48.8	5,009
Texas	15	64.5	2.0	4,299.9	624	3.4	42	20.22	65.9	2,205
Pennsylvania	19	43.4	1.3	2,282.6	432	2.4	23	10.66	37.3	1,769
New Jersey	15	41.8	1.3	2,788.7	310	1.7	21	16.95	29.5	4,816
North Carolina	8	29.5	0.9	3,685.2	232	1.3	29	12.96	32.8	2,129
New York	14	28.0	0.9	2,002.0	209	1.1	15	13.10	36.6	2,708
Florida	14	17.2	0.5	1,230.1	137	0.7	10	14.76	36.0	1,964

Source: 2002 *Economic Census*. The states are in descending order of shipments or establishments (if shipment data are missing for the majority). The symbol (D) appears when data are withheld to prevent disclosure of competitive information. States marked with (D) are sorted by number of establishments. A dash (-) indicates that the data element cannot be calculated. Data may not show all states active in the NAICS category. All data available at the time of publication are shown.

NAICS 334513 - INSTRUMENTS FOR MEASURING PROCESS VARIABLES

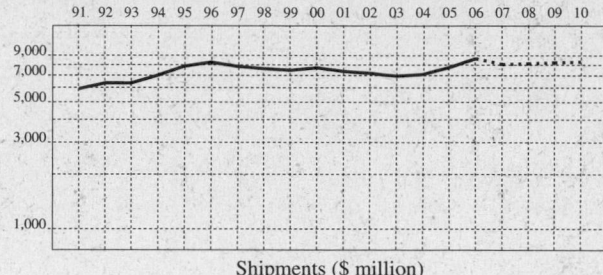

Shipments ($ million)

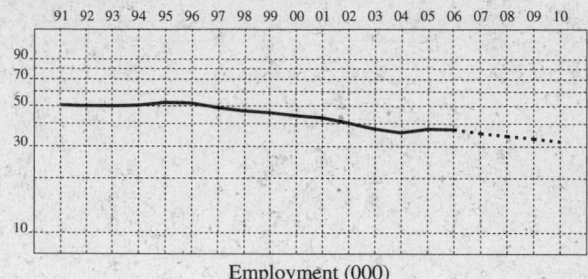

Employment (000)

GENERAL STATISTICS

Year	Companies	Establishments Total	Establishments with 20 or more employees	Employment Total (000)	Employment Production Workers (000)	Employment Hours (Mil)	Compensation Payroll ($ mil)	Compensation Wages ($/hr)	Production Cost of Materials	Production Value Added by Manufacture	Production Value of Shipments	Production Capital Invest.
1991		789	360	50.4	23.7	47.2	1,654.6	11.39	2,078.8	3,765.7	5,903.5	346.8
1992	817	885	358	50.1	24.0	47.3	1,764.8	12.32	2,137.7	4,182.9	6,360.4	158.1
1993		906	370	50.0	23.6	47.1	1,790.4	12.32	2,118.8	4,238.0	6,356.1	133.3
1994		908	378	50.4	24.3	50.5	1,876.8	12.31	2,446.7	4,568.6	7,012.1	226.9
1995		947	402	52.3	25.9	52.4	1,901.9	12.84	2,896.7	4,998.5	7,864.9	224.0
1996		1,040	402	51.8	24.6	49.6	1,974.7	13.01	3,109.1	5,171.2	8,270.9	231.1
1997	922	1,000	409	49.0	21.6	41.8	1,996.2	15.03	2,784.2	5,046.0	7,850.9	208.4
1998		1,025	404	47.0	22.0	42.7	2,014.0	16.16	2,858.6	4,761.8	7,621.2	305.7
1999		1,000	387	45.9	20.4	40.7	1,959.6	16.16	2,893.0	4,581.3	7,482.8	219.8
2000		968	366	44.2	19.6	39.1	1,945.7	16.71	2,948.0	4,801.6	7,715.5	174.8
2001		994	367	43.0	18.7	37.4	1,936.3	17.24	2,776.3	4,567.2	7,376.6	158.1
2002	905	986	359	40.3	18.5	36.4	1,845.1	17.12	2,727.0	4,418.8	7,204.9	171.9
2003		967	349	37.4	16.7	33.4	1,866.9	16.75	2,652.7	4,295.8	6,950.5	110.3
2004		1,004	339	35.7	16.2	33.5	1,859.7	17.81	2,810.9	4,299.1	7,110.4	132.8
2005		1,015	344	37.4	16.3	33.6	2,064.7	18.75	3,188.7	4,590.7	7,767.9	239.8
2006		1,045P	356P	37.2	17.5	35.3	2,109.5	17.99	3,349.4	5,361.7	8,670.0	174.9
2007		1,056P	354P	35.4P	15.5P	31.2P	2,042.6P	19.48P	3,117.1P	4,989.8P	8,068.7P	157.4P
2008		1,066P	351P	34.2P	14.8P	30.0P	2,058.1P	19.98P	3,150.0P	5,042.5P	8,153.8P	152.3P
2009		1,077P	349P	33.1P	14.2P	28.7P	2,073.7P	20.48P	3,182.9P	5,095.2P	8,239.0P	147.2P
2010		1,087P	347P	31.9P	13.5P	27.5P	2,089.3P	20.98P	3,215.8P	5,147.8P	8,324.1P	142.1P

Sources: 1992, 1997, 2002 *Economic Census*; other years, up to 2006, are from the *Annual Survey of Manufactures*. Establishment counts for non-Census years are from *County Business Patterns*; 1997 and 2002 values are from the 1997 and 2002 censuses respectively, reported in the Federal Government's NAICS format. Other years were originally reported in equivalent SIC format. 'P's show projections by the editors.

INDICES OF CHANGE

Year	Companies	Establishments Total	Establishments with 20 or more employees	Employment Total (000)	Employment Production Workers (000)	Employment Hours (Mil)	Compensation Payroll ($ mil)	Compensation Wages ($/hr)	Production Cost of Materials	Production Value Added by Manufacture	Production Value of Shipments	Production Capital Invest.
1992	90	90	100	124	130	130	96	72	78	95	88	92
1997	102	101	114	122	117	115	108	88	102	114	109	121
2001		101	102	107	101	103	105	101	102	103	102	92
2002	100	100	100	100	100	100	100	100	100	100	100	100
2003		98	97	93	90	92	101	98	97	97	96	64
2004		102	94	89	88	92	101	104	103	97	99	77
2005		103	96	93	88	92	112	110	117	104	108	139
2006		106P	99P	92	95	97	114	105	123	121	120	102
2007		107P	98P	88P	84P	86P	111P	114P	114P	113P	112P	92P
2008		108P	98P	85P	80P	82P	112P	117P	116P	114P	113P	89P
2009		109P	97P	82P	77P	79P	112P	120P	117P	115P	114P	86P
2010		110P	97P	79P	73P	76P	113P	123P	118P	116P	116P	83P

Sources: Same as General Statistics. Values reflect change from the base year, 2002. Values above 100 mean greater than 2002, values below 100 mean less than 2002, and the values of 100 in other years means the same as 2002. 'P's show projections by the editors.

SELECTED RATIOS

For 2002	Avg. of All Manufact.	Analyzed Industry	Index	For 2002	Avg. of All Manufact.	Analyzed Industry	Index
Employees per Establishment	42	41	97	Value Added per Production Worker	182,367	238,854	131
Payroll per Establishment	1,639,184	1,871,298	114	Cost per Establishment	5,769,015	2,765,720	48
Payroll per Employee	39,053	45,784	117	Cost per Employee	137,446	67,667	49
Production Workers per Establishment	30	19	64	Cost per Production Worker	195,506	147,405	75
Wages per Establishment	694,845	632,016	91	Shipments per Establishment	11,158,348	7,307,201	65
Wages per Production Worker	23,548	33,685	143	Shipments per Employee	265,847	178,782	67
Hours per Production Worker	1,980	1,968	99	Shipments per Production Worker	378,144	389,454	103
Wages per Hour	11.89	17.12	144	Investment per Establishment	361,338	174,341	48
Value Added per Establishment	5,381,325	4,481,542	83	Investment per Employee	8,609	4,266	50
Value Added per Employee	128,210	109,648	86	Investment per Production Worker	12,245	9,292	76

Sources: Same as General Statistics. The 'Average of All Manufacturing' column represents the average of all manufacturing industries reported for the most recent complete year available. The Index shows the relationship between the Average and the Analyzed Industry. For example, 100 means that they are equal; 500 that the Analyzed Industry is five times the average; 50 means that the Analyzed Industry is half the national average. The abbreviation 'na' is used to show that data are 'not available'. Ratios shown for 2002, the last complete census year.

LEADING COMPANIES Number shown: **75**   Total sales ($ mil): **59,195**   Total employment (000): **198.6**

Company Name	Address				CEO Name	Phone	Co. Type	Sales ($ mil)	Empl. (000)
L-3 Communications Holdings	600 3rd Ave.	New York	NY	10016		212-697-1111	P	13,961	63.7
Eastman Kodak Co.	343 State St.	Rochester	NY	14650		716-724-4000	P	10,301	26.9
Lexmark International Inc.	740 New Circle Rd.	Lexington	KY	40550	Paul J. Curlander	859-232-2000	P	4,974	13.8
KLA-Tencor Corp.	160 Rio Robles	San Jose	CA	95134	Edward W. Barnholt	408-875-3000	P	2,731	6.0
AMETEK Inc.	PO Box 1764	Paoli	PA	19301	Frank S. Hermance	610-647-2121	P	2,137	10.4
Roper Industries Inc.	6901 Professional	Sarasota	FL	34240		941-556-2601	P	2,102	7.1
Bombardier Transport. Holdings	1501 Lebanon Ch.	Pittsburgh	PA	15236	Raymond Betler	412-655-5700	R	2,037*	0.9
PerkinElmer Inc.	940 Winter St.	Waltham	MA	02451	Robert F. Friel	781-663-6900	P	1,787	8.7
Dresser-Rand Group Inc.	1200 W S Houston	Houston	TX	77043	Vince Volpe	713-467-2221	P	1,665	6.0
Rainin Instrument L.L.C.	PO Box 4026	Woburn	MA	01888	Kenneth Rainin	510-564-1600	R	1,590*	0.1
K and L Microwave Inc.	2250 Northwood Dr.	Salisbury	MD	21801	Darby Kruger	410-749-2424	S	1,339*	0.5
Esterline Technologies Corp.	500 108th Ave. NE	Bellevue	WA	98004	Robert W. Cremin	425-453-9400	P	1,267	8.2
Omron Healthcare Inc.	1200 Lakeside Dr.	Deerfield	IL	60015		847-680-6200	R	872*	0.1
Invensys Systems Inc.	15345 Barranca	Irvine	CA	92618		949-885-0700	R	850*	0.2
MKS Instruments Inc.	90 Industrial Way	Wilmington	MA	01887	Leo Berlinghieri	978-284-4000	P	783	3.0
Wesco Acquistion Partners Inc.	PO Box 924068	Houston	TX	77292	Ronnie Davis	713-688-5551	R	543*	<0.1
Aeroflex Inc.	PO Box 6022	Plainview	NY	11803	Harvey R. Blau	516-694-6700	R	537*	2.6
UOP L.L.C.	25 E Algonquin Rd.	Des Plaines	IL	60017	Carlos Guimaraes	847-391-2000	R	500*	4.0
TAC L.L.C.	PO Box 2940	Loves Park	IL	61132	Enrique Santacana	815-637-3000	S	444*	0.5
Liebert Corp.	PO Box 29186	Columbus	OH	43229	Robert Bauer	614-888-0246	S	440*	5.0
Sypris Solutions Inc.	101 Bullitt Ln.	Louisville	KY	40222	Jeffrey T. Gill	502-329-2000	P	436	2.1
Dionex Corp.	PO Box 3603	Sunnyvale	CA	94088	Lukas Braunschweiler	408-737-0700	P	327	1.1
BAE Systems Platform Solutions	600 Main St.	Johnson City	NY	13790	Michael Heffron	607-770-2000	D	294*	1.6
Veeder-Root Co.	PO Box 2003	Simsbury	CT	06070	Brian Burnett	860-651-2700	S	282*	0.6
BEI Technologies Inc.	1 Post St., 2500	San Francisco	CA	94104	Charles Crocker	805-552-3599	S	281	1.0
ABB Industrial Systems Inc.	579 Exec Campus	Westerville	OH	43082	Fred Kindle	614-818-6300	S	250*	1.5
Heraeus Electro-Nite Co.	1 Summit Sq.	Langhorne	PA	19047	Michael Midash	215-944-9000	R	246*	0.4
Cognex International Inc.	1 Vision Dr.	Natick	MA	01760	Robert J. Shillman	508-650-3000	S	238*	0.6
INFICON Holding AG	2 Technology Pl.	East Syracuse	NY	13057	Paul E. Otth	315-434-1100	P	237	0.7
Cognex Corp.	1 Vision Dr.	Natick	MA	01760	Jerald Fishman	508-650-3000	P	226	0.8
Smartronix Inc.	22685 Three Notch	California	MD	20619	M. Arshed Javaid	301-737-2800	R	221*	0.4
AAI Corp.	PO Box 126	Hunt Valley	MD	21030		410-666-1400	S	219*	1.8
Raven Industries Inc.	PO Box 5107	Sioux Falls	SD	57117	Conrad J. Hoigaard	605-336-2750	P	217	0.9
K-Tron International Inc.	PO Box 888	Pitman	NJ	08071	Edward B. Cloues II	856-589-0500	P	202	0.7
QED Environmental Systems Inc.	PO Box 3726	Ann Arbor	MI	48106	Michael Cross	734-995-2547	R	192*	<0.1
Real Time Laboratories L.L.C.	990 S Rogers Cir.	Boca Raton	FL	33487		561-988-8826	R	190*	<0.1
Hurco Companies Inc.	1 Technology Way	Indianapolis	IN	46268	Michael Doar	317-293-5309	P	188	0.4
Lee Co.	PO Box 424	Westbrook	CT	06498		860-399-6281	R	183*	0.8
Oerlikon USA Holding Inc.	615 Epsilon Dr.	Pittsburgh	PA	15238	James Brissenden	724-327-5700	R	172*	0.2
Emerson Control Techniques	12005 Technology	Eden Prairie	MN	55344	Paul Shuter	952-995-8000	S	171*	0.2
Barksdale Inc.	PO Box 58843	Los Angeles	CA	90058	Ian Dodd	323-589-6181	S	168*	0.2
Vishay Dale Electronics Inc.	1122 23rd St.	Columbus	NE	68601	Gerald Paul	402-564-3131	S	162*	0.5
Keithley Int'l Investment	28775 Aurora Rd.	Solon	OH	44139	Joseph Keithley	440-248-0400	S	155	0.7
LTX Corp.	825 University Ave.	Norwood	MA	02062	Roger W. Blethen	781-461-1000	P	148	0.5
Keithley Instruments Inc.	28775 Aurora Rd.	Solon	OH	44139		440-248-0400	P	144	0.7
OYO Geospace Corp.	7007 Pinemont Dr.	Houston	TX	77040	Gary D. Owens	713-986-4444	P	138	1.2
TSI Inc.	500 Cardigan Rd.	St. Paul	MN	55126	James Doubles	612-483-0900	R	133*	0.8
ENGlobal Construction Resource	3155 Executive Blvd	Beaumont	TX	77705	Jimmie N. Carpenter	409-840-2500	S	128*	0.3
A and B Process Systems Corp.	PO Box 86	Stratford	WI	54484	A J. Hilgemann	715-687-4332	R	128*	0.2
National Tank Co.	2950 N Loop W, 750	Houston	TX	77092	John Clarke	713-683-9292	S	125*	1.0
Meggitt-U.S.A. Inc.	1955 N Surveyor	Simi Valley	CA	93063	John Stobie	805-526-5700	S	120*	1.2
Fisher Pierce	54 Commercial St.	Raynham	MA	02767	H. Lawerence Culp, Jr	508-821-1579	S	117*	0.2
Bristol Babcock Inc.	1100 Buckingham	Watertown	CT	06795	John Kelly	860-945-2200	S	115*	0.3
Rudolph Technologies Inc.	PO Box 1000	Flanders	NJ	07836	Paul F. McLaughlin	973-691-1300	P	106	0.6
ITW Hobart Brothers Co.	101 Trade Sq. E	Troy	OH	45373		937-332-4000	S	102*	0.5
Howard Miller Clock Co.	860 E Main Ave.	Zeeland	MI	49464	Howard Miller	616-772-9131	R	98*	0.4
First Technology	228 NE Road	Standish	ME	04084	David MeMeo	248-353-6200	S	97*	1.2
Cleveland Motion Controls Inc.	7550 Hub Pkwy.	Cleveland	OH	44125	Wayne Foley	216-524-8800	S	95*	0.1
International Motion Control	369 Franklin St.	Buffalo	NY	14202	Patrick Lee	716-855-2500	R	95*	<0.1
Alstom Power Conversion	610 Epsilon Dr.	Pittsburgh	PA	15238	Torspen Astrom	412-967-0765	S	93*	0.2
Interstate Electronics Corp.	PO Box 3117	Anaheim	CA	92803	Robert Huffman	714-758-0500	S	90*	0.6
Phoenix International	1441 44th St. NW	Fargo	ND	58102			R	87*	0.2
Daniel Measurement and Control	PO Box 19097	Houston	TX	77224	Joe Vasvily	713-467-6000	S	79*	0.5
Wika Instrument Corp.	1000 Wiegand Blvd.	Lawrenceville	GA	30043	Alexander Wiegand	770-513-8200	R	79*	0.5
Lionheart Technologies Inc.	PO Box 998	Winooski	VT	05404	Norman Alpert	802-655-4040	R	78*	0.2
Sensidyne Inc.	16333 Bay Vista Dr.	Clearwater	FL	33760	Halvor Anderson	727-530-3602	R	76*	0.5
OI Analytical	PO Box 9010	College Station	TX	77842	Bruce Lancaster	979-690-1711	S	72*	0.2
Weldmation Inc.	31720 Stephenson	Madison Heights	MI	48071	Arthur Kelsey	248-585-0010	R	71*	0.4
Interstates Control Systems	PO Box 260	Sioux Center	IA	51250	Larry Herder	712-722-1663	R	70*	<0.1
Meggitt Safety Systems	1955 N Surveyor	Simi Valley	CA	93063		805-526-5700	S	69*	0.5
Dwyer Instruments Inc.	PO Box 373	Michigan City	IN	46361	Stephen Clark	219-879-8868	R	69*	0.2
ERC Parts Inc.	4001 Cobb Intl Blvd	Kennesaw	GA	30152	Charles Rollins	770-984-0276	R	66*	<0.1
K-Tron America Inc.	PO Box 888	Pitman	NJ	08071	Edward Cloues	856-589-0500	S	65*	0.5
YSI Inc.	1700 Brannum Ln.	Yellow Springs	OH	45387	Richard Omlor	937-767-7241	R	64*	0.1
Advanced Control Systems Inc.	PO Box 922548	Norcross	GA	30010	John Muench	770-446-8854	R	64*	<0.1

Source: Ward's Business Directory of U.S. Private and Public Companies, Volumes 1 and 2, 2008. The company type code used is as follows: P - Public, R - Private, S - Subsidiary, D - Division, J - Joint Venture, A - Affiliate, G - Group. Sales are in millions of dollars, employees are in thousands. An asterisk (*) indicates an estimated sales volume. The symbol < stands for 'less than'. Company names and addresses are truncated, in some cases, to fit into the available space.

MATERIALS CONSUMED

Material	Quantity	Delivered Cost ($ million)
Printed ciruit boards (without inserted components) for electronic circuitry	(X)	56.0
Printed circuit assemblies, loaded boards, and modules	(X)	126.1
Semiconductors (incl. transistors, diodes, rectifiers, and integrated circuits), for electronic circuitry	(X)	35.9
Capacitors for electronic circuitry	(X)	8.2
Resistors for electronic circuitry	(X)	(D)
All other miscellaneous components and accessories for electronic circuitry (exc. tubes)	(X)	(D)
Current-carrying wiring devices	(X)	25.9
Electrical transmission, distribution, and control equipment	(X)	54.9
Electronic computer equipment	(X)	34.7
Electrical instrument mechanisms and meter movements	(X)	23.7
All other miscellaneous electrical measuring instruments and parts	(X)	75.4
Plastics resins consumed in the form of granules, pellets, etc.	(X)	14.4
Fabricated plastics products (exc. gaskets, hoses, and belting)	(X)	28.8
Sheet metal products (excluding stampings)	(X)	41.5
Metal stampings	(X)	24.8
Other fabricated metal products (exc. forgings, metal stampings, and sheet metal products)	(X)	97.7
Forgings	(X)	10.3
Castings, rough and semifinished	(X)	58.0
Metal shapes and forms (exc. castings, forgings, fabr. metal products)	(X)	26.1
Steel shapes and forms (exc. castings, forgings, fabr. metal products)	(X)	65.1
Aluminum and aluminum-base alloy shapes and forms (exc. castings, forgings, fabr. metal products)	(X)	26.2
Other nonferrous shapes and forms (exc. castings, forgings, fabricated metal products)	(X)	5.5
Copper and copper-base alloy shapes and forms (exc. castings, forgings, fabr. metal products)	(X)	14.0
Glass and glass products (excluding windows and mirrors)	(X)	10.4
Insulated wire and cable (including magnet wire)	(X)	16.9
Metal bolts, nuts, screws, and other screw machine products	(X)	26.4
Optical instruments and lenses (exc. sighting, tracking, and fire control)	(X)	19.6
Electronic communication equipment	(X)	17.4
Fractional horsepower electric motors (less than 1 hp)	(X)	4.1
Liquid crystal display screens (LCD), including LED	(X)	24.7
Paper and paperboard containers (incl. shipping sacks and other paper packaging supplies)	(X)	18.5
All other materials, components, parts, containers, and supplies	(X)	379.6
Materials, ingredients, containers, and supplies, nsk	(X)	877.3

Source: 2002 *Economic Census*. Explanation of symbols used: (D): Withheld to avoid disclosure of competitive data; na: Not available; (S): Withheld because statistical norms were not met; (X): Not applicable; (Z): Less than half the unit shown; nec: Not elsewhere classified; nsk: Not specified by kind; - : zero; p : 10-19 percent estimated; q : 20-29 percent estimated.

PRODUCT SHARE DETAILS

Product or Product Class Shipments	Mil. $	Product or Product Class Shipments	Mil. $
PROCESS CONTROL INSTRUMENTS	6,965.3		

Source: 2002 *Economic Census*. The values are product shipments in millions of dollars for 2002. Total product shipments may be lower or higher than industry shipments. See Introduction for a full discussion. Values of indented subcategories are summed in the main heading(s). The symbol (D) appears when data are withheld to prevent disclosure of competitive information. The abbreviation nsk stands for 'not specified by kind' and nec for 'not elsewhere classified'. A dash (-) means zero.

INPUTS AND OUTPUTS FOR INDUSTRIAL PROCESS VARIABLE INSTRUMENTS MANUFACTURING

Economic Sector or Industry Providing Inputs	%	Sector	Economic Sector or Industry Buying Outputs	%	Sector
Compensation of employees	33.8		Exports of goods & services	39.8	Cap Inv
Management of companies & enterprises	9.3	Services	Private fixed investment	36.2	
Lessors of nonfinancial assets	4.2	Fin/R.E.	Basic inorganic chemicals, nec	5.3	Manufg.
Wholesale trade	3.9	Trade	S/L govt. invest., other	1.8	S/L Govt
Printed circuit assemblies (electronic assemblies)	3.2	Manufg.	Plastics products, nec	1.6	Manufg.
Software publishers	2.9	Services	S/L govt. invest., education	1.6	S/L Govt
Scientific research & development services	2.5	Services	Coating, engraving, heat treating & allied activities	1.3	Manufg.
Electricity & signal testing instruments	2.1	Manufg.	Retail trade	1.2	Trade
Electronic components, nec	1.9	Manufg.	Search, detection, & navigation instruments	0.8	Manufg.
Iron & steel mills & ferroalloys	1.9	Manufg.	Totalizing fluid meters & counting devices	0.8	Manufg.
Real estate	1.3	Fin/R.E.	Printing	0.8	Manufg.
Plastics products, nec	1.3	Manufg.	Semiconductors & related devices	0.8	Manufg.
Bare printed circuit boards	1.2	Manufg.	Industrial process variable instruments	0.6	Manufg.
Advertising & related services	1.2	Services	Federal government, investment, national defense	0.5	Fed Govt
Machine shops	0.9	Manufg.	Plastics materials & resins	0.5	Manufg.
Industrial process variable instruments	0.9	Manufg.	Personal services, nec	0.4	Services
Turned products & screws, nuts, & bolts	0.9	Manufg.	Other S/L govt. enterprises	0.4	S/L Govt
Securities, commodity contracts, investments	0.9	Fin/R.E.	Directories, mailing lists, & other publishers	0.4	Services
Custom computer programming services	0.9	Services	Waste management & remediation services	0.3	Services
Ornamental & architectural metal products	0.8	Manufg.	Fabricated metals, nec	0.3	Manufg.
Semiconductors & related devices	0.8	Manufg.	General S/L govt. services	0.3	S/L Govt
Alumina refining & primary aluminum production	0.7	Manufg.	Book publishers	0.2	Services
Telecommunications	0.7	Services	Business support services	0.2	Services

Continued on next page.

INPUTS AND OUTPUTS FOR INDUSTRIAL PROCESS VARIABLE INSTRUMENTS MANUFACTURING - Continued

Economic Sector or Industry Providing Inputs	%	Sector	Economic Sector or Industry Buying Outputs	%	Sector
Legal services	0.7	Services	Wholesale trade	0.2	Trade
Food services & drinking places	0.7	Services	Periodical publishers	0.2	Services
Ferrous metal foundries	0.7	Manufg.	Software publishers	0.2	Services
Crowns & closures & metal stamping	0.7	Manufg.	Industrial gases	0.2	Manufg.
Power generation & supply	0.6	Util.	Internet publishing & broadcasting	0.2	Services
Monetary authorities/depository credit intermediation	0.6	Fin/R.E.	Machine shops	0.2	Manufg.
Coating, engraving, heat treating & allied activities	0.6	Manufg.	Relay & industrial controls	0.1	Manufg.
Nonferrous metal foundries	0.6	Manufg.	Support services, nec	0.1	Services
Wiring devices	0.6	Manufg.	Automotive repair & maintenance, ex. car washes	0.1	Services
Hotels & motels, including casino hotels	0.6	Services	Basic organic chemicals, nec	0.1	Manufg.
Relay & industrial controls	0.6	Manufg.	Federal government, investment, nondefense	0.1	Fed Govt
Architectural, engineering, & related services	0.6	Services	Services to buildings & dwellings	0.1	Services
Copper rolling, drawing, extruding, & alloying	0.6	Manufg.	Internet service providers & web search portals	0.1	Services
Electronic capacitors, resistors, coils, transformers	0.6	Manufg.			
Data processing, hosting, & related services	0.5	Services			
Management, scientific, & technical consulting	0.5	Services			
Laminated plastics plates, sheets, & shapes	0.5	Manufg.			
Air transportation	0.4	Util.			
Computer terminals & peripherals	0.4	Manufg.			
Truck transportation	0.4	Util.			
Paperboard containers	0.4	Manufg.			
Professional, scientific, technical services, nec	0.4	Services			
Other computer related services, including facilities	0.4	Services			
Automotive equipment rental & leasing	0.4	Fin/R.E.			
Accounting, tax preparation, bookkeeping, & payroll	0.4	Services			
Noncomparable imports	0.3	Foreign			
Warehousing & storage	0.3	Util.			
Plastics materials & resins	0.3	Manufg.			
Taxes on production & imports, less subsidies	0.3				
Broadcast & wireless communications equipment	0.3	Manufg.			
Forging, stamping, & sintering, nec	0.3	Manufg.			
Fabricated metals, nec	0.2	Manufg.			
Valve & fittings other than plumbing	0.2	Manufg.			
Retail trade	0.2	Trade			
Services to buildings & dwellings	0.2	Services			
Commercial & industrial machinery rental & leasing	0.2	Fin/R.E.			
Cutting tools & machine tool accessories	0.2	Manufg.			
Aluminum products from purchased aluminum	0.2	Manufg.			
Maintenance/repair of nonresidential structures	0.2	Construct.			
Optical instruments & lenses	0.2	Manufg.			
Motor vehicle parts	0.2	Manufg.			
Transit & ground passenger transportation	0.2	Util.			
Communication & energy wires & cables	0.2	Manufg.			
Ball & roller bearings	0.2	Manufg.			
Computer system design services	0.1	Services			
Handtools	0.1	Manufg.			
Employment services	0.1	Services			
Automotive repair & maintenance, ex. car washes	0.1	Services			
Glass products from purchased glass	0.1	Manufg.			
Business support services	0.1	Services			
Natural gas distribution	0.1	Util.			
Nondepository credit intermediation activities	0.1	Fin/R.E.			

Source: *Benchmark Input-Output Accounts for the U.S. Economy, 2002*, U.S. Department of Commerce, Washington, D.C., January 2008. The abbreviation nec stands for 'not elsewhere classified'.

OCCUPATIONS EMPLOYED BY NAVIGATIONAL, MEASURING, MEDICAL, & CONTROL INSTRUMENTS

Occupation	% of Total 2006	Change to 2016	Occupation	% of Total 2006	Change to 2016
Electrical & electronic equipment assemblers	7.1	-23.4	First-line supervisors/managers of production workers	2.1	-4.3
Team assemblers	5.3	-4.3	Engineers, nec	1.9	-4.3
Electromechanical equipment assemblers	3.6	-4.3	Purchasing agents, exc wholesale, retail, & farm	1.9	-4.3
Electrical engineers	3.3	-4.3	Machinists	1.8	0.5
Computer software engineers, applications	2.9	14.9	General & operations managers	1.7	-13.8
Aerospace engineers	2.9	0.5	Sales representatives, wholesale & manufacturing, tech	1.6	-4.3
Mechanical engineers	2.8	-4.3	Executive secretaries & administrative assistants	1.5	-4.3
Electrical & electronic engineering technicians	2.7	-4.3	Customer service representatives	1.3	5.3
Computer software engineers, systems software	2.7	5.3	Office clerks, general	1.2	-5.7
Industrial engineers	2.5	16.3	Shipping, receiving, & traffic clerks	1.2	-7.9
Inspectors, testers, sorters, samplers, & weighers	2.4	-9.7	Accountants & auditors	1.2	-4.3
Engineering managers	2.4	-4.3	Production, planning, & expediting clerks	1.2	-4.3
Electronics engineers, exc computer	2.2	-4.3			

Source: *Industry-Occupation Matrix*, Bureau of Labor Statistics, December 4, 2007. These data are reported based on 4-digit NAICS categories but have been matched to corresponding 6-digit NAICS industry codes. The change reported for each occupation to the year 2016 is a percent of growth or decline as estimated by the Bureau of Labor Statistics. The abbreviation nec stands for 'not elsewhere classified'.

LOCATION BY STATE AND REGIONAL CONCENTRATION

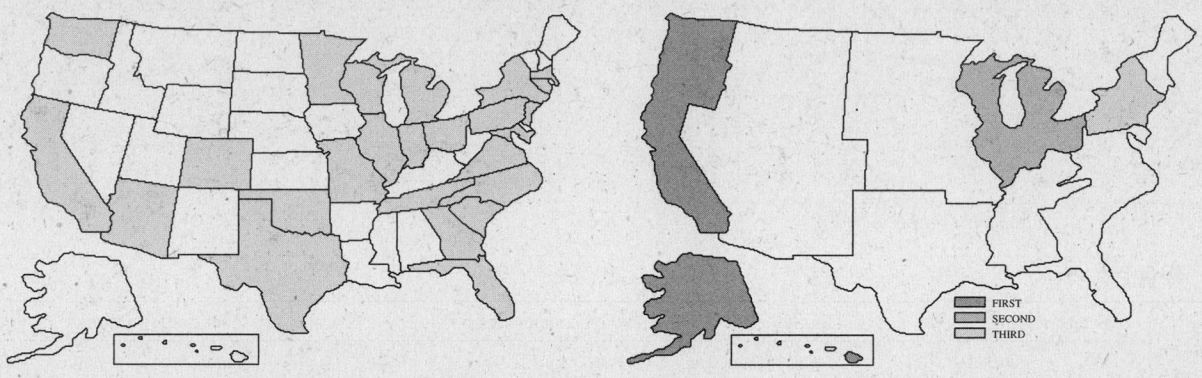

FIRST
SECOND
THIRD

INDUSTRY DATA BY STATE

State	Establish-ments	Shipments			Employment				Cost as % of Shipments	Investment per Employee ($)
		Total ($ mil)	% of U.S.	Per Establ.	Total Number	% of U.S.	Per Establ.	Wages ($/hour)		
California	172	923.3	12.8	5,368.3	5,255	13.0	31	18.05	34.9	6,356
Massachusetts	40	784.2	10.9	19,604.7	4,387	10.9	110	18.37	34.2	2,327
Pennsylvania	61	752.4	10.4	12,334.5	4,357	10.8	71	17.50	42.0	4,174
Texas	89	641.7	8.9	7,209.7	3,457	8.6	39	15.43	42.7	5,754
Ohio	56	508.8	7.1	9,086.0	2,913	7.2	52	18.86	32.4	4,034
Connecticut	40	415.2	5.8	10,378.8	2,343	5.8	59	18.20	42.2	2,662
Minnesota	30	396.8	5.5	13,227.8	2,223	5.5	74	21.62	32.3	7,641
Illinois	40	267.1	3.7	6,677.3	1,659	4.1	41	17.03	38.9	2,664
Georgia	21	238.5	3.3	11,357.0	1,202	3.0	57	13.07	48.9	4,133
New York	35	235.7	3.3	6,735.3	1,262	3.1	36	14.87	35.1	2,372
Colorado	24	225.3	3.1	9,385.5	977	2.4	41	18.08	26.3	8,382
Michigan	46	225.3	3.1	4,897.8	1,261	3.1	27	19.74	34.1	3,777
Arizona	14	175.6	2.4	12,541.7	442	1.1	32	17.97	60.3	3,337
New Jersey	34	142.6	2.0	4,194.6	766	1.9	23	20.94	34.3	11,678
Wisconsin	23	123.5	1.7	5,367.7	665	1.6	29	14.14	59.8	2,343
Oklahoma	10	122.8	1.7	12,279.1	828	2.1	83	16.64	61.7	2,475
Indiana	18	98.7	1.4	5,482.8	637	1.6	35	12.54	36.3	1,322
Missouri	15	88.3	1.2	5,883.5	564	1.4	38	15.00	38.7	1,894
Florida	24	87.5	1.2	3,647.6	553	1.4	23	14.47	38.5	3,311
Tennessee	13	84.5	1.2	6,501.1	645	1.6	50	14.82	39.4	1,735
Virginia	17	69.3	1.0	4,077.4	405	1.0	24	14.29	28.1	1,602
Maryland	10	27.9	0.4	2,785.1	188	0.5	19	14.90	33.2	1,872
Washington	16	27.5	0.4	1,719.9	179	0.4	11	16.25	37.3	3,469
South Carolina	6	24.3	0.3	4,053.8	132	0.3	22	14.19	32.2	3,258
North Carolina	21	23.7	0.3	1,128.8	211	0.5	10	12.89	35.8	2,076

Source: 2002 *Economic Census*. The states are in descending order of shipments or establishments (if shipment data are missing for the majority). The symbol (D) appears when data are withheld to prevent disclosure of competitive information. States marked with (D) are sorted by number of establishments. A dash (-) indicates that the data element cannot be calculated. Data may not show all states active in the NAICS category. All data available at the time of publication are shown.

NAICS 334514 - TOTALIZING FLUID METER AND COUNTING DEVICE MANUFACTURING

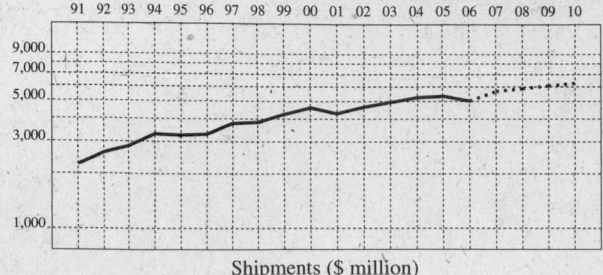

Shipments ($ million)

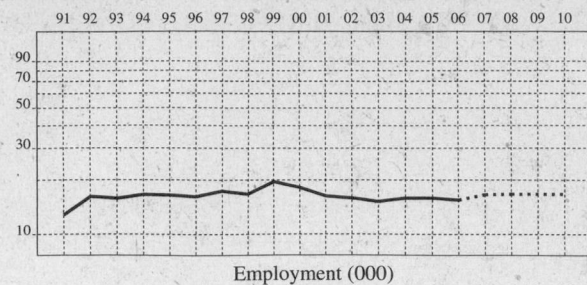

Employment (000)

GENERAL STATISTICS

Year	Companies	Establishments		Employment			Compensation		Production ($ million)			
		Total	with 20 or more employees	Total (000)	Production Workers (000)	Hours (Mil)	Payroll ($ mil)	Wages ($/hr)	Cost of Materials	Value Added by Manufacture	Value of Shipments	Capital Invest.
1991		164	63	12.8	8.3	16.3	388.2	13.13	986.9	1,260.1	2,246.8	81.8
1992	181	193	74	16.2	11.3	21.6	533.7	15.36	1,117.5	1,469.2	2,601.5	74.1
1993		197	78	15.8	10.7	22.0	554.1	15.55	1,333.3	1,486.3	2,823.8	76.1
1994		201	80	16.6	11.8	25.0	607.4	16.70	1,466.8	1,861.7	3,299.8	92.3
1995		200	86	16.5	12.0	23.9	627.6	18.18	1,501.9	1,716.6	3,255.7	93.7
1996		216	88	16.2	11.7	22.9	615.3	18.27	1,596.3	1,707.5	3,294.2	97.6
1997	211	223	100	17.4	12.1	23.8	684.4	17.62	1,771.6	2,000.0	3,773.3	116.8
1998		225	93	16.7	11.7	23.6	695.8	17.90	1,836.1	2,018.2	3,840.6	131.3
1999		212	90	19.6	11.9	25.1	937.1	19.93	2,183.2	2,051.2	4,248.2	128.1
2000		205	90	18.2	11.9	24.9	895.1	21.30	2,496.7	2,126.7	4,614.4	116.8
2001		203	91	16.3	10.4	20.2	730.7	19.79	2,299.6	1,996.6	4,292.8	75.6
2002	221	233	91	15.9	10.1	19.2	715.6	19.81	2,778.2	1,885.3	4,655.6	90.5
2003		249	97	15.2	9.1	17.7	667.9	19.02	2,743.0	2,142.7	4,934.7	70.3
2004		248	95	15.9	10.2	20.1	732.8	18.58	3,142.0	2,102.5	5,244.9	69.6
2005		260	101	15.9	9.9	19.9	773.1	18.19	3,152.1	2,185.9	5,334.3	124.1
2006		254P	103P	15.5	9.5	18.9	780.8	18.38	2,950.1	2,080.2	5,022.4	89.6
2007		259P	105P	16.6P	10.2P	20.2P	853.4P	20.50P	3,330.8P	2,348.7P	5,670.6P	100.0P
2008		264P	107P	16.7P	10.1P	20.0P	873.4P	20.80P	3,448.5P	2,431.6P	5,870.9P	100.6P
2009		269P	109P	16.7P	10.0P	19.9P	893.4P	21.10P	3,566.2P	2,514.6P	6,071.2P	101.1P
2010		274P	111P	16.7P	9.9P	19.7P	913.3P	21.40P	3,683.9P	2,597.6P	6,271.6P	101.6P

Sources: 1992, 1997, 2002 *Economic Census*; other years, up to 2006, are from the *Annual Survey of Manufactures*. Establishment counts for non-Census years are from *County Business Patterns*; 1997 and 2002 values are from the 1997 and 2002 censuses respectively, reported in the Federal Government's NAICS format. Other years were originally reported in equivalent SIC format. 'P's show projections by the editors.

INDICES OF CHANGE

Year	Companies	Establishments		Employment			Compensation		Production ($ million)			
		Total	with 20 or more employees	Total (000)	Production Workers (000)	Hours (Mil)	Payroll ($ mil)	Wages ($/hr)	Cost of Materials	Value Added by Manufacture	Value of Shipments	Capital Invest.
1992	82	83	81	102	112	113	75	78	40	78	56	82
1997	95	96	110	109	120	124	96	89	64	106	81	129
2001		87	100	103	103	105	102	100	83	106	92	84
2002	100	100	100	100	100	100	100	100	100	100	100	100
2003		107	107	96	90	92	93	96	99	114	106	78
2004		106	104	100	101	105	102	94	113	112	113	77
2005		112	111	100	98	104	108	92	113	116	115	137
2006		109P	113P	97	94	98	109	93	106	110	108	99
2007		111P	116P	104P	101P	105P	119P	103P	120P	125P	122P	110P
2008		113P	118P	105P	100P	104P	122P	105P	124P	129P	126P	111P
2009		115P	120P	105P	99P	104P	125P	107P	128P	133P	130P	112P
2010		118P	122P	105P	98P	103P	128P	108P	133P	138P	135P	112P

Sources: Same as General Statistics. Values reflect change from the base year, 2002. Values above 100 mean greater than 2002, values below 100 mean less than 2002, and the values of 100 in other years means the same as 2002. 'P's show projections by the editors.

SELECTED RATIOS

For 2002	Avg. of All Manufact.	Analyzed Industry	Index	For 2002	Avg. of All Manufact.	Analyzed Industry	Index
Employees per Establishment	42	68	163	Value Added per Production Worker	182,367	186,663	102
Payroll per Establishment	1,639,184	3,071,245	187	Cost per Establishment	5,769,015	11,923,605	207
Payroll per Employee	39,053	45,006	115	Cost per Employee	137,446	174,730	127
Production Workers per Establishment	30	43	147	Cost per Production Worker	195,506	275,069	141
Wages per Establishment	694,845	1,632,412	235	Shipments per Establishment	11,158,348	19,981,116	179
Wages per Production Worker	23,548	37,659	160	Shipments per Employee	265,847	292,805	110
Hours per Production Worker	1,980	1,901	96	Shipments per Production Worker	378,144	460,950	122
Wages per Hour	11.89	19.81	167	Investment per Establishment	361,338	388,412	107
Value Added per Establishment	5,381,325	8,091,416	150	Investment per Employee	8,609	5,692	66
Value Added per Employee	128,210	118,572	92	Investment per Production Worker	12,245	8,960	73

Sources: Same as General Statistics. The 'Average of All Manufacturing' column represents the average of all manufacturing industries reported for the most recent complete year available. The Index shows the relationship between the Average and the Analyzed Industry. For example, 100 means that they are equal; 500 that the Analyzed Industry is five times the average; 50 means that the Analyzed Industry is half the national average. The abbreviation 'na' is used to show that data are 'not available'. Ratios shown for 2002, the last complete census year.

LEADING COMPANIES Number shown: **75**   Total sales ($ mil): **17,838**   Total employment (000): **63.0**

Company Name	Address				CEO Name	Phone	Co. Type	Sales ($ mil)	Empl. (000)
Danaher Corp.	2099 Penn. Avenue	Washington	DC	20006	H. Lawrence Culp Jr.	202-828-0850	P	11,026	50.0
Danaher Industrial Controls	1675 Delany Rd.	Gurnee	IL	60031	Larry Culp	847-662-2666	S	3,567*	2.4
Elster Amco Water Inc.	PO Box 1852	Ocala	FL	34478	James Gardiner	352-732-4670	R	585*	0.2
Sensus Precision Die Casting	232 Hopkinsville Rd	Russellville	KY	42276	Stephen C. Larkin	270-726-0235	S	456*	0.3
Yokogawa Industrial Automation	2 Dart Rd.	Newnan	GA	30265	Kiyoshi Makino	770-254-0400	R	244*	0.7
Badger Meter Inc.	PO Box 245036	Milwaukee	WI	53224		414-355-0400	P	235	1.1
TSI Inc.	500 Cardigan Rd.	St. Paul	MN	55126	James Doubles	612-483-0900	R	133*	0.8
Mid-South Electronics Inc.	2600 E Meighan	Gadsden	AL	35903	Harold Weaver	256-492-8997	R	111*	0.4
Curtis Instruments Inc.	200 Kisco Ave.	Mount Kisco	NY	10549		914-666-2971	R	100*	0.2
Daniel Measurement and Control	PO Box 19097	Houston	TX	77224	Joe Vasvily	713-467-6000	S	79*	0.5
Delta Scientific Corp.	40355 Delta Ln.	Palmdale	CA	93551	Harry D. Dickinson	661-575-1100	R	69*	0.3
Avg Advanced Technologies L.P.	343 Saint Paul Blvd	Carol Stream	IL	60188		630-668-3900	R	65*	<0.1
ARC-Tronics Inc.	1150 Pagni Dr.	Elk Grove Vlg	IL	60007	Conrad Goeringer	847-437-0211	R	59*	0.3
Thomas G Faria Corp.	PO Box 983	Uncasville	CT	06382	David Blackburn	860-848-9271	R	57*	0.3
Great Plains Industries Inc.	PO Box 8901	Wichita	KS	67208	Grant Nutter	316-686-7361	R	54*	0.3
HACH Ultra Analytics	481 California Ave.	Grants Pass	OR	97526	Simon Appleby		S	54*	0.2
Designatronics Inc.	PO Box 5416	New Hyde Park	NY	11042		516-328-3300	R	51*	0.3
Actaris US Gas Inc.	970 Hwy. 127 N	Owenton	KY	40359	Bill Shepard	502-484-5747	R	43*	0.2
Auto Meter Products Inc.	413 W Elm St.	Sycamore	IL	60178	Jeff King	815-895-8141	R	43*	0.2
Thermo Electron, Process Instr	9303 W S Houston	Houston	TX	77099		713-272-0404	D	33*	0.3
Pemberton Fabricators Inc.	PO Box 227	Rancocas	NJ	08073	Robert Murnan	609-267-0922	R	32*	<0.1
Ludlum Measurements Inc.	PO Box 810	Sweetwater	TX	79556	Donald Ludlum	325-235-5494	R	30*	0.3
Creative Apparel Associates	PO Box 208	Belfast	ME	04915		207-342-5830	R	30*	<0.1
Liquid Controls Corp.	105 Albrecht Dr.	Lake Bluff	IL	60044	Michael Schneider	847-295-1050	D	29*	0.2
Thermo Polysonics Inc.	1410 Gillingham	Sugar Land	TX	77478	Marijn E. Dekkers	713-272-0404	S	28*	<0.1
Fluid Components International	1755 La Costa Mdw.	San Marcos	CA	92078	Daniel McQueen	760-744-6950	R	25*	0.2
Actaris Liquid Measurement	1310 Emerald Rd.	Greenwood	SC	29646	Chuck Strawn	864-223-1212	R	25*	0.1
Precipart Corp.	90 Finn Ct.	Farmingdale	NY	11735	Lloyd Miller	631-694-3100	R	23*	0.1
Duncan Parking Technologies	PO Box 849	Harrison	AR	72602	Mike Nickolaus	870-741-5481	R	22*	0.1
ENM Company Inc.	5617 N NW Hwy.	Chicago	IL	60646	Nicholas Polydoris	773-775-8400	R	22*	0.1
Schenck Accurate Inc.	PO Box 208	Whitewater	WI	53190	Gregory Fream	262-473-2441	R	21*	0.1
GE Reuter-Stokes Inc.	8499 Darrow Rd.	Twinsburg	OH	44087		330-425-3755	S	21*	0.2
Acteras US Liquid Measurement	1310 Emerald Rd.	Greenwood	SC	29646		864-223-1212	D	21*	0.1
Mectrol Corp.	20 Northwestern Dr.	Salem	NH	03079	Klaus Faber	603-685-0404	R	20*	<0.1
Peek Traffic Inc.	2511 Corporate Way	Palmetto	FL	34221	Leslie Jezuit	941-366-8770	S	19*	0.1
Sentry Equipment Corp.	PO Box 127	Oconomowoc	WI	53066	Mike Farrell	262-567-7256	R	19*	<0.1
Tri-Continent Scientific Inc.	12555 Loma Rica	Grass Valley	CA	95945	Brenton Hanlon	530-273-8389	R	18*	<0.1
POM Inc.	PO Box 430	Russellville	AR	72811	Seth Ward	479-968-2880	R	17*	<0.1
Sonin Inc.	15105-D John J. Del	Charlotte	NC	28277	Chris Tufo	704-540-9000	R	17*	<0.1
Gurley Precision Instruments	514 Fulton St.	Troy	NY	12180	Patrick Brady	518-272-6300	R	16*	0.1
DCI Inc.	846 N Mart-Way Ct.	Olathe	KS	66061	Karl Gemperli	913-982-5672	S	15*	0.1
Lake Shore Cryotronics Inc.	575 McCorkle Blvd.	Westerville	OH	43082		614-891-2243	R	15*	0.1
Dieterich Standard Inc.	PO Box 9000	Boulder	CO	80301		303-530-9600	S	14*	0.1
Blue-White Industries Ltd.	5300 Business Dr.	Huntington Bch	CA	92649	Robert Gledhill	714-893-8529	R	14*	<0.1
Sparling Instruments Inc.	4097 Temple City	El Monte	CA	91731	Steve Kim	626-444-0571	R	14*	<0.1
Minks Engineering Inc.	2700 Partin Sttlmnt	Kissimmee	FL	34744	Floyd Minks	407-847-4200	R	13*	<0.1
Monarch International Inc.	15 Columbia Dr.	Amherst	NH	03031	Kenneth Grabeau	603-883-3390	R	13*	<0.1
Spartanics Ltd.	3605 Edison Pl.	Rolling Mdws	IL	60008	Thomas Kleeman	847-394-5700	R	11*	<0.1
Royal Design and Manufacturing	32401 Stephenson	Madison Heights	MI	48071	Rodney Paulick	248-588-0110	R	11*	<0.1
Mindrum Precision Products	10000 4th St.	R Cucamonga	CA	91730	Diane Mindrum	909-989-1728	R	11*	<0.1
Teledyne Electr. Tech Hastings	PO Box 1436	Hampton	VA	23661		757-723-6531	D	10*	0.1
Commercial Electric Products	1738 E 30th St.	Cleveland	OH	44114	Robert Meyer	216-241-2886	R	10*	<0.1
Redington Counters Inc.	PO Box 608	Windsor	CT	06095	William Little	860-688-6205	R	10*	<0.1
AmTote International Inc.	11200 Pepper Rd.	Hunt Valley	MD	21031	Steve Keech	410-771-8700	R	10*	<0.1
Wavecrest Corp.	7610 Executive Dr.	Eden Prairie	MN	55344		952-831-0030	R	10*	<0.1
7-SIGMA Inc.	2843 26th Ave. S	Minneapolis	MN	55406	Kristian Wyrobek	612-722-5358	R	9*	<0.1
Magnetic Instrumentation Inc.	8431 Castlewood Dr.	Indianapolis	IN	46250	G. Bradley	317-842-7500	R	9*	<0.1
Torrington Research Co.	PO Box 536	Torrington	CT	06790	Roger Dickinson	860-489-0489	R	9*	<0.1
ERDCO Engineering Corp.	PO Box 6318	Evanston	IL	60204	Bruce Nesvig	847-328-0550	R	8*	<0.1
Melland Gear and Instrument	225 Engineers Rd.	Hauppauge	NY	11788	Richard Coronato	631-234-0100	R	8*	<0.1
Techno Inc.	PO Box 5416	New Hyde Park	NY	11042	George Klein	516-328-3970	S	8*	<0.1
FloScan Instrument Company	3016 NE Blakeley St	Seattle	WA	98105	Charles Wurster	206-524-6625	R	7*	<0.1
Management Systems Inc.	2629 Redwing Rd.	Fort Collins	CO	80527	Mitchell Gross	970-223-1530	R	7*	<0.1
World Wide Plastics Inc.	250 Andrews Rd.	Trevose	PA	19053	Donald Frick	215-357-0893	R	7*	<0.1
Master Meter Inc.	101 Regency Pkwy.	Mansfield	TX	76063	Jerry Potter	817-842-8000	R	7*	<0.1
LFG and e International Inc.	PO Box 430	Alpine	CA	91903	Ronald Brookshire	619-593-3690	R	7*	<0.1
Bidwell Industrial Group Inc.	2055 S Main St.	Middletown	CT	06457	Donald Bidwell	860-346-9283	R	6*	<0.1
Midwest Computer Register	PO Box 376	Hampton	IA	50441	Maurice Vosburg	641-456-4847	R	6*	<0.1
Parkeon Inc.	40 Twosome Dr., 7	Moorestown	NJ	08057	Yves Chambeau	856-234-8000	R	6*	<0.1
Roxar Inc.	14701 St. Marys Ln.	Houston	TX	77079	Sandy Esselmont	713-482-6400	R	6*	<0.1
SRI Connector Gage Company	751 N Dr. Ste. 12	Melbourne	FL	32934	James Twombly	321-259-9688	R	6*	<0.1
Waukee Engineering Company	5600 W Florist Ave.	Milwaukee	WI	53218	Andreas Melville	414-462-8200	R	6*	<0.1
Kelley Instrument Machine Inc.	PO Box 5368	Texarkana	TX	75505	William Kelley	903-832-3332	R	6*	<0.1
HF Scientific Inc.	3170 Metro Pky.	Fort Myers	FL	33916	Patrick O'Keefe	239-337-2116	S	6*	<0.1
Delmhorst Instrument Co.	51 Indian Ln. E	Towaco	NJ	07082	Aristide Laurenzi	973-334-2557	R	6*	<0.1

Source: Ward's Business Directory of U.S. Private and Public Companies, Volumes 1 and 2, 2008. The company type code used is as follows: P - Public, R - Private, S - Subsidiary, D - Division, J - Joint Venture, A - Affiliate, G - Group. Sales are in millions of dollars, employees are in thousands. An asterisk (*) indicates an estimated sales volume. The symbol < stands for 'less than'. Company names and addresses are truncated, in some cases, to fit into the available space.

MATERIALS CONSUMED

Material	Quantity	Delivered Cost ($ million)
Printed ciruit boards (without inserted components) for electronic circuitry	(X)	80.1
Printed circuit assemblies, loaded boards, and modules	(X)	83.1
Semiconductors (incl. transistors, diodes, rectifiers, and integrated circuits), for electronic circuitry	(X)	79.4
Capacitors for electronic circuitry	(X)	7.8
Resistors for electronic circuitry	(X)	5.7
All other miscellaneous components and accessories for electronic circuitry (exc. tubes)	(X)	57.7
Current-carrying wiring devices	(X)	6.3
Electrical transmission, distribution, and control equipment	(X)	26.1
Electrical instrument mechanisms and meter movements	(X)	28.0
All other miscellaneous electrical measuring instruments and parts	(X)	13.5
Plastics resins consumed in the form of granules, pellets, etc.	(X)	18.3
Fabricated plastics products (exc. gaskets, hoses, and belting)	(X)	63.2
Sheet metal products (excluding stampings)	(X)	13.0
Metal stampings	(X)	8.5
Other fabricated metal products (exc. forgings, metal stampings, and sheet metal products)	(X)	14.7
Forgings	(X)	(D)
Castings, rough and semifinished	(X)	56.8
Metal shapes and forms (exc. castings, forgings, fabr. metal products)	(X)	11.7
Steel shapes and forms (exc. castings, forgings, fabr. metal products)	(X)	5.8
Aluminum and aluminum-base alloy shapes and forms (exc. castings, forgings, fabr. metal products)	(X)	2.3
Other nonferrous shapes and forms (exc. castings, forgings, fabricated metal products)	(X)	1.6
Copper and copper-base alloy shapes and forms (exc. castings, forgings, fabr. metal products)	(X)	(D)
Glass and glass products (excluding windows and mirrors)	(X)	1.4
Insulated wire and cable (including magnet wire)	(X)	6.4
Metal bolts, nuts, screws, and other screw machine products	(X)	14.2
Optical instruments and lenses (exc. sighting, tracking, and fire control)	(X)	(D)
Electronic communication equipment	(X)	5.9
Fractional horsepower electric motors (less than 1 hp)	(X)	1.5
Liquid crystal display screens (LCD), including LED	(X)	3.3
Paper and paperboard containers (incl. shipping sacks and other paper packaging supplies)	(X)	5.0
All other materials, components, parts, containers, and supplies	(X)	496.1
Materials, ingredients, containers, and supplies, nsk	(X)	1,524.7

Source: 2002 *Economic Census*. Explanation of symbols used: (D): Withheld to avoid disclosure of competitive data; na: Not available; (S): Withheld because statistical norms were not met; (X): Not applicable; (Z): Less than half the unit shown; nec: Not elsewhere classified; nsk: Not specified by kind; - : zero; p : 10-19 percent estimated; q : 20-29 percent estimated.

PRODUCT SHARE DETAILS

Product or Product Class Shipments	Mil. $	Product or Product Class Shipments	Mil. $
TOTALIZING FLUID METERS AND COUNTING DEVICES	4,901.2	**Counting devices, excluding motor vehicle instruments**	**466.3**
		Motor vehicle instruments	2,919.8
Integrating and totalizing meters for gas and liquids	**1,359.2**	**Totalizing fluid meters and counting devices, nsk, total**	**155.9**

Source: 2002 *Economic Census*. The values are product shipments in millions of dollars for 2002. Total product shipments may be lower or higher than industry shipments. See Introduction for a full discussion. Values of indented subcategories are summed in the main heading(s). The symbol (D) appears when data are withheld to prevent disclosure of competitive information. The abbreviation nsk stands for 'not specified by kind' and nec for 'not elsewhere classified'. A dash (-) means zero.

INPUTS AND OUTPUTS FOR TOTALIZING FLUID METERS & COUNTING DEVICES

Economic Sector or Industry Providing Inputs	%	Sector	Economic Sector or Industry Buying Outputs	%	Sector
Compensation of employees	20.5		Light truck & utility vehicles	29.6	Manufg.
Software publishers	13.6	Services	Private fixed investment	22.0	
Management of companies & enterprises	7.1	Services	Automobiles	10.0	Manufg.
Wholesale trade	5.7	Trade	Other S/L govt. enterprises	9.5	S/L Govt
Plastics products, nec	4.9	Manufg.	Exports of goods & services	5.1	Cap Inv
Printed circuit assemblies (electronic assemblies)	4.8	Manufg.	S/L govt. invest., other	3.6	S/L Govt
Bare printed circuit boards	4.4	Manufg.	Basic organic chemicals, nec	3.5	Manufg.
Semiconductors & related devices	4.3	Manufg.	S/L govt. passenger transit	2.3	S/L Govt
Electronic components, nec	3.2	Manufg.	Food services & drinking places	1.9	Services
Electricity & signal testing instruments	2.2	Manufg.	Retail trade	1.7	Trade
Scientific research & development services	2.0	Services	Water, sewage and other systems	1.2	Util.
Industrial process variable instruments	1.7	Manufg.	Heavy duty trucks	0.9	Manufg.
Ferrous metal foundries	1.7	Manufg.	Natural gas distribution	0.9	Util.
Nonferrous metal foundries	1.5	Manufg.	Plastics materials & resins	0.8	Manufg.
Lessors of nonfinancial assets	1.2	Fin/R.E.	Telecommunications	0.7	Services
Retail trade	1.2	Trade	S/L govt. invest., education	0.7	S/L Govt
Plastics materials & resins	1.0	Manufg.	Waste management & remediation services	0.7	Services
Iron & steel mills & ferroalloys	0.9	Manufg.	Nursing & residential care facilities	0.6	Services
Turned products & screws, nuts, & bolts	0.9	Manufg.	Wholesale trade	0.6	Trade
Electronic capacitors, resistors, coils, transformers	0.8	Manufg.	General Federal government services, nondefense	0.4	Fed Govt
Ornamental & architectural metal products	0.6	Manufg.	Scientific research & development services	0.4	Services

Continued on next page.

INPUTS AND OUTPUTS FOR TOTALIZING FLUID METERS & COUNTING DEVICES - Continued

Economic Sector or Industry Providing Inputs	%	Sector	Economic Sector or Industry Buying Outputs	%	Sector
Machine shops	0.6	Manufg.	Power generation & supply	0.4	Util.
Crowns & closures & metal stamping	0.6	Manufg.	Community food, housing, relief, & rehabilitation	0.3	Services
Copper rolling, drawing, extruding, & alloying	0.6	Manufg.	Industrial gases	0.3	Manufg.
Real estate	0.6	Fin/R.E.	Automotive repair & maintenance, ex. car washes	0.2	Services
Truck transportation	0.5	Util.	Totalizing fluid meters & counting devices	0.2	Manufg.
Relay & industrial controls	0.4	Manufg.	Residential structures, nec	0.2	Construct.
Advertising & related services	0.4	Services	Architectural, engineering, & related services	0.2	Services
Power generation & supply	0.4	Util.	Residential permanent site structures	0.2	Construct.
Wiring devices	0.4	Manufg.	Hospitals	0.1	Services
Telecommunications	0.4	Services			
Custom computer programming services	0.4	Services			
Forging, stamping, & sintering, nec	0.3	Manufg.			
Plastics packaging materials, film & sheet	0.3	Manufg.			
Coating, engraving, heat treating & allied activities	0.3	Manufg.			
Taxes on production & imports, less subsidies	0.3				
Specialized design services	0.3	Services			
Cutting tools & machine tool accessories	0.3	Manufg.			
Legal services	0.3	Services			
Architectural, engineering, & related services	0.3	Services			
Paperboard containers	0.3	Manufg.			
Employment services	0.3	Services			
Totalizing fluid meters & counting devices	0.3	Manufg.			
Alumina refining & primary aluminum production	0.2	Manufg.			
Broadcast & wireless communications equipment	0.2	Manufg.			
Fabricated metals, nec	0.2	Manufg.			
Business support services	0.2	Services			
Securities, commodity contracts, investments	0.2	Fin/R.E.			
Warehousing & storage	0.2	Util.			
Monetary authorities/depository credit intermediation	0.2	Fin/R.E.			
Automotive equipment rental & leasing	0.2	Fin/R.E.			
Aluminum products from purchased aluminum	0.1	Manufg.			
Communication & energy wires & cables	0.1	Manufg.			
Accounting, tax preparation, bookkeeping, & payroll	0.1	Services			
Support services, nec	0.1	Services			
Air transportation	0.1	Util.			
Paperboard mills	0.1	Manufg.			
Data processing, hosting, & related services	0.1	Services			
Professional, scientific, technical services, nec	0.1	Services			
Investigation & security services	0.1	Services			
Chemical products & preparations, nec	0.1	Manufg.			
Natural gas distribution	0.1	Util.			
Other computer related services, including facilities	0.1	Services			
Food services & drinking places	0.1	Services			

Source: Benchmark Input-Output Accounts for the U.S. Economy, 2002, U.S. Department of Commerce, Washington, D.C., January 2008. The abbreviation nec stands for 'not elsewhere classified'.

OCCUPATIONS EMPLOYED BY NAVIGATIONAL, MEASURING, MEDICAL, & CONTROL INSTRUMENTS

Occupation	% of Total 2006	Change to 2016	Occupation	% of Total 2006	Change to 2016
Electrical & electronic equipment assemblers	7.1	-23.4	First-line supervisors/managers of production workers	2.1	-4.3
Team assemblers	5.3	-4.3	Engineers, nec	1.9	-4.3
Electromechanical equipment assemblers	3.6	-4.3	Purchasing agents, exc wholesale, retail, & farm	1.9	-4.3
Electrical engineers	3.3	-4.3	Machinists	1.8	0.5
Computer software engineers, applications	2.9	14.9	General & operations managers	1.7	-13.8
Aerospace engineers	2.9	0.5	Sales representatives, wholesale & manufacturing, tech	1.6	-4.3
Mechanical engineers	2.8	-4.3	Executive secretaries & administrative assistants	1.5	-4.3
Electrical & electronic engineering technicians	2.7	-4.3	Customer service representatives	1.3	5.3
Computer software engineers, systems software	2.7	5.3	Office clerks, general	1.2	-5.7
Industrial engineers	2.5	16.3	Shipping, receiving, & traffic clerks	1.2	-7.9
Inspectors, testers, sorters, samplers, & weighers	2.4	-9.7	Accountants & auditors	1.2	-4.3
Engineering managers	2.4	-4.3	Production, planning, & expediting clerks	1.2	-4.3
Electronics engineers, exc computer	2.2	-4.3			

Source: Industry-Occupation Matrix, Bureau of Labor Statistics, December 4, 2007. These data are reported based on 4-digit NAICS categories but have been matched to corresponding 6-digit NAICS industry codes. The change reported for each occupation to the year 2016 is a percent of growth or decline as estimated by the Bureau of Labor Statistics. The abbreviation nec stands for 'not elsewhere classified'.

LOCATION BY STATE AND REGIONAL CONCENTRATION

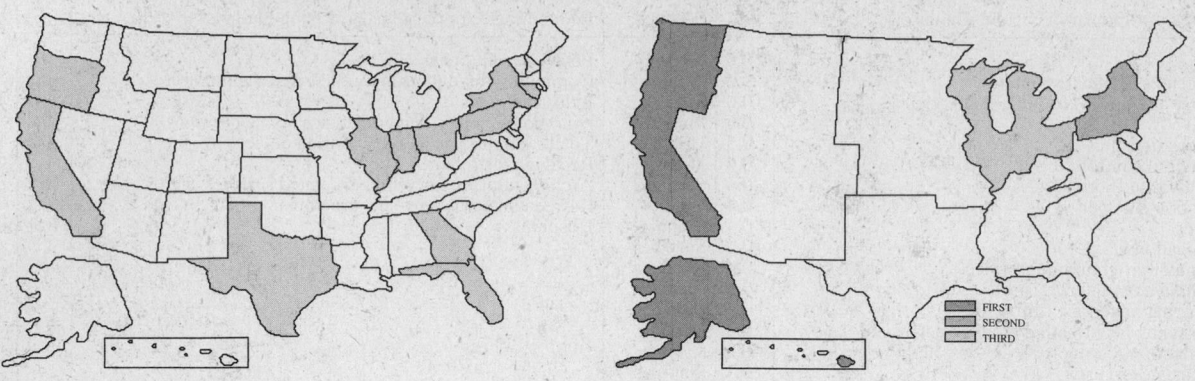

INDUSTRY DATA BY STATE

State	Establish-ments	Shipments			Employment				Cost as % of Shipments	Investment per Employee ($)
		Total ($ mil)	% of U.S.	Per Establ.	Total Number	% of U.S.	Per Establ.	Wages ($/hour)		
Pennsylvania	21	443.9	9.5	21,136.3	1,624	10.2	77	18.86	58.5	8,977
Ohio	13	204.5	4.4	15,730.5	732	4.6	56	12.49	80.5	11,301
California	34	172.7	3.7	5,078.7	1,300	8.2	38	21.56	47.8	2,660
Illinois	13	135.3	2.9	10,405.8	609	3.8	47	17.07	40.7	3,663
Georgia	8	102.0	2.2	12,744.2	564	3.5	71	14.57	50.3	3,222
Texas	17	96.2	2.1	5,657.0	492	3.1	29	20.90	44.1	4,392
Florida	8	83.7	1.8	10,464.4	319	2.0	40	17.41	58.3	11,097
New York	15	53.7	1.2	3,577.6	275	1.7	18	23.18	58.8	2,549
Indiana	5	35.7	0.8	7,137.2	307	1.9	61	17.47	47.4	3,143
Connecticut	10	30.1	0.6	3,005.5	244	1.5	24	15.39	45.8	2,131
Oregon	5	29.3	0.6	5,852.4	303	1.9	61	15.77	52.8	1,548

Source: 2002 *Economic Census*. The states are in descending order of shipments or establishments (if shipment data are missing for the majority). The symbol (D) appears when data are withheld to prevent disclosure of competitive information. States marked with (D) are sorted by number of establishments. A dash (-) indicates that the data element cannot be calculated. Data may not show all states active in the NAICS category. All data available at the time of publication are shown.

NAICS 334515 - INSTRUMENT MANUFACTURING FOR MEASURING AND TESTING ELECTRICITY AND ELECTRICAL SIGNALS

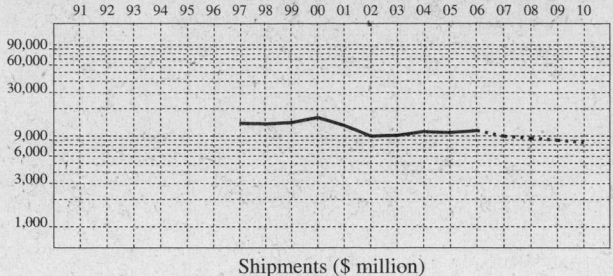

Shipments ($ million)

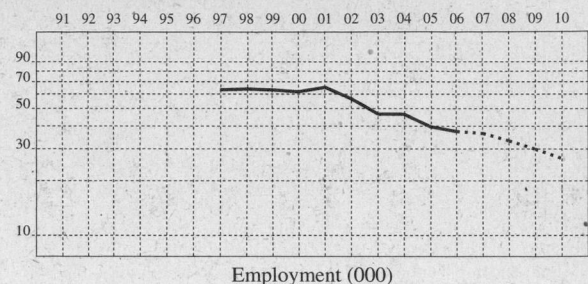

Employment (000)

GENERAL STATISTICS

Year	Com-panies	Establishments		Employment			Compensation		Production ($ million)			
		Total	with 20 or more employees	Total (000)	Production Workers (000)	Hours (Mil)	Payroll ($ mil)	Wages ($/hr)	Cost of Materials	Value Added by Manufacture	Value of Shipments	Capital Invest.
1997	759	825	366	63.3	29.5	60.8	3,000.8	16.91	5,122.6	8,831.5	13,849.7	667.6
1998		838	360	64.0	28.7	59.5	3,222.9	17.66	4,772.8	8,755.0	13,610.1	647.6
1999		824	359	63.2	27.0	51.8	3,143.8	18.64	5,161.0	9,010.4	14,079.6	662.8
2000		791	354	61.8	25.8	51.1	3,421.8	18.94	5,821.2	10,346.8	16,002.8	794.6
2001		769	346	65.4	24.3	47.1	3,607.0	20.39	4,880.7	8,236.5	13,110.0	1,115.9
2002	728	791	294	56.6	19.3	38.3	3,280.9	21.01	3,721.6	6,053.9	9,977.8	467.6
2003		807	307	46.7	16.2	28.5	3,134.3	21.74	3,472.7	6,612.2	10,130.2	503.0
2004		795	316	46.6	14.4	28.8	3,197.9	21.63	3,542.6	7,565.0	11,175.2	406.2
2005		796	298	39.7	14.1	28.9	3,045.1	22.49	3,753.0	7,294.7	10,920.7	627.8
2006		781P	286P	37.4	12.7	26.3	3,099.1	22.78	4,298.6	7,283.4	11,444.3	499.2
2007		776P	277P	36.5P	9.5P	18.2P	3,172.8P	23.91P	3,720.5P	6,303.9P	9,905.2P	490.6P
2008		772P	267P	33.2P	7.4P	13.9P	3,165.0P	24.58P	3,548.1P	6,011.7P	9,446.1P	463.5P
2009		767P	258P	29.9P	5.3P	9.6P	3,157.3P	25.25P	3,375.6P	5,719.5P	8,987.0P	436.5P
2010		762P	248P	26.6P	3.2P	5.2P	3,149.5P	25.92P	3,203.2P	5,427.4P	8,528.0P	409.5P

Sources: 1997 and 2002 *Economic Census*; other years, up to 2006, are from *Annual Survey of Manufactures*. Establishment counts for non-Census years are from *County Business Patterns*; 1997 and 2002 values are from the 1997 and 2002 censuses, respectively. 'P's show projections by the editors.

INDICES OF CHANGE

Year	Com-panies	Establishments		Employment			Compensation		Production ($ million)			
		Total	with 20 or more employees	Total (000)	Production Workers (000)	Hours (Mil)	Payroll ($ mil)	Wages ($/hr)	Cost of Materials	Value Added by Manufacture	Value of Shipments	Capital Invest.
1997	104	104	124	112	153	159	91	80	138	146	139	143
1998		106	122	113	149	155	98	84	128	145	136	138
1999		104	122	112	140	135	96	89	139	149	141	142
2000		100	120	109	134	133	104	90	156	171	160	170
2001		97	118	116	126	123	110	97	131	136	131	239
2002	100	100	100	100	100	100	100	100	100	100	100	100
2003		102	104	83	84	74	96	103	93	109	102	108
2004		101	107	82	75	75	97	103	95	125	112	87
2005		101	101	70	73	75	93	107	101	120	109	134
2006		99P	97P	66	66	69	94	108	116	120	115	107
2007		98P	94P	64P	49P	48P	97P	114P	100P	104P	99P	105P
2008		98P	91P	59P	38P	36P	96P	117P	95P	99P	95P	99P
2009		97P	88P	53P	27P	25P	96P	120P	91P	94P	90P	93P
2010		96P	84P	47P	17P	14P	96P	123P	86P	90P	85P	88P

Sources: Same as General Statistics. Values reflect change from the base year, 2002. Values above 100 mean greater than 2002, values below 100 mean less than 2002, and the values of 100 in other years means the same as 2002. 'P's show projections by the editors.

SELECTED RATIOS

For 2002	Avg. of All Manufact.	Analyzed Industry	Index	For 2002	Avg. of All Manufact.	Analyzed Industry	Index
Employees per Establishment	42	72	170	Value Added per Production Worker	182,367	313,674	172
Payroll per Establishment	1,639,184	4,147,788	253	Cost per Establishment	5,769,015	4,704,930	82
Payroll per Employee	39,053	57,966	148	Cost per Employee	137,446	65,753	48
Production Workers per Establishment	30	24	83	Cost per Production Worker	195,506	192,829	99
Wages per Establishment	694,845	1,017,298	146	Shipments per Establishment	11,158,348	12,614,159	113
Wages per Production Worker	23,548	41,693	177	Shipments per Employee	265,847	176,286	66
Hours per Production Worker	1,980	1,984	100	Shipments per Production Worker	378,144	516,984	137
Wages per Hour	11.89	21.01	177	Investment per Establishment	361,338	591,150	164
Value Added per Establishment	5,381,325	7,653,477	142	Investment per Employee	8,609	8,261	96
Value Added per Employee	128,210	106,959	83	Investment per Production Worker	12,245	24,228	198

Sources: Same as General Statistics. The 'Average of All Manufacturing' column represents the average of all manufacturing industries reported for the most recent complete year available. The Index shows the relationship between the Average and the Analyzed Industry. For example, 100 means that they are equal; 500 that the Analyzed Industry is five times the average; 50 means that the Analyzed Industry is half the national average. The abbreviation 'na' is used to show that data are 'not available'. Ratios shown for 2002, the last complete census year.

LEADING COMPANIES Number shown: 75 Total sales ($ mil): 63,986 Total employment (000): 204.6

Company Name	Address				CEO Name	Phone	Co. Type	Sales ($ mil)	Empl. (000)
L-3 Communications Holdings	600 3rd Ave.	New York	NY	10016		212-697-1111	P	13,961	63.7
Eastman Kodak Co.	343 State St.	Rochester	NY	14650		716-724-4000	P	10,301	26.9
ITT Corp.	4 W Red Oak Ln.	White Plains	NY	10604		914-641-2000	P	9,003	39.7
Agilent Technologies Inc.	5301 Stevens Creek	Santa Clara	CA	95051	Patrick J. Byrne	408-345-8886	P	5,420	19.2
Carl Zeiss IMT Corp.	6250 Sycamore N	Osseo	MN	55369	Gregory Lee	763-744-2400	R	4,420*	0.1
Snap-On Inc.	PO Box 1410	Kenosha	WI	53141	Tim Chambers	262-656-5200	P	2,841	11.6
Wakefield Thermal Solutions	33 Bridge St.	Pelham	NH	03076	Robert Streiter	603-635-2800	S	2,398*	0.1
DENSO Manufacturing Tennessee	1720 Rbrt C Jackson	Maryville	TN	37801	Mack Hattori	865-982-7000	S	2,231*	2.0
ECS. Inc International	1105 S Ridgeview	Olathe	KS	66062	Patricia S. Taylor	913-782-7787	R	1,689*	0.5
Tektronix Inc	PO Box 500	Beaverton	OR	97077		503-627-7111	P	1,105	4.4
Teradyne Inc.	600 Riverpark Dr.	North Reading	MA	01864	James Bagley	978-370-2700	P	1,102	3.6
GenCorp Inc.	PO Box 537012	Sacramento	CA	95853	Terry L. Hall	916-355-4000	P	745	3.3
FlexStar Technology Inc.	47323 Warm Springs	Fremont	CA	94539	Eric Vergari	510-440-0170	R	622*	<0.1
UOP L.L.C.	25 E Algonquin Rd.	Des Plaines	IL	60017	Carlos Guimaraes	847-391-2000	R	500*	4.0
Anritsu Co.	490 Jarvis Dr.	Morgan Hill	CA	95037		408-778-2000	R	472*	0.5
Credence Systems Corp.	1421 California	Milpitas	CA	95035		408-635-4300	P	461	1.5
Analogic Corp.	8 Centennial Dr.	Peabody	MA	01960	Bernard Gordon	978-977-3000	P	341	1.5
Nidec-Shimpo America Corp.	1701 Glenlake Ave.	Itasca	IL	60143	Yoshio Takahara	630-924-7138	R	256*	<0.1
Electro Rent Corporation Data	6060 Sepulveda	Van Nuys	CA	91411	William Weitzman	818-787-2100	D	256*	0.4
ABB Industrial Systems Inc.	579 Exec Campus	Westerville	OH	43082	Fred Kindle	614-818-6300	S	250*	1.5
Heraeus Electro-Nite Co.	1 Summit Sq.	Langhorne	PA	19047	Michael Midash	215-944-9000	R	246*	0.4
Cohu Inc.	12367 Crosthwaite	Poway	CA	92064	James A. Donahue	858-848-8100	P	245*	1.0
Raven Industries Inc.	PO Box 5107	Sioux Falls	SD	57117	Conrad J. Hoigaard	605-336-2750	P	217	0.9
Mitutoyo America Corp.	965 Corporate Blvd.	Aurora	IL	60504		630-820-9666	R	198*	0.2
EXFO America Inc.	3701 Plano Pkwy.	Plano	TX	75075	Germain Lamonde	972-907-1505	R	197*	0.2
Ideal Industries Inc.	Becker Pl.	Sycamore	IL	60178	Dave Juday		R	192*	1.7
Simpson Electric Co.	PO Box 99	Lac d Flambeau	WI	54538	Richard Schermetzler	715-588-3311	R	182*	0.1
Spirent Communications	1325 Borregas Ave.	Sunnyvale	CA	94089	Barry Phelps	408-752-7100	S	180*	0.3
Ixia	26601 W Agoura	Calabasas	CA	91302	Jean-Claude Asscher	818-871-1800	P	174	0.8
Hittite Microwave Corp.	20 Alpha Rd.	Chelmsford	MA	01824	Yalcin Ayasli	978-250-3343	P	156	0.3
Keithley Int'l Investment	28775 Aurora Rd.	Solon	OH	44139	Joseph Keithley	440-248-0400	S	155	0.7
LeCroy Corp.	700 Chestnut Ridge	Chestnut Ridge	NY	10977	Charles Dickinson	845-425-2000	P	152	0.4
LTX Corp.	825 University Ave.	Norwood	MA	02062	Roger W. Blethen	781-461-1000	P	148	0.5
Keithley Instruments Inc.	28775 Aurora Rd.	Solon	OH	44139		440-248-0400	P	144	0.7
TSI Inc.	500 Cardigan Rd.	St. Paul	MN	55126	James Doubles	612-483-0900	P	133*	0.8
SigmaTel Inc.	1601 S Mo Pac	Austin	TX	78746		512-381-3700	P	127	0.4
MCL Inc.	PO Box 3287	Chicago	IL	60678	Arthur Faverio	630-759-9500	R	122*	0.5
Fisher Pierce	54 Commercial St.	Raynham	MA	02767	H. Lawerence Culp, Jr	508-821-1579	S	117*	0.2
Bristol Babcock Inc.	1100 Buckingham	Watertown	CT	06795	John Kelly	860-945-2200	S	115*	0.3
International Transducer Corp.	869 Ward Dr.	Santa Barbara	CA	93111		805-683-2575	S	104*	0.5
ADE Corp.	80 Wilson Way	Westwood	MA	02090	Landon T. Clay	781-467-3500	S	103	0.4
Curtis Instruments Inc.	200 Kisco Ave.	Mount Kisco	NY	10549		914-666-2971	R	100*	0.2
Triton Services Inc.	17001 Science Dr.	Bowie	MD	20715	Stephen E. Hincks	301-809-6834	R	92*	0.2
Fluke Networks	PO Box 777	Everett	WA	98206	Chris O'Dell	425-347-6100	S	91*	0.5
ESA Biosciences Inc.	22 Alpha Rd.	Chelmsford	MA	01824	Walter Giusto	978-250-7000	R	90*	<0.1
Cascade Microtech Inc.	2430 NW 206th	Beaverton	OR	97006		503-601-1000	P	90	0.4
Allied Motion Technologies	23 Inverness Way E	Englewood	CO	80112	Eugene E. Prince	303-799-8520	P	85	0.5
Milbank Manufacturing Co.	PO Box 419028	Kansas City	MO	64141		816-483-5314	R	79*	0.4
Cherry Electrical Products	11200 88th Ave.	Pleasant Pr	WI	53158	Peter B. Cherry	262-942-6500	S	77*	0.7
Delta Design Inc.	12367 Crosthwaite	Poway	CA	92064	James Donahue	858-848-8000	S	77*	0.5
Photon Dynamics Inc.	5970 Optical Ct.	San Jose	CA	95138	Jeffrey A. Hawthorne	408-226-9900	P	74	0.3
Clover Systems	26241 Enterprise Ct	Lake Forest	CA	92630	Gordon Rudd	949-598-0800	R	74*	0.1
OI Analytical	PO Box 9010	College Station	TX	77842	Bruce Lancaster	979-690-1711	S	72*	0.2
Lansdale Semiconductor Inc.	2412 W Huntington	Tempe	AZ	85282	Dale Lillard	602-438-0123	R	71*	<0.1
Barnstead-Thermolyne Corp.	PO Box 797	Dubuque	IA	52004		563-556-2241	S	70*	0.5
Transcat Inc.	35 Vantage Point Dr	Rochester	NY	14624	Charles Hadeed	585-352-7777	P	67	0.2
Boonton Electronics Corp.	PO BOX 465	Parsippany	NJ	07054	Paul Genova	973-386-9696	S	63*	0.1
inTEST Corp.	7 Esterbrook Ln.	Cherry Hill	NJ	08003	Alyn R. Holt	856-424-6886	P	62	0.2
Ametek Drexelbrook	205 Keith Valley Rd	Horsham	PA	19044	Frank Hermance	215-674-1234	D	60*	0.2
Anderson Electronics Inc.	PO Box 89	Hollidaysburg	PA	16648	William Anderson	814-695-4428	R	57*	<0.1
Frequency Electronics Inc.	55 Charls Lindbergh	Mitchell Field	NY	11553	Martin B. Bloch	516-794-4500	P	56	0.5
Cyberex L.L.C.	5900 Eastport Blvd.	Richmond	VA	23231	Kurt Gallo	804-236-3300	S	56*	0.4
Foerster Instruments Inc.	140 Industry Dr.	Pittsburgh	PA	15275	Matt Davin	412-788-8976	R	56*	<0.1
CEM Corp.	PO Box 200	Matthews	NC	28106	Michael J. Collins	704-821-7015	P	55	0.2
Rohde and Schwarz Inc.	8661A Robert Fulton	Columbia	MD	21046	Christian Leicher	410-910-7800	S	54*	0.1
Wireless Telecom Group Inc.	25 Eastmans Rd.	Parsippany	NJ	07054	Paul Genova	201-386-9696	P	54	0.2
Ledtronics Inc.	23105 Kashiwa Ct.	Torrance	CA	90505		310-534-1505	R	51*	0.1
Specialized Products Co.	PO Box 201546	Southlake	TX	76092	Pete Smith		R	50*	0.1
Avtron Manufacturing Inc.	7900 E Pleasant Vly	Cleveland	OH	44131	Robert Fritz	216-642-1230	R	48*	0.2
Trans-Coil Inc.	7878 N 86th St.	Milwaukee	WI	53224	Steve Cobb	414-357-4480	R	48*	<0.1
Trio-Tech International	14731 Califa St.	Van Nuys	CA	91411	A. Charles Wilson	818-787-7000	P	47	0.7
Emrise Corp.	9485 Haven Ave.	R Cucamonga	CA	91730		909-987-9220	P	46	0.3
AMETEK/Dixson	287 27 Road	Grand Junction	CO	81503		970-242-8863	P	44*	0.3
Jameco Electronics Inc.	1355 Shoreway Rd.	Belmont	CA	94002	Bob Croshaw	650-592-8097	R	43*	0.1
Plastronics Socket Company	2601 Texas Dr.	Irving	TX	75062	Wayne Pfaff	972-258-2580	R	43*	<0.1

Source: *Ward's Business Directory of U.S. Private and Public Companies*, Volumes 1 and 2, 2008. The company type code used is as follows: P - Public, R - Private, S - Subsidiary, D - Division, J - Joint Venture, A - Affiliate, G - Group. Sales are in millions of dollars, employees are in thousands. An asterisk (*) indicates an estimated sales volume. The symbol < stands for 'less than'. Company names and addresses are truncated, in some cases, to fit into the available space.

MATERIALS CONSUMED

Material	Quantity	Delivered Cost ($ million)
Printed ciruit boards (without inserted components) for electronic circuitry	(X)	199.0
Printed circuit assemblies, loaded boards, and modules	(X)	302.2
Semiconductors (incl. transistors, diodes, rectifiers, and integrated circuits), for electronic circuitry	(X)	167.9
Capacitors for electronic circuitry	(X)	25.6
Resistors for electronic circuitry	(X)	35.1
All other miscellaneous components and accessories for electronic circuitry (exc. tubes)	(X)	228.5
Current-carrying wiring devices	(X)	21.3
Electrical transmission, distribution, and control equipment	(X)	152.2
Electronic computer equipment	(X)	21.4
Electrical instrument mechanisms and meter movements	(X)	23.0
All other miscellaneous electrical measuring instruments and parts	(X)	443.3
Plastics resins consumed in the form of granules, pellets, etc.	(X)	7.7
Fabricated plastics products (exc. gaskets, hoses, and belting)	(X)	47.7
Sheet metal products (excluding stampings)	(X)	27.5
Metal stampings	(X)	21.9
Other fabricated metal products (exc. forgings, metal stampings, and sheet metal products)	(X)	23.1
Castings, rough and semifinished	(X)	9.9
Metal shapes and forms (exc. castings, forgings, fabr. metal products)	(X)	6.0
Steel shapes and forms (exc. castings, forgings, fabr. metal products)	(X)	8.2
Aluminum and aluminum-base alloy shapes and forms (exc. castings, forgings, fabr. metal products)	(X)	3.6
Other nonferrous shapes and forms (exc. castings, forgings, fabricated metal products)	(X)	2.1
Copper and copper-base alloy shapes and forms (exc. castings, forgings, fabr. metal products)	(X)	2.5
Glass and glass products (excluding windows and mirrors)	(X)	5.9
Insulated wire and cable (including magnet wire)	(X)	14.4
Metal bolts, nuts, screws, and other screw machine products	(X)	9.0
Optical instruments and lenses (exc. sighting, tracking, and fire control)	(X)	7.7
Electronic communication equipment	(X)	19.4
Fractional horsepower electric motors (less than 1 hp)	(X)	2.8
Liquid crystal display screens (LCD), including LED	(X)	13.2
Paper and paperboard containers (incl. shipping sacks and other paper packaging supplies)	(X)	6.3
All other materials, components, parts, containers, and supplies	(X)	636.8
Materials, ingredients, containers, and supplies, nsk	(X)	901.7

Source: 2002 *Economic Census*. Explanation of symbols used: (D): Withheld to avoid disclosure of competitive data; na: Not available; (S): Withheld because statistical norms were not met; (X): Not applicable; (Z): Less than half the unit shown; nec: Not elsewhere classified; nsk: Not specified by kind; - : zero; p : 10-19 percent estimated; q : 20-29 percent estimated.

PRODUCT SHARE DETAILS

Product or Product Class Shipments	Mil. $	Product or Product Class Shipments	Mil. $
INSTRUMENTS FOR MEASURING AND TESTING ELECTRICITY AND ELECTRICAL SIGNALS	9,773.8	**instrument transformers**	8,134.1
Electrical integrating instruments	**623.5**	**Other instruments to measure electricity**	**379.5**
Test equipment for testing electrical, radio and communication circuits, and motors, except portable		**Instruments for measuring and testing electricity and electrical signals, nsk, total**	**636.7**

Source: 2002 *Economic Census*. The values are product shipments in millions of dollars for 2002. Total product shipments may be lower or higher than industry shipments. See Introduction for a full discussion. Values of indented subcategories are summed in the main heading(s). The symbol (D) appears when data are withheld to prevent disclosure of competitive information. The abbreviation nsk stands for 'not specified by kind' and nec for 'not elsewhere classified'. A dash (-) means zero.

INPUTS AND OUTPUTS FOR ELECTRICITY AND SIGNAL TESTING INSTRUMENTS

Economic Sector or Industry Providing Inputs	%	Sector	Economic Sector or Industry Buying Outputs	%	Sector
Compensation of employees	44.6		Exports of goods & services	39.8	Cap Inv
Electricity & signal testing instruments	6.7	Manufg.	Private fixed investment	31.4	
Software publishers	5.7	Services	Federal government, investment, national defense	13.8	Fed Govt
Printed circuit assemblies (electronic assemblies)	4.6	Manufg.	Electricity & signal testing instruments	5.5	Manufg.
Lessors of nonfinancial assets	3.9	Fin/R.E.	Search, detection, & navigation instruments	1.5	Manufg.
Wholesale trade	3.8	Trade	Industrial process variable instruments	1.2	Manufg.
Electronic components, nec	3.1	Manufg.	Broadcast & wireless communications equipment	0.9	Manufg.
Bare printed circuit boards	2.6	Manufg.	Totalizing fluid meters & counting devices	0.9	Manufg.
Semiconductors & related devices	2.2	Manufg.	Semiconductors & related devices	0.9	Manufg.
Real estate	1.3	Fin/R.E.	Watches, clocks, & related devices	0.8	Manufg.
Relay & industrial controls	1.1	Manufg.	Analytical laboratory instruments	0.7	Manufg.
Plastics products, nec	1.1	Manufg.	S/L govt. invest., other	0.4	S/L Govt
Advertising & related services	1.1	Services	Federal government, investment, nondefense	0.4	Fed Govt
Securities, commodity contracts, investments	1.0	Fin/R.E.	S/L govt. invest., education	0.2	S/L Govt
Electronic capacitors, resistors, coils, transformers	0.9	Manufg.	Electronic components, nec	0.2	Manufg.
Data processing, hosting, & related services	0.6	Services	Communications equipment, nec	0.2	Manufg.
Power generation & supply	0.6	Util.	Optical instruments & lenses	0.2	Manufg.
Scientific research & development services	0.6	Services	Automatic environmental controls	0.2	Manufg.
Custom computer programming services	0.5	Services	Electrical equipment & components, nec	0.1	Manufg.
Telecommunications	0.5	Services	Metal cutting & forming machine tools	0.1	Manufg.
Food services & drinking places	0.5	Services			

Continued on next page.

INPUTS AND OUTPUTS FOR ELECTRICITY AND SIGNAL TESTING INSTRUMENTS - Continued

Economic Sector or Industry Providing Inputs	%	Sector	Economic Sector or Industry Buying Outputs	%	Sector
Warehousing & storage	0.5	Util.			
Management of companies & enterprises	0.5	Services			
Monetary authorities/depository credit intermediation	0.5	Fin/R.E.			
Architectural, engineering, & related services	0.4	Services			
Professional, scientific, technical services, nec	0.4	Services			
Truck transportation	0.4	Util.			
Hotels & motels, including casino hotels	0.4	Services			
Crowns & closures & metal stamping	0.4	Manufg.			
Management, scientific, & technical consulting	0.3	Services			
Other computer related services, including facilities	0.3	Services			
Ornamental & architectural metal products	0.3	Manufg.			
Legal services	0.3	Services			
Accounting, tax preparation, bookkeeping, & payroll	0.3	Services			
Machine shops	0.3	Manufg.			
Taxes on production & imports, less subsidies	0.3				
Wiring devices	0.3	Manufg.			
Air transportation	0.3	Util.			
Automotive equipment rental & leasing	0.3	Fin/R.E.			
Analytical laboratory instruments	0.3	Manufg.			
Motor vehicle parts	0.2	Manufg.			
Computer terminals & peripherals	0.2	Manufg.			
Retail trade	0.2	Trade			
Iron & steel mills & ferroalloys	0.2	Manufg.			
Broadcast & wireless communications equipment	0.2	Manufg.			
Cutting tools & machine tool accessories	0.2	Manufg.			
Coating, engraving, heat treating & allied activities	0.2	Manufg.			
Turned products & screws, nuts, & bolts	0.2	Manufg.			
Copper rolling, drawing, extruding, & alloying	0.2	Manufg.			
Fabricated metals, nec	0.2	Manufg.			
Business support services	0.2	Services			
Services to buildings & dwellings	0.1	Services			
Noncomparable imports	0.1	Foreign			
Commercial & industrial machinery rental & leasing	0.1	Fin/R.E.			
Maintenance/repair of nonresidential structures	0.1	Construct.			
Computer system design services	0.1	Services			
Paperboard mills	0.1	Manufg.			

Source: Benchmark Input-Output Accounts for the U.S. Economy, 2002, U.S. Department of Commerce, Washington, D.C., January 2008. The abbreviation nec stands for 'not elsewhere classified'.

OCCUPATIONS EMPLOYED BY NAVIGATIONAL, MEASURING, MEDICAL, & CONTROL INSTRUMENTS

Occupation	% of Total 2006	Change to 2016	Occupation	% of Total 2006	Change to 2016
Electrical & electronic equipment assemblers	7.1	-23.4	First-line supervisors/managers of production workers	2.1	-4.3
Team assemblers	5.3	-4.3	Engineers, nec	1.9	-4.3
Electromechanical equipment assemblers	3.6	-4.3	Purchasing agents, exc wholesale, retail, & farm	1.9	-4.3
Electrical engineers	3.3	-4.3	Machinists	1.8	0.5
Computer software engineers, applications	2.9	14.9	General & operations managers	1.7	-13.8
Aerospace engineers	2.9	0.5	Sales representatives, wholesale & manufacturing, tech	1.6	-4.3
Mechanical engineers	2.8	-4.3	Executive secretaries & administrative assistants	1.5	-4.3
Electrical & electronic engineering technicians	2.7	-4.3	Customer service representatives	1.3	5.3
Computer software engineers, systems software	2.7	5.3	Office clerks, general	1.2	-5.7
Industrial engineers	2.5	16.3	Shipping, receiving, & traffic clerks	1.2	-7.9
Inspectors, testers, sorters, samplers, & weighers	2.4	-9.7	Accountants & auditors	1.2	-4.3
Engineering managers	2.4	-4.3	Production, planning, & expediting clerks	1.2	-4.3
Electronics engineers, exc computer	2.2	-4.3			

Source: Industry-Occupation Matrix, Bureau of Labor Statistics, December 4, 2007. These data are reported based on 4-digit NAICS categories but have been matched to corresponding 6-digit NAICS industry codes. The change reported for each occupation to the year 2016 is a percent of growth or decline as estimated by the Bureau of Labor Statistics. The abbreviation nec stands for 'not elsewhere classified'.

LOCATION BY STATE AND REGIONAL CONCENTRATION

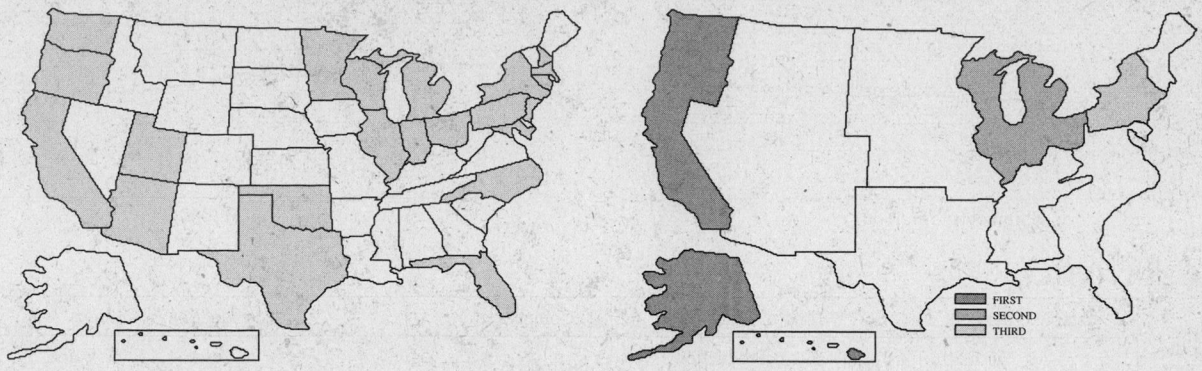

INDUSTRY DATA BY STATE

| State | Establish-ments | Shipments | | | Employment | | | | Cost as % of Shipments | Investment per Employee ($) |
		Total ($ mil)	% of U.S.	Per Establ.	Total Number	% of U.S.	Per Establ.	Wages ($/hour)		
California	217	3,728.9	37.4	17,183.7	20,261	35.8	93	25.18	35.5	7,387
Oregon	24	815.8	8.2	33,991.2	3,921	6.9	163	18.10	36.8	9,345
Massachusetts	40	787.3	7.9	19,681.5	4,506	8.0	113	26.31	41.7	8,111
Washington	17	602.1	6.0	35,416.5	2,792	4.9	164	15.92	34.5	7,138
Maryland	7	498.7	5.0	71,240.1	2,116	3.7	302	18.94	44.2	7,178
New York	40	399.4	4.0	9,983.8	2,404	4.2	60	15.23	43.2	3,997
Texas	55	306.1	3.1	5,565.0	1,812	3.2	33	17.48	45.4	12,265
Ohio	38	275.1	2.8	7,239.5	1,852	3.3	49	19.51	44.5	5,755
Indiana	12	224.6	2.3	18,713.3	1,106	2.0	92	17.53	41.9	3,746
North Carolina	10	164.5	1.6	16,451.7	868	1.5	87	15.82	49.5	5,006
New Hampshire	17	157.7	1.6	9,279.2	872	1.5	51	19.91	42.2	4,356
Illinois	19	112.5	1.1	5,920.1	663	1.2	35	16.11	35.5	3,804
Minnesota	18	112.4	1.1	6,242.4	795	1.4	44	22.29	29.4	4,482
Michigan	23	87.3	0.9	3,795.8	411	0.7	18	15.67	36.8	4,311
Arizona	24	83.5	0.8	3,477.2	672	1.2	28	15.88	31.8	4,067
New Jersey	33	80.3	0.8	2,432.0	429	0.8	13	19.34	30.1	3,117
Pennsylvania	22	78.0	0.8	3,543.7	451	0.8	20	18.10	36.8	2,412
Florida	27	73.0	0.7	2,703.0	557	1.0	21	16.45	25.4	2,199
Wisconsin	17	64.2	0.6	3,775.1	297	0.5	17	19.36	35.2	3,811
Oklahoma	9	38.9	0.4	4,318.3	305	0.5	34	17.28	36.2	2,200
Connecticut	8	38.3	0.4	4,792.4	324	0.6	41	17.47	54.3	6,182
Utah	6	16.5	0.2	2,747.7	246	0.4	41	12.04	36.6	1,187

Source: 2002 Economic Census. The states are in descending order of shipments or establishments (if shipment data are missing for the majority). The symbol (D) appears when data are withheld to prevent disclosure of competitive information. States marked with (D) are sorted by number of establishments. A dash (-) indicates that the data element cannot be calculated. Data may not show all states active in the NAICS category. All data available at the time of publication are shown.

NAICS 334516 - ANALYTICAL LABORATORY INSTRUMENT MANUFACTURING

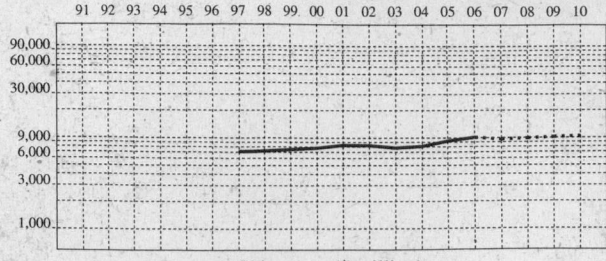

Shipments ($ million)

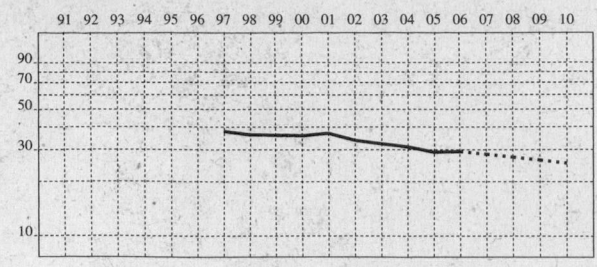

Employment (000)

GENERAL STATISTICS

Year	Companies	Establishments		Employment			Compensation		Production ($ million)			
		Total	with 20 or more employees	Total (000)	Production Workers (000)	Hours (Mil)	Payroll ($ mil)	Wages ($/hr)	Cost of Materials	Value Added by Manufacture	Value of Shipments	Capital Invest.
1997	629	669	241	37.9	14.2	29.1	1,771.2	17.67	2,869.0	4,249.8	7,117.9	207.4
1998		655	246	36.3	13.1	26.5	1,767.9	19.32	2,689.6	4,480.6	7,201.5	329.3
1999		633	247	36.1	13.1	27.0	1,784.7	16.83	2,775.2	4,715.0	7,509.4	305.7
2000		612	242	35.9	12.8	25.9	1,880.1	18.11	3,092.0	4,730.3	7,779.1	303.5
2001		595	236	37.0	12.9	25.5	2,124.9	19.07	3,551.1	4,723.1	8,350.4	315.2
2002	516	563	202	33.8	10.9	21.6	1,981.2	19.66	3,178.4	5,126.5	8,284.5	233.1
2003		558	221	32.3	11.4	22.6	1,985.0	18.83	2,898.0	4,932.9	7,810.4	342.0
2004		561	223	31.1	10.4	21.0	2,076.2	18.49	3,146.6	4,973.7	8,080.9	339.3
2005		572	219	29.1	9.7	19.9	2,004.3	19.68	3,338.9	5,972.5	9,276.0	250.1
2006		530P	210P	29.3	9.5	19.4	2,103.3	20.06	3,741.9	6,454.8	10,130.7	258.2
2007		515P	206P	28.3P	8.9P	17.9P	2,157.0P	19.94P	3,560.0P	6,141.0P	9,638.2P	291.9P
2008		501P	202P	27.3P	8.4P	16.9P	2,195.0P	20.15P	3,659.7P	6,312.9P	9,908.0P	292.5P
2009		486P	198P	26.3P	7.9P	15.8P	2,233.0P	20.37P	3,759.3P	6,484.9P	10,177.9P	293.1P
2010		472P	193P	25.3P	7.4P	14.7P	2,271.0P	20.58P	3,859.0P	6,656.8P	10,447.7P	293.7P

Sources: 1997 and 2002 *Economic Census*; other years, up to 2006, are from *Annual Survey of Manufactures*. Establishment counts for non-Census years are from *County Business Patterns*; 1997 and 2002 values are from the 1997 and 2002 censuses, respectively. 'P's show projections by the editors.

INDICES OF CHANGE

Year	Companies	Establishments		Employment			Compensation		Production ($ million)			
		Total	with 20 or more employees	Total (000)	Production Workers (000)	Hours (Mil)	Payroll ($ mil)	Wages ($/hr)	Cost of Materials	Value Added by Manufacture	Value of Shipments	Capital Invest.
1997	122	119	119	112	130	135	89	90	90	83	86	89
1998		116	122	107	120	123	89	98	85	87	87	141
1999		112	122	107	120	125	90	86	87	92	91	131
2000		109	120	106	117	120	95	92	97	92	94	130
2001		106	117	109	118	118	107	97	112	92	101	135
2002	100	100	100	100	100	100	100	100	100	100	100	100
2003		99	109	96	105	105	100	96	91	96	94	147
2004		100	110	92	95	97	105	94	99	97	98	146
2005		102	108	86	89	92	101	100	105	117	112	107
2006		94P	104P	87	87	90	106	102	118	126	122	111
2007		91P	102P	84P	82P	83P	109P	101P	112P	120P	116P	125P
2008		89P	100P	81P	77P	78P	111P	102P	115P	123P	120P	125P
2009		86P	98P	78P	72P	73P	113P	104P	118P	126P	123P	126P
2010		84P	96P	75P	68P	68P	115P	105P	121P	130P	126P	126P

Sources: Same as General Statistics. Values reflect change from the base year, 2002. Values above 100 mean greater than 2002, values below 100 mean less than 2002, and the values of 100 in other years means the same as 2002. 'P's show projections by the editors.

SELECTED RATIOS

For 2002	Avg. of All Manufact.	Analyzed Industry	Index	For 2002	Avg. of All Manufact.	Analyzed Industry	Index
Employees per Establishment	42	60	143	Value Added per Production Worker	182,367	470,321	258
Payroll per Establishment	1,639,184	3,519,005	215	Cost per Establishment	5,769,015	5,645,471	98
Payroll per Employee	39,053	58,615	150	Cost per Employee	137,446	94,036	68
Production Workers per Establishment	30	19	66	Cost per Production Worker	195,506	291,596	149
Wages per Establishment	694,845	754,274	109	Shipments per Establishment	11,158,348	14,715,631	132
Wages per Production Worker	23,548	38,959	165	Shipments per Employee	265,847	245,115	92
Hours per Production Worker	1,980	1,982	100	Shipments per Production Worker	378,144	760,083	201
Wages per Hour	11.89	19.66	165	Investment per Establishment	361,338	414,032	115
Value Added per Establishment	5,381,325	9,105,684	169	Investment per Employee	8,609	6,896	80
Value Added per Employee	128,210	151,672	118	Investment per Production Worker	12,245	21,385	175

Sources: Same as General Statistics. The 'Average of All Manufacturing' column represents the average of all manufacturing industries reported for the most recent complete year available. The Index shows the relationship between the Average and the Analyzed Industry. For example, 100 means that they are equal; 500 that the Analyzed Industry is five times the average; 50 means that the Analyzed Industry is half the national average. The abbreviation 'na' is used to show that data are 'not available'. Ratios shown for 2002, the last complete census year.

LEADING COMPANIES   Number shown: **75**   Total sales ($ mil): **64,740**   Total employment (000): **219.5**

Company Name	Address				CEO Name	Phone	Co. Type	Sales ($ mil)	Empl. (000)
Honeywell International Inc.	PO Box 4000	Morristown	NJ	07962	Adriane M. Brown	973-455-2000	P	34,589	122.0
Agilent Technologies Inc.	5301 Stevens Creek	Santa Clara	CA	95051	Patrick J. Byrne	408-345-8886	P	5,420	19.2
Beckman Coulter Inc.	PO Box 3100	Fullerton	CA	92834		714-871-4848	P	2,761	10.5
Wakefield Thermal Solutions	33 Bridge St.	Pelham	NH	03076	Robert Streiter	603-635-2800	S	2,398*	0.1
Applera Corp.	PO Box 5435	Norwalk	CT	06851		203-840-2000	P	2,133	5.5
Applied Biosystems Group	850 Lincoln Ctre Dr	Foster City	CA	94404	Tony L. White	650-638-5800	P	2,094	5.0
Millipore Corp.	290 Concord Rd.	Billerica	MA	01821	Dominique Baly	978-715-4321	P	1,532	6.1
Waters Corp.	34 Maple St.	Milford	MA	01757	D A. Berthiaume	508-478-2000	P	1,473	5.0
Bio-Rad Laboratories Inc.	1000 Alfrd Nobel Dr	Hercules	CA	94547	Norman Schwartz	510-724-7000	P	1,461	6.4
Varian Inc.	3120 Hansen Way	Palo Alto	CA	94304	Allen J. Lauer	650-213-8000	P	921	3.7
EDO Corp.	60 E 42nd St., 42nd	New York	NY	10165		212-716-2000	S	715	4.0
Cytyc Corp.	250 Campus Dr.	Marlborough	MA	01752		508-263-2900	P	608	1.5
Coherent Inc.	PO Box 54980	Santa Clara	CA	95056	John R. Ambroseo	408-764-4000	P	601	2.3
Ocean Optics Inc.	PO Box 2249	Dunedin	FL	34697	Michael Morris	727-733-2447	R	595*	<0.1
FEI Co.	5350 NE Dawson	Hillsboro	OR	97124		503-726-7500	P	593	1.8
Fisher Scientific	2000 Park Lane Dr.	Pittsburgh	PA	15275	David Dellapenta	412-490-8300	D	568	1.8
Bruker BioSciences Corp.	40 Manning Rd.	Billerica	MA	01821	Frank H. Laukien	978-663-3660	P	548	1.9
Integra LifeSciences Holdings	311 Enterprise Dr.	Plainsboro	NJ	08536		609-275-0500	P	419	1.8
Affymetrix Inc.	3420 Central Expy.	Santa Clara	CA	95051	Stephen P. A. Fodor	408-731-5000	P	371	1.1
Illumina Inc.	9885 Towne Centre	San Diego	CA	92121		858-202-4566	P	367	1.0
Biosite Inc.	9975 Summers Rdg	San Diego	CA	92121	Kim D. Blickenstaff	858-805-4808	P	309	1.0
Abbott Labs Diagnostic Div.	1921 Hurd Dr.	Irving	TX	75038	Miles White	972-518-6000	D	306*	2.0
ENGlobal Corp.	654 N Sam Houston	Houston	TX	77060	William Coskey	281-878-1000	P	303	2.1
Zeiss, Carl Inc.	1 Zeiss Dr.	Thornwood	NY	10594	Jim Kelly	914-681-7600	R	300*	1.7
Nova Biomedical Corp.	PO Box 9141	Waltham	MA	02454	Francis Manganaro	781-894-0800	R	266*	0.6
QED Environmental Systems Inc.	PO Box 3726	Ann Arbor	MI	48106	Michael Cross	734-995-2547	R	192*	<0.1
Molecular Devices Corp.	1311 Orleans Dr.	Sunnyvale	CA	94089	Blaine Bowman	408-747-1700	P	186*	0.6
Keithley Int'l Investment	28775 Aurora Rd.	Solon	OH	44139	Joseph Keithley	440-248-0400	S	155	0.7
Keithley Instruments Inc.	28775 Aurora Rd.	Solon	OH	44139		440-248-0400	P	144	0.7
Caliper Life Sciences Inc.	68 Elm Street	Hopkinton	MA	01748		508-435-9500	P	141	0.5
Pieratt's Inc.	110 S Mt. Tabor Rd.	Lexington	KY	40517	Bruce W. Pieratt	859-268-6200	R	134*	<0.1
Cepheid	904 Caribbean Dr.	Sunnyvale	CA	94089	John L. Bishop	408-541-4191	P	130	0.5
Bruker Daltonics Inc.	40 Manning Rd.	Billerica	MA	01821	Frank H. Laukien	978-663-3660	S	121*	0.7
Stratagene Cloning Systems	11011 N Torrey Pine	La Jolla	CA	92037	Joseph A. Sorge	858-373-6300	P	96	0.5
ESA Biosciences Inc.	22 Alpha Rd.	Chelmsford	MA	01824	Walter Giusto	978-250-7000	R	90*	<0.1
Thermo NORAN	5225 Verona Rd.	Madison	WI	53711	Brenda Wilcox	608-276-6100	S	85*	0.5
IRIS International Inc.	9172 Eton Ave.	Chatsworth	CA	91311	Kenneth R. Castleman	818-709-1244	P	84	0.3
Harvard Bioscience Inc.	84 October Hill Rd.	Holliston	MA	01746	Chane Graziano	508-893-8999	P	83	0.3
Topcon Technologies Inc.	37 W Century Rd.	Paramus	NJ	07652	Scott Hokari	201-261-9450	R	80*	<0.1
Ircon Inc.	7300 N Natchez	Niles	IL	60714	M Fay	847-967-5151	R	68*	<0.1
Clinical Data Inc.	1 Gateway Ctr.	Newton	MA	02458	Drew Fromkin	617-527-9933	P	64	0.5
YSI Inc.	1700 Brannum Ln.	Yellow Springs	OH	45387	Richard Omlor	937-767-7241	R	64*	0.1
Particle Measuring Systems	5475 Airport Blvd.	Boulder	CO	80301		303-443-7100	R	61*	0.2
Foerster Instruments Inc.	140 Industry Dr.	Pittsburgh	PA	15275	Matt Davin	412-788-8976	R	56*	<0.1
CEM Corp.	PO Box 200	Matthews	NC	28106	Michael J. Collins	704-821-7015	R	55	0.2
HACH Ultra Analytics	481 California Ave.	Grants Pass	OR	97526	Simon Appleby		S	54*	0.2
Union Biometrica Inc.	84 October Hill Rd.	Holliston	MA	01746	Chane Graziano	508-893-3115	S	48*	0.1
Sakura Finetek USA Inc.	1750 W 214th St.	Torrance	CA	90501	Anthony Marotti	310-972-7800	R	47*	0.1
Phenomenex Inc.	411 Madrid Ave.	Torrance	CA	90501	Farshad Mahjoor	310-212-0555	R	47*	0.3
Siemens Applied Automation	500 W Highway 60	Bartlesville	OK	74003	Riener Pallmann	918-662-7000	D	46*	0.3
Bioanalytical Systems Inc.	2701 Kent Ave.	West Lafayette	IN	47906		765-463-4527	P	45	0.3
Millipore Inc.	PO Box 11977	Cidra	PR	00739	Ricardo Lugo	787-747-8485	R	44*	0.1
Seiler Instrument and Mfg. Co.	170 E Kirkham Ave.	Saint Louis	MO	63119		314-968-2282	R	38*	0.1
Bruker Biospin Corp.	15 Fortune Dr.	Billerica	MA	01821		978-667-9580	R	37*	0.1
Poly-Vac Inc.	253 Abby Rd.	Manchester	NH	03103		603-647-7822	R	36*	0.2
Aperio Technologies Inc.	1430 Vantage Ct.	Vista	CA	92081	Dirk G. Soenksen	760-539-1100	R	34*	<0.1
Clarient Inc.	31 Columbia	Aliso Viejo	CA	92656	R A. Andrews Jr.	949-425-5700	P	34	0.2
Brookfield Engineering Labs	11 Commerce Blvd.	Middleboro	MA	02346	David Brookfield	508-946-6200	R	33*	0.2
Quantum Dot Corp.	26118 Research Pl.	Hayward	CA	94545	George Dunbar	510-887-8775	R	32*	<0.1
O.I. Corp.	PO Box 9010	College Station	TX	77842	Raymond Cabillot	979-690-1711	P	30	0.2
Ludlum Measurements Inc.	PO Box 810	Sweetwater	TX	79556	Donald Ludlum	325-235-5494	R	30*	0.3
Bruker Medical Inc.	15 Fortune Dr.	Billerica	MA	01821	Frank Laukien	978-667-9580	S	30*	0.2
Electronic Systems Engineering	1 E Eseco Rd.	Cushing	OK	74023	Arthur Kaminshine	918-225-1266	R	30*	<0.1
Heath Consultants Inc.	9030 W Monroe Rd.	Houston	TX	77061	Milton Heath	713-844-1300	R	29*	<0.1
Dako Colorado Inc.	4850 Innovation Dr.	Fort Collins	CO	80525	Patrik Dahlen	970-226-2200	R	28*	0.2
Horiba Instruments Inc.	17671 Armstrong	Irvine	CA	92614	Masayuki Adachi	949-250-4811	R	27*	<0.1
Nanogen Inc.	10398 Pac. Cntr Ct	San Diego	CA	92121	Howard C. Birndorf	858-410-4600	P	27	0.3
LI-COR Inc.	PO Box 4425	Lincoln	NE	68504	William Biggs	402-467-3576	R	26*	0.2
La Motte Chemical Products Co.	PO Box 329	Chestertown	MD	21620	David Motte	410-778-3100	R	25*	0.1
Bacharach Inc.	621 Hunt Valley Cir	New Kensington	PA	15068		724-334-5000	R	25*	0.2
Princeton Instruments Acton	15 Discovery Way	Acton	MA	01720	Don Templeman	978-263-3584	D	25*	<0.1
Rigaku Americas Corp.	9009 New Trails Dr.	The Woodlands	TX	77381		281-362-2300	R	24*	<0.1
TDK Corporation of America	1600 Feehanville Dr	Mount Prospect	IL	60056	Frank Avant	847-803-6100	S	24*	0.2
Thorlabs Inc.	PO Box 366	Newton	NJ	07860	Alex Cable	973-579-9014	R	24*	0.1
Analytica of Branford Inc.	29 Business Park Dr	Branford	CT	06405	Craig Whitehouse	203-488-8899	R	24*	0.1

Source: *Ward's Business Directory of U.S. Private and Public Companies*, Volumes 1 and 2, 2008. The company type code used is as follows: P - Public, R - Private, S - Subsidiary, D - Division, J - Joint Venture, A - Affiliate, G - Group. Sales are in millions of dollars, employees are in thousands. An asterisk (*) indicates an estimated sales volume. The symbol < stands for 'less than'. Company names and addresses are truncated, in some cases, to fit into the available space.

MATERIALS CONSUMED

Material	Quantity	Delivered Cost ($ million)
Printed ciruit boards (without inserted components) for electronic circuitry	(X)	48.7
Printed circuit assemblies, loaded boards, and modules	(X)	84.4
Semiconductors (incl. transistors, diodes, rectifiers, and integrated circuits), for electronic circuitry	(X)	36.7
Capacitors for electronic circuitry	(X)	10.4
Resistors for electronic circuitry	(X)	3.4
All other miscellaneous components and accessories for electronic circuitry (exc. tubes)	(X)	55.6
Current-carrying wiring devices	(X)	80.3
Electrical transmission, distribution, and control equipment	(X)	33.5
Electronic computer equipment	(X)	55.8
Electrical instrument mechanisms and meter movements	(X)	(D)
All other miscellaneous electrical measuring instruments and parts	(X)	32.2
Plastics resins consumed in the form of granules, pellets, etc.	(X)	10.0
Fabricated plastics products (exc. gaskets, hoses, and belting)	(X)	57.9
Sheet metal products (excluding stampings)	(X)	50.5
Metal stampings	(X)	5.9
Other fabricated metal products (exc. forgings, metal stampings, and sheet metal products)	(X)	56.0
Forgings	(X)	(D)
Castings, rough and semifinished	(X)	6.6
Metal shapes and forms (exc. castings, forgings, fabr. metal products)	(X)	18.9
Steel shapes and forms (exc. castings, forgings, fabr. metal products)	(X)	6.7
Aluminum and aluminum-base alloy shapes and forms (exc. castings, forgings, fabr. metal products)	(X)	5.0
Other nonferrous shapes and forms (exc. castings, forgings, fabricated metal products)	(X)	2.5
Copper and copper-base alloy shapes and forms (exc. castings, forgings, fabr. metal products)	(X)	0.5
Glass and glass products (excluding windows and mirrors)	(X)	9.7
Insulated wire and cable (including magnet wire)	(X)	10.6
Metal bolts, nuts, screws, and other screw machine products	(X)	10.0
Optical instruments and lenses (exc. sighting, tracking, and fire control)	(X)	40.9
Electronic communication equipment	(X)	(D)
Fractional horsepower electric motors (less than 1 hp)	(X)	11.2
Liquid crystal display screens (LCD), including LED	(X)	4.8
Paper and paperboard containers (incl. shipping sacks and other paper packaging supplies)	(X)	17.5
All other materials, components, parts, containers, and supplies	(X)	900.1
Materials, ingredients, containers, and supplies, nsk	(X)	970.7

Source: 2002 *Economic Census*. Explanation of symbols used: (D): Withheld to avoid disclosure of competitive data; na: Not available; (S): Withheld because statistical norms were not met; (X): Not applicable; (Z): Less than half the unit shown; nec: Not elsewhere classified; nsk: Not specified by kind; - : zero; p : 10-19 percent estimated; q : 20-29 percent estimated.

PRODUCT SHARE DETAILS

Product or Product Class Shipments	Mil. $	Product or Product Class Shipments	Mil. $
ANALYTICAL LABORATORY INSTRUMENTS	7,117.7	**Analytical and scientific instruments, except optical**	**7,117.7**

Source: 2002 *Economic Census*. The values are product shipments in millions of dollars for 2002. Total product shipments may be lower or higher than industry shipments. See Introduction for a full discussion. Values of indented subcategories are summed in the main heading(s). The symbol (D) appears when data are withheld to prevent disclosure of competitive information. The abbreviation nsk stands for 'not specified by kind' and nec for 'not elsewhere classified'. A dash (-) means zero.

INPUTS AND OUTPUTS FOR ANALYTICAL LABORATORY INSTRUMENT MANUFACTURING

Economic Sector or Industry Providing Inputs	%	Sector	Economic Sector or Industry Buying Outputs	%	Sector
Compensation of employees	31.2		Private fixed investment	53.8	
Management of companies & enterprises	12.1	Services	Exports of goods & services	29.7	Cap Inv
Software publishers	10.2	Services	Architectural, engineering, & related services	4.6	Services
Wholesale trade	3.7	Trade	Home health care services	3.2	Services
Scientific research & development services	3.4	Services	S/L govt. invest., education	2.1	S/L Govt
Plastics products, nec	3.0	Manufg.	Change in private inventories	0.9	In House
Lessors of nonfinancial assets	2.8	Fin/R.E.	Other S/L govt. enterprises	0.8	S/L Govt
Printed circuit assemblies (electronic assembiles)	2.3	Manufg.	Laboratory apparatus & furniture	0.8	Manufg.
Wiring devices	1.7	Manufg.	Aircraft	0.6	Manufg.
Ornamental & architectural metal products	1.4	Manufg.	Search, detection, & navigation instruments	0.6	Manufg.
Advertising & related services	1.3	Services	Elementary & secondary schools	0.4	Services
Electronic components, nec	1.3	Manufg.	Physician, dentist, other health practitioner offices	0.4	Services
Chemical products & preparations, nec	1.2	Manufg.	General Federal government services, nondefense	0.3	Fed Govt
Electricity & signal testing instruments	1.1	Manufg.	Electricity & signal testing instruments	0.3	Manufg.
Bare printed circuit boards	1.0	Manufg.	Analytical laboratory instruments	0.2	Manufg.
Real estate	1.0	Fin/R.E.	Medical & diagnostic labs & outpatient services	0.2	Services
Semiconductors & related devices	0.7	Manufg.	Legal services	0.2	Services
Pressed & blown glass & glassware, nec	0.7	Manufg.	Surgical appliances & supplies	0.1	Manufg.
Computer terminals & peripherals	0.7	Manufg.	Computer system design services	0.1	Services
Management, scientific, & technical consulting	0.6	Services	Professional, scientific, technical services, nec	0.1	Services
Telecommunications	0.6	Services	S/L govt. invest., other	0.1	S/L Govt
Machine shops	0.6	Manufg.			

Continued on next page.

INPUTS AND OUTPUTS FOR ANALYTICAL LABORATORY INSTRUMENT MANUFACTURING - Continued

Economic Sector or Industry Providing Inputs	%	Sector	Economic Sector or Industry Buying Outputs	%	Sector
Iron & steel mills & ferroalloys	0.5	Manufg.			
Securities, commodity contracts, investments	0.5	Fin/R.E.			
Custom computer programming services	0.5	Services			
Legal services	0.5	Services			
Warehousing & storage	0.4	Util.			
Relay & industrial controls	0.4	Manufg.			
Taxes on production & imports, less subsidies	0.4				
Monetary authorities/depository credit intermediation	0.4	Fin/R.E.			
Coating, engraving, heat treating & allied activities	0.4	Manufg.			
Food services & drinking places	0.4	Services			
Architectural, engineering, & related services	0.4	Services			
Turned products & screws, nuts, & bolts	0.4	Manufg.			
Optical instruments & lenses	0.4	Manufg.			
Paperboard containers	0.4	Manufg.			
Retail trade	0.4	Trade			
Power generation & supply	0.4	Util.			
Truck transportation	0.4	Util.			
Data processing, hosting, & related services	0.3	Services			
Hotels & motels, including casino hotels	0.3	Services			
Broadcast & wireless communications equipment	0.3	Manufg.			
Electronic capacitors, resistors, coils, transformers	0.3	Manufg.			
Accounting, tax preparation, bookkeeping, & payroll	0.3	Services			
Air transportation	0.3	Util.			
Analytical laboratory instruments	0.3	Manufg.			
Professional, scientific, technical services, nec	0.3	Services			
Other computer related services, including facilities	0.2	Services			
Motors & generators	0.2	Manufg.			
Fabricated metals, nec	0.2	Manufg.			
Motor vehicle parts	0.2	Manufg.			
Plastics materials & resins	0.2	Manufg.			
Plastics packaging materials, film & sheet	0.2	Manufg.			
Services to buildings & dwellings	0.2	Services			
Automotive equipment rental & leasing	0.2	Fin/R.E.			
Maintenance/repair of nonresidential structures	0.2	Construct.			
Alumina refining & primary aluminum production	0.2	Manufg.			
Copper rolling, drawing, extruding, & alloying	0.2	Manufg.			
Noncomparable imports	0.2	Foreign			
Crowns & closures & metal stamping	0.1	Manufg.			
Employment services	0.1	Services			
Business support services	0.1	Services			
Valve & fittings other than plumbing	0.1	Manufg.			
Paperboard mills	0.1	Manufg.			
Aluminum products from purchased aluminum	0.1	Manufg.			
Automotive repair & maintenance, ex. car washes	0.1	Services			
Glass products from purchased glass	0.1	Manufg.			

Source: Benchmark Input-Output Accounts for the U.S. Economy, 2002, U.S. Department of Commerce, Washington, D.C., January 2008. The abbreviation nec stands for 'not elsewhere classified'.

OCCUPATIONS EMPLOYED BY NAVIGATIONAL, MEASURING, MEDICAL, & CONTROL INSTRUMENTS

Occupation	% of Total 2006	Change to 2016	Occupation	% of Total 2006	Change to 2016
Electrical & electronic equipment assemblers	7.1	-23.4	First-line supervisors/managers of production workers	2.1	-4.3
Team assemblers	5.3	-4.3	Engineers, nec	1.9	-4.3
Electromechanical equipment assemblers	3.6	-4.3	Purchasing agents, exc wholesale, retail, & farm	1.9	-4.3
Electrical engineers	3.3	-4.3	Machinists	1.8	0.5
Computer software engineers, applications	2.9	14.9	General & operations managers	1.7	-13.8
Aerospace engineers	2.9	0.5	Sales representatives, wholesale & manufacturing, tech	1.6	-4.3
Mechanical engineers	2.8	-4.3	Executive secretaries & administrative assistants	1.5	-4.3
Electrical & electronic engineering technicians	2.7	-4.3	Customer service representatives	1.3	5.3
Computer software engineers, systems software	2.7	5.3	Office clerks, general	1.2	-5.7
Industrial engineers	2.5	16.3	Shipping, receiving, & traffic clerks	1.2	-7.9
Inspectors, testers, sorters, samplers, & weighers	2.4	-9.7	Accountants & auditors	1.2	-4.3
Engineering managers	2.4	-4.3	Production, planning, & expediting clerks	1.2	-4.3
Electronics engineers, exc computer	2.2	-4.3			

Source: Industry-Occupation Matrix, Bureau of Labor Statistics, December 4, 2007. These data are reported based on 4-digit NAICS categories but have been matched to corresponding 6-digit NAICS industry codes. The change reported for each occupation to the year 2016 is a percent of growth or decline as estimated by the Bureau of Labor Statistics. The abbreviation nec stands for 'not elsewhere classified'.

LOCATION BY STATE AND REGIONAL CONCENTRATION

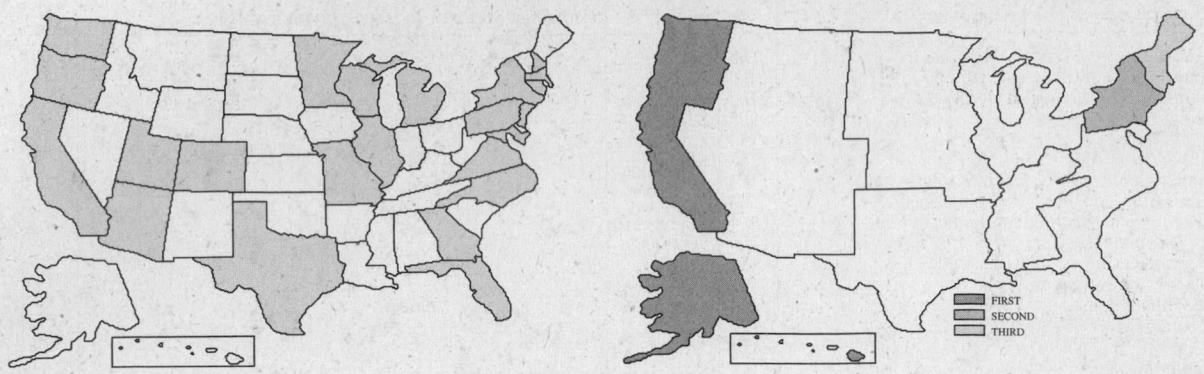

INDUSTRY DATA BY STATE

| State | Establish-ments | Shipments | | | Employment | | | | Cost as % of Shipments | Investment per Employee ($) |
		Total ($ mil)	% of U.S.	Per Establ.	Total Number	% of U.S.	Per Establ.	Wages ($/hour)		
California	121	3,591.0	43.3	29,677.9	11,111	32.8	92	22.89	40.0	10,406
Massachusetts	42	990.1	12.0	23,574.6	3,467	10.2	83	19.53	27.3	11,425
Texas	39	447.5	5.4	11,474.6	3,184	9.4	82	16.45	44.7	3,066
Florida	24	391.5	4.7	16,312.3	1,092	3.2	46	19.28	36.9	3,542
Minnesota	10	329.5	4.0	32,947.8	1,051	3.1	105	26.44	27.8	4,439
Pennsylvania	32	292.6	3.5	9,144.0	1,472	4.3	46	15.52	51.8	6,470
New Jersey	23	286.1	3.5	12,439.2	1,207	3.6	52	17.60	42.8	4,274
Wisconsin	11	231.7	2.8	21,062.4	1,035	3.1	94	19.43	38.1	5,614
Connecticut	13	224.6	2.7	17,274.8	1,457	4.3	112	20.83	52.0	380
Michigan	15	214.2	2.6	14,283.1	1,242	3.7	83	16.45	28.9	4,376
Colorado	18	200.9	2.4	11,163.8	1,022	3.0	57	18.90	35.3	4,577
Illinois	16	123,1	1.5	7,691.7	480	1.4	30	15.89	36.3	3,058
New York	26	110.2	1.3	4,239.8	653	1.9	25	17.06	41.1	2,848
Maryland	12	86.2	1.0	7,185.4	311	0.9	26	11.75	63.9	16,582
North Carolina	11	58.2	0.7	5,291.1	290	0.9	26	31.82	35.1	1,500
Georgia	6	55.3	0.7	9,213.8	339	1.0	57	15.28	27.5	5,236
Oregon	9	54.9	0.7	6,101.9	390	1.2	43	15.59	34.6	879
Arizona	9	50.2	0.6	5,582.0	225	0.7	25	18.48	36.2	2,933
Utah	8	46.1	0.6	5,759.9	232	0.7	29	18.12	32.4	5,315
Washington	14	41.3	0.5	2,950.1	243	0.7	17	23.02	64.0	6,695
New Hampshire	8	34.9	0.4	4,359.5	243	0.7	30	17.14	26.7	3,119
Missouri	7	23.5	0.3	3,355.6	111	0.3	16	18.20	32.6	4,405
Virginia	8	17.6	0.2	2,198.0	112	0.3	14	22.43	58.4	1,741

Source: 2002 *Economic Census*. The states are in descending order of shipments or establishments (if shipment data are missing for the majority). The symbol (D) appears when data are withheld to prevent disclosure of competitive information. States marked with (D) are sorted by number of establishments. A dash (-) indicates that the data element cannot be calculated. Data may not show all states active in the NAICS category. All data available at the time of publication are shown.

NAICS 334517 - IRRADIATION APPARATUS MANUFACTURING

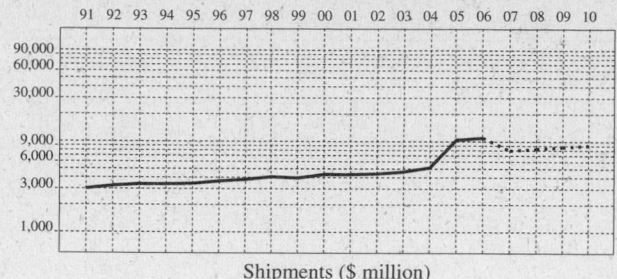

Shipments ($ million)

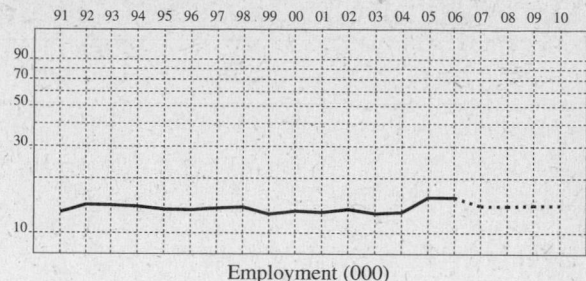

Employment (000)

GENERAL STATISTICS

Year	Com-panies	Establishments		Employment			Compensation		Production ($ million)			
		Total	with 20 or more employees	Total (000)	Production Workers (000)	Hours (Mil)	Payroll ($ mil)	Wages ($/hr)	Cost of Materials	Value Added by Manufacture	Value of Shipments	Capital Invest.
1991		93	48	13.0	6.6	13.1	483.8	14.37	1,321.2	1,683.9	3,011.4	65.3
1992	110	128	65	14.3	7.1	14.3	562.7	14.79	1,302.0	1,871.4	3,235.0	63.6
1993		132	60	14.2	6.9	13.7	572.9	15.44	1,586.2	1,770.8	3,372.3	85.6
1994		129	62	14.0	6.6	13.6	598.7	15.28	1,638.0	1,704.9	3,373.1	84.8
1995		130	62	13.5	6.4	13.9	590.9	15.39	1,662.7	1,748.9	3,422.7	93.5
1996		154	66	13.4	6.3	13.5	618.1	16.05	1,805.5	1,835.6	3,633.9	60.0
1997	136	154	73	13.7	5.7	12.3	631.7	15.82	1,839.1	1,978.0	3,797.8	75.9
1998		164	71	13.9	5.7	12.5	692.3	16.26	1,834.0	2,243.4	4,061.9	72.2
1999		163	71	12.7	5.1	11.9	689.8	17.03	1,664.9	2,249.9	3,948.8	121.9
2000		155	68	13.2	4.9	10.8	694.3	18.12	2,069.8	2,255.3	4,329.2	128.8
2001		160	70	13.0	4.9	10.2	706.5	20.52	2,141.8	2,150.0	4,324.6	103.8
2002	153	169	72	13.5	4.7	9.4	796.8	20.68	2,098.5	2,338.8	4,395.3	92.7
2003		171	66	12.8	4.7	9.8	903.9	20.88	2,237.5	2,391.1	4,631.4	58.9
2004		173	65	13.0	5.0	10.3	939.3	22.64	2,453.3	2,711.2	5,149.7	113.6
2005		168	68	15.7	5.4	11.2	1,253.7	27.33	4,379.3	6,403.7	10,414.0	218.2
2006		185P	73P	15.7	5.3	10.7	1,352.0	28.02	4,845.1	6,153.0	10,949.8	277.7
2007		190P	73P	14.1P	4.4P	9.4P	1,141.1P	25.72P	3,513.7P	4,462.2P	7,941.0P	178.4P
2008		194P	74P	14.1P	4.3P	9.1P	1,186.5P	26.55P	3,679.7P	4,673.0P	8,316.0P	186.8P
2009		199P	75P	14.2P	4.1P	8.8P	1,231.9P	27.38P	3,845.6P	4,883.7P	8,691.0P	195.2P
2010		203P	76P	14.2P	4.0P	8.6P	1,277.2P	28.21P	4,011.6P	5,094.5P	9,066.1P	203.6P

Sources: 1992, 1997, 2002 *Economic Census*; other years, up to 2006, are from the *Annual Survey of Manufactures*. Establishment counts for non-Census years are from *County Business Patterns*; 1997 and 2002 values are from the 1997 and 2002 censuses respectively, reported in the Federal Government's NAICS format. Other years were originally reported in equivalent SIC format. 'P's show projections by the editors.

INDICES OF CHANGE

Year	Com-panies	Establishments		Employment			Compensation		Production ($ million)			
		Total	with 20 or more employees	Total (000)	Production Workers (000)	Hours (Mil)	Payroll ($ mil)	Wages ($/hr)	Cost of Materials	Value Added by Manufacture	Value of Shipments	Capital Invest.
1992	72	76	90	106	151	152	71	72	62	80	74	69
1997	89	91	101	101	121	131	79	76	88	85	86	82
2001		95	97	96	104	109	89	99	102	92	98	112
2002	100	100	100	100	100	100	100	100	100	100	100	100
2003		101	92	95	100	104	113	101	107	102	105	64
2004		102	90	96	106	110	118	109	117	116	117	123
2005		99	94	116	115	119	157	132	209	274	237	235
2006		110P	101P	116	113	114	170	135	231	263	249	300
2007		112P	102P	104P	94P	100P	143P	124P	167P	191P	181P	192P
2008		115P	103P	104P	91P	97P	149P	128P	175P	200P	189P	202P
2009		118P	104P	105P	87P	94P	155P	132P	183P	209P	198P	211P
2010		120P	105P	105P	85P	91P	160P	136P	191P	218P	206P	220P

Sources: Same as General Statistics. Values reflect change from the base year, 2002. Values above 100 mean greater than 2002, values below 100 mean less than 2002, and the values of 100 in other years means the same as 2002. 'P's show projections by the editors.

SELECTED RATIOS

For 2002	Avg. of All Manufact.	Analyzed Industry	Index	For 2002	Avg. of All Manufact.	Analyzed Industry	Index
Employees per Establishment	42	80	190	Value Added per Production Worker	182,367	497,617	273
Payroll per Establishment	1,639,184	4,714,793	288	Cost per Establishment	5,769,015	12,417,160	215
Payroll per Employee	39,053	59,022	151	Cost per Employee	137,446	155,444	113
Production Workers per Establishment	30	28	94	Cost per Production Worker	195,506	446,489	228
Wages per Establishment	694,845	1,150,249	166	Shipments per Establishment	11,158,348	26,007,692	233
Wages per Production Worker	23,548	41,360	176	Shipments per Employee	265,847	325,578	122
Hours per Production Worker	1,980	2,000	101	Shipments per Production Worker	378,144	935,170	247
Wages per Hour	11.89	20.68	174	Investment per Establishment	361,338	548,521	152
Value Added per Establishment	5,381,325	13,839,053	257	Investment per Employee	8,609	6,867	80
Value Added per Employee	128,210	173,244	135	Investment per Production Worker	12,245	19,723	161

Sources: Same as General Statistics. The 'Average of All Manufacturing' column represents the average of all manufacturing industries reported for the most recent complete year available. The Index shows the relationship between the Average and the Analyzed Industry. For example, 100 means that they are equal; 500 that the Analyzed Industry is five times the average; 50 means that the Analyzed Industry is half the national average. The abbreviation 'na' is used to show that data are 'not available'. Ratios shown for 2002, the last complete census year.

LEADING COMPANIES   Number shown: **75**   Total sales ($ mil): **290,361**   Total employment (000): **647.8**

Company Name	Address				CEO Name	Phone	Co. Type	Sales ($ mil)	Empl. (000)
General Electric Co.	3135 Easton Tpk.	Fairfield	CT	06828		203-373-2211	P	172,738	327.0
3M Co.	3M Ctr.	St. Paul	MN	55144	George W. Buckley	651-733-2204	P	24,462	76.2
Eli Lilly and Co.	Lilly Corporate Ctr	Indianapolis	IN	46285		317-276-2000	P	18,634	40.6
Medtronic Inc.	710 Medtronic Pky.	Minneapolis	MN	55432		763-514-4000	P	12,299	38.0
Eastman Kodak Co.	343 State St.	Rochester	NY	14650		716-724-4000	P	10,301	26.9
Medtronic AVE Inc.	3576 Unocal Pl.	Santa Rosa	CA	95403	William Hawkins	707-525-0111	S	10,054	21.5
Siemens Medical Solutions USA	51 Valley Stream Pk	Malvern	PA	19355	Thomas McCausland	610-219-6300	S	9,135*	13.0
Stryker Corp.	PO Box 4085	Kalamazoo	MI	49003		616-385-2600	P	6,001	16.0
St. Jude Medical Inc.	1 Lillehei Plz.	St. Paul	MN	55117		651-483-2000	P	3,779	12.0
Guidant Corp.	PO Box 44906	St. Paul	MN	55112	James M. Cornelius	651-582-4000	P	3,551	13.0
C.R. Bard Inc.	730 Central Ave.	Murray Hill	NJ	07974		908-277-8000	P	2,202	10.2
Varian Medical Systems Inc.	3100 Hansen Way	Palo Alto	CA	94304	Timothy Guertin	650-493-4000	P	1,777	4.5
Cadwell Laboratories Inc.	909 N Kellogg St.	Kennewick	WA	99336	Carl Cadwell	509-735-6481	R	1,583*	<0.1
Respironics Inc.	1010 Murry Ridge	Murrysville	PA	15668	Gerald E. McGinnis	724-387-5200	P	1,195	4.9
Sulzer Inc.	555 5th Ave., 15th	New York	NY	10017	Kelli Edell	212-949-0999	S	1,000*	4.5
Omron Healthcare Inc.	1200 Lakeside Dr.	Deerfield	IL	60015		847-680-6200	R	872*	0.1
Acuson Corp.	1220 Charleston Rd.	Mountain View	CA	94043	Klaus Hambuechen	650-969-9112	R	782*	1.0
Hologic Inc.	35 Crosby Dr.	Bedford	MA	01730	Robert A. Cascella	781-999-7300	P	738	3.6
CONMED Corp.	525 French Rd.	Utica	NY	13502	Eugene R. Corasanti	315-797-8375	P	694	3.2
Coherent Inc.	PO Box 54980	Santa Clara	CA	95056	John R. Ambroseo	408-764-4000	P	601	2.3
Gambro Renal Products Inc.	10810 W Collins	Lakewood	CO	80215	Kevin Smith	303-232-6800	R	482*	<0.1
Terumo Cardiovascular Systems	6200 Jackson Rd.	Ann Arbor	MI	48103	Mark Sutter	734-663-4145	R	481*	0.3
Datascope Corp.	14 Philips Pky.	Montvale	NJ	07645		201-391-8100	P	379	1.2
ZOLL Medical Corp.	269 Mill Rd.	Chelmsford	MA	01824		978-421-9655	P	310	1.3
ArthroCare Corp.	7500 Rialto Blvd.	Austin	TX	78735	Michael A. Baker	512-391-3900	P	308	1.1
Zeiss, Carl Inc.	1 Zeiss Dr.	Thornwood	NY	10594	Jim Kelly	914-681-7600	R	300*	1.7
GE OEC Medical Systems Inc.	384 Wright Brothers	Salt Lake City	UT	84116	Ruben Beruman	801-328-9300	S	298*	1.0
Olympus America Inc.	3500 Corporate	Center Valley	PA	18034	F. Mark Gumz	484-896-5000	S	259*	1.7
SpaceLabs Medical Inc.	PO Box 7018	Issaquah	WA	98027	Deepak Chopra	425-657-7200	D	246*	1.2
Thoratec Corp.	6101 Stoneridge Dr.	Pleasanton	CA	94588	Gary F. Burbach	925-847-8600	P	235	1.2
Roche Diagnostics Corp.	9115 Hague Rd.	Indianapolis	IN	46250	Tiffany Olson	317-521-2000	S	215	2.0
SonoSite Inc.	21919 30th Dr. SE	Bothell	WA	98021	Kirby L. Cramer	425-951-1200	P	205	0.6
Del Medical Imaging Corp.	11550 W King St.	Franklin Park	IL	60131	Walter Schneider	847-288-7000	D	194*	0.1
Cardiac Science Corp.	3303 Monte Villa	Bothell	WA	98021	John R. Hinson	425-402-2000	P	182	0.6
Spectra-Physics Lasers Inc.	PO Box 7013	Mountain View	CA	94039	Bruce Craig	650-961-2550	S	175*	1.0
American Science & Engineering	829 Middlesex Tpke.	Billerica	MA	01821	Anthony R. Fabiano	978-262-8700	P	153	0.3
Candela Corp.	530 Boston Post Rd.	Wayland	MA	01778		508-358-7400	P	149	0.4
HealthTronics Inc.	1301 S Capital - TX	Austin	TX	78746	R. Steven Hicks	512-328-2892	P	140	0.4
Medrad Inc.	1 Medrad Dr.	Indianola	PA	15051	John Friel	412-767-2400	R	137*	0.8
Cyberonics Inc.	100 Cyberonics Blvd	Houston	TX	77058	Daniel J. Moore	281-228-7200	P	131	0.5
Cynosure Inc.	5 Carlisle Rd.	Westford	MA	01886	Michael R. Davin	978-256-4200	P	124	0.3
Laserscope Inc.	3070 Orchard Dr.	San Jose	CA	95134		408-943-0636	S	122*	0.3
Advanced Neuromodulation Sys.	6901 Preston Rd.	Plano	TX	75024	C G. Chavez	972-309-8000	S	121	0.5
Candela Skin Care Centers Inc.	530 Boston Post Rd.	Wayland	MA	01778	Gerard E. Puorro	508-358-7400	P	120*	0.2
Natus Medical Inc.	1501 Industrial Rd.	San Carlos	CA	94070	Robert Gunst	650-802-0400	P	118	0.4
Home Diagnostics Inc.	2400 NW 55th Ct.	Fort Lauderdale	FL	33309	J. Richard Damron Jr.	954-677-9201	P	113	0.5
Lake Region Manufacturing Inc.	340 Lake Hazeltine	Chaska	MN	55318	Joseph Fleischhacker	952-448-5111	R	109*	0.5
Pyxis Corp.	3750 Torrey View	San Diego	CA	92130	Kerry Clark	858-480-6000	S	108*	0.6
Bruker AXS Inc.	5465 E Cheryl Pky.	Madison	WI	53711	Frank H. Laukien	608-276-3000	S	104*	0.6
Cutera Inc.	3240 Bayshore Blvd.	Brisbane	CA	94005	Kevin P. Connors	415-657-5500	P	102	0.2
Aspect Medical Systems Inc.	1 Upland Rd.	Norwood	MA	02062	Nassib Chamoun	617-559-7000	P	97	0.3
Dornier Medtech	1155 Roberts Blvd.	Kennesaw	GA	30144	Bryan Walsh	770-426-1315	R	96*	0.5
Compex Technologies Inc.	1811 Old Hwy. 8	New Brighton	MN	55112	Dan W. Gladney	651-631-0590	R	95*	0.6
DMS Imaging Inc.	11600 96th Ave. N	Maple Grove	MN	55369	Mark A. Doda	763-315-1947	S	89*	0.3
Abaxis Inc.	3240 Whipple Rd.	Union City	CA	94587		510-675-6500	P	86	0.3
Fibercor Div.	14605 28th Ave. N	Plymouth	MN	55447	Roy Malkin	763-553-3300	D	86*	0.4
Astra Tech Inc.	890 Winter St., 310	Waltham	MA	02451	Niklas Lidskog	781-890-6800	S	86*	0.2
AngioCare Corp.	680 Vaqueros Ave.	Sunnyvale	CA	94085	Michael A. Baker	408-736-0224	S	85*	0.2
Roho Group Inc.	PO Box 658	Belleville	IL	62222	Robert Graebe	618-277-9150	R	84*	0.2
Dunlee Inc.	555 N Commerce St.	Aurora	IL	60504		630-585-2000	D	78*	0.3
EBI L.P.	100 Interpace Pky.	Parsippany	NJ	07054	Daniel Hann	973-299-9300	S	75*	0.3
Applied Medical Resources	22872 Ave. Empresa	R St Margarita	CA	92688	Said Hilal	949-713-8000	R	74*	0.3
BSN-Jobst Inc.	PO Box 471048	Charlotte	NC	28247	Maurizio Ballicu	704-554-9933	R	72*	0.2
Minntech Corp.	14605 28th Ave. N	Minneapolis	MN	55447	Roy Malkin	763-553-3300	S	71*	0.3
Cholestech Corp.	3347 Investment	Hayward	CA	94545	John H. Landon	510-732-7200	P	70	0.2
Canberra Albuquerque Inc.	PO Box 10300	Albuquerque	NM	87184	Steven Kadner	505-828-9100	R	67*	<0.1
Spectranetics Corp.	96 Talamine Ct.	Colorado Spgs	CO	80907	E J. Geisenheimer	719-633-8333	P	64	0.3
Thermage Inc.	25881 Indu. Blvd.	Hayward	CA	94545	Stephen J. Fanning	510-782-2886	P	63	0.2
Draeger Medical Systems Inc.	6 Tech Dr.	Andover	MA	01810	Bill Isenberg	978-907-7500	S	63*	0.3
NxStage Medical Inc.	439 S Union St.	Lawrence	MA	01843	Jeffrey H. Burbank	978-687-4700	P	60	1.5
Allstates Worldcargo Inc.	4 Lakeside Dr. S	Forked River	NJ	08731	Sam DiGiralomo	609-693-5950	R	60*	<0.1
Hospital Systems Inc.	750 Garcia Ave.	Pittsburg	CA	94565	David Miller	925-427-7800	R	60*	<0.1
SensorMedics Corp.	22745 Savi Ranch	Yorba Linda	CA	92887	Randy Thurman	714-283-1830	S	59*	0.3
Karl Storz Imaging Inc.	175 Cremona Dr.	Goleta	CA	93117		805-968-5563	R	55*	0.3
Orex Computed Radiography Ltd.	2000 Cmmnwealth	Auburndale	MA	02466	Antonio M. Perez	617-244-9000	S	52*	<0.1

Source: Ward's Business Directory of U.S. Private and Public Companies, Volumes 1 and 2, 2008. The company type code used is as follows: P - Public, R - Private, S - Subsidiary, D - Division, J - Joint Venture, A - Affiliate, G - Group. Sales are in millions of dollars, employees are in thousands. An asterisk (*) indicates an estimated sales volume. The symbol < stands for 'less than'. Company names and addresses are truncated, in some cases, to fit into the available space.

MATERIALS CONSUMED

Material	Quantity	Delivered Cost ($ million)
Metal bolts, nuts, screws, and other screw machine products	(X)	12.2
Metal stampings	(X)	(D)
All other fabricated metal products (excluding forgings)	(X)	77.4
Forgings	(X)	(D)
Castings, rough and semifinished	(X)	(D)
Stainless steel shapes and forms (exc. castings, forgings, fabr. metal products)	(X)	8.9
Other steel shapes and forms (exc. castings, forgings, fabr. metal products)	(X)	11.7
Nonferrous shapes and forms	(X)	(D)
Transmittal, industrial, and special-purpose electron tubes (exc. X-ray)	(X)	59.7
Semiconductors (incl. transistors, diodes, rectifiers, and integrated circuits), for electronic circuitry	(X)	50.6
Capacitors for electronic circuitry	(X)	6.6
Resistors for electronic circuitry	(X)	9.5
Connectors for electronic circuitry	(X)	4.9
Other electronic components and accessories	(X)	93.8
Insulated wire and cable (excluding magnet wire)	(X)	27.7
Plastics products consumed in the form of sheets, rods, etc.	(X)	10.9
Paperboard containers, boxes, and corrugated paperboard	(X)	5.6
All other materials, components, parts, containers, and supplies	(X)	423.1
Materials, ingredients, containers, and supplies, nsk	(X)	930.0

Source: 2002 Economic Census. Explanation of symbols used: (D): Withheld to avoid disclosure of competitive data; na: Not available; (S): Withheld because statistical norms were not met; (X): Not applicable; (Z): Less than half the unit shown; nec: Not elsewhere classified; nsk: Not specified by kind; - : zero; p : 10-19 percent estimated; q : 20-29 percent estimated.

PRODUCT SHARE DETAILS

Product or Product Class Shipments	Mil. $	Product or Product Class Shipments	Mil. $
IRRADIATION APPARATUS Irradiation (ionizing radiation) equipment, including x-ray,	4,181.0	beta ray, gamma ray, and nuclear	4,181.0

Source: 2002 Economic Census. The values are product shipments in millions of dollars for 2002. Total product shipments may be lower or higher than industry shipments. See Introduction for a full discussion. Values of indented subcategories are summed in the main heading(s). The symbol (D) appears when data are withheld to prevent disclosure of competitive information. The abbreviation nsk stands for 'not specified by kind' and nec for 'not elsewhere classified'. A dash (-) means zero.

INPUTS AND OUTPUTS FOR IRRADIATION APPARATUS MANUFACTURING

Economic Sector or Industry Providing Inputs	%	Sector	Economic Sector or Industry Buying Outputs	%	Sector
Compensation of employees	21.6		Private fixed investment	61.1	
Management of companies & enterprises	8.5	Services	Exports of goods & services	23.2	Cap Inv
Computer terminals & peripherals	7.1	Manufg.	Physician, dentist, other health practitioner offices	7.2	Services
Wholesale trade	6.8	Trade	General Federal government services, nondefense	1.9	Fed Govt
Software publishers	5.4	Services	Change in private inventories	1.7	In House
Printed circuit assemblies (electronic assemblies)	4.1	Manufg.	Federal government, investment, national defense	1.7	Fed Govt
Forging, stamping, & sintering, nec	3.3	Manufg.	Medical & diagnostic labs & outpatient services	1.5	Services
Electron tubes	2.6	Manufg.	Federal government, investment, nondefense	0.9	Fed Govt
Scientific research & development services	2.4	Services	S/L govt. invest., other	0.6	S/L Govt
Semiconductors & related devices	2.1	Manufg.			
Crowns & closures & metal stamping	1.6	Manufg.			
Turned products & screws, nuts, & bolts	1.4	Manufg.			
Computer storage devices	1.1	Manufg.			
Machine shops	0.9	Manufg.			
Iron & steel mills & ferroalloys	0.8	Manufg.			
Advertising & related services	0.8	Services			
Copper rolling, drawing, extruding, & alloying	0.7	Manufg.			
Real estate	0.7	Fin/R.E.			
Coating, engraving, heat treating & allied activities	0.7	Manufg.			
Electronic capacitors, resistors, coils, transformers	0.6	Manufg.			
Plastics packaging materials, film & sheet	0.6	Manufg.			
Custom roll forming	0.5	Manufg.			
Bare printed circuit boards	0.5	Manufg.			
Legal services	0.5	Services			
Communication & energy wires & cables	0.5	Manufg.			
Truck transportation	0.5	Util.			
Watches, clocks, & related devices	0.4	Manufg.			
Lessors of nonfinancial assets	0.3	Fin/R.E.			
Warehousing & storage	0.3	Util.			
Power generation & supply	0.3	Util.			
Securities, commodity contracts, investments	0.3	Fin/R.E.			
Telecommunications	0.3	Services			
Metal cans, boxes, & other containers (light gauge)	0.3	Manufg.			
Automotive equipment rental & leasing	0.3	Fin/R.E.			
Paperboard containers	0.3	Manufg.			
Electronic connectors	0.3	Manufg.			

Continued on next page.

INPUTS AND OUTPUTS FOR IRRADIATION APPARATUS MANUFACTURING - Continued

Economic Sector or Industry Providing Inputs	%	Sector	Economic Sector or Industry Buying Outputs	%	Sector
Fabricated metals, nec	0.2	Manufg.			
Electronic components, nec	0.2	Manufg.			
Accounting, tax preparation, bookkeeping, & payroll	0.2	Services			
Ferrous metal foundries	0.2	Manufg.			
Plate work & fabricated structural products	0.2	Manufg.			
Nonferrous metal foundries	0.2	Manufg.			
Management, scientific, & technical consulting	0.2	Services			
Ball & roller bearings	0.2	Manufg.			
Handtools	0.2	Manufg.			
Noncomparable imports	0.2	Foreign			
Data processing, hosting, & related services	0.2	Services			
Taxes on production & imports, less subsidies	0.1				
Commercial & industrial machinery rental & leasing	0.1	Fin/R.E.			
Valve & fittings other than plumbing	0.1	Manufg.			
Monetary authorities/depository credit intermediation	0.1	Fin/R.E.			
Other computer related services, including facilities	0.1	Services			
Relay & industrial controls	0.1	Manufg.			

Source: Benchmark Input-Output Accounts for the U.S. Economy, 2002, U.S. Department of Commerce, Washington, D.C., January 2008. The abbreviation nec stands for 'not elsewhere classified'.

OCCUPATIONS EMPLOYED BY NAVIGATIONAL, MEASURING, MEDICAL, & CONTROL INSTRUMENTS

Occupation	% of Total 2006	Change to 2016	Occupation	% of Total 2006	Change to 2016
Electrical & electronic equipment assemblers	7.1	-23.4	First-line supervisors/managers of production workers	2.1	-4.3
Team assemblers	5.3	-4.3	Engineers, nec	1.9	-4.3
Electromechanical equipment assemblers	3.6	-4.3	Purchasing agents, exc wholesale, retail, & farm	1.9	-4.3
Electrical engineers	3.3	-4.3	Machinists	1.8	0.5
Computer software engineers, applications	2.9	14.9	General & operations managers	1.7	-13.8
Aerospace engineers	2.9	0.5	Sales representatives, wholesale & manufacturing, tech	1.6	-4.3
Mechanical engineers	2.8	-4.3	Executive secretaries & administrative assistants	1.5	-4.3
Electrical & electronic engineering technicians	2.7	-4.3	Customer service representatives	1.3	5.3
Computer software engineers, systems software	2.7	5.3	Office clerks, general	1.2	-5.7
Industrial engineers	2.5	16.3	Shipping, receiving, & traffic clerks	1.2	-7.9
Inspectors, testers, sorters, samplers, & weighers	2.4	-9.7	Accountants & auditors	1.2	-4.3
Engineering managers	2.4	-4.3	Production, planning, & expediting clerks	1.2	-4.3
Electronics engineers, exc computer	2.2	-4.3			

Source: Industry-Occupation Matrix, Bureau of Labor Statistics, December 4, 2007. These data are reported based on 4-digit NAICS categories but have been matched to corresponding 6-digit NAICS industry codes. The change reported for each occupation to the year 2016 is a percent of growth or decline as estimated by the Bureau of Labor Statistics. The abbreviation nec stands for 'not elsewhere classified'.

LOCATION BY STATE AND REGIONAL CONCENTRATION

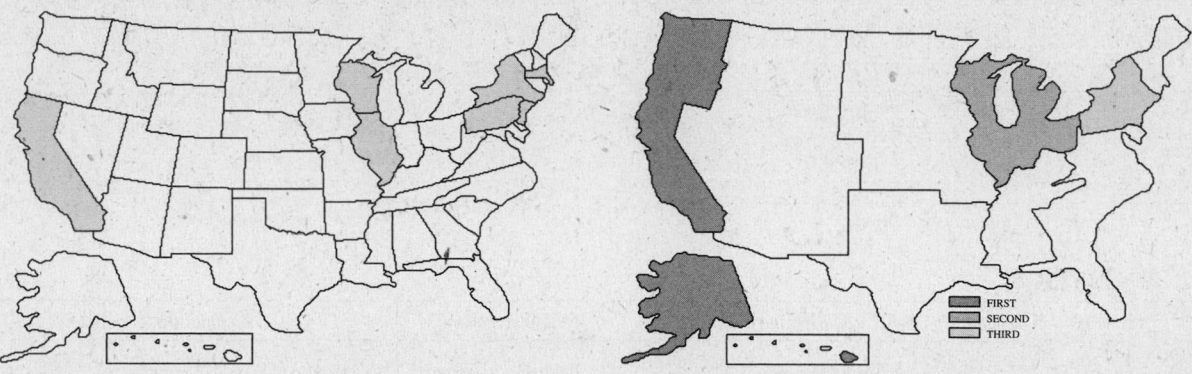

INDUSTRY DATA BY STATE

State	Establish-ments	Shipments			Employment				Cost as % of Shipments	Investment per Employee ($)
		Total ($ mil)	% of U.S.	Per Establ.	Total Number	% of U.S.	Per Establ.	Wages ($/hour)		
California	33	1,471.7	33.5	44,598.2	4,880	36.2	148	28.89	47.6	6,891
Massachusetts	16	561.7	12.8	35,108.7	2,381	17.7	149	15.41	38.7	5,698
Illinois	22	533.0	12.1	24,227.8	1,571	11.6	71	21.35	53.3	4,377
New York	9	82.6	1.9	9,173.3	419	3.1	47	12.86	38.5	4,232
Wisconsin	5	69.7	1.6	13,938.6	301	2.2	60	14.28	33.2	9,535
New Jersey	8	41.4	0.9	5,174.6	190	1.4	24	16.92	33.7	9,663
Pennsylvania	6	33.9	0.8	5,644.3	140	1.0	23	15.47	44.7	4,550

Source: 2002 *Economic Census*. The states are in descending order of shipments or establishments (if shipment data are missing for the majority). The symbol (D) appears when data are withheld to prevent disclosure of competitive information. States marked with (D) are sorted by number of establishments. A dash (-) indicates that the data element cannot be calculated. Data may not show all states active in the NAICS category. All data available at the time of publication are shown.

NAICS 334518 - WATCH, CLOCK, AND PARTS MANUFACTURING

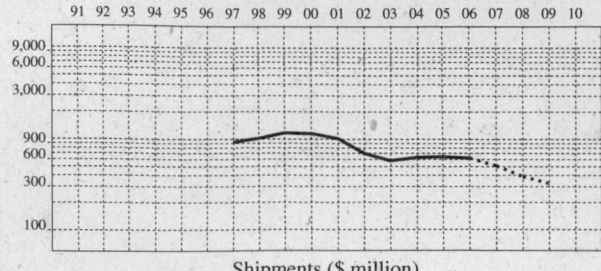

Shipments ($ million)

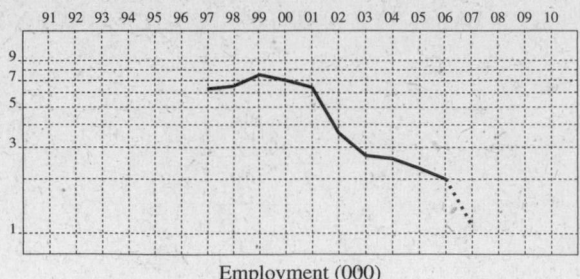

Employment (000)

GENERAL STATISTICS

Year	Com-panies	Establishments		Employment			Compensation		Production ($ million)			
		Total	with 20 or more employees	Total (000)	Production Workers (000)	Hours (Mil)	Payroll ($ mil)	Wages ($/hr)	Cost of Materials	Value Added by Manufacture	Value of Shipments	Capital Invest.
1997	144	145	44	6.3	4.5	9.2	178.5	10.14	380.5	536.9	921.3	26.2
1998		172	69	6.5	4.5	9.6	199.4	10.34	425.1	598.5	1,020.8	30.9
1999		139	48	7.5	5.3	10.5	211.2	10.31	445.2	771.9	1,168.4	37.7
2000		133	42	7.0	4.3	11.1	218.2	9.39	463.5	695.1	1,150.6	44.1
2001		128	42	6.4	3.8	8.3	200.2	11.93	452.8	568.4	1,018.2	23.6
2002	124	126	38	3.6	2.4	4.8	125.5	13.30	288.4	419.3	699.6	9.4
2003		121	37	2.7	1.8	3.6	97.0	13.04	226.7	348.6	579.1	4.4
2004		120	37	2.6	1.8	3.6	102.3	15.62	243.7	397.0	630.3	5.0
2005		115	36	2.3	1.5	3.0	98.4	17.06	236.8	412.0	641.1	7.7
2006		107P	31P	2.0	1.3	2.5	92.4	17.66	230.2	402.9	621.6	5.0
2007		101P	28P	1.1P	0.6P	1.1P	70.2P	18.00P	188.6P	330.0P	509.1P	
2008		91P	23P				40.3P	19.86P	143.3P	250.8P	387.0P	
2009		85P	21P				25.3P	20.79P	120.7P	211.2P	325.9P	
2010												

Sources: 1997 and 2002 *Economic Census*; other years, up to 2006, are from *Annual Survey of Manufactures*. Establishment counts for non-Census years are from *County Business Patterns*; 1997 and 2002 values are from the 1997 and 2002 censuses, respectively. 'P's show projections by the editors.

INDICES OF CHANGE

Year	Com-panies	Establishments		Employment			Compensation		Production ($ million)			
		Total	with 20 or more employees	Total (000)	Production Workers (000)	Hours (Mil)	Payroll ($ mil)	Wages ($/hr)	Cost of Materials	Value Added by Manufacture	Value of Shipments	Capital Invest.
1997	116	115	116	175	188	192	142	76	132	128	132	279
1998		137	182	181	188	200	159	78	147	143	146	329
1999		110	126	208	221	219	168	78	154	184	167	401
2000		106	111	194	179	231	174	71	161	166	164	469
2001		102	111	178	158	173	160	90	157	136	146	251
2002	100	100	100	100	100	100	100	100	100	100	100	100
2003		96	97	75	75	75	77	98	79	83	83	47
2004		95	97	72	75	75	82	117	85	95	90	53
2005		91	95	64	63	63	78	128	82	98	92	82
2006		85P	81P	56	54	52	74	133	80	96	89	53
2007		80P	74P	31P	25P	23P	56P	135P	65P	79P	73P	
2008		72P	61P				32P	149P	50P	60P	55P	
2009		68P	54P				20P	156P	42P	50P	47P	
2010												

Sources: Same as General Statistics. Values reflect change from the base year, 2002. Values above 100 mean greater than 2002, values below 100 mean less than 2002, and the values of 100 in other years means the same as 2002. 'P's show projections by the editors.

SELECTED RATIOS

For 2002	Avg. of All Manufact.	Analyzed Industry	Index	For 2002	Avg. of All Manufact.	Analyzed Industry	Index
Employees per Establishment	42	29	68	Value Added per Production Worker	182,367	174,708	96
Payroll per Establishment	1,639,184	996,032	61	Cost per Establishment	5,769,015	2,288,889	40
Payroll per Employee	39,053	34,861	89	Cost per Employee	137,446	80,111	58
Production Workers per Establishment	30	19	65	Cost per Production Worker	195,506	120,167	61
Wages per Establishment	694,845	506,667	73	Shipments per Establishment	11,158,348	5,552,381	50
Wages per Production Worker	23,548	26,600	113	Shipments per Employee	265,847	194,333	73
Hours per Production Worker	1,980	2,000	101	Shipments per Production Worker	378,144	291,500	77
Wages per Hour	11.89	13.30	112	Investment per Establishment	361,338	74,603	21
Value Added per Establishment	5,381,325	3,327,778	62	Investment per Employee	8,609	2,611	30
Value Added per Employee	128,210	116,472	91	Investment per Production Worker	12,245	3,917	32

Sources: Same as General Statistics. The 'Average of All Manufacturing' column represents the average of all manufacturing industries reported for the most recent complete year available. The Index shows the relationship between the Average and the Analyzed Industry. For example, 100 means that they are equal; 500 that the Analyzed Industry is five times the average; 50 means that the Analyzed Industry is half the national average. The abbreviation 'na' is used to show that data are 'not available'. Ratios shown for 2002, the last complete census year.

LEADING COMPANIES   Number shown: 75   Total sales ($ mil): 64,881   Total employment (000): 162.8

Company Name	Address				CEO Name	Phone	Co. Type	Sales ($ mil)	Empl. (000)
Xerox Corp.	PO Box 1600	Stamford	CT	06904		203-968-3000	P	17,288	57.4
Canon U.S.A. Inc.	1 Canon Plz.	Lake Success	NY	11042	Yoroku Adachi	516-328-5000	S	10,745*	11.0
Triangle Suspension Systems	PO Box 425	Du Bois	PA	15801	Greg Maffia	814-375-7211	R	7,000*	0.2
Pitney Bowes Inc.	1 Elmcroft Rd.	Stamford	CT	06926	Michael J. Critelli	203-356-5000	P	6,130	26.3
Lexmark International Inc.	740 New Circle Rd.	Lexington	KY	40550	Paul J. Curlander	859-232-2000	P	4,974	13.8
Harris Corp.	1025 W NASA	Melbourne	FL	32919		321-727-9100	P	4,243	16.0
Oce-USA Inc.	5450 N Cumberland	Chicago	IL	60656	Jan Dix	773-714-8500	S	3,671*	3.1
ACCO Brands Corp.	300 Tower Pkwy.	Lincolnshire	IL	60069	David Campbell		P	1,939	6.0
Stenograph L.L.C.	1500 Bishop Ct.	Mount Prospect	IL	60056		847-803-1400	R	1,560*	0.2
Fossil Inc.	2280 N Greenville	Richardson	TX	75082	Michael W. Barnes	972-234-2525	P	1,433	6.0
Standard Register Co.	PO Box 1167	Dayton	OH	45401		937-221-1000	P	865	3.8
White Systems Inc.	30 Boright Ave.	Kenilworth	NJ	07033	Richard Paolino	908-272-6700	S	673*	0.3
Movado Group Inc.	650 From Rd.	Paramus	NJ	07652	Efraim Grinberg	201-267-8000	P	533	1.3
Swatch Group (US) Inc.	1200 Harbor Blvd.	Weehawken	NJ	07087	Nicolas G. Hayek	201-271-1400	S	322*	0.7
Toshiba America Info. Systems	PO Box 19724	Irvine	CA	92623		949-583-3000	S	290*	1.7
Ricoh Electronics Inc.	2320 Redhill Ave.	Santa Ana	CA	92705	Shunsuke Nakanishi	949-250-7440	R	276*	1.1
Brother Industries Inc.	7819 N Brother Blvd	Bartlett	TN	38133	Hiromi Gunji	901-377-7777	R	258*	1.2
Kern-Liebers USA Inc.	PO Box 396	Holland	OH	43528	Lothar Bauerle	419-865-2437	R	178*	<0.1
Digi International Inc.	11001 Bren Rd. E	Minnetonka	MN	55343	Joseph T. Dunsmore	952-912-3444	P	173	0.6
Bulman Products Inc.	1650 McReynolds	Grand Rapids	MI	49504		616-363-4416	R	124*	<0.1
Chestnut Group Inc.	115 Bloomingdale	Wayne	PA	19087	Park Blatchford	610-688-3300	R	122*	0.4
Peterson American Co.	21200 Telegraph Rd.	Southfield	MI	48034	Eric C. Peterson	248-799-5400	R	100*	1.0
Howard Miller Clock Co.	860 E Main Ave.	Zeeland	MI	49464	Howard Miller	616-772-9131	R	98*	0.4
Vulcan Inc.	PO Box 1850	Foley	AL	36536	Robert W. Lee	251-943-7000	R	96*	0.3
Swiss Army Brands Inc.	PO Box 874	Shelton	CT	06484		203-929-6391	S	93*	0.3
Hyson Products	10367 Brecksvil Rd.	Brecksville	OH	44141	Regis Minerd	440-526-5900	D	91*	0.7
Midwest Trophy Manufacturing	PO Box 15659	Oklahoma City	OK	73155		405-670-4545	R	82*	0.5
Cummins-Allison Corp.	PO Box 339	Mount Prospect	IL	60056	John Jones	847-299-9550	R	67*	0.2
Standard Steel Specialty Co.	PO Box 20	Beaver Falls	PA	15010	Robert Conley	724-846-7600	S	67*	0.3
ECRM Inc.	554 Clark Rd.	Tewksbury	MA	01876	Richard Black	978-851-0207	R	63*	0.2
Mid-West Spring and Stamping	1404 Joliet Rd., C	Romeoville	IL	60446	Michael B. Curran		R	62*	0.5
Uttermost Company Inc.	PO Box 558	Rocky Mount	VA	24151	Mac Cooper	540-483-5103	R	62*	0.3
Amano Cincinnati Inc.	140 Harrison Ave.	Roseland	NJ	07068	Osamu Okagaki	973-403-1900	R	56*	0.1
Koh-I-Noor Inc.	1 River Rd.	Leeds	MA	01053		413-584-5446	R	53*	0.4
Franklin Electronic Publishers	1 Franklin Plz.	Burlington	NJ	08016	Barry J. Lipsky	609-386-2500	P	52	0.2
Seiko Corporation of America	1111 Macarthur	Mahwah	NJ	07430		201-529-5730	S	51*	0.5
Bal-Seal Engineering Co.	19650 Pauling	Foothill Ranch	CA	92610	Peter Balsells	949-460-2100	R	46*	0.3
American Thermoform Corp.	1758 Brackett St.	La Verne	CA	91750		909-593-6711	R	45*	<0.1
Int'l Staple and Machine	PO Box 629	Butler	PA	16003	Farhad Gerannayeh		R	40*	0.2
Varitronic Systems Inc.	6835 Winnetka Cir.	Brooklyn Park	MN	55428	Frank Jaehnert	763-536-6400	D	38*	0.3
Graphic Enterprises Inc.	3874 Highland Park	North Canton	OH	44720	Jason Parikh		R	37*	0.3
Newbold Corp.	450 Weaver St.	Rocky Mount	VA	24151	Robert Scott	540-489-4400	R	36*	0.2
Caldwell Manufacturing Co.	PO Box 92891	Rochester	NY	14692	Edward Boucher	585-352-3790	R	35*	0.1
Gunther International Ltd.	1 Winnenden Rd.	Norwich	CT	06360	Marc I. Perkins	860-823-1427	R	34	0.2
Gr Spring and Stamping Inc.	PO Box 141397	Grand Rapids	MI	49514	James Zawacki	616-453-4491	R	32*	0.3
JD Norman Industries Inc.	787 W Belden Ave.	Addison	IL	60101		630-458-3700	R	31*	<0.1
Quality Spring Togo Inc.	355 Jay St.	Coldwater	MI	49036	Mark Katayama	517-278-2391	R	28*	0.2
New Products International	1 Alpine Ct.	Chestnut Ridge	NY	10977	Giora Tamir	845-352-9700	R	28*	<0.1
Wire Products Company Inc.	14601 Indu. Pkwy.	Cleveland	OH	44135	Scot Kennedy	216-267-0777	R	28*	0.2
Mapes Piano String Co.	PO Box 700	Elizabethton	TN	37644		423-543-3195	R	26*	0.2
Connecticut Spring & Stamping	48 Spring Ln.	Farmington	CT	06032	William Stevenson	860-677-1341	R	26*	0.2
Mid Continent Spring Co.	PO Box 649	Hopkinsville	KY	42241	Donald Langhi	270-885-8433	R	25*	0.2
Control Module Inc.	227 Brainard Rd.	Enfield	CT	06082	Jana Moak	860-745-2433	R	25*	<0.1
S and S Time Corp.	1381 N 108th E Ave.	Tulsa	OK	74116	VI Schulmeier	918-437-3572	R	25*	<0.1
Perfection Spring and Stamping	PO Box 275	Mount Prospect	IL	60056	David Kahn	847-437-3900	R	23*	0.1
Dudek and Bock Spring Mfg.	5100 W Roosevelt	Chicago	IL	60644	John Dudek	773-379-4100	R	23*	0.2
Exacto Spring Corp.	PO Box 24	Grafton	WI	53024	Greg Heitz	262-377-3970	R	23*	0.2
Spring Draco Manufacturing Co.	7042 Long Dr.	Houston	TX	77087	Barry Drager	713-645-4973	R	22*	0.2
Spring Rowley and Stamping	PO Box 276	Bristol	CT	06011	Stanley Bitel	860-582-8175	R	21*	0.2
Selco Custom Time Corp.	8909 E 21st St.	Tulsa	OK	74129	Larry Abels	918-622-6100	R	21*	<0.1
Takane USA Inc.	18640 Crenshaw	Torrance	CA	90504	Kenji Hanaoka	310-538-4920	R	20*	0.1
E Gluck Corp.	2910 Thomson Ave.	Long Island Cty	NY	11101	Eugen Gluck	718-784-0700	R	20*	0.4
Riddles Group Inc.	PO Box 5600	Rapid City	SD	57709	Brett Riddle	605-343-2226	R	20*	0.3
inc.jet Inc.	1 Winnenden Rd.	Norwich	CT	06360	Marc Perkins	860-823-3090	R	20*	<0.1
Winamac Coil Spring Inc.	PO Box 278	Kewanna	IN	46939	Daniel Pesaresi	574-653-2186	R	20*	0.2
StockerYale Inc.	32 Hampshire Rd.	Salem	NH	03079	Mark W. Blodgett	603-893-8778	P	19	0.2
Heidelberg/Baumfolder Corp.	1660 Campbell Rd.	Sidney	OH	45365	Ulrik Nygaard	937-492-1281	S	19*	<0.1
Fraen Corp.	80 Newcrossing Rd.	Reading	MA	01867	Charles Fuller	781-942-2223	R	19*	0.1
Accu-Time Systems Inc.	420 Somers Rd.	Ellington	CT	06029	Peter DiMaria	860-870-5000	R	18	<0.1
Deltrol Controls	PO Box 343915	Milwaukee	WI	53234	Josh Ferrer	414-671-6800	S	18*	0.3
Twist Inc.	PO Box 177	Jamestown	OH	45335	Joe Wright	937-675-9581	R	18*	0.1
Gb Instruments Inc.	1143 W Newport	Deerfield Beach	FL	33442	Maurice Rochman	954-596-5000	R	17*	<0.1
Card Technology Corp.	70 Eisenhower Dr.	Paramus	NJ	07652		201-845-7373	R	16*	0.1
Helical Products Company Inc.	PO Box 1069	Santa Maria	CA	93456	Herbert Merrell	805-928-3851	R	16*	0.1
Smalley Steel Ring Co.	555 Oakwood Rd.	Lake Zurich	IL	60047	Charles Greenhill	847-719-5900	R	16*	0.1

Source: Ward's Business Directory of U.S. Private and Public Companies, Volumes 1 and 2, 2008. The company type code used is as follows: P - Public, R - Private, S - Subsidiary, D - Division, J - Joint Venture, A - Affiliate, G - Group. Sales are in millions of dollars, employees are in thousands. An asterisk (*) indicates an estimated sales volume. The symbol < stands for 'less than'. Company names and addresses are truncated, in some cases, to fit into the available space.

MATERIALS CONSUMED

Material	Quantity	Delivered Cost ($ million)
Metal shapes and forms (exc. castings, forgings, fabr. metal products)	(X)	0.5
Castings, rough and semifinished	(X)	(D)
Other fabricated metal products (exc. castings and forgings)	(X)	3.5
Forgings	(X)	(D)
Printed ciruit boards (without inserted components) for electronic circuitry	(X)	(D)
Printed computer processors for electronic circuitry	(X)	(D)
Resistors for electronic circuitry	(X)	1.6
Capacitors for electronic circuitry	(X)	2.6
Other components and accessories, for electronic circuitry (coils, transformers, etc.), excluding tubes	(X)	9.8
Electric motors and generators	(X)	3.6
Domestic (made in the United States) watch movements/modules	(X)	0.5
Imported (not made in the United States) watch movements and modules	(X)	8.2
Domestic (made in the United States) watchcases	(X)	(D)
Imported (not made in the United States) watchcases	(X)	(D)
Domestic (made in the United States) watch parts (exc. movements and face crystals)	(X)	(D)
Imported (not made in the United States) watch parts, excluding movements and face crystals	(X)	2.2
Watchbands	(X)	0.3
Face crystals	(X)	(D)
Precious metals (gold, platinum, etc.), all forms (incl. ingot, sheet, strip, solder, plating, electrodes, etc.)	(X)	(D)
Steel, aluminum, and other metal electronic enclosures	(X)	8.6
Plastics electronic enclosures	(X)	7.0
Batteries, primary	(X)	1.2
Metal bolts, nuts, screws, and other screw machine products	(X)	1.6
Plastics resins consumed in the form of granules, pellets, etc.	(X)	(D)
Appliance outlets and other current-carrying wiring devices	(X)	(D)
Paperboard containers, boxes, and corrugated paperboard	(X)	5.3
All other materials, components, parts, containers, and supplies	(X)	68.5
Materials, ingredients, containers, and supplies, nsk	(X)	81.3

Source: 2002 Economic Census. Explanation of symbols used: (D): Withheld to avoid disclosure of competitive data; na: Not available; (S): Withheld because statistical norms were not met; (X): Not applicable; (Z): Less than half the unit shown; nec: Not elsewhere classified; nsk: Not specified by kind; - : zero; p : 10-19 percent estimated; q : 20-29 percent estimated.

PRODUCT SHARE DETAILS

Product or Product Class Shipments	Mil. $	Product or Product Class Shipments	Mil. $
WATCHES, CLOCKS, AND PARTS	638.2	Other complete clocks, excluding alarm clocks	22.9
Watches, watchcases, movements, and modules (including watch parts)	**113.6**	Household timing mechanisms, excluding time recording and time stamp machines	(D)
Watches	48.3	Commercial timing mechanisms, excluding time recording and time stamp machines	7.9
Watchcases, movements and modules (including watch parts)	9.1	Time recording and time stamp machines and devices	213.8
Lapidary work, including cutting, engraving, and polishing precious stones, diamonds, semiprecious stones, natural pearls, and cultured pearls, for use as watch jewels	56.2	Other timing mechanisms (including military), excluding time recording and time stamp machines	(D)
Clocks, timing mechanisms, time recording and time stamp devices, time switches, clock movements, and clock cases (including parts)	**507.5**	Timers and switch clocks with clock or watch movements or modules having dials or displays for telling time of day	15.7
		Clock movements and modules, complete	13.0
Alarm clocks, excluding clock timers and timing mechanisms	46.6	Chronometers	14.8
Household wall clocks, excluding alarm clocks	31.3	Other clock parts (except timing motors), clock and watch springs, and parts and attachments for time recording and time stamp devices	13.2
All other household clocks, excluding alarm clocks	102.0	**Watches, clocks, and parts, nsk, total**	**17.2**

Source: 2002 Economic Census. The values are product shipments in millions of dollars for 2002. Total product shipments may be lower or higher than industry shipments. See Introduction for a full discussion. Values of indented subcategories are summed in the main heading(s). The symbol (D) appears when data are withheld to prevent disclosure of competitive information. The abbreviation nsk stands for 'not specified by kind' and nec for 'not elsewhere classified'. A dash (-) means zero.

INPUTS AND OUTPUTS FOR WATCHES, CLOCKS, & OTHER MEASURING DEVICES

Economic Sector or Industry Providing Inputs	%	Sector	Economic Sector or Industry Buying Outputs	%	Sector
Compensation of employees	34.4		Personal consumption expenditures	30.4	
Management of companies & enterprises	10.7	Services	Private fixed investment	26.1	
Software publishers	7.9	Services	Exports of goods & services	17.4	Cap Inv
Wholesale trade	3.7	Trade	Aircraft	8.2	Manufg.
Lessors of nonfinancial assets	3.4	Fin/R.E.	General Federal government services, nondefense	3.7	Fed Govt
Scientific research & development services	3.0	Services	General S/L govt. services	2.0	S/L Govt
Printed circuit assemblies (electronic assemblies)	2.9	Manufg.	General Federal government services, defense	1.7	Fed Govt
Plastics products, nec	1.5	Manufg.	S/L govt. invest., other	1.3	S/L Govt
Electricity & signal testing instruments	1.5	Manufg.	Search, detection, & navigation instruments	1.2	Manufg.
Real estate	1.3	Fin/R.E.	Other S/L govt. enterprises	1.1	S/L Govt
Iron & steel mills & ferroalloys	1.2	Manufg.	Watches, clocks, & related devices	0.6	Manufg.

Continued on next page.

INPUTS AND OUTPUTS FOR WATCHES, CLOCKS, & OTHER MEASURING DEVICES - Continued

Economic Sector or Industry Providing Inputs	%	Sector	Economic Sector or Industry Buying Outputs	%	Sector
Advertising & related services	1.2	Services	Household laundry equipment	0.5	Manufg.
Semiconductors & related devices	1.1	Manufg.	Architectural, engineering, & related services	0.5	Services
Watches, clocks, & related devices	1.0	Manufg.	Household cooking appliances	0.5	Manufg.
Turned products & screws, nuts, & bolts	0.9	Manufg.	Tobacco products	0.5	Manufg.
Electronic components, nec	0.9	Manufg.	Asphalt paving mixtures & blocks	0.4	Manufg.
Electronic capacitors, resistors, coils, transformers	0.8	Manufg.	Change in private inventories	0.4	In House
Computer terminals & peripherals	0.8	Manufg.	Wood containers & pallets	0.4	Manufg.
Ornamental & architectural metal products	0.7	Manufg.	Computer system design services	0.3	Services
Wiring devices	0.7	Manufg.	Civic, social, & professional organizations	0.3	Services
Machine shops	0.7	Manufg.	Wholesale trade	0.2	Trade
Legal services	0.7	Services	Irradiation apparatus	0.2	Manufg.
Securities, commodity contracts, investments	0.7	Fin/R.E.	S/L govt. invest., education	0.2	S/L Govt
Bare printed circuit boards	0.6	Manufg.	Scientific research & development services	0.2	Services
Power generation & supply	0.6	Util.	Household refrigerators & home freezers	0.2	Manufg.
Architectural, engineering, & related services	0.6	Services	Major household appliances, nec	0.1	Manufg.
Telecommunications	0.5	Services	Commercial & health care structures	0.1	Construct.
Computer storage devices	0.5	Manufg.	Management of companies & enterprises	0.1	Services
Custom computer programming services	0.5	Services	Nonresidential structures, nec	0.1	Construct.
Monetary authorities/depository credit intermediation	0.5	Fin/R.E.	Personal & household goods repair/maintenance	0.1	Services
Coating, engraving, heat treating & allied activities	0.5	Manufg.	Retail trade	0.1	Trade
Chemical products & preparations, nec	0.4	Manufg.			
Food services & drinking places	0.4	Services			
Plastics materials & resins	0.4	Manufg.			
Data processing, hosting, & related services	0.4	Services			
Accounting, tax preparation, bookkeeping, & payroll	0.4	Services			
Copper rolling, drawing, extruding, & alloying	0.4	Manufg.			
Professional, scientific, technical services, nec	0.4	Services			
Hotels & motels, including casino hotels	0.4	Services			
Other computer related services, including facilities	0.3	Services			
Warehousing & storage	0.3	Util.			
Employment services	0.3	Services			
Truck transportation	0.3	Util.			
Paperboard containers	0.3	Manufg.			
Taxes on production & imports, less subsidies	0.3				
Primary nonferrous metal, ex. copper & aluminum	0.3	Manufg.			
Automotive equipment rental & leasing	0.3	Fin/R.E.			
Motors & generators	0.3	Manufg.			
Management, scientific, & technical consulting	0.3	Services			
Air transportation	0.3	Util.			
Ferrous metal foundries	0.3	Manufg.			
Specialized design services	0.3	Services			
Nonferrous metal foundries	0.2	Manufg.			
Alumina refining & primary aluminum production	0.2	Manufg.			
Noncomparable imports	0.2	Foreign			
Communication & energy wires & cables	0.2	Manufg.			
Fabricated metals, nec	0.2	Manufg.			
Cutting tools & machine tool accessories	0.2	Manufg.			
Business support services	0.2	Services			
Relay & industrial controls	0.2	Manufg.			
Services to buildings & dwellings	0.2	Services			
Maintenance/repair of nonresidential structures	0.2	Construct.			
Aluminum products from purchased aluminum	0.2	Manufg.			
Retail trade	0.2	Trade			
Broadcast & wireless communications equipment	0.1	Manufg.			
Commercial & industrial machinery rental & leasing	0.1	Fin/R.E.			
Valve & fittings other than plumbing	0.1	Manufg.			
Support services, nec	0.1	Services			
Crowns & closures & metal stamping	0.1	Manufg.			
Computer system design services	0.1	Services			
Paperboard mills	0.1	Manufg.			
Automotive repair & maintenance, ex. car washes	0.1	Services			
Forging, stamping, & sintering, nec	0.1	Manufg.			
Investigation & security services	0.1	Services			
Commercial & industrial equipment repair/maintenance	0.1	Services			

Source: Benchmark Input-Output Accounts for the U.S. Economy, 2002, U.S. Department of Commerce, Washington D.C., January 2008. User should note that this Input-Output table is not for this particular narrowly defined industry but for a larger aggregate. Input and Output data for Watches, Clocks, & Other Measuring Devices include Input and Output data for the Annual Survey of Manufactures' NAICS industries 334518 and 334519. The abbreviation nec stands for 'not elsewhere classified'.

OCCUPATIONS EMPLOYED BY NAVIGATIONAL, MEASURING, MEDICAL, & CONTROL INSTRUMENTS

Occupation	% of Total 2006	Change to 2016	Occupation	% of Total 2006	Change to 2016
Electrical & electronic equipment assemblers	7.1	-23.4	First-line supervisors/managers of production workers	2.1	-4.3
Team assemblers	5.3	-4.3	Engineers, nec	1.9	-4.3
Electromechanical equipment assemblers	3.6	-4.3	Purchasing agents, exc wholesale, retail, & farm	1.9	-4.3
Electrical engineers	3.3	-4.3	Machinists	1.8	0.5
Computer software engineers, applications	2.9	14.9	General & operations managers	1.7	-13.8
Aerospace engineers	2.9	0.5	Sales representatives, wholesale & manufacturing, tech	1.6	-4.3
Mechanical engineers	2.8	-4.3	Executive secretaries & administrative assistants	1.5	-4.3
Electrical & electronic engineering technicians	2.7	-4.3	Customer service representatives	1.3	5.3
Computer software engineers, systems software	2.7	5.3	Office clerks, general	1.2	-5.7
Industrial engineers	2.5	16.3	Shipping, receiving, & traffic clerks	1.2	-7.9
Inspectors, testers, sorters, samplers, & weighers	2.4	-9.7	Accountants & auditors	1.2	-4.3
Engineering managers	2.4	-4.3	Production, planning, & expediting clerks	1.2	-4.3
Electronics engineers, exc computer	2.2	-4.3			

Source: Industry-Occupation Matrix, Bureau of Labor Statistics, December 4, 2007. These data are reported based on 4-digit NAICS categories but have been matched to corresponding 6-digit NAICS industry codes. The change reported for each occupation to the year 2016 is a percent of growth or decline as estimated by the Bureau of Labor Statistics. The abbreviation nec stands for 'not elsewhere classified'.

LOCATION BY STATE AND REGIONAL CONCENTRATION

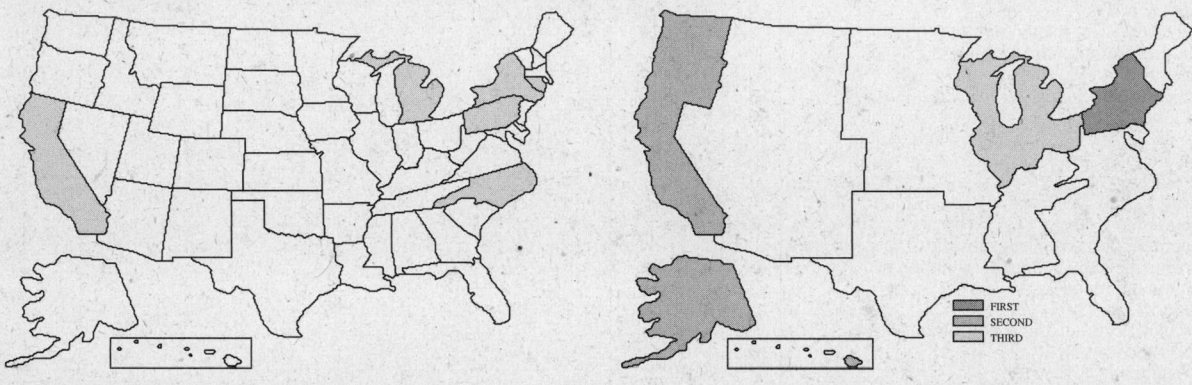

FIRST
SECOND
THIRD

INDUSTRY DATA BY STATE

State	Establish-ments	Shipments			Employment				Cost as % of Shipments	Investment per Employee ($)
		Total ($ mil)	% of U.S.	Per Establ.	Total Number	% of U.S.	Per Establ.	Wages ($/hour)		
Michigan	7	116.8	16.7	16,691.0	737	20.6	105	16.15	43.8	1,285
New York	15	78.1	11.2	5,205.2	255	7.1	17	14.54	64.3	5,573
California	20	77.2	11.0	3,860.2	497	13.9	25	10.01	46.8	3,284
Connecticut	7	26.8	3.8	3,824.4	113	3.2	16	15.08	33.6	1,743
North Carolina	3	26.2	3.7	8,745.0	134	3.7	45	14.15	51.6	2,463
Pennsylvania	10	11.7	1.7	1,173.6	142	4.0	14	9.75	40.5	4,077

Source: 2002 *Economic Census*. The states are in descending order of shipments or establishments (if shipment data are missing for the majority). The symbol (D) appears when data are withheld to prevent disclosure of competitive information. States marked with (D) are sorted by number of establishments. A dash (-) indicates that the data element cannot be calculated. Data may not show all states active in the NAICS category. All data available at the time of publication are shown.

NAICS 334519 - MEASURING AND CONTROLLING DEVICE MANUFACTURING NEC

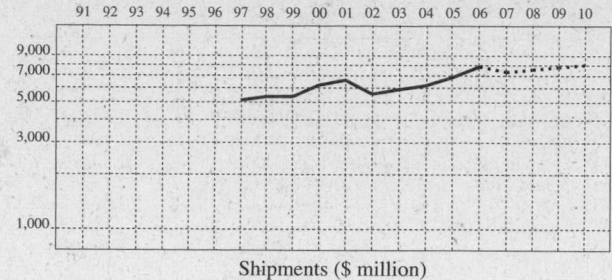

Shipments ($ million)

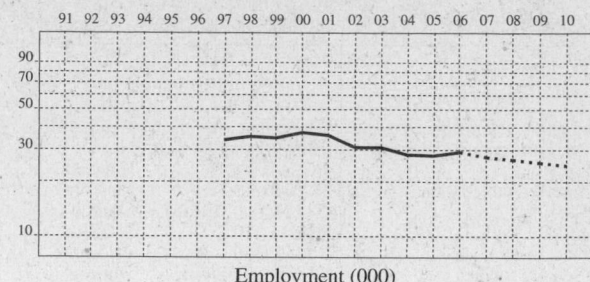

Employment (000)

GENERAL STATISTICS

Year	Com-panies	Establishments		Employment			Compensation		Production ($ million)			
		Total	with 20 or more employees	Total (000)	Production Workers (000)	Hours (Mil)	Payroll ($ mil)	Wages ($/hr)	Cost of Materials	Value Added by Manufacture	Value of Shipments	Capital Invest.
1997	833	858	332	33.9	18.0	35.0	1,358.0	14.81	1,975.3	3,123.4	5,120.7	135.3
1998		873	331	35.4	18.0	36.1	1,477.2	15.78	2,080.3	3,331.9	5,368.8	164.5
1999		859	324	34.8	17.6	32.4	1,468.2	16.11	2,136.1	3,230.3	5,376.4	158.3
2000		843	328	37.3	18.6	35.2	1,674.7	16.47	2,487.8	3,904.8	6,228.9	195.1
2001		830	315	36.0	18.0	34.3	1,697.9	16.62	2,668.4	3,998.0	6,617.3	121.9
2002	783	825	283	30.9	14.5	27.7	1,548.6	18.10	2,186.8	3,313.5	5,557.1	133.9
2003		770	270	30.9	14.5	28.9	1,610.3	18.10	2,245.0	3,655.0	5,890.5	105.0
2004		771	274	28.2	12.8	26.2	1,570.3	19.48	2,379.9	3,885.0	6,191.3	112.5
2005		779	281	27.9	13.4	27.6	1,666.0	21.91	2,689.2	4,308.0	6,869.9	190.6
2006		755P	260P	29.2	14.4	29.7	1,831.0	23.03	2,896.6	5,100.7	7,867.1	186.3
2007		741P	251P	27.4P	12.5P	25.9P	1,781.8P	22.71P	2,706.1P	4,765.2P	7,349.6P	155.5P
2008		728P	243P	26.5P	11.9P	24.9P	1,816.6P	23.56P	2,789.1P	4,911.5P	7,575.2P	156.4P
2009		714P	234P	25.5P	11.2P	23.9P	1,851.4P	24.41P	2,872.2P	5,057.7P	7,800.8P	157.4P
2010		700P	225P	24.6P	10.6P	22.9P	1,886.3P	25.26P	2,955.3P	5,204.0P	8,026.4P	158.3P

Sources: 1997 and 2002 *Economic Census*; other years, up to 2006, are from *Annual Survey of Manufactures*. Establishment counts for non-Census years are from *County Business Patterns*; 1997 and 2002 values are from the 1997 and 2002 censuses, respectively. 'P's show projections by the editors.

INDICES OF CHANGE

Year	Com-panies	Establishments		Employment			Compensation		Production ($ million)			
		Total	with 20 or more employees	Total (000)	Production Workers (000)	Hours (Mil)	Payroll ($ mil)	Wages ($/hr)	Cost of Materials	Value Added by Manufacture	Value of Shipments	Capital Invest.
1997	106	104	117	110	124	126	88	82	90	94	92	101
1998		106	117	115	124	130	95	87	95	101	97	123
1999		104	114	113	121	117	95	89	98	97	97	118
2000		102	116	121	128	127	108	91	114	118	112	146
2001		101	111	117	124	124	110	92	122	121	119	91
2002	100	100	100	100	100	100	100	100	100	100	100	100
2003		93	95	100	100	104	104	100	103	110	106	78
2004		93	97	91	88	95	101	108	109	117	111	84
2005		94	99	90	92	100	108	121	123	130	124	142
2006		92P	92P	94	99	107	118	127	132	154	142	139
2007		90P	89P	89P	86P	94P	115P	125P	124P	144P	132P	116P
2008		88P	86P	86P	82P	90P	117P	130P	128P	148P	136P	117P
2009		87P	83P	83P	77P	86P	120P	135P	131P	153P	140P	118P
2010		85P	80P	80P	73P	83P	122P	140P	135P	157P	144P	118P

Sources: Same as General Statistics. Values reflect change from the base year, 2002. Values above 100 mean greater than 2002, values below 100 mean less than 2002, and the values of 100 in other years means the same as 2002. 'P's show projections by the editors.

SELECTED RATIOS

For 2002	Avg. of All Manufact.	Analyzed Industry	Index	For 2002	Avg. of All Manufact.	Analyzed Industry	Index
Employees per Establishment	42	37	89	Value Added per Production Worker	182,367	228,517	125
Payroll per Establishment	1,639,184	1,877,091	115	Cost per Establishment	5,769,015	2,650,667	46
Payroll per Employee	39,053	50,117	128	Cost per Employee	137,446	70,770	51
Production Workers per Establishment	30	18	60	Cost per Production Worker	195,506	150,814	77
Wages per Establishment	694,845	607,721	87	Shipments per Establishment	11,158,348	6,735,879	60
Wages per Production Worker	23,548	34,577	147	Shipments per Employee	265,847	179,841	68
Hours per Production Worker	1,980	1,910	96	Shipments per Production Worker	378,144	383,248	101
Wages per Hour	11.89	18.10	152	Investment per Establishment	361,338	162,303	45
Value Added per Establishment	5,381,325	4,016,364	75	Investment per Employee	8,609	4,333	50
Value Added per Employee	128,210	107,233	84	Investment per Production Worker	12,245	9,234	75

Sources: Same as General Statistics. The 'Average of All Manufacturing' column represents the average of all manufacturing industries reported for the most recent complete year available. The Index shows the relationship between the Average and the Analyzed Industry. For example, 100 means that they are equal; 500 that the Analyzed Industry is five times the average; 50 means that the Analyzed Industry is half the national average. The abbreviation 'na' is used to show that data are 'not available'. Ratios shown for 2002, the last complete census year.

LEADING COMPANIES Number shown: **75** Total sales ($ mil): **39,942** Total employment (000): **155.6**

Company Name	Address				CEO Name	Phone	Co. Type	Sales ($ mil)	Empl. (000)
Thermo Fisher Scientific Inc.	81 Wyman St.	Waltham	MA	02451	Marijn E. Dekkers	781-622-1000	P	9,746	33.0
Hi-Stat Manufacturing Company	28001 Cabot Dr.	Novi	MI	48377	John Corey	248-489-9300	D	3,194*	5.0
Snap-On Inc.	PO Box 1410	Kenosha	WI	53141	Tim Chambers	262-656-5200	P	2,841	11.6
Vishay Intertechnology Inc.	PO Box 4004	Malvern	PA	19355	Gerald Paul	610-644-1300	P	2,833	27.9
Hubbell Inc.	584 Derby Milford	Orange	CT	06477		203-799-4100	P	2,534	11.5
Rainin Instrument L.L.C.	PO Box 4026	Woburn	MA	01888	Kenneth Rainin	510-564-1600	R	1,590*	0.1
Dresser Inc.	15455 Dallas Pkwy.	Addison	TX	75001		972-361-9800	S	1,343*	6.0
Orbital Sciences Corp.	21839 Atlantic Blvd	Dulles	VA	20166		703-406-5000	P	1,084	2.8
Trimble Navigation Ltd.	935 Stewart Dr.	Sunnyvale	CA	94085	Steven W. Berglund	408-481-8000	P	940	2.8
Cubic Corp.	PO Box 85587	San Diego	CA	92186	Gerald Dinkel	858-277-6780	P	890	6.0
Omron Healthcare Inc.	1200 Lakeside Dr.	Deerfield	IL	60015		847-680-6200	R	872*	0.1
MKS Instruments Inc.	90 Industrial Way	Wilmington	MA	01887	Leo Berlinghieri	978-284-4000	P	783	3.0
Input/Output Inc.	2105 CityWest Blvd.	Houston	TX	77042	James M. Lapeyre Jr.	281-933-3339	P	504	1.0
UOP L.L.C.	25 E Algonquin Rd.	Des Plaines	IL	60017	Carlos Guimaraes	847-391-2000	R	500*	4.0
Liebert Corp.	PO Box 29186	Columbus	OH	43229	Robert Bauer	614-888-0246	S	440*	5.0
MTS Systems Corp.	14000 Technology	Eden Prairie	MN	55344	Sidney W. Emery Jr.	952-937-4000	P	421	1.6
Global Charter S.A.	12300 Parc Crest Dr	Stafford	TX	77477	Robert P. Peebler	281-933-3339	S	403*	0.8
I/O Sensors Inc.	12300 Parc Crest Dr	Stafford	TX	77477	Robert P. Peebler	281-933-3339	S	403*	0.8
IPOP Management Inc.	12300 Parc Crest Dr	Stafford	TX	77477	Robert P. Peebler	281-933-3339	S	403*	0.8
I/O Exploration Products USA	12300 Parc Crest Dr	Stafford	TX	77477	Robert P. Peebler	281-933-3339	S	391*	0.8
I/O of Austin Inc.	12300 Parc Crest Dr	Stafford	TX	77477	Robert P. Peebler	281-933-3339	S	391*	0.8
Raytheon Electronic Systems	PO Box 902	El Segundo	CA	90245	Jack Kelbe	310-647-0445	R	255*	1.6
ABB Industrial Systems Inc.	579 Exec Campus	Westerville	OH	43082	Fred Kindle	614-818-6300	S	250*	1.5
Cohu Inc.	12367 Crosthwaite	Poway	CA	92064	James A. Donahue	858-848-8100	P	245*	1.0
Yokogawa Industrial Automation	2 Dart Rd.	Newnan	GA	30265	Kiyoshi Makino	770-254-0400	R	244*	0.7
I/O Eastern Inc.	12300 Parc Crest Dr	Stafford	TX	77477	Robert P. Peebler	281-933-3339	S	240*	0.5
I/O Geoview Inc.	12300 Parc Crest Dr	Stafford	TX	77477	Robert P. Peebler	281-933-3339	S	240*	0.5
I/O International Inc.	12300 Parc Crest Dr	Stafford	TX	77477	Robert P. Peebler	281-933-3339	S	240*	0.5
Smartronix Inc.	22685 Three Notch	California	MD	20619	M. Arshed Javaid	301-737-2800	R	221*	0.4
General Atomics	PO Box 85608	San Diego	CA	92186	James Blue	858-455-3000	R	219*	1.0
Measurement Specialties Inc.	1000 Lucas Way	Hampton	VA	23666	Frank D. Guidone	757-766-1500	P	200	2.2
Sparton Corp.	2400 E Ganson St.	Jackson	MI	49202	D W. Hockenbrocht	517-787-8600	P	200	1.2
Mitutoyo America Corp.	965 Corporate Blvd.	Aurora	IL	60504		630-820-9666	R	198*	0.2
Framatome ANP Inc.	PO Box 10935	Lynchburg	VA	24506	Tom Christopher	434-832-3000	S	198*	1.8
Faro Technologies Inc.	125 Technology Pk.	Lake Mary	FL	32746	Jay Freeland	407-333-9911	P	192	0.8
Geospace Engineering Resources	7007 Pinemont Dr.	Houston	TX	77040	Gary Owens	713-986-4444	S	187*	0.4
Simpson Electric Co.	PO Box 99	Lac d Flambeau	WI	54538	Richard Schermetzler	715-588-3311	R	182*	0.1
Barksdale Inc.	PO Box 58843	Los Angeles	CA	90058	Ian Dodd	323-589-6181	S	168*	0.2
Special Devices Inc.	14370 White Sage	Moorpark	CA	93021	Tom W. Cresante	805-553-1200	R	163*	0.8
Keithley Int'l Investment	28775 Aurora Rd.	Solon	OH	44139	Joseph Keithley	440-248-0400	S	155	0.7
Instron Corp.	825 University Ave.	Norwood	MA	02062	James O. Garrison	781-828-5000	R	155*	1.2
Transistor Devices Inc.	36 Newburgh Rd.	Hackettstown	NJ	07840	Richard Blake	973-267-1900	R	151*	0.1
Nanometrics Inc.	1550 Buckeye Dr.	Milpitas	CA	95035		408-435-9600	P	146	0.5
Keithley Instruments Inc.	28775 Aurora Rd.	Solon	OH	44139		440-248-0400	P	144	0.7
Media Recovery Inc.	PO Box 1407	Graham	TX	76450	Tim Smith	940-549-5462	R	143*	<0.1
Fairfield Industries Inc.	14100 SW Freeway	Sugar Land	TX	77478	Walter Pharris	281-275-7500	R	140*	0.4
Great Neck Saw Manufacturers	PO Box 3	Mineola	NY	11501		516-746-5352	R	138*	0.4
OYO Geospace Corp.	7007 Pinemont Dr.	Houston	TX	77040	Gary D. Owens	713-986-4444	P	138	1.2
SGS US Testing Company Inc.	291 Fairfield Ave.	Fairfield	NJ	07004	Christian Jilch	973-575-5252	R	137*	<0.1
TSI Inc.	500 Cardigan Rd.	St. Paul	MN	55126	James Doubles	612-483-0900	R	133*	0.8
Charles Machine Works Inc.	PO Box 66	Perry	OK	73077	Ed Malzahn	580-336-4402	R	132*	1.2
Electronic Warfare Associates	13873 Park Ctr. Rd.	Herndon	VA	20171	Doug Armstrong	703-904-5700	R	129*	1.0
Howard Miller Clock Co.	860 E Main Ave.	Zeeland	MI	49464	Howard Miller	616-772-9131	R	98*	0.4
First Technology	228 NE Road	Standish	ME	04084	David MeMeo	248-353-6200	S	97*	1.2
International Motion Control	369 Franklin St.	Buffalo	NY	14202	Patrick Lee	716-855-2500	R	95*	<0.1
Martin Engineering	1 Martin Pl.	Neponset	IL	61345		309-594-2384	R	94*	0.5
Fluke Networks	PO Box 777	Everett	WA	98206	Chris O'Dell	425-347-6100	S	91*	0.5
Cascade Microtech Inc.	2430 NW 206th	Beaverton	OR	97006	Robert Cronin	503-601-1000	P	90	0.4
Landauer Inc.	2 Science Rd.	Glenwood	IL	60425		708-755-7000	P	84	0.4
Topcon Technologies Inc.	37 W Century Rd.	Paramus	NJ	07652	Scott Hokari	201-261-9450	R	80*	<0.1
Adesta Communications Inc.	1200 Landmark Ctr.	Omaha	NE	68102	Bob Sommerfeld	402-233-7700	R	78*	0.2
TomoTherapy Inc.	1240 Deming Way	Madison	WI	53717		608-824-2800	P	76	0.5
Multilink Inc.	PO Box 955	Elyria	OH	44036		440-366-6966	R	76*	0.1
Horiba Stec Inc.	3265 Scott Blvd.	Santa Clara	CA	95054	Masami Maeda	408-730-8795	R	73*	<0.1
Barnstead-Thermolyne Corp.	PO Box 797	Dubuque	IA	52004		563-556-2241	S	70*	0.5
Interstates Control Systems	PO Box 260	Sioux Center	IA	51250	Larry Herder	712-722-1663	R	70*	<0.1
Dwyer Instruments Inc.	PO Box 373	Michigan City	IN	46361	Stephen Clark	219-879-8868	R	69*	0.2
Stone Construction Equipment	PO Box 150	Honeoye	NY	14471	Robert Fien	585-229-5141	R	69*	0.2
RAE Systems Inc.	3775 N 1st Street	San Jose	CA	95134	Robert I. Chen	408-952-8200	P	68	0.8
Ircon Inc.	7300 N Natchez	Niles	IL	60714	M Fay	847-967-5151	R	68*	<0.1
Tyco Integrated Cable Systems	PO Box 479	Portsmouth	NH	03802		603-436-6100	R	64*	0.2
Boonton Electronics Corp.	PO BOX 465	Parsippany	NJ	07054	Paul Genova	973-386-9696	S	63*	0.1
MTI Instruments Inc.	325 Washington	Albany	NY	12205	Steven N. Fischer	518-218-2550	S	62*	0.1
Ametek Drexelbrook	205 Keith Valley Rd	Horsham	PA	19044	Frank Hermance	215-674-1234	D	60*	0.2
JAE Electronics Inc.	142 Technology Dr.	Irvine	CA	92618	Shinsuke Takahashi	949-753-2600	R	60*	<0.1

Source: Ward's Business Directory of U.S. Private and Public Companies, Volumes 1 and 2, 2008. The company type code used is as follows: P - Public, R - Private, S - Subsidiary, D - Division, J - Joint Venture, A - Affiliate, G - Group. Sales are in millions of dollars, employees are in thousands. An asterisk (*) indicates an estimated sales volume. The symbol < stands for 'less than'. Company names and addresses are truncated, in some cases, to fit into the available space.

MATERIALS CONSUMED

Material	Quantity	Delivered Cost ($ million)
Printed ciruit boards (without inserted components) for electronic circuitry	(X)	21.4
Printed circuit assemblies, loaded boards, and modules	(X)	92.0
Semiconductors (incl. transistors, diodes, rectifiers, and integrated circuits), for electronic circuitry	(X)	34.8
Capacitors for electronic circuitry	(X)	7.2
Resistors for electronic circuitry	(X)	7.1
All other miscellaneous components and accessories for electronic circuitry (exc. tubes)	(X)	26.2
Current-carrying wiring devices	(X)	24.9
Electrical transmission, distribution, and control equipment	(X)	8.3
Electronic computing equipment	(X)	(D)
Electrical instrument mechanisms and meter movements	(X)	19.3
All other miscellaneous electrical measuring instruments and parts	(X)	38.5
Plastics resins consumed in the form of granules, pellets, etc.	(X)	3.4
Fabricated plastics products (exc. gaskets, hoses, and belting)	(X)	17.3
Sheet metal products (excluding stampings)	(X)	20.7
Metal stampings	(X)	4.0
Other fabricated metal products (exc. forgings, metal stampings, and sheet metal products)	(X)	46.9
Forgings	(X)	2.3
Castings, rough and semifinished	(X)	(D)
Metal shapes and forms (exc. castings, forgings, fabr. metal products)	(X)	10.8
Steel shapes and forms (exc. castings, forgings, fabr. metal products)	(X)	24.4
Aluminum and aluminum-base alloy shapes and forms (exc. castings, forgings, fabr. metal products)	(X)	6.2
Other nonferrous shapes and forms (exc. castings, forgings, fabricated metal products)	(X)	2.5
Copper and copper-base alloy shapes and forms (exc. castings, forgings, fabr. metal products)	(X)	0.7
Glass and glass products (excluding windows and mirrors)	(X)	3.8
Insulated wire and cable (including magnet wire)	(X)	20.5
Metal bolts, nuts, screws, and other screw machine products	(X)	26.0
Optical instruments and lenses (exc. sighting, tracking, and fire control)	(X)	3.9
Electronic communication equipment	(X)	7.5
Fractional horsepower electric motors (less than 1 hp)	(X)	6.5
Liquid crystal display screens (LCD), including LED	(X)	5.7
Paper and paperboard containers (incl. shipping sacks and other paper packaging supplies)	(X)	5.8
All other materials, components, parts, containers, and supplies	(X)	552.7
Materials, ingredients, containers, and supplies, nsk	(X)	726.5

Source: 2002 *Economic Census*. Explanation of symbols used: (D): Withheld to avoid disclosure of competitive data; na: Not available; (S): Withheld because statistical norms were not met; (X): Not applicable; (Z): Less than half the unit shown; nec: Not elsewhere classified; nsk: Not specified by kind; - : zero; p : 10-19 percent estimated; q : 20-29 percent estimated.

PRODUCT SHARE DETAILS

Product or Product Class Shipments	Mil. $	Product or Product Class Shipments	Mil. $
MEASURING AND CONTROLLING DEVICES, NEC	5,009.7	purpose instruments and equipment, except medical thermometers	1,351.7
Aircraft engine instruments, except flight	**811.0**	Survey and drafting instruments and apparatus, including	
Physical properties testing and inspection equipment and kinematic testing and measuring equipment	**1,717.9**	photogrammetric equipment	254.0
Nuclear radiation detection and monitoring instruments	**504.8**	Measuring and controlling devices, nec, nsk, total	370.3
Commercial, geophysical, meteorological, and general-			

Source: 2002 *Economic Census*. The values are product shipments in millions of dollars for 2002. Total product shipments may be lower or higher than industry shipments. See Introduction for a full discussion. Values of indented subcategories are summed in the main heading(s). The symbol (D) appears when data are withheld to prevent disclosure of competitive information. The abbreviation nsk stands for 'not specified by kind' and nec for 'not elsewhere classified'. A dash (-) means zero.

INPUTS AND OUTPUTS FOR WATCHES, CLOCKS, & OTHER MEASURING DEVICES

Economic Sector or Industry Providing Inputs	%	Sector	Economic Sector or Industry Buying Outputs	%	Sector
Compensation of employees	34.4		Personal consumption expenditures	30.4	
Management of companies & enterprises	10.7	Services	Private fixed investment	26.1	
Software publishers	7.9	Services	Exports of goods & services	17.4	Cap Inv
Wholesale trade	3.7	Trade	Aircraft	8.2	Manufg.
Lessors of nonfinancial assets	3.4	Fin/R.E.	General Federal government services, nondefense	3.7	Fed Govt
Scientific research & development services	3.0	Services	General S/L govt. services	2.0	S/L Govt
Printed circuit assemblies (electronic assemblies)	2.9	Manufg.	General Federal government services, defense	1.7	Fed Govt
Plastics products, nec	1.5	Manufg.	S/L govt. invest., other	1.3	S/L Govt
Electricity & signal testing instruments	1.5	Manufg.	Search, detection, & navigation instruments	1.2	Manufg.
Real estate	1.3	Fin/R.E.	Other S/L govt. enterprises	1.1	S/L Govt
Iron & steel mills & ferroalloys	1.2	Manufg.	Watches, clocks, & related devices	0.6	Manufg.
Advertising & related services	1.2	Services	Household laundry equipment	0.5	Manufg.
Semiconductors & related devices	1.1	Manufg.	Architectural, engineering, & related services	0.5	Services
Watches, clocks, & related devices	1.0	Manufg.	Household cooking appliances	0.5	Manufg.
Turned products & screws, nuts, & bolts	0.9	Manufg.	Tobacco products	0.5	Manufg.
Electronic components, nec	0.9	Manufg.	Asphalt paving mixtures & blocks	0.4	Manufg.
Electronic capacitors, resistors, coils, transformers	0.8	Manufg.	Change in private inventories	0.4	In House
Computer terminals & peripherals	0.8	Manufg.	Wood containers & pallets	0.4	Manufg.

Continued on next page.

INPUTS AND OUTPUTS FOR WATCHES, CLOCKS, & OTHER MEASURING DEVICES - Continued

Economic Sector or Industry Providing Inputs	%	Sector	Economic Sector or Industry Buying Outputs	%	Sector
Ornamental & architectural metal products	0.7	Manufg.	Computer system design services	0.3	Services
Wiring devices	0.7	Manufg.	Civic, social, & professional organizations	0.3	Services
Machine shops	0.7	Manufg.	Wholesale trade	0.2	Trade
Legal services	0.7	Services	Irradiation apparatus	0.2	Manufg.
Securities, commodity contracts, investments	0.7	Fin/R.E.	S/L govt. invest., education	0.2	S/L Govt
Bare printed circuit boards	0.6	Manufg.	Scientific research & development services	0.2	Services
Power generation & supply	0.6	Util.	Household refrigerators & home freezers	0.2	Manufg.
Architectural, engineering, & related services	0.6	Services	Major household appliances, nec	0.1	Manufg.
Telecommunications	0.5	Services	Commercial & health care structures	0.1	Construct.
Computer storage devices	0.5	Manufg.	Management of companies & enterprises	0.1	Services
Custom computer programming services	0.5	Services	Nonresidential structures, nec	0.1	Construct.
Monetary authorities/depository credit intermediation	0.5	Fin/R.E.	Personal & household goods repair/maintenance	0.1	Services
Coating, engraving, heat treating & allied activities	0.5	Manufg.	Retail trade	0.1	Trade
Chemical products & preparations, nec	0.4	Manufg.			
Food services & drinking places	0.4	Services			
Plastics materials & resins	0.4	Manufg.			
Data processing, hosting, & related services	0.4	Services			
Accounting, tax preparation, bookkeeping, & payroll	0.4	Services			
Copper rolling, drawing, extruding, & alloying	0.4	Manufg.			
Professional, scientific, technical services, nec	0.4	Services			
Hotels & motels, including casino hotels	0.4	Services			
Other computer related services, including facilities	0.3	Services			
Warehousing & storage	0.3	Util.			
Employment services	0.3	Services			
Truck transportation	0.3	Util.			
Paperboard containers	0.3	Manufg.			
Taxes on production & imports, less subsidies	0.3				
Primary nonferrous metal, ex. copper & aluminum	0.3	Manufg.			
Automotive equipment rental & leasing	0.3	Fin/R.E.			
Motors & generators	0.3	Manufg.			
Management, scientific, & technical consulting	0.3	Services			
Air transportation	0.3	Util.			
Ferrous metal foundries	0.3	Manufg.			
Specialized design services	0.3	Services			
Nonferrous metal foundries	0.2	Manufg.			
Alumina refining & primary aluminum production	0.2	Manufg.			
Noncomparable imports	0.2	Foreign			
Communication & energy wires & cables	0.2	Manufg.			
Fabricated metals, nec	0.2	Manufg.			
Cutting tools & machine tool accessories	0.2	Manufg.			
Business support services	0.2	Services			
Relay & industrial controls	0.2	Manufg.			
Services to buildings & dwellings	0.2	Services			
Maintenance/repair of nonresidential structures	0.2	Construct.			
Aluminum products from purchased aluminum	0.2	Manufg.			
Retail trade	0.2	Trade			
Broadcast & wireless communications equipment	0.1	Manufg.			
Commercial & industrial machinery rental & leasing	0.1	Fin/R.E.			
Valve & fittings other than plumbing	0.1	Manufg.			
Support services, nec	0.1	Services			
Crowns & closures & metal stamping	0.1	Manufg.			
Computer system design services	0.1	Services			
Paperboard mills	0.1	Manufg.			
Automotive repair & maintenance, ex. car washes	0.1	Services			
Forging, stamping, & sintering, nec	0.1	Manufg.			
Investigation & security services	0.1	Services			
Commercial & industrial equipment repair/maintenance	0.1	Services			

Source: Benchmark Input-Output Accounts for the U.S. Economy, 2002, U.S. Department of Commerce, Washington D.C., January 2008. *User should note that this Input-Output table is not for this particular narrowly defined industry but for a larger aggregate. Input and Output data for* Watches, Clocks, & Other Measuring Devices *include Input and Output data for the* Annual Survey of Manufactures' *NAICS industries 334518 and 334519.* The abbreviation nec stands for 'not elsewhere classified'.

OCCUPATIONS EMPLOYED BY NAVIGATIONAL, MEASURING, MEDICAL, & CONTROL INSTRUMENTS

Occupation	% of Total 2006	Change to 2016	Occupation	% of Total 2006	Change to 2016
Electrical & electronic equipment assemblers	7.1	-23.4	First-line supervisors/managers of production workers	2.1	-4.3
Team assemblers	5.3	-4.3	Engineers, nec	1.9	-4.3
Electromechanical equipment assemblers	3.6	-4.3	Purchasing agents, exc wholesale, retail, & farm	1.9	-4.3
Electrical engineers	3.3	-4.3	Machinists	1.8	0.5
Computer software engineers, applications	2.9	14.9	General & operations managers	1.7	-13.8
Aerospace engineers	2.9	0.5	Sales representatives, wholesale & manufacturing, tech	1.6	-4.3
Mechanical engineers	2.8	-4.3	Executive secretaries & administrative assistants	1.5	-4.3
Electrical & electronic engineering technicians	2.7	-4.3	Customer service representatives	1.3	5.3
Computer software engineers, systems software	2.7	5.3	Office clerks, general	1.2	-5.7
Industrial engineers	2.5	16.3	Shipping, receiving, & traffic clerks	1.2	-7.9
Inspectors, testers, sorters, samplers, & weighers	2.4	-9.7	Accountants & auditors	1.2	-4.3
Engineering managers	2.4	-4.3	Production, planning, & expediting clerks	1.2	-4.3
Electronics engineers, exc computer	2.2	-4.3			

Source: Industry-Occupation Matrix, Bureau of Labor Statistics, December 4, 2007. These data are reported based on 4-digit NAICS categories but have been matched to corresponding 6-digit NAICS industry codes. The change reported for each occupation to the year 2016 is a percent of growth or decline as estimated by the Bureau of Labor Statistics. The abbreviation nec stands for 'not elsewhere classified'.

LOCATION BY STATE AND REGIONAL CONCENTRATION

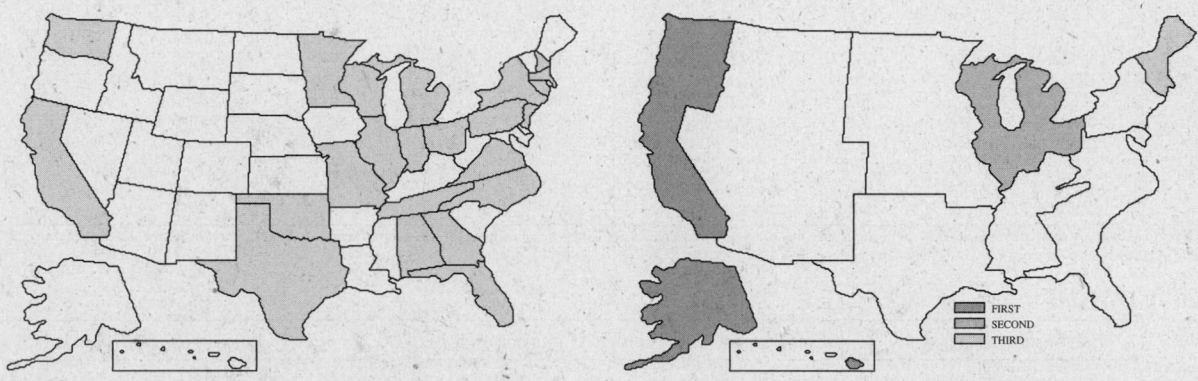

FIRST
SECOND
THIRD

INDUSTRY DATA BY STATE

State	Establishments	Shipments Total ($ mil)	Shipments % of U.S.	Shipments Per Establ.	Employment Total Number	Employment % of U.S.	Employment Per Establ.	Employment Wages ($/hour)	Cost as % of Shipments	Investment per Employee ($)
California	135	918.5	16.5	6,804.0	4,786	15.5	35	17.42	35.6	5,491
Minnesota	21	544.9	9.8	25,945.7	2,495	8.1	119	22.76	46.3	3,332
Texas	66	520.8	9.4	7,891.6	2,387	7.7	36	17.38	50.5	4,401
Massachusetts	59	431.2	7.8	7,309.2	2,708	8.8	46	20.15	36.2	2,366
New York	40	352.1	6.3	8,802.7	2,116	6.8	53	19.05	35.0	6,204
Ohio	52	273.4	4.9	5,257.5	1,427	4.6	27	16.80	36.8	4,994
Pennsylvania	46	224.1	4.0	4,871.4	1,606	5.2	35	17.65	34.2	2,415
Connecticut	31	222.2	4.0	7,167.9	1,290	4.2	42	21.75	26.9	2,296
Illinois	30	195.7	3.5	6,522.9	1,022	3.3	34	17.43	41.9	2,897
Indiana	19	194.3	3.5	10,224.1	774	2.5	41	21.07	42.9	8,886
Florida	35	135.3	2.4	3,864.3	1,125	3.6	32	10.83	39.7	2,060
Michigan	47	127.8	2.3	2,719.0	997	3.2	21	18.75	33.3	2,606
Washington	32	96.5	1.7	3,015.6	636	2.1	20	19.84	24.3	2,469
Tennessee	9	74.2	1.3	8,247.6	403	1.3	45	16.80	29.6	3,015
Wisconsin	12	63.5	1.1	5,295.8	323	1.0	27	11.16	36.0	9,653
North Carolina	10	60.7	1.1	6,074.5	564	1.8	56	14.40	26.2	2,727
New Hampshire	11	55.6	1.0	5,052.1	375	1.2	34	17.09	26.6	6,739
New Jersey	15	47.2	0.8	3,147.8	337	1.1	22	18.62	46.7	3,611
Oklahoma	10	30.9	0.6	3,087.5	202	0.7	20	19.13	47.1	3,307
Alabama	5	29.2	0.5	5,843.6	192	0.6	38	16.66	29.4	3,917
Virginia	11	24.2	0.4	2,196.0	161	0.5	15	27.85	35.2	5,217
Georgia	6	22.1	0.4	3,677.8	101	0.3	17	13.88	41.5	4,158
Missouri	6	16.3	0.3	2,714.3	137	0.4	23	15.60	20.9	1,723

Source: 2002 *Economic Census*. The states are in descending order of shipments or establishments (if shipment data are missing for the majority). The symbol (D) appears when data are withheld to prevent disclosure of competitive information. States marked with (D) are sorted by number of establishments. A dash (-) indicates that the data element cannot be calculated. Data may not show all states active in the NAICS category. All data available at the time of publication are shown.

NAICS 334611 - SOFTWARE REPRODUCING

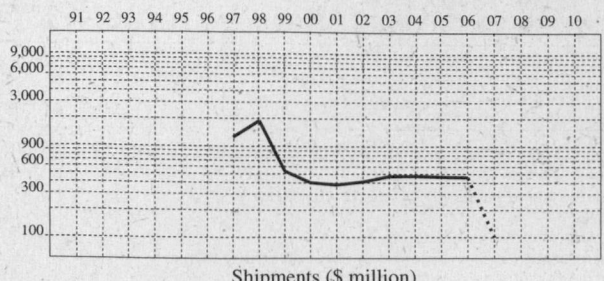

Shipments ($ million)

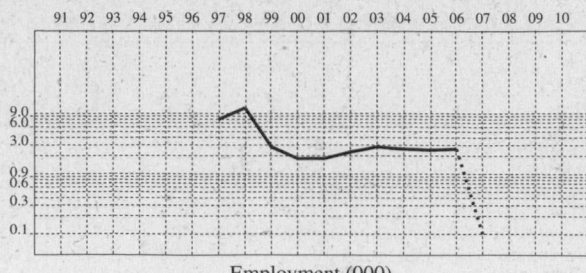

Employment (000)

GENERAL STATISTICS

Year	Companies	Establishments		Employment			Compensation		Production ($ million)			
		Total	with 20 or more employees	Total (000)	Production Workers (000)	Hours (Mil)	Payroll ($ mil)	Wages ($/hr)	Cost of Materials	Value Added by Manufacture	Value of Shipments	Capital Invest.
1997	112	124	49	8.0	4.4	10.1	310.9	19.67	438.3	819.1	1,258.4	133.6
1998		93	42	12.4	6.4	13.3	466.1	15.47	648.7	1,256.1	1,889.3	104.7
1999		104	45	2.8	2.5	4.8	98.9	15.56	169.1	370.5	535.3	71.3
2000		98	39	1.8	1.8	3.4	80.4	17.06	149.6	253.9	403.4	47.7
2001		143	34	1.8	1.8	3.3	64.8	17.20	130.3	248.9	382.2	36.5
2002	185	190	26	2.3	1.6	2.8	97.5	19.70	150.2	260.4	410.7	18.6
2003		198	19	2.8	2.4	4.2	110.1	19.26	175.7	295.5	471.7	15.5
2004		201	22	2.6	1.7	3.2	118.3	20.13	176.3	298.7	474.6	26.0
2005		213	28	2.5	1.6	3.2	116.7	19.01	181.8	284.0	465.2	25.3
2006		232P	16P	2.6	1.6	3.1	126.3	18.66	182.5	274.6	458.2	32.0
2007		248P	13P	0.1P	0.5P	0.5P	29.4P	19.76P	39.9P	60.1P	100.2P	
2008		264P	9P		0.2P		5.8P	20.05P				
2009		280P	6P					20.34P				
2010		296P	2P					20.63P				

Sources: 1997 and 2002 *Economic Census*; other years, up to 2006, are from *Annual Survey of Manufactures*. Establishment counts for non-Census years are from *County Business Patterns*; 1997 and 2002 values are from the 1997 and 2002 censuses, respectively. 'P's show projections by the editors.

INDICES OF CHANGE

Year	Companies	Establishments		Employment			Compensation		Production ($ million)			
		Total	with 20 or more employees	Total (000)	Production Workers (000)	Hours (Mil)	Payroll ($ mil)	Wages ($/hr)	Cost of Materials	Value Added by Manufacture	Value of Shipments	Capital Invest.
1997	61	65	188	348	275	361	319	100	292	315	306	718
1998		49	162	539	400	475	478	79	432	482	460	563
1999		55	173	122	156	171	101	79	113	142	130	383
2000		52	150	78	113	121	82	87	100	98	98	256
2001		75	131	78	113	118	66	87	87	96	93	196
2002	100	100	100	100	100	100	100	100	100	100	100	100
2003		104	73	122	150	150	113	98	117	113	115	83
2004		106	85	113	106	114	121	102	117	115	116	140
2005		112	108	109	100	114	120	96	121	109	113	136
2006		122P	63P	113	100	111	130	95	122	105	112	172
2007		130P	50P	4P	31P	18P	30P	100P	27P	23P	24P	
2008		139P	36P		13P		6P	102P				
2009		147P	23P					103P				
2010		156P	9P					105P				

Sources: Same as General Statistics. Values reflect change from the base year, 2002. Values above 100 mean greater than 2002, values below 100 mean less than 2002, and the values of 100 in other years means the same as 2002. 'P's show projections by the editors.

SELECTED RATIOS

For 2002	Avg. of All Manufact.	Analyzed Industry	Index	For 2002	Avg. of All Manufact.	Analyzed Industry	Index
Employees per Establishment	42	12	29	Value Added per Production Worker	182,367	162,750	89
Payroll per Establishment	1,639,184	513,158	31	Cost per Establishment	5,769,015	790,526	14
Payroll per Employee	39,053	42,391	109	Cost per Employee	137,446	65,304	48
Production Workers per Establishment	30	8	29	Cost per Production Worker	195,506	93,875	48
Wages per Establishment	694,845	290,316	42	Shipments per Establishment	11,158,348	2,161,579	19
Wages per Production Worker	23,548	34,475	146	Shipments per Employee	265,847	178,565	67
Hours per Production Worker	1,980	1,750	88	Shipments per Production Worker	378,144	256,688	68
Wages per Hour	11.89	19.70	166	Investment per Establishment	361,338	97,895	27
Value Added per Establishment	5,381,325	1,370,526	25	Investment per Employee	8,609	8,087	94
Value Added per Employee	128,210	113,217	88	Investment per Production Worker	12,245	11,625	95

Sources: Same as General Statistics. The 'Average of All Manufacturing' column represents the average of all manufacturing industries reported for the most recent complete year available. The Index shows the relationship between the Average and the Analyzed Industry. For example, 100 means that they are equal; 500 that the Analyzed Industry is five times the average; 50 means that the Analyzed Industry is half the national average. The abbreviation 'na' is used to show that data are 'not available'. Ratios shown for 2002, the last complete census year.

LEADING COMPANIES

Number shown: **75**   Total sales ($ mil): **546,347**   Total employment (000): **1,345.4**

Company Name	Address				CEO Name	Phone	Co. Type	Sales ($ mil)	Empl. (000)
Hewlett-Packard Co.	3000 Hanover St.	Palo Alto	CA	94304		650-857-1501	P	104,286	172.0
International Bus. Machines	1 New Orchard Rd.	Armonk	NY	10504		914-499-1900	P	98,786	329.4
Dell Inc.	1 Dell Way	Round Rock	TX	78682	Michael R. Cannon	512-338-4400	P	57,420	90.5
Microsoft Corp.	1 Microsoft Way	Redmond	WA	98052	Steven A. Ballmer		P	51,122	79.0
Cisco Systems Inc.	170 W Tasman Dr.	San Jose	CA	95134		408-526-4000	P	34,922	61.5
Apple Inc.	1 Infinite Loop	Cupertino	CA	95014	Bill Campbell	408-996-1010	P	24,006	21.6
Computer Sciences Corp.	2100 E Grand Ave.	El Segundo	CA	90245		310-615-0311	P	14,855	79.0
Sun Microsystems Inc.	4150 Network Cir.	Santa Clara	CA	95054		650-960-1300	P	13,873	34.2
EMC Corp.	176 South St.	Hopkinton	MA	01748		508-435-1000	P	13,230	31.1
Seagate Technology	920 Disc Dr.	Scotts Valley	CA	95066	Stephen Luczo	831-438-6550	P	11,360	54.0
Hitachi Global Storage Tech.	5600 Cottle Rd.	San Jose	CA	95193	Hiroaki Nakanishi	408-717-5000	J	9,450*	21.0
Siemens Medical Solutions USA	51 Valley Stream Pk	Malvern	PA	19355	Thomas McCausland	610-219-6300	S	9,135*	13.0
First American Corp.	1 First Am. Way	Santa Ana	CA	92707		714-800-3000	P	8,196	37.4
ALLTEL Corp.	1 Allied Dr.	Little Rock	AR	72202		501-905-8000	R	7,884	14.9
McGraw-Hill Companies Inc.	PO Box 182604	Columbus	OH	43272			P	6,772	21.2
Henry Schein Inc.	135 Duryea Rd.	Melville	NY	11747	Stanley M. Bergman	631-843-5500	P	5,920	12.0
Corning Inc.	1 Riverfront Plz.	Corning	NY	14831	James R. Houghton	607-974-9000	P	5,860	24.5
Unisys Corp.	Unisys Way	Blue Bell	PA	19424		215-986-4011	P	5,653	30.0
Symantec Corp.	20330 Stevens Creek	Cupertino	CA	95014		408-517-8000	P	5,199	17.1
Rockwell Automation Inc.	777 E Wisconsin	Milwaukee	WI	53202		414-212-5800	P	5,004	20.0
NCR Corp.	1700 S Patterson	Dayton	OH	45479		937-445-5000	P	4,970	23.2
Hasbro Inc.	PO Box 1059	Pawtucket	RI	02861		401-431-8697	P	3,838	5.9
Diebold Inc.	PO Box 3077	North Canton	OH	44720		330-490-4000	P	2,906	15.5
Network Appliance Inc.	495 E Java Dr.	Sunnyvale	CA	94089		408-822-6000	P	2,804	6.6
Follett Corp.	2233 West Street	River Grove	IL	60171	Christopher Traut	708-583-2000	R	2,370	8.3
Scholastic Corp.	557 Broadway	New York	NY	10012		212-343-6100	P	2,179	6.7
Xilinx Inc.	2100 Logic Dr.	San Jose	CA	95124		408-559-7778	P	1,843	3.4
Ingram Industries Inc.	PO Box 23049	Nashville	TN	37202	Martha R. Ingram	615-298-8200	R	1,696*	5.2
Palm Inc.	950 W Maude Ave.	Sunnyvale	CA	94085	Eric Benhamou	408-617-7000	P	1,561	1.2
Itron Inc.	2111 N Molter Rd.	Liberty Lake	WA	99019		509-924-9900	P	1,464	2.4
Reinhart Institutional Foods	1500 Saint James St	La Crosse	WI	54602	Mark Drazkowski	608-782-2660	S	1,463*	2.0
AVX Corp.	PO Box 867	Myrtle Beach	SC	29578	John S. Gilbertson	843-448-9411	P	1,333	13.0
ADC Telecommunications Inc.	PO Box 1101	Minneapolis	MN	55440		952-938-8080	P	1,322	9.1
F. Dohmen Co.	N11120 Stonewood	Germantown	WI	53022	John Dohmen	262-251-6420	R	1,300*	0.5
Houghton Mifflin Co.	222 Berkeley St.	Boston	MA	02116	Anthony Lucki	617-351-5000	S	1,282*	3.1
3Com Corp.	350 Campus Dr.	Marlborough	MA	01752	Eric A. Benhamou	508-323-5000	P	1,268	6.3
Kaman Corp.	PO Box 1	Bloomfield	CT	06002		860-243-7100	P	1,086	3.6
Harland Clarke	2939 Miller Rd.	Decatur	GA	30035	John Heald	770-981-9460	S	1,050	5.4
Hughes Network Systems Inc.	11717 Exploratn Ln.	Germantown	MD	20876	Pradman P. Kaul	301-428-5500	S	975*	1.5
Corbis Corp.	15395 SE 30th Pl.,	Bellevue	WA	98007	Bill Gates	206-373-6000	R	939*	1.0
Zebra Technologies Corp.	333 Corp. Woods	Vernon Hills	IL	60061	Edward L. Kaplan	847-634-6700	P	760	2.8
Polaroid Holding Co.	1265 Main St.	Waltham	MA	02451	Jacque A. Nasser	781-386-2000	S	753	3.4
National Instruments Corp.	11500 N MoPac	Austin	TX	78759		512-338-9119	P	740	4.1
IHS Inc.	15 Inverness Way E	Englewood	CO	80112	Bruce Langsen	303-790-0600	P	688	3.0
White Systems Inc.	30 Boright Ave.	Kenilworth	NJ	07033	Richard Paolino	908-272-6700	S	673*	0.3
Polaroid Corp.	300 Baker Ave.	Concord	MA	01742	Bob Gregerson	781-386-2000	P	664*	3.0
Electronics For Imaging Inc.	303 Velocity Way	Foster City	CA	94404	Guy Gecht	650-357-3500	P	621	2.0
Intuitive Surgical Inc.	950 Kifer Rd.	Sunnyvale	CA	94086		408-523-2100	P	601	0.8
QLogic Corp.	26650 Aliso Viejo	Aliso Viejo	CA	92656	H.K. Desai	949-389-6000	P	587	1.0
VeriFone Holdings Inc.	2099 Gateway Pl.	San Jose	CA	95110	Douglas G. Bergeron	408-232-7800	P	581	1.3
Stratus Technologies Inc.	111 Powdermill Rd.	Maynard	MA	01754	Stephen Kiely	978-461-7000	R	569*	2.3
HLTH Corp.	669 River Dr.	Elmwood Park	NJ	07407	Martin J. Wygod	201-703-3400	P	527	2.5
Mirapoint Inc.	909 Hermosa Ct.	Sunnyvale	CA	94085	Barry M. Ariko	408-720-3700	R	519*	0.2
Zoran Corp.	1390 Kifer Rd.	Sunnyvale	CA	94086	Levy Gerzberg	408-523-6500	P	507	1.4
SunGard Corbel Inc.	PO Box 47470	Jacksonville	FL	32247	Don Mackanos	904-399-5888	S	505*	0.2
Morningstar Inc.	225 W Wacker Dr.	Chicago	IL	60606	Chris Boruff	312-696-6000	P	435	1.7
FileNet Corp.	3565 Harbor Blvd.	Costa Mesa	CA	92626	Lee D. Roberts	714-327-3400	S	422	1.7
Mestek Inc.	260 N Elm St.	Westfield	MA	01085	R. Bruce Dewey	413-568-9571	R	372*	2.6
Standard Microsystems Corp.	80 Arkay Dr.	Hauppauge	NY	11788	Steven J. Bilodeau	631-435-6000	P	371	0.8
Allied Telesyn International	19800 N Creek Pky.	Bothell	WA	98011			S	350*	1.2
Silicon Graphics Inc.	1140 E Arques Ave.	Sunnyvale	CA	94085	Robert Ewald	650-960-1980	P	341	1.6
Carbo Ceramics Inc.	6565 MacArthur	Irving	TX	75039	Gary Kolstad	972-401-0090	P	340	0.8
TransCore Holdings Inc.	19111 Dallas Pky.	Dallas	TX	75287	John Worthington	972-387-8197	R	338*	1.8
BancTec Inc.	2701 E Grauwyler	Irving	TX	75061	J. Coley Clark	972-821-4000	S	325*	2.7
Sonus Networks Inc.	7 Technology Park	Westford	MA	01886	Hassan Ahmed	978-614-8100	P	320	0.9
ADC Broadband Access Systems	PO Box 1181	Minneapolis	MN	55440		952-938-8080	S	316*	7.5
Harmonic Inc.	549 Baltic Way	Sunnyvale	CA	94089	Patrick Harshman	408-542-2500	P	312	0.6
RSA Security Inc.	174 Middlesex Tpk.	Bedford	MA	01730	A. W. Coviello, Jr.	781-515-5000	D	310	1.3
eProduction Solutions Inc.	22001 N Park Dr.	Kingwood	TX	77339	Dharmesh Mehta	281-348-1000	R	298*	1.0
Itronix Corp.	12825 E Mirabeau	Spokane Valley	WA	99216		509-624-6600	S	285*	0.5
AllScripts Healthcare Solution	222 Mrchandse Mrt	Chicago	IL	60654		847-680-3515	P	282	1.2
EDO Reconnaissance/Surveillan.	18705 Madrone Pky.	Morgan Hill	CA	95037	James Smith	408-201-8000	S	267*	0.3
Synaptics Inc.	3120 Scott Blvd.	Santa Clara	CA	95054	Federico Faggin	408-454-5100	P	267	0.3
SafeNet Inc.	4690 Millennium Dr.	Belcamp	MD	21017	Chris Fedde	410-931-7500	S	263	1.0
Adaptec Inc.	691 S Milpitas Blvd	Milpitas	CA	95035	D. Scott Mercer	408-945-8600	P	255	0.6

Source: Ward's Business Directory of U.S. Private and Public Companies, Volumes 1 and 2, 2008. The company type code used is as follows: P - Public, R - Private, S - Subsidiary, D - Division, J - Joint Venture, A - Affiliate, G - Group. Sales are in millions of dollars, employees are in thousands. An asterisk (*) indicates an estimated sales volume. The symbol < stands for 'less than'. Company names and addresses are truncated, in some cases, to fit into the available space.

MATERIALS CONSUMED
No Materials Consumed data available for this industry.

PRODUCT SHARE DETAILS

Product or Product Class Shipments	Mil. $	Product or Product Class Shipments	Mil. $
SOFTWARE REPRODUCING	579.5		

Source: 2002 *Economic Census*. The values are product shipments in millions of dollars for 2002. Total product shipments may be lower or higher than industry shipments. See Introduction for a full discussion. Values of indented subcategories are summed in the main heading(s). The symbol (D) appears when data are withheld to prevent disclosure of competitive information. The abbreviation nsk stands for 'not specified by kind' and nec for 'not elsewhere classified'. A dash (-) means zero.

INPUTS AND OUTPUTS FOR SOFTWARE, AUDIO, AND VIDEO MEDIA REPRODUCING

Economic Sector or Industry Providing Inputs	%	Sector	Economic Sector or Industry Buying Outputs	%	Sector
Compensation of employees	26.9		Motion picture & video industries	20.6	Services
Management of companies & enterprises	10.8	Services	Sound recording industries	9.9	Services
Magnetic & optical recording media	4.9	Manufg.	Advertising & related services	7.7	Services
Lessors of nonfinancial assets	4.5	Fin/R.E.	Travel arrangement & reservation services	7.3	Services
Paperboard mills	4.2	Manufg.	Electronic computers	6.6	Manufg.
Plastics products, nec	3.7	Manufg.	Support services, nec	6.6	Services
Plastics materials & resins	3.6	Manufg.	Investigation & security services	4.8	Services
Plastics packaging materials, film & sheet	3.4	Manufg.	Photographic services	4.6	Services
Scientific research & development services	3.1	Services	Internet service providers & web search portals	4.3	Services
Wholesale trade	3.0	Trade	Exports of goods & services	4.3	Cap Inv
Software publishers	2.8	Services	Telecommunications	2.9	Services
Software, audio, and video media reproducing	1.8	Manufg.	General S/L govt. services	2.2	S/L Govt
Semiconductors & related devices	1.6	Manufg.	Legal services	2.0	Services
Power generation & supply	1.3	Util.	Software, audio, and video media reproducing	1.7	Manufg.
Real estate	1.2	Fin/R.E.	Professional, scientific, technical services, nec	1.5	Services
Custom computer programming services	0.9	Services	Other S/L govt. enterprises	1.5	S/L Govt
Securities, commodity contracts, investments	0.9	Fin/R.E.	Tobacco products	1.4	Manufg.
Advertising & related services	0.7	Services	Computer storage devices	1.3	Manufg.
Printed circuit assemblies (electronic assemblies)	0.7	Manufg.	Cable & other subscription programming	1.2	Services
Unlaminated plastics profile shapes	0.6	Manufg.	Scientific research & development services	1.0	Services
Taxes on production & imports, less subsidies	0.6		Accounting, tax preparation, bookkeeping, & payroll	0.9	Services
Monetary authorities/depository credit intermediation	0.6	Fin/R.E.	General Federal government services, nondefense	0.7	Fed Govt
Automotive equipment rental & leasing	0.5	Fin/R.E.	Asphalt paving mixtures & blocks	0.6	Manufg.
Truck transportation	0.5	Util.	Computer system design services	0.5	Services
Management, scientific, & technical consulting	0.5	Services	Wood containers & pallets	0.5	Manufg.
Coating, engraving, heat treating & allied activities	0.5	Manufg.	Educational services, nec	0.5	Services
Architectural, engineering, & related services	0.5	Services	Employment services	0.5	Services
Professional, scientific, technical services, nec	0.5	Services	Office administrative services	0.4	Services
Telecommunications	0.5	Services	Business support services	0.4	Services
Bare printed circuit boards	0.4	Manufg.	Management, scientific, & technical consulting	0.3	Services
Maintenance/repair of nonresidential structures	0.4	Construct.	Search, detection, & navigation instruments	0.3	Manufg.
Machine shops	0.4	Manufg.	Vending, commercial, industrial, office machinery	0.2	Manufg.
Services to buildings & dwellings	0.4	Services	Radio & television broadcasting	0.2	Services
Legal services	0.3	Services	Food services & drinking places	0.1	Services
Accounting, tax preparation, bookkeeping, & payroll	0.3	Services	Computer terminals & peripherals	0.1	Manufg.
Warehousing & storage	0.3	Util.	Physician, dentist, other health practitioner offices	0.1	Services
Paperboard containers	0.3	Manufg.			
Data processing, hosting, & related services	0.3	Services			
Fabricated metals, nec	0.3	Manufg.			
Noncomparable imports	0.3	Foreign			
Commercial & industrial machinery rental & leasing	0.3	Fin/R.E.			
Rail transportation	0.3	Util.			
Food services & drinking places	0.3	Services			
Other computer related services, including facilities	0.3	Services			
Employment services	0.2	Services			
Automotive repair & maintenance, ex. car washes	0.2	Services			
Commercial & industrial equipment repair/maintenance	0.2	Services			
Business support services	0.2	Services			
Laminated plastics plates, sheets, & shapes	0.2	Manufg.			
Natural gas distribution	0.2	Util.			
Hotels & motels, including casino hotels	0.2	Services			
Air transportation	0.1	Util.			
Specialized design services	0.1	Services			
Electronic & precision equipment repair/maintenance	0.1	Services			

Source: Benchmark Input-Output Accounts for the U.S. Economy, 2002, U.S. Department of Commerce, Washington D.C., January 2008. *User should note that this Input-Output table is not for this particular narrowly defined industry but for a larger aggregate. Input and Output data for* Software, Audio, and Video Media Reproducing *include Input and Output data for the* Annual Survey of Manufactures' *NAICS industries 334611 and 334612.* The abbreviation nec stands for 'not elsewhere classified'.

OCCUPATIONS EMPLOYED BY MANUFACTURING & REPRODUCING MAGNETIC & OPTICAL MEDIA

Occupation	% of Total 2006	Change to 2016	Occupation	% of Total 2006	Change to 2016
Packers & packagers, hand	4.6	-21.4	General & operations managers	1.5	-11.6
Team assemblers	4.4	-1.7	Computer-controlled machine tool operators	1.5	8.1
Computer support specialists	4.0	-1.7	Maintenance & repair workers, general	1.4	-1.7
Production workers, nec	3.8	-3.6	Industrial truck & tractor operators	1.3	-11.6
Molding, coremaking, & casting machine operators	3.1	-11.6	Industrial machinery mechanics	1.3	13.0
Customer service representatives	3.0	8.1	Electrical & electronic engineering technicians	1.2	-1.7
Computer software engineers, applications	2.9	17.9	Office clerks, general	1.2	-3.2
Machine feeders & offbearers	2.3	-11.6	Accountants & auditors	1.2	-1.7
First-line supervisors/managers of production workers	2.1	-1.7	Packaging & filling machine operators & tenders	1.1	-11.6
Inspectors, testers, sorters, samplers, & weighers	2.1	-7.4	Computer specialists, nec	1.1	-1.8
Computer software engineers, systems software	2.1	8.1	Graphic designers	1.1	-1.7
Shipping, receiving, & traffic clerks	1.9	-5.5	Bookkeeping, accounting, & auditing clerks	1.1	-1.7
Computer programmers	1.9	-21.4	Film & video editors	1.1	-1.7
Computer systems analysts	1.7	8.1	Helpers--Production workers	1.1	-1.7
Sales reps, wholesale & manufacturing, exc tech	1.6	-1.7	Industrial engineers	1.0	19.3

Source: *Industry-Occupation Matrix*, Bureau of Labor Statistics, December 4, 2007. These data are reported based on 4-digit NAICS categories but have been matched to corresponding 6-digit NAICS industry codes. The change reported for each occupation to the year 2016 is a percent of growth or decline as estimated by the Bureau of Labor Statistics. The abbreviation nec stands for 'not elsewhere classified'.

LOCATION BY STATE AND REGIONAL CONCENTRATION

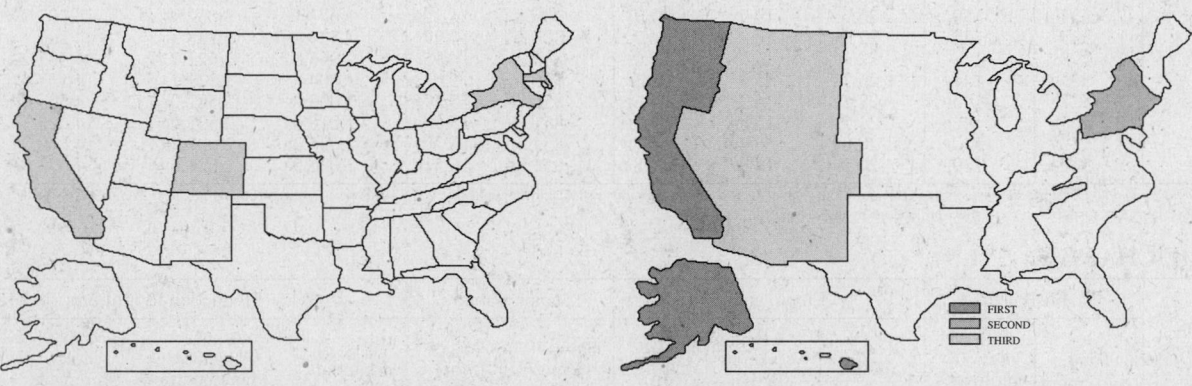

FIRST
SECOND
THIRD

INDUSTRY DATA BY STATE

State	Establish-ments	Shipments			Employment				Cost as % of Shipments	Investment per Employee ($)
		Total ($ mil)	% of U.S.	Per Establ.	Total Number	% of U.S.	Per Establ.	Wages ($/hour)		
California	38	123.8	30.1	3,257.3	616	27.0	16	21.00	38.4	7,213
Massachusetts	5	61.1	14.9	12,218.8	357	15.6	71	16.16	34.6	8,910
Colorado	8	18.1	4.4	2,261.6	105	4.6	13	20.33	34.9	4,295
New York	10	18.1	4.4	1,805.7	141	6.2	14	26.48	37.8	1,887

Source: 2002 *Economic Census*. The states are in descending order of shipments or establishments (if shipment data are missing for the majority). The symbol (D) appears when data are withheld to prevent disclosure of competitive information. States marked with (D) are sorted by number of establishments. A dash (-) indicates that the data element cannot be calculated. Data may not show all states active in the NAICS category. All data available at the time of publication are shown.

NAICS 334612 - PRERECORDED COMPACT DISC (EXCEPT SOFTWARE), TAPE, AND RECORD REPRODUCING

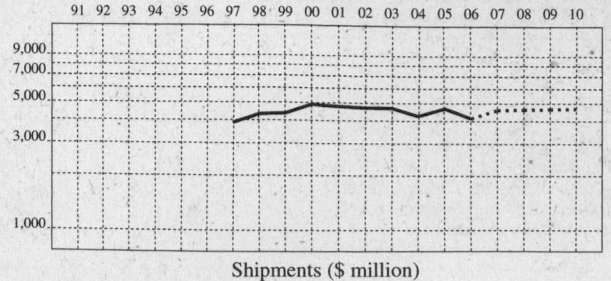

Shipments ($ million)

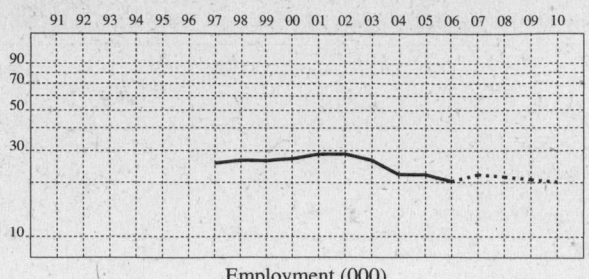

Employment (000)

GENERAL STATISTICS

Year	Companies	Establishments		Employment			Compensation		Production ($ million)			
		Total	with 20 or more employees	Total (000)	Production Workers (000)	Hours (Mil)	Payroll ($ mil)	Wages ($/hr)	Cost of Materials	Value Added by Manufacture	Value of Shipments	Capital Invest.
1997	495	531	150	25.6	19.7	40.7	756.9	12.77	1,432.3	2,418.9	3,870.1	282.5
1998		550	155	26.5	20.5	42.1	808.9	12.94	1,602.6	2,702.7	4,315.7	353.2
1999		534	150	26.4	19.3	40.8	832.8	13.10	1,742.2	2,615.5	4,364.3	383.4
2000		547	150	27.1	20.4	42.0	883.4	13.74	1,985.7	2,913.4	4,894.2	374.0
2001		567	151	28.7	20.2	43.4	936.6	13.31	1,903.8	2,861.4	4,781.9	387.9
2002	528	576	173	28.8	21.2	44.8	976.9	13.72	1,690.8	3,025.6	4,715.8	249.8
2003		532	159	26.6	19.9	41.7	909.1	14.12	1,673.5	3,032.9	4,703.0	277.5
2004		537	144	22.2	16.8	36.7	804.7	14.27	1,534.4	2,723.3	4,261.1	185.1
2005		498	128	22.1	16.6	35.0	810.2	14.95	2,066.8	2,621.7	4,687.2	180.2
2006		529P	144P	20.3	15.3	31.1	765.6	16.03	1,804.6	2,323.1	4,141.6	260.1
2007		527P	143P	22.1P	16.3P	34.6P	850.7P	15.59P	2,005.7P	2,582.0P	4,603.1P	199.0P
2008		524P	142P	21.5P	15.8P	33.7P	851.0P	15.90P	2,016.0P	2,595.2P	4,626.7P	181.8P
2009		522P	140P	20.8P	15.4P	32.7P	851.4P	16.20P	2,026.2P	2,608.4P	4,650.2P	164.7P
2010		519P	139P	20.2P	14.9P	31.8P	851.8P	16.51P	2,036.5P	2,621.6P	4,673.8P	147.5P

Sources: 1997 and 2002 *Economic Census*; other years, up to 2006, are from *Annual Survey of Manufactures*. Establishment counts for non-Census years are from *County Business Patterns*; 1997 and 2002 values are from the 1997 and 2002 censuses, respectively. 'P's show projections by the editors.

INDICES OF CHANGE

Year	Companies	Establishments		Employment			Compensation		Production ($ million)			
		Total	with 20 or more employees	Total (000)	Production Workers (000)	Hours (Mil)	Payroll ($ mil)	Wages ($/hr)	Cost of Materials	Value Added by Manufacture	Value of Shipments	Capital Invest.
1997	94	92	87	89	93	91	77	93	85	80	82	113
1998		95	90	92	97	94	83	94	95	89	92	141
1999		93	87	92	91	91	85	95	103	86	93	153
2000		95	87	94	96	94	90	100	117	96	104	150
2001		98	87	100	95	97	96	97	113	95	101	155
2002	100	100	100	100	100	100	100	100	100	100	100	100
2003		92	92	92	94	93	93	103	99	100	100	111
2004		93	83	77	79	82	82	104	91	90	90	74
2005		86	74	77	78	78	83	109	122	87	99	72
2006		92P	83P	70	72	69	78	117	107	77	88	104
2007		91P	83P	77P	77P	77P	87P	114P	119P	85P	98P	80P
2008		91P	82P	75P	75P	75P	87P	116P	119P	86P	98P	73P
2009		91P	81P	72P	73P	73P	87P	118P	120P	86P	99P	66P
2010		90P	80P	70P	70P	71P	87P	120P	120P	87P	99P	59P

Sources: Same as General Statistics. Values reflect change from the base year, 2002. Values above 100 mean greater than 2002, values below 100 mean less than 2002, and the values of 100 in other years means the same as 2002. 'P's show projections by the editors.

SELECTED RATIOS

For 2002	Avg. of All Manufact.	Analyzed Industry	Index	For 2002	Avg. of All Manufact.	Analyzed Industry	Index
Employees per Establishment	42	50	119	Value Added per Production Worker	182,367	142,717	78
Payroll per Establishment	1,639,184	1,696,007	103	Cost per Establishment	5,769,015	2,935,417	51
Payroll per Employee	39,053	33,920	87	Cost per Employee	137,446	58,708	43
Production Workers per Establishment	30	37	125	Cost per Production Worker	195,506	79,755	41
Wages per Establishment	694,845	1,067,111	154	Shipments per Establishment	11,158,348	8,187,153	73
Wages per Production Worker	23,548	28,993	123	Shipments per Employee	265,847	163,743	62
Hours per Production Worker	1,980	2,113	107	Shipments per Production Worker	378,144	222,443	59
Wages per Hour	11.89	13.72	115	Investment per Establishment	361,338	433,681	120
Value Added per Establishment	5,381,325	5,252,778	98	Investment per Employee	8,609	8,674	101
Value Added per Employee	128,210	105,056	82	Investment per Production Worker	12,245	11,783	96

Sources: Same as General Statistics. The 'Average of All Manufacturing' column represents the average of all manufacturing industries reported for the most recent complete year available. The Index shows the relationship between the Average and the Analyzed Industry. For example, 100 means that they are equal; 500 that the Analyzed Industry is five times the average; 50 means that the Analyzed Industry is half the national average. The abbreviation 'na' is used to show that data are 'not available'. Ratios shown for 2002, the last complete census year.

LEADING COMPANIES   Number shown: 75   Total sales ($ mil): **48,942**   Total employment (000): **173.7**

Company Name	Address				CEO Name	Phone	Co. Type	Sales ($ mil)	Empl. (000)
Walt Disney Co.	500 S Buena Vista	Burbank	CA	91521	Andy Bird	818-560-1000	P	35,510	133.0
Bertelsmann Inc.	1540 Broadway	New York	NY	10036	Joel Klein	212-782-1000	R	4,154*	<0.1
Univision Communications Inc.	1999 Ave. of Stars	Los Angeles	CA	90067	Adam Chesnoff	310-556-7665	R	2,073	4.2
Universal Studios Inc.	100 Universal City	Universal City	CA	91608	Ron Meyer	818-777-1000	S	2,070*	15.0
Sony Music Entertainment Inc.	550 Madison Ave.	New York	NY	10022	Mike Bebel	212-833-8000	S	1,500*	10.0
AandE Television Networks	235 E 45th St.	New York	NY	10017	Abbe Raven	212-210-1400	J	625	0.6
Lagoon Corp.	PO Box 696	Farmington	UT	84025	David Freed	801-451-8000	R	436*	2.0
Capitol Records Inc.	1750 N Vine St.	Hollywood	CA	90028	Andrew Slater	323-462-6252	R	286*	0.2
Muzak L.L.C.	3318 Lakemont	Fort Mill	SC	29708	Stephen Villa	803-396-3000	S	247*	1.3
Thomas Nelson Inc.	PO Box 141000	Nashville	TN	37214	Michael S. Hyatt	615-889-9000	R	238	0.6
Panavision International L.P.	6219 De Soto Ave.	Woodland Hills	CA	91367	Bob Beitcher	818-316-1000	S	194*	1.2
Sony Disc Manufacturing	123 International W	Springfield	OR	97477	Cliff Horton	541-988-8000	S	183*	0.4
Audio-Video-Color Corp.	20550 Denker Ave.	Torrance	CA	90501	Moshe Begim	310-533-5811	R	154*	0.2
Integrity Media Inc.	PO Box 851389	Mobile	AL	36685	P. Michael Coleman	251-633-9000	R	85*	0.3
Cinram Inc.	1600 Rich Rd.	Richmond	IN	47374	Isidore Philosophe	765-962-9511	S	84*	0.7
Amer. Printing House For Blind	PO Box 6085	Louisville	KY	40206		502-895-2405	R	80*	0.3
Concord Music Group Inc.	100 N Crescent Dr.	Beverly Hills	CA	90210	Glen Barros	310-385-4455	R	77*	0.1
Integrity Music	PO Box 851389	Mobile	AL	36685	Michael Coleman	251-633-9000	S	67*	0.1
Allied Vaughn	7951 Computer Ave.	Minneapolis	MN	55435		952-832-3100	R	59*	0.3
Pamplin Entertainment Corp.	10209 SE Dvsion St.	Portland	OR	97266	Andrea Marek	503-251-1597	S	59*	0.1
Motown Record Company L.P.	1755 Broadway, 6th	New York	NY	10019	Dan Leighton.	212-841-8600	S	46*	0.1
American Multimedia Inc.	2609 Tucker St. Ext	Burlington	NC	27215	Bill Brit	336-229-5554	R	44*	0.3
Topics Entertainment Inc.	1600 SW 43rd St.	Renton	WA	98055	Greg James	425-656-3621	R	38*	<0.1
Tape Specialty Inc.	24831 Ave. Tibbitts	Valencia	CA	91355	Steven Feldman	661-702-9030	R	37*	<0.1
Hollywood Film Co.	9265 Borden Ave.	Sun Valley	CA	91352	Vincent Carabello	818-683-1130	R	34*	0.1
Educational Insights Inc.	18730 S Wilmington	R Dominguez	CA	90220	G. Reid Calcott	310-884-2000	S	30*	0.3
Singing Machine Company Inc.	6601 Lyons Rd.	Coconut Creek	FL	33073		954-596-1000	P	27	<0.1
Magnetix Corp.	3600 Ecommerce Pl.	Orlando	FL	32808	William Hohns	407-926-2400	R	27*	0.2
Chapman/Leonard Studio Equip.	12950 Raymer St.	N Hollywood	CA	91605	Leonard Chapman	818-764-6726	R	25*	0.2
Rainbo Record Manufacturing	8960 Eton Ave.	Canoga Park	CA	91304	Steve Sheldon	818-280-1100	R	23*	<0.1
On-Board Media Inc.	1691 Michigan Ave.	Miami Beach	FL	33139	Robert Eichner	305-673-0400	R	21*	<0.1
Voice of God Recording Inc.	PO Box 950	Jeffersonville	IN	47131	Joseph Branham	812-256-1177	R	21*	<0.1
Optical Disc Solutions Inc.	1767 Sheridan St.	Richmond	IN	47374	Fred Austerman	765-935-7574	R	18*	0.1
Hollywood Records	500 S Buena Vista	Burbank	CA	91521	Bob Cavallo	818-560-5670	R	16*	<0.1
Dorling Kindersley Publishing	375 Hudson St. Frnt	New York	NY	10014	Tom Altier	212-213-4800	R	16*	<0.1
Post Asylum	5642 Dyer Street	Dallas	TX	75206	Donald Stokes	214-363-0162	R	16*	<0.1
US Optical Disc Inc.	1 Eagle Dr.	Sanford	ME	04073	Timothy Roy	207-324-1124	R	15*	<0.1
Fantasy Inc.	2600 10th St.	Berkeley	CA	94710	Ralph Kaffel	510-549-2500	R	15*	0.1
HD Studios	23689 Indu. Prk Dr.	Farmington Hls	MI	48335	Steven D. Wild	248-471-6010	R	15*	<0.1
World Media Group Inc.	6737 E 30th St.	Indianapolis	IN	46219	Jeff Mellentine	317-549-8484	R	14*	<0.1
Windswept Holdings L.L.C.	9320 Wilshire Blvd.	Beverly Hills	CA	90212	Evan Medow	310-550-1500	R	13*	<0.1
CD Video Manufacturing Corp.	12650 Westminster	Santa Ana	CA	92706	Minh Nguyen	714-265-0770	R	13*	<0.1
Victory Studios	2247 15th Ave. W	Seattle	WA	98119	Conrad Denke	206-282-1776	R	13*	<0.1
Michele Audio Corp. of America	PO Box 566	Massena	NY	13662	Ginette Gramuglia	315-769-2448	R	11*	<0.1
Axcel Photonics Inc.	45 Bartlett St.	Marlborough	MA	01752	Jim Hsieh	508-481-9200	R	11*	<0.1
DVC Inc.	7301 E 46th St.	Indianapolis	IN	46226		317-544-2150	R	11*	<0.1
Professional Video Supply Inc.	9201 Cody St.	Shawnee Msn	KS	66214	Brad Bartholomew	913-492-1787	R	11*	<0.1
Ultra Stereo Labs Inc.	181 Bonetti Dr.	San Luis Obispo	CA	93401	Jack Cashin	805-549-0161	R	10*	<0.1
AMA Printing Finishing Inc.	PO Box 7535	Waco	TX	76714	Marsh Shaw	254-776-8860	R	9*	<0.1
Builders Publishing Company	11221 Roe Ave. 1A	Shawnee Msn	KS	66211	Stephen Small	913-385-0884	R	9*	<0.1
Nelson White Systems Inc.	8725A Loch Raven	Baltimore	MD	21286	Arlene Wilder	410-668-9628	R	9*	<0.1
Advanced Digital Media	21329 Nordhoff St.	Chatsworth	CA	91311	Patricia Ratner	818-882-3095	R	8*	<0.1
Abkco Music and Records Inc.	1700 Broadway, 41st	New York	NY	10019	Allen Klein	212-399-0300	R	8*	<0.1
Vicom Inc.	1866 Fernandz Juncs	San Juan	PR	00909	Salvatore Nolfo	787-728-5252	R	8*	<0.1
Machine Head	1410 Abbot Kinney	Venice	CA	90291	Stephen Dewey	310-392-8393	R	8*	<0.1
Vision's Edge Inc.	3502 Limerick Dr.	Tallahassee	FL	32309	Dacques Viker	850-386-4573	R	8*	<0.1
Tri State Metrovision Inc.	271 Rte. 46, F108	Fairfield	NJ	07004		973-276-8000	R	8*	<0.1
Good News Broadcasting Assoc.	PO Box 82808	Lincoln	NE	68501	Woodrow Kroll	402-464-7200	R	7*	<0.1
Cubist Media Group	234 Market St.	Philadelphia	PA	19106		215-765-7000	R	7*	<0.1
Rainbo Record	8960 Eton Ave.	Canoga Park	CA	91304	Steve Sheldon	818-341-1124	S	7*	<0.1
Synchronicity Mastering Svcs	5447 W 700 S Ste. C	Salt Lake City	UT	84104		801-533-0301	R	7*	<0.1
HAVE Inc.	350 Power Ave.	Hudson	NY	12534	Nancy Gordon	518-828-2000	R	7*	<0.1
Trudy Corp.	PO Box 679	Norwalk	CT	06856	Ashley C. Andersen	203-846-2274	P	6	<0.1
Scott Resources Inc.	PO Box 2121	Fort Collins	CO	80522	Mike Anderson	970-484-7445	D	6*	<0.1
Talking Devices Co.	37 Brown St.	Weaverville	NC	28787	Lad Ottofy	828-658-0660	R	6*	<0.1
Milliken Publishing Co.	3190 Rider Trail S	Earth City	MO	63045	Thomas Moore	314-991-4220	R	5*	<0.1
HDMG	6573 City W Pky.	Eden Prairie	MN	55344		952-943-1711	R	5*	<0.1
California Magnetics	7898 Ostrow St., H	San Diego	CA	92111	Don Nuzzo	858-576-0291	R	5*	<0.1
Joey Records Inc.	6703 W Commerce	San Antonio	TX	78227	Joe Lopez	210-432-7893	R	5*	<0.1
K-Tel International Inc.	2491 Xenium Ln. N	Plymouth	MN	55441	Philip Kives	763-559-5566	P	5	<0.1
CBD Inc.	1185 Jansen Farm Ct	Elgin	IL	60123	Thom Carpenter	847-741-2233	R	5*	<0.1
Covenant Communications Inc.	PO Box 416	American Fork	UT	84003	Lewis Kofford	801-756-9966	R	5*	<0.1
Imtek L.L.C.	2075 High Hill Rd.	Bridgeport	NJ	08014		856-467-0047	R	5*	<0.1
Studio One Midwest Inc.	74 Leonard Wood	Battle Creek	MI	49037	Michael Clark	269-962-2124	R	4*	<0.1
Metrolpolis Mastering L.P.	88 10th Ave. 6W	New York	NY	10011		212-604-9433	R	4*	<0.1

Source: Ward's Business Directory of U.S. Private and Public Companies, Volumes 1 and 2, 2008. The company type code used is as follows: P - Public, R - Private, S - Subsidiary, D - Division, J - Joint Venture, A - Affiliate, G - Group. Sales are in millions of dollars, employees are in thousands. An asterisk (*) indicates an estimated sales volume. The symbol < stands for 'less than'. Company names and addresses are truncated, in some cases, to fit into the available space.

MATERIALS CONSUMED

Material	Quantity	Delivered Cost ($ million)
Blank magnetic tape, audio use	(X)	161.8
Record blanks, audio	(X)	3.1
Compact disc blanks for audio and computer use	(X)	44.2
Empty tape cassettes and cartridges	(X)	117.0
Plastics products consumed in the form of sheets, rods, etc.	(X)	123.2
Plastics resins consumed in the form of granules, pellets, etc.	(X)	110.9
Paper and paperboard products (album covers, sleeves, etc.)	(X)	107.9
All other materials, components, parts, containers, and supplies	(X)	262.7
Materials, ingredients, containers, and supplies, nsk	(X)	491.0

Source: 2002 *Economic Census*. Explanation of symbols used: (D): Withheld to avoid disclosure of competitive data; na: Not available; (S): Withheld because statistical norms were not met; (X): Not applicable; (Z): Less than half the unit shown; nec: Not elsewhere classified; nsk: Not specified by kind; - : zero; p : 10-19 percent estimated; q : 20-29 percent estimated.

PRODUCT SHARE DETAILS

Product or Product Class Shipments	Mil. $	Product or Product Class Shipments	Mil. $
PRERECORDED COMPACT DISCS (EXCEPT		12 inch	32.3
SOFTWARE), TAPES, AND RECORDS	4,194.5	Audio discs and records long playing (LP), excluding	
Prerecorded compact disc, (except software), tape, and		digitally mastered records for consumer use	8.3
record reproducing	**4,194.5**	Audio discs and records compact disc (CD) singles-	
Audio discs, records, and compact discs (CD), full-length	1,212.6	maxisingles	42.8
Audio tapes, cassette, full-length	195.0	Other audio discs or records, including digitally	
Reproduction of video recording media	2,045.5	mastered records for consumer use, and master	
Video discs, including laser	907.5	records used to press commercial records	(D)
Video tapes	1,138.0	Audio tapes, cassette singles-maxisingles	(D)
All other reproduction of recording media	140.6	Other audio tapes, including 8-track and DAT	(D)
Audio discs and records vinyl singles, including 7 and		Reproduction of recording media, nsk, total	600.8

Source: 2002 *Economic Census*. The values are product shipments in millions of dollars for 2002. Total product shipments may be lower or higher than industry shipments. See Introduction for a full discussion. Values of indented subcategories are summed in the main heading(s). The symbol (D) appears when data are withheld to prevent disclosure of competitive information. The abbreviation nsk stands for 'not specified by kind' and nec for 'not elsewhere classified'. A dash (-) means zero.

INPUTS AND OUTPUTS FOR SOFTWARE, AUDIO, AND VIDEO MEDIA REPRODUCING

Economic Sector or Industry Providing Inputs	%	Sector	Economic Sector or Industry Buying Outputs	%	Sector
Compensation of employees	26.9		Motion picture & video industries	20.6	Services
Management of companies & enterprises	10.8	Services	Sound recording industries	9.9	Services
Magnetic & optical recording media	4.9	Manufg.	Advertising & related services	7.7	Services
Lessors of nonfinancial assets	4.5	Fin/R.E.	Travel arrangement & reservation services	7.3	Services
Paperboard mills	4.2	Manufg.	Electronic computers	6.6	Manufg.
Plastics products, nec	3.7	Manufg.	Support services, nec	6.6	Services
Plastics materials & resins	3.6	Manufg.	Investigation & security services	4.8	Services
Plastics packaging materials, film & sheet	3.4	Manufg.	Photographic services	4.6	Services
Scientific research & development services	3.1	Services	Internet service providers & web search portals	4.3	Services
Wholesale trade	3.0	Trade	Exports of goods & services	4.3	Cap Inv
Software publishers	2.8	Services	Telecommunications	2.9	Services
Software, audio, and video media reproducing	1.8	Manufg.	General S/L govt. services	2.2	S/L Govt
Semiconductors & related devices	1.6	Manufg.	Legal services	2.0	Services
Power generation & supply	1.3	Util.	Software, audio, and video media reproducing	1.7	Manufg.
Real estate	1.2	Fin/R.E.	Professional, scientific, technical services, nec	1.5	Services
Custom computer programming services	0.9	Services	Other S/L govt. enterprises	1.5	S/L Govt
Securities, commodity contracts, investments	0.9	Fin/R.E.	Tobacco products	1.4	Manufg.
Advertising & related services	0.7	Services	Computer storage devices	1.3	Manufg.
Printed circuit assemblies (electronic assemblies)	0.7	Manufg.	Cable & other subscription programming	1.2	Services
Unlaminated plastics profile shapes	0.6	Manufg.	Scientific research & development services	1.0	Services
Taxes on production & imports, less subsidies	0.6		Accounting, tax preparation, bookkeeping, & payroll	0.9	Services
Monetary authorities/depository credit intermediation	0.6	Fin/R.E.	General Federal government services, nondefense	0.7	Fed Govt
Automotive equipment rental & leasing	0.5	Fin/R.E.	Asphalt paving mixtures & blocks	0.6	Manufg.
Truck transportation	0.5	Util.	Computer system design services	0.5	Services
Management, scientific, & technical consulting	0.5	Services	Wood containers & pallets	0.5	Manufg.
Coating, engraving, heat treating & allied activities	0.5	Manufg.	Educational services, nec	0.5	Services
Architectural, engineering, & related services	0.5	Services	Employment services	0.5	Services
Professional, scientific, technical services, nec	0.5	Services	Office administrative services	0.4	Services
Telecommunications	0.5	Services	Business support services	0.4	Services
Bare printed circuit boards	0.4	Manufg.	Management, scientific, & technical consulting	0.3	Services
Maintenance/repair of nonresidential structures	0.4	Construct.	Search, detection, & navigation instruments	0.3	Manufg.
Machine shops	0.4	Manufg.	Vending, commercial, industrial, office machinery	0.2	Manufg.
Services to buildings & dwellings	0.4	Services	Radio & television broadcasting	0.2	Services
Legal services	0.3	Services	Food services & drinking places	0.1	Services
Accounting, tax preparation, bookkeeping, & payroll	0.3	Services	Computer terminals & peripherals	0.1	Manufg.
Warehousing & storage	0.3	Util.	Physician, dentist, other health practitioner offices	0.1	Services

Continued on next page.

INPUTS AND OUTPUTS FOR SOFTWARE, AUDIO, AND VIDEO MEDIA REPRODUCING - Continued

Economic Sector or Industry Providing Inputs	%	Sector	Economic Sector or Industry Buying Outputs	%	Sector
Paperboard containers	0.3	Manufg.			
Data processing, hosting, & related services	0.3	Services			
Fabricated metals, nec	0.3	Manufg.			
Noncomparable imports	0.3	Foreign			
Commercial & industrial machinery rental & leasing	0.3	Fin/R.E.			
Rail transportation	0.3	Util.			
Food services & drinking places	0.3	Services			
Other computer related services, including facilities	0.3	Services			
Employment services	0.2	Services			
Automotive repair & maintenance, ex. car washes	0.2	Services			
Commercial & industrial equipment repair/maintenance	0.2	Services			
Business support services	0.2	Services			
Laminated plastics plates, sheets, & shapes	0.2	Manufg.			
Natural gas distribution	0.2	Util.			
Hotels & motels, including casino hotels	0.2	Services			
Air transportation	0.1	Util.			
Specialized design services	0.1	Services			
Electronic & precision equipment repair/maintenance	0.1	Services			

Source: Benchmark Input-Output Accounts for the U.S. Economy, 2002, U.S. Department of Commerce, Washington D.C., January 2008. User should note that this Input-Output table is not for this particular narrowly defined industry but for a larger aggregate. Input and Output data for Software, Audio, and Video Media Reproducing include Input and Output data for the Annual Survey of Manufactures' NAICS industries 334611 and 334612. The abbreviation nec stands for 'not elsewhere classified'.

OCCUPATIONS EMPLOYED BY MANUFACTURING & REPRODUCING MAGNETIC & OPTICAL MEDIA

Occupation	% of Total 2006	Change to 2016	Occupation	% of Total 2006	Change to 2016
Packers & packagers, hand	4.6	-21.4	General & operations managers	1.5	-11.6
Team assemblers	4.4	-1.7	Computer-controlled machine tool operators	1.5	8.1
Computer support specialists	4.0	-1.7	Maintenance & repair workers, general	1.4	-1.7
Production workers, nec	3.8	-3.6	Industrial truck & tractor operators	1.3	-11.6
Molding, coremaking, & casting machine operators	3.1	-11.6	Industrial machinery mechanics	1.3	13.0
Customer service representatives	3.0	8.1	Electrical & electronic engineering technicians	1.2	-1.7
Computer software engineers, applications	2.9	17.9	Office clerks, general	1.2	-3.2
Machine feeders & offbearers	2.3	-11.6	Accountants & auditors	1.2	-1.7
First-line supervisors/managers of production workers	2.1	-1.7	Packaging & filling machine operators & tenders	1.1	-11.6
Inspectors, testers, sorters, samplers, & weighers	2.1	-7.4	Computer specialists, nec	1.1	-1.8
Computer software engineers, systems software	2.1	8.1	Graphic designers	1.1	-1.7
Shipping, receiving, & traffic clerks	1.9	-5.5	Bookkeeping, accounting, & auditing clerks	1.1	-1.7
Computer programmers	1.9	-21.4	Film & video editors	1.1	-1.7
Computer systems analysts	1.7	8.1	Helpers--Production workers	1.1	-1.7
Sales reps, wholesale & manufacturing, exc tech	1.6	-1.7	Industrial engineers	1.0	19.3

Source: Industry-Occupation Matrix, Bureau of Labor Statistics, December 4, 2007. These data are reported based on 4-digit NAICS categories but have been matched to corresponding 6-digit NAICS industry codes. The change reported for each occupation to the year 2016 is a percent of growth or decline as estimated by the Bureau of Labor Statistics. The abbreviation nec stands for 'not elsewhere classified'.

LOCATION BY STATE AND REGIONAL CONCENTRATION

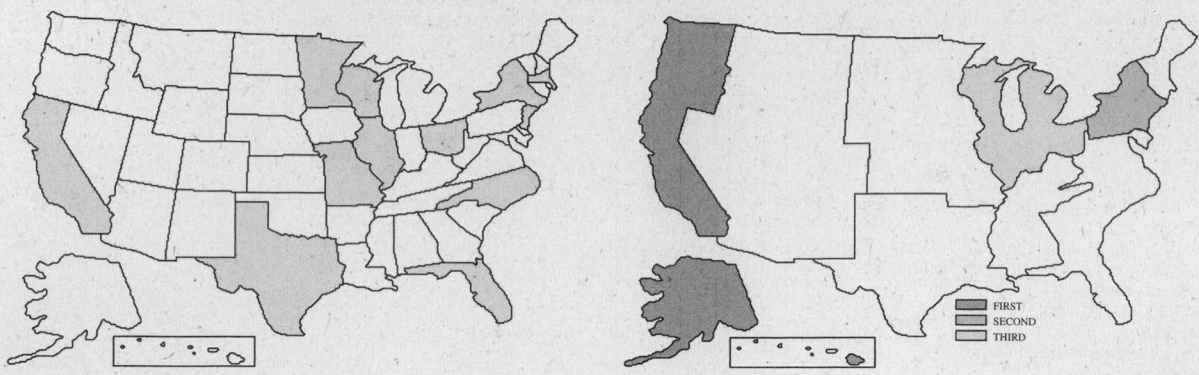

INDUSTRY DATA BY STATE

| State | Establish-ments | Shipments | | | Employment | | | | Cost as % of Shipments | Investment per Employee ($) |
		Total ($ mil)	% of U.S.	Per Establ.	Total Number	% of U.S.	Per Establ.	Wages ($/hour)		
California	147	843.0	17.9	5,734.8	5,830	20.3	40	13.81	39.0	10,919
Illinois	28	310.3	6.6	11,081.4	2,378	8.3	85	14.54	36.8	3,841
North Carolina	10	279.5	5.9	27,951.8	2,067	7.2	207	13.55	45.4	6,390
New York	63	194.9	4.1	3,093.3	1,489	5.2	24	14.54	29.9	4,716
New Jersey	18	167.9	3.6	9,325.8	875	3.0	49	12.64	34.4	7,296
Massachusetts	18	83.0	1.8	4,610.2	640	2.2	36	13.23	36.4	3,370
Florida	27	75.6	1.6	2,800.1	792	2.8	29	12.02	34.5	1,678
Texas	27	73.1	1.6	2,707.9	606	2.1	22	11.72	38.0	2,266
Ohio	10	64.7	1.4	6,473.6	441	1.5	44	14.29	21.7	1,823
Minnesota	11	53.0	1.1	4,813.8	398	1.4	36	14.37	42.4	1,967
Wisconsin	9	34.0	0.7	3,780.1	162	0.6	18	13.80	21.1	3,321
Missouri	9	15.0	0.3	1,663.9	107	0.4	12	10.79	43.1	6,570

Source: 2002 *Economic Census*. The states are in descending order of shipments or establishments (if shipment data are missing for the majority). The symbol (D) appears when data are withheld to prevent disclosure of competitive information. States marked with (D) are sorted by number of establishments. A dash (-) indicates that the data element cannot be calculated. Data may not show all states active in the NAICS category. All data available at the time of publication are shown.

NAICS 334613 - MAGNETIC AND OPTICAL RECORDING MEDIA MANUFACTURING

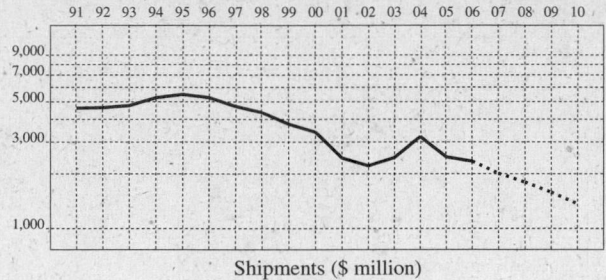

Shipments ($ million)

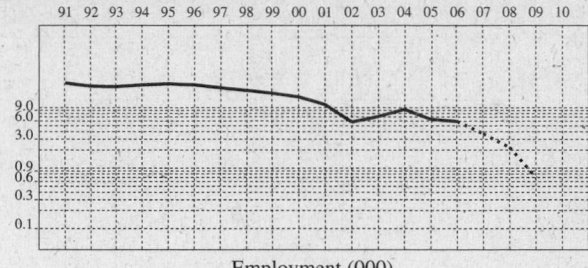

Employment (000)

GENERAL STATISTICS

Year	Com-panies	Establishments		Employment			Compensation		Production ($ million)			
		Total	with 20 or more employees	Total (000)	Production Workers (000)	Hours (Mil)	Payroll ($ mil)	Wages ($/hr)	Cost of Materials	Value Added by Manufacture	Value of Shipments	Capital Invest.
1991		243	103	25.4	16.1	33.2	734.7	11.24	2,734.8	1,959.9	4,615.9	305.2
1992	239	261	97	22.6	15.1	32.2	695.0	11.30	2,513.6	2,091.5	4,641.3	394.2
1993		261	93	22.2	15.0	31.2	689.6	12.18	2,406.1	2,388.0	4,765.5	337.9
1994		262	81	23.7	15.5	30.3	778.5	14.16	2,637.5	2,615.2	5,256.3	325.7
1995		263	91	24.7	17.2	32.5	816.2	13.97	2,711.2	2,787.8	5,481.5	388.9
1996		268	83	23.7	16.7	31.3	844.6	14.81	2,827.6	2,455.0	5,271.5	522.5
1997	241	258	75	21.3	14.7	30.3	814.7	13.76	2,427.6	2,323.5	4,721.3	439.9
1998		252	71	19.2	12.8	27.1	715.9	14.52	2,117.8	2,242.3	4,358.6	311.4
1999		262	66	17.2	11.4	23.9	681.4	14.91	1,818.9	1,902.5	3,763.6	304.1
2000		256	64	15.0	9.6	19.0	611.5	15.99	1,947.6	1,440.6	3,401.6	261.3
2001		253	64	11.2	6.7	14.6	513.1	17.04	1,402.1	989.9	2,448.0	140.0
2002	169	173	35	5.8	4.0	8.5	250.6	17.44	947.5	1,240.2	2,219.0	83.2
2003		172	35	7.1	4.7	9.3	395.3	24.19	1,121.0	1,319.5	2,456.4	102.8
2004		152	35	9.4	5.6	10.7	640.8	23.86	2,003.6	1,178.4	3,207.9	226.3
2005		148	36	6.4	3.4	7.2	449.5	21.40	1,735.9	731.6	2,478.6	168.0
2006		170P	27P	5.9	2.9	6.2	418.4	20.98	1,719.1	662.0	2,345.6	277.8
2007		163P	22P	3.7P	1.8P	3.8P	400.8P	23.09P	1,476.4P	568.5P	2,014.4P	147.1P
2008		155P	17P	2.2P	0.8P	1.7P	374.1P	23.88P	1,319.0P	507.9P	1,799.7P	130.6P
2009		147P	12P	0.7P			347.4P	24.68P	1,161.6P	447.3P	1,584.9P	114.2P
2010		139P	7P				320.6P	25.47P	1,004.2P	386.7P	1,370.2P	97.7P

Sources: 1992, 1997, 2002 *Economic Census*; other years, up to 2006, are from the *Annual Survey of Manufactures.* Establishment counts for non-Census years are from *County Business Patterns*; 1997 and 2002 values are from the 1997 and 2002 censuses respectively, reported in the Federal Government's NAICS format. Other years were originally reported in equivalent SIC format. 'P's show projections by the editors.

INDICES OF CHANGE

Year	Com-panies	Establishments		Employment			Compensation		Production ($ million)			
		Total	with 20 or more employees	Total (000)	Production Workers (000)	Hours (Mil)	Payroll ($ mil)	Wages ($/hr)	Cost of Materials	Value Added by Manufacture	Value of Shipments	Capital Invest.
1992	141	151	277	390	378	379	277	65	265	169	209	474
1997	143	149	214	367	368	356	325	79	256	187	213	529
2001		146	183	193	168	172	205	98	148	80	110	168
2002	100	100	100	100	100	100	100	100	100	100	100	100
2003		99	100	122	118	109	158	139	118	106	111	124
2004		88	100	162	140	126	256	137	211	95	145	272
2005		86	103	110	85	85	179	123	183	59	112	202
2006		98P	78P	102	73	73	167	120	181	53	106	334
2007		94P	63P	64P	45P	45P	160P	132P	156P	46P	91P	177P
2008		89P	49P	38P	20P	20P	149P	137P	139P	41P	81P	157P
2009		85P	34P	12P			139P	142P	123P	36P	71P	137P
2010		81P	19P				128P	146P	106P	31P	62P	117P

Sources: Same as General Statistics. Values reflect change from the base year, 2002. Values above 100 mean greater than 2002, values below 100 mean less than 2002, and the values of 100 in other years means the same as 2002. 'P's show projections by the editors.

SELECTED RATIOS

For 2002	Avg. of All Manufact.	Analyzed Industry	Index	For 2002	Avg. of All Manufact.	Analyzed Industry	Index
Employees per Establishment	42	34	80	Value Added per Production Worker	182,367	310,050	170
Payroll per Establishment	1,639,184	1,448,555	88	Cost per Establishment	5,769,015	5,476,879	95
Payroll per Employee	39,053	43,207	111	Cost per Employee	137,446	163,362	119
Production Workers per Establishment	30	23	78	Cost per Production Worker	195,506	236,875	121
Wages per Establishment	694,845	856,879	123	Shipments per Establishment	11,158,348	12,826,590	115
Wages per Production Worker	23,548	37,060	157	Shipments per Employee	265,847	382,586	144
Hours per Production Worker	1,980	2,125	107	Shipments per Production Worker	378,144	554,750	147
Wages per Hour	11.89	17.44	147	Investment per Establishment	361,338	480,925	133
Value Added per Establishment	5,381,325	7,168,786	133	Investment per Employee	8,609	14,345	167
Value Added per Employee	128,210	213,828	167	Investment per Production Worker	12,245	20,800	170

Sources: Same as General Statistics. The 'Average of All Manufacturing' column represents the average of all manufacturing industries reported for the most recent complete year available. The Index shows the relationship between the Average and the Analyzed Industry. For example, 100 means that they are equal; 500 that the Analyzed Industry is five times the average; 50 means that the Analyzed Industry is half the national average. The abbreviation 'na' is used to show that data are 'not available'. Ratios shown for 2002, the last complete census year.

1337

LEADING COMPANIES   Number shown: 75   Total sales ($ mil): 33,102   Total employment (000): 107.5

Company Name	Address				CEO Name	Phone	Co. Type	Sales ($ mil)	Empl. (000)
3M Co.	3M Ctr.	St. Paul	MN	55144	George W. Buckley	651-733-2204	P	24,462	76.2
Imation Corp.	1 Imation Pl.	Oakdale	MN	55128		651-704-4000	P	2,062	2.3
Ascent Media DVD	201 Santa Monica	Santa Monica	CA	90401		310-899-7200	R	1,680*	4.0
Sony Music Entertainment Inc.	550 Madison Ave.	New York	NY	10022	Mike Bebel	212-833-8000	S	1,500*	10.0
WD Media Inc.	20511 Lk Forest Dr.	Lake Forest	CA	92630	John F. Coyne	408-576-2000	S	943*	8.4
IPC Communication Services	501 Colonial Dr.	Saint Joseph	MI	49085	Ken Kozminski	269-983-7105	S	300*	0.3
JVC Disc America Co.	2 JVC Rd.	Tuscaloosa	AL	35405	Koichi Yamane	205-256-1111	S	182*	0.5
Quantum3D Inc.	6330 San Ignacio	San Jose	CA	95119	Gordon Campbell	408-361-9999	R	166*	0.1
American Media International	2609 Tucker St. Ext	Burlington	NC	27215	Richard Clark		R	126*	0.3
R!OT	702 Arizona Ave.	Santa Monica	CA	90401	Bob Saloman	310-434-6000	R	125*	0.3
Enovation Graphic Systems Inc.	200 Summit Lake	Valhalla	NY	10595	Shigetaka Komori	914-789-8100	S	111*	0.3
Cogent Inc.	209 Fair Oaks Ave.	South Pasadena	CA	91030	Ming Hseih	626-799-8090	P	106	0.3
Cinram Inc.	1600 Rich Rd.	Richmond	IN	47374	Isidore Philosophe	765-962-9511	S	84*	0.7
Panasonic Disc Services Corp.	20608 Madrona Ave.	Torrance	CA	90503		310-783-4800	R	84*	0.2
Reel Picture	5330 Eastgate Mall	San Diego	CA	92121	David Smitjkozick	858-587-0301	R	84*	0.2
DVS InteleStream	2600 W Olive Ave.	Burbank	CA	91505	Richard Appell	818-566-4151	R	83*	0.2
OEM Inc.	PO Box 7206	Charlotte	NC	28241		704-504-1877	R	67*	0.1
Digital Excellence Inc.	300 York Ave.	Saint Paul	MN	55101	Richard Stevens	651-772-5100	S	60*	0.1
Disctronics	2800 Summit Ave.	Plano	TX	75074	Dave Littlefield	972-881-8800	R	50*	0.1
L-3 Telemetry-West, Conic	9020 Balboa Ave.	San Diego	CA	92123		858-694-7500	D	42*	0.4
Crest National	PO Box 68057	Anaheim	CA	92807	Ryan Stain	714-666-2266	R	42*	0.1
Digital Audio Disc Corp (DADC)	1800 N Fruitridge	Terre Haute	IN	47804	Dieter Daum	812-462-8100	R	42*	0.1
Bethesda Softworks/Media Tech.	1370 Piccard Dr.	Rockville	MD	20850	Christoper Weaver	301-926-8300	R	32*	<0.1
Magnetix Corp.	3600 Ecommerce Pl.	Orlando	FL	32808	William Hohns	407-926-2400	R	27*	0.2
Hello World Communications	118 W 22nd St.	New York	NY	10011	Ann Chitwood	212-243-8800	R	26*	<0.1
EchoData Group	855 Fox Chase	Coatesville	PA	19320	C. R. Nocella	610-466-2100	R	25*	<0.1
Action Duplication Inc.	8 Union Hill Rd.	W Conshohckn	PA	19428	Joel Levitt	610-828-7580	R	24*	<0.1
Digigraphics Inc.	2639 Minnehaha	Minneapolis	MN	55406	Bob Remakel	612-721-2434	R	24*	<0.1
US DigitalMedia	1929 W Lone Cactus	Phoenix	AZ	85027	Chris Pignotti	623-587-4900	R	23*	<0.1
Data Management Internationale	55 Lukens Dr.	New Castle	DE	19720	Carol Swezey	302-656-1151	R	21*	<0.1
Qualstar Corp.	3990-B Heritg Oak	Simi Valley	CA	93063	William J. Gervais	805-583-7744	P	21	<0.1
Chicago Recording Co.	232 E Ohio St.	Chicago	IL	60611	Alan Kubicka	312-822-9333	R	20*	<0.1
Metters Industries Inc.	8200 Greensboro Dr.	McLean	VA	22102	Samuel Metters	703-821-3300	R	19*	0.2
Acoustech Mastering	486 Dawson Dr.	Camarillo	CA	93012		805-484-2747	R	17*	<0.1
Nuvidia	9258 Bond St.	Overland Park	KS	66214	Thomas P. Doyle	913-599-5200	R	17*	<0.1
SOA Software Inc.	12100 Wilshire Blvd	Los Angeles	CA	90025	Paul Gigg	310-826-1317	R	16*	<0.1
Agile Network L.L.C.	6209 Mid Rivrs Mall	Saint Charles	MO	63304		636-300-0912	R	15*	<0.1
US Optical Disc Inc.	1 Eagle Dr.	Sanford	ME	04073	Timothy Roy	207-324-1124	R	15*	<0.1
3M Visual Systems Div.	6801 River Place	Austin	TX	78726	Robert Morrison	512-984-1800	R	15*	0.1
HD Studios	23689 Indu. Prk Dr.	Farmington Hls	MI	48335	Steven D. Wild	248-471-6010	R	15*	<0.1
Global Information Distrib.	2635 Zanker Rd.	San Jose	CA	95134	Ernstfried Driesen	408-232-5528	R	14*	<0.1
4M Systems Inc.	4655 Old Ironsides	Santa Clara	CA	95054	Stephen Grey	408-970-8505	R	14*	<0.1
CD Video Manufacturing Corp.	12650 Westminster	Santa Ana	CA	92706	Minh Nguyen	714-265-0770	R	13*	<0.1
Vigobyte International Corp.	360 N Pastoria Ave.	Sunnyvale	CA	94085	Bob Wong	408-773-2900	R	13*	<0.1
Oasis CD Manufacturing	PO Box 214	Sperryville	VA	22740	Micah Solomon	540-987-8810	R	13*	<0.1
Victory Studios	2247 15th Ave. W	Seattle	WA	98119	Conrad Denke	206-282-1776	R	13*	<0.1
Now Disc	3875 S American	Idaho Falls	ID	83402	Brian Powell	208-552-1720	R	13*	<0.1
Trutone Inc.	321 W 44th St.	New York	NY	10036	Carl Rowatti	212-265-5636	R	12*	<0.1
Michele Audio Corp. of America	PO Box 566	Massena	NY	13662	Ginette Gramuglia	315-769-2448	R	11*	<0.1
GoldenRom Inc.	3 Vertical Dr.	Canonsburg	PA	15317	Derek Signorini	724-746-5807	R	11*	<0.1
Corporate Duplication Solution	375 North St.	Teterboro	NJ	07608	Anthony Chinni	201-342-3060	R	11*	<0.1
Formats Unlimited Inc.	121 Carolyn Blvd.	E Farmingdale	NY	11735	Joyce Cosentino	631-249-9200	R	11*	<0.1
5.1 Entertainment Group L.L.C.	2231 S Carmelina	W Los Angeles	CA	90064	John Trickett	310-207-5181	R	11*	<0.1
Promedia Digital	3777 Business Park	Columbus	OH	43204	Joe Chylik	614-274-1600	R	11*	<0.1
ISODISC/Software Services Grp	7030 N 97th Cir.	Omaha	NE	68122	Alan D Kegel	402-453-1699	R	10*	<0.1
Precision Powerhouse	911 Second St. S	Minneapolis	MN	55415	Daniel Piepho	612-333-9111	S	10*	<0.1
Design Video Communications	7301 E 46th St.	Indianapolis	IN	46226	Jad Porter	317-544-2150	R	9*	<0.1
Dove Enterprises	4520 Hudson Dr.	Stow	OH	44224	Larry Adams	330-928-9160	R	9*	<0.1
Datasis Corp.	1687 Elmhurst Rd.	Elk Grove Vlg	IL	60007	Bob Thomas	847-427-0909	R	9*	<0.1
Advanced Digital Media	21329 Nordhoff St.	Chatsworth	CA	91311	Patricia Ratner	818-882-3095	R	8*	<0.1
bitMAX L.L.C.	6255 Sunset Blvd.	Hollywood	CA	90028	Richard Martin	323-957-9797	R	8*	<0.1
Diversified Systems Group Inc.	14816 NE 95th	Redmond	WA	98052	Bob Sambrook	425-947-1500	R	8*	<0.1
All Pro Solutions Inc.	5542 Brisa St., F	Livermore	CA	94550	Tibi Czentye	925-447-8484	R	8*	<0.1
Error Free Software L.L.C.	200 S Wacker Dr.	Chicago	IL	60606	Alexei Gitter	312-461-0300	R	8*	<0.1
Optical Disc Corp.	10415 Slusher Dr.	Santa Fe Spgs	CA	90670		562-946-3050	R	8*	<0.1
Wholesale Tape and Supply Co.	2841 Hickory Valley	Chattanooga	TN	37421	Michael Salley	423-894-9427	R	7*	<0.1
Getecha Incorporated USA	2914 Bus. One Dr.	Kalamazoo	MI	49048	Chris Koffend	269-373-8896	R	7*	<0.1
Rainbo Record	8960 Eton Ave.	Canoga Park	CA	91304	Steve Sheldon	818-341-1124	S	7*	<0.1
Renaissance Prof Training Prog	3914 154th Ave. SE	Bellevue	WA	98006	Bob Applegate	425-922-6198	R	7*	<0.1
Talking Devices Co.	37 Brown St.	Weaverville	NC	28787	Lad Ottofy	828-658-0660	R	6*	<0.1
Vinyl Art Inc.	15300 28th Ave. N	Minneapolis	MN	55447	Robert Roy	763-559-4443	R	6*	<0.1
Star-Byte Inc.	611 Jeffers Cir.	Exton	PA	19341	Steve Derstine		R	6*	<0.1
White Graphics Inc. (WGI)	1411 Ctre Circle Dr	Downers Grove	IL	60515	Richard White	630-629-9300	R	6*	<0.1
WRS Motion Picture and Video	1000 Napor Blvd.	Pittsburgh	PA	15205	F. Jack Naper	412-937-1200	R	6*	<0.1
Spectrum Digital Services	600 Northshore Dr.	Hartland	WI	53029	Russell S. Gnant	262-369-1577	R	6*	<0.1

Source: Ward's Business Directory of U.S. Private and Public Companies, Volumes 1 and 2, 2008. The company type code used is as follows: P - Public, R - Private, S - Subsidiary, D - Division, J - Joint Venture, A - Affiliate, G - Group. Sales are in millions of dollars, employees are in thousands. An asterisk (*) indicates an estimated sales volume. The symbol < stands for 'less than'. Company names and addresses are truncated, in some cases, to fit into the available space.

MATERIALS CONSUMED

Material	Quantity	Delivered Cost ($ million)
Paperboard containers, boxes, and corrugated paperboard	(X)	8.7
Plastics resins consumed in the form of granules, pellets, etc.	(X)	26.6
Fabricated plastics products (exc. gaskets, hoses, and belting)	(X)	9.7
Plastics products consumed in the form of sheets, rods, etc.	(X)	133.9
Metal bolts, nuts, screws, and other screw machine products	(X)	(D)
Other fabricated metal products (exc. castings and forgings)	(X)	(D)
Aluminum and aluminum-base alloy shapes and forms (exc. castings, forgings, fabr. metal products)	(X)	(D)
Other nonferrous shapes and forms (exc. castings, forgings, fabricated metal products)	(X)	(D)
Ferrites (powder and paste)	(X)	(D)
All other materials, components, parts, containers, and supplies	(X)	566.0
Materials, ingredients, containers, and supplies, nsk	(X)	77.6

Source: 2002 *Economic Census*. Explanation of symbols used: (D): Withheld to avoid disclosure of competitive data; na: Not available; (S): Withheld because statistical norms were not met; (X): Not applicable; (Z): Less than half the unit shown; nec: Not elsewhere classified; nsk: Not specified by kind; - : zero; p : 10-19 percent estimated; q : 20-29 percent estimated.

PRODUCT SHARE DETAILS

Product or Product Class Shipments	Mil. $	Product or Product Class Shipments	Mil. $
UNRECORDED MAGNETIC AND OPTICAL DISCS AND TAPES	2,520.0	including reels, cassettes, cartridges, and video	1,606.9
Magnetic and optical recording media, unrecorded	**2,520.0**	All other magnetic and optical recording media, unrecorded	542.4
Magnetic and optical recording media, unrecorded disks	174.7	Unrecorded magnetic and optical discs and tapes, nsk, total	196.0
Magnetic and optical recording media, unrecorded tapes,			

Source: 2002 *Economic Census*. The values are product shipments in millions of dollars for 2002. Total product shipments may be lower or higher than industry shipments. See Introduction for a full discussion. Values of indented subcategories are summed in the main heading(s). The symbol (D) appears when data are withheld to prevent disclosure of competitive information. The abbreviation nsk stands for 'not specified by kind' and nec for 'not elsewhere classified'. A dash (-) means zero.

INPUTS AND OUTPUTS FOR MAGNETIC AND OPTICAL RECORDING MEDIA MANUFACTURING

Economic Sector or Industry Providing Inputs	%	Sector	Economic Sector or Industry Buying Outputs	%	Sector
Compensation of employees	15.1		Exports of goods & services	15.7	Cap Inv
Software publishers	10.1	Services	Food services & drinking places	11.3	Services
Plastics products, nec	5.8	Manufg.	Personal consumption expenditures	10.8	
Wholesale trade	5.8	Trade	Hotels & motels, including casino hotels	10.2	Services
Plastics packaging materials, film & sheet	5.1	Manufg.	Software publishers	5.7	Services
Management of companies & enterprises	4.9	Services	Software, audio, and video media reproducing	4.9	Manufg.
Chemical products & preparations, nec	3.4	Manufg.	Retail trade	3.9	Trade
Aluminum products from purchased aluminum	2.9	Manufg.	Wholesale trade	3.6	Trade
Noncomparable imports	1.7	Foreign	Private fixed investment	3.5	
Magnetic & optical recording media	1.4	Manufg.	General Federal government services, defense	3.4	Fed Govt
Turned products & screws, nuts, & bolts	1.4	Manufg.	Hospitals	2.9	Services
Scientific research & development services	1.4	Services	Accounting, tax preparation, bookkeeping, & payroll	2.9	Services
Automotive equipment rental & leasing	1.3	Fin/R.E.	General Federal government services, nondefense	2.7	Fed Govt
Plastics materials & resins	1.1	Manufg.	Physician, dentist, other health practitioner offices	2.2	Services
Power generation & supply	0.9	Util.	Telecommunications	1.5	Services
Printed circuit assemblies (electronic assemblies)	0.9	Manufg.	Warehousing & storage	1.3	Util.
Unlaminated plastics profile shapes	0.8	Manufg.	Architectural, engineering, & related services	1.2	Services
Semiconductors & related devices	0.8	Manufg.	Monetary authorities/depository credit intermediation	0.8	Fin/R.E.
Iron & steel mills & ferroalloys	0.7	Manufg.	Motor vehicle parts	0.8	Manufg.
Commercial & industrial machinery rental & leasing	0.7	Fin/R.E.	Magnetic & optical recording media	0.7	Manufg.
Alumina refining & primary aluminum production	0.6	Manufg.	Religious organizations	0.7	Services
Truck transportation	0.6	Util.	Nondepository credit intermediation activities	0.6	Fin/R.E.
Real estate	0.5	Fin/R.E.	Pipeline transportation	0.5	Util.
Paperboard containers	0.4	Manufg.	Data processing, hosting, & related services	0.5	Services
Machine shops	0.4	Manufg.	Nursing & residential care facilities	0.5	Services
Advertising & related services	0.4	Services	Civic, social, & professional organizations	0.5	Services
Electronic components, nec	0.4	Manufg.	Environmental & other technical consulting services	0.5	Services
Natural gas distribution	0.3	Util.	Medical & diagnostic labs & outpatient services	0.4	Services
Electronic capacitors, resistors, coils, transformers	0.3	Manufg.	Personal services, nec	0.4	Services
Laminated plastics plates, sheets, & shapes	0.3	Manufg.	Business support services	0.4	Services
Electronic connectors	0.3	Manufg.	Internet service providers & web search portals	0.4	Services
Maintenance/repair of nonresidential structures	0.3	Construct.	Accommodations, nec	0.3	Services
Management, scientific, & technical consulting	0.3	Services	Amusement & recreation, nec	0.3	Services
Relay & industrial controls	0.3	Manufg.	Computer system design services	0.3	Services
Cutting tools & machine tool accessories	0.3	Manufg.	Natural gas distribution	0.2	Util.
Securities, commodity contracts, investments	0.2	Fin/R.E.	Insurance agencies, brokerages, & related activities	0.2	Fin/R.E.
Services to buildings & dwellings	0.2	Services	Cable & other subscription programming	0.2	Services
Electron tubes	0.2	Manufg.	Grantmaking, giving, & social advocacy organizations	0.2	Services
Nonferrous metal foundries	0.2	Manufg.	Transit & ground passenger transportation	0.2	Util.
Coating, engraving, heat treating & allied activities	0.2	Manufg.	Legal services	0.2	Services

Continued on next page.

INPUTS AND OUTPUTS FOR MAGNETIC AND OPTICAL RECORDING MEDIA MANUFACTURING - Continued

Economic Sector or Industry Providing Inputs	%	Sector	Economic Sector or Industry Buying Outputs	%	Sector
Motor vehicle parts	0.2	Manufg.	Scientific research & development services	0.2	Services
Electrical equipment & components, nec	0.2	Manufg.	General S/L govt. services	0.1	S/L Govt
Taxes on production & imports, less subsidies	0.2		Fitness & recreational sports centers	0.1	Services
Warehousing & storage	0.2	Util.			
Automotive repair & maintenance, ex. car washes	0.2	Services			
Commercial & industrial equipment repair/maintenance	0.1	Services			
Legal services	0.1	Services			
Data processing, hosting, & related services	0.1	Services			
Abrasive products	0.1	Manufg.			
Accounting, tax preparation, bookkeeping, & payroll	0.1	Services			
Custom roll forming	0.1	Manufg.			
Employment services	0.1	Services			
Paperboard mills	0.1	Manufg.			
Petroleum lubricating oil & grease	0.1	Manufg.			
Specialized design services	0.1	Services			

Source: Benchmark Input-Output Accounts for the U.S. Economy, 2002, U.S. Department of Commerce, Washington, D.C., January 2008. The abbreviation nec stands for 'not elsewhere classified'.

OCCUPATIONS EMPLOYED BY MANUFACTURING & REPRODUCING MAGNETIC & OPTICAL MEDIA

Occupation	% of Total 2006	Change to 2016	Occupation	% of Total 2006	Change to 2016
Packers & packagers, hand	4.6	-21.4	General & operations managers	1.5	-11.6
Team assemblers	4.4	-1.7	Computer-controlled machine tool operators	1.5	8.1
Computer support specialists	4.0	-1.7	Maintenance & repair workers, general	1.4	-1.7
Production workers, nec	3.8	-3.6	Industrial truck & tractor operators	1.3	-11.6
Molding, coremaking, & casting machine operators	3.1	-11.6	Industrial machinery mechanics	1.3	13.0
Customer service representatives	3.0	8.1	Electrical & electronic engineering technicians	1.2	-1.7
Computer software engineers, applications	2.9	17.9	Office clerks, general	1.2	-3.2
Machine feeders & offbearers	2.3	-11.6	Accountants & auditors	1.2	-1.7
First-line supervisors/managers of production workers	2.1	-1.7	Packaging & filling machine operators & tenders	1.1	-11.6
Inspectors, testers, sorters, samplers, & weighers	2.1	-7.4	Computer specialists, nec	1.1	-1.8
Computer software engineers, systems software	2.1	8.1	Graphic designers	1.1	-1.7
Shipping, receiving, & traffic clerks	1.9	-5.5	Bookkeeping, accounting, & auditing clerks	1.1	-1.7
Computer programmers	1.9	-21.4	Film & video editors	1.1	-1.7
Computer systems analysts	1.7	8.1	Helpers--Production workers	1.1	-1.7
Sales reps, wholesale & manufacturing, exc tech	1.6	-1.7	Industrial engineers	1.0	19.3

Source: Industry-Occupation Matrix, Bureau of Labor Statistics, December 4, 2007. These data are reported based on 4-digit NAICS categories but have been matched to corresponding 6-digit NAICS industry codes. The change reported for each occupation to the year 2016 is a percent of growth or decline as estimated by the Bureau of Labor Statistics. The abbreviation nec stands for 'not elsewhere classified'.

LOCATION BY STATE AND REGIONAL CONCENTRATION

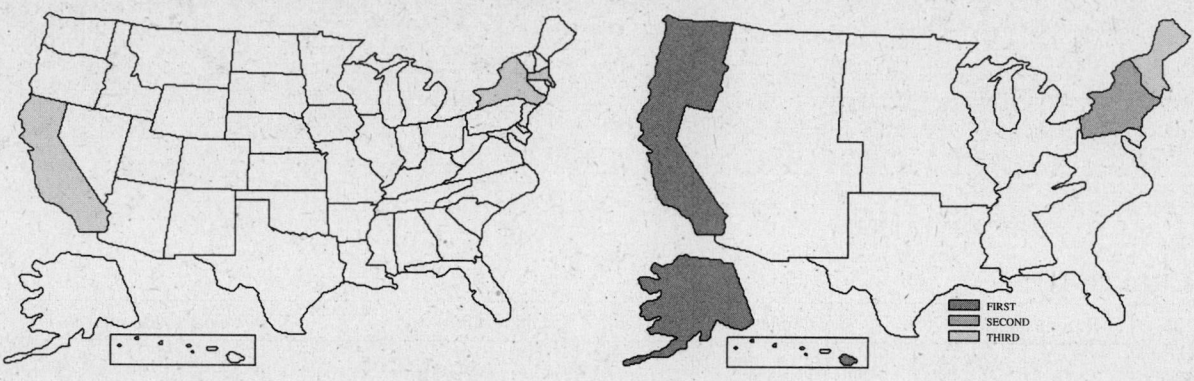

FIRST
SECOND
THIRD

INDUSTRY DATA BY STATE

| State | Establish-ments | Shipments | | | Employment | | | | Cost as % of Shipments | Investment per Employee ($) |
		Total ($ mil)	% of U.S.	Per Establ.	Total Number	% of U.S.	Per Establ.	Wages ($/hour)		
California	59	927.9	41.8	15,727.3	2,548	44.3	43	17.21	38.8	15,158
Massachusetts	5	113.8	5.1	22,753.4	250	4.3	50	23.14	71.2	6,864
New York	15	103.0	4.6	6,864.7	414	7.2	28	20.73	45.4	8,263

Source: 2002 *Economic Census*. The states are in descending order of shipments or establishments (if shipment data are missing for the majority). The symbol (D) appears when data are withheld to prevent disclosure of competitive information. States marked with (D) are sorted by number of establishments. A dash (-) indicates that the data element cannot be calculated. Data may not show all states active in the NAICS category. All data available at the time of publication are shown.

NAICS 335110 - ELECTRIC LAMP BULB AND PARTS MANUFACTURING

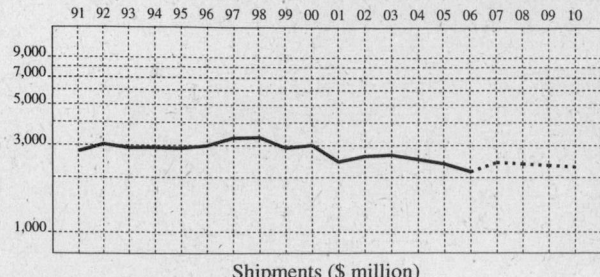

Shipments ($ million)

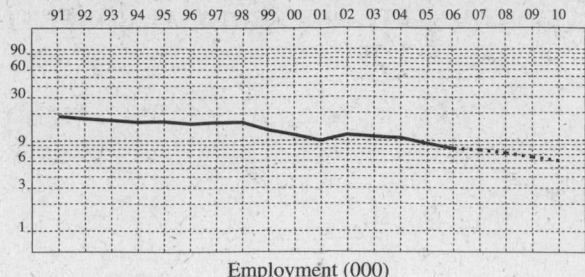

Employment (000)

GENERAL STATISTICS

| Year | Com-panies | Establishments | | Employment | | | Compensation | | Production ($ million) | | | |
		Total	with 20 or more employees	Total (000)	Production Workers (000)	Hours (Mil)	Payroll ($ mil)	Wages ($/hr)	Cost of Materials	Value Added by Manufacture	Value of Shipments	Capital Invest.
1991		128	75	18.6	15.6	33.0	486.8	11.68	898.4	1,863.0	2,772.9	105.4
1992	76	105	66	17.5	14.7	29.3	510.7	13.86	955.6	2,067.5	3,026.9	99.6
1993		103	65	16.8	14.2	26.8	514.9	15.59	981.5	1,911.3	2,900.6	115.7
1994		110	66	16.0	13.5	28.1	514.8	14.89	1,006.0	1,902.0	2,915.0	110.1
1995		107	63	16.2	13.9	29.0	539.1	15.26	1,060.9	1,833.4	2,888.9	157.5
1996		113	64	15.3	13.0	27.0	518.6	15.59	1,031.7	1,941.5	2,984.8	145.7
1997	53	81	55	15.8	13.4	28.3	572.5	16.59	1,184.5	2,114.5	3,299.5	173.9
1998		90	57	15.9	13.1	27.1	556.5	16.48	1,126.2	2,177.4	3,321.0	143.9
1999		94	56	13.0	11.1	23.9	497.4	17.54	950.0	1,896.4	2,907.4	84.5
2000		92	51	11.5	10.5	22.4	516.6	19.40	977.1	2,041.5	3,012.8	121.6
2001		95	51	9.9	9.0	17.3	443.5	20.98	846.2	1,586.6	2,441.4	108.9
2002	56	80	48	11.5	9.5	18.7	486.2	20.25	883.1	1,747.0	2,615.0	76.9
2003		87	53	11.0	9.2	18.1	492.2	20.69	950.6	1,727.3	2,655.0	54.8
2004		97	54	10.7	8.9	19.3	521.5	20.39	897.1	1,623.7	2,516.2	61.3
2005		95	52	9.3	7.6	16.0	495.1	23.13	1,013.6	1,381.8	2,380.0	56.9
2006		83P	46P	8.2	6.7	13.6	449.9	24.90	962.1	1,195.7	2,155.1	63.6
2007		81P	45P	7.9P	6.7P	13.9P	484.0P	24.14P	1,081.5P	1,344.1P	2,422.6P	64.5P
2008		79P	43P	7.3P	6.1P	12.8P	481.3P	24.87P	1,061.7P	1,319.5P	2,378.3P	59.7P
2009		77P	42P	6.6P	5.6P	11.6P	478.6P	25.60P	1,041.9P	1,294.9P	2,333.9P	54.9P
2010		75P	40P	6.0P	5.0P	10.5P	475.8P	26.33P	1,022.1P	1,270.3P	2,289.6P	50.2P

Sources: 1992, 1997, 2002 *Economic Census*; other years, up to 2006, are from the *Annual Survey of Manufactures*. Establishment counts for non-Census years are from *County Business Patterns*; 1997 and 2002 values are from the 1997 and 2002 censuses respectively, reported in the Federal Government's NAICS format. Other years were originally reported in equivalent SIC format. 'P's show projections by the editors.

INDICES OF CHANGE

| Year | Com-panies | Establishments | | Employment | | | Compensation | | Production ($ million) | | | |
		Total	with 20 or more employees	Total (000)	Production Workers (000)	Hours (Mil)	Payroll ($ mil)	Wages ($/hr)	Cost of Materials	Value Added by Manufacture	Value of Shipments	Capital Invest.
1992	136	131	138	152	155	157	105	68	108	118	116	130
1997	95	101	115	137	141	151	118	82	134	121	126	226
2001		119	106	86	95	93	91	104	96	91	93	142
2002	100	100	100	100	100	100	100	100	100	100	100	100
2003		109	110	96	97	97	101	102	108	99	102	71
2004		121	113	93	94	103	107	101	102	93	96	80
2005		119	108	81	80	86	102	114	115	79	91	74
2006		104P	96P	71	71	73	93	123	109	68	82	83
2007		101P	93P	69P	71P	74P	100P	119P	122P	77P	93P	84P
2008		99P	90P	63P	64P	68P	99P	123P	120P	76P	91P	78P
2009		96P	87P	57P	59P	62P	98P	126P	118P	74P	89P	71P
2010		94P	84P	52P	53P	56P	98P	130P	116P	73P	88P	65P

Sources: Same as General Statistics. Values reflect change from the base year, 2002. Values above 100 mean greater than 2002, values below 100 mean less than 2002, and the values of 100 in other years means the same as 2002. 'P's show projections by the editors.

SELECTED RATIOS

For 2002	Avg. of All Manufact.	Analyzed Industry	Index	For 2002	Avg. of All Manufact.	Analyzed Industry	Index
Employees per Establishment	42	144	342	Value Added per Production Worker	182,367	183,895	101
Payroll per Establishment	1,639,184	6,077,500	371	Cost per Establishment	5,769,015	11,038,750	191
Payroll per Employee	39,053	42,278	108	Cost per Employee	137,446	76,791	56
Production Workers per Establishment	30	119	402	Cost per Production Worker	195,506	92,958	48
Wages per Establishment	694,845	4,733,438	681	Shipments per Establishment	11,158,348	32,687,500	293
Wages per Production Worker	23,548	39,861	169	Shipments per Employee	265,847	227,391	86
Hours per Production Worker	1,980	1,968	99	Shipments per Production Worker	378,144	275,263	73
Wages per Hour	11.89	20.25	170	Investment per Establishment	361,338	961,250	266
Value Added per Establishment	5,381,325	21,837,500	406	Investment per Employee	8,609	6,687	78
Value Added per Employee	128,210	151,913	118	Investment per Production Worker	12,245	8,095	66

Sources: Same as General Statistics. The 'Average of All Manufacturing' column represents the average of all manufacturing industries reported for the most recent complete year available. The Index shows the relationship between the Average and the Analyzed Industry. For example, 100 means that they are equal; 500 that the Analyzed Industry is five times the average; 50 means that the Analyzed Industry is half the national average. The abbreviation 'na' is used to show that data are 'not available'. Ratios shown for 2002, the last complete census year.

LEADING COMPANIES   Number shown: **75**   Total sales ($ mil): **2,131**   Total employment (000): **7.9**

Company Name	Address				CEO Name	Phone	Co. Type	Sales ($ mil)	Empl. (000)
Lighting Science Group Corp.	2100 McKinney Ave.	Dallas	TX	75201	Govi Rao	214-382-3630	P	436	<0.1
PerkinElmer OptoElectronics	44370 Christy St.	Fremont	CA	94538	John A. Roush	510-979-6500	D	110*	0.3
Venture Lighting International	10295 Philipp Pky.	Streetsboro	OH	44241	Wayne Hellman	440-248-3510	S	99*	0.3
Lights of America Inc.	611 Reyes Dr.	Walnut	CA	91789	Usman Vakil	909-594-7883	R	93*	0.5
Westinghouse Lighting Corp.	12401 McNulty Rd.	Philadelphia	PA	19154	Raymond Angelo	215-671-2000	R	92*	0.1
Barnstead-Thermolyne Corp.	PO Box 797	Dubuque	IA	52004		563-556-2241	S	70*	0.5
Elmet Technologies Corp.	1560 Lisbon St.	Lewiston	ME	04240	John S. Jensen	207-784-3591	S	55	0.3
Ledtronics Inc.	23105 Kashiwa Ct.	Torrance	CA	90505		310-534-1505	R	51*	0.1
Light Sources Inc.	PO Box 948	Orange	CT	06477	Christian Sauska	203-799-7877	R	48*	0.2
Dasol Inc.	PO Box 2065	Gardena	CA	90247	David Smith	310-327-6700	R	47*	0.2
Whelen Engineering Company	PO Box 1236	Charlestown	NH	03603	John Olson	860-526-9504	R	44*	0.3
Light Process Co.	1631 Gillingham	Sugar Land	TX	77478	Michael Hirsch	281-530-3600	R	40*	0.1
HIDirect Inc.	32000 Aurora Rd.	Solon	OH	44139	Wayne C. Hellman	440-519-0500	S	39*	0.1
Gty Industries	12881 Bradley Ave.	Sylmar	CA	91342	Craig Jennings	818-362-9465	R	33*	0.2
Luminator Holding L.P.	PO Box 278	Plano	TX	75086		972-424-6511	R	33*	0.2
Wide-Lite	PO Box 606	San Marcos	TX	78667	Travis King	512-392-5821	D	33*	0.2
Robert Abbey Inc.	3166 Main Ave. SE	Hickory	NC	28602	Jeffrey Rose	828-322-3480	R	32*	0.2
Anthony California Inc.	4980 Eucalyptus	Chino	CA	91710	James Chang	909-627-0351	R	31*	<0.1
Ross Lighting Corp.	PO Box 1065	Jesup	GA	31598	Marvin Ross	912-530-8200	R	31*	0.2
Hamamatsu Corp.	PO Box 6910	Bridgewater	NJ	08807	Akira Hiruma	908-231-0960	R	29*	<0.1
Trojan Inc.	198 Trojan St.	Mount Sterling	KY	40353	Danny Duzyk	859-498-0526	R	29*	0.1
Stylecraft Lamps Inc.	PO Box 347	Hernando	MS	38632	Jimmy Webster	662-429-5279	R	29*	0.2
St George Crystal Ltd.	PO Box 709	Jeannette	PA	15644	Richard Rifenburgh	724-523-6501	R	27*	0.2
Eye Lighting Int'l of N Amer.	9150 Hendricks Rd.	Mentor	OH	44060	Tsuneo Kobayashi	440-350-7000	R	27*	0.2
Musco Corp.	100 1st Ave. W	Oskaloosa	IA	52577	Joe Crookham	641-673-0411	R	26*	0.1
Junction City Wire Harness	PO Box 45	Junction City	KS	66441	Chester Sliski	785-762-4400	R	25*	0.1
EGL Company Inc.	100 Industrial Rd.	Berkeley Hts	NJ	07922	Harold Cortese	908-508-1111	R	23*	0.1
Dolan-Jenner Industries Inc.	159 Swanson Rd.	Boxborough	MA	01719	Mike Balas	978-263-1400	S	22*	0.2
Weinstock Lamp Company Inc.	3430 Steinway St.	Long Island Cty	NY	11101	Morris Weinstock	718-729-4848	R	21*	<0.1
Altman Stage Lighting Co.	57 Alexander St.	Yonkers	NY	10701	Robert Altman	914-476-7987	R	21*	0.1
Satco Products Inc.	110 Heartland Blvd.	Brentwood	NY	11717	Herbert Gildin	631-243-2022	R	20*	<0.1
Tork Inc.	1 Grove St.	Mount Vernon	NY	10550	Sam Shankar	914-664-3542	R	18*	0.1
Lumitex Inc.	8443 Dow Cir.	Strongsville	OH	44136	Peter Broer	440-243-8401	R	16*	<0.1
Pent Plastics Inc.	PO Box 668	Avilla	IN	46710	Rick Nowels	260-897-3775	R	15*	0.1
Amglo Kemlite Laboratories	215 Gateway Rd.	Bensenville	IL	60106	James Hyland	630-350-9470	R	15*	<0.1
Metro-Mark Inc.	11574 Encore Cir.	Hopkins	MN	55343	Steve Comer	952-912-1700	R	14*	<0.1
Lowel-Light Manufacturing Inc.	140 58th St., 8C	Brooklyn	NY	11220	Marvin Seligman	718-921-0600	R	14*	<0.1
Jelight Company Inc.	2 Mason	Irvine	CA	92618	Marinko Jelic	949-380-8774	R	14*	<0.1
Superior Quartz Products Inc.	2701 Baglyos Cir.	Bethlehem	PA	18020	Dennis Losco	610-317-3450	R	14*	<0.1
Pauluhn Electric Manufacturing	1616 N Main Street	Pearland	TX	77581	Peter Guile	281-485-4311	S	13*	<0.1
Rueff Lighting Co.	523 E Broadway	Louisville	KY	40202	William P. Rueff	502-583-1617	R	13*	<0.1
Hallmark Manufacturing Company	PO Box 2313	Chatsworth	CA	91313		818-885-5010	R	13*	0.1
HH Fluorescent Parts Inc.	PO Box 65	Cheltenham	PA	19012	Robert Hillen	215-379-2750	R	12*	<0.1
American Light Bulb Mfg.	105 American St.	Mullins	SC	29574	Ray Schlosser	843-464-0755	R	12*	<0.1
Environ. Lighting Concepts	1214 W Cass St.	Tampa	FL	33606	Fred Mendelsohn	813-621-0058	R	12*	<0.1
Ramco Industries	420 Roske Dr.	Elkhart	IN	46516	Greg Bland	574-389-0040	R	12*	<0.1
Union City Filament Corp.	PO Box 777	Ridgefield	NJ	07657	Joseph Celia	201-945-3366	R	11*	<0.1
Sunnex Inc.	3 Huron Dr.	Natick	MA	01760	Lars-Arne Lundholm	508-651-0009	R	10*	<0.1
Hanovia Specialty Lighting	825 Lehigh Ave.	Union	NJ	07083		908-688-0050	R	10*	<0.1
Westron Corp.	3590 Oceanside Rd.	Oceanside	NY	11572	Hershel Allerhand	516-678-2300	R	10*	<0.1
Kesio Inc.	2 Ascension	Irvine	CA	92612	Hsin Zengchen	949-725-0382	R	10*	<0.1
National Biological Corp.	1532 Enterprise Pky	Twinsburg	OH	44087	Mark Friedman	330-425-3535	R	9*	<0.1
Baader-Brown Manufacturing Co.	4220 S Jamestown	Springfield	OH	45502	Jenny Baader	937-323-6017	R	9*	<0.1
Dazor Manufacturing Corp.	11721 Dunlap Ind	Maryland Hgts	MO	63043	Stan Hogrebe	314-652-2400	R	9*	<0.1
LaMar Lighting Company Inc.	PO Box 9013	Farmingdale	NY	11735	Barry Kugel	631-777-7700	R	9*	<0.1
Lime Energy Co.	1280 Landmeier Rd.	Elk Grove Vlg	IL	60007	David Asplund	847-437-1666	P	8	<0.1
US Miniature Lamps Inc.	PO Box 6325	Fishers	IN	46038	Noah Stodghill	317-577-4003	R	8*	<0.1
Don-Ell Corp.	8450 Central Ave.	Toledo	OH	43560	Donald R. Sell	419-841-1828	R	8*	<0.1
Lamp Recyclers of Louisiana	46257 Morris Rd.	Hammond	LA	70401	Art Shilling	985-878-3333	R	8*	<0.1
Ric-Lo Productions Ltd.	PO Box D	Sugar Loaf	NY	10981	Richard Logothetis	845-469-2285	R	7*	<0.1
Litetronics International Inc.	4101 W 123rd St.	Chicago	IL	60803	Robert Sorensen	708-389-8000	R	7*	<0.1
Malcolite Corp.	PO Box 569	Monterey Park	CA	91754	Jason Howard	847-562-1350	R	6*	<0.1
USPAR Enterprises Inc.	13404 Monte Vista	Chino	CA	91710	Khalid Parekh	909-591-7506	R	6*	<0.1
Atlantic Ultraviolet Corp.	375 Marcus Blvd.	Hauppauge	NY	11788	Hilary Boehme	631-273-0500	R	6*	<0.1
Alert Stamping & Manufacturing	24500 Solon Rd.	Cleveland	OH	44146	Paul Blanch	440-232-5020	R	6*	<0.1
Interlectric Corp.	1401 Lexington Ave.	Warren	PA	16365	Steven Rothenberg	814-723-6061	R	6*	0.1
Rockscapes L.L.C.	8749 Shirley Ave.	Northridge	CA	91324	Perry Romano	818-704-5195	R	6*	<0.1
Hoosier Fire Equipment Inc.	4009 Montdale Park	Valparaiso	IN	46383	Nick Swartz	219-462-1707	R	6*	<0.1
MKS Inc.	7 N Industrial Blvd	Bridgeton	NJ	08302	Ken Brattlie	856-451-5545	R	5*	<0.1
Solar Kinetics Inc.	3878 Oak Lawn	Dallas	TX	75219	David White	972-556-2376	R	5*	<0.1
Carlisle and Finch Co.	4562 W Mitchell	Cincinnati	OH	45232	Brent Finch	513-681-6080	R	5*	<0.1
Radiant Thermal Products Co.	640 W 1st Ave.	Roselle	NJ	07203	Albert Maglio	908-241-7700	R	5*	<0.1
Xenonics Holdings Inc.	2236 Rutherford Rd.	Carlsbad	CA	92008	Chuck Hunter	760-438-4004	P	5	<0.1
Medallion Lighting Corp.	PO Box 51	Mentor	OH	44061	William Knuff	440-255-8383	R	5*	<0.1
Art Specialty Company Inc.	3421 W 48th Pl.	Chicago	IL	60632	Mary Holewinski	773-927-2711	R	4*	<0.1

Source: Ward's Business Directory of U.S. Private and Public Companies, Volumes 1 and 2, 2008. The company type code used is as follows: P - Public, R - Private, S - Subsidiary, D - Division, J - Joint Venture, A - Affiliate, G - Group. Sales are in millions of dollars, employees are in thousands. An asterisk (*) indicates an estimated sales volume. The symbol < stands for 'less than'. Company names and addresses are truncated, in some cases, to fit into the available space.

MATERIALS CONSUMED

Material	Quantity	Delivered Cost ($ million)
Glass and glass products (including lamp bulb blanks)	(X)	256.7
Paper and paperboard containers (incl. shipping sacks and other paper packaging supplies)	(X)	90.1
Industrial inorganic chemicals	(X)	53.3
Nonferrous metal wire	(X)	104.7
Electric lamp (bulb) bases	(X)	84.0
All other materials, components, parts, containers, and supplies	(X)	140.7
Materials, ingredients, containers, and supplies, nsk	(X)	17.2

Source: 2002 *Economic Census*. Explanation of symbols used: (D): Withheld to avoid disclosure of competitive data; na: Not available; (S): Withheld because statistical norms were not met; (X): Not applicable; (Z): Less than half the unit shown; nec: Not elsewhere classified; nsk: Not specified by kind; - : zero; p : 10-19 percent estimated; q : 20-29 percent estimated.

PRODUCT SHARE DETAILS

Product or Product Class Shipments	Mil. $	Product or Product Class Shipments	Mil. $
ELECTRIC LAMP BULBS AND PARTS	2,472.2	Electric lamp (bulbs and tubes) components (bases, supports, lead-in, filaments, etc., but excluding lamp bulb blanks)	308.1
Electric lamp bulbs and tubes (including sealed beam lamp bulbs)	2,155.8	Electric lamp bulbs and parts, nsk, total	8.3

Source: 2002 *Economic Census*. The values are product shipments in millions of dollars for 2002. Total product shipments may be lower or higher than industry shipments. See Introduction for a full discussion. Values of indented subcategories are summed in the main heading(s). The symbol (D) appears when data are withheld to prevent disclosure of competitive information. The abbreviation nsk stands for 'not specified by kind' and nec for 'not elsewhere classified'. A dash (-) means zero.

INPUTS AND OUTPUTS FOR ELECTRIC LAMP BULB AND PART MANUFACTURING

Economic Sector or Industry Providing Inputs	%	Sector	Economic Sector or Industry Buying Outputs	%	Sector
Compensation of employees	26.5		Personal consumption expenditures	28.4	
Wholesale trade	6.8	Trade	General S/L govt. services	20.7	S/L Govt
Management of companies & enterprises	5.2	Services	Exports of goods & services	11.8	Cap Inv
Glass products from purchased glass	4.2	Manufg.	General Federal government services, nondefense	7.7	Fed Govt
Nonferrous metal (ex. copper & aluminum) processing	3.6	Manufg.	Wholesale trade	3.7	Trade
Pressed & blown glass & glassware, nec	3.5	Manufg.	Lighting fixtures	3.4	Manufg.
Paperboard containers	3.2	Manufg.	Light truck & utility vehicles	3.4	Manufg.
Electric lamp bulbs & parts	2.8	Manufg.	Automobiles	3.1	Manufg.
Flat glass	1.4	Manufg.	Motor vehicle parts	2.4	Manufg.
Power generation & supply	1.1	Util.	Electric lamp bulbs & parts	1.8	Manufg.
Basic inorganic chemicals, nec	0.9	Manufg.	Elementary & secondary schools	1.6	Services
Truck transportation	0.6	Util.	Change in private inventories	1.3	In House
Machine shops	0.6	Manufg.	Services to buildings & dwellings	0.9	Services
Lessors of nonfinancial assets	0.5	Fin/R.E.	Food services & drinking places	0.7	Services
Securities, commodity contracts, investments	0.5	Fin/R.E.	Management of companies & enterprises	0.6	Services
Semiconductors & related devices	0.4	Manufg.	Retail trade	0.4	Trade
Printed circuit assemblies (electronic assemblies)	0.4	Manufg.	Heavy duty trucks	0.4	Manufg.
Chemical products & preparations, nec	0.4	Manufg.	Nonresidential structures, nec	0.4	Construct.
Natural gas distribution	0.4	Util.	Residential permanent site structures	0.4	Construct.
Scientific research & development services	0.3	Services	Warehousing & storage	0.3	Util.
Adhesives	0.3	Manufg.	Management, scientific, & technical consulting	0.3	Services
Coating, engraving, heat treating & allied activities	0.3	Manufg.	Hospitals	0.3	Services
Noncomparable imports	0.3	Foreign	Colleges, universities, & professional schools	0.2	Services
Advertising & related services	0.3	Services	Ice cream & frozen desserts	0.2	Manufg.
Maintenance/repair of nonresidential structures	0.3	Construct.	Natural gas distribution	0.2	Util.
Industrial gases	0.3	Manufg.	Maintenance/repair of nonresidential structures	0.2	Construct.
Services to buildings & dwellings	0.2	Services	Snack food	0.2	Manufg.
Plastics products, nec	0.2	Manufg.	Residential structures, nec	0.2	Construct.
Real estate	0.2	Fin/R.E.	Commercial & health care structures	0.2	Construct.
Cutting tools & machine tool accessories	0.2	Manufg.	Owner-occupied dwellings	0.2	
Warehousing & storage	0.2	Util.	Automotive repair & maintenance, ex. car washes	0.2	Services
Automotive repair & maintenance, ex. car washes	0.2	Services	Breweries	0.2	Manufg.
Specialized design services	0.2	Services	Toilet preparations	0.2	Manufg.
Retail trade	0.2	Trade	Cookies, crackers, & pasta	0.1	Manufg.
Commercial & industrial equipment repair/maintenance	0.2	Services	Canned & dehydrated fruits & vegetables	0.1	Manufg.
Professional, scientific, technical services, nec	0.1	Services	Confectionery products, chocolate	0.1	Manufg.
Paper bag & coated paper, nec	0.1	Manufg.	Civic, social, & professional organizations	0.1	Services
Alkalies & chlorine	0.1	Manufg.	Soft drinks & ice	0.1	Manufg.
Fabricated metals, nec	0.1	Manufg.	Other S/L govt. enterprises	0.1	S/L Govt
Waste management & remediation services	0.1	Services	Scientific research & development services	0.1	Services
			Soap & cleaning compounds	0.1	Manufg.
			Architectural, engineering, & related services	0.1	Services
			Hotels & motels, including casino hotels	0.1	Services

Source: *Benchmark Input-Output Accounts for the U.S. Economy, 2002*, U.S. Department of Commerce, Washington, D.C., January 2008. The abbreviation nec stands for 'not elsewhere classified'.

OCCUPATIONS EMPLOYED BY ELECTRIC LIGHTING EQUIPMENT MANUFACTURING

Occupation	% of Total 2006	Change to 2016	Occupation	% of Total 2006	Change to 2016
Team assemblers	18.6	-25.3	Machinists	1.5	-21.5
Electrical & electronic equipment assemblers	7.8	-40.2	Coating, painting, & spraying machine operators	1.5	-29.0
First-line supervisors/managers of production workers	3.4	-25.3	Stock clerks & order fillers	1.4	-37.5
Sales reps, wholesale & manufacturing, exc tech	2.6	-25.3	Industrial truck & tractor operators	1.4	-32.7
Inspectors, testers, sorters, samplers, & weighers	2.5	-29.5	Bookkeeping, accounting, & auditing clerks	1.3	-25.3
Shipping, receiving, & traffic clerks	2.4	-28.1	Packaging & filling machine operators & tenders	1.3	-32.7
Customer service representatives	2.2	-17.8	Production workers, nec	1.3	-26.6
Laborers & freight, stock, & material movers, hand	2.1	-32.7	Grinding, lapping, polishing machine tool operators	1.3	-27.5
Cutting, punching, & press machine operators	2.1	-32.7	Purchasing agents, exc wholesale, retail, & farm	1.1	-25.3
Maintenance & repair workers, general	1.8	-25.3	Office clerks, general	1.0	-26.4
Packers & packagers, hand	1.6	-40.2	Electrical engineers	1.0	-25.3
General & operations managers	1.5	-32.7			

Source: *Industry-Occupation Matrix*, Bureau of Labor Statistics, December 4, 2007. These data are reported based on 4-digit NAICS categories but have been matched to corresponding 6-digit NAICS industry codes. The change reported for each occupation to the year 2016 is a percent of growth or decline as estimated by the Bureau of Labor Statistics. The abbreviation nec stands for 'not elsewhere classified'.

LOCATION BY STATE AND REGIONAL CONCENTRATION

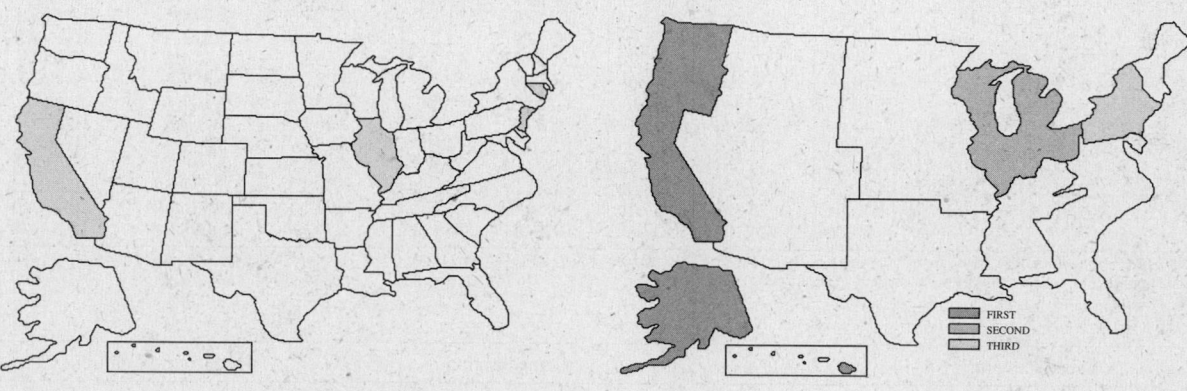

FIRST
SECOND
THIRD

INDUSTRY DATA BY STATE

State	Establish-ments	Shipments			Employment				Cost as % of Shipments	Investment per Employee ($)
		Total ($ mil)	% of U.S.	Per Establ.	Total Number	% of U.S.	Per Establ.	Wages ($/hour)		
Connecticut	3	71.7	2.7	23,885.0	537	4.7	179	10.58	31.7	2,291
Illinois	5	59.2	2.3	11,839.2	585	5.1	117	20.56	42.9	6,277
California	10	30.0	1.1	2,998.1	221	1.9	22	10.78	31.2	2,118
New Jersey	4	10.9	0.4	2,715.3	112	1.0	28	13.89	25.3	634

Source: 2002 *Economic Census*. The states are in descending order of shipments or establishments (if shipment data are missing for the majority). The symbol (D) appears when data are withheld to prevent disclosure of competitive information. States marked with (D) are sorted by number of establishments. A dash (-) indicates that the data element cannot be calculated. Data may not show all states active in the NAICS category. All data available at the time of publication are shown.

NAICS 33512M - LIGHTING FIXTURE MANUFACTURING*

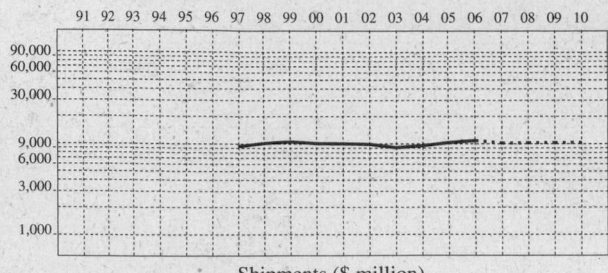

Shipments ($ million)

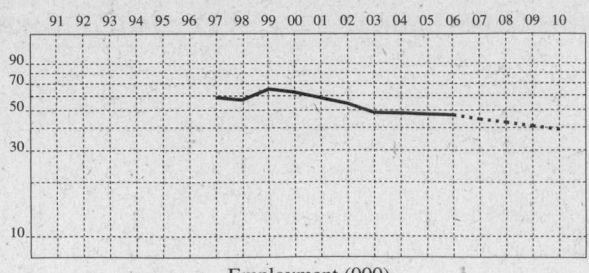

Employment (000)

GENERAL STATISTICS

Year	Companies	Establishments		Employment			Compensation		Production ($ million)			
		Total	with 20 or more employees	Total (000)	Production Workers (000)	Hours (Mil)	Payroll ($ mil)	Wages ($/hr)	Cost of Materials	Value Added by Manufacture	Value of Shipments	Capital Invest.
1997	1,173	1,242	492	58.8	42.1	83.5	1,619.4	10.62	4,514.3	4,879.2	9,383.9	232.7
1998		1,263	499	57.0	41.9	87.1	1,613.9	10.54	4,789.6	5,339.7	10,159.0	261.1
1999		1,239	490	65.3	45.5	88.3	1,870.2	11.02	5,093.1	5,462.6	10,554.7	310.1
2000		1,215	475	62.7	43.6	82.6	1,831.6	11.87	4,814.5	5,378.9	10,116.5	264.4
2001		1,212	466	58.3	39.9	76.0	1,792.9	12.28	4,664.0	5,371.4	10,056.7	215.1
2002	1,092	1,155	456	54.3	37.8	75.2	1,753.7	12.36	4,432.6	5,454.5	9,889.8	197.0
2003		1,147	440	48.3	33.2	66.6	1,635.9	12.71	4,221.9	4,884.8	9,102.7	146.2
2004		1,119	428	48.1	32.3	67.0	1,723.1	13.51	4,434.3	5,149.1	9,554.3	169.8
2005		1,110	424	47.5	31.5	66.1	1,806.3	14.05	4,769.6	5,632.8	10,335.2	163.7
2006		1,089P	413P	47.0	31.5	66.5	1,874.0	14.05	4,990.7	5,994.4	10,868.5	192.2
2007		1,069P	403P	44.5P	29.0P	60.7P	1,828.0P	14.65P	4,690.6P	5,633.9P	10,214.9P	144.5P
2008		1,049P	393P	42.7P	27.4P	58.0P	1,841.8P	15.08P	4,708.4P	5,655.3P	10,253.6P	131.7P
2009		1,029P	383P	40.8P	25.8P	55.2P	1,855.6P	15.51P	4,726.1P	5,676.6P	10,292.3P	118.8P
2010		1,009P	373P	39.0P	24.1P	52.4P	1,869.4P	15.93P	4,743.9P	5,698.0P	10,331.0P	106.0P

Sources: 1997 and 2002 *Economic Census*; other years, up to 2006, are from *Annual Survey of Manufactures*. Establishment counts for non-Census years are from *County Business Patterns*; 1997 and 2002 values are from the 1997 and 2002 censuses, respectively. 'P's show projections by the editors.

INDICES OF CHANGE

Year	Companies	Establishments		Employment			Compensation		Production ($ million)			
		Total	with 20 or more employees	Total (000)	Production Workers (000)	Hours (Mil)	Payroll ($ mil)	Wages ($/hr)	Cost of Materials	Value Added by Manufacture	Value of Shipments	Capital Invest.
1997	107	108	108	108	111	111	92	86	102	89	95	118
1998		109	109	105	111	116	92	85	108	98	103	133
1999		107	107	120	120	117	107	89	115	100	107	157
2000		105	104	115	115	110	104	96	109	99	102	134
2001		105	102	107	106	101	102	99	105	98	102	109
2002	100	100	100	100	100	100	100	100	100	100	100	100
2003		99	96	89	88	89	93	103	95	90	92	74
2004		97	94	89	85	89	98	109	100	94	97	86
2005		96	93	87	83	88	103	114	108	103	105	83
2006		94P	91P	87	83	88	107	114	113	110	110	98
2007		93P	88P	82P	77P	81P	104P	119P	106P	103P	103P	73P
2008		91P	86P	79P	72P	77P	105P	122P	106P	104P	104P	67P
2009		89P	84P	75P	68P	73P	106P	125P	107P	104P	104P	60P
2010		87P	82P	72P	64P	70P	107P	129P	107P	104P	104P	54P

Sources: Same as General Statistics. Values reflect change from the base year, 2002. Values above 100 mean greater than 2002, values below 100 mean less than 2002, and the values of 100 in other years means the same as 2002. 'P's show projections by the editors.

SELECTED RATIOS

For 2002	Avg. of All Manufact.	Analyzed Industry	Index	For 2002	Avg. of All Manufact.	Analyzed Industry	Index
Employees per Establishment	42	47	112	Value Added per Production Worker	182,367	144,299	79
Payroll per Establishment	1,639,184	1,518,355	93	Cost per Establishment	5,769,015	3,837,749	67
Payroll per Employee	39,053	32,297	83	Cost per Employee	137,446	81,632	59
Production Workers per Establishment	30	33	111	Cost per Production Worker	195,506	117,265	60
Wages per Establishment	694,845	804,738	116	Shipments per Establishment	11,158,348	8,562,597	77
Wages per Production Worker	23,548	24,589	104	Shipments per Employee	265,847	182,133	69
Hours per Production Worker	1,980	1,989	100	Shipments per Production Worker	378,144	261,635	69
Wages per Hour	11.89	12.36	104	Investment per Establishment	361,338	170,563	47
Value Added per Establishment	5,381,325	4,722,511	88	Investment per Employee	8,609	3,628	42
Value Added per Employee	128,210	100,451	78	Investment per Production Worker	12,245	5,212	43

Sources: Same as General Statistics. The 'Average of All Manufacturing' column represents the average of all manufacturing industries reported for the most recent complete year available. The Index shows the relationship between the Average and the Analyzed Industry. For example, 100 means that they are equal; 500 that the Analyzed Industry is five times the average; 50 means that the Analyzed Industry is half the national average. The abbreviation 'na' is used to show that data are 'not available'. Ratios shown for 2002, the last complete census year.

*Equivalent to Federal Government NAICS 335121, 335122, 335129.

LEADING COMPANIES   Number shown: 75   Total sales ($ mil): 407,954   Total employment (000): 896.0

Company Name	Address				CEO Name	Phone	Co. Type	Sales ($ mil)	Empl. (000)
General Electric Co.	3135 Easton Tpk.	Fairfield	CT	06828		203-373-2211	P	172,738	327.0
McKesson Corp.	1 Post St.	San Francisco	CA	94104	John H. Hammergren	415-983-8300	P	92,977	31.8
Emerson Electric	PO Box 4100	St. Louis	MO	63136	L.C. Barrett	314-553-2000	P	22,572	137.7
CP and P Inc.	133 Peachtree St.	Atlanta	GA	30303	Jospeh Moller	404-652-4000	S	16,083*	55.0
Truck-Lite Company Inc.	PO Box 387	Jamestown	NY	14702	Brian Kupchella	716-665-6214	R	7,160*	0.6
Boon Edam Tomsed	420 McKinney Pky.	Lillington	NC	27546	Tom DeVine	910-814-3800	R	7,005*	0.1
Etec Systems Inc.	PO Box 58039	Santa Clara	CA	95052		408-727-5555	S	6,992	12.2
Cooper Industries Ltd.	PO Box 4446	Houston	TX	77210	Kirk S. Hachigian	713-209-8400	P	5,903	31.5
Stanley Works	PO Box 700	New Britain	CT	06053		860-225-5111	P	4,484	18.4
Energizer Holdings Inc.	533 Maryville Univ.	St. Louis	MO	63141		314-985-2000	P	3,365	11.1
Milliken Chemical	PO Box 1926	Spartanburg	SC	29304	Ashley Allen	864-503-2200	R	3,317*	10.0
Greenlee Inc.	1300 Hutton, 110	Carrollton	TX	75006	Robert J. Ready	972-466-1133	S	3,131*	1.4
Arco Auto and Marine Products	3921 Navy Blvd.	Pensacola	FL	32507	Ron Miller	850-455-5476	R	3,015	<0.1
Exide Technologies	13000 Deerfield Pky	Alpharetta	GA	30004		678-566-9000	P	2,940	13.9
Diebold Inc.	PO Box 3077	North Canton	OH	44720		330-490-4000	P	2,906	15.5
GE Water and Process Tech.	4636 Somerton Rd.	Trevose	PA	19053	Jeff Garwood	215-355-3300	S	2,748*	8.0
Flow Systems	PO Box 1069	St. Helena Is	SC	29920	James Barrett	843-838-6699	R	2,681*	<0.1
International Game Technology	PO Box 10580	Reno	NV	89510	G. Thomas Baker	775-448-7777	P	2,621	5.4
Hubbell Inc.	584 Derby Milford	Orange	CT	06477		203-799-4100	P	2,534	11.5
Acuity Brands Inc.	1170 Peachtree St.	Atlanta	GA	30309	John K. Morgan	404-853-1400	P	2,531	10.0
Lockheed Martin Enterpr. Info.	12506 Lk Underhill	Orlando	FL	32825	Robert J. Stevens	407-306-1000	S	2,383*	4.0
NTK Holdings Inc.	50 Kennedy Plz.	Providence	RI	02903	Richard L. Bready	401-751-1600	S	2,218	9.8
Spectrum Brands Inc.	6 Concourse Pky.	Atlanta	GA	30328	John D. Bowlin	770-829-6200	P	1,995	7.1
Scientific-Atlanta Inc.	PO Box 465447	Lawrenceville	GA	30042		770-236-5000	S	1,910	7.7
American Greetings Corp.	1 American Rd.	Cleveland	OH	44144		216-252-7300	P	1,745	28.9
National Service Industries	1420 Peachtree St.	Atlanta	GA	30309	Carol Ellis Morgan	404-853-1000	R	1,650*	22.0
Genlyte Group Inc.	10350 Ormsby Prk	Louisville	KY	40223	Larry K. Powers	502-420-9500	P	1,485	6.4
Osram Sylvania Inc.	100 Endicott St.	Danvers	MA	01923		978-777-1900	S	1,476*	10.0
JDS Uniphase Corp.	430 N McCarthy	Milpitas	CA	95035	Martin A. Kaplan	408-546-5000	P	1,397*	7.0
Rittal Corp.	1 Rittal Pl.	Springfield	OH	45504	Carie Ray	937-399-0500	R	1,268*	0.6
Blyth Inc.	1 E Weaver St.	Greenwich	CT	06831		203-661-1926	P	1,221	4.0
Longaberger Co.	1500 E Main St.	Newark	OH	43055	Jim Klein	740-322-5000	R	1,206*	8.7
Lancaster Colony Corp.	37 W Broad St.	Columbus	OH	43215	John B. Gerlach, Jr.	614-224-7141	P	1,091	5.6
Syngenta Seeds Inc. - NK	PO Box 959	Minneapolis	MN	55440	Jeff Cox	763-593-7333	S	1,044*	1.3
Brady Corp.	PO Box 571	Milwaukee	WI	53201		414-358-6600	P	1,018	8.0
Travel Tags Inc.	5842 Carmen Ave.	Inver Grove Hts	MN	55076	Barb Cederberg	651-450-1201	R	763*	0.3
Ceradyne Inc.	3169 Red Hill Ave.	Costa Mesa	CA	92626		714-549-0421	P	757	2.5
Oldenburg Group Inc.	1717 W Civic Dr.	Glendale	WI	53209	Wayne C. Oldenburg	414-977-1717	R	720*	1.2
East Penn Manufacturing Co.	PO Box 147	Lyon Station	PA	19536			R	716*	5.0
Suntory Water Group Inc.	5660 New Northside	Atlanta	GA	30328	Stewart E. Allen	770-933-1400	S	688*	5.5
Yankee Candle Company Inc.	16 Yankee Candle	South Deerfield	MA	01373	Harlan M. Kent	413-665-8306	R	688	4.1
Alliance Gaming Corp.	6601 S Bermuda Rd.	Las Vegas	NV	89119	Richard M. Haddrill	702-584-7700	P	682	2.3
Oregon Cutting Systems Group	PO Box 22127	Portland	OR	97269	Jim Oscermanc	503-653-8881	D	674*	1.0
United Industrial Corp.	PO Box 126	Hunt Valley	MD	21030	W. G. Lichtenstein	410-628-3500	S	564	2.3
Mid-South Industries Inc.	PO Box 322	Gadsden	AL	35902	Larry Ferguson	256-494-1302	R	563*	1.6
Lamson and Sessions Co.	25701 Science Park	Cleveland	OH	44122		216-464-3400	S	561	1.3
WMS Industries Inc.	800 S Northpoint	Waukegan	IL	60085	Brian R. Gamache	847-785-3000	P	539	1.4
C and D Technologies Inc.	PO Box 3053	Blue Bell	PA	19422	Jeffrey A. Graves	215-619-2700	P	525	2.9
Overhead Door Corp.	2501 St. Hwy. 121	Lewisville	TX	75022	Howard Simons		R	508*	0.1
Koken Manufacturing Company	PO Box 265	Saint Louis	MO	63166	Masahiro Kanaya	314-231-7383	R	458*	<0.1
Camber Corp.	22289 Exploration	Lexington Park	MD	20653	Joseph Alexander	301-862-4577	R	447*	0.8
Arden Companies	18000 W 9 Mile Rd.	Southfield	MI	48075	Robert S. Sachs	248-355-1101	R	424*	1.2
Rofin-Sinar Technologies Inc.	40984 Concept Dr.	Plymouth	MI	48170	Gunther Braun	734-455-5400	P	421	1.4
Link Simulation and Training	PO Box 5328	Arlington	TX	76005	John McNellis	817-619-3536	D	415*	0.8
WMS Gaming Inc.	3401 N California	Chicago	IL	60618	Brian R. Gamache	773-961-1620	S	398*	0.8
Coleman Company Inc.	258 Beacon Street	Somerset	PA	15501	Bill Phillips		S	389*	2.3
Amscan Holdings Inc.	80 Grasslands Rd.	Elmsford	NY	10523	James Harrison	914-345-2020	R	386*	2.0
Rofin-Sinar Inc.	40984 Concept Dr.	Plymouth	MI	48170	Gunther Braun	734-455-5400	P	375	1.4
Totes-Isotoner Corp.	9655 International	Cincinnati	OH	45246	Douglas Gernert	513-682-8200	R	358*	1.1
UNICEF	333 E 38th St., 6th	New York	NY	10016	Charles Lyons	212-326-7000	R	352*	1.0
LSI Industries Inc.	PO Box 42728	Cincinnati	OH	45242	Wilfred OGara	513-793-3200	P	338	1.6
Greenlee Lighting L.P.	1300 Hutton, 110	Carrollton	TX	75006	Robert J. Ready	972-466-1133	S	324*	1.4
LSI Kentucky L.L.C.	3871 Turkeyfoot Rd.	Erlanger	KY	41018	Robert J. Ready	859-342-2273	S	324*	1.4
Prescolite Inc.	101 Corporate Dr.	Spartanburg	SC	29303	Jim Duggar	864-599-6000	S	300*	2.2
Russ Berrie and Company Inc.	111 Bauer Dr.	Oakland	NJ	07436	Andrew R. Gatto	201-337-9000	P	295	1.0
AZZ Inc.	1300 S Universty Dr	Fort Worth	TX	76107	David H. Dingus	817-810-0095	P	260	1.0
Electro Scientific Industries	13900 NW Sci Pk	Portland	OR	97229		503-641-4141	P	251	0.6
Juno Lighting Inc.	PO Box 5065	Des Plaines	IL	60017		847-827-9880	S	242*	1.0
Columbia Lighting Inc.	PO Box 2787	Spokane	WA	99220	Timothy Powers	509-924-7000	S	230*	1.4
Preformed Line Products Co.	660 Beta Dr.	Cleveland	OH	44101	Robert Ruhlman	440-461-5200	P	217	1.5
Oil-Dri Corporation of America	410 N Michigan	Chicago	IL	60611		312-321-1515	P	212	0.8
FlightSafety International	Marine Air Terminal	Flushing	NY	11371	A.L. Ueltschi	718-565-4100	D	200*	1.5
Day-Timers Inc.	1 Willow Ln.	East Texas	PA	18046	Bob Dorney		S	200*	1.3
Panavision International L.P.	6219 De Soto Ave.	Woodland Hills	CA	91367	Bob Beitcher	818-316-1000	S	194*	1.2
IPG Photonics Corp.	50 Old Webster Rd.	Oxford	MA	01540	V. P. Gapontsev	508-373-1100	P	189	1.3

Source: Ward's Business Directory of U.S. Private and Public Companies, Volumes 1 and 2, 2008. The company type code used is as follows: P - Public, R - Private, S - Subsidiary, D - Division, J - Joint Venture, A - Affiliate, G - Group. Sales are in millions of dollars, employees are in thousands. An asterisk (*) indicates an estimated sales volume. The symbol < stands for 'less than'. Company names and addresses are truncated, in some cases, to fit into the available space.

MATERIALS CONSUMED FOR RESIDENTIAL ELECTRIC LIGHTING FIXTURE MANUFACTURING

Material	Quantity	Delivered Cost ($ million)
Plastics resins consumed in the form of granules, pellets, etc.	(X)	27.9
Plastics products consumed in the form of sheets, rods, etc.	(X)	6.9
Paperboard containers, boxes, and corrugated paperboard	(X)	30.6
Specialty transformers and fluorescent ballasts	(X)	23.0
Current-carrying wiring devices	(X)	20.8
Electric lamp bulbs	(X)	12.3
Flat glass (plate, float, and sheet)	(X)	6.0
Fabricated plastics products (excluding gaskets)	(X)	7.8
Insulated wire and cable (including magnet wire)	(X)	6.7
Metal bolts, nuts, screws, and other screw machine products	(X)	7.4
Metal poles	(X)	4.3
All other fabricated metal products (excluding forgings)	(X)	22.7
Forgings	(X)	(D)
Iron and steel castings (rough and semifinished)	(X)	10.7
Aluminum and aluminum-base alloy castings (rough and semifinished)	(X)	5.7
Other nonferrous metal castings, rough or semifinished (inc. aluminum)	(X)	(D)
Steel sheet and strip (including tinplate)	(X)	13.8
Steel wire and wire products	(X)	4.6
All other steel mill shapes and forms (exc. castings and forgings)	(X)	7.5
Aluminum and aluminum-base alloy sheet, plate, foil, and welded tubing	(X)	9.0
Aluminum and aluminum-base alloy extruded shapes (rod, bar, pipe, tube, etc.)	(X)	4.2
Other aluminum and aluminum-base alloy shapes and forms (exc. castings, forgings, fabr. metal products)	(X)	4.8
Copper and copper-base alloy shapes and forms (exc. castings, forgings, fabr. metal products)	(X)	4.1
Other nonferrous shapes and forms (exc. castings, forgings, fabricated metal products)	(X)	2.4
Lamp shades	(X)	18.9
All other materials, components, parts, containers, and supplies	(X)	356.2
Materials, ingredients, containers, and supplies, nsk	(X)	112.3

Source: 2002 *Economic Census*. Explanation of symbols used: (D): Withheld to avoid disclosure of competitive data; na: Not available; (S): Withheld because statistical norms were not met; (X): Not applicable; (Z): Less than half the unit shown; nec: Not elsewhere classified; nsk: Not specified by kind; - : zero; p : 10-19 percent estimated; q : 20-29 percent estimated.

MATERIALS CONSUMED FOR NONRESIDENTIAL ELECTRIC LIGHTING FIXTURE MANUFACTURING

Material	Quantity	Delivered Cost ($ million)
Plastics resins consumed in the form of granules, pellets, etc.	(X)	7.6
Plastics products consumed in the form of sheets, rods, etc.	(X)	61.9
Paperboard containers, boxes, and corrugated paperboard	(X)	58.6
Specialty transformers and fluorescent ballasts	(X)	409.8
Current-carrying wiring devices	(X)	36.5
Electric lamp bulbs	(X)	47.7
Flat glass (plate, float, and sheet)	(X)	8.2
Fabricated plastics products (excluding gaskets)	(X)	16.3
Insulated wire and cable (including magnet wire)	(X)	13.9
Metal bolts, nuts, screws, and other screw machine products	(X)	45.3
Metal poles	(X)	10.2
All other fabricated metal products (excluding forgings)	(X)	66.7
Forgings	(X)	17.0
Iron and steel castings (rough and semifinished)	(X)	11.5
Aluminum and aluminum-base alloy castings (rough and semifinished)	(X)	34.4
Other nonferrous metal castings, rough or semifinished (inc. aluminum)	(X)	3.1
Steel sheet and strip (including tinplate)	(X)	121.3
Steel wire and wire products	(X)	15.8
All other steel mill shapes and forms (exc. castings and forgings)	(X)	50.2
Aluminum and aluminum-base alloy sheet, plate, foil, and welded tubing	(X)	43.2
Aluminum and aluminum-base alloy extruded shapes (rod, bar, pipe, tube, etc.)	(X)	15.9
Other aluminum and aluminum-base alloy shapes and forms (exc. castings, forgings, fabr. metal products)	(X)	18.3
Copper and copper-base alloy shapes and forms (exc. castings, forgings, fabr. metal products)	(X)	5.6
Other nonferrous shapes and forms (exc. castings, forgings, fabricated metal products)	(X)	2.6
Lamp shades	(X)	1.8
All other materials, components, parts, containers, and supplies	(X)	336.5
Materials, ingredients, containers, and supplies, nsk	(X)	47.0

Source: 2002 *Economic Census*. Explanation of symbols used: (D): Withheld to avoid disclosure of competitive data; na: Not available; (S): Withheld because statistical norms were not met; (X): Not applicable; (Z): Less than half the unit shown; nec: Not elsewhere classified; nsk: Not specified by kind; - : zero; p : 10-19 percent estimated; q : 20-29 percent estimated.

MATERIALS CONSUMED FOR LIGHTING EQUIPMENT MANUFACTURING NEC

Material	Quantity	Delivered Cost ($ million)
Plastics resins consumed in the form of granules, pellets, etc.	(X)	20.1
Plastics products consumed in the form of sheets, rods, etc.	(X)	25.4
Paperboard containers, boxes, and corrugated paperboard	(X)	39.1
Specialty transformers and fluorescent ballasts	(X)	111.7
Current-carrying wiring devices	(X)	37.4
Electric lamp bulbs	(X)	74.6
Flat glass (plate, float, and sheet)	(X)	18.4
Fabricated plastics products (excluding gaskets)	(X)	49.0
Insulated wire and cable (including magnet wire)	(X)	21.9
Metal bolts, nuts, screws, and other screw machine products	(X)	28.0
Metal poles	(X)	33.9
All other fabricated metal products (excluding forgings)	(X)	52.6
Forgings	(X)	18.2
Iron and steel castings (rough and semifinished)	(X)	16.8
Aluminum and aluminum-base alloy castings (rough and semifinished)	(X)	58.5
Other nonferrous metal castings, rough or semifinished (inc. aluminum)	(X)	7.4
Steel sheet and strip (including tinplate)	(X)	19.0
Steel wire and wire products	(X)	4.0
All other steel mill shapes and forms (exc. castings and forgings)	(X)	12.5
Aluminum and aluminum-base alloy sheet, plate, foil, and welded tubing	(X)	34.2
Aluminum and aluminum-base alloy extruded shapes (rod, bar, pipe, tube, etc.)	(X)	25.1
Other aluminum and aluminum-base alloy shapes and forms (exc. castings, forgings, fabr. metal products)	(X)	9.5
Copper and copper-base alloy shapes and forms (exc. castings, forgings, fabr. metal products)	(X)	5.7
Other nonferrous shapes and forms (exc. castings, forgings, fabricated metal products)	(X)	6.4
Lamp shades	(X)	1.0
All other materials, components, parts, containers, and supplies	(X)	794.9
Materials, ingredients, containers, and supplies, nsk	(X)	50.4

Source: 2002 Economic Census. Explanation of symbols used: (D): Withheld to avoid disclosure of competitive data; na: Not available; (S): Withheld because statistical norms were not met; (X): Not applicable; (Z): Less than half the unit shown; nec: Not elsewhere classified; nsk: Not specified by kind; - : zero; p : 10-19 percent estimated; q : 20-29 percent estimated.

PRODUCT SHARE DETAILS FOR RESIDENTIAL ELECTRIC LIGHTING FIXTURE MANUFACTURING

Product or Product Class Shipments	Mil. $	Product or Product Class Shipments	Mil. $
RESIDENTIAL ELECTRIC LIGHTING FIXTURES	1,970.6	Other residential-type incandescent portable lamps (including desk and boudior lamps), complete with shade	88.8
Residential-type electric lighting fixtures (except portable), including parts and accessories	**1,268.9**	Residential-type incandescent portable lamps sold without shade	20.7
Residential-type portable lighting fixtures, including parts and accessories	**631.0**	Residential-type fluorescent portable lamps	5.3
Residential-type incandescent portable floor lamps, complete with shade	241.6	Paper or textile lamp shades	41.9
Residential-type incandescent portable wall lamps (including adjustable types), complete with shade	57.4	Parts and accessories for residential-type portable lighting fixtures	10.2
Residential-type incandescent portable table lamps (excluding desk lamps), complete with shade	165.3	**Residential electric lighting fixtures, nsk, total**	**70.6**

Source: 2002 Economic Census. The values are product shipments in millions of dollars for 2002. Total product shipments may be lower or higher than industry shipments. See Introduction for a full discussion. Values of indented subcategories are summed in the main heading(s). The symbol (D) appears when data are withheld to prevent disclosure of competitive information. The abbreviation nsk stands for 'not specified by kind' and nec for 'not elsewhere classified'. A dash (-) means zero.

PRODUCT SHARE DETAILS FOR NONRESIDENTIAL ELECTRIC LIGHTING FIXTURE MANUFACTURING

Product or Product Class Shipments	Mil. $	Product or Product Class Shipments	Mil. $
COMMERCIAL, INDUSTRIAL, AND INSTITUTIONAL ELECTRIC LIGHTING FIXTURES	4,033.7	**Industrial-type electric lighting fixtures, including parts and accessories**	**747.1**
Commercial and institutional-type electric lighting fixtures, including parts and accessories	**3,169.2**	**Commercial, industrial, and institutional electric lighting fixtures, nsk, total**	**117.3**

Source: 2002 Economic Census. The values are product shipments in millions of dollars for 2002. Total product shipments may be lower or higher than industry shipments. See Introduction for a full discussion. Values of indented subcategories are summed in the main heading(s). The symbol (D) appears when data are withheld to prevent disclosure of competitive information. The abbreviation nsk stands for 'not specified by kind' and nec for 'not elsewhere classified'. A dash (-) means zero.

PRODUCT SHARE DETAILS FOR LIGHTING EQUIPMENT MANUFACTURING NEC

Product or Product Class Shipments	Mil. $	Product or Product Class Shipments	Mil. $
LIGHTING EQUIPMENT, NEC	3,483.2	Other electric lighting equipment (including mercury and sodium vapor, and ultraviolet and infrared health lamp fixtures), except street and highway lighting equipment and signs	186.6
Outdoor lighting equipment (including parts and accessories)	**1,879.1**		
Electric and nonelectric lighting equipment, nec (including parts and accessories)	**1,494.2**	Electric fireplace logs	(D)
Electric and nonelectric lighting equipment, nec (including parts and accessories)	1,491.1	Parts and accessories for all other miscellaneous electric lighting fixtures	125.6
Rechargeable battery-operated incandescent hand portable lighting equipment, excluding parts and accessories	134.1	Electric trouble lighting equipment	(D)
Incandescent hand portable flashlights and flashlight lanterns, except rechargeable battery-operated	347.1	Nonelectric lighting fixtures and equipment, complete units (including lamps and lanterns using kerosene, gasoline, propane, butane, etc., and carbide lamps of all types)	33.6
Other incandescent hand portable lighting equipment (miners' lights, emergency warning lights, generator flashlights, etc.), except rechargeable battery-operated	115.9	Electric insect killers	14.8
		Electric insect repellent lamps	(D)
Other incandescent lighting equipment, including marine markers and beacons	122.1	Parts and accessories for nonelectric lighting equipment (including reflectors and fittings, incandescent mantles, etc.)	66.8
Other fluorescent electric lighting equipment, complete units, including processing and technical equipment	101.6	Electric and nonelectric lighting equipment, nec, nsk	3.2
		Other lighting equipment, nec, nsk, total	**109.8**

Source: 2002 *Economic Census*. The values are product shipments in millions of dollars for 2002. Total product shipments may be lower or higher than industry shipments. See Introduction for a full discussion. Values of indented subcategories are summed in the main heading(s). The symbol (D) appears when data are withheld to prevent disclosure of competitive information. The abbreviation nsk stands for 'not specified by kind' and nec for 'not elsewhere classified'. A dash (-) means zero.

INPUTS AND OUTPUTS FOR LIGHTING FIXTURE MANUFACTURING

Economic Sector or Industry Providing Inputs	%	Sector	Economic Sector or Industry Buying Outputs	%	Sector
Compensation of employees	23.8		Personal consumption expenditures	15.2	
Wholesale trade	7.2	Trade	Nonresidential structures, nec	14.6	Construct.
Management of companies & enterprises	5.3	Services	Manufacturing structures	12.0	Construct.
Power, distribution, & specialty transformers	5.3	Manufg.	Residential permanent site structures	9.9	Construct.
Aluminum products from purchased aluminum	2.6	Manufg.	Commercial & health care structures	7.8	Construct.
Iron & steel mills & ferroalloys	2.5	Manufg.	General S/L govt. services	5.2	S/L Govt
Paperboard containers	1.7	Manufg.	Exports of goods & services	4.4	Cap Inv
Nonferrous metal foundries	1.7	Manufg.	Private fixed investment	4.2	
Turned products & screws, nuts, & bolts	1.5	Manufg.	Residential structures, nec	3.3	Construct.
Electric lamp bulbs & parts	1.4	Manufg.	Maintenance/repair of nonresidential structures	3.1	Construct.
Wiring devices	1.2	Manufg.	Other S/L govt. enterprises	2.8	S/L Govt
Plastics products, nec	1.2	Manufg.	Owner-occupied dwellings	2.1	
Plastics packaging materials, film & sheet	1.2	Manufg.	Hunting and trapping	1.2	Agric.
Advertising & related services	1.2	Services	Railroad rolling stock	1.0	Manufg.
Paints & coatings	1.1	Manufg.	Lighting fixtures	0.7	Manufg.
Lighting fixtures	1.1	Manufg.	Food services & drinking places	0.6	Services
Lessors of nonfinancial assets	1.0	Fin/R.E.	Natural gas distribution	0.6	Util.
Semiconductors & related devices	1.0	Manufg.	Scientific research & development services	0.6	Services
Printed circuit assemblies (electronic assemblies)	0.9	Manufg.	Waste management & remediation services	0.5	Services
Real estate	0.9	Fin/R.E.	Hospitals	0.5	Services
Truck transportation	0.8	Util.	Investigation & security services	0.5	Services
Plastics materials & resins	0.7	Manufg.	Steel products from purchased steel	0.5	Manufg.
Securities, commodity contracts, investments	0.7	Fin/R.E.	Hotels & motels, including casino hotels	0.4	Services
Machine shops	0.7	Manufg.	Nursing & residential care facilities	0.4	Services
Fabricated pipes & pipe fittings	0.6	Manufg.	Services to buildings & dwellings	0.4	Services
Copper rolling, drawing, extruding, & alloying	0.5	Manufg.	Engine equipment, nec	0.4	Manufg.
Retail trade	0.5	Trade	Plastics products, nec	0.4	Manufg.
Power generation & supply	0.5	Util.	Telecommunications	0.4	Services
Ferrous metal foundries	0.5	Manufg.	Management of companies & enterprises	0.4	Services
Specialized design services	0.5	Services	Colleges, universities, & professional schools	0.3	Services
Coating, engraving, heat treating & allied activities	0.5	Manufg.	Tobacco products	0.3	Manufg.
Petroleum lubricating oil & grease	0.5	Manufg.	Retail trade	0.3	Trade
Forging, stamping, & sintering, nec	0.4	Manufg.	Semiconductors & related devices	0.3	Manufg.
Legal services	0.4	Services	Maintenance/repair of residential structures	0.2	Construct.
Flat glass	0.4	Manufg.	Oil & gas well drilling	0.2	Mining
Scientific research & development services	0.4	Services	Architectural, engineering, & related services	0.2	Services
Monetary authorities/depository credit intermediation	0.3	Fin/R.E.	Change in private inventories	0.2	In House
Architectural, engineering, & related services	0.3	Services	Oil & gas operations services	0.2	Mining
Employment services	0.3	Services	Real estate	0.2	Fin/R.E.
Professional, scientific, technical services, nec	0.3	Services	Civic, social, & professional organizations	0.2	Services
Taxes on production & imports, less subsidies	0.3		Asphalt paving mixtures & blocks	0.2	Manufg.
Steel products from purchased steel	0.3	Manufg.	Motor vehicle parts	0.2	Manufg.
Noncomparable imports	0.3	Foreign	S/L govt. passenger transit	0.2	S/L Govt
Telecommunications	0.3	Services	Manufactured homes & mobile homes	0.2	Manufg.
Postal service	0.2	Util.	Motor vehicle bodies	0.2	Manufg.
Paper mills	0.2	Manufg.	Legal services	0.1	Services
Fabricated metals, nec	0.2	Manufg.	Coal	0.1	Mining
Data processing, hosting, & related services	0.2	Services	Amusement parks, arcades, & gambling	0.1	Services
Accounting, tax preparation, bookkeeping, & payroll	0.2	Services	Professional, scientific, technical services, nec	0.1	Services

Continued on next page.

INPUTS AND OUTPUTS FOR LIGHTING FIXTURE MANUFACTURING - Continued

Economic Sector or Industry Providing Inputs	%	Sector	Economic Sector or Industry Buying Outputs	%	Sector
Warehousing & storage	0.2	Util.			
Automotive equipment rental & leasing	0.2	Fin/R.E.			
Soap & cleaning compounds	0.2	Manufg.			
Communication & energy wires & cables	0.2	Manufg.			
Metal cans, boxes, & other containers (light gauge)	0.2	Manufg.			
Natural gas distribution	0.2	Util.			
Food services & drinking places	0.2	Services			
Relay & industrial controls	0.2	Manufg.			
Nonferrous metal (ex. copper & aluminum) processing	0.2	Manufg.			
Unlaminated plastics profile shapes	0.2	Manufg.			
Alumina refining & primary aluminum production	0.1	Manufg.			
Paperboard mills	0.1	Manufg.			
Services to buildings & dwellings	0.1	Services			
Maintenance/repair of nonresidential structures	0.1	Construct.			
Bare printed circuit boards	0.1	Manufg.			
Business support services	0.1	Services			
Cutting tools & machine tool accessories	0.1	Manufg.			
Plate work & fabricated structural products	0.1	Manufg.			
Commercial & industrial machinery rental & leasing	0.1	Fin/R.E.			
Crowns & closures & metal stamping	0.1	Manufg.			
Laminated plastics plates, sheets, & shapes	0.1	Manufg.			
Hotels & motels, including casino hotels	0.1	Services			
Chemical products & preparations, nec	0.1	Manufg.			

Source: Benchmark Input-Output Accounts for the U.S. Economy, 2002, U.S. Department of Commerce, Washington, D.C., January 2008. The abbreviation nec stands for 'not elsewhere classified'.

OCCUPATIONS EMPLOYED BY ELECTRIC LIGHTING EQUIPMENT MANUFACTURING

Occupation	% of Total 2006	Change to 2016	Occupation	% of Total 2006	Change to 2016
Team assemblers	18.6	-25.3	Machinists	1.5	-21.5
Electrical & electronic equipment assemblers	7.8	-40.2	Coating, painting, & spraying machine operators	1.5	-29.0
First-line supervisors/managers of production workers	3.4	-25.3	Stock clerks & order fillers	1.4	-37.5
Sales reps, wholesale & manufacturing, exc tech	2.6	-25.3	Industrial truck & tractor operators	1.4	-32.7
Inspectors, testers, sorters, samplers, & weighers	2.5	-29.5	Bookkeeping, accounting, & auditing clerks	1.3	-25.3
Shipping, receiving, & traffic clerks	2.4	-28.1	Packaging & filling machine operators & tenders	1.3	-32.7
Customer service representatives	2.2	-17.8	Production workers, nec	1.3	-26.6
Laborers & freight, stock, & material movers, hand	2.1	-32.7	Grinding, lapping, polishing machine tool operators	1.3	-27.5
Cutting, punching, & press machine operators	2.1	-32.7	Purchasing agents, exc wholesale, retail, & farm	1.1	-25.3
Maintenance & repair workers, general	1.8	-25.3	Office clerks, general	1.0	-26.4
Packers & packagers, hand	1.6	-40.2	Electrical engineers	1.0	-25.3
General & operations managers	1.5	-32.7			

Source: Industry-Occupation Matrix, Bureau of Labor Statistics, December 4, 2007. These data are reported based on 4-digit NAICS categories but have been matched to corresponding 6-digit NAICS industry codes. The change reported for each occupation to the year 2016 is a percent of growth or decline as estimated by the Bureau of Labor Statistics. The abbreviation nec stands for 'not elsewhere classified'.

LOCATION BY STATE AND REGIONAL CONCENTRATION

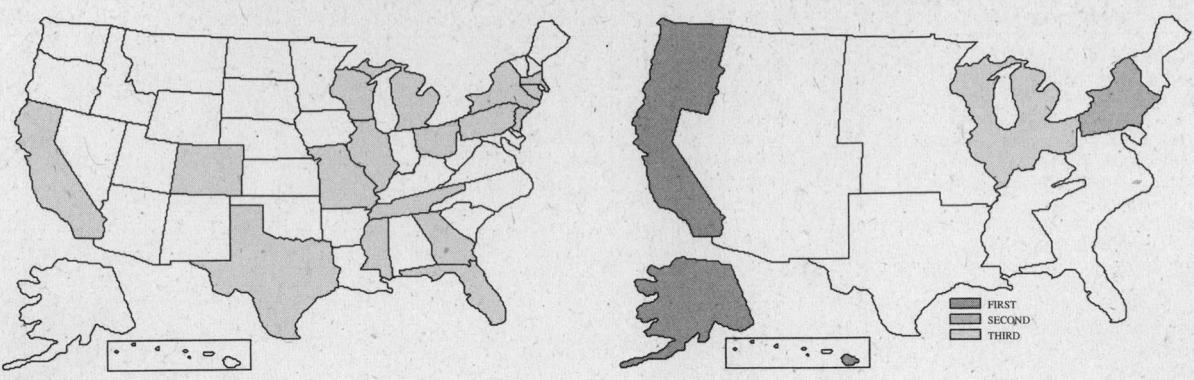

INDUSTRY DATA BY STATE

| State | Establish-ments | Shipments | | | Employment | | | | Cost as % of Shipments | Investment per Employee ($) |
		Total ($ mil)	% of U.S.	Per Establ.	Total Number	% of U.S.	Per Establ.	Wages ($/hour)		
California	250	1,492.7	15.1	5,970.9	9,588	17.7	38	11.96	46.3	2,846
Illinois	68	965.0	9.8	14,190.5	4,814	8.9	71	12.36	37.3	1,688
Pennsylvania	36	543.4	5.5	15,094.7	2,681	4.9	74	10.62	60.8	2,443
New Jersey	56	404.4	4.1	7,221.2	2,155	4.0	38	11.57	47.2	1,586
Ohio	19	391.1	4.0	20,584.4	1,383	2.5	73	11.59	37.1	4,341
New York	58	339.1	3.4	5,846.0	2,420	4.5	42	14.55	38.9	6,521
Massachusetts	10	222.6	2.3	22,257.3	1,179	2.2	118	13.47	43.5	2,315
Tennessee	10	162.4	1.6	16,236.5	863	1.6	86	14.03	55.3	9,352
Wisconsin	10	149.4	1.5	14,938.5	770	1.4	77	13.77	56.5	2,497
Texas	22	138.3	1.4	6,286.3	888	1.6	40	9.83	48.1	6,856
Connecticut	17	117.0	1.2	6,881.7	656	1.2	39	11.77	47.9	2,401
Georgia	9	86.2	0.9	9,576.2	884	1.6	98	9.46	44.4	1,400
Missouri	7	82.7	0.8	11,820.1	538	1.0	77	12.91	45.1	4,056
Colorado	4	62.1	0.6	15,533.3	223	0.4	56	12.61	31.9	2,018
Michigan	7	24.0	0.2	3,434.9	107	0.2	15	12.01	30.9	1,093
Florida	15	16.6	0.2	1,109.9	146	0.3	10	12.20	41.9	1,432
Mississippi	5	12.7	0.1	2,547.0	125	0.2	25	14.22	36.5	1,120

Source: 2002 *Economic Census*. The states are in descending order of shipments or establishments (if shipment data are missing for the majority). The symbol (D) appears when data are withheld to prevent disclosure of competitive information. States marked with (D) are sorted by number of establishments. A dash (-) indicates that the data element cannot be calculated. Data may not show all states active in the NAICS category. All data available at the time of publication are shown.

NAICS 33521M - SMALL ELECTRICAL APPLIANCE MANUFACTURING*

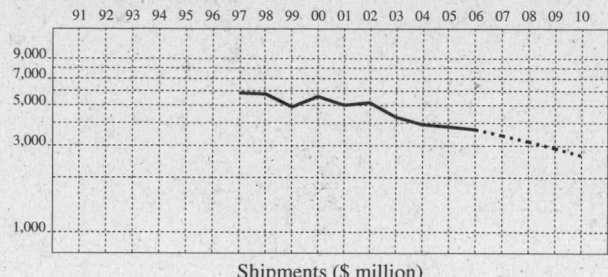

Shipments ($ million)

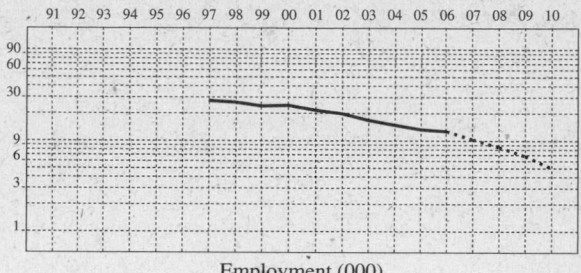

Employment (000)

GENERAL STATISTICS

| Year | Com-panies | Establishments | | Employment | | | Compensation | | Production ($ million) | | | |
		Total	with 20 or more employees	Total (000)	Production Workers (000)	Hours (Mil)	Payroll ($ mil)	Wages ($/hr)	Cost of Materials	Value Added by Manufacture	Value of Shipments	Capital Invest.
1997	144	171	89	27.4	20.0	37.5	748.2	11.58	3,023.5	2,811.1	5,832.8	171.3
1998		189	99	26.4	19.6	37.4	743.0	11.55	3,291.0	2,503.2	5,757.9	174.9
1999		191	91	24.0	18.2	33.8	677.4	11.89	2,496.7	2,394.2	4,892.6	126.5
2000		194	92	24.4	18.3	36.4	754.0	12.67	2,857.9	2,703.8	5,578.9	160.4
2001		190	90	21.6	15.9	31.7	668.8	12.84	2,536.1	2,444.9	5,003.4	133.5
2002	118	138	66	19.8	14.8	27.8	651.6	13.90	2,518.7	2,686.9	5,165.7	128.0
2003		163	73	16.8	12.7	23.4	556.8	14.18	2,223.0	2,084.7	4,304.5	95.2
2004		154	66	14.9	11.5	21.8	509.1	14.28	2,034.0	1,882.4	3,922.9	60.9
2005		155	67	13.3	9.7	19.1	463.7	14.54	2,007.7	1,639.3	3,804.7	56.7
2006		148P	61P	12.7	9.9	19.3	473.1	15.13	1,991.4	1,716.6	3,678.1	57.7
2007		144P	57P	10.3P	8.0P	15.7P	428.5P	15.60P	1,845.3P	1,590.7P	3,408.3P	37.2P
2008		139P	52P	8.5P	6.7P	13.3P	392.9P	16.03P	1,708.9P	1,473.1P	3,156.4P	22.8P
2009		134P	48P	6.8P	5.4P	10.9P	357.2P	16.46P	1,572.5P	1,355.5P	2,904.4P	8.4P
2010		130P	44P	5.0P	4.2P	8.5P	321.6P	16.88P	1,436.1P	1,237.9P	2,652.5P	

Sources: 1997 and 2002 *Economic Census*; other years, up to 2006, are from *Annual Survey of Manufactures*. Establishment counts for non-Census years are from *County Business Patterns*; 1997 and 2002 values are from the 1997 and 2002 censuses, respectively. 'P's show projections by the editors.

INDICES OF CHANGE

| Year | Com-panies | Establishments | | Employment | | | Compensation | | Production ($ million) | | | |
		Total	with 20 or more employees	Total (000)	Production Workers (000)	Hours (Mil)	Payroll ($ mil)	Wages ($/hr)	Cost of Materials	Value Added by Manufacture	Value of Shipments	Capital Invest.
1997	122	124	135	138	135	135	115	83	120	105	113	134
1998		137	150	133	132	135	114	83	131	93	111	137
1999		138	138	121	123	122	104	86	99	89	95	99
2000		141	139	123	124	131	116	91	113	101	108	125
2001		138	136	109	107	114	103	92	101	91	97	104
2002	100	100	100	100	100	100	100	100	100	100	100	100
2003		118	111	85	86	84	85	102	88	78	83	74
2004		112	100	75	78	78	78	103	81	70	76	48
2005		112	102	67	66	69	71	105	80	61	74	44
2006		107P	92P	64	67	69	73	109	79	64	71	45
2007		104P	86P	52P	54P	56P	66P	112P	73P	59P	66P	29P
2008		101P	79P	43P	45P	48P	60P	115P	68P	55P	61P	18P
2009		97P	73P	34P	36P	39P	55P	118P	62P	50P	56P	7P
2010		94P	67P	25P	28P	31P	49P	121P	57P	46P	51P	

Sources: Same as General Statistics. Values reflect change from the base year, 2002. Values above 100 mean greater than 2002, values below 100 mean less than 2002, and the values of 100 in other years means the same as 2002. 'P's show projections by the editors.

SELECTED RATIOS

For 2002	Avg. of All Manufact.	Analyzed Industry	Index	For 2002	Avg. of All Manufact.	Analyzed Industry	Index
Employees per Establishment	42	143	342	Value Added per Production Worker	182,367	181,547	100
Payroll per Establishment	1,639,184	4,721,739	288	Cost per Establishment	5,769,015	18,251,449	316
Payroll per Employee	39,053	32,909	84	Cost per Employee	137,446	127,207	93
Production Workers per Establishment	30	107	363	Cost per Production Worker	195,506	170,182	87
Wages per Establishment	694,845	2,800,145	403	Shipments per Establishment	11,158,348	37,432,609	335
Wages per Production Worker	23,548	26,109	111	Shipments per Employee	265,847	260,894	98
Hours per Production Worker	1,980	1,878	95	Shipments per Production Worker	378,144	349,034	92
Wages per Hour	11.89	13.90	117	Investment per Establishment	361,338	927,536	257
Value Added per Establishment	5,381,325	19,470,290	362	Investment per Employee	8,609	6,465	75
Value Added per Employee	128,210	135,702	106	Investment per Production Worker	12,245	8,649	71

Sources: Same as General Statistics. The 'Average of All Manufacturing' column represents the average of all manufacturing industries reported for the most recent complete year available. The Index shows the relationship between the Average and the Analyzed Industry. For example, 100 means that they are equal; 500 that the Analyzed Industry is five times the average; 50 means that the Analyzed Industry is half the national average. The abbreviation 'na' is used to show that data are 'not available'. Ratios shown for 2002, the last complete census year.

*Equivalent to Federal Government NAICS 335211, 335212.

LEADING COMPANIES   Number shown: **75**   Total sales ($ mil): **237,438**   Total employment (000): **507.2**

Company Name	Address				CEO Name	Phone	Co. Type	Sales ($ mil)	Empl. (000)
General Electric Co.	3135 Easton Tpk.	Fairfield	CT	06828		203-373-2211	P	172,738	327.0
Raytheon Co.	870 Winter St.	Waltham	MA	02451		781-522-3000	P	21,301	72.1
TUTCO Inc.	500 Gould Dr.	Cookeville	TN	38506		931-432-4141	R	9,602*	0.5
Black and Decker Corp.	101 Schilling Rd.	Hunt Valley	MD	21031	Nolan D. Archibald	410-716-3900	P	6,563	25.0
Jarden Consumer Solutions	2381 Executive Ctr.	Boca Raton	FL	33431	Andrew Hill	561-912-4100	S	4,420*	13.0
NACCO Industries Inc.	5875 Landerbrook	Mayfield Hgts	OH	44124		440-449-9600	P	3,603	10.2
A.O. Smith Corp.	PO Box 245008	Milwaukee	WI	53224		414-359-4000	P	2,312	16.8
NTK Holdings Inc.	50 Kennedy Plz.	Providence	RI	02903	Richard L. Bready	401-751-1600	S	2,218	9.8
Dekko Technologies L.L.C.	PO Box 337	North Webster	IN	46555	Steven Hankinf	574-834-2818	R	2,130*	0.1
Sharp Manufacturing Co.	4050 S Mendenhall	Memphis	TN	38115	Saiko Hanatani	901-795-6510	S	1,508*	0.8
Jacuzzi Brands Inc.	777 S Flagler Dr.	W Palm Bch	FL	33401		561-514-3838	S	1,202	4.5
Simmons Co.	1 Concourse Pky.	Atlanta	GA	30328	Charles R. Eitel	770-512-7700	R	855	3.0
Alpine Industries Inc.	310 T. Elmer Cox Dr	Greeneville	TN	37745	William Converse	423-638-7246	R	749*	1.0
Freshflush L.L.C.	5980 Miami Lakes	Miami Lakes	FL	33014	Harry Shulman	305-362-2611	S	673*	0.3
Water Pik Technologies Inc.	1730 E Prospect Rd.	Fort Collins	CO	80553	Richard Bisson	970-484-1352	R	647*	0.6
Applica Inc.	3633 Flamingo Rd.	Miramar	FL	33027		954-883-1000	S	556	0.3
Salton Inc.	1955 W Field Ct.	Lake Forest	IL	60045	Leonhard Dreimann	847-803-4600	P	523	1.0
Eureka Co.	PO Box 3900	Peoria	IL	61612	Marty Holleran		S	450*	2.5
National Presto Industries	3925 N Hastings	Eau Claire	WI	54703	Maryjo Cohen	715-839-2121	P	421	1.0
Royal Appliance Manufacturing	7005 Cochran Rd.	Glenwillow	OH	44139	Paul R. D'Alora	440-996-2000	S	404*	0.6
Tatung Company of America Inc.	2850 El Presidio St	Long Beach	CA	90810	Andrew Sun	310-637-2105	S	355*	0.3
American Water Heater Co.	PO Box 4056	Johnson City	TN	37602	Robert Trudeau	423-283-8000	R	278*	<0.1
Aerus L.L.C.	300 E Valley Dr.	Bristol	VA	24201	Jim Scott		S	250*	5.0
iRobot Inc.	63 S Ave.	Burlington	MA	01803	Colin Angle	781-345-0200	P	249	0.4
Blendtec Inc.	1206 S 1680 W	Orem	UT	84058	Tom Dickson	801-222-0888	D	248*	0.1
Oreck Corp.	100 Plantation Rd.	Harahan	LA	70123		504-733-8761	R	192*	0.3
Knight Inc.	20531 Crescent Bay	Lake Forest	CA	92630	George Noa	949-595-4800	S	189*	0.1
Stanley Steemer International	PO Box 8004	Dublin	OH	43016	Wesley Bates	614-764-2007	R	178*	0.3
Ronco Inventions L.L.C.	PO Box 4052	Beverly Hills	CA	90213	Ron Popeil		R	173*	0.2
Melitta North America Inc.	13925 58th St. N	Clearwater	FL	33760	Martin Miller	727-535-2111	R	169*	0.1
Bissell Inc.	PO Box 1888	Grand Rapids	MI	49501	Mark Bissell	616-453-4451	R	162*	0.5
Cobra Electronics Corp.	6500 W Cortland St.	Chicago	IL	60707	James Bazet	773-889-8870	P	154	0.2
Tacony Corp.	1760 Gilsinn Ln.	Fenton	MO	63026		636-349-3000	R	120*	0.3
P and F Industries Inc.	445 Broadhollow	Melville	NY	11747	Richard A. Horowitz	631-694-9800	P	112	0.2
Dometic Corp.	PO Box 490	Elkhart	IN	46516	John Waters	574-294-2511	S	110*	0.6
Oasis Corp.	265 N Hamilton Rd.	Columbus	OH	43213	Romanie Gilliland	614-861-1350	S	92*	0.5
Hamilton Beach/Proctor-Silex	234 Springs Rd.	Washington	NC	27889	Michael Morecroft		S	83*	0.3
Dacor Inc.	950 S Raymond	Pasadena	CA	91105	Ric Brutocao	626-799-1000	R	82*	0.5
Lakewood Engineering and Mfg.	501 N Sacramento	Chicago	IL	60612	D Hirschsield	773-722-4300	R	82*	0.4
Wilen Companies Inc.	3760 Southside Ind.	Atlanta	GA	30354	Jeffrey Alder	404-366-2111	D	80*	0.4
Tri-Tech Laboratories Inc.	1000 Robins Rd.	Lynchburg	VA	24504	Ronald Rodgers	434-845-7073	R	68*	0.2
Western Industries Inc.	W156 Pilgrim	Menomonee Fls	WI	53051	Tom Hall	262-251-1915	R	67*	0.6
Singer Sewing Co.	PO Box 7017	La Vergne	TN	37086	Stephen H. Goodman	615-213-0880	R	66*	<0.1
Springfield Wire Inc.	PO Box 638	Springfield	MA	01102	William Bradford	413-781-6950	R	66*	0.3
Boyd Coffee Co.	19730 NE Sandy	Portland	OR	97230	Richard Boyd	503-666-4545	R	59*	0.2
GMI Holdings Inc.	22790 Lake Park	Alliance	OH	44601	Carl Adrien	330-821-5360	S	54*	0.3
Remington Products Company	PO Box 44960	Madison	WI	53744	David Jones		S	51*	0.3
National Refrigeration Co.	PO Box 148	Honea Path	SC	29654	James Kaufman	864-369-1665	R	50*	0.2
Wilbur Curtis Company Inc.	6913 W Acco Street	Montebello	CA	90640	Robert Curtis	323-837-2300	R	49*	0.3
Varian Vacuum Technologies	121 Hartwell Ave.	Lexington	MA	02421	Allen Lauer	781-861-7200	D	49*	0.2
Andis Co.	PO Box 85005	Racine	WI	53408	Matthew Andis	262-884-2600	R	45*	0.4
Ecoquest Manufacturing Inc.	310 T Elmer Cox	Greeneville	TN	37743	Michael Jackson	423-798-6488	R	41*	0.2
Cleveland Range Co.	1333 E 179th St.	Cleveland	OH	44110	Rick Cutler	216-481-4900	S	39*	0.2
HMI Industries Inc.	13325 Darice Pky.	Strongsville	OH	44149	Kirk W. Foley	440-846-7800	R	32	0.1
EdgeCraft Corp.	825 Southwood Rd.	Avondale	PA	19311	Daniel Friel	610-268-0500	R	31*	0.1
Battle Creek Equipment Co.	307 W Jackson St.	Battle Creek	MI	49037	John Doty	269-962-6181	R	30*	<0.1
Anaheim Manufacturing Company	PO Box 4146	Anaheim	CA	92803		714-524-7770	R	30*	0.1
Lee Industries Inc.	PO Box 688	Philipsburg	PA	16866	Robert Montler	814-342-0461	R	29*	0.2
Atlanta Attachement Co.	362 Industrial Park	Lawrenceville	GA	30045	Elvin Price	770-963-7369	R	26*	0.2
Presto Manufacturing Co.	PO Box 10057	Jackson	MS	39286		601-366-3481	S	24*	0.2
K-TEC Inc.	1206 S 1680 W	Orem	UT	84058	Thomas Dickson	801-222-0888	R	24*	0.1
Fka Distributing Co.	3000 N Pontiac Trl.	Commerce Twp	MI	48390	Ron Ferber	248-863-3000	R	23*	0.2
Douglas Quikut	PO Box 29	Walnut Ridge	AR	72476	Warren E. Buffett		D	22*	<0.1
Cadet Manufacturing Co.	PO Box 1675	Vancouver	WA	98668	Richard Anderson	360-693-2505	R	22*	0.1
Metal Ware Corp.	PO Box 237	Two Rivers	WI	54241	Wesley Drumm	920-793-1368	R	20*	0.1
Rama Corp.	600 W Esplanade	San Jacinto	CA	92583	Marco Renshaw	951-654-7351	R	20*	0.1
Hybrinetics Inc.	PO Box 14399	Santa Rosa	CA	95402	Richard Rosa	707-585-0333	R	19*	<0.1
Fostoria Industries Inc.	1200 N Main St.	Fostoria	OH	44830	Larry Dunlap	419-435-9201	S	19*	0.1
Joseph Enterprises Inc.	425 California St.	San Francisco	CA	94104	Joe Pedott	415-397-6992	R	19*	<0.1
Jump River Electric Coop.	PO Box 99	Ladysmith	WI	54848	John Kmosena	715-532-5524	R	19*	<0.1
Vaughn Manufacturing Corp.	PO Box 5431	Salisbury	MA	01952	James Vaughn	978-462-6683	R	19*	<0.1
Dominick Terzuoli	163 13th Street	Brooklyn	NY	11215	Dominick Terzuoli	718-499-9717	R	19*	<0.1
Bertolotti's Ceres Disposal	PO Box 127	Ceres	CA	95307	Bert Bertolotti	209-537-8000	R	18*	<0.1
Accu Therm Inc.	PO Box 249	Monroe City	MO	63456	Charles Bindemann	573-735-1060	R	18*	0.1
LCAR	2650 W 35th Ave.	Gary	IN	46408		219-884-1138	R	17*	0.5

Source: Ward's Business Directory of U.S. Private and Public Companies, Volumes 1 and 2, 2008. The company type code used is as follows: P - Public, R - Private, S - Subsidiary, D - Division, J - Joint Venture, A - Affiliate, G - Group. Sales are in millions of dollars, employees are in thousands. An asterisk (*) indicates an estimated sales volume. The symbol < stands for 'less than'. Company names and addresses are truncated, in some cases, to fit into the available space.

MATERIALS CONSUMED FOR ELECTRIC HOUSEWARES AND HOUSEHOLD FAN MANUFACTURING

Material	Quantity	Delivered Cost ($ million)
Metal stampings	(X)	27.4
Metal bolts, nuts, screws, and other screw machine products	(X)	11.5
All other fabricated metal products (excluding forgings)	(X)	10.1
Iron and steel castings (rough and semifinished)	(X)	(D)
Aluminum and aluminum-base alloy castings (rough and semifinished)	(X)	10.1
Other nonferrous metal castings, rough or semifinished (inc. aluminum)	(X)	(D)
Steel sheet and strip (including tinplate)	(X)	29.7
All other steel shapes and forms (exc. castings, forgings, fabr. metal products)	(X)	(D)
Aluminum and aluminum-base alloy shapes and forms (exc. castings, forgings, fabr. metal products)	(X)	4.5
Other nonferrous shapes and forms (exc. castings, forgings, fabricated metal products)	(X)	(D)
Nonferrous wire and cable (incl. magnet wire, bare wire or insulated wire, etc.)	(X)	5.9
Fractional horsepower electric motors and generators (less than 1 hp)	(X)	106.0
Integral horsepower electric motors and generators (1 hp or more)	(X)	(D)
Paper and paperboard containers (incl. shipping sacks and other paper packaging supplies)	(X)	43.9
Electrical transmission, distribution, and control equipment	(X)	(D)
Current-carrying wiring devices	(X)	(D)
Timing mechanisms (excluding microprocessors)	(X)	(D)
Automatic temperature controls (thermostats, regulators, etc.)	(X)	27.0
Paints, varnishes, stains, lacquers, shellacs, japans, enamels, etc.	(X)	10.1
Fabricated rubber products (exc. tires, tubes, hoses, belting, and gaskets)	(X)	1.2
Rubber and plastics hose and belting	(X)	(D)
Plastics products consumed in the form of sheets, rods, etc.	(X)	27.5
Plastics resins consumed in the form of granules, pellets, etc.	(X)	36.6
Complete flexible cord sets	(X)	8.2
Resistors, capacitors, transformers, electron tubes, semiconductors, and other electronic components	(X)	11.5
Mineral wool insulation (fibrous glass, rock wool, etc.)	(X)	(D)
All other materials, components, parts, containers, and supplies	(X)	180.7
Materials, ingredients, containers, and supplies, nsk	(X)	199.3

Source: 2002 *Economic Census*. Explanation of symbols used: (D): Withheld to avoid disclosure of competitive data; na: Not available; (S): Withheld because statistical norms were not met; (X): Not applicable; (Z): Less than half the unit shown; nec: Not elsewhere classified; nsk: Not specified by kind; - : zero; p : 10-19 percent estimated; q : 20-29 percent estimated.

MATERIALS CONSUMED FOR HOUSEHOLD VACUUM CLEANER MANUFACTURING

Material	Quantity	Delivered Cost ($ million)
Metal stampings	(X)	14.5
Metal fabricated nonelectric wire products (except forgings)	(X)	(D)
Metal bolts, nuts, screws, and other screw machine products	(X)	15.7
All other fabricated metal products (excluding forgings)	(X)	5.6
Forgings	(X)	(D)
Iron and steel castings (rough and semifinished)	(X)	(D)
Aluminum and aluminum-base alloy castings (rough and semifinished)	(X)	(D)
Other nonferrous metal castings, rough or semifinished (inc. aluminum)	(X)	(D)
Steel bars, bar shapes, and plates (exc. castings, forgings, fabr. metal products)	(X)	(D)
Steel sheet and strip (including tinplate)	(X)	(D)
All other steel shapes and forms (exc. castings, forgings, fabr. metal products)	(X)	(D)
Aluminum and aluminum-base alloy shapes and forms (exc. castings, forgings, fabr. metal products)	(X)	(D)
Nonferrous wire and cable (incl. magnet wire, bare wire or insulated wire, etc.)	(X)	(D)
Fractional horsepower electric motors and generators (less than 1 hp)	(X)	78.0
Integral horsepower electric motors and generators (1 hp or more)	(X)	77.5
Paper and paperboard containers (incl. shipping sacks and other paper packaging supplies)	(X)	50.2
Electrical transmission, distribution, and control equipment	(X)	5.1
Current-carrying wiring devices	(X)	(D)
Automatic temperature controls (thermostats, regulators, etc.)	(X)	(D)
Paints, varnishes, stains, lacquers, shellacs, japans, enamels, etc.	(X)	(D)
Fabricated rubber products (exc. tires, tubes, hoses, belting, and gaskets)	(X)	(D)
Rubber and plastics hose and belting	(X)	57.4
Plastics products consumed in the form of sheets, rods, etc.	(X)	132.9
Plastics resins consumed in the form of granules, pellets, etc.	(X)	132.0
Complete flexible cord sets	(X)	19.4
Resistors, capacitors, transformers, electron tubes, semiconductors, and other electronic components	(X)	18.6
All other materials, components, parts, containers, and supplies	(X)	246.0
Materials, ingredients, containers, and supplies, nsk	(X)	157.5

Source: 2002 *Economic Census*. Explanation of symbols used: (D): Withheld to avoid disclosure of competitive data; na: Not available; (S): Withheld because statistical norms were not met; (X): Not applicable; (Z): Less than half the unit shown; nec: Not elsewhere classified; nsk: Not specified by kind; - : zero; p : 10-19 percent estimated; q : 20-29 percent estimated.

PRODUCT SHARE DETAILS FOR ELECTRIC HOUSEWARES AND HOUSEHOLD FAN MANUFACTURING

Product or Product Class Shipments	Mil. $	Product or Product Class Shipments	Mil. $
ELECTRIC HOUSEWARES AND HOUSEHOLD FANS	1,993.2	appliances	65.2
Electric fans, except industrial-type	**662.8**	Parts for household electric fans	7.2
Small electric household appliances, except fans and wall		Parts for other small household electric appliances	58.0
and baseboard heating units for permanent installation	**1,254.1**	**Electric housewares and household fans, nsk, total**	**11.0**
Parts and attachments for small household electric			

Source: 2002 *Economic Census*. The values are product shipments in millions of dollars for 2002. Total product shipments may be lower or higher than industry shipments. See Introduction for a full discussion. Values of indented subcategories are summed in the main heading(s). The symbol (D) appears when data are withheld to prevent disclosure of competitive information. The abbreviation nsk stands for 'not specified by kind' and nec for 'not elsewhere classified'. A dash (-) means zero.

PRODUCT SHARE DETAILS FOR HOUSEHOLD VACUUM CLEANER MANUFACTURING

Product or Product Class Shipments	Mil. $	Product or Product Class Shipments	Mil. $
HOUSEHOLD VACUUM CLEANERS	2,277.6	Parts for household type vacuum cleaners, including	
Household vacuum cleaners, including parts and attachments	**(D)**	central system parts	123.9
Household vacuum cleaners, complete power units,		Household vacuum cleaners, upright-stick type, including	
central system type	(D)	parts, nsk	16.7
Household vacuum cleaners, hand type	(D)	**Floor waxing and floor polishing machines and parts**	**(D)**
Household vacuum cleaners, upright-stick type	1,246.9	Parts for floor waxing and floor polishing machines	(D)
Other household vacuum cleaners, general purpose		Floor waxing and floor polishing machines	(D)
types, including utility and canister tank types	193.9	**Household vacuum cleaners, including parts and**	
Attachments and cleaning tools for household vacuum		**attachments, nsk, total**	**8.1**
cleaners, including central system attachments	81.3		

Source: 2002 *Economic Census*. The values are product shipments in millions of dollars for 2002. Total product shipments may be lower or higher than industry shipments. See Introduction for a full discussion. Values of indented subcategories are summed in the main heading(s). The symbol (D) appears when data are withheld to prevent disclosure of competitive information. The abbreviation nsk stands for 'not specified by kind' and nec for 'not elsewhere classified'. A dash (-) means zero.

INPUTS AND OUTPUTS FOR SMALL ELECTRICAL APPLIANCE MANUFACTURING

Economic Sector or Industry Providing Inputs	%	Sector	Economic Sector or Industry Buying Outputs	%	Sector
Compensation of employees	20.8		Personal consumption expenditures	72.2	
Motors & generators	6.5	Manufg.	Exports of goods & services	8.5	Cap Inv
Plastics products, nec	6.1	Manufg.	Residential permanent site structures	4.8	Construct.
Wholesale trade	5.8	Trade	Personal care services	2.6	Services
Management of companies & enterprises	4.1	Services	Private fixed investment	2.4	
Plastics materials & resins	3.8	Manufg.	Nonresidential structures, nec	1.2	Construct.
Plastics packaging materials, film & sheet	3.3	Manufg.	Change in private inventories	1.1	In House
Advertising & related services	2.3	Services	S/L govt. invest., education	1.1	S/L Govt
Paperboard containers	2.3	Manufg.	Personal & household goods repair/maintenance	1.0	Services
Rubber & plastics hose & belting	1.5	Manufg.	Commercial & health care structures	1.0	Construct.
Iron & steel mills & ferroalloys	1.4	Manufg.	Educational services, nec	0.6	Services
Crowns & closures & metal stamping	1.2	Manufg.	Residential structures, nec	0.6	Construct.
Truck transportation	1.2	Util.	Plastics products, nec	0.6	Manufg.
Wiring devices	1.0	Manufg.	Maintenance/repair of nonresidential structures	0.6	Construct.
Automatic environmental controls	0.8	Manufg.	S/L govt. invest., other	0.3	S/L Govt
Turned products & screws, nuts, & bolts	0.8	Manufg.	Owner-occupied dwellings	0.3	
Copper rolling, drawing, extruding, & alloying	0.7	Manufg.	Telecommunications	0.2	Services
Semiconductors & related devices	0.6	Manufg.	Retail trade	0.1	Trade
Nonferrous metal foundries	0.6	Manufg.	Elementary & secondary schools	0.1	Services
Unlaminated plastics profile shapes	0.6	Manufg.			
Nonmetallic minerals, nec	0.6	Mining			
Power generation & supply	0.5	Util.			
Taxes on production & imports, less subsidies	0.4				
Real estate	0.4	Fin/R.E.			
Paints & coatings	0.4	Manufg.			
Postal service	0.4	Util.			
Printed circuit assemblies (electronic assemblies)	0.4	Manufg.			
Legal services	0.3	Services			
Noncomparable imports	0.3	Foreign			
Securities, commodity contracts, investments	0.3	Fin/R.E.			
Scientific research & development services	0.3	Services			
Relay & industrial controls	0.3	Manufg.			
Rail transportation	0.3	Util.			
Watches, clocks, & related devices	0.2	Manufg.			
Machine shops	0.2	Manufg.			
Ferrous metal foundries	0.2	Manufg.			
Laminated plastics plates, sheets, & shapes	0.2	Manufg.			
Lessors of nonfinancial assets	0.2	Fin/R.E.			
Nonferrous metal (ex. copper & aluminum) processing	0.2	Manufg.			
Automotive equipment rental & leasing	0.2	Fin/R.E.			
Maintenance/repair of nonresidential structures	0.2	Construct.			
Accounting, tax preparation, bookkeeping, & payroll	0.1	Services			
Cutting tools & machine tool accessories	0.1	Manufg.			

Continued on next page.

INPUTS AND OUTPUTS FOR SMALL ELECTRICAL APPLIANCE MANUFACTURING - Continued

Economic Sector or Industry Providing Inputs	%	Sector	Economic Sector or Industry Buying Outputs	%	Sector
Employment services	0.1	Services			
Telecommunications	0.1	Services			
Warehousing & storage	0.1	Util.			
Alumina refining & primary aluminum production	0.1	Manufg.			
Coating, engraving, heat treating & allied activities	0.1	Manufg.			
Natural gas distribution	0.1	Util.			
Services to buildings & dwellings	0.1	Services			
Electronic capacitors, resistors, coils, transformers	0.1	Manufg.			
Petroleum lubricating oil & grease	0.1	Manufg.			

Source: Benchmark Input-Output Accounts for the U.S. Economy, 2002, U.S. Department of Commerce, Washington, D.C., January 2008. The abbreviation nec stands for 'not elsewhere classified'.

OCCUPATIONS EMPLOYED BY HOUSEHOLD APPLIANCE MANUFACTURING

Occupation	% of Total 2006	Change to 2016	Occupation	% of Total 2006	Change to 2016
Team assemblers	25.6	-24.3	Customer service representatives	1.9	-16.8
Industrial truck & tractor operators	3.6	-31.9	Mechanical engineers	1.8	-24.3
Laborers & freight, stock, & material movers, hand	3.5	-31.9	Production workers, nec	1.6	-25.7
First-line supervisors/managers of production workers	3.4	-24.3	Maintenance & repair workers, general	1.4	-24.3
Cutting, punching, & press machine operators	3.3	-31.9	Electrical & electronic equipment assemblers	1.1	-39.5
Inspectors, testers, sorters, samplers, & weighers	3.0	-28.6	Coating, painting, & spraying machine operators	1.0	-28.1
Welders, cutters, solderers, & brazers	2.0	-19.5			

Source: Industry-Occupation Matrix, Bureau of Labor Statistics, December 4, 2007. These data are reported based on 4-digit NAICS categories but have been matched to corresponding 6-digit NAICS industry codes. The change reported for each occupation to the year 2016 is a percent of growth or decline as estimated by the Bureau of Labor Statistics. The abbreviation nec stands for 'not elsewhere classified'.

LOCATION BY STATE AND REGIONAL CONCENTRATION

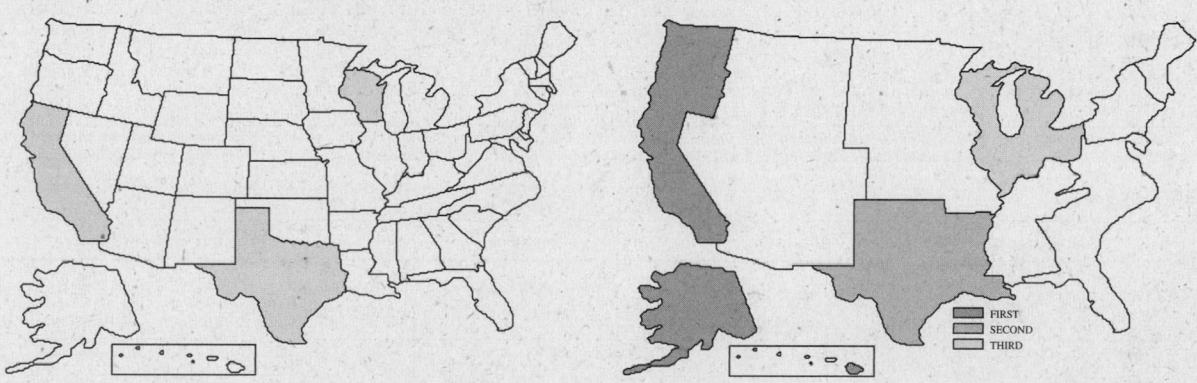

INDUSTRY DATA BY STATE

State	Establish- ments	Shipments			Employment				Cost as % of Shipments	Investment per Employee ($)
		Total ($ mil)	% of U.S.	Per Establ.	Total Number	% of U.S.	Per Establ.	Wages ($/hour)		
Wisconsin	6	453.7	8.8	75,622.5	1,678	8.5	280	19.15	48.5	2,616
Texas	7	139.3	2.7	19,902.7	776	3.9	111	9.21	63.7	4,995
California	14	23.7	0.5	1,695.9	152	0.8	11	9.09	44.1	2,618

Source: 2002 Economic Census. The states are in descending order of shipments or establishments (if shipment data are missing for the majority). The symbol (D) appears when data are withheld to prevent disclosure of competitive information. States marked with (D) are sorted by number of establishments. A dash (-) indicates that the data element cannot be calculated. Data may not show all states active in the NAICS category. All data available at the time of publication are shown.

NAICS 335221 - HOUSEHOLD COOKING APPLIANCE MANUFACTURING

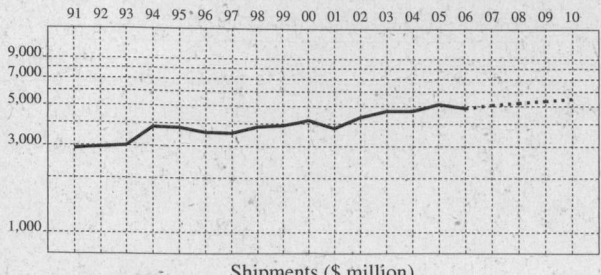

Shipments ($ million)

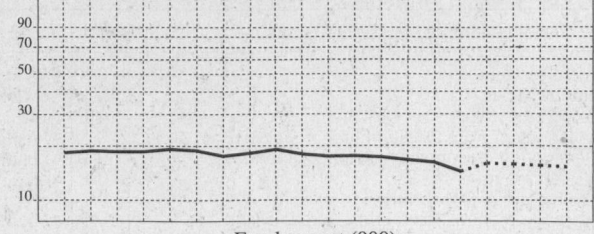

Employment (000)

GENERAL STATISTICS

Year	Companies	Establishments Total	Establishments with 20 or more employees	Employment Total (000)	Employment Production Workers (000)	Employment Hours (Mil)	Compensation Payroll ($ mil)	Compensation Wages ($/hr)	Production ($ million) Cost of Materials	Production ($ million) Value Added by Manufacture	Production ($ million) Value of Shipments	Production ($ million) Capital Invest.
1991		90	53	18.4	14.8	28.0	401.5	9.95	1,801.0	1,091.2	2,890.7	95.7
1992	80	89	43	18.8	15.0	29.9	437.0	9.81	1,811.7	1,141.4	2,950.0	82.9
1993		98	42	18.6	14.9	29.6	461.1	10.34	1,741.5	1,330.7	3,010.2	82.6
1994		97	43	18.6	15.0	30.2	491.2	10.69	1,922.1	1,908.0	3,813.9	101.6
1995		100	49	19.2	15.2	29.5	504.3	10.82	2,030.2	1,745.1	3,788.2	116.8
1996		103	48	18.9	14.7	29.4	517.4	11.30	2,190.8	1,288.0	3,564.7	144.2
1997	78	84	46	17.6	14.4	30.1	480.9	11.02	1,754.6	1,779.3	3,540.2	135.3
1998		96	51	18.2	15.3	29.8	523.1	11.98	2,225.7	1,705.0	3,849.2	214.3
1999		100	49	19.1	16.4	33.7	555.3	11.70	2,285.4	1,564.4	3,915.5	119.4
2000		91	48	18.0	15.3	32.2	512.2	11.06	2,387.4	1,699.7	4,179.0	120.5
2001		100	47	17.5	14.8	30.0	493.6	11.64	2,390.3	1,326.7	3,773.4	101.8
2002	87	97	46	17.6	14.4	26.9	487.3	12.54	2,737.5	1,612.2	4,339.1	112.2
2003		105	56	17.3	14.5	27.5	491.3	12.85	2,964.4	1,680.3	4,691.7	154.6
2004		117	52	16.7	14.1	28.4	506.8	13.44	3,184.1	1,535.3	4,699.5	116.8
2005		124	48	16.2	14.1	28.1	491.1	13.64	3,420.2	1,710.2	5,120.9	90.1
2006		112P	51P	14.4	12.7	24.6	439.7	13.84	3,248.9	1,627.6	4,864.3	84.5
2007		113P	51P	16.0P	14.0P	27.8P	508.0P	13.85P	3,390.8P	1,698.7P	5,076.8P	122.0P
2008		115P	52P	15.8P	13.9P	27.6P	510.4P	14.11P	3,480.4P	1,743.6P	5,210.9P	122.6P
2009		116P	52P	15.6P	13.8P	27.4P	512.9P	14.37P	3,570.0P	1,788.4P	5,345.0P	123.2P
2010		118P	52P	15.4P	13.7P	27.3P	515.3P	14.63P	3,659.5P	1,833.3P	5,479.1P	123.8P

Sources: 1992, 1997, 2002 *Economic Census*; other years, up to 2006, are from the *Annual Survey of Manufactures*. Establishment counts for non-Census years are from *County Business Patterns*; 1997 and 2002 values are from the 1997 and 2002 censuses respectively, reported in the Federal Government's NAICS format. Other years were originally reported in equivalent SIC format. 'P's show projections by the editors.

INDICES OF CHANGE

Year	Companies	Establishments Total	Establishments with 20 or more employees	Employment Total (000)	Employment Production Workers (000)	Employment Hours (Mil)	Compensation Payroll ($ mil)	Compensation Wages ($/hr)	Production ($ million) Cost of Materials	Production ($ million) Value Added by Manufacture	Production ($ million) Value of Shipments	Production ($ million) Capital Invest.
1992	92	92	93	107	104	111	90	78	66	71	68	74
1997	90	87	100	100	100	112	99	88	64	110	82	121
2001		103	102	99	103	112	101	93	87	82	87	91
2002	100	100	100	100	100	100	100	100	100	100	100	100
2003		108	122	98	101	102	101	102	108	104	108	138
2004		121	113	95	98	106	104	107	116	95	108	104
2005		128	104	92	98	104	101	109	125	106	118	80
2006		115P	111P	82	88	91	90	110	119	101	112	75
2007		117P	111P	91P	97P	103P	104P	110P	124P	105P	117P	109P
2008		118P	112P	90P	97P	103P	105P	113P	127P	108P	120P	109P
2009		120P	113P	89P	96P	102P	105P	115P	130P	111P	123P	110P
2010		122P	114P	88P	95P	101P	106P	117P	134P	114P	126P	110P

Sources: Same as General Statistics. Values reflect change from the base year, 2002. Values above 100 mean greater than 2002, values below 100 mean less than 2002, and the values of 100 in other years means the same as 2002. 'P's show projections by the editors.

SELECTED RATIOS

For 2002	Avg. of All Manufact.	Analyzed Industry	Index	For 2002	Avg. of All Manufact.	Analyzed Industry	Index
Employees per Establishment	42	181	432	Value Added per Production Worker	182,367	111,958	61
Payroll per Establishment	1,639,184	5,023,711	306	Cost per Establishment	5,769,015	28,221,649	489
Payroll per Employee	39,053	27,687	71	Cost per Employee	137,446	155,540	113
Production Workers per Establishment	30	148	503	Cost per Production Worker	195,506	190,104	97
Wages per Establishment	694,845	3,477,588	500	Shipments per Establishment	11,158,348	44,732,990	401
Wages per Production Worker	23,548	23,425	99	Shipments per Employee	265,847	246,540	93
Hours per Production Worker	1,980	1,868	94	Shipments per Production Worker	378,144	301,326	80
Wages per Hour	11.89	12.54	105	Investment per Establishment	361,338	1,156,701	320
Value Added per Establishment	5,381,325	16,620,619	309	Investment per Employee	8,609	6,375	74
Value Added per Employee	128,210	91,602	71	Investment per Production Worker	12,245	7,792	64

Sources: Same as General Statistics. The 'Average of All Manufacturing' column represents the average of all manufacturing industries reported for the most recent complete year available. The Index shows the relationship between the Average and the Analyzed Industry. For example, 100 means that they are equal; 500 that the Analyzed Industry is five times the average; 50 means that the Analyzed Industry is half the national average. The abbreviation 'na' is used to show that data are 'not available'. Ratios shown for 2002, the last complete census year.

LEADING COMPANIES   Number shown: **36**   Total sales ($ mil): **25,086**   Total employment (000): **91.6**

Company Name	Address				CEO Name	Phone	Co. Type	Sales ($ mil)	Empl. (000)
Whirlpool Corp.	Whirlpool Center	Benton Harbor	MI	49022		269-923-5000	P	19,408	73.0
NACCO Industries Inc.	5875 Landerbrook	Mayfield Hgts	OH	44124		440-449-9600	P	3,603	10.2
Salton Inc.	1955 W Field Ct.	Lake Forest	IL	60045	Leonhard Dreimann	847-803-4600	P	523	1.0
Lifetime Brands Inc.	1000 Stewart Ave.	Garden City	NY	11530	Jeffrey Siegel	516-683-6000	P	494	1.5
Coleman Company Inc.	258 Beacon Street	Somerset	PA	15501	Bill Phillips		S	389*	2.3
Unaka Company Inc.	1500 Industrial Rd.	Greeneville	TN	37745	Robert Austin	423-639-1171	R	89*	0.8
Dacor Inc.	950 S Raymond	Pasadena	CA	91105	Ric Brutocao	626-799-1000	R	82*	0.5
Brinkmann, J Baxter Intl.	4215 McEwen Rd.	Dallas	TX	75244	Baxter Brinkmann	972-387-4939	R	69*	<0.1
Little Tikes Commercial Inc.	PO Box 897	Farmington	MO	63640		573-756-4591	S	56*	0.5
Peerless-Premier Appliance Co.	PO Box 387	Belleville	IL	62222	Joseph Geary	618-233-0475	R	50*	0.3
Weber-Stephen Products Co.	200 E Daniels Rd.	Palatine	IL	60067		847-934-5700	R	37*	0.3
Keurig Inc.	101 Edgewater Dr.	Wakefield	MA	01880	Nick Lazaris	781-246-3466	S	37	<0.1
Empire Comfort Systems Inc.	PO Box 529	Belleville	IL	62222	Brian Bauer	618-233-7420	R	30*	0.2
Meco Corp.	1500 Industrial Rd.	Greeneville	TN	37745	Robert Austin	423-639-1171	R	22*	0.1
Metal Ware Corp.	PO Box 237	Two Rivers	WI	54241	Wesley Drumm	920-793-1368	R	20*	0.1
Traeger Pellet Grills L.L.C.	990 N 1st Street	Silverton	OR	97381		503-845-9234	R	20*	<0.1
Thermal Engineering Corp.	PO Box 868	Columbia	SC	29202	William Best	803-783-0750	R	18*	0.1
United States Stove Co.	227 Industrial Park	South Pittsburg	TN	37380	Charles Layman		R	17*	0.1
Fiesta Gas Grills L.L.C.	1 Fiesta Dr.	Dickson	TN	37055		615-446-1800	R	16*	<0.1
Strategic Products Inc.	5100 Laguna Vista	Melbourne	FL	32934	Art Markuson	321-752-0441	R	15*	<0.1
American Harvest Inc.	PO Box 237	Two Rivers	WI	54241	Wess Drumm	920-793-1368	S	15*	<0.1
BB Robertson Co.	5003 Meadowland	Marion	IL	62959	Mike Robertson	618-997-9348	BB	8*	<0.1
Masterbuilt Manufacturing Inc.	450 Brown Ave.	Columbus	GA	31906	John Lemore	706-327-5622	R	7*	<0.1
Island Bbqs and Fireside	29360 Hunco Way	Lake Elsinore	CA	92530	Matt Doll	951-245-5340	R	7*	<0.1
KRH Thermal Systems L.L.C.	17462 Armstrong	Irvine	CA	92614		949-250-4477	R	6*	<0.1
David B Knight and Associates	333 N Main St.	Cape Girardeau	MO	63701	David Knight	573-334-6512	R	6*	<0.1
Oscarware Inc.	PO Box 40	Bonnieville	KY	42713	Debra Dudley	270-531-2860	R	6*	<0.1
Cervitor Kitchens Inc.	10775 Lower Azusa	El Monte	CA	91731	Mary Crowley	626-443-0184	R	5*	<0.1
Kenyon International Inc.	PO Box 925	Clinton	CT	06413	Phillip Williams	860-664-4906	R	5*	<0.1
Metal Fusion Inc.	712 Saint George	Jefferson	LA	70121	Norman Bourgeois	504-736-0201	R	5*	<0.1
Modern Home Products Corp.	150 Ram Rd.	Antioch	IL	60002	Ted Koziol	847-395-6556	R	5*	<0.1
Thermodyne Food Service Prods	4418 New Haven	Fort Wayne	IN	46803	Vincent Tippmann	260-428-2535	R	4*	<0.1
Berwick Lighting Corp.	335 S Poplar St.	Berwick	PA	18603	Frank Bedosky	570-759-0346	R	3*	<0.1
Traeger Industries Inc.	PO Box 829	Mount Angel	OR	97362	Joseph Traeger	503-845-9234	R	3*	<0.1
Applied Research Laboratories	5371 NW 161st St.	Hialeah	FL	33014	Alan Sukert	305-624-4800	R	3*	<0.1
Deluxe Equipment Company Inc.	4414 28th St. W	Bradenton	FL	34207	Gib Smith	941-753-4184	R	2	<0.1

Source: Ward's Business Directory of U.S. Private and Public Companies, Volumes 1 and 2, 2008. The company type code used is as follows: P - Public, R - Private, S - Subsidiary, D - Division, J - Joint Venture, A - Affiliate, G - Group. Sales are in millions of dollars, employees are in thousands. An asterisk (*) indicates an estimated sales volume. The symbol < stands for 'less than'. Company names and addresses are truncated, in some cases, to fit into the available space.

MATERIALS CONSUMED

Material	Quantity	Delivered Cost ($ million)
Metal stampings	(X)	258.3
Metal bolts, nuts, screws, and other screw machine products	(X)	43.1
All other fabricated metal products (excluding forgings)	(X)	213.7
Forgings	(X)	(D)
Iron and steel castings (rough and semifinished)	(X)	49.1
Aluminum and aluminum-base alloy castings (rough and semifinished)	(X)	89.8
Other nonferrous metal castings, rough or semifinished (inc. aluminum)	(X)	(D)
Steel bars, bar shapes, and plates (exc. castings, forgings, fabr. metal products)	(X)	3.1
Steel sheet and strip (including tinplate)	(X)	199.2
All other steel shapes and forms (exc. castings, forgings, fabr. metal products)	(X)	78.5
Aluminum and aluminum-base alloy shapes and forms (exc. castings, forgings, fabr. metal products)	(X)	36.6
Other nonferrous shapes and forms (exc. castings, forgings, fabricated metal products)	(X)	15.3
Nonferrous wire and cable (incl. magnet wire, bare wire or insulated wire, etc.)	(X)	9.1
Fractional horsepower electric motors and generators (less than 1 hp)	(X)	23.0
Integral horsepower electric motors and generators (1 hp or more)	(X)	(D)
Paper and paperboard containers (incl. shipping sacks and other paper packaging supplies)	(X)	104.1
Electrical transmission, distribution, and control equipment	(X)	158.1
Current-carrying wiring devices	(X)	62.2
Timing mechanisms (excluding microprocessors)	(X)	(D)
Automatic temperature controls (thermostats, regulators, etc.)	(X)	80.0
Paints, varnishes, stains, lacquers, shellacs, japans, enamels, etc.	(X)	49.0
Fabricated rubber products (exc. tires, tubes, hoses, belting, and gaskets)	(X)	5.9
Rubber and plastics hose and belting	(X)	(D)
Plastics products consumed in the form of sheets, rods, etc.	(X)	112.1
Plastics resins consumed in the form of granules, pellets, etc.	(X)	(D)
Complete flexible cord sets	(X)	(D)
Resistors, capacitors, transformers, electron tubes, semiconductors, and other electronic components	(X)	124.2
Mineral wool insulation (fibrous glass, rock wool, etc.)	(X)	121.3
All other materials, components, parts, containers, and supplies	(X)	564.5
Materials, ingredients, containers, and supplies, nsk	(X)	131.7

Source: 2002 *Economic Census*. Explanation of symbols used: (D): Withheld to avoid disclosure of competitive data; na: Not available; (S): Withheld because statistical norms were not met; (X): Not applicable; (Z): Less than half the unit shown; nec: Not elsewhere classified; nsk: Not specified by kind; - : zero; p : 10-19 percent estimated; q : 20-29 percent estimated.

PRODUCT SHARE DETAILS

Product or Product Class Shipments	Mil. $	Product or Product Class Shipments	Mil. $
HOUSEHOLD COOKING APPLIANCES	4,138.5	equipment	802.1
Electric household ranges, ovens, surface cooking units, and equipment, including microwave ovens	**2,075.8**	Parts and accessories for gas household ranges and ovens, such as burners, rotisseries, oven racks, broiler pans, etc.	46.2
Electric household ranges, ovens, surface cooking units, and equipment	1,973.7	**Other household ranges and cooking equipment**	**1,182.5**
Parts and accessories for electric household ranges and ovens, such as burners, rotisseries, oven racks, broiler pans, etc., sold separately	102.1	Other household ranges and cooking equipment (except gas and electric), and outdoor cooking equipment	1,116.2
Gas household ranges, ovens, surface cooking units, and equipment, including parts and accessories	**848.3**	Parts and accessories for outdoor and other cooking equipment, sold separately	66.4
Gas household ranges, ovens, surface cooking units, and		**Household cooking appliances, nsk, total**	**31.8**

Source: 2002 *Economic Census*. The values are product shipments in millions of dollars for 2002. Total product shipments may be lower or higher than industry shipments. See Introduction for a full discussion. Values of indented subcategories are summed in the main heading(s). The symbol (D) appears when data are withheld to prevent disclosure of competitive information. The abbreviation nsk stands for 'not specified by kind' and nec for 'not elsewhere classified'. A dash (-) means zero.

INPUTS AND OUTPUTS FOR HOUSEHOLD COOKING APPLIANCE MANUFACTURING

Economic Sector or Industry Providing Inputs	%	Sector	Economic Sector or Industry Buying Outputs	%	Sector
Compensation of employees	16.0		Personal consumption expenditures	64.3	
Wholesale trade	6.9	Trade	Private fixed investment	24.7	
Crowns & closures & metal stamping	6.8	Manufg.	Exports of goods & services	4.3	Cap Inv
Plastics products, nec	6.4	Manufg.	Personal & household goods repair/maintenance	2.1	Services
Iron & steel mills & ferroalloys	5.9	Manufg.	Change in private inventories	1.2	In House
Management of companies & enterprises	3.3	Services	Commercial & industrial machinery rental & leasing	0.9	Fin/R.E.
Mineral wool	3.1	Manufg.	Retail trade	0.8	Trade
Semiconductors & related devices	2.5	Manufg.	S/L govt. invest., education	0.8	S/L Govt
Relay & industrial controls	2.3	Manufg.	S/L govt. invest., other	0.2	S/L Govt
Paperboard containers	2.3	Manufg.	Manufactured homes & mobile homes	0.2	Manufg.
Plastics packaging materials, film & sheet	2.3	Manufg.	Federal government, investment, national defense	0.2	Fed Govt
Nonferrous metal foundries	2.1	Manufg.	Motor homes	0.1	Manufg.
Automatic environmental controls	2.0	Manufg.	Wholesale trade	0.1	Trade
Paints & coatings	1.9	Manufg.			
Turned products & screws, nuts, & bolts	1.5	Manufg.			
Wiring devices	1.4	Manufg.			
Advertising & related services	1.2	Services			
Watches, clocks, & related devices	1.1	Manufg.			
Machine shops	1.1	Manufg.			
Ferrous metal foundries	1.0	Manufg.			
Truck transportation	0.9	Util.			
Coating, engraving, heat treating & allied activities	0.9	Manufg.			
Alumina refining & primary aluminum production	0.8	Manufg.			
Motors & generators	0.5	Manufg.			
Software publishers	0.5	Services			
Power generation & supply	0.4	Util.			
Metal cans, boxes, & other containers (light gauge)	0.4	Manufg.			
Electronic capacitors, resistors, coils, transformers	0.4	Manufg.			
Printed circuit assemblies (electronic assemblies)	0.4	Manufg.			
Unlaminated plastics profile shapes	0.4	Manufg.			
Lessors of nonfinancial assets	0.4	Fin/R.E.			
Fabricated metals, nec	0.3	Manufg.			
Securities, commodity contracts, investments	0.3	Fin/R.E.			
Real estate	0.3	Fin/R.E.			
Natural gas distribution	0.3	Util.			
Aluminum products from purchased aluminum	0.3	Manufg.			
Plate work & fabricated structural products	0.3	Manufg.			
Automotive equipment rental & leasing	0.2	Fin/R.E.			
Ball & roller bearings	0.2	Manufg.			
Handtools	0.2	Manufg.			
Valve & fittings other than plumbing	0.2	Manufg.			
Nonferrous metal (ex. copper & aluminum) processing	0.2	Manufg.			
Custom roll forming	0.2	Manufg.			
Scientific research & development services	0.2	Services			
Taxes on production & imports, less subsidies	0.2				
Specialized design services	0.2	Services			
Maintenance/repair of nonresidential structures	0.2	Construct.			
Bare printed circuit boards	0.2	Manufg.			
Postal service	0.2	Util.			
Services to buildings & dwellings	0.2	Services			
Rail transportation	0.1	Util.			
Legal services	0.1	Services			
Laminated plastics plates, sheets, & shapes	0.1	Manufg.			
Commercial & industrial machinery rental & leasing	0.1	Fin/R.E.			
Management, scientific, & technical consulting	0.1	Services			
Rubber & plastics hose & belting	0.1	Manufg.			
Warehousing & storage	0.1	Util.			

Continued on next page.

INPUTS AND OUTPUTS FOR HOUSEHOLD COOKING APPLIANCE MANUFACTURING - Continued

Economic Sector or Industry Providing Inputs	%	Sector	Economic Sector or Industry Buying Outputs	%	Sector
Architectural, engineering, & related services	0.1	Services			
Automotive repair & maintenance, ex. car washes	0.1	Services			
Electronic components, nec	0.1	Manufg.			
Springs & wire products	0.1	Manufg.			
Petroleum lubricating oil & grease	0.1	Manufg.			

Source: Benchmark Input-Output Accounts for the U.S. Economy, 2002, U.S. Department of Commerce, Washington, D.C., January 2008. The abbreviation nec stands for 'not elsewhere classified'.

OCCUPATIONS EMPLOYED BY HOUSEHOLD APPLIANCE MANUFACTURING

Occupation	% of Total 2006	Change to 2016	Occupation	% of Total 2006	Change to 2016
Team assemblers	25.6	-24.3	Customer service representatives	1.9	-16.8
Industrial truck & tractor operators	3.6	-31.9	Mechanical engineers	1.8	-24.3
Laborers & freight, stock, & material movers, hand	3.5	-31.9	Production workers, nec	1.6	-25.7
First-line supervisors/managers of production workers	3.4	-24.3	Maintenance & repair workers, general	1.4	-24.3
Cutting, punching, & press machine operators	3.3	-31.9	Electrical & electronic equipment assemblers	1.1	-39.5
Inspectors, testers, sorters, samplers, & weighers	3.0	-28.6	Coating, painting, & spraying machine operators	1.0	-28.1
Welders, cutters, solderers, & brazers	2.0	-19.5			

Source: Industry-Occupation Matrix, Bureau of Labor Statistics, December 4, 2007. These data are reported based on 4-digit NAICS categories but have been matched to corresponding 6-digit NAICS industry codes. The change reported for each occupation to the year 2016 is a percent of growth or decline as estimated by the Bureau of Labor Statistics. The abbreviation nec stands for 'not elsewhere classified'.

LOCATION BY STATE AND REGIONAL CONCENTRATION

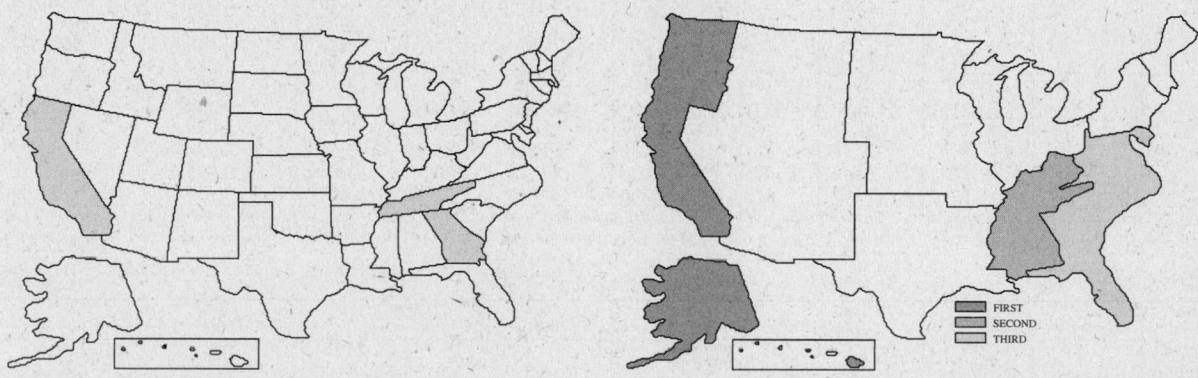

INDUSTRY DATA BY STATE

State	Establish-ments	Shipments Total ($ mil)	Shipments % of U.S.	Shipments Per Establ.	Employment Total Number	Employment % of U.S.	Employment Per Establ.	Wages ($/hour)	Cost as % of Shipments	Investment per Employee ($)
Tennessee	10	1,377.9	31.8	137,785.7	6,091	34.6	609	12.74	66.6	6,629
Georgia	9	1,107.0	25.5	122,994.7	4,069	23.1	452	13.31	70.6	7,681
California	15	253.3	5.8	16,885.6	1,288	7.3	86	9.29	43.1	2,109

Source: 2002 Economic Census. The states are in descending order of shipments or establishments (if shipment data are missing for the majority). The symbol (D) appears when data are withheld to prevent disclosure of competitive information. States marked with (D) are sorted by number of establishments. A dash (-) indicates that the data element cannot be calculated. Data may not show all states active in the NAICS category. All data available at the time of publication are shown.

NAICS 335222 - HOUSEHOLD REFRIGERATOR AND HOME FREEZER MANUFACTURING

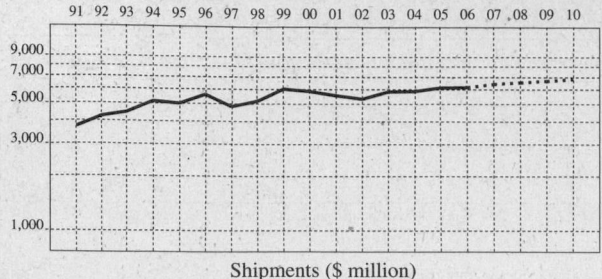

Shipments ($ million)

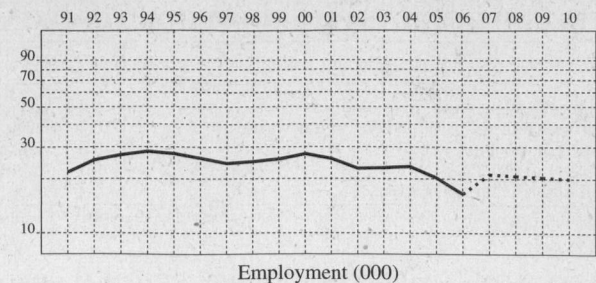

Employment (000)

GENERAL STATISTICS

Year	Companies	Establishments Total	Establishments with 20 or more employees	Employment Total (000)	Employment Production Workers (000)	Employment Hours (Mil)	Compensation Payroll ($ mil)	Compensation Wages ($/hr)	Cost of Materials	Value Added by Manufacture	Value of Shipments	Capital Invest.
1991		48	22	21.8	17.8	35.8	605.5	12.85	2,238.4	1,386.9	3,721.3	168.7
1992	52	58	19	25.4	21.4	41.5	719.0	12.81	2,596.6	1,629.1	4,232.4	187.4
1993		54	22	27.1	22.5	42.6	741.5	13.21	2,883.7	1,602.4	4,463.1	139.9
1994		53	22	28.3	23.9	46.3	817.6	13.43	3,329.7	1,909.7	5,149.1	170.5
1995		61	26	27.6	22.7	43.7	834.3	14.12	3,365.4	1,609.4	5,005.6	175.6
1996		66	29	26.1	21.9	41.2	809.6	15.04	3,350.2	2,156.0	5,604.6	191.2
1997	19	25	21	24.4	21.4	40.9	794.4	15.76	2,896.7	1,925.4	4,825.6	92.7
1998		26	20	24.9	22.1	42.4	837.3	16.25	3,182.1	2,035.9	5,188.2	108.5
1999		27	22	25.7	22.6	44.1	873.7	15.96	3,471.2	2,585.7	6,038.5	166.0
2000		29	23	27.4	24.1	45.9	978.2	17.17	3,643.2	2,349.8	5,863.7	248.0
2001		33	23	25.8	22.6	43.5	910.6	17.04	3,405.5	2,018.1	5,561.6	197.0
2002	16	23	19	22.8	19.9	37.2	796.2	17.36	3,199.9	2,045.7	5,332.3	148.6
2003		29	23	23.0	20.2	37.0	797.3	17.58	3,265.5	2,548.6	5,834.7	131.8
2004		25	21	23.4	20.1	36.0	812.9	18.50	3,597.2	2,284.5	5,872.2	125.4
2005		29	20	20.3	17.5	32.3	716.7	18.36	3,564.9	2,565.8	6,144.0	69.0
2006		18P	21P	16.5	14.7	26.8	673.8	20.90	3,277.9	2,854.8	6,171.4	57.2
2007		16P	21P	21.2P	18.9P	34.5P	825.2P	20.08P	3,414.9P	2,974.1P	6,429.4P	106.6P
2008		13P	21P	20.8P	18.7P	33.8P	828.8P	20.56P	3,484.7P	3,034.9P	6,560.7P	101.7P
2009		10P	21P	20.4P	18.4P	33.2P	832.3P	21.04P	3,554.4P	3,095.6P	6,692.1P	96.8P
2010		8P	21P	20.0P	18.2P	32.6P	835.9P	21.52P	3,624.2P	3,156.4P	6,823.4P	91.8P

Sources: 1992, 1997, 2002 *Economic Census*; other years, up to 2006, are from the *Annual Survey of Manufactures*. Establishment counts for non-Census years are from *County Business Patterns*; 1997 and 2002 values are from the 1997 and 2002 censuses respectively, reported in the Federal Government's NAICS format. Other years were originally reported in equivalent SIC format. 'P's show projections by the editors.

INDICES OF CHANGE

Year	Companies	Establishments Total	Establishments with 20 or more employees	Employment Total (000)	Employment Production Workers (000)	Employment Hours (Mil)	Compensation Payroll ($ mil)	Compensation Wages ($/hr)	Cost of Materials	Value Added by Manufacture	Value of Shipments	Capital Invest.
1992	325	252	100	111	108	112	90	74	81	80	79	126
1997	119	109	111	107	108	110	100	91	91	94	90	62
2001		143	121	113	114	117	114	98	106	99	104	133
2002	100	100	100	100	100	100	100	100	100	100	100	100
2003		126	121	101	102	99	100	101	102	125	109	89
2004		109	111	103	101	97	102	107	112	112	110	84
2005		126	105	89	88	87	90	106	111	125	115	46
2006		79P	112P	72	74	72	85	120	102	140	116	38
2007		67P	112P	93P	95P	93P	104P	116P	107P	145P	121P	72P
2008		56P	111P	91P	94P	91P	104P	118P	109P	148P	123P	68P
2009		45P	111P	89P	92P	89P	105P	121P	111P	151P	126P	65P
2010		33P	110P	88P	91P	88P	105P	124P	113P	154P	128P	62P

Sources: Same as General Statistics. Values reflect change from the base year, 2002. Values above 100 mean greater than 2002, values below 100 mean less than 2002, and the values of 100 in other years means the same as 2002. 'P's show projections by the editors.

SELECTED RATIOS

For 2002	Avg. of All Manufact.	Analyzed Industry	Index	For 2002	Avg. of All Manufact.	Analyzed Industry	Index
Employees per Establishment	42	991	2,362	Value Added per Production Worker	182,367	102,799	56
Payroll per Establishment	1,639,184	34,617,391	2,112	Cost per Establishment	5,769,015	139,126,087	2,412
Payroll per Employee	39,053	34,921	89	Cost per Employee	137,446	140,346	102
Production Workers per Establishment	30	865	2,932	Cost per Production Worker	195,506	160,799	82
Wages per Establishment	694,845	28,077,913	4,041	Shipments per Establishment	11,158,348	231,839,130	2,078
Wages per Production Worker	23,548	32,452	138	Shipments per Employee	265,847	233,873	88
Hours per Production Worker	1,980	1,869	94	Shipments per Production Worker	378,144	267,955	71
Wages per Hour	11.89	17.36	146	Investment per Establishment	361,338	6,460,870	1,788
Value Added per Establishment	5,381,325	88,943,478	1,653	Investment per Employee	8,609	6,518	76
Value Added per Employee	128,210	89,724	70	Investment per Production Worker	12,245	7,467	61

Sources: Same as General Statistics. The 'Average of All Manufacturing' column represents the average of all manufacturing industries reported for the most recent complete year available. The Index shows the relationship between the Average and the Analyzed Industry. For example, 100 means that they are equal; 500 that the Analyzed Industry is five times the average; 50 means that the Analyzed Industry is half the national average. The abbreviation 'na' is used to show that data are 'not available'. Ratios shown for 2002, the last complete census year.

LEADING COMPANIES   Number shown: 22   Total sales ($ mil): 21,743   Total employment (000): 78.6

Company Name	Address				CEO Name	Phone	Co. Type	Sales ($ mil)	Empl. (000)
Whirlpool Corp.	Whirlpool Center	Benton Harbor	MI	49022	James Bakke	269-923-5000	P	19,408	73.0
Sub-Zero Inc.	4717 Hammersley	Madison	WI	53711	James Bakke	608-271-2233	R	758*	3.0
Norcold Inc.	PO Box 180	Sidney	OH	45365	Jack Tierney	937-497-3080	S	600*	0.3
Thetford Corp.	PO Box 1285	Ann Arbor	MI	48106	Michael Harris	734-769-6000	R	600*	0.2
Delfield Co.	980 S Isabella Rd.	Mt. Pleasant	MI	48858	Kevin Clark	989-773-7981	D	108*	0.7
National Refrigeration Co.	PO Box 148	Honea Path	SC	29654	James Kaufman	864-369-1665	R	50*	0.2
Kolpak Walk-Ins	2915 Tennessee	Parsons	TN	38363	Alex Best	715-425-6741	S	42*	0.2
U-Line Corp.	PO Box 245040	Milwaukee	WI	53224	Philip Uihlein	414-354-0300	R	40*	0.2
Cleveland Range Co.	1333 E 179th St.	Cleveland	OH	44110	Rick Cutler	216-481-4900	S	39*	0.2
Champion Industries Inc.	PO Box 4149	Winston-Salem	NC	27115	Hank Holt	336-661-1556	R	28*	0.1
Equipment Brokers Inc.	720 Northwestern	Audubon	IA	50025	Jorge Defarias	712-563-4623	R	28*	0.1
BB Robertson Co.	5003 Meadowland	Marion	IL	62959	Mike Robertson	618-997-9348	R	8*	<0.1
HA Phillips and Co.	1612 Louise Dr.	South Elgin	IL	60177		847-289-0050	R	6*	<0.1
Cervitor Kitchens Inc.	10775 Lower Azusa	El Monte	CA	91731	Mary Crowley	626-443-0184	R	5*	<0.1
Forma-Kool Manufacturing Inc.	46880 Continental	Chesterfield	MI	48047	Andrew Tassopoulos	586-949-4813	R	5*	<0.1
Coldvault L.L.C.	PO Box 1690	Henderson	TX	75653		903-657-2377	R	4*	<0.1
Scientemp Corp.	3565 S Adrian Hwy.	Adrian	MI	49221	Howard Tenniswood	517-263-6020	R	4*	<0.1
B Frank Inc.	300 71st St., 435	Miami Beach	FL	33141	Bernard Frank	305-861-8227	R	3*	<0.1
Sun Frost	PO Box 1101	Arcata	CA	95518	Larry Schussler	707-822-9095	R	3*	<0.1
Applied Research Laboratories	5371 NW 161st St.	Hialeah	FL	33014	Alan Sukert	305-624-4800	R	3*	<0.1
Acme Kitchenettes Corp.	PO Box 348	Hudson	NY	12534	Nick Peros	518-828-4191	R	3*	<0.1
Medelco Inc.	2 Corporate Dr.	Trumbull	CT	06611	Walter Wolczek	203-445-0640	R	1*	<0.1

Source: *Ward's Business Directory of U.S. Private and Public Companies*, Volumes 1 and 2, 2008. The company type code used is as follows: P - Public, R - Private, S - Subsidiary, D - Division, J - Joint Venture, A - Affiliate, G - Group. Sales are in millions of dollars, employees are in thousands. An asterisk (*) indicates an estimated sales volume. The symbol < stands for 'less than'. Company names and addresses are truncated, in some cases, to fit into the available space.

MATERIALS CONSUMED

Material	Quantity	Delivered Cost ($ million)
Metal stampings	(X)	112.1
Metal bolts, nuts, screws, and other screw machine products	(X)	25.7
All other fabricated metal products (excluding forgings)	(X)	62.4
Iron and steel castings (rough and semifinished)	(X)	(D)
Aluminum and aluminum-base alloy castings (rough and semifinished)	(X)	11.7
Other nonferrous metal castings, rough or semifinished (inc. aluminum)	(X)	6.7
Steel bars, bar shapes, and plates (exc. castings, forgings, fabr. metal products)	(X)	(D)
Steel sheet and strip (including tinplate)	(X)	209.5
All other steel shapes and forms (exc. castings, forgings, fabr. metal products)	(X)	184.1
Aluminum and aluminum-base alloy shapes and forms (exc. castings, forgings, fabr. metal products)	(X)	(D)
Other nonferrous shapes and forms (exc. castings, forgings, fabricated metal products)	(X)	44.9
Nonferrous wire and cable (incl. magnet wire, bare wire or insulated wire, etc.)	(X)	44.5
Fractional horsepower electric motors and generators (less than 1 hp)	(X)	222.4
Paper and paperboard containers (incl. shipping sacks and other paper packaging supplies)	(X)	119.1
Electrical transmission, distribution, and control equipment	(X)	161.1
Current-carrying wiring devices	(X)	51.1
Timing mechanisms (excluding microprocessors)	(X)	20.6
Automatic temperature controls (thermostats, regulators, etc.)	(X)	42.9
Paints, varnishes, stains, lacquers, shellacs, japans, enamels, etc.	(X)	33.9
Fabricated rubber products (exc. tires, tubes, hoses, belting, and gaskets)	(X)	23.7
Rubber and plastics hose and belting	(X)	29.9
Plastics products consumed in the form of sheets, rods, etc.	(X)	525.9
Plastics resins consumed in the form of granules, pellets, etc.	(X)	222.6
Complete flexible cord sets	(X)	27.4
Resistors, capacitors, transformers, electron tubes, semiconductors, and other electronic components	(X)	83.9
Mineral wool insulation (fibrous glass, rock wool, etc.)	(X)	6.6
All other materials, components, parts, containers, and supplies	(X)	653.6
Materials, ingredients, containers, and supplies, nsk	(X)	76.9

Source: 2002 *Economic Census*. Explanation of symbols used: (D): Withheld to avoid disclosure of competitive data; na: Not available; (S): Withheld because statistical norms were not met; (X): Not applicable; (Z): Less than half the unit shown; nec: Not elsewhere classified; nsk: Not specified by kind; - : zero; p : 10-19 percent estimated; q : 20-29 percent estimated.

PRODUCT SHARE DETAILS

Product or Product Class Shipments	Mil. $	Product or Product Class Shipments	Mil. $
HOUSEHOLD REFRIGERATORS, FREEZERS, PARTS AND ATTACHMENTS	5,140.5	**Parts and attachments for household refrigerators and freezers**	(D)
Household refrigerators, including combination refrigerator-freezers	4,632.5	**Household refrigerators, freezers, parts and attachments, nsk, total**	0.4
Household food freezers, complete units	(D)		

Source: 2002 *Economic Census*. The values are product shipments in millions of dollars for 2002. Total product shipments may be lower or higher than industry shipments. See Introduction for a full discussion. Values of indented subcategories are summed in the main heading(s). The symbol (D) appears when data are withheld to prevent disclosure of competitive information. The abbreviation nsk stands for 'not specified by kind' and nec for 'not elsewhere classified'. A dash (-) means zero.

INPUTS AND OUTPUTS FOR HOUSEHOLD REFRIGERATOR AND HOME FREEZER MANUFACTURING

Economic Sector or Industry Providing Inputs	%	Sector	Economic Sector or Industry Buying Outputs	%	Sector
Compensation of employees	22.2		Personal consumption expenditures	58.1	
Wholesale trade	7.8	Trade	Private fixed investment	26.8	
Plastics packaging materials, film & sheet	7.3	Manufg.	Exports of goods & services	10.0	Cap Inv.
Iron & steel mills & ferroalloys	6.1	Manufg.	Personal & household goods repair/maintenance	1.5	Services
AC, refrigeration, and warm air heating equipment	6.0	Manufg.	S/L govt. invest., education	1.3	S/L Govt
Management of companies & enterprises	4.2	Services	S/L govt. invest., other	0.6	S/L Govt
Motors & generators	3.5	Manufg.	Change in private inventories	0.5	In House
Plastics materials & resins	3.3	Manufg.	Manufactured homes & mobile homes	0.5	Manufg.
Plastics products, nec	2.6	Manufg.	Motor homes	0.3	Manufg.
Crowns & closures & metal stamping	2.1	Manufg.	Travel trailers & campers	0.2	Manufg.
Rubber products, nec	2.0	Manufg.	Retail trade	0.1	Trade
Paperboard containers	1.9	Manufg.			
Relay & industrial controls	1.8	Manufg.			
Semiconductors & related devices	1.3	Manufg.			
Unlaminated plastics profile shapes	1.3	Manufg.			
Truck transportation	1.0	Util.			
Wiring devices	0.8	Manufg.			
Paints & coatings	0.8	Manufg.			
Automatic environmental controls	0.8	Manufg.			
Nonferrous metal (ex. copper & aluminum) processing	0.8	Manufg.			
Turned products & screws, nuts, & bolts	0.5	Manufg.			
Rubber & plastics hose & belting	0.5	Manufg.			
Aluminum products from purchased aluminum	0.5	Manufg.			
Power generation & supply	0.5	Util.			
Alumina refining & primary aluminum production	0.5	Manufg.			
Copper rolling, drawing, extruding, & alloying	0.4	Manufg.			
Laminated plastics plates, sheets, & shapes	0.4	Manufg.			
Machine shops	0.3	Manufg.			
Nonferrous metal foundries	0.3	Manufg.			
Printed circuit assemblies (electronic assemblies)	0.3	Manufg.			
Specialized design services	0.3	Services			
Lessors of nonfinancial assets	0.3	Fin/R.E.			
Watches, clocks, & related devices	0.3	Manufg.			
Advertising & related services	0.3	Services			
Electronic capacitors, resistors, coils, transformers	0.3	Manufg.			
Scientific research & development services	0.3	Services			
Rail transportation	0.2	Util.			
Coating, engraving, heat treating & allied activities	0.2	Manufg.			
Postal service	0.2	Util.			
Taxes on production & imports, less subsidies	0.2				
Employment services	0.2	Services			
Securities, commodity contracts, investments	0.2	Fin/R.E.			
Software publishers	0.2	Services			
Custom roll forming	0.2	Manufg.			
Architectural, engineering, & related services	0.2	Services			
Business support services	0.2	Services			
Maintenance/repair of nonresidential structures	0.2	Construct.			
Legal services	0.1	Services			
Warehousing & storage	0.1	Util.			
Natural gas distribution	0.1	Util.			
Electronic components, nec	0.1	Manufg.			
Services to buildings & dwellings	0.1	Services			
Noncomparable imports	0.1	Foreign			
Mineral wool	0.1	Manufg.			
Management, scientific, & technical consulting	0.1	Services			
Monetary authorities/depository credit intermediation	0.1	Fin/R.E.			

Source: Benchmark Input-Output Accounts for the U.S. Economy, 2002, U.S. Department of Commerce, Washington, D.C., January 2008. The abbreviation nec stands for 'not elsewhere classified'.

OCCUPATIONS EMPLOYED BY HOUSEHOLD APPLIANCE MANUFACTURING

Occupation	% of Total 2006	Change to 2016	Occupation	% of Total 2006	Change to 2016
Team assemblers	25.6	-24.3	Customer service representatives	1.9	-16.8
Industrial truck & tractor operators	3.6	-31.9	Mechanical engineers	1.8	-24.3
Laborers & freight, stock, & material movers, hand	3.5	-31.9	Production workers, nec	1.6	-25.7
First-line supervisors/managers of production workers	3.4	-24.3	Maintenance & repair workers, general	1.4	-24.3
Cutting, punching, & press machine operators	3.3	-31.9	Electrical & electronic equipment assemblers	1.1	-39.5
Inspectors, testers, sorters, samplers, & weighers	3.0	-28.6	Coating, painting, & spraying machine operators	1.0	-28.1
Welders, cutters, solderers, & brazers	2.0	-19.5			

Source: Industry-Occupation Matrix, Bureau of Labor Statistics, December 4, 2007. These data are reported based on 4-digit NAICS categories but have been matched to corresponding 6-digit NAICS industry codes. The change reported for each occupation to the year 2016 is a percent of growth or decline as estimated by the Bureau of Labor Statistics. The abbreviation nec stands for 'not elsewhere classified'.

INDUSTRY DATA BY STATE

State-level data are not available.

NAICS 335224 - HOUSEHOLD LAUNDRY EQUIPMENT MANUFACTURING

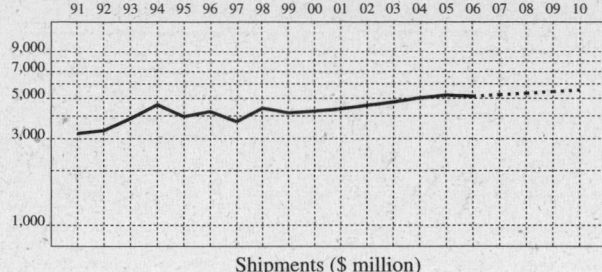

Shipments ($ million)

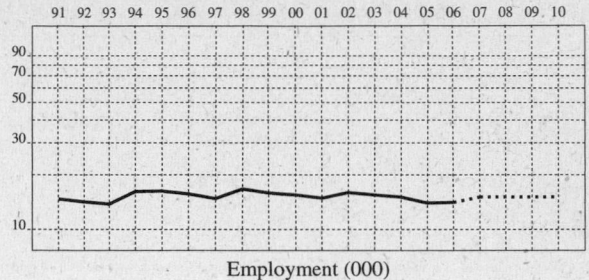

Employment (000)

GENERAL STATISTICS

Year	Com-panies	Establishments		Employment			Compensation		Production ($ million)			
		Total	with 20 or more employees	Total (000)	Production Workers (000)	Hours (Mil)	Payroll ($ mil)	Wages ($/hr)	Cost of Materials	Value Added by Manufacture	Value of Shipments	Capital Invest.
1991		18	14	14.7	12.4	24.5	413.3	13.65	1,654.3	1,517.6	3,205.7	82.2
1992	10	17	15	14.2	12.1	24.8	423.1	13.71	1,721.2	1,545.2	3,328.5	93.6
1993		17	13	13.8	11.9	24.2	440.7	14.76	2,170.0	1,761.9	3,871.3	73.5
1994		21	14	16.2	12.9	25.3	537.2	15.15	2,327.2	2,290.0	4,612.1	79.6
1995		25	18	16.3	12.9	24.5	521.0	15.14	2,206.6	1,749.3	3,968.8	146.1
1996		23	19	15.7	12.9	25.4	501.0	15.48	2,382.2	1,863.6	4,232.9	149.5
1997	10	17	15	14.8	12.9	25.1	480.1	15.71	2,081.2	1,668.4	3,723.4	37.4
1998		21	13	16.7	14.3	26.3	565.2	16.67	2,316.7	2,106.0	4,421.4	84.6
1999		23	14	15.9	14.0	26.5	554.1	16.41	2,245.3	1,921.5	4,163.3	99.8
2000		23	14	15.5	13.3	25.5	568.9	16.83	2,395.3	1,731.2	4,252.7	78.7
2001		24	15	14.9	12.8	25.3	541.0	16.62	2,555.8	1,856.7	4,380.8	97.0
2002	13	18	13	16.0	13.6	26.2	622.0	17.46	2,494.3	2,094.4	4,576.3	80.4
2003		22	15	15.5	13.1	25.0	572.1	17.43	2,607.3	2,147.3	4,767.1	72.0
2004		24	15	15.1	12.9	24.5	552.9	17.33	2,619.0	2,381.7	5,030.7	61.8
2005		23	17	14.0	12.3	23.0	502.1	17.14	2,707.7	2,513.3	5,202.0	80.3
2006		24P	15P	14.1	12.4	23.5	571.5	19.75	3,138.8	2,056.3	5,129.3	95.5
2007		24P	15P	15.1P	13.2P	24.7P	599.3P	18.83P	3,197.4P	2,094.7P	5,225.1P	78.8P
2008		24P	15P	15.1P	13.2P	24.6P	608.3P	19.14P	3,263.8P	2,138.2P	5,333.5P	77.7P
2009		25P	15P	15.1P	13.2P	24.6P	617.2P	19.44P	3,330.1P	2,181.6P	5,441.8P	76.6P
2010		25P	15P	15.1P	13.3P	24.6P	626.2P	19.75P	3,396.4P	2,225.0P	5,550.2P	75.5P

Sources: 1992, 1997, 2002 *Economic Census*; other years, up to 2006, are from the *Annual Survey of Manufactures*. Establishment counts for non-Census years are from *County Business Patterns*; 1997 and 2002 values are from the 1997 and 2002 censuses respectively, reported in the Federal Government's NAICS format. Other years were originally reported in equivalent SIC format. 'P's show projections by the editors.

INDICES OF CHANGE

Year	Com-panies	Establishments		Employment			Compensation		Production ($ million)			
		Total	with 20 or more employees	Total (000)	Production Workers (000)	Hours (Mil)	Payroll ($ mil)	Wages ($/hr)	Cost of Materials	Value Added by Manufacture	Value of Shipments	Capital Invest.
1992	77	94	115	89	89	95	68	79	69	74	73	116
1997	77	94	115	93	95	96	77	90	83	80	81	47
2001		133	115	93	94	97	87	95	102	89	96	121
2002	100	100	100	100	100	100	100	100	100	100	100	100
2003		122	115	97	96	95	92	100	105	103	104	90
2004		133	115	94	95	94	89	99	105	114	110	77
2005		128	131	88	90	88	81	98	109	120	114	100
2006		132P	116P	88	91	90	92	113	126	98	112	119
2007		134P	117P	94P	97P	94P	96P	108P	128P	100P	114P	98P
2008		136P	117P	94P	97P	94P	98P	110P	131P	102P	117P	97P
2009		137P	117P	94P	97P	94P	99P	111P	134P	104P	119P	95P
2010		139P	117P	94P	98P	94P	101P	113P	136P	106P	121P	94P

Sources: Same as General Statistics. Values reflect change from the base year, 2002. Values above 100 mean greater than 2002, values below 100 mean less than 2002, and the values of 100 in other years means the same as 2002. 'P's show projections by the editors.

SELECTED RATIOS

For 2002	Avg. of All Manufact.	Analyzed Industry	Index	For 2002	Avg. of All Manufact.	Analyzed Industry	Index
Employees per Establishment	42	889	2,118	Value Added per Production Worker	182,367	154,000	84
Payroll per Establishment	1,639,184	34,555,556	2,108	Cost per Establishment	5,769,015	138,572,222	2,402
Payroll per Employee	39,053	38,875	100	Cost per Employee	137,446	155,894	113
Production Workers per Establishment	30	756	2,560	Cost per Production Worker	195,506	183,404	94
Wages per Establishment	694,845	25,414,000	3,658	Shipments per Establishment	11,158,348	254,238,889	2,278
Wages per Production Worker	23,548	33,636	143	Shipments per Employee	265,847	286,019	108
Hours per Production Worker	1,980	1,926	97	Shipments per Production Worker	378,144	336,493	89
Wages per Hour	11.89	17.46	147	Investment per Establishment	361,338	4,466,667	1,236
Value Added per Establishment	5,381,325	116,355,556	2,162	Investment per Employee	8,609	5,025	58
Value Added per Employee	128,210	130,900	102	Investment per Production Worker	12,245	5,912	48

Sources: Same as General Statistics. The 'Average of All Manufacturing' column represents the average of all manufacturing industries reported for the most recent complete year available. The Index shows the relationship between the Average and the Analyzed Industry. For example, 100 means that they are equal; 500 that the Analyzed Industry is five times the average; 50 means that the Analyzed Industry is half the national average. The abbreviation 'na' is used to show that data are 'not available'. Ratios shown for 2002, the last complete census year.

LEADING COMPANIES   Number shown: **6**   Total sales ($ mil): **19,460**   Total employment (000): **73.2**

Company Name	Address				CEO Name	Phone	Co. Type	Sales ($ mil)	Empl. (000)
Whirlpool Corp.	Whirlpool Center	Benton Harbor	MI	49022		269-923-5000	P	19,408	73.0
Dryclean USA Inc.	290 NE 68th St.	Miami	FL	33138		305-758-0066	P	23	<0.1
Cuda Cleaning Systems Inc.	51804 Industrial Dr	Calumet	MI	49913	Andy Gale	906-482-1600	S	10*	<0.1
Staber Industries Inc.	4800 Homer Ohio	Groveport	OH	43125	William Staber	614-836-5995	R	9*	<0.1
Iron-A-Way Inc.	220 W Jackson St.	Morton	IL	61550	Reginald Smidt	309-266-7232	R	8*	<0.1
Keltner Research Inc.	1501 W Campus Dr.	Littleton	CO	80120	Steven Keltner	303-795-9024	R	3*	<0.1

Source: *Ward's Business Directory of U.S. Private and Public Companies*, Volumes 1 and 2, 2008. The company type code used is as follows: P - Public, R - Private, S - Subsidiary, D - Division, J - Joint Venture, A - Affiliate, G - Group. Sales are in millions of dollars, employees are in thousands. An asterisk (*) indicates an estimated sales volume. The symbol < stands for 'less than'. Company names and addresses are truncated, in some cases, to fit into the available space.

MATERIALS CONSUMED

Material	Quantity	Delivered Cost ($ million)
Metal stampings	(X)	55.6
Metal bolts, nuts, screws, and other screw machine products	(X)	47.2
All other fabricated metal products (excluding forgings)	(X)	42.8
Forgings	(X)	(D)
Iron and steel castings (rough and semifinished)	(X)	98.6
Aluminum and aluminum-base alloy castings (rough and semifinished)	(X)	27.6
Other nonferrous metal castings, rough or semifinished (inc. aluminum)	(X)	(D)
Steel bars, bar shapes, and plates (exc. castings, forgings, fabr. metal products)	(X)	(D)
Steel sheet and strip (including tinplate)	(X)	311.6
All other steel shapes and forms (exc. castings, forgings, fabr. metal products)	(X)	(D)
Aluminum and aluminum-base alloy shapes and forms (exc. castings, forgings, fabr. metal products)	(X)	40.8
Other nonferrous shapes and forms (exc. castings, forgings, fabricated metal products)	(X)	(D)
Nonferrous wire and cable (incl. magnet wire, bare wire or insulated wire, etc.)	(X)	(D)
Fractional horsepower electric motors and generators (less than 1 hp)	(X)	(D)
Integral horsepower electric motors and generators (1 hp or more)	(X)	232.4
Paper and paperboard containers (incl. shipping sacks and other paper packaging supplies)	(X)	79.6
Electrical transmission, distribution, and control equipment	(X)	143.8
Current-carrying wiring devices	(X)	45.9
Timing mechanisms (excluding microprocessors)	(X)	80.9
Automatic temperature controls (thermostats, regulators, etc.)	(X)	86.0
Paints, varnishes, stains, lacquers, shellacs, japans, enamels, etc.	(X)	68.3
Fabricated rubber products (exc. tires, tubes, hoses, belting, and gaskets)	(X)	(D)
Rubber and plastics hose and belting	(X)	55.9
Plastics products consumed in the form of sheets, rods, etc.	(X)	154.0
Plastics resins consumed in the form of granules, pellets, etc.	(X)	58.5
Complete flexible cord sets	(X)	(D)
Resistors, capacitors, transformers, electron tubes, semiconductors, and other electronic components	(X)	130.3
Mineral wool insulation (fibrous glass, rock wool, etc.)	(X)	6.2
All other materials, components, parts, containers, and supplies	(X)	278.4
Materials, ingredients, containers, and supplies, nsk	(X)	51.9

Source: 2002 *Economic Census*. Explanation of symbols used: (D): Withheld to avoid disclosure of competitive data; na: Not available; (S): Withheld because statistical norms were not met; (X): Not applicable; (Z): Less than half the unit shown; nec: Not elsewhere classified; nsk: Not specified by kind; - : zero; p : 10-19 percent estimated; q : 20-29 percent estimated.

PRODUCT SHARE DETAILS

Product or Product Class Shipments	Mil. $	Product or Product Class Shipments	Mil. $
HOUSEHOLD LAUNDRY EQUIPMENT	4,569.5	noncoin-operated washing machines, dryers, and combinations	4,427.4
Household laundry machines	**4,569.5**		
Household laundry machines, parts, accessories, and attachments	4,568.3	Parts, accessories, and attachments for household laundry equipment, sold separately	140.9
Household laundry machines, including both coin- and		Household laundry equipment, nsk, total	1.1

Source: 2002 *Economic Census*. The values are product shipments in millions of dollars for 2002. Total product shipments may be lower or higher than industry shipments. See Introduction for a full discussion. Values of indented subcategories are summed in the main heading(s). The symbol (D) appears when data are withheld to prevent disclosure of competitive information. The abbreviation nsk stands for 'not specified by kind' and nec for 'not elsewhere classified'. A dash (-) means zero.

INPUTS AND OUTPUTS FOR HOUSEHOLD LAUNDRY EQUIPMENT MANUFACTURING

Economic Sector or Industry Providing Inputs	%	Sector	Economic Sector or Industry Buying Outputs	%	Sector
Compensation of employees	23.3		Personal consumption expenditures	75.1	
Motors & generators	9.9	Manufg.	Exports of goods & services	11.9	Cap Inv
Iron & steel mills & ferroalloys	7.1	Manufg.	Private fixed investment	8.8	
Wholesale trade	7.1	Trade	Dry-cleaning & laundry services	2.6	Services
Management of companies & enterprises	5.1	Services	S/L govt. invest., education	0.6	S/L Govt
Plastics packaging materials, film & sheet	2.8	Manufg.	Change in private inventories	0.5	In House
Semiconductors & related devices	2.7	Manufg.	Retail trade	0.2	Trade
Automatic environmental controls	2.1	Manufg.	Other S/L govt. enterprises	0.2	S/L Govt
Relay & industrial controls	2.1	Manufg.	Household laundry equipment	0.2	Manufg.
Ferrous metal foundries	1.9	Manufg.			
Paperboard containers	1.7	Manufg.			
Paints & coatings	1.6	Manufg.			
Watches, clocks, & related devices	1.5	Manufg.			
Crowns & closures & metal stamping	1.5	Manufg.			
Rubber & plastics hose & belting	1.3	Manufg.			
Plastics materials & resins	1.2	Manufg.			
Turned products & screws, nuts, & bolts	1.1	Manufg.			
Wiring devices	1.0	Manufg.			
Alumina refining & primary aluminum production	0.9	Manufg.			
Truck transportation	0.8	Util.			
Nonferrous metal foundries	0.7	Manufg.			
Unlaminated plastics profile shapes	0.5	Manufg.			
Power generation & supply	0.4	Util.			
Electronic capacitors, resistors, coils, transformers	0.3	Manufg.			
Scientific research & development services	0.3	Services			
Machine shops	0.3	Manufg.			
Natural gas distribution	0.2	Util.			
Household laundry equipment	0.2	Manufg.			
Rail transportation	0.2	Util.			
Coating, engraving, heat treating & allied activities	0.2	Manufg.			
Advertising & related services	0.2	Services			
Laminated plastics plates, sheets, & shapes	0.2	Manufg.			
Warehousing & storage	0.2	Util.			
Mineral wool	0.2	Manufg.			
Taxes on production & imports, less subsidies	0.1				
Maintenance/repair of nonresidential structures	0.1	Construct.			
Noncomparable imports	0.1	Foreign			
Real estate	0.1	Fin/R.E.			
Services to buildings & dwellings	0.1	Services			

Source: Benchmark Input-Output Accounts for the U.S. Economy, 2002, U.S. Department of Commerce, Washington, D.C., January 2008. The abbreviation nec stands for 'not elsewhere classified'.

OCCUPATIONS EMPLOYED BY HOUSEHOLD APPLIANCE MANUFACTURING

Occupation	% of Total 2006	Change to 2016	Occupation	% of Total 2006	Change to 2016
Team assemblers	25.6	-24.3	Customer service representatives	1.9	-16.8
Industrial truck & tractor operators	3.6	-31.9	Mechanical engineers	1.8	-24.3
Laborers & freight, stock, & material movers, hand	3.5	-31.9	Production workers, nec	1.6	-25.7
First-line supervisors/managers of production workers	3.4	-24.3	Maintenance & repair workers, general	1.4	-24.3
Cutting, punching, & press machine operators	3.3	-31.9	Electrical & electronic equipment assemblers	1.1	-39.5
Inspectors, testers, sorters, samplers, & weighers	3.0	-28.6	Coating, painting, & spraying machine operators	1.0	-28.1
Welders, cutters, solderers, & brazers	2.0	-19.5			

Source: Industry-Occupation Matrix, Bureau of Labor Statistics, December 4, 2007. These data are reported based on 4-digit NAICS categories but have been matched to corresponding 6-digit NAICS industry codes. The change reported for each occupation to the year 2016 is a percent of growth or decline as estimated by the Bureau of Labor Statistics. The abbreviation nec stands for 'not elsewhere classified'.

INDUSTRY DATA BY STATE

State-level data are not available.

NAICS 335228 - MAJOR HOUSEHOLD APPLIANCE MANUFACTURING NEC

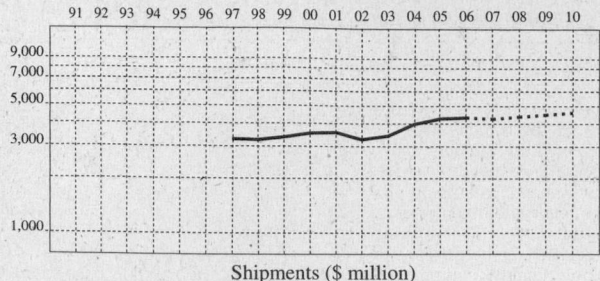

Shipments ($ million)

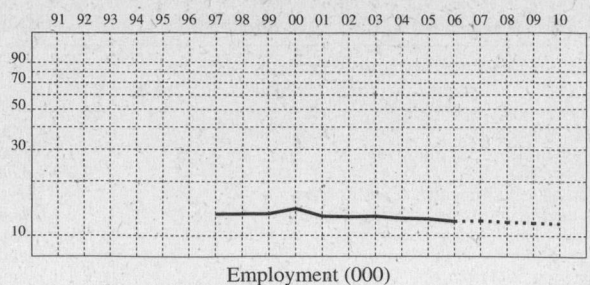

Employment (000)

GENERAL STATISTICS

| Year | Com-panies | Establishments | | Employment | | | Compensation | | Production ($ million) | | | |
		Total	with 20 or more employees	Total (000)	Production Workers (000)	Hours (Mil)	Payroll ($ mil)	Wages ($/hr)	Cost of Materials	Value Added by Manufacture	Value of Shipments	Capital Invest.
1997	28	31	27	13.2	11.2	22.4	424.1	14.47	1,466.2	1,800.5	3,280.9	65.0
1998		38	27	13.2	11.2	21.9	421.0	14.81	1,572.8	1,682.1	3,255.1	68.2
1999		40	24	13.2	11.1	22.6	452.5	15.17	1,736.4	1,624.8	3,362.3	85.8
2000		40	25	14.1	11.8	23.2	474.6	14.88	1,786.2	1,778.4	3,540.7	88.2
2001		41	26	12.8	10.4	21.5	472.3	15.41	1,772.5	1,796.8	3,579.7	95.5
2002	32	34	25	12.7	10.6	21.9	457.0	15.84	1,572.4	1,702.3	3,278.8	129.0
2003		41	26	12.8	10.5	21.0	467.6	16.29	1,948.6	1,505.1	3,428.1	192.5
2004		37	26	12.5	10.2	20.4	473.7	17.10	2,027.6	1,954.7	3,975.8	86.6
2005		39	28	12.4	10.2	20.8	484.1	17.23	2,215.8	2,061.8	4,263.5	93.4
2006		40P	26P	12.0	10.3	21.4	485.9	17.54	2,330.1	2,004.2	4,319.4	105.6
2007		40P	27P	12.1P	10.0P	20.6P	496.9P	17.84P	2,296.0P	1,974.9P	4,256.2P	130.7P
2008		41P	27P	11.9P	9.8P	20.4P	503.3P	18.19P	2,357.6P	2,027.9P	4,370.4P	136.1P
2009		41P	27P	11.8P	9.7P	20.2P	509.8P	18.55P	2,419.2P	2,080.8P	4,484.5P	141.5P
2010		42P	27P	11.7P	9.5P	20.0P	516.3P	18.91P	2,480.8P	2,133.8P	4,598.7P	146.9P

Sources: 1997 and 2002 *Economic Census*; other years, up to 2006, are from *Annual Survey of Manufactures*. Establishment counts for non-Census years are from *County Business Patterns*; 1997 and 2002 values are from the 1997 and 2002 censuses, respectively. 'P's show projections by the editors.

INDICES OF CHANGE

| Year | Com-panies | Establishments | | Employment | | | Compensation | | Production ($ million) | | | |
		Total	with 20 or more employees	Total (000)	Production Workers (000)	Hours (Mil)	Payroll ($ mil)	Wages ($/hr)	Cost of Materials	Value Added by Manufacture	Value of Shipments	Capital Invest.
1997	88	91	108	104	106	102	93	91	93	106	100	50
1998		112	108	104	106	100	92	93	100	99	99	53
1999		118	96	104	105	103	99	96	110	95	103	67
2000		118	100	111	111	106	104	94	114	104	108	68
2001		121	104	101	98	98	103	97	113	106	109	74
2002	100	100	100	100	100	100	100	100	100	100	100	100
2003		121	104	101	99	96	102	103	124	88	105	149
2004		109	104	98	96	93	104	108	129	115	121	67
2005		115	112	98	96	95	106	109	141	121	130	72
2006		118P	106P	94	97	98	106	111	148	118	132	82
2007		119P	106P	95P	94P	94P	109P	113P	146P	116P	130P	101P
2008		120P	106P	94P	92P	93P	110P	115P	150P	119P	133P	106P
2009		121P	107P	93P	92P	92P	112P	117P	154P	122P	137P	110P
2010		122P	107P	92P	90P	91P	113P	119P	158P	125P	140P	114P

Sources: Same as General Statistics. Values reflect change from the base year, 2002. Values above 100 mean greater than 2002, values below 100 mean less than 2002, and the values of 100 in other years means the same as 2002. 'P's show projections by the editors.

SELECTED RATIOS

For 2002	Avg. of All Manufact.	Analyzed Industry	Index	For 2002	Avg. of All Manufact.	Analyzed Industry	Index
Employees per Establishment	42	374	890	Value Added per Production Worker	182,367	160,594	88
Payroll per Establishment	1,639,184	13,441,176	820	Cost per Establishment	5,769,015	46,247,059	802
Payroll per Employee	39,053	35,984	92	Cost per Employee	137,446	123,811	90
Production Workers per Establishment	30	312	1,057	Cost per Production Worker	195,506	148,340	76
Wages per Establishment	694,845	10,202,824	1,468	Shipments per Establishment	11,158,348	96,435,294	864
Wages per Production Worker	23,548	32,726	139	Shipments per Employee	265,847	258,173	97
Hours per Production Worker	1,980	2,066	104	Shipments per Production Worker	378,144	309,321	82
Wages per Hour	11.89	15.84	133	Investment per Establishment	361,338	3,794,118	1,050
Value Added per Establishment	5,381,325	50,067,647	930	Investment per Employee	8,609	10,157	118
Value Added per Employee	128,210	134,039	105	Investment per Production Worker	12,245	12,170	99

Sources: Same as General Statistics. The 'Average of All Manufacturing' column represents the average of all manufacturing industries reported for the most recent complete year available. The Index shows the relationship between the Average and the Analyzed Industry. For example, 100 means that they are equal; 500 that the Analyzed Industry is five times the average; 50 means that the Analyzed Industry is half the national average. The abbreviation 'na' is used to show that data are 'not available'. Ratios shown for 2002, the last complete census year.

LEADING COMPANIES   Number shown: **41**   Total sales ($ mil): **181,292**   Total employment (000): **358.9**

Company Name	Address				CEO Name	Phone	Co. Type	Sales ($ mil)	Empl. (000)
General Electric Co.	3135 Easton Tpk.	Fairfield	CT	06828		203-373-2211	P	172,738	327.0
A.O. Smith Corp.	PO Box 245008	Milwaukee	WI	53224		414-359-4000	P	2,312	16.8
NTK Holdings Inc.	50 Kennedy Plz.	Providence	RI	02903	Richard L. Bready	401-751-1600	S	2,218	9.8
Sharp Manufacturing Co.	4050 S Mendenhall	Memphis	TN	38115	Saiko Hanatani	901-795-6510	S	1,508*	0.8
Freshflush L.L.C.	5980 Miami Lakes	Miami Lakes	FL	33014	Harry Shulman	305-362-2611	S	673*	0.3
Salton Inc.	1955 W Field Ct.	Lake Forest	IL	60045	Leonhard Dreimann	847-803-4600	P	523	1.0
American Water Heater Co.	PO Box 4056	Johnson City	TN	37602	Robert Trudeau	423-283-8000	R	278*	<0.1
Knight Inc.	20531 Crescent Bay	Lake Forest	CA	92630	George Noa	949-595-4800	S	189*	0.1
Cobra Electronics Corp.	6500 W Cortland St.	Chicago	IL	60707	James Bazet	773-889-8870	P	154	0.2
Tacony Corp.	1760 Gilsinn Ln.	Fenton	MO	63026		636-349-3000	R	120*	0.3
P and F Industries Inc.	445 Broadhollow	Melville	NY	11747	Richard A. Horowitz	631-694-9800	P	112	0.2
Dacor Inc.	950 S Raymond	Pasadena	CA	91105	Ric Brutocao	626-799-1000	R	82*	0.5
Singer Sewing Co.	PO Box 7017	La Vergne	TN	37086	Stephen H. Goodman	615-213-0880	R	66*	<0.1
National Refrigeration Co.	PO Box 148	Honea Path	SC	29654	James Kaufman	864-369-1665	R	50*	0.2
Anaheim Manufacturing Company	PO Box 4146	Anaheim	CA	92803		714-524-7770	R	30*	0.1
Atlanta Attachement Co.	362 Industrial Park	Lawrenceville	GA	30045	Elvin Price	770-963-7369	R	26*	0.2
Joseph Enterprises Inc.	425 California St.	San Francisco	CA	94104	Joe Pedott	415-397-6992	R	19*	<0.1
Jump River Electric Coop.	PO Box 99	Ladysmith	WI	54848	John Kmosena	715-532-5524	R	19*	<0.1
Vaughn Manufacturing Corp.	PO Box 5431	Salisbury	MA	01952	James Vaughn	978-462-6683	R	19*	<0.1
Bertolotti's Ceres Disposal	PO Box 127	Ceres	CA	95307	Bert Bertolotti	209-537-8000	R	18*	<0.1
LCAR	2650 W 35th Ave.	Gary	IN	46408		219-884-1138	R	17*	0.5
Innova Electronics Corp.	17291 Mt. Herrmann	Fountain Valley	CA	92708	Ieon Chen	714-241-6800	R	17*	<0.1
Sanyo Fisher Corp.	21605 Plummer St.	Chatsworth	CA	91311	Shin Oka	818-998-7322	S	14*	0.1
Cemline Corp.	PO Box 55	Cheswick	PA	15024	Charles Chappell	724-274-5430	R	13*	<0.1
Bock Water Heaters Inc.	PO Box 8632	Madison	WI	53708	Donna Sheehan	608-257-2225	R	10*	<0.1
Water Heater Innovations Inc.	3107 Sibley Mem	Eagan	MN	55121		651-688-8827	R	10*	<0.1
Eemax Inc.	353 Christian St.	Oxford	CT	06478	David Corrado	203-267-7890	R	9*	<0.1
WECO Industries Inc.	2777 Washington	Bellwood	IL	60104	Steve Kligis	708-547-6661	R	7*	<0.1
Old Dutch International Ltd.	421 N Midland Ave.	Saddle Brook	NJ	07663	Ben Kan	201-794-6262	R	6*	<0.1
AMI Inc.	PO Box 1782	Stanwood	WA	98292		360-629-9269	R	6	<0.1
Tilia Inc.	PO Box 194530	San Francisco	CA	94119	Linda S. Graebner	415-371-7200	S	5*	<0.1
Greenway Home Services L.L.C.	3910 Windolyn Cir.	Memphis	TN	38133		901-381-9001	R	5*	<0.1
Nolting Manufacturing Inc.	1265 Hawkeye Dr.	Hiawatha	IA	52233	Daniel Terrill	319-378-0999	R	4*	<0.1
Therma-Flow Inc.	PO Box 416	Watertown	MA	02471	Edwin Hill	617-924-3877	R	3*	<0.1
Jado Sewing Machine Inc.	4008 22nd St., 5	Long Island Cty	NY	11101	Onik Balian	718-784-2314	R	3*	<0.1
Hammbros Inc.	401 Rockcrest Rd.	Mc Kinney	TX	75071	Johnny Hamm	972-548-0975	R	2*	<0.1
Camatron Sewing Machine Inc.	42 Bergenwood Rd.	Fairview	NJ	07022	Robert Ross	201-941-5116	R	2*	<0.1
Gammill Quilting Machine Co.	PO Box 230	West Plains	MO	65775	Kenneth Gammill	417-256-5919	R	1*	<0.1
A-1 Quilting Machine Inc.	3232 E Evans Rd.	Springfield	MO	65804	Stewart Plank	417-883-6883	R	1*	<0.1
Cremer, William C and Son Inc.	PO Box 293	Reading	PA	19603	William Cremer	610-929-0545	R	1*	<0.1
Dan-Ray Machine Company Inc.	PO Box 1447	Haverhill	MA	01831	Daniel Germaine	978-374-7611	R	1*	<0.1

Source: Ward's Business Directory of U.S. Private and Public Companies, Volumes 1 and 2, 2008. The company type code used is as follows: P - Public, R - Private, S - Subsidiary, D - Division, J - Joint Venture, A - Affiliate, G - Group. Sales are in millions of dollars, employees are in thousands. An asterisk (*) indicates an estimated sales volume. The symbol < stands for 'less than'. Company names and addresses are truncated, in some cases, to fit into the available space.

MATERIALS CONSUMED

Material	Quantity	Delivered Cost ($ million)
Metal stampings	(X)	88.5
Metal wire racks, grills, springs, and other fabricated nonelectric wire products	(X)	28.6
Metal bolts, nuts, screws, and other screw machine products	(X)	21.0
All other fabricated metal products (excluding forgings)	(X)	40.4
Forgings	(X)	(D)
Iron and steel castings (rough and semifinished)	(X)	(D)
Aluminum and aluminum-base alloy castings (rough and semifinished)	(X)	(D)
Other nonferrous metal castings, rough or semifinished (inc. aluminum)	(X)	3.5
Steel bars, bar shapes, and plates (exc. castings, forgings, fabr. metal products)	(X)	(D)
Steel sheet and strip (including tinplate)	(X)	128.6
All other steel shapes and forms (exc. castings, forgings, fabr. metal products)	(X)	35.7
Aluminum and aluminum-base alloy shapes and forms (exc. castings, forgings, fabr. metal products)	(X)	8.5
Other nonferrous shapes and forms (exc. castings, forgings, fabricated metal products)	(X)	(D)
Nonferrous wire and cable (incl. magnet wire, bare wire or insulated wire, etc.)	(X)	10.8
Fractional horsepower electric motors and generators (less than 1 hp)	(X)	76.2
Integral horsepower electric motors and generators (1 hp or more)	(X)	(D)
Paper and paperboard containers (incl. shipping sacks and other paper packaging supplies)	(X)	68.9
Electrical transmission, distribution, and control equipment	(X)	49.8
Current-carrying wiring devices	(X)	37.0
Timing mechanisms (excluding microprocessors)	(X)	(D)
Automatic temperature controls (thermostats, regulators, etc.)	(X)	135.2
Paints, varnishes, stains, lacquers, shellacs, japans, enamels, etc.	(X)	21.7
Fabricated rubber products (exc. tires, tubes, hoses, belting, and gaskets)	(X)	(D)
Rubber and plastics hose and belting	(X)	26.6
Plastics products consumed in the form of sheets, rods, etc.	(X)	79.4
Plastics resins consumed in the form of granules, pellets, etc.	(X)	108.6

Continued on next page.

MATERIALS CONSUMED - Continued

Material	Quantity	Delivered Cost ($ million)
Complete flexible cord sets	(X)	(D)
Resistors, capacitors, transformers, electron tubes, semiconductors, and other electronic components	(X)	63.4
Mineral wool insulation (fibrous glass, rock wool, etc.)	(X)	27.2
All other materials, components, parts, containers, and supplies	(X)	331.4
Materials, ingredients, containers, and supplies, nsk	(X)	18.6

Source: 2002 *Economic Census*. Explanation of symbols used: (D): Withheld to avoid disclosure of competitive data; na: Not available; (S): Withheld because statistical norms were not met; (X): Not applicable; (Z): Less than half the unit shown; nec: Not elsewhere classified; nsk: Not specified by kind; - : zero; p : 10-19 percent estimated; q : 20-29 percent estimated.

PRODUCT SHARE DETAILS

Product or Product Class Shipments	Mil. $	Product or Product Class Shipments	Mil. $
OTHER MAJOR HOUSEHOLD APPLIANCES	3,037.2	appliances, nec (excluding parts)	1,764.5
Household water heaters, electric, for permanent installation	**562.2**	Parts for household dishwashing machines, food waste	
Household water heaters, except electric	**664.7**	disposers and trash compactors, and other major	
Household appliances and parts, nec	**1,809.2**	household appliances, nec	44.7
Household dishwashing machines, food waste disposers		**Other major household appliances, nsk, total**	**1.2**
and trash compactors, and other major household			

Source: 2002 *Economic Census*. The values are product shipments in millions of dollars for 2002. Total product shipments may be lower or higher than industry shipments. See Introduction for a full discussion. Values of indented subcategories are summed in the main heading(s). The symbol (D) appears when data are withheld to prevent disclosure of competitive information. The abbreviation nsk stands for 'not specified by kind' and nec for 'not elsewhere classified'. A dash (-) means zero.

INPUTS AND OUTPUTS FOR OTHER MAJOR HOUSEHOLD APPLIANCE MANUFACTURING

Economic Sector or Industry Providing Inputs	%	Sector	Economic Sector or Industry Buying Outputs	%	Sector
Compensation of employees	18.9		Personal consumption expenditures	39.8	
Wholesale trade	5.4	Trade	Residential permanent site structures	15.7	Construct.
Plastics products, nec	5.1	Manufg.	Private fixed investment	14.3	
Iron & steel mills & ferroalloys	4.4	Manufg.	Exports of goods & services	7.8	Cap Inv
Automatic environmental controls	3.9	Manufg.	Residential structures, nec	6.7	Construct.
Management of companies & enterprises	3.8	Services	Manufactured homes & mobile homes	3.5	Manufg.
Crowns & closures & metal stamping	2.7	Manufg.	Travel trailers & campers	2.4	Manufg.
Plastics materials & resins	2.6	Manufg.	Motor homes	2.1	Manufg.
Motors & generators	2.2	Manufg.	Commercial & health care structures	1.9	Construct.
Paperboard containers	1.8	Manufg.	Retail trade	1.9	Trade
Plastics packaging materials, film & sheet	1.7	Manufg.	Maintenance/repair of residential structures	1.3	Construct.
Semiconductors & related devices	1.5	Manufg.	Owner-occupied dwellings	1.2	
Truck transportation	1.3	Util.	Change in private inventories	0.9	In House
Turned products & screws, nuts, & bolts	1.2	Manufg.	Nonresidential structures, nec	0.4	Construct.
Lessors of nonfinancial assets	1.2	Fin/R.E.	Personal & household goods repair/maintenance	0.2	Services
Wiring devices	1.0	Manufg.	Real estate	0.1	Fin/R.E.
Paints & coatings	0.9	Manufg.			
Relay & industrial controls	0.9	Manufg.			
Springs & wire products	0.8	Manufg.			
Mineral wool	0.8	Manufg.			
Securities, commodity contracts, investments	0.8	Fin/R.E.			
Rubber & plastics hose & belting	0.7	Manufg.			
Management, scientific, & technical consulting	0.7	Services			
Advertising & related services	0.6	Services			
Nonmetallic minerals, nec	0.5	Mining			
Power generation & supply	0.5	Util.			
Monetary authorities/depository credit intermediation	0.4	Fin/R.E.			
Watches, clocks, & related devices	0.4	Manufg.			
Specialized design services	0.4	Services			
Nonferrous metal foundries	0.4	Manufg.			
Architectural, engineering, & related services	0.4	Services			
Professional, scientific, technical services, nec	0.4	Services			
Printed circuit assemblies (electronic assemblies)	0.3	Manufg.			
Machine shops	0.3	Manufg.			
Postal service	0.3	Util.			
Nonferrous metal (ex. copper & aluminum) processing	0.3	Manufg.			
Unlaminated plastics profile shapes	0.3	Manufg.			
Copper rolling, drawing, extruding, & alloying	0.3	Manufg.			
Forging, stamping, & sintering, nec	0.3	Manufg.			
Rail transportation	0.3	Util.			
Scientific research & development services	0.3	Services			
Maintenance/repair of nonresidential structures	0.2	Construct.			
Natural gas distribution	0.2	Util.			
Taxes on production & imports, less subsidies	0.2				
Coating, engraving, heat treating & allied activities	0.2	Manufg.			
Aluminum products from purchased aluminum	0.2	Manufg.			

Continued on next page.

INPUTS AND OUTPUTS FOR OTHER MAJOR HOUSEHOLD APPLIANCE MANUFACTURING - Continued

Economic Sector or Industry Providing Inputs	%	Sector	Economic Sector or Industry Buying Outputs	%	Sector
Data processing, hosting, & related services	0.2	Services			
Alumina refining & primary aluminum production	0.2	Manufg.			
Food services & drinking places	0.2	Services			
Services to buildings & dwellings	0.2	Services			
Ferrous metal foundries	0.2	Manufg.			
Telecommunications	0.2	Services			
Legal services	0.2	Services			
Software publishers	0.2	Services			
Electronic components, nec	0.2	Manufg.			
Automotive equipment rental & leasing	0.2	Fin/R.E.			
Automotive repair & maintenance, ex. car washes	0.2	Services			
Business support services	0.1	Services			
Accounting, tax preparation, bookkeeping, & payroll	0.1	Services			
Noncomparable imports	0.1	Foreign			
Warehousing & storage	0.1	Util.			
Electronic capacitors, resistors, coils, transformers	0.1	Manufg.			
Commercial & industrial equipment repair/maintenance	0.1	Services			
Hotels & motels, including casino hotels	0.1	Services			
Air transportation	0.1	Util.			
Employment services	0.1	Services			
Real estate	0.1	Fin/R.E.			
Petroleum lubricating oil & grease	0.1	Manufg.			
Laminated plastics plates, sheets, & shapes	0.1	Manufg.			

Source: Benchmark Input-Output Accounts for the U.S. Economy, 2002, U.S. Department of Commerce, Washington, D.C., January 2008. The abbreviation nec stands for 'not elsewhere classified'.

OCCUPATIONS EMPLOYED BY HOUSEHOLD APPLIANCE MANUFACTURING

Occupation	% of Total 2006	Change to 2016	Occupation	% of Total 2006	Change to 2016
Team assemblers	25.6	-24.3	Customer service representatives	1.9	-16.8
Industrial truck & tractor operators	3.6	-31.9	Mechanical engineers	1.8	-24.3
Laborers & freight, stock, & material movers, hand	3.5	-31.9	Production workers, nec	1.6	-25.7
First-line supervisors/managers of production workers	3.4	-24.3	Maintenance & repair workers, general	1.4	-24.3
Cutting, punching, & press machine operators	3.3	-31.9	Electrical & electronic equipment assemblers	1.1	-39.5
Inspectors, testers, sorters, samplers, & weighers	3.0	-28.6	Coating, painting, & spraying machine operators	1.0	-28.1
Welders, cutters, solderers, & brazers	2.0	-19.5			

Source: Industry-Occupation Matrix, Bureau of Labor Statistics, December 4, 2007. These data are reported based on 4-digit NAICS categories but have been matched to corresponding 6-digit NAICS industry codes. The change reported for each occupation to the year 2016 is a percent of growth or decline as estimated by the Bureau of Labor Statistics. The abbreviation nec stands for 'not elsewhere classified'.

INDUSTRY DATA BY STATE

State-level data are not available.

NAICS 335311 - POWER, DISTRIBUTION, AND SPECIALTY TRANSFORMER MANUFACTURING

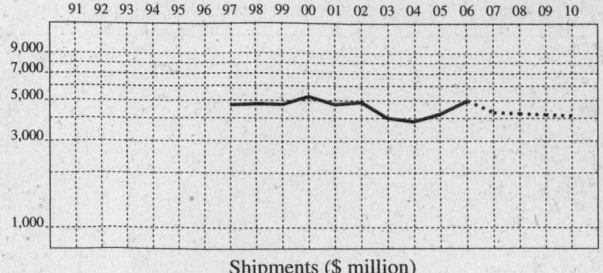

Shipments ($ million)

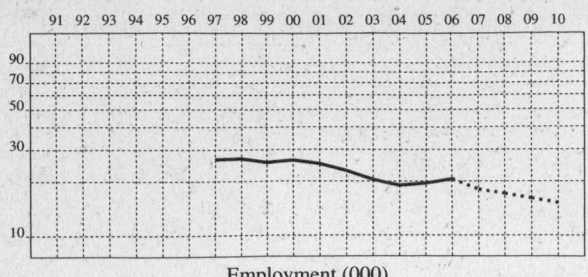

Employment (000)

GENERAL STATISTICS

Year	Com-panies	Establishments		Employment			Compensation		Production ($ million)			
		Total	with 20 or more employees	Total (000)	Production Workers (000)	Hours (Mil)	Payroll ($ mil)	Wages ($/hr)	Cost of Materials	Value Added by Manufacture	Value of Shipments	Capital Invest.
1997	276	318	148	26.6	19.9	41.0	819.6	12.52	2,169.9	2,558.9	4,716.2	131.8
1998		315	147	26.8	19.8	40.0	831.0	12.73	2,343.3	2,476.4	4,779.1	140.9
1999		306	149	25.5	18.7	40.0	839.3	12.66	2,337.4	2,439.7	4,760.6	100.2
2000		296	147	26.2	19.2	38.8	890.2	13.64	2,557.6	2,745.3	5,250.4	100.8
2001		296	148	25.0	17.8	33.8	864.4	15.12	2,389.7	2,299.2	4,756.5	77.0
2002	259	296	140	22.9	16.3	31.1	848.8	15.64	2,250.4	2,613.5	4,896.5	78.4
2003		289	129	20.5	14.9	29.1	754.6	15.07	1,987.7	2,016.9	4,008.7	31.6
2004		269	118	19.0	13.8	28.2	748.5	15.77	1,971.4	1,846.5	3,841.4	39.8
2005		280	132	19.5	14.5	29.7	781.4	15.99	2,167.7	2,111.7	4,231.6	38.9
2006		269P	123P	20.6	15.4	31.6	863.3	16.47	2,597.1	2,456.6	4,985.4	65.6
2007		264P	120P	18.0P	13.1P	26.1P	796.4P	17.19P	2,241.6P	2,120.3P	4,302.9P	19.9P
2008		258P	117P	17.1P	12.4P	24.6P	791.4P	17.66P	2,211.3P	2,091.7P	4,244.8P	8.9P
2009		253P	113P	16.1P	11.7P	23.1P	786.4P	18.14P	2,181.0P	2,063.0P	4,186.7P	
2010		248P	110P	15.2P	11.0P	21.6P	781.3P	18.62P	2,150.7P	2,034.4P	4,128.6P	

Sources: 1997 and 2002 *Economic Census*; other years, up to 2006, are from *Annual Survey of Manufactures*. Establishment counts for non-Census years are from *County Business Patterns*; 1997 and 2002 values are from the 1997 and 2002 censuses, respectively. 'P's show projections by the editors.

INDICES OF CHANGE

Year	Com-panies	Establishments		Employment			Compensation		Production ($ million)			
		Total	with 20 or more employees	Total (000)	Production Workers (000)	Hours (Mil)	Payroll ($ mil)	Wages ($/hr)	Cost of Materials	Value Added by Manufacture	Value of Shipments	Capital Invest.
1997	107	107	106	116	122	132	97	80	96	98	96	168
1998		106	105	117	121	129	98	81	104	95	98	180
1999		103	106	111	115	129	99	81	104	93	97	128
2000		100	105	114	118	125	105	87	114	105	107	129
2001		100	106	109	109	109	102	97	106	88	97	98
2002	100	100	100	100	100	100	100	100	100	100	100	100
2003		98	92	90	91	94	89	96	88	77	82	40
2004		91	84	83	85	91	88	101	88	71	78	51
2005		95	94	85	89	95	92	102	96	81	86	50
2006		91P	88P	90	94	102	102	105	115	94	102	84
2007		89P	86P	79P	80P	84P	94P	110P	100P	81P	88P	25P
2008		87P	83P	75P	76P	79P	93P	113P	98P	80P	87P	11P
2009		85P	81P	70P	72P	74P	93P	116P	97P	79P	86P	
2010		84P	79P	66P	67P	69P	92P	119P	96P	78P	84P	

Sources: Same as General Statistics. Values reflect change from the base year, 2002. Values above 100 mean greater than 2002, values below 100 mean less than 2002, and the values of 100 in other years means the same as 2002. 'P's show projections by the editors.

SELECTED RATIOS

For 2002	Avg. of All Manufact.	Analyzed Industry	Index	For 2002	Avg. of All Manufact.	Analyzed Industry	Index
Employees per Establishment	42	77	184	Value Added per Production Worker	182,367	160,337	88
Payroll per Establishment	1,639,184	2,867,568	175	Cost per Establishment	5,769,015	7,602,703	132
Payroll per Employee	39,053	37,066	95	Cost per Employee	137,446	98,271	71
Production Workers per Establishment	30	55	187	Cost per Production Worker	195,506	138,061	71
Wages per Establishment	694,845	1,643,257	236	Shipments per Establishment	11,158,348	16,542,230	148
Wages per Production Worker	23,548	29,841	127	Shipments per Employee	265,847	213,821	80
Hours per Production Worker	1,980	1,908	96	Shipments per Production Worker	378,144	300,399	79
Wages per Hour	11.89	15.64	132	Investment per Establishment	361,338	264,865	73
Value Added per Establishment	5,381,325	8,829,392	164	Investment per Employee	8,609	3,424	40
Value Added per Employee	128,210	114,127	89	Investment per Production Worker	12,245	4,810	39

Sources: Same as General Statistics. The 'Average of All Manufacturing' column represents the average of all manufacturing industries reported for the most recent complete year available. The Index shows the relationship between the Average and the Analyzed Industry. For example, 100 means that they are equal; 500 that the Analyzed Industry is five times the average; 50 means that the Analyzed Industry is half the national average. The abbreviation 'na' is used to show that data are 'not available'. Ratios shown for 2002, the last complete census year.

LEADING COMPANIES   Number shown: **75**   Total sales ($ mil): **47,907**   Total employment (000): **139.5**

Company Name	Address				CEO Name	Phone	Co. Type	Sales ($ mil)	Empl. (000)
Impulse NC Inc.	100 Impulse Way	Mount Olive	NC	28365	Terry Derrico	919-658-2200	R	7,000*	0.2
Cooper Industries Ltd.	PO Box 4446	Houston	TX	77210	Kirk S. Hachigian	713-209-8400	P	5,903	31.5
Lincoln Electric Co.	22801 St. Clair Ave	Cleveland	OH	44117		216-481-8100	S	5,398*	7.0
SPX Corp.	13515 Ballnyn Corp.	Charlotte	NC	28277		704-752-4400	P	4,822	17.8
Stoody Co.	5557 Nashville Rd.	Bowling Green	KY	42101	Paul D. Melnuk	270-781-9777	S	1,537*	3.0
Thermadyne Manufacturing	101 S Hanley Rd.	St. Louis	MO	63105	Paul D. Melnuk	314-721-5573	S	1,537*	3.0
Marison Cylinder Co.	101 S Hanley Rd.	St. Louis	MO	63105	Paul D. Melnuk	314-721-5573	S	1,530*	3.0
Modern Engineering Company	US Highway I-55 S	Gallman	MS	39077	Paul D. Melnuk	601-892-3500	S	1,530*	3.0
Thermadyne Industries Inc.	16052 Swingley	Chesterfield	MO	63017	Paul D. Melnuk	314-721-5573	S	1,530*	3.0
Thermal Dynamics Corp.	Industrial Part #D	West Lebanon	NH	03784	Paul D. Melnuk	603-298-5711	S	1,530*	3.0
Victor Coyne International	101 S Hanley Rd.	St. Louis	MO	63105	Paul D. Melnuk	314-721-5573	S	1,530*	3.0
Victor Gas Systems Inc.	960 Brookroad, 1	Conshohocken	PA	19428	Paul D. Melnuk	314-721-5573	S	1,530*	3.0
Square D Co.	1415 S Roselle Rd.	Palatine	IL	60067	John Guerdan	847-397-2600	S	1,271*	18.0
Universal Lighting Techn.	26 Century Blvd.	Nashville	TN	37214		615-316-5100	S	1,040*	0.1
EFD Inc.	977 Waterman Ave.	East Providence	RI	02914	Peter Lambert	401-434-1680	S	972*	0.3
Sumitomo Machinery Corporation	4200 Holland Blvd.	Chesapeake	VA	23323	Nobuhiko Kawamura	757-485-3355	R	749*	0.2
Progressive Tool & Ind./Wisne	21000 Telegraph Rd.	Southfield	MI	48034	Robert Stoutenburg	248-353-8888	D	733*	5.5
NCH Corp.	PO Box 152170	Irving	TX	75015		972-438-0211	S	688*	8.5
Powell Industries Inc.	PO Box 12818	Houston	TX	77217		713-944-6900	P	564	2.1
Power-One Inc.	740 Calle Plano	Camarillo	CA	93012		805-987-8741	P	512	4.2
Belkin Corp.	PO Box 5649	Compton	CA	90220	Chet Pipkin	310-604-2347	R	460*	1.0
Panamax	1690 Corporate Cir.	Petaluma	CA	94954	Bill Pollock		R	372*	0.1
FANUC Robotics America Inc.	3900 W Hamlin Rd.	Rochester Hills	MI	48309		248-377-7000	R	361*	0.9
Spence Engineering Company	PO Box 230	Walden	NY	12586		845-778-5566	S	329*	0.2
Multiquip Inc.	PO Box 6254	Carson	CA	90749	Roger Euliss	310-537-3700	R	317*	0.3
Americor Electronics Ltd.	675 S Lively Blvd.	Elk Grove Vlg	IL	60007	Troy Gunnin	847-956-6200	R	247*	<0.1
Body Glove International	201 Herondo St.	Redondo Beach	CA	90277		310-374-3441	R	200*	<0.1
Airgas Mid South Inc.	31 N Peoria Ave.	Tulsa	OK	74120	Mike Duvall	918-585-2611	S	191*	0.7
Central Wire Industries Ltd.	370 Franklin Tpke.	Mahwah	NJ	07430	Thierry Cremailh	201-529-0900	R	167*	<0.1
GE Drives and Controls Inc.	1501 Roanoke Blvd.	Salem	VA	24153	Jeff Immelt	540-387-7000	R	159*	0.9
Hi-Lex Controls Inc.	152 Simpson Dr.	Litchfield	MI	49252	Robert Chrysler	517-542-2955	R	153*	0.5
Deloro Stellite Company Inc.	1201 Eisenhower Dr.	Goshen	IN	46526	Mark Aldridge	574-534-2585	R	153*	1.2
Transistor Devices Inc.	36 Newburgh Rd.	Hackettstown	NJ	07840	Richard Blake	973-267-1900	R	151*	0.1
Norco Inc.	1125 W Amity Rd.	Boise	ID	83705	Ned Pontious	208-336-1643	R	151*	0.5
Babcock Inc.	14930 E Alondra	La Mirada	CA	90638	Richard Dixon	714-994-6500	R	145*	0.2
Gentex Corp.	324 Main Street	Simpson	PA	18407	L. Peter Frieder Jr.	570-282-3550	R	113*	0.6
Carling Technologies Inc.	60 Johnson Ave.	Plainville	CT	06062		860-793-9266	R	110*	0.2
Piller Inc.	45 Turner Rd.	Middletown	NY	10941	Michael Barron	845-695-5300	R	105*	<0.1
Mining Controls Inc.	PO Box 1141	Beckley	WV	25802	Randall Hurst	304-252-6243	R	104*	0.6
ITW Hobart Brothers Co.	101 Trade Sq. E	Troy	OH	45373		937-332-4000	S	102*	0.5
Phillips Service Industries	11878 Hubbard St.	Livonia	MI	48150	Scott Phillips	734-853-5000	R	92*	0.7
Acme Electric Corp.	4815 W 5th St.	Lumberton	NC	28358	Robert J. McKenna	910-738-4251	S	89*	0.7
Delta Star Inc.	270 Industrial Rd.	San Carlos	CA	94070	Ivan Tepper	650-508-2850	R	83*	0.2
V and F Transformer Corp.	PO Box 8449	Bartlett	IL	60103	Francis Foderaro	630-497-8070	R	82*	0.1
Central Moloney Inc.	PO Box 6608	Pine Bluff	AR	71611		870-247-5320	R	78*	0.7
Suhner Manufacturing Inc.	PO Box 1367	Rome	GA	30162	Paul Luthi	706-235-8046	R	77*	0.2
Waukesha Electric Systems Inc.	400 S Prairie Ave.	Waukesha	WI	53186	Myron Bechtel		R	72*	0.5
Weldmation Inc.	31720 Stephenson	Madison Heights	MI	48071	Arthur Kelsey	248-585-0010	R	71*	0.4
Emhart Teknologies Inc.	PO Box 868	Mount Clemens	MI	48046	Paul A. Gustafson	586-949-0440	S	70*	0.5
Solomon Corp.	PO Box 245	Solomon	KS	67480	Phillip Hemmer	785-655-2191	R	67*	0.3
Valley National Gases Inc.	200 W Beau St.	Washington	PA	15301	James P. Hart	724-228-3000	S	67*	0.2
Cyberex L.L.C.	5900 Eastport Blvd.	Richmond	VA	23231	Kurt Gallo	804-236-3300	S	56*	0.4
Solder Station-One	2231 Cape Cod	Santa Ana	CA	92703	Lawerence S. Adelson	714-558-1019	S	55*	<0.1
Spellman High Voltage Electr.	475 Wireless Blvd.	Hauppauge	NY	11788	Loren Skeist	631-630-3000	R	55*	0.5
Nelson Stud Welding Inc.	PO Box 4019	Elyria	OH	44036	Ken Caratelli	440-329-0400	R	54*	0.4
California Natural Products	PO Box 1219	Lathrop	CA	95330	Pat Mitchell	209-858-2525	R	52*	0.2
Russound Fmp Inc.	5 Forbes Rd. Ste. 1	Newmarket	NH	03857	Maureen Baldwin	603-659-5170	R	51*	0.2
Pauwels Transformers Inc.	1 Pauwels Dr.	Washington	MO	63090	Victor Pauwels	636-239-9300	R	50*	0.3
Welding Technology Corp.	150 E St Charles Rd	Carol Stream	IL	60188	Durrell Miller	630-462-8250	R	48*	0.2
Trans-Coil Inc.	7878 N 86th St.	Milwaukee	WI	53224	Steve Cobb	414-357-4480	R	48*	<0.1
Virginia Transformer Corp.	220 Glade View Dr.	Roanoke	VA	24012	Prabhat Jain	540-345-9892	R	46*	0.3
Robertson Transformer Co.	13611 Thornton Rd.	Blue Island	IL	60406	Gregory Traphagen	708-388-2315	R	44*	0.3
Intermatic Inc.	7777 Winn Rd.	Spring Grove	IL	60081	Douglas Kinney	815-675-2321	R	43*	0.8
Paslin Co.	25411 Ryan Rd.	Warren	MI	48091	Charles Pasque	586-758-0200	R	43*	0.3
Int'l Rectifier HiRel Products	205 Crawford St.	Leominster	MA	01453	Alex Lidow	978-534-5776	S	42*	0.3
Int'l Power Technologies	3603 S Via Terra St	Salt Lake City	UT	84115		801-224-4828	R	42*	<0.1
Beckwith Electric Company Inc.	6190-118th Ave. N	Largo	FL	33773	Bob Beckwith	727-544-2326	R	41*	0.1
Porcelain Products Co.	225 N Patterson St.	Carey	OH	43316	Morris Murphy	419-396-7621	R	40*	0.4
Forney Industries Inc.	PO Box 563	Fort Collins	CO	80521	Steve Anderson	970-482-7271	R	38*	0.5
Ault Inc.	7105 Northland Ter.	Minneapolis	MN	55428	Frederick M. Green	763-592-1900	R	37	0.7
Pacific Transformer Corp.	5399 E Hunter Ave.	Anaheim	CA	92807	Pat Thomas	714-779-0450	R	36*	0.2
Zareba Systems Inc.	13705 26th Ave. N	Minneapolis	MN	55441		763-551-1125	P	36	0.1
American Torch Tip Co.	6212 29th St. E	Bradenton	FL	34203	John Walters	941-753-7557	R	36*	0.2
Actown-Electrocoil Inc.	PO Box 248	Spring Grove	IL	60081	David Weisberg	815-675-6641	R	35*	0.2
Kepco Inc.	13138 Sanford Ave.	Flushing	NY	11355	Martin Kupferberg	718-461-7000	R	35*	0.2

Source: Ward's Business Directory of U.S. Private and Public Companies, Volumes 1 and 2, 2008. The company type code used is as follows: P - Public, R - Private, S - Subsidiary, D - Division, J - Joint Venture, A - Affiliate, G - Group. Sales are in millions of dollars, employees are in thousands. An asterisk (*) indicates an estimated sales volume. The symbol < stands for 'less than'. Company names and addresses are truncated, in some cases, to fit into the available space.

MATERIALS CONSUMED

Material	Quantity	Delivered Cost ($ million)
Metal bolts, nuts, screws, and other screw machine products	(X)	11.3
Forgings .... 1,000 s tons	(S)	2.0
Other fabricated metal products (exc. castings and forgings)	(X)	33.9
Aluminum and aluminum-base alloy sheet, plate, foil, and welded tubing ...... mil lb	(S)	33.6
Paints, varnishes, stains, lacquers, shellacs, japans, etc. ...... 1,000 gallons	(S)	19.2
Copper and copper-base alloy shapes and forms (exc. castings, forgings, fabr. metal products)	(X)	36.6
Other nonferrous shapes and forms (exc. castings, forgings, fabricated metal products)	(X)	11.1
Electrical industrial capacitors, resistors, rheostats, and coil windings	(X)	87.5
Castings, rough and semifinished	(X)	18.6
Steel shapes and forms (exc. castings, forgings, fabr. metal products)	(X)	466.7
All other aluminum and aluminum-base alloy shapes and forms (exc. castings, forgings, fabr. metal products)	(X)	15.7
Magnet wire	(X)	191.7
Insulated wire and cable (excluding magnet wire)	(X)	43.1
Refined petroleum products (transformer oils, lubricating oils and greases, etc.)	(X)	70.1
Porcelain, steatite, and other ceramic electrical products	(X)	60.3
Paper and paperboard products	(X)	34.0
Current-carrying wiring devices	(X)	25.5
All other materials, components, parts, containers, and supplies	(X)	397.7
Materials, ingredients, containers, and supplies, nsk	(X)	485.2

Source: 2002 *Economic Census*. Explanation of symbols used: (D): Withheld to avoid disclosure of competitive data; na: Not available; (S): Withheld because statistical norms were not met; (X): Not applicable; (Z): Less than half the unit shown; nec: Not elsewhere classified; nsk: Not specified by kind; - : zero; p : 10-19 percent estimated; q : 20-29 percent estimated.

PRODUCT SHARE DETAILS

Product or Product Class Shipments	Mil. $	Product or Product Class Shipments	Mil. $
POWER, DISTRIBUTION, AND SPECIALTY TRANSFORMERS	4,656.8	kVA, OA (167,000 kVA, top FOA), liquid-immersed	53.8
Power and distribution transformers, except parts	**2,309.0**	Large power transformers without load-tap-changing, 30,001 kVA, OA (50,001 kVA, top FOA) to 100,000 kVA, OA (167,000 kVA, top FOA), liquid-immersed	(D)
Distribution transformers, overhead type, single-phase, liquid-immersed; 500 kVA and smaller	477.4	Large power transformers with load-tap-changing, 100,001 kVA, OA (167,001 kVA, top FOA) and larger, liquid-immersed	(D)
Distribution transformers, compartmentalized pad-mounted, single-phase, liquid-immersed; 500 kVA and smaller	295.6	Large power transformers without load-tap-changing, 100,001 kVA, OA (167,001 kVA, top FOA) and larger, liquid-immersed	(D)
Other distribution transformers, including network transformers, single-phase, and liquid-immersed (all voltages)	358.3	Power and distribution transformers, except parts, nsk	39.8
Distribution transformers, subsurface and subway types, single-phase, liquid-immersed; 500 kVA and smaller	(D)	**Specialty transformers, except fluorescent lamp ballasts**	**355.1**
Distribution three-phase transformers, 500 kVA and smaller, liquid-immersed (all voltages)	178.7	Specialty transformers	338.2
Distribution network transformers, all ratings, excluding network protectors	(D)	Open core and coil units, excluding machine tool control transformers and all units end-bell enclosed (250 VA and under)	31.4
Distribution transformers, single-phase and three-phase, pad-mounted (dry); 500 kVA and smaller	114.7	Machine tool control transformers	31.0
Small conventional and power transformers; single- and three-phase (all voltages); primary and secondary unit substations	712.3	Transformers for arc welders	(D)
		Indoor and outdoor current instrument transformers	(D)
		Indoor and outdoor voltage instrument transformers	57.9
		High intensity discharge lamp transformers (ballasts)	(D)
Small power transformers, compartmentalized pad-mounted and subsurface underground and conventional subway type, 501 kVA through 2500 kVA liquid-immersed	278.4	All other specialty transformers, excluding internal combustion engine ignition	144.0
Small conventional transformers and autotransformers, single-and three-phase, all voltages, primary unit and single circuit unit substations, 501 kVA through 2500 kVA liquid-immersed	58.2	Specialty transformers, except fluorescent lamp ballast, nsk	16.9
		Fluorescent lamp ballasts	**831.4**
Small power transformers, single- and three-phase, all voltages, liquid-immersed conventionals, primary unit and single circuit unit substations, 2501 kVA through 10,000 kVA	202.6	**Commercial, institutional, and industrial general-purpose transformers, all voltages**	**261.1**
Dry-type small conventional power transformers, primary unit substation, and core and coil units, single-and three-phase, all voltages	75.3	Commercial, institutional, and industrial general-purpose transformers	251.1
		Single- and three-phase, 3 kVA and below, all voltages	87.0
Secondary unit substation power transformers, liquid-immersed, all kVA ratings	56.3	Single- and three-phase, 3.01 kVA through 15 kVA, all voltages	37.9
Secondary unit substation power transformers, dry-type, all kVA ratings	41.6	Single- and three-phase, 15.01 kVA through 100 kVA, all voltages	48.7
Large liquid-immersed power transformers with and without load-tap-changing	425.6	Single- and three-phase, 100.01 kVA and above, all voltages	17.3
		Other commercial, institutional, and industrial general-purpose transformers	60.3
Large power transformers with load-tap-changing, 10,001 kVA, OA to 30,000 kVA, OA (50,000 kVA, top FOA), liquid-immersed	153.9	Commercial, institutional, and industrial general-purpose transformers, all voltages, nsk	10.0
Large power transformers without load-tap-changing, 10,001 kVA, OA to 30,000 kVA, OA (50,000 kVA, top FOA), liquid-immersed	81.8	**Power regulators, boosters, and other transformers and parts for all transformers**	**674.0**
		Power regulators, boosters, and other transformers and parts for all transformers	646.3
Large power transformers with load-tap-changing, 30,001 kVA, OA (50,000 kVA, top FOA) to 100,000		Transmission and distribution voltage regulators, boosters, and other special-purpose transformers	479.3
		Parts, subassemblies and accessories for all transformers	167.0
		Power regulators, boosters, and other transformers and parts for all transformers, nsk	27.7
		Power, distribution, and specialty transformers, nsk, total	**226.2**

Source: 2002 *Economic Census*. The values are product shipments in millions of dollars for 2002. Total product shipments may be lower or higher than industry shipments. See Introduction for a full discussion. Values of indented subcategories are summed in the main heading(s). The symbol (D) appears when data are withheld to prevent disclosure of competitive information. The abbreviation nsk stands for 'not specified by kind' and nec for 'not elsewhere classified'. A dash (-) means zero.

INPUTS AND OUTPUTS FOR POWER, DISTRIBUTION, & SPECIALTY TRANSFORMERS

Economic Sector or Industry Providing Inputs	%	Sector	Economic Sector or Industry Buying Outputs	%	Sector
Compensation of employees	26.2		Private fixed investment	58.9	
Iron & steel mills & ferroalloys	11.8	Manufg.	Lighting fixtures	8.7	Manufg.
Copper rolling, drawing, extruding, & alloying	7.3	Manufg.	Exports of goods & services	6.6	Cap Inv
Wholesale trade	7.3	Trade	S/L govt. invest., other	4.5	S/L Govt
Management of companies & enterprises	5.9	Services	Electromedical & electrotherapeutic apparatus	2.5	Manufg.
Petroleum lubricating oil & grease	1.9	Manufg.	S/L govt. invest., education	2.0	S/L Govt
Pottery, ceramics, and plumbing fixtures	1.8	Manufg.	Wood windows & doors & millwork	1.8	Manufg.
Aluminum products from purchased aluminum	1.3	Manufg.	Signs	1.5	Manufg.
Noncomparable imports	1.3	Foreign	Packaging machinery	1.3	Manufg.
Electronic capacitors, resistors, coils, transformers	1.2	Manufg.	Commercial & health care structures	1.2	Construct.
Electrical equipment & components, nec	1.2	Manufg.	Arms, ordnance, & accessories	0.9	Manufg.
Truck transportation	1.0	Util.	Ammunition	0.8	Manufg.
Paper mills	0.9	Manufg.	General Federal government services, nondefense	0.7	Fed Govt
Paints & coatings	0.9	Manufg.	Federal government, investment, nondefense	0.6	Fed Govt
Wiring devices	0.8	Manufg.	Motors & generators	0.6	Manufg.
Advertising & related services	0.7	Services	Wholesale trade	0.6	Trade
Power generation & supply	0.7	Util.	Nonresidential structures, nec	0.5	Construct.

Continued on next page.

INPUTS AND OUTPUTS FOR POWER, DISTRIBUTION, & SPECIALTY TRANSFORMERS - Continued

Economic Sector or Industry Providing Inputs	%	Sector	Economic Sector or Industry Buying Outputs	%	Sector
Lessors of nonfinancial assets	0.6	Fin/R.E.	Broadcast & wireless communications equipment	0.4	Manufg.
Turned products & screws, nuts, & bolts	0.6	Manufg.	Military armored vehicles, tanks, & tank components	0.4	Manufg.
Securities, commodity contracts, investments	0.5	Fin/R.E.	Paints & coatings	0.4	Manufg.
Communication & energy wires & cables	0.5	Manufg.	Material handling equipment	0.3	Manufg.
Real estate	0.5	Fin/R.E.	Legal services	0.3	Services
Paperboard containers	0.5	Manufg.	Industrial molds	0.3	Manufg.
Semiconductors & related devices	0.4	Manufg.	Other S/L govt. enterprises	0.3	S/L Govt
Printed circuit assemblies (electronic assemblies)	0.4	Manufg.	Professional, scientific, technical services, nec	0.2	Services
Plastics products, nec	0.4	Manufg.	Services to buildings & dwellings	0.2	Services
Scientific research & development services	0.4	Services	Accounting, tax preparation, bookkeeping, & payroll	0.2	Services
Machine shops	0.4	Manufg.	Personal consumption expenditures	0.1	
Taxes on production & imports, less subsidies	0.3		Facilities support services	0.1	Services
Nonferrous metal (ex. copper & aluminum) processing	0.3	Manufg.	Management, scientific, & technical consulting	0.1	Services
Ferrous metal foundries	0.3	Manufg.	Rail transportation	0.1	Util.
Retail trade	0.3	Trade	Power, distribution, & specialty transformers	0.1	Manufg.
Rail transportation	0.3	Util.			
Automotive equipment rental & leasing	0.3	Fin/R.E.			
Nonferrous metal foundries	0.2	Manufg.			
Software publishers	0.2	Services			
Natural gas distribution	0.2	Util.			
Coating, engraving, heat treating & allied activities	0.2	Manufg.			
Warehousing & storage	0.2	Util.			
Maintenance/repair of nonresidential structures	0.2	Construct.			
Legal services	0.2	Services			
Specialized design services	0.2	Services			
Alumina refining & primary aluminum production	0.2	Manufg.			
Monetary authorities/depository credit intermediation	0.2	Fin/R.E.			
Services to buildings & dwellings	0.2	Services			
Employment services	0.2	Services			
Professional, scientific, technical services, nec	0.2	Services			
Architectural, engineering, & related services	0.2	Services			
Power, distribution, & specialty transformers	0.1	Manufg.			
Accounting, tax preparation, bookkeeping, & payroll	0.1	Services			
Data processing, hosting, & related services	0.1	Services			
Commercial & industrial machinery rental & leasing	0.1	Fin/R.E.			
Postal service	0.1	Util.			
Business support services	0.1	Services			
Telecommunications	0.1	Services			
Cutting tools & machine tool accessories	0.1	Manufg.			
Food services & drinking places	0.1	Services			
Automotive repair & maintenance, ex. car washes	0.1	Services			
Plastics packaging materials, film & sheet	0.1	Manufg.			

Source: Benchmark Input-Output Accounts for the U.S. Economy, 2002, U.S. Department of Commerce, Washington, D.C., January 2008. The abbreviation nec stands for 'not elsewhere classified'.

OCCUPATIONS EMPLOYED BY ELECTRICAL EQUIPMENT MANUFACTURING

Occupation	% of Total 2006	Change to 2016	Occupation	% of Total 2006	Change to 2016
Electrical & electronic equipment assemblers	15.2	-32.0	Shipping, receiving, & traffic clerks	1.7	-18.2
Team assemblers	10.7	-15.0	Industrial engineers	1.5	3.2
Coil winders, tapers, & finishers	4.9	-32.0	Mechanical engineers	1.4	-15.0
First-line supervisors/managers of production workers	3.3	-15.0	Assemblers & fabricators, nec	1.3	-23.5
Inspectors, testers, sorters, samplers, & weighers	2.9	-19.9	Maintenance & repair workers, general	1.3	-15.0
Electromechanical equipment assemblers	2.7	-15.0	Purchasing agents, exc wholesale, retail, & farm	1.2	-15.0
Electrical engineers	2.6	-15.0	General & operations managers	1.2	-23.5
Cutting, punching, & press machine operators	2.5	-23.5	Bookkeeping, accounting, & auditing clerks	1.1	-15.0
Machinists	2.3	-10.8	Electronics engineers, exc computer	1.1	-15.0
Welders, cutters, solderers, & brazers	2.1	-9.6	Customer service representatives	1.1	-6.5
Computer-controlled machine tool operators	1.7	-6.5	Electrical & electronics drafters	1.1	-15.0
Electrical & electronic engineering technicians	1.7	-15.0			

Source: Industry-Occupation Matrix, Bureau of Labor Statistics, December 4, 2007. These data are reported based on 4-digit NAICS categories but have been matched to corresponding 6-digit NAICS industry codes. The change reported for each occupation to the year 2016 is a percent of growth or decline as estimated by the Bureau of Labor Statistics. The abbreviation nec stands for 'not elsewhere classified'.

LOCATION BY STATE AND REGIONAL CONCENTRATION

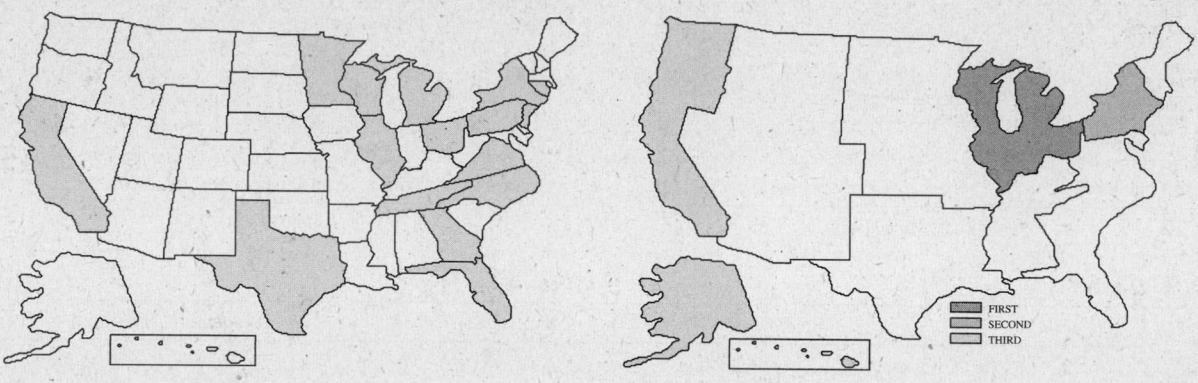

INDUSTRY DATA BY STATE

| State | Establish-ments | Shipments | | | Employment | | | | Cost as % of Shipments | Investment per Employee ($) |
		Total ($ mil)	% of U.S.	Per Establ.	Total Number	% of U.S.	Per Establ.	Wages ($/hour)		
Wisconsin	10	868.7	17.7	86,871.7	2,458	10.7	246	16.94	35.9	2,393
Virginia	11	413.9	8.5	37,626.8	1,724	7.5	157	14.37	39.9	6,503
Illinois	22	397.6	8.1	18,072.3	1,492	6.5	68	12.04	32.2	1,434
California	37	271.7	5.5	7,343.9	1,702	7.4	46	19.35	49.1	1,815
Tennessee	8	252.5	5.2	31,558.9	1,045	4.6	131	15.28	48.8	2,992
North Carolina	8	202.6	4.1	25,327.6	943	4.1	118	15.16	46.3	2,032
New Jersey	20	194.9	4.0	9,743.5	804	3.5	40	13.52	49.0	1,022
Georgia	5	186.6	3.8	37,326.8	995	4.3	199	14.24	57.3	2,472
Texas	26	132.2	2.7	5,086.4	696	3.0	27	12.25	57.1	5,463
Pennsylvania	12	121.6	2.5	10,129.4	530	2.3	44	14.25	49.0	1,985
Florida	10	78.2	1.6	7,816.9	671	2.9	67	10.41	35.8	1,678
Ohio	14	69.8	1.4	4,983.6	481	2.1	34	8.91	47.1	4,268
Connecticut	10	55.5	1.1	5,554.6	431	1.9	43	9.55	44.4	3,868
New York	10	45.9	0.9	4,585.9	381	1.7	38	13.31	39.4	2,955
Michigan	6	27.8	0.6	4,630.5	188	0.8	31	15.29	33.2	3,436
Minnesota	10	24.1	0.5	2,408.3	134	0.6	13	15.31	46.7	4,664

Source: 2002 *Economic Census*. The states are in descending order of shipments or establishments (if shipment data are missing for the majority). The symbol (D) appears when data are withheld to prevent disclosure of competitive information. States marked with (D) are sorted by number of establishments. A dash (-) indicates that the data element cannot be calculated. Data may not show all states active in the NAICS category. All data available at the time of publication are shown.

NAICS 335312 - MOTOR AND GENERATOR MANUFACTURING

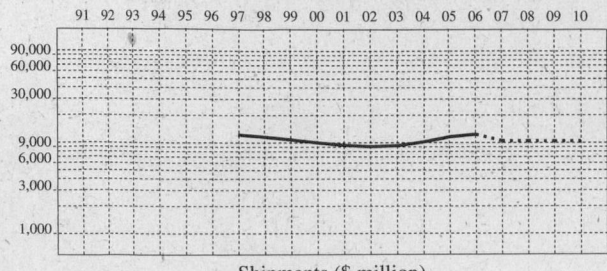

Shipments ($ million)

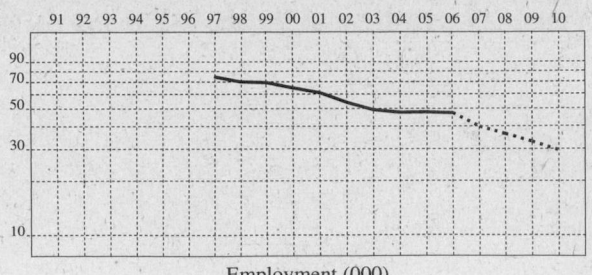

Employment (000)

GENERAL STATISTICS

| Year | Com-panies | Establishments | | Employment | | | Compensation | | Production ($ million) | | | |
		Total	with 20 or more employees	Total (000)	Production Workers (000)	Hours (Mil)	Payroll ($ mil)	Wages ($/hr)	Cost of Materials	Value Added by Manufacture	Value of Shipments	Capital Invest.
1997	563	724	367	74.7	58.3	116.7	2,184.4	12.59	6,041.7	6,191.5	12,247.9	322.3
1998		734	364	70.1	55.3	105.6	2,149.6	13.79	5,738.4	5,993.8	11,594.8	393.7
1999		704	353	69.3	54.0	106.1	2,131.9	13.27	5,425.6	5,404.4	10,815.0	257.9
2000		684	336	64.8	49.7	96.9	2,021.3	13.22	4,853.0	5,150.5	10,018.3	231.7
2001		659	336	61.0	45.9	89.9	1,929.4	13.35	4,514.8	4,866.8	9,389.6	208.2
2002	470	594	308	54.1	40.8	79.0	1,802.7	14.67	4,267.8	4,747.7	9,079.1	214.8
2003		582	298	49.2	36.3	72.5	1,726.7	15.23	4,472.4	4,863.2	9,271.4	154.7
2004		561	291	47.6	34.7	68.5	1,714.8	15.89	4,924.1	5,339.7	10,178.4	369.1
2005		541	279	47.8	34.2	68.2	1,836.2	16.59	5,993.3	5,608.4	11,598.8	196.8
2006		511P	267P	47.3	34.3	68.1	1,816.0	16.54	6,839.9	5,635.2	12,334.8	261.1
2007		484P	255P	39.8P	27.5P	54.8P	1,644.5P	17.03P	5,816.2P	4,791.8P	10,488.7P	207.8P
2008		458P	243P	36.3P	24.4P	48.9P	1,592.3P	17.49P	5,799.6P	4,778.2P	10,458.8P	198.1P
2009		431P	231P	32.9P	21.4P	43.0P	1,540.1P	17.95P	5,783.1P	4,764.5P	10,429.0P	188.4P
2010		405P	219P	29.5P	18.3P	37.1P	1,488.0P	18.41P	5,766.5P	4,750.9P	10,399.1P	178.7P

Sources: 1997 and 2002 *Economic Census*; other years, up to 2006, are from *Annual Survey of Manufactures*. Establishment counts for non-Census years are from *County Business Patterns*; 1997 and 2002 values are from the 1997 and 2002 censuses, respectively. 'P's show projections by the editors.

INDICES OF CHANGE

| Year | Com-panies | Establishments | | Employment | | | Compensation | | Production ($ million) | | | |
		Total	with 20 or more employees	Total (000)	Production Workers (000)	Hours (Mil)	Payroll ($ mil)	Wages ($/hr)	Cost of Materials	Value Added by Manufacture	Value of Shipments	Capital Invest.
1997	120	122	119	138	143	148	121	86	142	130	135	150
1998		124	118	130	136	134	119	94	134	126	128	183
1999		119	115	128	132	134	118	90	127	114	119	120
2000		115	109	120	122	123	112	90	114	108	110	108
2001		111	109	113	113	114	107	91	106	103	103	97
2002	100	100	100	100	100	100	100	100	100	100	100	100
2003		98	97	91	89	92	96	104	105	102	102	72
2004		94	94	88	85	87	95	108	115	112	112	172
2005		91	91	88	84	86	102	113	140	118	128	92
2006		86P	87P	87	84	86	101	113	160	119	136	122
2007		81P	83P	74P	67P	69P	91P	116P	136P	101P	116P	97P
2008		77P	79P	67P	60P	62P	88P	119P	136P	101P	115P	92P
2009		73P	75P	61P	52P	54P	85P	122P	136P	100P	115P	88P
2010		68P	71P	55P	45P	47P	83P	125P	135P	100P	115P	83P

Sources: Same as General Statistics. Values reflect change from the base year, 2002. Values above 100 mean greater than 2002, values below 100 mean less than 2002, and the values of 100 in other years means the same as 2002. 'P's show projections by the editors.

SELECTED RATIOS

For 2002	Avg. of All Manufact.	Analyzed Industry	Index	For 2002	Avg. of All Manufact.	Analyzed Industry	Index
Employees per Establishment	42	91	217	Value Added per Production Worker	182,367	116,365	64
Payroll per Establishment	1,639,184	3,034,848	185	Cost per Establishment	5,769,015	7,184,848	125
Payroll per Employee	39,053	33,322	85	Cost per Employee	137,446	78,887	57
Production Workers per Establishment	30	69	233	Cost per Production Worker	195,506	104,603	54
Wages per Establishment	694,845	1,951,061	281	Shipments per Establishment	11,158,348	15,284,680	137
Wages per Production Worker	23,548	28,405	121	Shipments per Employee	265,847	167,821	63
Hours per Production Worker	1,980	1,936	98	Shipments per Production Worker	378,144	222,527	59
Wages per Hour	11.89	14.67	123	Investment per Establishment	361,338	361,616	100
Value Added per Establishment	5,381,325	7,992,761	149	Investment per Employee	8,609	3,970	46
Value Added per Employee	128,210	87,758	68	Investment per Production Worker	12,245	5,265	43

Sources: Same as General Statistics. The 'Average of All Manufacturing' column represents the average of all manufacturing industries reported for the most recent complete year available. The Index shows the relationship between the Average and the Analyzed Industry. For example, 100 means that they are equal; 500 that the Analyzed Industry is five times the average; 50 means that the Analyzed Industry is half the national average. The abbreviation 'na' is used to show that data are 'not available'. Ratios shown for 2002, the last complete census year.

LEADING COMPANIES   Number shown: **75**   Total sales ($ mil): **282,913**   Total employment (000): **747.7**

Company Name	Address				CEO Name	Phone	Co. Type	Sales ($ mil)	Empl. (000)
General Electric Co.	3135 Easton Tpk.	Fairfield	CT	06828		203-373-2211	P	172,738	327.0
Emerson Electric	PO Box 4100	St. Louis	MO	63136	L.C. Barrett	314-553-2000	P	22,572	137.7
Cummins Inc.	PO Box 3005	Columbus	IN	47202		812-377-5000	P	13,048	37.8
Canon U.S.A. Inc.	1 Canon Plz.	Lake Success	NY	11042	Yoroku Adachi	516-328-5000	S	10,745*	11.0
Perfection Hy-Test Company	100 Perfection Way	Timmonsville	SC	29161		843-326-5544	R	7,000*	0.2
ArvinMeritor Inc.	2135 W Maple Rd.	Troy	MI	48084		248-435-1000	P	6,449	18.0
Corning Inc.	1 Riverfront Plz.	Corning	NY	14831	James R. Houghton	607-974-9000	P	5,860	24.5
Lincoln Electric Co.	22801 St. Clair Ave	Cleveland	OH	44117		216-481-8100	S	5,398*	7.0
Rockwell Automation Inc.	777 E Wisconsin	Milwaukee	WI	53202		414-212-5800	P	5,004	20.0
SPX Corp.	13515 Ballnyn Corp.	Charlotte	NC	28277		704-752-4400	P	4,822	17.8
Kohler Co.	444 Highland Dr.	Kohler	WI	53044	Herbert Kohler	920-457-4441	R	4,061*	33.0
Crane Co.	100 First Stamford	Stamford	CT	06902	Thomas Craney	203-363-7300	P	2,619	12.0
A.O. Smith Corp.	PO Box 245008	Milwaukee	WI	53224		414-359-4000	P	2,312	16.8
AMETEK Inc.	PO Box 1764	Paoli	PA	19301	Frank S. Hermance	610-647-2121	P	2,137	10.4
Baldor Electric Co.	PO Box 2400	Fort Smith	AR	72902		479-646-4711	P	1,825	8.1
Regal-Beloit Corp.	200 State St.	Beloit	WI	53511		608-364-8800	P	1,803	17.9
Globe Motors	2275 Stanley Ave.	Dayton	OH	45404	Jean-Claude Page	937-228-3171	S	1,671*	0.9
Teco Holdings USA Inc.	5100 N I H 35, N	Round Rock	TX	78681	H Meng	512-255-4141	R	1,240*	0.3
Remy International Inc.	2902 Enterprise Dr.	Anderson	IN	46013	Thomas J. Synder	765-778-6499	S	1,218*	7.9
Tecumseh Products Co.	100 E Patterson St.	Tecumseh	MI	49286	Edwin Bunker	517-423-8411	P	1,133	10.3
TriMas Corp.	39400 Woodward	Bloomfield Hls	MI	48304	Grant Beard	248-631-5450	P	1,068	5.1
ASMO North Carolina Inc.	470 Crawford Rd.	Statesville	NC	28625	Yutaka Kuroyanagi	704-878-6663	R	812*	0.8
Franklin Electric Company Inc.	400 E Spring St.	Bluffton	IN	46714		219-824-2900	P	602	3.2
TAC L.L.C.	PO Box 2940	Loves Park	IL	61132	Enrique Santacana	815-637-3000	S	444*	0.5
Warner Electric	449 Gardner St.	South Beloit	IL	61080		815-389-3771	R	439	0.3
Johnson Outdoors Inc.	555 Main St.	Racine	WI	53403	H. P. Johnson-Leipold	262-631-6600	P	432	1.4
Cme L.L.C.	2945 Three Leaves	Mount Pleasant	MI	48858		989-773-0377	R	317*	0.4
Toshiba International Corp.	13131 W Little York	Houston	TX	77241	Hideya Sakaida	713-466-0277	S	263*	1.0
Texas Genco Services L.P.	1301 McKinney St.	Houston	TX	77010		713-795-6000	R	246*	1.5
Penn Engineering and Mfg.	PO Box 1000	Danboro	PA	18916	Charlie Grigg	215-766-8853	R	239*	1.4
Revak Turbomachinery Services	PO Box 1645	La Porte	TX	77572	Lynn Revak	281-474-4458	R	207*	0.1
Lindgren R.F. Enclosures Inc.	1301 Arrow Pnt Dr.	Cedar Park	TX	78613	Bruce Butler	512-531-6400	S	206*	0.1
EMA Corp.	PO Box 1764	Paoli	PA	19301	Frank S. Hermance	610-647-2121	S	197*	0.1
Cummins Npower	1600 Buerkle Rd.	White Bear Lake	MN	55110	Jim Andrews	651-636-1000	S	195*	0.1
AMETEK Lamb Electric	PO Box 1599	Kent	OH	44240		330-673-3451	D	188*	1.4
Advanced D.C. Motors Inc.	6268 E Molloy Rd.	East Syracuse	NY	13057	James Jackson	315-434-9303	S	186*	0.2
SL Industries Inc.	520 Fellowship Rd.	Mount Laurel	NJ	08054	Steven Gilliatt	856-727-1500	P	177	1.9
Riverside Engineering	400 21st St.	Moline	IL	61265	Bart Mitchell	309-764-2020	D	161*	0.3
Wacker Corp.	N92 Anthony	Menomonee Fls	WI	53051	Christopher Barnard	262-255-0500	R	156*	0.5
Voss Equipment Inc.	15241 S Cmmercial	Harvey	IL	60426	Darrell Davis	708-596-7000	R	138*	<0.1
Tampa Armature Works Inc.	6312 78th Street	Riverview	FL	33578	James Turner	813-621-5661	R	137*	0.2
YMH Torrance Inc.	1495 Hawkeye Dr.	Hiawatha	IA	52233	Steve Gallagher	319-247-6039	R	130*	<0.1
Carolina Tractor/CAT	PO Box 1095	Charlotte	NC	28201	Edward Weisiger	704-596-6700	R	127*	0.7
Danfoss Inc.	7941 Corporate Dr.	Baltimore	MD	21236	Jorgen Clausen	410-931-8250	R	125*	0.1
MCL Inc.	PO Box 3287	Chicago	IL	60678	Arthur Faverio	630-759-9500	R	122*	0.5
Generac Power Systems Inc.	PO Box 8	Waukesha	WI	53189		262-544-4811	R	104*	0.5
Motor Products	PO Box 127	Owosso	MI	48867	Bill Stout	989-725-5151	S	103*	0.2
MCG Inc.	1500 N Front St.	New Ulm	MN	56073	Francis Tedesco	507-233-7000	R	103*	<0.1
Nidec America Corp.	318 Industrial Ln.	Torrington	CT	06790	Thomas Keenan	860-482-4422	R	97*	0.1
Winegard Co.	3000 Kirkwood St.	Burlington	IA	52601		319-754-0600	R	96*	0.4
L and S Electric Inc.	5101 Mesker St.	Schofield	WI	54476		715-359-3155	R	89*	0.3
Cummins Southeastern Power	PO Box 11737	Tampa	FL	33680	Richard Stohler	813-621-7202	S	86*	0.3
Alma Products Co.	2000 Michigan Ave.	Alma	MI	48801	Alan Galtan	989-463-1151	R	82*	<0.1
RAM Industries Inc.	PO Box 629	Leesport	PA	19533		610-916-3939	R	75*	0.3
Ideal Electrical Co.	330 E 1st St.	Mansfield	OH	44902	Michael Vucelic	419-522-3611	R	74*	0.5
Dreisilker Electric Motors	352 Roosevelt Rd.	Glen Ellyn	IL	60137	Leo Dreisilker	630-469-7510	R	69*	0.1
Keb America Inc.	5100 Valley Indust.	Shakopee	MN	55379	Andy Delius	952-224-1400	R	68*	<0.1
Peerless-Winsmith Inc.	172 Eaton St.	Springville	NY	14141	David McCann	716-592-9310	S	64*	0.8
Boonton Electronics Corp.	PO BOX 465	Parsippany	NJ	07054	Paul Genova	973-386-9696	S	63*	0.1
Contours Ltd.	PO Box 608	Orrville	OH	44667		330-683-5060	S	61*	0.2
Bodine Electric Co.	2500 W Bradley Pl.	Chicago	IL	60618	John Bodine	773-478-3515	R	60*	0.3
Cyberex L.L.C.	5900 Eastport Blvd.	Richmond	VA	23231	Kurt Gallo	804-236-3300	S	56*	0.4
Sloan Valve Co.	10500 Seymour Ave.	Franklin Park	IL	60131	Charles Allen	847-671-4300	R	50*	<0.1
Morrell Inc.	3333 Bald Mtn. Rd.	Auburn Hills	MI	48326	Steven Tallman	248-373-1600	S	50*	0.1
Aeroflex Laboratories Inc.	35 S Service Rd.	Plainview	NY	11803	Harvey R. Blau	516-694-6700	S	50*	0.4
McMillan Electric Co.	400 Best Rd.	Woodville	WI	54028	Douglas McMillan	715-698-2488	R	49*	0.3
ENI Products Group	100 Highpower Rd.	Rochester	NY	14623	Leo Berlinghieri	585-427-8300	S	49*	0.3
Kato Engineering Inc.	PO Box 8447	Mankato	MN	56002		507-625-4011	S	46*	0.3
Robertson Transformer Co.	13611 Thornton Rd.	Blue Island	IL	60406	Gregory Traphagen	708-388-2315	R	44*	0.3
Auburn Armature Inc.	PO Box 870	Auburn	NY	13021	Michael Capocefalo	315-253-9721	R	44*	<0.1
Tigerpoly Manufacturing Inc.	6231 Enterprise Pkw	Grove City	OH	43123		614-871-0045	R	44*	0.3
Orion South Inc.	PO Box 1850	Gretna	LA	70054	Thomas Reagan	504-368-9760	R	42*	<0.1
Tri-State Armature/Electr Wrks	PO Box 466	Memphis	TN	38101	Lonnie Loeffel	901-527-8412	R	42*	0.2
Johnson Electric Automotive	47660 Halyard Dr.	Plymouth	MI	48170		734-392-5300	S	42*	0.3
Stature Electric Inc.	PO Box 6660	Watertown	NY	13601	Richard D. Smith	315-782-5910	S	42*	0.3

Source: Ward's Business Directory of U.S. Private and Public Companies, Volumes 1 and 2, 2008. The company type code used is as follows: P - Public, R - Private, S - Subsidiary, D - Division, J - Joint Venture, A - Affiliate, G - Group. Sales are in millions of dollars, employees are in thousands. An asterisk (*) indicates an estimated sales volume. The symbol < stands for 'less than'. Company names and addresses are truncated, in some cases, to fit into the available space.

MATERIALS CONSUMED

Material	Quantity	Delivered Cost ($ million)
Metal stampings	(X)	129.5
Metal bolts, nuts, screws, and other screw machine products	(X)	82.9
All other fabricated metal products (excluding forgings)	(X)	93.0
Forgings	(X)	13.4
Iron and steel castings (rough and semifinished)	(X)	83.7
Aluminum and aluminum-base alloy castings (rough and semifinished)	(X)	71.1
Other nonferrous metal castings, rough or semifinished (inc. aluminum)	(X)	13.4
Steel bars, bar shapes, and plates (exc. castings, forgings, fabr. metal products)	(X)	55.8
Steel sheet and strip (including tinplate)	(X)	278.8
Steel wire and wire products	(X)	17.1
All other steel shapes and forms (exc. castings, forgings, fabr. metal products)	(X)	70.3
Copper and copper-base alloy bare wire for electrical conduction only	(X)	5.0
Copper and copper-base alloy rod, bar, and mechanical wire	(X)	17.9
All other copper and copper-base alloy shapes and forms (exc. castings, forgings, fabr. metal products)	(X)	28.0
Aluminum and aluminum-base alloy shapes and forms (exc. castings, forgings, fabr. metal products)	(X)	46.5
Other nonferrous shapes and forms (exc. castings, forgings, fabricated metal products)	(X)	12.2
Magnet wire	(X)	183.7
Insulated copper wire and cable (excluding magnet wire)	(X)	45.1
Primary aluminum and aluminum-base alloy refinery shapes	(X)	10.9
Diesel and semidiesel engines	(X)	209.5
Gasoline and other carburetor engines	(X)	142.3
Fractional horsepower electric motors (less than 1 hp)	(X)	41.8
Integral horsepower electric motors and generators (1 hp or more)	(X)	25.6
Ball and roller bearings (mounted or unmounted)	(X)	53.0
Plain bearings and bushings	(X)	18.4
Mechanical speed changers, gears, and industrial high-speed drives	(X)	20.9
Semiconductors (incl. transistors, diodes, rectifiers, and integrated circuits), for electronic circuitry	(X)	45.1
Carbon brushes	(X)	19.3
Ceramic magnets (ferrite)	(X)	23.4
Plastics products consumed in the form of sheets, rods, etc.	(X)	45.8
Plastics resins consumed in the form of granules, pellets, etc.	(X)	23.8
Paints, varnishes, stains, lacquers, shellacs, japans, enamels, etc.	(X)	21.3
Electrical industrial capacitors, resistors, rheostats, and coil windings	(X)	72.4
Electrical transmission, distribution, and control equipment	(X)	72.7
Paperboard containers, boxes, and corrugated paperboard	(X)	37.4
All other materials, components, parts, containers, and supplies	(X)	1,185.9
Materials, ingredients, containers, and supplies, nsk	(X)	619.7

Source: 2002 Economic Census. Explanation of symbols used: (D): Withheld to avoid disclosure of competitive data; na: Not available; (S): Withheld because statistical norms were not met; (X): Not applicable; (Z): Less than half the unit shown; nec: Not elsewhere classified; nsk: Not specified by kind; - : zero; p : 10-19 percent estimated; q : 20-29 percent estimated.

PRODUCT SHARE DETAILS

Product or Product Class Shipments	Mil. $	Product or Product Class Shipments	Mil. $
MOTORS AND GENERATORS	9,008.1	Fractional motor generator sets and other rotating equipment, including hermetics	482.7
Fractional horsepower motors (rated at less than 746 watts) (excluding hermetics)	2,988.8	Integral motor generator sets and other rotating equipment, including hermetics	534.3
Integral horsepower motors and generators other than for land transportation equipment (rated at 746 watts or more)	1,732.6	Parts, supplies for motors, generators, generator sets, and other rotating equipment, excluding motors for built-in jobs	695.6
Land transportation motors, generators, and control equipment, excluding parts	197.3	Armature rewinding on a factory basis	64.9
Prime mover generator sets, except steam or hydraulic turbine	1,776.3	Motors and generators, nsk, total	535.7

Source: 2002 Economic Census. The values are product shipments in millions of dollars for 2002. Total product shipments may be lower or higher than industry shipments. See Introduction for a full discussion. Values of indented subcategories are summed in the main heading(s). The symbol (D) appears when data are withheld to prevent disclosure of competitive information. The abbreviation nsk stands for 'not specified by kind' and nec for 'not elsewhere classified'. A dash (-) means zero.

INPUTS AND OUTPUTS FOR MOTOR AND GENERATOR MANUFACTURING

Economic Sector or Industry Providing Inputs	%	Sector	Economic Sector or Industry Buying Outputs	%	Sector
Compensation of employees	27.1		Exports of goods & services	17.1	Cap Inv
Iron & steel mills & ferroalloys	6.0	Manufg.	Private fixed investment	13.6	
Wholesale trade	5.5	Trade	AC, refrigeration, and warm air heating equipment	6.8	Manufg.
Management of companies & enterprises	5.4	Services	Pumps & pumping equipment	3.4	Manufg.
Copper rolling, drawing, extruding, & alloying	3.5	Manufg.	Engine equipment, nec	2.6	Manufg.
Engine equipment, nec	2.9	Manufg.	Household laundry equipment	2.4	Manufg.
Motors & generators	2.1	Manufg.	Residential permanent site structures	2.2	Construct.
Crowns & closures & metal stamping	2.0	Manufg.	Wholesale trade	2.1	Trade
Motor vehicle parts	2.0	Manufg.	S/L govt. invest., other	2.1	S/L Govt
Noncomparable imports	1.7	Foreign	S/L govt. passenger transit	2.0	S/L Govt

Continued on next page.

INPUTS AND OUTPUTS FOR MOTOR AND GENERATOR MANUFACTURING - Continued

Economic Sector or Industry Providing Inputs	%	Sector	Economic Sector or Industry Buying Outputs	%	Sector
Turned products & screws, nuts, & bolts	1.6	Manufg.	Small electrical applicances	2.0	Manufg.
Pottery, ceramics, and plumbing fixtures	1.2	Manufg.	Other S/L govt. enterprises	1.5	S/L Govt
Nonferrous metal foundries	1.2	Manufg.	Industrial machinery, nec	1.4	Manufg.
Ferrous metal foundries	1.0	Manufg.	Electromedical & electrotherapeutic apparatus	1.4	Manufg.
Truck transportation	0.8	Util.	Material handling equipment	1.3	Manufg.
Ball & roller bearings	0.8	Manufg.	Motors & generators	1.3	Manufg.
Alumina refining & primary aluminum production	0.8	Manufg.	Household refrigerators & home freezers	1.3	Manufg.
Gaskets, packing, & sealing devices	0.8	Manufg.	Hardware	1.2	Manufg.
Communication & energy wires & cables	0.8	Manufg.	Nonresidential structures, nec	1.2	Construct.
Plastics packaging materials, film & sheet	0.7	Manufg.	Truck transportation	1.2	Util.
Power generation & supply	0.7	Util.	Commercial & service industry machinery, nec	1.1	Manufg.
Relay & industrial controls	0.7	Manufg.	S/L govt. invest., education	1.1	S/L Govt
Printed circuit assemblies (electronic assembles)	0.7	Manufg.	Automotive repair & maintenance, ex. car washes	1.1	Services
Semiconductors & related devices	0.6	Manufg.	Motor vehicle parts	1.1	Manufg.
Electronic capacitors, resistors, coils, transformers	0.5	Manufg.	General purpose machinery, nec	1.0	Manufg.
Plastics products, nec	0.5	Manufg.	Air purification & ventilation equipment	1.0	Manufg.
Software publishers	0.5	Services	Power-driven handtools	1.0	Manufg.
Paperboard containers	0.5	Manufg.	Air & gas compressors	1.0	Manufg.
Paints & coatings	0.5	Manufg.	Commercial & industrial equipment repair/maintenance	0.9	Services
Machine shops	0.5	Manufg.	Machine shops	0.9	Manufg.
Electrical equipment & components, nec	0.4	Manufg.	Personal consumption expenditures	0.8	
Advertising & related services	0.4	Services	Construction machinery	0.8	Manufg.
Real estate	0.4	Fin/R.E.	Retail trade	0.8	Trade
Power, distribution, & specialty transformers	0.4	Manufg.	Semiconductors & related devices	0.8	Manufg.
Speed changers, industrial high-speed drives, & gears	0.4	Manufg.	Fabricated metals, nec	0.8	Manufg.
Taxes on production & imports, less subsidies	0.4		Federal government, investment, national defense	0.7	Fed Govt
Mechanical power transmission equipment	0.4	Manufg.	Railroad rolling stock	0.7	Manufg.
Retail trade	0.3	Trade	Commercial & health care structures	0.7	Construct.
Scientific research & development services	0.3	Services	General S/L govt. services	0.6	S/L Govt
Coating, engraving, heat treating & allied activities	0.3	Manufg.	Natural gas distribution	0.6	Util.
Plastics materials & resins	0.3	Manufg.	Telephone apparatus	0.6	Manufg.
Natural gas distribution	0.3	Util.	Residential structures, nec	0.6	Construct.
Carbon & graphite products	0.3	Manufg.	Surgical appliances & supplies	0.6	Manufg.
Automotive equipment rental & leasing	0.2	Fin/R.E.	Vending, commercial, industrial, office machinery	0.6	Manufg.
Maintenance/repair of nonresidential structures	0.2	Construct.	Computer terminals & peripherals	0.6	Manufg.
Warehousing & storage	0.2	Util.	Major household appliances, nec	0.5	Manufg.
Steel products from purchased steel	0.2	Manufg.	Maintenance/repair of nonresidential structures	0.5	Construct.
Forging, stamping, & sintering, nec	0.2	Manufg.	Rolling mill & other metalworking machinery	0.5	Manufg.
Services to buildings & dwellings	0.2	Services	Semiconductor machinery	0.5	Manufg.
Aluminum products from purchased aluminum	0.2	Manufg.	Search, detection, & navigation instruments	0.4	Manufg.
Cutting tools & machine tool accessories	0.2	Manufg.	Laboratory apparatus & furniture	0.4	Manufg.
Nonferrous metal (ex. copper & aluminum) processing	0.2	Manufg.	Packaging machinery	0.4	Manufg.
Telecommunications	0.1	Services	Fluid power process machinery	0.4	Manufg.
Management, scientific, & technical consulting	0.1	Services	Plastics & rubber industry machinery	0.4	Manufg.
Rail transportation	0.1	Util.	Boat building	0.4	Manufg.
Postal service	0.1	Util.	Transit & ground passenger transportation	0.4	Util.
Electronic components, nec	0.1	Manufg.	Metal cutting & forming machine tools	0.3	Manufg.
Automotive repair & maintenance, ex. car washes	0.1	Services	Valve & fittings other than plumbing	0.3	Manufg.
Ornamental & architectural metal products	0.1	Manufg.	Speed changers, industrial high-speed drives, & gears	0.3	Manufg.
Commercial & industrial machinery rental & leasing	0.1	Fin/R.E.	Heating equipment (except warm air furnaces)	0.3	Manufg.
Accounting, tax preparation, bookkeeping, & payroll	0.1	Services	Mining & oil & gas field machinery	0.3	Manufg.
Legal services	0.1	Services	Electronic & precision equipment repair/maintenance	0.3	Services
Commercial & industrial equipment repair/maintenance	0.1	Services	Ship building & repairing	0.3	Manufg.
Petroleum lubricating oil & grease	0.1	Manufg.	General Federal government services, defense	0.2	Fed Govt
Metal cans, boxes, & other containers (light gauge)	0.1	Manufg.	Turbines & turbine generator set units	0.2	Manufg.
Paperboard mills	0.1	Manufg.	Architectural, engineering, & related services	0.2	Services
			Farm machinery & equipment	0.2	Manufg.
			Telecommunications	0.2	Services
			Scientific research & development services	0.2	Services
			Surgical & medical instrument	0.2	Manufg.
			Household cooking appliances	0.1	Manufg.
			Owner-occupied dwellings	0.1	
			Analytical laboratory instruments	0.1	Manufg.
			Federal government, investment, nondefense	0.1	Fed Govt
			Maintenance/repair of residential structures	0.1	Construct.
			Watches, clocks, & related devices	0.1	Manufg.
			Computer storage devices	0.1	Manufg.
			Electrical equipment & components, nec	0.1	Manufg.
			Nondepository credit intermediation activities	0.1	Fin/R.E.
			Couriers & messengers	0.1	Util.

Source: Benchmark Input-Output Accounts for the U.S. Economy, 2002, U.S. Department of Commerce, Washington, D.C., January 2008. The abbreviation nec stands for 'not elsewhere classified'.

OCCUPATIONS EMPLOYED BY ELECTRICAL EQUIPMENT MANUFACTURING

Occupation	% of Total 2006	Change to 2016	Occupation	% of Total 2006	Change to 2016
Electrical & electronic equipment assemblers	15.2	-32.0	Shipping, receiving, & traffic clerks	1.7	-18.2
Team assemblers	10.7	-15.0	Industrial engineers	1.5	3.2
Coil winders, tapers, & finishers	4.9	-32.0	Mechanical engineers	1.4	-15.0
First-line supervisors/managers of production workers	3.3	-15.0	Assemblers & fabricators, nec	1.3	-23.5
Inspectors, testers, sorters, samplers, & weighers	2.9	-19.9	Maintenance & repair workers, general	1.3	-15.0
Electromechanical equipment assemblers	2.7	-15.0	Purchasing agents, exc wholesale, retail, & farm	1.2	-15.0
Electrical engineers	2.6	-15.0	General & operations managers	1.2	-23.5
Cutting, punching, & press machine operators	2.5	-23.5	Bookkeeping, accounting, & auditing clerks	1.1	-15.0
Machinists	2.3	-10.8	Electronics engineers, exc computer	1.1	-15.0
Welders, cutters, solderers, & brazers	2.1	-9.6	Customer service representatives	1.1	-6.5
Computer-controlled machine tool operators	1.7	-6.5	Electrical & electronics drafters	1.1	-15.0
Electrical & electronic engineering technicians	1.7	-15.0			

Source: Industry-Occupation Matrix, Bureau of Labor Statistics, December 4, 2007. These data are reported based on 4-digit NAICS categories but have been matched to corresponding 6-digit NAICS industry codes. The change reported for each occupation to the year 2016 is a percent of growth or decline as estimated by the Bureau of Labor Statistics. The abbreviation nec stands for 'not elsewhere classified'.

LOCATION BY STATE AND REGIONAL CONCENTRATION

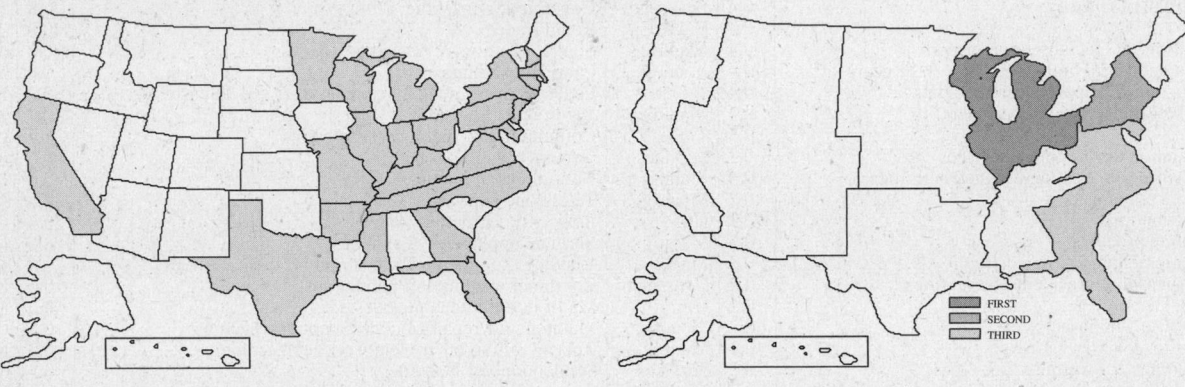

FIRST
SECOND
THIRD

INDUSTRY DATA BY STATE

State	Establish- ments	Shipments Total ($ mil)	Shipments % of U.S.	Shipments Per Establ.	Employment Total Number	Employment % of U.S.	Employment Per Establ.	Wages ($/hour)	Cost as % of Shipments	Investment per Employee ($)
Wisconsin	39	1,168.9	12.9	29,971.6	5,794	10.7	149	14.03	53.8	2,433
Arkansas	16	910.5	10.0	56,908.6	4,684	8.7	293	14.17	39.1	3,753
Minnesota	18	775.4	8.5	43,076.1	2,769	5.1	154	22.04	66.2	4,214
Georgia	13	592.9	6.5	45,610.0	1,878	3.5	144	14.41	43.0	4,471
Ohio	40	577.8	6.4	14,445.9	4,704	8.7	118	15.93	43.1	5,601
Missouri	13	567.4	6.2	43,647.6	3,700	6.8	285	12.78	42.2	6,656
North Carolina	20	536.7	5.9	26,833.3	2,803	5.2	140	13.42	58.4	4,598
Texas	29	431.5	4.8	14,879.0	1,848	3.4	64	15.92	43.6	3,668
Kentucky	11	342.5	3.8	31,136.4	2,179	4.0	198	13.12	53.2	4,924
Illinois	31	331.8	3.7	10,703.4	2,412	4.5	78	15.83	35.7	5,068
Tennessee	24	315.4	3.5	13,142.7	3,050	5.6	127	14.02	46.7	5,223
Mississippi	12	301.0	3.3	25,082.2	2,026	3.7	169	10.84	42.4	3,420
Indiana	29	279.9	3.1	9,650.9	2,681	5.0	92	16.29	38.9	2,634
Pennsylvania	25	223.3	2.5	8,931.8	1,672	3.1	67	15.98	37.6	3,857
California	56	203.1	2.2	3,626.3	1,487	2.7	27	14.38	38.2	2,915
New York	28	188.1	2.1	6,719.5	1,733	3.2	62	11.82	40.5	1,628
Michigan	20	152.5	1.7	7,623.7	1,106	2.0	55	13.07	48.1	3,219
Virginia	13	149.8	1.7	11,524.9	1,109	2.0	85	16.79	28.4	4,453
Massachusetts	13	111.5	1.2	8,575.0	823	1.5	63	21.52	49.8	3,650
Connecticut	9	96.5	1.1	10,716.8	483	0.9	54	14.93	66.4	3,547
New Jersey	16	51.9	0.6	3,245.2	370	0.7	23	16.92	42.1	3,803
New Hampshire	6	27.3	0.3	4,555.3	219	0.4	37	23.60	32.5	1,598
Florida	12	27.0	0.3	2,247.6	223	0.4	19	16.26	41.4	3,726
Maryland	4	20.4	0.2	5,104.2	174	0.3	43	22.92	24.6	2,333

Source: 2002 *Economic Census*. The states are in descending order of shipments or establishments (if shipment data are missing for the majority). The symbol (D) appears when data are withheld to prevent disclosure of competitive information. States marked with (D) are sorted by number of establishments. A dash (-) indicates that the data element cannot be calculated. Data may not show all states active in the NAICS category. All data available at the time of publication are shown.

NAICS 335313 - SWITCHGEAR AND SWITCHBOARD APPARATUS MANUFACTURING

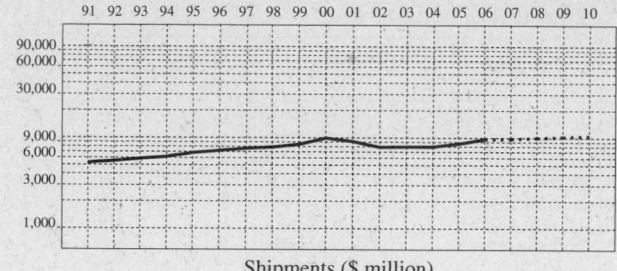

Shipments ($ million)

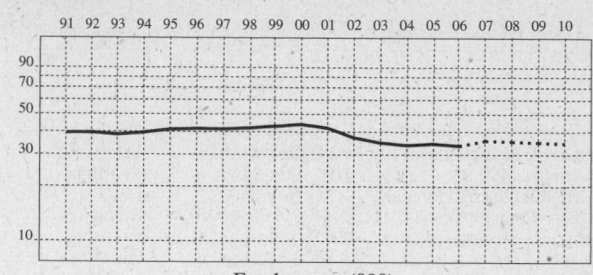

Employment (000)

GENERAL STATISTICS

Year	Companies	Establishments		Employment			Compensation		Production ($ million)			
		Total	with 20 or more employees	Total (000)	Production Workers (000)	Hours (Mil)	Payroll ($ mil)	Wages ($/hr)	Cost of Materials	Value Added by Manufacture	Value of Shipments	Capital Invest.
1991		480	245	39.4	26.2	51.3	1,100.4	11.52	2,137.7	3,084.2	5,280.6	114.5
1992	441	533	241	39.5	26.3	52.8	1,167.0	12.15	2,240.6	3,277.7	5,527.7	118.4
1993		522	237	38.5	25.7	50.0	1,185.9	12.89	2,396.1	3,443.6	5,849.0	120.2
1994		528	242	39.5	27.2	54.5	1,250.9	13.25	2,552.4	3,614.9	6,140.2	145.7
1995		532	247	41.1	28.7	58.1	1,329.2	13.29	2,741.0	4,083.3	6,796.8	151.9
1996		571	243	41.5	29.0	58.7	1,397.0	13.61	3,021.3	4,187.0	7,184.2	164.0
1997	501	583	241	41.3	28.9	59.3	1,454.2	14.32	3,194.4	4,420.3	7,613.9	195.4
1998		590	246	41.9	29.5	61.3	1,508.0	14.29	3,449.2	4,458.3	7,877.2	206.4
1999		587	243	42.9	30.2	62.2	1,606.8	14.84	3,767.7	4,702.7	8,466.4	175.2
2000		578	256	43.9	31.7	62.7	1,676.9	15.44	4,871.3	5,011.7	9,898.6	193.3
2001		580	258	41.9	30.1	58.7	1,585.8	15.51	4,439.8	4,666.6	9,112.7	196.8
2002	446	528	220	37.2	25.9	51.3	1,449.6	16.22	3,558.3	4,294.5	7,894.2	191.4
2003		535	213	34.9	23.9	48.1	1,474.7	17.43	3,484.6	4,505.1	7,976.8	112.0
2004		535	218	33.8	23.0	47.6	1,473.0	17.32	3,570.6	4,407.4	7,991.4	106.5
2005		555	224	34.4	23.0	46.6	1,568.3	18.62	4,092.7	4,567.8	8,627.2	111.4
2006		571P	226P	33.5	23.6	47.8	1,582.0	18.57	4,859.4	4,894.7	9,647.8	164.6
2007		574P	224P	35.8P	25.2P	51.3P	1,677.7P	18.83P	4,911.4P	4,947.1P	9,751.1P	161.9P
2008		576P	223P	35.4P	25.0P	50.9P	1,707.3P	19.29P	5,037.8P	5,074.4P	10,002.1P	162.7P
2009		579P	221P	35.0P	24.8P	50.5P	1,737.0P	19.74P	5,164.3P	5,201.8P	10,253.1P	163.6P
2010		582P	220P	34.6P	24.6P	50.1P	1,766.7P	20.20P	5,290.7P	5,329.1P	10,504.0P	164.5P

Sources: 1992, 1997, 2002 *Economic Census*; other years, up to 2006, are from the *Annual Survey of Manufactures*. Establishment counts for non-Census years are from *County Business Patterns*; 1997 and 2002 values are from the 1997 and 2002 censuses respectively, reported in the Federal Government's NAICS format. Other years were originally reported in equivalent SIC format. 'P's show projections by the editors.

INDICES OF CHANGE

Year	Companies	Establishments		Employment			Compensation		Production ($ million)			
		Total	with 20 or more employees	Total (000)	Production Workers (000)	Hours (Mil)	Payroll ($ mil)	Wages ($/hr)	Cost of Materials	Value Added by Manufacture	Value of Shipments	Capital Invest.
1992	99	101	110	106	102	103	81	75	63	76	70	62
1997	112	110	110	111	112	116	100	88	90	103	96	102
2001		110	117	113	116	114	109	96	125	109	115	103
2002	100	100	100	100	100	100	100	100	100	100	100	100
2003		101	97	94	92	94	102	107	98	105	101	59
2004		101	99	91	89	93	102	107	100	103	101	56
2005		105	102	92	89	91	108	115	115	106	109	58
2006		108P	103P	90	91	93	109	114	137	114	122	86
2007		109P	102P	96P	97P	100P	116P	116P	138P	115P	124P	85P
2008		109P	101P	95P	97P	99P	118P	119P	142P	118P	127P	85P
2009		110P	101P	94P	96P	98P	120P	122P	145P	121P	130P	85P
2010		110P	100P	93P	95P	98P	122P	125P	149P	124P	133P	86P

Sources: Same as General Statistics. Values reflect change from the base year, 2002. Values above 100 mean greater than 2002, values below 100 mean less than 2002, and the values of 100 in other years means the same as 2002. 'P's show projections by the editors.

SELECTED RATIOS

For 2002	Avg. of All Manufact.	Analyzed Industry	Index	For 2002	Avg. of All Manufact.	Analyzed Industry	Index
Employees per Establishment	42	70	168	Value Added per Production Worker	182,367	165,811	91
Payroll per Establishment	1,639,184	2,745,455	167	Cost per Establishment	5,769,015	6,739,205	117
Payroll per Employee	39,053	38,968	100	Cost per Employee	137,446	95,653	70
Production Workers per Establishment	30	49	166	Cost per Production Worker	195,506	137,386	70
Wages per Establishment	694,845	1,575,920	227	Shipments per Establishment	11,158,348	14,951,136	134
Wages per Production Worker	23,548	32,127	136	Shipments per Employee	265,847	212,210	80
Hours per Production Worker	1,980	1,981	100	Shipments per Production Worker	378,144	304,795	81
Wages per Hour	11.89	16.22	136	Investment per Establishment	361,338	362,500	100
Value Added per Establishment	5,381,325	8,133,523	151	Investment per Employee	8,609	5,145	60
Value Added per Employee	128,210	115,444	90	Investment per Production Worker	12,245	7,390	60

Sources: Same as General Statistics. The 'Average of All Manufacturing' column represents the average of all manufacturing industries reported for the most recent complete year available. The Index shows the relationship between the Average and the Analyzed Industry. For example, 100 means that they are equal; 500 that the Analyzed Industry is five times the average; 50 means that the Analyzed Industry is half the national average. The abbreviation 'na' is used to show that data are 'not available'. Ratios shown for 2002, the last complete census year.

LEADING COMPANIES   Number shown: **75**   Total sales ($ mil): **21,514**   Total employment (000): **97.4**

Company Name	Address				CEO Name	Phone	Co. Type	Sales ($ mil)	Empl. (000)
Federal-Mogul Corp.	PO Box 1966	Detroit	MI	48235	Jose Maria Alapont	248-354-7700	P	6,914	43.1
Caribe General Electric Prods	PO Box 41306	San Juan	PR	00940		787-774-0202	R	1,558*	3.0
Cutler-Hammer de P.R.	PO Box 336	Toa Baja	PR	00951		787-794-1818	R	1,351*	2.6
Leviton Manufacturing Company	PO Box 630087	Little Neck	NY	11363	Donald Hendler	718-229-4040	R	800*	0.7
Siemens Pwr Transm./Distrib.	4700 Falls of Neuse	Raleigh	NC	27609	David Pacyna	919-325-7000	S	648*	1.0
Powell-Process Systems Inc.	8550 Mosley Dr.	Houston	TX	77075	Thomas Powell	713-944-6900	S	606*	1.1
Powell Energy Systems Inc.	8550 Mosley Dr.	Houston	TX	77075	Thomas Powell	713-944-6900	S	577*	1.0
Powell Industries Inc.	PO Box 12818	Houston	TX	77217		713-944-6900	P	564	2.1
Littelfuse Inc.	800 E Northwest	Des Plaines	IL	60016		847-824-1188	P	536	6.6
Power-One Inc.	740 Calle Plano	Camarillo	CA	93012		805-987-8741	P	512	4.2
ADTRAN Inc.	901 Explorer Blvd.	Huntsville	AL	35806	Thomas Stanton	256-963-8000	P	477	1.6
Mitsubishi Electric Pwr Prods	530 Keystone Dr.	Warrendale	PA	15086	John Greaf	724-772-2555	R	450*	0.2
Liebert Corp.	PO Box 29186	Columbus	OH	43229	Robert Bauer	614-888-0246	S	440*	5.0
Cherry Corp.	10411 Corporate Dr.	Pleasant Pr	WI	53158	Peter B. Cherry	262-942-6500	R	411*	3.9
Marquardt Switches Inc.	2711 US Rte. 20	Cazenovia	NY	13035	Michael Beckett	315-655-8050	R	338*	0.2
S and C Electric Co.	6601 N Ridge Blvd.	Chicago	IL	60626	John Estey	773-338-1000	R	289*	1.7
Aromat Corp.	629 Central Ave.	New Providence	NJ	07974	Kazushige Nishida	908-464-3550	S	234*	1.0
Winona Watlow Inc.	PO Box 5580	Winona	MN	55987	Peter Desloge	507-454-5300	R	202*	0.3
Framatome ANP Inc.	PO Box 10935	Lynchburg	VA	24506	Tom Christopher	434-832-3000	S	198*	1.8
Motion Holdings Inc.	11380 White Rock	Rancho Cordova	CA	95742	Randy Bays	916-463-9200	S	195*	0.4
Simpson Electric Co.	PO Box 99	Lac d Flambeau	WI	54538	Richard Schermetzler	715-588-3311	R	182*	0.1
On-Line Power Corp.	5701 Smithway St.	Commerce	CA	90040	Abblid Gourgerchian	323-721-5017	R	181*	0.2
Vishay Dale Electronics Inc.	1122 23rd St.	Columbus	NE	68601	Gerald Paul	402-564-3131	S	162*	0.5
Cantata Technology Inc.	410 1st Ave.	Needham	MA	02494	Timothy Murray	781-449-4100	S	159*	0.4
Takkt America Holding Inc.	770 S 70th St.	Milwaukee	WI	53214	George Gayier	414-443-1700	R	156*	0.8
Hi-Lex Controls Inc.	152 Simpson Dr.	Litchfield	MI	49252	Robert Chrysler	517-542-2955	R	153*	0.5
Powell Electrical Mfg.	PO Box 12818	Houston	TX	77217	Thomas Powell	713-944-6900	S	149*	0.9
Babcock Inc.	14930 E Alondra	La Mirada	CA	90638	Richard Dixon	714-994-6500	R	145*	0.2
Calix	1035 N McDowell	Petaluma	CA	94954	Carl Russo	707-766-3000	R	144*	0.3
Micro Craft Inc.	41129 Jo Dr.	Novi	MI	48375	William Brown	248-476-6510	R	143*	<0.1
Mil-Con Inc.	555 Pond Dr.	Wood Dale	IL	60191	Bernard Machura	630-595-2366	R	113*	0.2
Carling Technologies Inc.	60 Johnson Ave.	Plainville	CT	06062		860-793-9266	R	110*	0.2
Mining Controls Inc.	PO Box 1141	Beckley	WV	25802	Randall Hurst	304-252-6243	R	104*	0.6
Electric Materials Co.	PO Box 390	North East	PA	16428	Douglas Winner	814-725-9621	R	100*	0.3
Shoretel Inc.	960 Stewart Dr.	Sunnyvale	CA	94085	John W. Combs	408-331-3300	R	98	0.3
First Technology	228 NE Road	Standish	ME	04084	David MeMeo	248-353-6200	S	97*	1.2
Axesstel Inc.	6815 Flanders Dr.	San Diego	CA	92121		858-625-2100	P	96	<0.1
Russelectric Inc.	99 Industrial Park	Hingham	MA	02043	Raymond Russell	781-749-6000	R	95*	0.2
Electrical Power Products Inc.	1800 Hull Ave.	Des Moines	IA	50313	Terry Nelson	515-262-8161	R	92*	0.5
L and S Electric Inc.	5101 Mesker St.	Schofield	WI	54476		715-359-3155	R	89*	0.3
RAM Industries Inc.	PO Box 629	Leesport	PA	19533		610-916-3939	R	75*	0.3
Ideal Electrical Co.	330 E 1st St.	Mansfield	OH	44902	Michael Vucelic	419-522-3611	R	74*	0.5
Powercon Corp.	PO Box 477	Severn	MD	21144	Ralph Siegel	410-551-6500	R	72*	0.4
Siemon Co.	PO Box 400	Watertown	CT	06795	Carl Siemon	860-945-4200	R	70*	0.5
W-Industries Inc.	11500 Charles Rd.	Houston	TX	77041	Rick Lynn	713-466-9463	R	70*	0.2
Motion Control Engineering	11380 White Rock	Rancho Cordova	CA	95742		916-463-9200	R	68*	0.4
Westwood Corp.	12402 E 60th St.	Tulsa	OK	74146	Ernest H. McKee	918-250-4411	S	64*	0.3
Advanced Control Systems Inc.	PO Box 922548	Norcross	GA	30010	John Muench	770-446-8854	R	64*	<0.1
Thomas G Faria Corp.	PO Box 983	Uncasville	CT	06382	David Blackburn	860-848-9271	R	57*	0.3
Grayhill Inc.	PO Box 10373	La Grange	IL	60525	Gene Hill	708-354-1040	R	56*	0.5
Datalux Corp.	155 Aviation Dr.	Winchester	VA	22602		540-662-4500	R	56*	0.1
Justcom Tech Inc.	2283 Paragon Dr.	San Jose	CA	95131	Genny Wu	408-392-9998	R	55*	0.3
Hooper Corporation	PO Box 7455	Madison	WI	53707	Fred Davie	608-249-0451	R	50*	0.4
Cole Hersee Co.	20 Old Colony Ave.	Boston	MA	02127	Robert Mayer	617-268-2100	R	50*	0.3
Carbone Lorraine North America	400 Myrtle Ave.	Boonton	NJ	07005	Michel Coniglio	973-541-4720	R	50*	<0.1
M and G Electronics Corp.	PO Box 8187	Virginia Beach	VA	23450	Mark Garcea	757-468-6000	R	49*	0.3
Innova Electronics L.P.	8383 N S Houston	Houston	TX	77064	Trey Cook	281-897-0422	R	47*	0.2
Beckwith Electric Company Inc.	6190-118th Ave. N	Largo	FL	33773	Bob Beckwith	727-544-2326	R	41*	0.1
Engineered Fluid Inc.	PO Box 723	Centralia	IL	62801	John Goodspeed	618-533-1351	R	40*	0.1
Paneltec Inc.	1277 Reamwood	Sunnyvale	CA	94089		408-745-8555	S	39*	0.3
TII Network Technologies Inc.	1385 Akron St.	Copiague	NY	11726		631-789-5000	P	39	<0.1
Technology Research Corp.	5250 140th Ave. N	Clearwater	FL	33760	Owen Farren	727-535-0572	P	38	0.4
Commerce Controls Inc.	41069 Vincenti Ct.	Novi	MI	48375	Harold Gardynik	248-476-1442	R	37*	0.2
Forney Corp.	3405 Wiley Post Rd.	Carrollton	TX	75006	John Conroy	972-458-6100	S	36*	0.2
Leitch Inc.	920 Corporate Ln.	Chesapeake	VA	23320	Timothy Thorsteinson	757-548-2300	S	35*	<0.1
Hermetic Switch Inc.	PO Box 2220	Chickasha	OK	73023	Thomas Posey	405-224-4046	R	34*	0.3
Systems Control	PO Box 788	Iron Mountain	MI	49801	Dave Brule, Sr.	906-774-0440	R	34*	0.2
Components Corp. of America	717 N Harwood St.	Dallas	TX	75201	Richard Hoestery	214-969-0166	R	34*	<0.1
Luminator Holding L.P.	PO Box 278	Plano	TX	75086		972-424-6511	R	33*	0.2
Hydra-Electric Co.	PO Box 7724	Burbank	CA	91510	Henry Acuff	818-843-6211	R	31*	0.2
Capco Inc.	PO Box 1028	Grand Junction	CO	81502		970-243-8750	R	31*	0.2
Cooper Industries Bussmann Div	PO Box 14460	St. Louis	MO	63178	H. John Riley Jr.	630-394-2877	D	30*	0.3
Trilithic Inc.	9710 Park Davis Dr.	Indianapolis	IN	46235	Terry Bush	317-895-3600	R	29*	0.1
Liquid Controls Corp.	105 Albrecht Dr.	Lake Bluff	IL	60044	Michael Schneider	847-295-1050	D	29*	0.2
Btx Technologies Inc.	5 Skyline Dr.	Hawthorne	NY	10532	Greg Schwartz	914-592-1800	R	29*	<0.1

Source: Ward's Business Directory of U.S. Private and Public Companies, Volumes 1 and 2, 2008. The company type code used is as follows: P - Public, R - Private, S - Subsidiary, D - Division, J - Joint Venture, A - Affiliate, G - Group. Sales are in millions of dollars, employees are in thousands. An asterisk (*) indicates an estimated sales volume. The symbol < stands for 'less than'. Company names and addresses are truncated, in some cases, to fit into the available space.

MATERIALS CONSUMED

Material	Quantity	Delivered Cost ($ million)
Sheet metal products (excluding stampings)	(X)	86.7
Metal bolts, nuts, screws, and other screw machine products	(X)	79.8
All other fabricated metal products (excluding forgings)	(X)	161.1
Forgings	(X)	7.1
Castings, rough and semifinished	(X)	65.2
Steel bars, bar shapes, and plates (exc. castings, forgings, fabr. metal products)	(X)	13.6
Steel sheet and strip (including tinplate)	(X)	72.4
Steel structural shapes and sheet piling (exc. castings, forgings, fabr. metal products)	(X)	3.1
All other steel shapes and forms (exc. castings, forgings, fabr. metal products)	(X)	49.2
Nonferrous metal smelter and refinery shapes, incl. precious metal	(X)	56.3
Aluminum and aluminum-base alloy shapes and forms (exc. wire, castings, forgings, fabr. metal products)	(X)	59.2
Copper and copper-base alloy shapes and forms (exc. wire, castings, forgings, and fabricated metal products)	(X)	147.0
All other nonferrous shapes and forms (exc. castings, forgings, fabr. metal products)	(X)	51.4
Nonferrous wire and cable (incl. magnet wire, bare wire or insulated wire, etc.)	(X)	23.3
Industrial electrical control equipment purchased from other companies	(X)	254.5
Industrial electrical control equipment received from other plants of the same company	(X)	355.7
Porcelain, steatite, and other ceramic electrical products	(X)	33.5
Plastics products consumed in the form of sheets, rods, etc.	(X)	82.2
Plastics resins consumed in the form of granules, pellets, etc.	(X)	43.9
Switches (excluding snap, toggle and push, and circuit breakers)	(X)	62.4
Resistors, capacitors, transformers, and other electronic-type components (exc. electron tubes and semiconductors)	(X)	104.8
Printed ciruit boards (without inserted components) for electronic circuitry	(X)	50.9
Semiconductors, microprocessors, memory, ASICs, etc.	(X)	13.2
All other materials, components, parts, containers, and supplies	(X)	564.7
Materials, ingredients, containers, and supplies, nsk	(X)	655.6

Source: 2002 Economic Census. Explanation of symbols used: (D): Withheld to avoid disclosure of competitive data; na: Not available; (S): Withheld because statistical norms were not met; (X): Not applicable; (Z): Less than half the unit shown; nec: Not elsewhere classified; nsk: Not specified by kind; - : zero; p : 10-19 percent estimated; q : 20-29 percent estimated.

PRODUCT SHARE DETAILS

Product or Product Class Shipments	Mil. $	Product or Product Class Shipments	Mil. $
SWITCHGEAR AND SWITCHBOARD APPARATUS	7,398.3	Molded case circuit breakers, 1000 volts or less	1,288.8
Power circuit breakers, all voltages	696.8	Duct, including plug-in units and accessories, 1000 volts or less	210.4
Low voltage panelboards and distribution boards and other switching and interrupting devices, 1000 volts or less	2,063.7	Switchgear, except ducts and relays	2,261.7
Fuses and fuse equipment, less than 2300 volts, except power distribution cut-outs	477.4	Switchgear and switchboard apparatus, nsk, total	399.5

Source: 2002 Economic Census. The values are product shipments in millions of dollars for 2002. Total product shipments may be lower or higher than industry shipments. See Introduction for a full discussion. Values of indented subcategories are summed in the main heading(s). The symbol (D) appears when data are withheld to prevent disclosure of competitive information. The abbreviation nsk stands for 'not specified by kind' and nec for 'not elsewhere classified'. A dash (-) means zero.

INPUTS AND OUTPUTS FOR SWITCHGEAR AND SWITCHBOARD APPARATUS MANUFACTURING

Economic Sector or Industry Providing Inputs	%	Sector	Economic Sector or Industry Buying Outputs	%	Sector
Compensation of employees	25.5		Private fixed investment	28.9	
Wholesale trade	7.1	Trade	Exports of goods & services	11.6	Cap Inv
Relay & industrial controls	6.9	Manufg.	Owner-occupied dwellings	10.8	
Management of companies & enterprises	5.1	Services	Nonresidential structures, nec	5.9	Construct.
Switchgear & switchboard apparatus	3.2	Manufg.	Residential permanent site structures	4.3	Construct.
Primary smelting & refining of copper	2.8	Manufg.	Residential structures, nec	4.3	Construct.
Iron & steel mills & ferroalloys	1.9	Manufg.	Telecommunications	3.2	Services
Printed circuit assemblies (electronic assemblies)	1.7	Manufg.	Food services & drinking places	3.2	Services
Turned products & screws, nuts, & bolts	1.5	Manufg.	Switchgear & switchboard apparatus	2.4	Manufg.
Ornamental & architectural metal products	1.1	Manufg.	General Federal government services, defense	2.1	Fed Govt
Plastics packaging materials, film & sheet	1.1	Manufg.	Commercial & health care structures	2.0	Construct.
Aluminum products from purchased aluminum	1.1	Manufg.	Relay & industrial controls	1.8	Manufg.
Noncomparable imports	1.0	Foreign	Facilities support services	1.7	Services
Nonferrous metal (ex. copper & aluminum) processing	0.9	Manufg.	Maintenance/repair of nonresidential structures	1.4	Construct.
Paints & coatings	0.8	Manufg.	Plastics products, nec	1.2	Manufg.
Machine shops	0.7	Manufg.	Federal government, investment, nondefense	1.2	Fed Govt
Bare printed circuit boards	0.7	Manufg.	Legal services	1.1	Services
Plastics materials & resins	0.6	Manufg.	S/L govt. invest., other	1.1	S/L Govt
Truck transportation	0.6	Util.	Other S/L govt. enterprises	0.9	S/L Govt
Coating, engraving, heat treating & allied activities	0.5	Manufg.	Professional, scientific, technical services, nec	0.8	Services
Gaskets, packing, & sealing devices	0.5	Manufg.	Natural gas distribution	0.8	Util.
Pottery, ceramics, and plumbing fixtures	0.5	Manufg.	Computer terminals & peripherals	0.8	Manufg.
Ferrous metal foundries	0.5	Manufg.	Engine equipment, nec	0.6	Manufg.
Power generation & supply	0.5	Util.	Railroad rolling stock	0.6	Manufg.
Semiconductors & related devices	0.4	Manufg.	Architectural, engineering, & related services	0.6	Services
Nonferrous metal foundries	0.4	Manufg.	Semiconductors & related devices	0.6	Manufg.

Continued on next page.

INPUTS AND OUTPUTS FOR SWITCHGEAR AND SWITCHBOARD APPARATUS MANUFACTURING - Continued

Economic Sector or Industry Providing Inputs	%	Sector	Economic Sector or Industry Buying Outputs	%	Sector
Lessors of nonfinancial assets	0.4	Fin/R.E.	Internet service providers & web search portals	0.5	Services
Taxes on production & imports, less subsidies	0.4		Accounting, tax preparation, bookkeeping, & payroll	0.5	Services
Custom roll forming	0.4	Manufg.	Personal consumption expenditures	0.5	
Real estate	0.4	Fin/R.E.	General Federal government services, nondefense	0.4	Fed Govt
Scientific research & development services	0.3	Services	Retail trade	0.3	Trade
Securities, commodity contracts, investments	0.3	Fin/R.E.	Civic, social, & professional organizations	0.3	Services
Advertising & related services	0.3	Services	Employment services	0.3	Services
Metal cans, boxes, & other containers (light gauge)	0.2	Manufg.	Data processing, hosting, & related services	0.2	Services
Fabricated metals, nec	0.2	Manufg.	Motor vehicle parts	0.2	Manufg.
Crowns & closures & metal stamping	0.2	Manufg.	Office administrative services	0.2	Services
Management, scientific, & technical consulting	0.2	Services	Search, detection, & navigation instruments	0.2	Manufg.
Warehousing & storage	0.2	Util.	Business support services	0.2	Services
Unlaminated plastics profile shapes	0.2	Manufg.	Management, scientific, & technical consulting	0.2	Services
Automotive equipment rental & leasing	0.2	Fin/R.E.	Rail transportation	0.2	Util.
Maintenance/repair of nonresidential structures	0.2	Construct.	Wholesale trade	0.2	Trade
Telecommunications	0.2	Services	Scientific research & development services	0.2	Services
Plate work & fabricated structural products	0.1	Manufg.	Maintenance/repair of residential structures	0.1	Construct.
Services to buildings & dwellings	0.1	Services	Waste management & remediation services	0.1	Services
Monetary authorities/depository credit intermediation	0.1	Fin/R.E.	Investigation & security services	0.1	Services
Ball & roller bearings	0.1	Manufg.	Real estate	0.1	Fin/R.E.
Forging, stamping, & sintering, nec	0.1	Manufg.	Manufacturing structures	0.1	Construct.
Natural gas distribution	0.1	Util.	Commercial & industrial machinery rental & leasing	0.1	Fin/R.E.
Handtools	0.1	Manufg.			
Professional, scientific, technical services, nec	0.1	Services			
Paperboard containers	0.1	Manufg.			
Accounting, tax preparation, bookkeeping, & payroll	0.1	Services			
Data processing, hosting, & related services	0.1	Services			
Rail transportation	0.1	Util.			
Postal service	0.1	Util.			

Source: Benchmark Input-Output Accounts for the U.S. Economy, 2002, U.S. Department of Commerce, Washington, D.C., January 2008. The abbreviation nec stands for 'not elsewhere classified'.

OCCUPATIONS EMPLOYED BY ELECTRICAL EQUIPMENT MANUFACTURING

Occupation	% of Total 2006	Change to 2016	Occupation	% of Total 2006	Change to 2016
Electrical & electronic equipment assemblers	15.2	-32.0	Shipping, receiving, & traffic clerks	1.7	-18.2
Team assemblers	10.7	-15.0	Industrial engineers	1.5	3.2
Coil winders, tapers, & finishers	4.9	-32.0	Mechanical engineers	1.4	-15.0
First-line supervisors/managers of production workers	3.3	-15.0	Assemblers & fabricators, nec	1.3	-23.5
Inspectors, testers, sorters, samplers, & weighers	2.9	-19.9	Maintenance & repair workers, general	1.3	-15.0
Electromechanical equipment assemblers	2.7	-15.0	Purchasing agents, exc wholesale, retail, & farm	1.2	-15.0
Electrical engineers	2.6	-15.0	General & operations managers	1.2	-23.5
Cutting, punching, & press machine operators	2.5	-23.5	Bookkeeping, accounting, & auditing clerks	1.1	-15.0
Machinists	2.3	-10.8	Electronics engineers, exc computer	1.1	-15.0
Welders, cutters, solderers, & brazers	2.1	-9.6	Customer service representatives	1.1	-6.5
Computer-controlled machine tool operators	1.7	-6.5	Electrical & electronics drafters	1.1	-15.0
Electrical & electronic engineering technicians	1.7	-15.0			

Source: Industry-Occupation Matrix, Bureau of Labor Statistics, December 4, 2007. These data are reported based on 4-digit NAICS categories but have been matched to corresponding 6-digit NAICS industry codes. The change reported for each occupation to the year 2016 is a percent of growth or decline as estimated by the Bureau of Labor Statistics. The abbreviation nec stands for 'not elsewhere classified'.

LOCATION BY STATE AND REGIONAL CONCENTRATION

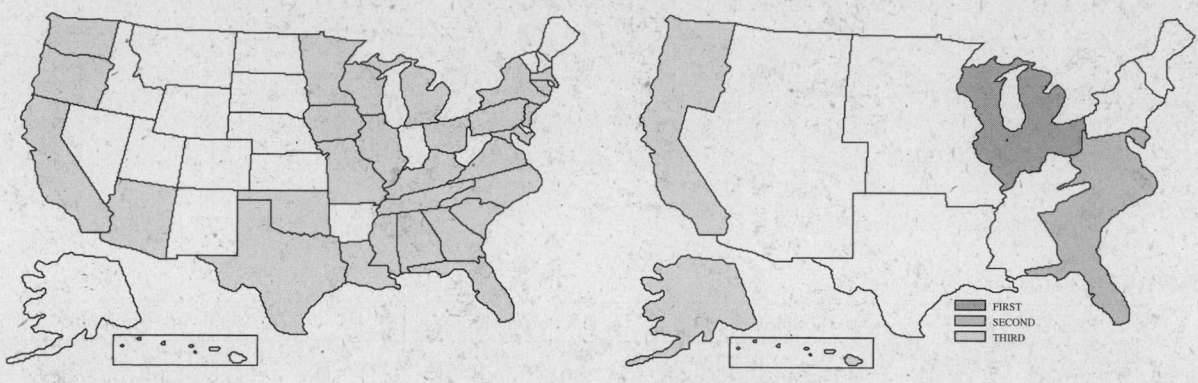

FIRST
SECOND
THIRD

INDUSTRY DATA BY STATE

| State | Establish-ments | Shipments | | | Employment | | | | Cost as % of Shipments | Investment per Employee ($) |
		Total ($ mil)	% of U.S.	Per Establ.	Total Number	% of U.S.	Per Establ.	Wages ($/hour)		
Illinois	41	1,142.4	14.5	27,863.0	5,604	15.1	137	15.77	40.2	9,125
Texas	32	630.5	8.0	19,702.2	2,812	7.6	88	13.83	45.0	4,136
South Carolina	10	506.7	6.4	50,669.8	2,293	6.2	229	15.05	52.2	2,727
Pennsylvania	26	496.5	6.3	19,094.9	2,020	5.4	78	19.27	49.6	1,940
Iowa	6	470.9	6.0	78,476.5	1,451	3.9	242	30.86	55.1	6,952
Kentucky	10	449.6	5.7	44,957.4	1,568	4.2	157	18.87	32.8	3,342
Ohio	43	428.7	5.4	9,968.9	2,240	6.0	52	18.39	37.4	3,291
California	56	388.2	4.9	6,932.1	2,202	5.9	39	15.42	43.6	4,538
North Carolina	22	308.3	3.9	14,012.6	1,726	4.6	78	17.34	56.1	19,614
Tennessee	13	290.5	3.7	22,349.7	1,143	3.1	88	16.75	44.6	3,055
Missouri	13	269.9	3.4	20,763.7	1,190	3.2	92	14.65	33.0	2,839
Georgia	20	244.8	3.1	12,239.9	1,154	3.1	58	13.47	48.2	5,673
Florida	16	190.0	2.4	11,878.1	957	2.6	60	14.31	61.3	1,823
Wisconsin	18	188.4	2.4	10,466.7	816	2.2	45	16.44	39.9	1,498
Massachusetts	7	186.1	2.4	26,581.1	745	2.0	106	24.32	33.6	4,587
Mississippi	6	152.0	1.9	25,336.8	428	1.2	71	14.72	57.0	4,514
Minnesota	16	123.1	1.6	7,692.9	685	1.8	43	16.81	52.3	3,028
New York	21	114.5	1.5	5,451.7	783	2.1	37	15.12	43.3	7,004
Connecticut	9	107.6	1.4	11,958.8	1,140	3.1	127	14.46	27.5	1,381
Michigan	29	90.6	1.1	3,123.9	717	1.9	25	15.17	46.1	11,409
New Jersey	16	88.1	1.1	5,507.7	533	1.4	33	21.89	33.6	1,927
Oklahoma	8	63.9	0.8	7,986.1	311	0.8	39	13.80	53.8	1,537
Maryland	5	53.8	0.7	10,754.8	569	1.5	114	5.53	43.7	650
Oregon	5	39.3	0.5	7,867.8	192	0.5	38	15.36	48.8	2,198
Virginia	8	38.7	0.5	4,837.7	228	0.6	28	11.89	55.6	1,351
Alabama	9	33.2	0.4	3,690.0	170	0.5	19	13.19	61.7	10,606
Washington	10	25.7	0.3	2,574.8	111	0.3	11	15.97	43.0	1,991
Louisiana	6	24.7	0.3	4,117.5	211	0.6	35	16.11	50.8	1,801
Arizona	8	23.2	0.3	2,904.5	132	0.4	16	16.49	59.6	4,939

Source: 2002 *Economic Census*. The states are in descending order of shipments or establishments (if shipment data are missing for the majority). The symbol (D) appears when data are withheld to prevent disclosure of competitive information. States marked with (D) are sorted by number of establishments. A dash (-) indicates that the data element cannot be calculated. Data may not show all states active in the NAICS category. All data available at the time of publication are shown.

NAICS 335314 - RELAY AND INDUSTRIAL CONTROL MANUFACTURING

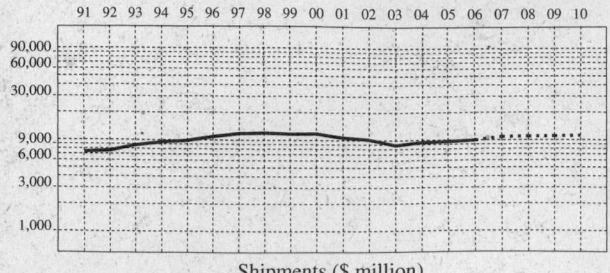

Shipments ($ million)

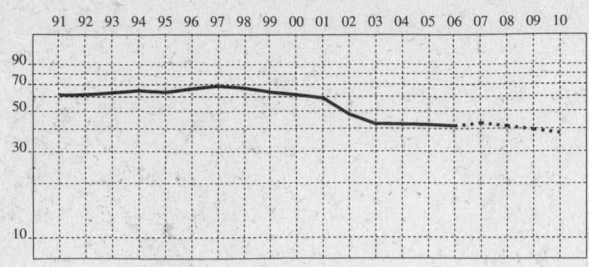

Employment (000)

GENERAL STATISTICS

Year	Companies	Establishments		Employment			Compensation		Production ($ million)			
		Total	with 20 or more employees	Total (000)	Production Workers (000)	Hours (Mil)	Payroll ($ mil)	Wages ($/hr)	Cost of Materials	Value Added by Manufacture	Value of Shipments	Capital Invest.
1991		1,074	438	61.2	35.3	72.3	1,798.7	10.37	3,072.8	4,289.2	7,378.6	196.4
1992	1,168	1,242	448	61.6	35.2	66.7	1,846.1	10.96	3,025.8	4,548.6	7,573.1	218.5
1993		1,221	450	63.1	37.2	68.3	1,928.8	11.58	3,442.2	5,275.5	8,726.7	217.0
1994		1,215	451	64.8	37.6	73.3	2,121.8	12.15	3,955.3	5,559.7	9,473.4	260.5
1995		1,162	445	63.4	37.2	72.6	2,172.7	12.39	4,258.3	5,616.9	9,840.5	304.6
1996		1,279	460	66.2	38.6	73.4	2,324.8	12.82	4,661.9	6,246.5	10,862.3	280.4
1997	1,244	1,323	481	68.6	38.9	71.3	2,434.5	13.65	5,626.5	6,160.8	11,781.7	339.1
1998		1,324	481	67.0	37.0	69.0	2,525.2	14.26	5,584.6	6,282.6	12,014.6	417.4
1999		1,285	467	63.7	36.5	66.9	2,493.3	15.18	5,480.2	6,082.1	11,655.7	275.0
2000		1,243	454	61.5	34.7	62.3	2,485.4	15.98	5,573.7	6,181.4	11,768.3	236.2
2001		1,216	451	59.0	30.9	53.9	2,280.7	16.29	5,102.4	5,507.4	10,674.7	220.5
2002	1,058	1,137	369	47.9	25.4	46.6	2,034.3	15.12	4,689.3	5,443.6	10,178.3	208.5
2003		1,082	367	42.4	22.7	42.8	1,839.9	14.56	3,966.3	4,848.2	8,812.4	141.1
2004		1,078	359	42.3	21.7	41.3	1,882.0	14.95	4,215.9	5,187.8	9,427.2	124.7
2005		1,075	346	42.1	22.1	44.2	2,047.9	15.56	4,603.6	5,018.1	9,621.5	132.7
2006		1,142P	376P	41.4	22.7	45.6	2,079.0	15.92	4,614.6	5,445.8	9,947.5	163.9
2007		1,135P	369P	42.9P	22.1P	41.0P	2,177.3P	16.94P	5,025.3P	5,930.5P	10,832.9P	169.6P
2008		1,128P	362P	41.2P	21.0P	38.7P	2,181.3P	17.30P	5,071.7P	5,985.2P	10,932.8P	162.1P
2009		1,121P	355P	39.5P	19.8P	36.4P	2,185.3P	17.66P	5,118.0P	6,039.9P	11,032.7P	154.5P
2010		1,114P	349P	37.8P	18.6P	34.1P	2,189.2P	18.02P	5,164.4P	6,094.6P	11,132.6P	147.0P

Sources: 1992, 1997, 2002 *Economic Census*; other years, up to 2006, are from the *Annual Survey of Manufactures*. Establishment counts for non-Census years are from *County Business Patterns*; 1997 and 2002 values are from the 1997 and 2002 censuses respectively, reported in the Federal Government's NAICS format. Other years were originally reported in equivalent SIC format. 'P's show projections by the editors.

INDICES OF CHANGE

Year	Companies	Establishments		Employment			Compensation		Production ($ million)			
		Total	with 20 or more employees	Total (000)	Production Workers (000)	Hours (Mil)	Payroll ($ mil)	Wages ($/hr)	Cost of Materials	Value Added by Manufacture	Value of Shipments	Capital Invest.
1992	110	109	121	129	139	143	91	72	65	84	74	105
1997	118	116	130	143	153	153	120	90	120	113	116	163
2001		107	122	123	122	116	112	108	109	101	105	106
2002	100	100	100	100	100	100	100	100	100	100	100	100
2003		95	99	89	89	92	90	96	85	89	87	68
2004		95	97	88	85	89	93	99	90	95	93	60
2005		95	94	88	87	95	101	103	98	92	95	64
2006		100P	102P	86	89	98	102	105	98	100	98	79
2007		100P	100P	90P	87P	88P	107P	112P	107P	109P	106P	81P
2008		99P	98P	86P	83P	83P	107P	114P	108P	110P	107P	78P
2009		99P	96P	82P	78P	78P	107P	117P	109P	111P	108P	74P
2010		98P	94P	79P	73P	73P	108P	119P	110P	112P	109P	71P

Sources: Same as General Statistics. Values reflect change from the base year, 2002. Values above 100 mean greater than 2002, values below 100 mean less than 2002, and the values of 100 in other years means the same as 2002. 'P's show projections by the editors.

SELECTED RATIOS

For 2002	Avg. of All Manufact.	Analyzed Industry	Index	For 2002	Avg. of All Manufact.	Analyzed Industry	Index
Employees per Establishment	42	42	100	Value Added per Production Worker	182,367	214,315	118
Payroll per Establishment	1,639,184	1,789,182	109	Cost per Establishment	5,769,015	4,124,274	71
Payroll per Employee	39,053	42,470	109	Cost per Employee	137,446	97,898	71
Production Workers per Establishment	30	22	76	Cost per Production Worker	195,506	184,618	94
Wages per Establishment	694,845	619,694	89	Shipments per Establishment	11,158,348	8,951,891	80
Wages per Production Worker	23,548	27,740	118	Shipments per Employee	265,847	212,491	80
Hours per Production Worker	1,980	1,835	93	Shipments per Production Worker	378,144	400,720	106
Wages per Hour	11.89	15.12	127	Investment per Establishment	361,338	183,377	51
Value Added per Establishment	5,381,325	4,787,687	89	Investment per Employee	8,609	4,353	51
Value Added per Employee	128,210	113,645	89	Investment per Production Worker	12,245	8,209	67

Sources: Same as General Statistics. The 'Average of All Manufacturing' column represents the average of all manufacturing industries reported for the most recent complete year available. The Index shows the relationship between the Average and the Analyzed Industry. For example, 100 means that they are equal; 500 that the Analyzed Industry is five times the average; 50 means that the Analyzed Industry is half the national average. The abbreviation 'na' is used to show that data are 'not available'. Ratios shown for 2002, the last complete census year.

LEADING COMPANIES   Number shown: **75**   Total sales ($ mil): **140,256**   Total employment (000): **594.0**

Company Name	Address				CEO Name	Phone	Co. Type	Sales ($ mil)	Empl. (000)
Johnson Controls Inc.	PO Box 591	Milwaukee	WI	53201		414-524-1200	P	34,624	140.0
Emerson Electric	PO Box 4100	St. Louis	MO	63136	L.C. Barrett	314-553-2000	P	22,572	137.7
Texas Instruments Inc.	PO Box 660199	Dallas	TX	75266	Thomas Engibous	972-995-2011	P	13,835	30.2
Eaton Corp.	1111 Superior Ave.	Cleveland	OH	44114		216-523-5000	P	13,033	60.0
Danaher Corp.	2099 Penn. Avenue	Washington	DC	20006	H. Lawrence Culp Jr.	202-828-0850	P	11,026	50.0
Rockwell Automation Inc.	777 E Wisconsin	Milwaukee	WI	53202		414-212-5800	P	5,004	20.0
SPX Corp.	13515 Ballnyn Corp.	Charlotte	NC	28277		704-752-4400	P	4,822	17.8
Rockwell Collins Inc.	400 Collins Rd. NE	Cedar Rapids	IA	52498		319-295-1000	P	4,415	19.5
Kohler Co.	444 Highland Dr.	Kohler	WI	53044	Herbert Kohler	920-457-4441	R	4,061*	33.0
Hamilton Sundstrand Corp.	1 Hamilton Rd.	Windsor Locks	CT	06096	Ronald F. McKenna	860-654-6000	S	3,600*	16.0
Arco Auto and Marine Products	3921 Navy Blvd.	Pensacola	FL	32507	Ron Miller	850-455-5476	R	3,015	<0.1
Hubbell Inc.	584 Derby Milford	Orange	CT	06477		203-799-4100	P	2,534	11.5
DENSO Manufacturing Tennessee	1720 Rbrt C Jackson	Maryville	TN	37801	Mack Hattori	865-982-7000	S	2,231*	2.0
Teleflex Inc.	155 S Limerick Rd.	Limerick	PA	19468	Jeffrey P. Black	610-948-5100	P	1,934	14.0
Caribe General Electric Prods	PO Box 41306	San Juan	PR	00940		787-774-0202	R	1,558*	3.0
Remy International Inc.	2902 Enterprise Dr.	Anderson	IN	46013	Thomas J. Synder	765-778-6499	S	1,218*	7.9
Plant Engineering Consultants	521 Airport Rd.	Chattanooga	TN	37421	William T. Fejes jr	423-892-7654	S	1,027*	0.9
Siemens Pwr Transm./Distrib.	4700 Falls of Neuse	Raleigh	NC	27609	David Pacyna	919-325-7000	S	648*	1.0
Franklin Electric Company Inc.	400 E Spring St.	Bluffton	IN	46714		219-824-2900	P	602	3.2
Wesco Acquistion Partners Inc.	PO Box 924068	Houston	TX	77292	Ronnie Davis	713-688-5551	R	543*	<0.1
Power-One Inc.	740 Calle Plano	Camarillo	CA	93012		805-987-8741	P	512	4.2
TAC L.L.C.	PO Box 2940	Loves Park	IL	61132	Enrique Santacana	815-637-3000	S	444*	0.5
Warner Electric	449 Gardner St.	South Beloit	IL	61080		815-389-3771	R	439	0.3
Omron Electronics L.L.C.	1 E Commerce Dr.	Schaumburg	IL	60173	Gary Bauer	847-843-7900	S	350*	0.5
Marquardt Switches Inc.	2711 US Rte. 20	Cazenovia	NY	13035	Michael Beckett	315-655-8050	R	338*	0.2
Poly-Flex Circuits Inc.	28 Kenney Dr.	Cranston	RI	02920	Dennis Carvalho	401-463-3180	S	281*	0.3
Raytheon Electronic Systems	PO Box 902	El Segundo	CA	90245	Jack Kelbe	310-647-0445	R	255*	1.6
ABB Industrial Systems Inc.	579 Exec Campus	Westerville	OH	43082	Fred Kindle	614-818-6300	R	250*	1.5
Yokogawa Industrial Automation	2 Dart Rd.	Newnan	GA	30265	Kiyoshi Makino	770-254-0400	R	244*	0.7
Aromat Corp.	629 Central Ave.	New Providence	NJ	07974	Kazushige Nishida	908-464-3550	S	234*	1.0
BLD Products Ltd.	534 E 48th St.	Holland	MI	49423	Scott Bye	616-395-5600	S	213*	0.2
API Delevan	270 Quaker Rd.	East Aurora	NY	14052		716-652-3600	S	195*	1.8
Knight Inc.	20531 Crescent Bay	Lake Forest	CA	92630	George Noa	949-595-4800	S	189*	0.1
Simpson Electric Co.	PO Box 99	Lac d Flambeau	WI	54538	Richard Schermetzler	715-588-3311	R	182*	0.1
Emerson Control Techniques	12005 Technology	Eden Prairie	MN	55344	Paul Shuter	952-995-8000	S	171*	0.2
Hi-Lex Controls Inc.	152 Simpson Dr.	Litchfield	MI	49252	Robert Chrysler	517-542-2955	R	153*	0.5
ACK Controls Inc.	PO Box 1297	Glasgow	KY	42142	Ryuichi Kinase	270-678-6200	R	153*	0.4
Transistor Devices Inc.	36 Newburgh Rd.	Hackettstown	NJ	07840	Richard Blake	973-267-1900	R	151*	0.1
SMC Corporation of America	PO Box 26640	Indianapolis	IN	46226	Yoshiki Takada	317-899-4440	R	151*	0.3
Danfoss Inc.	7941 Corporate Dr.	Baltimore	MD	21236	Jorgen Clausen	410-931-8250	R	125*	0.1
SFA Inc.	2200 Defense Hwy.	Crofton	MD	21114		301-858-1230	R	124*	<0.1
Fisher Pierce	54 Commercial St.	Raynham	MA	02767	H. Lawerence Culp, Jr	508-821-1579	S	117*	0.2
Centrilift	200 W Stuart Roosa	Claremore	OK	74017	Chad Deaton	918-341-9600	D	115*	1.5
Bristol Babcock Inc.	1100 Buckingham	Watertown	CT	06795	John Kelly	860-945-2200	S	115*	0.3
Novar Controls Corp.	6060 Rockside Wds	Cleveland	OH	44131	Dean Lindstorm		R	113*	0.1
Meter Devices Company Inc.	PO Box 6382	Canton	OH	44706	Jack Roessner	330-455-0301	R	111*	0.6
Lutron Electronics Company	7200 Suter Rd.	Coopersburg	PA	18036	John Longenderfer	610-282-3800	R	110*	0.5
Magnetic Power Systems Inc.	PO Box 26508	Oklahoma City	OK	73126	Bruce Ryan	405-755-1600	R	105*	0.7
GE Control Products	709 W Wall St.	Morrison	IL	61270	Jeffrey R. Immelt	815-772-1100	R	104*	0.5
Melling Tool Co.	PO Box 1188	Jackson	MI	49204	David Horthrop	517-787-8172	R	100*	0.3
Cleveland Motion Controls Inc.	7550 Hub Pkwy.	Cleveland	OH	44125	Wayne Foley	216-524-8800	S	95*	0.1
Apsco Inc.	3700 Ln. Rd. Ext.	Perry	OH	44081	Steven Schmidt	440-352-8961	R	94*	0.4
Electrical Power Products Inc.	1800 Hull Ave.	Des Moines	IA	50313	Terry Nelson	515-262-8161	R	92*	0.5
Acme Electric Corp.	4815 W 5th St.	Lumberton	NC	28358	Robert J. McKenna	910-738-4251	S	89*	0.7
L and S Electric Inc.	5101 Mesker St.	Schofield	WI	54476		715-359-3155	R	89*	0.3
Phoenix International	1441 44th St. NW	Fargo	ND	58102			R	87*	0.2
Hi-Lex Corp.	5200 Wayne Rd.	Battle Creek	MI	49015	Katsuaki Shima	269-968-0781	R	82*	0.5
BENSHAW Inc.	1659 E Sutter Rd.	Glenshaw	PA	15116	Francis Livingston	412-487-8235	R	82*	<0.1
Minarik Corp.	905 E Thompson	Glendale	CA	91201	Patrick Frater	818-637-7500	R	79*	0.2
Ideal Electrical Co.	330 E 1st St.	Mansfield	OH	44902	Michael Vucelic	419-522-3611	R	74*	0.5
Networks Electronic Corp.	9750 DeSoto Ave.	Chatsworth	CA	91311	Tamara Christen	818-341-0440	R	73*	0.1
W-Industries Inc.	11500 Charles Rd.	Houston	TX	77041	Rick Lynn	713-466-9463	R	70*	0.2
Dwyer Instruments Inc.	PO Box 373	Michigan City	IN	46361	Stephen Clark	219-879-8868	R	69*	0.2
Kelco Industries Inc.	9210 Country Club	Woodstock	IL	60098	Kevin Kelly	815-338-5521	R	66*	<0.1
Avg Advanced Technologies L.P.	343 Saint Paul Blvd	Carol Stream	IL	60188		630-668-3900	R	65*	0.3
Limitorque Corp.	PO Box 11318	Lynchburg	VA	24506		434-528-4400	S	65*	0.3
Micro Dynamics Corp.	6201 Bury Dr.	Eden Prairie	MN	55346	Michael Brown	952-941-8071	R	63*	<0.1
Therm-O-Disc Inc.	1320 S Main St.	Mansfield	OH	44907	Peter Loconto	419-525-8500	S	61*	1.0
Bodine Electric Co.	2500 W Bradley Pl.	Chicago	IL	60618	John Bodine	773-478-3515	R	60*	0.3
Ametek Drexelbrook	205 Keith Valley Rd	Horsham	PA	19044	Frank Hermance	215-674-1234	D	60*	0.2
Henschel Inc.	9 Malcolm Hoyt Dr.	Newburyport	MA	01950	Don S. Roussinos	978-462-2400	S	60*	0.2
Young and Franklin Inc.	942 Old Liverpool	Liverpool	NY	13088	Dudley Johnson	315-457-3110	R	60*	0.1
Automotive Remanufacturers	3250 S 76th St.	Philadelphia	PA	19153	Carol Mancini	215-492-6330	R	59*	0.3
Evans Tempcon Inc.	701 Ann St. NW	Grand Rapids	MI	49504		616-361-2681	R	59*	0.4
Travis Pattern and Foundry	PO Box 6325	Spokane	WA	99217	Travis Garske	509-466-3545	R	58*	0.2

Source: Ward's Business Directory of U.S. Private and Public Companies, Volumes 1 and 2, 2008. The company type code used is as follows: P - Public, R - Private, S - Subsidiary, D - Division, J - Joint Venture, A - Affiliate, G - Group. Sales are in millions of dollars, employees are in thousands. An asterisk (*) indicates an estimated sales volume. The symbol < stands for 'less than'. Company names and addresses are truncated, in some cases, to fit into the available space.

MATERIALS CONSUMED

Material	Quantity	Delivered Cost ($ million)
Sheet metal products (excluding stampings)	(X)	79.4
Metal bolts, nuts, screws, and other screw machine products	(X)	30.1
All other fabricated metal products (excluding forgings)	(X)	85.2
Forgings	(X)	2.7
Castings, rough and semifinished	(X)	26.1
Steel bars, bar shapes, and plates (exc. castings, forgings, fabr. metal products)	(X)	13.4
Steel sheet and strip (including tinplate)	(X)	20.8
Steel structural shapes and sheet piling (exc. castings, forgings, fabr. metal products)	(X)	4.1
All other steel shapes and forms (exc. castings, forgings, fabr. metal products)	(X)	19.4
Nonferrous metal smelter and refinery shapes, incl. precious metal	(X)	13.3
Aluminum and aluminum-base alloy shapes and forms (exc. wire, castings, forgings, fabr. metal products)	(X)	16.0
Copper and copper-base alloy shapes and forms (exc. wire, castings, forgings, and fabricated metal products)	(X)	19.7
All other nonferrous shapes and forms (exc. castings, forgings, fabr. metal products)	(X)	3.4
Nonferrous wire and cable (incl. magnet wire, bare wire or insulated wire, etc.)	(X)	38.7
Industrial electrical control equipment purchased from other companies	(X)	484.1
Industrial electrical control equipment received from other plants of the same company	(X)	281.6
Porcelain, steatite, and other ceramic electrical products	(X)	4.1
Plastics products consumed in the form of sheets, rods, etc.	(X)	31.3
Plastics resins consumed in the form of granules, pellets, etc.	(X)	25.8
Switches (excluding snap, toggle and push, and circuit breakers)	(X)	64.5
Resistors, capacitors, transformers, and other electronic-type components (exc. electron tubes and semiconductors)	(X)	165.8
Printed ciruit boards (without inserted components) for electronic circuitry	(X)	135.7
Semiconductors, microprocessors, memory, ASICs, etc.	(X)	198.9
All other materials, components, parts, containers, and supplies	(X)	699.4
Materials, ingredients, containers, and supplies, nsk	(X)	1,035.2

Source: 2002 *Economic Census*. Explanation of symbols used: (D): Withheld to avoid disclosure of competitive data; na: Not available; (S): Withheld because statistical norms were not met; (X): Not applicable; (Z): Less than half the unit shown; nec: Not elsewhere classified; nsk: Not specified by kind; - : zero; p : 10-19 percent estimated; q : 20-29 percent estimated.

PRODUCT SHARE DETAILS

Product or Product Class Shipments	Mil. $	Product or Product Class Shipments	Mil. $
RELAYS AND INDUSTRIAL CONTROLS	8,731.8	**General-purpose industrial controls**	**3,747.3**
Relays for electronic circuitry, industrial control, overload,		**Parts for industrial controls and motor-control accessories**	**537.1**
and switchgear type	**625.8**	**Relays and industrial controls, nsk, total**	**928.7**
Specific-purpose industrial controls	**2,893.0**		

Source: 2002 *Economic Census*. The values are product shipments in millions of dollars for 2002. Total product shipments may be lower or higher than industry shipments. See Introduction for a full discussion. Values of indented subcategories are summed in the main heading(s). The symbol (D) appears when data are withheld to prevent disclosure of competitive information. The abbreviation nsk stands for 'not specified by kind' and nec for 'not elsewhere classified'. A dash (-) means zero.

INPUTS AND OUTPUTS FOR RELAY AND INDUSTRIAL CONTROL MANUFACTURING

Economic Sector or Industry Providing Inputs	%	Sector	Economic Sector or Industry Buying Outputs	%	Sector
Compensation of employees	29.4		Exports of goods & services	13.9	Cap Inv
Relay & industrial controls	11.0	Manufg.	Private fixed investment	8.1	
Wholesale trade	9.3	Trade	Relay & industrial controls	7.9	Manufg.
Management of companies & enterprises	6.1	Services	Switchgear & switchboard apparatus	4.3	Manufg.
Printed circuit assemblies (electronic assemblies)	5.4	Manufg.	Plastics products, nec	4.1	Manufg.
Switchgear & switchboard apparatus	2.1	Manufg.	Federal government, investment, national defense	2.4	Fed Govt
Bare printed circuit boards	2.0	Manufg.	Material handling equipment	2.2	Manufg.
Gaskets, packing, & sealing devices	1.1	Manufg.	Search, detection, & navigation instruments	2.2	Manufg.
Noncomparable imports	1.1	Foreign	S/L govt. invest., other	2.2	S/L Govt
Ornamental & architectural metal products	1.1	Manufg.	Basic inorganic chemicals, nec	2.0	Manufg.
Iron & steel mills & ferroalloys	0.9	Manufg.	Motor vehicle parts	2.0	Manufg.
Turned products & screws, nuts, & bolts	0.8	Manufg.	Railroad rolling stock	1.9	Manufg.
Nonferrous metal (ex. copper & aluminum) processing	0.7	Manufg.	AC, refrigeration, and warm air heating equipment	1.7	Manufg.
Real estate	0.7	Fin/R.E.	General Federal government services, nondefense	1.7	Fed Govt
Advertising & related services	0.6	Services	S/L govt. passenger transit	1.7	S/L Govt
Semiconductors & related devices	0.6	Manufg.	Industrial machinery, nec	1.4	Manufg.
Machine shops	0.6	Manufg.	Semiconductor machinery	1.3	Manufg.
Plastics packaging materials, film & sheet	0.5	Manufg.	Plastics materials & resins	1.2	Manufg.
Truck transportation	0.5	Util.	Warehousing & storage	1.0	Util.
Primary smelting & refining of copper	0.4	Manufg.	Wholesale trade	1.0	Trade
Plastics materials & resins	0.4	Manufg.	Construction machinery	1.0	Manufg.
Power generation & supply	0.4	Util.	Electricity & signal testing instruments	0.9	Manufg.
Scientific research & development services	0.4	Services	Metal cutting & forming machine tools	0.9	Manufg.
Coating, engraving, heat treating & allied activities	0.3	Manufg.	General Federal government services, defense	0.8	Fed Govt
Telecommunications	0.2	Services	Rolling mill & other metalworking machinery	0.8	Manufg.
Cutting tools & machine tool accessories	0.2	Manufg.	Household cooking appliances	0.8	Manufg.
Warehousing & storage	0.2	Util.	General purpose machinery, nec	0.8	Manufg.
Chemical products & preparations, nec	0.2	Manufg.	Household refrigerators & home freezers	0.8	Manufg.

Continued on next page.

INPUTS AND OUTPUTS FOR RELAY AND INDUSTRIAL CONTROL MANUFACTURING - Continued

Economic Sector or Industry Providing Inputs	%	Sector	Economic Sector or Industry Buying Outputs	%	Sector
Taxes on production & imports, less subsidies	0.2		Steel products from purchased steel	0.8	Manufg.
Automotive equipment rental & leasing	0.2	Fin/R.E.	Electrical equipment & components, nec	0.7	Manufg.
Aluminum products from purchased aluminum	0.2	Manufg.	Petroleum refineries	0.6	Manufg.
Ferrous metal foundries	0.2	Manufg.	General S/L govt. services	0.6	S/L Govt
Nonferrous metal foundries	0.2	Manufg.	Electromedical & electrotherapeutic apparatus	0.6	Manufg.
Industrial process variable instruments	0.2	Manufg.	Packaging machinery	0.6	Manufg.
Legal services	0.1	Services	Plastics & rubber industry machinery	0.6	Manufg.
Postal service	0.1	Util.	Household laundry equipment	0.6	Manufg.
Gold, silver, & other metal ore	0.1	Mining	Other S/L govt. enterprises	0.6	S/L Govt
Maintenance/repair of nonresidential structures	0.1	Construct.	Computer terminals & peripherals	0.6	Manufg
Accounting, tax preparation, bookkeeping, & payroll	0.1	Services	Air & gas compressors	0.6	Manufg.
Motor vehicle parts	0.1	Manufg.	Soft drinks & ice	0.6	Manufg.
Metal cans, boxes, & other containers (light gauge)	0.1	Manufg.	Pumps & pumping equipment	0.6	Manufg.
Securities, commodity contracts, investments	0.1	Fin/R.E.	Printing	0.5	Manufg.
Management, scientific, & technical consulting	0.1	Services	Poultry processing	0.5	Manufg.
Fabricated metals, nec	0.1	Manufg.	Chemical products & preparations, nec	0.5	Manufg.
Services to buildings & dwellings	0.1	Services	Motors & generators	0.5	Manufg.
Commercial & industrial machinery rental & leasing	0.1	Fin/R.E.	Printed circuit assemblies (electronic assemblies)	0.5	Manufg.
Custom roll forming	0.1	Manufg.	Paper mills	0.5	Manufg.
Crowns & closures & metal stamping	0.1	Manufg.	Commercial & service industry machinery, nec	0.5	Manufg.
Paperboard containers	0.1	Manufg.	Paperboard containers	0.4	Manufg.
			Basic organic chemicals, nec	0.4	Manufg.
			Urethane & other foam products (except polystrene)	0.4	Manufg.
			Truck transportation	0.4	Util.
			Iron & steel mills & ferroalloys	0.4	Manufg.
			Industrial process variable instruments	0.3	Manufg.
			Ship building & repairing	0.3	Manufg.
			Commercial & industrial equipment repair/maintenance	0.3	Services
			Electron tubes	0.3	Manufg.
			Apparel knitting mills	0.3	Manufg.
			Analytical laboratory instruments	0.3	Manufg.
			Aluminum products from purchased aluminum	0.3	Manufg.
			Major household appliances, nec	0.2	Manufg.
			Cheese	0.2	Manufg.
			Breweries	0.2	Manufg.
			Plate work & fabricated structural products	0.2	Manufg.
			Ornamental & architectural metal products	0.2	Manufg.
			Wineries	0.2	Manufg.
			Bread & bakery products	0.2	Manufg.
			Soybean & oilseed processing	0.2	Manufg.
			Heavy duty trucks	0.2	Manufg.
			Fluid milk & butter	0.2	Manufg.
			Industrial process furnaces & ovens	0.2	Manufg.
			Bare printed circuit boards	0.2	Manufg.
			Mining & oil & gas field machinery	0.2	Manufg.
			Cookies, crackers, & pasta	0.2	Manufg.
			Telecommunications	0.2	Services
			Electronic components, nec	0.2	Manufg.
			Vending, commercial, industrial, office machinery	0.2	Manufg.
			Wood windows & doors & millwork	0.2	Manufg.
			Totalizing fluid meters & counting devices	0.2	Manufg.
			Waste management & remediation services	0.2	Services
			Surgical appliances & supplies	0.2	Manufg.
			Dry, condensed, & evaporated dairy products	0.2	Manufg.
			Telephone apparatus	0.1	Manufg.
			Handtools	0.1	Manufg.
			Special tools, dies, jigs, & fixtures	0.1	Manufg.
			Coated & laminated paper & packaging materials	0.1	Manufg.
			Farm machinery & equipment	0.1	Manufg.
			Pharmaceutical preparations	0.1	Manufg.
			Frozen food	0.1	Manufg.
			Sanitary paper products	0.1	Manufg.
			Lighting fixtures	0.1	Manufg.
			Automatic environmental controls	0.1	Manufg.
			Transit & ground passenger transportation	0.1	Util.
			Coating, engraving, heat treating & allied activities	0.1	Manufg.
			Ready-mix concrete	0.1	Manufg.
			Carpet & rug mills	0.1	Manufg.
			Paperboard mills	0.1	Manufg.
			Air purification & ventilation equipment	0.1	Manufg.
			Valve & fittings other than plumbing	0.1	Manufg.
			Snack food	0.1	Manufg.
			Nonferrous metal (ex. copper & aluminum) processing	0.1	Manufg.
			Semiconductors & related devices	0.1	Manufg.
			Watches, clocks, & related devices	0.1	Manufg.
			Turned products & screws, nuts, & bolts	0.1	Manufg.
			Glass products from purchased glass	0.1	Manufg.
			Rubber products, nec	0.1	Manufg.
			S/L govt. invest., education	0.1	S/L Govt
			Wet corn milling	0.1	Manufg.

Continued on next page.

INPUTS AND OUTPUTS FOR RELAY AND INDUSTRIAL CONTROL MANUFACTURING - Continued

Economic Sector or Industry Providing Inputs	%	Sector	Economic Sector or Industry Buying Outputs	%	Sector
			Architectural, engineering, & related services	0.1	Services
			Fabricated metals, nec	0.1	Manufg.
			Wiring devices	0.1	Manufg.
			Turbines & turbine generator set units	0.1	Manufg.

Source: *Benchmark Input-Output Accounts for the U.S. Economy, 2002*, U.S. Department of Commerce, Washington, D.C., January 2008. The abbreviation nec stands for 'not elsewhere classified'.

OCCUPATIONS EMPLOYED BY ELECTRICAL EQUIPMENT MANUFACTURING

Occupation	% of Total 2006	Change to 2016	Occupation	% of Total 2006	Change to 2016
Electrical & electronic equipment assemblers	15.2	-32.0	Shipping, receiving, & traffic clerks	1.7	-18.2
Team assemblers	10.7	-15.0	Industrial engineers	1.5	3.2
Coil winders, tapers, & finishers	4.9	-32.0	Mechanical engineers	1.4	-15.0
First-line supervisors/managers of production workers	3.3	-15.0	Assemblers & fabricators, nec	1.3	-23.5
Inspectors, testers, sorters, samplers, & weighers	2.9	-19.9	Maintenance & repair workers, general	1.3	-15.0
Electromechanical equipment assemblers	2.7	-15.0	Purchasing agents, exc wholesale, retail, & farm	1.2	-15.0
Electrical engineers	2.6	-15.0	General & operations managers	1.2	-23.5
Cutting, punching, & press machine operators	2.5	-23.5	Bookkeeping, accounting, & auditing clerks	1.1	-15.0
Machinists	2.3	-10.8	Electronics engineers, exc computer	1.1	-15.0
Welders, cutters, solderers, & brazers	2.1	-9.6	Customer service representatives	1.1	-6.5
Computer-controlled machine tool operators	1.7	-6.5	Electrical & electronics drafters	1.1	-15.0
Electrical & electronic engineering technicians	1.7	-15.0			

Source: *Industry-Occupation Matrix*, Bureau of Labor Statistics, December 4, 2007. These data are reported based on 4-digit NAICS categories but have been matched to corresponding 6-digit NAICS industry codes. The change reported for each occupation to the year 2016 is a percent of growth or decline as estimated by the Bureau of Labor Statistics. The abbreviation nec stands for 'not elsewhere classified'.

LOCATION BY STATE AND REGIONAL CONCENTRATION

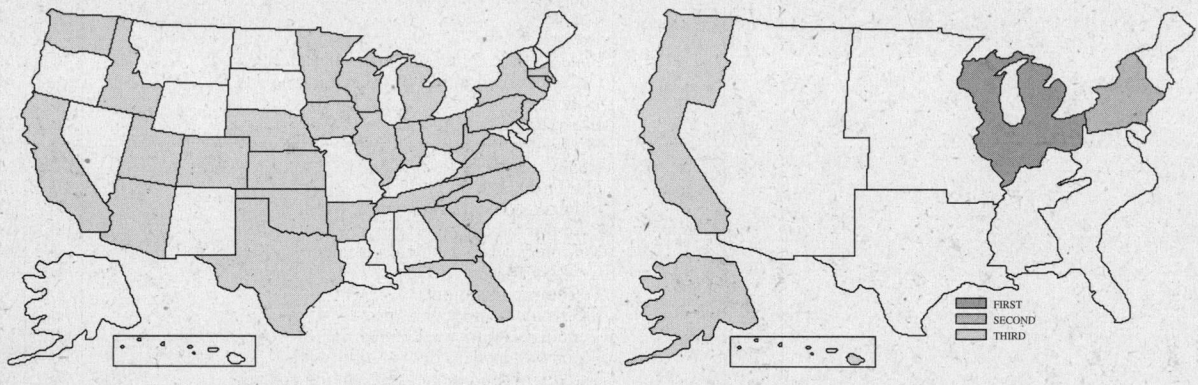

FIRST
SECOND
THIRD

INDUSTRY DATA BY STATE

State	Establish-ments	Shipments			Employment				Cost as % of Shipments	Investment per Employee ($)
		Total ($ mil)	% of U.S.	Per Establ.	Total Number	% of U.S.	Per Establ.	Wages ($/hour)		
Wisconsin	50	1,739.9	17.1	34,798.9	8,325	17.4	167	20.23	61.1	4,710
North Carolina	32	1,143.5	11.2	35,733.7	4,246	8.9	133	16.82	50.1	3,648
Ohio	67	1,051.7	10.3	15,696.6	2,124	4.4	32	14.36	35.2	1,881
Virginia	25	926.1	9.1	37,042.2	3,084	6.4	123	18.82	30.8	3,104
California	129	607.4	6.0	4,708.8	4,742	9.9	37	13.59	36.6	2,363
Georgia	19	512.4	5.0	26,966.8	1,365	2.9	72	13.83	50.4	1,849
Illinois	89	498.8	4.9	5,604.1	2,759	5.8	31	15.86	50.9	2,079
Massachusetts	39	411.3	4.0	10,545.0	2,415	5.0	62	15.22	41.8	3,772
Pennsylvania	56	407.7	4.0	7,280.6	1,722	3.6	31	12.29	58.7	15,575
New York	71	368.7	3.6	5,193.5	2,432	5.1	34	12.57	40.8	3,165
Texas	66	301.9	3.0	4,573.7	1,252	2.6	19	12.73	48.5	4,589
Minnesota	34	238.5	2.3	7,015.9	1,532	3.2	45	14.10	45.9	16,345
Michigan	68	209.8	2.1	3,085.9	1,483	3.1	22	18.88	42.7	2,442
South Carolina	10	194.5	1.9	19,449.9	1,084	2.3	108	16.50	47.5	1,724

Continued on next page.

INDUSTRY DATA BY STATE - Continued

State	Establish- ments	Shipments			Employment				Cost as % of Shipments	Investment per Employee ($)
		Total ($ mil)	% of U.S.	Per Establ.	Total Number	% of U.S.	Per Establ.	Wages ($/hour)		
Florida	46	178.4	1.8	3,877.7	1,066	2.2	23	13.44	41.1	7,987
New Jersey	40	169.8	1.7	4,246.0	989	2.1	25	10.57	42.9	2,056
Iowa	8	149.8	1.5	18,727.6	660	1.4	83	21.98	30.1	979
Connecticut	40	134.8	1.3	3,370.4	1,093	2.3	27	16.00	39.1	1,723
Indiana	27	109.9	1.1	4,069.9	837	1.7	31	11.98	49.1	4,579
Washington	29	94.1	0.9	3,243.9	529	1.1	18	15.49	43.7	4,892
Colorado	16	78.9	0.8	4,934.3	516	1.1	32	10.82	48.1	1,926
Utah	7	51.8	0.5	7,406.3	173	0.4	25	10.79	44.7	4,462
Kansas	9	49.7	0.5	5,527.6	397	0.8	44	13.73	37.8	2,350
Arkansas	6	45.5	0.4	7,581.3	155	0.3	26	11.64	54.2	3,219
West Virginia	6	23.0	0.2	3,831.2	153	0.3	25	14.19	46.3	1,190
Tennessee	12	22.5	0.2	1,877.2	180	0.4	15	13.15	33.5	2,572
Oklahoma	10	21.6	0.2	2,156.9	158	0.3	16	11.71	25.6	2,620
Rhode Island	8	18.0	0.2	2,253.7	146	0.3	18	8.08	31.2	3,795
Arizona	9	16.0	0.2	1,780.1	122	0.3	14	8.59	38.9	1,828
Nebraska	5	15.4	0.2	3,080.8	276	0.6	55	6.47	22.7	772
Idaho	7	12.9	0.1	1,838.4	153	0.3	22	18.17	36.1	647

Source: 2002 *Economic Census*. The states are in descending order of shipments or establishments (if shipment data are missing for the majority). The symbol (D) appears when data are withheld to prevent disclosure of competitive information. States marked with (D) are sorted by number of establishments. A dash (-) indicates that the data element cannot be calculated. Data may not show all states active in the NAICS category. All data available at the time of publication are shown.

NAICS 335911 - STORAGE BATTERY MANUFACTURING

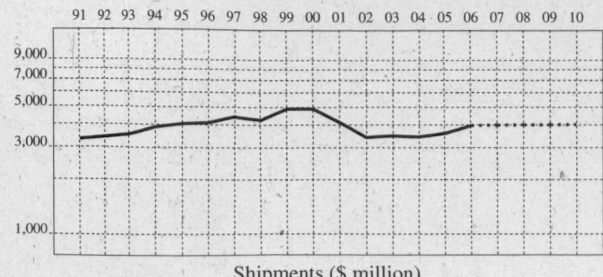

Shipments ($ million)

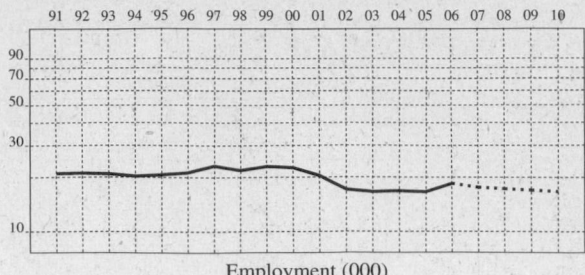

Employment (000)

GENERAL STATISTICS

Year	Companies	Establishments Total	Establishments with 20 or more employees	Employment Total (000)	Employment Production Workers (000)	Employment Hours (Mil)	Compensation Payroll ($ mil)	Compensation Wages ($/hr)	Production Cost of Materials	Production Value Added by Manufacture	Production Value of Shipments	Production Capital Invest.
1991		149	92	21.0	16.6	33.8	579.9	12.56	1,740.6	1,577.1	3,313.3	110.1
1992	110	154	91	21.1	16.9	33.5	596.7	12.77	1,633.3	1,774.0	3,409.5	120.0
1993		146	91	20.9	16.9	34.2	613.1	13.16	1,711.1	1,805.1	3,520.3	111.9
1994		142	90	20.3	16.5	35.5	663.6	14.04	1,891.2	2,023.6	3,877.2	158.5
1995		140	88	20.7	17.1	34.1	683.1	14.77	1,947.2	2,125.5	4,048.1	178.5
1996		141	90	21.3	17.7	35.6	702.8	14.92	1,949.4	2,175.6	4,110.0	199.4
1997	93	135	88	23.2	18.7	37.4	787.7	15.66	2,238.9	2,171.6	4,422.7	171.7
1998		132	86	21.9	17.8	36.7	751.9	15.33	2,222.1	2,039.9	4,252.5	121.6
1999		137	86	23.0	18.5	38.6	817.5	15.05	2,399.3	2,504.7	4,904.1	192.3
2000		138	86	22.6	18.3	38.0	813.3	15.18	2,563.2	2,345.1	4,890.7	237.9
2001		138	83	20.4	15.7	30.8	737.9	16.29	2,280.6	1,756.5	4,132.2	118.7
2002	97	130	81	17.1	13.0	27.3	642.9	15.66	1,930.5	1,471.1	3,415.4	85.8
2003		130	78	16.6	12.7	26.9	649.6	15.96	1,904.2	1,579.4	3,486.4	120.5
2004		129	77	16.8	12.8	26.4	672.4	16.86	1,927.4	1,483.6	3,433.8	91.0
2005		121	77	16.6	12.5	26.7	697.0	16.44	1,989.2	1,611.2	3,597.1	85.6
2006		124P	77P	18.5	14.3	30.2	759.2	16.43	2,320.4	1,697.4	3,965.7	108.0
2007		122P	76P	17.6P	13.4P	28.2P	755.0P	17.26P	2,336.0P	1,708.8P	3,992.4P	115.3P
2008		120P	74P	17.3P	13.1P	27.6P	761.7P	17.51P	2,340.7P	1,712.3P	4,000.4P	112.6P
2009		119P	73P	17.0P	12.8P	27.1P	768.4P	17.77P	2,345.5P	1,715.7P	4,008.5P	109.9P
2010		117P	72P	16.7P	12.4P	26.5P	775.1P	18.03P	2,350.2P	1,719.2P	4,016.6P	107.2P

Sources: 1992, 1997, 2002 *Economic Census*; other years, up to 2006, are from the *Annual Survey of Manufactures*. Establishment counts for non-Census years are from *County Business Patterns*; 1997 and 2002 values are from the 1997 and 2002 censuses respectively, reported in the Federal Government's NAICS format. Other years were originally reported in equivalent SIC format. 'P's show projections by the editors.

INDICES OF CHANGE

Year	Companies	Establishments Total	Establishments with 20 or more employees	Employment Total (000)	Employment Production Workers (000)	Employment Hours (Mil)	Compensation Payroll ($ mil)	Compensation Wages ($/hr)	Production Cost of Materials	Production Value Added by Manufacture	Production Value of Shipments	Production Capital Invest.
1992	113	118	112	123	130	123	93	82	85	121	100	140
1997	96	104	109	136	144	137	123	100	116	148	129	200
2001		106	102	119	121	113	115	104	118	119	121	138
2002	100	100	100	100	100	100	100	100	100	100	100	100
2003		100	96	97	98	99	101	102	99	107	102	140
2004		99	95	98	98	97	105	108	100	101	101	106
2005		93	95	97	96	98	108	105	103	110	105	100
2006		95P	95P	108	110	111	118	105	120	115	116	126
2007		94P	93P	103P	103P	103P	117P	110P	121P	116P	117P	134P
2008		92P	92P	101P	101P	101P	118P	112P	121P	116P	117P	131P
2009		91P	90P	99P	98P	99P	120P	113P	121P	117P	117P	128P
2010		90P	89P	98P	95P	97P	121P	115P	122P	117P	118P	125P

Sources: Same as General Statistics. Values reflect change from the base year, 2002. Values above 100 mean greater than 2002, values below 100 mean less than 2002, and the values of 100 in other years means the same as 2002. 'P's show projections by the editors.

SELECTED RATIOS

For 2002	Avg. of All Manufact.	Analyzed Industry	Index	For 2002	Avg. of All Manufact.	Analyzed Industry	Index
Employees per Establishment	42	132	313	Value Added per Production Worker	182,367	113,162	62
Payroll per Establishment	1,639,184	4,945,385	302	Cost per Establishment	5,769,015	14,850,000	257
Payroll per Employee	39,053	37,596	96	Cost per Employee	137,446	112,895	82
Production Workers per Establishment	30	100	339	Cost per Production Worker	195,506	148,500	76
Wages per Establishment	694,845	3,288,600	473	Shipments per Establishment	11,158,348	26,272,308	235
Wages per Production Worker	23,548	32,886	140	Shipments per Employee	265,847	199,731	75
Hours per Production Worker	1,980	2,100	106	Shipments per Production Worker	378,144	262,723	69
Wages per Hour	11.89	15.66	132	Investment per Establishment	361,338	660,000	183
Value Added per Establishment	5,381,325	11,316,154	210	Investment per Employee	8,609	5,018	58
Value Added per Employee	128,210	86,029	67	Investment per Production Worker	12,245	6,600	54

Sources: Same as General Statistics. The 'Average of All Manufacturing' column represents the average of all manufacturing industries reported for the most recent complete year available. The Index shows the relationship between the Average and the Analyzed Industry. For example, 100 means that they are equal; 500 that the Analyzed Industry is five times the average; 50 means that the Analyzed Industry is half the national average. The abbreviation 'na' is used to show that data are 'not available'. Ratios shown for 2002, the last complete census year.

LEADING COMPANIES   Number shown: 67   Total sales ($ mil): 53,953   Total employment (000): 208.2

Company Name	Address				CEO Name	Phone	Co. Type	Sales ($ mil)	Empl. (000)
Johnson Controls Inc.	PO Box 591	Milwaukee	WI	53201		414-524-1200	P	34,624	140.0
Gillette Co.	PO Box 720	Boston	MA	02217	James M. Kilts	617-421-7000	S	10,477	28.7
Exide Technologies	13000 Deerfield Pky	Alpharetta	GA	30004		678-566-9000	P	2,940	13.9
Spectrum Brands Inc.	6 Concourse Pky.	Atlanta	GA	30328	John D. Bowlin	770-829-6200	P	1,995	7.1
EaglePicher Corp.	2424 John Daly Rd.	Inkster	MI	48141	Donald L. Runkle	313-278-5956	R	1,244*	4.2
Remy International Inc.	2902 Enterprise Dr.	Anderson	IN	46013	Thomas J. Snyder	765-778-6499	S	1,218*	7.9
Belkin Corp.	PO Box 5649	Compton	CA	90220	Chet Pipkin	310-604-2347	R	460*	1.0
Energy Conversion Devices Inc.	2956 Waterview Dr.	Rochester Hills	MI	48309	Mark Morelli	248-293-0440	P	114	1.2
Crown Battery Manufacturing	PO Box 990	Fremont	OH	43420	Hal Hawk	419-334-7181	R	84*	0.3
Innergy Power Corp.	9375 Customhouse	San Diego	CA	92154	Dan Lankford	619-710-0758	R	67*	<0.1
Trojan Battery Co.	12380 Clark St.	Santa Fe Spgs	CA	90670	Richard Godber	562-946-8381	R	60*	0.4
Centurion Wireless Tech.	PO Box 82846	Lincoln	NE	68501	Magnus Tannfelt	402-325-3100	R	60*	0.3
EnerSys Energy Products Inc.	2366 Bernville Rd.	Reading	PA	19605	John Craig	660-208-1991	S	55*	0.4
FuelCell Energy Inc.	3 Great Pasture Rd.	Danbury	CT	06810	Daniel Brdar	203-825-6000	P	48	0.4
Arotech Corp.	1229 Oak Valley Dr.	Ann Arbor	MI	48108	Robert S. Ehrlich		P	43	0.3
Power Battery Company Inc.	25 McLean Blvd.	Paterson	NJ	07514	William Rasmussen	973-523-8630	R	37*	0.2
Mathews Associates Inc.	220 Power Ct.	Sanford	FL	32771	Daniel Perreault	407-323-3390	R	30*	0.2
Bulldog Battery Corp.	PO Box 766	Wabash	IN	46992	Norman Benjamin	260-563-0551	R	28*	<0.1
Multiplier Industries Corp.	PO Box 630	Mount Kisco	NY	10549	Walter Ullrich	914-241-9510	R	27*	<0.1
Storage Battery Systems Inc.	N56 Ridgewood	Menomonee Fls	WI	53051	Scott Rubenzer	262-703-5800	R	25*	<0.1
Superior Battery Manufacturing	PO Box 1010	Russell Springs	KY	42642	Randolph Hart	270-866-6056	R	24*	0.1
Ramcar Batteries Inc.	2700 Carrier Ave.	Los Angeles	CA	90040	Clifford Crowe	323-726-1212	R	22*	0.1
HM Electronics Inc.	14110 Stowe Dr.	Poway	CA	92064	Mitzi Dominguez	858-535-6000	R	21*	0.2
EFI Electronics Corp.	1751 S 4800 W	Salt Lake City	UT	84104	Todd Dauphinais	801-977-9009	S	20*	0.1
Quantum Instruments Inc.	10 Commerce Dr.	Hauppauge	NY	11788	Steven Victor	631-656-7400	R	18*	<0.1
Fedco Electronics Inc.	PO Box 1403	Fond du Lac	WI	54936			R	18*	<0.1
Battery Handling Systems Inc.	PO Box 28990	Saint Louis	MO	63132	W Huber	314-423-7091	R	17*	<0.1
Advanced Battery Technologies	21 W 39th St., 2A	New York	NY	10018	Zhiguo Fu	212-391-2752	P	16	<0.1
BST Systems Inc.	78 Plainfield Pke.	Plainfield	CT	06374	Max Solis	860-564-4078	R	14*	<0.1
Yardney Technical Products	82 Mechanic St., 2	Pawcatuck	CT	06379	Richard Scibelli	860-599-1100	R	14*	<0.1
EAC Corp.	380 N Street	Teterboro	NJ	07608	Mark Schmit	201-288-4477	R	13*	0.1
Teledyne Contin. Motors, Batt.	PO Box 7950	Redlands	CA	92375		909-793-3131	S	11*	<0.1
Energy Technologies Inc.	219 Park Ave. E	Mansfield	OH	44902	Paul Madden	419-522-4444	R	10*	<0.1
Interspace Battery Inc.	2009 W S Brnrdino	West Covina	CA	91790	Donald Godber	626-813-1234	R	8*	<0.1
R and D Batteries Inc.	PO Box 5007	Burnsville	MN	55337	Randall Noddings	952-890-0629	R	8*	<0.1
Harding Energy Inc.	509 E Ellis Rd.	Muskegon	MI	49441	David Clow	231-798-7033	R	7*	<0.1
Dantona Industries Inc.	3051 Burns Ave.	Wantagh	NY	11793	Sal Dantona	516-783-5050	R	7*	<0.1
Ace Hobby Distributors Inc.	2055 Main St.	Irvine	CA	92614	Aling Lai	949-833-0088	R	7*	<0.1
Industrial Battery Engineering	9121 De Garmo	Sun Valley	CA	91352	Birger Holmquist	818-767-7067	R	6*	<0.1
American Battery Corp.	525 W Washington	Escondido	CA	92025	Dennis Loso	760-746-8010	R	6*	<0.1
Nilar Inc.	7388 S Revere	Englewood	CO	80112	Norma Vickers	303-662-8891	R	4*	<0.1
Avex Electronics Corp.	PO Box 1026	Bensalem	PA	19020	Michael Hasness	215-638-3300	R	4*	<0.1
New ERA Technologies Co.	23935 Madison St.	Torrance	CA	90505	John Cartier	310-373-8894	R	3*	<0.1
Graywacke Engineering Inc.	201 E 5th St., 100	Mansfield	OH	44902	Scott Huffman	419-525-3888	R	3*	<0.1
Lithium House Inc.	7122 Sophia Ave.	Van Nuys	CA	91406	Chase Haba	818-909-3440	R	3*	<0.1
Page One Science Inc.	1321 Powhatan St.	Alexandria	VA	22314	Marshall Soghoian	703-684-6222	R	3*	<0.1
Span Inc.	5605 W 73rd St.	Indianapolis	IN	46278	William Baker	317-347-2646	R	2*	<0.1
Battery Systems of America	2029 Chatsworth Rd.	Carrollton	TX	75007	James Wood	972-492-2327	R	2*	<0.1
Bell City Battery Mfg. Inc.	915 S Charles St.	Belleville	IL	62220	Jeanith Miller	618-234-7272	R	2*	<0.1
Aristo-Craft Inc.	698 S 21st St.	Irvington	NJ	07111	Lewis Polk	973-351-9800	R	2*	<0.1
Keystone Battery	35 Holton St.	Winchester	MA	01890	Barry Faye	781-729-8333	R	2*	<0.1
API Inc.	4025 NE Lakewood	Lees Summit	MO	64064	Edward Rafter	816-795-0208	R	2*	<0.1
Astro Flight Inc.	13311 Beach Ave.	Marina Del Rey	CA	90292	Robert Boucher	310-821-0291	R	2*	<0.1
Cell Phone Battery Warehouse	1020 Whisper. Pns	Grass Valley	CA	95945		530-273-2312	R	2*	<0.1
Magnevolt Inc.	PO Box 58099	Raleigh	NC	27658	William Davidson	919-790-9686	R	2*	<0.1
Uninterruptible Power Products	1567 W 11th Dr.	Friendship	WI	53934	Gary Jungwirth	608-339-2151	R	2*	<0.1
Hedb Corp.	3355 Woodward	Santa Clara	CA	95054	Adrian Zolla	408-980-1877	R	2*	<0.1
Red Line Research Laboratories	10845 Wheatlands	Santee	CA	92071	Steve Leiserson	619-562-7591	R	2*	<0.1
Transdigm Inc.	1301 E 9th St.	Cleveland	OH	44114	Nicholas Howley	216-289-4939	R	1*	<0.1
Nolan Power Group	21448 Marion Ln.	Mandeville	LA	70471		985-867-4821	R	1*	<0.1
Advanced Battery Systems Inc.	516 Bedford St.	E Bridgewater	MA	02333	Brian Kmito	508-378-2284	R	1*	<0.1
Battery Pros Inc.	PO Box 54	Horseshoe Bch	FL	32648	Patti Novack	352-498-2477	R	1*	<0.1
Int'l Marketing Concepts	903 Dell Ave.	Campbell	CA	95008	Ronald Evans	408-874-0800	R	1*	<0.1
MP Batteries Inc.	PO Box 181	Clarence Center	NY	14032	Terry Stornelli	716-741-2178	R	1*	<0.1
Rolls Battery of New England	7 Oak Street	Salem	MA	01970		978-745-3333	R	1*	<0.1
Sky Power Battery L.L.C.	81 N Maple Ave.	Ridgewood	NJ	07450		201-444-3232	R	1*	<0.1
All Power Battery Inc.	1387 Clarendon	Canton	OH	44710	William Ferris	330-453-5236	R	1*	<0.1

Source: Ward's Business Directory of U.S. Private and Public Companies, Volumes 1 and 2, 2008. The company type code used is as follows: P - Public, R - Private, S - Subsidiary, D - Division, J - Joint Venture, A - Affiliate, G - Group. Sales are in millions of dollars, employees are in thousands. An asterisk (*) indicates an estimated sales volume. The symbol < stands for 'less than'. Company names and addresses are truncated, in some cases, to fit into the available space.

MATERIALS CONSUMED

Material	Quantity	Delivered Cost ($ million)
Metal stampings	(X)	5.5
All other fabricated metal products (excluding forgings)	(X)	33.1
Forgings	(X)	(D)
Castings, rough and semifinished	(X)	2.0
Refined unalloyed lead shapes and forms (exc. castings, forgings, fabr. metal products)	(X)	370.7
Antimonial lead	(X)	272.8
Lead-calcium alloyed	(X)	147.4
Steel sheet and strip (including tinplate)	(X)	(D)
All other steel shapes and forms (exc. castings, forgings, fabr. metal products)	(X)	2.7
Zinc and zinc-base alloy shapes and forms (exc. castings, forgings, fabr. metal products)	(X)	(D)
Litharge	(X)	24.6
Sulfuric acid, new and spent (100 percent H2SO4)	(X)	29.1
Other industrial inorganic chemicals (incl. mercury and silver oxide)	(X)	14.8
Plastics resins consumed in the form of granules, pellets, etc.	(X)	17.2
Plastics products consumed in the form of sheets, rods, etc.	(X)	74.3
Fabricated plastics products (excluding gaskets)	(X)	218.3
Paperboard containers, boxes, and corrugated paperboard	(X)	38.2
Carbon and graphite electrodes and other products for electrical use	(X)	(D)
Metal powders	(X)	45.0
All other materials, components, parts, containers, and supplies	(X)	304.4
Materials, ingredients, containers, and supplies, nsk	(X)	143.9

Source: 2002 *Economic Census*. Explanation of symbols used: (D): Withheld to avoid disclosure of competitive data; na: Not available; (S): Withheld because statistical norms were not met; (X): Not applicable; (Z): Less than half the unit shown; nec: Not elsewhere classified; nsk: Not specified by kind; - : zero; p : 10-19 percent estimated; q : 20-29 percent estimated.

PRODUCT SHARE DETAILS

Product or Product Class Shipments	Mil. $	Product or Product Class Shipments	Mil. $
STORAGE BATTERIES	3,285.5	than BCI dimensional size group 8D (1.5 cu ft or .042 cu m and smaller)	57.7
Storage batteries, lead acid type, Battery Council International dimensional size group 8D (1.5 cu ft or .042 cu m and smaller)	**2,087.5**	All other lead acid storage batteries, larger than BCI dimensional size group 8D (1.6 cu ft or .042 cu m)	497.4
Starting, lighting, and ignition (SLI) type lead acid storage batteries for original equipment, BCI dimensional size group 8D (1.5 cu ft or .042 cu m and smaller)	(D)	Communication lead acid storage batteries (central office telephone supervisory equipment, telemetering, and microwave), larger than BCI dimensional size group 8D (1.5 cu ft or .042 cu m and smaller)	208.9
Starting, lighting, and ignition (SLI) type lead acid storage batteries for replacement, BCI dimensional size group 8D (1.5 cu ft or .042 cu m and smaller)	1,185.8	Standby emergency power lead acid storage batteries, larger than BCI dimensional size group 8D (1.5 cu ft or .042 cu m and smaller)	211.3
Lead acid storage batteries other than (SLI) type, BCI dimensional size group 8D (1.5 cu ft or .042 cu m and smaller)	(D)	All other lead acid storage batteries, larger than BCI dimensional size group 8D (1.5 cu ft or .042 cu m and smaller), including starting, lighting, and ignition (SLI type)	77.3
Storage batteries, lead acid type, larger than Battery Council International dimensional size group 8D (1.5 cu ft or .042 cu m and smaller)	**863.0**	**Storage batteries, except lead acid, including parts for all storage batteries**	**262.8**
Motive power type lead acid storage batteries, larger than BCI dimensional size group 8D (1.5 cu ft or .042 cu m), including mining and industrial locomotive	365.6	Storage batteries except lead acid	251.4
		Nickel cadmium storage batteries (sealed or vented)	125.9
Motive power type lead acid storage batteries for industrial trucks, larger than BCI dimensional size group 8D (1.5 cu ft or .042 cu m and smaller)	307.8	Storage batteries other than nickel cadmium or lead acid	125.5
All other motive power type lead acid storage batteries, including mining and industrial locomotive, larger		Parts for all storage batteries, excluding cases and containers	11.5
		Storage batteries, nsk, total	**72.2**

Source: 2002 *Economic Census*. The values are product shipments in millions of dollars for 2002. Total product shipments may be lower or higher than industry shipments. See Introduction for a full discussion. Values of indented subcategories are summed in the main heading(s). The symbol (D) appears when data are withheld to prevent disclosure of competitive information. The abbreviation nsk stands for 'not specified by kind' and nec for 'not elsewhere classified'. A dash (-) means zero.

INPUTS AND OUTPUTS FOR STORAGE BATTERY MANUFACTURING

Economic Sector or Industry Providing Inputs	%	Sector	Economic Sector or Industry Buying Outputs	%	Sector
Compensation of employees	26.8		Personal consumption expenditures	26.1	
Primary nonferrous metal, ex. copper & aluminum	20.7	Manufg.	Exports of goods & services	10.9	Cap Inv
Management of companies & enterprises	5.3	Services	Other S/L govt. enterprises	8.4	S/L Govt
Plastics products, nec	4.9	Manufg.	Light truck & utility vehicles	7.2	Manufg.
Wholesale trade	4.8	Trade	Private fixed investment	6.2	
Power generation & supply	2.2	Util.	Retail trade	4.8	Trade
Plastics packaging materials, film & sheet	1.9	Manufg.	Automotive repair & maintenance, ex. car washes	3.7	Services
Lessors of nonfinancial assets	1.6	Fin/R.E.	Power-driven handtools	2.2	Manufg.
Noncomparable imports	1.5	Foreign	Automobiles	1.8	Manufg.
Retail trade	1.5	Trade	Material handling equipment	1.7	Manufg.
Securities, commodity contracts, investments	1.2	Fin/R.E.	Construction machinery	1.6	Manufg.
Paperboard containers	1.1	Manufg.	Farm machinery & equipment	1.6	Manufg.

Continued on next page.

INPUTS AND OUTPUTS FOR STORAGE BATTERY MANUFACTURING - Continued

Economic Sector or Industry Providing Inputs	%	Sector	Economic Sector or Industry Buying Outputs	%	Sector
Basic inorganic chemicals, nec	1.0	Manufg.	Change in private inventories	1.5	In House
Truck transportation	1.0	Util.	General S/L govt. services	1.5	S/L Govt
Maintenance/repair of nonresidential structures	0.9	Construct.	Waste management & remediation services	1.4	Services
Nonferrous metal (ex. copper & aluminum) processing	0.9	Manufg.	Architectural, engineering, & related services	1.4	Services
Services to buildings & dwellings	0.8	Services	Tobacco products	1.4	Manufg.
Iron & steel mills & ferroalloys	0.8	Manufg.	Asphalt paving mixtures & blocks	1.1	Manufg.
Synthetic dyes & pigments	0.7	Manufg.	Computer system design services	1.0	Services
Monetary authorities/depository credit intermediation	0.7	Fin/R.E.	Grains	1.0	Agric.
Architectural, engineering, & related services	0.6	Services	Oil & gas well drilling	0.9	Mining
Automotive repair & maintenance, ex. car washes	0.6	Services	Wholesale trade	0.8	Trade
Professional, scientific, technical services, nec	0.6	Services	Hunting and trapping	0.7	Agric.
Natural gas distribution	0.5	Util.	Heavy duty trucks	0.6	Manufg.
Advertising & related services	0.5	Services	Miscellaneous crops	0.6	Agric.
Commercial & industrial equipment repair/maintenance	0.5	Services	Dairy cattle & milk	0.6	Agric.
Semiconductors & related devices	0.5	Manufg.	Scientific research & development services	0.5	Services
Plastics materials & resins	0.5	Manufg.	Wood containers & pallets	0.5	Manufg.
Printed circuit assemblies (electronic assemblies)	0.4	Manufg.	Residential structures, nec	0.5	Construct.
Laminated plastics plates, sheets, & shapes	0.4	Manufg.	Oilseeds	0.5	Agric.
Taxes on production & imports, less subsidies	0.4		Oil & gas operations services	0.4	Mining
Data processing, hosting, & related services	0.4	Services	Livestock, nec	0.4	Agric.
Scientific research & development services	0.4	Services	Child day care services	0.4	Services
Real estate	0.4	Fin/R.E.	Monetary authorities/depository credit intermediation	0.4	Fin/R.E.
Food services & drinking places	0.4	Services	Securities, commodity contracts, investments	0.3	Fin/R.E.
Machine shops	0.3	Manufg.	Nondepository credit intermediation activities	0.3	Fin/R.E.
Unlaminated plastics profile shapes	0.3	Manufg.	Maintenance/repair of nonresidential structures	0.3	Construct.
Management, scientific, & technical consulting	0.3	Services	Nonresidential structures, nec	0.3	Construct.
Legal services	0.3	Services	Truck transportation	0.3	Util.
Coating, engraving, heat treating & allied activities	0.2	Manufg.	Management of companies & enterprises	0.3	Services
Warehousing & storage	0.2	Util.	Individual & family services	0.3	Services
Telecommunications	0.2	Services	Vegetables and melons	0.3	Agric.
Accounting, tax preparation, bookkeeping, & payroll	0.2	Services	Greenhouse & nursery products	0.3	Agric.
Storage batteries	0.2	Manufg.	Natural gas distribution	0.3	Util.
Automotive equipment rental & leasing	0.2	Fin/R.E.	Residential permanent site structures	0.3	Construct.
Hotels & motels, including casino hotels	0.2	Services	Fruit	0.2	Agric.
Crowns & closures & metal stamping	0.2	Manufg.	Amusement & recreation, nec	0.2	Services
Forging, stamping, & sintering, nec	0.2	Manufg.	Real estate	0.2	Fin/R.E.
Rail transportation	0.2	Util.	Cotton	0.2	Agric.
Motor vehicle parts	0.1	Manufg.	Food services & drinking places	0.1	Services
Business support services	0.1	Services	Sugar crops	0.1	Agric.
Electronic & precision equipment repair/maintenance	0.1	Services	Storage batteries	0.1	Manufg.
Nondepository credit intermediation activities	0.1	Fin/R.E.	Automotive equipment rental & leasing	0.1	Fin/R.E.
Other computer related services, including facilities	0.1	Services	Commercial & health care structures	0.1	Construct.
Air transportation	0.1	Util.			
Personal & household goods repair/maintenance	0.1	Services			
Waste management & remediation services	0.1	Services			
Turned products & screws, nuts, & bolts	0.1	Manufg.			
Chemical products & preparations, nec	0.1	Manufg.			

Source: Benchmark Input-Output Accounts for the U.S. Economy, 2002, U.S. Department of Commerce, Washington, D.C., January 2008. The abbreviation nec stands for 'not elsewhere classified'.

OCCUPATIONS EMPLOYED BY OTHER ELECTRICAL EQUIPMENT & COMPONENT MANUFACTURING

Occupation	% of Total 2006	Change to 2016	Occupation	% of Total 2006	Change to 2016
Team assemblers	14.6	-7.3	Customer service representatives	1.4	1.9
Electrical & electronic equipment assemblers	9.0	-25.9	Electrical engineers	1.2	-7.3
Extruding & drawing machine operators & tenders	3.8	-7.3	Sales reps, wholesale & manufacturing, exc tech	1.2	-7.3
First-line supervisors/managers of production workers	3.7	-7.3	Plating & coating machine operators & tenders	1.2	-3.3
Inspectors, testers, sorters, samplers, & weighers	3.3	-12.6	Tool & die makers	1.1	-2.7
Cutting, punching, & press machine operators	2.8	-16.6	Mechanical engineers	1.1	-7.3
Shipping, receiving, & traffic clerks	2.4	-10.8	Multiple machine tool operators & tenders	1.1	1.9
Maintenance & repair workers, general	2.4	-7.3	Sales representatives, wholesale & manufacturing, tech	1.1	-7.3
Molding, coremaking, & casting machine operators	2.4	-16.6	Packers & packagers, hand	1.1	-25.9
Machinists	2.2	-2.7	Office clerks, general	1.0	-8.7
Helpers--Production workers	2.0	-7.3	Industrial production managers	1.0	-7.3
Laborers & freight, stock, & material movers, hand	1.9	-16.6	Packaging & filling machine operators & tenders	1.0	-16.6
Industrial truck & tractor operators	1.6	-16.6	Electromechanical equipment assemblers	1.0	-7.3
Industrial engineers	1.4	12.5	Computer-controlled machine tool operators	1.0	1.9
General & operations managers	1.4	-16.6	Bookkeeping, accounting, & auditing clerks	1.0	-7.3

Source: Industry-Occupation Matrix, Bureau of Labor Statistics, December 4, 2007. These data are reported based on 4-digit NAICS categories but have been matched to corresponding 6-digit NAICS industry codes. The change reported for each occupation to the year 2016 is a percent of growth or decline as estimated by the Bureau of Labor Statistics. The abbreviation nec stands for 'not elsewhere classified'.

LOCATION BY STATE AND REGIONAL CONCENTRATION

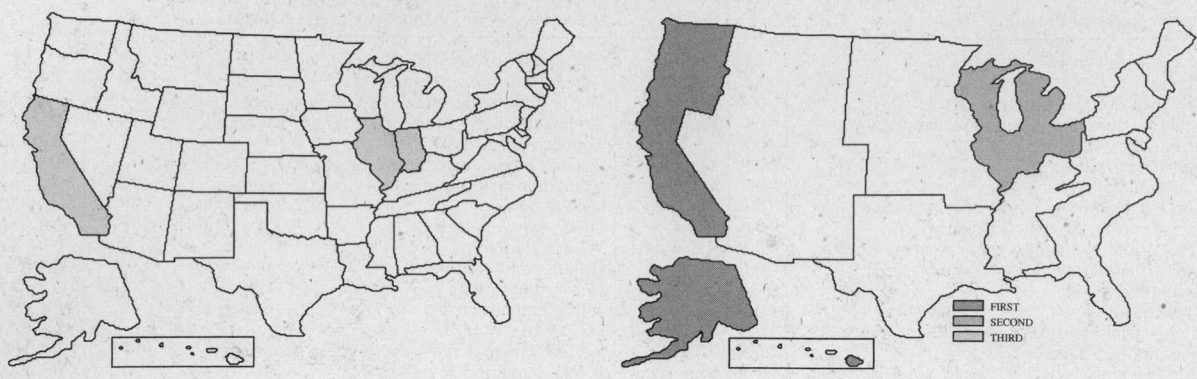

INDUSTRY DATA BY STATE

State	Establish-ments	Shipments			Employment				Cost as % of Shipments	Investment per Employee ($)
		Total ($ mil)	% of U.S.	Per Establ.	Total Number	% of U.S.	Per Establ.	Wages ($/hour)		
California	20	398.0	11.7	19,898.1	1,591	9.3	80	15.49	54.0	3,035
Illinois	10	163.5	4.8	16,351.9	632	3.7	63	15.00	54.5	7,416
Indiana	3	88.6	2.6	29,521.0	382	2.2	127	14.72	40.5	4,924

Source: 2002 *Economic Census*. The states are in descending order of shipments or establishments (if shipment data are missing for the majority). The symbol (D) appears when data are withheld to prevent disclosure of competitive information. States marked with (D) are sorted by number of establishments. A dash (-) indicates that the data element cannot be calculated. Data may not show all states active in the NAICS category. All data available at the time of publication are shown.

NAICS 335912 - PRIMARY BATTERY MANUFACTURING

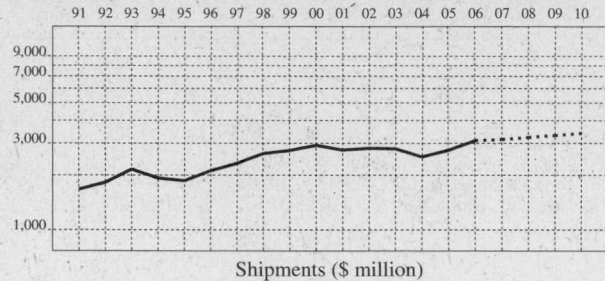

Shipments ($ million)

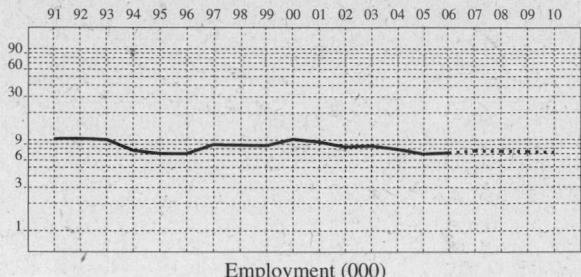

Employment (000)

GENERAL STATISTICS

Year	Companies	Establishments		Employment			Compensation		Production ($ million)			
		Total	with 20 or more employees	Total (000)	Production Workers (000)	Hours (Mil)	Payroll ($ mil)	Wages ($/hr)	Cost of Materials	Value Added by Manufacture	Value of Shipments	Capital Invest.
1991		71	38	10.3	7.9	16.6	250.3	10.11	863.7	787.3	1,672.3	38.9
1992	53	68	32	10.4	7.9	16.0	271.9	11.23	933.9	871.0	1,823.7	52.5
1993		60	31	10.1	7.7	15.8	275.0	11.91	1,159.3	1,006.2	2,158.2	76.2
1994		56	30	7.7	6.4	11.9	211.4	12.82	1,041.3	891.0	1,925.9	80.6
1995		56	34	7.1	6.0	11.2	216.9	14.06	1,025.3	833.1	1,864.7	105.2
1996		55	32	7.1	5.9	10.8	238.7	15.72	1,097.5	1,020.4	2,116.1	112.1
1997	34	45	23	8.9	6.8	13.0	281.5	14.41	995.1	1,349.0	2,322.9	130.2
1998		45	24	8.8	6.7	13.6	310.0	15.00	1,181.5	1,460.4	2,634.0	116.2
1999		44	22	8.7	7.0	13.8	331.5	16.26	1,203.4	1,538.5	2,738.9	143.0
2000		44	22	10.2	7.9	15.5	369.9	15.55	1,281.0	1,699.4	2,925.1	158.3
2001		46	22	9.5	7.3	13.9	367.4	17.19	1,226.8	1,494.6	2,753.6	123.6
2002	31	42	23	8.4	6.6	13.2	306.7	15.73	1,117.3	1,691.8	2,816.0	83.4
2003		47	25	8.6	6.6	12.7	330.1	16.96	1,228.3	1,555.9	2,800.0	56.0
2004		48	23	7.9	5.8	10.9	338.2	19.16	1,220.6	1,301.9	2,527.3	72.9
2005		52	28	7.0	5.5	11.1	316.8	18.97	1,392.3	1,366.5	2,749.6	61.3
2006		40P	20P	7.2	5.8	11.9	320.2	17.88	1,579.7	1,572.3	3,104.4	58.5
2007		38P	20P	7.6P	5.9P	11.4P	358.0P	19.66P	1,602.1P	1,594.6P	3,148.3P	93.9P
2008		37P	19P	7.5P	5.8P	11.2P	365.2P	20.19P	1,644.9P	1,637.2P	3,232.5P	94.1P
2009		35P	18P	7.4P	5.7P	11.0P	372.5P	20.71P	1,687.7P	1,679.8P	3,316.6P	94.4P
2010		34P	17P	7.2P	5.6P	10.8P	379.8P	21.24P	1,730.5P	1,722.4P	3,400.7P	94.6P

Sources: 1992, 1997, 2002 *Economic Census*; other years, up to 2006, are from the *Annual Survey of Manufactures*. Establishment counts for non-Census years are from *County Business Patterns*; 1997 and 2002 values are from the 1997 and 2002 censuses respectively, reported in the Federal Government's NAICS format. Other years were originally reported in equivalent SIC format. 'P's show projections by the editors.

INDICES OF CHANGE

Year	Companies	Establishments		Employment			Compensation		Production ($ million)			
		Total	with 20 or more employees	Total (000)	Production Workers (000)	Hours (Mil)	Payroll ($ mil)	Wages ($/hr)	Cost of Materials	Value Added by Manufacture	Value of Shipments	Capital Invest.
1992	171	162	139	124	120	121	89	71	84	51	65	63
1997	110	107	100	106	103	98	92	92	89	80	82	156
2001		110	96	113	111	105	120	109	110	88	98	148
2002	100	100	100	100	100	100	100	100	100	100	100	100
2003		112	109	102	100	96	108	108	110	92	99	67
2004		114	100	94	88	83	110	122	109	77	90	87
2005		124	122	83	83	84	103	121	125	81	98	74
2006		95P	89P	86	88	90	104	114	141	93	110	70
2007		91P	85P	90P	89P	86P	117P	125P	143P	94P	112P	113P
2008		87P	81P	89P	88P	85P	119P	128P	147P	97P	115P	113P
2009		84P	78P	88P	86P	83P	121P	132P	151P	99P	118P	113P
2010		80P	74P	86P	85P	82P	124P	135P	155P	102P	121P	113P

Sources: Same as General Statistics. Values reflect change from the base year, 2002. Values above 100 mean greater than 2002, values below 100 mean less than 2002, and the values of 100 in other years means the same as 2002. 'P's show projections by the editors.

SELECTED RATIOS

For 2002	Avg. of All Manufact.	Analyzed Industry	Index	For 2002	Avg. of All Manufact.	Analyzed Industry	Index
Employees per Establishment	42	200	476	Value Added per Production Worker	182,367	256,333	141
Payroll per Establishment	1,639,184	7,302,381	445	Cost per Establishment	5,769,015	26,602,381	461
Payroll per Employee	39,053	36,512	93	Cost per Employee	137,446	133,012	97
Production Workers per Establishment	30	157	533	Cost per Production Worker	195,506	169,288	87
Wages per Establishment	694,845	4,943,714	711	Shipments per Establishment	11,158,348	67,047,619	601
Wages per Production Worker	23,548	31,460	134	Shipments per Employee	265,847	335,238	126
Hours per Production Worker	1,980	2,000	101	Shipments per Production Worker	378,144	426,667	113
Wages per Hour	11.89	15.73	132	Investment per Establishment	361,338	1,985,714	550
Value Added per Establishment	5,381,325	40,280,952	749	Investment per Employee	8,609	9,929	115
Value Added per Employee	128,210	201,405	157	Investment per Production Worker	12,245	12,636	103

Sources: Same as General Statistics. The 'Average of All Manufacturing' column represents the average of all manufacturing industries reported for the most recent complete year available. The Index shows the relationship between the Average and the Analyzed Industry. For example, 100 means that they are equal; 500 that the Analyzed Industry is five times the average; 50 means that the Analyzed Industry is half the national average. The abbreviation 'na' is used to show that data are 'not available'. Ratios shown for 2002, the last complete census year.

1399

LEADING COMPANIES   Number shown: **28**   Total sales ($ mil): **46,309**   Total employment (000): **185.9**

Company Name	Address				CEO Name	Phone	Co. Type	Sales ($ mil)	Empl. (000)
Johnson Controls Inc.	PO Box 591	Milwaukee	WI	53201		414-524-1200	P	34,624	140.0
Energizer Battery Co.	533 Maryville Univ.	St. Louis	MO	63141	Ward Klein	314-985-2000	S	3,807*	10.0
Exide Technologies	13000 Deerfield Pky	Alpharetta	GA	30004		678-566-9000	P	2,940	13.9
Spectrum Brands Inc.	6 Concourse Pky.	Atlanta	GA	30328	John D. Bowlin	770-829-6200	P	1,995	7.1
EaglePicher Corp.	2424 John Daly Rd.	Inkster	MI	48141	Donald L. Runkle	313-278-5956	R	1,244*	4.2
East Penn Manufacturing Co.	PO Box 147	Lyon Station	PA	19536			R	716*	5.0
Greatbatch Inc.	9645 Wehrle Dr.	Clarence	NY	14031		716-759-5600	P	319	2.4
Ultralife Batteries Inc.	2000 Technology	Newark	NY	14513		315-332-7100	P	138	1.1
Deepsea Power and Light Inc.	3855 Ruffin Rd.	San Diego	CA	92123	Mark Olsson	858-576-1261	R	75*	0.2
Ovonic Battery Co.	2968 Waterview Dr.	Rochester Hills	MI	48309	James Metzger	248-293-0440	S	64*	0.3
Trojan Battery Co.	12380 Clark St.	Santa Fe Spgs	CA	90670	Richard Godber	562-946-8381	R	60*	0.4
Nuvera Fuel Cells Inc.	20 Acorn Park	Cambridge	MA	02140	Roberto Cordaro	617-245-7500	R	60*	0.1
FuelCell Energy Inc.	3 Great Pasture Rd.	Danbury	CT	06810	Daniel Brdar	203-825-6000	P	48	0.4
Anton Bauer Inc.	14 Progress Dr.	Shelton	CT	06484	Alexander Desorbo	203-929-1100	R	34*	0.1
Bulldog Battery Corp.	PO Box 766	Wabash	IN	46992	Norman Benjamin	260-563-0551	R	28*	<0.1
Adva-Lite Inc.	PO Box 12289	St Petersburg	FL	33733	Keith Olivit	727-546-5483	R	22*	0.1
Bright Star Industries Inc.	380 Stewart Rd.	Wilkes Barre	PA	18706		570-825-1900	R	21*	<0.1
Bren-Tronics Inc.	10 Brayton Ct.	Commack	NY	11725	William Ehman	631-499-5155	R	20*	0.1
Battery Handling Systems Inc.	PO Box 28990	Saint Louis	MO	63132	W Huber	314-423-7091	R	17*	<0.1
BST Systems Inc.	78 Plainfield Pke.	Plainfield	CT	06374	Max Solis	860-564-4078	R	14*	<0.1
China Digital Communications	225 S Lake Ave.	Pasadena	CA	91101	Zhongan Xu	626-432-5427	P	12	<0.1
Lind Electronics Inc.	6414 Cambridge St.	Minneapolis	MN	55426	LeRoy Lind	952-927-6303	R	11*	<0.1
Co-Ax Technology Inc.	29401 Ambina Dr.	Solon	OH	44139	Hassan Varghai	440-914-9200	R	11*	<0.1
Spectrum Batteries Inc.	6910 Sprigg St.	Fulshear	TX	77441	Jim Dutchak	281-533-9596	R	10*	<0.1
R and D Batteries Inc.	PO Box 5007	Burnsville	MN	55337	Randall Noddings	952-890-0629	R	8*	<0.1
TAE Trans Atlantic Electronics	PO Box 817	Deer Park	NY	11729	Harry English	631-595-9206	R	6*	<0.1
Electro Energy Inc.	30 Shelter Rock Rd.	Danbury	CT	06810	Martin G. Klein	203-797-2699	P	5	<0.1
Uninterruptible Power Products	1567 W 11th Dr.	Friendship	WI	53934	Gary Jungwirth	608-339-2151	R	2*	<0.1

Source: Ward's Business Directory of U.S. Private and Public Companies, Volumes 1 and 2, 2008. The company type code used is as follows: P - Public, R - Private, S - Subsidiary, D - Division, J - Joint Venture, A - Affiliate, G - Group. Sales are in millions of dollars, employees are in thousands. An asterisk (*) indicates an estimated sales volume. The symbol < stands for 'less than'. Company names and addresses are truncated, in some cases, to fit into the available space.

MATERIALS CONSUMED

Material	Quantity	Delivered Cost ($ million)
Metal stampings	(X)	137.7
All other fabricated metal products (excluding forgings)	(X)	49.7
Castings, rough and semifinished	(X)	(D)
Refined unalloyed lead shapes and forms (exc. castings, forgings, fabr. metal products)	(X)	(D)
Lead-calcium alloyed	(X)	(D)
Steel sheet and strip (including tinplate)	(X)	28.6
All other steel shapes and forms (exc. castings, forgings, fabr. metal products)	(X)	(D)
Zinc and zinc-based alloy shapes and forms (exc. castings, forgings, fabr. metal products)	(X)	88.0
Litharge	(X)	(D)
Other industrial inorganic chemicals (incl. mercury and silver oxide)	(X)	(D)
Plastics resins consumed in the form of granules, pellets, etc.	(X)	3.8
Plastics products consumed in the form of sheets, rods, etc.	(X)	35.5
Fabricated plastics products (excluding gaskets)	(X)	47.9
Paperboard containers, boxes, and corrugated paperboard	(X)	46.0
Carbon and graphite electrodes and other products for electrical use	(X)	46.9
Metal powders	(X)	58.0
All other materials, components, parts, containers, and supplies	(X)	462.4
Materials, ingredients, containers, and supplies, nsk	(X)	29.3

Source: 2002 *Economic Census*. Explanation of symbols used: (D): Withheld to avoid disclosure of competitive data; na: Not available; (S): Withheld because statistical norms were not met; (X): Not applicable; (Z): Less than half the unit shown; nec: Not elsewhere classified; nsk: Not specified by kind; - : zero; p : 10-19 percent estimated; q : 20-29 percent estimated.

PRODUCT SHARE DETAILS

Product or Product Class Shipments	Mil. $	Product or Product Class Shipments	Mil. $
PRIMARY BATTERIES	2,781.8	Button and coin primary battery cells	224.9
Round and prismatic primary battery cells	2,462.2	Silver oxide button and coin primary battery cells	(D)
Alkaline manganese round and prismatic primary battery cells	1,392.3	Alkaline manganese button and coin primary battery cells	(D)
Zinc carbon round and prismatic primary battery cells	(D)	Zinc air button and coin primary battery cells	137.4
Mercuric oxide round and prismatic primary battery cells	-	Lithium button and coin primary battery cells	(D)
Lithium round and prismatic primary battery cells	(D)	All other button and coin primary battery cells	(D)
All other round and prismatic battery cells	878.6	Parts for primary batteries, excluding cases and containers	83.9
		Primary batteries, nsk, total	10.8

Source: 2002 *Economic Census*. The values are product shipments in millions of dollars for 2002. Total product shipments may be lower or higher than industry shipments. See Introduction for a full discussion. Values of indented subcategories are summed in the main heading(s). The symbol (D) appears when data are withheld to prevent disclosure of competitive information. The abbreviation nsk stands for 'not specified by kind' and nec for 'not elsewhere classified'. A dash (-) means zero.

INPUTS AND OUTPUTS FOR PRIMARY BATTERY MANUFACTURING

Economic Sector or Industry Providing Inputs	%	Sector	Economic Sector or Industry Buying Outputs	%	Sector
Compensation of employees	15.2		Personal consumption expenditures	78.1	
Crowns & closures & metal stamping	6.7	Manufg.	Exports of goods & services	13.3	Cap Inv
Nonferrous metal (ex. copper & aluminum) processing	4.9	Manufg.	Change in private inventories	1.6	In House
Wholesale trade	4.0	Trade	General S/L govt. services	1.4	S/L Govt
Iron & steel mills & ferroalloys	3.0	Manufg.	Telecommunications	1.2	Services
Management of companies & enterprises	2.9	Services	General Federal government services, defense	0.9	Fed Govt
Carbon & graphite products	2.1	Manufg.	Wholesale trade	0.8	Trade
Paperboard containers	2.1	Manufg.	Primary batteries	0.4	Manufg.
Plastics products, nec	1.8	Manufg.	Air transportation	0.3	Util.
Plastics packaging materials, film & sheet	1.6	Manufg.	S/L govt. passenger transit	0.2	S/L Govt
Semiconductors & related devices	1.3	Manufg.	Personal & household goods repair/maintenance	0.1	Services
Printed circuit assemblies (electronic assembiles)	1.2	Manufg.	Retail trade	0.1	Trade
Machine shops	0.9	Manufg.	Lighting fixtures	0.1	Manufg.
Primary nonferrous metal, ex. copper & aluminum	0.8	Manufg.	Wineries	0.1	Manufg.
Truck transportation	0.8	Util.	Motor vehicle parts	0.1	Manufg.
Retail trade	0.6	Trade			
Power generation & supply	0.6	Util.			
Coating, engraving, heat treating & allied activities	0.5	Manufg.			
Synthetic dyes & pigments	0.5	Manufg.			
Primary batteries	0.5	Manufg.			
Cutting tools & machine tool accessories	0.4	Manufg.			
Taxes on production & imports, less subsidies	0.4				
Turned products & screws, nuts, & bolts	0.3	Manufg.			
Petroleum lubricating oil & grease	0.3	Manufg.			
Noncomparable imports	0.3	Foreign			
Maintenance/repair of nonresidential structures	0.3	Construct.			
Ferrous metal foundries	0.2	Manufg.			
Advertising & related services	0.2	Services			
Paper mills	0.2	Manufg.			
Unlaminated plastics profile shapes	0.2	Manufg.			
Nonferrous metal foundries	0.2	Manufg.			
Metal cans, boxes, & other containers (light gauge)	0.2	Manufg.			
Services to buildings & dwellings	0.2	Services			
Laminated plastics plates, sheets, & shapes	0.2	Manufg.			
Chemical products & preparations, nec	0.2	Manufg.			
Relay & industrial controls	0.2	Manufg.			
Scientific research & development services	0.2	Services			
Bare printed circuit boards	0.2	Manufg.			
Fabricated metals, nec	0.2	Manufg.			
Paperboard mills	0.2	Manufg.			
Plastics materials & resins	0.2	Manufg.			
Automotive repair & maintenance, ex. car washes	0.2	Services			
Accounting, tax preparation, bookkeeping, & payroll	0.2	Services			
Basic inorganic chemicals, nec	0.2	Manufg.			
Plate work & fabricated structural products	0.1	Manufg.			
Commercial & industrial equipment repair/maintenance	0.1	Services			
Valve & fittings other than plumbing	0.1	Manufg.			
Legal services	0.1	Services			
Ball & roller bearings	0.1	Manufg.			
Handtools	0.1	Manufg.			

Source: *Benchmark Input-Output Accounts for the U.S. Economy, 2002*, U.S. Department of Commerce, Washington, D.C., January 2008. The abbreviation nec stands for 'not elsewhere classified'.

OCCUPATIONS EMPLOYED BY OTHER ELECTRICAL EQUIPMENT & COMPONENT MANUFACTURING

Occupation	% of Total 2006	Change to 2016	Occupation	% of Total 2006	Change to 2016
Team assemblers	14.6	-7.3	Customer service representatives	1.4	1.9
Electrical & electronic equipment assemblers	9.0	-25.9	Electrical engineers	1.2	-7.3
Extruding & drawing machine operators & tenders	3.8	-7.3	Sales reps, wholesale & manufacturing, exc tech	1.2	-7.3
First-line supervisors/managers of production workers	3.7	-7.3	Plating & coating machine operators & tenders	1.2	-3.3
Inspectors, testers, sorters, samplers, & weighers	3.3	-12.6	Tool & die makers	1.1	-2.7
Cutting, punching, & press machine operators	2.8	-16.6	Mechanical engineers	1.1	-7.3
Shipping, receiving, & traffic clerks	2.4	-10.8	Multiple machine tool operators & tenders	1.1	1.9
Maintenance & repair workers, general	2.4	-7.3	Sales representatives, wholesale & manufacturing, tech	1.1	-7.3
Molding, coremaking, & casting machine operators	2.4	-16.6	Packers & packagers, hand	1.1	-25.9
Machinists	2.2	-2.7	Office clerks, general	1.0	-8.7
Helpers--Production workers	2.0	-7.3	Industrial production managers	1.0	-7.3
Laborers & freight, stock, & material movers, hand	1.9	-16.6	Packaging & filling machine operators & tenders	1.0	-16.6
Industrial truck & tractor operators	1.6	-16.6	Electromechanical equipment assemblers	1.0	-7.3
Industrial engineers	1.4	12.5	Computer-controlled machine tool operators	1.0	1.9
General & operations managers	1.4	-16.6	Bookkeeping, accounting, & auditing clerks	1.0	-7.3

Source: *Industry-Occupation Matrix*, Bureau of Labor Statistics, December 4, 2007. These data are reported based on 4-digit NAICS categories but have been matched to corresponding 6-digit NAICS industry codes. The change reported for each occupation to the year 2016 is a percent of growth or decline as estimated by the Bureau of Labor Statistics. The abbreviation nec stands for 'not elsewhere classified'.

INDUSTRY DATA BY STATE

State-level data are not available.

NAICS 33592M - COMMUNICATION AND ENERGY WIRE AND CABLE MANUFACTURING*

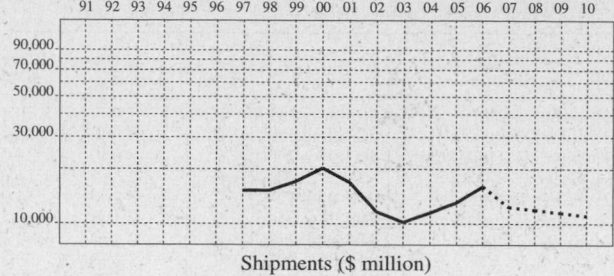

Shipments ($ million)

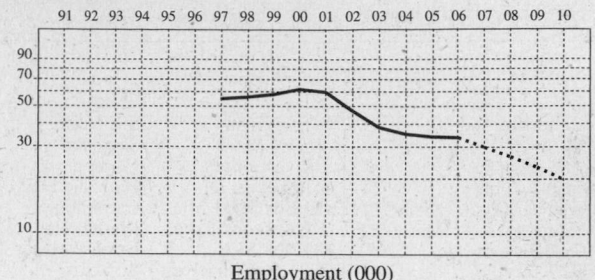

Employment (000)

GENERAL STATISTICS

Year	Companies	Establishments		Employment			Compensation		Production ($ million)			
		Total	with 20 or more employees	Total (000)	Production Workers (000)	Hours (Mil)	Payroll ($ mil)	Wages ($/hr)	Cost of Materials	Value Added by Manufacture	Value of Shipments	Capital Invest.
1997	228	313	300	54.9	39.6	83.7	1,897.6	13.73	9,081.0	6,213.2	15,249.9	608.8
1998		413	309	56.1	40.2	86.9	2,003.7	13.99	8,767.9	6,515.5	15,270.0	754.2
1999		421	305	58.0	42.6	89.7	2,108.4	14.66	10,398.8	6,711.9	17,126.5	852.5
2000		447	303	62.0	46.2	97.4	2,300.7	14.49	11,984.1	8,422.5	20,270.0	881.4
2001		447	309	59.8	42.3	85.1	2,159.0	14.98	9,516.1	7,348.5	16,885.3	871.4
2002	348	452	291	47.1	32.9	66.1	1,752.8	15.35	6,714.2	4,857.9	11,659.6	313.8
2003		458	276	38.4	27.7	57.1	1,515.1	15.86	5,902.4	4,307.2	10,220.0	198.8
2004		434	248	35.3	25.5	52.4	1,437.0	17.18	6,993.4	4,716.2	11,533.6	240.0
2005		411	254	34.1	24.8	51.5	1,462.3	17.62	8,413.3	4,806.2	13,135.7	163.5
2006		466P	252P	33.7	25.0	51.1	1,514.0	18.04	10,751.2	5,632.2	16,041.4	250.6
2007		475P	245P	29.9P	21.7P	43.2P	1,369.7P	18.30P	8,288.8P	4,342.2P	12,367.3P	79.3P
2008		484P	237P	26.6P	19.3P	37.9P	1,288.7P	18.79P	7,999.7P	4,190.8P	11,936.1P	0.3P
2009		493P	230P	23.3P	17.0P	32.7P	1,207.7P	19.28P	7,710.7P	4,039.4P	11,504.8P	
2010		502P	223P	20.0P	14.6P	27.4P	1,126.7P	19.78P	7,421.7P	3,888.0P	11,073.5P	

Sources: 1997 and 2002 *Economic Census*; other years, up to 2006, are from *Annual Survey of Manufactures*. Establishment counts for non-Census years are from *County Business Patterns*; 1997 and 2002 values are from the 1997 and 2002 censuses, respectively. 'P's show projections by the editors.

INDICES OF CHANGE

Year	Companies	Establishments		Employment			Compensation		Production ($ million)			
		Total	with 20 or more employees	Total (000)	Production Workers (000)	Hours (Mil)	Payroll ($ mil)	Wages ($/hr)	Cost of Materials	Value Added by Manufacture	Value of Shipments	Capital Invest.
1997	66	69	103	117	120	127	108	89	135	128	131	194
1998		91	106	119	122	131	114	91	131	134	131	240
1999		93	105	123	129	136	120	96	155	138	147	272
2000		99	104	132	140	147	131	94	178	173	174	281
2001		99	106	127	129	129	123	98	142	151	145	278
2002	100	100	100	100	100	100	100	100	100	100	100	100
2003		101	95	82	84	86	86	103	88	89	88	63
2004		96	85	75	78	79	82	112	104	97	99	76
2005		91	87	72	75	78	83	115	125	99	113	52
2006		103P	87P	72	76	77	86	118	160	116	138	80
2007		105P	84P	63P	66P	65P	78P	119P	123P	89P	106P	25P
2008		107P	82P	56P	59P	57P	74P	122P	119P	86P	102P	
2009		109P	79P	49P	52P	49P	69P	126P	115P	83P	99P	
2010		111P	77P	42P	44P	41P	64P	129P	111P	80P	95P	

Sources: Same as General Statistics. Values reflect change from the base year, 2002. Values above 100 mean greater than 2002, values below 100 mean less than 2002, and the values of 100 in other years means the same as 2002. 'P's show projections by the editors.

SELECTED RATIOS

For 2002	Avg. of All Manufact.	Analyzed Industry	Index	For 2002	Avg. of All Manufact.	Analyzed Industry	Index
Employees per Establishment	42	104	248	Value Added per Production Worker	182,367	147,657	81
Payroll per Establishment	1,639,184	3,877,876	237	Cost per Establishment	5,769,015	14,854,425	257
Payroll per Employee	39,053	37,214	95	Cost per Employee	137,446	142,552	104
Production Workers per Establishment	30	73	247	Cost per Production Worker	195,506	204,079	104
Wages per Establishment	694,845	2,244,768	323	Shipments per Establishment	11,158,348	25,795,575	231
Wages per Production Worker	23,548	30,840	131	Shipments per Employee	265,847	247,550	93
Hours per Production Worker	1,980	2,009	101	Shipments per Production Worker	378,144	354,395	94
Wages per Hour	11.89	15.35	129	Investment per Establishment	361,338	694,248	192
Value Added per Establishment	5,381,325	10,747,566	200	Investment per Employee	8,609	6,662	77
Value Added per Employee	128,210	103,140	80	Investment per Production Worker	12,245	9,538	78

Sources: Same as General Statistics. The 'Average of All Manufacturing' column represents the average of all manufacturing industries reported for the most recent complete year available. The Index shows the relationship between the Average and the Analyzed Industry. For example, 100 means that they are equal; 500 that the Analyzed Industry is five times the average; 50 means that the Analyzed Industry is half the national average. The abbreviation 'na' is used to show that data are 'not available'. Ratios shown for 2002, the last complete census year.

*Equivalent to Federal Government NAICS 335921, 335929.

LEADING COMPANIES   Number shown: 75   Total sales ($ mil): 45,103   Total employment (000): 104.0

Company Name	Address				CEO Name	Phone	Co. Type	Sales ($ mil)	Empl. (000)
Harbour Industries Inc.	PO Box 188	Shelburne	VT	05482	Dennis Dodd	802-985-3311	R	7,000*	<0.1
Kerite Co.	49 Day Street	Seymour	CT	06483	John Degray	203-888-2591	R	7,000*	<0.1
Corning Inc.	1 Riverfront Plz.	Corning	NY	14831	James R. Houghton	607-974-9000	P	5,860	24.5
General Cable Corp.	4 Tesseneer Dr.	Highland Hgts	KY	41076	Gregory B. Kenny	859-572-8000	P	4,615	11.8
Southwire Co.	PO Box 1000	Carrollton	GA	30112	Stuart Thorn	770-832-4242	R	3,200*	4.2
Andrew Corp.	3 Westbrook Corp.	Westchester	IL	60154	Ralph E. Faison	708-236-6600	S	2,195	11.8
Dekko Technologies L.L.C.	PO Box 337	North Webster	IN	46555	Steven Hankinf	574-834-2818	R	2,130*	0.1
Belden CDT Inc.	7701 Forsyth Blvd.	St. Louis	MO	63105		314-854-8000	P	2,033	8.3
W.L. Gore and Associates Inc.	PO Box 9206	Newark	DE	19714	Terri Kelly	410-506-7787	R	1,670*	7.3
JDS Uniphase Corp.	430 N McCarthy	Milpitas	CA	95035	Martin A. Kaplan	408-546-5000	P	1,397*	7.0
Leviton Manufacturing Company	PO Box 630087	Little Neck	NY	11363	Donald Hendler	718-229-4040	R	800*	0.7
East Penn Manufacturing Co.	PO Box 147	Lyon Station	PA	19536			R	716*	5.0
Judd Wire Inc.	124 Tpke. Rd.	Turners Falls	MA	01376	Hidetoshi Kinuta	413-863-4357	R	650*	0.2
Accellent Corp.	PO Box 26992	Collegeville	PA	19426	Kenneth Freeman	610-489-0300	S	474	1.3
JBL Professional Inc.	8400 Balboa Blvd.	Northridge	CA	91329	John Carpanini	818-894-8850	S	443*	1.8
Handy and Harman	555 Theodore Fremd	Rye	NY	10580	Jeffrey A. Svoboda	914-921-5200	S	326*	<0.1
Olympic Manufacturing Group	153 Bowles Rd.	Agawam	MA	01001			S	291*	0.3
Lynn Products Inc.	2645 W 237th St.	Torrance	CA	90505	Hsinyu Lin	310-530-5966	R	287*	1.0
Intercon 1	1120 Wayzata E	Wayzata	MN	55391	M. J. Degen	218-828-3157	D	245*	1.0
Ensign-Bickford Industries	PO Box 7	Simsbury	CT	06070	Bob Lepossky	860-843-2000	R	185*	0.6
Phelps Dodge Magnet Wire Co.	806 Douglas Rd.	Coral Gables	FL	33134	Don Disque	305-648-8000	S	170*	1.3
Draka USA Corp.	9 Forge Park	Franklin	MA	02038	Joe Dixon	508-520-1200	S	170*	0.9
Central Wire Industries Ltd.	370 Franklin Tpke.	Mahwah	NJ	07430	Thierry Cremailh	201-529-0900	R	167*	<0.1
PolyVision Corp.	3970 Johns Creek Ct	Suwanee	GA	30024	Michael H. Dunn	678-542-3100	S	153*	1.1
ACK Controls Inc.	PO Box 1297	Glasgow	KY	42142	Ryuichi Kinase	270-678-6200	R	153*	0.4
Okonite Company Inc.	PO Box 340	Ramsey	NJ	07446	A Coppola	201-825-0300	R	130*	0.2
Nexans USA Inc.	PO Box 60339	Charlotte	NC	28260	Kevin Cyr	717-354-6200	R	121*	0.5
Centrilift	200 W Stuart Roosa	Claremore	OK	74017	Chad Deaton	918-341-9600	D	115*	1.5
Aetna Insulated Wire Co.	1537 Air Rail Ave.	Virginia Beach	VA	23455	Walt Smith		R	96*	0.3
Multiplex Inc.	5000 Hadley Rd.	S Plainfield	NJ	07080	Christopher Peterson	908-757-8817	R	85*	0.3
Hi-Lex Corp.	5200 Wayne Rd.	Battle Creek	MI	49015	Katsuaki Shima	269-968-0781	R	82*	0.5
FLX Micro Inc.	4415 Euclid Ave.	Cleveland	OH	44103	Gary Johnson	216-431-3356	R	79*	<0.1
AFC Cable Systems Inc.	272 Duchaine Blvd.	New Bedford	MA	02745	Bob Tereira	508-998-1131	S	76*	1.3
Horizon Music Inc.	3581 Larch Ln.	Jackson	MO	63755	Dale Williams	573-651-6500	R	74*	0.3
Pyott-Boone Electronics Inc.	PO Box 809	Tazewell	VA	24651	Donald Fetterolf	276-988-5505	R	73*	0.2
Monster Cable Products Inc.	455 Valley Dr.	Brisbane	CA	94005	Noel Lee	415-840-2000	R	72*	0.5
Siemon Co.	PO Box 400	Watertown	CT	06795	Carl Siemon	860-945-4200	R	70*	0.5
Meggitt Safety Systems	1955 N Surveyor	Simi Valley	CA	93063		805-526-5700	S	69*	0.5
Phifer Inc.	PO Box 1700	Tuscaloosa	AL	35403	Beverly Phifer	205-345-2120	R	66*	0.9
Aved Electronics Inc.	59 Technology Dr.	Lowell	MA	01851	Ralph Santosuosso	978-453-6393	R	66*	<0.1
Crest Electronics Inc.	PO Box 727	Dassel	MN	55325	Larry Lautt	320-275-3382	R	66*	<0.1
New York Wire Co.	PO Box 866	Mount Wolf	PA	17347	Barry Douglas	717-266-5626	R	65*	0.5
Hendrix Wire and Cable Inc.	53 Old Wilton Rd.	Milford	NH	03055	Thomas Brennan	603-673-2040	R	64*	0.2
Tyco Integrated Cable Systems	PO Box 479	Portsmouth	NH	03802		603-436-6100	R	64*	0.2
ARC-Tronics Inc.	1150 Pagni Dr.	Elk Grove Vlg	IL	60007	Conrad Goeringer	847-437-0211	R	59*	0.3
LGC Wireless Inc.	2540 Junction Ave.	San Jose	CA	95134	Ian Sugarbroad	408-952-2400	S	58*	<0.1
Champlain Cable Corp.	175 Hercules Dr.	Colchester	VT	05446	Richard Hall	802-655-2121	S	55*	0.3
Wyre-Wynd	77 Anthony St.	Jewett City	CT	06351		860-376-2516	D	52*	0.2
Morrell Inc.	3333 Bald Mtn. Rd.	Auburn Hills	MI	48326	Steven Tallman	248-373-1600	R	50*	0.1
Amphenol Interconnect Products	20 Valley St.	Endicott	NY	13760		607-754-4444	S	50*	0.2
M and G Electronics Corp.	PO Box 8187	Virginia Beach	VA	23450	Mark Garcea	757-468-6000	R	49*	0.3
BIW Cable Systems Inc.	22 Joseph E Warner	North Dighton	MA	02764		508-822-5444	D	48*	0.3
Optical Cable Corp.	5290 Concourse Dr.	Roanoke	VA	24019	Randall Frazier	540-265-0690	P	45	0.2
Alan Wire Company Inc.	830 S W Street	Sikeston	MO	63801	Alan Keenan	573-471-9548	R	43*	0.1
New England Wire Tchnlgs Corp.	PO Box 264	Lisbon	NH	03585	Richard Johns	603-838-6625	R	43*	0.3
Ortronics Inc.	125 Eugene Oneill	New London	CT	06320	Tom Goetter	860-445-3900	R	43*	0.3
Isotec Inc.	1780 Birchwood	Des Plaines	IL	60018	Gary Geppert	847-299-9299	R	42*	0.1
Tappan Wire and Cable Inc.	616 Rte. 303	Blauvelt	NY	10913	Sidney Grant	845-353-9000	R	40*	0.2
Audio Authority Corp.	2048 Mercer Rd.	Lexington	KY	40511	Jonathan Sisk	859-233-4599	R	39*	<0.1
Nichols Wire Inc.	1547 Helton Dr.	Florence	AL	35630	Earl Thomason	256-764-4271	R	38*	0.1
Kalas Manufacturing Inc.	PO Box 328	Denver	PA	17517	Richard Witwer	717-336-5575	R	38*	0.1
Draka Cableteq USA	PO Box 347	Schuylkill Hvn	PA	17972	Joseph Dickson	570-385-4381	R	38*	0.1
Alpha Wire Co.	711 Lidgerwood	Elizabeth	NJ	07207		908-925-8000	R	36*	0.2
Trilogy Communications Inc.	2910 Hwy. 80 E	Pearl	MS	39208	Shinn Lee	601-932-4461	R	35*	0.1
Miller Electric Co.	2501 St. Marys Ave.	Omaha	NE	68105	Don Fitzpatrick	402-341-6479	R	35*	0.2
Comtran Corp.	1 Main St., Ste. 2	Whitinsville	MA	01588	David Allegrezza	508-234-6256	R	35*	0.1
Oklahoma Steel and Wire Co.	PO Box 220	Madill	OK	73446		580-795-7311	R	34*	0.3
Whirlwind Music Distributors	99 Ling Rd.	Rochester	NY	14612	Michael Laiacona	585-663-8820	R	34*	0.1
Applied Fiber Telecom	251 Walnut Ave. S	Leesburg	GA	31763		229-759-8301	R	32*	0.1
Tol-O-Matic Inc.	3800 Cnty Rd 116	Hamel	MN	55340	William Toles	763-478-8000	R	31*	0.2
Cordset Designs Inc.	PO Box 650	Pink Hill	NC	28572	Steven Peltz	252-568-4001	R	30*	0.1
Computer Crafts Inc.	PO Box 264	Hawthorne	NJ	07507	Donald Harkins	973-423-3500	R	29*	0.3
CS Business Systems Inc.	1236 Main St.	Buffalo	NY	14209	Michael Choo	716-886-6521	R	27*	<0.1
Radix Wire Company Inc.	26000 Lakeland	Cleveland	OH	44132	Charles Vermerris	216-731-9191	R	26*	<0.1
Therm-O-Link Inc.	10513 Freedom St.	Garrettsville	OH	44231	David Campbell	330-527-2124	R	26*	0.1

Source: Ward's Business Directory of U.S. Private and Public Companies, Volumes 1 and 2, 2008. The company type code used is as follows: P - Public, R - Private, S - Subsidiary, D - Division, J - Joint Venture, A - Affiliate, G - Group. Sales are in millions of dollars, employees are in thousands. An asterisk (*) indicates an estimated sales volume. The symbol < stands for 'less than'. Company names and addresses are truncated, in some cases, to fit into the available space.

MATERIALS CONSUMED FOR FIBER OPTIC CABLE MANUFACTURING

Material		Quantity	Delivered Cost ($ million)
Bare steel wire	1,000 s tons	(D)	(D)
All other steel shapes and forms (exc. castings, forgings, fabricated metal products, and bare wire)		(X)	2.4
Insulated copper wire and cable		(X)	(D)
All other copper and copper-base alloy shapes and forms (incl. wire bar)	mil lb	(D)	(D)
All other aluminum and aluminum-base alloy shapes and forms (exc. castings, forgings, fabr. metal products)	mil lb	(D)	(D)
Plastics resins consumed in the form of granules, pellets, etc.		(X)	29.8
Synthetic rubber		(X)	(D)
All other chemicals and allied products (exc. plastics resins and synthetic rubber)	mil lb	(D)	(D)
Optical fiber, data and nondata transmission		(X)	231.1
Plastics products consumed in the form of sheets, rods, etc.		(X)	(D)
Cotton yarns		(X)	(D)
Connectors		(X)	8.9
All other materials, components, parts, containers, and supplies		(X)	159.9
Materials, ingredients, containers, and supplies, nsk		(X)	184.3

Source: 2002 *Economic Census*. Explanation of symbols used: (D): Withheld to avoid disclosure of competitive data; na: Not available; (S): Withheld because statistical norms were not met; (X): Not applicable; (Z): Less than half the unit shown; nec: Not elsewhere classified; nsk: Not specified by kind; - : zero; p : 10-19 percent estimated; q : 20-29 percent estimated.

MATERIALS CONSUMED FOR COMMUNICATION AND ENERGY WIRE MANUFACTURING NEC

Material		Quantity	Delivered Cost ($ million)
Bare steel wire	1,000 s tons	34.8q	38.0
All other steel shapes and forms (exc. castings, forgings, fabricated metal products, and bare wire)		(X)	26.5
Unalloyed copper and copper-base alloy rods	mil lb	1,029.0q	860.2
Alloyed copper and copper-base alloy rods	mil lb	(S)	75.4
Copper and copper-base alloy wire for redrawing	mil lb	257.7q	221.0
Bare copper and copper-base alloy wire, electrical (exc. wire for redrawing)	mil lb	666.5	598.4
Insulated copper wire and cable		(X)	369.7
Copper and copper-base alloy cathodes	1,000 s tons	(D)	(D)
All other copper and copper-base alloy shapes and forms (incl. wire bar)	mil lb	(S)	172.6
Aluminum and aluminum-base alloy rods	mil lb	(S)	210.0
Aluminum and aluminum-base alloy wire for redrawing	mil lb	18.5p	16.6
Bare aluminum and aluminum-base alloy wire (exc. wire for redrawing)	mil lb	15.5	24.9
All other aluminum and aluminum-base alloy shapes and forms (exc. castings, forgings, fabr. metal products)	mil lb	68.7p	86.9
Refined unalloyed tin shapes and forms (exc. castings, forgings, fabr. metal products)		(X)	(D)
All other nonferrous shapes and forms (exc. castings, forgings, fabr. metal products)	mil lb	(S)	51.3
Plastics resins consumed in the form of granules, pellets, etc.		(X)	591.1
Plastics products consumed in the form of sheets, rods, etc.		(X)	127.3
Synthetic rubber		(X)	(D)
Natural rubber		(X)	(D)
All other chemicals and allied products (exc. plastics resins and synthetic rubber)	mil lb	30.6	39.3
Optical fiber, data and nondata transmission		(X)	11.9
Fiberglass insulating materials		(X)	3.5
All other stone, clay, glass, and concrete products		(X)	(D)
Cotton yarns		(X)	3.4
Connectors		(X)	56.3
All other materials, components, parts, containers, and supplies		(X)	1,161.8
Materials, ingredients, containers, and supplies, nsk		(X)	536.2

Source: 2002 *Economic Census*. Explanation of symbols used: (D): Withheld to avoid disclosure of competitive data; na: Not available; (S): Withheld because statistical norms were not met; (X): Not applicable; (Z): Less than half the unit shown; nec: Not elsewhere classified; nsk: Not specified by kind; - : zero; p : 10-19 percent estimated; q : 20-29 percent estimated.

PRODUCT SHARE DETAILS FOR FIBER OPTIC CABLE MANUFACTURING

Product or Product Class Shipments	Mil. $	Product or Product Class Shipments	Mil. $
FIBER OPTIC CABLE	1,420.0	Fiber optic cable, all other applications	44.0
Fiber optic cable, communication applications	1,243.6		

Source: 2002 *Economic Census*. The values are product shipments in millions of dollars for 2002. Total product shipments may be lower or higher than industry shipments. See Introduction for a full discussion. Values of indented subcategories are summed in the main heading(s). The symbol (D) appears when data are withheld to prevent disclosure of competitive information. The abbreviation nsk stands for 'not specified by kind' and nec for 'not elsewhere classified'. A dash (-) means zero.

PRODUCT SHARE DETAILS FOR COMMUNICATION AND ENERGY WIRE MANUFACTURING NEC

Product or Product Class Shipments	Mil. $	Product or Product Class Shipments	Mil. $
OTHER COMMUNICATION AND ENERGY WIRES	9,603.9	Control and signal wire and cable, made from nonferrous metals (purchased wire)	252.0
Power wire and cable, made from nonferrous metals (purchased wire)	1,450.0	Building wire and cable, made from nonferrous metals (purchased wire)	2,456.3
Electronic wire and cable, made from nonferrous metals (purchased wire)	2,795.6	Other insulated wire and cable, including automotive, made from nonferrous metals (purchased wire)	657.7
Telephone and telegraph wire and cable, made from nonferrous metals (purchased wire)	1,360.9	Other communication and energy wires, nsk, total	631.5

Source: 2002 *Economic Census*. The values are product shipments in millions of dollars for 2002. Total product shipments may be lower or higher than industry shipments. See Introduction for a full discussion. Values of indented subcategories are summed in the main heading(s). The symbol (D) appears when data are withheld to prevent disclosure of competitive information. The abbreviation nsk stands for 'not specified by kind' and nec for 'not elsewhere classified'. A dash (-) means zero.

INPUTS AND OUTPUTS FOR COMMUNICATION AND ENERGY WIRE AND CABLE

Economic Sector or Industry Providing Inputs	%	Sector	Economic Sector or Industry Buying Outputs	%	Sector
Compensation of employees	21.0		Exports of goods & services	13.7	Cap Inv
Copper rolling, drawing, extruding, & alloying	16.1	Manufg.	Telecommunications	12.4	Services
Wholesale trade	6.3	Trade	Residential permanent site structures	7.3	Construct.
Communication & energy wires & cables	5.6	Manufg.	Nonresidential structures, nec	6.6	Construct.
Plastics materials & resins	5.3	Manufg.	Food services & drinking places	5.8	Services
Primary smelting & refining of copper	4.8	Manufg.	Residential structures, nec	4.6	Construct.
Management of companies & enterprises	4.5	Services	Communication & energy wires & cables	4.5	Manufg.
Glass products from purchased glass	3.3	Manufg.	Commercial & health care structures	4.0	Construct.
Aluminum products from purchased aluminum	2.9	Manufg.	Architectural, engineering, & related services	3.1	Services
Miscellaneous wood products	1.5	Manufg.	Maintenance/repair of nonresidential structures	2.4	Construct.
Plastics packaging materials, film & sheet	1.1	Manufg.	Motor vehicle parts	2.3	Manufg.
Truck transportation	1.1	Util.	Owner-occupied dwellings	2.2	
Power generation & supply	1.0	Util.	Search, detection, & navigation instruments	1.8	Manufg.
Noncomparable imports	0.8	Foreign	Computer system design services	1.7	Services
Wiring devices	0.6	Manufg.	Plumbing fixture fittings & trim	1.5	Manufg.
Machine shops	0.6	Manufg.	Telephone apparatus	1.4	Manufg.
Lessors of nonfinancial assets	0.5	Fin/R.E.	Commercial & service industry machinery, nec	1.3	Manufg.
Advertising & related services	0.5	Services	Natural gas distribution	1.3	Util.
Real estate	0.5	Fin/R.E.	Copper rolling, drawing, extruding, & alloying	1.2	Manufg.
Semiconductors & related devices	0.5	Manufg.	Engine equipment, nec	1.2	Manufg.
Printed circuit assemblies (electronic assemblies)	0.5	Manufg.	Private fixed investment	1.2	
Paints & coatings	0.5	Manufg.	Nonferrous metal (ex. copper & aluminum) processing	1.2	Manufg.
Securities, commodity contracts, investments	0.4	Fin/R.E.	Valve & fittings other than plumbing	1.2	Manufg.
Steel products from purchased steel	0.4	Manufg.	Aircraft	0.8	Manufg.
Taxes on production & imports, less subsidies	0.3		Motor vehicle bodies	0.8	Manufg.
Coating, engraving, heat treating & allied activities	0.3	Manufg.	Aircraft parts & auxiliary equipment, nec	0.7	Manufg.
Synthetic rubber	0.3	Manufg.	Plastics products, nec	0.7	Manufg.
Scientific research & development services	0.3	Services	Federal government, investment, nondefense	0.7	Fed Govt
Primary nonferrous metal, ex. copper & aluminum	0.3	Manufg.	Legal services	0.6	Services
Rail transportation	0.3	Util.	Fabricated metals, nec	0.5	Manufg.
Legal services	0.3	Services	Federal government, investment, national defense	0.5	Fed Govt
Chemical products & preparations, nec	0.3	Manufg.	Motors & generators	0.5	Manufg.
Natural gas distribution	0.3	Util.	Other S/L govt. enterprises	0.5	S/L Govt
Iron & steel mills & ferroalloys	0.2	Manufg.	Retail trade	0.5	Trade
Architectural, engineering, & related services	0.2	Services	Maintenance/repair of residential structures	0.5	Construct.
Monetary authorities/depository credit intermediation	0.2	Fin/R.E.	Professional, scientific, technical services, nec	0.5	Services
Maintenance/repair of nonresidential structures	0.2	Construct.	Electromedical & electrotherapeutic apparatus	0.4	Manufg.
Basic organic chemicals, nec	0.2	Manufg.	Electronic components, nec	0.4	Manufg.
Custom roll forming	0.2	Manufg.	Vending, commercial, industrial, office machinery	0.3	Manufg.
Automotive equipment rental & leasing	0.2	Fin/R.E.	Semiconductors & related devices	0.3	Manufg.
Telecommunications	0.2	Services	Accounting, tax preparation, bookkeeping, & payroll	0.3	Services
Services to buildings & dwellings	0.2	Services	Computer terminals & peripherals	0.3	Manufg.
Nonferrous metal (ex. copper & aluminum) processing	0.2	Manufg.	AC, refrigeration, and warm air heating equipment	0.3	Manufg.
Food services & drinking places	0.2	Services	Broadcast & wireless communications equipment	0.3	Manufg.
Cutting tools & machine tool accessories	0.2	Manufg.	Federal electric utilities	0.3	Fed Govt
Professional, scientific, technical services, nec	0.2	Services	Electronic connectors	0.2	Manufg.
Warehousing & storage	0.2	Util.	Hardware	0.2	Manufg.
Unlaminated plastics profile shapes	0.2	Manufg.	Civic, social, & professional organizations	0.2	Services
Accounting, tax preparation, bookkeeping, & payroll	0.2	Services	Wholesale trade	0.2	Trade
Data processing, hosting, & related services	0.2	Services	Electrical equipment & components, nec	0.2	Manufg.
Management, scientific, & technical consulting	0.2	Services	Machine shops	0.2	Manufg.
Air transportation	0.1	Util.	Wiring devices	0.2	Manufg.
Automotive repair & maintenance, ex. car washes	0.1	Services	General Federal government services, defense	0.2	Fed Govt
Postal service	0.1	Util.	Electronic & precision equipment repair/maintenance	0.2	Services
Hotels & motels, including casino hotels	0.1	Services	Irradiation apparatus	0.2	Manufg.
Business support services	0.1	Services	Electronic capacitors, resistors, coils, transformers	0.2	Manufg.
Commercial & industrial equipment repair/maintenance	0.1	Services	Employment services	0.2	Services
Motor vehicle parts	0.1	Manufg.	Scientific research & development services	0.1	Services
Fabricated metals, nec	0.1	Manufg.	Power, distribution, & specialty transformers	0.1	Manufg.
Employment services	0.1	Services	Lighting fixtures	0.1	Manufg.
Specialized design services	0.1	Services	Commercial & industrial machinery rental & leasing	0.1	Fin/R.E.

Continued on next page.

INPUTS AND OUTPUTS FOR COMMUNICATION AND ENERGY WIRE AND CABLE - Continued

Economic Sector or Industry Providing Inputs	%	Sector	Economic Sector or Industry Buying Outputs	%	Sector
Paperboard containers	0.1	Manufg.	Manufacturing structures	0.1	Construct.
Commercial & industrial machinery rental & leasing	0.1	Fin/R.E.	Springs & wire products	0.1	Manufg.
Relay & industrial controls	0.1	Manufg.	Printed circuit assemblies (electronic assembiles)	0.1	Manufg.
			Office administrative services	0.1	Services
			Individual & family services	0.1	Services
			Business support services	0.1	Services
			Watches, clocks, & related devices	0.1	Manufg.
			Audio & video equipment	0.1	Manufg.
			Management, scientific, & technical consulting	0.1	Services

Source: Benchmark Input-Output Accounts for the U.S. Economy, 2002, U.S. Department of Commerce, Washington, D.C., January 2008. The abbreviation nec stands for 'not elsewhere classified'.

OCCUPATIONS EMPLOYED BY OTHER ELECTRICAL EQUIPMENT & COMPONENT MANUFACTURING

Occupation	% of Total 2006	Change to 2016	Occupation	% of Total 2006	Change to 2016
Team assemblers	14.6	-7.3	Customer service representatives	1.4	1.9
Electrical & electronic equipment assemblers	9.0	-25.9	Electrical engineers	1.2	-7.3
Extruding & drawing machine operators & tenders	3.8	-7.3	Sales reps, wholesale & manufacturing, exc tech	1.2	-7.3
First-line supervisors/managers of production workers	3.7	-7.3	Plating & coating machine operators & tenders	1.2	-3.3
Inspectors, testers, sorters, samplers, & weighers	3.3	-12.6	Tool & die makers	1.1	-2.7
Cutting, punching, & press machine operators	2.8	-16.6	Mechanical engineers	1.1	-7.3
Shipping, receiving, & traffic clerks	2.4	-10.8	Multiple machine tool operators & tenders	1.1	1.9
Maintenance & repair workers, general	2.4	-7.3	Sales representatives, wholesale & manufacturing, tech	1.1	-7.3
Molding, coremaking, & casting machine operators	2.4	-16.6	Packers & packagers, hand	1.1	-25.9
Machinists	2.2	-2.7	Office clerks, general	1.0	-8.7
Helpers--Production workers	2.0	-7.3	Industrial production managers	1.0	-7.3
Laborers & freight, stock, & material movers, hand	1.9	-16.6	Packaging & filling machine operators & tenders	1.0	-16.6
Industrial truck & tractor operators	1.6	-16.6	Electromechanical equipment assemblers	1.0	-7.3
Industrial engineers	1.4	12.5	Computer-controlled machine tool operators	1.0	1.9
General & operations managers	1.4	-16.6	Bookkeeping, accounting, & auditing clerks	1.0	-7.3

Source: Industry-Occupation Matrix, Bureau of Labor Statistics, December 4, 2007. These data are reported based on 4-digit NAICS categories but have been matched to corresponding 6-digit NAICS industry codes. The change reported for each occupation to the year 2016 is a percent of growth or decline as estimated by the Bureau of Labor Statistics. The abbreviation nec stands for 'not elsewhere classified'.

LOCATION BY STATE AND REGIONAL CONCENTRATION

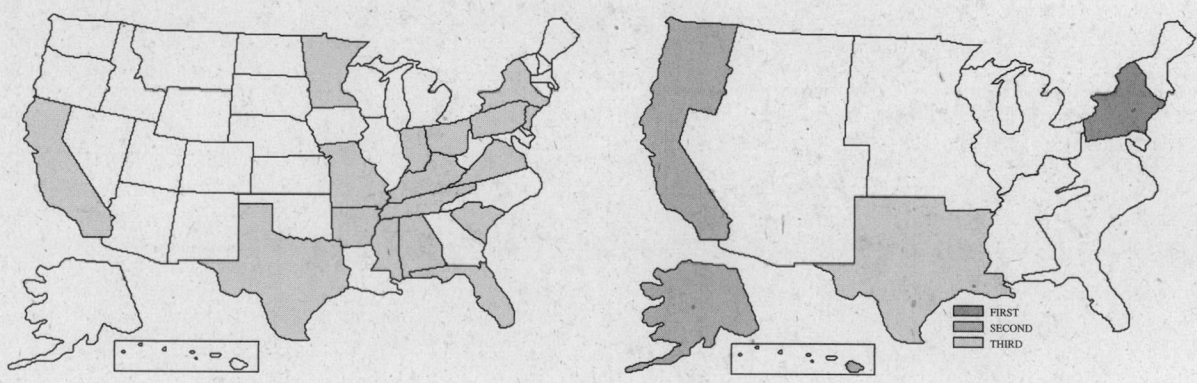

INDUSTRY DATA BY STATE

State	Establish-ments	Shipments			Employment				Cost as % of Shipments	Investment per Employee ($)
		Total ($ mil)	% of U.S.	Per Establ.	Total Number	% of U.S.	Per Establ.	Wages ($/hour)		
California	64	868.7	7.5	13,572.8	3,555	7.6	56	14.64	49.8	7,315
Texas	23	831.6	7.1	36,158.6	3,097	6.6	135	12.61	64.4	9,472
Indiana	17	607.0	5.2	35,703.9	2,123	4.5	125	15.57	57.3	3,702
Pennsylvania	21	588.2	5.0	28,007.6	2,599	5.5	124	13.57	60.3	3,158
New York	28	489.6	4.2	17,485.2	1,991	4.2	71	16.35	58.5	3,805

Continued on next page.

INDUSTRY DATA BY STATE - Continued

State	Establish-ments	Shipments			Employment				Cost as % of Shipments	Investment per Employee ($)
		Total ($ mil)	% of U.S.	Per Establ.	Total Number	% of U.S.	Per Establ.	Wages ($/hour)		
Kentucky	7	483.8	4.1	69,115.6	1,659	3.5	237	16.19	46.2	5,992
South Carolina	8	371.4	3.2	46,425.6	1,104	2.3	138	19.41	61.3	11,771
Alabama	6	353.7	3.0	58,955.0	930	2.0	155	13.76	63.9	3,762
Missouri	5	302.2	2.6	60,433.0	685	1.5	137	14.03	69.5	3,873
Virginia	5	235.0	2.0	46,992.6	1,109	2.4	222	17.01	65.4	1,752
Mississippi	6	218.5	1.9	36,421.2	950	2.0	158	15.30	59.3	3,708
Arkansas	6	216.2	1.9	36,034.5	918	2.0	153	13.93	57.3	4,790
New Jersey	16	188.8	1.6	11,800.1	504	1.1	32	15.71	67.2	1,857
Tennessee	5	169.5	1.5	33,891.6	714	1.5	143	11.13	38.2	24,200
Florida	12	138.0	1.2	11,496.8	989	2.1	82	12.45	60.1	2,369
Ohio	10	60.4	0.5	6,038.2	226	0.5	23	12.49	63.0	3,332
Minnesota	5	17.8	0.2	3,553.4	179	0.4	36	8.19	38.9	1,145

Source: 2002 Economic Census. The states are in descending order of shipments or establishments (if shipment data are missing for the majority). The symbol (D) appears when data are withheld to prevent disclosure of competitive information. States marked with (D) are sorted by number of establishments. A dash (-) indicates that the data element cannot be calculated. Data may not show all states active in the NAICS category. All data available at the time of publication are shown.

NAICS 33593M - WIRING DEVICE MANUFACTURING*

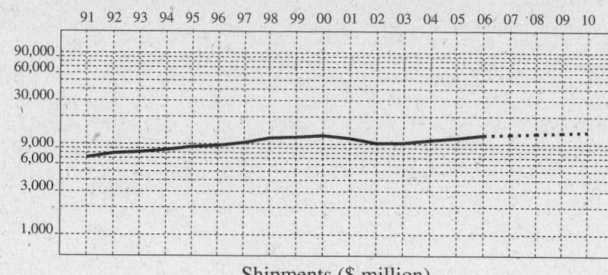

Shipments ($ million)

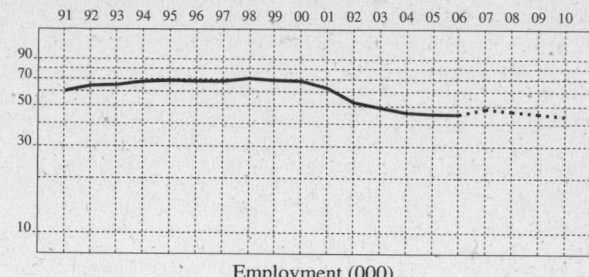

Employment (000)

GENERAL STATISTICS

Year	Companies	Establishments Total	Establishments with 20 or more employees	Employment Total (000)	Employment Production Workers (000)	Employment Hours (Mil)	Compensation Payroll ($ mil)	Compensation Wages ($/hr)	Production Cost of Materials	Production Value Added by Manufacture	Production Value of Shipments	Capital Invest.
1991		649	387	60.0	42.9	85.0	1,527.7	10.48	2,855.1	4,190.6	7,084.8	180.6
1992	583	695	398	64.3	46.0	93.1	1,714.4	10.75	3,140.1	4,753.4	7,891.8	204.9
1993		686	400	64.9	46.7	92.5	1,744.2	10.95	3,356.3	4,704.4	8,124.2	208.5
1994		677	394	67.7	49.0	99.4	1,854.0	10.94	3,524.0	5,090.5	8,606.9	239.3
1995		689	407	68.7	50.0	98.9	1,896.4	11.34	3,812.2	5,497.1	9,281.7	243.8
1996		729	398	68.1	49.9	98.3	1,985.7	11.84	4,033.9	5,550.8	9,617.9	280.1
1997	615	739	399	68.1	49.9	99.2	2,070.3	12.43	4,311.7	6,010.6	10,329.2	380.7
1998		752	404	70.6	51.3	103.6	2,166.5	12.58	4,682.1	6,911.4	11,664.4	380.5
1999		750	386	69.1	50.9	101.8	2,189.7	12.73	4,647.8	7,312.4	11,930.2	390.5
2000		765	399	68.5	50.3	98.2	2,232.9	13.10	4,886.7	7,587.3	12,420.6	381.5
2001		743	390	62.9	44.9	87.2	2,134.2	13.48	4,550.8	6,914.6	11,543.1	297.3
2002	524	625	316	52.5	37.1	70.0	1,866.2	15.04	4,010.6	6,154.5	10,201.0	282.2
2003		655	338	49.1	33.9	66.4	1,849.5	15.56	4,119.0	6,099.8	10,260.0	200.4
2004		627	309	46.1	31.5	61.9	1,836.9	16.20	4,445.8	6,619.3	10,993.2	186.2
2005		605	311	45.3	30.7	61.5	1,887.2	16.70	4,895.4	6,741.8	11,588.9	264.9
2006		669P	326P	45.1	30.9	63.2	1,966.3	16.85	5,422.2	7,069.6	12,448.5	312.5
2007		666P	320P	48.4P	33.5P	65.8P	2,068.2P	17.04P	5,539.8P	7,223.0P	12,718.6P	308.7P
2008		663P	313P	46.9P	32.4P	63.4P	2,084.2P	17.50P	5,666.4P	7,388.0P	13,009.1P	312.5P
2009		660P	307P	45.5P	31.2P	61.0P	2,100.1P	17.95P	5,792.9P	7,553.0P	13,299.6P	316.2P
2010		657P	301P	44.0P	30.0P	58.6P	2,116.1P	18.40P	5,919.5P	7,718.0P	13,590.2P	319.9P

Sources: 1992, 1997, 2002 *Economic Census*; other years, up to 2006, are from the *Annual Survey of Manufactures*. Establishment counts for non-Census years are from *County Business Patterns*; 1997 and 2002 values are from the 1997 and 2002 censuses respectively, reported in the Federal Government's NAICS format. Other years were originally reported in equivalent SIC format. 'P's show projections by the editors.

INDICES OF CHANGE

Year	Companies	Establishments Total	Establishments with 20 or more employees	Employment Total (000)	Employment Production Workers (000)	Employment Hours (Mil)	Compensation Payroll ($ mil)	Compensation Wages ($/hr)	Production Cost of Materials	Production Value Added by Manufacture	Production Value of Shipments	Capital Invest.
1992	111	111	126	122	124	133	92	71	78	77	77	73
1997	117	118	126	130	135	142	111	83	108	98	101	135
2001		119	123	120	121	125	114	90	113	112	113	105
2002	100	100	100	100	100	100	100	100	100	100	100	100
2003		105	107	94	91	95	99	103	103	99	101	71
2004		100	98	88	85	88	98	108	111	108	108	66
2005		97	98	86	83	88	101	111	122	110	114	94
2006		107P	103P	86	83	90	105	112	135	115	122	111
2007		106P	101P	92P	90P	94P	111P	113P	138P	117P	125P	109P
2008		106P	99P	89P	87P	91P	112P	116P	141P	120P	128P	111P
2009		106P	97P	87P	84P	87P	113P	119P	144P	123P	130P	112P
2010		105P	95P	84P	81P	84P	113P	122P	148P	125P	133P	113P

Sources: Same as General Statistics. Values reflect change from the base year, 2002. Values above 100 mean greater than 2002, values below 100 mean less than 2002, and the values of 100 in other years means the same as 2002. 'P's show projections by the editors.

SELECTED RATIOS

For 2002	Avg. of All Manufact.	Analyzed Industry	Index	For 2002	Avg. of All Manufact.	Analyzed Industry	Index
Employees per Establishment	42	84	200	Value Added per Production Worker	182,367	165,889	91
Payroll per Establishment	1,639,184	2,985,920	182	Cost per Establishment	5,769,015	6,416,960	111
Payroll per Employee	39,053	35,547	91	Cost per Employee	137,446	76,392	56
Production Workers per Establishment	30	59	201	Cost per Production Worker	195,506	108,102	55
Wages per Establishment	694,845	1,684,480	242	Shipments per Establishment	11,158,348	16,321,600	146
Wages per Production Worker	23,548	28,377	121	Shipments per Employee	265,847	194,305	73
Hours per Production Worker	1,980	1,887	95	Shipments per Production Worker	378,144	274,960	73
Wages per Hour	11.89	15.04	126	Investment per Establishment	361,338	451,520	125
Value Added per Establishment	5,381,325	9,847,200	183	Investment per Employee	8,609	5,375	62
Value Added per Employee	128,210	117,229	91	Investment per Production Worker	12,245	7,606	62

Sources: Same as General Statistics. The 'Average of All Manufacturing' column represents the average of all manufacturing industries reported for the most recent complete year available. The Index shows the relationship between the Average and the Analyzed Industry. For example, 100 means that they are equal; 500 that the Analyzed Industry is five times the average; 50 means that the Analyzed Industry is half the national average. The abbreviation 'na' is used to show that data are 'not available'. Ratios shown for 2002, the last complete census year.

*Equivalent to Federal Government NAICS 335931, 335932.

LEADING COMPANIES Number shown: 75   Total sales ($ mil): **107,381**   Total employment (000): **176.3**

Company Name	Address				CEO Name	Phone	Co. Type	Sales ($ mil)	Empl. (000)
Technitrol Delaware Inc.	3411 Silverside Rd.	Wilmington	DE	19810	James M. Papada	302-478-8271	S	67,716*	22.8
Kohler Co.	444 Highland Dr.	Kohler	WI	53044	Herbert Kohler	920-457-4441	R	4,061*	33.0
Phoenix Contact Services Inc.	PO Box 4100	Harrisburg	PA	17111	Jack Nehlig	717-944-1300	R	3,873*	0.3
Kalmar Industries USA L.L.C.	415 E Dundee St.	Ottawa	KS	66067		785-242-2200	R	3,320*	0.3
Molex Inc.	2222 Wellington Ct.	Lisle	IL	60532		630-969-4550	P	3,266	33.2
Hi-Stat Manufacturing Company	28001 Cabot Dr.	Novi	MI	48377	John Corey	248-489-9300	D	3,194*	5.0
Hubbell Inc.	584 Derby Milford	Orange	CT	06477		203-799-4100	P	2,534	11.5
Thomas and Betts Corp.	8155 T and B Blvd.	Memphis	TN	38125	T. Kevin Dunnigan	901-252-8000	P	2,137	11.0
Dekko Technologies L.L.C.	PO Box 337	North Webster	IN	46555	Steven Hankinf	574-834-2818	R	2,130*	0.1
Panduit Corp.	17301 Ridgeland	Tinley Park	IL	60477	John Caveney		R	1,306*	4.0
3Com Corp.	350 Campus Dr.	Marlborough	MA	01752	Eric A. Benhamou	508-323-5000	P	1,268	6.3
Nesco Inc.	6140 Parkland Blvd.	Mayfield Hgts	OH	44124	Robert J. Tomsich	440-461-6000	R	1,133*	10.3
Bogan Inc.	1500 Chester Pk.	Eddystone	PA	19022	Michael J. Hall	610-876-9292	S	1,072*	3.3
NGK-Locke Inc.	2525 Insulator Dr.	Baltimore	MD	21230	Shun Matsushita	410-347-1700	S	941*	3.7
Leviton Manufacturing Company	PO Box 630087	Little Neck	NY	11363	Donald Hendler	718-229-4040	R	800*	0.7
East Penn Manufacturing Co.	PO Box 147	Lyon Station	PA	19536			R	716*	5.0
Thomas and Betts Caribe Inc.	PO Box 4058	Vega Baja	PR	00693	J David Parkinson	787-855-3046	R	572*	0.6
Wesco Acquistion Partners Inc.	PO Box 924068	Houston	TX	77292	Ronnie Davis	713-688-5551	R	543*	<0.1
TRAM Inc.	47200 Port Street	Plymouth	MI	48170	Yoshihei Iida	734-254-8500	R	477*	0.1
Cherry Corp.	10411 Corporate Dr.	Pleasant Pr	WI	53158	Peter B. Cherry	262-942-6500	R	411*	3.9
Cinch Connectors Inc.	1700 S Finley Rd.	Lombard	IL	60148	Michael Murray	630-705-6000	R	406*	0.1
RMS Co.	8600 Evergreen Blvd	Coon Rapids	MN	55433	Arthur Mouyard	763-786-1520	S	400*	0.3
Aromat Corp.	629 Central Ave.	New Providence	NJ	07974	Kazushige Nishida	908-464-3550	S	234*	1.0
Ideal Industries Inc.	Becker Pl.	Sycamore	IL	60178	Dave Juday		R	192*	1.7
Transpo Trading Inc.	2150 Brengle Ave.	Orlando	FL	32808		407-298-4563	R	179*	0.3
SL Industries Inc.	520 Fellowship Rd.	Mount Laurel	NJ	08054	Steven Gilliatt	856-727-1500	P	177	1.9
Seacon Phoenix Inc.	PO Box 2236	Westerly	RI	02891	Frank Ravenelle	401-596-6658	S	171*	0.2
Barksdale Inc.	PO Box 58843	Los Angeles	CA	90058	Ian Dodd	323-589-6181	S	168*	0.2
Geo Space L.P.	7007 Pinemont	Houston	TX	77040		713-986-4444	S	162*	0.3
Bergquist Company Inc.	18930 W 78th St.	Chanhassen	MN	55317	Carl Bergquist	952-835-2322	R	152*	0.1
Micro Craft Inc.	41129 Jo Dr.	Novi	MI	48375	William Brown	248-476-6510	R	143*	<0.1
Arlington Industries	1 Stauffer Ind.Park	Scranton	PA	18517	Thomas Stark	570-562-0270	R	136*	0.3
Western Tube and Conduit Corp.	PO Box 2720	Long Beach	CA	90801	Yuzo Oishi	310-537-6300	R	133*	0.3
Thermon Industries Inc.	PO Box 609	San Marcos	TX	78667	Mark Burdick	512-396-5801	R	125*	0.1
Nexans USA Inc.	PO Box 60339	Charlotte	NC	28260	Kevin Cyr	717-354-6200	R	121*	0.5
VeriFone Inc.	300 Park Place Blvd	Clearwater	FL	33759	Douglas G. Bergeron	727-953-4000	S	121*	0.9
Ppc	6176 E Molloy Rd.	East Syracuse	NY	13057	Jhon Mezzalingua	315-431-7200	R	118*	0.9
Fusite	6000 Fernview Ave.	Cincinnati	OH	45212		513-731-2020	R	115*	0.8
Wauconda Tool and Engineering	821 W Algonquin	Algonquin	IL	60102	Chuck Burnside	847-658-4588	R	112*	<0.1
Meter Devices Company Inc.	PO Box 6382	Canton	OH	44706	Jack Roessner	330-455-0301	R	111*	0.6
Carling Technologies Inc.	60 Johnson Ave.	Plainville	CT	06062		860-793-9266	R	110*	0.2
Glastic Corp.	4321 Glenridge Rd.	Cleveland	OH	44121	Richard Crawford	216-486-0100	R	101*	0.2
Erico Products Inc.	31700 Solon Rd.	Solon	OH	44139	William Roj	440-248-0100	S	100*	<0.1
Woven Electronics L.L.C.	PO Box 367	Greenville	SC	29602	Henry Little	864-233-6740	R	100*	<0.1
ELDEC Corp.	PO Box 97027	Lynnwood	WA	98046	David Bender	425-743-8321	S	94*	0.6
Tri-Star Electronics Int'l	2201 Rosecrans Ave.	El Segundo	CA	90245	Terry Jarnigan	310-536-0444	D	90*	0.3
Wago Corp.	PO Box 1015	Germantown	WI	53022	Thomas Artman	262-255-6222	R	90*	0.1
Aubrey Silvey Enterprises Inc.	371 Hamp Jones Rd.	Carrollton	GA	30117	Tommy Muse	770-834-0738	R	89*	0.2
Whitney Blake Co.	PO Box 579	Bellows Falls	VT	05101	Sheldon Scott	802-463-9558	R	85*	0.1
NACOM Corp.	375 Airport Rd.	Griffin	GA	30224	Riku Yakazi	770-467-9545	R	85*	0.5
Atlantic Teleconnect Inc.	2529 Commerce	North Port	FL	34286	Ric Galberaith		R	84*	<0.1
Cherry Electrical Products	11200 88th Ave.	Pleasant Pr	WI	53158	Peter B. Cherry	262-942-6500	S	77*	0.7
Penn-Union Corp.	229 Waterford St.	Edinboro	PA	16412		814-734-1631	R	76*	0.2
AFC Cable Systems Inc.	272 Duchaine Blvd.	New Bedford	MA	02745	Bob Tereira	508-998-1131	S	76*	1.3
Deutsch Engin. Connecting Dev.	700 S Hathaway St.	Banning	CA	92220		951-849-7844	R	72*	0.5
Siemon Co.	PO Box 400	Watertown	CT	06795	Carl Siemon	860-945-4200	R	70*	0.5
SEA CON/Brantner & Associates	1240 Vernon Way	El Cajon	CA	92020		619-562-7071	R	69*	0.4
Ramp Industries Inc.	1 N Floral Ave.	Binghamton	NY	13905	Michael Pandich	607-729-5256	R	68*	0.3
Switchcraft Inc.	5555 N Elston Ave.	Chicago	IL	60630	Keith Bandolik	773-792-2700	R	64*	0.5
Dayton-Granger Inc.	PO Box 350550	Fort Lauderdale	FL	33335	Gibbons Cline	954-768-0224	R	60*	0.3
Thomas G Faria Corp.	PO Box 983	Uncasville	CT	06382	David Blackburn	860-848-9271	R	57*	0.3
Grayhill Inc.	PO Box 10373	La Grange	IL	60525	Gene Hill	708-354-1040	R	56*	0.5
Heller Performance Polymers	7227 W Doe Ave.	Visalia	CA	93291	Herbert Heller	559-651-2091	S	56*	0.2
Datalux Corp.	155 Aviation Dr.	Winchester	VA	22602		540-662-4500	R	56*	0.1
Fargo Assembly Co.	PO Box 2340	Fargo	ND	58108	Ron Bergan	701-298-3803	R	56*	0.3
Syncro Corp.	PO Box 890	Arab	AL	35016	Edwin Childress	256-586-6045	R	52*	0.2
Nsi Industries L.L.C.	PO Box 2725	Huntersville	NC	28070		704-439-2420	R	52*	0.2
Cole Hersee Co.	20 Old Colony Ave.	Boston	MA	02127	Robert Mayer	617-268-2100	R	50*	0.3
Connector Manufacturing Co.	3501 Symmes Rd.	Hamilton	OH	45015	William Boehm	513-860-4455	R	50*	0.2
M and G Electronics Corp.	PO Box 8187	Virginia Beach	VA	23450	Mark Garcea	757-468-6000	R	49*	0.3
Synovis Interventional Solut.	475 Apollo Dr.	Lino Lakes	MN	55014	Mary L. Frick	651-792-8500	S	49*	0.2
Park Enterprises	PO Box 60947	Rochester	NY	14606	Sook Park	585-546-4200	R	48*	0.3
Dura-Line Corp.	835 Innovation Dr.	Knoxville	TN	37932	Paresh Chari		S	48*	0.4
FCI Electronics Inc.	825 Old Trail Rd.	Etters	PA	17319	Alain Bugat	717-938-7200	S	48*	0.2
Wilco Wire Technology Inc.	1035 Mission Ct.	Fremont	CA	94539	Judy Wilson	510-249-9000	R	47*	<0.1

Source: *Ward's Business Directory of U.S. Private and Public Companies*, Volumes 1 and 2, 2008. The company type code used is as follows: P - Public, R - Private, S - Subsidiary, D - Division, J - Joint Venture, A - Affiliate, G - Group. Sales are in millions of dollars, employees are in thousands. An asterisk (*) indicates an estimated sales volume. The symbol < stands for 'less than'. Company names and addresses are truncated, in some cases, to fit into the available space.

MATERIALS CONSUMED FOR CURRENT-CARRYING WIRING DEVICE MANUFACTURING

Material	Quantity	Delivered Cost ($ million)
Metal stampings	(X)	81.7
Metal bolts, nuts, screws, and other screw machine products	(X)	85.2
All other fabricated metal products (excluding forgings)	(X)	45.3
Forgings	(X)	2.0
Iron and steel castings (rough and semifinished)	(X)	8.4
Aluminum and aluminum-base alloy castings (rough and semifinished)	(X)	25.0
Copper and copper-base alloy castings (rough and semifinished)	(X)	8.0
Other nonferrous castings (rough and semifinished)	(X)	9.4
Steel bars, bar shapes, and plates (exc. castings, forgings, fabr. metal products)	(X)	5.9
Steel sheet and strip (including tinplate)	(X)	29.9
All other steel shapes and forms (exc. castings, forgings, fabr. metal products)	(X)	14.8
Copper and copper-base alloy rod, bar, and bar shapes (exc. castings, forgings, fabr. metal products)	(X)	30.8
Copper and copper-base alloy plate, sheet, and strip (incl. military cups and discs)	(X)	47.0
All other copper and copper-base alloy mill shapes and forms (exc. castings and forgings)	(X)	38.2
Aluminum and aluminum-base alloy shapes and forms (exc. castings, forgings, fabr. metal products)	(X)	42.9
Other nonferrous shapes and forms (exc. castings, forgings, fabricated metal products)	(X)	22.2
Plastics resins consumed in the form of granules, pellets, etc.	(X)	152.5
Plastics products consumed in the form of sheets, rods, etc.	(X)	131.5
Current-carrying wiring devices	(X)	163.6
Precious metals (gold, platinum, etc.), all forms (incl. ingot, sheet, strip, solder, plating, electrodes, etc.)	(X)	59.7
Insulated wire and cable (excluding magnet wire)	(X)	42.6
Semiconductors (incl. transistors, diodes, rectifiers, and integrated circuits), for electronic circuitry	(X)	144.7
Paper and paperboard containers (incl. shipping sacks and other paper packaging supplies)	(X)	39.8
All other materials, components, parts, containers, and supplies	(X)	754.4
Materials, ingredients, containers, and supplies, nsk	(X)	22.9

Source: 2002 *Economic Census*. Explanation of symbols used: (D): Withheld to avoid disclosure of competitive data; na: Not available; (S): Withheld because statistical norms were not met; (X): Not applicable; (Z): Less than half the unit shown; nec: Not elsewhere classified; nsk: Not specified by kind; - : zero; p : 10-19 percent estimated; q : 20-29 percent estimated.

MATERIALS CONSUMED FOR NONCURRENT-CARRYING WIRING DEVICE MANUFACTURING

Material	Quantity	Delivered Cost ($ million)
Metal stampings	(X)	22.4
Metal bolts, nuts, screws, and other screw machine products	(X)	32.0
All other fabricated metal products (excluding forgings)	(X)	13.6
Forgings	(X)	(D)
Iron and steel castings (rough and semifinished)	(X)	125.5
Aluminum and aluminum-base alloy castings (rough and semifinished)	(X)	16.7
Copper and copper-base alloy castings (rough and semifinished)	(X)	2.4
Other nonferrous castings (rough and semifinished)	(X)	8.0
Steel bars, bar shapes, and plates (exc. castings, forgings, fabr. metal products)	(X)	57.2
Steel sheet and strip (including tinplate)	(X)	291.2
All other steel shapes and forms (exc. castings, forgings, fabr. metal products)	(X)	21.9
Copper and copper-base alloy rod, bar, and bar shapes (exc. castings, forgings, fabr. metal products)	(X)	(D)
Copper and copper-base alloy plate, sheet, and strip (incl. military cups and discs)	(X)	2.9
All other copper and copper-base alloy mill shapes and forms (exc. castings and forgings)	(X)	2.2
Aluminum and aluminum-base alloy shapes and forms (exc. castings, forgings, fabr. metal products)	(X)	52.5
Other nonferrous shapes and forms (exc. castings, forgings, fabricated metal products)	(X)	(D)
Plastics resins consumed in the form of granules, pellets, etc.	(X)	320.8
Plastics products consumed in the form of sheets, rods, etc.	(X)	11.4
Current-carrying wiring devices	(X)	13.2
Precious metals (gold, platinum, etc.), all forms (incl. ingot, sheet, strip, solder, plating, electrodes, etc.)	(X)	(D)
Insulated wire and cable (excluding magnet wire)	(X)	19.2
Semiconductors (incl. transistors, diodes, rectifiers, and integrated circuits), for electronic circuitry	(X)	(D)
Paper and paperboard containers (incl. shipping sacks and other paper packaging supplies)	(X)	25.3
All other materials, components, parts, containers, and supplies	(X)	221.0
Materials, ingredients, containers, and supplies, nsk	(X)	19.8

Source: 2002 *Economic Census*. Explanation of symbols used: (D): Withheld to avoid disclosure of competitive data; na: Not available; (S): Withheld because statistical norms were not met; (X): Not applicable; (Z): Less than half the unit shown; nec: Not elsewhere classified; nsk: Not specified by kind; - : zero; p : 10-19 percent estimated; q : 20-29 percent estimated.

PRODUCT SHARE DETAILS FOR CURRENT-CARRYING WIRING DEVICE MANUFACTURING

Product or Product Class Shipments	Mil. $	Product or Product Class Shipments	Mil. $
CURRENT-CARRYING WIRING DEVICES	5,582.4	Current-carrying metal contacts, including precious metal	219.0
Current-carrying lampholders	151.1	Current-carrying wire connectors for electrical circuitry	1,275.8
Current-carrying general- and special-purpose convenience and power outlets (excluding pin-and-sleeve type)	302.4	All other miscellaneous current-carrying wiring devices (attachments, plug caps, connector bodies, lighting arrestors, etc.)	1,562.9
Current-carrying switches for electrical circuitry (including vehicular switches)	1,830.3	Current-carrying wiring devices, nsk, total	241.0

Source: 2002 *Economic Census*. The values are product shipments in millions of dollars for 2002. Total product shipments may be lower or higher than industry shipments. See Introduction for a full discussion. Values of indented subcategories are summed in the main heading(s). The symbol (D) appears when data are withheld to prevent disclosure of competitive information. The abbreviation nsk stands for 'not specified by kind' and nec for 'not elsewhere classified'. A dash (-) means zero.

PRODUCT SHARE DETAILS FOR NONCURRENT-CARRYING WIRING DEVICE MANUFACTURING

Product or Product Class Shipments	Mil. $	Product or Product Class Shipments	Mil. $
NONCURRENT-CARRYING WIRING DEVICES	3,573.1	Other noncurrent-carrying wiring devices and supplies	
Noncurrent-carrying pole and transmission line hardware .	603.8	(boxes, covers, bar hangers, etc.)	763.6
Noncurrent-carrying electrical conduit and conduit fittings,		Noncurrent-carrying wiring devices, nsk, total	78.7
including plastics conduit and conduit fittings	2,126.9		

Source: 2002 *Economic Census*. The values are product shipments in millions of dollars for 2002. Total product shipments may be lower or higher than industry shipments. See Introduction for a full discussion. Values of indented subcategories are summed in the main heading(s). The symbol (D) appears when data are withheld to prevent disclosure of competitive information. The abbreviation nsk stands for 'not specified by kind' and nec for 'not elsewhere classified'. A dash (-) means zero.

INPUTS AND OUTPUTS FOR WIRING DEVICE MANUFACTURING

Economic Sector or Industry Providing Inputs	%	Sector	Economic Sector or Industry Buying Outputs	%	Sector
Compensation of employees	25.5		Exports of goods & services	14.9	Cap Inv
Management of companies & enterprises	5.0	Services	Residential permanent site structures	14.8	Construct.
Wholesale trade	4.7	Trade	Residential structures, nec	7.4	Construct.
Plastics materials & resins	4.5	Manufg.	Motor vehicle parts	7.0	Manufg.
Iron & steel mills & ferroalloys	4.0	Manufg.	Nonresidential structures, nec	6.7	Construct.
Turned products & screws, nuts, & bolts	2.1	Manufg.	Owner-occupied dwellings	6.6	
Wiring devices	1.9	Manufg.	Commercial & health care structures	5.1	Construct.
Semiconductors & related devices	1.6	Manufg.	Private fixed investment	2.6	
Copper rolling, drawing, extruding, & alloying	1.6	Manufg.	Maintenance/repair of nonresidential structures	2.3	Construct.
Plastics packaging materials, film & sheet	1.5	Manufg.	Wiring devices	1.8	Manufg.
Crowns & closures & metal stamping	1.3	Manufg.	Aircraft	1.5	Manufg.
Ferrous metal foundries	1.2	Manufg.	AC, refrigeration, and warm air heating equipment	1.4	Manufg.
Alumina refining & primary aluminum production	1.0	Manufg.	Analytical laboratory instruments	1.3	Manufg.
Power generation & supply	1.0	Util.	Retail trade	1.3	Trade
Printed circuit assemblies (electronic assemblies)	0.8	Manufg.	Search, detection, & navigation instruments	1.3	Manufg.
Lessors of nonfinancial assets	0.8	Fin/R.E.	Commercial & service industry machinery, nec	1.2	Manufg.
Nonferrous metal foundries	0.8	Manufg.	Semiconductors & related devices	1.1	Manufg.
Advertising & related services	0.7	Services	Lighting fixtures	1.1	Manufg.
Paperboard containers	0.7	Manufg.	Travel trailers & campers	1.0	Manufg.
Primary nonferrous metal, ex. copper & aluminum	0.7	Manufg.	Vending, commercial, industrial, office machinery	1.0	Manufg.
Truck transportation	0.6	Util.	Motor homes	1.0	Manufg.
Securities, commodity contracts, investments	0.6	Fin/R.E.	Maintenance/repair of residential structures	0.9	Construct.
Machine shops	0.5	Manufg.	Audio & video equipment	0.8	Manufg.
Real estate	0.5	Fin/R.E.	General Federal government services, nondefense	0.7	Fed Govt
Noncomparable imports	0.5	Foreign	Computer terminals & peripherals	0.7	Manufg.
Primary smelting & refining of copper	0.5	Manufg.	Electrical equipment & components, nec	0.7	Manufg.
Cutting tools & machine tool accessories	0.5	Manufg.	Communication & energy wires & cables	0.6	Manufg.
Nonferrous metal (ex. copper & aluminum) processing	0.4	Manufg.	Telecommunications	0.6	Services
Architectural, engineering, & related services	0.4	Services	Wholesale trade	0.6	Trade
Scientific research & development services	0.3	Services	Household cooking appliances	0.5	Manufg.
Legal services	0.3	Services	Computer storage devices	0.5	Manufg.
Postal service	0.3	Util.	Other S/L govt. enterprises	0.5	S/L Govt
Specialized design services	0.3	Services	Manufacturing structures	0.5	Construct.
Maintenance/repair of nonresidential structures	0.3	Construct.	Engine equipment, nec	0.5	Manufg.
Monetary authorities/depository credit intermediation	0.3	Fin/R.E.	Watches, clocks, & related devices	0.5	Manufg.
Employment services	0.3	Services	Broadcast & wireless communications equipment	0.4	Manufg.
Communication & energy wires & cables	0.3	Manufg.	Household refrigerators & home freezers	0.4	Manufg.
Services to buildings & dwellings	0.2	Services	Real estate	0.4	Fin/R.E.
Taxes on production & imports, less subsidies	0.2		Industrial process variable instruments	0.4	Manufg.
Professional, scientific, technical services, nec	0.2	Services	Small electrical applicances	0.4	Manufg.
Coating, engraving, heat treating & allied activities	0.2	Manufg.	Colleges, universities, & professional schools	0.4	Services
Rail transportation	0.2	Util.	Surgical appliances & supplies	0.4	Manufg.
Unlaminated plastics profile shapes	0.2	Manufg.	Electronic components, nec	0.3	Manufg.
Business support services	0.2	Services	Household laundry equipment	0.3	Manufg.
Automotive equipment rental & leasing	0.2	Fin/R.E.	Major household appliances, nec	0.3	Manufg.
Bare printed circuit boards	0.2	Manufg.	Power, distribution, & specialty transformers	0.3	Manufg.
Telecommunications	0.2	Services	Electricity & signal testing instruments	0.3	Manufg.
Forging, stamping, & sintering, nec	0.2	Manufg.	Telephone apparatus	0.3	Manufg.
Warehousing & storage	0.2	Util.	Automatic environmental controls	0.3	Manufg.
Natural gas distribution	0.2	Util.	Air purification & ventilation equipment	0.3	Manufg.
Abrasive products	0.2	Manufg.	Food services & drinking places	0.3	Services
Automotive repair & maintenance, ex. car washes	0.2	Services	Electronic connectors	0.3	Manufg.
Data processing, hosting, & related services	0.2	Services	Data processing, hosting, & related services	0.3	Services
Aluminum products from purchased aluminum	0.1	Manufg.	Surgical & medical instrument	0.2	Manufg.
Management, scientific, & technical consulting	0.1	Services	Laboratory apparatus & furniture	0.2	Manufg.
Commercial & industrial equipment repair/maintenance	0.1	Services	Electronic & precision equipment repair/maintenance	0.2	Services
Accounting, tax preparation, bookkeeping, & payroll	0.1	Services	Manufactured homes & mobile homes	0.2	Manufg.
Support services, nec	0.1	Services	Totalizing fluid meters & counting devices	0.2	Manufg.
Chemical products & preparations, nec	0.1	Manufg.	Printed circuit assemblies (electronic assemblies)	0.2	Manufg.
Relay & industrial controls	0.1	Manufg.	Electronic capacitors, resistors, coils, transformers	0.1	Manufg.
Food services & drinking places	0.1	Services	Musical instruments	0.1	Manufg.
Paperboard mills	0.1	Manufg.	Commercial & industrial machinery rental & leasing	0.1	Fin/R.E.
Motor vehicle parts	0.1	Manufg.	General purpose machinery, nec	0.1	Manufg.
Investigation & security services	0.1	Services	Commercial & industrial equipment repair/maintenance	0.1	Services

Continued on next page.

INPUTS AND OUTPUTS FOR WIRING DEVICE MANUFACTURING - Continued

Economic Sector or Industry Providing Inputs	%	Sector	Economic Sector or Industry Buying Outputs	%	Sector
Commercial & industrial machinery rental & leasing	0.1	Fin/R.E.	Natural gas distribution	0.1	Util.
Plastics products, nec	0.1	Manufg.			

Source: Benchmark Input-Output Accounts for the U.S. Economy, 2002, U.S. Department of Commerce, Washington, D.C., January 2008. The abbreviation nec stands for 'not elsewhere classified'.

OCCUPATIONS EMPLOYED BY OTHER ELECTRICAL EQUIPMENT & COMPONENT MANUFACTURING

Occupation	% of Total 2006	Change to 2016	Occupation	% of Total 2006	Change to 2016
Team assemblers	14.6	-7.3	Customer service representatives	1.4	1.9
Electrical & electronic equipment assemblers	9.0	-25.9	Electrical engineers	1.2	-7.3
Extruding & drawing machine operators & tenders	3.8	-7.3	Sales reps, wholesale & manufacturing, exc tech	1.2	-7.3
First-line supervisors/managers of production workers	3.7	-7.3	Plating & coating machine operators & tenders	1.2	-3.3
Inspectors, testers, sorters, samplers, & weighers	3.3	-12.6	Tool & die makers	1.1	-2.7
Cutting, punching, & press machine operators	2.8	-16.6	Mechanical engineers	1.1	-7.3
Shipping, receiving, & traffic clerks	2.4	-10.8	Multiple machine tool operators & tenders	1.1	1.9
Maintenance & repair workers, general	2.4	-7.3	Sales representatives, wholesale & manufacturing, tech	1.1	-7.3
Molding, coremaking, & casting machine operators	2.4	-16.6	Packers & packagers, hand	1.1	-25.9
Machinists	2.2	-2.7	Office clerks, general	1.0	-8.7
Helpers--Production workers	2.0	-7.3	Industrial production managers	1.0	-7.3
Laborers & freight, stock, & material movers, hand	1.9	-16.6	Packaging & filling machine operators & tenders	1.0	-16.6
Industrial truck & tractor operators	1.6	-16.6	Electromechanical equipment assemblers	1.0	-7.3
Industrial engineers	1.4	12.5	Computer-controlled machine tool operators	1.0	1.9
General & operations managers	1.4	-16.6	Bookkeeping, accounting, & auditing clerks	1.0	-7.3

Source: Industry-Occupation Matrix, Bureau of Labor Statistics, December 4, 2007. These data are reported based on 4-digit NAICS categories but have been matched to corresponding 6-digit NAICS industry codes. The change reported for each occupation to the year 2016 is a percent of growth or decline as estimated by the Bureau of Labor Statistics. The abbreviation nec stands for 'not elsewhere classified'.

LOCATION BY STATE AND REGIONAL CONCENTRATION

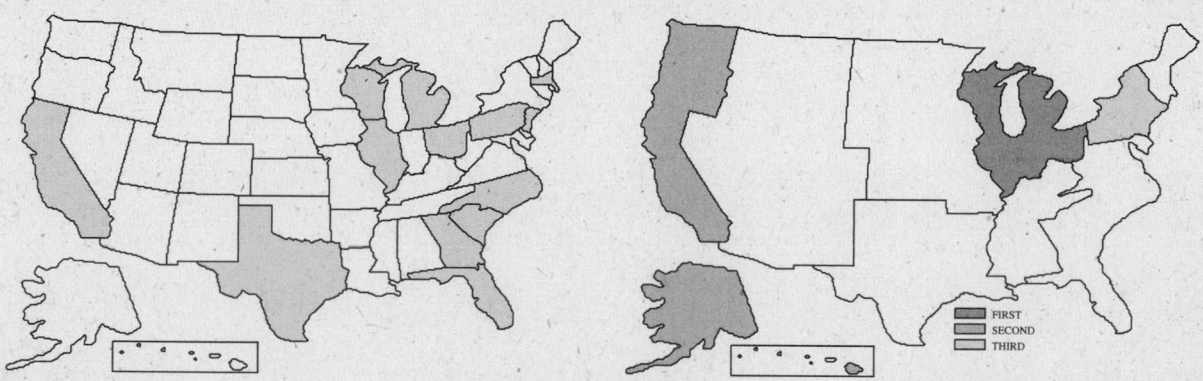

FIRST
SECOND
THIRD

INDUSTRY DATA BY STATE

State	Establish-ments	Shipments			Employment				Cost as % of Shipments	Investment per Employee ($)
		Total ($ mil)	% of U.S.	Per Establ.	Total Number	% of U.S.	Per Establ.	Wages ($/hour)		
Illinois	58	1,014.2	9.9	17,485.8	5,161	9.8	89	15.73	43.0	6,780
Pennsylvania	41	884.0	8.7	21,561.8	4,133	7.9	101	15.95	42.8	5,768
California	76	667.3	6.5	8,780.7	3,375	6.4	44	14.52	45.1	4,216
Ohio	45	651.1	6.4	14,469.2	4,030	7.7	90	15.22	53.3	4,613
Massachusetts	27	542.7	5.3	20,101.5	3,170	6.0	117	14.38	41.0	2,607
North Carolina	11	392.8	3.9	35,707.3	3,524	6.7	320	12.94	32.4	1,904
Texas	33	356.6	3.5	10,805.5	1,547	2.9	47	13.44	48.7	9,647
Michigan	21	277.2	2.7	13,200.8	1,719	3.3	82	14.33	46.0	3,472
Wisconsin	10	272.0	2.7	27,195.5	1,242	2.4	124	18.70	48.0	2,895
Florida	25	252.3	2.5	10,092.0	1,697	3.2	68	13.40	46.6	11,045
Georgia	16	172.0	1.7	10,750.9	1,382	2.6	86	11.98	53.4	1,161

Continued on next page.

INDUSTRY DATA BY STATE - Continued

State	Establish-ments	Shipments			Employment				Cost as % of Shipments	Investment per Employee ($)
		Total ($ mil)	% of U.S.	Per Establ.	Total Number	% of U.S.	Per Establ.	Wages ($/hour)		
New Jersey	22	148.2	1.5	6,737.5	878	1.7	40	12.94	51.3	8,274
South Carolina	4	22.8	0.2	5,704.5	202	0.4	51	14.42	56.5	1,891

Source: 2002 *Economic Census*. The states are in descending order of shipments or establishments (if shipment data are missing for the majority). The symbol (D) appears when data are withheld to prevent disclosure of competitive information. States marked with (D) are sorted by number of establishments. A dash (-) indicates that the data element cannot be calculated. Data may not show all states active in the NAICS category. All data available at the time of publication are shown.

NAICS 335991 - CARBON AND GRAPHITE PRODUCT MANUFACTURING

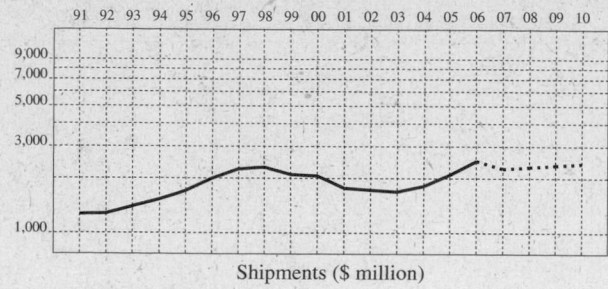

Shipments ($ million)

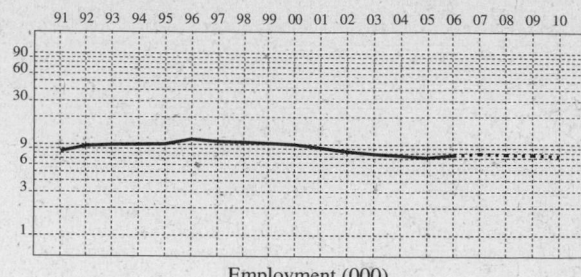

Employment (000)

GENERAL STATISTICS

Year	Companies	Establishments		Employment			Compensation		Production ($ million)			
		Total	with 20 or more employees	Total (000)	Production Workers (000)	Hours (Mil)	Payroll ($ mil)	Wages ($/hr)	Cost of Materials	Value Added by Manufacture	Value of Shipments	Capital Invest.
1991		97	59	8.4	6.0	13.0	279.9	13.68	585.9	684.8	1,266.9	66.0
1992	86	110	67	9.6	7.0	14.4	286.6	12.85	561.2	724.2	1,276.4	43.6
1993		108	64	9.9	7.4	15.9	300.9	12.69	612.5	788.7	1,397.7	40.3
1994		101	60	10.0	7.3	15.5	329.9	13.87	699.6	844.4	1,527.0	50.4
1995		109	69	10.1	7.5	15.5	328.0	13.75	750.9	955.1	1,704.6	94.1
1996		113	67	11.4	8.5	17.6	391.6	14.44	849.3	1,168.1	1,994.9	92.6
1997	99	125	72	10.8	8.0	17.7	406.9	14.92	1,044.5	1,224.2	2,249.2	179.0
1998		129	77	10.6	7.9	17.1	397.0	15.66	1,054.7	1,278.0	2,302.0	141.5
1999		140	81	10.3	7.6	16.4	378.5	15.07	1,007.6	1,037.1	2,099.0	89.7
2000		143	80	10.0	7.3	15.9	371.0	15.01	1,038.8	1,026.2	2,062.0	80.8
2001		141	78	9.2	6.8	14.7	342.4	14.66	872.8	903.2	1,767.5	57.7
2002	104	129	75	8.4	6.2	14.4	337.4	14.61	797.3	916.2	1,724.9	100.4
2003		147	74	7.9	5.8	12.3	327.6	16.16	753.1	886.7	1,687.9	51.4
2004		141	67	7.6	5.6	12.1	346.2	17.16	795.7	1,015.7	1,814.9	67.3
2005		139	68	7.2	5.1	11.3	336.5	18.11	1,023.6	1,090.0	2,098.4	93.0
2006		152P	77P	7.6	5.4	11.5	367.1	19.81	1,211.0	1,334.7	2,494.8	300.3
2007		156P	78P	7.9P	5.7P	12.7P	372.1P	18.11P	1,096.6P	1,208.6P	2,259.0P	146.6P
2008		159P	79P	7.7P	5.6P	12.4P	375.2P	18.46P	1,120.4P	1,234.8P	2,308.1P	152.4P
2009		162P	80P	7.6P	5.5P	12.2P	378.3P	18.81P	1,144.2P	1,261.1P	2,357.2P	158.3P
2010		166P	81P	7.4P	5.4P	12.0P	381.5P	19.16P	1,168.0P	1,287.4P	2,406.3P	164.2P

Sources: 1992, 1997, 2002 *Economic Census*; other years, up to 2006, are from the *Annual Survey of Manufactures*. Establishment counts for non-Census years are from *County Business Patterns*; 1997 and 2002 values are from the 1997 and 2002 censuses respectively, reported in the Federal Government's NAICS format. Other years were originally reported in equivalent SIC format. 'P's show projections by the editors.

INDICES OF CHANGE

Year	Companies	Establishments		Employment			Compensation		Production ($ million)			
		Total	with 20 or more employees	Total (000)	Production Workers (000)	Hours (Mil)	Payroll ($ mil)	Wages ($/hr)	Cost of Materials	Value Added by Manufacture	Value of Shipments	Capital Invest.
1992	83	85	89	114	113	100	85	88	70	79	74	43
1997	95	97	96	129	129	123	121	102	131	134	130	178
2001		109	104	110	110	102	101	100	109	99	102	57
2002	100	100	100	100	100	100	100	100	100	100	100	100
2003		114	99	94	94	85	97	111	94	97	98	51
2004		109	89	90	90	84	103	117	100	111	105	67
2005		108	91	86	82	78	100	124	128	119	122	93
2006		118P	103P	90	87	80	109	136	152	146	145	299
2007		121P	104P	94P	92P	88P	110P	124P	138P	132P	131P	146P
2008		123P	105P	92P	90P	86P	111P	126P	141P	135P	134P	152P
2009		126P	106P	90P	89P	85P	112P	129P	144P	138P	137P	158P
2010		129P	107P	88P	87P	83P	113P	131P	146P	141P	140P	164P

Sources: Same as General Statistics. Values reflect change from the base year, 2002. Values above 100 mean greater than 2002, values below 100 mean less than 2002, and the values of 100 in other years means the same as 2002. 'P' show projections by the editors.

SELECTED RATIOS

For 2002	Avg. of All Manufact.	Analyzed Industry	Index	For 2002	Avg. of All Manufact.	Analyzed Industry	Index
Employees per Establishment	42	65	155	Value Added per Production Worker	182,367	147,774	81
Payroll per Establishment	1,639,184	2,615,504	160	Cost per Establishment	5,769,015	6,180,620	107
Payroll per Employee	39,053	40,167	103	Cost per Employee	137,446	94,917	69
Production Workers per Establishment	30	48	163	Cost per Production Worker	195,506	128,597	66
Wages per Establishment	694,845	1,630,884	235	Shipments per Establishment	11,158,348	13,371,318	120
Wages per Production Worker	23,548	33,933	144	Shipments per Employee	265,847	205,345	77
Hours per Production Worker	1,980	2,323	117	Shipments per Production Worker	378,144	278,210	74
Wages per Hour	11.89	14.61	123	Investment per Establishment	361,338	778,295	215
Value Added per Establishment	5,381,325	7,102,326	132	Investment per Employee	8,609	11,952	139
Value Added per Employee	128,210	109,071	85	Investment per Production Worker	12,245	16,194	132

Sources: Same as General Statistics. The 'Average of All Manufacturing' column represents the average of all manufacturing industries reported for the most recent complete year available. The Index shows the relationship between the Average and the Analyzed Industry. For example, 100 means that they are equal; 500 that the Analyzed Industry is five times the average; 50 means that the Analyzed Industry is half the national average. The abbreviation 'na' is used to show that data are 'not available'. Ratios shown for 2002, the last complete census year.

LEADING COMPANIES   Number shown: **73**   Total sales ($ mil): **11,551**   Total employment (000): **17.4**

Company Name	Address				CEO Name	Phone	Co. Type	Sales ($ mil)	Empl. (000)
Cabot Corp.	2 Seaport Ln., 1300	Boston	MA	02210		617-345-0100	P	2,616	4.3
Morgan Adv. Materials/Tech.	441 Hall Ave.	Saint Marys	PA	15857	David Cooper	814-781-1573	R	1,320*	0.3
Nat'l Electrical Carbon Prods	PO Box 1056	Greenville	SC	29602		864-458-7777	R	1,320*	0.2
Fulmer Company L.L.C.	3004 Venture Ct.	Export	PA	15632	Leo Eger	724-325-7140	R	1,320*	<0.1
Koppers Inc.	436 7th Ave.	Pittsburgh	PA	15219	Robert Cizik	412-227-2001	R	1,160	2.0
Graftech International Ltd.	12900 Snow Rd.	Parma	OH	44130		216-676-2000	P	1,005	2.6
Continental Carbon Co.	16850 Park Row	Houston	TX	77084	Leslie Koo	281-647-3700	R	523*	0.1
Graphel Corp.	PO Box 369	West Chester	OH	45071	Cliff Kersker	513-779-6166	R	337*	0.1
Horsehead Holding Corp.	300 Frankfort Rd.	Monaca	PA	15061	James M. Hensler	724-774-1020	S	264	1.0
Metaullics Systems Div/Pyrotek	31935 Aurora Rd.	Cleveland	OH	44139	Alan Roy	440-349-8800	R	250*	<0.1
Brillion Iron Works Inc.	200 Park Ave.	Brillion	WI	54110		920-756-2121	S	158*	1.0
American Spring Wire Corp.	PO Box 46510	Cleveland	OH	44146		216-292-4620	R	153*	0.2
Zoltek Companies Inc.	3101 McKelvey Rd.	Bridgeton	MO	63044		314-291-5110	P	151	1.3
N American Hoganas Holdings	PO Box 509	Hollsopple	PA	15935	Stan Kvist	814-479-2551	R	131*	<0.1
SGL Technic Inc/Polycarbon Div	28176 Ave. Stanford	Valencia	CA	91355	Mark Kokosinski	661-257-0500	D	65*	0.1
Helwig Carbon Products Inc.	PO Box 240160	Milwaukee	WI	53224	Jay Koenitzer	414-354-2411	R	58*	0.3
Advanced Ceramics Corp.	22557 W Lunn Rd.	Strongsville	OH	44149	John Krenicki	440-878-5700	S	53*	0.3
Carbone Lorraine North America	400 Myrtle Ave.	Boonton	NJ	07005	Michel Coniglio	973-541-4720	R	50*	<0.1
Portland Forge	PO Box 905	Portland	IN	47371	Patrick W. Bennett	260-726-8121	S	38*	0.2
Kaydon Ring and Seal Inc.	PO Box 626	Baltimore	MD	21203		410-547-7700	S	35*	0.3
CG Electrodes L.L.C.	800 Theresia St.	Saint Marys	PA	15857	David Jardini	814-834-2801	R	29*	0.1
Metallized Carbon Corp.	19 S Water St.	Ossining	NY	10562	Bruce Neri	914-941-3738	R	29*	0.1
St Marys Carbon Company Inc.	259 Eberl St.	Saint Marys	PA	15857	Harold Lanzel	814-781-7333	R	27*	0.2
Schunk Graphite Technology	W146 Held	Menomonee Fls	WI	53051	Heinz Volk	262-253-8720	R	26*	0.1
Graphite Engineering and Sales	PO Box 637	Greenville	MI	48838	Todd Taylor	616-754-5671	R	24*	0.1
B. A. E Sys. Composite Struct.	1095 Columbia St.	Brea	CA	92821		714-990-6300	R	23*	0.1
Nat'l Electrical Carbon Prods	200 N Town St.	Fostoria	OH	44830		419-435-8182	S	21*	0.1
Asbury Carbons Inc.	PO Box 144	Asbury	NJ	08802	Marvin Riddle	908-537-2155	R	20*	<0.1
Stein Seal Co.	PO Box 316	Kulpsville	PA	19443	Philip Stein	215-256-0201	R	20*	0.2
Asbury Graphite Mills Inc.	PO Box 144	Asbury	NJ	08802		908-537-2155	S	18*	0.2
FSR Inc.	244 Bergen Blvd.	West Paterson	NJ	07424	William Fitzsimmons	973-785-4347	R	18*	<0.1
TYK AMERICA Inc.	301 Brickyard Rd.	Clairton	PA	15025	Kenichi Sasaki	412-384-4259	R	17*	<0.1
Mill-Rose Co.	7995 Tyler Blvd.	Mentor	OH	44060	Paul Miller	440-255-9171	R	16*	0.2
Graphite Sales Inc.	16710 W Prk Cir Dr	Chagrin Falls	OH	44023	George Hanna	440-543-8221	R	15*	0.1
Micro-Tronics Inc.	2905 S Potter Dr.	Tempe	AZ	85282	Robert Marusiak	602-437-8995	R	15*	0.1
CompositAir	12827 E Imperial	Santa Fe Spgs	CA	90670	Michael T. Furry	562-944-3281	D	14*	0.1
Maclean Quality Composites	3392 W 8600 S	West Jordan	UT	84088		801-565-8003	R	14*	0.1
Hoyt Corp.	520 S Dean St.	Englewood	NJ	07631	Donald McGuire	201-894-0707	R	12*	<0.1
Weaver Industries Inc.	PO Box 326	Denver	PA	17517	John Weaver	717-336-7507	R	12*	<0.1
Tris USA Inc.	PO Box 1290	Athens	AL	35612	Kiroshi Sasaki	256-233-2511	R	11*	<0.1
Car-Graph Inc.	1545 W Elna Rae St.	Tempe	AZ	85281	Charles Lindbloom	480-894-1356	R	11*	<0.1
Applied Composite Technology	PO Box Hc 13	Fayette	UT	84630	Roland Christensen	435-528-7199	R	11*	<0.1
Metaullics Systems Company	2040 Cory Dr.	Sanborn	NY	14132		716-731-3221	S	10*	<0.1
NAC Carbon Products Inc.	PO Box 436	Punxsutawney	PA	15767	William Deeley	814-938-7450	R	10*	<0.1
Carbon Fiber Technology L.L.C.	1375 Union Dr.	Evanston	WY	82930	Steven Russell	307-789-2499	R	10*	<0.1
MWI Inc.	1269 Brighton Hen	Rochester	NY	14623	David Mc Mahon	585-424-4204	R	9*	<0.1
Advance Carbon Products Inc.	2036 National Ave.	Hayward	CA	94545	Ronald Crader	510-293-5930	R	8*	<0.1
Performance Composites Inc.	1418 S Alameda St.	Compton	CA	90221	Francis Hu	310-328-6661	R	8*	<0.1
Saturn Industries Inc.	PO Box 367	Hudson	NY	12534	John Lee	518-828-9956	R	6*	<0.1
EDM Supplies Inc.	9806 Everest St.	Downey	CA	90242	David Muhs	562-803-6563	R	6*	<0.1
Jensen's Inc.	PO Box 320	Shelbyville	TN	37162	Aksel Jensen	931-684-5021	R	6*	<0.1
Bay Carbon Inc.	PO Box 205	Bay City	MI	48707	William Clare	989-686-8090	R	5*	<0.1
Thresh Hold Rehabilitation	1554 W Carroll Ave.	Chicago	IL	60607		312-850-2219	R	5*	<0.1
Zook Enterprises Inc.	PO Box 419	Chagrin Falls	OH	44022	Richard Varos	440-543-1010	R	5*	<0.1
Cummings-Moore Graphite Co.	1646 N Green St.	Detroit	MI	48209	Michael Mares	313-841-1615	R	5*	<0.1
Kbr Inc.	2000 W Gaylord St.	Long Beach	CA	90813	David McMahon	562-436-9281	R	5*	<0.1
Applied Composites Engineering	705 S Girls School	Indianapolis	IN	46231	Leigh Sargent	317-243-4225	R	5*	<0.1
Innovative Composite Engineer.	PO Box 1218	White Salmon	WA	98672	Steve Maier	509-493-4484	R	5*	<0.1
Sherbrooke Metals	37552 N Ind Pkwy	Willoughby	OH	44094	Randy Spoth	440-942-3520	R	5*	<0.1
ROC Industries Inc.	1605 Brittmoore Rd.	Houston	TX	77043	Pamela Carlson	713-468-7744	R	4*	<0.1
Micron Research Corp.	PO Box 269	Emporium	PA	15834	David Trinkley	814-486-2444	R	4*	<0.1
South-Land Carbon Products	PO Box 170799	Birmingham	AL	35217	Raymond Lilly	205-841-8799	R	4*	<0.1
AMS Seals Inc.	500 Chaddick Dr.	Wheeling	IL	60090	Dieter Ade	847-215-7333	R	3*	<0.1
Slade Inc.	181 Crawford Rd.	Statesville	NC	28625	Ward Crosier	704-873-1366	R	3*	<0.1
Applied Sciences Inc.	PO Box 579	Cedarville	OH	45314	Max Lake	937-766-2020	R	3*	<0.1
Caldwell Corp.	PO Box 230	Emporium	PA	15834	Joseph Caldwell	814-486-3493	R	3*	<0.1
Hausermann Die and Machine Co.	300 W Laura Dr.	Addison	IL	60101	Marten Hausermann	630-543-6688	R	2*	<0.1
Graphite Electrodes Ltd.	1311 N Sherman St.	Bay City	MI	48708	Patrick Martin	989-893-3635	R	2*	<0.1
Joshua L.L.C.	90 Hamilton St.	New Haven	CT	06511		203-624-0080	R	2*	<0.1
Structural Lining Systems Inc.	2815 Charles Page	Tulsa	OK	74127	Roger Walker	918-584-2220	R	1*	<0.1
Citizens Mechanical Services	6805 Hillsdale Ct.	Indianapolis	IN	46250		317-595-3000	R	1*	<0.1
Graphite Die Mold	18 Airline Rd.	Durham	CT	06422	Fred Wallman	860-349-4444	R	1*	<0.1
Ohio Carbon Blank Inc.	PO Box 714093	Columbus	OH	43271	Scott Boncha	440-953-9302	R	1*	<0.1

Source: Ward's Business Directory of U.S. Private and Public Companies, Volumes 1 and 2, 2008. The company type code used is as follows: P - Public, R - Private, S - Subsidiary, D - Division, J - Joint Venture, A - Affiliate, G - Group. Sales are in millions of dollars, employees are in thousands. An asterisk (*) indicates an estimated sales volume. The symbol < stands for 'less than'. Company names and addresses are truncated, in some cases, to fit into the available space.

MATERIALS CONSUMED

Material	Quantity	Delivered Cost ($ million)
Castings, rough and semifinished	(X)	(D)
Nonferrous shapes and forms	(X)	(D)
Pitch	(X)	50.8
Coke (petroleum, metallurgical, etc.), used as raw material	(X)	171.8
Natural graphite	(X)	6.8
Artificial graphite	(X)	39.0
Carbon, ground or treated	(X)	33.6
All other materials, components, parts, containers, and supplies	(X)	200.5
Materials, ingredients, containers, and supplies, nsk	(X)	99.2

Source: 2002 Economic Census. Explanation of symbols used: (D): Withheld to avoid disclosure of competitive data; na: Not available; (S): Withheld because statistical norms were not met; (X): Not applicable; (Z): Less than half the unit shown; nec: Not elsewhere classified; nsk: Not specified by kind; - : zero; p : 10-19 percent estimated; q : 20-29 percent estimated.

PRODUCT SHARE DETAILS

Product or Product Class Shipments	Mil. $	Product or Product Class Shipments	Mil. $
CARBON AND GRAPHITE PRODUCTS	1,593.6	All other carbon and graphite products, except refractories, for mechanical uses, rotor vanes, and other uses where motion is between two parts, except metallic oilless bearings	96.6
Carbon and graphite electrodes for electric furnaces and electrolytic cell use	**740.3**		
Carbon electrodes for electric furnaces and electrolytic cell use	188.3	All other carbon and graphite products, except refractories, for aerospace uses, including machined and unmachined stock not included elsewhere	(D)
Graphite electrodes for electric furnaces and electrolytic cell use	552.0		
All other carbon and graphite products	**810.2**	All other carbon and graphite paste products, except refractories, for all other uses (including chemical, metallurgical, etc.)	(D)
Carbon and graphite brushes, contacts, and brush plates	195.0		
Carbon and graphite fibers	209.3	All other carbon and graphite products, except refractories, for all other uses (including chemical, metallurgical, etc.)	130.6
All other carbon and graphite products, except refractories	395.4		
All other carbon and graphite products, except refractories, for electrical uses, including welding products, illuminating carbons, battery (except silver or other metal contacts)	94.8	All other carbon and graphite products, nsk	10.6
		Carbon and graphite products, nsk, total	**43.1**

Source: 2002 Economic Census. The values are product shipments in millions of dollars for 2002. Total product shipments may be lower or higher than industry shipments. See Introduction for a full discussion. Values of indented subcategories are summed in the main heading(s). The symbol (D) appears when data are withheld to prevent disclosure of competitive information. The abbreviation nsk stands for 'not specified by kind' and nec for 'not elsewhere classified'. A dash (-) means zero.

INPUTS AND OUTPUTS FOR CARBON AND GRAPHITE PRODUCT MANUFACTURING

Economic Sector or Industry Providing Inputs	%	Sector	Economic Sector or Industry Buying Outputs	%	Sector
Compensation of employees	27.7		Exports of goods & services	18.9	Cap Inv
Petroleum & coal products, nec	8.2	Manufg.	Iron & steel mills & ferroalloys	12.4	Manufg.
Management of companies & enterprises	5.6	Services	Alumina refining & primary aluminum production	12.3	Manufg.
Truck transportation	4.5	Util.	Aircraft parts & auxiliary equipment, nec	11.8	Manufg.
Basic organic chemicals, nec	3.8	Manufg.	Legal services	5.7	Services
Ground or treated mineral & earth	3.0	Manufg.	Other S/L govt. enterprises	4.8	S/L Govt
Wholesale trade	3.0	Trade	Professional, scientific, technical services, nec	4.2	Services
Power generation & supply	3.0	Util.	Basic organic chemicals, nec	3.5	Manufg.
Nonmetallic mineral products, nec	2.8	Manufg.	Transit & ground passenger transportation	3.5	Util.
Rail transportation	2.3	Util.	Primary batteries	3.0	Manufg.
Natural gas distribution	1.8	Util.	Accounting, tax preparation, bookkeeping, & payroll	2.6	Services
Chemical products & preparations, nec	1.6	Manufg.	Urethane & other foam products (except polystrene)	1.9	Manufg.
Carbon & graphite products	1.1	Manufg.	Ferrous metal foundries	1.6	Manufg.
Plastics packaging materials, film & sheet	1.0	Manufg.	Employment services	1.5	Services
Semiconductors & related devices	0.9	Manufg.	Motors & generators	1.2	Manufg.
Printed circuit assemblies (electronic assembiles)	0.9	Manufg.	Tobacco products	1.2	Manufg.
Machine shops	0.7	Manufg.	Office administrative services	1.1	Services
Coating, engraving, heat treating & allied activities	0.6	Manufg.	Business support services	1.0	Services
Noncomparable imports	0.6	Foreign	Architectural, engineering, & related services	0.9	Services
Taxes on production & imports, less subsidies	0.5		Management, scientific, & technical consulting	0.9	Services
Unlaminated plastics profile shapes	0.5	Manufg.	Carbon & graphite products	0.9	Manufg.
Securities, commodity contracts, investments	0.4	Fin/R.E.	Asphalt paving mixtures & blocks	0.8	Manufg.
Fabricated metals, nec	0.4	Manufg.	Waste management & remediation services	0.7	Services
Legal services	0.4	Services	Wood containers & pallets	0.7	Manufg.
Advertising & related services	0.3	Services	Services to buildings & dwellings	0.6	Services
Real estate	0.3	Fin/R.E.	Scientific research & development services	0.6	Services
Scientific research & development services	0.3	Services	Computer system design services	0.4	Services
Lessors of nonfinancial assets	0.3	Fin/R.E.	Steel products from purchased steel	0.3	Manufg.
Specialized design services	0.3	Services	Industrial gases	0.3	Manufg.
Employment services	0.3	Services	Scenic & sightseeing transport & related services	0.3	Util.
Maintenance/repair of nonresidential structures	0.3	Construct.	Air transportation	0.2	Util.
Pipeline transportation	0.3	Util.	S/L govt. electric utilities	0.1	S/L Govt

Continued on next page.

INPUTS AND OUTPUTS FOR CARBON AND GRAPHITE PRODUCT MANUFACTURING - Continued

Economic Sector or Industry Providing Inputs	%	Sector	Economic Sector or Industry Buying Outputs	%	Sector
Architectural, engineering, & related services	0.2	Services			
Business support services	0.2	Services			
Custom roll forming	0.2	Manufg.			
Services to buildings & dwellings	0.2	Services			
Telecommunications	0.2	Services			
Automotive equipment rental & leasing	0.2	Fin/R.E.			
Warehousing & storage	0.2	Util.			
Management, scientific, & technical consulting	0.2	Services			
Accounting, tax preparation, bookkeeping, & payroll	0.2	Services			
Automotive repair & maintenance, ex. car washes	0.2	Services			
Support services, nec	0.2	Services			
Commercial & industrial equipment repair/maintenance	0.1	Services			
Paperboard mills	0.1	Manufg.			
Relay & industrial controls	0.1	Manufg.			
Ferrous metal foundries	0.1	Manufg.			
Water transportation	0.1	Util.			
Bare printed circuit boards	0.1	Manufg.			
Cutting tools & machine tool accessories	0.1	Manufg.			
Paperboard containers	0.1	Manufg.			
Commercial & industrial machinery rental & leasing	0.1	Fin/R.E.			
Investigation & security services	0.1	Services			
Nonferrous metal foundries	0.1	Manufg.			
Turned products & screws, nuts, & bolts	0.1	Manufg.			

Source: Benchmark Input-Output Accounts for the U.S. Economy, 2002, U.S. Department of Commerce, Washington, D.C., January 2008. The abbreviation nec stands for 'not elsewhere classified'.

OCCUPATIONS EMPLOYED BY OTHER ELECTRICAL EQUIPMENT & COMPONENT MANUFACTURING

Occupation	% of Total 2006	Change to 2016	Occupation	% of Total 2006	Change to 2016
Team assemblers	14.6	-7.3	Customer service representatives	1.4	1.9
Electrical & electronic equipment assemblers	9.0	-25.9	Electrical engineers	1.2	-7.3
Extruding & drawing machine operators & tenders	3.8	-7.3	Sales reps, wholesale & manufacturing, exc tech	1.2	-7.3
First-line supervisors/managers of production workers	3.7	-7.3	Plating & coating machine operators & tenders	1.2	-3.3
Inspectors, testers, sorters, samplers, & weighers	3.3	-12.6	Tool & die makers	1.1	-2.7
Cutting, punching, & press machine operators	2.8	-16.6	Mechanical engineers	1.1	-7.3
Shipping, receiving, & traffic clerks	2.4	-10.8	Multiple machine tool operators & tenders	1.1	1.9
Maintenance & repair workers, general	2.4	-7.3	Sales representatives, wholesale & manufacturing, tech	1.1	-7.3
Molding, coremaking, & casting machine operators	2.4	-16.6	Packers & packagers, hand	1.1	-25.9
Machinists	2.2	-2.7	Office clerks, general	1.0	-8.7
Helpers--Production workers	2.0	-7.3	Industrial production managers	1.0	-7.3
Laborers & freight, stock, & material movers, hand	1.9	-16.6	Packaging & filling machine operators & tenders	1.0	-16.6
Industrial truck & tractor operators	1.6	-16.6	Electromechanical equipment assemblers	1.0	-7.3
Industrial engineers	1.4	12.5	Computer-controlled machine tool operators	1.0	1.9
General & operations managers	1.4	-16.6	Bookkeeping, accounting, & auditing clerks	1.0	-7.3

Source: Industry-Occupation Matrix, Bureau of Labor Statistics, December 4, 2007. These data are reported based on 4-digit NAICS categories but have been matched to corresponding 6-digit NAICS industry codes. The change reported for each occupation to the year 2016 is a percent of growth or decline as estimated by the Bureau of Labor Statistics. The abbreviation nec stands for 'not elsewhere classified'.

LOCATION BY STATE AND REGIONAL CONCENTRATION

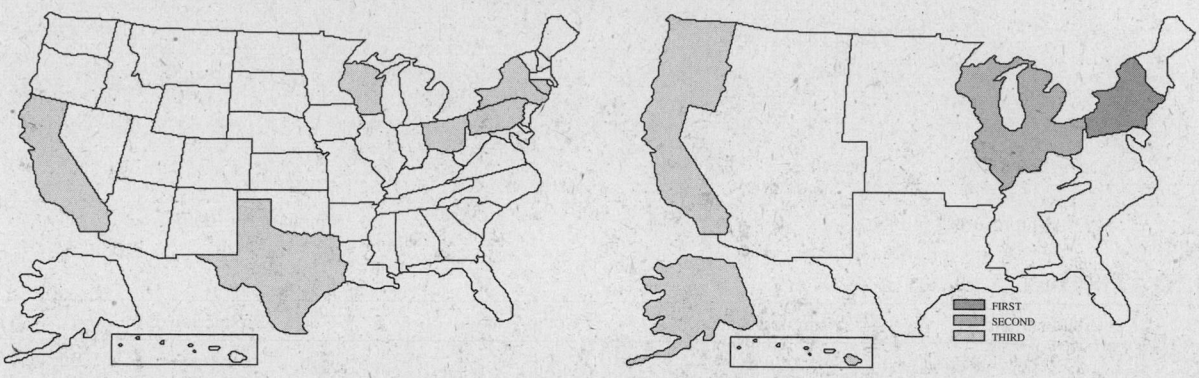

FIRST
SECOND
THIRD

INDUSTRY DATA BY STATE

| State | Establish-ments | Shipments | | | Employment | | | | Cost as % of Shipments | Investment per Employee ($) |
		Total ($ mil)	% of U.S.	Per Establ.	Total Number	% of U.S.	Per Establ.	Wages ($/hour)		
Pennsylvania	18	262.3	15.2	14,573.3	1,587	19.0	88	14.39	37.7	9,579
New York	5	121.1	7.0	24,229.2	504	6.0	101	14.92	69.3	4,954
California	13	101.5	5.9	7,809.6	297	3.5	23	19.65	57.5	9,061
Ohio	12	69.0	4.0	5,751.3	463	5.5	39	10.36	46.5	2,410
Wisconsin	3	66.4	3.9	22,148.3	487	5.8	162	13.59	42.6	2,659
Texas	6	57.0	3.3	9,502.2	394	4.7	66	12.72	32.0	3,525
Connecticut	5	20.0	1.2	4,004.4	138	1.6	28	17.27	40.3	3,710

Source: 2002 *Economic Census*. The states are in descending order of shipments or establishments (if shipment data are missing for the majority). The symbol (D) appears when data are withheld to prevent disclosure of competitive information. States marked with (D) are sorted by number of establishments. A dash (-) indicates that the data element cannot be calculated. Data may not show all states active in the NAICS category. All data available at the time of publication are shown.

NAICS 335999 - ELECTRICAL EQUIPMENT AND COMPONENT MANUFACTURING NEC

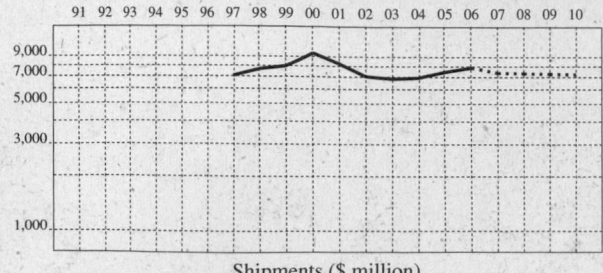

Shipments ($ million)

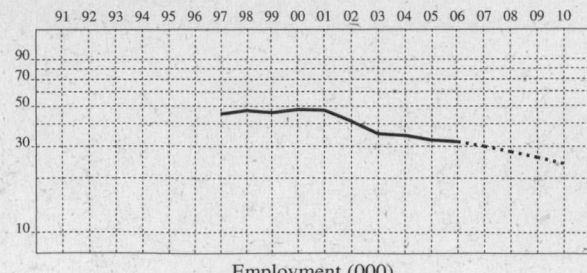

Employment (000)

GENERAL STATISTICS

Year	Companies	Establishments		Employment			Compensation		Production ($ million)			
		Total	with 20 or more employees	Total (000)	Production Workers (000)	Hours (Mil)	Payroll ($ mil)	Wages ($/hr)	Cost of Materials	Value Added by Manufacture	Value of Shipments	Capital Invest.
1997	932	976	455	45.2	28.4	53.9	1,521.4	12.29	3,290.5	3,773.9	7,035.6	231.4
1998		990	451	47.2	29.8	56.7	1,625.7	12.33	3,486.2	4,159.1	7,683.6	284.3
1999		1,016	437	46.0	28.1	55.3	1,663.3	12.42	3,665.9	4,361.1	7,982.0	211.8
2000		1,019	412	47.8	28.9	56.5	1,830.3	13.16	4,492.4	5,029.1	9,394.4	271.7
2001		979	414	47.4	28.5	55.5	1,742.1	12.78	4,073.3	4,145.8	8,254.7	271.5
2002	957	1,003	367	41.2	24.4	48.8	1,661.7	14.00	3,012.3	4,031.7	7,057.3	276.2
2003		864	341	35.2	20.7	41.9	1,534.9	14.72	2,845.6	4,023.5	6,832.1	301.4
2004		899	338	34.5	19.8	39.9	1,616.7	16.34	2,940.2	3,993.3	6,932.2	216.0
2005		847	328	32.4	18.4	36.9	1,558.1	16.97	3,145.9	4,315.0	7,477.8	164.0
2006		862P	303P	31.8	18.4	36.2	1,589.9	17.01	3,379.1	4,569.8	7,882.1	252.1
2007		844P	285P	30.0P	16.5P	34.0P	1,599.2P	17.55P	3,167.3P	4,283.3P	7,388.0P	230.0P
2008		825P	267P	28.0P	15.1P	31.4P	1,592.8P	18.16P	3,146.6P	4,255.4P	7,339.8P	226.7P
2009		807P	249P	26.1P	13.6P	28.8P	1,586.4P	18.77P	3,125.9P	4,227.4P	7,291.6P	223.4P
2010		788P	231P	24.1P	12.2P	26.2P	1,580.0P	19.38P	3,105.3P	4,199.5P	7,243.4P	220.2P

Sources: 1997 and 2002 *Economic Census*; other years, up to 2006, are from *Annual Survey of Manufactures*. Establishment counts for non-Census years are from *County Business Patterns*; 1997 and 2002 values are from the 1997 and 2002 censuses, respectively. 'P's show projections by the editors.

INDICES OF CHANGE

Year	Companies	Establishments		Employment			Compensation		Production ($ million)			
		Total	with 20 or more employees	Total (000)	Production Workers (000)	Hours (Mil)	Payroll ($ mil)	Wages ($/hr)	Cost of Materials	Value Added by Manufacture	Value of Shipments	Capital Invest.
1997	97	97	124	110	116	110	92	88	109	94	100	84
1998		99	123	115	122	116	98	88	116	103	109	103
1999		101	119	112	115	113	100	89	122	108	113	77
2000		102	112	116	118	116	110	94	149	125	133	98
2001		98	113	115	117	114	105	91	135	103	117	98
2002	100	100	100	100	100	100	100	100	100	100	100	100
2003		86	93	85	85	86	92	105	94	100	97	109
2004		90	92	84	81	82	97	117	98	99	98	78
2005		84	89	79	75	76	94	121	104	107	106	59
2006		86P	83P	77	75	74	96	122	112	113	112	91
2007		84P	78P	73P	68P	70P	96P	125P	105P	106P	105P	83P
2008		82P	73P	68P	62P	64P	96P	130P	104P	106P	104P	82P
2009		80P	68P	63P	56P	59P	95P	134P	104P	105P	103P	81P
2010		79P	63P	58P	50P	54P	95P	138P	103P	104P	103P	80P

Sources: Same as General Statistics. Values reflect change from the base year, 2002. Values above 100 mean greater than 2002, values below 100 mean less than 2002, and the values of 100 in other years means the same as 2002. 'P's show projections by the editors.

SELECTED RATIOS

For 2002	Avg. of All Manufact.	Analyzed Industry	Index	For 2002	Avg. of All Manufact.	Analyzed Industry	Index
Employees per Establishment	42	41	98	Value Added per Production Worker	182,367	165,234	91
Payroll per Establishment	1,639,184	1,656,730	101	Cost per Establishment	5,769,015	3,003,290	52
Payroll per Employee	39,053	40,333	103	Cost per Employee	137,446	73,114	53
Production Workers per Establishment	30	24	82	Cost per Production Worker	195,506	123,455	63
Wages per Establishment	694,845	681,157	98	Shipments per Establishment	11,158,348	7,036,191	63
Wages per Production Worker	23,548	28,000	119	Shipments per Employee	265,847	171,294	64
Hours per Production Worker	1,980	2,000	101	Shipments per Production Worker	378,144	289,234	76
Wages per Hour	11.89	14.00	118	Investment per Establishment	361,338	275,374	76
Value Added per Establishment	5,381,325	4,019,641	75	Investment per Employee	8,609	6,704	78
Value Added per Employee	128,210	97,857	76	Investment per Production Worker	12,245	11,320	92

Sources: Same as General Statistics. The 'Average of All Manufacturing' column represents the average of all manufacturing industries reported for the most recent complete year available. The Index shows the relationship between the Average and the Analyzed Industry. For example, 100 means that they are equal; 500 that the Analyzed Industry is five times the average; 50 means that the Analyzed Industry is half the national average. The abbreviation 'na' is used to show that data are 'not available'. Ratios shown for 2002, the last complete census year.

LEADING COMPANIES   Number shown: **75**   Total sales ($ mil): **269,789**   Total employment (000): **666.6**

Company Name	Address				CEO Name	Phone	Co. Type	Sales ($ mil)	Empl. (000)
General Electric Co.	3135 Easton Tpk.	Fairfield	CT	06828		203-373-2211	P	172,738	327.0
Emerson Electric	PO Box 4100	St. Louis	MO	63136	L.C. Barrett	314-553-2000	P	22,572	137.7
Nypro Inc.	101 Union St.	Clinton	MA	01510	Ted Lapres	978-365-9721	R	10,030*	17.0
Boon Edam Tomsed	420 McKinney Pky.	Lillington	NC	27546	Tom DeVine	910-814-3800	R	7,005*	0.1
Etec Systems Inc.	PO Box 58039	Santa Clara	CA	95052		408-727-5555	S	6,992	12.2
Cooper Industries Ltd.	PO Box 4446	Houston	TX	77210	Kirk S. Hachigian	713-209-8400	P	5,903	31.5
Stanley Works	PO Box 700	New Britain	CT	06053		860-225-5111	P	4,484	18.4
Cytec Industries Inc.	5 Garret Mtn. Plz.	West Paterson	NJ	07424		973-357-3100	P	3,504	6.8
Arco Auto and Marine Products	3921 Navy Blvd.	Pensacola	FL	32507	Ron Miller	850-455-5476	R	3,015	<0.1
Exide Technologies	13000 Deerfield Pky	Alpharetta	GA	30004		678-566-9000	P	2,940	13.9
Diebold Inc.	PO Box 3077	North Canton	OH	44720		330-490-4000	P	2,906	15.5
Flow Systems	PO Box 1069	St. Helena Is	SC	29920	James Barrett	843-838-6699	R	2,681*	<0.1
Lockheed Martin Enterpr. Info.	12506 Lk Underhill	Orlando	FL	32825	Robert J. Stevens	407-306-1000	S	2,383*	4.0
NTK Holdings Inc.	50 Kennedy Plz.	Providence	RI	02903	Richard L. Bready	401-751-1600	S	2,218	9.8
Spectrum Brands Inc.	6 Concourse Pky.	Atlanta	GA	30328	John D. Bowlin	770-829-6200	P	1,995	7.1
American Power Conversion	132 Fairgrounds Rd.	West Kingston	RI	02892	Rodger B. Dowdell Jr.	401-789-5735	S	1,980	7.6
Scientific-Atlanta Inc.	PO Box 465447	Lawrenceville	GA	30042		770-236-5000	S	1,910	7.7
JDS Uniphase Corp.	430 N McCarthy	Milpitas	CA	95035	Martin A. Kaplan	408-546-5000	P	1,397*	7.0
Rittal Corp.	1 Rittal Pl.	Springfield	OH	45504	Carie Ray	937-399-0500	R	1,268*	0.6
Woodward Governor Co.	PO Box 1519	Fort Collins	CO	80522	Thomas A. Gendron	970-482-5811	P	1,042	3.4
East Penn Manufacturing Co.	PO Box 147	Lyon Station	PA	19536			R	716*	5.0
United Industrial Corp.	PO Box 126	Hunt Valley	MD	21030	W. G. Lichtenstein	410-628-3500	S	564	2.3
Lamson and Sessions Co.	25701 Science Park	Cleveland	OH	44122		216-464-3400	S	561	1.3
Lepel Corp.	200 Executive Dr.	Edgewood	NY	11717	Vladimir Pilic	631-586-3300	R	556*	<0.1
Aeroflex Inc.	PO Box 6022	Plainview	NY	11803	Harvey R. Blau	516-694-6700	R	537*	2.6
C and D Technologies Inc.	PO Box 3053	Blue Bell	PA	19422	Jeffrey A. Graves	215-619-2700	P	525	2.9
Overhead Door Corp.	2501 St. Hwy. 121	Lewisville	TX	75022	Howard Simons		R	508*	0.1
Camber Corp.	22289 Exploration	Lexington Park	MD	20653	Joseph Alexander	301-862-4577	R	447*	0.8
Rofin-Sinar Technologies Inc.	40984 Concept Dr.	Plymouth	MI	48170	Gunther Braun	734-455-5400	P	421	1.4
Link Simulation and Training	PO Box 5328	Arlington	TX	76005	John McNellis	817-619-3536	D	415*	0.8
Rofin-Sinar Inc.	40984 Concept Dr.	Plymouth	MI	48170	Gunther Braun	734-455-5400	S	375	1.4
Tatung Company of America Inc.	2850 El Presidio St	Long Beach	CA	90810	Andrew Sun	310-637-2105	S	355*	0.3
Electro Scientific Industries	13900 NW Sci Pk	Portland	OR	97229		503-641-4141	P	251	0.6
Lynch Systems Inc.	601 Independent St.	Bainbridge	GA	39817	Brian Fabacher	229-248-2345	S	235*	0.4
Preformed Line Products Co.	660 Beta Dr.	Cleveland	OH	44101	Robert Ruhlman	440-461-5200	P	217	1.5
FlightSafety International	Marine Air Terminal	Flushing	NY	11371	A.L. Ueltsbi	718-565-4100	D	200*	1.5
IPG Photonics Corp.	50 Old Webster Rd.	Oxford	MA	01540	V. P. Gapontsev	508-373-1100	P	189	1.3
Spectra-Physics Lasers Inc.	PO Box 7013	Mountain View	CA	94039	Bruce Craig	650-961-2550	S	175*	1.0
FlightSafety International	PO Box 12304	Wichita	KS	67209	Albert Ueltschi	316-220-3100	S	170*	1.2
Paige Electric Company L.P.	PO Box 368	Union	NJ	07083		908-687-7810	R	165*	<0.1
Excel Technology Inc.	41 Research Way	East Setauket	NY	11733	Antoine Dominic	631-784-6175	P	160	0.7
Techko Inc.	9767 Research Dr.	Irvine	CA	92618	Joseph Ko	949-486-0678	R	154*	1.0
QUANTUM Fuel Sys. Tech. WW	17872 Cartwright Rd	Irvine	CA	92614	Alan P. Niedzwiecki	949-399-4500	P	147	0.5
Micro Craft Inc.	41129 Jo Dr.	Novi	MI	48375	William Brown	248-476-6510	R	143*	<0.1
Spectrum Control Inc.	8031 Avonia Rd.	Fairview	PA	16415		814-474-2207	P	126	1.5
Zero Manufacturing Inc.	500 W 200 N	North Salt Lake	UT	84054	Stephen Henderson	801-298-5900	S	123*	0.3
Fisher Pierce	54 Commercial St.	Raynham	MA	02767	H. Lawerence Culp, Jr	508-821-1579	S	117*	0.2
Interpoint Corp.	PO Box 97005	Redmond	WA	98073	Doug Spittel	425-882-3100	S	105*	0.4
Piller Inc.	45 Turner Rd.	Middletown	NY	10941	Michael Barron	845-695-5300	R	105*	<0.1
Mining Controls Inc.	PO Box 1141	Beckley	WV	25802	Randall Hurst	304-252-6243	R	104*	0.6
MCG Inc.	1500 N Front St.	New Ulm	MN	56073	Francis Tedesco	507-233-7000	R	103*	<0.1
Erico Products Inc.	31700 Solon Rd.	Solon	OH	44139	William Roj	440-248-0100	S	100*	<0.1
Cubic Defense Systems Inc.	PO Box 85587	San Diego	CA	92186	Gerald Dinkel	858-277-6780	S	100*	0.9
Sypris Electronics L.L.C.	10901 N McKinley	Tampa	FL	33612	Bob Sanders	813-972-6000	S	100*	0.7
Curtis Instruments Inc.	200 Kisco Ave.	Mount Kisco	NY	10549		914-666-2971	R	100*	0.2
Tri-Star Electronics Int'l	2201 Rosecrans Ave.	El Segundo	CA	90245	Terry Jarnigan	310-536-0444	D	90*	0.3
Aubrey Silvey Enterprises Inc.	371 Hamp Jones Rd.	Carrollton	GA	30117	Tommy Muse	770-834-0738	R	89*	0.2
Acme Electric Corp.	4815 W 5th St.	Lumberton	NC	28358	Robert J. McKenna	910-738-4251	S	89*	0.7
Carlon Chimes Co.	25701 Science Park	Cleveland	OH	44122	M. J. Merriman, Jr.	216-464-3400	S	86*	0.2
Static Control Components Inc.	PO Box 152	Sanford	NC	27331		919-774-3808	R	82*	1.2
Firearms Training Systems Inc.	7340 McGinnis Fry	Suwanee	GA	30024	Ronovan R. Mohling	770-813-0180	S	79	0.4
Synrad Inc.	4600 Campus Pl.	Mukilteo	WA	98275	Dave Clarke	425-349-3500	S	76*	0.2
Carrier Access Corp.	5395 Pearl Pky	Boulder	CO	80301		303-442-5455	P	75	0.3
Sonatech Inc.	879 Ward Dr.	Santa Barbara	CA	93111	Robert Carlson	805-683-1431	S	73*	0.5
Evergreen Solar Inc.	138 Bartlett St.	Marlboro	MA	01752	Richard M. Feldt	508-357-2221	P	70	0.4
Biolase Technology Inc.	4 Cromwell	Irvine	CA	92618		949-361-1200	R	70	0.2
Sling Media Inc.	1051 E Hillsdale	Foster City	CA	94404	Blake Krikorian	650-293-8000	R	69*	0.1
Schumacher Electric Corp.	801 E Business Ctr.	Mount Prospect	IL	60056	Donald Schumacher	847-385-1600	R	69*	<0.1
Cain Electrical Supply Corp.	PO Box 2158	Big Spring	TX	79721	Tom R. Ross	432-263-8421	R	67*	0.3
Tollgrade Communications Inc.	493 Nixon Rd.	Cheswick	PA	15024	Daniel P. Barry	412-820-1400	P	67	0.3
International Laser Group Inc.	PO Box 686	Woodland Hills	CA	91365	Cindy Michaels	818-888-0400	R	65*	0.2
Tonoga Inc.	PO Box 69	Petersburg	NY	12138	Andrew Russell	518-658-3202	R	62*	0.2
PI Manufacturing Corp.	20732 Currier Rd.	Walnut	CA	91789	Bill Chang	909-598-3718	R	61*	<0.1
Austin International Inc.	7 Ross Cannon St.	York	SC	29745	Randy Austin	803-628-0035	R	61*	0.1
Nuvera Fuel Cells Inc.	20 Acorn Park	Cambridge	MA	02140	Roberto Cordaro	617-245-7500	R	60*	0.1

Source: Ward's Business Directory of U.S. Private and Public Companies, Volumes 1 and 2, 2008. The company type code used is as follows: P - Public, R - Private, S - Subsidiary, D - Division, J - Joint Venture, A - Affiliate, G - Group. Sales are in millions of dollars, employees are in thousands. An asterisk (*) indicates an estimated sales volume. The symbol < stands for 'less than'. Company names and addresses are truncated, in some cases, to fit into the available space.

MATERIALS CONSUMED

Material	Quantity	Delivered Cost ($ million)
Metal bolts, nuts, screws, and other screw machine products	(X)	15.5
Forgings	(X)	1.0
Castings, rough and semifinished	(X)	5.5
Steel shapes and forms (exc. castings, forgings, fabr. metal products)	(X)	16.1
Copper and copper-base alloy shapes and forms (exc. castings, forgings, fabr. metal products)	(X)	7.3
Aluminum and aluminum-base alloy shapes and forms (exc. castings, forgings, fabr. metal products)	(X)	33.8
Other nonferrous shapes and forms (exc. castings, forgings, fabricated metal products)	(X)	10.7
Metal stampings	(X)	36.7
Sheet metal products (excluding stampings)	(X)	36.5
Other fabricated metal products (excluding forgings)	(X)	59.2
Fabricated plastics products (exc. gaskets, hoses, and belting)	(X)	16.7
Capacitors for electronic circuitry	(X)	29.2
Resistors for electronic circuitry	(X)	13.0
Printed ciruit boards (without inserted components) for electronic circuitry	(X)	31.5
Printed circuit assemblies, loaded boards, and modules	(X)	132.5
Semiconductors (incl. transistors, diodes, rectifiers, and integrated circuits), for electronic circuitry	(X)	48.8
All other miscellaneous components and accessories for electronic circuitry (exc. tubes)	(X)	124.3
Insulated wire and cable (including magnet wire)	(X)	49.0
Industrial electrical control equipment	(X)	51.1
Current-carrying wiring devices	(X)	47.5
Fractional horsepower electric motors (less than 1 hp)	(X)	(D)
Electronic communication equipment	(X)	(D)
Electrical instrument mechanisms and meter movements	(X)	11.2
Optical instruments and lenses (exc. sighting, tracking, and fire control)	(X)	33.9
Paper and paperboard containers (incl. shipping sacks and other paper packaging supplies)	(X)	13.8
All other materials, components, parts, containers, and supplies	(X)	958.7
Materials, ingredients, containers, and supplies, nsk	(X)	688.4

Source: 2002 *Economic Census*. Explanation of symbols used: (D): Withheld to avoid disclosure of competitive data; na: Not available; (S): Withheld because statistical norms were not met; (X): Not applicable; (Z): Less than half the unit shown; nec: Not elsewhere classified; nsk: Not specified by kind; - : zero; p : 10-19 percent estimated; q : 20-29 percent estimated.

PRODUCT SHARE DETAILS

Product or Product Class Shipments	Mil. $	Product or Product Class Shipments	Mil. $
ELECTRICAL EQUIPMENT AND COMPONENTS, NEC	7,276.2	Other rectifying (power conversion) apparatus, except for electronic circuitry	419.4
Capacitors for industrial use (except for electronic circuitry)	**147.6**	Rectifying apparatus, nsk	12.3
Capacitors for industrial use (except for electronic circuitry)	146.4	**Other electrical equipment for industrial use, except for electronic circuitry**	**473.5**
Shunt and series power capacitors, units, and equipment, one-half kVA or more, and accessories for industrial use (except for electronic circuitry)	99.7	Electrical coil windings for industrial use	50.9
		Surge suppressors for industrial use	61.5
Other capacitors (except electrolytic) including AC, general-purpose motors and controls, and high intensity discharge lighting for industrial use (except for electronic circuitry)	46.7	Cathodic protection equipment for industrial use	79.2
		All other electrical equipment for industrial use, nec, including electrical discharge equipment	281.9
Capacitors for industrial use (except for electronic circuitry), nsk	1.2	**Laser generator power supplies and components**	**903.8**
Rectifying apparatus	**2,030.0**	**All other laser systems and equipment**	**176.1**
Semiconductor power conversion apparatus, except for electronic circuitry	618.9	**Ultrasonic equipment (except medical and dental)**	**224.8**
Semiconductor battery chargers, automotive	208.5	**All other apparatus wire and cordage manufactured from purchased insulated wire (except wiring harnesses and fiber optic)**	**93.1**
Semiconductor battery chargers, industrial and railroad	122.6	**All other electrical equipment and components, nec, except for industrial use**	**218.6**
Semiconductor high-voltage power supplies in excess of 2 kV, 100 kW or less	269.6	Electric gongs, chimes, bells, etc.	(D)
Semiconductor high-voltage power supplies in excess of 2 kV, more than 100 kW	18.2	Electrical door openers, except garage door openers	(D)
		Surge suppressors designed for equipment operating on 110-120 volt circuits	86.4
All other AC to DC semiconductor power conversion and rectifying apparatus, except for electronic circuitry	1,398.8	All other electrical equipment and components, nec, except for industrial use, nsk	1.0
All other AC to DC semiconductor power conversion apparatus	337.4	**All other miscellaneous electronic systems and equipment, including automatic garage door openers and amplifiers**	**1,613.6**
Uninterruptible power supply (UPS) systems	642.0	**Electrical equipment and components, nec, nsk, total**	**1,395.1**

Source: 2002 *Economic Census*. The values are product shipments in millions of dollars for 2002. Total product shipments may be lower or higher than industry shipments. See Introduction for a full discussion. Values of indented subcategories are summed in the main heading(s). The symbol (D) appears when data are withheld to prevent disclosure of competitive information. The abbreviation nsk stands for 'not specified by kind' and nec for 'not elsewhere classified'. A dash (-) means zero.

INPUTS AND OUTPUTS FOR ALL OTHER ELECTRICAL EQUIPMENT & COMPONENTS

Economic Sector or Industry Providing Inputs	%	Sector	Economic Sector or Industry Buying Outputs	%	Sector
Compensation of employees	30.5		Private fixed investment	45.8	
Management of companies & enterprises	7.2	Services	Exports of goods & services	26.9	Cap Inv
Wholesale trade	5.5	Trade	Personal consumption expenditures	7.1	
Electrical equipment & components, nec	4.6	Manufg.	Electrical equipment & components, nec	3.1	Manufg.
Printed circuit assemblies (electronic assemblies)	3.3	Manufg.	Federal government, investment, national defense	3.0	Fed Govt
Electronic components, nec	2.4	Manufg.	Electromedical & electrotherapeutic apparatus	1.2	Manufg.
Electronic connectors	1.7	Manufg.	Rail transportation	1.1	Util.
Noncomparable imports	1.5	Foreign	Other S/L govt. enterprises	1.0	S/L Govt
Lessors of nonfinancial assets	1.5	Fin/R.E.	General Federal government services, nondefense	1.0	Fed Govt
Electronic capacitors, resistors, coils, transformers	1.4	Manufg.	Retail trade	0.9	Trade
Turned products & screws, nuts, & bolts	1.3	Manufg.	Automotive repair & maintenance, ex. car washes	0.8	Services
Advertising & related services	1.3	Services	Electronic computers	0.7	Manufg.
Relay & industrial controls	1.3	Manufg.	Residential structures, nec	0.6	Construct.
Wiring devices	1.0	Manufg.	S/L govt. invest., education	0.6	S/L Govt
Crowns & closures & metal stamping	1.0	Manufg.	Search, detection, & navigation instruments	0.6	Manufg.
Semiconductors & related devices	1.0	Manufg.	Power, distribution, & specialty transformers	0.5	Manufg.
Real estate	1.0	Fin/R.E.	Commercial & health care structures	0.4	Construct.
Securities, commodity contracts, investments	0.9	Fin/R.E.	Wholesale trade	0.4	Trade
Legal services	0.8	Services	Motors & generators	0.4	Manufg.
Architectural, engineering, & related services	0.8	Services	S/L govt. invest., other	0.4	S/L Govt
Copper rolling, drawing, extruding, & alloying	0.8	Manufg.	Commercial & service industry machinery, nec	0.3	Manufg.
Alumina refining & primary aluminum production	0.8	Manufg.	General Federal government services, defense	0.3	Fed Govt
Ornamental & architectural metal products	0.7	Manufg.	Residential permanent site structures	0.3	Construct.
Specialized design services	0.7	Services	Computer terminals & peripherals	0.2	Manufg.
Bare printed circuit boards	0.7	Manufg.	General purpose machinery, nec	0.2	Manufg.
Employment services	0.6	Services	Computer storage devices	0.2	Manufg.
Gold, silver, & other metal ore	0.6	Mining	Electronic & precision equipment repair/maintenance	0.2	Services
Machine shops	0.6	Manufg.	Semiconductors & related devices	0.2	Manufg.
Management, scientific, & technical consulting	0.6	Services	Scientific research & development services	0.2	Services
Monetary authorities/depository credit intermediation	0.6	Fin/R.E.	Motor vehicle parts	0.1	Manufg.
Power generation & supply	0.5	Util.	Telecommunications	0.1	Services
Business support services	0.5	Services	Nonresidential structures, nec	0.1	Construct.
Scientific research & development services	0.5	Services	Federal government, investment, nondefense	0.1	Fed Govt
Professional, scientific, technical services, nec	0.5	Services			
Telecommunications	0.5	Services			
Taxes on production & imports, less subsidies	0.4				
Communication & energy wires & cables	0.4	Manufg.			
Plastics products, nec	0.4	Manufg.			
Accounting, tax preparation, bookkeeping, & payroll	0.4	Services			
Data processing, hosting, & related services	0.4	Services			
Support services, nec	0.4	Services			
Optical instruments & lenses	0.4	Manufg.			
Truck transportation	0.4	Util.			
Automotive equipment rental & leasing	0.4	Fin/R.E.			
Coating, engraving, heat treating & allied activities	0.4	Manufg.			
Electron tubes	0.3	Manufg.			
Iron & steel mills & ferroalloys	0.3	Manufg.			
Warehousing & storage	0.3	Util.			
Paperboard containers	0.3	Manufg.			
Food services & drinking places	0.3	Services			
Investigation & security services	0.3	Services			
Plastics packaging materials, film & sheet	0.3	Manufg.			
Motors & generators	0.2	Manufg.			
Cutting tools & machine tool accessories	0.2	Manufg.			
Electricity & signal testing instruments	0.2	Manufg.			
Nonferrous metal (ex. copper & aluminum) processing	0.2	Manufg.			
Metal cans, boxes, & other containers (light gauge)	0.2	Manufg.			
Commercial & industrial machinery rental & leasing	0.2	Fin/R.E.			
Chemical products & preparations, nec	0.2	Manufg.			
Hotels & motels, including casino hotels	0.2	Services			
Postal service	0.2	Util.			
Services to buildings & dwellings	0.2	Services			
Other computer related services, including facilities	0.1	Services			
Fabricated metals, nec	0.1	Manufg.			
Maintenance/repair of nonresidential structures	0.1	Construct.			
Retail trade	0.1	Trade			
Air transportation	0.1	Util.			
Environmental & other technical consulting services	0.1	Services			
Paperboard mills	0.1	Manufg.			
Facilities support services	0.1	Services			
Nondepository credit intermediation activities	0.1	Fin/R.E.			

Source: Benchmark Input-Output Accounts for the U.S. Economy, 2002, U.S. Department of Commerce, Washington, D.C., January 2008. The abbreviation nec stands for 'not elsewhere classified'.

OCCUPATIONS EMPLOYED BY OTHER ELECTRICAL EQUIPMENT & COMPONENT MANUFACTURING

Occupation	% of Total 2006	Change to 2016	Occupation	% of Total 2006	Change to 2016
Team assemblers	14.6	-7.3	Customer service representatives	1.4	1.9
Electrical & electronic equipment assemblers	9.0	-25.9	Electrical engineers	1.2	-7.3
Extruding & drawing machine operators & tenders	3.8	-7.3	Sales reps, wholesale & manufacturing, exc tech	1.2	-7.3
First-line supervisors/managers of production workers	3.7	-7.3	Plating & coating machine operators & tenders	1.2	-3.3
Inspectors, testers, sorters, samplers, & weighers	3.3	-12.6	Tool & die makers	1.1	-2.7
Cutting, punching, & press machine operators	2.8	-16.6	Mechanical engineers	1.1	-7.3
Shipping, receiving, & traffic clerks	2.4	-10.8	Multiple machine tool operators & tenders	1.1	1.9
Maintenance & repair workers, general	2.4	-7.3	Sales representatives, wholesale & manufacturing, tech	1.1	-7.3
Molding, coremaking, & casting machine operators	2.4	-16.6	Packers & packagers, hand	1.1	-25.9
Machinists	2.2	-2.7	Office clerks, general	1.0	-8.7
Helpers--Production workers	2.0	-7.3	Industrial production managers	1.0	-7.3
Laborers & freight, stock, & material movers, hand	1.9	-16.6	Packaging & filling machine operators & tenders	1.0	-16.6
Industrial truck & tractor operators	1.6	-16.6	Electromechanical equipment assemblers	1.0	-7.3
Industrial engineers	1.4	12.5	Computer-controlled machine tool operators	1.0	1.9
General & operations managers	1.4	-16.6	Bookkeeping, accounting, & auditing clerks	1.0	-7.3

Source: *Industry-Occupation Matrix*, Bureau of Labor Statistics, December 4, 2007. These data are reported based on 4-digit NAICS categories but have been matched to corresponding 6-digit NAICS industry codes. The change reported for each occupation to the year 2016 is a percent of growth or decline as estimated by the Bureau of Labor Statistics. The abbreviation nec stands for 'not elsewhere classified'.

LOCATION BY STATE AND REGIONAL CONCENTRATION

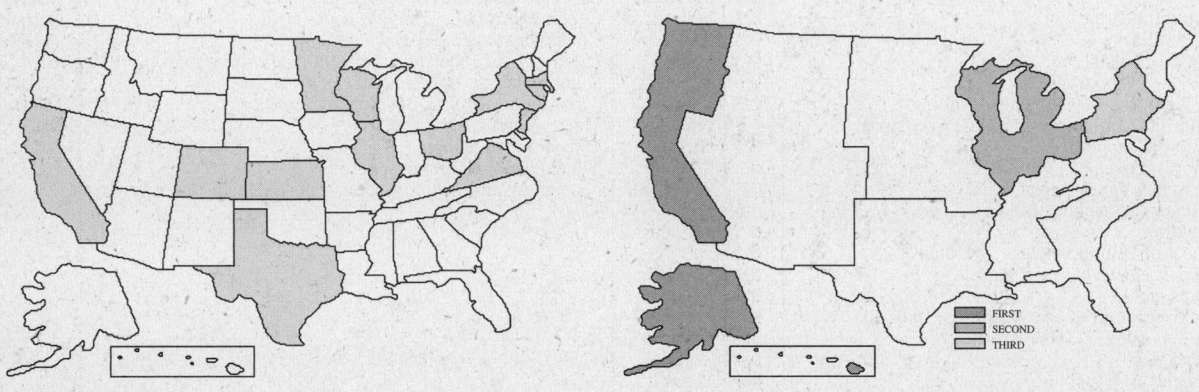

FIRST
SECOND
THIRD

INDUSTRY DATA BY STATE

State	Establish-ments	Shipments			Employment				Cost as % of Shipments	Investment per Employee ($)
		Total ($ mil)	% of U.S.	Per Establ.	Total Number	% of U.S.	Per Establ.	Wages ($/hour)		
California	184	1,809.1	25.6	9,831.9	9,941	24.1	54	14.20	38.4	14,378
New York	49	462.6	6.6	9,441.3	2,380	5.8	49	17.12	39.4	2,887
Illinois	71	400.2	5.7	5,637.3	2,376	5.8	33	12.73	51.7	2,569
Ohio	41	366.8	5.2	8,946.2	1,830	4.4	45	13.92	24.0	4,720
Connecticut	30	365.7	5.2	12,188.4	2,503	6.1	83	16.41	32.2	3,306
Massachusetts	46	321.8	4.6	6,996.0	2,648	6.4	58	17.69	49.0	6,017
Minnesota	27	285.6	4.0	10,576.0	1,456	3.5	54	12.21	59.9	9,230
Texas	61	222.0	3.1	3,639.8	1,265	3.1	21	14.69	43.8	2,553
Wisconsin	29	204.0	2.9	7,033.8	1,072	2.6	37	12.56	49.5	2,936
New Jersey	44	167.3	2.4	3,803.1	1,538	3.7	35	15.38	36.4	1,684
Virginia	12	140.9	2.0	11,742.8	837	2.0	70	12.72	33.7	2,679
Kansas	10	50.3	0.7	5,027.0	248	0.6	25	10.01	33.7	2,827
Colorado	20	39.4	0.6	1,969.6	307	0.7	15	13.48	49.1	5,524

Source: 2002 *Economic Census*. The states are in descending order of shipments or establishments (if shipment data are missing for the majority). The symbol (D) appears when data are withheld to prevent disclosure of competitive information. States marked with (D) are sorted by number of establishments. A dash (-) indicates that the data element cannot be calculated. Data may not show all states active in the NAICS category. All data available at the time of publication are shown.

NAICS 336111 - AUTOMOBILE MANUFACTURING

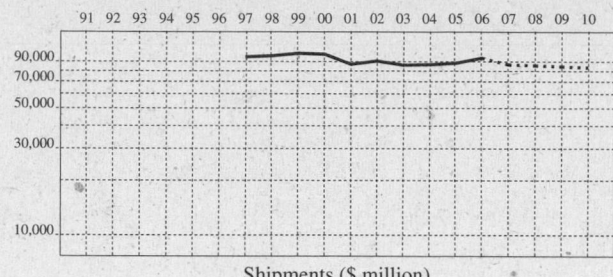

Shipments ($ million)

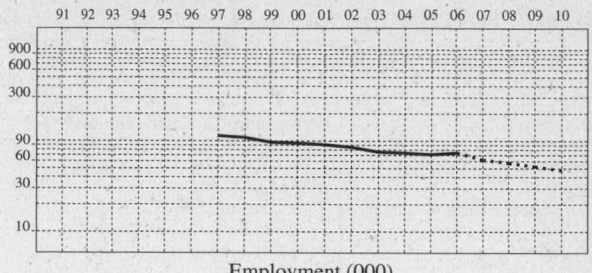

Employment (000)

GENERAL STATISTICS

Year	Companies	Establishments		Employment			Compensation		Production ($ million)			
		Total	with 20 or more employees	Total (000)	Production Workers (000)	Hours (Mil)	Payroll ($ mil)	Wages ($/hr)	Cost of Materials	Value Added by Manufacture	Value of Shipments	Capital Invest.
1997	174	194	72	114.1	98.0	197.6	6,412.0	26.30	66,546.2	28,954.6	95,385.6	3,506.8
1998		216	86	109.2	92.5	180.1	6,054.3	26.80	69,454.3	27,124.9	96,707.9	3,173.6
1999		218	76	96.7	84.1	170.9	5,861.2	28.87	69,514.4	30,302.7	99,802.5	1,760.0
2000		217	77	94.7	82.2	168.4	6,013.1	30.07	69,748.7	29,035.2	98,760.0	1,984.0
2001	161	221	74	91.1	78.6	159.6	5,387.8	27.85	61,248.3	25,773.4	87,046.3	2,261.3
2002		176	52	85.8	75.1	143.1	5,495.2	33.15	61,556.2	29,200.0	90,713.3	2,091.3
2003		172	52	76.0	65.7	126.1	5,224.1	34.99	63,960.4	22,305.2	86,218.5	2,114.7
2004		183	60	74.3	64.1	120.3	5,305.3	37.21	63,802.9	23,149.1	86,818.4	2,391.5
2005		180	68	71.5	60.8	124.4	5,353.2	36.19	63,817.2	24,518.0	88,366.0	2,542.0
2006		173P	55P	74.3	64.0	126.3	5,352.1	35.91	68,898.0	25,261.8	94,229.4	1,794.4
2007		169P	52P	62.3P	53.8P	104.1P	4,996.3P	38.87P	63,477.2P	23,274.2P	86,815.6P	1,813.5P
2008		164P	49P	57.4P	49.7P	95.4P	4,878.2P	40.16P	62,734.2P	23,001.8P	85,799.3P	1,713.8P
2009		159P	46P	52.6P	45.6P	86.8P	4,760.1P	41.46P	61,991.1P	22,729.4P	84,783.1P	1,614.1P
2010		154P	43P	47.8P	41.4P	78.1P	4,642.0P	42.76P	61,248.1P	22,456.9P	83,766.9P	1,514.4P

Sources: 1997 and 2002 *Economic Census*; other years, up to 2006, are from *Annual Survey of Manufactures*. Establishment counts for non-Census years are from *County Business Patterns*; 1997 and 2002 values are from the 1997 and 2002 censuses, respectively. 'P's show projections by the editors.

INDICES OF CHANGE

Year	Companies	Establishments		Employment			Compensation		Production ($ million)			
		Total	with 20 or more employees	Total (000)	Production Workers (000)	Hours (Mil)	Payroll ($ mil)	Wages ($/hr)	Cost of Materials	Value Added by Manufacture	Value of Shipments	Capital Invest.
1997	108	110	138	133	130	138	117	79	108	99	105	168
1998		123	165	127	123	126	110	81	113	93	107	152
1999		124	146	113	112	119	107	87	113	104	110	84
2000		123	148	110	109	118	109	91	113	99	109	95
2001		126	142	106	105	112	98	84	99	88	96	108
2002	100	100	100	100	100	100	100	100	100	100	100	100
2003		98	100	89	87	88	95	106	104	76	95	101
2004		104	115	87	85	84	97	112	104	79	96	114
2005		102	131	83	81	87	97	109	104	84	97	122
2006		99P	105P	87	85	88	97	108	112	87	104	86
2007		96P	100P	73P	72P	73P	91P	117P	103P	80P	96P	87P
2008		93P	94P	67P	66P	67P	89P	121P	102P	79P	95P	82P
2009		90P	89P	61P	61P	61P	87P	125P	101P	78P	93P	77P
2010		88P	84P	56P	55P	55P	84P	129P	99P	77P	92P	72P

Sources: Same as General Statistics. Values reflect change from the base year, 2002. Values above 100 mean greater than 2002, values below 100 mean less than 2002, and the values of 100 in other years means the same as 2002. 'P's show projections by the editors.

SELECTED RATIOS

For 2002	Avg. of All Manufact.	Analyzed Industry	Index	For 2002	Avg. of All Manufact.	Analyzed Industry	Index
Employees per Establishment	42	488	1,161	Value Added per Production Worker	182,367	388,815	213
Payroll per Establishment	1,639,184	31,222,727	1,905	Cost per Establishment	5,769,015	349,751,136	6,063
Payroll per Employee	39,053	64,047	164	Cost per Employee	137,446	717,438	522
Production Workers per Establishment	30	427	1,446	Cost per Production Worker	195,506	819,656	419
Wages per Establishment	694,845	26,953,210	3,879	Shipments per Establishment	11,158,348	515,416,477	4,619
Wages per Production Worker	23,548	63,166	268	Shipments per Employee	265,847	1,057,265	398
Hours per Production Worker	1,980	1,905	96	Shipments per Production Worker	378,144	1,207,900	319
Wages per Hour	11.89	33.15	279	Investment per Establishment	361,338	11,882,386	3,288
Value Added per Establishment	5,381,325	165,909,091	3,083	Investment per Employee	8,609	24,374	283
Value Added per Employee	128,210	340,326	265	Investment per Production Worker	12,245	27,847	227

Sources: Same as General Statistics. The 'Average of All Manufacturing' column represents the average of all manufacturing industries reported for the most recent complete year available. The Index shows the relationship between the Average and the Analyzed Industry. For example, 100 means that they are equal; 500 that the Analyzed Industry is five times the average; 50 means that the Analyzed Industry is half the national average. The abbreviation 'na' is used to show that data are 'not available'. Ratios shown for 2002, the last complete census year.

LEADING COMPANIES   Number shown: 75   Total sales ($ mil): 607,362   Total employment (000): 1,074.8

Company Name	Address				CEO Name	Phone	Co. Type	Sales ($ mil)	Empl. (000)
General Motors Corp.	300 Renaissance Ctr	Detroit	MI	48265		313-556-5000	P	181,122	266.0
Ford Motor Co.	1 American Rd.	Dearborn	MI	48126		313-322-3000	P	172,455	246.0
United Technologies Corp.	1 Financial Plz.	Hartford	CT	06101	Mario Abajo	860-728-7000	P	47,829	225.6
Chrysler L.L.C.	1000 Chrysler Dr.	Auburn Hills	MI	48326	Thomas W. LaSorda	248-576-5741	S	45,237*	84.4
American Honda Motor Company	1919 Torrance Blvd.	Torrance	CA	90501	Koichi Kondo	310-783-2000	S	42,539	25.0
PACCAR Inc.	PO Box 1518	Bellevue	WA	98009		425-468-7400	P	15,220	21.8
Ford VAC Corp.	1 American Rd.	Dearborn	MI	48121	William J. Ford	313-322-3000	S	15,105*	1.9
Dana Corp.	PO Box 1000	Toledo	OH	43697	Michael J. Burns	419-535-4500	P	8,504	45.0
Triangle Suspension Systems	PO Box 425	Du Bois	PA	15801	Greg Maffia	814-375-7211	R	7,000*	0.2
Oshkosh Truck Corp.	PO Box 2566	Oshkosh	WI	54903	Robert G. Bohn	920-235-9150	P	6,307	14.2
Toyota Motor Mfg. N America	25 Atlantic Ave.	Erlanger	KY	41018	Masamoto Amezawa	859-746-4000	S	6,120*	7.5
Honda of America Manufacturing	24000 Honda Pkwy.	Marysville	OH	43040	Takeo Fukui	937-642-5000	S	5,090*	13.0
Mack Trucks Inc.	PO Box M	Allentown	PA	18105		610-709-3011	R	4,324*	0.8
Toyota Motor Mfg, Kentucky	PO Box 2700	Georgetown	KY	40324	Steven Angelo	502-868-2000	R	4,181*	5.0
New United Motor Manufacturing	45500 Fremont	Fremont	CA	94538	Bruce Walker	510-498-5500	J	4,080*	5.0
Saturn Corp.	PO Box 1502	Spring Hill	TN	37174		931-486-5000	S	3,901	9.6
Motors Insurance Corp.	PO Box 66937	St. Louis	MO	63166	Gary Kuzumi		S	3,849*	2.2
Thor Industries Inc.	PO Box 629	Jackson Center	OH	45334		937-596-6849	P	3,066	9.1
AutoAlliance International	1 International Dr.	Flat Rock	MI	48134	Phillip G. Spender	734-782-7800	J	3,019*	3.7
Freightliner L.L.C.	PO Box 3849	Portland	OR	97208	Chris Patterson	503-745-8000	S	2,734*	14.0
BMW of North America L.L.C.	PO Box 1227	Westwood	NJ	07675	Thomas Purves	201-307-4000	S	2,690*	1.0
Nissan North America Inc.	333 Commerce St.	Nashville	TN	37201	Carlos Ghosn	615-725-1000	S	2,148	14.0
Renco Group Inc.	30 Rockefeller Plz.	New York	NY	10112	Ira Leno Rennert	212-541-6000	R	1,900	9.4
Thor America Inc.	37 Old 522	Middleburg	PA	17842	W. F. B. Thompson	570-837-1663	S	1,592*	8.5
Aero Coach Inc.	Hickory Hill Rd.	Longview	TX	75601	W. F. B. Thompson	903-663-7699	S	1,313*	7.5
Monaco Coach Corp.	91320 Coburg Indust	Coburg	OR	97408		541-686-8011	P	1,298	5.3
Federal Signal Corp.	1415 W 22nd St.	Oak Brook	IL	60523	James C. Janning	630-954-2000	P	1,268	5.5
Mitsubishi Motors N America	PO Box 6014	Cypress	CA	90630	Hiroshi Harunari	714-372-6000	S	1,198	3.6
International Truck and Engine	PO Box 1488	Warrenville	IL	60555	Daniel C. Ustian	630-753-5000	S	1,114*	1.7
Spartan Motors Chassis Inc.	1165 Reynolds Rd.	Charlotte	MI	48813	John Sztykiel	517-543-6400	S	1,030*	0.8
Toyota Motor Mfg. W Virginia	1 Sugar Maple Ln.	Buffalo	WV	25033	Laquita Harris	304-937-7000	S	901*	0.9
North American Bus Industries	106 National Dr.	Anniston	AL	36207		256-831-4296	R	886*	0.6
Utilimaster Corp.	PO Box 585	Wakarusa	IN	46573	Lawrence Doyle	574-862-4561	R	836*	1.0
Spartan Motors Inc.	PO Box 440	Charlotte	MI	48813		517-543-6400	P	682	1.4
Airstream Inc.	PO Box 629	Jackson Center	OH	45334	Bpob Wheeler	937-596-6111	S	622*	0.5
Purdy Motor S.A.	CC Aventura 100	San Jose	PR	00930	John Kilmer	506-287-4230	S	509*	0.4
Coachmen Industries Inc.	PO Box 3300	Elkhart	IN	46515	Richard M. Lavers	574-262-0123	P	481	2.7
Ford of North Miami Beach	2198 NE 163rd St.	N Miami Bch	FL	33162		305-493-5000	R	447*	0.3
Reinke Manufacturing Company	PO Box 566	Deshler	NE	68340	Chris Roth	402-365-7251	R	335*	0.4
Wheeled Coach Industries Corp.	2737 Forsyth Rd.	Winter Park	FL	32792	Robert Collins	407-677-7777	S	326*	0.4
Jefferson Industries Corp.	6670 State Rte.	West Jefferson	OH	43162	Hideo Hayashi	614-879-5300	R	309*	0.4
ASC Inc.	1 ASC Ctr.	Southgate	MI	48195	Paul Wilbur	734-285-4911	R	300*	1.0
Elgin Sweeper Co.	1300 W Bartlett Rd.	Elgin	IL	60120	Mark Weber	847-741-5370	S	286*	0.3
SanduskyAthol International	3130 W Monroe St.	Sandusky	OH	44870	Jack Givens	419-627-3200	R	266*	0.2
Allianz Sweeper Co.	4651 Schaefer Ave.	Chino	CA	91710	Gabriel Charky	909-613-5600	R	233*	0.1
Braun Industries Inc.	1170 Production Dr.	Van Wert	OH	45891	Phillip Braun	419-232-7020	R	223*	0.2
Collins Industries Inc.	PO Box 648	Hutchinson	KS	67502	Don L. Collins	620-663-5551	S	208	1.0
Cheetah Chassis Corp.	PO Box 388	Berwick	PA	18603	Frank Katz	570-752-2708	R	167*	0.2
Ferrara Fire Apparatus Inc.	PO Box 249	Holden	LA	70744	Christopher Ferrara	225-567-7100	R	159*	0.3
Midwest Stamping Inc.	3455 Briarfield	Maumee	OH	43537	Ronald L. Thompson	419-724-6970	R	155*	0.6
VSV Group	1110 DI Dr.	Elkhart	IN	46514	Mark Grossbauer	574-264-7511	R	148*	0.5
Smeal Fire Apparatus Co.	PO Box 8	Snyder	NE	68664	Delwin Smeal	402-568-2224	R	139*	0.3
Freightliner Specialty Vehicle	2300 S 13th St.	Clinton	OK	73601	Tim Sinor	580-323-4100	R	123*	0.2
Schwarze Industries Inc.	1055 Jordan Rd.	Huntsville	AL	35811	Ronald A. Robinson	256-851-1200	S	122*	0.2
Excellance Inc.	453 Lanier Rd.	Madison	AL	35758	Charles Epps	256-772-9321	R	112*	<0.1
Executive Coach Builders Inc.	4400 W Production	Springfield	MO	65803	David Bakare	417-935-2233	R	104*	<0.1
Louis Berkman Company Inc.	PO Box 820	Steubenville	OH	43952	Louis Berkman	740-283-3722	R	82*	<0.1
Alfa Leisure Inc.	1612 S Cucamonga	Ontario	CA	91761	Johnnie R. Crean	909-628-5574	R	75*	0.7
FWD Seagrave Holdings L.P.	105 E 12th St.	Clintonville	WI	54929		715-823-2141	R	72*	0.4
Custom Coach International	PO Box 869	Pawhuska	OK	74056	Ray Smith	918-287-4445	R	71*	<0.1
Temic Automotive of N America	21440 Lake Cook	Barrington	IL	60010		847-862-6300	R	71*	0.4
Sutphen Corp.	PO Box 158	Amlin	OH	43002		614-889-1005	R	71*	<0.1
Foretravel Inc.	1221 NW Stallings	Nacogdoches	TX	75964		936-564-8367	R	68*	0.3
Accubuilt Inc.	4707 E Kearney St.	Springfield	MO	65803	Dan Mitchell	417-864-4411	R	67*	<0.1
Amerigon Inc.	21680 Haggerty Rd.	Northville	MI	48167	Daniel R. Coker	248-504-0500	P	64	<0.1
Alpine Armoring Inc.	570 Herndon Pkwy.	Herndon	VA	20170	Fred Khoroushi	703-471-0009	R	56*	<0.1
Super Products Corp.	PO Box 270128	Milwaukee	WI	53227	Henry Rowan	262-784-7100	R	51*	0.1
Super Vacuum Manufacturing Co.	PO Box 87	Loveland	CO	80539	Roger Weinmeister	970-667-5146	R	51*	0.1
E-ONE	1601 SW 37 Ave.	Ocala	FL	34474	Mark Gastafin	352-237-1122	D	44*	0.3
Arotech Corp.	1229 Oak Valley Dr.	Ann Arbor	MI	48108	Robert S. Ehrlich		P	43	0.3
Schwartz Industries Inc.	1055 Jordan Rd.	Huntsville	AL	35811	Jim Morris	256-851-1200	R	40*	0.2
AGM Automotive Inc.	1000 E Whitcomb	Madison Heights	MI	48071		248-776-0600	R	33*	<0.1
Pemberton Fabricators Inc.	PO Box 227	Rancocas	NJ	08073	Robert Murnan	609-267-0922	R	32*	<0.1
Phoenix U S A Inc.	PO Box 40	Cookeville	TN	38503	James Wright	931-526-6128	R	30*	<0.1
Special Projects Inc.	45901 Helm St.	Plymouth	MI	48170	Kenneth Yanez	734-455-7130	R	29*	<0.1

Source: *Ward's Business Directory of U.S. Private and Public Companies*, Volumes 1 and 2, 2008. The company type code used is as follows: P - Public, R - Private, S - Subsidiary, D - Division, J - Joint Venture, A - Affiliate, G - Group. Sales are in millions of dollars, employees are in thousands. An asterisk (*) indicates an estimated sales volume. The symbol < stands for 'less than'. Company names and addresses are truncated, in some cases, to fit into the available space.

MATERIALS CONSUMED

Material	Quantity	Delivered Cost ($ million)
Gasoline engines and parts specially designed for gasoline engines	(X)	9,919.8
Diesel engines and parts specially designed for diesel engines	(X)	(D)
Drive train components and parts	(X)	6,020.7
Car bodies	(X)	1,118.3
Refrigeration compressors, compressor units, condensing units, and other heat transfer equipment	(X)	1,499.4
Shocks, struts, and other suspension equipment and parts	(X)	3,456.6
Exhaust systems and parts	(X)	1,843.6
Machine tool accessories, including cutting tools	(X)	16.2
Fluid power pumps, motors, and hydrostatic transmissions	(X)	459.9
Fluid power valves (hydraulic and pneumatic)	(X)	53.5
Fluid power cylinders and rotary actuators (hydraulic and pneumatic)	(X)	130.9
Fluid power hose, tube fittings, and assemblies (hydraulic and pneumatic)	(X)	153.3
Fluid power filters (hydraulic and pneumatic)	(X)	20.9
Other transportation related fluid power products, hydraulic and pneumatic	(X)	(D)
Automotive stampings (inc. body parts, hubcaps, fenders, etc.)	(X)	4,168.7
Steel springs (excluding wire)	(X)	58.2
Motor vehicle metal hardware (lock units, etc.), exc. forgings	(X)	473.2
Metal bolts, nuts, screws, and other screw machine products	(X)	674.0
Other fabricated metal products (excluding forgings)	(X)	746.8
Forgings	(X)	(D)
Castings, rough and semifinished	(X)	(D)
Metal shapes and forms (exc. castings, forgings, fabr. metal products)	(X)	(D)
Ball and roller bearings (mounted or unmounted)	(X)	59.7
Pneumatic tires and inner tubes	(X)	920.7
Rubber and plastics hose and belting	(X)	158.4
Fabricated rubber products (exc. tires, tubes, hoses, belting, and gaskets)	(X)	152.7
Gaskets (all types), and packing and sealing devices	(X)	232.7
Fabricated plastics products (exc. gaskets, hoses, and belting)	(X)	806.1
Glass and glass products (including windows and mirrors)	(X)	1,698.9
Seats (purchased separately) for automobiles, trucks, and buses	(X)	2,566.8
Seat covers, seat belts, and shoulder harnesses	(X)	416.8
Automotive air bag assemblies and parts	(X)	733.8
Automotive trimmings, textile (panels, headliners, etc.)	(X)	3,773.4
Carpeting	(X)	369.6
Ceramic and ceramic composite parts, components, and accessories	(X)	(D)
Glues and adhesives	(X)	16.3
Paints, varnishes, stains, lacquers, shellacs, japans, enamels, etc.	(X)	321.6
Engine electrical equipment (incl. spark plugs, magnetos, generators, starters, etc.)	(X)	520.2
Motor vehicle lighting fixtures, excluding auto lamps	(X)	525.0
Automotive lamps (bulbs and sealed beams)	(X)	162.0
Storage batteries, automotive	(X)	96.0
Automotive radios and loudspeakers	(X)	1,104.4
Motor vehicle clusters, meters, and gauges, excluding electrical	(X)	645.4
Semiconductors and related devices and electronic control modules	(X)	1,209.9
Purchased computers for incorporation into motor vehicles, trucks, and buses	(X)	193.3
All other materials, components, parts, containers, and supplies	(X)	9,769.1
Materials, ingredients, containers, and supplies, nsk	(X)	2,166.7

Source: 2002 *Economic Census*. Explanation of symbols used: (D): Withheld to avoid disclosure of competitive data; na: Not available; (S): Withheld because statistical norms were not met; (X): Not applicable; (Z): Less than half the unit shown; nec: Not elsewhere classified; nsk: Not specified by kind; - : zero; p : 10-19 percent estimated; q : 20-29 percent estimated.

PRODUCT SHARE DETAILS

Product or Product Class Shipments	Mil. $	Product or Product Class Shipments	Mil. $
AUTOMOBILES	85,841.1	Complete passenger vehicles, knockdown or assembled, passenger car chassis, and nonarmored military	
Complete passenger vehicles, knockdown or assembled, passenger car chassis, and nonarmored military automobiles	**85,841.1**	automobiles	85,158.5
		Automobiles, nsk, total	682.6

Source: 2002 *Economic Census*. The values are product shipments in millions of dollars for 2002. Total product shipments may be lower or higher than industry shipments. See Introduction for a full discussion. Values of indented subcategories are summed in the main heading(s). The symbol (D) appears when data are withheld to prevent disclosure of competitive information. The abbreviation nsk stands for 'not specified by kind' and nec for 'not elsewhere classified'. A dash (-) means zero.

INPUTS AND OUTPUTS FOR AUTOMOBILE MANUFACTURING

Economic Sector or Industry Providing Inputs	%	Sector	Economic Sector or Industry Buying Outputs	%	Sector
Motor vehicle parts	45.3	Manufg.	Personal consumption expenditures	46.7	
Compensation of employees	8.7		Private fixed investment	43.5	
Wholesale trade	5.7	Trade	Exports of goods & services	4.2	Cap Inv
Management of companies & enterprises	3.3	Services	Change in private inventories	4.0	In House
Noncomparable imports	1.7	Foreign	S/L govt. invest., other	0.9	S/L Govt
Semiconductors & related devices	1.4	Manufg.	S/L govt. invest., education	0.5	S/L Govt

Continued on next page.

INPUTS AND OUTPUTS FOR AUTOMOBILE MANUFACTURING - Continued

Economic Sector or Industry Providing Inputs	%	Sector	Economic Sector or Industry Buying Outputs	%	Sector
Glass products from purchased glass	1.3	Manufg.	Federal government, investment, nondefense	0.2	Fed Govt
Motor vehicle bodies	1.2	Manufg.			
Audio & video equipment	1.1	Manufg.			
Engine equipment, nec	1.1	Manufg.			
Tires	1.0	Manufg.			
Truck transportation	0.9	Util.			
Plastics products, nec	0.9	Manufg.			
Totalizing fluid meters & counting devices	0.7	Manufg.			
Leather & hide tanning & finishing	0.6	Manufg.			
Textile product mills, nec	0.6	Manufg.			
Turned products & screws, nuts, & bolts	0.6	Manufg.			
Hardware	0.5	Manufg.			
Carpet & rug mills	0.5	Manufg.			
Pressed & blown glass & glassware, nec	0.5	Manufg.			
Paperboard containers	0.3	Manufg.			
Paints & coatings	0.3	Manufg.			
Fluid power process machinery	0.3	Manufg.			
Rubber products, nec	0.3	Manufg.			
Scientific research & development services	0.3	Services			
Ornamental & architectural metal products	0.2	Manufg.			
Valve & fittings other than plumbing	0.2	Manufg.			
Computer terminals & peripherals	0.2	Manufg.			
Power generation & supply	0.2	Util.			
Gaskets, packing, & sealing devices	0.2	Manufg.			
Rail transportation	0.2	Util.			
Machine shops	0.2	Manufg.			
Electronic computers	0.2	Manufg.			
Taxes on production & imports, less subsidies	0.2				
Mechanical power transmission equipment	0.2	Manufg.			
AC, refrigeration, and warm air heating equipment	0.2	Manufg.			
Springs & wire products	0.2	Manufg.			
Coating, engraving, heat treating & allied activities	0.2	Manufg.			
Rubber & plastics hose & belting	0.2	Manufg.			
Electric lamp bulbs & parts	0.1	Manufg.			
Real estate	0.1	Fin/R.E.			
Automotive equipment rental & leasing	0.1	Fin/R.E.			
Natural gas distribution	0.1	Util.			
Storage batteries	0.1	Manufg.			

Source: Benchmark Input-Output Accounts for the U.S. Economy, 2002, U.S. Department of Commerce, Washington, D.C., January 2008. The abbreviation nec stands for 'not elsewhere classified'.

OCCUPATIONS EMPLOYED BY MOTOR VEHICLE MANUFACTURING

Occupation	% of Total 2006	Change to 2016	Occupation	% of Total 2006	Change to 2016
Team assemblers	24.3	-0.4	Maintenance & repair workers, general	2.1	-3.1
Assemblers & fabricators, nec	18.7	-12.8	Laborers & freight, stock, & material movers, hand	1.8	-12.8
First-line supervisors/managers of production workers	2.8	-3.1	Industrial truck & tractor operators	1.5	-12.8
Inspectors, testers, sorters, samplers, & weighers	2.7	-8.6	Welders, cutters, solderers, & brazers	1.3	3.1
Painters, transportation equipment	2.2	-3.1	Industrial machinery mechanics	1.2	11.4

Source: Industry-Occupation Matrix, Bureau of Labor Statistics, December 4, 2007. These data are reported based on 4-digit NAICS categories but have been matched to corresponding 6-digit NAICS industry codes. The change reported for each occupation to the year 2016 is a percent of growth or decline as estimated by the Bureau of Labor Statistics. The abbreviation nec stands for 'not elsewhere classified'.

LOCATION BY STATE AND REGIONAL CONCENTRATION

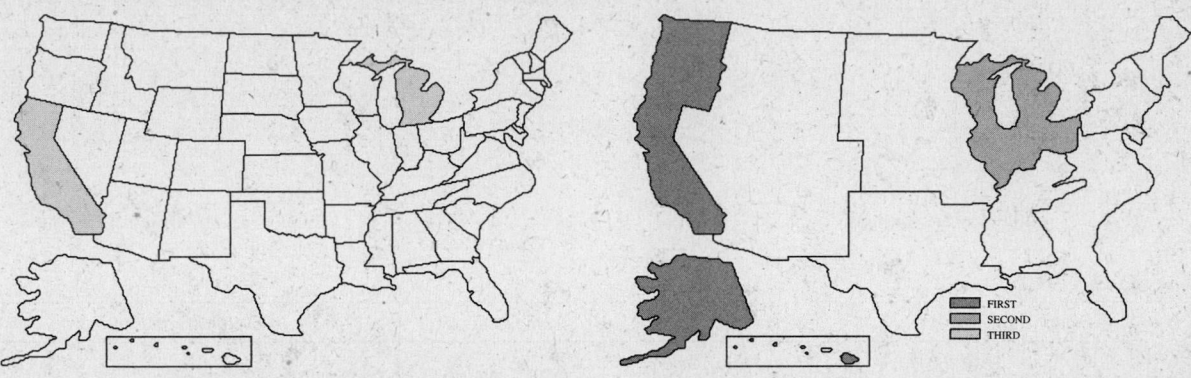

FIRST
SECOND
THIRD

INDUSTRY DATA BY STATE

State	Establish-ments	Shipments			Employment				Cost as % of Shipments	Investment per Employee ($)
		Total ($ mil)	% of U.S.	Per Establ.	Total Number	% of U.S.	Per Establ.	Wages ($/hour)		
Michigan	22	33,968.0	37.4	1,543,998.0	27,673	32.2	1,258	34.37	63.1	17,296
California	28	3,088.7	3.4	110,311.7	6,068	7.1	217	36.70	72.9	7,229

Source: 2002 Economic Census. The states are in descending order of shipments or establishments (if shipment data are missing for the majority). The symbol (D) appears when data are withheld to prevent disclosure of competitive information. States marked with (D) are sorted by number of establishments. A dash (-) indicates that the data element cannot be calculated. Data may not show all states active in the NAICS category. All data available at the time of publication are shown.

NAICS 336112 - LIGHT TRUCK AND UTILITY VEHICLE MANUFACTURING

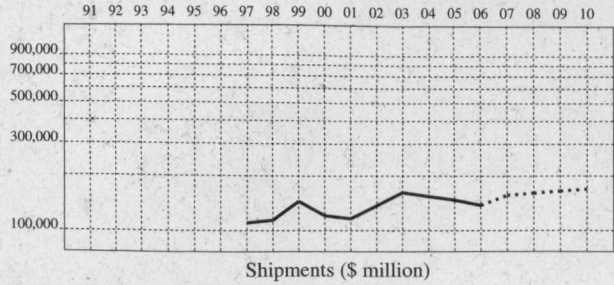

Shipments ($ million)

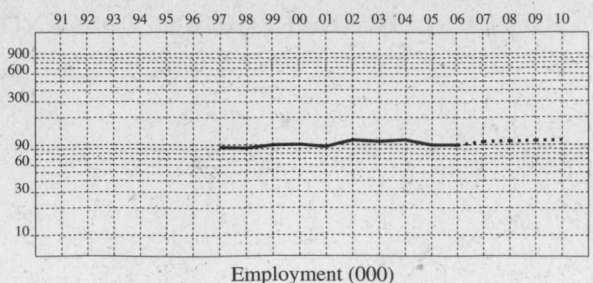

Employment (000)

GENERAL STATISTICS

| Year | Companies | Establishments | | Employment | | | Compensation | | Production ($ million) | | | |
		Total	with 20 or more employees	Total (000)	Production Workers (000)	Hours (Mil)	Payroll ($ mil)	Wages ($/hr)	Cost of Materials	Value Added by Manufacture	Value of Shipments	Capital Invest.
1997	85	112	40	94.0	86.5	180.3	5,362.0	26.29	70,927.3	39,539.8	110,400.2	1,769.5
1998		108	39	92.2	84.5	172.0	5,464.2	28.08	81,186.0	33,284.8	114,494.8	2,078.7
1999		111	46	99.3	90.5	199.6	6,820.1	30.19	103,247.5	42,081.4	145,329.0	2,769.5
2000		107	44	100.8	90.3	189.1	6,934.2	32.15	93,504.0	27,845.3	121,185.4	2,495.3
2001		100	43	95.5	86.5	176.1	6,047.0	29.93	90,378.3	25,983.0	116,468.1	1,695.0
2002	69	97	41	112.7	102.0	209.1	7,822.1	33.38	96,387.6	40,607.9	137,069.6	2,591.6
2003		101	46	108.7	99.3	205.4	7,992.0	34.49	108,129.1	54,204.1	162,240.6	2,889.3
2004		92	46	112.6	101.8	209.5	8,283.7	34.77	110,607.2	43,950.4	154,475.3	2,135.4
2005		101	54	99.6	88.7	183.5	7,432.4	35.52	108,615.4	39,200.7	147,633.6	1,544.2
2006		93P	51P	99.2	88.4	174.4	7,167.3	35.73	102,733.9	35,769.4	138,223.3	2,120.2
2007		91P	52P	108.3P	96.7P	195.2P	8,342.2P	37.73P	116,799.6P	40,666.7P	157,147.9P	2,153.0P
2008		89P	53P	109.6P	97.6P	196.2P	8,598.5P	38.77P	119,826.0P	41,720.5P	161,219.9P	2,142.8P
2009		87P	54P	110.8P	98.5P	197.1P	8,854.8P	39.80P	122,852.5P	42,774.2P	165,291.9P	2,132.6P
2010		85P	55P	112.1P	99.3P	198.1P	9,111.2P	40.83P	125,879.0P	43,828.0P	169,363.9P	2,122.5P

Sources: 1997 and 2002 *Economic Census*; other years, up to 2006, are from *Annual Survey of Manufactures*. Establishment counts for non-Census years are from *County Business Patterns*; 1997 and 2002 values are from the 1997 and 2002 censuses, respectively. 'P's show projections by the editors.

INDICES OF CHANGE

| Year | Companies | Establishments | | Employment | | | Compensation | | Production ($ million) | | | |
		Total	with 20 or more employees	Total (000)	Production Workers (000)	Hours (Mil)	Payroll ($ mil)	Wages ($/hr)	Cost of Materials	Value Added by Manufacture	Value of Shipments	Capital Invest.
1997	123	115	98	83	85	86	69	79	74	97	81	68
1998		111	95	82	83	82	70	84	84	82	84	80
1999		114	112	88	89	95	87	90	107	104	106	107
2000		110	107	89	89	90	89	96	97	69	88	96
2001		103	105	85	85	84	77	90	94	64	85	65
2002	100	100	100	100	100	100	100	100	100	100	100	100
2003		104	112	96	97	98	102	103	112	133	118	111
2004		95	112	100	100	100	106	104	115	108	113	82
2005		104	132	88	87	88	95	106	113	97	108	60
2006		96P	123P	88	87	83	92	107	107	88	101	82
2007		94P	126P	96P	95P	93P	107P	113P	121P	100P	115P	83P
2008		92P	129P	97P	96P	94P	110P	116P	124P	103P	118P	83P
2009		90P	132P	98P	97P	94P	113P	119P	127P	105P	121P	82P
2010		88P	135P	99P	97P	95P	116P	122P	131P	108P	124P	82P

Sources: Same as General Statistics. Values reflect change from the base year, 2002. Values above 100 mean greater than 2002, values below 100 mean less than 2002, and the values of 100 in other years means the same as 2002. 'P's show projections by the editors.

SELECTED RATIOS

For 2002	Avg. of All Manufact.	Analyzed Industry	Index	For 2002	Avg. of All Manufact.	Analyzed Industry	Index
Employees per Establishment	42	1,162	2,768	Value Added per Production Worker	182,367	398,117	218
Payroll per Establishment	1,639,184	80,640,206	4,920	Cost per Establishment	5,769,015	993,686,598	17,225
Payroll per Employee	39,053	69,406	178	Cost per Employee	137,446	855,258	622
Production Workers per Establishment	30	1,052	3,564	Cost per Production Worker	195,506	944,976	483
Wages per Establishment	694,845	71,956,268	10,356	Shipments per Establishment	11,158,348	1,413,088,660	12,664
Wages per Production Worker	23,548	68,429	291	Shipments per Employee	265,847	1,216,234	457
Hours per Production Worker	1,980	2,050	104	Shipments per Production Worker	378,144	1,343,820	355
Wages per Hour	11.89	33.38	281	Investment per Establishment	361,338	26,717,526	7,394
Value Added per Establishment	5,381,325	418,638,144	7,779	Investment per Employee	8,609	22,996	267
Value Added per Employee	128,210	360,319	281	Investment per Production Worker	12,245	25,408	207

Sources: Same as General Statistics. The 'Average of All Manufacturing' column represents the average of all manufacturing industries reported for the most recent complete year available. The Index shows the relationship between the Average and the Analyzed Industry. For example, 100 means that they are equal; 500 that the Analyzed Industry is five times the average; 50 means that the Analyzed Industry is half the national average. The abbreviation 'na' is used to show that data are 'not available'. Ratios shown for 2002, the last complete census year.

LEADING COMPANIES   Number shown: **75**   Total sales ($ mil): **607,362**   Total employment (000): **1,074.8**

Company Name	Address				CEO Name	Phone	Co. Type	Sales ($ mil)	Empl. (000)
General Motors Corp.	300 Renaissance Ctr	Detroit	MI	48265		313-556-5000	P	181,122	266.0
Ford Motor Co.	1 American Rd.	Dearborn	MI	48126		313-322-3000	P	172,455	246.0
United Technologies Corp.	1 Financial Plz.	Hartford	CT	06101	Mario Abajo	860-728-7000	P	47,829	225.6
Chrysler L.L.C.	1000 Chrysler Dr.	Auburn Hills	MI	48326	Thomas W. LaSorda	248-576-5741	S	45,237*	84.4
American Honda Motor Company	1919 Torrance Blvd.	Torrance	CA	90501	Koichi Kondo	310-783-2000	S	42,539	25.0
PACCAR Inc.	PO Box 1518	Bellevue	WA	98009		425-468-7400	P	15,220	21.8
Ford VAC Corp.	1 American Rd.	Dearborn	MI	48121	William J. Ford	313-322-3000	P	15,105*	1.9
Dana Corp.	PO Box 1000	Toledo	OH	43697	Michael J. Burns	419-535-4500	P	8,504	45.0
Triangle Suspension Systems	PO Box 425	Du Bois	PA	15801	Greg Maffia	814-375-7211	R	7,000*	0.2
Oshkosh Truck Corp.	PO Box 2566	Oshkosh	WI	54903	Robert G. Bohn	920-235-9150	P	6,307	14.2
Toyota Motor Mfg. N America	25 Atlantic Ave.	Erlanger	KY	41018	Masamoto Amezawa	859-746-4000	S	6,120*	7.5
Honda of America Manufacturing	24000 Honda Pkwy.	Marysville	OH	43040	Takeo Fukui	937-642-5000	S	5,090*	13.0
Mack Trucks Inc.	PO Box M	Allentown	PA	18105		610-709-3011	R	4,324*	0.8
Toyota Motor Mfg, Kentucky	PO Box 2700	Georgetown	KY	40324	Steven Angelo	502-868-2000	R	4,181*	5.0
New United Motor Manufacturing	45500 Fremont	Fremont	CA	94538	Bruce Walker	510-498-5500	J	4,080*	5.0
Saturn Corp.	PO Box 1502	Spring Hill	TN	37174		931-486-5000	S	3,901	9.6
Motors Insurance Corp.	PO Box 66937	St. Louis	MO	63166	Gary Kuzumi		S	3,849*	2.2
Thor Industries Inc.	PO Box 629	Jackson Center	OH	45334		937-596-6849	P	3,066	9.1
AutoAlliance International	1 International Dr.	Flat Rock	MI	48134	Phillip G. Spender	734-782-7800	J	3,019*	3.7
Freightliner L.L.C.	PO Box 3849	Portland	OR	97208	Chris Patterson	503-745-8000	S	2,734*	14.0
BMW of North America L.L.C.	PO Box 1227	Westwood	NJ	07675	Thomas Purves	201-307-4000	S	2,690*	1.0
Nissan North America Inc.	333 Commerce St.	Nashville	TN	37201	Carlos Ghosn	615-725-1000	S	2,148	14.0
Renco Group Inc.	30 Rockefeller Plz.	New York	NY	10112	Ira Leno Rennert	212-541-6000	R	1,900	9.4
Thor America Inc.	37 Old 522	Middleburg	PA	17842	W F. B. Thompson	570-837-1663	S	1,592*	8.5
Aero Coach Inc.	Hickory Hill Rd.	Longview	TX	75601	W F. B. Thompson	903-663-7699	S	1,313*	7.5
Monaco Coach Corp.	91320 Coburg Indust	Coburg	OR	97408		541-686-8011	P	1,298	5.3
Federal Signal Corp.	1415 W 22nd St.	Oak Brook	IL	60523	James C. Janning	630-954-2000	P	1,268	5.5
Mitsubishi Motors N America	PO Box 6014	Cypress	CA	90630	Hiroshi Harunari	714-372-6000	S	1,198	3.6
International Truck and Engine	PO Box 1488	Warrenville	IL	60555	Daniel C. Ustian	630-753-5000	S	1,114*	1.7
Spartan Motors Chassis Inc.	1165 Reynolds Rd.	Charlotte	MI	48813	John Sztykiel	517-543-6400	S	1,030*	0.8
Toyota Motor Mfg. W Virginia	1 Sugar Maple Ln.	Buffalo	WV	25033	Laquita Harris	304-937-7000	S	901*	0.9
North American Bus Industries	106 National Dr.	Anniston	AL	36207		256-831-4296	R	886*	0.6
Utilimaster Corp.	PO Box 585	Wakarusa	IN	46573	Lawrence Doyle	574-862-4561	R	836*	1.0
Spartan Motors Inc.	PO Box 440	Charlotte	MI	48813		517-543-6400	P	682	1.4
Airstream Inc.	PO Box 629	Jackson Center	OH	45334	Bpob Wheeler	937-596-6111	S	622*	0.5
Purdy Motor S.A.	CC Aventura 100	San Jose	PR	00930	John Kilmer	506-287-4230	S	509*	0.4
Coachmen Industries Inc.	PO Box 3300	Elkhart	IN	46515	Richard M. Lavers	574-262-0123	P	481	2.7
Ford of North Miami Beach	2198 NE 163rd St.	N Miami Bch	FL	33162		305-493-5000	R	447*	0.3
Reinke Manufacturing Company	PO Box 566	Deshler	NE	68340	Chris Roth	402-365-7251	R	335*	0.4
Wheeled Coach Industries Corp.	2737 Forsyth Rd.	Winter Park	FL	32792	Robert Collins	407-677-7777	S	326*	0.4
Jefferson Industries Corp.	6670 State Rte.	West Jefferson	OH	43162	Hideo Hayashi	614-879-5300	R	309*	0.4
ASC Inc.	1 ASC Ctr.	Southgate	MI	48195	Paul Wilbur	734-285-4911	S	300*	1.0
Elgin Sweeper Co.	1300 W Bartlett Rd.	Elgin	IL	60120	Mark Weber	847-741-5370	S	286*	0.3
SanduskyAthol International	3130 W Monroe St.	Sandusky	OH	44870	Jack Givens	419-627-3200	R	266*	0.2
Allianz Sweeper Co.	4651 Schaefer Ave.	Chino	CA	91710	Gabriel Charky	909-613-5600	R	233*	0.1
Braun Industries Inc.	1170 Production Dr.	Van Wert	OH	45891	Phillip Braun	419-232-7020	R	223*	0.2
Collins Industries Inc.	PO Box 648	Hutchinson	KS	67502	Don L. Collins	620-663-5551	S	208	1.0
Cheetah Chassis Corp.	PO Box 388	Berwick	PA	18603	Frank Katz	570-752-2708	R	167*	0.2
Ferrara Fire Apparatus Inc.	PO Box 249	Holden	LA	70744	Christopher Ferrara	225-567-7100	R	159*	0.3
Midwest Stamping Inc.	3455 Briarfield	Maumee	OH	43537	Ronald L. Thompson	419-724-6970	R	155*	0.6
VSV Group	1110 DI Dr.	Elkhart	IN	46514	Mark Grossbauer	574-264-7511	R	148*	0.5
Smeal Fire Apparatus Co.	PO Box 8	Snyder	NE	68664	Delwin Smeal	402-568-2224	R	139*	0.3
Freightliner Specialty Vehicle	2300 S 13th St.	Clinton	OK	73601	Tim Sinor	580-323-4100	R	123*	0.2
Schwarze Industries Inc.	1055 Jordan Rd.	Huntsville	AL	35811	Ronald A. Robinson	256-851-1200	S	122*	0.2
Excellance Inc.	453 Lanier Rd.	Madison	AL	35758	Charles Epps	256-772-9321	R	112*	<0.1
Executive Coach Builders Inc.	4400 W Production	Springfield	MO	65803	David Bakare	417-935-2233	R	104*	0.1
Louis Berkman Company Inc.	PO Box 820	Steubenville	OH	43952	Louis Berkman	740-283-3722	R	82*	<0.1
Alfa Leisure Inc.	1612 S Cucamonga	Ontario	CA	91761	Johnnie R. Crean	909-628-5574	R	75*	0.7
FWD Seagrave Holdings L.P.	105 E 12th St.	Clintonville	WI	54929		715-823-2141	R	72*	0.4
Custom Coach International	PO Box 869	Pawhuska	OK	74056	Ray Smith	918-287-4445	R	71*	<0.1
Temic Automotive of N America	21440 Lake Cook	Barrington	IL	60010		847-862-6300	R	71*	0.4
Sutphen Corp.	PO Box 158	Amlin	OH	43002		614-889-1005	R	71*	<0.1
Foretravel Inc.	1221 NW Stallings	Nacogdoches	TX	75964		936-564-8367	R	68*	0.3
Accubuilt Inc.	4707 E Kearney St.	Springfield	MO	65803	Dan Mitchell	417-864-4411	R	67*	<0.1
Amerigon Inc.	21680 Haggerty Rd.	Northville	MI	48167	Daniel R. Coker	248-504-0500	P	64	<0.1
Alpine Armoring Inc.	570 Herndon Pkwy.	Herndon	VA	20170	Fred Khoroushi	703-471-0009	R	56*	<0.1
Super Products Corp.	PO Box 270128	Milwaukee	WI	53227	Henry Rowan	262-784-7100	R	51*	0.1
Super Vacuum Manufacturing Co.	PO Box 87	Loveland	CO	80539	Roger Weinmeister	970-667-5146	R	51*	0.1
E-ONE	1601 SW 37 Ave.	Ocala	FL	34474	Mark Gastafin	352-237-1122	D	44*	0.3
Arotech Corp.	1229 Oak Valley Dr.	Ann Arbor	MI	48108	Robert S. Ehrlich		P	43	0.3
Schwartz Industries Inc.	1055 Jordan Rd.	Huntsville	AL	35811	Jim Morris	256-851-1200	R	40*	0.2
AGM Automotive Inc.	1000 E Whitcomb	Madison Heights	MI	48071		248-776-0600	R	33*	<0.1
Pemberton Fabricators Inc.	PO Box 227	Rancocas	NJ	08073	Robert Murnan	609-267-0922	R	32*	<0.1
Phoenix U S A Inc.	PO Box 40	Cookeville	TN	38503	James Wright	931-526-6128	R	30*	<0.1
Special Projects Inc.	45901 Helm St.	Plymouth	MI	48170	Kenneth Yanez	734-455-7130	R	29*	<0.1

Source: *Ward's Business Directory of U.S. Private and Public Companies*, Volumes 1 and 2, 2008. The company type code used is as follows: P - Public, R - Private, S - Subsidiary, D - Division, J - Joint Venture, A - Affiliate, G - Group. Sales are in millions of dollars, employees are in thousands. An asterisk (*) indicates an estimated sales volume. The symbol < stands for 'less than'. Company names and addresses are truncated, in some cases, to fit into the available space.

MATERIALS CONSUMED

Material	Quantity	Delivered Cost ($ million)
Gasoline engines and parts specially designed for gasoline engines	(X)	14,729.4
Diesel engines and parts specially designed for diesel engines	(X)	2,434.4
Drive train components and parts	(X)	12,285.5
Car bodies	(X)	(D)
Refrigeration compressors, compressor units, condensing units, and other heat transfer equipment	(X)	3,086.5
Shocks, struts, and other suspension equipment and parts	(X)	5,960.1
Exhaust systems and parts	(X)	2,885.0
Machine tool accessories, including cutting tools	(X)	(D)
Fluid power pumps, motors, and hydrostatic transmissions	(X)	505.4
Fluid power valves (hydraulic and pneumatic)	(X)	(D)
Fluid power cylinders and rotary actuators (hydraulic and pneumatic)	(X)	(D)
Fluid power hose, tube fittings, and assemblies (hydraulic and pneumatic)	(X)	(D)
Fluid power filters (hydraulic and pneumatic)	(X)	20.6
Other transportation related fluid power products, hydraulic and pneumatic	(X)	(D)
Automotive stampings (inc. body parts, hubcaps, fenders, etc.)	(X)	6,750.9
Steel springs (excluding wire)	(X)	477.9
Motor vehicle metal hardware (lock units, etc.), exc. forgings	(X)	711.2
Metal bolts, nuts, screws, and other screw machine products	(X)	740.6
Other fabricated metal products (excluding forgings)	(X)	1,420.0
Forgings	(X)	25.6
Castings, rough and semifinished	(X)	70.5
Metal shapes and forms (exc. castings, forgings, fabr. metal products)	(X)	1,101.4
Ball and roller bearings (mounted or unmounted)	(X)	25.6
Pneumatic tires and inner tubes	(X)	2,026.8
Rubber and plastics hose and belting	(X)	666.2
Fabricated rubber products (exc. tires, tubes, hoses, belting, and gaskets)	(X)	(D)
Gaskets (all types), and packing and sealing devices	(X)	(D)
Fabricated plastics products (exc. gaskets, hoses, and belting)	(X)	1,953.7
Glass and glass products (including windows and mirrors)	(X)	2,092.5
Seats (purchased separately) for automobiles, trucks, and buses	(X)	7,222.5
Seat covers, seat belts, and shoulder harnesses	(X)	581.5
Automotive air bag assemblies and parts	(X)	1,074.1
Automotive trimmings, textile (panels, headliners, etc.)	(X)	4,501.4
Carpeting	(X)	847.8
Ceramic and ceramic composite parts, components, and accessories	(X)	(D)
Glues and adhesives	(X)	(D)
Paints, varnishes, stains, lacquers, shellacs, japans, enamels, etc.	(X)	674.7
Engine electrical equipment (incl. spark plugs, magnetos, generators, starters, etc.)	(X)	2,445.5
Motor vehicle lighting fixtures, excluding auto lamps	(X)	616.7
Automotive lamps (bulbs and sealed beams)	(X)	178.8
Storage batteries, automotive	(X)	387.9
Automotive radios and loudspeakers	(X)	1,754.3
Motor vehicle clusters, meters, and gauges, excluding electrical	(X)	1,954.7
Semiconductors and related devices and electronic control modules	(X)	(D)
Purchased computers for incorporation into motor vehicles, trucks, and buses	(X)	307.5
All other materials, components, parts, containers, and supplies	(X)	4,529.0
Materials, ingredients, containers, and supplies, nsk	(X)	2,378.9

Source: 2002 *Economic Census*. Explanation of symbols used: (D): Withheld to avoid disclosure of competitive data; na: Not available; (S): Withheld because statistical norms were not met; (X): Not applicable; (Z): Less than half the unit shown; nec: Not elsewhere classified; nsk: Not specified by kind; - : zero; p : 10-19 percent estimated; q : 20-29 percent estimated.

PRODUCT SHARE DETAILS

Product or Product Class Shipments	Mil. $	Product or Product Class Shipments	Mil. $
LIGHT TRUCKS AND UTILITY VEHICLES	134,629.0	Trucks, truck tractors, and bus chassis (chassis of own manufacture) 14,000 lb or less, including minivans and sport utility vehicles	
Trucks, truck tractors, and bus chassis (chassis of own manufacture) 14,000 lb or less, including minivans and sport utility vehicles	**134,629.0**	sport utility vehicles	134,396.0
		Light trucks and utility vehicles, nsk, total	233.1

Source: 2002 *Economic Census*. The values are product shipments in millions of dollars for 2002. Total product shipments may be lower or higher than industry shipments. See Introduction for a full discussion. Values of indented subcategories are summed in the main heading(s). The symbol (D) appears when data are withheld to prevent disclosure of competitive information. The abbreviation nsk stands for 'not specified by kind' and nec for 'not elsewhere classified'. A dash (-) means zero.

INPUTS AND OUTPUTS FOR LIGHT TRUCK AND UTILITY VEHICLE MANUFACTURING

Economic Sector or Industry Providing Inputs	%	Sector	Economic Sector or Industry Buying Outputs	%	Sector
Motor vehicle parts	47.2	Manufg.	Personal consumption expenditures	56.9	
Compensation of employees	8.4		Private fixed investment	30.5	
Wholesale trade	5.8	Trade	Exports of goods & services	8.2	Cap Inv
Management of companies & enterprises	3.5	Services	Change in private inventories	2.7	In House
Semiconductors & related devices	1.9	Manufg.	S/L govt. invest., other	1.0	S/L Govt
Engine equipment, nec	1.6	Manufg.	S/L govt. invest., education	0.3	S/L Govt

Continued on next page.

INPUTS AND OUTPUTS FOR LIGHT TRUCK AND UTILITY VEHICLE MANUFACTURING - Continued

Economic Sector or Industry Providing Inputs	%	Sector	Economic Sector or Industry Buying Outputs	%	Sector
Plastics products, nec	1.5	Manufg.	Federal government, investment, nondefense	0.2	Fed Govt
Tires	1.4	Manufg.	Federal government, investment, national defense	0.1	Fed Govt
Totalizing fluid meters & counting devices	1.4	Manufg.			
Audio & video equipment	1.1	Manufg.			
Glass products from purchased glass	1.1	Manufg.			
Truck transportation	1.0	Util.			
Motor vehicle bodies	0.9	Manufg.			
Carpet & rug mills	0.6	Manufg.			
Noncomparable imports	0.6	Foreign			
Valve & fittings other than plumbing	0.6	Manufg.			
Hardware	0.5	Manufg.			
Rubber & plastics hose & belting	0.4	Manufg.			
Paints & coatings	0.4	Manufg.			
Turned products & screws, nuts, & bolts	0.4	Manufg.			
Springs & wire products	0.4	Manufg.			
Adhesives	0.4	Manufg.			
Iron & steel mills & ferroalloys	0.4	Manufg.			
Pressed & blown glass & glassware, nec	0.4	Manufg.			
Paperboard containers	0.4	Manufg.			
Fluid power process machinery	0.3	Manufg.			
Leather & hide tanning & finishing	0.3	Manufg.			
Storage batteries	0.3	Manufg.			
Manufacturing, nec	0.3	Manufg.			
Scientific research & development services	0.2	Services			
Machine shops	0.2	Manufg.			
Rubber products, nec	0.2	Manufg.			
Power generation & supply	0.2	Util.			
Rail transportation	0.2	Util.			
Computer terminals & peripherals	0.2	Manufg.			
Coating, engraving, heat treating & allied activities	0.2	Manufg.			
Electronic computers	0.2	Manufg.			
AC, refrigeration, and warm air heating equipment	0.2	Manufg.			
Mechanical power transmission equipment	0.2	Manufg.			
Plastics packaging materials, film & sheet	0.2	Manufg.			
Aluminum products from purchased aluminum	0.1	Manufg.			
Natural gas distribution	0.1	Util.			

Source: Benchmark Input-Output Accounts for the U.S. Economy, 2002, U.S. Department of Commerce, Washington, D.C., January 2008. The abbreviation nec stands for 'not elsewhere classified'.

OCCUPATIONS EMPLOYED BY MOTOR VEHICLE MANUFACTURING

Occupation	% of Total 2006	Change to 2016	Occupation	% of Total 2006	Change to 2016
Team assemblers	24.3	-0.4	Maintenance & repair workers, general	2.1	-3.1
Assemblers & fabricators, nec	18.7	-12.8	Laborers & freight, stock, & material movers, hand	1.8	-12.8
First-line supervisors/managers of production workers	2.8	-3.1	Industrial truck & tractor operators	1.5	-12.8
Inspectors, testers, sorters, samplers, & weighers	2.7	-8.6	Welders, cutters, solderers, & brazers	1.3	3.1
Painters, transportation equipment	2.2	-3.1	Industrial machinery mechanics	1.2	11.4

Source: Industry-Occupation Matrix, Bureau of Labor Statistics, December 4, 2007. These data are reported based on 4-digit NAICS categories but have been matched to corresponding 6-digit NAICS industry codes. The change reported for each occupation to the year 2016 is a percent of growth or decline as estimated by the Bureau of Labor Statistics. The abbreviation nec stands for 'not elsewhere classified'.

LOCATION BY STATE AND REGIONAL CONCENTRATION

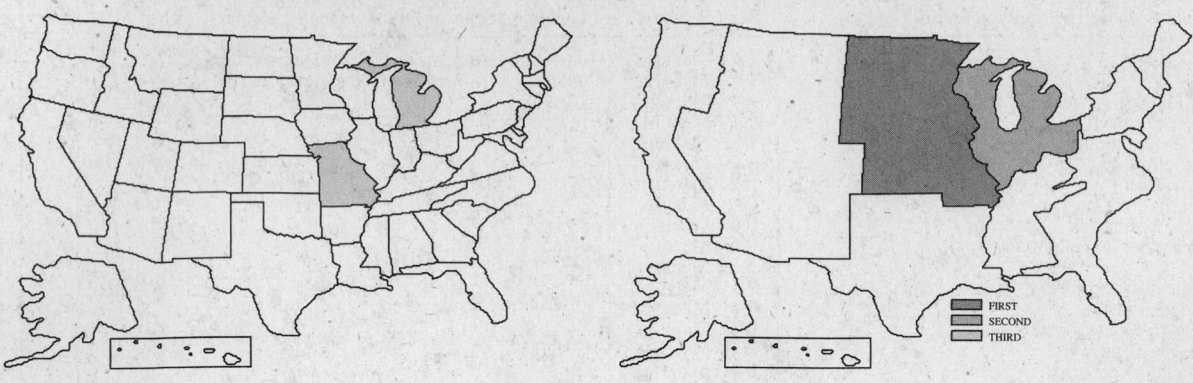

INDUSTRY DATA BY STATE

| State | Establish-ments | Shipments | | | Employment | | | | Cost as % of Shipments | Investment per Employee ($) |
		Total ($ mil)	% of U.S.	Per Establ.	Total Number	% of U.S.	Per Establ.	Wages ($/hour)		
Michigan	6	24,269.0	17.7	4,044,825.0	18,642	16.5	3,107	34.56	73.2	4,020
Missouri	8	20,622.3	15.0	2,577,785.6	17,320	15.4	2,165	32.90	80.0	7,203

Source: 2002 *Economic Census*. The states are in descending order of shipments or establishments (if shipment data are missing for the majority). The symbol (D) appears when data are withheld to prevent disclosure of competitive information. States marked with (D) are sorted by number of establishments. A dash (-) indicates that the data element cannot be calculated. Data may not show all states active in the NAICS category. All data available at the time of publication are shown.

NAICS 336120 - HEAVY DUTY TRUCK MANUFACTURING

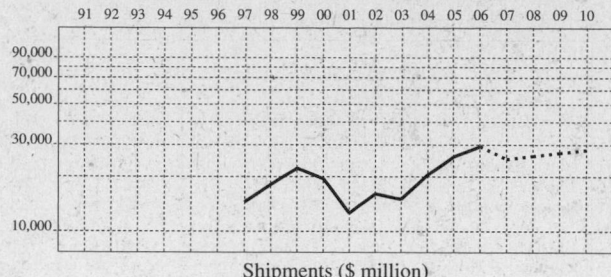

Shipments ($ million)

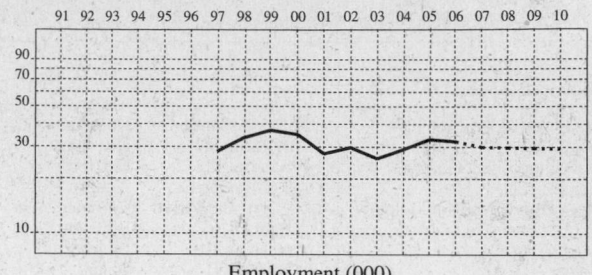

Employment (000)

GENERAL STATISTICS

| Year | Com-panies | Establishments | | Employment | | | Compensation | | Production ($ million) | | | |
		Total	with 20 or more employees	Total (000)	Production Workers (000)	Hours (Mil)	Payroll ($ mil)	Wages ($/hr)	Cost of Materials	Value Added by Manufacture	Value of Shipments	Capital Invest.
1997	75	84	41	28.2	22.9	45.6	1,190.2	20.51	10,306.4	4,205.8	14,490.3	130.3
1998		87	42	33.6	27.6	53.4	1,439.2	20.86	12,253.5	5,878.9	18,121.9	131.5
1999		89	43	37.0	30.3	60.9	1,732.5	21.76	17,273.6	5,040.6	22,268.4	244.0
2000		86	47	35.0	28.4	52.0	1,619.4	22.62	14,818.9	4,747.2	19,528.0	298.4
2001		89	48	27.5	21.1	37.5	1,211.9	22.27	10,064.1	2,416.5	12,613.4	504.9
2002	81	99	54	29.8	22.7	42.1	1,228.9	20.43	13,188.7	2,878.5	16,100.7	158.4
2003		94	55	25.9	20.2	36.4	1,099.5	20.67	12,363.1	2,739.3	15,022.1	163.5
2004		102	61	29.1	23.2	41.4	1,316.8	22.56	16,789.4	3,696.6	20,422.1	161.3
2005		99	60	33.0	26.8	46.9	1,445.7	22.36	22,002.9	3,887.1	25,844.4	196.9
2006		103P	64P	32.2	26.5	46.1	1,495.6	23.91	24,389.5	5,004.1	29,389.1	128.2
2007		105P	67P	30.0P	23.9P	40.2P	1,350.4P	23.04P	20,755.0P	4,258.4P	25,009.5P	187.5P
2008		107P	69P	29.8P	23.7P	39.1P	1,345.4P	23.27P	21,604.4P	4,432.7P	26,033.1P	183.1P
2009		109P	72P	29.6P	23.5P	38.0P	1,340.4P	23.50P	22,453.8P	4,606.9P	27,056.6P	178.7P
2010		111P	75P	29.4P	23.3P	36.9P	1,335.4P	23.72P	23,303.2P	4,781.2P	28,080.2P	174.4P

Sources: 1997 and 2002 *Economic Census*; other years, up to 2006, are from *Annual Survey of Manufactures*, Establishment counts for non-Census years are from *County Business Patterns*; 1997 and 2002 values are from the 1997 and 2002 censuses, respectively. 'P's show projections by the editors.

INDICES OF CHANGE

| Year | Com-panies | Establishments | | Employment | | | Compensation | | Production ($ million) | | | |
		Total	with 20 or more employees	Total (000)	Production Workers (000)	Hours (Mil)	Payroll ($ mil)	Wages ($/hr)	Cost of Materials	Value Added by Manufacture	Value of Shipments	Capital Invest.
1997	93	85	76	95	101	108	97	100	78	146	90	82
1998		88	78	113	122	127	117	102	93	204	113	83
1999		90	80	124	133	145	141	107	131	175	138	154
2000		87	87	117	125	124	132	111	112	165	121	188
2001		90	89	92	93	89	99	109	76	84	78	319
2002	100	100	100	100	100	100	100	100	100	100	100	100
2003		95	102	87	89	86	89	101	94	95	93	103
2004		103	113	98	102	98	107	110	127	128	127	102
2005		100	111	111	118	111	118	109	167	135	161	124
2006		104P	118P	108	117	110	122	117	185	174	183	81
2007		106P	123P	101P	105P	95P	110P	113P	157P	148P	155P	118P
2008		108P	128P	100P	104P	93P	109P	114P	164P	154P	162P	116P
2009		110P	133P	99P	104P	90P	109P	115P	170P	160P	168P	113P
2010		112P	138P	99P	103P	88P	109P	116P	177P	166P	174P	110P

Sources: Same as General Statistics. Values reflect change from the base year, 2002. Values above 100 mean greater than 2002, values below 100 mean less than 2002, and the values of 100 in other years means the same as 2002. 'P's show projections by the editors.

SELECTED RATIOS

For 2002	Avg. of All Manufact.	Analyzed Industry	Index	For 2002	Avg. of All Manufact.	Analyzed Industry	Index
Employees per Establishment	42	301	717	Value Added per Production Worker	182,367	126,806	70
Payroll per Establishment	1,639,184	12,413,131	757	Cost per Establishment	5,769,015	133,219,192	2,309
Payroll per Employee	39,053	41,238	106	Cost per Employee	137,446	442,574	322
Production Workers per Establishment	30	229	777	Cost per Production Worker	195,506	581,000	297
Wages per Establishment	694,845	8,687,909	1,250	Shipments per Establishment	11,158,348	162,633,333	1,458
Wages per Production Worker	23,548	37,890	161	Shipments per Employee	265,847	540,292	203
Hours per Production Worker	1,980	1,855	94	Shipments per Production Worker	378,144	709,282	188
Wages per Hour	11.89	20.43	172	Investment per Establishment	361,338	1,600,000	443
Value Added per Establishment	5,381,325	29,075,758	540	Investment per Employee	8,609	5,315	62
Value Added per Employee	128,210	96,594	75	Investment per Production Worker	12,245	6,978	57

Sources: Same as General Statistics. The 'Average of All Manufacturing' column represents the average of all manufacturing industries reported for the most recent complete year available. The Index shows the relationship between the Average and the Analyzed Industry. For example, 100 means that they are equal; 500 that the Analyzed Industry is five times the average; 50 means that the Analyzed Industry is half the national average. The abbreviation 'na' is used to show that data are 'not available'. Ratios shown for 2002, the last complete census year.

LEADING COMPANIES   Number shown: 75   Total sales ($ mil): 607,362   Total employment (000): 1,074.8

Company Name	Address				CEO Name	Phone	Co. Type	Sales ($ mil)	Empl. (000)
General Motors Corp.	300 Renaissance Ctr	Detroit	MI	48265		313-556-5000	P	181,122	266.0
Ford Motor Co.	1 American Rd.	Dearborn	MI	48126		313-322-3000	P	172,455	246.0
United Technologies Corp.	1 Financial Plz.	Hartford	CT	06101	Mario Abajo	860-728-7000	P	47,829	225.6
Chrysler L.L.C.	1000 Chrysler Dr.	Auburn Hills	MI	48326	Thomas W. LaSorda	248-576-5741	S	45,237*	84.4
American Honda Motor Company	1919 Torrance Blvd.	Torrance	CA	90501	Koichi Kondo	310-783-2000	S	42,539	25.0
PACCAR Inc.	PO Box 1518	Bellevue	WA	98009		425-468-7400	P	15,220	21.8
Ford VAC Corp.	1 American Rd.	Dearborn	MI	48121	William J. Ford	313-322-3000	S	15,105*	1.9
Dana Corp.	PO Box 1000	Toledo	OH	43697	Michael J. Burns	419-535-4500	P	8,504	45.0
Triangle Suspension Systems	PO Box 425	Du Bois	PA	15801	Greg Maffia	814-375-7211	R	7,000*	0.2
Oshkosh Truck Corp.	PO Box 2566	Oshkosh	WI	54903	Robert G. Bohn	920-235-9150	P	6,307	14.2
Toyota Motor Mfg. N America	25 Atlantic Ave.	Erlanger	KY	41018	Masamoto Amezawa	859-746-4000	S	6,120*	7.5
Honda of America Manufacturing	24000 Honda Pkwy.	Marysville	OH	43040	Takeo Fukui	937-642-5000	S	5,090*	13.0
Mack Trucks Inc.	PO Box M	Allentown	PA	18105		610-709-3011	R	4,324*	0.8
Toyota Motor Mfg, Kentucky	PO Box 2700	Georgetown	KY	40324	Steven Angelo	502-868-2000	R	4,181*	5.0
New United Motor Manufacturing	45500 Fremont	Fremont	CA	94538	Bruce Walker	510-498-5500	J	4,080*	5.0
Saturn Corp.	PO Box 1502	Spring Hill	TN	37174		931-486-5000	S	3,901	9.6
Motors Insurance Corp.	PO Box 66937	St. Louis	MO	63166	Gary Kuzumi		S	3,849*	2.2
Thor Industries Inc.	PO Box 629	Jackson Center	OH	45334		937-596-6849	P	3,066	9.1
AutoAlliance International	1 International Dr.	Flat Rock	MI	48134	Phillip G. Spender	734-782-7800	J	3,019*	3.7
Freightliner L.L.C.	PO Box 3849	Portland	OR	97208	Chris Patterson	503-745-8000	S	2,734*	14.0
BMW of North America L.L.C.	PO Box 1227	Westwood	NJ	07675	Thomas Purves	201-307-4000	S	2,690*	1.0
Nissan North America Inc.	333 Commerce St.	Nashville	TN	37201	Carlos Ghosn	615-725-1000	S	2,148	14.0
Renco Group Inc.	30 Rockefeller Plz.	New York	NY	10112	Ira Leno Rennert	212-541-6000	R	1,900	9.4
Thor America Inc.	37 Old 522	Middleburg	PA	17842	W F. B. Thompson	570-837-1663	S	1,592*	8.5
Aero Coach Inc.	Hickory Hill Rd.	Longview	TX	75601	W F. B. Thompson	903-663-7699	S	1,313*	7.5
Monaco Coach Corp.	91320 Coburg Indust	Coburg	OR	97408		541-686-8011	P	1,298	5.3
Federal Signal Corp.	1415 W 22nd St.	Oak Brook	IL	60523	James C. Janning	630-954-2000	P	1,268	5.5
Mitsubishi Motors N America	PO Box 6014	Cypress	CA	90630	Hiroshi Harunari	714-372-6000	S	1,198	3.6
International Truck and Engine	PO Box 1488	Warrenville	IL	60555	Daniel C. Ustian	630-753-5000	S	1,114*	1.7
Spartan Motors Chassis Inc.	1165 Reynolds Rd.	Charlotte	MI	48813	John Sztykiel	517-543-6400	S	1,030*	0.8
Toyota Motor Mfg. W Virginia	1 Sugar Maple Ln.	Buffalo	WV	25033	Laquita Harris	304-937-7000	S	901*	0.9
North American Bus Industries	106 National Dr.	Anniston	AL	36207		256-831-4296	R	886*	0.6
Utilimaster Corp.	PO Box 585	Wakarusa	IN	46573	Lawrence Doyle	574-862-4561	R	836*	1.0
Spartan Motors Inc.	PO Box 440	Charlotte	MI	48813		517-543-6400	P	682	1.4
Airstream Inc.	PO Box 629	Jackson Center	OH	45334	Bpob Wheeler	937-596-6111	S	622*	0.5
Purdy Motor S.A.	CC Aventura 100	San Jose	PR	00930	John Kilmer	506-287-4230	S	509*	0.4
Coachmen Industries Inc.	PO Box 3300	Elkhart	IN	46515	Richard M. Lavers	574-262-0123	P	481	2.7
Ford of North Miami Beach	2198 NE 163rd St.	N Miami Bch	FL	33162		305-493-5000	R	447*	0.3
Reinke Manufacturing Company	PO Box 566	Deshler	NE	68340	Chris Roth	402-365-7251	R	335*	0.4
Wheeled Coach Industries Corp.	2737 Forsyth Rd.	Winter Park	FL	32792	Robert Collins	407-677-7777	S	326*	0.4
Jefferson Industries Corp.	6670 State Rte.	West Jefferson	OH	43162	Hideo Hayashi	614-879-5300	R	309*	0.4
ASC Inc.	1 ASC Ctr.	Southgate	MI	48195	Paul Wilbur	734-285-4911	S	300*	1.0
Elgin Sweeper Co.	1300 W Bartlett Rd.	Elgin	IL	60120	Mark Weber	847-741-5370	S	286*	0.3
SanduskyAthol International	3130 W Monroe St.	Sandusky	OH	44870	Jack Givens	419-627-3200	R	266*	0.2
Allianz Sweeper Co.	4651 Schaefer Ave.	Chino	CA	91710	Gabriel Charky	909-613-5600	R	233*	0.1
Braun Industries Inc.	1170 Production Dr.	Van Wert	OH	45891	Phillip Braun	419-232-7020	R	223*	0.2
Collins Industries Inc.	PO Box 648	Hutchinson	KS	67502	Don L. Collins	620-663-5551	S	208	1.0
Cheetah Chassis Corp.	PO Box 388	Berwick	PA	18603	Frank Katz	570-752-2708	R	167*	0.2
Ferrara Fire Apparatus Inc.	PO Box 249	Holden	LA	70744	Christopher Ferrara	225-567-7100	R	159*	0.3
Midwest Stamping Inc.	3455 Briarfield	Maumee	OH	43537	Ronald L. Thompson	419-724-6970	R	155*	0.6
VSV Group	1110 DI Dr.	Elkhart	IN	46514	Mark Grossbauer	574-264-7511	R	148*	0.5
Smeal Fire Apparatus Co.	PO Box 8	Snyder	NE	68664	Delwin Smeal	402-568-2224	R	139*	0.3
Freightliner Specialty Vehicle	2300 S 13th St.	Clinton	OK	73601	Tim Sinor	580-323-4100	R	123*	0.2
Schwarze Industries Inc.	1055 Jordan Rd.	Huntsville	AL	35811	Ronald A. Robinson	256-851-1200	S	122*	0.2
Excallance Inc.	453 Lanier Rd.	Madison	AL	35758	Charles Epps	256-772-9321	R	112*	<0.1
Executive Coach Builders Inc.	4400 W Production	Springfield	MO	65803	David Bakare	417-935-2233	R	104*	0.1
Louis Berkman Company Inc.	PO Box 820	Steubenville	OH	43952	Louis Berkman	740-283-3722	R	82*	<0.1
Alfa Leisure Inc.	1612 S Cucamonga	Ontario	CA	91761	Johnnie R. Crean	909-628-5574	R	75*	0.7
FWD Seagrave Holdings L.P.	105 E 12th St.	Clintonville	WI	54929		715-823-2141	R	72*	0.4
Custom Coach International	PO Box 869	Pawhuska	OK	74056	Ray Smith	918-287-4445	R	71*	<0.1
Temic Automotive of N America	21440 Lake Cook	Barrington	IL	60010		847-862-6300	R	71*	0.4
Sutphen Corp.	PO Box 158	Amlin	OH	43002		614-889-1005	R	71*	<0.1
Foretravel Inc.	1221 NW Stallings	Nacogdoches	TX	75964		936-564-8367	R	68*	0.3
Accubuilt Inc.	4707 E Kearney St.	Springfield	MO	65803	Dan Mitchell	417-864-4411	R	67*	<0.1
Amerigon Inc.	21680 Haggerty Rd.	Northville	MI	48167	Daniel R. Coker	248-504-0500	P	64	<0.1
Alpine Armoring Inc.	570 Herndon Pkwy.	Herndon	VA	20170	Fred Khoroushi	703-471-0009	R	56*	<0.1
Super Products Corp.	PO Box 270128	Milwaukee	WI	53227	Henry Rowan	262-784-7100	R	51*	0.1
Super Vacuum Manufacturing Co.	PO Box 87	Loveland	CO	80539	Roger Weinmeister	970-667-5146	R	51*	0.1
E-ONE	1601 SW 37 Ave.	Ocala	FL	34474	Mark Gastafin	352-237-1122	D	44*	0.3
Arotech Corp.	1229 Oak Valley Dr.	Ann Arbor	MI	48108	Robert S. Ehrlich		P	43	0.3
Schwartz Industries Inc.	1055 Jordan Rd.	Huntsville	AL	35811	Jim Morris	256-851-1200	R	40*	0.2
AGM Automotive Inc.	1000 E Whitcomb	Madison Heights MI		48071		248-776-0600	R	33*	<0.1
Pemberton Fabricators Inc.	PO Box 227	Rancocas	NJ	08073	Robert Murnan	609-267-0922	R	32*	<0.1
Phoenix U S A Inc.	PO Box 40	Cookeville	TN	38503	James Wright	931-526-6128	R	30*	<0.1
Special Projects Inc.	45901 Helm St.	Plymouth	MI	48170	Kenneth Yanez	734-455-7130	R	29*	<0.1

Source: Ward's Business Directory of U.S. Private and Public Companies, Volumes 1 and 2, 2008. The company type code used is as follows: P - Public, R - Private, S - Subsidiary, D - Division, J - Joint Venture, A - Affiliate, G - Group. Sales are in millions of dollars, employees are in thousands. An asterisk (*) indicates an estimated sales volume. The symbol < stands for 'less than'. Company names and addresses are truncated, in some cases, to fit into the available space.

MATERIALS CONSUMED

Material	Quantity	Delivered Cost ($ million)
Gasoline engines and parts specially designed for gasoline engines	(X)	(D)
Diesel engines and parts specially designed for diesel engines	(X)	1,723.9
Drive train components and parts	(X)	1,095.2
Car bodies	(X)	(D)
Refrigeration compressors, compressor units, condensing units, and other heat transfer equipment	(X)	127.9
Shocks, struts, and other suspension equipment and parts	(X)	208.8
Exhaust systems and parts	(X)	45.1
Machine tool accessories, including cutting tools	(X)	4.3
Fluid power pumps, motors, and hydrostatic transmissions	(X)	36.9
Fluid power valves (hydraulic and pneumatic)	(X)	20.7
Fluid power cylinders and rotary actuators (hydraulic and pneumatic)	(X)	8.7
Fluid power hose, tube fittings, and assemblies (hydraulic and pneumatic)	(X)	39.6
Fluid power filters (hydraulic and pneumatic)	(X)	16.9
Other transportation related fluid power products, hydraulic and pneumatic	(X)	(D)
Automotive stampings (inc. body parts, hubcaps, fenders, etc.)	(X)	169.4
Steel springs (excluding wire)	(X)	34.5
Motor vehicle metal hardware (lock units, etc.), exc. forgings	(X)	35.4
Metal bolts, nuts, screws, and other screw machine products	(X)	118.3
Other fabricated metal products (excluding forgings)	(X)	158.6
Forgings	(X)	(D)
Castings, rough and semifinished	(X)	(D)
Metal shapes and forms (exc. castings, forgings, fabr. metal products)	(X)	57.0
Ball and roller bearings (mounted or unmounted)	(X)	10.3
Pneumatic tires and inner tubes	(X)	201.2
Rubber and plastics hose and belting	(X)	47.2
Fabricated rubber products (exc. tires, tubes, hoses, belting, and gaskets)	(X)	24.5
Gaskets (all types), and packing and sealing devices	(X)	5.6
Fabricated plastics products (exc. gaskets, hoses, and belting)	(X)	28.1
Glass and glass products (including windows and mirrors)	(X)	43.3
Seats (purchased separately) for automobiles, trucks, and buses	(X)	67.2
Seat covers, seat belts, and shoulder harnesses	(X)	8.0
Automotive air bag assemblies and parts	(X)	(D)
Automotive trimmings, textile (panels, headliners, etc.)	(X)	87.3
Carpeting	(X)	(D)
Glues and adhesives	(X)	4.2
Paints, varnishes, stains, lacquers, shellacs, japans, enamels, etc.	(X)	69.4
Engine electrical equipment (incl. spark plugs, magnetos, generators, starters, etc.)	(X)	78.4
Motor vehicle lighting fixtures, excluding auto lamps	(X)	28.1
Automotive lamps (bulbs and sealed beams)	(X)	18.2
Storage batteries, automotive	(X)	29.8
Automotive radios and loudspeakers	(X)	16.9
Motor vehicle clusters, meters, and gauges, excluding electrical	(X)	51.7
Semiconductors and related devices and electronic control modules	(X)	56.1
Purchased computers for incorporation into motor vehicles, trucks, and buses	(X)	(D)
All other materials, components, parts, containers, and supplies	(X)	6,693.6
Materials, ingredients, containers, and supplies, nsk	(X)	1,045.2

Source: 2002 *Economic Census*. Explanation of symbols used: (D): Withheld to avoid disclosure of competitive data; na: Not available; (S): Withheld because statistical norms were not met; (X): Not applicable; (Z): Less than half the unit shown; nec: Not elsewhere classified; nsk: Not specified by kind; - : zero; p : 10-19 percent estimated; q : 20-29 percent estimated.

PRODUCT SHARE DETAILS

Product or Product Class Shipments	Mil. $	Product or Product Class Shipments	Mil. $
HEAVY DUTY TRUCKS AND BUSES	16,522.0	of own manufacture)	1,737.5
Trucks, truck tractors, and bus chassis (chassis of own manufacture) 14,001 to 33,000 lb	3,543.2	Buses, including military (except trolley buses) (chassis of own manufacture)	1,475.7
Trucks, truck tractors, and bus chassis (chassis of own manufacture) 33,001 lb or more	10,351.8	Firefighting vehicles (chassis of own manufacture)	261.8
Buses, including military and firefighting vehicles (chassis of own manufacture)	2,404.7	Buses, including military and firefighting vehicles (chassis of own manufacture), nsk	667.2
Buses, including military and firefighting vehicles (chassis		**Heavy duty trucks and buses, nsk, total**	**222.4**

Source: 2002 *Economic Census*. The values are product shipments in millions of dollars for 2002. Total product shipments may be lower or higher than industry shipments. See Introduction for a full discussion. Values of indented subcategories are summed in the main heading(s). The symbol (D) appears when data are withheld to prevent disclosure of competitive information. The abbreviation nsk stands for 'not specified by kind' and nec for 'not elsewhere classified'. A dash (-) means zero.

INPUTS AND OUTPUTS FOR HEAVY DUTY TRUCK MANUFACTURING

Economic Sector or Industry Providing Inputs	%	Sector	Economic Sector or Industry Buying Outputs	%	Sector
Motor vehicle parts	29.8	Manufg.	Private fixed investment	53.9	
Engine equipment, nec	20.2	Manufg.	S/L govt. invest., other	19.6	S/L Govt
Compensation of employees	11.9		Exports of goods & services	10.6	Cap Inv
Wholesale trade	7.5	Trade	Motor homes	4.4	Manufg.
Mechanical power transmission equipment	4.5	Manufg.	S/L govt. invest., education	2.9	S/L Govt
Management of companies & enterprises	3.3	Services	Motor vehicle bodies	2.3	Manufg.
AC, refrigeration, and warm air heating equipment	1.5	Manufg.	Federal government, investment, national defense	2.1	Fed Govt
Tires	1.4	Manufg.	Federal government, investment, nondefense	1.9	Fed Govt
Rubber products, nec	1.4	Manufg.	Construction machinery	0.7	Manufg.
Turned products & screws, nuts, & bolts	1.4	Manufg.	Change in private inventories	0.5	In House
Natural gas distribution	1.1	Util.	Travel trailers & campers	0.4	Manufg.
Software publishers	1.1	Services	Automotive repair & maintenance, ex. car washes	0.3	Services
Truck transportation	0.7	Util.	Retail trade	0.3	Trade
Paperboard containers	0.7	Manufg.			
Paints & coatings	0.6	Manufg.			
Semiconductors & related devices	0.6	Manufg.			
Nonwoven fabric mills	0.5	Manufg.			
Noncomparable imports	0.5	Foreign			
Valve & fittings other than plumbing	0.4	Manufg.			
Printed circuit assemblies (electronic assemblies)	0.4	Manufg.			
Fluid power process machinery	0.4	Manufg.			
Totalizing fluid meters & counting devices	0.4	Manufg.			
Plastics packaging materials, film & sheet	0.4	Manufg.			
Rubber & plastics hose & belting	0.4	Manufg.			
Scientific research & development services	0.3	Services			
Machine shops	0.3	Manufg.			
Springs & wire products	0.3	Manufg.			
Hardware	0.3	Manufg.			
Iron & steel mills & ferroalloys	0.3	Manufg.			
Plastics products, nec	0.3	Manufg.			
Glass products from purchased glass	0.2	Manufg.			
Coating, engraving, heat treating & allied activities	0.2	Manufg.			
Computer terminals & peripherals	0.2	Manufg.			
Power generation & supply	0.2	Util.			
Textile product mills, nec	0.2	Manufg.			
Maintenance/repair of nonresidential structures	0.2	Construct.			
Storage batteries	0.2	Manufg.			
Services to buildings & dwellings	0.2	Services			
Relay & industrial controls	0.2	Manufg.			
Automotive equipment rental & leasing	0.2	Fin/R.E.			
Ornamental & architectural metal products	0.1	Manufg.			
Rail transportation	0.1	Util.			
Advertising & related services	0.1	Services			
Automotive repair & maintenance, ex. car washes	0.1	Services			
Ball & roller bearings	0.1	Manufg.			
General purpose machinery, nec	0.1	Manufg.			
Audio & video equipment	0.1	Manufg.			
Commercial & industrial equipment repair/maintenance	0.1	Services			
Taxes on production & imports, less subsidies	0.1				
Pressed & blown glass & glassware, nec	0.1	Manufg.			
Electric lamp bulbs & parts	0.1	Manufg.			

Source: Benchmark Input-Output Accounts for the U.S. Economy, 2002, U.S. Department of Commerce, Washington, D.C., January 2008. The abbreviation nec stands for 'not elsewhere classified'.

OCCUPATIONS EMPLOYED BY MOTOR VEHICLE MANUFACTURING

Occupation	% of Total 2006	Change to 2016	Occupation	% of Total 2006	Change to 2016
Team assemblers	24.3	-0.4	Maintenance & repair workers, general	2.1	-3.1
Assemblers & fabricators, nec	18.7	-12.8	Laborers & freight, stock, & material movers, hand	1.8	-12.8
First-line supervisors/managers of production workers	2.8	-3.1	Industrial truck & tractor operators	1.5	-12.8
Inspectors, testers, sorters, samplers, & weighers	2.7	-8.6	Welders, cutters, solderers, & brazers	1.3	3.1
Painters, transportation equipment	2.2	-3.1	Industrial machinery mechanics	1.2	11.4

Source: Industry-Occupation Matrix, Bureau of Labor Statistics, December 4, 2007. These data are reported based on 4-digit NAICS categories but have been matched to corresponding 6-digit NAICS industry codes. The change reported for each occupation to the year 2016 is a percent of growth or decline as estimated by the Bureau of Labor Statistics. The abbreviation nec stands for 'not elsewhere classified'.

LOCATION BY STATE AND REGIONAL CONCENTRATION

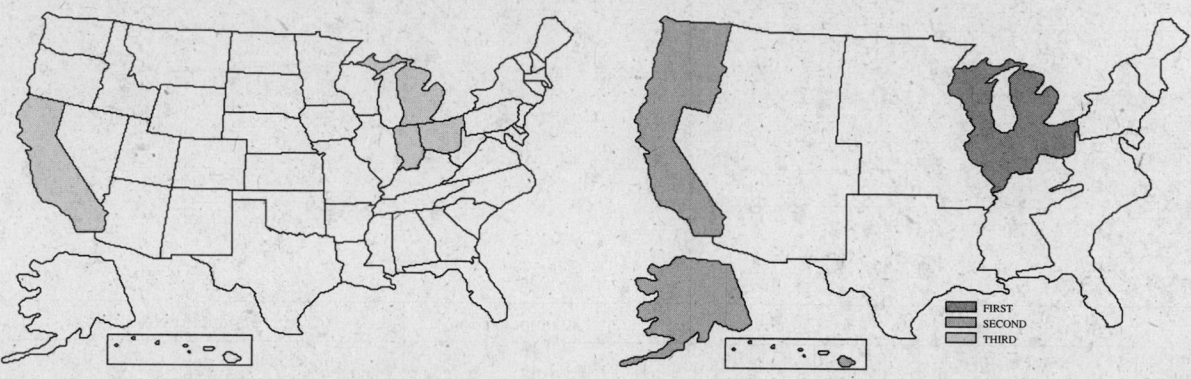

INDUSTRY DATA BY STATE

State	Establish-ments	Shipments			Employment				Cost as % of Shipments	Investment per Employee ($)
		Total ($ mil)	% of U.S.	Per Establ.	Total Number	% of U.S.	Per Establ.	Wages ($/hour)		
Ohio	10	2,722.8	16.9	272,280.2	4,562	15.3	456	24.72	74.5	2,617
Indiana	8	586.7	3.6	73,337.0	834	2.8	104	10.50	72.8	5,146
California	10	485.0	3.0	48,501.9	1,065	3.6	107	16.27	66.6	3,283
Michigan	5	288.7	1.8	57,735.8	897	3.0	179	7.14	80.2	1,913

Source: 2002 *Economic Census*. The states are in descending order of shipments or establishments (if shipment data are missing for the majority). The symbol (D) appears when data are withheld to prevent disclosure of competitive information. States marked with (D) are sorted by number of establishments. A dash (-) indicates that the data element cannot be calculated. Data may not show all states active in the NAICS category. All data available at the time of publication are shown.

NAICS 336211 - MOTOR VEHICLE BODY AND TRAILER MANUFACTURING

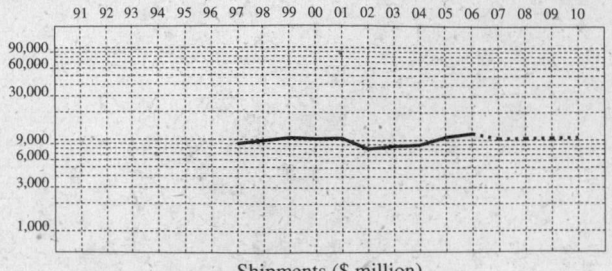

Shipments ($ million)

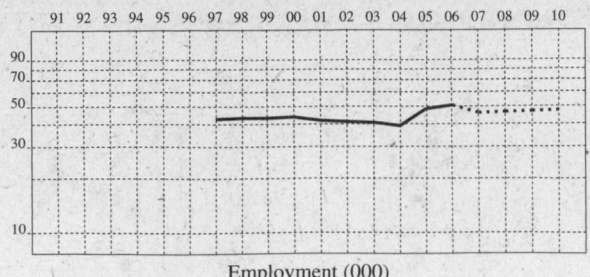

Employment (000)

GENERAL STATISTICS

| Year | Companies | Establishments | | Employment | | | Compensation | | Production ($ million) | | | |
		Total	with 20 or more employees	Total (000)	Production Workers (000)	Hours (Mil)	Payroll ($ mil)	Wages ($/hr)	Cost of Materials	Value Added by Manufacture	Value of Shipments	Capital Invest.
1997	749	808	339	42.7	32.5	65.3	1,227.5	12.83	5,968.5	2,962.8	8,934.8	228.2
1998		814	360	43.3	32.9	66.4	1,267.0	12.87	6,404.3	2,982.9	9,696.0	136.0
1999		832	360	43.2	33.8	68.6	1,374.0	13.77	6,779.3	3,825.9	10,520.3	152.7
2000		822	364	43.8	33.6	66.9	1,423.9	14.19	6,546.8	3,843.9	10,334.9	303.7
2001		811	368	41.8	30.9	60.2	1,325.2	14.11	6,659.3	3,873.0	10,534.7	320.0
2002	759	847	367	41.2	30.9	61.1	1,419.6	15.31	5,288.8	2,741.7	8,028.3	149.9
2003		837	375	40.7	30.9	63.0	1,450.5	15.29	5,392.9	3,252.8	8,597.5	179.5
2004		826	367	39.1	29.9	60.8	1,459.9	15.89	5,401.6	3,466.1	8,861.0	152.0
2005		814	362	48.4	36.3	72.8	1,807.8	16.47	6,490.5	4,411.8	10,797.0	149.8
2006		831P	375P	50.7	38.3	80.5	1,933.2	16.06	6,903.1	4,928.7	11,738.6	150.1
2007		833P	377P	46.1P	34.6P	71.0P	1,826.9P	16.99P	6,097.4P	4,353.4P	10,368.5P	153.8P
2008		835P	380P	46.5P	34.9P	71.8P	1,892.0P	17.41P	6,157.7P	4,396.5P	10,471.1P	146.8P
2009		836P	382P	47.0P	35.2P	72.6P	1,957.1P	17.83P	6,218.0P	4,439.6P	10,573.7P	139.8P
2010		838P	384P	47.5P	35.5P	73.3P	2,022.2P	18.25P	6,278.4P	4,482.7P	10,676.3P	132.8P

Sources: 1997 and 2002 *Economic Census*; other years, up to 2006, are from *Annual Survey of Manufactures*. Establishment counts for non-Census years are from *County Business Patterns*; 1997 and 2002 values are from the 1997 and 2002 censuses, respectively. 'P's show projections by the editors.

INDICES OF CHANGE

| Year | Companies | Establishments | | Employment | | | Compensation | | Production ($ million) | | | |
		Total	with 20 or more employees	Total (000)	Production Workers (000)	Hours (Mil)	Payroll ($ mil)	Wages ($/hr)	Cost of Materials	Value Added by Manufacture	Value of Shipments	Capital Invest.
1997	99	95	92	104	105	107	86	84	113	108	111	152
1998		96	98	105	106	109	89	84	121	109	121	91
1999		98	98	105	109	112	97	90	128	140	131	102
2000		97	99	106	109	109	100	93	124	140	129	203
2001		96	100	101	100	99	93	92	126	141	131	213
2002	100	100	100	100	100	100	100	100	100	100	100	100
2003		99	102	99	100	103	102	100	102	119	107	120
2004		98	100	95	97	100	103	104	102	126	110	101
2005		96	99	117	117	119	127	108	123	161	134	100
2006		98P	102P	123	124	132	136	105	131	180	146	100
2007		98P	103P	112P	112P	116P	129P	111P	115P	159P	129P	103P
2008		99P	103P	113P	113P	118P	133P	114P	116P	160P	130P	98P
2009		99P	104P	114P	114P	119P	138P	116P	118P	162P	132P	93P
2010		99P	105P	115P	115P	120P	142P	119P	119P	164P	133P	89P

Sources: Same as General Statistics. Values reflect change from the base year, 2002. Values above 100 mean greater than 2002, values below 100 mean less than 2002, and the values of 100 in other years means the same as 2002. 'P's show projections by the editors.

SELECTED RATIOS

For 2002	Avg. of All Manufact.	Analyzed Industry	Index	For 2002	Avg. of All Manufact.	Analyzed Industry	Index
Employees per Establishment	42	49	116	Value Added per Production Worker	182,367	88,728	49
Payroll per Establishment	1,639,184	1,676,033	102	Cost per Establishment	5,769,015	6,244,156	108
Payroll per Employee	39,053	34,456	88	Cost per Employee	137,446	128,369	93
Production Workers per Establishment	30	36	124	Cost per Production Worker	195,506	171,159	88
Wages per Establishment	694,845	1,104,417	159	Shipments per Establishment	11,158,348	9,478,512	85
Wages per Production Worker	23,548	30,273	129	Shipments per Employee	265,847	194,862	73
Hours per Production Worker	1,980	1,977	100	Shipments per Production Worker	378,144	259,816	69
Wages per Hour	11.89	15.31	129	Investment per Establishment	361,338	176,978	49
Value Added per Establishment	5,381,325	3,236,954	60	Investment per Employee	8,609	3,638	42
Value Added per Employee	128,210	66,546	52	Investment per Production Worker	12,245	4,851	40

Sources: Same as General Statistics. The 'Average of All Manufacturing' column represents the average of all manufacturing industries reported for the most recent complete year available. The Index shows the relationship between the Average and the Analyzed Industry. For example, 100 means that they are equal; 500 that the Analyzed Industry is five times the average; 50 means that the Analyzed Industry is half the national average. The abbreviation 'na' is used to show that data are 'not available'. Ratios shown for 2002, the last complete census year.

LEADING COMPANIES

Number shown: **75**   Total sales ($ mil): **944,449**   Total employment (000): **2,238.2**

Company Name	Address				CEO Name	Phone	Co. Type	Sales ($ mil)	Empl. (000)
General Motors Corp.	300 Renaissance Ctr	Detroit	MI	48265		313-556-5000	P	181,122	266.0
Ford Motor Co.	1 American Rd.	Dearborn	MI	48126		313-322-3000	P	172,455	246.0
United Technologies Corp.	1 Financial Plz.	Hartford	CT	06101	Mario Abajo	860-728-7000	P	47,829	225.6
Chrysler L.L.C.	1000 Chrysler Dr.	Auburn Hills	MI	48326	Thomas W. LaSorda	248-576-5741	S	45,237*	84.4
American Honda Motor Company	1919 Torrance Blvd.	Torrance	CA	90501	Koichi Kondo	310-783-2000	S	42,539	25.0
Honeywell International Inc.	PO Box 4000	Morristown	NJ	07962	Adriane M. Brown	973-455-2000	P	34,589	122.0
ArvinMeritor OE L.L.C.	950 W 450 S, Bldg.	Columbus	IN	47201	C. G. McClure Jr.	812-341-2000	S	23,491*	32.0
Delphi Corp.	5725 Delphi Dr.	Troy	MI	48098	Voker J. Barth	248-813-2000	P	22,383	169.5
Lear Corp.	PO Box 5008	Southfield	MI	48086	Jim Brackenbury	248-447-1500	P	15,995	91.0
PACCAR Inc.	PO Box 1518	Bellevue	WA	98009		425-468-7400	P	15,220	21.8
Ford VAC Corp.	1 American Rd.	Dearborn	MI	48121	William J. Ford	313-322-3000	S	15,105*	1.9
TRW Automotive Holdings Inc.	12001 Tech Cntr Dr.	Livonia	MI	48150		734-855-2600	P	14,702	66.3
Textron Inc.	40 Westminster St.	Providence	RI	02903		401-421-2800	P	13,225	44.0
Cummins Inc.	PO Box 3005	Columbus	IN	47202		812-377-5000	P	13,048	37.8
Eaton Corp.	1111 Superior Ave.	Cleveland	OH	44114		216-523-5000	P	13,033	60.0
Navistar International Corp.	PO Box 1488	Warrenville	IL	60555		630-753-5000	P	12,153	14.8
Visteon Corp.	1 Village Center Dr	Van Buren Twp	MI	48111		313-755-2800	P	11,266	41.5
Parker Hannifin Corp.	6035 Parkland Blvd.	Cleveland	OH	44124	Lee Banks	216-896-3000	P	10,718	57.3
Acument Global Technologies	840 W Long Lake	Troy	MI	48098	Joseph Gray	248-813-6329	S	10,080*	9.0
ITT Corp.	4 W Red Oak Ln.	White Plains	NY	10604		914-641-2000	P	9,003	39.7
Dana Corp.	PO Box 1000	Toledo	OH	43697	Michael J. Burns	419-535-4500	P	8,504	45.0
American Standard Inc.	PO Box 6820	Piscataway	NJ	08855		732-980-3000	S	7,614*	67.0
Neapco L.L.C.	PO Box 399	Pottstown	PA	19464		610-323-6000	R	7,580*	0.3
Trane Inc.	PO Box 6820	Piscataway	NJ	08855		732-980-6000	P	7,450	29.6
Triangle Suspension Systems	PO Box 425	Du Bois	PA	15801	Greg Maffia	814-375-7211	R	7,000*	0.2
Perfection Hy-Test Company	100 Perfection Way	Timmonsville	SC	29161		843-326-5544	R	7,000*	0.2
Penn Machine Co.	106 Station St.	Johnstown	PA	15905	H Wiegand	814-288-1547	R	7,000*	<0.1
Federal-Mogul Corp.	PO Box 1966	Detroit	MI	48235	Jose Maria Alapont	248-354-7700	P	6,914	43.1
Robert Bosch Corp.	2800 S 25th Ave.	Broadview	IL	60155	Kurt W. Liedtke	708-865-5200	S	6,782*	25.0
ArvinMeritor Inc.	2135 W Maple Rd.	Troy	MI	48084		248-435-1000	P	6,449	18.0
Oshkosh Truck Corp.	PO Box 2566	Oshkosh	WI	54903	Robert G. Bohn	920-235-9150	P	6,307	14.2
Tenneco Inc.	500 N Field Dr.	Lake Forest	IL	60045		847-482-5000	P	6,184	21.0
Toyota Motor Mfg. N America	25 Atlantic Ave.	Erlanger	KY	41018	Masamoto Amezawa	859-746-4000	S	6,120*	7.5
Guardian Industries Corp.	2300 Harmon Rd.	Auburn Hills	MI	48326	William M. Davidson	248-340-1800	R	5,330	19.0
BorgWarner Inc.	3850 Hamlin Rd.	Auburn Hills	MI	48326		248-754-9200	P	5,329	17.7
Autoliv ASP Inc.	3350 Airport Rd.	Ogden	UT	84405	Leonard Barton	801-625-4800	S	5,301*	3.7
Honda of America Manufacturing	24000 Honda Pkwy.	Marysville	OH	43040	Takeo Fukui	937-642-5000	S	5,090*	13.0
Carlisle Tire and Wheel Co.	23 Windham Blvd.	Aiken	SC	29805	Barry Littrell	803-643-2900	S	4,822*	0.6
Karl Schmidt Unisia Inc.	1731 Industrial Pky	Marinette	WI	54143	Frank Pohlmann	715-732-0181	R	4,640*	0.9
Pioneer Automotive Tech.	100 S Pioneer Blvd.	Springboro	OH	45066	Steve Moerner	937-746-6600	R	4,610*	0.3
Toledo Trans-Kit Inc.	13515 Ballnyn Corp.	Charlotte	NC	28277	C. J. Kearney	704-752-4400	S	4,372	23.8
Mack Trucks Inc.	PO Box M	Allentown	PA	18105		610-709-3011	R	4,324*	0.8
Toyota Motor Mfg, Kentucky	PO Box 2700	Georgetown	KY	40324	Steven Angelo	502-868-2000	S	4,181*	5.0
CCI Manufacturing Inc.	2624 Joe Field Rd.	Dallas	TX	75229	Steve Bond	972-488-8131	R	4,143*	0.1
New United Motor Manufacturing	45500 Fremont	Fremont	CA	94538	Bruce Walker	510-498-5500	J	4,080*	5.0
Saturn Corp.	PO Box 1502	Spring Hill	TN	37174		931-486-5000	S	3,901	9.6
Motors Insurance Corp.	PO Box 66937	St. Louis	MO	63166	Gary Kuzumi		S	3,849*	2.2
Kalmar Industries USA L.L.C.	415 E Dundee St.	Ottawa	KS	66067		785-242-2200	R	3,320*	0.3
American Axle & Mfg Holdings	1 Dauch Dr.	Detroit	MI	48211	Richard E. Dauch	313-974-2000	P	3,248	10.0
Hi-Stat Manufacturing Company	28001 Cabot Dr.	Novi	MI	48377	John Corey	248-489-9300	D	3,194*	5.0
Thor Industries Inc.	PO Box 629	Jackson Center	OH	45334		937-596-6849	P	3,066	9.1
Amsted Industries Inc.	2 Prudential Plaza	Chicago	IL	60601	W. Robert Reum	312-645-1700	R	3,050	9.9
AutoAlliance International	1 International Dr.	Flat Rock	MI	48134	Phillip G. Spender	734-782-7800	J	3,019*	3.7
TAG Holdings L.L.C.	2075 W Big Beaver	Troy	MI	48084	J. B. Anderson, Jr.	248-822-8056	R	2,904*	2.5
Freightliner L.L.C.	PO Box 3849	Portland	OR	97208	Chris Patterson	503-745-8000	S	2,734*	14.0
BMW of North America L.L.C.	PO Box 1227	Westwood	NJ	07675	Thomas Purves	201-307-4000	S	2,690*	1.0
Crane Co.	100 First Stamford	Stamford	CT	06902	Thomas Craney	203-363-7300	P	2,619	12.0
Consolidated Metco Inc.	PO Box 83201	Portland	OR	97283		503-286-5741	R	2,510*	0.1
Pall Corp.	2200 Northern Blvd.	East Hills	NY	11548	Eric Krasnoff	516-484-5400	P	2,250	10.8
DENSO Manufacturing Tennessee	1720 Rbrt C Jackson	Maryville	TN	37801	Mack Hattori	865-982-7000	S	2,231*	2.0
Sequa Corp.	200 Park Ave.	New York	NY	10166	Gail Binderman	212-986-5500	P	2,183	10.2
Affinia Group Inc.	1101 Technology	Ann Arbor	MI	48108		734-827-5400	P	2,160	12.4
Nissan North America Inc.	333 Commerce St.	Nashville	TN	37201	Carlos Ghosn	615-725-1000	S	2,148	14.0
Dura Automotive Systems Inc.	2791 Research Dr.	Rochester Hills	MI	48309	Lawrence A. Denton	248-299-7500	P	2,091	15.4
Heil Co.	5751 Cornelison Rd.	Chattanooga	TN	37411	Michael G. Jobe	423-899-9100	S	2,085*	1.6
Hayes Lemmerz International	15300 Centennial Dr	Northville	MI	48167	Fred Bentley	734-737-5000	P	2,039	11.0
Cooper Tire and Rubber Co.	701 Lima Ave.	Findlay	OH	45840	Roy V. Armes	419-423-1321	P	2,036	13.6
ZF Group N American Operations	15811 Centennial Dr	Northville	MI	48168	Julio Caspari	734-416-6200	R	1,949*	5.5
Sypris Technologies Marion	1550 Marion-Agosta	Marion	OH	43301	Jeffrey T. Gill	740-383-2111	S	1,920*	2.6
Renco Group Inc.	30 Rockefeller Plz.	New York	NY	10112	Ira Leno Rennert	212-541-6000	R	1,900	9.4
Hutchinson FTS Inc.	1835 Technology	Troy	MI	48083	Paul Campbell	248-589-7710	R	1,863*	<0.1
ADVICS North America Inc.	45300 Polaris Ct.	Plymouth	MI	48170	Haruhiko Saito	734-414-5100	S	1,810*	<0.1
Regal-Beloit Corp.	200 State St.	Beloit	WI	53511		608-364-8800	P	1,803	17.9
Bose Corp.	The Mountain	Framingham	MA	01701	Amar G. Bose	508-879-7330	R	1,800	8.0
Modine Manufacturing Co.	1500 DeKoven Ave.	Racine	WI	53403	Richard J. Doyle	262-636-1200	P	1,758	7.7

Source: Ward's Business Directory of U.S. Private and Public Companies, Volumes 1 and 2, 2008. The company type code used is as follows: P - Public, R - Private, S - Subsidiary, D - Division, J - Joint Venture, A - Affiliate, G - Group. Sales are in millions of dollars, employees are in thousands. An asterisk (*) indicates an estimated sales volume. The symbol < stands for 'less than'. Company names and addresses are truncated, in some cases, to fit into the available space.

MATERIALS CONSUMED

Material	Quantity	Delivered Cost ($ million)
Purchased chassis for vehicles (excluding passenger cars)	(X)	570.7
Truck bodies	(X)	77.1
Transmissions and parts	(X)	45.8
Car bodies	(X)	(D)
Shocks, struts, and other suspension equipment and parts	(X)	42.4
Automotive stampings (inc. body parts, hubcaps, fenders, etc.)	(X)	(D)
Motor vehicle metal hardware (lock units, etc.), exc. forgings	(X)	29.1
Metal bolts, nuts, screws, and other screw machine products	(X)	39.8
Other fabricated metal products (excluding forgings)	(X)	96.0
Forgings	(X)	(D)
Castings, rough and semifinished	(X)	47.3
Fluid power products	(X)	162.4
Pneumatic tires and inner tubes	(X)	12.1
Fabricated plastics products (exc. gaskets, hoses, and belting)	(X)	24.1
Glass and glass products (including windows and mirrors)	(X)	19.3
Seats (purchased separately) for automobiles, trucks, and buses	(X)	36.1
Paints, varnishes, stains, lacquers, shellacs, japans, enamels, etc.	(X)	50.0
Motor vehicle lighting fixtures, excluding auto lamps	(X)	37.5
Automotive lamps (bulbs and sealed beams)	(X)	2.6
Steel bars, bar shapes, and plates (exc. castings, forgings, fabr. metal products)	(X)	41.7
Steel sheet and strip (including tinplate)	(X)	107.4
Steel structural shapes and sheet piling (exc. castings, forgings, fabr. metal products)	(X)	16.0
All other steel shapes and forms (exc. castings, forgings, fabr. metal products)	(X)	44.2
Aluminum and aluminum-base alloy sheet, plate, foil, and welded tubing	(X)	71.7
Aluminum and aluminum-base alloy extruded shapes (rod, bar, pipe, tube, etc.)	(X)	55.3
Other aluminum and aluminum-base alloy shapes and forms (exc. castings, forgings, fabr. metal products)	(X)	13.0
Other nonferrous shapes and forms (exc. castings, forgings, fabricated metal products)	(X)	3.0
Rough and dressed lumber	(X)	41.1
Other motor vehicle wheel parts, metal (axles, brakes, etc.)	(X)	56.1
All other materials, components, parts, containers, and supplies	(X)	2,741.3
Materials, ingredients, containers, and supplies, nsk	(X)	146.3

Source: 2002 *Economic Census*. Explanation of symbols used: (D): Withheld to avoid disclosure of competitive data; na: Not available; (S): Withheld because statistical norms were not met; (X): Not applicable; (Z): Less than half the unit shown; nec: Not elsewhere classified; nsk: Not specified by kind; - : zero; p : 10-19 percent estimated; q : 20-29 percent estimated.

PRODUCT SHARE DETAILS

Product or Product Class Shipments	Mil. $	Product or Product Class Shipments	Mil. $
MOTOR VEHICLE BODIES	7,730.1	car bodies for sale separately	(D)
Bus bodies and truck cable for sale separately	**1,408.0**	Kit cars	18.1
Bus bodies for sale separately	1,203.8	Motor vehicle fifth wheels, new	99.9
School bus bodies for sale separately	1,061.7	All other truck and vehicle bodies for sale separately	173.7
Other bus bodies for sale separately	142.1	**Buses and firefighting vehicles, complete, manufactured on purchased chassis**	**1,668.9**
Truck cabs for sale separately	204.2	Buses, complete, manufactured on purchased chassis	833.4
Van bodies for sale separately	**433.6**	Firefighting vehicles, complete, manufactured on purchased chassis	835.5
Van bodies, walk-in, for sale separately	142.6	Firefighting vehicles, complete, 19,000 lb or less, manufactured on purchased chassis	37.2
Van bodies with separate cab for sale separately	291.0		
Van bodies, insulated, for sale separately	72.7	Firefighting vehicles, complete, greater than 19,000 lb, manufactured on purchased chassis	798.3
Van bodies, dry freight, for sale separately	186.7	**Other trucks, complete, manufactured on purchased chassis**	**1,503.6**
Van bodies, parcel delivery, for sale separately	26.7	Other trucks, complete, manufactured on purchased chassis	1,028.5
Other van bodies with separate cab for sale separately	4.9		
Other truck and vehicle bodies for sale separately, including dumptruck lifting mechanisms and kit cars	**1,961.9**	Ambulance and rescue vehicles, complete, manufactured on purchased chassis	166.2
Tank bodies for sale separately	62.5	Vans, complete, manufactured on purchased chassis	86.9
Front loading garbage and refuse truck bodies (packer-types) for sale separately	31.2	Tank trucks, complete, manufactured on purchased chassis	(D)
Rear loading garbage and refuse truck bodies (packer-types) for sale separately	74.8	Utility line service trucks, complete, manufactured on purchased chassis	110.7
Side loading garbage and refuse truck bodies (packer-types) for sale separately	68.8	Other mobile service type trucks, complete, manufactured on purchased chassis	283.4
Other garbage and refuse truck bodies for sale separately	37.7	All other trucks designed primarily for transporting persons or goods, manufactured on purchased chassis	96.9
Beverage truck bodies for sale separately	89.5	All other trucks not designed primarily for transporting persons or goods, manufactured on purchased chassis	244.5
Dump truck bodies for sale separately	188.3	Upfitting	472.0
Dump truck lifting mechanisms	41.0	Other trucks, complete, manufactured on purchased chassis, nsk	3.1
Stake and platform truck bodies for sale separately	67.7	**Motor vehicle bodies, nsk, total**	**754.0**
Utility line service truck bodies for sale separately	171.5		
Other mobile service type truck bodies for sale separately	92.9		
Wrecker truck bodies for sale separately	(D)		
Ambulance and rescue vehicle bodies for sale separately	103.7		
Light truck (minivan, SUV, pickup truck) and passenger			

Source: 2002 *Economic Census*. The values are product shipments in millions of dollars for 2002. Total product shipments may be lower or higher than industry shipments. See Introduction for a full discussion. Values of indented subcategories are summed in the main heading(s). The symbol (D) appears when data are withheld to prevent disclosure of competitive information. The abbreviation nsk stands for 'not specified by kind' and nec for 'not elsewhere classified'. A dash (-) means zero.

INPUTS AND OUTPUTS FOR MOTOR VEHICLE BODY MANUFACTURING

Economic Sector or Industry Providing Inputs	%	Sector	Economic Sector or Industry Buying Outputs	%	Sector
Compensation of employees	21.5		Private fixed investment	35.2	
Management of companies & enterprises	7.5	Services	Light truck & utility vehicles	22.5	Manufg.
Heavy duty trucks	6.4	Manufg.	Automobiles	20.3	Manufg.
Motor vehicle parts	5.1	Manufg.	Exports of goods & services	10.6	Cap Inv
Wholesale trade	5.0	Trade	Motor vehicle bodies	3.9	Manufg.
Iron & steel mills & ferroalloys	3.4	Manufg.	Federal government, investment, nondefense	2.0	Fed Govt
Aluminum products from purchased aluminum	3.4	Manufg.	Retail trade	1.6	Trade
Motor vehicle bodies	2.4	Manufg.	Change in private inventories	1.3	In House
Ornamental & architectural metal products	1.4	Manufg.	Construction machinery	0.9	Manufg.
Rubber & plastics hose & belting	1.4	Manufg.	Automotive repair & maintenance, ex. car washes	0.5	Services
Communication & energy wires & cables	1.3	Manufg.	Personal consumption expenditures	0.4	
Turned products & screws, nuts, & bolts	1.3	Manufg.	Wholesale trade	0.2	Trade
Textile product mills, nec	1.1	Manufg.	Heavy duty trucks	0.2	Manufg.
Fluid power process machinery	1.1	Manufg.	Truck trailers	0.1	Manufg.
Rubber products, nec	1.1	Manufg.	General Federal government services, nondefense	0.1	Fed Govt
General purpose machinery, nec	1.0	Manufg.			
Paints & coatings	1.0	Manufg.			
Coating, engraving, heat treating & allied activities	0.9	Manufg.			
Truck transportation	0.8	Util.			
Springs & wire products	0.8	Manufg.			
Scientific research & development services	0.8	Services			
Valve & fittings other than plumbing	0.7	Manufg.			
Glass products from purchased glass	0.7	Manufg.			
Lessors of nonfinancial assets	0.6	Fin/R.E.			
Semiconductors & related devices	0.5	Manufg.			
Machine shops	0.5	Manufg.			
Cutting tools & machine tool accessories	0.5	Manufg.			
Real estate	0.5	Fin/R.E.			
Printed circuit assemblies (electronic assemblies)	0.5	Manufg.			
Securities, commodity contracts, investments	0.5	Fin/R.E.			
Sawmills & wood preservation	0.4	Manufg.			
Advertising & related services	0.4	Services			
Hardware	0.4	Manufg.			
Paperboard containers	0.4	Manufg.			
Abrasive products	0.4	Manufg.			
Software publishers	0.3	Services			
Power generation & supply	0.3	Util.			
Ferrous metal foundries	0.3	Manufg.			
Plastics products, nec	0.3	Manufg.			
Architectural, engineering, & related services	0.3	Services			
Professional, scientific, technical services, nec	0.3	Services			
Lighting fixtures	0.3	Manufg.			
Nonferrous metal foundries	0.3	Manufg.			
Specialized design services	0.2	Services			
Retail trade	0.2	Trade			
Warehousing & storage	0.2	Util.			
Taxes on production & imports, less subsidies	0.2				
Automotive equipment rental & leasing	0.2	Fin/R.E.			
Rail transportation	0.2	Util.			
Legal services	0.2	Services			
Accounting, tax preparation, bookkeeping, & payroll	0.2	Services			
Food services & drinking places	0.2	Services			
Telecommunications	0.2	Services			
Tires	0.2	Manufg.			
Natural gas distribution	0.1	Util.			
Data processing, hosting, & related services	0.1	Services			
Air transportation	0.1	Util.			
Metal cans, boxes, & other containers (light gauge)	0.1	Manufg.			
Services to buildings & dwellings	0.1	Services			

Source: Benchmark Input-Output Accounts for the U.S. Economy, 2002, U.S. Department of Commerce, Washington, D.C., January 2008. The abbreviation nec stands for 'not elsewhere classified'.

OCCUPATIONS EMPLOYED BY MOTOR VEHICLE BODY & TRAILER MANUFACTURING

Occupation	% of Total 2006	Change to 2016	Occupation	% of Total 2006	Change to 2016
Team assemblers	24.6	0.2	Laborers & freight, stock, & material movers, hand	1.8	-11.9
Welders, cutters, solderers, & brazers	11.6	4.1	Industrial truck & tractor operators	1.7	-11.9
First-line supervisors/managers of production workers	4.1	-2.2	Welding, soldering, & brazing machine operators	1.4	10.0
Structural metal fabricators & fitters	3.0	-2.2	Maintenance & repair workers, general	1.3	-2.2
Helpers--Production workers	2.9	-2.2	Production workers, nec	1.3	-4.0
Painters, transportation equipment	2.5	-11.9	Machinists	1.3	2.7
Sales reps, wholesale & manufacturing, exc tech	2.0	-2.2	Shipping, receiving, & traffic clerks	1.2	-5.8
Cutting, punching, & press machine operators	2.0	-11.9	Office clerks, general	1.2	-3.6
Inspectors, testers, sorters, samplers, & weighers	1.8	-7.7	Fiberglass laminators & fabricators	1.1	-2.2

Source: *Industry-Occupation Matrix*, Bureau of Labor Statistics, December 4, 2007. These data are reported based on 4-digit NAICS categories but have been matched to corresponding 6-digit NAICS industry codes. The change reported for each occupation to the year 2016 is a percent of growth or decline as estimated by the Bureau of Labor Statistics. The abbreviation nec stands for 'not elsewhere classified'.

LOCATION BY STATE AND REGIONAL CONCENTRATION

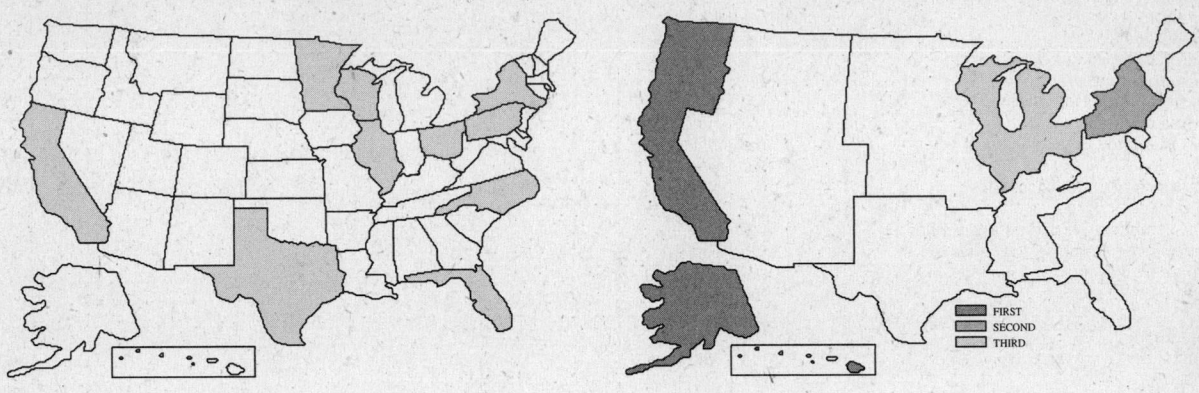

INDUSTRY DATA BY STATE

State	Establish-ments	Shipments Total ($ mil)	Shipments % of U.S.	Shipments Per Establ.	Employment Total Number	Employment % of U.S.	Employment Per Establ.	Wages ($/hour)	Cost as % of Shipments	Investment per Employee ($)
North Carolina	37	876.4	10.9	23,686.8	3,473	8.4	94	17.87	83.9	14,376
Pennsylvania	64	670.3	8.3	10,473.7	3,960	9.6	62	15.07	64.4	1,914
Wisconsin	23	601.4	7.5	26,146.0	3,094	7.5	135	17.84	58.5	2,428
Minnesota	20	593.9	7.4	29,694.4	1,780	4.3	89	18.10	73.9	4,043
California	110	369.5	4.6	3,358.8	2,515	6.1	23	14.13	57.5	1,889
Ohio	41	362.6	4.5	8,843.6	2,183	5.3	53	17.75	59.3	2,353
Florida	21	319.1	4.0	15,197.2	2,101	5.1	100	13.30	55.8	1,494
Texas	44	285.7	3.6	6,493.4	1,646	4.0	37	13.97	54.5	2,583
Illinois	25	276.2	3.4	11,049.5	1,372	3.3	55	17.34	52.5	3,091
New York	42	244.0	3.0	5,808.6	1,237	3.0	29	14.25	72.3	1,498

Source: 2002 *Economic Census*. The states are in descending order of shipments or establishments (if shipment data are missing for the majority). The symbol (D) appears when data are withheld to prevent disclosure of competitive information. States marked with (D) are sorted by number of establishments. A dash (-) indicates that the data element cannot be calculated. Data may not show all states active in the NAICS category. All data available at the time of publication are shown.

NAICS 336212 - TRUCK TRAILER MANUFACTURING

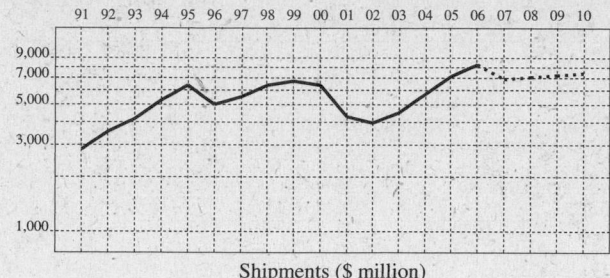

Shipments ($ million)

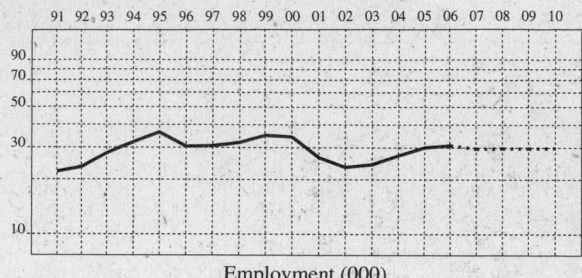

Employment (000)

GENERAL STATISTICS

Year	Com-panies	Establishments Total	Establishments with 20 or more employees	Employment Total (000)	Employment Production Workers (000)	Employment Hours (Mil)	Compensation Payroll ($ mil)	Compensation Wages ($/hr)	Production ($ million) Cost of Materials	Production Value Added by Manufacture	Production Value of Shipments	Capital Invest.
1991		327	169	22.1	16.9	34.5	515.2	9.97	2,066.4	742.0	2,832.4	45.6
1992	310	339	157	23.4	18.7	38.4	565.9	10.34	2,459.0	1,093.5	3,545.5	30.9
1993		351	160	27.9	23.0	47.8	692.1	10.58	3,105.6	1,070.5	4,172.2	66.7
1994		355	158	32.1	26.6	56.0	812.1	10.71	3,821.6	1,487.1	5,273.7	116.1
1995		353	180	36.3	30.3	62.0	910.7	10.80	4,572.4	1,890.6	6,381.5	110.1
1996		392	189	30.4	24.6	49.7	799.3	11.20	3,581.6	1,411.7	4,993.7	79.2
1997	354	388	181	30.6	25.6	50.4	835.3	11.45	3,764.7	1,785.3	5,500.5	89.5
1998		410	187	31.9	26.7	53.0	906.0	12.15	4,290.5	2,118.8	6,380.4	139.1
1999		392	184	35.0	29.8	59.7	988.5	12.38	4,423.2	2,362.5	6,721.8	167.0
2000		394	191	34.3	28.9	58.5	1,026.4	13.24	4,172.9	2,218.5	6,379.7	122.1
2001		393	182	26.4	20.8	42.2	824.7	13.73	2,777.1	1,490.7	4,295.7	71.6
2002	361	397	176	23.4	18.8	36.4	719.2	14.06	2,489.8	1,439.9	3,959.4	53.4
2003		394	178	24.2	20.0	40.7	785.0	14.27	2,838.8	1,653.3	4,501.5	61.6
2004		408	178	27.1	22.5	45.5	875.0	14.41	3,863.0	1,827.2	5,695.0	126.5
2005		391	185	30.0	24.9	50.4	1,014.7	15.29	4,898.8	2,292.0	7,144.9	108.2
2006		418P	189P	30.8	26.0	52.8	1,064.8	15.52	5,417.5	2,892.4	8,276.5	130.6
2007		423P	190P	29.6P	24.8P	49.6P	1,024.5P	15.79P	4,508.8P	2,407.3P	6,888.3P	121.6P
2008		428P	192P	29.7P	24.9P	49.8P	1,047.0P	16.18P	4,625.1P	2,469.3P	7,065.9P	124.8P
2009		433P	193P	29.7P	25.0P	49.9P	1,069.5P	16.56P	4,741.4P	2,531.4P	7,243.5P	127.9P
2010		438P	195P	29.8P	25.1P	50.0P	1,092.0P	16.95P	4,857.6P	2,593.5P	7,421.2P	131.0P

Sources: 1992, 1997, 2002 *Economic Census*; other years, up to 2006, are from the *Annual Survey of Manufactures*. Establishment counts for non-Census years are from *County Business Patterns*; 1997 and 2002 values are from the 1997 and 2002 censuses respectively, reported in the Federal Government's NAICS format. Other years were originally reported in equivalent SIC format. 'P's show projections by the editors.

INDICES OF CHANGE

Year	Com-panies	Establishments Total	Establishments with 20 or more employees	Employment Total (000)	Employment Production Workers (000)	Employment Hours (Mil)	Compensation Payroll ($ mil)	Compensation Wages ($/hr)	Production ($ million) Cost of Materials	Production Value Added by Manufacture	Production Value of Shipments	Capital Invest.
1992	86	85	89	100	99	105	79	74	99	76	90	58
1997	98	98	103	131	136	138	116	81	151	124	139	168
2001		99	103	113	111	116	115	98	112	104	108	134
2002	100	100	100	100	100	100	100	100	100	100	100	100
2003		99	101	103	106	112	109	101	114	115	114	115
2004		103	101	116	120	125	122	102	155	127	144	237
2005		98	105	128	132	138	141	109	197	159	180	203
2006		105P	107P	132	138	145	148	110	218	201	209	245
2007		107P	108P	126P	132P	136P	142P	112P	181P	167P	174P	228P
2008		108P	109P	127P	132P	137P	146P	115P	186P	171P	178P	234P
2009		109P	110P	127P	133P	137P	149P	118P	190P	176P	183P	240P
2010		110P	111P	127P	134P	137P	152P	121P	195P	180P	187P	245P

Sources: Same as General Statistics. Values reflect change from the base year, 2002. Values above 100 mean greater than 2002, values below 100 mean less than 2002, and the values of 100 in other years means the same as 2002. 'P's show projections by the editors.

SELECTED RATIOS

For 2002	Avg. of All Manufact.	Analyzed Industry	Index	For 2002	Avg. of All Manufact.	Analyzed Industry	Index
Employees per Establishment	42	59	140	Value Added per Production Worker	182,367	76,590	42
Payroll per Establishment	1,639,184	1,811,587	111	Cost per Establishment	5,769,015	6,271,537	109
Payroll per Employee	39,053	30,735	79	Cost per Employee	137,446	106,402	77
Production Workers per Establishment	30	47	160	Cost per Production Worker	195,506	132,436	68
Wages per Establishment	694,845	1,289,128	186	Shipments per Establishment	11,158,348	9,973,300	89
Wages per Production Worker	23,548	27,223	116	Shipments per Employee	265,847	169,205	64
Hours per Production Worker	1,980	1,936	98	Shipments per Production Worker	378,144	210,606	56
Wages per Hour	11.89	14.06	118	Investment per Establishment	361,338	134,509	37
Value Added per Establishment	5,381,325	3,626,952	67	Investment per Employee	8,609	2,282	27
Value Added per Employee	128,210	61,534	48	Investment per Production Worker	12,245	2,840	23

Sources: Same as General Statistics. The 'Average of All Manufacturing' column represents the average of all manufacturing industries reported for the most recent complete year available. The Index shows the relationship between the Average and the Analyzed Industry. For example, 100 means that they are equal; 500 that the Analyzed Industry is five times the average; 50 means that the Analyzed Industry is half the national average. The abbreviation 'na' is used to show that data are 'not available'. Ratios shown for 2002, the last complete census year.

LEADING COMPANIES   Number shown: 75   Total sales ($ mil): 15,901   Total employment (000): 45.6

Company Name	Address				CEO Name	Phone	Co. Type	Sales ($ mil)	Empl. (000)
Terex Corp.	200 Nyala Farm Rd.	Westport	CT	06880		203-222-7170	P	9,138	21.0
Wabash National Corp.	PO Box 6129	Lafayette	IN	47903	Richard Giromini	765-771-5300	P	1,103	3.1
International Industries Inc.	PO Box 1210	Gilbert	WV	25621		304-664-3227	R	835*	0.5
Utility Trailer Manufacturing	PO Box 1299	City of Industry	CA	91748	Paul Bennett	626-965-1541	R	742*	3.6
Lufkin Industries Inc.	PO Box 849	Lufkin	TX	75902		936-634-2211	P	597	2.7
Saf-Holland USA Inc.	PO Box 425	Muskegon	MI	49443	Timothy Hemingway	231-773-3271	R	321*	0.3
Featherlite Inc.	PO Box 320	Cresco	IA	52136	Conrad D. Clement	563-547-6000	S	225	1.3
Jost International Corp.	1770 Hayes St.	Grand Haven	MI	49417	Lee Brace	616-846-7700	R	185*	<0.1
Trailmobile Inc.	100 N Field Dr, 355	Lake Forest	IL	60045	Edward Wanandi	847-504-2000	R	141*	0.6
Ranew's Truck and Equipment	1308 Highway 41 N	Milner	GA	30257		770-227-4688	R	138*	0.1
Beall Trailers of Montana Inc.	PO Box 2543	Billings	MT	59103	Jerry Beall	406-252-7163	S	113*	0.8
Fontaine International Inc.	5000 Grantswood	Irondale	AL	35210	Brian Ballard	205-421-4300	S	113*	0.4
STI Holdings Inc.	PO Box 606	Stoughton	WI	53589	Donald Wahlin	608-873-2500	R	97*	0.1
Mickey Truck Bodies Inc.	PO Box 2044	High Point	NC	27261		336-882-6806	R	90*	0.5
Beall Corp.	PO Box 17095	Portland	OR	97217	James Beall	503-735-2110	R	87*	<0.1
Wells Cargo Inc.	PO Box 728	Elkhart	IN	46515		574-264-9661	R	86*	0.1
Pace American Inc.	11550 Harter Dr.	Middlebury	IN	46540	Mitchell Bender	574-825-7223	R	81*	0.2
East Manufacturing Corp.	PO Box 277	Randolph	OH	44265	Howard Booher	330-325-9921	R	78*	0.4
Boydstun Metal Works Inc.	9125 N Time Oil Rd.	Portland	OR	97203	Robert Boydstun	503-285-3515	R	76*	0.4
Wilson Trailer Co.	PO Box 2616	Sioux City	IA	51106	Wilson Persinger	712-252-6500	R	76*	0.5
Southern Fabricators Inc.	4768 Hungerford	Memphis	TN	38118	Greg Langston	901-363-1571	R	72*	0.7
Mac Trailer Manufacturing Inc.	14599 Commerce NE	Alliance	OH	44601	Michael Conny	330-823-9900	R	72*	0.4
McKenzie Tank Lines Inc.	PO Box 1200	Tallahassee	FL	32302	Joseph Audie	850-576-1221	R	72*	<0.1
Road Systems Inc.	2001 S Benton St.	Searcy	AR	72143		501-279-0991	S	70*	0.2
Action Equipment Co.	2350 Arrowhead Rd.	Moundridge	KS	67107	Mark Ellingson	620-345-2811	R	69*	<0.1
Contract Manufacturer L.L.C.	200 County Rd.	Madill	OK	73446	Ronald Jackson	580-795-5536	R	56*	0.3
Reliance Trailer Company	3025 S Geiger Blvd.	Spokane	WA	99224		509-455-8650	R	50*	0.3
Johnson Truck Bodies Inc.	215 E Allen St.	Rice Lake	WI	54868		715-234-7071	S	48*	0.3
RC Tway Co.	PO Box 17185	Louisville	KY	40217		502-637-2551	R	46*	0.4
Western Trailer Co.	PO Box 5598	Boise	ID	83705	Jerry Whitehead	208-344-2539	R	46*	0.3
4-Star Trailers Inc.	PO Box 75395	Oklahoma City	OK	73147	Kenneth Waller	405-324-7827	R	45*	0.3
Sooner Trailer Manufacturing	1515 McCurdy	Duncan	OK	73533	Jim Garis		R	43*	0.3
Merritt Equipment Co.	9339 US Hwy. 85	Henderson	CO	80640	Everett Merritt	303-289-2286	R	41*	0.2
Whiting Door Manufacturing	PO Box 388	Akron	NY	14001	Donald Whiting	716-542-5427	R	41*	0.3
Austin-Westran L.L.C.	PO Box 921	Byron	IL	61010		815-234-2811	R	39*	0.2
Ledwell and Son Enterprises	PO Box 1106	Texarkana	TX	75504	Lloy Ledwell	903-838-6531	R	38*	0.2
Sooner Trailer Manufacturing	900 Exiss Blvd.	El Reno	OK	73036	Jim Garis	405-262-6471	R	36*	0.2
Benson Manufacturing Inc.	PO Box 970	Mineral Wells	WV	26150	James Harless	304-489-9020	R	34*	0.2
Mechanical Products Mfg. Co.	832 Fairground Rd.	Lucasville	OH	45648		740-259-6444	R	34*	0.3
E.D. Etnyre and Co.	1333 S Daysville Rd	Oregon	IL	61061	Tom Brown	815-732-2116	R	34*	0.3
Kiefer Built L.L.C.	PO Box 88	Kanawha	IA	50447	Brad Henning	641-762-3201	R	31*	0.2
Brenner Tank L.L.C.	PO Box 670	Fond du Lac	WI	54936		920-922-5020	R	30*	0.2
VE Enterprises Inc.	PO Box 369	Springer	OK	73458	Lonnie Whatley	580-653-2171	R	30*	<0.1
Clement Industries Inc.	PO Box 914	Minden	LA	71058	Glen Hicks	318-377-2776	R	29*	0.1
Reliance Trailer Manufacturing	7911 Redwood Dr.	Cotati	CA	94931	Brian Ling	707-795-0081	R	29*	0.2
WW-Trailer Manufacturers Inc.	PO Box 807	Madill	OK	73446	H Watkins	580-795-5571	R	26*	0.2
Wabash Wood Products	PO Box 597	Harrison	AR	72602		870-741-6644	S	22*	0.3
Talbert Manufacturing Inc.	1628 W State Rd.	Rensselaer	IN	47978	Rick Odle	219-866-7141	R	22*	0.2
Kandi Kountry Express Ltd.	61381 US Hwy. 12	Litchfield	MN	55355	Brian Weseman	320-693-7900	R	20*	<0.1
Manac Trailers USA Inc.	Drawer K	Oran	MO	63771	Charles Dutil	573-262-2166	R	20*	0.1
UNI-Form Components Corp.	10703 Sheldon Rd.	Houston	TX	77044		281-456-9310	S	18*	0.1
Cherokee Industries Inc.	RR 890430	Oklahoma City	OK	73189	Thomas Welchel	405-691-8222	R	18*	0.1
Trinity Trailer Manufacturing	8200 S Eisenman	Boise	ID	83716	Pete Eisenman	208-336-3666	R	18*	0.1
CEI Equipment Company Inc.	PO Box 8090	Cedar Rapids	IA	52408	Don Gaddis	319-396-7336	R	18*	<0.1
Cooperative Bright Inc.	803 W Seale St.	Nacogdoches	TX	75964	Charles Bright	936-564-8378	R	17*	0.2
Construction Trailer Special.	2535 Rose Pkwy.	Sikeston	MO	63801	Spencer Taylor	573-481-0941	R	17*	<0.1
Unique Functional Products	135 Sunshine Ln.	San Marcos	CA	92069	Bernhardt Goettker	760-744-1610	R	17*	<0.1
Pierce Manufacturing Inc.	PO Box 2017	Appleton	WI	54912	John Randjelovic	920-832-3000	R	16*	0.1
Van Nu Technology Inc.	PO Box 2293	Mansfield	TX	76063	Fred Ufolla	817-477-1734	R	16*	<0.1
Rockland Products Inc.	4060 Iberia Ave.	Rockland	WI	54653	Phillip Sykes	608-269-8347	R	14*	<0.1
Warren Manufacturing Inc.	1008 37th St. N	Birmingham	AL	35234	Russell Warren	205-591-3002	R	14*	<0.1
Lakes Enterprises Inc.	1300 38th Ave. W	Spencer	IA	51301		712-262-2992	S	13*	<0.1
Hillsboro Industries Inc.	220 Industrial Rd.	Hillsboro	KS	67063	Robert Klein	620-947-3127	R	13*	<0.1
Capital Industrial Inc.	2649 R W Johnson	Tumwater	WA	98512	Janette Nieman	360-786-1890	R	12*	<0.1
Gooseneck Trailer Mfg. Co.	PO Box 832	Bryan	TX	77806	David Carrabba	979-778-0034	R	12*	0.1
Dakota Manufacturing Company	PO Box 1188	Mitchell	SD	57301	Dean Oehlerking	605-996-5571	R	12*	0.1
VANCO USA L.L.C.	1170 F Columbus	Bordentown	NJ	08505	Carl Massaro	609-499-4141	R	12*	<0.1
X-L Specialized Trailers Inc.	PO Box 400	Manchester	IA	52057	George Wall	319-283-4468	R	11*	<0.1
Play'mor Trailers Inc.	PO Box 128	Westphalia	MO	65085	John Willibrand	573-455-2387	R	11*	<0.1
Industrial Hardwood Products	2720 N Service Dr.	Red Wing	MN	55066	Marcus Chorney	651-388-6150	R	11*	<0.1
PAMCO Inc.	PO Box 298	Oskaloosa	IA	52577	Dennis Palmer	641-672-2576	R	10*	<0.1
Truck Equipment Service Co.	800 Oak Street	Lincoln	NE	68521	Ernest Churda	402-476-3225	R	9*	<0.1
Summit Trailer Sales Inc.	1 Summit Plz.	Summit Station	PA	17979	Charles Pishock	570-754-3511	R	9*	<0.1
Wilkens Industries Inc.	184 County Rd. 22	Morris	MN	56267		320-589-1971	R	9*	<0.1
Calutech Mobile Solutions Inc.	3550 179th St., C	Hammond	IN	46323	C. A. Mitchell Jr.	219-845-1695	R	8*	<0.1

Source: *Ward's Business Directory of U.S. Private and Public Companies*, Volumes 1 and 2, 2008. The company type code used is as follows: P - Public, R - Private, S - Subsidiary, D - Division, J - Joint Venture, A - Affiliate, G - Group. Sales are in millions of dollars, employees are in thousands. An asterisk (*) indicates an estimated sales volume. The symbol < stands for 'less than'. Company names and addresses are truncated, in some cases, to fit into the available space.

MATERIALS CONSUMED

Material	Quantity	Delivered Cost ($ million)
Purchased chassis for vehicles (excluding passenger cars)	(X)	1.1
Truck bodies	(X)	2.2
Transmissions and parts	(X)	(D)
Car bodies	(X)	(D)
Shocks, struts, and other suspension equipment and parts	(X)	91.5
Automotive stampings (inc. body parts, hubcaps, fenders, etc.)	(X)	0.6
Motor vehicle metal hardware (lock units, etc.), exc. forgings	(X)	8.5
Metal bolts, nuts, screws, and other screw machine products	(X)	39.0
Other fabricated metal products (excluding forgings)	(X)	42.8
Forgings	(X)	4.0
Castings, rough and semifinished	(X)	7.2
Fluid power products	(X)	46.4
Pneumatic tires and inner tubes	(X)	104.4
Fabricated plastics products (exc. gaskets, hoses, and belting)	(X)	12.0
Glass and glass products (including windows and mirrors)	(X)	(D)
Seats (purchased separately) for automobiles, trucks, and buses	(X)	(D)
Paints, varnishes, stains, lacquers, shellacs, japans, enamels, etc.	(X)	30.5
Motor vehicle lighting fixtures, excluding auto lamps	(X)	19.4
Automotive lamps (bulbs and sealed beams)	(X)	1.8
Steel bars, bar shapes, and plates (exc. castings, forgings, fabr. metal products)	(X)	66.1
Steel sheet and strip (including tinplate)	(X)	61.5
Steel structural shapes and sheet piling (exc. castings, forgings, fabr. metal products)	(X)	14.0
All other steel shapes and forms (exc. castings, forgings, fabr. metal products)	(X)	15.1
Aluminum and aluminum-base alloy sheet, plate, foil, and welded tubing	(X)	137.0
Aluminum and aluminum-base alloy extruded shapes (rod, bar, pipe, tube, etc.)	(X)	129.0
Other aluminum and aluminum-base alloy shapes and forms (exc. castings, forgings, fabr. metal products)	(X)	9.2
Other nonferrous shapes and forms (exc. castings, forgings, fabricated metal products)	(X)	2.1
Rough and dressed lumber	(X)	60.5
All other materials, components, parts, containers, and supplies	(X)	388.0
Materials, ingredients, containers, and supplies, nsk	(X)	1,050.3

Source: 2002 *Economic Census*. Explanation of symbols used: (D): Withheld to avoid disclosure of competitive data; na: Not available; (S): Withheld because statistical norms were not met; (X): Not applicable; (Z): Less than half the unit shown; nec: Not elsewhere classified; nsk: Not specified by kind; - : zero; p : 10-19 percent estimated; q : 20-29 percent estimated.

PRODUCT SHARE DETAILS

Product or Product Class Shipments	Mil. $	Product or Product Class Shipments	Mil. $
TRUCK TRAILERS	3,819.3	Truck trailers and chassis, with axle rating of less than 10,000 lb	181.9
Truck trailers and chassis, with axle rating of 10,000 lb or more	3,358.2	Truck trailers, nsk, total	279.2

Source: 2002 *Economic Census*. The values are product shipments in millions of dollars for 2002. Total product shipments may be lower or higher than industry shipments. See Introduction for a full discussion. Values of indented subcategories are summed in the main heading(s). The symbol (D) appears when data are withheld to prevent disclosure of competitive information. The abbreviation nsk stands for 'not specified by kind' and nec for 'not elsewhere classified'. A dash (-) means zero.

INPUTS AND OUTPUTS FOR TRUCK TRAILER MANUFACTURING

Economic Sector or Industry Providing Inputs	%	Sector	Economic Sector or Industry Buying Outputs	%	Sector
Compensation of employees	23.5		Private fixed investment	85.6	
Motor vehicle parts	12.8	Manufg.	Exports of goods & services	8.6	Cap Inv
Aluminum products from purchased aluminum	9.1	Manufg.	Federal government, investment, national defense	3.9	Fed Govt
Management of companies & enterprises	7.4	Services	Construction machinery	0.9	Manufg.
Wholesale trade	5.8	Trade	Federal government, investment, nondefense	0.4	Fed Govt
Iron & steel mills & ferroalloys	5.0	Manufg.	Change in private inventories	0.3	In House
Tires	4.4	Manufg.	Truck trailers	0.2	Manufg.
Travel trailers & campers	3.3	Manufg.	General Federal government services, nondefense	0.2	Fed Govt
Sawmills & wood preservation	2.1	Manufg.			
Paints & coatings	1.7	Manufg.			
AC, refrigeration, and warm air heating equipment	1.6	Manufg.			
Turned products & screws, nuts, & bolts	1.5	Manufg.			
Fluid power process machinery	1.5	Manufg.			
Retail trade	1.4	Trade			
Rubber products, nec	1.1	Manufg.			
Truck transportation	1.1	Util.			
Wood windows & doors & millwork	0.9	Manufg.			
Securities, commodity contracts, investments	0.8	Fin/R.E.			
Scientific research & development services	0.7	Services			
Valve & fittings other than plumbing	0.7	Manufg.			
Real estate	0.7	Fin/R.E.			
Lessors of nonfinancial assets	0.7	Fin/R.E.			
Software publishers	0.5	Services			

Continued on next page.

INPUTS AND OUTPUTS FOR TRUCK TRAILER MANUFACTURING - Continued

Economic Sector or Industry Providing Inputs	%	Sector	Economic Sector or Industry Buying Outputs	%	Sector
Power generation & supply	0.5	Util.			
Plastics products, nec	0.5	Manufg.			
Machine shops	0.5	Manufg.			
Hardware	0.4	Manufg.			
Coating, engraving, heat treating & allied activities	0.3	Manufg.			
Advertising & related services	0.3	Services			
Taxes on production & imports, less subsidies	0.3				
Automotive equipment rental & leasing	0.3	Fin/R.E.			
Monetary authorities/depository credit intermediation	0.3	Fin/R.E.			
Semiconductors & related devices	0.3	Manufg.			
Paperboard containers	0.3	Manufg.			
Truck trailers	0.3	Manufg.			
Legal services	0.3	Services			
Printed circuit assemblies (electronic assemblies)	0.3	Manufg.			
Rail transportation	0.3	Util.			
General purpose machinery, nec	0.2	Manufg.			
Nonferrous metal (ex. copper & aluminum) processing	0.2	Manufg.			
Maintenance/repair of nonresidential structures	0.2	Construct.			
Telecommunications	0.2	Services			
Services to buildings & dwellings	0.2	Services			
Accounting, tax preparation, bookkeeping, & payroll	0.2	Services			
Ornamental & architectural metal products	0.2	Manufg.			
Natural gas distribution	0.2	Util.			
Architectural, engineering, & related services	0.2	Services			
Commercial & industrial machinery rental & leasing	0.2	Fin/R.E.			
Food services & drinking places	0.2	Services			
Motor vehicle bodies	0.1	Manufg.			
Professional, scientific, technical services, nec	0.1	Services			
Ferrous metal foundries	0.1	Manufg.			
Specialized design services	0.1	Services			
Alumina refining & primary aluminum production	0.1	Manufg.			
Fabricated metals, nec	0.1	Manufg.			
Nonferrous metal foundries	0.1	Manufg.			
Automotive repair & maintenance, ex. car washes	0.1	Services			
Metal cans, boxes, & other containers (light gauge)	0.1	Manufg.			
Cutting tools & machine tool accessories	0.1	Manufg.			
Employment services	0.1	Services			
Business support services	0.1	Services			
Commercial & industrial equipment repair/maintenance	0.1	Services			

Source: Benchmark Input-Output Accounts for the U.S. Economy, 2002, U.S. Department of Commerce, Washington, D.C., January 2008. The abbreviation nec stands for 'not elsewhere classified'.

OCCUPATIONS EMPLOYED BY MOTOR VEHICLE BODY & TRAILER MANUFACTURING

Occupation	% of Total 2006	Change to 2016	Occupation	% of Total 2006	Change to 2016
Team assemblers	24.6	0.2	Laborers & freight, stock, & material movers, hand	1.8	-11.9
Welders, cutters, solderers, & brazers	11.6	4.1	Industrial truck & tractor operators	1.7	-11.9
First-line supervisors/managers of production workers	4.1	-2.2	Welding, soldering, & brazing machine operators	1.4	10.0
Structural metal fabricators & fitters	3.0	-2.2	Maintenance & repair workers, general	1.3	-2.2
Helpers--Production workers	2.9	-2.2	Production workers, nec	1.3	-4.0
Painters, transportation equipment	2.5	-11.9	Machinists	1.3	2.7
Sales reps, wholesale & manufacturing, exc tech	2.0	-2.2	Shipping, receiving, & traffic clerks	1.2	-5.8
Cutting, punching, & press machine operators	2.0	-11.9	Office clerks, general	1.2	-3.6
Inspectors, testers, sorters, samplers, & weighers	1.8	-7.7	Fiberglass laminators & fabricators	1.1	-2.2

Source: Industry-Occupation Matrix, Bureau of Labor Statistics, December 4, 2007. These data are reported based on 4-digit NAICS categories but have been matched to corresponding 6-digit NAICS industry codes. The change reported for each occupation to the year 2016 is a percent of growth or decline as estimated by the Bureau of Labor Statistics. The abbreviation nec stands for 'not elsewhere classified'.

LOCATION BY STATE AND REGIONAL CONCENTRATION

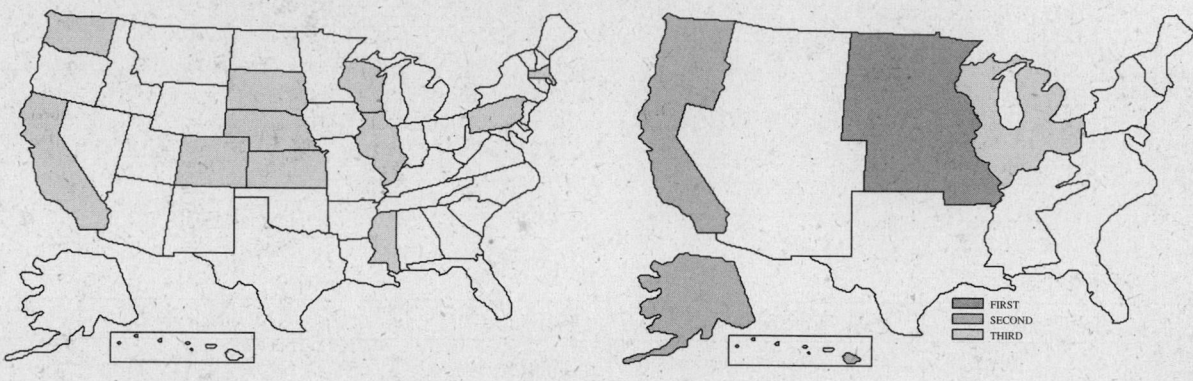

INDUSTRY DATA BY STATE

| State | Establish-ments | Shipments | | | Employment | | | | Cost as % of Shipments | Investment per Employee ($) |
		Total ($ mil)	% of U.S.	Per Establ.	Total Number	% of U.S.	Per Establ.	Wages ($/hour)		
Wisconsin	16	168.1	4.2	10,505.6	1,015	4.3	63	13.74	69.7	871
Pennsylvania	20	161.6	4.1	8,078.6	955	4.1	48	14.82	61.1	2,487
Nebraska	10	145.4	3.7	14,542.3	662	2.8	66	11.64	64.4	1,282
Illinois	5	132.3	3.3	26,450.0	644	2.7	129	11.86	59.1	898
California	20	115.3	2.9	5,767.2	756	3.2	38	14.40	66.3	1,692
South Dakota	8	107.8	2.7	13,480.5	608	2.6	76	13.97	55.5	2,692
Kansas	11	74.5	1.9	6,768.6	553	2.4	50	15.19	58.1	3,081
Mississippi	7	64.4	1.6	9,203.0	321	1.4	46	10.20	65.5	564
Colorado	6	62.4	1.6	10,407.0	383	1.6	64	12.79	68.4	1,875
Massachusetts	5	32.8	0.8	6,562.8	166	0.7	33	20.39	54.3	880
Washington	7	16.9	0.4	2,408.0	120	0.5	17	16.95	65.5	1,617

Source: 2002 *Economic Census*. The states are in descending order of shipments or establishments (if shipment data are missing for the majority). The symbol (D) appears when data are withheld to prevent disclosure of competitive information. States marked with (D) are sorted by number of establishments. A dash (-) indicates that the data element cannot be calculated. Data may not show all states active in the NAICS category. All data available at the time of publication are shown.

NAICS 336213 - MOTOR HOME MANUFACTURING

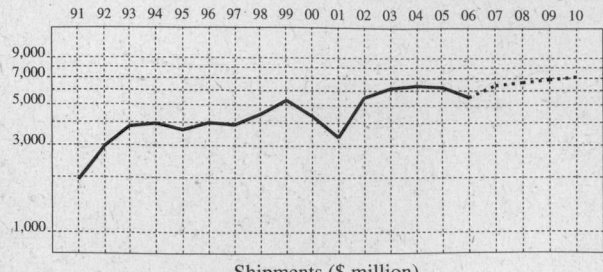

Shipments ($ million)

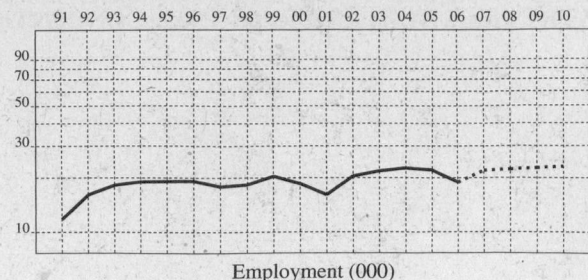

Employment (000)

GENERAL STATISTICS

| Year | Companies | Establishments | | Employment | | | Compensation | | Production ($ million) | | | |
		Total	with 20 or more employees	Total (000)	Production Workers (000)	Hours (Mil)	Payroll ($ mil)	Wages ($/hr)	Cost of Materials	Value Added by Manufacture	Value of Shipments	Capital Invest.
1991		144	70	11.8	9.5	18.4	259.9	9.30	1,334.3	631.9	1,935.4	17.2
1992	122	145	83	16.1	13.1	24.9	367.3	9.89	2,063.3	842.9	2,960.9	19.0
1993		124	69	18.2	15.1	27.7	438.8	10.75	2,810.2	957.6	3,795.0	23.4
1994		121	70	19.0	15.9	30.0	494.9	11.09	2,893.3	1,077.6	3,954.9	40.5
1995		110	70	19.1	16.0	29.2	480.1	10.83	2,614.5	973.3	3,640.3	29.3
1996		112	67	19.2	15.4	30.1	530.8	11.43	2,866.0	1,148.1	3,986.0	34.9
1997	74	86	49	17.9	14.8	29.6	503.3	11.92	2,679.8	1,228.5	3,895.4	50.2
1998		85	46	18.3	15.2	29.2	542.2	13.03	3,126.5	1,340.3	4,465.8	32.4
1999		88	46	20.4	16.7	33.2	651.7	13.55	3,695.1	1,688.9	5,311.0	44.3
2000		92	47	18.5	15.3	27.0	556.3	13.67	3,051.7	1,353.2	4,364.7	44.7
2001		93	45	16.1	13.1	22.8	501.9	15.20	2,359.0	812.4	3,344.5	20.1
2002	82	93	50	20.4	16.5	30.8	708.9	15.82	3,658.8	1,863.5	5,498.0	51.0
2003		91	50	21.8	18.0	31.9	758.0	16.88	4,120.1	2,059.7	6,162.8	56.1
2004		103	58	22.6	18.7	36.2	828.3	16.26	4,310.3	2,195.7	6,356.8	80.3
2005		98	50	22.1	18.0	33.5	777.9	16.46	4,124.4	2,138.3	6,250.8	53.3
2006		79P	41P	18.9	15.4	30.4	729.1	17.49	3,733.3	1,768.9	5,518.7	25.7
2007		76P	39P	22.0P	18.0P	33.7P	830.0P	18.10P	4,344.9P	2,058.7P	6,422.8P	56.6P
2008		72P	37P	22.3P	18.3P	34.3P	860.5P	18.66P	4,500.7P	2,132.5P	6,653.1P	58.6P
2009		69P	35P	22.7P	18.6P	34.8P	891.1P	19.22P	4,656.5P	2,206.3P	6,883.4P	60.7P
2010		65P	33P	23.1P	18.9P	35.4P	921.6P	19.78P	4,812.3P	2,280.2P	7,113.8P	62.8P

Sources: 1992, 1997, 2002 *Economic Census*; other years, up to 2006, are from the *Annual Survey of Manufactures*. Establishment counts for non-Census years are from *County Business Patterns*; 1997 and 2002 values are from the 1997 and 2002 censuses respectively, reported in the Federal Government's NAICS format. Other years were originally reported in equivalent SIC format. 'P's show projections by the editors.

INDICES OF CHANGE

| Year | Companies | Establishments | | Employment | | | Compensation | | Production ($ million) | | | |
		Total	with 20 or more employees	Total (000)	Production Workers (000)	Hours (Mil)	Payroll ($ mil)	Wages ($/hr)	Cost of Materials	Value Added by Manufacture	Value of Shipments	Capital Invest.
1992	149	156	166	79	79	81	52	63	56	45	54	37
1997	90	92	98	88	90	96	71	75	73	66	71	98
2001		100	90	79	79	74	71	96	64	44	61	39
2002	100	100	100	100	100	100	100	100	100	100	100	100
2003		98	100	107	109	104	107	107	113	111	112	110
2004		111	116	111	113	118	117	103	118	118	116	157
2005		105	100	108	109	109	110	104	113	115	114	105
2006		85P	83P	93	93	99	103	111	102	95	100	50
2007		81P	79P	108P	109P	109P	117P	114P	119P	110P	117P	111P
2008		78P	74P	109P	111P	111P	121P	118P	123P	114P	121P	115P
2009		74P	70P	111P	113P	113P	126P	121P	127P	118P	125P	119P
2010		70P	66P	113P	115P	115P	130P	125P	132P	122P	129P	123P

Sources: Same as General Statistics. Values reflect change from the base year, 2002. Values above 100 mean greater than 2002, values below 100 mean less than 2002, and the values of 100 in other years means the same as 2002. 'P's show projections by the editors.

SELECTED RATIOS

For 2002	Avg. of All Manufact.	Analyzed Industry	Index	For 2002	Avg. of All Manufact.	Analyzed Industry	Index
Employees per Establishment	42	219	523	Value Added per Production Worker	182,367	112,939	62
Payroll per Establishment	1,639,184	7,622,581	465	Cost per Establishment	5,769,015	39,341,935	682
Payroll per Employee	39,053	34,750	89	Cost per Employee	137,446	179,353	130
Production Workers per Establishment	30	177	601	Cost per Production Worker	195,506	221,745	113
Wages per Establishment	694,845	5,239,312	754	Shipments per Establishment	11,158,348	59,118,280	530
Wages per Production Worker	23,548	29,531	125	Shipments per Employee	265,847	269,510	101
Hours per Production Worker	1,980	1,867	94	Shipments per Production Worker	378,144	333,212	88
Wages per Hour	11.89	15.82	133	Investment per Establishment	361,338	548,387	152
Value Added per Establishment	5,381,325	20,037,634	372	Investment per Employee	8,609	2,500	29
Value Added per Employee	128,210	91,348	71	Investment per Production Worker	12,245	3,091	25

Sources: Same as General Statistics. The 'Average of All Manufacturing' column represents the average of all manufacturing industries reported for the most recent complete year available. The Index shows the relationship between the Average and the Analyzed Industry. For example, 100 means that they are equal; 500 that the Analyzed Industry is five times the average; 50 means that the Analyzed Industry is half the national average. The abbreviation 'na' is used to show that data are not available. Ratios shown for 2002, the last complete census year.

LEADING COMPANIES Number shown: 30 Total sales ($ mil): 19,539 Total employment (000): 88.7

Company Name	Address				CEO Name	Phone	Co. Type	Sales ($ mil)	Empl. (000)
Thor Industries Inc.	PO Box 629	Jackson Center	OH	45334		937-596-6849	P	3,066	9.1
Fleetwood Enterprises Inc.	PO Box 7638	Riverside	CA	92513		951-351-3500	P	2,008	9.3
Thor America Inc.	37 Old 522	Middleburg	PA	17842	W. F. B. Thompson	570-837-1663	S	1,592*	8.5
ElDorado National California	13900 Sycamore	Chino	CA	91710	W. F. B. Thompson	909-591-9557	S	1,491*	8.5
ElDorado National Kansas Inc.	1655 Wall Street	Salina	KS	67401	W. F. B. Thompson	785-827-1033	S	1,491*	8.5
General Coach America Inc.	419 W Pike St.	Jackson Center	OH	45334	W. F. B. Thompson	937-596-6849	S	1,491*	8.5
Thor California Inc.	14255 Elsworth St.	Moreno Valley	CA	92553	W. F. B. Thompson	909-697-4190	S	1,489*	8.5
Aero Coach Inc.	Hickory Hill Rd.	Longview	TX	75601	W. F. B. Thompson	903-663-7699	S	1,313*	7.5
Monaco Coach Corp.	91320 Coburg Indust	Coburg	OR	97408		541-686-8011	P	1,298	5.3
Winnebago Industries Inc.	PO Box 152	Forest City	IA	50436		641-585-3535	P	870	3.3
Airstream Inc.	PO Box 629	Jackson Center	OH	45334	Bpob Wheeler	937-596-6111	S	622*	0.5
Jayco Inc.	PO Box 460	Middlebury	IN	46540	Derald Bontrager	574-825-5861	R	585*	1.6
Coachmen Industries Inc.	PO Box 3300	Elkhart	IN	46515	Richard M. Lavers	574-262-0123	P	481	2.7
National RV Holdings Inc.	3411 N Perris Blvd.	Perris	CA	92571	Bradley Albrechtsen	951-943-6007	P	397	0.9
Fleetwood Motor Homes/Indiana	PO Box 31	Decatur	IN	46733	Thomas Pitcher	260-728-2121	D	277*	1.2
Newmar Corp.	PO Box 30	Nappanee	IN	46550	Matthew Miller	574-773-7791	R	218*	1.0
National RV Inc.	3411 N Perris Blvd.	Perris	CA	92571	Bradley Albrechtsen	951-943-6007	S	184*	1.0
Gulf Stream Coach Inc.	PO Box 1005	Nappanee	IN	46550		574-773-7761	R	150*	0.1
Tiffin Motor Homes Inc.	105 2nd St.	Red Bay	AL	35582	Robert Tiffin	256-356-8661	R	119*	0.5
SMC Corp.	PO Box 5639	Bend	OR	97708	John Napute	541-686-8011	S	100*	0.6
Four Winds International Inc.	PO Box 1486	Elkhart	IN	46515	Wade F.B. Thompson	574-266-1111	S	75*	0.3
Marathon Coach Inc.	91333 Coburg Indust	Coburg	OR	97408	Robert Schoellhorn	541-343-9991	R	72*	0.3
Foretravel Inc.	1221 NW Stallings	Nacogdoches	TX	75964		936-564-8367	R	68*	0.3
Dynamax Corp.	PO Box 1948	Elkhart	IN	46515	Dewayne Creighton	574-262-3474	R	33*	0.2
Southern Comfort Conversions	PO Box 748	Pinson	AL	35126		205-856-4800	R	26*	0.2
Associated Partnership Ltd.	6591 Hwy. 13 W	Savage	MN	55378	Du Wade Harris	952-890-7851	R	11*	0.1
Colfax Country RV L.L.C.	8615 Triad Dr.	Colfax	NC	27235		336-996-6661	S	6*	<0.1
Kingsley Coach Inc.	25820 7th St. W	Zimmerman	MN	55398	Allan Smethers	763-856-3733	P	3	<0.1
Gresham Driving Aids Inc.	PO Box 930334	Wixom	MI	48393	William Dillon	248-624-1533	R	2*	<0.1
Viking Recreational Vehicles	PO Box 549	Centreville	MI	49032		269-467-6321	S	1*	0.3

Source: Ward's Business Directory of U.S. Private and Public Companies, Volumes 1 and 2, 2008. The company type code used is as follows: P - Public, R - Private, S - Subsidiary, D - Division, J - Joint Venture, A - Affiliate, G - Group. Sales are in millions of dollars, employees are in thousands. An asterisk (*) indicates an estimated sales volume. The symbol < stands for 'less than'. Company names and addresses are truncated, in some cases, to fit into the available space.

MATERIALS CONSUMED

Material	Quantity	Delivered Cost ($ million)
Other metal vehicular parts, metal (trailer axles, wheels, etc.)	(X)	219.8
Pneumatic tires and inner tubes	(X)	8.5
Purchased chassis for motor homes	(X)	952.2
Household appliances, excluding air conditioners	(X)	122.3
Air-conditioning equipment	(X)	37.6
Metal heating equipment (excluding electric)	(X)	8.6
Metal doors and door units, windows and window units	(X)	33.9
Metal plumbing fixtures, fittings, and trim (including enameled)	(X)	21.3
Sheet metal products (excluding stampings)	(X)	15.9
Metal bolts, nuts, screws, and other screw machine products	(X)	13.7
Other fabricated metal products (excluding forgings)	(X)	54.8
Forgings	(X)	(D)
Castings, rough and semifinished	(X)	(D)
Steel shapes and forms (exc. castings, forgings, fabr. metal products)	(X)	37.8
Aluminum and aluminum-base alloy shapes and forms (exc. castings, forgings, fabr. metal products)	(X)	59.7
Other nonferrous shapes and forms (exc. castings, forgings, fabricated metal products)	(X)	14.6
Current-carrying wiring devices	(X)	93.7
Plywood	(X)	33.7
Lumber, dressed	(X)	36.8
Millwork, wood (wood doors, window sash, moldings, cabinets)	(X)	47.0
Glass and glass products (including windows and mirrors)	(X)	30.9
Fabricated plastics products (excluding gaskets)	(X)	39.4
Plastics products consumed in the form of sheets, rods, etc.	(X)	33.1
Plastics resins consumed in the form of granules, pellets, etc.	(X)	10.9
Paints, varnishes, stains, lacquers, shellacs, japans, enamels, etc.	(X)	41.7
Carpeting	(X)	22.8
Curtains and draperies	(X)	38.1
Molded composites	(X)	37.5
All other materials, components, parts, containers, and supplies	(X)	862.3
Materials, ingredients, containers, and supplies, nsk	(X)	589.8

Source: 2002 Economic Census. Explanation of symbols used: (D): Withheld to avoid disclosure of competitive data; na: Not available; (S): Withheld because statistical norms were not met; (X): Not applicable; (Z): Less than half the unit shown; nec: Not elsewhere classified; nsk: Not specified by kind; - : zero; p : 10-19 percent estimated; q : 20-29 percent estimated.

PRODUCT SHARE DETAILS

Product or Product Class Shipments	Mil. $	Product or Product Class Shipments	Mil. $
MOTOR HOMES	5,110.1	chassis	675.0
Motor homes built on purchased chassis . . .	**5,110.1**	Van camper (type B) motor homes built on purchased	
Motor homes built on purchased chassis. . . .	5,019.1	chassis.	29.0
Conventional (type A) motor homes built on purchased		Converted vans not qualifying as van campers (type B)	
chassis.	4,123.1	motor homes built on purchased chassis	192.1
Chopped van (type C) motor homes built on purchased		Motor homes, nsk, total	90.9

Source: 2002 *Economic Census*. The values are product shipments in millions of dollars for 2002. Total product shipments may be lower or higher than industry shipments. See Introduction for a full discussion. Values of indented subcategories are summed in the main heading(s). The symbol (D) appears when data are withheld to prevent disclosure of competitive information. The abbreviation nsk stands for 'not specified by kind' and nec for 'not elsewhere classified'. A dash (-) means zero.

INPUTS AND OUTPUTS FOR MOTOR HOME MANUFACTURING

Economic Sector or Industry Providing Inputs	%	Sector	Economic Sector or Industry Buying Outputs	%	Sector
Heavy duty trucks	17.9	Manufg.	Personal consumption expenditures	86.3	
Compensation of employees	16.1		Change in private inventories	5.6	In House
Wood windows & doors & millwork	7.6	Manufg.	Private fixed investment	3.6	
Wholesale trade	6.3	Trade	Exports of goods & services	3.5	Cap Inv
Management of companies & enterprises	5.4	Services	Motor homes	1.1	Manufg.
Motor vehicle parts	4.5	Manufg.			
AC, refrigeration, and warm air heating equipment	2.5	Manufg.			
Wiring devices	1.8	Manufg.			
Rubber products, nec	1.6	Manufg.			
Major household appliances, nec	1.4	Manufg.			
Truck transportation	1.3	Util.			
Plastics products, nec	1.2	Manufg.			
Paints & coatings	1.2	Manufg.			
Alumina refining & primary aluminum production	1.2	Manufg.			
Motor homes	1.1	Manufg.			
Ornamental & architectural metal products	1.0	Manufg.			
Crowns & closures & metal stamping	1.0	Manufg.			
Advertising & related services	0.9	Services			
Water, sewage and other systems	0.9	Util.			
Plastics packaging materials, film & sheet	0.7	Manufg.			
Curtain & linen mills	0.7	Manufg.			
Sawmills & wood preservation	0.7	Manufg.			
Iron & steel mills & ferroalloys	0.6	Manufg.			
Veneer & plywood	0.6	Manufg.			
Basic organic chemicals, nec	0.6	Manufg.			
Software publishers	0.6	Services			
Scientific research & development services	0.5	Services			
Lessors of nonfinancial assets	0.5	Fin/R.E.			
Carpet & rug mills	0.4	Manufg.			
Securities, commodity contracts, investments	0.4	Fin/R.E.			
Semiconductors & related devices	0.4	Manufg.			
Paperboard containers	0.4	Manufg.			
Retail trade	0.4	Trade			
Printed circuit assemblies (electronic assemblies)	0.4	Manufg.			
Turned products & screws, nuts, & bolts	0.4	Manufg.			
Machine shops	0.4	Manufg.			
Plumbing fixture fittings & trim	0.4	Manufg.			
Household refrigerators & home freezers	0.3	Manufg.			
Warehousing & storage	0.3	Util.			
Glass products from purchased glass	0.3	Manufg.			
Aluminum products from purchased aluminum	0.3	Manufg.			
Rail transportation	0.3	Util.			
Legal services	0.3	Services			
Coating, engraving, heat treating & allied activities	0.3	Manufg.			
Real estate	0.2	Fin/R.E.			
Pressed & blown glass & glassware, nec	0.2	Manufg.			
Plastics materials & resins	0.2	Manufg.			
Power generation & supply	0.2	Util.			
Tires	0.2	Manufg.			
Accounting, tax preparation, bookkeeping, & payroll	0.2	Services			
Cutting tools & machine tool accessories	0.2	Manufg.			
Heating equipment (except warm air furnaces)	0.2	Manufg.			
Household cooking appliances	0.2	Manufg.			
Architectural, engineering, & related services	0.1	Services			
Abrasive products	0.1	Manufg.			
Data processing, hosting, & related services	0.1	Services			
Taxes on production & imports, less subsidies	0.1				
Relay & industrial controls	0.1	Manufg.			
Transportation equipment, nec	0.1	Manufg.			
Telecommunications	0.1	Services			

Source: Benchmark Input-Output Accounts for the U.S. Economy, 2002, U.S. Department of Commerce, Washington, D.C., January 2008. The abbreviation nec stands for 'not elsewhere classified'.

OCCUPATIONS EMPLOYED BY MOTOR VEHICLE BODY & TRAILER MANUFACTURING

Occupation	% of Total 2006	Change to 2016	Occupation	% of Total 2006	Change to 2016
Team assemblers	24.6	0.2	Laborers & freight, stock, & material movers, hand	1.8	-11.9
Welders, cutters, solderers, & brazers	11.6	4.1	Industrial truck & tractor operators	1.7	-11.9
First-line supervisors/managers of production workers	4.1	-2.2	Welding, soldering, & brazing machine operators	1.4	10.0
Structural metal fabricators & fitters	3.0	-2.2	Maintenance & repair workers, general	1.3	-2.2
Helpers--Production workers	2.9	-2.2	Production workers, nec	1.3	-4.0
Painters, transportation equipment	2.5	-11.9	Machinists	1.3	2.7
Sales reps, wholesale & manufacturing, exc tech	2.0	-2.2	Shipping, receiving, & traffic clerks	1.2	-5.8
Cutting, punching, & press machine operators	2.0	-11.9	Office clerks, general	1.2	-3.6
Inspectors, testers, sorters, samplers, & weighers	1.8	-7.7	Fiberglass laminators & fabricators	1.1	-2.2

Source: Industry-Occupation Matrix, Bureau of Labor Statistics, December 4, 2007. These data are reported based on 4-digit NAICS categories but have been matched to corresponding 6-digit NAICS industry codes. The change reported for each occupation to the year 2016 is a percent of growth or decline as estimated by the Bureau of Labor Statistics. The abbreviation nec stands for 'not elsewhere classified'.

LOCATION BY STATE AND REGIONAL CONCENTRATION

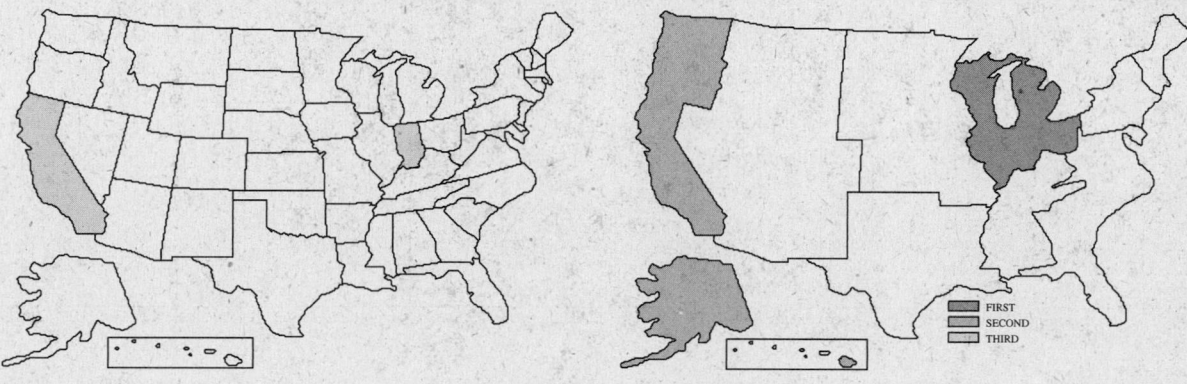

FIRST
SECOND
THIRD

INDUSTRY DATA BY STATE

State	Establish-ments	Shipments			Employment				Cost as % of Shipments	Investment per Employee ($)
		Total ($ mil)	% of U.S.	Per Establ.	Total Number	% of U.S.	Per Establ.	Wages ($/hour)		
Indiana	31	2,607.6	47.4	84,114.9	7,492	36.7	242	19.22	70.0	3,071
California	10	640.4	11.6	64,037.2	2,638	12.9	264	13.45	65.3	1,653

Source: 2002 *Economic Census.* The states are in descending order of shipments or establishments (if shipment data are missing for the majority). The symbol (D) appears when data are withheld to prevent disclosure of competitive information. States marked with (D) are sorted by number of establishments. A dash (-) indicates that the data element cannot be calculated. Data may not show all states active in the NAICS category. All data available at the time of publication are shown.

NAICS 336214 - TRAVEL TRAILER AND CAMPER MANUFACTURING

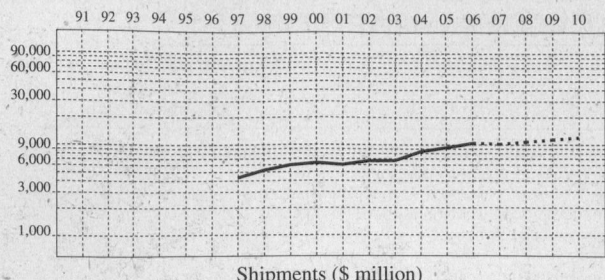

Shipments ($ million)

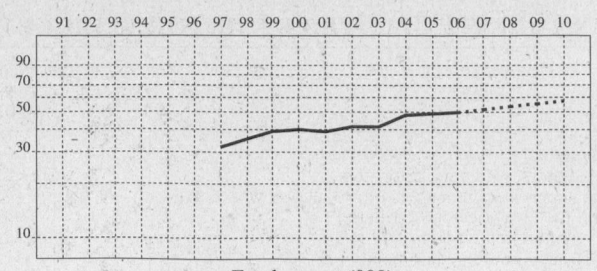

Employment (000)

GENERAL STATISTICS

Year	Companies	Establishments Total	Establishments with 20 or more employees	Employment Total (000)	Employment Production Workers (000)	Employment Hours (Mil)	Compensation Payroll ($ mil)	Compensation Wages ($/hr)	Production ($ million) Cost of Materials	Production ($ million) Value Added by Manufacture	Production ($ million) Value of Shipments	Production ($ million) Capital Invest.
1997	748	806	311	32.0	25.9	49.3	770.5	10.69	2,725.0	1,624.8	4,339.8	73.2
1998		807	312	35.5	29.2	56.6	916.0	11.23	3,253.8	2,032.4	5,247.1	70.3
1999		791	324	39.1	32.6	63.4	1,095.5	12.10	3,680.4	2,281.6	5,966.1	99.6
2000		773	327	40.0	33.2	63.5	1,199.4	12.84	3,884.1	2,455.7	6,291.2	117.6
2001		765	327	38.9	32.3	60.7	1,155.6	13.09	3,724.5	2,241.3	6,034.4	91.7
2002	733	809	338	41.5	33.4	64.7	1,321.1	14.34	4,089.2	2,586.2	6,649.6	73.7
2003		820	328	41.4	33.5	67.4	1,350.4	14.42	3,970.4	2,707.1	6,719.2	91.7
2004		858	363	48.0	37.7	76.8	1,632.7	15.25	5,211.2	3,265.3	8,403.7	78.3
2005		861	374	49.0	39.3	78.2	1,680.6	15.52	5,889.7	3,450.4	9,343.4	79.9
2006		849P	369P	49.8	40.8	80.7	1,848.9	16.51	6,651.1	3,892.9	10,476.9	87.0
2007		857P	376P	51.7P	41.5P	83.3P	1,909.1P	17.07P	6,484.0P	3,795.1P	10,213.6P	85.9P
2008		865P	383P	53.6P	42.9P	86.5P	2,020.4P	17.70P	6,861.0P	4,015.8P	10,807.6P	85.9P
2009		872P	390P	55.4P	44.3P	89.6P	2,131.7P	18.33P	7,238.0P	4,236.4P	11,401.5P	85.8P
2010		880P	397P	57.3P	45.8P	92.7P	2,243.0P	18.96P	7,615.1P	4,457.1P	11,995.4P	85.7P

Sources: 1997 and 2002 *Economic Census*; other years, up to 2006, are from *Annual Survey of Manufactures*. Establishment counts for non-Census years are from *County Business Patterns*; 1997 and 2002 values are from the 1997 and 2002 censuses, respectively. 'P's show projections by the editors.

INDICES OF CHANGE

Year	Companies	Establishments Total	Establishments with 20 or more employees	Employment Total (000)	Employment Production Workers (000)	Employment Hours (Mil)	Compensation Payroll ($ mil)	Compensation Wages ($/hr)	Production ($ million) Cost of Materials	Production ($ million) Value Added by Manufacture	Production ($ million) Value of Shipments	Production ($ million) Capital Invest.
1997	102	100	92	77	78	76	58	75	67	63	65	99
1998		100	92	86	87	87	69	78	80	79	79	95
1999		98	96	94	98	98	83	84	90	88	90	135
2000		96	97	96	99	98	91	90	95	95	95	160
2001		95	97	94	97	94	87	91	91	87	91	124
2002	100	100	100	100	100	100	100	100	100	100	100	100
2003		101	97	100	100	104	102	101	97	105	101	124
2004		106	107	116	113	119	124	106	127	126	126	106
2005		106	111	118	118	121	127	108	144	133	141	108
2006		105P	109P	120	122	125	140	115	163	151	158	118
2007		106P	111P	125P	124P	129P	145P	119P	159P	147P	154P	117P
2008		107P	113P	129P	128P	134P	153P	123P	168P	155P	163P	117P
2009		108P	115P	133P	133P	138P	161P	128P	177P	164P	171P	116P
2010		109P	118P	138P	137P	143P	170P	132P	186P	172P	180P	116P

Sources: Same as General Statistics. Values reflect change from the base year, 2002. Values above 100 mean greater than 2002, values below 100 mean less than 2002, and the values of 100 in other years means the same as 2002. 'P's show projections by the editors.

SELECTED RATIOS

For 2002	Avg. of All Manufact.	Analyzed Industry	Index	For 2002	Avg. of All Manufact.	Analyzed Industry	Index
Employees per Establishment	42	51	122	Value Added per Production Worker	182,367	77,431	42
Payroll per Establishment	1,639,184	1,633,004	100	Cost per Establishment	5,769,015	5,054,635	88
Payroll per Employee	39,053	31,834	82	Cost per Employee	137,446	98,535	72
Production Workers per Establishment	30	41	140	Cost per Production Worker	195,506	122,431	63
Wages per Establishment	694,845	1,146,845	165	Shipments per Establishment	11,158,348	8,219,530	74
Wages per Production Worker	23,548	27,778	118	Shipments per Employee	265,847	160,231	60
Hours per Production Worker	1,980	1,937	98	Shipments per Production Worker	378,144	199,090	53
Wages per Hour	11.89	14.34	121	Investment per Establishment	361,338	91,100	25
Value Added per Establishment	5,381,325	3,196,786	59	Investment per Employee	8,609	1,776	21
Value Added per Employee	128,210	62,318	49	Investment per Production Worker	12,245	2,207	18

Sources: Same as General Statistics. The 'Average of All Manufacturing' column represents the average of all manufacturing industries reported for the most recent complete year available. The Index shows the relationship between the Average and the Analyzed Industry. For example, 100 means that they are equal; 500 that the Analyzed Industry is five times the average; 50 means that the Analyzed Industry is half the national average. The abbreviation 'na' is used to show that data are 'not available'. Ratios shown for 2002, the last complete census year.

LEADING COMPANIES   Number shown: 75   Total sales ($ mil): **69,441**   Total employment (000): **113.9**

Company Name	Address				CEO Name	Phone	Co. Type	Sales ($ mil)	Empl. (000)
American Honda Motor Company	1919 Torrance Blvd.	Torrance	CA	90501	Koichi Kondo	310-783-2000	S	42,539	25.0
Nordic Group of Companies Ltd.	414 Broadway, 200	Baraboo	WI	53913	William R. Sauey	608-356-0136	R	2,706*	2.5
Dutchmen Manufacturing Inc.	813 W Brooklyn St.	Syracuse	IN	46567	W F. B. Thompson	574-457-8385	S	2,065*	8.5
Fleetwood Enterprises Inc.	PO Box 7638	Riverside	CA	92513		951-351-3500	P	2,008	9.3
Polaris Industries Inc.	2100 Hwy. 55	Medina	MN	55340		763-542-0500	P	1,780	3.2
Kawasaki Motors Manufacturing	PO Box 81469	Lincoln	NE	68501		402-476-6600	S	1,758*	1.3
Thor America Inc.	37 Old 522	Middleburg	PA	17842	W F. B. Thompson	570-837-1663	S	1,592*	8.5
ElDorado National California	13900 Sycamore	Chino	CA	91710	W F. B. Thompson	909-591-9557	S	1,491*	8.5
ElDorado National Kansas Inc.	1655 Wall Street	Salina	KS	67401	W F. B. Thompson	785-827-1033	S	1,491*	8.5
Thor California Inc.	14255 Elsworth St.	Moreno Valley	CA	92553	W F. B. Thompson	909-697-4190	S	1,489*	8.5
Tri-Con Industries Ltd.	4000 NW 44th St.	Lincoln	NE	68524		402-470-3311	R	1,450*	0.3
TriMas Corp.	39400 Woodward	Bloomfield Hls	MI	48304	Grant Beard	248-631-5450	P	1,068	5.1
International Industries Inc.	PO Box 1210	Gilbert	WV	25621		304-664-3227	R	835*	0.5
Arctic Cat Inc.	PO Box 810	Thief River Fls	MN	56701		218-681-8558	P	782	1.8
Airstream Inc.	PO Box 629	Jackson Center	OH	45334	Bpob Wheeler	937-596-6111	S	622*	0.5
Jayco Inc.	PO Box 460	Middlebury	IN	46540	Derald Bontrager	574-825-5861	R	585*	1.6
Thule Towing Systems L.L.C.	32501 Dequindre	Madison Heights	MI	48071	George Caplea	248-588-6900	R	582*	0.2
Coachmen Industries Inc.	PO Box 3300	Elkhart	IN	46515	Richard M. Lavers	574-262-0123	P	481	2.7
Skyline Corp.	PO Box 743	Elkhart	IN	46515	Arthur J. Decio	574-294-6521	P	366	2.3
Truck Accessories Group Inc.	PO Box 1128	Elkhart	IN	46515	John Poindexter	574-522-5337	R	331*	0.3
Columbia Parcar Florida	PO Box 60	Reedsburg	WI	53959		608-524-8888	R	256*	<0.1
Textron Turf-Care & Specialty	2166-A W Park Ct.	Stone Mountain	GA	30087	Jon Carlson	770-949-9316	R	243*	1.2
Newmar Corp.	PO Box 30	Nappanee	IN	46550	Matthew Miller	574-773-7791	R	218*	1.0
MasterCraft Boat Company Inc.	100 Cherokee Cv Dr.	Vonore	TN	37885		423-884-2221	R	199*	0.6
Drago Supply Company Inc.	740 Houston Ave.	Port Arthur	TX	77640	Joseph P. Drago	409-983-4911	R	164*	0.2
Gulf Stream Coach Inc.	PO Box 1005	Nappanee	IN	46550		574-773-7761	R	150*	0.1
Draw-Tite Inc.	47774 Anchor Ct. W	Plymouth	MI	48170	Thomas Benson	734-656-3000	R	141*	0.8
Quixote Corp.	35 E Wacker Dr.	Chicago	IL	60601	Leslie J. Jezuit	312-467-6755	P	138	0.7
Penda Corp.	PO Box 449	Portage	WI	53901	Uls Buergel	608-742-5301	R	103*	0.1
Skyline Corp. Nomad Div.	PO Box 360	McMinnville	OR	97128	Thomas G. Deranek	503-472-3101	S	101*	0.1
Fleetwood Folding Trailers	PO Box 111	Somerset	PA	15501	Eldin Smith	814-445-9661	S	90*	0.6
Wilderness Western Holdings	PO Box 9547	Yakima	WA	98909	Ronald Doyle	509-457-4133	R	82*	0.6
Weekend Warrior Trailers Inc.	1320 W Oleander	Perris	CA	92571	Mark Warmoth	951-940-5556	R	78*	0.4
Kzrv L.P.	985 N 900 W	Shipshewana	IN	46565	Daryl Zook	260-768-4016	R	72*	0.5
Northwood Manufacturing Inc.	PO Box 3359	La Grande	OR	97850	Ron Nash	541-962-6274	R	68*	0.4
EZ Loader Boat Trailers Inc.	PO Box 3263	Spokane	WA	99220	Randy Johnson	509-489-0181	R	66*	0.1
Dynamic Corp.	Box 67	Montmorenci	IN	47962	Debbie Fleming	765-583-4406	S	57*	<0.1
Contract Manufacturer L.L.C.	200 County Rd.	Madill	OK	73446	Ronald Jackson	580-795-5536	R	56*	0.3
Midwest Industries Inc.	PO Box 235	Ida Grove	IA	51445	Andy Brosius	712-364-3365	R	54*	0.3
ARE Inc.	PO Box 1100	Massillon	OH	44648	Ralph Gatti	330-359-5450	R	53*	0.4
EZ Way Inc.	PO Box 89	Clarinda	IA	51632	Bill Lisle	712-542-5102	R	52*	0.3
Teton Homes Corp.	PO Box 2349	Mills	WY	82644	Charles Larkin	307-235-1525	R	49*	0.2
Travel Supreme Inc.	PO Box 610	Wakarusa	IN	46573	Glen Troyer	574-862-4484	R	44*	0.3
Arctic Cat Sales Inc.	601 Brooks Ave. S	Thief River Fls	MN	56701	Christopher Twomey	218-681-8558	S	44*	0.2
Sooner Trailer Manufacturing	1515 McCurdy	Duncan	OK	73533	Jim Garis		R	43*	0.3
Fleetwood Travel Trailers/CA	PO Box 810	Rialto	CA	92377		909-874-2223	S	43*	0.3
Dethmers Manufacturing Co.	PO Box 189	Boyden	IA	51234	James Koerselman	712-725-2311	R	42*	0.3
Lance Camper Manufacturing	43120 Venture St.	Lancaster	CA	93535	Jack Cole	661-949-3322	R	41*	0.3
Komfort Corp.	12628 SE Jennifer	Clackamas	OR	97015	Wade F.B. Thompson	503-722-5199	S	39*	0.3
RV Sunnybrook Inc.	PO Box 2001	Middlebury	IN	46540	Elvie Frey	574-825-5250	R	38*	0.3
20th Century Fiberglass Inc.	1131 D I Dr.	Elkhart	IN	46514	Steven Robinson	574-264-7528	R	37*	0.3
Custom Fibreglass Mfg. Co.	PO Box 121	Long Beach	CA	90801	Hartmut Schroeder	562-432-5454	R	35*	0.3
Karavan Trailers Inc.	PO Box 27	Fox Lake	WI	53933	Scott Boyd	920-928-6200	R	34*	0.3
Chief Automotive Systems Inc.	PO Box 1368	Grand Island	NE	68801	Randy Gard	308-384-9747	S	34*	0.2
Nu-WA Industries Inc.	3701 S Johnson Rd.	Chanute	KS	66720	Neil Ford	620-431-2088	R	33*	0.2
Dynamax Corp.	PO Box 1948	Elkhart	IN	46515	Dewayne Creighton	574-262-3474	R	33*	0.2
Carriage Inc.	PO Box 246	Millersburg	IN	46543	Glenn Cushman	574-642-3622	R	31*	0.2
Vanguard L.L.C.	PO Box 802	Colon	MI	49040		269-432-3271	R	27*	0.2
Rolligon Corp.	6740 Hwy. 30	Anderson	TX	77830	Mike Dearing	936-873-2600	R	27*	0.1
Sunline Coach Co.	245 S Muddy Creek	Denver	PA	17517	Joe Bocaro	717-336-2858	R	27*	0.2
Magic Tilt Trailers Inc.	2161 Lions Club Rd.	Clearwater	FL	33764	Craig Blawson	727-535-5561	R	26*	<0.1
WW-Trailer Manufacturers Inc.	PO Box 807	Madill	OK	73446	H Watkins	580-795-5571	R	26*	0.2
Lippert Components Inc.	2375 Tamiami Trl.	Naples	FL	34103	Jason D. Lippert	574-971-4100	S	25*	0.1
Peterson Industries Inc.	616 E Hwy. 36	Smith Center	KS	66967	Vaughn Peterson	785-282-6825	R	20*	0.2
Femco Inc.	500 N US Hwy 81	McPherson	KS	67460	Rodney Borman	620-241-3513	R	20*	<0.1
AL-KO KOBER Corp.	PO Box 1367	Elkhart	IN	46515	Elwood Smith	574-294-6651	S	20*	0.1
T.J.T. Inc.	PO Box 278	Emmett	ID	83617		208-365-5321	P	18	<0.1
Playbuoy Pontoon Manufacturing	PO Box 698	Alma	MI	48801	Jim Wolf	989-463-2112	R	18*	0.1
Pierce Manufacturing Inc.	PO Box 2017	Appleton	WI	54912	John Randjelovic	920-832-3000	R	16*	0.1
MGS Inc.	178 Muddy Creek	Denver	PA	17517	Andrew Gehman	717-336-7528	R	16*	0.1
IPV Inc.	PO Box 232	Vivian	LA	71082	William Parker	318-375-3241	R	16*	0.1
Leitner-Poma of America Inc.	2510 Foresight Cir.	Grand Junction	CO	81505	Anton Sebber	970-241-4442	R	15*	<0.1
Shelby Industries L.L.C.	PO Box 308	Shelbyville	KY	40066	Lalit Sarin	502-633-2040	R	15*	<0.1
Chariot Eagle Inc.	931 NW 37th Ave.	Ocala	FL	34475	Robert Holliday	352-629-7007	R	14*	0.2
HLT Ltd.	PO Box 569	Humboldt	IA	50548	Carl Crewson	515-332-1802	R	14*	0.1

Source: Ward's Business Directory of U.S. Private and Public Companies, Volumes 1 and 2, 2008. The company type code used is as follows: P - Public, R - Private, S - Subsidiary, D - Division, J - Joint Venture, A - Affiliate, G - Group. Sales are in millions of dollars, employees are in thousands. An asterisk (*) indicates an estimated sales volume. The symbol < stands for 'less than'. Company names and addresses are truncated, in some cases, to fit into the available space.

MATERIALS CONSUMED

Material	Quantity	Delivered Cost ($ million)
Other metal vehicular parts, metal (trailer axles, wheels, etc.)	(X)	275.9
Pneumatic tires and inner tubes	(X)	64.4
Purchased chassis for motor homes	(X)	60.3
Household appliances, excluding air conditioners	(X)	96.1
Air-conditioning equipment	(X)	50.3
Metal heating equipment (excluding electric)	(X)	25.8
Metal doors and door units, windows and window units	(X)	81.7
Metal plumbing fixtures, fittings, and trim (including enameled)	(X)	20.6
Sheet metal products (excluding stampings)	(X)	64.5
Metal bolts, nuts, screws, and other screw machine products	(X)	36.7
Other fabricated metal products (excluding forgings)	(X)	69.0
Forgings	(X)	3.2
Castings, rough and semifinished	(X)	6.6
Steel shapes and forms (exc. castings, forgings, fabr. metal products)	(X)	165.4
Aluminum and aluminum-base alloy shapes and forms (exc. castings, forgings, fabr. metal products)	(X)	190.8
Other nonferrous shapes and forms (exc. castings, forgings, fabricated metal products)	(X)	10.8
Current-carrying wiring devices	(X)	70.4
Plywood	(X)	100.7
Lumber, dressed	(X)	62.1
Millwork, wood (wood doors, window sash, moldings, cabinets)	(X)	53.5
Glass and glass products (including windows and mirrors)	(X)	68.0
Fabricated plastics products (excluding gaskets)	(X)	33.5
Plastics products consumed in the form of sheets, rods, etc.	(X)	38.6
Plastics resins consumed in the form of granules, pellets, etc.	(X)	17.5
Paints, varnishes, stains, lacquers, shellacs, japans, enamels, etc.	(X)	38.5
Carpeting	(X)	25.5
Curtains and draperies	(X)	35.4
Molded composites	(X)	34.3
All other materials, components, parts, containers, and supplies	(X)	559.9
Materials, ingredients, containers, and supplies, nsk	(X)	1,577.3

Source: 2002 *Economic Census*. Explanation of symbols used: (D): Withheld to avoid disclosure of competitive data; na: Not available; (S): Withheld because statistical norms were not met; (X): Not applicable; (Z): Less than half the unit shown; nec: Not elsewhere classified; nsk: Not specified by kind; - : zero; p : 10-19 percent estimated; q : 20-29 percent estimated.

PRODUCT SHARE DETAILS

Product or Product Class Shipments	Mil. $	Product or Product Class Shipments	Mil. $
TRAVEL TRAILERS AND CAMPERS	6,745.0	Automobile and light truck mobile equipment trailers 26,000 lb or less GVW	136.3
Travel trailers	**3,403.0**	Other automobile and light truck trailers 26,000 lb or less GVW, including general utility, commercial display, etc., for transport of goods	369.9
Conventional travel trailers, up to 24 ft 11 in.(7.595 m) in length	537.8		
Conventional travel trailers, less than 20 ft (6.096 m) in length	144.0	Other automobile and light truck trailers 26,000 lb or less GVW, including general utility, commercial display, etc., for other uses	360.6
Conventional travel trailers, 20 ft (6.096 m) to 24 ft 11 in. (7.595 m) in length	393.8		
Conventional travel trailers, 25 ft (7.620 m) to 29 ft 11 in. (9.118 m) in length	842.5	Automobile and light truck trailers 26,001 lbs or more GVW	34.0
Conventional travel trailers, 30 ft (9.144 m) or more in length, including park models	471.4	Automobile and light truck trailers, nsk	151.0
		Camping trailers, campers, pickup covers, and parts	**988.8**
Fifth wheel travel trailers, less than 30 ft (9.144 m) in length	613.6	Folddown camping trailers	229.6
		Truck (pickup) campers (for sliding on and off trucks), caps, or box covers	378.8
Fifth wheel travel trailers, 30 ft (9.144 m) or more in length	835.3	Truck (pickup) campers (for sliding on and off trucks), excluding parts	117.5
Travel trailers, nsk	102.4	Truck (pickup) caps and box covers, excluding parts	261.2
Automobile and light truck trailers	**1,769.4**	Other parts for travel and camping trailers (including bodies and chassis), and parts for pickup campers and caps (excluding appliances and furnishings)	338.6
Automobile and light truck trailers	1,618.4		
Automobile and light truck horse trailers 26,000 lb or less GVW, excluding those pulled by truck tractors	407.5	Camping trailers, campers, pickup covers, and parts, nsk	41.9
Automobile and light truck boat trailers 26,000 lb or less GVW	310.3	**Travel trailers and campers, nsk, total**	**583.8**

Source: 2002 *Economic Census*. The values are product shipments in millions of dollars for 2002. Total product shipments may be lower or higher than industry shipments. See Introduction for a full discussion. Values of indented subcategories are summed in the main heading(s). The symbol (D) appears when data are withheld to prevent disclosure of competitive information. The abbreviation nsk stands for 'not specified by kind' and nec for 'not elsewhere classified'. A dash (-) means zero.

INPUTS AND OUTPUTS FOR TRAVEL TRAILER AND CAMPER MANUFACTURING

Economic Sector or Industry Providing Inputs	%	Sector	Economic Sector or Industry Buying Outputs	%	Sector
Compensation of employees	24.3		Personal consumption expenditures	64.7	
Motor vehicle parts	6.3	Manufg.	Private fixed investment	10.4	
Wholesale trade	6.0	Trade	Exports of goods & services	5.9	Cap Inv
Travel trailers & campers	4.6	Manufg.	Travel trailers & campers	4.3	Manufg.
Alumina refining & primary aluminum production	4.2	Manufg.	Change in private inventories	4.0	In House
Ornamental & architectural metal products	3.3	Manufg.	General S/L govt. services	3.7	S/L Govt
Management of companies & enterprises	3.2	Services	Services to buildings & dwellings	2.5	Services
Iron & steel mills & ferroalloys	3.1	Manufg.	Truck trailers	1.8	Manufg.
Rubber products, nec	3.0	Manufg.	Waste management & remediation services	1.6	Services
AC, refrigeration, and warm air heating equipment	2.2	Manufg.	Spectator sports	0.3	Services
Veneer & plywood	2.2	Manufg.	Scientific research & development services	0.2	Services
Transportation equipment, nec	2.1	Manufg.	Other S/L govt. enterprises	0.2	S/L Govt
Wiring devices	1.6	Manufg.	S/L govt. electric utilities	0.2	S/L Govt
Tires	1.5	Manufg.			
Water, sewage and other systems	1.4	Util.			
Major household appliances, nec	1.3	Manufg.			
Truck transportation	1.3	Util.			
Heavy duty trucks	1.3	Manufg.			
Sawmills & wood preservation	1.2	Manufg.			
Plastics products, nec	1.2	Manufg.			
Wood windows & doors & millwork	1.2	Manufg.			
Advertising & related services	1.1	Services			
Lessors of nonfinancial assets	1.0	Fin/R.E.			
Paints & coatings	0.9	Manufg.			
Turned products & screws, nuts, & bolts	0.9	Manufg.			
Scientific research & development services	0.9	Services			
Securities, commodity contracts, investments	0.8	Fin/R.E.			
Crowns & closures & metal stamping	0.7	Manufg.			
Curtain & linen mills	0.7	Manufg.			
Plastics packaging materials, film & sheet	0.7	Manufg.			
Glass products from purchased glass	0.7	Manufg.			
Real estate	0.6	Fin/R.E.			
Architectural, engineering, & related services	0.6	Services			
Monetary authorities/depository credit intermediation	0.6	Fin/R.E.			
Carpet & rug mills	0.6	Manufg.			
Pressed & blown glass & glassware, nec	0.6	Manufg.			
Heating equipment (except warm air furnaces)	0.5	Manufg.			
Professional, scientific, technical services, nec	0.5	Services			
Basic organic chemicals, nec	0.5	Manufg.			
Aluminum products from purchased aluminum	0.4	Manufg.			
Machine shops	0.4	Manufg.			
Plumbing fixture fittings & trim	0.4	Manufg.			
Semiconductors & related devices	0.4	Manufg.			
Paperboard containers	0.3	Manufg.			
Plastics materials & resins	0.3	Manufg.			
Power generation & supply	0.3	Util.			
Printed circuit assemblies (electronic assemblies)	0.3	Manufg.			
Coating, engraving, heat treating & allied activities	0.3	Manufg.			
Management, scientific, & technical consulting	0.3	Services			
Legal services	0.3	Services			
Taxes on production & imports, less subsidies	0.3				
Accounting, tax preparation, bookkeeping, & payroll	0.3	Services			
Rail transportation	0.2	Util.			
Warehousing & storage	0.2	Util.			
Telecommunications	0.2	Services			
Flat glass	0.2	Manufg.			
Household refrigerators & home freezers	0.2	Manufg.			
Automotive equipment rental & leasing	0.2	Fin/R.E.			
Data processing, hosting, & related services	0.2	Services			
Food services & drinking places	0.2	Services			
Natural gas distribution	0.2	Util.			
Business support services	0.2	Services			
Employment services	0.2	Services			
Specialized design services	0.2	Services			
Services to buildings & dwellings	0.2	Services			
Maintenance/repair of nonresidential structures	0.1	Construct.			
Hotels & motels, including casino hotels	0.1	Services			
Unlaminated plastics profile shapes	0.1	Manufg.			
Waste management & remediation services	0.1	Services			
Air transportation	0.1	Util.			
Metal cans, boxes, & other containers (light gauge)	0.1	Manufg.			
Fabricated metals, nec	0.1	Manufg.			
Commercial & industrial machinery rental & leasing	0.1	Fin/R.E.			

Source: Benchmark Input-Output Accounts for the U.S. Economy, 2002, U.S. Department of Commerce, Washington, D.C., January 2008. The abbreviation nec stands for 'not elsewhere classified'.

OCCUPATIONS EMPLOYED BY MOTOR VEHICLE BODY & TRAILER MANUFACTURING

Occupation	% of Total 2006	Change to 2016	Occupation	% of Total 2006	Change to 2016
Team assemblers	24.6	0.2	Laborers & freight, stock, & material movers, hand	1.8	-11.9
Welders, cutters, solderers, & brazers	11.6	4.1	Industrial truck & tractor operators	1.7	-11.9
First-line supervisors/managers of production workers	4.1	-2.2	Welding, soldering, & brazing machine operators	1.4	10.0
Structural metal fabricators & fitters	3.0	-2.2	Maintenance & repair workers, general	1.3	-2.2
Helpers--Production workers	2.9	-2.2	Production workers, nec	1.3	-4.0
Painters, transportation equipment	2.5	-11.9	Machinists	1.3	2.7
Sales reps, wholesale & manufacturing, exc tech	2.0	-2.2	Shipping, receiving, & traffic clerks	1.2	-5.8
Cutting, punching, & press machine operators	2.0	-11.9	Office clerks, general	1.2	-3.6
Inspectors, testers, sorters, samplers, & weighers	1.8	-7.7	Fiberglass laminators & fabricators	1.1	-2.2

Source: *Industry-Occupation Matrix*, Bureau of Labor Statistics, December 4, 2007. These data are reported based on 4-digit NAICS categories but have been matched to corresponding 6-digit NAICS industry codes. The change reported for each occupation to the year 2016 is a percent of growth or decline as estimated by the Bureau of Labor Statistics. The abbreviation nec stands for 'not elsewhere classified'.

LOCATION BY STATE AND REGIONAL CONCENTRATION

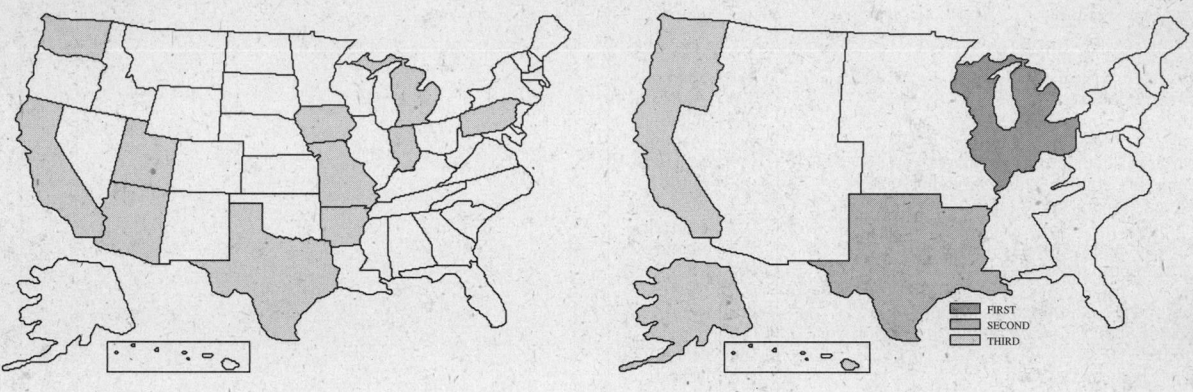

FIRST
SECOND
THIRD

INDUSTRY DATA BY STATE

State	Establish-ments	Shipments Total ($ mil)	Shipments % of U.S.	Shipments Per Establ.	Employment Total Number	Employment % of U.S.	Employment Per Establ.	Wages ($/hour)	Cost as % of Shipments	Investment per Employee ($)
Indiana	99	2,708.0	40.7	27,353.5	12,700	30.6	128	18.32	65.3	1,521
California	72	626.8	9.4	8,706.2	4,021	9.7	56	11.16	61.6	1,858
Texas	79	387.1	5.8	4,899.9	3,151	7.6	40	11.58	61.9	2,210
Pennsylvania	31	292.3	4.4	9,429.2	2,021	4.9	65	10.96	56.1	1,535
Iowa	21	269.2	4.0	12,819.8	1,933	4.7	92	14.01	56.6	3,100
Michigan	32	176.0	2.6	5,499.4	1,201	2.9	38	14.69	59.1	1,544
Missouri	33	74.5	1.1	2,258.2	655	1.6	20	10.82	65.0	2,041
Utah	12	66.1	1.0	5,508.5	527	1.3	44	11.20	61.0	5,226
Washington	14	45.3	0.7	3,234.8	275	0.7	20	14.11	69.5	1,360
Arkansas	12	41.0	0.6	3,416.4	331	0.8	28	10.37	62.1	1,133
Arizona	14	20.8	0.3	1,487.2	190	0.5	14	10.00	56.4	1,316

Source: 2002 *Economic Census*. The states are in descending order of shipments or establishments (if shipment data are missing for the majority). The symbol (D) appears when data are withheld to prevent disclosure of competitive information. States marked with (D) are sorted by number of establishments. A dash (-) indicates that the data element cannot be calculated. Data may not show all states active in the NAICS category. All data available at the time of publication are shown.

NAICS 33631M - MOTOR VEHICLE GASOLINE ENGINE AND ENGINE PARTS MANUFACTURING*

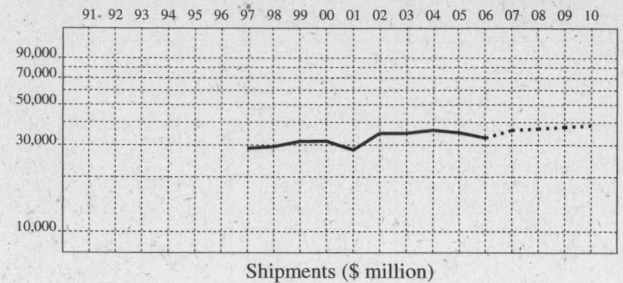

Shipments ($ million)

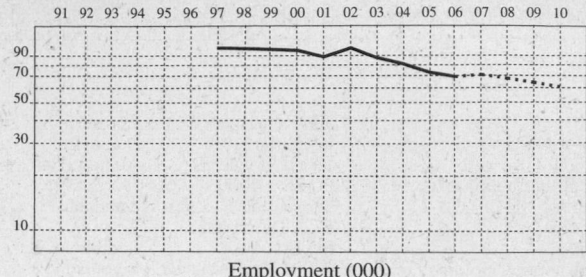

Employment (000)

GENERAL STATISTICS

Year	Companies	Establishments		Employment			Compensation		Production ($ million)			
		Total	with 20 or more employees	Total (000)	Production Workers (000)	Hours (Mil)	Payroll ($ mil)	Wages ($/hr)	Cost of Materials	Value Added by Manufacture	Value of Shipments	Capital Invest.
1997	933	1,022	330	99.4	81.1	168.2	4,238.7	19.27	19,010.1	9,685.0	28,755.1	1,962.6
1998		1,048	339	98.6	80.1	165.0	4,214.6	19.36	18,741.5	10,680.2	29,398.6	1,798.5
1999		1,003	341	97.5	80.2	172.9	4,727.0	21.45	19,896.9	11,471.8	31,395.1	1,464.4
2000		982	352	96.3	79.5	169.8	4,723.2	21.80	19,916.0	11,596.6	31,455.8	1,334.1
2001		984	340	88.7	73.0	149.4	4,287.9	22.23	18,285.2	9,764.1	28,201.6	1,514.8
2002	948	1,050	321	98.9	81.2	149.7	4,753.9	24.67	22,650.6	12,262.2	34,817.8	1,274.2
2003		1,042	329	87.7	68.6	144.3	4,770.7	24.65	22,102.4	12,670.4	34,786.9	1,150.3
2004		1,021	314	81.1	63.3	131.4	4,500.7	25.68	21,813.9	14,330.7	36,257.6	1,003.5
2005		1,005	301	73.0	56.6	120.7	4,223.1	25.65	21,271.1	13,918.9	35,087.9	1,428.4
2006		1,017P	309P	69.1	53.2	113.9	3,927.0	25.36	19,469.1	13,555.7	32,835.0	1,225.0
2007		1,017P	305P	70.7P	54.2P	112.4P	4,327.7P	27.38P	21,473.0P	14,951.0P	36,214.7P	1,004.7P
2008		1,017P	301P	67.4P	51.0P	105.9P	4,307.9P	28.17P	21,895.2P	15,244.9P	36,926.6P	930.0P
2009		1,017P	297P	64.1P	47.8P	99.3P	4,288.1P	28.97P	22,317.3P	15,538.8P	37,638.5P	855.3P
2010		1,017P	293P	60.7P	44.7P	92.8P	4,268.3P	29.76P	22,739.4P	15,832.7P	38,350.4P	780.6P

Sources: 1997 and 2002 *Economic Census*; other years, up to 2006, are from *Annual Survey of Manufactures*. Establishment counts for non-Census years are from *County Business Patterns*; 1997 and 2002 values are from the 1997 and 2002 censuses, respectively. 'P's show projections by the editors.

INDICES OF CHANGE

Year	Companies	Establishments		Employment			Compensation		Production ($ million)			
		Total	with 20 or more employees	Total (000)	Production Workers (000)	Hours (Mil)	Payroll ($ mil)	Wages ($/hr)	Cost of Materials	Value Added by Manufacture	Value of Shipments	Capital Invest.
1997	98	97	103	101	100	112	89	78	84	79	83	154
1998		100	106	100	99	110	89	78	83	87	84	141
1999		96	106	99	99	115	99	87	88	94	90	115
2000		94	110	97	98	113	99	88	88	95	90	105
2001		94	106	90	90	100	90	90	81	80	81	119
2002	100	100	100	100	100	100	100	100	100	100	100	100
2003		99	102	89	84	96	100	100	98	103	100	90
2004		97	98	82	78	88	95	104	96	117	104	79
2005		96	94	74	70	81	89	104	94	114	101	112
2006		97P	96P	70	66	76	83	103	86	111	94	96
2007		97P	95P	71P	67P	75P	91P	111P	95P	122P	104P	79P
2008		97P	94P	68P	63P	71P	91P	114P	97P	124P	106P	73P
2009		97P	92P	65P	59P	66P	90P	117P	99P	127P	108P	67P
2010		97P	91P	61P	55P	62P	90P	121P	100P	129P	110P	61P

Sources: Same as General Statistics. Values reflect change from the base year, 2002. Values above 100 mean greater than 2002, values below 100 mean less than 2002, and the values of 100 in other years means the same as 2002. 'P's show projections by the editors.

SELECTED RATIOS

For 2002	Avg. of All Manufact.	Analyzed Industry	Index	For 2002	Avg. of All Manufact.	Analyzed Industry	Index
Employees per Establishment	42	94	224	Value Added per Production Worker	182,367	151,012	83
Payroll per Establishment	1,639,184	4,527,524	276	Cost per Establishment	5,769,015	21,572,000	374
Payroll per Employee	39,053	48,068	123	Cost per Employee	137,446	229,025	167
Production Workers per Establishment	30	77	262	Cost per Production Worker	195,506	278,948	143
Wages per Establishment	694,845	3,517,237	506	Shipments per Establishment	11,158,348	33,159,810	297
Wages per Production Worker	23,548	45,482	193	Shipments per Employee	265,847	352,051	132
Hours per Production Worker	1,980	1,844	93	Shipments per Production Worker	378,144	428,791	113
Wages per Hour	11.89	24.67	207	Investment per Establishment	361,338	1,213,524	336
Value Added per Establishment	5,381,325	11,678,286	217	Investment per Employee	8,609	12,884	150
Value Added per Employee	128,210	123,986	97	Investment per Production Worker	12,245	15,692	128

Sources: Same as General Statistics. The 'Average of All Manufacturing' column represents the average of all manufacturing industries reported for the most recent complete year available. The Index shows the relationship between the Average and the Analyzed Industry. For example, 100 means that they are equal; 500 that the Analyzed Industry is five times the average; 50 means that the Analyzed Industry is half the national average. The abbreviation 'na' is used to show that data are 'not available'. Ratios shown for 2002, the last complete census year.

*Equivalent to Federal Government NAICS 336311, 336312.

LEADING COMPANIES   Number shown: **75**   Total sales ($ mil): **786,437**   Total employment (000): **1,870.9**

Company Name	Address				CEO Name	Phone	Co. Type	Sales ($ mil)	Empl. (000)
General Motors Corp.	300 Renaissance Ctr	Detroit	MI	48265		313-556-5000	P	181,122	266.0
Ford Motor Co.	1 American Rd.	Dearborn	MI	48126		313-322-3000	P	172,455	246.0
Chrysler L.L.C.	1000 Chrysler Dr.	Auburn Hills	MI	48326	Thomas W. LaSorda	248-576-5741	S	45,237*	84.4
Honeywell International Inc.	PO Box 4000	Morristown	NJ	07962	Adriane M. Brown	973-455-2000	P	34,589	122.0
ArvinMeritor OE L.L.C.	950 W 450 S, Bldg.	Columbus	IN	47201	C. G. McClure Jr.	812-341-2000	S	23,491*	32.0
Delphi Corp.	5725 Delphi Dr.	Troy	MI	48098	Voker J. Barth	248-813-2000	P	22,383	169.5
Lear Corp.	PO Box 5008	Southfield	MI	48086	Jim Brackenbury	248-447-1500	P	15,995	91.0
TRW Automotive Holdings Inc.	12001 Tech Cntr Dr.	Livonia	MI	48150		734-855-2600	P	14,702	66.3
Textron Inc.	40 Westminster St.	Providence	RI	02903		401-421-2800	P	13,225	44.0
Cummins Inc.	PO Box 3005	Columbus	IN	47202		812-377-5000	P	13,048	37.8
Eaton Corp.	1111 Superior Ave.	Cleveland	OH	44114		216-523-5000	P	13,033	60.0
Visteon Corp.	1 Village Center Dr	Van Buren Twp	MI	48111		313-755-2800	P	11,266	41.5
Parker Hannifin Corp.	6035 Parkland Blvd.	Cleveland	OH	44124	Lee Banks	216-896-3000	P	10,718	57.3
Acument Global Technologies	840 W Long Lake	Troy	MI	48098	Joseph Gray	248-813-6329	S	10,080*	9.0
ITT Corp.	4 W Red Oak Ln.	White Plains	NY	10604		914-641-2000	P	9,003	39.7
Dana Corp.	PO Box 1000	Toledo	OH	43697	Michael J. Burns	419-535-4500	P	8,504	45.0
Neapco L.L.C.	PO Box 399	Pottstown	PA	19464		610-323-6000	R	7,580*	0.3
Trane Inc.	PO Box 6820	Piscataway	NJ	08855		732-980-6000	P	7,450	29.6
Triangle Suspension Systems	PO Box 425	Du Bois	PA	15801	Greg Maffia	814-375-7211	R	7,000*	0.2
Perfection Hy-Test Company	100 Perfection Way	Timmonsville	SC	29161		843-326-5544	R	7,000*	0.2
Penn Machine Co.	106 Station St.	Johnstown	PA	15905	H Wiegand	814-288-1547	R	7,000*	<0.1
Federal-Mogul Corp.	PO Box 1966	Detroit	MI	48235	Jose Maria Alapont	248-354-7700	P	6,914	43.1
Robert Bosch Corp.	2800 S 25th Ave.	Broadview	IL	60155	Kurt W. Liedtke	708-865-5200	S	6,782*	25.0
ArvinMeritor Inc.	2135 W Maple Rd.	Troy	MI	48084		248-435-1000	P	6,449	18.0
Tenneco Inc.	500 N Field Dr.	Lake Forest	IL	60045		847-482-5000	P	6,184	21.0
Toyota Motor Mfg. N America	25 Atlantic Ave.	Erlanger	KY	41018	Masamoto Amezawa	859-746-4000	S	6,120*	7.5
Guardian Industries Corp.	2300 Harmon Rd.	Auburn Hills	MI	48326	William M. Davidson	248-340-1800	R	5,330	19.0
BorgWarner Inc.	3850 Hamlin Rd.	Auburn Hills	MI	48326		248-754-9200	P	5,329	17.7
Autoliv ASP Inc.	3350 Airport Rd.	Ogden	UT	84405	Leonard Barton	801-625-4800	S	5,301*	3.7
Carlisle Tire and Wheel Co.	23 Windham Blvd.	Aiken	SC	29805	Barry Littrell	803-643-2900	S	4,822*	0.6
Karl Schmidt Unisia Inc.	1731 Industrial Pky	Marinette	WI	54143	Frank Pohlmann	715-732-0181	R	4,640*	0.9
Pioneer Automotive Tech.	100 S Pioneer Blvd.	Springboro	OH	45066	Steve Moerner	937-746-6600	R	4,610*	0.3
Toledo Trans-Kit Inc.	13515 Ballnyn Corp.	Charlotte	NC	28277	C. J. Kearney	704-752-4400	S	4,372	23.8
Mack Trucks Inc.	PO Box M	Allentown	PA	18105		610-709-3011	R	4,324*	0.8
New United Motor Manufacturing	45500 Fremont	Fremont	CA	94538	Bruce Walker	510-498-5500	J	4,080*	5.0
Kalmar Industries USA L.L.C.	415 E Dundee St.	Ottawa	KS	66067		785-242-2200	R	3,320*	0.3
American Axle & Mfg Holdings	1 Dauch Dr.	Detroit	MI	48211	Richard E. Dauch	313-974-2000	P	3,248	10.0
Hi-Stat Manufacturing Company	28001 Cabot Dr.	Novi	MI	48377	John Corey	248-489-9300	D	3,194*	5.0
Amsted Industries Inc.	2 Prudential Plaza	Chicago	IL	60601	W. Robert Reum	312-645-1700	R	3,050	9.9
AutoAlliance International	1 International Dr.	Flat Rock	MI	48134	Phillip G. Spender	734-782-7800	J	3,019*	3.7
TAG Holdings L.L.C.	2075 W Big Beaver	Troy	MI	48084	J. B. Anderson, Jr.	248-822-8056	R	2,904*	2.5
Crane Co.	100 First Stamford	Stamford	CT	06902	Thomas Craney	203-363-7300	P	2,619	12.0
Consolidated Metco Inc.	PO Box 83201	Portland	OR	97283		503-286-5741	R	2,510*	0.1
Pall Corp.	2200 Northern Blvd.	East Hills	NY	11548	Eric Krasnoff	516-484-5400	P	2,250	10.8
DENSO Manufacturing Tennessee	1720 Rbrt C Jackson	Maryville	TN	37801	Mack Hattori	865-982-7000	S	2,231*	2.0
Sequa Corp.	200 Park Ave.	New York	NY	10166	Gail Binderman	212-986-5500	P	2,183	10.2
Affinia Group Inc.	1101 Technology	Ann Arbor	MI	48108		734-827-5400	P	2,160	12.4
Dura Automotive Systems Inc.	2791 Research Dr.	Rochester Hills	MI	48309	Lawrence A. Denton	248-299-7500	P	2,091	15.4
Hayes Lemmerz International	15300 Centennial Dr	Northville	MI	48167	Fred Bentley	734-737-5000	P	2,039	11.0
Cooper Tire and Rubber Co.	701 Lima Ave.	Findlay	OH	45840	Roy V. Armes	419-423-1321	P	2,036	13.6
Sauer-Danfoss Inc.	250 Pkwy. Dr., 270	Lincolnshire	IL	60069	David J. Anderson	515-239-6000	P	1,973	9.8
ZF Group N American Operations	15811 Centennial Dr	Northville	MI	48168	Julio Caspari	734-416-6200	R	1,949*	5.5
Sypris Technologies Marion	1550 Marion-Agosta	Marion	OH	43301	Jeffrey T. Gill	740-383-2111	S	1,920*	2.6
Hutchinson FTS Inc.	1835 Technology	Troy	MI	48083	Paul Campbell	248-589-7710	R	1,863*	<0.1
ADVICS North America Inc.	45300 Polaris Ct.	Plymouth	MI	48170	Haruhiko Saito	734-414-5100	S	1,810*	<0.1
Regal-Beloit Corp.	200 State St.	Beloit	WI	53511		608-364-8800	P	1,803	17.9
Bose Corp.	The Mountain	Framingham	MA	01701	Amar G. Bose	508-879-7330	R	1,800	8.0
Modine Manufacturing Co.	1500 DeKoven Ave.	Racine	WI	53403	Richard J. Doyle	262-636-1200	P	1,758	7.7
Siemens VDO Automotive Corp.	2400 Executive Hill	Auburn Hills	MI	48326	John Sanderson	248-209-4000	S	1,738*	10.0
Solvay America Inc.	3333 Richmond	Houston	TX	77098	David G. Birney	713-525-6000	S	1,611*	4.0
Neoplan USA Corp.	12015 E 46th Ave.	Denver	CO	80239	Harold Boade	303-451-5305	R	1,610*	<0.1
Hitachi Cable Indiana Inc.	5300 Grant Line Rd.	New Albany	IN	47150	Kenji Nakata	812-945-9011	R	1,590*	<0.1
Actuant Corp.	13000 W Slvr Spring	Butler	WI	53007	Bob Arzbaecher	414-352-4160	P	1,459	6.3
Accuride Corp.	PO Box 15600	Evansville	IN	47716	Terry Keating	812-962-5000	P	1,408	4.6
Morgan Adv. Materials/Tech.	441 Hall Ave.	Saint Marys	PA	15857	David Cooper	814-781-1573	R	1,320*	0.3
Inergy Automotive Systems	2710 Bellingham Dr.	Troy	MI	48083	James Squatrito	248-743-5700	R	1,257*	0.2
RBS Global Inc.	4701 W Greenfield	Milwaukee	WI	53214	Robert Hitt	414-643-3000	R	1,256	5.7
EaglePicher Corp.	2424 John Daly Rd.	Inkster	MI	48141	Donald L. Runkle	313-278-5956	R	1,244*	4.2
Remy International Inc.	2902 Enterprise Dr.	Anderson	IN	46013	Thomas J. Synder	765-778-6499	S	1,218*	7.9
Mark IV Industries Inc.	PO Box 810	Amherst	NY	14226		716-689-4972	R	1,215*	8.1
Adams Rite Manufacturing Co.	260 W Santa Fe St.	Pomona	CA	91767	Peter Adams	909-632-2300	R	1,201*	0.2
Noranda Aluminum Inc.	801 Crescent Centre	Franklin	TN	37067	William Brooks	615-771-5700	R	1,170*	<0.1
Tecumseh Products Co.	100 E Patterson St.	Tecumseh	MI	49286	Edwin Bunker	517-423-8411	P	1,133	10.3
Axiom Automotive Technologies	1 PPG Pl., 3150	Pittsburgh	PA	15222	Greg Gyllstorm	412-545-8100	R	1,110*	1.7
Key Safety Systems Inc.	7000 Nineteen Mile	Sterling Hgts	MI	48314	Jason Luo	586-726-3800	S	1,030	8.7

Source: Ward's Business Directory of U.S. Private and Public Companies, Volumes 1 and 2, 2008. The company type code used is as follows: P - Public, R - Private, S - Subsidiary, D - Division, J - Joint Venture, A - Affiliate, G - Group. Sales are in millions of dollars, employees are in thousands. An asterisk (*) indicates an estimated sales volume. The symbol < stands for 'less than'. Company names and addresses are truncated, in some cases, to fit into the available space.

MATERIALS CONSUMED FOR CARBURETOR, PISTON, PISTON RING, AND VALVE MANUFACTURING

Material	Quantity	Delivered Cost ($ million)
Metal bolts, nuts, screws, and other screw machine products	(X)	1.4
Other fabricated metal products (exc. castings and forgings)	(X)	3.7
Iron and steel castings (rough and semifinished)	(X)	128.0
Aluminum and aluminum-base alloy castings (rough and semifinished)	(X)	194.3
Other nonferrous metal castings, rough or semifinished (inc. aluminum)	(X)	(D)
Steel bars, bar shapes, and plates (exc. castings, forgings, fabr. metal products)	(X)	27.0
All other steel shapes and forms (exc. castings, forgings, fabr. metal products)	(X)	(D)
Aluminum and aluminum-base alloy shapes and forms (exc. castings, forgings, fabr. metal products)	(X)	4.5
Other nonferrous shapes and forms (exc. castings, forgings, fabricated metal products)	(X)	(D)
Paperboard containers, boxes, and corrugated paperboard	(X)	2.6
Flexible packaging materials	(X)	0.9
Gaskets (all types), and packing and sealing devices	(X)	1.4
All other materials, components, parts, containers, and supplies	(X)	79.4
Materials, ingredients, containers, and supplies, nsk	(X)	27.4

Source: 2002 *Economic Census*. Explanation of symbols used: (D): Withheld to avoid disclosure of competitive data; na: Not available; (S): Withheld because statistical norms were not met; (X): Not applicable; (Z): Less than half the unit shown; nec: Not elsewhere classified; nsk: Not specified by kind; - : zero; p : 10-19 percent estimated; q : 20-29 percent estimated.

MATERIALS CONSUMED FOR GASOLINE ENGINE AND ENGINE PARTS MANUFACTURING

Material	Quantity	Delivered Cost ($ million)
Iron and steel castings (rough and semifinished)	(X)	3,852.0
Aluminum and aluminum-base alloy castings (rough and semifinished)	(X)	1,365.8
Other nonferrous metal castings, rough or semifinished (inc. aluminum)	(X)	56.1
Steel bars, bar shapes, and plates (exc. castings, forgings, fabr. metal products)	(X)	153.8
Steel sheet and strip (including tinplate)	(X)	38.5
All other steel shapes and forms (exc. castings, forgings, fabr. metal products)	(X)	111.0
Copper and copper-base alloy shapes and forms (exc. castings, forgings, fabr. metal products)	(X)	25.4
Aluminum and aluminum-base alloy shapes and forms (exc. castings, forgings, fabr. metal products)	(X)	116.3
Other nonferrous shapes and forms (exc. castings, forgings, fabricated metal products)	(X)	17.8
Ball and roller bearings (mounted or unmounted)	(X)	192.5
Fabricated plastics products (exc. gaskets, hoses, and belting)	(X)	234.2
Plastics products consumed in the form of sheets, rods, etc.	(X)	104.4
Plastics resins consumed in the form of granules, pellets, etc.	(X)	125.8
Fabricated rubber products (exc. tires, tubes, hoses, belting, and gaskets)	(X)	14.0
Rubber and plastics hose and belting	(X)	77.6
Ceramic raw materials (incl. powders, chemicals, and fibers)	(X)	(D)
Ceramic and ceramic composite parts, components, and accessories	(X)	(D)
Gaskets (all types), and packing and sealing devices	(X)	210.4
Paints, varnishes, stains, lacquers, shellacs, japans, enamels, etc.	(X)	(D)
Glues and adhesives	(X)	5.6
Flexible packaging materials	(X)	12.0
Paper and paperboard containers	(X)	44.9
Spark plugs for internal combustion engines	(X)	65.9
Generators for internal combustion engines	(X)	(D)
Starting motors for internal combustion engines	(X)	19.6
Distributors for internal combustion engines	(X)	14.5
Ignition coils for internal combustion engines	(X)	104.8
Ignition harness and cable sets for internal combustion engines	(X)	53.7
All other engine electrical equipment for internal combustion engines	(X)	140.7
Magnetos, magneto-dynamos, and magnetic flywheels for internal combustion engines	(X)	(D)
Turbochargers	(X)	(D)
Injection fuel pumps	(X)	115.8
Machined engine blocks	(X)	(D)
Resistors for electronic circuitry	(X)	(D)
Capacitors for electronic circuitry	(X)	(D)
Semiconductors (incl. transistors, diodes, rectifiers, and integrated circuits), for electronic circuitry	(X)	26.6
Used engine electrical equipment for rebuilding, or to be used in rebuilding (starting motors, generators, etc.)	(X)	(D)
All other miscellaneous components and accessories for electronic circuitry (exc. tubes)	(X)	507.7
Core parts purchased for use in remanufacturing and rebuilding	(X)	442.9
Printed ciruit boards (without inserted components) for electronic circuitry	(X)	15.0
Metal bolts, nuts, screws, and other screw machine products	(X)	293.5
Other fabricated metal products (exc. fluid power and forgings)	(X)	1,595.7
Forgings	(X)	239.6
Insulated wire and cable (excluding magnet wire)	(X)	(D)
Magnet wire	(X)	2.2
Mechanical speed changers, gears, and industrial high-speed drives	(X)	(D)
Fluid power pumps, motors, and hydrostatic transmissions	(X)	963.8
Fluid power valves (hydraulic and pneumatic)	(X)	408.3
Fluid power cylinders and rotary actuators (hydraulic and pneumatic)	(X)	(D)
Fluid power hose, tube fittings, and assemblies (hydraulic and pneumatic)	(X)	77.1
Fluid power filters (hydraulic and pneumatic)	(X)	68.5
Other transportation related fluid power products, hydraulic and pneumatic	(X)	69.2
Automotive stampings (inc. body parts, hubcaps, fenders, etc.)	(X)	415.7
Current-carrying wiring devices	(X)	50.4
Other chemicals and allied products	(X)	33.3

Continued on next page.

MATERIALS CONSUMED FOR GASOLINE ENGINE AND ENGINE PARTS MANUFACTURING - Continued

Material	Quantity	Delivered Cost ($ million)
All other materials, components, parts, containers, and supplies	(X)	6,745.5
Materials, ingredients, containers, and supplies, nsk	(X)	965.2

Source: 2002 *Economic Census*. Explanation of symbols used: (D): Withheld to avoid disclosure of competitive data; na: Not available; (S): Withheld because statistical norms were not met; (X): Not applicable; (Z): Less than half the unit shown; nec: Not elsewhere classified; nsk: Not specified by kind; - : zero; p : 10-19 percent estimated; q : 20-29 percent estimated.

PRODUCT SHARE DETAILS FOR CARBURETOR, PISTON, PISTON RING, AND VALVE MANUFACTURING

Product or Product Class Shipments	Mil. $	Product or Product Class Shipments	Mil. $
CARBURETORS, PISTONS, PISTON RINGS AND VALVES	2,238.2	All other engine pistons, all types (machined), except rough castings	71.3
Carburetors, new and rebuilt (all types)	**415.5**	Piston rings, all types	(D)
Carburetors, new and rebuilt, except parts	(D)	Oil type piston rings for motor vehicle engines (passenger car, truck, and bus), all types	252.6
Carburetors for motor vehicle engines (passenger car, truck, and bus), new, all types	(D)	All other oil type engine piston rings	(D)
All other carburetors, new, all types	(D)	Compression type piston rings for motor vehicle engines (passenger car, truck, and bus), all types	32.2
Carburetors, rebuilt, all types	49.5	All other compression type engine piston rings	63.1
Parts for carburetors (excluding gaskets and screw machine products)	(D)	Engine piston pins	(D)
Carburetors, new and rebuilt (all types), nsk	16.3	Pistons, piston rings, and piston pins (engine), nsk	33.9
Pistons, piston rings, and piston pins (engine)	**1,317.3**	**Valves (engine intake and exhaust)**	**426.1**
Pistons, all types	762.7	Intake and exhaust valves for all engines	422.0
Pistons for motor vehicle engines (passenger car, truck, and bus), all types (machined), except rough castings	691.5	Valves (engine intake and exhaust), nsk	4.1
		Carburetors, pistons, piston rings and valves, nsk, total	**79.3**

Source: 2002 *Economic Census*. The values are product shipments in millions of dollars for 2002. Total product shipments may be lower or higher than industry shipments. See Introduction for a full discussion. Values of indented subcategories are summed in the main heading(s). The symbol (D) appears when data are withheld to prevent disclosure of competitive information. The abbreviation nsk stands for 'not specified by kind' and nec for 'not elsewhere classified'. A dash (-) means zero.

PRODUCT SHARE DETAILS FOR GASOLINE ENGINE AND ENGINE PARTS MANUFACTURING

Product or Product Class Shipments	Mil. $	Product or Product Class Shipments	Mil. $
GASOLINE ENGINES AND ENGINE PARTS	31,259.9	Gasoline engine valve guides, seats, and tappets, new, for motor vehicles	404.7
Gasoline engines and gasoline engine parts for motor vehicles, new	**29,669.6**	Gasoline engine flywheels and flexplates, new, for motor vehicles	(D)
Gasoline engines, new (with or without cylinder heads, fuel pumps, water pumps, and other standard accessories), for motor vehicles	20,078.0	Gasoline engine timing gears, sprockets, and chains, new, for motor vehicles	(D)
Gasoline engine fuel injection systems, new, for motor vehicles	1,515.4	Gasoline engine main engine bearings (halves), new, for motor vehicles	71.3
Gasoline engine fuel and water pump assemblies (excluding kits), new, for motor vehicles	1,186.6	Gasoline engine connecting rod, engine bearings (halves), new, for motor vehicles	192.7
Gasoline engine fuel pump assemblies (excluding kits), new, for motor vehicles	871.6	Other gasoline engine bearings (halves) (balance shaft, camshaft, etc.), new, for motor vehicles	295.5
Gasoline engine water pump assemblies (excluding kits), new, for motor vehicles	315.1	Gasoline engine oil pumps, new, for motor vehicles	249.4
Gasoline engine cooling fans and thermostats, new, for motor vehicles	744.5	Gasoline engine PCV (positive crankcase ventilation) valves, new, for motor vehicles	17.3
Gasoline engine cooling fans (including hubs and clutches), new, for motor vehicles	(D)	All other parts and accessories for gasoline engines, new, for motor vehicles	2,681.9
Gasoline engine thermostats (engine cooling system), new, for motor vehicles	(D)	Gasoline engines and gasoline engine parts for motor vehicles, new, nsk	142.7
All other gasoline engines and gasoline engine parts for motor vehicles, new	6,002.3	**Gasoline engines and engine parts for motor vehicles, rebuilt**	**656.7**
Gasoline engine intake manifolds, new, for motor vehicles	937.8	Gasoline engines and engine parts for motor vehicles, rebuilt	419.9
Gasoline engine exhaust manifolds, new, for motor vehicles	137.3	Motor vehicle fuel pumps, rebuilt	3.6
Gasoline engine crankshafts, new, for motor vehicles	55.6	Motor vehicle water pumps, rebuilt	17.7
Gasoline engine camshafts, new, for motor vehicles	221.9	Car and light truck gasoline engines, rebuilt	270.1
Gasoline engine rocker arms and parts, new, for motor vehicles	188.6	Heavy truck and bus gasoline engines, rebuilt	28.7
		Other rebuilt engine parts and components	99.9
		Other rebuilt engine and engine parts, nsk	236.8
		Gasoline engines and engine parts, nsk, total	**933.6**

Source: 2002 *Economic Census*. The values are product shipments in millions of dollars for 2002. Total product shipments may be lower or higher than industry shipments. See Introduction for a full discussion. Values of indented subcategories are summed in the main heading(s). The symbol (D) appears when data are withheld to prevent disclosure of competitive information. The abbreviation nsk stands for 'not specified by kind' and nec for 'not elsewhere classified'. A dash (-) means zero.

INPUTS AND OUTPUTS FOR MOTOR VEHICLE PARTS MANUFACTURING

Economic Sector or Industry Providing Inputs	%	Sector	Economic Sector or Industry Buying Outputs	%	Sector
Compensation of employees	22.8		Light truck & utility vehicles	25.3	Manufg.
Motor vehicle parts	10.7	Manufg.	Automobiles	15.8	Manufg.
Management of companies & enterprises	7.0	Services	Exports of goods & services	13.9	Cap Inv
Wholesale trade	5.3	Trade	Motor vehicle parts	8.5	Manufg.
Iron & steel mills & ferroalloys	5.0	Manufg.	Retail trade	7.4	Trade
Nonferrous metal foundries	2.6	Manufg.	Personal consumption expenditures	4.1	
Ferrous metal foundries	2.4	Manufg.	Automotive repair & maintenance, ex. car washes	2.9	Services
Plate work & fabricated structural products	1.9	Manufg.	Truck transportation	2.2	Util.
Turned products & screws, nuts, & bolts	1.9	Manufg.	General S/L govt. services	2.0	S/L Govt
Machine shops	1.5	Manufg.	Heavy duty trucks	1.9	Manufg.
Plastics products, nec	1.4	Manufg.	Wholesale trade	1.5	Trade
Truck transportation	1.1	Util.	Transit & ground passenger transportation	0.8	Util.
Retail trade	1.0	Trade	Change in private inventories	0.7	In House
Electronic components, nec	0.9	Manufg.	Postal service	0.6	Util.
Custom roll forming	0.9	Manufg.	General Federal government services, defense	0.6	Fed Govt
Coating, engraving, heat treating & allied activities	0.9	Manufg.	Residential structures, nec	0.6	Construct.
Crowns & closures & metal stamping	0.8	Manufg.	Residential permanent site structures	0.6	Construct.
Rubber products, nec	0.7	Manufg.	Nonresidential structures, nec	0.5	Construct.
Semiconductors & related devices	0.7	Manufg.	Lawn & garden equipment	0.4	Manufg.
Plastics packaging materials, film & sheet	0.7	Manufg.	Boat building	0.4	Manufg.
Scientific research & development services	0.7	Services	Construction machinery	0.4	Manufg.
Power generation & supply	0.7	Util.	S/L govt. passenger transit	0.4	S/L Govt
Leather & hide tanning & finishing	0.7	Manufg.	Transportation equipment, nec	0.3	Manufg.
Ball & roller bearings	0.7	Manufg.	Engine equipment, nec	0.3	Manufg.
Valve & fittings other than plumbing	0.6	Manufg.	Food services & drinking places	0.3	Services
Textile & fabric finishing mills	0.6	Manufg.	Waste management & remediation services	0.3	Services
Lessors of nonfinancial assets	0.5	Fin/R.E.	Aircraft	0.3	Manufg.
Fluid power process machinery	0.5	Manufg.	Services to buildings & dwellings	0.3	Services
Taxes on production & imports, less subsidies	0.5		Oil & gas extraction	0.2	Mining
Plastics materials & resins	0.5	Manufg.	Commercial & health care structures	0.2	Construct.
Ornamental & architectural metal products	0.5	Manufg.	Farm machinery & equipment	0.2	Manufg.
Gaskets, packing, & sealing devices	0.5	Manufg.	Management of companies & enterprises	0.2	Services
Securities, commodity contracts, investments	0.5	Fin/R.E.	Truck trailers	0.2	Manufg.
Noncomparable imports	0.5	Foreign	Warehousing & storage	0.2	Util.
Urethane & other foam products (except polystrene)	0.4	Manufg.	Motor vehicle bodies	0.2	Manufg.
Printed circuit assemblies (electronic assembles)	0.4	Manufg.	Travel trailers & campers	0.2	Manufg.
Alumina refining & primary aluminum production	0.4	Manufg.	Scientific research & development services	0.2	Services
Bare printed circuit boards	0.4	Manufg.	Maintenance/repair of nonresidential structures	0.2	Construct.
Paints & coatings	0.4	Manufg.	Private fixed investment	0.2	
Wiring devices	0.4	Manufg.	Couriers & messengers	0.1	Util.
Fabricated metals, nec	0.4	Manufg.	Individual & family services	0.1	Services
Copper rolling, drawing, extruding, & alloying	0.3	Manufg.	Scenic & sightseeing transport & related services	0.1	Util.
Advertising & related services	0.3	Services	Car washes	0.1	Services
Metal cans, boxes, & other containers (light gauge)	0.3	Manufg.	Automotive equipment rental & leasing	0.1	Fin/R.E.
Real estate	0.3	Fin/R.E.	Crowns & closures & metal stamping	0.1	Manufg.
Speed changers, industrial high-speed drives, & gears	0.3	Manufg.	Material handling equipment	0.1	Manufg.
Primary nonferrous metal, ex. copper & aluminum	0.3	Manufg.			
Paperboard containers	0.3	Manufg.			
Maintenance/repair of nonresidential structures	0.3	Construct.			
Gold, silver, & other metal ore	0.3	Mining			
Services to buildings & dwellings	0.2	Services			
Aluminum products from purchased aluminum	0.2	Manufg.			
Nonferrous metal (ex. copper & aluminum) processing	0.2	Manufg.			
Forging, stamping, & sintering, nec	0.2	Manufg.			
Rubber & plastics hose & belting	0.2	Manufg.			
Natural gas distribution	0.2	Util.			
Rail transportation	0.2	Util.			
Monetary authorities/depository credit intermediation	0.2	Fin/R.E.			
Handtools	0.2	Manufg.			
Automotive equipment rental & leasing	0.2	Fin/R.E.			
Professional, scientific, technical services, nec	0.2	Services			
Basic organic chemicals, nec	0.2	Manufg.			
Warehousing & storage	0.2	Util.			
Legal services	0.2	Services			
Food services & drinking places	0.2	Services			
Communication & energy wires & cables	0.2	Manufg.			
Automotive repair & maintenance, ex. car washes	0.2	Services			
Management, scientific, & technical consulting	0.2	Services			
Engine equipment, nec	0.2	Manufg.			
Wood windows & doors & millwork	0.2	Manufg.			
Veneer & plywood	0.2	Manufg.			
Telecommunications	0.2	Services			
Accounting, tax preparation, bookkeeping, & payroll	0.1	Services			
Commercial & industrial equipment repair/maintenance	0.1	Services			
Architectural, engineering, & related services	0.1	Services			
Artificial & synthetic fibers & filaments	0.1	Manufg.			
Air transportation	0.1	Util.			
Cutting tools & machine tool accessories	0.1	Manufg.			
Employment services	0.1	Services			
Chemical products & preparations, nec	0.1	Manufg.			

Continued on next page.

INPUTS AND OUTPUTS FOR MOTOR VEHICLE PARTS MANUFACTURING - Continued

Economic Sector or Industry Providing Inputs	%	Sector	Economic Sector or Industry Buying Outputs	%	Sector
Data processing, hosting, & related services	0.1	Services			
Specialized design services	0.1	Services			
Relay & industrial controls	0.1	Manufg.			
Business support services	0.1	Services			
Fiber, yarn, & thread mills	0.1	Manufg.			
Hotels & motels, including casino hotels	0.1	Services			
Electronic capacitors, resistors, coils, transformers	0.1	Manufg.			
Wood containers & pallets	0.1	Manufg.			
Waste management & remediation services	0.1	Services			
Springs & wire products	0.1	Manufg.			
Automatic environmental controls	0.1	Manufg.			

Source: Benchmark Input-Output Accounts for the U.S. Economy, 2002, U.S. Department of Commerce, Washington D.C., January 2008. User should note that this Input-Output table is not for this particular narrowly defined industry but for a larger aggregate. Input and Output data for Motor Vehicle Parts Manufacturing include Input and Output data for the Annual Survey of Manufactures' NAICS industries 33631M, 33632M, 336330, 336340, 336350, 336360, 336370, 336391, and 336399. The abbreviation nec stands for 'not elsewhere classified'.

OCCUPATIONS EMPLOYED BY MOTOR VEHICLE PARTS MANUFACTURING

Occupation	% of Total 2006	Change to 2016	Occupation	% of Total 2006	Change to 2016
Team assemblers	15.2	-19.2	Welders, cutters, solderers, & brazers	1.9	-15.3
Cutting, punching, & press machine operators	4.2	-28.4	Molding, coremaking, & casting machine operators	1.8	-28.4
Machinists	3.8	-16.4	Welding, soldering, & brazing machine operators	1.6	-10.5
Inspectors, testers, sorters, samplers, & weighers	3.5	-24.9	Industrial machinery mechanics	1.5	-8.4
First-line supervisors/managers of production workers	3.3	-20.4	Helpers--Production workers	1.5	-20.4
Assemblers & fabricators, nec	3.2	-28.4	Mechanical engineers	1.4	-20.4
Multiple machine tool operators & tenders	2.6	-12.4	Electrical & electronic equipment assemblers	1.4	-36.3
Tool & die makers	2.6	-16.4	Lathe & turning machine tool operators & tenders	1.3	-28.4
Industrial truck & tractor operators	2.6	-28.4	Shipping, receiving, & traffic clerks	1.3	-23.4
Laborers & freight, stock, & material movers, hand	2.1	-28.4	Electricians	1.3	-17.4
Industrial engineers	2.1	-3.3	Grinding, lapping, polishing machine tool operators	1.2	-22.8
Maintenance & repair workers, general	2.0	-20.4	Engine & other machine assemblers	1.1	-20.4
Production workers, nec	2.0	-21.9	Drilling & boring machine tool operators	1.1	-28.4
Computer-controlled machine tool operators	1.9	-12.4	Production, planning, & expediting clerks	1.1	-20.4

Source: Industry-Occupation Matrix, Bureau of Labor Statistics, December 4, 2007. These data are reported based on 4-digit NAICS categories but have been matched to corresponding 6-digit NAICS industry codes. The change reported for each occupation to the year 2016 is a percent of growth or decline as estimated by the Bureau of Labor Statistics. The abbreviation nec stands for 'not elsewhere classified'.

LOCATION BY STATE AND REGIONAL CONCENTRATION

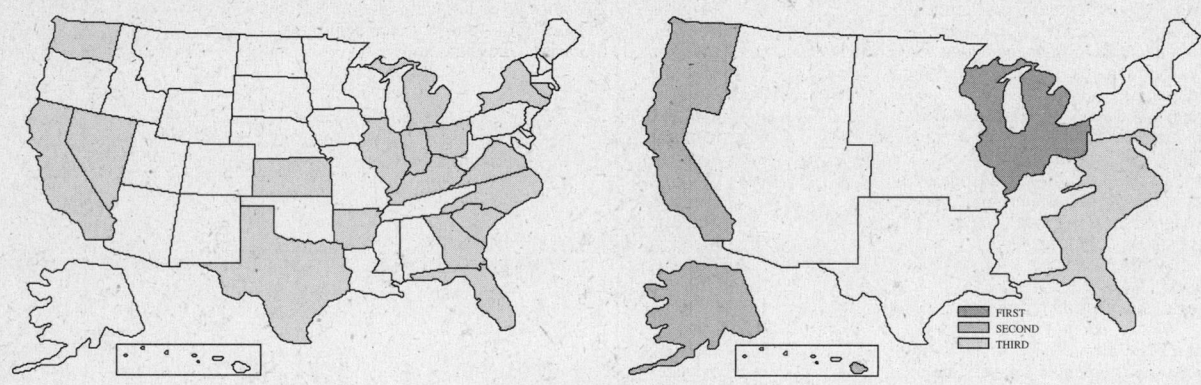

INDUSTRY DATA BY STATE

State	Establish-ments	Shipments Total ($ mil)	% of U.S.	Per Establ.	Employment Total Number	% of U.S.	Per Establ.	Wages ($/hour)	Cost as % of Shipments	Investment per Employee ($)
Michigan	119	13,289.5	38.2	111,676.3	32,241	32.6	271	30.00	65.3	11,518
Ohio	47	5,937.4	17.1	126,327.5	15,658	15.8	333	27.48	81.6	14,773
New York	40	3,747.6	10.8	93,689.2	7,439	7.5	186	28.87	58.6	30,269
Indiana	36	2,191.3	6.3	60,869.3	6,830	6.9	190	17.39	64.7	9,225
South Carolina	13	955.4	2.7	73,491.2	2,748	2.8	211	20.68	51.8	13,241

Continued on next page.

INDUSTRY DATA BY STATE - Continued

| State | Establish-ments | Shipments | | | Employment | | | | Cost as % of Shipments | Investment per Employee ($) |
		Total ($ mil)	% of U.S.	Per Establ.	Total Number	% of U.S.	Per Establ.	Wages ($/hour)		
Kentucky	15	603.6	1.7	40,240.3	1,789	1.8	119	23.56	90.2	12,707
California	166	573.1	1.6	3,452.4	3,749	3.8	23	17.85	49.8	11,123
Texas	56	533.2	1.5	9,520.7	1,616	1.6	29	19.30	72.4	13,134
Illinois	33	435.9	1.3	13,208.6	1,457	1.5	44	16.29	50.6	4,815
North Carolina	32	433.7	1.2	13,552.7	2,000	2.0	63	17.41	39.9	8,095
Virginia	19	337.1	1.0	17,742.5	1,821	1.8	96	17.04	40.6	8,992
Georgia	22	336.8	1.0	15,310.2	1,835	1.9	83	28.64	64.3	7,928
Arkansas	13	248.5	0.7	19,118.0	1,130	1.1	87	10.67	58.5	7,699
Connecticut	10	214.8	0.6	21,483.5	904	0.9	90	15.83	61.6	5,971
Florida	34	161.5	0.5	4,749.4	684	0.7	20	21.01	62.4	5,231
Washington	22	40.6	0.1	1,843.2	284	0.3	13	18.36	65.6	3,581
Nevada	4	36.5	0.1	9,119.5	279	0.3	70	11.04	31.2	681
Kansas	8	29.2	0.1	3,654.0	197	0.2	25	13.24	66.5	1,386

Source: 2002 *Economic Census*. The states are in descending order of shipments or establishments (if shipment data are missing for the majority). The symbol (D) appears when data are withheld to prevent disclosure of competitive information. States marked with (D) are sorted by number of establishments. A dash (-) indicates that the data element cannot be calculated. Data may not show all states active in the NAICS category. All data available at the time of publication are shown.

NAICS 33632M - MOTOR VEHICLE ELECTRICAL AND ELECTRONIC EQUIPMENT MANUFACTURING*

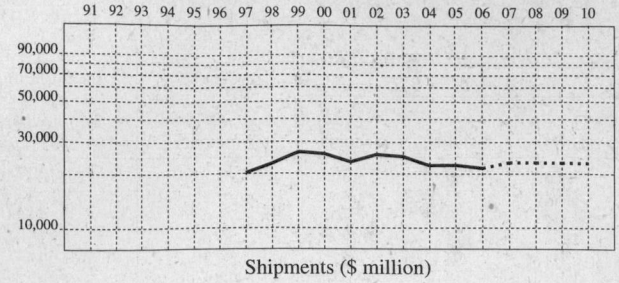

Shipments ($ million)

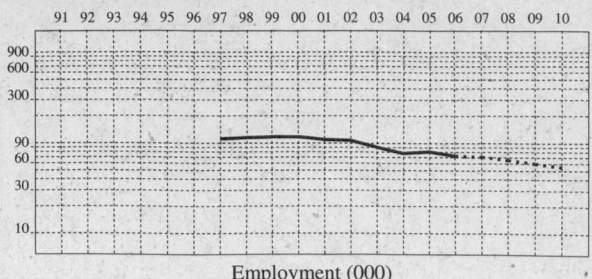

Employment (000)

GENERAL STATISTICS

| Year | Com-panies | Establishments | | Employment | | | Compensation | | Production ($ million) | | | |
		Total	with 20 or more employees	Total (000)	Production Workers (000)	Hours (Mil)	Payroll ($ mil)	Wages ($/hr)	Cost of Materials	Value Added by Manufacture	Value of Shipments	Capital Invest.
1997	1,049	1,127	509	112.1	88.3	171.3	3,687.6	15.02	11,503.0	8,634.3	20,255.8	909.2
1998		1,135	524	115.0	88.4	173.1	3,928.3	15.34	12,342.8	10,555.5	22,793.4	832.3
1999		1,109	508	117.5	90.0	171.6	4,359.6	17.52	14,402.2	11,753.7	26,321.7	826.4
2000		1,072	505	117.7	85.8	165.3	4,549.0	18.11	14,308.4	11,513.4	25,768.1	655.7
2001		1,034	494	109.5	80.6	152.7	4,312.4	18.38	13,221.4	10,006.8	23,310.0	617.1
2002	792	877	383	107.2	78.2	150.5	4,196.3	17.28	12,511.5	13,183.5	25,657.1	731.6
2003		880	407	90.8	66.5	130.4	3,876.4	18.69	12,402.8	12,657.1	24,962.1	690.9
2004		854	393	77.5	55.9	109.7	3,320.2	17.98	10,823.6	11,479.2	22,274.7	535.7
2005		828	376	80.9	58.3	116.7	3,566.4	18.43	12,422.3	10,000.1	22,359.6	715.6
2006		766P	351P	72.6	52.7	106.9	3,349.8	19.51	12,163.1	9,376.3	21,530.6	706.1
2007		722P	331P	70.8P	49.1P	98.5P	3,484.5P	19.79P	13,065.3P	10,071.8P	23,127.7P	592.8P
2008		677P	310P	65.5P	44.5P	90.0P	3,406.2P	20.19P	13,024.7P	10,040.5P	23,055.7P	569.3P
2009		632P	289P	60.2P	39.8P	81.6P	3,328.0P	20.58P	12,984.0P	10,009.1P	22,983.8P	545.8P
2010		587P	268P	54.9P	35.2P	73.2P	3,249.8P	20.97P	12,943.4P	9,977.8P	22,911.9P	522.3P

Sources: 1997 and 2002 *Economic Census*; other years, up to 2006, are from *Annual Survey of Manufactures*. Establishment counts for non-Census years are from *County Business Patterns*; 1997 and 2002 values are from the 1997 and 2002 censuses, respectively. 'P's show projections by the editors.

INDICES OF CHANGE

| Year | Com-panies | Establishments | | Employment | | | Compensation | | Production ($ million) | | | |
		Total	with 20 or more employees	Total (000)	Production Workers (000)	Hours (Mil)	Payroll ($ mil)	Wages ($/hr)	Cost of Materials	Value Added by Manufacture	Value of Shipments	Capital Invest.
1997	132	129	133	105	113	114	88	87	92	65	79	124
1998		129	137	107	113	115	94	89	99	80	89	114
1999		126	133	110	115	114	104	101	115	89	103	113
2000		122	132	110	110	110	108	105	114	87	100	90
2001		118	129	102	103	101	103	106	106	76	91	84
2002	100	100	100	100	100	100	100	100	100	100	100	100
2003		100	106	85	85	87	92	108	99	96	97	94
2004		97	103	72	71	73	79	104	87	87	87	73
2005		94	98	75	75	78	85	107	99	76	87	98
2006		87P	92P	68	67	71	80	113	97	71	84	97
2007		82P	86P	66P	63P	65P	83P	115P	104P	76P	90P	81P
2008		77P	81P	61P	57P	60P	81P	117P	104P	76P	90P	78P
2009		72P	75P	56P	51P	54P	79P	119P	104P	76P	90P	75P
2010		67P	70P	51P	45P	49P	77P	121P	103P	76P	89P	71P

Sources: Same as General Statistics. Values reflect change from the base year, 2002. Values above 100 mean greater than 2002, values below 100 mean less than 2002, and the values of 100 in other years means the same as 2002. 'P's show projections by the editors.

SELECTED RATIOS

For 2002	Avg. of All Manufact.	Analyzed Industry	Index	For 2002	Avg. of All Manufact.	Analyzed Industry	Index
Employees per Establishment	42	122	291	Value Added per Production Worker	182,367	168,587	92
Payroll per Establishment	1,639,184	4,784,835	292	Cost per Establishment	5,769,015	14,266,249	247
Payroll per Employee	39,053	39,145	100	Cost per Employee	137,446	116,712	85
Production Workers per Establishment	30	89	302	Cost per Production Worker	195,506	159,994	82
Wages per Establishment	694,845	2,965,382	427	Shipments per Establishment	11,158,348	29,255,530	262
Wages per Production Worker	23,548	33,256	141	Shipments per Employee	265,847	239,339	90
Hours per Production Worker	1,980	1,925	97	Shipments per Production Worker	378,144	328,096	87
Wages per Hour	11.89	17.28	145	Investment per Establishment	361,338	834,208	231
Value Added per Establishment	5,381,325	15,032,497	279	Investment per Employee	8,609	6,825	79
Value Added per Employee	128,210	122,980	96	Investment per Production Worker	12,245	9,355	76

Sources: Same as General Statistics. The 'Average of All Manufacturing' column represents the average of all manufacturing industries reported for the most recent complete year available. The Index shows the relationship between the Average and the Analyzed Industry. For example, 100 means that they are equal; 500 that the Analyzed Industry is five times the average; 50 means that the Analyzed Industry is half the national average. The abbreviation 'na' is used to show that data are 'not available'. Ratios shown for 2002, the last complete census year.

*Equivalent to Federal Government NAICS 336321, 336322.

LEADING COMPANIES   Number shown: **75**   Total sales ($ mil): **997,289**   Total employment (000): **2,120.5**

Company Name	Address				CEO Name	Phone	Co. Type	Sales ($ mil)	Empl. (000)
General Motors Corp.	300 Renaissance Ctr	Detroit	MI	48265		313-556-5000	P	181,122	266.0
Ford Motor Co.	1 American Rd.	Dearborn	MI	48126		313-322-3000	P	172,455	246.0
Technitrol Delaware Inc.	3411 Silverside Rd.	Wilmington	DE	19810	James M. Papada	302-478-8271	S	67,716*	22.8
Chrysler L.L.C.	1000 Chrysler Dr.	Auburn Hills	MI	48326	Thomas W. LaSorda	248-576-5741	S	45,237*	84.4
Honeywell International Inc.	PO Box 4000	Morristown	NJ	07962	Adriane M. Brown	973-455-2000	P	34,589	122.0
General Dynamics Corp.	2941 Fairview Park	Falls Church	VA	22042	Nicholas D. Chabraja	703-876-3000	P	27,240	83.5
ArvinMeritor OE L.L.C.	950 W 450 S, Bldg.	Columbus	IN	47201	C. G. McClure Jr.	812-341-2000	S	23,491*	32.0
Delphi Corp.	5725 Delphi Dr.	Troy	MI	48098	Voker J. Barth	248-813-2000	P	22,383	169.5
Raytheon Co.	870 Winter St.	Waltham	MA	02451		781-522-3000	P	21,301	72.1
ITT Federal Services Corp.	4410 E Fountain	Colorado Spgs	CO	80916	Steven Loranger	719-591-3600	S	20,690*	7.0
Mars Inc.	6885 Elm Street	Mc Lean	VA	22101	John F. Mars	703-821-4900	R	18,462*	40.0
Lear Corp.	PO Box 5008	Southfield	MI	48086	Jim Brackenbury	248-447-1500	P	15,995	91.0
Computer Sciences Corp.	2100 E Grand Ave.	El Segundo	CA	90245		310-615-0311	P	14,855	79.0
TRW Automotive Holdings Inc.	12001 Tech Cntr Dr.	Livonia	MI	48150		734-855-2600	P	14,702	66.3
Textron Inc.	40 Westminster St.	Providence	RI	02903		401-421-2800	P	13,225	44.0
Cummins Inc.	PO Box 3005	Columbus	IN	47202		812-377-5000	P	13,048	37.8
Eaton Corp.	1111 Superior Ave.	Cleveland	OH	44114		216-523-5000	P	13,033	60.0
Visteon Corp.	1 Village Center Dr	Van Buren Twp	MI	48111		313-755-2800	P	11,266	41.5
Parker Hannifin Corp.	6035 Parkland Blvd.	Cleveland	OH	44124	Lee Banks	216-896-3000	P	10,718	57.3
Acument Global Technologies	840 W Long Lake	Troy	MI	48098	Joseph Gray	248-813-6329	S	10,080*	9.0
ITT Corp.	4 W Red Oak Ln.	White Plains	NY	10604		914-641-2000	P	9,003	39.7
Dana Corp.	PO Box 1000	Toledo	OH	43697	Michael J. Burns	419-535-4500	P	8,504	45.0
Neapco L.L.C.	PO Box 399	Pottstown	PA	19464		610-323-6000	R	7,580*	0.3
Ball Corp.	PO Box 5000	Broomfield	CO	80021	R. David Hoover	303-469-3131	P	7,475	15.5
Trane Inc.	PO Box 6820	Piscataway	NJ	08855		732-980-6000	P	7,450	29.6
Truck-Lite Company Inc.	PO Box 387	Jamestown	NY	14702	Brian Kupchella	716-665-6214	R	7,160*	0.6
Triangle Suspension Systems	PO Box 425	Du Bois	PA	15801	Greg Maffia	814-375-7211	R	7,000*	0.2
Perfection Hy-Test Company	100 Perfection Way	Timmonsville	SC	29161		843-326-5544	R	7,000*	0.2
Penn Machine Co.	106 Station St.	Johnstown	PA	15905	H Wiegand	814-288-1547	R	7,000*	<0.1
Federal-Mogul Corp.	PO Box 1966	Detroit	MI	48235	Jose Maria Alapont	248-354-7700	P	6,914	43.1
Robert Bosch Corp.	2800 S 25th Ave.	Broadview	IL	60155	Kurt W. Liedtke	708-865-5200	S	6,782*	25.0
ArvinMeritor Inc.	2135 W Maple Rd.	Troy	MI	48084		248-435-1000	P	6,449	18.0
Tenneco Inc.	500 N Field Dr.	Lake Forest	IL	60045		847-482-5000	P	6,184	21.0
Toyota Motor Mfg. N America	25 Atlantic Ave.	Erlanger	KY	41018	Masamoto Amezawa	859-746-4000	S	6,120*	7.5
Order-Matic Corp.	PO Box 25463	Oklahoma City	OK	73125	Bill Cunningham	405-672-1487	R	5,787	0.2
Allegheny Technologies Inc.	1000 Six PPG Pl.	Pittsburgh	PA	15222		412-394-2800	P	5,453	9.5
Guardian Industries Corp.	2300 Harmon Rd.	Auburn Hills	MI	48326	William M. Davidson	248-340-1800	R	5,330	19.0
BorgWarner Inc.	3850 Hamlin Rd.	Auburn Hills	MI	48326		248-754-9200	P	5,329	17.7
Autoliv ASP Inc.	3350 Airport Rd.	Ogden	UT	84405	Leonard Barton	801-625-4800	S	5,301*	3.7
Magna Donnelly Corp.	600 Wilshire Dr.	Troy	MI	48084	Carlos Mazzorin	248-729-2400	R	4,906*	<0.1
Carlisle Tire and Wheel Co.	23 Windham Blvd.	Aiken	SC	29805	Barry Littrell	803-643-2900	S	4,822*	0.6
Flextronics	2090 Fortune Dr.	San Jose	CA	95131	Mike McNamara	408-576-7000	S	4,699*	1.5
Marathon Redevelopment Corp.	200 State St.	Beloit	WI	53511	Henry W. Knueppel	608-364-8800	S	4,669*	10.0
LSI Marcole Inc.	1108 Oakdale St.	Manchester	TN	37355	Robert J. Ready	931-723-4442	R	4,643*	1.4
Karl Schmidt Unisia Inc.	1731 Industrial Pky	Marinette	WI	54143	Frank Pohlmann	715-732-0181	R	4,640*	0.9
Pioneer Automotive Tech.	100 S Pioneer Blvd.	Springboro	OH	45066	Steve Moerner	937-746-6600	R	4,610*	0.3
Toledo Trans-Kit Inc.	13515 Ballnyn Corp.	Charlotte	NC	28277	C. J. Kearney	704-752-4400	S	4,372	23.8
Mack Trucks Inc.	PO Box M	Allentown	PA	18105		610-709-3011	R	4,324*	0.8
Oki Data Americas Inc.	2000 Bishops Gate	Mount Laurel	NJ	08054	Stewart Krentzman	856-235-2600	S	4,260*	0.5
Harris Corp.	1025 W NASA	Melbourne	FL	32919		321-727-9100	P	4,243	16.0
New United Motor Manufacturing	45500 Fremont	Fremont	CA	94538	Bruce Walker	510-498-5500	J	4,080*	5.0
Sparton Electronics	PO Box 788	De Leon Springs	FL	32130	D W. Hockenbrocht	386-985-4631	S	3,491*	1.0
Kalmar Industries USA L.L.C.	415 E Dundee St.	Ottawa	KS	66067		785-242-2200	R	3,320*	0.3
American Axle & Mfg Holdings	1 Dauch Dr.	Detroit	MI	48211	Richard E. Dauch	313-974-2000	P	3,248	10.0
Hi-Stat Manufacturing Company	28001 Cabot Dr.	Novi	MI	48377	John Corey	248-489-9300	D	3,194*	5.0
Amsted Industries Inc.	2 Prudential Plaza	Chicago	IL	60601	W. Robert Reum	312-645-1700	R	3,050	9.9
AutoAlliance International	1 International Dr.	Flat Rock	MI	48134	Phillip G. Spender	734-782-7800	J	3,019*	3.7
Arco Auto and Marine Products	3921 Navy Blvd.	Pensacola	FL	32507	Ron Miller	850-455-5476	R	3,015	<0.1
Benchmark Electronics Inc.	3000 Technology	Angleton	TX	77515		979-849-6550	P	2,916	10.9
TAG Holdings L.L.C.	2075 W Big Beaver	Troy	MI	48084	J. B. Anderson, Jr.	248-822-8056	R	2,904*	2.5
Crane Co.	100 First Stamford	Stamford	CT	06902	Thomas Craney	203-363-7300	P	2,619	12.0
I/O Marine Systems Inc.	5200 Toler St.	Harahan	LA	70123	Robert P. Peebler	504-733-6061	S	2,610*	0.8
I/O Nevada L.L.C.	12300 Parc Crest Dr	Stafford	TX	77477	Robert P. Peebler	281-933-3339	S	2,610*	0.8
I/O Texas L.P.	12300 Parc Crest Dr	Stafford	TX	77477	Robert P. Peebler	281-933-3339	S	2,610*	0.8
Hubbell Inc.	584 Derby Milford	Orange	CT	06477		203-799-4100	P	2,534	11.5
Consolidated Metco Inc.	PO Box 83201	Portland	OR	97283		503-286-5741	R	2,510*	0.1
I/O Marine Systems Ltd.	5200 Toler St.	Harahan	LA	70123	Robert P. Peebler	504-733-6061	S	2,444*	0.8
Wakefield Thermal Solutions	33 Bridge St.	Pelham	NH	03076	Robert Streiter	603-635-2800	S	2,398*	0.1
Pall Corp.	2200 Northern Blvd.	East Hills	NY	11548	Eric Krasnoff	516-484-5400	P	2,250	10.8
DENSO Manufacturing Tennessee	1720 Rbrt C Jackson	Maryville	TN	37801	Mack Hattori	865-982-7000	S	2,231*	2.0
Sequa Corp.	200 Park Ave.	New York	NY	10166	Gail Binderman	212-986-5500	P	2,183	10.2
Affinia Group Inc.	1101 Technology	Ann Arbor	MI	48108		734-827-5400	P	2,160	12.4
Red Rocket Inc.	5217 Verdugo Way	Camarillo	CA	93012	James B. Schutz	805-409-0909	R	2,146*	0.7
Dura Automotive Systems Inc.	2791 Research Dr.	Rochester Hills	MI	48309	Lawrence A. Denton	248-299-7500	P	2,091	15.4
Hayes Lemmerz International	15300 Centennial Dr	Northville	MI	48167	Fred Bentley	734-737-5000	P	2,039	11.0

Source: Ward's Business Directory of U.S. Private and Public Companies, Volumes 1 and 2, 2008. The company type code used is as follows: P - Public, R - Private, S - Subsidiary, D - Division, J - Joint Venture, A - Affiliate, G - Group. Sales are in millions of dollars, employees are in thousands. An asterisk (*) indicates an estimated sales volume. The symbol < stands for 'less than'. Company names and addresses are truncated, in some cases, to fit into the available space.

MATERIALS CONSUMED FOR VEHICULAR LIGHTING EQUIPMENT MANUFACTURING

Material	Quantity	Delivered Cost ($ million)
Specialty transformers and fluorescent ballasts	(X)	3.7
Current-carrying wiring devices	(X)	130.3
Electric lamp bulbs	(X)	111.0
Flat glass (plate, float, and sheet)	(X)	1.1
Plastics resins consumed in the form of granules, pellets, etc.	(X)	224.2
Plastics products consumed in the form of sheets, rods, etc.	(X)	81.7
Fabricated plastics products (excluding gaskets)	(X)	121.0
Insulated wire and cable (including magnet wire)	(X)	27.8
Paperboard containers, boxes, and corrugated paperboard	(X)	33.9
Metal bolts, nuts, screws, and other screw machine products	(X)	52.9
Metal poles	(X)	(D)
All other fabricated metal products (excluding forgings)	(X)	66.5
Iron and steel castings (rough and semifinished)	(X)	(D)
Aluminum and aluminum-base alloy castings (rough and semifinished)	(X)	2.7
Other nonferrous metal castings, rough or semifinished (inc. aluminum)	(X)	(D)
Steel sheet and strip (including tinplate)	(X)	2.1
Steel wire and wire products	(X)	0.7
All other steel mill shapes and forms (exc. castings and forgings)	(X)	2.2
Aluminum and aluminum-base alloy sheet, plate, foil, and welded tubing	(X)	4.3
Aluminum and aluminum-base alloy extruded shapes (rod, bar, pipe, tube, etc.)	(X)	4.5
Other aluminum and aluminum-base alloy shapes and forms (exc. castings, forgings, fabr. metal products)	(X)	2.3
Copper and copper-base alloy shapes and forms (exc. castings, forgings, fabr. metal products)	(X)	(D)
Other nonferrous shapes and forms (exc. castings, forgings, fabricated metal products)	(X)	(D)
Lamp shades	(X)	(D)
All other materials, components, parts, containers, and supplies	(X)	222.3
Materials, ingredients, containers, and supplies, nsk	(X)	163.9

Source: 2002 *Economic Census*. Explanation of symbols used: (D): Withheld to avoid disclosure of competitive data; na: Not available; (S): Withheld because statistical norms were not met; (X): Not applicable; (Z): Less than half the unit shown; nec: Not elsewhere classified; nsk: Not specified by kind; - : zero; p : 10-19 percent estimated; q : 20-29 percent estimated.

MATERIALS CONSUMED FOR MOTOR VEHICLE ELECTRICAL & ELECTRONIC EQUIPMENT NEC

Material	Quantity	Delivered Cost ($ million)
Iron and steel castings (rough and semifinished)	(X)	225.2
Aluminum and aluminum-base alloy castings (rough and semifinished)	(X)	277.5
Other nonferrous metal castings, rough or semifinished (inc. aluminum)	(X)	16.7
Steel bars, bar shapes, and plates (exc. castings, forgings, fabr. metal products)	(X)	5.8
Steel sheet and strip (including tinplate)	(X)	13.6
All other steel shapes and forms (exc. castings, forgings, fabr. metal products)	(X)	58.3
Copper and copper-base alloy shapes and forms (exc. castings, forgings, fabr. metal products)	(X)	119.2
Aluminum and aluminum-base alloy shapes and forms (exc. castings, forgings, fabr. metal products)	(X)	25.5
Other nonferrous shapes and forms (exc. castings, forgings, fabricated metal products)	(X)	(D)
Ball and roller bearings (mounted or unmounted)	(X)	34.8
Fabricated plastics products (exc. gaskets, hoses, and belting)	(X)	270.4
Plastics products consumed in the form of sheets, rods, etc.	(X)	68.9
Plastics resins consumed in the form of granules, pellets, etc.	(X)	106.1
Fabricated rubber products (exc. tires, tubes, hoses, belting, and gaskets)	(X)	17.5
Rubber and plastics hose and belting	(X)	(D)
Ceramic raw materials (incl. powders, chemicals, and fibers)	(X)	(D)
Ceramic and ceramic composite parts, components, and accessories	(X)	(D)
Gaskets (all types), and packing and sealing devices	(X)	(D)
Paints, varnishes, stains, lacquers, shellacs, japans, enamels, etc.	(X)	7.9
Glues and adhesives	(X)	6.6
Flexible packaging materials	(X)	4.3
Paper and paperboard containers	(X)	43.1
Spark plugs for internal combustion engines	(X)	(D)
Generators for imternal combustion engines	(X)	33.0
Starting motors for internal combustion engines	(X)	58.4
Distributors for internal combustion engines	(X)	(D)
Ignition coils for internal combustion engines	(X)	51.1
Ignition harness and cable sets for internal combustion engines	(X)	37.0
All other engine electrical equipment for internal combustion engines	(X)	(D)
Magnetos, magneto-dynamos, and magnetic flywheels for internal combustion engines	(X)	20.7
Injection fuel pumps	(X)	(D)
Resistors for electronic circuitry	(X)	55.1
Capacitors for electronic circuitry	(X)	69.2
Semiconductors (incl. transistors, diodes, rectifiers, and integrated circuits), for electronic circuitry	(X)	847.0
Used engine electrical equipment for rebuilding, or to be used in rebuilding (starting motors, generators, etc.)	(X)	(D)
All other miscellaneous components and accessories for electronic circuitry (exc. tubes)	(X)	481.0
Core parts purchased for use in remanufacturing and rebuilding	(X)	393.7
Printed ciruit boards (without inserted components) for electronic circuitry	(X)	646.6
Metal bolts, nuts, screws, and other screw machine products	(X)	138.4
Other fabricated metal products (exc. fluid power and forgings)	(X)	169.2
Forgings	(X)	(D)
Insulated wire and cable (excluding magnet wire)	(X)	77.4
Magnet wire	(X)	31.8

Continued on next page.

MATERIALS CONSUMED FOR MOTOR VEHICLE ELECTRICAL & ELECTRONIC EQUIPMENT NEC - Continued

Material	Quantity	Delivered Cost ($ million)
Mechanical speed changers, gears, and industrial high-speed drives	(X)	0.4
Fluid power pumps, motors, and hydrostatic transmissions	(X)	179.9
Fluid power valves (hydraulic and pneumatic)	(X)	3.1
Fluid power cylinders and rotary actuators (hydraulic and pneumatic)	(X)	(D)
Fluid power hose, tube fittings, and assemblies (hydraulic and pneumatic)	(X)	34.6
Fluid power filters (hydraulic and pneumatic)	(X)	8.9
Other transportation related fluid power products, hydraulic and pneumatic	(X)	(D)
Automotive stampings (inc. body parts, hubcaps, fenders, etc.)	(X)	92.5
Current-carrying wiring devices	(X)	178.8
Other chemicals and allied products	(X)	8.6
All other materials, components, parts, containers, and supplies	(X)	1,582.9
Materials, ingredients, containers, and supplies, nsk	(X)	1,368.5

Source: 2002 *Economic Census*. Explanation of symbols used: (D): Withheld to avoid disclosure of competitive data; na: Not available; (S): Withheld because statistical norms were not met; (X): Not applicable; (Z): Less than half the unit shown; nec: Not elsewhere classified; nsk: Not specified by kind; - : zero; p : 10-19 percent estimated; q : 20-29 percent estimated.

PRODUCT SHARE DETAILS FOR VEHICULAR LIGHTING EQUIPMENT MANUFACTURING

Product or Product Class Shipments	Mil. $	Product or Product Class Shipments	Mil. $
VEHICULAR LIGHTING EQUIPMENT	2,423.8	lighting and headlights	1,063.2
Vehicular lighting equipment, electric (including parts and accessories)	**2,423.8**	Truck lighting equipment, except emergency lighting and headlights	404.8
Vehicular lighting equipment, electric (including parts and accessories)	2,405.7	Emergency vehicle lighting (autos and trucks)	290.1
		Headlights (autos and trucks)	647.6
Automobile lighting equipment, except emergency		Vehicular lighting equipment, nsk, total	18.2

Source: 2002 *Economic Census*. The values are product shipments in millions of dollars for 2002. Total product shipments may be lower or higher than industry shipments. See Introduction for a full discussion. Values of indented subcategories are summed in the main heading(s). The symbol (D) appears when data are withheld to prevent disclosure of competitive information. The abbreviation nsk stands for 'not specified by kind' and nec for 'not elsewhere classified'. A dash (-) means zero.

PRODUCT SHARE DETAILS FOR MOTOR VEHICLE ELECTRICAL & ELECTRONIC EQUIPMENT NEC

Product or Product Class Shipments	Mil. $	Product or Product Class Shipments	Mil. $
MOTOR VEHICLE ELECTRICAL AND ELECTRONIC EQUIPMENT, NEC	17,581.8	All other complete engine electrical and electronic equipment	2,349.9
Ignition harness and cable sets	**1,145.5**	Electrical distributors (all types)	44.7
Ignition harness sets, all types	820.9	Magnetos, magneto-dynamos, and magnetic flywheels	(D)
Automotive-type ignition harness sets	762.3	All other complete ignition equipment, including electronic ignitions	(D)
Other ignition harness sets, including tractor, stationary engine, and aircraft	58.7	All other complete electrical and electronic equipment for internal combustion engines	1,035.0
Engine electrical cable sets, all types	289.5	Complete engine electrical equipment, nec, nsk	1.8
Automotive-type engine electrical cable sets	194.6	**Parts for engine electrical and electronic equipment**	**373.1**
Aircraft and other type engine electrical cable sets	94.9	Armatures, field coils, and drive-end housings for cranking motors	(D)
Ignition harness and cable sets, nsk	35.0	Armatures and field coils for alternators and generators	9.8
Battery charging alternators, generators, and regulators	**1,670.7**	Ignition distributor heads and rotors	65.0
New battery charging alternators and generators for internal combustion engines	1,387.3	Ignition distributor breaker point sets	(D)
New automotive battery charging alternators and generators for internal combustion engines	1,359.9	Ignition distributor condensers (capacitors)	(D)
All other new battery charging alternators and generators for internal combustion engines, new	27.4	Other parts for engine electrical and-or electronic equipment	128.4
Rebuilt battery charging alternators and generators for internal combustion engines, all types, and regulators for alternators and generators	242.8	Parts for engine electrical and electronic equipment, nsk	24.5
		Motor vehicle electrical and electronic equipment	**6,125.0**
Rebuilt battery charging alternators and generators for internal combustion engines, all types	205.0	Motor vehicle cruise control units, new	294.5
		Motor vehicle permanent defrosters, new	-
Regulators for battery charging alternators and generators (new and rebuilt)	37.8	Motor vehicle wiring harness sets, except ignition, new	1,787.0
Battery charging alternators, generators, and regulators, nsk	40.6	Motor vehicle windshield washer-wiper mechanisms, including washer pumps, new	936.3
		Motor vehicle block and battery heaters, new	(D)
Cranking motors (starters)	**2,203.8**	Other motor vehicle heaters and other heater parts, new	99.4
New starting (engine cranking) motors	1,880.5	Electronic control modular chips for motor vehicles	1,182.2
Rebuilt starting (engine cranking) motors, all types	302.8	Motor vehicle instrument board assemblies, new	49.3
Cranking motors (starters), nsk	20.5	Other motor vehicle electrical and electronic equipment, except engine electrical equipment, new	1,239.7
Spark plugs (all types)	**507.3**	Cruise control units, rebuilt	(D)
Complete engine electrical equipment, nec	**4,506.0**	Windshield washer-wiper units, rebuilt	(D)
Electrical ignition coils (all types) for complete engines	860.6	Other electrical equipment, except engine electrical equipment, rebuilt	507.8
Electronic systems for complete engine control, using computers or microprocessors	1,293.7	**Motor vehicle electrical and electronic equipment, nsk, total**	**1,050.5**

Source: 2002 *Economic Census*. The values are product shipments in millions of dollars for 2002. Total product shipments may be lower or higher than industry shipments. See Introduction for a full discussion. Values of indented subcategories are summed in the main heading(s). The symbol (D) appears when data are withheld to prevent disclosure of competitive information. The abbreviation nsk stands for 'not specified by kind' and nec for 'not elsewhere classified'. A dash (-) means zero.

INPUTS AND OUTPUTS FOR MOTOR VEHICLE PARTS MANUFACTURING

Economic Sector or Industry Providing Inputs	%	Sector	Economic Sector or Industry Buying Outputs	%	Sector
Compensation of employees	22.8		Light truck & utility vehicles	25.3	Manufg.
Motor vehicle parts	10.7	Manufg.	Automobiles	15.8	Manufg.
Management of companies & enterprises	7.0	Services	Exports of goods & services	13.9	Cap Inv
Wholesale trade	5.3	Trade	Motor vehicle parts	8.5	Manufg.
Iron & steel mills & ferroalloys	5.0	Manufg.	Retail trade	7.4	Trade
Nonferrous metal foundries	2.6	Manufg.	Personal consumption expenditures	4.1	
Ferrous metal foundries	2.4	Manufg.	Automotive repair & maintenance, ex. car washes	2.9	Services
Plate work & fabricated structural products	1.9	Manufg.	Truck transportation	2.2	Util.
Turned products & screws, nuts, & bolts	1.9	Manufg.	General S/L govt. services	2.0	S/L Govt
Machine shops	1.5	Manufg.	Heavy duty trucks	1.9	Manufg.
Plastics products, nec	1.4	Manufg.	Wholesale trade	1.5	Trade
Truck transportation	1.1	Util.	Transit & ground passenger transportation	0.8	Util.
Retail trade	1.0	Trade	Change in private inventories	0.7	In House
Electronic components, nec	0.9	Manufg.	Postal service	0.6	Util.
Custom roll forming	0.9	Manufg.	General Federal government services, defense	0.6	Fed Govt
Coating, engraving, heat treating & allied activities	0.9	Manufg.	Residential structures, nec	0.6	Construct.
Crowns & closures & metal stamping	0.8	Manufg.	Residential permanent site structures	0.6	Construct.
Rubber products, nec	0.7	Manufg.	Nonresidential structures, nec	0.5	Construct.
Semiconductors & related devices	0.7	Manufg.	Lawn & garden equipment	0.4	Manufg.
Plastics packaging materials, film & sheet	0.7	Manufg.	Boat building	0.4	Manufg.
Scientific research & development services	0.7	Services	Construction machinery	0.4	Manufg.
Power generation & supply	0.7	Util.	S/L govt. passenger transit	0.4	S/L Govt
Leather & hide tanning & finishing	0.7	Manufg.	Transportation equipment, nec	0.3	Manufg.
Ball & roller bearings	0.7	Manufg.	Engine equipment, nec	0.3	Manufg.
Valve & fittings other than plumbing	0.6	Manufg.	Food services & drinking places	0.3	Services
Textile & fabric finishing mills	0.6	Manufg.	Waste management & remediation services	0.3	Services
Lessors of nonfinancial assets	0.5	Fin/R.E.	Aircraft	0.3	Manufg.
Fluid power process machinery	0.5	Manufg.	Services to buildings & dwellings	0.3	Services
Taxes on production & imports, less subsidies	0.5		Oil & gas extraction	0.2	Mining
Plastics materials & resins	0.5	Manufg.	Commercial & health care structures	0.2	Construct.
Ornamental & architectural metal products	0.5	Manufg.	Farm machinery & equipment	0.2	Manufg.
Gaskets, packing, & sealing devices	0.5	Manufg.	Management of companies & enterprises	0.2	Services
Securities, commodity contracts, investments	0.5	Fin/R.E.	Truck trailers	0.2	Manufg.
Noncomparable imports	0.5	Foreign	Warehousing & storage	0.2	Util.
Urethane & other foam products (except polystrene)	0.4	Manufg.	Motor vehicle bodies	0.2	Manufg.
Printed circuit assemblies (electronic assembles)	0.4	Manufg.	Travel trailers & campers	0.2	Manufg.
Alumina refining & primary aluminum production	0.4	Manufg.	Scientific research & development services	0.2	Services
Bare printed circuit boards	0.4	Manufg.	Maintenance/repair of nonresidential structures	0.2	Construct.
Paints & coatings	0.4	Manufg.	Private fixed investment	0.2	
Wiring devices	0.4	Manufg.	Couriers & messengers	0.1	Util.
Fabricated metals, nec	0.4	Manufg.	Individual & family services	0.1	Services
Copper rolling, drawing, extruding, & alloying	0.3	Manufg.	Scenic & sightseeing transport & related services	0.1	Util.
Advertising & related services	0.3	Services	Car washes	0.1	Services
Metal cans, boxes, & other containers (light gauge)	0.3	Manufg.	Automotive equipment rental & leasing	0.1	Fin/R.E.
Real estate	0.3	Fin/R.E.	Crowns & closures & metal stamping	0.1	Manufg.
Speed changers, industrial high-speed drives, & gears	0.3	Manufg.	Material handling equipment	0.1	Manufg.
Primary nonferrous metal, ex. copper & aluminum	0.3	Manufg.			
Paperboard containers	0.3	Manufg.			
Maintenance/repair of nonresidential structures	0.3	Construct.			
Gold, silver, & other metal ore	0.3	Mining			
Services to buildings & dwellings	0.2	Services			
Aluminum products from purchased aluminum	0.2	Manufg.			
Nonferrous metal (ex. copper & aluminum) processing	0.2	Manufg.			
Forging, stamping, & sintering, nec	0.2	Manufg.			
Rubber & plastics hose & belting	0.2	Manufg.			
Natural gas distribution	0.2	Util.			
Rail transportation	0.2	Util.			
Monetary authorities/depository credit intermediation	0.2	Fin/R.E.			
Handtools	0.2	Manufg.			
Automotive equipment rental & leasing	0.2	Fin/R.E.			
Professional, scientific, technical services, nec	0.2	Services			
Basic organic chemicals, nec	0.2	Manufg.			
Warehousing & storage	0.2	Util.			
Legal services	0.2	Services			
Food services & drinking places	0.2	Services			
Communication & energy wires & cables	0.2	Manufg.			
Automotive repair & maintenance, ex. car washes	0.2	Services			
Management, scientific, & technical consulting	0.2	Services			
Engine equipment, nec	0.2	Manufg.			
Wood windows & doors & millwork	0.2	Manufg.			
Veneer & plywood	0.2	Manufg.			
Telecommunications	0.2	Services			
Accounting, tax preparation, bookkeeping, & payroll	0.1	Services			
Commercial & industrial equipment repair/maintenance	0.1	Services			
Architectural, engineering, & related services	0.1	Services			
Artificial & synthetic fibers & filaments	0.1	Manufg.			
Air transportation	0.1	Util.			
Cutting tools & machine tool accessories	0.1	Manufg.			
Employment services	0.1	Services			
Chemical products & preparations, nec	0.1	Manufg.			

Continued on next page.

INPUTS AND OUTPUTS FOR MOTOR VEHICLE PARTS MANUFACTURING - Continued

Economic Sector or Industry Providing Inputs	%	Sector	Economic Sector or Industry Buying Outputs	%	Sector
Data processing, hosting, & related services	0.1	Services			
Specialized design services	0.1	Services			
Relay & industrial controls	0.1	Manufg.			
Business support services	0.1	Services			
Fiber, yarn, & thread mills	0.1	Manufg.			
Hotels & motels, including casino hotels	0.1	Services			
Electronic capacitors, resistors, coils, transformers	0.1	Manufg.			
Wood containers & pallets	0.1	Manufg.			
Waste management & remediation services	0.1	Services			
Springs & wire products	0.1	Manufg.			
Automatic environmental controls	0.1	Manufg.			

Source: *Benchmark Input-Output Accounts for the U.S. Economy, 2002*, U.S. Department of Commerce, Washington D.C., January 2008. *User should note that this Input-Output table is* not *for this particular narrowly defined industry but for a larger aggregate. Input and Output data for* Motor Vehicle Parts Manufacturing *include Input and Output data for the* Annual Survey of Manufactures' *NAICS industries 33631M, 33632M, 336330, 336340, 336350, 336360, 336370, 336391, and 336399. The abbreviation nec stands for 'not elsewhere classified'.*

OCCUPATIONS EMPLOYED BY MOTOR VEHICLE PARTS MANUFACTURING

Occupation	% of Total 2006	Change to 2016	Occupation	% of Total 2006	Change to 2016
Team assemblers	15.2	-19.2	Welders, cutters, solderers, & brazers	1.9	-15.3
Cutting, punching, & press machine operators	4.2	-28.4	Molding, coremaking, & casting machine operators	1.8	-28.4
Machinists	3.8	-16.4	Welding, soldering, & brazing machine operators	1.6	-10.5
Inspectors, testers, sorters, samplers, & weighers	3.5	-24.9	Industrial machinery mechanics	1.5	-8.4
First-line supervisors/managers of production workers	3.3	-20.4	Helpers--Production workers	1.5	-20.4
Assemblers & fabricators, nec	3.2	-28.4	Mechanical engineers	1.4	-20.4
Multiple machine tool operators & tenders	2.6	-12.4	Electrical & electronic equipment assemblers	1.4	-36.3
Tool & die makers	2.6	-16.4	Lathe & turning machine tool operators & tenders	1.3	-28.4
Industrial truck & tractor operators	2.6	-28.4	Shipping, receiving, & traffic clerks	1.3	-23.4
Laborers & freight, stock, & material movers, hand	2.1	-28.4	Electricians	1.3	-17.4
Industrial engineers	2.1	-3.3	Grinding, lapping, polishing machine tool operators	1.2	-22.8
Maintenance & repair workers, general	2.0	-20.4	Engine & other machine assemblers	1.1	-20.4
Production workers, nec	2.0	-21.9	Drilling & boring machine tool operators	1.1	-28.4
Computer-controlled machine tool operators	1.9	-12.4	Production, planning, & expediting clerks	1.1	-20.4

Source: *Industry-Occupation Matrix*, Bureau of Labor Statistics, December 4, 2007. These data are reported based on 4-digit NAICS categories but have been matched to corresponding 6-digit NAICS industry codes. The change reported for each occupation to the year 2016 is a percent of growth or decline as estimated by the Bureau of Labor Statistics. The abbreviation nec stands for 'not elsewhere classified'.

LOCATION BY STATE AND REGIONAL CONCENTRATION

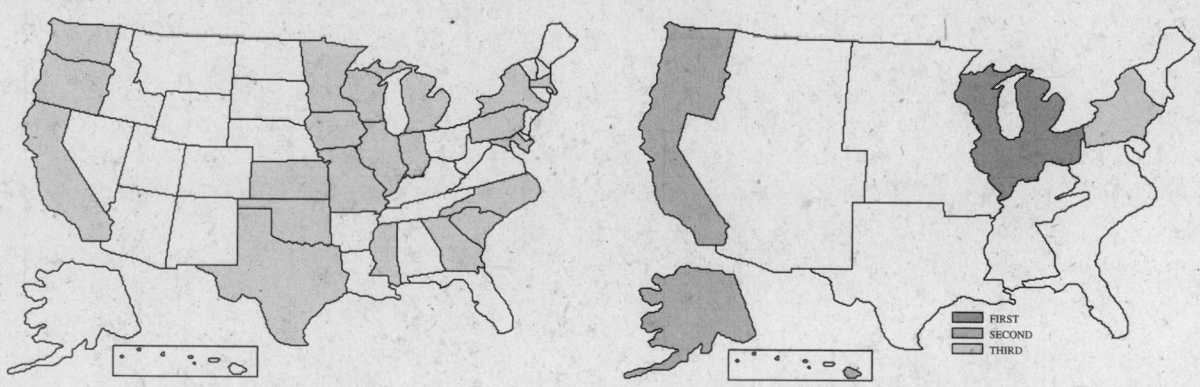

FIRST
SECOND
THIRD

INDUSTRY DATA BY STATE

State	Establish-ments	Shipments			Employment				Cost as % of Shipments	Investment per Employee ($)
		Total ($ mil)	% of U.S.	Per Establ.	Total Number	% of U.S.	Per Establ.	Wages ($/hour)		
Indiana	60	5,695.1	22.2	94,918.3	15,908	14.8	265	20.54	36.5	9,484
Michigan	64	2,812.4	11.0	43,943.7	17,687	16.5	276	17.45	43.0	5,520
Texas	52	1,219.4	4.8	23,449.1	4,229	3.9	81	14.13	51.8	10,513
New York	37	935.7	3.6	25,288.7	3,413	3.2	92	24.02	48.7	5,951
Illinois	53	923.5	3.6	17,424.7	4,256	4.0	80	11.57	46.6	6,531

Continued on next page.

INDUSTRY DATA BY STATE - Continued

State	Establish-ments	Shipments			Employment				Cost as % of Shipments	Investment per Employee ($)
		Total ($ mil)	% of U.S.	Per Establ.	Total Number	% of U.S.	Per Establ.	Wages ($/hour)		
Pennsylvania	33	917.0	3.6	27,787.4	4,522	4.2	137	14.07	52.4	3,222
Wisconsin	24	841.0	3.3	35,042.5	2,406	2.2	100	18.13	49.6	3,708
Massachusetts	20	678.6	2.6	33,931.4	2,533	2.4	127	9.24	38.0	8,386
California	100	669.9	2.6	6,699.5	3,534	3.3	35	13.29	49.4	4,808
North Carolina	10	466.5	1.8	46,650.8	1,404	1.3	140	10.36	56.4	8,293
Mississippi	15	400.8	1.6	26,722.9	3,304	3.1	220	14.12	64.7	5,955
South Carolina	12	376.9	1.5	31,408.8	1,883	1.8	157	12.23	56.0	3,102
Oklahoma	11	277.4	1.1	25,216.4	1,787	1.7	162	34.16	45.1	1,359
Kansas	14	259.1	1.0	18,503.9	1,284	1.2	92	13.67	58.5	1,410
Georgia	18	241.5	0.9	13,416.9	1,737	1.6	97	12.02	60.6	3,756
Iowa	15	204.5	0.8	13,636.5	1,054	1.0	70	16.70	33.8	5,040
Missouri	20	165.0	0.6	8,249.1	988	0.9	49	10.11	46.5	4,535
Maryland	3	128.5	0.5	42,822.3	741	0.7	247	14.11	33.4	3,709
Washington	18	111.6	0.4	6,199.4	509	0.5	28	13.85	45.5	4,426
Minnesota	11	109.1	0.4	9,914.9	1,020	1.0	93	10.98	56.3	2,218
Oregon	14	77.3	0.3	5,519.2	355	0.3	25	21.91	42.8	2,882

Source: 2002 Economic Census. The states are in descending order of shipments or establishments (if shipment data are missing for the majority). The symbol (D) appears when data are withheld to prevent disclosure of competitive information. States marked with (D) are sorted by number of establishments. A dash (-) indicates that the data element cannot be calculated. Data may not show all states active in the NAICS category. All data available at the time of publication are shown.

NAICS 336330 - MOTOR VEHICLE STEERING AND SUSPENSION COMPONENT (EXCEPT SPRING) MANUFACTURING

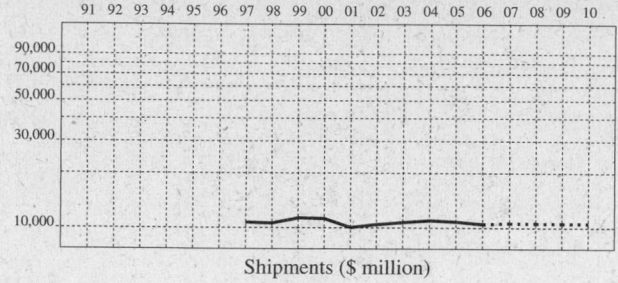

Shipments ($ million)

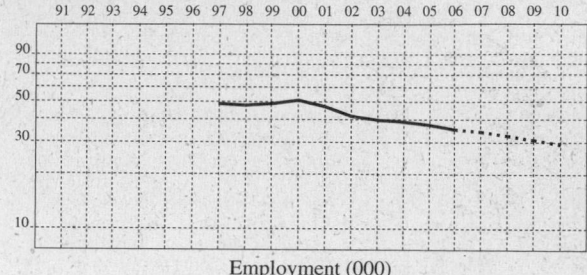

Employment (000)

GENERAL STATISTICS

Year	Companies	Establishments Total	Establishments with 20 or more employees	Employment Total (000)	Employment Production Workers (000)	Employment Hours (Mil)	Compensation Payroll ($ mil)	Compensation Wages ($/hr)	Production Cost of Materials	Production Value Added by Manufacture	Production Value of Shipments	Production Capital Invest.
1997	183	211	108	48.6	40.1	87.0	2,323.6	20.78	5,473.7	5,262.0	10,702.7	551.3
1998		211	110	47.7	39.1	85.5	2,269.8	20.76	5,423.7	5,117.6	10,589.8	583.4
1999		212	113	48.7	40.5	90.1	2,508.8	21.89	5,701.0	5,645.6	11,316.3	553.2
2000		207	115	51.0	41.7	87.1	2,505.8	22.03	5,896.5	5,332.4	11,239.7	482.1
2001		204	112	47.0	38.2	79.0	2,207.3	20.64	5,424.1	4,591.1	10,043.8	539.2
2002	196	236	129	41.7	33.3	68.9	2,048.1	21.64	5,518.0	4,937.7	10,438.4	403.3
2003		233	132	39.7	31.6	70.3	1,917.8	20.49	5,752.7	4,986.6	10,696.6	364.2
2004		229	136	38.9	30.9	65.9	1,918.1	21.61	6,130.2	4,828.4	10,982.4	317.2
2005		246	140	37.4	29.6	59.0	1,857.9	22.73	6,486.5	4,331.6	10,789.3	334.3
2006		243P	143P	35.3	28.0	56.8	1,785.0	22.34	6,595.3	3,923.7	10,489.9	298.9
2007		248P	148P	34.3P	26.7P	53.7P	1,714.0P	22.25P	6,673.8P	3,970.4P	10,614.8P	253.2P
2008		252P	152P	32.6P	25.1P	49.8P	1,637.6P	22.39P	6,660.8P	3,962.7P	10,594.0P	218.8P
2009		256P	156P	30.9P	23.5P	45.9P	1,561.2P	22.53P	6,647.7P	3,954.9P	10,573.3P	184.3P
2010		261P	160P	29.2P	22.0P	42.1P	1,484.7P	22.67P	6,634.7P	3,947.1P	10,552.6P	149.9P

Sources: 1997 and 2002 *Economic Census*; other years, up to 2006, are from *Annual Survey of Manufactures*. Establishment counts for non-Census years are from *County Business Patterns*; 1997 and 2002 values are from the 1997 and 2002 censuses, respectively. 'P's show projections by the editors.

INDICES OF CHANGE

Year	Companies	Establishments Total	Establishments with 20 or more employees	Employment Total (000)	Employment Production Workers (000)	Employment Hours (Mil)	Compensation Payroll ($ mil)	Compensation Wages ($/hr)	Production Cost of Materials	Production Value Added by Manufacture	Production Value of Shipments	Production Capital Invest.
1997	93	89	84	117	120	126	113	96	99	107	103	137
1998		89	85	114	117	124	111	96	98	104	101	145
1999		90	88	117	122	131	122	101	103	114	108	137
2000		88	89	122	125	126	122	102	107	108	108	120
2001		86	87	113	115	115	108	95	98	93	96	134
2002	100	100	100	100	100	100	100	100	100	100	100	100
2003		99	102	95	95	102	94	95	104	101	102	90
2004		97	105	93	93	96	94	100	111	98	105	79
2005		104	109	90	89	86	91	105	118	88	103	83
2006		103P	111P	85	84	82	87	103	120	79	100	74
2007		105P	114P	82P	80P	78P	84P	103P	121P	80P	102P	63P
2008		107P	118P	78P	75P	72P	80P	103P	121P	80P	101P	54P
2009		109P	121P	74P	71P	67P	76P	104P	120P	80P	101P	46P
2010		111P	124P	70P	66P	61P	72P	105P	120P	80P	101P	37P

Sources: Same as General Statistics. Values reflect change from the base year, 2002. Values above 100 mean greater than 2002, values below 100 mean less than 2002, and the values of 100 in other years means the same as 2002. 'P's show projections by the editors.

SELECTED RATIOS

For 2002	Avg. of All Manufact.	Analyzed Industry	Index	For 2002	Avg. of All Manufact.	Analyzed Industry	Index
Employees per Establishment	42	177	421	Value Added per Production Worker	182,367	148,279	81
Payroll per Establishment	1,639,184	8,678,390	529	Cost per Establishment	5,769,015	23,381,356	405
Payroll per Employee	39,053	49,115	126	Cost per Employee	137,446	132,326	96
Production Workers per Establishment	30	141	478	Cost per Production Worker	195,506	165,706	85
Wages per Establishment	694,845	6,317,780	909	Shipments per Establishment	11,158,348	44,230,508	396
Wages per Production Worker	23,548	44,775	190	Shipments per Employee	265,847	250,321	94
Hours per Production Worker	1,980	2,069	104	Shipments per Production Worker	378,144	313,465	83
Wages per Hour	11.89	21.64	182	Investment per Establishment	361,338	1,708,898	473
Value Added per Establishment	5,381,325	20,922,458	389	Investment per Employee	8,609	9,671	112
Value Added per Employee	128,210	118,410	92	Investment per Production Worker	12,245	12,111	99

Sources: Same as General Statistics. The 'Average of All Manufacturing' column represents the average of all manufacturing industries reported for the most recent complete year available. The Index shows the relationship between the Average and the Analyzed Industry. For example, 100 means that they are equal; 500 that the Analyzed Industry is five times the average; 50 means that the Analyzed Industry is half the national average. The abbreviation 'na' is used to show that data are 'not available'. Ratios shown for 2002, the last complete census year.

LEADING COMPANIES   Number shown: **75**   Total sales ($ mil): **785,184**   Total employment (000): **1,861.6**

Company Name	Address				CEO Name	Phone	Co. Type	Sales ($ mil)	Empl. (000)
General Motors Corp.	300 Renaissance Ctr	Detroit	MI	48265		313-556-5000	P	181,122	266.0
Ford Motor Co.	1 American Rd.	Dearborn	MI	48126		313-322-3000	P	172,455	246.0
Chrysler L.L.C.	1000 Chrysler Dr.	Auburn Hills	MI	48326	Thomas W. LaSorda	248-576-5741	S	45,237*	84.4
Honeywell International Inc.	PO Box 4000	Morristown	NJ	07962	Adriane M. Brown	973-455-2000	P	34,589	122.0
ArvinMeritor OE L.L.C.	950 W 450 S, Bldg.	Columbus	IN	47201	C. G. McClure Jr.	812-341-2000	S	23,491*	32.0
Delphi Corp.	5725 Delphi Dr.	Troy	MI	48098	Voker J. Barth	248-813-2000	P	22,383	169.5
Lear Corp.	PO Box 5008	Southfield	MI	48086	Jim Brackenbury	248-447-1500	P	15,995	91.0
TRW Automotive Holdings Inc.	12001 Tech Cntr Dr.	Livonia	MI	48150		734-855-2600	P	14,702	66.3
Textron Inc.	40 Westminster St.	Providence	RI	02903		401-421-2800	P	13,225	44.0
Cummins Inc.	PO Box 3005	Columbus	IN	47202		812-377-5000	P	13,048	37.8
Eaton Corp.	1111 Superior Ave.	Cleveland	OH	44114		216-523-5000	P	13,033	60.0
Visteon Corp.	1 Village Center Dr	Van Buren Twp	MI	48111		313-755-2800	P	11,266	41.5
Parker Hannifin Corp.	6035 Parkland Blvd.	Cleveland	OH	44124	Lee Banks	216-896-3000	P	10,718	57.3
Acument Global Technologies	840 W Long Lake	Troy	MI	48098	Joseph Gray	248-813-6329	S	10,080*	9.0
ITT Corp.	4 W Red Oak Ln.	White Plains	NY	10604		914-641-2000	P	9,003	39.7
Dana Corp.	PO Box 1000	Toledo	OH	43697	Michael J. Burns	419-535-4500	P	8,504	45.0
Neapco L.L.C.	PO Box 399	Pottstown	PA	19464		610-323-6000	R	7,580*	0.3
Trane Inc.	PO Box 6820	Piscataway	NJ	08855		732-980-6000	P	7,450	29.6
Triangle Suspension Systems	PO Box 425	Du Bois	PA	15801	Greg Maffia	814-375-7211	R	7,000*	0.2
Perfection Hy-Test Company	100 Perfection Way	Timmonsville	SC	29161		843-326-5544	R	7,000*	0.2
Penn Machine Co.	106 Station St.	Johnstown	PA	15905	H Wiegand	814-288-1547	R	7,000*	<0.1
Federal-Mogul Corp.	PO Box 1966	Detroit	MI	48235	Jose Maria Alapont	248-354-7700	P	6,914	43.1
Robert Bosch Corp.	2800 S 25th Ave.	Broadview	IL	60155	Kurt W. Liedtke	708-865-5200	S	6,782*	25.0
ArvinMeritor Inc.	2135 W Maple Rd.	Troy	MI	48084		248-435-1000	P	6,449	18.0
Tenneco Inc.	500 N Field Dr.	Lake Forest	IL	60045		847-482-5000	P	6,184	21.0
Toyota Motor Mfg. N America	25 Atlantic Ave.	Erlanger	KY	41018	Masamoto Amezawa	859-746-4000	S	6,120*	7.5
Guardian Industries Corp.	2300 Harmon Rd.	Auburn Hills	MI	48326	William M. Davidson	248-340-1800	R	5,330	19.0
BorgWarner Inc.	3850 Hamlin Rd.	Auburn Hills	MI	48326		248-754-9200	P	5,329	17.7
Autoliv ASP Inc.	3350 Airport Rd.	Ogden	UT	84405	Leonard Barton	801-625-4800	S	5,301*	3.7
Carlisle Tire and Wheel Co.	23 Windham Blvd.	Aiken	SC	29805	Barry Littrell	803-643-2900	S	4,822*	0.6
Karl Schmidt Unisia Inc.	1731 Industrial Pky	Marinette	WI	54143	Frank Pohlmann	715-732-0181	R	4,640*	0.9
Pioneer Automotive Tech.	100 S Pioneer Blvd.	Springboro	OH	45066	Steve Moerner	937-746-6600	R	4,610*	0.3
Toledo Trans-Kit Inc.	13515 Ballnyn Corp.	Charlotte	NC	28277	C. J. Kearney	704-752-4400	S	4,372	23.8
Mack Trucks Inc.	PO Box M	Allentown	PA	18105		610-709-3011	R	4,324*	0.8
New United Motor Manufacturing	45500 Fremont	Fremont	CA	94538	Bruce Walker	510-498-5500	J	4,080*	5.0
Kalmar Industries USA L.L.C.	415 E Dundee St.	Ottawa	KS	66067		785-242-2200	R	3,320*	0.3
American Axle & Mfg Holdings	1 Dauch Dr.	Detroit	MI	48211	Richard E. Dauch	313-974-2000	P	3,248	10.0
Hi-Stat Manufacturing Company	28001 Cabot Dr.	Novi	MI	48377	John Corey	248-489-9300	D	3,194*	5.0
Amsted Industries Inc.	2 Prudential Plaza	Chicago	IL	60601	W. Robert Reum	312-645-1700	R	3,050	9.9
AutoAlliance International	1 International Dr.	Flat Rock	MI	48134	Phillip G. Spender	734-782-7800	J	3,019*	3.7
TAG Holdings L.L.C.	2075 W Big Beaver	Troy	MI	48084	J. B. Anderson, Jr.	248-822-8056	R	2,904*	2.5
Crane Co.	100 First Stamford	Stamford	CT	06902	Thomas Craney	203-363-7300	P	2,619	12.0
Consolidated Metco Inc.	PO Box 83201	Portland	OR	97283		503-286-5741	R	2,510*	0.1
Pall Corp.	2200 Northern Blvd.	East Hills	NY	11548	Eric Krasnoff	516-484-5400	P	2,250	10.8
DENSO Manufacturing Tennessee	1720 Rbrt C Jackson	Maryville	TN	37801	Mack Hattori	865-982-7000	S	2,231*	2.0
Sequa Corp.	200 Park Ave.	New York	NY	10166	Gail Binderman	212-986-5500	P	2,183	10.2
Affinia Group Inc.	1101 Technology	Ann Arbor	MI	48108		734-827-5400	Affinia	2,160	12.4
Dura Automotive Systems Inc.	2791 Research Dr.	Rochester Hills	MI	48309	Lawrence A. Denton	248-299-7500	P	2,091	15.4
Hayes Lemmerz International	15300 Centennial Dr	Northville	MI	48167	Fred Bentley	734-737-5000	P	2,039	11.0
Cooper Tire and Rubber Co.	701 Lima Ave.	Findlay	OH	45840	Roy V. Armes	419-423-1321	P	2,036	13.6
ZF Group N American Operations	15811 Centennial Dr	Northville	MI	48168	Julio Caspari	734-416-6200	R	1,949*	5.5
Sypris Technologies Marion	1550 Marion-Agosta	Marion	OH	43301	Jeffrey T. Gill	740-383-2111	S	1,920*	2.6
Hutchinson FTS Inc.	1835 Technology	Troy	MI	48083	Paul Campbell	248-589-7710	R	1,863*	<0.1
ADVICS North America Inc.	45300 Polaris Ct.	Plymouth	MI	48170	Haruhiko Saito	734-414-5100	S	1,810*	<0.1
Regal-Beloit Corp.	200 State St.	Beloit	WI	53511		608-364-8800	P	1,803	17.9
Bose Corp.	The Mountain	Framingham	MA	01701	Amar G. Bose	508-879-7330	R	1,800	8.0
Modine Manufacturing Co.	1500 DeKoven Ave.	Racine	WI	53403	Richard J. Doyle	262-636-1200	P	1,758	7.7
Siemens VDO Automotive Corp.	2400 Executive Hill	Auburn Hills	MI	48326	John Sanderson	248-209-4000	S	1,738*	10.0
Solvay America Inc.	3333 Richmond	Houston	TX	77098	David G. Birney	713-525-6000	S	1,611*	4.0
Neoplan USA Corp.	12015 E 46th Ave.	Denver	CO	80239	Harold Boade	303-451-5305	R	1,610*	<0.1
Hitachi Cable Indiana Inc.	5300 Grant Line Rd.	New Albany	IN	47150	Kenji Nakata	812-945-9011	R	1,590*	<0.1
Actuant Corp.	13000 W Slvr Spring	Butler	WI	53007	Bob Arzbaecher	414-352-4160	P	1,459	6.3
Accuride Corp.	PO Box 15600	Evansville	IN	47716	Terry Keating	812-962-5000	P	1,408	4.6
Inergy Automotive Systems	2710 Bellingham Dr.	Troy	MI	48083	James Squatrito	248-743-5700	R	1,257*	0.2
RBS Global Inc.	4701 W Greenfield	Milwaukee	WI	53214	Robert Hitt	414-643-3000	R	1,256	5.7
EaglePicher Corp.	2424 John Daly Rd.	Inkster	MI	48141	Donald L. Runkle	313-278-5956	R	1,244*	4.2
Remy International Inc.	2902 Enterprise Dr.	Anderson	IN	46013	Thomas J. Synder	765-778-6499	S	1,218*	7.9
Mark IV Industries Inc.	PO Box 810	Amherst	NY	14226		716-689-4972	R	1,215*	8.1
Adams Rite Manufacturing Co.	260 W Santa Fe St.	Pomona	CA	91767	Peter Adams	909-632-2300	R	1,201*	0.2
Noranda Aluminum Inc.	801 Crescent Centre	Franklin	TN	37067	William Brooks	615-771-5700	R	1,170*	<0.1
Tecumseh Products Co.	100 E Patterson St.	Tecumseh	MI	49286	Edwin Bunker	517-423-8411	P	1,133	10.3
Axiom Automotive Technologies	1 PPG Pl., 3150	Pittsburgh	PA	15222	Greg Gyllstorm	412-545-8100	R	1,110*	1.7
Key Safety Systems Inc.	7000 Nineteen Mile	Sterling Hgts	MI	48314	Jason Luo	586-726-3800	S	1,030	8.7
Spartan Motors Chassis Inc.	1165 Reynolds Rd.	Charlotte	MI	48813	John Sztykiel	517-543-6400	S	1,030*	0.8
Zf Lemforder Corp.	15811 Centennial Dr	Northville	MI	48168	Reinhard Buhl	734-416-6200	R	1,009*	<0.1

Source: Ward's Business Directory of U.S. Private and Public Companies, Volumes 1 and 2, 2008. The company type code used is as follows: P - Public, R - Private, S - Subsidiary, D - Division, J - Joint Venture, A - Affiliate, G - Group. Sales are in millions of dollars, employees are in thousands. An asterisk (*) indicates an estimated sales volume. The symbol < stands for 'less than'. Company names and addresses are truncated, in some cases, to fit into the available space.

MATERIALS CONSUMED

Material	Quantity	Delivered Cost ($ million)
Iron and steel castings (rough and semifinished)	(X)	600.9
Aluminum and aluminum-base alloy castings (rough and semifinished)	(X)	122.6
Other nonferrous metal castings, rough or semifinished (inc. aluminum)	(X)	(D)
Steel bars, bar shapes, and plates (exc. castings, forgings, fabr. metal products)	(X)	265.7
Steel sheet and strip (including tinplate)	(X)	166.7
All other steel shapes and forms (exc. castings, forgings, fabr. metal products)	(X)	137.7
Copper and copper-base alloy shapes and forms (exc. castings, forgings, fabr. metal products)	(X)	(D)
Aluminum and aluminum-base alloy shapes and forms (exc. castings, forgings, fabr. metal products)	(X)	2.6
Other nonferrous shapes and forms (exc. castings, forgings, fabricated metal products)	(X)	(D)
Ball and roller bearings (mounted or unmounted)	(X)	124.3
Fabricated plastics products (exc. gaskets, hoses, and belting)	(X)	81.0
Plastics products consumed in the form of sheets, rods, etc.	(X)	28.9
Plastics resins consumed in the form of granules, pellets, etc.	(X)	16.4
Fabricated rubber products (exc. tires, tubes, hoses, belting, and gaskets)	(X)	144.9
Rubber and plastics hose and belting	(X)	28.0
Ceramic raw materials (incl. powders, chemicals, and fibers)	(X)	(D)
Ceramic and ceramic composite parts, components, and accessories	(X)	(D)
Gaskets (all types), and packing and sealing devices	(X)	37.5
Paints, varnishes, stains, lacquers, shellacs, japans, enamels, etc.	(X)	26.5
Glues and adhesives	(X)	2.4
Flexible packaging materials	(X)	11.6
Paper and paperboard containers	(X)	16.5
Ignition coils for internal combustion engines	(X)	(D)
Ignition harness and cable sets for internal combustion engines	(X)	(D)
All other engine electrical equipment for internal combustion engines	(X)	(D)
Semiconductors (incl. transistors, diodes, rectifiers, and integrated circuits), for electronic circuitry	(X)	(D)
All other miscellaneous components and accessories for electronic circuitry (exc. tubes)	(X)	178.1
Core parts purchased for use in remanufacturing and rebuilding	(X)	213.1
Metal bolts, nuts, screws, and other screw machine products	(X)	105.9
Other fabricated metal products (exc. fluid power and forgings)	(X)	560.1
Forgings	(X)	188.0
Insulated wire and cable (excluding magnet wire)	(X)	(D)
Magnet wire	(X)	(D)
Fluid power pumps, motors, and hydrostatic transmissions	(X)	(D)
Fluid power valves (hydraulic and pneumatic)	(X)	(D)
Fluid power cylinders and rotary actuators (hydraulic and pneumatic)	(X)	(D)
Fluid power hose, tube fittings, and assemblies (hydraulic and pneumatic)	(X)	85.2
Fluid power filters (hydraulic and pneumatic)	(X)	0.4
Other transportation related fluid power products, hydraulic and pneumatic	(X)	1.5
Automotive stampings (inc. body parts, hubcaps, fenders, etc.)	(X)	129.8
Current-carrying wiring devices	(X)	(D)
Other chemicals and allied products	(X)	25.4
All other materials, components, parts, containers, and supplies	(X)	906.6
Materials, ingredients, containers, and supplies, nsk	(X)	688.1

Source: 2002 *Economic Census*. Explanation of symbols used: (D): Withheld to avoid disclosure of competitive data; na: Not available; (S): Withheld because statistical norms were not met; (X): Not applicable; (Z): Less than half the unit shown; nec: Not elsewhere classified; nsk: Not specified by kind; - : zero; p : 10-19 percent estimated; q : 20-29 percent estimated.

PRODUCT SHARE DETAILS

Product or Product Class Shipments	Mil. $	Product or Product Class Shipments	Mil. $
MOTOR VEHICLE STEERING AND SUSPENSION COMPONENTS, EXCEPT SPRINGS	10,590.5	Motor vehicle power steering hose assemblies, new	(D)
Motor vehicle steering and suspension components, new	**10,267.9**	Other motor vehicle steering and suspension components, new	2,637.4
Motor vehicle shock absorbers, new	830.0	Motor vehicle steering and suspension components, new, nsk	4.7
Motor vehicle tie rod ends, new	253.4	**Motor vehicle steering and suspension components, rebuilt**	**182.1**
Motor vehicle steering idler arms, drag links, and control arms, new	761.2	Motor vehicle steering and suspension components, rebuilt	181.5
Motor vehicle steering wheels, columns, and gearboxes, new	2,343.2	Motor vehicle power steering pumps, rebuilt	76.5
Other motor vehicle steering and suspension components, including motor vehicle ball joints, new	6,075.5	Motor vehicle rack and pinion steering assemblies, rebuilt	48.4
Motor vehicle ball joints, new	245.1	Other rebuilt steering and suspension components, rebuilt	56.5
Motor vehicle struts, new	702.2	Motor vehicle steering and suspension components, rebuilt, nsk	0.6
Motor vehicle rack and pinion steering gears, new	1,284.5	**Motor vehicle steering and suspension components, except springs, nsk, total**	**140.5**
Motor vehicle integral and manual steering gears, new	506.3		
Motor vehicle power steering pumps, new	(D)		

Source: 2002 *Economic Census*. The values are product shipments in millions of dollars for 2002. Total product shipments may be lower or higher than industry shipments. See Introduction for a full discussion. Values of indented subcategories are summed in the main heading(s). The symbol (D) appears when data are withheld to prevent disclosure of competitive information. The abbreviation nsk stands for 'not specified by kind' and nec for 'not elsewhere classified'. A dash (-) means zero.

INPUTS AND OUTPUTS FOR MOTOR VEHICLE PARTS MANUFACTURING

Economic Sector or Industry Providing Inputs	%	Sector	Economic Sector or Industry Buying Outputs	%	Sector
Compensation of employees	22.8		Light truck & utility vehicles	25.3	Manufg.
Motor vehicle parts	10.7	Manufg.	Automobiles	15.8	Manufg.
Management of companies & enterprises	7.0	Services	Exports of goods & services	13.9	Cap Inv
Wholesale trade	5.3	Trade	Motor vehicle parts	8.5	Manufg.
Iron & steel mills & ferroalloys	5.0	Manufg.	Retail trade	7.4	Trade
Nonferrous metal foundries	2.6	Manufg.	Personal consumption expenditures	4.1	
Ferrous metal foundries	2.4	Manufg.	Automotive repair & maintenance, ex. car washes	2.9	Services
Plate work & fabricated structural products	1.9	Manufg.	Truck transportation	2.2	Util.
Turned products & screws, nuts, & bolts	1.9	Manufg.	General S/L govt. services	2.0	S/L Govt
Machine shops	1.5	Manufg.	Heavy duty trucks	1.9	Manufg.
Plastics products, nec	1.4	Manufg.	Wholesale trade	1.5	Trade
Truck transportation	1.1	Util.	Transit & ground passenger transportation	0.8	Util.
Retail trade	1.0	Trade	Change in private inventories	0.7	In House
Electronic components, nec	0.9	Manufg.	Postal service	0.6	Util.
Custom roll forming	0.9	Manufg.	General Federal government services, defense	0.6	Fed Govt
Coating, engraving, heat treating & allied activities	0.9	Manufg.	Residential structures, nec	0.6	Construct.
Crowns & closures & metal stamping	0.8	Manufg.	Residential permanent site structures	0.6	Construct.
Rubber products, nec	0.7	Manufg.	Nonresidential structures, nec	0.5	Construct.
Semiconductors & related devices	0.7	Manufg.	Lawn & garden equipment	0.4	Manufg.
Plastics packaging materials, film & sheet	0.7	Manufg.	Boat building	0.4	Manufg.
Scientific research & development services	0.7	Services	Construction machinery	0.4	Manufg.
Power generation & supply	0.7	Util.	S/L govt. passenger transit	0.4	S/L Govt
Leather & hide tanning & finishing	0.7	Manufg.	Transportation equipment, nec	0.3	Manufg.
Ball & roller bearings	0.7	Manufg.	Engine equipment, nec	0.3	Manufg.
Valve & fittings other than plumbing	0.6	Manufg.	Food services & drinking places	0.3	Services
Textile & fabric finishing mills	0.6	Manufg.	Waste management & remediation services	0.3	Services
Lessors of nonfinancial assets	0.5	Fin/R.E.	Aircraft	0.3	Manufg.
Fluid power process machinery	0.5	Manufg.	Services to buildings & dwellings	0.3	Services
Taxes on production & imports, less subsidies	0.5		Oil & gas extraction	0.2	Mining
Plastics materials & resins	0.5	Manufg.	Commercial & health care structures	0.2	Construct.
Ornamental & architectural metal products	0.5	Manufg.	Farm machinery & equipment	0.2	Manufg.
Gaskets, packing, & sealing devices	0.5	Manufg.	Management of companies & enterprises	0.2	Services
Securities, commodity contracts, investments	0.5	Fin/R.E.	Truck trailers	0.2	Manufg.
Noncomparable imports	0.5	Foreign	Warehousing & storage	0.2	Util.
Urethane & other foam products (except polystrene)	0.4	Manufg.	Motor vehicle bodies	0.2	Manufg.
Printed circuit assemblies (electronic assembiles)	0.4	Manufg.	Travel trailers & campers	0.2	Manufg.
Alumina refining & primary aluminum production	0.4	Manufg.	Scientific research & development services	0.2	Services
Bare printed circuit boards	0.4	Manufg.	Maintenance/repair of nonresidential structures	0.2	Construct.
Paints & coatings	0.4	Manufg.	Private fixed investment	0.2	
Wiring devices	0.4	Manufg.	Couriers & messengers	0.1	Util.
Fabricated metals, nec	0.4	Manufg.	Individual & family services	0.1	Services
Copper rolling, drawing, extruding, & alloying	0.3	Manufg.	Scenic & sightseeing transport & related services	0.1	Util.
Advertising & related services	0.3	Services	Car washes	0.1	Services
Metal cans, boxes, & other containers (light gauge)	0.3	Manufg.	Automotive equipment rental & leasing	0.1	Fin/R.E.
Real estate	0.3	Fin/R.E.	Crowns & closures & metal stamping	0.1	Manufg.
Speed changers, industrial high-speed drives, & gears	0.3	Manufg.	Material handling equipment	0.1	Manufg.
Primary nonferrous metal, ex. copper & aluminum	0.3	Manufg.			
Paperboard containers	0.3	Manufg.			
Maintenance/repair of nonresidential structures	0.3	Construct.			
Gold, silver, & other metal ore	0.3	Mining			
Services to buildings & dwellings	0.2	Services			
Aluminum products from purchased aluminum	0.2	Manufg.			
Nonferrous metal (ex. copper & aluminum) processing	0.2	Manufg.			
Forging, stamping, & sintering, nec	0.2	Manufg.			
Rubber & plastics hose & belting	0.2	Manufg.			
Natural gas distribution	0.2	Util.			
Rail transportation	0.2	Util.			
Monetary authorities/depository credit intermediation	0.2	Fin/R.E.			
Handtools	0.2	Manufg.			
Automotive equipment rental & leasing	0.2	Fin/R.E.			
Professional, scientific, technical services, nec	0.2	Services			
Basic organic chemicals, nec	0.2	Manufg.			
Warehousing & storage	0.2	Util.			
Legal services	0.2	Services			
Food services & drinking places	0.2	Services			
Communication & energy wires & cables	0.2	Manufg.			
Automotive repair & maintenance, ex. car washes	0.2	Services			
Management, scientific, & technical consulting	0.2	Services			
Engine equipment, nec	0.2	Manufg.			
Wood windows & doors & millwork	0.2	Manufg.			
Veneer & plywood	0.2	Manufg.			
Telecommunications	0.2	Services			
Accounting, tax preparation, bookkeeping, & payroll	0.1	Services			
Commercial & industrial equipment repair/maintenance	0.1	Services			
Architectural, engineering, & related services	0.1	Services			
Artificial & synthetic fibers & filaments	0.1	Manufg.			
Air transportation	0.1	Util.			
Cutting tools & machine tool accessories	0.1	Manufg.			
Employment services	0.1	Services			
Chemical products & preparations, nec	0.1	Manufg.			

Continued on next page.

INPUTS AND OUTPUTS FOR MOTOR VEHICLE PARTS MANUFACTURING - Continued

Economic Sector or Industry Providing Inputs	%	Sector	Economic Sector or Industry Buying Outputs	%	Sector
Data processing, hosting, & related services	0.1	Services			
Specialized design services	0.1	Services			
Relay & industrial controls	0.1	Manufg.			
Business support services	0.1	Services			
Fiber, yarn, & thread mills	0.1	Manufg.			
Hotels & motels, including casino hotels	0.1	Services			
Electronic capacitors, resistors, coils, transformers	0.1	Manufg.			
Wood containers & pallets	0.1	Manufg.			
Waste management & remediation services	0.1	Services			
Springs & wire products	0.1	Manufg.			
Automatic environmental controls	0.1	Manufg.			

Source: Benchmark Input-Output Accounts for the U.S. Economy, 2002, U.S. Department of Commerce, Washington D.C., January 2008. User should note that this Input-Output table is not for this particular narrowly defined industry but for a larger aggregate. Input and Output data for Motor Vehicle Parts Manufacturing include Input and Output data for the Annual Survey of Manufactures' NAICS industries 33631M, 33632M, 336330, 336340, 336350, 336360, 336370, 336391, and 336399. The abbreviation nec stands for 'not elsewhere classified'.

OCCUPATIONS EMPLOYED BY MOTOR VEHICLE PARTS MANUFACTURING

Occupation	% of Total 2006	Change to 2016	Occupation	% of Total 2006	Change to 2016
Team assemblers	15.2	-19.2	Welders, cutters, solderers, & brazers	1.9	-15.3
Cutting, punching, & press machine operators	4.2	-28.4	Molding, coremaking, & casting machine operators	1.8	-28.4
Machinists	3.8	-16.4	Welding, soldering, & brazing machine operators	1.6	-10.5
Inspectors, testers, sorters, samplers, & weighers	3.5	-24.9	Industrial machinery mechanics	1.5	-8.4
First-line supervisors/managers of production workers	3.3	-20.4	Helpers--Production workers	1.5	-20.4
Assemblers & fabricators, nec	3.2	-28.4	Mechanical engineers	1.4	-20.4
Multiple machine tool operators & tenders	2.6	-12.4	Electrical & electronic equipment assemblers	1.4	-36.3
Tool & die makers	2.6	-16.4	Lathe & turning machine tool operators & tenders	1.3	-28.4
Industrial truck & tractor operators	2.6	-28.4	Shipping, receiving, & traffic clerks	1.3	-23.4
Laborers & freight, stock, & material movers, hand	2.1	-28.4	Electricians	1.3	-17.4
Industrial engineers	2.1	-3.3	Grinding, lapping, polishing machine tool operators	1.2	-22.8
Maintenance & repair workers, general	2.0	-20.4	Engine & other machine assemblers	1.1	-20.4
Production workers, nec	2.0	-21.9	Drilling & boring machine tool operators	1.1	-28.4
Computer-controlled machine tool operators	1.9	-12.4	Production, planning, & expediting clerks	1.1	-20.4

Source: Industry-Occupation Matrix, Bureau of Labor Statistics, December 4, 2007. These data are reported based on 4-digit NAICS categories but have been matched to corresponding 6-digit NAICS industry codes. The change reported for each occupation to the year 2016 is a percent of growth or decline as estimated by the Bureau of Labor Statistics. The abbreviation nec stands for 'not elsewhere classified'.

LOCATION BY STATE AND REGIONAL CONCENTRATION

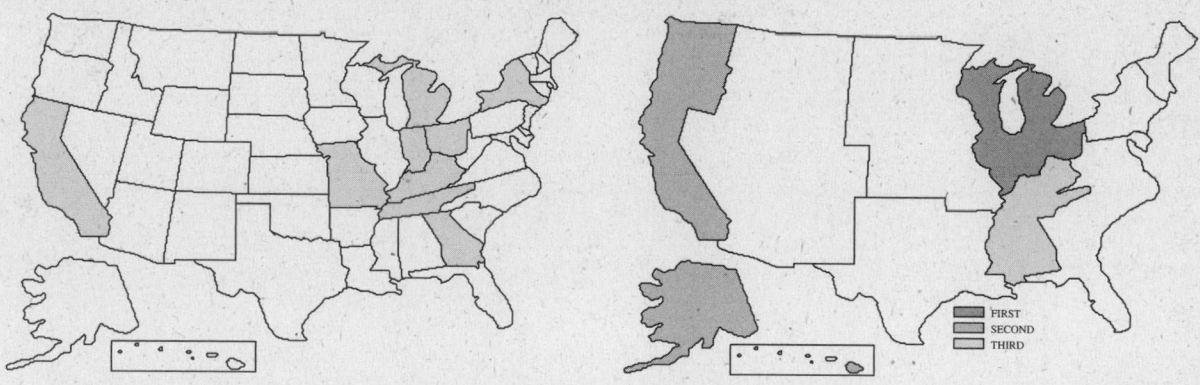

INDUSTRY DATA BY STATE

State	Establish-ments	Shipments			Employment				Cost as % of Shipments	Investment per Employee ($)
		Total ($ mil)	% of U.S.	Per Establ.	Total Number	% of U.S.	Per Establ.	Wages ($/hour)		
Michigan	29	2,472.3	23.7	85,251.4	9,220	22.1	318	28.91	50.6	5,038
Indiana	24	2,143.9	20.5	89,327.3	7,635	18.3	318	24.88	56.6	13,035
Ohio	23	1,520.9	14.6	66,125.0	5,958	14.3	259	17.13	48.1	13,699
Tennessee	12	1,116.1	10.7	93,005.9	4,159	10.0	347	17.62	54.6	11,003
Kentucky	8	652.2	6.2	81,526.8	2,296	5.5	287	16.41	68.4	16,400

Continued on next page.

INDUSTRY DATA BY STATE - Continued

State	Establish-ments	Shipments			Employment				Cost as % of Shipments	Investment per Employee ($)
		Total ($ mil)	% of U.S.	Per Establ.	Total Number	% of U.S.	Per Establ.	Wages ($/hour)		
Georgia	6	240.0	2.3	39,998.8	1,065	2.6	177	14.27	73.4	3,586
Missouri	11	129.8	1.2	11,801.5	912	2.2	83	14.11	48.0	2,594
California	30	94.8	0.9	3,158.4	460	1.1	15	23.19	51.5	4,991
New York	7	42.2	0.4	6,023.3	294	0.7	42	14.15	60.9	8,269

Source: 2002 Economic Census. The states are in descending order of shipments or establishments (if shipment data are missing for the majority). The symbol (D) appears when data are withheld to prevent disclosure of competitive information. States marked with (D) are sorted by number of establishments. A dash (-) indicates that the data element cannot be calculated. Data may not show all states active in the NAICS category. All data available at the time of publication are shown.

NAICS 336340 - MOTOR VEHICLE BRAKE SYSTEM MANUFACTURING

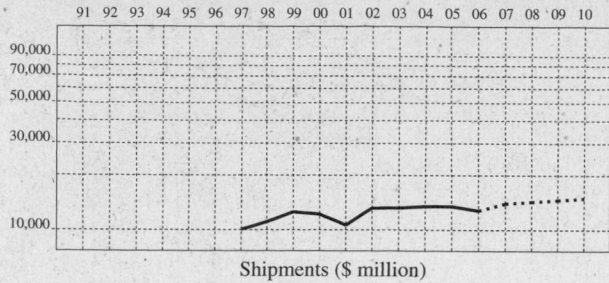

Shipments ($ million)

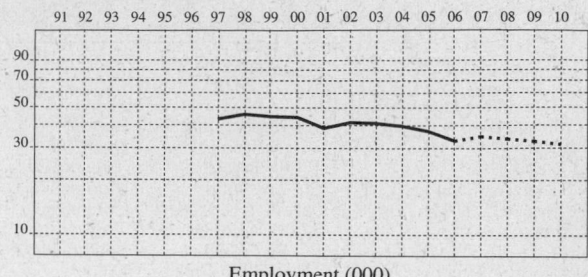

Employment (000)

GENERAL STATISTICS

Year	Com-panies	Establishments		Employment			Compensation		Production ($ million)			
		Total	with 20 or more employees	Total (000)	Production Workers (000)	Hours (Mil)	Payroll ($ mil)	Wages ($/hr)	Cost of Materials	Value Added by Manufacture	Value of Shipments	Capital Invest.
1997	204	269	170	43.1	33.5	72.1	1,486.1	14.57	6,407.9	3,618.2	10,033.3	484.3
1998		282	167	45.8	36.8	73.1	1,551.5	15.46	6,906.8	4,140.4	11,075.7	505.2
1999		278	164	44.6	34.9	72.0	1,690.9	16.98	7,764.2	4,761.7	12,548.9	406.2
2000		266	158	44.3	35.0	66.5	1,610.5	17.13	7,585.6	4,766.4	12,201.0	455.0
2001		260	152	38.7	29.5	59.6	1,420.1	16.59	6,343.2	4,259.5	10,635.6	384.8
2002	207	275	159	41.5	33.2	70.5	1,632.2	16.83	7,484.4	5,757.0	13,193.2	568.7
2003		262	163	41.1	32.1	66.7	1,599.9	16.32	8,331.0	4,895.5	13,227.3	423.3
2004		262	161	39.7	31.5	64.0	1,587.4	17.09	8,167.1	5,346.1	13,493.8	461.2
2005		251	157	37.2	28.7	59.3	1,524.8	17.19	8,239.5	5,277.4	13,486.7	360.4
2006		254P	155P	32.9	25.3	52.5	1,355.7	17.09	7,758.2	5,033.3	12,781.1	299.8
2007		252P	154P	34.8P	27.0P	55.6P	1,489.3P	17.63P	8,498.0P	5,513.3P	13,999.9P	357.9P
2008		249P	153P	33.7P	26.0P	53.8P	1,479.0P	17.83P	8,689.2P	5,637.3P	14,314.9P	343.9P
2009		247P	152P	32.6P	25.1P	51.9P	1,468.7P	18.03P	8,880.4P	5,761.4P	14,629.9P	329.9P
2010		244P	151P	31.4P	24.2P	50.1P	1,458.5P	18.23P	9,071.6P	5,885.4P	14,944.8P	315.9P

Sources: 1997 and 2002 *Economic Census*; other years, up to 2006, are from *Annual Survey of Manufactures*. Establishment counts for non-Census years are from *County Business Patterns*; 1997 and 2002 values are from the 1997 and 2002 censuses, respectively. 'P's show projections by the editors.

INDICES OF CHANGE

Year	Com-panies	Establishments		Employment			Compensation		Production ($ million)			
		Total	with 20 or more employees	Total (000)	Production Workers (000)	Hours (Mil)	Payroll ($ mil)	Wages ($/hr)	Cost of Materials	Value Added by Manufacture	Value of Shipments	Capital Invest.
1997	99	98	107	104	101	102	91	87	86	63	76	85
1998		103	105	110	111	104	95	92	92	72	84	89
1999		101	103	107	105	102	104	101	104	83	95	71
2000		97	99	107	105	94	99	102	101	83	92	80
2001		95	96	93	89	85	87	99	85	74	81	68
2002	100	100	100	100	100	100	100	100	100	100	100	100
2003		95	103	99	97	95	98	97	111	85	100	74
2004		95	101	96	95	91	97	102	109	93	102	81
2005		91	99	90	86	84	93	102	110	92	102	63
2006		92P	98P	79	76	74	83	102	104	87	97	53
2007		92P	97P	84P	81P	79P	91P	105P	114P	96P	106P	63P
2008		91P	96P	81P	78P	76P	91P	106P	116P	98P	109P	60P
2009		90P	95P	79P	76P	74P	90P	107P	119P	100P	111P	58P
2010		89P	95P	76P	73P	71P	89P	108P	121P	102P	113P	56P

Sources: Same as General Statistics. Values reflect change from the base year, 2002. Values above 100 mean greater than 2002, values below 100 mean less than 2002, and the values of 100 in other years means the same as 2002. 'P's show projections by the editors.

SELECTED RATIOS

For 2002	Avg. of All Manufact.	Analyzed Industry	Index	For 2002	Avg. of All Manufact.	Analyzed Industry	Index
Employees per Establishment	42	151	360	Value Added per Production Worker	182,367	173,404	95
Payroll per Establishment	1,639,184	5,935,273	362	Cost per Establishment	5,769,015	27,216,000	472
Payroll per Employee	39,053	39,330	101	Cost per Employee	137,446	180,347	131
Production Workers per Establishment	30	121	409	Cost per Production Worker	195,506	225,434	115
Wages per Establishment	694,845	4,314,600	621	Shipments per Establishment	11,158,348	47,975,273	430
Wages per Production Worker	23,548	35,738	152	Shipments per Employee	265,847	317,908	120
Hours per Production Worker	1,980	2,123	107	Shipments per Production Worker	378,144	397,386	105
Wages per Hour	11.89	16.83	142	Investment per Establishment	361,338	2,068,000	572
Value Added per Establishment	5,381,325	20,934,545	389	Investment per Employee	8,609	13,704	159
Value Added per Employee	128,210	138,723	108	Investment per Production Worker	12,245	17,130	140

Sources: Same as General Statistics. The 'Average of All Manufacturing' column represents the average of all manufacturing industries reported for the most recent complete year available. The Index shows the relationship between the Average and the Analyzed Industry. For example, 100 means that they are equal; 500 that the Analyzed Industry is five times the average; 50 means that the Analyzed Industry is half the national average. The abbreviation 'na' is used to show that data are 'not available'. Ratios shown for 2002, the last complete census year.

LEADING COMPANIES   Number shown: 75   Total sales ($ mil): 786,144   Total employment (000): 1,865.2

Company Name	Address				CEO Name	Phone	Co. Type	Sales ($ mil)	Empl. (000)
General Motors Corp.	300 Renaissance Ctr	Detroit	MI	48265		313-556-5000	P	181,122	266.0
Ford Motor Co.	1 American Rd.	Dearborn	MI	48126		313-322-3000	P	172,455	246.0
Chrysler L.L.C.	1000 Chrysler Dr.	Auburn Hills	MI	48326	Thomas W. LaSorda	248-576-5741	S	45,237*	84.4
Honeywell International Inc.	PO Box 4000	Morristown	NJ	07962	Adriane M. Brown	973-455-2000	P	34,589	122.0
ArvinMeritor OE L.L.C.	950 W 450 S, Bldg.	Columbus	IN	47201	C. G. McClure Jr.	812-341-2000	S	23,491*	32.0
Delphi Corp.	5725 Delphi Dr.	Troy	MI	48098	Voker J. Barth	248-813-2000	P	22,383	169.5
Lear Corp.	PO Box 5008	Southfield	MI	48086	Jim Brackenbury	248-447-1500	P	15,995	91.0
TRW Automotive Holdings Inc.	12001 Tech Cntr Dr.	Livonia	MI	48150		734-855-2600	P	14,702	66.3
Textron Inc.	40 Westminster St.	Providence	RI	02903		401-421-2800	P	13,225	44.0
Cummins Inc.	PO Box 3005	Columbus	IN	47202		812-377-5000	P	13,048	37.8
Eaton Corp.	1111 Superior Ave.	Cleveland	OH	44114		216-523-5000	P	13,033	60.0
Visteon Corp.	1 Village Center Dr	Van Buren Twp	MI	48111		313-755-2800	P	11,266	41.5
Parker Hannifin Corp.	6035 Parkland Blvd.	Cleveland	OH	44124	Lee Banks	216-896-3000	P	10,718	57.3
Acument Global Technologies	840 W Long Lake	Troy	MI	48098	Joseph Gray	248-813-6329	S	10,080*	9.0
ITT Corp.	4 W Red Oak Ln.	White Plains	NY	10604		914-641-2000	P	9,003	39.7
Dana Corp.	PO Box 1000	Toledo	OH	43697	Michael J. Burns	419-535-4500	P	8,504	45.0
Neapco L.L.C.	PO Box 399	Pottstown	PA	19464		610-323-6000	R	7,580*	0.3
Trane Inc.	PO Box 6820	Piscataway	NJ	08855		732-980-6000	P	7,450	29.6
Triangle Suspension Systems	PO Box 425	Du Bois	PA	15801	Greg Maffia	814-375-7211	R	7,000*	0.2
Perfection Hy-Test Company	100 Perfection Way	Timmonsville	SC	29161		843-326-5544	R	7,000*	0.2
Penn Machine Co.	106 Station St.	Johnstown	PA	15905	H Wiegand	814-288-1547	R	7,000*	<0.1
Federal-Mogul Corp.	PO Box 1966	Detroit	MI	48235	Jose Maria Alapont	248-354-7700	P	6,914	43.1
Robert Bosch Corp.	2800 S 25th Ave.	Broadview	IL	60155	Kurt W. Liedtke	708-865-5200	S	6,782*	25.0
ArvinMeritor Inc.	2135 W Maple Rd.	Troy	MI	48084		248-435-1000	P	6,449	18.0
Tenneco Inc.	500 N Field Dr.	Lake Forest	IL	60045		847-482-5000	P	6,184	21.0
Toyota Motor Mfg. N America	25 Atlantic Ave.	Erlanger	KY	41018	Masamoto Amezawa	859-746-4000	S	6,120*	7.5
Guardian Industries Corp.	2300 Harmon Rd.	Auburn Hills	MI	48326	William M. Davidson	248-340-1800	R	5,330	19.0
BorgWarner Inc.	3850 Hamlin Rd.	Auburn Hills	MI	48326		248-754-9200	P	5,329	17.7
Autoliv ASP Inc.	3350 Airport Rd.	Ogden	UT	84405	Leonard Barton	801-625-4800	S	5,301*	3.7
Carlisle Tire and Wheel Co.	23 Windham Blvd.	Aiken	SC	29805	Barry Littrell	803-643-2900	S	4,822*	0.6
Karl Schmidt Unisia Inc.	1731 Industrial Pky	Marinette	WI	54143	Frank Pohlmann	715-732-0181	R	4,640*	0.9
Pioneer Automotive Tech.	100 S Pioneer Blvd.	Springboro	OH	45066	Steve Moerner	937-746-6600	R	4,610*	0.3
Toledo Trans-Kit Inc.	13515 Ballnyn Corp.	Charlotte	NC	28277	C. J. Kearney	704-752-4400	S	4,372	23.8
Mack Trucks Inc.	PO Box M	Allentown	PA	18105		610-709-3011	R	4,324*	0.8
New United Motor Manufacturing	45500 Fremont	Fremont	CA	94538	Bruce Walker	510-498-5500	J	4,080*	5.0
Kalmar Industries USA L.L.C.	415 E Dundee St.	Ottawa	KS	66067		785-242-2200	R	3,320*	0.3
American Axle & Mfg Holdings	1 Dauch Dr.	Detroit	MI	48211	Richard E. Dauch	313-974-2000	P	3,248	10.0
Hi-Stat Manufacturing Company	28001 Cabot Dr.	Novi	MI	48377	John Corey	248-489-9300	D	3,194*	5.0
Amsted Industries Inc.	2 Prudential Plaza	Chicago	IL	60601	W. Robert Reum	312-645-1700	R	3,050	9.9
AutoAlliance International	1 International Dr.	Flat Rock	MI	48134	Phillip G. Spender	734-782-7800	J	3,019*	3.7
TAG Holdings L.L.C.	2075 W Big Beaver	Troy	MI	48084	J. B. Anderson, Jr.	248-822-8056	R	2,904*	2.5
Crane Co.	100 First Stamford	Stamford	CT	06902	Thomas Craney	203-363-7300	P	2,619	12.0
Consolidated Metco Inc.	PO Box 83201	Portland	OR	97283		503-286-5741	R	2,510*	0.1
Pall Corp.	2200 Northern Blvd.	East Hills	NY	11548	Eric Krasnoff	516-484-5400	P	2,250	10.8
DENSO Manufacturing Tennessee	1720 Rbrt C Jackson	Maryville	TN	37801	Mack Hattori	865-982-7000	S	2,231*	2.0
Sequa Corp.	200 Park Ave.	New York	NY	10166	Gail Binderman	212-986-5500	P	2,183	10.2
Affinia Group Inc.	1101 Technology	Ann Arbor	MI	48108		734-827-5400	P	2,160	12.4
Dura Automotive Systems Inc.	2791 Research Dr.	Rochester Hills	MI	48309	Lawrence A. Denton	248-299-7500	P	2,091	15.4
Hayes Lemmerz International	15300 Centennial Dr	Northville	MI	48167	Fred Bentley	734-737-5000	P	2,039	11.0
Cooper Tire and Rubber Co.	701 Lima Ave.	Findlay	OH	45840	Roy V. Armes	419-423-1321	P	2,036	13.6
G-I Holdings Corp.	1361 Alps Rd.	Wayne	NJ	07470	Samuel Heyman	973-628-3000	R	1,970	3.6
ZF Group N American Operations	15811 Centennial Dr	Northville	MI	48168	Julio Caspari	734-416-6200	R	1,949*	5.5
Sypris Technologies Marion	1550 Marion-Agosta	Marion	OH	43301	Jeffrey T. Gill	740-383-2111	S	1,920*	2.6
Hutchinson FTS Inc.	1835 Technology	Troy	MI	48083	Paul Campbell	248-589-7710	R	1,863*	<0.1
ADVICS North America Inc.	45300 Polaris Ct.	Plymouth	MI	48170	Haruhiko Saito	734-414-5100	S	1,810*	<0.1
Regal-Beloit Corp.	200 State St.	Beloit	WI	53511		608-364-8800	P	1,803	17.9
Bose Corp.	The Mountain	Framingham	MA	01701	Amar G. Bose	508-879-7330	R	1,800	8.0
Modine Manufacturing Co.	1500 DeKoven Ave.	Racine	WI	53403	Richard J. Doyle	262-636-1200	P	1,758	7.7
Siemens VDO Automotive Corp.	2400 Executive Hill	Auburn Hills	MI	48326	John Sanderson	248-209-4000	S	1,738*	10.0
Solvay America Inc.	3333 Richmond	Houston	TX	77098	David G. Birney	713-525-6000	S	1,611*	4.0
Neoplan USA Corp.	12015 E 46th Ave.	Denver	CO	80239	Harold Boade	303-451-5305	R	1,610*	<0.1
Hitachi Cable Indiana Inc.	5300 Grant Line Rd.	New Albany	IN	47150	Kenji Nakata	812-945-9011	R	1,590*	<0.1
Actuant Corp.	13000 W Slvr Spring	Butler	WI	53007	Bob Arzbaecher	414-352-4160	P	1,459	6.3
Accuride Corp.	PO Box 15600	Evansville	IN	47716	Terry Keating	812-962-5000	P	1,408	4.6
Inergy Automotive Systems	2710 Bellingham Dr.	Troy	MI	48083	James Squatrito	248-743-5700	R	1,257*	0.2
RBS Global Inc.	4701 W Greenfield	Milwaukee	WI	53214	Robert Hitt	414-643-3000	R	1,256	5.7
EaglePicher Corp.	2424 John Daly Rd.	Inkster	MI	48141	Donald L. Runkle	313-278-5956	R	1,244*	4.2
Remy International Inc.	2902 Enterprise Dr.	Anderson	IN	46013	Thomas J. Snyder	765-778-6499	S	1,218*	7.9
Mark IV Industries Inc.	PO Box 810	Amherst	NY	14226		716-689-4972	R	1,215*	8.1
Adams Rite Manufacturing Co.	260 W Santa Fe St.	Pomona	CA	91767	Peter Adams	909-632-2300	R	1,201*	0.2
Noranda Aluminum Inc.	801 Crescent Centre	Franklin	TN	37067	William Brooks	615-771-5700	R	1,170*	<0.1
Tecumseh Products Co.	100 E Patterson St.	Tecumseh	MI	49286	Edwin Bunker	517-423-8411	P	1,133	10.3
Axiom Automotive Technologies	1 PPG Pl., 3150	Pittsburgh	PA	15222	Greg Gyllstorm	412-545-8100	R	1,110*	1.7
Key Safety Systems Inc.	7000 Nineteen Mile	Sterling Hgts	MI	48314	Jason Luo	586-726-3800	S	1,030	8.7
Spartan Motors Chassis Inc.	1165 Reynolds Rd.	Charlotte	MI	48813	John Sztykiel	517-543-6400	S	1,030*	0.8

Source: Ward's Business Directory of U.S. Private and Public Companies, Volumes 1 and 2, 2008. The company type code used is as follows: P - Public, R - Private, S - Subsidiary, D - Division, J - Joint Venture, A - Affiliate, G - Group. Sales are in millions of dollars, employees are in thousands. An asterisk (*) indicates an estimated sales volume. The symbol < stands for 'less than'. Company names and addresses are truncated, in some cases, to fit into the available space.

MATERIALS CONSUMED

Material	Quantity	Delivered Cost ($ million)
Iron and steel castings (rough and semifinished)	(X)	1,189.2
Aluminum and aluminum-base alloy castings (rough and semifinished)	(X)	95.3
Other nonferrous metal castings, rough or semifinished (inc. aluminum)	(X)	(D)
Steel bars, bar shapes, and plates (exc. castings, forgings, fabr. metal products)	(X)	39.4
Steel sheet and strip (including tinplate)	(X)	43.1
All other steel shapes and forms (exc. castings, forgings, fabr. metal products)	(X)	187.9
Copper and copper-base alloy shapes and forms (exc. castings, forgings, fabr. metal products)	(X)	7.9
Aluminum and aluminum-base alloy shapes and forms (exc. castings, forgings, fabr. metal products)	(X)	80.0
Other nonferrous shapes and forms (exc. castings, forgings, fabricated metal products)	(X)	73.6
Ball and roller bearings (mounted or unmounted)	(X)	(D)
Fabricated plastics products (exc. gaskets, hoses, and belting)	(X)	62.6
Plastics products consumed in the form of sheets, rods, etc.	(X)	(D)
Plastics resins consumed in the form of granules, pellets, etc.	(X)	19.8
Fabricated rubber products (exc. tires, tubes, hoses, belting, and gaskets)	(X)	59.9
Rubber and plastics hose and belting	(X)	23.8
Ceramic raw materials (incl. powders, chemicals, and fibers)	(X)	24.3
Ceramic and ceramic composite parts, components, and accessories	(X)	(D)
Gaskets (all types), and packing and sealing devices	(X)	69.0
Paints, varnishes, stains, lacquers, shellacs, japans, enamels, etc.	(X)	5.3
Glues and adhesives	(X)	6.2
Flexible packaging materials	(X)	10.6
Paper and paperboard containers	(X)	35.0
Spark plugs for internal combustion engines	(X)	(D)
Starting motors for internal combustion engines	(X)	(D)
Ignition harness and cable sets for internal combustion engines	(X)	(D)
All other engine electrical equipment for internal combustion engines	(X)	(D)
Resistors for electronic circuitry	(X)	(D)
Capacitors for electronic circuitry	(X)	(D)
Semiconductors (incl. transistors, diodes, rectifiers, and integrated circuits), for electronic circuitry	(X)	(D)
All other miscellaneous components and accessories for electronic circuitry (exc. tubes)	(X)	27.4
Core parts purchased for use in remanufacturing and rebuilding	(X)	330.3
Printed ciruit boards (without inserted components) for electronic circuitry	(X)	(D)
Metal bolts, nuts, screws, and other screw machine products	(X)	217.0
Other fabricated metal products (exc. fluid power and forgings)	(X)	177.7
Forgings	(X)	185.2
Insulated wire and cable (excluding magnet wire)	(X)	16.4
Magnet wire	(X)	(D)
Mechanical speed changers, gears, and industrial high-speed drives	(X)	(D)
Fluid power pumps, motors, and hydrostatic transmissions	(X)	12.1
Fluid power valves (hydraulic and pneumatic)	(X)	17.1
Fluid power cylinders and rotary actuators (hydraulic and pneumatic)	(X)	40.9
Fluid power hose, tube fittings, and assemblies (hydraulic and pneumatic)	(X)	31.4
Fluid power filters (hydraulic and pneumatic)	(X)	(D)
Other transportation related fluid power products, hydraulic and pneumatic	(X)	1.0
Automotive stampings (inc. body parts, hubcaps, fenders, etc.)	(X)	388.5
Current-carrying wiring devices	(X)	7.3
Other chemicals and allied products	(X)	104.9
All other materials, components, parts, containers, and supplies	(X)	1,603.6
Materials, ingredients, containers, and supplies, nsk	(X)	1,031.8

Source: 2002 *Economic Census*. Explanation of symbols used: (D): Withheld to avoid disclosure of competitive data; na: Not available; (S): Withheld because statistical norms were not met; (X): Not applicable; (Z): Less than half the unit shown; nec: Not elsewhere classified; nsk: Not specified by kind; - : zero; p : 10-19 percent estimated; q : 20-29 percent estimated.

PRODUCT SHARE DETAILS

Product or Product Class Shipments	Mil. $	Product or Product Class Shipments	Mil. $
MOTOR VEHICLE BRAKE SYSTEMS	12,119.2	separately, new	414.8
Motor vehicle brake parts and assemblies, new	**11,486.2**	Motor vehicle air brake power actuation units, new	232.9
Motor vehicle wheel brake and master brake cylinders, sold separately, new	348.9	Motor vehicle hydraulic brake power actuation units, new	462.4
Motor vehicle wheel brake cylinders, sold separately, new	142.4	Motor vehicle vacuum brake power actuation units, new	(D)
Motor vehicle master brake cylinders, sold separately, new	206.5	Automotive brake hose assemblies, new	244.9
		Other motor vehicle brake parts, new	1,832.8
Motor vehicle brake assemblies (drum), including backing plates, shoes, linings (except asbestos), cylinders, etc., sold together, new	2,800.5	Motor vehicle brake parts and assemblies, new, nsk	19.5
		Motor vehicle brake parts and assemblies, rebuilt	**407.4**
Motor vehicle brake assemblies (disc-caliper), including rotors, calipers, pads (except asbestos), cylinders, etc., sold together, new	2,102.6	Motor vehicle brake parts and assemblies, rebuilt	395.0
		Motor vehicle brake shoe assemblies (drum brake), rebuilt	78.7
Motor vehicle brake drums (with or without hub), sold separately, new	484.9	Motor vehicle brake caliper assemblies (disc brake), rebuilt	169.6
Motor vehicle brake rotors-discs (with or without hub), sold separately, new	1,186.9	Motor vehicle brake master cylinders, rebuilt	(D)
		Motor vehicle air brake power actuation units, rebuilt	(D)
Motor vehicle metallic or semimetallic brake linings, except asbestos, new	382.7	Motor vehicle vacuum brake power actuation units, rebuilt	(D)
Other motor vehicle brake parts and assemblies, new	4,160.2	Motor vehicle hydraulic brake power actuation units, rebuilt	(D)
Motor vehicle brake valves, new	(D)	Other rebuilt brake systems and parts	52.9
Motor vehicle brake shoes (with or without lining), sold		Motor vehicle brake parts and assemblies, rebuilt, nsk	12.4
		Motor vehicle brake systems, nsk, total	**225.6**

Source: 2002 *Economic Census*. The values are product shipments in millions of dollars for 2002. Total product shipments may be lower or higher than industry shipments. See Introduction for a full discussion. Values of indented subcategories are summed in the main heading(s). The symbol (D) appears when data are withheld to prevent disclosure of competitive information. The abbreviation nsk stands for 'not specified by kind' and nec for 'not elsewhere classified'. A dash (-) means zero.

INPUTS AND OUTPUTS FOR MOTOR VEHICLE PARTS MANUFACTURING

Economic Sector or Industry Providing Inputs	%	Sector	Economic Sector or Industry Buying Outputs	%	Sector
Compensation of employees	22.8		Light truck & utility vehicles	25.3	Manufg.
Motor vehicle parts	10.7	Manufg.	Automobiles	15.8	Manufg.
Management of companies & enterprises	7.0	Services	Exports of goods & services	13.9	Cap Inv
Wholesale trade	5.3	Trade	Motor vehicle parts	8.5	Manufg.
Iron & steel mills & ferroalloys	5.0	Manufg.	Retail trade	7.4	Trade
Nonferrous metal foundries	2.6	Manufg.	Personal consumption expenditures	4.1	
Ferrous metal foundries	2.4	Manufg.	Automotive repair & maintenance, ex. car washes	2.9	Services
Plate work & fabricated structural products	1.9	Manufg.	Truck transportation	2.2	Util.
Turned products & screws, nuts, & bolts	1.9	Manufg.	General S/L govt. services	2.0	S/L Govt
Machine shops	1.5	Manufg.	Heavy duty trucks	1.9	Manufg.
Plastics products, nec	1.4	Manufg.	Wholesale trade	1.5	Trade
Truck transportation	1.1	Util.	Transit & ground passenger transportation	0.8	Util.
Retail trade	1.0	Trade	Change in private inventories	0.7	In House
Electronic components, nec	0.9	Manufg.	Postal service	0.6	Util.
Custom roll forming	0.9	Manufg.	General Federal government services, defense	0.6	Fed Govt
Coating, engraving, heat treating & allied activities	0.9	Manufg.	Residential structures, nec	0.6	Construct.
Crowns & closures & metal stamping	0.8	Manufg.	Residential permanent site structures	0.6	Construct.
Rubber products, nec	0.7	Manufg.	Nonresidential structures, nec	0.5	Construct.
Semiconductors & related devices	0.7	Manufg.	Lawn & garden equipment	0.4	Manufg.
Plastics packaging materials, film & sheet	0.7	Manufg.	Boat building	0.4	Manufg.
Scientific research & development services	0.7	Services	Construction machinery	0.4	Manufg.
Power generation & supply	0.7	Util.	S/L govt. passenger transit	0.4	S/L Govt
Leather & hide tanning & finishing	0.7	Manufg.	Transportation equipment, nec	0.3	Manufg.
Ball & roller bearings	0.7	Manufg.	Engine equipment, nec	0.3	Manufg.
Valve & fittings other than plumbing	0.6	Manufg.	Food services & drinking places	0.3	Services
Textile & fabric finishing mills	0.6	Manufg.	Waste management & remediation services	0.3	Services
Lessors of nonfinancial assets	0.5	Fin/R.E.	Aircraft	0.3	Manufg.
Fluid power process machinery	0.5	Manufg.	Services to buildings & dwellings	0.3	Services
Taxes on production & imports, less subsidies	0.5		Oil & gas extraction	0.2	Mining
Plastics materials & resins	0.5	Manufg.	Commercial & health care structures	0.2	Construct.
Ornamental & architectural metal products	0.5	Manufg.	Farm machinery & equipment	0.2	Manufg.
Gaskets, packing, & sealing devices	0.5	Manufg.	Management of companies & enterprises	0.2	Services
Securities, commodity contracts, investments	0.5	Fin/R.E.	Truck trailers	0.2	Manufg.
Noncomparable imports	0.5	Foreign	Warehousing & storage	0.2	Util.
Urethane & other foam products (except polystrene)	0.4	Manufg.	Motor vehicle bodies	0.2	Manufg.
Printed circuit assemblies (electronic assemblies)	0.4	Manufg.	Travel trailers & campers	0.2	Manufg.
Alumina refining & primary aluminum production	0.4	Manufg.	Scientific research & development services	0.2	Services
Bare printed circuit boards	0.4	Manufg.	Maintenance/repair of nonresidential structures	0.2	Construct.
Paints & coatings	0.4	Manufg.	Private fixed investment	0.2	
Wiring devices	0.4	Manufg.	Couriers & messengers	0.1	Util.
Fabricated metals, nec	0.4	Manufg.	Individual & family services	0.1	Services
Copper rolling, drawing, extruding, & alloying	0.3	Manufg.	Scenic & sightseeing transport & related services	0.1	Util.
Advertising & related services	0.3	Services	Car washes	0.1	Services
Metal cans, boxes, & other containers (light gauge)	0.3	Manufg.	Automotive equipment rental & leasing	0.1	Fin/R.E.
Real estate	0.3	Fin/R.E.	Crowns & closures & metal stamping	0.1	Manufg.

Continued on next page.

INPUTS AND OUTPUTS FOR MOTOR VEHICLE PARTS MANUFACTURING - Continued

Economic Sector or Industry Providing Inputs	%	Sector	Economic Sector or Industry Buying Outputs	%	Sector
Speed changers, industrial high-speed drives, & gears	0.3	Manufg.	Material handling equipment	0.1	Manufg.
Primary nonferrous metal, ex. copper & aluminum	0.3	Manufg.			
Paperboard containers	0.3	Manufg.			
Maintenance/repair of nonresidential structures	0.3	Construct.			
Gold, silver, & other metal ore	0.3	Mining			
Services to buildings & dwellings	0.2	Services			
Aluminum products from purchased aluminum	0.2	Manufg.			
Nonferrous metal (ex. copper & aluminum) processing	0.2	Manufg.			
Forging, stamping, & sintering, nec	0.2	Manufg.			
Rubber & plastics hose & belting	0.2	Manufg.			
Natural gas distribution	0.2	Util.			
Rail transportation	0.2	Util.			
Monetary authorities/depository credit intermediation	0.2	Fin/R.E.			
Handtools	0.2	Manufg.			
Automotive equipment rental & leasing	0.2	Fin/R.E.			
Professional, scientific, technical services, nec	0.2	Services			
Basic organic chemicals, nec	0.2	Manufg.			
Warehousing & storage	0.2	Util.			
Legal services	0.2	Services			
Food services & drinking places	0.2	Services			
Communication & energy wires & cables	0.2	Manufg.			
Automotive repair & maintenance, ex. car washes	0.2	Services			
Management, scientific, & technical consulting	0.2	Services			
Engine equipment, nec	0.2	Manufg.			
Wood windows & doors & millwork	0.2	Manufg.			
Veneer & plywood	0.2	Manufg.			
Telecommunications	0.2	Services			
Accounting, tax preparation, bookkeeping, & payroll	0.1	Services			
Commercial & industrial equipment repair/maintenance	0.1	Services			
Architectural, engineering, & related services	0.1	Services			
Artificial & synthetic fibers & filaments	0.1	Manufg.			
Air transportation	0.1	Util.			
Cutting tools & machine tool accessories	0.1	Manufg.			
Employment services	0.1	Services			
Chemical products & preparations, nec	0.1	Manufg.			
Data processing, hosting, & related services	0.1	Services			
Specialized design services	0.1	Services			
Relay & industrial controls	0.1	Manufg.			
Business support services	0.1	Services			
Fiber, yarn, & thread mills	0.1	Manufg.			
Hotels & motels, including casino hotels	0.1	Services			
Electronic capacitors, resistors, coils, transformers	0.1	Manufg.			
Wood containers & pallets	0.1	Manufg.			
Waste management & remediation services	0.1	Services			
Springs & wire products	0.1	Manufg.			
Automatic environmental controls	0.1	Manufg.			

Source: Benchmark Input-Output Accounts for the U.S. Economy, 2002, U.S. Department of Commerce, Washington D.C., January 2008. User should note that this Input-Output table is not for this particular narrowly defined industry but for a larger aggregate. Input and Output data for Motor Vehicle Parts Manufacturing include Input and Output data for the Annual Survey of Manufactures' NAICS industries 33631M, 33632M, 336330, 336340, 336350, 336360, 336370, 336391, and 336399. The abbreviation nec stands for 'not elsewhere classified'.

OCCUPATIONS EMPLOYED BY MOTOR VEHICLE PARTS MANUFACTURING

Occupation	% of Total 2006	Change to 2016	Occupation	% of Total 2006	Change to 2016
Team assemblers	15.2	-19.2	Welders, cutters, solderers, & brazers	1.9	-15.3
Cutting, punching, & press machine operators	4.2	-28.4	Molding, coremaking, & casting machine operators	1.8	-28.4
Machinists	3.8	-16.4	Welding, soldering, & brazing machine operators	1.6	-10.5
Inspectors, testers, sorters, samplers, & weighers	3.5	-24.9	Industrial machinery mechanics	1.5	-8.4
First-line supervisors/managers of production workers	3.3	-20.4	Helpers--Production workers	1.5	-20.4
Assemblers & fabricators, nec	3.2	-28.4	Mechanical engineers	1.4	-20.4
Multiple machine tool operators & tenders	2.6	-12.4	Electrical & electronic equipment assemblers	1.4	-36.3
Tool & die makers	2.6	-16.4	Lathe & turning machine tool operators & tenders	1.3	-28.4
Industrial truck & tractor operators	2.6	-28.4	Shipping, receiving, & traffic clerks	1.3	-23.4
Laborers & freight, stock, & material movers, hand	2.1	-28.4	Electricians	1.3	-17.4
Industrial engineers	2.1	-3.3	Grinding, lapping, polishing machine tool operators	1.2	-22.8
Maintenance & repair workers, general	2.0	-20.4	Engine & other machine assemblers	1.1	-20.4
Production workers, nec	2.0	-21.9	Drilling & boring machine tool operators	1.1	-28.4
Computer-controlled machine tool operators	1.9	-12.4	Production, planning, & expediting clerks	1.1	-20.4

Source: Industry-Occupation Matrix, Bureau of Labor Statistics, December 4, 2007. These data are reported based on 4-digit NAICS categories but have been matched to corresponding 6-digit NAICS industry codes. The change reported for each occupation to the year 2016 is a percent of growth or decline as estimated by the Bureau of Labor Statistics. The abbreviation nec stands for 'not elsewhere classified'.

LOCATION BY STATE AND REGIONAL CONCENTRATION

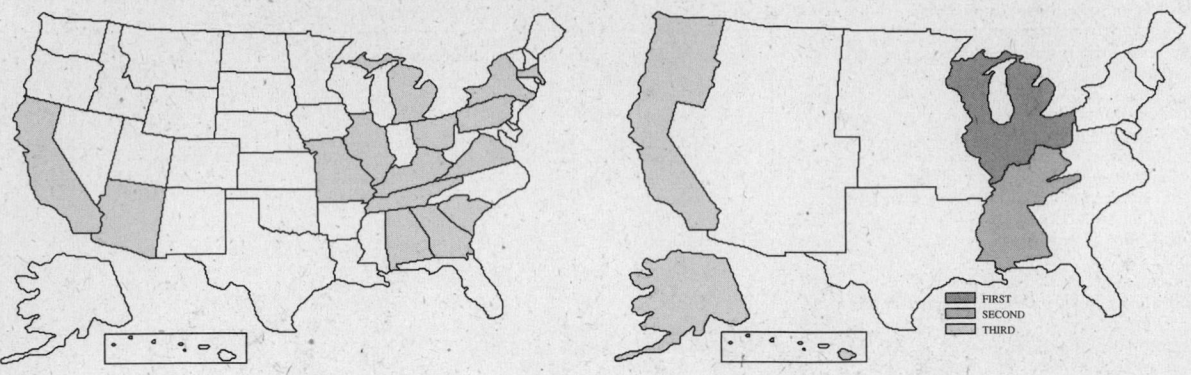

INDUSTRY DATA BY STATE

State	Establish-ments	Shipments			Employment				Cost as % of Shipments	Investment per Employee ($)
		Total ($ mil)	% of U.S.	Per Establ.	Total Number	% of U.S.	Per Establ.	Wages ($/hour)		
Michigan	33	3,039.0	23.0	92,089.8	5,298	12.8	161	21.07	48.2	18,403
Ohio	33	2,679.8	20.3	81,204.6	8,944	21.6	271	18.20	60.7	12,543
South Carolina	8	1,600.5	12.1	200,059.6	4,396	10.6	550	18.42	55.9	15,081
Kentucky	15	1,060.6	8.0	70,704.8	3,817	9.2	254	11.92	47.9	22,447
Tennessee	15	1,001.5	7.6	66,766.9	3,160	7.6	211	22.73	59.0	11,660
Illinois	14	460.7	3.5	32,906.0	1,999	4.8	143	14.57	63.8	3,597
Missouri	14	357.1	2.7	25,509.8	2,243	5.4	160	13.47	46.8	9,127
Pennsylvania	8	267.2	2.0	33,406.0	1,468	3.5	183	18.51	48.5	7,822
Alabama	5	194.8	1.5	38,952.8	956	2.3	191	13.52	56.9	2,735
Virginia	7	189.1	1.4	27,007.6	1,316	3.2	188	14.58	39.6	7,157
California	26	165.1	1.3	6,351.4	756	1.8	29	11.75	65.3	5,024
Georgia	5	118.7	0.9	23,744.0	883	2.1	177	11.94	38.4	9,933
New York	10	61.7	0.5	6,168.1	367	0.9	37	13.01	50.1	7,398
Arizona	7	31.4	0.2	4,491.0	150	0.4	21	13.39	54.1	7,680
Massachusetts	6	27.8	0.2	4,625.3	254	0.6	42	11.98	56.2	1,079

Source: 2002 *Economic Census*. The states are in descending order of shipments or establishments (if shipment data are missing for the majority). The symbol (D) appears when data are withheld to prevent disclosure of competitive information. States marked with (D) are sorted by number of establishments. A dash (-) indicates that the data element cannot be calculated. Data may not show all states active in the NAICS category. All data available at the time of publication are shown.

NAICS 336350 - MOTOR VEHICLE TRANSMISSION AND POWER TRAIN PARTS

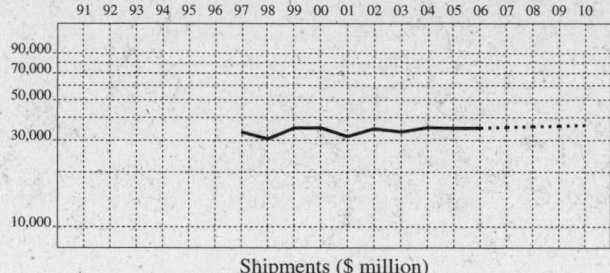

Shipments ($ million)

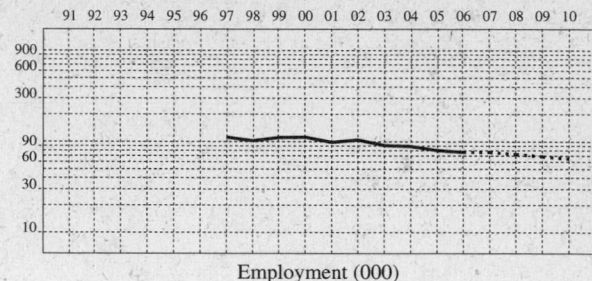

Employment (000)

GENERAL STATISTICS

Year	Com-panies	Establishments		Employment			Compensation		Production ($ million)			
		Total	with 20 or more employees	Total (000)	Production Workers (000)	Hours (Mil)	Payroll ($ mil)	Wages ($/hr)	Cost of Materials	Value Added by Manufacture	Value of Shipments	Capital Invest.
1997	429	524	258	112.0	88.9	197.0	5,516.8	21.51	19,567.9	13,711.1	33,288.1	1,876.8
1998		550	259	102.5	84.6	192.9	5,183.0	21.35	18,948.6	11,807.1	30,516.0	2,247.3
1999		532	262	111.3	91.2	208.7	5,913.3	22.82	20,303.0	14,675.7	35,003.9	1,924.7
2000		509	261	112.2	91.9	202.8	6,147.0	24.30	20,777.6	14,533.1	35,102.6	1,808.5
2001		507	253	98.8	79.3	171.2	5,178.1	23.48	17,775.2	13,304.8	31,466.0	1,619.0
2002	433	542	260	104.7	85.7	183.5	5,649.6	24.47	20,542.6	14,276.4	34,725.6	1,561.5
2003		536	265	91.1	74.1	161.1	5,493.9	26.92	20,032.6	13,593.4	33,360.7	1,192.8
2004		534	265	89.2	72.2	162.6	5,863.8	28.35	21,421.7	13,620.8	35,239.7	1,327.2
2005		533	262	80.5	66.2	147.3	5,200.9	27.98	20,844.2	14,169.5	34,943.5	1,367.1
2006		532P	264P	76.9	62.7	138.8	5,193.1	29.73	19,883.8	15,004.7	34,973.7	1,617.3
2007		533P	265P	76.7P	62.8P	137.0P	5,383.2P	30.32P	20,111.7P	15,176.7P	35,374.5P	1,207.9P
2008		533P	265P	72.8P	59.7P	129.9P	5,355.8P	31.27P	20,268.0P	15,294.6P	35,649.5P	1,126.8P
2009		534P	266P	68.9P	56.7P	122.7P	5,328.3P	32.22P	20,424.4P	15,412.6P	35,924.5P	1,045.6P
2010		534P	266P	65.1P	53.6P	115.5P	5,300.9P	33.17P	20,580.7P	15,530.6P	36,199.5P	964.5P

Sources: 1997 and 2002 *Economic Census*; other years, up to 2006, are from *Annual Survey of Manufactures*. Establishment counts for non-Census years are from *County Business Patterns*; 1997 and 2002 values are from the 1997 and 2002 censuses, respectively. 'P's show projections by the editors.

INDICES OF CHANGE

Year	Com-panies	Establishments		Employment			Compensation		Production ($ million)			
		Total	with 20 or more employees	Total (000)	Production Workers (000)	Hours (Mil)	Payroll ($ mil)	Wages ($/hr)	Cost of Materials	Value Added by Manufacture	Value of Shipments	Capital Invest.
1997	99	97	99	107	104	107	98	88	95	96	96	120
1998		101	100	98	99	105	92	87	92	83	88	144
1999		98	101	106	106	114	105	93	99	103	101	123
2000		94	100	107	107	111	109	99	101	102	101	116
2001		94	97	94	93	93	92	96	87	93	91	104
2002	100	100	100	100	100	100	100	100	100	100	100	100
2003		99	102	87	86	88	97	110	98	95	96	76
2004		99	102	85	84	89	104	116	104	95	101	85
2005		98	101	77	77	80	92	114	101	99	101	88
2006		98P	101P	73	73	76	92	121	97	105	101	104
2007		98P	102P	73P	73P	75P	95P	124P	98P	106P	102P	77P
2008		98P	102P	70P	70P	71P	95P	128P	99P	107P	103P	72P
2009		98P	102P	66P	66P	67P	94P	132P	99P	108P	103P	67P
2010		99P	102P	62P	63P	63P	94P	136P	100P	109P	104P	62P

Sources: Same as General Statistics. Values reflect change from the base year, 2002. Values above 100 mean greater than 2002, values below 100 mean less than 2002, and the values of 100 in other years means the same as 2002. 'P's show projections by the editors.

SELECTED RATIOS

For 2002	Avg. of All Manufact.	Analyzed Industry	Index	For 2002	Avg. of All Manufact.	Analyzed Industry	Index
Employees per Establishment	42	193	460	Value Added per Production Worker	182,367	166,586	91
Payroll per Establishment	1,639,184	10,423,616	636	Cost per Establishment	5,769,015	37,901,476	657
Payroll per Employee	39,053	53,960	138	Cost per Employee	137,446	196,204	143
Production Workers per Establishment	30	158	536	Cost per Production Worker	195,506	239,704	123
Wages per Establishment	694,845	8,284,585	1,192	Shipments per Establishment	11,158,348	64,069,373	574
Wages per Production Worker	23,548	52,395	223	Shipments per Employee	265,847	331,668	125
Hours per Production Worker	1,980	2,141	108	Shipments per Production Worker	378,144	405,200	107
Wages per Hour	11.89	24.47	206	Investment per Establishment	361,338	2,880,996	797
Value Added per Establishment	5,381,325	26,340,221	489	Investment per Employee	8,609	14,914	173
Value Added per Employee	128,210	136,355	106	Investment per Production Worker	12,245	18,221	149

Sources: Same as General Statistics. The 'Average of All Manufacturing' column represents the average of all manufacturing industries reported for the most recent complete year available. The Index shows the relationship between the Average and the Analyzed Industry. For example, 100 means that they are equal; 500 that the Analyzed Industry is five times the average; 50 means that the Analyzed Industry is half the national average. The abbreviation 'na' is used to show that data are 'not available'. Ratios shown for 2002, the last complete census year.

LEADING COMPANIES   Number shown: 75   Total sales ($ mil): 785,184   Total employment (000): 1,861.6

Company Name	Address				CEO Name	Phone	Co. Type	Sales ($ mil)	Empl. (000)
General Motors Corp.	300 Renaissance Ctr	Detroit	MI	48265		313-556-5000	P	181,122	266.0
Ford Motor Co.	1 American Rd.	Dearborn	MI	48126		313-322-3000	P	172,455	246.0
Chrysler L.L.C.	1000 Chrysler Dr.	Auburn Hills	MI	48326	Thomas W. LaSorda	248-576-5741	S	45,237*	84.4
Honeywell International Inc.	PO Box 4000	Morristown	NJ	07962	Adriane M. Brown	973-455-2000	P	34,589	122.0
ArvinMeritor OE L.L.C.	950 W. 450 S, Bldg.	Columbus	IN	47201	C. G. McClure Jr.	812-341-2000	S	23,491*	32.0
Delphi Corp.	5725 Delphi Dr.	Troy	MI	48098	Voker J. Barth	248-813-2000	P	22,383	169.5
Lear Corp.	PO Box 5008	Southfield	MI	48086	Jim Brackenbury	248-447-1500	P	15,995	91.0
TRW Automotive Holdings Inc.	12001 Tech Cntr Dr.	Livonia	MI	48150		734-855-2600	P	14,702	66.3
Textron Inc.	40 Westminster St.	Providence	RI	02903		401-421-2800	P	13,225	44.0
Cummins Inc.	PO Box 3005	Columbus	IN	47202		812-377-5000	P	13,048	37.8
Eaton Corp.	1111 Superior Ave.	Cleveland	OH	44114		216-523-5000	P	13,033	60.0
Visteon Corp.	1 Village Center Dr	Van Buren Twp	MI	48111		313-755-2800	P	11,266	41.5
Parker Hannifin Corp.	6035 Parkland Blvd.	Cleveland	OH	44124	Lee Banks	216-896-3000	P	10,718	57.3
Acument Global Technologies	840 W Long Lake	Troy	MI	48098	Joseph Gray	248-813-6329	S	10,080*	9.0
ITT Corp.	4 W Red Oak Ln.	White Plains	NY	10604		914-641-2000	P	9,003	39.7
Dana Corp.	PO Box 1000	Toledo	OH	43697	Michael J. Burns	419-535-4500	P	8,504	45.0
Neapco L.L.C.	PO Box 399	Pottstown	PA	19464		610-323-6000	R	7,580*	0.3
Trane Inc.	PO Box 6820	Piscataway	NJ	08855		732-980-6000	P	7,450	29.6
Triangle Suspension Systems	PO Box 425	Du Bois	PA	15801	Greg Maffia	814-375-7211	R	7,000*	0.2
Perfection Hy-Test Company	100 Perfection Way	Timmonsville	SC	29161		843-326-5544	R	7,000*	0.2
Penn Machine Co.	106 Station St.	Johnstown	PA	15905	H Wiegand	814-288-1547	R	7,000*	<0.1
Federal-Mogul Corp.	PO Box 1966	Detroit	MI	48235	Jose Maria Alapont	248-354-7700	P	6,914	43.1
Robert Bosch Corp.	2800 S 25th Ave.	Broadview	IL	60155	Kurt W. Liedtke	708-865-5200	S	6,782*	25.0
ArvinMeritor Inc.	2135 W Maple Rd.	Troy	MI	48084		248-435-1000	P	6,449	18.0
Tenneco Inc.	500 N Field Dr.	Lake Forest	IL	60045		847-482-5000	P	6,184	21.0
Toyota Motor Mfg. N America	25 Atlantic Ave.	Erlanger	KY	41018	Masamoto Amezawa	859-746-4000	S	6,120*	7.5
Guardian Industries Corp.	2300 Harmon Rd.	Auburn Hills	MI	48326	William M. Davidson	248-340-1800	R	5,330	19.0
BorgWarner Inc.	3850 Hamlin Rd.	Auburn Hills	MI	48326		248-754-9200	P	5,329	17.7
Autoliv ASP Inc.	3350 Airport Rd.	Ogden	UT	84405	Leonard Barton	801-625-4800	S	5,301*	3.7
Carlisle Tire and Wheel Co.	23 Windham Blvd.	Aiken	SC	29805	Barry Littrell	803-643-2900	S	4,822*	0.6
Karl Schmidt Unisia Inc.	1731 Industrial Pky	Marinette	WI	54143	Frank Pohlmann	715-732-0181	R	4,640*	0.9
Pioneer Automotive Tech.	100 S Pioneer Blvd.	Springboro	OH	45066	Steve Moerner	937-746-6600	R	4,610*	0.3
Toledo Trans-Kit Inc.	13515 Ballnyn Corp.	Charlotte	NC	28277	C. J. Kearney	704-752-4400	S	4,372	23.8
Mack Trucks Inc.	PO Box M	Allentown	PA	18105		610-709-3011	R	4,324*	0.8
New United Motor Manufacturing	45500 Fremont	Fremont	CA	94538	Bruce Walker	510-498-5500	J	4,080*	5.0
Kalmar Industries USA L.L.C.	415 E Dundee St.	Ottawa	KS	66067		785-242-2200	R	3,320*	0.3
American Axle & Mfg Holdings	1 Dauch Dr.	Detroit	MI	48211	Richard E. Dauch	313-974-2000	P	3,248	10.0
Hi-Stat Manufacturing Company	28001 Cabot Dr.	Novi	MI	48377	John Corey	248-489-9300	D	3,194*	5.0
Amsted Industries Inc.	2 Prudential Plaza	Chicago	IL	60601	W. Robert Reum	312-645-1700	R	3,050	9.9
AutoAlliance International	1 International Dr.	Flat Rock	MI	48134	Phillip G. Spender	734-782-7800	J	3,019*	3.7
TAG Holdings L.L.C.	2075 W Big Beaver	Troy	MI	48084	J. B. Anderson, Jr.	248-822-8056	R	2,904*	2.5
Crane Co.	100 First Stamford	Stamford	CT	06902	Thomas Craney	203-363-7300	P	2,619	12.0
Consolidated Metco Inc.	PO Box 83201	Portland	OR	97283		503-286-5741	R	2,510*	0.1
Pall Corp.	2200 Northern Blvd.	East Hills	NY	11548	Eric Krasnoff	516-484-5400	P	2,250	10.8
DENSO Manufacturing Tennessee	1720 Rbrt C Jackson	Maryville	TN	37801	Mack Hattori	865-982-7000	S	2,231*	2.0
Sequa Corp.	200 Park Ave.	New York	NY	10166	Gail Binderman	212-986-5500	P	2,183	10.2
Affinia Group Inc.	1101 Technology	Ann Arbor	MI	48108		734-827-5400	P	2,160	12.4
Dura Automotive Systems Inc.	2791 Research Dr.	Rochester Hills	MI	48309	Lawrence A. Denton	248-299-7500	P	2,091	15.4
Hayes Lemmerz International	15300 Centennial Dr	Northville	MI	48167	Fred Bentley	734-737-5000	P	2,039	11.0
Cooper Tire and Rubber Co.	701 Lima Ave.	Findlay	OH	45840	Roy V. Armes	419-423-1321	P	2,036	13.6
ZF Group N American Operations	15811 Centennial Dr	Northville	MI	48168	Julio Caspari	734-416-6200	R	1,949*	5.5
Sypris Technologies Marion	1550 Marion-Agosta	Marion	OH	43301	Jeffrey T. Gill	740-383-2111	S	1,920*	2.6
Hutchinson FTS Inc.	1835 Technology	Troy	MI	48083	Paul Campbell	248-589-7710	R	1,863*	<0.1
ADVICS North America Inc.	45300 Polaris Ct.	Plymouth	MI	48170	Haruhiko Saito	734-414-5100	S	1,810*	<0.1
Regal-Beloit Corp.	200 State St.	Beloit	WI	53511		608-364-8800	P	1,803	17.9
Bose Corp.	The Mountain	Framingham	MA	01701	Amar G. Bose	508-879-7330	R	1,800	8.0
Modine Manufacturing Co.	1500 DeKoven Ave.	Racine	WI	53403	Richard J. Doyle	262-636-1200	P	1,758	7.7
Siemens VDO Automotive Corp.	2400 Executive Hill	Auburn Hills	MI	48326	John Sanderson	248-209-4000	S	1,738*	10.0
Solvay America Inc.	3333 Richmond	Houston	TX	77098	David G. Birney	713-525-6000	S	1,611*	4.0
Neoplan USA Corp.	12015 E 46th Ave.	Denver	CO	80239	Harold Boade	303-451-5305	R	1,610*	<0.1
Hitachi Cable Indiana Inc.	5300 Grant Line Rd.	New Albany	IN	47150	Kenji Nakata	812-945-9011	R	1,590*	<0.1
Actuant Corp.	13000 W Slvr Spring	Butler	WI	53007	Bob Arzbaecher	414-352-4160	P	1,459	6.3
Accuride Corp.	PO Box 15600	Evansville	IN	47716	Terry Keating	812-962-5000	P	1,408	4.6
Inergy Automotive Systems	2710 Bellingham Dr.	Troy	MI	48083	James Squatrito	248-743-5700	R	1,257*	0.2
RBS Global Inc.	4701 W Greenfield	Milwaukee	WI	53214	Robert Hitt	414-643-3000	R	1,256	5.7
EaglePicher Corp.	2424 John Daly Rd.	Inkster	MI	48141	Donald L. Runkle	313-278-5956	R	1,244*	4.2
Remy International Inc.	2902 Enterprise Dr.	Anderson	IN	46013	Thomas J. Synder	765-778-6499	S	1,218*	7.9
Mark IV Industries Inc.	PO Box 810	Amherst	NY	14226		716-689-4972	R	1,215*	8.1
Adams Rite Manufacturing Co.	260 W Santa Fe St.	Pomona	CA	91767	Peter Adams	909-632-2300	R	1,201*	0.3
Noranda Aluminum Inc.	801 Crescent Centre	Franklin	TN	37067	William Brooks	615-771-5700	R	1,170*	<0.1
Tecumseh Products Co.	100 E Patterson St.	Tecumseh	MI	49286	Edwin Bunker	517-423-8411	P	1,133	10.3
Axiom Automotive Technologies	1 PPG Pl., 3150	Pittsburgh	PA	15222	Greg Gyllstorm	412-545-8100	R	1,110*	1.7
Key Safety Systems Inc.	7000 Nineteen Mile	Sterling Hgts	MI	48314	Jason Luo	586-726-3800	S	1,030*	8.7
Spartan Motors Chassis Inc.	1165 Reynolds Rd.	Charlotte	MI	48813	John Sztykiel	517-543-6400	S	1,030*	0.8
Zf Lemforder Corp.	15811 Centennial Dr	Northville	MI	48168	Reinhard Buhl	734-416-6200	R	1,009*	<0.1

Source: Ward's Business Directory of U.S. Private and Public Companies, Volumes 1 and 2, 2008. The company type code used is as follows: P - Public, R - Private, S - Subsidiary, D - Division, J - Joint Venture, A - Affiliate, G - Group. Sales are in millions of dollars, employees are in thousands. An asterisk (*) indicates an estimated sales volume. The symbol < stands for 'less than'. Company names and addresses are truncated, in some cases, to fit into the available space.

MATERIALS CONSUMED

Material	Quantity	Delivered Cost ($ million)
Iron and steel castings (rough and semifinished)	(X)	2,348.1
Aluminum and aluminum-base alloy castings (rough and semifinished)	(X)	1,444.4
Other nonferrous metal castings, rough or semifinished (inc. aluminum)	(X)	(D)
Steel bars, bar shapes, and plates (exc. castings, forgings, fabr. metal products)	(X)	475.9
Steel sheet and strip (including tinplate)	(X)	167.7
All other steel shapes and forms (exc. castings, forgings, fabr. metal products)	(X)	604.8
Copper and copper-base alloy shapes and forms (exc. castings, forgings, fabr. metal products)	(X)	15.1
Aluminum and aluminum-base alloy shapes and forms (exc. castings, forgings, fabr. metal products)	(X)	149.1
Other nonferrous shapes and forms (exc. castings, forgings, fabricated metal products)	(X)	(D)
Ball and roller bearings (mounted or unmounted)	(X)	379.6
Fabricated plastics products (exc. gaskets, hoses, and belting)	(X)	99.2
Plastics products consumed in the form of sheets, rods, etc.	(X)	11.2
Plastics resins consumed in the form of granules, pellets, etc.	(X)	26.7
Fabricated rubber products (exc. tires, tubes, hoses, belting, and gaskets)	(X)	53.8
Rubber and plastics hose and belting	(X)	(D)
Ceramic raw materials (incl. powders, chemicals, and fibers)	(X)	(D)
Ceramic and ceramic composite parts, components, and accessories	(X)	(D)
Gaskets (all types), and packing and sealing devices	(X)	129.1
Paints, varnishes, stains, lacquers, shellacs, japans, enamels, etc.	(X)	(D)
Glues and adhesives	(X)	6.6
Flexible packaging materials	(X)	6.4
Paper and paperboard containers	(X)	27.5
Starting motors for internal combustion engines	(X)	(D)
Ignition harness and cable sets for internal combustion engines	(X)	(D)
All other engine electrical equipment for internal combustion engines	(X)	79.9
Resistors for electronic circuitry	(X)	(D)
Capacitors for electronic circuitry	(X)	(D)
Semiconductors (incl. transistors, diodes, rectifiers, and integrated circuits), for electronic circuitry	(X)	(D)
All other miscellaneous components and accessories for electronic circuitry (exc. tubes)	(X)	531.8
Core parts purchased for use in remanufacturing and rebuilding	(X)	877.4
Printed ciruit boards (without inserted components) for electronic circuitry	(X)	0.6
Metal bolts, nuts, screws, and other screw machine products	(X)	405.7
Other fabricated metal products (exc. fluid power and forgings)	(X)	2,939.3
Forgings	(X)	1,377.0
Insulated wire and cable (excluding magnet wire)	(X)	(D)
Magnet wire	(X)	4.5
Mechanical speed changers, gears, and industrial high-speed drives	(X)	492.8
Fluid power pumps, motors, and hydrostatic transmissions	(X)	(D)
Fluid power valves (hydraulic and pneumatic)	(X)	55.0
Fluid power cylinders and rotary actuators (hydraulic and pneumatic)	(X)	0.8
Fluid power hose, tube fittings, and assemblies (hydraulic and pneumatic)	(X)	23.9
Fluid power filters (hydraulic and pneumatic)	(X)	15.6
Other transportation related fluid power products, hydraulic and pneumatic	(X)	(D)
Automotive stampings (inc. body parts, hubcaps, fenders, etc.)	(X)	608.9
Current-carrying wiring devices	(X)	162.8
Other chemicals and allied products	(X)	51.3
All other materials, components, parts, containers, and supplies	(X)	3,733.4
Materials, ingredients, containers, and supplies, nsk	(X)	700.7

Source: 2002 *Economic Census*. Explanation of symbols used: (D): Withheld to avoid disclosure of competitive data; na: Not available; (S): Withheld because statistical norms were not met; (X): Not applicable; (Z): Less than half the unit shown; nec: Not elsewhere classified; nsk: Not specified by kind; - : zero; p : 10-19 percent estimated; q : 20-29 percent estimated.

PRODUCT SHARE DETAILS

Product or Product Class Shipments	Mil. $	Product or Product Class Shipments	Mil. $
MOTOR VEHICLE TRANSMISSIONS AND POWER TRAIN PARTS	34,639.9	Motor vehicle clutch disc and facing assemblies, new	746.8
Motor vehicle drive train components, except wheels and brakes, new	**33,342.1**	Motor vehicle gear shifters, new	220.3
Car and light truck transmissions (except auxiliary and parts), new	10,540.4	Motor vehicle drive shafts, new	1,997.7
		Motor vehicle universal joints, new	182.3
		Motor vehicle wheel hubs, sold separately, new	532.3
Car and light truck manual transmissions (except auxiliary and parts), new	1,565.1	Other motor vehicle drive train components, except wheels and brakes, new	1,538.6
Car and light truck automatic transmissions (except auxiliary and parts), new	8,975.3	Motor vehicle drive train components, new, nsk	92.4
		Motor vehicle drive train components, rebuilt	**885.8**
Heavy truck and bus transmissions, new	3,128.7	Motor vehicle drive drain components, rebuilt	880.2
Heavy truck and bus manual transmissions (except auxiliary and parts), new	(D)	Motor vehicle clutch discs and pressure plates, rebuilt	28.5
Heavy truck and bus automatic transmissions (except auxiliary and parts), new	(D)	Car and light truck automatic transmissions, including drive lines and axles, rebuilt	668.7
Parts for manual and automatic transmissions, new	3,200.7	Car and light truck manual (standard) transmissions, including drive lines and axles, rebuilt	(D)
Parts for manual transmissions, new	413.8	Heavy truck and bus transmissions, including drive lines and axles, rebuilt	(D)
Parts for automatic transmissions, new	2,786.9	Other rebuilt transmission parts including clutch and facing assemblies, gear shifters, universal joints, and wheel hubs	46.5
Motor vehicle axles and axle parts, new	10,921.1		
Motor vehicle axles, new	9,577.1	Other rebuilt drive train parts and components	59.8
Motor vehicle axle parts, new	1,344.0	Motor vehicle drive train components, rebuilt, nsk	5.6
Other motor vehicle drive train components, except wheels and brakes, new	5,459.0	**Motor vehicle transmissions and power train parts, nsk, total**	**411.9**
Motor vehicle transaxles, new	241.0		

Source: 2002 *Economic Census*. The values are product shipments in millions of dollars for 2002. Total product shipments may be lower or higher than industry shipments. See Introduction for a full discussion. Values of indented subcategories are summed in the main heading(s). The symbol (D) appears when data are withheld to prevent disclosure of competitive information. The abbreviation nsk stands for 'not specified by kind' and nec for 'not elsewhere classified'. A dash (-) means zero.

INPUTS AND OUTPUTS FOR MOTOR VEHICLE PARTS MANUFACTURING

Economic Sector or Industry Providing Inputs	%	Sector	Economic Sector or Industry Buying Outputs	%	Sector
Compensation of employees	22.8		Light truck & utility vehicles	25.3	Manufg.
Motor vehicle parts	10.7	Manufg.	Automobiles	15.8	Manufg.
Management of companies & enterprises	7.0	Services	Exports of goods & services	13.9	Cap Inv
Wholesale trade	5.3	Trade	Motor vehicle parts	8.5	Manufg.
Iron & steel mills & ferroalloys	5.0	Manufg.	Retail trade	7.4	Trade
Nonferrous metal foundries	2.6	Manufg.	Personal consumption expenditures	4.1	
Ferrous metal foundries	2.4	Manufg.	Automotive repair & maintenance, ex. car washes	2.9	Services
Plate work & fabricated structural products	1.9	Manufg.	Truck transportation	2.2	Util.
Turned products & screws, nuts, & bolts	1.9	Manufg.	General S/L govt. services	2.0	S/L Govt
Machine shops	1.5	Manufg.	Heavy duty trucks	1.9	Manufg.
Plastics products, nec	1.4	Manufg.	Wholesale trade	1.5	Trade
Truck transportation	1.1	Util.	Transit & ground passenger transportation	0.8	Util.
Retail trade	1.0	Trade	Change in private inventories	0.7	In House
Electronic components, nec	0.9	Manufg.	Postal service	0.6	Util.
Custom roll forming	0.9	Manufg.	General Federal government services, defense	0.6	Fed Govt
Coating, engraving, heat treating & allied activities	0.9	Manufg.	Residential structures, nec	0.6	Construct.
Crowns & closures & metal stamping	0.8	Manufg.	Residential permanent site structures	0.6	Construct.
Rubber products, nec	0.7	Manufg.	Nonresidential structures, nec	0.5	Construct.
Semiconductors & related devices	0.7	Manufg.	Lawn & garden equipment	0.4	Manufg.
Plastics packaging materials, film & sheet	0.7	Manufg.	Boat building	0.4	Manufg.
Scientific research & development services	0.7	Services	Construction machinery	0.4	Manufg.
Power generation & supply	0.7	Util.	S/L govt. passenger transit	0.4	S/L Govt
Leather & hide tanning & finishing	0.7	Manufg.	Transportation equipment, nec	0.3	Manufg.
Ball & roller bearings	0.7	Manufg.	Engine equipment, nec	0.3	Manufg.
Valve & fittings other than plumbing	0.6	Manufg.	Food services & drinking places	0.3	Services
Textile & fabric finishing mills	0.6	Manufg.	Waste management & remediation services	0.3	Services
Lessors of nonfinancial assets	0.5	Fin/R.E.	Aircraft	0.3	Manufg.
Fluid power process machinery	0.5	Manufg.	Services to buildings & dwellings	0.3	Services
Taxes on production & imports, less subsidies	0.5		Oil & gas extraction	0.2	Mining
Plastics materials & resins	0.5	Manufg.	Commercial & health care structures	0.2	Construct.
Ornamental & architectural metal products	0.5	Manufg.	Farm machinery & equipment	0.2	Manufg.
Gaskets, packing, & sealing devices	0.5	Manufg.	Management of companies & enterprises	0.2	Services
Securities, commodity contracts, investments	0.5	Fin/R.E.	Truck trailers	0.2	Manufg.
Noncomparable imports	0.5	Foreign	Warehousing & storage	0.2	Util.
Urethane & other foam products (except polystrene)	0.4	Manufg.	Motor vehicle bodies	0.2	Manufg.
Printed circuit assemblies (electronic assembiles)	0.4	Manufg.	Travel trailers & campers	0.2	Manufg.
Alumina refining & primary aluminum production	0.4	Manufg.	Scientific research & development services	0.2	Services
Bare printed circuit boards	0.4	Manufg.	Maintenance/repair of nonresidential structures	0.2	Construct.
Paints & coatings	0.4	Manufg.	Private fixed investment	0.2	
Wiring devices	0.4	Manufg.	Couriers & messengers	0.1	Util.
Fabricated metals, nec	0.4	Manufg.	Individual & family services	0.1	Services
Copper rolling, drawing, extruding, & alloying	0.3	Manufg.	Scenic & sightseeing transport & related services	0.1	Util.
Advertising & related services	0.3	Services	Car washes	0.1	Services
Metal cans, boxes, & other containers (light gauge)	0.3	Manufg.	Automotive equipment rental & leasing	0.1	Fin/R.E.
Real estate	0.3	Fin/R.E.	Crowns & closures & metal stamping	0.1	Manufg.

Continued on next page.

INPUTS AND OUTPUTS FOR MOTOR VEHICLE PARTS MANUFACTURING - Continued

Economic Sector or Industry Providing Inputs	%	Sector	Economic Sector or Industry Buying Outputs	%	Sector
Speed changers, industrial high-speed drives, & gears	0.3	Manufg.	Material handling equipment	0.1	Manufg.
Primary nonferrous metal, ex. copper & aluminum	0.3	Manufg.			
Paperboard containers	0.3	Manufg.			
Maintenance/repair of nonresidential structures	0.3	Construct.			
Gold, silver, & other metal ore	0.3	Mining			
Services to buildings & dwellings	0.2	Services			
Aluminum products from purchased aluminum	0.2	Manufg.			
Nonferrous metal (ex. copper & aluminum) processing	0.2	Manufg.			
Forging, stamping, & sintering, nec	0.2	Manufg.			
Rubber & plastics hose & belting	0.2	Manufg.			
Natural gas distribution	0.2	Util.			
Rail transportation	0.2	Util.			
Monetary authorities/depository credit intermediation	0.2	Fin/R.E.			
Handtools	0.2	Manufg.			
Automotive equipment rental & leasing	0.2	Fin/R.E.			
Professional, scientific, technical services, nec	0.2	Services			
Basic organic chemicals, nec	0.2	Manufg.			
Warehousing & storage	0.2	Util.			
Legal services	0.2	Services			
Food services & drinking places	0.2	Services			
Communication & energy wires & cables	0.2	Manufg.			
Automotive repair & maintenance, ex. car washes	0.2	Services			
Management, scientific, & technical consulting	0.2	Services			
Engine equipment, nec	0.2	Manufg.			
Wood windows & doors & millwork	0.2	Manufg.			
Veneer & plywood	0.2	Manufg.			
Telecommunications	0.2	Services			
Accounting, tax preparation, bookkeeping, & payroll	0.1	Services			
Commercial & industrial equipment repair/maintenance	0.1	Services			
Architectural, engineering, & related services	0.1	Services			
Artificial & synthetic fibers & filaments	0.1	Manufg.			
Air transportation	0.1	Util.			
Cutting tools & machine tool accessories	0.1	Manufg.			
Employment services	0.1	Services			
Chemical products & preparations, nec	0.1	Manufg.			
Data processing, hosting, & related services	0.1	Services			
Specialized design services	0.1	Services			
Relay & industrial controls	0.1	Manufg.			
Business support services	0.1	Services			
Fiber, yarn, & thread mills	0.1	Manufg.			
Hotels & motels, including casino hotels	0.1	Services			
Electronic capacitors, resistors, coils, transformers	0.1	Manufg.			
Wood containers & pallets	0.1	Manufg.			
Waste management & remediation services	0.1	Services			
Springs & wire products	0.1	Manufg.			
Automatic environmental controls	0.1	Manufg.			

Source: Benchmark Input-Output Accounts for the U.S. Economy, 2002, U.S. Department of Commerce, Washington D.C., January 2008. User should note that this Input-Output table is not for this particular narrowly defined industry but for a larger aggregate. Input and Output data for Motor Vehicle Parts Manufacturing include Input and Output data for the Annual Survey of Manufactures' NAICS industries 33631M, 33632M, 336330, 336340, 336350, 336360, 336370, 336391, and 336399. The abbreviation nec stands for 'not elsewhere classified'.

OCCUPATIONS EMPLOYED BY MOTOR VEHICLE PARTS MANUFACTURING

Occupation	% of Total 2006	Change to 2016	Occupation	% of Total 2006	Change to 2016
Team assemblers	15.2	-19.2	Welders, cutters, solderers, & brazers	1.9	-15.3
Cutting, punching, & press machine operators	4.2	-28.4	Molding, coremaking, & casting machine operators	1.8	-28.4
Machinists	3.8	-16.4	Welding, soldering, & brazing machine operators	1.6	-10.5
Inspectors, testers, sorters, samplers, & weighers	3.5	-24.9	Industrial machinery mechanics	1.5	-8.4
First-line supervisors/managers of production workers	3.3	-20.4	Helpers--Production workers	1.5	-20.4
Assemblers & fabricators, nec	3.2	-28.4	Mechanical engineers	1.4	-20.4
Multiple machine tool operators & tenders	2.6	-12.4	Electrical & electronic equipment assemblers	1.4	-36.3
Tool & die makers	2.6	-16.4	Lathe & turning machine tool operators & tenders	1.3	-28.4
Industrial truck & tractor operators	2.6	-28.4	Shipping, receiving, & traffic clerks	1.3	-23.4
Laborers & freight, stock, & material movers, hand	2.1	-28.4	Electricians	1.3	-17.4
Industrial engineers	2.1	-3.3	Grinding, lapping, polishing machine tool operators	1.2	-22.8
Maintenance & repair workers, general	2.0	-20.4	Engine & other machine assemblers	1.1	-20.4
Production workers, nec	2.0	-21.9	Drilling & boring machine tool operators	1.1	-28.4
Computer-controlled machine tool operators	1.9	-12.4	Production, planning, & expediting clerks	1.1	-20.4

Source: Industry-Occupation Matrix, Bureau of Labor Statistics, December 4, 2007. These data are reported based on 4-digit NAICS categories but have been matched to corresponding 6-digit NAICS industry codes. The change reported for each occupation to the year 2016 is a percent of growth or decline as estimated by the Bureau of Labor Statistics. The abbreviation nec stands for 'not elsewhere classified'.

LOCATION BY STATE AND REGIONAL CONCENTRATION

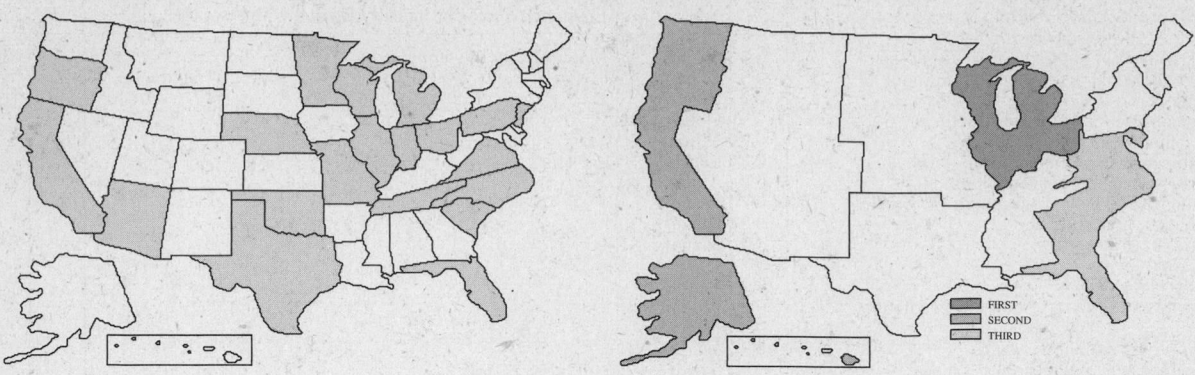

INDUSTRY DATA BY STATE

State	Establish-ments	Shipments			Employment				Cost as % of Shipments	Investment per Employee ($)
		Total ($ mil)	% of U.S.	Per Establ.	Total Number	% of U.S.	Per Establ.	Wages ($/hour)		
Michigan	67	10,223.6	29.4	152,591.7	28,615	27.3	427	28.54	60.7	12,893
Indiana	42	7,001.6	20.2	166,705.2	21,078	20.1	502	27.80	52.7	23,448
Ohio	41	5,360.1	15.4	130,734.4	17,925	17.1	437	26.15	63.0	14,462
North Carolina	27	2,340.6	6.7	86,690.7	6,019	5.8	223	13.58	60.6	15,553
South Carolina	14	783.3	2.3	55,947.0	2,754	2.6	197	14.26	66.1	7,660
Virginia	10	773.2	2.2	77,319.3	1,374	1.3	137	17.24	78.0	4,183
Illinois	29	597.5	1.7	20,603.4	2,774	2.7	96	18.57	42.0	6,176
Missouri	17	518.4	1.5	30,491.3	1,713	1.6	101	12.47	70.6	8,920
Pennsylvania	16	328.4	0.9	20,522.9	1,428	1.4	89	20.65	52.0	9,572
California	69	295.4	0.9	4,281.6	1,710	1.6	25	9.70	57.4	3,122
Tennessee	13	278.0	0.8	21,388.5	1,069	1.0	82	21.77	58.0	5,357
Oklahoma	10	241.7	0.7	24,166.6	1,345	1.3	134	12.20	54.6	5,720
Nebraska	3	143.2	0.4	47,739.0	403	0.4	134	12.82	45.0	2,757
Wisconsin	14	133.7	0.4	9,552.5	793	0.8	57	21.81	15.2	904
Minnesota	7	119.1	0.3	17,007.1	434	0.4	62	17.35	57.6	2,986
Texas	22	94.5	0.3	4,295.4	562	0.5	26	14.88	46.0	8,335
Oregon	6	94.2	0.3	15,703.7	349	0.3	58	26.08	41.5	1,564
Arizona	12	34.5	0.1	2,872.1	208	0.2	17	13.71	43.3	12,760
New Jersey	5	32.0	0.1	6,391.0	290	0.3	58	14.35	30.7	2,162
Florida	13	22.0	0.1	1,695.7	128	0.1	10	18.78	43.7	4,422

Source: 2002 *Economic Census*. The states are in descending order of shipments or establishments (if shipment data are missing for the majority). The symbol (D) appears when data are withheld to prevent disclosure of competitive information. States marked with (D) are sorted by number of establishments. A dash (-) indicates that the data element cannot be calculated. Data may not show all states active in the NAICS category. All data available at the time of publication are shown.

NAICS 336360 - MOTOR VEHICLE SEATING AND INTERIOR TRIM MANUFACTURING

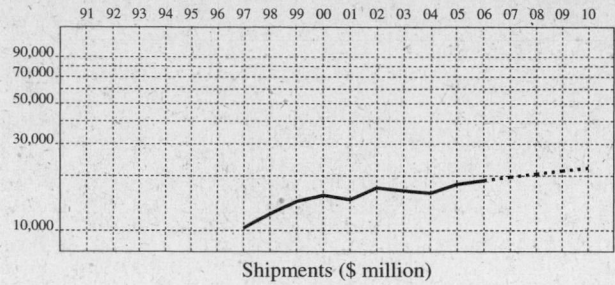

Shipments ($ million)

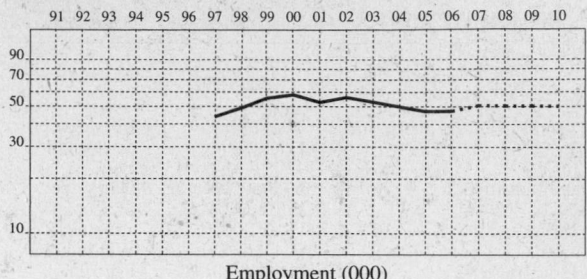

Employment (000)

GENERAL STATISTICS

Year	Com-panies	Establishments		Employment			Compensation		Production ($ million)			
		Total	with 20 or more employees	Total (000)	Production Workers (000)	Hours (Mil)	Payroll ($ mil)	Wages ($/hr)	Cost of Materials	Value Added by Manufacture	Value of Shipments	Capital Invest.
1997	281	355	186	43.9	35.3	72.7	1,429.2	14.10	6,652.0	3,669.8	10,326.7	310.7
1998		366	203	48.9	39.4	80.9	1,636.3	14.31	8,191.8	4,181.2	12,379.7	333.0
1999		350	198	55.5	44.7	92.5	1,972.1	15.14	9,393.5	5,104.5	14,463.5	353.2
2000		335	199	58.0	45.8	92.4	2,028.7	15.24	10,591.0	5,100.7	15,652.1	306.0
2001		338	197	52.7	42.3	79.7	1,674.6	14.76	10,441.5	4,351.1	14,813.9	250.0
2002	287	384	229	56.2	43.5	81.6	2,042.1	17.11	12,168.6	5,027.8	17,206.5	335.4
2003		392	232	53.0	40.3	79.8	2,088.3	17.64	11,301.1	5,282.6	16,580.6	295.4
2004		407	239	50.0	36.9	74.8	2,028.7	17.83	11,655.7	4,453.5	16,104.4	286.1
2005		399	231	47.1	34.3	66.1	1,975.5	19.20	13,699.5	4,335.3	18,001.3	276.8
2006		406P	245P	47.3	33.5	66.7	1,943.3	18.34	14,243.9	4,621.7	18,865.5	211.0
2007		413P	251P	50.6P	36.1P	69.3P	2,142.9P	19.55P	14,918.4P	4,840.6P	19,758.9P	243.3P
2008		420P	258P	50.4P	35.4P	67.6P	2,190.4P	20.12P	15,511.4P	5,033.0P	20,544.2P	233.8P
2009		427P	264P	50.3P	34.8P	65.9P	2,237.8P	20.70P	16,104.3P	5,225.3P	21,329.6P	224.3P
2010		434P	271P	50.2P	34.1P	64.2P	2,285.3P	21.28P	16,697.3P	5,417.7P	22,114.9P	214.7P

Sources: 1997 and 2002 *Economic Census*; other years, up to 2006, are from *Annual Survey of Manufactures*. Establishment counts for non-Census years are from *County Business Patterns*; 1997 and 2002 values are from the 1997 and 2002 censuses, respectively. 'P's show projections by the editors.

INDICES OF CHANGE

Year	Com-panies	Establishments		Employment			Compensation		Production ($ million)			
		Total	with 20 or more employees	Total (000)	Production Workers (000)	Hours (Mil)	Payroll ($ mil)	Wages ($/hr)	Cost of Materials	Value Added by Manufacture	Value of Shipments	Capital Invest.
1997	98	92	81	78	81	89	70	82	55	73	60	93
1998		95	89	87	91	99	80	84	67	83	72	99
1999		91	86	99	103	113	97	88	77	102	84	105
2000		87	87	103	105	113	99	89	87	101	91	91
2001		88	86	94	97	98	82	86	86	87	86	75
2002	100	100	100	100	100	100	100	100	100	100	100	100
2003		102	101	94	93	98	102	103	93	105	96	88
2004		106	104	89	85	92	99	104	96	89	94	85
2005		104	101	84	79	81	97	112	113	86	105	83
2006		106P	107P	84	77	82	95	107	117	92	110	63
2007		108P	110P	90P	83P	85P	105P	114P	123P	96P	115P	73P
2008		109P	113P	90P	81P	83P	107P	118P	127P	100P	119P	70P
2009		111P	115P	90P	80P	81P	110P	121P	132P	104P	124P	67P
2010		113P	118P	89P	78P	79P	112P	124P	137P	108P	129P	64P

Sources: Same as General Statistics. Values reflect change from the base year, 2002. Values above 100 mean greater than 2002, values below 100 mean less than 2002, and the values of 100 in other years means the same as 2002. 'P's show projections by the editors.

SELECTED RATIOS

For 2002	Avg. of All Manufact.	Analyzed Industry	Index	For 2002	Avg. of All Manufact.	Analyzed Industry	Index
Employees per Establishment	42	146	349	Value Added per Production Worker	182,367	115,582	63
Payroll per Establishment	1,639,184	5,317,969	324	Cost per Establishment	5,769,015	31,689,063	549
Payroll per Employee	39,053	36,336	93	Cost per Employee	137,446	216,523	158
Production Workers per Establishment	30	113	384	Cost per Production Worker	195,506	279,738	143
Wages per Establishment	694,845	3,635,875	523	Shipments per Establishment	11,158,348	44,808,594	402
Wages per Production Worker	23,548	32,096	136	Shipments per Employee	265,847	306,165	115
Hours per Production Worker	1,980	1,876	95	Shipments per Production Worker	378,144	395,552	105
Wages per Hour	11.89	17.11	144	Investment per Establishment	361,338	873,438	242
Value Added per Establishment	5,381,325	13,093,229	243	Investment per Employee	8,609	5,968	69
Value Added per Employee	128,210	89,463	70	Investment per Production Worker	12,245	7,710	63

Sources: Same as General Statistics. The 'Average of All Manufacturing' column represents the average of all manufacturing industries reported for the most recent complete year available. The Index shows the relationship between the Average and the Analyzed Industry. For example, 100 means that they are equal; 500 that the Analyzed Industry is five times the average; 50 means that the Analyzed Industry is half the national average. The abbreviation 'na' is used to show that data are 'not available'. Ratios shown for 2002, the last complete census year.

LEADING COMPANIES   Number shown: **75**   Total sales ($ mil): **84,180**   Total employment (000): **366.4**

Company Name	Address				CEO Name	Phone	Co. Type	Sales ($ mil)	Empl. (000)
Johnson Controls Inc.	PO Box 591	Milwaukee	WI	53201		414-524-1200	P	34,624	140.0
Lear Corp.	PO Box 5008	Southfield	MI	48086	Jim Brackenbury	248-447-1500	P	15,995	91.0
Amsafe Inc.	1043 N 47th Ave.	Phoenix	AZ	85043	Ken Beckemeyer	602-850-2850	R	7,000*	0.2
Hillenbrand Industries Inc.	1069 State Rte 46E	Batesville	IN	47006		812-934-7000	P	2,024	9.9
Kellwood Co.	PO Box 14374	St. Louis	MO	63178		314-576-3100	P	1,962	28.0
Herman Miller Inc.	PO Box 302	Zeeland	MI	49464		616-654-3000	P	1,919	6.4
BE Aerospace Inc.	1400 Corp. Ctr. Way	Wellington	FL	33414	Michael B. Baughan	561-791-5000	P	1,678	5.1
Tri-Con Industries Ltd.	4000 NW 44th St.	Lincoln	NE	68524		402-470-3311	R	1,450*	0.3
Carter's Inc.	1170 Peachtree St.	Atlanta	GA	30309	Frederick J. Rowan II	404-745-2700	P	1,412	7.6
Hill-Rom Company Inc.	1069 SR 46 E	Batesville	IN	47006	Peter H. Soderberg	812-934-7000	S	1,192*	6.5
Findlay Industries Inc.	4000 Fostoria Ave.	Findlay	OH	45840	Philip D. Gardner	419-422-1302	R	1,141*	5.0
Haworth Inc.	1 Haworth Ctr.	Holland	MI	49423	Franco Bianchi	616-393-3000	R	1,120*	8.0
Steiner Corp.	PO Box 2317	Salt Lake City	UT	84110	Kevin Steiner	801-328-8831	R	855*	12.0
Travel Tags Inc.	5842 Carmen Ave.	Inver Grove Hts	MN	55076	Barb Cederberg	651-450-1201	R	763*	0.3
Fenner Inc.	8720 Red Oak Blvd.	Charlotte	NC	28217	Nick Hobson	704-973-2158	R	701*	<0.1
Commercial Vehicle Group Inc.	6530 W Campus Ovl	New Albany	OH	43054	Gordon Boyd	614-289-5360	P	697	6.4
Parkdale Mills Inc.	PO Box 1787	Gastonia	NC	28053	Anderson D. Warlick	704-874-5000	R	686*	2.5
Pioneer Aerospace Corp.	PO Box 207	South Windsor	CT	06074	Ernie Haas	860-528-0092	R	638*	<0.1
Krueger International Inc.	PO Box 8100	Green Bay	WI	54308	Richard J. Resch	920-468-8100	R	600*	4.0
Sauder Woodworking Co.	PO Box 156	Archbold	OH	43502	Kevin Sauder	419-446-2711	R	525*	3.0
Advanced Accessory Holdings	12900 Hall Rd.	Sterling Hgts	MI	48313	Alan C. Johnson	586-997-2900	R	443	2.3
Johnson Outdoors Inc.	555 Main St.	Racine	WI	53403	H. P. Johnson-Leipold	262-631-6600	P	432	1.4
G-III Apparel Group Ltd.	512 7th Ave.	New York	NY	10018	Morris Goldfarb	212-403-0500	P	427	0.5
Flexsteel Industries Inc.	PO Box 877	Dubuque	IA	52004	Bruce Boylen	563-556-7730	P	425	2.3
Bing Group L.L.C.	11500 Oakland St.	Detroit	MI	48211	David Bing	313-867-3700	R	411*	1.1
Coleman Company Inc.	258 Beacon Street	Somerset	PA	15501	Bill Phillips		S	389*	2.3
Virco Manufacturing Corp.	PO Box 44846	Los Angeles	CA	90044		310-533-0474	P	223	1.2
Advanced Component Tech.	PO Box 168	Northwood	IA	50459	Robert Kluver	641-324-2231	S	217*	0.9
Sauder Manufacturing Co.	PO Box 230	Archbold	OH	43502	Virgil Miller	419-445-7670	R	184*	0.2
Berwick Offray L.L.C.	PO Box 428	Berwick	PA	18603	Scott Shea	570-752-5934	S	180*	1.5
Lifetime Products Inc.	PO Box 160010	Clearfield	UT	84016		801-776-1532	R	177*	0.3
Tachi-S Engineering USA Inc.	23227 Commerce	Farmington Hls	MI	48335		248-478-5050	R	177*	<0.1
Annin and Co.	55 Locust Ave.	Roseland	NJ	07068	C.R. Beard Jr.	973-228-9400	R	173*	0.4
Da-Lite Screen Company Inc.	PO Box 137	Warsaw	IN	46581	Richard E. Lundin	574-267-8101	R	170*	0.6
Shelby Williams Industries	150 S Williams	Morristown	TN	37813	Franklin Jacobs	423-586-7000	S	166*	1.7
Avedon Engineering Inc.	PO Box 1018	Longmont	CO	80502	Ray Avedon	303-772-2633	R	159*	0.2
Bridgewater Interiors L.L.C.	4617 W Fort St.	Detroit	MI	48209	John Barth	313-842-3300	J	147*	0.3
Setex Inc.	1111 McKinley Rd.	Saint Marys	OH	45885	Mutsumi Gamou	419-394-7800	S	140*	0.6
Cranston Print Works Co.	1381 Cranston St.	Cranston	RI	02920	F Rockefeller	401-943-4800	R	129*	0.6
Superior Uniform Group Inc.	10055 Seminole	Seminole	FL	33772	Gerald M. Benstock	727-397-9611	P	128	0.7
Manufacturers Industrial Group	PO Box 1048	Lexington	TN	38351		731-967-0001	R	120*	0.9
Vox Medica Inc.	601 Walnut St.	Philadelphia	PA	19106	Donald Phillips	215-238-8500	R	115*	0.1
Gentex Corp.	324 Main Street	Simpson	PA	18407	L. Peter Frieder Jr.	570-282-3550	R	113*	0.6
Irwin Seating Co.	PO Box 2429	Grand Rapids	MI	49501	Earle Irwin	616-574-7400	R	104*	0.7
Toyo Seat USA Corp.	2155 S Almont Ave.	Imlay City	MI	48444	Seizo Yamaguchi	810-724-0300	R	93*	0.2
Brodart Co.	500 Arch St.	Williamsport	PA	17701	Arthur Brody		R	92*	1.0
Blacksheep Inc.	3220 W Gentry	Tyler	TX	75702	Bob Archer	903-592-3853	S	90*	0.5
Hollywood Ribbon Industries	PO Box 63187	Los Angeles	CA	90063	Jim Scott		R	87*	0.2
Kaufman Container Company Inc.	PO Box 35902	Cleveland	OH	44135		216-898-2000	R	76*	<0.1
Safe Reflections Inc.	3220 N Granada	St. Paul	MN	55128	Robert Koppes	651-773-8199	R	76*	<0.1
Augusta Sportswear Inc.	PO Box 14939	Augusta	GA	30919	Brian Marks	706-860-4633	R	74*	0.4
Sharpline Converting Inc.	PO Box 9608	Wichita	KS	67277		316-722-9080	R	72*	0.3
Magnet L.L.C.	PO Box 605	Washington	MO	63090	Bill Korowitz	636-239-5661	R	71*	0.3
Decrane Aircraft Seating Co.	PO Box 129	Peshtigo	WI	54157		715-582-4517	R	70*	0.3
Dallas Manufacturing Company	PO Box 891101	Dallas	TX	75389		972-716-4200	S	69*	<0.1
Joe's Jeans Inc.	5901 Eastern Ave.	Commerce	CA	90040	Marc Crossman	323-837-3700	P	63	<0.1
Mity Enterprises Inc.	1301 W 400 N	Orem	UT	84057	Randall Hales	801-224-0589	P	60	0.4
Landscape Structures Inc.	PO Box 198	Delano	MN	55328	Barbara King	763-972-3391	R	60*	0.4
Wincraft Inc.	PO Box 888	Winona	MN	55987	Theodore Biesanz	507-454-5510	R	59*	0.2
Western Badge and Trophy Co.	831 Monterey Pass	Monterey Park	CA	91754	Wesley Ru	323-735-1201	R	59*	<0.1
Nixon Uniform Service Inc.	2925 Northeast Blvd	Wilmington	DE	19802	Murray Berstein	302-764-7550	R	54*	0.3
Decorator Industries Inc.	10011 Pines Blvd.	Pembroke Pines	FL	33024		954-436-8909	P	52	0.7
Whirley Industries Inc.	PO Box 988	Warren	PA	16365		814-723-7600	R	50*	0.3
Tesco Industries Inc.	1035 E Hacienda	Bellville	TX	77418			R	49*	0.1
Security Textile Corp.	1457 E Wash. Blvd.	Los Angeles	CA	90021	Brian Weitman	213-746-0850	R	48*	<0.1
Faurecia Automotive Seating	12209 Chandler Dr.	Walton	KY	41094	Jacques Lemorvan	859-485-1700	R	48*	0.2
Plymold Furnishing Solutions	615 Centennial Dr.	Kenyon	MN	55946	Stephen Sheppard	507-789-5111	R	46*	0.2
American Seating Co.	401 Americn Seating	Grand Rapids	MI	49504	Edward Clark	616-732-6600	R	45*	0.4
Wilcox Press Inc.	PO Box 9	Ithaca	NY	14851		607-272-1212	R	42*	0.3
B and B Concrete Company Inc.	PO Box 407	Tupelo	MS	38802	Henry C. Brevard Jr.	662-842-6312	R	42*	0.1
Brittany Dyeing and Printing	PO Box 3106	New Bedford	MA	02741	Kenneth Joblon	508-999-3281	R	41*	0.3
Lewisburg Seating Systems Inc.	1801 Childress Rd.	Lewisburg	TN	37091			S	41*	0.2
Crystal Springs Printworks	PO Box 750	Chickamauga	GA	30707	Frank Pierce	706-375-2125	R	41*	0.2
Racemark International L.P.	1 Racemark Way	Malta	NY	12020		518-899-6611	R	41*	0.2
Anomatic Corp.	1650 Tamarack Rd.	Newark	OH	43055	William Rusch	740-522-2203	R	40*	0.5

Source: Ward's Business Directory of U.S. Private and Public Companies, Volumes 1 and 2, 2008. The company type code used is as follows: P - Public, R - Private, S - Subsidiary, D - Division, J - Joint Venture, A - Affiliate, G - Group. Sales are in millions of dollars, employees are in thousands. An asterisk (*) indicates an estimated sales volume. The symbol < stands for 'less than'. Company names and addresses are truncated, in some cases, to fit into the available space.

MATERIALS CONSUMED

Material	Quantity	Delivered Cost ($ million)
Polyester broadwoven fabrics (piece goods)	(X)	194.9
Cotton broadwoven fabrics (piece goods)	(X)	9.8
Rayon and acetate broadwoven fabrics (piece goods)	(X)	(D)
Nylon broadwoven fabrics (piece goods)	(X)	8.4
Uncoated broadwoven fabrics for upholstery	(X)	213.9
Other broadwoven fabrics (piece goods)	(X)	256.8
Narrow fabrics (12 inches or less in width)	(X)	(D)
Yarn, all fibers	(X)	234.6
Fabrics (plastics coated, impregnated, and laminated)	(X)	375.7
Leather and other material cut stock and findings	(X)	1,340.0
Manmade fibers, staple, and tow	(X)	149.0
Plastics resins consumed in the form of granules, pellets, etc.	(X)	197.3
Plastics products consumed in the form of sheets, rods, etc.	(X)	602.2
Metal stampings	(X)	729.3
All other fabricated metal products (exc. castings and forgings)	(X)	1,071.6
Castings, rough and semifinished	(X)	4.8
Steel sheet and strip (including tinplate)	(X)	60.1
All other steel shapes and forms (exc. castings, forgings, fabr. metal products)	(X)	107.8
Aluminum and aluminum-base alloy sheet, plate, foil, and welded tubing	(X)	24.1
Hardwood lumber, rough and dressed	(X)	2.0
Plastics furniture parts and components	(X)	138.2
Formed and slab stock for pillows, cushions, seating, etc. (urethane)	(X)	477.3
Furniture and builders' hardware (incl. cabinet hardware, casters, glides, handles, hinges, locks, etc.)	(X)	21.0
Paperboard containers, boxes, and corrugated paperboard	(X)	31.8
All other materials, components, parts, containers, and supplies	(X)	4,624.5
Materials, ingredients, containers, and supplies, nsk	(X)	1,029.3

Source: 2002 *Economic Census*. Explanation of symbols used: (D): Withheld to avoid disclosure of competitive data; na: Not available; (S): Withheld because statistical norms were not met; (X): Not applicable; (Z): Less than half the unit shown; nec: Not elsewhere classified; nsk: Not specified by kind; - : zero; p : 10-19 percent estimated; q : 20-29 percent estimated.

PRODUCT SHARE DETAILS

Product or Product Class Shipments	Mil. $	Product or Product Class Shipments	Mil. $
MOTOR VEHICLE SEATING AND INTERIOR TRIM	16,762.1	automobiles, trucks, buses, and van conversions	8,857.8
Automobile trimmings	**4,487.2**	Seats for aircraft	604.0
Fabricated seat or safety belts, including shoulder harnesses		**Fabricated automobile seat covers and tire covers**	**615.2**
(except leather)	**758.3**	**Metal motor vehicle seat frames**	**1,149.8**
Seats for public conveyance and aircraft	**9,461.8**	**Motor vehicle seating and interior trim, nsk, total**	**289.8**
Seats for public conveyances (except aircraft), including			

Source: 2002 *Economic Census*. The values are product shipments in millions of dollars for 2002. Total product shipments may be lower or higher than industry shipments. See Introduction for a full discussion. Values of indented subcategories are summed in the main heading(s). The symbol (D) appears when data are withheld to prevent disclosure of competitive information. The abbreviation nsk stands for 'not specified by kind' and nec for 'not elsewhere classified'. A dash (-) means zero.

INPUTS AND OUTPUTS FOR MOTOR VEHICLE PARTS MANUFACTURING

Economic Sector or Industry Providing Inputs	%	Sector	Economic Sector or Industry Buying Outputs	%	Sector
Compensation of employees	22.8		Light truck & utility vehicles	25.3	Manufg.
Motor vehicle parts	10.7	Manufg.	Automobiles	15.8	Manufg.
Management of companies & enterprises	7.0	Services	Exports of goods & services	13.9	Cap Inv
Wholesale trade	5.3	Trade	Motor vehicle parts	8.5	Manufg.
Iron & steel mills & ferroalloys	5.0	Manufg.	Retail trade	7.4	Trade
Nonferrous metal foundries	2.6	Manufg.	Personal consumption expenditures	4.1	
Ferrous metal foundries	2.4	Manufg.	Automotive repair & maintenance, ex. car washes	2.9	Services
Plate work & fabricated structural products	1.9	Manufg.	Truck transportation	2.2	Util.
Turned products & screws, nuts, & bolts	1.9	Manufg.	General S/L govt. services	2.0	S/L Govt
Machine shops	1.5	Manufg.	Heavy duty trucks	1.9	Manufg.
Plastics products, nec	1.4	Manufg.	Wholesale trade	1.5	Trade
Truck transportation	1.1	Util.	Transit & ground passenger transportation	0.8	Util.
Retail trade	1.0	Trade	Change in private inventories	0.7	In House
Electronic components, nec	0.9	Manufg.	Postal service	0.6	Util.
Custom roll forming	0.9	Manufg.	General Federal government services, defense	0.6	Fed Govt
Coating, engraving, heat treating & allied activities	0.9	Manufg.	Residential structures, nec	0.6	Construct.
Crowns & closures & metal stamping	0.8	Manufg.	Residential permanent site structures	0.6	Construct.
Rubber products, nec	0.7	Manufg.	Nonresidential structures, nec	0.5	Construct.
Semiconductors & related devices	0.7	Manufg.	Lawn & garden equipment	0.4	Manufg.
Plastics packaging materials, film & sheet	0.7	Manufg.	Boat building	0.4	Manufg.
Scientific research & development services	0.7	Services	Construction machinery	0.4	Manufg.
Power generation & supply	0.7	Util.	S/L govt. passenger transit	0.4	S/L Govt
Leather & hide tanning & finishing	0.7	Manufg.	Transportation equipment, nec	0.3	Manufg.
Ball & roller bearings	0.7	Manufg.	Engine equipment, nec	0.3	Manufg.
Valve & fittings other than plumbing	0.6	Manufg.	Food services & drinking places	0.3	Services

Continued on next page.

INPUTS AND OUTPUTS FOR MOTOR VEHICLE PARTS MANUFACTURING - Continued

Economic Sector or Industry Providing Inputs	%	Sector	Economic Sector or Industry Buying Outputs	%	Sector
Textile & fabric finishing mills	0.6	Manufg.	Waste management & remediation services	0.3	Services
Lessors of nonfinancial assets	0.5	Fin/R.E.	Aircraft	0.3	Manufg.
Fluid power process machinery	0.5	Manufg.	Services to buildings & dwellings	0.3	Services
Taxes on production & imports, less subsidies	0.5		Oil & gas extraction	0.2	Mining
Plastics materials & resins	0.5	Manufg.	Commercial & health care structures	0.2	Construct.
Ornamental & architectural metal products	0.5	Manufg.	Farm machinery & equipment	0.2	Manufg.
Gaskets, packing, & sealing devices	0.5	Manufg.	Management of companies & enterprises	0.2	Services
Securities, commodity contracts, investments	0.5	Fin/R.E.	Truck trailers	0.2	Manufg.
Noncomparable imports	0.5	Foreign	Warehousing & storage	0.2	Util.
Urethane & other foam products (except polystrene)	0.4	Manufg.	Motor vehicle bodies	0.2	Manufg.
Printed circuit assemblies (electronic assembles)	0.4	Manufg.	Travel trailers & campers	0.2	Manufg.
Alumina refining & primary aluminum production	0.4	Manufg.	Scientific research & development services	0.2	Services
Bare printed circuit boards	0.4	Manufg.	Maintenance/repair of nonresidential structures	0.2	Construct.
Paints & coatings	0.4	Manufg.	Private fixed investment	0.2	
Wiring devices	0.4	Manufg.	Couriers & messengers	0.1	Util.
Fabricated metals, nec	0.4	Manufg.	Individual & family services	0.1	Services
Copper rolling, drawing, extruding, & alloying	0.3	Manufg.	Scenic & sightseeing transport & related services	0.1	Util.
Advertising & related services	0.3	Services	Car washes	0.1	Services
Metal cans, boxes, & other containers (light gauge)	0.3	Manufg.	Automotive equipment rental & leasing	0.1	Fin/R.E.
Real estate	0.3	Fin/R.E.	Crowns & closures & metal stamping	0.1	Manufg.
Speed changers, industrial high-speed drives, & gears	0.3	Manufg.	Material handling equipment	0.1	Manufg.
Primary nonferrous metal, ex. copper & aluminum	0.3	Manufg.			
Paperboard containers	0.3	Manufg.			
Maintenance/repair of nonresidential structures	0.3	Construct.			
Gold, silver, & other metal ore	0.3	Mining			
Services to buildings & dwellings	0.2	Services			
Aluminum products from purchased aluminum	0.2	Manufg.			
Nonferrous metal (ex. copper & aluminum) processing	0.2	Manufg.			
Forging, stamping, & sintering, nec	0.2	Manufg.			
Rubber & plastics hose & belting	0.2	Manufg.			
Natural gas distribution	0.2	Util.			
Rail transportation	0.2	Util.			
Monetary authorities/depository credit intermediation	0.2	Fin/R.E.			
Handtools	0.2	Manufg.			
Automotive equipment rental & leasing	0.2	Fin/R.E.			
Professional, scientific, technical services, nec	0.2	Services			
Basic organic chemicals, nec	0.2	Manufg.			
Warehousing & storage	0.2	Util.			
Legal services	0.2	Services			
Food services & drinking places	0.2	Services			
Communication & energy wires & cables	0.2	Manufg.			
Automotive repair & maintenance, ex. car washes	0.2	Services			
Management, scientific, & technical consulting	0.2	Services			
Engine equipment, nec	0.2	Manufg.			
Wood windows & doors & millwork	0.2	Manufg.			
Veneer & plywood	0.2	Manufg.			
Telecommunications	0.2	Services			
Accounting, tax preparation, bookkeeping, & payroll	0.1	Services			
Commercial & industrial equipment repair/maintenance	0.1	Services			
Architectural, engineering, & related services	0.1	Services			
Artificial & synthetic fibers & filaments	0.1	Manufg.			
Air transportation	0.1	Util.			
Cutting tools & machine tool accessories	0.1	Manufg.			
Employment services	0.1	Services			
Chemical products & preparations, nec	0.1	Manufg.			
Data processing, hosting, & related services	0.1	Services			
Specialized design services	0.1	Services			
Relay & industrial controls	0.1	Manufg.			
Business support services	0.1	Services			
Fiber, yarn, & thread mills	0.1	Manufg.			
Hotels & motels, including casino hotels	0.1	Services			
Electronic capacitors, resistors, coils, transformers	0.1	Manufg.			
Wood containers & pallets	0.1	Manufg.			
Waste management & remediation services	0.1	Services			
Springs & wire products	0.1	Manufg.			
Automatic environmental controls	0.1	Manufg.			

Source: Benchmark Input-Output Accounts for the U.S. Economy, 2002, U.S. Department of Commerce, Washington D.C., January 2008. *User should note that this Input-Output table is not for this particular narrowly defined industry but for a larger aggregate. Input and Output data for* Motor Vehicle Parts Manufacturing *include Input and Output data for the* Annual Survey of Manufactures' *NAICS industries 33631M, 33632M, 336330, 336340, 336350, 336360, 336370, 336391, and 336399. The abbreviation nec stands for 'not elsewhere classified'.*

OCCUPATIONS EMPLOYED BY MOTOR VEHICLE PARTS MANUFACTURING

Occupation	% of Total 2006	Change to 2016	Occupation	% of Total 2006	Change to 2016
Team assemblers	15.2	-19.2	Welders, cutters, solderers, & brazers	1.9	-15.3
Cutting, punching, & press machine operators	4.2	-28.4	Molding, coremaking, & casting machine operators	1.8	-28.4
Machinists	3.8	-16.4	Welding, soldering, & brazing machine operators	1.6	-10.5
Inspectors, testers, sorters, samplers, & weighers	3.5	-24.9	Industrial machinery mechanics	1.5	-8.4
First-line supervisors/managers of production workers	3.3	-20.4	Helpers--Production workers	1.5	-20.4
Assemblers & fabricators, nec	3.2	-28.4	Mechanical engineers	1.4	-20.4
Multiple machine tool operators & tenders	2.6	-12.4	Electrical & electronic equipment assemblers	1.4	-36.3
Tool & die makers	2.6	-16.4	Lathe & turning machine tool operators & tenders	1.3	-28.4
Industrial truck & tractor operators	2.6	-28.4	Shipping, receiving, & traffic clerks	1.3	-23.4
Laborers & freight, stock, & material movers, hand	2.1	-28.4	Electricians	1.3	-17.4
Industrial engineers	2.1	-3.3	Grinding, lapping, polishing machine tool operators	1.2	-22.8
Maintenance & repair workers, general	2.0	-20.4	Engine & other machine assemblers	1.1	-20.4
Production workers, nec	2.0	-21.9	Drilling & boring machine tool operators	1.1	-28.4
Computer-controlled machine tool operators	1.9	-12.4	Production, planning, & expediting clerks	1.1	-20.4

Source: Industry-Occupation Matrix, Bureau of Labor Statistics, December 4, 2007. These data are reported based on 4-digit NAICS categories but have been matched to corresponding 6-digit NAICS industry codes. The change reported for each occupation to the year 2016 is a percent of growth or decline as estimated by the Bureau of Labor Statistics. The abbreviation nec stands for 'not elsewhere classified'.

LOCATION BY STATE AND REGIONAL CONCENTRATION

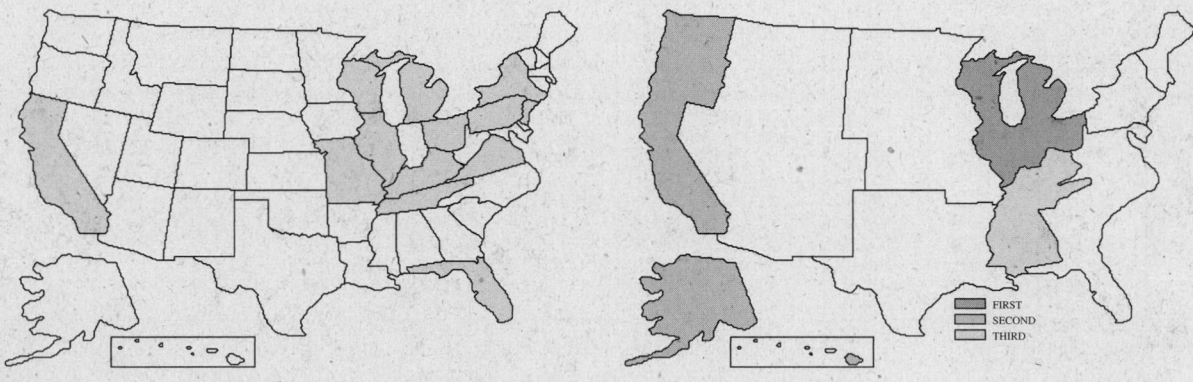

FIRST
SECOND
THIRD

INDUSTRY DATA BY STATE

State	Establish- ments	Shipments Total ($ mil)	Shipments % of U.S.	Shipments Per Establ.	Employment Total Number	Employment % of U.S.	Employment Per Establ.	Wages ($/hour)	Cost as % of Shipments	Investment per Employee ($)
Michigan	58	5,125.7	29.8	88,373.8	16,936	30.1	292	18.51	69.2	3,983
Ohio	29	2,225.7	12.9	76,748.8	7,003	12.5	241	16.00	73.2	8,430
Kentucky	12	1,449.3	8.4	120,776.7	3,707	6.6	309	15.28	82.7	8,192
Missouri	13	1,145.6	6.7	88,123.3	2,543	4.5	196	25.34	73.9	4,411
Tennessee	16	975.5	5.7	60,966.7	3,899	6.9	244	11.98	64.8	14,170
Illinois	9	648.4	3.8	72,042.8	1,665	3.0	185	14.12	71.7	6,903
Wisconsin	9	610.4	3.5	67,818.8	1,643	2.9	183	22.11	74.2	4,565
California	52	459.4	2.7	8,835.3	2,442	4.3	47	14.07	51.4	3,381
Virginia	5	254.3	1.5	50,866.2	1,100	2.0	220	17.28	64.7	3,520
New Jersey	5	126.3	0.7	25,266.0	362	0.6	72	17.51	70.8	1,459
Pennsylvania	8	81.8	0.5	10,226.6	582	1.0	73	20.33	46.5	5,395
New York	7	48.8	0.3	6,976.4	365	0.6	52	12.55	42.6	8,318
Florida	18	36.3	0.2	2,018.7	346	0.6	19	10.04	59.1	1,355

Source: 2002 Economic Census. The states are in descending order of shipments or establishments (if shipment data are missing for the majority). The symbol (D) appears when data are withheld to prevent disclosure of competitive information. States marked with (D) are sorted by number of establishments. A dash (-) indicates that the data element cannot be calculated. Data may not show all states active in the NAICS category. All data available at the time of publication are shown.

NAICS 336370 - MOTOR VEHICLE METAL STAMPING

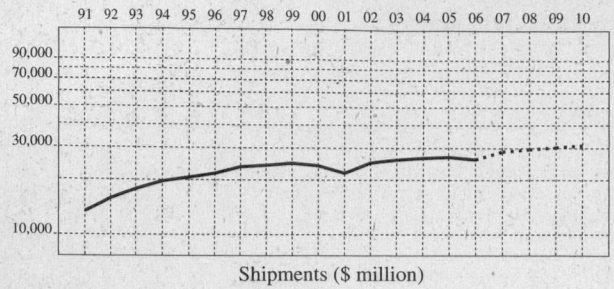

Shipments ($ million)

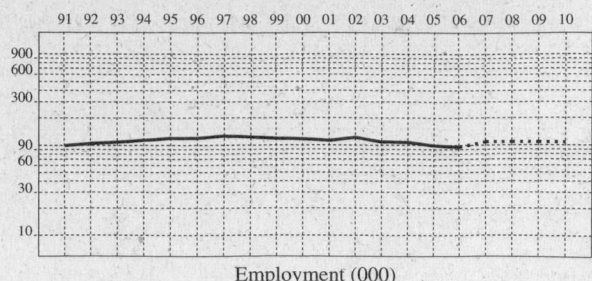

Employment (000)

GENERAL STATISTICS

| Year | Com-panies | Establishments | | Employment | | | Compensation | | Production ($ million) | | | |
		Total	with 20 or more employees	Total (000)	Production Workers (000)	Hours (Mil)	Payroll ($ mil)	Wages ($/hr)	Cost of Materials	Value Added by Manufacture	Value of Shipments	Capital Invest.
1991		644	450	99.3	82.1	169.1	3,680.6	17.23	7,700.0	5,662.7	13,403.6	722.0
1992	585	700	506	105.2	87.1	184.0	4,098.9	17.76	8,598.1	7,241.8	15,821.4	519.9
1993		693	483	108.7	91.8	199.7	4,410.2	17.82	9,689.4	8,126.8	17,780.8	842.3
1994		673	497	114.0	95.4	212.5	4,882.2	18.42	10,641.5	9,074.9	19,652.8	1,201.1
1995		689	526	119.4	100.0	215.7	5,139.7	18.88	11,593.1	9,091.4	20,638.9	1,443.3
1996		712	523	119.5	100.5	217.8	5,123.7	18.42	11,691.5	10,056.8	21,691.6	1,212.6
1997	663	809	581	126.5	105.1	226.4	5,640.2	19.52	12,674.2	10,907.0	23,624.7	1,515.6
1998		789	568	123.2	101.2	215.5	5,461.8	19.13	12,686.7	11,489.7	24,127.0	1,382.4
1999		784	560	118.7	100.4	217.2	5,927.9	21.74	12,870.1	11,920.0	24,775.9	1,582.4
2000		754	556	117.0	98.4	207.8	6,027.1	23.17	12,775.0	11,203.8	24,025.6	1,445.0
2001		740	532	112.5	94.0	190.6	5,391.8	22.50	11,835.5	9,899.5	21,858.3	1,322.8
2002	666	798	533	121.6	100.3	187.4	5,648.7	23.59	12,805.7	12,144.4	24,899.8	1,023.5
2003		790	585	108.9	89.2	190.2	5,898.0	24.38	13,067.9	12,761.1	25,857.0	1,938.9
2004		788	573	107.5	88.9	183.9	5,930.5	25.52	13,462.4	13,014.6	26,450.6	1,016.3
2005		792	583	99.4	81.0	170.9	5,461.1	25.01	14,758.6	12,065.7	26,781.4	946.2
2006		823P	596P	95.4	77.7	161.8	5,116.5	24.80	14,093.0	11,880.2	25,978.1	1,114.1
2007		832P	603P	109.2P	89.8P	183.9P	6,135.5P	26.28P	15,607.9P	13,157.3P	28,770.7P	1,421.5P
2008		842P	610P	108.9P	89.3P	182.3P	6,240.8P	26.89P	16,018.7P	13,503.5P	29,527.7P	1,447.4P
2009		852P	618P	108.5P	88.9P	180.8P	6,346.2P	27.50P	16,429.4P	13,849.7P	30,284.8P	1,473.2P
2010		862P	625P	108.1P	88.5P	179.3P	6,451.5P	28.10P	16,840.1P	14,196.0P	31,041.9P	1,499.1P

Sources: 1992, 1997, 2002 *Economic Census*; other years, up to 2006, are from the *Annual Survey of Manufactures*. Establishment counts for non-Census years are from *County Business Patterns*; 1997 and 2002 values are from the 1997 and 2002 censuses respectively, reported in the Federal Government's NAICS format. Other years were originally reported in equivalent SIC format. 'P's show projections by the editors.

INDICES OF CHANGE

| Year | Com-panies | Establishments | | Employment | | | Compensation | | Production ($ million) | | | |
		Total	with 20 or more employees	Total (000)	Production Workers (000)	Hours (Mil)	Payroll ($ mil)	Wages ($/hr)	Cost of Materials	Value Added by Manufacture	Value of Shipments	Capital Invest.
1992	88	88	95	87	87	98	73	75	67	60	64	51
1997	100	101	109	104	105	121	100	83	99	90	95	148
2001		93	100	93	94	102	95	95	92	82	88	129
2002	100	100	100	100	100	100	100	100	100	100	100	100
2003		99	110	90	89	101	104	103	102	105	104	189
2004		99	108	88	89	98	105	108	105	107	106	99
2005		99	109	82	81	91	97	106	115	99	108	92
2006		103P	112P	78	77	86	91	105	110	98	104	109
2007		104P	113P	90P	90P	98P	109P	111P	122P	108P	116P	139P
2008		106P	115P	90P	89P	97P	110P	114P	125P	111P	119P	141P
2009		107P	116P	89P	89P	96P	112P	117P	128P	114P	122P	144P
2010		108P	117P	89P	88P	96P	114P	119P	132P	117P	125P	146P

Sources: Same as General Statistics. Values reflect change from the base year, 2002. Values above 100 mean greater than 2002, values below 100 mean less than 2002, and the values of 100 in other years means the same as 2002. 'P's show projections by the editors.

SELECTED RATIOS

For 2002	Avg. of All Manufact.	Analyzed Industry	Index	For 2002	Avg. of All Manufact.	Analyzed Industry	Index
Employees per Establishment	42	152	363	Value Added per Production Worker	182,367	121,081	66
Payroll per Establishment	1,639,184	7,078,571	432	Cost per Establishment	5,769,015	16,047,243	278
Payroll per Employee	39,053	46,453	119	Cost per Employee	137,446	105,310	77
Production Workers per Establishment	30	126	426	Cost per Production Worker	195,506	127,674	65
Wages per Establishment	694,845	5,539,807	797	Shipments per Establishment	11,158,348	31,202,757	280
Wages per Production Worker	23,548	44,075	187	Shipments per Employee	265,847	204,768	77
Hours per Production Worker	1,980	1,868	94	Shipments per Production Worker	378,144	248,253	66
Wages per Hour	11.89	23.59	198	Investment per Establishment	361,338	1,282,581	355
Value Added per Establishment	5,381,325	15,218,546	283	Investment per Employee	8,609	8,417	98
Value Added per Employee	128,210	99,872	78	Investment per Production Worker	12,245	10,204	83

Sources: Same as General Statistics. The 'Average of All Manufacturing' column represents the average of all manufacturing industries reported for the most recent complete year available. The Index shows the relationship between the Average and the Analyzed Industry. For example, 100 means that they are equal; 500 that the Analyzed Industry is five times the average; 50 means that the Analyzed Industry is half the national average. The abbreviation 'na' is used to show that data are 'not available'. Ratios shown for 2002, the last complete census year.

LEADING COMPANIES Number shown: **75** Total sales ($ mil): **44,491** Total employment (000): **148.2**

Company Name	Address				CEO Name	Phone	Co. Type	Sales ($ mil)	Empl. (000)
Lear Corp.	PO Box 5008	Southfield	MI	48086	Jim Brackenbury	248-447-1500	P	15,995	91.0
PACCAR Inc.	PO Box 1518	Bellevue	WA	98009		425-468-7400	P	15,220	21.8
Toyota Motor Mfg. N America	25 Atlantic Ave.	Erlanger	KY	41018	Masamoto Amezawa	859-746-4000	S	6,120*	7.5
Tower Automotive L.L.C.	27175 Haggerty Rd.	Novi	MI	48377		248-675-6000	R	2,539	10.5
Northern Stamping Inc.	6600 Chapek Pkwy.	Cleveland	OH	44125		216-883-8888	R	410*	0.2
Feintool US Operations Inc.	11280 Cornell Park	Cincinnati	OH	45242	Richard Surico	513-247-0110	R	408*	0.3
JSJ Corp.	700 Robbins Rd.	Grand Haven	MI	49417	Martin Johnson	616-842-6350	R	295*	<0.1
Pridgeon and Clay Inc.	50 Cottage Grove St	Grand Rapids	MI	49507	Donald Clay	616-241-5675	R	207*	0.8
Ogihara America Corp.	1480 McPherson Pk	Howell	MI	48843	Tokio Ogihara	517-548-4900	R	202*	0.5
Yorozu Automotive Tennessee	395 Mt View Indust.	Morrison	TN	37357	Yusuke Kawada	931-668-7700	R	187*	1.0
Guelph Tool Sales Inc.	24150 Gibson Dr.	Warren	MI	48089	Robert Ireland	586-755-3333	R	168*	0.9
MPI International Inc.	2129 Austin Ave.	Rochester	MI	48309		248-853-9010	S	157*	1.0
Eagle Bend Manufacturing Inc.	1000 Jd Yarnell Ind	Clinton	TN	37716		865-457-3800	R	118*	0.6
Spartanburg Automotive Steel	PO Box 6428	Spartanburg	SC	29304	John Byers	864-585-5211	R	115*	0.6
Duffy Tool & Stamping Ltd.	PO Box 2128	Muncie	IN	47307	Greggory Notestine	765-288-1941	R	113*	0.2
Unipres USA Inc.	PO Box 799	Portland	TN	37148		615-325-7311	R	112*	0.6
Colfor Manufacturing Inc.	PO Box 485	Malvern	OH	44644	Richard Dauch	330-863-0404	S	100*	0.7
Gill Industries Inc.	5271 Plainfield Ave	Grand Rapids	MI	49525		616-559-2700	R	88*	0.1
Motor City Stampings Inc.	47783 Gratiot Ave.	Chesterfield	MI	48051	Judith Kucway	586-949-8420	R	84*	0.5
PK USA Inc.	600 Northridge Dr.	Shelbyville	IN	46176	Hirosige Kakudo	317-398-6909	R	76*	0.3
Stanco Metal Products Inc.	PO Box 307	Grand Haven	MI	49417	Warren Stansberry	616-842-5000	R	69*	<0.1
Challenge Manufacturing Co.	PO Box 1049	Holland	MI	49422	Bruce Vor Broker	616-735-6500	R	66*	0.5
Hatch Stamping Co.	635 E Industrial Dr	Chelsea	MI	48118	Daniel Craig	734-475-8628	R	63*	0.2
Lenawee Stamping Corp.	1200 E Chicago	Tecumseh	MI	49286	Allan Power	517-423-2400	R	62*	0.3
Lapeer Metal Stamping Co.	930 S Saginaw St.	Lapeer	MI	48446	Gerald Diez	810-664-8588	R	60*	0.3
Select International Corp.	PO Box 887	Dayton	OH	45401	Robert Whited	937-233-9191	R	59*	<0.1
Checker Motors Corp.	2016 N Pitcher St.	Kalamazoo	MI	49007	David R. Markin	269-343-6121	R	50*	0.4
Ki Corp.	501 Mayde Rd.	Berea	KY	40403		859-986-1420	R	45*	0.2
SFI of Tennessee L.L.C.	4768 Hungerford	Memphis	TN	38118		901-363-1571	R	45*	0.2
Manter Technologies Corp.	7177 Marine City	Marine City	MI	48039	Bill Manter	810-765-8000	R	44*	0.2
Landmark Manufacturing Corp.	28100 Quick Ave.	Gallatin	MO	64640	Donald Critten	660-663-2185	R	43*	0.3
Handy & Harman Electronic Mat.	231 Ferris Ave.	East Providence	RI	02916		401-434-6543	S	43*	0.2
Oakwood Metal Fabricating Co.	1100 Oakwood	Dearborn	MI	48124	Richard Audi	313-561-7740	R	43*	<0.1
AJ Rose Manufacturing Co.	38000 Chester Rd.	Avon	OH	44011	John Warnkey	440-934-7700	R	42*	0.2
Heritage Products Inc.	2000 Smith Ave.	Crawfordsville	IN	47933	Takaya Yunoki	765-364-9002	R	40*	0.2
Alken-Ziegler Inc.	406 S Park Dr.	Kalkaska	MI	49646	Gilbert Ziegler	231-258-4906	R	40*	0.2
Guardian Automotive	2300 Harmon Rd.	Auburn Hills	MI	48326	Jim Davis	248-340-1800	D	39*	0.2
Q3 Industries Inc.	PO Box 28309	Columbus	OH	43228	Francis Price	614-870-0195	R	35*	0.2
Wren Industries Inc.	PO Box 24009	Dayton	OH	45424	George Derr	937-667-4403	R	33*	0.2
Su-Dan Co.	1853 Rochester Ind.	Rochester Hills	MI	48309	Dennis Keat	248-651-6035	R	33*	<0.1
Concord Tool and Manufacturing	118 N Groesbeck	Mount Clemens	MI	48043	Mark Dichtel	586-465-6537	R	31*	0.2
Wellington Industries Inc.	39555 S Interst 94	Belleville	MI	48111	Marvin Tyghem	734-942-1060	R	30*	0.3
Anchor Tool and Die Co.	11830 Brookpark	Cleveland	OH	44130		216-362-1850	R	30*	0.3
Unipres Southeast USA Inc.	1001 Fountain Dr.	Forest	MS	39074	Takayuki Nitta	601-469-0234	R	30*	0.2
Delaco Steel Corp.	8111 Tireman Ave.	Dearborn	MI	48126	Gerald Diez	313-491-1200	R	30*	<0.1
Advance Engineering Co.	12025 Dixie	Redford	MI	48239	George Helms	313-537-3500	R	29*	<0.1
Automatic Spring Products	803 Taylor Ave.	Grand Haven	MI	49417	Steve Moreland	616-842-7800	R	29*	0.2
York Corrugating Co.	PO Box 1192	York	PA	17405	Kim Raub	717-845-3511	R	28*	<0.1
WICO Metal Products Company	23500 Sherwood	Warren	MI	48091	Richard Brodie	586-755-9600	R	28*	0.2
Modern Metal Products Co.	726 Beacon St.	Loves Park	IL	61111	Michael Anderson	815-877-9571	R	28*	0.3
BAE Industries Inc.	24400 Sherwood	Center Line	MI	48015	Jessee Lopez	586-754-3000	R	27*	0.3
Global Advanced Products	30707 Commerce	Chesterfield	MI	48051		586-749-6800	R	26*	0.1
Dixien L.L.C.	PO Box 337	Forest Park	GA	30298	Juan Garcia	404-366-7427	R	26*	0.2
Quality Metalcraft Inc.	33355 Glendale St.	Livonia	MI	48150	Alexander Chetcuti	734-261-6700	R	26*	0.3
Dickey-Grabler Co.	PO Box 5870	Cleveland	OH	44194	William Primrose	216-961-4172	R	25*	0.2
E and G Classics Inc.	8910 McGaw Ct.	Columbia	MD	21045	David Eash	410-381-4900	R	24*	0.1
Perfection Spring and Stamping	PO Box 275	Mount Prospect	IL	60056	David Kahn	847-437-3900	R	23*	0.1
Logghe Stamping Co.	16711 Thirteen Mile	Fraser	MI	48026		586-293-2250	R	23*	<0.1
Ohio Stamping and Machine	PO Box 1846	Springfield	OH	45501	Daniel McGregor	937-322-3880	R	22*	0.1
Yachiyo Mfg. of Alabama L.L.C.	990 Duncan Farms	Steele	AL	35987		256-538-1974	R	22*	0.1
AMG Industries Inc.	200 Commerce Dr.	Mount Vernon	OH	43050	David Mc Elroy	740-397-4044	R	22*	0.1
Angell-Demmell North America	1516 Stanley Ave.	Dayton	OH	45404	Richard Anglin	937-461-5800	R	21*	<0.1
AWP Industries Inc.	616 Industrial Park	Frankfort	KY	40601	Craig Chamberlin	502-695-0070	R	21*	0.1
New Center Stamping Inc.	950 E Milwaukee St.	Detroit	MI	48211	Ronald Hall	313-872-1722	R	20*	0.1
Taylor Metal Products Co.	700 Springmill St.	Mansfield	OH	44903	Richard Taylor	419-522-0751	R	20*	0.2
Washers Inc.	33375 Glendale St.	Livonia	MI	48150	George Strumbos	734-523-9000	R	20*	0.1
Hamlin Tool and Machine Comp.	1671 E Hamlin Rd.	Rochester	MI	48307	Patrick Pihjalic	248-651-6302	R	20*	0.1
Quaker Manufacturing Corp.	PO Box 449	Salem	OH	44460		330-337-6883	R	19*	0.2
Inalfa SSI Roof Systems L.L.C.	12500 E 9 Mile Rd.	Warren	MI	48089		586-758-6620	R	19*	0.1
Stamco Industries Inc.	26650 Lakeland	Cleveland	OH	44132	William Sopko	216-731-9333	R	19*	0.1
Superior Cam Inc.	31240 Stephenson	Madison Heights	MI	48071	John Basso	248-588-1100	R	19*	0.1
Utica Metal Products Inc.	1526 Lincoln Ave.	Utica	NY	13502	Charles Fields	315-732-6163	R	19*	0.1
Fab-All Manufacturing Inc.	645 Executive Dr.	Troy	MI	48083	Josef Hubert	248-585-6700	R	18*	<0.1
MTD Technologies Inc.	5201 102nd Ave.	Pinellas Park	FL	33782	Dennis Ruppel	727-546-2446	R	17*	<0.1
Powerlasers Corp.	PO Box 939	Pioneer	OH	43554	Joe Neri	419-737-3180	R	17*	<0.1

Source: Ward's Business Directory of U.S. Private and Public Companies, Volumes 1 and 2, 2008: The company type code used is as follows: P - Public, R - Private, S - Subsidiary, D - Division, J - Joint Venture, A - Affiliate, G - Group. Sales are in millions of dollars, employees are in thousands. An asterisk (*) indicates an estimated sales volume. The symbol < stands for 'less than'. Company names and addresses are truncated, in some cases, to fit into the available space.

MATERIALS CONSUMED

Material	Quantity		Delivered Cost ($ million)
Metal bolts, nuts, screws, and other screw machine products		(X)	354.8
All other steel shapes and forms (exc. castings, forgings, fabr. metal products)		(X)	(D)
Other fabricated metal products (exc. castings and forgings)		(X)	483.0
Iron and steel castings (rough and semifinished)		(X)	415.6
Nonferrous (aluminum, copper, etc.) castings (rough and semifinished)		(X)	22.7
Forgings		(X)	(D)
Steel bars and bar shapes (exc. castings, forgings, fabr. metal products)		(X)	82.6
Steel sheet and strip (including tinplate)	1,000 s tons	8,352.8q	5,672.5
Steel plate		(X)	15.1
Steel wire and wire products		(X)	46.5
Steel tinplate, tin free steel, terneplate, and blackplate	1,000 s tons	(S)	11.0
All other steel shapes and forms (exc. castings, forgings, fabr. metal products)		(X)	427.6
Copper and copper-base alloy shapes and forms (exc. castings, forgings, fabr. metal products)		(X)	42.4
Aluminum and aluminum-base alloy sheet, plate, foil, and welded tubing		(X)	188.9
Aluminum and aluminum-base alloy extruded shapes (rod, bar, pipe, tube, etc.)	mil lb	43.0	57.6
Other aluminum and aluminum-base alloy shapes and forms (exc. castings, forgings, fabr. metal products)		(X)	23.8
Other nonferrous shapes and forms (exc. castings, forgings, fabricated metal products)		(X)	14.3
Plastics resins consumed in the form of granules, pellets, etc.		(X)	28.5
Paints, varnishes, stains, lacquers, shellacs, japans, enamels, etc.		(X)	26.0
All other chemicals and allied products		(X)	11.1
Plastics products consumed in the form of sheets, rods, etc.		(X)	37.1
Paperboard containers, boxes, and corrugated paperboard		(X)	76.4
Other paper and paperboard products		(X)	(D)
Special dies, tools, die sets, jigs, and fixtures (exc. cutting tools)		(X)	20.5
All other materials, components, parts, containers, and supplies		(X)	1,934.6
Materials, ingredients, containers, and supplies, nsk		(X)	1,783.6

Source: 2002 *Economic Census*. Explanation of symbols used: (D): Withheld to avoid disclosure of competitive data; na: Not available; (S): Withheld because statistical norms were not met; (X): Not applicable; (Z): Less than half the unit shown; nec: Not elsewhere classified; nsk: Not specified by kind; - : zero; p : 10-19 percent estimated; q : 20-29 percent estimated.

PRODUCT SHARE DETAILS

Product or Product Class Shipments	Mil. $	Product or Product Class Shipments	Mil. $
AUTOMOTIVE JOB STAMPINGS	24,038.3		

Source: 2002 *Economic Census*. The values are product shipments in millions of dollars for 2002. Total product shipments may be lower or higher than industry shipments. See Introduction for a full discussion. Values of indented subcategories are summed in the main heading(s). The symbol (D) appears when data are withheld to prevent disclosure of competitive information. The abbreviation nsk stands for 'not specified by kind' and nec for 'not elsewhere classified'. A dash (-) means zero.

INPUTS AND OUTPUTS FOR MOTOR VEHICLE PARTS MANUFACTURING

Economic Sector or Industry Providing Inputs	%	Sector	Economic Sector or Industry Buying Outputs	%	Sector
Compensation of employees	22.8		Light truck & utility vehicles	25.3	Manufg.
Motor vehicle parts	10.7	Manufg.	Automobiles	15.8	Manufg.
Management of companies & enterprises	7.0	Services	Exports of goods & services	13.9	Cap Inv
Wholesale trade	5.3	Trade	Motor vehicle parts	8.5	Manufg.
Iron & steel mills & ferroalloys	5.0	Manufg.	Retail trade	7.4	Trade
Nonferrous metal foundries	2.6	Manufg.	Personal consumption expenditures	4.1	
Ferrous metal foundries	2.4	Manufg.	Automotive repair & maintenance, ex. car washes	2.9	Services
Plate work & fabricated structural products	1.9	Manufg.	Truck transportation	2.2	Util.
Turned products & screws, nuts, & bolts	1.9	Manufg.	General S/L govt. services	2.0	S/L Govt
Machine shops	1.5	Manufg.	Heavy duty trucks	1.9	Manufg.
Plastics products, nec	1.4	Manufg.	Wholesale trade	1.5	Trade
Truck transportation	1.1	Util.	Transit & ground passenger transportation	0.8	Util.
Retail trade	1.0	Trade	Change in private inventories	0.7	In House
Electronic components, nec	0.9	Manufg.	Postal service	0.6	Util.
Custom roll forming	0.9	Manufg.	General Federal government services, defense	0.6	Fed Govt
Coating, engraving, heat treating & allied activities	0.9	Manufg.	Residential structures, nec	0.6	Construct.
Crowns & closures & metal stamping	0.8	Manufg.	Residential permanent site structures	0.6	Construct.
Rubber products, nec	0.7	Manufg.	Nonresidential structures, nec	0.5	Construct.
Semiconductors & related devices	0.7	Manufg.	Lawn & garden equipment	0.4	Manufg.
Plastics packaging materials, film & sheet	0.7	Manufg.	Boat building	0.4	Manufg.
Scientific research & development services	0.7	Services	Construction machinery	0.4	Manufg.
Power generation & supply	0.7	Util.	S/L govt. passenger transit	0.4	S/L Govt
Leather & hide tanning & finishing	0.7	Manufg.	Transportation equipment, nec	0.3	Manufg.
Ball & roller bearings	0.7	Manufg.	Engine equipment, nec	0.3	Manufg.
Valve & fittings other than plumbing	0.6	Manufg.	Food services & drinking places	0.3	Services
Textile & fabric finishing mills	0.6	Manufg.	Waste management & remediation services	0.3	Services
Lessors of nonfinancial assets	0.5	Fin/R.E.	Aircraft	0.3	Manufg.
Fluid power process machinery	0.5	Manufg.	Services to buildings & dwellings	0.3	Services
Taxes on production & imports, less subsidies	0.5		Oil & gas extraction	0.2	Mining
Plastics materials & resins	0.5	Manufg.	Commercial & health care structures	0.2	Construct.

Continued on next page.

INPUTS AND OUTPUTS FOR MOTOR VEHICLE PARTS MANUFACTURING - Continued

Economic Sector or Industry Providing Inputs	%	Sector	Economic Sector or Industry Buying Outputs	%	Sector
Ornamental & architectural metal products	0.5	Manufg.	Farm machinery & equipment	0.2	Manufg.
Gaskets, packing, & sealing devices	0.5	Manufg.	Management of companies & enterprises	0.2	Services
Securities, commodity contracts, investments	0.5	Fin/R.E.	Truck trailers	0.2	Manufg.
Noncomparable imports	0.5	Foreign	Warehousing & storage	0.2	Util.
Urethane & other foam products (except polystrene)	0.4	Manufg.	Motor vehicle bodies	0.2	Manufg.
Printed circuit assemblies (electronic assemblies)	0.4	Manufg.	Travel trailers & campers	0.2	Manufg.
Alumina refining & primary aluminum production	0.4	Manufg.	Scientific research & development services	0.2	Services
Bare printed circuit boards	0.4	Manufg.	Maintenance/repair of nonresidential structures	0.2	Construct.
Paints & coatings	0.4	Manufg.	Private fixed investment	0.2	
Wiring devices	0.4	Manufg.	Couriers & messengers	0.1	Util.
Fabricated metals, nec	0.4	Manufg.	Individual & family services	0.1	Services
Copper rolling, drawing, extruding, & alloying	0.3	Manufg.	Scenic & sightseeing transport & related services	0.1	Util.
Advertising & related services	0.3	Services	Car washes	0.1	Services
Metal cans, boxes, & other containers (light gauge)	0.3	Manufg.	Automotive equipment rental & leasing	0.1	Fin/R.E.
Real estate	0.3	Fin/R.E.	Crowns & closures & metal stamping	0.1	Manufg.
Speed changers, industrial high-speed drives, & gears	0.3	Manufg.	Material handling equipment	0.1	Manufg.
Primary nonferrous metal, ex. copper & aluminum	0.3	Manufg.			
Paperboard containers	0.3	Manufg.			
Maintenance/repair of nonresidential structures	0.3	Construct.			
Gold, silver, & other metal ore	0.3	Mining			
Services to buildings & dwellings	0.2	Services			
Aluminum products from purchased aluminum	0.2	Manufg.			
Nonferrous metal (ex. copper & aluminum) processing	0.2	Manufg.			
Forging, stamping, & sintering, nec	0.2	Manufg.			
Rubber & plastics hose & belting	0.2	Manufg.			
Natural gas distribution	0.2	Util.			
Rail transportation	0.2	Util.			
Monetary authorities/depository credit intermediation	0.2	Fin/R.E.			
Handtools	0.2	Manufg.			
Automotive equipment rental & leasing	0.2	Fin/R.E.			
Professional, scientific, technical services, nec	0.2	Services			
Basic organic chemicals, nec	0.2	Manufg.			
Warehousing & storage	0.2	Util.			
Legal services	0.2	Services			
Food services & drinking places	0.2	Services			
Communication & energy wires & cables	0.2	Manufg.			
Automotive repair & maintenance, ex. car washes	0.2	Services			
Management, scientific, & technical consulting	0.2	Services			
Engine equipment, nec	0.2	Manufg.			
Wood windows & doors & millwork	0.2	Manufg.			
Veneer & plywood	0.2	Manufg.			
Telecommunications	0.2	Services			
Accounting, tax preparation, bookkeeping, & payroll	0.1	Services			
Commercial & industrial equipment repair/maintenance	0.1	Services			
Architectural, engineering, & related services	0.1	Services			
Artificial & synthetic fibers & filaments	0.1	Manufg.			
Air transportation	0.1	Util.			
Cutting tools & machine tool accessories	0.1	Manufg.			
Employment services	0.1	Services			
Chemical products & preparations, nec	0.1	Manufg.			
Data processing, hosting, & related services	0.1	Services			
Specialized design services	0.1	Services			
Relay & industrial controls	0.1	Manufg.			
Business support services	0.1	Services			
Fiber, yarn, & thread mills	0.1	Manufg.			
Hotels & motels, including casino hotels	0.1	Services			
Electronic capacitors, resistors, coils, transformers	0.1	Manufg.			
Wood containers & pallets	0.1	Manufg.			
Waste management & remediation services	0.1	Services			
Springs & wire products	0.1	Manufg.			
Automatic environmental controls	0.1	Manufg.			

Source: Benchmark Input-Output Accounts for the U.S. Economy, 2002, U.S. Department of Commerce, Washington D.C., January 2008. User should note that this Input-Output table is not for this particular narrowly defined industry but for a larger aggregate. Input and Output data for Motor Vehicle Parts Manufacturing include Input and Output data for the Annual Survey of Manufactures' NAICS industries 33631M, 33632M, 336330, 336340, 336350, 336360, 336370, 336391, and 336399. The abbreviation nec stands for 'not elsewhere classified'.

OCCUPATIONS EMPLOYED BY MOTOR VEHICLE PARTS MANUFACTURING

Occupation	% of Total 2006	Change to 2016	Occupation	% of Total 2006	Change to 2016
Team assemblers	15.2	-19.2	Welders, cutters, solderers, & brazers	1.9	-15.3
Cutting, punching, & press machine operators	4.2	-28.4	Molding, coremaking, & casting machine operators	1.8	-28.4
Machinists	3.8	-16.4	Welding, soldering, & brazing machine operators	1.6	-10.5
Inspectors, testers, sorters, samplers, & weighers	3.5	-24.9	Industrial machinery mechanics	1.5	-8.4
First-line supervisors/managers of production workers	3.3	-20.4	Helpers--Production workers	1.5	-20.4
Assemblers & fabricators, nec	3.2	-28.4	Mechanical engineers	1.4	-20.4
Multiple machine tool operators & tenders	2.6	-12.4	Electrical & electronic equipment assemblers	1.4	-36.3
Tool & die makers	2.6	-16.4	Lathe & turning machine tool operators & tenders	1.3	-28.4
Industrial truck & tractor operators	2.6	-28.4	Shipping, receiving, & traffic clerks	1.3	-23.4
Laborers & freight, stock, & material movers, hand	2.1	-28.4	Electricians	1.3	-17.4
Industrial engineers	2.1	-3.3	Grinding, lapping, polishing machine tool operators	1.2	-22.8
Maintenance & repair workers, general	2.0	-20.4	Engine & other machine assemblers	1.1	-20.4
Production workers, nec	2.0	-21.9	Drilling & boring machine tool operators	1.1	-28.4
Computer-controlled machine tool operators	1.9	-12.4	Production, planning, & expediting clerks	1.1	-20.4

Source: Industry-Occupation Matrix, Bureau of Labor Statistics, December 4, 2007. These data are reported based on 4-digit NAICS categories but have been matched to corresponding 6-digit NAICS industry codes. The change reported for each occupation to the year 2016 is a percent of growth or decline as estimated by the Bureau of Labor Statistics. The abbreviation nec stands for 'not elsewhere classified'.

LOCATION BY STATE AND REGIONAL CONCENTRATION

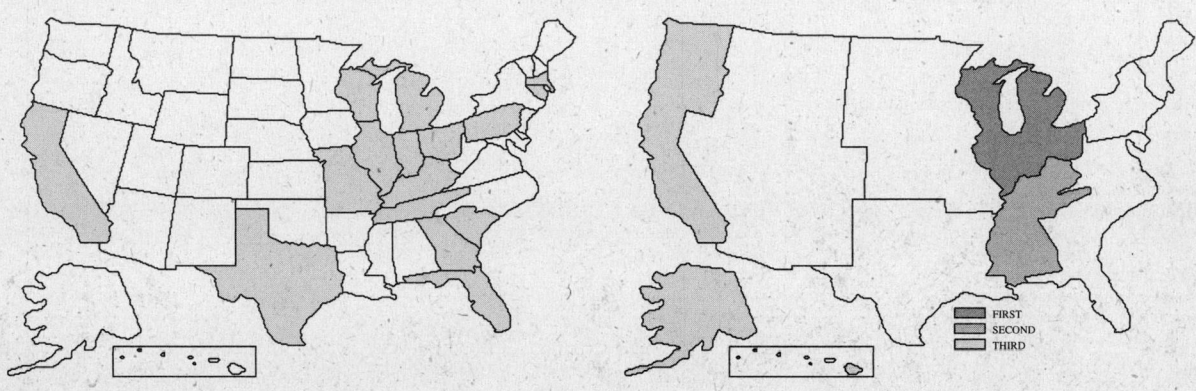

FIRST
SECOND
THIRD

INDUSTRY DATA BY STATE

State	Establish-ments	Shipments			Employment				Cost as % of Shipments	Investment per Employee ($)
		Total ($ mil)	% of U.S.	Per Establ.	Total Number	% of U.S.	Per Establ.	Wages ($/hour)		
Michigan	284	10,443.1	41.9	36,771.5	49,458	40.7	174	25.84	52.9	7,761
Ohio	159	6,326.1	25.4	39,787.0	30,088	24.7	189	25.29	48.7	9,878
Indiana	50	2,170.4	8.7	43,407.6	10,021	8.2	200	23.15	51.3	6,389
Kentucky	17	1,194.3	4.8	70,254.8	4,513	3.7	265	16.23	51.8	10,017
Illinois	53	702.7	2.8	13,257.7	3,760	3.1	71	19.82	49.7	16,046
Tennessee	23	532.6	2.1	23,154.8	2,830	2.3	123	20.00	58.1	21,528
South Carolina	9	418.0	1.7	46,449.6	1,422	1.2	158	17.89	60.7	18,098
Pennsylvania	18	291.9	1.2	16,215.5	1,778	1.5	99	27.78	41.3	2,456
California	31	243.8	1.0	7,865.6	2,198	1.8	71	13.67	53.7	5,590
Wisconsin	17	181.8	0.7	10,694.8	1,353	1.1	80	12.74	45.3	3,834
Georgia	10	175.7	0.7	17,571.6	1,090	0.9	109	13.89	53.5	7,912
Missouri	11	123.8	0.5	11,255.3	733	0.6	67	16.31	49.1	4,030
Connecticut	12	91.8	0.4	7,652.6	510	0.4	43	26.19	36.1	3,533
Florida	11	90.3	0.4	8,207.0	983	0.8	89	11.46	49.6	2,985
Texas	12	84.2	0.3	7,013.2	359	0.3	30	15.65	51.7	2,880
Massachusetts	10	57.1	0.2	5,714.3	423	0.3	42	20.45	45.1	2,225

Source: 2002 Economic Census. The states are in descending order of shipments or establishments (if shipment data are missing for the majority). The symbol (D) appears when data are withheld to prevent disclosure of competitive information. States marked with (D) are sorted by number of establishments. A dash (-) indicates that the data element cannot be calculated. Data may not show all states active in the NAICS category. All data available at the time of publication are shown.

NAICS 336391 - MOTOR VEHICLE AIR-CONDITIONING MANUFACTURING

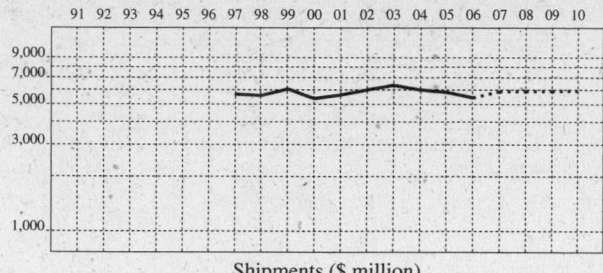

Shipments ($ million)

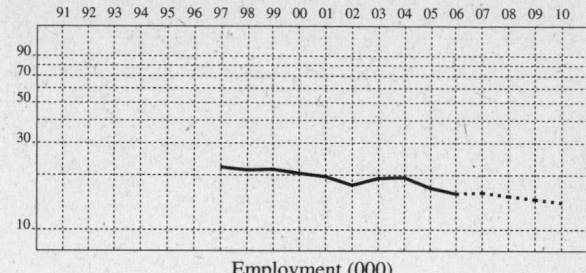

Employment (000)

GENERAL STATISTICS

Year	Com-panies	Establishments		Employment			Compensation		Production ($ million)			
		Total	with 20 or more employees	Total (000)	Production Workers (000)	Hours (Mil)	Payroll ($ mil)	Wages ($/hr)	Cost of Materials	Value Added by Manufacture	Value of Shipments	Capital Invest.
1997	60	62	38	22.1	17.9	39.6	1,067.1	20.90	2,895.6	2,720.0	5,665.0	188.6
1998		62	37	21.3	17.4	38.4	999.1	19.68	3,002.0	2,606.7	5,568.5	259.4
1999		70	39	21.5	17.8	39.8	1,169.7	22.26	3,363.2	2,713.6	6,065.4	360.8
2000		69	40	20.4	16.9	35.3	1,058.1	22.58	3,173.0	2,175.1	5,364.7	243.1
2001		69	36	19.6	16.0	32.0	1,054.3	24.95	3,287.9	2,355.1	5,623.1	248.5
2002	74	81	42	17.6	14.1	28.3	857.7	22.45	3,546.8	2,438.3	5,987.7	212.0
2003		87	38	19.2	15.3	30.3	947.4	21.96	3,951.7	2,399.9	6,355.3	135.5
2004		86	41	19.4	15.2	29.9	954.5	22.57	3,804.0	2,221.2	6,008.1	115.2
2005		80	42	17.0	13.1	26.4	822.9	21.57	3,708.4	2,092.6	5,820.3	132.3
2006		90P	42P	15.8	12.3	24.8	795.7	22.12	3,212.5	2,249.6	5,430.3	183.7
2007		93P	42P	16.0P	12.3P	23.0P	796.6P	22.82P	3,477.9P	2,435.4P	5,878.8P	123.9P
2008		96P	43P	15.3P	11.7P	21.2P	764.6P	22.95P	3,487.5P	2,442.2P	5,895.2P	108.6P
2009		99P	43P	14.7P	11.0P	19.5P	732.6P	23.08P	3,497.2P	2,449.0P	5,911.6P	93.3P
2010		103P	43P	14.1P	10.4P	17.8P	700.6P	23.21P	3,506.9P	2,455.8P	5,927.9P	78.0P

Sources: 1997 and 2002 *Economic Census*; other years, up to 2006, are from *Annual Survey of Manufactures*. Establishment counts for non-Census years are from *County Business Patterns*; 1997 and 2002 values are from the 1997 and 2002 censuses, respectively. 'P's show projections by the editors.

INDICES OF CHANGE

Year	Com-panies	Establishments		Employment			Compensation		Production ($ million)			
		Total	with 20 or more employees	Total (000)	Production Workers (000)	Hours (Mil)	Payroll ($ mil)	Wages ($/hr)	Cost of Materials	Value Added by Manufacture	Value of Shipments	Capital Invest.
1997	81	77	90	126	127	140	124	93	82	112	95	89
1998		77	88	121	123	136	116	88	85	107	93	122
1999		86	93	122	126	141	136	99	95	111	101	170
2000		85	95	116	120	125	123	101	89	89	90	115
2001		85	86	111	113	113	123	111	93	97	94	117
2002	100	100	100	100	100	100	100	100	100	100	100	100
2003		107	90	109	109	107	110	98	111	98	106	64
2004		106	98	110	108	106	111	101	107	91	100	54
2005		99	100	97	93	93	96	96	105	86	97	62
2006		111P	99P	90	87	88	93	99	91	92	91	87
2007		115P	100P	91P	87P	81P	93P	102P	98P	100P	98P	58P
2008		119P	101P	87P	83P	75P	89P	102P	98P	100P	98P	51P
2009		123P	102P	84P	78P	69P	85P	103P	99P	100P	99P	44P
2010		127P	103P	80P	74P	63P	82P	103P	99P	101P	99P	37P

Sources: Same as General Statistics. Values reflect change from the base year, 2002. Values above 100 mean greater than 2002, values below 100 mean less than 2002, and the values of 100 in other years means the same as 2002. 'P's show projections by the editors.

SELECTED RATIOS

For 2002	Avg. of All Manufact.	Analyzed Industry	Index	For 2002	Avg. of All Manufact.	Analyzed Industry	Index
Employees per Establishment	42	217	518	Value Added per Production Worker	182,367	172,929	95
Payroll per Establishment	1,639,184	10,588,889	646	Cost per Establishment	5,769,015	43,787,654	759
Payroll per Employee	39,053	48,733	125	Cost per Employee	137,446	201,523	147
Production Workers per Establishment	30	174	590	Cost per Production Worker	195,506	251,546	129
Wages per Establishment	694,845	7,843,642	1,129	Shipments per Establishment	11,158,348	73,922,222	662
Wages per Production Worker	23,548	45,059	191	Shipments per Employee	265,847	340,210	128
Hours per Production Worker	1,980	2,007	101	Shipments per Production Worker	378,144	424,660	112
Wages per Hour	11.89	22.45	189	Investment per Establishment	361,338	2,617,284	724
Value Added per Establishment	5,381,325	30,102,469	559	Investment per Employee	8,609	12,045	140
Value Added per Employee	128,210	138,540	108	Investment per Production Worker	12,245	15,035	123

Sources: Same as General Statistics. The 'Average of All Manufacturing' column represents the average of all manufacturing industries reported for the most recent complete year available. The Index shows the relationship between the Average and the Analyzed Industry. For example, 100 means that they are equal; 500 that the Analyzed Industry is five times the average; 50 means that the Analyzed Industry is half the national average. The abbreviation 'na' is used to show that data are 'not available'. Ratios shown for 2002, the last complete census year.

LEADING COMPANIES   Number shown: **75**   Total sales ($ mil): **155,967**   Total employment (000): **627.5**

Company Name	Address				CEO Name	Phone	Co. Type	Sales ($ mil)	Empl. (000)
United Technologies Corp.	1 Financial Plz.	Hartford	CT	06101	Mario Abajo	860-728-7000	P	47,829	225.6
Danaher Corp.	2099 Penn. Avenue	Washington	DC	20006	H. Lawrence Culp Jr.	202-828-0850	P	11,026	50.0
Carrier Corp.	One Carrier Pl.	Farmington	CT	06034	Geraud Darnis		S	10,600	4.3
American Standard Inc.	PO Box 6820	Piscataway	NJ	08855		732-980-3000	S	7,614*	67.0
Trane Inc.	PO Box 6820	Piscataway	NJ	08855		732-980-6000	P	7,450	29.6
Dover Corp.	280 Park Ave.	New York	NY	10017		212-922-1640	P	7,226	33.4
Trane	4 Wood Hollow Rd.	Piscataway	NJ	08855		973-887-8800	S	6,020	27.1
Hussmann Corp.	12999 St. Chrles Rd	Bridgeton	MO	63044	Dennis Gibson	314-291-2000	S	4,623*	8.0
York International Corp.	PO Box 1592	York	PA	17405		717-771-7890	S	4,510	23.2
PepsiAmericas Inc.	4000 Dain Rauscher	Minneapolis	MN	55402		612-661-4000	P	4,480	20.7
Marley-Wylain Co.	13515 Ballnyn Corp.	Charlotte	NC	28277	C. J. Kearney	704-752-4400	S	4,372*	23.8
Manitowoc Company Inc.	PO Box 66	Manitowoc	WI	54221		920-684-4410	P	4,005	10.5
Lennox International Inc.	PO Box 799900	Dallas	TX	75379	Todd M. Bluedorn	972-497-5000	P	3,750	15.0
Siemens Power Generation Inc.	4400 N Alafaya Trl.	Orlando	FL	32826	Randy Zwirn	407-736-2000	S	3,081*	3.0
Cornelius IMI Inc.	101 Broadway St. W	Osseo	MN	55369	Richard Barkley	763-488-8200	R	2,840*	0.3
Baltimore Aircoil Company Inc.	PO Box 7322	Baltimore	MD	21227	Steven Duerwachter	410-799-6200	R	2,510*	0.2
NTK Holdings Inc.	50 Kennedy Plz.	Providence	RI	02903	Richard L. Bready	401-751-1600	S	2,218	9.8
Goodman Global Inc.	2550 North Loop W	Houston	TX	77092	Charles A. Carroll	713-861-2500	S	1,795	4.9
Engineered Support Systems	201 Evans Ln.	St. Louis	MO	63121	Nicholas Innerbichler	314-553-4000	S	1,736	5.7
Formtek Inc.	260 N Elm St.	Westfield	MA	01085	John E. Reed	413-568-9571	S	1,530*	2.6
Connell L.P.	1 International Pl.	Boston	MA	02110	Margot C. Connell	617-737-2700	R	1,429*	2.0
Sanden of America Inc.	601 Sanden Blvd.	Wylie	TX	75098	Kazuhiko Arai	972-442-8400	S	1,420*	<0.1
Tecumseh Products Co.	100 E Patterson St.	Tecumseh	MI	49286	Edwin Bunker	517-423-8411	P	1,133	10.3
Behr Climate Systems Inc.	5020 Augusta Dr.	Fort Worth	TX	76106		817-624-7273	R	885*	0.2
McQuay International	13600 Indu Prk Blvd	Minneapolis	MN	55441	Ho Nyuk Chow	763-553-5330	S	838*	5.0
Enodis Corp.	2227 Welbilt Blvd.	New Port Richey	FL	34655	Peter Brooks	727-375-7010	S	650*	3.0
Axair Nortec Inc.	PO Box 698	Ogdensburg	NY	13669	URS Schenk	315-425-1255	R	627*	<0.1
Standex International Corp.	6 Manor Pky.	Salem	NH	03079	Roger L. Fix	603-893-9701	P	621	5.4
Middleby Corp.	1400 Toastmaster Dr	Elgin	IL	60120	Selim A. Bassoul	847-741-3300	P	501	1.7
LSB Industries Inc.	16 S Penn. Avenue	Oklahoma City	OK	73107	Jack E. Golsen	405-235-4546	P	492	1.6
Elkay Manufacturing Co.	2222 Camden Ct.	Oak Brook	IL	60523	Ronald Katz	630-574-8484	R	470*	3.6
Luwa Inc.	3901 Westpoint Blvd	Winston-Salem	NC	27103		336-760-3111	R	448*	0.1
Liebert Corp.	PO Box 29186	Columbus	OH	43229	Robert Bauer	614-888-0246	S	440*	5.0
Proliance International Inc.	100 Gando Dr.	New Haven	CT	06513	Barry R. Banducci	203-401-6450	P	416	2.0
Lan-Leasing Inc.	6655 Lancer Blvd.	San Antonio	TX	78219	Chris Hughes	210-310-7000	R	386*	0.7
Nordyne Inc.	8000 Phoenix Pkwy.	O Fallon	MO	63366	David Lagrand	636-561-7300	S	377*	1.8
Mestek Inc.	260 N Elm St.	Westfield	MA	01085	R. Bruce Dewey	413-568-9571	R	372*	2.6
FES Systems Inc.	PO Box 2306	York	PA	17405	Ronald Eberhard	717-767-6411	R	347*	0.2
Reddy Ice Holdings Inc.	8750 N Central Expy	Dallas	TX	75231	William P. Brick	214-526-6740	P	339	1.5
TOPP Portable Air	12 Crozerville Rd.	Aston	PA	19014	Dan Topp	610-459-5515	R	303*	<0.1
Mammoth Inc.	101 W 82nd St.	Chaska	MN	55318	David J. Huntley	952-361-2711	S	299*	0.4
Fedders Corp.	PO Box 813	Liberty Corner	NJ	07938	Michael Giordano	908-604-8686	P	279	2.0
AAON Inc.	2425 S Yukon Ave.	Tulsa	OK	74107	N H. Asbjornson	918-583-2266	P	263	1.4
Michigan Automotive Compressor	2400 N Dearing Rd.	Parma	MI	49269	Hiroyo Kono	517-622-7000	R	231*	0.8
Thermo Products L.L.C.	PO Box 217	North Judson	IN	46366		574-896-2133	R	218*	0.1
Krack Corp.	401 S Rohlwing Rd.	Addison	IL	60101	Herbert Henkel	630-629-7500	S	199*	0.3
Carrier Refrigeration	One Carrier Pl.	Farmington	CT	06034	Geraud Darnis	860-674-3000	D	175*	0.3
Lancer Corp.	PO Box 131425	San Antonio	TX	78219		210-310-7000	S	157*	1.5
Igloo Products Corp.	PO Box 19322	Houston	TX	77224	Jonathan Godshall	713-584-6800	R	150*	1.5
Ultra Air Products Inc.	3309 John Conley	Lapeer	MI	48446	Don Swanson	810-667-6800	R	136*	0.7
Danfoss Inc.	7941 Corporate Dr.	Baltimore	MD	21236	Jorgen Clausen	410-931-8250	R	125*	0.1
Idleaire Technologies Corp.	410 N Cedar Bluff	Knoxville	TN	37923	Michael Crabtree	865-342-3600	R	113*	0.5
ATCO Rubber Products Inc.	7101 Atco Dr.	Fort Worth	TX	76118	Charles Anderson	817-595-2894	R	113*	0.6
AIRXCEL Inc.	PO Box 4020	Wichita	KS	67204	Melvin Adams	316-832-3400	R	111*	0.2
Dometic Corp.	PO Box 490	Elkhart	IN	46516	John Waters	574-294-2511	S	110*	0.6
Delfield Co.	980 S Isabella Rd.	Mt. Pleasant	MI	48858	Kevin Clark	989-773-7981	D	108*	0.7
Standex Int'l Federal Indust.	215 Federal Ave.	Belleville	WI	53508	Jerry Jansen		D	106*	0.2
AdobeAir Inc.	1450 E Grant St.	Phoenix	AZ	85034		602-257-0060	R	105*	0.6
EvapCo Inc.	5151 Allendale Ln.	Taneytown	MD	21787	Wilson Bradley	410-756-2600	R	96*	0.2
Beverage-Air Co.	PO Box 5932	Spartanburg	SC	29304	Tim Grob		D	93*	0.1
Oasis Corp.	265 N Hamilton Rd.	Columbus	OH	43213	Romanie Gilliland	614-861-1350	R	92*	0.5
Chatleff Controls Inc.	PO Box 1350	Buda	TX	78610	Raymond Henderson	512-295-2217	R	86*	0.5
J.B. Industries Inc.	PO Box 1180	Aurora	IL	60507	Jeff Cherif	630-851-9444	R	84*	<0.1
Alma Products Co.	2000 Michigan Ave.	Alma	MI	48801	Alan Galtan	989-463-1151	R	82*	<0.1
Enviro Systems Inc.	12037 N Hwy 99	Seminole	OK	74868	Craig Froelich	405-382-0731	R	80*	0.1
Manitowoc Ice Inc.	2110 S 26th St.	Manitowoc	WI	54220	Dan Brandel	920-682-0161	S	77*	0.4
Lasko Products Inc.	820 Lincoln Ave.	West Chester	PA	19380	Oscar Lasko	610-692-7400	R	74*	0.2
Climate Master Inc.	7300 SW 44th St.	Oklahoma City	OK	73179	Dan Ellis	405-745-6000	S	70*	0.3
Kelco Industries Inc.	9210 Country Club	Woodstock	IL	60098	Kevin Kelly	815-338-5521	R	66*	<0.1
Henry Technologies Inc.	1 ABC Pkwy.	Beloit	WI	53511	Charlie Graham	608-361-4400	R	62*	<0.1
Water Services of America Inc.	2018 S 1st St.	Milwaukee	WI	53207	Kaveh Someah	414-481-4120	R	61*	0.2
Slant Fin Corp.	100 Forest Dr.	Greenvale	NY	11548	Donald Brown	516-484-2600	R	60*	0.4
Technical Chemical Co.	PO Box 139	Cleburne	TX	76033	Howard Dudley	817-645-6088	R	60*	0.1
Astro Air Inc.	1653 N Bolton St.	Jacksonville	TX	75766	Rex Dacus	903-586-3691	R	59*	0.3
Evans Tempcon Inc.	701 Ann St. NW	Grand Rapids	MI	49504		616-361-2681	R	59*	0.4

Source: Ward's Business Directory of U.S. Private and Public Companies, Volumes 1 and 2, 2008. The company type code used is as follows: P - Public, R - Private, S - Subsidiary, D - Division, J - Joint Venture, A - Affiliate, G - Group. Sales are in millions of dollars, employees are in thousands. An asterisk (*) indicates an estimated sales volume. The symbol < stands for 'less than'. Company names and addresses are truncated, in some cases, to fit into the available space.

MATERIALS CONSUMED

Material	Quantity	Delivered Cost ($ million)
Refrigeration compressors, compressor units, condensing units, and other heat transfer equipment	(X)	568.5
Fractional horsepower electric timing motors (less than 1 hp)	(X)	2.9
Fractional horsepower electric motors (less than 1 hp), exc. timing motors	(X)	(D)
Integral horsepower electric motors and generators (1 hp or more)	(X)	(D)
Fans and blowers	(X)	21.6
Electrical transmission, distribution, and control equipment	(X)	(D)
Current-carrying wiring devices	(X)	88.4
Automatic temperature controls (thermostats, regulators, etc.)	(X)	(D)
Ball and roller bearings (mounted or unmounted)	(X)	85.6
Metal bolts, nuts, screws, and other screw machine products	(X)	145.2
Metal stampings	(X)	(D)
Metal hardware (inc. hinges, handles, locks, casters, etc.)	(X)	(D)
Metal pipe, valves, and pipe fittings (excluding forgings)	(X)	17.5
All other fabricated metal products (excluding forgings)	(X)	(D)
Forgings	(X)	58.7
Iron and steel castings (rough and semifinished)	(X)	(D)
Aluminum and aluminum-base alloy castings (rough and semifinished)	(X)	(D)
Steel bars, bar shapes, and plates (exc. castings, forgings, fabr. metal products)	(X)	15.7
Steel sheet and strip (including tinplate)	(X)	5.7
Steel wire and wire products	(X)	(D)
All other steel shapes and forms (exc. castings, forgings, fabr. metal products)	(X)	15.9
Copper and copper-base alloy pipe and tube (exc. castings, forgings, fabr. metal products)	(X)	7.1
All other copper and copper-base alloy shapes and forms (exc. castings, forgings, fabr. metal products)	(X)	(D)
Aluminum and aluminum-base alloy sheet, plate, foil, and welded tubing	(X)	(D)
All other aluminum and aluminum-base alloy shapes and forms (exc. castings, forgings, fabr. metal products)	(X)	(D)
Other nonferrous shapes and forms (exc. castings, forgings, fabricated metal products)	(X)	3.7
Paper and paperboard containers (incl. shipping sacks and other paper packaging supplies)	(X)	18.2
Wooden containers, complete (incl. combination wood and paperboard)	(X)	(D)
Paints, varnishes, stains, lacquers, shellacs, japans, enamels, etc.	(X)	2.3
Refrigerant gases and other synthetic organic chemicals	(X)	2.6
Plastics resins consumed in the form of granules, pellets, etc.	(X)	(D)
Plastics products consumed in the form of sheets, rods, etc.	(X)	44.8
Fabricated plastics products (exc. gaskets, hoses, and belting)	(X)	75.1
Rubber and plastics hose and belting	(X)	110.8
Gaskets (all types) and asbestos packing	(X)	28.1
Mineral wool insulation (fibrous glass, rock wool, etc.)	(X)	(D)
All other materials, components, parts, containers, and supplies	(X)	861.2
Materials, ingredients, containers, and supplies, nsk	(X)	17.3

Source: 2002 *Economic Census*. Explanation of symbols used: (D): Withheld to avoid disclosure of competitive data; na: Not available; (S): Withheld because statistical norms were not met; (X): Not applicable; (Z): Less than half the unit shown; nec: Not elsewhere classified; nsk: Not specified by kind; - : zero; p : 10-19 percent estimated; q : 20-29 percent estimated.

PRODUCT SHARE DETAILS

Product or Product Class Shipments	Mil. $	Product or Product Class Shipments	Mil. $
MOTOR VEHICLE AIR-CONDITIONING UNITS AND SYSTEMS	4,664.2	buses	162.9
Motor vehicle mechanical air-conditioning systems	**2,940.3**	Other motor vehicle mechanical air-conditioning systems	628.1
Motor vehicle mechanical air-conditioning systems for passenger automobiles	2,149.3	**Automotive air-conditioning compressors (open-type, with or without motor)**	**1,707.2**
Motor vehicle mechanical air-conditioning systems for		**Motor vehicle air-conditioning units and systems, nsk, total**	**16.7**

Source: 2002 *Economic Census*. The values are product shipments in millions of dollars for 2002. Total product shipments may be lower or higher than industry shipments. See Introduction for a full discussion. Values of indented subcategories are summed in the main heading(s). The symbol (D) appears when data are withheld to prevent disclosure of competitive information. The abbreviation nsk stands for 'not specified by kind' and nec for 'not elsewhere classified'. A dash (-) means zero.

INPUTS AND OUTPUTS FOR MOTOR VEHICLE PARTS MANUFACTURING

Economic Sector or Industry Providing Inputs	%	Sector	Economic Sector or Industry Buying Outputs	%	Sector
Compensation of employees	22.8		Light truck & utility vehicles	25.3	Manufg.
Motor vehicle parts	10.7	Manufg.	Automobiles	15.8	Manufg.
Management of companies & enterprises	7.0	Services	Exports of goods & services	13.9	Cap Inv
Wholesale trade	5.3	Trade	Motor vehicle parts	8.5	Manufg.
Iron & steel mills & ferroalloys	5.0	Manufg.	Retail trade	7.4	Trade
Nonferrous metal foundries	2.6	Manufg.	Personal consumption expenditures	4.1	
Ferrous metal foundries	2.4	Manufg.	Automotive repair & maintenance, ex. car washes	2.9	Services
Plate work & fabricated structural products	1.9	Manufg.	Truck transportation	2.2	Util.
Turned products & screws, nuts, & bolts	1.9	Manufg.	General S/L govt. services	2.0	S/L Govt
Machine shops	1.5	Manufg.	Heavy duty trucks	1.9	Manufg.
Plastics products, nec	1.4	Manufg.	Wholesale trade	1.5	Trade
Truck transportation	1.1	Util.	Transit & ground passenger transportation	0.8	Util.
Retail trade	1.0	Trade	Change in private inventories	0.7	In House

Continued on next page.

INPUTS AND OUTPUTS FOR MOTOR VEHICLE PARTS MANUFACTURING - Continued

Economic Sector or Industry Providing Inputs	%	Sector	Economic Sector or Industry Buying Outputs	%	Sector
Electronic components, nec	0.9	Manufg.	Postal service	0.6	Util.
Custom roll forming	0.9	Manufg.	General Federal government services, defense	0.6	Fed Govt
Coating, engraving, heat treating & allied activities	0.9	Manufg.	Residential structures, nec	0.6	Construct.
Crowns & closures & metal stamping	0.8	Manufg.	Residential permanent site structures	0.6	Construct.
Rubber products, nec	0.7	Manufg.	Nonresidential structures, nec	0.5	Construct.
Semiconductors & related devices	0.7	Manufg.	Lawn & garden equipment	0.4	Manufg.
Plastics packaging materials, film & sheet	0.7	Manufg.	Boat building	0.4	Manufg.
Scientific research & development services	0.7	Services	Construction machinery	0.4	Manufg.
Power generation & supply	0.7	Util.	S/L govt. passenger transit	0.4	S/L Govt
Leather & hide tanning & finishing	0.7	Manufg.	Transportation equipment, nec	0.3	Manufg.
Ball & roller bearings	0.7	Manufg.	Engine equipment, nec	0.3	Manufg.
Valve & fittings other than plumbing	0.6	Manufg.	Food services & drinking places	0.3	Services
Textile & fabric finishing mills	0.6	Manufg.	Waste management & remediation services	0.3	Services
Lessors of nonfinancial assets	0.5	Fin/R.E.	Aircraft	0.3	Manufg.
Fluid power process machinery	0.5	Manufg.	Services to buildings & dwellings	0.3	Services
Taxes on production & imports, less subsidies	0.5		Oil & gas extraction	0.2	Mining
Plastics materials & resins	0.5	Manufg.	Commercial & health care structures	0.2	Construct.
Ornamental & architectural metal products	0.5	Manufg.	Farm machinery & equipment	0.2	Manufg.
Gaskets, packing, & sealing devices	0.5	Manufg.	Management of companies & enterprises	0.2	Services
Securities, commodity contracts, investments	0.5	Fin/R.E.	Truck trailers	0.2	Manufg.
Noncomparable imports	0.5	Foreign	Warehousing & storage	0.2	Util.
Urethane & other foam products (except polystrene)	0.4	Manufg.	Motor vehicle bodies	0.2	Manufg.
Printed circuit assemblies (electronic assemblies)	0.4	Manufg.	Travel trailers & campers	0.2	Manufg.
Alumina refining & primary aluminum production	0.4	Manufg.	Scientific research & development services	0.2	Services
Bare printed circuit boards	0.4	Manufg.	Maintenance/repair of nonresidential structures	0.2	Construct.
Paints & coatings	0.4	Manufg.	Private fixed investment	0.2	
Wiring devices	0.4	Manufg.	Couriers & messengers	0.1	Util.
Fabricated metals, nec	0.4	Manufg.	Individual & family services	0.1	Services
Copper rolling, drawing, extruding, & alloying	0.3	Manufg.	Scenic & sightseeing transport & related services	0.1	Util.
Advertising & related services	0.3	Services	Car washes	0.1	Services
Metal cans, boxes, & other containers (light gauge)	0.3	Manufg.	Automotive equipment rental & leasing	0.1	Fin/R.E.
Real estate	0.3	Fin/R.E.	Crowns & closures & metal stamping	0.1	Manufg.
Speed changers, industrial high-speed drives, & gears	0.3	Manufg.	Material handling equipment	0.1	Manufg.
Primary nonferrous metal, ex. copper & aluminum	0.3	Manufg.			
Paperboard containers	0.3	Manufg.			
Maintenance/repair of nonresidential structures	0.3	Construct.			
Gold, silver, & other metal ore	0.3	Mining			
Services to buildings & dwellings	0.2	Services			
Aluminum products from purchased aluminum	0.2	Manufg.			
Nonferrous metal (ex. copper & aluminum) processing	0.2	Manufg.			
Forging, stamping, & sintering, nec	0.2	Manufg.			
Rubber & plastics hose & belting	0.2	Manufg.			
Natural gas distribution	0.2	Util.			
Rail transportation	0.2	Util.			
Monetary authorities/depository credit intermediation	0.2	Fin/R.E.			
Handtools	0.2	Manufg.			
Automotive equipment rental & leasing	0.2	Fin/R.E.			
Professional, scientific, technical services, nec	0.2	Services			
Basic organic chemicals, nec	0.2	Manufg.			
Warehousing & storage	0.2	Util.			
Legal services	0.2	Services			
Food services & drinking places	0.2	Services			
Communication & energy wires & cables	0.2	Manufg.			
Automotive repair & maintenance, ex. car washes	0.2	Services			
Management, scientific, & technical consulting	0.2	Services			
Engine equipment, nec	0.2	Manufg.			
Wood windows & doors & millwork	0.2	Manufg.			
Veneer & plywood	0.2	Manufg.			
Telecommunications	0.2	Services			
Accounting, tax preparation, bookkeeping, & payroll	0.1	Services			
Commercial & industrial equipment repair/maintenance	0.1	Services			
Architectural, engineering, & related services	0.1	Services			
Artificial & synthetic fibers & filaments	0.1	Manufg.			
Air transportation	0.1	Util.			
Cutting tools & machine tool accessories	0.1	Manufg.			
Employment services	0.1	Services			
Chemical products & preparations, nec	0.1	Manufg.			
Data processing, hosting, & related services	0.1	Services			
Specialized design services	0.1	Services			
Relay & industrial controls	0.1	Manufg.			
Business support services	0.1	Services			
Fiber, yarn, & thread mills	0.1	Manufg.			
Hotels & motels, including casino hotels	0.1	Services			
Electronic capacitors, resistors, coils, transformers	0.1	Manufg.			
Wood containers & pallets	0.1	Manufg.			
Waste management & remediation services	0.1	Services			
Springs & wire products	0.1	Manufg.			
Automatic environmental controls	0.1	Manufg.			

Source: Benchmark Input-Output Accounts for the U.S. Economy, 2002, U.S. Department of Commerce, Washington D.C., January 2008. User should note that this Input-Output table is not for this particular narrowly defined industry but for a larger aggregate. Input and Output data for Motor Vehicle Parts Manufacturing include Input and Output data for the Annual Survey of Manufactures' NAICS industries 33631M, 33632M, 336330, 336340, 336350, 336360, 336370, 336391, and 336399. The abbreviation nec stands for 'not elsewhere classified'.

OCCUPATIONS EMPLOYED BY MOTOR VEHICLE PARTS MANUFACTURING

Occupation	% of Total 2006	Change to 2016	Occupation	% of Total 2006	Change to 2016
Team assemblers	15.2	-19.2	Welders, cutters, solderers, & brazers	1.9	-15.3
Cutting, punching, & press machine operators	4.2	-28.4	Molding, coremaking, & casting machine operators	1.8	-28.4
Machinists	3.8	-16.4	Welding, soldering, & brazing machine operators	1.6	-10.5
Inspectors, testers, sorters, samplers, & weighers	3.5	-24.9	Industrial machinery mechanics	1.5	-8.4
First-line supervisors/managers of production workers	3.3	-20.4	Helpers--Production workers	1.5	-20.4
Assemblers & fabricators, nec	3.2	-28.4	Mechanical engineers	1.4	-20.4
Multiple machine tool operators & tenders	2.6	-12.4	Electrical & electronic equipment assemblers	1.4	-36.3
Tool & die makers	2.6	-16.4	Lathe & turning machine tool operators & tenders	1.3	-28.4
Industrial truck & tractor operators	2.6	-28.4	Shipping, receiving, & traffic clerks	1.3	-23.4
Laborers & freight, stock, & material movers, hand	2.1	-28.4	Electricians	1.3	-17.4
Industrial engineers	2.1	-3.3	Grinding, lapping, polishing machine tool operators	1.2	-22.8
Maintenance & repair workers, general	2.0	-20.4	Engine & other machine assemblers	1.1	-20.4
Production workers, nec	2.0	-21.9	Drilling & boring machine tool operators	1.1	-28.4
Computer-controlled machine tool operators	1.9	-12.4	Production, planning, & expediting clerks	1.1	-20.4

Source: Industry-Occupation Matrix, Bureau of Labor Statistics, December 4, 2007. These data are reported based on 4-digit NAICS categories but have been matched to corresponding 6-digit NAICS industry codes. The change reported for each occupation to the year 2016 is a percent of growth or decline as estimated by the Bureau of Labor Statistics. The abbreviation nec stands for 'not elsewhere classified'.

LOCATION BY STATE AND REGIONAL CONCENTRATION

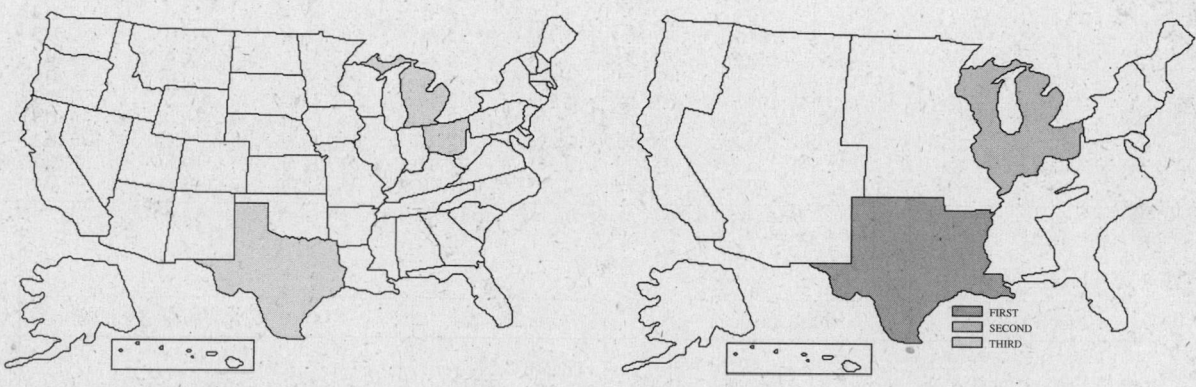

INDUSTRY DATA BY STATE

State	Establish-ments	Shipments			Employment				Cost as % of Shipments	Investment per Employee ($)
		Total ($ mil)	% of U.S.	Per Establ.	Total Number	% of U.S.	Per Establ.	Wages ($/hour)		
Michigan	7	2,010.6	33.6	287,228.7	3,436	19.6	491	25.02	60.2	24,726
Ohio	7	1,018.1	17.0	145,439.6	2,364	13.5	338	21.02	38.0	14,382
Texas	23	614.2	10.3	26,704.8	2,013	11.5	88	22.57	74.5	19,129

Source: 2002 Economic Census. The states are in descending order of shipments or establishments (if shipment data are missing for the majority). The symbol (D) appears when data are withheld to prevent disclosure of competitive information. States marked with (D) are sorted by number of establishments. A dash (-) indicates that the data element cannot be calculated. Data may not show all states active in the NAICS category. All data available at the time of publication are shown.

NAICS 336399 - MOTOR VEHICLE PARTS MANUFACTURING NEC

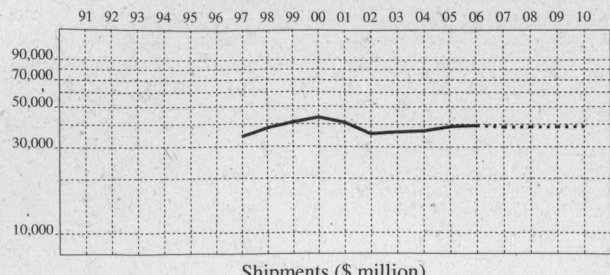

Shipments ($ million)

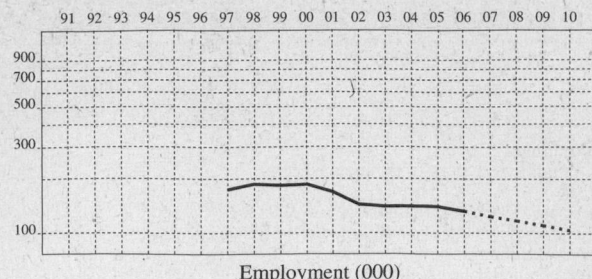

Employment (000)

GENERAL STATISTICS

Year	Companies	Establishments		Employment			Compensation		Production ($ million)			
		Total	with 20 or more employees	Total (000)	Production Workers (000)	Hours (Mil)	Payroll ($ mil)	Wages ($/hr)	Cost of Materials	Value Added by Manufacture	Value of Shipments	Capital Invest.
1997	1,272	1,507	787	174.5	139.5	274.3	5,485.0	14.07	18,958.4	15,116.5	34,067.6	1,690.3
1998		1,488	800	186.6	149.4	295.5	6,138.5	14.63	21,180.3	16,792.1	38,027.5	1,889.4
1999		1,478	788	183.7	146.7	297.6	6,337.0	14.83	23,587.7	17,379.7	40,906.2	1,993.1
2000		1,427	769	185.6	147.8	295.3	6,667.3	15.47	25,309.2	18,259.8	43,526.3	2,133.7
2001		1,390	730	168.6	131.5	254.4	5,974.2	14.97	24,691.0	16,000.2	40,886.5	1,894.3
2002	1,172	1,447	741	144.1	113.9	225.7	5,129.1	15.57	19,746.9	15,766.0	35,449.1	1,365.5
2003		1,429	750	140.3	108.3	220.4	5,132.6	15.78	20,700.8	15,523.2	36,355.1	1,227.3
2004		1,487	769	140.8	110.6	224.9	5,317.7	16.52	21,217.2	15,512.0	36,779.4	1,208.9
2005		1,490	786	140.4	110.9	221.5	5,407.6	16.76	23,726.8	15,098.5	38,835.5	1,198.1
2006		1,448P	752P	132.3	105.3	210.0	5,233.0	17.35	24,597.0	14,852.2	39,400.8	1,228.4
2007		1,445P	749P	123.8P	96.6P	194.8P	5,084.5P	17.41P	24,113.1P	14,560.0P	38,625.7P	1,044.1P
2008		1,443P	745P	117.2P	91.2P	184.5P	4,975.9P	17.74P	24,136.1P	14,573.9P	38,662.5P	946.1P
2009		1,440P	742P	110.7P	85.8P	174.1P	4,867.2P	18.07P	24,159.1P	14,587.8P	38,699.3P	848.1P
2010		1,438P	739P	104.2P	80.3P	163.7P	4,758.5P	18.40P	24,182.0P	14,601.6P	38,736.1P	750.1P

Sources: 1997 and 2002 *Economic Census*; other years, up to 2006, are from *Annual Survey of Manufactures*. Establishment counts for non-Census years are from *County Business Patterns*; 1997 and 2002 values are from the 1997 and 2002 censuses, respectively. 'P's show projections by the editors.

INDICES OF CHANGE

Year	Companies	Establishments		Employment			Compensation		Production ($ million)			
		Total	with 20 or more employees	Total (000)	Production Workers (000)	Hours (Mil)	Payroll ($ mil)	Wages ($/hr)	Cost of Materials	Value Added by Manufacture	Value of Shipments	Capital Invest.
1997	109	104	106	121	122	122	107	90	96	96	96	124
1998		103	108	129	131	131	120	94	107	107	107	138
1999		102	106	127	129	132	124	95	119	110	115	146
2000		99	104	129	130	131	130	99	128	116	123	156
2001		96	99	117	115	113	116	96	125	101	115	139
2002	100	100	100	100	100	100	100	100	100	100	100	100
2003		99	101	97	95	98	100	101	105	98	103	90
2004		103	104	98	97	100	104	106	107	98	104	89
2005		103	106	97	97	98	105	108	120	96	110	88
2006		100P	101P	92	92	93	102	111	125	94	111	90
2007		100P	101P	86P	85P	86P	99P	112P	122P	92P	109P	76P
2008		100P	101P	81P	80P	82P	97P	114P	122P	92P	109P	69P
2009		100P	100P	77P	75P	77P	95P	116P	122P	93P	109P	62P
2010		99P	100P	72P	71P	73P	93P	118P	122P	93P	109P	55P

Sources: Same as General Statistics. Values reflect change from the base year, 2002. Values above 100 mean greater than 2002, values below 100 mean less than 2002, and the values of 100 in other years means the same as 2002. 'P's show projections by the editors.

SELECTED RATIOS

For 2002	Avg. of All Manufact.	Analyzed Industry	Index	For 2002	Avg. of All Manufact.	Analyzed Industry	Index
Employees per Establishment	42	100	237	Value Added per Production Worker	182,367	138,420	76
Payroll per Establishment	1,639,184	3,544,644	216	Cost per Establishment	5,769,015	13,646,786	237
Payroll per Employee	39,053	35,594	91	Cost per Employee	137,446	137,036	100
Production Workers per Establishment	30	79	267	Cost per Production Worker	195,506	173,371	89
Wages per Establishment	694,845	2,428,576	350	Shipments per Establishment	11,158,348	24,498,341	220
Wages per Production Worker	23,548	30,853	131	Shipments per Employee	265,847	246,003	93
Hours per Production Worker	1,980	1,982	100	Shipments per Production Worker	378,144	311,230	82
Wages per Hour	11.89	15.57	131	Investment per Establishment	361,338	943,677	261
Value Added per Establishment	5,381,325	10,895,646	202	Investment per Employee	8,609	9,476	110
Value Added per Employee	128,210	109,410	85	Investment per Production Worker	12,245	11,989	98

Sources: Same as General Statistics. The 'Average of All Manufacturing' column represents the average of all manufacturing industries reported for the most recent complete year available. The Index shows the relationship between the Average and the Analyzed Industry. For example, 100 means that they are equal; 500 that the Analyzed Industry is five times the average; 50 means that the Analyzed Industry is half the national average. The abbreviation 'na' is used to show that data are 'not available'. Ratios shown for 2002, the last complete census year.

LEADING COMPANIES   Number shown: 75   Total sales ($ mil): **909,339**   Total employment (000): **2,198.3**

Company Name	Address				CEO Name	Phone	Co. Type	Sales ($ mil)	Empl. (000)
General Motors Corp.	300 Renaissance Ctr	Detroit	MI	48265		313-556-5000	P	181,122	266.0
Ford Motor Co.	1 American Rd.	Dearborn	MI	48126		313-322-3000	P	172,455	246.0
Chrysler L.L.C.	1000 Chrysler Dr.	Auburn Hills	MI	48326	Thomas W. LaSorda	248-576-5741	S	45,237*	84.4
Caterpillar Inc.	100 NE Adams St.	Peoria	IL	61629		309-675-1000	P	44,958	101.3
Honeywell International Inc.	PO Box 4000	Morristown	NJ	07962	Adriane M. Brown	973-455-2000	P	34,589	122.0
General Dynamics Corp.	2941 Fairview Park	Falls Church	VA	22042	Nicholas D. Chabraja	703-876-3000	P	27,240	83.5
ArvinMeritor OE L.L.C.	950 W 450 S, Bldg.	Columbus	IN	47201	C. G. McClure Jr.	812-341-2000	S	23,491*	32.0
Delphi Corp.	5725 Delphi Dr.	Troy	MI	48098	Voker J. Barth	248-813-2000	P	22,383	169.5
Lear Corp.	PO Box 5008	Southfield	MI	48086	Jim Brackenbury	248-447-1500	P	15,995	91.0
TRW Automotive Holdings Inc.	12001 Tech Cntr Dr.	Livonia	MI	48150		734-855-2600	P	14,702	66.3
Textron Inc.	40 Westminster St.	Providence	RI	02903		401-421-2800	P	13,225	44.0
Cummins Inc.	PO Box 3005	Columbus	IN	47202		812-377-5000	P	13,048	37.8
Eaton Corp.	1111 Superior Ave.	Cleveland	OH	44114		216-523-5000	P	13,033	60.0
Navistar International Corp.	PO Box 1488	Warrenville	IL	60555		630-753-5000	P	12,153	14.8
Visteon Corp.	1 Village Center Dr	Van Buren Twp	MI	48111		313-755-2800	P	11,266	41.5
GE Aircraft Engines	1 Neumann Way	Cincinnati	OH	45215	Scott C. Donnelly	513-243-2000	D	11,181*	26.5
Parker Hannifin Corp.	6035 Parkland Blvd.	Cleveland	OH	44124	Lee Banks	216-896-3000	P	10,718	57.3
Acument Global Technologies	840 W Long Lake	Troy	MI	48098	Joseph Gray	248-813-6329	S	10,080*	9.0
Applied Materials Inc.	PO Box 58039	Santa Clara	CA	95052		408-727-5555	P	9,735	15.3
ITT Corp.	4 W Red Oak Ln.	White Plains	NY	10604		914-641-2000	P	9,003	39.7
Dana Corp.	PO Box 1000	Toledo	OH	43697	Michael J. Burns	419-535-4500	P	8,504	45.0
Neapco L.L.C.	PO Box 399	Pottstown	PA	19464		610-323-6000	R	7,580*	0.3
Prager Inc.	PO Box 61670	New Orleans	LA	70161	Jennifer McKnight	504-524-2363	R	7,580*	<0.1
Trane Inc.	PO Box 6820	Piscataway	NJ	08855		732-980-6000	P	7,450	29.6
Triangle Suspension Systems	PO Box 425	Du Bois	PA	15801	Greg Maffia	814-375-7211	R	7,000*	0.2
Perfection Hy-Test Company	100 Perfection Way	Timmonsville	SC	29161		843-326-5544	R	7,000*	0.2
Penn Machine Co.	106 Station St.	Johnstown	PA	15905	H Wiegand	814-288-1547	R	7,000*	<0.1
Federal-Mogul Corp.	PO Box 1966	Detroit	MI	48235	Jose Maria Alapont	248-354-7700	P	6,914	43.1
Robert Bosch Corp.	2800 S 25th Ave.	Broadview	IL	60155	Kurt W. Liedtke	708-865-5200	S	6,782*	25.0
ArvinMeritor Inc.	2135 W Maple Rd.	Troy	MI	48084		248-435-1000	P	6,449	18.0
Tenneco Inc.	500 N Field Dr.	Lake Forest	IL	60045		847-482-5000	P	6,184	21.0
Toyota Motor Mfg. N America	25 Atlantic Ave.	Erlanger	KY	41018	Masamoto Amezawa	859-746-4000	S	6,120*	7.5
Brunswick Corp.	1 N Field Ct.	Lake Forest	IL	60045		847-735-4700	P	5,671	27.1
Guardian Industries Corp.	2300 Harmon Rd.	Auburn Hills	MI	48326	William M. Davidson	248-340-1800	R	5,330	19.0
BorgWarner Inc.	3850 Hamlin Rd.	Auburn Hills	MI	48326		248-754-9200	P	5,329	17.7
Autoliv ASP Inc.	3350 Airport Rd.	Ogden	UT	84405	Leonard Barton	801-625-4800	S	5,301*	3.7
Carlisle Tire and Wheel Co.	23 Windham Blvd.	Aiken	SC	29805	Barry Littrell	803-643-2900	S	4,822*	0.6
Cameron International Corp.	1333 W Loop S	Houston	TX	77027	Sheldon R. Erikson	713-513-3300	P	4,666	15.4
Karl Schmidt Unisia Inc.	1731 Industrial Pky	Marinette	WI	54143	Frank Pohlmann	715-732-0181	R	4,640*	0.9
Pioneer Automotive Tech.	100 S Pioneer Blvd.	Springboro	OH	45066	Steve Moerner	937-746-6600	R	4,610*	0.3
Toledo Trans-Kit Inc.	13515 Ballnyn Corp.	Charlotte	NC	28277	C. J. Kearney	704-752-4400	S	4,372	23.8
Mack Trucks Inc.	PO Box M	Allentown	PA	18105		610-709-3011	R	4,324*	0.8
New United Motor Manufacturing	45500 Fremont	Fremont	CA	94538	Bruce Walker	510-498-5500	J	4,080*	5.0
Kohler Co.	444 Highland Dr.	Kohler	WI	53044	Herbert Kohler	920-457-4441	R	4,061*	33.0
Harsco Corp.	PO Box 8888	Camp Hill	PA	17001	S. D. Fazzolari	717-763-7064	P	3,688	21.5
Kalmar Industries USA L.L.C.	415 E Dundee St.	Ottawa	KS	66067		785-242-2200	R	3,320*	0.3
American Axle & Mfg Holdings	1 Dauch Dr.	Detroit	MI	48211	Richard E. Dauch	313-974-2000	P	3,248	10.0
Hi-Stat Manufacturing Company	28001 Cabot Dr.	Novi	MI	48377	John Corey	248-489-9300	D	3,194*	5.0
Amsted Industries Inc.	2 Prudential Plaza	Chicago	IL	60601	W. Robert Reum	312-645-1700	R	3,050	9.9
AutoAlliance International	1 International Dr.	Flat Rock	MI	48134	Phillip G. Spender	734-782-7800	J	3,019*	3.7
Diebold Inc.	PO Box 3077	North Canton	OH	44720		330-490-4000	P	2,906	15.5
TAG Holdings L.L.C.	2075 W Big Beaver	Troy	MI	48084	J. B. Anderson, Jr.	248-822-8056	R	2,904*	2.5
Crane Co.	100 First Stamford	Stamford	CT	06902	Thomas Craney	203-363-7300	P	2,619	12.0
O'Reilly Automotive Inc.	233 S Patterson Ave	Springfield	MO	65802	Greg Henslee	417-862-6708	P	2,522	18.5
Consolidated Metco Inc.	PO Box 83201	Portland	OR	97283		503-286-5741	R	2,510*	0.1
Pall Corp.	2200 Northern Blvd.	East Hills	NY	11548	Eric Krasnoff	516-484-5400	P	2,250	10.8
DENSO Manufacturing Tennessee	1720 Rbrt C Jackson	Maryville	TN	37801	Mack Hattori	865-982-7000	S	2,231*	2.0
Sequa Corp.	200 Park Ave.	New York	NY	10166	Gail Binderman	212-986-5500	P	2,183	10.2
Affinia Group Inc.	1101 Technology	Ann Arbor	MI	48108		734-827-5400	P	2,160	12.4
Dura Automotive Systems Inc.	2791 Research Dr.	Rochester Hills	MI	48309	Lawrence A. Denton	248-299-7500	P	2,091	15.4
Hayes Lemmerz International	15300 Centennial Dr	Northville	MI	48167	Fred Bentley	734-737-5000	P	2,039	11.0
Cooper Tire and Rubber Co.	701 Lima Ave.	Findlay	OH	45840	Roy V. Armes	419-423-1321	P	2,036	13.6
American Power Conversion	132 Fairgrounds Rd.	West Kingston	RI	02892	Rodger B. Dowdell Jr.	401-789-5735	S	1,980	7.6
ZF Group N American Operations	15811 Centennial Dr	Northville	MI	48168	Julio Caspari	734-416-6200	R	1,949*	5.5
Teleflex Inc.	155 S Limerick Rd.	Limerick	PA	19468	Jeffrey P. Black	610-948-5100	P	1,934	14.0
Sypris Technologies Marion	1550 Marion-Agosta	Marion	OH	43301	Jeffrey T. Gill	740-383-2111	S	1,920*	2.6
Schuler Inc.	7145 Commerce	Canton	MI	48187	Timothy McCaughey	734-207-7200	R	1,874*	<0.1
Hutchinson FTS Inc.	1835 Technology	Troy	MI	48083	Paul Campbell	248-589-7710	S	1,863*	<0.1
ADVICS North America Inc.	45300 Polaris Ct.	Plymouth	MI	48170	Haruhiko Saito	734-414-5100	S	1,810*	<0.1
Regal-Beloit Corp.	200 State St.	Beloit	WI	53511		608-364-8800	P	1,803	17.9
Bose Corp.	The Mountain	Framingham	MA	01701	Amar G. Bose	508-879-7330	R	1,800	8.0
Detroit Diesel Corp.	13400 W Outer Dr.	Detroit	MI	48239	Robert R. Allran	313-592-5266	S	1,787*	5.0
Weir Spm	7701 Skyline Park	Fort Worth	TX	76108	Steve Noon	817-246-2461	R	1,770*	0.3
Modine Manufacturing Co.	1500 DeKoven Ave.	Racine	WI	53403	Richard J. Doyle	262-636-1200	P	1,758	7.7
Siemens VDO Automotive Corp.	2400 Executive Hill	Auburn Hills	MI	48326	John Sanderson	248-209-4000	S	1,738*	10.0

Source: Ward's Business Directory of U.S. Private and Public Companies, Volumes 1 and 2, 2008. The company type code used is as follows: P - Public, R - Private, S - Subsidiary, D - Division, J - Joint Venture, A - Affiliate, G - Group. Sales are in millions of dollars, employees are in thousands. An asterisk (*) indicates an estimated sales volume. The symbol < stands for 'less than'. Company names and addresses are truncated, in some cases, to fit into the available space.

MATERIALS CONSUMED

Material	Quantity	Delivered Cost ($ million)
Iron and steel castings (rough and semifinished)	(X)	615.1
Aluminum and aluminum-base alloy castings (rough and semifinished)	(X)	355.3
Other nonferrous metal castings, rough or semifinished (inc. aluminum)	(X)	56.0
Steel bars, bar shapes, and plates (exc. castings, forgings, fabr. metal products)	(X)	124.0
Steel sheet and strip (including tinplate)	(X)	599.6
All other steel shapes and forms (exc. castings, forgings, fabr. metal products)	(X)	314.6
Copper and copper-base alloy shapes and forms (exc. castings, forgings, fabr. metal products)	(X)	44.2
Aluminum and aluminum-base alloy shapes and forms (exc. castings, forgings, fabr. metal products)	(X)	348.9
Other nonferrous shapes and forms (exc. castings, forgings, fabricated metal products)	(X)	92.8
Ball and roller bearings (mounted or unmounted)	(X)	30.8
Fabricated plastics products (exc. gaskets, hoses, and belting)	(X)	286.7
Plastics products consumed in the form of sheets, rods, etc.	(X)	111.8
Plastics resins consumed in the form of granules, pellets, etc.	(X)	273.3
Fabricated rubber products (exc. tires, tubes, hoses, belting, and gaskets)	(X)	57.7
Rubber and plastics hose and belting	(X)	46.1
Ceramic raw materials (incl. powders, chemicals, and fibers)	(X)	(D)
Ceramic and ceramic composite parts, components, and accessories	(X)	(D)
Gaskets (all types), and packing and sealing devices	(X)	67.6
Paints, varnishes, stains, lacquers, shellacs, japans, enamels, etc.	(X)	202.1
Glues and adhesives	(X)	29.6
Flexible packaging materials	(X)	41.6
Paper and paperboard containers	(X)	180.2
Spark plugs for internal combustion engines	(X)	(D)
Starting motors for internal combustion engines	(X)	(D)
Distributors for internal combustion engines	(X)	(D)
All other engine electrical equipment for internal combustion engines	(X)	(D)
Resistors for electronic circuitry	(X)	(D)
Capacitors for electronic circuitry	(X)	1.2
Semiconductors (incl. transistors, diodes, rectifiers, and integrated circuits), for electronic circuitry	(X)	(D)
All other miscellaneous components and accessories for electronic circuitry (exc. tubes)	(X)	99.2
Core parts purchased for use in remanufacturing and rebuilding	(X)	1,559.3
Printed ciruit boards (without inserted components) for electronic circuitry	(X)	(D)
Metal bolts, nuts, screws, and other screw machine products	(X)	935.9
Other fabricated metal products (exc. fluid power and forgings)	(X)	1,555.1
Forgings	(X)	71.3
Insulated wire and cable (excluding magnet wire)	(X)	50.4
Mechanical speed changers, gears, and industrial high-speed drives	(X)	(D)
Fluid power pumps, motors, and hydrostatic transmissions	(X)	134.0
Fluid power valves (hydraulic and pneumatic)	(X)	2.3
Fluid power cylinders and rotary actuators (hydraulic and pneumatic)	(X)	4.5
Fluid power hose, tube fittings, and assemblies (hydraulic and pneumatic)	(X)	103.9
Fluid power filters (hydraulic and pneumatic)	(X)	13.6
Other transportation related fluid power products, hydraulic and pneumatic	(X)	2.0
Automotive stampings (inc. body parts, hubcaps, fenders, etc.)	(X)	1,618.3
Current-carrying wiring devices	(X)	103.8
Other chemicals and allied products	(X)	88.5
All other materials, components, parts, containers, and supplies	(X)	5,191.3
Materials, ingredients, containers, and supplies, nsk	(X)	2,270.6

Source: 2002 *Economic Census.* Explanation of symbols used: (D): Withheld to avoid disclosure of competitive data; na: Not available; (S): Withheld because statistical norms were not met; (X): Not applicable; (Z): Less than half the unit shown; nec: Not elsewhere classified; nsk: Not specified by kind; - : zero; p : 10-19 percent estimated; q : 20-29 percent estimated.

PRODUCT SHARE DETAILS

Product or Product Class Shipments	Mil. $	Product or Product Class Shipments	Mil. $
MOTOR VEHICLE PARTS, NEC	36,834.0	Motor vehicle wheels, new, nsk	65.0
Filters for internal combustion engines and motor vehicles, new	**2,811.0**	**Trailer hitches for travel trailers, automobile trailers, and light duty truck trailers**	**322.8**
Filters for internal combustion engines and motor vehicles, new	2,767.9	**Motor vehicle parts and accessories, new and rebuilt, nec**	**20,839.4**
Oil filters for internal combustion engines and motor vehicles, new, light-duty (car and light truck)	875.1	Motor vehicle bumper assemblies, bumpers, and parts, new	1,322.7
Oil filters for internal combustion engines and motor vehicles, new, heavy-duty	350.9	Motor vehicle bumper assemblies, bumpers, and parts for cars and light trucks (10,000 lb GVW and less), new	1,228.6
Fuel filters for internal combustion engines and motor vehicles, new, light-duty (car and light truck)	279.5	Motor vehicle bumper assemblies, bumpers, and parts for heavy trucks (greater than 10,000 lb GVW), new	94.0
Fuel filters for internal combustion engines and motor vehicles, new, heavy-duty	252.5	Motor vehicle frames, new	1,938.7
Air filters for internal combustion engines and motor vehicles, new, light-duty (car and light truck)	398.3	Motor vehicle fuel tanks, new	543.6
Air filters for internal combustion engines and motor vehicles, new, heavy-duty	388.5	Radiators, radiator shells and cores, new	1,546.3
Other filters for internal combustion engines and motor vehicles, new, including coolant and hydraulic	222.9	Gasoline engine radiators, complete, new for motor vehicles	1,149.4
Filters for internal combustion engines and motor vehicles, new, nsk	43.2	Gasoline engine radiator shells and cores, new for motor vehicles	207.2
Exhaust system parts, new	**7,194.5**	Stationary engine radiators for internal combustion engines, except aircraft and gasoline automotive engines and gas turbines	189.7
Exhaust system parts, new	7,183.7	All other motor vehicle parts, new and rebuilt	15,404.6
Exhaust system mufflers, including standard, sports or glass pack, and resonators, new, for motor vehicles	1,918.4	Motor vehicle air-conditioning hose assemblies, new	423.4
Exhaust system pipes, including exhaust, intermediate, connecting, crossover, tail, and side pipes	1,721.0	Motor vehicle windshield wiper blades, new	136.8
Exhaust system catalytic converters, new, for motor vehicles	3,544.3	Truck and trailer liftgates, new	(D)
		Motor vehicle convertible tops, new	230.3
Exhaust system parts, new, nsk	10.7	Motor vehicle sunroofs and parts, new	494.9
Motor vehicle wheels, new	**2,665.7**	Motor vehicle doors, new	190.1
Motor vehicle wheels, new	2,600.8	Motor vehicle air bag assemblies and parts, new	3,294.4
Car and light truck wheels, steel, new	440.3	Motor vehicle heater cores, new	(D)
Car and light truck wheels, aluminum, new	1,726.1	Luggage and utility racks	344.8
Other car and light truck wheels, including combination, new	202.3	All other motor vehicle parts and accessories, new	9,780.6
		Other motor vehicle parts, excluding carburetors and engine electrical equipment, rebuilt	390.2
Heavy truck and bus type wheels, including those for truck trailers and trailer coaches	232.1	All other motor vehicle parts and accessories, new and rebuilt, nsk	83.5
		Motor vehicle parts, nec, nsk, total	**3,000.5**

Source: 2002 Economic Census. The values are product shipments in millions of dollars for 2002. Total product shipments may be lower or higher than industry shipments. See Introduction for a full discussion. Values of indented subcategories are summed in the main heading(s). The symbol (D) appears when data are withheld to prevent disclosure of competitive information. The abbreviation nsk stands for 'not specified by kind' and nec for 'not elsewhere classified'. A dash (-) means zero.

INPUTS AND OUTPUTS FOR MOTOR VEHICLE PARTS MANUFACTURING

Economic Sector or Industry Providing Inputs	%	Sector	Economic Sector or Industry Buying Outputs	%	Sector
Compensation of employees	22.8		Light truck & utility vehicles	25.3	Manufg.
Motor vehicle parts	10.7	Manufg.	Automobiles	15.8	Manufg.
Management of companies & enterprises	7.0	Services	Exports of goods & services	13.9	Cap Inv
Wholesale trade	5.3	Trade	Motor vehicle parts	8.5	Manufg.
Iron & steel mills & ferroalloys	5.0	Manufg.	Retail trade	7.4	Trade
Nonferrous metal foundries	2.6	Manufg.	Personal consumption expenditures	4.1	
Ferrous metal foundries	2.4	Manufg.	Automotive repair & maintenance, ex. car washes	2.9	Services
Plate work & fabricated structural products	1.9	Manufg.	Truck transportation	2.2	Util.
Turned products & screws, nuts, & bolts	1.9	Manufg.	General S/L govt. services	2.0	S/L Govt
Machine shops	1.5	Manufg.	Heavy duty trucks	1.9	Manufg.
Plastics products, nec	1.4	Manufg.	Wholesale trade	1.5	Trade
Truck transportation	1.1	Util.	Transit & ground passenger transportation	0.8	Util.
Retail trade	1.0	Trade	Change in private inventories	0.7	In House
Electronic components, nec	0.9	Manufg.	Postal service	0.6	Util.
Custom roll forming	0.9	Manufg.	General Federal government services, defense	0.6	Fed Govt
Coating, engraving, heat treating & allied activities	0.9	Manufg.	Residential structures, nec	0.6	Construct.
Crowns & closures & metal stamping	0.8	Manufg.	Residential permanent site structures	0.6	Construct.
Rubber products, nec	0.7	Manufg.	Nonresidential structures, nec	0.5	Construct.
Semiconductors & related devices	0.7	Manufg.	Lawn & garden equipment	0.4	Manufg.
Plastics packaging materials, film & sheet	0.7	Manufg.	Boat building	0.4	Manufg.
Scientific research & development services	0.7	Services	Construction machinery	0.4	Manufg.
Power generation & supply	0.7	Util.	S/L govt. passenger transit	0.4	S/L Govt
Leather & hide tanning & finishing	0.7	Manufg.	Transportation equipment, nec	0.3	Manufg.
Ball & roller bearings	0.7	Manufg.	Engine equipment, nec	0.3	Manufg.
Valve & fittings other than plumbing	0.6	Manufg.	Food services & drinking places	0.3	Services
Textile & fabric finishing mills	0.6	Manufg.	Waste management & remediation services	0.3	Services
Lessors of nonfinancial assets	0.5	Fin/R.E.	Aircraft	0.3	Manufg.
Fluid power process machinery	0.5	Manufg.	Services to buildings & dwellings	0.3	Services
Taxes on production & imports, less subsidies	0.5		Oil & gas extraction	0.2	Mining
Plastics materials & resins	0.5	Manufg.	Commercial & health care structures	0.2	Construct.
Ornamental & architectural metal products	0.5	Manufg.	Farm machinery & equipment	0.2	Manufg.

Continued on next page.

INPUTS AND OUTPUTS FOR MOTOR VEHICLE PARTS MANUFACTURING - Continued

Economic Sector or Industry Providing Inputs	%	Sector	Economic Sector or Industry Buying Outputs	%	Sector
Gaskets, packing, & sealing devices	0.5	Manufg.	Management of companies & enterprises	0.2	Services
Securities, commodity contracts, investments	0.5	Fin/R.E.	Truck trailers	0.2	Manufg.
Noncomparable imports	0.5	Foreign	Warehousing & storage	0.2	Util.
Urethane & other foam products (except polystrene)	0.4	Manufg.	Motor vehicle bodies	0.2	Manufg.
Printed circuit assemblies (electronic assemblies)	0.4	Manufg.	Travel trailers & campers	0.2	Manufg.
Alumina refining & primary aluminum production	0.4	Manufg.	Scientific research & development services	0.2	Services
Bare printed circuit boards	0.4	Manufg.	Maintenance/repair of nonresidential structures	0.2	Construct.
Paints & coatings	0.4	Manufg.	Private fixed investment	0.2	
Wiring devices	0.4	Manufg.	Couriers & messengers	0.1	Util.
Fabricated metals, nec	0.4	Manufg.	Individual & family services	0.1	Services
Copper rolling, drawing, extruding, & alloying	0.3	Manufg.	Scenic & sightseeing transport & related services	0.1	Util.
Advertising & related services	0.3	Services	Car washes	0.1	Services
Metal cans, boxes, & other containers (light gauge)	0.3	Manufg.	Automotive equipment rental & leasing	0.1	Fin/R.E.
Real estate	0.3	Fin/R.E.	Crowns & closures & metal stamping	0.1	Manufg.
Speed changers, industrial high-speed drives, & gears	0.3	Manufg.	Material handling equipment	0.1	Manufg.
Primary nonferrous metal, ex. copper & aluminum	0.3	Manufg.			
Paperboard containers	0.3	Manufg.			
Maintenance/repair of nonresidential structures	0.3	Construct.			
Gold, silver, & other metal ore	0.3	Mining			
Services to buildings & dwellings	0.2	Services			
Aluminum products from purchased aluminum	0.2	Manufg.			
Nonferrous metal (ex. copper & aluminum) processing	0.2	Manufg.			
Forging, stamping, & sintering, nec	0.2	Manufg.			
Rubber & plastics hose & belting	0.2	Manufg.			
Natural gas distribution	0.2	Util.			
Rail transportation	0.2	Util.			
Monetary authorities/depository credit intermediation	0.2	Fin/R.E.			
Handtools	0.2	Manufg.			
Automotive equipment rental & leasing	0.2	Fin/R.E.			
Professional, scientific, technical services, nec	0.2	Services			
Basic organic chemicals, nec	0.2	Manufg.			
Warehousing & storage	0.2	Util.			
Legal services	0.2	Services			
Food services & drinking places	0.2	Services			
Communication & energy wires & cables	0.2	Manufg.			
Automotive repair & maintenance, ex. car washes	0.2	Services			
Management, scientific, & technical consulting	0.2	Services			
Engine equipment, nec	0.2	Manufg.			
Wood windows & doors & millwork	0.2	Manufg.			
Veneer & plywood	0.2	Manufg.			
Telecommunications	0.2	Services			
Accounting, tax preparation, bookkeeping, & payroll	0.1	Services			
Commercial & industrial equipment repair/maintenance	0.1	Services			
Architectural, engineering, & related services	0.1	Services			
Artificial & synthetic fibers & filaments	0.1	Manufg.			
Air transportation	0.1	Util.			
Cutting tools & machine tool accessories	0.1	Manufg.			
Employment services	0.1	Services			
Chemical products & preparations, nec	0.1	Manufg.			
Data processing, hosting, & related services	0.1	Services			
Specialized design services	0.1	Services			
Relay & industrial controls	0.1	Manufg.			
Business support services	0.1	Services			
Fiber, yarn, & thread mills	0.1	Manufg.			
Hotels & motels, including casino hotels	0.1	Services			
Electronic capacitors, resistors, coils, transformers	0.1	Manufg.			
Wood containers & pallets	0.1	Manufg.			
Waste management & remediation services	0.1	Services			
Springs & wire products	0.1	Manufg.			
Automatic environmental controls	0.1	Manufg.			

Source: *Benchmark Input-Output Accounts for the U.S. Economy, 2002*, U.S. Department of Commerce, Washington D.C., January 2008. *User should note that this Input-Output table is* not *for this particular narrowly defined industry but for a larger aggregate. Input and Output data for* Motor Vehicle Parts Manufacturing *include Input and Output data for the* Annual Survey of Manufactures' *NAICS industries 33631M, 33632M, 336330, 336340, 336350, 336360, 336370, 336391, and 336399. The abbreviation nec stands for 'not elsewhere classified'.*

OCCUPATIONS EMPLOYED BY MOTOR VEHICLE PARTS MANUFACTURING

Occupation	% of Total 2006	Change to 2016	Occupation	% of Total 2006	Change to 2016
Team assemblers	15.2	-19.2	Welders, cutters, solderers, & brazers	1.9	-15.3
Cutting, punching, & press machine operators	4.2	-28.4	Molding, coremaking, & casting machine operators	1.8	-28.4
Machinists	3.8	-16.4	Welding, soldering, & brazing machine operators	1.6	-10.5
Inspectors, testers, sorters, samplers, & weighers	3.5	-24.9	Industrial machinery mechanics	1.5	-8.4
First-line supervisors/managers of production workers	3.3	-20.4	Helpers--Production workers	1.5	-20.4
Assemblers & fabricators, nec	3.2	-28.4	Mechanical engineers	1.4	-20.4
Multiple machine tool operators & tenders	2.6	-12.4	Electrical & electronic equipment assemblers	1.4	-36.3
Tool & die makers	2.6	-16.4	Lathe & turning machine tool operators & tenders	1.3	-28.4
Industrial truck & tractor operators	2.6	-28.4	Shipping, receiving, & traffic clerks	1.3	-23.4
Laborers & freight, stock, & material movers, hand	2.1	-28.4	Electricians	1.3	-17.4
Industrial engineers	2.1	-3.3	Grinding, lapping, polishing machine tool operators	1.2	-22.8
Maintenance & repair workers, general	2.0	-20.4	Engine & other machine assemblers	1.1	-20.4
Production workers, nec	2.0	-21.9	Drilling & boring machine tool operators	1.1	-28.4
Computer-controlled machine tool operators	1.9	-12.4	Production, planning, & expediting clerks	1.1	-20.4

Source: Industry-Occupation Matrix, Bureau of Labor Statistics, December 4, 2007. These data are reported based on 4-digit NAICS categories but have been matched to corresponding 6-digit NAICS industry codes. The change reported for each occupation to the year 2016 is a percent of growth or decline as estimated by the Bureau of Labor Statistics. The abbreviation nec stands for 'not elsewhere classified'.

LOCATION BY STATE AND REGIONAL CONCENTRATION

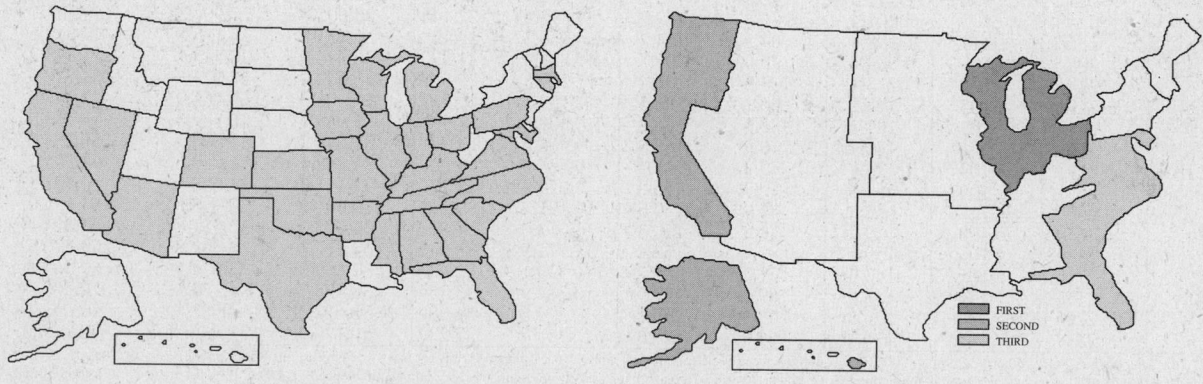

FIRST
SECOND
THIRD

INDUSTRY DATA BY STATE

State	Establish-ments	Shipments			Employment				Cost as % of Shipments	Investment per Employee ($)
		Total ($ mil)	% of U.S.	Per Establ.	Total Number	% of U.S.	Per Establ.	Wages ($/hour)		
Michigan	199	7,050.7	19.9	35,430.6	25,703	17.8	129	19.51	60.8	9,664
Indiana	93	3,837.7	10.8	41,265.3	14,991	10.4	161	14.83	59.9	6,438
Ohio	122	3,390.1	9.6	27,787.5	12,048	8.4	99	15.89	65.0	17,573
Tennessee	62	2,827.5	8.0	45,605.0	10,804	7.5	174	12.54	55.1	7,861
California	208	2,058.2	5.8	9,895.1	12,958	9.0	62	13.06	46.9	5,299
Wisconsin	42	2,021.7	5.7	48,135.7	5,089	3.5	121	18.95	34.2	5,792
Kentucky	41	1,558.0	4.4	38,000.9	7,062	4.9	172	15.25	62.1	20,192
Illinois	55	1,397.8	3.9	25,414.1	6,119	4.2	111	15.27	37.9	11,599
North Carolina	37	1,064.0	3.0	28,756.3	5,779	4.0	156	16.59	42.3	13,114
Missouri	31	1,046.1	3.0	33,743.7	4,334	3.0	140	14.63	59.8	6,235
Pennsylvania	33	752.8	2.1	22,811.2	1,793	1.2	54	13.64	65.3	10,997
South Carolina	21	704.1	2.0	33,526.8	2,580	1.8	123	15.38	65.5	10,119
Georgia	31	576.1	1.6	18,583.3	2,784	1.9	90	14.31	57.8	5,385
Alabama	21	573.3	1.6	27,301.3	1,394	1.0	66	13.72	57.3	22,367
Arizona	27	555.1	1.6	20,558.0	1,804	1.3	67	15.78	62.2	9,379
Iowa	16	444.6	1.3	27,784.5	2,361	1.6	148	14.36	41.5	3,776
Virginia	14	356.0	1.0	25,425.9	1,657	1.2	118	11.77	43.3	5,180
Arkansas	9	342.5	1.0	38,060.9	2,294	1.6	255	13.28	43.1	12,390
Texas	63	327.6	0.9	5,199.8	2,528	1.8	40	14.56	45.7	5,585
Kansas	13	263.9	0.7	20,300.8	1,279	0.9	98	14.61	56.1	11,287
Mississippi	9	254.8	0.7	28,311.2	1,202	0.8	134	13.89	48.8	10,439
Oregon	27	247.5	0.7	9,165.6	1,082	0.8	40	24.37	38.4	5,544
Florida	39	246.2	0.7	6,311.7	1,744	1.2	45	9.25	56.3	9,351
Oklahoma	14	197.6	0.6	14,112.4	1,037	0.7	74	14.57	81.9	2,831
Colorado	16	197.2	0.6	12,324.5	1,146	0.8	72	15.22	50.1	2,342
Connecticut	11	134.4	0.4	12,217.2	562	0.4	51	18.36	35.9	2,799
Minnesota	19	70.2	0.2	3,693.7	460	0.3	24	13.75	63.0	4,637
Maryland	7	47.5	0.1	6,787.9	313	0.2	45	14.72	43.5	1,885
Massachusetts	11	40.0	0.1	3,635.0	226	0.2	21	13.97	53.8	5,752
Nevada	7	26.4	0.1	3,765.3	179	0.1	26	12.99	62.6	19,168

Source: 2002 Economic Census. The states are in descending order of shipments or establishments (if shipment data are missing for the majority). The symbol (D) appears when data are withheld to prevent disclosure of competitive information. States marked with (D) are sorted by number of establishments. A dash (-) indicates that the data element cannot be calculated. Data may not show all states active in the NAICS category. All data available at the time of publication are shown.

NAICS 336411 - AIRCRAFT MANUFACTURING

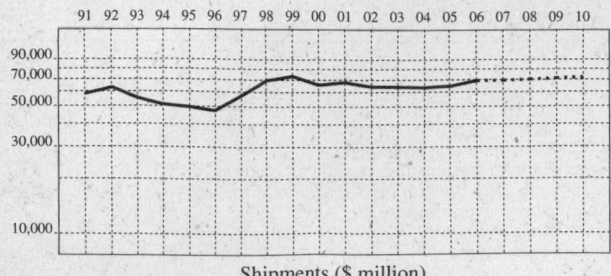

Shipments ($ million)

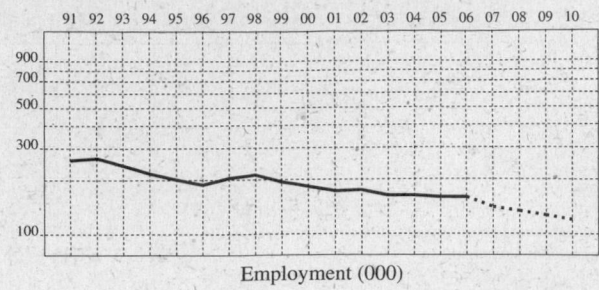

Employment (000)

GENERAL STATISTICS

| Year | Com-panies | Establishments | | Employment | | | Compensation | | Production ($ million) | | | |
		Total	with 20 or more employees	Total (000)	Production Workers (000)	Hours (Mil)	Payroll ($ mil)	Wages ($/hr)	Cost of Materials	Value Added by Manufacture	Value of Shipments	Capital Invest.
1991		198	94	258.3	125.3	244.8	10,324.1	17.82	36,077.2	23,090.6	58,090.2	1,046.1
1992	151	182	103	264.9	122.1	227.0	11,498.9	19.98	36,133.3	25,157.1	62,980.8	1,661.3
1993		260	116	241.2	104.4	198.7	10,790.0	19.90	33,206.4	22,903.3	55,119.8	1,154.4
1994		204	104	217.9	92.8	172.7	10,312.1	20.77	25,778.3	23,606.4	50,944.0	872.2
1995		224	105	201.4	86.4	159.7	9,893.6	22.14	25,005.7	20,904.3	49,504.1	628.3
1996		255	111	188.3	84.5	164.7	9,839.3	23.12	26,131.1	25,136.8	47,312.6	622.2
1997	173	205	109	204.4	98.6	208.7	10,888.8	21.32	36,344.0	20,545.1	56,843.2	774.9
1998		228	110	213.1	106.2	200.4	11,289.8	24.02	40,572.4	36,025.7	69,540.6	904.4
1999		229	105	194.2	96.1	196.5	10,709.9	23.81	37,308.3	33,462.9	73,397.5	767.8
2000		244	102	183.1	86.8	185.2	10,409.5	24.33	33,969.2	26,227.0	65,783.5	616.9
2001		259	101	172.7	78.9	165.0	9,468.6	23.77	36,048.7	31,668.9	67,853.0	569.1
2002	184	219	104	174.7	79.2	161.4	9,786.0	23.62	34,768.2	28,740.6	64,355.2	912.7
2003		264	109	162.8	79.7	156.9	10,059.9	28.72	32,111.2	31,058.5	64,108.5	694.9
2004		266	112	162.8	82.9	150.6	10,191.2	30.44	30,661.9	30,195.8	63,475.0	891.6
2005		265	98	159.2	78.6	150.3	11,063.0	34.50	34,973.0	32,487.8	64,624.4	1,064.6
2006		267P	106P	159.1	81.4	153.4	11,141.5	33.54	37,514.3	33,547.8	69,100.5	983.5
2007		271P	106P	140.3P	71.5P	142.2P	10,393.1P	32.42P	37,659.3P	33,677.5P	69,367.6P	734.5P
2008		275P	106P	133.6P	69.0P	137.7P	10,382.9P	33.35P	38,165.7P	34,130.3P	70,300.4P	716.7P
2009		279P	106P	126.8P	66.5P	133.1P	10,372.8P	34.28P	38,672.1P	34,583.1P	71,233.1P	699.0P
2010		283P	106P	120.1P	64.0P	128.6P	10,362.7P	35.22P	39,178.4P	35,036.0P	72,165.8P	681.2P

Sources: 1992, 1997, 2002 *Economic Census*; other years, up to 2006, are from the *Annual Survey of Manufactures*. Establishment counts for non-Census years are from *County Business Patterns*; 1997 and 2002 values are from the 1997 and 2002 censuses respectively, reported in the Federal Government's NAICS format. Other years were originally reported in equivalent SIC format. 'P's show projections by the editors.

INDICES OF CHANGE

| Year | Com-panies | Establishments | | Employment | | | Compensation | | Production ($ million) | | | |
		Total	with 20 or more employees	Total (000)	Production Workers (000)	Hours (Mil)	Payroll ($ mil)	Wages ($/hr)	Cost of Materials	Value Added by Manufacture	Value of Shipments	Capital Invest.
1992	82	83	99	152	154	141	118	85	104	88	98	182
1997	94	94	105	117	124	129	111	90	105	71	88	85
2001		118	97	99	100	102	97	101	104	110	105	62
2002	100	100	100	100	100	100	100	100	100	100	100	100
2003		121	105	93	101	97	103	122	92	108	100	76
2004		121	108	93	105	93	104	129	88	105	99	98
2005		121	94	91	99	93	113	146	101	113	100	117
2006		122P	102P	91	103	95	114	142	108	117	107	108
2007		124P	102P	80P	90P	88P	106P	137P	108P	117P	108P	80P
2008		126P	102P	76P	87P	85P	106P	141P	110P	119P	109P	79P
2009		127P	102P	73P	84P	82P	106P	145P	111P	120P	111P	77P
2010		129P	102P	69P	81P	80P	106P	149P	113P	122P	112P	75P

Sources: Same as General Statistics. Values reflect change from the base year, 2002. Values above 100 mean greater than 2002, values below 100 mean less than 2002, and the values of 100 in other years means the same as 2002. 'P's show projections by the editors.

SELECTED RATIOS

For 2002	Avg. of All Manufact.	Analyzed Industry	Index	For 2002	Avg. of All Manufact.	Analyzed Industry	Index
Employees per Establishment	42	798	1,901	Value Added per Production Worker	182,367	362,886	199
Payroll per Establishment	1,639,184	44,684,932	2,726	Cost per Establishment	5,769,015	158,758,904	2,752
Payroll per Employee	39,053	56,016	143	Cost per Employee	137,446	199,017	145
Production Workers per Establishment	30	362	1,226	Cost per Production Worker	195,506	438,992	225
Wages per Establishment	694,845	17,407,616	2,505	Shipments per Establishment	11,158,348	293,859,361	2,634
Wages per Production Worker	23,548	48,135	204	Shipments per Employee	265,847	368,376	139
Hours per Production Worker	1,980	2,038	103	Shipments per Production Worker	378,144	812,566	215
Wages per Hour	11.89	23.62	199	Investment per Establishment	361,338	4,167,580	1,153
Value Added per Establishment	5,381,325	131,235,616	2,439	Investment per Employee	8,609	5,224	61
Value Added per Employee	128,210	164,514	128	Investment per Production Worker	12,245	11,524	94

Sources: Same as General Statistics. The 'Average of All Manufacturing' column represents the average of all manufacturing industries reported for the most recent complete year available. The Index shows the relationship between the Average and the Analyzed Industry. For example, 100 means that they are equal; 500 that the Analyzed Industry is five times the average; 50 means that the Analyzed Industry is half the national average. The abbreviation 'na' is used to show that data are 'not available'. Ratios shown for 2002, the last complete census year.

LEADING COMPANIES   Number shown: 58   Total sales ($ mil): 301,855   Total employment (000): 663.7

Company Name	Address				CEO Name	Phone	Co. Type	Sales ($ mil)	Empl. (000)
Sikorsky Aircraft Corp.	PO Box 9729	Stratford	CT	06615	Jeffrey P. Pino	203-386-4000	S	84,245*	6.0
Boeing Co.	100 N Riverside Plz	Chicago	IL	60606		312-544-2000	P	66,387	159.3
Lockheed Martin Corp.	6801 Rockledge Dr.	Bethesda	MD	20817	Richard F. Ambrose	301-897-6000	P	41,862	140.0
Northrop Grumman Corp.	1840 Century Park E	Los Angeles	CA	90067		310-553-6262	P	32,018	122.6
Raytheon Co.	870 Winter St.	Waltham	MA	02451		781-522-3000	P	21,301	72.1
Boeing Integrated Defense Sys.	PO Box 516	St. Louis	MO	63166	James Albaugh	314-232-0232	D	17,354*	72.0
Textron Inc.	40 Westminster St.	Providence	RI	02903		401-421-2800	P	13,225	44.0
Airlog Part Sales Inc.	224 Rue De Jean	Lafayette	LA	70505	Kenneth M. Jones	337-233-1221	S	5,124*	3.3
Cessna Aircraft Co.	PO Box 7706	Wichita	KS	67277	Jack J. Pelton	316-517-6000	S	5,091*	10.0
Learjet Inc.	PO Box 7707	Wichita	KS	67277	Jim Ziegler	316-946-2000	R	2,867*	0.8
Gulfstream Aerospace Corp.	PO Box 2206	Savannah	GA	31402	Bryan Moss	912-965-3000	S	2,670*	8.0
American Eurocopter L.L.C.	2701 N Forum Dr.	Grand Prairie	TX	75052	Marc Paganini	972-641-0000	R	2,554*	9.1
Flight Options	26180 Curtiss Wrght	Cleveland	OH	44143	S. Michael Scheeringa	216-261-3880	S	2,477*	1.8
Kaman Corp.	PO Box 1	Bloomfield	CT	06002		860-243-7100	P	1,086	3.6
Dassault Falcon Jet Corp.	200 Riser Road, 200	S Hackensack	NJ	07606	John Rosanvallon	201-440-6700	S	1,008*	1.9
Mooney Airplane Company Inc.	L Schreiner Field	Kerrville	TX	78028	Dennis E. Ferguson	830-896-6000	S	478*	0.3
Kaman Aerospace Corp.	PO Box 2	Bloomfield	CT	06002	Sal Bordanelero	860-242-4461	D	349*	1.4
Adam Aircraft Inc.	12876 E Jamison Cir	Englewood	CO	80112	Duncan B. Koerbel	303-406-5900	R	220*	0.2
Robinson Helicopter Co.	2901 Airport Dr.	Torrance	CA	90505	Rogelio Pena	310-539-0508	R	200*	1.2
Midcoast Aviation Inc.	6400 C Steinberg	E Saint Louis	IL	62206		618-646-8000	S	185*	0.6
Alabama Aircraft Industries	1943 N 50th St.	Birmingham	AL	35212	Ronald A. Aramini	205-592-0011	P	161	1.5
Groen Brothers Aviation USA	2640 W California	Salt Lake City	UT	84104	Jay Groen	801-973-0177	S	146*	0.1
Huck International Aerospace	3724 E Columbia St.	Tucson	AZ	85714		520-519-7400	D	67*	0.2
Tcom L.P.	7115 Thomas Edison	Columbia	MD	21046		410-312-2315	R	59*	<0.1
Dakota Aircraft Corp.	4515 Taylor Cir.	Duluth	MN	55811	Allan Klapmeier	218-727-2737	R	59*	0.2
Aurora Flight Sciences Corp.	9950 Wakeman Dr.	Manassas	VA	20110		703-369-3633	R	51*	0.1
Bizjet Intl. Sales and Support	3515 N Sheridan Rd.	Tulsa	OK	74115	Bernd Kowalewski	918-832-7733	R	45*	0.3
Mooney Aerospace Group Ltd.	165 Al Mooney N	Kerrville	TX	78028	Dennis Ferguson	830-896-6000	R	42	0.4
Schweizer Aircraft Corp.	1250 Schweizer Rd.	Horseheads	NY	14845	Paul Schweizer	607-739-3821	S	35*	0.5
LMI Finishing Inc.	2104 N 170th E Ave.	Tulsa	OK	74116		918-438-2122	S	34*	0.1
Aircraft Investor Resources	22590 Nelson Rd.	Bend	OR	97701		541-318-8849	R	34*	0.1
Hiller Aircraft Corp.	925 M Street	Firebaugh	CA	93622		559-565-5959	R	29*	<0.1
Techsphere Systems Int'l	750 Hammond Dr.	Atlanta	GA	30328	William Robinson	404-446-2203	S	29*	<0.1
Enstrom Helicopter Corp.	PO Box 490	Menominee	MI	49858	Jerry Mullins	906-863-1200	R	28*	0.1
Pacific Jet Inc.	16644 Roscoe Blvd.	Van Nuys	CA	91406	Tim Prero	818-989-4700	R	28*	0.1
Snow Aviation International	7201 Paul Tibbets	Columbus	OH	43217	Harry Snow	614-492-7669	R	28*	0.1
Agusta Aerospace Corp.	PO Box 16002	Philadelphia	PA	19114	Vruno Cellenne	215-281-1400	R	25*	<0.1
Maule Air Inc.	2099 Ga Hwy. 133 S	Moultrie	GA	31788	June Maule	229-985-2045	R	24*	<0.1
Aerostar International Inc.	PO Box 5057	Sioux Falls	SD	57117	Mark West	605-331-3500	S	22	0.3
Thrush Aircraft Inc.	PO Box 3149	Albany	GA	31706	William Bays	229-883-1440	R	20*	<0.1
Marsh Aviation Co.	5060 E Falcon Dr.	Mesa	AZ	85215	Edward Allen	480-832-3770	R	19*	0.1
Basler Turbo Conversions	PO Box 2305	Oshkosh	WI	54903		920-236-7820	R	18*	<0.1
D.P. Associates Inc.	3401 Columbia Pke.	Arlington	VA	22204	D. J. Patterson Jr.	703-521-6236	S	18*	0.3
Aviat Aircraft Inc.	PO Box 1240	Afton	WY	83110	Stuart Horn	307-885-3151	R	18*	<0.1
Butler National Corp.	19920 W 161st St.	Olathe	KS	66062		913-780-9595	P	15	<0.1
Norcimbus F Crawford IV Inc.	3451 E Harbour Dr.	Phoenix	AZ	85034	John Wheeler	602-437-8500	R	14*	<0.1
Commander Premier Aircraft	20 Stanford Dr.	Farmington	CT	06032	Joel M. Hartstone	573-332-0880	R	12*	<0.1
Helicomb International Inc.	1402 S 69th E Ave.	Tulsa	OK	74112	Robert Austin	918-835-3999	R	11*	0.1
Avcon Industries	PO Box 748	Newton	KS	67114	Curtis Beadle	316-284-2842	S	11*	<0.1
Mingo Manufacturing Inc.	PO Box 30	Owasso	OK	74055	Terry Ingle	918-272-1151	R	10*	<0.1
Flanagan Brothers Inc.	PO Box 396	Glastonbury	CT	06033	Kenneth Flanagan	860-633-9474	R	8*	<0.1
STW Composites Inc.	1624 Flight Line	Mojave	CA	93501	Burt Rutan	661-824-4541	S	7*	<0.1
Amco Precision Tools Inc.	PO Box 442	Berlin	CT	06037	Aldo Zovich	860-828-5640	R	7*	<0.1
Northwest Helicopters Inc.	3725 N Boyer Ave.	Sandpoint	ID	83864	Brian Reynolds	208-265-9859	R	7*	<0.1
Kestrel Aircraft Co.	1600 Westheimer	Norman	OK	73070	M. M. Humphreys	405-573-0090	R	5*	<0.1
B and F Design Incorp	187 Stamm Rd.	Newington	CT	06111	Raymond Forgione	860-665-0062	R	4*	<0.1
Groen Brothers Aviation Inc.	2640 W California	Salt Lake City	UT	84104	David Groen	801-973-0177	P	3	<0.1
Ramec Engineering	1736 W 130th St.	Gardena	CA	90249	Leonard Roberts	310-532-2573	R	1*	<0.1

Source: Ward's Business Directory of U.S. Private and Public Companies, Volumes 1 and 2, 2008. The company type code used is as follows: P - Public, R - Private, S - Subsidiary, D - Division, J - Joint Venture, A - Affiliate, G - Group. Sales are in millions of dollars, employees are in thousands. An asterisk (*) indicates an estimated sales volume. The symbol < stands for 'less than'. Company names and addresses are truncated, in some cases, to fit into the available space.

MATERIALS CONSUMED

Material	Quantity	Delivered Cost ($ million)
Aircraft engines	(X)	6,760.8
Aircraft engine parts (excluding instruments)	(X)	708.1
Structural fuselage components (excluding instruments)	(X)	(D)
Structural empennage (tail) components (exc. instruments)	(X)	(D)
Structural wing components (excluding instruments)	(X)	(D)
Structural landing gear components	(X)	(D)
Other structural components (airframe) (exc. instruments)	(X)	(D)
Aircraft propellers and parts	(X)	8.9
Aircraft seats	(X)	79.0

Continued on next page.

MATERIALS CONSUMED - Continued

Material	Quantity	Delivered Cost ($ million)
Radio communication systems and equipment (microwave, UHF, etc.)	(X)	600.3
Navigational systems and equipment (NAVAIDS)	(X)	250.6
Search, detection, tracking, and electronic communication systems and equipment (RADAR, SONAR, and optical)	(X)	(D)
Flight, navigational, airframe, and engine indicators, instruments, and clusters (incl. sensors, displays, etc.)	(X)	666.0
Resistors, capacitors, transformers, electron tubes, semiconductors, and other electronic components	(X)	935.9
Resin matrix composites	(X)	100.8
Other matrix composites (ceramic, carbon, metal, etc.)	(X)	59.6
Complete mechanical, hydraulic and pneumatic subassemblies	(X)	(D)
Fluid power pumps, motors, and hydrostatic transmissions	(X)	(D)
Fluid power valves (excluding complete assemblies)	(X)	98.9
Fluid power hose, tube fittings, and assemblies (hydraulic and pneumatic)	(X)	89.4
Fluid power cylinders and rotary actuators (exc. complete assemblies)	(X)	(D)
Fluid power filters (hydraulic and pneumatic)	(X)	(D)
Other transportation related fluid power products, hydraulic and pneumatic	(X)	(D)
Ball and roller bearings (mounted or unmounted)	(X)	60.0
Cutting tools for machine tools	(X)	(D)
Aircraft metal hardware (excluding forgings)	(X)	(D)
Metal bolts, nuts, screws, and other screw machine products	(X)	124.9
Other fabricated metal products (exc. fluid power and forgings)	(X)	166.1
Iron and steel forgings	(X)	6.4
Aluminum and aluminum-base alloy forgings	(X)	15.9
Titanium and titanium-base alloy forgings	(X)	(D)
Other forgings	(X)	-
Iron and steel castings (rough and semifinished)	(X)	4.7
Aluminum and aluminum-base alloy castings (rough and semifinished)	(X)	30.2
Other nonferrous metal castings, rough or semifinished (inc. aluminum)	(X)	(D)
Steel bars, bar shapes, and plates (exc. castings, forgings, fabr. metal products)	(X)	(D)
Steel sheet and strip (including tinplate)	(X)	(D)
All other steel shapes and forms (exc. castings, forgings, fabr. metal products)	(X)	(D)
Aluminum and aluminum-base alloy sheet, plate, foil, and welded tubing	(X)	59.9
All other aluminum and aluminum-base alloy shapes and forms (exc. castings, forgings, fabr. metal products)	(X)	(D)
Copper and copper-base alloy shapes and forms (exc. castings, forgings, fabr. metal products)	(X)	(D)
Titanium and titanium-base alloy shapes and forms (exc. castings, forgings, fabr. metal products)	(X)	(D)
Other nonferrous shapes and forms (exc. castings, forgings, fabricated metal products)	(X)	(D)
Paints, varnishes, stains, lacquers, shellacs, japans, enamels, etc.	(X)	33.9
All other materials, components, parts, containers, and supplies	(X)	2,914.3
Materials, ingredients, containers, and supplies, nsk	(X)	8,942.0

Source: 2002 Economic Census. Explanation of symbols used: (D): Withheld to avoid disclosure of competitive data; na: Not available; (S): Withheld because statistical norms were not met; (X): Not applicable; (Z): Less than half the unit shown; nec: Not elsewhere classified; nsk: Not specified by kind; - : zero; p : 10-19 percent estimated; q : 20-29 percent estimated.

PRODUCT SHARE DETAILS

Product or Product Class Shipments	Mil. $	Product or Product Class Shipments	Mil. $
AIRCRAFT	59,778.2	accepted aircraft, nsk	434.6
Military aircraft	**14,468.0**	**Other aeronautical services on complete aircraft, nec**	**3,770.8**
Civilian aircraft	**35,267.0**	Other aeronautical services on complete aircraft, nec	3,675.9
Modification, conversion, and overhaul of previously accepted aircraft	**6,203.3**	Research and development on complete aircraft for military customers	1,842.8
Modification, conversion, and overhaul of previously accepted aircraft	5,768.7	All other aeronautical services on complete aircraft for military customers	734.5
Modification, conversion, and overhaul of U.S. military aircraft and all other aircraft built to military specifications	3,448.6	Research and development on complete aircraft for civilian customers	(D)
Modification, conversion, and overhaul of previously accepted aircraft for civilian customers	2,320.1	All other aeronautical services on complete aircraft for civilian customers	(D)
Modification, conversion, and overhaul of previously		Other aeronautical services on complete aircraft, nec, nsk	94.9
		Aircraft, nsk, total	**69.1**

Source: 2002 Economic Census. The values are product shipments in millions of dollars for 2002. Total product shipments may be lower or higher than industry shipments. See Introduction for a full discussion. Values of indented subcategories are summed in the main heading(s). The symbol (D) appears when data are withheld to prevent disclosure of competitive information. The abbreviation nsk stands for 'not specified by kind' and nec for 'not elsewhere classified'. A dash (-) means zero.

INPUTS AND OUTPUTS FOR AIRCRAFT MANUFACTURING

Economic Sector or Industry Providing Inputs	%	Sector	Economic Sector or Industry Buying Outputs	%	Sector
Compensation of employees	22.1		Private fixed investment	35.6	
Aircraft parts & auxiliary equipment, nec	14.1	Manufg.	Exports of goods & services	34.5	Cap Inv
Aircraft engine & engine parts	13.7	Manufg.	General Federal government services, defense	15.9	Fed Govt
Management of companies & enterprises	6.5	Services	Federal government, investment, national defense	11.5	Fed Govt
Search, detection, & navigation instruments	6.3	Manufg.	Air transportation	0.9	Util.
Wholesale trade	2.9	Trade	Personal consumption expenditures	0.7	

Continued on next page.

INPUTS AND OUTPUTS FOR AIRCRAFT MANUFACTURING - Continued

Economic Sector or Industry Providing Inputs	%	Sector	Economic Sector or Industry Buying Outputs	%	Sector
Broadcast & wireless communications equipment	2.0	Manufg.	Aircraft	0.4	Manufg.
Semiconductors & related devices	1.7	Manufg.	Couriers & messengers	0.2	Util.
Iron & steel mills & ferroalloys	1.5	Manufg.	General Federal government services, nondefense	0.2	Fed Govt
Watches, clocks, & related devices	1.3	Manufg.	Federal government, investment, nondefense	0.1	Fed Govt
Motor vehicle parts	1.0	Manufg.			
Valve & fittings other than plumbing	0.8	Manufg.			
Truck transportation	0.7	Util.			
Fluid power process machinery	0.6	Manufg.			
Scientific research & development services	0.6	Services			
Plastics products, nec	0.6	Manufg.			
Custom computer programming services	0.5	Services			
Aircraft	0.4	Manufg.			
Advertising & related services	0.4	Services			
Carpet & rug mills	0.4	Manufg.			
Lessors of nonfinancial assets	0.4	Fin/R.E.			
Aluminum products from purchased aluminum	0.4	Manufg.			
Automotive equipment rental & leasing	0.3	Fin/R.E.			
Power generation & supply	0.3	Util.			
Hardware	0.3	Manufg.			
Specialized design services	0.3	Services			
Printed circuit assemblies (electronic assemblies)	0.3	Manufg.			
Securities, commodity contracts, investments	0.3	Fin/R.E.			
Wiring devices	0.3	Manufg.			
Turned products & screws, nuts, & bolts	0.3	Manufg.			
Management, scientific, & technical consulting	0.2	Services			
Air transportation	0.2	Util.			
Chemical products & preparations, nec	0.2	Manufg.			
Other computer related services, including facilities	0.2	Services			
Warehousing & storage	0.2	Util.			
Data processing, hosting, & related services	0.2	Services			
Paperboard containers	0.2	Manufg.			
Communication & energy wires & cables	0.2	Manufg.			
Telecommunications	0.2	Services			
Legal services	0.2	Services			
Architectural, engineering, & related services	0.2	Services			
Commercial & industrial machinery rental & leasing	0.2	Fin/R.E.			
Copper rolling, drawing, extruding, & alloying	0.2	Manufg.			
Machine shops	0.2	Manufg.			
Employment services	0.1	Services			
Real estate	0.1	Fin/R.E.			
Ball & roller bearings	0.1	Manufg.			
Noncomparable imports	0.1	Foreign			
Business support services	0.1	Services			
Maintenance/repair of nonresidential structures	0.1	Construct.			
Professional, scientific, technical services, nec	0.1	Services			
Services to buildings & dwellings	0.1	Services			
Forging, stamping, & sintering, nec	0.1	Manufg.			
General purpose machinery, nec	0.1	Manufg.			
Accounting, tax preparation, bookkeeping, & payroll	0.1	Services			
Sand, gravel, clay, & refractory minerals	0.1	Mining			
Taxes on production & imports, less subsidies	0.1				
Coating, engraving, heat treating & allied activities	0.1	Manufg.			

Source: Benchmark Input-Output Accounts for the U.S. Economy, 2002, U.S. Department of Commerce, Washington, D.C., January 2008. The abbreviation nec stands for 'not elsewhere classified'.

OCCUPATIONS EMPLOYED BY AEROSPACE PRODUCT & PARTS MANUFACTURING

Occupation	% of Total 2006	Change to 2016	Occupation	% of Total 2006	Change to 2016
Aerospace engineers	9.3	6.9	Management analysts	1.8	1.8
Aircraft structure & systems assemblers	5.2	12.0	Engineers, nec	1.8	1.8
Aircraft mechanics & service technicians	4.4	22.2	Production, planning, & expediting clerks	1.6	1.8
Machinists	3.8	6.9	Industrial engineering technicians	1.5	12.0
Inspectors, testers, sorters, samplers, & weighers	3.5	-4.0	Team assemblers	1.5	1.8
Industrial engineers	3.1	23.7	Executive secretaries & administrative assistants	1.4	1.8
Computer software engineers, applications	2.5	22.2	Computer-controlled machine tool operators	1.1	12.0
Mechanical engineers	2.3	1.8	Computer software engineers, systems software	1.1	12.0
Engineering managers	2.2	12.0	Engineering technicians, exc drafters, nec	1.1	1.8
Purchasing agents, exc wholesale, retail, & farm	2.0	1.8	Industrial production managers	1.0	1.8
First-line supervisors/managers of production workers	2.0	1.8	Stock clerks & order fillers	1.0	-14.8
Business operation specialists, nec	1.9	12.0			

Source: Industry-Occupation Matrix, Bureau of Labor Statistics, December 4, 2007. These data are reported based on 4-digit NAICS categories but have been matched to corresponding 6-digit NAICS industry codes. The change reported for each occupation to the year 2016 is a percent of growth or decline as estimated by the Bureau of Labor Statistics. The abbreviation nec stands for 'not elsewhere classified'.

LOCATION BY STATE AND REGIONAL CONCENTRATION

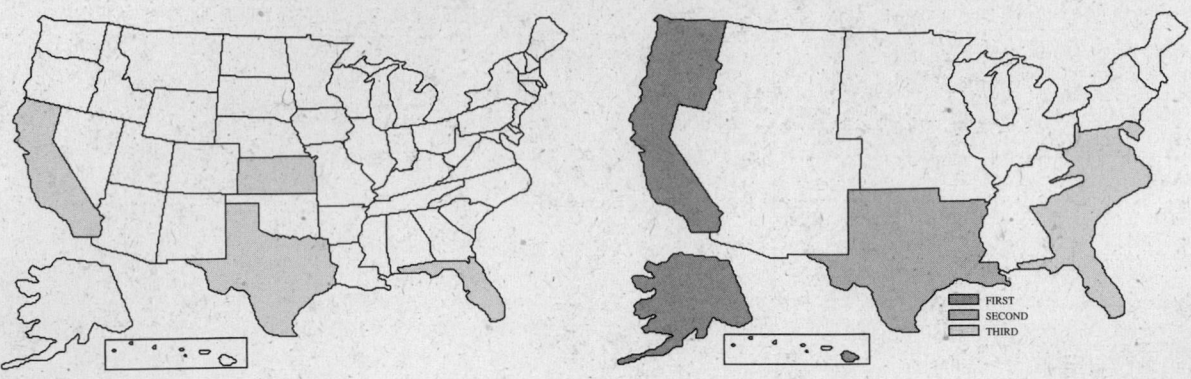

INDUSTRY DATA BY STATE

State	Establish-ments	Shipments			Employment				Cost as % of Shipments	Investment per Employee ($)
		Total ($ mil)	% of U.S.	Per Establ.	Total Number	% of U.S.	Per Establ.	Wages ($/hour)		
Kansas	9	6,834.4	10.6	759,381.8	22,593	12.9	2,510	18.74	41.0	8,133
Texas	25	5,668.2	8.8	226,728.3	21,183	12.1	847	29.11	52.6	7,864
California	29	4,579.7	7.1	157,919.0	25,824	14.8	890	33.06	51.3	2,822
Florida	21	903.0	1.4	42,999.0	3,302	1.9	157	23.43	40.1	5,962

Source: 2002 *Economic Census*. The states are in descending order of shipments or establishments (if shipment data are missing for the majority). The symbol (D) appears when data are withheld to prevent disclosure of competitive information. States marked with (D) are sorted by number of establishments. A dash (-) indicates that the data element cannot be calculated. Data may not show all states active in the NAICS category. All data available at the time of publication are shown.

NAICS 336412 - AIRCRAFT ENGINE AND ENGINE PARTS MANUFACTURING

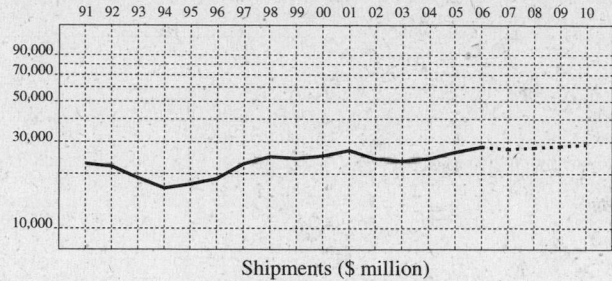

Shipments ($ million)

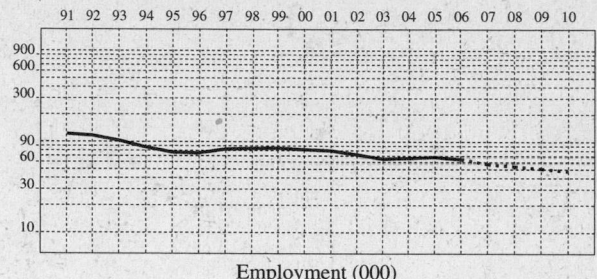

Employment (000)

GENERAL STATISTICS

Year	Com-panies	Establishments		Employment			Compensation		Production ($ million)			
		Total	with 20 or more employees	Total (000)	Production Workers (000)	Hours (Mil)	Payroll ($ mil)	Wages ($/hr)	Cost of Materials	Value Added by Manufacture	Value of Shipments	Capital Invest.
1991		437	287	122.3	67.3	141.6	4,822.0	15.56	10,078.5	12,278.1	22,746.2	770.6
1992	338	442	281	116.7	64.2	130.8	4,851.7	16.97	9,019.2	11,445.4	21,968.5	590.2
1993		423	271	102.9	53.6	111.0	4,142.9	17.15	8,873.8	10,047.1	18,946.1	439.5
1994		410	250	86.9	46.4	94.5	3,786.0	18.02	8,455.3	7,956.5	16,663.7	437.7
1995		395	241	76.3	41.9	92.7	3,618.4	18.17	8,466.4	9,061.3	17,519.4	475.0
1996		355	239	75.1	41.4	85.5	3,639.9	19.98	9,758.3	9,036.7	18,769.2	485.0
1997	279	370	248	82.9	48.1	98.6	4,234.1	19.60	11,347.7	11,572.5	22,659.5	679.8
1998		371	240	84.6	49.4	103.8	4,292.0	19.59	12,031.5	12,959.9	24,868.5	733.4
1999		382	244	85.1	49.6	99.1	4,520.8	20.04	12,040.0	11,724.6	24,343.0	787.1
2000		388	257	82.0	47.2	94.7	4,503.8	21.27	12,430.5	12,633.2	25,124.7	695.5
2001		392	251	79.9	47.4	94.0	4,514.5	22.43	13,055.3	14,092.3	26,969.3	895.7
2002	297	412	249	72.3	40.6	83.0	4,113.3	23.31	11,629.5	12,358.8	24,246.4	829.7
2003		411	252	65.0	37.4	76.2	3,926.6	24.88	10,624.6	12,804.7	23,538.8	672.2
2004		410	240	66.4	37.5	75.4	4,077.7	26.48	11,232.8	12,983.0	24,279.5	435.6
2005		417	249	68.1	39.6	79.2	4,309.9	27.44	13,233.1	13,402.5	26,337.7	550.4
2006		392P	238P	64.4	37.8	77.4	4,384.2	27.82	14,818.1	13,303.2	28,180.9	451.7
2007		391P	236P	56.9P	34.3P	68.2P	4,181.3P	27.90P	14,391.9P	12,920.6P	27,370.4P	638.1P
2008		390P	234P	53.8P	32.8P	64.9P	4,175.1P	28.69P	14,665.5P	13,166.2P	27,890.7P	640.2P
2009		389P	232P	50.7P	31.4P	61.6P	4,169.0P	29.48P	14,939.1P	13,411.8P	28,411.0P	642.2P
2010		388P	230P	47.6P	29.9P	58.3P	4,162.8P	30.27P	15,212.7P	13,657.5P	28,931.4P	644.3P

Sources: 1992, 1997, 2002 *Economic Census*; other years, up to 2006, are from the *Annual Survey of Manufactures*. Establishment counts for non-Census years are from *County Business Patterns*; 1997 and 2002 values are from the 1997 and 2002 censuses respectively, reported in the Federal Government's NAICS format. Other years were originally reported in equivalent SIC format. 'P's show projections by the editors.

INDICES OF CHANGE

Year	Com-panies	Establishments		Employment			Compensation		Production ($ million)			
		Total	with 20 or more employees	Total (000)	Production Workers (000)	Hours (Mil)	Payroll ($ mil)	Wages ($/hr)	Cost of Materials	Value Added by Manufacture	Value of Shipments	Capital Invest.
1992	114	107	113	161	158	158	118	73	78	93	91	71
1997	94	90	100	115	118	119	103	84	98	94	93	82
2001		95	101	111	117	113	110	96	112	114	111	108
2002	100	100	100	100	100	100	100	100	100	100	100	100
2003		100	101	90	92	92	95	107	91	104	97	81
2004		100	96	92	92	91	99	114	97	105	100	53
2005		101	100	94	98	95	105	118	114	108	109	66
2006		95P	95P	89	93	93	107	119	127	108	116	54
2007		95P	95P	79P	84P	82P	102P	120P	124P	105P	113P	77P
2008		95P	94P	74P	81P	78P	102P	123P	126P	107P	115P	77P
2009		94P	93P	70P	77P	74P	101P	126P	128P	109P	117P	77P
2010		94P	92P	66P	74P	70P	101P	130P	131P	111P	119P	78P

Sources: Same as General Statistics. Values reflect change from the base year, 2002. Values above 100 mean greater than 2002, values below 100 mean less than 2002, and the values of 100 in other years means the same as 2002. 'P's show projections by the editors.

SELECTED RATIOS

For 2002	Avg. of All Manufact.	Analyzed Industry	Index	For 2002	Avg. of All Manufact.	Analyzed Industry	Index
Employees per Establishment	42	175	418	Value Added per Production Worker	182,367	304,404	167
Payroll per Establishment	1,639,184	9,983,738	609	Cost per Establishment	5,769,015	28,226,942	489
Payroll per Employee	39,053	56,892	146	Cost per Employee	137,446	160,851	117
Production Workers per Establishment	30	99	334	Cost per Production Worker	195,506	286,441	147
Wages per Establishment	694,845	4,695,947	676	Shipments per Establishment	11,158,348	58,850,485	527
Wages per Production Worker	23,548	47,653	202	Shipments per Employee	265,847	335,358	126
Hours per Production Worker	1,980	2,044	103	Shipments per Production Worker	378,144	597,202	158
Wages per Hour	11.89	23.31	196	Investment per Establishment	361,338	2,013,835	557
Value Added per Establishment	5,381,325	29,997,087	557	Investment per Employee	8,609	11,476	133
Value Added per Employee	128,210	170,938	133	Investment per Production Worker	12,245	20,436	167

Sources: Same as General Statistics. The 'Average of All Manufacturing' column represents the average of all manufacturing industries reported for the most recent complete year available. The Index shows the relationship between the Average and the Analyzed Industry. For example, 100 means that they are equal; 500 that the Analyzed Industry is five times the average; 50 means that the Analyzed Industry is half the national average. The abbreviation 'na' is used to show that data are 'not available'. Ratios shown for 2002, the last complete census year.

LEADING COMPANIES   Number shown: 75   Total sales ($ mil): 345,748   Total employment (000): 902.5

Company Name	Address				CEO Name	Phone	Co. Type	Sales ($ mil)	Empl. (000)
General Electric Co.	3135 Easton Tpk.	Fairfield	CT	06828		203-373-2211	P	172,738	327.0
Boeing Co.	100 N Riverside Plz	Chicago	IL	60606		312-544-2000	P	66,387	159.3
United Technologies Corp.	1 Financial Plz.	Hartford	CT	06101	Mario Abajo	860-728-7000	P	47,829	225.6
Textron Inc.	40 Westminster St.	Providence	RI	02903		401-421-2800	P	13,225	44.0
GE Aircraft Engines	1 Neumann Way	Cincinnati	OH	45215	Scott C. Donnelly	513-243-2000	D	11,181*	26.5
Pratt and Whitney	400 Main Street	East Hartford	CT	06108	Stephen Finger	860-565-4321	S	7,670*	30.0
Goodrich Corp.	4 Coliseum Centre	Charlotte	NC	28217		704-423-7000	P	6,392	23.4
Precision Castparts Corp.	4650 SW Macadam	Portland	OR	97201		503-417-4800	P	5,361	19.8
Hamilton Sundstrand Corp.	1 Hamilton Rd.	Windsor Locks	CT	06096	Ronald F. McKenna	860-654-6000	S	3,600*	16.0
B/E Aerospace Machined Prods.	2555 Birch St.	Vista	CA	92083	Robert Khoury	760-599-1130	S	2,385*	3.5
Vought Aircraft Industries	PO Box 655907	Dallas	TX	75265	Elmer Doty	972-946-2011	S	1,577*	6.0
EaglePicher Corp.	2424 John Daly Rd.	Inkster	MI	48141	Donald L. Runkle	313-278-5956	R	1,244*	4.2
GKN Aerospace Chem-Tronics	PO Box 1604	El Cajon	CA	92022		619-448-2320	R	931*	0.9
Turbomeca Engine Corp.	2709 Forum Dr.	Grand Prairie	TX	75052	Russ Spray	972-606-7600	S	704*	0.3
HEICO Corp.	3000 Taft St.	Hollywood	FL	33021	L A. Mendelson	954-987-4000	P	508	2.2
Int'l Airmotive Holding Co.	PO Box 36199	Dallas	TX	75235	Hugh McElory	214-956-3000	R	500*	<0.1
TECT Utica Corp.	2 Halsey Rd.	Whitesboro	NY	13492	Ron Cable	315-768-8070	R	356*	1.3
Williams International Company	PO Box 200	Walled Lake	MI	48390		248-624-5200	R	300*	0.6
West Star Aviation Inc.	796 Heritage Way	Grand Junction	CO	81506	Bob Rasberry	970-243-7500	R	223*	0.3
SL Industries Inc.	520 Fellowship Rd.	Mount Laurel	NJ	08054	Steven Gilliatt	856-727-1500	P	177	1.9
Jet Avion Corp.	3000 Taft St.	Hollywood	FL	33021	Eric Mendelson	954-987-6101	S	175*	0.2
NORDAM Group Inc.	PO Box 3365	Tulsa	OK	74101		918-587-4105	R	169*	1.3
Chromalloy Georgia	30 Dart Rd.	Newnan	GA	30265	Chris Richardson	770-254-6200	D	124*	0.2
First Aviation Services Inc.	15 Riverside Ave.	Westport	CT	06880	Aaron Hollander	203-291-3300	P	119	0.2
International Motion Control	369 Franklin St.	Buffalo	NY	14202	Patrick Lee	716-855-2500	R	95*	<0.1
Meyer Tool Inc.	PO Box 25098	Cincinnati	OH	45225	Arlyn Easton	513-853-4400	R	89*	0.7
SIFCO Industries Inc.	970 E 64th St.	Cleveland	OH	44103	Jeffrey Gotschall	216-881-8600	P	87	0.4
Pemco World Air Services	100 Pemco Dr.	Dothan	AL	36303	Wake Smith		S	80*	0.6
Windsor Airmotive	7 Connecticut S Dr.	East Granby	CT	06026	Patrick Dempsey	860-653-5531	D	69*	0.1
Aeronca Inc.	2320 Wedekind Dr.	Middletown	OH	45042		513-422-2751	R	68*	0.3
Electro-Methods Inc.	PO Box 54	South Windsor	CT	06074	Randy Fries	860-289-8661	R	55*	0.2
Therm Inc.	PO Box 220	Ithaca	NY	14851	Robert Sprole	607-272-8500	R	55*	0.2
Gentz Industries L.L.C.	25250 Easy St.	Warren	MI	48089	Donald Duckett	586-772-2500	R	51*	0.2
Niles Precision Co.	PO Box 548	Niles	MI	49120	James Skalla	269-683-0585	R	48*	0.2
Exotic Metals Forming Company	5411 S 226th St.	Kent	WA	98032		253-395-3710	R	47*	0.3
Fairchild Controls Corp.	540 Highland St.	Frederick	MD	21701	Scott Selle	301-228-3400	R	45*	0.2
Palmer Manufacturing Company	PO Box K	Malden	MA	02148		781-321-0480	R	45*	0.2
Wood Group Pratt and Whitney	PO Box 3425	Windsor Locks	CT	06096		860-623-3366	R	45*	<0.1
Delta Industries	39 Bradley Park Rd.	East Granby	CT	06026	William Evans	860-653-5041	R	42*	0.2
Beacon Group Inc.	85 Granby St.	Bloomfield	CT	06002	Robert Sarkisian	860-242-3453	R	41*	0.1
Budney Industries Inc.	PO Box 1316	Berlin	CT	06037	Michael Budney	860-828-1950	R	41*	0.2
Cfan Co.	1000 Technology	San Marcos	TX	78666	Robert Baeumel	512-353-2832	R	41*	0.2
Dyna-Empire Inc.	1075 Stewart Ave.	Garden City	NY	11530	Patrick Carthy	516-222-2700	R	40*	0.1
Middleton Aerospace Corp.	20 Computer Dr.	Haverhill	MA	01832	Richard Neill	978-774-6000	R	40*	0.1
Senior Aerospace Jet Products	9106 Balboa Ave.	San Diego	CA	92123	Ronald Blair	858-278-8400	R	39*	0.1
Edac Technologies Corp.	1806 New Britain	Farmington	CT	06032	Dominick A. Pagano	860-678-8140	P	38	0.2
Berkshire Industries Inc.	PO Box 828	Westfield	MA	01086	Eckard Brause	413-568-8676	R	36*	0.1
Danville Metal Stamping Co.	20 Oakwood Ave.	Danville	IL	61832	Judd Beck	217-446-0647	R	34*	<0.1
Moeller Aerospace Technology	8725 Moeller Dr.	Harbor Springs	MI	49740	Daniel Moellering	231-347-9575	R	34*	0.1
Champion Air Compressors	PO Box 4024	Quincy	IL	62305		815-875-3321	S	32*	0.2
Pointe Precision Inc.	2675 Precision Dr.	Plover	WI	54467	Joseph Kinsella	715-342-5100	R	32*	0.1
Rich Technology International	28 Pond View Dr.	Scarborough	ME	04074	Allen Estes	207-883-7424	R	30*	0.1
Snow Aviation International	7201 Paul Tibbets	Columbus	OH	43217	Harry Snow	614-492-7669	R	28*	0.1
Barnes Aerospace/Adv. Fabric.	169 Kennedy Rd.	Windsor	CT	06095	Patrick Dempsey	860-298-7740	D	26*	0.1
Capo Industries Inc.	5498 Vine St.	Chino	CA	91710	Dave Feltch	909-627-2723	R	26*	<0.1
Birken Manufacturing Co.	PO Box 65	Bloomfield	CT	06002	Gary Greenberg	860-242-2211	R	25*	<0.1
Kreisler Manufacturing Corp.	180 Van Riper Ave.	Elmwood Park	NJ	07407	Wallace N. Kelly	201-791-0700	P	24	0.2
Tech Development Inc.	PO Box 13557	Dayton	OH	45413		937-898-9600	R	24*	<0.1
Arrow Gear Company Inc.	2301 Curtiss St.	Downers Grove	IL	60515	Joseph Arvin	630-969-7640	R	23*	0.2
Twigg Corp.	659 E York St.	Martinsville	IN	46151		765-342-7126	R	22*	<0.1
Welded Ring Products Company	2180 W 114th St.	Cleveland	OH	44102	James Janosek	216-961-3800	R	22*	<0.1
GE Tri-Remanufacturing Inc.	3390 E Locust St.	Terre Haute	IN	47803		812-234-5889	S	21*	<0.1
A.O. Sherman L.L.C.	2 Research Dr.	Shelton	CT	06484		203-929-8300	S	20*	<0.1
Precision Machine Works Inc.	PO Box 1115	Tacoma	WA	98401	David Baublits	253-272-5119	R	20*	0.1
Stein Seal Co.	PO Box 316	Kulpsville	PA	19443	Philip Stein	215-256-0201	R	20*	0.2
Ferrotherm Corp.	4758 Warner Rd.	Cleveland	OH	44125	Haakon Egeland	216-883-9350	R	20*	0.1
Smith West Inc.	404 W Guadalupe	Tempe	AZ	85283	John Mohnach	480-839-0501	R	20*	<0.1
Basler Turbo Conversions	PO Box 2305	Oshkosh	WI	54903		920-236-7820	R	18*	<0.1
Dynatech International Corp.	1 Rodeo Dr.	Brentwood	NY	11717	Terry Clark	631-243-1700	R	18*	<0.1
Norris Precision Manufacturing	PO Box 1968	Pinellas Park	FL	33780	Arthur Norris	727-572-6330	R	18*	<0.1
BH Aircraft Company Inc.	2230 Smithtown	Lk Ronkonkoma	NY	11779	Daniel Kearns	631-981-4200	R	17*	0.1
Kerns Manufacturing Corp.	3714 29th St.	Long Island Cty	NY	11101	Louis Srybnik	718-784-4044	R	16*	<0.1
Winslow Automatics Inc.	23 Saint Claire Ave	New Britain	CT	06051	Janusz Podlasek	860-225-6321	R	16*	<0.1
Scot Inc.	2525 Curtiss St.	Downers Grove	IL	60515	William Currer	630-969-0620	R	16*	<0.1
Reliable Manufacturing Company	125 Highland Prk Dr	Bloomfield	CT	06002	Mark Gregoreti	860-242-5591	R	15*	<0.1

Source: Ward's Business Directory of U.S. Private and Public Companies, Volumes 1 and 2, 2008. The company type code used is as follows: P - Public, R - Private, S - Subsidiary, D - Division, J - Joint Venture, A - Affiliate, G - Group. Sales are in millions of dollars, employees are in thousands. An asterisk (*) indicates an estimated sales volume. The symbol < stands for 'less than'. Company names and addresses are truncated, in some cases, to fit into the available space.

MATERIALS CONSUMED

Material	Quantity	Delivered Cost ($ million)
Aircraft engines	(X)	(D)
Aircraft engine parts (excluding instruments)	(X)	5,189.7
Structural fuselage components (excluding instruments)	(X)	0.6
Structural empennage (tail) components (exc. instruments)	(X)	(D)
Structural wing components (excluding instruments)	(X)	(D)
Structural landing gear components	(X)	(D)
Other structural components (airframe) (exc. instruments)	(X)	(D)
Aircraft propellers and parts	(X)	0.5
Radio communication systems and equipment (microwave, UHF, etc.)	(X)	(D)
Navigational systems and equipment (NAVAIDS)	(X)	(D)
Search, detection, tracking, and electronic communication systems and equipment (RADAR, SONAR, and optical)	(X)	(D)
Flight, navigational, airframe, and engine indicators, instruments, and clusters (incl. sensors, displays, etc.)	(X)	(D)
Resistors, capacitors, transformers, electron tubes, semiconductors, and other electronic components	(X)	84.6
Resin matrix composites	(X)	10.0
Other matrix composites (ceramic, carbon, metal, etc.)	(X)	23.7
Complete mechanical, hydraulic and pneumatic subassemblies	(X)	71.7
Fluid power pumps, motors, and hydrostatic transmissions	(X)	(D)
Fluid power valves (excluding complete assemblies)	(X)	(D)
Fluid power hose, tube fittings, and assemblies (hydraulic and pneumatic)	(X)	12.2
Fluid power cylinders and rotary actuators (exc. complete assemblies)	(X)	1.5
Fluid power filters (hydraulic and pneumatic)	(X)	2.1
Other transportation related fluid power products, hydraulic and pneumatic	(X)	(D)
Ball and roller bearings (mounted or unmounted)	(X)	38.0
Cutting tools for machine tools	(X)	26.5
Aircraft metal hardware (excluding forgings)	(X)	(D)
Metal bolts, nuts, screws, and other screw machine products	(X)	40.7
Other fabricated metal products (exc. fluid power and forgings)	(X)	35.5
Iron and steel forgings	(X)	80.4
Aluminum and aluminum-base alloy forgings	(X)	39.8
Titanium and titanium-base alloy forgings	(X)	156.8
Other forgings	(X)	67.6
Iron and steel castings (rough and semifinished)	(X)	266.9
Aluminum and aluminum-base alloy castings (rough and semifinished)	(X)	23.4
Other nonferrous metal castings, rough or semifinished (inc. aluminum)	(X)	83.9
Steel bars, bar shapes, and plates (exc. castings, forgings, fabr. metal products)	(X)	37.2
Steel sheet and strip (including tinplate)	(X)	42.9
All other steel shapes and forms (exc. castings, forgings, fabr. metal products)	(X)	13.1
Aluminum and aluminum-base alloy sheet, plate, foil, and welded tubing	(X)	5.0
All other aluminum and aluminum-base alloy shapes and forms (exc. castings, forgings, fabr. metal products)	(X)	11.5
Copper and copper-base alloy shapes and forms (exc. castings, forgings, fabr. metal products)	(X)	2.0
Titanium and titanium-base alloy shapes and forms (exc. castings, forgings, fabr. metal products)	(X)	30.7
Other nonferrous shapes and forms (exc. castings, forgings, fabricated metal products)	(X)	28.3
Paints, varnishes, stains, lacquers, shellacs, japans, enamels, etc.	(X)	1.2
All other materials, components, parts, containers, and supplies	(X)	226.1
Materials, ingredients, containers, and supplies, nsk	(X)	1,694.7

Source: 2002 *Economic Census*. Explanation of symbols used: (D): Withheld to avoid disclosure of competitive data; na: Not available; (S): Withheld because statistical norms were not met; (X): Not applicable; (Z): Less than half the unit shown; nec: Not elsewhere classified; nsk: Not specified by kind; - : zero; p : 10-19 percent estimated; q : 20-29 percent estimated.

PRODUCT SHARE DETAILS

Product or Product Class Shipments	Mil. $	Product or Product Class Shipments	Mil. $
AIRCRAFT ENGINES AND ENGINE PARTS	21,267.7	specifications	517.3
Military aircraft engines (and any other aircraft engines built to military specifications)	**1,805.0**	All other aeronautical services on civilian aircraft engines	2,394.0
Civilian aircraft engines	**5,949.9**	Aeronautical services on aircraft engines, nsk	264.7
Aeronautical services on aircraft engines	**3,539.7**	**Aircraft engine parts and accessories**	**9,578.8**
Aeronautical services on aircraft engines	3,275.0	Parts and accessories for spark ignition reciprocating and rotary internal combustion military aircraft engines	1,044.6
Research and development work on U.S. military aircraft engines and all other engines built to military specifications	(D)	Parts and accessories for other military aircraft engines	1,270.7
Research and development work on civilian aircraft engines	(D)	Parts and accessories for spark ignition reciprocating and rotary internal combustion civilian aircraft engines	3,270.4
All other aeronautical services on U.S. military aircraft engines and all other engines built to military		Parts and accessories for other civilian aircraft engines	3,706.6
		Aircraft engine parts and accessories, nsk	286.6
		Aircraft engines and engine parts, nsk, total	**394.3**

Source: 2002 *Economic Census*. The values are product shipments in millions of dollars for 2002. Total product shipments may be lower or higher than industry shipments. See Introduction for a full discussion. Values of indented subcategories are summed in the main heading(s). The symbol (D) appears when data are withheld to prevent disclosure of competitive information. The abbreviation nsk stands for 'not specified by kind' and nec for 'not elsewhere classified'. A dash (-) means zero.

INPUTS AND OUTPUTS FOR AIRCRAFT ENGINE AND ENGINE PARTS MANUFACTURING

Economic Sector or Industry Providing Inputs	%	Sector	Economic Sector or Industry Buying Outputs	%	Sector
Aircraft engine & engine parts	27.0	Manufg.	Exports of goods & services	40.3	Cap Inv
Compensation of employees	25.1		Aircraft	30.3	Manufg.
Management of companies & enterprises	7.7	Services	Aircraft engine & engine parts	21.1	Manufg.
Hardware	2.1	Manufg.	Federal government, investment, national defense	3.0	Fed Govt
Aircraft parts & auxiliary equipment, nec	1.5	Manufg.	General Federal government services, defense	2.6	Fed Govt
Forging, stamping, & sintering, nec	1.5	Manufg.	Private fixed investment	1.3	
Wholesale trade	1.5	Trade	Aircraft parts & auxiliary equipment, nec	0.5	Manufg.
Management, scientific, & technical consulting	1.4	Services	Scientific research & development services	0.3	Services
Legal services	1.1	Services	General Federal government services, nondefense	0.3	Fed Govt
Search, detection, & navigation instruments	1.1	Manufg.	Air transportation	0.2	Util.
Ferrous metal foundries	1.0	Manufg.			
Valve & fittings other than plumbing	0.9	Manufg.			
Scientific research & development services	0.8	Services			
Specialized design services	0.7	Services			
Rubber products, nec	0.6	Manufg.			
Business support services	0.6	Services			
Truck transportation	0.6	Util.			
Employment services	0.6	Services			
Lessors of nonfinancial assets	0.6	Fin/R.E.			
Power generation & supply	0.6	Util.			
Securities, commodity contracts, investments	0.5	Fin/R.E.			
Nonferrous metal foundries	0.5	Manufg.			
Fluid power process machinery	0.4	Manufg.			
Architectural, engineering, & related services	0.4	Services			
Iron & steel mills & ferroalloys	0.4	Manufg.			
Semiconductors & related devices	0.4	Manufg.			
Monetary authorities/depository credit intermediation	0.4	Fin/R.E.			
Broadcast & wireless communications equipment	0.3	Manufg.			
Advertising & related services	0.3	Services			
Support services, nec	0.3	Services			
Professional, scientific, technical services, nec	0.3	Services			
Real estate	0.3	Fin/R.E.			
Telecommunications	0.3	Services			
Investigation & security services	0.2	Services			
Custom computer programming services	0.2	Services			
Taxes on production & imports, less subsidies	0.2				
Data processing, hosting, & related services	0.2	Services			
Accounting, tax preparation, bookkeeping, & payroll	0.2	Services			
Noncomparable imports	0.2	Foreign			
Warehousing & storage	0.2	Util.			
Food services & drinking places	0.2	Services			
Natural gas distribution	0.2	Util.			
Turned products & screws, nuts, & bolts	0.2	Manufg.			
Ball & roller bearings	0.2	Manufg.			
Other computer related services, including facilities	0.2	Services			
Air transportation	0.2	Util.			
Maintenance/repair of nonresidential structures	0.2	Construct.			
Environmental & other technical consulting services	0.2	Services			
Services to buildings & dwellings	0.2	Services			
Office administrative services	0.2	Services			
Motor vehicle parts	0.2	Manufg.			
Automotive equipment rental & leasing	0.1	Fin/R.E.			
Nonferrous metal (ex. copper & aluminum) processing	0.1	Manufg.			
Hotels & motels, including casino hotels	0.1	Services			
Printed circuit assemblies (electronic assemblies)	0.1	Manufg.			
Aluminum products from purchased aluminum	0.1	Manufg.			
Cutting tools & machine tool accessories	0.1	Manufg.			
Facilities support services	0.1	Services			
Sand, gravel, clay, & refractory minerals	0.1	Mining			
Automotive repair & maintenance, ex. car washes	0.1	Services			

Source: Benchmark Input-Output Accounts for the U.S. Economy, 2002, U.S. Department of Commerce, Washington, D.C., January 2008. The abbreviation nec stands for 'not elsewhere classified'.

OCCUPATIONS EMPLOYED BY AEROSPACE PRODUCT & PARTS MANUFACTURING

Occupation	% of Total 2006	Change to 2016	Occupation	% of Total 2006	Change to 2016
Aerospace engineers	9.3	6.9	Management analysts	1.8	1.8
Aircraft structure & systems assemblers	5.2	12.0	Engineers, nec	1.8	1.8
Aircraft mechanics & service technicians	4.4	22.2	Production, planning, & expediting clerks	1.6	1.8
Machinists	3.8	6.9	Industrial engineering technicians	1.5	12.0
Inspectors, testers, sorters, samplers, & weighers	3.5	-4.0	Team assemblers	1.5	1.8
Industrial engineers	3.1	23.7	Executive secretaries & administrative assistants	1.4	1.8
Computer software engineers, applications	2.5	22.2	Computer-controlled machine tool operators	1.1	12.0
Mechanical engineers	2.3	1.8	Computer software engineers, systems software	1.1	12.0
Engineering managers	2.2	12.0	Engineering technicians, exc drafters, nec	1.1	1.8
Purchasing agents, exc wholesale, retail, & farm	2.0	1.8	Industrial production managers	1.0	1.8
First-line supervisors/managers of production workers	2.0	1.8	Stock clerks & order fillers	1.0	-14.8
Business operation specialists, nec	1.9	12.0			

Source: Industry-Occupation Matrix, Bureau of Labor Statistics, December 4, 2007. These data are reported based on 4-digit NAICS categories but have been matched to corresponding 6-digit NAICS industry codes. The change reported for each occupation to the year 2016 is a percent of growth or decline as estimated by the Bureau of Labor Statistics. The abbreviation nec stands for 'not elsewhere classified'.

LOCATION BY STATE AND REGIONAL CONCENTRATION

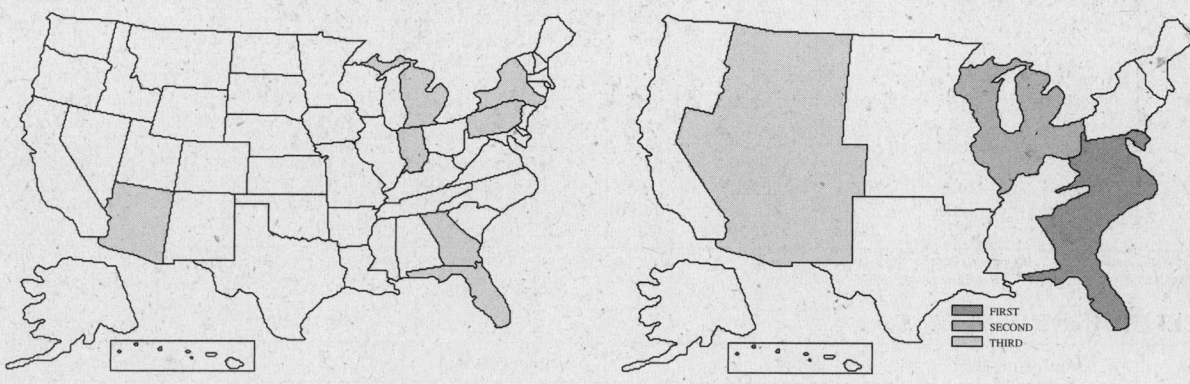

INDUSTRY DATA BY STATE

State	Establish-ments	Shipments Total ($ mil)	% of U.S.	Per Establ.	Employment Total Number	% of U.S.	Per Establ.	Wages ($/hour)	Cost as % of Shipments	Investment per Employee ($)
Arizona	28	2,992.1	12.3	106,860.9	5,577	7.7	199	20.56	32.2	7,321
Indiana	14	1,749.4	7.2	124,956.2	5,815	8.0	415	32.64	34.5	5,793
Michigan	21	463.1	1.9	22,051.2	3,160	4.4	150	28.16	40.1	9,253
New York	19	430.0	1.8	22,632.8	2,846	3.9	150	16.58	39.9	6,309
Georgia	9	369.5	1.5	41,060.3	1,948	2.7	216	15.23	37.6	3,068
Florida	27	325.8	1.3	12,065.3	1,633	2.3	60	16.81	45.9	5,175
Pennsylvania	9	281.6	1.2	31,287.1	1,211	1.7	135	20.25	71.8	4,430

Source: 2002 Economic Census. The states are in descending order of shipments or establishments (if shipment data are missing for the majority). The symbol (D) appears when data are withheld to prevent disclosure of competitive information. States marked with (D) are sorted by number of establishments. A dash (-) indicates that the data element cannot be calculated. Data may not show all states active in the NAICS category. All data available at the time of publication are shown.

NAICS 336413 - AIRCRAFT PARTS AND AUXILIARY EQUIPMENT MANUFACTURING NEC

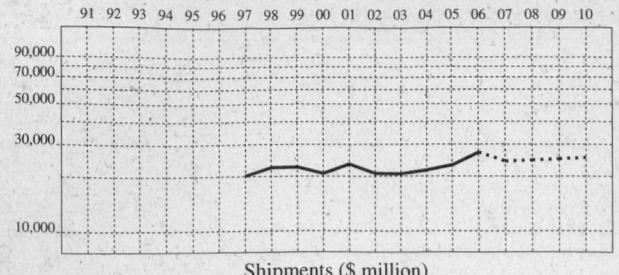

Shipments ($ million)

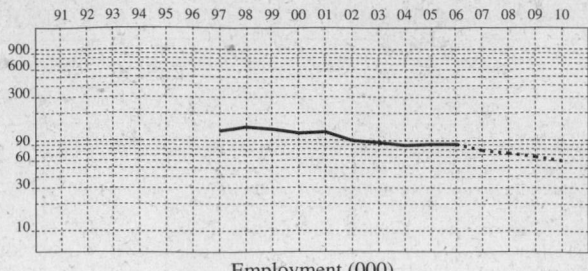

Employment (000)

GENERAL STATISTICS

Year	Com-panies	Establishments		Employment			Compensation		Production ($ million)			
		Total	with 20 or more employees	Total (000)	Production Workers (000)	Hours (Mil)	Payroll ($ mil)	Wages ($/hr)	Cost of Materials	Value Added by Manufacture	Value of Shipments	Capital Invest.
1997	1,051	1,138	458	127.7	73.7	157.1	5,737.8	19.34	7,480.1	13,279.7	20,073.1	925.1
1998		1,128	476	141.0	82.7	180.3	6,464.8	19.26	8,830.0	14,361.2	22,402.7	975.2
1999		1,134	469	132.7	74.8	155.3	6,306.3	20.77	8,747.8	13,046.8	22,500.7	782.7
2000		1,106	455	119.7	70.7	148.7	6,048.1	22.11	8,608.4	11,868.7	20,750.1	581.8
2001		1,058	455	123.0	71.6	150.4	6,438.9	22.13	9,314.2	13,903.0	23,403.8	594.0
2002	759	854	382	99.4	53.0	111.5	5,306.4	23.44	7,262.5	13,203.2	20,772.0	570.7
2003		807	373	95.2	51.4	107.2	5,269.4	22.85	7,751.5	12,515.0	20,620.6	492.0
2004		816	386	89.0	45.9	93.8	5,255.1	24.74	7,526.3	14,253.1	21,598.1	557.9
2005		797	406	91.3	47.8	96.9	5,291.8	23.89	8,351.3	14,565.6	23,099.7	550.5
2006		715P	367P	91.4	49.4	98.2	5,710.1	26.18	10,469.7	17,348.0	27,093.4	926.5
2007		661P	355P	78.0P	39.3P	77.1P	5,210.0P	26.38P	9,370.6P	15,526.7P	24,249.0P	549.7P
2008		608P	342P	72.0P	35.2P	67.5P	5,105.9P	27.09P	9,512.3P	15,761.6P	24,615.9P	523.2P
2009		555P	330P	66.0P	31.0P	57.9P	5,001.7P	27.81P	9,654.1P	15,996.5P	24,982.7P	496.7P
2010		501P	317P	60.0P	26.9P	48.3P	4,897.6P	28.52P	9,795.8P	16,231.4P	25,349.5P	470.2P

Sources: 1997 and 2002 *Economic Census*; other years, up to 2006, are from *Annual Survey of Manufactures*. Establishment counts for non-Census years are from *County Business Patterns*; 1997 and 2002 values are from the 1997 and 2002 censuses, respectively. 'P's show projections by the editors.

INDICES OF CHANGE

Year	Com-panies	Establishments		Employment			Compensation		Production ($ million)			
		Total	with 20 or more employees	Total (000)	Production Workers (000)	Hours (Mil)	Payroll ($ mil)	Wages ($/hr)	Cost of Materials	Value Added by Manufacture	Value of Shipments	Capital Invest.
1997	138	133	120	128	139	141	108	83	103	101	97	162
1998		132	125	142	156	162	122	82	122	109	108	171
1999		133	123	134	141	139	119	89	120	99	108	137
2000		130	119	120	133	133	114	94	119	90	100	102
2001		124	119	124	135	135	121	94	128	105	113	104
2002	100	100	100	100	100	100	100	100	100	100	100	100
2003		94	98	96	97	96	99	97	107	95	99	86
2004		96	101	90	87	84	99	106	104	108	104	98
2005		93	106	92	90	87	100	102	115	110	111	96
2006		84P	96P	92	93	88	108	112	144	131	130	162
2007		77P	93P	78P	74P	69P	98P	113P	129P	118P	117P	96P
2008		71P	90P	72P	66P	61P	96P	116P	131P	119P	119P	92P
2009		65P	86P	66P	58P	52P	94P	119P	133P	121P	120P	87P
2010		59P	83P	60P	51P	43P	92P	122P	135P	123P	122P	82P

Sources: Same as General Statistics. Values reflect change from the base year, 2002. Values above 100 mean greater than 2002, values below 100 mean less than 2002, and the values of 100 in other years means the same as 2002. 'P's show projections by the editors.

SELECTED RATIOS

For 2002	Avg. of All Manufact.	Analyzed Industry	Index	For 2002	Avg. of All Manufact.	Analyzed Industry	Index
Employees per Establishment	42	116	277	Value Added per Production Worker	182,367	249,117	137
Payroll per Establishment	1,639,184	6,213,583	379	Cost per Establishment	5,769,015	8,504,098	147
Payroll per Employee	39,053	53,384	137	Cost per Employee	137,446	73,063	53
Production Workers per Establishment	30	62	210	Cost per Production Worker	195,506	137,028	70
Wages per Establishment	694,845	3,060,375	440	Shipments per Establishment	11,158,348	24,323,185	218
Wages per Production Worker	23,548	49,312	209	Shipments per Employee	265,847	208,974	79
Hours per Production Worker	1,980	2,104	106	Shipments per Production Worker	378,144	391,925	104
Wages per Hour	11.89	23.44	197	Investment per Establishment	361,338	668,267	185
Value Added per Establishment	5,381,325	15,460,422	287	Investment per Employee	8,609	5,741	67
Value Added per Employee	128,210	132,829	104	Investment per Production Worker	12,245	10,768	88

Sources: Same as General Statistics. The 'Average of All Manufacturing' column represents the average of all manufacturing industries reported for the most recent complete year available. The Index shows the relationship between the Average and the Analyzed Industry. For example, 100 means that they are equal; 500 that the Analyzed Industry is five times the average; 50 means that the Analyzed Industry is half the national average. The abbreviation 'na' is used to show that data are 'not available'. Ratios shown for 2002, the last complete census year.

LEADING COMPANIES   Number shown: 75   Total sales ($ mil): **244,977**   Total employment (000): **782.6**

Company Name	Address				CEO Name	Phone	Co. Type	Sales ($ mil)	Empl. (000)
Boeing Co.	100 N Riverside Plz	Chicago	IL	60606		312-544-2000	P	66,387	159.3
Lockheed Martin Corp.	6801 Rockledge Dr	Bethesda	MD	20817	Richard F. Ambrose	301-897-6000	P	41,862	140.0
Northrop Grumman Corp.	1840 Century Park E	Los Angeles	CA	90067		310-553-6262	P	32,018	122.6
Raytheon Co.	870 Winter St.	Waltham	MA	02451		781-522-3000	P	21,301	72.1
Textron Inc.	40 Westminster St.	Providence	RI	02903		401-421-2800	P	13,225	44.0
Parker Hannifin Corp.	6035 Parkland Blvd.	Cleveland	OH	44124	Lee Banks	216-896-3000	P	10,718	57.3
Pratt and Whitney	400 Main Street	East Hartford	CT	06108	Stephen Finger	860-565-4321	S	7,670*	30.0
Goodrich Corp.	4 Coliseum Centre	Charlotte	NC	28217		704-423-7000	P	6,392	23.4
Allegheny Technologies Inc.	1000 Six PPG Pl.	Pittsburgh	PA	15222		412-394-2800	P	5,453	9.5
Rockwell Collins Inc.	400 Collins Rd. NE	Cedar Rapids	IA	52498		319-295-1000	P	4,415	19.5
Spirit AeroSystems Holdings	3801 S Oliver	Wichita	KS	67210	Jeffrey L. Turner	316-526-9000	P	3,861	13.1
Hamilton Sundstrand Corp.	1 Hamilton Rd.	Windsor Locks	CT	06096	Ronald F. McKenna	860-654-6000	S	3,600*	16.0
Crane Co.	100 First Stamford	Stamford	CT	06902	Thomas Craney	203-363-7300	P	2,619	12.0
Apph Wichita Inc.	1445 S Sierra Dr.	Wichita	KS	67209	Dan Kilby	316-943-5752	R	2,590*	<0.1
Smith Industries Inc.	14200 Roosevlt Blvd	Clearwater	FL	33762	Vic Bonneau	727-531-7781	R	2,125*	10.0
Precise Machine Co.	2215 River Hill Rd.	Irving	TX	75061	Ronald S. Saks	972-438-3995	S	1,708*	0.7
Precise Machine Partners	3600 Mueller Rd.	St. Charles	MO	63301	Ronald S. Saks	636-946-6525	S	1,708*	0.7
Vought Aircraft Industries	PO Box 655907	Dallas	TX	75265	Elmer Doty	972-946-2011	S	1,577*	6.0
AAR Manufacturing Inc.	1100 N Wood Dale	Wood Dale	IL	60191	David Storch	630-227-2000	S	1,526*	3.5
AAR Corp.	1100 N Wood Dale	Wood Dale	IL	60191	Ira A. Eichner	630-227-2000	P	1,061	3.9
C and D Zodiac Inc.	5701 Bolsa Ave.	Huntington Bch	CA	92647		714-934-0000	R	1,045*	0.5
L-3 Display Systems	1355 Bluegrass Lake	Alpharetta	GA	30004		770-752-7000	S	998*	0.3
Triumph Group Inc.	1550 Liberty Ridge	Wayne	PA	19087	John M. Brasch	610-251-1000	P	955	5.1
Dow-United Tech. Compos. Prods	3951 Al Hwy. 229 S	Tallassee	AL	36078	Anthony Cacace	334-283-9200	R	886*	0.7
Sub-Zero Inc.	4717 Hammersley	Madison	WI	53711	James Bakke	608-271-2233	R	758*	3.0
Ducommun Technologies	23301 Wilmington	Carson	CA	90745		310-513-7280	S	539*	0.2
Stellex Aerospace	3 Werner Way	Lebanon	NJ	08833	Jay Fitzsimmons	908-437-4170	R	429*	0.5
K and F Industries Inc.	50 Main St., 4th	White Plains	NY	10606	Kenneth M. Schwartz	914-448-2700	S	424	1.4
Luxfer Inc.	3016 Kansas Ave.	Riverside	CA	92507	John Rhodes	951-684-5110	R	400*	<0.1
Air Methods Corp.	7301 S Peoria St.	Englewood	CO	80112		303-792-7400	P	396	2.7
Ducommun Inc.	23301 Wilmington	Carson	CA	90745	Joseph C. Berenato	310-513-7280	P	367	1.9
Kaman Aerospace Corp.	PO Box 2	Bloomfield	CT	06002	Sal Bordanelero	860-242-4461	D	349*	1.4
Wall Colmonoy Corp.	101 West Girard	Madison Heights	MI	48071		248-585-6400	R	336*	0.3
Pall Aeropower Corp.	1054 Ridge Rd.	New Port Richey	FL	34654	Jim Wester	727-849-9999	S	271*	0.5
Aerotech World Trade Corp.	11 New King St.	White Plains	NY	10604	Jan Endresen	914-681-3000	R	269*	<0.1
General Atomics Aeronaut. Sys.	16761 Via D Campo	San Diego	CA	92127	Thomas J. Cassidy Jr.	858-455-2810	S	262*	2.3
Hydro-Aire Inc.	PO Box 7722	Burbank	CA	91510		818-526-2600	S	254*	0.6
Korry Electronics Co.	901 Dexter Ave. N	Seattle	WA	98109	Frank Houston	206-281-1300	S	242*	0.6
Hawk Corp.	200 Public Sq.	Cleveland	OH	44114		216-861-3553	P	212	1.1
Edwards and Associates Inc.	PO Box 3689	Bristol	TN	37625	Phil Dieterich	423-538-5111	R	212*	0.4
Avox Systems Inc.	225 Erie Street	Lancaster	NY	14086		716-683-5100	S	201*	1.0
Van's Aircraft Inc.	14401 NE Keil Rd.	Aurora	OR	97002	Richard VanGrunsven	503-678-6545	R	200*	<0.1
General Dynamics Armament/Tech	4 LakePointe Plz.	Charlotte	NC	28217	Linda Hudson	703-714-8000	S	198*	1.2
Lee Co.	PO Box 424	Westbrook	CT	06498		860-399-6281	R	183*	0.8
Carleton Technologies Inc.	10 Cobham Dr.	Orchard Park	NY	14127	Padraig Cawdery	716-662-0006	R	183*	0.2
NORDAM Group Inc.	PO Box 3365	Tulsa	OK	74101		918-587-4105	R	169*	1.3
LMI Aerospace Inc.	PO Box 900	St. Charles	MO	63302	Joseph Burstein	636-946-6525	P	169	1.3
Alabama Aircraft Industries	1943 N 50th St.	Birmingham	AL	35212	Ronald A. Aramini	205-592-0011	P	161	1.5
Astronics Corp.	130 Commerce Way	East Aurora	NY	14052	Peter J. Gundermann	716-805-1599	P	158	0.8
Radiant Power Corp.	6416 Parkland Dr.	Sarasota	FL	34243	Victor Mendelson	941-739-3200	S	141*	<0.1
Ellanef Manufacturing Corp.	9711 50th Ave.	Corona	NY	11368	Murray Edwards	718-699-4000	R	131*	0.2
HR Textron Inc.	25200 Rye Cyn. Rd.	Santa Clarita	CA	91355	Richard Millman	661-294-6000	S	112*	0.9
Aim Aviation Inc.	PO Box 9011	Renton	WA	98057	Mark Potensky	425-235-2750	R	104*	0.1
Kurt Manufacturing Company	5280 Main St. NE	Fridley	MN	55421		763-572-1500	R	101*	0.3
Woven Electronics L.L.C.	PO Box 367	Greenville	SC	29602	Henry Little	864-233-6740	R	100*	<0.1
Parker Hannifin Racor Div.	PO Box 3208	Modesto	CA	95353		209-521-7860	D	98*	0.8
Arrowhead Products Corp.	4411 Katella Ave.	Los Alamitos	CA	90720		714-828-7770	R	94*	0.6
Audio International Inc.	7300 Industry Dr.	N Little Rock	AR	72117		501-955-2929	R	86*	0.1
Hawker Pacific Aerospace	11240 Sherman Way	Sun Valley	CA	91352	Richard Fortner	818-765-6201	R	79*	0.5
Breeze-Eastern Corp.	PO Box 3300	Union	NJ	07083	John Dalton	908-686-4000	P	73	0.2
Meggitt Safety Systems	1955 N Surveyor	Simi Valley	CA	93063		805-526-5700	S	69*	0.5
Aeronca Inc.	2320 Wedekind Dr.	Middletown	OH	45042		513-422-2751	R	68*	0.3
Huck International Aerospace	3724 E Columbia St.	Tucson	AZ	85714		520-519-7400	D	67*	0.2
Young and Franklin Inc.	942 Old Liverpool	Liverpool	NY	13088	Dudley Johnson	315-457-3110	R	60*	<0.1
Jonal Laboratories Inc.	PO Box 743	Meriden	CT	06450	Marc Nemeth	203-634-4444	R	55*	<0.1
Electro-Methods Inc.	PO Box 54	South Windsor	CT	06074	Randy Fries	860-289-8661	R	55*	0.2
Philadelphia Bourse Inc.	4601 Forbes Blvd.	Lanham	MD	20706	John Hozik	301-731-0811	R	53*	0.1
EADS Barfield Inc.	PO Box 25367	Miami	FL	33102	Frederic Denise	305-876-1678	S	52*	0.3
FMC Corp. Airline Prods & Sys.	7300 Presidents Dr.	Orlando	FL	32809	Charles Cannon	407-851-3377	D	52*	0.3
Alinabal Inc.	28 Woodmont Rd.	Milford	CT	06460	Sam Bergami	203-877-3241	R	49*	0.3
Triumph Fabrications Hot Sprgs	1923 Central Ave.	Hot Springs	AR	71901	Tony Johnson	501-321-9325	S	48*	0.3
Niles Precision Co.	PO Box 548	Niles	MI	49120	James Skalla	269-683-0585	R	48*	0.2
K and D Plastics Holdings L.P.	4430 W Hwy. 82	Gainesville	TX	76240		940-668-7015	R	48*	<0.1
Monogram Systems	PO Box 11189	Carson	CA	90749	Mike Rozenblatt	310-884-7000	R	47*	0.3
Arkwin Industries Inc.	686 Main Street	Westbury	NY	11590	Daniel Berlin	516-333-2640	R	47*	0.3

Source: Ward's Business Directory of U.S. Private and Public Companies, Volumes 1 and 2, 2008. The company type code used is as follows: P - Public, R - Private, S - Subsidiary, D - Division, J - Joint Venture, A - Affiliate, G - Group. Sales are in millions of dollars, employees are in thousands. An asterisk (*) indicates an estimated sales volume. The symbol < stands for 'less than'. Company names and addresses are truncated, in some cases, to fit into the available space.

MATERIALS CONSUMED

Material	Quantity	Delivered Cost ($ million)
Aircraft engines	(X)	(D)
Aircraft engine parts (excluding instruments)	(X)	(D)
Structural fuselage components (excluding instruments)	(X)	12.2
Structural empennage (tail) components (exc. instruments)	(X)	0.2
Structural wing components (excluding instruments)	(X)	2.9
Structural landing gear components	(X)	399.8
Other structural components (airframe) (exc. instruments)	(X)	85.2
Aircraft propellers and parts	(X)	28.6
Aircraft seats	(X)	1.9
Radio communication systems and equipment (microwave, UHF, etc.)	(X)	1.2
Navigational systems and equipment (NAVAIDS)	(X)	(D)
Search, detection, tracking, and electronic communication systems and equipment (RADAR, SONAR, and optical)	(X)	(D)
Flight, navigational, airframe, and engine indicators, instruments, and clusters (incl. sensors, displays, etc.)	(X)	3.1
Resistors, capacitors, transformers, electron tubes, semiconductors, and other electronic components	(X)	86.7
Resin matrix composites	(X)	35.1
Other matrix composites (ceramic, carbon, metal, etc.)	(X)	218.2
Complete mechanical, hydraulic and pneumatic subassemblies	(X)	37.2
Fluid power pumps, motors, and hydrostatic transmissions	(X)	18.4
Fluid power valves (excluding complete assemblies)	(X)	19.6
Fluid power hose, tube fittings, and assemblies (hydraulic and pneumatic)	(X)	(D)
Fluid power cylinders and rotary actuators (exc. complete assemblies)	(X)	(D)
Fluid power filters (hydraulic and pneumatic)	(X)	(D)
Other transportation related fluid power products, hydraulic and pneumatic	(X)	14.7
Ball and roller bearings (mounted or unmounted)	(X)	28.9
Cutting tools for machine tools	(X)	14.6
Aircraft metal hardware (excluding forgings)	(X)	183.9
Metal bolts, nuts, screws, and other screw machine products	(X)	96.4
Other fabricated metal products (exc. fluid power and forgings)	(X)	251.9
Iron and steel forgings	(X)	13.2
Aluminum and aluminum-base alloy forgings	(X)	46.7
Titanium and titanium-base alloy forgings	(X)	(D)
Other forgings	(X)	33.2
Iron and steel castings (rough and semifinished)	(X)	14.7
Aluminum and aluminum-base alloy castings (rough and semifinished)	(X)	33.8
Other nonferrous metal castings, rough or semifinished (inc. aluminum)	(X)	6.9
Steel bars, bar shapes, and plates (exc. castings, forgings, fabr. metal products)	(X)	15.0
Steel sheet and strip (including tinplate)	(X)	14.1
All other steel shapes and forms (exc. castings, forgings, fabr. metal products)	(X)	8.9
Aluminum and aluminum-base alloy sheet, plate, foil, and welded tubing	(X)	272.6
All other aluminum and aluminum-base alloy shapes and forms (exc. castings, forgings, fabr. metal products)	(X)	99.1
Copper and copper-base alloy shapes and forms (exc. castings, forgings, fabr. metal products)	(X)	(D)
Titanium and titanium-base alloy shapes and forms (exc. castings, forgings, fabr. metal products)	(X)	65.7
Other nonferrous shapes and forms (exc. castings, forgings, fabricated metal products)	(X)	21.0
Paints, varnishes, stains, lacquers, shellacs, japans, enamels, etc.	(X)	31.7
All other materials, components, parts, containers, and supplies	(X)	1,316.6
Materials, ingredients, containers, and supplies, nsk	(X)	2,412.2

Source: 2002 Economic Census. Explanation of symbols used: (D): Withheld to avoid disclosure of competitive data; na: Not available; (S): Withheld because statistical norms were not met; (X): Not applicable; (Z): Less than half the unit shown; nec: Not elsewhere classified; nsk: Not specified by kind; - : zero; p : 10-19 percent estimated; q : 20-29 percent estimated.

PRODUCT SHARE DETAILS

Product or Product Class Shipments	Mil. $	Product or Product Class Shipments	Mil. $
AIRCRAFT PARTS AND AUXILIARY EQUIPMENT, NEC	21,324.2	Aircraft mechanical power transmission equipment for military aircraft and other aircraft built to military specifications	1,014.2
Aircraft propellers and helicopter rotors	**512.3**		
Complete aircraft propellers, excluding helicopter rotors	59.3	Aircraft mechanical power transmission equipment for civilian aircraft	912.1
Aircraft propeller blades	41.8		
Aircraft propeller parts, except propeller blades	75.7	Aircraft landing gear for civilian and military aircraft	3,424.8
Helicopter rotors and parts	335.5	Aircraft landing gear for military aircraft and other aircraft built to military specifications	572.5
Research and development on aircraft parts (except engines)	**604.5**		
Research and development on U.S. military aircraft parts (except engines) and all other aircraft parts built to military specifications	562.6	Aircraft landing gear for civilian aircraft	2,852.3
		Other aircraft subassemblies and parts for military aircraft and other aircraft built to military specifications	5,148.9
Research and development on civilian aircraft parts (except engines)	41.9	Other aircraft subassemblies and parts for civilian aircraft	8,565.4
Aircraft parts and auxiliary equipment, except hydraulic and pneumatic subassemblies and engines	**19,072.8**	Aircraft parts and auxiliary equipment, except hydraulic and pneumatic subassemblies and engines, nsk	7.3
Aircraft mechanical power transmission equipment for civilian and military aircraft	1,926.3	**Aircraft parts and auxiliary equipment, nec, nsk, total**	**1,134.6**

Source: 2002 Economic Census. The values are product shipments in millions of dollars for 2002. Total product shipments may be lower or higher than industry shipments. See Introduction for a full discussion. Values of indented subcategories are summed in the main heading(s). The symbol (D) appears when data are withheld to prevent disclosure of competitive information. The abbreviation nsk stands for 'not specified by kind' and nec for 'not elsewhere classified'. A dash (-) means zero.

INPUTS AND OUTPUTS FOR OTHER AIRCRAFT PARTS AND AUXILIARY EQUIPMENT MANUFACTURING

Economic Sector or Industry Providing Inputs	%	Sector	Economic Sector or Industry Buying Outputs	%	Sector
Compensation of employees	37.0		Exports of goods & services	49.4	Cap Inv
Management of companies & enterprises	10.8	Services	Aircraft	34.5	Manufg.
Aircraft parts & auxiliary equipment, nec	4.2	Manufg.	General Federal government services, defense	6.2	Fed Govt
Plastics products, nec	3.3	Manufg.	Aircraft parts & auxiliary equipment, nec	3.3	Manufg.
Truck transportation	2.8	Util.	Air transportation	3.3	Util.
Plate work & fabricated structural products	2.5	Manufg.	Aircraft engine & engine parts	1.3	Manufg.
Wholesale trade	2.5	Trade	Retail trade	0.8	Trade
Aluminum products from purchased aluminum	2.2	Manufg.	Scenic & sightseeing transport & related services	0.4	Util.
Sand, gravel, clay, & refractory minerals	1.6	Mining	Wholesale trade	0.3	Trade
Carbon & graphite products	1.2	Manufg.	General Federal government services, nondefense	0.3	Fed Govt
Hardware	1.2	Manufg.			
Power generation & supply	1.1	Util.			
Forging, stamping, & sintering, nec	1.1	Manufg.			
Scientific research & development services	1.1	Services			
Turned products & screws, nuts, & bolts	1.0	Manufg.			
Specialized design services	0.8	Services			
Architectural, engineering, & related services	0.8	Services			
Aircraft engine & engine parts	0.7	Manufg.			
Lessors of nonfinancial assets	0.7	Fin/R.E.			
Employment services	0.6	Services			
Real estate	0.6	Fin/R.E.			
Securities, commodity contracts, investments	0.6	Fin/R.E.			
Legal services	0.6	Services			
Business support services	0.6	Services			
Valve & fittings other than plumbing	0.6	Manufg.			
Iron & steel mills & ferroalloys	0.6	Manufg.			
Search, detection, & navigation instruments	0.5	Manufg.			
Semiconductors & related devices	0.5	Manufg.			
Machine shops	0.5	Manufg.			
Electronic connectors	0.5	Manufg.			
Communication & energy wires & cables	0.5	Manufg.			
Advertising & related services	0.5	Services			
Monetary authorities/depository credit intermediation	0.4	Fin/R.E.			
Fabricated pipes & pipe fittings	0.4	Manufg.			
Coating, engraving, heat treating & allied activities	0.4	Manufg.			
Support services, nec	0.4	Services			
Warehousing & storage	0.4	Util.			
Natural gas distribution	0.3	Util.			
Professional, scientific, technical services, nec	0.3	Services			
Investigation & security services	0.3	Services			
Taxes on production & imports, less subsidies	0.3				
Ball & roller bearings	0.3	Manufg.			
Rail transportation	0.3	Util.			
Automotive equipment rental & leasing	0.3	Fin/R.E.			
Nonferrous metal foundries	0.3	Manufg.			
Custom computer programming services	0.3	Services			
Data processing, hosting, & related services	0.3	Services			
Food services & drinking places	0.3	Services			
Printed circuit assemblies (electronic assemblies)	0.2	Manufg.			
Chemical products & preparations, nec	0.2	Manufg.			
Alumina refining & primary aluminum production	0.2	Manufg.			
Paints & coatings	0.2	Manufg.			
Telecommunications	0.2	Services			
Accounting, tax preparation, bookkeeping, & payroll	0.2	Services			
Industrial gases	0.2	Manufg.			
Noncomparable imports	0.2	Foreign			
Fluid power process machinery	0.2	Manufg.			
Hotels & motels, including casino hotels	0.2	Services			
Air transportation	0.2	Util.			
Services to buildings & dwellings	0.2	Services			
Commercial & industrial machinery rental & leasing	0.1	Fin/R.E.			
Paperboard containers	0.1	Manufg.			
Maintenance/repair of nonresidential structures	0.1	Construct.			
Other computer related services, including facilities	0.1	Services			
Facilities support services	0.1	Services			
Fabricated metals, nec	0.1	Manufg.			
Petroleum refineries	0.1	Manufg.			
Metal cans, boxes, & other containers (light gauge)	0.1	Manufg.			
Management, scientific, & technical consulting	0.1	Services			
Crowns & closures & metal stamping	0.1	Manufg.			

Source: Benchmark Input-Output Accounts for the U.S. Economy, 2002, U.S. Department of Commerce, Washington, D.C., January 2008. The abbreviation nec stands for 'not elsewhere classified'.

OCCUPATIONS EMPLOYED BY AEROSPACE PRODUCT & PARTS MANUFACTURING

Occupation	% of Total 2006	Change to 2016	Occupation	% of Total 2006	Change to 2016
Aerospace engineers	9.3	6.9	Management analysts	1.8	1.8
Aircraft structure & systems assemblers	5.2	12.0	Engineers, nec	1.8	1.8
Aircraft mechanics & service technicians	4.4	22.2	Production, planning, & expediting clerks	1.6	1.8
Machinists	3.8	6.9	Industrial engineering technicians	1.5	12.0
Inspectors, testers, sorters, samplers, & weighers	3.5	-4.0	Team assemblers	1.5	1.8
Industrial engineers	3.1	23.7	Executive secretaries & administrative assistants	1.4	1.8
Computer software engineers, applications	2.5	22.2	Computer-controlled machine tool operators	1.1	12.0
Mechanical engineers	2.3	1.8	Computer software engineers, systems software	1.1	12.0
Engineering managers	2.2	12.0	Engineering technicians, exc drafters, nec	1.1	1.8
Purchasing agents, exc wholesale, retail, & farm	2.0	1.8	Industrial production managers	1.0	1.8
First-line supervisors/managers of production workers	2.0	1.8	Stock clerks & order fillers	1.0	-14.8
Business operation specialists, nec	1.9	12.0			

Source: Industry-Occupation Matrix, Bureau of Labor Statistics, December 4, 2007. These data are reported based on 4-digit NAICS categories but have been matched to corresponding 6-digit NAICS industry codes. The change reported for each occupation to the year 2016 is a percent of growth or decline as estimated by the Bureau of Labor Statistics. The abbreviation nec stands for 'not elsewhere classified'.

LOCATION BY STATE AND REGIONAL CONCENTRATION

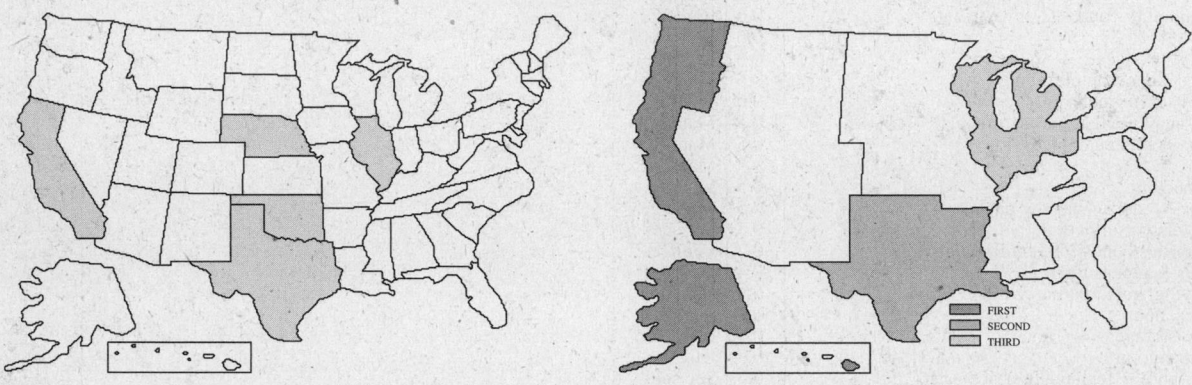

FIRST
SECOND
THIRD

INDUSTRY DATA BY STATE

State	Establish-ments	Shipments			Employment				Cost as % of Shipments	Investment per Employee ($)
		Total ($ mil)	% of U.S.	Per Establ.	Total Number	% of U.S.	Per Establ.	Wages ($/hour)		
California	179	5,584.7	26.9	31,199.4	24,567	24.7	137	23.53	30.3	7,927
Texas	74	1,408.9	6.8	19,038.6	8,498	8.6	115	27.06	34.1	5,103
Illinois	12	1,369.8	6.6	114,147.7	4,184	4.2	349	21.16	25.9	4,721
Oklahoma	26	821.3	4.0	31,588.0	3,489	3.5	134	25.38	61.2	6,301
Nebraska	3	47.1	0.2	15,695.3	451	0.5	150	18.84	39.3	4,135

Source: 2002 Economic Census. The states are in descending order of shipments or establishments (if shipment data are missing for the majority). The symbol (D) appears when data are withheld to prevent disclosure of competitive information. States marked with (D) are sorted by number of establishments. A dash (-) indicates that the data element cannot be calculated. Data may not show all states active in the NAICS category. All data available at the time of publication are shown.

NAICS 336414 - GUIDED MISSILE AND SPACE VEHICLE MANUFACTURING

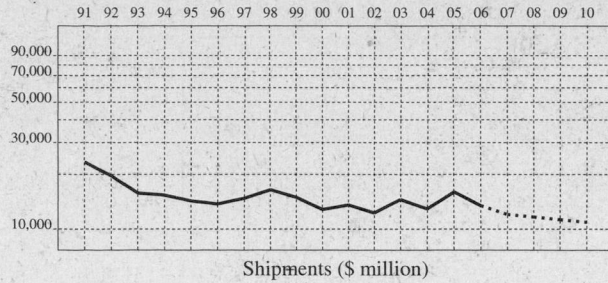

Shipments ($ million)

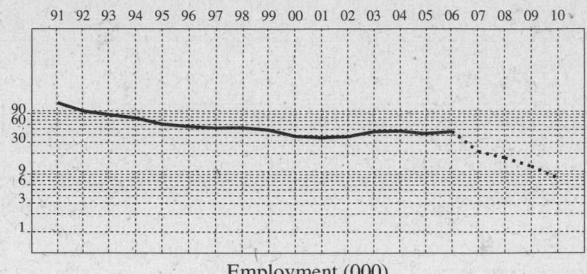

Employment (000)

GENERAL STATISTICS

Year	Com- panies	Establishments		Employment			Compensation		Production ($ million)			
		Total	with 20 or more employees	Total (000)	Production Workers (000)	Hours (Mil)	Payroll ($ mil)	Wages ($/hr)	Cost of Materials	Value Added by Manufacture	Value of Shipments	Capital Invest.
1991		44	41	135.8	45.0	91.3	6,025.5	19.07	8,219.7	13,550.9	23,399.3	449.9
1992	23	38	31	100.1	31.5	57.8	4,722.2	22.23	6,788.9	11,080.9	19,675.1	306.7
1993		35	28	86.6	27.6	53.1	4,017.6	20.88	5,804.5	10,090.2	15,799.6	307.6
1994		33	28	76.8	25.0	49.8	3,806.2	21.02	6,277.0	10,120.5	15,396.9	329.0
1995		33	26	60.8	20.0	43.4	3,401.3	20.65	6,462.1	7,770.2	14,315.2	293.7
1996		29	22	55.7	18.6	36,8	3,323.4	21.81	6,659.1	7,470.1	13,777.3	367.3
1997	15	22	18	52.2	18.7	36.5	3,156.2	22.59	5,598.0	8,583.0	14,791.5	634.2
1998		22	17	53.1	18.0	34.7	3,429.4	25.01	6,697.4	9,950.0	16,475.7	700.2
1999		21	17	48.7	14.9	30.6	3,517.5	26.67	6,166.0	11,739.8	14,963.3	906.2
2000		17	14	38.3	13.4	24.9	2,682.1	27.38	4,385.5	6,644.6	12,831.9	320.0
2001		18	14	36.6	12.5	23.7	2,821.1	29.14	5,207.9	10,251.0	13,600.5	271.6
2002	12	19	16	37.9	14.1	26.4	2,889.3	32.11	5,466.7	6,818.0	12,288.6	359.9
2003		19	17	46.0	15.0	30.3	3,409.3	32.25	6,278.3	8,163.1	14,558.3	438.1
2004		31	24	46.8	15.2	31.2	3,644.4	32.84	5,490.3	7,679.7	12,935.8	318.3
2005		24	21	42.7	14.2	28.7	3,629.5	37.04	8,536.2	7,658.6	16,028.8	402.6
2006		16P	13P	46.0	15.1	30.0	3,743.6	37.26	5,586.2	8,091.5	13,470.6	425.5
2007		15P	11P	21.4P	7.5P	15.1P	2,844.4P	37.13P	4,995.5P	7,235.9P	12,046.2P	442.3P
2008		13P	10P	16.8P	6.1P	12.3P	2,751.0P	38.36P	4,838.3P	7,008.2P	11,667.1P	444.1P
2009		12P	9P	12.2P	4.6P	9.4P	2,657.5P	39.58P	4,681.0P	6,780.4P	11,287.9P	445.9P
2010		10P	8P	7.7P	3.2P	6.6P	2,564.1P	40.80P	4,523.8P	6,552.6P	10,908.7P	447.7P

Sources: 1992, 1997, 2002 *Economic Census*; other years, up to 2006, are from the *Annual Survey of Manufactures*. Establishment counts for non-Census years are from *County Business Patterns*; 1997 and 2002 values are from the 1997 and 2002 censuses respectively, reported in the Federal Government's NAICS format. Other years were originally reported in equivalent SIC format. 'P's show projections by the editors.

INDICES OF CHANGE

Year	Com- panies	Establishments		Employment			Compensation		Production ($ million)			
		Total	with 20 or more employees	Total (000)	Production Workers (000)	Hours (Mil)	Payroll ($ mil)	Wages ($/hr)	Cost of Materials	Value Added by Manufacture	Value of Shipments	Capital Invest.
1992	192	200	194	264	223	219	163	69	124	163	160	85
1997	125	116	113	138	133	138	109	70	102	126	120	176
2001		95	88	97	89	90	98	91	95	150	111	75
2002	100	100	100	100	100	100	100	100	100	100	100	100
2003		100	106	121	106	115	118	100	115	120	118	122
2004		163	150	123	108	118	126	102	100	113	105	88
2005		126	131	113	101	109	126	115	156	112	130	112
2006		84P	79P	121	107	114	130	116	102	119	110	118
2007		76P	71P	56P	53P	57P	98P	116P	91P	106P	98P	123P
2008		69P	64P	44P	43P	47P	95P	119P	89P	103P	95P	123P
2009		62P	56P	32P	33P	36P	92P	123P	86P	99P	92P	124P
2010		55P	49P	20P	23P	25P	89P	127P	83P	96P	89P	124P

Sources: Same as General Statistics. Values reflect change from the base year, 2002. Values above 100 mean greater than 2002, values below 100 mean less than 2002, and the values of 100 in other years means the same as 2002. 'P's show projections by the editors.

SELECTED RATIOS

For 2002	Avg. of All Manufact.	Analyzed Industry	Index	For 2002	Avg. of All Manufact.	Analyzed Industry	Index
Employees per Establishment	42	1,995	4,752	Value Added per Production Worker	182,367	483,546	265
Payroll per Establishment	1,639,184	152,068,421	9,277	Cost per Establishment	5,769,015	287,721,053	4,987
Payroll per Employee	39,053	76,235	195	Cost per Employee	137,446	144,240	105
Production Workers per Establishment	30	742	2,515	Cost per Production Worker	195,506	387,709	198
Wages per Establishment	694,845	44,616,000	6,421	Shipments per Establishment	11,158,348	646,768,421	5,796
Wages per Production Worker	23,548	60,121	255	Shipments per Employee	265,847	324,237	122
Hours per Production Worker	1,980	1,872	95	Shipments per Production Worker	378,144	871,532	230
Wages per Hour	11.89	32.11	270	Investment per Establishment	361,338	18,942,105	5,242
Value Added per Establishment	5,381,325	358,842,105	6,668	Investment per Employee	8,609	9,496	110
Value Added per Employee	128,210	179,894	140	Investment per Production Worker	12,245	25,525	208

Sources: Same as General Statistics. The 'Average of All Manufacturing' column represents the average of all manufacturing industries reported for the most recent complete year available. The Index shows the relationship between the Average and the Analyzed Industry. For example, 100 means that they are equal; 500 that the Analyzed Industry is five times the average; 50 means that the Analyzed Industry is half the national average. The abbreviation 'na' is used to show that data are 'not available'. Ratios shown for 2002, the last complete census year.

LEADING COMPANIES   Number shown: **10**   Total sales ($ mil): **162,981**   Total employment (000): **505.3**

Company Name	Address				CEO Name	Phone	Co. Type	Sales ($ mil)	Empl. (000)
Boeing Co.	100 N Riverside Plz	Chicago	IL	60606		312-544-2000	P	66,387	159.3
Lockheed Martin Corp.	6801 Rockledge Dr.	Bethesda	MD	20817	Richard F. Ambrose	301-897-6000	P	41,862	140.0
Northrop Grumman Corp.	1840 Century Park E	Los Angeles	CA	90067		310-553-6262	P	32,018	122.6
Raytheon Co.	870 Winter St.	Waltham	MA	02451		781-522-3000	P	21,301	72.1
Northrop Grumman Space Tech.	1 Space Park Dr.	Redondo Beach	CA	90278	Wes Bush	310-812-4321	S	1,000*	9.3
Alabama Aircraft Industries	1943 N 50th St.	Birmingham	AL	35212	Ronald A. Aramini	205-592-0011	P	161	1.5
L'Garde Inc.	15181 Woodlawn	Tustin	CA	92780	Gayle Bilyeu	714-259-0771	R	142*	<0.1
Spacehab Inc.	12130 Highway 3	Webster	TX	77598		713-558-5000	P	53	0.2
SpaceDev Inc.	13855 Stowe Dr.	Poway	CA	92064	Mark Sirangelo	858-375-2000	P	33	0.2
GASL Inc.	77 Raynor Ave.	Ronkonkoma	NY	11779	A. Castrogiovanni	631-737-6100	S	25*	<0.1

Source: Ward's Business Directory of U.S. Private and Public Companies, Volumes 1 and 2, 2008. The company type code used is as follows: P - Public, R - Private, S - Subsidiary, D - Division, J - Joint Venture, A - Affiliate, G - Group. Sales are in millions of dollars, employees are in thousands. An asterisk (*) indicates an estimated sales volume. The symbol < stands for 'less than'. Company names and addresses are truncated, in some cases, to fit into the available space.

MATERIALS CONSUMED

Material	Quantity	Delivered Cost ($ million)
Guided missile and space vehicle engines and parts	(X)	(D)
Guided missile and space vehicle airframe parts	(X)	(D)
Radio communication systems and equipment (microwave, UHF, etc.)	(X)	(D)
Navigational systems and equipment (NAVAIDS)	(X)	(D)
Flight, navigational, airframe, and engine indicators, instruments, and clusters (incl. sensors, displays, etc.)	(X)	(D)
Resin matrix composites	(X)	(D)
Other matrix composites (ceramic, carbon, metal, etc.)	(X)	(D)
Metal bolts, nuts, screws, and other screw machine products	(X)	(D)
Iron and steel forgings	(X)	(D)
Iron and steel castings (rough and semifinished)	(X)	(D)
Aluminum and aluminum-base alloy castings (rough and semifinished)	(X)	(D)
All other materials, components, parts, containers, and supplies	(X)	1,056.2
Materials, ingredients, containers, and supplies, nsk	(X)	410.2

Source: 2002 *Economic Census*. Explanation of symbols used: (D): Withheld to avoid disclosure of competitive data; na: Not available; (S): Withheld because statistical norms were not met; (X): Not applicable; (Z): Less than half the unit shown; nec: Not elsewhere classified; nsk: Not specified by kind; - : zero; p : 10-19 percent estimated; q : 20-29 percent estimated.

PRODUCT SHARE DETAILS

Product or Product Class Shipments	Mil. $	Product or Product Class Shipments	Mil. $
GUIDED MISSILES AND SPACE VEHICLES	10,204.2	All other services on complete space vehicles for U.S. Government military customers	166.6
Complete guided missiles	**3,654.9**	All other services on complete space vehicles for other	
Research and development on complete guided missiles	**785.5**	customers	(D)
Other services on complete guided missiles	**55.4**	All other services on complete space vehicles, nsk	32.2
Complete space vehicles (excluding propulsion systems)	**4,473.4**	**Guided missiles and space vehicles, nsk, total**	**1.5**
Research and development on complete space vehicles	**(D)**		
All other services on complete space vehicles	**(D)**		

Source: 2002 *Economic Census*. The values are product shipments in millions of dollars for 2002. Total product shipments may be lower or higher than industry shipments. See Introduction for a full discussion. Values of indented subcategories are summed in the main heading(s). The symbol (D) appears when data are withheld to prevent disclosure of competitive information. The abbreviation nsk stands for 'not specified by kind' and nec for 'not elsewhere classified'. A dash (-) means zero.

INPUTS AND OUTPUTS FOR GUIDED MISSILE AND SPACE VEHICLE MANUFACTURING

Economic Sector or Industry Providing Inputs	%	Sector	Economic Sector or Industry Buying Outputs	%	Sector
Compensation of employees	31.0		General Federal government services, defense	48.0	Fed Govt
Guided missile & space vehicle parts	11.1	Manufg.	Federal government, investment, national defense	26.4	Fed Govt
Management of companies & enterprises	9.4	Services	Federal government, investment, nondefense	11.9	Fed Govt
Specialized design services	3.6	Services	Exports of goods & services	4.0	Cap Inv
Guided missiles & space vehicles	3.5	Manufg.	Guided missiles & space vehicles	3.9	Manufg.
Employment services	2.9	Services	Change in private inventories	2.2	In House
Business support services	2.3	Services	General Federal government services, nondefense	1.5	Fed Govt
Valve & fittings other than plumbing	2.0	Manufg.	Scientific research & development services	1.4	Services
Architectural, engineering, & related services	2.0	Services	Private fixed investment	0.7	
Semiconductors & related devices	1.8	Manufg.			
Support services, nec	1.6	Services			
Legal services	1.5	Services			
Wholesale trade	1.3	Trade			
Coating, engraving, heat treating & allied activities	1.3	Manufg.			

Continued on next page.

INPUTS AND OUTPUTS FOR GUIDED MISSILE AND SPACE VEHICLE MANUFACTURING - Continued

Economic Sector or Industry Providing Inputs	%	Sector	Economic Sector or Industry Buying Outputs	%	Sector
Investigation & security services	1.2	Services			
Securities, commodity contracts, investments	1.1	Fin/R.E.			
Lessors of nonfinancial assets	1.1	Fin/R.E.			
Broadcast & wireless communications equipment	1.0	Manufg.			
Scientific research & development services	1.0	Services			
Forging, stamping, & sintering, nec	0.9	Manufg.			
Plate work & fabricated structural products	0.8	Manufg.			
Monetary authorities/depository credit intermediation	0.6	Fin/R.E.			
Gaskets, packing, & sealing devices	0.6	Manufg.			
Facilities support services	0.6	Services			
Real estate	0.6	Fin/R.E.			
Management, scientific, & technical consulting	0.6	Services			
Truck transportation	0.5	Util.			
Professional, scientific, technical services, nec	0.5	Services			
Machine shops	0.5	Manufg.			
Search, detection, & navigation instruments	0.5	Manufg.			
Power generation & supply	0.5	Util.			
Food services & drinking places	0.4	Services			
Basic organic chemicals, nec	0.4	Manufg.			
Advertising & related services	0.4	Services			
Plastics products, nec	0.4	Manufg.			
Warehousing & storage	0.3	Util.			
Fluid power process machinery	0.3	Manufg.			
Hotels & motels, including casino hotels	0.3	Services			
Air transportation	0.3	Util.			
Alumina refining & primary aluminum production	0.2	Manufg.			
Accounting, tax preparation, bookkeeping, & payroll	0.2	Services			
Chemical products & preparations, nec	0.2	Manufg.			
Automotive equipment rental & leasing	0.2	Fin/R.E.			
Telecommunications	0.2	Services			
Fabricated metals, nec	0.2	Manufg.			
Iron & steel mills & ferroalloys	0.1	Manufg.			
Data processing, hosting, & related services	0.1	Services			
Other computer related services, including facilities	0.1	Services			
Nondepository credit intermediation activities	0.1	Fin/R.E.			
Natural gas distribution	0.1	Util.			

Source: Benchmark Input-Output Accounts for the U.S. Economy, 2002, U.S. Department of Commerce, Washington, D.C., January 2008. The abbreviation nec stands for 'not elsewhere classified'.

OCCUPATIONS EMPLOYED BY AEROSPACE PRODUCT & PARTS MANUFACTURING

Occupation	% of Total 2006	Change to 2016	Occupation	% of Total 2006	Change to 2016
Aerospace engineers	9.3	6.9	Management analysts	1.8	1.8
Aircraft structure & systems assemblers	5.2	12.0	Engineers, nec	1.8	1.8
Aircraft mechanics & service technicians	4.4	22.2	Production, planning, & expediting clerks	1.6	1.8
Machinists	3.8	6.9	Industrial engineering technicians	1.5	12.0
Inspectors, testers, sorters, samplers, & weighers	3.5	-4.0	Team assemblers	1.5	1.8
Industrial engineers	3.1	23.7	Executive secretaries & administrative assistants	1.4	1.8
Computer software engineers, applications	2.5	22.2	Computer-controlled machine tool operators	1.1	12.0
Mechanical engineers	2.3	1.8	Computer software engineers, systems software	1.1	12.0
Engineering managers	2.2	12.0	Engineering technicians, exc drafters, nec	1.1	1.8
Purchasing agents, exc wholesale, retail, & farm	2.0	1.8	Industrial production managers	1.0	1.8
First-line supervisors/managers of production workers	2.0	1.8	Stock clerks & order fillers	1.0	-14.8
Business operation specialists, nec	1.9	12.0			

Source: Industry-Occupation Matrix, Bureau of Labor Statistics, December 4, 2007. These data are reported based on 4-digit NAICS categories but have been matched to corresponding 6-digit NAICS industry codes. The change reported for each occupation to the year 2016 is a percent of growth or decline as estimated by the Bureau of Labor Statistics. The abbreviation nec stands for 'not elsewhere classified'.

INDUSTRY DATA BY STATE

State-level data are not available.

NAICS 336415 - GUIDED MISSILE AND SPACE VEHICLE PROPULSION PARTS

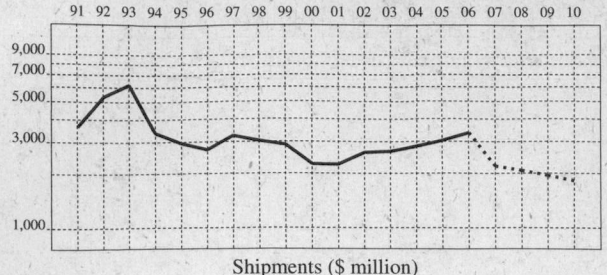

Shipments ($ million)

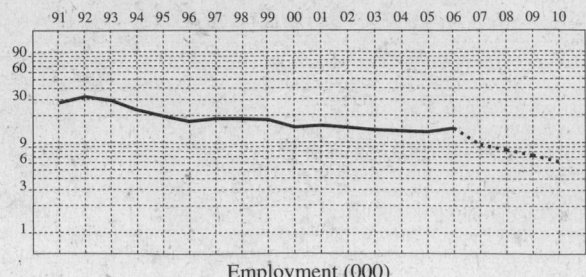

Employment (000)

GENERAL STATISTICS

Year	Companies	Establishments		Employment			Compensation		Production ($ million)			
		Total	with 20 or more employees	Total (000)	Production Workers (000)	Hours (Mil)	Payroll ($ mil)	Wages ($/hr)	Cost of Materials	Value Added by Manufacture	Value of Shipments	Capital Invest.
1991		37	30	27.7	9.5	17.7	1,166.6	19.05	1,230.4	2,345.8	3,657.9	102.3
1992	30	42	33	32.3	13.4	20.9	1,495.6	23.74	2,181.3	2,819.0	5,328.1	128.2
1993		39	31	29.2	8.9	15.8	1,401.1	22.03	1,255.6	4,282.2	6,201.0	85.4
1994		37	29	22.8	7.8	14.1	1,126.6	22.10	1,148.0	2,184.8	3,373.6	68.9
1995		34	26	19.6	6.7	13.6	996.9	19.60	945.0	1,943.5	2,953.6	48.8
1996		31	23	17.2	5.5	10.8	916.5	20.61	913.8	1,858.5	2,715.0	77.5
1997	19	28	22	18.5	8.3	16.5	1,066.1	23.15	1,124.8	2,134.7	3,239.0	89.3
1998		29	23	18.4	7.8	15.6	1,068.8	23.63	968.9	2,139.1	3,030.1	124.8
1999		29	23	17.9	7.6	15.5	1,038.5	23.60	921.6	1,996.1	2,879.8	162.0
2000		22	17	14.7	6.5	13.6	898.3	22.56	707.5	1,656.3	2,258.2	101.6
2001		24	18	15.3	6.3	13.2	1,021.0	22.11	665.8	1,447.4	2,244.4	97.7
2002	17	27	21	14.6	5.6	11.5	990.2	25.22	731.2	1,862.1	2,619.6	106.7
2003		27	20	13.8	5.0	10.8	979.6	24.15	647.8	2,017.1	2,653.8	79.8
2004		31	22	13.5	4.8	10.6	1,026.4	24.60	711.6	1,859.2	2,819.5	64.5
2005		32	20	13.3	4.8	10.4	1,046.9	26.47	871.7	2,156.5	3,035.9	81.5
2006		24P	17P	14.5	4.7	9.5	1,051.1	29.16	1,034.5	2,354.8	3,357.2	82.4
2007		23P	16P	9.5P	3.8P	9.3P	917.3P	26.72P	678.2P	1,543.7P	2,200.8P	88.1P
2008		22P	15P	8.4P	3.4P	8.8P	898.1P	27.13P	639.3P	1,455.2P	2,074.7P	87.5P
2009		22P	14P	7.3P	3.0P	8.2P	878.8P	27.54P	600.4P	1,366.8P	1,948.6P	86.8P
2010		21P	13P	6.2P	2.6P	7.7P	859.6P	27.95P	561.6P	1,278.3P	1,822.4P	86.1P

Sources: 1992, 1997, 2002 *Economic Census*; other years, up to 2006, are from the *Annual Survey of Manufactures*. Establishment counts for non-Census years are from *County Business Patterns*; 1997 and 2002 values are from the 1997 and 2002 censuses respectively, reported in the Federal Government's NAICS format. Other years were originally reported in equivalent SIC format. 'P's show projections by the editors.

INDICES OF CHANGE

Year	Companies	Establishments		Employment			Compensation		Production ($ million)			
		Total	with 20 or more employees	Total (000)	Production Workers (000)	Hours (Mil)	Payroll ($ mil)	Wages ($/hr)	Cost of Materials	Value Added by Manufacture	Value of Shipments	Capital Invest.
1992	176	156	157	221	239	182	151	94	298	151	203	120
1997	112	104	105	127	148	143	108	92	154	115	124	84
2001		89	86	105	113	115	103	88	91	78	86	92
2002	100	100	100	100	100	100	100	100	100	100	100	100
2003		100	95	95	89	94	99	96	89	108	101	75
2004		115	105	92	86	92	104	98	97	100	108	60
2005		119	95	91	86	90	106	105	119	116	116	76
2006		90P	79P	99	84	83	106	116	141	126	128	77
2007		86P	74P	65P	68P	81P	93P	106P	93P	83P	84P	83P
2008		83P	70P	58P	61P	77P	91P	108P	87P	78P	79P	82P
2009		80P	65P	50P	54P	71P	89P	109P	82P	73P	74P	81P
2010		76P	61P	42P	46P	67P	87P	111P	77P	69P	70P	81P

Sources: Same as General Statistics. Values reflect change from the base year, 2002. Values above 100 mean greater than 2002, values below 100 mean less than 2002, and the values of 100 in other years means the same as 2002. 'P's show projections by the editors.

SELECTED RATIOS

For 2002	Avg. of All Manufact.	Analyzed Industry	Index	For 2002	Avg. of All Manufact.	Analyzed Industry	Index
Employees per Establishment	42	541	1,288	Value Added per Production Worker	182,367	332,518	182
Payroll per Establishment	1,639,184	36,674,074	2,237	Cost per Establishment	5,769,015	27,081,481	469
Payroll per Employee	39,053	67,822	174	Cost per Employee	137,446	50,082	36
Production Workers per Establishment	30	207	703	Cost per Production Worker	195,506	130,571	67
Wages per Establishment	694,845	10,741,852	1,546	Shipments per Establishment	11,158,348	97,022,222	870
Wages per Production Worker	23,548	51,791	220	Shipments per Employee	265,847	179,425	67
Hours per Production Worker	1,980	2,054	104	Shipments per Production Worker	378,144	467,786	124
Wages per Hour	11.89	25.22	212	Investment per Establishment	361,338	3,951,852	1,094
Value Added per Establishment	5,381,325	68,966,667	1,282	Investment per Employee	8,609	7,308	85
Value Added per Employee	128,210	127,541	99	Investment per Production Worker	12,245	19,054	156

Sources: Same as General Statistics. The 'Average of All Manufacturing' column represents the average of all manufacturing industries reported for the most recent complete year available. The Index shows the relationship between the Average and the Analyzed Industry. For example, 100 means that they are equal; 500 that the Analyzed Industry is five times the average; 50 means that the Analyzed Industry is half the national average. The abbreviation 'na' is used to show that data are 'not available'. Ratios shown for 2002, the last complete census year.

LEADING COMPANIES   Number shown: **7**   Total sales ($ mil): **4,258**   Total employment (000): **23.5**

Company Name	Address				CEO Name	Phone	Co. Type	Sales ($ mil)	Empl. (000)
Sequa Corp.	200 Park Ave.	New York	NY	10166	Gail Binderman	212-986-5500	P	2,183	10.2
Northrop Grumman Space Tech.	1 Space Park Dr.	Redondo Beach	CA	90278	Wes Bush	310-812-4321	S	1,000*	9.3
GenCorp Inc.	PO Box 537012	Sacramento	CA	95853	Terry L. Hall	916-355-4000	P	745	3.3
Williams International Company	PO Box 200	Walled Lake	MI	48390		248-624-5200	R	300*	0.6
Vitron Acqusition L.L.C.	18008 N Black Cyn.	Phoenix	AZ	85053		602-548-9661	R	19*	0.1
Atlantic Research Liquid Prop.	6686 Walmore Rd.	Niagara Falls	NY	14304		716-731-6000	D	7*	<0.1
Innovation Marine Corp.	8011 15th St. E	Sarasota	FL	34243	Richard Lamore	941-355-7852	R	3*	<0.1

Source: Ward's Business Directory of U.S. Private and Public Companies, Volumes 1 and 2, 2008. The company type code used is as follows: P - Public, R - Private, S - Subsidiary, D - Division, J - Joint Venture, A - Affiliate, G - Group. Sales are in millions of dollars, employees are in thousands. An asterisk (*) indicates an estimated sales volume. The symbol < stands for 'less than'. Company names and addresses are truncated, in some cases, to fit into the available space.

MATERIALS CONSUMED

Material	Quantity	Delivered Cost ($ million)
Guided missile and space vehicle engines and parts	(X)	(D)
Guided missile and space vehicle propulsion units and parts	(X)	160.3
Guided missile and space vehicle airframe parts	(X)	(D)
Radio communication systems and equipment (microwave, UHF, etc.)	(X)	(D)
Navigational systems and equipment (NAVAIDS)	(X)	(D)
Resistors, capacitors, transformers, electron tubes, semiconductors, and other electronic components	(X)	0.8
Resin matrix composites	(X)	(D)
Other matrix composites (ceramic, carbon, metal, etc.)	(X)	(D)
Complete mechanical, hydraulic and pneumatic subassemblies	(X)	(D)
Fluid power products	(X)	(D)
Metal bolts, nuts, screws, and other screw machine products	(X)	2.3
Other fabricated metal products (exc. fluid power products and forgings)	(X)	(D)
Iron and steel forgings	(X)	(D)
Nonferrous forgings	(X)	(D)
Iron and steel castings (rough and semifinished)	(X)	3.7
Aluminum and aluminum-base alloy castings (rough and semifinished)	(X)	(D)
Other nonferrous metal castings, rough or semifinished (inc. aluminum)	(X)	(D)
Metal shapes and forms (exc. castings, forgings, fabr. metal products)	(X)	(D)
Chemicals, all types (including propellants)	(X)	31.2
All other materials, components, parts, containers, and supplies	(X)	259.8
Materials, ingredients, containers, and supplies, nsk	(X)	22.6

Source: 2002 *Economic Census*. Explanation of symbols used: (D): Withheld to avoid disclosure of competitive data; na: Not available; (S): Withheld because statistical norms were not met; (X): Not applicable; (Z): Less than half the unit shown; nec: Not elsewhere classified; nsk: Not specified by kind; - : zero; p : 10-19 percent estimated; q : 20-29 percent estimated.

PRODUCT SHARE DETAILS

Product or Product Class Shipments	Mil. $	Product or Product Class Shipments	Mil. $
GUIDED MISSILE AND SPACE VEHICLE PROPULSION UNITS AND PROPULSION UNIT PARTS	3,390.3	customers	18.2
Complete missiles, space vehicle engines, and propulsion units	**2,177.3**	**Other services on complete missiles, space vehicle engines, and propulsion units**	**287.0**
Complete missiles, space vehicle engines, and propulsion units for U.S. Government military customers	1,133.8	**Missile and space vehicle engine and propulsion parts and accessories**	**238.3**
Complete missiles, space vehicle engines, and propulsion units for U.S. Government nonmilitary customers	734.0	Missile and space vehicle engine and propulsion parts and accessories	233.6
Complete missiles, space vehicle engines, and propulsion units for other customers	309.5	Missile and space vehicle engine and propulsion parts and accessories for U.S. Government military customers	136.8
Research and development on complete missiles, space vehicle engines, and propulsion units	**681.9**	Missile and space vehicle engine and propulsion parts and accessories for U.S. Government nonmilitary customers	(D)
Research and development on complete missiles, space vehicle engines, and propulsion units for U.S. Government military customers	580.6	Missile and space vehicle engine and propulsion parts and accessories for other customers	(D)
Research and development on complete missiles, space vehicle engines, and propulsion units for U.S. Government nonmilitary customers	83.1	Missile and space vehicle engine and propulsion parts and accessories, nsk	4.7
Research and development on complete missiles, space vehicle engines, and propulsion units for other		**Guided missile and space vehicle propulsion units and propulsion unit parts, nsk, total**	**5.9**

Source: 2002 *Economic Census*. The values are product shipments in millions of dollars for 2002. Total product shipments may be lower or higher than industry shipments. See Introduction for a full discussion. Values of indented subcategories are summed in the main heading(s). The symbol (D) appears when data are withheld to prevent disclosure of competitive information. The abbreviation nsk stands for 'not specified by kind' and nec for 'not elsewhere classified'. A dash (-) means zero.

INPUTS AND OUTPUTS FOR GUIDED MISSILE & SPACE VEHICLE PARTS

Economic Sector or Industry Providing Inputs	%	Sector	Economic Sector or Industry Buying Outputs	%	Sector
Compensation of employees	49.7		Guided missiles & space vehicles	22.6	Manufg.
Guided missile & space vehicle parts	13.3	Manufg.	Exports of goods & services	22.2	Cap Inv
Management of companies & enterprises	6.6	Services	Federal government, investment, nondefense	21.2	Fed Govt
Software publishers	3.2	Services	General Federal government services, defense	17.5	Fed Govt
Scientific research & development services	1.5	Services	General Federal government services, nondefense	8.3	Fed Govt
Power generation & supply	1.4	Util.	Guided missile & space vehicle parts	7.6	Manufg.
Printed circuit assemblies (electronic assemblies)	1.0	Manufg.	Scientific research & development services	0.3	Services
Wholesale trade	0.9	Trade	Architectural, engineering, & related services	0.3	Services
Taxes on production & imports, less subsidies	0.7				
Advertising & related services	0.7	Services			
Paints & coatings	0.7	Manufg.			
Truck transportation	0.6	Util.			
Machine shops	0.6	Manufg.			
Semiconductors & related devices	0.6	Manufg.			
Securities, commodity contracts, investments	0.6	Fin/R.E.			
Legal services	0.6	Services			
Real estate	0.6	Fin/R.E.			
Warehousing & storage	0.6	Util.			
Nonferrous metal foundries	0.5	Manufg.			
Lessors of nonfinancial assets	0.5	Fin/R.E.			
Specialized design services	0.5	Services			
Chemical products & preparations, nec	0.5	Manufg.			
Employment services	0.5	Services			
Forging, stamping, & sintering, nec	0.5	Manufg.			
Basic organic chemicals, nec	0.4	Manufg.			
Coating, engraving, heat treating & allied activities	0.4	Manufg.			
Business support services	0.4	Services			
Maintenance/repair of nonresidential structures	0.4	Construct.			
Ferrous metal foundries	0.4	Manufg.			
Natural gas distribution	0.4	Util.			
Paperboard containers	0.3	Manufg.			
Data processing, hosting, & related services	0.3	Services			
Management, scientific, & technical consulting	0.3	Services			
Services to buildings & dwellings	0.3	Services			
Automotive equipment rental & leasing	0.3	Fin/R.E.			
Architectural, engineering, & related services	0.3	Services			
Valve & fittings other than plumbing	0.3	Manufg.			
Telecommunications	0.3	Services			
Iron & steel mills & ferroalloys	0.3	Manufg.			
Basic inorganic chemicals, nec	0.3	Manufg.			
Support services, nec	0.2	Services			
Accounting, tax preparation, bookkeeping, & payroll	0.2	Services			
Sand, gravel, clay, & refractory minerals	0.2	Mining			
Automotive repair & maintenance, ex. car washes	0.2	Services			
Fabricated metals, nec	0.2	Manufg.			
Investigation & security services	0.2	Services			
Commercial & industrial equipment repair/maintenance	0.2	Services			
Other computer related services, including facilities	0.2	Services			
Commercial & industrial machinery rental & leasing	0.2	Fin/R.E.			
Monetary authorities/depository credit intermediation	0.2	Fin/R.E.			
Paperboard mills	0.1	Manufg.			
Professional, scientific, technical services, nec	0.1	Services			
Turned products & screws, nuts, & bolts	0.1	Manufg.			
Rubber products, nec	0.1	Manufg.			
Electronic & precision equipment repair/maintenance	0.1	Services			
Food services & drinking places	0.1	Services			

Source: Benchmark Input-Output Accounts for the U.S. Economy, 2002, U.S. Department of Commerce, Washington D.C., January 2008. User should note that this Input-Output table is not for this particular narrowly defined industry but for a larger aggregate. Input and Output data for Guided Missile & Space Vehicle Parts include Input and Output data for the Annual Survey of Manufactures' NAICS industries 336415 and 336419. The abbreviation nec stands for 'not elsewhere classified'.

OCCUPATIONS EMPLOYED BY AEROSPACE PRODUCT & PARTS MANUFACTURING

Occupation	% of Total 2006	Change to 2016	Occupation	% of Total 2006	Change to 2016
Aerospace engineers	9.3	6.9	Management analysts	1.8	1.8
Aircraft structure & systems assemblers	5.2	12.0	Engineers, nec	1.8	1.8
Aircraft mechanics & service technicians	4.4	22.2	Production, planning, & expediting clerks	1.6	1.8
Machinists	3.8	6.9	Industrial engineering technicians	1.5	12.0
Inspectors, testers, sorters, samplers, & weighers	3.5	-4.0	Team assemblers	1.5	1.8
Industrial engineers	3.1	23.7	Executive secretaries & administrative assistants	1.4	1.8
Computer software engineers, applications	2.5	22.2	Computer-controlled machine tool operators	1.1	12.0
Mechanical engineers	2.3	1.8	Computer software engineers, systems software	1.1	12.0
Engineering managers	2.2	12.0	Engineering technicians, exc drafters, nec	1.1	1.8
Purchasing agents, exc wholesale, retail, & farm	2.0	1.8	Industrial production managers	1.0	1.8
First-line supervisors/managers of production workers	2.0	1.8	Stock clerks & order fillers	1.0	-14.8
Business operation specialists, nec	1.9	12.0			

Source: *Industry-Occupation Matrix*, Bureau of Labor Statistics, December 4, 2007. These data are reported based on 4-digit NAICS categories but have been matched to corresponding 6-digit NAICS industry codes. The change reported for each occupation to the year 2016 is a percent of growth or decline as estimated by the Bureau of Labor Statistics. The abbreviation nec stands for 'not elsewhere classified'.

LOCATION BY STATE AND REGIONAL CONCENTRATION

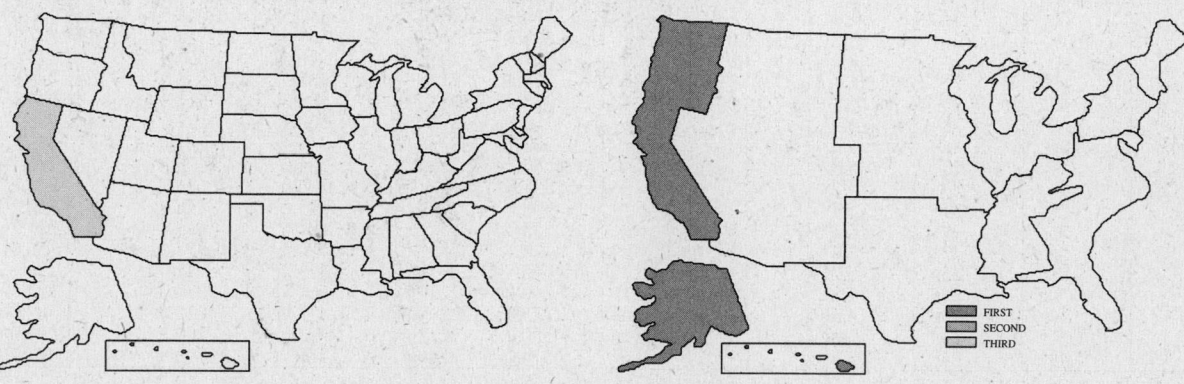

FIRST
SECOND
THIRD

INDUSTRY DATA BY STATE

State	Establishments	Shipments			Employment				Cost as % of Shipments	Investment per Employee ($)
		Total ($ mil)	% of U.S.	Per Establ.	Total Number	% of U.S.	Per Establ.	Wages ($/hour)		
California	7	1,158.3	44.2	165,465.0	6,862	46.9	980	29.88	23.1	8,823

Source: 2002 *Economic Census*. The states are in descending order of shipments or establishments (if shipment data are missing for the majority). The symbol (D) appears when data are withheld to prevent disclosure of competitive information. States marked with (D) are sorted by number of establishments. A dash (-) indicates that the data element cannot be calculated. Data may not show all states active in the NAICS category. All data available at the time of publication are shown.

NAICS 336419 - GUIDED MISSILE AND SPACE VEHICLE PARTS

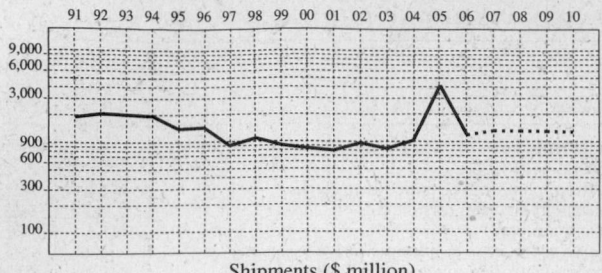

Shipments ($ million)

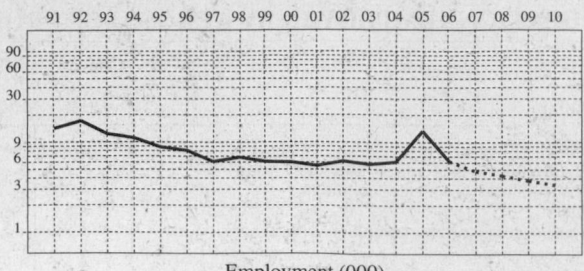

Employment (000)

GENERAL STATISTICS

Year	Com-panies	Establishments		Employment			Compensation		Production ($ million)			
		Total	with 20 or more employees	Total (000)	Production Workers (000)	Hours (Mil)	Payroll ($ mil)	Wages ($/hr)	Cost of Materials	Value Added by Manufacture	Value of Shipments	Capital Invest.
1991		53	34	14.2	7.7	14.5	558.2	18.36	752.5	1,206.4	1,907.3	31.4
1992	54	60	37	17.2	7.7	15.0	694.5	18.09	643.8	1,456.4	2,070.7	41.0
1993		63	40	12.3	5.6	11.1	532.6	19.95	778.3	1,289.2	2,014.9	25.3
1994		60	31	11.1	5.5	11.6	520.3	20.48	813.5	1,045.8	1,944.4	38.3
1995		49	26	8.8	4.6	9.1	394.1	21.49	564.0	852.0	1,397.9	37.0
1996		45	24	8.1	4.8	10.0	391.8	20.98	546.6	657.4	1,435.9	45.0
1997	47	49	26	6.1	4.2	8.5	278.4	21.01	365.5	538.3	898.8	28.8
1998		47	23	6.8	4.6	9.4	303.3	20.73	458.3	613.2	1,086.1	39.0
1999		50	28	6.1	4.8	9.6	288.3	22.11	320.2	577.4	903.8	15.8
2000		46	26	6.0	4.7	9.2	302.1	23.05	316.4	504.4	839.7	10.5
2001		41	23	5.5	4.1	8.4	277.7	22.32	324.0	476.9	796.1	20.5
2002	52	54	27	6.2	2.9	6.0	321.0	18.47	306.0	684.7	963.8	18.0
2003		56	31	5.7	3.1	6.4	308.6	17.61	273.0	576.9	830.2	12.0
2004		55	29	6.1	3.6	6.9	355.4	20.59	407.6	623.4	1,021.2	25.0
2005		58	32	13.4	4.0	7.3	1,034.1	25.56	2,600.3	1,818.8	4,156.0	331.7
2006		50P	25P	6.2	3.5	6.7	365.1	21.84	451.2	742.0	1,184.1	39.5
2007		50P	25P	4.8P	2.6P	5.1P	390.8P	22.33P	504.7P	830.0P	1,324.5P	89.0P
2008		50P	25P	4.3P	2.4P	4.6P	385.9P	22.52P	498.4P	819.6P	1,307.9P	93.9P
2009		50P	24P	3.8P	2.1P	4.1P	380.9P	22.70P	492.0P	809.2P	1,291.3P	98.8P
2010		49P	24P	3.4P	1.9P	3.6P	376.0P	22.88P	485.7P	798.8P	1,274.7P	103.7P

Sources: 1992, 1997, 2002 *Economic Census*; other years, up to 2006, are from the *Annual Survey of Manufactures*. Establishment counts for non-Census years are from *County Business Patterns*; 1997 and 2002 values are from the 1997 and 2002 censuses respectively, reported in the Federal Government's NAICS format. Other years were originally reported in equivalent SIC format. 'P's show projections by the editors.

INDICES OF CHANGE

Year	Com-panies	Establishments		Employment			Compensation		Production ($ million)			
		Total	with 20 or more employees	Total (000)	Production Workers (000)	Hours (Mil)	Payroll ($ mil)	Wages ($/hr)	Cost of Materials	Value Added by Manufacture	Value of Shipments	Capital Invest.
1992	104	111	137	277	266	250	216	98	210	213	215	228
1997	90	91	96	98	145	142	87	114	119	79	93	160
2001		76	85	89	141	140	87	121	106	70	83	114
2002	100	100	100	100	100	100	100	100	100	100	100	100
2003		104	115	92	107	107	96	95	89	84	86	67
2004		102	107	98	124	115	111	111	133	91	106	139
2005		107	119	216	138	122	322	138	850	266	431	1,843
2006		93P	94P	100	121	112	114	118	147	108	123	219
2007		93P	93P	77P	90P	85P	122P	121P	165P	121P	137P	494P
2008		92P	91P	69P	83P	77P	120P	122P	163P	120P	136P	522P
2009		92P	90P	61P	72P	68P	119P	123P	161P	118P	134P	549P
2010		91P	88P	55P	66P	60P	117P	124P	159P	117P	132P	576P

Sources: Same as General Statistics. Values reflect change from the base year, 2002. Values above 100 mean greater than 2002, values below 100 mean less than 2002; and the values of 100 in other years means the same as 2002. 'P's show projections by the editors.

SELECTED RATIOS

For 2002	Avg. of All Manufact.	Analyzed Industry	Index	For 2002	Avg. of All Manufact.	Analyzed Industry	Index
Employees per Establishment	42	115	274	Value Added per Production Worker	182,367	236,103	129
Payroll per Establishment	1,639,184	5,944,444	363	Cost per Establishment	5,769,015	5,666,667	98
Payroll per Employee	39,053	51,774	133	Cost per Employee	137,446	49,355	36
Production Workers per Establishment	30	54	182	Cost per Production Worker	195,506	105,517	54
Wages per Establishment	694,845	2,052,222	295	Shipments per Establishment	11,158,348	17,848,148	160
Wages per Production Worker	23,548	38,214	162	Shipments per Employee	265,847	155,452	58
Hours per Production Worker	1,980	2,069	104	Shipments per Production Worker	378,144	332,345	88
Wages per Hour	11.89	18.47	155	Investment per Establishment	361,338	333,333	92
Value Added per Establishment	5,381,325	12,679,630	236	Investment per Employee	8,609	2,903	34
Value Added per Employee	128,210	110,435	86	Investment per Production Worker	12,245	6,207	51

Sources: Same as General Statistics. The 'Average of All Manufacturing' column represents the average of all manufacturing industries reported for the most recent complete year available. The Index shows the relationship between the Average and the Analyzed Industry. For example, 100 means that they are equal; 500 that the Analyzed Industry is five times the average; 50 means that the Analyzed Industry is half the national average. The abbreviation 'na' is used to show that data are 'not available'. Ratios shown for 2002, the last complete census year.

LEADING COMPANIES Number shown: **75**   Total sales ($ mil): **134,637**   Total employment (000): **429.0**

Company Name	Address				CEO Name	Phone	Co. Type	Sales ($ mil)	Empl. (000)
Boeing Co.	100 N Riverside Plz	Chicago	IL	60606		312-544-2000	P	66,387	159.3
Boeing Integrated Defense Sys.	PO Box 516	St. Louis	MO	63166	James Albaugh	314-232-0232	D	17,354*	72.0
L-3 Communications Holdings	600 3rd Ave.	New York	NY	10016		212-697-1111	P	13,961	63.7
Textron Inc.	40 Westminster St.	Providence	RI	02903		401-421-2800	P	13,225	44.0
Ball Corp.	PO Box 5000	Broomfield	CO	80021	R. David Hoover	303-469-3131	P	7,475	15.5
Hamilton Sundstrand Corp.	1 Hamilton Rd.	Windsor Locks	CT	06096	Ronald F. McKenna	860-654-6000	S	3,600*	16.0
Crane Co.	100 First Stamford	Stamford	CT	06902	Thomas Craney	203-363-7300	P	2,619	11.0
Sequa Corp.	200 Park Ave.	New York	NY	10166	Gail Binderman	212-986-5500	P	2,183	10.2
Orbital Sciences Corp.	21839 Atlantic Blvd	Dulles	VA	20166		703-406-5000	P	1,084	2.8
MRC Bearings	402 Chandler St.	Jamestown	NY	14701		716-661-2600	S	1,012*	1.6
Northrop Grumman Space Tech.	1 Space Park Dr.	Redondo Beach	CA	90278	Wes Bush	310-812-4321	S	1,000*	9.3
GenCorp Inc.	PO Box 537012	Sacramento	CA	95853	Terry L. Hall	916-355-4000	P	745	3.3
Ball Aerospace & Technologies	PO Box 1062	Boulder	CO	80306		303-939-4000	S	672*	3.0
RMS Co.	8600 Evergreen Blvd	Coon Rapids	MN	55433	Arthur Mouyard	763-786-1520	S	400*	0.3
TECT Utica Corp.	2 Halsey Rd.	Whitesboro	NY	13492	Ron Cable	315-768-8070	R	356*	1.3
Telex Communications Inc.	12000 Portland Ave.	Burnsville	MN	55337	R V. Malpocher	952-884-4051	R	308*	3.0
BAE Systems Platform Solutions	600 Main St.	Johnson City	NY	13790	Michael Heffron	607-770-2000	D	294*	1.6
Astronautics Corp. of America	PO Box 523	Milwaukee	WI	53201	Michael Russek	414-449-4000	R	233*	0.5
Barnes Aerospace Corp.	169 Kennedy Rd.	Windsor	CT	06095	Patrick Dempsey	860-298-7740	D	230*	1.0
Aerostructures Corp.	1431 Vultee Blvd.	Nashville	TN	37217	Elmer Doty	615-361-2000	R	181*	1.4
Ellanef Manufacturing Corp.	9711 50th Ave.	Corona	NY	11368	Murray Edwards	718-699-4000	R	131*	0.2
Woven Electronics L.L.C.	PO Box 367	Greenville	SC	29602	Henry Little	864-233-6740	R	100*	<0.1
Hoke Inc.	PO Box 4866	Spartanburg	SC	29305	David A. Bloss	864-574-7966	S	86*	0.5
Meggitt Safety Systems	1955 N Surveyor	Simi Valley	CA	93063		805-526-5700	S	69*	0.5
Pratt and Whitney Rocketdyne	PO Box 49028	San Jose	CA	95161		408-779-9121	D	56*	0.3
Spacehab Inc.	12130 Highway 3	Webster	TX	77598		713-558-5000	P	53	0.2
Gentz Industries L.L.C.	25250 Easy St.	Warren	MI	48089	Donald Duckett	586-772-2500	R	51*	0.2
Palmer Manufacturing Company	PO Box K	Malden	MA	02148		781-321-0480	R	45*	0.2
AHF-Ducommun	PO Box 2310	Gardena	CA	90247	Tony Reardon	310-380-5390	R	37*	0.3
Schweizer Aircraft Corp.	1250 Schweizer Rd.	Horseheads	NY	14845	Paul Schweizer	607-739-3821	S	35*	0.5
Circle Seal Controls Inc.	PO Box 3300	Corona	CA	92878	Carl Nasca	951-270-6200	D	33*	0.3
Certified Fabricators Inc.	6530 Altura Blvd.	Buena Park	CA	90620	Joseph Lauderdale	714-670-1491	S	29*	0.2
Heizer Aerospace Inc.	8750 Pevely Indust.	Pevely	MO	63070	Charles Heizer	636-475-6300	R	28*	0.2
GS Precision Inc.	101 John Seitz Dr.	Brattleboro	VT	05301	George Schneeberger	802-257-5200	R	25*	0.2
Mayday Manufacturing Co.	1500 Interstate 35W	Denton	TX	76207	James Nelson	940-898-8301	R	24*	0.2
Major Tool and Machine Inc.	1458 E 19th St.	Indianapolis	IN	46218	Stephen Weyreter	317-636-6433	R	23*	0.3
Millat Industries Corp.	4901 Croftshire Dr.	Dayton	OH	45440	Gregory Millat	937-434-6666	R	23*	0.1
AC Inc.	PO Box 17069	Huntsville	AL	35810	George Smith	256-851-9020	R	23*	0.1
B.A. E Sys. Composite Struct.	1095 Columbia St.	Brea	CA	92821		714-990-6300	R	23*	0.1
Astro Aerospace	6384 Via Real	Carpinteria	CA	93013	Chris Yamada	805-684-6641	S	22*	0.1
Kreisler Industrial Corp.	180 Van Riper Ave.	Elmwood Park	NJ	07407		201-791-0700	R	21*	0.1
Hi-Shear Technology Corp.	24225 Garnier St.	Torrance	CA	90505	Thomas R. Mooney	310-784-2100	P	21	0.1
Morris Bean and Co.	777 E Hyde Rd.	Yellow Springs	OH	45387	Edward Myers	937-767-7301	R	20*	0.2
Tayco Engineering Inc.	PO Box 6034	Cypress	CA	90630	Jay Chung	714-952-2240	R	19*	0.1
Frontier Electronic Systems	PO Box 1023	Stillwater	OK	74076	Peggy Shreve	405-624-1769	R	19*	0.1
Western Methods Machinery	2344 Pullman St.	Santa Ana	CA	92705	Mark Heasley	949-252-6600	R	19*	0.1
Braxton Manufacturing Company	PO Box 429	Watertown	CT	06795	Joseph Triano	860-274-6781	R	18*	0.2
Accra Manufacturing Inc.	17703 15th Ave. SE	Bothell	WA	98012	Joseph Rieger	425-424-1000	R	15*	<0.1
Trigon Holding Inc.	124 Hidden Vly Rd.	Canonsburg	PA	15317	Peter Stephans	724-941-5540	R	15*	<0.1
Maine Machine Products Co.	PO Box 260	South Paris	ME	04281	Roland Sutton	207-743-6344	R	14*	0.2
Precision Aerospace L.L.C.	3011 W Windsor	Phoenix	AZ	85009		602-352-8658	R	13*	<0.1
Haynes Corp.	3581 Mercantile Ave	Naples	FL	34104	James Dixon	239-643-3013	R	13*	<0.1
Fiber Materials Inc.	5 Morin Street	Biddeford	ME	04005	Walter Lachman	207-282-5911	R	12*	0.1
AMRO Fabricating Corp.	1430 Adelia Ave.	South El Monte	CA	91733	Aquilina Hutton	626-579-2200	R	12*	<0.1
Morton Grinding Inc.	17341 Sierra Hwy.	Santa Clarita	CA	91351	Wallace Morton	661-298-0895	R	12*	0.1
Meriden Manufacturing Inc.	PO Box 694	Meriden	CT	06450	Sharon Fox	203-237-7481	R	11*	<0.1
Aero Panel Corp.	661 Myrtle Ave.	Boonton	NJ	07005		973-335-9636	R	11*	<0.1
Composites Horizons Inc.	1471 W Indu Prk St	Covina	CA	91722	Jeff Hynes	626-331-0861	R	10*	0.1
Ithaco Space Systems Inc.	950 Danby Rd., 100	Ithaca	NY	14850		607-272-7640	S	10*	<0.1
Sterling Engineering Corp.	PO Box 559	Winsted	CT	06098	John Lavieri	860-379-3366	R	10*	<0.1
Rooke Corp.	7230 Fulton Ave.	N Hollywood	CA	91605		818-982-6700	R	8*	<0.1
Competitive Engineering Inc.	3371 E Hemisphere	Tucson	AZ	85706	Don Martin	520-746-0270	R	8*	<0.1
Quintus Inc.	PO Box 3930	Camp Verde	AZ	86322	Richard Cook	928-567-3833	R	8*	<0.1
K and G Manufacturing Co.	PO Box 187	Faribault	MN	55021	Thomas Gerbig	507-334-5501	R	8*	<0.1
Ion Corp.	5474 Feltl Rd.	Minnetonka	MN	55343		952-936-9490	R	8*	<0.1
Industrial Quartz Corp.	7552 Saint Clair	Mentor	OH	44060	Richard Intihar	440-942-0909	R	7*	<0.1
American Automated Engineering	5382 Argosy Ave.	Huntington Bch	CA	92649	Kenneth Christensen	714-898-9951	R	7*	<0.1
Attco Machine Products Inc.	2411 Foundation Dr.	South Bend	IN	46628	Richard Verwilst	574-234-1063	R	7*	<0.1
Prec. Fabricating & Cleaning	3975 E Railroad Ave	Cocoa	FL	32926	Russell Gray	321-635-2000	R	7*	<0.1
Heartland Enterprises Ltd.	1039 Kerr Rd.	Fredericksburg	TX	78624		830-997-9434	R	7*	<0.1
Stewart Manufacturing Company	1620 W Knudsen Dr.	Phoenix	AZ	85027	Patrick Stewart	623-582-2261	R	7*	<0.1
Swissline Products Inc.	23 Ashton Pkwy.	Cumberland	RI	02864	David Chenevert	401-333-8888	R	7*	<0.1
Advance Mfg, Engin. & Design	PO Box 130317	Ann Arbor	MI	48113	Glen Theisen	734-665-8181	R	7*	<0.1
Saturn Industries Inc.	PO Box 367	Hudson	NY	12534	John Lee	518-828-9956	R	6*	<0.1
Merritt Tool Company Inc.	PO Box 1209	Kilgore	TX	75663	A Merritt	903-983-1592	R	6*	<0.1

Source: Ward's Business Directory of U.S. Private and Public Companies, Volumes 1 and 2, 2008. The company type code used is as follows: P - Public, R - Private, S - Subsidiary, D - Division, J - Joint Venture, A - Affiliate, G - Group. Sales are in millions of dollars, employees are in thousands. An asterisk (*) indicates an estimated sales volume. The symbol < stands for 'less than'. Company names and addresses are truncated, in some cases, to fit into the available space.

MATERIALS CONSUMED

Material	Quantity	Delivered Cost ($ million)
Guided missile and space vehicle airframe parts	(X)	(D)
Resistors, capacitors, transformers, electron tubes, semiconductors, and other electronic components	(X)	(D)
Resin matrix composites	(X)	(D)
Other matrix composites (ceramic, carbon, metal, etc.)	(X)	(D)
Metal bolts, nuts, screws, and other screw machine products	(X)	0.3
Iron and steel forgings	(X)	(D)
Nonferrous forgings	(X)	(D)
Iron and steel castings (rough and semifinished)	(X)	(D)
Aluminum and aluminum-base alloy castings (rough and semifinished)	(X)	(D)
Metal shapes and forms (exc. castings, forgings, fabr. metal products)	(X)	(D)
Chemicals, all types (including propellants)	(X)	0.1
All other materials, components, parts, containers, and supplies	(X)	106.5
Materials, ingredients, containers, and supplies, nsk	(X)	95.2

Source: 2002 *Economic Census*. Explanation of symbols used: (D): Withheld to avoid disclosure of competitive data; na: Not available; (S): Withheld because statistical norms were not met; (X): Not applicable; (Z): Less than half the unit shown; nec: Not elsewhere classified; nsk: Not specified by kind; - : zero; p : 10-19 percent estimated; q : 20-29 percent estimated.

PRODUCT SHARE DETAILS

Product or Product Class Shipments	Mil. $	Product or Product Class Shipments	Mil. $
GUIDED MISSILE AND SPACE VEHICLE PARTS AND AUXILIARY EQUIPMENT, NEC	2,858.9	Research and development on missile and space vehicle parts and components, nec	204.2
Missile and space vehicle components, parts, and subassemblies	**2,601.9**	Research and development on missile and space vehicle airframes and space capsules for U.S. Government military customers	7.6
Missile and space vehicle airframes and space capsules for U.S. Government military customers	(D)	All other research and development on missile and space vehicle parts and components for U.S. Government military customers	110.6
All other missile and space vehicle components, parts, and subassemblies for U.S. Government military customers	1,333.5		
Missile and space vehicle components, parts, and subassemblies for U.S. Government nonmilitary customers	(D)	Research and development on missile and space vehicle parts and components for U.S. Government nonmilitary customers	(D)
Missile and space vehicle components, parts, and subassemblies for other customers	218.8	Research and development on missile and space vehicle parts and components for other customers	(D)
Missile and space vehicle components, parts, and subassemblies, nsk	278.7	Research and development on missile and space vehicle parts and components, nec, nsk	1.3
Research and development on missile and space vehicle parts and components, nec	**205.5**	**Guided missile and space vehicle parts and auxiliary equipment, nec, nsk, total**	**51.5**

Source: 2002 *Economic Census*. The values are product shipments in millions of dollars for 2002. Total product shipments may be lower or higher than industry shipments. See Introduction for a full discussion. Values of indented subcategories are summed in the main heading(s). The symbol (D) appears when data are withheld to prevent disclosure of competitive information. The abbreviation nsk stands for 'not specified by kind' and nec for 'not elsewhere classified'. A dash (-) means zero.

INPUTS AND OUTPUTS FOR GUIDED MISSILE & SPACE VEHICLE PARTS

Economic Sector or Industry Providing Inputs	%	Sector	Economic Sector or Industry Buying Outputs	%	Sector
Compensation of employees	49.7		Guided missiles & space vehicles	22.6	Manufg.
Guided missile & space vehicle parts	13.3	Manufg.	Exports of goods & services	22.2	Cap Inv
Management of companies & enterprises	6.6	Services	Federal government, investment, nondefense	21.2	Fed Govt
Software publishers	3.2	Services	General Federal government services, defense	17.5	Fed Govt
Scientific research & development services	1.5	Services	General Federal government services, nondefense	8.3	Fed Govt
Power generation & supply	1.4	Util.	Guided missile & space vehicle parts	7.6	Manufg.
Printed circuit assemblies (electronic assembiles)	1.0	Manufg.	Scientific research & development services	0.3	Services
Wholesale trade	0.9	Trade	Architectural, engineering, & related services	0.3	Services
Taxes on production & imports, less subsidies	0.7				
Advertising & related services	0.7	Services			
Paints & coatings	0.7	Manufg.			
Truck transportation	0.6	Util.			
Machine shops	0.6	Manufg.			
Semiconductors & related devices	0.6	Manufg.			
Securities, commodity contracts, investments	0.6	Fin/R.E.			
Legal services	0.6	Services			
Real estate	0.6	Fin/R.E.			
Warehousing & storage	0.6	Util.			
Nonferrous metal foundries	0.5	Manufg.			
Lessors of nonfinancial assets	0.5	Fin/R.E.			
Specialized design services	0.5	Services			
Chemical products & preparations, nec	0.5	Manufg.			
Employment services	0.5	Services			
Forging, stamping, & sintering, nec	0.5	Manufg.			
Basic organic chemicals, nec	0.4	Manufg.			
Coating, engraving, heat treating & allied activities	0.4	Manufg.			

Continued on next page.

INPUTS AND OUTPUTS FOR GUIDED MISSILE & SPACE VEHICLE PARTS - Continued

Economic Sector or Industry Providing Inputs	%	Sector	Economic Sector or Industry Buying Outputs	%	Sector
Business support services	0.4	Services			
Maintenance/repair of nonresidential structures	0.4	Construct.			
Ferrous metal foundries	0.4	Manufg.			
Natural gas distribution	0.4	Util.			
Paperboard containers	0.3	Manufg.			
Data processing, hosting, & related services	0.3	Services			
Management, scientific, & technical consulting	0.3	Services			
Services to buildings & dwellings	0.3	Services			
Automotive equipment rental & leasing	0.3	Fin/R.E.			
Architectural, engineering, & related services	0.3	Services			
Valve & fittings other than plumbing	0.3	Manufg.			
Telecommunications	0.3	Services			
Iron & steel mills & ferroalloys	0.3	Manufg.			
Basic inorganic chemicals, nec	0.3	Manufg.			
Support services, nec	0.2	Services			
Accounting, tax preparation, bookkeeping, & payroll	0.2	Services			
Sand, gravel, clay, & refractory minerals	0.2	Mining			
Automotive repair & maintenance, ex. car washes	0.2	Services			
Fabricated metals, nec	0.2	Manufg.			
Investigation & security services	0.2	Services			
Commercial & industrial equipment repair/maintenance	0.2	Services			
Other computer related services, including facilities	0.2	Services			
Commercial & industrial machinery rental & leasing	0.2	Fin/R.E.			
Monetary authorities/depository credit intermediation	0.2	Fin/R.E.			
Paperboard mills	0.1	Manufg.			
Professional, scientific, technical services, nec	0.1	Services			
Turned products & screws, nuts, & bolts	0.1	Manufg.			
Rubber products, nec	0.1	Manufg.			
Electronic & precision equipment repair/maintenance	0.1	Services			
Food services & drinking places	0.1	Services			

Source: Benchmark Input-Output Accounts for the U.S. Economy, 2002, U.S. Department of Commerce, Washington D.C., January 2008. User should note that this Input-Output table is not for this particular narrowly defined industry but for a larger aggregate. Input and Output data for Guided Missile & Space Vehicle Parts include Input and Output data for the Annual Survey of Manufactures' NAICS industries 336415 and 336419. The abbreviation nec stands for 'not elsewhere classified'.

OCCUPATIONS EMPLOYED BY AEROSPACE PRODUCT & PARTS MANUFACTURING

Occupation	% of Total 2006	Change to 2016	Occupation	% of Total 2006	Change to 2016
Aerospace engineers	9.3	6.9	Management analysts	1.8	1.8
Aircraft structure & systems assemblers	5.2	12.0	Engineers, nec	1.8	1.8
Aircraft mechanics & service technicians	4.4	22.2	Production, planning, & expediting clerks	1.6	1.8
Machinists	3.8	6.9	Industrial engineering technicians	1.5	12.0
Inspectors, testers, sorters, samplers, & weighers	3.5	-4.0	Team assemblers	1.5	1.8
Industrial engineers	3.1	23.7	Executive secretaries & administrative assistants	1.4	1.8
Computer software engineers, applications	2.5	22.2	Computer-controlled machine tool operators	1.1	12.0
Mechanical engineers	2.3	1.8	Computer software engineers, systems software	1.1	12.0
Engineering managers	2.2	12.0	Engineering technicians, exc drafters, nec	1.1	1.8
Purchasing agents, exc wholesale, retail, & farm	2.0	1.8	Industrial production managers	1.0	1.8
First-line supervisors/managers of production workers	2.0	1.8	Stock clerks & order fillers	1.0	-14.8
Business operation specialists, nec	1.9	12.0			

Source: Industry-Occupation Matrix, Bureau of Labor Statistics, December 4, 2007. These data are reported based on 4-digit NAICS categories but have been matched to corresponding 6-digit NAICS industry codes. The change reported for each occupation to the year 2016 is a percent of growth or decline as estimated by the Bureau of Labor Statistics. The abbreviation nec stands for 'not elsewhere classified'.

INDUSTRY DATA BY STATE

State-level data are not available.

NAICS 336510 - RAILROAD ROLLING STOCK MANUFACTURING

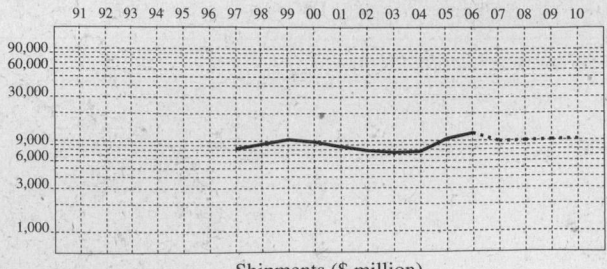

Shipments ($ million)

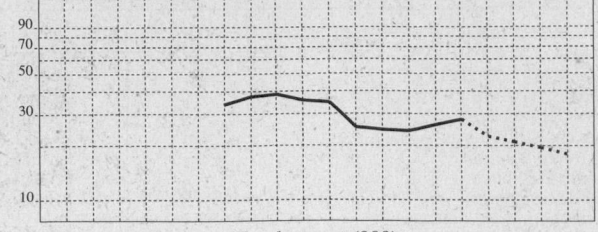

Employment (000)

GENERAL STATISTICS

| Year | Companies | Establishments | | Employment | | | Compensation | | Production ($ million) | | | |
		Total	with 20 or more employees	Total (000)	Production Workers (000)	Hours (Mil)	Payroll ($ mil)	Wages ($/hr)	Cost of Materials	Value Added by Manufacture	Value of Shipments	Capital Invest.
1997	173	230	145	33.8	23.8	53.0	1,313.6	14.92	5,068.9	3,329.6	8,219.1	197.2
1998		236	152	37.4	26.6	55.2	1,440.1	15.38	5,427.6	3,848.4	9,256.8	201.6
1999		241	154	38.5	27.9	59.9	1,533.0	15.50	5,869.5	4,460.7	10,352.3	219.5
2000		227	146	35.6	24.9	57.3	1,480.2	15.22	5,376.3	4,360.1	9,722.4	203.0
2001		218	142	34.7	24.0	48.7	1,449.8	16.41	4,571.1	3,850.2	8,603.8	169.6
2002	148	199	116	25.3	15.6	30.6	1,195.1	20.65	4,013.3	3,741.7	7,793.4	124.3
2003		194	103	24.5	15.4	30.0	1,156.1	19.58	4,269.4	2,909.8	7,404.8	96.2
2004		198	115	24.1	15.5	30.9	1,123.1	19.69	4,472.0	3,216.7	7,566.1	111.3
2005		202	120	26.0	17.8	34.2	1,188.7	20.60	6,539.3	3,679.6	10,465.3	124.8
2006		187P	104P	27.9	19.4	37.1	1,328.9	21.76	7,779.3	4,479.4	12,082.3	272.4
2007		181P	98P	22.5P	14.4P	25.9P	1,157.6P	22.52P	6,351.3P	3,657.1P	9,864.4P	146.4P
2008		176P	93P	21.0P	13.2P	22.6P	1,127.9P	23.34P	6,435.3P	3,705.5P	9,994.9P	141.8P
2009		170P	87P	19.5P	12.0P	19.4P	1,098.2P	24.17P	6,519.4P	3,753.9P	10,125.5P	137.1P
2010		164P	81P	18.0P	10.8P	16.1P	1,068.5P	25.00P	6,603.4P	3,802.3P	10,256.0P	132.5P

Sources: 1997 and 2002 *Economic Census*; other years, up to 2006, are from *Annual Survey of Manufactures*. Establishment counts for non-Census years are from *County Business Patterns*; 1997 and 2002 values are from the 1997 and 2002 censuses, respectively. 'P's show projections by the editors.

INDICES OF CHANGE

| Year | Companies | Establishments | | Employment | | | Compensation | | Production ($ million) | | | |
		Total	with 20 or more employees	Total (000)	Production Workers (000)	Hours (Mil)	Payroll ($ mil)	Wages ($/hr)	Cost of Materials	Value Added by Manufacture	Value of Shipments	Capital Invest.
1997	117	116	125	134	153	173	110	72	126	89	105	159
1998		119	131	148	171	180	121	74	135	103	119	162
1999		121	133	152	179	196	128	75	146	119	133	177
2000		114	126	141	160	187	124	74	134	117	125	163
2001		110	122	137	154	159	121	79	114	103	110	136
2002	100	100	100	100	100	100	100	100	100	100	100	100
2003		97	89	97	99	98	97	95	106	78	95	77
2004		99	99	95	99	101	94	95	111	86	97	90
2005		102	103	103	114	112	99	100	163	98	134	100
2006		94P	90P	110	124	121	111	105	194	120	155	219
2007		91P	85P	89P	92P	85P	97P	109P	158P	98P	127P	118P
2008		88P	80P	83P	85P	74P	94P	113P	160P	99P	128P	114P
2009		85P	75P	77P	77P	63P	92P	117P	162P	100P	130P	110P
2010		82P	70P	71P	69P	53P	89P	121P	165P	102P	132P	107P

Sources: Same as General Statistics. Values reflect change from the base year, 2002. Values above 100 mean greater than 2002, values below 100 mean less than 2002, and the values of 100 in other years means the same as 2002. 'P's show projections by the editors.

SELECTED RATIOS

For 2002	Avg. of All Manufact.	Analyzed Industry	Index	For 2002	Avg. of All Manufact.	Analyzed Industry	Index
Employees per Establishment	42	127	303	Value Added per Production Worker	182,367	239,853	132
Payroll per Establishment	1,639,184	6,005,528	366	Cost per Establishment	5,769,015	20,167,337	350
Payroll per Employee	39,053	47,237	121	Cost per Employee	137,446	158,628	115
Production Workers per Establishment	30	78	266	Cost per Production Worker	195,506	257,263	132
Wages per Establishment	694,845	3,175,327	457	Shipments per Establishment	11,158,348	39,162,814	351
Wages per Production Worker	23,548	40,506	172	Shipments per Employee	265,847	308,040	116
Hours per Production Worker	1,980	1,962	99	Shipments per Production Worker	378,144	499,577	132
Wages per Hour	11.89	20.65	174	Investment per Establishment	361,338	624,623	173
Value Added per Establishment	5,381,325	18,802,513	349	Investment per Employee	8,609	4,913	57
Value Added per Employee	128,210	147,893	115	Investment per Production Worker	12,245	7,968	65

Sources: Same as General Statistics. The 'Average of All Manufacturing' column represents the average of all manufacturing industries reported for the most recent complete year available. The Index shows the relationship between the Average and the Analyzed Industry. For example, 100 means that they are equal; 500 that the Analyzed Industry is five times the average; 50 means that the Analyzed Industry is half the national average. The abbreviation 'na' is used to show that data are 'not available'. Ratios shown for 2002, the last complete census year.

LEADING COMPANIES   Number shown: 75   Total sales ($ mil): 355,291   Total employment (000): 625.3

Company Name	Address				CEO Name	Phone	Co. Type	Sales ($ mil)	Empl. (000)
General Motors Corp.	300 Renaissance Ctr	Detroit	MI	48265		313-556-5000	P	181,122	266.0
Caterpillar Inc.	100 NE Adams St.	Peoria	IL	61629		309-675-1000	P	44,958	101.3
APAC Inc.	900 Ashwood Pkwy.	Atlanta	GA	30338	Garry Higdem	770-392-5300	S	25,170*	1.5
Deere and Co.	1 John Deere Pl.	Moline	IL	61265		309-765-8000	P	24,082	52.0
PACCAR Inc.	PO Box 1518	Bellevue	WA	98009		425-468-7400	P	15,220	21.8
Terex Corp.	200 Nyala Farm Rd.	Westport	CT	06880		203-222-7170	P	9,138	21.0
Dover Corp.	280 Park Ave.	New York	NY	10017		212-922-1640	P	7,226	33.4
Union Tank Car Co.	175 W Jackson Blvd.	Chicago	IL	60604	Kenneth Fischl	312-431-3111	R	7,000*	0.2
General Cable Corp.	4 Tesseneer Dr.	Highland Hgts	KY	41076	Gregory B. Kenny	859-572-8000	P	4,615	11.8
Manitowoc Company Inc.	PO Box 66	Manitowoc	WI	54221		920-684-4410	P	4,005	10.5
Trinity Industries Inc.	2525 Stemmons	Dallas	TX	75207		214-631-4420	P	3,833	14.4
Washington Group International	PO Box 73	Boise	ID	83729		208-386-5000	D	3,398	25.0
JLG Industries Inc.	1 Jlg Dr.	McConnellsburg	PA	17233		717-485-5161	S	2,289	4.1
Rowan Companies Inc.	2800 Post Oak Blvd.	Houston	TX	77056		713-621-7800	P	2,095	5.7
Bombardier Transport. Holdings	1501 Lebanon Ch.	Pittsburgh	PA	15236	Raymond Betler	412-655-5700	R	2,037*	0.9
Heico Holding Inc.	2626 Warrenville Rd	Downers Grove	IL	60515	Michael Heisley	630-353-5000	R	1,560*	<0.1
Westinghouse Air Brake Techn.	1001 Air Brake Ave.	Wilmerding	PA	15148	William E. Kassling	412-825-1000	P	1,360	6.0
Greenbrier Companies Inc.	1 Centerpointe Dr.	Lake Oswego	OR	97035	Alejandro Centurion	503-684-7000	P	1,224	4.2
Progress Rail Services Corp.	PO Box 1037	Albertville	AL	35950		256-593-1260	S	1,200	3.8
Astec Industries Inc.	1725 Shepherd Rd.	Chattanooga	TN	37421	J. Don Brock	423-899-5898	P	869	1.0
GE Transportation Systems	2901 East Lake Rd.	Erie	PA	16531	William Yuskovic	814-875-2234	S	747*	8.0
Komatsu America International	1701 W Golf Rd.	Rolling Mdws	IL	60008	David W. Grzelak	847-437-5800	S	634*	4.6
Columbus McKinnon Corp.	140 J J Audubon Pky	Amherst	NY	14228	Herbert P. Ladds Jr.	716-689-5400	P	590	3.3
ACF Industries Inc.	101 Clark St.	St. Charles	MO	63301	Carl C. Icahn	636-949-2399	R	579*	0.5
Motive Power, Inc.	4600 Apple St.	Boise	ID	83716	Albert Neupaver	208-947-4800	S	544*	0.3
L.B. Foster Co.	415 Holiday Dr.	Pittsburgh	PA	15220	Stan Hasselbusch	412-928-3400	P	509	0.7
JCB Inc.	2000 Bamford Blvd.	Pooler	GA	31322	Helmut Peters	912-447-2000	R	501*	0.3
McNeilus Companies Inc.	113 Conner Rd.	Villa Rica	GA	30180	Micheal Wuest	770-459-6005	S	485*	1.0
Dayton Superior Corp.	7777 Washing. Vlg	Dayton	OH	45459	J.A. Ciccarelli	937-428-6360	P	483	1.6
Ballantine Inc.	840 McKinley St.	Anoka	MN	55303	Joe Newfield	763-427-3959	S	483*	<0.1
Freedom Forge Corp.	500 N Walnut St.	Burnham	PA	17009	Michael Farrell	717-248-4911	S	480*	3.3
Schwing America Inc.	5900 Centerville Rd	Saint Paul	MN	55127	Thomas Anderson	651-429-0999	R	453*	0.6
Madill Equipment US Inc.	552 Hendrickson Dr.	Kalama	WA	98625	Gil Schmunk	360-673-5236	R	397*	<0.1
ESCO Corp.	PO Box 10123	Portland	OR	97296		503-228-2141	R	352*	0.8
Link-Belt Construction Equip.	PO Box 13600	Lexington	KY	40583	Chuck Martz	859-263-5200	R	349*	0.7
Multiquip Inc.	PO Box 6254	Carson	CA	90749	Roger Euliss	310-537-3700	R	317*	0.3
Kuhn Knight Inc.	1501 W 7th Ave.	Brodhead	WI	53520	Thierry Krier	608-897-2131	R	305*	0.2
Caterpillar Paving Products	PO Box 1362	Minneapolis	MN	55440	James Owens	763-425-4100	S	295*	0.6
P and H Mining Equipment Inc.	PO Box 310	Milwaukee	WI	53201	Mark Readinger	414-671-4400	S	272*	0.9
Gunderson Rail Services	4012 NW Front St.	Portland	OR	97210		503-972-5950	S	260*	1.4
A.S.V. Inc.	PO Box 5160	Grand Rapids	MN	55744	Richard Benson	218-327-3434	P	246	0.3
Vermeer Manufacturing Company	PO Box 200	Pella	IA	50219	Mary Andringa	641-628-3141	R	238*	2.0
Coe Manufacturing Company Inc.	PO Box 520	Painesville	OH	44077	Shawn Casey	440-352-9381	R	236*	0.1
Vmv Enterprises Inc.	1300 Kentucky Ave.	Paducah	KY	42003	Robert Pedersen	270-444-4555	R	189*	1.0
Altec Industries Inc.	PO Box 10264	Birmingham	AL	35202		205-991-7733	R	173*	<0.1
Wacker Corp.	N92 Anthony	Menomonee Fls	WI	53051	Christopher Barnard	262-255-0500	R	156*	0.5
Compaction America Inc.	2000 Kentville Rd.	Kewanee	IL	61443	Robert Patterson	309-853-3571	D	134*	0.4
Universal De Cristo	840 25th Ave.	Bellwood	IL	60104	Thomas Fahey	708-544-4255	R	134*	0.3
Charles Machine Works Inc.	PO Box 66	Perry	OK	73077	Ed Malzahn	580-336-4402	R	132*	1.2
Protection Services Inc.	635 Lucknow Rd.	Harrisburg	PA	17110	Douglas Danko	717-236-9307	R	127*	0.1
JH Fletcher and Co.	PO Box 2187	Huntington	WV	25722	Sammons Duncan	304-525-7811	R	120*	0.2
Hoge Warren Zimmermann Co.	40 W Crescentville	Cincinnati	OH	45246	Robert Hoge	513-618-0300	R	112*	<0.1
Psp Industries Inc.	9885 Doerr Ln.	Schertz	TX	78154	Andrew Easton	210-651-9595	R	105*	<0.1
Loram Maintenance of Way Inc.	PO Box 188	Hamel	MN	55340	Paul Wilson	763-478-6014	R	100*	0.2
Portec Rail Products Inc.	PO Box 38250	Pittsburgh	PA	15238	Richard Jarosinsk	412-782-6000	P	99	0.3
Besser Co.	801 Johnson St.	Alpena	MI	49707	Kevin Curtis	989-354-4111	R	99*	0.4
Gardner Asphalt Inc.	PO Box 5449	Tampa	FL	33675	Raymond Hyer	813-248-2101	R	99*	<0.1
Angus Industries Inc.	PO Box 610	Watertown	SD	57201	Robert Kluver	605-886-5681	R	96*	0.3
Neil F Lampson Inc.	PO Box 6510	Kennewick	WA	99336	William Lampson	509-586-0411	R	96*	0.2
Godbersen-Smith Construction	PO Box 151	Ida Grove	IA	51445	Gary Godbersen	712-364-3347	R	90*	0.3
Deere-Hitachi Construct Mach.	PO Box 1187	Kernersville	NC	27285	Al Seeba	336-996-8100	J	89*	0.4
A.S.V. Distribution Inc.	PO Box 5160	Grand Rapids	MN	55744	Gary Lemke	218-327-3434	S	89*	0.2
White Construction Company	PO Box 790	Chiefland	FL	32644	Luther White	352-493-1444	R	83*	0.1
Dynapac	PO Box 615	Schertz	TX	78154	Bruce Trusedale	210-474-5770	R	83*	<0.1
H and L Tooth Co.	PO Box 48	Owasso	OK	74055	Richard Launder	918-272-0951	R	81*	<0.1
Patent Construction Systems	1 Mack Centre Dr.	Paramus	NJ	07652		201-261-5600	D	77*	0.7
Gencor Industries Inc.	5201 N Orng Blssm	Orlando	FL	32810	Marc G. Elliot	407-290-6000	P	75	0.3
Stone Construction Equipment	PO Box 150	Honeoye	NY	14471	Robert Fien	585-229-5141	R	69*	0.2
Braden Carco Gearmatic Winch	PO Box 547	Broken Arrow	OK	74013	Mark Pigott	918-251-8511	D	66*	0.3
Compressed Air Systems Inc.	9303 Stannum St.	Tampa	FL	33619	Richard Hall	813-626-8177	R	62*	<0.1
TMF Center Inc.	300 W Washington	Williamsport	IN	47993	Lloyd Gowen	765-762-1000	R	62*	0.2
Ellcon-National Inc.	PO Box 9377	Greenville	SC	29604		864-277-5000	R	61*	0.3
P.A. Landers Inc.	PO Box 217	Hanover	MA	02339	Preston Landers	781-826-8818	R	60*	<0.1
Kershaw Manufacturing Co.	PO Box 244100	Montgomery	AL	36124		334-215-1000	S	60*	0.3
Allied Systems Co.	21433 SW Oregon	Sherwood	OR	97140		503-625-2560	R	59*	0.3

Source: *Ward's Business Directory of U.S. Private and Public Companies*, Volumes 1 and 2, 2008. The company type code used is as follows: P - Public, R - Private, S - Subsidiary, D - Division, J - Joint Venture, A - Affiliate, G - Group. Sales are in millions of dollars, employees are in thousands. An asterisk (*) indicates an estimated sales volume. The symbol < stands for 'less than'. Company names and addresses are truncated, in some cases, to fit into the available space.

MATERIALS CONSUMED

Material	Quantity	Delivered Cost ($ million)
Metal bolts, nuts, screws, and other screw machine products	(X)	17.5
Fluid power products	(X)	67.8
Forgings	(X)	56.9
Other fabricated metal products (exc. fluid power products and forgings)	(X)	80.5
Iron and steel castings (rough and semifinished)	(X)	286.0
Steel bars, bar shapes, and plates (exc. castings, forgings, fabr. metal products)	(X)	56.1
Steel sheet and strip (including tinplate)	(X)	14.3
Steel structural shapes and sheet piling (exc. castings, forgings, fabr. metal products)	(X)	(D)
All other steel shapes and forms (exc. castings, forgings, fabr. metal products)	(X)	24.7
Nonferrous shapes and forms	(X)	14.4
Nonferrous (aluminum, copper, etc.) castings (rough and semifinished)	(X)	18.0
Roller bearings (mounted or unmounted)	(X)	53.4
Plain bearings and bushings	(X)	8.2
Mechanical speed changers, gears, and industrial high-speed drives	(X)	25.7
Railway electrical control equipment	(X)	(D)
Brake equipment, truck assemblies, and other coupling devices, etc.	(X)	181.0
All other materials, components, parts, containers, and supplies	(X)	1,635.4
Materials, ingredients, containers, and supplies, nsk	(X)	513.0

Source: 2002 Economic Census. Explanation of symbols used: (D): Withheld to avoid disclosure of competitive data; na: Not available; (S): Withheld because statistical norms were not met; (X): Not applicable; (Z): Less than half the unit shown; nec: Not elsewhere classified; nsk: Not specified by kind; - : zero; p : 10-19 percent estimated; q : 20-29 percent estimated.

PRODUCT SHARE DETAILS

Product or Product Class Shipments	Mil. $	Product or Product Class Shipments	Mil. $
RAILROAD EQUIPMENT	6,319.2	for all railcars, and other work and service railway vehicles (excluding locomotive cranes)	973.9
Locomotives, both new and rebuilt, and parts	**2,452.6**	Railway maintenance of way equipment (rail layers,	
Locomotives, both new and rebuilt, and parts	2,439.8	ballast spreaders, etc.), excluding rail cars	109.4
Diesel-electric locomotives, new and rebuilt	2,057.9	Other work and service railroad vehicles (excluding	
Parts for locomotives, except fuel lubricating and		locomotive cranes)	(D)
cooling medium pumps	381.9	Airbrake equipment for railroad and streetcars	(D)
Locomotives, both new and rebuilt, and parts, nsk	12.8	Other brake equipment for railroad and streetcars	40.4
New freight train and passenger train cars, excluding parts	**1,269.1**	Hooks and other coupling devices, buffers, and parts	
Rebuilt street, subway, trolley, and rapid transit cars, and parts	**2,491.4**	thereof for railroad and streetcars	81.1
Rebuilt street, subway, trolley, and rapid transit cars, and		Other railroad and streetcar parts and accessories,	
parts	1,502.5	including truck assemblies	606.6
Rebuilt passenger and freight train cars	564.5	Parts for railway maintenance of way equipment	62.0
Rebuilt self-propelled and nonself-propelled streetcars,		Street, subway, trolley, and rapid transit cars, all rebuilt	
subway cars, and rapid transit cars	938.0	railcars, and parts for all railcars, nsk	14.9
Railway maintenance of way equipment and parts, parts		**Railroad equipment, nsk, total**	**106.0**

Source: 2002 Economic Census. The values are product shipments in millions of dollars for 2002. Total product shipments may be lower or higher than industry shipments. See Introduction for a full discussion. Values of indented subcategories are summed in the main heading(s). The symbol (D) appears when data are withheld to prevent disclosure of competitive information. The abbreviation nsk stands for 'not specified by kind' and nec for 'not elsewhere classified'. A dash (-) means zero.

INPUTS AND OUTPUTS FOR RAILROAD ROLLING STOCK MANUFACTURING

Economic Sector or Industry Providing Inputs	%	Sector	Economic Sector or Industry Buying Outputs	%	Sector
Compensation of employees	21.9		Private fixed investment	52.4	
Railroad rolling stock	9.4	Manufg.	Rail transportation	16.5	Util.
Management of companies & enterprises	6.6	Services	Exports of goods & services	10.8	Cap Inv
Plate work & fabricated structural products	6.3	Manufg.	Railroad rolling stock	8.8	Manufg.
Wholesale trade	4.7	Trade	S/L govt. invest., other	7.4	S/L Govt
Relay & industrial controls	3.1	Manufg.	Construction machinery	1.0	Manufg.
Iron & steel mills & ferroalloys	2.4	Manufg.	S/L govt. passenger transit	0.8	S/L Govt
Lighting fixtures	2.1	Manufg.	Scenic & sightseeing transport & related services	0.8	Util.
Springs & wire products	2.0	Manufg.	Federal government, investment, national defense	0.6	Fed Govt
Primary smelting & refining of copper	1.7	Manufg.	Wholesale trade	0.2	Trade
Textile product mills, nec	1.4	Manufg.	Coal	0.1	Mining
Motors & generators	1.4	Manufg.	Federal government, investment, nondefense	0.1	Fed Govt
Fluid power process machinery	1.3	Manufg.	Residential permanent site structures	0.1	Construct.
Paints & coatings	1.2	Manufg.			
Software publishers	0.9	Services			
Ball & roller bearings	0.9	Manufg.			
Switchgear & switchboard apparatus	0.8	Manufg.			
Truck transportation	0.8	Util.			
Noncomparable imports	0.8	Foreign			
Forging, stamping, & sintering, nec	0.8	Manufg.			
Rubber & plastics hose & belting	0.7	Manufg.			
Scientific research & development services	0.7	Services			
Lessors of nonfinancial assets	0.6	Fin/R.E.			

Continued on next page.

INPUTS AND OUTPUTS FOR RAILROAD ROLLING STOCK MANUFACTURING - Continued

Economic Sector or Industry Providing Inputs	%	Sector	Economic Sector or Industry Buying Outputs	%	Sector
Securities, commodity contracts, investments	0.6	Fin/R.E.			
Speed changers, industrial high-speed drives, & gears	0.5	Manufg.			
Turned products & screws, nuts, & bolts	0.5	Manufg.			
Ferrous metal foundries	0.5	Manufg.			
Semiconductors & related devices	0.5	Manufg.			
Rubber products, nec	0.4	Manufg.			
Printed circuit assemblies (electronic assemblies)	0.4	Manufg.			
Machine shops	0.4	Manufg.			
Architectural, engineering, & related services	0.4	Services			
Valve & fittings other than plumbing	0.4	Manufg.			
Power generation & supply	0.4	Util.			
Paperboard containers	0.3	Manufg.			
Real estate	0.3	Fin/R.E.			
Automotive equipment rental & leasing	0.3	Fin/R.E.			
Nonferrous metal foundries	0.3	Manufg.			
Coating, engraving, heat treating & allied activities	0.3	Manufg.			
Advertising & related services	0.3	Services			
Telecommunications	0.2	Services			
Food services & drinking places	0.2	Services			
Custom roll forming	0.2	Manufg.			
Natural gas distribution	0.2	Util.			
Taxes on production & imports, less subsidies	0.2				
Air transportation	0.2	Util.			
Mechanical power transmission equipment	0.2	Manufg.			
Legal services	0.2	Services			
Data processing, hosting, & related services	0.2	Services			
Warehousing & storage	0.2	Util.			
Commercial & industrial machinery rental & leasing	0.2	Fin/R.E.			
Accounting, tax preparation, bookkeeping, & payroll	0.2	Services			
Motor vehicle parts	0.1	Manufg.			
General purpose machinery, nec	0.1	Manufg.			
Hotels & motels, including casino hotels	0.1	Services			
Services to buildings & dwellings	0.1	Services			
Rail transportation	0.1	Util.			
Maintenance/repair of nonresidential structures	0.1	Construct.			
Monetary authorities/depository credit intermediation	0.1	Fin/R.E.			
Other computer related services, including facilities	0.1	Services			
Abrasive products	0.1	Manufg.			

Source: Benchmark Input-Output Accounts for the U.S. Economy, 2002, U.S. Department of Commerce, Washington, D.C., January 2008: The abbreviation nec stands for 'not elsewhere classified'.

OCCUPATIONS EMPLOYED BY RAILROAD ROLLING STOCK MANUFACTURING

Occupation	% of Total 2006	Change to 2016	Occupation	% of Total 2006	Change to 2016
Welders, cutters, solderers, & brazers	17.4	-11.9	Maintenance & repair workers, general	2.3	-17.2
Rail car repairers	5.9	-17.2	Mechanical engineers	1.9	-17.2
Team assemblers	5.6	-17.2	Multiple machine tool operators & tenders	1.8	-8.9
Machinists	4.3	-13.0	Industrial truck & tractor operators	1.6	-25.4
First-line supervisors/managers of production workers	4.2	-17.2	Laborers & freight, stock, & material movers, hand	1.6	-25.4
Inspectors, testers, sorters, samplers, & weighers	3.6	-21.9	Computer-controlled machine tool operators	1.4	-8.9
Painters, transportation equipment	3.2	-17.2	General & operations managers	1.0	-25.4
Helpers--Production workers	3.1	-17.2			

Source: Industry-Occupation Matrix, Bureau of Labor Statistics, December 4, 2007. These data are reported based on 4-digit NAICS categories but have been matched to corresponding 6-digit NAICS industry codes. The change reported for each occupation to the year 2016 is a percent of growth or decline as estimated by the Bureau of Labor Statistics. The abbreviation nec stands for 'not elsewhere classified'.

LOCATION BY STATE AND REGIONAL CONCENTRATION

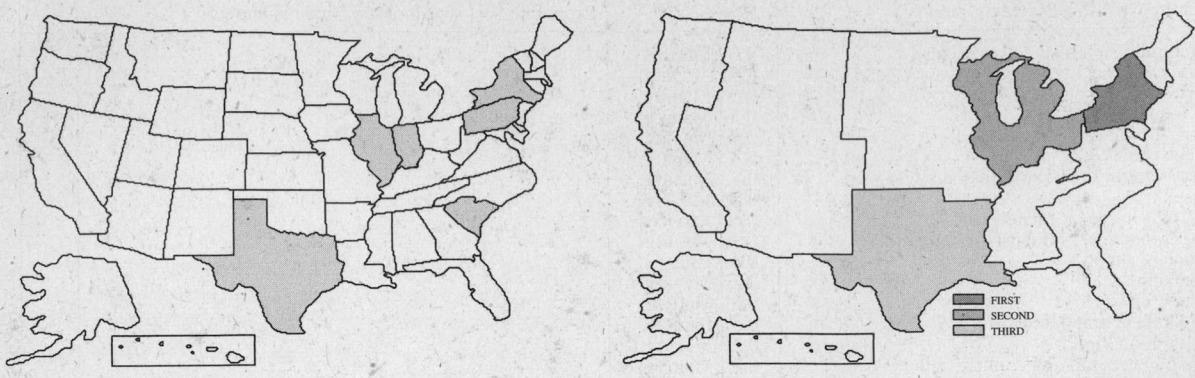

INDUSTRY DATA BY STATE

| State | Establish-ments | Shipments | | | Employment | | | | Cost as % of Shipments | Investment per Employee ($) |
		Total ($ mil)	% of U.S.	Per Establ.	Total Number	% of U.S.	Per Establ.	Wages ($/hour)		
Pennsylvania	30	2,772.8	35.6	92,427.9	9,080	35.9	303	24.56	52.9	5,069
Illinois	32	1,705.9	21.9	53,309.4	3,961	15.7	124	24.06	57.0	3,014
New York	14	914.0	11.7	65,283.9	2,029	8.0	145	16.37	48.5	7,960
South Carolina	9	272.8	3.5	30,307.9	1,047	4.1	116	17.03	49.2	12,819
Indiana	6	173.1	2.2	28,842.0	1,125	4.4	188	17.18	56.4	7,002
Texas	9	171.7	2.2	19,075.6	772	3.1	86	14.51	68.3	3,547

Source: 2002 *Economic Census*. The states are in descending order of shipments or establishments (if shipment data are missing for the majority). The symbol (D) appears when data are withheld to prevent disclosure of competitive information. States marked with (D) are sorted by number of establishments. A dash (-) indicates that the data element cannot be calculated. Data may not show all states active in the NAICS category. All data available at the time of publication are shown.

NAICS 336611 - SHIP BUILDING AND REPAIRING

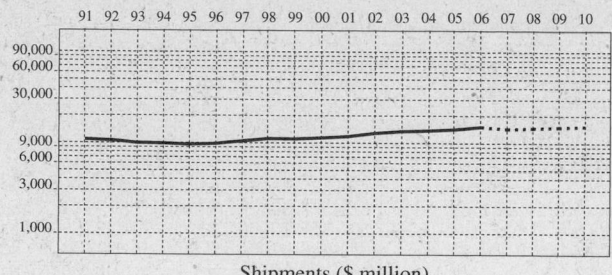

Shipments ($ million)

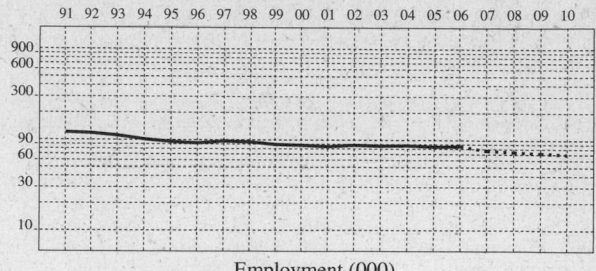

Employment (000)

GENERAL STATISTICS

Year	Companies	Establishments Total	Establishments with 20 or more employees	Employment Total (000)	Employment Production Workers (000)	Employment Hours (Mil)	Compensation Payroll ($ mil)	Compensation Wages ($/hr)	Production Cost of Materials	Production Value Added by Manufacture	Production Value of Shipments	Capital Invest.
1991		551	269	120.8	90.1	183.9	3,679.8	12.97	4,494.7	6,354.2	10,848.8	172.2
1992	562	598	267	118.3	87.1	176.8	3,624.1	12.98	4,065.2	6,543.2	10,608.3	128.4
1993		613	269	111.5	81.9	159.0	3,362.6	13.45	4,006.8	5,957.2	9,964.0	155.8
1994		582	243	101.5	75.6	151.7	3,311.1	13.98	4,103.7	5,760.3	9,864.0	140.7
1995		561	246	95.4	70.5	139.0	3,221.8	14.76	3,866.3	5,719.6	9,585.9	231.6
1996		628	251	92.1	68.4	137.9	3,175.2	14.39	4,364.7	5,446.7	9,811.3	241.6
1997	648	696	276	96.5	71.2	142.8	3,338.4	15.04	4,286.7	6,154.7	10,441.4	243.7
1998		699	281	94.8	67.3	135.4	3,347.5	14.92	4,414.3	6,729.0	11,143.2	248.8
1999		681	254	89.0	61.0	124.7	3,336.6	15.80	4,742.2	6,328.8	11,071.0	285.9
2000		682	261	87.5	64.7	128.7	3,435.8	17.72	5,055.9	6,324.2	11,380.1	414.3
2001		675	261	84.5	63.5	127.2	3,439.5	18.26	5,364.7	6,438.1	11,802.8	328.2
2002	586	639	224	87.7	62.2	116.4	3,628.4	19.49	4,365.6	8,449.0	12,814.6	279.2
2003		620	234	86.2	61.7	119.0	3,692.0	19.89	4,805.8	8,679.7	13,485.5	238.3
2004		640	236	87.1	60.4	117.8	3,772.6	19.59	5,132.7	8,573.3	13,706.0	176.6
2005		642	226	84.4	58.5	117.3	3,790.3	19.78	5,454.6	8,736.3	14,190.9	221.4
2006		679P	233P	85.3	59.2	116.3	4,042.8	21.83	5,764.9	9,337.5	15,102.4	170.7
2007		685P	231P	76.4P	52.6P	102.1P	3,762.3P	21.60P	5,480.3P	8,876.5P	14,356.7P	274.9P
2008		691P	228P	74.2P	50.7P	98.0P	3,791.7P	22.19P	5,603.4P	9,076.0P	14,679.4P	280.3P
2009		696P	226P	71.9P	48.8P	93.9P	3,821.1P	22.78P	5,726.6P	9,275.5P	15,002.1P	285.6P
2010		702P	223P	69.7P	46.9P	89.8P	3,850.5P	23.38P	5,849.8P	9,475.0P	15,324.8P	290.9P

Sources: 1992, 1997, 2002 *Economic Census*; other years, up to 2006, are from the *Annual Survey of Manufactures*. Establishment counts for non-Census years are from *County Business Patterns*; 1997 and 2002 values are from the 1997 and 2002 censuses respectively, reported in the Federal Government's NAICS format. Other years were originally reported in equivalent SIC format. 'P's show projections by the editors.

INDICES OF CHANGE

Year	Companies	Establishments Total	Establishments with 20 or more employees	Employment Total (000)	Employment Production Workers (000)	Employment Hours (Mil)	Compensation Payroll ($ mil)	Compensation Wages ($/hr)	Production Cost of Materials	Production Value Added by Manufacture	Production Value of Shipments	Capital Invest.
1992	96	94	119	135	140	152	100	67	93	77	83	46
1997	111	109	123	110	114	123	92	77	98	73	81	87
2001		106	117	96	102	109	95	94	123	76	92	118
2002	100	100	100	100	100	100	100	100	100	100	100	100
2003		97	104	98	99	102	102	102	110	103	105	85
2004		100	105	99	97	101	104	101	118	101	107	63
2005		100	101	96	94	101	104	101	125	103	111	79
2006		106P	104P	97	95	100	111	112	132	111	118	61
2007		107P	103P	87P	85P	88P	104P	111P	126P	105P	112P	98P
2008		108P	102P	85P	82P	84P	105P	114P	128P	107P	115P	100P
2009		109P	101P	82P	78P	81P	105P	117P	131P	110P	117P	102P
2010		110P	100P	79P	75P	77P	106P	120P	134P	112P	120P	104P

Sources: Same as General Statistics. Values reflect change from the base year, 2002. Values above 100 mean greater than 2002, values below 100 mean less than 2002, and the values of 100 in other years means the same as 2002. 'P's show projections by the editors.

SELECTED RATIOS

For 2002	Avg. of All Manufact.	Analyzed Industry	Index	For 2002	Avg. of All Manufact.	Analyzed Industry	Index
Employees per Establishment	42	137	327	Value Added per Production Worker	182,367	135,836	74
Payroll per Establishment	1,639,184	5,678,247	346	Cost per Establishment	5,769,015	6,831,925	118
Payroll per Employee	39,053	41,373	106	Cost per Employee	137,446	49,779	36
Production Workers per Establishment	30	97	330	Cost per Production Worker	195,506	70,186	36
Wages per Establishment	694,845	3,550,291	511	Shipments per Establishment	11,158,348	20,054,147	180
Wages per Production Worker	23,548	36,473	155	Shipments per Employee	265,847	146,119	55
Hours per Production Worker	1,980	1,871	95	Shipments per Production Worker	378,144	206,023	54
Wages per Hour	11.89	19.49	164	Investment per Establishment	361,338	436,933	121
Value Added per Establishment	5,381,325	13,222,222	246	Investment per Employee	8,609	3,184	37
Value Added per Employee	128,210	96,340	75	Investment per Production Worker	12,245	4,489	37

Sources: Same as General Statistics. The 'Average of All Manufacturing' column represents the average of all manufacturing industries reported for the most recent complete year available. The Index shows the relationship between the Average and the Analyzed Industry. For example, 100 means that they are equal; 500 that the Analyzed Industry is five times the average; 50 means that the Analyzed Industry is half the national average. The abbreviation 'na' is used to show that data are 'not available'. Ratios shown for 2002, the last complete census year.

1543

LEADING COMPANIES   Number shown: **75**   Total sales ($ mil): **43,884**   Total employment (000): **158.6**

Company Name	Address				CEO Name	Phone	Co. Type	Sales ($ mil)	Empl. (000)
General Dynamics Corp.	2941 Fairview Park	Falls Church	VA	22042	Nicholas D. Chabraja	703-876-3000	P	27,240	83.5
Manitowoc Company Inc.	PO Box 66	Manitowoc	WI	54221		920-684-4410	P	4,005	10.5
Trinity Industries Inc.	2525 Stemmons	Dallas	TX	75207		214-631-4420	P	3,833	14.4
Newport News Shipbuilding Inc.	4101 Washington	Newport News	VA	23607		757-380-2000	S	2,316*	19.0
National Steel & Shipbuilding	PO Box 85278	San Diego	CA	92186	Fred Harris	619-544-3400	S	1,819*	5.0
Tidewater Inc.	601 Poydras St.	New Orleans	LA	70130		504-568-1010	P	1,125	8.0
American Commercial Lines	1701 E Market St.	Jeffersonville	IN	47130	Mark R. Holden	812-288-0100	P	943	2.8
Gunderson Rail Services	4012 NW Front St.	Portland	OR	97210		503-972-5950	S	260*	1.4
Bollinger Shipyards Inc.	PO Box 250	Lockport	LA	70374	Donald Bollinger	985-532-2554	R	222*	0.6
Manitowoc Marine Group L.L.C.	1600 Ely Street	Marinette	WI	54143	Robert P. Herre	715-735-9341	S	209*	0.7
Keppel Amfels Inc.	PO Box 3107	Brownsville	TX	78523	C Ho	956-831-8220	R	183*	1.5
Todd Shipyards Corp.	PO Box 3806	Seattle	WA	98124	Patrick W. Hodgson	206-623-1635	P	126	0.8
Conrad Industries Inc.	1100 Brashear Ave.	Morgan City	LA	70381	John P. Conrad Jr.	985-702-0195	P	122	0.5
B.A. E Sys Norfolk Ship Repair	PO Box 2100	Norfolk	VA	23501	William Clifford	757-494-4000	R	109*	1.0
Metro Machine Corp.	PO Box 1860	Norfolk	VA	23501	Paul Reason	757-543-6801	R	101*	0.5
Diversified Group Inc.	PO Box 23890	New Orleans	LA	70183	Danny Hughes	504-733-2800	R	85*	0.3
Fountain Powerboat Industries	PO Box 457	Washington	NC	27889	Reginald Fountain	252-672-5419	P	69	0.3
Detyens Shipyards Inc.	1670 Drydock Ave.	N Charleston	SC	29405	D. Loy Stewart, Jr.	843-308-8000	R	66*	0.8
Mc Ginnis Inc.	PO Box 534	South Point	OH	45680	C. Douglas Mc Ginn	740-377-4391	R	61*	0.2
US Marine Inc.	PO Box 307	Bayou La Batre	AL	36509	Brett Dungan	251-824-4151	R	60*	<0.1
North American Shipbuilding	PO Box 580	Larose	LA	70373	Gary Chouest	985-693-4072	R	58*	0.5
Atlantic Marine Alabama L.L.C.	PO Box 3202	Mobile	AL	36652		251-690-7100	R	54*	0.5
Tecnico Corp.	831 Industrial Ave.	Chesapeake	VA	23324	Michael Torrech	757-545-4013	R	52*	0.4
Caddell Dry Dock and Repair	PO Box 327	Staten Island	NY	10310	John Caddell	718-442-2112	R	51*	0.3
Gulf Marine Repair Corp.	1200 Sertoma Dr.	Tampa	FL	33605	Aaron W. Hendry	813-247-3153	R	51*	0.2
Key West Boats Inc.	PO Box 399	Ridgeville	SC	29472	William Holseberg	843-873-0112	R	40*	0.1
Quality Shipyards L.L.C.	PO Box 1817	Houma	LA	70361		985-876-4846	S	38*	0.3
Marine Hydraulics Int'l	543 E Indian River	Norfolk	VA	23523	Gary Brandt	757-545-6400	R	29*	<0.1
Fraser Shipyards Inc.	PO Box 997	Superior	WI	54880		715-394-7787	R	28*	0.1
Cascade General Inc.	PO Box 4367	Portland	OR	97208	Frank Foti	503-285-1111	R	27*	0.3
Tampa Bay Shipbuilding/Repair	1130 McClosky	Tampa	FL	33605	Walter Hartley	813-248-9310	R	27*	0.3
Dakota Creek Industries Inc.	PO Box 218	Anacortes	WA	98221	Richard Nelson	360-293-9575	R	27*	0.2
Pacific Ship Repair & Fabric.	PO Box 13428	San Diego	CA	92170	Gary Thomas	619-232-3200	R	25*	0.3
Derecktor, Robert E. Inc.	311 E Boston Post	Mamaroneck	NY	10543	Paul Derecktor	914-698-5020	R	22*	0.1
Twin Brothers Marine L.L.C.	PO Box 2426	Morgan City	LA	70381		337-923-4981	R	22*	0.2
Lyon Shipyard Inc.	PO Box 2180	Norfolk	VA	23501	George Lyon	757-622-4661	R	21*	0.2
Swiftship Shipbuilders L.L.C.	PO Box 2869	Morgan City	LA	70381	Calvin Leleux	985-384-1700	R	20*	0.2
B.A. E Systems Hawaii Shipyard	3049 Ualena St.	Honolulu	HI	96819	Roger Kubischta	808-836-7776	R	18*	0.2
Metal Trades Inc.	PO Box 129	Hollywood	SC	29449	Russell Corbin	843-889-6442	R	18*	0.2
B.A. E San Fran. Ship Repair	PO Box 7644	San Francisco	CA	94120	Joseph O'Rourke	415-861-7447	R	16*	0.2
Leevac Industries L.L.C.	PO Box 1190	Jennings	LA	70546		337-824-2210	R	16*	0.2
Main Iron Works L.L.C.	PO Box 1918	Houma	LA	70361		985-876-6302	R	14*	0.1
Columbia Group Inc.	1201 M St. SE	Washington	DC	20003	Norman Witbeck	202-546-1435	R	14*	<0.1
Buck Kreihs Marine Repair	PO Box 53305	New Orleans	LA	70153	William Baraldi	504-524-7681	R	13*	0.1
Raffield Fisheries Inc.	PO Box 309	Port Saint Joe	FL	32457	Carl Raffield	850-229-8229	R	13*	<0.1
Christensen Shipyards Ltd.	4400 SE Columbia	Vancouver	WA	98661	Joe Foggia	360-695-3238	R	12*	0.2
Fetzer W H and Sons Mfg.	PO Box 45	Plymouth	OH	44865	William Fetzer	419-687-8237	R	12*	<0.1
JM Martinac Shipbuilding Corp.	401 E 15th St.	Tacoma	WA	98421	Joseph Martinac	253-572-4005	R	11*	0.1
Marine Construction and Design	4259 22nd Ave. W	Seattle	WA	98199	Peter Schmidt	206-285-3200	R	11*	0.1
Owl International Inc.	4701 S 16th St.	Philadelphia	PA	19112		215-897-5976	R	11*	0.1
Robert E Derecktor Inc.	311 E Boston Post	Mamaroneck	NY	10543	Paul Derecktor	914-698-5020	R	11*	<0.1
Alaska Ship and Drydock Inc.	PO Box 9470	Ketchikan	AK	99901	Randall Johnson	907-225-7199	R	10*	<0.1
Pacific Marine and Supply Co.	841 Bishop St.	Honolulu	HI	96813	Steven Loui	808-531-7001	R	10*	<0.1
Marisco Ltd.	91-607 Malakole St.	Kapolei	HI	96707	Alfred Anawati	808-682-1333	R	9*	0.1
Marine Industrial Fabrication	PO Box 9218	New Iberia	LA	70562	R Burton	337-369-7004	R	9*	<0.1
Zidell Marine Corp.	3121 SW Moody	Portland	OR	97239	Jay Zidell	503-228-8691	R	9*	<0.1
Offshore Express Inc.	PO Box 2666	Houma	LA	70361	Harlan Belanger	985-868-5950	R	8*	<0.1
Pacific Seacraft Corp.	1301 E Orngthorpe	Fullerton	CA	92831	Geoffrey Emery	714-879-1610	R	8*	<0.1
Larson Al Boat Shop	1046 S Seaside Ave.	San Pedro	CA	90731		310-514-4100	R	8*	<0.1
Navatek Ltd.	PO Box 29816	Honolulu	HI	96820	Steven Loui	808-531-7001	S	7*	<0.1
York Goltens-New Corp.	160 Van Brunt St.	Brooklyn	NY	11231	Norman Golten	718-855-7200	R	7*	<0.1
B and A Marine Company Inc.	75 Huntington St.	Brooklyn	NY	11231	Bill Crokos	718-875-6700	R	6*	<0.1
St Augustine Marine Canvas	164 Nix Boat Yard	Saint Augustine	FL	32084	Joseph Bowman	904-826-3591	R	6*	<0.1
B & D Marine & Indust. Boilers	3567 Meeting St. Rd	N Charleston	SC	29405	Phyllis Faircloth	843-747-0951	R	6*	<0.1
Hendry Corp.	PO Box 75036	Tampa	FL	33675	Aaron Hendry	813-241-9206	R	5*	<0.1
Marine Industries Northwest	PO Box 1275	Tacoma	WA	98401	Don Slater	253-627-9136	R	5*	<0.1
Navtec Inc.	351 New Whitfield	Guilford	CT	06437		203-458-3163	R	5*	<0.1
Newbrook Machine Corp.	PO Box 231	Silver Creek	NY	14136	Christopher Lanski	716-934-2644	R	5*	<0.1
Treadwell Corp.	PO Box 458	Thomaston	CT	06787	John Johnson	860-283-8251	R	5*	<0.1
Weedon Engineering Co.	5105 Buffalo Ave.	Jacksonville	FL	32206	James Weedon	904-355-8411	R	4*	<0.1
Excelco Developments Inc.	PO Box 230	Silver Creek	NY	14136	Christopher Lanski	716-934-2651	R	4*	<0.1
Rigdon Marine L.L.C.	100 James Dr., 250	St. Rose	LA	70087	Larry Rigdon	713-236-9100	R	4*	<0.1
Puglia Engineering Inc.	201 Harris Ave.	Bellingham	WA	98225		360-647-0080	R	4*	<0.1
Intracoastal City Dry Dock	18938 Live Oak Rd.	Abbeville	LA	70510	Lewis Faciane	337-893-4184	R	3*	<0.1
Akerue Industries L.L.C.	90 McMillen Rd.	Antioch	IL	60002		847-395-3300	R	3*	<0.1

Source: Ward's Business Directory of U.S. Private and Public Companies, Volumes 1 and 2, 2008. The company type code used is as follows: P - Public, R - Private, S - Subsidiary, D - Division, J - Joint Venture, A - Affiliate, G - Group. Sales are in millions of dollars, employees are in thousands. An asterisk (*) indicates an estimated sales volume. The symbol < stands for 'less than'. Company names and addresses are truncated, in some cases, to fit into the available space.

MATERIALS CONSUMED

Material	Quantity	Delivered Cost ($ million)
Diesel and semidiesel engines	(X)	73.6
Steam engines and turbines	(X)	(D)
Integral horsepower electric motors and generators (1 hp or more)	(X)	13.3
Engine electrical equipment (incl. spark plugs, magnetos, generators, starters, etc.)	(X)	11.3
Mechanical speed changers, gears, and industrial high-speed drives	(X)	25.7
Industrial controls	(X)	13.9
Fluid power pumps, motors, and hydrostatic transmissions	(X)	81.0
Fluid power valves (hydraulic and pneumatic)	(X)	52.9
Fluid power cylinders and rotary actuators (hydraulic and pneumatic)	(X)	(D)
Fluid power hose, tube fittings, and assemblies (hydraulic and pneumatic)	(X)	26.6
Fluid power filters (hydraulic and pneumatic)	(X)	2.0
Other transportation related fluid power products, hydraulic and pneumatic	(X)	9.7
Metal boilers, condensers, and parts (excluding forgings)	(X)	(D)
Metal bolts, nuts, screws, and other screw machine products	(X)	18.0
Other fabricated metal products (exc. fluid power products and forgings)	(X)	41.4
Forgings	(X)	5.3
Aluminum and aluminum-base alloy forgings	(X)	109.6
Castings, rough and semifinished	(X)	9.8
Steel bars, bar shapes, and plates (exc. castings, forgings, fabr. metal products)	(X)	139.5
Steel sheet and strip (including tinplate)	(X)	12.5
Steel structural shapes and sheet piling (exc. castings, forgings, fabr. metal products)	(X)	7.2
All other steel shapes and forms (exc. castings, forgings, fabr. metal products)	(X)	7.7
Aluminum and aluminum-base alloy sheet, plate, foil, and welded tubing	(X)	16.7
Other aluminum and aluminum-base alloy shapes and forms (exc. castings, forgings, fabr. metal products)	(X)	0.8
Other nonferrous shapes and forms (exc. castings, forgings, fabricated metal products)	(X)	2.6
Construction machinery and parts (shipwinches, cranes, derricks, etc.)	(X)	(D)
Paints, varnishes, stains, lacquers, shellacs, japans, enamels, etc.	(X)	38.9
Lumber, dressed	(X)	12.0
All other materials, components, parts, containers, and supplies	(X)	1,159.4
Materials, ingredients, containers, and supplies, nsk	(X)	1,815.7

Source: 2002 *Economic Census*. Explanation of symbols used: (D): Withheld to avoid disclosure of competitive data; na: Not available; (S): Withheld because statistical norms were not met; (X): Not applicable; (Z): Less than half the unit shown; nec: Not elsewhere classified; nsk: Not specified by kind; - : zero; p : 10-19 percent estimated; q : 20-29 percent estimated.

PRODUCT SHARE DETAILS

Product or Product Class Shipments	Mil. $	Product or Product Class Shipments	Mil. $
SHIP BUILDING AND REPAIRING	12,315.3	the Coast Guard, new construction	305.4
Nonpropelled ships and barges, new construction	**755.9**	Nonmilitary self-propelled commercial fishing trawlers, new construction	46.7
Nonpropelled ships and barges, new construction	754.8	Other nonmilitary self-propelled commercial fishing vessels and seiners, new construction	20.8
Military and nonmilitary nonpropelled barges, all types, new construction	466.4	Nonmilitary self-propelled tugboats and towboats and integrated tug-barge combinations, new construction	193.9
Military and nonmilitary nonpropelled drilling-production platforms, new construction	253.2	Nonmilitary self-propelled ferryboats, new construction	65.5
Other military and nonmilitary nonpropelled ships (including dredges and floating docks), new construction	35.2	Nonmilitary self-propelled support vessels for offshore drilling and mining, new construction	267.5
Nonpropelled ships, new construction, nsk	1.1	Other nonmilitary ships, including container and trailer ships, dry bulk carriers, and tankers	615.0
Military, self-propelled ships, including combat ships, troop transport vessels, fleet auxiliaries, and service craft, new construction	**(D)**	**Ship repair, military**	**(D)**
		Ship repair, nonmilitary	**615.9**
Nonmilitary self-propelled ships, new construction	**1,514.9**	Ship conversions and reconversions, nonmilitary	180.9
Nonmilitary self-propelled yachts, 65 ft or more in length requiring a professional crew as specified by		All other ship repairs, nonmilitary	435.0
		Ship building and repairing, nsk, total	**434.1**

Source: 2002 *Economic Census*. The values are product shipments in millions of dollars for 2002. Total product shipments may be lower or higher than industry shipments. See Introduction for a full discussion. Values of indented subcategories are summed in the main heading(s). The symbol (D) appears when data are withheld to prevent disclosure of competitive information. The abbreviation nsk stands for 'not specified by kind' and nec for 'not elsewhere classified'. A dash (-) means zero.

INPUTS AND OUTPUTS FOR SHIP BUILDING AND REPAIRING

Economic Sector or Industry Providing Inputs	%	Sector	Economic Sector or Industry Buying Outputs	%	Sector
Compensation of employees	38.5		Federal government, investment, national defense	50.3	Fed Govt
Engine equipment, nec	5.3	Manufg.	Private fixed investment	19.0	
Wholesale trade	3.6	Trade	General Federal government services, defense	13.9	Fed Govt
Management of companies & enterprises	3.4	Services	Exports of goods & services	7.4	Cap Inv
Lessors of nonfinancial assets	2.3	Fin/R.E.	Water transportation	6.6	Util.
Iron & steel mills & ferroalloys	2.1	Manufg.	Fishing	0.9	Agric.
Valve & fittings other than plumbing	1.9	Manufg.	Federal government, investment, nondefense	0.8	Fed Govt
Management, scientific, & technical consulting	1.8	Services	S/L govt. invest., other	0.6	S/L Govt
Scientific research & development services	1.6	Services	Scenic & sightseeing transport & related services	0.3	Util.

Continued on next page.

INPUTS AND OUTPUTS FOR SHIP BUILDING AND REPAIRING - Continued

Economic Sector or Industry Providing Inputs	%	Sector	Economic Sector or Industry Buying Outputs	%	Sector
Forging, stamping, & sintering, nec	1.5	Manufg.	Ship building & repairing	0.2	Manufg.
Securities, commodity contracts, investments	1.5	Fin/R.E.			
Turbines & turbine generator set units	1.5	Manufg.			
Mechanical power transmission equipment	1.3	Manufg.			
Architectural, engineering, & related services	1.2	Services			
Unlaminated plastics profile shapes	1.1	Manufg.			
Monetary authorities/depository credit intermediation	1.0	Fin/R.E.			
Plate work & fabricated structural products	0.9	Manufg.			
Plastics products, nec	0.8	Manufg.			
Search, detection, & navigation instruments	0.8	Manufg.			
Professional, scientific, technical services, nec	0.8	Services			
Business support services	0.8	Services			
Fluid power process machinery	0.7	Manufg.			
Data processing, hosting, & related services	0.7	Services			
Power generation & supply	0.7	Util.			
Legal services	0.7	Services			
Employment services	0.6	Services			
Paints & coatings	0.6	Manufg.			
Specialized design services	0.6	Services			
Pressed & blown glass & glassware, nec	0.6	Manufg.			
Taxes on production & imports, less subsidies	0.6				
Software publishers	0.6	Services			
Food services & drinking places	0.5	Services			
Semiconductors & related devices	0.5	Manufg.			
Construction machinery	0.5	Manufg.			
Truck transportation	0.5	Util.			
Printed circuit assemblies (electronic assemblies)	0.5	Manufg.			
Advertising & related services	0.5	Services			
Plastics packaging materials, film & sheet	0.5	Manufg.			
Accounting, tax preparation, bookkeeping, & payroll	0.5	Services			
Real estate	0.4	Fin/R.E.			
Speed changers, industrial high-speed drives, & gears	0.4	Manufg.			
Hotels & motels, including casino hotels	0.4	Services			
Turned products & screws, nuts, & bolts	0.4	Manufg.			
Other computer related services, including facilities	0.4	Services			
Telecommunications	0.3	Services			
Services to buildings & dwellings	0.3	Services			
Maintenance/repair of nonresidential structures	0.3	Construct.			
Warehousing & storage	0.3	Util.			
Nondepository credit intermediation activities	0.3	Fin/R.E.			
Relay & industrial controls	0.3	Manufg.			
Support services, nec	0.3	Services			
Machine shops	0.3	Manufg.			
Air transportation	0.3	Util.			
Motors & generators	0.3	Manufg.			
Aluminum products from purchased aluminum	0.3	Manufg.			
Automotive equipment rental & leasing	0.3	Fin/R.E.			
Motor vehicle parts	0.3	Manufg.			
Investigation & security services	0.3	Services			
Paperboard containers	0.2	Manufg.			
Nonferrous metal (ex. copper & aluminum) processing	0.2	Manufg.			
Office administrative services	0.2	Services			
Environmental & other technical consulting services	0.2	Services			
Dry-cleaning & laundry services	0.2	Services			
Waste management & remediation services	0.2	Services			
Automotive repair & maintenance, ex. car washes	0.2	Services			
Computer system design services	0.2	Services			
Ship building & repairing	0.2	Manufg.			
Coating, engraving, heat treating & allied activities	0.2	Manufg.			
Commercial & industrial equipment repair/maintenance	0.2	Services			
Textile bag & canvas mills	0.2	Manufg.			
Sawmills & wood preservation	0.2	Manufg.			
Boat building	0.2	Manufg.			
Commercial & industrial machinery rental & leasing	0.1	Fin/R.E.			
Travel arrangement & reservation services	0.1	Services			
Natural gas distribution	0.1	Util.			
Civic, social, & professional organizations	0.1	Services			
Cutting tools & machine tool accessories	0.1	Manufg.			
Rubber products, nec	0.1	Manufg.			
Transit & ground passenger transportation	0.1	Util.			

Source: Benchmark Input-Output Accounts for the U.S. Economy, 2002, U.S. Department of Commerce, Washington, D.C., January 2008. The abbreviation nec stands for 'not elsewhere classified'.

OCCUPATIONS EMPLOYED BY SHIP & BOAT BUILDING

Occupation	% of Total 2006	Change to 2016	Occupation	% of Total 2006	Change to 2016
Fiberglass laminators & fabricators	8.5	11.9	Painters, transportation equipment	1.5	11.9
Welders, cutters, solderers, & brazers	6.6	19.1	Painters, construction & maintenance	1.4	10.2
Team assemblers	6.4	11.9	Laborers & freight, stock, & material movers, hand	1.3	0.7
First-line supervisors/managers of production workers	4.2	11.9	Inspectors, testers, sorters, samplers, & weighers	1.3	5.5
Carpenters	4.0	11.9	Sheet metal workers	1.2	9.8
Plumbers, pipefitters, & steamfitters	3.4	11.9	Maintenance & repair workers, general	1.2	11.9
Structural metal fabricators & fitters	2.9	11.9	Grinding & polishing workers, hand	1.2	11.9
Machinists	2.4	17.5	Office clerks, general	1.1	10.3
Electricians	2.4	16.1	Stock clerks & order fillers	1.1	-6.3
Helpers--Production workers	1.8	11.9	Welding, soldering, & brazing machine operators	1.1	25.9
Production, planning, & expediting clerks	1.7	11.9	Riggers	1.1	0.7
Assemblers & fabricators, nec	1.6	0.7			

Source: Industry-Occupation Matrix, Bureau of Labor Statistics, December 4, 2007. These data are reported based on 4-digit NAICS categories but have been matched to corresponding 6-digit NAICS industry codes. The change reported for each occupation to the year 2016 is a percent of growth or decline as estimated by the Bureau of Labor Statistics. The abbreviation nec stands for 'not elsewhere classified'.

LOCATION BY STATE AND REGIONAL CONCENTRATION

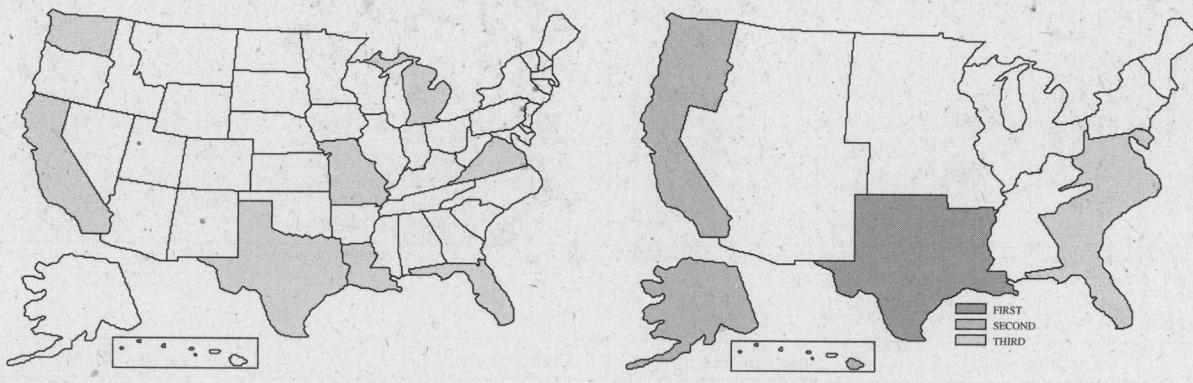

FIRST
SECOND
THIRD

INDUSTRY DATA BY STATE

State	Establish-ments	Shipments			Employment				Cost as % of Shipments	Investment per Employee ($)
		Total ($ mil)	% of U.S.	Per Establ.	Total Number	% of U.S.	Per Establ.	Wages ($/hour)		
Virginia	33	3,138.3	24.5	95,101.2	20,077	22.9	608	21.73	17.3	2,019
Louisiana	77	1,772.6	13.8	23,020.5	12,821	14.6	167	17.42	51.7	2,521
California	65	1,007.6	7.9	15,501.9	6,568	7.5	101	17.21	48.7	6,798
Washington	57	435.0	3.4	7,631.8	3,191	3.6	56	20.23	32.5	2,745
Texas	68	323.2	2.5	4,752.5	2,851	3.3	42	17.88	36.4	3,963
Florida	68	285.9	2.2	4,203.8	2,478	2.8	36	19.02	38.8	2,320
Missouri	9	96.1	0.7	10,672.6	870	1.0	97	14.71	48.0	2,656
Michigan	7	4.9	<0.1	697.7	41	<0.1	6	24.10	36.2	2,341

Source: 2002 *Economic Census.* The states are in descending order of shipments or establishments (if shipment data are missing for the majority). The symbol (D) appears when data are withheld to prevent disclosure of competitive information. States marked with (D) are sorted by number of establishments. A dash (-) indicates that the data element cannot be calculated. Data may not show all states active in the NAICS category. All data available at the time of publication are shown.

NAICS 336612 - BOAT BUILDING

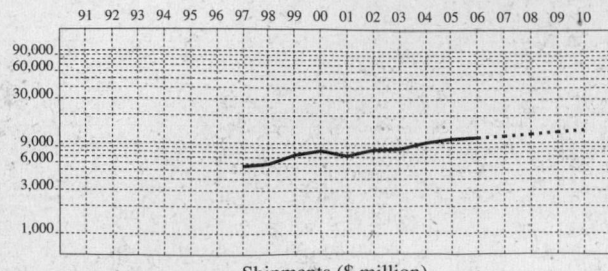

Shipments ($ million)

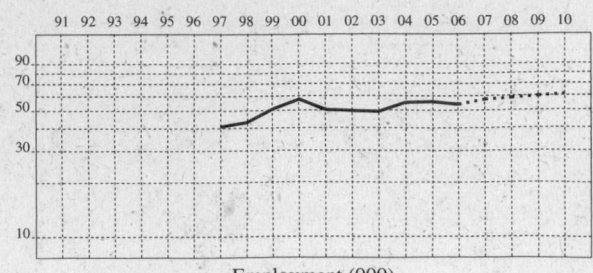

Employment (000)

GENERAL STATISTICS

| Year | Companies | Establishments | | Employment | | | Compensation | | Production ($ million) | | | |
		Total	with 20 or more employees	Total (000)	Production Workers (000)	Hours (Mil)	Payroll ($ mil)	Wages ($/hr)	Cost of Materials	Value Added by Manufacture	Value of Shipments	Capital Invest.
1997	984	1,041	301	40.9	32.8	62.6	1,025.5	11.04	3,207.1	2,378.5	5,556.1	121.9
1998		1,135	332	43.0	34.9	68.8	1,113.8	11.28	3,202.1	2,768.7	5,938.6	263.0
1999		1,098	323	50.9	41.8	83.2	1,371.3	11.65	4,103.2	3,413.1	7,436.0	231.7
2000		1,081	335	57.4	47.2	93.1	1,576.5	12.13	4,712.9	3,689.1	8,282.9	189.0
2001		1,140	333	50.2	40.2	77.8	1,385.8	12.44	4,013.9	3,200.7	7,239.3	147.6
2002	1,063	1,123	329	49.6	38.8	76.9	1,463.7	13.47	4,631.6	3,798.2	8,429.7	163.5
2003		1,119	322	49.0	37.5	79.6	1,532.8	13.52	4,610.8	3,981.2	8,592.0	137.0
2004		1,153	329	55.1	42.4	88.1	1,733.8	13.82	5,436.5	4,575.4	10,011.9	181.7
2005		1,157	336	55.7	43.2	90.2	1,803.5	13.95	6,393.3	4,646.7	11,040.0	210.3
2006		1,167P	337P	53.9	42.0	85.8	1,842.4	15.03	6,643.7	4,734.8	11,378.4	219.5
2007		1,177P	339P	57.3P	43.9P	92.0P	1,949.6P	15.19P	6,905.9P	4,921.6P	11,827.4P	190.5P
2008		1,187P	341P	58.5P	44.5P	94.1P	2,034.0P	15.62P	7,270.7P	5,181.7P	12,452.3P	191.2P
2009		1,197P	343P	59.7P	45.2P	96.1P	2,118.5P	16.04P	7,635.6P	5,441.7P	13,077.2P	191.9P
2010		1,207P	345P	60.9P	45.9P	98.2P	2,203.0P	16.47P	8,000.5P	5,701.7P	13,702.1P	192.7P

Sources: 1997 and 2002 *Economic Census*; other years, up to 2006, are from *Annual Survey of Manufactures*. Establishment counts for non-Census years are from *County Business Patterns*; 1997 and 2002 values are from the 1997 and 2002 censuses, respectively. 'P's show projections by the editors.

INDICES OF CHANGE

| Year | Companies | Establishments | | Employment | | | Compensation | | Production ($ million) | | | |
		Total	with 20 or more employees	Total (000)	Production Workers (000)	Hours (Mil)	Payroll ($ mil)	Wages ($/hr)	Cost of Materials	Value Added by Manufacture	Value of Shipments	Capital Invest.
1997	93	93	91	82	85	81	70	82	69	63	66	75
1998		101	101	87	90	89	76	84	69	73	70	161
1999		98	98	103	108	108	94	86	89	90	88	142
2000		96	102	116	122	121	108	90	102	97	98	116
2001		102	101	101	104	101	95	92	87	84	86	90
2002	100	100	100	100	100	100	100	100	100	100	100	100
2003		100	98	99	97	104	105	100	100	105	102	84
2004		103	100	111	109	115	118	103	117	120	119	111
2005		103	102	112	111	117	123	104	138	122	131	129
2006		104P	102P	109	108	112	126	112	143	125	135	134
2007		105P	103P	116P	113P	120P	133P	113P	149P	130P	140P	117P
2008		106P	104P	118P	115P	122P	139P	116P	157P	136P	148P	117P
2009		107P	104P	120P	116P	125P	145P	119P	165P	143P	155P	117P
2010		107P	105P	123P	118P	128P	151P	122P	173P	150P	163P	118P

Sources: Same as General Statistics. Values reflect change from the base year, 2002. Values above 100 mean greater than 2002, values below 100 mean less than 2002, and the values of 100 in other years means the same as 2002. 'P's show projections by the editors.

SELECTED RATIOS

For 2002	Avg. of All Manufact.	Analyzed Industry	Index	For 2002	Avg. of All Manufact.	Analyzed Industry	Index
Employees per Establishment	42	44	105	Value Added per Production Worker	182,367	97,892	54
Payroll per Establishment	1,639,184	1,303,384	80	Cost per Establishment	5,769,015	4,124,310	71
Payroll per Employee	39,053	29,510	76	Cost per Employee	137,446	93,379	68
Production Workers per Establishment	30	35	117	Cost per Production Worker	195,506	119,371	61
Wages per Establishment	694,845	922,389	133	Shipments per Establishment	11,158,348	7,506,411	67
Wages per Production Worker	23,548	26,697	113	Shipments per Employee	265,847	169,954	64
Hours per Production Worker	1,980	1,982	100	Shipments per Production Worker	378,144	217,260	57
Wages per Hour	11.89	13.47	113	Investment per Establishment	361,338	145,592	40
Value Added per Establishment	5,381,325	3,382,191	63	Investment per Employee	8,609	3,296	38
Value Added per Employee	128,210	76,577	60	Investment per Production Worker	12,245	4,214	34

Sources: Same as General Statistics. The 'Average of All Manufacturing' column represents the average of all manufacturing industries reported for the most recent complete year available. The Index shows the relationship between the Average and the Analyzed Industry. For example, 100 means that they are equal; 500 that the Analyzed Industry is five times the average; 50 means that the Analyzed Industry is half the national average. The abbreviation 'na' is used to show that data are 'not available'. Ratios shown for 2002, the last complete census year.

LEADING COMPANIES   Number shown: **75**   Total sales ($ mil): **48,022**   Total employment (000): **163.7**

Company Name	Address				CEO Name	Phone	Co. Type	Sales ($ mil)	Empl. (000)
General Dynamics Corp.	2941 Fairview Park	Falls Church	VA	22042	Nicholas D. Chabraja	703-876-3000	P	27,240	83.5
Brunswick Corp.	1 N Field Ct.	Lake Forest	IL	60045		847-735-4700	P	5,671	27.1
Polaris Industries Inc.	2100 Hwy. 55	Medina	MN	55340		763-542-0500	P	1,780	3.2
Bass Pro Shops Inc.	2500 E Kearney	Springfield	MO	65803	James Hagale	417-873-5000	R	1,662*	12.5
Newpark Shipholding Texas L.P.	3850 N Causeway	Metairie	LA	70002	James D. Cole	504-838-8222	S	1,320*	1.7
Genmar Holdings Inc.	80 S 8th St., 2900	Minneapolis	MN	55402	Roger R. Cloutier II	612-337-1965	R	1,254*	5.7
Chaparral Marine Inc.	2170 Piedmont NE	Atlanta	GA	30324	Richard A. Hubbell	404-321-7910	S	972*	1.2
Robalo Acquisition Company	PO Box 928	Nashville	GA	31639	Richard A. Hubbell	229-686-2700	S	891*	1.1
Genmar Transportation Inc.	2900 Ids Ctr. 80th	Minneapolis	MN	55402	Irwin Jacobs	612-339-7600	R	705*	<0.1
RPC Inc.	2170 Piedmont NE	Atlanta	GA	30324	Richard A. Hubbell	404-321-2140	P	690	2.4
Carver Boat Corporation L.L.C.	PO Box 1010	Pulaski	WI	54162		920-822-3214	R	679*	0.9
Bombardier Motor Corp. of Amer.	10101 Science Dr.	Sturtevant	WI	53177	Laurent Beaudoin	262-884-5000	S	518*	0.7
Triton Boat Company L.P.	15 Blue Grass Dr.	Ashland City	TN	37015	Earl Bentz	615-792-6767	R	346*	0.5
Marine Products Corp.	2801 Buford Hwy.	Atlanta	GA	30329	Richard A. Hubbell	404-321-7910	P	261	1.1
Skeeter Products Inc.	PO Box 230	Kilgore	TX	75663		903-984-0541	R	254*	0.2
Viking Yacht Co.	The Bass Riv RR 9	New Gretna	NJ	08224	Robert Healey	609-296-6000	R	217*	1.3
MasterCraft Boat Company Inc.	100 Cherokee Cv Dr.	Vonore	TN	37885		423-884-2221	R	199*	0.6
Bombardier Motor Corp. of Amer	250 Sea Horse Dr.	Waukegan	IL	60085	Laurent Beaudoin	847-689-6000	S	185*	0.3
Roberts Company Inc.	PO Box 1109	Winterville	NC	28590	John Roberts	252-355-9353	R	163*	0.3
Windway Capital Corp.	630 Riverfront Dr.	Sheboygan	WI	53081	Terry Kohler	920-457-8600	R	138*	1.6
Malibu Boats L.L.C.	1 Malibu Ct.	Merced	CA	95341		209-383-7469	R	131*	0.3
Conrad Industries Inc.	1100 Brashear Ave.	Morgan City	LA	70381	John P. Conrad Jr.	985-702-0195	P	122	0.5
Larson Glastron Boats Inc.	700 P Larson Mem	Little Falls	MN	56345	Jeffery Olson	320-632-5481	S	119*	0.9
Four Winns Boats L.L.C.	925 Frisbie St.	Cadillac	MI	49601		231-775-1351	R	115*	0.9
Wood Manufacturing Company	PO Box 179	Flippin	AR	72634	Randy Hopper	870-453-2222	S	115*	0.9
Sea Fox Boat Company Inc.	2550 Hwy. 52	Moncks Corner	SC	29461		843-761-6090	R	114*	0.2
B. A. E Sys Norfolk Ship Repair	PO Box 2100	Norfolk	VA	23501	William Clifford	757-494-4000	R	109*	1.0
KCS International Inc.	PO Box 78	Oconto	WI	54153		920-834-2211	R	94*	0.6
Regal Marine Industries Inc.	2300 Jetport Dr.	Orlando	FL	32809	Duane Kuck	407-851-4360	R	86*	0.7
S2 Yachts Inc.	725 E 40th St.	Holland	MI	49423		616-392-7163	R	85*	0.6
Fiberglass Engineering Inc.	1715 N 8th St.	Neodesha	KS	66757	William StClair	620-325-2653	R	78*	0.7
Crownline Boats Inc.	11884 Country Club	West Frankfort	IL	62896	James Claxton	618-937-6426	R	75*	0.6
Mainship Corp.	255 Diesel Rd.	Saint Augustine	FL	32084	Bill Finney	904-829-0500	R	73*	0.3
Hunter Marine Corp.	PO Box 1030	Alachua	FL	32616	Daniel Jett	386-462-3077	R	73*	<0.1
Seabring Marine Industries	1579 SW 18th St.	Williston	FL	32696	Robert Pita	352-528-2628	R	71*	0.5
Dallas Manufacturing Company	PO Box 891101	Dallas	TX	75389		972-716-4200	S	69*	<0.1
Glastron Inc.	PO Box 460	Little Falls	MN	56345	Jeffrey Olson	320-632-8395	S	67*	0.8
Rinker Boat Company L.L.C.	300 W Chicago St.	Syracuse	IN	46567		574-457-5731	R	61*	0.5
Kent Sporting Goods Company	433 Park Ave.	New London	OH	44851	Robert Tipton	419-929-7021	R	59*	0.1
Boston Whaler Inc.	100 Whaler Way	Edgewater	FL	32141	John Ward	386-428-0057	D	58*	0.5
Bertram Yacht Inc.	PO Box 520774	Miami	FL	33152	Joe Bubenzer	305-633-8011	R	54*	0.4
Delta Marine Industries Inc.	1608 S 96th St.	Seattle	WA	98108	Ivor Jones	206-763-2383	R	54*	0.4
Destination Outdoors Inc.	111 Kayaker Way	Easley	SC	29642	John Rukavina	864-859-7518	R	47*	0.3
Chris Craft Corp.	8161 15th St. E	Sarasota	FL	34243	Stephen Heese	941-351-4900	R	46*	0.3
Shipbuilders of Wisconsin Inc.	1811 Spring St.	Manitowoc	WI	54220	David Ross	920-684-1600	R	42*	0.2
Silverton Marine Corp.	301 Riverside Dr.	Millville	NJ	08332	John Luhrs	856-825-4117	R	41*	0.3
Tracker Marine L.L.C.	1402 Killingsworth	Bolivar	MO	65613		417-326-8770	R	41*	0.3
Key West Boats Inc.	PO Box 399	Ridgeville	SC	29472	William Holseberg	843-873-0112	R	40*	0.1
Quality Shipyards L.L.C.	PO Box 1817	Houma	LA	70361		985-876-4846	S	38*	0.3
Catalina Yachts Inc.	21200 Victory Blvd.	Woodland Hills	CA	91367	Frank Butler	818-884-7700	R	37*	0.3
Alumacraft Boat Co.	315 Saint Julien St	Saint Peter	MN	56082	David Benbow	507-931-1050	R	35*	0.1
Colonna's Shipyard Inc.	400 E Indian Rvr Rd	Norfolk	VA	23523	Tom Godfrey	757-545-2414	R	34*	0.3
Carolina Skiff L.L.C.	3231 Fulford Rd.	Waycross	GA	31503	Joseph Kirkland	912-287-0547	R	34*	0.3
Vivian Industries Inc.	PO Box 232	Vivian	LA	71082	William Parker	318-375-3241	R	33*	0.2
Skipperliner Industries Inc.	127 Marina Dr.	La Crosse	WI	54603	Noel Jordan	608-784-5110	R	32*	0.1
PFC Inc.	PO Box 669	Hartsville	SC	29551	James Fink	843-383-4507	R	32*	0.2
Westport Shipyard Inc.	PO Box 308	Westport	WA	98595		360-268-1800	R	29*	0.3
Contender Boats Inc.	1820 SE 38th Ave.	Homestead	FL	33035	Joseph Neber	305-230-1600	R	27*	0.2
Dakota Creek Industries Inc.	PO Box 218	Anacortes	WA	98221	Richard Nelson	360-293-9575	R	27*	0.2
Ocean Yachts Inc.	PO Box 312	Egg Harbor City	NJ	08215	John Leek	609-965-4616	R	27*	0.2
Skier's Choice Inc.	1717 Henry G Ln St.	Maryville	TN	37801	Rick Tinker	865-856-3035	R	27*	0.2
Summit Marine L.L.C.	PO Box 21	Aberdeen	MS	39730		662-369-5870	R	27*	0.2
Maverick Boat Company Inc.	3207 Indust. 29th	Fort Pierce	FL	34946	Douglas Deal	772-465-0631	R	26*	0.2
Parker Marine Enterprises Inc.	PO Box 2129	Beaufort	NC	28516	Linwood Parker	252-728-5621	R	26*	0.2
Rybovich Spencer	4200 N Flagler Dr.	W Palm Bch	FL	33407	Edward L. Bronstien	561-844-1800	R	25*	0.2
Beneteau USA Inc.	1313 West Hwy 76	Marion	SC	29571		843-805-5000	S	25	0.2
Ebbtide Corp.	2545 Jones Creek Rd	White Bluff	TN	37187	Thomas Trabue	615-797-3193	R	24*	0.2
Crane Interiors Inc.	PO Box 459	Woodbury	TN	37190	Larry Bucklin	615-563-4800	R	23*	0.2
Stardust Cruisers Inc.	2300 E Highway 90	Monticello	KY	42633	Robert Meacham	606-348-8466	R	23*	0.2
Marine Travelift Inc.	PO Box 66	Sturgeon Bay	WI	54235	Gerald Lamer	920-743-6202	R	23*	0.1
Bradford Yacht Limited Inc.	3051 W State Rd. 84	Fort Lauderdale	FL	33312	Dieter Cosman	954-791-3800	R	22*	0.2
Derecktor, Robert E. Inc.	311 E Boston Post	Mamaroneck	NY	10543	Paul Derecktor	914-698-5020	R	22*	0.1
Knight and Carver YachtCenter	1313 Bay Marina Dr.	National City	CA	91950	Sampson Brown	619-336-4141	R	22*	0.2
Premier Marine Inc.	PO Box 509	Wyoming	MN	55092	Robert Menne	651-462-2880	R	21*	0.2
Sumerset Acquisition L.L.C.	200 Sumerset Blvd.	Somerset	KY	42501	Steve Lochmueller	606-679-9393	R	20*	0.2

Source: *Ward's Business Directory of U.S. Private and Public Companies*, Volumes 1 and 2, 2008. The company type code used is as follows: P - Public, R - Private, S - Subsidiary, D - Division, J - Joint Venture, A - Affiliate, G - Group. Sales are in millions of dollars, employees are in thousands. An asterisk (*) indicates an estimated sales volume. The symbol < stands for 'less than'. Company names and addresses are truncated, in some cases, to fit into the available space.

MATERIALS CONSUMED

Material	Quantity	Delivered Cost ($ million)
Diesel and semidiesel engines	(X)	159.9
Gasoline and other internal combustion engines	(X)	701.6
Integral horsepower electric motors and generators (1 hp or more)	(X)	35.3
Boat propellers	(X)	15.0
Marine metal hardware (incl. shackles, rope shackles, rope sockets, tackle blocks), excluding forgings	(X)	81.9
Metal bolts, nuts, screws, and other screw machine products	(X)	20.9
Other fabricated metal products (excluding forgings)	(X)	21.8
Forgings	(X)	7.6
Castings, rough and semifinished	(X)	14.3
Steel shapes and forms (exc. castings, forgings, fabr. metal products)	(X)	12.2
Aluminum and aluminum-base alloy sheet, plate, foil, and welded tubing	(X)	79.4
Aluminum and aluminum-base alloy extruded shapes (rod, bar, pipe, tube, etc.)	(X)	41.8
Other aluminum and aluminum-base alloy shapes and forms (exc. castings, forgings, fabr. metal products)	(X)	16.1
Other nonferrous shapes and forms (exc. castings, forgings, fabricated metal products)	(X)	6.8
Plastics resins consumed in the form of granules, pellets, etc.	(X)	144.2
Plastics products consumed in the form of sheets, rods, etc.	(X)	52.8
Glass fiber (textile type, bonded mat type, etc.)	(X)	119.5
Lumber, dressed	(X)	22.7
Plywood	(X)	56.2
Carpeting	(X)	30.3
Canvas products	(X)	58.3
Paints, varnishes, stains, lacquers, shellacs, japans, enamels, etc.	(X)	34.3
Marine nautical and navigation equipment operating by radio signal	(X)	33.4
Bilge pumps	(X)	11.6
All other materials, components, parts, containers, and supplies	(X)	732.1
Materials, ingredients, containers, and supplies, nsk	(X)	1,667.3

Source: 2002 *Economic Census*. Explanation of symbols used: (D): Withheld to avoid disclosure of competitive data; na: Not available; (S): Withheld because statistical norms were not met; (X): Not applicable; (Z): Less than half the unit shown; nec: Not elsewhere classified; nsk: Not specified by kind; - : zero; p : 10-19 percent estimated; q : 20-29 percent estimated.

PRODUCT SHARE DETAILS

Product or Product Class Shipments	Mil. $	Product or Product Class Shipments	Mil. $
BOAT BUILDING	7,803.0	(professional crew not required by Coast Guard)	1,086.5
Outboard motorboats, including commercial and military (except sailboats and lifeboats)	**2,611.6**	Other inboard motorboats, including commercial and military (except sailboats and lifeboats)	517.6
Outboard wood or metal motorboats, including commercial and military (except sailboats and lifeboats)	1,138.6	Inboard runabouts	356.8
Outboard wood or metal runabouts	(D)	Other inboard motorboats (including houseboats)	160.8
Outboard wood or metal utility boats	(D)	Inboard motorboats, including commercial and military (except sailboats and lifeboats), nsk	140.3
Outboard wood or metal pontoon boats	363.7	**Inboard-outdrive boats, including commercial and military (except sailboats and lifeboats)**	**1,579.5**
Outboard wood or metal bass boats	152.1	Inboard-outdrive cabin cruisers	330.8
Outboard wood or metal fish and ski boats	178.9	Other inboard-outdrive boats, including commercial and military (except sailboats and lifeboats)	1,218.2
Outboard wood or metal other fish boats	205.6	Inboard-outdrive houseboats	75.7
Other outboard wood or metal motorboats, including cabin cruisers and center consoles	18.2	Inboard-outdrive runabouts	670.1
Outboard plastics (reinforced), fiberglass motorboats, including commercial and military (except sailboats and lifeboats)	1,156.0	Inboard-outdrive fish boats	78.5
		Other inboard-outdrive boats, including center consoles	393.9
Outboard plastics (reinforced), fiberglass runabouts	159.9	Inboard-outdrive boats, including commercial and military (except sailboats and lifeboats), nsk	30.5
Outboard plastics (reinforced), fiberglass utility boats	(D)	**All other boats, except military and commercial**	**473.3**
Outboard plastics (reinforced), fiberglass cabin cruisers	176.1	Sailboats without auxiliary motor, all sizes, except military and commercial	42.6
Outboard plastics (reinforced), fiberglass center console motorboats	244.7	Sailboats with auxiliary motor, not more than 6.5 m (21.33 ft) in length, except military and commercial	(D)
Outboard plastics (reinforced), fiberglass deck boats	(D)	Sailboats with auxiliary motor, more than 6.5 m (21.33 ft) but not more than 9.0 m (29.53 ft) in length, except military and commercial	(D)
Outboard plastics (reinforced), fiberglass fish and ski boats (except bass boats)	223.7	Sailboats with auxiliary motor, more than 9.0 m (29.53 ft) but not more than 12.0 m (39.03 ft) in length, except military and commercial	98.2
Outboard plastics (reinforced), fiberglass other fish boats (except bass boats)	153.7	Sailboats with auxiliary motor, more than 12.0 m (39.03 ft) in length, except military and commercial	106.1
Other plastics (reinforced), fiberglass outboard motorboats	75.0	Canoes made from all types of materials, except military and commercial	60.1
Outboard plastics (reinforced), fiberglass bass boats	301.9	Hovercraft (professional crew not required by Coast Guard) and all other miscellaneous boats, excluding military and commercial	133.0
Outboard motorboats, including commercial and military (except sailboats and lifeboats), nsk	15.1	**Boat building, nsk, total**	**782.1**
Inboard motorboats, including commercial and military (except sailboats and lifeboats)	**2,356.5**		
Inboard cabin cruisers, including commercial and military (except sailboats and lifeboats)	1,698.6		
Inboard cabin cruisers, less than 40 ft (12.19 m) in length	612.1		
Inboard cabin cruisers, 40 ft (12.19 m) or more in length			

Source: 2002 *Economic Census*. The values are product shipments in millions of dollars for 2002. Total product shipments may be lower or higher than industry shipments. See Introduction for a full discussion. Values of indented subcategories are summed in the main heading(s). The symbol (D) appears when data are withheld to prevent disclosure of competitive information. The abbreviation nsk stands for 'not specified by kind' and nec for 'not elsewhere classified'. A dash (-) means zero.

INPUTS AND OUTPUTS FOR BOAT BUILDING

Economic Sector or Industry Providing Inputs	%	Sector	Economic Sector or Industry Buying Outputs	%	Sector
Compensation of employees	23.2		Personal consumption expenditures	73.3	
Motor vehicle parts	11.8	Manufg.	Private fixed investment	10.9	
Management of companies & enterprises	7.4	Services	Exports of goods & services	8.9	Cap Inv
Retail trade	5.4	Trade	Federal government, investment, national defense	3.0	Fed Govt
Engine equipment, nec	4.3	Manufg.	Change in private inventories	1.2	In House
Wholesale trade	4.1	Trade	General Federal government services, nondefense	0.9	Fed Govt
Aluminum products from purchased aluminum	3.1	Manufg.	Other S/L govt. enterprises	0.6	S/L Govt
Plastics materials & resins	2.7	Manufg.	Boat building	0.4	Manufg.
Textile bag & canvas mills	2.2	Manufg.	Water transportation	0.3	Util.
Software publishers	1.8	Services	S/L govt. invest., other	0.3	S/L Govt
Hardware	1.8	Manufg.	Ship building & repairing	0.2	Manufg.
Advertising & related services	1.5	Services			
Pressed & blown glass & glassware, nec	1.4	Manufg.			
Veneer & plywood	1.1	Manufg.			
Plastics packaging materials, film & sheet	1.1	Manufg.			
Lessors of nonfinancial assets	1.1	Fin/R.E.			
Plate work & fabricated structural products	1.0	Manufg.			
Securities, commodity contracts, investments	0.9	Fin/R.E.			
Paints & coatings	0.8	Manufg.			
Truck transportation	0.8	Util.			
Scientific research & development services	0.8	Services			
Search, detection, & navigation instruments	0.7	Manufg.			
Motors & generators	0.7	Manufg.			
Turned products & screws, nuts, & bolts	0.6	Manufg.			
Carpet & rug mills	0.6	Manufg.			
Semiconductors & related devices	0.6	Manufg.			
Monetary authorities/depository credit intermediation	0.6	Fin/R.E.			
Printed circuit assemblies (electronic assembles)	0.6	Manufg.			
Real estate	0.5	Fin/R.E.			
Professional, scientific, technical services, nec	0.5	Services			
Paperboard containers	0.5	Manufg.			
Taxes on production & imports, less subsidies	0.5				
Boat building	0.5	Manufg.			
Sawmills & wood preservation	0.4	Manufg.			
Power generation & supply	0.4	Util.			
Legal services	0.4	Services			
Fabricated metals, nec	0.3	Manufg.			
Machine shops	0.3	Manufg.			
Automotive equipment rental & leasing	0.2	Fin/R.E.			
Accounting, tax preparation, bookkeeping, & payroll	0.2	Services			
Iron & steel mills & ferroalloys	0.2	Manufg.			
Pumps & pumping equipment	0.2	Manufg.			
Food services & drinking places	0.2	Services			
Telecommunications	0.2	Services			
Warehousing & storage	0.2	Util.			
Rubber products, nec	0.2	Manufg.			
Data processing, hosting, & related services	0.2	Services			
Natural gas distribution	0.2	Util.			
Rail transportation	0.2	Util.			
Coating, engraving, heat treating & allied activities	0.2	Manufg.			
Unlaminated plastics profile shapes	0.2	Manufg.			
Forging, stamping, & sintering, nec	0.2	Manufg.			
Management, scientific, & technical consulting	0.2	Services			
Services to buildings & dwellings	0.2	Services			
Ferrous metal foundries	0.1	Manufg.			
Nonferrous metal foundries	0.1	Manufg.			
Architectural, engineering, & related services	0.1	Services			
Relay & industrial controls	0.1	Manufg.			
Commercial & industrial machinery rental & leasing	0.1	Fin/R.E.			
Maintenance/repair of nonresidential structures	0.1	Construct.			
Alumina refining & primary aluminum production	0.1	Manufg.			
Cutting tools & machine tool accessories	0.1	Manufg.			
Air transportation	0.1	Util.			
Hotels & motels, including casino hotels	0.1	Services			
Waste management & remediation services	0.1	Services			
Other computer related services, including facilities	0.1	Services			

Source: Benchmark Input-Output Accounts for the U.S. Economy, 2002, U.S. Department of Commerce, Washington, D.C., January 2008. The abbreviation nec stands for 'not elsewhere classified'.

OCCUPATIONS EMPLOYED BY SHIP & BOAT BUILDING

Occupation	% of Total 2006	Change to 2016	Occupation	% of Total 2006	Change to 2016
Fiberglass laminators & fabricators	8.5	11.9	Painters, transportation equipment	1.5	11.9
Welders, cutters, solderers, & brazers	6.6	19.1	Painters, construction & maintenance	1.4	10.2
Team assemblers	6.4	11.9	Laborers & freight, stock, & material movers, hand	1.3	0.7
First-line supervisors/managers of production workers	4.2	11.9	Inspectors, testers, sorters, samplers, & weighers	1.3	5.5
Carpenters	4.0	11.9	Sheet metal workers	1.2	9.8
Plumbers, pipefitters, & steamfitters	3.4	11.9	Maintenance & repair workers, general	1.2	11.9
Structural metal fabricators & fitters	2.9	11.9	Grinding & polishing workers, hand	1.2	11.9
Machinists	2.4	17.5	Office clerks, general	1.1	10.3
Electricians	2.4	16.1	Stock clerks & order fillers	1.1	-6.3
Helpers--Production workers	1.8	11.9	Welding, soldering, & brazing machine operators	1.1	25.9
Production, planning, & expediting clerks	1.7	11.9	Riggers	1.1	0.7
Assemblers & fabricators, nec	1.6	0.7			

Source: Industry-Occupation Matrix, Bureau of Labor Statistics, December 4, 2007. These data are reported based on 4-digit NAICS categories but have been matched to corresponding 6-digit NAICS industry codes. The change reported for each occupation to the year 2016 is a percent of growth or decline as estimated by the Bureau of Labor Statistics. The abbreviation nec stands for 'not elsewhere classified'.

LOCATION BY STATE AND REGIONAL CONCENTRATION

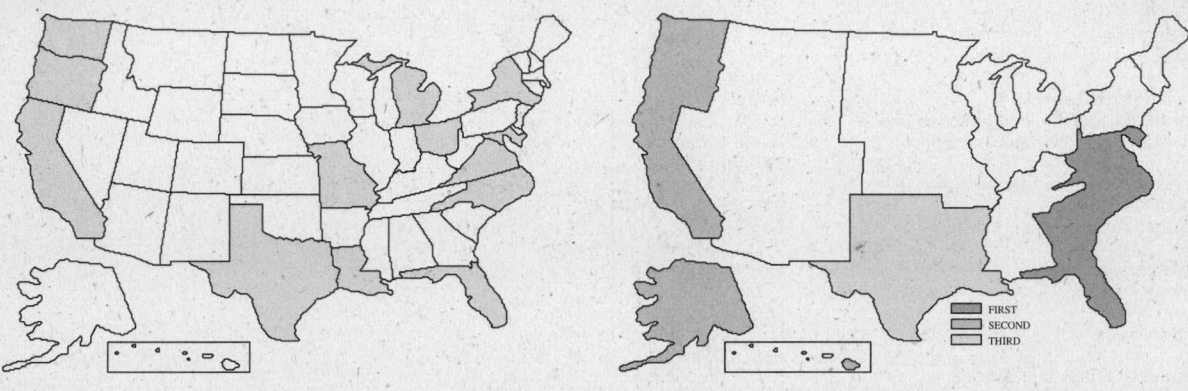

FIRST
SECOND
THIRD

INDUSTRY DATA BY STATE

State	Establish-ments	Shipments Total ($ mil)	Shipments % of U.S.	Shipments Per Establ.	Employment Total Number	Employment % of U.S.	Employment Per Establ.	Wages ($/hour)	Cost as % of Shipments	Investment per Employee ($)
Florida	236	1,761.3	20.9	7,463.0	10,486	21.1	44	13.48	52.9	2,690
North Carolina	53	526.4	6.2	9,932.0	3,387	6.8	64	12.88	49.2	5,127
Michigan	26	373.5	4.4	14,364.7	1,953	3.9	75	14.79	58.8	2,266
Missouri	20	371.6	4.4	18,580.9	1,863	3.8	93	10.31	45.0	1,769
California	80	332.0	3.9	4,149.8	2,319	4.7	29	13.59	50.0	2,904
Washington	85	300.6	3.6	3,536.5	2,778	5.6	33	13.76	46.4	3,285
Maryland	29	165.0	2.0	5,688.1	794	1.6	27	13.03	59.9	7,064
Oregon	25	146.5	1.7	5,859.3	870	1.8	35	12.34	55.8	1,979
Louisiana	36	122.4	1.5	3,401.2	990	2.0	28	13.55	55.2	2,585
Texas	41	118.7	1.4	2,894.6	565	1.1	14	14.79	53.5	2,851
Ohio	12	68.5	0.8	5,707.2	453	0.9	38	12.78	78.2	3,196
Virginia	22	34.9	0.4	1,586.9	382	0.8	17	14.36	51.1	1,599
New York	20	18.8	0.2	941.8	156	0.3	8	13.75	46.0	9,718

Source: 2002 Economic Census. The states are in descending order of shipments or establishments (if shipment data are missing for the majority). The symbol (D) appears when data are withheld to prevent disclosure of competitive information. States marked with (D) are sorted by number of establishments. A dash (-) indicates that the data element cannot be calculated. Data may not show all states active in the NAICS category. All data available at the time of publication are shown.

NAICS 336991 - MOTORCYCLE, BICYCLE, AND PARTS MANUFACTURING

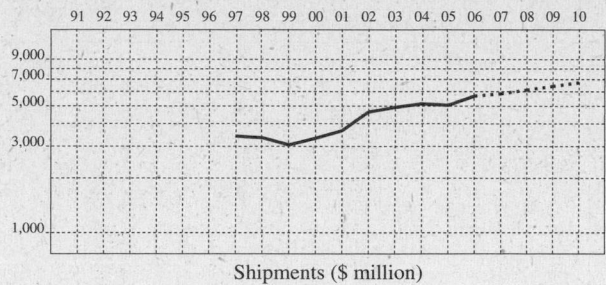

Shipments ($ million)

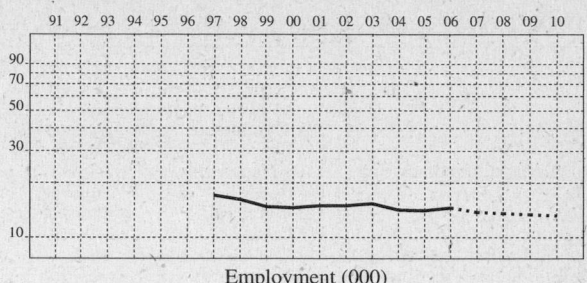

Employment (000)

GENERAL STATISTICS

| Year | Companies | Establishments | | Employment | | | Compensation | | Production ($ million) | | | |
		Total	with 20 or more employees	Total (000)	Production Workers (000)	Hours (Mil)	Payroll ($ mil)	Wages ($/hr)	Cost of Materials	Value Added by Manufacture	Value of Shipments	Capital Invest.
1997	371	387	98	17.1	12.7	24.3	567.5	15.03	1,797.5	1,617.5	3,411.7	104.6
1998		391	97	16.2	11.7	22.9	620.3	15.90	1,740.7	1,589.6	3,343.8	131.8
1999		402	99	14.8	10.3	19.3	576.1	16.95	1,599.8	1,476.9	3,054.7	117.5
2000		410	103	14.6	10.6	19.4	583.9	19.71	1,664.6	1,630.6	3,320.9	113.3
2001		390	103	15.0	10.8	19.7	639.3	21.25	1,814.6	1,832.6	3,657.0	130.1
2002	346	355	86	15.0	11.6	22.9	629.9	19.52	2,435.6	2,121.4	4,631.6	308.5
2003		387	94	15.4	12.4	23.6	666.9	20.32	2,849.8	2,096.0	4,916.5	152.2
2004		415	103	14.2	10.9	21.5	626.3	21.18	2,979.2	2,168.7	5,144.3	100.0
2005		441	99	14.1	10.6	20.5	630.6	21.00	3,155.1	1,961.9	5,051.2	137.0
2006		414P	98P	14.6	10.7	21.0	705.6	21.71	3,552.4	2,210.7	5,674.3	81.1
2007		418P	98P	13.8P	10.7P	20.9P	684.8P	23.16P	3,654.9P	2,274.5P	5,838.1P	138.7P
2008		421P	97P	13.6P	10.6P	20.7P	695.8P	23.87P	3,839.1P	2,389.1P	6,132.2P	138.9P
2009		425P	97P	13.4P	10.5P	20.6P	706.7P	24.58P	4,023.2P	2,503.7P	6,426.3P	139.1P
2010		428P	97P	13.2P	10.4P	20.5P	717.7P	25.29P	4,207.3P	2,618.2P	6,720.4P	139.3P

Sources: 1997 and 2002 *Economic Census*; other years, up to 2006, are from *Annual Survey of Manufactures*. Establishment counts for non-Census years are from *County Business Patterns*; 1997 and 2002 values are from the 1997 and 2002 censuses, respectively. 'P's show projections by the editors.

INDICES OF CHANGE

| Year | Companies | Establishments | | Employment | | | Compensation | | Production ($ million) | | | |
		Total	with 20 or more employees	Total (000)	Production Workers (000)	Hours (Mil)	Payroll ($ mil)	Wages ($/hr)	Cost of Materials	Value Added by Manufacture	Value of Shipments	Capital Invest.
1997	107	109	114	114	109	106	90	77	74	76	74	34
1998		110	113	108	101	100	98	81	71	75	72	43
1999		113	115	99	89	84	91	87	66	70	66	38
2000		115	120	97	91	85	93	101	68	77	72	37
2001		110	120	100	93	86	101	109	75	86	79	42
2002	100	100	100	100	100	100	100	100	100	100	100	100
2003		109	109	103	107	103	106	104	117	99	106	49
2004		117	120	95	94	94	99	109	122	102	111	32
2005		124	115	94	91	90	100	108	130	92	109	44
2006		117P	113P	97	92	92	112	111	146	104	123	26
2007		118P	113P	92P	92P	91P	109P	119P	150P	107P	126P	45P
2008		119P	113P	91P	91P	90P	110P	122P	158P	113P	132P	45P
2009		120P	113P	89P	91P	90P	112P	126P	165P	118P	139P	45P
2010		121P	113P	88P	90P	90P	114P	130P	173P	123P	145P	45P

Sources: Same as General Statistics. Values reflect change from the base year, 2002. Values above 100 mean greater than 2002, values below 100 mean less than 2002, and the values of 100 in other years means the same as 2002. 'P's show projections by the editors.

SELECTED RATIOS

For 2002	Avg. of All Manufact.	Analyzed Industry	Index	For 2002	Avg. of All Manufact.	Analyzed Industry	Index
Employees per Establishment	42	42	101	Value Added per Production Worker	182,367	182,879	100
Payroll per Establishment	1,639,184	1,774,366	108	Cost per Establishment	5,769,015	6,860,845	119
Payroll per Employee	39,053	41,993	108	Cost per Employee	137,446	162,373	118
Production Workers per Establishment	30	33	111	Cost per Production Worker	195,506	209,966	107
Wages per Establishment	694,845	1,259,177	181	Shipments per Establishment	11,158,348	13,046,761	117
Wages per Production Worker	23,548	38,535	164	Shipments per Employee	265,847	308,773	116
Hours per Production Worker	1,980	1,974	100	Shipments per Production Worker	378,144	399,276	106
Wages per Hour	11.89	19.52	164	Investment per Establishment	361,338	869,014	240
Value Added per Establishment	5,381,325	5,975,775	111	Investment per Employee	8,609	20,567	239
Value Added per Employee	128,210	141,427	110	Investment per Production Worker	12,245	26,595	217

Sources: Same as General Statistics. The 'Average of All Manufacturing' column represents the average of all manufacturing industries reported for the most recent complete year available. The Index shows the relationship between the Average and the Analyzed Industry. For example, 100 means that they are equal; 500 that the Analyzed Industry is five times the average; 50 means that the Analyzed Industry is half the national average. The abbreviation 'na' is used to show that data are 'not available'. Ratios shown for 2002, the last complete census year.

LEADING COMPANIES   Number shown: **75**   Total sales ($ mil): **36,757**   Total employment (000): **88.4**

Company Name	Address				CEO Name	Phone	Co. Type	Sales ($ mil)	Empl. (000)
Mattel Inc.	333 Continental	El Segundo	CA	90245	Robert A. Eckert	310-252-2000	P	5,970	31.0
Harley-Davidson Inc.	PO Box 453	Milwaukee	WI	53201	Jeffrey L. Bleustein	414-342-4680	P	5,727	9.0
Honda of America Manufacturing	24000 Honda Pkwy.	Marysville	OH	43040	Takeo Fukui	937-642-5000	S	5,090*	13.0
Hasbro Inc.	PO Box 1059	Pawtucket	RI	02861		401-431-8697	P	3,838	5.9
HCAC Inc.	225 Byers Rd.	Miamisburg	OH	45342	Paul R. D'Aloia	937-866-6251	S	2,991*	1.1
BMW of North America L.L.C.	PO Box 1227	Westwood	NJ	07675	Thomas Purves	201-307-4000	S	2,690*	1.0
Kawasaki Motors Manufacturing	PO Box 81469	Lincoln	NE	68501		402-476-6600	S	1,758*	1.3
Sony Music Entertainment Inc.	550 Madison Ave.	New York	NY	10022	Mike Bebel	212-833-8000	S	1,500*	10.0
Tri-Con Industries Ltd.	4000 NW 44th St.	Lincoln	NE	68524		402-470-3311	R	1,450*	0.3
JAKKS Pacific Inc.	22619 Pacific Coast	Malibu	CA	90265	Stephen G. Berman	310-456-7799	P	857	0.6
Plaid Enterprises Inc.	PO Box 7600	Norcross	GA	30091	Michael McCooey	678-291-8100	R	600*	0.2
Speedway Motorsports Inc.	PO Box 600	Concord	NC	28026	O. Bruton Smith	704-455-3239	P	562	1.0
LeapFrog Enterprises Inc.	6401 Hollis St.	Emeryville	CA	94608	Steven B. Fink	510-420-5000	P	445	0.9
Marvel Entertainment Group	417 5th Ave.	New York	NY	10016	Morton Handel	212-576-4000	S	352	0.3
Newman Technology Inc.	100 Cairns Rd.	Mansfield	OH	44903	Noriyoshi Asami	419-525-1856	R	167*	0.9
Fisher-Price Inc.	636 Girard Ave.	East Aurora	NY	14052	Neil Friedman	716-687-3000	S	165*	0.9
Exx Inc.	1350 E Flamingo	Las Vegas	NV	89119		702-598-3223	P	159	0.8
First Years Inc.	100 Tec. Center Dr.	Stoughton	MA	02072	Curtis Stoelting	781-341-6250	S	150*	0.2
Battat Inc.	PO Box 1264	Plattsburgh	NY	12901	Joe Battat	518-562-2200	R	146*	0.2
Revell-Monogram L.L.C.	725 Landwehr Rd.	Northbrook	IL	60062		847-770-6100	R	122*	<0.1
K and N Engineering Inc.	PO Box 1329	Riverside	CA	92502	Jerry Mall	951-826-4100	R	109*	0.6
Peg-Perego USA Inc.	3625 Independence	Fort Wayne	IN	46808		260-482-8191	R	100*	0.1
Mad Catz Interactive Inc.	7480 Mission Vly	San Diego	CA	92108	Patrick S. Brigham	619-683-9830	P	100	0.1
Pioneer National Latex Inc.	246 E 4th St.	Ashland	OH	44805		419-289-3300	R	98*	0.1
Summit Products Inc.	PO Box 620	Trussville	AL	35173		205-661-1774	R	87*	<0.1
United States Playing Card Co.	4590 Beech St.	Cincinnati	OH	45212	Greg Simko	513-396-5700	S	81*	0.6
Gaming Partners International	1700 S Indu. Rd.	Las Vegas	NV	89102	Gerard P. Charlier	702-384-2425	P	74	0.8
American Ironhorse Motorcycle	4600 Blue Mound	Fort Worth	TX	76106	Dwayne Moyers	817-665-2000	R	74*	0.3
AW Faber-Castell USA Inc.	9450 Allen Dr.	Cleveland	OH	44125	Jamie Gallagher	216-643-4660	R	59*	0.1
Ff Acquisition Corp.	PO Box 1296	West Point	MS	39773	Alex Garcia	662-494-4732	R	57*	0.4
American Educational Products	401 W Hickory St.	Fort Collins	CO	80522	Michael Anderson	970-484-7445	R	55*	0.2
Markland Industries Inc.	1111 E McFadden	Santa Ana	CA	92705	Donald Markland	714-245-4923	R	49*	0.3
Steve Jackson Games Inc.	PO Box 18957	Austin	TX	78760	Steve Jackson	512-447-7866	R	48*	<0.1
Shimano American Corp.	PO Box 19615	Irvine	CA	92618	Yozo Shimano	949-951-5003	S	46*	0.1
Swing-A-Way Products L.L.C.	4100 Beck Ave.	Saint Louis	MO	63116		314-773-1487	S	46*	<0.1
Wellman Products Group	920 Lake Rd.	Medina	OH	44256	Steve Campbell		S	45*	0.3
Paladin Holdings Inc.	344 Woodridge	Kingsport	TN	37664	Larry Lunan	423-247-9560	P	43	0.9
Performance Machine Inc.	6892 Marlin Cir.	La Palma	CA	90623	Nancy Sands	714-523-3000	R	40*	0.2
Custom Chrome Manufacturing	16100 Jacqueline Ct	Morgan Hill	CA	95037	Dan Cook	408-825-5000	R	40*	0.2
Corbin Pacific Inc.	2360 Technology	Hollister	CA	95023	Michael Hanagan	831-634-1100	R	36*	0.2
American Plastic Toys Inc.	PO Box 100	Walled Lake	MI	48390	John Gessert	248-624-4881	R	33*	0.2
Step2 Company L.L.C.	10010 A Hudson	Streetsboro	OH	44241		330-656-0440	R	30*	0.5
Educational Insights Inc.	18730 S Wilmington	R Dominguez	CA	90220	G. Reid Calcott	310-884-2000	S	30*	0.3
Big Fish Games Inc.	1501 4th Ave., 800	Seattle	WA	98101	Jeremy Lewis	206-282-4923	R	30	0.1
FMF Racing	18033 S Santa Fe	E R Domingz	CA	90221	Don Emler	310-631-4363	R	30*	0.2
Sun Metal Products Inc.	2156 N Detroit St.	Warsaw	IN	46580	Robert Piecuch	574-267-3281	R	30*	0.2
Small World Kids Inc.	5711 Buckingham	Culver City	CA	90230	Debra Fine	310-645-9680	P	28	<0.1
Athearn Inc.	1550 Glenn Curtiss	Carson	CA	90746	Tim Geddes	310-763-7140	R	26*	0.2
Thiessen Products Inc.	555 Dawson Dr.	Camarillo	CA	93012	Jim Thiessen	805-482-6913	R	25*	0.1
Cmsi Inc.	PO Box 969	Preston	WA	98050	Thomas Lynott	425-222-7738	R	25*	<0.1
Ohio Art Co.	PO Box 111	Bryan	OH	43506	William C. Killgallon	419-636-3141	P	25	0.2
Persons-Majestic Manufacturing	PO Box 370	Huron	OH	44839	Richard D. Sanderson	419-433-9057	S	24*	0.2
Poof Slinky Inc.	PO Box 701394	Plymouth	MI	48170	Raymo Dallavecchia	734-454-9552	R	23*	<0.1
Extron Logistics L.L.C.	47550 Kato Rd.	Fremont	CA	94538		510-353-0177	R	23*	0.2
Mag-Nif Inc.	PO Box 720	Mentor	OH	44061	William Knox	440-255-9366	R	23*	0.2
Wm. K. Walthers Inc.	5601 W Florist Ave.	Milwaukee	WI	53218	Philip Walthers	414-527-0770	R	22*	0.2
Litespeed Racing Components	PO Box 22666	Chattanooga	TN	37422	Mark Lynskey	423-238-5530	R	22*	0.2
Western Synthetic Fiber Inc.	966 Sandhill Ave.	Carson	CA	90746	Ken Hardin	310-767-1000	R	22*	<0.1
Vari-Wall Tube Specialists	PO Box 340	Columbiana	OH	44408	Randall Alexoff	330-482-0000	R	20*	0.1
Klein Bicycle Corp. of WA	801 W Madison St.	Waterloo	WI	53594	John Burke	920-478-4676	R	20*	0.1
Rowe International Inc.	1500 Union Ave. SE	Grand Rapids	MI	49507	Douglas Johnson	616-243-3633	R	19*	0.1
DS Manufacturing Inc.	67 5th St. NE	Pine Island	MN	55963	James Preisler	507-356-8322	R	18*	<0.1
Poolmaster Inc.	PO Box 340308	Sacramento	CA	95834	Lee Tager	916-567-9800	R	18*	<0.1
Imperial Toy L.L.C.	PO Box 21068	Los Angeles	CA	90021	Arthur Hirsch	213-489-2100	R	18*	0.1
Kids II Inc.	555 N Point Ctr. E	Alpharetta	GA	30022	Ryan Gunnigle	770-751-0442	R	16*	0.1
National Cycle Inc.	PO Box 158	Maywood	IL	60153	Barry Willey	708-343-0400	R	16*	<0.1
Bucilla Corp.	1 Oak Ridge Rd.	Hazleton	PA	18202	Michael McCooey	570-384-2525	S	15*	0.1
Decipher Inc.	259 Granby St., 100	Norfolk	VA	23510	Warren Holland	757-664-1111	R	15*	0.1
Universal Manufacturing Co.	5450 Deramus	Kansas City	MO	64120	Jim Lepore	816-231-2771	R	15*	0.3
Buffalo Games Inc.	220 James E Casey	Buffalo	NY	14206	Paul Dedrick	716-827-8393	R	13*	<0.1
Atlas Model Railroad Company	378 Florence Ave.	Hillside	NJ	07205	Diane Haedrich	908-687-0880	R	12*	<0.1
Playmobil USA Inc.	PO Box 877	Dayton	NJ	08810		609-395-5566	R	12*	<0.1
Lone Star Racing Inc.	1424 E Broadway	Phoenix	AZ	85040	Tom Fisher	602-243-7437	R	12*	<0.1
Radio Sound Inc.	1713 Cobalt Dr.	Louisville	KY	40299	Wood Northup	502-267-6768	R	12*	<0.1
SwimWays Corp.	5816 Ward Ct.	Virginia Beach	VA	23455	David Arias	757-460-1156	R	11*	<0.1

Source: Ward's Business Directory of U.S. Private and Public Companies, Volumes 1 and 2, 2008. The company type code used is as follows: P - Public, R - Private, S - Subsidiary, D - Division, J - Joint Venture, A - Affiliate, G - Group. Sales are in millions of dollars, employees are in thousands. An asterisk (*) indicates an estimated sales volume. The symbol < stands for 'less than'. Company names and addresses are truncated, in some cases, to fit into the available space.

MATERIALS CONSUMED

Material	Quantity	Delivered Cost ($ million)
Bicycle frames, forks, and parts	(X)	93.2
Bicycle wheel rims and spokes	(X)	37.3
Bicycle seats (saddles)	(X)	(D)
Pneumatic tires and inner tubes	(X)	39.0
Other bicycle parts	(X)	261.9
Fabricated metal products (excluding forgings)	(X)	303.1
Forgings	(X)	(D)
Castings, rough and semifinished	(X)	(D)
Metal shapes and forms (exc. castings, forgings, fabr. metal products)	(X)	(D)
All other materials, components, parts, containers, and supplies	(X)	777.9
Materials, ingredients, containers, and supplies, nsk	(X)	274.3

Source: 2002 *Economic Census*. Explanation of symbols used: (D): Withheld to avoid disclosure of competitive data; na: Not available; (S): Withheld because statistical norms were not met; (X): Not applicable; (Z): Less than half the unit shown; nec: Not elsewhere classified; nsk: Not specified by kind; - : zero; p : 10-19 percent estimated; q : 20-29 percent estimated.

PRODUCT SHARE DETAILS

Product or Product Class Shipments	Mil. $	Product or Product Class Shipments	Mil. $
MOTORCYCLES, BICYCLES, AND PARTS	4,242.8	Wheel rims and spokes for bicycles, unicycles, and adult tricycles	10.2
Bicycles and parts, except children's two-wheel sidewalk cycles with solid or semipneumatic tires	**845.2**	Seats (saddles) for bicycles, unicycles, and adult tricycles	46.6
Bicycles and parts, except children's two-wheel sidewalk cycles with solid or semipneumatic tires	845.2	Pedals and crankgear and similar parts for bicycles, unicycles, and adult tricycles	(D)
Bicycles, complete, wheels of all diameter and all speeds (including lightweight, road, mountain, all-terrain, and cruiser-type)	548.0	Other parts for bicycles, unicycles, and adult tricycles (including hubs, brakes, freewheel sprocket wheels, and parts thereof)	111.1
Other cycles including unicycles, adult tricycles, and children's tricycles of metal tubular construction (except children's sidewalk bikes with solid or semipneumatic tires)	(D)	Bicycles and parts, except children's two-wheel sidewalk cycles with solid or semipneumatic tires, nsk	0.1
Frames, forks, and similar parts for bicycles, unicycles, and adult tricycles	104.9	**Motorcycles, including three-wheel, motorbikes, motor scooters, mopeds, and parts (including sidecars)**	**3,162.2**
		Motorcycles, bicycles, and parts, nsk, total	**235.4**

Source: 2002 *Economic Census*. The values are product shipments in millions of dollars for 2002. Total product shipments may be lower or higher than industry shipments. See Introduction for a full discussion. Values of indented subcategories are summed in the main heading(s). The symbol (D) appears when data are withheld to prevent disclosure of competitive information. The abbreviation nsk stands for 'not specified by kind' and nec for 'not elsewhere classified'. A dash (-) means zero.

INPUTS AND OUTPUTS FOR MOTORCYCLE, BICYCLE, AND PARTS MANUFACTURING

Economic Sector or Industry Providing Inputs	%	Sector	Economic Sector or Industry Buying Outputs	%	Sector
Compensation of employees	20.1		Personal consumption expenditures	71.7	
Motorcycles, bicycles, & parts	10.6	Manufg.	Exports of goods & services	9.9	Cap Inv
Iron & steel mills & ferroalloys	6.9	Manufg.	Motorcycles, bicycles, & parts	5.6	Manufg.
Wholesale trade	5.9	Trade	Retail trade	4.1	Trade
Management of companies & enterprises	5.8	Services	S/L govt. invest., other	2.4	S/L Govt
Aluminum products from purchased aluminum	5.6	Manufg.	Private fixed investment	2.3	
Software publishers	2.7	Services	Personal & household goods repair/maintenance	2.0	Services
Machine shops	2.0	Manufg.	Change in private inventories	1.7	In House
Paperboard mills	1.8	Manufg.	Child day care services	0.2	Services
Coating, engraving, heat treating & allied activities	1.5	Manufg.			
Lessors of nonfinancial assets	1.4	Fin/R.E.			
Alumina refining & primary aluminum production	1.1	Manufg.			
Tires	1.1	Manufg.			
Securities, commodity contracts, investments	1.0	Fin/R.E.			
Ferrous metal foundries	1.0	Manufg.			
Nonferrous metal foundries	0.9	Manufg.			
Turned products & screws, nuts, & bolts	0.9	Manufg.			
Architectural, engineering, & related services	0.9	Services			
Truck transportation	0.9	Util.			
Semiconductors & related devices	0.8	Manufg.			
Printed circuit assemblies (electronic assemblies)	0.8	Manufg.			
Metal cans, boxes, & other containers (light gauge)	0.7	Manufg.			
Advertising & related services	0.7	Services			
Fabricated metals, nec	0.6	Manufg.			
Paperboard containers	0.6	Manufg.			
Scientific research & development services	0.6	Services			
Valve & fittings other than plumbing	0.5	Manufg.			
Plate work & fabricated structural products	0.5	Manufg.			
Real estate	0.5	Fin/R.E.			
Crowns & closures & metal stamping	0.4	Manufg.			
Primary nonferrous metal, ex. copper & aluminum	0.4	Manufg.			
Ball & roller bearings	0.4	Manufg.			

Continued on next page.

INPUTS AND OUTPUTS FOR MOTORCYCLE, BICYCLE, AND PARTS MANUFACTURING - Continued

Economic Sector or Industry Providing Inputs	%	Sector	Economic Sector or Industry Buying Outputs	%	Sector
Power generation & supply	0.4	Util.			
Legal services	0.4	Services			
Handtools	0.4	Manufg.			
Custom roll forming	0.3	Manufg.			
Food services & drinking places	0.3	Services			
Nonferrous metal (ex. copper & aluminum) processing	0.3	Manufg.			
Accounting, tax preparation, bookkeeping, & payroll	0.2	Services			
Services to buildings & dwellings	0.2	Services			
Rail transportation	0.2	Util.			
Data processing, hosting, & related services	0.2	Services			
Employment services	0.2	Services			
Lighting fixtures	0.2	Manufg.			
Telecommunications	0.2	Services			
Maintenance/repair of nonresidential structures	0.2	Construct.			
Management, scientific, & technical consulting	0.2	Services			
Natural gas distribution	0.2	Util.			
Specialized design services	0.2	Services			
Business support services	0.2	Services			
Springs & wire products	0.2	Manufg.			
Warehousing & storage	0.2	Util.			
Monetary authorities/depository credit intermediation	0.2	Fin/R.E.			
Hotels & motels, including casino hotels	0.1	Services			
Other computer related services, including facilities	0.1	Services			
Automotive equipment rental & leasing	0.1	Fin/R.E.			
Air transportation	0.1	Util.			
Automotive repair & maintenance, ex. car washes	0.1	Services			
Taxes on production & imports, less subsidies	0.1				
Cutlery, utensils, pots, & pans	0.1	Manufg.			
Commercial & industrial equipment repair/maintenance	0.1	Services			

Source: Benchmark Input-Output Accounts for the U.S. Economy, 2002, U.S. Department of Commerce, Washington, D.C., January 2008. The abbreviation nec stands for 'not elsewhere classified'.

OCCUPATIONS EMPLOYED BY OTHER TRANSPORTATION EQUIPMENT MANUFACTURING

Occupation	% of Total 2006	Change to 2016	Occupation	% of Total 2006	Change to 2016
Team assemblers	17.5	0.4	Laborers & freight, stock, & material movers, hand	1.6	-9.6
Welders, cutters, solderers, & brazers	7.5	6.8	Industrial engineers	1.4	22.0
Cutting, punching, & press machine operators	3.9	-9.6	Painters, transportation equipment	1.4	0.4
First-line supervisors/managers of production workers	3.3	0.4	Fiberglass laminators & fabricators	1.3	0.4
Grinding, lapping, polishing machine tool operators	3.3	-2.6	Purchasing agents, exc wholesale, retail, & farm	1.2	0.4
Inspectors, testers, sorters, samplers, & weighers	2.6	-5.3	Maintenance & repair workers, general	1.1	0.4
Assemblers & fabricators, nec	1.9	-9.6	Production, planning, & expediting clerks	1.1	0.4
Shipping, receiving, & traffic clerks	1.8	-3.4	Tool & die makers	1.1	5.4
Sales reps, wholesale & manufacturing, exc tech	1.8	0.4	Office clerks, general	1.1	-1.1
Engine & other machine assemblers	1.6	0.4	General & operations managers	1.1	-9.6
Industrial truck & tractor operators	1.6	-9.6	Bookkeeping, accounting, & auditing clerks	1.0	0.4
Structural metal fabricators & fitters	1.6	0.4			

Source: Industry-Occupation Matrix, Bureau of Labor Statistics, December 4, 2007. These data are reported based on 4-digit NAICS categories but have been matched to corresponding 6-digit NAICS industry codes. The change reported for each occupation to the year 2016 is a percent of growth or decline as estimated by the Bureau of Labor Statistics. The abbreviation nec stands for 'not elsewhere classified'.

LOCATION BY STATE AND REGIONAL CONCENTRATION

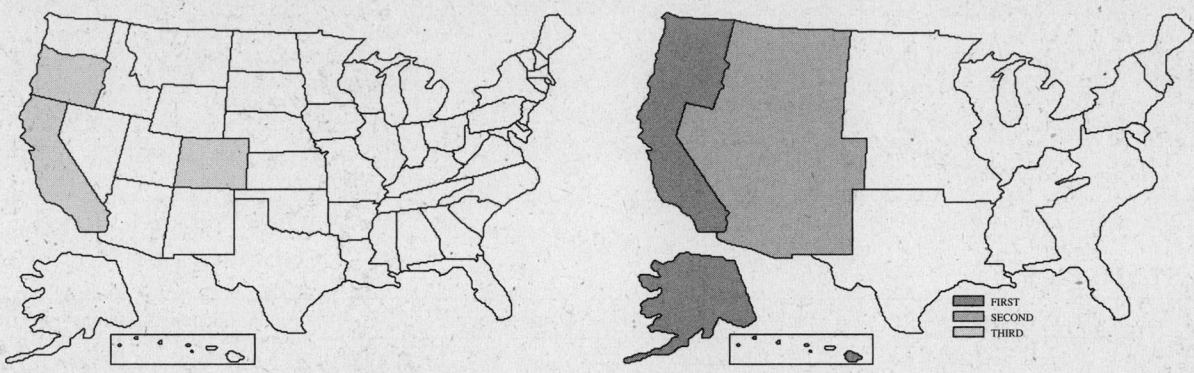

FIRST
SECOND
THIRD

INDUSTRY DATA BY STATE

State	Establish-ments	Shipments			Employment				Cost as % of Shipments	Investment per Employee ($)
		Total ($ mil)	% of U.S.	Per Establ.	Total Number	% of U.S.	Per Establ.	Wages ($/hour)		
California	133	563.7	12.2	4,238.0	3,607	24.0	27	17.96	45.7	3,439
Colorado	12	54.5	1.2	4,544.4	359	2.4	30	20.35	23.3	1,827
Oregon	17	31.0	0.7	1,821.5	248	1.7	15	16.01	34.6	6,536

Source: 2002 *Economic Census*. The states are in descending order of shipments or establishments (if shipment data are missing for the majority). The symbol (D) appears when data are withheld to prevent disclosure of competitive information. States marked with (D) are sorted by number of establishments. A dash (-) indicates that the data element cannot be calculated. Data may not show all states active in the NAICS category. All data available at the time of publication are shown.

NAICS 336992 - MILITARY ARMORED VEHICLE, TANK, AND TANK COMPONENT MANUFACTURING

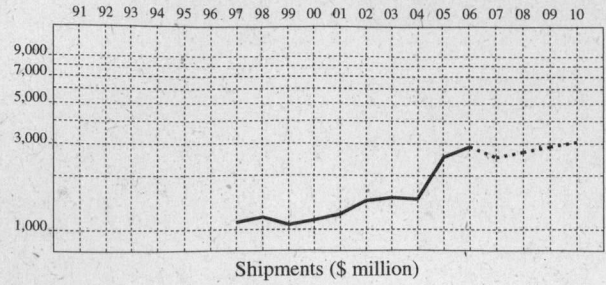

Shipments ($ million)

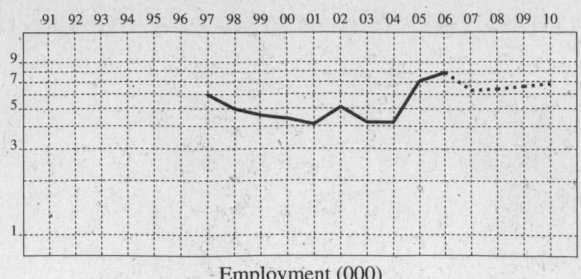

Employment (000)

GENERAL STATISTICS

Year	Com- panies	Establishments		Employment			Compensation		Production ($ million)			
		Total	with 20 or more employees	Total (000)	Production Workers (000)	Hours (Mil)	Payroll ($ mil)	Wages ($/hr)	Cost of Materials	Value Added by Manufacture	Value of Shipments	Capital Invest.
1997	39	44	23	6.0	2.9	5.4	238.2	19.93	495.7	552.8	1,095.4	17.3
1998		52	26	5.0	2.3	4.9	258.0	21.34	443.8	730.7	1,172.7	15.7
1999		52	28	4.6	2.2	4.6	264.3	20.60	425.4	668.9	1,064.8	17.4
2000		53	25	4.4	2.1	4.3	251.4	20.90	387.5	719.0	1,128.6	16.8
2001		48	25	4.1	2.0	3.9	252.1	25.10	474.4	810.7	1,221.2	15.1
2002	31	39	24	5.1	2.5	5.3	282.4	21.51	662.5	818.0	1,450.9	13.9
2003		43	29	4.2	2.2	4.2	247.7	24.81	628.5	864.8	1,508.8	22.0
2004		49	31	4.2	2.3	4.4	253.8	23.86	558.8	914.6	1,477.8	18.4
2005		53	36	7.1	4.4	8.6	387.5	21.51	1,151.7	1,392.7	2,539.0	33.1
2006		48P	33P	7.9	4.9	9.8	463.1	21.88	1,407.3	1,526.0	2,890.8	50.1
2007		48P	34P	6.3P	3.9P	7.7P	386.4P	23.58P	1,230.2P	1,333.9P	2,526.9P	36.5P
2008		48P	35P	6.4P	4.1P	8.1P	404.0P	23.85P	1,316.2P	1,427.2P	2,703.6P	39.2P
2009		47P	37P	6.6P	4.3P	8.5P	421.5P	24.11P	1,402.2P	1,520.5P	2,880.4P	41.8P
2010		47P	38P	6.8P	4.5P	8.9P	439.1P	24.37P	1,488.2P	1,613.8P	3,057.1P	44.5P

Sources: 1997 and 2002 *Economic Census*; other years, up to 2006, are from *Annual Survey of Manufactures*. Establishment counts for non-Census years are from *County Business Patterns*; 1997 and 2002 values are from the 1997 and 2002 censuses, respectively. 'P's show projections by the editors.

INDICES OF CHANGE

Year	Com- panies	Establishments		Employment			Compensation		Production ($ million)			
		Total	with 20 or more employees	Total (000)	Production Workers (000)	Hours (Mil)	Payroll ($ mil)	Wages ($/hr)	Cost of Materials	Value Added by Manufacture	Value of Shipments	Capital Invest.
1997	126	113	96	118	116	102	84	93	75	68	75	124
1998		133	108	98	92	92	91	99	67	89	81	113
1999		133	117	90	88	87	94	96	64	82	73	125
2000		136	104	86	84	81	89	97	58	88	78	121
2001		123	104	80	80	74	89	117	72	99	84	109
2002	100	100	100	100	100	100	100	100	100	100	100	100
2003		110	121	82	88	79	88	115	95	106	104	158
2004		126	129	82	92	83	90	111	84	112	102	132
2005		136	150	139	176	162	137	100	174	170	175	238
2006		122P	138P	155	196	185	164	102	212	187	199	360
2007		122P	143P	124P	156P	145P	137P	110P	186P	163P	174P	263P
2008		122P	148P	125P	164P	153P	143P	111P	199P	174P	186P	282P
2009		122P	152P	129P	172P	160P	149P	112P	212P	186P	199P	301P
2010		122P	157P	133P	180P	168P	155P	113P	225P	197P	211P	320P

Sources: Same as General Statistics. Values reflect change from the base year, 2002. Values above 100 mean greater than 2002, values below 100 mean less than 2002, and the values of 100 in other years means the same as 2002. 'P's show projections by the editors.

SELECTED RATIOS

For 2002	Avg. of All Manufact.	Analyzed Industry	Index	For 2002	Avg. of All Manufact.	Analyzed Industry	Index
Employees per Establishment	42	131	312	Value Added per Production Worker	182,367	327,200	179
Payroll per Establishment	1,639,184	7,241,026	442	Cost per Establishment	5,769,015	16,987,179	294
Payroll per Employee	39,053	55,373	142	Cost per Employee	137,446	129,902	95
Production Workers per Establishment	30	64	217	Cost per Production Worker	195,506	265,000	136
Wages per Establishment	694,845	2,923,154	421	Shipments per Establishment	11,158,348	37,202,564	333
Wages per Production Worker	23,548	45,601	194	Shipments per Employee	265,847	284,490	107
Hours per Production Worker	1,980	2,120	107	Shipments per Production Worker	378,144	580,360	153
Wages per Hour	11.89	21.51	181	Investment per Establishment	361,338	356,410	99
Value Added per Establishment	5,381,325	20,974,359	390	Investment per Employee	8,609	2,725	32
Value Added per Employee	128,210	160,392	125	Investment per Production Worker	12,245	5,560	45

Sources: Same as General Statistics. The 'Average of All Manufacturing' column represents the average of all manufacturing industries reported for the most recent complete year available. The Index shows the relationship between the Average and the Analyzed Industry. For example, 100 means that they are equal; 500 that the Analyzed Industry is five times the average; 50 means that the Analyzed Industry is half the national average. The abbreviation 'na' is used to show that data are 'not available'. Ratios shown for 2002, the last complete census year.

LEADING COMPANIES   Number shown: **75**   Total sales ($ mil): **637,469**   Total employment (000): **1,168.0**

Company Name	Address				CEO Name	Phone	Co. Type	Sales ($ mil)	Empl. (000)
General Motors Corp.	300 Renaissance Ctr	Detroit	MI	48265		313-556-5000	P	181,122	266.0
Ford Motor Co.	1 American Rd.	Dearborn	MI	48126		313-322-3000	P	172,455	246.0
United Technologies Corp.	1 Financial Plz.	Hartford	CT	06101	Mario Abajo	860-728-7000	P	47,829	225.6
Chrysler L.L.C.	1000 Chrysler Dr.	Auburn Hills	MI	48326	Thomas W. LaSorda	248-576-5741	S	45,237*	84.4
American Honda Motor Company	1919 Torrance Blvd.	Torrance	CA	90501	Koichi Kondo	310-783-2000	S	42,539	25.0
General Dynamics Corp.	2941 Fairview Park	Falls Church	VA	22042	Nicholas D. Chabraja	703-876-3000	P	27,240	83.5
PACCAR Inc.	PO Box 1518	Bellevue	WA	98009		425-468-7400	P	15,220	21.8
Ford VAC Corp.	1 American Rd.	Dearborn	MI	48121	William J. Ford	313-322-3000	S	15,105*	1.9
Dana Corp.	PO Box 1000	Toledo	OH	43697	Michael J. Burns	419-535-4500	P	8,504	45.0
Triangle Suspension Systems	PO Box 425	Du Bois	PA	15801	Greg Maffia	814-375-7211	R	7,000*	0.2
Oshkosh Truck Corp.	PO Box 2566	Oshkosh	WI	54903	Robert G. Bohn	920-235-9150	P	6,307	14.2
Toyota Motor Mfg. N America	25 Atlantic Ave.	Erlanger	KY	41018	Masamoto Amezawa	859-746-4000	S	6,120*	7.5
Honda of America Manufacturing	24000 Honda Pkwy.	Marysville	OH	43040	Takeo Fukui	937-642-5000	S	5,090*	13.0
Mack Trucks Inc.	PO Box M	Allentown	PA	18105		610-709-3011	R	4,324*	0.8
Toyota Motor Mfg, Kentucky	PO Box 2700	Georgetown	KY	40324	Steven Angelo	502-868-2000	R	4,181*	5.0
New United Motor Manufacturing	45500 Fremont	Fremont	CA	94538	Bruce Walker	510-498-5500	J	4,080*	5.0
Saturn Corp.	PO Box 1502	Spring Hill	TN	37174		931-486-5000	S	3,901	9.6
Motors Insurance Corp.	PO Box 66937	St. Louis	MO	63166	Gary Kuzumi		S	3,849*	2.2
Thor Industries Inc.	PO Box 629	Jackson Center	OH	45334		937-596-6849	P	3,066	9.1
AutoAlliance International	1 International Dr.	Flat Rock	MI	48134	Phillip G. Spender	734-782-7800	J	3,019*	3.7
Freightliner L.L.C.	PO Box 3849	Portland	OR	97208	Chris Patterson	503-745-8000	S	2,734*	14.0
BMW of North America L.L.C.	PO Box 1227	Westwood	NJ	07675	Thomas Purves	201-307-4000	S	2,690*	1.0
Nissan North America Inc.	333 Commerce St.	Nashville	TN	37201	Carlos Ghosn	615-725-1000	S	2,148	14.0
Heil Co.	5751 Cornelison Rd.	Chattanooga	TN	37411	Michael G. Jobe	423-899-9100	S	2,085*	1.6
Renco Group Inc.	30 Rockefeller Plz.	New York	NY	10112	Ira Leno Rennert	212-541-6000	R	1,900	9.4
Thor America Inc.	37 Old 522	Middleburg	PA	17842	W. F. B. Thompson	570-837-1663	S	1,592*	8.5
Aero Coach Inc.	Hickory Hill Rd.	Longview	TX	75601	W. F. B. Thompson	903-663-7699	S	1,313*	7.5
Monaco Coach Corp.	91320 Coburg Indust	Coburg	OR	97408		541-686-8011	P	1,298	5.3
Federal Signal Corp.	1415 W 22nd St.	Oak Brook	IL	60523	James C. Janning	630-954-2000	P	1,268	5.5
Mitsubishi Motors N America	PO Box 6014	Cypress	CA	90630	Hiroshi Harunari	714-372-6000	S	1,198	3.6
International Truck and Engine	PO Box 1488	Warrenville	IL	60555	Daniel C. Ustian	630-753-5000	S	1,114*	1.7
Spartan Motors Chassis Inc.	1165 Reynolds Rd.	Charlotte	MI	48813	John Sztykiel	517-543-6400	S	1,030*	0.8
Toyota Motor Mfg. W Virginia	1 Sugar Maple Ln.	Buffalo	WV	25033	Laquita Harris	304-937-7000	S	901*	0.9
North American Bus Industries	106 National Dr.	Anniston	AL	36207		256-831-4296	R	886*	0.6
Utilimaster Corp.	PO Box 585	Wakarusa	IN	46573	Lawrence Doyle	574-862-4561	R	836*	1.0
Spartan Motors Inc.	PO Box 440	Charlotte	MI	48813		517-543-6400	P	682	1.4
General Dynamics Land Systems	PO Box 2074	Warren	MI	48090		586-825-4000	S	674*	7.4
Airstream Inc.	PO Box 629	Jackson Center	OH	45334	Bpob Wheeler	937-596-6111	S	622*	0.5
Purdy Motor S.A.	CC Aventura 100	San Jose	PR	00930	John Kilmer	506-287-4230	S	509*	0.4
Coachmen Industries Inc.	PO Box 3300	Elkhart	IN	46515	Richard M. Lavers	574-262-0123	P	481	2.7
Ford of North Miami Beach	2198 NE 163rd St.	N Miami Bch	FL	33162		305-493-5000	R	447*	0.3
Reinke Manufacturing Company	PO Box 566	Deshler	NE	68340	Chris Roth	402-365-7251	R	335*	0.4
Wheeled Coach Industries Corp.	2737 Forsyth Rd.	Winter Park	FL	32792	Robert Collins	407-677-7777	S	326*	0.4
Jefferson Industries Corp.	6670 State Rte.	West Jefferson	OH	43162	Hideo Hayashi	614-879-5300	R	309*	0.4
ASC Inc.	1 ASC Ctr.	Southgate	MI	48195	Paul Wilbur	734-285-4911	S	300*	1.0
Elgin Sweeper Co.	1300 W Bartlett Rd.	Elgin	IL	60120	Mark Weber	847-741-5370	S	286*	0.3
SanduskyAthol International	3130 W Monroe St.	Sandusky	OH	44870	Jack Givens	419-627-3200	R	266*	0.2
Allianz Sweeper Co.	4651 Schaefer Ave.	Chino	CA	91710	Gabriel Charky	909-613-5600	S	233*	0.1
Braun Industries Inc.	1170 Production Dr.	Van Wert	OH	45891	Phillip Braun	419-232-7020	R	223*	0.2
Collins Industries Inc.	PO Box 648	Hutchinson	KS	67502	Don L. Collins	620-663-5551	S	208	1.0
Cheetah Chassis Corp.	PO Box 388	Berwick	PA	18603	Frank Katz	570-752-2708	R	167*	0.2
Ferrara Fire Apparatus Inc.	PO Box 249	Holden	LA	70744	Christopher Ferrara	225-567-7100	R	159*	0.3
Midwest Stamping Inc.	3455 Briarfield	Maumee	OH	43537	Ronald L. Thompson	419-724-6970	R	155*	0.6
VSV Group	1110 DI Dr.	Elkhart	IN	46514	Mark Grossbauer	574-264-7511	R	148*	0.5
B.A. E Sys. Land & Armaments	PO Box 15512	York	PA	17405		717-225-8000	R	148*	0.8
Smeal Fire Apparatus Co.	PO Box 8	Snyder	NE	68664	Delwin Smeal	402-568-2224	R	139*	0.3
Palomar Medical Technologies	82 Cambridge St.	Burlington	MA	01803	Joseph P. Caruso	781-993-2300	P	124	0.3
Freightliner Specialty Vehicle	2300 S 13th St.	Clinton	OK	73601	Tim Sinor	580-323-4100	S	123*	0.2
Schwarze Industries Inc.	1055 Jordan Rd.	Huntsville	AL	35811	Ronald A. Robinson	256-851-1200	S	122*	0.2
Excellance Inc.	453 Lanier Rd.	Madison	AL	35758	Charles Epps	256-772-9321	R	112*	<0.1
Executive Coach Builders Inc.	4400 W Production	Springfield	MO	65803	David Bakare	417-935-2233	R	104*	0.1
Louis Berkman Company Inc.	PO Box 820	Steubenville	OH	43952	Louis Berkman	740-283-3722	R	82*	<0.1
Alfa Leisure Inc.	1612 S Cucamonga	Ontario	CA	91761	Johnnie R. Crean	909-628-5574	R	75*	0.7
FWD Seagrave Holdings L.P.	105 E 12th St.	Clintonville	WI	54929		715-823-2141	R	72*	0.4
Custom Coach International	PO Box 869	Pawhuska	OK	74056	Ray Smith	918-287-4445	R	71*	<0.1
Temic Automotive of N America	21440 Lake Cook	Barrington	IL	60010		847-862-6300	R	71*	0.4
Sutphen Corp.	PO Box 158	Amlin	OH	43002		614-889-1005	R	71*	<0.1
Foretravel Inc.	1221 NW Stallings	Nacogdoches	TX	75964		936-564-8367	R	68*	0.3
Accubuilt Inc.	4707 E Kearney St.	Springfield	MO	65803	Dan Mitchell	417-864-4411	R	67*	<0.1
Amerigon Inc.	21680 Haggerty Rd.	Northville	MI	48167	Daniel R. Coker	248-504-0500	P	64	<0.1
Alpine Armoring Inc.	570 Herndon Pkwy.	Herndon	VA	20170	Fred Khoroushi	703-471-0009	R	56*	<0.1
Super Products Corp.	PO Box 270128	Milwaukee	WI	53227	Henry Rowan	262-784-7100	R	51*	0.1
Super Vacuum Manufacturing Co.	PO Box 87	Loveland	CO	80539	Roger Weinmeister	970-667-5146	R	51*	0.1
E-ONE	1601 SW 37 Ave.	Ocala	FL	34474	Mark Gastafin	352-237-1122	D	44*	0.3
Arotech Corp.	1229 Oak Valley Dr.	Ann Arbor	MI	48108	Robert S. Ehrlich		P	43	0.3

Source: Ward's Business Directory of U.S. Private and Public Companies, Volumes 1 and 2, 2008. The company type code used is as follows: P - Public, R - Private, S - Subsidiary, D - Division, J - Joint Venture, A - Affiliate, G - Group. Sales are in millions of dollars, employees are in thousands. An asterisk (*) indicates an estimated sales volume. The symbol < stands for 'less than'. Company names and addresses are truncated, in some cases, to fit into the available space.

MATERIALS CONSUMED

Material	Quantity	Delivered Cost ($ million)
Metal bolts, nuts, screws, and other screw machine products	(X)	44.5
Other fabricated metal products (exc. castings and forgings)	(X)	115.7
Iron and steel castings (rough and semifinished)	(X)	8.9
Aluminum and aluminum-base alloy castings (rough and semifinished)	(X)	1.8
Iron and steel forgings	(X)	(D)
Aluminum and aluminum-base alloy forgings	(X)	(D)
Other nonferrous forgings	(X)	(D)
Steel shapes and forms (exc. castings, forgings, fabr. metal products)	(X)	43.2
Copper and copper-base alloy shapes and forms (exc. castings, forgings, fabr. metal products)	(X)	(D)
Aluminum and aluminum-base alloy shapes and forms (exc. castings, forgings, fabr. metal products)	(X)	(D)
Other nonferrous shapes and forms (exc. castings, forgings, fabricated metal products)	(X)	(D)
Plastics resins consumed in the form of granules, pellets, etc.	(X)	(D)
Fabricated plastics products (excluding gaskets)	(X)	(D)
Electronic, hydraulic, and mechanical subassemblies	(X)	(D)
Rough and dressed lumber	(X)	(D)
Other chemicals and allied products	(X)	(D)
Machine tool accessories, including cutting tools	(X)	0.1
Paperboard containers, boxes, and corrugated paperboard	(X)	0.1
All other materials, components, parts, containers, and supplies	(X)	194.8
Materials, ingredients, containers, and supplies, nsk	(X)	43.2

Source: 2002 *Economic Census*. Explanation of symbols used: (D): Withheld to avoid disclosure of competitive data; na: Not available; (S): Withheld because statistical norms were not met; (X): Not applicable; (Z): Less than half the unit shown; nec: Not elsewhere classified; nsk: Not specified by kind; - : zero; p : 10-19 percent estimated; q : 20-29 percent estimated.

PRODUCT SHARE DETAILS

Product or Product Class Shipments	Mil. $	Product or Product Class Shipments	Mil. $
MILITARY ARMORED VEHICLES, TANKS, AND TANK COMPONENTS	1,745.5	combat vehicles and armored utility vehicles, including parts	901.5
Tanks and parts	821.4	Military armored vehicles, tank, and tank components	22.6
Self-propelled weapons and parts and other full-tracked			

Source: 2002 *Economic Census*. The values are product shipments in millions of dollars for 2002. Total product shipments may be lower or higher than industry shipments. See Introduction for a full discussion. Values of indented subcategories are summed in the main heading(s). The symbol (D) appears when data are withheld to prevent disclosure of competitive information. The abbreviation nsk stands for 'not specified by kind' and nec for 'not elsewhere classified'. A dash (-) means zero.

INPUTS AND OUTPUTS FOR MILITARY ARMORED VEHICLE, TANK, & TANK COMPONENT

Economic Sector or Industry Providing Inputs	%	Sector	Economic Sector or Industry Buying Outputs	%	Sector
Compensation of employees	24.9		Federal government, investment, national defense	63.4	Fed Govt
Ornamental & architectural metal products	12.4	Manufg.	Exports of goods & services	30.9	Cap Inv
Management of companies & enterprises	7.7	Services	Military armored vehicles, tanks, & tank components	4.0	Manufg.
Military armored vehicles, tanks, & tank components	5.4	Manufg.	Change in private inventories	1.5	In House
Wholesale trade	5.1	Trade	Scientific research & development services	0.2	Services
Turned products & screws, nuts, & bolts	3.1	Manufg.			
Iron & steel mills & ferroalloys	2.1	Manufg.			
Machine shops	1.6	Manufg.			
Power, distribution, & specialty transformers	1.5	Manufg.			
Coating, engraving, heat treating & allied activities	1.2	Manufg.			
Plastics products, nec	0.9	Manufg.			
Alumina refining & primary aluminum production	0.9	Manufg.			
Lessors of nonfinancial assets	0.9	Fin/R.E.			
Sawmills & wood preservation	0.8	Manufg.			
Copper rolling, drawing, extruding, & alloying	0.8	Manufg.			
Scientific research & development services	0.8	Services			
Nonferrous metal (ex. copper & aluminum) processing	0.8	Manufg.			
Real estate	0.8	Fin/R.E.			
Plastics materials & resins	0.7	Manufg.			
Securities, commodity contracts, investments	0.7	Fin/R.E.			
Truck transportation	0.6	Util.			
Power generation & supply	0.6	Util.			
Management, scientific, & technical consulting	0.5	Services			
Metal cans, boxes, & other containers (light gauge)	0.5	Manufg.			
Monetary authorities/depository credit intermediation	0.5	Fin/R.E.			
Fabricated metals, nec	0.5	Manufg.			
Advertising & related services	0.4	Services			
Crowns & closures & metal stamping	0.4	Manufg.			
Ferrous metal foundries	0.4	Manufg.			
Professional, scientific, technical services, nec	0.4	Services			
Valve & fittings other than plumbing	0.4	Manufg.			
Ball & roller bearings	0.3	Manufg.			
Handtools	0.3	Manufg.			

Continued on next page.

INPUTS AND OUTPUTS FOR MILITARY ARMORED VEHICLE, TANK, & TANK COMPONENT - Continued

Economic Sector or Industry Providing Inputs	%	Sector	Economic Sector or Industry Buying Outputs	%	Sector
Basic inorganic chemicals, nec	0.3	Manufg.			
Printed circuit assemblies (electronic assemblies)	0.3	Manufg.			
Plate work & fabricated structural products	0.3	Manufg.			
Taxes on production & imports, less subsidies	0.3				
Basic organic chemicals, nec	0.3	Manufg.			
Warehousing & storage	0.3	Util.			
Semiconductors & related devices	0.2	Manufg.			
Custom roll forming	0.2	Manufg.			
Data processing, hosting, & related services	0.2	Services			
Accounting, tax preparation, bookkeeping, & payroll	0.2	Services			
Business support services	0.2	Services			
Automotive equipment rental & leasing	0.2	Fin/R.E.			
Legal services	0.2	Services			
Food services & drinking places	0.2	Services			
Springs & wire products	0.2	Manufg.			
Employment services	0.1	Services			
Natural gas distribution	0.1	Util.			
Services to buildings & dwellings	0.1	Services			
Maintenance/repair of nonresidential structures	0.1	Construct.			
Telecommunications	0.1	Services			
Architectural, engineering, & related services	0.1	Services			
Other computer related services, including facilities	0.1	Services			
Nonferrous metal foundries	0.1	Manufg.			
Rail transportation	0.1	Util.			
Specialized design services	0.1	Services			
Support services, nec	0.1	Services			

Source: Benchmark Input-Output Accounts for the U.S. Economy, 2002, U.S. Department of Commerce, Washington, D.C., January 2008. The abbreviation nec stands for 'not elsewhere classified'.

OCCUPATIONS EMPLOYED BY OTHER TRANSPORTATION EQUIPMENT MANUFACTURING

Occupation	% of Total 2006	Change to 2016	Occupation	% of Total 2006	Change to 2016
Team assemblers	17.5	0.4	Laborers & freight, stock, & material movers, hand	1.6	-9.6
Welders, cutters, solderers, & brazers	7.5	6.8	Industrial engineers	1.4	22.0
Cutting, punching, & press machine operators	3.9	-9.6	Painters, transportation equipment	1.4	0.4
First-line supervisors/managers of production workers	3.3	0.4	Fiberglass laminators & fabricators	1.3	0.4
Grinding, lapping, polishing machine tool operators	3.3	-2.6	Purchasing agents, exc wholesale, retail, & farm	1.2	0.4
Inspectors, testers, sorters, samplers, & weighers	2.6	-5.3	Maintenance & repair workers, general	1.1	0.4
Assemblers & fabricators, nec	1.9	-9.6	Production, planning, & expediting clerks	1.1	0.4
Shipping, receiving, & traffic clerks	1.8	-3.4	Tool & die makers	1.1	5.4
Sales reps, wholesale & manufacturing, exc tech	1.8	0.4	Office clerks, general	1.1	-1.1
Engine & other machine assemblers	1.6	0.4	General & operations managers	1.1	-9.6
Industrial truck & tractor operators	1.6	-9.6	Bookkeeping, accounting, & auditing clerks	1.0	0.4
Structural metal fabricators & fitters	1.6	0.4			

Source: Industry-Occupation Matrix, Bureau of Labor Statistics, December 4, 2007. These data are reported based on 4-digit NAICS categories but have been matched to corresponding 6-digit NAICS industry codes. The change reported for each occupation to the year 2016 is a percent of growth or decline as estimated by the Bureau of Labor Statistics. The abbreviation nec stands for 'not elsewhere classified'.

LOCATION BY STATE AND REGIONAL CONCENTRATION

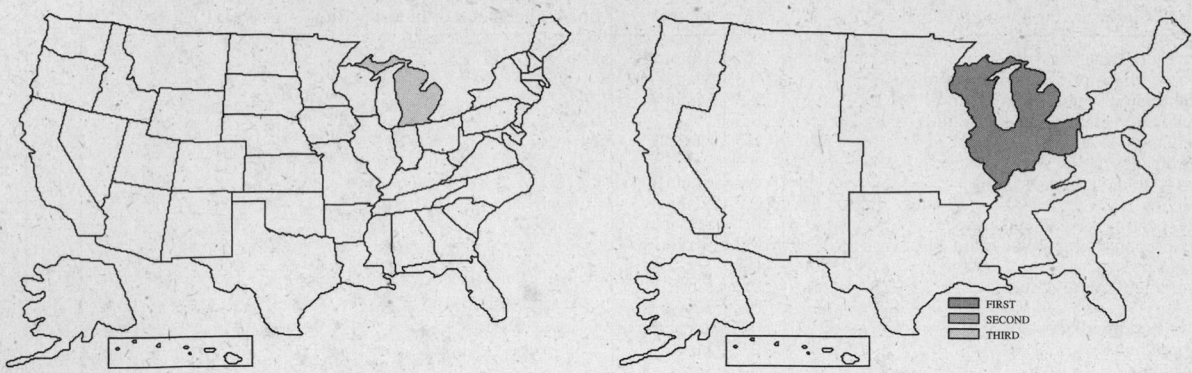

INDUSTRY DATA BY STATE

| State | Establish-ments | Shipments | | | Employment | | | | Cost as % of Shipments | Investment per Employee ($) |
		Total ($ mil)	% of U.S.	Per Establ.	Total Number	% of U.S.	Per Establ.	Wages ($/hour)		
Michigan	11	97.0	6.7	8,821.9	522	10.2	47	16.63	48.2	6,130

Source: 2002 *Economic Census*. The states are in descending order of shipments or establishments (if shipment data are missing for the majority). The symbol (D) appears when data are withheld to prevent disclosure of competitive information. States marked with (D) are sorted by number of establishments. A dash (-) indicates that the data element cannot be calculated. Data may not show all states active in the NAICS category. All data available at the time of publication are shown.

NAICS 336999 - TRANSPORTATION EQUIPMENT MANUFACTURING NEC

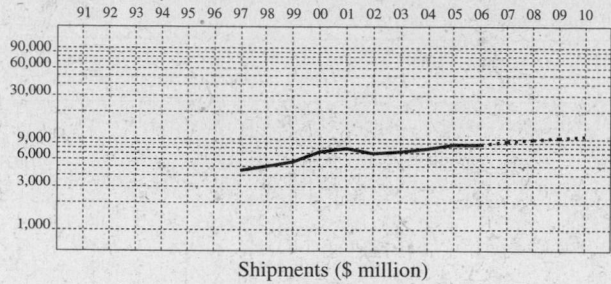

Shipments ($ million)

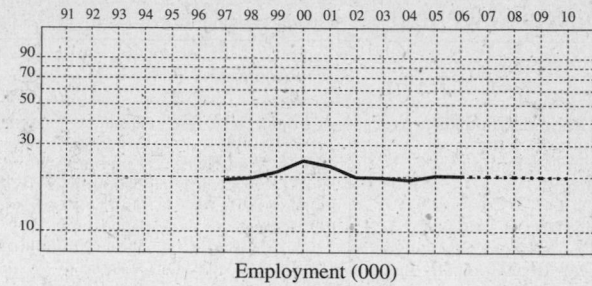

Employment (000)

GENERAL STATISTICS

Year	Com- panies	Establishments		Employment			Compensation		Production ($ million)			
		Total	with 20 or more employees	Total (000)	Production Workers (000)	Hours (Mil)	Payroll ($ mil)	Wages ($/hr)	Cost of Materials	Value Added by Manufacture	Value of Shipments	Capital Invest.
1997	353	374	136	19.3	13.9	24.9	504.9	11.70	2,875.9	1,679.5	4,527.4	97.2
1998		400	140	19.7	14.1	25.9	578.0	12.30	3,236.0	1,769.8	5,032.9	122.3
1999		386	138	21.3	15.4	29.1	644.0	12.69	3,766.2	1,876.8	5,644.9	106.3
2000		378	144	24.5	18.3	35.9	771.7	13.18	5,116.7	2,154.6	7,258.3	116.7
2001		366	133	22.9	17.3	34.4	753.0	13.50	5,322.8	2,581.1	7,928.9	122.4
2002	420	431	91	19.9	14.6	27.5	625.5	14.23	4,260.3	2,664.4	6,958.9	195.0
2003		396	98	19.8	14.2	27.0	680.4	15.05	4,822.3	2,435.5	7,280.2	194.8
2004		401	93	19.2	14.3	26.0	665.2	15.77	5,219.0	2,574.1	7,844.7	184.1
2005		438	101	20.3	15.1	28.3	760.6	15.71	5,857.3	2,862.8	8,688.3	180.4
2006		424P	85P	20.2	14.9	28.7	759.7	15.25	6,009.0	2,688.6	8,696.2	165.8
2007		430P	78P	20.2P	15.1P	28.8P	783.5P	16.52P	6,513.4P	2,914.3P	9,426.1P	205.8P
2008		435P	71P	20.1P	15.0P	28.8P	803.4P	16.99P	6,819.9P	3,051.4P	9,869.8P	216.3P
2009		441P	64P	20.0P	15.0P	28.9P	823.2P	17.46P	7,126.5P	3,188.6P	10,313.4P	226.7P
2010		447P	57P	19.9P	15.0P	28.9P	843.1P	17.93P	7,433.0P	3,325.8P	10,757.1P	237.1P

Sources: 1997 and 2002 *Economic Census*; other years, up to 2006, are from *Annual Survey of Manufactures*. Establishment counts for non-Census years are from *County Business Patterns*; 1997 and 2002 values are from the 1997 and 2002 censuses, respectively. 'P's show projections by the editors.

INDICES OF CHANGE

Year	Com- panies	Establishments		Employment			Compensation		Production ($ million)			
		Total	with 20 or more employees	Total (000)	Production Workers (000)	Hours (Mil)	Payroll ($ mil)	Wages ($/hr)	Cost of Materials	Value Added by Manufacture	Value of Shipments	Capital Invest.
1997	84	87	149	97	95	91	81	82	68	63	65	50
1998		93	154	99	97	94	92	86	76	66	72	63
1999		90	152	107	105	106	103	89	88	70	81	55
2000		88	158	123	125	131	123	93	120	81	104	60
2001		85	146	115	118	125	120	95	125	97	114	63
2002	100	100	100	100	100	100	100	100	100	100	100	100
2003		92	108	99	97	98	109	106	113	91	105	100
2004		93	102	96	98	95	106	111	123	97	113	94
2005		102	111	102	103	103	122	110	137	107	125	93
2006		98P	93P	102	102	104	121	107	141	101	125	85
2007		100P	86P	102P	103P	105P	125P	116P	153P	109P	135P	106P
2008		101P	78P	101P	103P	105P	128P	119P	160P	115P	142P	111P
2009		102P	70P	101P	103P	105P	132P	123P	167P	120P	148P	116P
2010		104P	63P	100P	103P	105P	135P	126P	174P	125P	155P	122P

Sources: Same as General Statistics. Values reflect change from the base year, 2002. Values above 100 mean greater than 2002, values below 100 mean less than 2002, and the values of 100 in other years means the same as 2002. 'P's show projections by the editors.

SELECTED RATIOS

For 2002	Avg. of All Manufact.	Analyzed Industry	Index	For 2002	Avg. of All Manufact.	Analyzed Industry	Index
Employees per Establishment	42	46	110	Value Added per Production Worker	182,367	182,493	100
Payroll per Establishment	1,639,184	1,451,276	89	Cost per Establishment	5,769,015	9,884,687	171
Payroll per Employee	39,053	31,432	80	Cost per Employee	137,446	214,085	156
Production Workers per Establishment	30	34	115	Cost per Production Worker	195,506	291,801	149
Wages per Establishment	694,845	907,947	131	Shipments per Establishment	11,158,348	16,145,940	145
Wages per Production Worker	23,548	26,803	114	Shipments per Employee	265,847	349,693	132
Hours per Production Worker	1,980	1,884	95	Shipments per Production Worker	378,144	476,637	126
Wages per Hour	11.89	14.23	120	Investment per Establishment	361,338	452,436	125
Value Added per Establishment	5,381,325	6,181,903	115	Investment per Employee	8,609	9,799	114
Value Added per Employee	128,210	133,889	104	Investment per Production Worker	12,245	13,356	109

Sources: Same as General Statistics. The 'Average of All Manufacturing' column represents the average of all manufacturing industries reported for the most recent complete year available. The Index shows the relationship between the Average and the Analyzed Industry. For example, 100 means that they are equal; 500 that the Analyzed Industry is five times the average; 50 means that the Analyzed Industry is half the national average. The abbreviation 'na' is used to show that data are 'not available'. Ratios shown for 2002, the last complete census year.

LEADING COMPANIES   Number shown: **63**   Total sales ($ mil): **9,872**   Total employment (000): **21.5**

Company Name	Address				CEO Name	Phone	Co. Type	Sales ($ mil)	Empl. (000)
Nordic Group of Companies Ltd.	414 Broadway, 200	Baraboo	WI	53913	William R. Sauey	608-356-0136	R	2,706*	2.5
Polaris Industries Inc.	2100 Hwy. 55	Medina	MN	55340		763-542-0500	P	1,780	3.2
Tri-Con Industries Ltd.	4000 NW 44th St.	Lincoln	NE	68524		402-470-3311	R	1,450*	0.3
TriMas Corp.	39400 Woodward	Bloomfield Hls	MI	48304	Grant Beard	248-631-5450	P	1,068	5.1
Arctic Cat Inc.	PO Box 810	Thief River Fls	MN	56701		218-681-8558	P	782	1.8
Columbia Parcar Florida	PO Box 60	Reedsburg	WI	53959		608-524-8888	R	256*	<0.1
Textron Turf-Care & Specialty	2166-A W Park Ct.	Stone Mountain	GA	30087	Jon Carlson	770-498-9316	R	243*	1.2
MasterCraft Boat Company Inc.	100 Cherokee Cv Dr.	Vonore	TN	37885		423-884-2221	R	199*	0.6
Drago Supply Company Inc.	740 Houston Ave.	Port Arthur	TX	77640	Joseph P. Drago	409-983-4911	R	164*	0.2
Draw-Tite Inc.	47774 Anchor Ct. W	Plymouth	MI	48170	Thomas Benson	734-656-3000	R	141*	0.8
Quixote Corp.	35 E Wacker Dr.	Chicago	IL	60601	Leslie J. Jezuit	312-467-6755	P	138	0.7
EZ Loader Boat Trailers Inc.	PO Box 3263	Spokane	WA	99220	Randy Johnson	509-489-0181	R	66*	0.1
Dynamic Corp.	Box 67	Montmorenci	IN	47962	Debbie Fleming	765-583-4406	S	57*	<0.1
Contract Manufacturer L.L.C.	200 County Rd.	Madill	OK	73446	Ronald Jackson	580-795-5536	R	56*	0.3
Midwest Industries Inc.	PO Box 235	Ida Grove	IA	51445	Andy Brosius	712-364-3365	R	54*	0.3
EZ Way Inc.	PO Box 89	Clarinda	IA	51632	Bill Lisle	712-542-5102	R	52*	0.3
Teton Homes Corp.	PO Box 2349	Mills	WY	82644	Charles Larkin	307-235-1525	R	49*	0.2
Arctic Cat Sales Inc.	601 Brooks Ave. S	Thief River Fls	MN	56701	Christopher Twomey	218-681-8558	S	44*	0.2
Sooner Trailer Manufacturing	1515 McCurdy	Duncan	OK	73533	Jim Garis		R	43*	0.3
Dethmers Manufacturing Co.	PO Box 189	Boyden	IA	51234	James Koerselman	712-725-2311	R	42*	0.3
Karavan Trailers Inc.	PO Box 27	Fox Lake	WI	53933	Scott Boyd	920-928-6200	R	34*	0.3
Chief Automotive Systems Inc.	PO Box 1368	Grand Island	NE	68801	Randy Gard	308-384-9747	S	34*	0.2
Rolligon Corp.	6740 Hwy. 30	Anderson	TX	77830	Mike Dearing	936-873-2600	R	27*	<0.1
Magic Tilt Trailers Inc.	2161 Lions Club Rd.	Clearwater	FL	33764	Craig Blawson	727-535-5561	R	26*	<0.1
WW-Trailer Manufacturers Inc.	PO Box 807	Madill	OK	73446	H Watkins	580-795-5571	R	26*	0.2
Femco Inc.	500 N US Hwy 81	McPherson	KS	67460	Rodney Borman	620-241-3513	R	20*	<0.1
AL-KO KOBER Corp.	PO Box 1367	Elkhart	IN	46515	Elwood Smith	574-294-6651	S	20*	0.1
T.J.T. Inc.	PO Box 278	Emmett	ID	83617		208-365-5321	P	18	<0.1
Playbuoy Pontoon Manufacturing	PO Box 698	Alma	MI	48801	Jim Wolf	989-463-2112	R	18*	0.1
MGS Inc.	178 Muddy Creek	Denver	PA	17517	Andrew Gehman	717-336-7528	R	16*	0.1
IPV Inc.	PO Box 232	Vivian	LA	71082	William Parker	318-375-3241	R	16*	0.1
Leitner-Poma of America Inc.	2510 Foresight Cir.	Grand Junction	CO	81505	Anton Sebber	970-241-4442	R	15*	<0.1
Shelby Industries L.L.C.	PO Box 308	Shelbyville	KY	40066	Lalit Sarin	502-633-2040	R	15*	<0.1
HLT Ltd.	PO Box 569	Humboldt	IA	50548	Carl Crewson	515-332-1802	R	14*	0.1
Load Rite Trailers Inc.	265 Lincoln Hwy.	Fairless Hills	PA	19030	Bill Merkel	215-949-0500	R	14*	0.1
Performance Metal Works Inc.	PO Box 1338	Winnsboro	TX	75494	Royce Patterson	903-967-2622	R	14*	<0.1
Sundowner Trailers Inc.	1110 County Rd 6	Elkhart	IN	46514	Larry Shipman	574-262-1523	R	14*	0.1
Triton Corp.	857 W State St.	Hartford	WI	53027		262-670-6514	R	14*	0.1
Charmac Inc.	PO Box 205	Twin Falls	ID	83303	Lloyd Casperson	208-733-5241	R	12*	<0.1
Cleveland Hardware and Forging	3270 E 79th St.	Cleveland	OH	44104	William Hoban	216-641-5200	R	11*	<0.1
Scaletta Moloney Armoring	6755 S Belt Cir. Dr	Bedford Park	IL	60638	Joseph Scaletta	708-924-0099	R	10*	0.1
Intermountain Design Inc.	2190 S 3270 W	Salt Lake City	UT	84119	Lloyd Barney	801-972-5252	R	8*	<0.1
Croft Trailer Supply Inc.	PO Box 300320	Kansas City	MO	64130	Sandy Jones	816-861-1001	R	7*	<0.1
CCI Manufacturing Inc.	1770 E Smith St.	Warsaw	IN	46580	Kevin Deardorff	574-267-6900	D	7*	<0.1
Erskine Attachments Inc.	PO Box 1083	Alexandria	MN	56308	Todd Olson	218-687-4045	R	7*	<0.1
Quality S Manufacturing Inc.	PO Box 23910	Phoenix	AZ	85063	Dennis Weir	602-233-3499	R	7*	<0.1
Olympic Fiberglass Industries	PO Box 920	Rochester	IN	46975	William Adams	574-223-3101	R	7*	<0.1
Green Valley Manufacturing	100 Green Valley Dr	Mount Zion	IL	62549	Robert Johnston	217-864-4125	R	6*	<0.1
Western Construction Component	9484 Mission Park	Santee	CA	92071	George Wilson	619-596-5696	R	5*	<0.1
J-Rod Inc.	398 N Interstate 35	Red Oak	TX	75154	Raymon Hunt	972-617-3770	R	5*	<0.1
Rush Gold Inc.	920 Stone Hill Rd.	Denver	PA	17517	Glenn Hyneman	717-738-1849	R	5*	<0.1
Spreuer and Son Inc.	115 E Spring St.	LaGrange	IN	46761	Ron Troyer	260-463-3513	R	5*	<0.1
Silver Star Trailers	PO Box 1214	Ridgeland	SC	29936		843-726-8676	R	4*	<0.1
Crozier Trucking	42009 US 70 W	Portales	NM	88130	Gerald Crozier	505-356-8528	R	4*	<0.1
Quadra Manufacturing Inc.	PO Box 536	White Pigeon	MI	49099	Eugene Lehman	269-483-9633	R	4*	<0.1
Jerald Inc.	3050 Wagner Rd.	Waterloo	IA	50703	Todd Gordon	319-234-6195	R	3*	<0.1
Currahee Trailers Inc.	850 Tommy Irvin	Mount Airy	GA	30563	Chet Barrett	706-754-5396	R	3*	<0.1
Custom Fiberglass Molding Inc.	E5880 Little River	Weyauwega	WI	54983	Richard Discher	920-867-2606	R	2*	<0.1
Land and Sea Inc.	PO Box 96	North Salem	NH	03073	Bob Bergeron	603-329-5645	R	2*	<0.1
Mirage Enterprises Inc.	2212 Industrial Rd.	Nampa	ID	83687	Dale Swikert	208-461-7776	R	2*	<0.1
CCE Technologies Inc.	PO Box 1686	Centralia	IL	62801	Cynthia Pitts	618-533-9010	R	1*	<0.1
Wheelit Inc.	PO Box 352800	Toledo	OH	43635	Thomas Skilliter	419-531-4900	R	1*	<0.1
Pacific Engineering and Mfg.	317 Sandy Bend Rd.	Castle Rock	WA	98611	Richard Moss	360-274-8323	R	1*	<0.1

Source: *Ward's Business Directory of U.S. Private and Public Companies*, Volumes 1 and 2, 2008. The company type code used is as follows: P - Public, R - Private, S - Subsidiary, D - Division, J - Joint Venture, A - Affiliate, G - Group. Sales are in millions of dollars, employees are in thousands. An asterisk (*) indicates an estimated sales volume. The symbol < stands for 'less than'. Company names and addresses are truncated, in some cases, to fit into the available space.

MATERIALS CONSUMED

Material	Quantity	Delivered Cost ($ million)
Other metal vehicular parts, metal (trailer axles, wheels, etc.)	(X)	272.1
Gasoline internal combustion engines	(X)	660.5
Pneumatic tires and inner tubes	(X)	52.8
Plastics products consumed in the form of sheets, rods, etc.	(X)	264.7

Continued on next page.

MATERIALS CONSUMED - Continued

Material	Quantity	Delivered Cost ($ million)
Paints, varnishes, stains, lacquers, shellacs, japans, enamels, etc.	(X)	27.8
Fabricated metal products (excluding forgings)	(X)	285.9
Forgings	(X)	47.5
Castings, rough and semifinished	(X)	73.6
Steel bars, bar shapes, and plates (exc. castings, forgings, fabr. metal products)	(X)	57.4
Steel sheet and strip (including tinplate)	(X)	(D)
Steel structural shapes and sheet piling (exc. castings, forgings, fabr. metal products)	(X)	(D)
All other steel shapes and forms (exc. castings, forgings, fabr. metal products)	(X)	24.6
Aluminum and aluminum-base alloy shapes and forms (exc. castings, forgings, fabr. metal products)	(X)	28.0
Other nonferrous shapes and forms (exc. castings, forgings, fabricated metal products)	(X)	7.1
All other materials, components, parts, containers, and supplies	(X)	1,703.7
Materials, ingredients, containers, and supplies, nsk	(X)	430.4

Source: 2002 *Economic Census*. Explanation of symbols used: (D): Withheld to avoid disclosure of competitive data; na: Not available; (S): Withheld because statistical norms were not met; (X): Not applicable; (Z): Less than half the unit shown; nec: Not elsewhere classified; nsk: Not specified by kind; - : zero; p : 10-19 percent estimated; q : 20-29 percent estimated.

PRODUCT SHARE DETAILS

Product or Product Class Shipments	Mil. $	Product or Product Class Shipments	Mil. $
TRANSPORTATION EQUIPMENT, NEC	6,952.3	Parts for all-terrain vehicles	467.5
Self-propelled golf carts and industrial in-plant personnel carriers, and parts	**968.6**	Other transportation equipment, including snowmobiles and personal watercraft	1,493.4
Self-propelled golf carts (electric and gasoline) for carrying passengers and-or industrial in-plant personnel carriers	727.2	Snowmobiles	(D)
		Personal watercraft	287.9
Parts for self-propelled golf carts and industrial in-plant personnel carriers	241.4	Other transportation equipment, nec	(D)
		Parts for automobile and light truck trailers and other transportation equipment	327.1
Transportation equipment, nec, including all-terrain vehicles	**5,728.4**	Transportation equipment, nec, including all-terrain vehicles, nsk	5.8
All-terrain vehicles, gasoline and electric, for transport of people or goods, designed to traverse all types of terrain	3,434.6	**Transportation equipment, nec, nsk, total**	**255.2**

Source: 2002 *Economic Census*. The values are product shipments in millions of dollars for 2002. Total product shipments may be lower or higher than industry shipments. See Introduction for a full discussion. Values of indented subcategories are summed in the main heading(s). The symbol (D) appears when data are withheld to prevent disclosure of competitive information. The abbreviation nsk stands for 'not specified by kind' and nec for 'not elsewhere classified'. A dash (-) means zero.

INPUTS AND OUTPUTS FOR ALL OTHER TRANSPORTATION EQUIPMENT MANUFACTURING

Economic Sector or Industry Providing Inputs	%	Sector	Economic Sector or Industry Buying Outputs	%	Sector
Motor vehicle parts	12.7	Manufg.	Personal consumption expenditures	56.2	
Compensation of employees	12.6		Private fixed investment	21.5	
Wholesale trade	5.5	Trade	Transportation equipment, nec	4.8	Manufg.
Transportation equipment, nec	5.1	Manufg.	General Federal government services, defense	3.7	Fed Govt
Rubber products, nec	5.0	Manufg.	Exports of goods & services	3.3	Cap Inv
Fabricated metals, nec	4.9	Manufg.	Transit & ground passenger transportation	2.3	Util.
Plastics packaging materials, film & sheet	3.9	Manufg.	Travel trailers & campers	2.0	Manufg.
Management of companies & enterprises	3.8	Services	S/L govt. invest., education	1.6	S/L Govt
Retail trade	3.6	Trade	Retail trade	0.9	Trade
Iron & steel mills & ferroalloys	3.3	Manufg.	Federal government, investment, national defense	0.9	Fed Govt
Paints & coatings	1.4	Manufg.	Handtools	0.5	Manufg.
Machine shops	1.3	Manufg.	Change in private inventories	0.5	In House
Engine equipment, nec	1.0	Manufg.	Scenic & sightseeing transport & related services	0.2	Util.
Tires	0.9	Manufg.	Nonresidential structures, nec	0.2	Construct.
Coating, engraving, heat treating & allied activities	0.9	Manufg.	Waste management & remediation services	0.1	Services
Truck transportation	0.9	Util.	Services to buildings & dwellings	0.1	Services
Forging, stamping, & sintering, nec	0.8	Manufg.	Amusement & recreation, nec	0.1	Services
Semiconductors & related devices	0.7	Manufg.	Wholesale trade	0.1	Trade
Printed circuit assemblies (electronic assemblies)	0.7	Manufg.	Truck transportation	0.1	Util.
Ferrous metal foundries	0.6	Manufg.	S/L govt. invest., other	0.1	S/L Govt
Paperboard containers	0.6	Manufg.			
Unlaminated plastics profile shapes	0.6	Manufg.			
Advertising & related services	0.6	Services			
Software publishers	0.6	Services			
Nonferrous metal foundries	0.6	Manufg.			
Turned products & screws, nuts, & bolts	0.6	Manufg.			
Alumina refining & primary aluminum production	0.5	Manufg.			
Lessors of nonfinancial assets	0.5	Fin/R.E.			
Metal cans, boxes, & other containers (light gauge)	0.4	Manufg.			
Scientific research & development services	0.4	Services			
Securities, commodity contracts, investments	0.4	Fin/R.E.			
Valve & fittings other than plumbing	0.3	Manufg.			
Plate work & fabricated structural products	0.3	Manufg.			

Continued on next page.

INPUTS AND OUTPUTS FOR ALL OTHER TRANSPORTATION EQUIPMENT MANUFACTURING - Continued

Economic Sector or Industry Providing Inputs	%	Sector	Economic Sector or Industry Buying Outputs	%	Sector
Legal services	0.3	Services			
Real estate	0.3	Fin/R.E.			
Crowns & closures & metal stamping	0.3	Manufg.			
Power generation & supply	0.2	Util.			
Ball & roller bearings	0.2	Manufg.			
Professional, scientific, technical services, nec	0.2	Services			
Handtools	0.2	Manufg.			
Laminated plastics plates, sheets, & shapes	0.2	Manufg.			
Architectural, engineering, & related services	0.2	Services			
Aluminum products from purchased aluminum	0.2	Manufg.			
Custom roll forming	0.2	Manufg.			
Taxes on production & imports, less subsidies	0.2				
Relay & industrial controls	0.2	Manufg.			
Natural gas distribution	0.1	Util.			
Specialized design services	0.1	Services			
Employment services	0.1	Services			
Rail transportation	0.1	Util.			
Automotive equipment rental & leasing	0.1	Fin/R.E.			
Business support services	0.1	Services			
Accounting, tax preparation, bookkeeping, & payroll	0.1	Services			
Springs & wire products	0.1	Manufg.			
Services to buildings & dwellings	0.1	Services			
Paperboard mills	0.1	Manufg.			

Source: Benchmark Input-Output Accounts for the U.S. Economy, 2002, U.S. Department of Commerce, Washington, D.C., January 2008. The abbreviation nec stands for 'not elsewhere classified'.

OCCUPATIONS EMPLOYED BY OTHER TRANSPORTATION EQUIPMENT MANUFACTURING

Occupation	% of Total 2006	Change to 2016	Occupation	% of Total 2006	Change to 2016
Team assemblers	17.5	0.4	Laborers & freight, stock, & material movers, hand	1.6	-9.6
Welders, cutters, solderers, & brazers	7.5	6.8	Industrial engineers	1.4	22.0
Cutting, punching, & press machine operators	3.9	-9.6	Painters, transportation equipment	1.4	0.4
First-line supervisors/managers of production workers	3.3	0.4	Fiberglass laminators & fabricators	1.3	0.4
Grinding, lapping, polishing machine tool operators	3.3	-2.6	Purchasing agents, exc wholesale, retail, & farm	1.2	0.4
Inspectors, testers, sorters, samplers, & weighers	2.6	-5.3	Maintenance & repair workers, general	1.1	0.4
Assemblers & fabricators, nec	1.9	-9.6	Production, planning, & expediting clerks	1.1	0.4
Shipping, receiving, & traffic clerks	1.8	-3.4	Tool & die makers	1.1	5.4
Sales reps, wholesale & manufacturing, exc tech	1.8	0.4	Office clerks, general	1.1	-1.1
Engine & other machine assemblers	1.6	0.4	General & operations managers	1.1	-9.6
Industrial truck & tractor operators	1.6	-9.6	Bookkeeping, accounting, & auditing clerks	1.0	0.4
Structural metal fabricators & fitters	1.6	0.4			

Source: Industry-Occupation Matrix, Bureau of Labor Statistics, December 4, 2007. These data are reported based on 4-digit NAICS categories but have been matched to corresponding 6-digit NAICS industry codes. The change reported for each occupation to the year 2016 is a percent of growth or decline as estimated by the Bureau of Labor Statistics. The abbreviation nec stands for 'not elsewhere classified'.

LOCATION BY STATE AND REGIONAL CONCENTRATION

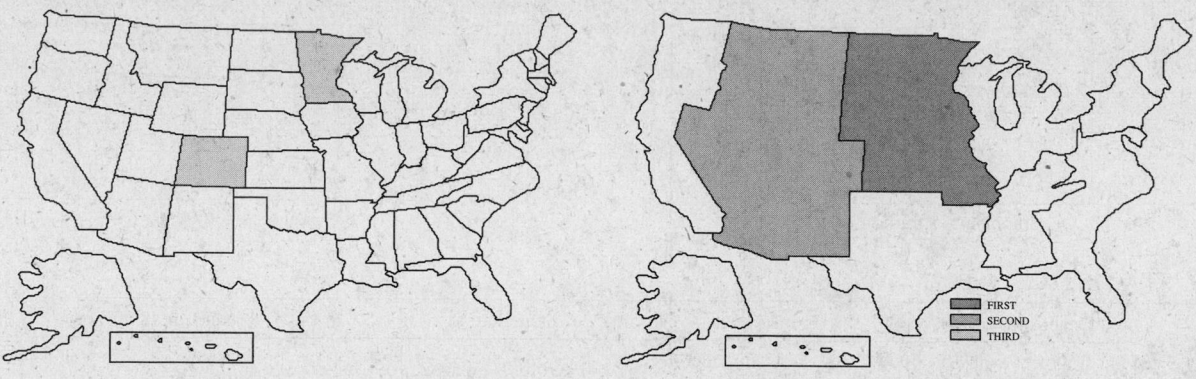

INDUSTRY DATA BY STATE

| State | Establish-ments | Shipments | | | Employment | | | | Cost as % of Shipments | Investment per Employee ($) |
		Total ($ mil)	% of U.S.	Per Establ.	Total Number	% of U.S.	Per Establ.	Wages ($/hour)		
Minnesota	21	1,954.0	28.1	93,045.7	3,421	17.2	163	13.47	58.0	8,789
Colorado	9	28.7	0.4	3,189.8	136	0.7	15	16.49	46.5	4,625

Source: 2002 *Economic Census*. The states are in descending order of shipments or establishments (if shipment data are missing for the majority). The symbol (D) appears when data are withheld to prevent disclosure of competitive information. States marked with (D) are sorted by number of establishments. A dash (-) indicates that the data element cannot be calculated. Data may not show all states active in the NAICS category. All data available at the time of publication are shown.

NAICS 337110 - WOOD KITCHEN CABINET AND COUNTER TOP MANUFACTURING

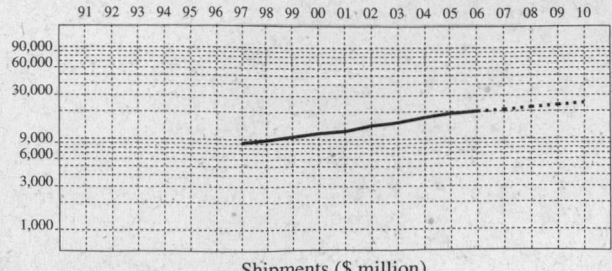

Shipments ($ million)

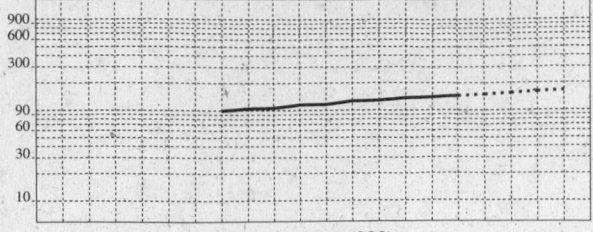

Employment (000)

GENERAL STATISTICS

Year	Companies	Establishments		Employment			Compensation		Production ($ million)			
		Total	with 20 or more employees	Total (000)	Production Workers (000).	Hours (Mil)	Payroll ($ mil)	Wages ($/hr)	Cost of Materials	Value Added by Manufacture	Value of Shipments	Capital Invest.
1997	7,875	7,962	834	99.1	79.5	151.1	2,315.7	10.86	3,891.4	5,181.2	9,071.5	248.2
1998		7,891	890	104.9	85.4	164.7	2,486.5	10.76	4,278.3	5,536.7	9,805.4	243.0
1999		7,749	943	106.6	84.8	170.7	2,774.2	11.27	4,470.4	6,211.7	10,664.7	368.3
2000		7,585	1,009	115.3	91.2	175.7	3,045.3	12.04	4,864.3	6,897.1	11,690.0	358.1
2001		8,176	1,076	115.8	91.7	180.8	3,169.5	12.11	5,038.3	7,333.6	12,333.6	333.1
2002	9,457	9,557	1,071	126.2	100.2	195.1	3,619.6	12.89	5,602.3	8,497.1	14,102.3	443.0
2003		9,126	1,028	128.0	102.5	206.1	3,773.4	12.71	6,061.6	9,259.2	15,267.1	476.8
2004		9,339	1,082	136.8	106.4	216.6	4,198.4	13.48	6,899.0	10,420.2	17,212.0	412.9
2005		9,473	1,117	139.3	109.9	229.9	4,445.8	13.66	7,713.8	11,364.1	18,994.9	475.6
2006		9,799P	1,167P	145.0	113.9	234.3	4,723.7	14.09	8,257.1	11,849.3	20,124.2	594.0
2007		10,051P	1,200P	150.1P	117.6P	243.8P	4,960.0P	14.49P	8,573.2P	12,302.8P	20,894.5P	576.3P
2008		10,303P	1,232P	155.3P	121.4P	253.2P	5,233.6P	14.88P	9,093.0P	13,048.8P	22,161.4P	609.2P
2009		10,555P	1,264P	160.5P	125.3P	262.5P	5,507.1P	15.26P	9,612.8P	13,794.8P	23,428.3P	642.1P
2010		10,807P	1,297P	165.7P	129.1P	271.8P	5,780.7P	15.64P	10,132.6P	14,540.7P	24,695.2P	675.0P

Sources: 1997 and 2002 *Economic Census*; other years, up to 2006, are from *Annual Survey of Manufactures*. Establishment counts for non-Census years are from *County Business Patterns*; 1997 and 2002 values are from the 1997 and 2002 censuses, respectively. 'P's show projections by the editors.

INDICES OF CHANGE

Year	Companies	Establishments		Employment			Compensation		Production ($ million)			
		Total	with 20 or more employees	Total (000)	Production Workers (000)	Hours (Mil)	Payroll ($ mil)	Wages ($/hr)	Cost of Materials	Value Added by Manufacture	Value of Shipments	Capital Invest.
1997	83	83	78	79	79	77	64	84	69	61	64	56
1998		83	83	83	85	84	69	83	76	65	70	55
1999		81	88	84	85	87	77	87	80	73	76	83
2000		79	94	91	91	90	84	93	87	81	83	81
2001		86	100	92	92	93	88	94	90	86	87	75
2002	100	100	100	100	100	100	100	100	100	100	100	100
2003		95	96	101	102	106	104	99	108	109	108	108
2004		98	101	108	106	111	116	105	123	123	122	93
2005		99	104	110	110	118	123	106	138	134	135	107
2006		103P	109P	115	114	120	131	109	147	139	143	134
2007		105P	112P	119P	117P	125P	137P	112P	153P	145P	148P	130P
2008		108P	115P	123P	121P	130P	145P	115P	162P	154P	157P	138P
2009		110P	118P	127P	125P	135P	152P	118P	172P	162P	166P	145P
2010		113P	121P	131P	129P	139P	160P	121P	181P	171P	175P	152P

Sources: Same as General Statistics. Values reflect change from the base year, 2002. Values above 100 mean greater than 2002, values below 100 mean less than 2002, and the values of 100 in other years means the same as 2002. 'P's show projections by the editors.

SELECTED RATIOS

For 2002	Avg. of All Manufact.	Analyzed Industry	Index	For 2002	Avg. of All Manufact.	Analyzed Industry	Index
Employees per Establishment	42	13	31	Value Added per Production Worker	182,367	84,801	47
Payroll per Establishment	1,639,184	378,738	23	Cost per Establishment	5,769,015	586,199	10
Payroll per Employee	39,053	28,681	73	Cost per Employee	137,446	44,392	32
Production Workers per Establishment	30	10	36	Cost per Production Worker	195,506	55,911	29
Wages per Establishment	694,845	263,141	38	Shipments per Establishment	11,158,348	1,475,599	13
Wages per Production Worker	23,548	25,098	107	Shipments per Employee	265,847	111,746	42
Hours per Production Worker	1,980	1,947	98	Shipments per Production Worker	378,144	140,742	37
Wages per Hour	11.89	12.89	108	Investment per Establishment	361,338	46,353	13
Value Added per Establishment	5,381,325	889,097	17	Investment per Employee	8,609	3,510	41
Value Added per Employee	128,210	67,330	53	Investment per Production Worker	12,245	4,421	36

Sources: Same as General Statistics. The 'Average of All Manufacturing' column represents the average of all manufacturing industries reported for the most recent complete year available. The Index shows the relationship between the Average and the Analyzed Industry. For example, 100 means that they are equal; 500 that the Analyzed Industry is five times the average; 50 means that the Analyzed Industry is half the national average. The abbreviation 'na' is used to show that data are 'not available'. Ratios shown for 2002, the last complete census year.

LEADING COMPANIES   Number shown: **75**   Total sales ($ mil): **130,897**   Total employment (000): **440.6**

Company Name	Address				CEO Name	Phone	Co. Type	Sales ($ mil)	Empl. (000)
Staples Inc.	PO Box 9328	Framingham	MA	01702		508-253-5000	P	19,373	75.6
Office Depot Inc.	2200 O Germantwn	Delray Beach	FL	33445		561-266-4800	P	15,528	49.0
OfficeMax Inc.	263 Shuman Blvd.	Naperville	IL	60563	Dorrit Bern	630-438-7800	P	15,528	49.0
Masco Corp.	21001 Van Born Rd.	Taylor	MI	48180	Ronald W. Ayers	313-274-7400	P	11,770	52.0
Fortune Brands Inc.	520 Lake Cook Rd.	Deerfield	IL	60015	Bruce A. Carbonari	847-484-4400	P	8,563	31.0
LA Darling Co.	1401 Hwy. 49B	Paragould	AR	72450		870-239-9564	R	7,000*	1.0
Silver King Refrigeration Inc.	1600 Xenium Ln. N	Plymouth	MN	55441	Korey Kohl	763-553-1881	S	7,000*	<0.1
IKEA North America	1000 IKEA Dr.	Elizabeth	NJ	07202	Anders Dahlvig	908-352-3270	R	5,937*	8.0
Hussmann Corp.	12999 St. Chrles Rd	Bridgeton	MO	63044	Dennis Gibson	314-291-2000	S	4,623*	8.0
Leggett and Platt Inc.	PO Box 757	Carthage	MO	64836		417-358-8131	P	4,306	24.0
Euromarket Design Inc.	1250 Techny Rd.	Northbrook	IL	60062	Gordon Segal	847-272-2888	R	2,215*	7.0
Farmer Furniture	PO Box 1140	Dublin	GA	31040		478-272-4000	R	1,961*	1.4
Pier 1 Imports Inc.	100 Pier 1 Pl.	Fort Worth	TX	76102		817-252-8000	P	1,623	15.4
Rooms To Go Inc.	11540 Hwy. 92 E	Seffner	FL	33584	Jeffrey Seaman	813-623-5400	R	1,596*	6.5
Builders FirstSource Inc.	2001 Bryan St.	Dallas	TX	75201	Paul Levy	214-880-3500	P	1,593	4.9
Aaron Rents Inc.	309 E Paces Ferry	Atlanta	GA	30305	R. C. Loudermilk Sr.	404-231-0011	P	1,495	9.6
EBSCO Industries Inc.	PO Box 1943	Birmingham	AL	35201	Dixon Brooke Jr.	205-991-6600	R	1,400*	5.0
Haworth Inc.	1 Haworth Ctr.	Holland	MI	49423	Franco Bianchi	616-393-3000	R	1,120*	8.0
Knoll Inc.	1235 Water St.	East Greenville	PA	18041	Andrew B. Cogan	215-679-7991	P	1,056	4.3
Cost Plus Inc.	200 4th St.	Oakland	CA	94607	Barry J. Feld	510-893-7300	P	1,040	6.7
Schottenstein Stores Corp.	1800 Moler Rd.	Columbus	OH	43207	Jay L. Schottenstein	614-221-9200	R	953*	7.6
Pan-Oston Co.	6944 Louisville Rd.	Bowling Green	KY	42101	John Kelly	270-783-3900	R	903*	0.3
Haverty Furniture Companies	780 Johnson Frry Rd	Atlanta	GA	30342		404-443-2900	P	859	4.5
Levitz Furniture	300 Crossways Park	Woodbury	NY	11797	Alan Rosenberg	516-496-9560	S	840*	4.5
Restoration Hardware Inc.	15 Koch Rd., Ste. J	Corte Madera	CA	94925	Gary G. Friedman	415-924-1005	P	713	3.8
Holmes Lumber and Building Ctr	6139 State Rte. 39	Millersburg	OH	44654	Paul Miller	330-674-9060	R	689*	0.1
Levin Furniture	609 W Main St.	Mt. Pleasant	PA	15666	Robert Levin	724-872-2050	R	557*	0.4
Bombay Company Inc.	PO Box 161009	Fort Worth	TX	76161	David B. Stewart	817-347-8200	P	536	4.5
Yorktowne Inc.	PO Box 231	Red Lion	PA	17356	Stanley Bandur	717-244-4011	R	534*	0.3
Art Van Furniture Inc.	6500 E 14 Mile Rd.	Warren	MI	48092	Art Van Elslander	586-939-0800	R	531*	3.5
Sauder Woodworking Co.	PO Box 156	Archbold	OH	43502	Kevin Sauder	419-446-2711	R	525*	3.0
Kraftmaid Cabinetry Inc.	PO Box 1055	Middlefield	OH	44062	Mike Newton	440-632-5333	S	511*	3.1
Elkay Manufacturing Co.	2222 Camden Ct.	Oak Brook	IL	60523	Ronald Katz	630-574-8484	R	470*	3.6
Lozier Corp.	PO Box 3448	Omaha	NE	68103	Sheri Andrews	402-457-8000	R	411*	1.1
Amer. TV & Appliance/Madison	2404 W Beltline	Madison	WI	53713	Douglas Reuhl	608-271-1000	R	400*	2.0
CORT Furniture Rental Corp.	11250 Waples Mill	Fairfax	VA	22030	Paul N. Arnold	703-968-8500	S	375*	3.0
Rose Furniture	PO Box 1829	High Point	NC	27261	Robert Kester	336-886-6050	R	327*	0.3
Rowe Companies	1650 Tysons Blvd.	McLean	VA	22102	Gerald M. Birnbach	703-847-8670	R	301	2.4
Prestige Cabinets Inc.	PO Box 340	Neodesha	KS	66757	Ronald Simon	620-325-8500	R	269*	0.3
Raymour and Flanigan Furniture	7230 Morgan Rd.	Liverpool	NY	13090	Neil Goldberg	315-453-2500	R	258*	3.8
Wood-Mode Inc.	PO Box 900	Kreamer	PA	17833	Robert Gronlund	570-374-2711	R	258*	<0.1
BJ Tidwell Industries Inc.	PO Box 200850	San Antonio	TX	78220		210-225-0290	R	255*	2.4
Dearden's Inc.	700 S Main St.	Los Angeles	CA	90014	Raquel Bensimon	213-362-9600	R	249*	0.5
Francisco Mendoza Inc.	PO Box 373430	Cayey	PR	00737	F. Mendoza Rivera	787-738-2112	R	245*	0.4
Jordan's Furniture Inc.	100 Stockwell Dr.	Avon	MA	02322	Barry Tattelman	508-580-4600	S	214*	1.4
Design Within Reach Inc.	225 Bush Street	San Francisco	CA	94104	Ray Brunner	415-248-5397	P	194	0.4
Morris Kirschman and Company	PO Box 26427	New Orleans	LA	70186	Arnold Kirschman	504-947-6673	R	186*	0.3
Sauder Manufacturing Co.	PO Box 230	Archbold	OH	43502	Virgil Miller	419-445-7670	R	184*	0.2
Nebraska Furniture Mart Inc.	PO Box 2335	Omaha	NE	68103	Ron Blumkins	402-255-6327	S	180*	1.2
Office Resources Inc.	374 Congress St.	Boston	MA	02210		617-423-9100	R	175*	0.2
Lexington Furniture Industries	PO Box 1008	Lexington	NC	27293	Asher Lepkin	336-474-5300	R	167*	0.3
Vermont Country Store	5650 Main Street	Manchester Ctr	VT	05255	Lyman Orton	802-362-8460	R	167*	1.0
Knape and Vogt Manufacturing	2700 Oak Indu. Dr.	Grand Rapids	MI	49505	William R. Dutmers	616-459-3311	R	157	0.6
Canyon Creek Cabinet Co.	16726 Tye St. SE	Monroe	WA	98272	Bill Weaver	206-674-0800	R	155*	0.4
Wickes Furniture Company Inc.	250 S Gary Ave.	Carol Stream	IL	60188	John Disa		R	150*	1.5
Norwalk Furniture Corp.	100 Furniture Pkwy.	Norwalk	OH	44857	James Gerken	419-668-4461	R	147*	0.9
Reface Inc.	2248 Dabney Rd.	Richmond	VA	23230	Murray H. Gross	804-359-9001	S	144*	0.7
Marlo Furniture Company Inc.	725 Rockville Pke.	Rockville	MD	20852	Neal Glickfield	301-738-9000	R	138*	0.7
Jennifer Convertibles Inc.	419 Crossways Park	Woodbury	NY	11797	Harley J. Greenfield	516-496-1900	P	137	0.5
Rotman's	725 Southbridge St.	Worcester	MA	01610	Steve Rotman	508-755-5276	R	135*	0.2
U.S. Remodelers Inc.	1884 S Elmhurst Rd.	Mount Prospect	IL	60056	Murray H. Gross	847-758-2310	S	128	0.6
Muebleria Berrios Inc.	PO Box 674	Cidra	PR	00739	Efrain Rivera	787-752-6020	R	128	0.7
Leath Furniture Inc.	4370 Peachtree Rd.	Atlanta	GA	30319	Ronald D. Phillips	404-848-0880	R	118*	0.8
Big Sandy Furniture Inc.	8375 Gallia Pike	Franklin Furnace	OH	45629	John C. Stewart Jr.	740-574-2113	R	112*	0.7
Porter of Racine	301 6th Street	Racine	WI	53403	H.R. Waters	262-633-6363	R	110*	<0.1
Gallery Furniture Inc.	6006 N Fwy.	Houston	TX	77076	Jim McIngvale	713-694-5570	R	105*	0.3
Marsh Pottery L.L.C.	3775 Ave / Carolina	Fort Mill	SC	29708	Tim Marsh	803-548-7075	R	105*	0.3
Goodman's Inc.	PO Box 13289	Phoenix	AZ	85002	Adam Goodman	602-263-1110	R	101*	0.1
Grand Home Furnishings	4235 Electric Rd SW	Roanoke	VA	24014	G. B. Cartledge Jr.	540-776-7000	R	100*	0.8
Woodcraft Industries Inc.	525 Lincoln Ave. SE	Saint Cloud	MN	56304	John Fitzpatrick	320-252-1503	R	99*	0.6
Howard Miller Clock Co.	860 E Main Ave.	Zeeland	MI	49464	Howard Miller	616-772-9131	R	98*	0.4
Bertch Cabinet Manufacturing	PO Box 2280	Waterloo	IA	50704	Gary Bertch	319-296-2987	R	96*	0.3
Wellborn Cabinet Inc.	PO Box 1210	Ashland	AL	36251		256-354-7151	R	93*	1.2
Brodart Co.	500 Arch St.	Williamsport	PA	17701	Arthur Brody		R	92*	1.0
Schewel Furniture Company Inc.	PO Box 1600	Lynchburg	VA	24505	Marc A. Schewel	434-845-2326	R	86*	0.7

Source: *Ward's Business Directory of U.S. Private and Public Companies*, Volumes 1 and 2, 2008. The company type code used is as follows: P - Public, R - Private, S - Subsidiary, D - Division, J - Joint Venture, A - Affiliate, G - Group. Sales are in millions of dollars, employees are in thousands. An asterisk (*) indicates an estimated sales volume. The symbol < stands for 'less than'. Company names and addresses are truncated, in some cases, to fit into the available space.

MATERIALS CONSUMED

Material	Quantity	Delivered Cost ($ million)
Hardwood cut stock and dimension (excluding furniture frames)	(X)	223.3
Hardwood veneer	(X)	85.2
Hardwood plywood	(X)	235.0
Softwood plywood	(X)	18.4
Particleboard (reconstituted wood)	(X)	293.2
Hardboard	(X)	30.4
Medium density fiberboard (MDF)	(X)	90.1
Paperboard containers, boxes, and corrugated paperboard	(X)	110.3
Hardwood lumber, rough and dressed	(X)	760.8
Softwood lumber, rough and dressed	(X)	29.0
Adhesives and sealants	(X)	33.9
Paints, varnishes, stains, lacquers, shellacs, japans, enamels, etc.	(X)	113.1
Plastics laminated sheets	(X)	147.6
Plastics furniture parts and components	(X)	8.0
Furniture and builders' hardware (incl. cabinet hardware, casters, glides, handles, hinges, locks, etc.)	(X)	235.3
Wood furniture frames	(X)	239.0
All other materials, components, parts, containers, and supplies	(X)	1,035.2
Materials, ingredients, containers, and supplies, nsk	(X)	1,443.4

Source: 2002 *Economic Census*. Explanation of symbols used: (D): Withheld to avoid disclosure of competitive data; na: Not available; (S): Withheld because statistical norms were not met; (X): Not applicable; (Z): Less than half the unit shown; nec: Not elsewhere classified; nsk: Not specified by kind; - : zero; p : 10-19 percent estimated; q : 20-29 percent estimated.

PRODUCT SHARE DETAILS

Product or Product Class Shipments	Mil. $	Product or Product Class Shipments	Mil. $
WOOD KITCHEN CABINETS AND COUNTERTOPS	13,394.3	sold directly to consumer	726.2
Wood kitchen cabinets and cabinetwork, stock line	**4,496.3**	Wood vanities and other cabinetwork, custom, except	
Wood kitchen cabinets and cabinetwork, stock line	4,409.7	sold directly to consumer	109.6
Wood kitchen cabinets and cabinetwork, stock line, plastics laminated	482.7	Vanities and other cabinetwork, except sold directly to consumer, nsk	119.4
Other wood kitchen cabinets and cabinetwork, stock line	3,927.0	**Wood and plastics laminated wood kitchen cabinet tops**	**694.6**
Wood kitchen cabinets and cabinetwork, stock line, nsk	86.6	Wood and plastics laminated wood kitchen cabinet tops	609.6
Wood kitchen cabinets and cabinetwork, custom, except sold directly to customer at retail	**1,422.9**	Wood and plastics laminated wood stock line kitchen cabinet tops	310.5
Wood kitchen cabinets and cabinetwork, custom, except sold directly to customer at retail	1,343.3	Wood and plastics laminated wood custom kitchen cabinet tops	299.1
Wood kitchen cabinets and cabinetwork, custom, except plastics laminated, except sold directly to customer at retail	991.9	Wood and plastics laminated wood kitchen cabinet tops, nsk	85.0
Wood kitchen cabinets and cabinetwork, custom, plastics laminated, except sold directly to customer at retail	351.4	**Wood and plastics laminated wood bathroom vanity tops**	**166.9**
Wood kitchen cabinets and cabinetwork, custom, except sold directly to customer at retail, nsk	79.6	Wood and plastics laminated wood bathroom vanity tops	105.8
Wood vanities and other cabinetwork, except sold directly to consumer	**955.2**	Wood and plastics laminated wood stock line bathroom vanity tops	51.7
Wood vanities and other cabinetwork, except sold directly to consumer	835.8	Wood and plastics laminated wood custom bathroom vanity tops	54.0
Wood vanities and other cabinetwork, stock line, except		Wood and plastics laminated wood bathroom vanity tops, nsk	61.1
		Wood kitchen cabinets, bathroom vanities, and related cabinetwork (permanent installation), custom, sold directly to customer at retail	**2,956.0**
		Wood kitchen cabinets and countertops, nsk, total	**2,702.3**

Source: 2002 *Economic Census*. The values are product shipments in millions of dollars for 2002. Total product shipments may be lower or higher than industry shipments. See Introduction for a full discussion. Values of indented subcategories are summed in the main heading(s). The symbol (D) appears when data are withheld to prevent disclosure of competitive information. The abbreviation nsk stands for 'not specified by kind' and nec for 'not elsewhere classified'. A dash (-) means zero.

INPUTS AND OUTPUTS FOR WOOD KITCHEN CABINET AND COUNTERTOP MANUFACTURING

Economic Sector or Industry Providing Inputs	%	Sector	Economic Sector or Industry Buying Outputs	%	Sector
Compensation of employees	31.3		Owner-occupied dwellings	33.0	
Sawmills & wood preservation	9.0	Manufg.	Residential permanent site structures	24.7	Construct.
Wholesale trade	4.5	Trade	Private fixed investment	10.4	
Reconstituted wood products	4.3	Manufg.	Residential structures, nec	5.4	Construct.
Advertising & related services	3.1	Services	Commercial & health care structures	4.2	Construct.
Veneer & plywood	3.0	Manufg.	Food services & drinking places	3.6	Services
Showcases, partitions, shelving, and lockers	2.6	Manufg.	Other S/L govt. enterprises	3.0	S/L Govt
Management of companies & enterprises	2.1	Services	Maintenance/repair of residential structures	1.6	Construct.
Professional, scientific, technical services, nec	2.1	Services	Maintenance/repair of nonresidential structures	1.2	Construct.
Real estate	1.8	Fin/R.E.	Engine equipment, nec	1.2	Manufg.
Telecommunications	1.8	Services	Plastics products, nec	1.1	Manufg.
Truck transportation	1.7	Util.	Retail trade	1.1	Trade
Plastics products, nec	1.6	Manufg.	Manufactured homes & mobile homes	1.0	Manufg.

Continued on next page.

INPUTS AND OUTPUTS FOR WOOD KITCHEN CABINET AND COUNTERTOP MANUFACTURING - Continued

Economic Sector or Industry Providing Inputs	%	Sector	Economic Sector or Industry Buying Outputs	%	Sector
Securities, commodity contracts, investments	1.5	Fin/R.E.	Motor vehicle parts	0.9	Manufg.
Data processing, hosting, & related services	1.2	Services	Nonresidential structures, nec	0.7	Construct.
Maintenance/repair of nonresidential structures	1.2	Construct.	Telecommunications	0.6	Services
Paints & coatings	1.1	Manufg.	Custom architectural woodwork & millwork	0.6	Manufg.
Laminated plastics plates, sheets, & shapes	1.1	Manufg.	Wood kitchen cabinets & countertops	0.5	Manufg.
Paperboard containers	1.1	Manufg.	Data processing, hosting, & related services	0.5	Services
Scientific research & development services	1.1	Services	Semiconductors & related devices	0.5	Manufg.
Miscellaneous wood products	1.1	Manufg.	Change in private inventories	0.5	In House
Services to buildings & dwellings	1.0	Services	Civic, social, & professional organizations	0.5	Services
Retail trade	1.0	Trade	Computer terminals & peripherals	0.4	Manufg.
Food services & drinking places	0.9	Services	Commercial & industrial machinery rental & leasing	0.4	Fin/R.E.
Hotels & motels, including casino hotels	0.8	Services	Prefabricated wood buildings	0.4	Manufg.
Waste management & remediation services	0.8	Services	Real estate	0.3	Fin/R.E.
Other computer related services, including facilities	0.8	Services	Physician, dentist, other health practitioner offices	0.3	Services
Accounting, tax preparation, bookkeeping, & payroll	0.7	Services	Exports of goods & services	0.3	Cap Inv
Hardware	0.7	Manufg.	Wholesale trade	0.2	Trade
Automotive repair & maintenance, ex. car washes	0.7	Services	Individual & family services	0.2	Services
Monetary authorities/depository credit intermediation	0.7	Fin/R.E.	Child day care services	0.1	Services
Semiconductors & related devices	0.7	Manufg.	Natural gas distribution	0.1	Util.
Power generation & supply	0.7	Util.	Amusement & recreation, nec	0.1	Services
Printed circuit assemblies (electronic assemblies)	0.6	Manufg.			
Commercial & industrial equipment repair/maintenance	0.6	Services			
Air transportation	0.6	Util.			
Wood kitchen cabinets & countertops	0.6	Manufg.			
Taxes on production & imports, less subsidies	0.5				
Architectural, engineering, & related services	0.5	Services			
Coating, engraving, heat treating & allied activities	0.4	Manufg.			
Automotive equipment rental & leasing	0.4	Fin/R.E.			
Rail transportation	0.4	Util.			
Support services, nec	0.4	Services			
Computer system design services	0.4	Services			
Legal services	0.4	Services			
Lessors of nonfinancial assets	0.3	Fin/R.E.			
Machine shops	0.3	Manufg.			
Adhesives	0.3	Manufg.			
Nondepository credit intermediation activities	0.3	Fin/R.E.			
Business support services	0.3	Services			
Warehousing & storage	0.3	Util.			
Travel arrangement & reservation services	0.3	Services			
Civic, social, & professional organizations	0.3	Services			
Water, sewage and other systems	0.2	Util.			
Commercial & industrial machinery rental & leasing	0.2	Fin/R.E.			
Transit & ground passenger transportation	0.2	Util.			
Natural gas distribution	0.2	Util.			
Other S/L govt. enterprises	0.2	S/L Govt			
Electronic & precision equipment repair/maintenance	0.2	Services			
Internet service providers & web search portals	0.2	Services			
Plastics packaging materials, film & sheet	0.2	Manufg.			
Personal & household goods repair/maintenance	0.1	Services			
Motor vehicle parts	0.1	Manufg.			
Management, scientific, & technical consulting	0.1	Services			
Fabricated metals, nec	0.1	Manufg.			
Wood windows & doors & millwork	0.1	Manufg.			
Paperboard mills	0.1	Manufg.			

Source: Benchmark Input-Output Accounts for the U.S. Economy, 2002, U.S. Department of Commerce, Washington, D.C., January 2008. The abbreviation nec stands for 'not elsewhere classified'.

OCCUPATIONS EMPLOYED BY HOUSEHOLD & INSTITUTIONAL FURNITURE & KITCHEN CABINETS

Occupation	% of Total 2006	Change to 2016	Occupation	% of Total 2006	Change to 2016
Cabinetmakers & bench carpenters	19.2	2.6	Customer service representatives	1.1	1.2
Team assemblers	7.0	-9.6	Bookkeeping, accounting, & auditing clerks	1.0	-5.2
Woodworking machine operators & tenders, exc sawing	5.7	2.2	Assemblers & fabricators, nec	1.0	-20.6
Upholsterers	5.3	-16.5	Maintenance & repair workers, general	1.0	-7.3
Sewing machine operators	4.0	-16.2	Machine feeders & offbearers	1.0	-18.6
First-line supervisors/managers of production workers	3.8	-7.2	Industrial truck & tractor operators	0.8	-22.0
Carpenters	3.8	4.1	Truck drivers, light or delivery services	0.8	-2.6
Laborers & freight, stock, & material movers, hand	3.3	-17.9	Cutting, punching, & press machine operators	0.8	-27.9
Helpers--Production workers	3.2	-9.7	Cutters & trimmers, hand	0.7	-10.2
Furniture finishers	3.2	-10.6	Secretaries, exc legal, medical, & executive	0.7	-14.4
Coating, painting, & spraying machine operators	2.0	-5.7	Welders, cutters, solderers, & brazers	0.7	-18.2
Sawing machine setters, operators, & tenders, wood	1.9	4.0	Industrial production managers	0.6	-8.8
Sales reps, wholesale & manufacturing, exc tech	1.8	-4.1	Production, planning, & expediting clerks	0.6	-8.9
Office clerks, general	1.4	-4.1	Stock clerks & order fillers	0.6	-25.1
Inspectors, testers, sorters, samplers, & weighers	1.3	-16.0	Retail salespersons	0.6	-6.9
General & operations managers	1.3	-14.7	Truck drivers, heavy & tractor-trailer	0.6	-7.3
Packers & packagers, hand	1.2	-32.8	Painting, coating, & decorating workers	0.6	-10.0
Shipping, receiving, & traffic clerks	1.2	-16.4	Order clerks	0.5	-37.0
Grinding & polishing workers, hand	1.1	-2.3	Janitors & cleaners, exc maids & housekeeping cleaners	0.5	-7.2

Source: Industry-Occupation Matrix, Bureau of Labor Statistics, December 4, 2007. These data are reported based on 4-digit NAICS categories but have been matched to corresponding 6-digit NAICS industry codes. The change reported for each occupation to the year 2016 is a percent of growth or decline as estimated by the Bureau of Labor Statistics. The abbreviation nec stands for 'not elsewhere classified'.

LOCATION BY STATE AND REGIONAL CONCENTRATION

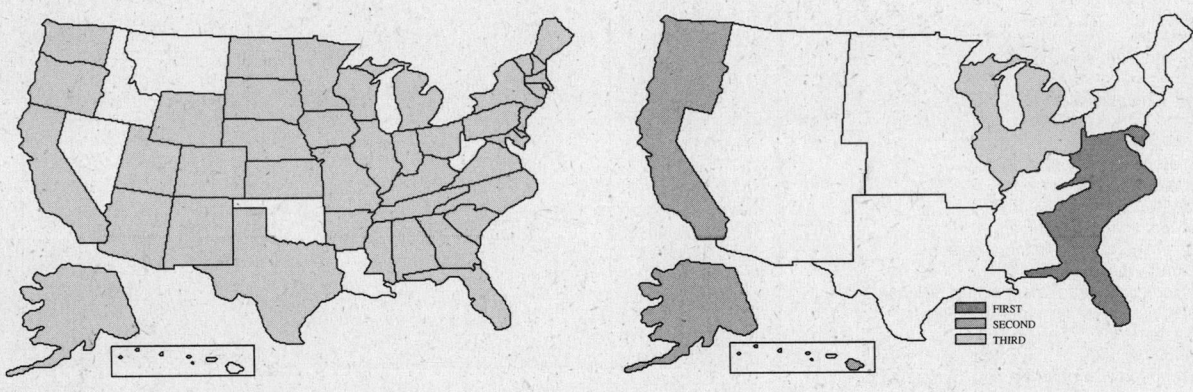

FIRST
SECOND
THIRD

INDUSTRY DATA BY STATE

State	Establish-ments	Shipments Total ($ mil)	Shipments % of U.S.	Shipments Per Establ.	Employment Total Number	Employment % of U.S.	Employment Per Establ.	Employment Wages ($/hour)	Cost as % of Shipments	Investment per Employee ($)
Ohio	335	1,520.0	10.8	4,537.4	8,160	6.5	24	12.78	41.1	3,032
California	1,159	1,391.6	9.9	1,200.7	14,032	11.1	12	13.44	36.3	2,456
Pennsylvania	373	1,016.0	7.2	2,723.9	8,748	6.9	23	14.30	37.0	2,754
Texas	495	1,006.8	7.1	2,034.0	10,644	8.4	22	11.03	44.2	5,463
Indiana	208	978.2	6.9	4,702.8	6,547	5.2	31	14.00	36.9	3,902
Florida	719	517.3	3.7	719.5	5,573	4.4	8	12.36	40.7	2,077
Illinois	346	507.7	3.6	1,467.4	4,703	3.7	14	13.22	38.4	2,112
Virginia	259	490.3	3.5	1,893.1	2,895	2.3	11	13.21	43.7	1,708
Georgia	357	464.3	3.3	1,300.5	3,689	2.9	10	12.88	44.5	2,293
Minnesota	327	463.8	3.3	1,418.3	4,255	3.4	13	14.33	34.8	2,336
North Carolina	325	417.0	3.0	1,282.9	3,833	3.0	12	11.74	48.0	4,544
Alabama	242	405.5	2.9	1,675.6	3,858	3.1	16	12.09	40.8	4,470
Michigan	209	357.0	2.5	1,708.3	2,426	1.9	12	13.97	44.5	2,535
Arizona	163	347.0	2.5	2,129.1	2,591	2.1	16	12.63	42.4	9,699
Iowa	98	338.4	2.4	3,453.6	3,158	2.5	32	12.94	41.4	2,807
New York	456	331.9	2.4	727.9	3,402	2.7	7	13.43	37.6	1,992
Kansas	99	327.4	2.3	3,306.9	3,314	2.6	33	11.91	35.9	3,134
Wisconsin	253	311.2	2.2	1,230.0	3,326	2.6	13	13.40	37.0	5,523
Oregon	204	296.7	2.1	1,454.5	2,506	2.0	12	12.55	39.4	7,391
Washington	247	288.2	2.0	1,166.9	3,605	2.9	15	12.61	36.8	1,852
Missouri	235	213.5	1.5	908.4	2,657	2.1	11	13.30	36.1	3,978
New Jersey	231	191.7	1.4	829.7	2,003	1.6	9	14.47	41.5	2,654
Utah	170	183.3	1.3	1,078.3	2,342	1.9	14	12.35	38.3	2,897
Tennessee	222	181.2	1.3	816.0	2,043	1.6	9	11.63	43.7	1,791

Continued on next page.

INDUSTRY DATA BY STATE - Continued

| State | Establish-ments | Shipments | | | Employment | | | | Cost as % of Shipments | Investment per Employee ($) |
		Total ($ mil)	% of U.S.	Per Establ.	Total Number	% of U.S.	Per Establ.	Wages ($/hour)		
Connecticut	134	154.5	1.1	1,153.3	1,401	1.1	10	13.74	35.2	8,283
Colorado	169	145.8	1.0	862.5	1,611	1.3	10	12.83	38.1	2,103
Kentucky	106	114.0	0.8	1,075.4	1,408	1.1	13	11.70	48.1	1,960
Massachusetts	153	107.8	0.8	704.8	1,129	0.9	7	14.66	37.6	2,471
South Dakota	36	92.8	0.7	2,578.6	1,066	0.8	30	11.60	40.9	4,341
Nebraska	54	86.2	0.6	1,596.7	673	0.5	12	12.31	37.8	5,156
Maryland	131	77.1	0.5	588.6	912	0.7	7	13.16	38.4	1,923
South Carolina	151	69.8	0.5	462.2	855	0.7	6	12.14	40.2	2,558
Mississippi	71	55.6	0.4	782.6	593	0.5	8	11.95	48.1	1,578
Arkansas	104	53.9	0.4	518.5	709	0.6	7	10.38	39.0	2,158
New Hampshire	43	37.4	0.3	870.7	400	0.3	9	15.93	30.7	2,327
North Dakota	35	33.8	0.2	966.1	273	0.2	8	12.39	23.4	4,190
New Mexico	59	25.7	0.2	435.2	362	0.3	6	12.40	36.4	2,580
Rhode Island	19	17.4	0.1	917.6	159	0.1	8	13.13	51.2	1,352
Maine	45	13.9	0.1	309.9	178	0.1	4	12.55	40.3	1,444
Alaska	26	12.4	0.1	476.1	105	0.1	4	12.62	47.5	2,876
Vermont	22	11.7	0.1	532.4	115	0.1	5	13.86	35.6	3,574
Delaware	17	11.6	0.1	681.5	130	0.1	8	11.28	40.0	4,092
Wyoming	21	10.1	0.1	480.4	120	0.1	6	10.26	30.7	7,983

Source: 2002 *Economic Census*. The states are in descending order of shipments or establishments (if shipment data are missing for the majority). The symbol (D) appears when data are withheld to prevent disclosure of competitive information. States marked with (D) are sorted by number of establishments. A dash (-) indicates that the data element cannot be calculated. Data may not show all states active in the NAICS category. All data available at the time of publication are shown.

NAICS 337121 - UPHOLSTERED HOUSEHOLD FURNITURE MANUFACTURING

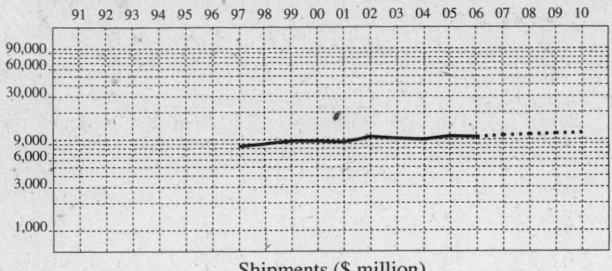

Shipments ($ million)

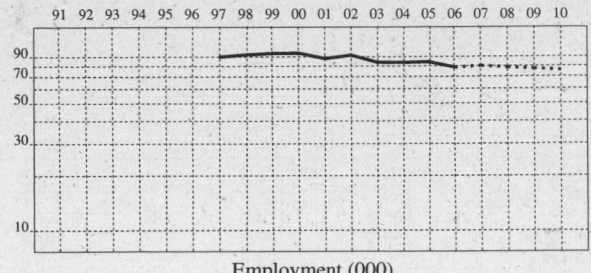

Employment (000)

GENERAL STATISTICS

Year	Com-panies	Establishments		Employment			Compensation		Production ($ million)			
		Total	with 20 or more employees	Total (000)	Production Workers (000)	Hours (Mil)	Payroll ($ mil)	Wages ($/hr)	Cost of Materials	Value Added by Manufacture	Value of Shipments	Capital Invest.
1997	1,565	1,706	534	90.0	77.4	144.2	2,022.6	10.65	4,321.7	4,082.2	8,398.7	104.8
1998		1,748	522	92.4	79.7	151.2	2,099.6	10.68	4,759.4	4,213.3	8,971.5	108.5
1999		1,675	522	94.0	80.9	154.5	2,273.9	11.22	4,998.1	4,624.5	9,601.0	170.4
2000		1,621	512	94.2	80.4	150.8	2,325.7	11.63	5,073.4	4,562.9	9,608.4	146.0
2001		1,585	489	88.0	74.9	138.5	2,190.0	11.64	4,870.6	4,450.9	9,318.3	95.0
2002	1,686	1,946	564	91.8	77.3	145.1	2,436.6	12.51	5,431.2	5,272.8	10,683.7	173.4
2003		1,813	530	83.9	70.1	135.9	2,285.2	12.37	5,373.5	4,868.3	10,235.6	91.4
2004		1,740	518	83.7	68.0	131.4	2,254.4	12.73	5,141.7	4,839.6	9,979.3	108.5
2005		1,593	484	84.2	69.0	138.8	2,419.5	13.07	5,642.8	5,218.4	10,816.8	77.8
2006		1,725P	507P	78.6	64.8	132.0	2,347.1	13.33	5,568.2	5,037.0	10,615.2	115.3
2007		1,727P	505P	80.1P	64.9P	130.6P	2,438.4P	13.70P	5,817.1P	5,262.1P	11,089.7P	101.9P
2008		1,729P	503P	78.7P	63.2P	128.4P	2,469.8P	14.01P	5,937.9P	5,371.4P	11,320.0P	98.8P
2009		1,731P	500P	77.2P	61.5P	126.3P	2,501.3P	14.32P	6,058.7P	5,480.7P	11,550.3P	95.7P
2010		1,733P	498P	75.8P	59.8P	124.2P	2,532.7P	14.64P	6,179.5P	5,590.0P	11,780.6P	92.6P

Sources: 1997 and 2002 *Economic Census*; other years, up to 2006, are from *Annual Survey of Manufactures*. Establishment counts for non-Census years are from *County Business Patterns*; 1997 and 2002 values are from the 1997 and 2002 censuses, respectively. 'P's show projections by the editors.

INDICES OF CHANGE

Year	Com-panies	Establishments		Employment			Compensation		Production ($ million)			
		Total	with 20 or more employees	Total (000)	Production Workers (000)	Hours (Mil)	Payroll ($ mil)	Wages ($/hr)	Cost of Materials	Value Added by Manufacture	Value of Shipments	Capital Invest.
1997	93	88	95	98	100	99	83	85	80	77	79	60
1998		90	93	101	103	104	86	85	88	80	84	63
1999		86	93	102	105	106	93	90	92	88	90	98
2000		83	91	103	104	104	95	93	93	87	90	84
2001		81	87	96	97	95	90	93	90	84	87	55
2002	100	100	100	100	100	100	100	100	100	100	100	100
2003		93	94	91	91	94	94	99	99	92	96	53
2004		89	92	91	88	91	93	102	95	92	93	63
2005		82	86	92	89	96	99	104	104	99	101	45
2006		89P	90P	86	84	91	96	107	103	96	99	66
2007		89P	90P	87P	84P	90P	100P	110P	107P	100P	104P	59P
2008		89P	89P	86P	82P	88P	101P	112P	109P	102P	106P	57P
2009		89P	89P	84P	80P	87P	103P	114P	112P	104P	108P	55P
2010		89P	88P	83P	77P	86P	104P	117P	114P	106P	110P	53P

Sources: Same as General Statistics. Values reflect change from the base year, 2002. Values above 100 mean greater than 2002, values below 100 mean less than 2002, and the values of 100 in other years means the same as 2002. 'P's show projections by the editors.

SELECTED RATIOS

For 2002	Avg. of All Manufact.	Analyzed Industry	Index	For 2002	Avg. of All Manufact.	Analyzed Industry	Index
Employees per Establishment	42	47	112	Value Added per Production Worker	182,367	68,212	37
Payroll per Establishment	1,639,184	1,252,107	76	Cost per Establishment	5,769,015	2,790,956	48
Payroll per Employee	39,053	26,542	68	Cost per Employee	137,446	59,163	43
Production Workers per Establishment	30	40	135	Cost per Production Worker	195,506	70,261	36
Wages per Establishment	694,845	932,786	134	Shipments per Establishment	11,158,348	5,490,082	49
Wages per Production Worker	23,548	23,483	100	Shipments per Employee	265,847	116,380	44
Hours per Production Worker	1,980	1,877	95	Shipments per Production Worker	378,144	138,211	37
Wages per Hour	11.89	12.51	105	Investment per Establishment	361,338	89,106	25
Value Added per Establishment	5,381,325	2,709,558	50	Investment per Employee	8,609	1,889	22
Value Added per Employee	128,210	57,438	45	Investment per Production Worker	12,245	2,243	18

Sources: Same as General Statistics. The 'Average of All Manufacturing' column represents the average of all manufacturing industries reported for the most recent complete year available. The Index shows the relationship between the Average and the Analyzed Industry. For example, 100 means that they are equal; 500 that the Analyzed Industry is five times the average; 50 means that the Analyzed Industry is half the national average. The abbreviation 'na' is used to show that data are 'not available'. Ratios shown for 2002, the last complete census year.

LEADING COMPANIES   Number shown: **75**   Total sales ($ mil): **101,978**   Total employment (000): **413.5**

Company Name	Address				CEO Name	Phone	Co. Type	Sales ($ mil)	Empl. (000)
Staples Inc.	PO Box 9328	Framingham	MA	01702		508-253-5000	P	19,373	75.6
Office Depot Inc.	2200 O Germantwn	Delray Beach	FL	33445		561-266-4800	P	15,528	49.0
OfficeMax Inc.	263 Shuman Blvd.	Naperville	IL	60563	Dorrit Bern	630-438-7800	P	15,528	49.0
IKEA North America	1000 IKEA Dr.	Elizabeth	NJ	07202	Anders Dahlvig	908-352-3270	R	5,937*	8.0
Leggett and Platt Inc.	PO Box 757	Carthage	MO	64836		417-358-8131	P	4,306	24.0
Kohler Co.	444 Highland Dr.	Kohler	WI	53044	Herbert Kohler	920-457-4441	R	4,061*	33.0
Armstrong World Industries	PO Box 3001	Lancaster	PA	17604	Michael D. Lockhart	717-397-0611	R	3,550	12.9
Euromarket Design Inc.	1250 Techny Rd.	Northbrook	IL	60062	Gordon Segal	847-272-2888	R	2,215*	7.0
Furniture Brands International	101 S Hanley Rd.	St. Louis	MO	63105	John T. Foy	314-863-1100	P	2,082	11.9
Hillenbrand Industries Inc.	1069 State Rte 46E	Batesville	IN	47006		812-934-7000	P	2,024	9.9
Farmer Furniture	PO Box 1140	Dublin	GA	31040		478-272-4000	R	1,961*	1.4
Sealy Corp.	Sealy Dr., 1 Ofc Pk	Trinity	NC	27370	Ronald L. Jones	336-861-3500	P	1,702	6.1
Pier 1 Imports Inc.	100 Pier 1 Pl.	Fort Worth	TX	76102		817-252-8000	P	1,623	15.4
La-Z-Boy Inc.	PO Box 2390	Monroe	MI	48161	K.L. Darrow	734-242-1444	P	1,617	11.7
Rooms To Go Inc.	11540 Hwy. 92 E	Seffner	FL	33584	Jeffrey Seaman	813-623-5400	R	1,596*	6.5
Aaron Rents Inc.	309 E Paces Ferry	Atlanta	GA	30305	R. C. Loudermilk Sr.	404-231-0011	P	1,495	9.6
Tempur-Pedic International	1713 Jaggie Fox	Lexington	KY	40511	H. Thomas Bryant	859-259-0754	P	1,107	1.4
Cost Plus Inc.	200 4th St.	Oakland	CA	94607	Barry J. Feld	510-893-7300	P	1,040	6.7
Schottenstein Stores Corp.	1800 Moler Rd.	Columbus	OH	43207	Jay L. Schottenstein	614-221-9200	R	953*	7.6
Haverty Furniture Companies	780 Johnson Frry Rd	Atlanta	GA	30342		404-443-2900	P	859	4.5
Simmons Co.	1 Concourse Pky.	Atlanta	GA	30328	Charles R. Eitel	770-512-7700	R	855	3.0
Levitz Furniture	300 Crossways Park	Woodbury	NY	11797	Alan Rosenberg	516-496-9560	S	840*	4.5
Select Comfort Corp.	6105 Trenton Ln. N	Minneapolis	MN	55442	W R. McLaughlin	763-551-7000	P	799	3.2
Ashley Furniture Industries	1 Ashley Way	Arcadia	WI	54612	Ronald G. Wanek	608-323-3377	R	761*	4.0
Restoration Hardware Inc.	15 Koch Rd., Ste. J	Corte Madera	CA	94925	Gary G. Friedman	415-924-1005	P	713	3.8
Levin Furniture	609 W Main St.	Mt. Pleasant	PA	15666	Robert Levin	724-872-2050	R	557*	0.4
Bombay Company Inc.	PO Box 161009	Fort Worth	TX	76161	David B. Stewart	817-347-8200	P	536	4.5
Art Van Furniture Inc.	6500 E 14 Mile Rd.	Warren	MI	48092	Art Van Elslander	586-939-0800	R	531*	3.5
Flexsteel Industries Inc.	PO Box 877	Dubuque	IA	52004	Bruce Boylen	563-556-7730	P	425	2.3
Amer. TV & Appliance/Madison	2404 W Beltline	Madison	WI	53713	Douglas Reuhl	608-271-1000	R	400*	2.0
CORT Furniture Rental Corp.	11250 Waples Mill	Fairfax	VA	22030	Paul N. Arnold	703-968-8500	S	375*	3.0
Rose Furniture	PO Box 1829	High Point	NC	27261	Robert Kester	336-886-6050	R	327*	0.3
Rowe Companies	1650 Tysons Blvd.	McLean	VA	22102	Gerald M. Birnbach	703-847-8670	R	301	2.4
Serta Inc.	5401 Trillium Blvd.	Hoffman Estates	IL	60192		847-645-0200	R	268*	<0.1
Raymour and Flanigan Furniture	7230 Morgan Rd.	Liverpool	NY	13090	Neil Goldberg	315-453-2500	R	258*	3.8
Dearden's Inc.	700 S Main St.	Los Angeles	CA	90014	Raquel Bensimon	213-362-9600	R	249*	0.5
Francisco Mendoza Inc.	PO Box 373430	Cayey	PR	00737	F. Mendoza Rivera	787-738-2112	R	245*	0.4
Berkline Benchcraft Holdings	PO Box 6003	Morristown	TN	37815		423-585-1500	R	240*	<0.1
Jordan's Furniture Inc.	100 Stockwell Dr.	Avon	MA	02322	Barry Tattelman	508-580-4600	S	214*	1.4
Design Within Reach Inc.	225 Bush Street	San Francisco	CA	94104	Ray Brunner	415-248-5397	P	194	0.4
Morris Kirschman and Company	PO Box 26427	New Orleans	LA	70186	Arnold Kirschman	504-947-6673	R	186*	0.3
Sauder Manufacturing Co.	PO Box 230	Archbold	OH	43502	Virgil Miller	419-445-7670	R	184*	0.2
Nebraska Furniture Mart Inc.	PO Box 2335	Omaha	NE	68103	Ron Blumkins	402-255-6327	S	180*	1.2
Office Resources Inc.	374 Congress St.	Boston	MA	02210		617-423-9100	R	175*	0.2
Lexington Furniture Industries	PO Box 1008	Lexington	NC	27293	Asher Lepkin	336-474-5300	R	167*	0.3
Vermont Country Store	5650 Main Street	Manchester Ctr	VT	05255	Lyman Orton	802-362-8460	R	167*	1.0
Chromcraft Revington Inc.	1330 Win Hentschel	West Lafayette	IN	47906	B. M. Anderson-Ray	765-807-2640	P	160	0.9
Rowe Furniture Inc.	2121 Gardner St.	Elliston	VA	24087	Gerald Birnbach	540-444-7693	R	159*	1.7
McGuire Furniture Company Inc.	1201 Bryant St.	San Francisco	CA	94103	Sarah Garcia	415-626-1414	R	155*	0.2
Wickes Furniture Company Inc.	250 S Gary Ave.	Carol Stream	IL	60188	John Disa		R	150*	1.5
Norwalk Furniture Corp.	100 Furniture Pkwy.	Norwalk	OH	44857	James Gerken	419-668-4461	R	147*	0.9
Marlo Furniture Company Inc.	725 Rockville Pke.	Rockville	MD	20852	Neal Glickfield	301-738-9000	R	138*	0.7
Jennifer Convertibles Inc.	419 Crossways Park	Woodbury	NY	11797	Harley J. Greenfield	516-496-1900	P	137	0.5
Rotman's	725 Southbridge St.	Worcester	MA	01610	Steve Rotman	508-755-5276	R	135*	0.2
Muebleria Berrios Inc.	PO Box 674	Cidra	PR	00739	Efrain Rivera	787-752-6020	R	128	0.7
Bernhardt Furniture Company	PO Box 740	Lenoir	NC	28645	Alexander Bernhardt	828-758-9811	R	123*	0.2
Leath Furniture Inc.	4370 Peachtree Rd.	Atlanta	GA	30319	Ronald D. Phillips	404-848-0880	R	118*	0.8
Hickory White Co.	PO Box 998	Hickory	NC	28603	Jim Adams	828-322-8624	S	115*	0.3
Big Sandy Furniture Inc.	8375 Gallia Pike	Franklin Furnace	OH	45629	John C. Stewart Jr.	740-574-2113	R	112*	0.7
Porter of Racine	301 6th Street	Racine	WI	53403	H.R. Waters	262-633-6363	R	110*	<0.1
Schnadig Corp.	1111 E Touhy Ave.	Des Plaines	IL	60018	Donald Belgrad	847-803-6000	R	107*	<0.1
Gallery Furniture Inc.	6006 N Fwy.	Houston	TX	77076	Jim McIingvale	713-694-5570	R	105*	0.3
Marsh Pottery L.L.C.	3775 Ave / Carolina	Fort Mill	SC	29708	Tim Marsh	803-548-7075	R	105*	0.3
Goodman's Inc.	PO Box 13289	Phoenix	AZ	85002	Adam Goodman	602-263-1110	R	101*	0.1
Bridon-American Corp.	PO Box 6000	Wilkes Barre	PA	18773	John Churchfield	570-822-3349	R	101*	0.4
Grand Home Furnishings	4235 Electric Rd SW	Roanoke	VA	24014	G. B. Cartledge Jr.	540-776-7000	R	100*	0.8
Stryker Medical	3800 E Centre Ave.	Portage	MI	49002	Stephen MacMillan	269-329-2100	D	96*	0.7
Sherrill Furniture Company	PO Box 189	Hickory	NC	28603		828-322-2640	R	89*	0.5
Schewel Furniture Company Inc.	PO Box 1600	Lynchburg	VA	24505	Marc A. Schewel	434-845-2326	R	86*	0.7
Peoploungers Inc.	PO Box 429	Nettleton	MS	38858	James Green	662-963-7301	R	85*	0.9
Spiller Spring Co.	2216 S 24th St.	Sheboygan	WI	53081	Donald Coleman	920-457-3649	R	85*	0.2
Patio Enclosures Inc.	700 Highland Rd. E	Macedonia	OH	44056		330-468-0700	R	84*	0.2
Lack Valley Stores Ltd.	1300 San Patricia D	Pharr	TX	78577	Lee Aaronson	956-702-3361	R	82*	0.3
Interior Investments L.L.C.	625 Heathrow Dr.	Lincolnshire	IL	60069		847-325-1000	R	81*	<0.1
United Furniture Industries	PO Box 308	Okolona	MS	38860	David Belford	662-257-1811	R	81*	0.9

Source: Ward's Business Directory of U.S. Private and Public Companies, Volumes 1 and 2, 2008. The company type code used is as follows: P - Public, R - Private, S - Subsidiary, D - Division, J - Joint Venture, A - Affiliate, G - Group. Sales are in millions of dollars, employees are in thousands. An asterisk (*) indicates an estimated sales volume. The symbol < stands for 'less than'. Company names and addresses are truncated, in some cases, to fit into the available space.

MATERIALS CONSUMED

Material	Quantity	Delivered Cost ($ million)
Hardwood lumber, rough and dressed	(X)	154.8
Softwood lumber, rough and dressed	(X)	57.1
Hardwood cut stock and dimension (excluding furniture frames)	(X)	89.5
Softwood plywood	(X)	53.2
Hardwood plywood	(X)	125.6
Hardwood veneer	(X)	6.3
Particleboard (reconstituted wood)	(X)	2.9
Medium density fiberboard (MDF)	(X)	1.2
Hardboard	(X)	0.9
Wood furniture frames	(X)	299.9
Woven cotton upholstery fabrics (excluding ticking)	(X)	312.3
Other woven upholstery fabrics (rayon, nylon, etc.), exc. ticking	(X)	802.0
Paddings, battings, and fillings (exc. rubber and plastics foam)	(X)	253.7
Coated and laminated fabrics (including vinyl coated)	(X)	184.8
Springs, innerspring units, and box spring constructions	(X)	102.1
Furniture and builders' hardware (incl. cabinet hardware, casters, glides, handles, hinges, locks, etc.)	(X)	126.3
Constructions (sleeper mechanisms), dual purpose sleep furniture	(X)	69.1
Foam cores for mattresses, including latex (exc. topper pads)	(X)	42.9
Formed and slab stock for pillows, cushions, seating, etc. (urethane)	(X)	387.7
Paints, varnishes, stains, lacquers, shellacs, japans, enamels, etc.	(X)	7.8
Adhesives and sealants	(X)	7.3
Plastics resins consumed in the form of granules, pellets, etc.	(X)	0.7
Plastics laminated sheets	(X)	2.3
Metal stampings	(X)	(D)
Other fabricated metal products (including forgings)	(X)	26.9
Castings, rough and semifinished	(X)	0.3
Steel sheet and strip (including tinplate)	(X)	(D)
All other steel shapes and forms (exc. castings, forgings, fabr. metal products)	(X)	(D)
Aluminum and aluminum-base alloy sheet, plate, foil, and welded tubing	(X)	(D)
All other aluminum and aluminum-base alloy shapes and forms (exc. castings, forgings, fabr. metal products)	(X)	(D)
Plastics furniture parts and components	(X)	24.4
Flat glass (plate, float, and sheet)	(X)	0.9
Mirrors, framed and unframed	(X)	0.2
Paperboard containers, boxes, and corrugated paperboard	(X)	95.5
All other materials, components, parts, containers, and supplies	(X)	865.0
Materials, ingredients, containers, and supplies, nsk	(X)	860.7

Source: 2002 *Economic Census.* Explanation of symbols used: (D): Withheld to avoid disclosure of competitive data; na: Not available; (S): Withheld because statistical norms were not met; (X): Not applicable; (Z): Less than half the unit shown; nec: Not elsewhere classified; nsk: Not specified by kind; - : zero; p : 10-19 percent estimated; q : 20-29 percent estimated.

PRODUCT SHARE DETAILS

Product or Product Class Shipments	Mil. $	Product or Product Class Shipments	Mil. $
UPHOLSTERED HOUSEHOLD FURNITURE	10,305.5	variable height adjustment, excluding swivel rockers, not custom sold at retail	146.3
Upholstered household furniture, except dual-purpose sleep furniture	**8,789.9**	Other upholstered wood household chairs, except dining room, kitchen, reclining, rocking, and swivel chairs, not custom sold at retail	956.3
Upholstered wood household sofas, davenports, settees, and loveseats, excluding chairs sold as part of suites and sectional sofa pieces, not custom sold at retail	4,430.3	Other upholstered wood household chairs, except dining room and kitchen chairs with upholstered seats or backs	419.2
Upholstered wood household sectional sofa pieces, including pieces seating one person, except dual-purpose sleep furniture, not custom sold at retail	673.3	Custom upholstered wood household furniture sold directly to the customer at retail, except dining room and kitchen chairs with upholstered seats or backs	325.9
Upholstered wood household rockers, including swivel rockers, not custom sold at retail	282.5	Upholstered wood household furniture, except dual-purpose sleep furniture, nsk	234.0
Upholstered wood household reclining chairs, not custom sold at retail	1,322.0	**Upholstered household furniture, except wood**	**76.5**
Upholstered wood household swivel chairs with variable height adjustment and other upholstered wood household chairs and furniture, except dual-purpose sleep furniture	1,847.8	**Dual-purpose sleep furniture, including convertible sofas, jackknife sofa beds and chair beds, studio couches, and futons shipped with frames, not custom sold at retail**	**501.6**
Upholstered wood household swivel chairs with		**Upholstered household furniture, nsk, total**	**937.5**

Source: 2002 *Economic Census.* The values are product shipments in millions of dollars for 2002. Total product shipments may be lower or higher than industry shipments. See Introduction for a full discussion. Values of indented subcategories are summed in the main heading(s). The symbol (D) appears when data are withheld to prevent disclosure of competitive information. The abbreviation nsk stands for 'not specified by kind' and nec for 'not elsewhere classified'. A dash (-) means zero.

INPUTS AND OUTPUTS FOR UPHOLSTERED HOUSEHOLD FURNITURE MANUFACTURING

Economic Sector or Industry Providing Inputs	%	Sector	Economic Sector or Industry Buying Outputs	%	Sector
Compensation of employees	29.2		Personal consumption expenditures	91.9	
Broadwoven fabric mills	9.1	Manufg.	Private fixed investment	5.2	
Urethane & other foam products (except polystrene)	8.2	Manufg.	Exports of goods & services	1.6	Cap Inv
Wholesale trade	6.1	Trade	Manufactured homes & mobile homes	0.3	Manufg.
Showcases, partitions, shelving, and lockers	3.7	Manufg.	Change in private inventories	0.3	In House
Sawmills & wood preservation	3.0	Manufg.	S/L govt. invest., education	0.3	S/L Govt
Textile product mills, nec	2.5	Manufg.	Upholstered household furniture	0.2	Manufg.
Management of companies & enterprises	2.4	Services			
Hardware	2.2	Manufg.			
Fabric coating mills	2.0	Manufg.			
Truck transportation	1.9	Util.			
Veneer & plywood	1.9	Manufg.			
Textile & fabric finishing mills	1.7	Manufg.			
Springs & wire products	1.3	Manufg.			
Paperboard containers	1.1	Manufg.			
Plastics products, nec	1.0	Manufg.			
Advertising & related services	0.8	Services			
Real estate	0.8	Fin/R.E.			
Securities, commodity contracts, investments	0.7	Fin/R.E.			
Retail trade	0.6	Trade			
Iron & steel mills & ferroalloys	0.6	Manufg.			
Aluminum products from purchased aluminum	0.5	Manufg.			
Power generation & supply	0.5	Util.			
Monetary authorities/depository credit intermediation	0.5	Fin/R.E.			
Crowns & closures & metal stamping	0.4	Manufg.			
Professional, scientific, technical services, nec	0.4	Services			
Specialized design services	0.4	Services			
Mattresses	0.4	Manufg.			
Semiconductors & related devices	0.3	Manufg.			
Warehousing & storage	0.3	Util.			
Upholstered household furniture	0.3	Manufg.			
Automotive equipment rental & leasing	0.3	Fin/R.E.			
Printed circuit assemblies (electronic assembles)	0.3	Manufg.			
Motor vehicle parts	0.2	Manufg.			
Accounting, tax preparation, bookkeeping, & payroll	0.2	Services			
Abrasive products	0.2	Manufg.			
Taxes on production & imports, less subsidies	0.2				
Data processing, hosting, & related services	0.2	Services			
Plastics packaging materials, film & sheet	0.2	Manufg.			
Machine shops	0.2	Manufg.			
Rail transportation	0.2	Util.			
Legal services	0.2	Services			
Food services & drinking places	0.2	Services			
Services to buildings & dwellings	0.2	Services			
Telecommunications	0.2	Services			
Maintenance/repair of nonresidential structures	0.1	Construct.			
Commercial & industrial machinery rental & leasing	0.1	Fin/R.E.			
Architectural, engineering, & related services	0.1	Services			
Coating, engraving, heat treating & allied activities	0.1	Manufg.			
Alumina refining & primary aluminum production	0.1	Manufg.			
Other computer related services, including facilities	0.1	Services			
Air transportation	0.1	Util.			

Source: Benchmark Input-Output Accounts for the U.S. Economy, 2002, U.S. Department of Commerce, Washington, D.C., January 2008. The abbreviation nec stands for 'not elsewhere classified'.

OCCUPATIONS EMPLOYED BY HOUSEHOLD & INSTITUTIONAL FURNITURE

Occupation	% of Total 2006	Change to 2016	Occupation	% of Total 2006	Change to 2016
Upholsterers	10.1	-16.5	Sales reps, wholesale & manufacturing, exc tech	1.4	-23.9
Cabinetmakers & bench carpenters	8.6	-23.9	Carpenters	1.4	-23.9
Team assemblers	7.8	-23.9	Cutting, punching, & press machine operators	1.3	-31.5
Sewing machine operators	7.5	-16.3	Assemblers & fabricators, nec	1.3	-31.5
Woodworking machine operators & tenders, exc sawing	5.6	-16.3	Welders, cutters, solderers, & brazers	1.3	-19.0
Furniture finishers	3.8	-23.9	Coating, painting, & spraying machine operators	1.2	-27.7
First-line supervisors/managers of production workers	3.8	-23.9	General & operations managers	1.1	-31.5
Helpers--Production workers	3.7	-23.9	Cutters & trimmers, hand	1.1	-16.3
Laborers & freight, stock, & material movers, hand	3.5	-31.5	Industrial truck & tractor operators	1.1	-31.5
Packers & packagers, hand	1.8	-39.1	Customer service representatives	1.1	-16.3
Sawing machine setters, operators, & tenders, wood	1.7	-16.3	Machine feeders & offbearers	1.1	-31.5
Inspectors, testers, sorters, samplers, & weighers	1.6	-28.2	Office clerks, general	1.0	-25.0
Shipping, receiving, & traffic clerks	1.6	-26.8			

Source: Industry-Occupation Matrix, Bureau of Labor Statistics, December 4, 2007. These data are reported based on 4-digit NAICS categories but have been matched to corresponding 6-digit NAICS industry codes. The change reported for each occupation to the year 2016 is a percent of growth or decline as estimated by the Bureau of Labor Statistics. The abbreviation nec stands for 'not elsewhere classified'.

LOCATION BY STATE AND REGIONAL CONCENTRATION

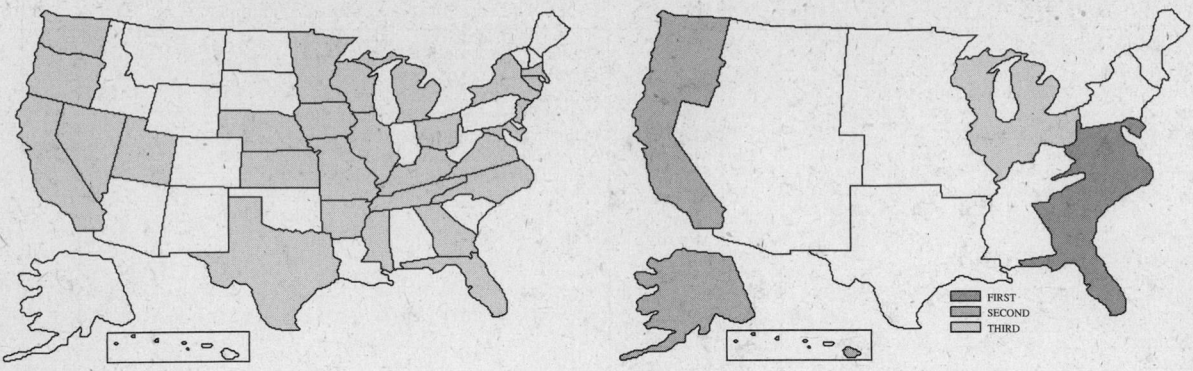

FIRST
SECOND
THIRD

INDUSTRY DATA BY STATE

| State | Establish-ments | Shipments | | | Employment | | | | Cost as % of Shipments | Investment per Employee ($) |
		Total ($ mil)	% of U.S.	Per Establ.	Total Number	% of U.S.	Per Establ.	Wages ($/hour)		
North Carolina	287	2,807.4	26.3	9,781.9	26,431	28.8	92	12.86	47.7	1,913
Mississippi	116	2,269.3	21.2	19,562.8	18,994	20.7	164	13.22	57.8	1,499
California	340	1,142.2	10.7	3,359.5	9,936	10.8	29	11.73	49.7	1,539
Tennessee	46	1,002.7	9.4	21,797.4	9,454	10.3	206	12.39	46.5	1,058
Texas	94	365.2	3.4	3,885.0	2,967	3.2	32	10.89	44.9	1,920
Missouri	30	286.6	2.7	9,554.2	2,365	2.6	79	13.60	38.4	661
Illinois	88	207.4	1.9	2,356.5	1,309	1.4	15	11.85	49.2	3,086
Virginia	53	203.9	1.9	3,847.3	1,916	2.1	36	10.90	49.1	12,448
New York	102	175.7	1.6	1,722.1	1,338	1.5	13	11.88	54.4	2,074
Utah	20	172.8	1.6	8,637.9	1,211	1.3	61	12.97	71.2	966
Arkansas	11	154.1	1.4	14,004.6	913	1.0	83	10.80	50.7	1,220
Ohio	57	148.3	1.4	2,601.5	1,217	1.3	21	14.66	47.9	1,675
Florida	107	139.4	1.3	1,303.1	1,141	1.2	11	12.25	51.0	1,649
Iowa	9	136.5	1.3	15,171.9	1,362	1.5	151	14.83	52.1	993
Georgia	32	117.8	1.1	3,680.4	868	0.9	27	10.55	54.4	2,950
Minnesota	39	98.4	0.9	2,524.2	712	0.8	18	11.88	51.5	2,178
Oregon	38	91.3	0.9	2,402.9	903	1.0	24	10.05	53.3	1,939
New Jersey	33	57.2	0.5	1,734.1	409	0.4	12	13.04	48.3	1,956
Wisconsin	30	56.3	0.5	1,875.4	600	0.7	20	11.37	47.2	2,553
Massachusetts	29	54.9	0.5	1,891.8	462	0.5	16	12.77	40.2	1,058
Michigan	40	52.9	0.5	1,322.8	434	0.5	11	12.08	50.3	2,099
Washington	23	28.9	0.3	1,257.8	281	0.3	12	12.64	47.7	1,836
Maryland	11	27.6	0.3	2,510.7	407	0.4	37	8.53	49.7	1,128
Kansas	9	23.4	0.2	2,600.9	259	0.3	29	10.45	60.7	1,764
Kentucky	12	20.8	0.2	1,736.0	195	0.2	16	9.06	49.8	1,313
Nevada	12	16.3	0.2	1,359.7	107	0.1	9	11.63	51.3	2,336
Connecticut	15	13.6	0.1	906.8	125	0.1	8	12.88	44.9	1,432
Nebraska	5	6.2	0.1	1,243.0	105	0.1	21	10.14	54.7	952

Source: 2002 *Economic Census*. The states are in descending order of shipments or establishments (if shipment data are missing for the majority). The symbol (D) appears when data are withheld to prevent disclosure of competitive information. States marked with (D) are sorted by number of establishments. A dash (-) indicates that the data element cannot be calculated. Data may not show all states active in the NAICS category. All data available at the time of publication are shown.

NAICS 337122 - NONUPHOLSTERED WOOD HOUSEHOLD FURNITURE MANUFACTURING

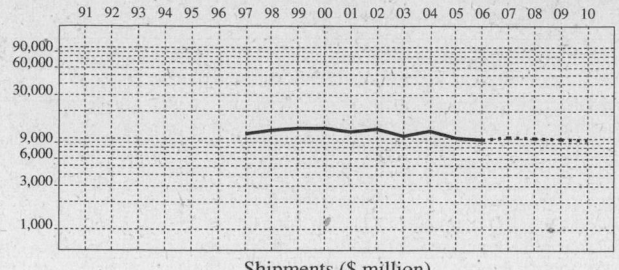

Shipments ($ million)

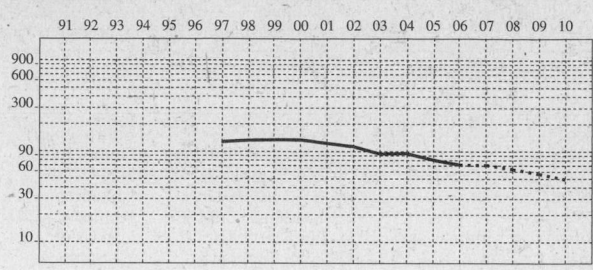

Employment (000)

GENERAL STATISTICS

Year	Companies	Establishments		Employment			Compensation		Production ($ million)			
		Total	with 20 or more employees	Total (000)	Production Workers (000)	Hours (Mil)	Payroll ($ mil)	Wages ($/hr)	Cost of Materials	Value Added by Manufacture	Value of Shipments	Capital Invest.
1997	3,678	3,849	743	127.7	110.6	213.4	2,677.6	9.52	5,377.6	5,874.7	11,252.7	296.6
1998		3,888	760	132.4	116.0	233.5	2,922.4	9.68	5,867.5	6,574.0	12,372.7	274.0
1999		3,839	754	134.2	116.9	231.1	3,058.2	10.17	6,148.5	7,012.9	12,995.8	346.6
2000		3,826	762	133.9	116.4	222.7	3,100.6	10.37	6,146.5	6,904.3	12,990.6	279.2
2001		3,913	724	122.8	106.0	196.8	2,817.1	10.63	5,483.1	6,261.1	11,860.9	238.5
2002	3,975	4,114	687	113.2	95.9	184.9	2,784.2	11.28	5,154.9	7,717.8	12,726.6	220.4
2003		4,003	623	94.3	79.5	154.6	2,446.7	11.63	4,759.9	5,835.7	10,678.4	137.4
2004		3,916	605	95.3	78.6	157.4	2,514.8	11.91	5,067.1	7,095.8	12,086.8	155.2
2005		3,771	558	81.0	65.7	130.6	2,201.7	12.04	4,613.3	5,524.1	10,165.2	127.4
2006		3,934P	562P	71.5	58.1	112.0	2,058.8	13.09	4,667.4	4,941.8	9,721.5	144.4
2007		3,941P	537P	71.0P	56.5P	109.8P	2,147.4P	13.09P	4,972.4P	5,264.8P	10,356.8P	95.4P
2008		3,947P	511P	63.8P	49.6P	96.3P	2,054.5P	13.47P	4,856.5P	5,142.0P	10,115.3P	72.4P
2009		3,954P	485P	56.6P	42.7P	82.9P	1,961.6P	13.84P	4,740.5P	5,019.2P	9,873.8P	49.4P
2010		3,960P	459P	49.4P	35.8P	69.5P	1,868.7P	14.21P	4,624.6P	4,896.4P	9,632.3P	26.4P

Sources: 1997 and 2002 *Economic Census*; other years, up to 2006, are from *Annual Survey of Manufactures*. Establishment counts for non-Census years are from *County Business Patterns*; 1997 and 2002 values are from the 1997 and 2002 censuses, respectively. 'P's show projections by the editors.

INDICES OF CHANGE

Year	Companies	Establishments		Employment			Compensation		Production ($ million)			
		Total	with 20 or more employees	Total (000)	Production Workers (000)	Hours (Mil)	Payroll ($ mil)	Wages ($/hr)	Cost of Materials	Value Added by Manufacture	Value of Shipments	Capital Invest.
1997	93	94	108	113	115	115	96	84	104	76	88	135
1998		95	111	117	121	126	105	86	114	85	97	124
1999		93	110	119	122	125	110	90	119	91	102	157
2000		93	111	118	121	120	111	92	119	89	102	127
2001		95	105	108	111	106	101	94	106	81	93	108
2002	100	100	100	100	100	100	100	100	100	100	100	100
2003		97	91	83	83	84	88	103	92	76	84	62
2004		95	88	84	82	85	90	106	98	92	95	70
2005		92	81	72	69	71	79	107	89	72	80	58
2006		96P	82P	63	61	61	74	116	91	64	76	66
2007		96P	78P	63P	59P	59P	77P	116P	96P	68P	81P	43P
2008		96P	74P	56P	52P	52P	74P	119P	94P	67P	79P	33P
2009		96P	71P	50P	45P	45P	70P	123P	92P	65P	78P	22P
2010		96P	67P	44P	37P	38P	67P	126P	90P	63P	76P	12P

Sources: Same as General Statistics. Values reflect change from the base year, 2002. Values above 100 mean greater than 2002, values below 100 mean less than 2002, and the values of 100 in other years means the same as 2002. 'P's show projections by the editors.

SELECTED RATIOS

For 2002	Avg. of All Manufact.	Analyzed Industry	Index	For 2002	Avg. of All Manufact.	Analyzed Industry	Index
Employees per Establishment	42	28	66	Value Added per Production Worker	182,367	80,478	44
Payroll per Establishment	1,639,184	676,762	41	Cost per Establishment	5,769,015	1,253,014	22
Payroll per Employee	39,053	24,595	63	Cost per Employee	137,446	45,538	33
Production Workers per Establishment	30	23	79	Cost per Production Worker	195,506	53,753	27
Wages per Establishment	694,845	506,969	73	Shipments per Establishment	11,158,348	3,093,486	28
Wages per Production Worker	23,548	21,748	92	Shipments per Employee	265,847	112,426	42
Hours per Production Worker	1,980	1,928	97	Shipments per Production Worker	378,144	132,707	35
Wages per Hour	11.89	11.28	95	Investment per Establishment	361,338	53,573	15
Value Added per Establishment	5,381,325	1,875,984	35	Investment per Employee	8,609	1,947	23
Value Added per Employee	128,210	68,178	53	Investment per Production Worker	12,245	2,298	19

Sources: Same as General Statistics. The 'Average of All Manufacturing' column represents the average of all manufacturing industries reported for the most recent complete year available. The Index shows the relationship between the Average and the Analyzed Industry. For example, 100 means that they are equal; 500 that the Analyzed Industry is five times the average; 50 means that the Analyzed Industry is half the national average. The abbreviation 'na' is used to show that data are 'not available'. Ratios shown for 2002, the last complete census year.

LEADING COMPANIES   Number shown: **75**   Total sales ($ mil): **92,911**   Total employment (000): **371.8**

Company Name	Address				CEO Name	Phone	Co. Type	Sales ($ mil)	Empl. (000)
Staples Inc.	PO Box 9328	Framingham	MA	01702		508-253-5000	P	19,373	75.6
Office Depot Inc.	2200 O Germantwn	Delray Beach	FL	33445		561-266-4800	P	15,528	49.0
OfficeMax Inc.	263 Shuman Blvd.	Naperville	IL	60563	Dorrit Bern	630-438-7800	P	15,528	49.0
IKEA North America	1000 IKEA Dr.	Elizabeth	NJ	07202	Anders Dahlvig	908-352-3270	R	5,937*	8.0
Kohler Co.	444 Highland Dr.	Kohler	WI	53044	Herbert Kohler	920-457-4441	R	4,061*	33.0
Armstrong World Industries	PO Box 3001	Lancaster	PA	17604	Michael D. Lockhart	717-397-0611	P	3,550	12.9
Euromarket Design Inc.	1250 Techny Rd.	Northbrook	IL	60062	Gordon Segal	847-272-2888	R	2,215*	7.0
Furniture Brands International	101 S Hanley Rd.	St. Louis	MO	63105	John T. Foy	314-863-1100	P	2,082	11.9
Farmer Furniture	PO Box 1140	Dublin	GA	31040		478-272-4000	R	1,961*	1.4
Pier 1 Imports Inc.	100 Pier 1 Pl.	Fort Worth	TX	76102		817-252-8000	P	1,623	15.4
Rooms To Go Inc.	11540 Hwy. 92 E	Seffner	FL	33584	Jeffrey Seaman	813-623-5400	R	1,596*	6.5
Aaron Rents Inc.	309 E Paces Ferry	Atlanta	GA	30305	R. C. Loudermilk Sr.	404-231-0011	P	1,495	9.6
Cost Plus Inc.	200 4th St.	Oakland	CA	94607	Barry J. Feld	510-893-7300	P	1,040	6.7
Ethan Allen Interiors Inc.	PO Box 1966	Danbury	CT	06813		203-743-8000	P	1,005	6.4
Schottenstein Stores Corp.	1800 Moler Rd.	Columbus	OH	43207	Jay L. Schottenstein	614-221-9200	R	953*	7.6
Haverty Furniture Companies	780 Johnson Frry Rd	Atlanta	GA	30342		404-443-2900	P	859	4.5
Simmons Co.	1 Concourse Pky.	Atlanta	GA	30328	Charles R. Eitel	770-512-7700	R	855	3.0
Levitz Furniture	300 Crossways Park	Woodbury	NY	11797	Alan Rosenberg	516-496-9560	S	840*	4.5
Ashley Furniture Industries	1 Ashley Way	Arcadia	WI	54612	Ronald G. Wanek	608-323-3377	R	761*	4.0
Restoration Hardware Inc.	15 Koch Rd., Ste. J	Corte Madera	CA	94925	Gary G. Friedman	415-924-1005	P	713	3.8
Levin Furniture	609 W Main St.	Mt. Pleasant	PA	15666	Robert Levin	724-872-2050	R	557*	0.4
Bombay Company Inc.	PO Box 161009	Fort Worth	TX	76161	David B. Stewart	817-347-8200	P	536	4.5
Art Van Furniture Inc.	6500 E 14 Mile Rd.	Warren	MI	48092	Art Van Elslander	586-939-0800	R	531*	3.5
Sauder Woodworking Co.	PO Box 156	Archbold	OH	43502	Kevin Sauder	419-446-2711	R	525*	3.0
Amer. TV & Appliance/Madison	2404 W Beltline	Madison	WI	53713	Douglas Reuhl	608-271-1000	R	400*	2.0
CORT Furniture Rental Corp.	11250 Waples Mill	Fairfax	VA	22030	Paul N. Arnold	703-968-8500	S	375*	3.0
Hooker Furniture Corp.	PO Box 4708	Martinsville	VA	24115		276-632-0459	P	350	1.1
Rose Furniture	PO Box 1829	High Point	NC	27261	Robert Kester	336-886-6050	R	327*	0.3
Stanley Furniture Company Inc.	1641 Fairystone Prk	Stanleytown	VA	24168		276-627-2000	P	308	2.2
Rowe Companies	1650 Tysons Blvd.	McLean	VA	22102	Gerald M. Birnbach	703-847-8670	R	301	2.4
Bassett Furniture Industries	PO Box 626	Bassett	VA	24055	Paul Fulton	276-629-6000	P	295	1.4
Raymour and Flanigan Furniture	7230 Morgan Rd.	Liverpool	NY	13090	Neil Goldberg	315-453-2500	R	258*	3.8
Dearden's Inc.	700 S Main St.	Los Angeles	CA	90014	Raquel Bensimon	213-362-9600	R	249*	0.5
Francisco Mendoza Inc.	PO Box 373430	Cayey	PR	00737	F. Mendoza Rivera	787-738-2112	R	245*	0.4
Pulaski Furniture Corp.	PO Box 1371	Pulaski	VA	24301	Lawerance E. Webb	540-980-7330	R	230*	2.5
O'Sullivan Industries Inc.	1900 Gulf Street	Lamar	MO	64759	Daniel F. O'Sullivan	417-682-3322	S	222*	1.3
Swaner Hardwood Company Inc.	5 W Magnolia Blvd.	Burbank	CA	91502	Gary Swaner	818-849-6761	R	217*	0.2
Jordan's Furniture Inc.	100 Stockwell Dr.	Avon	MA	02322	Barry Tattelman	508-580-4600	S	214*	1.4
Design Within Reach Inc.	225 Bush Street	San Francisco	CA	94104	Ray Brunner	415-248-5397	P	194	0.4
Morris Kirschman and Company	PO Box 26427	New Orleans	LA	70186	Arnold Kirschman	504-947-6673	R	186*	0.3
Sauder Manufacturing Co.	PO Box 230	Archbold	OH	43502	Virgil Miller	419-445-7670	R	184*	0.2
Progressive Furniture Inc.	PO Box 308	Archbold	OH	43502	Dennis Ammons	419-446-4500	R	184*	<0.1
Nebraska Furniture Mart Inc.	PO Box 2335	Omaha	NE	68103	Ron Blumkins	402-255-6327	S	180*	1.2
Lifetime Products Inc.	PO Box 160010	Clearfield	UT	84016		801-776-1532	R	177*	0.3
Office Resources Inc.	374 Congress St.	Boston	MA	02210		617-423-9100	R	175*	0.2
Lexington Furniture Industries	PO Box 1008	Lexington	NC	27293	Asher Lepkin	336-474-5300	R	167*	0.3
Vermont Country Store	5650 Main Street	Manchester Ctr	VT	05255	Lyman Orton	802-362-8460	R	167*	1.0
Chromcraft Revington Inc.	1330 Win Hentschel	West Lafayette	IN	47906	B. M. Anderson-Ray	765-807-2640	P	160	0.9
McGuire Furniture Company Inc.	1201 Bryant St.	San Francisco	CA	94103	Sarah Garcia	415-626-1414	R	155*	0.2
Cox Industries Inc.	PO Box 1124	Orangeburg	SC	29116	William Cox	803-534-7467	R	152*	0.1
Wickes Furniture Company Inc.	250 S Gary Ave.	Carol Stream	IL	60188	John Disa		R	150*	1.5
Norwalk Furniture Corp.	100 Furniture Pkwy.	Norwalk	OH	44857	James Gerken	419-668-4461	R	147*	0.9
Marlo Furniture Company Inc.	725 Rockville Pke.	Rockville	MD	20852	Neal Glickfield	301-738-9000	R	138*	0.7
Jennifer Convertibles Inc.	419 Crossways Park	Woodbury	NY	11797	Harley J. Greenfield	516-496-1900	P	137	0.5
Rotman's	725 Southbridge St.	Worcester	MA	01610	Steve Rotman	508-755-5276	R	135*	0.2
Muebleria Berrios Inc.	PO Box 674	Cidra	PR	00739	Efrain Rivera	787-752-6020	R	128	0.7
Bernhardt Furniture Company	PO Box 740	Lenoir	NC	28645	Alexander Bernhardt	828-758-9811	R	123*	0.2
Leath Furniture Inc.	4370 Peachtree Rd.	Atlanta	GA	30319	Ronald D. Phillips	404-848-0880	R	118*	0.8
Hickory White Co.	PO Box 998	Hickory	NC	28603	Jim Adams	828-322-8624	S	115*	0.3
Big Sandy Furniture Inc.	8375 Gallia Pike	Franklin Furnace	OH	45629	John C. Stewart Jr.	740-574-2113	R	112*	0.7
Porter of Racine	301 6th Street	Racine	WI	53403	H.R. Waters	262-633-6363	R	110*	<0.1
Gallery Furniture Inc.	6006 N Fwy.	Houston	TX	77076	Jim McIingvale	713-694-5570	R	105*	0.3
Marsh Pottery L.L.C.	3775 Ave / Carolina	Fort Mill	SC	29708	Tim Marsh	803-548-7075	R	105*	0.3
Goodman's Inc.	PO Box 13289	Phoenix	AZ	85002	Adam Goodman	602-263-1110	R	101*	0.1
Bush Industries Inc.	PO Box 460	Jamestown	NY	14702	James L. Sherbert	716-665-2510	R	100*	0.9
Grand Home Furnishings	4235 Electric Rd SW	Roanoke	VA	24014	G. B. Cartledge Jr.	540-776-7000	R	100*	0.8
Howard Miller Clock Co.	860 E Main Ave.	Zeeland	MI	49464	Howard Miller	616-772-9131	R	98*	0.4
Whittier Wood Products Co.	3787 W 1st Ave.	Eugene	OR	97402	Scott Whittier		R	96*	0.5
Wellborn Cabinet Inc.	PO Box 1210	Ashland	AL	36251		256-354-7151	R	93*	1.2
Sherrill Furniture Company	PO Box 189	Hickory	NC	28603		828-322-2640	R	89*	0.5
Schewel Furniture Company Inc.	PO Box 1600	Lynchburg	VA	24505	Marc A. Schewel	434-845-2326	R	86*	0.7
Patio Enclosures Inc.	700 Highland Rd. E	Macedonia	OH	44056		330-468-0700	R	84*	0.2
Ofs Brands Holdings Inc.	PO Box 100	Huntingburg	IN	47542	Joseph Bellino	812-683-4848	R	83*	0.1
Lack Valley Stores Ltd.	1300 San Patricia D	Pharr	TX	78577	Lee Aaronson	956-702-3361	R	82*	0.7
Interior Investments L.L.C.	625 Heathrow Dr.	Lincolnshire	IL	60069		847-325-1000	R	81*	<0.1

Source: Ward's Business Directory of U.S. Private and Public Companies, Volumes 1 and 2, 2008. The company type code used is as follows: P - Public, R - Private, S - Subsidiary, D - Division, J - Joint Venture, A - Affiliate, G - Group. Sales are in millions of dollars; employees are in thousands. An asterisk (*) indicates an estimated sales volume. The symbol < stands for 'less than'. Company names and addresses are truncated, in some cases, to fit into the available space.

MATERIALS CONSUMED

Material	Quantity	Delivered Cost ($ million)
Hardwood lumber, rough and dressed	(X)	514.2
Softwood lumber, rough and dressed	(X)	160.2
Hardwood cut stock and dimension (excluding furniture frames)	(X)	222.4
Softwood plywood	(X)	56.2
Hardwood plywood	(X)	114.2
Hardwood veneer	(X)	124.7
Particleboard (reconstituted wood)	(X)	266.4
Medium density fiberboard (MDF)	(X)	100.2
Hardboard	(X)	88.9
Wood furniture frames	(X)	71.6
Woven cotton upholstery fabrics (excluding ticking)	(X)	6.9
Other woven upholstery fabrics (rayon, nylon, etc.), exc. ticking	(X)	26.2
Paddings, battings, and fillings (exc. rubber and plastics foam)	(X)	9.9
Coated and laminated fabrics (including vinyl coated)	(X)	3.5
Springs, innerspring units, and box spring constructions	(X)	9.5
Furniture and builders' hardware (incl. cabinet hardware, casters, glides, handles, hinges, locks, etc.)	(X)	267.0
Constructions (sleeper mechanisms), dual purpose sleep furniture	(X)	1.3
Foam cores for mattresses, including latex (exc. topper pads)	(X)	7.2
Formed and slab stock for pillows, cushions, seating, etc. (urethane)	(X)	10.7
Paints, varnishes, stains, lacquers, shellacs, japans, enamels, etc.	(X)	93.4
Adhesives and sealants	(X)	76.4
Plastics resins consumed in the form of granules, pellets, etc.	(X)	3.8
Plastics laminated sheets	(X)	69.7
Metal stampings	(X)	4.7
Other fabricated metal products (including forgings)	(X)	12.2
Castings, rough and semifinished	(X)	2.3
Steel sheet and strip (including tinplate)	(X)	1.3
All other steel shapes and forms (exc. castings, forgings, fabr. metal products)	(X)	1.6
Aluminum and aluminum-base alloy sheet, plate, foil, and welded tubing	(X)	1.4
All other aluminum and aluminum-base alloy shapes and forms (exc. castings, forgings, fabr. metal products)	(X)	2.6
Plastics furniture parts and components	(X)	24.5
Flat glass (plate, float, and sheet)	(X)	33.2
Mirrors, framed and unframed	(X)	67.7
Paperboard containers, boxes, and corrugated paperboard	(X)	229.5
All other materials, components, parts, containers, and supplies	(X)	343.7
Materials, ingredients, containers, and supplies, nsk	(X)	1,054.1

Source: 2002 *Economic Census.* Explanation of symbols used: (D): Withheld to avoid disclosure of competitive data; na: Not available; (S): Withheld because statistical norms were not met; (X): Not applicable; (Z): Less than half the unit shown; nec: Not elsewhere classified; nsk: Not specified by kind; - : zero; p : 10-19 percent estimated; q : 20-29 percent estimated.

PRODUCT SHARE DETAILS

Product or Product Class Shipments	Mil. $	Product or Product Class Shipments	Mil. $
NONUPHOLSTERED WOOD HOUSEHOLD FURNITURE	11,456.9	Other nonupholstered wood bedroom furniture	729.3
Wood living room, library, family room, and den furniture, nonupholstered, except custom sold at retail	**3,429.8**	Armoires, chifforobes, wardrobe, and wardrobe-type cabinets	235.8
Tables (all types), except card and telephone tables and not custom sold at retail	791.9	Cedar chests	13.8
		Night tables and stands	312.6
Cabinets, desks, credenzas, bookcases, bookshelves, and wall units, except custom sold at retail	1,145.3	Other nonupholstered wood bedroom furniture (bed rails, chairs, commodes, and valet stands	167.1
Cabinets, including audio and television, excluding custom sold at retail	307.6	Wood bedroom furniture, except custom sold at retail, nsk	6.7
Wood household desks, except custom sold at retail	221.9	**Infants' and children's wood furniture, except custom sold at retail**	**419.3**
Credenzas, bookcases, and bookshelves, except wall units, not custom sold at retail	163.7	Infants' and children's wood furniture, except custom sold at retail	418.4
Wall units (desk, bookcase, and storage type), except custom sold at retail	452.0	Cribs, including springs sold as part of the crib	147.9
Other nonupholstered wood household furniture, except dining room and kitchen chairs, not custom sold at retail	1,326.8	Other infants' and children's wood bedroom furniture, including youth beds	246.5
Chairs, except dining room, kitchen, and rocking chairs, not custom sold at retail	124.8	Other infants' and children's nonupholstered wood furniture, including wood seating such as chairs, high chairs, and nursery seats	24.0
Rocking chairs, except custom sold at retail	14.9	Infants' and children's wood furniture, nsk	0.9
Other seating, except benches, loveseats, settees, and stools, not custom sold at retail	67.3	**Wood outdoor furniture, unpainted wood furniture, and ready-to-assemble wood furniture, except custom sold at retail**	**1,901.9**
Other nonupholstered furniture (bars, breakfronts, hanging shelves, and magazine racks), not custom sold at retail	1,119.8	Wood outdoor furniture, unpainted wood furniture, and ready-to-assemble wood furniture	1,852.4
Wood living room, library, family room, and den furniture, not custom sold at retail, nsk	165.8	Porch, lawn, beach, and similar wood outdoor furniture	82.7
Wood dining room and kitchen furniture, except kitchen cabinets, not custom sold at retail	**1,619.1**	Unpainted wood furniture, assembled (furniture-in-the-white), including bookcases, chairs, tables, desks, vanities, etc.	61.6
Tables, 30 x 40 in. or greater	626.7	Ready-to-assemble wood household seating, unpainted and finished, sold in kits	108.2
Dining room chairs	446.0	Ready-to-assemble wood kitchen furniture, unpainted and finished, sold in kits	141.6
Other wood dining room and kitchen furniture	473.8	Ready-to-assemble wood bedroom furniture, unpainted and finished, sold in kits	121.1
Buffets and servers	151.6	Ready-to-assemble wood home entertainment centers, unpainted and finished, sold in kits	354.4
China and corner cabinets	131.8	Ready-to-assemble wood shelving, unpainted and finished, sold in kits	143.7
Other nonupholstered wood dining and kitchen furniture, nec	190.3	Ready-to-assemble wood home-office computer furniture, unpainted and finished, sold in kits	556.9
Wood dining room and kitchen furniture, except kitchen cabinets, nsk	72.6	Other ready-to-assemble wood furniture, unpainted and finished, sold in kits	282.1
Wood bedroom furniture, except custom sold at retail	**2,858.5**	Wood outdoor furniture, unpainted wood furniture, and ready-to-assemble wood furniture, nsk	49.5
Wood beds and headboards, except cribs, cradles, hollywood beds, and youth beds	1,128.7	**Custom nonupholstered wood household furniture sold directly to the customer at retail**	**88.7**
Beds, except bunk beds, cribs, cradles, headboards, headboard beds, hollywood beds, water beds, and youth beds	558.9	**Nonupholstered wood household furniture, nsk, total**	**1,139.7**
Headboards and headboard beds, including padded	489.0		
Bunk beds, except mattresses and detachable springs	(D)		
Conventional wood waterbeds	(D)		
Wood bedroom dressers, dressing tables, and vanities	558.3		
Wood bedroom chests of drawers	435.5		

Source: 2002 *Economic Census*. The values are product shipments in millions of dollars for 2002. Total product shipments may be lower or higher than industry shipments. See Introduction for a full discussion. Values of indented subcategories are summed in the main heading(s). The symbol (D) appears when data are withheld to prevent disclosure of competitive information. The abbreviation nsk stands for 'not specified by kind' and nec for 'not elsewhere classified'. A dash (-) means zero.

INPUTS AND OUTPUTS FOR NONUPHOLSTERED WOOD HOUSEHOLD FURNITURE

Economic Sector or Industry Providing Inputs	%	Sector	Economic Sector or Industry Buying Outputs	%	Sector
Compensation of employees	31.0		Personal consumption expenditures	89.3	
Sawmills & wood preservation	8.4	Manufg.	Private fixed investment	4.7	
Reconstituted wood products	5.0	Manufg.	Exports of goods & services	3.2	Cap Inv
Wholesale trade	4.4	Trade	Change in private inventories	1.1	In House
Veneer & plywood	2.9	Manufg.	S/L govt. invest., education	-0.8	S/L Govt
Management of companies & enterprises	2.6	Services	Nonupholstered wood household furniture	0.3	Manufg.
Paperboard containers	2.4	Manufg.	Manufactured homes & mobile homes	0.2	Manufg.
Advertising & related services	1.9	Services	S/L govt. invest., other	0.2	S/L Govt
Plastics products, nec	1.7	Manufg.	Federal government, investment, nondefense	0.2	Fed Govt
Truck transportation	1.6	Util.			
Retail trade	1.2	Trade			
Showcases, partitions, shelving, and lockers	1.1	Manufg.			
Power generation & supply	1.1	Util.			
Paints & coatings	1.0	Manufg.			
Real estate	0.9	Fin/R.E.			
Hardware	0.9	Manufg.			
Glass products from purchased glass	0.8	Manufg.			
Adhesives	0.8	Manufg.			
Securities, commodity contracts, investments	0.7	Fin/R.E.			
Laminated plastics plates, sheets, & shapes	0.6	Manufg.			
Monetary authorities/depository credit intermediation	0.5	Fin/R.E.			

Continued on next page.

INPUTS AND OUTPUTS FOR NONUPHOLSTERED WOOD HOUSEHOLD FURNITURE - Continued

Economic Sector or Industry Providing Inputs	%	Sector	Economic Sector or Industry Buying Outputs	%	Sector
Nonupholstered wood household furniture	0.4	Manufg.			
Taxes on production & imports, less subsidies	0.4				
Professional, scientific, technical services, nec	0.4	Services			
Accounting, tax preparation, bookkeeping, & payroll	0.4	Services			
Rail transportation	0.4	Util.			
Specialized design services	0.4	Services			
Warehousing & storage	0.3	Util.			
Automotive equipment rental & leasing	0.3	Fin/R.E.			
Flat glass	0.3	Manufg.			
Semiconductors & related devices	0.3	Manufg.			
Maintenance/repair of nonresidential structures	0.3	Construct.			
Food services & drinking places	0.3	Services			
Legal services	0.3	Services			
Printed circuit assemblies (electronic assemblies)	0.3	Manufg.			
Services to buildings & dwellings	0.3	Services			
Data processing, hosting, & related services	0.3	Services			
Broadwoven fabric mills	0.2	Manufg.			
Telecommunications	0.2	Services			
Natural gas distribution	0.2	Util.			
Urethane & other foam products (except polystrene)	0.2	Manufg.			
Noncomparable imports	0.2	Foreign			
Architectural, engineering, & related services	0.2	Services			
Abrasive products	0.2	Manufg.			
Hotels & motels, including casino hotels	0.2	Services			
Automotive repair & maintenance, ex. car washes	0.2	Services			
Commercial & industrial machinery rental & leasing	0.2	Fin/R.E.			
Air transportation	0.1	Util.			
Commercial & industrial equipment repair/maintenance	0.1	Services			
Other computer related services, including facilities	0.1	Services			
Management, scientific, & technical consulting	0.1	Services			
Lessors of nonfinancial assets	0.1	Fin/R.E.			
Wood windows & doors & millwork	0.1	Manufg.			
Motor vehicle parts	0.1	Manufg.			
Springs & wire products	0.1	Manufg.			
Support services, nec	0.1	Services			
Business support services	0.1	Services			
Wood kitchen cabinets & countertops	0.1	Manufg.			

Source: Benchmark Input-Output Accounts for the U.S. Economy, 2002, U.S. Department of Commerce, Washington, D.C., January 2008. The abbreviation nec stands for 'not elsewhere classified'.

OCCUPATIONS EMPLOYED BY HOUSEHOLD & INSTITUTIONAL FURNITURE

Occupation	% of Total 2006	Change to 2016	Occupation	% of Total 2006	Change to 2016
Upholsterers	10.1	-16.5	Sales reps, wholesale & manufacturing, exc tech	1.4	-23.9
Cabinetmakers & bench carpenters	8.6	-23.9	Carpenters	1.4	-23.9
Team assemblers	7.8	-23.9	Cutting, punching, & press machine operators	1.3	-31.5
Sewing machine operators	7.5	-16.3	Assemblers & fabricators, nec	1.3	-31.5
Woodworking machine operators & tenders, exc sawing	5.6	-16.3	Welders, cutters, solderers, & brazers	1.3	-19.0
Furniture finishers	3.8	-23.9	Coating, painting, & spraying machine operators	1.2	-27.7
First-line supervisors/managers of production workers	3.8	-23.9	General & operations managers	1.1	-31.5
Helpers--Production workers	3.7	-23.9	Cutters & trimmers, hand	1.1	-16.3
Laborers & freight, stock, & material movers, hand	3.5	-31.5	Industrial truck & tractor operators	1.1	-31.5
Packers & packagers, hand	1.8	-39.1	Customer service representatives	1.1	-16.3
Sawing machine setters, operators, & tenders, wood	1.7	-16.3	Machine feeders & offbearers	1.1	-31.5
Inspectors, testers, sorters, samplers, & weighers	1.6	-28.2	Office clerks, general	1.0	-25.0
Shipping, receiving, & traffic clerks	1.6	-26.8			

Source: Industry-Occupation Matrix, Bureau of Labor Statistics, December 4, 2007. These data are reported based on 4-digit NAICS categories but have been matched to corresponding 6-digit NAICS industry codes. The change reported for each occupation to the year 2016 is a percent of growth or decline as estimated by the Bureau of Labor Statistics. The abbreviation nec stands for 'not elsewhere classified'.

LOCATION BY STATE AND REGIONAL CONCENTRATION

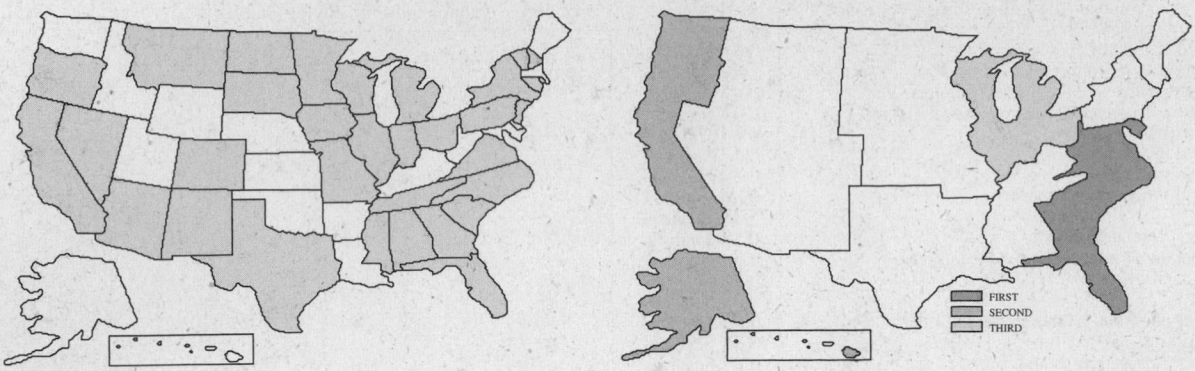

INDUSTRY DATA BY STATE

| State | Establish-ments | Shipments | | | Employment | | | | Cost as % of Shipments | Investment per Employee ($) |
		Total ($ mil)	% of U.S.	Per Establ.	Total Number	% of U.S.	Per Establ.	Wages ($/hour)		
North Carolina	205	2,565.2	20.2	12,513.3	24,530	21.7	120	11.42	44.3	1,639
California	568	1,242.0	9.8	2,186.6	13,506	11.9	24	10.38	44.3	1,616
New Jersey	88	1,021.6	8.0	11,609.2	673	0.6	8	11.21	4.5	1,847
Virginia	109	796.9	6.3	7,310.7	8,885	7.9	82	11.62	40.1	1,430
New York	288	736.5	5.8	2,557.3	7,315	6.5	25	13.30	35.5	1,998
Ohio	180	637.7	5.0	3,542.7	4,357	3.8	24	10.35	47.2	1,718
Wisconsin	108	597.9	4.7	5,536.0	4,311	3.8	40	10.60	53.6	2,970
Mississippi	32	475.5	3.7	14,859.3	3,761	3.3	118	12.55	46.9	2,035
Missouri	66	385.4	3.0	5,838.9	3,033	2.7	46	12.25	45.2	2,034
Alabama	60	380.7	3.0	6,345.6	2,616	2.3	44	10.40	40.6	4,322
Indiana	94	354.6	2.8	3,772.1	3,358	3.0	36	13.49	44.6	1,016
Pennsylvania	185	345.2	2.7	1,866.0	3,675	3.2	20	11.28	48.7	2,365
Vermont	49	341.9	2.7	6,977.2	2,560	2.3	52	12.73	22.8	1,865
Arizona	108	292.2	2.3	2,705.7	3,734	3.3	35	10.01	51.8	1,337
Tennessee	67	241.2	1.9	3,600.4	2,320	2.0	35	10.03	48.5	3,487
Michigan	100	225.3	1.8	2,253.5	2,449	2.2	24	11.49	44.5	3,806
Oregon	72	208.9	1.6	2,900.8	1,319	1.2	18	11.73	35.9	3,231
Georgia	98	197.6	1.6	2,015.9	1,862	1.6	19	9.72	39.6	4,506
Florida	252	170.4	1.3	676.1	1,783	1.6	7	10.70	45.4	2,473
Illinois	137	165.2	1.3	1,206.1	1,643	1.5	12	10.93	48.0	1,679
Texas	203	119.2	0.9	587.4	1,383	1.2	7	10.88	43.9	1,303
South Carolina	40	114.9	0.9	2,871.5	1,516	1.3	38	8.71	43.8	1,414
Colorado	78	92.7	0.7	1,187.8	1,299	1.1	17	11.56	26.7	761
Minnesota	76	49.5	0.4	651.0	594	0.5	8	11.51	41.3	1,975
New Hampshire	40	39.0	0.3	975.7	550	0.5	14	10.79	56.7	1,131
Connecticut	40	32.7	0.3	817.5	330	0.3	8	13.22	52.4	1,806
Iowa	34	32.3	0.3	950.8	417	0.4	12	10.95	17.4	544
Nevada	17	25.6	0.2	1,503.7	153	0.1	9	9.56	48.2	3,660
New Mexico	36	18.0	0.1	500.8	216	0.2	6	11.54	46.5	1,037
South Dakota	9	16.0	0.1	1,774.8	176	0.2	20	11.35	37.7	750
Montana	35	15.7	0.1	449.8	225	0.2	6	10.38	42.7	4,231
Rhode Island	8	9.9	0.1	1,243.2	139	0.1	17	10.34	34.2	4,086
North Dakota	10	8.8	0.1	882.3	243	0.2	24	5.90	31.2	173

Source: 2002 *Economic Census.* The states are in descending order of shipments or establishments (if shipment data are missing for the majority). The symbol (D) appears when data are withheld to prevent disclosure of competitive information. States marked with (D) are sorted by number of establishments. A dash (-) indicates that the data element cannot be calculated. Data may not show all states active in the NAICS category. All data available at the time of publication are shown.

NAICS 337127 - INSTITUTIONAL FURNITURE MANUFACTURING

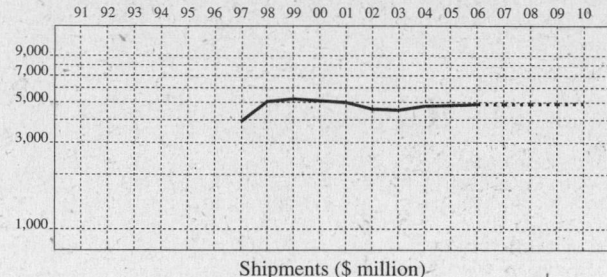

Shipments ($ million)

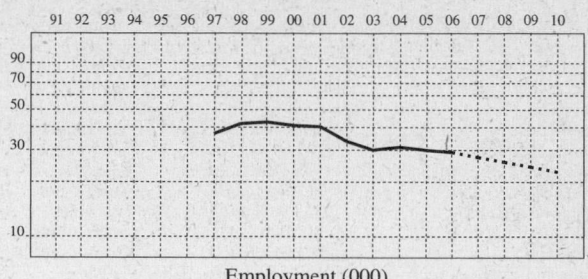

Employment (000)

GENERAL STATISTICS

Year	Companies	Establishments		Employment			Compensation		Production ($ million)			
		Total	with 20 or more employees	Total (000)	Production Workers (000)	Hours (Mil)	Payroll ($ mil)	Wages ($/hr)	Cost of Materials	Value Added by Manufacture	Value of Shipments	Capital Invest.
1997	965	997	366	36.9	27.5	50.9	974.6	11.73	1,839.6	2,077.1	3,917.9	118.1
1998		986	364	41.9	31.1	61.3	1,173.2	11.49	2,305.3	2,753.6	5,051.8	150.9
1999		987	373	42.8	32.2	63.2	1,250.7	11.90	2,311.7	2,898.3	5,216.2	141.7
2000		925	361	41.0	29.8	60.0	1,254.3	12.30	2,328.3	2,777.5	5,098.1	167.4
2001		912	354	40.4	29.6	58.6	1,203.8	12.48	2,228.9	2,737.1	4,993.9	115.6
2002	687	725	303	33.5	24.6	48.9	1,051.3	12.92	1,925.4	2,658.5	4,582.0	128.7
2003		708	305	30.1	21.8	43.9	972.1	13.32	1,896.4	2,619.3	4,527.7	105.9
2004		684	293	31.2	22.7	48.2	1,097.6	13.53	2,048.4	2,770.7	4,760.3	101.1
2005		705	293	30.0	22.1	44.3	1,089.4	14.96	2,232.2	2,593.7	4,810.6	106.7
2006		612P	276P	29.2	21.8	43.0	1,105.8	15.85	2,253.8	2,647.5	4,870.0	68.1
2007		564P	265P	27.4P	20.0P	41.5P	1,078.3P	15.48P	2,251.7P	2,645.0P	4,865.4P	82.6P
2008		517P	253P	25.8P	18.8P	39.5P	1,071.2P	15.92P	2,258.6P	2,653.2P	4,880.5P	75.8P
2009		470P	242P	24.3P	17.6P	37.5P	1,064.1P	16.37P	2,265.6P	2,661.4P	4,895.5P	68.9P
2010		423P	230P	22.8P	16.5P	35.6P	1,057.0P	16.81P	2,272.5P	2,669.5P	4,910.5P	62.0P

Sources: 1997 and 2002 *Economic Census*; other years, up to 2006, are from *Annual Survey of Manufactures*. Establishment counts for non-Census years are from *County Business Patterns*; 1997 and 2002 values are from the 1997 and 2002 censuses, respectively. 'P's show projections by the editors.

INDICES OF CHANGE

Year	Companies	Establishments		Employment			Compensation		Production ($ million)			
		Total	with 20 or more employees	Total (000)	Production Workers (000)	Hours (Mil)	Payroll ($ mil)	Wages ($/hr)	Cost of Materials	Value Added by Manufacture	Value of Shipments	Capital Invest.
1997	140	138	121	110	112	104	93	91	96	78	86	92
1998		136	120	125	126	125	112	89	120	104	110	117
1999		136	123	128	131	129	119	92	120	109	114	110
2000		128	119	122	121	123	119	95	121	104	111	130
2001		126	117	121	120	120	115	97	116	103	109	90
2002	100	100	100	100	100	100	100	100	100	100	100	100
2003		98	101	90	89	90	92	103	98	99	99	82
2004		94	97	93	92	99	104	105	106	104	104	79
2005		97	97	90	90	91	104	116	116	98	105	83
2006		84P	91P	87	89	88	105	123	117	100	106	53
2007		78P	87P	82P	81P	85P	103P	120P	117P	99P	106P	64P
2008		71P	84P	77P	76P	81P	102P	123P	117P	100P	107P	59P
2009		65P	80P	73P	72P	77P	101P	127P	118P	100P	107P	54P
2010		58P	76P	68P	67P	73P	101P	130P	118P	100P	107P	48P

Sources: Same as General Statistics. Values reflect change from the base year, 2002. Values above 100 mean greater than 2002, values below 100 mean less than 2002, and the values of 100 in other years means the same as 2002. 'P's show projections by the editors.

SELECTED RATIOS

For 2002	Avg. of All Manufact.	Analyzed Industry	Index	For 2002	Avg. of All Manufact.	Analyzed Industry	Index
Employees per Establishment	42	46	110	Value Added per Production Worker	182,367	108,069	59
Payroll per Establishment	1,639,184	1,450,069	88	Cost per Establishment	5,769,015	2,655,724	46
Payroll per Employee	39,053	31,382	80	Cost per Employee	137,446	57,475	42
Production Workers per Establishment	30	34	115	Cost per Production Worker	195,506	78,268	40
Wages per Establishment	694,845	871,432	125	Shipments per Establishment	11,158,348	6,320,000	57
Wages per Production Worker	23,548	25,682	109	Shipments per Employee	265,847	136,776	51
Hours per Production Worker	1,980	1,988	100	Shipments per Production Worker	378,144	186,260	49
Wages per Hour	11.89	12.92	109	Investment per Establishment	361,338	177,517	49
Value Added per Establishment	5,381,325	3,666,897	68	Investment per Employee	8,609	3,842	45
Value Added per Employee	128,210	79,358	62	Investment per Production Worker	12,245	5,232	43

Sources: Same as General Statistics. The 'Average of All Manufacturing' column represents the average of all manufacturing industries reported for the most recent complete year available. The Index shows the relationship between the Average and the Analyzed Industry. For example, 100 means that they are equal; 500 that the Analyzed Industry is five times the average; 50 means that the Analyzed Industry is half the national average. The abbreviation 'na' is used to show that data are 'not available'. Ratios shown for 2002, the last complete census year.

LEADING COMPANIES   Number shown: **75**   Total sales ($ mil): **215,525**   Total employment (000): **564.1**

Company Name	Address				CEO Name	Phone	Co. Type	Sales ($ mil)	Empl. (000)
McKesson Corp.	1 Post St.	San Francisco	CA	94104	John H. Hammergren	415-983-8300	P	92,977	31.8
Johnson Controls Inc.	PO Box 591	Milwaukee	WI	53201		414-524-1200	P	34,624	140.0
CP and P Inc.	133 Peachtree St.	Atlanta	GA	30303	Jospeh Moller	404-652-4000	S	16,083*	55.0
Lear Corp.	PO Box 5008	Southfield	MI	48086	Jim Brackenbury	248-447-1500	P	15,995	91.0
Energizer Holdings Inc.	533 Maryville Univ.	St. Louis	MO	63141		314-985-2000	P	3,365	11.1
Milliken Chemical	PO Box 1926	Spartanburg	SC	29304	Ashley Allen	864-503-2200	R	3,317*	10.0
Steelcase Inc.	PO Box 1967	Grand Rapids	MI	49501	James P. Hackett	616-247-2710	P	3,097	13.0
GE Water and Process Tech.	4636 Somerton Rd.	Trevose	PA	19053	Jeff Garwood	215-355-3300	S	2,748*	8.0
International Game Technology	PO Box 10580	Reno	NV	89510	G. Thomas Baker	775-448-7777	P	2,621	5.4
HNI Corp.	PO Box 1109	Muscatine	IA	52761	Timothy Anderson	563-264-7400	P	2,571	14.2
Furniture Brands International	101 S Hanley Rd.	St. Louis	MO	63105	John T. Foy	314-863-1100	P	2,082	11.9
Hillenbrand Industries Inc.	1069 State Rte 46E	Batesville	IN	47006		812-934-7000	P	2,024	9.9
Herman Miller Inc.	PO Box 302	Zeeland	MI	49464		616-654-3000	P	1,919	6.4
HON Co.	PO Box 1109	Muscatine	IA	52761	Eric Jungbluth	563-264-7100	S	1,789*	9.8
American Greetings Corp.	1 American Rd.	Cleveland	OH	44144		216-252-7300	P	1,745	28.9
BE Aerospace Inc.	1400 Corp. Ctr. Way	Wellington	FL	33414	Michael B. Baughan	561-791-5000	P	1,678	5.1
Kinetic Concepts Inc.	PO Box 659508	San Antonio	TX	78265	Catherine M. Burzik	210-524-9000	P	1,610	6.4
Tri-Con Industries Ltd.	4000 NW 44th St.	Lincoln	NE	68524		402-470-3311	R	1,450*	0.3
Blyth Inc.	1 E Weaver St.	Greenwich	CT	06831		203-661-1926	P	1,221	4.0
Longaberger Co.	1500 E Main St.	Newark	OH	43055	Jim Klein	740-322-5000	R	1,206*	8.7
Hill-Rom Company Inc.	1069 SR 46 E	Batesville	IN	47006	Peter H. Soderberg	812-934-7000	S	1,192*	6.5
Haworth Inc.	1 Haworth Ctr.	Holland	MI	49423	Franco Bianchi	616-393-3000	R	1,120*	8.0
Lancaster Colony Corp.	37 W Broad St.	Columbus	OH	43215	John B. Gerlach, Jr.	614-224-7141	P	1,091	5.6
Knoll Inc.	1235 Water St.	East Greenville	PA	18041	Andrew B. Cogan	215-679-7991	P	1,056	4.3
Syngenta Seeds Inc. - NK	PO Box 959	Minneapolis	MN	55440	Jeff Cox	763-593-7333	S	1,044*	1.3
Brady Corp.	PO Box 571	Milwaukee	WI	53201		414-358-6600	P	1,018	8.0
Travel Tags Inc.	5842 Carmen Ave.	Inver Grove Hts	MN	55076	Barb Cederberg	651-450-1201	R	763*	0.3
Ceradyne Inc.	3169 Red Hill Ave.	Costa Mesa	CA	92626		714-549-0421	P	757	2.5
Suntory Water Group Inc.	5660 New Northside	Atlanta	GA	30328	Stewart E. Allen	770-933-1400	R	688*	5.5
Yankee Candle Company Inc.	16 Yankee Candle	South Deerfield	MA	01373	Harlan M. Kent	413-665-8306	R	688	4.1
Alliance Gaming Corp.	6601 S Bermuda Rd.	Las Vegas	NV	89119	Richard M. Haddrill	702-584-7700	P	682	2.3
Oregon Cutting Systems Group	PO Box 22127	Portland	OR	97269	Jim Oscermanc	503-653-8881	D	674*	1.0
Krueger International Inc.	PO Box 8100	Green Bay	WI	54308	Richard J. Resch	920-468-8100	R	600*	4.0
Mid-South Industries Inc.	PO Box 322	Gadsden	AL	35902	Larry Ferguson	256-494-1302	R	563*	1.6
WMS Industries Inc.	800 S Northpoint	Waukegan	IL	60085	Brian R. Gamache	847-785-3000	P	539	1.4
Sauder Woodworking Co.	PO Box 156	Archbold	OH	43502	Kevin Sauder	419-446-2711	R	525*	3.0
Koken Manufacturing Company	PO Box 265	Saint Louis	MO	63166	Masahiro Kanaya	314-231-7383	R	458*	<0.1
Flexsteel Industries Inc.	PO Box 877	Dubuque	IA	52004	Bruce Boylen	563-556-7730	P	425	2.3
Arden Companies	18000 W 9 Mile Rd.	Southfield	MI	48075	Robert S. Sachs	248-355-1101	R	424*	1.2
Bing Group L.L.C.	11500 Oakland St.	Detroit	MI	48211	David Bing	313-867-3700	R	411*	1.1
WMS Gaming Inc.	3401 N California	Chicago	IL	60618	Brian R. Gamache	773-961-1620	S	398*	0.8
Amscan Holdings Inc.	80 Grasslands Rd.	Elmsford	NY	10523	James Harrison	914-345-2020	R	386*	2.0
Totes-Isotoner Corp.	9655 International	Cincinnati	OH	45246	Douglas Gernert	513-682-8200	R	358*	1.1
UNICEF	333 E 38th St., 6th	New York	NY	10016	Charles Lyons	212-326-7000	R	352*	1.0
Hooker Furniture Corp.	PO Box 4708	Martinsville	VA	24115		276-632-0459	P	350	1.1
Edsal Manufacturing Company	4400 S Packers Ave.	Chicago	IL	60609	Bruce Saltzberg	773-254-0600	R	300*	1.2
Russ Berrie and Company Inc.	111 Bauer Dr.	Oakland	NJ	07436	Andrew R. Gatto	201-337-9000	P	295	1.0
Pulaski Furniture Corp.	PO Box 1371	Pulaski	VA	24301	Lawerance E. Webb	540-980-7330	R	230*	2.5
Virco Manufacturing Corp.	PO Box 44846	Los Angeles	CA	90044		310-533-0474	P	223	1.2
Advanced Component Tech.	PO Box 168	Northwood	IA	50459	Robert Kluver	641-324-2231	S	217*	0.9
Oil-Dri Corporation of America	410 N Michigan	Chicago	IL	60611		312-321-1515	P	212	0.8
Day-Timers Inc.	1 Willow Ln.	East Texas	PA	18046	Bob Dorney		S	200*	1.3
Sauder Manufacturing Co.	PO Box 230	Archbold	OH	43502	Virgil Miller	419-445-7670	R	184*	0.2
Shuffle Master Inc.	1106 Palms Airport	Las Vegas	NV	89119		702-897-7150	P	179	0.6
Lifetime Products Inc.	PO Box 160010	Clearfield	UT	84016		801-776-1532	R	177*	0.3
Tachi-S Engineering USA Inc.	23227 Commerce	Farmington Hls	MI	48335		248-478-5050	R	177*	<0.1
Da-Lite Screen Company Inc.	PO Box 137	Warsaw	IN	46581	Richard E. Lundin	574-267-8101	R	170*	0.6
Shelby Williams Industries	150 S Williams	Morristown	TN	37813	Franklin Jacobs	423-586-7000	R	166*	1.7
Blackbourn Media Packaging	200 4th Ave. N	Edgerton	MN	56128	Don Taft	507-442-4311	S	166*	0.3
Midway Games Inc.	2704 W Roscoe St.	Chicago	IL	60618	David F. Zucker	773-961-2222	P	157	0.7
Midwest Stamping Inc.	3455 Briarfield	Maumee	OH	43537	Ronald L. Thompson	419-724-6970	R	155*	0.6
LG Seeds Inc.	22827 Shissler Rd.	Elmwood	IL	61529	Craig Anderson	309-742-8802	R	154*	0.1
Commercial Furniture Group	10650 Gateway	St. Louis	MO	63132	Seamus Bateson	314-991-9200	R	153*	0.8
Setex Inc.	1111 McKinley Rd.	Saint Marys	OH	45885	Mutsumi Gamou	419-394-7800	S	140*	0.6
Flextronics International NC	130 Mosswood	Youngsville	NC	27596	Richard L. Sharp	919-556-7881	S	138*	0.5
Bally Gaming Systems Inc.	6601 Bermuda Rd.	Las Vegas	NV	89119		702-896-7700	S	135*	2.3
Manufacturers Industrial Group	PO Box 1048	Lexington	TN	38351		731-967-0001	R	120*	0.9
Delfield Co.	980 S Isabella Rd.	Mt. Pleasant	MI	48858	Kevin Clark	989-773-7981	D	108*	0.7
Irwin Seating Co.	PO Box 2429	Grand Rapids	MI	49501	Earle Irwin	616-574-7400	R	104*	0.7
American Biophysics Corp.	140 Frenchtown Rd.	N Kingstown	RI	02852	Raymond Iannetta	401-884-3500	R	102*	0.2
Sierra Design Group	300 Sierra Manor Dr	Reno	NV	89511	Robert Luciano	775-850-1500	S	101*	0.1
Franklin Mint Co.	US Rte. One	Media	PA	19091	Bruce Newman	610-459-6000	R	97*	1.1
Stryker Medical	3800 E Centre Ave.	Portage	MI	49002	Stephen MacMillan	269-329-2100	D	96*	0.7
Stack On Products Co.	PO Box 489	Wauconda	IL	60084			R	94*	0.3
Toyo Seat USA Corp.	2155 S Almont Ave.	Imlay City	MI	48444	Seizo Yamaguchi	810-724-0300	R	93*	0.2

Source: Ward's Business Directory of U.S. Private and Public Companies, Volumes 1 and 2, 2008. The company type code used is as follows: P - Public, R - Private, S - Subsidiary, D - Division, J - Joint Venture, A - Affiliate, G - Group. Sales are in millions of dollars, employees are in thousands. An asterisk (*) indicates an estimated sales volume. The symbol < stands for 'less than'. Company names and addresses are truncated, in some cases, to fit into the available space.

MATERIALS CONSUMED

Material	Quantity	Delivered Cost ($ million)
Metal stampings	(X)	4.4
Other fabricated metal products (including forgings)	(X)	20.7
Castings, rough and semifinished	(X)	4.5
Steel sheet and strip (including tinplate)	(X)	55.8
All other steel shapes and forms (exc. castings, forgings, fabr. metal products)	(X)	37.8
Aluminum and aluminum-base alloy sheet, plate, foil, and welded tubing	(X)	13.3
All other aluminum and aluminum-base alloy shapes and forms (exc. castings, forgings, fabr. metal products)	(X)	20.8
Hardwood lumber, rough and dressed	(X)	47.2
Softwood lumber, rough and dressed	(X)	6.1
Hardwood cut stock and dimension (excluding furniture frames)	(X)	29.9
Softwood plywood	(X)	12.1
Hardwood plywood	(X)	23.2
Hardwood veneer	(X)	13.5
Particleboard (reconstituted wood)	(X)	23.4
Medium density fiberboard (MDF)	(X)	7.6
Wood furniture frames	(X)	19.9
Plastics laminated sheets	(X)	30.8
Plastics furniture parts and components	(X)	54.0
Formed and slab stock for pillows, cushions, seating, etc. (urethane)	(X)	6.9
Coated and laminated fabrics (including vinyl coated)	(X)	10.7
Woven cotton upholstery fabrics (excluding ticking)	(X)	7.8
Other woven upholstery fabrics (rayon, nylon, etc.), exc. ticking	(X)	10.5
Paints, varnishes, stains, lacquers, shellacs, japans, enamels, etc.	(X)	18.8
Adhesives and sealants	(X)	6.0
Furniture and builders' hardware (incl. cabinet hardware, casters, glides, handles, hinges, locks, etc.)	(X)	40.2
Paperboard containers, boxes, and corrugated paperboard	(X)	28.3
All other materials, components, parts, containers, and supplies	(X)	637.4
Materials, ingredients, containers, and supplies, nsk	(X)	353.6

Source: 2002 Economic Census. Explanation of symbols used: (D): Withheld to avoid disclosure of competitive data; na: Not available; (S): Withheld because statistical norms were not met; (X): Not applicable; (Z): Less than half the unit shown; nec: Not elsewhere classified; nsk: Not specified by kind; - : zero; p : 10-19 percent estimated; q : 20-29 percent estimated.

PRODUCT SHARE DETAILS

Product or Product Class Shipments	Mil. $	Product or Product Class Shipments	Mil. $
INSTITUTIONAL FURNITURE	4,138.8	Other public building chairs, including auditorium, barber, beauty, freestanding, theater, and institutional chairs and seats	78.5
School furniture, except stone and concrete, excluding library furniture	**764.1**	Stadium and bleacher seating, including grandstands	233.4
School single-pupil units and nonfolding chairs, excluding library	259.1	Other public building and related furniture, including church furniture (altars, lecterns, pulpits), except pews and bar, bowling center, cafeteria, restaurant, and school furniture	334.9
School single-pupil units, excluding library	143.3		
School chairs, all-purpose (nonfolding), excluding library	115.8	Public building furniture, except bar, bowling center, cafeteria, school and restaurant furniture, nsk	26.9
School storage units and furniture except single-pupil units and chairs (excluding library)	491.9	**Bar, bowling center, cafeteria, and restaurant furniture**	**897.0**
School storage cabinets, excluding library	132.0	Bar, bowling center, cafeteria, and restaurant furniture	813.7
Other school furniture (designed specifically for use in schools)	359.9	Bar, bowling center, cafeteria, and restaurant upholstered wood chairs and stools	149.9
School furniture, except stone and concrete (excluding library furniture), nsk	13.1	Bar, bowling center, cafeteria, and restaurant nonupholstered wood chairs and stools	28.9
Public building furniture, except bar, bowling center, cafeteria, school and restaurant furniture	**1,311.1**	Bar, bowling center, cafeteria, and restaurant metal chairs and stools	81.3
Public building furniture, except bar, bowling center, cafeteria, school and restaurant furniture	1,284.2	Bar, bowling center, cafeteria, and restaurant bars and booths, including back bars	116.5
Library furniture, including chairs, charging desks, study carrels, reading tables, etc.	88.3	Other bar, bowling center, cafeteria, and restaurant furniture, including lunchroom tables	437.1
Church pews	64.8	Bar, bowling center, cafeteria, and restaurant furniture, nsk	83.3
Folding tables, including folding banquet tables, except bar, bowling center, cafeteria, library, restaurant, and school	136.8	**Other furniture, nec**	**543.0**
Fixed chairs and seats, including theater, auditorium, and institutional	248.9	Other furniture, nec	501.4
		Industrial work benches and stools	171.2
Portable folding chairs, single and ganged theater, auditorium, and institutional	48.9	Other furniture, including ship furniture and amusement game cabinets	330.2
Stacking chairs and seats, including theater, auditorium, and institutional (except bar, bowling center, cafeteria, library, school, and restaurant)	49.6	Other furniture and fixtures, nsk	41.6
		Institutional furniture, nsk, total	**623.6**

Source: 2002 Economic Census. The values are product shipments in millions of dollars for 2002. Total product shipments may be lower or higher than industry shipments. See Introduction for a full discussion. Values of indented subcategories are summed in the main heading(s). The symbol (D) appears when data are withheld to prevent disclosure of competitive information. The abbreviation nsk stands for 'not specified by kind' and nec for 'not elsewhere classified'. A dash (-) means zero.

INPUTS AND OUTPUTS FOR INSTITUTIONAL FURNITURE MANUFACTURING

Economic Sector or Industry Providing Inputs	%	Sector	Economic Sector or Industry Buying Outputs	%	Sector
Compensation of employees	30.0		Private fixed investment	72.0	
Iron & steel mills & ferroalloys	4.7	Manufg.	S/L govt. invest., education	11.1	S/L Govt
Wholesale trade	4.3	Trade	Exports of goods & services	6.4	Cap Inv
Showcases, partitions, shelving, and lockers	2.9	Manufg.	Nonresidential structures, nec	3.2	Construct.
Sawmills & wood preservation	2.8	Manufg.	Commercial & health care structures	2.5	Construct.
Plastics products, nec	2.5	Manufg.	S/L govt. invest., other	1.6	S/L Govt
Management of companies & enterprises	2.4	Services	Institutional furniture	1.3	Manufg.
Institutional furniture	1.9	Manufg.	Personal consumption expenditures	0.6	
Real estate	1.8	Fin/R.E.	Change in private inventories	0.6	In House
Veneer & plywood	1.7	Manufg.	Personal care services	0.2	Services
Aluminum products from purchased aluminum	1.7	Manufg.			
Paints & coatings	1.6	Manufg.			
Truck transportation	1.5	Util.			
Securities, commodity contracts, investments	1.3	Fin/R.E.			
Retail trade	1.3	Trade			
Semiconductors & related devices	1.2	Manufg.			
Reconstituted wood products	1.2	Manufg.			
Printed circuit assemblies (electronic assembles)	1.2	Manufg.			
Paperboard containers	1.1	Manufg.			
Advertising & related services	1.0	Services			
Professional, scientific, technical services, nec	1.0	Services			
Monetary authorities/depository credit intermediation	0.9	Fin/R.E.			
Laminated plastics plates, sheets, & shapes	0.9	Manufg.			
Power generation & supply	0.7	Util.			
Specialized design services	0.6	Services			
Manufacturing, nec	0.6	Manufg.			
Urethane & other foam products (except polystrene)	0.5	Manufg.			
Food services & drinking places	0.5	Services			
Accounting, tax preparation, bookkeeping, & payroll	0.5	Services			
Hardware	0.5	Manufg.			
Broadwoven fabric mills	0.5	Manufg.			
Telecommunications	0.4	Services			
Data processing, hosting, & related services	0.4	Services			
Automotive equipment rental & leasing	0.4	Fin/R.E.			
Machine shops	0.4	Manufg.			
Fabric coating mills	0.4	Manufg.			
Architectural, engineering, & related services	0.4	Services			
Hotels & motels, including casino hotels	0.4	Services			
Legal services	0.3	Services			
Nondepository credit intermediation activities	0.3	Fin/R.E.			
Taxes on production & imports, less subsidies	0.3				
Lessors of nonfinancial assets	0.3	Fin/R.E.			
Warehousing & storage	0.3	Util.			
Abrasive products	0.3	Manufg.			
Coating, engraving, heat treating & allied activities	0.3	Manufg.			
Alumina refining & primary aluminum production	0.3	Manufg.			
Management, scientific, & technical consulting	0.3	Services			
Stone mining & quarrying	0.3	Mining			
Air transportation	0.3	Util.			
Natural gas distribution	0.2	Util.			
Motor vehicle parts	0.2	Manufg.			
Rail transportation	0.2	Util.			
Adhesives	0.2	Manufg.			
Crowns & closures & metal stamping	0.2	Manufg.			
Commercial & industrial machinery rental & leasing	0.2	Fin/R.E.			
Scientific research & development services	0.2	Services			
Services to buildings & dwellings	0.2	Services			
Other computer related services, including facilities	0.2	Services			
Maintenance/repair of nonresidential structures	0.2	Construct.			
Business support services	0.2	Services			
Bare printed circuit boards	0.2	Manufg.			
Paperboard mills	0.2	Manufg.			
Ornamental & architectural metal products	0.1	Manufg.			
Noncomparable imports	0.1	Foreign			
Relay & industrial controls	0.1	Manufg.			
Chemical products & preparations, nec	0.1	Manufg.			
Waste management & remediation services	0.1	Services			
Automotive repair & maintenance, ex. car washes	0.1	Services			
Civic, social, & professional organizations	0.1	Services			

Source: Benchmark Input-Output Accounts for the U.S. Economy, 2002, U.S. Department of Commerce, Washington, D.C., January 2008. The abbreviation nec stands for 'not elsewhere classified'.

OCCUPATIONS EMPLOYED BY HOUSEHOLD & INSTITUTIONAL FURNITURE

Occupation	% of Total 2006	Change to 2016	Occupation	% of Total 2006	Change to 2016
Upholsterers	10.1	-16.5	Sales reps, wholesale & manufacturing, exc tech	1.4	-23.9
Cabinetmakers & bench carpenters	8.6	-23.9	Carpenters	1.4	-23.9
Team assemblers	7.8	-23.9	Cutting, punching, & press machine operators	1.3	-31.5
Sewing machine operators	7.5	-16.3	Assemblers & fabricators, nec	1.3	-31.5
Woodworking machine operators & tenders, exc sawing	5.6	-16.3	Welders, cutters, solderers, & brazers	1.3	-19.0
Furniture finishers	3.8	-23.9	Coating, painting, & spraying machine operators	1.2	-27.7
First-line supervisors/managers of production workers	3.8	-23.9	General & operations managers	1.1	-31.5
Helpers--Production workers	3.7	-23.9	Cutters & trimmers, hand	1.1	-16.3
Laborers & freight, stock, & material movers, hand	3.5	-31.5	Industrial truck & tractor operators	1.1	-31.5
Packers & packagers, hand	1.8	-39.1	Customer service representatives	1.1	-16.3
Sawing machine setters, operators, & tenders, wood	1.7	-16.3	Machine feeders & offbearers	1.1	-31.5
Inspectors, testers, sorters, samplers, & weighers	1.6	-28.2	Office clerks, general	1.0	-25.0
Shipping, receiving, & traffic clerks	1.6	-26.8			

Source: *Industry-Occupation Matrix*, Bureau of Labor Statistics, December 4, 2007. These data are reported based on 4-digit NAICS categories but have been matched to corresponding 6-digit NAICS industry codes. The change reported for each occupation to the year 2016 is a percent of growth or decline as estimated by the Bureau of Labor Statistics. The abbreviation nec stands for 'not elsewhere classified'.

LOCATION BY STATE AND REGIONAL CONCENTRATION

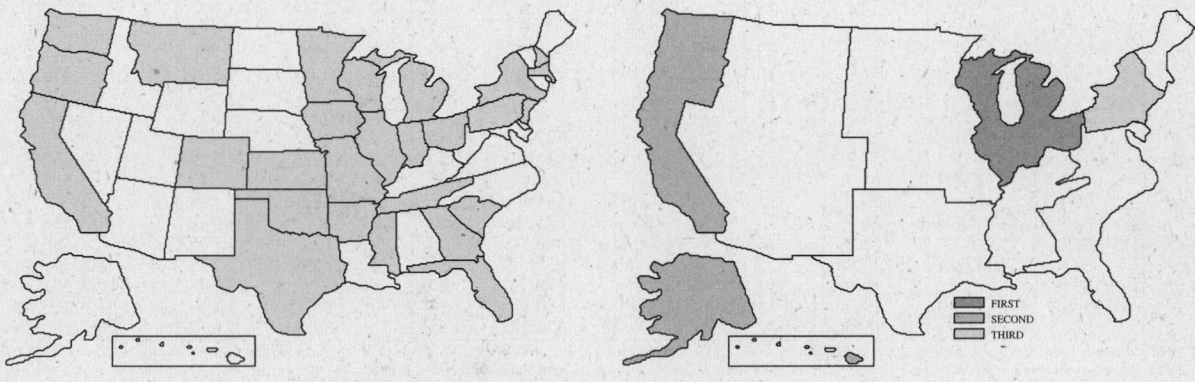

FIRST
SECOND
THIRD

INDUSTRY DATA BY STATE

State	Establish-ments	Shipments			Employment				Cost as % of Shipments	Investment per Employee ($)
		Total ($ mil)	% of U.S.	Per Establ.	Total Number	% of U.S.	Per Establ.	Wages ($/hour)		
Mississippi	13	453.3	9.9	34,872.0	2,379	7.1	183	9.39	41.0	2,951
Michigan	39	388.2	8.5	9,953.5	2,394	7.1	61	15.30	44.1	6,388
Tennessee	25	346.3	7.6	13,853.8	2,937	8.8	117	11.70	43.9	1,826
California	100	329.8	7.2	3,298.3	2,848	8.5	28	13.59	37.3	2,242
Texas	45	313.2	6.8	6,959.1	2,391	7.1	53	10.76	52.8	3,779
Arkansas	15	253.7	5.5	16,910.2	1,800	5.4	120	14.34	33.0	3,188
Wisconsin	27	252.7	5.5	9,361.0	1,732	5.2	64	14.20	39.9	7,003
Pennsylvania	36	206.7	4.5	5,741.9	1,428	4.3	40	12.54	41.1	10,608
Minnesota	17	193.7	4.2	11,392.9	1,410	4.2	83	18.30	33.9	1,647
Illinois	39	190.3	4.2	4,878.3	1,359	4.1	35	13.60	40.2	4,042
Florida	37	151.8	3.3	4,103.9	1,018	3.0	28	13.33	38.9	2,097
Massachusetts	18	136.0	3.0	7,553.4	970	2.9	54	14.32	47.4	4,353
Ohio	28	128.3	2.8	4,581.9	987	2.9	35	13.52	38.4	3,073
Missouri	15	98.2	2.1	6,548.7	666	2.0	44	13.45	36.0	2,746
South Carolina	8	86.2	1.9	10,775.6	512	1.5	64	13.79	64.0	2,939
Washington	12	73.5	1.6	6,125.3	546	1.6	46	12.92	40.1	1,784
New Jersey	18	70.5	1.5	3,916.2	498	1.5	28	13.23	36.7	8,382
Kansas	7	68.2	1.5	9,747.1	521	1.6	74	15.44	13.5	866
New York	42	68.1	1.5	1,622.0	667	2.0	16	13.15	44.8	2,243
Indiana	14	63.8	1.4	4,557.4	468	1.4	33	15.35	44.9	4,350
Georgia	16	59.6	1.3	3,723.8	655	2.0	41	13.91	33.2	1,166
Oregon	10	28.4	0.6	2,840.6	261	0.8	26	14.00	42.0	1,632
Colorado	5	25.5	0.6	5,103.2	243	0.7	49	12.32	41.6	1,309
Iowa	7	21.6	0.5	3,081.4	135	0.4	19	14.44	37.3	2,793
Oklahoma	4	11.0	0.2	2,758.0	151	0.5	38	7.23	16.2	2,172
New Hampshire	6	10.8	0.2	1,792.5	115	0.3	19	12.62	47.9	948
Montana	5	9.5	0.2	1,906.8	107	0.3	21	9.03	39.9	2,093

Source: 2002 *Economic Census*. The states are in descending order of shipments or establishments (if shipment data are missing for the majority). The symbol (D) appears when data are withheld to prevent disclosure of competitive information. States marked with (D) are sorted by number of establishments. A dash (-) indicates that the data element cannot be calculated. Data may not show all states active in the NAICS category. All data available at the time of publication are shown.

NAICS 33712N - HOUSEHOLD NONUPHOLSTERED FURNITURE NEC*

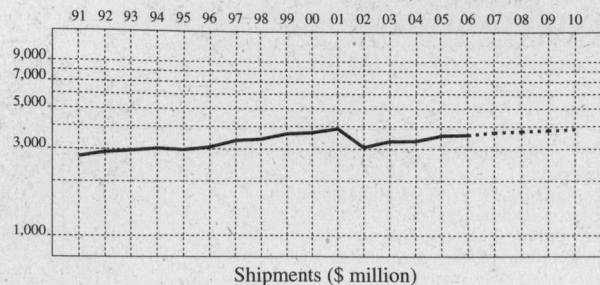

Shipments ($ million)

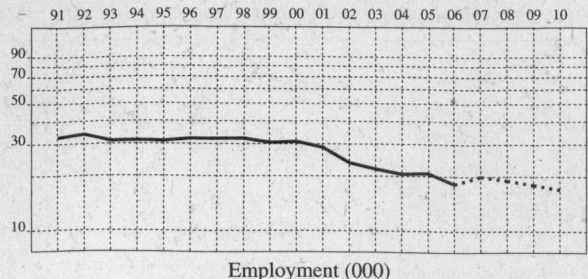

Employment (000)

GENERAL STATISTICS

Year	Com-panies	Establishments		Employment			Compensation		Production ($ million)			
		Total	with 20 or more employees	Total (000)	Production Workers (000)	Hours (Mil)	Payroll ($ mil)	Wages ($/hr)	Cost of Materials	Value Added by Manufacture	Value of Shipments	Capital Invest.
1991		588	246	32.6	27.0	51.0	601.1	8.05	1,418.3	1,333.3	2,736.9	45.5
1992	624	658	253	33.9	27.5	52.2	665.3	8.70	1,453.2	1,449.3	2,890.6	51.5
1993		639	238	31.2	25.0	49.4	626.9	8.82	1,497.5	1,469.9	2,948.3	46.8
1994		654	243	31.4	25.3	49.3	642.5	9.06	1,628.9	1,393.1	3,032.6	70.8
1995		650	226	31.1	25.1	50.0	658.9	9.08	1,623.0	1,357.4	2,978.3	139.7
1996		696	215	32.1	26.3	52.8	680.9	8.88	1,608.2	1,454.0	3,079.7	68.6
1997	697	734	219	32.1	25.8	50.4	709.6	9.57	1,641.0	1,700.8	3,341.8	97.8
1998		723	217	32.2	26.1	52.8	726.4	9.74	1,701.0	1,704.7	3,410.1	104.1
1999		727	232	30.5	24.9	50.3	726.1	9.56	1,857.1	1,812.9	3,642.4	88.0
2000		727	229	30.9	25.1	48.6	739.9	10.13	1,890.0	1,851.6	3,699.8	80.8
2001		785	226	28.7	23.0	44.4	727.1	10.45	1,985.0	1,900.4	3,886.9	72.5
2002	741	768	201	23.7	18.9	36.5	635.7	11.54	1,439.2	1,619.8	3,066.2	62.9
2003		771	192	21.9	17.2	35.4	607.6	11.65	1,758.2	1,546.5	3,301.7	43.1
2004		784	178	20.6	15.5	31.6	587.9	12.16	1,938.3	1,379.0	3,317.9	51.4
2005		815	168	20.8	15.7	30.6	605.5	12.38	1,854.7	1,739.2	3,553.9	49.6
2006		827P	180P	18.2	13.9	27.0	563.7	12.93	1,917.6	1,715.1	3,583.9	49.8
2007		841P	175P	20.0P	15.3P	30.7P	632.5P	12.76P	1,980.6P	1,771.4P	3,701.6P	60.9P
2008		855P	171P	19.0P	14.4P	29.1P	629.7P	13.07P	2,007.2P	1,795.2P	3,751.3P	59.8P
2009		869P	166P	18.0P	13.5P	27.4P	626.9P	13.38P	2,033.7P	1,819.0P	3,800.9P	58.7P
2010		883P	161P	17.0P	12.7P	25.8P	624.1P	13.68P	2,060.3P	1,842.7P	3,850.6P	57.6P

Sources: 1992, 1997, 2002 *Economic Census*; other years, up to 2006, are from the *Annual Survey of Manufactures*. Establishment counts for non-Census years are from *County Business Patterns*; 1997 and 2002 values are from the 1997 and 2002 censuses respectively, reported in the Federal Government's NAICS format. Other years were originally reported in equivalent SIC format. 'P's show projections by the editors.

INDICES OF CHANGE

Year	Com-panies	Establishments		Employment			Compensation		Production ($ million)			
		Total	with 20 or more employees	Total (000)	Production Workers (000)	Hours (Mil)	Payroll ($ mil)	Wages ($/hr)	Cost of Materials	Value Added by Manufacture	Value of Shipments	Capital Invest.
1992	84	86	126	143	146	143	105	75	101	89	94	82
1997	94	96	109	135	137	138	112	83	114	105	109	155
2001		102	112	121	122	122	114	91	138	117	127	115
2002	100	100	100	100	100	100	100	100	100	100	100	100
2003		100	96	92	91	97	96	101	122	95	108	69
2004		102	89	87	82	87	92	105	135	85	108	82
2005		106	84	88	83	84	95	107	129	107	116	79
2006		108P	90P	77	74	74	89	112	133	106	117	79
2007		109P	87P	84P	81P	84P	99P	111P	138P	109P	121P	97P
2008		111P	85P	80P	76P	80P	99P	113P	139P	111P	122P	95P
2009		113P	82P	76P	71P	75P	99P	116P	141P	112P	124P	93P
2010		115P	80P	72P	67P	71P	98P	119P	143P	114P	126P	92P

Sources: Same as General Statistics. Values reflect change from the base year, 2002. Values above 100 mean greater than 2002, values below 100 mean less than 2002, and the values of 100 in other years means the same as 2002. 'P's show projections by the editors.

SELECTED RATIOS

For 2002	Avg. of All Manufact.	Analyzed Industry	Index	For 2002	Avg. of All Manufact.	Analyzed Industry	Index
Employees per Establishment	42	31	74	Value Added per Production Worker	182,367	85,704	47
Payroll per Establishment	1,639,184	827,734	50	Cost per Establishment	5,769,015	1,873,958	32
Payroll per Employee	39,053	26,823	69	Cost per Employee	137,446	60,726	44
Production Workers per Establishment	30	25	83	Cost per Production Worker	195,506	76,148	39
Wages per Establishment	694,845	548,451	79	Shipments per Establishment	11,158,348	3,992,448	36
Wages per Production Worker	23,548	22,286	95	Shipments per Employee	265,847	129,376	49
Hours per Production Worker	1,980	1,931	98	Shipments per Production Worker	378,144	162,233	43
Wages per Hour	11.89	11.54	97	Investment per Establishment	361,338	81,901	23
Value Added per Establishment	5,381,325	2,109,115	39	Investment per Employee	8,609	2,654	31
Value Added per Employee	128,210	68,346	53	Investment per Production Worker	12,245	3,328	27

Sources: Same as General Statistics. The 'Average of All Manufacturing' column represents the average of all manufacturing industries reported for the most recent complete year available. The Index shows the relationship between the Average and the Analyzed Industry. For example, 100 means that they are equal; 500 that the Analyzed Industry is five times the average; 50 means that the Analyzed Industry is half the national average. The abbreviation 'na' is used to show that data are 'not available'. Ratios shown for 2002, the last complete census year.

*Equivalent to Federal Government NAICS 337124, 337125, 337129.

LEADING COMPANIES   Number shown: 75   Total sales ($ mil): 17,443   Total employment (000): 95.0

Company Name	Address				CEO Name	Phone	Co. Type	Sales ($ mil)	Empl. (000)
Leggett and Platt Inc.	PO Box 757	Carthage	MO	64836	Herbert Kohler	417-358-8131	P	4,306	24.0
Kohler Co.	444 Highland Dr.	Kohler	WI	53044	Herbert Kohler	920-457-4441	R	4,061*	33.0
H.T. Hackney Co.	PO Box 238	Knoxville	TN	37901	William B. Sansom	865-546-1291	R	3,550*	3.6
CC Industries Inc.	222 N La Salle St.	Chicago	IL	60601	William H. Crown	312-855-4000	S	1,560*	6.0
Eddie Bauer Holdings Inc.	15010 NE 36th St.	Redmond	WA	98052	Neil Fiske	425-755-6100	P	1,013	9.6
Flexsteel Industries Inc.	PO Box 877	Dubuque	IA	52004	Bruce Boylen	563-556-7730	P	425	2.3
Rowe Companies	1650 Tysons Blvd.	McLean	VA	22102	Gerald M. Birnbach	703-847-8670	R	301	2.4
Progressive Furniture Inc.	PO Box 308	Archbold	OH	43502	Dennis Ammons	419-446-4500	R	184*	<0.1
Lifetime Products Inc.	PO Box 160010	Clearfield	UT	84016		801-776-1532	R	177*	0.3
Canyon Creek Cabinet Co.	16726 Tye St. SE	Monroe	WA	98272	Bill Weaver	206-674-0800	R	155*	0.4
McGuire Furniture Company Inc.	1201 Bryant St.	San Francisco	CA	94103	Sarah Garcia	415-626-1414	R	155*	0.2
Unaka Company Inc.	1500 Industrial Rd.	Greeneville	TN	37745	Robert Austin	423-639-1171	R	89*	0.8
Suncast Corp.	701 N Kirk Rd.	Batavia	IL	60510	Thomas Tisbo	630-879-2050	R	88*	0.8
Viking Aluminum Products Inc.	33 John Street	New Britain	CT	06051		860-225-6478	R	60*	0.5
Little Tikes Commercial Inc.	PO Box 897	Farmington	MO	63640		573-756-4591	S	56*	0.5
JL Audio Inc.	103 N Commerce	Hollywood	FL	33025	Andrew Oxenhorn	954-443-1100	R	51*	0.2
Kay Home Products Inc.	90 McMillen Rd.	Antioch	IL	60002	Jack Rosen		R	48*	0.4
La Barge Inc.	2427 Penny Rd.	High Point	NC	27265	Jeff Young	336-812-2400	R	47*	0.1
Syroco Inc.	7528 State Fair	Baldwinsville	NY	13027	Raymond P. Carrock	315-635-9911	S	45*	0.4
Tropitone Furniture Company	5 Marconi	Irvine	CA	92618	Michael Echolds	949-951-2010	R	38*	0.3
Beck & Son, Clayborne C	9117 Jeffersn Davis	Fredericksburg	VA	22407	Ronald Beck	540-898-0401	R	34*	<0.1
Eagle Industries L.L.C.	PO Box 9697	Bowling Green	KY	42102	Herb Holtzman	270-843-3363	R	33*	0.8
Golden West Equipment Inc.	1000 S Euclid St.	La Habra	CA	90631	Michael Kennedy	714-879-3850	R	33*	<0.1
Corsican Table Co.	PO Box 58647	Los Angeles	CA	90058		323-587-3101	R	32*	0.2
Minson Corp.	1 Minson Way	Montebello	CA	90640	Jennifer Chen	323-513-1041	R	32*	0.3
Cramco Inc.	2200 E Ann Street	Philadelphia	PA	19134	Paul Cramer	215-427-9500	R	32*	0.2
Contemporary Products of TX	PO Box 510	Walburg	TX	78673	Ken Lucas	512-476-6660	R	31*	<0.1
Arte De Mexico Inc.	1000 Chestnut St.	Burbank	CA	91506	Gerald Stoffers	818-753-4559	R	30*	<0.1
Durham Manufacturing Co.	PO Box 230	Durham	CT	06422		860-349-3427	R	30*	0.2
Bohn and Dawson Inc.	3500 Tree Ct. Ind.	Saint Louis	MO	63122	Steven Hurster	636-225-5011	R	30*	0.2
Kessler Industries Inc.	PO Box 17549	El Paso	TX	79917	Calvin Kessler	915-591-8161	R	29*	0.3
Braxton Culler Inc.	PO Box 248	High Point	NC	27261	Braxton Culler	336-861-5800	R	29*	0.2
Woodharbor Doors and Cabinetry	3277 9th St. SW	Mason City	IA	50401	Curtis Lewerke	641-423-0444	R	25*	0.5
Swaim Inc.	PO Box 4189	High Point	NC	27263	Andy Swaim	336-885-6131	R	24*	0.2
Brown Jordan Co.	9860 Gidley St.	El Monte	CA	91731	Rob Ginn	626-443-8971	R	24*	0.2
Smith Brothers of Berne Inc.	PO Box 270	Berne	IN	46711	Steven Lehman	260-589-2131	R	23*	0.2
Meco Corp.	1500 Industrial Rd.	Greeneville	TN	37745	Robert Austin	423-639-1171	R	22*	0.1
Akro-Mils Corp.	PO Box 989	Akron	OH	44309		330-253-5592	D	22*	0.2
Dehler Manufacturing Company	5801 W Dickens	Chicago	IL	60639	Morton Herman	773-637-1666	R	21*	0.2
Reyes Industries Inc.	1554 Cantrell Dr.	San Antonio	TX	78221	Fernando Reyes	210-924-3190	R	20*	0.3
Hc Holdings L.L.C.	PO Box 350	Wadena	MN	56482	John Sundet	218-631-1000	R	20*	0.2
Pacific Precision Metals Inc.	601 S Vincent Ave.	Azusa	CA	91702	John Wallace	626-334-0361	D	20*	0.3
Fredman Brothers Furniture Co.	PO Box 512	Collinsville	IL	62234	Alvin Fredman	314-426-3999	R	20*	0.3
U-Han Inc.	10212 Denton Dr.	Dallas	TX	75220	Kil Yoo	214-654-0554	R	19*	<0.1
All-Luminum Products Inc.	10981 Decatur Rd.	Philadelphia	PA	19154	Warren Cohen	215-632-2800	R	19*	0.2
Flanders Industries Inc.	PO Box 1788	Fort Smith	AR	72902	Don Flanders	479-785-2351	R	19*	0.1
Sunterrace Casual Furniture	2369 Charles Raper	Stanley	NC	28164	Travis Boyd	704-263-1967	R	19*	0.2
Church Chair Industries Inc.	PO Box 990	Shannon	GA	30172	Dean Sammons	706-235-0115	R	19*	0.2
Parker House Manufacturing Co.	505 W Foothill Blvd	Azusa	CA	91702		626-812-0262	R	18*	<0.1
Nichols and Stone Co.	PO Box 527	Gardner	MA	01440	Carlton Nichols	978-632-2770	R	18*	0.3
Loewenstein Inc.	1801 N Andrews	Pompano Beach	FL	33069	Craig Watts	954-960-1100	S	17*	0.2
Capris Furniture Industries	1401 NW 27th Ave.	Ocala	FL	34475	Pedro Interian	352-629-8889	R	17*	0.2
Nambe L.L.C.	PO Box 15070	Santa Fe	NM	87592		505-471-2912	R	16*	0.2
ALP Lighting & Ceiling Prods	1401 Blairs Bridge	Lithia Springs	GA	30122		770-819-7880	R	15*	0.1
Pavilion Furniture Inc.	16200 NW 49th	Hialeah	FL	33014	Michael Buzzella	305-823-3480	R	15*	0.1
Steve's Plating Corp.	3111 N S Fernando	Burbank	CA	91504	Terry Knezevich	818-842-2184	R	15*	0.1
Victor Martin Inc.	PO Box 58647	Los Angeles	CA	90058	Martin Perfit	323-587-3101	R	15*	0.1
Alladin Investments Inc.	140 Industrial Dr.	Surgoinsville	TN	37873	Allen Vogel	423-345-2351	R	15*	0.1
Mastercraft Inc.	PO Box 97	LaGrange	IN	46761	Clifton Reynolds	260-463-8702	R	14*	0.2
Knox County ARC	2525 N 6th St.	Vincennes	IN	47591	Michael Carney	812-895-0059	R	13*	0.5
California Furniture Collections	9340 Dowdy Dr.	San Diego	CA	92126	Eric Vogt	858-693-6000	R	13*	0.1
Comfort Designs Inc.	1167 N Wash. St.	Wilkes Barre	PA	18705	John Graham	570-270-9172	R	13*	0.1
Hanco Inc.	PO Box 48	Peru	IN	46970	Kim Regan	765-473-6691	R	12*	0.1
Johnston Casuals Furniture	PO Box 668	N Wilkesboro	NC	28659	Joseph Johnston	336-838-5178	R	11*	0.1
Rosedale Fabricators L.L.C.	PO Box 2572	Jackson	MS	39207		601-355-0260	R	11*	0.1
Quality Musical Systems Inc.	PO Box 850	Candler	NC	28715	Daniel Wilson	828-667-5719	R	10*	<0.1
Metal Fabricating Corp.	10408 Berea Rd.	Cleveland	OH	44102	Bernard Golias	216-631-2480	R	10*	<0.1
Sound-Craft Systems Inc.	1584 Petit Jean Mtn	Morrilton	AR	72110	Bruce McCullough	501-727-5476	R	9*	<0.1
American Stitchco Inc.	4662 Hwy. 62 W	Mountain Home	AR	72653	Steve Luelf	870-425-7777	R	8*	0.1
A Diamond Productions Inc.	2150 Cesar Chavez	San Francisco	CA	94124	Suzanne Diamond	415-920-6800	R	8*	<0.1
Sharut Furniture Inc.	220 Passaic St.	Passaic	NJ	07055	Elliot Bissu	973-473-1000	R	7*	0.1
Custom Shoppe	300 Air Park Dr.	Watertown	WI	53094	Frank Krejci	920-262-9700	R	7*	0.1
Hard Manufacturing Company	230 Grider St.	Buffalo	NY	14215	William Godin	716-893-1800	R	7*	<0.1
Vitro Products Inc.	PO Box 470159	Saint Louis	MO	63147	Stephen Scott	314-241-2265	R	6*	<0.1
Prime Time Products Inc.	1536 Jones St.	Brawley	CA	92227	Dan Hammond	760-351-2690	R	6*	<0.1

Source: Ward's Business Directory of U.S. Private and Public Companies, Volumes 1 and 2, 2008. The company type code used is as follows: P - Public, R - Private, S - Subsidiary, D - Division, J - Joint Venture, A - Affiliate, G - Group. Sales are in millions of dollars, employees are in thousands. An asterisk (*) indicates an estimated sales volume. The symbol < stands for 'less than'. Company names and addresses are truncated, in some cases, to fit into the available space.

MATERIALS CONSUMED FOR METAL HOUSEHOLD FURNITURE MANUFACTURING

Material	Quantity	Delivered Cost ($ million)
Softwood lumber, rough and dressed	(X)	2.4
Softwood plywood	(X)	0.3
Particleboard (reconstituted wood)	(X)	1.1
Woven cotton upholstery fabrics (excluding ticking)	(X)	(D)
Other woven upholstery fabrics (rayon, nylon, etc.), exc. ticking	(X)	21.4
Coated and laminated fabrics (including vinyl coated)	(X)	13.7
Furniture and builders' hardware (incl. cabinet hardware, casters, glides, handles, hinges, locks, etc.)	(X)	19.4
Formed and slab stock for pillows, cushions, seating, etc. (urethane)	(X)	2.8
Paints, varnishes, stains, lacquers, shellacs, japans, enamels, etc.	(X)	9.7
Plastics resins consumed in the form of granules, pellets, etc.	(X)	(D)
Metal stampings	(X)	7.1
Other fabricated metal products (including forgings)	(X)	95.3
Castings, rough and semifinished	(X)	6.2
Steel sheet and strip (including tinplate)	(X)	34.5
All other steel shapes and forms (exc. castings, forgings, fabr. metal products)	(X)	37.3
Aluminum and aluminum-base alloy sheet, plate, foil, and welded tubing	(X)	26.7
All other aluminum and aluminum-base alloy shapes and forms (exc. castings, forgings, fabr. metal products)	(X)	(D)
Plastics furniture parts and components	(X)	12.0
Flat glass (plate, float, and sheet)	(X)	4.8
Paperboard containers, boxes, and corrugated paperboard	(X)	23.7
All other materials, components, parts, containers, and supplies	(X)	167.6
Materials, ingredients, containers, and supplies, nsk	(X)	229.3

Source: 2002 *Economic Census*. Explanation of symbols used: (D): Withheld to avoid disclosure of competitive data; na: Not available; (S): Withheld because statistical norms were not met; (X): Not applicable; (Z): Less than half the unit shown; nec: Not elsewhere classified; nsk: Not specified by kind; - : zero; p : 10-19 percent estimated; q : 20-29 percent estimated.

MATERIALS CONSUMED FOR HOUSEHOLD FURNITURE (EXCEPT WOOD AND METAL)

Material	Quantity	Delivered Cost ($ million)
Wood furniture frames	(X)	14.6
Woven cotton upholstery fabrics (excluding ticking)	(X)	3.6
Other woven upholstery fabrics (rayon, nylon, etc.), exc. ticking	(X)	5.8
Paddings, battings, and fillings (exc. rubber and plastics foam)	(X)	4.5
Furniture and builders' hardware (incl. cabinet hardware, casters, glides, handles, hinges, locks, etc.)	(X)	2.5
Formed and slab stock for pillows, cushions, seating, etc. (urethane)	(X)	(D)
Paints, varnishes, stains, lacquers, shellacs, japans, enamels, etc.	(X)	3.1
Plastics resins consumed in the form of granules, pellets, etc.	(X)	85.3
Plastics laminated sheets	(X)	(D)
Plastics furniture parts and components	(X)	(D)
Flat glass (plate, float, and sheet)	(X)	1.3
Paperboard containers, boxes, and corrugated paperboard	(X)	6.2
All other materials, components, parts, containers, and supplies	(X)	65.2
Materials, ingredients, containers, and supplies, nsk	(X)	56.9

Source: 2002 *Economic Census*. Explanation of symbols used: (D): Withheld to avoid disclosure of competitive data; na: Not available; (S): Withheld because statistical norms were not met; (X): Not applicable; (Z): Less than half the unit shown; nec: Not elsewhere classified; nsk: Not specified by kind; - : zero; p : 10-19 percent estimated; q : 20-29 percent estimated.

MATERIALS CONSUMED FOR WOOD TV, RADIO, & SEWING MACHINE CABINETS

Material	Quantity	Delivered Cost ($ million)
Hardwood lumber, rough and dressed	(X)	6.3
Hardwood cut stock and dimension (excluding furniture frames)	(X)	5.7
Hardwood plywood	(X)	1.1
Hardwood veneer	(X)	(D)
Particleboard (reconstituted wood)	(X)	25.4
Medium density fiberboard (MDF)	(X)	(D)
Hardboard	(X)	(D)
Furniture and builders' hardware (incl. cabinet hardware, casters, glides, handles, hinges, locks, etc.)	(X)	11.4
Paints, varnishes, stains, lacquers, shellacs, japans, enamels, etc.	(X)	4.1
Paperboard containers, boxes, and corrugated paperboard	(X)	3.8
All other materials, components, parts, containers, and supplies	(X)	30.0
Materials, ingredients, containers, and supplies, nsk	(X)	35.6

Source: 2002 *Economic Census*. Explanation of symbols used: (D): Withheld to avoid disclosure of competitive data; na: Not available; (S): Withheld because statistical norms were not met; (X): Not applicable; (Z): Less than half the unit shown; nec: Not elsewhere classified; nsk: Not specified by kind; - : zero; p : 10-19 percent estimated; q : 20-29 percent estimated.

PRODUCT SHARE DETAILS FOR METAL HOUSEHOLD FURNITURE MANUFACTURING

Product or Product Class Shipments	Mil. $	Product or Product Class Shipments	Mil. $
METAL HOUSEHOLD FURNITURE	1,800.3	Other nonupholstered cast and wrought iron porch, lawn, and outdoor furniture, including gliders, hammocks, swings, and tables	(D)
Household dining room and kitchen furniture, metal	**176.0**	Other beach, garden, porch, lawn, outdoor and casual furniture, including picnic tables, metal	(D)
Tubular metal breakfast, dinette, and dining tables, sold as part of a set	27.5	Beach, porch, lawn, outdoor and casual furniture, metal, nsk	2.5
Tubular nonupholstered metal breakfast, dinette, and dining tables, sold as part of a set	42.6	**Other nonupholstered metal household furniture**	**425.2**
Tubular metal breakfast, dinette, and dining tables (not sold with a set)	13.5	Metal army cots, folding cots, rollable cots, other metal beds and metal bed frames	233.0
Tubular nonupholstered breakfast, dinette, and dining chairs (not sold with a set)	10.1	Metal army cots, folding cots, rollable cots, and other metal beds	18.0
Other nonupholstered metal household dining room and kitchen furniture, including cabinets, hostess carts, and padded and plain stools	82.2	Metal bed frames, including complete metal bed frames, sold separately, with or without a headboard	215.0
Beach, garden, porch, lawn, outdoor and casual furniture, metal	**674.6**	Other nonupholstered metal household furniture, nec	192.2
		Medicine cabinets, including insert-type and wall-type	70.7
Tubular nonupholstered aluminum benches, chairs, chaise lounges, rockers, and settees	183.3	Metal infants' car seats	-
Other metal outdoor and casual furniture	488.9	Other nonupholstered metal household infants' and children's furniture, including chairs, high chairs, playpens, play yards, portable cribs, and tables	(D)
Other nonupholstered tubular aluminum porch, lawn, outdoor, and casual furniture, including gliders, swings, hammocks, and tables	106.9	Other nonupholstered metal household furniture, including folding trays	(D)
Nonupholstered cast and wrought iron chairs, rockers, benches, chaise lounges, and settees	150.3	**Metal household furniture, nsk, total**	**524.5**

Source: 2002 *Economic Census*. The values are product shipments in millions of dollars for 2002. Total product shipments may be lower or higher than industry shipments. See Introduction for a full discussion. Values of indented subcategories are summed in the main heading(s). The symbol (D) appears when data are withheld to prevent disclosure of competitive information. The abbreviation nsk stands for 'not specified by kind' and nec for 'not elsewhere classified'. A dash (-) means zero.

PRODUCT SHARE DETAILS FOR HOUSEHOLD FURNITURE (EXCEPT WOOD AND METAL)

Product or Product Class Shipments	Mil. $	Product or Product Class Shipments	Mil. $
HOUSEHOLD FURNITURE, EXCEPT WOOD AND METAL	561.8	rattan, reed, wicker, and willow	66.2
Plastic cabinets, including audio and television cabinets, except cabinets used as housings	99.2	Other nonupholstered household furniture, except wood and metal	209.9
Nonupholstered household furniture made of rattan, reed, wicker, and willow	148.2	Plastics infants' car seats	(D)
Rattan, reed, wicker, and willow seating	46.2	Other plastics household furniture, including other plastics seating, except cabinets used as housings	87.2
Rattan, reed, wicker, and willow laundry hampers	35.8	Other nonupholstered household furniture, nec	(D)
Other nonupholstered household furniture made of		Household furniture, except wood and metal, nsk, total	104.5

Source: 2002 *Economic Census*. The values are product shipments in millions of dollars for 2002. Total product shipments may be lower or higher than industry shipments. See Introduction for a full discussion. Values of indented subcategories are summed in the main heading(s). The symbol (D) appears when data are withheld to prevent disclosure of competitive information. The abbreviation nsk stands for 'not specified by kind' and nec for 'not elsewhere classified'. A dash (-) means zero.

PRODUCT SHARE DETAILS FOR WOOD TV, RADIO, & SEWING MACHINE CABINETS

Product or Product Class Shipments	Mil. $	Product or Product Class Shipments	Mil. $
WOOD TELEVISION, RADIO, AND SEWING MACHINE CABINETS	378.7	machine cabinets	192.0
Wood television, radio, and sewing machine cabinets used as housings	**378.7**	Wood audio cabinets, including radio, stereo, phonograph, and speaker cabinets, used as housings	141.1
Wood television cabinets and combinations (television, stereo, and radio)	121.9	Other wood cabinets used as housings, including wood sewing machine cabinets	50.9
Wood audio cabinets, (including radio, stereo, phonograph), speaker cabinets, and wood sewing		Wood television, radio, and sewing machine cabinets, nsk, total	64.8

Source: 2002 *Economic Census*. The values are product shipments in millions of dollars for 2002. Total product shipments may be lower or higher than industry shipments. See Introduction for a full discussion. Values of indented subcategories are summed in the main heading(s). The symbol (D) appears when data are withheld to prevent disclosure of competitive information. The abbreviation nsk stands for 'not specified by kind' and nec for 'not elsewhere classified'. A dash (-) means zero.

INPUTS AND OUTPUTS FOR METAL AND OTHER HOUSEHOLD FURNITURE MANUFACTURING

Economic Sector or Industry Providing Inputs	%	Sector	Economic Sector or Industry Buying Outputs	%	Sector
Compensation of employees	25.6		Personal consumption expenditures	84.1	
Plastics materials & resins	6.0	Manufg.	Private fixed investment	5.1	
Wholesale trade	5.1	Trade	Exports of goods & services	2.4	Cap Inv
Iron & steel mills & ferroalloys	3.4	Manufg.	Audio & video equipment	1.4	Manufg.
Aluminum products from purchased aluminum	3.0	Manufg.	Surgical appliances & supplies	1.3	Manufg.

Continued on next page.

INPUTS AND OUTPUTS FOR METAL AND OTHER HOUSEHOLD FURNITURE MANUFACTURING - Continued

Economic Sector or Industry Providing Inputs	%	Sector	Economic Sector or Industry Buying Outputs	%	Sector
Laminated plastics plates, sheets, & shapes	2.4	Manufg.	S/L govt. invest., education	1.3	S/L Govt
Broadwoven fabric mills	2.0	Manufg.	Surgical & medical instrument	0.8	Manufg.
Management of companies & enterprises	1.9	Services	Broadcast & wireless communications equipment	0.7	Manufg.
Sawmills & wood preservation	1.9	Manufg.	Search, detection, & navigation instruments	0.6	Manufg.
Forestry products	1.9	Agric.	Metal & other household furniture	0.5	Manufg.
Paperboard containers	1.6	Manufg.	S/L govt. invest., other	0.5	S/L Govt
Paints & coatings	1.4	Manufg.	Electron tubes	0.2	Manufg.
Real estate	1.4	Fin/R.E.	Communications equipment, nec	0.2	Manufg.
Machine shops	1.3	Manufg.	Residential permanent site structures	0.2	Construct.
Advertising & related services	1.3	Services	Aircraft	0.1	Manufg.
Plastics products, nec	1.3	Manufg.	Federal government, investment, nondefense	0.1	Fed Govt
Securities, commodity contracts, investments	1.1	Fin/R.E.			
Truck transportation	1.1	Util.			
Coating, engraving, heat treating & allied activities	1.1	Manufg.			
Semiconductors & related devices	0.9	Manufg.			
Showcases, partitions, shelving, and lockers	0.9	Manufg.			
Printed circuit assemblies (electronic assembles)	0.9	Manufg.			
Power generation & supply	0.9	Util.			
Metal & other household furniture	0.9	Manufg.			
Alumina refining & primary aluminum production	0.7	Manufg.			
Monetary authorities/depository credit intermediation	0.7	Fin/R.E.			
Retail trade	0.7	Trade			
Fabric coating mills	0.6	Manufg.			
Crowns & closures & metal stamping	0.6	Manufg.			
Specialized design services	0.6	Services			
Turned products & screws, nuts, & bolts	0.6	Manufg.			
Professional, scientific, technical services, nec	0.6	Services			
Urethane & other foam products (except polystrene)	0.6	Manufg.			
Architectural, engineering, & related services	0.6	Services			
Fabricated metals, nec	0.5	Manufg.			
Abrasive products	0.5	Manufg.			
Hardware	0.4	Manufg.			
Miscellaneous wood products	0.4	Manufg.			
Metal cans, boxes, & other containers (light gauge)	0.4	Manufg.			
Legal services	0.4	Services			
Automotive equipment rental & leasing	0.4	Fin/R.E.			
Data processing, hosting, & related services	0.4	Services			
Management, scientific, & technical consulting	0.4	Services			
Food services & drinking places	0.4	Services			
Natural gas distribution	0.3	Util.			
Petroleum lubricating oil & grease	0.3	Manufg.			
Rail transportation	0.3	Util.			
Taxes on production & imports, less subsidies	0.3				
Accounting, tax preparation, bookkeeping, & payroll	0.3	Services			
Telecommunications	0.3	Services			
Plastics packaging materials, film & sheet	0.3	Manufg.			
Wood windows & doors & millwork	0.3	Manufg.			
Flat glass	0.3	Manufg.			
Forging, stamping, & sintering, nec	0.3	Manufg.			
Handtools	0.3	Manufg.			
Plate work & fabricated structural products	0.3	Manufg.			
Services to buildings & dwellings	0.3	Services			
Warehousing & storage	0.3	Util.			
Maintenance/repair of nonresidential structures	0.2	Construct.			
Hotels & motels, including casino hotels	0.2	Services			
Textile product mills, nec	0.2	Manufg.			
Ball & roller bearings	0.2	Manufg.			
Business support services	0.2	Services			
Commercial & industrial machinery rental & leasing	0.2	Fin/R.E.			
Other computer related services, including facilities	0.2	Services			
Air transportation	0.2	Util.			
Ferrous metal foundries	0.2	Manufg.			
Custom roll forming	0.2	Manufg.			
Employment services	0.2	Services			
Valve & fittings other than plumbing	0.2	Manufg.			
Waste management & remediation services	0.2	Services			
Automotive repair & maintenance, ex. car washes	0.1	Services			
Material handling equipment	0.1	Manufg.			
Motor vehicle parts	0.1	Manufg.			
Nonferrous metal foundries	0.1	Manufg.			
Insurance carriers	0.1	Fin/R.E.			
Noncomparable imports	0.1	Foreign			
Paperboard mills	0.1	Manufg.			
Commercial & industrial equipment repair/maintenance	0.1	Services			
Nondepository credit intermediation activities	0.1	Fin/R.E.			
Support services, nec	0.1	Services			
Scientific research & development services	0.1	Services			

Source: Benchmark Input-Output Accounts for the U.S. Economy, 2002, U.S. Department of Commerce, Washington, D.C., January 2008. The abbreviation nec stands for 'not elsewhere classified'.

OCCUPATIONS EMPLOYED BY HOUSEHOLD & INSTITUTIONAL FURNITURE

Occupation	% of Total 2006	Change to 2016	Occupation	% of Total 2006	Change to 2016
Upholsterers	10.1	-16.5	Sales reps, wholesale & manufacturing, exc tech	1.4	-23.9
Cabinetmakers & bench carpenters	8.6	-23.9	Carpenters	1.4	-23.9
Team assemblers	7.8	-23.9	Cutting, punching, & press machine operators	1.3	-31.5
Sewing machine operators	7.5	-16.3	Assemblers & fabricators, nec	1.3	-31.5
Woodworking machine operators & tenders, exc sawing	5.6	-16.3	Welders, cutters, solderers, & brazers	1.3	-19.0
Furniture finishers	3.8	-23.9	Coating, painting, & spraying machine operators	1.2	-27.7
First-line supervisors/managers of production workers	3.8	-23.9	General & operations managers	1.1	-31.5
Helpers--Production workers	3.7	-23.9	Cutters & trimmers, hand	1.1	-16.3
Laborers & freight, stock, & material movers, hand	3.5	-31.5	Industrial truck & tractor operators	1.1	-31.5
Packers & packagers, hand	1.8	-39.1	Customer service representatives	1.1	-16.3
Sawing machine setters, operators, & tenders, wood	1.7	-16.3	Machine feeders & offbearers	1.1	-31.5
Inspectors, testers, sorters, samplers, & weighers	1.6	-28.2	Office clerks, general	1.0	-25.0
Shipping, receiving, & traffic clerks	1.6	-26.8			

Source: Industry-Occupation Matrix, Bureau of Labor Statistics, December 4, 2007. These data are reported based on 4-digit NAICS categories but have been matched to corresponding 6-digit NAICS industry codes. The change reported for each occupation to the year 2016 is a percent of growth or decline as estimated by the Bureau of Labor Statistics. The abbreviation nec stands for 'not elsewhere classified'.

LOCATION BY STATE AND REGIONAL CONCENTRATION

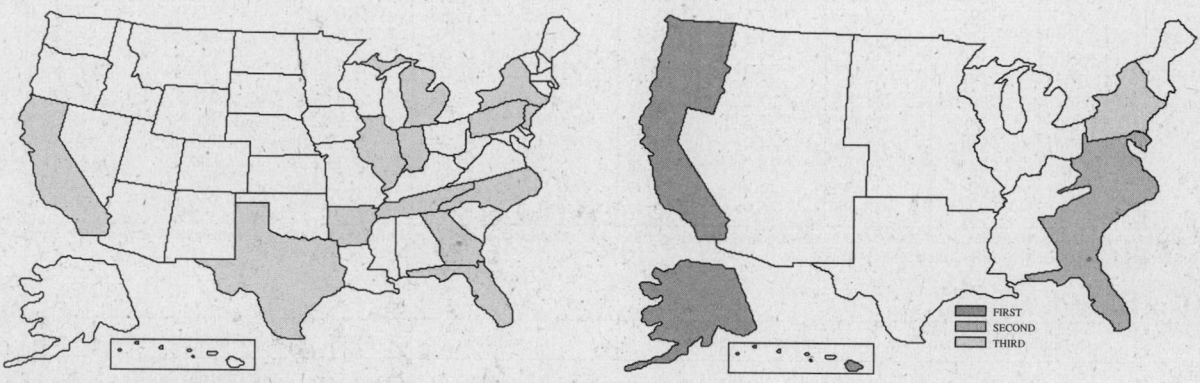

FIRST
SECOND
THIRD

INDUSTRY DATA BY STATE

State	Establish-ments	Shipments			Employment				Cost as % of Shipments	Investment per Employee ($)
		Total ($ mil)	% of U.S.	Per Establ.	Total Number	% of U.S.	Per Establ.	Wages ($/hour)		
California	176	591.5	19.3	3,360.6	5,115	21.6	29	11.66	44.6	2,810
Pennsylvania	26	207.5	6.8	7,982.4	1,199	5.1	46	11.49	47.2	3,007
North Carolina	23	204.4	6.7	8,884.8	1,805	7.6	78	9.96	51.0	1,798
Florida	55	148.3	4.8	2,696.2	1,372	5.8	25	10.66	43.1	900
Texas	22	96.5	3.1	4,388.1	776	3.3	35	11.43	49.9	1,566
Illinois	18	80.9	2.6	4,493.9	697	2.9	39	10.60	42.6	3,110
Georgia	13	76.8	2.5	5,906.1	221	0.9	17	10.45	52.1	4,765
New York	23	59.1	1.9	2,570.7	531	2.2	23	13.39	39.8	661
Indiana	9	58.6	1.9	6,508.0	482	2.0	54	9.64	34.8	1,936
New Jersey	8	45.3	1.5	5,666.9	263	1.1	33	13.81	60.5	1,837
Michigan	12	31.8	1.0	2,652.8	323	1.4	27	12.69	56.0	966
Arkansas	7	31.1	1.0	4,445.4	333	1.4	48	10.12	32.6	865
Tennessee	9	17.5	0.6	1,941.1	212	0.9	24	8.61	57.3	486

Source: 2002 *Economic Census.* The states are in descending order of shipments or establishments (if shipment data are missing for the majority). The symbol (D) appears when data are withheld to prevent disclosure of competitive information. States marked with (D) are sorted by number of establishments. A dash (-) indicates that the data element cannot be calculated. Data may not show all states active in the NAICS category. All data available at the time of publication are shown.

NAICS 337212 - CUSTOM ARCHITECTURAL WOODWORK AND MILLWORK MANUFACTURING

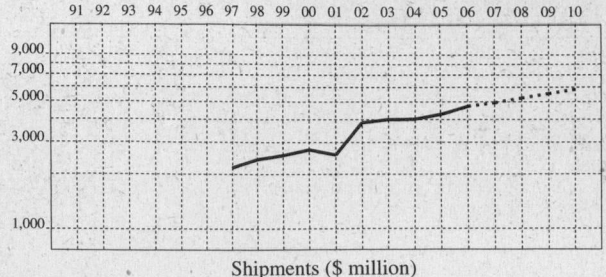

Shipments ($ million)

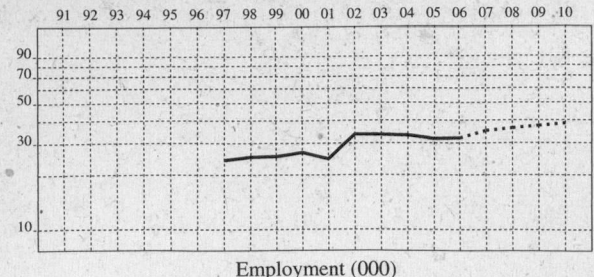

Employment (000)

GENERAL STATISTICS

| Year | Com-panies | Establishments | | Employment | | | Compensation | | Production ($ million) | | | |
		Total	with 20 or more employees	Total (000)	Production Workers (000)	Hours (Mil)	Payroll ($ mil)	Wages ($/hr)	Cost of Materials	Value Added by Manufacture	Value of Shipments	Capital Invest.
1997	1,090	1,100	368	24.2	17.3	32.5	709.4	13.10	838.1	1,328.8	2,168.8	56.0
1998		1,069	372	25.2	17.4	34.6	793.4	12.94	920.8	1,499.4	2,419.3	45.2
1999		1,054	372	25.4	17.8	34.8	804.2	13.56	909.9	1,644.5	2,544.4	61.0
2000		1,035	377	26.7	19.1	36.3	890.0	13.98	1,009.1	1,743.9	2,732.5	68.0
2001		1,165	382	24.6	17.2	33.1	796.5	13.58	1,034.7	1,528.3	2,559.8	44.6
2002	1,543	1,557	516	33.6	23.1	45.3	1,214.6	15.30	1,440.7	2,408.5	3,846.5	85.5
2003		1,553	507	33.4	23.5	48.1	1,235.5	15.23	1,508.3	2,492.6	4,007.0	54.2
2004		1,520	488	33.1	23.0	46.0	1,290.9	16.02	1,635.9	2,421.2	4,022.4	76.6
2005		1,554	502	31.7	22.0	44.4	1,317.4	16.37	1,718.6	2,561.7	4,273.3	62.0
2006		1,680P	539P	32.0	22.5	45.1	1,400.1	17.17	1,942.1	2,800.8	4,728.8	76.1
2007		1,759P	561P	35.1P	24.4P	49.5P	1,504.3P	17.34P	2,031.9P	2,930.4P	4,947.6P	75.5P
2008		1,837P	582P	36.2P	25.2P	51.3P	1,587.7P	17.81P	2,152.7P	3,104.5P	5,241.6P	77.7P
2009		1,915P	604P	37.3P	25.9P	53.0P	1,671.2P	18.29P	2,273.5P	3,278.7P	5,535.7P	80.0P
2010		1,993P	626P	38.4P	26.7P	54.7P	1,754.7P	18.76P	2,394.2P	3,452.8P	5,829.7P	82.3P

Sources: 1997 and 2002 *Economic Census*; other years, up to 2006, are from *Annual Survey of Manufactures*. Establishment counts for non-Census years are from *County Business Patterns*; 1997 and 2002 values are from the 1997 and 2002 censuses, respectively. 'P's show projections by the editors.

INDICES OF CHANGE

| Year | Com-panies | Establishments | | Employment | | | Compensation | | Production ($ million) | | | |
		Total	with 20 or more employees	Total (000)	Production Workers (000)	Hours (Mil)	Payroll ($ mil)	Wages ($/hr)	Cost of Materials	Value Added by Manufacture	Value of Shipments	Capital Invest.
1997	71	71	71	72	75	72	58	86	58	55	56	65
1998		69	72	75	75	76	65	85	64	62	63	53
1999		68	72	76	77	77	66	89	63	68	66	71
2000		66	73	79	83	80	73	91	70	72	71	80
2001		75	74	73	74	73	66	89	72	63	67	52
2002	100	100	100	100	100	100	100	100	100	100	100	100
2003		100	98	99	102	106	102	100	105	103	104	63
2004		98	95	99	100	102	106	105	114	101	105	90
2005		100	97	94	95	98	108	107	119	106	111	73
2006		108P	105P	95	97	100	115	112	135	116	123	89
2007		113P	109P	104P	106P	109P	124P	113P	141P	122P	129P	88P
2008		118P	113P	108P	109P	113P	131P	116P	149P	129P	136P	91P
2009		123P	117P	111P	112P	117P	138P	120P	158P	136P	144P	94P
2010		128P	121P	114P	116P	121P	144P	123P	166P	143P	152P	96P

Sources: Same as General Statistics. Values reflect change from the base year, 2002. Values above 100 mean greater than 2002, values below 100 mean less than 2002, and the values of 100 in other years means the same as 2002. 'P's show projections by the editors.

SELECTED RATIOS

For 2002	Avg. of All Manufact.	Analyzed Industry	Index	For 2002	Avg. of All Manufact.	Analyzed Industry	Index
Employees per Establishment	42	22	51	Value Added per Production Worker	182,367	104,264	57
Payroll per Establishment	1,639,184	780,090	48	Cost per Establishment	5,769,015	925,305	16
Payroll per Employee	39,053	36,149	93	Cost per Employee	137,446	42,878	31
Production Workers per Establishment	30	15	50	Cost per Production Worker	195,506	62,368	32
Wages per Establishment	694,845	445,145	64	Shipments per Establishment	11,158,348	2,470,456	22
Wages per Production Worker	23,548	30,004	127	Shipments per Employee	265,847	114,479	43
Hours per Production Worker	1,980	1,961	99	Shipments per Production Worker	378,144	166,515	44
Wages per Hour	11.89	15.30	129	Investment per Establishment	361,338	54,913	15
Value Added per Establishment	5,381,325	1,546,885	29	Investment per Employee	8,609	2,545	30
Value Added per Employee	128,210	71,682	56	Investment per Production Worker	12,245	3,701	30

Sources: Same as General Statistics. The 'Average of All Manufacturing' column represents the average of all manufacturing industries reported for the most recent complete year available. The Index shows the relationship between the Average and the Analyzed Industry. For example, 100 means that they are equal; 500 that the Analyzed Industry is five times the average; 50 means that the Analyzed Industry is half the national average. The abbreviation 'na' is used to show that data are 'not available'. Ratios shown for 2002, the last complete census year.

LEADING COMPANIES Number shown: **75**   Total sales ($ mil): **43,723**   Total employment (000): **124.3**

Company Name	Address				CEO Name	Phone	Co. Type	Sales ($ mil)	Empl. (000)
Masco Corp.	21001 Van Born Rd.	Taylor	MI	48180	Ronald W. Ayers	313-274-7400	P	11,770	52.0
LA Darling Co.	1401 Hwy. 49B	Paragould	AR	72450		870-239-9564	R	7,000*	1.0
Silver King Refrigeration Inc.	1600 Xenium Ln. N	Plymouth	MN	55441	Korey Kohl	763-553-1881	S	7,000*	<0.1
Hussmann Corp.	12999 St. Chrles Rd	Bridgeton	MO	63044	Dennis Gibson	314-291-2000	S	4,623*	8.0
Leggett and Platt Inc.	PO Box 757	Carthage	MO	64836		417-358-8131	P	4,306	24.0
Builders FirstSource Inc.	2001 Bryan St.	Dallas	TX	75201	Paul Levy	214-880-3500	P	1,593	4.9
EBSCO Industries Inc.	PO Box 1943	Birmingham	AL	35201	Dixon Brooke Jr.	205-991-6600	R	1,400*	5.0
Haworth Inc.	1 Haworth Ctr.	Holland	MI	49423	Franco Bianchi	616-393-3000	R	1,120*	8.0
Knoll Inc.	1235 Water St.	East Greenville	PA	18041	Andrew B. Cogan	215-679-7991	P	1,056	4.3
Pan-Oston Co.	6944 Louisville Rd.	Bowling Green	KY	42101	John Kelly	270-783-3900	R	903*	0.3
Sauder Woodworking Co.	PO Box 156	Archbold	OH	43502	Kevin Sauder	419-446-2711	R	525*	3.0
Lozier Corp.	PO Box 3448	Omaha	NE	68103	Sheri Andrews	402-457-8000	R	411*	1.1
Lexington Furniture Industries	PO Box 1008	Lexington	NC	27293	Asher Lepkin	336-474-5300	R	167*	0.3
Knape and Vogt Manufacturing	2700 Oak Indu. Dr.	Grand Rapids	MI	49505	William R. Dutmers	616-459-3311	R	157	0.6
Brodart Co.	500 Arch St.	Williamsport	PA	17701	Arthur Brody		R	92*	1.0
Streater Inc.	411 S 1st Ave.	Albert Lea	MN	56007	John Mulvihill	507-373-0611	S	74*	0.7
Goebel Fixture Co.	528 S Dale St.	Hutchinson	MN	55350		320-587-2112	R	69*	0.2
Cape Cod Lumber Company Inc.	PO Box 968	Abington	MA	02351	Harvey Hurvitz	781-878-0715	R	68*	<0.1
Hirsh Industries Inc.	11229 Aurora Ave.	Des Moines	IA	50322	Douglas Smith	515-299-3200	R	57*	<0.1
Stevens Industries Inc.	PO Box 206	Teutopolis	IL	62467	Thomas Wegman	217-540-3100	R	50*	0.6
Kenney Manufacturing Co.	1000 Jefferson Blvd	Warwick	RI	02886	G Kenney	401-739-2200	R	49*	0.5
Counterpoint Distributors	1205 5th St. SW	Canton	OH	44707	Cindy Guest	330-455-7000	R	45*	<0.1
Borroughs Corp.	3002 N Burdick St.	Kalamazoo	MI	49004	Tim Tyler	269-342-0161	R	45*	0.3
Marco Display Specialists, GP	PO Box 123439	Fort Worth	TX	76121	Darrell Cooper	817-244-8300	R	44*	0.3
Grandview Products Co.	PO Box 874	Parsons	KS	67357	Emil Zetmeir	620-421-6950	R	41*	0.3
Steel King Industries Inc.	2700 Chamber St.	Stevens Point	WI	54481	Jay Anderson	715-341-3120	R	40*	0.1
Bargreen-Ellingson Inc.	6626 Tacoma Mall	Tacoma	WA	98409	Paul Ellingson	253-475-9201	R	39*	<0.1
Wenger Corp.	PO Box 448	Owatonna	MN	55060	William Beer	507-455-4100	R	37*	0.5
Store Kraft Manufacturing Co.	PO Box 807	Beatrice	NE	68310	James Evans	402-223-2348	R	37*	0.4
MII Inc.	2100 5th St.	Lincoln	IL	62656	Ronald McComas	217-735-1241	R	35*	<0.1
Boden Store Fixtures Inc.	PO Box 301009	Portland	OR	97294	Carl Boden	503-252-4728	R	33*	<0.1
LaFata Cabinet Shop	50905 Hayes Rd.	Shelby Twp	MI	48315	Peter Fata	586-247-1140	R	32*	0.1
Marlite Inc.	PO Box 250	Dover	OH	44622	John Popa	330-343-6621	R	29*	0.3
Harbor Industries Inc.	14130 172nd Ave.	Grand Haven	MI	49417		616-842-5330	R	29*	0.1
Hamilton Fixture Co.	3550 Symmes Rd.	Hamilton	OH	45015		513-870-8700	R	28*	0.3
Design Fabricators Inc.	12777 Claud Ct.	Thornton	CO	80241	Scott Stewart	303-661-9800	S	26*	0.3
Resnick Supermarket Equipment	PO Box Q	Mountain Dale	NY	12763	Daniel Resnick	845-434-8200	R	25*	<0.1
Panel Specialists Inc.	PO Box 968	Temple	TX	76503	Hal Martin	254-774-9800	R	24*	<0.1
Kent Corp.	PO Box 170399	Birmingham	AL	35217	M Oztekin	205-853-3420	R	23*	0.2
Jahabow Industries Inc.	1004 Industrial Dr.	Owensville	MO	65066	Ed Ryan	573-437-4151	R	22*	0.1
Precision Countertops Inc.	PO Box 1265	Tualatin	OR	97062	Marcus Neff	503-692-6660	R	22*	<0.1
Top Master Inc.	2844 Roe Ln.	Kansas City	KS	66103	Mike Kaufmann	913-492-3030	R	22*	0.2
Abex Display Systems Inc.	7101 Fair Ave.	N Hollywood	CA	91605	Robbie Blumenfeld	818-503-0999	R	22*	0.1
Handy Store Fixtures Inc.	337 Sherman Ave.	Newark	NJ	07114	Marc Kurland	973-242-1600	R	21*	0.2
King Load Manufacturing Co.	PO Box 40606	Jacksonville	FL	32203	Charlie Chupp	904-354-8882	R	21*	0.2
Structural Concepts Corp.	888 E Porter Rd.	Muskegon	MI	49441	James Doss	231-798-8888	R	21*	0.2
Rynone Manufacturing Corp.	PO Box 128	Sayre	PA	18840	Richard Rynone	570-888-5272	R	21*	0.1
Bishop Fixture and Millwork	101 Eagle Dr.	Balsam Lake	WI	54810	Hubert Nelson	715-485-9312	R	21*	0.2
The Miller Group	1555 L Williams	Fenton	MO	63026	Randy Cook		R	20*	0.2
Russ Bassett Corp.	8189 Byron Rd.	Whittier	CA	90606	Mike Dressendorfer	562-945-2445	R	20*	0.1
Pacific Home Products Inc.	PO Box 55188	Hayward	CA	94545	Wesley Moore	510-293-6909	R	19*	<0.1
Reconditioned Systems Inc.	2636 S Wilson St.	Tempe	AZ	85282	Dirk D. Anderson	480-968-1772	P	19	0.1
Middlebury Hardwood Products	PO Box 1429	Middlebury	IN	46540	Charles Lamb	574-825-9524	R	19*	0.1
LSI Corporation of America	2100 Xenium Ln. N	Plymouth	MN	55441		763-559-4664	R	18*	0.2
Westmark Products Inc.	PO Box 44040	Tacoma	WA	98444	Dennis Milsten	253-531-3470	R	18*	0.2
Felbro Inc.	3666 E Olympic	Los Angeles	CA	90023	Norman Feldner	323-263-8686	R	17*	0.2
Quality Custom Cabinetry Inc.	PO Box 189	New Holland	PA	17557	Glen Good	717-661-6900	R	16*	<0.1
Fetzers Inc.	6223 Double Eagle	Salt Lake City	UT	84118	Wallace Fetzer	801-484-6103	R	16*	0.1
National Partitions/Interiors	10300 Goldenfern	Knoxville	TN	37931	Anthony D'Andrea	865-670-2100	R	16*	0.2
Spectrum Industries Inc.	PO Box 400	Chippewa Falls	WI	54729	David Hancock	715-723-6750	R	16*	0.2
Alexander Plastics Inc.	11937 Denton Dr.	Dallas	TX	75234	Ben Goldfarb	972-241-4171	R	15*	0.2
Columbus Show Case Co.	4401 Equity Dr.	Columbus	OH	43228	Carl Aschinger	614-850-1460	R	15*	0.2
AGR of Florida Inc.	PO Box 10158	Jacksonville	FL	32247	George Shami	904-733-9393	R	15*	<0.1
Synsor Corp.	1920 Merrill Creek	Everett	WA	98203	Gary Bullock	425-551-1300	R	15*	<0.1
CIP International Inc.	9575 Le Saint Dr.	Fairfield	OH	45014	Kathleen Huff	513-874-9925	R	15*	<0.1
Worden Co.	199 E 17th St.	Holland	MI	49423	William Hendrick	616-392-1848	R	14*	0.1
J and W Counter Tops Inc.	600 N Street	Springfield	IL	62704	Walter Justison	217-544-0876	R	14*	<0.1
Panelfold Inc.	PO Box 680130	Miami	FL	33168	Guy Dixon	305-688-3501	R	14*	0.2
Northwestern Inc.	15054 Oxnard St.	Van Nuys	CA	91411	C. Wayne Noecker	818-786-1581	R	14*	<0.1
Wine Cellar Innovations	4575 Eastern Ave.	Cincinnati	OH	45226	James Deckebach	513-321-3733	R	14*	0.2
Bay View Industries Inc.	7821 S 10th St.	Oak Creek	WI	53154	Eugene Plitt	414-764-2120	R	14*	0.2
Ghent Manufacturing Inc.	2999 Henkle Dr.	Lebanon	OH	45036	George Leasure	513-932-3445	R	14*	0.1
Wood Designs L.L.C.	5500 SW 38th St.	Oklahoma City	OK	73179		405-680-3000	R	14*	0.2
Northway Industries Inc.	PO Box 277	Middleburg	PA	17842	C Battram	570-837-1564	R	13*	0.1
Process Displays Co.	7108 31st Ave. N	Minneapolis	MN	55427	Peter Strommen	763-546-1133	R	13*	0.1

Source: Ward's Business Directory of U.S. Private and Public Companies, Volumes 1 and 2, 2008. The company type code used is as follows: P - Public, R - Private, S - Subsidiary, D - Division, J - Joint Venture, A - Affiliate, G - Group. Sales are in millions of dollars, employees are in thousands. An asterisk (*) indicates an estimated sales volume. The symbol < stands for 'less than'. Company names and addresses are truncated, in some cases, to fit into the available space.

MATERIALS CONSUMED

Material	Quantity	Delivered Cost ($ million)
Metal stampings	(X)	1.2
Other fabricated metal products (including forgings)	(X)	37.8
Steel sheet and strip (including tinplate)	(X)	7.4
All other steel shapes and forms (exc. castings, forgings, fabr. metal products)	(X)	12.6
Aluminum and aluminum-base alloy sheet, plate, foil, and welded tubing	(X)	4.1
All other aluminum and aluminum-base alloy shapes and forms (exc. castings, forgings, fabr. metal products)	(X)	8.5
Hardwood lumber, rough and dressed	(X)	85.2
Softwood lumber, rough and dressed	(X)	10.1
Hardwood cut stock and dimension (excluding furniture frames)	(X)	16.9
Softwood plywood	(X)	11.2
Hardwood plywood	(X)	48.5
Hardwood veneer	(X)	42.5
Particleboard (reconstituted wood)	(X)	66.6
Medium density fiberboard (MDF)	(X)	38.6
Hardboard	(X)	12.8
Plastics resins consumed in the form of granules, pellets, etc.	(X)	4.7
Plastics laminated sheets	(X)	84.5
Plastics furniture parts and components	(X)	13.9
Flat glass (plate, float, and sheet)	(X)	9.0
Mirrors, framed and unframed	(X)	3.6
Paints, varnishes, stains, lacquers, shellacs, japans, enamels, etc.	(X)	16.3
Adhesives and sealants	(X)	6.7
Furniture and builders' hardware (incl. cabinet hardware, casters, glides, handles, hinges, locks, etc.)	(X)	40.5
Paperboard containers, boxes, and corrugated paperboard	(X)	9.8
All other materials, components, parts, containers, and supplies	(X)	96.4
Materials, ingredients, containers, and supplies, nsk	(X)	479.1

Source: 2002 Economic Census. Explanation of symbols used: (D): Withheld to avoid disclosure of competitive data; na: Not available; (S): Withheld because statistical norms were not met; (X): Not applicable; (Z): Less than half the unit shown; nec: Not elsewhere classified; nsk: Not specified by kind; - : zero; p : 10-19 percent estimated; q : 20-29 percent estimated.

PRODUCT SHARE DETAILS

Product or Product Class Shipments	Mil. $	Product or Product Class Shipments	Mil. $
CUSTOM ARCHITECTURAL WOODWORK, MILLWORK, AND FIXTURES	3,601.7	Custom architectural woodwork, millwork, and fixtures, except kitchen cabinet tops and bathroom vanity tops	3,043.8
Custom architectural woodwork, millwork, and fixtures	3,601.7		

Source: 2002 Economic Census. The values are product shipments in millions of dollars for 2002. Total product shipments may be lower or higher than industry shipments. See Introduction for a full discussion. Values of indented subcategories are summed in the main heading(s). The symbol (D) appears when data are withheld to prevent disclosure of competitive information. The abbreviation nsk stands for 'not specified by kind' and nec for 'not elsewhere classified'. A dash (-) means zero.

INPUTS AND OUTPUTS FOR CUSTOM ARCHITECTURAL WOODWORK & MILLWORK

Economic Sector or Industry Providing Inputs	%	Sector	Economic Sector or Industry Buying Outputs	%	Sector
Compensation of employees	30.7		Private fixed investment	63.2	
Wholesale trade	4.9	Trade	Residential permanent site structures	21.0	Construct.
Plastics products, nec	3.3	Manufg.	S/L govt. invest., education	6.3	S/L Govt
Iron & steel mills & ferroalloys	3.3	Manufg.	S/L govt. invest., other	6.2	S/L Govt
Reconstituted wood products	2.7	Manufg.	Exports of goods & services	1.4	Cap Inv
Veneer & plywood	2.5	Manufg.	Custom architectural woodwork & millwork	0.5	Manufg.
Management of companies & enterprises	2.4	Services	Personal consumption expenditures	0.5	
Sawmills & wood preservation	2.0	Manufg.	Federal government, investment, nondefense	0.3	Fed Govt
Retail trade	1.9	Trade	Change in private inventories	0.2	In House
Hardware	1.5	Manufg.	Owner-occupied dwellings	0.1	
Laminated plastics plates, sheets, & shapes	1.5	Manufg.			
Paints & coatings	1.3	Manufg.			
Real estate	1.2	Fin/R.E.			
Truck transportation	1.2	Util.			
Paperboard containers	1.1	Manufg.			
Securities, commodity contracts, investments	1.1	Fin/R.E.			
Crowns & closures & metal stamping	1.0	Manufg.			
Advertising & related services	0.8	Services			
Showcases, partitions, shelving, and lockers	0.8	Manufg.			
Broadwoven fabric mills	0.8	Manufg.			
Monetary authorities/depository credit intermediation	0.7	Fin/R.E.			
Fabric coating mills	0.7	Manufg.			
Wood kitchen cabinets & countertops	0.6	Manufg.			
Power generation & supply	0.6	Util.			
Custom architectural woodwork & millwork	0.6	Manufg.			
Professional, scientific, technical services, nec	0.6	Services			
Aluminum products from purchased aluminum	0.5	Manufg.			
Semiconductors & related devices	0.5	Manufg.			
Textile & fabric finishing mills	0.5	Manufg.			

Continued on next page.

INPUTS AND OUTPUTS FOR CUSTOM ARCHITECTURAL WOODWORK & MILLWORK - Continued

Economic Sector or Industry Providing Inputs	%	Sector	Economic Sector or Industry Buying Outputs	%	Sector
Rubber products, nec	0.4	Manufg.			
Urethane & other foam products (except polystrene)	0.4	Manufg.			
Printed circuit assemblies (electronic assembles)	0.4	Manufg.			
Legal services	0.4	Services			
Machine shops	0.4	Manufg.			
Telecommunications	0.4	Services			
Specialized design services	0.3	Services			
Food services & drinking places	0.3	Services			
Automotive equipment rental & leasing	0.3	Fin/R.E.			
Taxes on production & imports, less subsidies	0.3				
Data processing, hosting, & related services	0.3	Services			
Accounting, tax preparation, bookkeeping, & payroll	0.3	Services			
Warehousing & storage	0.3	Util.			
Coating, engraving, heat treating & allied activities	0.3	Manufg.			
Maintenance/repair of nonresidential structures	0.3	Construct.			
Services to buildings & dwellings	0.3	Services			
Management, scientific, & technical consulting	0.2	Services			
Natural gas distribution	0.2	Util.			
Architectural, engineering, & related services	0.2	Services			
Rail transportation	0.2	Util.			
Other computer related services, including facilities	0.2	Services			
Adhesives	0.2	Manufg.			
Hotels & motels, including casino hotels	0.2	Services			
Textile product mills, nec	0.2	Manufg.			
Commercial & industrial machinery rental & leasing	0.2	Fin/R.E.			
Automotive repair & maintenance, ex. car washes	0.2	Services			
Abrasive products	0.2	Manufg.			
Alumina refining & primary aluminum production	0.2	Manufg.			
Turned products & screws, nuts, & bolts	0.1	Manufg.			
Air transportation	0.1	Util.			
Commercial & industrial equipment repair/maintenance	0.1	Services			
Nondepository credit intermediation activities	0.1	Fin/R.E.			
Flat glass	0.1	Manufg.			
Waste management & remediation services	0.1	Services			
Metal cans, boxes, & other containers (light gauge)	0.1	Manufg.			

Source: Benchmark Input-Output Accounts for the U.S. Economy, 2002, U.S. Department of Commerce, Washington, D.C., January 2008. The abbreviation nec stands for 'not elsewhere classified'.

OCCUPATIONS EMPLOYED BY OFFICE FURNITURE (INCLUDING FIXTURES) MANUFACTURING

Occupation	% of Total 2006	Change to 2016	Occupation	% of Total 2006	Change to 2016
Cabinetmakers & bench carpenters	11.1	-6.0	General & operations managers	1.7	-15.4
Team assemblers	9.5	-6.0	Industrial truck & tractor operators	1.6	-15.4
Woodworking machine operators & tenders, exc sawing	5.0	3.4	Sawing machine setters, operators, & tenders, wood	1.6	3.4
First-line supervisors/managers of production workers	4.0	-6.0	Packers & packagers, hand	1.6	-24.8
Cutting, punching, & press machine operators	3.2	-15.4	Shipping, receiving, & traffic clerks	1.6	-9.5
Laborers & freight, stock, & material movers, hand	3.0	-15.4	Multiple machine tool operators & tenders	1.3	3.4
Welders, cutters, solderers, & brazers	2.8		Office clerks, general	1.3	-7.4
Furniture finishers	2.7	-6.0	Customer service representatives	1.3	3.4
Helpers--Production workers	2.5	-6.0	Bookkeeping, accounting, & auditing clerks	1.1	-6.0
Assemblers & fabricators, nec	2.5	-15.4	Industrial engineers	1.1	14.2
Sales reps, wholesale & manufacturing, exc tech	2.4	-6.0	Maintenance & repair workers, general	1.1	-6.0
Carpenters	2.2	-6.0	Molding, coremaking, & casting machine operators	1.1	-15.4
Coating, painting, & spraying machine operators	1.8	-10.7			

Source: Industry-Occupation Matrix, Bureau of Labor Statistics, December 4, 2007. These data are reported based on 4-digit NAICS categories but have been matched to corresponding 6-digit NAICS industry codes. The change reported for each occupation to the year 2016 is a percent of growth or decline as estimated by the Bureau of Labor Statistics. The abbreviation nec stands for 'not elsewhere classified'.

LOCATION BY STATE AND REGIONAL CONCENTRATION

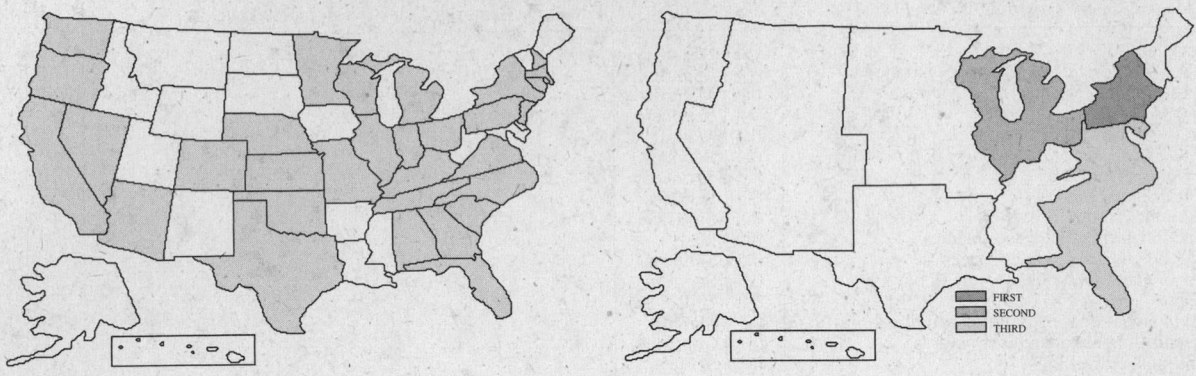

FIRST
SECOND
THIRD

INDUSTRY DATA BY STATE

| State | Establish-ments | Shipments | | | Employment | | | | Cost as % of Shipments | Investment per Employee ($) |
		Total ($ mil)	% of U.S.	Per Establ.	Total Number	% of U.S.	Per Establ.	Wages ($/hour)		
California	140	408.4	10.6	2,916.9	3,326	9.9	24	16.67	35.6	2,080
New York	136	304.7	7.9	2,240.4	2,230	6.6	16	17.96	39.1	2,382
Ohio	62	226.8	5.9	3,658.0	1,832	5.5	30	14.79	43.4	2,973
Texas	84	201.3	5.2	2,396.1	1,792	5.3	21	13.87	34.8	2,674
Pennsylvania	85	178.6	4.6	2,101.0	1,646	4.9	19	14.09	39.0	4,555
North Carolina	51	164.0	4.3	3,215.5	1,292	3.8	25	12.28	48.9	1,582
Massachusetts	57	155.0	4.0	2,718.6	1,269	3.8	22	16.82	35.4	3,500
Wisconsin	43	154.4	4.0	3,590.4	1,216	3.6	28	15.08	42.0	3,194
Illinois	56	150.7	3.9	2,691.1	1,155	3.4	21	18.25	33.8	2,183
Minnesota	41	148.7	3.9	3,627.8	1,064	3.2	26	16.74	38.6	2,195
New Jersey	53	107.5	2.8	2,027.8	951	2.8	18	17.63	36.1	1,623
Washington	42	106.9	2.8	2,544.7	911	2.7	22	15.20	31.1	1,311
Oregon	25	102.0	2.7	4,078.2	807	2.4	32	15.20	29.7	4,320
Florida	71	95.9	2.5	1,350.8	895	2.7	13	12.78	35.3	1,902
Georgia	43	90.9	2.4	2,113.5	803	2.4	19	13.83	34.6	1,792
Missouri	30	82.1	2.1	2,736.5	506	1.5	17	18.04	43.0	2,077
Colorado	39	81.2	2.1	2,080.9	698	2.1	18	15.91	37.3	3,146
Michigan	42	81.1	2.1	1,930.1	787	2.3	19	15.41	36.9	2,579
Virginia	41	80.9	2.1	1,974.2	824	2.5	20	14.26	37.7	1,352
Tennessee	31	64.9	1.7	2,093.4	696	2.1	22	13.17	33.6	2,741
Connecticut	34	62.4	1.6	1,835.4	688	2.0	20	15.30	33.9	1,863
Rhode Island	11	62.0	1.6	5,640.5	582	1.7	53	18.33	32.5	1,905
Indiana	32	61.9	1.6	1,934.1	594	1.8	19	14.92	36.0	2,488
Arizona	27	59.7	1.6	2,211.6	590	1.8	22	14.72	37.6	6,641
Oklahoma	15	53.0	1.4	3,530.9	422	1.3	28	12.85	36.1	3,763
Alabama	18	44.3	1.2	2,461.9	432	1.3	24	13.47	43.5	5,005
Nevada	11	41.3	1.1	3,751.2	434	1.3	39	16.44	34.1	1,585
South Carolina	24	38.1	1.0	1,587.5	448	1.3	19	15.00	24.3	1,076
Kentucky	15	34.0	0.9	2,268.3	385	1.1	26	13.71	39.2	1,387
Kansas	15	29.8	0.8	1,984.0	258	0.8	17	16.39	43.9	1,872
New Hampshire	10	23.9	0.6	2,388.4	210	0.6	21	16.64	41.6	2,752
Nebraska	7	21.7	0.6	3,103.0	282	0.8	40	13.55	35.9	741

Source: 2002 *Economic Census*. The states are in descending order of shipments or establishments (if shipment data are missing for the majority). The symbol (D) appears when data are withheld to prevent disclosure of competitive information. States marked with (D) are sorted by number of establishments. A dash (-) indicates that the data element cannot be calculated. Data may not show all states active in the NAICS category. All data available at the time of publication are shown.

NAICS 337215 - SHOWCASE, PARTITION, SHELVING, AND LOCKER MANUFACTURING

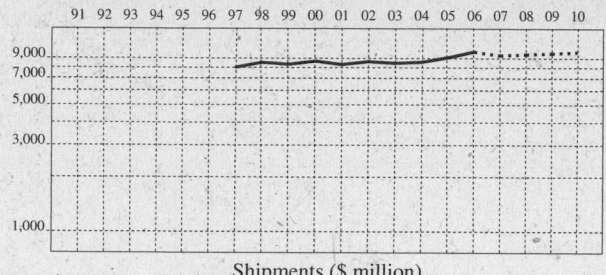

Shipments ($ million)

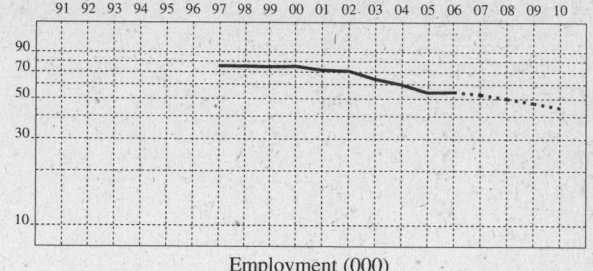

Employment (000)

GENERAL STATISTICS

| Year | Com-panies | Establishments | | Employment | | | Compensation | | Production ($ million) | | | |
		Total	with 20 or more employees	Total (000)	Production Workers (000)	Hours (Mil)	Payroll ($ mil)	Wages ($/hr)	Cost of Materials	Value Added by Manufacture	Value of Shipments	Capital Invest.
1997	2,076	2,156	812	75.4	57.8	109.7	2,084.6	11.74	3,526.3	4,491.1	8,006.3	222.4
1998		2,116	810	75.3	57.9	111.4	2,182.8	12.06	3,932.8	4,637.9	8,526.7	325.7
1999		2,105	816	74.8	58.1	117.3	2,199.0	12.13	3,518.6	4,867.3	8,350.4	332.1
2000		2,076	817	75.3	58.1	112.9	2,269.3	12.80	3,595.9	5,134.3	8,670.4	298.6
2001		2,028	794	71.8	53.1	100.8	2,193.1	13.47	3,524.0	4,768.0	8,328.1	232.8
2002	1,795	1,890	771	71.0	53.3	102.8	2,195.3	13.12	3,917.3	4,729.1	8,631.3	204.7
2003		1,830	712	64.1	48.0	98.0	2,115.1	13.19	3,907.9	4,521.2	8,464.7	199.7
2004		1,828	699	59.8	45.6	92.1	2,033.8	13.62	4,034.8	4,632.0	8,584.5	156.5
2005		1,789	675	54.1	42.0	85.9	1,970.8	14.55	4,551.3	4,608.5	9,098.1	143.4
2006		1,724P	673P	54.4	42.5	86.4	2,018.1	14.78	5,102.7	4,720.9	9,776.1	192.0
2007		1,673P	654P	52.7P	40.3P	83.2P	2,013.9P	14.91P	4,873.2P	4,508.6P	9,336.5P	139.0P
2008		1,622P	635P	50.0P	38.2P	79.8P	1,993.5P	15.24P	4,939.0P	4,569.4P	9,462.4P	122.4P
2009		1,571P	616P	47.3P	36.1P	76.4P	1,973.1P	15.56P	5,004.7P	4,630.3P	9,588.4P	105.7P
2010		1,520P	597P	44.6P	34.0P	73.0P	1,952.6P	15.88P	5,070.5P	4,691.1P	9,714.4P	89.0P

Sources: 1997 and 2002 *Economic Census*; other years, up to 2006, are from *Annual Survey of Manufactures*. Establishment counts for non-Census years are from *County Business Patterns*; 1997 and 2002 values are from the 1997 and 2002 censuses, respectively. 'P's show projections by the editors.

INDICES OF CHANGE

| Year | Com-panies | Establishments | | Employment | | | Compensation | | Production ($ million) | | | |
		Total	with 20 or more employees	Total (000)	Production Workers (000)	Hours (Mil)	Payroll ($ mil)	Wages ($/hr)	Cost of Materials	Value Added by Manufacture	Value of Shipments	Capital Invest.
1997	116	114	105	106	108	107	95	89	90	95	93	109
1998		112	105	106	109	108	99	92	100	98	99	159
1999		111	106	105	109	114	100	92	90	103	97	162
2000		110	106	106	109	110	103	98	92	109	100	146
2001		107	103	101	100	98	100	103	90	101	96	114
2002	100	100	100	100	100	100	100	100	100	100	100	100
2003		97	92	90	90	95	96	101	100	96	98	98
2004		97	91	84	86	90	93	104	103	98	99	76
2005		95	88	76	79	84	90	111	116	97	105	70
2006		91P	87P	77	80	84	92	113	130	100	113	94
2007		89P	85P	74P	76P	81P	92P	114P	124P	95P	108P	68P
2008		86P	82P	70P	72P	78P	91P	116P	126P	97P	110P	60P
2009		83P	80P	67P	68P	74P	90P	119P	128P	98P	111P	52P
2010		80P	77P	63P	64P	71P	89P	121P	129P	99P	113P	43P

Sources: Same as General Statistics. Values reflect change from the base year, 2002. Values above 100 mean greater than 2002, values below 100 mean less than 2002, and the values of 100 in other years means the same as 2002. 'P's show projections by the editors.

SELECTED RATIOS

For 2002	Avg. of All Manufact.	Analyzed Industry	Index	For 2002	Avg. of All Manufact.	Analyzed Industry	Index
Employees per Establishment	42	38	90	Value Added per Production Worker	182,367	88,726	49
Payroll per Establishment	1,639,184	1,161,534	71	Cost per Establishment	5,769,015	2,072,646	36
Payroll per Employee	39,053	30,920	79	Cost per Employee	137,446	55,173	40
Production Workers per Establishment	30	28	96	Cost per Production Worker	195,506	73,495	38
Wages per Establishment	694,845	713,617	103	Shipments per Establishment	11,158,348	4,566,825	41
Wages per Production Worker	23,548	25,305	107	Shipments per Employee	265,847	121,568	46
Hours per Production Worker	1,980	1,929	97	Shipments per Production Worker	378,144	161,938	43
Wages per Hour	11.89	13.12	110	Investment per Establishment	361,338	108,307	30
Value Added per Establishment	5,381,325	2,502,169	46	Investment per Employee	8,609	2,883	33
Value Added per Employee	128,210	66,607	52	Investment per Production Worker	12,245	3,841	31

Sources: Same as General Statistics. The 'Average of All Manufacturing' column represents the average of all manufacturing industries reported for the most recent complete year available. The Index shows the relationship between the Average and the Analyzed Industry. For example, 100 means that they are equal; 500 that the Analyzed Industry is five times the average; 50 means that the Analyzed Industry is half the national average. The abbreviation 'na' is used to show that data are 'not available'. Ratios shown for 2002, the last complete census year.

LEADING COMPANIES   Number shown: 75   Total sales ($ mil): 109,224   Total employment (000): 359.7

Company Name	Address				CEO Name	Phone	Co. Type	Sales ($ mil)	Empl. (000)
Weyerhaeuser Co.	PO Box 9777	Federal Way	WA	98003		253-924-2345	P	16,308	37.9
Masco Corp.	21001 Van Born Rd.	Taylor	MI	48180	Ronald W. Ayers	313-274-7400	P	11,770	52.0
Fortune Brands Inc.	520 Lake Cook Rd.	Deerfield	IL	60015	Bruce A. Carbonari	847-484-4400	P	8,563	31.0
LA Darling Co.	1401 Hwy. 49B	Paragould	AR	72450		870-239-9564	R	7,000*	1.0
Silver King Refrigeration Inc.	1600 Xenium Ln. N	Plymouth	MN	55441	Korey Kohl	763-553-1881	S	7,000*	<0.1
BorgWarner Inc.	3850 Hamlin Rd.	Auburn Hills	MI	48326		248-754-9200	P	5,329	17.7
Hussmann Corp.	12999 St. Chrles Rd	Bridgeton	MO	63044	Dennis Gibson	314-291-2000	S	4,623*	8.0
Leggett and Platt Inc.	PO Box 757	Carthage	MO	64836		417-358-8131	P	4,306	24.0
Flowserve Corp.	5215 N O'Connor	Irving	TX	75039		972-443-6500	P	3,763	15.0
DCI Marketing Inc.	PO Box 514010	Milwaukee	WI	53203	Joseph Asfour	414-228-7000	R	2,840*	0.2
HNI Corp.	PO Box 1109	Muscatine	IA	52761	Timothy Anderson	563-264-7400	P	2,571	14.2
JELD-WEN Inc.	PO Box 1329	Klamath Falls	OR	97601	Richard Wendt	541-882-3451	R	2,476*	23.8
Herman Miller Inc.	PO Box 302	Zeeland	MI	49464		616-654-3000	P	1,919	6.4
Unarco Material Handling Inc.	PO Box 547	Springfield	TN	37172		615-384-3531	R	1,890*	0.4
Hope Lumber and Supply Co.	12215 E 61st St.	Broken Arrow	OK	74012	Jim Cavanaugh	918-249-0909	R	1,690*	<0.1
Potlatch Corp.	601 W Riverside	Spokane	WA	99201	Michael Covey	509-835-1500	P	1,654	3.8
Builders FirstSource Inc.	2001 Bryan St.	Dallas	TX	75201	Paul Levy	214-880-3500	P	1,593	4.9
Barnes Group Inc.	PO Box 489	Bristol	CT	06011	Thomas Barnes	860-583-7070	P	1,539	6.7
Valmont Industries Inc.	1 Valmont Plz.	Omaha	NE	68154	Mogens C. Bay	402-963-1000	P	1,500	6.0
EBSCO Industries Inc.	PO Box 1943	Birmingham	AL	35201	Dixon Brooke Jr.	205-991-6600	R	1,400*	5.0
Columbia Forest Products Inc.	222 SW Columbia	Portland	OR	97201	Harry L. Demorest	503-224-5300	R	1,181*	4.5
Haworth Inc.	1 Haworth Ctr.	Holland	MI	49423	Franco Bianchi	616-393-3000	R	1,120*	8.0
Knoll Inc.	1235 Water St.	East Greenville	PA	18041	Andrew B. Cogan	215-679-7991	P	1,056	4.3
BWAY Holding Co.	8607 Roberts Dr.	Atlanta	GA	30350	Jean-Pierre M. Ergas	770-645-4800	P	959	2.5
United Components Inc.	14601 Hwy 41 N	Evansville	IN	47725	Bruce Zorich	812-867-4156	S	906	6.8
Pan-Oston Co.	6944 Louisville Rd.	Bowling Green	KY	42101	John Kelly	270-783-3900	R	903*	0.3
Raybestos Products Co.	1204 Darlington Ave	Crawfordsville	IN	47933	Larry S. Singleton	765-362-3500	S	701*	5.3
Commercial Vehicle Group Inc.	6530 W Campus Ovl	New Albany	OH	43054	Gordon Boyd	614-289-5360	P	697	6.4
Holmes Lumber and Building Ctr	6139 State Rte. 39	Millersburg	OH	44654	Paul Miller	330-674-9060	R	689*	0.1
White Systems Inc.	30 Boright Ave.	Kenilworth	NJ	07033	Richard Paolino	908-272-6700	S	673*	0.3
Ameron International Corp.	245 S Los Robles	Pasadena	CA	91101	James Marlen	626-683-4000	P	631	2.8
Performance Contracting Group	16400 College Blvd.	Lenexa	KS	66219	Craig Davis	913-888-8600	R	600*	5.7
UNICOR	320 1st St. NW	Washington	DC	20534	Steve Schwalb	202-305-3500	R	567*	21.0
Sauder Woodworking Co.	PO Box 156	Archbold	OH	43502	Kevin Sauder	419-446-2711	R	525*	3.0
Cascade Corp.	PO Box 20187	Portland	OR	97294		503-669-6300	P	479	2.1
Wood Structures Inc.	PO Box 347	Biddeford	ME	04005	Frank Paul	207-282-7556	R	464*	<0.1
Bing Group L.L.C.	11500 Oakland St.	Detroit	MI	48211	David Bing	313-867-3700	R	411*	1.1
Lozier Corp.	PO Box 3448	Omaha	NE	68103	Sheri Andrews	402-457-8000	R	411*	1.1
O.C. Tanner Recognition Co.	1930 S State St.	Salt Lake City	UT	84115	Kent H. Murdock	801-486-2430	R	319*	1.8
Edsal Manufacturing Company	4400 S Packers Ave.	Chicago	IL	60609	Bruce Saltzberg	773-254-0600	R	300*	1.2
Intermagnetics General Corp.	PO Box 461	Latham	NY	12110	Leo Blecher	518-782-1122	R	265	1.1
Martco L.P.	PO Box 1110	Alexandria	LA	71309		318-448-0405	R	263*	<0.1
C. Cowles and Co.	83 Water St.	New Haven	CT	06511	Lawrence C. Moon Jr.	203-865-3110	R	260*	0.2
Autocam Corp.	4070 E Paris Ave SE	Kentwood	MI	49512	John C. Kennedy	616-698-0707	S	230*	2.3
Raytech Corp.	4 Corporate Dr.	Shelton	CT	06484		203-925-8023	R	227	1.7
Nielsen and Bainbridge	40 Eisenhower Dr.	Paramus	NJ	07653	Jack Forbes	201-368-9191	R	219*	0.9
Liberty Diversified Industries	5600 Hwy. 169 N	New Hope	MN	55428	Benjamin Fiterman	763-536-6600	R	219*	<0.1
JCM Industries Inc.	PO Box 1220	Nash	TX	75569	Ronald Collins	903-832-2581	R	218*	0.2
Defiance Metal Products Co.	PO Box 447	Defiance	OH	43512		419-784-5332	R	211*	1.7
Darlington Veneer Company Inc.	PO Box 1087	Darlington	SC	29540	John Ramsey	843-393-3861	R	203*	0.2
Burgess-Norton Manufacturing	737 Peyton St.	Geneva	IL	60134	John Carroll	630-232-4100	S	199*	0.9
General Dynamics Armament/Tech	4 LakePointe Plz.	Charlotte	NC	28217	Linda Hudson	703-714-8000	S	198*	1.2
Frazier Industrial Company	PO Box F	Long Valley	NJ	07853	Donald Frazier	908-876-3001	R	173*	0.1
Da-Lite Screen Company Inc.	PO Box 137	Warsaw	IN	46581	Richard E. Lundin	574-267-8101	R	170*	0.6
Sun Hydraulics Corp.	1500 W Univ. Pkwy.	Sarasota	FL	34243	Allen J. Carlson	941-362-1200	P	167	0.7
Lexington Furniture Industries	PO Box 1008	Lexington	NC	27293	Asher Lepkin	336-474-5300	R	167*	0.3
Morton Metalcraft Co.	PO Box 729	Welcome	NC	27374	William Morton	336-731-5700	S	161*	1.4
Knape and Vogt Manufacturing	2700 Oak Indu. Dr.	Grand Rapids	MI	49505	William R. Dutmers	616-459-3311	R	157	0.6
Eastern Co.	PO Box 460	Naugatuck	CT	06770	Leonard F. Leganza	203-729-2255	P	156	0.7
Deloro Stellite Company Inc.	1201 Eisenhower Dr.	Goshen	IN	46526	Mark Aldridge	574-534-2585	R	153*	1.2
Teak Isle Inc.	401 Capitol Ct.	Ocoee	FL	34761	Patrick Brown	407-656-8885	R	150*	0.2
Norwalk Furniture Corp.	100 Furniture Pkwy.	Norwalk	OH	44857	James Gerken	419-668-4461	R	147*	0.9
Bridgewater Interiors L.L.C.	4617 W Fort St.	Detroit	MI	48209	John Barth	313-842-3300	J	147*	0.3
EFCO Corp.	1800 NE Broadway	Des Moines	IA	50313	Chris Fuldnet	515-266-1141	R	144*	1.0
Atek Manufacturing L.L.C.	PO Box 403	Brainerd	MN	56401	Christy Bieber Orris	218-829-1481	R	140*	0.3
Latrobe Specialty Steel Co.	PO Box 31	Latrobe	PA	15650	Hans J. Sack	724-537-7711	R	130*	0.8
A and B Process Systems Corp.	PO Box 86	Stratford	WI	54484	A J. Hilgemann	715-687-4332	R	128*	0.2
Chestnut Group Inc.	115 Bloomingdale	Wayne	PA	19087	Park Blatchford	610-688-3300	R	122*	0.4
Manufacturers Industrial Group	PO Box 1048	Lexington	TN	38351		731-967-0001	R	120*	0.9
Steelcraft Manufacturing Co.	9017 Blue Ash Rd.	Cincinnati	OH	45242	Chris Mosby	513-745-6400	D	119*	1.0
McDonough Corp.	15150 N Hayden Rd.	Scottsdale	AZ	85260	Dale Knight	602-544-5900	R	119*	<0.1
Waterloo Industries Inc.	PO Box 2095	Waterloo	IA	50703	John M. Trebel	319-235-7131	D	108*	1.0
Glen Oak Lumber and Milling	N2885 County Rd. F	Montello	WI	53949		608-297-2161	R	105*	0.1
Barbour Corp.	PO Box 2158	Brockton	MA	02305	Richard Hynes	508-583-8200	R	103*	0.2
Kurt Manufacturing Company	5280 Main St. NE	Fridley	MN	55421		763-572-1500	R	101*	0.3

Source: Ward's Business Directory of U.S. Private and Public Companies, Volumes 1 and 2, 2008. The company type code used is as follows: P - Public, R - Private, S - Subsidiary, D - Division, J - Joint Venture, A - Affiliate, G - Group. Sales are in millions of dollars, employees are in thousands. An asterisk (*) indicates an estimated sales volume. The symbol < stands for 'less than'. Company names and addresses are truncated, in some cases, to fit into the available space.

MATERIALS CONSUMED

Material	Quantity	Delivered Cost ($ million)
Metal stampings	(X)	29.6
Other fabricated metal products (including forgings)	(X)	95.8
Castings, rough and semifinished	(X)	5.7
Steel sheet and strip (including tinplate)	(X)	378.5
All other steel shapes and forms (exc. castings, forgings, fabr. metal products)	(X)	209.8
Aluminum and aluminum-base alloy sheet, plate, foil, and welded tubing	(X)	35.8
All other aluminum and aluminum-base alloy shapes and forms (exc. castings, forgings, fabr. metal products)	(X)	29.7
Hardwood lumber, rough and dressed	(X)	102.6
Softwood lumber, rough and dressed	(X)	19.6
Hardwood cut stock and dimension (excluding furniture frames)	(X)	39.4
Softwood plywood	(X)	13.5
Hardwood plywood	(X)	93.5
Hardwood veneer	(X)	15.9
Particleboard (reconstituted wood)	(X)	66.0
Medium density fiberboard (MDF)	(X)	68.4
Hardboard	(X)	34.7
Wood furniture frames	(X)	10.6
Plastics resins consumed in the form of granules, pellets, etc.	(X)	94.1
Plastics laminated sheets	(X)	69.3
Plastics furniture parts and components	(X)	14.8
Paddings, battings, and fillings (exc. rubber and plastics foam)	(X)	6.9
Coated and laminated fabrics (including vinyl coated)	(X)	5.0
Other woven upholstery fabrics (rayon, nylon, etc.), exc. ticking	(X)	8.8
Flat glass (plate, float, and sheet)	(X)	17.8
Mirrors, framed and unframed	(X)	6.7
Paints, varnishes, stains, lacquers, shellacs, japans, enamels, etc.	(X)	74.7
Adhesives and sealants	(X)	10.0
Furniture and builders' hardware (incl. cabinet hardware, casters, glides, handles, hinges, locks, etc.)	(X)	69.2
Paperboard containers, boxes, and corrugated paperboard	(X)	75.6
All other materials, components, parts, containers, and supplies	(X)	660.9
Materials, ingredients, containers, and supplies, nsk	(X)	967.5

Source: 2002 *Economic Census*. Explanation of symbols used: (D): Withheld to avoid disclosure of competitive data; na: Not available; (S): Withheld because statistical norms were not met; (X): Not applicable; (Z): Less than half the unit shown; nec: Not elsewhere classified; nsk: Not specified by kind; - : zero; p : 10-19 percent estimated; q : 20-29 percent estimated.

PRODUCT SHARE DETAILS

Product or Product Class Shipments	Mil. $	Product or Product Class Shipments	Mil. $
SHOWCASES, PARTITIONS, SHELVING, AND LOCKERS . .	8,173.3	Shelving and lockers, nonwood, nsk	3.0
Wood partitions, shelving, and lockers, except custom	**198.4**	**Storage racks and accessories, nonwood**	**919.7**
Prefabricated wood partitions (assembled and knock-		Storage racks and accessories, nonwood	867.6
down), and wood shelving and lockers, except custom . .	174.6	Drive-in, drive-thru, and gravity conveyor storage racks,	
Wood partitions, prefabricated (assembled and knock-		nonwood	170.4
down), except custom	18.3	Cantilever storage racks, nonwood	23.9
Wood shelving, except custom	115.4	Portable stacking racks and frames, nonwood . . .	78.7
Wood lockers, except custom	40.8	Stacker racks, nonwood	56.2
Wood partitions, shelving, and lockers, nsk	23.8	Storage racks and accessories for trucks and vans,	
Wood bank, office, store, and related fixtures, except custom .	**1,383.7**	nonwood	145.6
Wood bank, office, store, and related fixtures, except		Other norwood storage racks and accessories, including	
custom	1,354.7	conventional pallet racks and accessories, nonwood . .	392.8
Wood retail store walls and wall fixtures, except custom . .	163.5	Storage racks and accessories, nonwood, nsk . . .	52.1
Wood retail store center floor tables and gondolas,		**Nonwood bank, office, store, and related fixtures**	**1,298.5**
except custom	86.4	Custom retail store fixtures, nonwood	500.8
Other wood retail store fixtures, including display cases,		Manufacturers' standard retail store fixtures, nonwood . . .	401.0
except custom	474.7	Other bank, office, store, and related fixtures, nonwood . . .	371.9
Other wood bank, office, store, and related table and		Other bank, office, store, and related table and display	
display fixtures, except custom	130.4	fixtures, nonwood	146.2
Wood bank, office, store, and related cabinets, except		Bank, office, store, and related cabinets, including floor	
custom, including floor and wall cabinets	176.5	and wall cabinets, nonwood	137.2
Wood office, store, and related counters, except custom . .	57.1	Other bank, office, store, and related fixtures, including	
Other wood bank, office, store, and related wood		cashier stands, nonwood	88.5
fixtures, except custom, including cashier stands and		Bank, office, store, and related fixtures, nonwood, nsk . . .	24.8
wood and plastics laminated wood stock line fixture		**Wood furniture frames**	**260.0**
tops	266.1	Wood furniture frames	258.3
Wood bank, office, store, and related fixtures, except		Wood furniture frames for household seating furniture . .	220.0
custom, nsk	29.0	Other wood furniture frames	38.2
Prefabricated partitions, assembled and knock-down,		Wood furniture frames, nsk	1.8
nonwood	**243.1**	**Hardwood and softwood furniture dimension fully machined**	
Prefabricated partitions, assembled and knock-down,		**ready for assembly**	**1,013.7**
nonwood.	215.7	Hardwood furniture dimension fully machined ready for	
Toilet partitions, nonwood	110.0	assembly, for cabinets	304.5
Movable partitions, except freestanding, nonwood . . .	84.6	Hardwood furniture dimension fully machined ready for	
Other partitions (excluding accordion and folding-door		assembly, not for cabinets	100.8
type), nonwood	21.1	Softwood fully machined furniture dimension	9.4
Partitions, prefabricated (assembled or knock-down),		Finished plastics furniture parts, including plastics	
nonwood, nsk	27.4	furniture frames	304.3
Shelving and lockers, nonwood	**1,124.7**	Other metal furniture parts for household furniture	
Commercial shelving (factory, store, etc.), nonwood . .	680.8	(household furniture frames, box spring frames, and	
Bookstacks, other shelving, and lockers, nonwood . . .	440.9	sleeper mechanisms), except metal furniture hardware . .	168.6
Bookstacks (library, office, and school), nonwood . . .	3.9	Other metal furniture parts, nec, except metal furniture	
Other shelving, including shelving for correspondence,		hardware	126.0
computer tapes and disks, microfilm, etc., nonwood . .	106.5	**Showcases, partitions, shelving, and lockers, nsk, total** . . .	**1,731.5**
Lockers, nonwood	330.6		

Source: 2002 *Economic Census*. The values are product shipments in millions of dollars for 2002. Total product shipments may be lower or higher than industry shipments. See Introduction for a full discussion. Values of indented subcategories are summed in the main heading(s). The symbol (D) appears when data are withheld to prevent disclosure of competitive information. The abbreviation nsk stands for 'not specified by kind' and nec for 'not elsewhere classified'. A dash (-) means zero.

INPUTS AND OUTPUTS FOR SHOWCASE, PARTITION, SHELVING, AND LOCKER MANUFACTURING

Economic Sector or Industry Providing Inputs	%	Sector	Economic Sector or Industry Buying Outputs	%	Sector
Compensation of employees	32.8		Private fixed investment	54.0	
Iron & steel mills & ferroalloys	11.2	Manufg.	Commercial & health care structures	8.0	Construct.
Wholesale trade	5.0	Trade	Personal consumption expenditures	5.4	
Reconstituted wood products	3.1	Manufg.	Exports of goods & services	4.0	Cap Inv
Management of companies & enterprises	2.7	Services	Upholstered household furniture	3.5	Manufg.
Sawmills & wood preservation	2.5	Manufg.	Wood kitchen cabinets & countertops	3.5	Manufg.
Paints & coatings	2.2	Manufg.	Retail trade	3.2	Trade
Veneer & plywood	1.9	Manufg.	S/L govt. invest., education	3.0	S/L Govt
Showcases, partitions, shelving, and lockers	1.9	Manufg.	Wholesale trade	1.7	Trade
Real estate	1.5	Fin/R.E.	Showcases, partitions, shelving, and lockers	1.5	Manufg.
Plastics materials & resins	1.5	Manufg.	Independent artists, writers, & performers	1.4	Services
Truck transportation	1.5	Util.	Institutional furniture	1.2	Manufg.
Paperboard containers	1.3	Manufg.	Nonupholstered wood household furniture	1.2	Manufg.
Securities, commodity contracts, investments	1.2	Fin/R.E.	Custom architectural woodwork & millwork	1.1	Manufg.
Aluminum products from purchased aluminum	1.2	Manufg.	Hospitals	0.9	Services
Textile & fabric finishing mills	1.1	Manufg.	S/L govt. invest., other	0.8	S/L Govt
Advertising & related services	1.1	Services	Nonresidential structures, nec	0.8	Construct.
Power generation & supply	1.0	Util.	Amusement & recreation, nec	0.7	Services
Laminated plastics plates, sheets, & shapes	0.9	Manufg.	Signs	0.7	Manufg.
Plastics products, nec	0.9	Manufg.	Personal & household goods repair/maintenance	0.4	Services
Monetary authorities/depository credit intermediation	0.8	Fin/R.E.	Medical & diagnostic labs & outpatient services	0.3	Services
Crowns & closures & metal stamping	0.7	Manufg.	Other S/L govt. enterprises	0.3	S/L Govt
Semiconductors & related devices	0.7	Manufg.	Residential permanent site structures	0.3	Construct.
Professional, scientific, technical services, nec	0.6	Services	Metal & other household furniture	0.2	Manufg.
Printed circuit assemblies (electronic assemblies)	0.6	Manufg.	Specialized design services	0.2	Services

Continued on next page.

INPUTS AND OUTPUTS FOR SHOWCASE, PARTITION, SHELVING, AND LOCKER MANUFACTURING - Continued

Economic Sector or Industry Providing Inputs	%	Sector	Economic Sector or Industry Buying Outputs	%	Sector
Retail trade	0.6	Trade	Change in private inventories	0.2	In House
Machine shops	0.5	Manufg.	Scientific research & development services	0.2	Services
Accounting, tax preparation, bookkeeping, & payroll	0.5	Services	Turned products & screws, nuts, & bolts	0.2	Manufg.
Food services & drinking places	0.5	Services	Federal government, investment, nondefense	0.1	Fed Govt
Data processing, hosting, & related services	0.5	Services	Motor vehicle parts	0.1	Manufg.
Taxes on production & imports, less subsidies	0.5		Manufacturing structures	0.1	Construct.
Legal services	0.4	Services	Management, scientific, & technical consulting	0.1	Services
Rail transportation	0.4	Util.			
Telecommunications	0.4	Services			
Natural gas distribution	0.4	Util.			
Hardware	0.4	Manufg.			
Automotive equipment rental & leasing	0.4	Fin/R.E.			
Coating, engraving, heat treating & allied activities	0.4	Manufg.			
Architectural, engineering, & related services	0.3	Services			
Hotels & motels, including casino hotels	0.3	Services			
Warehousing & storage	0.3	Util.			
Services to buildings & dwellings	0.3	Services			
Maintenance/repair of nonresidential structures	0.3	Construct.			
Nondepository credit intermediation activities	0.3	Fin/R.E.			
Air transportation	0.3	Util.			
Flat glass	0.3	Manufg.			
Ornamental & architectural metal products	0.2	Manufg.			
Other computer related services, including facilities	0.2	Services			
Abrasive products	0.2	Manufg.			
Commercial & industrial machinery rental & leasing	0.2	Fin/R.E.			
Scientific research & development services	0.2	Services			
Management, scientific, & technical consulting	0.2	Services			
Alumina refining & primary aluminum production	0.2	Manufg.			
Automotive repair & maintenance, ex. car washes	0.2	Services			
Turned products & screws, nuts, & bolts	0.2	Manufg.			
Adhesives	0.2	Manufg.			
Commercial & industrial equipment repair/maintenance	0.2	Services			
Motor vehicle parts	0.2	Manufg.			
Miscellaneous wood products	0.2	Manufg.			
Business support services	0.2	Services			
Metal cans, boxes, & other containers (light gauge)	0.1	Manufg.			
Waste management & remediation services	0.1	Services			
Glass products from purchased glass	0.1	Manufg.			
Fabricated metals, nec	0.1	Manufg.			
Textile product mills, nec	0.1	Manufg.			
Noncomparable imports	0.1	Foreign			

Source: Benchmark Input-Output Accounts for the U.S. Economy, 2002, U.S. Department of Commerce, Washington, D.C., January 2008. The abbreviation nec stands for 'not elsewhere classified'.

OCCUPATIONS EMPLOYED BY OFFICE FURNITURE (INCLUDING FIXTURES) MANUFACTURING

Occupation	% of Total 2006	Change to 2016	Occupation	% of Total 2006	Change to 2016
Cabinetmakers & bench carpenters	11.1	-6.0	General & operations managers	1.7	-15.4
Team assemblers	9.5	-6.0	Industrial truck & tractor operators	1.6	-15.4
Woodworking machine operators & tenders, exc sawing	5.0	3.4	Sawing machine setters, operators, & tenders, wood	1.6	3.4
First-line supervisors/managers of production workers	4.0	-6.0	Packers & packagers, hand	1.6	-24.8
Cutting, punching, & press machine operators	3.2	-15.4	Shipping, receiving, & traffic clerks	1.6	-9.5
Laborers & freight, stock, & material movers, hand	3.0	-15.4	Multiple machine tool operators & tenders	1.3	3.4
Welders, cutters, solderers, & brazers	2.8		Office clerks, general	1.3	-7.4
Furniture finishers	2.7	-6.0	Customer service representatives	1.3	3.4
Helpers--Production workers	2.5	-6.0	Bookkeeping, accounting, & auditing clerks	1.1	-6.0
Assemblers & fabricators, nec	2.5	-15.4	Industrial engineers	1.1	14.2
Sales reps, wholesale & manufacturing, exc tech	2.4	-6.0	Maintenance & repair workers, general	1.1	-6.0
Carpenters	2.2	-6.0	Molding, coremaking, & casting machine operators	1.1	-15.4
Coating, painting, & spraying machine operators	1.8	-10.7			

Source: Industry-Occupation Matrix, Bureau of Labor Statistics, December 4, 2007. These data are reported based on 4-digit NAICS categories but have been matched to corresponding 6-digit NAICS industry codes. The change reported for each occupation to the year 2016 is a percent of growth or decline as estimated by the Bureau of Labor Statistics. The abbreviation nec stands for 'not elsewhere classified'.

LOCATION BY STATE AND REGIONAL CONCENTRATION

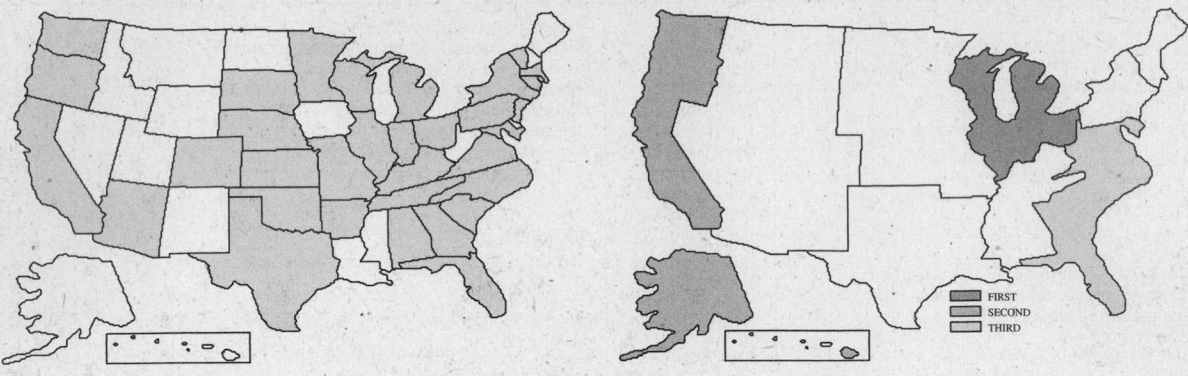

INDUSTRY DATA BY STATE

| State | Establish-ments | Shipments | | | Employment | | | | Cost as % of Shipments | Investment per Employee ($) |
		Total ($ mil)	% of U.S.	Per Establ.	Total Number	% of U.S.	Per Establ.	Wages ($/hour)		
Illinois	98	975.7	11.3	9,956.6	6,700	9.4	68	13.05	45.9	1,772
California	263	910.8	10.6	3,463.0	6,914	9.7	26	13.25	45.2	1,749
Michigan	92	519.6	6.0	5,647.5	4,151	5.8	45	15.79	49.1	3,248
Indiana	50	496.5	5.8	9,929.1	3,668	5.2	73	12.12	55.0	2,594
New York	137	455.1	5.3	3,322.1	3,770	5.3	28	14.28	42.8	1,748
Texas	85	420.1	4.9	4,941.8	3,252	4.6	38	13.08	49.5	5,329
Pennsylvania	83	410.6	4.8	4,946.6	3,216	4.5	39	13.64	41.9	2,727
Ohio	90	363.0	4.2	4,033.3	3,123	4.4	35	14.93	44.1	2,508
North Carolina	159	354.4	4.1	2,228.8	3,800	5.4	24	11.49	38.3	4,304
Georgia	59	340.6	3.9	5,773.1	2,780	3.9	47	11.97	48.3	5,389
Tennessee	32	329.4	3.8	10,292.9	2,578	3.6	81	11.60	48.4	3,331
Minnesota	59	273.7	3.2	4,638.3	2,335	3.3	40	17.30	41.2	2,910
Alabama	21	245.9	2.8	11,709.3	1,831	2.6	87	11.77	37.8	3,481
Nebraska	9	243.7	2.8	27,076.7	1,114	1.6	124	15.83	33.3	3,228
Wisconsin	49	203.0	2.4	4,143.1	1,721	2.4	35	14.36	43.8	2,485
Missouri	35	173.0	2.0	4,944.0	2,053	2.9	59	11.49	50.3	2,021
Colorado	23	161.9	1.9	7,037.8	1,237	1.7	54	14.08	36.0	2,890
Arkansas	14	161.2	1.9	11,512.9	1,537	2.2	110	11.91	56.6	4,031
New Jersey	57	155.2	1.8	2,722.8	1,656	2.3	29	12.26	46.6	1,705
Florida	66	153.2	1.8	2,321.1	1,730	2.4	26	12.76	44.4	1,975
Kentucky	22	147.6	1.7	6,709.5	1,359	1.9	62	12.33	48.2	4,706
Washington	40	130.7	1.5	3,268.6	956	1.3	24	16.47	45.8	5,157
South Carolina	11	76.3	0.9	6,934.3	607	0.9	55	12.17	61.5	2,517
Virginia	21	72.7	0.8	3,461.9	718	1.0	34	11.12	39.2	1,359
Massachusetts	28	66.4	0.8	2,371.3	535	0.8	19	15.32	46.9	2,222
Kansas	13	65.3	0.8	5,025.0	643	0.9	49	13.01	36.1	1,044
Connecticut	27	61.7	0.7	2,285.5	471	0.7	17	15.50	40.6	2,123
Oklahoma	15	58.2	0.7	3,876.7	551	0.8	37	11.18	33.2	2,479
Maryland	21	56.6	0.7	2,693.9	484	0.7	23	15.50	43.3	1,709
Oregon	39	53.7	0.6	1,376.3	556	0.8	14	12.88	34.2	1,320
Rhode Island	19	50.1	0.6	2,634.3	554	0.8	29	10.98	38.5	982
Arizona	22	33.6	0.4	1,525.9	373	0.5	17	16.59	42.4	1,169
South Dakota	8	22.2	0.3	2,779.5	200	0.3	25	12.26	56.8	4,220
Vermont	6	18.6	0.2	3,096.3	181	0.3	30	11.14	35.4	1,343

Source: 2002 *Economic Census*. The states are in descending order of shipments or establishments (if shipment data are missing for the majority). The symbol (D) appears when data are withheld to prevent disclosure of competitive information. States marked with (D) are sorted by number of establishments. A dash (-) indicates that the data element cannot be calculated. Data may not show all states active in the NAICS category. All data available at the time of publication are shown.

NAICS 33721N - OFFICE FURNITURE MANUFACTURING*

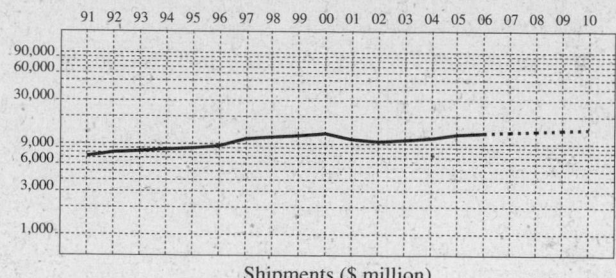

Shipments ($ million)

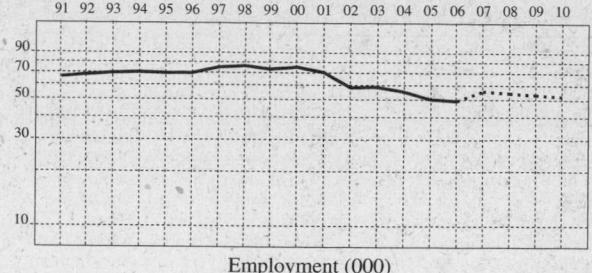

Employment (000)

GENERAL STATISTICS

Year	Companies	Establishments Total	Establishments with 20 or more employees	Employment Total (000)	Employment Production Workers (000)	Employment Hours (Mil)	Compensation Payroll ($ mil)	Compensation Wages ($/hr)	Production Cost of Materials	Production Value Added by Manufacture	Production Value of Shipments	Production Capital Invest.
1991		893	408	66.1	47.8	96.9	1,761.3	10.91	3,083.3	4,128.3	7,262.9	172.6
1992	938	1,021	414	67.9	50.4	108.4	1,866.8	10.83	3,359.4	4,634.0	8,007.7	201.5
1993		1,011	421	69.5	52.2	111.3	1,950.6	11.19	3,508.2	4,751.6	8,265.1	234.8
1994		974	419	70.2	53.3	114.5	2,021.6	11.16	3,652.8	5,040.5	8,663.1	243.4
1995		972	430	69.5	53.7	112.4	2,062.7	11.70	3,732.9	5,201.2	8,943.4	303.1
1996		1,025	434	69.5	53.3	114.6	2,172.4	11.86	4,011.4	5,447.1	9,443.8	358.3
1997	941	1,034	439	74.8	57.0	119.6	2,401.9	12.70	4,582.4	6,729.1	11,339.4	431.5
1998		1,020	438	76.3	59.4	117.4	2,513.4	13.36	4,605.5	7,308.4	11,900.3	525.0
1999		982	439	73.2	55.6	113.1	2,549.3	13.98	4,787.4	7,599.3	12,309.3	486.3
2000		925	421	75.2	57.7	118.8	2,656.4	14.01	4,904.5	8,141.4	12,998.3	490.6
2001		920	425	70.3	52.3	107.9	2,548.7	14.22	4,309.0	6,958.5	11,229.3	314.7
2002	807	882	352	58.2	43.6	85.8	2,079.6	14.54	4,083.1	6,528.2	10,608.3	236.8
2003		838	330	58.6	40.2	79.4	2,072.5	15.10	4,122.4	6,913.0	11,023.5	166.2
2004		823	320	55.4	37.9	78.2	2,080.0	15.42	4,304.5	7,211.6	11,520.5	132.0
2005		794	313	50.2	36.3	75.8	1,977.7	15.84	4,875.6	7,788.7	12,660.1	212.9
2006		840P	343P	49.2	36.5	77.1	2,014.5	16.57	5,157.5	8,017.1	13,161.4	202.6
2007		828P	336P	55.6P	40.4P	81.6P	2,294.6P	16.69P	5,283.6P	8,213.2P	13,483.3P	272.4P
2008		815P	329P	54.4P	39.3P	79.2P	2,309.2P	17.08P	5,417.3P	8,421.0P	13,824.4P	269.8P
2009		803P	322P	53.2P	38.3P	76.8P	2,323.8P	17.48P	5,551.0P	8,628.8P	14,165.6P	267.2P
2010		790P	315P	52.0P	37.3P	74.4P	2,338.4P	17.87P	5,684.7P	8,836.6P	14,506.7P	264.6P

Sources: 1992, 1997, 2002 *Economic Census*; other years, up to 2006, are from the *Annual Survey of Manufactures*. Establishment counts for non-Census years are from *County Business Patterns*; 1997 and 2002 values are from the 1997 and 2002 censuses respectively, reported in the Federal Government's NAICS format. Other years were originally reported in equivalent SIC format. 'P's show projections by the editors.

INDICES OF CHANGE

Year	Companies	Establishments Total	Establishments with 20 or more employees	Employment Total (000)	Employment Production Workers (000)	Employment Hours (Mil)	Compensation Payroll ($ mil)	Compensation Wages ($/hr)	Production Cost of Materials	Production Value Added by Manufacture	Production Value of Shipments	Production Capital Invest.
1992	116	116	118	117	116	126	90	74	82	71	75	85
1997	117	117	125	129	131	139	115	87	112	103	107	182
2001		104	121	121	120	126	123	98	106	107	106	133
2002	100	100	100	100	100	100	100	100	100	100	100	100
2003		95	94	101	92	93	100	104	101	106	104	70
2004		93	91	95	87	91	100	106	105	110	109	56
2005		90	89	86	83	88	95	109	119	119	119	90
2006		95P	98P	85	84	90	97	114	126	123	124	86
2007		94P	95P	96P	93P	95P	110P	115P	129P	126P	127P	115P
2008		92P	93P	93P	90P	92P	111P	117P	133P	129P	130P	114P
2009		91P	91P	91P	88P	90P	112P	120P	136P	132P	134P	113P
2010		90P	89P	89P	86P	87P	112P	123P	139P	135P	137P	112P

Sources: Same as General Statistics. Values reflect change from the base year, 2002. Values above 100 mean greater than 2002, values below 100 mean less than 2002, and the values of 100 in other years means the same as 2002. 'P's show projections by the editors.

SELECTED RATIOS

For 2002	Avg. of All Manufact.	Analyzed Industry	Index	For 2002	Avg. of All Manufact.	Analyzed Industry	Index
Employees per Establishment	42	66	157	Value Added per Production Worker	182,367	149,729	82
Payroll per Establishment	1,639,184	2,357,823	144	Cost per Establishment	5,769,015	4,629,365	80
Payroll per Employee	39,053	35,732	91	Cost per Employee	137,446	70,156	51
Production Workers per Establishment	30	49	168	Cost per Production Worker	195,506	93,649	48
Wages per Establishment	694,845	1,414,435	204	Shipments per Establishment	11,158,348	12,027,551	108
Wages per Production Worker	23,548	28,613	122	Shipments per Employee	265,847	182,273	69
Hours per Production Worker	1,980	1,968	99	Shipments per Production Worker	378,144	243,310	64
Wages per Hour	11.89	14.54	122	Investment per Establishment	361,338	268,481	74
Value Added per Establishment	5,381,325	7,401,587	138	Investment per Employee	8,609	4,069	47
Value Added per Employee	128,210	112,168	87	Investment per Production Worker	12,245	5,431	44

Sources: Same as General Statistics. The 'Average of All Manufacturing' column represents the average of all manufacturing industries reported for the most recent complete year available. The Index shows the relationship between the Average and the Analyzed Industry. For example, 100 means that they are equal; 500 that the Analyzed Industry is five times the average; 50 means that the Analyzed Industry is half the national average. The abbreviation 'na' is used to show that data are 'not available'. Ratios shown for 2002, the last complete census year.

*Equivalent to Federal Government NAICS 337211, 337214.

LEADING COMPANIES   Number shown: 75   Total sales ($ mil): 26,834   Total employment (000): 157.2

Company Name	Address				CEO Name	Phone	Co. Type	Sales ($ mil)	Empl. (000)
Steelcase Inc.	PO Box 1967	Grand Rapids	MI	49501	James P. Hackett	616-247-2710	P	3,097	13.0
HNI Corp.	PO Box 1109	Muscatine	IA	52761	Timothy Anderson	563-264-7400	P	2,571	14.2
Hillenbrand Industries Inc.	1069 State Rte 46E	Batesville	IN	47006		812-934-7000	P	2,024	9.9
Herman Miller Inc.	PO Box 302	Zeeland	MI	49464		616-654-3000	P	1,919	6.4
HON Co.	PO Box 1109	Muscatine	IA	52761	Eric Jungbluth	563-264-7100	S	1,789*	9.8
La-Z-Boy Inc.	PO Box 2390	Monroe	MI	48161	K.L. Darrow	734-242-1444	P	1,617	11.7
Aaron Rents Inc.	309 E Paces Ferry	Atlanta	GA	30305	R. C. Loudermilk Sr.	404-231-0011	P	1,495	9.6
EBSCO Industries Inc.	PO Box 1943	Birmingham	AL	35201	Dixon Brooke Jr.	205-991-6600	R	1,400*	5.0
Kimball International Inc.	1600 Royal St.	Jasper	IN	47549		812-482-1600	P	1,287	7.6
Haworth Inc.	1 Haworth Ctr.	Holland	MI	49423	Franco Bianchi	616-393-3000	R	1,120*	8.0
Knoll Inc.	1235 Water St.	East Greenville	PA	18041	Andrew B. Cogan	215-679-7991	P	1,056	4.3
Ashley Furniture Industries	1 Ashley Way	Arcadia	WI	54612	Ronald G. Wanek	608-323-3377	R	761*	4.0
Krueger International Inc.	PO Box 8100	Green Bay	WI	54308	Richard J. Resch	920-468-8100	R	600*	4.0
UNICOR	320 1st St. NW	Washington	DC	20534	Steve Schwalb	202-305-3500	R	567*	21.0
Smead Manufacturing Co.	600 Smead Blvd.	Hastings	MN	55033	S Hoffman Avent	651-437-4111	R	550	2.6
Sauder Woodworking Co.	PO Box 156	Archbold	OH	43502	Kevin Sauder	419-446-2711	R	525*	3.0
Hooker Furniture Corp.	PO Box 4708	Martinsville	VA	24115		276-632-0459	P	350	1.1
Edsal Manufacturing Company	4400 S Packers Ave.	Chicago	IL	60609	Bruce Saltzberg	773-254-0600	R	300*	1.2
JSJ Corp.	700 Robbins Rd.	Grand Haven	MI	49417	Martin Johnson	616-842-6350	R	295*	<0.1
Carolina Mills Inc.	PO Box 157	Maiden	NC	28650	S. G. Dobbins Jr.	828-428-9911	R	206*	1.2
Shelby Williams Industries	150 S Williams	Morristown	TN	37813	Franklin Jacobs	423-586-7000	S	166*	1.7
Chromcraft Revington Inc.	1330 Win Hentschel	West Lafayette	IN	47906	B. M. Anderson-Ray	765-807-2640	P	160	0.9
Canyon Creek Cabinet Co.	16726 Tye St. SE	Monroe	WA	98272	Bill Weaver	206-674-0800	R	155*	0.4
PolyVision Corp.	3970 Johns Creek Ct	Suwanee	GA	30024	Michael H. Dunn	678-542-3100	S	153*	1.1
Allsteel Inc.	2210 2nd Ave.	Muscatine	IA	52761	Stan A. Askren	563-262-4800	S	149*	1.4
Ivan Allen Furniture Co.	730 Peachtree St.	Atlanta	GA	30308	H. Inman Allen	404-760-8700	R	144*	0.8
Bernhardt Furniture Company	PO Box 740	Lenoir	NC	28645	Alexander Bernhardt	828-758-9811	R	123*	0.2
TAB Products Co.	605 Fourth St.	Mayville	WI	53050	Bill Graham	920-387-3131	R	115*	0.8
Fire King International L.L.C.	PO Box 559	New Albany	IN	47151		812-948-8400	R	100*	0.4
Global Industrial Equipment	11 Harbor Park Dr.	Port Washington	NY	11050	Richard Leeds	516-625-6200	S	93*	0.3
Ofs Brands Holdings Inc.	PO Box 100	Huntingburg	IN	47542	Joseph Bellino	812-683-4848	R	83*	0.1
Paoli Inc.	PO Box 30	Paoli	IN	47454	Thomas A. Tolone	812-865-1525	S	82*	0.7
Lyon Workspace Products L.L.C.	PO Box 671	Aurora	IL	60507		630-892-8941	R	76*	0.6
Eagle Manufacturing Inc.	2400 Charles St.	Wellsburg	WV	26070	James Paull	304-737-3171	R	73*	0.2
Tennsco Corp.	PO Box 1888	Dickson	TN	37056	Stuart Speyer	615-446-8000	R	71*	0.6
Goebel Fixture Co.	528 S Dale St.	Hutchinson	MN	55350		320-587-2112	R	69*	0.2
Hekman Furniture Co.	1400 Buchanan SW	Grand Rapids	MI	49507	Jack Miller	616-452-1411	S	62*	0.3
Bretford Manufacturing Inc.	11000 Seymour Ave.	Schiller Park	IL	60131	Mikel Briggs	847-678-2545	R	61*	0.6
Mity Enterprises Inc.	1301 W 400 N	Orem	UT	84057	Randall Hales	801-224-0589	P	60	0.4
Herman Miller Greenhouse	10201 Adams St.	Holland	MI	49424	Michael Volkema	616-654-3000	S	60*	0.6
AC Furniture Company Inc.	PO Box 200	Axton	VA	24054		276-650-3356	R	57*	0.1
Hirsh Industries Inc.	11229 Aurora Ave.	Des Moines	IA	50322	Douglas Smith	515-299-3200	R	57*	<0.1
John D Brush Company Inc.	900 Linden Ave.	Rochester	NY	14625	Douglas Brush	585-381-4900	R	50*	0.4
Schwab Corp.	PO Box 5088	Lafayette	IN	47903	Donald Ehrlich	765-447-9470	R	50*	<0.1
Tesco Industries Inc.	1035 E Hacienda	Bellville	TX	77418			R	49*	0.1
La Barge Inc.	2427 Penny Rd.	High Point	NC	27265	Jeff Young	336-812-2400	R	47*	0.1
American Seating Co.	401 Americn Seating	Grand Rapids	MI	49504	Edward Clark	616-732-6600	R	45*	0.4
Borroughs Corp.	3002 N Burdick St.	Kalamazoo	MI	49004	Tim Tyler	269-342-0161	R	45*	0.3
Marco Display Specialists, GP	PO Box 123439	Fort Worth	TX	76121	Darrell Cooper	817-244-8300	R	44*	0.3
Norstar Office Products Inc.	5353 Jillson St.	Commerce	CA	90040	Willaim Huang	323-262-1919	R	39*	<0.1
Maxon Furniture Inc.	660 SW 39th St.	Renton	WA	98057	Jean Reynolds	253-395-4457	S	38*	0.2
Adair Office Furniture Centers	14941 E Northam St.	La Mirada	CA	91324		562-926-6642	R	38*	<0.1
GF Office Furniture Limited	525 Steam Plant Rd.	Gallatin	TN	37066		615-452-9120	R	36*	0.3
Harden Furniture Company Inc.	8550 Mill Pond Way	Mc Connellsvlle	NY	13401	Gregory Harden	315-245-1000	R	35*	0.5
Jasper Seating Company Inc.	PO Box 231	Jasper	IN	47547	Michael Elliott	812-482-3204	R	35*	<0.1
MII Inc.	2100 5th St.	Lincoln	IL	62656	Ronald McComas	217-735-1241	R	35*	0.2
Suburban Surgical Co.	275 12th St., A	Wheeling	IL	60090	James Pinkerman	847-537-9320	R	34*	0.2
Richards-Wilcox Inc.	600 S Lake St.	Aurora	IL	60506	Manfred Haiderer	630-897-6951	R	34*	0.3
Stylex Inc.	PO Box 5038	Riverside	NJ	08075	John Golden	856-461-5600	R	34*	0.2
Balt Inc.	2885 Lorraine Ave.	Temple	TX	76501	Lorraine Moore	254-778-4727	R	33*	0.1
Aspen Furniture L.L.C.	2929 NW Grand	Phoenix	AZ	85017	Richard McMillan	602-233-0224	R	30*	0.3
Arte De Mexico Inc.	1000 Chestnut St.	Burbank	CA	91506	Gerald Stoffers	818-753-4559	R	30*	<0.1
Scott Rice Co.	7501 N Broadway	Oklahoma City	OK	73116	James Hackett	405-848-2224	S	30*	<0.1
Durham Manufacturing Co.	PO Box 230	Durham	CT	06422		860-349-3427	R	30*	0.2
Child Craft Industries Inc.	1010 Keller Dr. NE	New Salisbury	IN	47161	William Suvak	812-206-2200	R	29*	0.3
Trendway Corp.	PO Box 9016	Holland	MI	49422	Mark Groulx	616-399-3900	R	29*	0.3
Henkel-Harris Company Inc.	PO Box 2170	Winchester	VA	22604	William Henkel	540-667-4900	R	29*	0.3
Office Star Products	PO Box 3520	Ontario	CA	91761	Rick Blumenthal	909-930-2000	R	28*	0.1
Michigan Tube Swagers/Fabric.	7100 Industrial Dr.	Temperance	MI	48182	Paul Swy	734-847-3875	R	28*	0.3
Hickory Business Furniture	PO Box 8	Hickory	NC	28603	Kevin Stark	828-328-2064	S	26*	0.3
Jofco Inc.	PO Box 71	Jasper	IN	47547	Bill Rubino	812-482-5154	R	26	0.3
Ergotron Inc.	1181 Trapp Rd.	Eagan	MN	55121	Joel Hazzard	651-681-7600	R	26*	0.2
Correctional Ind. Georgia Adm.	2984 Clifton Sprngs	Decatur	GA	30034		404-244-5100	R	26*	<0.1
Classic Leather Inc.	PO Box 2404	Hickory	NC	28603	Thomas Shores	828-328-2046	R	26*	0.4
Woodharbor Doors and Cabinetry	3277 9th St. SW	Mason City	IA	50401	Curtis Lewerke	641-423-0444	R	25*	0.5

Source: Ward's Business Directory of U.S. Private and Public Companies, Volumes 1 and 2, 2008. The company type code used is as follows: P - Public, R - Private, S - Subsidiary, D - Division, J - Joint Venture, A - Affiliate, G - Group. Sales are in millions of dollars, employees are in thousands. An asterisk (*) indicates an estimated sales volume. The symbol < stands for 'less than'. Company names and addresses are truncated, in some cases, to fit into the available space.

MATERIALS CONSUMED FOR WOOD OFFICE FURNITURE MANUFACTURING

Material	Quantity	Delivered Cost ($ million)
Metal stampings	(X)	8.3
Other fabricated metal products (including forgings)	(X)	9.7
Castings, rough and semifinished	(X)	3.5
Steel sheet and strip (including tinplate)	(X)	7.9
All other steel shapes and forms (exc. castings, forgings, fabr. metal products)	(X)	9.4
Aluminum and aluminum-base alloy sheet, plate, foil, and welded tubing	(X)	2.1
Hardwood lumber, rough and dressed	(X)	55.0
Softwood lumber, rough and dressed	(X)	6.2
Hardwood cut stock and dimension (excluding furniture frames)	(X)	48.1
Softwood plywood	(X)	2.7
Hardwood plywood	(X)	56.6
Hardwood veneer	(X)	49.5
Particleboard (reconstituted wood)	(X)	63.6
Medium density fiberboard (MDF)	(X)	8.4
Hardboard	(X)	4.3
Wood furniture frames	(X)	14.1
Plastics resins consumed in the form of granules, pellets, etc.	(X)	4.6
Plastics laminated sheets	(X)	61.1
Plastics furniture parts and components	(X)	6.5
Formed and slab stock for pillows, cushions, seating, etc. (urethane)	(X)	9.1
Paddings, battings, and fillings (exc. rubber and plastics foam)	(X)	5.8
Coated and laminated fabrics (including vinyl coated)	(X)	10.5
Woven cotton upholstery fabrics (excluding ticking)	(X)	10.3
Other woven upholstery fabrics (rayon, nylon, etc.), exc. ticking	(X)	31.2
Flat glass (plate, float, and sheet)	(X)	8.0
Paints, varnishes, stains, lacquers, shellacs, japans, enamels, etc.	(X)	60.6
Adhesives and sealants	(X)	4.5
Furniture and builders' hardware (incl. cabinet hardware, casters, glides, handles, hinges, locks, etc.)	(X)	125.3
Paperboard containers, boxes, and corrugated paperboard	(X)	40.5
All other materials, components, parts, containers, and supplies	(X)	77.8
Materials, ingredients, containers, and supplies, nsk	(X)	194.6

Source: 2002 *Economic Census*. Explanation of symbols used: (D): Withheld to avoid disclosure of competitive data; na: Not available; (S): Withheld because statistical norms were not met; (X): Not applicable; (Z): Less than half the unit shown; nec: Not elsewhere classified; nsk: Not specified by kind; - : zero; p : 10-19 percent estimated; q : 20-29 percent estimated.

MATERIALS CONSUMED FOR OFFICE FURNITURE (EXCEPT WOOD) MANUFACTURING

Material	Quantity	Delivered Cost ($ million)
Metal stampings	(X)	99.0
Other fabricated metal products (including forgings)	(X)	107.9
Castings, rough and semifinished	(X)	12.3
Steel sheet and strip (including tinplate)	(X)	340.8
All other steel shapes and forms (exc. castings, forgings, fabr. metal products)	(X)	61.9
Aluminum and aluminum-base alloy sheet, plate, foil, and welded tubing	(X)	18.8
All other aluminum and aluminum-base alloy shapes and forms (exc. castings, forgings, fabr. metal products)	(X)	43.0
Hardwood lumber, rough and dressed	(X)	7.3
Softwood lumber, rough and dressed	(X)	(D)
Hardwood cut stock and dimension (excluding furniture frames)	(X)	17.8
Hardwood plywood	(X)	12.1
Hardwood veneer	(X)	(D)
Particleboard (reconstituted wood)	(X)	62.1
Medium density fiberboard (MDF)	(X)	5.3
Hardboard	(X)	(D)
Wood furniture frames	(X)	(D)
Plastics laminated sheets	(X)	66.9
Plastics furniture parts and components	(X)	268.5
Formed and slab stock for pillows, cushions, seating, etc. (urethane)	(X)	23.4
Paddings, battings, and fillings (exc. rubber and plastics foam)	(X)	20.0
Coated and laminated fabrics (including vinyl coated)	(X)	(D)
Woven cotton upholstery fabrics (excluding ticking)	(X)	19.8
Other woven upholstery fabrics (rayon, nylon, etc.), exc. ticking	(X)	70.5
Paints, varnishes, stains, lacquers, shellacs, japans, enamels, etc.	(X)	69.5
Adhesives and sealants	(X)	10.6
Furniture and builders' hardware (incl. cabinet hardware, casters, glides, handles, hinges, locks, etc.)	(X)	220.3
Paperboard containers, boxes, and corrugated paperboard	(X)	90.5
All other materials, components, parts, containers, and supplies	(X)	412.2
Materials, ingredients, containers, and supplies, nsk	(X)	359.8

Source: 2002 *Economic Census*. Explanation of symbols used: (D): Withheld to avoid disclosure of competitive data; na: Not available; (S): Withheld because statistical norms were not met; (X): Not applicable; (Z): Less than half the unit shown; nec: Not elsewhere classified; nsk: Not specified by kind; - : zero; p : 10-19 percent estimated; q : 20-29 percent estimated.

PRODUCT SHARE DETAILS FOR WOOD OFFICE FURNITURE MANUFACTURING

Product or Product Class Shipments	Mil. $	Product or Product Class Shipments	Mil. $
WOOD OFFICE FURNITURE	2,860.5	credenzas and files	120.1
Wood office seating, including upholstered	**566.8**	Wood office files, vertical, horizontal, and other, and	
Wood office seating, including upholstered	564.8	wood office tables	348.5
Wood office seating, including upholstered, task and		Wood office files, vertical, letter and legal	44.4
general office chairs	266.9	Wood office files, horizontal-lateral, letter and legal	50.3
Wood office seating, including upholstered, side and		Wood office work and conference tables	190.2
arm chairs	140.1	Other wood office files and tables, including wood	
Wood office seating, including upholstered, lounge		equipment support tables	63.6
seating	97.5	Wood office storage units, files, and tables, nsk	3.3
Other wood office seating, including stacking chairs and		**Wood office panel and desking systems furniture, and all**	
other upholstered chairs	60.2	**other wood office furniture, nec**	**744.3**
Wood office seating, including upholstered, nsk	2.0	Wood panel and desking systems and accessories	741.4
Wood office desks and extensions	**614.1**	Wood office furniture panel systems, including	
Wood office desks and extensions	606.2	accessories and components	319.7
Wood office desks	542.6	Wood office furniture desking systems, including	
Wood office desk extensions	63.6	accessories and components	159.1
Wood office desks and extensions, nsk	7.9	All other wood office furniture, nec	262.7
Wood office storage units, files, and tables	**660.8**	Wood office panel and desking systems and all other	
Wood office credenzas	188.9	wood furniture, nec, nsk	2.8
Wood office bookcases and other storage units, except		**Wood office furniture, nsk, total**	**274.4**

Source: 2002 *Economic Census*. The values are product shipments in millions of dollars for 2002. Total product shipments may be lower or higher than industry shipments. See Introduction for a full discussion. Values of indented subcategories are summed in the main heading(s). The symbol (D) appears when data are withheld to prevent disclosure of competitive information. The abbreviation nsk stands for 'not specified by kind' and nec for 'not elsewhere classified'. A dash (-) means zero.

PRODUCT SHARE DETAILS FOR OFFICE FURNITURE (EXCEPT WOOD) MANUFACTURING

Product or Product Class Shipments	Mil. $	Product or Product Class Shipments	Mil. $
OFFICE FURNITURE, EXCEPT WOOD	7,170.5	Office files, horizontal-lateral, letter and legal, nonwood	786.4
Office seating, including upholstered, nonwood	**2,156.9**	All other office files, nonwood	363.4
Office seating, including upholstered, nonwood, task and		Office storage credenzas, bookcases, storage units, and	
general office chairs	1,763.5	tables, nonwood	731.5
Office seating, including upholstered, nonwood, side and		Office storage units, including bookcases and credenzas	412.4
arm chairs, lounge seating, stacking chairs	389.1	Office tables, work and conference, nonwood	237.4
Office seating, including upholstered, nonwood, side		Office tables, equipment supporting, nonwood	57.1
and arm chairs	196.5	Other office tables, nonwood	24.6
Office seating, including upholstered, nonwood,		Office storage units, files, and tables, nonwood, nsk	2.6
stacking chairs	118.1	**Office furniture panel systems, desk systems and other office**	
Office seating, including upholstered, nonwood, lounge		**furniture, nonwood, nec**	**2,154.4**
seating	74.5	Desking systems, accessories and components, and all	
Office seating, including upholstered, nonwood, nsk	4.2	other office furniture, nonwood	444.8
Office desks and extensions, nonwood	**280.5**	Desking systems, accessories and components,	
Office desks and extensions, nonwood	276.1	nonwood	266.3
Office desks, nonwood	238.3	All other office furniture, nonwood, nec	178.5
Office desk extensions, nonwood	37.8	Panel systems, accessories and components, nonwood	1,700.9
Office desks and extensions, nonwood, nsk	4.4	Office panel and desking systems and all other office	
Office storage units, files, and tables, nonwood	**2,315.8**	furniture, nonwood, nec, nsk	8.8
Office files, vertical, letter and legal, nonwood	432.0	**Office furniture, except wood, nsk, total**	**262.8**

Source: 2002 *Economic Census*. The values are product shipments in millions of dollars for 2002. Total product shipments may be lower or higher than industry shipments. See Introduction for a full discussion. Values of indented subcategories are summed in the main heading(s). The symbol (D) appears when data are withheld to prevent disclosure of competitive information. The abbreviation nsk stands for 'not specified by kind' and nec for 'not elsewhere classified'. A dash (-) means zero.

INPUTS AND OUTPUTS FOR OFFICE FURNITURE MANUFACTURING

Economic Sector or Industry Providing Inputs	%	Sector	Economic Sector or Industry Buying Outputs	%	Sector
Compensation of employees	24.2		Audio & video equipment	65.1	Manufg.
Reconstituted wood products	13.1	Manufg.	Personal consumption expenditures	15.0	
Veneer & plywood	5.3	Manufg.	Musical instruments	10.0	Manufg.
Wholesale trade	3.7	Trade	Broadcast & wireless communications equipment	2.9	Manufg.
Sawmills & wood preservation	2.7	Manufg.	Surgical & medical instrument	2.5	Manufg.
Management of companies & enterprises	2.0	Services	Electron tubes	1.5	Manufg.
Truck transportation	1.8	Util.	Nonresidential structures, nec	0.8	Construct.
Plastics products, nec	1.5	Manufg.	Exports of goods & services	0.8	Cap Inv
Retail trade	1.1	Trade	Search, detection, & navigation instruments	0.7	Manufg.
Paints & coatings	1.1	Manufg.	Scientific research & development services	0.4	Services
Paperboard containers	1.0	Manufg.	Aircraft parts & auxiliary equipment, nec	0.2	Manufg.
Real estate	1.0	Fin/R.E.	Specialized design services	0.2	Services
Hardware	0.8	Manufg.			
Power generation & supply	0.8	Util.			
Specialized design services	0.6	Services			
Semiconductors & related devices	0.6	Manufg.			
Employment services	0.5	Services			

Continued on next page.

INPUTS AND OUTPUTS FOR OFFICE FURNITURE MANUFACTURING - Continued

Economic Sector or Industry Providing Inputs	%	Sector	Economic Sector or Industry Buying Outputs	%	Sector
Printed circuit assemblies (electronic assemblies)	0.5	Manufg.			
Securities, commodity contracts, investments	0.5	Fin/R.E.			
Legal services	0.5	Services			
Business support services	0.4	Services			
Architectural, engineering, & related services	0.4	Services			
Coating, engraving, heat treating & allied activities	0.3	Manufg.			
Advertising & related services	0.3	Services			
Professional, scientific, technical services, nec	0.3	Services			
Support services, nec	0.3	Services			
Abrasive products	0.3	Manufg.			
Machine shops	0.3	Manufg.			
Automotive equipment rental & leasing	0.2	Fin/R.E.			
Fabricated metals, nec	0.2	Manufg.			
Material handling equipment	0.2	Manufg.			
Rail transportation	0.2	Util.			
Warehousing & storage	0.2	Util.			
Investigation & security services	0.2	Services			
Accounting, tax preparation, bookkeeping, & payroll	0.1	Services			
Commercial & industrial machinery rental & leasing	0.1	Fin/R.E.			
Maintenance/repair of nonresidential structures	0.1	Construct.			
Monetary authorities/depository credit intermediation	0.1	Fin/R.E.			
Natural gas distribution	0.1	Util.			
Services to buildings & dwellings	0.1	Services			
Data processing, hosting, & related services	0.1	Services			
Facilities support services	0.1	Services			
Paperboard mills	0.1	Manufg.			
Wood windows & doors & millwork	0.1	Manufg.			

Source: Benchmark Input-Output Accounts for the U.S. Economy, 2002, U.S. Department of Commerce, Washington, D.C., January 2008. The abbreviation nec stands for 'not elsewhere classified'.

OCCUPATIONS EMPLOYED BY OFFICE FURNITURE (INCLUDING FIXTURES) MANUFACTURING

Occupation	% of Total 2006	Change to 2016	Occupation	% of Total 2006	Change to 2016
Cabinetmakers & bench carpenters	11.1	-6.0	General & operations managers	1.7	-15.4
Team assemblers	9.5	-6.0	Industrial truck & tractor operators	1.6	-15.4
Woodworking machine operators & tenders, exc sawing	5.0	3.4	Sawing machine setters, operators, & tenders, wood	1.6	3.4
First-line supervisors/managers of production workers	4.0	-6.0	Packers & packagers, hand	1.6	-24.8
Cutting, punching, & press machine operators	3.2	-15.4	Shipping, receiving, & traffic clerks	1.6	-9.5
Laborers & freight, stock, & material movers, hand	3.0	-15.4	Multiple machine tool operators & tenders	1.3	3.4
Welders, cutters, solderers, & brazers	2.8		Office clerks, general	1.3	-7.4
Furniture finishers	2.7	-6.0	Customer service representatives	1.3	3.4
Helpers--Production workers	2.5	-6.0	Bookkeeping, accounting, & auditing clerks	1.1	-6.0
Assemblers & fabricators, nec	2.5	-15.4	Industrial engineers	1.1	14.2
Sales reps, wholesale & manufacturing, exc tech	2.4	-6.0	Maintenance & repair workers, general	1.1	-6.0
Carpenters	2.2	-6.0	Molding, coremaking, & casting machine operators	1.1	-15.4
Coating, painting, & spraying machine operators	1.8	-10.7			

Source: Industry-Occupation Matrix, Bureau of Labor Statistics, December 4, 2007. These data are reported based on 4-digit NAICS categories but have been matched to corresponding 6-digit NAICS industry codes. The change reported for each occupation to the year 2016 is a percent of growth or decline as estimated by the Bureau of Labor Statistics. The abbreviation nec stands for 'not elsewhere classified'.

LOCATION BY STATE AND REGIONAL CONCENTRATION

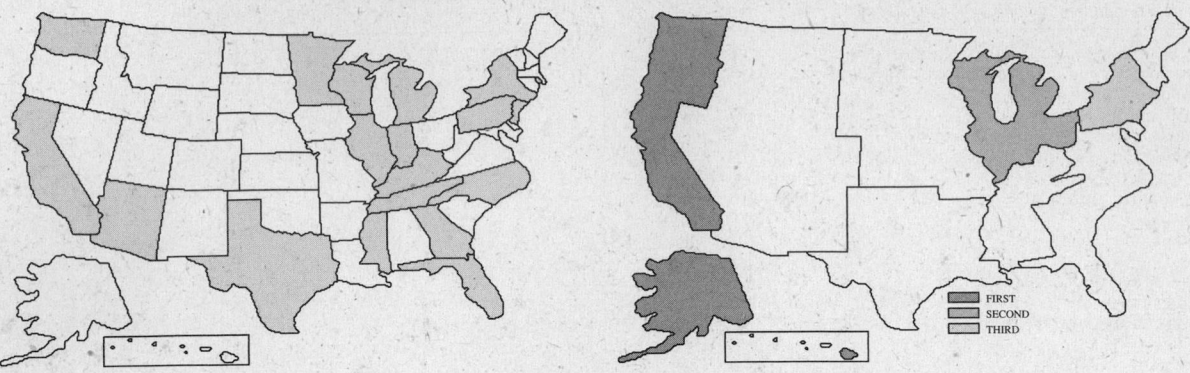

INDUSTRY DATA BY STATE

| State | Establish-ments | Shipments | | | Employment | | | | Cost as % of Shipments | Investment per Employee ($) |
		Total ($ mil)	% of U.S.	Per Establ.	Total Number	% of U.S.	Per Establ.	Wages ($/hour)		
Michigan	58	3,863.7	36.4	66,615.4	16,487	28.3	284	16.51	38.1	6,561
California	144	721.7	6.8	5,011.9	5,256	9.0	37	13.06	35.2	3,369
Indiana	38	636.8	6.0	16,758.5	4,890	8.4	129	13.49	42.7	2,101
Pennsylvania	31	587.7	5.5	18,956.5	2,681	4.6	86	15.10	44.8	6,214
North Carolina	53	554.1	5.2	10,454.2	4,627	7.9	87	13.19	36.8	2,226
Wisconsin	23	381.4	3.6	16,584.3	1,954	3.4	85	14.35	38.0	2,904
New York	58	296.0	2.8	5,103.6	2,219	3.8	38	15.18	34.6	1,569
Georgia	13	293.7	2.8	22,594.4	989	1.7	76	15.97	37.1	3,488
Illinois	34	218.1	2.1	6,413.7	1,696	2.9	50	12.68	39.7	3,041
Texas	38	180.9	1.7	4,760.3	1,236	2.1	33	12.55	38.8	5,755
New Jersey	26	169.5	1.6	6,519.2	937	1.6	36	15.07	39.6	2,543
Minnesota	32	168.6	1.6	5,268.5	1,161	2.0	36	15.36	39.4	1,702
Tennessee	18	131.2	1.2	7,291.1	992	1.7	55	12.13	33.4	1,499
Kentucky	9	113.8	1.1	12,643.8	900	1.5	100	14.38	41.3	1,428
Florida	43	95.2	0.9	2,214.2	780	1.3	18	12.11	55.4	1,669
Washington	25	85.9	0.8	3,436.8	673	1.2	27	14.36	35.7	2,520
Mississippi	7	57.6	0.5	8,229.7	370	0.6	53	11.76	36.6	3,378
Arizona	9	14.7	0.1	1,628.7	179	0.3	20	11.07	38.1	1,419
Rhode Island	3	11.9	0.1	3,964.3	195	0.3	65	14.41	36.3	2,708

Source: 2002 Economic Census. The states are in descending order of shipments or establishments (if shipment data are missing for the majority). The symbol (D) appears when data are withheld to prevent disclosure of competitive information. States marked with (D) are sorted by number of establishments. A dash (-) indicates that the data element cannot be calculated. Data may not show all states active in the NAICS category. All data available at the time of publication are shown.

NAICS 337910 - MATTRESS MANUFACTURING

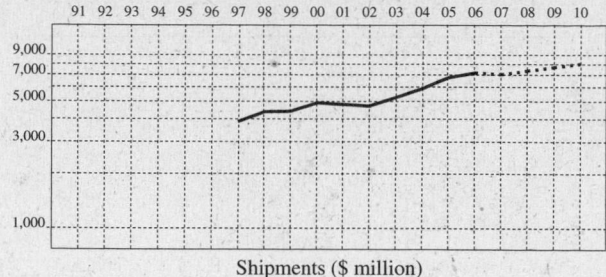

Shipments ($ million)

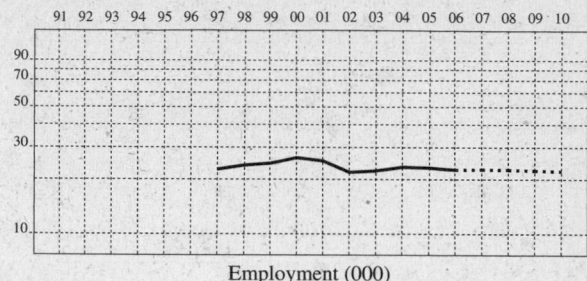

Employment (000)

GENERAL STATISTICS

| Year | Companies | Establishments | | Employment | | | Compensation | | Production ($ million) | | | |
		Total	with 20 or more employees	Total (000)	Production Workers (000)	Hours (Mil)	Payroll ($ mil)	Wages ($/hr)	Cost of Materials	Value Added by Manufacture	Value of Shipments	Capital Invest.
1997	624	702	280	22.7	17.0	33.3	602.6	10.95	1,953.5	1,918.8	3,869.1	124.8
1998		696	289	23.9	18.0	36.4	663.0	11.13	2,144.1	2,248.6	4,382.8	78.2
1999		685	302	24.5	18.7	37.1	689.9	11.40	2,184.1	2,243.5	4,413.2	94.0
2000		661	297	26.3	20.6	40.4	755.9	11.60	2,396.2	2,519.8	4,906.0	98.2
2001		639	285	25.3	19.7	38.7	744.7	11.92	2,300.0	2,520.2	4,814.7	50.0
2002	508	585	252	21.9	17.0	37.6	728.9	12.16	2,158.1	2,565.8	4,716.7	79.0
2003		571	277	22.3	17.5	35.3	776.8	14.01	2,395.3	2,869.1	5,248.4	64.8
2004		584	274	23.4	18.1	36.9	837.7	14.36	2,578.8	3,297.7	5,864.0	61.7
2005		567	283	23.2	18.1	36.6	853.0	14.98	3,159.3	3,612.0	6,762.3	101.7
2006		534P	271P	22.6	17.5	35.3	874.0	15.68	3,300.3	3,890.2	7,188.0	65.0
2007		514P	269P	22.7P	17.9P	36.8P	904.6P	15.88P	3,232.4P	3,810.2P	7,040.2P	61.5P
2008		495P	267P	22.6P	17.8P	36.8P	932.2P	16.43P	3,384.7P	3,989.6P	7,371.8P	57.9P
2009		475P	265P	22.4P	17.8P	36.9P	959.9P	16.99P	3,536.9P	4,169.1P	7,703.3P	54.2P
2010		455P	263P	22.2P	17.7P	36.9P	987.5P	17.55P	3,689.1P	4,348.6P	8,034.9P	50.5P

Sources: 1997 and 2002 *Economic Census*; other years, up to 2006, are from *Annual Survey of Manufactures*. Establishment counts for non-Census years are from *County Business Patterns*; 1997 and 2002 values are from the 1997 and 2002 censuses, respectively. 'P's show projections by the editors.

INDICES OF CHANGE

| Year | Companies | Establishments | | Employment | | | Compensation | | Production ($ million) | | | |
		Total	with 20 or more employees	Total (000)	Production Workers (000)	Hours (Mil)	Payroll ($ mil)	Wages ($/hr)	Cost of Materials	Value Added by Manufacture	Value of Shipments	Capital Invest.
1997	123	120	111	104	100	89	83	90	91	75	82	158
1998		119	115	109	106	97	91	92	99	88	93	99
1999		117	120	112	110	99	95	94	101	87	94	119
2000		113	118	120	121	107	104	95	111	98	104	124
2001		109	113	116	116	103	102	98	107	98	102	63
2002	100	100	100	100	100	100	100	100	100	100	100	100
2003		98	110	102	103	94	107	115	111	112	111	82
2004		100	109	107	106	98	115	118	119	129	124	78
2005		97	112	106	106	97	117	123	146	141	143	129
2006		91P	108P	103	103	94	120	129	153	152	152	82
2007		88P	107P	104P	105P	98P	124P	131P	150P	148P	149P	78P
2008		85P	106P	103P	105P	98P	128P	135P	157P	155P	156P	73P
2009		81P	105P	102P	105P	98P	132P	140P	164P	162P	163P	69P
2010		78P	104P	101P	104P	98P	135P	144P	171P	169P	170P	64P

Sources: Same as General Statistics. Values reflect change from the base year, 2002. Values above 100 mean greater than 2002, values below 100 mean less than 2002, and the values of 100 in other years means the same as 2002. 'P's show projections by the editors.

SELECTED RATIOS

For 2002	Avg. of All Manufact.	Analyzed Industry	Index	For 2002	Avg. of All Manufact.	Analyzed Industry	Index
Employees per Establishment	42	37	89	Value Added per Production Worker	182,367	150,929	83
Payroll per Establishment	1,639,184	1,245,983	76	Cost per Establishment	5,769,015	3,689,060	64
Payroll per Employee	39,053	33,283	85	Cost per Employee	137,446	98,543	72
Production Workers per Establishment	30	29	98	Cost per Production Worker	195,506	126,947	65
Wages per Establishment	694,845	781,566	112	Shipments per Establishment	11,158,348	8,062,735	72
Wages per Production Worker	23,548	26,895	114	Shipments per Employee	265,847	215,374	81
Hours per Production Worker	1,980	2,212	112	Shipments per Production Worker	378,144	277,453	73
Wages per Hour	11.89	12.16	102	Investment per Establishment	361,338	135,043	37
Value Added per Establishment	5,381,325	4,385,983	82	Investment per Employee	8,609	3,607	42
Value Added per Employee	128,210	117,160	91	Investment per Production Worker	12,245	4,647	38

Sources: Same as General Statistics. The 'Average of All Manufacturing' column represents the average of all manufacturing industries reported for the most recent complete year available. The Index shows the relationship between the Average and the Analyzed Industry. For example, 100 means that they are equal; 500 that the Analyzed Industry is five times the average; 50 means that the Analyzed Industry is half the national average. The abbreviation 'na' is used to show that data are 'not available'. Ratios shown for 2002, the last complete census year.

LEADING COMPANIES   Number shown: **54**   Total sales ($ mil): **12,242**   Total employment (000): **54.6**

Company Name	Address				CEO Name	Phone	Co. Type	Sales ($ mil)	Empl. (000)
Leggett and Platt Inc.	PO Box 757	Carthage	MO	64836		417-358-8131	P	4,306	24.0
Hillenbrand Industries Inc.	1069 State Rte 46E	Batesville	IN	47006		812-934-7000	P	2,024	9.9
Sealy Corp.	Sealy Dr., 1 Ofc Pk	Trinity	NC	27370	Ronald L. Jones	336-861-3500	P	1,702	6.1
Tempur-Pedic International	1713 Jaggie Fox	Lexington	KY	40511	H. Thomas Bryant	859-259-0754	P	1,107	1.4
Simmons Co.	1 Concourse Pky.	Atlanta	GA	30328	Charles R. Eitel	770-512-7700	R	855	3.0
Select Comfort Corp.	6105 Trenton Ln. N	Minneapolis	MN	55442	W R. McLaughlin	763-551-7000	P	799	3.2
Serta Inc.	5401 Trillium Blvd.	Hoffman Estates	IL	60192		847-645-0200	R	268*	<0.1
Bridon-American Corp.	PO Box 6000	Wilkes Barre	PA	18773	John Churchfield	570-822-3349	R	101*	0.4
Stryker Medical	3800 E Centre Ave.	Portage	MI	49002	Stephen MacMillan	269-329-2100	D	96*	0.7
Spiller Spring Co.	2216 S 24th St.	Sheboygan	WI	53081	Donald Coleman	920-457-3649	R	85*	0.2
Mattress Discounters Corp.	9822 Fallard Ct.	Upper Marlboro	MD	20772		301-856-6755	R	66*	<0.1
Winston-Salem Ind. For Blind	7730 N Point Blvd.	Winston-Salem	NC	27106	Daniel Boucher	336-759-0551	R	57*	0.3
Fraenkel Wholesale Furniture	PO Box 15385	Baton Rouge	LA	70895	Brian Akchin	225-275-8111	R	56*	0.3
Craftmatic Organization Inc.	2500 Interplex Dr.	Langhorne	PA	19053	Stanley Kraftsow	215-639-1310	R	52*	0.2
Corsicana Bedding Inc.	PO Box 1050	Corsicana	TX	75151	Carroll Moran	903-872-2591	R	48*	0.2
Jamison Bedding Inc.	PO Box 681948	Franklin	TN	37068	Frank Gorrell	615-794-1883	R	42*	<0.1
Blue Bell Mattress Company	PO Box 546	Windsor	CT	06095	Jonah Byer	860-688-6496	R	37*	0.2
Kolcraft Enterprises Inc.	1100 W Monroe St.	Chicago	IL	60607	Sanfred Koltun	312-361-6315	R	34*	<0.1
Child Craft Industries Inc.	1010 Keller Dr. NE	New Salisbury	IN	47161	William Suvak	812-206-2200	R	29*	0.3
Kingsdown Inc.	PO Box 388	Mebane	NC	27302	Patrick Flippin	919-563-3531	R	29*	0.2
Paramount Industrial Company	1112 Kingwood	Norfolk	VA	23502	Arthur Diamonstein	757-855-3321	R	27*	0.2
Chestnut Ridge Foam Inc.	PO Box 781	Latrobe	PA	15650	Larry Garrity	724-537-9000	R	26*	0.2
SICO America Inc.	7525 Cahill Rd.	Minneapolis	MN	55439	Jerel Danielson	952-941-1700	R	25*	0.2
Foam Rubber Products Inc.	PO Box 525	New Castle	IN	47362	Frank Nold	765-521-2000	R	23*	0.1
Sealy Mattress Company of NJ	PO Box 1520	Paterson	NJ	07544	Walter Hertz	973-345-8800	R	20*	0.1
Ther-A-Pedic Sleep Products	1375 Jersey Ave.	N Brunswick	NJ	08902	Stuart Carlitz	732-628-0800	R	20*	0.1
Serta Restokraft Mattress Co.	38025 Jay Kay Dr.	Romulus	MI	48174	Lawrence Kraft	734-727-9000	R	19*	0.1
Nichols and Stone Co.	PO Box 527	Gardner	MA	01440	Carlton Nichols	978-632-2770	R	18*	0.3
Omaha Bedding Co.	PO Box 27396	Omaha	NE	68127	Irving Veitzer	402-733-8600	R	17*	0.1
Dreamline Manufacturing Inc.	PO Box 1250	Cabot	AR	72023	D Tipton	501-843-3585	R	16*	<0.1
Spring Air Mattress Corp.	PO Box 20028	Greensboro	NC	27420	Frank Grove	336-272-1141	R	16*	<0.1
Clearwater Mattress Company	1185 Gooden Xing	Largo	FL	33778	Mel Jones	727-479-1600	R	16*	<0.1
Dynasty Consolidated Ind.	4646 Harry Hines	Dallas	TX	75235	Amir Sunderji	214-630-3132	R	15*	0.1
Standard Mattress Co.	PO Box 89	Hartford	CT	06141	Robert Naboicheck	860-549-2000	R	15*	<0.1
Home Style Industries	PO Box 1500	Nampa	ID	83652	Randy Raptosh	208-466-8481	R	14*	0.2
Mastercraft Inc.	PO Box 97	LaGrange	IN	46761	Clifton Reynolds	260-463-8702	R	14*	0.2
Specialized Plastic Sealings	1420 E Greene St.	Carlsbad	NM	88220	Joyce Springer	575-887-8853	R	14*	<0.1
Finegood Holdings Inc.	1118 E 223rd St.	Carson	CA	90745	Daniel Finegood	310-549-2160	R	13*	0.2
Lions Volunteer Blind Ind.	PO Box 706	Morristown	TN	37815	Fred Overbay	423-586-3922	R	12*	0.1
Dixie Bedding Corp.	4800 NW 37th Ave.	Miami	FL	33142	Dan Kamis	305-634-1505	R	11*	0.1
Land and Sky Inc.	1401 W Bond Cir.	Lincoln	NE	68521	Ronald Larson	402-470-2468	R	10*	0.1
LaCrosse Furniture Co.	PO Box 99	La Crosse	KS	67548	Chris Podschun	785-222-2541	R	10*	0.1
Spring Air Partners - CA	111 Baldwin Park	City of Industry	CA	91746	Earl Kluft	626-369-4701	R	10*	<0.1
Mississippi Ind. For The Blind	PO Box 4417	Jackson	MS	39296		601-984-3200	R	10*	0.2
A Diamond Productions Inc.	2150 Cesar Chavez	San Francisco	CA	94124	Suzanne Diamond	415-920-6800	R	8*	<0.1
Hard Manufacturing Company	230 Grider St.	Buffalo	NY	14215	William Godin	716-893-1800	R	7*	<0.1
Goldstar U S A Inc.	2705 Pacific Ave.	Tacoma	WA	98402	Vern Padgett	253-627-4000	R	7*	<0.1
Springco Bedding Co.	1207 W Crosby Rd.	Carrollton	TX	75006	Larry Bannister	972-242-7666	R	7*	<0.1
Mattress Holding Corp.	5815 Gulf Fwy.	Houston	TX	77023	Gary T. Fazio	713-923-1090	R	6	0.6
Norka Futon	143 W Market St.	Akron	OH	44303		330-253-9330	R	6*	<0.1
Calhoun Manufacturing Co.	1008 Watkins Rd.	Battle Creek	MI	49015	Robert Nisbet	269-962-0948	R	6*	<0.1
Popular Mattress Factory Inc.	1049 Eastside Rd.	El Paso	TX	79915	George Yapor	915-774-4212	R	5*	<0.1
Blue Ridge Products Company	PO Box 2028	Hickory	NC	28603	Charles Ingle	828-322-7990	R	5*	<0.1
Comfortex Inc.	PO Box 850	Winona	MN	55987	Mike Murphy	507-454-6579	R	3*	<0.1

Source: Ward's Business Directory of U.S. Private and Public Companies, Volumes 1 and 2, 2008. The company type code used is as follows: P - Public, R - Private, S - Subsidiary, D - Division, J - Joint Venture, A - Affiliate, G - Group. Sales are in millions of dollars, employees are in thousands. An asterisk (*) indicates an estimated sales volume. The symbol < stands for 'less than'. Company names and addresses are truncated, in some cases, to fit into the available space.

MATERIALS CONSUMED

Material	Quantity	Delivered Cost ($ million)
Hardwood dimension and parts (including wood furniture frames)	(X)	71.8
Plastics products consumed in the form of sheets, rods, etc.	(X)	25.2
Springs, innerspring units, and box spring constructions	(X)	501.9
Foam cores for mattresses, including latex (exc. topper pads)	(X)	60.9
Woven upholstery fabrics (cotton, nylon, polyester, rayon, etc.), excluding ticking	(X)	63.8
Ticking (mattress)	(X)	258.3
Cotton linters and waste	(X)	24.7
Foam padding (excluding mattress cores)	(X)	286.6
Insulators (all types), exc. cotton felt (purchased premade)	(X)	72.3
Other cushioning materials (purchased premade)	(X)	28.6
All other materials, components, parts, containers, and supplies	(X)	247.0
Materials, ingredients, containers, and supplies, nsk	(X)	426.3

Source: 2002 Economic Census. Explanation of symbols used: (D): Withheld to avoid disclosure of competitive data; na: Not available; (S): Withheld because statistical norms were not met; (X): Not applicable; (Z): Less than half the unit shown; nec: Not elsewhere classified; nsk: Not specified by kind; - : zero; p : 10-19 percent estimated; q : 20-29 percent estimated.

PRODUCT SHARE DETAILS

Product or Product Class Shipments	Mil. $	Product or Product Class Shipments	Mil. $
MATTRESSES	4,585.8	excluding innerspring units and those incorporated into hybrid-type flotation and electric adjustable ensembles	1,154.5
Innerspring mattresses, excluding crib-size, including those with polyurethane or rubber topper pads and those sold as part of hollywood beds, excluding inserts	**2,717.2**	Spring foundations, excluding innerspring units and those incorporated into hybrid-type flotation and adjustable ensembles	1,016.0
Other mattresses, including crib mattresses and mattress inserts	**355.6**	Foam foundations, excluding those incorporated into hybrid-type flotation and adjustable ensembles	30.4
Other mattresses, including crib mattresses, foam core mattresses other than crib-size, inflatable air chambered, and mattress inserts	354.2	Other foundations, including platform, excluding those incorporated into hybrid-type flotation, air, and adjustable ensembles	108.1
Crib mattresses, including crib-size mattresses made with polyurethane, latex foam, hair, and cotton felt	97.4	Foundations, excluding innerspring units and those incorporated into hybrid-type flotation and adjustable ensembles, nsk	0.3
Foam core mattresses, other than crib-size	115.9	**Sleep system ensembles and mattresses, excluding conventional waterbeds**	**77.1**
Other mattresses, including inflatable air chambered, cotton felt, hair, etc. (excludes hybrid-type flotation and electric adjustable ensembles)	59.9	Hybrid-type sleep system flotation ensembles, excluding conventional waterbeds	(D)
Mattress inserts for dual-purpose sleep furniture (innerspring and foam) and mattresses for futons	81.0	Electric adjustable sleep system ensemble, excluding hospital and conventional waterbeds	(D)
Other mattresses, including crib mattresses and mattress inserts, nsk	1.4	Sleep system ensembles and mattresses, excluding conventional waterbeds, nsk	-
Foundations, excluding innerspring units and those incorporated into hybrid-type flotation and electric adjustable ensembles	**1,154.8**	**Mattresses, nsk, total**	**281.2**
Foundations, including spring, foam and platform,			

Source: 2002 *Economic Census*. The values are product shipments in millions of dollars for 2002. Total product shipments may be lower or higher than industry shipments. See Introduction for a full discussion. Values of indented subcategories are summed in the main heading(s). The symbol (D) appears when data are withheld to prevent disclosure of competitive information. The abbreviation nsk stands for 'not specified by kind' and nec for 'not elsewhere classified'. A dash (-) means zero.

INPUTS AND OUTPUTS FOR MATTRESS MANUFACTURING

Economic Sector or Industry Providing Inputs	%	Sector	Economic Sector or Industry Buying Outputs	%	Sector
Compensation of employees	19.4		Personal consumption expenditures	87.3	
Springs & wire products	12.7	Manufg.	Private fixed investment	5.6	
Urethane & other foam products (except polystrene)	11.6	Manufg.	S/L govt. invest., education	2.1	S/L Govt
Advertising & related services	4.8	Services	Mattresses	2.0	Manufg.
Wholesale trade	4.4	Trade	Exports of goods & services	1.2	Cap Inv
Broadwoven fabric mills	3.9	Manufg.	S/L govt. invest., other	0.9	S/L Govt
Scenic & sightseeing transport & related services	3.3	Util.	Upholstered household furniture	0.7	Manufg.
Mattresses	2.0	Manufg.	Change in private inventories	0.2	In House
Truck transportation	1.6	Util.			
Wood windows & doors & millwork	1.5	Manufg.			
Management of companies & enterprises	1.5	Services			
Nonwoven fabric mills	1.2	Manufg.			
Rubber products, nec	1.2	Manufg.			
Real estate	1.2	Fin/R.E.			
Fiber, yarn, & thread mills	1.1	Manufg.			
Securities, commodity contracts, investments	1.0	Fin/R.E.			
Taxes on production & imports, less subsidies	0.9				
Monetary authorities/depository credit intermediation	0.8	Fin/R.E.			
Professional, scientific, technical services, nec	0.6	Services			
Plastics packaging materials, film & sheet	0.5	Manufg.			
Textile product mills, nec	0.5	Manufg.			
Food services & drinking places	0.5	Services			
Data processing, hosting, & related services	0.4	Services			
Hotels & motels, including casino hotels	0.4	Services			
Semiconductors & related devices	0.3	Manufg.			
Accounting, tax preparation, bookkeeping, & payroll	0.3	Services			
Power generation & supply	0.3	Util.			
Printed circuit assemblies (electronic assemblies)	0.3	Manufg.			
Automotive equipment rental & leasing	0.3	Fin/R.E.			
Telecommunications	0.3	Services			
Air transportation	0.3	Util.			
Coating, engraving, heat treating & allied activities	0.2	Manufg.			
Architectural, engineering, & related services	0.2	Services			
Legal services	0.2	Services			
Lessors of nonfinancial assets	0.2	Fin/R.E.			
Paperboard containers	0.2	Manufg.			
Services to buildings & dwellings	0.2	Services			
Warehousing & storage	0.2	Util.			
Machine shops	0.2	Manufg.			
Maintenance/repair of nonresidential structures	0.2	Construct.			
Other computer related services, including facilities	0.2	Services			
Business support services	0.2	Services			
Commercial & industrial machinery rental & leasing	0.2	Fin/R.E.			
Fabricated metals, nec	0.2	Manufg.			
Motor vehicle parts	0.1	Manufg.			
Automotive repair & maintenance, ex. car washes	0.1	Services			
Nondepository credit intermediation activities	0.1	Fin/R.E.			

Source: *Benchmark Input-Output Accounts for the U.S. Economy, 2002*, U.S. Department of Commerce, Washington, D.C., January 2008. The abbreviation nec stands for 'not elsewhere classified'.

OCCUPATIONS EMPLOYED BY OTHER FURNITURE RELATED PRODUCT MANUFACTURING

Occupation	% of Total 2006	Change to 2016	Occupation	% of Total 2006	Change to 2016
Team assemblers	22.1	4.4	Truck drivers, light or delivery services	1.9	4.4
Sewing machine operators	8.7	4.4	Upholsterers	1.8	-5.0
Assemblers & fabricators, nec	3.9	-6.0	Inspectors, testers, sorters, samplers, & weighers	1.6	-1.6
First-line supervisors/managers of production workers	3.5	4.4	Retail salespersons	1.4	4.4
Cutting, punching, & press machine operators	3.5	-6.0	Packaging & filling machine operators & tenders	1.4	-6.0
Sales reps, wholesale & manufacturing, exc tech	3.5	4.4	Maintenance & repair workers, general	1.4	4.4
Laborers & freight, stock, & material movers, hand	3.0	-6.0	General & operations managers	1.4	-6.0
Customer service representatives	2.6	14.8	Packers & packagers, hand	1.3	-16.5
Shipping, receiving, & traffic clerks	2.0	0.5	Industrial truck & tractor operators	1.2	-6.0
Truck drivers, heavy & tractor-trailer	2.0	4.4	Office clerks, general	1.1	2.8
Helpers--Production workers	2.0	4.4	Bookkeeping, accounting, & auditing clerks	1.1	4.4

Source: Industry-Occupation Matrix, Bureau of Labor Statistics, December 4, 2007. These data are reported based on 4-digit NAICS categories but have been matched to corresponding 6-digit NAICS industry codes. The change reported for each occupation to the year 2016 is a percent of growth or decline as estimated by the Bureau of Labor Statistics. The abbreviation nec stands for 'not elsewhere classified'.

LOCATION BY STATE AND REGIONAL CONCENTRATION

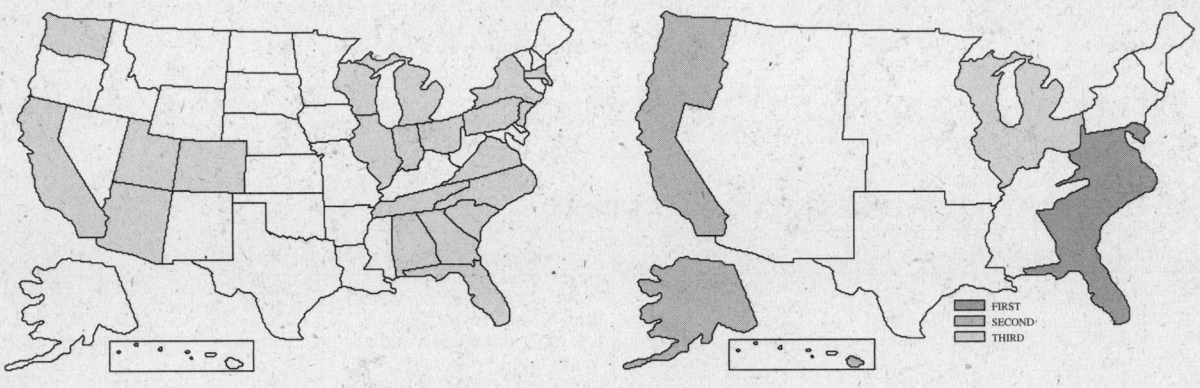

FIRST
SECOND
THIRD

INDUSTRY DATA BY STATE

State	Establish-ments	Shipments			Employment				Cost as % of Shipments	Investment per Employee ($)
		Total ($ mil)	% of U.S.	Per Establ.	Total Number	% of U.S.	Per Establ.	Wages ($/hour)		
California	88	714.9	15.2	8,124.0	3,002	13.7	34	13.85	45.3	2,293
Florida	44	312.9	6.6	7,111.5	1,510	6.9	34	11.79	50.0	2,483
New Jersey	15	296.0	6.3	19,735.9	1,288	5.9	86	13.62	43.5	11,155
Virginia	14	227.2	4.8	16,225.3	788	3.6	56	15.24	42.0	10,721
North Carolina	24	214.3	4.5	8,927.8	1,407	6.4	59	13.30	50.1	1,851
Massachusetts	10	192.7	4.1	19,266.4	764	3.5	76	15.22	44.5	2,411
Ohio	13	190.4	4.0	14,649.8	788	3.6	61	17.11	43.3	2,938
Pennsylvania	21	173.8	3.7	8,276.0	793	3.6	38	13.82	46.2	5,532
Wisconsin	14	173.3	3.7	12,378.6	397	1.8	28	14.87	40.9	6,957
Georgia	19	173.2	3.7	9,118.2	747	3.4	39	14.20	44.5	1,470
Illinois	28	167.2	3.5	5,972.2	830	3.8	30	7.41	46.9	2,705
New York	23	157.9	3.3	6,865.7	716	3.3	31	10.81	43.7	1,504
Washington	14	100.4	2.1	7,174.4	430	2.0	31	13.19	42.0	2,340
Arizona	14	98.3	2.1	7,020.0	390	1.8	28	15.19	44.8	1,882
Michigan	19	92.2	2.0	4,850.4	592	2.7	31	11.97	44.7	3,115
Indiana	14	89.4	1.9	6,388.0	594	2.7	42	10.62	44.6	1,354
Alabama	15	81.4	1.7	5,424.8	493	2.2	33	11.21	47.6	1,144
Tennessee	16	80.6	1.7	5,035.6	454	2.1	28	9.96	53.3	4,313
Colorado	7	77.7	1.6	11,098.4	316	1.4	45	13.67	51.6	7,715
Utah	12	48.7	1.0	4,058.3	437	2.0	36	11.07	52.1	1,556
South Carolina	4	28.7	0.6	7,168.7	263	1.2	66	9.92	61.4	3,221

Source: 2002 *Economic Census*. The states are in descending order of shipments or establishments (if shipment data are missing for the majority). The symbol (D) appears when data are withheld to prevent disclosure of competitive information. States marked with (D) are sorted by number of establishments. A dash (-) indicates that the data element cannot be calculated. Data may not show all states active in the NAICS category. All data available at the time of publication are shown.

NAICS 337920 - BLIND AND SHADE MANUFACTURING

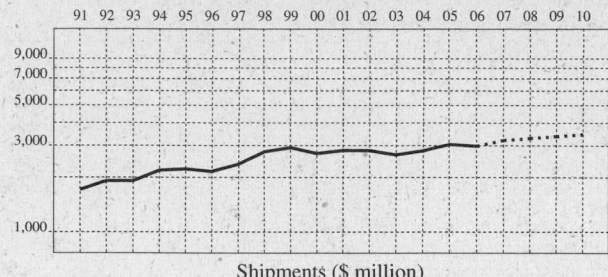

Shipments ($ million)

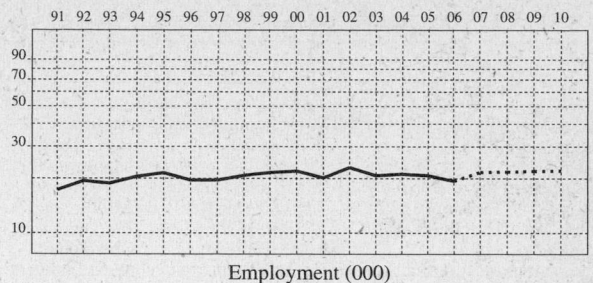

Employment (000)

GENERAL STATISTICS

Year	Companies	Establishments		Employment			Compensation		Production ($ million)			
		Total	with 20 or more employees	Total (000)	Production Workers (000)	Hours (Mil)	Payroll ($ mil)	Wages ($/hr)	Cost of Materials	Value Added by Manufacture	Value of Shipments	Capital Invest.
1991		505	137	17.3	12.2	24.7	341.6	8.27	778.0	928.0	1,712.5	24.9
1992	502	556	157	19.4	13.0	26.3	395.5	8.38	941.2	959.9	1,915.6	27.6
1993		536	137	18.8	12.6	26.0	390.9	8.40	959.5	957.9	1,914.7	21.9
1994		515	145	20.5	14.0	27.8	436.7	9.03	1,085.3	1,114.5	2,191.1	24.6
1995		506	142	21.5	15.3	29.4	424.4	8.77	1,188.0	1,032.1	2,229.2	36.0
1996		493	142	19.6	13.6	27.9	413.1	8.91	1,144.2	1,010.9	2,158.8	30.5
1997	442	486	146	19.6	13.8	28.1	435.0	9.34	1,210.6	1,147.3	2,363.9	44.4
1998		470	144	20.8	14.9	29.9	487.1	10.22	1,445.2	1,333.6	2,775.3	62.7
1999		463	143	21.6	15.2	28.7	556.2	11.17	1,566.3	1,375.4	2,921.4	77.8
2000		467	145	22.0	15.3	29.2	575.6	11.19	1,434.6	1,291.1	2,713.1	65.8
2001		470	140	20.2	14.0	25.8	559.7	12.18	1,433.8	1,390.8	2,821.7	81.1
2002	458	500	158	23.0	15.6	28.4	619.0	11.89	1,467.3	1,321.6	2,813.8	123.7
2003		503	151	20.8	14.6	27.4	560.6	11.17	1,305.8	1,368.5	2,668.9	48.2
2004		517	154	21.2	14.4	28.0	603.4	11.47	1,443.1	1,373.6	2,805.5	44.5
2005		502	149	20.8	14.0	27.9	634.7	12.45	1,569.0	1,501.8	3,046.0	48.5
2006		480P	151P	19.4	13.1	25.8	621.7	12.85	1,484.8	1,484.4	2,979.5	46.9
2007		478P	152P	21.7P	14.9P	28.1P	670.3P	13.10P	1,598.1P	1,597.7P	3,206.9P	75.7P
2008		476P	153P	21.8P	14.9P	28.1P	690.0P	13.42P	1,639.5P	1,639.0P	3,289.9P	78.6P
2009		473P	153P	22.0P	15.0P	28.2P	709.6P	13.74P	1,680.8P	1,680.4P	3,372.8P	81.6P
2010		471P	154P	22.1P	15.1P	28.3P	729.2P	14.06P	1,722.1P	1,721.7P	3,455.8P	84.5P

Sources: 1992, 1997, 2002 *Economic Census*; other years, up to 2006, are from the *Annual Survey of Manufactures*. Establishment counts for non-Census years are from *County Business Patterns*; 1997 and 2002 values are from the 1997 and 2002 censuses respectively, reported in the Federal Government's NAICS format. Other years were originally reported in equivalent SIC format. 'P's show projections by the editors.

INDICES OF CHANGE

Year	Companies	Establishments		Employment			Compensation		Production ($ million)			
		Total	with 20 or more employees	Total (000)	Production Workers (000)	Hours (Mil)	Payroll ($ mil)	Wages ($/hr)	Cost of Materials	Value Added by Manufacture	Value of Shipments	Capital Invest.
1992	110	111	99	84	83	93	64	70	64	73	68	22
1997	97	97	92	85	88	99	70	79	83	87	84	36
2001		94	89	88	90	91	90	102	98	105	100	66
2002	100	100	100	100	100	100	100	100	100	100	100	100
2003		101	96	90	94	96	91	94	89	104	95	39
2004		103	97	92	92	99	97	96	98	104	100	36
2005		100	94	90	90	98	103	105	107	114	108	39
2006		96P	96P	84	84	91	100	108	101	112	106	38
2007		96P	96P	94P	96P	99P	108P	110P	109P	121P	114P	61P
2008		95P	97P	95P	96P	99P	111P	113P	112P	124P	117P	64P
2009		95P	97P	96P	96P	99P	115P	116P	115P	127P	120P	66P
2010		94P	97P	96P	97P	100P	118P	118P	117P	130P	123P	68P

Sources: Same as General Statistics. Values reflect change from the base year, 2002. Values above 100 mean greater than 2002, values below 100 mean less than 2002, and the values of 100 in other years means the same as 2002. 'P's show projections by the editors.

SELECTED RATIOS

For 2002	Avg. of All Manufact.	Analyzed Industry	Index	For 2002	Avg. of All Manufact.	Analyzed Industry	Index
Employees per Establishment	42	46	110	Value Added per Production Worker	182,367	84,718	46
Payroll per Establishment	1,639,184	1,238,000	76	Cost per Establishment	5,769,015	2,934,600	51
Payroll per Employee	39,053	26,913	69	Cost per Employee	137,446	63,796	46
Production Workers per Establishment	30	31	106	Cost per Production Worker	195,506	94,058	48
Wages per Establishment	694,845	675,352	97	Shipments per Establishment	11,158,348	5,627,600	50
Wages per Production Worker	23,548	21,646	92	Shipments per Employee	265,847	122,339	46
Hours per Production Worker	1,980	1,821	92	Shipments per Production Worker	378,144	180,372	48
Wages per Hour	11.89	11.89	100	Investment per Establishment	361,338	247,400	68
Value Added per Establishment	5,381,325	2,643,200	49	Investment per Employee	8,609	5,378	62
Value Added per Employee	128,210	57,461	45	Investment per Production Worker	12,245	7,929	65

Sources: Same as General Statistics. The 'Average of All Manufacturing' column represents the average of all manufacturing industries reported for the most recent complete year available. The Index shows the relationship between the Average and the Analyzed Industry. For example, 100 means that they are equal; 500 that the Analyzed Industry is five times the average; 50 means that the Analyzed Industry is half the national average. The abbreviation 'na' is used to show that data are 'not available'. Ratios shown for 2002, the last complete census year.

LEADING COMPANIES   Number shown: **38**   Total sales ($ mil): **10,764**   Total employment (000): **39.3**

Company Name	Address				CEO Name	Phone	Co. Type	Sales ($ mil)	Empl. (000)
Newell Rubbermaid Inc.	10B Glenlake Pkwy.	Atlanta	GA	30328	Crandall C. Bowles	770-407-3800	P	6,407	22.0
Springs Global US Inc.	PO Box 70	Fort Mill	SC	29716	Crandall C. Bowles	803-547-1500	R	1,081*	8.0
Comfortex Corp.	21 Elm St.	Maplewood	NY	12189	Thomas Marusak	518-273-3333	R	933*	0.5
Douglas Hunter Fabrication Co.	2315 Luna Rd. Ste.	Carrollton	TX	75006	Marv Hopkins	972-484-9771	R	933*	<0.1
Springs Window Fashions L.L.C.	7549 Graber Rd.	Middleton	WI	53562	Scott Fawcett	608-836-1011	R	377*	0.9
Royal Window Coverings L.P.	PO Box 629	Plaquemine	LA	70765	Douglas Dunsmuir	281-447-6686	R	122*	1.0
Draper Inc.	411 S Pearl St.	Spiceland	IN	47385	John Pidgeon	765-987-7999	R	121*	0.5
Lafayette Venetian Blind Inc.	PO Box 2838	West Lafayette	IN	47996	Joseph Morgan	765-464-2500	R	81*	0.9
Abbott Bamboo Inc.	195 Raritan Ctr Pky	Edison	NJ	08837	Joel Botwick	732-225-2330	R	76*	0.6
3 Day Blinds Inc.	2220 E Cerritos Ave	Anaheim	CA	92806	Jim Buch	714-634-4600	R	70*	1.2
Carole Fabrics Corp.	PO Box 1436	Augusta	GA	30903	W 'Bill' Geiger	706-863-4742	R	69*	0.5
Skagfield Corp.	PO Box 6566	Tallahassee	FL	32314	Hilmar Skagfield	850-878-1144	R	61*	0.5
Next Day Blinds Corp.	8251 Preston Ct.	Jessup	MD	20794	Steve Freishtat	240-568-8800	R	53*	0.2
Kenney Manufacturing Co.	1000 Jefferson Blvd	Warwick	RI	02886	G Kenney	401-739-2200	R	49*	0.5
Mariak Industries Inc.	1609 Lockness Pl.	Torrance	CA	90501	Leonard Elinson	310-517-8800	R	43*	0.1
Shade Paterson	781 River Street	Paterson	NJ	07524	Richard Cohlm	973-684-2200	R	30*	0.1
Marietta Drapery/Window Cover.	PO Box 569	Marietta	GA	30061	Andrew Bentley	770-428-3335	R	26*	<0.1
Kreative Kamaaina Enterprises	1804 Hart St.	Honolulu	HI	96819		808-841-8731	R	23*	<0.1
Designs By Mark Inc.	2900 S Fairview St.	Santa Ana	CA	92704	Robert Jackowski	714-641-1411	R	18*	0.2
Steven Fabrics Co.	600 Hoover St. NE	Minneapolis	MN	55413	Richard Schommer	612-781-6671	R	18*	0.2
Summit Door Inc.	130 Eva St.	Saint Paul	MN	55107	Keith Pollari	651-292-9711	R	18*	<0.1
Sunshine Drapery Company Inc.	11800 Adie Rd.	Maryland Hgts	MO	63043	Bruce Bernstein	314-569-2980	R	17*	0.2
Home Style Industries	PO Box 1500	Nampa	ID	83653	Randy Raptosh	208-466-8481	R	14*	0.2
Designer Blinds of Omaha Inc.	PO Box 27459	Omaha	NE	68127	Lloyd Woodworth	402-331-2283	R	14*	0.2
Amer. Drapery Blind & Carpet	PO Box 896	Renton	WA	98057	Donald Richmond	425-255-3893	R	13*	0.1
Suncoast Window Treatments	14105 McCormick	Tampa	FL	33626	Mike Conforti	813-855-4441	R	13*	0.2
Tentina Window Fashions Inc.	PO Box 615	Lindenhurst	NY	11757	Andrea Miritello	631-957-9585	R	13*	0.1
C-Mor Co.	7 Jewell St.	Garfield	NJ	07026		973-478-3900	R	12*	0.1
Selective Enterprises Inc.	PO Box 410149	Charlotte	NC	28241	John Hawkins	704-588-3310	R	11*	0.1
S Morantz Inc.	9984 Gantry Rd.	Philadelphia	PA	19115	Stan Morantz	215-969-0266	R	9*	<0.1
Hob Enterprises L.L.C.	21518 Bridge St.	Southfield	MI	48033		248-357-4710	R	9*	0.1
American Window Concepts	908 W Rd. Ste. B	Houston	TX	77038	Minh Nguyen	281-999-9002	R	9*	<0.1
Alfred's Heatheranncreations	1580 Sunflower	Costa Mesa	CA	92626	Pat Cochrane	714-434-4838	R	6*	<0.1
Beauti-Vue Products Corp.	8555 194th Ave.	Bristol	WI	53104	Jim Grumbeck	262-857-2306	R	5*	<0.1
Aero Drapery Corp.	3525 State Rd. 32 W	Westfield	IN	46074	Mark Hopper	317-896-2521	R	5*	<0.1
B and D Precision Tools Inc.	2367 W 8th Ln.	Hialeah	FL	33010	Heliodoro Duran	305-885-1583	R	2*	<0.1
Techniku Inc.	325 Intrlcken Pkwy.	Broomfield	CO	80021	Robert Collett	303-355-9347	R	2*	<0.1
Bautech Inc.	1550 N Old Rand	Wauconda	IL	60084	John Karas	847-526-1515	R	1*	<0.1

Source: Ward's Business Directory of U.S. Private and Public Companies, Volumes 1 and 2, 2008. The company type code used is as follows: P - Public, R - Private, S - Subsidiary, D - Division, J - Joint Venture, A - Affiliate, G - Group. Sales are in millions of dollars, employees are in thousands. An asterisk (*) indicates an estimated sales volume. The symbol < stands for 'less than'. Company names and addresses are truncated, in some cases, to fit into the available space.

MATERIALS CONSUMED

Material	Quantity	Delivered Cost ($ million)
Fabricated metal products, including forgings	(X)	38.8
Steel shapes and forms (exc. castings, forgings, fabr. metal products)	(X)	33.3
Aluminum and aluminum-base alloy sheet, plate, foil, and welded tubing	(X)	66.7
All other aluminum and aluminum-base alloy shapes and forms (exc. castings, forgings, fabr. metal products)	(X)	81.7
Plastics coated fabrics and shade cloth	(X)	194.6
Plastics products consumed in the form of sheets, rods, etc.	(X)	134.9
Paperboard containers, boxes, and corrugated paperboard	(X)	35.0
All other materials, components, parts, containers, and supplies	(X)	214.3
Materials, ingredients, containers, and supplies, nsk	(X)	383.8

Source: 2002 *Economic Census*. Explanation of symbols used: (D): Withheld to avoid disclosure of competitive data; na: Not available; (S): Withheld because statistical norms were not met; (X): Not applicable; (Z): Less than half the unit shown; nec: Not elsewhere classified; nsk: Not specified by kind; - : zero; p : 10-19 percent estimated; q : 20-29 percent estimated.

PRODUCT SHARE DETAILS

Product or Product Class Shipments	Mil. $	Product or Product Class Shipments	Mil. $
BLINDS AND SHADES	2,444.8	wood	572.1
Window shades and window shade accessories and rollers	**512.9**	Venetian blind components and parts	117.0
Plastics window shades	72.4	Venetian blinds, including components and parts, nsk	59.4
Other window shades, including window shades made of canvas, other fabric, and paper	418.9	**Other blinds and shades, including curtain and drapery fixtures, poles, and rods**	**771.6**
Window shade accessories and rollers sold separately	21.6	Other blinds and shades, excluding canvas and other fabric awnings	509.6
Venetian blinds, including components and parts	**982.2**	Curtain and drapery fixtures, poles, and rods, except window shade accessories and rollers	262.0
Aluminum-slat venetian blinds, complete, vertical and horizontal	233.8	**Blinds and shades, nsk, total**	**178.1**
Other Venetian blinds, complete, including horizontal and vertical and Venetian blinds made of plastics, steel, and			

Source: 2002 *Economic Census*. The values are product shipments in millions of dollars for 2002. Total product shipments may be lower or higher than industry shipments. See Introduction for a full discussion. Values of indented subcategories are summed in the main heading(s). The symbol (D) appears when data are withheld to prevent disclosure of competitive information. The abbreviation nsk stands for 'not specified by kind' and nec for 'not elsewhere classified'. A dash (-) means zero.

INPUTS AND OUTPUTS FOR BLIND AND SHADE MANUFACTURING

Economic Sector or Industry Providing Inputs	%	Sector	Economic Sector or Industry Buying Outputs	%	Sector
Compensation of employees	31.1		Personal consumption expenditures	79.2	
Fabric coating mills	10.3	Manufg.	Private fixed investment	14.3	
Aluminum products from purchased aluminum	7.2	Manufg.	S/L govt. invest., education	1.6	S/L Govt
Wholesale trade	6.8	Trade	Commercial & health care structures	0.8	Construct.
Plastics packaging materials, film & sheet	5.9	Manufg.	Exports of goods & services	0.8	Cap Inv
Rubber products, nec	4.4	Manufg.	Change in private inventories	0.7	In House
Management of companies & enterprises	2.5	Services	Blinds & shades	0.6	Manufg.
Advertising & related services	2.3	Services	Amusement & recreation, nec	0.3	Services
Paperboard containers	1.9	Manufg.	S/L govt. invest., other	0.3	S/L Govt
Real estate	1.9	Fin/R.E.	Residential structures, nec	0.2	Construct.
Miscellaneous wood products	1.9	Manufg.	Residential permanent site structures	0.2	Construct.
Alumina refining & primary aluminum production	1.6	Manufg.	Vegetables and melons	0.2	Agric.
Iron & steel mills & ferroalloys	1.6	Manufg.	Ship building & repairing	0.2	Manufg.
Truck transportation	1.2	Util.	Scenic & sightseeing transport & related services	0.2	Util.
Unlaminated plastics profile shapes	1.1	Manufg.	Retail trade	0.1	Trade
Securities, commodity contracts, investments	1.0	Fin/R.E.	Fruit	0.1	Agric.
Blinds & shades	0.8	Manufg.			
Monetary authorities/depository credit intermediation	0.7	Fin/R.E.			
Architectural, engineering, & related services	0.6	Services			
Telecommunications	0.6	Services			
Machine shops	0.6	Manufg.			
Professional, scientific, technical services, nec	0.5	Services			
Power generation & supply	0.5	Util.			
Taxes on production & imports, less subsidies	0.5				
Semiconductors & related devices	0.5	Manufg.			
Printed circuit assemblies (electronic assemblies)	0.4	Manufg.			
Coating, engraving, heat treating & allied activities	0.4	Manufg.			
Food services & drinking places	0.4	Services			
Laminated plastics plates, sheets, & shapes	0.4	Manufg.			
Data processing, hosting, & related services	0.3	Services			
Warehousing & storage	0.3	Util.			
Accounting, tax preparation, bookkeeping, & payroll	0.3	Services			
Legal services	0.3	Services			
Hotels & motels, including casino hotels	0.3	Services			
Management, scientific, & technical consulting	0.3	Services			
Turned products & screws, nuts, & bolts	0.2	Manufg.			
Automotive equipment rental & leasing	0.2	Fin/R.E.			
Air transportation	0.2	Util.			
Services to buildings & dwellings	0.2	Services			
Other computer related services, including facilities	0.2	Services			
Abrasive products	0.2	Manufg.			
Maintenance/repair of nonresidential structures	0.2	Construct.			
Metal cans, boxes, & other containers (light gauge)	0.2	Manufg.			
Fabricated metals, nec	0.2	Manufg.			
Crowns & closures & metal stamping	0.1	Manufg.			
Forging, stamping, & sintering, nec	0.1	Manufg.			
Commercial & industrial machinery rental & leasing	0.1	Fin/R.E.			
Plate work & fabricated structural products	0.1	Manufg.			
Nondepository credit intermediation activities	0.1	Fin/R.E.			
Automotive repair & maintenance, ex. car washes	0.1	Services			
Ball & roller bearings	0.1	Manufg.			
Business support services	0.1	Services			
Handtools	0.1	Manufg.			
Rail transportation	0.1	Util.			

Source: Benchmark Input-Output Accounts for the U.S. Economy, 2002, U.S. Department of Commerce, Washington, D.C., January 2008. The abbreviation nec stands for 'not elsewhere classified'.

OCCUPATIONS EMPLOYED BY OTHER FURNITURE RELATED PRODUCT MANUFACTURING

Occupation	% of Total 2006	Change to 2016	Occupation	% of Total 2006	Change to 2016
Team assemblers	22.1	4.4	Truck drivers, light or delivery services	1.9	4.4
Sewing machine operators	8.7	4.4	Upholsterers	1.8	-5.0
Assemblers & fabricators, nec	3.9	-6.0	Inspectors, testers, sorters, samplers, & weighers	1.6	-1.6
First-line supervisors/managers of production workers	3.5	4.4	Retail salespersons	1.4	4.4
Cutting, punching, & press machine operators	3.5	-6.0	Packaging & filling machine operators & tenders	1.4	-6.0
Sales reps, wholesale & manufacturing, exc tech	3.5	4.4	Maintenance & repair workers, general	1.4	4.4
Laborers & freight, stock, & material movers, hand	3.0	-6.0	General & operations managers	1.4	-6.0
Customer service representatives	2.6	14.8	Packers & packagers, hand	1.3	-16.5
Shipping, receiving, & traffic clerks	2.0	0.5	Industrial truck & tractor operators	1.2	-6.0
Truck drivers, heavy & tractor-trailer	2.0	4.4	Office clerks, general	1.1	2.8
Helpers--Production workers	2.0	4.4	Bookkeeping, accounting, & auditing clerks	1.1	4.4

Source: *Industry-Occupation Matrix*, Bureau of Labor Statistics, December 4, 2007. These data are reported based on 4-digit NAICS categories but have been matched to corresponding 6-digit NAICS industry codes. The change reported for each occupation to the year 2016 is a percent of growth or decline as estimated by the Bureau of Labor Statistics. The abbreviation nec stands for 'not elsewhere classified'.

LOCATION BY STATE AND REGIONAL CONCENTRATION

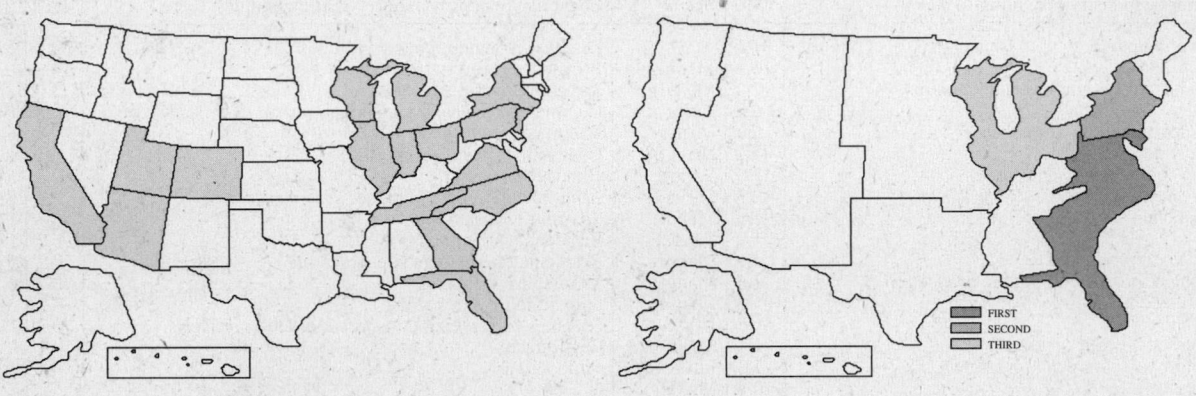

FIRST
SECOND
THIRD

INDUSTRY DATA BY STATE

State	Establish-ments	Shipments			Employment				Cost as % of Shipments	Investment per Employee ($)
		Total ($ mil)	% of U.S.	Per Establ.	Total Number	% of U.S.	Per Establ.	Wages ($/hour)		
California	72	577.8	20.5	8,025.7	4,062	17.7	56	10.55	45.5	2,775
Illinois	28	295.0	10.5	10,535.8	1,407	6.1	50	11.53	60.0	1,928
Florida	79	212.9	7.6	2,695.3	1,887	8.2	24	10.50	53.2	2,759
New York	44	174.6	6.2	3,967.6	1,197	5.2	27	11.44	50.5	3,222
Pennsylvania	18	164.1	5.8	9,118.4	1,295	5.6	72	14.22	53.9	1,941
Wisconsin	13	114.9	4.1	8,835.9	1,661	7.2	128	21.41	66.9	3,881
Indiana	11	111.9	4.0	10,173.4	1,336	5.8	121	12.31	54.6	1,263
New Jersey	17	86.3	3.1	5,076.8	791	3.4	47	9.89	54.3	1,083
Utah	8	80.4	2.9	10,052.3	704	3.1	88	12.47	43.7	3,774
Georgia	8	53.7	1.9	6,712.6	344	1.5	43	12.29	29.1	567
North Carolina	13	37.0	1.3	2,845.6	256	1.1	20	11.55	51.1	1,891
Michigan	12	33.5	1.2	2,794.5	989	4.3	82	13.54	59.4	488
Ohio	13	29.6	1.1	2,280.7	330	1.4	25	14.39	50.1	2,688
Arizona	13	25.3	0.9	1,948.8	227	1.0	17	8.44	42.2	4,088
Tennessee	5	18.9	0.7	3,787.8	210	0.9	42	9.37	49.0	1,014
Colorado	8	15.6	0.6	1,948.5	185	0.8	23	11.97	44.0	962
Virginia	8	14.7	0.5	1,841.1	122	0.5	15	10.49	45.4	3,254

Source: 2002 *Economic Census*. The states are in descending order of shipments or establishments (if shipment data are missing for the majority). The symbol (D) appears when data are withheld to prevent disclosure of competitive information. States marked with (D) are sorted by number of establishments. A dash (-) indicates that the data element cannot be calculated. Data may not show all states active in the NAICS category. All data available at the time of publication are shown.

NAICS 339111 - LABORATORY APPARATUS AND FURNITURE MANUFACTURING

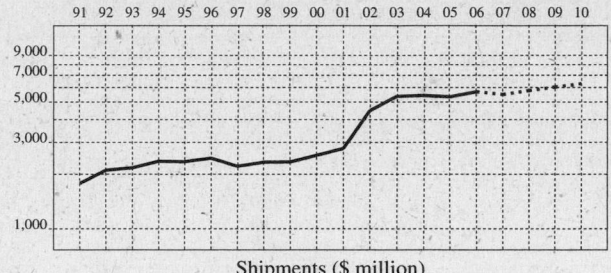

Shipments ($ million)

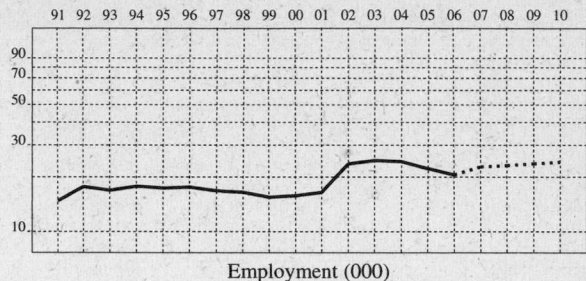

Employment (000)

GENERAL STATISTICS

| Year | Com-panies | Establishments | | Employment | | | Compensation | | Production ($ million) | | | |
		Total	with 20 or more employees	Total (000)	Production Workers (000)	Hours (Mil)	Payroll ($ mil)	Wages ($/hr)	Cost of Materials	Value Added by Manufacture	Value of Shipments	Capital Invest.
1991		246	123	14.8	6.9	14.6	485.7	11.41	650.5	1,100.1	1,782.5	52.7
1992	330	342	143	17.7	9.0	18.4	571.6	11.63	817.1	1,314.9	2,106.0	55.4
1993		346	143	16.9	8.2	16.7	567.1	11.86	818.3	1,364.3	2,172.7	42.9
1994		336	139	17.8	8.8	17.9	603.2	11.89	913.3	1,399.0	2,360.5	39.7
1995		344	137	17.4	8.9	17.9	603.4	12.56	926.7	1,427.8	2,349.3	45.0
1996		362	140	17.6	8.7	18.7	620.0	12.32	983.7	1,487.2	2,454.6	48.0
1997	373	384	152	16.8	9.1	18.2	616.8	13.62	909.8	1,291.4	2,213.7	59.8
1998		378	154	16.5	9.0	17.5	630.4	13.55	938.3	1,390.3	2,331.4	67.3
1999		382	158	15.5	8.6	17.0	642.5	15.31	1,000.3	1,318.4	2,339.6	58.8
2000		377	164	15.8	9.1	18.1	716.4	15.63	1,058.1	1,540.0	2,546.1	105.9
2001		369	158	16.5	9.4	19.1	765.1	15.51	1,127.4	1,680.9	2,772.4	94.7
2002	402	425	202	23.7	12.6	25.9	1,075.6	15.51	1,745.6	2,749.7	4,480.6	109.7
2003		414	190	24.7	13.4	27.7	1,153.5	16.34	1,931.5	3,442.3	5,374.8	89.1
2004		422	185	24.4	12.3	25.0	1,180.5	17.55	2,063.6	3,311.5	5,429.1	98.1
2005		434	188	22.3	11.8	23.6	1,124.2	18.80	2,034.6	3,316.8	5,342.8	103.1
2006		445P	196P	20.6	11.2	22.9	1,073.6	18.91	2,147.4	3,576.4	5,689.3	89.3
2007		454P	201P	22.8P	12.5P	25.3P	1,177.4P	18.93P	2,075.3P	3,456.4P	5,498.4P	110.4P
2008		463P	205P	23.2P	12.8P	25.9P	1,224.5P	19.45P	2,175.9P	3,623.8P	5,764.8P	114.9P
2009		473P	210P	23.7P	13.2P	26.6P	1,271.7P	19.97P	2,276.4P	3,791.3P	6,031.1P	119.4P
2010		482P	215P	24.2P	13.5P	27.2P	1,318.8P	20.49P	2,377.0P	3,958.7P	6,297.5P	123.8P

Sources: 1992, 1997, 2002 *Economic Census*; other years, up to 2006, are from the *Annual Survey of Manufactures*. Establishment counts for non-Census years are from *County Business Patterns*; 1997 and 2002 values are from the 1997 and 2002 censuses respectively, reported in the Federal Government's NAICS format. Other years were originally reported in equivalent SIC format. 'P's show projections by the editors.

INDICES OF CHANGE

| Year | Com-panies | Establishments | | Employment | | | Compensation | | Production ($ million) | | | |
		Total	with 20 or more employees	Total (000)	Production Workers (000)	Hours (Mil)	Payroll ($ mil)	Wages ($/hr)	Cost of Materials	Value Added by Manufacture	Value of Shipments	Capital Invest.
1992	82	80	71	75	71	71	53	75	47	48	47	51
1997	93	90	75	71	72	70	57	88	52	47	49	55
2001		87	78	70	75	74	71	100	65	61	62	86
2002	100	100	100	100	100	100	100	100	100	100	100	100
2003		97	94	104	106	107	107	105	111	125	120	81
2004		99	92	103	98	97	110	113	118	120	121	89
2005		102	93	94	94	91	105	121	117	121	119	94
2006		105P	97P	87	89	88	100	122	123	130	127	81
2007		107P	99P	96P	99P	98P	109P	122P	119P	126P	123P	101P
2008		109P	102P	98P	102P	100P	114P	125P	125P	132P	129P	105P
2009		111P	104P	100P	105P	103P	118P	129P	130P	138P	135P	109P
2010		113P	106P	102P	107P	105P	123P	132P	136P	144P	141P	113P

Sources: Same as General Statistics. Values reflect change from the base year, 2002. Values above 100 mean greater than 2002, values below 100 mean less than 2002, and the values of 100 in other years means the same as 2002. 'P's show projections by the editors.

SELECTED RATIOS

For 2002	Avg. of All Manufact.	Analyzed Industry	Index	For 2002	Avg. of All Manufact.	Analyzed Industry	Index
Employees per Establishment	42	56	133	Value Added per Production Worker	182,367	218,230	120
Payroll per Establishment	1,639,184	2,530,824	154	Cost per Establishment	5,769,015	4,107,294	71
Payroll per Employee	39,053	45,384	116	Cost per Employee	137,446	73,654	54
Production Workers per Establishment	30	30	100	Cost per Production Worker	195,506	138,540	71
Wages per Establishment	694,845	945,198	136	Shipments per Establishment	11,158,348	10,542,588	94
Wages per Production Worker	23,548	31,882	135	Shipments per Employee	265,847	189,055	71
Hours per Production Worker	1,980	2,056	104	Shipments per Production Worker	378,144	355,603	94
Wages per Hour	11.89	15.51	130	Investment per Establishment	361,338	258,118	71
Value Added per Establishment	5,381,325	6,469,882	120	Investment per Employee	8,609	4,629	54
Value Added per Employee	128,210	116,021	90	Investment per Production Worker	12,245	8,706	71

Sources: Same as General Statistics. The 'Average of All Manufacturing' column represents the average of all manufacturing industries reported for the most recent complete year available. The Index shows the relationship between the Average and the Analyzed Industry. For example, 100 means that they are equal; 500 that the Analyzed Industry is five times the average; 50 means that the Analyzed Industry is half the national average. The abbreviation 'na' is used to show that data are 'not available'. Ratios shown for 2002, the last complete census year.

LEADING COMPANIES   Number shown: **75**   Total sales ($ mil): **5,228**   Total employment (000): **16.6**

Company Name	Address				CEO Name	Phone	Co. Type	Sales ($ mil)	Empl. (000)
Rainin Instrument L.L.C.	PO Box 4026	Woburn	MA	01888	Kenneth Rainin	510-564-1600	R	1,590*	0.1
MKS Instruments Inc.	90 Industrial Way	Wilmington	MA	01887	Leo Berlinghieri	978-284-4000	P	783	3.0
Fisher Scientific	2000 Park Lane Dr.	Pittsburgh	PA	15275	David Dellapenta	412-490-8300	D	568	1.8
Newport Corp.	1791 Deere Ave.	Irvine	CA	92606	Michael ONeill	949-863-3144	P	445	2.0
Venturedyne Ltd.	600 College Ave.	Pewaukee	WI	53072		262-691-9900	R	147*	1.3
Alltech Inc.	3031 Catnip Hill Rd	Nicholasville	KY	40356		859-885-9613	R	121*	0.2
Sarstedt Inc.	PO Box 468	Newton	NC	28658		828-465-4000	R	103*	0.2
Kewaunee Scientific Corp.	PO Box 1842	Statesville	NC	28687		704-873-7202	P	81	0.6
New Brunswick Scientific Co.	PO Box 4005	Edison	NJ	08818		732-287-1200	P	76	0.4
Barnstead-Thermolyne Corp.	PO Box 797	Dubuque	IA	52004		563-556-2241	S	70*	0.5
Ircon Inc.	7300 N Natchez	Niles	IL	60714	M Fay	847-967-5151	R	68*	<0.1
CEM Corp.	PO Box 200	Matthews	NC	28106	Michael J. Collins	704-821-7015	R	55	0.2
IKA-Works Inc.	2635 Northchase	Wilmington	NC	28405		910-452-7059	R	46*	<0.1
Bioanalytical Systems Inc.	2701 Kent Ave.	West Lafayette	IN	47906		765-463-4527	P	45	0.3
Restek Corp.	110 Benner Cir.	Bellefonte	PA	16823	Don Chandless	814-353-1300	R	43	0.2
Misonix Inc.	1938 New Hwy.	Farmingdale	NY	11735	Gary Gelman	631-694-9555	P	42	0.2
Molecular Bio-Products Inc.	9880 Mesa Rim Rd.	San Diego	CA	92121	Larry Scaramella		S	36*	0.3
NuAire Inc.	2100 Fernbrook Ln.	Plymouth	MN	55447		763-553-1270	R	36*	0.2
Rhea Campbell Manufacturing	1865 Hwy. 641 N	Paris	TN	38242		731-642-4251	R	32*	0.3
Kurt J Lesker Co.	1925 Rte. 51 Ste. 1	Clairton	PA	15025	Kurt Lesker	412-233-0801	R	32*	0.2
Atlas Material Testing Tech	4114 N Ravenswood	Chicago	IL	60613	William Lane	773-327-4520	R	30*	0.2
Bel-Art Products Inc.	6 Industrial Rd.	Pequannock	NJ	07440	David Landsberger	973-694-0500	R	29*	0.1
Dako Colorado Inc.	4850 Innovation Dr.	Fort Collins	CO	80525	Patrik Dahlen	970-226-2200	R	28*	0.2
Labcon, North America	3700 Lakeville Hwy.	Petaluma	CA	94954		707-766-2100	S	25*	0.2
Chemineer Inc.	PO Box 1123	Dayton	OH	45401		937-454-3200	S	22*	0.2
Boekel Industries Inc.	855 Penn. Blvd.	Feastrvl Trevose	PA	19053	Leo Synnestvedt	215-396-8200	R	21*	0.2
Buehler Ltd.	PO Box 1	Lake Bluff	IL	60044	David N. Farr	847-295-6500	S	21	0.2
Mechanical Equipment Company	12505 Reed Rd.	Sugar Land	TX	77478	George Gsell	281-276-7600	R	21*	<0.1
Parr Instrument Co.	211 53rd Street	Moline	IL	61265	Michael Steffenson	309-762-7716	R	20*	<0.1
Case Systems Inc.	PO Box 2044	Midland	MI	48641	Robert Bowden	989-496-9510	R	19*	0.2
Tri-Continent Scientific Inc.	12555 Loma Rica	Grass Valley	CA	95945	Brenton Hanlon	530-273-8389	R	18*	<0.1
Preston Industries Inc.	6600 W Touhy Ave.	Niles	IL	60714	Philip Preston	847-647-0611	R	18*	0.1
Collegedale Casework Inc.	PO Box 810	Collegedale	TN	37315	James C Wardlaw	423-238-4131	R	18*	0.1
ThermoGenesis Corp.	2711 Citrus Rd.	Rancho Cordova	CA	95742	William Osgood	916-858-5100	P	17	<0.1
QualMark Corp.	4580 Florence St.	Denver	CO	80238	Charles D. Johnston	303-254-8800	P	16	<0.1
Humboldt Manufacturing Co.	7300 W Agatite Ave.	Chicago	IL	60706	Dennis Burgess	708-456-6300	R	16*	<0.1
Hemosense Inc.	651 River Oaks Pky.	San Jose	CA	95134	James Merselis	408-719-1393	P	16	<0.1
Henry Troemner L.L.C.	PO Box 87	Thorofare	NJ	08086		856-686-1600	R	16*	0.2
Balance Technology Inc.	7035 Jo Mar Dr.	Whitmore Lake	MI	48189	Thomas Plunkett	734-769-2100	R	16*	0.1
Alpha Resources Inc.	PO Box 199	Stevensville	MI	49127	Philip Lunsford	269-465-5559	R	16*	<0.1
Magenta Corp.	3800 N Milwaukee	Chicago	IL	60641	Michael Illenberger	773-777-5050	R	16*	0.1
KNF Neuberger Inc.	2 Black Forest Rd.	Trenton	NJ	08691	Martin Becker	609-890-8889	R	16*	<0.1
AGR of Florida Inc.	PO Box 10158	Jacksonville	FL	32247	George Shami	904-733-9393	R	15*	<0.1
Baker Company Inc.	PO Box E	Sanford	ME	04073	Dennis Eagleson	207-324-8773	R	15*	0.1
Grieve Corp.	500 Hart Rd.	Round Lake	IL	60073	Pat Calabrese	847-546-8225	R	15*	<0.1
Helmer Inc.	15425 Herriman	Noblesville	IN	46060	David Helmer	317-773-9073	R	15*	<0.1
Tomtec Inc.	1000 Sherman Ave.	Hamden	CT	06514	Thomas Astle	203-281-6790	R	14*	<0.1
Fts Systems Inc.	PO Box 158	Stone Ridge	NY	12484	Claus Kinder	845-687-5300	R	14*	<0.1
SKC Inc.	863 Valley View Rd.	Eighty Four	PA	15330	Lloyd Guild	724-941-9701	R	14*	<0.1
Bnz Materials Inc.	6901 S Pierce St.	Littleton	CO	80128	J Hulce	303-978-1199	R	14*	<0.1
Western Slate Co.	365 Keyes Ave.	Hampshire	IL	60140	Jeff Pope	847-683-4400	R	13*	<0.1
Genomic Solutions Inc.	4355 Varsity Dr.	Ann Arbor	MI	48108	Robert G. Shepler	734-975-4800	S	13*	0.1
MFIC Corp.	PO Box 9101	Newton	MA	02464	Robert P. Bruno	617-969-5452	P	13	<0.1
Commonwealth Technology Inc.	5875 Barclay Dr.	Alexandria	VA	22315	James Sawyer	703-719-6800	R	13*	<0.1
Rheodyne L.P.	600 Park Ct.	Rohnert Park	CA	94928	Jeff Cannon	707-588-2000	S	12*	0.1
Spectracom Corp.	95 Methodist Hill	Rochester	NY	14623	George Gazarek	585-321-5800	R	12*	<0.1
Lamson and Goodnow Mfg. Co.	15 Greenfield St.	Greenfield	MA	01301	Ross Anderson	413-774-9830	R	12*	<0.1
Sartorius Tcc Co.	6542 Fig Street	Arvada	CO	80004	Scott Schuler	303-431-7255	R	11*	<0.1
BSI Corp.	52 E Centre St.	Nutley	NJ	07110	Jeremy Linder	973-667-8400	R	11*	<0.1
Carver Inc.	PO Box 544	Wabash	IN	46992		260-563-7577	R	11*	<0.1
Genevac Inc.	707 Executive Blvd.	Valley Cottage	NY	10989	Paul M. Montrone	845-267-2211	S	11*	<0.1
Leonard Peterson and Company	PO Box 2277	Auburn	AL	36831	Roger Lethander	334-821-6832	R	11*	0.1
WL Walker Company Inc.	1009 S Main St.	Tulsa	OK	74119	Anne Bracket	918-583-3109	R	11*	<0.1
Tecan Systems	2450 Zanker Rd.	San Jose	CA	95131	Stephen Levers	408-953-3100	R	11*	0.1
Schroer Manufacturing Co.	511 Osage Ave.	Kansas City	KS	66105	Joseph Schroer	913-281-1500	R	10*	0.1
Finish Thompson Inc.	921 Greengarden	Erie	PA	16501	David Bowes	814-455-4478	R	9*	<0.1
So-Low Environmental Equipment	10310 Spartan Dr.	Cincinnati	OH	45215	Walter Schum	513-772-9410	R	9*	<0.1
Spex Sampleprep L.L.C.	203 Norcross Ave.	Metuchen	NJ	08840		732-549-7144	R	9*	<0.1
Thoren Caging Systems Inc.	PO Box 586	Hazleton	PA	18201	Sally Thomas	570-455-5041	R	9*	<0.1
Paragon Furniture L.P.	2224 E Randol Mill	Arlington	TX	76011		817-633-3242	R	9*	<0.1
Applied Test Systems Inc.	348 New Castle Rd.	Butler	PA	16001	Floyd Ganassi	724-283-1212	R	9*	<0.1
Parter Medical Products Inc.	17015 Kingsview	Carson	CA	90746	Parviz Hassanzadeh	310-327-4417	R	8*	<0.1
Metuchen Scientific Inc.	203 Norcross Ave.	Metuchen	NJ	08840	Michel Baudron	732-549-7144	R	8*	<0.1
Eye Design L.L.C.	220 W 5th Ave.	Collegeville	PA	19426		610-409-1900	R	8*	<0.1
Ncl of Wisconsin Inc.	PO Box 8	Birnamwood	WI	54414	Emily Tobisch	715-449-2673	R	8*	<0.1

Source: Ward's Business Directory of U.S. Private and Public Companies, Volumes 1 and 2, 2008. The company type code used is as follows: P - Public, R - Private, S - Subsidiary, D - Division, J - Joint Venture, A - Affiliate, G - Group. Sales are in millions of dollars, employees are in thousands. An asterisk (*) indicates an estimated sales volume. The symbol < stands for 'less than'. Company names and addresses are truncated, in some cases, to fit into the available space.

MATERIALS CONSUMED

Material	Quantity	Delivered Cost ($ million)
Printed ciruit boards (without inserted components) for electronic circuitry	(X)	65.6
Printed circuit assemblies, loaded boards, and modules	(X)	45.1
Resistors, capacitors, transformers, electron tubes, semiconductors, and other electronic components	(X)	33.1
Current-carrying wiring devices	(X)	23.1
Electric motors and generators	(X)	56.4
Metal bolts, nuts, screws, and other screw machine products	(X)	11.6
Other fabricated metal products (exc. bolts, nuts, washers, etc.)	(X)	56.4
Iron and steel castings (rough and semifinished)	(X)	29.7
Nonferrous (aluminum, copper, etc.) castings (rough and semifinished)	(X)	17.9
Steel shapes and forms (exc. castings, forgings, fabr. metal products)	(X)	27.1
Nonferrous shapes and forms	(X)	22.6
Plastics resins consumed in the form of granules, pellets, etc.	(X)	66.1
Plastics products consumed in the form of sheets, rods, etc.	(X)	14.4
Fabricated plastics products	(X)	57.9
Fabricated rubber products (exc. tires, tubes, hoses, belting, and gaskets)	(X)	(D)
Surgical and orthopedic supplies	(X)	(D)
Sheet metal products (excluding stampings)	(X)	78.8
Adhesives and sealants	(X)	6.9
Paperboard containers, boxes, and corrugated paperboard	(X)	61.7
Paper and paperboard products	(X)	4.3
All other materials, components, parts, containers, and supplies	(X)	562.4
Materials, ingredients, containers, and supplies, nsk	(X)	135.2

Source: 2002 *Economic Census*. Explanation of symbols used: (D): Withheld to avoid disclosure of competitive data; na: Not available; (S): Withheld because statistical norms were not met; (X): Not applicable; (Z): Less than half the unit shown; nec: Not elsewhere classified; nsk: Not specified by kind; - : zero; p : 10-19 percent estimated; q : 20-29 percent estimated.

PRODUCT SHARE DETAILS

Product or Product Class Shipments	Mil. $	Product or Product Class Shipments	Mil. $
LABORATORY AND HOSPITAL APPARATUS AND FURNITURE	4,187.2	chairs)	104.9
Hospital beds	**766.2**	Other hospital furniture (back rests, bassinets, cases, chart racks, and other tables), except hospital beds,	
Hospital furniture	**886.3**	operating room furniture, and patient room furniture	577.0
Hospital furniture	879.5	Hospital furniture, nsk	6.8
Hospital operating room furniture, including cabinets,		**Laboratory apparatus and furniture**	**2,320.0**
cases, and tables	197.6	Laboratory furniture and parts sold separately	366.4
Hospital patient room furniture, including cabinets,		Laboratory and scientific apparatus	1,953.6
desks, dressers, and over-bed tables (except beds and		**Laboratory and hospital apparatus and furniture, nsk, total**	**214.7**

Source: 2002 *Economic Census*. The values are product shipments in millions of dollars for 2002. Total product shipments may be lower or higher than industry shipments. See Introduction for a full discussion. Values of indented subcategories are summed in the main heading(s). The symbol (D) appears when data are withheld to prevent disclosure of competitive information. The abbreviation nsk stands for 'not specified by kind' and nec for 'not elsewhere classified'. A dash (-) means zero.

INPUTS AND OUTPUTS FOR LABORATORY APPARATUS AND FURNITURE MANUFACTURING

Economic Sector or Industry Providing Inputs	%	Sector	Economic Sector or Industry Buying Outputs	%	Sector
Compensation of employees	32.0		Private fixed investment	77.1	
Wholesale trade	4.0	Trade	S/L govt. invest., other	7.5	S/L Govt
Management of companies & enterprises	3.4	Services	Exports of goods & services	5.8	Cap Inv
Hotels & motels, including casino hotels	3.0	Services	S/L govt. invest., education	3.1	S/L Govt
Food services & drinking places	3.0	Services	Personal consumption expenditures	3.0	
Veneer & plywood	2.5	Manufg.	Laboratory apparatus & furniture	0.9	Manufg.
Ornamental & architectural metal products	1.9	Manufg.	General Federal government services, nondefense	0.5	Fed Govt
Real estate	1.9	Fin/R.E.	Change in private inventories	0.4	In House
Analytical laboratory instruments	1.8	Manufg.	Hospitals	0.3	Services
Plastics products, nec	1.6	Manufg.	Nonresidential structures, nec	0.3	Construct.
Paperboard containers	1.5	Manufg.	General Federal government services, defense	0.2	Fed Govt
Bare printed circuit boards	1.5	Manufg.	Surgical appliances & supplies	0.2	Manufg.
Plastics materials & resins	1.5	Manufg.	Physician, dentist, other health practitioner offices	0.2	Services
Motors & generators	1.3	Manufg.			
Telecommunications	1.2	Services			
Advertising & related services	1.2	Services			
Printed circuit assemblies (electronic assemblies)	1.2	Manufg.			
Laboratory apparatus & furniture	1.0	Manufg.			
Legal services	0.9	Services			
Transit & ground passenger transportation	0.8	Util.			
Iron & steel mills & ferroalloys	0.8	Manufg.			
Business support services	0.8	Services			
Semiconductors & related devices	0.7	Manufg.			
Machine shops	0.7	Manufg.			
Ferrous metal foundries	0.6	Manufg.			

Continued on next page.

INPUTS AND OUTPUTS FOR LABORATORY APPARATUS AND FURNITURE MANUFACTURING - Continued

Economic Sector or Industry Providing Inputs	%	Sector	Economic Sector or Industry Buying Outputs	%	Sector
Plastics packaging materials, film & sheet	0.6	Manufg.			
Surgical & medical instrument	0.6	Manufg.			
Truck transportation	0.6	Util.			
Wiring devices	0.6	Manufg.			
Taxes on production & imports, less subsidies	0.5				
Air transportation	0.5	Util.			
Scientific research & development services	0.5	Services			
Custom roll forming	0.5	Manufg.			
Nonferrous metal foundries	0.5	Manufg.			
Retail trade	0.4	Trade			
Coating, engraving, heat treating & allied activities	0.4	Manufg.			
Power generation & supply	0.4	Util.			
Turned products & screws, nuts, & bolts	0.4	Manufg.			
Data processing, hosting, & related services	0.3	Services			
Warehousing & storage	0.3	Util.			
Management, scientific, & technical consulting	0.3	Services			
Accounting, tax preparation, bookkeeping, & payroll	0.3	Services			
Cutting tools & machine tool accessories	0.3	Manufg.			
Surgical appliances & supplies	0.3	Manufg.			
Chemical products & preparations, nec	0.3	Manufg.			
Spectator sports	0.2	Services			
Investigation & security services	0.2	Services			
Fitness & recreational sports centers	0.2	Services			
Lessors of nonfinancial assets	0.2	Fin/R.E.			
Professional, scientific, technical services, nec	0.2	Services			
Maintenance/repair of nonresidential structures	0.2	Construct.			
Automotive equipment rental & leasing	0.2	Fin/R.E.			
Adhesives	0.2	Manufg.			
Monetary authorities/depository credit intermediation	0.2	Fin/R.E.			
Services to buildings & dwellings	0.2	Services			
Rail transportation	0.2	Util.			
Computer terminals & peripherals	0.2	Manufg.			
Custom computer programming services	0.1	Services			
Valve & fittings other than plumbing	0.1	Manufg.			
Natural gas distribution	0.1	Util.			
Amusement & recreation, nec	0.1	Services			
Automotive repair & maintenance, ex. car washes	0.1	Services			
Laminated plastics plates, sheets, & shapes	0.1	Manufg.			
Unlaminated plastics profile shapes	0.1	Manufg.			
Other computer related services, including facilities	0.1	Services			
Personal & household goods repair/maintenance	0.1	Services			

Source: Benchmark Input-Output Accounts for the U.S. Economy, 2002, U.S. Department of Commerce, Washington, D.C., January 2008. The abbreviation nec stands for 'not elsewhere classified'.

OCCUPATIONS EMPLOYED BY MEDICAL EQUIPMENT & SUPPLIES MANUFACTURING

Occupation	% of Total 2006	Change to 2016	Occupation	% of Total 2006	Change to 2016
Dental laboratory technicians	12.2	2.3	Assemblers & fabricators, nec	1.4	-7.9
Team assemblers	11.0	2.3	Sales reps, wholesale & manufacturing, exc tech	1.3	2.3
First-line supervisors/managers of production workers	3.0	2.3	Helpers--Production workers	1.3	2.3
Inspectors, testers, sorters, samplers, & weighers	3.0	-3.6	Truck drivers, light or delivery services	1.2	2.3
Customer service representatives	2.2	12.5	Packaging & filling machine operators & tenders	1.2	-7.9
Medical appliance technicians	2.0	8.3	Bookkeeping, accounting, & auditing clerks	1.2	2.3
Packers & packagers, hand	1.9	-18.2	Multiple machine tool operators & tenders	1.1	12.5
Shipping, receiving, & traffic clerks	1.9	-1.6	Maintenance & repair workers, general	1.1	2.3
Machinists	1.7	7.4	Stock clerks & order fillers	1.1	-14.4
Molding, coremaking, & casting machine operators	1.6	-7.9	Mechanical engineers	1.1	2.3
Sales representatives, wholesale & manufacturing, tech	1.6	2.3	Laborers & freight, stock, & material movers, hand	1.1	-7.9
General & operations managers	1.5	-7.9	Computer-controlled machine tool operators	1.1	12.5
Sewing machine operators	1.5	2.3	Executive secretaries & administrative assistants	1.1	2.3
Industrial engineers	1.5	24.2	Cutting, punching, & press machine operators	1.1	-7.9
Office clerks, general	1.5	0.8			

Source: Industry-Occupation Matrix, Bureau of Labor Statistics, December 4, 2007. These data are reported based on 4-digit NAICS categories but have been matched to corresponding 6-digit NAICS industry codes. The change reported for each occupation to the year 2016 is a percent of growth or decline as estimated by the Bureau of Labor Statistics. The abbreviation nec stands for 'not elsewhere classified'.

LOCATION BY STATE AND REGIONAL CONCENTRATION

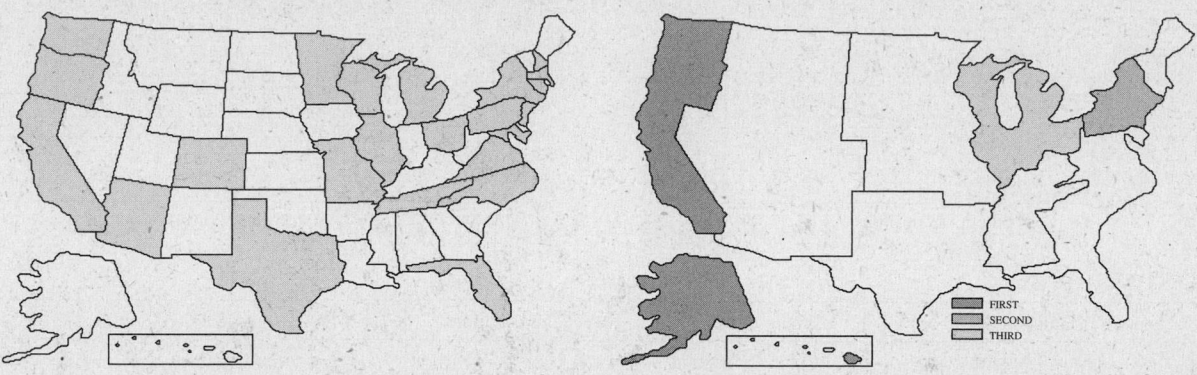

INDUSTRY DATA BY STATE

| State | Establish-ments | Shipments | | | Employment | | | | Cost as % of Shipments | Investment per Employee ($) |
		Total ($ mil)	% of U.S.	Per Establ.	Total Number	% of U.S.	Per Establ.	Wages ($/hour)		
California	77	938.8	21.0	12,192.2	4,467	18.8	58	14.89	37.3	6,194
Ohio	15	331.9	7.4	22,125.9	1,917	8.1	128	17.46	38.6	4,957
Wisconsin	15	276.4	6.2	18,428.7	1,933	8.1	129	15.49	40.3	3,703
New York	26	239.6	5.3	9,214.4	1,471	6.2	57	15.77	37.9	2,046
Massachusetts	25	180.2	4.0	7,209.0	922	3.9	37	19.11	34.9	3,843
Pennsylvania	37	176.5	3.9	4,769.3	1,223	5.2	33	14.40	37.7	4,443
Texas	15	175.3	3.9	11,683.8	754	3.2	50	15.86	48.2	5,444
New Jersey	23	162.7	3.6	7,074.6	1,365	5.7	59	15.87	39.5	4,952
Connecticut	10	143.1	3.2	14,310.1	446	1.9	45	23.45	64.4	10,260
New Hampshire	6	129.2	2.9	21,531.8	910	3.8	152	13.51	42.3	4,693
Michigan	19	122.6	2.7	6,450.7	848	3.6	45	12.64	39.2	1,599
Illinois	13	108.8	2.4	8,372.8	655	2.8	50	14.91	34.9	6,027
North Carolina	8	107.9	2.4	13,488.6	735	3.1	92	14.41	46.2	3,396
Minnesota	8	70.3	1.6	8,793.1	503	2.1	63	14.73	38.9	6,606
Colorado	9	57.1	1.3	6,341.3	367	1.5	41	19.41	40.1	3,428
Missouri	10	36.4	0.8	3,635.1	283	1.2	28	12.55	43.4	2,127
Virginia	8	31.7	0.7	3,966.1	199	0.8	25	15.42	41.3	2,889
Washington	9	31.2	0.7	3,464.6	254	1.1	28	14.11	44.4	965
Florida	14	27.8	0.6	1,986.8	228	1.0	16	12.37	34.3	4,031
Oregon	11	23.5	0.5	2,135.3	240	1.0	22	10.57	44.3	2,758
Maryland	10	16.2	0.4	1,618.0	130	0.5	13	15.61	26.1	1,454
Tennessee	6	11.2	0.2	1,859.5	109	0.5	18	21.33	44.0	6,963
Arizona	5	10.3	0.2	2,064.6	103	0.4	21	17.85	33.6	1,757

Source: 2002 *Economic Census*. The states are in descending order of shipments or establishments (if shipment data are missing for the majority). The symbol (D) appears when data are withheld to prevent disclosure of competitive information. States marked with (D) are sorted by number of establishments. A dash (-) indicates that the data element cannot be calculated. Data may not show all states active in the NAICS category. All data available at the time of publication are shown.

NAICS 339112 - SURGICAL AND MEDICAL INSTRUMENT MANUFACTURING

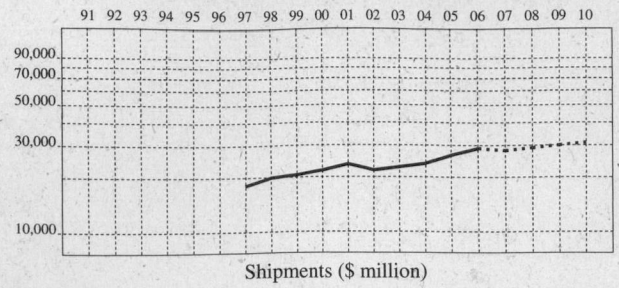

Shipments ($ million)

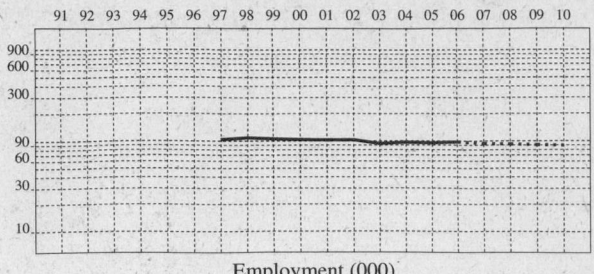

Employment (000)

GENERAL STATISTICS

Year	Com-panies	Establishments		Employment			Compensation		Production ($ million)			
		Total	with 20 or more employees	Total (000)	Production Workers (000)	Hours (Mil)	Payroll ($ mil)	Wages ($/hr)	Cost of Materials	Value Added by Manufacture	Value of Shipments	Capital Invest.
1997	1,454	1,591	591	104.1	62.5	124.2	3,971.8	12.72	5,108.0	12,931.8	18,026.9	721.7
1998		1,586	593	108.8	65.2	124.6	4,257.1	13.93	5,673.8	14,311.8	19,940.7	712.2
1999		1,568	601	106.0	62.0	118.7	4,294.5	14.53	5,500.3	15,307.7	20,624.4	832.4
2000		1,480	587	103.7	58.3	112.1	4,421.6	14.82	5,717.3	16,317.8	21,778.2	919.3
2001		1,433	576	102.3	58.6	113.0	4,636.7	15.16	6,783.8	16,880.6	23,559.2	1,066.0
2002	1,216	1,352	601	103.1	57.7	115.3	4,581.6	15.48	6,541.0	15,079.8	21,819.4	930.7
2003		1,272	567	93.8	54.0	106.5	4,402.6	14.92	6,583.5	16,334.2	22,719.2	736.3
2004		1,256	566	96.6	52.6	110.7	4,733.3	16.79	6,804.0	17,000.4	23,742.6	829.1
2005		1,289	562	95.2	51.7	107.7	4,928.9	17.40	7,289.8	19,368.2	26,484.0	849.5
2006		1,182P	562P	98.0	53.8	108.4	5,460.4	18.05	8,002.5	21,039.2	28,883.5	1,002.3
2007		1,133P	558P	93.6P	49.9P	103.6P	5,241.6P	18.19P	7,784.7P	20,466.6P	28,097.4P	952.8P
2008		1,085P	553P	92.3P	48.4P	101.7P	5,363.9P	18.70P	8,053.7P	21,173.7P	29,068.2P	969.7P
2009		1,036P	549P	90.9P	47.0P	99.8P	5,486.2P	19.21P	8,322.7P	21,880.9P	30,039.0P	986.6P
2010		988P	545P	89.5P	45.6P	97.9P	5,608.5P	19.72P	8,591.6P	22,588.1P	31,009.9P	1,003.5P

Sources: 1997 and 2002 *Economic Census*; other years, up to 2006, are from *Annual Survey of Manufactures*. Establishment counts for non-Census years are from *County Business Patterns*; 1997 and 2002 values are from the 1997 and 2002 censuses, respectively. 'P's show projections by the editors.

INDICES OF CHANGE

Year	Com-panies	Establishments		Employment			Compensation		Production ($ million)			
		Total	with 20 or more employees	Total (000)	Production Workers (000)	Hours (Mil)	Payroll ($ mil)	Wages ($/hr)	Cost of Materials	Value Added by Manufacture	Value of Shipments	Capital Invest.
1997	120	118	98	101	108	108	87	82	78	86	83	78
1998		117	99	106	113	108	93	90	87	95	91	77
1999		116	100	103	107	103	94	94	84	102	95	89
2000		109	98	101	101	97	97	96	87	108	100	99
2001		106	96	99	102	98	101	98	104	112	108	115
2002	100	100	100	100	100	100	100	100	100	100	100	100
2003		94	94	91	94	92	96	96	101	108	104	79
2004		93	94	94	91	96	103	108	104	113	109	89
2005		95	94	92	90	93	108	112	111	128	121	91
2006		87P	93P	95	93	94	119	117	122	140	132	108
2007		84P	93P	91P	86P	90P	114P	118P	119P	136P	129P	102P
2008		80P	92P	90P	84P	88P	117P	121P	123P	140P	133P	104P
2009		77P	91P	88P	81P	87P	120P	124P	127P	145P	138P	106P
2010		73P	91P	87P	79P	85P	122P	127P	131P	150P	142P	108P

Sources: Same as General Statistics. Values reflect change from the base year, 2002. Values above 100 mean greater than 2002, values below 100 mean less than 2002, and the values of 100 in other years means the same as 2002. 'P's show projections by the editors.

SELECTED RATIOS

For 2002	Avg. of All Manufact.	Analyzed Industry	Index	For 2002	Avg. of All Manufact.	Analyzed Industry	Index
Employees per Establishment	42	76	182	Value Added per Production Worker	182,367	261,348	143
Payroll per Establishment	1,639,184	3,388,757	207	Cost per Establishment	5,769,015	4,838,018	84
Payroll per Employee	39,053	44,438	114	Cost per Employee	137,446	63,443	46
Production Workers per Establishment	30	43	145	Cost per Production Worker	195,506	113,362	58
Wages per Establishment	694,845	1,320,151	190	Shipments per Establishment	11,158,348	16,138,609	145
Wages per Production Worker	23,548	30,933	131	Shipments per Employee	265,847	211,633	80
Hours per Production Worker	1,980	1,998	101	Shipments per Production Worker	378,144	378,153	100
Wages per Hour	11.89	15.48	130	Investment per Establishment	361,338	688,388	191
Value Added per Establishment	5,381,325	11,153,698	207	Investment per Employee	8,609	9,027	105
Value Added per Employee	128,210	146,264	114	Investment per Production Worker	12,245	16,130	132

Sources: Same as General Statistics. The 'Average of All Manufacturing' column represents the average of all manufacturing industries reported for the most recent complete year available. The Index shows the relationship between the Average and the Analyzed Industry. For example, 100 means that they are equal; 500 that the Analyzed Industry is five times the average; 50 means that the Analyzed Industry is half the national average. The abbreviation 'na' is used to show that data are 'not available'. Ratios shown for 2002, the last complete census year.

LEADING COMPANIES   Number shown: **75**   Total sales ($ mil): **192,076**   Total employment (000): **613.8**

Company Name	Address				CEO Name	Phone	Co. Type	Sales ($ mil)	Empl. (000)
Abbott Laboratories	100 Abbott Park Rd.	Abbott Park	IL	60064		847-937-6100	P	25,914	68.0
Eli Lilly and Co.	Lilly Corporate Ctr	Indianapolis	IN	46285		317-276-2000	P	18,634	40.6
Abbott Diabetes Care	1360 S Loop Rd.	Alameda	CA	94502	Ed Fiorentino		S	18,514*	60.0
Medtronic Inc.	710 Medtronic Pky.	Minneapolis	MN	55432		763-514-4000	P	12,299	38.0
Baxter International Inc.	1 Baxter Pky.	Deerfield	IL	60015		847-948-2000	P	11,263	46.0
Medtronic AVE Inc.	3576 Unocal Pl.	Santa Rosa	CA	95403	William Hawkins	707-525-0111	S	10,054	21.5
Thermo Fisher Scientific Inc.	81 Wyman St.	Waltham	MA	02451	Marijn E. Dekkers	781-622-1000	P	9,746	33.0
Boston Scientific Corp.	1 Boston Scientific	Natick	MA	01760		508-650-8000	P	8,357	27.5
Becton, Dickinson and Co.	1 Becton Dr.	Franklin Lakes	NJ	07417		201-847-6800	P	6,360	28.0
Stryker Corp.	PO Box 4085	Kalamazoo	MI	49003		616-385-2600	P	6,001	16.0
Guidant Corp.	PO Box 44906	St. Paul	MN	55112	James M. Cornelius	651-582-4000	S	3,551	13.0
Genzyme Corp.	500 Kendall St.	Cambridge	MA	02142		617-252-7500	P	3,458	10.0
Hi-Stat Manufacturing Company	28001 Cabot Dr.	Novi	MI	48377	John Corey	248-489-9300	D	3,194*	5.0
Snap-On Inc.	PO Box 1410	Kenosha	WI	53141	Tim Chambers	262-656-5200	P	2,841	11.6
Vishay Intertechnology Inc.	PO Box 4004	Malvern	PA	19355	Gerald Paul	610-644-1300	P	2,833	27.9
Hubbell Inc.	584 Derby Milford	Orange	CT	06477		203-799-4100	P	2,534	11.5
Medline Industries Inc.	1 Medline Pl.	Mundelein	IL	60060	Charles S. Mills	847-949-5500	R	2,450	4.9
C.R. Bard Inc.	730 Central Ave.	Murray Hill	NJ	07974		908-277-8000	P	2,202	10.2
Biomet Inc.	PO Box 587	Warsaw	IN	46581	Jeffrey R. Binder	574-267-6639	R	2,026	4.1
Cordis Endovascular Systems	14201 NW 60th	Miami Lakes	FL	33014	Rick Anderson	786-313-2000	S	1,974*	7.0
Teleflex Inc.	155 S Limerick Rd.	Limerick	PA	19468	Jeffrey P. Black	610-948-5100	P	1,934	14.0
DENTSPLY International Inc.	PO Box 872	York	PA	17405		717-845-7511	P	1,811	8.5
Rainin Instrument L.L.C.	PO Box 4026	Woburn	MA	01888	Kenneth Rainin	510-564-1600	R	1,590*	0.1
Cadwell Laboratories Inc.	909 N Kellogg St.	Kennewick	WA	99336	Carl Cadwell	509-735-6481	R	1,583*	<0.1
GF Health Products Inc.	2935 Northeast Pky.	Atlanta	GA	30360	Michael A. Joffred		R	1,457*	2.2
Dresser Inc.	15455 Dallas Pkwy.	Addison	TX	75001	Charles Immel	972-361-9800	S	1,343*	6.0
STERIS Corp.	5960 Heisley Rd.	Mentor	OH	44060	Charles Immel	440-354-2600	P	1,197	5.1
Respironics Inc.	1010 Murry Ridge	Murrysville	PA	15668	Gerald E. McGinnis	724-387-5200	P	1,195	4.9
United States Surgical Corp.	150 Glover Ave.	Norwalk	CT	06850	Allen Panzer	203-845-1000	S	1,172*	5.8
Edwards Lifesciences Corp.	1 Edwards Way	Irvine	CA	92614		949-250-2500	P	1,091	5.6
Advanced Medical Optics Inc.	PO Box 25162	Santa Ana	CA	92705	William Grant	714-247-8200	P	1,091	4.1
Orbital Sciences Corp.	21839 Atlantic Blvd	Dulles	VA	20166		703-406-5000	P	1,084	2.8
Varian Oncology Systems	3100 Hansen Way	Palo Alto	CA	94304	Timothy Guertin	650-493-4000	D	1,046*	3.6
Trimble Navigation Ltd.	935 Stewart Dr.	Sunnyvale	CA	94085	Steven W. Berglund	408-481-8000	P	940	2.8
Cubic Corp.	PO Box 85587	San Diego	CA	92186	Gerald Dinkel	858-277-6780	P	890	6.0
Omron Healthcare Inc.	1200 Lakeside Dr.	Deerfield	IL	60015		847-680-6200	R	872*	0.5
Nephros Inc.	3960 Broadway	New York	NY	10032	Norman J. Barta	212-781-5113	P	794	<0.1
MKS Instruments Inc.	90 Industrial Way	Wilmington	MA	01887	Leo Berlinghieri	978-284-4000	P	783	3.0
ResMed Inc.	14040 Danielson St.	Poway	CA	92064	Peter C. Farrell	858-746-2400	P	716	2.7
CONMED Corp.	525 French Rd.	Utica	NY	13502	Eugene R. Corasanti	315-797-8375	P	694	3.2
PolyMedica Corp.	701 Edgewater Dr.	Wakefield	MA	01880	Patrick T. Ryan	781-486-8111	P	676	2.2
B. Braun Inc.	PO Box 4027	Bethlehem	PA	18018	Carroll Neubauer	610-997-4253	S	630*	1.6
Cook Group Inc.	PO Box 489	Bloomington	IN	47402	William A. Cook	812-339-2235	R	615	4.0
VIASYS Healthcare Inc.	227 Washington St.	Conshohocken	PA	19428	Lori Cross	610-862-0800	P	610	2.4
Intuitive Surgical Inc.	950 Kifer Rd.	Sunnyvale	CA	94086		408-523-2100	P	601	0.8
BD Medical Systems	1 Becton Dr.	Franklin Lakes	NJ	07417	Edward Ludwig	201-847-6800	D	577*	1.2
Input/Output Inc.	2105 CityWest Blvd.	Houston	TX	77042	James M. Lapeyre Jr.	281-933-3339	P	504	1.0
UOP L.L.C.	25 E Algonquin Rd.	Des Plaines	IL	60017	Carlos Guimaraes	847-391-2000	R	500*	4.0
Arrow International Inc.	PO Box 12888	Reading	PA	19612	Carl Anderson	610-378-0131	S	482	4.0
Terumo Cardiovascular Systems	6200 Jackson Rd.	Ann Arbor	MI	48103	Mark Sutter	734-663-4145	R	481*	0.3
Haemonetics Corp.	400 Wood Rd.	Braintree	MA	02184		781-848-7100	P	450	1.8
Liebert Corp.	PO Box 29186	Columbus	OH	43229	Robert Bauer	614-888-0246	S	440*	5.0
Baxter Healthcare Corporation	PO Box 1389	Aibonito	PR	00705		787-753-8021	R	423*	1.3
MTS Systems Corp.	14000 Technology	Eden Prairie	MN	55344	Sidney W. Emery Jr.	952-937-4000	P	421	1.6
Kyphon Inc.	1221 Crossman Ave.	Sunnyvale	CA	94089		408-548-6500	P	408	1.1
Global Charter S.A.	12300 Parc Crest Dr	Stafford	TX	77477	Robert P. Peebler	281-933-3339	S	403*	0.8
I/O Sensors Inc.	12300 Parc Crest Dr	Stafford	TX	77477	Robert P. Peebler	281-933-3339	S	403*	0.8
IPOP Management Inc.	12300 Parc Crest Dr	Stafford	TX	77477	Robert P. Peebler	281-933-3339	S	403*	0.8
RMS Co.	8600 Evergreen Blvd	Coon Rapids	MN	55433	Arthur Mouyard	763-786-1520	S	400*	0.3
Arthrex Inc.	1370 Creekside Blvd	Naples	FL	34108	Reinhold Schmieding	239-643-5553	R	400*	0.2
Synthes USA L.P.	1302 Wrights Ln. E	West Chester	PA	19380		610-719-5000	R	393*	0.3
I/O Exploration Products USA	12300 Parc Crest Dr	Stafford	TX	77477	Robert P. Peebler	281-933-3339	S	391*	0.8
I/O of Austin Inc.	12300 Parc Crest Dr	Stafford	TX	77477	Robert P. Peebler	281-933-3339	S	391*	0.8
Datascope Corp.	14 Philips Pky.	Montvale	NJ	07645		201-391-8100	P	379	1.2
Recon Optical Inc.	550 W NW Hwy.	Barrington	IL	60010		847-381-2400	R	344*	0.2
GSI Group Inc.	39 Manning Rd.	Billerica	MA	01821	Sergio Edelstein	978-439-5511	P	318	1.4
Biosite Inc.	9975 Summers Rdg	San Diego	CA	92121	Kim D. Blickenstaff	858-805-4808	P	309	1.0
Abbott Labs Diagnostic Div.	1921 Hurd Dr.	Irving	TX	75038	Miles White	972-518-6000	D	306*	2.0
B Braun/McGaw of Puerto Rico	PO Box 729	Sabana Grande	PR	00637	James Sweeney	787-873-4600	R	301*	0.9
Zeiss, Carl Inc.	1 Zeiss Dr.	Thornwood	NY	10594	Jim Kelly	914-681-7600	R	300*	1.7
Medtronic MiniMed Inc.	18000 Devonshire St	Northridge	CA	91325	Jeff McCaulley	818-362-5958	S	287*	1.5
Nektar Therapeutics	150 Industrial Rd.	San Carlos	CA	94070	Robert Chess	650-631-3100	P	273	0.6
Getinge USA Inc.	1777 E Henrietta Rd	Rochester	NY	14623	Andrew Csery	585-475-1400	R	263*	0.2
DMS Holdings Inc.	1931 Norman Dr. S	Waukegan	IL	60085	Michael Mazza	847-680-6811	R	257*	0.1
Raytheon Electronic Systems	PO Box 902	El Segundo	CA	90245	Jack Kelbe	310-647-0445	R	255*	1.6

Source: Ward's Business Directory of U.S. Private and Public Companies, Volumes 1 and 2, 2008. The company type code used is as follows: P - Public, R - Private, S - Subsidiary, D - Division, J - Joint Venture, A - Affiliate, G - Group. Sales are in millions of dollars, employees are in thousands. An asterisk (*) indicates an estimated sales volume. The symbol < stands for 'less than'. Company names and addresses are truncated, in some cases, to fit into the available space.

MATERIALS CONSUMED

Material	Quantity	Delivered Cost ($ million)
Printed ciruit boards (without inserted components) for electronic circuitry	(X)	9.6
Printed circuit assemblies, loaded boards, and modules	(X)	53.2
Resistors, capacitors, transformers, electron tubes, semiconductors, and other electronic components	(X)	100.1
Current-carrying wiring devices	(X)	20.1
Electric motors and generators	(X)	18.5
Metal bolts, nuts, screws, and other screw machine products	(X)	31.2
Other fabricated metal products (exc. bolts, nuts, washers, etc.)	(X)	98.3
Iron and steel castings (rough and semifinished)	(X)	25.2
Nonferrous (aluminum, copper, etc.) castings (rough and semifinished)	(X)	15.0
Steel shapes and forms (exc. castings, forgings, fabr. metal products)	(X)	48.1
Nonferrous shapes and forms	(X)	22.4
Nonwoven fabrics	(X)	11.7
Broadwoven fabrics	(X)	4.6
Plastics resins consumed in the form of granules, pellets, etc.	(X)	165.4
Plastics products consumed in the form of sheets, rods, etc.	(X)	282.9
Fabricated plastics products	(X)	557.5
Fabricated rubber products (exc. tires, tubes, hoses, belting, and gaskets)	(X)	60.8
Surgical and orthopedic supplies	(X)	1,071.0
Sheet metal products (excluding stampings)	(X)	32.0
Adhesives and sealants	(X)	21.2
Paperboard containers, boxes, and corrugated paperboard	(X)	100.6
Paper and paperboard products	(X)	36.9
All other materials, components, parts, containers, and supplies	(X)	1,272.9
Materials, ingredients, containers, and supplies, nsk	(X)	1,245.6

Source: 2002 *Economic Census*. Explanation of symbols used: (D): Withheld to avoid disclosure of competitive data; na: Not available; (S): Withheld because statistical norms were not met; (X): Not applicable; (Z): Less than half the unit shown; nec: Not elsewhere classified; nsk: Not specified by kind; - : zero; p : 10-19 percent estimated; q : 20-29 percent estimated.

PRODUCT SHARE DETAILS

Product or Product Class Shipments	Mil. $	Product or Product Class Shipments	Mil. $
SURGICAL AND MEDICAL INSTRUMENTS	20,482.7	Medical and surgical hypodermic needles	352.6
Orthopedic and surgical instruments	4,662.3	Medical and surgical blood transfusion and IV equipment, including blood donor kits	1,313.6
Surgical instruments, including suture needles and ear, eye, nose, and throat instruments	3,667.2	Medical and surgical catheters	2,720.1
Orthopedic instruments, excluding ear, eye, nose, and throat instruments	995.1	Other medical and surgical apparatus and instruments, excluding parts	4,498.1
Medical and surgical diagnostic apparatus, except electromedical diagnostic apparatus	3,030.8	Medical and surgical anesthetic apparatus and instruments	681.5
Medical and surgical metabolism and blood pressure diagnostic apparatus, except electromedical diagnostic apparatus	298.5	Medical and surgical bone nails, plates, and screws, and other internal fixation devices	1,276.0
		Medical and surgical mechanical therapy apparatus	212.7
Other medical and surgical diagnostic apparatus, including optical diagnostic apparatus, excluding electromedical diagnostic apparatus	2,732.3	Other medical and surgical apparatus and instruments, excluding parts	2,327.9
Medical and surgical syringes and hypodermic needles	1,545.5	Parts for medical and surgical apparatus and instruments	942.3
Medical and surgical syringes	1,192.9	Surgical and medical instruments, nsk, total	1,770.0

Source: 2002 *Economic Census*. The values are product shipments in millions of dollars for 2002. Total product shipments may be lower or higher than industry shipments. See Introduction for a full discussion. Values of indented subcategories are summed in the main heading(s). The symbol (D) appears when data are withheld to prevent disclosure of competitive information. The abbreviation nsk stands for 'not specified by kind' and nec for 'not elsewhere classified'. A dash (-) means zero.

INPUTS AND OUTPUTS FOR SURGICAL AND MEDICAL INSTRUMENT MANUFACTURING

Economic Sector or Industry Providing Inputs	%	Sector	Economic Sector or Industry Buying Outputs	%	Sector
Compensation of employees	28.0		Private fixed investment	48.9	
Surgical & medical instrument	5.1	Manufg.	Exports of goods & services	16.0	Cap Inv
Wholesale trade	4.1	Trade	Hospitals	7.7	Services
Management of companies & enterprises	3.1	Services	Physician, dentist, other health practitioner offices	7.4	Services
Plastics products, nec	3.0	Manufg.	General S/L govt. services	5.5	S/L Govt
Surgical appliances & supplies	2.8	Manufg.	Surgical & medical instrument	4.0	Manufg.
Plastics packaging materials, film & sheet	1.7	Manufg.	Surgical appliances & supplies	2.3	Manufg.
Lessors of nonfinancial assets	1.1	Fin/R.E.	Medical & diagnostic labs & outpatient services	2.1	Services
Truck transportation	1.1	Util.	Ophthalmic goods	1.0	Manufg.
Advertising & related services	1.1	Services	S/L govt. invest., other	0.8	S/L Govt
Textile & fabric finishing mills	1.0	Manufg.	Nursing & residential care facilities	0.7	Services
Securities, commodity contracts, investments	1.0	Fin/R.E.	Personal consumption expenditures	0.6	
Plastics materials & resins	0.9	Manufg.	Federal government, investment, national defense	0.6	Fed Govt
Retail trade	0.9	Trade	Veterinary services	0.5	Services
Legal services	0.8	Services	General Federal government services, defense	0.5	Fed Govt
Real estate	0.8	Fin/R.E.	General Federal government services, nondefense	0.4	Fed Govt
Monetary authorities/depository credit intermediation	0.7	Fin/R.E.	S/L govt. invest., education	0.3	S/L Govt

Continued on next page.

INPUTS AND OUTPUTS FOR SURGICAL AND MEDICAL INSTRUMENT MANUFACTURING - Continued

Economic Sector or Industry Providing Inputs	%	Sector	Economic Sector or Industry Buying Outputs	%	Sector
Synthetic rubber	0.7	Manufg.	Home health care services	0.3	Services
Paperboard containers	0.6	Manufg.	Community food, housing, relief, & rehabilitation	0.2	Services
Noncomparable imports	0.6	Foreign	Individual & family services	0.2	Services
Semiconductors & related devices	0.6	Manufg.			
Professional, scientific, technical services, nec	0.6	Services			
Turned products & screws, nuts, & bolts	0.5	Manufg.			
Specialized design services	0.5	Services			
Power generation & supply	0.5	Util.			
Management, scientific, & technical consulting	0.5	Services			
Telecommunications	0.4	Services			
Machine shops	0.4	Manufg.			
Taxes on production & imports, less subsidies	0.4				
Printed circuit assemblies (electronic assemblies)	0.4	Manufg.			
Accounting, tax preparation, bookkeeping, & payroll	0.3	Services			
Food services & drinking places	0.3	Services			
Warehousing & storage	0.3	Util.			
Data processing, hosting, & related services	0.3	Services			
Automotive equipment rental & leasing	0.3	Fin/R.E.			
Unlaminated plastics profile shapes	0.3	Manufg.			
Laminated plastics plates, sheets, & shapes	0.3	Manufg.			
Iron & steel mills & ferroalloys	0.3	Manufg.			
Architectural, engineering, & related services	0.2	Services			
Coating, engraving, heat treating & allied activities	0.2	Manufg.			
Paper mills	0.2	Manufg.			
Scientific research & development services	0.2	Services			
Services to buildings & dwellings	0.2	Services			
Other computer related services, including facilities	0.2	Services			
Hotels & motels, including casino hotels	0.2	Services			
Metal & other household furniture	0.2	Manufg.			
Ornamental & architectural metal products	0.2	Manufg.			
Maintenance/repair of nonresidential structures	0.2	Construct.			
Fabricated metals, nec	0.2	Manufg.			
Air transportation	0.2	Util.			
Commercial & industrial machinery rental & leasing	0.1	Fin/R.E.			
Ferrous metal foundries	0.1	Manufg.			
Abrasive products	0.1	Manufg.			
Business support services	0.1	Services			
Adhesives	0.1	Manufg.			
Wiring devices	0.1	Manufg.			
Cutting tools & machine tool accessories	0.1	Manufg.			
Custom roll forming	0.1	Manufg.			
Motors & generators	0.1	Manufg.			
Nondepository credit intermediation activities	0.1	Fin/R.E.			
Automotive repair & maintenance, ex. car washes	0.1	Services			

Source: *Benchmark Input-Output Accounts for the U.S. Economy, 2002*, U.S. Department of Commerce, Washington, D.C., January 2008. The abbreviation nec stands for 'not elsewhere classified'.

OCCUPATIONS EMPLOYED BY MEDICAL EQUIPMENT & SUPPLIES MANUFACTURING

Occupation	% of Total 2006	Change to 2016	Occupation	% of Total 2006	Change to 2016
Dental laboratory technicians	12.2	2.3	Assemblers & fabricators, nec	1.4	-7.9
Team assemblers	11.0	2.3	Sales reps, wholesale & manufacturing, exc tech	1.3	2.3
First-line supervisors/managers of production workers	3.0	2.3	Helpers--Production workers	1.3	2.3
Inspectors, testers, sorters, samplers, & weighers	3.0	-3.6	Truck drivers, light or delivery services	1.2	2.3
Customer service representatives	2.2	12.5	Packaging & filling machine operators & tenders	1.2	-7.9
Medical appliance technicians	2.0	8.3	Bookkeeping, accounting, & auditing clerks	1.2	2.3
Packers & packagers, hand	1.9	-18.2	Multiple machine tool operators & tenders	1.1	12.5
Shipping, receiving, & traffic clerks	1.9	-1.6	Maintenance & repair workers, general	1.1	2.3
Machinists	1.7	7.4	Stock clerks & order fillers	1.1	-14.4
Molding, coremaking, & casting machine operators	1.6	-7.9	Mechanical engineers	1.1	2.3
Sales representatives, wholesale & manufacturing, tech	1.6	2.3	Laborers & freight, stock, & material movers, hand	1.1	-7.9
General & operations managers	1.5	-7.9	Computer-controlled machine tool operators	1.1	12.5
Sewing machine operators	1.5	2.3	Executive secretaries & administrative assistants	1.1	2.3
Industrial engineers	1.5	24.2	Cutting, punching, & press machine operators	1.1	-7.9
Office clerks, general	1.5	0.8			

Source: *Industry-Occupation Matrix*, Bureau of Labor Statistics, December 4, 2007. These data are reported based on 4-digit NAICS categories but have been matched to corresponding 6-digit NAICS industry codes. The change reported for each occupation to the year 2016 is a percent of growth or decline as estimated by the Bureau of Labor Statistics. The abbreviation nec stands for 'not elsewhere classified'.

LOCATION BY STATE AND REGIONAL CONCENTRATION

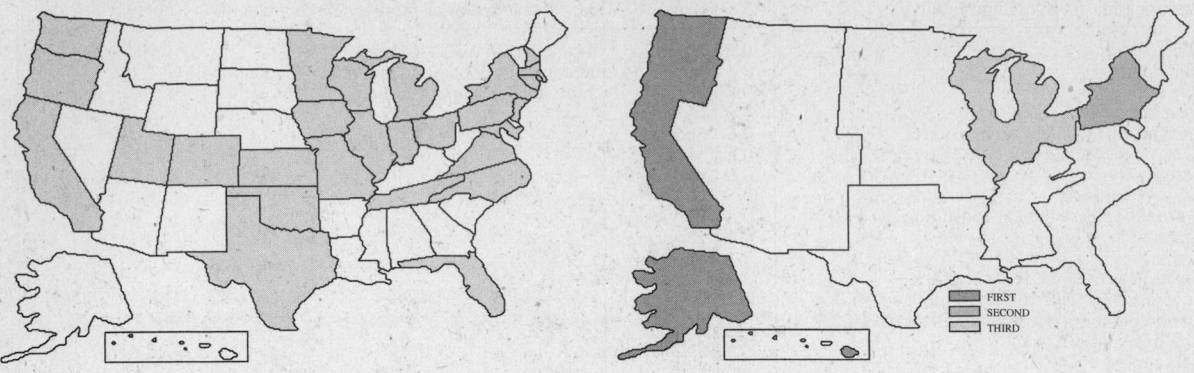

FIRST
SECOND
THIRD

INDUSTRY DATA BY STATE

| State | Establish-ments | Shipments | | | Employment | | | | Cost as % of Shipments | Investment per Employee ($) |
		Total ($ mil)	% of U.S.	Per Establ.	Total Number	% of U.S.	Per Establ.	Wages ($/hour)		
California	264	4,607.0	21.1	17,450.8	20,682	20.1	78	16.22	31.8	11,657
Massachusetts	92	1,836.1	8.4	19,958.0	8,361	8.1	91	14.91	27.5	7,570
Pennsylvania	72	1,633.9	7.5	22,692.5	8,555	8.3	119	19.81	30.0	7,694
Florida	75	1,135.7	5.2	15,142.4	6,627	6.4	88	14.35	25.8	10,803
New York	69	1,091.5	5.0	15,819.2	6,872	6.7	100	13.43	37.5	7,150
Minnesota	66	1,047.8	4.8	15,876.2	6,669	6.5	101	16.89	29.2	9,596
Connecticut	39	1,043.6	4.8	26,758.1	4,273	4.1	110	16.47	38.7	7,193
Texas	59	741.6	3.4	12,570.0	3,797	3.7	64	15.96	35.8	6,608
North Carolina	31	680.8	3.1	21,961.3	2,736	2.7	88	13.37	26.2	9,201
Colorado	33	662.4	3.0	20,072.2	2,366	2.3	72	13.76	15.1	7,259
New Jersey	59	631.8	2.9	10,708.3	2,724	2.6	46	14.53	22.3	6,437
Utah	19	594.7	2.7	31,298.5	2,883	2.8	152	12.29	27.1	10,917
Wisconsin	27	529.3	2.4	19,602.0	1,735	1.7	64	17.20	33.1	7,984
Ohio	45	457.5	2.1	10,167.4	3,217	3.1	71	13.60	26.6	6,048
Indiana	39	382.3	1.8	9,802.8	3,016	2.9	77	14.34	41.5	2,564
Michigan	32	346.0	1.6	10,813.7	1,260	1.2	39	14.63	24.7	8,373
New Hampshire	18	303.9	1.4	16,883.8	1,661	1.6	92	17.14	34.0	9,463
Illinois	45	247.5	1.1	5,500.8	1,605	1.6	36	13.89	30.1	12,193
Missouri	26	235.2	1.1	9,047.4	1,527	1.5	59	19.67	23.5	4,050
Washington	34	218.1	1.0	6,414.9	900	0.9	26	15.64	27.9	9,100
Kansas	7	213.1	1.0	30,437.6	255	0.2	36	16.37	6.2	7,863
Maryland	24	143.0	0.7	5,957.7	1,118	1.1	47	14.63	29.7	18,895
Tennessee	23	140.3	0.6	6,101.6	559	0.5	24	12.40	23.6	6,517
Oklahoma	8	85.7	0.4	10,715.1	355	0.3	44	12.76	59.0	4,394
Virginia	7	76.2	0.3	10,888.6	346	0.3	49	13.32	41.4	3,610
Oregon	19	57.8	0.3	3,044.7	325	0.3	17	17.85	22.1	14,480
Iowa	8	39.6	0.2	4,950.4	364	0.4	46	10.48	32.0	2,165
Rhode Island	7	27.7	0.1	3,951.7	226	0.2	32	15.69	29.2	4,115

Source: 2002 *Economic Census*. The states are in descending order of shipments or establishments (if shipment data are missing for the majority). The symbol (D) appears when data are withheld to prevent disclosure of competitive information. States marked with (D) are sorted by number of establishments. A dash (-) indicates that the data element cannot be calculated. Data may not show all states active in the NAICS category. All data available at the time of publication are shown.

NAICS 339113 - SURGICAL APPLIANCE AND SUPPLIES MANUFACTURING

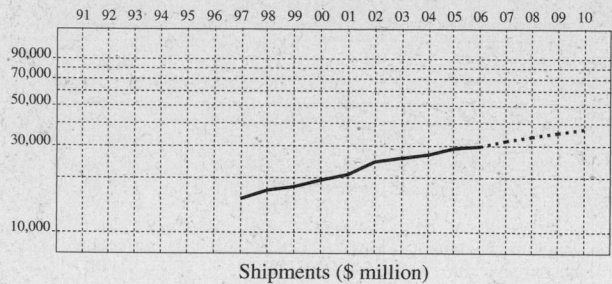

Shipments ($ million)

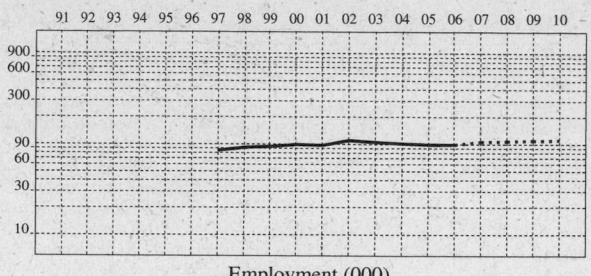

Employment (000)

GENERAL STATISTICS

| Year | Companies | Establishments | | Employment | | | Compensation | | Production ($ million) | | | |
		Total	with 20 or more employees	Total (000)	Production Workers (000)	Hours (Mil)	Payroll ($ mil)	Wages ($/hr)	Cost of Materials	Value Added by Manufacture	Value of Shipments	Capital Invest.
1997	1,512	1,649	603	84.6	53.4	100.4	2,962.5	12.55	5,279.7	9,965.5	15,322.7	565.0
1998		1,637	611	91.6	57.4	109.8	3,488.6	13.16	5,804.1	11,331.7	17,044.0	801.7
1999		1,611	603	93.8	59.3	112.9	3,540.5	13.56	6,069.1	11,981.1	17,846.2	763.0
2000		1,612	610	99.0	62.0	118.2	3,860.5	13.37	6,359.0	13,218.7	19,453.2	724.6
2001		1,599	606	96.9	59.2	115.5	3,858.5	13.49	6,587.2	14,356.2	20,859.5	770.1
2002	1,607	1,845	648	109.9	65.0	128.5	4,431.0	14.41	7,325.5	17,259.0	24,515.1	808.0
2003		1,844	650	105.7	65.7	133.8	4,723.5	14.35	7,546.3	19,036.0	25,705.6	750.3
2004		1,842	626	101.2	57.0	116.1	4,699.4	15.81	8,070.9	18,828.4	26,799.3	919.3
2005		1,858	618	98.8	56.3	115.0	5,016.5	16.43	8,881.6	20,407.1	29,038.6	1,140.3
2006		1,901P	639P	98.9	57.1	113.9	5,347.2	17.48	9,383.4	21,094.5	29,795.2	1,170.7
2007		1,937P	643P	106.3P	60.3P	124.2P	5,563.3P	17.21P	10,083.3P	22,668.0P	32,017.7P	1,131.9P
2008		1,973P	647P	107.9P	60.5P	125.6P	5,812.4P	17.71P	10,620.4P	23,875.4P	33,723.1P	1,184.7P
2009		2,009P	651P	109.4P	60.6P	127.0P	6,061.6P	18.21P	11,157.5P	25,082.8P	35,428.5P	1,237.6P
2010		2,044P	655P	110.9P	60.8P	128.4P	6,310.8P	18.70P	11,694.6P	26,290.2P	37,133.9P	1,290.4P

Sources: 1997 and 2002 *Economic Census*; other years, up to 2006, are from *Annual Survey of Manufactures*. Establishment counts for non-Census years are from *County Business Patterns*; 1997 and 2002 values are from the 1997 and 2002 censuses, respectively. 'P's show projections by the editors.

INDICES OF CHANGE

| Year | Companies | Establishments | | Employment | | | Compensation | | Production ($ million) | | | |
		Total	with 20 or more employees	Total (000)	Production Workers (000)	Hours (Mil)	Payroll ($ mil)	Wages ($/hr)	Cost of Materials	Value Added by Manufacture	Value of Shipments	Capital Invest.
1997	94	89	93	77	82	78	67	87	72	58	63	70
1998		89	94	83	88	85	79	91	79	66	70	99
1999		87	93	85	91	88	80	94	83	69	73	94
2000		87	94	90	95	92	87	93	87	77	79	90
2001		87	94	88	91	90	87	94	90	83	85	95
2002	100	100	100	100	100	100	100	100	100	100	100	100
2003		100	100	96	101	104	107	100	103	110	105	93
2004		100	97	92	88	90	106	110	110	109	109	114
2005		101	95	90	87	89	113	114	121	118	118	141
2006		103P	99P	90	88	89	121	121	128	122	122	145
2007		105P	99P	97P	93P	97P	126P	119P	138P	131P	131P	140P
2008		107P	100P	98P	93P	98P	131P	123P	145P	138P	138P	147P
2009		109P	100P	100P	93P	99P	137P	126P	152P	145P	145P	153P
2010		111P	101P	101P	94P	100P	142P	130P	160P	152P	151P	160P

Sources: Same as General Statistics. Values reflect change from the base year, 2002. Values above 100 mean greater than 2002, values below 100 mean less than 2002, and the values of 100 in other years means the same as 2002. 'P's show projections by the editors.

SELECTED RATIOS

For 2002	Avg. of All Manufact.	Analyzed Industry	Index	For 2002	Avg. of All Manufact.	Analyzed Industry	Index
Employees per Establishment	42	60	142	Value Added per Production Worker	182,367	265,523	146
Payroll per Establishment	1,639,184	2,401,626	147	Cost per Establishment	5,769,015	3,970,461	69
Payroll per Employee	39,053	40,318	103	Cost per Employee	137,446	66,656	48
Production Workers per Establishment	30	35	119	Cost per Production Worker	195,506	112,700	58
Wages per Establishment	694,845	1,003,623	144	Shipments per Establishment	11,158,348	13,287,317	119
Wages per Production Worker	23,548	28,487	121	Shipments per Employee	265,847	223,067	84
Hours per Production Worker	1,980	1,977	100	Shipments per Production Worker	378,144	377,155	100
Wages per Hour	11.89	14.41	121	Investment per Establishment	361,338	437,940	121
Value Added per Establishment	5,381,325	9,354,472	174	Investment per Employee	8,609	7,352	85
Value Added per Employee	128,210	157,043	122	Investment per Production Worker	12,245	12,431	102

Sources: Same as General Statistics. The 'Average of All Manufacturing' column represents the average of all manufacturing industries reported for the most recent complete year available. The Index shows the relationship between the Average and the Analyzed Industry. For example, 100 means that they are equal; 500 that the Analyzed Industry is five times the average; 50 means that the Analyzed Industry is half the national average. The abbreviation 'na' is used to show that data are 'not available'. Ratios shown for 2002, the last complete census year.

LEADING COMPANIES   Number shown: **75**   Total sales ($ mil): **278,598**   Total employment (000): **784.7**

Company Name	Address				CEO Name	Phone	Co. Type	Sales ($ mil)	Empl. (000)
Johnson & Johnson	1 Johnsn & Johnsn	New Brunswick	NJ	08901		732-524-0400	P	61,095	119.2
Pfizer Inc.	235 E 42nd St.	New York	NY	10017		212-573-2323	P	48,418	86.6
Kimberly-Clark Corp.	PO Box 619100	Dallas	TX	75261		972-281-1200	P	18,266	53.0
Schering-Plough Corp.	2000 Galloping Hill	Kenilworth	NJ	07033		908-298-4000	P	12,690	55.0
Medtronic Inc.	710 Medtronic Pky.	Minneapolis	MN	55432		763-514-4000	P	12,299	38.0
Baxter International Inc.	1 Baxter Pky.	Deerfield	IL	60015		847-948-2000	P	11,263	46.0
Medtronic AVE Inc.	3576 Unocal Pl.	Santa Rosa	CA	95403	William Hawkins	707-525-0111	S	10,054	21.5
Covidien	15 Hampshire St.	Mansfield	MA	02048	Richard Meelia	508-261-8000	R	10,000	43.0
Siemens Medical Solutions USA	51 Valley Stream Pk	Malvern	PA	19355	Thomas McCausland	610-219-6300	S	9,135*	13.0
Encon Safety Products	PO Box 3826	Houston	TX	77253	David Key	713-466-1449	R	7,970*	<0.1
Becton, Dickinson and Co.	1 Becton Dr.	Franklin Lakes	NJ	07417		201-847-6800	P	6,360	28.0
Stryker Corp.	PO Box 4085	Kalamazoo	MI	49003		616-385-2600	P	6,001	16.0
Zimmer Holdings Inc.	PO Box 708	Warsaw	IN	46580	David Dvorak	574-267-6131	P	3,898	7.6
St. Jude Medical Inc.	1 Lillehei Plz.	St. Paul	MN	55117		651-483-2000	P	3,779	12.0
Cintas Corp.	PO Box 625737	Cincinnati	OH	45262		513-459-1200	P	3,707	34.0
Steelcase Inc.	PO Box 1967	Grand Rapids	MI	49501	James P. Hackett	616-247-2710	P	3,097	13.0
HNI Corp.	PO Box 1109	Muscatine	IA	52761	Timothy Anderson	563-264-7400	P	2,571	14.2
Medline Industries Inc.	1 Medline Pl.	Mundelein	IL	60060	Charles S. Mills	847-949-5500	R	2,450	4.9
Bausch and Lomb Inc.	1 Bausch Lomb Pl.	Rochester	NY	14604		585-338-6000	P	2,292	13.0
C.R. Bard Inc.	730 Central Ave.	Murray Hill	NJ	07974		908-277-8000	P	2,202	10.2
Furniture Brands International	101 S Hanley Rd.	St. Louis	MO	63105	John T. Foy	314-863-1100	P	2,082	11.9
Biomet Inc.	PO Box 587	Warsaw	IN	46581	Jeffrey R. Binder	574-267-6639	R	2,026	4.1
Hillenbrand Industries Inc.	1069 State Rte 46E	Batesville	IN	47006		812-934-7000	P	2,024	9.9
Herman Miller Inc.	PO Box 302	Zeeland	MI	49464		616-654-3000	P	1,919	6.4
DENTSPLY International Inc.	PO Box 872	York	PA	17405		717-845-7511	P	1,811	8.5
HON Co.	PO Box 1109	Muscatine	IA	52761		563-264-7100	S	1,789*	9.8
Kinetic Concepts Inc.	PO Box 659508	San Antonio	TX	78265	Catherine M. Burzik	210-524-9000	P	1,610	6.4
Invacare Corp.	PO Box 4028	Elyria	OH	44036	Gerald B. Blouch	440-329-6000	P	1,602	5.7
GF Health Products Inc.	2935 Northeast Pky.	Atlanta	GA	30360	Michael A. Joffred		R	1,457*	2.2
Hartmann-Conco Inc.	481 Lakeshore	Rock Hill	SC	29730	John Gilbert	803-325-7600	R	1,431*	<0.1
STERIS Corp.	5960 Heisley Rd.	Mentor	OH	44060	Charles Immel	440-354-2600	P	1,197	5.1
Respironics Inc.	1010 Murry Ridge	Murrysville	PA	15668	Gerald E. McGinnis	724-387-5200	P	1,195	4.9
Hill-Rom Company Inc.	1069 SR 46 E	Batesville	IN	47006	Peter H. Soderberg	812-934-7000	S	1,192*	6.5
United States Surgical Corp.	150 Glover Ave.	Norwalk	CT	06850	Allen Panzer	203-845-1000	S	1,172*	5.8
Guidant's Cardiac Rhythm Manag	4100 Hamline	St. Paul	MN	55112	Fred McCoy	651-582-4000	S	1,130*	5.0
Haworth Inc.	1 Haworth Ctr.	Holland	MI	49423	Franco Bianchi	616-393-3000	R	1,120*	8.0
Knoll Inc.	1235 Water St.	East Greenville	PA	18041	Andrew B. Cogan	215-679-7991	P	1,056	4.3
Sulzer Inc.	555 5th Ave., 15th	New York	NY	10017	Kelli Edell	212-949-0999	S	1,000*	4.5
Mine Safety Appliances Co.	PO Box 426	Pittsburgh	PA	15230		412-967-3000	P	914	4.9
Barden Corp.	PO Box 2449	Danbury	CT	06813	John McCloskey	203-744-2211	R	776*	0.3
CONMED Corp.	525 French Rd.	Utica	NY	13502	Eugene R. Corasanti	315-797-8375	P	694	3.2
Hanger Orthopedic Group Inc.	2 Bethesda Mtro Ctr	Bethesda	MD	20814	Thomas F. Kirk	301-986-0701	P	637	3.4
B. Braun Inc.	PO Box 4027	Bethlehem	PA	18018	Carroll Neubauer	610-997-4253	S	630*	1.6
Cook Group Inc.	PO Box 489	Bloomington	IN	47402	William A. Cook	812-339-2235	R	615	4.0
Intuitive Surgical Inc.	950 Kifer Rd.	Sunnyvale	CA	94086		408-523-2100	P	601	0.8
Cotton Goods Manufacturing Co.	259 N California	Chicago	IL	60612	Edward J. Lewis	773-265-0088	R	525*	<0.1
Medtronic Sofamor Danek Inc.	1800 Pyramid Pl.	Memphis	TN	38132	Michael Demane	901-396-2695	S	470*	1.5
Amer. Med. Systems Holdings	10700 Bren Rd. W	Minnetonka	MN	55343		952-930-6000	P	464	1.2
Aearo Technologies Inc.	5457 W 79th St.	Indianapolis	IN	46268	Michael A. McLain	317-692-6666	R	423	1.7
Ethicon Johnson/Johnson Prof.	Rd. 183 KM 8.3	San Lorenzo	PR	00754		787-783-7070	P	400*	1.2
DJ Orthopedics L.L.C.	1430 Decision St.	Vista	CA	92081	Leslie H. Cross	760-727-1280	S	400*	1.2
Synthes USA L.P.	1302 Wrights Ln. E	West Chester	PA	19380		610-719-5000	R	393*	0.3
Datascope Corp.	14 Philips Pky.	Montvale	NJ	07645		201-391-8100	P	379	1.2
FLA Orthopedics Inc.	2881 Corporate Way	Miramar	FL	33025	E Slautterback	954-704-4484	R	370*	0.1
TECT Utica Corp.	2 Halsey Rd.	Whitesboro	NY	13492	Ron Cable	315-768-8070	R	356*	1.3
Hooker Furniture Corp.	PO Box 4708	Martinsville	VA	24115		276-632-0459	P	350	1.1
Wright Medical Group Inc.	5677 Airline Rd.	Arlington	TN	38002	F. Barry Bays	901-867-9971	P	339	1.1
Ethicon Endo-Surgery Inc.	4545 Creek Rd.	Cincinnati	OH	45242	Bob Salerno		S	324*	2.0
DHB Industries Inc.	2102 SW 2nd Street	Pompano Beach	FL	33069	Larry Ellis	954-630-0900	P	321	1.3
Mentor Corp.	201 Mentor Dr.	Santa Barbara	CA	93111		805-879-6000	P	302	1.0
Edsal Manufacturing Company	4400 S Packers Ave.	Chicago	IL	60609	Bruce Saltzberg	773-254-0600	R	300*	1.2
Kayser-Roth Corp.	PO Box 26530	Greensboro	NC	27415		336-852-2030	R	288*	0.2
Medtronic MiniMed Inc.	18000 Devonshire St	Northridge	CA	91325	Jeff McCaulley	818-362-5958	S	287*	1.5
Align Technology Inc.	881 Martin Ave.	Santa Clara	CA	95050		408-470-1000	P	284	1.3
Getinge USA Inc.	1777 E Henrietta Rd	Rochester	NY	14623	Andrew Csery	585-475-1400	R	263*	0.2
Hoveround Corp.	2151 Whitfield Ind.	Sarasota	FL	34243	Thomas Kruse	941-739-6200	R	257*	0.3
Linvatec Corp.	11311 Concept Blvd.	Largo	FL	33773	Gerald Woodard		S	248*	1.1
Smith and Nephew Inc.	1450 E Brooks Rd.	Memphis	TN	38116	Davin Illingsworth	901-396-2121	R	235*	0.1
Pulaski Furniture Corp.	PO Box 1371	Pulaski	VA	24301	Lawerance E. Webb	540-980-7330	R	230*	2.5
Medical Action Industries Inc.	800 Prime Pl.	Hauppauge	NY	11788	Paul D. Meringolo	631-231-4600	P	217	0.7
Avox Systems Inc.	225 Erie Street	Lancaster	NY	14086		716-683-5100	S	201*	1.0
Davis and Geck Inc.	PO Box 45	Manati	PR	00674			R	200*	0.6
BG Sulzle Inc.	1 Needle Ln.	North Syracuse	NY	13212		315-454-3221	R	191*	1.1
Hollister Inc.	2000 Hollister Dr.	Libertyville	IL	60048	Alan Herbert	847-680-1000	R	183*	0.3
Othy Inc.	486 W 350 N	Warsaw	IN	46582	John Byrd	574-267-8700	R	172*	1.0

Source: Ward's Business Directory of U.S. Private and Public Companies, Volumes 1 and 2, 2008. The company type code used is as follows: P - Public, R - Private, S - Subsidiary, D - Division, J - Joint Venture, A - Affiliate, G - Group. Sales are in millions of dollars, employees are in thousands. An asterisk (*) indicates an estimated sales volume. The symbol < stands for 'less than'. Company names and addresses are truncated, in some cases, to fit into the available space.

MATERIALS CONSUMED

Material	Quantity	Delivered Cost ($ million)
Printed ciruit boards (without inserted components) for electronic circuitry	(X)	(D)
Printed circuit assemblies, loaded boards, and modules	(X)	63.6
Resistors, capacitors, transformers, electron tubes, semiconductors, and other electronic components	(X)	35.8
Current-carrying wiring devices	(X)	33.3
Electric motors and generators	(X)	72.7
Metal bolts, nuts, screws, and other screw machine products	(X)	59.8
Other fabricated metal products (exc. bolts, nuts, washers, etc.)	(X)	191.1
Iron and steel castings (rough and semifinished)	(X)	140.2
Nonferrous (aluminum, copper, etc.) castings (rough and semifinished)	(X)	31.3
Steel shapes and forms (exc. castings, forgings, fabr. metal products)	(X)	143.5
Nonferrous shapes and forms	(X)	62.8
Nonwoven fabrics	(X)	195.1
Broadwoven fabrics	(X)	269.0
Plastics resins consumed in the form of granules, pellets, etc.	(X)	171.7
Plastics products consumed in the form of sheets, rods, etc.	(X)	210.5
Fabricated plastics products	(X)	246.9
Fabricated rubber products (exc. tires, tubes, hoses, belting, and gaskets)	(X)	35.3
Surgical and orthopedic supplies	(X)	691.8
Sheet metal products (excluding stampings)	(X)	(D)
Adhesives and sealants	(X)	76.2
Paperboard containers, boxes, and corrugated paperboard	(X)	134.3
Paper and paperboard products	(X)	71.0
All other materials, components, parts, containers, and supplies	(X)	1,652.0
Materials, ingredients, containers, and supplies, nsk	(X)	1,387.0

Source: 2002 Economic Census. Explanation of symbols used: (D): Withheld to avoid disclosure of competitive data; na: Not available; (S): Withheld because statistical norms were not met; (X): Not applicable; (Z): Less than half the unit shown; nec: Not elsewhere classified; nsk: Not specified by kind; - : zero; p : 10-19 percent estimated; q : 20-29 percent estimated.

PRODUCT SHARE DETAILS

Product or Product Class Shipments	Mil. $	Product or Product Class Shipments	Mil. $
SURGICAL APPLIANCES AND SUPPLIES	22,843.5	supplies, nec	687.7
Medical and surgical appliances and supplies, including orthopedic, prosthetic, and therapeutic appliances and supplies	**18,847.6**	Surgical kits	677.1
		Stents	2,023.4
Artificial joints and limbs	3,992.1	Other medical and surgical appliances and supplies, except parts	3,001.2
Artificial joints	3,853.1	Parts for medical and surgical appliances and supplies	314.9
Artificial limbs	139.0	All other surgical appliances and supplies, nec	2,265.1
Other orthopedic and prosthetic appliances	2,406.4	Sterile surgical sutures	358.6
Orthopedic and prosthetic mechanical braces	303.6	Rubber medical and surgical gloves, including rubber household gloves	113.9
Orthopedic and prosthetic elastic braces, suspensories, and supports	217.4	Breathing devices (incubators, inhalators, respirators, resuscitators), except anesthetic apparatus	728.2
Orthopedic and prosthetic elastic stockings	66.5	Wheelchairs	520.4
Orthopedic and prosthetic splints and trusses	50.9	Other patient transport devices (stretchers, tables, and wheeled chairs), except wheelchairs	544.0
Orthopedic and prosthetic crutches, canes, and other walking assistance appliances	49.0	Medical and surgical appliances and supplies, including orthopedic, prosthetic, and therapeutic appliances and supplies, nsk	1,397.7
Orthopedic and prosthetic arch supports and other foot appliances	266.7		
Intraocular lenses	130.7	**Personal industrial and nonindustrial safety equipment and clothing**	**2,671.2**
Other orthopedic and prosthetic appliances, including surgical corsets	1,321.5	Personal safety equipment and clothing	2,307.6
Surgical dressings	1,601.0	Respiratory protection equipment, including abrasive masks, canister masks, and gas masks	684.7
Surgical dressings, elastic bandages	(D)	Industrial helmets (hardhats)	173.0
Surgical dressings, other bandages, including muslin and plaster of Paris, except self-adhering bandages	(D)	Eye and face protection equipment, including face shields, masks, and welding helmets, except eye protectors and industrial goggles	195.0
Surgical dressings, adhesive plaster, medicated and nonmedicated, including self-adhering bandages	293.5	Industrial rubber gloves	37.3
Surgical dressings, gauze, absorbent and packing	101.4	Other protective clothing (except footwear and gloves), including rubber and rubberized protective clothing	738.2
Surgical dressings, cotton, sterile and nonsterile, including cotton balls	192.5	First aid, snake bite, and burn kits, including household and industrial kits	45.4
Other surgical dressings, including compresses, pads, and sponges	630.1	Other personal safety equipment, including life preservers (except cork life preservers) and auto racing and motorcycle helmets	434.1
Disposable surgical drapes, including obstetric and operating room packs	448.0	Personal industrial and nonindustrial safety equipment, nsk	363.5
Other medical and surgical appliances and supplies	6,737.2	**Surgical appliances and supplies, nsk, total**	**1,324.8**
Hydrotherapy appliances, including full body and limb-tanks	33.0		
Other therapeutic appliances and supplies, except electromedical and hydrotherapy appliances and			

Source: 2002 Economic Census. The values are product shipments in millions of dollars for 2002. Total product shipments may be lower or higher than industry shipments. See Introduction for a full discussion. Values of indented subcategories are summed in the main heading(s). The symbol (D) appears when data are withheld to prevent disclosure of competitive information. The abbreviation nsk stands for 'not specified by kind' and nec for 'not elsewhere classified'. A dash (-) means zero.

INPUTS AND OUTPUTS FOR SURGICAL APPLIANCE AND SUPPLIES MANUFACTURING

Economic Sector or Industry Providing Inputs	%	Sector	Economic Sector or Industry Buying Outputs	%	Sector
Compensation of employees	25.0		Personal consumption expenditures	21.7	
Wholesale trade	4.4	Trade	Exports of goods & services	13.3	Cap Inv
Management of companies & enterprises	2.7	Services	Hospitals	11.9	Services
Surgical & medical instrument	2.6	Manufg.	General S/L govt. services	11.5	S/L Govt
Advertising & related services	2.6	Services	Physician, dentist, other health practitioner offices	11.3	Services
Surgical appliances & supplies	2.6	Manufg.	Private fixed investment	11.2	
Textile & fabric finishing mills	2.0	Manufg.	Nursing & residential care facilities	2.8	Services
Plastics products, nec	1.2	Manufg.	Medical & diagnostic labs & outpatient services	2.3	Services
Plastics packaging materials, film & sheet	1.1	Manufg.	Surgical appliances & supplies	2.3	Manufg.
Synthetic rubber	1.1	Manufg.	Surgical & medical instrument	2.3	Manufg.
Lessors of nonfinancial assets	1.0	Fin/R.E.	S/L govt. invest., other	1.7	S/L Govt
Truck transportation	1.0	Util.	Waste management & remediation services	1.1	Services
Nonwoven fabric mills	1.0	Manufg.	Services to buildings & dwellings	0.9	Services
Securities, commodity contracts, investments	0.8	Fin/R.E.	Veterinary services	0.6	Services
Plastics materials & resins	0.8	Manufg.	Change in private inventories	0.6	In House
Legal services	0.8	Services	General Federal government services, nondefense	0.6	Fed Govt
Paperboard containers	0.7	Manufg.	Ophthalmic goods	0.5	Manufg.
Management, scientific, & technical consulting	0.7	Services	Scientific research & development services	0.4	Services
Iron & steel mills & ferroalloys	0.7	Manufg.	Community food, housing, relief, & rehabilitation	0.3	Services
Monetary authorities/depository credit intermediation	0.7	Fin/R.E.	Individual & family services	0.3	Services
Ferrous metal foundries	0.7	Manufg.	Federal government, investment, nondefense	0.3	Fed Govt
Lime & gypsum products	0.7	Manufg.	Other S/L govt. enterprises	0.3	S/L Govt
Real estate	0.6	Fin/R.E.	S/L govt. electric utilities	0.2	S/L Govt
Turned products & screws, nuts, & bolts	0.6	Manufg.	Nonmetallic mineral products, nec	0.2	Manufg.
Professional, scientific, technical services, nec	0.5	Services	Architectural, engineering, & related services	0.1	Services
Machine shops	0.5	Manufg.	General Federal government services, defense	0.1	Fed Govt
Power generation & supply	0.4	Util.	Dental equipment & supplies	0.1	Manufg.
Adhesives	0.4	Manufg.			
Electromedical & electrotherapeutic apparatus	0.4	Manufg.			
Retail trade	0.4	Trade			
Optical instruments & lenses	0.4	Manufg.			
Telecommunications	0.4	Services			
Accounting, tax preparation, bookkeeping, & payroll	0.4	Services			
Motors & generators	0.4	Manufg.			
Printed circuit assemblies (electronic assemblies)	0.4	Manufg.			
Paper mills	0.3	Manufg.			
Food services & drinking places	0.3	Services			
Noncomparable imports	0.3	Foreign			
Coating, engraving, heat treating & allied activities	0.3	Manufg.			
Nonferrous metal (ex. copper & aluminum) processing	0.3	Manufg.			
Taxes on production & imports, less subsidies	0.3				
Data processing, hosting, & related services	0.3	Services			
Custom roll forming	0.3	Manufg.			
Metal & other household furniture	0.3	Manufg.			
Hotels & motels, including casino hotels	0.3	Services			
Warehousing & storage	0.2	Util.			
Architectural, engineering, & related services	0.2	Services			
Air transportation	0.2	Util.			
Services to buildings & dwellings	0.2	Services			
Automotive equipment rental & leasing	0.2	Fin/R.E.			
Scientific research & development services	0.2	Services			
Semiconductors & related devices	0.2	Manufg.			
Wiring devices	0.2	Manufg.			
Nonferrous metal foundries	0.2	Manufg.			
Unlaminated plastics profile shapes	0.2	Manufg.			
Other computer related services, including facilities	0.2	Services			
Maintenance/repair of nonresidential structures	0.2	Construct.			
Fabricated metals, nec	0.2	Manufg.			
Bare printed circuit boards	0.2	Manufg.			
Electronic capacitors, resistors, coils, transformers	0.2	Manufg.			
Business support services	0.2	Services			
Ornamental & architectural metal products	0.1	Manufg.			
Forging, stamping, & sintering, nec	0.1	Manufg.			
Laminated plastics plates, sheets, & shapes	0.1	Manufg.			
Valve & fittings other than plumbing	0.1	Manufg.			
Metal cans, boxes, & other containers (light gauge)	0.1	Manufg.			
Natural gas distribution	0.1	Util.			
Automotive repair & maintenance, ex. car washes	0.1	Services			

Source: Benchmark Input-Output Accounts for the U.S. Economy, 2002, U.S. Department of Commerce, Washington, D.C., January 2008. The abbreviation nec stands for 'not elsewhere classified'.

OCCUPATIONS EMPLOYED BY MEDICAL EQUIPMENT & SUPPLIES MANUFACTURING

Occupation	% of Total 2006	Change to 2016	Occupation	% of Total 2006	Change to 2016
Dental laboratory technicians	12.2	2.3	Assemblers & fabricators, nec	1.4	-7.9
Team assemblers	11.0	2.3	Sales reps, wholesale & manufacturing, exc tech	1.3	2.3
First-line supervisors/managers of production workers	3.0	2.3	Helpers--Production workers	1.3	2.3
Inspectors, testers, sorters, samplers, & weighers	3.0	-3.6	Truck drivers, light or delivery services	1.2	2.3
Customer service representatives	2.2	12.5	Packaging & filling machine operators & tenders	1.2	-7.9
Medical appliance technicians	2.0	8.3	Bookkeeping, accounting, & auditing clerks	1.2	2.3
Packers & packagers, hand	1.9	-18.2	Multiple machine tool operators & tenders	1.1	12.5
Shipping, receiving, & traffic clerks	1.9	-1.6	Maintenance & repair workers, general	1.1	2.3
Machinists	1.7	7.4	Stock clerks & order fillers	1.1	-14.4
Molding, coremaking, & casting machine operators	1.6	-7.9	Mechanical engineers	1.1	2.3
Sales representatives, wholesale & manufacturing, tech	1.6	2.3	Laborers & freight, stock, & material movers, hand	1.1	-7.9
General & operations managers	1.5	-7.9	Computer-controlled machine tool operators	1.1	12.5
Sewing machine operators	1.5	2.3	Executive secretaries & administrative assistants	1.1	2.3
Industrial engineers	1.5	24.2	Cutting, punching, & press machine operators	1.1	-7.9
Office clerks, general	1.5	0.8			

Source: *Industry-Occupation Matrix*, Bureau of Labor Statistics, December 4, 2007. These data are reported based on 4-digit NAICS categories but have been matched to corresponding 6-digit NAICS industry codes. The change reported for each occupation to the year 2016 is a percent of growth or decline as estimated by the Bureau of Labor Statistics. The abbreviation nec stands for 'not elsewhere classified'.

LOCATION BY STATE AND REGIONAL CONCENTRATION

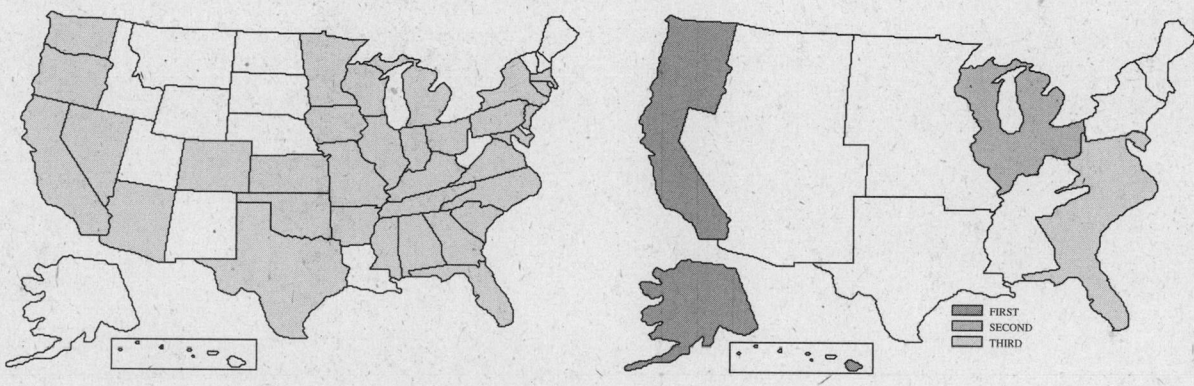

FIRST
SECOND
THIRD

INDUSTRY DATA BY STATE

State	Establish-ments	Shipments			Employment				Cost as % of Shipments	Investment per Employee ($)
		Total ($ mil)	% of U.S.	Per Establ.	Total Number	% of U.S.	Per Establ.	Wages ($/hour)		
California	256	4,283.2	17.5	16,731.1	19,127	17.4	75	14.45	24.0	5,227
Indiana	39	2,806.5	11.4	71,960.6	6,617	6.0	170	16.66	15.9	22,581
New Jersey	52	2,078.5	8.5	39,970.8	8,755	8.0	168	17.02	27.0	6,221
Pennsylvania	108	1,567.2	6.4	14,510.9	6,911	6.3	64	13.02	49.3	6,134
Texas	127	1,394.6	5.7	10,981.0	7,038	6.4	55	13.95	33.8	5,579
Ohio	88	1,295.8	5.3	14,725.3	6,212	5.7	71	13.79	38.5	5,640
Florida	120	1,275.9	5.2	10,632.3	7,263	6.6	61	13.77	21.1	6,289
Tennessee	40	999.3	4.1	24,983.6	4,020	3.7	100	13.82	26.2	17,769
Massachusetts	46	777.5	3.2	16,902.3	3,613	3.3	79	15.47	22.0	5,635
Michigan	63	708.5	2.9	11,246.0	2,972	2.7	47	15.36	35.6	5,232
Georgia	32	688.2	2.8	21,505.1	2,582	2.3	81	14.50	38.4	6,118
North Carolina	53	685.2	2.8	12,927.7	3,332	3.0	63	12.07	46.0	6,874
Arizona	40	674.4	2.8	16,860.6	2,683	2.4	67	22.49	25.4	5,449
New York	123	567.9	2.3	4,617.2	3,808	3.5	31	12.43	38.1	5,392
Minnesota	51	536.1	2.2	10,511.9	3,032	2.8	59	15.30	29.4	6,522
South Carolina	17	397.2	1.6	23,367.3	1,397	1.3	82	12.35	35.0	9,312
Virginia	34	328.4	1.3	9,658.5	1,271	1.2	37	14.91	44.2	9,714
Illinois	62	290.5	1.2	4,685.9	2,218	2.0	36	10.92	37.1	4,606
Missouri	37	256.8	1.0	6,939.2	1,200	1.1	32	13.84	34.2	3,972
Wisconsin	37	212.2	0.9	5,734.1	1,591	1.4	43	13.74	32.0	3,591
Alabama	29	132.9	0.5	4,582.2	1,235	1.1	43	11.52	39.1	7,681
Connecticut	27	129.6	0.5	4,798.5	688	0.6	25	12.13	42.7	6,904
Kentucky	24	126.9	0.5	5,285.5	783	0.7	33	11.31	50.7	2,562
Washington	34	122.5	0.5	3,603.9	857	0.8	25	14.98	35.1	7,292
Maryland	30	121.1	0.5	4,036.0	596	0.5	20	17.52	40.1	3,164
Colorado	40	105.4	0.4	2,634.2	1,064	1.0	27	12.39	41.2	13,208
Rhode Island	10	77.3	0.3	7,731.9	432	0.4	43	12.04	43.5	6,491
Oklahoma	11	65.5	0.3	5,952.3	295	0.3	27	19.58	15.0	6,332

Continued on next page.

INDUSTRY DATA BY STATE - Continued

State	Establish- ments	Shipments			Employment				Cost as % of Shipments	Investment per Employee ($)
		Total ($ mil)	% of U.S.	Per Establ.	Total Number	% of U.S.	Per Establ.	Wages ($/hour)		
Mississippi	16	63.3	0.3	3,958.7	660	0.6	41	11.32	40.6	3,826
Kansas	14	56.1	0.2	4,006.1	323	0.3	23	11.55	37.3	3,062
Oregon	23	34.8	0.1	1,514.0	258	0.2	11	13.32	37.7	3,849
Arkansas	19	32.3	0.1	1,700.4	203	0.2	11	21.18	38.9	3,197
Nevada	12	21.1	0.1	1,758.1	103	0.1	9	10.63	25.7	6,524
Iowa	13	14.1	0.1	1,088.4	126	0.1	10	9.70	33.6	4,857

Source: 2002 *Economic Census*. The states are in descending order of shipments or establishments (if shipment data are missing for the majority). The symbol (D) appears when data are withheld to prevent disclosure of competitive information. States marked with (D) are sorted by number of establishments. A dash (-) indicates that the data element cannot be calculated. Data may not show all states active in the NAICS category. All data available at the time of publication are shown.

NAICS 339114 - DENTAL EQUIPMENT AND SUPPLIES MANUFACTURING

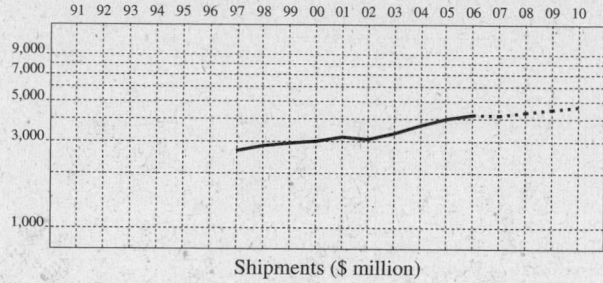

Shipments ($ million)

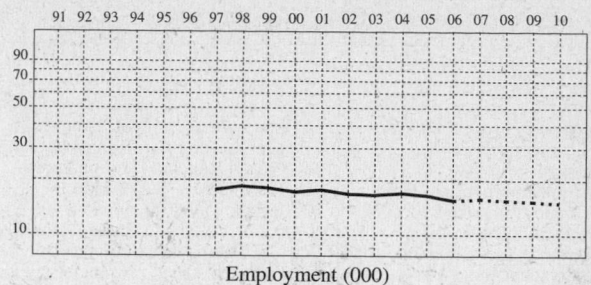

Employment (000)

GENERAL STATISTICS

| Year | Companies | Establishments | | Employment | | | Compensation | | Production ($ million) | | | |
		Total	with 20 or more employees	Total (000)	Production Workers (000)	Hours (Mil)	Payroll ($ mil)	Wages ($/hr)	Cost of Materials	Value Added by Manufacture	Value of Shipments	Capital Invest.
1997	852	876	141	17.7	11.6	21.5	594.3	13.00	950.5	1,736.4	2,662.0	71.6
1998		890	144	18.5	12.1	22.9	644.0	13.11	1,028.3	1,782.8	2,836.9	85.7
1999		879	141	18.1	11.5	21.9	662.5	13.33	1,056.3	1,893.9	2,932.0	80.5
2000		842	136	17.2	10.7	20.6	656.7	14.10	1,079.4	1,911.2	3,008.4	82.3
2001		831	143	17.7	11.0	21.3	696.8	14.54	1,157.1	2,040.7	3,174.5	122.3
2002	852	875	150	16.8	9.9	17.2	678.3	15.90	1,099.8	2,013.5	3,087.2	144.6
2003		818	152	16.6	9.9	18.5	707.4	15.22	1,102.4	2,204.5	3,326.2	86.9
2004		802	143	17.0	9.6	18.4	737.4	16.11	1,274.7	2,389.6	3,673.0	60.5
2005		788	141	16.5	9.7	19.1	734.7	16.44	1,457.1	2,583.0	4,001.1	86.2
2006		786P	146P	15.5	9.2	18.4	755.5	17.56	1,428.0	2,808.4	4,207.5	71.3
2007		774P	147P	15.8P	8.8P	17.2P	773.2P	17.70P	1,418.2P	2,789.1P	4,178.5P	87.1P
2008		762P	147P	15.5P	8.5P	16.7P	788.9P	18.20P	1,472.9P	2,896.8P	4,339.9P	86.7P
2009		751P	148P	15.3P	8.2P	16.2P	804.7P	18.70P	1,527.7P	3,004.5P	4,501.3P	86.3P
2010		739P	148P	15.0P	7.9P	15.7P	820.4P	19.21P	1,582.5P	3,112.3P	4,662.7P	85.9P

Sources: 1997 and 2002 *Economic Census*; other years, up to 2006, are from *Annual Survey of Manufactures*. Establishment counts for non-Census years are from *County Business Patterns*; 1997 and 2002 values are from the 1997 and 2002 censuses, respectively. 'P's show projections by the editors.

INDICES OF CHANGE

| Year | Companies | Establishments | | Employment | | | Compensation | | Production ($ million) | | | |
		Total	with 20 or more employees	Total (000)	Production Workers (000)	Hours (Mil)	Payroll ($ mil)	Wages ($/hr)	Cost of Materials	Value Added by Manufacture	Value of Shipments	Capital Invest.
1997	100	100	94	105	117	125	88	82	86	86	86	50
1998		102	96	110	122	133	95	82	93	89	92	59
1999		100	94	108	116	127	98	84	96	94	95	56
2000		96	91	102	108	120	97	89	98	95	97	57
2001		95	95	105	111	124	103	91	105	101	103	85
2002	100	100	100	100	100	100	100	100	100	100	100	100
2003		93	101	99	100	108	104	96	100	109	108	60
2004		92	95	101	97	107	109	101	116	119	119	42
2005		90	94	98	98	111	108	103	132	128	130	60
2006		90P	97P	92	93	107	111	110	130	139	136	49
2007		88P	98P	94P	89P	100P	114P	111P	129P	139P	135P	60P
2008		87P	98P	92P	86P	97P	116P	114P	134P	144P	141P	60P
2009		86P	99P	91P	83P	94P	119P	118P	139P	144P	146P	60P
2010		84P	99P	89P	80P	91P	121P	121P	144P	155P	151P	59P

Sources: Same as General Statistics. Values reflect change from the base year, 2002. Values above 100 mean greater than 2002, values below 100 mean less than 2002, and the values of 100 in other years means the same as 2002. 'P's show projections by the editors.

SELECTED RATIOS

For 2002	Avg. of All Manufact.	Analyzed Industry	Index	For 2002	Avg. of All Manufact.	Analyzed Industry	Index
Employees per Establishment	42	19	46	Value Added per Production Worker	182,367	203,384	112
Payroll per Establishment	1,639,184	775,200	47	Cost per Establishment	5,769,015	1,256,914	22
Payroll per Employee	39,053	40,375	103	Cost per Employee	137,446	65,464	48
Production Workers per Establishment	30	11	38	Cost per Production Worker	195,506	111,091	57
Wages per Establishment	694,845	312,549	45	Shipments per Establishment	11,158,348	3,528,229	32
Wages per Production Worker	23,548	27,624	117	Shipments per Employee	265,847	183,762	69
Hours per Production Worker	1,980	1,737	88	Shipments per Production Worker	378,144	311,838	82
Wages per Hour	11.89	15.90	134	Investment per Establishment	361,338	165,257	46
Value Added per Establishment	5,381,325	2,301,143	43	Investment per Employee	8,609	8,607	100
Value Added per Employee	128,210	119,851	93	Investment per Production Worker	12,245	14,606	119

Sources: Same as General Statistics. The 'Average of All Manufacturing' column represents the average of all manufacturing industries reported for the most recent complete year available. The Index shows the relationship between the Average and the Analyzed Industry. For example, 100 means that they are equal; 500 that the Analyzed Industry is five times the average; 50 means that the Analyzed Industry is half the national average. The abbreviation 'na' is used to show that data are 'not available'. Ratios shown for 2002, the last complete census year.

LEADING COMPANIES   Number shown: 75   Total sales ($ mil): 35,366   Total employment (000): 118.2

Company Name	Address				CEO Name	Phone	Co. Type	Sales ($ mil)	Empl. (000)
3M Co.	3M Ctr.	St. Paul	MN	55144	George W. Buckley	651-733-2204	P	24,462	76.2
Bausch and Lomb Inc.	1 Bausch Lomb Pl.	Rochester	NY	14604		585-338-6000	P	2,292	13.0
Nobel Biocare Inc.	22715 Savi Ranch	Yorba Linda	CA	92887	Heliane Canepa	714-282-4800	R	2,054*	1.3
DENTSPLY International Inc.	PO Box 872	York	PA	17405		717-845-7511	P	1,811	8.5
Darby Group Companies Inc.	300 Jericho Quadrnl	Jericho	NY	11753	Carl Ashkin	516-683-1800	R	670*	1.4
Sirona Dental Systems Inc.	30-00 47th Ave.	Long Island Cty	NY	11101	Jost Fischer		P	660	2.0
Sybron Dental Specialties Inc.	1717 W Collins Ave.	Orange	CA	92867	Floyd W. Pickrell Jr.	714-516-7400	S	650	4.1
Ivoclar Vivadent Inc.	175 Pineview Dr.	Amherst	NY	14228	Robert A. Ganley	716-691-0010	R	524	2.2
Koken Manufacturing Company	PO Box 265	Saint Louis	MO	63166	Masahiro Kanaya	314-231-7383	R	458*	<0.1
Getinge USA Inc.	1777 E Henrietta Rd	Rochester	NY	14623	Andrew Csery	585-475-1400	R	263*	0.2
A-DEC Inc.	PO Box 111	Newberg	OR	97132	George Austin	503-538-9471	R	149*	1.0
Fujinon Inc.	10 Highpoint Dr.	Wayne	NJ	07470	Takeshi Higuchi	973-633-5600	R	85*	0.1
Ormco Corp.	1717 W Collins Ave.	Orange	CA	92867	Don Tuttle	714-516-7400	S	84*	1.2
Den-Mat Corp.	PO Box 1729	Santa Maria	CA	93456	Robert Ibsen	805-922-8491	R	83*	0.5
Kyocera Tycom North America	17862 Fitch	Irvine	CA	92614	Scott Yardley	949-955-0800	S	81*	0.3
Biolase Technology Inc.	4 Cromwell	Irvine	CA	92618		949-361-1200	P	70	0.2
Midmark Corp.	PO Box 286	Versailles	OH	45380	Anne Klamar	937-526-3662	R	65*	0.6
Peter Brasseler Holdings L.P.	1 Brasseler Blvd.	Savannah	GA	31419		912-925-8525	R	63*	0.2
Gudebrod Inc.	PO Box 3178	Pottstown	PA	19464	Edward John	610-327-4050	R	58*	0.2
Hu-Friedy Manufacturing Co.	3232 N Rockwell St.	Chicago	IL	60618	Ronald Saslow	773-975-6100	R	55*	0.4
Argen Corp.	5855 Oberlin Dr.	San Diego	CA	92121		858-455-7900	R	46*	0.1
Jeneric Pentron Inc.	PO Box 724	Wallingford	CT	06492	Gordon Cohen	203-265-3886	R	30*	0.2
RMO Inc.	PO Box 17085	Denver	CO	80217	Martin Brusse	303-592-8200	R	30*	0.2
Mycone Dental Supply Company	616 Hollywood Ave.	Cherry Hill	NJ	08002	Cary Robinson	856-663-4700	R	29*	0.2
GS Precision Inc.	101 John Seitz Dr.	Brattleboro	VT	05301	George Schneeberger	802-257-5200	R	25*	0.2
Whip-Mix Corp.	PO Box 17183	Louisville	KY	40217	Allen Steinbock	502-637-1451	R	25*	0.2
Den-Tal-Ez Inc.	101 Lindenwood Dr.	Malvern	PA	19355	Jeffrey Perelman	610-725-8004	R	23*	<0.1
Unicep Packaging Inc.	1702 Industrial Dr.	Sandpoint	ID	83864	John Snedden	208-265-9696	R	21*	0.1
Dental Components Inc.	305 N Springbrook	Newberg	OR	97132		503-538-8343	R	21*	0.1
Heraeus Kulzer Inc.	4315 S Lafayette	South Bend	IN	46614	Gerrit Steen	574-291-0661	R	18*	0.1
Pulse Technologies Inc.	2000 AM Dr.	Quakertown	PA	18951	Robert S. Walsh Sr.	267-733-0200	R	17*	0.1
CMP Industries Inc.	413 N Pearl St.	Albany	NY	12207	William Regan	518-434-3147	R	17*	<0.1
Spartan Ultrasonics Inc.	1663 Fenton Bus Prk	Fenton	MO	63026	Richard Maheu	636-343-8300	R	16*	<0.1
Winslow Automatics Inc.	23 Saint Claire Ave	New Britain	CT	06051	Janusz Podlasek	860-225-6321	R	16*	<0.1
JM Murray Center Inc.	PO Box 589	Cortland	NY	13045	Richard Benchley	607-756-9913	R	15*	0.1
Centrix Inc.	770 River Rd.	Shelton	CT	06484	William Dragan	203-929-5582	R	15*	0.1
Aseptico Inc.	PO Box 1548	Woodinville	WA	98072	Douglas Kazen	425-487-3157	R	15*	0.1
Bisco Inc.	1100 W Irving Park	Schaumburg	IL	60193	Byoung Suh	847-534-6000	R	15*	0.1
North Star Orthodontics Inc.	PO Box 146	Park Rapids	MN	56470	John Kelly	218-732-9503	R	15*	0.1
Sunoptic Technologies L.L.C.	6018 Bowdendale	Jacksonville	FL	32216		904-737-7611	R	15*	<0.1
DENTSPLY Rinn	1212 Abbott Dr.	Elgin	IL	60123	Gary Kunkle	847-742-1115	S	14*	0.1
Parkell Products Inc.	300 Executive Dr.	Edgewood	NY	11717	Karen Mitchell	631-249-1134	R	14*	0.1
Lares Research	295 Lockheed Ave.	Chico	CA	95973	Craig Lares	530-345-1767	R	13*	<0.1
Rafi Systems Inc.	750 N Diamond Bar	Diamond Bar	CA	91765	Kusum Rafiquzza	909-593-8124	R	13*	<0.1
Nu Life Restorations of L I	PO Box 297	West Hempstead	NY	11552	Mark Marinbach	516-489-5200	R	13*	<0.1
Issaquah Dental Lab Inc.	640 NW Gilman	Issaquah	WA	98027	Larry Searles	425-392-5125	R	12*	<0.1
Sultan Healthcare Inc.	85 W Forest Ave.	Englewood	NJ	07631		201-871-1232	R	11*	<0.1
Royal Dental Manufacturing	12414 Highway 99	Everett	WA	98204	Harold Tai	425-743-0988	R	10*	<0.1
CMP Industries L.L.C.	PO Box 350	Albany	NY	12201	Devon Howe	518-434-3147	R	10*	<0.1
Moyco Precision Abrasives Inc.	200 Commerce Dr.	Montgomryville	PA	18936	Jose Alfonso	215-855-4300	S	10*	<0.1
Dux Industries Inc.	600 E Hueneme Rd.	Oxnard	CA	93033	Don Porteous	805-488-1122	R	10*	<0.1
Pulpdent Corp.	PO Box 780	Watertown	MA	02471	Harold Berk	617-926-6666	R	10*	<0.1
Biotec Inc.	652 E Main Ave.	Zeeland	MI	49464	Charles Pree	616-772-2133	R	9*	<0.1
Confi-Dental Products Co.	416 S Taylor Ave.	Louisville	CO	80027	Kent Chiu	303-665-7535	R	9*	<0.1
Selane Products Inc.	PO Box 4184	Van Nuys	CA	91409	John Christian	818-998-7460	R	9*	<0.1
Jensen Industries Slc Inc.	PO Box 514	North Haven	CT	06473	David Stine	203-239-2090	R	9*	<0.1
Imaging Sciences International	1910 N Penn Rd.	Hatfield	PA	19440	Henry Tancredi	215-997-5666	R	9*	<0.1
Ottawa Dental Labs Inc.	PO Box 771	Ottawa	IL	61350	Lucian Caruso	815-434-0655	R	8*	0.1
Columbia Dentoform Corp.	3424 Hunterspoint	Long Island Cty	NY	11101	Carl Bredco	718-482-1569	R	8*	<0.1
Boyd Industries Inc.	12900 44th St. N	Clearwater	FL	33762	Bruce Livingston	727-561-9292	R	8*	<0.1
Dexta Corp.	962 Kaiser Rd.	Napa	CA	94558	Mark Rusin	707-255-2454	R	8*	<0.1
Syracuse Forge Inc.	606 Factory Ave.	Syracuse	NY	13208	Brent Driscoll	315-455-8155	S	8*	<0.1
Buffalo Dental Manufacturing	PO Box 678	Syosset	NY	11791	Donald Nevin	516-496-7200	R	7*	<0.1
CDB Corp.	9201 Indust. Blvd.	Leland	NC	28451	H Heipl	910-383-6464	R	7*	<0.1
Lesam Inc.	2701 Bartram Rd.	Bristol	PA	19007		215-785-1600	R	7*	<0.1
Lite Specialty Metal Works	29600 SW Seely	Wilsonville	OR	97070	Art Blumenkron	503-685-9212	R	7*	<0.1
Calton Dental Lab	119 SE 11th Ave.	Gainesville	FL	32601	Larry Calton	352-376-3041	R	7*	<0.1
Orthopli Corp.	10061 Sandmeyer	Philadelphia	PA	19116	William Tippy	215-671-1000	R	7*	<0.1
Dental Art Laboratories Inc.	PO Box 22032	Lansing	MI	48909	Richard Blundy	517-485-2200	R	6*	<0.1
Handler Manufacturing Company	PO Box 520	Westfield	NJ	07091	William Lehman	908-233-7796	R	6*	<0.1
Restore Medical Inc.	2800 Patton Rd.	St. Paul	MN	55113	J. Robert Paulsen Jr.	651-634-3111	P	6	<0.1
Dyna Flex of Missouri L.P.	PO Box 142399	Saint Louis	MO	63114	Daryl Buddemeyer	314-426-4020	R	6*	<0.1
Ortho Arch Laboratory Inc.	PO Box 600	Kingsford Hgts	IN	46346	Jeffrey Maki	219-393-5591	R	6*	<0.1
Proma Inc.	730 Kingshill Pl.	Carson	CA	90746	Harold Tai	310-327-0035	R	6*	<0.1
Edmonds Dental Prosthetics	PO Box 10387	Springfield	MO	65808	Bobby Edmonds	417-881-8572	R	6*	<0.1

Source: Ward's Business Directory of U.S. Private and Public Companies, Volumes 1 and 2, 2008. The company type code used is as follows: P - Public, R - Private, S - Subsidiary, D - Division, J - Joint Venture, A - Affiliate, G - Group. Sales are in millions of dollars, employees are in thousands. An asterisk (*) indicates an estimated sales volume. The symbol < stands for 'less than'. Company names and addresses are truncated, in some cases, to fit into the available space.

MATERIALS CONSUMED

Material	Quantity	Delivered Cost ($ million)
Steel shapes and forms (exc. castings, forgings, fabr. metal products)	(X)	10.4
Fabricated metal products (excluding forgings)	(X)	50.1
Precious metals (gold, platinum, etc.), all forms (incl. ingot, sheet, strip, solder, plating, electrodes, etc.)	(X)	232.2
Chemical, all types (including resins)	(X)	47.5
Resistors, capacitors, transformers, electron tubes, semiconductors, and other electronic components	(X)	19.9
Fabricated plastics products (excluding gaskets)	(X)	35.2
Paperboard containers, boxes, and corrugated paperboard	(X)	30.8
All other materials, components, parts, containers, and supplies	(X)	202.5
Materials, ingredients, containers, and supplies, nsk	(X)	169.4

Source: 2002 *Economic Census*. Explanation of symbols used: (D): Withheld to avoid disclosure of competitive data; na: Not available; (S): Withheld because statistical norms were not met; (X): Not applicable; (Z): Less than half the unit shown; nec: Not elsewhere classified; nsk: Not specified by kind; - : zero; p : 10-19 percent estimated; q : 20-29 percent estimated.

PRODUCT SHARE DETAILS

Product or Product Class Shipments	Mil. $	Product or Product Class Shipments	Mil. $
DENTAL EQUIPMENT AND SUPPLIES	2,850.5	Other dental professional supplies	450.0
Dental professional equipment and supplies	**1,893.9**	Dental professional equipment and supplies, nsk	63.1
Professional dental equipment	658.3	**Dental laboratory equipment and supplies**	**651.0**
Dental chairs	137.2	Dental laboratory equipment and supplies	645.2
Dental instrument delivery systems, dental units	113.4	Dental laboratory equipment (furnaces, casting	
Dental hand pieces	118.6	machines, lathes, benches, polishing units, flasks,	
Dental hand instruments (forceps and pliers, broaches,		blow pipes, etc)	67.9
cutting instruments, etc)	155.2	Dental laboratory supplies, precious metals	260.5
Other dental professional equipment, including dental		Dental laboratory supplies, nonprecious metals	49.9
lasers, excluding x-ray	134.0	Artificial teeth not customized for individual application	
Professional dental supplies	1,172.5	(excluding dentures)	14.6
Dental burs, diamond points, abrasive points, wheels,		Other dental laboratory supplies not customized for	
disks, and similar tools for use with dental hand		individual application (waxes, gypsums, crowns,	
pieces	133.9	dentures, and other orthodontic appliances, except	
Dental alloys for amalgams	88.0	artificial teeth)	252.4
Dental impression materials (alginates, silicones, etc)	168.1	Dental laboratory equipment and supplies, nsk	5.7
Dental cements and other nonmetallic filling materials	332.6	**Dental equipment and supplies, nsk, total**	**305.6**

Source: 2002 *Economic Census*. The values are product shipments in millions of dollars for 2002. Total product shipments may be lower or higher than industry shipments. See Introduction for a full discussion. Values of indented subcategories are summed in the main heading(s). The symbol (D) appears when data are withheld to prevent disclosure of competitive information. The abbreviation nsk stands for 'not specified by kind' and nec for 'not elsewhere classified'. A dash (-) means zero.

INPUTS AND OUTPUTS FOR DENTAL EQUIPMENT AND SUPPLIES MANUFACTURING

Economic Sector or Industry Providing Inputs	%	Sector	Economic Sector or Industry Buying Outputs	%	Sector
Compensation of employees	28.4		Physician, dentist, other health practitioner offices	44.5	Services
Primary nonferrous metal, ex. copper & aluminum	8.9	Manufg.	Private fixed investment	26.3	
Wholesale trade	3.9	Trade	Exports of goods & services	15.5	Cap Inv
Lime & gypsum products	3.2	Manufg.	Dental laboratories	7.2	Manufg.
Management of companies & enterprises	3.1	Services	Federal government, investment, nondefense	2.4	Fed Govt
Advertising & related services	2.6	Services	Change in private inventories	1.3	In House
Paperboard containers	1.3	Manufg.	General S/L govt. services	1.1	S/L Govt
Plastics products, nec	1.2	Manufg.	S/L govt. invest., other	0.7	S/L Govt
Lessors of nonfinancial assets	1.1	Fin/R.E.	Dental equipment & supplies	0.6	Manufg.
Basic organic chemicals, nec	1.1	Manufg.	Federal government, investment, national defense	0.5	Fed Govt
Securities, commodity contracts, investments	1.1	Fin/R.E.			
Real estate	1.1	Fin/R.E.			
Truck transportation	0.9	Util.			
Surgical appliances & supplies	0.9	Manufg.			
Architectural, engineering, & related services	0.8	Services			
Semiconductors & related devices	0.8	Manufg.			
Legal services	0.8	Services			
Monetary authorities/depository credit intermediation	0.8	Fin/R.E.			
Dental equipment & supplies	0.7	Manufg.			
Gold, silver, & other metal ore	0.7	Mining			
Dry-cleaning & laundry services	0.7	Services			
Machine shops	0.7	Manufg.			
Management, scientific, & technical consulting	0.6	Services			
Printed circuit assemblies (electronic assemblies)	0.6	Manufg.			
Professional, scientific, technical services, nec	0.6	Services			
Taxes on production & imports, less subsidies	0.6				
Accounting, tax preparation, bookkeeping, & payroll	0.6	Services			
Turned products & screws, nuts, & bolts	0.5	Manufg.			
Telecommunications	0.5	Services			
Noncomparable imports	0.5	Foreign			

Continued on next page.

INPUTS AND OUTPUTS FOR DENTAL EQUIPMENT AND SUPPLIES MANUFACTURING - Continued

Economic Sector or Industry Providing Inputs	%	Sector	Economic Sector or Industry Buying Outputs	%	Sector
Coating, engraving, heat treating & allied activities	0.5	Manufg.			
Power generation & supply	0.4	Util.			
Iron & steel mills & ferroalloys	0.4	Manufg.			
Retail trade	0.4	Trade			
Nonferrous metal foundries	0.4	Manufg.			
Food services & drinking places	0.3	Services			
Data processing, hosting, & related services	0.3	Services			
Automotive equipment rental & leasing	0.3	Fin/R.E.			
Warehousing & storage	0.3	Util.			
Basic inorganic chemicals, nec	0.2	Manufg.			
Hotels & motels, including casino hotels	0.2	Services			
Rail transportation	0.2	Util.			
Scientific research & development services	0.2	Services			
Services to buildings & dwellings	0.2	Services			
Chemical products & preparations, nec	0.2	Manufg.			
Other computer related services, including facilities	0.2	Services			
Metal cans, boxes, & other containers (light gauge)	0.2	Manufg.			
Business support services	0.2	Services			
Maintenance/repair of nonresidential structures	0.2	Construct.			
Air transportation	0.2	Util.			
Fabricated metals, nec	0.2	Manufg.			
Commercial & industrial machinery rental & leasing	0.2	Fin/R.E.			
Valve & fittings other than plumbing	0.1	Manufg.			
Crowns & closures & metal stamping	0.1	Manufg.			
Nondepository credit intermediation activities	0.1	Fin/R.E.			
Employment services	0.1	Services			
Plate work & fabricated structural products	0.1	Manufg.			
Plastics packaging materials, film & sheet	0.1	Manufg.			
Ball & roller bearings	0.1	Manufg.			

Source: Benchmark Input-Output Accounts for the U.S. Economy, 2002, U.S. Department of Commerce, Washington, D.C., January 2008. The abbreviation nec stands for 'not elsewhere classified'.

OCCUPATIONS EMPLOYED BY MEDICAL EQUIPMENT & SUPPLIES MANUFACTURING

Occupation	% of Total 2006	Change to 2016	Occupation	% of Total 2006	Change to 2016
Dental laboratory technicians	12.2	2.3	Assemblers & fabricators, nec	1.4	-7.9
Team assemblers	11.0	2.3	Sales reps, wholesale & manufacturing, exc tech	1.3	2.3
First-line supervisors/managers of production workers	3.0	2.3	Helpers--Production workers	1.3	2.3
Inspectors, testers, sorters, samplers, & weighers	3.0	-3.6	Truck drivers, light or delivery services	1.2	2.3
Customer service representatives	2.2	12.5	Packaging & filling machine operators & tenders	1.2	-7.9
Medical appliance technicians	2.0	8.3	Bookkeeping, accounting, & auditing clerks	1.2	2.3
Packers & packagers, hand	1.9	-18.2	Multiple machine tool operators & tenders	1.1	12.5
Shipping, receiving, & traffic clerks	1.9	-1.6	Maintenance & repair workers, general	1.1	2.3
Machinists	1.7	7.4	Stock clerks & order fillers	1.1	-14.4
Molding, coremaking, & casting machine operators	1.6	-7.9	Mechanical engineers	1.1	2.3
Sales representatives, wholesale & manufacturing, tech	1.6	2.3	Laborers & freight, stock, & material movers, hand	1.1	-7.9
General & operations managers	1.5	-7.9	Computer-controlled machine tool operators	1.1	12.5
Sewing machine operators	1.5	2.3	Executive secretaries & administrative assistants	1.1	2.3
Industrial engineers	1.5	24.2	Cutting, punching, & press machine operators	1.1	-7.9
Office clerks, general	1.5	0.8			

Source: Industry-Occupation Matrix, Bureau of Labor Statistics, December 4, 2007. These data are reported based on 4-digit NAICS categories but have been matched to corresponding 6-digit NAICS industry codes. The change reported for each occupation to the year 2016 is a percent of growth or decline as estimated by the Bureau of Labor Statistics. The abbreviation nec stands for 'not elsewhere classified'.

LOCATION BY STATE AND REGIONAL CONCENTRATION

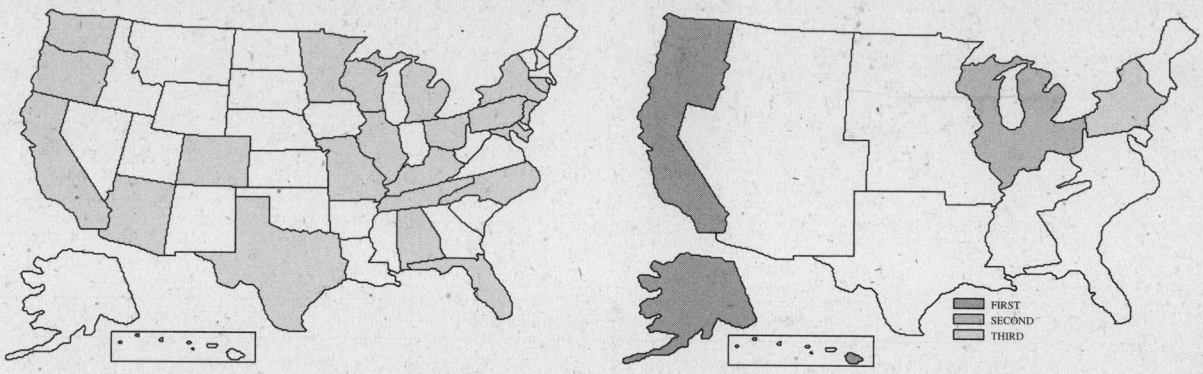

FIRST
SECOND
THIRD

INDUSTRY DATA BY STATE

State	Establish-ments	Shipments			Employment				Cost as % of Shipments	Investment per Employee ($)
		Total ($ mil)	% of U.S.	Per Establ.	Total Number	% of U.S.	Per Establ.	Wages ($/hour)		
California	171	1,025.0	33.2	5,994.4	3,209	19.1	19	18.33	40.5	7,656
Illinois	48	276.0	8.9	5,749.8	1,316	7.9	27	17.03	35.1	7,831
Oregon	35	245.3	7.9	7,008.7	1,408	8.4	40	16.18	27.4	8,732
Pennsylvania	33	177.8	5.8	5,388.8	1,010	6.0	31	16.21	36.8	3,188
New York	53	138.4	4.5	2,611.1	579	3.5	11	16.71	55.1	14,040
Connecticut	10	123.1	4.0	12,308.3	552	3.3	55	14.99	48.9	9,038
Michigan	34	106.3	3.4	3,126.6	415	2.5	12	27.21	34.1	2,366
New Jersey	34	98.5	3.2	2,895.9	898	5.4	26	15.05	22.8	9,862
Wisconsin	16	72.3	2.3	4,520.8	388	2.3	24	16.62	16.5	3,631
Colorado	26	56.9	1.8	2,189.2	518	3.1	20	21.39	47.0	4,948
Washington	23	48.5	1.6	2,109.5	351	2.1	15	16.60	33.8	2,524
Missouri	16	48.4	1.6	3,023.1	306	1.8	19	15.41	22.4	4,072
Tennessee	11	39.5	1.3	3,592.9	409	2.4	37	11.21	27.4	5,670
Florida	43	37.4	1.2	870.0	436	2.6	10	15.95	25.0	1,922
Texas	41	36.1	1.2	880.3	350	2.1	9	15.02	32.5	1,709
Alabama	9	28.1	0.9	3,126.1	139	0.8	15	11.35	47.9	8,496
Ohio	26	26.5	0.9	1,017.8	252	1.5	10	17.55	30.4	2,075
Kentucky	5	24.1	0.8	4,825.0	219	1.3	44	13.44	31.9	2,315
Minnesota	19	18.6	0.6	979.6	192	1.1	10	15.22	33.9	2,583
North Carolina	19	17.2	0.6	903.4	135	0.8	7	13.72	33.4	3,837
Arizona	16	8.2	0.3	511.4	119	0.7	7	16.92	30.1	2,496
Maryland	12	7.1	0.2	594.1	136	0.8	11	16.71	25.3	1,221

Source: 2002 *Economic Census*. The states are in descending order of shipments or establishments (if shipment data are missing for the majority). The symbol (D) appears when data are withheld to prevent disclosure of competitive information. States marked with (D) are sorted by number of establishments. A dash (-) indicates that the data element cannot be calculated. Data may not show all states active in the NAICS category. All data available at the time of publication are shown.

NAICS 339115 - OPHTHALMIC GOODS MANUFACTURING

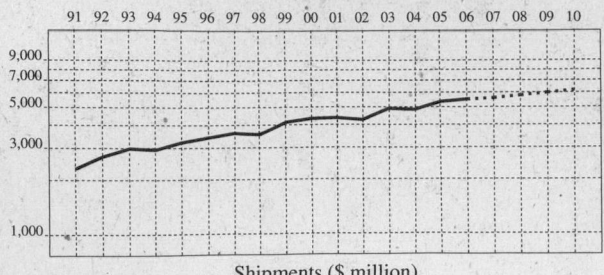

Shipments ($ million)

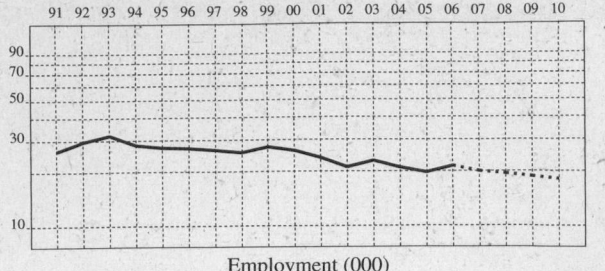

Employment (000)

GENERAL STATISTICS

Year	Companies	Establishments Total	Establishments with 20 or more employees	Employment Total (000)	Employment Production Workers (000)	Employment Hours (Mil)	Compensation Payroll ($ mil)	Compensation Wages ($/hr)	Production Cost of Materials	Production Value Added by Manufacture	Production Value of Shipments	Capital Invest.
1991				26.2	17.2	34.8	626.9	9.64	666.4	1,645.2	2,313.0	120.0
1992	526	569	150	29.6	19.9	40.2	716.3	9.59	748.0	1,950.6	2,692.1	202.4
1993				32.0	21.6	41.7	796.7	9.86	838.2	2,173.4	2,983.9	192.4
1994				28.2	18.8	36.4	719.1	10.09	865.9	2,095.6	2,928.5	200.3
1995				27.3	17.3	33.9	715.6	10.39	947.1	2,254.4	3,212.6	217.8
1996				27.0	17.0	34.6	756.5	10.36	1,020.4	2,390.2	3,416.9	196.7
1997	520	575	159	26.4	17.9	36.4	814.2	12.55	1,084.1	2,511.3	3,607.8	213.7
1998		553	156	25.5	17.1	33.4	786.6	12.48	1,152.0	2,448.1	3,540.4	297.0
1999		542	152	27.4	18.6	35.6	860.5	12.88	1,329.1	2,815.3	4,129.7	296.1
2000		520	147	26.1	18.0	34.2	862.1	13.41	1,479.8	2,902.0	4,320.9	291.2
2001		515	147	23.8	17.0	31.2	868.0	14.63	1,603.8	2,801.3	4,356.2	264.4
2002	488	559	173	21.1	14.1	27.1	845.6	16.30	1,487.2	2,794.3	4,250.6	143.0
2003		559	179	22.9	14.6	28.7	896.1	16.06	1,678.0	3,171.5	4,904.7	168.5
2004		567	175	21.0	12.7	25.8	872.9	17.31	1,647.6	3,199.1	4,837.1	241.7
2005		593	173	19.7	13.2	27.7	916.0	17.13	1,805.5	3,604.4	5,339.1	248.7
2006				21.4	14.4	27.4	964.2	17.00	1,615.0	3,979.1	5,498.0	283.2
2007				20.0P	13.3P	25.7P	960.7P	18.23P	1,640.2P	4,041.2P	5,583.8P	265.5P
2008				19.4P	12.9P	24.9P	978.0P	18.83P	1,698.5P	4,184.9P	5,782.4P	270.4P
2009				18.7P	12.4P	24.0P	995.4P	19.43P	1,756.9P	4,328.7P	5,981.0P	275.3P
2010				18.1P	12.0P	23.1P	1,012.7P	20.04P	1,815.2P	4,472.4P	6,179.6P	280.3P

Sources: 1992, 1997, 2002 *Economic Census*; other years, up to 2006, are from the *Annual Survey of Manufactures*. Establishment counts for non-Census years are from *County Business Patterns*; 1997 and 2002 values are from the 1997 and 2002 censuses respectively, reported in the Federal Government's NAICS format. Other years were originally reported in equivalent SIC format. 'P's show projections by the editors.

INDICES OF CHANGE

Year	Companies	Establishments Total	Establishments with 20 or more employees	Employment Total (000)	Employment Production Workers (000)	Employment Hours (Mil)	Compensation Payroll ($ mil)	Compensation Wages ($/hr)	Production Cost of Materials	Production Value Added by Manufacture	Production Value of Shipments	Capital Invest.
1992	108	102	87	140	141	148	85	59	50	70	63	142
1997	107	103	92	125	127	134	96	77	73	90	85	149
2001		92	85	113	121	115	103	90	108	100	102	185
2002	100	100	100	100	100	100	100	100	100	100	100	100
2003		100	103	109	104	106	106	99	113	113	115	118
2004		101	101	100	90	95	103	106	111	114	114	169
2005		106	100	93	94	102	108	105	121	129	126	174
2006				101	102	101	114	104	109	142	129	198
2007				95P	94P	95P	114P	112P	110P	145P	131P	186P
2008				92P	91P	92P	116P	116P	114P	150P	136P	189P
2009				89P	88P	89P	118P	119P	118P	155P	141P	193P
2010				86P	85P	85P	120P	123P	122P	160P	145P	196P

Sources: Same as General Statistics. Values reflect change from the base year, 2002. Values above 100 mean greater than 2002, values below 100 mean less than 2002, and the values of 100 in other years means the same as 2002. 'P's show projections by the editors.

SELECTED RATIOS

For 2002	Avg. of All Manufact.	Analyzed Industry	Index	For 2002	Avg. of All Manufact.	Analyzed Industry	Index
Employees per Establishment	42	38	90	Value Added per Production Worker	182,367	198,177	109
Payroll per Establishment	1,639,184	1,512,701	92	Cost per Establishment	5,769,015	2,660,465	46
Payroll per Employee	39,053	40,076	103	Cost per Employee	137,446	70,483	51
Production Workers per Establishment	30	25	85	Cost per Production Worker	195,506	105,475	54
Wages per Establishment	694,845	790,215	114	Shipments per Establishment	11,158,348	7,603,936	68
Wages per Production Worker	23,548	31,328	133	Shipments per Employee	265,847	201,450	76
Hours per Production Worker	1,980	1,922	97	Shipments per Production Worker	378,144	301,461	80
Wages per Hour	11.89	16.30	137	Investment per Establishment	361,338	255,814	71
Value Added per Establishment	5,381,325	4,998,748	93	Investment per Employee	8,609	6,777	79
Value Added per Employee	128,210	132,431	103	Investment per Production Worker	12,245	10,142	83

Sources: Same as General Statistics. The 'Average of All Manufacturing' column represents the average of all manufacturing industries reported for the most recent complete year available. The Index shows the relationship between the Average and the Analyzed Industry. For example, 100 means that they are equal; 500 that the Analyzed Industry is five times the average; 50 means that the Analyzed Industry is half the national average. The abbreviation 'na' is used to show that data are 'not available'. Ratios shown for 2002, the last complete census year.

LEADING COMPANIES Number shown: **75** Total sales ($ mil): **57,389** Total employment (000): **321.6**

Company Name	Address				CEO Name	Phone	Co. Type	Sales ($ mil)	Empl. (000)
Sears, Roebuck and Co.	3333 Beverly Rd.	Hoffman Estates	IL	60179		847-286-2500	S	30,030	247.0
Davis Vision Inc.	159 Express St.	Plainview	NY	11803	Joe Carlomusto	516-932-9500	R	9,840*	0.2
Allergan Inc.	PO Box 19534	Irvine	CA	92623		714-246-4500	P	3,939	7.9
Bausch and Lomb Inc.	1 Bausch Lomb Pl.	Rochester	NY	14604		585-338-6000	P	2,292	13.0
Custom Eyes Inc.	PO Box 546	Sauk Rapids	MN	56379		320-654-0573	S	1,630*	<0.1
Cooper Companies Inc.	21062 Bake Pky.	Lake Forest	CA	92630	Thomas Bender	949-597-4700	P	951	7.6
Essilor of America Inc.	PO Box 814689	Dallas	TX	75381	Laurent Vacherot	972-241-4141	R	866*	1.0
Oakley Inc.	1 Icon	Foothill Ranch	CA	92610		949-951-0991	S	768	3.4
Polaroid Holding Co.	1265 Main St.	Waltham	MA	02451	Jacque A. Nasser	781-386-2000	S	753	3.4
NCH Corp.	PO Box 152170	Irving	TX	75015		972-438-0211	R	688*	8.5
Polaroid Corp.	300 Baker Ave.	Concord	MA	01742	Bob Gregerson	781-386-2000	S	664*	3.0
Ocular Sciences Puerto Rico	Amuelas Industrial	Juana Diaz	PR	00795	Thomas Bender	787-260-0555	S	596*	2.6
Sola International Inc.	10590 W Ocean Air	San Diego	CA	92130	Jeremy C. Bishop	858-509-9899	R	550*	6.6
For Eyes Optical Co.	285 W 74th Pl.	Hialeah	FL	33014	Phillip Wolman	305-557-9004	R	438*	0.4
Marchon Eyewear Inc.	35 Hub Dr.	Melville	NY	11747	Al Berg	631-755-2020	R	317*	1.1
Ocular Sciences Inc. USA	1855 Gateway Blvd.	Concord	CA	94520	A. Thomas Bender		S	300*	2.5
1-800 CONTACTS Inc.	66 E Wadsworth Pk	Draper	UT	84020	Brian Bethers	801-924-9800	P	249	1.1
US Vision Inc.	1 Harmon Dr.	Glendora	NJ	08029	George T. Gorman	856-228-1000	R	171*	3.0
Walman Optical Co.	PO Box 9440	Minneapolis	MN	55440	Martin Bassett	612-520-6000	R	155*	0.2
Soderberg Inc.	PO Box 64313	Saint Paul	MN	55164	Craig Giles	651-291-1400	S	155*	0.1
Jackson Products Inc.	1859 Bowles Ave.	Fenton	MO	63026	David Gilchrist	636-717-6600	R	133*	<0.1
Sterling Optical	100 Quentin Rsevelt	Garden City	NY	11530	Christopher G. Payan	516-390-4500	S	129*	0.1
Lombart Instruments U.S.	5358 Robin Hood	Norfolk	VA	23513	Kenneth Lombart	757-853-8888	R	125*	0.1
Gentex Corp.	324 Main Street	Simpson	PA	18407	L. Peter Frieder Jr.	570-282-3550	R	113*	0.6
Titmus Optical Inc.	3811 Corporate Dr.	Petersburg	VA	23805	Thomas Goeltz	804-732-6121	S	88*	0.4
Suncoast Medical Clinic	601 7th St. S	St. Petersburg	FL	33701		727-894-1818	R	85*	0.3
Rosin Eyecare	6233 W Cermak Rd.	Berwyn	IL	60402	James Rosin	708-749-2020	R	82*	0.1
Spectera Inc.	2811 Lord Baltimore	Baltimore	MD	21244	David Hall	410-265-6033	S	74*	0.7
Nassau Lens Company Inc.	160 Legrand Ave.	Northvale	NJ	07647	Michael Pildes	201-767-8033	S	62*	0.4
Signet Armorlite Inc.	1001 Armorlite Dr.	San Marcos	CA	92069		760-744-4000	R	60*	0.4
STAAR Surgical Co.	1911 Walker Ave.	Monrovia	CA	91016	David Bailey	626-303-7902	P	59	0.4
Winston-Salem Ind. For Blind	7730 N Point Blvd.	Winston-Salem	NC	27106	Daniel Boucher	336-759-0551	R	57*	0.3
Luxottica USA Inc.	44 Harbor Park Dr.	Port Washington	NY	11050	L Del Vecchio	516-484-3800	S	49*	0.4
Twin City Optical Co.	5205 Hwy. 169 N	Minneapolis	MN	55442		763-551-2000	R	43*	0.4
Orange 21 Inc.	2070 Las Palmas Dr.	Carlsbad	CA	92009		760-804-8420	P	42	<0.1
Hilsinger Co.	PO Box 1538	Plainville	MA	02762	Robert Nahmias	508-699-4406	R	42*	0.2
Testrite Instrument Company	216 S Newman St.	Hackensack	NJ	07601	Harold Rubin	201-543-0240	R	37*	0.1
Uvex Safety Manufacturing Ltd.	10 Thurber Blvd.	Smithfield	RI	02917	Herve Meillat	401-232-1200	R	37*	0.3
Ciba Vision Puerto Rico Inc.	PO Box 1358	Cidra	PR	00739		787-739-8418	R	34*	0.1
Rodenstock Corp.	PO Box 8	Yauco	PR	00698	Antonio Oliver		S	34*	0.1
Sperian Fall Protection Inc.	900 Douglas Pke.	Smithfield	RI	02917	Henri-Dominiq Petit	401-232-1200	R	33*	<0.1
United Lens Company Inc.	259 Worcester St.	Southbridge	MA	01550	Albert Digregorio	508-765-5421	R	28*	0.2
Luzerne Optical Laboratories	PO Box 998	Wilkes Barre	PA	18703	John Dougherty	570-822-3183	R	25*	0.2
Signature Eyewear Inc.	498 N Oak St.	Inglewood	CA	90302	Michael Prince	310-330-2700	P	25	<0.1
Kollmorgen Electro-Optical	347 King Street	Northampton	MA	01060	Ken Bixby	413-586-2330	D	25*	0.3
Dr Bizer's Visionworld	516 E Hwy. 131	Clarksville	IN	47129		812-282-2020	R	25*	<0.1
Sterling Vision Kenoha Inc.	7532 Pershing Blvd.	Kenosha	WI	53142	Christopher Payan	262-694-2400	S	25*	<0.1
Riviera Trading Inc.	180 Madison Ave.	New York	NY	10016	Orville Ankarlo	212-949-9000	R	23*	<0.1
Emerging Vision Inc.	100 Quentin Rsevelt	Garden City	NY	11530	Alan Cohen	516-390-2106	P	22	0.1
Moc Acquisition Corp.	2360 59th St.	Saint Louis	MO	63110	Matt Iovaldi	314-533-2020	R	20*	0.2
New Era Optical Company Inc.	5575 N Lynch Ave.	Chicago	IL	60630	Herbert Natkin	773-725-9600	R	20*	0.2
Lobob Laboratories Inc.	1440 Atteberry Ln.	San Jose	CA	95131	Robert Lohr	408-432-0580	R	20*	<0.1
Sth Corp.	3630 W Miller Rd.	Garland	TX	75041	Richard Bullwinkle	972-543-2500	R	20*	0.1
21st Century Optics Inc.	4700 33rd St.	Long Island Cty	NY	11101	Ralph Woythaler	718-392-2310	S	19*	0.1
City Optical Company Inc.	2839 Lafayette Rd.	Indianapolis	IN	46222	Lawrence Tavel	317-924-1300	R	19*	<0.1
Parmelee Industries Inc.	PO Box 15965	Shawnee Msn	KS	66285	Alan Sankpill	913-599-5555	R	19*	<0.1
Artcraft Optical Company Inc.	57 Goodway Dr. S	Rochester	NY	14623	Thomas Eagle	585-546-6640	R	18*	0.1
Optical Supply Inc.	1526 Plainfield Ave	Grand Rapids	MI	49505	Hubert Sagnieres	616-361-6000	S	18*	0.1
Designs For Visions Inc.	760 Koehler Ave.	Ronkonkoma	NY	11779	Richard Feinbloom	631-585-3300	R	18*	0.1
Bartley Optical Sales Inc.	1300 W Optical Dr.	Azusa	CA	91702		626-969-6181	R	18*	<0.1
Rite-Style Optical Co.	PO Box 3068	Omaha	NE	68103	George Lee	402-492-8822	R	16*	0.1
Sunbelt USA Inc.	PO Box 2009	Upland	CA	91785	Roy Burchett	909-593-0500	R	15*	<0.1
Icare Industries Inc.	PO Box 84000	St. Petersburg	FL	33784	J. Scott Payne	727-526-0501	R	15*	0.2
Art Optical Contact Lens Inc.	PO Box 1848	Grand Rapids	MI	49501	Thomas Anastor	616-453-1888	R	15*	0.1
Mueller Optical Co.	PO Box 888	Columbia	IL	62236	Eric Mueller	618-281-3344	R	15*	<0.1
Fibre-Metal Products Co.	PO Box 248	Concordville	PA	19331	Charles Grandi	610-459-5300	R	14*	0.2
Cooperative Optical Services	2424 E 8 Mile Rd.	Detroit	MI	48234	Jackee Smith	313-366-5100	R	14*	<0.1
DFG Inc.	651 Critchlow Dr. 2	Ogden	UT	84404	Ken Barfield	801-773-4180	R	14*	0.1
Fosta-Tek Optics Inc.	320 Hamilton St.	Leominster	MA	01453	John Morrison	978-534-6511	R	14*	0.1
Lens C-C Inc.	PO Box 2198	San Leandro	CA	94577	Carl Moore	510-483-9400	R	14*	0.1
Zyloware Corp.	1136 46th Rd.	Long Island Cty	NY	11101	Christopher Shyer	718-392-3900	R	14*	0.1
Optovision Coating Labs Inc.	10510 Olympic Dr.	Dallas	TX	75220	Peter Zuccarelli	214-357-1717	R	14*	<0.1
Dioptics Medical Products Inc.	125 Venture Ln.	San Luis Obispo	CA	93401	Henry Lane	805-781-3300	R	14*	<0.1
Rafi Systems Inc.	750 N Diamond Bar	Diamond Bar	CA	91765	Kusum Rafiquzza	909-593-8124	R	13*	<0.1
Tri-Supreme Optical L.L.C.	91 Carolyn Blvd.	Farmingdale	NY	11735		631-249-2020	S	13*	<0.1

Source: Ward's Business Directory of U.S. Private and Public Companies, Volumes 1 and 2, 2008. The company type code used is as follows: P - Public, R - Private, S - Subsidiary, D - Division, J - Joint Venture, A - Affiliate, G - Group. Sales are in millions of dollars, employees are in thousands. An asterisk (*) indicates an estimated sales volume. The symbol < stands for 'less than'. Company names and addresses are truncated, in some cases, to fit into the available space.

MATERIALS CONSUMED

Material	Quantity	Delivered Cost ($ million)
Lens blanks, optical and ophthalmic	(X)	147.7
Lenses and prisms for optical instruments and sighting and fire control equipment	(X)	(D)
Plastics resins consumed in the form of granules, pellets, etc.	(X)	87.6
Plastics products consumed in the form of sheets, rods, etc.	(X)	29.3
Paperboard containers, boxes, and corrugated paperboard	(X)	(D)
All other materials, components, parts, containers, and supplies	(X)	616.0
Materials, ingredients, containers, and supplies, nsk	(X)	202.4

Source: 2002 *Economic Census.* Explanation of symbols used: (D): Withheld to avoid disclosure of competitive data; na: Not available; (S): Withheld because statistical norms were not met; (X): Not applicable; (Z): Less than half the unit shown; nec: Not elsewhere classified; nsk: Not specified by kind; - : zero; p : 10-19 percent estimated; q : 20-29 percent estimated.

PRODUCT SHARE DETAILS

Product or Product Class Shipments	Mil. $	Product or Product Class Shipments	Mil. $
OPHTHALMIC GOODS	3,879.4	**Contact lenses**	**1,853.0**
Ophthalmic fronts and temples	**67.6**	Hard contact lenses, except molded lens blanks	36.9
Ophthalmic fronts and temples	65.3	Soft contact lenses, except molded lens blanks	1,811.6
Plastic ophthalmic finished fronts	26.7	Contact lenses, nsk	4.5
Other ophthalmic finished fronts	27.1	**Ophthalmic goods and prescription ground eyeglass lenses**	**1,049.0**
Ophthalmic temples	11.5	Ophthalmic goods and prescription ground eyeglass	
Ophthalmic fronts and temples, nsk	2.3	lenses, except retailing eyeglasses in combination with	
Glass ophthalmic focal lenses	**59.4**	the grinding of the eyeglass lenses to order on the	
Glass ophthalmic lenses	58.3	premises	979.7
Glass ophthalmic single vision lenses (ground and		Industrial goggles, eye protectors, welding circles and	
polished and molded blanks), except prescription		plates, and mountings	140.5
ground eyeglass lenses and molded lens blanks	23.4	Ready-made antiglare glasses, including reading	
Glass ophthalmic multifocal lenses (finished,		glasses, sunglasses, and sungoggles	512.9
semifinished, and molded blanks), except prescription		Other ophthalmic goods, nec	208.1
ground eyeglass lenses and molded lens blanks	34.9	Prescription ground eyeglass lenses, except retailing	
Glass ophthalmic focal lenses, nsk	1.1	prescription eyeglasses in combination with the	
Plastics ophthalmic focal lenses	**480.6**	grinding of the eyeglass lenses to order on the	
Plastic single vision lenses, except prescription ground		premises	118.1
eyeglass lenses and molded lens blanks	209.0	Ophthalmic goods and prescription ground eyeglass	
Plastic multifocal lenses, except prescription ground		lenses, nsk	69.3
eyeglass lenses and molded lens blanks	218.2	**Ophthalmic goods, nsk, total**	**369.8**
Plastic ophthalmic focal lenses, nsk	53.3		

Source: 2002 *Economic Census.* The values are product shipments in millions of dollars for 2002. Total product shipments may be lower or higher than industry shipments. See Introduction for a full discussion. Values of indented subcategories are summed in the main heading(s). The symbol (D) appears when data are withheld to prevent disclosure of competitive information. The abbreviation nsk stands for 'not specified by kind' and nec for 'not elsewhere classified'. A dash (-) means zero.

INPUTS AND OUTPUTS FOR OPHTHALMIC GOODS MANUFACTURING

Economic Sector or Industry Providing Inputs	%	Sector	Economic Sector or Industry Buying Outputs	%	Sector
Compensation of employees	27.5		Personal consumption expenditures	85.1	
Surgical & medical instrument	5.7	Manufg.	Exports of goods & services	11.5	Cap Inv
Wholesale trade	3.1	Trade	Change in private inventories	1.0	In House
Advertising & related services	3.1	Services	Urethane & other foam products (except polystrene)	1.0	Manufg.
Optical instruments & lenses	3.1	Manufg.	Ophthalmic goods	0.3	Manufg.
Surgical appliances & supplies	2.7	Manufg.	Wholesale trade	0.2	Trade
Management of companies & enterprises	2.7	Services	Motor vehicle parts	0.1	Manufg.
Plastics products, nec	2.5	Manufg.	General S/L govt. services	0.1	S/L Govt
Plastics materials & resins	2.0	Manufg.			
Retail trade	1.9	Trade			
Truck transportation	1.0	Util.			
Paperboard containers	1.0	Manufg.			
Power generation & supply	0.8	Util.			
Real estate	0.8	Fin/R.E.			
Plastics packaging materials, film & sheet	0.7	Manufg.			
Noncomparable imports	0.6	Foreign			
Machine shops	0.6	Manufg.			
Nonwoven fabric mills	0.5	Manufg.			
Ophthalmic goods	0.5	Manufg.			
Semiconductors & related devices	0.4	Manufg.			
Maintenance/repair of nonresidential structures	0.4	Construct.			
Securities, commodity contracts, investments	0.4	Fin/R.E.			
Printed circuit assemblies (electronic assemblies)	0.4	Manufg.			
Lessors of nonfinancial assets	0.4	Fin/R.E.			
Synthetic rubber	0.4	Manufg.			
Services to buildings & dwellings	0.4	Services			
Automotive equipment rental & leasing	0.3	Fin/R.E.			
Coating, engraving, heat treating & allied activities	0.3	Manufg.			

Continued on next page.

INPUTS AND OUTPUTS FOR OPHTHALMIC GOODS MANUFACTURING - Continued

Economic Sector or Industry Providing Inputs	%	Sector	Economic Sector or Industry Buying Outputs	%	Sector
Cutting tools & machine tool accessories	0.3	Manufg.			
Glass products from purchased glass	0.3	Manufg.			
Automotive repair & maintenance, ex. car washes	0.3	Services			
Telecommunications	0.2	Services			
Warehousing & storage	0.2	Util.			
Abrasive products	0.2	Manufg.			
Commercial & industrial equipment repair/maintenance	0.2	Services			
Dental laboratories	0.2	Manufg.			
Commercial & industrial machinery rental & leasing	0.2	Fin/R.E.			
Motor vehicle parts	0.1	Manufg.			
Professional, scientific, technical services, nec	0.1	Services			
Scientific research & development services	0.1	Services			
Accounting, tax preparation, bookkeeping, & payroll	0.1	Services			
Data processing, hosting, & related services	0.1	Services			
Employment services	0.1	Services			
Chemical products & preparations, nec	0.1	Manufg.			
Legal services	0.1	Services			
Unlaminated plastics profile shapes	0.1	Manufg.			

Source: *Benchmark Input-Output Accounts for the U.S. Economy, 2002*, U.S. Department of Commerce, Washington, D.C., January 2008. The abbreviation nec stands for 'not elsewhere classified'.

OCCUPATIONS EMPLOYED BY MEDICAL EQUIPMENT & SUPPLIES MANUFACTURING

Occupation	% of Total 2006	Change to 2016	Occupation	% of Total 2006	Change to 2016
Dental laboratory technicians	12.2	2.3	Assemblers & fabricators, nec	1.4	-7.9
Team assemblers	11.0	2.3	Sales reps, wholesale & manufacturing, exc tech	1.3	2.3
First-line supervisors/managers of production workers	3.0	2.3	Helpers--Production workers	1.3	2.3
Inspectors, testers, sorters, samplers, & weighers	3.0	-3.6	Truck drivers, light or delivery services	1.2	2.3
Customer service representatives	2.2	12.5	Packaging & filling machine operators & tenders	1.2	-7.9
Medical appliance technicians	2.0	8.3	Bookkeeping, accounting, & auditing clerks	1.2	2.3
Packers & packagers, hand	1.9	-18.2	Multiple machine tool operators & tenders	1.1	12.5
Shipping, receiving, & traffic clerks	1.9	-1.6	Maintenance & repair workers, general	1.1	2.3
Machinists	1.7	7.4	Stock clerks & order fillers	1.1	-14.4
Molding, coremaking, & casting machine operators	1.6	-7.9	Mechanical engineers	1.1	2.3
Sales representatives, wholesale & manufacturing, tech	1.6	2.3	Laborers & freight, stock, & material movers, hand	1.1	-7.9
General & operations managers	1.5	-7.9	Computer-controlled machine tool operators	1.1	12.5
Sewing machine operators	1.5	2.3	Executive secretaries & administrative assistants	1.1	2.3
Industrial engineers	1.5	24.2	Cutting, punching, & press machine operators	1.1	-7.9
Office clerks, general	1.5	0.8			

Source: *Industry-Occupation Matrix*, Bureau of Labor Statistics, December 4, 2007. These data are reported based on 4-digit NAICS categories but have been matched to corresponding 6-digit NAICS industry codes. The change reported for each occupation to the year 2016 is a percent of growth or decline as estimated by the Bureau of Labor Statistics. The abbreviation nec stands for 'not elsewhere classified'.

LOCATION BY STATE AND REGIONAL CONCENTRATION

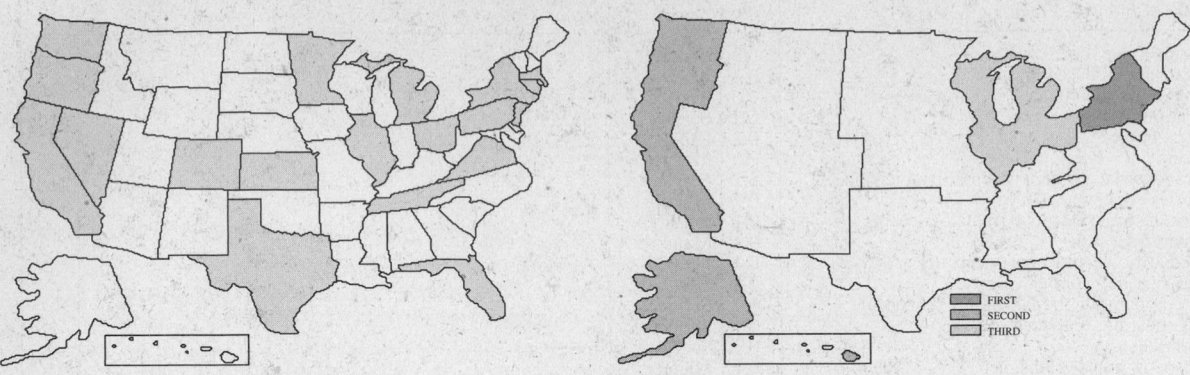

FIRST
SECOND
THIRD

INDUSTRY DATA BY STATE

| State | Establish-ments | Shipments | | | Employment | | | | Cost as % of Shipments | Investment per Employee ($) |
		Total ($ mil)	% of U.S.	Per Establ.	Total Number	% of U.S.	Per Establ.	Wages ($/hour)		
Florida	36	755.9	17.8	20,997.7	3,038	14.4	84	19.09	13.7	11,926
California	72	701.2	16.5	9,738.3	2,827	13.4	39	14.33	46.0	7,284
New York	45	320.3	7.5	7,117.1	1,827	8.7	41	15.09	27.9	2,771
Massachusetts	19	193.4	4.5	10,178.1	1,475	7.0	78	17.68	35.3	8,339
Minnesota	16	188.4	4.4	11,773.7	1,103	5.2	69	13.56	36.1	5,236
Texas	25	168.5	4.0	6,738.4	1,231	5.8	49	12.92	36.2	4,940
Rhode Island	7	124.1	2.9	17,734.4	575	2.7	82	15.59	28.5	6,440
Virginia	12	118.3	2.8	9,856.9	815	3.9	68	12.82	30.8	5,733
Illinois	24	104.0	2.4	4,332.8	965	4.6	40	15.00	38.9	11,973
Pennsylvania	35	86.3	2.0	2,466.1	671	3.2	19	15.16	27.9	3,724
Ohio	28	80.3	1.9	2,868.2	607	2.9	22	12.54	44.6	6,797
Tennessee	16	70.5	1.7	4,408.5	517	2.5	32	13.73	36.3	3,153
New Jersey	18	64.3	1.5	3,572.1	458	2.2	25	15.04	29.9	2,360
Michigan	18	49.7	1.2	2,761.8	398	1.9	22	15.32	31.3	3,583
Washington	12	45.2	1.1	3,762.6	306	1.5	25	13.18	36.5	3,340
Connecticut	5	37.1	0.9	7,416.0	232	1.1	46	16.56	57.3	10,983
Kansas	7	32.8	0.8	4,679.4	224	1.1	32	14.47	31.5	4,384
Oregon	12	29.7	0.7	2,473.1	226	1.1	19	16.99	33.5	3,394
Colorado	14	28.0	0.7	1,997.7	177	0.8	13	13.38	30.8	4,395
Nevada	3	23.1	0.5	7,703.7	139	0.7	46	16.92	46.0	6,324

Source: 2002 *Economic Census*. The states are in descending order of shipments or establishments (if shipment data are missing for the majority). The symbol (D) appears when data are withheld to prevent disclosure of competitive information. States marked with (D) are sorted by number of establishments. A dash (-) indicates that the data element cannot be calculated. Data may not show all states active in the NAICS category. All data available at the time of publication are shown.

NAICS 339116 - DENTAL LABORATORIES

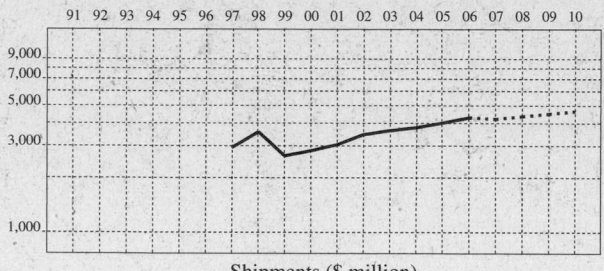

Shipments ($ million)

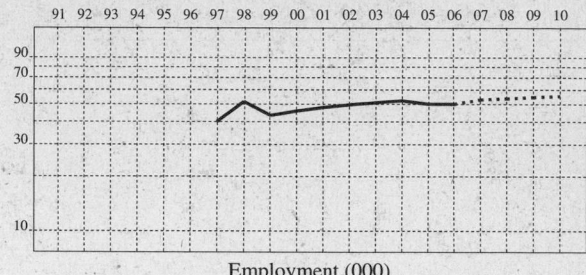

Employment (000)

GENERAL STATISTICS

| Year | Com-panies | Establishments | | Employment | | | Compensation | | Production ($ million) | | | |
		Total	with 20 or more employees	Total (000)	Production Workers (000)	Hours (Mil)	Payroll ($ mil)	Wages ($/hr)	Cost of Materials	Value Added by Manufacture	Value of Shipments	Capital Invest.
1997	7,473	7,566	325	40.1	29.7	49.3	999.8	12.68	780.2	2,118.0	2,931.8	73.7
1998		7,425	344	51.6	39.7	73.7	1,271.4	12.14	994.1	2,536.3	3,580.4	73.7
1999		7,345	365	43.4	32.9	61.7	1,155.7	12.86	583.4	2,049.3	2,640.5	83.0
2000		7,332	394	45.9	33.9	65.1	1,245.0	13.20	649.5	2,192.0	2,821.6	82.1
2001		7,404	408	48.0	35.2	72.2	1,345.7	12.80	670.1	2,397.5	3,044.3	78.8
2002	6,918	7,089	475	49.7	36.8	68.8	1,531.9	15.64	645.0	2,818.4	3,463.4	94.7
2003		6,989	425	51.0	37.6	72.4	1,604.9	15.13	671.5	2,951.5	3,641.2	115.7
2004		7,250	437	52.3	36.4	70.7	1,641.3	15.66	774.4	3,049.6	3,780.7	99.1
2005		7,225	425	50.2	34.7	64.6	1,687.8	17.41	866.8	3,163.7	4,017.6	116.7
2006		7,055P	473P	50.1	34.8	65.9	1,793.5	17.93	951.4	3,360.9	4,298.0	127.5
2007		7,007P	488P	53.0P	36.5P	71.4P	1,886.1P	18.10P	934.1P	3,299.7P	4,219.8P	127.2P
2008		6,960P	502P	53.8P	36.8P	72.3P	1,969.4P	18.75P	966.2P	3,413.2P	4,364.8P	133.2P
2009		6,913P	517P	54.7P	37.0P	73.2P	2,052.8P	19.40P	998.3P	3,526.6P	4,509.9P	139.2P
2010		6,865P	532P	55.5P	37.3P	74.1P	2,136.1P	20.05P	1,030.4P	3,640.0P	4,655.0P	145.1P

Sources: 1997 and 2002 *Economic Census*; other years, up to 2006, are from *Annual Survey of Manufactures*. Establishment counts for non-Census years are from *County Business Patterns*; 1997 and 2002 values are from the 1997 and 2002 censuses, respectively. 'P's show projections by the editors.

INDICES OF CHANGE

| Year | Com-panies | Establishments | | Employment | | | Compensation | | Production ($ million) | | | |
		Total	with 20 or more employees	Total (000)	Production Workers (000)	Hours (Mil)	Payroll ($ mil)	Wages ($/hr)	Cost of Materials	Value Added by Manufacture	Value of Shipments	Capital Invest.
1997	108	107	68	81	81	72	65	81	121	75	85	78
1998		105	72	104	108	107	83	78	154	90	103	78
1999		104	77	87	89	90	75	82	90	73	76	88
2000		103	83	92	92	95	81	84	101	78	81	87
2001		104	86	97	96	105	88	82	104	85	88	83
2002	100	100	100	100	100	100	100	100	100	100	100	100
2003		99	89	103	102	105	105	97	104	105	105	122
2004		102	92	105	99	103	107	100	120	108	109	105
2005		102	89	101	94	94	110	111	134	112	116	123
2006		100P	100P	101	95	96	117	115	148	119	124	135
2007		99P	103P	107P	99P	104P	123P	116P	145P	117P	122P	134P
2008		98P	106P	108P	100P	105P	129P	120P	150P	121P	126P	141P
2009		98P	109P	110P	101P	106P	134P	124P	155P	125P	130P	147P
2010		97P	112P	112P	101P	108P	139P	128P	160P	129P	134P	153P

Sources: Same as General Statistics. Values reflect change from the base year, 2002. Values above 100 mean greater than 2002, values below 100 mean less than 2002, and the values of 100 in other years means the same as 2002. 'P's show projections by the editors.

SELECTED RATIOS

For 2002	Avg. of All Manufact.	Analyzed Industry	Index	For 2002	Avg. of All Manufact.	Analyzed Industry	Index
Employees per Establishment	42	7	17	Value Added per Production Worker	182,367	76,587	42
Payroll per Establishment	1,639,184	216,095	13	Cost per Establishment	5,769,015	90,986	2
Payroll per Employee	39,053	30,823	79	Cost per Employee	137,446	12,978	9
Production Workers per Establishment	30	5	18	Cost per Production Worker	195,506	17,527	9
Wages per Establishment	694,845	151,789	22	Shipments per Establishment	11,158,348	488,560	4
Wages per Production Worker	23,548	29,240	124	Shipments per Employee	265,847	69,686	26
Hours per Production Worker	1,980	1,870	94	Shipments per Production Worker	378,144	94,114	25
Wages per Hour	11.89	15.64	132	Investment per Establishment	361,338	13,359	4
Value Added per Establishment	5,381,325	397,574	7	Investment per Employee	8,609	1,905	22
Value Added per Employee	128,210	56,708	44	Investment per Production Worker	12,245	2,573	21

Sources: Same as General Statistics. The 'Average of All Manufacturing' column represents the average of all manufacturing industries reported for the most recent complete year available. The Index shows the relationship between the Average and the Analyzed Industry. For example, 100 means that they are equal; 500 that the Analyzed Industry is five times the average; 50 means that the Analyzed Industry is half the national average. The abbreviation 'na' is used to show that data are 'not available'. Ratios shown for 2002, the last complete census year.

LEADING COMPANIES   Number shown: **42**   Total sales ($ mil): **190**   Total employment (000): **1.9**

Company Name	Address				CEO Name	Phone	Co. Type	Sales ($ mil)	Empl. (000)
Sharpe Dry Goods Co.	200 N Broadway St.	Checotah	OK	74426	Louis Sharpe IV	918-473-2233	R	60*	0.4
Issaquah Dental Lab Inc.	640 NW Gilman	Issaquah	WA	98027	Larry Searles	425-392-5125	R	12*	<0.1
Selane Products Inc.	PO Box 4184	Van Nuys	CA	91409	John Christian	818-998-7460	R	9*	<0.1
Ottawa Dental Labs Inc.	PO Box 771	Ottawa	IL	61350	Lucian Caruso	815-434-0655	R	8*	0.1
Dental Art Laboratories Inc.	PO Box 22032	Lansing	MI	48909	Richard Blundy	517-485-2200	R	6*	<0.1
Edmonds Dental Prosthetics	PO Box 10387	Springfield	MO	65808	Bobby Edmonds	417-881-8572	R	6*	<0.1
Harold A Burdette Dental Labs	PO Box 364	Birmingham	AL	35201	Harold Burdette	205-916-0887	R	5*	<0.1
Mason Dental Midwest Inc.	12752 Stark Rd.	Livonia	MI	48150	Gary Lockwood	734-525-1070	R	5*	<0.1
Orthodontic Technologies Inc.	PO Box 4871	Houston	TX	77210	Diane Johnson	713-861-0033	R	4*	<0.1
Bertram Dental Laboratory	PO Box 1853	Appleton	WI	54912	William Bertram	920-731-1483	R	4*	<0.1
TP Orthodontics Inc.	PO Box 742	Lodi	CA	95241		209-368-7545	R	4*	<0.1
Artistic Dental Studio Inc.	470 Woodcreek Dr.	Bolingbrook	IL	60440	Thom Goetz	630-679-8686	R	3*	<0.1
Dental Craft Corp.	PO Box 178	Ringwood	IL	60072	Jerome Wakitsch	815-385-7132	R	3*	<0.1
Myron's Dental Laboratories	PO Box 171458	Kansas City	KS	66117	Timothy Sigler	913-281-5552	R	3*	<0.1
Tincher Dental Laboratory	PO Box 18057	Charleston	WV	25303	George Obst	304-744-4671	R	3*	<0.1
Dental Prosthetic Services	PO Box 2939	Cedar Rapids	IA	52406	Dennis Becker	319-393-1990	R	3*	<0.1
Saylors Dental Laboratory Inc.	PO Box 410	Manassas	VA	20108	Robert Sayors	703-631-1875	R	3*	<0.1
Jasinski Dental Lab Inc.	1141 Smile Ln.	Lansdale	PA	19446	Hubert Jasinski	215-699-8861	R	3*	<0.1
Marque Dental Laboratory Inc.	PO Box 10278	Fargo	ND	58106	Darrell Fey	701-235-2932	R	3*	<0.1
Bay View Dental Laboratory	1207 Volvo Pkwy.	Chesapeake	VA	23320	Vernon Shafer	757-583-1787	R	3*	<0.1
Dental Ceramics Inc.	5299 98th Blvd.	Cleveland	OH	44125	John Lavicka	216-662-3123	R	3*	<0.1
Jackson Spah Dental Studio	PO Box 9659	Minneapolis	MN	55440	Gerald Jackson	763-785-2435	R	3*	<0.1
United Dental Laboratories	187 W Exchange St.	Akron	OH	44302	Richard Delapa	330-253-1810	R	3*	<0.1
Somer Inc.	11707 N Michigan	Zionsville	IN	46077	Larry Sowinski	317-873-1111	R	2*	<0.1
ADL Dental Laboratory	PO Box 34188	Louisville	KY	40232	Allan Morris	502-451-2200	R	2*	<0.1
Oratech Inc.	PO Box 13486	Springfield	IL	62791	Norman Ross	217-793-2735	R	2*	<0.1
Lactona Corp.	PO Box 428	Hatfield	PA	19440	Robert Goglia	215-692-9000	R	2*	<0.1
Encore Crown and Bridge Inc.	PO Box 1699	Plymouth	MA	02362	Steven Schilling	508-746-6025	R	2*	<0.1
Jochim Chrome Laboratory Inc.	PO Box 4058	Concord	CA	94524	Ron Dixon	925-676-9200	R	2*	<0.1
Allen Dental Laboratory Inc.	1405 E Berry St.	Fort Wayne	IN	46803	Stanley Ferguson	260-424-4846	R	2*	<0.1
Dental Professional Labs	8040 Cleveland Pl.	Merrillville	IN	46410	Michael Suris	219-769-6225	R	2*	<0.1
Littman Dental Laboratory Inc.	1209 Greenwood	Baltimore	MD	21208	Ronald Gill	410-486-0666	R	2*	<0.1
O'Guinn Corp.	10609 N Park Ave.	Indianapolis	IN	46280	Howard O'Guinn	317-848-1414	R	2*	<0.1
Midwest Dental Laboratories	1311 Baur Blvd.	Saint Louis	MO	63132	Frederick Bertram	314-991-0325	R	2*	<0.1
Berger Excel Dental Labs	1600 US Hwy. 130	N Brunswick	NJ	08902	Ronald Berger	732-422-4444	R	2*	<0.1
Conicella-Fessler Dental Lab.	409 Shadeland Ave.	Drexel Hill	PA	19026	Nicholas Conicella	610-622-3298	R	2*	<0.1
Lafayette Dental Laboratory	PO Box 5479	Lafayette	IN	47903	Randall Jackson	765-447-9341	R	2*	<0.1
Nakoma Dental Studio Ltd.	PO Box 7954	Madison	WI	53707	Terry Lueder	608-221-2229	R	2*	<0.1
American Dental Laboratory Co.	PO Box 1776	Memphis	TN	38101		901-345-1776	R	1*	<0.1
Space Maintainers of Mid West	PO Box 7212	Saint Louis	MO	63177	Mark Ohlendorf	314-533-3440	R	1*	<0.1
Leonard Greenberg Corp.	1581 Sprngfield Ave	Maplewood	NJ	07040	Leonard Greenberg	973-761-0032	R	1*	<0.1
Tanaka Dental Enterprises Inc.	5135 Golf Rd. Fl. 1	Skokie	IL	60077	Asami Tanaka	847-679-1610	R	1*	<0.1

Source: *Ward's Business Directory of U.S. Private and Public Companies*, Volumes 1 and 2, 2008. The company type code used is as follows: P - Public, R - Private, S - Subsidiary, D - Division, J - Joint Venture, A - Affiliate, G - Group. Sales are in millions of dollars, employees are in thousands. An asterisk (*) indicates an estimated sales volume. The symbol < stands for 'less than'. Company names and addresses are truncated, in some cases, to fit into the available space.

MATERIALS CONSUMED

Material	Quantity	Delivered Cost ($ million)
Steel shapes and forms (exc. castings, forgings, fabr. metal products)	(X)	4.9
Fabricated metal products (excluding forgings and castings)	(X)	15.8
Precious metals (gold, platinum, etc.), all forms (incl. ingot, sheet, strip, solder, plating, electrodes, etc.)	(X)	75.4
Chemical, all types (including resins)	(X)	13.3
Fabricated plastics products (excluding gaskets)	(X)	6.8
Resistors, capacitors, transformers, electron tubes, semiconductors, and other electronic components	(X)	1.2
Paperboard containers, boxes, and corrugated paperboard	(X)	3.1
All other materials, components, parts, containers, and supplies	(X)	72.5
Materials, ingredients, containers, and supplies, nsk	(X)	314.1

Source: 2002 *Economic Census*. Explanation of symbols used: (D): Withheld to avoid disclosure of competitive data; na: Not available; (S): Withheld because statistical norms were not met; (X): Not applicable; (Z): Less than half the unit shown; nec: Not elsewhere classified; nsk: Not specified by kind; - : zero; p : 10-19 percent estimated; q : 20-29 percent estimated.

PRODUCT SHARE DETAILS

Product or Product Class Shipments	Mil. $	Product or Product Class Shipments	Mil. $
DENTAL LABORATORIES	3,178.1	individual application (prescription basis)	1,973.9
Artificial teeth, bridges, crowns, dentures, and other orthodontic appliances that are customized for		Dental laboratories, nsk, total	1,204.2

Source: 2002 *Economic Census*. The values are product shipments in millions of dollars for 2002. Total product shipments may be lower or higher than industry shipments. See Introduction for a full discussion. Values of indented subcategories are summed in the main heading(s). The symbol (D) appears when data are withheld to prevent disclosure of competitive information. The abbreviation nsk stands for 'not specified by kind' and nec for 'not elsewhere classified'. A dash (-) means zero.

INPUTS AND OUTPUTS FOR DENTAL LABORATORIES

Economic Sector or Industry Providing Inputs	%	Sector	Economic Sector or Industry Buying Outputs	%	Sector
Compensation of employees	55.9		Physician, dentist, other health practitioner offices	98.5	Services
Dental equipment & supplies	7.6	Manufg.	Surgical appliances & supplies	0.5	Manufg.
Management of companies & enterprises	6.3	Services	Change in private inventories	0.4	In House
Wholesale trade	3.0	Trade	Ophthalmic goods	0.3	Manufg.
Primary nonferrous metal, ex. copper & aluminum	2.8	Manufg.	Exports of goods & services	0.2	Cap Inv
Real estate	1.7	Fin/R.E.			
Lessors of nonfinancial assets	1.1	Fin/R.E.			
Securities, commodity contracts, investments	1.1	Fin/R.E.			
Advertising & related services	1.0	Services			
Truck transportation	1.0	Util.			
Monetary authorities/depository credit intermediation	0.7	Fin/R.E.			
Accounting, tax preparation, bookkeeping, & payroll	0.7	Services			
Professional, scientific, technical services, nec	0.6	Services			
Automotive equipment rental & leasing	0.6	Fin/R.E.			
Warehousing & storage	0.6	Util.			
Data processing, hosting, & related services	0.5	Services			
Power generation & supply	0.4	Util.			
Taxes on production & imports, less subsidies	0.4				
Telecommunications	0.4	Services			
Scientific research & development services	0.4	Services			
Legal services	0.3	Services			
Food services & drinking places	0.3	Services			
Plastics products, nec	0.3	Manufg.			
Commercial & industrial machinery rental & leasing	0.3	Fin/R.E.			
Employment services	0.3	Services			
Business support services	0.3	Services			
Specialized design services	0.3	Services			
Architectural, engineering, & related services	0.2	Services			
Basic organic chemicals, nec	0.2	Manufg.			
Support services, nec	0.2	Services			
Hotels & motels, including casino hotels	0.2	Services			
Iron & steel mills & ferroalloys	0.2	Manufg.			
Machine shops	0.2	Manufg.			
Other computer related services, including facilities	0.2	Services			
Air transportation	0.2	Util.			
Services to buildings & dwellings	0.2	Services			
Coating, engraving, heat treating & allied activities	0.1	Manufg.			
Management, scientific, & technical consulting	0.1	Services			
Paperboard containers	0.1	Manufg.			
Maintenance/repair of nonresidential structures	0.1	Construct.			
Nondepository credit intermediation activities	0.1	Fin/R.E.			
Investigation & security services	0.1	Services			
Basic inorganic chemicals, nec	0.1	Manufg.			

Source: Benchmark Input-Output Accounts for the U.S. Economy, 2002, U.S. Department of Commerce, Washington, D.C., January 2008. The abbreviation nec stands for 'not elsewhere classified'.

OCCUPATIONS EMPLOYED BY MEDICAL EQUIPMENT & SUPPLIES MANUFACTURING

Occupation	% of Total 2006	Change to 2016	Occupation	% of Total 2006	Change to 2016
Dental laboratory technicians	12.2	2.3	Assemblers & fabricators, nec	1.4	-7.9
Team assemblers	11.0	2.3	Sales reps, wholesale & manufacturing, exc tech	1.3	2.3
First-line supervisors/managers of production workers	3.0	2.3	Helpers--Production workers	1.3	2.3
Inspectors, testers, sorters, samplers, & weighers	3.0	-3.6	Truck drivers, light or delivery services	1.2	2.3
Customer service representatives	2.2	12.5	Packaging & filling machine operators & tenders	1.2	-7.9
Medical appliance technicians	2.0	8.3	Bookkeeping, accounting, & auditing clerks	1.2	2.3
Packers & packagers, hand	1.9	-18.2	Multiple machine tool operators & tenders	1.1	12.5
Shipping, receiving, & traffic clerks	1.9	-1.6	Maintenance & repair workers, general	1.1	2.3
Machinists	1.7	7.4	Stock clerks & order fillers	1.1	-14.4
Molding, coremaking, & casting machine operators	1.6	-7.9	Mechanical engineers	1.1	2.3
Sales representatives, wholesale & manufacturing, tech	1.6	2.3	Laborers & freight, stock, & material movers, hand	1.1	-7.9
General & operations managers	1.5	-7.9	Computer-controlled machine tool operators	1.1	12.5
Sewing machine operators	1.5	2.3	Executive secretaries & administrative assistants	1.1	2.3
Industrial engineers	1.5	24.2	Cutting, punching, & press machine operators	1.1	-7.9
Office clerks, general	1.5	0.8			

Source: Industry-Occupation Matrix, Bureau of Labor Statistics, December 4, 2007. These data are reported based on 4-digit NAICS categories but have been matched to corresponding 6-digit NAICS industry codes. The change reported for each occupation to the year 2016 is a percent of growth or decline as estimated by the Bureau of Labor Statistics. The abbreviation nec stands for 'not elsewhere classified'.

LOCATION BY STATE AND REGIONAL CONCENTRATION

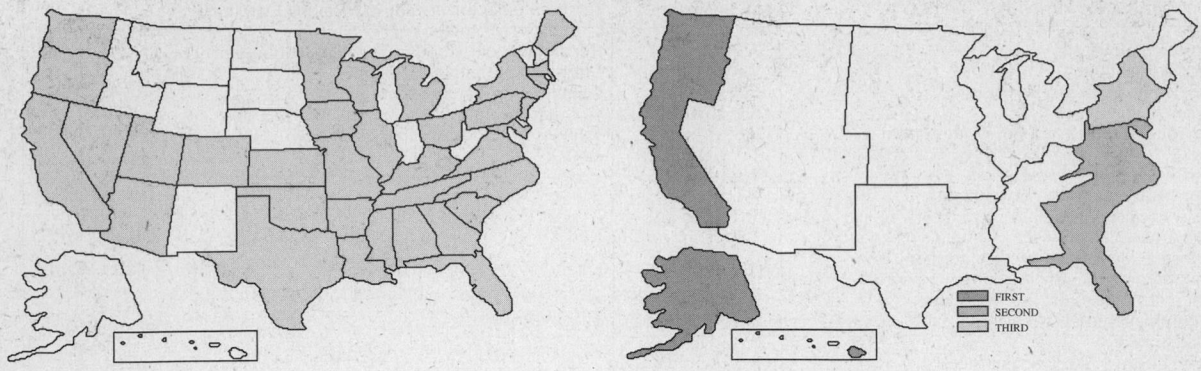

INDUSTRY DATA BY STATE

State	Establish-ments	Shipments			Employment				Cost as % of Shipments	Investment per Employee ($)
		Total ($ mil)	% of U.S.	Per Establ.	Total Number	% of U.S.	Per Establ.	Wages ($/hour)		
California	1,046	850.2	24.5	812.8	9,703	19.5	9	17.03	18.9	1,544
New York	437	224.5	6.5	513.7	3,148	6.3	7	14.82	20.0	3,750
Florida	518	155.4	4.5	300.0	2,536	5.1	5	14.92	20.0	1,867
Pennsylvania	231	154.0	4.4	666.5	1,869	3.8	8	14.84	17.2	3,482
Texas	376	142.9	4.1	380.1	2,318	4.7	6	14.77	20.8	1,904
Illinois	299	119.4	3.4	399.4	1,959	3.9	7	15.26	18.3	1,609
Michigan	222	114.7	3.3	516.7	1,730	3.5	8	16.55	18.5	1,710
Georgia	218	105.6	3.0	484.5	1,694	3.4	8	15.39	18.6	1,663
Minnesota	137	103.7	3.0	756.7	1,552	3.1	11	16.45	18.0	2,124
Washington	270	102.7	3.0	380.3	1,565	3.1	6	15.72	17.8	1,744
New Jersey	214	87.4	2.5	408.3	1,242	2.5	6	17.33	19.0	1,474
Wisconsin	130	84.9	2.5	652.9	1,301	2.6	10	14.50	17.8	1,224
Ohio	226	84.5	2.4	373.7	1,468	3.0	6	15.18	18.7	2,048
Massachusetts	145	81.3	2.3	560.5	1,253	2.5	9	15.90	19.4	1,682
North Carolina	234	74.4	2.1	317.9	1,181	2.4	5	15.46	17.5	1,565
Colorado	147	66.2	1.9	450.1	908	1.8	6	15.22	16.6	1,937
Oregon	134	62.8	1.8	468.3	952	1.9	7	15.48	17.6	1,943
Arizona	153	59.6	1.7	389.4	917	1.8	6	15.01	19.7	1,812
Utah	104	58.5	1.7	562.6	725	1.5	7	18.89	16.1	1,321
Missouri	141	57.9	1.7	410.5	986	2.0	7	15.73	17.8	1,256
Kansas	57	55.1	1.6	967.5	771	1.6	14	14.51	17.4	1,437
Connecticut	83	54.4	1.6	655.0	904	1.8	11	14.91	16.4	1,845
Virginia	152	46.5	1.3	306.2	751	1.5	5	15.62	18.8	2,979
Alabama	107	44.7	1.3	418.0	807	1.6	8	14.33	18.2	1,627
Maryland	110	34.3	1.0	312.1	521	1.0	5	15.83	18.7	1,889
Louisiana	82	33.1	1.0	403.8	578	1.2	7	14.06	20.5	1,651
Tennessee	131	32.4	0.9	247.3	552	1.1	4	14.78	18.2	1,953
Kentucky	81	31.9	0.9	393.2	435	0.9	5	16.01	16.7	1,959
Arkansas	52	26.0	0.8	500.3	361	0.7	7	14.80	17.6	1,510
Iowa	62	24.9	0.7	402.3	425	0.9	7	14.56	18.6	1,129
South Carolina	59	20.6	0.6	349.4	310	0.6	5	14.39	14.8	1,642
Oklahoma	70	18.5	0.5	263.7	318	0.6	5	14.47	18.1	1,591
Mississippi	49	17.2	0.5	350.2	273	0.5	6	12.95	18.5	2,048
Nevada	48	16.7	0.5	348.3	261	0.5	5	18.56	18.2	2,126
Maine	23	8.7	0.3	377.1	148	0.3	6	14.88	16.0	1,432

Source: 2002 *Economic Census*. The states are in descending order of shipments or establishments (if shipment data are missing for the majority). The symbol (D) appears when data are withheld to prevent disclosure of competitive information. States marked with (D) are sorted by number of establishments. A dash (-) indicates that the data element cannot be calculated. Data may not show all states active in the NAICS category. All data available at the time of publication are shown.

NAICS 33991M - JEWELRY AND SILVERWARE MANUFACTURING*

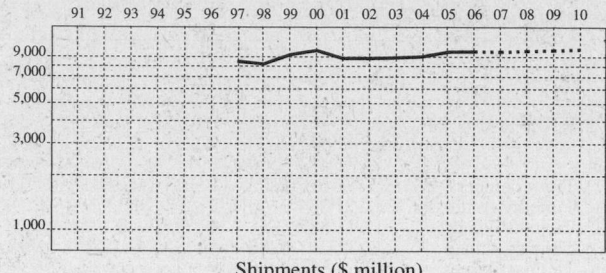

Shipments ($ million)

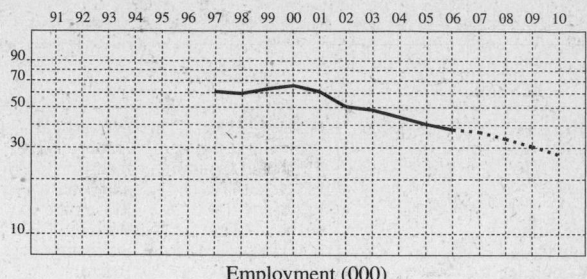

Employment (000)

GENERAL STATISTICS

| Year | Companies | Establishments | | Employment | | | Compensation | | Production ($ million) | | | |
		Total	with 20 or more employees	Total (000)	Production Workers (000)	Hours (Mil)	Payroll ($ mil)	Wages ($/hr)	Cost of Materials	Value Added by Manufacture	Value of Shipments	Capital Invest.
1997	3,747	3,770	564	61.0	43.1	77.5	1,532.4	10.91	4,472.1	4,066.3	8,501.2	114.0
1998		3,793	564	59.5	41.7	80.3	1,554.2	10.50	4,411.3	3,954.2	8,232.7	128.9
1999		3,718	560	63.2	43.9	81.1	1,671.2	11.35	5,116.4	4,229.0	9,258.4	130.0
2000		3,693	554	65.9	46.2	87.5	1,792.5	11.42	5,378.5	4,528.5	9,764.7	176.2
2001		3,505	528	61.0	42.6	80.7	1,657.5	11.35	4,802.5	3,998.5	8,845.3	147.3
2002	3,051	3,077	504	50.5	34.8	67.5	1,548.0	12.08	4,926.4	3,894.9	8,833.2	130.2
2003		2,985	458	48.4	33.2	63.5	1,530.8	12.71	4,787.3	4,163.3	8,925.9	112.0
2004		2,945	438	44.4	28.9	57.2	1,482.9	13.20	4,770.6	4,310.7	9,026.3	138.0
2005		2,807	394	40.5	25.6	51.4	1,425.8	13.69	5,220.9	4,605.9	9,603.1	131.5
2006		2,659P	398P	37.7	24.6	48.8	1,391.0	14.19	5,299.7	4,443.7	9,650.0	111.9
2007		2,518P	376P	36.6P	23.1P	47.4P	1,425.0P	14.33P	5,275.3P	4,423.2P	9,605.5P	126.3P
2008		2,377P	354P	33.5P	20.7P	43.3P	1,400.8P	14.73P	5,329.3P	4,468.5P	9,704.0P	125.3P
2009		2,236P	332P	30.5P	18.2P	39.3P	1,376.5P	15.13P	5,383.4P	4,513.9P	9,802.4P	124.3P
2010		2,094P	310P	27.5P	15.8P	35.3P	1,352.2P	15.52P	5,437.5P	4,559.2P	9,900.8P	123.2P

Sources: 1997 and 2002 *Economic Census*; other years, up to 2006, are from *Annual Survey of Manufactures*. Establishment counts for non-Census years are from *County Business Patterns*; 1997 and 2002 values are from the 1997 and 2002 censuses, respectively. 'P's show projections by the editors.

INDICES OF CHANGE

| Year | Companies | Establishments | | Employment | | | Compensation | | Production ($ million) | | | |
		Total	with 20 or more employees	Total (000)	Production Workers (000)	Hours (Mil)	Payroll ($ mil)	Wages ($/hr)	Cost of Materials	Value Added by Manufacture	Value of Shipments	Capital Invest.
1997	123	123	112	121	124	115	99	90	91	104	96	88
1998		123	112	118	120	119	100	87	90	102	93	99
1999		121	111	125	126	120	108	94	104	109	105	100
2000		120	110	130	133	130	116	95	109	116	111	135
2001		114	105	121	122	120	107	94	97	103	100	113
2002	100	100	100	100	100	100	100	100	100	100	100	100
2003		97	91	96	95	94	99	105	97	107	101	86
2004		96	87	88	83	85	96	109	97	111	102	106
2005		91	78	80	74	76	92	113	106	118	109	101
2006		86P	79P	75	71	72	90	117	108	114	109	86
2007		82P	75P	72P	66P	70P	92P	119P	107P	114P	109P	97P
2008		77P	70P	66P	59P	64P	90P	122P	108P	115P	110P	96P
2009		73P	66P	60P	52P	58P	89P	125P	109P	116P	111P	95P
2010		68P	62P	54P	45P	52P	87P	128P	110P	117P	112P	95P

Sources: Same as General Statistics. Values reflect change from the base year, 2002. Values above 100 mean greater than 2002, values below 100 mean less than 2002, and the values of 100 in other years means the same as 2002. 'P's show projections by the editors.

SELECTED RATIOS

For 2002	Avg. of All Manufact.	Analyzed Industry	Index	For 2002	Avg. of All Manufact.	Analyzed Industry	Index
Employees per Establishment	42	16	39	Value Added per Production Worker	182,367	111,922	61
Payroll per Establishment	1,639,184	503,087	31	Cost per Establishment	5,769,015	1,601,040	28
Payroll per Employee	39,053	30,653	78	Cost per Employee	137,446	97,552	71
Production Workers per Establishment	30	11	38	Cost per Production Worker	195,506	141,563	72
Wages per Establishment	694,845	264,998	38	Shipments per Establishment	11,158,348	2,870,718	26
Wages per Production Worker	23,548	23,431	100	Shipments per Employee	265,847	174,915	66
Hours per Production Worker	1,980	1,940	98	Shipments per Production Worker	378,144	253,828	67
Wages per Hour	11.89	12.08	102	Investment per Establishment	361,338	42,314	12
Value Added per Establishment	5,381,325	1,265,811	24	Investment per Employee	8,609	2,578	30
Value Added per Employee	128,210	77,127	60	Investment per Production Worker	12,245	3,741	31

Sources: Same as General Statistics. The 'Average of All Manufacturing' column represents the average of all manufacturing industries reported for the most recent complete year available. The Index shows the relationship between the Average and the Analyzed Industry. For example, 100 means that they are equal; 500 that the Analyzed Industry is five times the average; 50 means that the Analyzed Industry is half the national average. The abbreviation 'na' is used to show that data are 'not available'. Ratios shown for 2002, the last complete census year.

*Equivalent to Federal Government NAICS 339911, 339912, 339913, 339914.

LEADING COMPANIES   Number shown: **75**   Total sales ($ mil): **62,158**   Total employment (000): **234.7**

Company Name	Address				CEO Name	Phone	Co. Type	Sales ($ mil)	Empl. (000)
Ball Corp.	PO Box 5000	Broomfield	CO	80021	R. David Hoover	303-469-3131	P	7,475	15.5
BorgWarner Inc.	3850 Hamlin Rd.	Auburn Hills	MI	48326		248-754-9200	P	5,329	17.7
Flowserve Corp.	5215 N O'Connor	Irving	TX	75039		972-443-6500	P	3,763	15.0
Snap-On Inc.	PO Box 1410	Kenosha	WI	53141	Tim Chambers	262-656-5200	P	2,841	11.6
HNI Corp.	PO Box 1109	Muscatine	IA	52761	Timothy Anderson	563-264-7400	P	2,571	14.2
JELD-WEN Inc.	PO Box 1329	Klamath Falls	OR	97601	Richard Wendt	541-882-3451	R	2,476*	23.8
Metaldyne Corp.	47603 Halyard Dr.	Plymouth	MI	48170	Thomas Amato	734-207-6200	S	1,886	8.0
Barnes Group Inc.	PO Box 489	Bristol	CT	06011	Thomas Barnes	860-583-7070	P	1,539	6.7
Tang Industries Inc.	8960 Spanish Ridge	Las Vegas	NV	89148	Cyrus Tang	702-734-3700	R	1,500*	3.2
Valmont Industries Inc.	1 Valmont Plz.	Omaha	NE	68154	Mogens C. Bay	402-963-1000	P	1,500	6.0
H.B. Fuller Co.	PO Box 64683	St. Paul	MN	55164	Michele Volpi	651-236-5900	P	1,428	3.2
Turner Industries Ltd.	PO Box 2750	Baton Rouge	LA	70821	Roland M. Toups	225-922-5050	R	1,410	13.3
Rittal Corp.	1 Rittal Pl.	Springfield	OH	45504	Carie Ray	937-399-0500	R	1,268*	0.6
Visant Corp.	357 Main St.	Armonk	NY	10504	Marc Reisch	914-595-8200	S	1,187*	<0.1
Plastech Engineered Products	835 Mason Ave.	Dearborn	MI	48124	Julie Nguyen Brown	313-791-3001	R	1,070	4.8
MTD Products Inc.	PO Box 368022	Cleveland	OH	44136	Curtis E. Moll	330-225-2600	R	1,015*	6.7
Alcoa Closure Systems Intl	6625 Network Way	Indianapolis	IN	46278	V. Lance Mitchell	317-390-5000	S	980*	3.0
BWAY Holding Co.	8607 Roberts Dr.	Atlanta	GA	30350	Jean-Pierre M. Ergas	770-645-4800	P	959	2.5
United Components Inc.	14601 Hwy 41 N	Evansville	IN	47725	Bruce Zorich	812-867-4156	S	906	6.8
Masonite Door Corp.	1 N D Mabry Hwy	Tampa	FL	33609	Fred Lynch	813-877-2726	R	876*	<0.1
Maui Divers of Hawaii Ltd.	1451 S King St.	Honolulu	HI	96814	Robert Taylor	808-943-8316	R	824*	0.6
Jostens Inc.	3601 Minnesota Dr.	Minneapolis	MN	55435	Michael L. Bailey	952-830-3300	S	807*	6.7
Barden Corp.	PO Box 2449	Danbury	CT	06813	John McCloskey	203-744-2211	R	776*	0.3
Sub-Zero Inc.	4717 Hammersley	Madison	WI	53711	James Bakke	608-271-2233	R	758*	3.0
Raybestos Products Co.	1204 Darlington Ave	Crawfordsville	IN	47933	Larry S. Singleton	765-362-3500	S	701*	5.3
Shachihata Incorporated USA	PO Box 2017	Torrance	CA	90505	Shinkitiro Funahashi		S	700*	0.9
Commercial Vehicle Group Inc.	6530 W Campus Ovl	New Albany	OH	43054	Gordon Boyd	614-289-5360	P	697	6.4
Oregon Cutting Systems Group	PO Box 22127	Portland	OR	97269	Jim Oscermanc	503-653-8881	D	674*	1.0
Bachman Machine Co.	4321 N Broadway	St. Louis	MO	63147	William Bachman	314-231-4221	R	656*	0.1
Ameron International Corp.	245 S Los Robles	Pasadena	CA	91101	James Marlen	626-683-4000	P	631	2.8
Andin International Inc.	609 Greenwich St.	New York	NY	10014	Aya Azrielant	212-886-6000	R	625*	0.5
Performance Contracting Group	16400 College Blvd.	Lenexa	KS	66219	Craig Davis	913-888-8600	R	600*	5.7
Shiloh Industries Inc.	880 Steel Dr.	Valley City	OH	44280	Curtis Moll	330-558-2600	P	590	1.8
Cascade Corp.	PO Box 20187	Portland	OR	97294		503-669-6300	P	479	2.1
Matco Tools Corp.	4403 Allen Rd.	Stow	OH	44224		330-929-4949	D	467*	0.5
Ladish Company Inc.	5481 S Packard Ave.	Cudahy	WI	53110		414-747-2611	P	425	2.0
Bing Group L.L.C.	11500 Oakland St.	Detroit	MI	48211	David Bing	313-867-3700	R	411*	1.1
Northern Stamping Inc.	6600 Chapek Pkwy.	Cleveland	OH	44125		216-883-8888	R	410*	0.2
Feintool US Operations Inc.	11280 Cornell Park	Cincinnati	OH	45242	Richard Surico	513-247-0110	R	408*	0.3
ICO Global Services Inc.	1811 Bering Dr, 200	Houston	TX	77057	A. John Knapp, Jr.	713-351-4100	S	380*	0.9
Metokote Corp.	1340 Neubrecht Rd.	Lima	OH	45801	DeWayne Pinkstaff	419-996-7800	R	364*	1.0
Crown Group Inc.	2111 Wltr P Reuther	Warren	MI	48091		586-575-9800	R	362*	1.0
Skill Metalforming Technologies	16151 Puritas Ave.	Cleveland	OH	44135	Roger Kalski	216-267-8866	R	352*	0.1
Onedia Ltd.	PO Box 1	Oneida	NY	13421	James E. Joseph	315-361-3000	R	348	0.7
AAC Group Holding Corp.	7211 Circle S Rd.	Austin	TX	78745	Donald J. Percenti	512-444-0571	S	321	1.8
O.C. Tanner Recognition Co.	1930 S State St.	Salt Lake City	UT	84115	Kent H. Murdock	801-486-2430	R	319*	1.8
American Achievement Corp.	7211 Circle S Rd.	Austin	TX	78745	David G. Fiore	512-444-0571	S	275*	2.2
Intermagnetics General Corp.	PO Box 461	Latham	NY	12110	Leo Blecher	518-782-1122	R	265	1.1
Material Sciences Corp.	2200 E Pratt Blvd.	Elk Grove Vlg	IL	60007		847-439-2210	P	263	0.6
Consolidated Systems Inc.	PO Box 1756	Columbia	SC	29202	S Holtschlag	803-771-7920	R	262*	0.3
AZZ Inc.	1300 S Universty Dr	Fort Worth	TX	76107	David H. Dingus	817-810-0095	P	260	1.0
C. Cowles and Co.	83 Water St.	New Haven	CT	06511	Lawrence C. Moon Jr.	203-865-3110	R	260*	0.2
Things Remembered Inc.	5500 Avion Park Dr.	Cleveland	OH	44143	Suzanne Sutter	440-473-2000	S	240*	3.0
Autocam Corp.	4070 E Paris Ave SE	Kentwood	MI	49512	John C. Kennedy	616-698-0707	S	230*	2.3
Daman Industrial Services Inc.	PO Box 486	East Brady	PA	16028		724-526-5714	R	228*	<0.1
Raytech Corp.	4 Corporate Dr.	Shelton	CT	06484		203-925-8023	R	227	1.7
Elixir Industries	24800 Chrisanta Dr.	Mission Viejo	CA	92691	Christopher Sahm	949-860-5000	R	221*	<0.1
Nielsen and Bainbridge	40 Eisenhower Dr.	Paramus	NJ	07653	Jack Forbes	201-368-9191	R	219*	0.9
Defiance Metal Products Co.	PO Box 447	Defiance	OH	43512		419-784-5332	R	211*	1.7
Nicholas J Bouras Inc.	PO Box 662	Summit	NJ	07902	Nicholas Bouras	908-277-1617	R	204*	<0.1
Burgess-Norton Manufacturing	737 Peyton St.	Geneva	IL	60134	John Carroll	630-232-4100	S	199*	0.9
General Dynamics Armament/Tech	4 LakePointe Plz.	Charlotte	NC	28217	Linda Hudson	703-714-8000	S	198*	1.2
Adrian Steel Co.	906 James Street	Adrian	MI	49221		517-265-6194	R	196*	<0.1
Pumpkin Masters Holdings Inc.	1905 Sherman St.	Denver	CO	80203	Brian Fitzgerald	303-860-8006	S	195*	1.3
Precoat Metals	1310 Papin St.	St. Louis	MO	63103	Gerard M. Dombek	314-436-7010	S	191*	0.7
Engineered Materials/Solutions	2200 E Pratt Blvd.	Elk Grove Vlg	IL	60007	Cliff Nastas	847-439-2210	S	189*	0.6
Keymark Corp.	PO Box 626	Fonda	NY	12068	William Keller	518-853-3421	R	183*	0.9
Anstro Manufacturing Inc.	238 Wolcott Rd.	Wolcott	CT	06716	Robert Bosco	203-879-1423	R	182*	0.2
Norfolk Iron and Metal Co.	PO Box 1129	Norfolk	NE	68702	Richard Robinson	402-371-1810	R	180*	0.3
Wallace Silversmiths Inc.	175 McClellan Hwy.	East Boston	MA	02128	Bob Meers	617-561-2200	S	174*	0.3
Precision Resource Inc.	25 Forest Pkwy.	Shelton	CT	06484		203-925-0012	R	174*	0.2
Oerlikon USA Holding Inc.	615 Epsilon Dr.	Pittsburgh	PA	15238	James Brissenden	724-327-5700	R	172*	0.2
Sun Hydraulics Corp.	1500 W Univ. Pkwy.	Sarasota	FL	34243	Allen J. Carlson	941-362-1200	P	167	0.7
Templeton Coal Company Inc.	701 Wabash Ave.	Terre Haute	IN	47807	John Templeton	812-232-7037	R	166*	<0.1
Acheson Colloids Co.	1600 Washington	Port Huron	MI	48060		810-984-5581	S	165*	0.9

Source: Ward's Business Directory of U.S. Private and Public Companies, Volumes 1 and 2, 2008. The company type code used is as follows: P - Public, R - Private, S - Subsidiary, D - Division, J - Joint Venture, A - Affiliate, G - Group. Sales are in millions of dollars, employees are in thousands. An asterisk (*) indicates an estimated sales volume. The symbol < stands for 'less than'. Company names and addresses are truncated, in some cases, to fit into the available space.

MATERIALS CONSUMED FOR JEWELRY (EXCEPT COSTUME) MANUFACTURING

Material	Quantity	Delivered Cost ($ million)
Fabricated metal products, including forgings	(X)	85.9
Precious metals (gold, platinum, etc.), all forms (incl. ingot, sheet, strip, solder, plating, electrodes, etc.)	(X)	935.5
Other metal shapes and forms (including castings)	(X)	82.5
Precious, semiprecious, and synthetic stones and pearls (cut, polished, and drilled)	(X)	662.8
Jewelers' findings (joints, pins, clasps, chains, flat stock, etc.)	(X)	213.9
Other jewelry, silverware, and plated ware	(X)	36.8
All other materials, components, parts, containers, and supplies	(X)	187.9
Materials, ingredients, containers, and supplies, nsk	(X)	756.7

Source: 2002 *Economic Census*. Explanation of symbols used: (D): Withheld to avoid disclosure of competitive data; na: Not available; (S): Withheld because statistical norms were not met; (X): Not applicable; (Z): Less than half the unit shown; nec: Not elsewhere classified; nsk: Not specified by kind; - : zero; p : 10-19 percent estimated; q : 20-29 percent estimated.

MATERIALS CONSUMED FOR SILVERWARE AND HOLLOWWARE MANUFACTURING

Material	Quantity	Delivered Cost ($ million)
Fabricated metal products, including forgings	(X)	65.8
Other metal shapes and forms (including castings)	(X)	0.7
Precious metals (gold, platinum, etc.), all forms (incl. ingot, sheet, strip, solder, plating, electrodes, etc.)	(X)	19.7
All other materials, components, parts, containers, and supplies	(X)	92.5
Materials, ingredients, containers, and supplies, nsk	(X)	18.2

Source: 2002 *Economic Census*. Explanation of symbols used: (D): Withheld to avoid disclosure of competitive data; na: Not available; (S): Withheld because statistical norms were not met; (X): Not applicable; (Z): Less than half the unit shown; nec: Not elsewhere classified; nsk: Not specified by kind; - : zero; p : 10-19 percent estimated; q : 20-29 percent estimated.

MATERIALS CONSUMED FOR JEWELERS' MATERIAL AND LAPIDARY WORK MANUFACTURING

Material	Quantity	Delivered Cost ($ million)
Fabricated metal products, including forgings	(X)	25.6
Precious metals (gold, platinum, etc.), all forms (incl. ingot, sheet, strip, solder, plating, electrodes, etc.)	(X)	77.2
Other metal shapes and forms (including castings)	(X)	(D)
Precious, semiprecious, and synthetic stones and pearls (cut, polished, and drilled)	(X)	(D)
Jewelers' findings (joints, pins, clasps, chains, flat stock, etc.)	(X)	85.5
Other jewelry, silverware, and plated ware	(X)	(D)
All other materials, components, parts, containers, and supplies	(X)	33.9
Materials, ingredients, containers, and supplies, nsk	(X)	243.9

Source: 2002 *Economic Census*. Explanation of symbols used: (D): Withheld to avoid disclosure of competitive data; na: Not available; (S): Withheld because statistical norms were not met; (X): Not applicable; (Z): Less than half the unit shown; nec: Not elsewhere classified; nsk: Not specified by kind; - : zero; p : 10-19 percent estimated; q : 20-29 percent estimated.

MATERIALS CONSUMED FOR COSTUME JEWELRY AND NOVELTY MANUFACTURING

Material	Quantity	Delivered Cost ($ million)
Fabricated metal products, including forgings	(X)	16.4
Precious metals (gold, platinum, etc.), all forms (incl. ingot, sheet, strip, solder, plating, electrodes, etc.)	(X)	23.3
Other metal shapes and forms (including castings)	(X)	3.9
Precious, semiprecious, and synthetic stones and pearls (cut, polished, and drilled)	(X)	27.3
Jewelers' findings (joints, pins, clasps, chains, flat stock, etc.)	(X)	17.9
Other jewelry, silverware, and plated ware	(X)	12.5
All other materials, components, parts, containers, and supplies	(X)	29.2
Materials, ingredients, containers, and supplies, nsk	(X)	83.9

Source: 2002 *Economic Census*. Explanation of symbols used: (D): Withheld to avoid disclosure of competitive data; na: Not available; (S): Withheld because statistical norms were not met; (X): Not applicable; (Z): Less than half the unit shown; nec: Not elsewhere classified; nsk: Not specified by kind; - : zero; p : 10-19 percent estimated; q : 20-29 percent estimated.

PRODUCT SHARE DETAILS FOR JEWELRY (EXCEPT COSTUME) MANUFACTURING

Product or Product Class Shipments	Mil. $	Product or Product Class Shipments	Mil. $
JEWELRY, PRECIOUS METAL	5,522.4	platinum metals and karat gold clad to silver)	127.2
Jewelry, made of platinum metals and karat gold	**3,527.1**	Women's and children's jewelry (necklaces, bracelets and watch bracelets, brooches, pins, clips, earrings, lockets, etc) made of silver (including platinum metals and karat gold clad to silver), except rings, ring mountings	448.9
Wedding rings made of platinum metals and karat gold (complete)	728.7	Other jewelry made of silver	157.9
Women's and children's jewelry (necklaces, bracelets and watch bracelets, brooches, pins, clips, earrings, lockets, etc) made of platinum metals and karat gold, except rings and ring mountings	1,191.5	Jewelry made of silver (including platinum metals and karat gold clad to silver), nsk	33.4
Other rings made of platinum metals and karat gold	870.3	**Other jewelry, except costume**	**647.6**
College, fraternal, and school rings made of platinum metals and karat gold (complete)	331.9	Other jewelry, except costume	620.3
Other rings made of platinum metals and karat gold (complete)	538.4	Rings and ring mountings (except costume) made of precious metal clad to nonprecious metal	71.6
Other jewelry made of platinum metals and karat gold	518.6	Other women's and children's jewelry, except rings and ring mountings (necklaces, bracelets and watch bracelets, brooches, pins, clips, earrings, lockets, except costume) made of precious metal clad to nonprecious metal	88.2
Organizational jewelry made of platinum metals and karat gold, excluding rings and ring mountings	108.5	Other jewelry made of precious metals clad to nonprecious metal	57.6
All other jewelry made of platinum metals and karat gold, nec	410.1	Engraving and etching on precious metal jewelry	28.3
Ring mountings made of platinum metals and karat gold (sold separately)	114.5	Jewelry of semiprecious or precious stones, and natural or cultured pearls	374.6
Jewelry, made of platinum metals and karat gold, nsk	103.4	Other jewelry, except costume, nsk	27.3
Jewelry, made of silver (including platinum metals and karat gold clad to silver)	**767.3**	**Stamped metal coins, including stamped metal tokens**	**8.7**
Jewelry made of silver (including platinum metals and karat gold clad to silver)	733.9	**Jewelry, precious metal, nsk, total**	**571.6**
Rings and ring mountings made of silver (including			

Source: 2002 *Economic Census*. The values are product shipments in millions of dollars for 2002. Total product shipments may be lower or higher than industry shipments. See Introduction for a full discussion. Values of indented subcategories are summed in the main heading(s). The symbol (D) appears when data are withheld to prevent disclosure of competitive information. The abbreviation nsk stands for 'not specified by kind' and nec for 'not elsewhere classified'. A dash (-) means zero.

PRODUCT SHARE DETAILS FOR SILVERWARE AND HOLLOWWARE MANUFACTURING

Product or Product Class Shipments	Mil. $	Product or Product Class Shipments	Mil. $
SILVERWARE AND HOLLOWWARE	419.6	Other precious metal and pewter hollowware	74.7
Precious metal and pewter hollowware, including baby goods, ecclesiastical ware, novelties, toiletware, and trophies	**119.8**	Engraving and etching on precious metal and pewter hollowware, including nonprecious metal clad or plated to precious metal	5.6
Precious metal and pewter hollowware, including baby goods, ecclesiastical ware, novelties, toiletware, and trophies	118.9	Precious metal and pewter hollowware, nsk	0.9
Electrosilverplated hollowware, electrosilverplated to a precious metal or pewter base	11.3	**Precious metal and pewter flatware and cutlery, including all knives, forks, spoons, and carving sets made wholly of metal**	**266.5**
Solid pewter hollowware	27.4	**Silverware and hollowware, nsk, total**	**33.4**

Source: 2002 *Economic Census*. The values are product shipments in millions of dollars for 2002. Total product shipments may be lower or higher than industry shipments. See Introduction for a full discussion. Values of indented subcategories are summed in the main heading(s). The symbol (D) appears when data are withheld to prevent disclosure of competitive information. The abbreviation nsk stands for 'not specified by kind' and nec for 'not elsewhere classified'. A dash (-) means zero.

PRODUCT SHARE DETAILS FOR JEWELERS' MATERIAL AND LAPIDARY WORK MANUFACTURING

Product or Product Class Shipments	Mil. $	Product or Product Class Shipments	Mil. $
JEWELERS' MATERIALS AND LAPIDARY WORK	1,073.5	including platinum and karat gold clad or plated to silver	42.0
Lapidary work, except for watch jewels	**353.8**	Jewelers' findings and materials made of precious metals clad to nonprecious metal	161.1
Jewelers' findings and materials of precious metal	**587.7**	Jewelers' findings and materials of precious metal, nsk	1.5
Jewelers' findings and materials of precious metal	586.1	**Other jewelers' findings and materials including those made of precious metal plated to nonprecious metal**	**46.0**
Jewelers' machine chain made of platinum and karat gold	173.3	**Jewelers' materials and lapidary work**	**86.0**
Other jewelers' findings and materials made of platinum and karat gold	209.7		
Jewelers' findings and materials made of silver,			

Source: 2002 *Economic Census*. The values are product shipments in millions of dollars for 2002. Total product shipments may be lower or higher than industry shipments. See Introduction for a full discussion. Values of indented subcategories are summed in the main heading(s). The symbol (D) appears when data are withheld to prevent disclosure of competitive information. The abbreviation nsk stands for 'not specified by kind' and nec for 'not elsewhere classified'. A dash (-) means zero.

PRODUCT SHARE DETAILS FOR COSTUME JEWELRY AND NOVELTY MANUFACTURING

Product or Product Class Shipments	Mil. $	Product or Product Class Shipments	Mil. $
COSTUME JEWELRY AND NOVELTIES	797.3	mountings	52.6
Nonprecious metal jewelry, including jewelry made of		Other nonprecious metal jewelry, including jewelry	
precious metals plated to nonprecious metal	518.1	made of precious metals plated to nonprecious metal . .	19.3
Metal rings and ring mountings.	102.3	Other jewelry and costume novelties, including engraving	
Metal women's and children's jewelry, except rings and		and etching on other jewelry	125.1
ring mountings	343.8	Costume jewelry and novelties, nsk, total	154.1
Metal organizational jewelry, except rings and ring			

Source: 2002 *Economic Census.* The values are product shipments in millions of dollars for 2002. Total product shipments may be lower or higher than industry shipments. See Introduction for a full discussion. Values of indented subcategories are summed in the main heading(s). The symbol (D) appears when data are withheld to prevent disclosure of competitive information. The abbreviation nsk stands for 'not specified by kind' and nec for 'not elsewhere classified'. A dash (-) means zero.

INPUTS AND OUTPUTS FOR JEWELRY AND SILVERWARE MANUFACTURING

Economic Sector or Industry Providing Inputs	%	Sector	Economic Sector or Industry Buying Outputs	%	Sector
Compensation of employees	22.5		Personal consumption expenditures	79.0	
Jewelry & silverware	18.8	Manufg.	Exports of goods & services	9.1	Cap Inv
Primary nonferrous metal, ex. copper & aluminum	13.9	Manufg.	Jewelry & silverware	5.5	Manufg.
Wholesale trade	4.1	Trade	Wholesale trade	2.0	Trade
Truck transportation	3.0	Util.	Change in private inventories	1.6	In House
Management of companies & enterprises	2.5	Services	Retail trade	1.3	Trade
Nonferrous metal (ex. copper & aluminum) processing	1.8	Manufg.	Food services & drinking places	0.9	Services
Advertising & related services	1.7	Services	General S/L govt. services	0.3	S/L Govt
Noncomparable imports	1.0	Foreign	Abrasive products	0.1	Manufg.
Real estate	1.0	Fin/R.E.			
Lessors of nonfinancial assets	0.9	Fin/R.E.			
Machine shops	0.9	Manufg.			
Used & secondhand goods	0.9				
Securities, commodity contracts, investments	0.8	Fin/R.E.			
Manufacturing, nec	0.8	Manufg.			
Coating, engraving, heat treating & allied activities	0.6	Manufg.			
Monetary authorities/depository credit intermediation	0.6	Fin/R.E.			
Taxes on production & imports, less subsidies	0.5				
Legal services	0.5	Services			
Specialized design services	0.5	Services			
Semiconductors & related devices	0.5	Manufg.			
Professional, scientific, technical services, nec	0.4	Services			
Printed circuit assemblies (electronic assemblies)	0.4	Manufg.			
Architectural, engineering, & related services	0.4	Services			
Employment services	0.4	Services			
Abrasive products	0.4	Manufg.			
Paperboard containers	0.4	Manufg.			
Accounting, tax preparation, bookkeeping, & payroll	0.4	Services			
Turned products & screws, nuts, & bolts	0.4	Manufg.			
Business support services	0.4	Services			
Food services & drinking places	0.3	Services			
Power generation & supply	0.3	Util.			
Telecommunications	0.3	Services			
Automotive equipment rental & leasing	0.3	Fin/R.E.			
Air transportation	0.3	Util.			
Support services, nec	0.3	Services			
Cutting tools & machine tool accessories	0.3	Manufg.			
Metal cans, boxes, & other containers (light gauge)	0.3	Manufg.			
Fabricated metals, nec	0.2	Manufg.			
Warehousing & storage	0.2	Util.			
Hotels & motels, including casino hotels	0.2	Services			
Data processing, hosting, & related services	0.2	Services			
Forging, stamping, & sintering, nec	0.2	Manufg.			
Gold, silver, & other metal ore	0.2	Mining			
Plate work & fabricated structural products	0.2	Manufg.			
Scientific research & development services	0.2	Services			
Plastics products, nec	0.2	Manufg.			
Crowns & closures & metal stamping	0.2	Manufg.			
Investigation & security services	0.2	Services			
Other computer related services, including facilities	0.2	Services			
Ball & roller bearings	0.2	Manufg.			
Commercial & industrial machinery rental & leasing	0.2	Fin/R.E.			
Management, scientific, & technical consulting	0.1	Services			
Handtools	0.1	Manufg.			
Nondepository credit intermediation activities	0.1	Fin/R.E.			
Natural gas distribution	0.1	Util.			
Valve & fittings other than plumbing	0.1	Manufg.			
Services to buildings & dwellings	0.1	Services			
Custom roll forming	0.1	Manufg.			

Source: Benchmark Input-Output Accounts for the U.S. Economy, 2002, U.S. Department of Commerce, Washington, D.C., January 2008. The abbreviation nec stands for 'not elsewhere classified'.

OCCUPATIONS EMPLOYED BY JEWELRY & SILVERWARE MANUFACTURING

Occupation	% of Total 2006	Change to 2016	Occupation	% of Total 2006	Change to 2016
Team assemblers	5.5	-39.6	Assemblers & fabricators, nec	1.9	-45.6
First-line supervisors/managers of production workers	4.0	-39.6	Packers & packagers, hand	1.8	-51.6
Sales reps, wholesale & manufacturing, exc tech	3.6	-39.6	Helpers--Production workers	1.6	-39.6
Grinding, lapping, polishing machine tool operators	3.1	-41.4	Retail salespersons	1.6	-39.6
Customer service representatives	3.0	-33.5	Grinding & polishing workers, hand	1.5	-39.6
Etchers & engravers	2.8	-39.6	Order clerks	1.4	-60.7
Office clerks, general	2.8	-40.4	Molding, coremaking, & casting machine operators	1.4	-45.6
Bookkeeping, accounting, & auditing clerks	2.6	-39.6	First-line supervisors/managers of office workers	1.2	-43.7
Inspectors, testers, sorters, samplers, & weighers	2.4	-43.0	Production, planning, & expediting clerks	1.1	-39.6
Cutting, punching, & press machine operators	2.3	-45.6	Stock clerks & order fillers	1.1	-49.4
Shipping, receiving, & traffic clerks	2.2	-41.8	Tool & die makers	1.1	-36.5
General & operations managers	2.1	-45.6			

Source: *Industry-Occupation Matrix*, Bureau of Labor Statistics, December 4, 2007. These data are reported based on 4-digit NAICS categories but have been matched to corresponding 6-digit NAICS industry codes. The change reported for each occupation to the year 2016 is a percent of growth or decline as estimated by the Bureau of Labor Statistics. The abbreviation nec stands for 'not elsewhere classified'.

LOCATION BY STATE AND REGIONAL CONCENTRATION

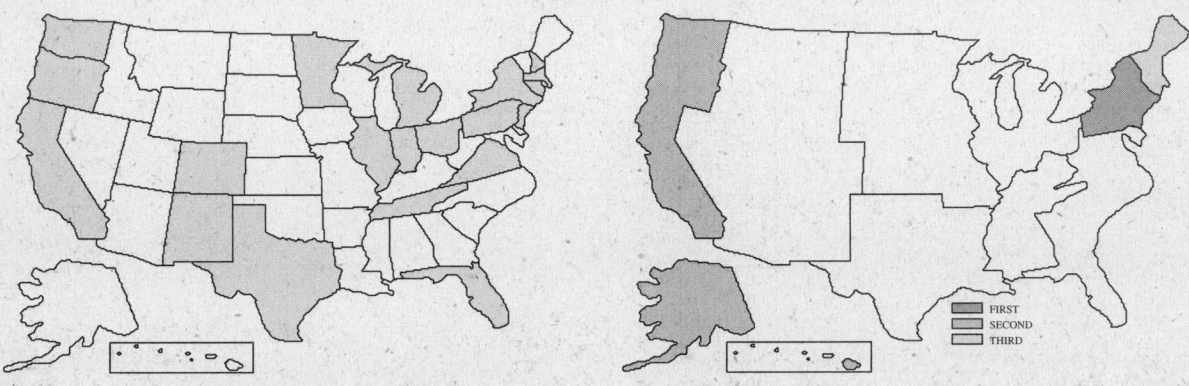

FIRST
SECOND
THIRD

INDUSTRY DATA BY STATE

State	Establish-ments	Shipments			Employment				Cost as % of Shipments	Investment per Employee ($)
		Total ($ mil)	% of U.S.	Per Establ.	Total Number	% of U.S.	Per Establ.	Wages ($/hour)		
New York	622	3,040.2	34.4	4,887.8	11,561	22.9	19	12.41	63.6	2,278
Rhode Island	257	1,106.2	12.5	4,304.3	6,752	13.4	26	11.56	47.7	3,005
California	525	909.4	10.3	1,732.2	5,792	11.5	11	11.30	53.8	2,083
Massachusetts	90	713.2	8.1	7,924.3	3,583	7.1	40	12.77	57.7	2,670
Texas	115	372.4	4.2	3,238.4	3,176	6.3	28	10.69	35.8	1,955
New Jersey	71	276.1	3.1	3,889.0	1,453	2.9	20	16.01	62.9	2,438
New Mexico	86	144.9	1.6	1,685.1	1,425	2.8	17	12.59	56.9	1,121
Illinois	40	111.8	1.3	2,794.7	634	1.3	16	12.26	58.7	3,002
Indiana	13	75.4	0.9	5,800.8	417	0.8	32	17.69	29.3	1,710
Ohio	40	46.7	0.5	1,167.6	274	0.5	7	10.96	56.9	1,318
Virginia	23	43.8	0.5	1,902.9	200	0.4	9	16.57	67.6	995
Florida	44	41.1	0.5	933.6	650	1.3	15	10.03	43.3	1,029
Tennessee	9	41.0	0.5	4,552.8	114	0.2	13	13.96	80.4	2,711
Minnesota	24	33.9	0.4	1,413.2	206	0.4	9	10.84	47.4	1,694
Colorado	32	23.6	0.3	737.2	207	0.4	6	13.44	44.2	918
New Hampshire	11	18.5	0.2	1,681.0	143	0.3	13	12.42	60.4	1,902
Washington	32	17.9	0.2	558.6	197	0.4	6	15.09	43.8	1,132
Oregon	22	17.2	0.2	779.9	171	0.3	8	9.38	44.5	1,421
Pennsylvania	9	13.6	0.2	1,514.2	123	0.2	14	11.13	65.6	3,073
Connecticut	11	11.6	0.1	1,052.7	120	0.2	11	10.45	51.4	2,167
Michigan	18	10.4	0.1	579.3	101	0.2	6	13.28	46.8	3,990

Source: 2002 *Economic Census*. The states are in descending order of shipments or establishments (if shipment data are missing for the majority). The symbol (D) appears when data are withheld to prevent disclosure of competitive information. States marked with (D) are sorted by number of establishments. A dash (-) indicates that the data element cannot be calculated. Data may not show all states active in the NAICS category. All data available at the time of publication are shown.

NAICS 339920 - SPORTING AND ATHLETIC GOODS MANUFACTURING

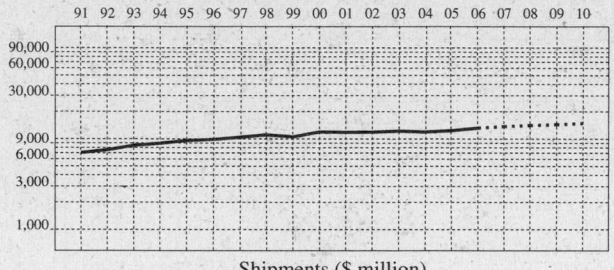

Shipments ($ million)

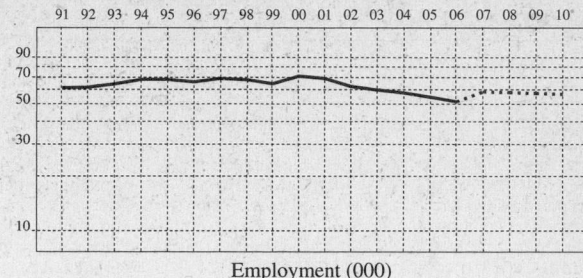

Employment (000)

GENERAL STATISTICS

| Year | Companies | Establishments | | Employment | | | Compensation | | Production ($ million) | | | |
		Total	with 20 or more employees	Total (000)	Production Workers (000)	Hours (Mil)	Payroll ($ mil)	Wages ($/hr)	Cost of Materials	Value Added by Manufacture	Value of Shipments	Capital Invest.
1991		1,881	499	61.3	45.4	90.3	1,247.3	8.20	3,287.4	3,753.6	7,035.7	138.2
1992	2,025	2,113	510	61.7	44.0	88.5	1,361.4	8.52	3,400.8	4,198.8	7,566.4	176.9
1993		2,204	556	64.4	46.8	93.7	1,438.4	8.74	3,834.1	4,626.0	8,459.4	217.7
1994		2,257	554	68.1	49.6	99.2	1,526.0	8.66	4,199.7	4,896.2	8,936.1	191.9
1995		2,255	584	68.2	49.3	98.0	1,607.4	9.28	4,467.5	5,122.0	9,588.0	225.6
1996		2,448	574	66.1	47.6	94.9	1,625.9	9.51	4,416.5	5,612.7	9,881.8	253.9
1997	2,480	2,565	570	68.9	50.1	96.8	1,799.9	10.38	4,679.1	5,773.7	10,458.2	344.2
1998		2,564	592	67.9	50.1	93.1	1,787.4	10.52	5,206.4	6,036.6	11,100.5	353.3
1999		2,496	571	64.6	46.4	88.3	1,796.6	11.06	5,031.8	5,600.9	10,550.6	410.9
2000		2,486	558	71.2	50.8	97.0	2,078.3	11.14	5,629.0	6,638.1	11,951.5	410.0
2001		2,433	535	69.1	48.6	94.9	2,088.4	11.35	5,564.3	6,233.7	11,844.9	457.7
2002	2,158	2,233	521	62.5	41.4	80.1	2,074.8	12.50	5,033.8	6,755.7	11,893.1	326.7
2003		2,182	506	59.8	39.2	77.7	2,037.5	13.08	5,273.9	7,017.6	12,225.6	290.0
2004		2,149	508	57.7	36.9	75.0	2,078.9	13.41	4,924.9	7,062.6	11,927.6	408.7
2005		2,052	480	54.7	34.2	69.1	2,061.2	14.01	5,103.2	7,432.6	12,352.4	458.9
2006		2,338P	521P	51.5	32.5	65.3	2,063.9	14.51	5,148.2	8,059.2	13,188.9	569.8
2007		2,344P	518P	58.5P	37.4P	73.2P	2,284.9P	14.58P	5,352.4P	8,378.8P	13,712.0P	516.0P
2008		2,350P	516P	57.9P	36.5P	71.5P	2,342.9P	15.01P	5,497.1P	8,605.4P	14,082.8P	538.2P
2009		2,357P	514P	57.3P	35.7P	69.8P	2,400.8P	15.43P	5,641.9P	8,832.0P	14,453.6P	560.4P
2010		2,363P	511P	56.7P	34.8P	68.1P	2,458.8P	15.86P	5,786.6P	9,058.6P	14,824.4P	582.6P

Sources: 1992, 1997, 2002 *Economic Census*; other years, up to 2006, are from the *Annual Survey of Manufactures*. Establishment counts for non-Census years are from *County Business Patterns*; 1997 and 2002 values are from the 1997 and 2002 censuses respectively, reported in the Federal Government's NAICS format. Other years were originally reported in equivalent SIC format. 'P's show projections by the editors.

INDICES OF CHANGE

| Year | Companies | Establishments | | Employment | | | Compensation | | Production ($ million) | | | |
		Total	with 20 or more employees	Total (000)	Production Workers (000)	Hours (Mil)	Payroll ($ mil)	Wages ($/hr)	Cost of Materials	Value Added by Manufacture	Value of Shipments	Capital Invest.
1992	94	95	98	99	106	110	66	68	68	62	64	54
1997	115	115	109	110	121	121	87	83	93	85	88	105
2001		109	103	111	117	118	101	91	111	92	100	140
2002	100	100	100	100	100	100	100	100	100	100	100	100
2003		98	97	96	95	97	98	105	105	104	103	89
2004		96	98	92	89	94	100	107	98	105	100	125
2005		92	92	88	83	86	99	112	101	110	104	140
2006		105P	100P	82	79	82	99	116	102	119	111	174
2007		105P	100P	94P	90P	91P	110P	117P	106P	124P	115P	158P
2008		105P	99P	93P	88P	89P	113P	120P	109P	127P	118P	165P
2009		106P	99P	92P	86P	87P	116P	123P	112P	131P	122P	172P
2010		106P	98P	91P	84P	85P	119P	127P	115P	134P	125P	178P

Sources: Same as General Statistics. Values reflect change from the base year, 2002. Values above 100 mean greater than 2002, values below 100 mean less than 2002, and the values of 100 in other years means the same as 2002. 'P's show projections by the editors.

SELECTED RATIOS

For 2002	Avg. of All Manufact.	Analyzed Industry	Index	For 2002	Avg. of All Manufact.	Analyzed Industry	Index
Employees per Establishment	42	28	67	Value Added per Production Worker	182,367	163,181	89
Payroll per Establishment	1,639,184	929,154	57	Cost per Establishment	5,769,015	2,254,277	39
Payroll per Employee	39,053	33,197	85	Cost per Employee	137,446	80,541	59
Production Workers per Establishment	30	19	63	Cost per Production Worker	195,506	121,589	62
Wages per Establishment	694,845	448,388	65	Shipments per Establishment	11,158,348	5,326,064	48
Wages per Production Worker	23,548	24,185	103	Shipments per Employee	265,847	190,290	72
Hours per Production Worker	1,980	1,935	98	Shipments per Production Worker	378,144	287,273	76
Wages per Hour	11.89	12.50	105	Investment per Establishment	361,338	146,305	40
Value Added per Establishment	5,381,325	3,025,392	56	Investment per Employee	8,609	5,227	61
Value Added per Employee	128,210	108,091	84	Investment per Production Worker	12,245	7,891	64

Sources: Same as General Statistics. The 'Average of All Manufacturing' column represents the average of all manufacturing industries reported for the most recent complete year available. The Index shows the relationship between the Average and the Analyzed Industry. For example, 100 means that they are equal; 500 that the Analyzed Industry is five times the average; 50 means that the Analyzed Industry is half the national average. The abbreviation 'na' is used to show that data are 'not available'. Ratios shown for 2002, the last complete census year.

LEADING COMPANIES   Number shown: 75   Total sales ($ mil): 65,414   Total employment (000): 227.3

Company Name	Address				CEO Name	Phone	Co. Type	Sales ($ mil)	Empl. (000)
Textron Inc.	40 Westminster St.	Providence	RI	02903		401-421-2800	P	13,225	44.0
Fortune Brands Inc.	520 Lake Cook Rd.	Deerfield	IL	60015	Bruce A. Carbonari	847-484-4400	P	8,563	31.0
Brunswick Corp.	1 N Field Ct.	Lake Forest	IL	60045		847-735-4700	P	5,671	27.1
AMF Bowling Centers Inc.	8100 AMF Dr.	Mechanicsville	VA	23111	Fred Hipp	804-559-8600	S	5,536*	9.8
Reebok International Ltd.	1895 JW Foster Blvd	Canton	MA	02021	Paul Fireman	781-401-5000	S	3,785	9.1
Quiksilver Inc.	15202 Graham St.	Huntington Bch	CA	92649		714-889-2200	P	2,426	9.2
Acushnet Co.	333 Bridge St.	Fairhaven	MA	02719	Walter R. Uihlein	508-979-2000	S	2,206*	4.6
Kellwood Co.	PO Box 14374	St. Louis	MO	63178		314-576-3100	P	1,962	28.0
Adidas Golf USA Inc.	5545 Fermi Ct.	Carlsbad	CA	92008		760-918-6000	R	1,932*	<0.1
Kawasaki Motors Manufacturing	PO Box 81469	Lincoln	NE	68501		402-476-6600	S	1,758*	1.3
Top-Flite Golf Co.	2180 Rutherford Rd.	Carlsbad	CA	92008	Bob Penicka		S	1,504*	3.2
EBSCO Industries Inc.	PO Box 1943	Birmingham	AL	35201	Dixon Brooke Jr.	205-991-6600	R	1,400*	5.0
K2 Inc.	5818 El Cam Real	Carlsbad	CA	92008	Martin E. Franklin	760-494-1000	P	1,395	5.0
Callaway Golf Co.	2180 Rutherford Rd.	Carlsbad	CA	92008	Ronald S. Beard	760-931-1771	P	1,125	3.0
ICON Health and Fitness Inc.	1500 South 1000 W	Logan	UT	84321	Scott Watterson	435-750-5000	D	900*	4.0
International Speedway Corp.	PO Box 2801	Daytona Beach	FL	32120	James C. France	386-254-2700	P	817	1.1
Icon Fitness Corp.	1500 S 1000 W	Logan	UT	84321	Scott R. Watterson	435-750-5000	R	781*	5.0
IHF Capital Inc.	1500 S 1000 W	Logan	UT	84321	Scott R. Watterson	435-750-5000	R	697*	4.5
Nautilus Inc.	16400 SE Nautilus D	Vancouver	WA	98683	Robert Falcone	360-859-2900	P	680	1.5
Under Armour Inc.	1020 Hull St., Fl 3	Baltimore	MD	21230	Kevin A. Plank	410-454-6428	P	607	1.4
Amer Holding Co.	8700 W Bryn Mawr	Chicago	IL	60631	Roger Talermo	773-714-6400	R	559*	0.3
Tommy Armour Golf Co.	225 Byers Rd.	Miamisburg	OH	45342	Paul R. D'Aloia	937-866-6251	S	538*	1.1
Huffy Corp.	225 Byers Rd.	Miamisburg	OH	45342	Michael Buenzow	937-865-2800	R	438*	1.1
Johnson Outdoors Inc.	555 Main St.	Racine	WI	53403	H. P. Johnson-Leipold	262-631-6600	P	432	1.4
Precor Inc.	PO Box 7202	Woodinville	WA	98072	Paul Byrne	425-486-9292	S	411	0.6
Coleman Company Inc.	258 Beacon Street	Somerset	PA	15501	Bill Phillips		S	389*	2.3
Golfsmith International, Inc.	11000 N IH-35	Austin	TX	78753	Jim Thompson	512-837-8810	P	388	1.7
Textron Turf-Care & Specialty	2166-A W Park Ct.	Stone Mountain	GA	30087	Jon Carlson	770-498-9316	R	243*	1.2
Sport Supply Group Inc.	1901 Diplomat Dr.	Farmers Branch	TX	75234	Geoffrey P. Jurick	972-406-3484	P	237	0.8
Bauer Nike Hockey Inc.	150 Ocean Rd.	Greenland	NH	03840	Chris Zimmerman	603-430-2111	S	226*	0.5
North Face Inc.	629 S Broadway St.	Boulder	CO	80305	Mike Egeck	303-499-1731	S	208*	0.7
Connor Sport Court Int'l	939 S 700 W	Salt Lake City	UT	84104	Ronald Cerny	801-972-0260	R	205*	0.1
Life Fitness Consumer Div.	10601 W Belmont	Franklin Park	IL	60131	Kevin Grodzki	847-288-3300	D	203*	0.4
Playcore Inc.	430 Chestnut St.	Chattanooga	TN	37402	Frederic L. Contino	423-756-0015	R	197*	1.1
Easton Technical Products Inc.	5040 Harold Gatty	Salt Lake City	UT	84116	Greg Easton	801-539-1400	R	188*	0.3
Lifetime Products Inc.	PO Box 160010	Clearfield	UT	84016		801-776-1532	R	177*	0.3
Louisville Bedding Company	10400 Bunsen Way	Louisville	KY	40299	John Minihan	502-491-3370	R	175*	0.3
Rawlings Sporting Goods Co.	1859 Intertech Dr.	Fenton	MO	63026	Robert Parish	636-349-3500	S	174*	0.9
Mizuno USA Inc.	4925 Avalon Ridge	Norcross	GA	30071		770-441-5553	R	150*	0.3
CYBEX International Inc.	10 Trotter Dr.	Medway	MA	02053	John Aglialoro	508-533-4300	P	147	0.5
Escalade Inc.	817 Maxwell St.	Evansville	IN	47711	Robert E. Griffin	812-467-4449	P	137	0.9
Wright and McGill Co.	PO Box 16011	Denver	CO	80216	John Jilling		R	126*	0.3
Century L.L.C.	1000 Century Blvd.	Oklahoma City	OK	73110	Lawrence Dillard	405-732-2226	R	125*	0.3
Worth Inc.	PO Box 88104	Tullahoma	TN	37388	Robert Parish	931-455-0691	S	114*	0.8
True Temper Sports Inc.	8275 Tournament	Memphis	TN	38125	Scott C. Hennessy	901-746-2000	S	111*	0.7
Bridgestone Golf Inc.	14230 Lochridge	Covington	GA	30014	Fhigeru Nakayama	770-787-7400	R	108*	0.2
Hornerxpress Inc.	5755 Powerline Rd.	Fort Lauderdale	FL	33309	William Kent	954-772-6966	R	100*	0.2
Flowtronex PSI Inc.	10661 Newkirk St.	Dallas	TX	75220	Dan Driscoll	214-357-1320	S	98*	0.2
Swiss Army Brands Inc.	PO Box 874	Shelton	CT	06484		203-929-6391	S	93*	0.3
Mayville Engineering Company	715 S Street	Mayville	WI	53050	Bob Kamphuis	920-387-4500	R	90*	0.5
Blacksheep Inc.	3220 W Gentry	Tyler	TX	75702	Bob Archer	903-592-3853	S	90*	0.5
Doskocil Manufacturing Company	PO Box 1246	Arlington	TX	76004	Gary S. Baughman	817-467-5116	R	90*	0.8
Miracle Recreation Equipment	878 Hwy. 60	Monett	MO	65708		417-235-6917	R	90*	0.5
Heartland Industries Inc.	6400 E 11 Mile Rd.	Warren	MI	48091		734-242-6900	S	89*	0.6
General Foam Plastics Corp.	3321 E Prncss Anne	Norfolk	VA	23502	Ascher Chase	757-857-0153	R	85*	0.4
Fox Pool of Lancaster Inc.	PO Box 549	York	PA	17405	Robert Seitz	717-764-8581	R	79*	<0.1
Adams Golf Inc.	2801 E Plano Pky.	Plano	TX	75074	Barney Adams	972-673-9000	P	76	0.1
Shakespeare Fishing Tackle	3801 Westmore Dr.	Columbia	SC	29223	Scott Hogsett	803-754-7000	D	75*	0.2
Aldila Inc.	13450 Stowe Dr.	Poway	CA	92064	Peter R. Mathewson	858-513-1801	P	72	2.6
Horizon Sports Technologies	8985 Crestmar Pt	San Diego	CA	92121	Randall Beck	858-689-0552	R	68*	0.5
D.M. Industries Ltd.	2320 NW 147th St.	Miami	FL	33054	Eric Dormoy	305-685-5739	R	63*	0.2
Ingear Corp.	650 W Lake Cook	Buffalo Grove	IL	60089	Lawrence Gutkin	847-821-9600	R	61*	<0.1
Landscape Structures Inc.	PO Box 198	Delano	MN	55328	Barbara King	763-972-3391	R	60*	0.4
Kent Sporting Goods Company	433 Park Ave.	New London	OH	44851	Robert Tipton	419-929-7021	R	59*	0.1
Connelly Skis Inc.	PO Box 716	Lynnwood	WA	98046		425-775-5416	S	59*	<0.1
Fownes Brothers and Company	16 E 34th St. Fl. 5	New York	NY	10016	Thomas Gluckman	212-683-0150	R	58*	<0.1
Ff Acquisition Corp.	PO Box 1296	West Point	MS	39773	Alex Garcia	662-494-4732	R	57*	0.4
Hunter's Specialties Inc.	6000 Huntington Ct.	Cedar Rapids	IA	52402	David Forbes	319-395-0321	R	57*	0.2
Little Tikes Commercial Inc.	PO Box 897	Farmington	MO	63640		573-756-4591	S	56*	0.5
Cascade Designs	4000 1st Ave. S	Seattle	WA	98134	Lee Formson	206-505-9500	R	54*	0.3
Grandoe Corp.	PO Box 713	Gloversville	NY	12078	Eric Friedman	518-725-8641	R	54*	0.3
Heartland Tanning Inc.	4251 NE Port Dr.	Lees Summit	MO	64064	Greg Henson	816-795-1414	R	54*	<0.1
Daiwa Corp.	12851 Midway Pl.	Cerritos	CA	90703	Kazuo Aoki	562-802-9589	R	51*	0.1
Pride Manufacturing Company	10 N Main St.	Burnham	ME	04922		207-487-3322	R	51*	0.1
Penn Racquet Sports	306 S 45th Ave.	Phoenix	AZ	85043	Dave Haggerty		S	50*	0.3

Source: Ward's Business Directory of U.S. Private and Public Companies, Volumes 1 and 2, 2008. The company type code used is as follows: P - Public, R - Private, S - Subsidiary, D - Division, J - Joint Venture, A - Affiliate, G - Group. Sales are in millions of dollars, employees are in thousands. An asterisk (*) indicates an estimated sales volume. The symbol < stands for 'less than'. Company names and addresses are truncated, in some cases, to fit into the available space.

MATERIALS CONSUMED

Material	Quantity	Delivered Cost ($ million)
Metal bolts, nuts, screws, and other screw machine products	(X)	67.9
Other fabricated metal products (exc. castings and forgings)	(X)	121.9
Aluminum and aluminum-base alloy castings (rough and semifinished)	(X)	72.4
Other castings (rough and semifinished)	(X)	89.6
Steel sheet and strip (including tinplate)	(X)	85.5
All other steel shapes and forms (exc. castings, forgings, fabr. metal products)	(X)	109.2
Aluminum and aluminum-base alloy sheet, plate, foil, and welded tubing	(X)	20.7
All other aluminum and aluminum-base alloy shapes and forms (exc. castings, forgings, fabr. metal products)	(X)	40.7
Other nonferrous shapes and forms (exc. castings, forgings, fabricated metal products)	(X)	10.8
Paints, varnishes, stains, lacquers, shellacs, japans, enamels, etc.	(X)	36.5
Plastics resins consumed in the form of granules, pellets, etc.	(X)	197.7
All other chemicals and allied products	(X)	44.1
Plastics products consumed in the form of sheets, rods, etc.	(X)	109.8
Broadwoven fabrics	(X)	101.7
Rough and dressed lumber	(X)	108.2
Parts, for sporting goods	(X)	401.5
Paperboard containers, boxes, and corrugated paperboard	(X)	127.4
All other materials, components, parts, containers, and supplies	(X)	875.7
Materials, ingredients, containers, and supplies, nsk	(X)	1,365.4

Source: 2002 Economic Census. Explanation of symbols used: (D): Withheld to avoid disclosure of competitive data; na: Not available; (S): Withheld because statistical norms were not met; (X): Not applicable; (Z): Less than half the unit shown; nec: Not elsewhere classified; nsk: Not specified by kind; - : zero; p : 10-19 percent estimated; q : 20-29 percent estimated.

PRODUCT SHARE DETAILS

Product or Product Class Shipments	Mil. $	Product or Product Class Shipments	Mil. $
SPORTING AND ATHLETIC GOODS	10,795.3	Gymnasium and exercise equipment, nsk	8.2
Fishing tackle and equipment	**647.3**	**Other sporting and athletic goods**	**3,328.3**
Fishing tackle and equipment	616.5	Other sporting and athletic goods	2,972.8
Fishing rods, except fishing rod and reel combinations	65.7	Billiard and pool tables	167.2
Fishing reels, except fishing rod and reel combinations	107.0	Other billiard and pool equipment, including balls and cues sold separately	30.2
Fishing rod and reel combinations	(D)	Bowling alleys and bowling pinsetters	22.0
Fish hooks (including snelled hooks)	(D)	Bowling balls	133.9
Fishing casting plugs, spinners, spoons, flies, lures, and similar artificial baits	191.7	Other bowling equipment (including pins), excluding apparel and shoes	150.0
Fishing tackle boxes	46.5	Sailboards and surfboards	37.2
Other fishing equipment, including creels, fish and bait buckets, floats, furnished lines, sinkers, snap swivels, etc	124.5	Water skis	33.0
		Rubber and rubberized dry and wet suits, scuba, skin diving, and other underwater sports equipment, except cameras and watches	55.0
Fishing tackle and equipment, nsk	30.8	Other water sports equipment, except cameras, watches, shoes, and apparel	103.5
Golf equipment, except apparel and shoes	**2,772.8**	Bicycle helmets	(D)
Golf balls	816.8	Other sports helmets, except auto racing, bicycle, and motorcycle helmets	184.2
Golf clubs, irons	709.0		
Golf clubs, woods, including metal woods	688.0	Body protective equipment for all sports, except helmets	69.5
Other golf equipment including bags, carts for carrying golf bags, excluding shoes and apparel	558.6	Metal baseball bats, including metal softball bats	111.7
Golf bags	106.5	Other baseball, football, soccer, softball, and track and field equipment, except apparel and shoes	538.4
Other golf equipment (carts for carrying golf bags, shafts sold as such, tees, etc), excluding shoes and apparel	452.1	Tennis equipment, except apparel, nets, and shoes	43.2
Golf equipment, nsk	0.5	Archery equipment	212.2
Playground equipment	**834.9**	In-line skates	(D)
Playground equipment	829.0	Wood and plastic skateboards	51.9
Home playground equipment, including swing sets, slides, seesaws, sandboxes, etc	376.0	Snowboards	(D)
Institutional and commercial playground equipment, heavy-duty (including swings, slides, etc)	453.0	Alpine and cross-country snow skis and other snow ski equipment, excluding apparel, body protective equipment, boots, helmets, and shoes	27.1
Playground equipment, nsk	5.9	Other winter sports equipment, including bobsleds, toboggans, ice skates, and hockey equipment (except apparel, body protective equiipment, boots, helmets, and shoes)	(D)
Gymnasium and exercise equipment	**2,232.1**		
Gymnasium and exercise equipment	2,223.9	Above-ground swimming pools, 15 ft or more in diameter, filtered, completely manufactured	210.4
Gymnasium and gymnastic apparatus and equipment (parallel and horizontal bars, balance beams, trampolines, mats, etc)	254.3	Other sporting and athletic equipment, including badminton, paint ball, racquetball, squash, and table tennis equipment and traditional (quads) and clamp-on roller skates and related equipment	533.3
Free weight lifting equipment (including belts, benches, and weights)	98.3	Other sporting and athletic goods, nsk	355.5
Training units and home gyms	254.4	**Sporting and athletic goods, nsk, total**	**979.8**
Treadmills	1,005.2		
Other exercise, health, and physical fitness equipment (including ab exercisers, cross-country ski exercisers, gliders and riders, rowing machines, and slant-boards)	611.7		

Source: 2002 Economic Census. The values are product shipments in millions of dollars for 2002. Total product shipments may be lower or higher than industry shipments. See Introduction for a full discussion. Values of indented subcategories are summed in the main heading(s). The symbol (D) appears when data are withheld to prevent disclosure of competitive information. The abbreviation nsk stands for 'not specified by kind' and nec for 'not elsewhere classified'. A dash (-) means zero.

INPUTS AND OUTPUTS FOR SPORTING AND ATHLETIC GOODS MANUFACTURING

Economic Sector or Industry Providing Inputs	%	Sector	Economic Sector or Industry Buying Outputs	%	Sector
Compensation of employees	23.3		Personal consumption expenditures	71.5	
Wholesale trade	5.1	Trade	Private fixed investment	10.1	
Sporting & athletic goods	4.1	Manufg.	Exports of goods & services	7.0	Cap Inv
Advertising & related services	3.6	Services	S/L govt. invest., education	3.7	S/L Govt
Iron & steel mills & ferroalloys	2.7	Manufg.	Sporting & athletic goods	2.8	Manufg.
Management of companies & enterprises	2.5	Services	General S/L govt. services	1.5	S/L Govt
Plastics materials & resins	2.4	Manufg.	Elementary & secondary schools	1.0	Services
Nonferrous metal foundries	2.3	Manufg.	Food services & drinking places	0.6	Services
Synthetic rubber	2.3	Manufg.	S/L govt. invest., other	0.5	S/L Govt
Paperboard containers	1.8	Manufg.	Amusement & recreation, nec	0.2	Services
Taxes on production & imports, less subsidies	1.5		Retail trade	0.1	Trade
Real estate	1.4	Fin/R.E.	Child day care services	0.1	Services
Plastics packaging materials, film & sheet	1.4	Manufg.			
Textile & fabric finishing mills	1.4	Manufg.			
Turned products & screws, nuts, & bolts	1.4	Manufg.			
Sawmills & wood preservation	1.3	Manufg.			
Plate work & fabricated structural products	1.3	Manufg.			
Lessors of nonfinancial assets	1.3	Fin/R.E.			
Securities, commodity contracts, investments	1.1	Fin/R.E.			
Truck transportation	1.1	Util.			
Professional, scientific, technical services, nec	1.0	Services			
Aluminum products from purchased aluminum	0.8	Manufg.			
Paints & coatings	0.8	Manufg.			
Metal cutting & forming machine tools	0.7	Manufg.			
Legal services	0.7	Services			
Coating, engraving, heat treating & allied activities	0.6	Manufg.			
Semiconductors & related devices	0.6	Manufg.			
Scenic & sightseeing transport & related services	0.6	Util.			
Printed circuit assemblies (electronic assembiles)	0.6	Manufg.			
Food services & drinking places	0.6	Services			
Cutting tools & machine tool accessories	0.6	Manufg.			
Machine shops	0.6	Manufg.			
Specialized design services	0.5	Services			
Leather products, nec	0.5	Manufg.			
Power generation & supply	0.5	Util.			
Telecommunications	0.5	Services			
Hotels & motels, including casino hotels	0.4	Services			
Accounting, tax preparation, bookkeeping, & payroll	0.4	Services			
Management, scientific, & technical consulting	0.4	Services			
Automotive equipment rental & leasing	0.4	Fin/R.E.			
Air transportation	0.3	Util.			
Data processing, hosting, & related services	0.3	Services			
Basic organic chemicals, nec	0.3	Manufg.			
Forestry products	0.3	Agric.			
Monetary authorities/depository credit intermediation	0.3	Fin/R.E.			
Warehousing & storage	0.2	Util.			
Architectural, engineering, & related services	0.2	Services			
Noncomparable imports	0.2	Foreign			
Miscellaneous wood products	0.2	Manufg.			
Unlaminated plastics profile shapes	0.2	Manufg.			
Rail transportation	0.2	Util.			
Natural gas distribution	0.2	Util.			
Alumina refining & primary aluminum production	0.2	Manufg.			
Other computer related services, including facilities	0.2	Services			
Scientific research & development services	0.2	Services			
Commercial & industrial machinery rental & leasing	0.2	Fin/R.E.			
Services to buildings & dwellings	0.2	Services			
Abrasive products	0.2	Manufg.			
Maintenance/repair of nonresidential structures	0.1	Construct.			
Business support services	0.1	Services			
Metal cans, boxes, & other containers (light gauge)	0.1	Manufg.			
Motor vehicle parts	0.1	Manufg.			
Fabricated metals, nec	0.1	Manufg.			
Crowns & closures & metal stamping	0.1	Manufg.			
Nondepository credit intermediation activities	0.1	Fin/R.E.			
Transit & ground passenger transportation	0.1	Util.			
Valve & fittings other than plumbing	0.1	Manufg.			

Source: *Benchmark Input-Output Accounts for the U.S. Economy, 2002*, U.S. Department of Commerce, Washington, D.C., January 2008. The abbreviation nec stands for 'not elsewhere classified'.

OCCUPATIONS EMPLOYED BY SPORTING AND ATHLETIC GOODS MANUFACTURING

No Occupation data available for this industry.

LOCATION BY STATE AND REGIONAL CONCENTRATION

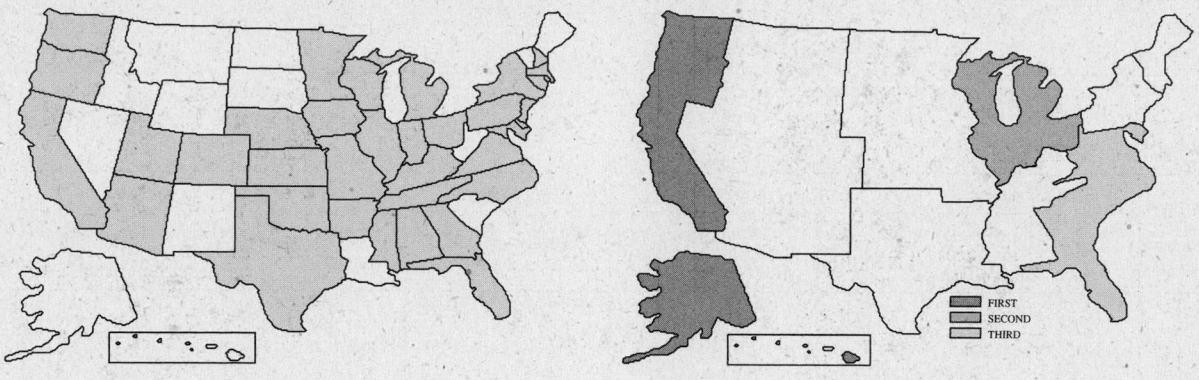

FIRST
SECOND
THIRD

INDUSTRY DATA BY STATE

| State | Establish-ments | Shipments | | | Employment | | | | Cost as % of Shipments | Investment per Employee ($) |
		Total ($ mil)	% of U.S.	Per Establ.	Total Number	% of U.S.	Per Establ.	Wages ($/hour)		
California	398	2,468.1	20.8	6,201.2	10,834	17.3	27	13.04	36.3	9,238
Utah	38	1,259.7	10.6	33,150.4	6,098	9.8	160	12.32	66.5	4,314
Massachusetts	43	880.6	7.4	20,479.0	3,463	5.5	81	16.25	20.6	5,697
Illinois	76	736.4	6.2	9,689.0	2,732	4.4	36	10.74	35.7	4,799
Texas	125	551.8	4.6	4,414.6	3,528	5.6	28	11.20	51.7	3,365
Missouri	67	447.1	3.8	6,672.7	2,810	4.5	42	11.36	40.7	4,465
Pennsylvania	70	435.9	3.7	6,226.5	2,302	3.7	33	12.26	45.2	4,761
Washington	98	435.3	3.7	4,442.1	2,492	4.0	25	12.03	47.1	2,451
Wisconsin	76	319.3	2.7	4,200.8	1,944	3.1	26	11.73	42.0	3,176
Arizona	37	309.2	2.6	8,355.9	1,913	3.1	52	13.07	39.4	6,651
Minnesota	75	277.4	2.3	3,698.9	1,929	3.1	26	16.66	42.8	6,228
Michigan	80	268.0	2.3	3,349.5	948	1.5	12	12.43	44.7	6,043
Indiana	41	235.1	2.0	5,733.4	1,236	2.0	30	11.29	54.3	3,782
Tennessee	29	233.6	2.0	8,053.8	1,143	1.8	39	10.04	54.8	3,996
Florida	149	219.1	1.8	1,470.8	1,500	2.4	10	11.48	46.0	2,375
Georgia	40	218.6	1.8	5,463.9	814	1.3	20	13.37	40.0	8,300
Virginia	22	211.1	1.8	9,597.6	1,101	1.8	50	12.97	35.3	15,621
New Jersey	39	190.4	1.6	4,883.2	817	1.3	21	12.42	43.7	2,435
New York	65	177.5	1.5	2,731.5	1,164	1.9	18	11.09	41.5	2,598
Oklahoma	28	169.9	1.4	6,068.2	1,066	1.7	38	11.99	50.1	7,013
Colorado	61	166.9	1.4	2,736.7	949	1.5	16	13.14	34.8	2,697
Alabama	39	153.4	1.3	3,932.7	951	1.5	24	13.10	37.5	3,341
Mississippi	28	129.9	1.1	4,637.6	879	1.4	31	17.76	21.8	3,217
Oregon	63	128.0	1.1	2,032.2	996	1.6	16	12.15	40.7	5,258
Arkansas	32	126.8	1.1	3,963.4	1,088	1.7	34	8.60	33.7	2,858
Ohio	58	108.2	0.9	1,865.9	663	1.1	11	13.01	47.7	2,164
Iowa	25	106.3	0.9	4,253.6	687	1.1	27	10.49	45.5	3,918
Kentucky	26	76.3	0.6	2,935.0	607	1.0	23	15.33	37.8	4,110
Connecticut	20	75.0	0.6	3,748.7	614	1.0	31	12.67	33.9	1,739
North Carolina	48	62.5	0.5	1,302.9	559	0.9	12	10.96	46.0	1,531
Nebraska	11	39.8	0.3	3,621.4	300	0.5	27	11.85	47.2	5,787
New Hampshire	7	27.6	0.2	3,940.4	140	0.2	20	9.98	18.8	564
Kansas	19	20.4	0.2	1,076.0	129	0.2	7	12.46	34.4	1,574
Maryland	13	17.3	0.1	1,331.5	125	0.2	10	9.34	37.3	5,296
Rhode Island	12	16.5	0.1	1,371.3	114	0.2	10	16.32	41.5	816
Delaware	5	14.1	0.1	2,810.8	178	0.3	36	7.78	46.1	416

Source: 2002 *Economic Census*. The states are in descending order of shipments or establishments (if shipment data are missing for the majority). The symbol (D) appears when data are withheld to prevent disclosure of competitive information. States marked with (D) are sorted by number of establishments. A dash (-) indicates that the data element cannot be calculated. Data may not show all states active in the NAICS category. All data available at the time of publication are shown.

NAICS 33993M - DOLL, TOY, AND GAME MANUFACTURING*

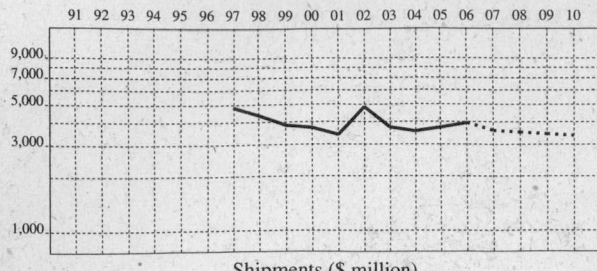
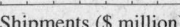

Shipments ($ million)

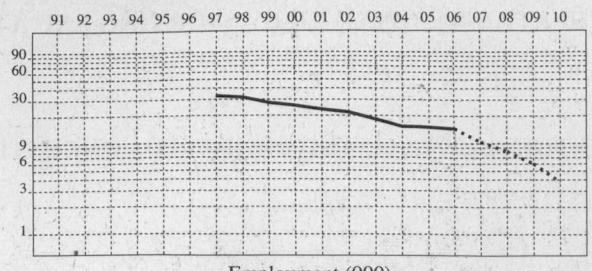

Employment (000)

GENERAL STATISTICS

Year	Com-panies	Establishments		Employment			Compensation		Production ($ million)			
		Total	with 20 or more employees	Total (000)	Production Workers (000)	Hours (Mil)	Payroll ($ mil)	Wages ($/hr)	Cost of Materials	Value Added by Manufacture	Value of Shipments	Capital Invest.
1997	992	1,021	242	32.8	24.1	44.5	830.9	10.65	1,975.4	2,866.7	4,835.4	137.4
1998		1,020	244	31.8	23.0	44.1	801.3	10.24	1,980.9	2,402.0	4,348.0	114.1
1999		1,017	225	27.6	19.7	38.1	701.1	10.57	1,807.3	2,014.4	3,832.3	126.1
2000		1,007	205	25.7	19.2	35.8	699.2	11.15	1,802.3	1,868.3	3,710.1	113.1
2001		958	201	23.4	16.6	30.5	668.7	11.50	1,585.5	1,772.0	3,389.0	93.2
2002	868	881	190	21.8	14.6	27.0	698.1	12.83	2,231.2	2,696.5	4,845.1	123.4
2003		857	182	18.3	12.6	23.9	597.7	12.42	1,668.4	2,009.4	3,729.2	79.1
2004		839	160	15.3	10.2	19.5	529.7	14.04	1,660.3	1,966.7	3,541.4	80.2
2005		811	151	15.1	9.6	18.0	563.7	14.76	1,900.3	2,012.9	3,721.7	69.5
2006		782P	140P	14.6	8.9	16.6	582.5	15.93	2,143.0	1,971.1	3,953.3	127.3
2007		752P	128P	10.4P	5.9P	10.9P	499.6P	15.80P	1,941.6P	1,785.8P	3,581.7P	82.9P
2008		721P	116P	8.2P	4.0P	7.5P	469.1P	16.41P	1,901.3P	1,748.8P	3,507.4P	78.6P
2009		691P	104P	6.0P	2.2P	4.1P	438.6P	17.03P	1,861.0P	1,711.7P	3,433.1P	74.3P
2010		660P	92P	3.8P	0.4P	0.6P	408.1P	17.65P	1,820.7P	1,674.7P	3,358.8P	70.1P

Sources: 1997 and 2002 *Economic Census*; other years, up to 2006, are from *Annual Survey of Manufactures*. Establishment counts for non-Census years are from *County Business Patterns*; 1997 and 2002 values are from the 1997 and 2002 censuses, respectively. 'P's show projections by the editors.

INDICES OF CHANGE

Year	Com-panies	Establishments		Employment			Compensation		Production ($ million)			
		Total	with 20 or more employees	Total (000)	Production Workers (000)	Hours (Mil)	Payroll ($ mil)	Wages ($/hr)	Cost of Materials	Value Added by Manufacture	Value of Shipments	Capital Invest.
1997	114	116	127	150	165	165	119	83	89	106	100	111
1998		116	128	146	158	163	115	80	89	89	90	92
1999		115	118	127	135	141	100	82	81	75	79	102
2000		114	108	118	132	133	100	87	81	69	77	92
2001		109	106	107	114	113	96	90	71	66	70	76
2002	100	100	100	100	100	100	100	100	100	100	100	100
2003		97	96	84	86	89	86	97	75	75	77	64
2004		95	84	70	70	72	76	109	74	73	73	65
2005		92	79	69	66	67	81	115	85	75	77	56
2006		89P	74P	67	61	61	83	124	96	73	82	103
2007		85P	68P	48P	40P	40P	72P	123P	87P	66P	74P	67P
2008		82P	61P	38P	27P	28P	67P	128P	85P	65P	72P	64P
2009		78P	55P	28P	15P	15P	63P	133P	83P	63P	71P	60P
2010		75P	49P	17P	3P	2P	58P	138P	82P	62P	69P	57P

Sources: Same as General Statistics. Values reflect change from the base year, 2002. Values above 100 mean greater than 2002, values below 100 mean less than 2002, and the values of 100 in other years means the same as 2002. 'P's show projections by the editors.

SELECTED RATIOS

For 2002	Avg. of All Manufact.	Analyzed Industry	Index	For 2002	Avg. of All Manufact.	Analyzed Industry	Index
Employees per Establishment	42	25	59	Value Added per Production Worker	182,367	184,692	101
Payroll per Establishment	1,639,184	792,395	48	Cost per Establishment	5,769,015	2,532,577	44
Payroll per Employee	39,053	32,023	82	Cost per Employee	137,446	102,349	74
Production Workers per Establishment	30	17	56	Cost per Production Worker	195,506	152,822	78
Wages per Establishment	694,845	393,201	57	Shipments per Establishment	11,158,348	5,499,546	49
Wages per Production Worker	23,548	23,727	101	Shipments per Employee	265,847	222,252	84
Hours per Production Worker	1,980	1,849	93	Shipments per Production Worker	378,144	331,856	88
Wages per Hour	11.89	12.83	108	Investment per Establishment	361,338	140,068	39
Value Added per Establishment	5,381,325	3,060,726	57	Investment per Employee	8,609	5,661	66
Value Added per Employee	128,210	123,693	96	Investment per Production Worker	12,245	8,452	69

Sources: Same as General Statistics. The 'Average of All Manufacturing' column represents the average of all manufacturing industries reported for the most recent complete year available. The Index shows the relationship between the Average and the Analyzed Industry. For example, 100 means that they are equal; 500 that the Analyzed Industry is five times the average; 50 means that the Analyzed Industry is half the national average. The abbreviation 'na' is used to show that data are 'not available'. Ratios shown for 2002, the last complete census year.

*Equivalent to Federal Government NAICS 339931, 339932.

LEADING COMPANIES Number shown: 75 Total sales ($ mil): **18,473** Total employment (000): **76.2**

Company Name	Address				CEO Name	Phone	Co. Type	Sales ($ mil)	Empl. (000)
Mattel Inc.	333 Continental	El Segundo	CA	90245	Robert A. Eckert	310-252-2000	P	5,970	31.0
Hasbro Inc.	PO Box 1059	Pawtucket	RI	02861		401-431-8697	P	3,838	5.9
Sony Music Entertainment Inc.	550 Madison Ave.	New York	NY	10022	Mike Bebel	212-833-8000	S	1,500*	10.0
JAKKS Pacific Inc.	22619 Pacific Coast	Malibu	CA	90265	Stephen G. Berman	310-456-7799	P	857	0.6
Ty Inc.	PO Box 5377	Oak Brook	IL	60522	H. Ty Warner	630-920-1515	R	750*	0.6
Plaid Enterprises Inc.	PO Box 7600	Norcross	GA	30091	Michael McCooey	678-291-8100	R	600*	0.2
Speedway Motorsports Inc.	PO Box 600	Concord	NC	28026	O. Bruton Smith	704-455-3223	P	562	1.0
Build-A-Bear Workshop Inc.	1954 Innerbelt Bus.	St. Louis	MO	63114	Maxine K. Clark	314-423-8000	P	474	7.2
LeapFrog Enterprises Inc.	6401 Hollis St.	Emeryville	CA	94608	Steven B. Fink	510-420-5000	P	445	0.9
Marvel Entertainment Group	417 5th Ave.	New York	NY	10016	Morton Handel	212-576-4000	S	352	0.9
Russ Berrie and Company Inc.	111 Bauer Dr.	Oakland	NJ	07436	Andrew R. Gatto	201-337-9000	P	295	1.0
Rainforest Cafe Inc.	1510 West Loop S	Houston	TX	77027	Tilman J. Fertitta		S	259*	6.8
Fisher-Price Inc.	636 Girard Ave.	East Aurora	NY	14052	Neil Friedman	716-687-3000	S	165*	0.9
Exx Inc.	1350 E Flamingo	Las Vegas	NV	89119		702-598-3223	P	159	0.8
First Years Inc.	100 Tec. Center Dr.	Stoughton	MA	02072	Curtis Stoelting	781-341-6250	S	150*	0.2
Battat Inc.	PO Box 1264	Plattsburgh	NY	12901	Joe Battat	518-562-2200	R	146*	0.2
Playmates Toys Inc.	611 Anton Blvd.	Costa Mesa	CA	92626	Charles Ip	714-428-2000	S	125*	<0.1
Revell-Monogram L.L.C.	725 Landwehr Rd.	Northbrook	IL	60062		847-770-6100	R	122*	<0.1
Peg-Perego USA Inc.	3625 Independence	Fort Wayne	IN	46808		260-482-8191	R	100*	0.1
Mad Catz Interactive Inc.	7480 Mission Vly	San Diego	CA	92108	Patrick S. Brigham	619-683-9830	P	100	0.1
Pioneer National Latex Inc.	246 E 4th St.	Ashland	OH	44805		419-289-3300	R	98*	0.1
Franklin Mint Co.	US Rte. One	Media	PA	19091	Bruce Newman	610-459-6000	R	97*	1.1
Summit Products Inc.	PO Box 620	Trussville	AL	35173		205-661-1774	R	87*	<0.1
United States Playing Card Co.	4590 Beech St.	Cincinnati	OH	45212	Greg Simko	513-396-5700	S	81*	0.6
Nancy Sales Company Inc.	PO Box 6477	Chelsea	MA	02150	Alton Lipkin	617-884-1700	R	77*	0.1
Gaming Partners International	1700 S Indu. Rd.	Las Vegas	NV	89102	Gerard P. Charlier	702-384-2425	P	74	0.8
AW Faber-Castell USA Inc.	9450 Allen Dr.	Cleveland	OH	44125	Jamie Gallagher	216-643-4660	R	59*	0.1
Ff Acquisition Corp.	PO Box 1296	West Point	MS	39773	Alex Garcia	662-494-4732	R	57*	0.4
Vermont Teddy Bear Company	PO Box 965	Shelburne	VT	05482		802-985-3001	R	56	0.3
American Educational Products	401 W Hickory St.	Fort Collins	CO	80522	Michael Anderson	970-484-7445	R	55*	0.2
Steve Jackson Games Inc.	PO Box 18957	Austin	TX	78760	Steve Jackson	512-447-7866	R	48*	<0.1
Swing-A-Way Products L.L.C.	4100 Beck Ave.	Saint Louis	MO	63116		314-773-1487	S	46*	<0.1
American Plastic Toys Inc.	PO Box 100	Walled Lake	MI	48390	John Gessert	248-624-4881	R	33*	0.2
Step2 Company L.L.C.	10010 A Hudson	Streetsboro	OH	44241		330-656-0440	R	30*	0.5
Educational Insights Inc.	18730 S Wilmington	R Dominguez	CA	90220	G. Reid Calcott	310-884-2000	S	30*	0.3
Big Fish Games Inc.	1501 4th Ave., 800	Seattle	WA	98101	Jeremy Lewis	206-282-4923	R	30	0.1
Small World Kids Inc.	5711 Buckingham	Culver City	CA	90230	Debra Fine	310-645-9680	P	28	<0.1
Athearn Inc.	1550 Glenn Curtiss	Carson	CA	90746	Tim Geddes	310-763-7140	R	26*	0.2
Ohio Art Co.	PO Box 111	Bryan	OH	43506	William C. Killgallon	419-636-3141	P	25	0.2
Poof Slinky Inc.	PO Box 701394	Plymouth	MI	48170	Raymo Dallavecchia	734-454-9552	R	23*	<0.1
Extron Logistics L.L.C.	47550 Kato Rd.	Fremont	CA	94538		510-353-0177	R	23*	0.2
Mag-Nif Inc.	PO Box 720	Mentor	OH	44061	William Knox	440-255-9366	R	23*	0.2
Wm. K. Walthers Inc.	5601 W Florist Ave.	Milwaukee	WI	53218	Philip Walthers	414-527-0770	R	22*	0.2
Western Synthetic Fiber Inc.	966 Sandhill Ave.	Carson	CA	90746	Ken Hardin	310-767-1000	R	22*	<0.1
Rowe International Inc.	1500 Union Ave. SE	Grand Rapids	MI	49507	Douglas Johnson	616-243-3633	R	19*	0.1
Poolmaster Inc.	PO Box 340308	Sacramento	CA	95834	Lee Tager	916-567-9800	R	18*	<0.1
Alexander Doll Company Inc.	615 W 131st St.	New York	NY	10027	Herbert Brown	212-283-5900	R	18*	0.2
Imperial Toy L.L.C.	PO Box 21068	Los Angeles	CA	90021	Arthur Hirsch	213-489-2100	R	18*	0.1
Middleton Doll Co.	1050 Walnut Rdge	Hartland	WI	53029	Salvatore L. Bando	262-369-8163	P	16	<0.1
Kids II Inc.	555 N Point Ctr. E	Alpharetta	GA	30022	Ryan Gunnigle	770-751-0442	R	16*	0.1
Bucilla Corp.	1 Oak Ridge Rd.	Hazleton	PA	18202	Michael McCooey	570-384-2525	S	15*	0.1
Decipher Inc.	259 Granby St., 100	Norfolk	VA	23510	Warren Holland	757-664-1111	R	15*	0.1
Universal Manufacturing Co.	5450 Deramus	Kansas City	MO	64120	Jim Lepore	816-231-2771	R	15*	0.3
Buffalo Games Inc.	220 James E Casey	Buffalo	NY	14206	Paul Dedrick	716-827-8393	R	13*	<0.1
Atlas Model Railroad Company	378 Florence Ave.	Hillside	NJ	07205	Diane Haedrich	908-687-0880	R	12*	<0.1
Playmobil USA Inc.	PO Box 877	Dayton	NJ	08810		609-395-5566	R	12*	<0.1
Gund Inc.	PO Box 852	Edison	NJ	08818	Jim Madonna	732-248-1500	R	12*	0.1
Plush Appeal L.L.C.	PO Box 19965	New Orleans	LA	70179		337-667-6866	R	12*	<0.1
SwimWays Corp.	5816 Ward Ct.	Virginia Beach	VA	23455	David Arias	757-460-1156	R	11*	<0.1
Accents Unlimited Inc.	5205 W Donges Bay	Mequon	WI	53092	Ron Creten	262-242-5205	R	10*	<0.1
Creations by Alan Stuart Inc.	49 W 38th St.	New York	NY	10018	Stuart Kalinsky	212-719-5511	R	10*	<0.1
Dolly Inc.	320 N 4th St.	Tipp City	OH	45371	Dennis Sullivan	937-667-5711	R	10*	<0.1
Hobby Products International	70 Icon	El Toro	CA	92610	Shawn Ireland	949-753-1099	R	10*	<0.1
Aqua-Leisure Industries Inc.	PO Box 239	Avon	MA	02322	Steven Berenson	508-587-5400	R	10*	<0.1
Fortunet Inc.	2950 Highland Dr.	Las Vegas	NV	89109	Yuri Itkis	702-796-9090	P	10	<0.1
Norscot Group Inc.	PO Box 998	Thiensville	WI	53092	Norman Stern	262-241-3313	R	9*	<0.1
Parris Manufacturing Co.	PO Box 338	Savannah	TN	38372	Craig Phillips	731-925-3918	R	8*	<0.1
N.H.S. Inc.	PO Box 2718	Santa Cruz	CA	95063		831-459-7800	R	8*	<0.1
Gayla Industries Inc.	PO Box 920800	Houston	TX	77292	Douglas Phillips	713-681-2411	R	8*	<0.1
Orange Products Inc.	1929 Vultee St.	Allentown	PA	18103	Paul Sachdev	610-791-9711	R	8*	<0.1
Action Products International	1101 N Keller Rd.	Orlando	FL	32810	Ronald S. Kaplan	407-481-8007	P	7	<0.1
Alexander Global Promotions	PO Box 52885	Bellevue	WA	98015	Malcolm Alexander	425-637-0610	R	7*	<0.1
Parma International Inc.	13927 Progress	North Royalton	OH	44133	Michael Macdowell	440-237-8650	R	7*	<0.1
Peltier Glass Company Inc.	1707 Boyce Ln.	Ottawa	IL	61350		815-433-0026	R	7*	<0.1
Chardan Corp.	705 S Union St.	Bryan	OH	43506	Daniel Johns	419-636-6900	R	6*	<0.1

Source: Ward's Business Directory of U.S. Private and Public Companies, Volumes 1 and 2, 2008. The company type code used is as follows: P - Public, R - Private, S - Subsidiary, D - Division, J - Joint Venture, A - Affiliate, G - Group. Sales are in millions of dollars, employees are in thousands. An asterisk (*) indicates an estimated sales volume. The symbol < stands for 'less than'. Company names and addresses are truncated, in some cases, to fit into the available space.

MATERIALS CONSUMED FOR DOLL AND STUFFED TOY MANUFACTURING

Material	Quantity	Delivered Cost ($ million)
Plastics products consumed in the form of sheets, rods, etc.	(X)	(D)
Broadwoven fabrics	(X)	1.9
Paperboard containers, boxes, and corrugated paperboard	(X)	0.7
Other paper products	(X)	(D)
Doll parts	(X)	16.1
All other materials, components, parts, containers, and supplies	(X)	12.0
Materials, ingredients, containers, and supplies, nsk	(X)	78.2

Source: 2002 *Economic Census*. Explanation of symbols used: (D): Withheld to avoid disclosure of competitive data; na: Not available; (S): Withheld because statistical norms were not met; (X): Not applicable; (Z): Less than half the unit shown; nec: Not elsewhere classified; nsk: Not specified by kind; - : zero; p : 10-19 percent estimated; q : 20-29 percent estimated.

MATERIALS CONSUMED FOR GAME, TOY, AND CHILDREN'S VEHICLE MANUFACTURING

Material	Quantity	Delivered Cost ($ million)
Fabricated metal products, including forgings	(X)	50.3
Steel shapes and forms (exc. castings, forgings, fabr. metal products)	(X)	4.3
Plastics resins consumed in the form of granules, pellets, etc.	(X)	139.3
Plastics products consumed in the form of sheets, rods, etc.	(X)	130.6
Broadwoven fabrics	(X)	11.3
Paperboard (news, chip, pasted, tablet, etc.), exc. for shipping	(X)	41.8
Paperboard containers, boxes, and corrugated paperboard	(X)	101.7
Other paper products	(X)	27.4
Lumber and wood products (excluding furniture)	(X)	18.9
Electronic components and accessories	(X)	35.1
All other materials, components, parts, containers, and supplies	(X)	336.5
Materials, ingredients, containers, and supplies, nsk	(X)	563.2

Source: 2002 *Economic Census*. Explanation of symbols used: (D): Withheld to avoid disclosure of competitive data; na: Not available; (S): Withheld because statistical norms were not met; (X): Not applicable; (Z): Less than half the unit shown; nec: Not elsewhere classified; nsk: Not specified by kind; - : zero; p : 10-19 percent estimated; q : 20-29 percent estimated.

PRODUCT SHARE DETAILS FOR DOLL AND STUFFED TOY MANUFACTURING

Product or Product Class Shipments	Mil. $	Product or Product Class Shipments	Mil. $
DOLLS AND STUFFED TOYS	276.1	Stuffed dolls	22.8
Dolls, toy animals, and action figures, not stuffed	96.5	Stuffed toy animals	84.3
Dolls, toy animals, and action figures, more than 13 in. in length (except stuffed)	60.6	Other stuffed toys	43.1
Dolls, toy animals, and action figures, 13 in. or less in length, including collectors' miniatures (except stuffed)	35.9	Parts for dolls, toy animals, and action figures, including accessories, clothes, and playsets for dolls, toy animals, and action figures	13.6
Stuffed toys and dolls	150.1	Dolls, stuffed toys, and parts and accessories for dolls and stuffed toys, nsk, total	15.8

Source: 2002 *Economic Census*. The values are product shipments in millions of dollars for 2002. Total product shipments may be lower or higher than industry shipments. See Introduction for a full discussion. Values of indented subcategories are summed in the main heading(s). The symbol (D) appears when data are withheld to prevent disclosure of competitive information. The abbreviation nsk stands for 'not specified by kind' and nec for 'not elsewhere classified'. A dash (-) means zero.

PRODUCT SHARE DETAILS FOR GAME, TOY, AND CHILDREN'S VEHICLE MANUFACTURING

Product or Product Class Shipments	Mil. $	Product or Product Class Shipments	Mil. $
GAMES, TOYS, AND CHILDREN'S VEHICLES	3,712.2	Models, craft kits and supplies, natural science kits and sets, and collectors' miniatures, nsk	1.7
Baby carriages and children's vehicles (including parts for children's vehicles sold separately), except bicycles with pneumatic tires	**444.3**	**Nonelectronic games and puzzles, including parts**	**472.3**
Baby carriages and strollers	(D)	Nonelectronic games and puzzles, including parts	471.3
Plastic tricycles, including chain and pedal driven	(D)	Board games	340.6
Parts for children's vehicles sold separately	(D)	Nonelectric sports-oriented action and skill games, including baseball and football action and skill games	33.3
Other children's vehicles (children's automobiles, scooters, tractors, wagons, baby walkers, and sleds), except bicycles with pneumatic tires	364.8	Nonelectric nonsports-oriented action and skill games	4.8
Models (operating and static), craft kits and supplies, natural science kits and sets, and collectors' miniatures	**482.7**	Puzzles	65.1
		Other nonelectric games	(D)
Models, including components and accessories	255.2	Nonelectronic games, nsk	1.0
Electrically operating model trains and railroads, including individual units, kits, sets, and accessories	103.3	**Other nonelectric toys, including parts**	**1,248.8**
Other operating models (boats, cars, and planes), including individual units, kits, sets, and accessories	76.5	Nonpowered transportation toys and toy sets	534.9
Plastics static models (boats, cars, planes, trains, and railroads), including individual units, kits, sets, and accessories	42.1	Plastics nonpowered transportation toys, nonriding, sold without accessories, more than 6 inches in length, except model kits	506.9
Other static models (boats, cars, planes, trains, and railroads), including individual units, kits, sets, and accessories	14.8	Other nonpowered transportation toys, nonriding, sold without accessories, more than 6 inches in length, except model kits	(D)
Components and accessories for models	18.5	Other nonpowered transportation toys and toy sets, nonriding (excluding model kits)	(D)
Craft kits and supplies, natural science kits and sets, and collectors' miniatures	225.8	Other preschool playsets and toys, excluding building toys and infant toys	71.7
Craft kits and supplies, individually packaged and in bulk (beadery, decoupage, embroidery, macrame, paint by number kits and supplies, except glass beads	179.8	Nonelectric toys, including parts, nec	519.0
Natural science kits and sets, including botanical, chemistry, electrical, and mineralogical kits and sets	(D)	Juvenile-scale sporting goods, gardening toys, sand toys, and inflatables (including water toys)	56.5
Collectors' miniatures, including aircraft, scale cars, historic figures, doll houses and accessories, and soldiers (except dolls)	(D)	Doll carriages, strollers, and carts	(D)
		All other nonelectric toys	433.8
		Parts for nonelectric toys	9.5
		Nonelectric toys, including parts, nec, nsk	0.3
		Electronic games and toys (excluding disks, tapes, and cartridges)	**817.1**
		Games, toys, and children's vehicles, nsk, total	**247.0**

Source: 2002 *Economic Census.* The values are product shipments in millions of dollars for 2002. Total product shipments may be lower or higher than industry shipments. See Introduction for a full discussion. Values of indented subcategories are summed in the main heading(s). The symbol (D) appears when data are withheld to prevent disclosure of competitive information. The abbreviation nsk stands for 'not specified by kind' and nec for 'not elsewhere classified'. A dash (-) means zero.

INPUTS AND OUTPUTS FOR DOLL, TOY, AND GAME MANUFACTURING

Economic Sector or Industry Providing Inputs	%	Sector	Economic Sector or Industry Buying Outputs	%	Sector
Compensation of employees	20.2		Personal consumption expenditures	92.3	
Plastics materials & resins	5.9	Manufg.	Exports of goods & services	3.3	Cap Inv
Plastics packaging materials, film & sheet	5.1	Manufg.	Change in private inventories	1.7	In House
Paperboard containers	4.8	Manufg.	General S/L govt. services	0.9	S/L Govt
Wholesale trade	2.9	Trade	Child day care services	0.7	Services
Management of companies & enterprises	2.4	Services	Dolls, toys, & games	0.4	Manufg.
Paperboard mills	2.0	Manufg.	Individual & family services	0.4	Services
Dolls, toys, & games	1.9	Manufg.			
Printed circuit assemblies (electronic assemblies)	1.7	Manufg.			
Noncomparable imports	1.6	Foreign			
Textile & fabric finishing mills	1.4	Manufg.			
Advertising & related services	1.3	Services			
Real estate	1.2	Fin/R.E.			
Converted paper products, nec	1.0	Manufg.			
Sawmills & wood preservation	1.0	Manufg.			
Truck transportation	0.9	Util.			
Semiconductors & related devices	0.9	Manufg.			
Unlaminated plastics profile shapes	0.9	Manufg.			
Securities, commodity contracts, investments	0.8	Fin/R.E.			
Taxes on production & imports, less subsidies	0.8				
Lessors of nonfinancial assets	0.8	Fin/R.E.			
Machine shops	0.8	Manufg.			
Plastics products, nec	0.7	Manufg.			
Power generation & supply	0.6	Util.			
Legal services	0.6	Services			
Coating, engraving, heat treating & allied activities	0.5	Manufg.			
Specialized design services	0.4	Services			
Monetary authorities/depository credit intermediation	0.4	Fin/R.E.			
Professional, scientific, technical services, nec	0.4	Services			
Automotive equipment rental & leasing	0.3	Fin/R.E.			
Broadwoven fabric mills	0.3	Manufg.			
Petroleum lubricating oil & grease	0.3	Manufg.			
Laminated plastics plates, sheets, & shapes	0.3	Manufg.			
Rail transportation	0.3	Util.			
Turned products & screws, nuts, & bolts	0.3	Manufg.			

Continued on next page.

INPUTS AND OUTPUTS FOR DOLL, TOY, AND GAME MANUFACTURING - Continued

Economic Sector or Industry Providing Inputs	%	Sector	Economic Sector or Industry Buying Outputs	%	Sector
Telecommunications	0.3	Services			
Accounting, tax preparation, bookkeeping, & payroll	0.3	Services			
Management, scientific, & technical consulting	0.2	Services			
Fiber, yarn, & thread mills	0.2	Manufg.			
Architectural, engineering, & related services	0.2	Services			
Warehousing & storage	0.2	Util.			
Bare printed circuit boards	0.2	Manufg.			
Fabricated metals, nec	0.2	Manufg.			
Food services & drinking places	0.2	Services			
Natural gas distribution	0.2	Util.			
Employment services	0.2	Services			
Metal cans, boxes, & other containers (light gauge)	0.2	Manufg.			
Iron & steel mills & ferroalloys	0.2	Manufg.			
Commercial & industrial machinery rental & leasing	0.2	Fin/R.E.			
Motor vehicle parts	0.2	Manufg.			
Data processing, hosting, & related services	0.2	Services			
Scientific research & development services	0.2	Services			
Services to buildings & dwellings	0.2	Services			
Maintenance/repair of nonresidential structures	0.2	Construct.			
Cutting tools & machine tool accessories	0.1	Manufg.			
Forging, stamping, & sintering, nec	0.1	Manufg.			
Crowns & closures & metal stamping	0.1	Manufg.			
Plate work & fabricated structural products	0.1	Manufg.			
Soap & cleaning compounds	0.1	Manufg.			
Textile bag & canvas mills	0.1	Manufg.			
Business support services	0.1	Services			
Ball & roller bearings	0.1	Manufg.			
Other computer related services, including facilities	0.1	Services			
Handtools	0.1	Manufg.			
Abrasive products	0.1	Manufg.			

Source: Benchmark Input-Output Accounts for the U.S. Economy, 2002, U.S. Department of Commerce, Washington, D.C., January 2008. The abbreviation nec stands for 'not elsewhere classified'.

OCCUPATIONS EMPLOYED BY DOLL, TOY, AND GAME MANUFACTURING

No Occupation data available for this industry.

LOCATION BY STATE AND REGIONAL CONCENTRATION

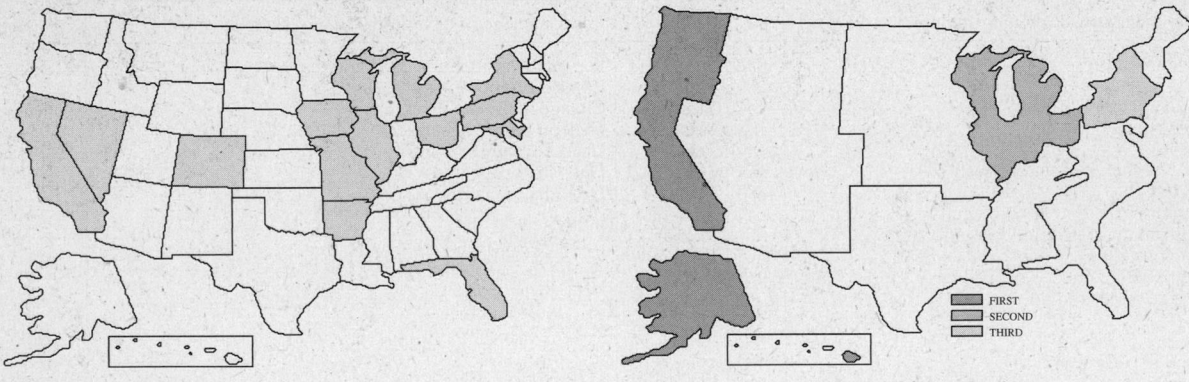

FIRST
SECOND
THIRD

INDUSTRY DATA BY STATE

State	Establish-ments	Shipments			Employment				Cost as % of Shipments	Investment per Employee ($)
		Total ($ mil)	% of U.S.	Per Establ.	Total Number	% of U.S.	Per Establ.	Wages ($/hour)		
California	140	941.7	19.4	6,726.4	3,514	16.1	25	12.10	44.4	2,620
Ohio	38	462.8	9.6	12,178.8	2,839	13.0	75	12.65	32.6	9,418
Illinois	35	224.7	4.6	6,419.3	865	4.0	25	12.94	54.5	12,554
Pennsylvania	43	179.4	3.7	4,171.4	1,110	5.1	26	11.70	46.6	1,758
New York	59	166.9	3.4	2,828.5	996	4.6	17	10.67	53.1	6,412
Nevada	10	165.0	3.4	16,501.1	416	1.9	42	13.90	32.6	18,442
Colorado	27	104.4	2.2	3,866.0	566	2.6	21	10.30	34.2	4,560
Missouri	25	85.5	1.8	3,419.8	317	1.5	13	12.83	49.5	11,543

Continued on next page.

INDUSTRY DATA BY STATE - Continued

State	Establish-ments	Shipments			Employment				Cost as % of Shipments	Investment per Employee ($)
		Total ($ mil)	% of U.S.	Per Establ.	Total Number	% of U.S.	Per Establ.	Wages ($/hour)		
Wisconsin	12	64.9	1.3	5,407.2	349	1.6	29	12.40	42.3	2,963
Maryland	12	53.8	1.1	4,487.2	195	0.9	16	19.65	68.7	1,918
Michigan	25	42.2	0.9	1,687.8	342	1.6	14	10.19	55.9	10,868
Florida	33	22.6	0.5	685.0	206	0.9	6	12.94	41.2	1,680
Arkansas	4	21.7	0.4	5,430.5	207	0.9	52	10.21	39.3	1,396
Iowa	10	18.0	0.4	1,803.8	137	0.6	14	9.84	44.0	1,460

Source: 2002 *Economic Census*. The states are in descending order of shipments or establishments (if shipment data are missing for the majority). The symbol (D) appears when data are withheld to prevent disclosure of competitive information. States marked with (D) are sorted by number of establishments. A dash (-) indicates that the data element cannot be calculated. Data may not show all states active in the NAICS category. All data available at the time of publication are shown.

NAICS 33994M - OFFICE SUPPLIES (EXCEPT PAPER) MANUFACTURING*

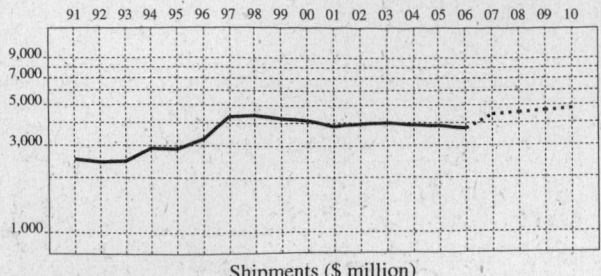

Shipments ($ million)

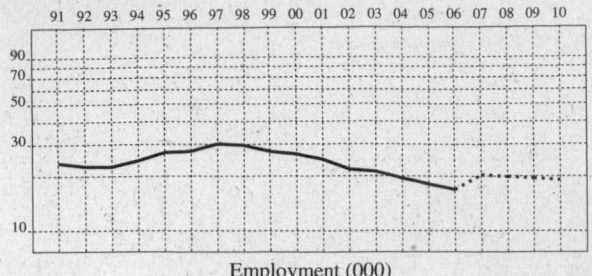

Employment (000)

GENERAL STATISTICS

| Year | Com-panies | Establishments | | Employment | | | Compensation | | Production ($ million) | | | |
		Total	with 20 or more employees	Total (000)	Production Workers (000)	Hours (Mil)	Payroll ($ mil)	Wages ($/hr)	Cost of Materials	Value Added by Manufacture	Value of Shipments	Capital Invest.
1991		830	212	23.7	16.6	32.8	515.1	8.81	1,173.9	1,355.4	2,519.8	63.3
1992	848	888	208	22.7	15.5	30.6	517.2	9.17	1,018.0	1,412.1	2,432.8	54.7
1993		875	218	22.6	15.7	31.0	541.1	9.53	1,103.3	1,328.2	2,457.5	61.5
1994		856	210	24.4	16.8	33.0	583.8	9.39	1,254.9	1,642.4	2,896.2	56.2
1995		846	205	27.0	19.5	36.7	626.6	9.62	1,244.5	1,736.8	2,872.8	56.7
1996		881	198	27.4	20.4	38.5	676.2	10.34	1,380.4	1,949.6	3,250.1	176.4
1997	1,002	1,037	227	30.1	21.2	42.1	786.6	11.20	1,765.1	2,597.8	4,332.7	120.5
1998		1,006	240	29.6	20.6	41.4	812.9	11.40	1,824.6	2,616.0	4,405.7	137.4
1999		988	231	27.3	19.5	37.4	767.2	12.16	1,706.9	2,497.6	4,235.0	130.3
2000		972	226	26.4	19.0	37.2	767.6	12.14	1,736.9	2,327.1	4,131.6	108.0
2001		918	205	24.7	17.6	34.0	739.3	12.14	1,501.2	2,322.5	3,834.7	106.1
2002	772	803	191	21.8	14.9	29.4	689.1	13.10	1,519.0	2,437.4	3,949.5	87.7
2003		784	180	21.2	14.1	27.8	737.4	13.68	1,613.3	2,380.6	3,990.5	71.8
2004		766	173	19.5	12.7	25.8	730.1	13.97	1,580.5	2,299.8	3,878.2	91.8
2005		736	161	18.1	11.3	22.9	701.9	14.53	1,595.8	2,259.7	3,840.8	72.1
2006		830P	184P	16.9	10.5	21.1	685.8	15.59	1,631.7	2,093.3	3,722.4	93.5
2007		824P	181P	20.4P	13.4P	26.7P	793.3P	15.37P	1,946.6P	2,497.2P	4,440.7P	105.2P
2008		818P	178P	19.9P	13.0P	26.0P	806.6P	15.81P	1,992.7P	2,556.4P	4,545.9P	106.6P
2009		812P	175P	19.5P	12.6P	25.3P	820.0P	16.24P	2,038.8P	2,615.5P	4,651.0P	108.0P
2010		806P	173P	19.1P	12.3P	24.6P	833.3P	16.68P	2,084.9P	2,674.6P	4,756.2P	109.5P

Sources: 1992, 1997, 2002 *Economic Census*; other years, up to 2006, are from the *Annual Survey of Manufactures*. Establishment counts for non-Census years are from *County Business Patterns*; 1997 and 2002 values are from the 1997 and 2002 censuses respectively, reported in the Federal Government's NAICS format. Other years were originally reported in equivalent SIC format. 'P's show projections by the editors.

INDICES OF CHANGE

| Year | Com-panies | Establishments | | Employment | | | Compensation | | Production ($ million) | | | |
		Total	with 20 or more employees	Total (000)	Production Workers (000)	Hours (Mil)	Payroll ($ mil)	Wages ($/hr)	Cost of Materials	Value Added by Manufacture	Value of Shipments	Capital Invest.
1992	110	111	109	104	104	104	75	70	67	58	62	62
1997	130	129	119	138	142	143	114	85	116	107	110	137
2001		114	107	113	118	116	107	93	99	95	97	121
2002	100	100	100	100	100	100	100	100	100	100	100	100
2003		98	94	97	95	95	107	104	106	98	101	82
2004		95	91	89	85	88	106	107	104	94	98	105
2005		92	84	83	76	78	102	111	105	93	97	82
2006		103P	96P	78	70	72	100	119	107	86	94	107
2007		103P	95P	94P	90P	91P	115P	117P	128P	102P	112P	120P
2008		102P	93P	91P	87P	88P	117P	121P	131P	105P	115P	122P
2009		101P	92P	89P	85P	86P	119P	124P	134P	107P	118P	123P
2010		100P	90P	88P	83P	84P	121P	127P	137P	110P	120P	125P

Sources: Same as General Statistics. Values reflect change from the base year, 2002. Values above 100 mean greater than 2002, values below 100 mean less than 2002, and the values of 100 in other years means the same as 2002. 'P's show projections by the editors.

SELECTED RATIOS

For 2002	Avg. of All Manufact.	Analyzed Industry	Index	For 2002	Avg. of All Manufact.	Analyzed Industry	Index
Employees per Establishment	42	27	65	Value Added per Production Worker	182,367	163,584	90
Payroll per Establishment	1,639,184	858,157	52	Cost per Establishment	5,769,015	1,891,656	33
Payroll per Employee	39,053	31,610	81	Cost per Employee	137,446	69,679	51
Production Workers per Establishment	30	19	63	Cost per Production Worker	195,506	101,946	52
Wages per Establishment	694,845	479,626	69	Shipments per Establishment	11,158,348	4,918,431	44
Wages per Production Worker	23,548	25,848	110	Shipments per Employee	265,847	181,170	68
Hours per Production Worker	1,980	1,973	100	Shipments per Production Worker	378,144	265,067	70
Wages per Hour	11.89	13.10	110	Investment per Establishment	361,338	109,215	30
Value Added per Establishment	5,381,325	3,035,367	56	Investment per Employee	8,609	4,023	47
Value Added per Employee	128,210	111,807	87	Investment per Production Worker	12,245	5,886	48

Sources: Same as General Statistics. The 'Average of All Manufacturing' column represents the average of all manufacturing industries reported for the most recent complete year available. The Index shows the relationship between the Average and the Analyzed Industry. For example, 100 means that they are equal; 500 that the Analyzed Industry is five times the average; 50 means that the Analyzed Industry is half the national average. The abbreviation 'na' is used to show that data are 'not available'. Ratios shown for 2002, the last complete census year.

*Equivalent to Federal Government NAICS 339941, 339942, 339943, 339944.

LEADING COMPANIES   Number shown: 75   Total sales ($ mil): **134,386**   Total employment (000): **491.6**

Company Name	Address				CEO Name	Phone	Co. Type	Sales ($ mil)	Empl. (000)
Johnson Controls Inc.	PO Box 591	Milwaukee	WI	53201		414-524-1200	P	34,624	140.0
Xerox Corp.	PO Box 1600	Stamford	CT	06904		203-968-3000	P	17,288	57.4
Lear Corp.	PO Box 5008	Southfield	MI	48086	Jim Brackenbury	248-447-1500	P	15,995	91.0
Canon U.S.A. Inc.	1 Canon Plz.	Lake Success	NY	11042	Yoroku Adachi	516-328-5000	S	10,745*	11.0
Newell Rubbermaid Inc.	10B Glenlake Pkwy.	Atlanta	GA	30328		770-407-3800	P	6,407	22.0
Pitney Bowes Inc.	1 Elmcroft Rd.	Stamford	CT	06926	Michael J. Critelli	203-356-5000	P	6,130	26.3
Lexmark International Inc.	740 New Circle Rd.	Lexington	KY	40550	Paul J. Curlander	859-232-2000	P	4,974	13.8
Harris Corp.	1025 W NASA	Melbourne	FL	32919		321-727-9100	P	4,243	16.0
Hallmark Cards Inc.	PO Box 419034	Kansas City	MO	64141		816-274-5111	R	4,100*	16.0
Oce-USA Inc.	5450 N Cumberland	Chicago	IL	60656	Jan Dix	773-714-8500	S	3,671*	3.1
Hillenbrand Industries Inc.	1069 State Rte 46E	Batesville	IN	47006		812-934-7000	P	2,024	9.9
ACCO Brands Corp.	300 Tower Pkwy.	Lincolnshire	IL	60069	David Campbell		P	1,939	6.0
Herman Miller Inc.	PO Box 302	Zeeland	MI	49464		616-654-3000	P	1,919	6.4
BE Aerospace Inc.	1400 Corp. Ctr. Way	Wellington	FL	33414	Michael B. Baughan	561-791-5000	P	1,678	5.1
Deluxe Corp.	3680 Victoria St. N	Shoreview	MN	55126		651-483-7111	P	1,606	7.6
Stenograph L.L.C.	1500 Bishop Ct.	Mount Prospect	IL	60056		847-803-1400	R	1,560*	0.2
Tri-Con Industries Ltd.	4000 NW 44th St.	Lincoln	NE	68524		402-470-3311	R	1,450*	0.3
Hill-Rom Company Inc.	1069 SR 46 E	Batesville	IN	47006	Peter H. Soderberg	812-934-7000	S	1,192*	6.5
Haworth Inc.	1 Haworth Ctr.	Holland	MI	49423	Franco Bianchi	616-393-3000	R	1,120*	8.0
Standard Register Co.	PO Box 1167	Dayton	OH	45401		937-221-1000	P	865	3.8
Schweitzer-Mauduit Int'l Inc.	100 N Point Ctr. E	Alpharetta	GA	30022	Wayne Deitrich	770-569-4272	P	715	3.5
Intertape Polymer Group	2000 S Beltline	Columbia	SC	29201	Melbourne Yull	803-376-5405	D	701*	2.6
Shachihata Incorporated USA	PO Box 2017	Torrance	CA	90505	Shinkitiro Funahashi		S	700*	0.9
White Systems Inc.	30 Boright Ave.	Kenilworth	NJ	07033	Richard Paolino	908-272-6700	S	673*	0.3
Krueger International Inc.	PO Box 8100	Green Bay	WI	54308	Richard J. Resch	920-468-8100	R	600*	4.0
Plaid Enterprises Inc.	PO Box 7600	Norcross	GA	30091	Michael McCooey	678-291-8100	R	600*	0.5
Rose Moon Inc.	6 Regent St.	Livingston	NJ	07039	Lawrence Rosen	973-535-1313	R	547*	<0.1
Sauder Woodworking Co.	PO Box 156	Archbold	OH	43502	Kevin Sauder	419-446-2711	R	525*	3.0
Flexsteel Industries Inc.	PO Box 877	Dubuque	IA	52004	Bruce Boylen	563-556-7730	P	425	2.3
Bing Group L.L.C.	11500 Oakland St.	Detroit	MI	48211	David Bing	313-867-3700	R	411*	1.1
Toshiba America Info. Systems	PO Box 19724	Irvine	CA	92623		949-583-3000	S	290*	1.7
Ricoh Electronics Inc.	2320 Redhill Ave.	Santa Ana	CA	92705	Shunsuke Nakanishi	949-250-7440	R	276*	1.1
Brother Industries Inc.	7819 N Brother Blvd	Bartlett	TN	38133	Hiromi Gunji	901-377-7777	R	258*	1.2
Virco Manufacturing Corp.	PO Box 44846	Los Angeles	CA	90044		310-533-0474	P	223	1.2
Advanced Component Tech.	PO Box 168	Northwood	IA	50459	Robert Kluver	641-324-2231	S	217*	0.9
Sauder Manufacturing Co.	PO Box 230	Archbold	OH	43502	Virgil Miller	419-445-7670	R	184*	0.2
Lifetime Products Inc.	PO Box 160010	Clearfield	UT	84016		801-776-1532	R	177*	0.3
Tachi-S Engineering USA Inc.	23227 Commerce	Farmington Hls	MI	48335		248-478-5050	R	177*	<0.1
Digi International Inc.	11001 Bren Rd. E	Minnetonka	MN	55343	Joseph T. Dunsmore	952-912-3444	P	173	0.6
Da-Lite Screen Company Inc.	PO Box 137	Warsaw	IN	46581	Richard E. Lundin	574-267-8101	R	170*	0.6
Shelby Williams Industries	150 S Williams	Morristown	TN	37813	Franklin Jacobs	423-586-7000	S	166*	1.7
A.T. Cross Co.	1 Albion Rd.	Lincoln	RI	02865	Russell A. Boss	401-333-1200	P	152	0.9
Setex Inc.	1111 McKinley Rd.	Saint Marys	OH	45885	Mutsumi Gamou	419-394-7800	S	140*	0.6
Weber Marking Systems Inc.	711 W Algonquin	Arlington Hts	IL	60005	Dennis McGrath	847-364-8500	R	134*	0.7
Bulman Products Inc.	1650 McReynolds	Grand Rapids	MI	49504		616-363-4416	R	124*	<0.1
Manufacturers Industrial Group	PO Box 1048	Lexington	TN	38351		731-967-0001	R	120*	0.9
Leach and Garner Co.	PO Box 200	North Attleboro	MA	02761		508-695-7800	R	113*	0.4
Irwin Seating Co.	PO Box 2429	Grand Rapids	MI	49501	Earle Irwin	616-574-7400	R	104*	0.7
Pamarco Technologies Inc.	235 E 11th Ave.	Roselle	NJ	07203	Richard Segel	908-241-1200	R	100*	0.7
Toyo Seat USA Corp.	2155 S Almont Ave.	Imlay City	MI	48444	Seizo Yamaguchi	810-724-0300	R	93*	0.2
Brodart Co.	500 Arch St.	Williamsport	PA	17701	Arthur Brody		R	92*	1.0
NER Data Products Inc.	307 S Delsea Dr.	Glassboro	NJ	08028	Francis C. Oatway	856-881-5524	R	92*	0.5
Dixon Ticonderoga Co.	195 Intl. Pkwy.	Heathrow	FL	32746	Richard Asta	407-829-9000	S	88*	1.4
Pentel of America Ltd.	2715 Columbia St.	Torrance	CA	90503	Yukio Horie	310-320-3831	R	86*	0.2
Diagraph Corp.	1 MO Research Park	Saint Charles	MO	63304		636-300-2000	R	84*	0.5
International Imaging Material	310 Commerce Dr.	Amherst	NY	14228		716-691-6333	R	73*	0.5
Inkcycle Inc.	11100 W 82nd St.	Shawnee Msn	KS	66214	Rick Krska	913-894-8387	R	72*	0.5
Decrane Aircraft Seating Co.	PO Box 129	Peshtigo	WI	54157		715-582-4517	R	70*	0.3
Cummins-Allison Corp.	PO Box 339	Mount Prospect	IL	60056	John Jones	847-299-9550	R	67*	0.2
Quoizel Inc.	6 Corporate Pkwy.	Goose Creek	SC	29445	Rick Seidman	631-273-2700	R	65*	0.4
ECRM Inc.	554 Clark Rd.	Tewksbury	MA	01876	Richard Black	978-851-0207	R	63*	0.2
Mity Enterprises Inc.	1301 W 400 N	Orem	UT	84057	Randall Hales	801-224-0589	P	60	0.4
Landscape Structures Inc.	PO Box 198	Delano	MN		Barbara King	763-972-3391	R	60*	0.4
Discount Labels Inc.	PO Box 709	New Albany	IN	47151	Paul V. Reilly		S	57*	<0.1
Amano Cincinnati Inc.	140 Harrison Ave.	Roseland	NJ	07068	Osamu Okagaki	973-403-1900	R	56*	0.1
Nu-Kote International Inc.	200 Beasley Dr.	Franklin	TN	37064	Ron Baiocchi	615-794-9000	R	54*	0.2
Koh-I-Noor Inc.	1 River Rd.	Leeds	MA	01053		413-584-5446	R	53*	0.4
Franklin Electronic Publishers	1 Franklin Plz.	Burlington	NJ	08016	Barry J. Lipsky	609-386-2500	P	52	0.2
West Point Products L.L.C.	PO Box 50	Valley Grove	WV	26060		304-547-1360	R	50*	0.2
Tesco Industries Inc.	1035 E Hacienda	Bellville	TX	77418			R	49*	0.1
Faurecia Automotive Seating	12209 Chandler Dr.	Walton	KY	41094	Jacques Lemorvan	859-485-1700	R	48*	0.2
Plymold Furnishing Solutions	615 Centennial Dr.	Kenyon	MN	55946	Stephen Sheppard	507-789-5111	R	46*	0.2
American Seating Co.	401 Americn Seating	Grand Rapids	MI	49504	Edward Clark	616-732-6600	R	45*	0.4
American Thermoform Corp.	1758 Brackett St.	La Verne	CA	91750		909-593-6711	R	45*	<0.1
Lewisburg Seating Systems Inc.	1801 Childress Rd.	Lewisburg	TN	37091			R	41*	0.2

Source: *Ward's Business Directory of U.S. Private and Public Companies*, Volumes 1 and 2, 2008. The company type code used is as follows: P - Public, R - Private, S - Subsidiary, D - Division, J - Joint Venture, A - Affiliate, G - Group. Sales are in millions of dollars, employees are in thousands. An asterisk (*) indicates an estimated sales volume. The symbol < stands for 'less than'. Company names and addresses are truncated, in some cases, to fit into the available space.

MATERIALS CONSUMED FOR PEN AND MECHANICAL PENCIL MANUFACTURING

Material	Quantity	Delivered Cost ($ million)
Lumber and wood products (excluding furniture)	(X)	(D)
Paperboard containers, boxes, and corrugated paperboard	(X)	13.8
Pigments, lakes, and toners (organic and inorganic)	(X)	(D)
Other chemicals and allied products	(X)	6.2
Plastics products consumed in the form of sheets, rods, etc.	(X)	20.8
Fabricated metal products, including forgings	(X)	11.8
Pens and mechanical pencils parts	(X)	125.2
All other materials, components, parts, containers, and supplies	(X)	155.1
Materials, ingredients, containers, and supplies, nsk	(X)	9.5

Source: 2002 Economic Census. Explanation of symbols used: (D): Withheld to avoid disclosure of competitive data; na: Not available; (S): Withheld because statistical norms were not met; (X): Not applicable; (Z): Less than half the unit shown; nec: Not elsewhere classified; nsk: Not specified by kind; - : zero; p : 10-19 percent estimated; q : 20-29 percent estimated.

MATERIALS CONSUMED FOR LEAD PENCIL AND ART GOOD MANUFACTURING

Material	Quantity	Delivered Cost ($ million)
Lumber and wood products (excluding furniture)	(X)	26.3
Paperboard containers, boxes, and corrugated paperboard	(X)	32.1
Pigments, lakes, and toners (organic and inorganic)	(X)	35.2
Other chemicals and allied products	(X)	32.8
Plastics products consumed in the form of sheets, rods, etc.	(X)	30.9
Fabricated metal products, including forgings	(X)	(D)
Pens and mechanical pencils parts	(X)	(D)
All other materials, components, parts, containers, and supplies	(X)	134.1
Materials, ingredients, containers, and supplies, nsk	(X)	134.7

Source: 2002 Economic Census. Explanation of symbols used: (D): Withheld to avoid disclosure of competitive data; na: Not available; (S): Withheld because statistical norms were not met; (X): Not applicable; (Z): Less than half the unit shown; nec: Not elsewhere classified; nsk: Not specified by kind; - : zero; p : 10-19 percent estimated; q : 20-29 percent estimated.

MATERIALS CONSUMED FOR MARKING DEVICE MANUFACTURING

Material	Quantity	Delivered Cost ($ million)
Lumber and wood products (excluding furniture)	(X)	10.3
Paperboard containers, boxes, and corrugated paperboard	(X)	3.1
Pigments, lakes, and toners (organic and inorganic)	(X)	(D)
Other chemicals and allied products	(X)	2.6
Plastics products consumed in the form of sheets, rods, etc.	(X)	7.4
Fabricated metal products, including forgings	(X)	1.4
Pens and mechanical pencils parts	(X)	(D)
All other materials, components, parts, containers, and supplies	(X)	70.2
Materials, ingredients, containers, and supplies, nsk	(X)	59.2

Source: 2002 Economic Census. Explanation of symbols used: (D): Withheld to avoid disclosure of competitive data; na: Not available; (S): Withheld because statistical norms were not met; (X): Not applicable; (Z): Less than half the unit shown; nec: Not elsewhere classified; nsk: Not specified by kind; - : zero; p : 10-19 percent estimated; q : 20-29 percent estimated.

MATERIALS CONSUMED FOR CARBON PAPER AND INKED RIBBON MANUFACTURING

Material	Quantity	Delivered Cost ($ million)
Textile fabrics	(X)	26.9
Paper, purchased (market)	(X)	9.2
Paperboard containers, boxes, and corrugated paperboard	(X)	6.3
Chemicals and allied products (incl. carbon black and printing inks)	(X)	83.3
All other materials, components, parts, containers, and supplies	(X)	58.4
Materials, ingredients, containers, and supplies, nsk	(X)	121.2

Source: 2002 Economic Census. Explanation of symbols used: (D): Withheld to avoid disclosure of competitive data; na: Not available; (S): Withheld because statistical norms were not met; (X): Not applicable; (Z): Less than half the unit shown; nec: Not elsewhere classified; nsk: Not specified by kind; - : zero; p : 10-19 percent estimated; q : 20-29 percent estimated.

PRODUCT SHARE DETAILS FOR PEN AND MECHANICAL PENCIL MANUFACTURING

Product or Product Class Shipments	Mil. $	Product or Product Class Shipments	Mil. $
PENS AND MECHANICAL PENCILS	1,281.2	**Other pens, mechanical pencils, and parts**	**189.2**
Pens	**581.9**	Other pens, mechanical pencils, and parts	188.5
Refillable ballpoint pens	164.2	Mechanical pencils, including clutch action and twist action	41.9
Nonrefillable ballpoint pens	327.5		
Roller pens	84.5	Refill cartridges for pens and markers	15.4
Pens, nsk	5.7	All other pens and mechanical pencil, pen, and marker parts (including pen points, renewal parts, fountain pens, desk sets, etc)	131.2
Markers	**477.2**		
Fine-point markers (thin-line writing pens)	158.0		
Broad-tipped markers (thick-line coloring pens and markers)	317.9	Other pens, mechanical pencils, and markers, and parts, nsk	0.7
Markers, nsk	1.3	**Pens and mechanical pencils, nsk, total**	**32.9**

Source: 2002 *Economic Census*. The values are product shipments in millions of dollars for 2002. Total product shipments may be lower or higher than industry shipments. See Introduction for a full discussion. Values of indented subcategories are summed in the main heading(s). The symbol (D) appears when data are withheld to prevent disclosure of competitive information. The abbreviation nsk stands for 'not specified by kind' and nec for 'not elsewhere classified'. A dash (-) means zero.

PRODUCT SHARE DETAILS FOR LEAD PENCIL AND ART GOOD MANUFACTURING

Product or Product Class Shipments	Mil. $	Product or Product Class Shipments	Mil. $
LEAD PENCILS AND ART GOODS	1,168.2	equipment, pantographs, and pyrography goods; excluding artists' crayons and other art materials, drawing and drafting tables and boards), except artist brushes	130.8
Nonmechanical (wood-cased) pencils, graphite and colored sticks, chalk, crayons, and blackboards	**494.4**		
Nonmechanical (wood-cased) pencils and graphite and colored sticks	(D)		
Nonmechanical (wood-cased) black graphite pencils	185.3	Other art materials (including modeling clay, other modeling material, chalk, watercolors, tempera colors, fingerpaint, block printing ink, etc), excluding drawing and india ink	272.3
Other nonmechanical (wood-cased) pencils and graphite and colored sticks, including colored and indelible nonmechanical pencils and refill sticks for mechanical pencils sold separately	(D)		
		Artists' equipment and materials, nsk	8.4
Crayons and chalk, except artists', including tailors' chalk	(D)	**Nonelectric office machines, including nonelectric gummed tape moisteners, paper cutters and trimmers, pencil sharpeners, perforators, punches, scalers for gummed tape, staple removers, and staplers**	**170.8**
Blackboards	96.0		
Artists' equipment and materials	**411.6**		
Artists' equipment (including children's school art		**Lead pencils and art goods, nsk, total**	**91.3**

Source: 2002 *Economic Census*. The values are product shipments in millions of dollars for 2002. Total product shipments may be lower or higher than industry shipments. See Introduction for a full discussion. Values of indented subcategories are summed in the main heading(s). The symbol (D) appears when data are withheld to prevent disclosure of competitive information. The abbreviation nsk stands for 'not specified by kind' and nec for 'not elsewhere classified'. A dash (-) means zero.

PRODUCT SHARE DETAILS FOR MARKING DEVICE MANUFACTURING

Product or Product Class Shipments	Mil. $	Product or Product Class Shipments	Mil. $
MARKING DEVICES	640.2	numerals, stamp pads, branding irons, etc	246.2
Plastics and rubber dies, hand stamps, typeholders, and permanently inked stamps	204.1	Metal hand stamps, steel incising and embossing dies, letter and figure stamps, type and type holders, steel embossing and incising numbering heads, and nonferrous types and dies	71.0
Plastics and rubber dies, hand stamps, and typeholders	118.2		
Plastics and rubber permanently inked stamps, except print dies	85.9		
Mechanical hand stamps, self-inkers including daters, time and numbering stamps, and metal and rubber wheel band goods	99.0	Other marking devices, including branding irons, embossing seals, figures, letters, numerals, stamp pads, and stencils	175.1
Other marking devices, such as stencils, letters, figures,		Marking devices, nsk, total	90.9

Source: 2002 *Economic Census*. The values are product shipments in millions of dollars for 2002. Total product shipments may be lower or higher than industry shipments. See Introduction for a full discussion. Values of indented subcategories are summed in the main heading(s). The symbol (D) appears when data are withheld to prevent disclosure of competitive information. The abbreviation nsk stands for 'not specified by kind' and nec for 'not elsewhere classified'. A dash (-) means zero.

PRODUCT SHARE DETAILS FOR CARBON PAPER AND INKED RIBBON MANUFACTURING

Product or Product Class Shipments	Mil. $	Product or Product Class Shipments	Mil. $
CARBON PAPER AND INKED RIBBONS	651.0	Other inked ribbons	77.1
Inked ribbons	**491.5**	Inked ribbons, nsk	4.7
Inked computer (electronic data processing) ribbons	372.3	**Carbon paper and stencil paper**	**93.2**
Other inked ribbons, including typewriter	114.6	**Carbon paper and inked ribbons, nsk, total**	**66.3**
Inked typewriter ribbons	37.5		

Source: 2002 *Economic Census*. The values are product shipments in millions of dollars for 2002. Total product shipments may be lower or higher than industry shipments. See Introduction for a full discussion. Values of indented subcategories are summed in the main heading(s). The symbol (D) appears when data are withheld to prevent disclosure of competitive information. The abbreviation nsk stands for 'not specified by kind' and nec for 'not elsewhere classified'. A dash (-) means zero.

INPUTS AND OUTPUTS FOR OFFICE SUPPLIES (EXCEPT PAPER) MANUFACTURING

Economic Sector or Industry Providing Inputs	%	Sector	Economic Sector or Industry Buying Outputs	%	Sector
Compensation of employees	25.3		Personal consumption expenditures	35.1	
Office supplies (except paper)	5.1	Manufg.	General S/L govt. services	15.0	S/L Govt
Wholesale trade	2.9	Trade	Exports of goods & services	7.5	Cap Inv
Truck transportation	2.6	Util.	Office supplies (except paper)	3.7	Manufg.
Management of companies & enterprises	2.4	Services	Hotels & motels, including casino hotels	2.9	Services
Basic organic chemicals, nec	2.4	Manufg.	Elementary & secondary schools	2.9	Services
Plastics packaging materials, film & sheet	1.9	Manufg.	Food services & drinking places	2.8	Services
Nonwoven fabric mills	1.9	Manufg.	Child day care services	2.7	Services
Synthetic dyes & pigments	1.9	Manufg.	Advertising & related services	1.8	Services
Paperboard containers	1.8	Manufg.	S/L govt. invest., education	1.4	S/L Govt
Sawmills & wood preservation	1.4	Manufg.	Retail trade	1.3	Trade
Nonmetallic minerals, nec	1.4	Mining	Data processing, hosting, & related services	1.3	Services
Advertising & related services	1.2	Services	Specialized design services	1.2	Services
Semiconductors & related devices	1.0	Manufg.	Warehousing & storage	1.0	Util.
Printed circuit assemblies (electronic assemblies)	1.0	Manufg.	Accounting, tax preparation, bookkeeping, & payroll	1.0	Services
Plastics products, nec	1.0	Manufg.	General Federal government services, nondefense	0.9	Fed Govt
Basic inorganic chemicals, nec	0.9	Manufg.	Legal services	0.9	Services
Real estate	0.9	Fin/R.E.	Physician, dentist, other health practitioner offices	0.9	Services
Securities, commodity contracts, investments	0.8	Fin/R.E.	Architectural, engineering, & related services	0.8	Services
Power generation & supply	0.7	Util.	Business support services	0.8	Services
Lessors of nonfinancial assets	0.6	Fin/R.E.	Educational services, nec	0.7	Services
Chemical products & preparations, nec	0.6	Manufg.	Wholesale trade	0.7	Trade
Machine shops	0.5	Manufg.	S/L govt. invest., other	0.7	S/L Govt
Rail transportation	0.4	Util.	Environmental & other technical consulting services	0.7	Services
Taxes on production & imports, less subsidies	0.4		Commercial & industrial machinery rental & leasing	0.6	Fin/R.E.
Architectural, engineering, & related services	0.4	Services	Motor vehicle parts	0.5	Manufg.
Paper mills	0.4	Manufg.	Monetary authorities/depository credit intermediation	0.5	Fin/R.E.
Adhesives	0.3	Manufg.	Civic, social, & professional organizations	0.5	Services
Cutting tools & machine tool accessories	0.3	Manufg.	Printing	0.5	Manufg.
Unlaminated plastics profile shapes	0.3	Manufg.	Hospitals	0.5	Services
Monetary authorities/depository credit intermediation	0.3	Fin/R.E.	Telecommunications	0.5	Services
Coating, engraving, heat treating & allied activities	0.3	Manufg.	Nonresidential structures, nec	0.4	Construct.
Rubber products, nec	0.3	Manufg.	Nondepository credit intermediation activities	0.4	Fin/R.E.
Ground or treated mineral & earth	0.3	Manufg.	Management, scientific, & technical consulting	0.3	Services
Automotive equipment rental & leasing	0.3	Fin/R.E.	Employment services	0.3	Services
Petroleum lubricating oil & grease	0.3	Manufg.	Medical & diagnostic labs & outpatient services	0.3	Services
Legal services	0.3	Services	Individual & family services	0.3	Services
Paints & coatings	0.3	Manufg.	Real estate	0.3	Fin/R.E.
Professional, scientific, technical services, nec	0.3	Services	Private fixed investment	0.2	
Iron & steel mills & ferroalloys	0.2	Manufg.	Independent artists, writers, & performers	0.2	Services
Abrasive products	0.2	Manufg.	Automotive equipment rental & leasing	0.2	Fin/R.E.
Paperboard mills	0.2	Manufg.	Securities, commodity contracts, investments	0.2	Fin/R.E.
Telecommunications	0.2	Services	Computer system design services	0.2	Services
Accounting, tax preparation, bookkeeping, & payroll	0.2	Services	Photographic services	0.2	Services
Warehousing & storage	0.2	Util.	Residential structures, nec	0.2	Construct.
Management, scientific, & technical consulting	0.2	Services	Residential permanent site structures	0.1	Construct.
Noncomparable imports	0.2	Foreign	Software publishers	0.1	Services
Scientific research & development services	0.2	Services	Scientific research & development services	0.1	Services
Data processing, hosting, & related services	0.2	Services	Scenic & sightseeing transport & related services	0.1	Util.
Natural gas distribution	0.2	Util.	Waste management & remediation services	0.1	Services
Textile & fabric finishing mills	0.2	Manufg.	Management of companies & enterprises	0.1	Services
Maintenance/repair of nonresidential structures	0.2	Construct.	Insurance agencies, brokerages, & related activities	0.1	Fin/R.E.
Services to buildings & dwellings	0.2	Services	Petroleum refineries	0.1	Manufg.
Employment services	0.1	Services	Amusement & recreation, nec	0.1	Services
Commercial & industrial machinery rental & leasing	0.1	Fin/R.E.	Community food, housing, relief, & rehabilitation	0.1	Services
Food services & drinking places	0.1	Services	Internet publishing & broadcasting	0.1	Services
Alkalies & chlorine	0.1	Manufg.			
Reconstituted wood products	0.1	Manufg.			
Artificial & synthetic fibers & filaments	0.1	Manufg.			
Laminated plastics plates, sheets, & shapes	0.1	Manufg.			
Business support services	0.1	Services			
Relay & industrial controls	0.1	Manufg.			
Turned products & screws, nuts, & bolts	0.1	Manufg.			
Nondepository credit intermediation activities	0.1	Fin/R.E.			
Automotive repair & maintenance, ex. car washes	0.1	Services			
Fabricated metals, nec	0.1	Manufg.			
Other computer related services, including facilities	0.1	Services			

Source: Benchmark Input-Output Accounts for the U.S. Economy, 2002, U.S. Department of Commerce, Washington, D.C., January 2008. The abbreviation nec stands for 'not elsewhere classified'.

OCCUPATIONS EMPLOYED BY OFFICE SUPPLIES (EXCEPT PAPER) MANUFACTURING

No Occupation data available for this industry.

LOCATION BY STATE AND REGIONAL CONCENTRATION

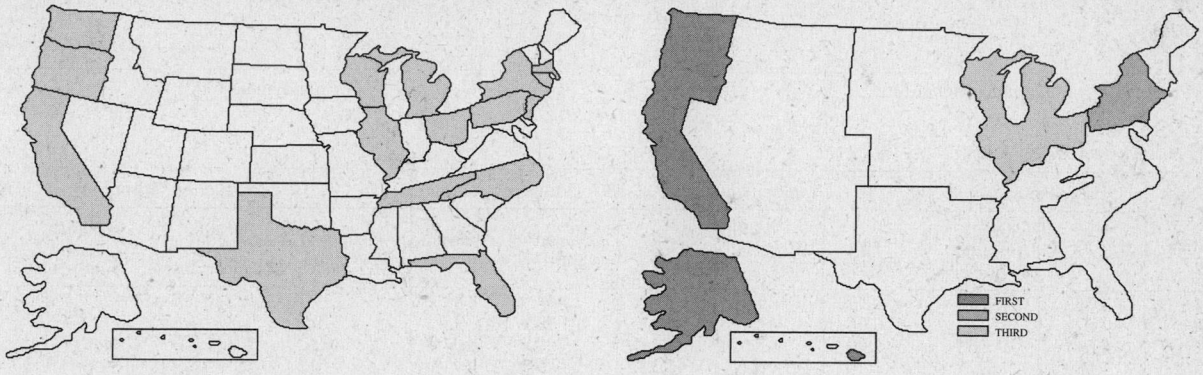

FIRST
SECOND
THIRD

INDUSTRY DATA BY STATE

State	Establish-ments	Shipments			Employment				Cost as % of Shipments	Investment per Employee ($)
		Total ($ mil)	% of U.S.	Per Establ.	Total Number	% of U.S.	Per Establ.	Wages ($/hour)		
California	120	379.6	9.6	3,163.6	2,865	13.1	24	14.16	42.9	5,371
Illinois	12	278.6	7.1	23,214.8	895	4.1	75	13.69	46.3	9,103
New York	55	240.6	6.1	4,375.0	1,611	7.4	29	13.66	41.5	4,436
Florida	32	214.7	5.4	6,708.5	1,242	5.7	39	14.65	36.2	1,862
Tennessee	7	152.8	3.9	21,833.9	1,015	4.7	145	14.43	44.0	2,807
New Jersey	45	119.8	3.0	2,662.8	896	4.1	20	11.73	42.7	3,958
Pennsylvania	10	85.4	2.2	8,541.6	326	1.5	33	15.66	72.1	4,479
Ohio	15	72.1	1.8	4,803.4	500	2.3	33	13.84	46.6	1,358
Oregon	8	35.4	0.9	4,429.3	211	1.0	26	10.72	49.4	2,521
Wisconsin	5	27.3	0.7	5,463.2	422	1.9	84	16.72	15.5	1,934
Washington	16	20.8	0.5	1,298.5	249	1.1	16	13.38	44.4	1,498
Texas	34	19.3	0.5	566.4	271	1.2	8	11.64	31.7	1,428
Michigan	17	17.1	0.4	1,004.2	160	0.7	9	13.44	38.4	800
Massachusetts	11	13.6	0.3	1,239.8	125	0.6	11	13.52	27.0	3,160
Connecticut	11	8.9	0.2	807.4	108	0.5	10	10.68	36.0	861
North Carolina	10	5.9	0.2	593.9	111	0.5	11	10.13	31.4	766

Source: 2002 *Economic Census*. The states are in descending order of shipments or establishments (if shipment data are missing for the majority). The symbol (D) appears when data are withheld to prevent disclosure of competitive information. States marked with (D) are sorted by number of establishments. A dash (-) indicates that the data element cannot be calculated. Data may not show all states active in the NAICS category. All data available at the time of publication are shown.

NAICS 339950 - SIGN MANUFACTURING

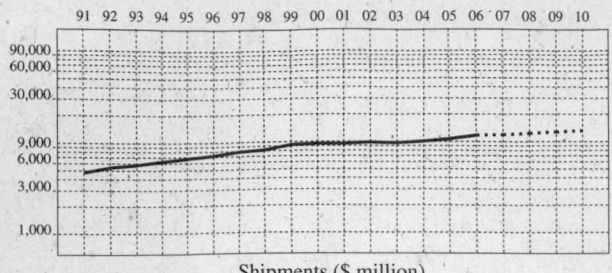

Shipments ($ million)

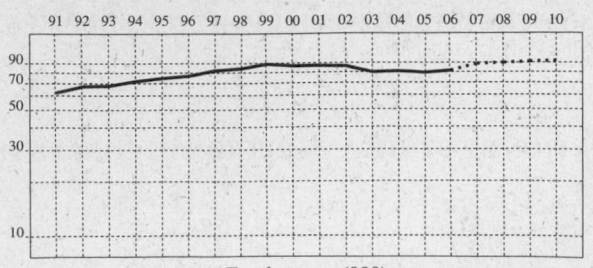

Employment (000)

GENERAL STATISTICS

| Year | Com-panies | Establishments | | Employment | | | Compensation | | Production ($ million) | | | |
		Total	with 20 or more employees	Total (000)	Production Workers (000)	Hours (Mil)	Payroll ($ mil)	Wages ($/hr)	Cost of Materials	Value Added by Manufacture	Value of Shipments	Capital Invest.
1991		3,766	766	62.2	39.5	79.2	1,453.9	8.92	2,237.7	2,529.5	4,755.0	105.0
1992	4,467	4,577	762	67.5	42.5	86.1	1,679.9	9.69	2,279.2	3,164.8	5,420.1	96.9
1993		4,617	768	68.0	43.6	86.7	1,728.0	10.09	2,462.5	3,350.0	5,777.3	106.7
1994		4,589	775	72.0	46.2	93.9	1,845.9	9.79	2,580.5	3,718.9	6,279.2	144.3
1995		4,885	832	74.8	47.7	96.1	1,972.4	10.15	2,782.1	3,992.6	6,735.5	238.7
1996		5,546	865	76.8	49.7	107.6	2,081.3	9.61	2,996.2	4,246.0	7,207.3	172.1
1997	5,559	5,690	928	82.2	53.5	102.4	2,367.3	11.70	3,314.8	4,551.6	7,856.6	236.5
1998		5,926	968	84.2	55.4	109.7	2,427.9	11.36	3,473.0	4,715.5	8,165.5	179.1
1999		6,007	1,008	89.0	57.6	112.9	2,714.7	12.00	3,942.5	5,381.2	9,268.7	307.2
2000		6,105	1,019	86.9	56.0	109.2	2,779.6	12.68	4,111.1	5,443.2	9,509.1	349.7
2001		6,041	1,011	87.1	55.0	108.8	2,815.7	12.80	4,103.6	5,403.6	9,517.4	290.3
2002	6,115	6,259	1,021	86.4	55.6	106.8	2,989.5	14.05	3,953.8	5,855.3	9,822.5	243.3
2003		6,263	1,002	80.0	50.9	100.9	2,900.2	13.77	3,882.5	5,825.5	9,683.0	162.9
2004		6,375	1,018	80.9	49.9	100.3	2,998.6	14.52	4,218.3	5,954.1	10,042.3	223.6
2005		6,308	987	79.4	49.2	97.2	3,010.5	14.86	4,671.8	6,118.8	10,725.8	216.9
2006		6,913P	1,091P	81.4	50.4	98.4	3,259.2	15.64	5,111.5	6,760.2	11,767.8	284.9
2007		7,086P	1,113P	88.8P	55.8P	109.1P	3,441.0P	15.72P	5,177.6P	6,847.6P	11,920.0P	294.9P
2008		7,259P	1,135P	90.0P	56.5P	110.2P	3,558.9P	16.16P	5,363.5P	7,093.4P	12,347.9P	304.9P
2009		7,432P	1,157P	91.2P	57.2P	111.3P	3,676.8P	16.60P	5,549.3P	7,339.2P	12,775.7P	314.9P
2010		7,604P	1,179P	92.3P	57.8P	112.4P	3,794.7P	17.04P	5,735.1P	7,585.0P	13,203.6P	324.9P

Sources: 1992, 1997, 2002 *Economic Census*; other years, up to 2006, are from the *Annual Survey of Manufactures*. Establishment counts for non-Census years are from *County Business Patterns*; 1997 and 2002 values are from the 1997 and 2002 censuses respectively, reported in the Federal Government's NAICS format. Other years were originally reported in equivalent SIC format. 'P's show projections by the editors.

INDICES OF CHANGE

| Year | Com-panies | Establishments | | Employment | | | Compensation | | Production ($ million) | | | |
		Total	with 20 or more employees	Total (000)	Production Workers (000)	Hours (Mil)	Payroll ($ mil)	Wages ($/hr)	Cost of Materials	Value Added by Manufacture	Value of Shipments	Capital Invest.
1992	73	73	75	78	76	81	56	69	58	54	55	40
1997	91	91	91	95	96	96	79	83	84	78	80	97
2001		97	99	101	99	102	94	91	104	92	97	119
2002	100	100	100	100	100	100	100	100	100	100	100	100
2003		100	98	93	92	94	97	98	98	99	99	67
2004		102	100	94	90	94	100	103	107	102	102	92
2005		101	97	92	88	91	101	106	118	105	109	89
2006		110P	107P	94	91	92	109	111	129	115	120	117
2007		113P	109P	103P	100P	102P	115P	112P	131P	117P	121P	121P
2008		116P	111P	104P	102P	103P	119P	115P	136P	121P	126P	125P
2009		119P	113P	106P	103P	104P	123P	118P	140P	125P	130P	129P
2010		121P	116P	107P	104P	105P	127P	121P	145P	130P	134P	134P

Sources: Same as General Statistics. Values reflect change from the base year, 2002. Values above 100 mean greater than 2002, values below 100 mean less than 2002, and the values of 100 in other years means the same as 2002. 'P's show projections by the editors.

SELECTED RATIOS

For 2002	Avg. of All Manufact.	Analyzed Industry	Index	For 2002	Avg. of All Manufact.	Analyzed Industry	Index
Employees per Establishment	42	14	33	Value Added per Production Worker	182,367	105,311	58
Payroll per Establishment	1,639,184	477,632	29	Cost per Establishment	5,769,015	631,698	11
Payroll per Employee	39,053	34,601	89	Cost per Employee	137,446	45,762	33
Production Workers per Establishment	30	9	30	Cost per Production Worker	195,506	71,112	36
Wages per Establishment	694,845	239,741	35	Shipments per Establishment	11,158,348	1,569,340	14
Wages per Production Worker	23,548	26,988	115	Shipments per Employee	265,847	113,686	43
Hours per Production Worker	1,980	1,921	97	Shipments per Production Worker	378,144	176,664	47
Wages per Hour	11.89	14.05	118	Investment per Establishment	361,338	38,872	11
Value Added per Establishment	5,381,325	935,501	17	Investment per Employee	8,609	2,816	33
Value Added per Employee	128,210	67,770	53	Investment per Production Worker	12,245	4,376	36

Sources: Same as General Statistics. The 'Average of All Manufacturing' column represents the average of all manufacturing industries reported for the most recent complete year available. The Index shows the relationship between the Average and the Analyzed Industry. For example, 100 means that they are equal; 500 that the Analyzed Industry is five times the average; 50 means that the Analyzed Industry is half the national average. The abbreviation 'na' is used to show that data are 'not available'. Ratios shown for 2002, the last complete census year.

LEADING COMPANIES

Number shown: **75**   Total sales ($ mil): **16,278**   Total employment (000): **70.3**

Company Name	Address				CEO Name	Phone	Co. Type	Sales ($ mil)	Empl. (000)
Hallmark Cards Inc.	PO Box 419034	Kansas City	MO	64141		816-274-5111	R	4,100*	16.0
DCI Marketing Inc.	PO Box 514010	Milwaukee	WI	53203	Joseph Asfour	414-228-7000	R	2,840*	0.2
Freeman Cos.	PO Box 650036	Dallas	TX	75265	Donald S. Freeman, Jr	214-670-9000	R	2,259*	3.8
American Greetings Corp.	1 American Rd.	Cleveland	OH	44144		216-252-7300	P	1,745	28.9
Lamar Advertising Co.	PO Box 66338	Baton Rouge	LA	70896	Kevin P. Reilly, Jr.	225-926-1000	P	1,210	3.2
Daktronics Inc.	PO Box 5128	Brookings	SD	57006	Aelred Kurtenbach	605-697-4000	P	433	3.2
Stoffel Seals Corp.	PO Box 825	Nyack	NY	10960	Charles Fuehrer	845-353-3800	R	370*	0.2
Rock-Tenn Converting Co.	5921 Grassy Creek	Winston-Salem	NC	27105	James L. Einstein	336-661-1700	S	187*	0.7
Everbrite L.L.C.	PO Box 20020	Milwaukee	WI	53220		414-529-3500	R	138*	0.1
Enterprise Products Inc.	6846 Suva St.	Bell Gardens	CA	90201	Ron Spicer	562-927-2515	R	134*	0.2
Persona Inc.	PO Box 210	Watertown	SD	57201	David Holien	605-882-2244	R	129*	0.2
Derse Inc.	1234 N 62nd St.	Milwaukee	WI	53213	Adam Beckett	414-257-2000	R	101*	0.1
Pop Displays USA L.L.C.	555 Tuckahoe Rd.	Yonkers	NY	10710		914-771-4200	R	86*	0.9
Camco Manufacturing Inc.	121 Landmark Dr.	Greensboro	NC	27409	Donald Caine	336-668-7661	R	84*	0.2
Icon Identity Solutions Inc.	1418 Elmhurst Rd.	Elk Grove Vlg	IL	60007	Greg Goulette	847-364-2250	R	83*	0.2
Alliance Display and Packaging	5950 Grassy Creek	Winston-Salem	NC	27105	James A. Rubright	336-661-1700	D	81*	0.3
World Manufacturing Inc.	350 Fischer Ave.	Costa Mesa	CA	92626	Michael Robinson	714-662-3539	R	78*	0.4
St Joseph Packaging Inc.	PO Box 579	Saint Joseph	MO	64502	Charles Hamilton	816-233-3181	R	77*	0.1
Vernon Co.	PO Box 600	Newton	IA	50208		641-792-9000	R	73*	0.7
Magnet L.L.C.	PO Box 605	Washington	MO	63090	Bill Korowitz	636-239-5661	R	71*	0.3
Ad Art Co.	3260 E 26th St.	Los Angeles	CA	90023	Joseph DeMarco	323-981-8941	R	68*	0.3
American Household Products	PO Box 310	Leeds	AL	35094	Burns Roensch	205-699-5144	R	68*	<0.1
Formetco Inc.	PO Box 1989	Duluth	GA	30096	Lawrence Garrett	770-476-7000	R	63*	0.1
Zippo Manufacturing Company	PO Box 364	Bradford	PA	16701	Greg Booth	814-368-2700	R	62*	0.8
Western Badge and Trophy Co.	831 Monterey Pass	Monterey Park	CA	91754	Wesley Ru	323-735-1201	R	59*	<0.1
Brede Exposition Service	2211 Broadway St.	Minneapolis	MN	55413	William C. Casey III	612-331-4540	R	54*	0.1
Imagepoint Inc.	PO Box 59043	Knoxville	TN	37950		865-251-1511	R	54*	0.3
Norampac New York City Inc.	55-15 Grand Ave.	Maspeth	NY	11378	Eric Laflamme	718-386-3200	S	53*	0.3
HB Stubbs Co.	27027 Mound Rd.	Warren	MI	48092	Scott Stubbs	586-574-9700	R	50*	0.2
Fluoresco Lighting-Sign Maint.	PO Box 27042	Tucson	AZ	85726	Ladd Kleiman	520-623-7953	R	49*	0.2
RTC Industries Inc.	2800 Golf Rd.	Rolling Mdws	IL	60008	Richard Nathan	847-640-2400	R	46*	0.2
Frank Mayer and Associates	PO Box 105	Grafton	WI	53024	Frank Mayer	262-377-4700	R	45*	<0.1
Marco Display Specialists, GP	PO Box 123439	Fort Worth	TX	76121	Darrell Cooper	817-244-8300	R	44*	0.3
Philadelphia Sign Co.	707 W Sprg Garden	Palmyra	NJ	08065	Bill Trucksess	856-829-1460	R	42*	0.3
Ideal Box Co.	4800 S Austin Ave.	Chicago	IL	60638	Scott Eisen	708-594-3100	R	41*	0.2
Longview Fibre Cntrl Container	PO Box 2008	Milwaukee	WI	53201	Richard Wollenberg	414-264-8100	D	39*	0.2
Mobile Media Inc.	7023 W Mill Rd.	Milwaukee	WI	53218	Larry Anthony	414-353-0511	R	38*	0.3
Prime Resources Corp.	1100 Boston Ave.	Bridgeport	CT	06610	Robert Brenner	203-331-9100	R	38*	0.4
Schult Industries L.L.C.	900 NW Hunter Dr.	Blue Springs	MO	64015		816-874-4600	R	38*	<0.1
Stouse Inc.	PO Box 3	Gardner	KS	66030	Bary Marquardt	913-764-5757	R	36*	0.3
Miller Dial Corp.	4400 Temple City	El Monte	CA	91731	Garrett Morelock	626-444-4555	R	36*	0.1
G and C Supply Company Inc.	1105 Hwy. Ste. 70A	Atwood	TN	38220	Kay Greenway	731-662-7193	R	36*	<0.1
Egads L.L.C.	3235 Polaris Ave.	Las Vegas	NV	89102		702-314-7777	R	34*	0.2
UPSHOT Direct Inc.	303 E Wacker Dr.	Chicago	IL	60601	Brian Kristofek	312-943-0900	S	33*	0.2
Russell and Miller Inc.	PO Box 2152	Santa Fe Spgs	CA	90670	Michael Wooten	562-946-6900	S	33*	<0.1
Econoco Corp.	PO Box 29	Hicksville	NY	11802	Barry Rosenberg	516-935-7700	R	32*	<0.1
Empire Screen Printing Inc.	PO Box 218	Onalaska	WI	54650	James Brush	608-783-3301	R	32*	0.3
Bullet Line Inc.	PO Box 694470	Miami	FL	33269	William Rosenfeld	305-623-9223	R	31*	0.3
Elderlee Inc.	PO Box 10	Oaks Corners	NY	14518	Robert Hirschman	315-789-6670	R	31*	0.1
Encore Image Group Inc.	1445 Sepulveda	Torrance	CA	90501	Kozell Boren	310-534-7500	R	31*	0.1
Moore Response Marketing Svcs	1200 Lakeside Dr.	Bannockburn	IL	60015	Mark Angelson	847-607-6000	S	31*	0.3
Dee Sign Co.	6163 Allen Rd.	West Chester	OH	45069	Braden Huenefeld	513-779-3333	R	31*	0.1
Jacobson, S I Manufacturing	1414 Jacobson Dr.	Waukegan	IL	60085	Larry Futterman	847-623-1414	R	31*	0.2
Peachtree Packaging Inc.	770 Marathon Pkwy.	Lawrenceville	GA	30045	Wayne Morrison	770-822-1304	R	31*	0.2
Metallics Inc.	PO Box 99	Onalaska	WI	54650	Doug Dale	608-781-5200	R	30*	0.2
Nelson Nameplate Co.	2800 Casitas Ave.	Los Angeles	CA	90039		323-663-3971	R	30*	0.3
SGI Integrated Graphic Systems	14902 Sommermyr	Houston	TX	77041		713-744-4100	D	30*	0.2
Noteworthy Industries Inc.	PO Box 490	Amsterdam	NY	12010	Carol Constantino	518-842-2660	R	30*	0.1
Display Specialties Inc.	9 Beacon Dr.	Wilder	KY	41076	Douglas Bray	859-781-7711	R	29*	<0.1
Harbor Industries Inc.	14130 172nd Ave.	Grand Haven	MI	49417		616-842-5330	R	29*	0.1
Adaptive Micro Systems Inc.	7840 N 86th St.	Milwaukee	WI	53224	William Latz	414-357-2020	R	28*	0.3
New England Wooden Ware Corp.	PO Box 508	Gardner	MA	01440	David Urquhart	978-632-3600	R	28*	0.1
Atlas Pen and Pencil Corp.	3040 N 29th Ave.	Hollywood	FL	33020		954-920-4444	R	27*	0.3
Display Systems Inc.	57-13 49th Street	Maspeth	NY	11378	Ben Weshler	718-628-2600	R	27*	0.2
International Patterns Inc.	50 Inez Dr.	Bay Shore	NY	11706	Shelley Beckwith	631-952-2000	R	26*	0.1
Correctional Ind. Georgia Adm.	2984 Clifton Sprngs	Decatur	GA	30034		404-244-5100	R	26*	<0.1
David Weber Co.	3500 Richmond St.	Philadelphia	PA	19134	James Doherty	215-426-3500	R	26*	0.1
Lone Star Corrugated Container	PO Box 177357	Irving	TX	75017	Jerry Hardison	972-579-1551	R	26*	0.1
Fellers Inc.	6566 E Skelly Dr.	Tulsa	OK	74145	Frank Fellers	918-621-4400	R	25*	0.1
Drake Co.	PO Box 7948	Houston	TX	77270	John Carrico	713-869-9121	R	25*	0.1
Morgan Signs Inc.	PO Box 77	State College	PA	16804	Marian Fredman	814-238-5051	R	25*	<0.1
Work Area Protection Corp.	PO Box 4087	St. Charles	IL	60174	Thomas Bednar	630-377-9100	S	24*	<0.1
Display Producers Inc.	1260 Zerega Ave.	Bronx	NY	10462	Robert Gottlieb	718-904-1200	R	24*	0.3
Gold Bond Inc.	PO Box 967	Hixson	TN	37343	Donald Godsey	423-842-5844	R	24*	0.2
Bennett Packaging/Kansas City	220 NW Space Ctr.	Lees Summit	MO	64064	Kathy Bennett	816-379-5001	R	24*	0.1

Source: *Ward's Business Directory of U.S. Private and Public Companies*, Volumes 1 and 2, 2008. The company type code used is as follows: P - Public, R - Private, S - Subsidiary, D - Division, J - Joint Venture, A - Affiliate, G - Group. Sales are in millions of dollars, employees are in thousands. An asterisk (*) indicates an estimated sales volume. The symbol < stands for 'less than'. Company names and addresses are truncated, in some cases, to fit into the available space.

MATERIALS CONSUMED

Material	Quantity	Delivered Cost ($ million)
Veneer and plywood	(X)	38.6
Paper and paperboard products (incl. paperboard boxes, etc.)	(X)	43.9
Plastics resins consumed in the form of granules, pellets, etc.	(X)	46.6
Paints, varnishes, stains, lacquers, shellacs, japans, enamels, etc.	(X)	37.9
Plastics products consumed in the form of sheets, rods, etc.	(X)	218.3
Metal hardware (inc. hinges, handles, locks, casters, etc.)	(X)	52.5
All other fabricated metal products (exc. castings and forgings)	(X)	174.2
Steel shapes and forms (exc. castings, forgings, fabr. metal products)	(X)	70.5
Nonferrous shapes and forms	(X)	68.8
Specialty transformers and fluorescent ballasts	(X)	51.0
Wood (excluding veneer and plywood)	(X)	35.4
Manufactured products used for advertising specialities	(X)	95.1
Textiles and fabrics	(X)	20.2
Printing inks	(X)	18.7
All other materials, components, parts, containers, and supplies	(X)	532.5
Materials, ingredients, containers, and supplies, nsk	(X)	1,627.7

Source: 2002 *Economic Census*. Explanation of symbols used: (D): Withheld to avoid disclosure of competitive data; na: Not available; (S): Withheld because statistical norms were not met; (X): Not applicable; (Z): Less than half the unit shown; nec: Not elsewhere classified; nsk: Not specified by kind; - : zero; p : 10-19 percent estimated; q : 20-29 percent estimated.

PRODUCT SHARE DETAILS

Product or Product Class Shipments	Mil. $	Product or Product Class Shipments	Mil. $
SIGNS	8,915.5	Nonelectric signs, including counter and floor displays, point-of-purchase, and other signs and displays	3,004.5
Electric signs	**2,586.8**	Nonelectric screen printed metal signs and displays	372.4
Luminous tubing electric signs (neon, argon, hydrogen, etc)	805.9	Other nonelectric metal signs and displays	565.6
Fluorescent lamp electric signs	653.0	Nonelectric screen printed wood signs and displays	90.8
Incandescent bulb electric signs and other electric signs	1,093.6	Other nonelectric wood signs and displays	259.7
Incandescent bulb, electronic variable message display signs	164.2	Nonelectric screen printed other than wood or metal signs and displays	262.9
Other incandescent bulb signs	116.7	Other printed or unprinted nonelectric other than wood or metal signs and displays	1,453.0
All other electric signs (including combinations of luminous fluorescent and incandescent)	812.7	Nonelectric signs, including counter and floor displays, point-of-purchase, and other signs and displays, nsk	61.8
Electric signs, nsk	34.2	**Advertising specialties**	**1,462.6**
Nonelectric signs, including counter and floor displays, point-of-purchase, and other signs and displays	**3,066.3**	**Signs, nsk, total**	**1,799.8**

Source: 2002 *Economic Census*. The values are product shipments in millions of dollars for 2002. Total product shipments may be lower or higher than industry shipments. See Introduction for a full discussion. Values of indented subcategories are summed in the main heading(s). The symbol (D) appears when data are withheld to prevent disclosure of competitive information. The abbreviation nsk stands for 'not specified by kind' and nec for 'not elsewhere classified'. A dash (-) means zero.

INPUTS AND OUTPUTS FOR SIGN MANUFACTURING

Economic Sector or Industry Providing Inputs	%	Sector	Economic Sector or Industry Buying Outputs	%	Sector
Compensation of employees	36.0		Private fixed investment	88.8	
Plastics products, nec	6.1	Manufg.	Signs	3.5	Manufg.
Management of companies & enterprises	4.1	Services	Nonresidential structures, nec	2.9	Construct.
Plastics packaging materials, film & sheet	4.0	Manufg.	Exports of goods & services	1.7	Cap Inv
Wholesale trade	3.6	Trade	Wholesale trade	1.0	Trade
Signs	2.4	Manufg.	Commercial & health care structures	0.6	Construct.
Taxes on production & imports, less subsidies	2.0		Monetary authorities/depository credit intermediation	0.5	Fin/R.E.
Real estate	1.8	Fin/R.E.	Nondepository credit intermediation activities	0.4	Fin/R.E.
Advertising & related services	1.5	Services	Securities, commodity contracts, investments	0.4	Fin/R.E.
Custom roll forming	1.4	Manufg.	Residential permanent site structures	0.1	Construct.
Iron & steel mills & ferroalloys	1.4	Manufg.			
Telecommunications	1.3	Services			
Machine shops	1.3	Manufg.			
Hardware	1.3	Manufg.			
Paints & coatings	1.2	Manufg.			
Lessors of nonfinancial assets	1.2	Fin/R.E.			
Textile & fabric finishing mills	1.1	Manufg.			
Accounting, tax preparation, bookkeeping, & payroll	1.1	Services			
Securities, commodity contracts, investments	1.1	Fin/R.E.			
Paperboard mills	1.0	Manufg.			
Plastics materials & resins	0.9	Manufg.			
Truck transportation	0.9	Util.			
Power, distribution, & specialty transformers	0.8	Manufg.			
Veneer & plywood	0.8	Manufg.			
Coating, engraving, heat treating & allied activities	0.8	Manufg.			
Showcases, partitions, shelving, and lockers	0.8	Manufg.			
Sawmills & wood preservation	0.7	Manufg.			

Continued on next page.

INPUTS AND OUTPUTS FOR SIGN MANUFACTURING - Continued

Economic Sector or Industry Providing Inputs	%	Sector	Economic Sector or Industry Buying Outputs	%	Sector
Monetary authorities/depository credit intermediation	0.7	Fin/R.E.			
Semiconductors & related devices	0.7	Manufg.			
Unlaminated plastics profile shapes	0.7	Manufg.			
Printed circuit assemblies (electronic assemblies)	0.7	Manufg.			
Data processing, hosting, & related services	0.7	Services			
Maintenance/repair of nonresidential structures	0.6	Construct.			
Professional, scientific, technical services, nec	0.6	Services			
Power generation & supply	0.6	Util.			
Food services & drinking places	0.6	Services			
Services to buildings & dwellings	0.6	Services			
Automotive equipment rental & leasing	0.5	Fin/R.E.			
Turned products & screws, nuts, & bolts	0.5	Manufg.			
Other computer related services, including facilities	0.4	Services			
Hotels & motels, including casino hotels	0.4	Services			
Abrasive products	0.4	Manufg.			
Nonwoven fabric mills	0.4	Manufg.			
Automotive repair & maintenance, ex. car washes	0.4	Services			
Cutting tools & machine tool accessories	0.4	Manufg.			
Legal services	0.4	Services			
Paperboard containers	0.4	Manufg.			
Warehousing & storage	0.3	Util.			
Scientific research & development services	0.3	Services			
Printing inks	0.3	Manufg.			
Commercial & industrial equipment repair/maintenance	0.3	Services			
Air transportation	0.3	Util.			
Metal cans, boxes, & other containers (light gauge)	0.3	Manufg.			
Architectural, engineering, & related services	0.3	Services			
Fabricated metals, nec	0.3	Manufg.			
Waste management & remediation services	0.3	Services			
Commercial & industrial machinery rental & leasing	0.3	Fin/R.E.			
Nonferrous metal (ex. copper & aluminum) processing	0.3	Manufg.			
Textile product mills, nec	0.3	Manufg.			
Handtools	0.2	Manufg.			
Laminated plastics plates, sheets, & shapes	0.2	Manufg.			
Crowns & closures & metal stamping	0.2	Manufg.			
Natural gas distribution	0.2	Util.			
Nondepository credit intermediation activities	0.2	Fin/R.E.			
Management, scientific, & technical consulting	0.2	Services			
Computer system design services	0.2	Services			
Ball & roller bearings	0.2	Manufg.			
Plate work & fabricated structural products	0.2	Manufg.			
Rail transportation	0.1	Util.			
Petroleum lubricating oil & grease	0.1	Manufg.			
Motor vehicle parts	0.1	Manufg.			
Business support services	0.1	Services			
Internet service providers & web search portals	0.1	Services			
Electronic & precision equipment repair/maintenance	0.1	Services			
Water, sewage and other systems	0.1	Util.			
Transit & ground passenger transportation	0.1	Util.			
Chemical products & preparations, nec	0.1	Manufg.			

Source: Benchmark Input-Output Accounts for the U.S. Economy, 2002, U.S. Department of Commerce, Washington, D.C., January 2008. The abbreviation nec stands for 'not elsewhere classified'.

OCCUPATIONS EMPLOYED BY SIGN MANUFACTURING

No Occupation data available for this industry.

LOCATION BY STATE AND REGIONAL CONCENTRATION

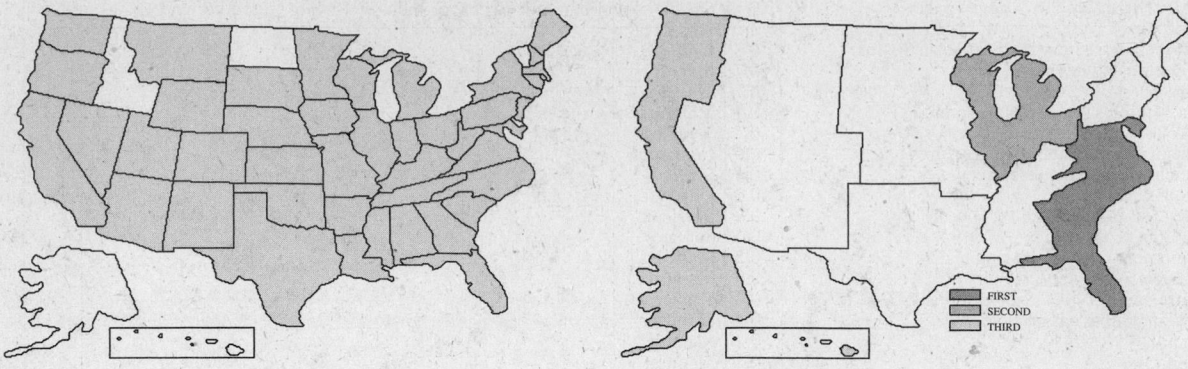

FIRST
SECOND
THIRD

INDUSTRY DATA BY STATE

| State | Establish-ments | Shipments | | | Employment | | | | Cost as % of Shipments | Investment per Employee ($) |
		Total ($ mil)	% of U.S.	Per Establ.	Total Number	% of U.S.	Per Establ.	Wages ($/hour)		
California	644	866.7	8.8	1,345.8	7,969	9.2	12	14.81	35.8	2,306
Illinois	246	683.6	7.0	2,778.8	4,641	5.4	19	15.24	43.3	2,980
New York	376	655.1	6.7	1,742.2	5,896	6.8	16	13.17	39.2	3,033
Texas	502	623.5	6.3	1,242.0	5,980	6.9	12	12.82	38.9	1,793
Ohio	290	552.4	5.6	1,904.7	4,956	5.7	17	13.70	38.2	1,985
Pennsylvania	239	510.3	5.2	2,135.2	4,015	4.6	17	15.65	37.5	1,877
New Jersey	179	469.7	4.8	2,624.0	3,512	4.1	20	14.10	38.7	2,569
Wisconsin	145	403.5	4.1	2,783.0	2,899	3.4	20	13.66	42.7	4,029
Florida	387	400.1	4.1	1,033.8	3,354	3.9	9	13.71	41.1	4,653
Michigan	217	369.0	3.8	1,700.6	2,783	3.2	13	15.23	42.9	2,148
Minnesota	136	329.7	3.4	2,424.5	2,620	3.0	19	15.07	40.4	2,299
Massachusetts	136	262.5	2.7	1,929.8	2,142	2.5	16	15.03	41.7	3,393
Missouri	137	256.3	2.6	1,871.1	2,523	2.9	18	12.97	40.8	2,294
Georgia	213	219.0	2.2	1,028.3	2,372	2.7	11	13.18	38.3	3,522
South Dakota	14	209.9	2.1	14,989.4	1,651	1.9	118	13.88	36.3	2,884
Arizona	118	198.2	2.0	1,679.3	1,410	1.6	12	14.63	47.9	2,643
Tennessee	120	190.7	1.9	1,589.0	2,045	2.4	17	17.54	50.3	1,654
North Carolina	180	186.5	1.9	1,035.8	1,727	2.0	10	16.22	38.5	2,211
Connecticut	75	185.7	1.9	2,476.1	1,725	2.0	23	10.51	44.0	6,772
Virginia	147	181.8	1.9	1,236.6	1,896	2.2	13	13.67	39.4	2,748
Indiana	152	179.0	1.8	1,177.4	1,811	2.1	12	14.09	45.3	3,025
Alabama	80	173.1	1.8	2,164.3	1,658	1.9	21	12.69	57.5	2,516
Nevada	64	164.5	1.7	2,570.8	1,493	1.7	23	17.23	35.0	4,697
Washington	152	149.0	1.5	980.6	1,390	1.6	9	15.61	37.5	2,106
Kentucky	78	136.0	1.4	1,743.4	1,091	1.3	14	12.65	47.9	5,042
Colorado	141	134.6	1.4	954.4	1,270	1.5	9	14.48	36.0	2,599
South Carolina	96	129.7	1.3	1,350.9	1,116	1.3	12	13.28	37.8	4,059
Oregon	113	114.0	1.2	1,008.8	1,150	1.3	10	14.90	34.7	2,094
Kansas	66	105.2	1.1	1,593.8	1,114	1.3	17	13.08	38.1	2,477
Maryland	120	100.7	1.0	839.5	1,071	1.2	9	13.67	35.8	2,226
Iowa	53	87.6	0.9	1,652.8	848	1.0	16	12.37	38.5	4,945
Rhode Island	27	77.1	0.8	2,854.5	803	0.9	30	10.99	41.2	2,872
Utah	72	74.3	0.8	1,031.8	690	0.8	10	14.25	43.3	1,964
Arkansas	50	50.1	0.5	1,002.2	478	0.6	10	12.28	41.0	4,897
Louisiana	57	46.6	0.5	817.8	514	0.6	9	12.73	41.1	2,105
Oklahoma	72	45.9	0.5	637.3	541	0.6	8	13.78	41.6	3,281
Mississippi	38	43.3	0.4	1,139.2	404	0.5	11	12.30	45.9	1,399
Nebraska	44	29.5	0.3	669.6	347	0.4	8	13.17	44.1	1,305
West Virginia	24	28.1	0.3	1,171.8	235	0.3	10	14.47	42.0	8,162
Maine	37	20.1	0.2	543.4	231	0.3	6	13.12	35.5	2,403
New Mexico	33	19.1	0.2	578.6	205	0.2	6	13.71	41.7	1,639
New Hampshire	42	17.4	0.2	414.7	178	0.2	4	16.32	38.7	1,466
Montana	25	12.2	0.1	488.4	124	0.1	5	17.52	37.2	1,944
Wyoming	8	8.4	0.1	1,046.7	120	0.1	15	12.59	33.2	1,817

Source: 2002 *Economic Census*. The states are in descending order of shipments or establishments (if shipment data are missing for the majority). The symbol (D) appears when data are withheld to prevent disclosure of competitive information. States marked with (D) are sorted by number of establishments. A dash (-) indicates that the data element cannot be calculated. Data may not show all states active in the NAICS category. All data available at the time of publication are shown.

NAICS 339991 - GASKET, PACKING, AND SEALING DEVICE MANUFACTURING

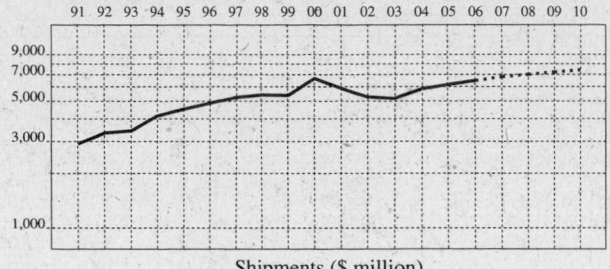

Shipments ($ million)

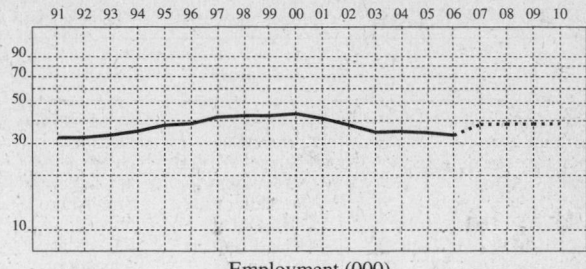

Employment (000)

GENERAL STATISTICS

| Year | Com-panies | Establishments | | Employment | | | Compensation | | Production ($ million) | | | |
		Total	with 20 or more employees	Total (000)	Production Workers (000)	Hours (Mil)	Payroll ($ mil)	Wages ($/hr)	Cost of Materials	Value Added by Manufacture	Value of Shipments	Capital Invest.
1991		503	271	32.3	23.2	46.8	809.3	10.23	1,246.3	1,665.8	2,911.1	72.0
1992	473	550	281	32.4	22.8	47.2	879.3	10.24	1,365.8	1,962.0	3,344.5	90.3
1993		551	278	33.4	23.6	48.6	912.1	10.50	1,421.2	2,009.1	3,433.8	77.6
1994		566	288	35.1	25.0	52.3	1,025.9	11.68	1,627.4	2,554.1	4,151.9	151.7
1995		584	295	37.8	27.2	56.3	1,128.9	11.70	1,906.2	2,647.5	4,518.7	151.1
1996		620	305	38.5	28.3	58.5	1,193.0	12.08	2,075.8	2,886.5	4,868.8	203.2
1997	558	662	317	41.9	30.1	62.7	1,287.5	12.15	2,134.4	3,101.1	5,240.5	203.9
1998		663	331	42.6	30.5	61.8	1,330.9	12.90	2,175.9	3,197.6	5,419.4	244.5
1999		650	322	42.7	31.0	63.5	1,381.4	13.00	2,230.5	3,132.2	5,377.0	228.5
2000		642	319	43.7	32.1	63.4	1,516.3	14.09	2,803.5	3,884.1	6,673.3	253.0
2001		616	308	41.2	29.9	60.1	1,452.5	14.18	2,545.6	3,337.3	5,878.0	215.4
2002	522	614	302	37.9	27.7	54.6	1,343.6	14.58	2,178.5	3,100.9	5,273.8	207.5
2003		619	302	34.6	24.9	52.2	1,333.0	15.21	2,148.3	3,049.4	5,178.2	147.5
2004		610	283	34.9	24.7	51.4	1,417.3	16.42	2,321.8	3,508.7	5,824.4	221.1
2005		595	287	34.4	23.8	49.3	1,391.7	15.95	2,497.5	3,674.7	6,166.0	189.9
2006		651P	310P	33.3	23.7	49.6	1,418.7	16.25	2,596.3	3,905.8	6,485.5	211.4
2007		657P	311P	38.2P	27.4P	56.1P	1,584.6P	16.92P	2,722.9P	4,096.3P	6,801.8P	248.2P
2008		662P	313P	38.3P	27.5P	56.3P	1,625.3P	17.36P	2,805.6P	4,220.6P	7,008.3P	256.3P
2009		668P	314P	38.4P	27.5P	56.4P	1,665.9P	17.80P	2,888.2P	4,345.0P	7,214.8P	264.4P
2010		674P	315P	38.5P	27.6P	56.6P	1,706.6P	18.24P	2,970.9P	4,469.3P	7,421.2P	272.5P

Sources: 1992, 1997, 2002 *Economic Census*; other years, up to 2006, are from the *Annual Survey of Manufactures*. Establishment counts for non-Census years are from *County Business Patterns*; 1997 and 2002 values are from the 1997 and 2002 censuses respectively, reported in the Federal Government's NAICS format. Other years were originally reported in equivalent SIC format. 'P's show projections by the editors.

INDICES OF CHANGE

| Year | Com-panies | Establishments | | Employment | | | Compensation | | Production ($ million) | | | |
		Total	with 20 or more employees	Total (000)	Production Workers (000)	Hours (Mil)	Payroll ($ mil)	Wages ($/hr)	Cost of Materials	Value Added by Manufacture	Value of Shipments	Capital Invest.
1992	91	90	93	85	82	86	65	70	63	63	63	44
1997	107	108	105	111	109	115	96	83	98	100	99	98
2001		100	102	109	108	110	108	97	117	108	111	104
2002	100	100	100	100	100	100	100	100	100	100	100	100
2003		101	100	91	90	96	99	104	99	98	98	71
2004		99	94	92	89	94	105	113	107	113	110	107
2005		97	95	91	86	90	104	109	115	119	117	92
2006		106P	103P	88	86	91	106	111	119	126	123	102
2007		107P	103P	101P	99P	103P	118P	116P	125P	132P	129P	120P
2008		108P	104P	101P	99P	103P	121P	119P	129P	136P	133P	124P
2009		109P	104P	101P	99P	103P	124P	122P	133P	140P	137P	127P
2010		110P	104P	102P	100P	104P	127P	125P	136P	144P	141P	131P

Sources: Same as General Statistics. Values reflect change from the base year, 2002. Values above 100 mean greater than 2002, values below 100 mean less than 2002, and the values of 100 in other years means the same as 2002. 'P's show projections by the editors.

SELECTED RATIOS

For 2002	Avg. of All Manufact.	Analyzed Industry	Index	For 2002	Avg. of All Manufact.	Analyzed Industry	Index
Employees per Establishment	42	62	147	Value Added per Production Worker	182,367	111,946	61
Payroll per Establishment	1,639,184	2,188,274	133	Cost per Establishment	5,769,015	3,548,046	62
Payroll per Employee	39,053	35,451	91	Cost per Employee	137,446	57,480	42
Production Workers per Establishment	30	45	153	Cost per Production Worker	195,506	78,646	40
Wages per Establishment	694,845	1,296,528	187	Shipments per Establishment	11,158,348	8,589,251	77
Wages per Production Worker	23,548	28,739	122	Shipments per Employee	265,847	139,150	52
Hours per Production Worker	1,980	1,971	100	Shipments per Production Worker	378,144	190,390	50
Wages per Hour	11.89	14.58	123	Investment per Establishment	361,338	337,948	94
Value Added per Establishment	5,381,325	5,050,326	94	Investment per Employee	8,609	5,475	64
Value Added per Employee	128,210	81,818	64	Investment per Production Worker	12,245	7,491	61

Sources: Same as General Statistics. The 'Average of All Manufacturing' column represents the average of all manufacturing industries reported for the most recent complete year available. The Index shows the relationship between the Average and the Analyzed Industry. For example, 100 means that they are equal; 500 that the Analyzed Industry is five times the average; 50 means that the Analyzed Industry is half the national average. The abbreviation 'na' is used to show that data are 'not available'. Ratios shown for 2002, the last complete census year.

LEADING COMPANIES   Number shown: **75**   Total sales ($ mil): **40,946**   Total employment (000): **104.7**

Company Name	Address				CEO Name	Phone	Co. Type	Sales ($ mil)	Empl. (000)
Macrotech Polyseal Inc.	PO Box 26627	Salt Lake City	UT	84126		801-973-9171	R	7,320*	0.2
Federal-Mogul Corp.	PO Box 1966	Detroit	MI	48235	Jose Maria Alapont	248-354-7700	P	6,914	43.1
International Seal Company	14 Sunset Way, B	Henderson	NV	89014	Skip Marvick	702-433-8433	R	6,470*	<0.1
InterTech Group Inc.	4838 Jenkins Ave.	N Charleston	SC	29405		843-744-5174	D	3,830	16.0
Epg Inc.	1780 Miller Pkwy.	Streetsboro	OH	44241	Michael Orazen	330-995-9725	R	3,720*	<0.1
Cooper-Standard Holdings Inc.	PO Box 8034	Novi	MI	48376	Ed Hasler	248-596-5900	R	2,164	16.3
Morgan Adv. Materials/Tech.	441 Hall Ave.	Saint Marys	PA	15857	David Cooper	814-781-1573	R	1,320*	0.3
Amesbury Group Inc.	57 S Hunt Rd.	Amesbury	MA	01913		978-388-0581	R	1,140*	<0.1
TriMas Corp.	39400 Woodward	Bloomfield Hls	MI	48304	Grant Beard	248-631-5450	P	1,068	5.1
EnPro Industries Inc.	5605 Carnegie Blvd.	Charlotte	NC	28209	William R. Holland	704-731-1500	P	1,030	4.4
Metzeler Auto. Profile Systems	900 E Whitcomb	Madison Heights	MI	48071	Thomas Wolanzyk	248-583-1122	R	860*	0.1
St-Gobain Performance Plastics	150 Dey Rd.	Wayne	NJ	07470	John Crowe	973-696-4700	S	703*	4.8
UTEX Industries Inc.	PO Box 940998	Houston	TX	77094	Michael Balas	713-467-1000	R	622*	<0.1
JMK International Inc.	4800 Bryant Irvin	Fort Worth	TX	76107	Mike Micallef	817-737-3703	R	459*	0.6
Lamons Metal Gasket Co.	7300 Airport Blvd.	Houston	TX	77061	Richard Owen	713-222-0284	R	365*	0.3
Garlock Sealing Technologies	1666 Division St.	Palmyra	NY	14522	Ernest F. Schaub	315-597-4811	D	354*	1.5
Hollingsworth and Vose Company	112 Washington St.	East Walpole	MA	02032		508-668-0295	R	251*	0.3
Crotty Corp.	854 E Chicago Rd.	Quincy	MI	49082	Keith Boyle	517-639-8787	R	127*	0.3
Holm Industries Inc.	PO Box 450	Scottsburg	IN	47170		812-752-2526	R	126*	0.3
Dana Corp. Plumley Div.	100 Plumley Dr.	Paris	TN	38242	Michael J. Burns	731-642-5582	J	123*	1.5
AW Chesterton Co.	PO Box 4004	Woburn	MA	01888	Richard Hoyle	781-438-7000	R	85*	<0.1
Forest City Technologies Inc.	PO Box 86	Wellington	OH	44090	John Cloud	440-647-2115	R	83*	0.1
Wika Instrument Corp.	1000 Wiegand Blvd.	Lawrenceville	GA	30043	Alexander Wiegand	770-513-8200	R	79*	0.5
Creative Foam Corp.	300 N Alloy Dr.	Fenton	MI	48430	Wayne Blessing	810-629-4149	R	78*	0.2
Sealing Devices Inc.	4400 Walden Ave.	Lancaster	NY	14086	Terry Galanis	716-684-7600	R	69*	0.1
GT Sales and Manufacturing	PO Box 9408	Wichita	KS	67277	N Onofrio	316-943-2171	R	65*	0.1
Uchiyama America Inc.	494 Arrington Bridg	Goldsboro	NC	27530	Masatomo Sueki	919-731-2364	R	61*	0.1
Toyo Seal America Corp.	225 Mooresville	Mooresville	NC	28115	Toru Nishioka	704-660-9062	R	60*	0.5
L and L Products Inc.	PO Box 308	Romeo	MI	48065	Claude Demby	586-336-1600	R	60*	0.4
John Crane Inc.	6400 W Oakton St.	Morton Grove	IL	60053	Bob Wasson	847-967-2400	S	57*	0.6
Precix Inc.	PO Box 6919	New Bedford	MA	02742	Mike Walther	508-998-4000	R	51*	0.3
Standco Industries Inc.	PO Box 87	Houston	TX	77001		713-224-6311	R	43*	0.3
Stemco Inc.	PO Box 1989	Longview	TX	75606	Jon Cox	903-758-9981	S	43*	0.3
Schlegel Systems Inc.	PO Box 23197	Rochester	NY	14692	Rich Koopman	585-427-7200	R	42*	0.2
Beacon Group Inc.	85 Granby St.	Bloomfield	CT	06002	Robert Sarkisian	860-242-3453	R	41*	0.1
BRC Rubber Group Inc.	PO Box 227	Churubusco	IN	46723	Charles Chaffee	260-693-2171	R	40*	0.3
Chardon Rubber Co.	373 Washington St.	Chardon	OH	44024	Jefferson Keener	440-285-2161	R	40*	0.2
Viziflex Seels Inc.	16 E Lafayette St.	Hackensack	NJ	07601	Michael Glicksman	201-487-8080	R	37*	<0.1
Kaydon Ring and Seal Inc.	PO Box 626	Baltimore	MD	21203		410-547-7700	S	35*	0.3
Parker Hannifin JBL Div.	PO Box 15009	Spartanburg	SC	29302		864-573-7332	D	35*	0.3
Industry Products Co.	PO Box 1158	Piqua	OH	45356	Linda Cleveland	937-778-0585	R	34*	0.3
Corpus Christi Gasket/Fastener	PO Box 4074	Corpus Christi	TX	78469	David Massie	361-884-6366	R	32*	0.1
Haynes Manufacturing Co.	24142 Detroit Rd.	Westlake	OH	44145	Beth Kloos	440-871-2188	R	31*	<0.1
Interface Sealing Solutions	410 S 1st Ave.	Marshalltown	IA	50158	Ron Kelling	641-752-6736	R	31*	0.1
Banks Brothers Corp.	24 Federal Plz.	Bloomfield	NJ	07003	Lawrence Banks	973-680-4488	R	31*	<0.1
Plastomer Corp.	37819 Schoolcraft	Livonia	MI	48150	Walter Baughman	734-464-0700	R	29*	0.2
Spirol International Corp.	30 Rock Ave.	Danielson	CT	06239	Haris Koehl	860-774-8571	R	29*	0.2
National Guard Products Inc.	PO Box 753430	Memphis	TN	38175	C Smith	901-795-6900	R	28*	0.2
Wire Products Company Inc.	14601 Indu. Pkwy.	Cleveland	OH	44135	Scot Kennedy	216-267-0777	R	28*	0.2
Rubberlite Inc.	PO Box 2965	Huntington	WV	25728	Allen Mayo	304-525-3116	R	27*	<0.1
Unique Fabricating Inc.	800 Standard Pkwy.	Auburn Hills	MI	48326	Douglas Stahl	248-853-2333	R	27*	0.3
Q'SO Inc.	5117 NE Pkwy.	Fort Worth	TX	76106	Fred Arnoldt	817-232-2026	R	27*	<0.1
Panhandle Packing and Gasket	PO Box 2154	Lubbock	TX	79408	Jay Newton	806-763-2801	R	27*	<0.1
St Marys Carbon Company Inc.	259 Eberl St.	Saint Marys	PA	15857	Harold Lanzel	814-781-7333	R	27*	0.2
Foamade Industries Inc.	2550 Auburn Ct.	Auburn Hills	MI	48326	Morris Rochlin	248-852-6010	R	26*	0.2
AGC Inc.	106 Evansville Ave.	Meriden	CT	06451	Walter Layman	203-235-3361	R	25*	0.2
Hanna Rubber Co.	1511 Baltimore Ave.	Kansas City	MO	64108	J Vandergrift	816-221-9600	R	25*	<0.1
Clark Seals L.L.C.	3824 S 79th E Ave.	Tulsa	OK	74145		918-664-0587	R	24*	<0.1
Flex-A-Seal Inc.	PO Box 184	Essex Junction	VT	05453	Hank Slauson	802-878-8307	R	24*	<0.1
MPD Inc.	316 E 9th St.	Owensboro	KY	42303	Gary Braswell	270-685-6200	R	24*	0.2
United Gasket Corp.	1633 S 55th Ave.	Cicero	IL	60804	Mark Pahios	708-656-3700	R	24*	<0.1
Ashtabula Rubber Co.	PO Box 398	Ashtabula	OH	44005	Nicholas Jammal	440-992-2195	R	24*	0.2
American National Rubber Co.	PO Box 878	Ceredo	WV	25507	Thomas Maxwell	304-453-1311	R	23*	0.1
Maxwell Technologies Inc.	5301 E River Rd.	Fridley	MN	55421		763-574-1613	R	23*	<0.1
Derby Cellular Products Inc.	PO Box 277	Derby	CT	06418	Allan Cribbines	203-735-4661	R	22*	0.2
Parco Inc.	1801 S Archibald	Ontario	CA	91761	Louis Burgener	909-947-2200	R	22*	0.2
Iten Industries Inc.	PO Box 2150	Ashtabula	OH	44005	Peter Huggins	440-997-6134	R	22*	0.2
CDI Seals Inc.	8103 Rankin Rd.	Humble	TX	77396		281-446-6662	R	22*	0.2
Fillipone Enterprises Inc.	2003 E 5th St., 1	Tempe	AZ	85281	Charles Fillipone	480-966-9311	R	21*	<0.1
Precision Associates Inc.	740 Washington	Minneapolis	MN	55401	Arnold Kadue	612-333-7464	R	20*	0.1
State Seal Co.	4135 E Wood St.	Phoenix	AZ	85040	Mike Curtis	602-437-1532	R	20*	<0.1
Stein Seal Co.	PO Box 316	Kulpsville	PA	19443	Philip Stein	215-256-0201	R	20*	0.2
Ferrotherm Corp.	4758 Warner Rd.	Cleveland	OH	44125	Haakon Egeland	216-883-9350	R	20*	0.1
Seal Methods Inc.	11915 Shoemaker	Santa Fe Spgs	CA	90670	Eugene Welter	562-944-0291	R	19*	<0.1
Hoosier Gasket Corp.	2400 Enterprise Prk	Indianapolis	IN	46218	Argyle Jackson	317-545-2000	R	19*	0.2

Source: Ward's Business Directory of U.S. Private and Public Companies, Volumes 1 and 2, 2008. The company type code used is as follows: P - Public, R - Private, S - Subsidiary, D - Division, J - Joint Venture, A - Affiliate, G - Group. Sales are in millions of dollars, employees are in thousands. An asterisk (*) indicates an estimated sales volume. The symbol < stands for 'less than'. Company names and addresses are truncated, in some cases, to fit into the available space.

MATERIALS CONSUMED

Material	Quantity	Delivered Cost ($ million)
Cork products	(X)	14.0
Building paper and board	(X)	40.8
Plastics resins consumed in the form of granules, pellets, etc.	(X)	121.9
Plastics products consumed in the form of sheets, rods, etc.	(X)	35.1
Synthetic rubber	(X)	221.3
Natural rubber	(X)	36.0
Fabricated rubber products (exc. tires, tubes, hoses, belting, and gaskets)	(X)	60.5
Gaskets (all types), and packing and sealing devices	(X)	244.6
Fabricated metal wire products (incl. wire rope, cable, springs, etc.)	(X)	47.9
All other fabricated metal products (including forgings)	(X)	113.8
Steel tinplate, tin free steel, terneplate, and blackplate	(X)	37.3
All other steel shapes and forms (exc. forgings and fabricated metal products)	(X)	85.8
Natural graphite	(X)	41.7
Carbon, ground or treated	(X)	20.8
All other materials, components, parts, containers, and supplies	(X)	511.0
Materials, ingredients, containers, and supplies, nsk	(X)	283.1

Source: 2002 Economic Census. Explanation of symbols used: (D): Withheld to avoid disclosure of competitive data; na: Not available; (S): Withheld because statistical norms were not met; (X): Not applicable; (Z): Less than half the unit shown; nec: Not elsewhere classified; nsk: Not specified by kind; - : zero; p : 10-19 percent estimated; q : 20-29 percent estimated.

PRODUCT SHARE DETAILS

Product or Product Class Shipments	Mil. $	Product or Product Class Shipments	Mil. $
GASKETS, PACKING, AND SEALING DEVICES	4,986.7	seals	343.7
Compression packings	**196.0**	Molded packings and seals, nsk	51.3
Synthetic fiber, plastics composition compression packings	122.3	**Metallic gaskets and machined seals**	**820.8**
All other compression packings, nec	70.6	Metallic gaskets and machined seals	816.2
Compression packings, nsk	3.0	Metallic spiral-wound gaskets	68.1
Nonmetallic gaskets and gasketing	**1,444.1**	Other metallic gaskets and machined seals, including	
Elastomeric gaskets and gasketing	480.0	metallic exclusion devices	748.1
Graphite gaskets and gasketing	181.3	Metallic gaskets and machined seals, nsk	4.6
Other nonmetallic gaskets and gasketing, nec	763.6	**Axial mechanical face seals, including parts**	**204.1**
Paper, felt base, and plant fiber gaskets and gasketing	163.2	Complete axial mechanical face seals	(D)
Cork and cork composition gaskets and gasketing	34.0	With single coil springs	75.0
Other nonmetallic gaskets and gasketing, nec	566.4	With multiple coil springs	34.3
Nonmetallic gaskets and gasketing, nsk	19.2	With bellows	(D)
Molded packings and seals	**1,324.4**	Clearance, labyrinth, and other axial mechanical face	
Molded O-rings (including spliced)	420.9	seals, nec	(D)
All other molded packings and seals	852.2	Parts for all axial mechanical face seals	(D)
Molded squeeze-type, solid-section ring seals (including rectangular seals, quad seals, D-rings, and T-rings) (excluding O-rings)	78.9	Axial mechanical face seals, including parts, nsk	4.3
		Rotary oil seals	**558.8**
		Rotary oil seals	541.0
Molded flexible seals, dual component-cushioned rings, backed, constrained, or loaded by an elastomeric ring	76.1	Bonded, sprung (spring-loaded) rotary oil seals	274.1
		Nonmetallic rotary oil seals	26.3
Molded flexible seals, single and multiple component lip-type, V-rings, V-ring sets, U-cup, collar seals, cup seals, flange seals, single-lip nonsymmetrical seals	263.9	Other rotary oil seals (unsprung bonded, displacement, inflatable, labyrinth, boundary lubrication, all-metallic, nonbonded-assembled, proximity, and unitized rotary oil seals)	240.5
Molded diaphragm seals	89.6	Rotary oil seals, nsk	17.8
All other molded packings and seals, including nonmetallic exclusion devices and leather and plastics		**Gaskets, packing, and sealing devices, nsk, total**	**438.6**

Source: 2002 Economic Census. The values are product shipments in millions of dollars for 2002. Total product shipments may be lower or higher than industry shipments. See Introduction for a full discussion. Values of indented subcategories are summed in the main heading(s). The symbol (D) appears when data are withheld to prevent disclosure of competitive information. The abbreviation nsk stands for 'not specified by kind' and nec for 'not elsewhere classified'. A dash (-) means zero.

INPUTS AND OUTPUTS FOR GASKET, PACKING, AND SEALING DEVICE MANUFACTURING

Economic Sector or Industry Providing Inputs	%	Sector	Economic Sector or Industry Buying Outputs	%	Sector
Compensation of employees	34.4		Motor vehicle parts	14.6	Manufg.
Gaskets, packing, & sealing devices	11.5	Manufg.	Exports of goods & services	12.6	Cap Inv
Synthetic rubber	4.6	Manufg.	Gaskets, packing, & sealing devices	9.1	Manufg.
Wholesale trade	3.7	Trade	Basic organic chemicals, nec	7.1	Manufg.
Management of companies & enterprises	3.6	Services	Retail trade	6.6	Trade
Plastics materials & resins	2.4	Manufg.	Valve & fittings other than plumbing	3.4	Manufg.
Iron & steel mills & ferroalloys	2.4	Manufg.	Pumps & pumping equipment	3.3	Manufg.
Truck transportation	1.6	Util.	Wholesale trade	3.1	Trade
Power generation & supply	1.3	Util.	Automobiles	2.7	Manufg.
Plastics packaging materials, film & sheet	1.2	Manufg.	Engine equipment, nec	2.6	Manufg.
Springs & wire products	1.2	Manufg.	Industrial machinery, nec	2.6	Manufg.
Lessors of nonfinancial assets	1.1	Fin/R.E.	Material handling equipment	2.5	Manufg.
Ground or treated mineral & earth	1.1	Manufg.	Personal consumption expenditures	2.2	

Continued on next page.

INPUTS AND OUTPUTS FOR GASKET, PACKING, AND SEALING DEVICE MANUFACTURING - Continued

Economic Sector or Industry Providing Inputs	%	Sector	Economic Sector or Industry Buying Outputs	%	Sector
Securities, commodity contracts, investments	1.0	Fin/R.E.	Fluid power process machinery	2.1	Manufg.
Paperboard mills	0.9	Manufg.	Mining & oil & gas field machinery	1.9	Manufg.
Real estate	0.8	Fin/R.E.	Air & gas compressors	1.7	Manufg.
Machine shops	0.8	Manufg.	Relay & industrial controls	1.6	Manufg.
Forestry products	0.7	Agric.	Commercial & service industry machinery, nec	1.6	Manufg.
Monetary authorities/depository credit intermediation	0.6	Fin/R.E.	AC, refrigeration, and warm air heating equipment	1.3	Manufg.
Plastics products, nec	0.6	Manufg.	Semiconductor machinery	1.3	Manufg.
Semiconductors & related devices	0.6	Manufg.	Oil & gas extraction	1.3	Mining
Professional, scientific, technical services, nec	0.5	Services	Light truck & utility vehicles	1.1	Manufg.
Printed circuit assemblies (electronic assemblies)	0.5	Manufg.	Guided missiles & space vehicles	1.1	Manufg.
Coating, engraving, heat treating & allied activities	0.5	Manufg.	Motors & generators	1.1	Manufg.
Taxes on production & imports, less subsidies	0.5		Oil & gas well drilling	0.7	Mining
Advertising & related services	0.5	Services	Architectural, engineering, & related services	0.7	Services
Telecommunications	0.4	Services	Lawn & garden equipment	0.7	Manufg.
Food services & drinking places	0.4	Services	Warehousing & storage	0.6	Util.
Rail transportation	0.3	Util.	Switchgear & switchboard apparatus	0.6	Manufg.
Natural gas distribution	0.3	Util.	Residential structures, nec	0.5	Construct.
Scenic & sightseeing transport & related services	0.3	Util.	Heating equipment (except warm air furnaces)	0.5	Manufg.
Architectural, engineering, & related services	0.3	Services	Oil & gas operations services	0.5	Mining
Legal services	0.3	Services	Photographic & photocopying equipment	0.5	Manufg.
Paperboard containers	0.3	Manufg.	Scientific research & development services	0.4	Services
Accounting, tax preparation, bookkeeping, & payroll	0.3	Services	Plastics & rubber industry machinery	0.4	Manufg.
Data processing, hosting, & related services	0.3	Services	Food services & drinking places	0.4	Services
Warehousing & storage	0.3	Util.	Nonresidential structures, nec	0.3	Construct.
Miscellaneous wood products	0.3	Manufg.	Optical instruments & lenses	0.3	Manufg.
Turned products & screws, nuts, & bolts	0.3	Manufg.	Air purification & ventilation equipment	0.3	Manufg.
Services to buildings & dwellings	0.3	Services	Change in private inventories	0.3	In House
Maintenance/repair of nonresidential structures	0.3	Construct.	Basic inorganic chemicals, nec	0.3	Manufg.
Cutting tools & machine tool accessories	0.2	Manufg.	Residential permanent site structures	0.3	Construct.
Abrasive products	0.2	Manufg.	General S/L govt. services	0.3	S/L Govt
Automotive equipment rental & leasing	0.2	Fin/R.E.	Turbines & turbine generator set units	0.2	Manufg.
Scientific research & development services	0.2	Services	Packaging machinery	0.2	Manufg.
Hotels & motels, including casino hotels	0.2	Services	Couriers & messengers	0.2	Util.
Specialized design services	0.2	Services	Heavy duty trucks	0.2	Manufg.
Metal cans, boxes, & other containers (light gauge)	0.2	Manufg.	Maintenance/repair of nonresidential structures	0.2	Construct.
Chemical products & preparations, nec	0.2	Manufg.	Death care services	0.2	Services
Unlaminated plastics profile shapes	0.2	Manufg.	Owner-occupied dwellings	0.2	
Business support services	0.2	Services	Truck transportation	0.1	Util.
Fabricated metals, nec	0.2	Manufg.	Coal	0.1	Mining
Noncomparable imports	0.2	Foreign	Transit & ground passenger transportation	0.1	Util.
Waste management & remediation services	0.2	Services	Miscellaneous mining services	0.1	Mining
Other computer related services, including facilities	0.2	Services			
Air transportation	0.2	Util.			
Automotive repair & maintenance, ex. car washes	0.2	Services			
Forging, stamping, & sintering, nec	0.1	Manufg.			
Support services, nec	0.1	Services			
Commercial & industrial equipment repair/maintenance	0.1	Services			
Management, scientific, & technical consulting	0.1	Services			
Plate work & fabricated structural products	0.1	Manufg.			
Ball & roller bearings	0.1	Manufg.			
Commercial & industrial machinery rental & leasing	0.1	Fin/R.E.			
Handtools	0.1	Manufg.			
Valve & fittings other than plumbing	0.1	Manufg.			
Rubber products, nec	0.1	Manufg.			
Crowns & closures & metal stamping	0.1	Manufg.			
Nondepository credit intermediation activities	0.1	Fin/R.E.			

Source: Benchmark Input-Output Accounts for the U.S. Economy, 2002, U.S. Department of Commerce, Washington, D.C., January 2008. The abbreviation nec stands for 'not elsewhere classified'.

OCCUPATIONS EMPLOYED BY GASKET, PACKING, AND SEALING DEVICE MANUFACTURING

No Occupation data available for this industry.

LOCATION BY STATE AND REGIONAL CONCENTRATION

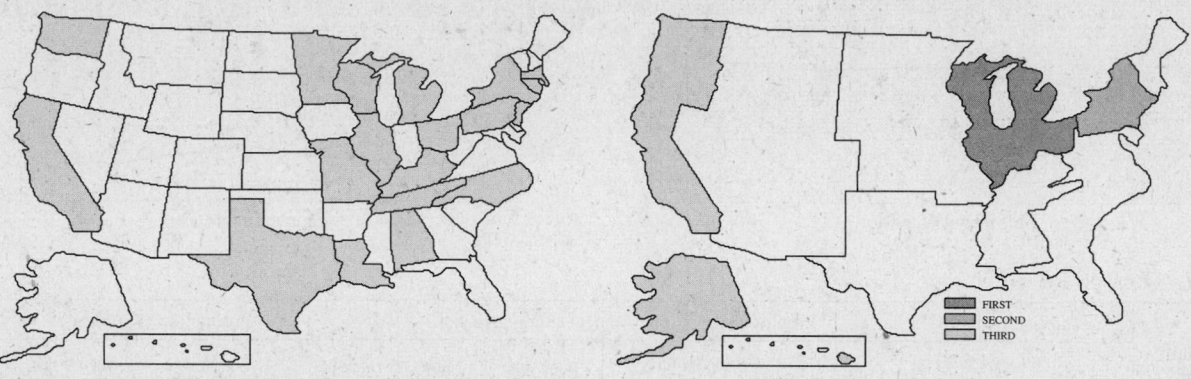

FIRST
SECOND
THIRD

INDUSTRY DATA BY STATE

| State | Establish-ments | Shipments | | | Employment | | | | Cost as % of Shipments | Investment per Employee ($) |
		Total ($ mil)	% of U.S.	Per Establ.	Total Number	% of U.S.	Per Establ.	Wages ($/hour)		
Texas	68	503.9	9.6	7,409.8	3,397	9.0	50	13.50	46.4	2,966
Illinois	37	497.7	9.4	13,450.1	3,792	10.0	102	17.60	49.8	3,858
California	72	411.0	7.8	5,708.3	3,259	8.6	45	15.91	30.1	2,628
New York	28	383.3	7.3	13,690.4	2,975	7.9	106	13.31	44.3	1,977
Ohio	43	356.8	6.8	8,298.1	2,864	7.6	67	15.44	39.7	7,344
Massachusetts	22	212.0	4.0	9,638.5	1,239	3.3	56	16.00	32.0	2,128
Tennessee	14	180.6	3.4	12,900.6	1,253	3.3	90	13.87	56.8	1,730
Pennsylvania	36	163.9	3.1	4,553.3	1,377	3.6	38	14.46	38.8	3,706
New Jersey	27	151.2	2.9	5,601.4	1,187	3.1	44	14.99	40.1	3,898
Kentucky	8	130.7	2.5	16,332.0	843	2.2	105	14.67	46.1	26,645
Minnesota	20	126.7	2.4	6,336.5	938	2.5	47	14.56	31.7	6,915
North Carolina	11	124.1	2.4	11,281.7	657	1.7	60	13.35	46.3	3,242
Michigan	26	120.4	2.3	4,629.2	907	2.4	35	14.29	36.5	1,619
Alabama	6	111.6	2.1	18,592.0	674	1.8	112	14.51	45.3	6,034
Wisconsin	18	83.7	1.6	4,649.6	729	1.9	41	15.30	42.7	2,911
Connecticut	15	75.0	1.4	5,001.8	697	1.8	46	13.08	34.8	3,723
Rhode Island	6	53.1	1.0	8,844.8	398	1.1	66	24.26	30.3	5,410
Missouri	12	42.4	0.8	3,530.2	295	0.8	25	14.15	35.9	3,488
Louisiana	9	36.5	0.7	4,053.8	274	0.7	30	12.70	39.4	2,434
Washington	10	16.6	0.3	1,660.8	170	0.4	17	16.60	34.7	2,024

Source: 2002 *Economic Census*. The states are in descending order of shipments or establishments (if shipment data are missing for the majority). The symbol (D) appears when data are withheld to prevent disclosure of competitive information. States marked with (D) are sorted by number of establishments. A dash (-) indicates that the data element cannot be calculated. Data may not show all states active in the NAICS category. All data available at the time of publication are shown.

NAICS 339992 - MUSICAL INSTRUMENT MANUFACTURING

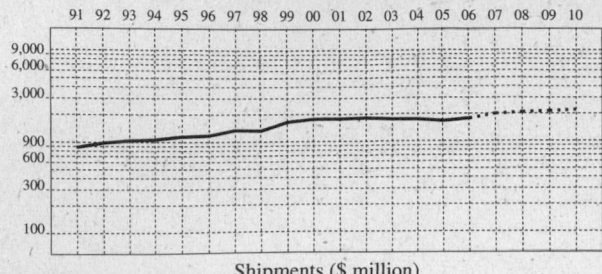

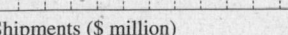

Shipments ($ million)

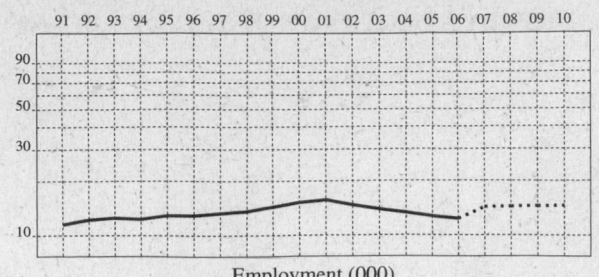

Employment (000)

GENERAL STATISTICS

| Year | Companies | Establishments | | Employment | | | Compensation | | Production ($ million) | | | |
		Total	with 20 or more employees	Total (000)	Production Workers (000)	Hours (Mil)	Payroll ($ mil)	Wages ($/hr)	Cost of Materials	Value Added by Manufacture	Value of Shipments	Capital Invest.
1991				11.5	8.7	17.4	238.1	8.90	349.2	536.3	881.3	12.6
1992	437	461	104	12.2	9.4	17.9	272.7	9.87	405.7	588.4	981.3	13.8
1993				12.5	9.7	18.9	290.0	10.14	411.6	629.8	1,036.8	17.1
1994				12.3	9.8	19.3	280.9	9.63	420.3	637.6	1,061.6	11.4
1995				12.9	10.4	19.7	312.7	10.61	497.4	689.9	1,144.1	23.7
1996				12.9	10.3	20.7	327.9	10.59	505.8	685.3	1,173.3	15.3
1997	548	571	104	13.3	10.8	21.8	359.1	11.12	493.0	843.4	1,339.1	34.6
1998		583	116	13.6	11.1	22.5	403.8	11.97	498.8	846.7	1,321.5	57.2
1999		618	112	14.4	11.5	22.2	413.3	12.52	660.6	1,000.2	1,648.1	73.4
2000		636	120	15.2	12.1	23.5	455.4	13.03	696.5	1,116.0	1,767.3	37.9
2001		622	123	15.7	12.6	24.2	477.3	13.47	707.4	1,099.6	1,777.4	40.0
2002	559	585	122	14.7	11.7	24.1	469.9	13.15	602.3	1,226.9	1,813.8	38.0
2003		608	125	13.9	11.1	21.6	454.3	14.33	571.2	1,177.8	1,749.6	24.8
2004		615	123	13.3	10.3	20.5	463.3	15.06	564.0	1,158.3	1,739.0	40.2
2005		604	123	12.7	9.7	19.8	478.6	15.59	632.7	1,000.8	1,664.3	30.4
2006				12.3	9.5	19.4	486.0	16.17	682.3	1,106.7	1,774.9	37.1
2007				14.3P	11.3P	22.7P	536.6P	16.24P	768.3P	1,246.2P	1,998.6P	46.8P
2008				14.4P	11.4P	22.9P	554.2P	16.71P	794.0P	1,287.9P	2,065.5P	48.6P
2009				14.5P	11.5P	23.1P	571.9P	17.17P	819.7P	1,329.6P	2,132.5P	50.4P
2010				14.6P	11.5P	23.3P	589.5P	17.64P	845.5P	1,371.4P	2,199.4P	52.1P

Sources: 1992, 1997, 2002 *Economic Census*; other years, up to 2006, are from the *Annual Survey of Manufactures*. Establishment counts for non-Census years are from *County Business Patterns*; 1997 and 2002 values are from the 1997 and 2002 censuses respectively, reported in the Federal Government's NAICS format. Other years were originally reported in equivalent SIC format. 'P's show projections by the editors.

INDICES OF CHANGE

| Year | Companies | Establishments | | Employment | | | Compensation | | Production ($ million) | | | |
		Total	with 20 or more employees	Total (000)	Production Workers (000)	Hours (Mil)	Payroll ($ mil)	Wages ($/hr)	Cost of Materials	Value Added by Manufacture	Value of Shipments	Capital Invest.
1992	78	79	85	83	80	74	58	75	67	48	54	36
1997	98	98	85	90	92	90	76	85	82	69	74	91
2001		106	101	107	108	100	102	102	117	90	98	105
2002	100	100	100	100	100	100	100	100	100	100	100	100
2003		104	102	95	95	90	97	109	95	96	96	65
2004		105	101	90	88	85	99	115	94	94	96	106
2005		103	101	86	83	82	102	119	105	82	92	80
2006				84	81	80	103	123	113	90	98	98
2007				97P	97P	94P	114P	123P	128P	102P	110P	123P
2008				98P	97P	95P	118P	127P	132P	105P	114P	128P
2009				99P	98P	96P	122P	131P	136P	108P	118P	133P
2010				99P	98P	97P	125P	134P	140P	112P	121P	137P

Sources: Same as General Statistics. Values reflect change from the base year, 2002. Values above 100 mean greater than 2002, values below 100 mean less than 2002, and the values of 100 in other years means the same as 2002. 'P's show projections by the editors.

SELECTED RATIOS

For 2002	Avg. of All Manufact.	Analyzed Industry	Index	For 2002	Avg. of All Manufact.	Analyzed Industry	Index
Employees per Establishment	42	25	60	Value Added per Production Worker	182,367	104,863	58
Payroll per Establishment	1,639,184	803,248	49	Cost per Establishment	5,769,015	1,029,573	18
Payroll per Employee	39,053	31,966	82	Cost per Employee	137,446	40,973	30
Production Workers per Establishment	30	20	68	Cost per Production Worker	195,506	51,479	26
Wages per Establishment	694,845	541,735	78	Shipments per Establishment	11,158,348	3,100,513	28
Wages per Production Worker	23,548	27,087	115	Shipments per Employee	265,847	123,388	46
Hours per Production Worker	1,980	2,060	104	Shipments per Production Worker	378,144	155,026	41
Wages per Hour	11.89	13.15	111	Investment per Establishment	361,338	64,957	18
Value Added per Establishment	5,381,325	2,097,265	39	Investment per Employee	8,609	2,585	30
Value Added per Employee	128,210	83,463	65	Investment per Production Worker	12,245	3,248	27

Sources: Same as General Statistics. The 'Average of All Manufacturing' column represents the average of all manufacturing industries reported for the most recent complete year available. The Index shows the relationship between the Average and the Analyzed Industry. For example, 100 means that they are equal; 500 that the Analyzed Industry is five times the average; 50 means that the Analyzed Industry is half the national average. The abbreviation 'na' is used to show that data are 'not available'. Ratios shown for 2002, the last complete census year.

LEADING COMPANIES   Number shown: **50**   Total sales ($ mil): **4,371**   Total employment (000): **24.3**

Company Name	Address				CEO Name	Phone	Co. Type	Sales ($ mil)	Empl. (000)
Sony Music Entertainment Inc.	550 Madison Ave.	New York	NY	10022	Mike Bebel	212-833-8000	S	1,500*	10.0
Kaman Corp.	PO Box 1	Bloomfield	CT	06002		860-243-7100	P	1,086	3.6
Steinway Musical Instruments	800 South St., 305	Waltham	MA	02453	Kyle R. Kirkland	781-894-9770	P	406	2.2
Kaman Aerospace Corp.	PO Box 2	Bloomfield	CT	06002	Sal Bordanelero	860-242-4461	D	349*	1.4
Fender Musical Instruments	8860 E Chaparral Rd	Scottsdale	AZ	85250		480-596-9690	R	196*	0.3
D'Addario and Company Inc.	PO Box 290	Farmingdale	NY	11735	James D'Addario	631-439-3300	R	120*	0.5
Gibson Guitar Corp.	309 Plus Park Blvd.	Nashville	TN	37217	Dave Berryman	615-871-4500	R	111*	<0.1
Baldwin Piano Inc.	PO Box 100087	Nashville	TN	37210	Henry E. Juszkiewicz	615-871-4500	S	86*	1.5
Line 6 Inc.	29901 Agoura Rd.	Agoura Hills	CA	91301	Mike Meunch	818-575-3600	R	40*	0.2
C.F. Martin and Company Inc.	PO Box 329	Nazareth	PA	18064	Chris Martin IV	610-759-2837	R	37*	0.6
Taylor-Listug Inc.	1980 Gillespie Way	El Cajon	CA	92020		619-258-1207	R	32*	0.3
Kawai America Corp.	PO Box 9045	R Dominguez	CA	90224	Hirotaka Kawai	310-631-1771	R	30*	0.2
Burgett Inc.	4111 N Freeway	Sacramento	CA	95834	Gary Burgett	916-567-9999	R	30*	0.1
Yamaha Music Manufacturing	100 Yamaha Park	Thomaston	GA	30286	Shinichi Minatodani	706-647-9601	R	27*	0.3
Mapes Piano String Co.	PO Box 700	Elizabethton	TN	37644		423-543-3195	R	26*	0.2
U.S. Music Corp.	444 E Courtland St.	Mundelein	IL	60060	Rudolph Schlacher	847-949-0444	R	23*	0.2
Paul Reed Smith Guitar Co.	380 Log Canoe Cir.	Stevensville	MD	21666		410-643-9970	R	19*	0.2
QRS Music Technologies Inc.	2011 Seward Ave.	Naples	FL	34102	Richard A. Dolan	239-597-5888	P	18	<0.1
Carson Industries Inc.	189 Foreman Rd.	Freeport	PA	16229	Harry Carson	724-295-5147	R	17*	0.2
Belco Works Inc.	340 Fox Shannon Pl.	St Clairsville	OH	43950		740-695-0500	R	17*	0.3
Rodgers Instruments L.L.C.	1300 NE 25th Ave.	Hillsboro	OR	97124	Dennis Houlihan	503-648-4181	R	16*	0.2
Ernie Ball Inc.	PO Box 4117	San Luis Obispo	CA	93403	Roland Ball	805-544-7726	R	15*	0.2
Lyon and Healy Harps Inc.	168 N Ogden Ave.	Chicago	IL	60607	Antonio Forero	312-786-1881	R	14*	0.1
Avedis Zildjian Co.	22 Longwater Dr.	Norwell	MA	02061	Craigie Zildjian	781-871-2200	R	13*	0.1
Fox Products Corp.	PO Box 347	South Whitley	IN	46787	Alan Fox	260-723-4888	R	13*	0.1
Sabine Inc.	13301 US Hwy. 441	Alachua	FL	32615	Doran Oster	386-418-2000	R	10*	<0.1
GHS Corp.	PO Box 136	Battle Creek	MI	49016	Robert Mc Fee	269-968-3351	R	10*	0.1
Ken-Tron Manufacturing Inc.	PO Box 21250	Owensboro	KY	42304	Robert Hudson	270-684-0431	R	10*	<0.1
E and O Mari Inc.	PO Box 869	Newburgh	NY	12551	Richard Cocco	845-562-4400	R	9*	<0.1
Gemeinhardt Company Inc.	PO Box 788	Elkhart	IN	46515		574-295-5280	R	9*	<0.1
Polytone Musical Instruments	6865 Vineland Ave.	N Hollywood	CA	91605	Thomas Gumina	818-760-2300	R	9*	<0.1
Ovation Instruments	PO Box 507	Bloomfield	CT	06002	Paul Kuhn	860-379-7575	D	8*	<0.1
Carvin Corp.	12340 World Trade	San Diego	CA	92128	Carson Kiesel	858-487-1600	R	8*	0.2
Schulmerich Carillons Inc.	PO Box 903	Sellersville	PA	18960	Nevin Scholl	215-257-2771	R	7*	<0.1
L.R. Baggs Co.	483 N Frontage Rd.	Nipomo	CA	93444	Lloyd Baggs	805-929-3545	R	7*	<0.1
Dean Markley Strings Inc.	3350 Scott Blvd.	Santa Clara	CA	95054	Dean Markley	408-988-2456	R	7*	<0.1
Commodore Criterion Spec. Bell	4312 2nd Ave.	Brooklyn	NY	11232	Abraham Damast	718-788-2600	R	7*	<0.1
Midi Music Center Inc.	PO Box 1270	La Grange Park	IL	60526	Naoki Mori	708-352-3388	R	6*	<0.1
IT Verdin Co.	444 Reading Rd.	Cincinnati	OH	45202	James Verdin	513-241-4010	R	4*	<0.1
Tech 21 USA Inc.	790 Bloomfield Ave.	Clifton	NJ	07012	Andrew Barta	973-777-6996	R	3*	<0.1
Santa Cruz Guitar Corp.	151 Harvey W Blvd.	Santa Cruz	CA	95060	Richard Hoover	831-425-0999	R	2*	<0.1
Calato, J D Manufacturing Co.	4501 Hyde Park	Niagara Falls	NY	14305	Carol Calato	716-285-3546	R	2*	<0.1
TEI Electronics Inc.	750 W 18th St.	Hialeah	FL	33010	Danilo Alonso	305-888-3980	R	2*	<0.1
Meisel Music Inc.	PO Box 90	Springfield	NJ	07081	Neil Lillian	973-379-5000	R	2*	<0.1
Artisan Instruments Inc.	6450 NE 183rd St.	Kenmore	WA	98028	H Carlson	425-486-6555	R	2*	<0.1
Acoustic Sciences Corp.	PO Box 1189	Eugene	OR	97440	Arthur Noxon	541-343-9727	R	2*	<0.1
Dave's Electronic Service Inc.	105 E Penn St.	Hoopeston	IL	60942	David Coffman	217-283-5010	R	1*	<0.1
Mike Balter Mallets	15 E Palatine Rd.	Prospect Hgts	IL	60070	Mike Balter	847-541-5777	R	1*	<0.1
L.A. Sax Co.	325 Nolan St.	San Antonio	TX	78202	James Gavigan	210-637-0414	S	1*	<0.1
Flex-Lite	3521 E Kilgore Rd.	Kalamazoo	MI	49001	Brian Barker	269-344-1662	R	1*	<0.1

Source: *Ward's Business Directory of U.S. Private and Public Companies*, Volumes 1 and 2, 2008. The company type code used is as follows: P - Public, R - Private, S - Subsidiary, D - Division, J - Joint Venture, A - Affiliate, G - Group. Sales are in millions of dollars, employees are in thousands. An asterisk (*) indicates an estimated sales volume. The symbol < stands for 'less than'. Company names and addresses are truncated, in some cases, to fit into the available space.

MATERIALS CONSUMED

Material	Quantity	Delivered Cost ($ million)
Rough and dressed lumber	(X)	78.6
Paperboard containers, boxes, and corrugated paperboard	(X)	11.3
Electronic components and accessories	(X)	45.7
Musical instruments parts (actions, strings, mouthpieces, etc.)	(X)	132.1
All other materials, components, parts, containers, and supplies	(X)	184.5
Materials, ingredients, containers, and supplies, nsk	(X)	72.3

Source: 2002 *Economic Census*. Explanation of symbols used: (D): Withheld to avoid disclosure of competitive data; na: Not available; (S): Withheld because statistical norms were not met; (X): Not applicable; (Z): Less than half the unit shown; nec: Not elsewhere classified; nsk: Not specified by kind; - : zero; p : 10-19 percent estimated; q : 20-29 percent estimated.

PRODUCT SHARE DETAILS

Product or Product Class Shipments	Mil. $	Product or Product Class Shipments	Mil. $
MUSICAL INSTRUMENTS	1,718.2	Electronic musical instruments, including electronic	
Nonelectronic pianos	**173.8**	pianos and synthesizers, except electronic organs	175.8
Vertical, upright, or console pianos	92.2	Other musical instruments, except electronic	761.7
Grand pianos	81.6	Woodwind musical instruments	156.4
Organs	**105.6**	Brass wind musical instruments	116.2
Organs	104.2	Nonelectronic fretted and string instruments (such as	
Pipe and reed organs	55.0	harps, harpsichords, guitars, banjos, etc)	349.6
Electronic organs	49.2	Percussion musical instruments (cymbals, drums,	
Organs, nsk	1.4	vibraphones (nonelectronic), etc)	103.9
Nonelectronic piano and organ parts, except benches	**49.9**	Other nonelectronic musical instruments, including	
Nonelectronic piano parts (actions, attachments, strings,		accordions, harmonicas, bagpipes, etc	35.6
tuning pins, etc.), except benches	36.6	Accessories and parts for other musical instruments	357.7
Organ parts, except benches	13.4	Other musical instruments and parts, nsk	25.9
Other musical instruments and parts	**1,321.1**	**Musical instruments, nsk, total**	**67.7**

Source: 2002 *Economic Census*. The values are product shipments in millions of dollars for 2002. Total product shipments may be lower or higher than industry shipments. See Introduction for a full discussion. Values of indented subcategories are summed in the main heading(s). The symbol (D) appears when data are withheld to prevent disclosure of competitive information. The abbreviation nsk stands for 'not specified by kind' and nec for 'not elsewhere classified'. A dash (-) means zero.

INPUTS AND OUTPUTS FOR MUSICAL INSTRUMENT MANUFACTURING

Economic Sector or Industry Providing Inputs	%	Sector	Economic Sector or Industry Buying Outputs	%	Sector
Compensation of employees	33.6		Personal consumption expenditures	62.2	
Musical instruments	7.3	Manufg.	Private fixed investment	13.9	
Sawmills & wood preservation	4.8	Manufg.	Exports of goods & services	8.4	Cap Inv
Wholesale trade	4.2	Trade	S/L govt. invest., education	7.0	S/L Govt
Management of companies & enterprises	3.6	Services	Musical instruments	4.3	Manufg.
Printed circuit assemblies (electronic assemblies)	3.0	Manufg.	Personal & household goods repair/maintenance	1.7	Services
Office furnitures	2.2	Manufg.	Commercial & industrial machinery rental & leasing	0.9	Fin/R.E.
Advertising & related services	2.0	Services	Wholesale trade	0.6	Trade
Truck transportation	1.4	Util.	General S/L govt. services	0.4	S/L Govt
Securities, commodity contracts, investments	1.4	Fin/R.E.	Retail trade	0.3	Trade
Lessors of nonfinancial assets	1.3	Fin/R.E.	Commercial & industrial equipment repair/maintenance	0.2	Services
Paints & coatings	1.2	Manufg.			
Architectural, engineering, & related services	1.1	Services			
Real estate	1.1	Fin/R.E.			
Monetary authorities/depository credit intermediation	0.9	Fin/R.E.			
Semiconductors & related devices	0.8	Manufg.			
Paperboard containers	0.8	Manufg.			
Wiring devices	0.8	Manufg.			
Power generation & supply	0.7	Util.			
Professional, scientific, technical services, nec	0.7	Services			
Machine shops	0.7	Manufg.			
Springs & wire products	0.5	Manufg.			
Coating, engraving, heat treating & allied activities	0.5	Manufg.			
Taxes on production & imports, less subsidies	0.4				
Noncomparable imports	0.4	Foreign			
Legal services	0.4	Services			
Accounting, tax preparation, bookkeeping, & payroll	0.4	Services			
Scientific research & development services	0.3	Services			
Warehousing & storage	0.3	Util.			
Cutting tools & machine tool accessories	0.3	Manufg.			
Abrasive products	0.3	Manufg.			
Nondepository credit intermediation activities	0.3	Fin/R.E.			
Bare printed circuit boards	0.3	Manufg.			
Data processing, hosting, & related services	0.3	Services			
Telecommunications	0.2	Services			
Automotive equipment rental & leasing	0.2	Fin/R.E.			
Food services & drinking places	0.2	Services			
Natural gas distribution	0.2	Util.			
Services to buildings & dwellings	0.2	Services			
Other computer related services, including facilities	0.2	Services			
Employment services	0.2	Services			
Specialized design services	0.2	Services			
Business support services	0.2	Services			
Fabricated metals, nec	0.2	Manufg.			
Air transportation	0.2	Util.			
Maintenance/repair of nonresidential structures	0.2	Construct.			
Rail transportation	0.2	Util.			
Hotels & motels, including casino hotels	0.1	Services			
Civic, social, & professional organizations	0.1	Services			
Commercial & industrial machinery rental & leasing	0.1	Fin/R.E.			
Paperboard mills	0.1	Manufg.			
Support services, nec	0.1	Services			
Management, scientific, & technical consulting	0.1	Services			

Source: Benchmark Input-Output Accounts for the U.S. Economy, 2002, U.S. Department of Commerce, Washington, D.C., January 2008. The abbreviation nec stands for 'not elsewhere classified'.

OCCUPATIONS EMPLOYED BY MUSICAL INSTRUMENT MANUFACTURING
No Occupation data available for this industry.

LOCATION BY STATE AND REGIONAL CONCENTRATION

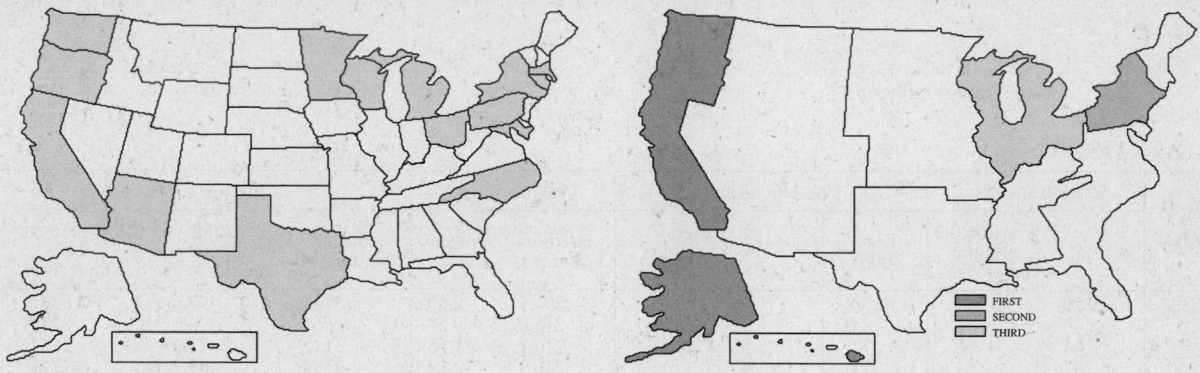

FIRST
SECOND
THIRD

INDUSTRY DATA BY STATE

State	Establish-ments	Shipments			Employment				Cost as % of Shipments	Investment per Employee ($)
		Total ($ mil)	% of U.S.	Per Establ.	Total Number	% of U.S.	Per Establ.	Wages ($/hour)		
California	89	471.1	26.0	5,292.7	2,996	20.3	34	10.21	28.7	3,112
New York	51	172.2	9.5	3,376.1	1,742	11.8	34	14.01	28.9	2,316
Pennsylvania	20	149.8	8.3	7,488.0	1,372	9.3	69	16.92	33.0	4,779
Massachusetts	27	81.5	4.5	3,020.1	517	3.5	19	14.43	25.5	2,662
Ohio	23	69.0	3.8	2,998.7	670	4.5	29	14.09	27.3	1,866
Michigan	16	59.9	3.3	3,745.4	440	3.0	28	16.62	52.8	1,677
Wisconsin	16	48.4	2.7	3,022.3	559	3.8	35	14.15	28.6	1,803
North Carolina	20	32.0	1.8	1,602.1	134	0.9	7	11.95	47.3	1,381
Washington	21	28.9	1.6	1,374.0	282	1.9	13	10.89	35.3	4,372
Maryland	13	28.3	1.6	2,176.4	229	1.6	18	17.66	29.9	1,729
Oregon	18	24.8	1.4	1,378.7	238	1.6	13	12.94	32.0	2,059
Texas	25	15.0	0.8	599.6	156	1.1	6	9.85	41.2	2,417
Connecticut	7	13.9	0.8	1,984.7	165	1.1	24	15.43	37.1	1,400
Arizona	9	11.4	0.6	1,261.3	162	1.1	18	9.49	26.7	1,333
Minnesota	20	6.0	0.3	301.6	111	0.8	6	10.57	34.4	1,108

Source: 2002 Economic Census. The states are in descending order of shipments or establishments (if shipment data are missing for the majority). The symbol (D) appears when data are withheld to prevent disclosure of competitive information. States marked with (D) are sorted by number of establishments. A dash (-) indicates that the data element cannot be calculated. Data may not show all states active in the NAICS category. All data available at the time of publication are shown.

NAICS 339993 - FASTENER, BUTTON, NEEDLE, AND PIN MANUFACTURING

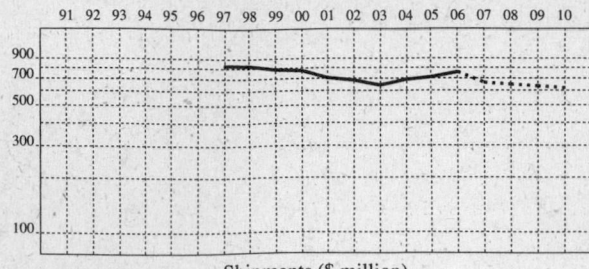

Shipments ($ million)

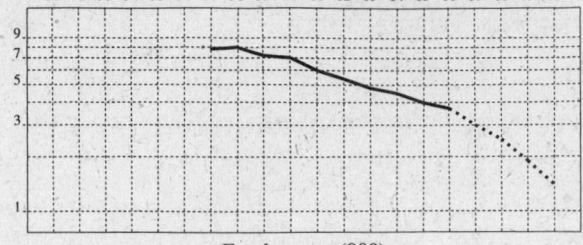

Employment (000)

GENERAL STATISTICS

Year	Companies	Establishments		Employment			Compensation		Production ($ million)			
		Total	with 20 or more employees	Total (000)	Production Workers (000)	Hours (Mil)	Payroll ($ mil)	Wages ($/hr)	Cost of Materials	Value Added by Manufacture	Value of Shipments	Capital Invest.
1997	237	250	71	7.8	5.6	12.7	206.1	9.63	344.8	494.6	828.5	48.5
1998		242	73	8.0	5.9	13.1	211.0	9.57	356.0	470.0	822.5	56.0
1999		244	68	7.2	5.5	11.5	213.1	11.66	312.2	471.9	785.0	62.3
2000		237	64	7.0	5.4	11.1	216.9	12.29	313.6	463.2	772.7	36.9
2001		216	59	6.0	4.3	8.7	185.4	12.13	283.7	423.7	704.3	30.2
2002	180	186	53	5.4	4.0	7.9	175.0	12.73	250.6	430.9	683.6	35.1
2003		188	52	4.8	3.5	7.4	163.2	12.66	243.2	394.3	642.0	39.0
2004		183	54	4.5	3.2	7.0	164.9	13.43	259.6	428.5	688.0	23.5
2005		181	52	4.0	2.8	6.3	159.4	14.84	269.8	441.1	710.2	23.9
2006		163P	46P	3.7	2.5	5.6	160.4	15.58	278.8	472.7	757.4	25.0
2007		153P	43P	3.0P	2.0P	4.3P	146.0P	15.82P	243.7P	413.1P	662.0P	17.4P
2008		142P	40P	2.5P	1.6P	3.4P	138.9P	16.43P	238.5P	404.3P	647.9P	13.7P
2009		132P	37P	1.9P	1.2P	2.5P	131.7P	17.04P	233.3P	395.6P	633.8P	9.9P
2010		122P	34P	1.4P	0.8P	1.6P	124.5P	17.66P	228.1P	386.8P	619.7P	6.2P

Sources: 1997 and 2002 *Economic Census*; other years, up to 2006, are from *Annual Survey of Manufactures*. Establishment counts for non-Census years are from *County Business Patterns*; 1997 and 2002 values are from the 1997 and 2002 censuses, respectively. 'P's show projections by the editors.

INDICES OF CHANGE

Year	Companies	Establishments		Employment			Compensation		Production ($ million)			
		Total	with 20 or more employees	Total (000)	Production Workers (000)	Hours (Mil)	Payroll ($ mil)	Wages ($/hr)	Cost of Materials	Value Added by Manufacture	Value of Shipments	Capital Invest.
1997	132	134	134	144	140	161	118	76	138	115	121	138
1998		130	138	148	148	166	121	75	142	109	120	160
1999		131	128	133	138	146	122	92	125	110	115	177
2000		127	121	130	135	141	124	97	125	107	113	105
2001		116	111	111	108	110	106	95	113	98	103	86
2002	100	100	100	100	100	100	100	100	100	100	100	100
2003		101	98	89	88	94	93	99	97	92	94	111
2004		98	102	83	80	89	94	105	104	99	101	67
2005		97	98	74	70	80	91	117	108	102	104	68
2006		88P	87P	69	63	71	92	122	111	110	111	71
2007		82P	81P	56P	50P	54P	83P	124P	97P	96P	97P	50P
2008		76P	76P	46P	40P	43P	79P	129P	95P	94P	95P	39P
2009		71P	70P	35P	30P	32P	75P	134P	93P	92P	93P	28P
2010		65P	65P	26P	20P	20P	71P	139P	91P	90P	91P	18P

Sources: Same as General Statistics. Values reflect change from the base year, 2002. Values above 100 mean greater than 2002, values below 100 mean less than 2002, and the values of 100 in other years means the same as 2002. 'P's show projections by the editors.

SELECTED RATIOS

For 2002	Avg. of All Manufact.	Analyzed Industry	Index	For 2002	Avg. of All Manufact.	Analyzed Industry	Index
Employees per Establishment	42	29	69	Value Added per Production Worker	182,367	107,725	59
Payroll per Establishment	1,639,184	940,860	57	Cost per Establishment	5,769,015	1,347,312	23
Payroll per Employee	39,053	32,407	83	Cost per Employee	137,446	46,407	34
Production Workers per Establishment	30	22	73	Cost per Production Worker	195,506	62,650	32
Wages per Establishment	694,845	540,683	78	Shipments per Establishment	11,158,348	3,675,269	33
Wages per Production Worker	23,548	25,142	107	Shipments per Employee	265,847	126,593	48
Hours per Production Worker	1,980	1,975	100	Shipments per Production Worker	378,144	170,900	45
Wages per Hour	11.89	12.73	107	Investment per Establishment	361,338	188,710	52
Value Added per Establishment	5,381,325	2,316,667	43	Investment per Employee	8,609	6,500	76
Value Added per Employee	128,210	79,796	62	Investment per Production Worker	12,245	8,775	72

Sources: Same as General Statistics. The 'Average of All Manufacturing' column represents the average of all manufacturing industries reported for the most recent complete year available. The Index shows the relationship between the Average and the Analyzed Industry. For example, 100 means that they are equal; 500 that the Analyzed Industry is five times the average; 50 means that the Analyzed Industry is half the national average. The abbreviation 'na' is used to show that data are 'not available'. Ratios shown for 2002, the last complete census year.

LEADING COMPANIES   Number shown: 54   Total sales ($ mil): 3,500   Total employment (000): 18.5

Company Name	Address				CEO Name	Phone	Co. Type	Sales ($ mil)	Empl. (000)
Brown Shoe Company Inc.	PO Box 29	St. Louis	MO	63166	Ronald A. Fromm	314-854-4000	P	2,471	12.7
Anstro Manufacturing Inc.	238 Wolcott Rd.	Wolcott	CT	06716	Robert Bosco	203-879-1423	R	182*	0.2
Aguadilla Shoe Corp.	Carr 111 Km 3.2	Aguadilla	PR	00603	Steven Duffy	787-891-0302	R	95*	0.4
QSN Manufacturing Inc.	1441 N Wood Dale	Wood Dale	IL	60191	Gary Mitchell	630-595-0000	R	92*	0.3
Avibank Manufacturing Inc.	11500 Sherman Way	N Hollywood	CA	91605	Dan Welter	818-392-2100	S	82*	0.4
Whitesell Corp.	PO Box 2570	Muscle Shoals	AL	35662		256-248-8500	R	52*	0.3
Scovill Fasteners Inc.	PO Box 44	Clarkesville	GA	30523		706-754-1000	R	48*	0.4
Agora Leather Products	2101 28th St. N	St. Petersburg	FL	33713	Subash Dave	727-321-0707	R	38*	0.3
Aplix Inc.	PO Box 7505	Charlotte	NC	28241	Patrick Billarant	704-588-1920	R	31*	0.3
Triad Fastener Corp.	PO Box 130	Alda	NE	68810	Richard Merrick	308-384-1780	R	26*	0.3
Lehigh Consumer Products Corp.	2834 Schoeneck Rd.	Macungie	PA	18062	Fred Keller	610-966-9702	S	25*	0.2
Stayfast Inc.	PO Box 456	Uriah	AL	36480	David Lindsay	251-862-5000	R	24*	0.2
Levcor International Inc.	1065 Ave of the Am.	New York	NY	10018	Robert A. Levison	212-354-8500	P	22	0.1
Rightway Fasteners Inc.	7945 S Intl. Dr.	Columbus	IN	47201	Kazumasa Arima	812-342-2700	R	21*	0.2
Braxton Manufacturing Company	PO Box 429	Watertown	CT	06795	Joseph Triano	860-274-6781	R	18*	0.2
Platt Brothers and Co.	PO Box 1030	Waterbury	CT	06721	James Behuniak	203-753-4194	R	18*	0.1
R-B Industries Inc.	6366 W Gross Pnt	Niles	IL	60714	Ronald Baade	847-647-5900	R	17*	<0.1
Ideal Fastener Corp.	PO Box 548	Oxford	NC	27565	Ralph Gut	919-693-3115	R	16*	0.2
Spencer Products Co.	1859 Summit Comm	Twinsburg	OH	44087	Robert Tuttle	330-487-5200	R	15*	<0.1
US Button Corp.	328 Kennedy Dr.	Putnam	CT	06260	Larry Jacobs	860-928-2707	R	15*	0.1
Brunner Manufacturing Company	PO Box 225	Mauston	WI	53948	Ronald Brunner	608-847-6667	R	14*	0.1
Handy Button Machine Co.	1750 N 25th Ave.	Melrose Park	IL	60160	Michael Baritz	708-450-9000	R	14*	0.1
Prym Dritz Corp.	PO Box 5028	Spartanburg	SC	29304	Johan Starrenburg		S	13*	0.1
Morton Grinding Inc.	17341 Sierra Hwy.	Santa Clarita	CA	91351	Wallace Morton	661-298-0895	R	12*	0.1
Dimcogray Corp.	900 Dimco Way	Dayton	OH	45458	Michael Sieron	937-433-7600	R	11*	<0.1
Bergamot Brass Works Inc.	820 E Wisconsin St.	Delavan	WI	53115	Daniel Baughman	262-728-5572	R	11*	0.1
SWD Inc.	910 S Stiles Dr.	Addison	IL	60101	Richard Delawder	630-543-3003	R	11*	0.1
Southeastern Bolt and Screw	PO Box 758	Birmingham	AL	35201	Walter Andrews	205-328-4551	R	7*	<0.1
AGE Manufacturers Inc.	10624 Ave. D	Brooklyn	NY	11236	Yosel Avtzon	718-927-0048	R	7*	<0.1
Foam Products Corp.	350 Beamer Rd. SW	Calhoun	GA	30701	Jerry Arnold	706-629-1256	R	7*	<0.1
Mac Neill Engineering Company	PO Box 735	Marlborough	MA	01752	Harris Macneill	508-481-8830	R	6*	<0.1
Punch Tech	2701 Busha Hwy.	Marysville	MI	48040	Richard Zenow	810-364-4811	R	6*	<0.1
Mark Eyelet Inc.	18 Park Rd.	Watertown	CT	06795	William Hamel	860-945-2681	R	5*	<0.1
Mona Slide Fasteners Inc.	4510 White Plains	Bronx	NY	10470	Joel Barrocas	718-325-7700	R	5*	<0.1
Ribco Manufacturing Inc.	192 Georgia Ave.	Providence	RI	02905	Kevin Redmond	401-467-4300	R	5*	<0.1
TOG Manufacturing Company Inc.	1454 S State St.	North Adams	MA	01247	John Alibozek	413-664-6711	R	5*	<0.1
WH Bagshaw Company Inc.	1 Pine St. Ext.	Nashua	NH	03060	Arron Bagshaw	603-883-7758	R	5*	<0.1
Mkt Fastening L.L.C.	1 Gunnebo Dr.	Lonoke	AR	72086	Bert Mayer	501-676-2222	R	5*	<0.1
Vermat Corp.	2101 S Hathaway St.	Santa Ana	CA	92705	Wendy Gustin	714-540-2846	R	5*	<0.1
OEMMCCO Inc.	9606 58th Pl.	Kenosha	WI	53144	Patricia Dihel	262-605-1170	R	4*	<0.1
Termax Corp.	1155 Rose Rd.	Lake Zurich	IL	60047	Micheal Smith	847-519-1500	R	4*	<0.1
Threaded Products Inc.	21050 N Brady St.	Davenport	IA	52804	Daniel Konrardy	563-386-1160	R	4*	<0.1
Chima Inc.	PO Box 6236	Reading	PA	19610	Douglas Heydt	610-372-6508	R	4*	<0.1
Marchel Industries Inc.	100 SW Dr.	Spartanburg	SC	29303	Ricky Pitts	864-574-6318	R	3*	<0.1
Eaglehead Manufacturing Co.	23555 Euclid Ave.	Euclid	OH	44117	Harris Phillips	216-692-1240	R	3*	<0.1
Badge Parts Inc.	1520 Paramount Dr.	Waukesha	WI	53186	Joseph Bruno	262-650-9991	R	3*	<0.1
Sure Foot Corp.	PO Box 12049	Grand Forks	ND	58208	Jon Larson	701-775-9560	R	3*	<0.1
Crumrine Manufacturing	145 Catron Dr.	Reno	NV	89512	Jeanne Lashelle	775-786-3712	R	3*	<0.1
Aero Assemblies Inc.	12012 12th Ave. S	Burnsville	MN	55337	Anthony Winick	952-894-5552	R	2*	<0.1
Snapco Manufacturing Corp.	140 Central Ave.	Hillside	NJ	07205	Arnold Spitz	973-282-0300	R	2*	<0.1
Leo F Maciver Company Inc.	PO Box 2086	Brockton	MA	02305	Don Iver	508-583-2501	R	2*	<0.1
Contract Stitching Inc.	PO Box 341	Saint Nazianz	WI	54232	Joan O'Leary	920-773-2820	R	2*	<0.1
Vel Tye L.L.C.	PO Box 5603	Virginia Beach	VA	23471	Steven Herring	757-318-7240	R	1*	<0.1
Midstate Precision Inc.	901 Highland Way	Grover Beach	CA	93433	Scott McGuire	805-481-6875	R	1*	<0.1

Source: Ward's Business Directory of U.S. Private and Public Companies, Volumes 1 and 2, 2008. The company type code used is as follows: P - Public, R - Private, S - Subsidiary, D - Division, J - Joint Venture, A - Affiliate, G - Group. Sales are in millions of dollars, employees are in thousands. An asterisk (*) indicates an estimated sales volume. The symbol < stands for 'less than'. Company names and addresses are truncated, in some cases, to fit into the available space.

MATERIALS CONSUMED

Material	Quantity	Delivered Cost ($ million)
Fabricated metal products, including forgings	(X)	7.7
Steel shapes and forms (exc. castings, forgings, fabr. metal products)	(X)	24.6
Aluminum and aluminum-base alloy shapes and forms (exc. castings, forgings, fabr. metal products)	(X)	(D)
Copper and copper-base alloy shapes and forms (exc. castings, forgings, fabr. metal products)	(X)	(D)
Plastics resins consumed in the form of granules, pellets, etc.	(X)	(D)
Cotton and manmade fiber fabrics, broadwoven and narrow woven	(X)	32.3
Buckles, button parts, buttons, fasteners, needles, pins, and zippers purchased for further manufacture or assembly	(X)	41.1
All other materials, components, parts, containers, and supplies	(X)	62.6
Materials, ingredients, containers, and supplies, nsk	(X)	9.1

Source: 2002 *Economic Census*. Explanation of symbols used: (D): Withheld to avoid disclosure of competitive data; na: Not available; (S): Withheld because statistical norms were not met; (X): Not applicable; (Z): Less than half the unit shown; nec: Not elsewhere classified; nsk: Not specified by kind; - : zero; p : 10-19 percent estimated; q : 20-29 percent estimated.

PRODUCT SHARE DETAILS

Product or Product Class Shipments	Mil. $	Product or Product Class Shipments	Mil. $
FASTENERS, BUTTONS, NEEDLES AND PINS	643.9	Plastics zippers and slide fasteners (except precious or semiprecious metals and precious or semiprecious stones).	15.9
Buttons and parts (except precious or semiprecious metals and precious or semiprecious stones) . . .	**217.9**	Zippers and slide fasteners (except precious or semiprecious metals and precious or semiprecious stones), nsk .	0.8
Buttons and parts (except precious or semiprecious metals and precious or semiprecious stones)	173.2	**Buckles, needles, pins, fasteners (except slide), and similar notions (except precious or semiprecious metals and precious or semiprecious stones)**	**222.6**
Metal and other buttons and parts (except precious or semiprecious metals and precious or semiprecious stones).	142.4	Buckles, needles, pins, fasteners (except slide), and similar notions (except precious or semiprecious metals and precious or semiprecious stones) . . .	218.5
Plastics buttons and parts (except precious or semiprecious metals and precious or semiprecious stones).	30.8	Buckles (including those covered with fabrics or other material (except precious or semiprecious metals and precious or semiprecious stones)	15.8
Buttons and parts (except precious or semiprecious metals and precious or semiprecious stones), nsk	44.7	Fasteners (except slide) (except precious or semiprecious metals and precious or semiprecious stones)	(D)
Zippers and slide fasteners (except precious or semiprecious metals and precious or semiprecious stones)	**133.3**	Needles, pins, fasteners (except slide), and similar notions, nsk	4.1
Zippers and slide fasteners (except precious or semiprecious metals and precious or semiprecious stones)	132.4	**Fasteners, buttons, needles, and pins, nsk, total**	**70.2**
Metal zippers and slide fasteners (except precious or semiprecious metals and precious or semiprecious stones).	116.5		

Source: 2002 *Economic Census*. The values are product shipments in millions of dollars for 2002. Total product shipments may be lower or higher than industry shipments. See Introduction for a full discussion. Values of indented subcategories are summed in the main heading(s). The symbol (D) appears when data are withheld to prevent disclosure of competitive information. The abbreviation nsk stands for 'not specified by kind' and nec for 'not elsewhere classified'. A dash (-) means zero.

INPUTS AND OUTPUTS FOR ALL OTHER MISCELLANEOUS MANUFACTURING

Economic Sector or Industry Providing Inputs	%	Sector	Economic Sector or Industry Buying Outputs	%	Sector
Compensation of employees	28.9		Personal consumption expenditures	51.1	
Wholesale trade	3.6	Trade	Private fixed investment	11.2	
Management of companies & enterprises	3.2	Services	Exports of goods & services	7.8	Cap Inv
Manufacturing, nec	2.9	Manufg.	Death care services	7.2	Services
Iron & steel mills & ferroalloys	2.9	Manufg.	Wholesale trade	3.4	Trade
Synthetic rubber	2.7	Manufg.	General S/L govt. services	2.9	S/L Govt
Machine shops	2.6	Manufg.	Manufacturing, nec	2.1	Manufg.
Paints & coatings	2.1	Manufg.	Light truck & utility vehicles	1.6	Manufg.
Plastics materials & resins	2.0	Manufg.	Food services & drinking places	1.4	Services
Sawmills & wood preservation	1.5	Manufg.	Women's & girls' cut & sew apparel	0.9	Manufg.
Reconstituted wood products	1.5	Manufg.	Curtain & linen mills	0.7	Manufg.
Real estate	1.5	Fin/R.E.	Retail trade	0.7	Trade
Plastics packaging materials, film & sheet	1.3	Manufg.	Men's & boys' cut & sew apparel	0.6	Manufg.
Truck transportation	1.2	Util.	Change in private inventories	0.6	In House
Paperboard containers	1.2	Manufg.	Grantmaking, giving, & social advocacy organizations	0.6	Services
Lessors of nonfinancial assets	0.9	Fin/R.E.	Cattle	0.4	Agric.
Semiconductors & related devices	0.9	Manufg.	Community food, housing, relief, & rehabilitation	0.4	Services
Fabricated metals, nec	0.8	Manufg.	Personal care services	0.4	Services
Coating, engraving, heat treating & allied activities	0.8	Manufg.	Civic, social, & professional organizations	0.3	Services
Alumina refining & primary aluminum production	0.8	Manufg.	Architectural, engineering, & related services	0.3	Services
Advertising & related services	0.8	Services	Elementary & secondary schools	0.3	Services
Securities, commodity contracts, investments	0.7	Fin/R.E.	Glass products from purchased glass	0.3	Manufg.
Unlaminated plastics profile shapes	0.7	Manufg.	Accounting, tax preparation, bookkeeping, & payroll	0.3	Services
Power generation & supply	0.7	Util.	Jewelry & silverware	0.3	Manufg.
Aluminum products from purchased aluminum	0.6	Manufg.	Federal government, investment, national defense	0.3	Fed Govt
Monetary authorities/depository credit intermediation	0.5	Fin/R.E.	Personal & household goods repair/maintenance	0.3	Services
Legal services	0.5	Services	Personal services, nec	0.2	Services
Hardware	0.5	Manufg.	Dry-cleaning & laundry services	0.2	Services
Turned products & screws, nuts, & bolts	0.5	Manufg.	Individual & family services	0.2	Services
Professional, scientific, technical services, nec	0.5	Services	Specialized design services	0.2	Services
Automotive equipment rental & leasing	0.4	Fin/R.E.	Motor vehicle parts	0.2	Manufg.
Printed circuit assemblies (electronic assemblies)	0.4	Manufg.	Child day care services	0.1	Services
Narrow fabric mills & schiffli embroidery	0.4	Manufg.	Nondepository credit intermediation activities	0.1	Fin/R.E.
Architectural, engineering, & related services	0.4	Services	Telecommunications	0.1	Services
Cutting tools & machine tool accessories	0.4	Manufg.	Institutional furniture	0.1	Manufg.
Miscellaneous wood products	0.3	Manufg.	Religious organizations	0.1	Services
Specialized design services	0.3	Services	Plastics materials & resins	0.1	Manufg.
Metal cans, boxes, & other containers (light gauge)	0.3	Manufg.	Tobacco products	0.1	Manufg.
Employment services	0.3	Services			
Warehousing & storage	0.3	Util.			
Accounting, tax preparation, bookkeeping, & payroll	0.3	Services			
Custom roll forming	0.3	Manufg.			
Greenhouse & nursery products	0.3	Agric.			
Telecommunications	0.3	Services			
Rail transportation	0.3	Util.			
Business support services	0.3	Services			
Taxes on production & imports, less subsidies	0.2				

Continued on next page.

INPUTS AND OUTPUTS FOR ALL OTHER MISCELLANEOUS MANUFACTURING - Continued

Economic Sector or Industry Providing Inputs	%	Sector	Economic Sector or Industry Buying Outputs	%	Sector
Forging, stamping, & sintering, nec	0.2	Manufg.			
Crowns & closures & metal stamping	0.2	Manufg.			
Natural gas distribution	0.2	Util.			
Commercial & industrial machinery rental & leasing	0.2	Fin/R.E.			
Management, scientific, & technical consulting	0.2	Services			
Food services & drinking places	0.2	Services			
Noncomparable imports	0.2	Foreign			
Plate work & fabricated structural products	0.2	Manufg.			
Data processing, hosting, & related services	0.2	Services			
Abrasive products	0.2	Manufg.			
Scientific research & development services	0.2	Services			
Ball & roller bearings	0.2	Manufg.			
Support services, nec	0.2	Services			
Postal service	0.2	Util.			
Wood windows & doors & millwork	0.2	Manufg.			
Handtools	0.2	Manufg.			
Copper rolling, drawing, extruding, & alloying	0.2	Manufg.			
Nonferrous metal foundries	0.2	Manufg.			
Services to buildings & dwellings	0.2	Services			
Textile & fabric finishing mills	0.2	Manufg.			
Air transportation	0.1	Util.			
Valve & fittings other than plumbing	0.1	Manufg.			
Maintenance/repair of nonresidential structures	0.1	Construct.			
Other computer related services, including facilities	0.1	Services			
Nonferrous metal (ex. copper & aluminum) processing	0.1	Manufg.			
Investigation & security services	0.1	Services			
Periodical publishers	0.1	Services			
Hotels & motels, including casino hotels	0.1	Services			

Source: Benchmark Input-Output Accounts for the U.S. Economy, 2002, U.S. Department of Commerce, Washington D.C., January 2008. User should note that this Input-Output table is not for this particular narrowly defined industry but for a larger aggregate. Input and Output data for All Other Miscellaneous Manufacturing include Input and Output data for the Annual Survey of Manufactures' NAICS industries 339993, 339995, and 339999. The abbreviation nec stands for 'not elsewhere classified'.

OCCUPATIONS EMPLOYED BY FASTENER, BUTTON, NEEDLE, AND PIN MANUFACTURING

No Occupation data available for this industry.

LOCATION BY STATE AND REGIONAL CONCENTRATION

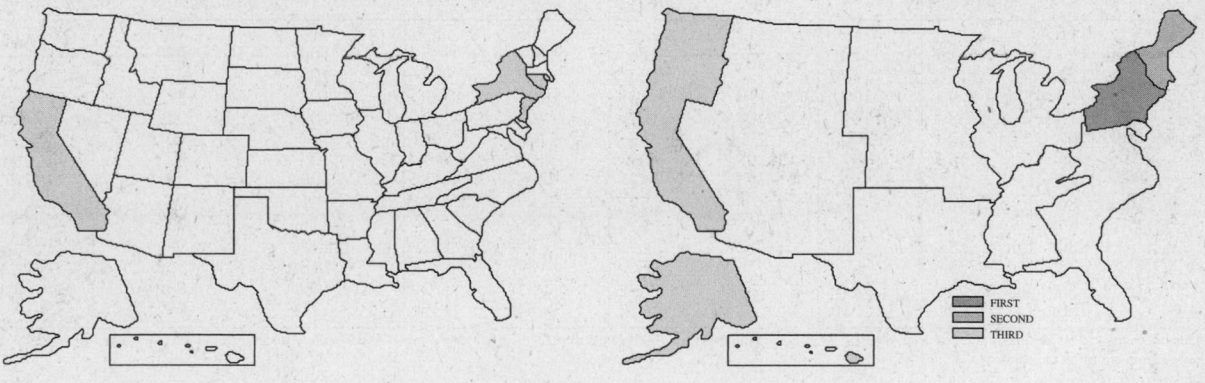

FIRST
SECOND
THIRD

INDUSTRY DATA BY STATE

State	Establish-ments	Shipments			Employment				Cost as % of Shipments	Investment per Employee ($)
		Total ($ mil)	% of U.S.	Per Establ.	Total Number	% of U.S.	Per Establ.	Wages ($/hour)		
Connecticut	16	75.3	11.0	4,704.4	772	14.4	48	13.68	28.4	7,184
California	23	52.7	7.7	2,289.3	545	10.1	24	12.02	30.3	3,897
New York	27	40.4	5.9	1,497.9	414	7.7	15	11.14	55.2	821
New Jersey	10	18.7	2.7	1,868.5	167	3.1	17	16.43	52.5	1,000
Rhode Island	8	12.6	1.8	1,573.4	184	3.4	23	10.37	35.5	1,511

Source: 2002 Economic Census. The states are in descending order of shipments or establishments (if shipment data are missing for the majority). The symbol (D) appears when data are withheld to prevent disclosure of competitive information. States marked with (D) are sorted by number of establishments. A dash (-) indicates that the data element cannot be calculated. Data may not show all states active in the NAICS category. All data available at the time of publication are shown.

NAICS 339994 - BROOM, BRUSH, AND MOP MANUFACTURING

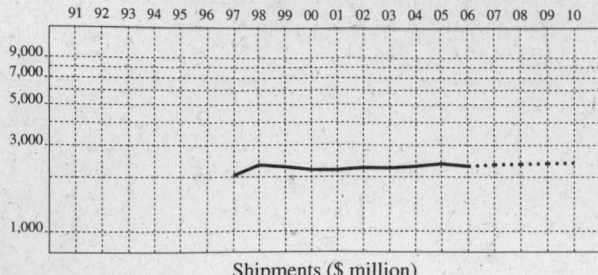

Shipments ($ million)

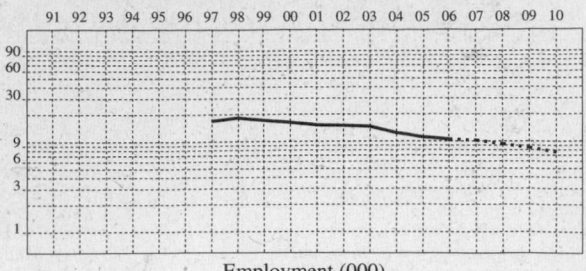

Employment (000)

GENERAL STATISTICS

| Year | Com-panies | Establishments | | Employment | | | Compensation | | Production ($ million) | | | |
		Total	with 20 or more employees	Total (000)	Production Workers (000)	Hours (Mil)	Payroll ($ mil)	Wages ($/hr)	Cost of Materials	Value Added by Manufacture	Value of Shipments	Capital Invest.
1997	308	333	151	17.0	12.8	24.7	438.9	10.68	918.7	1,132.8	2,035.8	90.0
1998		357	154	18.3	14.1	27.8	479.9	10.45	1,036.0	1,301.5	2,329.2	258.8
1999		354	157	17.2	13.3	26.9	469.5	10.70	1,008.5	1,271.5	2,266.9	88.2
2000		344	157	16.3	12.7	25.3	452.7	10.88	978.3	1,216.3	2,185.1	59.6
2001		334	142	15.2	11.9	23.6	431.6	11.01	946.8	1,243.2	2,180.7	63.3
2002	268	289	132	15.0	11.1	22.1	461.7	12.24	948.2	1,316.0	2,245.5	63.7
2003		277	129	14.6	10.9	22.8	460.0	12.09	1,005.5	1,237.6	2,243.0	57.3
2004		269	120	12.4	8.6	17.8	436.5	14.07	1,036.4	1,251.1	2,286.6	76.5
2005		248	106	11.1	7.5	15.6	399.6	14.55	1,148.4	1,245.2	2,364.8	48.0
2006		244P	108P	10.5	7.5	15.2	395.1	14.76	1,087.7	1,220.2	2,295.8	39.9
2007		230P	102P	10.2P	6.9P	14.7P	406.9P	15.05P	1,109.1P	1,244.2P	2,340.9P	18.1P
2008		217P	96P	9.3P	6.2P	13.3P	400.4P	15.58P	1,117.5P	1,253.6P	2,358.6P	6.1P
2009		203P	90P	8.5P	5.4P	11.9P	393.9P	16.10P	1,125.9P	1,263.0P	2,376.3P	
2010		190P	84P	7.6P	4.7P	10.6P	387.5P	16.63P	1,134.3P	1,272.4P	2,394.1P	

Sources: 1997 and 2002 *Economic Census*; other years, up to 2006, are from *Annual Survey of Manufactures*. Establishment counts for non-Census years are from *County Business Patterns*; 1997 and 2002 values are from the 1997 and 2002 censuses, respectively. 'P's show projections by the editors.

INDICES OF CHANGE

| Year | Com-panies | Establishments | | Employment | | | Compensation | | Production ($ million) | | | |
		Total	with 20 or more employees	Total (000)	Production Workers (000)	Hours (Mil)	Payroll ($ mil)	Wages ($/hr)	Cost of Materials	Value Added by Manufacture	Value of Shipments	Capital Invest.
1997	115	115	114	113	115	112	95	87	97	86	91	141
1998		124	117	122	127	126	104	85	109	99	104	406
1999		122	119	115	120	122	102	87	106	97	101	138
2000		119	119	109	114	114	98	89	103	92	97	94
2001		116	108	101	107	107	93	90	100	94	97	99
2002	100	100	100	100	100	100	100	100	100	100	100	100
2003		96	98	97	98	103	100	99	106	94	100	90
2004		93	91	83	77	81	95	115	109	95	102	120
2005		86	80	74	68	71	87	119	121	95	105	75
2006		84P	82P	70	68	69	86	121	115	93	102	63
2007		80P	78P	68P	62P	67P	88P	123P	117P	95P	104P	28P
2008		75P	73P	62P	56P	60P	87P	127P	118P	95P	105P	10P
2009		70P	68P	57P	49P	54P	85P	132P	119P	96P	106P	
2010		66P	64P	51P	42P	48P	84P	136P	120P	97P	107P	

Sources: Same as General Statistics. Values reflect change from the base year, 2002. Values above 100 mean greater than 2002, values below 100 mean less than 2002, and the values of 100 in other years means the same as 2002. 'P's show projections by the editors.

SELECTED RATIOS

For 2002	Avg. of All Manufact.	Analyzed Industry	Index	For 2002	Avg. of All Manufact.	Analyzed Industry	Index
Employees per Establishment	42	52	124	Value Added per Production Worker	182,367	118,559	65
Payroll per Establishment	1,639,184	1,597,578	97	Cost per Establishment	5,769,015	3,280,969	57
Payroll per Employee	39,053	30,780	79	Cost per Employee	137,446	63,213	46
Production Workers per Establishment	30	38	130	Cost per Production Worker	195,506	85,423	44
Wages per Establishment	694,845	936,000	135	Shipments per Establishment	11,158,348	7,769,896	70
Wages per Production Worker	23,548	24,370	103	Shipments per Employee	265,847	149,700	56
Hours per Production Worker	1,980	1,991	101	Shipments per Production Worker	378,144	202,297	53
Wages per Hour	11.89	12.24	103	Investment per Establishment	361,338	220,415	61
Value Added per Establishment	5,381,325	4,553,633	85	Investment per Employee	8,609	4,247	49
Value Added per Employee	128,210	87,733	68	Investment per Production Worker	12,245	5,739	47

Sources: Same as General Statistics. The 'Average of All Manufacturing' column represents the average of all manufacturing industries reported for the most recent complete year available. The Index shows the relationship between the Average and the Analyzed Industry. For example, 100 means that they are equal; 500 that the Analyzed Industry is five times the average; 50 means that the Analyzed Industry is half the national average. The abbreviation 'na' is used to show that data are 'not available'. Ratios shown for 2002, the last complete census year.

LEADING COMPANIES   Number shown: **75**   Total sales ($ mil): **32,205**   Total employment (000): **147.4**

Company Name	Address				CEO Name	Phone	Co. Type	Sales ($ mil)	Empl. (000)
Gillette Co.	PO Box 720	Boston	MA	02217	James M. Kilts	617-421-7000	S	10,477	28.7
Newell Rubbermaid Inc.	10B Glenlake Pkwy.	Atlanta	GA	30328		770-407-3800	P	6,407	22.0
Milliken and Co.	PO Box 1926	Spartanburg	SC	29304	Ashley Allen	864-503-2020	R	3,001*	10.0
Dallas Market Center Company	2100 Stemmons	Dallas	TX	75207	Bill Winsor	214-655-6100	R	1,973*	0.4
Kellwood Co.	PO Box 14374	St. Louis	MO	63178		314-576-3100	P	1,962	28.0
Springs Global US Inc.	PO Box 70	Fort Mill	SC	29716	Crandall C. Bowles	803-547-1500	R	1,081*	8.0
Eddie Bauer Holdings Inc.	15010 NE 36th St.	Redmond	WA	98052	Neil Fiske	425-755-6100	P	1,013	9.6
Simmons Co.	1 Concourse Pky.	Atlanta	GA	30328	Charles R. Eitel	770-512-7700	R	855	3.0
UNICOR	320 1st St. NW	Washington	DC	20534	Steve Schwalb	202-305-3500	R	567*	21.0
Cotton Goods Manufacturing Co.	259 N California	Chicago	IL	60612	Edward J. Lewis	773-265-0088	R	525*	<0.1
Arden Companies	18000 W 9 Mile Rd.	Southfield	MI	48075	Robert S. Sachs	248-355-1101	R	424*	1.2
Muralo Company Inc.	PO Box 455	Bayonne	NJ	07002	Ed Norton		R	389*	0.4
Jay Franco and Sons Inc.	295 5th Ave., 312	New York	NY	10016	Joseph A. Franco	212-679-3022	R	240*	0.1
American Woolen Company Inc.	PO Box 521399	Miami	FL	33152	Richard Marcus	305-635-4000	R	206*	1.5
Louisville Bedding Company	10400 Bunsen Way	Louisville	KY	40299	John Minihan	502-491-3370	R	175*	0.3
Best-Artex L.L.C.	PO Box 309	Highland	IL	62249	Charles Anderson	618-654-2113	S	172*	<0.1
CCP Industries Inc.	PO Box 6500	Cleveland	OH	44101	Richard Sims	440-449-6550	R	151*	0.1
First Years Inc.	100 Tec. Center Dr.	Stoughton	MA	02072	Curtis Stoelting	781-341-6250	S	150*	0.2
SK Textiles Inc.	2938 E 54th St.	Vernon	CA	90058	Robert Paul Schwartz	323-581-8986	R	143*	0.4
Pacific Coast Feather Co.	PO Box 80385	Seattle	WA	98108	Gerard Hanauer	206-624-1057	R	113*	0.2
Charles D Owen Manufacturing	PO Box 457	Swannanoa	NC	28778	Charles Owen	828-298-6802	R	101*	0.7
Roho Group Inc.	PO Box 658	Belleville	IL	62222	Robert Graebe	618-277-9150	R	84*	0.2
Brentwood Originals Inc.	PO Box 6272	Carson	CA	90749	Harold Alden	310-637-6804	S	81*	0.6
Miller Curtain Company Inc.	105 Riviera Dr.	San Antonio	TX	78213	Gerd Miller	210-483-1000	R	80*	1.1
Wilen Companies Inc.	3760 Southside Ind.	Atlanta	GA	30354	Jeffrey Alder	404-366-2111	D	80*	0.4
Royale Comfort Seating Inc.	PO Box 235	Taylorsville	NC	28681	Clyde Goble	828-632-2865	R	78*	0.1
Team Technologies Molding Inc.	5949 Commerce	Morristown	TN	37814	Steve Henrikson	423-587-2199	R	76*	0.3
Carole Fabrics Corp.	PO Box 1436	Augusta	GA	30903	W 'Bill' Geiger	706-863-4742	R	69*	0.5
Manual Woodworkers & Weavers	3737 Howard Gap	Hendersonville	NC	28792	Jay Zito	828-692-7333	R	68*	0.3
Bomaine Corp.	20731 S Fordyce	Carson	CA	90810	G.M. Bronstein	310-537-1979	R	67*	0.5
American Fiber and Finishing	PO Box 2488	Albemarle	NC	28002	P Keener	704-983-6102	R	58*	0.2
Winston-Salem Ind. For Blind	7730 N Point Blvd.	Winston-Salem	NC	27106	Daniel Boucher	336-759-0551	R	57*	0.3
Harper Brush Works Inc.	PO Box 608	Fairfield	IA	52556	Barry Harper	641-472-5186	R	55*	0.1
Franco Manufacturing Company	555 Prospect St.	Metuchen	NJ	08840	Louis Franco	732-494-0500	R	54*	0.2
Madison Industries Inc.	279 5th Ave.	New York	NY	10016	Michael Schwartz	212-679-5110	R	52*	<0.1
Fuller Brush Co.	1 Fuller Way	Great Bend	KS	67530	Norbert Schneider	620-792-1711	R	50*	0.5
Anderson Fabrics Inc.	PO Box 311	Blackduck	MN	56630	Ron Anderson	218-835-6677	R	46*	0.3
Sewing Source Inc.	PO Box 639	Spring Hope	NC	27882	Janet Sload	252-478-3900	R	46*	0.2
CHF Industries Inc.	PO Box 410727	Charlotte	NC	28241	Frank Foley	704-522-5000	R	46*	<0.1
Contec Inc.	PO Box 530	Spartanburg	SC	29304	John McBride	864-503-8333	R	43*	0.2
Forney Industries Inc.	PO Box 563	Fort Collins	CO	80521	Steve Anderson	970-482-7271	R	38*	0.5
Goodwill Ind./N New England	PO Box 8600	Portland	ME	04104		207-774-6323	R	38*	0.1
Wise Company Inc.	5535 Pleasant View	Memphis	TN	38134	James Freudenberg	901-388-0155	R	38*	<0.1
Croscill Inc.	261 5th Ave. Fl. 25	New York	NY	10016	Myron Kahn	212-689-7222	R	34*	<0.1
Quickie Manufacturing Corp.	PO Box 156	Riverton	NJ	08077	Peter Vosbikian	856-829-7900	R	33*	<0.1
Down-Lite International Inc.	8153 Duke Blvd.	Mason	OH	45040	Larry Werthaiser	513-229-3696	R	33*	0.2
Big Horn Inc.	PO Box 72965	Chattanooga	TN	37407	Mike Stocker	423-867-9901	R	31*	0.2
Libman Co.	220 N Sheldon St.	Arcola	IL	61910	Robert Libman	217-268-4200	R	30*	0.3
Irwin Manufacturing Corp.	PO Box 507	Ocilla	GA	31774	Jeff Heller	229-468-9481	R	30*	0.2
Layton Home Fashions Inc.	14546 N Lombard	Portland	OR	97203	Corey Faul	503-283-4864	R	28*	0.2
Tag Trade Associates Group	1730 W Wrightwood	Chicago	IL	60614	Karen Biedermann	773-871-1300	R	28*	<0.1
Monterey Inc.	PO Box 271	Janesville	WI	53547		608-754-2866	S	27*	0.2
Paramount Industrial Company	1112 Kingwood	Norfolk	VA	23502	Arthur Diamonstein	757-855-3321	R	27*	0.2
Saddle Barn Tack Distributors	PO Box 2465	Roswell	NM	88202	Marc Andrus	575-622-9344	R	27*	<0.1
Marietta Drapery/Window Cover.	PO Box 569	Marietta	GA	30061	Andrew Bentley	770-428-3335	R	26*	<0.1
Weiler Corp.	1 Weiler Dr.	Cresco	PA	18326	Richard Gommel	570-595-7495	R	26*	0.4
Chestnut Ridge Foam Inc.	PO Box 781	Latrobe	PA	15650	Larry Garrity	724-537-9000	R	26*	0.2
Tabb Textiles Company Inc.	PO Box 2707	Opelika	AL	36803	Alan Fenster	334-745-6762	R	26*	<0.1
Bardwil Industries Inc.	1071 Ave of the Am.	New York	NY	10018		212-944-1870	R	25*	0.2
Fabtex Inc.	111 Woodbine Ln.	Danville	PA	17821	Robert Snyder	570-275-7500	R	25*	0.1
Crane Interiors Inc.	PO Box 459	Woodbury	TN	37190	Larry Bucklin	615-563-4800	R	23*	0.2
Carolina North Lumber Co.	PO Box 340	Randleman	NC	27317	Bruce Hughes	336-498-6600	R	23*	0.2
Foam Rubber Products Inc.	PO Box 525	New Castle	IN	47362	Frank Nold	765-521-2000	R	23*	0.1
Fabricut Inc.	9303 E 46th St.	Tulsa	OK	74145	David Finer	918-622-7700	R	22*	0.3
Continental Commercial Prods	3760 Southside Ind.	Atlanta	GA	30354		404-366-2111	R	21*	0.2
Whiting Manufacturing Company	6975 Dixie Hwy.	Fairfield	OH	45014	Richard Whiting	513-874-8750	R	21*	0.2
Town and Country Linen Corp.	475 Oberlin Ave. S	Lakewood	NJ	08701	David Beyda	732-364-2000	R	21*	<0.1
Latex Foam International	510 River Rd.	Shelton	CT	06484	William Coffey	203-924-0700	R	20*	0.2
Lawnview Industries Inc.	PO Box 829	Urbana	OH	43078		937-653-5217	R	19*	0.2
John R Lyman Co.	PO Box 157	Chicopee	MA	01014	William Wright	413-598-8344	R	18*	0.1
American Uniform Co.	4363 Ocoee St. N	Cleveland	TN	37312	Gary Smith	423-476-6561	R	17*	0.2
Beacon Looms Inc.	411 Alfred Ave.	Teaneck	NJ	07666	Seymour Sadinoff	201-833-1600	R	17*	0.2
Bramson House Inc.	151 Albany Ave.	Freeport	NY	11520	Ellis Abramson	516-764-5006	R	17*	0.1
Easy Way Leisure Corp.	412 S Cooper Ave.	Cincinnati	OH	45215	Jon Randman	513-731-5640	R	17*	0.1
Park B. Smith Inc.	295 5th Ave.	New York	NY	10016	Park B. Smith	212-889-1818	R	16*	<0.1

Source: Ward's Business Directory of U.S. Private and Public Companies, Volumes 1 and 2, 2008. The company type code used is as follows: P - Public, R - Private, S - Subsidiary, D - Division, J - Joint Venture, A - Affiliate, G - Group. Sales are in millions of dollars, employees are in thousands. An asterisk (*) indicates an estimated sales volume. The symbol < stands for 'less than'. Company names and addresses are truncated, in some cases, to fit into the available space.

MATERIALS CONSUMED

Material	Quantity	Delivered Cost ($ million)
Plastics products consumed in the form of sheets, rods, etc.	(X)	60.6
Fabricated metal products, including forgings	(X)	18.1
Metal shapes and forms (exc. castings, forgings, fabr. metal products)	(X)	19.1
Yarns and textiles (cotton, wool, silk, and manmade fibers)	(X)	112.1
Wood brush handles and backs	(X)	55.9
Paperboard containers, boxes, and corrugated paperboard	(X)	50.7
Plastics resins consumed in the form of granules, pellets, etc.	(X)	45.0
Dressed hair (including bristle and horsehair)	(X)	16.5
All other materials, components, parts, containers, and supplies	(X)	312.0
Materials, ingredients, containers, and supplies, nsk	(X)	101.6

Source: 2002 *Economic Census*. Explanation of symbols used: (D): Withheld to avoid disclosure of competitive data; na: Not available; (S): Withheld because statistical norms were not met; (X): Not applicable; (Z): Less than half the unit shown; nec: Not elsewhere classified; nsk: Not specified by kind; - : zero; p : 10-19 percent estimated; q : 20-29 percent estimated.

PRODUCT SHARE DETAILS

Product or Product Class Shipments	Mil. $	Product or Product Class Shipments	Mil. $
BROOMS, BRUSHES, AND MOPS	2,065.4	Paint rollers, roller frames, and replacement rollers	222.5
Brooms, mops, and dusters	**536.0**	Paint and varnish brushes, rollers, and pads, nsk	6.6
Brooms	192.0	**Other brushes**	**876.0**
Household floor brooms	89.7	Personal brushes, including toothbrushes and hairbrushes	341.3
Other brooms (industrial brooms, whiskbrooms, toy brooms, hearth brooms, streetsweeping machine brooms, etc)	102.2	Toothbrushes	275.4
		Other personal brushes (including shaving brushes and hairbrushes)	65.9
Mops and dusters, including refills	299.3	Other brushes, including household, industrial and artists' brushes	489.5
Dry mops and dusters (excluding dusting cloths, including refills)	94.8	Household maintenance brushes (floor, scrub, dusting, window, etc), including any twisted-in-wire brushes	120.7
Wet mops (except sponge mops, including refills)	97.8	Industrial maintenance brushes (floor, scrub, dusting, window, etc), including any twisted-in-wire brushes	114.8
Sponge mops (including refills)	106.7		
Brooms, mops, and dusters, nsk	44.7	Industrial brushes (except maintenance) (including power-driven, rotary, end, cup, jewelers' and dentists' brushes, etc)	124.7
Paint and varnish brushes and paint holders, pads, roller frames, and rollers, including replacement rollers	**497.6**	Other brushes, including artists' brushes and hair pencils, except artists' airbrushes	129.3
Whitewash, kalsomine, paperhanging, marking, and stenciling brushes	213.8	Other brushes, nsk	45.2
Paint holders, pads, roller frames and rollers and replacement rollers	277.2	**Brooms, brushes, and mops, nsk, total**	**155.7**
Paint pads and holders	54.7		

Source: 2002 *Economic Census*. The values are product shipments in millions of dollars for 2002. Total product shipments may be lower or higher than industry shipments. See Introduction for a full discussion. Values of indented subcategories are summed in the main heading(s). The symbol (D) appears when data are withheld to prevent disclosure of competitive information. The abbreviation nsk stands for 'not specified by kind' and nec for 'not elsewhere classified'. A dash (-) means zero.

INPUTS AND OUTPUTS FOR BROOM, BRUSH, AND MOP MANUFACTURING

Economic Sector or Industry Providing Inputs	%	Sector	Economic Sector or Industry Buying Outputs	%	Sector
Compensation of employees	26.5		Personal consumption expenditures	44.9	
Truck transportation	12.2	Util.	General S/L govt. services	11.5	S/L Govt
Used & secondhand goods	4.7		Services to buildings & dwellings	5.1	Services
Fiber, yarn, & thread mills	4.4	Manufg.	Exports of goods & services	4.6	Cap Inv
Management of companies & enterprises	3.0	Services	Owner-occupied dwellings	3.8	
Wholesale trade	2.8	Trade	Residential permanent site structures	3.4	Construct.
Paperboard containers	2.2	Manufg.	Elementary & secondary schools	3.2	Services
Plastics packaging materials, film & sheet	2.2	Manufg.	Telecommunications	3.0	Services
Miscellaneous wood products	1.9	Manufg.	Wholesale trade	2.6	Trade
Plastics materials & resins	1.8	Manufg.	Food services & drinking places	1.9	Services
Advertising & related services	1.6	Services	Residential structures, nec	1.9	Construct.
Brooms, brushes, & mops	1.3	Manufg.	Plastics products, nec	1.8	Manufg.
Real estate	0.8	Fin/R.E.	Change in private inventories	1.1	In House
Manufacturing, nec	0.7	Manufg.	Brooms, brushes, & mops	1.0	Manufg.
Power generation & supply	0.6	Util.	Nonresidential structures, nec	0.8	Construct.
Taxes on production & imports, less subsidies	0.5		Civic, social, & professional organizations	0.6	Services
Iron & steel mills & ferroalloys	0.5	Manufg.	Commercial & health care structures	0.6	Construct.
Unlaminated plastics profile shapes	0.4	Manufg.	General Federal government services, nondefense	0.6	Fed Govt
Steel products from purchased steel	0.3	Manufg.	Maintenance/repair of nonresidential structures	0.5	Construct.
Machine shops	0.3	Manufg.	Miscellaneous crops	0.4	Agric.
Semiconductors & related devices	0.3	Manufg.	Semiconductors & related devices	0.4	Manufg.
Legal services	0.3	Services	Retail trade	0.4	Trade
Accounting, tax preparation, bookkeeping, & payroll	0.2	Services	Personal care services	0.3	Services
Warehousing & storage	0.2	Util.	Hospitals	0.3	Services
Securities, commodity contracts, investments	0.2	Fin/R.E.	Religious organizations	0.3	Services
Specialized design services	0.2	Services	Amusement & recreation, nec	0.2	Services
Printed circuit assemblies (electronic assemblies)	0.2	Manufg.	Cattle	0.2	Agric.

Continued on next page.

INPUTS AND OUTPUTS FOR BROOM, BRUSH, AND MOP MANUFACTURING - Continued

Economic Sector or Industry Providing Inputs	%	Sector	Economic Sector or Industry Buying Outputs	%	Sector
Automotive equipment rental & leasing	0.2	Fin/R.E.	Scientific research & development services	0.2	Services
Crowns & closures & metal stamping	0.2	Manufg.	Maintenance/repair of residential structures	0.2	Construct.
Employment services	0.2	Services	Natural gas distribution	0.2	Util.
Sawmills & wood preservation	0.2	Manufg.	Child day care services	0.2	Services
Maintenance/repair of nonresidential structures	0.2	Construct.	Business support services	0.2	Services
Coating, engraving, heat treating & allied activities	0.2	Manufg.	Support services, nec	0.2	Services
Natural gas distribution	0.2	Util.	Colleges, universities, & professional schools	0.1	Services
Services to buildings & dwellings	0.2	Services	Advertising & related services	0.1	Services
Telecommunications	0.2	Services	Dairy cattle & milk	0.1	Agric.
Business support services	0.2	Services	Data processing, hosting, & related services	0.1	Services
Aluminum products from purchased aluminum	0.1	Manufg.	Educational services, nec	0.1	Services
Scientific research & development services	0.1	Services	Printing	0.1	Manufg.
Laminated plastics plates, sheets, & shapes	0.1	Manufg.	Environmental & other technical consulting services	0.1	Services
Artificial & synthetic fibers & filaments	0.1	Manufg.	Veterinary services	0.1	Services
Management, scientific, & technical consulting	0.1	Services	Real estate	0.1	Fin/R.E.
Commercial & industrial machinery rental & leasing	0.1	Fin/R.E.	Breweries	0.1	Manufg.
Noncomparable imports	0.1	Foreign	Grains	0.1	Agric.
Automotive repair & maintenance, ex. car washes	0.1	Services			
Data processing, hosting, & related services	0.1	Services			
Rail transportation	0.1	Util.			
Cutting tools & machine tool accessories	0.1	Manufg.			

Source: Benchmark Input-Output Accounts for the U.S. Economy, 2002, U.S. Department of Commerce, Washington, D.C., January 2008. The abbreviation nec stands for 'not elsewhere classified'.

OCCUPATIONS EMPLOYED BY BROOM, BRUSH, AND MOP MANUFACTURING

No Occupation data available for this industry.

LOCATION BY STATE AND REGIONAL CONCENTRATION

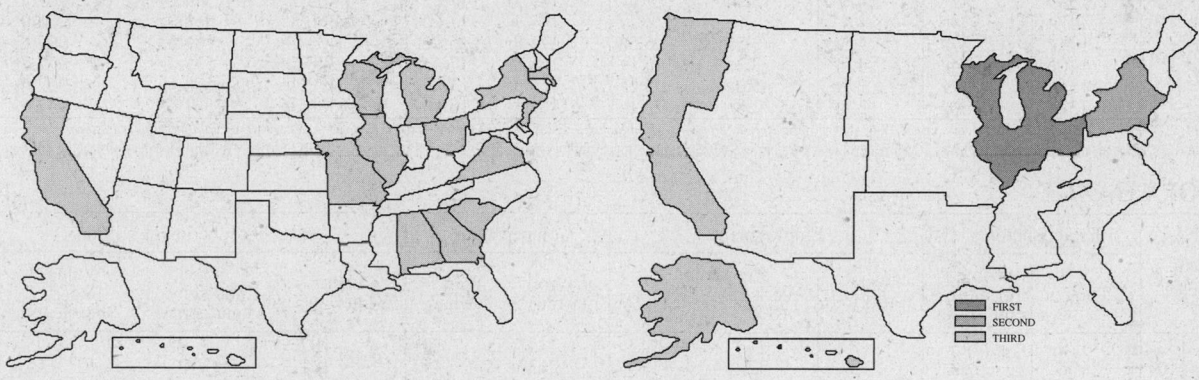

FIRST
SECOND
THIRD

INDUSTRY DATA BY STATE

State	Establish-ments	Shipments			Employment				Cost as % of Shipments	Investment per Employee ($)
		Total ($ mil)	% of U.S.	Per Establ.	Total Number	% of U.S.	Per Establ.	Wages ($/hour)		
Ohio	25	352.6	15.7	14,104.5	2,159	14.4	86	12.76	51.7	5,466
Illinois	20	212.6	9.5	10,631.0	1,447	9.7	72	13.20	32.9	4,845
Wisconsin	12	168.3	7.5	14,021.4	1,026	6.8	86	13.34	40.0	2,600
California	31	159.7	7.1	5,151.0	1,082	7.2	35	13.90	32.2	2,955
New York	21	78.0	3.5	3,716.3	727	4.9	35	10.06	42.8	2,435
Michigan	8	47.7	2.1	5,959.0	340	2.3	43	15.30	43.5	1,588
Georgia	7	46.7	2.1	6,668.4	414	2.8	59	11.05	47.8	1,867
Massachusetts	9	43.1	1.9	4,794.1	418	2.8	46	10.77	41.4	9,799
Missouri	10	42.0	1.9	4,201.4	313	2.1	31	11.41	34.6	2,316
New Jersey	14	36.8	1.6	2,630.4	275	1.8	20	12.00	45.0	3,487
South Carolina	6	28.9	1.3	4,809.5	238	1.6	40	8.04	58.1	483
Virginia	5	28.4	1.3	5,672.0	166	1.1	33	14.10	42.8	2,633
Alabama	4	12.3	0.5	3,070.5	122	0.8	30	8.76	54.6	3,336

Source: 2002 Economic Census. The states are in descending order of shipments or establishments (if shipment data are missing for the majority). The symbol (D) appears when data are withheld to prevent disclosure of competitive information. States marked with (D) are sorted by number of establishments. A dash (-) indicates that the data element cannot be calculated. Data may not show all states active in the NAICS category. All data available at the time of publication are shown.

NAICS 339995 - BURIAL CASKET MANUFACTURING

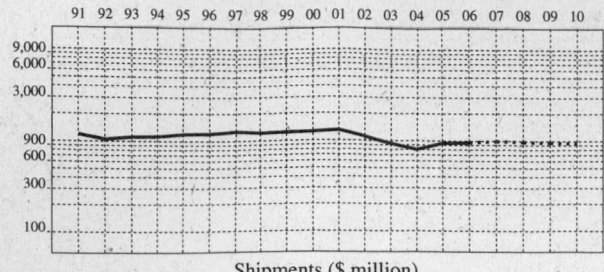

Shipments ($ million)

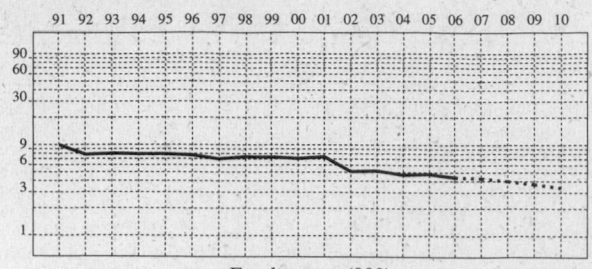

Employment (000)

GENERAL STATISTICS

| Year | Com-panies | Establishments | | Employment | | | Compensation | | Production ($ million) | | | |
		Total	with 20 or more employees	Total (000)	Production Workers (000)	Hours (Mil)	Payroll ($ mil)	Wages ($/hr)	Cost of Materials	Value Added by Manufacture	Value of Shipments	Capital Invest.
1991		209	77	9.9	7.7	16.2	237.8	9.27	554.3	644.2	1,193.7	29.1
1992	195	211	67	7.8	6.0	13.4	196.2	9.78	390.6	660.6	1,053.3	28.5
1993		197	70	8.0	6.3	13.6	202.0	9.98	431.9	693.5	1,118.6	27.2
1994		197	72	7.9	6.2	13.4	199.6	10.44	411.7	722.5	1,128.0	18.7
1995		195	61	7.9	6.3	12.9	205.0	11.38	404.8	797.5	1,196.0	28.3
1996		189	61	7.7	6.2	12.5	206.2	11.82	399.2	807.0	1,207.8	24.0
1997	163	177	53	7.0	5.2	10.6	212.5	13.71	384.4	882.9	1,271.2	27.4
1998		171	60	7.4	5.6	10.7	212.7	13.75	365.5	855.4	1,220.6	13.4
1999		172	56	7.3	5.3	10.6	211.3	13.03	358.1	873.1	1,238.7	17.8
2000		164	53	7.1	5.3	10.1	201.3	13.08	360.9	897.8	1,252.6	18.2
2001		160	53	7.4	5.7	10.5	210.4	13.02	383.1	921.0	1,300.4	18.1
2002	148	164	47	5.1	4.2	9.4	160.1	12.38	382.1	706.7	1,113.4	17.0
2003		164	47	5.2	4.3	8.7	177.5	14.91	336.2	587.3	935.8	13.9
2004		161	42	4.7	3.9	7.9	159.1	15.06	324.4	480.6	801.7	12.8
2005		158	42	4.8	3.9	7.9	189.2	17.02	405.2	544.2	947.7	12.7
2006		147P	39P	4.4	3.6	7.2	174.7	17.62	390.8	568.3	958.8	13.9
2007		144P	37P	4.3P	3.5P	6.6P	171.8P	16.96P	404.7P	588.5P	992.8P	10.5P
2008		140P	34P	4.0P	3.3P	6.1P	168.8P	17.44P	398.5P	579.5P	977.7P	9.3P
2009		136P	32P	3.7P	3.0P	5.6P	165.8P	17.92P	392.4P	570.6P	962.6P	8.2P
2010		132P	30P	3.4P	2.8P	5.1P	162.8P	18.40P	386.2P	561.6P	947.5P	7.1P

Sources: 1992, 1997, 2002 *Economic Census*; other years, up to 2006, are from the *Annual Survey of Manufactures*. Establishment counts for non-Census years are from *County Business Patterns*; 1997 and 2002 values are from the 1997 and 2002 censuses respectively, reported in the Federal Government's NAICS format. Other years were originally reported in equivalent SIC format. 'P's show projections by the editors.

INDICES OF CHANGE

| Year | Com-panies | Establishments | | Employment | | | Compensation | | Production ($ million) | | | |
		Total	with 20 or more employees	Total (000)	Production Workers (000)	Hours (Mil)	Payroll ($ mil)	Wages ($/hr)	Cost of Materials	Value Added by Manufacture	Value of Shipments	Capital Invest.
1992	132	129	143	153	143	143	123	79	102	93	95	168
1997	110	108	113	137	124	113	133	111	101	125	114	161
2001		98	113	145	136	112	131	105	100	130	117	106
2002	100	100	100	100	100	100	100	100	100	100	100	100
2003		100	100	102	102	93	111	120	88	83	84	82
2004		98	89	92	93	84	99	122	85	68	72	75
2005		96	89	94	93	84	118	137	106	77	85	75
2006		90P	83P	86	86	77	109	142	102	80	86	82
2007		88P	78P	84P	83P	70P	107P	137P	106P	83P	89P	62P
2008		85P	73P	78P	79P	65P	105P	141P	104P	82P	88P	55P
2009		83P	68P	73P	71P	60P	104P	145P	103P	81P	86P	48P
2010		80P	63P	67P	67P	54P	102P	149P	101P	79P	85P	42P

Sources: Same as General Statistics. Values reflect change from the base year, 2002. Values above 100 mean greater than 2002, values below 100 mean less than 2002, and the values of 100 in other years means the same as 2002. 'P's show projections by the editors.

SELECTED RATIOS

For 2002	Avg. of All Manufact.	Analyzed Industry	Index	For 2002	Avg. of All Manufact.	Analyzed Industry	Index
Employees per Establishment	42	31	74	Value Added per Production Worker	182,367	168,262	92
Payroll per Establishment	1,639,184	976,220	60	Cost per Establishment	5,769,015	2,329,878	40
Payroll per Employee	39,053	31,392	80	Cost per Employee	137,446	74,922	55
Production Workers per Establishment	30	26	87	Cost per Production Worker	195,506	90,976	47
Wages per Establishment	694,845	709,585	102	Shipments per Establishment	11,158,348	6,789,024	61
Wages per Production Worker	23,548	27,708	118	Shipments per Employee	265,847	218,314	82
Hours per Production Worker	1,980	2,238	113	Shipments per Production Worker	378,144	265,095	70
Wages per Hour	11.89	12.38	104	Investment per Establishment	361,338	103,659	29
Value Added per Establishment	5,381,325	4,309,146	80	Investment per Employee	8,609	3,333	39
Value Added per Employee	128,210	138,569	108	Investment per Production Worker	12,245	4,048	33

Sources: Same as General Statistics. The 'Average of All Manufacturing' column represents the average of all manufacturing industries reported for the most recent complete year available. The Index shows the relationship between the Average and the Analyzed Industry. For example, 100 means that they are equal; 500 that the Analyzed Industry is five times the average; 50 means that the Analyzed Industry is half the national average. The abbreviation 'na' is used to show that data are 'not available'. Ratios shown for 2002, the last complete census year.

LEADING COMPANIES   Number shown: 12   Total sales ($ mil): **5,359**   Total employment (000): **22.1**

Company Name	Address				CEO Name	Phone	Co. Type	Sales ($ mil)	Empl. (000)
Batesville Casket Company Inc.	1 Batesville Blvd.	Batesville	IN	47006	Kenneth Camp	812-934-7500	S	2,357*	3.8
Hillenbrand Industries Inc.	1069 State Rte 46E	Batesville	IN	47006		812-934-7000	P	2,024	9.9
Stewart Enterprises Inc.	1333 S Clearview Pk	Jefferson	LA	70121	Thomas Crawford	504-729-1400	P	523	5.5
York Group Inc.	2 NorthShore Center	Pittsburgh	PA	15212	Thomas J. Crawford	412-995-1600	S	196*	1.7
Aurora Casket Company Inc.	PO Box 29	Aurora	IN	47001	William Backman	812-926-1111	R	154*	0.5
Casket Shells Inc.	PO Box 172	Archbald	PA	18403	Joseph Semon	570-876-2642	R	32*	0.2
Astral Industries Inc.	PO Box 638	Lynn	IN	47355	Charles B. Shaw	765-874-2525	R	20*	0.2
JM Hutton Company Inc.	PO Box 129	Richmond	IN	47375	Anthony Wright	765-962-3591	R	15*	<0.1
Schuylkill Haven Casket Co.	PO Box 179	Schuylkill Hvn	PA	17972	Donald Houck	570-385-0296	R	15*	<0.1
Clark Grave Vault Co.	PO Box 8250	Columbus	OH	43201	David Beck	614-294-3761	R	11*	0.1
Freeman Metal Products Inc.	PO Box 785	Ahoskie	NC	27910	Morris Freeman	252-332-5390	R	9*	0.1
Greenwood Inc.	3901 N Vermilion St	Danville	IL	61834	D Darby-Walthall	217-442-9224	R	4*	<0.1

Source: *Ward's Business Directory of U.S. Private and Public Companies*, Volumes 1 and 2, 2008. The company type code used is as follows: P - Public, R - Private, S - Subsidiary, D - Division, J - Joint Venture, A - Affiliate, G - Group. Sales are in millions of dollars, employees are in thousands. An asterisk (*) indicates an estimated sales volume. The symbol < stands for 'less than'. Company names and addresses are truncated, in some cases, to fit into the available space.

MATERIALS CONSUMED

Material	Quantity	Delivered Cost ($ million)
Fabrics (cotton, wool, manmade fiber , etc.)	(X)	22.7
Rough and dressed lumber	(X)	25.1
Metal casket and casket shell hardware	(X)	62.1
Other fabricated metal products (exc. castings and forgings)	(X)	26.1
Steel shapes and forms (exc. castings, forgings, fabr. metal products)	(X)	135.7
Paints, varnishes, stains, lacquers, shellacs, japans, enamels, etc.	(X)	19.2
All other materials, components, parts, containers, and supplies	(X)	57.3
Materials, ingredients, containers, and supplies, nsk	(X)	12.3

Source: 2002 *Economic Census*. Explanation of symbols used: (D): Withheld to avoid disclosure of competitive data; na: Not available; (S): Withheld because statistical norms were not met; (X): Not applicable; (Z): Less than half the unit shown; nec: Not elsewhere classified; nsk: Not specified by kind; - : zero; p : 10-19 percent estimated; q : 20-29 percent estimated.

PRODUCT SHARE DETAILS

Product or Product Class Shipments	Mil. $	Product or Product Class Shipments	Mil. $
BURIAL CASKETS	1,100.3	Fiberboard, hardboard, and softwood (except pine) wood burial caskets and coffins, completely lined and	
Metal burial caskets and coffins completely lined and trimmed, adult sizes only	**778.7**	trimmed, adult sizes only	12.1
Steel burial caskets and coffins (excluding stainless steel)	544.8	Hardwood (including pine) burial caskets and coffins, completely lined and trimmed, adult sizes only	180.9
Other metal burial caskets and coffins (stainless steel, bronze, copper, etc)	233.4	Wood burial caskets and coffins, completely lined and trimmed, adult sizes only, nsk	0.3
Metal caskets and coffins completely lined and trimmed, adult sizes only, nsk	0.5	**Other burial caskets and coffins, burial boxes, and metal vaults, casket shells, casket shipping cases and containers,**	
Wood burial caskets and coffins, completely lined and trimmed, adult sizes only	**193.3**	**and children's caskets and coffins**	**74.2**
Wood burial caskets and coffins, completely lined and trimmed, adult sizes only	193.0	**Burial caskets, nsk, total**	**54.1**

Source: 2002 *Economic Census*. The values are product shipments in millions of dollars for 2002. Total product shipments may be lower or higher than industry shipments. See Introduction for a full discussion. Values of indented subcategories are summed in the main heading(s). The symbol (D) appears when data are withheld to prevent disclosure of competitive information. The abbreviation nsk stands for 'not specified by kind' and nec for 'not elsewhere classified'. A dash (-) means zero.

INPUTS AND OUTPUTS FOR ALL OTHER MISCELLANEOUS MANUFACTURING

Economic Sector or Industry Providing Inputs	%	Sector	Economic Sector or Industry Buying Outputs	%	Sector
Compensation of employees	28.9		Personal consumption expenditures	51.1	
Wholesale trade	3.6	Trade	Private fixed investment	11.2	
Management of companies & enterprises	3.2	Services	Exports of goods & services	7.8	Cap Inv
Manufacturing, nec	2.9	Manufg.	Death care services	7.2	Services
Iron & steel mills & ferroalloys	2.9	Manufg.	Wholesale trade	3.4	Trade
Synthetic rubber	2.7	Manufg.	General S/L govt. services	2.9	S/L Govt
Machine shops	2.6	Manufg.	Manufacturing, nec	2.1	Manufg.
Paints & coatings	2.1	Manufg.	Light truck & utility vehicles	1.6	Manufg.
Plastics materials & resins	2.0	Manufg.	Food services & drinking places	1.4	Services
Sawmills & wood preservation	1.5	Manufg.	Women's & girls' cut & sew apparel	0.9	Manufg.
Reconstituted wood products	1.5	Manufg.	Curtain & linen mills	0.7	Manufg.

Continued on next page.

INPUTS AND OUTPUTS FOR ALL OTHER MISCELLANEOUS MANUFACTURING - Continued

Economic Sector or Industry Providing Inputs	%	Sector	Economic Sector or Industry Buying Outputs	%	Sector
Real estate	1.5	Fin/R.E.	Retail trade	0.7	Trade
Plastics packaging materials, film & sheet	1.3	Manufg.	Men's & boys' cut & sew apparel	0.6	Manufg.
Truck transportation	1.2	Util.	Change in private inventories	0.6	In House
Paperboard containers	1.2	Manufg.	Grantmaking, giving, & social advocacy organizations	0.6	Services
Lessors of nonfinancial assets	0.9	Fin/R.E.	Cattle	0.4	Agric.
Semiconductors & related devices	0.9	Manufg.	Community food, housing, relief, & rehabilitation	0.4	Services
Fabricated metals, nec	0.8	Manufg.	Personal care services	0.4	Services
Coating, engraving, heat treating & allied activities	0.8	Manufg.	Civic, social, & professional organizations	0.3	Services
Alumina refining & primary aluminum production	0.8	Manufg.	Architectural, engineering, & related services	0.3	Services
Advertising & related services	0.8	Services	Elementary & secondary schools	0.3	Services
Securities, commodity contracts, investments	0.7	Fin/R.E.	Glass products from purchased glass	0.3	Manufg.
Unlaminated plastics profile shapes	0.7	Manufg.	Accounting, tax preparation, bookkeeping, & payroll	0.3	Services
Power generation & supply	0.7	Util.	Jewelry & silverware	0.3	Manufg.
Aluminum products from purchased aluminum	0.6	Manufg.	Federal government, investment, national defense	0.3	Fed Govt
Monetary authorities/depository credit intermediation	0.5	Fin/R.E.	Personal & household goods repair/maintenance	0.3	Services
Legal services	0.5	Services	Personal services, nec	0.2	Services
Hardware	0.5	Manufg.	Dry-cleaning & laundry services	0.2	Services
Turned products & screws, nuts, & bolts	0.5	Manufg.	Individual & family services	0.2	Services
Professional, scientific, technical services, nec	0.5	Services	Specialized design services	0.2	Services
Automotive equipment rental & leasing	0.4	Fin/R.E.	Motor vehicle parts	0.2	Manufg.
Printed circuit assemblies (electronic assemblies)	0.4	Manufg.	Child day care services	0.1	Services
Narrow fabric mills & schiffli embroidery	0.4	Manufg.	Nondepository credit intermediation activities	0.1	Fin/R.E.
Architectural, engineering, & related services	0.4	Services	Telecommunications	0.1	Services
Cutting tools & machine tool accessories	0.4	Manufg.	Institutional furniture	0.1	Manufg.
Miscellaneous wood products	0.3	Manufg.	Religious organizations	0.1	Services
Specialized design services	0.3	Services	Plastics materials & resins	0.1	Manufg.
Metal cans, boxes, & other containers (light gauge)	0.3	Manufg.	Tobacco products	0.1	Manufg.
Employment services	0.3	Services			
Warehousing & storage	0.3	Util.			
Accounting, tax preparation, bookkeeping, & payroll	0.3	Services			
Custom roll forming	0.3	Manufg.			
Greenhouse & nursery products	0.3	Agric.			
Telecommunications	0.3	Services			
Rail transportation	0.3	Util.			
Business support services	0.3	Services			
Taxes on production & imports, less subsidies	0.2				
Forging, stamping, & sintering, nec	0.2	Manufg.			
Crowns & closures & metal stamping	0.2	Manufg.			
Natural gas distribution	0.2	Util.			
Commercial & industrial machinery rental & leasing	0.2	Fin/R.E.			
Management, scientific, & technical consulting	0.2	Services			
Food services & drinking places	0.2	Services			
Noncomparable imports	0.2	Foreign			
Plate work & fabricated structural products	0.2	Manufg.			
Data processing, hosting, & related services	0.2	Services			
Abrasive products	0.2	Manufg.			
Scientific research & development services	0.2	Services			
Ball & roller bearings	0.2	Manufg.			
Support services, nec	0.2	Services			
Postal service	0.2	Util.			
Wood windows & doors & millwork	0.2	Manufg.			
Handtools	0.2	Manufg.			
Copper rolling, drawing, extruding, & alloying	0.2	Manufg.			
Nonferrous metal foundries	0.2	Manufg.			
Services to buildings & dwellings	0.2	Services			
Textile & fabric finishing mills	0.2	Manufg.			
Air transportation	0.1	Util.			
Valve & fittings other than plumbing	0.1	Manufg.			
Maintenance/repair of nonresidential structures	0.1	Construct.			
Other computer related services, including facilities	0.1	Services			
Nonferrous metal (ex. copper & aluminum) processing	0.1	Manufg.			
Investigation & security services	0.1	Services			
Periodical publishers	0.1	Services			
Hotels & motels, including casino hotels	0.1	Services			

Source: Benchmark Input-Output Accounts for the U.S. Economy, 2002, U.S. Department of Commerce, Washington D.C., January 2008. User should note that this Input-Output table is not for this particular narrowly defined industry but for a larger aggregate. Input and Output data for All Other Miscellaneous Manufacturing include Input and Output data for the Annual Survey of Manufactures' NAICS industries 339993, 339995, and 339999. The abbreviation nec stands for 'not elsewhere classified'.

OCCUPATIONS EMPLOYED BY BURIAL CASKET MANUFACTURING

No Occupation data available for this industry.

LOCATION BY STATE AND REGIONAL CONCENTRATION

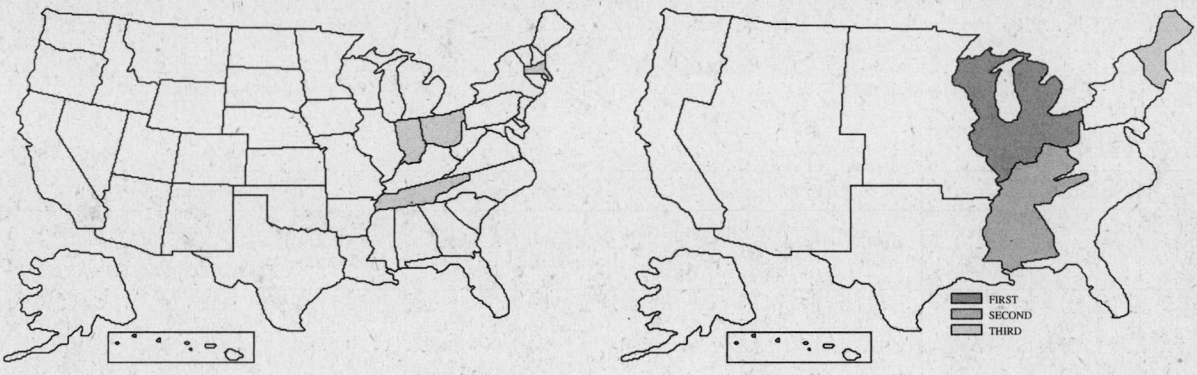

FIRST
SECOND
THIRD

INDUSTRY DATA BY STATE

| State | Establish-ments | Shipments | | | Employment | | | | Cost as % of Shipments | Investment per Employee ($) |
		Total ($ mil)	% of U.S.	Per Establ.	Total Number	% of U.S.	Per Establ.	Wages ($/hour)		
Indiana	20	511.2	45.9	25,561.2	1,870	36.9	94	12.64	33.1	2,605
Tennessee	7	171.9	15.4	24,556.4	730	14.4	104	13.85	30.4	1,084
Ohio	8	44.1	4.0	5,511.6	179	3.5	22	16.57	57.3	7,883
Massachusetts	4	13.8	1.2	3,447.3	166	3.3	42	11.71	33.1	928

Source: 2002 *Economic Census*. The states are in descending order of shipments or establishments (if shipment data are missing for the majority). The symbol (D) appears when data are withheld to prevent disclosure of competitive information. States marked with (D) are sorted by number of establishments. A dash (-) indicates that the data element cannot be calculated. Data may not show all states active in the NAICS category. All data available at the time of publication are shown.

NAICS 339999 - MISCELLANEOUS MANUFACTURING NEC

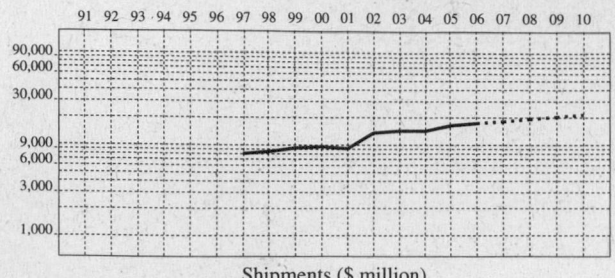

Shipments ($ million)

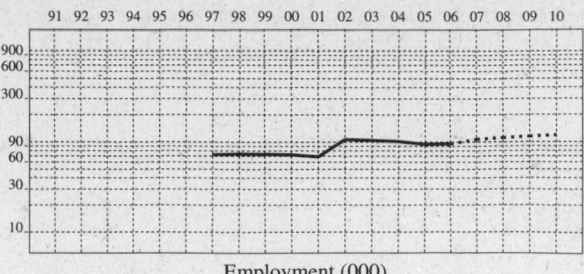

Employment (000)

GENERAL STATISTICS

| Year | Companies | Establishments | | Employment | | | Compensation | | Production ($ million) | | | |
		Total	with 20 or more employees	Total (000)	Production Workers (000)	Hours (Mil)	Payroll ($ mil)	Wages ($/hr)	Cost of Materials	Value Added by Manufacture	Value of Shipments	Capital Invest.
1997	2,635	2,691	672	72.6	51.8	103.6	1,763.9	9.20	3,712.9	4,351.0	8,046.1	370.2
1998		2,916	672	74.1	52.6	96.8	1,813.2	10.27	3,940.8	4,677.9	8,501.8	271.7
1999		2,879	686	73.6	51.2	97.7	1,973.3	10.68	4,455.4	4,934.5	9,317.2	326.9
2000		2,854	687	72.5	50.1	92.9	1,996.3	11.28	4,731.6	4,994.4	9,633.8	279.0
2001		2,764	656	69.0	46.0	86.6	2,090.9	11.42	4,651.5	4,460.0	9,162.9	311.0
2002	5,313	5,362	1,253	106.8	73.8	134.6	3,271.1	12.49	6,006.7	7,677.2	13,652.8	526.6
2003		4,598	1,078	104.6	71.1	135.3	3,416.8	12.59	6,264.5	8,075.9	14,359.3	397.7
2004		4,748	1,088	101.7	68.8	139.1	3,514.2	12.23	6,438.7	7,883.6	14,270.2	516.2
2005		4,692	1,075	95.0	63.6	127.9	3,498.8	13.48	6,910.1	9,785.3	16,450.0	638.0
2006		5,343P	1,225P	95.7	65.8	130.0	3,656.7	14.20	7,533.8	9,950.3	17,422.2	528.2
2007		5,667P	1,295P	107.5P	72.2P	142.4P	4,098.9P	14.46P	7,868.7P	10,392.7P	18,196.8P	600.0P
2008		5,991P	1,365P	111.3P	74.5P	147.4P	4,353.3P	14.94P	8,349.5P	11,027.7P	19,308.6P	633.4P
2009		6,316P	1,435P	115.1P	76.8P	152.5P	4,607.7P	15.43P	8,830.3P	11,662.7P	20,420.4P	666.7P
2010		6,640P	1,506P	119.0P	79.1P	157.6P	4,862.2P	15.92P	9,311.1P	12,297.7P	21,532.3P	700.1P

Sources: 1997 and 2002 *Economic Census*; other years, up to 2006, are from *Annual Survey of Manufactures*. Establishment counts for non-Census years are from *County Business Patterns*; 1997 and 2002 values are from the 1997 and 2002 censuses, respectively. 'P's show projections by the editors.

INDICES OF CHANGE

| Year | Companies | Establishments | | Employment | | | Compensation | | Production ($ million) | | | |
		Total	with 20 or more employees	Total (000)	Production Workers (000)	Hours (Mil)	Payroll ($ mil)	Wages ($/hr)	Cost of Materials	Value Added by Manufacture	Value of Shipments	Capital Invest.
1997	50	50	54	68	70	77	54	74	62	57	59	70
1998		54	54	69	71	72	55	82	66	61	62	52
1999		54	55	69	69	73	60	86	74	64	68	62
2000		53	55	68	68	69	61	90	79	65	71	53
2001		52	52	65	62	64	64	91	77	58	67	59
2002	100	100	100	100	100	100	100	100	100	100	100	100
2003		86	86	98	96	101	104	101	104	105	105	76
2004		89	87	95	93	103	107	98	107	103	105	98
2005		88	86	89	86	95	107	108	115	127	120	121
2006		100P	98P	90	89	97	112	114	125	130	128	100
2007		106P	103P	101P	98P	106P	125P	116P	131P	135P	133P	114P
2008		112P	109P	104P	101P	110P	133P	120P	139P	144P	141P	120P
2009		118P	115P	108P	104P	113P	141P	124P	147P	152P	150P	127P
2010		124P	120P	111P	107P	117P	149P	127P	155P	160P	158P	133P

Sources: Same as General Statistics. Values reflect change from the base year, 2002. Values above 100 mean greater than 2002, values below 100 mean less than 2002, and the values of 100 in other years means the same as 2002. 'P's show projections by the editors.

SELECTED RATIOS

For 2002	Avg. of All Manufact.	Analyzed Industry	Index	For 2002	Avg. of All Manufact.	Analyzed Industry	Index
Employees per Establishment	42	20	47	Value Added per Production Worker	182,367	104,027	57
Payroll per Establishment	1,639,184	610,052	37	Cost per Establishment	5,769,015	1,120,235	19
Payroll per Employee	39,053	30,628	78	Cost per Employee	137,446	56,243	41
Production Workers per Establishment	30	14	47	Cost per Production Worker	195,506	81,392	42
Wages per Establishment	694,845	313,531	45	Shipments per Establishment	11,158,348	2,546,214	23
Wages per Production Worker	23,548	22,780	97	Shipments per Employee	265,847	127,835	48
Hours per Production Worker	1,980	1,824	92	Shipments per Production Worker	378,144	184,997	49
Wages per Hour	11.89	12.49	105	Investment per Establishment	361,338	98,210	27
Value Added per Establishment	5,381,325	1,431,779	27	Investment per Employee	8,609	4,931	57
Value Added per Employee	128,210	71,884	56	Investment per Production Worker	12,245	7,136	58

Sources: Same as General Statistics. The 'Average of All Manufacturing' column represents the average of all manufacturing industries reported for the most recent complete year available. The Index shows the relationship between the Average and the Analyzed Industry. For example, 100 means that they are equal; 500 that the Analyzed Industry is five times the average; 50 means that the Analyzed Industry is half the national average. The abbreviation 'na' is used to show that data are 'not available'. Ratios shown for 2002, the last complete census year.

LEADING COMPANIES   Number shown: 75   Total sales ($ mil): 173,255   Total employment (000): 350.1

Company Name	Address				CEO Name	Phone	Co. Type	Sales ($ mil)	Empl. (000)
McKesson Corp.	1 Post St.	San Francisco	CA	94104	John H. Hammergren	415-983-8300	P	92,977	31.8
CP and P Inc.	133 Peachtree St.	Atlanta	GA	30303	Jospeh Moller	404-652-4000	S	16,083*	55.0
Georgia-Pacific Corp.	PO Box 105605	Atlanta	GA	30348	Mario Concha	404-652-4000	S	13,685*	50.0
Pro-Build Holdings	82 Devonshire	Boston	MA	02109	Paul Mucci		R	4,653*	17.0
Energizer Holdings Inc.	533 Maryville Univ.	St. Louis	MO	63141		314-985-2000	P	3,365	11.1
Milliken Chemical	PO Box 1926	Spartanburg	SC	29304	Ashley Allen	864-503-2200	R	3,317*	10.0
GE Water and Process Tech.	4636 Somerton Rd.	Trevose	PA	19053	Jeff Garwood	215-355-3300	S	2,748*	8.0
International Game Technology	PO Box 10580	Reno	NV	89510	G. Thomas Baker	775-448-7777	P	2,621	5.4
JELD-WEN Inc.	PO Box 1329	Klamath Falls	OR	97601	Richard Wendt	541-882-3451	R	2,476*	23.8
J.M. Huber Corp.	333 Thornall St.	Edison	NJ	08837	Peter T. Francis	732-549-8600	R	2,300*	5.0
American Greetings Corp.	1 American Rd.	Cleveland	OH	44144		216-252-7300	P	1,745	28.9
Potlatch Corp.	601 W Riverside	Spokane	WA	99201	Michael Covey	509-835-1500	P	1,654	3.8
Builders FirstSource Inc.	2001 Bryan St.	Dallas	TX	75201	Paul Levy	214-880-3500	P	1,593	4.9
Pella Corp.	102 Main St.	Pella	IA	50219	Charles S. Farver	641-628-1000	R	1,531*	10.6
Sierra Pacific Industries	PO Box 496028	Redding	CA	96049	A.A. Emmerson	530-378-8000	R	1,425*	3.9
Blyth Inc.	1 E Weaver St.	Greenwich	CT	06831		203-661-1926	P	1,221	4.0
Longaberger Co.	1500 E Main St.	Newark	OH	43055	Jim Klein	740-322-5000	R	1,206*	8.7
Koppers Inc.	436 7th Ave.	Pittsburgh	PA	15219	Robert Cizik	412-227-2001	R	1,160	2.0
Lancaster Colony Corp.	37 W Broad St.	Columbus	OH	43215	John B. Gerlach, Jr.	614-224-7141	P	1,091	5.6
Ply Gem Holdings Inc.	185 Platte Clay Way	Kearney	MO	64060	Frederick J. Iseman	816-903-6400	R	1,055	4.6
Syngenta Seeds Inc. - NK	PO Box 959	Minneapolis	MN	55440	Jeff Cox	763-593-7333	S	1,044*	1.3
Brady Corp.	PO Box 571	Milwaukee	WI	53201		414-358-6600	P	1,018	8.0
Simpson Manufacturing Company	5956 W Las Positas	Pleasanton	CA	94588	Thomas J. Fitzmyers	925-560-9000	P	817	2.7
Travel Tags Inc.	5842 Carmen Ave.	Inver Grove Hts	MN	55076	Barb Cederberg	651-450-1201	R	763*	0.3
Ceradyne Inc.	3169 Red Hill Ave.	Costa Mesa	CA	92626		714-549-0421	P	757	2.5
Suntory Water Group Inc.	5660 New Northside	Atlanta	GA	30328	Stewart E. Allen	770-933-1400	R	688*	5.5
Yankee Candle Company Inc.	16 Yankee Candle	South Deerfield	MA	01373	Harlan M. Kent	413-665-8306	R	688	4.1
Alliance Gaming Corp.	6601 S Bermuda Rd.	Las Vegas	NV	89119	Richard M. Haddrill	702-584-7700	P	682	2.3
Oregon Cutting Systems Group	PO Box 22127	Portland	OR	97269	Jim Oscermanc	503-653-8881	D	674*	1.0
Mid-South Industries Inc.	PO Box 322	Gadsden	AL	35902	Larry Ferguson	256-494-1302	R	563*	1.6
WMS Industries Inc.	800 S Northpoint	Waukegan	IL	60085	Brian R. Gamache	847-785-3000	P	539	1.4
Koken Manufacturing Company	PO Box 265	Saint Louis	MO	63166	Masahiro Kanaya	314-231-7383	R	458*	<0.1
Arden Companies	18000 W 9 Mile Rd.	Southfield	MI	48075	Robert S. Sachs	248-355-1101	R	424*	1.2
WMS Gaming Inc.	3401 N California	Chicago	IL	60618	Brian R. Gamache	773-961-1620	S	398*	0.8
Amscan Holdings Inc.	80 Grasslands Rd.	Elmsford	NY	10523	James Harrison	914-345-2020	R	386*	2.0
Totes-Isotoner Corp.	9655 International	Cincinnati	OH	45246	Douglas Gernert	513-682-8200	R	358*	1.1
UNICEF	333 E 38th St., 6th	New York	NY	10016	Charles Lyons	212-326-7000	R	352*	1.0
Trex Company Inc.	160 Exeter Dr.	Winchester	VA	22603		540-542-6300	P	329	0.8
Russ Berrie and Company Inc.	111 Bauer Dr.	Oakland	NJ	07436	Andrew R. Gatto	201-337-9000	P	295	1.0
Nielsen and Bainbridge	40 Eisenhower Dr.	Paramus	NJ	07653	Jack Forbes	201-368-9191	R	219*	0.9
Oil-Dri Corporation of America	410 N Michigan	Chicago	IL	60611		312-321-1515	P	212	0.8
Day-Timers Inc.	1 Willow Ln.	East Texas	PA	18046	Bob Dorney		S	200*	1.3
International Wood Industries	18101 SW Boons	Tualatin	OR	97062	Robert Rotticci	503-670-0365	R	185*	0.1
Shuffle Master Inc.	1106 Palms Airport	Las Vegas	NV	89119		702-897-7150	P	179	0.6
Annin and Co.	55 Locust Ave.	Roseland	NJ	07068	C.R. Beard Jr.	973-228-9400	R	173*	0.4
Blackbourn Media Packaging	200 4th Ave. N	Edgerton	MN	56128	Don Taft	507-442-4311	S	166*	0.3
Midway Games Inc.	2704 W Roscoe St.	Chicago	IL	60618	David F. Zucker	773-961-2222	P	157	0.7
Midwest Stamping Inc.	3455 Briarfield	Maumee	OH	43537	Ronald L. Thompson	419-724-6970	R	155*	0.6
LG Seeds Inc.	22827 Shissler Rd.	Elmwood	IL	61529	Craig Anderson	309-742-8802	R	154*	0.1
Flextronics International NC	130 Mosswood	Youngsville	NC	27596	Richard L. Sharp	919-556-7881	S	138*	0.5
Bally Gaming Systems Inc.	6601 Bermuda Rd.	Las Vegas	NV	89119		702-896-7700	S	135*	2.3
Enterprise Products Inc.	6846 Suva St.	Bell Gardens	CA	90201	Ron Spicer	562-927-2515	R	134*	0.2
American Biophysics Corp.	140 Frenchtown Rd.	N Kingstown	RI	02852	Raymond Iannetta	401-884-3500	R	102*	0.2
Sierra Design Group	300 Sierra Manor Dr	Reno	NV	89511	Robert Luciano	775-850-1500	S	101*	0.1
Adv. Environ. Recycling Tech.	PO Box 1237	Springdale	AR	72765	Joe G. Brooks	479-756-7400	P	98	0.7
RSG Forest Products Inc.	985 NW 2nd Street	Kalama	WA	98625	Robert Sanders	360-673-2825	R	97*	0.2
Franklin Mint Co.	US Rte. One	Media	PA	19091	Bruce Newman	610-459-6000	R	97*	1.1
Home Fragrance Holdings Inc.	411 N Sam Houston	Houston	TX	77060	Jon Godshall	832-554-4600	R	92*	0.4
Manke Lumber Company Inc.	1717 Marine View	Tacoma	WA	98422	Charles Manke	253-752-6252	R	91*	0.3
Wood Resources L.P.	1 Sound Shore Dr.	Greenwich	CT	06830	Richard Yarbrough	203-302-3343	R	90*	0.9
Ball Horticultural Co.	622 Town Rd.	West Chicago	IL	60185	Anna Caroline Ball	630-231-3600	R	90*	0.5
J.H. Baxter and Co.	PO Box 5902	San Mateo	CA	94402	G Baxter Krause	650-349-0201	R	86*	0.2
General Foam Plastics Corp.	3321 E Prncss Anne	Norfolk	VA	23502	Ascher Chase	757-857-0153	R	85*	0.4
Midwest Trophy Manufacturing	PO Box 15659	Oklahoma City	OK	73155		405-670-4545	R	82*	0.5
Amer. Printing House For Blind	PO Box 6085	Louisville	KY	40206		502-895-2405	R	80*	0.3
Wahl Clipper Corp.	PO Box 578	Sterling	IL	61081		815-625-6525	R	80*	0.7
Marquis Corp.	596 Hoffman Rd.	Independence	OR	97351	Jerry Lankheet	503-838-0888	R	79*	0.2
Cross Match Technologies Inc.	3950 RCA Blvd.	Palm Bch Gdns	FL	33410	James W. Ziglar	561-622-1650	R	76*	0.3
Polk Audio Inc.	5601 Metro Dr.	Baltimore	MD	21215	Mathew Polk	410-358-3600	R	73	0.1
Carris Reels Inc.	439 West Street	Rutland	VT	05701	Michael Curran	802-773-9111	R	71*	0.6
Caffco International	PO Box 3508	Montgomery	AL	36109		334-272-2140	R	71*	0.5
Progressive Gaming Int'l Corp.	920 Pilot Rd.	Las Vegas	NV	89119	Peter G. Boynton	702-896-3890	P	71	0.3
Dallas Manufacturing Company	PO Box 891101	Dallas	TX	75389		972-716-4200	S	69*	<0.1
Epolin Holding Corp.	358-364 Adams St.	Newark	NJ	07105	Greg Amato	973-465-9495	S	65*	<0.1
Leanin Tree Inc.	PO Box 9500	Boulder	CO	80301	Edward Trumble	303-530-1442	R	65*	0.2

Source: *Ward's Business Directory of U.S. Private and Public Companies*, Volumes 1 and 2, 2008. The company type code used is as follows: P - Public, R - Private, S - Subsidiary, D - Division, J - Joint Venture, A - Affiliate, G - Group. Sales are in millions of dollars, employees are in thousands. An asterisk (*) indicates an estimated sales volume. The symbol < stands for 'less than'. Company names and addresses are truncated, in some cases, to fit into the available space.

MATERIALS CONSUMED

Material	Quantity	Delivered Cost ($ million)
Rough and dressed lumber	(X)	144.1
Fabricated metal products, including forgings	(X)	414.3
Paperboard containers, boxes, and corrugated paperboard	(X)	115.5
Steel shapes and forms (exc. castings, forgings, fabr. metal products)	(X)	247.1
Aluminum and aluminum-base alloy shapes and forms (exc. castings, forgings, fabr. metal products)	(X)	84.9
Other nonferrous shapes and forms (exc. castings, forgings, fabricated metal products)	(X)	89.3
Plastics products consumed in the form of sheets, rods, etc.	(X)	159.9
Plastics resins consumed in the form of granules, pellets, etc.	(X)	124.1
All other materials, components, parts, containers, and supplies	(X)	1,625.6
Materials, ingredients, containers, and supplies, nsk	(X)	1,796.5

Source: 2002 *Economic Census*. Explanation of symbols used: (D): Withheld to avoid disclosure of competitive data; na: Not available; (S): Withheld because statistical norms were not met; (X): Not applicable; (Z): Less than half the unit shown; nec: Not elsewhere classified; nsk: Not specified by kind; - : zero; p : 10-19 percent estimated; q : 20-29 percent estimated.

PRODUCT SHARE DETAILS

Product or Product Class Shipments	Mil. $	Product or Product Class Shipments	Mil. $
ALL OTHER MISCELLANEOUS FABRICATIONS	12,174.4	Christmas	80.2
Chemical fire-extinguishing equipment and parts and attachments	**664.2**	Artificial flowers, fruits, and wreaths	92.4
Hand portable carbon dioxide fire extinguishers	17.3	Feathers and plumes	49.9
Hand portable dry chemical fire extinguishers	227.6	Artificial trees, flowers, fruits, and wreaths, including feathers and plumes, nsk	1.7
Other hand portable fire extinguishers (including foam, pressurized water, and halogenated agents)	47.0	**Mirror and picture frames, and framed pictures**	**1,368.8**
Fixed fire-extinguishing systems (except parts and attachments), including inert gas, dry and wet chemical, and other chemical fire-extinguishing equipment	(D)	Wood mirror and picture frames	439.9
		Wood-framed pictures	315.0
		Metal and plastics mirror and picture frames, including other framed pictures	599.7
Parts and attachments for chemical fire-extinguishing equipment	(D)	Metal mirror and picture frames	64.0
Coin-operated amusement machines, except jukeboxes	**886.7**	Plastics mirror and picture frames	209.1
Coin-operated arcade and amusement center type electronic games	136.1	Other framed pictures, including pictures framed with fiber, metal, and plastics	326.7
Other coin-operated amusement machines, including nonelectronic arcade games and parts for all arcade games	750.6	Mirror and picture frames and framed pictures, nsk	14.2
		All other miscellaneous fabricated products	**5,295.3**
Candles (including tapers)	**975.3**	All other miscellaneous fabricated products	5,185.4
Umbrellas and parasols (including parts)	**70.2**	Christmas tree ornaments and decorations, excluding glass and electric	59.4
Artificial trees, flowers, fruits, and wreaths, including feathers and plumes	**224.2**	Potpourri, including potpourri made from dried and chemically preserved flowers, foliage, fruits, and vines	66.0
Artificial trees, flowers, fruits, and wreaths, including feathers and plumes	222.5	Other miscellaneous fabricated products, including products made from a combination of materials	5,060.0
Artificial trees, all types (metal, plastics, etc), including		All other miscellaneous fabricated products, nsk	109.9
		All other miscellaneous fabrications, nsk, total	**2,689.8**

Source: 2002 *Economic Census*. The values are product shipments in millions of dollars for 2002. Total product shipments may be lower or higher than industry shipments. See Introduction for a full discussion. Values of indented subcategories are summed in the main heading(s). The symbol (D) appears when data are withheld to prevent disclosure of competitive information. The abbreviation nsk stands for 'not specified by kind' and nec for 'not elsewhere classified'. A dash (-) means zero.

INPUTS AND OUTPUTS FOR ALL OTHER MISCELLANEOUS MANUFACTURING

Economic Sector or Industry Providing Inputs	%	Sector	Economic Sector or Industry Buying Outputs	%	Sector
Compensation of employees	28.9		Personal consumption expenditures	51.1	
Wholesale trade	3.6	Trade	Private fixed investment	11.2	
Management of companies & enterprises	3.2	Services	Exports of goods & services	7.8	Cap Inv
Manufacturing, nec	2.9	Manufg.	Death care services	7.2	Services
Iron & steel mills & ferroalloys	2.9	Manufg.	Wholesale trade	3.4	Trade
Synthetic rubber	2.7	Manufg.	General S/L govt. services	2.9	S/L Govt
Machine shops	2.6	Manufg.	Manufacturing, nec	2.1	Manufg.
Paints & coatings	2.1	Manufg.	Light truck & utility vehicles	1.6	Manufg.
Plastics materials & resins	2.0	Manufg.	Food services & drinking places	1.4	Services
Sawmills & wood preservation	1.5	Manufg.	Women's & girls' cut & sew apparel	0.9	Manufg.
Reconstituted wood products	1.5	Manufg.	Curtain & linen mills	0.7	Manufg.
Real estate	1.5	Fin/R.E.	Retail trade	0.7	Trade
Plastics packaging materials, film & sheet	1.3	Manufg.	Men's & boys' cut & sew apparel	0.6	Manufg.
Truck transportation	1.2	Util.	Change in private inventories	0.6	In House
Paperboard containers	1.2	Manufg.	Grantmaking, giving, & social advocacy organizations	0.6	Services
Lessors of nonfinancial assets	0.9	Fin/R.E.	Cattle	0.4	Agric.
Semiconductors & related devices	0.9	Manufg.	Community food, housing, relief, & rehabilitation	0.4	Services
Fabricated metals, nec	0.8	Manufg.	Personal care services	0.4	Services
Coating, engraving, heat treating & allied activities	0.8	Manufg.	Civic, social, & professional organizations	0.3	Services
Alumina refining & primary aluminum production	0.8	Manufg.	Architectural, engineering, & related services	0.3	Services
Advertising & related services	0.8	Services	Elementary & secondary schools	0.3	Services

Continued on next page.

INPUTS AND OUTPUTS FOR ALL OTHER MISCELLANEOUS MANUFACTURING - Continued

Economic Sector or Industry Providing Inputs	%	Sector	Economic Sector or Industry Buying Outputs	%	Sector
Securities, commodity contracts, investments	0.7	Fin/R.E.	Glass products from purchased glass	0.3	Manufg.
Unlaminated plastics profile shapes	0.7	Manufg.	Accounting, tax preparation, bookkeeping, & payroll	0.3	Services
Power generation & supply	0.7	Util.	Jewelry & silverware	0.3	Manufg.
Aluminum products from purchased aluminum	0.6	Manufg.	Federal government, investment, national defense	0.3	Fed Govt
Monetary authorities/depository credit intermediation	0.5	Fin/R.E.	Personal & household goods repair/maintenance	0.3	Services
Legal services	0.5	Services	Personal services, nec	0.2	Services
Hardware	0.5	Manufg.	Dry-cleaning & laundry services	0.2	Services
Turned products & screws, nuts, & bolts	0.5	Manufg.	Individual & family services	0.2	Services
Professional, scientific, technical services, nec	0.5	Services	Specialized design services	0.2	Services
Automotive equipment rental & leasing	0.4	Fin/R.E.	Motor vehicle parts	0.2	Manufg.
Printed circuit assemblies (electronic assemblies)	0.4	Manufg.	Child day care services	0.1	Services
Narrow fabric mills & schiffli embroidery	0.4	Manufg.	Nondepository credit intermediation activities	0.1	Fin/R.E.
Architectural, engineering, & related services	0.4	Services	Telecommunications	0.1	Services
Cutting tools & machine tool accessories	0.4	Manufg.	Institutional furniture	0.1	Manufg.
Miscellaneous wood products	0.3	Manufg.	Religious organizations	0.1	Services
Specialized design services	0.3	Services	Plastics materials & resins	0.1	Manufg.
Metal cans, boxes, & other containers (light gauge)	0.3	Manufg.	Tobacco products	0.1	Manufg.
Employment services	0.3	Services			
Warehousing & storage	0.3	Util.			
Accounting, tax preparation, bookkeeping, & payroll	0.3	Services			
Custom roll forming	0.3	Manufg.			
Greenhouse & nursery products	0.3	Agric.			
Telecommunications	0.3	Services			
Rail transportation	0.3	Util.			
Business support services	0.3	Services			
Taxes on production & imports, less subsidies	0.2				
Forging, stamping, & sintering, nec	0.2	Manufg.			
Crowns & closures & metal stamping	0.2	Manufg.			
Natural gas distribution	0.2	Util.			
Commercial & industrial machinery rental & leasing	0.2	Fin/R.E.			
Management, scientific, & technical consulting	0.2	Services			
Food services & drinking places	0.2	Services			
Noncomparable imports	0.2	Foreign			
Plate work & fabricated structural products	0.2	Manufg.			
Data processing, hosting, & related services	0.2	Services			
Abrasive products	0.2	Manufg.			
Scientific research & development services	0.2	Services			
Ball & roller bearings	0.2	Manufg.			
Support services, nec	0.2	Services			
Postal service	0.2	Util.			
Wood windows & doors & millwork	0.2	Manufg.			
Handtools	0.2	Manufg.			
Copper rolling, drawing, extruding, & alloying	0.2	Manufg.			
Nonferrous metal foundries	0.2	Manufg.			
Services to buildings & dwellings	0.2	Services			
Textile & fabric finishing mills	0.2	Manufg.			
Air transportation	0.1	Util.			
Valve & fittings other than plumbing	0.1	Manufg.			
Maintenance/repair of nonresidential structures	0.1	Construct.			
Other computer related services, including facilities	0.1	Services			
Nonferrous metal (ex. copper & aluminum) processing	0.1	Manufg.			
Investigation & security services	0.1	Services			
Periodical publishers	0.1	Services			
Hotels & motels, including casino hotels	0.1	Services			

Source: Benchmark Input-Output Accounts for the U.S. Economy, 2002, U.S. Department of Commerce, Washington D.C., January 2008. *User should note that this Input-Output table is not for this particular narrowly defined industry, but for a larger aggregate. Input and Output data for* All Other Miscellaneous Manufacturing *include Input and Output data for the* Annual Survey of Manufactures' *NAICS industries 339993, 339995, and 339999.* The abbreviation nec stands for 'not elsewhere classified'.

OCCUPATIONS EMPLOYED BY MISCELLANEOUS MANUFACTURING NEC

No Occupation data available for this industry.

LOCATION BY STATE AND REGIONAL CONCENTRATION

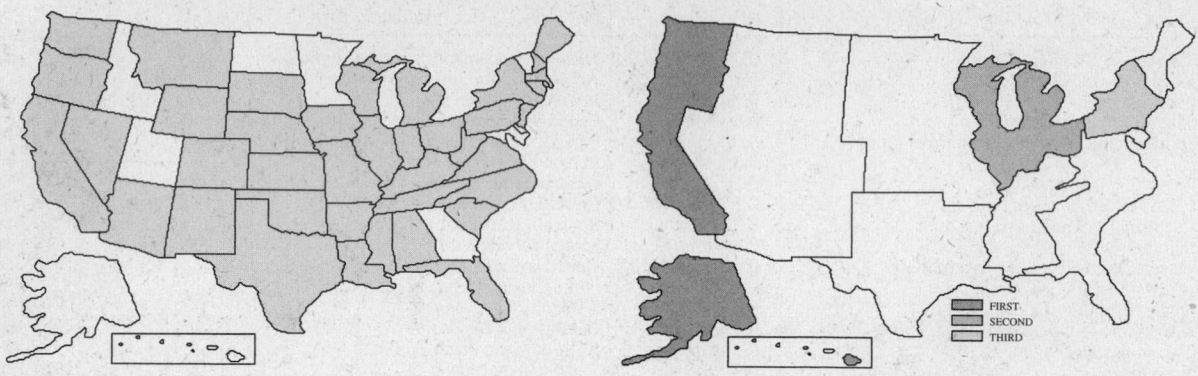

INDUSTRY DATA BY STATE

| State | Establish-ments | Shipments | | | Employment | | | | Cost as % of Shipments | Investment per Employee ($) |
		Total ($ mil)	% of U.S.	Per Establ.	Total Number	% of U.S.	Per Establ.	Wages ($/hour)		
California	845	1,938.0	14.2	2,293.5	16,026	15.0	19	11.71	42.7	3,455
Illinois	278	1,027.9	7.5	3,697.5	6,832	6.4	25	13.26	40.6	7,108
Texas	355	976.9	7.2	2,751.7	7,508	7.0	21	13.03	32.7	3,456
New York	359	829.5	6.1	2,310.6	7,688	7.2	21	11.24	44.9	4,276
Pennsylvania	276	794.4	5.8	2,878.3	5,619	5.3	20	13.62	40.3	4,867
North Carolina	148	773.1	5.7	5,223.9	4,237	4.0	29	12.72	47.2	3,287
Massachusetts	184	617.5	4.5	3,355.8	3,573	3.3	19	12.44	41.2	20,503
Nevada	44	580.9	4.3	13,202.6	4,001	3.7	91	16.49	82.8	8,435
Wisconsin	131	573.0	4.2	4,374.1	3,731	3.5	28	12.89	44.4	4,563
Ohio	222	565.8	4.1	2,548.5	4,460	4.2	20	12.17	44.0	3,056
Florida	254	429.4	3.1	1,690.4	4,103	3.8	16	12.59	43.0	3,192
Michigan	213	350.2	2.6	1,644.2	2,623	2.5	12	17.02	44.3	4,745
New Jersey	149	329.4	2.4	2,210.8	2,745	2.6	18	13.22	46.0	5,401
Kentucky	67	278.6	2.0	4,158.8	2,243	2.1	33	11.34	42.2	13,060
Indiana	117	258.0	1.9	2,205.1	2,212	2.1	19	14.40	39.2	14,769
Arkansas	42	241.5	1.8	5,750.6	2,169	2.0	52	8.83	50.4	2,695
Tennessee	79	239.7	1.8	3,033.9	1,953	1.8	25	13.05	35.0	2,965
Alabama	58	232.1	1.7	4,001.6	1,844	1.7	32	10.87	50.4	2,119
Washington	118	215.7	1.6	1,828.4	1,888	1.8	16	12.97	39.2	3,242
Arizona	88	188.7	1.4	2,143.9	1,682	1.6	19	11.60	43.5	2,482
Oklahoma	57	176.4	1.3	3,095.2	1,001	0.9	18	11.47	38.5	4,941
Missouri	96	172.8	1.3	1,800.4	1,844	1.7	19	10.60	39.9	1,976
Virginia	72	132.9	1.0	1,846.3	1,158	1.1	16	11.89	49.1	2,338
South Carolina	42	109.2	0.8	2,600.5	877	0.8	21	10.97	47.4	5,445
Rhode Island	45	108.2	0.8	2,403.5	636	0.6	14	11.86	49.6	3,039
Colorado	105	104.8	0.8	998.2	987	0.9	9	13.45	32.0	3,490
Connecticut	65	97.7	0.7	1,503.0	931	0.9	14	13.86	39.6	1,797
Iowa	45	89.8	0.7	1,996.2	732	0.7	16	11.85	41.6	2,160
Kansas	48	83.1	0.6	1,731.8	870	0.8	18	12.46	48.6	2,922
Oregon	97	79.6	0.6	820.5	903	0.8	9	13.00	37.2	4,334
Maine	36	69.8	0.5	1,937.5	825	0.8	23	11.53	40.5	2,645
Nebraska	20	58.5	0.4	2,924.2	555	0.5	28	11.68	41.5	3,422
New Hampshire	31	46.4	0.3	1,496.2	486	0.5	16	11.83	41.4	1,704
Mississippi	19	42.3	0.3	2,225.5	517	0.5	27	9.23	34.7	1,600
New Mexico	34	39.6	0.3	1,164.7	329	0.3	10	12.18	32.0	2,395
South Dakota	16	31.0	0.2	1,938.1	238	0.2	15	12.36	46.5	2,504
Louisiana	31	28.7	0.2	925.8	394	0.4	13	12.32	38.2	3,736
Montana	22	26.5	0.2	1,203.7	180	0.2	8	12.38	50.2	2,111
West Virginia	21	23.5	0.2	1,118.3	291	0.3	14	11.61	39.0	1,464
Wyoming	13	10.8	0.1	833.9	120	0.1	9	10.99	44.2	1,292

Source: 2002 *Economic Census*. The states are in descending order of shipments or establishments (if shipment data are missing for the majority). The symbol (D) appears when data are withheld to prevent disclosure of competitive information. States marked with (D) are sorted by number of establishments. A dash (-) indicates that the data element cannot be calculated. Data may not show all states active in the NAICS category. All data available at the time of publication are shown.